Oxford Dictionary of
National Biography

Volume 1

Oxford Dictionary of National Biography

IN ASSOCIATION WITH
The British Academy

From the earliest times to the year 2000

Edited by
H. C. G. Matthew
and
Brian Harrison

Volume 1
Aaron–Amory

OXFORD
UNIVERSITY PRESS

OXFORD
UNIVERSITY PRESS

Great Clarendon Street, Oxford OX2 6DP

Oxford University Press is a department of the University of Oxford.
It furthers the University's objective of excellence in research, scholarship,
and education by publishing worldwide in

Oxford New York

Auckland Bangkok Buenos Aires Cape Town
Chennai Dar es Salaam Delhi Hong Kong Istanbul Karachi
Kolkata Kuala Lumpur Madrid Melbourne Mexico City Mumbai Nairobi
São Paulo Shanghai Taipei Tokyo Toronto

Oxford is a registered trade mark of Oxford University Press
in the UK and in certain other countries

Published in the United States
by Oxford University Press Inc., New York

British Library Cataloguing in Publication Data
Data available

Library of Congress Cataloging in Publication Data
Oxford dictionary of national biography : in association with the British Academy :
from the earliest times to the year 2000 / edited by H.C.G. Matthew and Brian Harrison.
p. cm.
Rev. ed. of: Dictionary of national biography. 1885-1901.
Includes bibliographical references.
ISBN 0-19-861351-2 (246x189 mm hardcover : alk. paper)
1. Great Britain–Biography–Dictionaries. I. Matthew, H. C. G. (Henry Colin Gray)
II. Harrison, Brian Howard. III. British Academy. IV. Dictionary of national biography.
DA28.D4O95 2004
920.041–dc22

ISBN 0-19-861351-2 (this volume)
ISBN 0-19-861411-X (set of sixty volumes)

Text captured by Alliance Phototypesetters, Pondicherry
Illustrations reproduced and archived by
Alliance Graphics Ltd, UK
Typeset in OUP Swift by Interactive Sciences Limited, Gloucester
Printed in Great Britain on acid-free paper by
Butler and Tanner Ltd,
Frome, Somerset

INTRODUCTION

The *Oxford Dictionary of National Biography, in association with the British Academy* is the first point of reference for anyone interested in the lives of the peoples of the British Isles and their connections overseas, from the earliest times to the end of the year 2000. It is the product of research instituted at the University of Oxford and funded by the British Academy—Britain's national academy for the humanities and the social sciences—and by Oxford University Press. It is the achievement of 10,000 contributors and advisers, a worldwide community co-ordinated by project staff in Oxford.

The *Oxford DNB* aims to provide full, accurate, concise, and readable articles on noteworthy people in all walks of life, which present current scholarship in a form accessible to all. No living person is included: the *Dictionary*'s articles are confined to people who died before 31 December 2000. It covers people who were born and lived in the British Isles, people from the British Isles who achieved recognition in other countries, people who lived in territories formerly connected to the British Isles at a time when they were in contact with British rule, and people born elsewhere who settled in the British Isles for significant periods or whose visits enabled them to leave a mark on British life.

The *Oxford DNB* comprises 50,113 substantive articles in a single alphabetical sequence. 49,705 of these concern individuals, and 408 cover the lives of several people in a single entry under the name of a family or group—the Grey family, for example, or the Tolpuddle Martyrs. 5217 people appear in subsidiary notices forming part of another article. In total, the *Oxford DNB* includes lives of 54,922 people. It incorporates in rewritten or revised form all 38,607 lives contained in the *Dictionary of National Biography*, the precursor of the *Oxford DNB*, published between 1885 and 1900, and in its supplements, published between 1901 and 1996.

Articles in this dictionary present the lives of one or more persons written by one or more authors. They bear the names of those authors, and in the case of articles from the *DNB* that have been revised for the *Oxford DNB* the form of the signature indicates the fact of their revision. In addition to outlining a person's activities, character, and significance, each article aims to include, where feasible, certain standard facts about the person's life: dates and, as appropriate, places of key life events (such as birth, education, marriage, death, and burial), information about parents and spouses, and places of residence. All articles contain bibliographical sources. Further references are provided which list material that supplements the article

and may assist research: on archives, likenesses, and wealth at death.

Accompanying about one article in five is an image of the person who is the subject of the article—generally a portrait, but sometimes an effigy, coin, or other iconographic material. Selection of the 10,057 likenesses was organized by the National Portrait Gallery, drawing on its own collections and on about 1500 other sources. Chosen to ensure that their overall balance reflects coverage in the *Dictionary*, the images are wherever possible authentic likenesses taken from the life.

This introduction seeks to explain the historical context from which the *Oxford DNB* came, its gestation, its principles of inclusion, how its information was gathered, how it is presented, and how it has been compiled and published in printed and electronic forms.

History of the *DNB*

The *DNB* was from the outset a remarkable enterprise.[1] The publisher George Smith—of Smith, Elder & Co.—at first projected a dictionary of world biography, taking as his model the forty-volume *Biographie universelle* (Paris, 1843–63). In 1881–2 he discussed this idea with Leslie Stephen, who was then working with him as editor of the *Cornhill Magazine*, and in 1882 was persuaded to scale down his ambition and instead to fund a dictionary of British national biography. Stephen then resigned from editing the *Cornhill* to become the *DNB*'s first editor. Once a quarter from 1885 to 1900 the *DNB*'s sixty-three volumes successively rolled out from the presses in alphabetical order 'with unbroken punctuality',[2] as Sidney Lee (the *DNB*'s second editor) wrote in 1900, casting a sidelong glance at the slow progress made with similar publications elsewhere in Europe. The *DNB*'s 27,236 articles covered 29,333 people.[3] Lee counted 653 contributors, but identified 'one hundred regular and voluminous contributors' who 'have written nearly three-fourths of the whole'.[4] He rightly called it 'an undertaking of exceptional magnitude in the history of publishing',[5] and the organizational skill involved still seems impressive. Smith's feat was also philanthropic: he invested £70,000 in the *DNB*—the equivalent of about £5 million at the start of the twenty-first century.

The task taxed Stephen's health as well as Smith's funds, and in 1891 Stephen gave way to his successor as editor, Sidney Lee, who brought the planned project to fruition in 1900. However, by 1901 the *DNB*'s revision had already begun: three supplementary volumes to the original dictionary were published in that year. Again edited by Lee, these volumes included 965 articles covering 1007 people who had died between 1885 and 22 January 1901 (the date of Queen Victoria's death), together with others unintentionally omitted from earlier years. Given that the *DNB*'s volumes had been published quarterly in alphabetical order, material for the supplement at the end of this process was inevitably weighted heavily towards the alphabet's earlier letters. A volume of corrigenda to the entire dictionary was published in 1902, and some of the accumulated corrections to the articles in the *DNB*'s first edition and first supplement were incorporated into the main body of the work when Smith, Elder reissued the sixty-three original volumes and the three-volume supplement in twenty-two volumes during 1908–9.

Thereafter the original *DNB* remained unmodified, but chronological supplements on the recently deceased continued to be published between 1912 and 1996. The first of these covered people who died between 1901 and 1911, included 1632 articles on 1659 people, and was published by Smith, Elder in 1912; it was the last among Lee's heroic labours for the *Dictionary*. In 1917 the Smith family gave the *DNB* to the University of Oxford, which entrusted it to OUP. Thereafter OUP kept in print the twenty-two-volume set and the supplement for 1901 to 1911, and published nine further supplements under eight editors, adding a total of 5551 new articles on 5570 people who had died up to 31 December 1990. In 1975 OUP published a two-volume 'compact edition' of the *DNB* with supplements covering the period to 1960, micrographically reproduced. The volume entitled *Missing Persons* (1993), edited by Christine Nicholls, added 1082 articles on 1083 people who had been omitted from all earlier volumes up to 1985. In 1996 OUP also published the *DNB* complete up to 1985 on CD-ROM, and some selections of *DNB* articles were published separately in thematic print volumes between 1997 and 2002.[6] The *Concise DNB* up to 1900 had been published in 1903 as the *Index and Epitome*, a second part (covering 1901 to 1950) in 1961, with a revised version (1901 to 1970) in 1982, and a consolidated three-volume edition (from the earliest times to 1985) in 1992. The *DNB* (including all its supplements and *Missing Persons*) contained 36,466 articles on 38,652 people: of these, 45 had been entered twice, so the total number of lives included was 38,607.

Plans for a new DNB

Throughout the twentieth century the case for revising the *DNB* and its supplements steadily built up. Errata were collected at the Institute of Historical Research and for many years were published in its *Bulletin*. Yet errors and omissions could not be comprehensively corrected without resetting the entire dictionary, and OUP did not feel able to meet the huge cost of doing this, given contemporary printing methods—nor in the 1960s could it tempt subsidies from charitable foundations. By the 1980s far more than mere correction was needed, for the century-old work now required complete rejuvenation. Modern scholarship called for articles on new types of people and a fresh approach to those already there. *Missing Persons* made a start on gathering additional names, but the need

for revision could be met only by a completely new edition. This would have the ancillary advantage of restoring the continuous alphabetical sequence of names that had been cumulatively subverted by each supplement published from 1901 onwards. At this point OUP could perhaps have abandoned the entire venture as too costly, but in 1989 the delegates and senior officers of OUP identified a new *DNB* as 'an urgent priority'.[7]

An initiative was encouraged at this time by the advent of new technology and by OUP's experience of two comparable projects. In 1984 the Press had begun computerizing the *Oxford English Dictionary*. This entailed integrating the original text with its supplements, and the whole was published as a second edition in 1989, electronically on compact disc in 1992, and online in 2000. In 1986 a new *American National Biography* had been commissioned by the American Council of Learned Societies; it was published by OUP's New York office in twenty-four print volumes in 1999, and online in 2000. Key decision-makers in the initial phase of planning the *Oxford DNB* were Ivon Asquith (managing director of OUP's Arts and Reference Division, and later of the wider Academic Division), Nick Wilson (commercial director of the Arts and Reference Division, and formerly publishing editor responsible for the *DNB*), Sir Anthony Kenny (president of the British Academy and a delegate of OUP), and Sir Keith Thomas (a delegate of OUP and chairman of its finance committee).

Initial plans put to OUP's delegates in March 1990 envisaged editorial work continuing over twenty years through to 2010, and proceeding alongside publication of three volumes a year for fifteen years from 1995. External financial support was thought essential to fund the necessary research and writing, and in April 1990 the delegates asked the British Academy for help in securing government funding for those elements of the work. Under Sir Anthony Kenny the Academy endorsed the plan, and in January 1992 received for the purpose a substantially increased grant from what was then the Department of Education and Science. On 21 February 1992 the Academy's Council agreed to contribute towards research costs through an annual subvention to the University of Oxford. That subvention, set at £250,000 a year in 1992/3 and subsequently rising in line with inflation, made it possible formally to establish the project. A Supervisory Committee was appointed, with representation for the Academy, the University of Oxford, and (by invitation) the Royal Society (the members are listed on page xxi). Meeting at least once a year, it was chaired throughout its life from 1992 to 2004 by Sir Keith Thomas. The Committee exercised general oversight of the project, which then assumed the working name New Dictionary of National Biography.

The most crucial early decision was the appointment of the editor. The leading candidate identified in 1991 was Colin Matthew—then Fellow of St Hugh's College, Oxford—who co-edited or edited the last twelve volumes of W. E. Gladstone's diaries (14 volumes, 1968–94). At the end of February 1992 he was formally invited to become editor of the new venture, and in March 1992 the

University of Oxford announced the project's establishment under his leadership from September 1992. Comparing his task with that of the *DNB*'s first two editors, Matthew noted that the university-based professional expertise available to them had been small, whereas by the 1990s the pool of such authority in the British Isles, the United States, the Commonwealth, and continental Europe was vast; 'mobilising and coordinating this expertise', he wrote, 'will be a chief duty of the Editor'.[8]

Even before taking up his new role on 1 September 1992, Matthew started work on reconstituting the project's plan with Nick Wilson, who was the OUP director responsible for the project until 1997. The plan in 1992 still envisaged writing and publication extending over twenty years. After wide canvassing of specialist views about the *DNB*, and working closely with OUP and the chairman of the Supervisory Committee, Matthew rapidly made several important recommendations. The most far-reaching among them were that the project be completed in only twelve years instead of twenty, and that the *Dictionary* be published as a complete set rather than in instalments. Such a change carried practical consequences for the balance of funding: OUP would be able to take up only three-fifths of the promised public funds, would have to fund the large balance of research costs, and would have to forgo the income from publishing the *Dictionary* in instalments. None the less, the OUP delegates on 21 January 1993 approved the revised project plan, agreeing to proceed with the *Dictionary* 'as a service to scholarship, in no expectation of a commercial return'. Matthew asked the Supervisory Committee formally to record in its minutes his 'delight' at this decision. To the total government funding of £3.7 million which the *Oxford DNB* received between 1992 and 2004, OUP eventually added £19.2 million, and spent a further £3 million on the production costs of the complete print and online editions.

The detailed plans for the new dictionary—practical, financial, and intellectual—were outlined in the editor's report to the Supervisory Committee's meeting on 5 April 1993, and were approved collectively by the British Academy, the University of Oxford, and OUP at that meeting. Within the project thereafter Matthew's 'April report' provided an authoritative statement of objectives. He publicized his proposals more widely in his article for *History Today* in September 1993, in his presentations to conferences and institutions, and in his Leslie Stephen lecture at Cambridge in 1995 (published two years later). Contacts were established with other national biographical dictionaries and scholarly projects. Public discussion of the *Dictionary*'s aims continued in occasional interviews for newspapers and magazines; as Lee said of the *DNB*, the work was being 'conducted in the full light of day'.[9] All this lent the project a clear intellectual aim, and gave it the strong editorial momentum that became one of its defining features.

Behind his recommendations lay Matthew's judicious combination of scholarship and pragmatism. 'From my point of view as Editor', he wrote, 'it is important both that it be done well and that it be done.'[10] He found reassurance in Stephen's own view that 'great as is the difference between a good and a bad work of the kind, even a very defective performance is immensely superior to none at all'.[11]

Principles of inclusion

At an early stage in the planning, Matthew decided to retain in the new dictionary everyone in the *DNB* and its supplements. 'My approach to the *DNB* has been throughout conservative', he wrote in his internal report of April 1993, 'both as to the distribution of subjects and the content of individual articles'; the new dictionary was 'thus a development from the present *DNB*, not a *de novo* replacement of it'. He felt that the *DNB* was too valuable to set aside completely: the task for the makers of the new was not to start again, but rather to retain the *DNB*'s range and character while updating and extending it. All the *DNB*'s articles were to be rewritten or revised in the light of social and intellectual change since Stephen's day.[12] This decision immediately built into the new dictionary much of the pragmatism of the old.

All the plans for the *Oxford DNB* envisaged including many articles on lives absent from the *DNB*. Initial OUP estimates, informed by surveys of the *DNB* and by the experience of compiling *Missing Persons*, indicated the need to expand the number of articles by about a fifth; the 7500 new articles originally projected produced a total of some 45,000. Matthew's initial canvassing of specialists in 1992 subsequently identified more clearly the areas that needed strengthening. Allowance also had to be made for the people who died between 1991 and 2000. So Matthew adopted a target of 50,000 articles for the new dictionary, an increase of about 13,500 articles (37 per cent) over the total number of articles in the *DNB*.

His aim was to recapture the *DNB*'s late-Victorian breadth of selection in terms of numbers, fields of activity, and formal nationality. Matthew wrote of a 'return to the integrationalist approach of the original edition, in which many minor figures were included, often in half a column … We seek today to reflect in our extra entries the incorporation of areas of historical interest and significance which have developed since the 1880s.' The 'use of the *DNB* as a sort of establishment roll-call of national pre-eminence', he added, 'is recent and in my view undesirable'.[13] As he wrote later, the new dictionary 'is not merely a roll-call of the great and the good, but also a gallimaufry of the eccentric and the bad'.[14] Matthew also decided that the *Oxford DNB* should include a small number of articles about families and groups. This was an experimental feature, building again on the precedent of the *DNB*, which had treated a few medieval families in this way. These articles would reflect new attitudes to biography, much of whose interest, he wrote, 'springs from the tension between individual characteristics and development and the family, social and class background to which such characteristics relate. Biographical research increasingly takes the form of books about groups of people.'[15]

With the Oxford DNB's overall scope decided, detailed implementation required important subordinate decisions. It was decided to continue the DNB's policy of including no living person, and to choose 31 December 2000 as the terminal date—a century after the original DNB's coverage had ended. More difficult was nationality. Matthew felt that Stephen's title for the DNB was 'brilliant' because it did not require him to define nationality; like the queen's head on postage stamps, the DNB asserted nationality but carefully avoided defining it.[16] This allowed a policy on inclusion that would be, like Stephen's, pragmatic and flexible.[17] Neither the DNB's first article (on Jacques Abbadie, 1654?–1727) nor its penultimate article (on William Zuylestein, 1645–1709) centred upon a person born in Britain; both had settled there. Such an integrative policy on inclusion fitted well with the libertarian, free-trading, and internationalist outlook prevalent among late-Victorian Liberals, and was perhaps inevitable in a work whose articles included many people who lived in the British Isles long before any recognizable state existed there. The chronological span of the DNB and its supplements encompassed periods of Roman, Anglo-Saxon, Danish, Norman, and Angevin dominion; separate kingdoms within what became England, Ireland, Scotland, and Wales; and the subsequent dramatic expansion and contraction in British rule overseas. In preparing the Oxford DNB, Matthew proposed in his report of April 1993 to adopt a working definition of nationality, often implicit but unstated in the DNB, which treated the inhabitants of the British Isles as a 'nation-in-effect'. At the same time he emphasized the inherent pluralism of its constituent nationalities, and aimed to enhance the Dictionary's coverage of Ireland, Scotland, Wales, the Isle of Man, and the Channel Islands by including people from the regions of the British Isles and British territories overseas.

The DNB had included people who lived in overseas territories under British rule, and who might never have set foot in the British Isles. By occasionally including people such as Commonwealth prime ministers, the DNB supplements had continued this earlier practice, though on a more limited scale. As with all the people in the DNB, Matthew included them in the new dictionary, and in assessing the claims of further such entrants he was influenced by how far they had interacted with British concerns—by whether they were 'known to Whitehall'. This meant that people in overseas territories were not included if they were notable only within those areas or cultures. On the other hand, people who played some significant part in the territory's relations with British imperial power—whether as clients and government servants, or as opponents of that power—could still be considered for inclusion, as could those whose significance extended into British cultural and intellectual life. More articles on Eire since 1922 were warranted, both on the 'known-to-Whitehall' principle (given that Eire remained in the Commonwealth until 1949) and to accommodate people who had been British subjects during the creation of the new state. As for former colonial territories, the DNB tended to focus on the governments of

Australia, Canada, India, New Zealand, and South Africa. The Oxford DNB, while maintaining and increasing that coverage, aimed to extend the 'known-to-Whitehall' principle within other former colonial territories, such as those in other parts of Africa and in the Caribbean.

Both the DNB and the Oxford DNB have sought to reflect the full range of national life, and to include noteworthy people of all kinds. Influence—whether for good or ill—is the principal criterion for admission. Coverage includes many people of achievement, merit, or worth, but is by no means confined to them: it is concerned also with impact, which may sometimes stem from celebrity and even from notoriety. As Lee wrote of the DNB: 'Malefactors whose crimes excite a permanent interest have received hardly less attention than benefactors.' He also pointed out that the DNB included eleven articles 'on legendary personages or creatures of romance who have been mistaken for heroes of history',[18] citing among others King Arthur and Merlin. A century of scholarship has exposed more such figments (St Bega, for example), whose continued presence is, in a sense, accidental. But Matthew sought to augment the various examples inherited from the DNB with a small but significant selection of articles on imaginary or at best shadowy subjects with an iconic status in the nation's political or cultural life (for instance, Junius and Tommy Atkins), together with figures whose standing in the national past is entirely symbolic (such as Britannia and John Bull).

The plan for the Oxford DNB envisaged adding new people in every period (see Table 1 below) and in every field of activity, because 'even in well-covered areas time and changing historical interests have revealed gaps.[19] Matthew also sought to build up coverage in fields that were poorly represented in the DNB: women; people in business and the world of labour; Britain's Roman rulers (whose names were not only familiar to anyone interested in the British past but even, in the case of Hadrian's Wall, embedded in the landscape); pre-independence Americans; and twentieth-century subjects. In addition Matthew aimed to expand the coverage of people of note from the regions of the British Isles and British territories overseas; people born abroad who spent a significant part of their lives in Britain; visitors who became important observers or interpreters of British life; and Britons who lived in Europe and played a significant part in the life of their new country.

The twentieth century acquired more new entrants than any other. Quite apart from the need to include the lives of those who died between 1991 and 2000, for whom there had been no supplement, this increase sought to repair the reduced scale of the DNB's chronological supplements.[20] The DNB had included an annual average of about 160 people in the late-Victorian and Edwardian years, but in the chronological supplements covering those who died after 1911 this had fallen to about 80 a year. If the material in the DNB and its supplements was all to be included, the Oxford DNB needed to ensure that all periods were treated more consistently. In extending twentieth-century coverage, Matthew saw the need as being not only to expand existing categories and to include more new-comers from the general categories already identified for enlargement, but also to expand the treatment of such areas as technology, sport, media, and entertainment.

The shortage of articles on women, and the way their lives were treated, had come to seem perhaps the *DNB*'s most notorious weakness—and it was the one most frequently mentioned when opinions were canvassed on the need for a new dictionary. Women were scarce in the *DNB* partly because the division between 'public' and 'private' life had been particularly salient when it was being compiled. Many areas of women's activity were then categorized as private, thus seeming beyond the *Dictionary*'s remit. A century later this would no longer do, if only because the line between the private and the public had always been blurred, and had subsequently shifted markedly. Many pathways into public life led out of the Victorian woman's distinctive domestic role—nursing, voluntary work, and charity, to name only three. In selecting the *Oxford DNB*'s new lives, policy was set in such a way as to avoid limiting the recognition of women as valid candidates for inclusion (see Table 2 below).[21] The *Dictionary*'s advisers were urged to identify women who could justifiably be added, and in considering all articles to review the treatment of women's activities and influence.

The *DNB*'s view of 'public' activity had also limited its coverage of business and the world of labour. When it included businessmen and labour leaders, it often did so on the basis of their other or subsequent interests, such as politics or philanthropy. It was less interested in how entrepreneurs made their money than in how they spent it, and it assessed their significance accordingly. Nor could the *DNB*'s individualist format fully reflect the importance of family dynasties—a factor which accentuated the neglect of women in business and other contexts. Stephen's *DNB*, wrote Matthew in 1993, 'was … with a few exceptions for medieval families, a dictionary of individuals very individually handled'.[22] Yet many people deeply influence British society without leaving behind much evidence about their careers because their impact stems only from participating in a larger group. The *Dictionary*'s group and family articles offer a way of drawing in such people.

By identifying the gaps in the *DNB* that needed to be filled, editorial priorities could be established and practical limits set to the work. The initial allowances for new entrants were not based on any predetermined and immutable scheme for assigning space between component areas in relation to the work as a whole. The editorial plan, which inherited the *DNB*'s balance of selection, was designed to be flexible in the face of new perceptions as the work progressed. The overall balance of content was kept continuously under review, and new allocations were made as new recruits to the *Dictionary* were (or sometimes were not) found. Suggestions for new entrants arrived throughout the writing process, partly because the project team monitored many sources in pursuit of the overlooked. A few less important lives were commissioned but

were not completed for want of adequate information. Some newcomers were captured late in the project, thanks to a fortunate conjuncture of idea and contributor. Serendipity and practicalities, as well as accumulated editorial policies, inevitably influenced the final selection—a point which needs to be remembered by anyone embarking upon a quantitative survey of the *Dictionary*'s contents.

The shape of the articles

Matthew had a clear view of what an article in the *Dictionary* should be like: it 'should be accurate, informative, clear, and interesting to read. Its purpose is to give a complete and balanced account of the life and work of its subject by supplying both detailed personal information and a general assessment of the subject's significance.'[23] It should remain a literary text, while at the same time delivering essential factual information predictably. Authors were encouraged to write accessibly for the general reader, and to treat lives in the round rather than focus on one aspect to the exclusion of others. The article should take the form of a biographical narrative, as in the *DNB*, with some modifications to the earlier pattern: most notably an ampler treatment of context, a more integrated treatment of personal relationships, and (in longer articles) fuller attention to the person's long-term reputation. Within the general shape, however, many variations were possible, depending on subject matter. Matthew felt that simultaneous publication electronically and in print should not change the article's essential characteristic as 'primarily a piece of prose and not a database with prose added'.[24]

The *Oxford DNB*'s editorial aims and conventions were set out in *Notes for Contributors*, a booklet sent to all authors, which went through several editions between 1994 and 1998. Articles begin with the *DNB*'s customary opening: immediately after the entry name, life dates, and occupational statement, an account is given of the person's birth, parentage, and other family information. They usually place personal relationships in their chronological location rather than (as in the *DNB*) at the end of the article, and the account of death and burial generally occurs at or near the end. Longer articles are divided by subheadings, and normally end with an account of the subject's posthumous reputation—that is, with a summary of the person's continuing and often changing significance, including reference to drama, novels, films, television, and other popular media. The *Oxford DNB* has followed the twentieth-century supplements, however, in not including a complete list of a person's published works within the account of the life. Now that library catalogues are so abundant and full, the comprehensive booklists valued by the Victorians are no longer required. Instead, contributors have been encouraged to bring out in the text the significance of the person's principal publications.

As for the supporting apparatus at the foot of each article, the aim has been that of the *DNB*: to make it 'an indispensable condition that writers should append to each article a full list of the sources whence their information was derived'.[25] However, the wider range of sources available by the 1990s required a fuller and more exact bibliographical description, and more avenues of research were by then available on which readers sought guidance. So the *Oxford DNB* provides not only bibliographical sources, but also other relevant material not necessarily used directly in compiling the article: lists of the person's archives (paper, sound, and film), likenesses, and records of wealth at death.

What Matthew called 'the grammar of a *New DNB* article' was thus established—as relevant for an early Welsh saint as for a recent businessman.[26] Within this framework the individual authorial voice was prized. In December 1995, in the first *Newsletter* distributed to contributors, Matthew expressed a fear that authors might be 'a little too conscious of the dignity of a *DNB* article'; it was 'important not to be *too* academic', he said, for liveliness was 'a vital ingredient of a *DNB* article'. Contributors should not hesitate to record 'their candid assessment' of their subject, and significant anecdote was welcomed.[27] The treatment of personal matters was to be frank (though not prurient): 'the memoir is not a panegyric'.[28] Here, as elsewhere, Matthew was carrying forward *DNB* practice into a new context. At the dinner for the contributors held by George Smith at the Hotel Metropole on 8 July 1897, Canon Ainger had described the *DNB*'s tone as 'no flowers, by request'.[29] His dictum applies as much to the new dictionary as to the old.

Editorial structure and procedure

The decision to publish the new dictionary as a single entity within twelve years brought significant editorial benefits. It would now be easier to maintain the *Dictionary*'s coherence because it would emerge from a single generation of contributors, editors, and staff. To the editors of the *Encyclopaedia Britannica*'s eleventh edition, even fourteen years (1875–89) had seemed 'an impossible system', preventing any one editor from seeing the project through and denying the volumes 'proper unity of conception or uniformity of treatment'.[30] Matthew was determined to avoid such dangers. The decision to publish the *Dictionary* only when it was complete had the effect of emancipating the writing phase from the tyranny of the alphabet which had governed the *DNB*'s preparation from 1882 to 1900. Instead, the text could be prepared through mounting a series of what were in effect subordinate research projects on specific areas of subject matter, whose subdivisions could be monitored by specialists.

For Matthew the project for the new dictionary constituted 'a formidable challenge to our generation'.[31] It required a carefully considered editorial structure. This he devised in consultation with Nick Wilson and Robert Faber, the project editor, who was Matthew's first appointment to the project staff. Matthew aimed to secure an appropriate specialist level of advice and editing for every article, to make the editorial responsibility for it clear to

both staff and contributors, and to prevent duplication of work. He began by dividing the subject matter (the existing *DNB* articles to be reassessed, and the spaces available for new subjects) into twelve research areas. Each was treated as a separate sub-project, operating according to a separate timetable within the overall project, and each was supervised by one consultant editor, appointed by the editor (the consultant editors are listed on page xxi). The consultant editor proposed to the editor a strategy for improving the area's coverage, and also for reviewing completed work.

All the people included in the new dictionary were assigned to areas, defined chronologically and thematically. Everyone included up to 1500 formed a single area. Thereafter Matthew placed some people in thematic areas for specialist attention: art and architecture, 1500–2000; literature, 1500–1779; literature, 1780–2000; business and the world of labour, 1500–2000; science, 1500–2000; and medicine, 1500–2000. The remainder were divided into five 'general' chronological areas, one for each century from the sixteenth to the twentieth. Matthew and his successor as editor acted as consultant editor for the nineteenth and twentieth centuries. In addition to consultant editors for the twelve subject areas, Matthew appointed two consultant editors with responsibility not for specific articles but for aspects of the edition as a whole. The consultant editor for women was appointed to prompt and review women's inclusion in all subject areas; the consultant editor for likenesses supervised the selection of all the images used as illustrations.

Soon after being appointed, Matthew consulted academic advisers about the *DNB*'s strengths and weaknesses. In the first months after the start of the project in September 1992 the focus was on detailed planning (including the appointment of consultant editors), on circulating announcements, and on soliciting suggestions for entries and offers to contribute. Tens of thousands of questionnaires were circulated to the memberships of learned societies and readers of journals, and were distributed widely at conferences and through correspondence; all suggestions were registered for further assessment by editors. Responses to the questionnaires helped to shape many of the early strategic decisions. During this initial period Matthew appointed the first project staff: in addition to the project editor (who became project director in 1997), these were the project secretary and personal assistant to the editor (January 1993) and the research director (May 1993). He also began recruiting additional temporary or part-time help from among Oxford's graduate students. Their intelligent interest and willingness to work on a great variety of tasks, from research to keying in data to filing, proved important in completing the *Dictionary*. In May 1993 the staff moved into 37A St Giles', a house owned by OUP, which was thenceforward the new dictionary's base. As Matthew sometimes observed, its location half way between the Bodleian Library and OUP's headquarters in Great Clarendon Street symbolized the project's dual nature, and the collaboration between scholarly and publishing concerns that was integral to it.

Research began in earnest in the second half of 1993 on three areas chosen for the contrasting academic and practical challenges that they posed: the general nineteenth-century area, pre-1500, and business and the world of labour. Work started on other areas in 1994 (science), 1995 (medicine), 1996 (literature, 1780–2000), 1997 (art and architecture, general eighteenth century, general twentieth century), and 1998 (general seventeenth century, general sixteenth century, and literature, 1500–1779).

Although refined over time, the organization of research was essentially the same in each area. At the start of work on an area, its consultant editor reviewed its *DNB* coverage and content, and recommended a structure for subdividing it into 'blocks': that is, into smaller groups of people who fell into broadly similar fields of activity. Matthew allocated an allowance of new spaces to each consultant editor, who then distributed them between blocks. The consultant editor recommended specialists as associate editors, subsequently appointed by Matthew, to advise on each block. There were eventually 373 associate editors, whose names appear on pages xxii–xxiii. They advised on blocks ranging from 6 to 500 articles (the average block comprised about 140 articles). Their initial responsibilities were: first, to review each *DNB* article in the block, and recommend whether it should be replaced by a newly written article, revised substantially, or revised more lightly; second, to propose new people for inclusion, from the associate editor's own expertise and through assessing all the relevant suggestions for introducing new people into the *Dictionary*; and third, for each article to be included, to recommend a contributor, a word allowance, and whether an illustration should be sought.

At the start of work on each research area, Matthew (together with the research and project directors and the relevant consultant editor) appointed one or more research editors as the in-house staff for that area. Each block was assigned to one associate editor for specialist academic advice, and to one research editor on the staff of the *Oxford DNB*. In some cases, a research editor had responsibility for all the blocks in an area; the blocks in larger areas were divided between two or three research editors. The average remit of each research editor covered between two thousand and three thousand articles. The research editors, generally post-doctoral research scholars with an appropriate specialism, were central to the whole process of commissioning, researching for, and writing the *Dictionary*. Each brought distinctive and widening contacts to the task, for which substantial organizational and diplomatic skills were essential. Their core duty was to pilot each article from the commissioning stage onwards until it met the *Oxford DNB*'s editorial standards. They sometimes also acted as associate editors for blocks where they had specific expertise, and they contributed many articles. In-house staff revised or wrote some 9 per cent of the *Oxford DNB*'s articles.

No *DNB* supplement existed to cover people who died between 1991 and 2000. Although the careers of most who died in that period had been pursued many years earlier, such articles carried to an extreme the difficulty of writing about the recent past, where scholarship is usually thinner and perspective relatively lacking. The editor, in his capacity as consultant editor for the twentieth century, assumed direct oversight of these articles, working with a research editor who was appointed in July 1998. The procedure for dealing with the recently deceased grew out of the system for consulting panels of advisers that had been established by the editors of the *DNB*'s supplements; but this was extended in scale, geography, and expertise. Many potential candidates were identified as 'possibles' for inclusion through drawing upon newspaper obituaries, specialist journals, and suggestions. These were sorted into occupational groups, and guidance on selection within them usually came from practitioners eminent in their field. The number of advisers for each group ranged from three to more than twenty, depending on the group's size and diversity, and the editor's decision was based on collating all the advice received. The *Dictionary*'s advisers on the recently deceased, numbering some 400, have not been named publicly and were unpaid, but their anonymity should not allow their important services to go unrecognized.

For twelve years the consultant editors, associate editors, and advisers on the recent past shaped the editorial effort, forming an indispensable network of judgement and expertise. The *Oxford DNB* and its readers owe much to their labours.

Writing the *Dictionary*

After receiving the advice of consultant and associate editors on every article, the decision to commission a contributor for each article was taken in house, and the editor signed every invitation. Word limits and *Notes for Contributors* provided necessary discipline, especially in ensuring that comparable people received comparable coverage. The editors did not view the lengths initially prescribed as final: where a good case for changing them was made, word allowances were often adjusted. In addition to the text of the article, contributors provided a list of the sources and other references to be printed beneath it. They were asked also to provide an abstract of the essential life details covered in the text, such as date and place of birth, education, death, and burial; this recorded (with commentary where necessary) the sources used for each of these key events, and enabled editors to ensure that such details were covered as fully and reliably as possible. The aim throughout, as in the *DNB*, was to secure clear presentation, conciseness, predictable scope, well-balanced treatment, and the clear separation of fact from interpretation or speculation.

When commissioned to revise rather than rewrite an article, the author was asked to check the *DNB* text for accuracy, remove archaisms, reinforce both text (especially in respect of core biographical data) and bibliography, and if possible provide information about the person's archives, likenesses, and wealth at death. A revision could, however, become a rewriting when this seemed justified. Some articles in recent supplements, especially those on people who had died since 1970, were carried over to the *Oxford DNB* largely in their existing form. In such cases the original authors were given the opportunity, where possible, to update their articles so as to enhance historical perspective and enable them to merge unobtrusively into the single alphabetical sequence that covered the whole of British history.

A central task of authors—whether of new articles, replacements for old articles, or revisions—was to summarize and clarify the latest state of knowledge. Many authors and editors drew upon the vast amount of manuscript material which had become available in print since the *DNB*'s day, and many could capitalize upon their years of relevant research. While preparing their articles, some were inspired to embark upon further, separately published, studies. Contributors' research was supplemented centrally from the project's own resources organized under the research director, Elizabeth Baigent. These mainly comprised documentation on standard life events. Searches for birth, marriage, and death certificates were undertaken in collaboration with the four General Register Offices: England and Wales (from 1837); Scotland (from 1855); Ireland and subsequently Northern Ireland and Éire (from 1864). In addition, searches of Scottish parish registers from 1553 were undertaken through the Scottish GRO. All these materials were routinely requested by and were provided to contributors, or were incorporated by the editors into articles after delivery.

Considerable effort was made centrally to enhance the new reference sections appended to each article. For archives, this involved searching the National Register of Archives, the British Library National Sound Archive, and the British Film Institute National Film and Television Archive. For likenesses, the scholarly catalogues of the chief national galleries were searched. An extensive survey of British records of wealth at death was conducted, using the published calendars for England and Wales (from 1858), Scotland (from 1876), and Ireland (1858–1922), and, from 1922, the calendars for Northern Ireland and Éire. Much of the information about wealth at death comes from these public documents. For earlier periods wills primarily from the courts of Canterbury, London, and York were obtained from the Public Record Office (now the National Archives); contributors also supplied information from secondary sources and private information. As with all documentary evidence, information about wealth at death requires careful interpretation: the *Dictionary*'s aim is simply to present what is found in the public records.

The lists of sources provided by contributors were dealt with differently from the other reference sections, and consist not of comprehensive bibliographies but of the materials used by the contributors and editors when preparing the article. The *Oxford DNB*'s bibliographical lists include sources ranging from archival records through published material of every variety to videos, oral history interviews, inscriptions on monuments, and websites. Almost half a million individual citations are provided in the *Dictionary* and every main article cites at least one source. The project's bibliographic editors aimed to verify citations, resolve discrepant versions of sources appearing many times, and impose a consistent scheme of abbreviation where this could simplify citations and save space. With help from a powerful computer program, they could compare groups of similar citations and, after detailed research, edit them collectively.

Once delivered, each article was reviewed by the research editor, who co-ordinated its further editorial scrutiny. Among the *Oxford DNB*'s most important features was its monitoring process, both from inside the project and from outside expert advisers. The associate editors read all the articles in their block, except where the *DNB* article needed only light revision. They were asked to indicate whether they thought the draft article a fair and up-to-date account of the person's life and work, whether it successfully combined specialist scholarship with accessibility to a non-specialist, and whether its bibliography adequately represented past and present scholarship. Articles longer than 1250 words were also reviewed by the consultant editor, and those over 3000 words by the editor himself. In the light of their comments and advice, changes were implemented either by the research editor in house, or by the contributor; this stage involved much co-operation between authors and editors. The research editor then submitted the article, together with its supporting material and comments, to the editor for approval of its content. Every article received this final scrutiny, which often resulted in further amendments. It was then 'passed for content' either by the editor or by the research director, who for this purpose deputized for the editor in some parts of the *Dictionary*. Editorial approval of content was the major gateway in the article's journey from writing to publication, and marked the end of the research phase.

The advent in the 1990s of email, whose use Matthew actively promoted within the project, made it much easier to build up the network of personal relationships between contributors and project staff. Throughout the project both editors sought to strengthen relations with contributors not only by signing invitations to contribute, but also by writing the postcard informing them that their articles had been approved for publication. Periodic newsletters, sent to all contributors from December 1995, kept the contributors in touch with the project. So also did the editor's monthly website messages, which appeared from June 2000, and the Oxford-based 'DNB seminars' held from January 2002.

In all, the names of 9804 authors appear as contributing new material to the *Oxford DNB*, either as writing new articles or as revising existing ones; a further 2746 authors' names are given as having written material for the *DNB* which now appears in revised form. A separately published *Index of Contributors* accompanies the *Dictionary*; it lists all contributors, together with details of the articles they wrote or revised. The scale of the contributors' effort should be acknowledged. They received only modest financial reward for each article; the fees were in the nature of honoraria and could not reflect the effort expended. The contributors' role was not confined to writing: they often suggested new names for inclusion, and frequently put the editors in touch with other scholars working in their field. Many served the *Dictionary* in ways that went far beyond any call of duty, especially those who came to its aid in autumn and winter 2001–2 by taking on as yet unwritten articles, thereby ensuring that the overall deadline would be met. Others gave valuable specialist help with formulating the editorial conventions applied throughout the text—on such issues as transliteration, and the names of institutions, events, and places. To those whose contributions amounted to at least fifty articles or 50,000 words, and to others who undertook long-term research projects for the *Dictionary*, the editors offered the title of 'research associate'; their names are gratefully listed on page xxv. The new dictionary was, in short, a worldwide collaborative venture whose planning and execution involved a two-way traffic in ideas.

Selecting the images

In recommending the inclusion of images, Matthew diverged from the *DNB* in practice but not in spirit. In the 1880s it would have been difficult to include reproductions of likenesses on any large scale, he felt, 'both for technical printing reasons and because portrait research was at a very elementary stage'. None the less, the *DNB* had given 'as much visual information as it could about subjects, short of actually printing an image', through quoting descriptions of their physical appearance as a standard item and by providing much information about the character and location of their portraits. So the new dictionary's policy would be 'a natural extension of the first *DNB*'s approach to the definition of a subject's individuality'.[32]

In 1995 Peter Funnell of the National Portrait Gallery was appointed consultant editor for likenesses. Responsible to the *Dictionary*'s editor for policy and practice in selecting 10,000 images, he and two academic picture researchers based at the Gallery (listed on page xxiv) undertook a project that ran in parallel with the editorial work in Oxford. 'We have the opportunity of creating a national iconography', he wrote, 'and it is an opportunity which should be embraced with great excitement.'[33] The editor and research director identified the articles which would (if feasible) be illustrated, so that the selection of illustrations would reflect the *Dictionary*'s editorial aims, not the availability of images. There were two particular requirements: first, that the *Oxford DNB* should include images of the more familiar figures in the national past for whom readers would expect illustrations; and second, that new emphases within the *Dictionary* should be reinforced by highlighting some of the newly included—for example, people from the regions of the British Isles and British territories overseas, people in business, and women.

Each article chosen for illustration was to receive only one image (see Table 3 below). In selecting likenesses, the first objective was to ensure authenticity by establishing that the portrait did indeed represent the person intended. In the case of painted portraits, the aim was to locate the prime version—the original portrait done from the life—falling back on a contemporary version if documented, and only in exceptional cases settling for a later copy. Where there were several types of representation to choose from (paintings, photographs, prints, and sculpture, for example), selection reflected several considerations. Where possible, likenesses were chosen from the time of life when the persons concerned were most active in the role that had justified their inclusion in the *Dictionary*; named artists were usually preferred to the unknown; the work of the best artists was chosen above the inferior; and in some cases the rare image was preferred to the familiar. Caricatures were avoided. The likenesses reproduced in the *Dictionary* were to be 'visually rich as well as informative',[34] so selections were not restricted to head-and-shoulder or half-length studies. Full-length portraits were chosen where these seemed more revealing. Costume, background, accessories, and period stylization were seen, along with likeness, as part of what 'constitutes the portrait as a representation of a given individual'.[35] Consequently the reproductions included in the *Dictionary* show in almost all cases the complete original composition.

Lists of the articles selected by the editor and research director in Oxford for illustration were sent to Funnell's team. Suitable images were then sought, and a final recommendation of a single likeness was made. The editor accepted the team's recommendations with very few exceptions. Continuous monitoring ensured that the balance of likenesses reflected the *Dictionary*'s new emphases for inclusion of subjects. Contributors provided information about likenesses, and this was sent regularly to the picture researchers; the information proved most fruitful where authors had access to private information about images that was not available in the usual scholarly resources. Research and selection of images began in 1996 and was completed on schedule in March 2002. Half the images came from the National Portrait Gallery's own collections, or from collections administered by them, and the rest from many other sources—ranging from major galleries and museums to much smaller collections, specialist societies, and private individuals. Separate research was undertaken to select images for subjects active before 1500, and this secured different types of iconographic material, including coins, effigies, stained-glass windows, and illustrated manuscripts.

Clearing rights and obtaining original photographic materials from which to reproduce images from non-Gallery sources constituted a major task, which was undertaken as a sub-project from September 2000 by the Gallery's picture library team. The later stages were completed by the *Dictionary*'s administrative staff, who also managed the design, scanning, and final approval of the 10,057 images published, finishing in March 2003. In all, some 1500 rights-holders gave permission for likenesses to be reproduced. The *Dictionary* is deeply indebted to all rights-holders for their co-operation and generosity.

Research by the National Portrait Gallery's team illuminated the Gallery's own collection, as well as the complexity of the relationship between historically noteworthy activity, celebrity, and portraiture.

Organization and staff

The challenge confronting Matthew was not only scholarly but organizational. Like the *DNB*, the *Oxford DNB* was planned as an integrated writing and publishing venture. Newcomers to the project were routinely reminded that the central task was still, in the new venture, the same as it had been in the old: to persuade the right people to write the selected articles in the desired manner. Personal relationships remained of central importance within an inevitably complex administrative structure. But whereas late-Victorian intellectual life flourished within a relatively tight London-based world of gentlemanly leisure, co-ordinated through the London clubs and informal associations, the new dictionary operated within a much wider, international world of professional scholarship conducted mainly through universities. Co-ordination on a larger scale was now needed if a dictionary nearly twice the size of George Smith's *DNB* was to be produced in little more than half the time by fifteen times as many contributors distributed worldwide.

The publishing process also posed fundamental questions for OUP. Encouraged by the *Oxford English Dictionary*'s success when it was published on CD-ROM in 1992, plans for the *Oxford DNB* from 1993 envisaged publication in both printed and electronic forms. Yet in a period of rapid technological change, nobody could predict exactly how the *Dictionary* would best be published twelve years hence; nor could OUP wait until the entire text had been written before preparing it for publication. The strategy decided upon in 1992–4 was at that time ambitious: to prepare the new dictionary's material so that it could be used to produce any future form of publication, and to ensure that after 2004 the contents could be continuously corrected and expanded. No longer could it be allowed to suffer the *DNB*'s fate of cumulating decay. The text would first be edited, keyed, proofread, and stored in a permanent electronic form that could be edited within the project. Versions of it could later be produced for publication in whatever form required.

In planning the project's administrative structure, a complete view of the publishing cycle had to be taken: from first considering a person for inclusion in the *Dictionary* to completing the individual article and from there to producing a complete set of articles for publication. Central to the work was the project's database. Conceived by Robert Faber, it was designed and built by specialist OUP computing teams, who from 1998 formed a dedicated technology group on the project staff. As with the *Dictionary*'s administration in general, the database was designed to achieve three aims: to clarify the sequence of tasks and decisions from which the completed article emerged; to remove routine tasks from editors and specialist staff; and to make all the necessary information, including the entire *Dictionary* text, immediately available to everyone within the project. From 1992 database records were kept of every individual who had been included in the *DNB* and of every new candidate proposed for inclusion; the database helped staff to perform and monitor every subsequent stage of work. Each of the *Dictionary*'s 50,000 articles could be seen as an individual project—to be commissioned, delivered, edited, approved, and prepared for publication at the same time as thousands of other articles were proceeding through every stage in their journey towards publication.

The *Dictionary*'s text was an integral part of the database. OUP had keyed the *Concise DNB*'s articles in electronic form to create the consolidated print edition published in 1992, and when the new project began these texts were used to set up the initial database records for each person in the *DNB*. This made a brief digest of the *DNB*'s articles readily accessible to staff while the subject matter of the new dictionary was being sorted into research areas. The 33 million words of the complete *DNB* (including the supplements) were rekeyed for the new project from November 1992, so that from late in 1993 this text too could be incorporated into the database. It enabled staff to read, group, and print out any *DNB* articles that were needed for editorial review or for sending to contributors; this facility greatly accelerated assessment and commissioning. It also enabled OUP to prepare an electronic version of the *DNB* on CD-ROM, from which valuable lessons were learned about how to present biographical material in that form. From 1997 *Oxford DNB* text was also entered into the database, forming the primary version of completed material from which printed and electronic editions could later be prepared. Multiple forms of publication were made possible by the design and implementation of electronic coding; unlike traditional typesetting methods, this procedure remained within editorial control throughout. The coding was used to identify not only typographical appearance, but particular aspects of content, and it enabled detailed searching of text both by editors within the project and eventually also by readers of electronic editions.

Matthew had highlighted in his report of April 1993 the central importance of computer technology for completing the project. Immediate electronic access to both text and administrative information was essential to his strategy of research by subject area rather than by alphabet. Not only could previous texts be extracted from the alphabetical run: new texts could be entered, in any order, as and when articles were completed, and editors could survey the accumulating mosaic of the new dictionary when addressing its special editorial problems. Like the *Dictionary* itself, these problems were unusual in scale. First, given that the *Oxford DNB* covered the whole of British history, it had to accommodate all the requirements specific to detailed biographical research in every subject area and period. Second, inconsistencies of treatment between different fields of research, rendered more visible by modern electronic searching, frequently posed substantial academic questions. These could be solved only through close collaboration between production and research staff. Because the accumulated material remained manipulable in the database until shortly before publication, conventions could be revised at a late stage in the publication process, with access to much of the completed dictionary—an opportunity which few editors of previous large-scale works had enjoyed.

Such a structure of sequential but interlocking concerns called for staff who were both expert in their respective fields and willing to collaborate on the broader aims of the work. The project's full-time staff (listed on page xxiv) was divided formally between research staff, who were employees of the University of Oxford funded by OUP and the British Academy, and publishing staff employed by OUP. Yet both groups operated as a single project under the direction of the editor, who had oversight of both editorial and production concerns. In this he worked closely with the project director, whose role from start to finish was to manage the project's organization and resources, and to oversee its publication. At its greatest extent, in 2002, the project employed fifty-one people (twenty-nine University and twenty-two OUP staff) on a full-time basis, as well as up to a hundred freelance, part-time, and temporary staff (listed on page xxvi). The research director was responsible for overall research policy and university staffing matters. In addition to the research editors, whose numbers rose to twenty-three at the height of the work in 2001–2, the research staff included a research co-ordinator and two bibliographic editors. The research co-ordinator organized the central provision of research materials to contributors and staff, and later the retrospective editing of reference lists, while the bibliographic editors focused on standardizing citations in the lists of sources. From 2001 one research editor assumed additional responsibility, as publication editor, for organizing the research side of the overall editing process in its later stages.

The publishing staff, working under the project director, consisted of four groups overseen by the publishing administrator (responsible for all aspects of the *Dictionary*'s administration), the chief copy-editor (responsible for editorial conventions and their implementation through copy-editing and proofreading), the data manager (responsible for the structure of the *Dictionary*'s electronic data and its implementation through setting the text), and the technology manager (responsible for building and maintaining the project's information systems to specifications agreed with staff). The administrative and secretarial teams backed up both the research and production staff at every stage and provided contributors with an important point of contact. They organized the flow of work, tracked the progress of articles, and gathered illustrations; with each of the 50,000 articles passing through their hands at least ten times, they had to confront the demands involved in archiving all the project's materials in the 600 metres of filing that embody the *Dictionary*'s history.

The sequence of production

Once the editor had approved the individual article for content, it passed from research into production: that is, into its preparation for publication through copy-editing, typesetting, proofreading, and correction. Within the general framework that Matthew had established, research staff were generally concerned with the balance of coverage and the adequacy of articles individually and in smaller groups, whereas production staff focused more on integrating the separate articles into a consistent and efficient work of reference.

The definition of editorial practice began early in the project. At that point, research and publishing staff established conventions for those aspects of the material (such as names, titles, vital dates, occupations, and standard facts) that had to be consistently presented for people in all walks of life from the fourth century BC to the twentieth century AD. Working with the editors and outside specialist advisers, the chief copy-editor and her team of editorial managers articulated historical conventions, nomenclature, and orthography to meet the special requirements of each newly launched research area. The editorial managers supervised more than twenty professional freelance copy-editors who usually worked from home, though in the later stages some were based in house. Their task extended beyond the usual duties of correcting errors: they helped to implement editorial policy. Questions of content (for example, apparent inconsistency within an article or between related articles, newly encountered specialist usage in particular types of article, or obscure phrasing) were at first referred to research editors and then where necessary to contributors. Once copy-editing was finished, the editorial preparation of an article was complete.

The article was then 'captured' in electronic form under the control of the data management group. The texts of the articles were sent to Pondicherry in India in monthly batches to be keyed by the same company which during 1992–3 had keyed the text of the *DNB*. During keyboarding, operators both transcribed the edited text and introduced tags (or machine-readable codes) to identify some of its aspects. Tagging had a threefold aim: to identify material for particular typographic treatment when the text was printed out or displayed on screen; to identify particular categories of information (such as names, dates, and places) so that editors and readers could search for them in the electronic version; and to enable automated checking of material, whereby staff could ensure that articles were correctly identified and contained all necessary components. Almost 7 million tags were inserted into 55 million words of text. This material was then returned to Oxford on magnetic tape and was copied into the database.

Meanwhile the supporting materials for each article— the lists of sources and references, and the abstract of life events which contributors had submitted with their article texts—had been keyed directly into the database at the project office in Oxford by part-time staff. The software developed by the project's technical staff enabled the keyboarders to insert the necessary coding around each element of information. This coding complemented the codes applied in the text, and made it possible later to conduct detailed searching, cross-checking, and re-editing. When all components of the article had been captured in the database, proofs were sent to its contributor, who was asked to review editorial changes. A proof-reading team of between twenty and thirty professional freelances then collated amendments, checked tagging, and ensured that editorial conventions had been observed. Copy-editing and proofreading required frequent consultation between the research and production sides of the project. The article then went through successive stages of correction and checking until all changes had been approved and its production was complete.

As the database grew, staff reviewed editorial practice across the entire *Dictionary*. From 2001 a programme of retrospective editing was carried out to detect inconsistencies, to redefine standards for particular components of the entries, and to reassess some policies in response to feedback from inside and outside the project. At this stage, all the project's members collaborated closely on such tasks as standardizing the forms and presentation of names, titles, vital dates, occupational statements, place names, institutional names, religious affiliations, and references to published and other works. Purpose-built software, used in conjunction with the tags inserted into the text, enabled a small team of staff to apply decisions across large groups of articles in final preparation for publication.

Progress of the project, 1992–2004

'Our purpose is to match the legendary timetable of the first *DNB*', wrote Matthew in 1994, urging contributors to keep to their deadlines.[36] Geared from the outset to publication in 2004, the *Oxford DNB* rested upon a stable but adjustable overall plan, and advanced to publication through five main phases. In the first of these, during 1992–3, suggestions were gathered from many quarters, the editorial and project plans were completed, and the *DNB*'s entire text was entered into the project database.

The second phase, from September 1993 to the end of 1996, saw the main lines of work established. The first research editors started work in September 1993. Matthew had approved fewer than 900 articles by December 1994, but 12,000 by December 1996. Copy-editing began in 1994 with decisions on editorial conventions, by 1995 the freelance copy-editors were at work and the administrative structure was in place, and in 1996 picture research at the National Portrait Gallery began. The project staff grew from four early in 1993 to twenty-four by December 1996. The editorial system was now tried and tested, and the *Dictionary* was on course, but it needed more staff than had at first been anticipated. By May 1996 a revised project plan—the first to rest on experience of the research process—had been approved by the delegates of OUP and by the project's Supervisory Committee.

The third phase, from 1997 to 2002, brought significant acceleration. By March 1997 fewer than half the *Dictionary*'s 50,000 articles had been started, of which contributors had delivered 16,400. With the start of all the remaining research areas, the number of commissions accepted by contributors rose to a peak of 1000 a month between August and October 1998, and by spring 1999 the number of articles delivered had risen to 750 a month. Research editors moved between neighbouring research areas as one area closed down and another opened up, thereby diffusing experience within the project. With the start of capture and proofing in January 1997, production speeded up until material was simultaneously moving through every stage of production. Furthermore, with up to 1000 articles a month being entered in the database, the completed material was now itself becoming an aid to creating the new dictionary. In nearly six years between April 1997 and the end of 2002, more than half the *Dictionary* was started, more than 70 per cent approved by the editor, and its entire content captured in the project database. Staff numbers rose to a peak of fifty-one in autumn 2001, partly reflecting the formation of a dedicated technology group. In 1998–2000 this group renovated the project's information systems and began developing the new facilities required to finish the editing.

Colin Matthew's sudden death from a heart attack, on 29 October 1999, shook the project. The unexpected loss of its driving force might have been expected to stall the whole enterprise. Yet so successful had Matthew been in fostering confidence in the new dictionary and in planning its progress, that its staff, advisers, and contributors were able to maintain its momentum. At that point every area of research (including picture research) had been launched and reviewed, and contributors had delivered 35,000 articles; of these, the editor had approved 31,600, and 20,000 were already lodged in the database. Robert Faber led the team while a new editor was being appointed, and ensured that daily work continued virtually uninterrupted. The University and OUP then invited Brian Harrison—a tutorial fellow at Corpus Christi College, Oxford, and a historian of nineteenth- and twentieth-century Britain—to succeed Matthew. He took up his new duties on 17 January 2000. A further revised (and final) project plan, approved in the following November, was informed by extensive experience of production as well as of research, and the project was eventually completed within its provisions. The editor approved the text of the last article on 30 September 2002, as planned.

The project's fourth phase, the effort to finish the work, overlapped with the regular editing of articles between 1999 and 2003. From 1999 editorial and bibliographic staff started to reconcile discrepancies across the entire dictionary. Writing and editing reached their final stages in 2002. During the six months to March 2003, work reached a peak in all areas of production, and the final thousands of articles were captured and proofread. The project's administrators secured original images and rights to reproduce several thousand illustrations. In collaboration with the National Portrait Gallery team, editors produced the captions and credits for the images that were to be included in the edition. Technical preparations included creating and checking cross-references and other data, and settling the alphabetical ordering of articles. In January 2003 contributors had a final opportunity to see their articles on the project website, a process which brought in much new information that had become available since the articles had been completed. On 25 March 2003 the entire text was sent, with all the images, for final typesetting.

The last phase was publication. Starting early in 2002, the project's technology group, working with research and production staff, created a working prototype of an online edition. This made it possible to gather the views of many librarians and readers on how best to present the *Dictionary* in electronic form, and to specify the final online edition in late 2003. Meanwhile OUP staff completed typographic designs in 2002, and the *Dictionary*'s encoded data enabled the typesetters within two months to produce page proofs of its 60,000 text pages. From April to September 2003 a team of more than seventy freelance proofreaders, together with the project's research staff, read the entire text, which was then returned in corrected form to the typesetters in October. Project staff checked second and final page proofs from November 2003 to February 2004. Printing began on 8 January 2004.

Outcomes

'Facts and figures are in accord with the spirit of the Dictionary', wrote Lee, looking back in 1900 at the goal that had been reached 'after eighteen years of unremitting labour'.[37] We can now stand back from the *DNB*, its supplements, and the *Oxford DNB* and view them as a single, cumulating enterprise. Three main aspects of the new dictionary can appropriately be quantified here: its scope (lives covered in comparison with the *DNB*, and images included), the scale of its text, and the composition of its contributor network.

The 54,922 lives covered in the *Oxford DNB* (in 50,113 substantive articles) represent an increase of 16,315 over the 38,607 lives included in the entire *DNB*. The additions include 1897 lives of those who died between 1991 and 2000. The *Dictionary*'s chronological range is shown in Table 1. The earliest person included lived in the fourth century BC; the latest, by date of decease, died on 26 December 2000.

The number of women in the *Oxford DNB* who either receive articles in their own right or appear as co-subjects in articles on groups, families, or other individuals (see Table 2) has risen from 1758 in the *DNB* to 5627 in the *Oxford DNB*, and women comprise nearly a quarter of the newly included lives. Their proportion reaches a peak in the twentieth century, where they account for 18 per cent of all lives and 28 per cent of new entrants.

Table 3 shows the distribution of the 10,057 articles which are accompanied by images, by period, in relation to the total number of lives.

TABLE 1 Individual lives in the *DNB* and *Oxford DNB*, by year of death

years	DNB	added (% increase)	Oxford DNB
400–1 BC	4	7 (175)	11
AD 1–100	3	24 (800)	27
101–200	2	13 (650)	15
201–300	4	5 (125)	9
301–400	4	9 (225)	13
401–500	27	25 (93)	52
501–600	78	39 (50)	117
601–700	130	51 (39)	181
701–800	99	77 (78)	176
801–900	63	37 (59)	100
901–1000	75	33 (44)	108
1001–1100	175	41 (23)	216
1101–1200	386	178 (46)	564
1201–1300	552	267 (48)	819
1301–1400	691	363 (53)	1054
1401–1500	687	459 (67)	1146
1501–1600	2079	604 (29)	2683
1601–1700	5929	1317 (22)	7246
1701–1800	6022	1789 (30)	7811
1801–1900	13931	2845 (20)	16776
1901–2000	7666	8132 (106)	15798
TOTAL	38607	16315 (42)	54922

TABLE 2 Lives of women in the *DNB* and *Oxford DNB*, by year of death

years	DNB (% of all lives)	added	Oxford DNB (% of all lives)
400 BC–AD 500	2 (5)	5	7 (6)
501–1000	37 (8)	24	61 (9)
1001–1500	64 (3)	166	230 (6)
1501–1600	50 (2)	98	148 (6)
1601–1700	118 (2)	268	386 (5)
1701–1800	232 (4)	315	547 (7)
1801–1900	716 (5)	688	1404 (8)
1901–2000	539 (7)	2305	2844 (18)
TOTAL	1758 (5)	3869	5627 (10)

TABLE 3 Images in the *Oxford DNB*, by year of death

years	total lives	images (% of lives)
pre-1501	4608	191 (4)
1501–1600	2683	216 (8)
1601–1700	7246	869 (12)
1701–1800	7811	1188 (15)
1801–1900	16776	3026 (18)
1901–2000	15798	4567 (29)
TOTAL	54922	10057 (18)

As for the scale of the publication, the *Oxford DNB* contains 55 million words of text, and a further 7 million words of bibliographical and other references. Together with the images, about 200,000 words of captions, and an additional 130,000 words in cross-reference entries, the present sixty-volume printed edition comprises a total of 60,305 pages of dictionary text containing 62.5 million words (excluding the preliminary pages and picture credits found in each volume). The longest articles in the *Dictionary* have more than 30,000 words, and the shortest has fewer than 30; the average text is 1087 words. Nearly 29,000 articles provide information on archival deposits, a similar number list information about likenesses, and nearly 27,000 contain data on wealth at death.

Of the 38,607 persons whose lives appear in the *DNB* and its supplements, 36,589 now receive their own article in the *Oxford DNB*, while 2018 appear as subsidiary notices forming part of another article.[38] Four additional 'genealogical' articles in the *DNB* have matching family articles in the *Oxford DNB*.[39] So a total of 36,593 *Oxford DNB* articles take as their main subject lives or families previously included in the *DNB*. Of these, 22,879 (63 per cent) have been newly written for the *Oxford DNB* (including a few reworked by the original *DNB* contributor); 13,714 of them (37 per cent) have been revised. To the 22,879 newly written articles on *DNB* subjects have been added 13,520 new articles whose main subject was not in the *DNB*: this produces a total of 36,399 newly written articles in the *Oxford DNB*. The newly written articles represent nearly three-quarters of the new dictionary, and roughly match the number of articles contained in the entire *DNB*, including its supplements. In addition to the main articles on individuals, families, and groups, 9294 cross-reference entries direct readers from an alternative name to the name under which a person has been entered. Such entries are included for all individuals who feature as co-subjects within another article.

The geographical spread of the *Dictionary*'s contributors is illuminated by the project's records of postal addresses in March 2004. At that time, of the 9804 authors whose names appear as writers or revisers of material for the *Oxford DNB*, nearly three-quarters were based in the British Isles: 7026 in the United Kingdom and 252 in Ireland. Another 2526 contributors were recorded in forty-nine other countries: 1396 in the United States, and 391 in Canada; 302 in Australia, and 88 in New Zealand; then 52 in Germany, 50 in France, 32 in South Africa, 31 in Italy, 16 in India, and 12 in Japan; a total of 96 were based in countries in Europe other than those already mentioned, while 60 were in twenty other countries in the rest of the world.

The *Oxford DNB* has throughout been conceived as a national and international endeavour. Public funds helped to launch the research process in 1992. The continuous growth of the work has been made possible by the steadfast commitment of the delegates and senior officers of OUP, and of the relevant authorities in the British Academy and the University of Oxford; all these bodies were represented on the Supervisory Committee which guided the project throughout. The contribution of the National Portrait Gallery and of many other owners of images has already been gratefully acknowledged. In organizing the central work of the project, the editors have received generous help from numerous institutions and scholarly projects. These included the Royal Society, and the General Register Offices, archival authorities, and others already mentioned. Over a decade of research, however, so many others helped the editors in every way—from providing suggestions, to answering queries, to lending books—that it would be impossible to name them all.

These obligations, however, reflect only a small fraction of the support which has sustained the project in its widest sense. The advisory editors and contributors were drawn from practically every research and higher-education institution in Britain, from many such overseas, and from many archives, galleries, museums, societies, professional institutions, and companies—as well as from individuals with a purely private interest in scholarship. In turn, they drew upon the resources of an international network of research and public libraries, record offices, and other archives. The sheer scale of the help received in creating the *Oxford DNB* is therefore to be found threaded throughout the nearly half a million source references given by contributors in their articles.

Nobody who has been involved with the new dictionary believes it to be free from errors and gaps, and we who have created it accept responsibility for its defects. 'That there are errors in the Dictionary,' wrote Lee, 'those who have been most closely associated with its production are probably more conscious than other people.'[40] Matthew felt that the creators of what became the *Oxford DNB* should not seek perfection, for that would hinder completion: only through publication could the project's labours benefit readers. The *Oxford DNB*'s defects will gradually be corrected after September 2004 in response to changes in evidence, interpretation, and priorities. No longer does a century need to elapse before such improvements can be made. After 2004 it will, for the first time in its history, be continually refined and amplified in its online edition and printed supplements, and will gain further strength from the collaboration with readers and contributors which has moulded the *Dictionary* since its inception in 1882.

My predecessor, Colin Matthew, receives his own article in the *Oxford DNB*, but it needs to be said here that he had the vision, courage, and energy in 1992 to undertake a huge task, and early in his time as editor his recommendations prompted several difficult but crucial decisions that have subsequently been vindicated. His death was a tragedy for the entire project, but all who have worked on the *Dictionary* take pride and pleasure in its completion according to the specification and the timetable that he laid down.

BRIAN HARRISON

Oxford, March 2004

Notes

1   For a fuller account, see R. Faber and B. Harrison, 'The *Dictionary of National Biography*: a publishing history', *Lives in print: biography and the book trade from the middle ages to the 21st century,* ed. R. Myers, M. Harris, and G. Mandelbrote (2002), 171–92.

2   S. Lee, 'The Dictionary of National Biography: a statistical account', *Dictionary of National Biography*, 63 vols. (1885–1900), vol. 63, p. viii.

3   Numbers given here are based on analysis of the entire *DNB* text. They differ marginally from those given by Lee in his 'Statistical account', where the totals given are '27,195 . . . full substantive articles' supplying 'notices of 29,120 men and women' (Lee, 'Statistical account', x).

4   Lee, 'Statistical account', xv; but cf. G. Fenwick, *The contributors' index to the 'Dictionary of National Biography', 1885–1901* (1989), xxi.

5   Lee, 'Statistical account', v.

6   *Brief lives*, selected by Colin Matthew (1997); *Stage and screen lives*, selected by Michael Billington (2001); *Literary lives*, selected by John Sutherland (2001); *Political lives*, selected by Hugo Young (2001); *Secret lives*, selected by M. R. D. Foot (2002); *Musical lives*, selected by Nicholas Kenyon (2002); *Royal lives*, selected by Frank Prochaska (2002); and *Military lives*, selected by Hew Strachan (2002).

7   Faber and Harrison, 'The *Dictionary of National Biography*', 181.

8   H. C. G. Matthew, 'Editor's preliminary report', 29 June 1992, Oxford DNB archives, 2.

9   Lee, 'Statistical account', v.

10 H. C. G. Matthew, *Leslie Stephen and the 'New Dictionary of National Biography'* (1997), 37.

11 Quoted in Matthew, *Leslie Stephen*, 37.

12 For a fuller discussion of editorial priorities since 1882, see B. Harrison, 'The D.N.B. and comparative biography', *Comparative Criticism*, 25 (2003), 3–24.

13 H. C. G. Matthew, 'Editor's report', April 1993, Oxford DNB archives, 1, 16–17.

14 C. Matthew, 'How far have we got?', New Dictionary of National Biography, *Newsletter*, no. 1 (Dec 1995), 2.

15 Matthew, 'Editor's report', 9–10.

16 Matthew, 'Editor's report', 3.

17 H. C. G. Matthew, 'Dictionaries of national biography', *National biographies & national identity*, ed. I. McCalman, with J. Parvey and M. Cook (1996), 4.

18 Lee, 'Statistical account', x, xi.

19 Matthew, 'Editor's report', 15.

20 See Faber and Harrison, 'The *Dictionary of National Biography*', 176, 182–3.

21 J. Garnett, 'Women and gender in the *New DNB*', New Dictionary of National Biography, *Newsletter*, no. 1 (Dec 1995), 3.

22 Matthew, 'Editor's report', 9.

23 New Dictionary of National Biography, *Notes for contributors* (1994), 2.

24 Matthew, 'Editor's report', 6.

25 Lee, 'Statistical account', viii.

26 C. Matthew, 'Further down the road', New Dictionary of National Biography, *Newsletter*, no. 2 (Dec 1996), 1.

27 Matthew, 'How far have we got?', 2.

28 *Notes for contributors*, 8.

29 *The Times* (9 July 1897), 9.

30 'Editorial introduction', *Encyclopaedia Britannica*, 11th edn (1910–11), vol. 1, p. xii.

31 Matthew, *Leslie Stephen*, 37.

32 Matthew, 'Editor's report', 7.

33 P. Funnell, 'Report on a policy for likenesses', December 1995, Oxford DNB archives, 2; see also P. Funnell, 'National Portrait Gallery begins research on likenesses', New Dictionary of National Biography, *Newsletter*, no. 2 (Dec 1996), 2–3.

34 Funnell, 'Report on a policy for likenesses', 4.

35 Funnell, 'Report on a policy for likenesses', 5.

36 *Notes for contributors*, 29.

37 Lee, 'Statistical account', v.

38 Articles included in the *DNB* do not correspond in every case with those included in the *Oxford DNB* because scholars have revised their identification of some historical figures, and because the editors have changed the distribution of full and subsidiary lives.

39 There were ten such genealogical articles in the *DNB*, though Lee noted only five ('Statistical account', xi). The six entries not retained have been replaced by cross-reference entries, as the subsidiary subjects they included now appear elsewhere in the *Oxford DNB*.

40 Lee, 'Statistical account', xxii.

ASSOCIATE EDITORS

Simon Adams
Geoffrey Alderman
Richard Aldrich
Brian Allen
Brigid Allen
J. D. Alsop
Donna T. Andrew
Michael Armitage
John Armstrong
R. M. Armstrong
Alan Atkinson
G. E. Aylmer
Paul G. Bahn
Elizabeth Baigent
J. H. Baker
Malcolm Baker
William Baker
Stephen Banfield
Hannah Barker
Toby Barnard
Robert Bartlett
D. W. Bebbington
Ian F. W. Beckett
Victor Belcher
James Belich
Alan Bell
Gary M. Bell
Michael Beloff
J. A. Bennett
John Benson
Jonathan Benthall
G. R. Berridge
Virginia Berridge
Michael Bevan
Paul Bew
Michael Billington
Tom Bingham
William Birken
Virginia H. Blain
John Blair
Brian Bond
Mark Haworth-Booth
Brian Bowers
Roger Bowers
Gail Braybon
Francis J. Bremer
Martin Brett
Christopher Breward
John Broad
W. H. Brock

Christopher W. Brooks
Jane Brown
Judith M. Brown
Keith M. Brown
Robert Brown
Janet Browne
Phillip Buckner
Michael Burden
Arthur Burns
Colin Burrow
Martin Butler
Perry Butler
Duncan Bythell
John W. Cairns
Ian Campbell
J. Campbell
Bernard Capp
Christine Carpenter
Philip Carter
E. H. Chalus
Muriel E. Chamberlain
J. A. I. Champion
S. D. Chapman
Olive Checkland
John Childs
Wendy R. Childs
Ian Christie
Tony Claydon
Timothy Clayton
Malcolm Coe
Thomas Cogswell
Patrick Collinson
Howard Colvin
R. V. Comerford
Harold J. Cook
J. P. D. Cooper
Thomas N. Corns
Pietro Corsi
Marios Costambeys
J. Mordaunt Crook
David Crouch
Valentine Cunningham
M. C. Curthoys
Martin Daunton
R. G. Davies
R. R. Davies
John Davis
Adrian Desmond
H. T. Dickinson
R. B. Dobson

Thomas Donnelly
J. D. Douglas
A. A. M. Duncan
Marguerite W. Dupree
T. M. Charles-Edwards
Judy Egerton
Simon Eliot
Steven G. Ellis
Todd M. Endelman
Chris Evans
Kelvin Everest
Mordechai Feingold
Kenneth Fincham
Richard Fisher
Mary Fissell
David Fitzpatrick
Alan Ford
Richard Foulkes
Robin Frame
Peter France
Michael Freeden
I. Gadd
Denis Galligan
Jane Garnett
David Gates
Perry Gauci
Ian J. Gentles
Faye Getz
Mark Goldie
Julian Goodare
Eleanor Gordon
Warwick Gould
Alexander Grant
Douglas Gray
A. H. M. Kirk-Greene
Jack P. Greene
F. E. C. Gregory
Jeremy Gregory
Joseph Gross
R. Geraint Gruffydd
I. Grattan-Guinness
P. M. S. Hacker
D. R. Hainsworth
David J. Hall
Paul Hammond
June Hannam
Peter H. Hansen
Bob Harris
Tim Harris
Brian Harrison

Mark Harrison
Henry Mayr-Harting
R. R. K. Hartmann
Barbara F. Harvey
Adrian Hastings
Tony Hayter
D. W. Hayton
Felicity Heal
Mary Heimann
R. H. Helmholz
Simon Heneage
Cynthia B. Herrup
Richard Davenport-Hines
Derek Hirst
Daire Hogan
Peter Holman
Clive Holmes
J. C. Holt
Richard Holt
Tony Honoré
David Hopkins
Anthony Howard
Janet Howarth
Gerald M. D. Howat
David Howell
David Howlett
Pat Hudson
Ann Hughes
E. W. Ives
R. D. S. Jack
Geraint H. Jenkins
Ieuan Gwynedd Jones
Alon Kadish
David S. Katz
Jacqueline M. Kavanagh
N. H. Keeble
M. H. Keen
Gary Kelly
James Kelly
Simon Keynes
Matthew Kilburn
James Kirk
Peter G. Lake
Susan Lambert
William Lamont
Paul Langford
Eleri Larkum
Vivienne Larminie
Christopher Lawrence
Susan C. Lawrence

PROJECT STAFF

Project editor/Project director
Robert Faber, *1992–2004*

RESEARCH

Research director

Elizabeth Baigent, *1993–2003*

Research editors

R. M. Armstrong, *1998–2000*
P. R. S. Baker, *2000–2002*
Michael Bevan, *1995–2003*
Troy O. Bickham, *2000–2001*
Robert Brown, *1993–2003*
Alan Bryson, *2001–2003*
Philip Carter, *1997–2004*
   and Publication editor, *2001–2004*
M. Clare Loughlin-Chow, *1996–2000*
J. P. D. Cooper, *1998–2001*
Marios Costambeys, *1994–1997*
C. A. Creffield, *1996–1998*

M. C. Curthoys, *1993–2004*
I. Gadd, *2000–2002*
Joseph Gross, *1994–1997*
Mary Heimann, *1996–1997*
Matthew Kilburn, *1999–2004*
Eleri Larkum, *1998–2003*
Vivienne Larminie, *1998–2004*
Anita McConnell, *1994–2003*
Alex May, *1998–2004*
Rosemary Mitchell, *1993–1999*
Peter Osborne, *1996–1998*
Annette Peach, *1997–2003*
Jane Potter, *2000–2003*
K. D. Reynolds, *1993–2003*
S. J. Skedd, *1997–2002*
H. J. Spencer, *1998–2002*
Roger T. Stearn, *1994–2002*

Henry Summerson, *1993–2004*
Clare L. Taylor, *2001–2003*
Deborah Graham-Vernon, *1999–2002*
Tim Wales, *1998–2002*
S. M. Wynne, *2001–2002*

*Research co-ordinator and
   references editor*
Tony Shaw, *1996–1997*
Michael T. Thornhill, *1997–2002*

Bibliographic editors

Simon Lancaster, *1999–2003*

Veronica Hurst, *1999–2000*
R. Jayatilaka, *1997–1999*
J. E. Thurgood, *2000–2002*

PUBLISHING

Administration

Jo Payne, *1996–2004*

Sarah Clayton, *2001–2003*
Adam Gilbert, *2000–2004*
Catriona Haig, *2001–2004*
Penny Williams, *1997–1998*
Judith Wilson, *1998–2001*

Data management

Rupert Mann, *1996–2004*

Rachel Goodyear, *1997–2003*
John McManus, *1998–2004*
Lucie Middlemiss, *1998–2000*
Sara C. Oxtoby, *1996–1999*

Editorial

Rosemary Roberts, *1994–2004*

Sarah Brolly, *1994–2004*
Ralph Evans, *1998–2004*
Peter Damian-Grint, *1997–1998*
Peter Lynan, *2000–2004*
Claire MacRae, *1998–2004*

Secretarial

Katherine Manville, *1993–2003*

Silvia Lauzzana, *1997–1998*
Patricia Mortimer, *1997–1998*
Deborah Simpson, *1998–2004*
Lucy Stanford, *2000–2001*

Technology

James Piggot, *1998–2004*

Jason Arneil, *1998–2001*
Dan Barker, *1998–2004*
Elena Blanco, *2001–2003*
Jane Few, *1996–2004*
Paul Harrington, *1999–2004*
David Hope, *1999–2004*
Mike Monaghan, *1995–2004*
Paul Storey, *2000–2004*

PICTURE RESEARCH

In partnership with the National Portrait Gallery, London

Peter Funnell, *1995–2004*

Arianne Burnette, *1996–2004*   Carol Blackett-Ord, *1996–2004*

OXFORD UNIVERSITY PRESS STAFF

Marketing

Clare Bebber
Nicky Grimbly
Susanna Lob
Lisa Nachtigall
Rebecca Seger

*Print production
and design*

Nick Clarke
Louise Edwards
Michael Johnson
Paul Luna
Barry Townsend
Andy Williams

Technology (1992–7)

Laura Elliott
Ewen Fletcher
Ray Hawi
James Howes
Phil James

Lisa Pearce
Suzanne Pinnington
Chris Rust
Richard Sabido
Ian Wright

RESEARCH ASSOCIATES

Simon Adams
Sinéad Agnew
D. E. Allen
J. D. Alsop
Nigel Aston
Kaye Bagshaw
Anne Pimlott Baker
J. H. Baker
Olive Baldwin
R. C. D. Baldwin
Nilanjana Banerji
Frank Barlow
Toby Barnard
Alan Bell
J. M. Blatchly
Paul Brand
Marc Brodie
John W. Cairns
John Callow
John Cannon
Jeremy Catto
Timothy Clayton
R. J. Cleevely
Patrick Collinson
Richard Copsey
T. A. B. Corley
P. K. Crimmin
David Crouch
J. D. Davies
John Davis
Caroline Dodds
A. A. M. Duncan
Alexander Du Toit
T. M. Charles-Edwards
Isobel Falconer
James Falkner

Simon Fenwick
M. T. Flanagan
Yolanda Foote
Kurt Gänzl
J. Gilliland
David J. Golby
Richard L. Greaves
Antony Griffiths
John D. Haigh
Roy Martin Haines
Stuart Handley
John B. Hattendorf
Michael Hicks
Alison Hiley
Richard Davenport-Hines
Paul Hopkins
Rosemary Horrox
Gerald M. D. Howat
A. C. Howe
David Huddleston
Roger Hutchins
Ronald Hutton
John Ingamells
E. W. Ives
Michael Jinkins
Michael Jones
James Kelly
Sean Kelsey
Joya Knight
C. S. Knighton
Andrew Lambert
Caroline L. Leachman
Marie-Louise Legg
Page Life
Julian Lock
William C. Lowe

Maria Luddy
James Lunt
Shannon R. McBriar
Wallace T. MacCaffrey
Thomas M. McCoog
Alan Marshall
Rosalind K. Marshall
G. H. Martin
John Martin
M. J. Mercer
Eric Metcalfe
R. W. J. Michaelis
Delia Millar
Rebecca Mills
Lynn Milne
Hugh Mooney
Kenneth O. Morgan
John Morrill
A. J. A. Morris
Roger Morriss
G. Martin Murphy
Bernard Nurse
Sybil Oldfield
Ian L. O'Neill
John Orbell
C. H. H. Owen
Jonathan Parry
A. W. H. Pearsall
Lucy Peltz
John D. Pickles
M. H. Port
Mark Pottle
Wilfrid Prest
Katherine Prior
Brian Quintrell
V. M. Quirke

D. Ben Rees
Lionel Alexander Ritchie
Alan Ruston
Janette Ryan
James Sambrook
Christopher Saunders
Paul Seaward
Richard Sharp
Robert Sharp
William Joseph Sheils
Arthur Sherbo
Richard Smail
David L. Smith
Nicholas D. Smith
Jonathan Spain
W. A. Speck
David Steele
Megan A. Stephan
David Stevenson
John Sweetman
Stephen Taylor
Peter D. G. Thomas
F. M. L. Thompson
Peter Thomson
Roland Thorne
David E. Thornton
Jason Tomes
Anthony Tuck
Brett Usher
Wray Vamplew
Nicholas Vincent
Patrick Wallis
R. K. Webb
Ann Williams
Thelma Wilson
Stephen Wright

FREELANCE, TEMPORARY, AND PART-TIME STAFF

ADMINISTRATION

Kafui Afenyo, Abigail Armstrong, Sarah Ballard, Nilanjana Banerji, Emma Beecham, Ruth Bestwick, Claire Booth, Justain Bracken, Andrea Breen, Chris Bruner, M. A. Bryant, Sean Burges, Anke Büttner, Alexander Carnwath, Flora Carnwath, Katrina Chandler, Martin P. Chow, Chris Clark, Alex Cock, Jennifer Cottrill, Cecily Crampin, Gavin Cullen, Michael Deibert, Pauline Dilworth, Divya Dubey, Giana Elyea, Alison Falby, Kian Febrer, Michelle Febrer, Lucy Fry, Nile Gardiner, Keith Gibeling, Gillian Gilbert, Natasha Goddard, Lucinda Godwin, Alexandra Gooden, Claudia Gorman, Gudrun Heim, Jessica Hinings, B. W. Holden, Ian Honeyman (*University administrator*), Lisse Honeyman, Beth R. Howard, Samantha Jackson, C. J. B. Joseph, Natalia Kennedy, Hanna Lahdenpera, Elizabeth Larminie, Matthew Larminie, Rosy Lyne, Louise McCaul, Matthew McLennan, Paula McMahon, Jenna McRae, Victoria Markland, Katharine Martin, Anthony Maude, Katya Melluish, Llyr Meredith, Nichole Miller, Leila Mills, Caitlin Milne, Ross Molden, Sarah Moss, Sandra Neave, Lucas North, Claire Oxtoby, Natasha Peach, Michelle Pestana, Anthony Phipps, Alexia Pospieszczyk, Laura Priest, Eileen Protheroe, Geeta Rampal, Frances Richards, Bronwyn Rivers, Sophie Rogers, Fiona St George, James Saunders, Mark J. Schofield, Simi Shah, Anna Skinner, Jeremy Smith, Naomi Smith, Leah Sparks, Julie Squires, Ursula Steele, Deepthi Talwar, Stephen Thompson, Paul Vlitos, Rebecca Wall, Sarah Elizabeth Wall, Nicky Weiner, Emma Westney, Sophie Weston, Hannah Whale, Katarina Wihlborg, Stephen Wood, Ann-Katrin Ziser

BIBLIOGRAPHIC RESEARCH

Christine Ayorinde, K. Grudzien Baston, Larissa Douglass, Kathryn James, Nicholas Karn, John Lamont, Coral Lancaster, Juliet McMurren, Andreas Petzold, Dara Price, Mark Proudman, Shirley Stacey, Artemis Gause-Stamboulopoulou, Jane Stemp, Vassilis Vavoulis, Sally Vilain

COPY-EDITING AND PROOFREADING

Supervisory: Jill Bowie, Michael Durnin, Pia Eekelaar, Fiona Little, Nancy-Jane Rucker, Mary Shields

Jane Bainbridge, Colin Baldwin, Charlotte Barrow, Laurien Berkeley, Patricia Bird, Jonathan Blaney, Charlotte Boynton, Penelope Brading, Pat Bulhosen, Shirley Card, Katy Carter, Simon Charles, Fabia Claris, Hazel Clarke, Stella Clifford, Rachel Coldicutt, Gill Colver, Madaleine Combie, Katy Coutts, C. A. Creffield, Jonathan Crowther, Alison Curr, Philip Daniel, Joan Dearnley, Susan Dunsmore, Catherine Eastman, Jo Egré, Gillian Evans, John Forder, Carolyn Garwes, Kate Gaylor, Cheryl Gibson, Elizabeth Gibson, David Grant, Frances Grant, Rosemary Hamilton, Sara Hawker, Anne Hegerty, Elaine Henderson, Benjamin Hervey, Gerard M.-F. Hill, Philip Hillyer, Jane Horwood, Anna Howes, Jesse Ingham, Veronica Ions, Helen Jeffrey, Richard Jones, Simon Jones, Judy Kearns, Anne Kendall, Jill Leatherbarrow, Victoria Linklater, Julian Lock, Alaine Low, Sally McCann, Anne McConnell, Elizabeth McKim, Kirk Marlow, Daffodil Marriage, Helen Marriage, Desmond Marshall, Jacquie Meredith, Hazel Mills, Bernadette Mohan, Sarah Newton, Sheila Oakley, Ruth Ogden, Sara C. Oxtoby, Angela Partington, Sarah Patey, Jo Pearce, Stephanie Pickering, Merle Read, Kim Richardson, Caroline Richmond, Penny Rogers, Halina Sand, John Shales, Mary Sheridan, R .S. Simpson, Dorothy Mitchell Smith, Lynn Smith, Marija Đurić Speare, Artemis Gause-Stamboulopoulou, Jane Tait, Matthew Taylor, Penny Trumble, Ruth Walter, Jenny Ward, Gillian Wightwick, Seren Wildwood, Jennifer Wilson, Sheilagh Wilson, Sarah Yates

DATACAPTURE

George Balanos, Anthony Bale, Katerina Bantinaki, Anna Bayman, John Birchall, Jill Bowie, Adina Bradeanu, Alberto Corsin Jimenez, Leif Dixon, Stephen Eyre, Marcus B. S. Flavin, Melissa Ford, Ginny Gardner, Thomas Genrich, Paul Gibbard, Sophie Gibson, Tamara Griffin, Vincent Haig, David Boyd Haycock, Christopher Hayden, Laura Hodgson, Kerstin Hoge, Catherine L. Humphries, Sara Jansson, Sally Ann Jenkins, Prashant Kidambi, John Linstroth, Jennifer Linton, Myfanwy Lloyd, Elizabeth Lock, Julian Lock, Dominique Lussier, Gerard Mannion, Philippa Martindale, Arantza Mayo, Michelle O'Connell, Sarah Ogilvie, Emma Plaskitt, Hugh Roberts, Philip Schwyzer, Dania Sheldon, Clare L. Taylor

DESIGN AND IMAGES

Andrew Boag, Boag Associates, Simon Levy, Anne Lyons, Julia Molden

National Portrait Gallery staff
Robert Carr-Archer, Emma Butterfield, Jennifer Cozens, Stephanie-Suzanne Durante, Bernard Horrocks, Nicole Mendelsohn, Tom Morgan, Shruti Patel

RESEARCH

Marc Abbott, Sylvia Adams, Victoria Christine Appel, J. T. K. Bain, Rebecca Black, Hazel Brothers, Robin Burls, André Celtel, Victor William Cook, Urmila Dé, Caroline Dodds, Sara Rich Dorman, Jane Dyson, J. G. Elzinga, Jacqueline Fernholz, Matthew Fisher, Stephen Follows, David Ford, Melissa Ford, David J. Golby, Kelly Grovier, Vincent Haig, Benjamin Hervey, Laura Hodgson, Isobel Hurst, Gordon Keable, Alexis Kirschbaum, John Linstroth, Richard Lofthouse, Dominique Lussier, Shannon R. McBriar, Gerard McCoy, Gareth Mann, R. W. J. Michaelis, Katherine Mullin, E. L. O'Brien, Ian L. O'Neill, Laura Merino-Pastor, Siobhan Peiffer, Christine Petsoulas, Emma Plaskitt, Katy Plowright, Sebastian Pocicovich, Jane Slinn, Nicholas D. Smith, Christina Storey, Edward Taylor, Joy Wang

GUIDE TO ARTICLES

Entry names

Articles on individuals begin with the name under which the person is entered (the 'entry name'), which appears in bold type. The entry name generally consists of a surname and one or more forenames, presented in inverted order: Smith, John Edward. In some cases the entry name is a single main name (Henry), and sometimes it is followed by additional identification, such as an epithet (the Carthusian) or toponym (of Abingdon), which is given after the main name, in direct order.

People are entered under personal names, not under names derived from aristocratic titles or other honours. (Information about titles is given following the personal name: see further below.) Where alternatives exist, the entry name chosen is usually the person's full name at death. People are not generally entered under literary or other artistic pseudonyms, aliases adopted for purposes of deception or disguise, names in religion or saints' names, nicknames, or diminutive name forms. However, these names, and others that help to identify the subject, such as maiden names, former names, and variant spellings, are often given in square brackets after the entry name.

The choice of full personal name at death is varied in the following cases:

- monarchs and their consorts are entered under their regnal names (the full personal name is provided early in the text)
- royal children are entered under their names as known (again the full personal name is provided in the text)
- performers are entered under adopted names when such a name consists of a forename and surname and when it superseded and differs significantly from the subject's original name (Grant, Cary)
- married women who did not use a husband's name in pursuit of the activities for which they are known are entered under their maiden name, or under a former married name, as appropriate

The entry name may encompass a title that precedes the forenames (such as Sir, Dame, Lord, or Lady). Persons bearing the same entry name may sometimes be distinguished by upper-case roman numerals in parentheses, where these are customary in historical writing about the family concerned: Mortimer, Roger (III) de. If it is known that the first forename(s) given to a person were not used, these are shown in parentheses: Woolf, (Adeline) Virginia.

The spelling of an entry name generally follows that used in historical records and writings, and may not be the spelling that the person would have used in his or her lifetime. If the person's chosen spelling of the name is significant but is not that under which he or she is entered, it is given in brackets.

People in the British Isles who are not English are entered under the form of their name most likely to be found in the historical literature. Where it will be helpful for identification or to aid pronunciation, a Welsh or Gaelic entry name is followed by an Anglicized version in brackets; where a Scottish, Irish, or Welsh subject is entered under an Anglicized version of his or her name, the Gaelic or Welsh original is provided wherever possible. In articles on medieval people of Norman origin the prefix 'de' is generally used in a toponym where the person's connection with the place derives from birth or land-holding, and the prefix 'of' where it relates to the person's activity in that place. People of foreign origin are entered under the name form most commonly found in English-language writings.

Order within entry names

All entry names consisting of a forename and surname are inverted for ordering by surname: Smith, John Edward.

When a surname comprises more than one word (such as a double-barrelled name) the inverted form is generally entered under the final word of the surname:

Bannerman, Sir Henry Campbell-
Bentinck, (William) John Cavendish-Scott-
Dyck, Sir Anthony Van
Smith, (Lloyd) Logan Pearsall

This formulation provides a predictable finding-rule for complex names, which occur often; but it does not indicate the form of name by which a person was habitually known, which is made apparent in the text of the article.

A few names of non-English origin are entered under prefixes which, following standard practice in their country or language of origin, have been treated as an inseparable part of the surname. These prefixes are:

A'	Du	Le	Ní	St	Ua
À	I'	M'	O	Ste	
D'	L'	Mac	O'	T'	
Des	La	Mc	Ó	Te	

Along with those consisting of only a single name, the following kinds of name are entered in direct order:

- names of monarchs and royal children (Henry IV, Frederick Lewis)
- a single name followed by an epithet (Adam the Carthusian)

- a single name followed by a patronymic where the patronymic element changes in each generation depending on the name of the father (Anarawd ap Rhodri, Coirpre mac Néill, David fitz Gerald)
- a single name followed by a toponym for people living before 1066 (Eadric of Laxfield)

Special considerations apply in the period before 1500, when naming customs and language forms were very fluid. Exceptionally, no subject in the period to 1500 is entered under D', Des, Du, L', Le, or La. Names with toponyms up to 1066 are generally presented in direct order; in the period after 1066 the place name is treated as a surname, and for subjects dying in or after 1307 the particle is usually dropped (Abingdon, Henry).

Where a reader is likely to look for a person under a name other than the entry name a cross-reference entry is included to guide the reader to the name under which the person is entered. However, cross-reference entries are not generally given for compound surnames or for names containing prefixes, the entry points for which are invariable (see above).

The entry names of family articles consist of the surname and the word 'family'. The entry names of group articles are formulated in such a way as to make them most readily findable—sometimes in inverted order (Roman Britain, British leaders in) and sometimes in direct order (Tolpuddle Martyrs).

Order of articles

Articles are ordered alphabetically by entry name; those with identical entry names are then ordered chronologically by date of birth or equivalent (see further below).

Entry names are ordered alphabetically up to the first comma, which generally occurs after the surname (in names entered in the 'surname, forename' pattern). Those with identical surnames are then ordered by forename. Ordering is letter by letter (so Butler, Elizabeth, precedes Butler, Eliza Marian). Names starting M', Mac, and Mc are alphabetized as if they all began Mac. Names starting St and Ste are alphabetized as though they began Saint. The following are all ignored for ordering purposes: names in square brackets and parentheses, titles preceding forenames (such as Sir), apostrophes, hyphens, spaces, accents, and titles appearing after the entry name.

The following (abbreviated) sequence illustrates alphabetical ordering of surnames with forenames:

Cottnam, Deborah
Cotton, George Edward Lynch
Cotton, (Thomas) Henry
Cotton, Sir Henry John Stedman
Cotton [née Robson], Mary Ann
Cotton, Sir Robert
Cotton, Roger
Cotton, Sir St Vincent
Cotton, Stapleton

Entry names comprising single names (together with any subsequent qualifiers), which are given in direct order, are treated for ordering purposes as if the first word of the name was a surname. All such entry names precede entries in the usual 'surname, forename' pattern. Where the first words of such names are identical, they are ordered by any remaining words in the entry name. Single names (including entry surnames for families) are given first; then names qualified by roman numerals (mostly in the names of monarchs); then those with additional words, which are ordered letter by letter. The following (abbreviated) sequence illustrates alphabetical ordering of entry names in direct order:

Henry
Henry I
Henry II
Henry Benedict
Henry fitz Count
Henry Frederick
Henry of Almain
Henry of Lancaster
Henry, Augustine

Where articles bear the same entry name, they are ordered chronologically, by year of birth (or baptism). If persons of the same name also share the same year of birth, the articles are ordered by year of death. Where the year of birth is not known, it is assumed, for the sake of ordering, that the person was born sixty years before the date of death, if that is known. If a subject is dated only to a period in which he or she flourished, then it is assumed that this date falls in the middle of a sixty-year life span. If a subject is dated only by a period within which he or she was alive (such as '6th cent[ury].'), then it is assumed for ordering purposes that he or she was born at the beginning of that period. (For further information on presentation of life and activity dates, see below.) The following (abbreviated) sequence illustrates chronological ordering:

Richard [Richard of Dover] (d. 1184)
Richard [Richard Palmer] (d. 1195)
Richard (fl. 1216–1222)
Richard (1209–1272)
Richard [Richard of Conisbrough] (1385–1415)

Titles

If the subject of an entry bore an aristocratic title, details are given after the entry name. Where more than one title was held, the person's highest title at death is used; in a few instances where the person is chiefly known by a subsidiary or previous title, that is stated in addition to the title at death.

An ordinal number is given whenever possible for all male holders of peerage titles and baronetcies originating in the British Isles, unless the peerage title or baronetcy was created for and died with the subject, or was a courtesy title. Ordinal numbers place each holder of a peerage title in a line of hereditary succession; so Hugh Percy (1742–1817) is described as second duke of Northumberland and not fourth, for although three individuals before him had borne the title, he was the second holder of the dukedom created for his father in 1766.

Women holders of hereditary peerages are marked by the Latin term suo jure ('in her own right') to distinguish them from the wives of hereditary peers. Where a title of nobility is borne as a title of pretence, it is qualified with the word 'styled'. This applies if the subject previously held the peerage title or baronetcy legitimately and then forfeited it; if they assumed it as part of an unsuccessful claim to the title; or if they assumed it as an alias.

Foreign hereditary titles of nobility are included where the subject had a career that was spent largely or entirely outside the British Isles, where they were foreign nationals, or where there is otherwise good reason to know that the title was in everyday use. Countries of origin are given for foreign titles where it has been possible to establish them.

In general, editors have treated GEC, the *Scots peerage*, Burke's *Peerage*, and the *Handbook of British chronology* (3rd edn, 1986) as authorities in the naming and numbering of peerage titles. These have been supplemented by research undertaken by contributors and by *Oxford DNB* editors.

Cross-reference entries are included for all title names that differ from the personal names of the persons who bore them.

Life and activity dates

Life dates are given after the entry name and title (if any). Dates are given wherever possible as years of birth and death. Where a date of birth is unknown, a year of baptism may be given instead, prefixed '*bap.*'. If only a year of birth or of death is known, this is given alone, prefixed '*b.*' or '*d.*'. Years may be qualified by the addition of a question mark (meaning 'probably in the year given') or the prefix '*c.*' (Latin *circa*, 'about', meaning 'about the year given: perhaps before and perhaps after'). Dates before the common era are labelled BC, and thereafter dates up to the year 100 are labelled AD. Other qualifiers (such as 'in or before') are self-explanatory.

A person's birth or death may not be datable to a single year. A solidus ('/') indicates alternative years: Ballantine, James (1807/8–1877). This form commonly occurs where there is evidence only of the subject's age at the time of another datable life event (for example, matriculation at university, marriage, or death). A multiplication sign indicates a range of years during which the subject may have been born or may have died: Baartman, Sara (1777x88–1815/16). Where a birth or death date cannot be more precisely fixed a decade date (late 1070s, early 1780s) may be provided.

Where neither a birth nor death date is known, dates are given of a person's known activity, prefixed by *fl.* (Latin *floruit*: 'flourished'). 'Flourished' dates may relate to activity in a single year or over a range of years. The same qualifications of year values may be used with 'flourished' dates as with birth and death dates: Smith, Theodore (*fl. c.*1765–*c.*1810x23). Where the person's activities cannot be dated more precisely, a century date is given. For a subject whose existence is highly doubtful or who is proven not to have existed, dates are prefixed by *supp.* ('supposedly').

The dates of activity of a family are prefixed by *per.* ('in the period'), indicating that the entry covers only that part of the family's existence. The dates of activity of a group are prefixed by *act.* ('active'), indicating that the entry covers the years of the group's activity and not necessarily its complete history or the lifespans of all its members.

Occupation or field of interest

After the entry name, title (if any), and dates, the identification of the subject of the article is completed by a statement of the principal occupation, activities, or field of interest for which the person is included in the dictionary. Taken with the other information, the occupational descriptor is intended to help the reader to identify the person quickly and in a general context. It usually offers a generic rather than a specific description (for example, 'Church of England clergyman', not 'vicar of Knutsford'), and a factual rather than an evaluative statement (for example, 'radio producer and presenter', not 'pioneering broadcaster').

Article text

References in the article text to the subject of the article (and to other people mentioned) use the name by which they were known during the period under discussion, which may not be the same as the name under which they are entered. A person who changed her name on marriage may be referred to first by her maiden name and afterwards by her married name; similarly one who succeeded to an aristocratic title will be called by his or her personal name until the date of succession, but by the title name thereafter. Persons with double-barrelled or other complex surnames are referred to in the text by the whole of the surname appropriate for the time under discussion.

Co-subjects are introduced in the course of the article text and their entry names are always given in direct order. If the narrative does not permit reference to the co-subject by his or her formal name at death, a bracketed identity is provided, giving this name and a title (if any). The entry name of a co-subject always appears in bold type, whether in open text or brackets. The bracketed pointer '*see below*' is used to indicate that a person mentioned is a co-subject on whom the main information will be found later in that article.

Within a family article, persons of the same name are distinguished where necessary by lower-case roman numerals in brackets. Unlike upper-case roman numerals used in a few entry names and article texts, lower-case numerals are used solely for ease of reading and identification within the article, and do not indicate that the figures concerned are so known in the historical literature.

Dates are given throughout according to the modern practice of changing the year at 1 January; thus a date that might be given as 1 February 1521/2 is rendered 1 February 1522. Dates up to 2 September 1752 are old style, thereafter new style; generally the abbreviations OS and NS are not used except where events taking place outside the British Isles make this qualification desirable and the dating system in use is clear.

Quoted matter is, wherever possible, provided with a parenthetical reference to the source: a short reference (consisting, for example, of an author's name and a page reference, or a work title and a page reference) relates to a work to be found in the list of sources at the end of the article; where the work quoted is not otherwise a source of information for the article a citation sufficient to allow the reader to trace it is given in parentheses.

Abbreviations used in the text are listed under 'General abbreviations' in the 'List of abbreviations' at the beginning of each volume.

Cross-references in the text

In addition to their use in cross-reference entries, cross-references are included within article texts to direct readers to other relevant entries. Cross-references are included in normal text for the following purposes:

- to identify members of the subject's close family
- to identify more remote members of the subject's family whose connection with the subject's life or activities is significant
- to identify other entries in which significant coverage of the subject's life or activities may be found, such as the entry on a business partner
- to identify entries on persons with whom the subject may be confused

Cross-references are not included simply to draw attention to the existence of articles on other persons mentioned in the subject's article.

Where possible a cross-reference is signalled by an asterisk attached to the entry name in the open text; otherwise a formal cross-reference is given in inverted form in brackets, prefixed by *see* or *see under*, as appropriate; '*see under*' indicates that the cross-reference is to a co-subject found in the article under the specified entry name.

Signatures

The signature of the author of the article is given at the foot of the article text. The style of the signature shows whether the entry has been newly written for the *Oxford DNB* or taken from the *DNB* and revised. Where an author's name is followed by the annotation '*rev.*', he or she was the author of the *DNB* article, which has been revised for the *Oxford DNB*; the name of the reviser usually follows.

The position of the signature indicates the author's role as the writer of the memoir on the subject. The author also contributed all or part of the reference material that appears below the signature, but the project editors have verified and often supplemented these sections.

An *Index of Contributors* to the *Oxford DNB*, showing the entries that contributors have written and/or revised, has been provided in a separately published volume which accompanies the dictionary.

Reference material

The references supplied for each entry consist of:

Sources: a list of materials used in the preparation of the entry

Archives: a list of the main archival holdings of the subject's papers and other remains

Likenesses: a list of images of the subject

Wealth at death: a statement of the value of the subject's estate at the time of death

(See the 'Introduction' for further information on the content of these sections.)

In all reference sections items are deemed to relate to the subject (or, especially in the case of sources, to the entry as a whole) unless a co-subject's name is given as a bracketed annotation at the end of a citation; such a citation relates only to that co-subject.

Sources are generally presented in the order in which the author supplied them, reflecting their importance. Commonly cited works are abbreviated: the forms used are listed under 'Bibliographic abbreviations' in the 'List of abbreviations' at the beginning of each volume. The form 'personal knowledge' indicates that the author knew the subject of the article; 'private information' refers to information gained by the author through private research that remains unpublished. The date following such citations is the date of first publication of the *DNB* or *Oxford DNB* article based on such information, not the date at which the information was acquired.

Archival holdings are divided into three sections: general holdings (including papers and other remains), film and moving image materials, and sound materials; the general section may be further divided into holdings of greater and lesser importance. Generally holdings cited first and those cited without a personal name may be retrieved in the archive's indexes through the name of the subject of the article. Multiple entries in each archives section are ordered alphabetically by institutional name.

Likenesses are ordered chronologically by date of execution, thereafter alphabetically by the surname of the artist or other maker, thereafter by the description of the work ('photograph', 'sculpture', etc.). The bracketed annotation '*see illus.*' indicates that the item listed (or one item of a group cited collectively) is the picture reproduced in the article. The annotation '*see illus. in …*' indicates that the likeness is reproduced in another article.

Wealth at death is recorded in a standard form where an official action (such as the proving of a will or the making of an inventory) has taken place; multiple records may be given, and a source for the information is generally provided. Informal assessments may also be given.

Abbreviations used in the references sections for the names of archives, libraries, museums, and other repositories are listed under 'Institution abbreviations' in the 'List of abbreviations' at the beginning of each volume.

Images

If an article includes a reproduction of an image, it appears near the head of the article, with a short descriptive caption. Further details, such as the location of the original, may be found in the list of 'Likenesses'. The holder of copyright in the image reproduced is listed among the 'Picture credits' at the end of the relevant volume.

LIST OF ABBREVIATIONS

1. *General abbreviations*

AB	bachelor of arts
ABC	Australian Broadcasting Corporation
ABC TV	ABC Television
act.	active
A$	Australian dollar
AD	*anno domini*
AFC	Air Force Cross
AIDS	acquired immune deficiency syndrome
AK	Alaska
AL	Alabama
A level	advanced level [examination]
ALS	associate of the Linnean Society
AM	master of arts
AMICE	associate member of the Institution of Civil Engineers
ANZAC	Australian and New Zealand Army Corps
appx *pl.* appxs	appendix(es)
AR	Arkansas
ARA	associate of the Royal Academy
ARCA	associate of the Royal College of Art
ARCM	associate of the Royal College of Music
ARCO	associate of the Royal College of Organists
ARIBA	associate of the Royal Institute of British Architects
ARP	air-raid precautions
ARRC	associate of the Royal Red Cross
ARSA	associate of the Royal Scottish Academy
art.	article / item
ASC	Army Service Corps
Asch	Austrian Schilling
ASDIC	Antisubmarine Detection Investigation Committee
ATS	Auxiliary Territorial Service
ATV	Associated Television
Aug	August
AZ	Arizona
b.	born
BA	bachelor of arts
BA (Admin.)	bachelor of arts (administration)
BAFTA	British Academy of Film and Television Arts
BAO	bachelor of arts in obstetrics
bap.	baptized
BBC	British Broadcasting Corporation / Company
BC	before Christ
BCE	before the common (*or* Christian) era
BCE	bachelor of civil engineering
BCG	bacillus of Calmette and Guérin [inoculation against tuberculosis]
BCh	bachelor of surgery
BChir	bachelor of surgery
BCL	bachelor of civil law

BCnL	bachelor of canon law
BCom	bachelor of commerce
BD	bachelor of divinity
BEd	bachelor of education
BEng	bachelor of engineering
bk *pl.* bks	book(s)
BL	bachelor of law / letters / literature
BLitt	bachelor of letters
BM	bachelor of medicine
BMus	bachelor of music
BP	before present
BP	British Petroleum
Bros.	Brothers
BS	(1) bachelor of science; (2) bachelor of surgery; (3) British standard
BSc	bachelor of science
BSc (Econ.)	bachelor of science (economics)
BSc (Eng.)	bachelor of science (engineering)
bt	baronet
BTh	bachelor of theology
bur.	buried
C.	command [identifier for published parliamentary papers]
c.	*circa*
c.	*capitulum pl. capitula*: chapter(s)
CA	California
Cantab.	Cantabrigiensis
cap.	*capitulum pl. capitula*: chapter(s)
CB	companion of the Bath
CBE	commander of the Order of the British Empire
CBS	Columbia Broadcasting System
cc	cubic centimetres
C$	Canadian dollar
CD	compact disc
Cd	command [identifier for published parliamentary papers]
CE	Common (*or* Christian) Era
cent.	century
cf.	compare
CH	Companion of Honour
chap.	chapter
ChB	bachelor of surgery
CI	Imperial Order of the Crown of India
CIA	Central Intelligence Agency
CID	Criminal Investigation Department
CIE	companion of the Order of the Indian Empire
Cie	Compagnie
CLit	companion of literature
CM	master of surgery
cm	centimetre(s)

Cmd	command [identifier for published parliamentary papers]
CMG	companion of the Order of St Michael and St George
Cmnd	command [identifier for published parliamentary papers]
CO	Colorado
Co.	company
co.	county
col. *pl.* cols.	column(s)
Corp.	corporation
CSE	certificate of secondary education
CSI	companion of the Order of the Star of India
CT	Connecticut
CVO	commander of the Royal Victorian Order
cwt	hundredweight
$	(American) dollar
d.	(1) penny (pence); (2) died
DBE	dame commander of the Order of the British Empire
DCH	diploma in child health
DCh	doctor of surgery
DCL	doctor of civil law
DCnL	doctor of canon law
DCVO	dame commander of the Royal Victorian Order
DD	doctor of divinity
DE	Delaware
Dec	December
dem.	demolished
DEng	doctor of engineering
des.	destroyed
DFC	Distinguished Flying Cross
DipEd	diploma in education
DipPsych	diploma in psychiatry
diss.	dissertation
DL	deputy lieutenant
DLitt	doctor of letters
DLittCelt	doctor of Celtic letters
DM	(1) Deutschmark; (2) doctor of medicine; (3) doctor of musical arts
DMus	doctor of music
DNA	dioxyribonucleic acid
doc.	document
DOL	doctor of oriental learning
DPH	diploma in public health
DPhil	doctor of philosophy
DPM	diploma in psychological medicine
DSC	Distinguished Service Cross
DSc	doctor of science
DSc (Econ.)	doctor of science (economics)
DSc (Eng.)	doctor of science (engineering)
DSM	Distinguished Service Medal
DSO	companion of the Distinguished Service Order
DSocSc	doctor of social science
DTech	doctor of technology
DTh	doctor of theology
DTM	diploma in tropical medicine
DTMH	diploma in tropical medicine and hygiene
DU	doctor of the university
DUniv	doctor of the university
dwt	pennyweight
EC	European Community
ed. *pl.* eds.	edited / edited by / editor(s)
Edin.	Edinburgh
edn	edition
EEC	European Economic Community
EFTA	European Free Trade Association
EICS	East India Company Service
EMI	Electrical and Musical Industries (Ltd)
Eng.	English
enl.	enlarged
ENSA	Entertainments National Service Association
ep. *pl.* epp.	*epistola(e)*
ESP	extra-sensory perception
esp.	especially
esq.	esquire
est.	estimate / estimated
EU	European Union
ex	sold by (*lit.* out of)
excl.	excludes / excluding
exh.	exhibited
exh. cat.	exhibition catalogue
f. *pl.* ff.	following [pages]
FA	Football Association
FACP	fellow of the American College of Physicians
facs.	facsimile
FANY	First Aid Nursing Yeomanry
FBA	fellow of the British Academy
FBI	Federation of British Industries
FCS	fellow of the Chemical Society
Feb	February
FEng	fellow of the Fellowship of Engineering
FFCM	fellow of the Faculty of Community Medicine
FGS	fellow of the Geological Society
fig.	figure
FIMechE	fellow of the Institution of Mechanical Engineers
FL	Florida
fl.	*floruit*
FLS	fellow of the Linnean Society
FM	frequency modulation
fol. *pl.* fols.	folio(s)
Fr	French francs
Fr.	French
FRAeS	fellow of the Royal Aeronautical Society
FRAI	fellow of the Royal Anthropological Institute
FRAM	fellow of the Royal Academy of Music
FRAS	(1) fellow of the Royal Asiatic Society; (2) fellow of the Royal Astronomical Society
FRCM	fellow of the Royal College of Music
FRCO	fellow of the Royal College of Organists
FRCOG	fellow of the Royal College of Obstetricians and Gynaecologists
FRCP(C)	fellow of the Royal College of Physicians of Canada
FRCP (Edin.)	fellow of the Royal College of Physicians of Edinburgh
FRCP (Lond.)	fellow of the Royal College of Physicians of London
FRCPath	fellow of the Royal College of Pathologists
FRCPsych	fellow of the Royal College of Psychiatrists
FRCS	fellow of the Royal College of Surgeons
FRGS	fellow of the Royal Geographical Society
FRIBA	fellow of the Royal Institute of British Architects
FRICS	fellow of the Royal Institute of Chartered Surveyors
FRS	fellow of the Royal Society
FRSA	fellow of the Royal Society of Arts

FRSCM	fellow of the Royal School of Church Music
FRSE	fellow of the Royal Society of Edinburgh
FRSL	fellow of the Royal Society of Literature
FSA	fellow of the Society of Antiquaries
ft	foot *pl.* feet
FTCL	fellow of Trinity College of Music, London
ft-lb per min.	foot-pounds per minute [unit of horsepower]
FZS	fellow of the Zoological Society
GA	Georgia
GBE	knight or dame grand cross of the Order of the British Empire
GCB	knight grand cross of the Order of the Bath
GCE	general certificate of education
GCH	knight grand cross of the Royal Guelphic Order
GCHQ	government communications headquarters
GCIE	knight grand commander of the Order of the Indian Empire
GCMG	knight or dame grand cross of the Order of St Michael and St George
GCSE	general certificate of secondary education
GCSI	knight grand commander of the Order of the Star of India
GCStJ	bailiff or dame grand cross of the order of St John of Jerusalem
GCVO	knight or dame grand cross of the Royal Victorian Order
GEC	General Electric Company
Ger.	German
GI	government (*or* general) issue
GMT	Greenwich mean time
GP	general practitioner
GPU	[Soviet special police unit]
GSO	general staff officer
Heb.	Hebrew
HEICS	Honourable East India Company Service
HI	Hawaii
HIV	human immunodeficiency virus
HK$	Hong Kong dollar
HM	his / her majesty('s)
HMAS	his / her majesty's Australian ship
HMNZS	his / her majesty's New Zealand ship
HMS	his / her majesty's ship
HMSO	His / Her Majesty's Stationery Office
HMV	His Master's Voice
Hon.	Honourable
hp	horsepower
hr	hour(s)
HRH	his / her royal highness
HTV	Harlech Television
IA	Iowa
ibid.	*ibidem*: in the same place
ICI	Imperial Chemical Industries (Ltd)
ID	Idaho
IL	Illinois
illus.	illustration
illustr.	illustrated
IN	Indiana
in.	inch(es)
Inc.	Incorporated
incl.	includes / including
IOU	I owe you
IQ	intelligence quotient
Ir£	Irish pound
IRA	Irish Republican Army

ISO	companion of the Imperial Service Order
It.	Italian
ITA	Independent Television Authority
ITV	Independent Television
Jan	January
JP	justice of the peace
jun.	junior
KB	knight of the Order of the Bath
KBE	knight commander of the Order of the British Empire
KC	king's counsel
kcal	kilocalorie
KCB	knight commander of the Order of the Bath
KCH	knight commander of the Royal Guelphic Order
KCIE	knight commander of the Order of the Indian Empire
KCMG	knight commander of the Order of St Michael and St George
KCSI	knight commander of the Order of the Star of India
KCVO	knight commander of the Royal Victorian Order
keV	kilo-electron-volt
KG	knight of the Order of the Garter
KGB	[Soviet committee of state security]
KH	knight of the Royal Guelphic Order
KLM	Koninklijke Luchtvaart Maatschappij (Royal Dutch Air Lines)
km	kilometre(s)
KP	knight of the Order of St Patrick
KS	Kansas
KT	knight of the Order of the Thistle
kt	knight
KY	Kentucky
£	pound(s) sterling
£E	Egyptian pound
L	lira *pl.* lire
l. *pl.* ll.	line(s)
LA	Louisiana
LAA	light anti-aircraft
LAH	licentiate of the Apothecaries' Hall, Dublin
Lat.	Latin
lb	pound(s), unit of weight
LDS	licence in dental surgery
lit.	literally
LittB	bachelor of letters
LittD	doctor of letters
LKQCPI	licentiate of the King and Queen's College of Physicians, Ireland
LLA	lady literate in arts
LLB	bachelor of laws
LLD	doctor of laws
LLM	master of laws
LM	licentiate in midwifery
LP	long-playing record
LRAM	licentiate of the Royal Academy of Music
LRCP	licentiate of the Royal College of Physicians
LRCPS (Glasgow)	licentiate of the Royal College of Physicians and Surgeons of Glasgow
LRCS	licentiate of the Royal College of Surgeons
LSA	licentiate of the Society of Apothecaries
LSD	lysergic acid diethylamide
LVO	lieutenant of the Royal Victorian Order
M. *pl.* MM.	Monsieur *pl.* Messieurs
m	metre(s)

m. *pl.* mm.	membrane(s)
MA	(1) Massachusetts; (2) master of arts
MAI	master of engineering
MB	bachelor of medicine
MBA	master of business administration
MBE	member of the Order of the British Empire
MC	Military Cross
MCC	Marylebone Cricket Club
MCh	master of surgery
MChir	master of surgery
MCom	master of commerce
MD	(1) doctor of medicine; (2) Maryland
MDMA	methylenedioxymethamphetamine
ME	Maine
MEd	master of education
MEng	master of engineering
MEP	member of the European parliament
MG	Morris Garages
MGM	Metro-Goldwyn-Mayer
Mgr	Monsignor
MI	(1) Michigan; (2) military intelligence
MI1c	[secret intelligence department]
MI5	[military intelligence department]
MI6	[secret intelligence department]
MI9	[secret escape service]
MICE	member of the Institution of Civil Engineers
MIEE	member of the Institution of Electrical Engineers
min.	minute(s)
Mk	mark
ML	(1) licentiate of medicine; (2) master of laws
MLitt	master of letters
Mlle	Mademoiselle
mm	millimetre(s)
Mme	Madame
MN	Minnesota
MO	Missouri
MOH	medical officer of health
MP	member of parliament
m.p.h.	miles per hour
MPhil	master of philosophy
MRCP	member of the Royal College of Physicians
MRCS	member of the Royal College of Surgeons
MRCVS	member of the Royal College of Veterinary Surgeons
MRIA	member of the Royal Irish Academy
MS	(1) master of science; (2) Mississippi
MS *pl.* MSS	manuscript(s)
MSc	master of science
MSc (Econ.)	master of science (economics)
MT	Montana
MusB	bachelor of music
MusBac	bachelor of music
MusD	doctor of music
MV	motor vessel
MVO	member of the Royal Victorian Order
n. *pl.* nn.	note(s)
NAAFI	Navy, Army, and Air Force Institutes
NASA	National Aeronautics and Space Administration
NATO	North Atlantic Treaty Organization
NBC	National Broadcasting Corporation
NC	North Carolina
NCO	non-commissioned officer
ND	North Dakota
n.d.	no date
NE	Nebraska
nem. con.	*nemine contradicente*: unanimously
new ser.	new series
NH	New Hampshire
NHS	National Health Service
NJ	New Jersey
NKVD	[Soviet people's commissariat for internal affairs]
NM	New Mexico
nm	nanometre(s)
no. *pl.* nos.	number(s)
Nov	November
n.p.	no place [of publication]
NS	new style
NV	Nevada
NY	New York
NZBS	New Zealand Broadcasting Service
OBE	officer of the Order of the British Empire
obit.	obituary
Oct	October
OCTU	officer cadets training unit
OECD	Organization for Economic Co-operation and Development
OEEC	Organization for European Economic Co-operation
OFM	order of Friars Minor [Franciscans]
OFMCap	Ordine Frati Minori Cappucini: member of the Capuchin order
OH	Ohio
OK	Oklahoma
O level	ordinary level [examination]
OM	Order of Merit
OP	order of Preachers [Dominicans]
op. *pl.* opp.	opus *pl.* opera
OPEC	Organization of Petroleum Exporting Countries
OR	Oregon
orig.	original
os	old style
OSB	Order of St Benedict
OTC	Officers' Training Corps
OWS	Old Watercolour Society
Oxon.	Oxoniensis
p. *pl.* pp.	page(s)
PA	Pennsylvania
p.a.	per annum
para.	paragraph
PAYE	pay as you earn
pbk *pl.* pbks	paperback(s)
per.	[during the] period
PhD	doctor of philosophy
pl.	(1) plate(s); (2) plural
priv. coll.	private collection
pt *pl.* pts	part(s)
pubd	published
PVC	polyvinyl chloride
q. *pl.* qq.	(1) question(s); (2) quire(s)
QC	queen's counsel
R	rand
R.	Rex / Regina
r	recto
r.	reigned / ruled
RA	Royal Academy / Royal Academician

RAC	Royal Automobile Club	Skr	Swedish krona
RAF	Royal Air Force	Span.	Spanish
RAFVR	Royal Air Force Volunteer Reserve	SPCK	Society for Promoting Christian Knowledge
RAM	[member of the] Royal Academy of Music	SS	(1) Santissimi; (2) Schutzstaffel; (3) steam ship
RAMC	Royal Army Medical Corps	STB	bachelor of theology
RCA	Royal College of Art	STD	doctor of theology
RCNC	Royal Corps of Naval Constructors	STM	master of theology
RCOG	Royal College of Obstetricians and Gynaecologists	STP	doctor of theology
RDI	royal designer for industry	*supp.*	supposedly
RE	Royal Engineers	suppl. *pl.* suppls.	supplement(s)
repr. *pl.* reprs.	reprint(s) / reprinted	s.v.	*sub verbo* / *sub voce*: under the word / heading
repro.	reproduced	SY	steam yacht
rev.	revised / revised by / reviser / revision	TA	Territorial Army
Revd	Reverend	TASS	[Soviet news agency]
RHA	Royal Hibernian Academy	TB	tuberculosis (*lit.* tubercle bacillus)
RI	(1) Rhode Island; (2) Royal Institute of Painters in Water-Colours	TD	(1) *teachtaí dála* (member of the Dáil); (2) territorial decoration
RIBA	Royal Institute of British Architects	TN	Tennessee
RIN	Royal Indian Navy	TNT	trinitrotoluene
RM	Reichsmark	trans.	translated / translated by / translation / translator
RMS	Royal Mail steamer	TT	tourist trophy
RN	Royal Navy	TUC	Trades Union Congress
RNA	ribonucleic acid	TX	Texas
RNAS	Royal Naval Air Service	U-boat	*Unterseeboot*: submarine
RNR	Royal Naval Reserve	Ufa	Universum-Film AG
RNVR	Royal Naval Volunteer Reserve	UMIST	University of Manchester Institute of Science and Technology
RO	Record Office	UN	United Nations
r.p.m.	revolutions per minute	UNESCO	United Nations Educational, Scientific, and Cultural Organization
RRS	royal research ship		
Rs	rupees	UNICEF	United Nations International Children's Emergency Fund
RSA	(1) Royal Scottish Academician; (2) Royal Society of Arts		
RSPCA	Royal Society for the Prevention of Cruelty to Animals	unpubd	unpublished
		USS	United States ship
Rt Hon.	Right Honourable	UT	Utah
Rt Revd	Right Reverend	*v*	verso
RUC	Royal Ulster Constabulary	v.	versus
Russ.	Russian	VA	Virginia
RWS	Royal Watercolour Society	VAD	Voluntary Aid Detachment
S4C	Sianel Pedwar Cymru	VC	Victoria Cross
s.	shilling(s)	VE-day	victory in Europe day
s.a.	*sub anno*: under the year	Ven.	Venerable
SABC	South African Broadcasting Corporation	VJ-day	victory over Japan day
SAS	Special Air Service	vol. *pl.* vols.	volume(s)
SC	South Carolina	VT	Vermont
ScD	doctor of science	WA	Washington [state]
S$	Singapore dollar	WAAC	Women's Auxiliary Army Corps
SD	South Dakota	WAAF	Women's Auxiliary Air Force
sec.	second(s)	WEA	Workers' Educational Association
sel.	selected	WHO	World Health Organization
sen.	senior	WI	Wisconsin
Sept	September	WRAF	Women's Royal Air Force
ser.	series	WRNS	Women's Royal Naval Service
SHAPE	supreme headquarters allied powers, Europe	WV	West Virginia
SIDRO	Société Internationale d'Énergie Hydro-Électrique	WVS	Women's Voluntary Service
		WY	Wyoming
sig. *pl.* sigs.	signature(s)	¥	yen
sing.	singular	YMCA	Young Men's Christian Association
SIS	Secret Intelligence Service	YWCA	Young Women's Christian Association
SJ	Society of Jesus		

2. Institution abbreviations

All Souls Oxf.	All Souls College, Oxford
AM Oxf.	Ashmolean Museum, Oxford
Balliol Oxf.	Balliol College, Oxford
BBC WAC	BBC Written Archives Centre, Reading
Beds. & Luton ARS	Bedfordshire and Luton Archives and Record Service, Bedford
Berks. RO	Berkshire Record Office, Reading
BFI	British Film Institute, London
BFI NFTVA	British Film Institute, London, National Film and Television Archive
BGS	British Geological Survey, Keyworth, Nottingham
Birm. CA	Birmingham Central Library, Birmingham City Archives
Birm. CL	Birmingham Central Library
BL	British Library, London
BL NSA	British Library, London, National Sound Archive
BL OIOC	British Library, London, Oriental and India Office Collections
BLPES	London School of Economics and Political Science, British Library of Political and Economic Science
BM	British Museum, London
Bodl. Oxf.	Bodleian Library, Oxford
Bodl. RH	Bodleian Library of Commonwealth and African Studies at Rhodes House, Oxford
Borth. Inst.	Borthwick Institute of Historical Research, University of York
Boston PL	Boston Public Library, Massachusetts
Bristol RO	Bristol Record Office
Bucks. RLSS	Buckinghamshire Records and Local Studies Service, Aylesbury
CAC Cam.	Churchill College, Cambridge, Churchill Archives Centre
Cambs. AS	Cambridgeshire Archive Service
CCC Cam.	Corpus Christi College, Cambridge
CCC Oxf.	Corpus Christi College, Oxford
Ches. & Chester ALSS	Cheshire and Chester Archives and Local Studies Service
Christ Church Oxf.	Christ Church, Oxford
Christies	Christies, London
City Westm. AC	City of Westminster Archives Centre, London
CKS	Centre for Kentish Studies, Maidstone
CLRO	Corporation of London Records Office
Coll. Arms	College of Arms, London
Col. U.	Columbia University, New York
Cornwall RO	Cornwall Record Office, Truro
Courtauld Inst.	Courtauld Institute of Art, London
CUL	Cambridge University Library
Cumbria AS	Cumbria Archive Service
Derbys. RO	Derbyshire Record Office, Matlock
Devon RO	Devon Record Office, Exeter
Dorset RO	Dorset Record Office, Dorchester
Duke U.	Duke University, Durham, North Carolina
Duke U., Perkins L.	Duke University, Durham, North Carolina, William R. Perkins Library
Durham Cath. CL	Durham Cathedral, chapter library
Durham RO	Durham Record Office
DWL	Dr Williams's Library, London
Essex RO	Essex Record Office
E. Sussex RO	East Sussex Record Office, Lewes
Eton	Eton College, Berkshire
FM Cam.	Fitzwilliam Museum, Cambridge
Folger	Folger Shakespeare Library, Washington, DC
Garr. Club	Garrick Club, London
Girton Cam.	Girton College, Cambridge
GL	Guildhall Library, London
Glos. RO	Gloucestershire Record Office, Gloucester
Gon. & Caius Cam.	Gonville and Caius College, Cambridge
Gov. Art Coll.	Government Art Collection
GS Lond.	Geological Society of London
Hants. RO	Hampshire Record Office, Winchester
Harris Man. Oxf.	Harris Manchester College, Oxford
Harvard TC	Harvard Theatre Collection, Harvard University, Cambridge, Massachusetts, Nathan Marsh Pusey Library
Harvard U.	Harvard University, Cambridge, Massachusetts
Harvard U., Houghton L.	Harvard University, Cambridge, Massachusetts, Houghton Library
Herefs. RO	Herefordshire Record Office, Hereford
Herts. ALS	Hertfordshire Archives and Local Studies, Hertford
Hist. Soc. Penn.	Historical Society of Pennsylvania, Philadelphia
HLRO	House of Lords Record Office, London
Hult. Arch.	Hulton Archive, London and New York
Hunt. L.	Huntington Library, San Marino, California
ICL	Imperial College, London
Inst. CE	Institution of Civil Engineers, London
Inst. EE	Institution of Electrical Engineers, London
IWM	Imperial War Museum, London
IWM FVA	Imperial War Museum, London, Film and Video Archive
IWM SA	Imperial War Museum, London, Sound Archive
JRL	John Rylands University Library of Manchester
King's AC Cam.	King's College Archives Centre, Cambridge
King's Cam.	King's College, Cambridge
King's Lond.	King's College, London
King's Lond., Liddell Hart C.	King's College, London, Liddell Hart Centre for Military Archives
Lancs. RO	Lancashire Record Office, Preston
L. Cong.	Library of Congress, Washington, DC
Leics. RO	Leicestershire, Leicester, and Rutland Record Office, Leicester
Lincs. Arch.	Lincolnshire Archives, Lincoln
Linn. Soc.	Linnean Society of London
LMA	London Metropolitan Archives
LPL	Lambeth Palace, London
Lpool RO	Liverpool Record Office and Local Studies Service
LUL	London University Library
Magd. Cam.	Magdalene College, Cambridge
Magd. Oxf.	Magdalen College, Oxford
Man. City Gall.	Manchester City Galleries
Man. CL	Manchester Central Library
Mass. Hist. Soc.	Massachusetts Historical Society, Boston
Merton Oxf.	Merton College, Oxford
MHS Oxf.	Museum of the History of Science, Oxford
Mitchell L., Glas.	Mitchell Library, Glasgow
Mitchell L., NSW	State Library of New South Wales, Sydney, Mitchell Library
Morgan L.	Pierpont Morgan Library, New York
NA Canada	National Archives of Canada, Ottawa
NA Ire.	National Archives of Ireland, Dublin
NAM	National Army Museum, London
NA Scot.	National Archives of Scotland, Edinburgh
News Int. RO	News International Record Office, London
NG Ire.	National Gallery of Ireland, Dublin

NG Scot.	National Gallery of Scotland, Edinburgh
NHM	Natural History Museum, London
NL Aus.	National Library of Australia, Canberra
NL Ire.	National Library of Ireland, Dublin
NL NZ	National Library of New Zealand, Wellington
NL NZ, Turnbull L.	National Library of New Zealand, Wellington, Alexander Turnbull Library
NL Scot.	National Library of Scotland, Edinburgh
NL Wales	National Library of Wales, Aberystwyth
NMG Wales	National Museum and Gallery of Wales, Cardiff
NMM	National Maritime Museum, London
Norfolk RO	Norfolk Record Office, Norwich
Northants. RO	Northamptonshire Record Office, Northampton
Northumbd RO	Northumberland Record Office
Notts. Arch.	Nottinghamshire Archives, Nottingham
NPG	National Portrait Gallery, London
NRA	National Archives, London, Historical Manuscripts Commission, National Register of Archives
Nuffield Oxf.	Nuffield College, Oxford
N. Yorks. CRO	North Yorkshire County Record Office, Northallerton
NYPL	New York Public Library
Oxf. UA	Oxford University Archives
Oxf. U. Mus. NH	Oxford University Museum of Natural History
Oxon. RO	Oxfordshire Record Office, Oxford
Pembroke Cam.	Pembroke College, Cambridge
PRO	National Archives, London, Public Record Office
PRO NIre.	Public Record Office for Northern Ireland, Belfast
Pusey Oxf.	Pusey House, Oxford
RA	Royal Academy of Arts, London
Ransom HRC	Harry Ransom Humanities Research Center, University of Texas, Austin
RAS	Royal Astronomical Society, London
RBG Kew	Royal Botanic Gardens, Kew, London
RCP Lond.	Royal College of Physicians of London
RCS Eng.	Royal College of Surgeons of England, London
RGS	Royal Geographical Society, London
RIBA	Royal Institute of British Architects, London
RIBA BAL	Royal Institute of British Architects, London, British Architectural Library
Royal Arch.	Royal Archives, Windsor Castle, Berkshire [by gracious permission of her majesty the queen]
Royal Irish Acad.	Royal Irish Academy, Dublin
Royal Scot. Acad.	Royal Scottish Academy, Edinburgh
RS	Royal Society, London
RSA	Royal Society of Arts, London
RS Friends, Lond.	Religious Society of Friends, London
St Ant. Oxf.	St Antony's College, Oxford
St John Cam.	St John's College, Cambridge
S. Antiquaries, Lond.	Society of Antiquaries of London
Sci. Mus.	Science Museum, London
Scot. NPG	Scottish National Portrait Gallery, Edinburgh
Scott Polar RI	University of Cambridge, Scott Polar Research Institute
Sheff. Arch.	Sheffield Archives
Shrops. RRC	Shropshire Records and Research Centre, Shrewsbury
SOAS	School of Oriental and African Studies, London
Som. ARS	Somerset Archive and Record Service, Taunton
Staffs. RO	Staffordshire Record Office, Stafford

Suffolk RO	Suffolk Record Office
Surrey HC	Surrey History Centre, Woking
TCD	Trinity College, Dublin
Trinity Cam.	Trinity College, Cambridge
U. Aberdeen	University of Aberdeen
U. Birm.	University of Birmingham
U. Birm. L.	University of Birmingham Library
U. Cal.	University of California
U. Cam.	University of Cambridge
UCL	University College, London
U. Durham	University of Durham
U. Durham L.	University of Durham Library
U. Edin.	University of Edinburgh
U. Edin., New Coll.	University of Edinburgh, New College
U. Edin., New Coll. L.	University of Edinburgh, New College Library
U. Edin. L.	University of Edinburgh Library
U. Glas.	University of Glasgow
U. Glas. L.	University of Glasgow Library
U. Hull	University of Hull
U. Hull, Brynmor Jones L.	University of Hull, Brynmor Jones Library
U. Leeds	University of Leeds
U. Leeds, Brotherton L.	University of Leeds, Brotherton Library
U. Lond.	University of London
U. Lpool	University of Liverpool
U. Lpool L.	University of Liverpool Library
U. Mich.	University of Michigan, Ann Arbor
U. Mich., Clements L.	University of Michigan, Ann Arbor, William L. Clements Library
U. Newcastle	University of Newcastle upon Tyne
U. Newcastle, Robinson L.	University of Newcastle upon Tyne, Robinson Library
U. Nott.	University of Nottingham
U. Nott. L.	University of Nottingham Library
U. Oxf.	University of Oxford
U. Reading	University of Reading
U. Reading L.	University of Reading Library
U. St Andr.	University of St Andrews
U. St Andr. L.	University of St Andrews Library
U. Southampton	University of Southampton
U. Southampton L.	University of Southampton Library
U. Sussex	University of Sussex, Brighton
U. Texas	University of Texas, Austin
U. Wales	University of Wales
U. Warwick Mod. RC	University of Warwick, Coventry, Modern Records Centre
V&A	Victoria and Albert Museum, London
V&A NAL	Victoria and Albert Museum, London, National Art Library
Warks. CRO	Warwickshire County Record Office, Warwick
Wellcome L.	Wellcome Library for the History and Understanding of Medicine, London
Westm. DA	Westminster Diocesan Archives, London
Wilts. & Swindon RO	Wiltshire and Swindon Record Office, Trowbridge
Worcs. RO	Worcestershire Record Office, Worcester
W. Sussex RO	West Sussex Record Office, Chichester
W. Yorks. AS	West Yorkshire Archive Service
Yale U.	Yale University, New Haven, Connecticut
Yale U., Beinecke L.	Yale University, New Haven, Connecticut, Beinecke Rare Book and Manuscript Library
Yale U. CBA	Yale University, New Haven, Connecticut, Yale Center for British Art

3. Bibliographic abbreviations

Adams, *Drama*	W. D. Adams, *A dictionary of the drama*, 1: *A–G* (1904); 2: *H–Z* (1956) [vol. 2 microfilm only]
AFM	J O'Donovan, ed. and trans., *Annala rioghachta Eireann / Annals of the kingdom of Ireland by the four masters*, 7 vols. (1848–51); 2nd edn (1856); 3rd edn (1990)
Allibone, *Dict.*	S. A. Allibone, *A critical dictionary of English literature and British and American authors*, 3 vols. (1859–71); suppl. by J. F. Kirk, 2 vols. (1891)
ANB	J. A. Garraty and M. C. Carnes, eds., *American national biography*, 24 vols. (1999)
Anderson, *Scot. nat.*	W. Anderson, *The Scottish nation, or, The surnames, families, literature, honours, and biographical history of the people of Scotland*, 3 vols. (1859–63)
Ann. mon.	H. R. Luard, ed., *Annales monastici*, 5 vols., Rolls Series, 36 (1864–9)
Ann. Ulster	S. Mac Airt and G. Mac Niocaill, eds., *Annals of Ulster (to AD 1131)* (1983)
APC	*Acts of the privy council of England*, new ser., 46 vols. (1890–1964)
APS	*The acts of the parliaments of Scotland*, 12 vols. in 13 (1814–75)
Arber, *Regs. Stationers*	F. Arber, ed., *A transcript of the registers of the Company of Stationers of London, 1554–1640 AD*, 5 vols. (1875–94)
ArchR	*Architectural Review*
ASC	D. Whitelock, D. C. Douglas, and S. I. Tucker, ed. and trans., *The Anglo-Saxon Chronicle: a revised translation* (1961)
AS chart.	P. H. Sawyer, *Anglo-Saxon charters: an annotated list and bibliography*, Royal Historical Society Guides and Handbooks (1968)
AusDB	D. Pike and others, eds., *Australian dictionary of biography*, 16 vols. (1966–2002)
Baker, *Serjeants*	J. H. Baker, *The order of serjeants at law*, SeldS, suppl. ser., 5 (1984)
Bale, *Cat.*	J. Bale, *Scriptorum illustrium Maioris Brytannie, quam nunc Angliam et Scotiam vocant: catalogus*, 2 vols. in 1 (Basel, 1557–9); facs. edn (1971)
Bale, *Index*	J. Bale, *Index Britanniae scriptorum*, ed. R. L. Poole and M. Bateson (1902); facs. edn (1990)
BBCS	*Bulletin of the Board of Celtic Studies*
BDMBR	J. O. Baylen and N. J. Gossman, eds., *Biographical dictionary of modern British radicals*, 3 vols. in 4 (1979–88)
Bede, *Hist. eccl.*	*Bede's Ecclesiastical history of the English people*, ed. and trans. B. Colgrave and R. A. B. Mynors, OMT (1969); repr. (1991)
Bénézit, *Dict.*	E. Bénézit, *Dictionnaire critique et documentaire des peintres, sculpteurs, dessinateurs et graveurs*, 3 vols. (Paris, 1911–23); new edn, 8 vols. (1948–66), repr. (1966); 3rd edn, rev. and enl., 10 vols. (1976); 4th edn, 14 vols. (1999)
BIHR	*Bulletin of the Institute of Historical Research*
Birch, *Seals*	W. de Birch, *Catalogue of seals in the department of manuscripts in the British Museum*, 6 vols. (1887–1900)
Bishop Burnet's History	*Bishop Burnet's History of his own time*, ed. M. J. Routh, 2nd edn, 6 vols. (1833)
Blackwood	*Blackwood's [Edinburgh] Magazine*, 328 vols. (1817–1980)
Blain, Clements & Grundy, *Feminist comp.*	V. Blain, P. Clements, and I. Grundy, eds., *The feminist companion to literature in English* (1990)
BL cat.	*The British Library general catalogue of printed books* [in 360 vols. with suppls., also CD-ROM and online]
BMJ	*British Medical Journal*
Boase & Courtney, *Bibl. Corn.*	G. C. Boase and W. P. Courtney, *Bibliotheca Cornubiensis: a catalogue of the writings … of Cornishmen*, 3 vols. (1874–82)
Boase, *Mod. Eng. biog.*	F. Boase, *Modern English biography: containing many thousand concise memoirs of persons who have died since the year 1850*, 6 vols. (privately printed, Truro, 1892–1921); repr. (1965)
Boswell, *Life*	*Boswell's Life of Johnson: together with Journal of a tour to the Hebrides and Johnson's Diary of a journey into north Wales*, ed. G. B. Hill, enl. edn, rev. L. F. Powell, 6 vols. (1934–50); 2nd edn (1964); repr. (1971)
Brown & Stratton, *Brit. mus.*	J. D. Brown and S. S. Stratton, *British musical biography* (1897)
Bryan, *Painters*	M. Bryan, *A biographical and critical dictionary of painters and engravers*, 2 vols. (1816); new edn, ed. G. Stanley (1849); new edn, ed. R. E. Graves and W. Armstrong, 2 vols. (1886–9); [4th edn], ed. G. C. Williamson, 5 vols. (1903–5) [various reprs.]
Burke, *Gen. GB*	J. Burke, *A genealogical and heraldic history of the commoners of Great Britain and Ireland*, 4 vols. (1833–8); new edn as *A genealogical and heraldic dictionary of the landed gentry of Great Britain and Ireland*, 3 vols. (1843–9) [many later edns]
Burke, *Gen. Ire.*	J. B. Burke, *A genealogical and heraldic history of the landed gentry of Ireland* (1899); 2nd edn (1904); 3rd edn (1912); 4th edn (1958); 5th edn as *Burke's Irish family records* (1976)
Burke, *Peerage*	J. Burke, *A general* [later edns *A genealogical*] *and heraldic dictionary of the peerage and baronetage of the United Kingdom* [later edns *the British empire*] (1829–)
Burney, *Hist. mus.*	C. Burney, *A general history of music, from the earliest ages to the present period*, 4 vols. (1776–89)
Burtchaell & Sadleir, *Alum. Dubl.*	G. D. Burtchaell and T. U. Sadleir, *Alumni Dublinenses: a register of the students, graduates, and provosts of Trinity College* (1924); [2nd edn], with suppl., in 2 pts (1935)
Calamy rev.	A. G. Matthews, *Calamy revised* (1934); repr. (1988)
CCI	*Calendar of confirmations and inventories granted and given up in the several commissariots of Scotland* (1876–)
CCIR	*Calendar of the close rolls preserved in the Public Record Office*, 47 vols. (1892–1963)
CDS	J. Bain, ed., *Calendar of documents relating to Scotland*, 4 vols., PRO (1881–8); suppl. vol. 5, ed. G. G. Simpson and J. D. Galbraith [1986]
CEPR letters	W. H. Bliss, C. Johnson, and J. Twemlow, eds., *Calendar of entries in the papal registers relating to Great Britain and Ireland: papal letters* (1893–)
CGPLA	*Calendars of the grants of probate and letters of administration* [in 4 ser.: *England & Wales, Northern Ireland, Ireland*, and *Éire*]
Chambers, *Scots.*	R. Chambers, ed., *A biographical dictionary of eminent Scotsmen*, 4 vols. (1832–5)
Chancery records	chancery records pubd by the PRO
Chancery records (RC)	chancery records pubd by the Record Commissions

CIPM Calendar of inquisitions post mortem, [20 vols.], PRO (1904–); also Henry VII, 3 vols. (1898–1955)

Clarendon, *Hist. rebellion* E. Hyde, earl of Clarendon, The history of the rebellion and civil wars in England, 6 vols. (1888); repr. (1958) and (1992)

Cobbett, *Parl. hist.* W. Cobbett and J. Wright, eds., Cobbett's Parliamentary history of England, 36 vols. (1806–1820)

Colvin, *Archs.* H. Colvin, A biographical dictionary of British architects, 1600–1840, 3rd edn (1995)

Cooper, *Ath. Cantab.* C. H. Cooper and T. Cooper, Athenae Cantabrigienses, 3 vols. (1858–1913); repr. (1967)

CPR Calendar of the patent rolls preserved in the Public Record Office (1891–)

Crockford Crockford's Clerical Directory

CS Camden Society

CSP Calendar of state papers [in 11 ser.: domestic, Scotland, Scottish series, Ireland, colonial, Commonwealth, foreign, Spain [at Simancas], Rome, Milan, and Venice]

CYS Canterbury and York Society

DAB Dictionary of American biography, 21 vols. (1928–36), repr. in 11 vols. (1964); 10 suppls. (1944–96)

DBB D. J. Jeremy, ed., Dictionary of business biography, 5 vols. (1984–6)

DCB G. W. Brown and others, Dictionary of Canadian biography, [14 vols.] (1966–)

Debrett's Peerage Debrett's Peerage (1803–) [sometimes Debrett's Illustrated peerage]

Desmond, *Botanists* R. Desmond, Dictionary of British and Irish botanists and horticulturists (1977); rev. edn (1994)

Dir. Brit. archs. A. Felstead, J. Franklin, and L. Pinfield, eds., Directory of British architects, 1834–1900 (1993); 2nd edn, ed. A. Brodie and others, 2 vols. (2001)

DLB J. M. Bellamy and J. Saville, eds., Dictionary of labour biography, [10 vols.] (1972–)

DLitB Dictionary of Literary Biography

DNB Dictionary of national biography, 63 vols. (1885–1900), suppl., 3 vols. (1901); repr. in 22 vols. (1908–9); 10 further suppls. (1912–96); Missing persons (1993)

DNZB W. H. Oliver and C. Orange, eds., The dictionary of New Zealand biography, 5 vols. (1990–2000)

DSAB W. J. de Kock and others, eds., Dictionary of South African biography, 5 vols. (1968–87)

DSB C. C. Gillispie and F. L. Holmes, eds., Dictionary of scientific biography, 16 vols. (1970–80); repr. in 8 vols. (1981); 2 vol. suppl. (1990)

DSBB A. Slaven and S. Checkland, eds., Dictionary of Scottish business biography, 1860–1960, 2 vols. (1986–90)

DSCHT N. M. de S. Cameron and others, eds., Dictionary of Scottish church history and theology (1993)

Dugdale, *Monasticon* W. Dugdale, Monasticon Anglicanum, 3 vols. (1655–72); 2nd edn, 3 vols. (1661–82); new edn, ed. J. Caley, J. Ellis, and B. Bandinel, 6 vols. in 8 pts (1817–30); repr. (1846) and (1970)

DWB J. E. Lloyd and others, eds., Dictionary of Welsh biography down to 1940 (1959) [Eng. trans. of Y bywgraffiadur Cymreig hyd 1940, 2nd edn (1954)]

EdinR Edinburgh Review, or, Critical Journal

EETS Early English Text Society

Emden, *Cam.* A. B. Emden, A biographical register of the University of Cambridge to 1500 (1963)

Emden, *Oxf.* A. B. Emden, A biographical register of the University of Oxford to AD 1500, 3 vols. (1957–9); also A biographical register of the University of Oxford, AD 1501 to 1540 (1974)

EngHR English Historical Review

Engraved Brit. ports. F. M. O'Donoghue and H. M. Hake, Catalogue of engraved British portraits preserved in the department of prints and drawings in the British Museum, 6 vols. (1908–25)

ER The English Reports, 178 vols. (1900–32)

ESTC English short title catalogue, 1475–1800 [CD-ROM and online]

Evelyn, *Diary* The diary of John Evelyn, ed. E. S. De Beer, 6 vols. (1955); repr. (2000)

Farington, *Diary* The diary of Joseph Farington, ed. K. Garlick and others, 17 vols. (1978–98)

Fasti Angl. (Hardy) J. Le Neve, Fasti ecclesiae Anglicanae, ed. T. D. Hardy, 3 vols. (1854)

Fasti Angl., 1066–1300 [J. Le Neve], Fasti ecclesiae Anglicanae, 1066–1300, ed. D. E. Greenway and J. S. Barrow, [8 vols.] (1968–)

Fasti Angl., 1300–1541 [J. Le Neve], Fasti ecclesiae Anglicanae, 1300–1541, 12 vols. (1962–7)

Fasti Angl., 1541–1857 [J. Le Neve], Fasti ecclesiae Anglicanae, 1541–1857, ed. J. M. Horn, D. M. Smith, and D. S. Bailey, [9 vols.] (1969–)

Fasti Scot. H. Scott, Fasti ecclesiae Scoticanae, 3 vols. in 6 (1871); new edn, [11 vols.] (1915–)

FO List Foreign Office List

Fortescue, *Brit. army* J. W. Fortescue, A history of the British army, 13 vols. (1899–1930)

Foss, *Judges* E. Foss, The judges of England, 9 vols. (1848–64); repr. (1966)

Foster, *Alum. Oxon.* J. Foster, ed., Alumni Oxonienses: the members of the University of Oxford, 1715–1886, 4 vols. (1887–8); later edn (1891); also Alumni Oxonienses … 1500–1714, 4 vols. (1891–2); 8 vol. repr. (1968) and (2000)

Fuller, *Worthies* T. Fuller, The history of the worthies of England, 4 pts (1662); new edn, 2 vols., ed. J. Nichols (1811); new edn, 3 vols., ed. P. A. Nuttall (1840); repr. (1965)

GEC, *Baronetage* G. E. Cokayne, Complete baronetage, 6 vols. (1900–09); repr. (1983) [microprint]

GEC, *Peerage* G. E. C. [G. E. Cokayne], The complete peerage of England, Scotland, Ireland, Great Britain, and the United Kingdom, 8 vols. (1887–98); new edn, ed. V. Gibbs and others, 14 vols. in 15 (1910–98); microprint repr. (1982) and (1987)

Genest, *Eng. stage* J. Genest, Some account of the English stage from the Restoration in 1660 to 1830, 10 vols. (1832); repr. [New York, 1965]

Gillow, *Lit. biog. hist.* J. Gillow, A literary and biographical history or bibliographical dictionary of the English Catholics, from the breach with Rome, in 1534, to the present time, 5 vols. [1885–1902]; repr. (1961); repr. with preface by C. Gillow (1999)

Gir. Camb. opera Giraldi Cambrensis opera, ed. J. S. Brewer, J. F. Dimock, and G. F. Warner, 8 vols., Rolls Series, 21 (1861–91)

GJ Geographical Journal

Gladstone, *Diaries* — *The Gladstone diaries: with cabinet minutes and prime-ministerial correspondence*, ed. M. R. D. Foot and H. C. G. Matthew, 14 vols. (1968–94)

GM — *Gentleman's Magazine*

Graves, *Artists* — A. Graves, ed., *A dictionary of artists who have exhibited works in the principal London exhibitions of oil paintings from 1760 to 1880* (1884); new edn (1895); 3rd edn (1901); facs. edn (1969); repr. [1970], (1973), and (1984)

Graves, *Brit. Inst.* — A. Graves, *The British Institution, 1806–1867: a complete dictionary of contributors and their work from the foundation of the institution* (1875); facs. edn (1908); repr. (1969)

Graves, *RA exhibitors* — A. Graves, *The Royal Academy of Arts: a complete dictionary of contributors and their work from its foundation in 1769 to 1904*, 8 vols. (1905–6); repr. in 4 vols. (1970) and (1972)

Graves, *Soc. Artists* — A. Graves, *The Society of Artists of Great Britain, 1760–1791, the Free Society of Artists, 1761–1783: a complete dictionary* (1907); facs. edn (1969)

Greaves & Zaller, *BDBR* — R. L. Greaves and R. Zaller, eds., *Biographical dictionary of British radicals in the seventeenth century*, 3 vols. (1982–4)

Grove, *Dict. mus.* — G. Grove, ed., *A dictionary of music and musicians*, 5 vols. (1878–90); 2nd edn, ed. J. A. Fuller Maitland (1904–10); 3rd edn, ed. H. C. Colles (1927); 4th edn with suppl. (1940); 5th edn, ed. E. Blom, 9 vols. (1954); suppl. (1961) [see also *New Grove*]

Hall, *Dramatic ports.* — L. A. Hall, *Catalogue of dramatic portraits in the theatre collection of the Harvard College library*, 4 vols. (1930–34)

Hansard — *Hansard's parliamentary debates*, ser. 1–5 (1803–)

Highfill, Burnim & Langhans, *BDA* — P. H. Highfill, K. A. Burnim, and E. A. Langhans, *A biographical dictionary of actors, actresses, musicians, dancers, managers, and other stage personnel in London, 1660–1800*, 16 vols. (1973–93)

Hist. U. Oxf. — T. H. Aston, ed., *The history of the University of Oxford*, 8 vols. (1984–2000) [1: *The early Oxford schools*, ed. J. I. Catto (1984); 2: *Late medieval Oxford*, ed. J. I. Catto and R. Evans (1992); 3: *The collegiate university*, ed. J. McConica (1986); 4: *Seventeenth-century Oxford*, ed. N. Tyacke (1997); 5: *The eighteenth century*, ed. L. S. Sutherland and L. G. Mitchell (1986); 6–7: *Nineteenth-century Oxford*, ed. M. G. Brock and M. C. Curthoys (1997–2000); 8: *The twentieth century*, ed. B. Harrison (2000)]

HJ — *Historical Journal*

HMC — Historical Manuscripts Commission

Holdsworth, *Eng. law* — W. S. Holdsworth, *A history of English law*, ed. A. L. Goodhart and H. L. Hanbury, 17 vols. (1903–72)

HoP, Commons — *The history of parliament: the House of Commons* [1386–1421, ed. J. S. Roskell, L. Clark, and C. Rawcliffe, 4 vols. (1992); 1509–1558, ed. S. T. Bindoff, 3 vols. (1982); 1558–1603, ed. P. W. Hasler, 3 vols. (1981); 1660–1690, ed. B. D. Henning, 3 vols. (1983); 1690–1715, ed. D. W. Hayton, E. Cruickshanks, and S. Handley, 5 vols. (2002); 1715–1754, ed. R. Sedgwick, 2 vols. (1970); 1754–1790, ed. L. Namier and J. Brooke, 3 vols. (1964), repr. (1985); 1790–1820, ed. R. G. Thorne, 5 vols. (1986); in draft (used with permission): 1422–1504, 1604–1629, 1640–1660, and 1820–1832]

IGI — *International Genealogical Index*, Church of Jesus Christ of the Latterday Saints

ILN — *Illustrated London News*

IMC — Irish Manuscripts Commission

Irving, *Scots.* — J. Irving, ed., *The book of Scotsmen eminent for achievements in arms and arts, church and state, law, legislation and literature, commerce, science, travel and philanthropy* (1881)

JCS — *Journal of the Chemical Society*

JHC — *Journals of the House of Commons*

JHL — *Journals of the House of Lords*

John of Worcester, *Chron.* — *The chronicle of John of Worcester*, ed. R. R. Darlington and P. McGurk, trans. J. Bray and P. McGurk, 3 vols., OMT (1995–) [vol. 1 forthcoming]

Keeler, *Long Parliament* — M. F. Keeler, *The Long Parliament, 1640–1641: a biographical study of its members* (1954)

Kelly, *Handbk* — *The upper ten thousand: an alphabetical list of all members of noble families*, 3 vols. (1875–7); continued as *Kelly's handbook of the upper ten thousand for 1878* [1879], 2 vols. (1878–9); continued as *Kelly's handbook to the titled, landed and official classes*, 94 vols. (1880–1973)

LondG — *London Gazette*

LP Henry VIII — J. S. Brewer, J. Gairdner, and R. H. Brodie, eds., *Letters and papers, foreign and domestic, of the reign of Henry VIII*, 23 vols. in 38 (1862–1932); repr. (1965)

Mallalieu, *Watercolour artists* — H. L. Mallalieu, *The dictionary of British watercolour artists up to 1820*, 3 vols. (1976–90); vol. 1, 2nd edn (1986)

Memoirs FRS — *Biographical Memoirs of Fellows of the Royal Society*

MGH — Monumenta Germaniae Historica

MT — *Musical Times*

Munk, *Roll* — W. Munk, *The roll of the Royal College of Physicians of London*, 2 vols. (1861); 2nd edn, 3 vols. (1878)

N&Q — *Notes and Queries*

New Grove — S. Sadie, ed., *The new Grove dictionary of music and musicians*, 20 vols. (1980); 2nd edn, 29 vols. (2001) [also online edn; see also Grove, *Dict. mus.*]

Nichols, *Illustrations* — J. Nichols and J. B. Nichols, *Illustrations of the literary history of the eighteenth century*, 8 vols. (1817–58)

Nichols, *Lit. anecdotes* — J. Nichols, *Literary anecdotes of the eighteenth century*, 9 vols. (1812–16); facs. edn (1966)

Obits. FRS — *Obituary Notices of Fellows of the Royal Society*

O'Byrne, *Naval biog. dict.* — W. R. O'Byrne, *A naval biographical dictionary* (1849); repr. (1990); [2nd edn], 2 vols. (1861)

OHS — Oxford Historical Society

Old Westminsters — *The record of Old Westminsters*, 1–2, ed. G. F. R. Barker and A. H. Stenning (1928); suppl. 1, ed. J. B. Whitmore and G. R. Y. Radcliffe [1938]; 3, ed. J. B. Whitmore, G. R. Y. Radcliffe, and D. C. Simpson (1963); suppl. 2, ed. F. E. Pagan (1978); 4, ed. F. E. Pagan and H. E. Pagan (1992)

OMT — Oxford Medieval Texts

Ordericus Vitalis, *Eccl. hist.* — *The ecclesiastical history of Orderic Vitalis*, ed. and trans. M. Chibnall, 6 vols., OMT (1969–80); repr. (1990)

Paris, *Chron.* — *Matthaei Parisiensis, monachi sancti Albani, chronica majora*, ed. H. R. Luard, Rolls Series, 7 vols. (1872–83)

Parl. papers — *Parliamentary papers* (1801–)

PBA — *Proceedings of the British Academy*

Pepys, *Diary*	*The diary of Samuel Pepys*, ed. R. Latham and W. Matthews, 11 vols. (1970–83); repr. (1995) and (2000)
Pevsner	N. Pevsner and others, Buildings of England series
PICE	*Proceedings of the Institution of Civil Engineers*
Pipe rolls	*The great roll of the pipe for . . .*, PRSoc. (1884–)
PRO	Public Record Office
PRS	*Proceedings of the Royal Society of London*
PRSoc.	Pipe Roll Society
PTRS	*Philosophical Transactions of the Royal Society*
QR	*Quarterly Review*
RC	Record Commissions
Redgrave, *Artists*	S. Redgrave, *A dictionary of artists of the English school* (1874); rev. edn (1878); repr. (1970)
Reg. Oxf.	C. W. Boase and A. Clark, eds., *Register of the University of Oxford*, 5 vols., OHS, 1, 10–12, 14 (1885–9)
Reg. PCS	J. H. Burton and others, eds., *The register of the privy council of Scotland*, 1st ser., 14 vols. (1877–98); 2nd ser., 8 vols. (1899–1908); 3rd ser., [16 vols.] (1908–70)
Reg. RAN	H. W. C. Davis and others, eds., *Regesta regum Anglo-Normannorum, 1066–1154*, 4 vols. (1913–69)
RIBA Journal	*Journal of the Royal Institute of British Architects* [later *RIBA Journal*]
RotP	J. Strachey, ed., *Rotuli parliamentorum ut et petitiones, et placita in parliamento*, 6 vols. (1767–77)
RotS	D. Macpherson, J. Caley, and W. Illingworth, eds., *Rotuli Scotiae in Turri Londinensi et in domo capitulari Westmonasteriensi asservati*, 2 vols., RC, 14 (1814–19)
RS	Record(s) Society
Rymer, *Foedera*	T. Rymer and R. Sanderson, eds., *Foedera, conventiones, literae et cuiuscunque generis acta publica inter reges Angliae et alios quosvis imperatores, reges, pontifices, principes, vel communitates*, 20 vols. (1704–35); 2nd edn, 20 vols. (1726–35); 3rd edn, 10 vols. (1739–45); facs. edn (1967); new edn, ed. A. Clarke, J. Caley, and F. Holbrooke, 4 vols., RC, 50 (1816–30)
Sainty, *Judges*	J. Sainty, ed., *The judges of England, 1272–1990*, SeldS, suppl. ser., 10 (1993)
Sainty, *King's counsel*	J. Sainty, ed., *A list of English law officers and king's counsel*, SeldS, suppl. ser., 7 (1987)
SCH	Studies in Church History
Scots peerage	J. B. Paul, ed., *The Scots peerage, founded on Wood's edition of Sir Robert Douglas's Peerage of Scotland, containing an historical and genealogical account of the nobility of that kingdom*, 9 vols. (1904–14)
SeldS	Selden Society
SHR	*Scottish Historical Review*
State trials	T. B. Howell and T. J. Howell, eds., *Cobbett's Complete collection of state trials*, 34 vols. (1809–28)
STC, 1475–1640	A. W. Pollard, G. R. Redgrave, and others, eds., *A short-title catalogue of . . . English books . . . 1475–1640* (1926); 2nd edn, ed. W. A. Jackson, F. S. Ferguson, and K. F. Pantzer, 3 vols. (1976–91) [see also Wing, *STC*]
STS	Scottish Text Society
SurtS	Surtees Society
Symeon of Durham, *Opera*	*Symeonis monachi opera omnia*, ed. T. Arnold, 2 vols., Rolls Series, 75 (1882–5); repr. (1965)
Tanner, *Bibl. Brit.-Hib.*	T. Tanner, *Bibliotheca Britannico-Hibernica*, ed. D. Wilkins (1748); repr. (1963)
Thieme & Becker, *Allgemeines Lexikon*	U. Thieme, F. Becker, and H. Vollmer, eds., *Allgemeines Lexikon der bildenden Künstler von der Antike bis zur Gegenwart*, 37 vols. (Leipzig, 1907–50); repr. (1961–5), (1983), and (1992)
Thurloe, *State papers*	*A collection of the state papers of John Thurloe*, ed. T. Birch, 7 vols. (1742)
TLS	*Times Literary Supplement*
Tout, *Admin. hist.*	T. F. Tout, *Chapters in the administrative history of mediaeval England: the wardrobe, the chamber, and the small seals*, 6 vols. (1920–33); repr. (1967)
TRHS	*Transactions of the Royal Historical Society*
VCH	H. A. Doubleday and others, eds., *The Victoria history of the counties of England*, [88 vols.] (1900–)
Venn, *Alum. Cant.*	J. Venn and J. A. Venn, *Alumni Cantabrigienses: a biographical list of all known students, graduates, and holders of office at the University of Cambridge, from the earliest times to 1900*, 10 vols. (1922–54); repr. in 2 vols. (1974–8)
Vertue, *Note books*	[G. Vertue], *Note books*, ed. K. Esdaile, earl of Ilchester, and H. M. Hake, 6 vols., Walpole Society, 18, 20, 22, 24, 26, 30 (1930–55)
VF	*Vanity Fair*
Walford, *County families*	E. Walford, *The county families of the United Kingdom, or, Royal manual of the titled and untitled aristocracy of Great Britain and Ireland* (1860)
Walker rev.	A. G. Matthews, *Walker revised: being a revision of John Walker's Sufferings of the clergy during the grand rebellion, 1642–60* (1948); repr. (1988)
Walpole, *Corr.*	*The Yale edition of Horace Walpole's correspondence*, ed. W. S. Lewis, 48 vols. (1937–83)
Ward, *Men of the reign*	T. H. Ward, ed., *Men of the reign: a biographical dictionary of eminent persons of British and colonial birth who have died during the reign of Queen Victoria* (1885); repr. (Graz, 1968)
Waterhouse, *18c painters*	E. Waterhouse, *The dictionary of 18th century painters in oils and crayons* (1981); repr. as *British 18th century painters in oils and crayons* (1991), vol. 2 of *Dictionary of British art*
Watt, *Bibl. Brit.*	R. Watt, *Bibliotheca Britannica, or, A general index to British and foreign literature*, 4 vols. (1824) [many reprs.]
Wellesley index	W. E. Houghton, ed., *The Wellesley index to Victorian periodicals, 1824–1900*, 5 vols. (1966–89); new edn (1999) [CD-ROM]
Wing, *STC*	D. Wing, ed., *Short-title catalogue of . . . English books . . . 1641–1700*, 3 vols. (1945–51); 2nd edn (1972–88); rev. and enl. edn, ed. J. J. Morrison, C. W. Nelson, and M. Seccombe, 4 vols. (1994–8) [see also *STC, 1475–1640*]
Wisden	*John Wisden's Cricketer's Almanack*
Wood, *Ath. Oxon.*	A. Wood, *Athenae Oxonienses . . . to which are added the Fasti*, 2 vols. (1691–2); 2nd edn (1721); new edn, 4 vols., ed. P. Bliss (1813–20); repr. (1967) and (1969)
Wood, *Vic. painters*	C. Wood, *Dictionary of Victorian painters* (1971); 2nd edn (1978); 3rd edn as *Victorian painters*, 2 vols. (1995), vol. 4 of *Dictionary of British art*
WW	*Who's who* (1849–)
WWBMP	M. Stenton and S. Lees, eds., *Who's who of British members of parliament*, 4 vols. (1976–81)
WWW	*Who was who* (1929–)

Aaron, Richard Ithamar (1901–1987), philosopher, was born on 6 November 1901 at Upper Dulais, Blaendulais, Glamorgan, the son of William Aaron (1864–1937), a draper, and his wife, Margaret Griffith (d. 1940). He was brought up in Llwyfenni, Llangyfelach, Ynystawe, which was his home from 1910 to 1932, and received his secondary education at Ystalyfera grammar school, from where he went to the University of Wales, Cardiff, in 1918 to study history and philosophy. In 1923 he was elected to a fellowship of the University of Wales which enabled him to go to Oriel College, Oxford, where he was awarded the degree of DPhil (1928) for a dissertation entitled 'The history and value of the distinction between intellect and intuition'. His first appointment, in 1926, was as lecturer in the department of philosophy at the University of Wales, Swansea. However, upon the retirement of W. Jenkin Jones in 1932 Aaron was appointed to the chair of philosophy at the University of Wales, Aberystwyth, eventually settling at Bryn Hir, and later at Garth Celyn, St David's Road, Aberystwyth, where he remained until 1986, having retired in 1969. He was brought up in a staunchly Baptist home and remained a faithful member, attending the local church services throughout his life.

Aaron's early publications focused on epistemology and the history of ideas, but a lifelong interest in the philosophy of John Locke was aroused when, in 1935, he discovered the unresearched wealth of material preserved in the Lovelace collection including letters, notebooks, catalogues, and, most exciting of all, an early draft of Locke's *Essay Concerning Human Understanding*, hitherto presumed missing. His research in this area led to the publication, in 1937, of his book on the life and work of John Locke, a book which subsequently came to be recognized as the standard work on the subject. Aaron is critical of Locke's theories of knowledge and perception on several scores, but is sympathetic to his treatment of primary and secondary qualities, of the former in terms of ideas which resemble primary qualities, and of the latter as representing but not resembling powers of objects which depend on their primary qualities. The proofs for the first edition of *John Locke* were read by Rhiannon (Annie) Morgan (b. 1911), daughter of Dr Morgan John Morgan, a medical practitioner, of Aberystwyth. She and Aaron were married at the Bethel Baptist Chapel, Aberystwyth, on 28 July 1937. The two were ideally suited, lived happily, and had five children—three daughters and two sons.

Aaron maintained a lively interest in the welfare of his department, lecturing on a wide range of subjects, inviting famous visiting philosophers to his Philosophy Society, and, not to be forgotten, arranging an annual walk and picnic in the hinterland of Cardiganshire. Aaron was charmingly conservative in some ways. Christmas parties would feature parlour games and carols. He did not take to television until presented with one on his retirement. As for having a car, it was enough for him that his home was within walking distance of the college and the railway station.

Aaron continued to produce a steady flow of articles, including several in Welsh, and also a book in Welsh on the history of philosophy, *Hanes athroniaeth—o Descartes i Hegel* (1932). He loved his native land, but rather regretted that it could not boast a philosopher of the status of Locke, Berkeley, or Hume. He tried to promote interest in philosophizing in Welsh, and established a philosophy section of the University of Wales Guild of Graduates in 1932, a society which still exists, having conducted all its proceedings, which are published annually as *Efrydiau Athronyddol*, entirely in Welsh. Among his other articles are some concerned with the problem of universals— 'Two senses of the word universal' published in *Mind* (1939) and 'Our knowledge of universals' read to the British Academy and published in its *Proceedings*, volume 23 (1945).

Aaron's work on universals culminated in another substantial book, *The Theory of Universals* (1952). He attacks the notion of universals as Platonic forms, but is equally critical of Aristotelian realism about essences, as he is also of nominalism and conceptualism as theories of universals. He defends the notion of common qualities which he regards as identities; 'the colour of this postage stamp does not resemble the colour of the second stamp but is identical with it'. We grasp the concept of such a colour by abstracting—singling out the colour and thereby getting an image of it. There is, however, a second feature of Aaron's theory. He argues that grasping the meaning of a word such as 'house' is a matter of acquiring a disposition to use the word in a certain way as a result of familiarity with a recurring pattern. Aaron produced a second edition of his book on universals, and this includes an additional section dealing with the views of Frege.

Aaron continued publishing several articles in learned journals throughout the fifties. When the Joint Session of Mind and the Aristotelian Society was held in Aberystwyth in 1956 it fell to Aaron to give the inaugural lecture. The following year he was president of the Aristotelian Society. Earlier, in 1952–3, he was visiting professor at Yale University, where he was able to study Draft C of Locke's *Essay* at the Pierpont Morgan Library. The fruits of the study appeared, in 1955, as a substantial addition in the second edition of his *John Locke*. In the same year he was elected a member of the British Academy, and to the presidency of the Mind Association.

As chairman of the Central Advisory Council for Education (Wales), Aaron was responsible for the reports that came out in 1948, 1951, and 1953. The Council for Wales also produced three important reports during his chairmanship of that body. He served as vice-chairman of Coleg Harlech for many years, and also as chairman of the Library Advisory Council (Wales).

In 1967 Aaron published a second edition of *The Theory of Universals*, with a new preface, several additions, and whole chapters rewritten. The third edition of his book on Locke was ready in 1971, when his last book, *Knowing and the Function of Reason*, appeared. The book includes a wide-ranging discussion of the logical principles of non-contradiction, excluded middle, identity, of the use of language in speech and thought, and of substance and causality. Aaron's own view is that there is such a thing as fallible opinion, which is not satisfactory and less than we often have, but we can also conceive of infallible knowing, which, however, we never actually obtain. But, he maintains, there is something better than fallible opinion, which nevertheless falls short of infallible knowledge, namely, feeling sure—what Aaron also calls 'probable knowledge'.

Upon his retirement in 1969 Aaron taught for a semester at Carlton College, Minnesota. When he returned he was busy writing articles for the 1974 edition of *Encyclopaedia Britannica*. Eventually he succumbed to Alzheimer's disease, and was given the unstinting support of his family, particularly his wife, Rhiannon. He died peacefully at his home, 22 North Parade, Aberystwyth, on 29 March 1987, and was buried in the cemetery at Llanbadarn Road, Aberystwyth, on 4 April.   O. R. JONES

Sources O. R. Jones, 'Richard Ithamar Aaron, 1901–1987', *PBA*, 73 (1987), 375–90 · *The Aaron philosophy collection: the library of Professor Richard I. Aaron* (1987) [incl. memoir by I. Tipton and D. O. Thomas] · B. B. Thomas, 'Richard I. Aaron', *Efrydiau Athronyddol*, 32 (1969), 12–13 · *The Times* (1 April 1987) · W. C. Davies, 'Yr Oriel: Yr Athro R. I. Aaron, M. A., D.Phil.', *Tywysydd y plant*, 7, 5 (1960), 131–3 · b. cert. · m. cert. · personal knowledge (2004) · private information (2004)
Archives NL Wales, corresp. and papers | NL Wales, letters to Annie Hughes Griffiths and Thomas Iorworth Ellis · NL Wales, corresp. with Thomas Jones
Likenesses photograph, 1969, repro. in Thomas, 'Richard I. Aaron', frontispiece · photograph, 1987, repro. in Jones, *PBA*, pl. XXVIII; priv. coll.
Wealth at death £136,929: probate, 16 Dec 1987, *CGPLA Eng. & Wales*

Abbadie, Jacques [James] (*bap.* 1654?, *d.* 1727), Church of Ireland dean of Killaloe, was born in Nay in Béarn; he is most probably the Jacques Abbadie who was the third child of Violente de Fortaner and Pierre Abbadie, baptized on 27 April 1654. He received his early education at the local protestant school, which was overseen by the pastor and writer Jean de la Placette, and in 1673 went to the protestant academy of Montauban-Puylaurens, and then to the academy of Saumur to study theology. The divergent ethos of these two academies—on the one hand conservative and on the other liberal—left its mark on Abbadie's theological outlook.

By January 1679 Abbadie was in Paris, attached to the French Reformed church at Charenton as a candidate for ministry. The capital city offered Abbadie many opportunities to hear the sermons of the great preachers of the day, and he was particularly taken by the pulpit oratory of the Jesuit Louis Bourdaloue, which he sought to imitate. The ornate style Abbadie acquired in Paris soon earned him a reputation as an able preacher, but it was later one of the many sources of tension between him and some of the French protestant refugees in Ireland. He was awarded his doctorate in divinity at the academy of Sedan on 19 March 1680 and shortly afterwards accepted the invitation of the elector of Brandenburg, conveyed by Louis de Beauveau, count of Espence, to serve the French church in Berlin.

Abbadie preached there for the first time, as a candidate for ministry, on 2 May 1680, and after ordination on 4 September according to the rite of the German Reformed church became the pastor. He spent nine years in this position, although his official discharge was actually issued on 17/27 June 1690, some months after his departure. During his years in Berlin he published a number of works: two volumes of sermons, three occasional sermons, a eulogy of the great elector, a treatise on the eucharist, and his highly acclaimed apology of the Christian religion, the *Traité de la vérité de la religion chrétienne* (1684), which went into some thirty reprints, editions, and translations into English, German, Dutch, and Italian. When the edict of Nantes was revoked (17 October 1685) the elector of Brandenburg issued the edict of Potsdam (29 October 1685) inviting the French protestants to settle in his territories. Abbadie was sent on an official mission to the Netherlands with instructions to encourage as many as possible of the Huguenot refugees to settle in Brandenburg, which had been seriously depopulated by the Thirty Years' War. His return to Berlin in the spring of 1686 was marred by conflict in the French church, which by that time had four ministers in charge of a much larger membership. Friedrich Herman, duke of Schomberg, had arrived in Berlin on 24 April 1687, and when the great elector furnished William of Orange with a regiment led by the duke for the invasion of England, Abbadie may have been invited to accompany him as his personal chaplain. Disenchanted with Berlin, he left in the summer of 1689 and joined Schomberg on 1 September, although he was officially attached to the French regiment of horse. Abbadie was serving as the duke's chaplain, as he later observed, when Schomberg 'was killed upon the spot att the Boyne' (LPL, 'Dean Abbadie, his case'). Deprived of his patron, Abbadie left Ireland some time later for London, where he arrived on 10 or 11 July 1691.

Abbadie's reputation as a preacher and apologist had preceded him, and he was appointed shortly afterwards to a vacancy at the French episcopalian (conforming to the Anglican rite) church of the Savoy in Westminster. Abbadie remained in London for eight years and during this period published his treatise on moral philosophy, the *Art de se connoître soi-même* (1692), which he dedicated to Viscount Sydney, the short-lived lord lieutenant of Ireland. He also published three works in support of what he referred to as the 'hapy revolution' and the 'protestant succession' (LPL, 'Dean Abbadie, his case'); the most substantial of these, the *Défense de la nation britannique* (1692), also contains a justification of the penal laws in Ireland. It was the third of these works, the *Histoire de la dernière conspiration d'Angleterre* (1696), an account of the assassination attempt on William III (15 February 1696), which brought him the preferment for which he had long hoped.

On William III's instructions, Secretary Sir William Trumbull wrote to the lords justices of Ireland on 23 January 1697, informing them that the king had 'a very good opinion' of Abbadie and was 'so well pleased with some service done by him as to design him a recompense', and urged them 'to confer upon him some benefice in Ireland at the first opportunity' (*CSP dom.*, *1697*, 21, 378–9). Unfortunately, the first opportunity was the deanery of St Patrick's, the national Anglican cathedral in Dublin, and Abbadie's poor knowledge of English excluded him from such an important position. Instead he was made rector of Aglishmartin and Castlecomer, and vicar of Odogh, Ballyragget, and Donoughmore in the diocese of Ossory (7 March 1699), and, on 13 May 1699, installed as dean of Killaloe, in co. Clare, a vacancy which arose as a result of the promotion of Jerome Ryves to the deanery of St Patrick's. Abbadie, however, had nourished greater expectations, and he maintained until his death that his transfer to Ireland left him at a financial loss, given that he did not reside at any of these charges and was obliged to pay his replacements out of a relatively low income. He initially settled in Portarlington (1699–1703), Queen's county, where he could enjoy the company of the Huguenot veterans who had been settled there by Henri de Ruvigny, Lord Galway. Following the bitter controversy which divided the French community when conformity to Anglicanism was imposed on the French Reformed church by the bishop of Kildare, William Moreton, with, it was alleged, Abbadie's collaboration, he moved to Dublin. There he became embroiled in further controversy when William King, archbishop of Dublin, involved Abbadie in fruitless efforts to bring the French Reformed refugees into conformity with Anglicanism.

It is clear that Abbadie's reputation as a writer and preacher meant that he was a spiritual figurehead for the refugee community in England and particularly in Ireland, but there was also something about his personality which irritated his contemporaries and undermined the authority and leadership the Anglican authorities expected him to exercise. In Berlin and London his fellow ministers attributed the difficulties they experienced to Abbadie's ambition, but in Ireland, where tensions sometimes ran high between the Huguenots who conformed to the established church and those who chose to remain faithful to the Reformed tradition, his fellow refugees thought of him as arrogant and high-handed. His florid preaching style merely reinforced their view that Abbadie was determined to lord it over them, leaving behind the sobriety of his own tradition. Disappointed by this lack of recognition, Abbadie divided the last years of his life between Dublin, London, and Amsterdam, where he supervised the printing of his two final publications—treatises on the Reformed tradition and on the apocalypse. He died in London on 25 September 1727, embittered by his fruitless attempts to acquire a more lucrative benefice, and convinced that he had not been rewarded, as he thought he deserved, 'for true and constant zeal for the hapy revolution and the succession in the illustrious House of Hanover' ('Dean Abbadie, his case'). He was buried in Marylebone cemetery.   RUTH WHELAN

Sources minute books of the consistory of the French Church, 1672–90, Archiv der Französischen Kirche in Französischen Dom, Berlin · Abbadie's mission to Holland, report to the great elector, Französisches Kolonie-departement, Zentrales Staatsarchiv, Merseburg, 3b I, fas.7.1, fols. 20–22 · 'Dean Abbadie, his case', LPL, Fulham MSS, Gibson 1, fols. 1–2 · J. Abbadie, letter to W. King, 5 April 1704, TCD, MS, 1995–2008/1073 · R. Whelan, 'The dean of Killaloe: Jacques Abbadie', *Lias*, 14 (1987), 101–17 · R. Whelan, 'Points of view: Benjamin de Daillon, William Moreton and the Portarlington affair', *Proceedings of the Huguenot Society*, 26 (1994–7), 463–89 · R. Whelan, 'The Huguenots, the crown and the clergy: Ireland 1704', *Proceedings of the Huguenot Society*, 26 (1994–7), 601–10 · R. Whelan, 'Sanctified by the word: the Huguenots and Anglican liturgy', *Propagating the word of Irish dissent, 1650–1800*, ed. K. Herlihy (1998), 74–94
Likenesses allegorical portrait

Abbas Hilmi II [ʿAbbās Ḥilmi II] (**1874–1944**), last khedive of Egypt, was born on 14 July 1874 in Alexandria, Egypt, the son of Muhammad Tawfiq (1852–1892), sixth ruler of Egypt under the dynasty founded in 1811 by his great-great-grandfather Mehmet Ali, and Princess Emine Hanem (1858–1931), daughter of Ibrahim Ilhami Pasha and the granddaughter of Abbas I. He had a younger brother and three sisters. Egypt was officially part of the Ottoman empire, but was occupied and administered by Britain from 1882.

Brought up in the harem until he was eight, Abbas was subsequently educated at a specially built school next to the Abdin Palace in Cairo until 1883 and then in Switzerland before entering the Theresianum Academy, Vienna, in 1887. He gained a speaking knowledge of Arabic, English, French, and German alongside his Turkish mother tongue. His studies ended abruptly when his father died from pneumonia on 7 January 1892. A day later the Ottoman government recognized him, by virtue of primogeniture, as the new khedive (viceroy) of Egypt. Because he was not eighteen until July, there was uncertainty about whether he could immediately assume the throne. However, Britain wanted to avoid an interregnum and so his age was calculated by the Muslim calendar with its 354 days, making an immediate accession possible. The handsome young sovereign sported a pointed upturned moustache; official portraits depicted him in fez and uniform of the Ottoman ruling family.

As with his father, however, Abbas was allowed only to reign: Lord Cromer (Evelyn Baring), the British agent and consul-general, was the effective ruler of Egypt. But whereas Tawfiq had been grateful to Britain for saving his throne during the Urabi uprising of 1882, Abbas resented the foreign domination. His energetic pursuit of power brought him into conflict with the British residency, the equivalent of government house in a crown colony. In January 1893 he sacked a pro-British prime minister and installed one of his own choosing after Alfred Milner, a senior official in the residency, had advocated maintaining a 'veiled protectorate' in his book *England in Egypt*, published a month earlier. The ministerial crisis ended in a humiliating climb-down by Abbas but it nevertheless presented him as a potential ally for Egypt's nascent nationalist movement. His next showdown with the British occurred in January 1894 after he made disparaging remarks about the Egyptian army to its commander-in-chief Horatio Kitchener. With Kitchener threatening to resign, Britain issued a démarche to Abbas requiring him to retract the comments. The threat of deposition hung

Abbas Hilmi II
(1874–1944), by
Dittrich, pubd 1900

over all subsequent acts of misbehaviour. Kitchener never forgave Abbas and a lasting antipathy ensued. In public Cromer put the khedive's behaviour down to youthful exuberance; his private view was that the dynasty had long been degenerate.

Swayed by a corrupt and sycophantic court, Abbas developed a self-indulgent personality that made it difficult for him to sustain political alliances. He gave financial backing to nationalists but the ensuing relationships foundered because of disagreements over future constitutional arrangements. The khedive wanted a strong monarchy, not European-style democracy. The British exploited these differences to divide their enemies. As the defender of Islam in Egypt, Abbas cultivated contacts with religious leaders and one of his most stable friendships was with Sheikh Ali Yusef, who was known for his moderate views.

Abbas married Ikbal Hanim (1876–1941), a former member of his mother's household, on 19 February 1895; they had four daughters prior to the birth of a son and heir, Muhammad Abdel Moneim (d. 1979), on 20 February 1899; a second son was born three years later. In 1900 Abbas began an affair with Marianne Torok de Szendro (1874–1944), an American-born Hungarian countess whom he first met while studying in Vienna. Because of Tawfiq's stipulation that monogamous marriage was a requisite for Egypt's rulers in the modern age, a divorce from his wife was deemed necessary before a second marriage could take place. Chafing against this constraint, Abbas secretly married his lover (the date is unknown), witnessed only by two sheikhs. An official wedding took place on 28 February 1910, officiated by the grand mufti of Egypt. Because of its polygamous and morganatic nature, the event was again kept secret, aside from an entry for Torok in *Genealogisches Handbuch des Adels* (1911). This listed her as Princess Djavidan Hanem, wife of the khedive of Egypt. The marriage was dissolved in 1913.

Abbas's international policies involved a vain attempt to play off France and Turkey against Britain. In 1895–8 he

reluctantly agreed to the reconquest of the Sudan and he bitterly resented the ensuing Anglo-Egyptian condominium agreements of 1899. It was not that he sympathized with the Sudanese; rather, he believed that the Egyptians alone should control the Nile. (Towards the end of his life he formed the ridiculous view that Britain had gained control of Egypt and the Sudan by deliberately fomenting two supposedly anti-British uprisings, Urabi's in 1882 and the Mahdi's in 1885.) The Anglo-French entente of 1904—by which France recognized Britain's position in Egypt—prevented him from manipulating imperial rivalries. Abbas responded by helping establish a pressure group in London called the English Committee for Egypt, headed by J. M. Robertson MP. At the same time, however, he attempted to put his relations with Britain on a more cordial footing and accepted a British officer as an aide-de-camp.

Without French opinion to restrain him, Cromer became even more autocratic. The nationalist credentials of Abbas suffered as a consequence, especially after the Dinshwai incident in June 1906 when the British treated an affray with brutal severity. Cromer retired soon after; his replacement, Eldon Gorst, was on good terms with Abbas, having previously served in Egypt. It helped that both shared an interest in horse breeding. (A century later the khedive's name still figured prominently in Arabian breed history.) Gorst's remit was to increase the influence of the khedive in the context of greater authority for Egypt's political institutions, but the liberal approach unleashed nationalist pressures and Abbas's newly cosy relationship with the British residency made him unpopular. His most trusted political friend, Boutros Ghali, was assassinated in 1910 after he and Abbas supported Britain's plan to extend the Suez Canal Company's ninety-nine-year lease by another forty years. For a while it looked as though the edifice built by Cromer would collapse. The death of Gorst in July 1911 was a massive blow to Abbas. Not only did he lose one of his best friends (he had rushed to a deathbed meeting and later attended the funeral) but Gorst's replacement, Lord Kitchener, was his nemesis.

Kitchener's return to Egypt as consul-general in September marked a resumption of autocratic methods of imperial rule, aptly signalled by his arrival in a warship rather than the customary steamship. A policy of humiliating Abbas was systematically pursued: Kitchener, for instance, wore his field marshal's uniform for meetings rather than that of a minister-plenipotentiary. Matters became so fraught that Abbas insisted that every conversation be put into writing. In the summer of 1914 Abbas planned to visit London but Kitchener ensured that an audience with the king would not be forthcoming. To avoid this snub, Abbas went instead to his estates in Turkey. During a visit to Constantinople he was shot by a pro-Turkish Egyptian student; a facial wound was sustained making speech painful for several months.

Abbas was recuperating in Turkey when the First World War broke out. His attempts to return to Egypt were blocked by Kitchener on the ground that he was pro-

Ottoman, although it was not until 5 November that Britain declared war on the Ottoman empire. On 19 December, the day after Egypt became a British protectorate, Abbas was deposed in favour of his father's brother, Hussein Kamal. The title sultan replaced khedive in order to indicate the break with the Ottoman sultanate. Abbas never forgave his uncle for usurping him, and the family grievance was extended to Kamal's successor, Fuad. Cromer defended the deposition in his biography of Abbas (1915); a contrary perspective is given in A. H. Beaman's *The Dethronement of the Khedive* (1929). For the rest of the war Abbas sided with the central powers in the hope of reinstatement. He lived for a while in Vienna, where he was involved in efforts to maintain Italy's neutrality, and thereafter lived in Switzerland.

After the war Abbas unsuccessfully sought compensation from the British government for properties it had sequestrated. Further misfortune beset him in the early 1920s when his Turkish estates were confiscated. He continued to follow the political situation in Egypt and wrote a critical piece on the British relationship in 1930 entitled *A Few Words on the Anglo-Egyptian Settlement*. Lingering hopes of regaining the throne were only extinguished in 1931 when he renounced his claim in return for a pension from the Egyptian government worth £E30,000 per annum. Fuad was anxious to ensure that his son Farouk succeeded him. In the late 1930s Abbas worked on his memoirs (which were published posthumously). He remained in Switzerland during the Second World War and died aged seventy on 21 December 1944 in Geneva.

MICHAEL T. THORNHILL

Sources *The last khedive of Egypt: memoirs of Abbas Hilmi II*, ed. and trans. A. Sonbol (1998) · earl of Cromer, *Abbas II* (1915) · A. H. Beaman, *The dethronement of the khedive* (1929) · T. H. O'Brien, *Milner* (1979) · A. Goldschmidt, *Biographical dictionary of modern Egypt* (2000) · D. M. Mckale, 'Influence without power: the last khedive of Egypt and the great powers', *Middle Eastern Studies*, 33/1 · S. Raafat, 'From Mag-Arabs to Al-Magary', *Egyptian Mail* (13 April 1996) · S. Raafat, 'Queen for a day', *Al-Ahram Weekly* (6 Oct 1994)
Archives U. Durham L., personal and official papers | U. Durham L., Sudan archive, letters with R. Wingate
Likenesses Dittrich, photograph, pubd 1900, NPG [*see illus.*] · photographs, U. Durham L. · photographs, repro. in Sonbol, ed., *Last khedive of Egypt*

Abbatt [*née* Cobb], (**Norah**) **Marjorie** (1899–1991), promoter of toy design and businesswoman, was born on 18 March 1899 in Surbiton, Surrey, daughter of a well-to-do fur broker. She was educated at Roedean School, Brighton, and at Somerville College, Oxford; but her postgraduate studies at University College, London, intended to combine psychoanalysis and speech therapy, were interrupted by marriage to (Cyril) Paul Abbatt in December 1930. Paul Abbatt had been born on 19 July 1899 in Bromley Cross near Bolton, son of a Quaker family, and educated in Quaker schools and Trinity Hall, Cambridge (natural sciences), following which he had taught at another Quaker school, Sidcot, from 1922. From 1932, when their toy company was registered, they were known in the progressive education world as Paul and Marjorie Abbatt.

Marjorie Abbatt was a romantic idealist with a highly pragmatic centre; she respected Paul for his ideas and principles, but saw herself as getting on with the practicalities of their life together. Paul had been deeply influenced by the order of Woodcraft Chivalry (which had established a lodge at Sidcot), and they first met at the yearly folkmoot—to which Marjorie had been taken by a friend—in the scented pinewoods of Godshill, Hampshire, where Paul had been working for a term in the order's newly established forest school. Marjorie in her eighties described the experience as 'ecstatic'. Both were inspired by the order's educational ideal of children 'learning by doing'; determined to start a progressive school themselves, they set off on a year's 'honeymoon' to Vienna and Russia, armed only with a letter of introduction from Sir Charles Trevelyan (then president of the Board of Education), to study kindergarten methods. In Vienna especially they were impressed by the way children's play was taken seriously as a valid form of 'work', and by the innovative educationist Professor Cizek at the Vienna School of Arts and Crafts. They returned with a collection of experiential toys and were ready to be inspired still further by Susan Isaacs, writing of her experimental school in Cambridge: 'We see no reason to let the school and its conventions stand between the child and the real situations in the world' (S. Isaacs, Intellectual growth in young children, 1930, 21).

The couple's focus now changed, away from starting their own school and towards the toys themselves. They visited workshops and small factories at home and abroad to discover craftspeople in wood, and held a six-week exhibition (1932) in their flat in Bloomsbury, London, to test interest. Encouraged, they started a mail-order business in a room rented from the New Education Fellowship, produced a catalogue illustrated by the sculptor John Skeaping, and registered as 'designers, manufacturers and retailers of toys, educational materials etc'. From the beginning, the principles and coherence of design were clearly set out in their catalogues, as well as in occasional lectures, linked to the psychology of play. In both 1933 and 1934 their toys filled the nursery sections of exhibitions of British industrial art for the Design and Industries Association, associating them with important architects such as Erno Goldfinger; and in 1938 Goldfinger himself designed their shop-front and interior at 94 Wimpole Street, London, emphasizing the validity of a marriage between imaginative play and functional design.

The shop itself was never a runaway commercial success: indeed, Marjorie late in life lamented that they had never even drawn salaries from it, living on her inherited money; but it was always the ideas it represented that were important to the Abbatts. They worked nationally and internationally to produce bibliographies on toys and play and to establish accepted standards for toy design, later to include design for children with special needs. At the time of Paul's death, Marjorie was president of the International Council for Children's Play and had established the Children's Play Activities Trust to 'extend the understanding of play … promote the design of good toys, and encourage safe and adequate provision for children's play' (trust deed; priv. coll.). The trust still exists as a charitable fund with the same objectives, and was especially active during Marjorie's eighties and nineties, when she delighted in the schemes funded through her generosity: 'I am so happy about how many *different* things we do nowadays!' (personal knowledge).

The Abbatt climbing frame, designed in the early thirties, won the Observer design award in 1969. Marjorie Abbatt was made an honorary MA in her eighties by Nottingham University in recognition of her contribution to the study of children's play (1981); and in 1989 the Bethnal Green Museum of Childhood mounted 'A tribute to Marjorie Abbatt' as part of its 'Themes from the thirties' exhibition. The British Toymakers' Guild awards a prize every year, named in her honour, for the toy most likely to encourage imaginative play. Paul died in June 1971, after a two-year illness in which he lost his capacity for speech; Marjorie continued active to the age of ninety-two, and died at her home, 39 Diamond Court, Moreton Road, Summertown, Oxford, on 10 November 1991.

ELIZABETH NEWSON

Sources J. Welton, 'Paul and Marjorie Abbatt: the story and ideas behind Abbatt Toys', MA diss., U. Nott., 1980 [Welton's sources were a ser. of interviews with M. A. and significant others, and access to Abbatt papers] · E. Newson, 'Marjorie Abbatt: a working life in play', *The Guardian* (19 Nov 1991); repr. in *The Toymaker* (Nov 1993), 3–4 · minutes of Children's Play Activities Ltd, later CPA Trust Fund, May 1966–Dec 1993, priv. coll. · H. Pasierbska, *The Independent* (13 Nov 1991) · *CGPLA Eng. & Wales* (1992) · personal knowledge (2004)
Archives Bethnal Green Museum of Childhood, London, CPA records · priv. coll., archival material, incl. artefacts
Likenesses J. Bown, photograph (with P. Abbatt), repro. in 'Idealists in the Toy Shop', *The Observer* (2 Dec 1962) [interview] · photograph, repro. in *The Guardian*
Wealth at death £423,988: probate, 15 May 1992, *CGPLA Eng. & Wales*

Abberbury family (*per. c.*1270–*c.*1475), gentry, of Donnington, Berkshire, was for several generations a highly successful family. The rise and decline of the Abberburys is typical of the volatility of the fortunes of many later medieval gentry families. Established as early as 1208 as one of the leading freeholding families in the north Oxfordshire village of Adderbury, they owed their initial rise from the ranks of the substantial peasantry to Master **Thomas** [i] **Abberbury** (*d.* 1307). An Oxford graduate and ecclesiastical lawyer, Master Thomas already held a benefice in 1269 and pursued a successful career in the diocesan administration of York before transferring to the service of Edward I's notorious minister, Walter Langton, bishop of Coventry and Lichfield. As the bishop's agent in his many questionable land transactions, Master Thomas used his position to acquire two substantial groups of properties, one located around his birthplace in north Oxfordshire, the other at Donnington, near Newbury, Berkshire. On Thomas's death both groups of estates passed to his brother, Walter Abberbury (*d.* in or before 1316), who further consolidated the north Oxfordshire lands of the family, and then to Walter's son, **Sir Richard** [i] **Abberbury** (*d.* 1334). Richard Abberbury, elected MP for

Oxfordshire in October 1328 and appointed as sheriff for Oxfordshire and Berkshire in 1333–4, was the first lay member of the family to achieve some local prominence, but after his death a series of minorities and a reorganization of the family lands, which settled some of the Oxfordshire properties on a cadet branch, reduced the Abberburys' prominence once more. Following the death of **Sir John Abberbury** (*c.*1316–1346), Richard's son, at the siege of Calais, the family estates were eventually inherited by John's nephew, **Sir Richard** [ii] **Abberbury** (*c.*1330–1399). It was his ability and success, in war and at court, that firmly established the Abberburys as one of the leading gentry families of the Thames valley.

Sir Richard was a follower of Edward, the Black Prince. His service with the prince at Nájera and in the principality of Aquitaine, where he acted as seneschal of the Limousin, was rewarded with the grant of a retaining fee of £40 p.a. and appointment as 'first master' to the prince's son and heir, Richard of Bordeaux. When the young Richard became prince of Wales in 1376, Sir Richard acted as his chief steward of lands and, following the prince's accession to the throne, Abberbury was immediately appointed a knight of the new king's chamber. Apart from a brief spell of disfavour in 1387–8, when he was removed from the royal household by the lords appellant, Sir Richard remained active at court throughout Richard II's reign: a chamber knight until 1387, he also acted as chamberlain to Anne of Bohemia, the king's first wife, and as chief of her council until her death. Such service brought him a substantial income in grants and annuities—amounting to over £200 p.a., to add to the yield of his own estates, which was perhaps £150 p.a.—and allowed Sir Richard to acquire several new manors in Oxfordshire and Berkshire, with the result that by the 1390s the Abberburys were among the largest landowners in an area notably lacking in resident magnates. Nowhere was this new prominence more forcibly stated than at Donnington itself, where Sir Richard built a comfortable but still defensible castle, established and endowed a dependent priory of the Crutched Friars, and founded an almshouse for thirteen of his indigent tenants.

From his marriage to Agnes, a younger daughter of Sir William *Shareshull, Sir Richard had four children, two sons and two daughters, all of whom made solid matches among the local gentry. His sons, **Sir Richard** [iii] **Abberbury** (*d.* 1416) and **Thomas** [ii] **Abberbury** (*d.* 1416), followed their father into royal and princely service. Sir Richard the younger began his career in the service of John of Gaunt, duke of Lancaster, and rose to be chamberlain of the Lancastrian household during the duke's Castilian expedition. During the 1390s he gravitated towards the royal court, however, and was several times employed on diplomatic missions by Richard II, besides serving as knight of the shire for Berkshire in January 1394 and 1397. Thomas took longer to establish himself, but after a spell as an esquire of the royal household his future seemed secured by his appointment as master of the horse to Richard II's second wife, Isabella, in 1397. By the time of their father's death, early in 1399, a courtier dynasty seemed in prospect.

Yet the next few years brought the start of a swift decline in the fortunes of the Abberbury family. Thomas's career was cut short by the usurpation of Henry IV for, once Queen Isabella was returned to France in 1402, he was given no further employment at the Lancastrian court. The case of Sir Richard [iii] is more puzzling: he left England early in 1400 and seems subsequently to have returned only for the briefest stays. In 1408 he is described as 'on pilgrimage, beyond the great sea' (PRO, E 28/24/8); in 1415 he began to sell up his entire inheritance, disposing of some estates to his nephew, Sir Richard Arches, but selling the bulk of his lands to the rising star of local politics, Thomas Chaucer. Whether this change of life sprang from a fervent spirituality, political disgrace, or a principled unwillingness to serve a usurping king is unclear, but it is plain enough that the surviving members of the Abberbury family were unable to sustain their social position in the face of such a wholesale loss of influence and income. **Richard** [iv] **Abberbury** (*d*. after 1473), son of Thomas [ii], sought to rescue the situation in 1448 by re-entering the estates formerly granted to the Crutched Friars but his scheme, apparently instigated by William de la Pole, duke of Suffolk, failed; by 1465 the Berkshire lands of the family were reduced to a single tenement in Newbury. For the cadet branch of the family in Oxfordshire, who had never risen so high, the experience of decline was less dramatic but hardly less inexorable: John Abberbury of Cotesford (*d*. after 1421), descended from a younger son of Walter (*d*. in or before 1316), had been MP for Oxfordshire in 1394 and 1397 and was still acquiring lands early in the fifteenth century. Yet, here too, a gradual liquidation of the Abberbury estates was soon in train; by the 1450s even the family's original free tenement at Adderbury was lost to them.

Though the Abberburys' rise and fall was replicated many times among the gentry families of later medieval England, their transformation from one of the leading families of Oxfordshire and Berkshire to modest burgesses of Newbury within a single generation was unusually rapid. What lay at the root of their change of fortune remains imponderable but their history encapsulates many of the opportunities and pitfalls the later medieval gentry were required to negotiate.   SIMON WALKER

Sources PRO, C.133/26/8; C.135/37/20; C.135/81/4; CP 25(1)/189(14)/20, 46 · *Chancery records* · S. Walker, 'Sir Richard Abberbury and his kinsmen: the rise and fall of a gentry family', *Nottingham Medieval Studies*, 34 (1990), 113–40 · muniments, New College, Oxford, 10347, 10354, 10370–10373, 14025, 14034–14036 · HoP, *Commons, 1386–1421* · Emden, *Oxf.* · *The diplomatic correspondence of Richard II*, ed. E. Perroy, CS, 3rd ser., 48 (1933) · F. N. Macnamara, 'Donnington Castle and its ancient lords', *Berkshire Archaeological Journal*, 4 (1898), 49–60
Wealth at death £150–£200 p.a. in *c*.1400: PRO, C 133/26/8; C 135/37/20; C 135/81/4

Abberbury, Sir John (*c*.1316–1346). *See under* Abberbury family (*per. c*.1270–*c*.1475).

Abberbury, Sir Richard (*d*. 1334). *See under* Abberbury family (*per. c*.1270–*c*.1475).

Abberbury, Sir Richard (*c*.1330–1399). *See under* Abberbury family (*per. c*.1270–*c*.1475).

Abberbury, Sir Richard (*d*. 1416). *See under* Abberbury family (*per. c*.1270–*c*.1475).

Abberbury, Richard (*d*. after 1473). *See under* Abberbury family (*per. c*.1270–*c*.1475).

Abberbury, Thomas (*d*. 1307). *See under* Abberbury family (*per. c*.1270–*c*.1475).

Abberbury, Thomas (*d*. 1416). *See under* Abberbury family (*per. c*.1270–*c*.1475).

Abbey, Edwin Austin (1852–1911), illustrator and painter, was born at 315 Race Street, Philadelphia, Pennsylvania, on 1 April 1852, the eldest of the three children of William Maxwell Abbey (1827–1897), a merchant of French and English descent, and Margery Ann Kiple (1825–1880), who was descended from German and Irish immigrants. He was educated in Philadelphia at Mrs Elizabeth Hall's school (1859–62), the Jefferson and Randolph schools (1862–4), and Henry Gregory's academy (1864–8). From the age of fourteen he took drawing lessons from the landscape painter Isaac L. Williams. A year later, under the pen-name Yorick, he began sending humorous letters, riddles, and rebuses to *Oliver Optic's Magazine: Our Boys and Girls*. In 1868 he went to work for W. H. Van Ingen and H. M. Snyder, wood-engravers, and enrolled in evening classes at the Pennsylvania Academy of the Fine Arts, then in 1871 he took a job as staff illustrator for the publishers Harper & Brothers and moved to New York. There he made drawings for *Harper's Weekly* and *Harper's Monthly*, as well as for books, including Charles Dickens's *Christmas Stories* (1876). Among his colleagues at Harper's were Winslow Homer, Arthur B. Frost, and Howard Pyle.

Inspired by the English illustrators of the 1860s as well as Adolf Menzel and Daniel Vierge, Abbey developed a lively pen-and-ink style characterized by architectonic compositions, dazzling light effects, close attention to detail, and keen insight into human emotions. Like his illustrations, Abbey's watercolours of the 1870s were modelled on British examples. One of them, *Rustics Dancing in a Barn* (exh. American Water Color Society, 1876), was sold to a collector who reportedly mistook it for the work of an English artist. Another, *A Rose in October* (exh. American Water Color Society, 1878), depicted the kind of subject then popular in England: a woman in 1820s costume standing by a gate and surrounded by autumn foliage. Unfortunately the present locations of these watercolours are unknown. Abbey first encountered a significant number of British oil paintings in 1876 at the Centennial Exposition in Philadelphia, where he preferred the English pictures to the French. Attracted to the work of the Pre-Raphaelites, he was especially devoted to the poetry and art of Dante Gabriel Rossetti. In 1877 he joined the Tile Club in New York. Inspired by the English arts and crafts movement, the club met weekly to socialize and paint decorative ceramic tiles; members included Winslow Homer and William Merritt Chase, the sculptor Augustus Saint-Gaudens, and the architect Stanford White. In 1878 *Harper's Monthly* began the serial publication of Abbey's illustrations to the poetry of Robert Herrick; these were issued in book form in 1882. Meanwhile, in December 1878, Harper's sent Abbey to England to absorb its ambience at first hand. He left behind his family and friends, planning to stay abroad for a year. Instead he remained in England for most of the rest of his life, except for occasional trips to New York, which included an extended stay in 1881–2.

During his first decade in England, Abbey's life and work revolved around the nostalgic ideal of a quiet old-fashioned existence in the country. His independent watercolours of the 1880s—representing genteel figures in period dress, set in simple but refined rural interiors—were exhibited in London and New York. Prominent among these were *The Sisters* (exh. American Water Color Society, 1882), which is set in The Swan inn in Lechlade; *The Widower* (exh. Royal Institute of Painters in Water Colours, 1883), set in nearby Buscot rectory; and *An Old Song* (exh. Royal Institute of Painters in Water Colours, 1885), all three of which are now in the Yale University Art Gallery, New Haven, Connecticut. Abbey's illustrations—for travel features, contemporary fiction, and English literature—were serialized in *Harper's Monthly* and often published in book form: *Sketching Rambles in Holland* (written and co-illustrated by George H. Boughton, 1885); Oliver Goldsmith's *She Stoops to Conquer* (1886); two collections of old English ballads and poems, *Old Songs* (1889) and *The Quiet Life* (1890); and Goldsmith's *The Deserted Village* (1902). For research on these projects the artist spent time in various small towns in the midlands. In 1885 he joined the artists' colony in Broadway, Worcestershire, where his friends included the American painters Francis D. Millet and John Singer Sargent, the English illustrator Alfred Parsons, the writers Austin Dobson, Edmund Gosse, and Henry James, and the American actress Mary Anderson.

In 1888 Abbey began the first of four major Shakespearian projects: illustrations for the comedies, which were serialized in *Harper's Monthly*, then published in book form in 1896. This was followed by seven large Shakespearian oil paintings, notably *Richard, Duke of Gloucester, and the Lady Anne* (exh. RA, 1896), *Hamlet* (exh. RA, 1897; both Yale University Art Gallery, New Haven, Connecticut), *King Lear* (exh. RA, 1898; Metropolitan Museum of Art, New York), and *The Penance of Eleanor, Duchess of Gloucester* (exh. RA, 1900; Carnegie Museum of Art, Pittsburgh). In 1898 Abbey designed Henry Irving's abortive production of *Richard II*. His illustrations for Shakespeare's tragedies and histories were published in *Harper's Monthly* between 1902 and 1909 but never appeared in book form.

On 22 April 1890, in New York, Abbey married (Mary) Gertrude Mead (1851–1931), the daughter of a wealthy New York merchant, whom he had met in Broadway in spring 1888. Both were nearly forty years of age at the time of their marriage, and they remained childless. Ambitious and well educated, Gertrude Abbey encouraged her new husband to take on more challenging projects and secured for him a commission to paint murals on the theme *The Quest and Achievement of the Holy Grail* for the Delivery Room of the new Boston Public Library, designed by the architects McKim, Mead, and White. Abbey leased Morgan Hall, near Fairford, Gloucestershire, to accommodate work on the fifteen monumental canvases, which he completed in 1901. In the murals, as in Abbey's contemporaneous Shakespearian paintings, space is flattened and decorative and moods are high-keyed. Teeming crowds heighten the works' theatricality and project them as spectacles or public events. During the 1890s Abbey travelled to Italy, France, and Germany for research on the murals and other projects. In that period he also executed dozens of pastels, mostly showing single figures in medieval or eighteenth-century costume; these were sold to help finance work on the murals. In 1902 he received a more lucrative commission, for a series of enormous murals to decorate the new state capitol in Harrisburg, Pennsylvania, his native state. Its centrepiece is *The Apotheosis of Pennsylvania*, an omnium gatherum of figures drawn from the entire history of the state, which dominates the vast ornate chamber of the capitol's house of representatives. For Harrisburg, Abbey developed a more classicizing approach, one that not only embodied his own increasing academicism but also reflected a more general turn away from flat, decorative, two-dimensional art towards a more physically conceived, three-dimensional style.

Recognized as one of the leading artists of his time, Abbey was showered with honours and awards. In the United States he belonged to the American Water Color Society in New York (member, 1876), the American Academy in Rome (member, 1895), the National Academy of Design (associate, 1901; member, 1902), and the American Academy of Arts and Letters (member, 1904); he also received honorary degrees from Yale University (MA, 1897), and the University of Pennsylvania (LLD, 1902). In England he was elected to the Royal Academy (associate, 1896; member, 1898), the Royal Institute of Painters in Water Colours (member, 1883; resigned 1893), and the Royal Watercolour Society (member, 1895). In addition he won gold medals in numerous international expositions in Europe and the United States and was an honorary member of artists' academies in Paris, Munich, and Madrid. In 1903–4 he executed the official painting of the coronation of Edward VII (Royal Collection), a huge canvas involving more than a hundred individual portraits. The king recommended Abbey for a knighthood in 1907, but he declined the honour in order to retain his American citizenship.

Abbey died of cancer at his London residence, Chelsea Lodge, 42 Tite Street, Chelsea, on 1 August 1911; following cremation his ashes were buried on 3 August at Kingsbury Old Church, near Willesden. His widow oversaw his memorial exhibition at the Royal Academy early in 1912 and commissioned the two-volume biography by E. V. Lucas (1921) that remains the standard work on the artist.

After her death in 1931, her executors donated the more than 4000 works of art in her estate to the Yale University Art Gallery in New Haven, which is now the foremost repository of Abbey's work. LUCY OAKLEY

Sources E. V. Lucas, *Edwin Austin Abbey, royal academician*, 2 vols. (1921) · M. H. Spielmann, 'Edwin Austin Abbey', *Magazine of Art*, 23 (1898–9), 145–51, 193–8, 247–52, facing pp. 168, 199 · K. A. Foster and M. Quick, *Edwin Austin Abbey* (1973) · L. Oakley, *Unfaded pageant: Edwin Austin Abbey's Shakespeare subjects* (1994) · K. A. Foster, 'Edwin Austin Abbey', *American Art Review*, 1 (1974), 83–95 · M. Simpson, 'Windows on the past: Edwin Austin Abbey and Francis Davis Millet in Broadway', *American Art Journal*, 22 (1990), 65–89 · d. cert.
Archives Bodl. Oxf., letters to Lewis Harcourt · JRL, letters to M. H. Spielmann · LUL, letters to A. Dobson
Likenesses W. R. O'Donovan, bas-relief, 1876–9 (*Ye Tyle Manne*), Yale U. Art Gallery · J. S. Sargent, charcoal drawing, *c.*1889, Yale U. Art Gallery · G. F. Watts, charcoal drawing, 1893, Yale U. Art Gallery · E. O. Ford, bronze bust, exh. RA 1902 · W. Q. Orchardson, oils, 1909 · F. O. Salisbury, decorative panel, before 1916, Chelsea town hall; repro. in F. O. Salisbury, *The great artists of Chelsea* · T. Brock, bust, exh. RA 1917, British School in Rome · J. Bacon, sketch, Yale U. Art Gallery · Bassano, photograph · Elliott & Fry, photograph · Gribáyedoff, photograph · Gutekunst, photograph · F. Holler, photograph · J. E. Purdy, photograph · N. Sarony, photograph · Spy [L. Ward], chromolithograph caricature, NPG; repro. in *VF* (29 Dec 1898) · G. H. Swinsted, photograph · E. Walker, photograph · Window & Grove, photograph, NPG
Wealth at death £4868 4s. 9d.: probate, 3 April 1912, CGPLA Eng. & Wales

Abbey, John Roland (1894–1969), book collector, was born in Brighton on 23 November 1894, the eldest of three sons of William Henry Abbey, brewer, of Sedgwick Park, Horsham, and his wife, Florence, daughter of Henry Belcher, of Hove, Sussex. He was named John Rowland, but later dropped the 'w'.

In consequence of an accident which caused lasting damage to one elbow, Abbey was educated by a private tutor, Mr Möens, at Rottingdean, instead of at school. In November 1914 he was commissioned in the rifle brigade and served as a regimental officer on the western front for two years from September 1915. The 13th and 8th battalions, to which he was posted in succession, saw severe fighting and both suffered heavy casualties. During the capture of Flers on 15 September 1916, when he was temporarily in reserve, the 8th battalion lost all its officers except one. He spent five months in hospital and on sick leave after being gassed in November 1916, the only interval in this long term of active service. He was invalided home in October 1917 and demobilized in August 1919. His war experiences in France and Flanders, especially during the third battle of Ypres, remained a vivid memory even in old age. His younger brother Lieutenant Noel Roland Abbey was killed in action in France in 1918 while serving with the Grenadier Guards.

Abbey became a director of the Kemp Town brewery, Brighton, after leaving the army, and succeeded his father as chairman after the latter's death in 1943. The brewery was sold to Charrington's in 1954. On 7 June 1921 he married Lady Ursula Helen Cairns (*b.* 1899), second daughter of the fourth Earl Cairns. There were two daughters of the marriage. Abbey rejoined the rifle brigade in November

1939 and served for two years from 1941 as staff officer to the admiral-superintendent, Great Yarmouth, until his release in October 1943. In 1946 he was granted the honorary rank of major.

Abbey started to collect in 1929, buying initially the productions of the modern private presses, and eventually formed complete collections of books from the Kelmscott, Ashendene, and Gregynog presses. His Kelmscott books included the Bible in pigskin blind-tooled by the Doves bindery after a design by William Morris; the Gregynog books were all bound by the press bindery. Meanwhile he had become interested in modern bindings and in 1931 commissioned examples from Sybil Pye and R. de Coverley & Sons. The latter, on a copy of *Memoirs of an Infantry Officer*, by Siegfried Sassoon, bore Abbey's arms and was decorated to his design. His first antiquarian bindings were some modestly priced armorial examples from the Rosebery sale of 1933 but this part of the collection was rapidly built up between 1936 and 1938 with purchases from the Mensing, Moss, Aldenham, Schiff, and Cortlandt F. Bishop sales and ultimately numbered over 1300 works, including seven Groliers. Contemporary French binding, with its faultless technique, its air of luxury, and its bold colouring, gave him particular pleasure. In 1937 he ordered his first specimen from Paul Bonet, whom he regarded as the greatest living master of the craft, and eventually he owned 100 modern illustrated books, mostly in polychrome bindings by Bonet, Creuzevault, Martin, and other members of the Société de la Reliure Originale, acquired or commissioned on post-war visits to Paris.

Bindings, however, did not monopolize his interest or resources. From 1935, with the help of two booksellers, George Stephenson of Messrs Rimell, and later George Bates, of Hove, he collected English colour-plate books of the eighteenth and nineteenth centuries. Here he broke new ground by paying attention to many neglected minor works, to copies in the wrappered parts in which they were issued, and to original condition. The collection, eventually consisting of 1914 items, represented the most creative side of his connoisseurship.

In 1946 Abbey entered a new field by buying for £40,000 the collection of illuminated manuscripts, mostly written in Gothic or humanistic scripts, formed by C. H. St John Hornby, the founder of the Ashendene Press. With the help of a small but distinguished group from Sir Sydney Cockerell, of the fourteenth-century *Ruskin Hours* and the late and lavish *Monypenny Breviary* bought from a Hove collector, D. M. Colman, and of single purchases from booksellers and at auction, Abbey finally acquired 143 medieval and Renaissance manuscripts. This collection, however, although including many outstanding volumes, remained a somewhat heterogeneous assemblage, owing its excellence more to the taste of Hornby and Cockerell than to its owner's discrimination. The library reached its maximum size at Greyfriars, Storrington, in the mid-1950s, with the addition of many bibliographical works and private library catalogues—bought in part at the suggestion of A. N. L. Munby—and an almost complete set of Roxburghe Club publications.

Abbey made no pretensions to scholarship and knew no language except English. It was the appearance, not the contents, of books which appealed to him. He was, however, a keen reader and a tireless visitor to libraries and bookshops; he had an excellent visual memory and a flair for quality in bindings; and he was fortunate in being advised by distinguished scholars, notably G. D. Hobson and A. N. L. Munby. He admired bibliographical scholarship and wanted his collections to be of service to bibliographers. For this purpose he commissioned a series of handsomely produced catalogues; G. D. Hobson, *English Bindings, 1490–1940, in the Library of J. R. Abbey* (1940); A. R. A. Hobson, *French and Italian collectors and their bindings, illustrated from examples in the library of J. R. Abbey* (1953); J. J. G. Alexander and A. C. de la Mare, *The Italian Manuscripts in the Library of Major J. R. Abbey* (1969). The bindings he had commissioned both in Britain and on the continent were exhibited at the Arts Council in 1949 and 1965, and described in the exhibition catalogues. In early days he bought many damaged or over-restored specimens. But a post-war visit to Sir Robert Abdy's eighteenth-century morocco library at Newton Ferrers, in a room permanently curtained to prevent sunlight fading the spines, converted him to the French attitude to book collecting, in which quality and fine condition are the predominant considerations.

Having bought extensively in the buyer's market of the 1930s Abbey was not always able to resist the temptation of a profit when prices rose after the war. Through John Carter of Charles Scribner & Sons he sold the colour-plate collection to Paul Mellon before the last two volumes of the catalogue had appeared. It is now at Yale University. A small group of fine books went to H. P. Kraus, of New York, and his German bindings to the Württembergische Landesbibliothek, Stuttgart. The other bindings and the bibliography were auctioned in a series of four sales in 1965–7 for £378,313. In 1967 Abbey moved from Redlynch House, Salisbury (his residence since he left Storrington in Sussex in 1957), to a flat at 12 Hill Street, Mayfair. Here the medieval manuscripts, French illustrated books, and modern bindings were shelved. He died in London on 24 December 1969. With the exception of a select group of manuscripts retained by his family, the Kelmscott Press books, which he had given to Eton College Library, and a choice of six French bindings bequeathed to the British Museum, the remainder of the collection was dispersed in five further sales in 1970–75 for £993,509.

If not the most learned, Abbey was certainly the largest English book collector of his time. His colour-plate collection showed genuine originality and his catalogues represented real advances of knowledge. Although sometimes too ready to take offence in matters affecting his collection, he was of a naturally amiable disposition and a generous and charming host, always glad to welcome scholars or fellow collectors. He was responsible for the publication of three books, compiled by E. Jutro and other collaborators: *Scenery of Great Britain and Ireland in Aquatint and Lithography, 1770–1860* (1952); *Life in England, in Aquatint and Lithography 1770–1860* (1953); and *Travel in Aquatint and Lithography* (2 vols., 1956–7). His favourite pastime, next to book collecting, was croquet, a game he played with skill and enthusiasm. Abbey was appointed high sheriff of Sussex in 1945. ANTHONY HOBSON, *rev.*

Sources J. F. Hayward, 'Silver bindings from the Abbey collection', *The Connoisseur*, 130 (1952), 98–104 · A. R. A. Hobson and A. N. L. Munby, 'Contemporary collectors XXVI: John Roland Abbey', *Book Collector*, 10 (1961), 40–48 · *The Times* (29 Dec 1969) · *The Times* (3 Jan 1970) · private information (1981) · personal knowledge (1981) · Burke, *Peerage* (1980) · CGPLA Eng. & Wales (1970)
Archives BL, visitors' book, Add. MS 70608 | Bodl. Oxf., corresp. with J. W. Hely-Hutchinson
Likenesses E. Seago, portrait, priv. coll.
Wealth at death £659,627: probate, 6 Feb 1970, CGPLA Eng. & Wales

Abbo of Fleury [St Abbo of Fleury] (945×50–1004), abbot of St Benoît-sur-Loire, was a French monk influential, by both his presence in England and his writings, in the monastic revival of the late tenth century. He was born in the region of Orléans between 945 and 950. As a child he was put into the monastery of St Benoît-sur-Loire at Fleury, which claimed to possess the bones of St Benedict. Although he became a professed monk, he was educated not only at Fleury but also at the schools in Paris, Rheims (where his teachers included the mathematician Gerbert d'Aurillac, later Pope Sylvester II), and Orléans. After returning to Fleury, Abbo was put in charge of teaching and continued his studies, especially in the field of computistics. Probably his first work was a commentary on the *Calculus* of Victorius, which is noteworthy because of its attitude to the liberal arts and the light it sheds on the great library at Fleury, as well as for its scientific interest. At the abbey he would have met Englishmen who either visited or spent periods of time there as monks; notable in the latter category are Oswald (in 961 to become bishop of Worcester, and one of the prime movers of the monastic revival) and, somewhat later, Germanus, who after unsatisfactory stays at Oswald's foundations at Westbury, Ramsey, and Winchcombe, was driven into exile at Fleury from 975 to about 978, when he returned to Ramsey in Cambridgeshire.

These connections help to explain Abbo's sojourn in England from 985 to 987. Possibly to get away after failing to be elected abbot at Fleury, he accepted an invitation from Oswald to head the school at Ramsey. There a prominent pupil was Byrhtferth, a notable figure in the history of science and in particular of computation. Byrhtferth's celebrated *Manual* (or *Enchiridion*) owes a good deal to Abbo, and the splendid early twelfth-century copy of this (Oxford, St John's College MS 17) includes a computus heavily dependent on Abbo's works and four short treatises attributed to him.

While in England Abbo also came into contact with Dunstan, whose final three years as archbishop of Canterbury coincided with Abbo's stay at Ramsey. A notable outcome of their friendship was one of the key documents of English medieval hagiography, a *passio* for St Edmund, king of

East Anglia, killed by invading Danes in 869. This was composed by Abbo, at the request of the monks of Ramsey, after he had heard Dunstan tell the story of Edmund's death, ostensibly passed on from the martyr's aged armour-bearer. Although the putative facts are English (and less heavily embroidered than the legend was later to become), the literary echoes are strongly classical, especially Virgilian. A few years later Ælfric turned Abbo's *passio* into English prose, referring to its author as a 'highly learned monk'. Abbo also addressed to Dunstan three poems (including a triple acrostic called by Stubbs 'A curious specimen of misdirected ingenuity' (*Memorials of St Dunstan*, 410)) and about the year 1000 was sent, by the abbot of St Augustine's, Canterbury, the first prose life of Dunstan with a request that he versify it; this, however, was never accomplished.

An indication of the value Abbo placed on his time at Ramsey is the dedication to its monks of his *Quaestiones grammaticales*, the first work he wrote after returning to Fleury and in 988 being elected its abbot. This rather extensive treatise sheds valuable light on questions of tenth-century pronunciation as well as on Latin grammar; to what extent it represents problems posed by the monks of Ramsey is not clear.

From his lofty position as abbot of Fleury, Abbo took an active role both in efforts to intensify monastic reform along lines generally called Cluniac (Fleury, though not technically subject to the Burgundian monastery of Cluny, had close ties with that great house) and in struggles over the relative power of papal and royal authority, the latter being that of the new Capetian dynasty. He became involved with the bishop of Orléans in a heated battle over monastic exemption from episcopal control, and in the context of justifying his position articulated views which seem to point towards the well-known division of medieval society into those who worked, those who prayed, and those who fought. Attempting to intervene in a squabble between the monks of a small abbey dependent on Fleury (at La Réole in Gascony) and the local townspeople, he was fatally injured—having thus some grounds to be considered a martyr—and died there on 13 November 1004. He was buried at Fleury.

The literary efforts of Abbo's later years reflect largely the preoccupations of his abbatial office. Several letters survive, as do an apology (concerned mainly with his positions on church reform), a collection of canons which was to be influential on the more definitive collections of the next century, and an epitome of lives of the popes (perhaps drawn from the *Liber pontificalis*). There are also an important early work on logic, now known as *Syllogismorum categoricorum et hypotheticorum enodatio*, and a few further scientific works, mostly brief treatises on computistic and astronomical subjects. Some of these were known in England also, as witness the appearance of three of them in a New Minster, Winchester, manuscript of *c*.1025, interspersed among works by earlier writers on computistics (Cambridge, Trinity College, MS R.15.32/945).

One of the most versatile thinkers and writers of his time, Abbo put his mark on several areas of medieval life and thought, but none more so than in transmitting much that was valuable from the tradition of reformed French monasticism to the nascent monastic culture of late tenth-century England.   RICHARD W. PFAFF

Sources *Patrologia Latina*, 139 (1853), 417–578 [Abbo's *Opera* and *Vita* by Aimoin of Fleury] · Abbo of Fleury, *Questions grammaticales*, ed. A. Guerreau-Jalabert (1982) · M. Winterbottom, ed., *Life of St Edmund*, in M. Winterbottom, *Three lives of English saints* (1972) · *Abbonis Floriacensis opera inedita*, ed. A. van de Vyver and R. Raes, 1 (Bruges, 1966) · A. van de Vyver, 'Les œuvres inédites d'Abbon de Fleury', *Revue Bénédictine*, 47 (1935), 125–69 · H. Fichtenau, *Living in the tenth century*, trans. P. J. Geary (1991) · M. Mostert, 'Le séjour d'Abbon à Ramsey', *Bibliothèque de l'École de Chartes*, 144 (1986), 199–208 · P. S. Baker, 'Byrhtferth's *Enchiridion* and the computus in Oxford, St John's College 17', *Anglo-Saxon England*, 10 (1982), 123–41 · M. Lapidge, 'Abbot Germanus, Winchcombe, Ramsey and the Cambridge psalter', *Words, texts and manuscripts: studies in Anglo-Saxon culture presented to Helmut Gneuss on the occasion of his sixty-fifth birthday*, ed. M. Korhammer and others (1992), 99–129 · M. Huglo, 'D'Helisachar à Abbon de Fleury', *Revue Bénédictine*, 104 (1994), 204–30 · G. Duby, *The three orders: feudal society imagined*, trans. A. Goldhammer (1982), 87–92 · P. Cousin, *Abbon de Fleury-sur-Loire* (1954) · M. Mostert, *The political theology of Abbo of Fleury* (1987) · W. Stubbs, ed., *Memorials of St Dunstan, archbishop of Canterbury*, Rolls Series, 63 (1874), 410

Archives St John's College, Oxford, MS 17 · Trinity Cam., MS R.15.32/945

Abbot, Charles, first Baron Colchester (1757–1829), speaker of the House of Commons, was born on 14 October 1757 at Abingdon, Berkshire, the son of the Revd John Abbot (*d.* 1760), a fellow of Balliol College, Oxford, and rector of All Saints, Colchester, and his wife, Sarah, the daughter of Jonathan Farr, a citizen and draper of London. He was educated at Westminster School from 1763 and at Christ Church, Oxford, from 1776, winning the college prize for Latin verse in his first year and the chancellor's prize the year after. In 1778–9 he studied civil law in Geneva and obtained a doctorate, which was complemented by bachelor's and doctoral degrees in English civil law in 1783 and 1793. Elected Vinerian scholar by the University of Oxford in 1781, he was promoted to a residential fellowship in 1786. After being called to the bar from the Middle Temple in 1783 and joining the Oxford and Chester circuits, he surrendered his fellowship in 1792 to practise in the equity courts.

Although Abbot earned some £1500 per annum as a barrister, he found the work uncongenial. He had aimed at a mastership in chancery, but upon his elder brother's death in 1794 he opted instead to succeed him in the relatively undemanding office of clerk of the rules in king's bench, worth £2700 a year. Some contemporaries sneered at his decision to serve personally as clerk rather than through a deputy. This office, noted Sylvester Douglas, was 'scarcely compatible with the description of a gentleman' (NL Scot., Glenbervie MSS, diary, 7, fols. 26–31). But the lighter workload and financial security gave Abbot the opportunity to pursue his twin passions for the preservation of historical records and the promotion of administrative reform. In 1795 he published two treatises, *The Practice of the Chester Circuit* and *Rules and Orders on the Plea Side of King's Bench*. On 29 December 1796 he married Elizabeth

Charles Abbot, first Baron Colchester (1757–1829), by Sir
Thomas Lawrence, c.1824

(1760/61–1847), the daughter of Sir Philip Gibbes, first baronet, of Spring Head, Barbados, and his wife, Agnes Osborne. They had two sons.

Early parliamentary career, 1795–1802 Abbot sought entry into the Commons in 1790 and was involved in a double return, which was determined against him. His electoral patron was a former schoolfellow, the fifth duke of Leeds, who brought him in for Helston, Cornwall, at the next vacancy in June 1795. Abbot soon made it clear that he intended to pursue an independent political line, giving conspicuous support to the government's repressive legislation of 1795, notwithstanding his patron's opposition and a hostile petition from his constituents. Abbot's speech in favour of the Seditious Meetings Bill on 3 December earned the approbation of both king and prime minister. He also demonstrated a keen interest in the business of legislation, gaining the approval of the speaker, Henry Addington, who became one of his staunchest supporters. On 14 March 1796 Abbot proposed an inquiry into the manner of dealing with expiring laws. He chaired the subsequent committee and delivered the report in June which thereby established a rational system of annual tables so that no time-limited act should expire unnoticed. From 2 November he presided over a committee to regulate the promulgation of the statutes. His report delivered the following year saved £14,000 and enabled government offices and law courts to function more efficiently.

At the general election of 1796 Abbot retained Helston, having rejected offers to stand elsewhere. He chaired the select committee on finance between 1797 and 1798, presenting thirty-six reports, many of which he had drawn up himself. Resulting reforms such as the transfer of the salt revenue to the excise, the abolition of patent offices in the customs, and the establishment of a superannuation fund proved beneficial. However, Abbot's diligent but tactless investigations caused resentment, particularly within the judiciary. As a defender of Pitt's financial measures, he felt bound to support the Assessed Taxes Bill in 1797–8. This led to a breach with his electoral patron, but, when Abbot offered to resign his seat, Leeds backed down. In January 1799 Abbot moved for the production of annual accounts by the treasury and once again encountered resistance from vested interests; he nevertheless succeeded in establishing that such accounts should be presented annually.

In February 1800 Abbot initiated an inquiry into the preservation and publication of the public records, and he became a principal figure within the ensuing record commission. In May his earlier work on financial reforms culminated in a bill to charge public accountants with interest on their balances. The salutary effect of this reform, which ended a notorious abuse, was commended a decade later by the committee of public expenditure. He made another significant contribution in November by promoting a Population Bill, which established the first national census in 1801. Abbot had already set his sights on the speakership of the Commons, and it came as a blow when he was not recommended to the chair when Addington became premier in February 1801. After protracted negotiations, during which he insisted on compensation for surrendering his legal salary, Abbot went to Ireland as chief secretary to the lord lieutenant, the third earl of Hardwicke. His financial future was secured by a current salary of £5000 per annum plus a reversionary provision settled upon a sinecure. As the first Irish secretary after the union, Abbot was horrified at the corruption which had taken place under his predecessor, Lord Castlereagh. Abbot, however, did not blow the whistle on the illegal system of secret annuities. Instead he set about reforming Irish administrative procedures. As in England so in Ireland, Abbot's probing inquiries and dictatorial manner upset influential figures.

Speaker of the House of Commons, 1802–1817 Abbot left Ireland to become speaker of the Commons as a consequence of the death of Lord Clare, the Irish lord chancellor, in January 1802. Sir John Mitford, who had succeeded Addington in the speakership, received the Irish seals and Abbot was recalled from Dublin to occupy the vacant chair. Indeed, Abbot had so far alienated vested interests in Ireland that one cabinet member greeted his candidacy with relief: 'There is one good circumstance attending his appointment,' noted Lord Hobart, 'Ireland will get rid of him.' Abbot's proven ability, together with his loyalty to Addington, guaranteed his nomination. In recommending him to the cabinet the prime minister stated bluntly that 'Abbot may be described in a few words "He is a firm man and a very *little man*"' (Glenbervie MSS, diary, fols. 16–17). The king himself was hardly enthusiastic, and made it clear that Abbot's reforming zeal was not to the royal taste. Abbot was not to be permitted to 'attempt novelties', because these 'seldom succeed in the transaction of public business' (*The Public and Private Life of Lord Chancellor Eldon*, ed. H. Twiss, 3 vols., 1844, 1.402). On 11 February 1802 Abbot was elected speaker with only token opposition. There were, however, discontented mutterings about the appointment. Lord Chatham questioned whether Abbot possessed sufficient status for the chair; Lord Minto thought his manner was 'rather pert than dignified' with 'the *tournure* of a clerk … rather than of a Speaker' (NL Scot., Minto MSS, 11054, fol. 14); and George Tierney maintained that the choice had given rise to 'very general disgust' (Durham University Library, Grey MSS, Tierney to Grey, 11 Feb 1802). The strongest indication of hostility came from Lord Chancellor Eldon, who snubbed the speaker on his first official visit to the Lords by declining to offer any words of approbation, privately describing Abbot as 'the most improper appointment that could have been thought of'. Some wags contented themselves with caricaturing the scene of Abbot's installation in the speaker's chair, which it was thought would require 'a moveable bar … like that used to prevent children from falling out' and a 'screw-moveable bottom to it' (Glenbervie MSS, diary, 7, fol. 51).

In September 1802 Abbot purchased Kidbrook, Sussex, as his private residence, and at the general election he transferred his parliamentary seat to New Woodstock, Oxfordshire, under the patronage of the duke of Marlborough. Notwithstanding the earlier rumblings of dissatisfaction, there was no challenge to his re-election as speaker on 16 November 1802. Indeed, he was chosen without serious challenges in the next four parliaments. As speaker, Abbot set about remedying some of the administrative deficiencies which had irritated him when a member. He began the process of improving the printing of the *Votes*. These records, which should have provided a running digest of pending and forthcoming business, had always been sadly in arrears and therefore failing in their primary function. The reforms Abbot initiated in 1802–3—compressing the entries and speeding up printing—also saved £1000 a year. Delays were not entirely eliminated, but in 1817 further reforms were devised in conjunction with his secretary, John Rickman. Improvements were made to the printing of the current *Commons Journal*, together with the reprinting of all earlier volumes. Abbot set in train the recovery and reprinting of old parliamentary papers and the propagation and preservation of all new ones. The way in which bills and statutes were printed was rationalized: the contents of clauses were epitomized in the margin, bill titles were shortened, and useful additional information was included. Abbot was also the driving force behind the setting up of the private bill office in 1811. This was sorely needed because of the growing complexity of standing orders and the increase in the number of private bills. Henceforth, the office maintained a register of all private bills, showing the agents and detailing the legislative process. At each stage comparisons were made to monitor any changes. The office also provided information, such as notice of future proceedings, together with daily lists of committees sitting on private bills.

Although these achievements would have earned Abbot eventual recognition, he had already gained a formidable reputation for his conduct over the Melville affair of 1805. Lord Melville (formerly Henry Dundas) had been attacked in a series of resolutions by Samuel Whitbread on 8 April. Melville stood accused of having allowed subordinates to invest public funds for private gain. The debate ended in a tie and the speaker held the casting vote. Abbot is commonly remembered as having voted against Melville, finding him culpable of corruption. This conclusion is incorrect. Although Whitbread had touched upon various matters in his speech, the house could proceed to take decisions only on each resolution in turn. When the first came to be put, Pitt moved a destructive amendment, intending to refer the matter to a select committee. But he was persuaded that he should first move the previous question, and it was on this technical motion that the division was tied. Some reports were misleadingly phrased, going so far as to describe the speaker as voting in favour of Whitbread's censures. What actually occurred was a casting vote in favour of permitting the original motion to be put. Indeed Whitbread's first motion was simply a statement of fact. It stated that the Commons had resolved in 1782 that it would be advisable to reform the functioning of the office of treasurer of the navy by paying fixed salaries in lieu of fees and perquisites. Such a motion could not be directly negatived since it was true. Abbot's conception of the situation was crystal clear: there had been three strands to the charges against Melville, and the first two (namely the breaking of the law and Melville's conniving at profiteering) were 'confessed and established—and fit for the immediate judgement of the House' (Abbot, 1.548). The only topic needing further inquiry before a decision could be taken was whether Melville had participated in any profits. Quite properly, the speaker chose to stand aside and allow the house to vote on the first of Whitbread's motions, knowing that, if it was carried, the sense of the house would still have to be taken on the remaining nine resolutions. If any of these prejudged Melville, then members would be free to propose amendments or refer matters for further inquiry. Abbot's casting vote, therefore, was given not upon Melville's guilt but upon the merits of the question whether the house should be permitted to proceed to vote upon a matter of fact as a prelude to voting on a series of censure motions.

The speaker today is expected to refrain from politics, but in Abbot's day a limited degree of active engagement was tolerated, even expected. During committees of the whole house, when the chair was occupied by another member, the speaker might well contribute to general debate. This right was exercised sparingly, not least, as Abbot realized, because of the 'inconvenience of being precluded afterwards … from explaining or defending any opinions in any subsequent stage of discussion'. Where, however, he perceived 'subjects of a paramount importance', he considered it not only a 'personal duty' to deliver his sentiments, but rather 'in some degree an official duty' (*Hansard 1*, 14, 1809, 837).

On 1 June 1809 Abbot spoke in committee on John Curwen's bill against electoral corruption. After citing precedents ranging from the thirteenth to the eighteenth centuries, he stated that the abuses in question were 'not only offences by the law of Parliament, they have been long since adjudged to be criminal by the common law of the realm'. He argued that Curwen's bill 'should be in itself declaratory' and on these terms earnestly hoped for the bill's successful passage because he believed it 'indispensable to the honour of this House'. The speaker's conduct was widely praised. Several members prefaced their own comments with reference to his 'high authority', and one commended 'the manly, dignified, and constitutional part he had … taken' (*Hansard 1*, 14, 1809, 840, 841, 843, 846, 850). The following year Abbot was once more involved in controversy. On 6 April 1810 he issued a warrant for the arrest of the radical member Sir Francis Burdett for breach of privilege. Burdett had spoken in parliament against the arrest of a printer for criticizing the exclusion of strangers from a recent debate. Moreover, Burdett had arranged for the publication of his speech accompanied by an inflammatory address impugning the house for illegal conduct. This became a *cause célèbre* and three days of rioting took place before he submitted to arrest. A private prosecution was brought by Burdett against Abbot, who was granted a public defence by the attorney-general and acquitted in 1811. But the case was not finally resolved until Burdett's appeal was rejected by the Lords six years later.

During proceedings on the regency in 1810–11, Abbot initially maintained a strict silence. As he explained in a speech on 4 February 1811, the speaker 'will be more likely to render his services satisfactory and effectual, by forbearing to mix in general debate' (*Hansard 1*, 18, 1810–11, 1108). He intervened only at the point when the question was 'reduced to the single issue respecting the form of our proceedings'. He made an authoritative declaration that the house was 'legally assembled' because 'elected by the King's writ, prorogued by the King's commission, and met upon the day prescribed by the prorogation'. On the substantive question of how to substitute for the normal procedure of receiving the royal assent to legislation, he endorsed the ministerial suggestion to give assent by a commission of the great seal. The force of logic compelled him to favour restrictions because the office of regent must be defined and then modelled 'into something that is not the King', baldly stating that 'two Kings at a time we cannot have' (ibid., 18, 1810–11, 111).

In 1813 Abbot played a decisive role in thwarting Catholic emancipation. On 9 March he spoke in a committee on the state of the law, making a 'warning protest' against 'a sweeping repeal of all known securities' (*Hansard 1*, 24, 1812–13, 1205). Although willing to allow Catholics access to higher military office, he refused to countenance their admission to parliament. The decision of the committee went against him, however, and leave was granted to introduce a relief bill. He spoke against it at the committee stage on 24 May, playing upon traditional prejudices: that Catholics took oaths with mental reservations; that priests were notorious spies; and that a restored Catholic hierarchy would be beholden to the mandates of the pope. His proposed amendment to the bill was entirely destructive: that the words 'to sit and vote in either House of Parliament' be left out. It was passed in a full house by a majority of only four votes.

There was an embarrassing sequel to this episode. On 22 July 1813 Abbot performed his accustomed task of presenting supply bills for royal assent prior to the prorogation of parliament. It was traditional on such occasions for the speaker to deliver a short speech at the bar of the Lords. These formal orations rarely created controversy, but on this occasion Abbot blurred the distinction between his personal views and official duty. He referred to the house having adhered to 'those laws by which the throne, the Parliament, and the government of this country are made fundamentally Protestant' and having refused to consent 'to allow that those who acknowledge a foreign jurisdiction should be authorised to administer the powers and jurisdictions of this realm' (*Hansard 1*, 27, 1813–14, 475). This was inflammatory enough, but the suspicion that the regent had been active in canvassing against Catholic relief made matters worse, raising the constitutional spectre of crown interference in parliamentary proceedings. Abbot was subjected to a motion of censure on 22 April 1814, but was exonerated, partly because of speeches in his favour by Catholic sympathizers such as George Canning, but also because many members recognized his worth as speaker and were unwilling to risk losing him. His proven ability as chairman of the house was a decided advantage. One member, Frederick Douglas, stated that 'they would run the risk of losing a person whose services were so eminently valuable … they were not to forget how often his judgement had been advantageously exercised on behalf of the House' (*Hansard 1*, 27, 1813–14, 498).

Later career, 1817–1829 On 30 May 1817 Abbot resigned because of ill health. He had long suffered from stomach and urinary ailments, compounded by recurrent back pain and occasional bouts of fainting and sickness. These he had borne bravely and without interrupting the business of the house. But he was finally driven to resign by erysipelas, an inflammatory disease of the face. He was raised to the peerage as Baron Colchester on 3 June 1817 and received a pension of £4000 for himself and £3000 to his heir. From 1819 to 1822 he travelled in France and Italy. Occasionally rumoured for high office, he supported the Liverpool ministry and particularly his mentor Addington, now Lord Sidmouth. He died at Spring Gardens, Whitehall, on 7 May 1829, and was buried in Westminster Abbey on 14 May. He was succeeded by his eldest son, Charles Abbot, second Baron Colchester (1798–1867). Colchester's speakership had been distinguished by an unflagging determination to improve administrative functioning through rational reform. He had also ensured that his researches into the history of parliamentary procedure were carefully collated, preserved, and handed on to posterity through the medium of John Hatsell's revised *Precedents of Procedure* (1818). Abbot was the first speaker since Arthur Onslow to apply systematic analysis to the functioning of the chair, and his successors were greatly indebted to him.   CLARE WILKINSON

Sources *The diary and correspondence of Charles Abbot, Lord Colchester*, ed. Charles, Lord Colchester, 3 vols. (1861) • C. Wilkinson, 'The practice and procedure of the House of Commons, *c*.1784–1832', PhD diss., U. Wales, Aberystwyth, 1998 • E. Porritt and A. G. Porritt, *The unreformed House of Commons*, 2 vols. (1909) • J. Redlich, *The procedure of the House of Commons: a study of its history and present form*, 3 vols. (1908) • A. I. Dasent, *The speakers of the House of Commons* (1911) • M. MacDonagh, *The speaker of the house* (1914) • R. G. Thorne, 'Abbot, Charles', HoP, *Commons, 1754–90* • GEC, *Peerage* • Foster, *Alum. Oxon.* • DNB • *Hansard 1* (1809), vol. 14; (1810–11), vol. 18; (1812–13), vol. 24; (1813–14), vol. 27
Archives Lincoln's Inn, London, legal notebooks and papers • NL Scot., travel journals • PRO, corresp., journals, and parliamentary papers, PRO 30/9 | BL, letters to Lord Auckland, Add. MSS 34456–34458 • BL, letters to Samuel and Jeremy Bentham, Add. MSS 33537–33545 • BL, letters to Lord Grenville, Add. MS 58954 • BL, corresp. with Lord Hardwicke, Add. MSS 35643–35764 • BL, corresp. with second earl of Liverpool, Add. MSS 38248–38328, 38571 • BL, corresp. with Sir Robert Peel, Add. MSS 40221–40536, *passim* • BL, corresp. with C. P. Yorke, Add. MS 45037 • BL OIOC, letters to Lord Amherst, MS Eur. F 140 • Devon RO, corresp. with first Viscount Sidmouth, 152M • E. Sussex RO, letters to first earl of Sheffield • Hants. RO, corresp. with William Wickham, 38M49 • NA Scot., letters to Sir Alexander Hope • NA Scot., corresp. with Lord Melville • NL Scot., Glenbervie MSS, diary • RBG Kew, corresp. with Sir Joseph Banks • U. Durham L., letters to second Earl Grey
Likenesses T. Lawrence, portrait, *c*.1824, Palace of Westminster, London [*see illus.*] • portrait, NPG • portrait, Speaker's House

Abbot, Charles (1761–1817), botanist and entomologist, was born on 24 March 1761. He was educated at Winchester College and matriculated at New College, Oxford, in 1779, gaining his BA in 1783. He was a fellow of the college between 1781 and 1788, was awarded his MA in 1787, and his DD in 1802. He held the life-appointment of usher at Bedford School from 22 October 1787, where he seems to have been an impatient teacher, was vicar of Oakley Raynes and Goldington, Bedfordshire, and may also have been a chaplain to the duke of Bedford and to the marquess of Tweeddale. He married Sarah Harris of Chockenhall (Cherkenhill), Worcestershire, on 7 November 1787. Among his scientific colleagues, Abbot was a pleasant and enthusiastic friend, and he seems to have held whig sympathies.

In 1793 Abbot was elected fellow of the Linnean Society of London, sponsored by founder member James Dickson, nurseryman, and the Revd Thomas Orlebar Marsh of Felmersham, vicar of Stevington, Bedfordshire, botanist and antiquarian. In 1813 he was elected a fellow of the Society of Antiquaries. The Linnean Society possesses Abbot's manuscript 'Catalogus plantarum' (May 1795), a list of 956 plants of Bedfordshire; this preceded his *Flora Bedfordiensis* (20 November 1798), arranged according to the Linnaean system, and describing 1225 wild plants, with six plates by James Sowerby, to whom he sent specimens. The English text and portable, octavo format were intended to enable female readers to learn botany and make field studies. The countess of Upper Ossory lent Abbot her books; Abbot's wife prepared his herbarium, which was formerly conserved at Turvey Abbey and is now at the Luton Museum.

In 1807 Abbot discovered the helleborine, *Epipactis purpurata*, named and published by Sir James Edward Smith in *The English Flora* (4.41–2), where Smith also describes the Bedford willow, *Salix russelliana* (4.186–7), identified by Abbot as a distinct species. Abbot is also mentioned in contemporary entomological literature, for he possessed a large collection of insects. In 1798 he made the first captures in England of *Papilio paniscus*, the chequered skipper, and in Bedfordshire of *Papilio charlotta*, a fritillary, sending specimens to the lepidopterist Adrian Hardy Haworth FLS, who acknowledged them, and others, in *Prodromus lepidopterum Britannicorum* (1802). Abbot made contributions to *Magna Britannia* (1806, vol. 1, *Bedfordshire*), by D. and S. Lysons, and to the *General View of Agriculture in the County of Bedford* (1808) by the farmer Thomas Batchelor. He also published *Hymns* (1791), *Sermons* (1805; 1807), and *Verses* (1802; 1806; 1815). He died at his home in Bedford on 8 September 1817 and is believed to have been buried beside his wife in Great Malvern, Worcestershire.

                                                                    ENID SLATTER

Sources J. G. Dony, 'Bedfordshire naturalists, III — Charles Abbot (1761–1817)', *Journal of the Natural History Society and Field Club*, 1/3 (1948), 38–42 • J. Godber, *The Harpur Trust, 1552–1973* (1973) • J. Godber, *History of Bedfordshire, 1066–1888* (1969) • J. Sargeaunt and E. Hockliffe, *A history of Bedford School* (1925), 50–53, 57–8 • Desmond, *Botanists*, rev. edn • J. E. Smith, *Flora Britannica*, 3 vols. (1800–04) • A. H. Haworth, *Lepidoptera Britannica*, 4 parts (1803–28), pt 1 • 'Extracts from the minute book', *Transactions of the Linnean Society*, 5 (1800), 276 • Linn. Soc., Smith papers • J. E. Smith, J. Sowerby, and others, *English botany*, 36 vols. (1790–1814) • T. F. Kirby, *Winchester scholars: a list of the wardens, fellows, and scholars of … Winchester College* (1888) • Foster, *Alum. Oxon.* • L. R. Conisbee, *A Bedfordshire bibliography* (1962) • will, PRO, PROB 11/1597, sig. 502
Archives Bedford School, Bedford • Linn. Soc., catalogue of Bedfordshire plants • New College, Oxford • Oxf. U. Mus. NH, entomological calendar and his *Lepidoptera Anglica cum Libellulis* • Woburn Abbey, Bedfordshire | BL, T. O. Marsh MSS • Linn. Soc., corresp. with Sir James Smith • Luton Museum and Art Gallery, herbarium • NHM, corresp. with members of the Sowerby family
Wealth at death approx. £1500 from bequests

Abbot, George (1562–1633), archbishop of Canterbury, was born on 29 October 1562 in the parish of St Nicholas, Guildford, Surrey, the fourth of six sons of Maurice Abbot (1519/20–1606), shearman (clothworker), and Alice, *née* Marsh or March (1525/6–1606). His parents were committed protestants who, according to Daniel Featley, had converted to the new faith in Edward VI's reign, only to suffer persecution by John Story, chancellor of the diocese of London, under Mary Tudor. John Aubrey records a story that Abbot's mother, when pregnant with him, dreamed that her unborn son was destined for greatness, which 'made several people of quality offer themselves to be sponsors at the baptismal fount' (Aubrey, *Natural History*, 3.281) and later to pay for his university education, 'his father not being able' (Aubrey, *Brief Lives*, 1.24).

Education and writings Like his elder brother Robert *Abbot (1559/60–1618) and younger brother Maurice *Abbot (1565–1642), Abbot attended Guildford grammar school and, in September 1579, he followed Robert to

George Abbot (1562–1633), after unknown artist, 1623 [copy]

Balliol College, Oxford. He matriculated on 2 May 1581, graduated BA on 31 May 1582, and proceeded MA on 17 December 1585. On 29 November 1583 he was elected a probationary fellow of Balliol and was probably ordained about this time. He was active in college affairs, holding various offices including that of senior dean on four occasions between 1591 and 1597. In August 1592 Abbot took part in the moral theology disputation during Elizabeth I's visit to Oxford; in 1594 he received his BTh and in 1597 his DTh. Six theses which he debated as part of the form for his doctoral degree were published the following year as *Quaestiones sex*, and republished by Abraham Scultetus in Frankfurt in 1616, while for his other disputations Abbot characteristically chose to attack the Petrine commission and the papacy.

A steady stream of works appeared between 1598 and 1604. In 1594 Abbot had been licensed to preach by the university, and began to lecture each Thursday morning in the university church of St Mary on the book of Jonah to an audience of students and others, including 'the elder and strongest sort' (Abbot, *Exposition*, 636–7). Thirty sermons, delivered over the next five years, were printed in 1600 as *An Exposition upon the Prophet Jonah*. Abbot also contributed to three collections of university poems to mark the deaths of John Case and Elizabeth I and the accession of James I, and wrote *A Briefe Description of the Whole Worlde* (1599), presumably for the use of his students. Its mixture of fact and comment on geography, politics, and trade, with additional updated information, may explain why it became the most popular of his works, being regularly reprinted, and enlarged in 1605 and 1617. However, it was

not until 1634, after Abbot's death, that the book appeared under his name. The book's composition and enlargement indicates the broad intellectual tastes of its author. Abbot's library as archbishop was to be noted for its works on political theory, science, mathematics, and witchcraft, with a special accent on books relating to France.

In 1604 Abbot published *The Reasons which Doctour Hill hath Brought for the Upholding of Papistry … Unmasked*, a rebuttal of the seminarist's *A Quatron of Reasons* (1600). Abbot wrote the text about 1603, but its publication was delayed by illness and his responsibilities at Oxford and Winchester, and the book contained only ten of the sixteen projected 'reasons' or heads for rejecting Thomas Hill's hostile critique of English protestantism. His theological writings show Abbot to have been an evangelical Calvinist, embracing the doctrine of double predestination, and implacably opposed to the teachings and practices of the Roman church. He was later credited as the first writer to expose Robert Southwell's doctrine of equivocation, and could contrast the freedom of the gospel in England with the pre-Reformation church, when 'Antichrist … had dazeled the peoples eyes … when the decrees of popes, and the canons of councels, and customes and traditions, were in place of the written word' (Abbot, *Exposition*, 340). Ministers must fulfil their evangelical duty to protestants and Catholics alike and 'be diligent in preaching the gospell to such as wil heare, and in writing, for such as will reade, that they may know and beleeve and be saved' (Abbot, *Reasons*, sig. Ff2r). At the same time Abbot distanced himself from puritan calls for major reforms of the English church. He maintained that the office of bishop was apostolic, condemned the idea of a gadding ministry, and supported 'seemely conformity' in ceremony (ibid., 102), thereby distinguishing his position from that of more radical Oxford contemporaries such as Henry Airay and John Rainolds.

From don to primate, 1597–1611 Abbot's early advancement owed much to Thomas Sackville, Lord Buckhurst, and from 1604 earl of Dorset, chancellor of Oxford University from 1591 to 1608, whose chaplain Abbot became at some stage in the 1590s. In 1600 Abbot stated that he had enjoyed Buckhurst's favour 'these manie yeeres' (Abbot, *Exposition*, sig. A3v), though only from 1597 did he receive major preferment. That year he became master of University College, Oxford, which lay in the chancellor's gift, and in 1600, through Buckhurst's influence, was appointed dean of Winchester. Little is known of Abbot's thirteen years as master of University College beyond the fact that he attracted the devotion of pupils such as Sir Dudley Digges and Sir George Savile, who on his death in 1616 left his son in Abbot's care.

Abbot was thrice nominated by Buckhurst to be vice-chancellor, for the academic years of 1601–2, 1603–4, and 1605–6, and thereby was drawn into public affairs on the national stage. In January 1601 both Abbot and the vice-chancellor of Cambridge were invited by the citizens of London to judge whether or not Cheapside cross, which the diocesan bishop, Richard Bancroft, proposed to repair, should stand or be demolished. Abbot argued that its images representing God and the Holy Spirit were 'unlawful in true divinity' and that its crucifix was 'a ready way unto idolatry', which he suggested should be replaced with a 'pyramide', though magistrates, not 'inferiour men', were 'to redresse such enormities' (Abbot, *Cheapside Crosse Censured and Condemned*, 1641, 2, 7, 8, 10). Abbot's judgment was endorsed by five other Oxford theologians, including Airay and Rainolds; Bancroft was probably furious at their recommendation and, with the backing of the privy council, went ahead with the restoration of the cross. In September 1603, again as vice-chancellor, Abbot headed a university delegation to Woodstock to welcome the new king, James I, and later that year helped to secure parliamentary representation for Oxford University, as an inscription on his tomb proudly records. In January 1604 Abbot attended the Hampton Court conference, to which he made no recorded contribution, though in private he was later to slight the puritan case as 'the objections of some refragatory persons' (PRO, SP 105/95, fols. 28v–29). Their leader was Abbot's colleague John Rainolds, president of Corpus Christi College, who in the summer of 1605 resisted all attempts by Abbot, acting on royal instructions, to pressurize him to subscribe to canon 36 of 1604 and eventually escaped unpunished. Both were commissioned to assist with the new translation of the Bible, and Abbot was one of eight Oxford divines responsible for the gospels, Acts, and Revelation. During his final term as vice-chancellor Abbot oversaw the successful visit of James I to Oxford in August 1605.

These years also saw the first tensions between Abbot and Oxford divines such as John Howson and William Laud, whose ceremonialism, sacerdotalism, and criticism of Calvinist doctrine Abbot came to view as crypto-Catholicism. Howson, vice-chancellor in 1602–3, provoked controversy in a sermon he preached on 17 November 1602 in which he vigorously defended church festivals and emphasized the importance of communal prayer rather than preaching. Abbot's reaction was to attempt, with little obvious success, to turn Chancellor Buckhurst against Howson. In 1603 Laud, then a fellow of St John's, argued for the constant and perpetual visibility of the church and rejected the idea of the proto-protestant descent of the true church through groups like the Waldensians down to the Reformation, an unconventional view which angered and alarmed Abbot, who was at that very time staunchly defending such a descent in his attack on the Catholic Dr Hill; there is no sign that Abbot took any formal action against Laud but he 'thereupon conceived a strong grudge against him, which no tract of time could either abolish or diminish' (Heylyn, 54).

As dean of Winchester, Abbot sat in southern convocation, which in April 1606 passed a series of canons which were refused the royal assent, since the king objected to the doctrine of non-resistance to usurpers and judged that the clergy had 'dipped too deep in what all kings reserve among the *arcana imperii*' (Onslow, 13–14). The fact that the king expressed his views in a letter sent to Abbot indicates his rising stature at court, which was to sustain him on the death of Buckhurst, by now earl of Dorset, in 1608. Abbot

preached a lengthy sermon at his funeral in Westminster Abbey on 26 May, in which he praised Dorset's virtues and even quoted the deceased's confident affirmation in his will that he was an elect saint. The loss of his patron did not hinder Abbot's prospects, for almost immediately, and perhaps through royal influence, he became household chaplain to the earl of Dunbar, lord treasurer of Scotland, and accompanied him north in June 1608 at the head of a small group of English ministers. Dunbar convened a general assembly of the Scottish church at Linlithgow to confer on the full restoration of diocesan bishops, a scheme for which James VI and I had long been working. Abbot's combination of theological rectitude and advocacy of episcopacy undoubtedly furthered the royal project, and on 31 July the Scottish bishops wrote south to the king praising Abbot for 'ane excellent sermone in presens of the assemblie, quwhairby he persuadit ws michtilie to peace and luif [love] towards utheris [others]' (Botfield, 1.147). Abbot then travelled to Edinburgh, where he witnessed the legal proceedings against George Sprot, an accomplice in the Gowrie conspiracy against James VI of 1600, which some continued to maintain was a fiction invented by the crown to dispose of the Gowries. Abbot witnessed Sprot's execution on 12 August, and then wrote a preface to the official account, *The Examinations, Arraignment and Conviction of George Sprot*, to be published in London, in which he defended the king's version of the conspiracy, and argued that James's escape from assassination both in 1600 and in the Gunpowder Plot of 1605 was providential, 'to the enlarging of his Church, to the further ruine of Antichrist, to the uniting of kingdomes, [and] to the comfort of all the godly dispersed thorow Europe' (*The Examinations*, 33–4). This served to pinpoint Abbot's priorities, if not those of his master. A reward for such signal service was not long in coming.

In April 1608 Abbot was tipped for higher preferment, but in the event it was not until exactly a year later that he was nominated for the vacant see of Coventry and Lichfield, probably on the recommendation of Archbishop Bancroft, whose mistrust of Abbot dating back to their dispute over Cheapside cross in 1601 had faded, probably through the good offices of Thomas Ravis, Abbot's ally from Oxford and currently bishop of London. Abbot was consecrated on 3 December 1609 at Lambeth, only to be translated to London on 20 January 1610 following Ravis's unexpected death. At the same time Abbot resigned his mastership of University College, Oxford.

During 1610 Bancroft and Abbot established a brief but close partnership. They worked together in the House of Lords, opposing bills attacking clerical privileges, such as that against pluralism and non-residency which, Abbot claimed, 'will overthrow the universities and bring in barbarism and I know not what' (E. R. Foster, ed., *Proceedings in Parliament, 1610*, 1966, 1.73); instead, he argued that these problems were best solved by augmenting clerical incomes. On several occasions Abbot deputized for the ailing archbishop. On 21 October 1610, together with Andrewes of Ely, Neile of Rochester, and Thornborough of Worcester, Abbot consecrated three Scottish bishops, who were then to return home and consecrate their fellow bishops. Abbot was also assiduous in policing the Roman Catholic community in and around London and in September 1610 led his primary visitation of the diocese. Although Richard Rogers recorded in his diary that 'Dr. Abbot visited. No hurt done. *Laus deo*' (M. Knappen, ed., *Two Elizabethan Puritan Diaries*, 1966, 32), in the months following the visitation Abbot checked several persistent nonconformists. He personally suspended two ministers who refused to subscribe and conform, and warned William Gouge, curate of St Anne Blackfriars, to kneel at communion and to insist that his parishioners did likewise. Abbot also blocked the appointment of the radical William Ames as town preacher at Colchester, and urged the bailiffs to elect a 'temperate man who will preach Christ crucified to the saving of your souls and not move contentions about those things wherein by the laws of God and of this church he is bound to obey' (Essex RO, Morant MS, D/Y 2/2, p. 123). Their choice eventually fell on William Eyre, a graduate of the godly Emmanuel College, Cambridge, who also became Abbot's chaplain.

Archbishop Bancroft died on 2 November 1610 and, after much deliberation, in late February 1611 Abbot was chosen to succeed him. James I's decision caused much surprise, to contemporaries as to later generations, since Abbot, though bishop of London, was the most recent appointment to the episcopal bench and was preferred over such prominent colleagues as Andrewes of Ely, Bilson of Winchester, and Matthew of York. Indeed the king felt it necessary to explain his reasoning to the privy council, informing them that he was merely honouring the suit of his favourite the earl of Dunbar, who had died on 30 January 1611; it was rumoured that Dunbar had ordered that 'his hart should be putt into a cuppe of gold and presented to the kings majestie in sign of his loiall service, in recompence wherof he desired nothinge but his majestie wold … preferre Mr Abbots to the sea of Canterbury', a mawkish gesture which James may have found irresistible (Westminster Cathedral Archives, series A, xi, pp. 87–8). Harder headed considerations were at work, though: James was still mindful of Abbot's successful embassy to Scotland in 1608 so that his appointment might further Anglo-Scottish religious harmony, a point that Abbot underlined with a skilful letter to the king on 22 February 1611 expressing his concern about the Scottish church. Abbot's energetic pursuit of Catholic plots and plotters also commended itself to a king still reeling from the shock of the assassination of Henri IV of France the previous summer. Indeed, Abbot may well have dwelt on these threats in the sermon he preached before the king on 5 November 1610, the fifth anniversary of the discovery of the Gunpowder Plot. Abbot had the added advantage that he was Bancroft's choice as successor, and in his funeral sermon on 25 November 1610 praised Bancroft's opposition to presbyterianism and his restoration of Cheapside cross, thereby placing himself firmly in the conformist mainstream of the church. On 9 April 1611 Abbot was installed in Lambeth Palace, at forty-eight the youngest archbishop of Canterbury since the elevation of Thomas Cranmer in 1533.

Court and confessional politics, 1611–1617 On 23 June 1611 Abbot was sworn in as a privy councillor, and took full advantage of the opportunities which now opened up for political influence and intrigue in a court characterized by deepening personal and ideological tensions, especially after the death of Lord Treasurer Salisbury in 1612. For the next decade Abbot pursued a coherent set of confessional objectives: dynastic and political alliances with protestant powers abroad, robust opposition to Catholicism at home and overseas, and a reliance on regular parliaments to finance the king's domestic and foreign affairs. Abbot found allies in Prince Henry, Lord Chancellor Ellesmere, Sir Ralph Winwood, secretary of state from 1614 to 1617, Edward, Lord Zouche, and Queen Anne, but came into conflict with the crypto-Catholic earl of Northampton, his nephew the earl of Suffolk, and, from 1612, the current favourite, Sir Robert Carr. Abbot's stock with the king was at its highest in 1611–12, aided by an unblemished record and James's anxiety at Catholic plotting.

English Catholics were dismayed at Abbot's elevation, for, as one fairly observed in March 1611, 'he is the sorest enemie that ever we had' (Westminster Cathedral Archives, series A, x, p. 41). Using teams of spies, informers, and pursuivants, Abbot infiltrated Catholic circles, seized priests, and compiled dossiers on suspects. Catholics attending mass at foreign embassies in London found themselves under arrest, and Abbot pushed for the execution of imprisoned priests, writing in 1614 that he 'never tooke delight in spilling of blood, but the insolencies of such persons at home and abrode doth deserve some deeper castigation then heere is layd upon them' (PRO, SP 14/76/48). Converts from Catholicism such as John Copley and the ex-Jesuit John Salkeld were handsomely rewarded by Abbot, who, Sir Thomas Lake reported in 1614, 'hath of our own cuntry men many proselytes wherein he much glorieth' (PRO, SP 14/76/9). Particularly useful were those prepared to write against their co-religionists, such as the Benedictine Thomas Preston, who defended the oath of allegiance, which involved a denial of the pope's deposing power, to the considerable embarrassment of other Catholics. At the same time Abbot's Lambeth chaplains were busy writing anti-Roman polemic. One of them, Francis Mason, wrote the definitive vindication of the Anglican episcopal order in 1613, and the following year, in order to nail the Catholic claim that the episcopal succession had been broken in 1559, Abbot summoned four imprisoned priests to Lambeth to examine the entry in the register relating to Matthew Parker's consecration as archbishop. One of Abbot's minor successes was to persuade James I in 1613 that an alleged nunnery run by the Spanish noblewoman Luisa de Carvajal y Mendoca in Highgate was a danger to the state. James, smarting at the publication of the Jesuit Suarez's *Defensor fidei catholicae*, which defended tyrannicide, allowed the house to be raided and Carvajal was arrested. Despite the protests of the Spanish ambassador, Gondamar, the privy council insisted on Carvajal's expulsion, though she died before this could occur. Abbot also capitalized on James's desire to see Catholics take the oath of allegiance, and in 1611–12 had Lord and Lady Vaux and Lord Montagu imprisoned for their refusal. Each found a champion in the earl of Northampton, who secured their eventual release, and who as warden of the Cinque Ports did too little, in Abbot's opinion, to prevent the movement of Catholics in and out of the country. Earl and archbishop clashed over the king's various proposals in 1611–12 to find foreign Catholic spouses for Prince Henry and Princess Elizabeth, which Abbot resolutely opposed; these tensions came to a head in the autumn of 1612 when Abbot probably informed the king of North-ampton's Catholic leanings in order to block his appoint-ment to the vacant post of lord treasurer, and he may have condoned the libels against Northampton which ended in prosecution of a group of court officials in Star Chamber.

Abbot's commitment to the cause of international prot-estantism and his desire to intervene effectively in diplo-matic debates at court led him to correspond with sympa-thetic English diplomats stationed abroad: he regularly exchanged letters with William Trumbull, English agent at Brussels, Dudley Carleton, ambassador to Venice and then the United Provinces, Sir Thomas Roe in Hindustan and then Constantinople, and more intermittently with Ralph Winwood at The Hague, Sir Thomas Edmondes in Paris, and Sir Henry Wotton at Venice. For, as he wrote to Roe in 1617, 'as thinges now stand throughout the whole worlde, there is no place so remote, but that the consider-ation thereof is mediatly or immediatly of consequence to our affaires heere' (PRO, 14/90/34). Matters of inter-national trade, political alliances, and religious develop-ments were all grist to his confessional mill. Another resource that Abbot drew on was the library of more than 6000 books bequeathed to his successors at Lambeth by Richard Bancroft, which Abbot arranged to be catalogued in 1612. Abbot himself expanded the collection, eventu-ally donating more than 2000 books at his death in 1633, though as early as 1614 he could state with considerable satisfaction that his library was 'not much inferiour unto that … of any private man in Europe' (BL, Add. MS 72242, fol. 33r).

The nationwide shock at the unexpected death of Prince Henry in November 1612 was acutely felt by Abbot, who lost an invaluable political ally. Abbot attended the prince on his deathbed, and at his funeral on 7 December preached for two hours. More happily, the same month at Whitehall, Abbot betrothed Princess Elizabeth and the Elector Frederick of the Palatinate, leader of the Evangel-ical Union of German Protestants; the betrothal was a dyn-astic alliance which Abbot warmly welcomed, and the two were married on 14 February 1614. Abbot was close to Prin-cess Elizabeth—a correspondent in 1616 informed Abbot that, her family aside, 'she loveth noe man breathing soe well as shee doeth your grace' (PRO, SP 81/14/271)—and quickly won the friendship of the elector, who gave Abbot a gift of plate worth £1000 on their departure abroad.

Abbot's standing with the king was severely dented by his opposition to the Essex annulment in 1613. His enemies Northampton and Suffolk supported a proposed annulment of the marriage of the earl of Essex and of Suf-folk's daughter Frances Howard so that the latter might marry the favourite, Robert Carr, now earl of Somerset, and thereby cement a key political alliance. On 16 May 1613 Abbot was appointed to head a commission consist-ing of three other bishops—Lancelot Andrewes, Richard Neile, and John King—and six laymen to consider the case for an annulment on the grounds of Essex's impotency towards his wife. Abbot became convinced that the cause of non-consummation was not impotency but lack of affection, and belatedly realized that the king was deter-mined to push through the annulment. By July he was keen to resign from the commission, and having written to James outlining his objections he received a letter refut-ing them in which the king described Abbot's belief that scripture could settle all controversies as 'preposterous' and 'one of the puritans arguments' (State trials, 2.797). James suspected that Abbot's opposition was a matter not of conscience but of politics, in order to frustrate the Howards; on 25 September, following the addition of two compliant bishops—Thomas Bilson and John Buck-eridge—to the commission, the annulment was pro-nounced, with Abbot and Bishop King dissenting. The marriage of Somerset and Frances Howard went ahead on 26 December in the Chapel Royal, with Abbot looking on. By then he had written a vindication of his conduct, pri-marily for his own satisfaction, in which he related Bishop Neile's duplicitous behaviour, and the support he received from across the country, from other bishops, 'many godly preachers out of all parts', 'nobles', and 'worthy personages', was evidence of his emerging repu-tation as a staunch defender of morality and protestant-ism at court (ibid., 2.833). His stance had publicly embar-rassed and angered the king, who promptly awarded the vacant see of Lincoln not to Abbot's brother Robert, for whom it had been earmarked, but to Neile. Though Abbot did eventually regain favour, the intimacy of king and pri-mate was broken.

Abbot welcomed the decision to call parliament in 1614, and looked for a harmonious session and some effective action against Catholic recusants. He regretted its untimely dissolution, and attempted to ease the king's financial plight by organizing a voluntary contribution of plate from bishops and civil lawyers, heading the list with a gift of a basin and ewer worth £140, an example to be fol-lowed by many peers and courtiers. In September 1615, when the privy council broadly supported the idea of con-vening another parliament, Abbot declared that 'he had taken as great pleasure in this day's work as in any that ever he had been at in that place' (J. Spedding, ed., The Let-ters and the Life of Francis Bacon, 5, 1869, 205–6), though the king was not ultimately persuaded to summon one. The death of Northampton in June 1614 was followed by Suf-folk's promotion to the treasury, and Abbot chafed at the king's pursuit of a Spanish match for the young Prince Charles, complaining in August 1614 that 'wee are inchanted by the false, fradulent, and syren-like songs of Spaine' (BL, Add. MS 72242, fol. 33r), which he feared would provoke divine vengeance. His solution was to hatch a plot in April 1615 with the earl of Pembroke, abetted by Queen Anne, to replace Somerset with George Villiers in the king's affections, and break the influence of the Howard interest. In May 1615 Abbot, alluding to the scheme with guarded optimism, wrote that 'some beginning is made' so that 'our master may bee happy in his elder yeeres' (ibid., fol. 44r), which was soon completed by Villiers's charm and the revelation of Somerset's complicity in the Overbury murder. Temporarily Abbot's influence improved, for his ally Lord Zouche was appointed warden of the Cinque Ports that July, while his brother Robert was finally promoted, to the see of Salisbury, in December. Hopes for a sea change in royal policy were to be disappointed, however, as the king continued to pursue religious harmony as the threat from Catholicism receded in his mind. In March 1617 serious negotiations for a royal marriage opened with Spain, and Abbot, with several other allies, found himself excluded from proceedings. His initial warm relations with Villiers became strained as early as 1617 as he resented the favourite's wish to dominate patronage, and afterwards wrote that 'no man goeth free that doth not stoope saile to that castle' (PRO, SP 14/171/59).

Church government and the defence of doctrine, 1611–1617 Abbot was an active metropolitan. On 30 April 1611 he took over the presidency of the southern court of high commission, which met at Lambeth, and resumed his predecessor's campaign against the use of writs of prohibition from the common law courts in cases before the ecclesiastical courts. The dispute was heard before the privy council in May, when Abbot clashed with the lord chief justice, Sir Edward Coke, and it concluded with a promise from James to incorporate reforms into new letters patent for the high commission. In the event the common law judges were dissatisfied at the changes and refused to sit as commissioners. Under Abbot's leadership the court became notorious for its harsh punishments of negligent clergymen, which some contemporaries ascribed to Abbot's ignorance of the realities of parochial life, since he had never had an incumbency; however, his published sermons suggest that he was well aware of the problems that ministers could encounter from vexatious or litigious parishioners, and he evidently believed that scandalous conduct impugned the whole clerical estate and deserved the highest censures of deprivation and degradation.

In 1612–16 Abbot conducted his metropolitical visitation of the southern province, sending his visitors to every diocese except London. The visitation articles he drew up were the first to enquire if the communion table was 'used out of time of divine service, as is not agreeable to the holy use of it' (Fincham, *Visitation Articles*, 1.100) and if all the liturgical offices were performed. Churchwardens were ordered to compile an ecclesiastical terrier of lands belonging to their parish church, in accordance with canon 87 of 1604, a measure intended to prevent the further erosion of parochial property and incomes. Though the records are missing for some dioceses, in at least three—Gloucester (1612), Salisbury (1613), and Hereford

(1614)—non-preaching ministers were assigned exercises or tutors, a late revival of Elizabethan vocational training schemes.

This initiative was part of a wider attempt by Abbot to promote a learned and diligent preaching ministry. Abbot himself was always an active preacher, and, in contrast to his immediate predecessors and successor at Canterbury, filled a regular slot—Palm Sunday—on the roster of Lenten preachers before James I and then Charles I. His patronage went to evangelical Calvinists, among them the staunch Calvinist Daniel Featley, Sampson Price, lecturer at St Olave's, Southwark, and Thomas Myriell, preacher at Barnet, and he was influential in securing bishoprics for such like-minded Oxonians as John King, bishop of London 1611–21, and Miles Smith, bishop of Gloucester 1612–24.

Abbot's evangelism is the key to his moderation towards puritan nonconformists. The church could ill afford to lose some of its most committed preachers by a close scrutiny of their adherence to ecclesiastical discipline, and Abbot could happily endorse the view of James I that clerical subscription to canon 36 of 1604 was a sufficient check against militancy. On 24 May 1611 Abbot dispatched a series of instructions to the bishops of his province, among which was an order that they win round or else remove 'anie unconformable ministers that disturbe the peace of the Churche' (Fincham, *Visitation Articles*, 1.98), which was very much in line with his own work in London diocese in 1610–11. Minor infringements were treated more leniently. In 1613 Abbot's vicar-general told a nonconformist minister that he should wear the surplice most Sundays, rather than at every service; and for the godly diocese of Norwich in 1618 Abbot even toned down the ceremonial enquiries in his articles, and asked if the minister 'commonly weare the surplis', in sharp contrast to bishops such as Neile who asked if the garment were worn at divine service 'always and at every time both morning and evening' (ibid., 1.xix, 100). Though Abbot can be found acting harshly against eminent puritans such as Arthur Hildersham, who refused to subscribe and to co-operate by taking the *ex officio* oath in high commission, this was largely at the bidding of James I; within weeks of the king's death in 1625 Abbot licensed Hildersham to preach again.

Puritans, for Abbot, were a tiny minority of extremists, typified by the exiled theologian William Ames, whose anti-episcopal writings exasperated the archbishop. The real challenge, he believed, came from those who deviated from established doctrine rather than discipline. In 1611 Abbot learned from Matthew Slade and Sibrandus Lubbertus, fellow Calvinists in the United Provinces, of the impending election of Conrad Vorstius to the divinity chair at Leiden University. Given that Catholic apologists had linked Vorstius's heterodox views, including Arianism, with some of James I's writings, Abbot had little difficulty in persuading the king to vindicate his orthodoxy by opposing Vorstius's election, which led to a protracted royal intervention in Dutch politics. At the same time the king ordered the burning of Edward Wightman and Bartholomew Legate, in Abbot's words 'blasphemous heretikes' who, among other positions, had maintained Arianism; the archbishop strongly endorsed the decision, and ensured that his opponent Coke be excluded from the panel of judges to hear the cases 'for his singularitie in opinion' (J. P. Collier, ed., *The Egerton Papers*, CS, 1st ser., 1840, 446–8). The two were burnt in March 1612, the last time this sentence was carried out for heresy in England. Later that year Bishop John Jegon of Norwich wrote to Abbot for advice about the appropriate punishment for William Sayer, 'a desperate heretique' who held a mixture of Barrowist and Anabaptist views. Abbot listed the various options available to Jegon, and added that Sayer would only burn were he to 'denie something expressly conteyned in the three Creeds or foure first generall Counsells' of the church (CUL, MS Mm 6.58 ss. 7, fol. 2r). Abbot's hostility towards the Dutch Arminian party, which had sponsored Vorstius's election, was evident in 1613 when the eminent Arminian and jurist Hugo Grotius visited England. Abbot, according to Grotius, regarded him as 'practically a heretic' (Patterson, 145).

Abbot also kept an eagle eye on the burgeoning anti-Calvinist interest at Oxford University and at court. In December 1610 he nudged Lord Ellesmere, the new chancellor of Oxford, to denounce William Laud to the king, in the hope of undermining Laud's candidacy for the vacant presidency of St John's College, Oxford. With the protection of Neile, however, Laud was elected president after a bitterly contested election. Neile's circle, the future Durham House group, contained many divines whose views Abbot suspected, including Laud, Laud's old tutor, Bishop Buckeridge of Rochester, and Benjamin Carier, whose conversion to Roman Catholicism in 1613–14 seemed to vindicate the archbishop's opposition. Carier, according to Abbot, 'for many yeeres hath not ben held sound, but hollow and wavering, so that wee shall lose nothing by his departure', though he added that Carier was in touch with some 'hollow-harted people in England' (BL, Add. MS 72242, fols. 12r, 17v).

At Oxford, Abbot's Calvinist allies included his brother Robert, regius professor of divinity until 1615, Sebastian Benefield, his former chaplain and Lady Margaret professor of divinity, both of whom wrote major works against Arminianism, and William Godwin, dean of Christ Church. In 1612 Robert Abbot and Godwin censured John Howson, the former vice-chancellor, for his provocative sermons on some notes printed in the Genevan Bible, which he claimed were tainted with Arianism; in February 1615 Robert Abbot clashed with William Laud over doctrine, and in June the archbishop had both Howson and Laud summoned to a royal hearing. The case against Laud was dismissed, and the archbishop 'acknowledged his brothers error … and Dr Abotts him selfe asked pardon' (PRO, SP 14/80/124). Howson's defence before James and Abbot on 10 June is better documented. The archbishop presented sixteen charges against Howson stretching back over twenty-five years, which collectively presented Howson as a crypto-papist; Howson retaliated with the insinuation that Abbot was, or had been, a puritan. James, however, refused to draw these conclusions: Howson was acquitted, though he was instructed to preach more often against Catholicism, and four years later was given the bishopric of Oxford. The limit of Abbot's influence over James was clear to see, and by denouncing Howson to the king, the archbishop had inadvertently advanced his opponent's career.

On his promotion to Canterbury, Abbot had been twice charged by James I to 'carry my house nobly … and live like an archbishop' (*State trials*, 2.1471). Abbot's household was large, and in 1614 included thirty-three gentlemen waiters-in-ordinary, thirty-five yeomen-in-ordinary, and thirty-nine retainers as well as his 'Croydon familie' of eight (LPL, MS 1730, fol. 7r). He exercised the liberal hospitality expected of leading churchmen, spending about £40 a week on his kitchen to entertain courtiers, ambassadors, lawyers, and divines, and at the end of each law term Abbot would invite every gentleman from Kent then in London to 'a general entertainment' at Lambeth, 'where he feasted them with great bounty and familiarity' (Heylyn, 244). Abbot visited Canterbury for the first time in August 1615 in such state that it offended James I, according to hostile Catholic observers. Relations between the archbishop and the city corporation were initially warm, and Abbot paid for a stone conduit to be erected in the high street, but at some time before 1627 he quarrelled with the city fathers over the liberties of the archbishopric and withdrew his offer of an annuity for its maintenance.

As primate Abbot was visitor to two Oxford colleges, All Souls and Merton. At All Souls he watched carefully over the college's finances, enforced discipline, and probably chose two of his chaplains—Richard Mocket and Richard Astley—to serve as warden between 1614 and 1635. In 1616 Mocket published *De politia ecclesiae Anglicanae*, a description of Anglican doctrine and discipline, which he dedicated to Abbot. The book offended the king, for reasons which remain unclear, though it was reported to have 'passages derogatory to the kings prerogative' (BL, Add. MS 72275, fol. 5r) and offered a partisan interpretation under the guise of an uncontroversial account of the church's doctrine. The king ordered the book to be burnt, and in December 1616 Abbot had the humiliation of presiding over the ceremony at Lambeth. Abbot's influence at Oxford also extended to his old college of Balliol, where another chaplain, John Parkhurst, became master in 1617. Abbot gave money to the college and secured benefactions for it. However, one of these, the foundation of Thomas Tisdale (*d.* 1610) of Abingdon, though initially associated with Balliol, was in 1623 augmented by money from Richard Wightwick, and reassigned to found a new college, Pembroke, apparently with Abbot's acquiescence; Balliol was left owing the trustees £300, which Abbot refunded from his own pocket.

From 1612 Abbot was also chancellor of Trinity College, Dublin. Initially he criticized several statutes, viewing the provision for lay preaching as 'flat puritanical' (*The Whole Works of J. Ussher*, ed. C. R. Elrington and J. H. Todd, 17 vols.,

1847–64, 15.72), and he wrote to the archbishop of Dublin in April 1613 relating the king's anger that the surplice was omitted in the college chapel and in both cathedrals in Dublin. His concern at the weakness of Irish protestantism led him to press James I to recruit better bishops from England, but Abbot habitually left the Irish church alone. His relations with the Scottish church remained cordial, but for an awkward moment in July 1616 when, on the king's instructions, Abbot absolved the Catholic marquess of Huntly from a sentence of excommunication pronounced by the Scottish kirk, and was exposed to the accusation of unwarranted interference in the affairs of a sister church. Abbot had to pen a carefully worded explanation to Archbishop John Spottiswoode of St Andrews, assuring him that it was done on good advice and in a spirit of 'brotherly correspondency and unity of affection' (Botfield, 2.477).

In his relentless search for allies against Rome, Abbot was drawn towards the Greek Orthodox church and with James I's blessing established formal contact between the two churches. About 1615 he opened a correspondence with Cyril Lukaris, patriarch of Alexandria and afterwards of Constantinople, whom Abbot came to prize as a kindred spirit—an opponent of Rome and 'as wee terme him, a pure Calvinist' (Richardson, ed., *Negotiations*, 102). The two exchanged books and manuscripts and in 1617 arranged that a young Greek scholar, Metrophanes Kritopoulos, be admitted to study theology at Oxford, to be followed by several others over the next twenty years.

Abbot also played a supporting part in the defection to England of Marco Antonio de Dominis, formerly the Roman Catholic archbishop of Spalato. He arrived in London on 3 December 1616, initially as Abbot's guest at Lambeth, to be fêted by the king and the establishment. Abbot welcomed the first volume of his *De republica ecclesiastica* which he believed would make 'any understanding man … stagger in his popery' (BL, Add. MS 72242, fol. 64r); he and other councillors heard de Dominis preach at the Italian church on 30 November 1617, and a month later, to underline the English church's claims to Catholicity, de Dominis joined Abbot in consecrating two bishops at Lambeth. De Dominis was to return to the Roman fold in 1622, alienated by the widespread hostility towards Roman Catholicism of senior English protestants, of whom Abbot was clearly the ringleader; the archbishop, in turn, was to denounce him as an 'ungodly man' enticed away by promises of preferment in the Roman church (Richardson, ed., *Negotiations*, 102).

Church and state, 1618–1625 Abbot's brother Robert, bishop of Salisbury, died in March 1618. Robert had remarried after his consecration in December 1615, for which he had been sharply rebuked by his brother, who evidently held the scriptural injunction that a bishop should be the husband of one wife. According to one hostile contemporary the letter was 'so full of reproaches and revilings' (Heylyn, 75) that it hastened Robert's death. In May 1618 James I issued his Book of Sports which authorized some recreation on Sundays after divine service and thereby attacked puritan ideas about strict sabbath observance.

Though writers since 1706 have claimed that Abbot forbade the book to be read in his church at Croydon, there is no contemporary evidence to support this, and the confusion may have arisen from conflating Abbot's known sabbatarian sympathies with the widespread refusal to read the book on its reissue in October 1633, two months after Abbot's death. On the fall of Lord Treasurer Suffolk on charges of corruption in July 1618 Abbot headed a team of seven commissioners to run the treasury which, for the next two and a half years, struggled to introduce financial reform. In August 1619 Abbot confessed that 'as thinges now stand, it is the worst occupation that ever I was at' (BL, Add. MS 72242, fol. 86r). In 1618–20 Abbot masterminded the transmission, translation, and publication of Paolo Sarpi's *History of the Council of Trent*, a deeply critical account of the papacy. In 1618 Abbot sent the civil lawyer Nathaniel Brent to Venice to persuade Sarpi to hand over the manuscript, which was sent in weekly packets back to Lambeth. De Dominis added a dedication to the work, which was published in Italian in 1619, followed by English and Latin versions in 1620. The publication was a remarkable coup, which gained wide continental readership, with French and German translations quickly appearing, and Sarpi's account was not fully answered in print until the 1650s. In 1622 Abbot rewarded Brent with the wardenship of Merton College, Oxford, in the face of competition from a rival backed by Prince Charles; in February 1626 Brent married Abbot's niece Martha, and in 1628 became Abbot's vicar-general for the province of Canterbury.

By 1618 Abbot had become seriously perturbed at the worsening religious divisions between Calvinists and Arminians in the United Provinces, which he was inclined to attribute to the absence of a supreme governor and an episcopate, 'where there is no superior to direct, nor inferior to obey' (PRO, SP 105/95, fol. 4v). Abbot strongly backed the decision of Prince Maurice, leader of the Calvinists, to convene the Synod of Dort in 1618–19, an international meeting of divines to settle the disputed doctrinal controversies. He picked George Carleton to be one of the four English delegates and on the withdrawal of another, Joseph Hall, owing to ill health, ensured that Hall's place was taken by his chaplain, Thomas Goad, who 'could not but in my house be well acquainted with those Arminian businesses' (ibid., fol. 48v). Abbot had less success directing their deliberations. Though he had briefed the delegates before their departure, and thereafter exchanged letters with them, they adopted a moderate position on the doctrine of redemption, which was sanctioned by the king though it ran counter to Abbot's view. Nevertheless Abbot could take satisfaction from the confessional solidarity which the synod had symbolized, as well as its condemnation of Arminian teaching, a stance which at that date James I openly endorsed.

In 1614 Abbot had publicly resolved to found an almshouse in his native town at Guildford and, after collecting money for some years, on 6 April 1619 was able to lay the foundation stone of his hospital of the blessed Trinity. The completed building was to comprise a huge gatehouse, brick quadrangle, and projecting wings, which contained a chapel, hall, and accommodation, including rooms for the founder's private use. In 1622 Abbot obtained a royal charter for the hospital, and appointed his nephew, Richard Abbot, as its first master. It was endowed with an annual income of £300, £200 of which was to support a master, twelve brethren, and eight sisters, and the other £100 was intended to set some of the poor to work. As late as November 1629 Abbot was making arrangements for the construction of rooms to house 'manufacture to imploye them therein' (Palmer, 24), and acknowledged that his nephew's rule had not been entirely successful.

Abbot avidly followed the developing European crisis of 1618–19. He may well have advised Frederick V of the Palatinate to take the proffered throne of Bohemia in the belief that James I would not abandon his son-in-law were the Habsburgs to retaliate with military force. Frederick's election to the Bohemian crown and Bethlen Gabor's successes against the Habsburgs in Hungary he viewed in apocalyptic terms, and he wrote to Secretary Sir Robert Naunton in September 1619 urging England to lead a protestant crusade against the Habsburgs. As for financing a war, 'parliament is the old and honourable way' (Onslow, 29–30), though the king might contemplate, he suggested, pawning or selling his jewels stored in the Tower of London. In more sober moments he also proposed an alliance with Catholic Savoy and Venice, fellow opponents of Spain.

Abbot's voice now carried little weight with the king, and he was weakened further by his strained relations with Buckingham, and the loss of key court allies: Winwood had died in October 1617, Bishop James Montagu in July 1618, and Queen Anne (whose funeral sermon he preached on 13 May at Westminster Abbey) in March 1619. Abbot thus could do nothing to prevent the king attempting to solve the crisis through mediation and an intensified pursuit of a Spanish match, and Abbot had to content himself with organizing a public collection for the Palatinate in January 1620. Nevertheless Abbot stayed in close touch with Christoph von Dohna, Frederick V's emissary in London, discussed developments with the Venetian ambassador, and exchanged several letters with Christian IV of Denmark, whose support for the reformed religion much impressed Abbot; by contrast, he believed that James overestimated his influence with the Spanish, and ridiculed the idea that through negotiations 'wee shall have such fruites of their pure love toward us that in the conclusion wee shall do what wee please' (BL, Add. MS 72242, fol. 91v). The expulsion of Frederick V from Bohemia in November 1620 by Spanish troops confirmed Abbot's worst fears and he informed Christian IV that if Spanish victories were to continue 'our *Rex Pacificus*' would be driven to war (*46th Report*, 47). Early in 1621 Abbot was in serious political trouble, accused of aiding Dohna's protest to James I at his inaction and backing Naunton's scheme to substitute a French for a Spanish dynastic match. Abbot was threatened with house arrest, but cleared his name; in June it was again rumoured that he was confined to Lambeth, at precisely the time that the

king was trying to suppress public criticism of his foreign diplomacy. Abbot survived, but at the cost, it seems, of surrendering his active role in confessional politics, and his correspondence with diplomats at home and abroad was curtailed. As he informed Trumbull in July 1622, 'there is reason of forbearance of letters till some things bee settled' (BL, Add. MS 72242, fol. 93r).

In late July 1621 Abbot went to stay with Lord Zouche at Bramshill, Hampshire, where he was to consecrate his chapel. Abbot suffered from gout and the stone and since 1616, on the advice of his physician, had hunted in the summer months, at Nonsuch, Wimbledon, and elsewhere. On 24 July Abbot shot an arrow from his crossbow which accidentally wounded a keeper, Peter Hawkins, who died shortly afterwards. It was a devastating misfortune, which a contemporary noted 'hath peerced his grace in the very marrowe of his bones' (BL, Add. MS 72272, fol. 119v), and Abbot himself acknowledged that it exposed him to 'the rejoycing of the papist, the insulting of the puritan, the greefe of my freendes, the contentment of ill-willers' (PRO, SP 14/122/97). Crucially the king, a keen huntsman himself, was sympathetic, and immediately entrusted Abbot with the care of the privy seal while the earl of Worcester was absent from London. However, the Sorbonne declared Abbot to be guilty of canonical irregularity, while three bishops-elect, John Williams, Valentine Carey, and William Laud, refused to accept consecration from a 'man of blood' (Welsby, 94); probably as a result, in early October, James referred the matter to a commission of bishops and lawyers to consider Abbot's irregularity and the scandal which the manslaughter had occasioned. Abbot himself drew up an apology in his own hand, which on 8 October was sent to Sir Henry Spelman, the prominent lawyer, whose answer maintained that Abbot was by canon law irregular. The commission took their time deliberating, in the course of which Abbot found unexpected support from Bishop Lancelot Andrewes, and eventually it recommended that the king authorize a dispensation from any irregularity, which was signed by James on 24 December 1621. Though Abbot was acquitted the accident cast a long shadow over the remainder of his life. He settled an annuity of £20 on the widow of Peter Hawkins, but had to endure many taunts: in 1623 de Dominis, now abroad, branded him a murderer, while a group of women surrounded his coach at Croydon on one occasion and, when Abbot complained, up went the shout 'you had best to shoot an arrow at us' (Fuller, 6.44, n. f).

With his pacific diplomacy under sustained attack from the pulpit and press, on 4 August 1622 James I issued six directions to regulate preaching. Preachers were to avoid matters of state and the difficult doctrine of predestination, which had been much discussed since the Synod of Dort; they were also to omit attacks on puritans or Catholics, and to devote Sunday afternoons to preaching or teaching on the catechism. On 12 August Abbot circulated the instructions to the bishops, with a brief covering note. The directions proved controversial, since they appeared at precisely the time that the king had also suspended penal laws against Roman Catholics and released Catholic priests from prison, so that on 4 September Abbot was forced to write again and at much length to stem the flow of this criticism. He did so in terms rather different from those used by James to explain the directions: the order was necessary to stop the defections to popery and separation, and far from restraining preaching, 'his majesty doth expect at our hands that it should encrease the number of sermons' through the profitable exposition of the catechism on Sunday afternoons (Fincham, *Visitation Articles*, 1.214). Thus Abbot's public support was secured by giving an evangelical cast to an unpalatable restraint on the pulpit.

Privately Abbot was aghast at the expedition of Prince Charles and Buckingham to Madrid in 1623 to win the Spanish infanta, which he feared would be 'the most doefull accident unto us that hath befallen in this later age of the worlde' (Richardson, ed., *Negotiations*, 252). Publicly, when preaching before James I on Palm Sunday 1623, he criticized older men who grew uncertain in their religion, thereby 'to leave theyr posteritye after them, in doubtes and waveringes [as to] which were the best', and women who 'came to heare masses, and soe chaunged theyr relligion', clear allusions, respectively, to the king and to Buckingham's mother, who had recently converted to Roman Catholicism, but James chose to ignore these pointed comments (BL, Stowe MS 743, fol. 52). On 20 July privy councillors were summoned to accept the articles of the Spanish marriage treaty, and Abbot, after protesting vigorously against a general toleration of Catholicism, fell into line and took his oath to the articles. James regarded this as a small victory for him: 'Now I must tell you miracles', he wrote to Charles and Buckingham the following day, 'our great primate hath behaved himself wonderful well in this business' (G. Akrigg, ed., *Letters of King James VI and I*, 1984, 417–18); others, such as Simonds D'Ewes, were critical of Abbot's consent. Within days, however, there appeared a spurious version of Abbot's speech to James, which roundly condemned the proposed toleration by which 'you labour to set up that most damnable and heretical doctrine of the Church of Rome, the whore of Babylon' (Onslow, 35). The 'speech' was very widely circulated, and though Abbot privately assured the king that he was not its author, publicly he took care not to dissociate himself from it, since he accepted its broad argument and saw it as a device to restore his standing among godly protestants such as D'Ewes. The return of Charles and Buckingham empty-handed from Spain in October caused nationwide rejoicing, and Abbot was the first to welcome them back to London.

The parliament of 1624 saw an alliance of the prince and Buckingham with anti-Spanish MPs and lords to press the king to break the match and declare war on Spain. Abbot was busy on their behalf, and on 13 March presented the petition from both houses to James, promising supply were he to declare war on Spain. Its preamble, which Abbot had composed, claimed that the king had recognized the insincerity of the Spanish, for which he was sharply rebuked by James. Eight days later Abbot used his Lenten sermon to press for stricter measures against Catholic recusants and to invoke the memory of victory over the Spanish Armada in 1588. Abbot also encouraged the Commons to investigate Richard Montagu's anti-Calvinist book, *A New Gag for an Old Goose*; with the king's permission he then summoned the author to urge him to remove the offensive passages, advice which Montagu ignored, and chose instead to compose the inflammatory *Appello Caesarem*, which was printed in 1625. Overall, though, Abbot was well satisfied with this session of parliament, with the termination of the Spanish match, the grant of supply for military aid to the protestant cause abroad, and a proclamation against recusants as well as the enactment of new laws against monopolists, concealers, and others 'so that the commonwealth is like to reape much benefitt' (Richardson, ed., *Negotiations*, 253). The same year a chapter from Abbot's book of 1604 against Dr Hill was published anonymously, though with his archiepiscopal arms on the title page. While *A Treatise of the Perpetuall Visibilitie and Succession of the True Church in All Ages* contributed to an active debate between Catholics and English protestants, its hostility to Rome and its claim of doctrinal bonds between proto-protestants and their Reformation successors identified clearly England's friends and enemies in the current European conflict. Its anonymity is a measure of Abbot's vulnerability and the king, for one, was sceptical of its authorship.

The unwanted archbishop, 1625–1633 Abbot was at Theobalds to witness the last hours of James I, who died on 27 March 1625. His personal influence with Charles I was slight, notwithstanding their political alliance in the parliament of 1624, for there was no personal warmth between them to counteract the hostility from Buckingham and Laud, both firmly in the new king's favour. Abbot's request to Charles for stronger measures against Catholics was brushed aside, while Buckingham saw him as a troublemaker in the parliament of 1625. Without the king's backing Abbot was unable to take effective action against Richard Montagu, despite promptings from his allies in the Commons, and he was excluded from a panel of bishops subsequently convened to review Montagu's work. Despite his unwavering support for foreign protestants Abbot was forced to act with great circumspection, so that in June 1625, when he received an envoy from the Huguenot leader, the duc de Soubise, he begged him to conceal the knowledge of his visit. Abbot presided at Charles's coronation on 2 February 1626, and crowned the new king, although the organization of the service fell to Laud. He attended parliament in 1626, but owing to illness he had to be carried into the Lords and was permitted to speak sitting; and recurrent poor health, as well as political isolation, kept Abbot from court in 1626–7, an absence which led to charges that he was fomenting faction at Lambeth. Ecclesiastical patronage was passing into the hands of Laud, and Abbot complained that he had no more knowledge of promotions 'than if I had dwelt at Venice, and understood of them but by some Gazette' (*State trials*, 2.1475). Abbot's Lenten sermon in 1627 was provocative, though the text has not survived. In May the privy council suppressed Henry Burton's anti-Roman tract, *The Baiting of the Popes Bull* (1627), which the author had dedicated to Buckingham, and it was rumoured that Abbot would face censure since one of his chaplains had licensed its publication.

In the event Abbot was already facing a showdown with Charles I. In the spring of 1627 the king ordered him to license a sermon by Robert Sibthorpe in favour of the forced loan. Although Abbot had private reservations about the propriety of the loan, he publicly supported its collection and chaired a meeting at Lambeth to organize payment in Surrey. However, Sibthorpe's arguments in favour of absolute obedience Abbot would not endorse and he feared that Buckingham 'had a purpose to turn upside down the laws, and the whole fundamental courses, and liberties of the subject' (*State trials*, 2.1477). According to Bishop Samuel Harsnett, Abbot 'grewe so passionate and discontent, it was not possible for him to subsist' (BL, Add. MS 39948, fol. 187). On Abbot's refusal the sermon was licensed by Bishop George Montaigne of London on 10 May; in early July, Abbot was banished to his manor of Ford in Kent and in October his metropolitical authority was entrusted to five bishops including Laud.

While at Ford, Abbot preached regularly and wrote a narrative of the whole affair, placing the blame for his troubles on Buckingham. At the opening of the parliament of 1628 Abbot was warned by Charles to stay in Kent, but he was recalled after petitioning from the upper house, and took his seat on 28 March. Abbot backed the petition of right and criticized the 'new counsels' of 1626–8 that had precipitated this crisis between king and subject. In June he delivered a magnificent censure of 'this miserable man' Roger Maynwaring who, like Sibthorpe, had preached 'impious and false' doctrine in favour of the loan (Johnson, *Proceedings*, 5.623, 634). Parliament was prorogued in late June, and only in December was Abbot restored to his jurisdiction and to his place on the privy council, one of a number of gestures which the king made in preparation for the forthcoming session. Abbot never again attended the council: despite the assassination of Buckingham in August 1628 his enemies Laud and Neile were now both councillors, and he was not welcome at the board. However, his stance won the respect of some of the crown's critics, and in 1629 he was invited to stand as godfather to the son of the earl of Lincoln, who had openly opposed the forced loan.

Ecclesiastical affairs were now firmly in the hands of Abbot's opponents. The royal instructions to bishops of December 1629 were drawn up by Laud and Harsnett, though Abbot was sent a draft and at his suggestion a clause was inserted that bishops should not waste woods attached to their temporalities. He had little sympathy for the measures they contained against lecturers, and relicensed Alexander Udney and Herbert Palmer after they had been suspended by his subordinates for breaking the instructions. Abbot's report to the king on the observance of the instructions in 1632 was brief, complacent about puritan nonconformity, and chiefly concerned at the activities of Roman Catholics.

The archbishop, however, was not entirely a broken reed. He also remained active on the high commission at Lambeth, though Laud, sitting beside him as a fellow commissioner, was often the more vigorous and forceful of the two. Abbot also allowed Calvinist writings through the press, and in effect pursued a rival licensing policy to that operated by first Montaigne then Laud as bishops of London. As early as 1627 the earl of Clare observed that 'what Canterbury stopps from the press, London letts go' (Seddon, 2.352); his chaplains licensed at least three books by William Prynne, most notoriously his *Histrio-mastix* of 1632; and when in May 1631 an Oxford don, William Page, submitted to Abbot a defence of the canonical duty to bow at the name of Jesus against Prynne's writings, he was warned off publishing 'a theme of so small necessity and of so great heate and distemper' (LPL, MS 943, p. 97). Laud, recently elected chancellor of Oxford, promptly authorized its publication there. In 1630–31 Abbot welcomed John Dury's project of a reconciliation between protestant churches, though he could do little more than allow Dury to collect signatures to his *Instrumentum theologorum Anglorum*, which expressed support for his mission. Nor did Abbot neglect his academic responsibilities. In 1627 he supervised the election of William Bedell as provost of Trinity College, Dublin, 'a man of great worth', as he told the fellows, whom he urged to attract more native Irish to the college (TCD, MS MUN/P/1/181). In January 1628, during his sequestration in Kent, Abbot upbraided the fellows of All Souls, Oxford, for converting the surplus of corn rents into a dividend rather than distributing it as poor relief. Five years later, in January 1633, he reproved them for 'that intolerable liberty as to tear off the doors and gates' of the college during the Christmas festivities (Welsby, 142–3).

Abbot never married. He died at Croydon Palace on 4 August 1633, and the chief mourner at his funeral on 3–4 September was his nemesis and nominated successor, William Laud. Abbot was buried on 4 September at Holy Trinity, Guildford, where his brother and executor, Sir Maurice Abbot, erected a splendid canopied tomb, adorned with eleven allegorical figures. His will, drawn up on 25 July 1632, contained numerous legacies to servants and relations, as well as one of £100 to Princess Elizabeth, and concluded with a prayer 'beseeching Almighty God to increase the number of his faithful' and 'to abate more and more daily the strength of antichrist and popery' (Onslow, 71–2).

Abbot's posthumous reputation has never been high. Laudian writers such as Peter Heylyn criticized his indulgence towards puritan nonconformists, while more moderate commentators such as Thomas Fuller censured the harsh discipline he administered at high commission against wayward ministers. A more sympathetic view came from the earl of Clare, who wrote in August 1633 that Abbot 'was a timorous weake man, yet was he orthodoxe, and hindered muche ill' (Seddon, 3.397). Yet as recently as the 1950s and 1960s Abbot was stigmatized as 'indifferent, negligent, secular' (H. Trevor-Roper, *Historical*

Essays, 1957, 135), while Paul Welsby, his modern biographer, saw him as an ecclesiastical misfit, 'unwanted' by both James I and Charles I. Since then a growing appreciation of the relative stability and inclusiveness of the Jacobean church has seen Abbot's stock rise.

Abbot's measured tolerance of nonconformity and his commitment to evangelism through clerical patronage and personal preaching exemplifies the dominant churchmanship among Jacobean bishops. His visitations proposed practical solutions to long-standing problems. Vocational training schemes tackled inadequate learning among the clergy, and the provision of terriers was a safeguard against the loss of parochial revenues. Though no disciplinarian over ritual Abbot was severe on ministers convicted of scandalous behaviour and was prepared to deprive and degrade notorious offenders. As a feared opponent of both Roman Catholics and anti-Calvinists, Abbot attempted to uphold a narrow view of protestant doctrine. At court he was an outspoken champion of the cause of international protestantism, and a tireless administrator, whether serving on the privy council or the treasury commission. Abbot was also an effective parliamentarian, co-operating with clients and allies in the House of Commons, and working sedulously for regular and harmonious meetings. In short, Abbot's reputation for doctrinal rectitude and his evangelical churchmanship made him an important figure in James I's inclusive ecclesiastical establishment, as a counterweight to other political and religious viewpoints, whether pro-Spanish or anti-Calvinist. The significance of Abbot's primacy rests in his vigorous espousal of protestant views which, while they remained popular in the wider country, became less influential at court as James I's reign progressed and were increasingly marginalized after the accession of Charles I. That Abbot's political achievements were so slight can be attributed to some naïve manoeuvring in court politics, especially his failure to maintain an amicable relationship with his erstwhile protégé Buckingham; but more damaging were James I's steady movement away from Abbot's anti-Catholic agenda in the years after 1611 and Charles I's deep antipathy to Abbot's views and values. His exclusion from power and favour after 1625 demonstrated the narrowing base of the new ecclesiastical order at court, though Abbot remained an irritant until his death, and not until Laud's elevation to Canterbury in September 1633 was Laudian control over the press, high commission, and dioceses secure.　KENNETH FINCHAM

Sources R. A. Christophers, *George Abbot, archbishop of Canterbury, 1562–1633: a bibliography* (1966) • A. Onslow, *The life of Dr George Abbot, lord archbishop of Canterbury* (1777) • K. Fincham, 'Prelacy and politics: Archbishop Abbot's defence of protestant orthodoxy', *Historical Research*, 61 (1988), 36–64 • K. Fincham, *Prelate as pastor: the episcopate of James I* (1990) • S. Holland, 'Archbishop Abbot and the problem of puritanism', *HJ*, 37 (1994), 23–43 • S. M. Holland, 'Archbishop George Abbot: a study in ecclesiastical statesmanship', PhD diss., U. Lond., 1991 • P. A. Welsby, *George Abbot, the unwanted archbishop, 1562–1633* (1962) • N. Tyacke, *Anti-Calvinists: the rise of English Arminianism, c.1590–1640* (1987) • P. Heylyn, *Cyprianus Anglicus* (1668) • T. W. King, 'Some remarks on a brass plate formerly in the church of Holy Trinity at Guildford', *Surrey Archaeological Collections*, 3 (1865), 254–66 • Abbot's domestic accounts, 1614–23, LPL, MS 1730 • LPL, Laud papers, MS 943 • BL, Trumbull papers, Add. MSS 72242, 72275, 72415 • state papers, domestic, James I, PRO, SP 14 • *State trials* • 'John Howson's answer to Archbishop Abbot's accusations at his "trial" before James I', ed. N. W. S. Cranfield and K. Fincham, *Camden miscellany, XXIX*, CS, 4th ser., 34 (1987) • B. Botfield, ed., *Original letters relating to ecclesiastical affairs of Scotland*, 2 vols. (1851) • F. Heal, 'The archbishops of Canterbury and the practice of hospitality', *Journal of Ecclesiastical History*, 33 (1982), 544–63 • P. E. McCullough, *Sermons at court: politics and religion in Elizabethan and Jacobean preaching* (1998) [incl. CD-ROM] • W. B. Patterson, *James VI and I and the reunion of Christendom* (1997) • K. Fincham, ed., *Visitation articles and injunctions of the early Stuart church*, 1 (1994) • *Report of the Deputy Keeper of the Public Records*, 46 (1885), 37–49 • Dudley Carleton's letter-book, 1616–19, PRO, SP 105/95 • Roman Catholic newsletters, Westminster Cathedral Archives, series A • P. Palmer, 'Mr Jasper Yardley, second master of Abbot's hospital, Guildford', *Surrey Archaeological Collections*, 31 (1918), 23–7 • J. Aubrey, *The natural history and antiquities of the county of Surrey*, 3 (1718), 280–1 • *Brief lives, chiefly of contemporaries, set down by John Aubrey, between the years 1669 and 1696*, ed. A. Clark, 1 (1898), 24 • T. Fuller, *The church history of Britain*, ed. J. S. Brewer, new edn, 6 vols. (1845), vols. 2, 6 • S. R. Gardiner, *Reports of cases in the courts of star chamber and high commission*, CS, 39 (1886) • R. C. Johnson and others, eds., *Proceedings in parliament, 1628*, 5 (1983) • P. R. Seddon, ed., *Letters of John Holles, 1587–1637*, 2–3, Thoroton Society, 3, 5, 6 (1983–8) • J. Burke, 'Archbishop Abbot's tomb at Guildford', *Journal of the Warburg and Courtauld Institutes*, 12 (1949), 179–88 • H. C. Davis, *A history of Balliol College* (1963) • *The negotiations of Sir Thomas Roe, in his embassy to the Ottoman Porte, from … 1621 to 1628*, ed. S. Richardson (1740)

Archives BL, letters and papers, Add. MSS 5750, 5822, 5956, 6095–6097, 6115, 6177–6178, 6394 • BL, papers • CUL, corresp. and papers • Inner Temple, London, papers • LPL, domestic accounts and list of mourners attending his funeral, MSS 1730, 3153 | BL, Trumbull papers, papers relating to his accidental killing of a keeper at Bramshill Park • Bodl. Oxf., Tanner MSS, corresp.

Likenesses attrib. R. Lockey, portrait, after 1609, Wolfson College, Cambridge • S. de Passe, line engraving, 1616, NPG • oils, 1623, Abbot's Hospital, Guildford • oils, c.1623, Fulham Palace, London • oils, copy, 1623, NPG [*see illus.*] • Christmas Brothers, tomb effigy, 1635, Holy Trinity, Guildford

Wealth at death moderately wealthy: Onslow, *The life*

Abbot, George. *See* Abbott, George (1604–1649).

Abbot, John (1587/8–*c*.1650), Roman Catholic priest and poet, is of unknown parentage and is variously recorded as 'of London' and 'of Leicester'. He was born a protestant, and was reputedly a nephew of George Abbot, who became archbishop of Canterbury in 1611, and of Robert Abbot, master of Balliol College, Oxford, and bishop of Salisbury. Abbot matriculated at Balliol on 16 November 1604 at the age of sixteen; he studied logic and philosophy and was made BA on 20 April 1608. During his subsequent travels on the continent he visited the English Jesuits at St Omer and was converted to Roman Catholicism. He then went to Spain where he was admitted to St Alban's College, Valladolid, on 16 November 1609. From there he went to Douai, to the English College, where he was ordained a priest on 14 June at Louvain; he left to enter the Society of Jesus on 3 August of the same year.

Abbot returned to England, to the English mission, perhaps in 1615, where he went under the names of Ashton, and John and Augustine Rivers. About 1621 he appears to have left the Jesuit order and become a secular priest. He was captured by the king's pursuivant, John Gray, in 1635 and imprisoned in the Gatehouse at Westminster but was released within the year. In 1637 he was arrested again, and it appears that he was kept in prison for the remainder of his life. He was tried at the Old Bailey in 1641 and, with six other priests, condemned to death. However, because of political struggles between the king and parliament, the execution was not carried out; and he died in Newgate about 1650.

Abbot is best-known today for his poems about the war in heaven and the temptation and fall of Adam and Eve contained in his *Devout Rhapsodies* (2 vols., 1647), poems which have been seen as significant contemporary English anticipations of Milton's *Paradise Lost*. In volume 1, Abbot's poem about the war in heaven presents that event in the form of a satiric epic. His account of the temptation of Eve is a satire on women and includes a treatment of Adam's psychology similar to Milton's, and volume 2 considers the fall of man and its effects, including a quarrel between Adam and Eve which parallels the quarrel in Milton's version. Both volumes of this work contain many topical allusions and offer accounts of the injustices and deprivations that Abbot and others faced during imprisonment. His other works include *Jesus Praefigured* (1623), a poem on the name of Jesus dedicated jointly to Prince Charles and to the Spanish infanta. The dedication was dated from the convent of St John the Baptist at Antwerp on 12 November 1623. In 1645 he published *The Sad Condition of a Distracted Kingdome*, a poem on the destruction brought about by the civil wars, and four years later published *Ka mee and I'le ka thee* (the title is a proverb meaning 'one good turn deserves another'), a plea for toleration of Catholics. He was at one time credited with the authorship of James Shirley's tragedy *The Traytor*.

RICHARD D. JORDAN

Sources D. M. Rogers, 'John Abbot (1588–?1650)', *Biographical Studies*, 1 (1951–2), 22–33 · D. M. Rogers, 'John Abbot: further notes on his life and writings', *Biographical Studies*, 1 (1951–2), 245–50 · H. Foley, ed., *Records of the English province of the Society of Jesus*, 7 vols. in 8 (1875–83) · R. D. Jordan, 'John Abbot's 1647 "Paradise Lost"', *Milton Quarterly*, 22 (1986), 48–51 · R. Challoner, *Memoirs of missionary priests*, 2 vols. (1741–2), vol. 2 · Foster, *Alum. Oxon.* · E. Henson, ed., *The registers of the English College at Valladolid, 1589–1862*, Catholic RS, 30 (1930) · Gillow, *Lit. biog. hist.*, vol. 1 · T. M. McCoog, *English and Welsh Jesuits, 1555–1650*, 1, Catholic RS, 74 (1994) · *DNB*

Abbot, John (1751–1840?), naturalist and artist, born at Bennet Street, St James, London, on 1 June 1751, was the second of the five children of John Abbot (d. 1787), a prosperous attorney, and his wife, Ann Clousinger. As a youth, Abbot developed a passion for entomology and for drawing, an enthusiasm that was supported by his father, who retained Jacob Bonneau, an accomplished draughtsman, as an art instructor for his son. The elder Abbot also bought illustrated works of natural history, including George Edwards's four-volume classic, *A Natural History of Uncommon Birds* (1743–51), which exerted a major stylistic influence on his son. The Abbots received as a gift a copy of Mark Catesby's *Natural History of Carolina, Florida, and the Bahama Islands* (1731–43), a work that probably contributed to Abbot's later decision to move to America. As a teenager, Abbot achieved a remarkable mastery of artistic

technique, and by 1770 was invited to exhibit his watercolour drawings of British insects at the Society of Artists of Great Britain, of which he was an honorary member. Apprenticed to his father as a law clerk in 1769, Abbot found that legal matters were 'little to my liking when my thoughts was ingrossed by Natural history'; and in the same year he firmly resolved to pursue natural history as a career, after being awestruck by the vast entomological collections of Dru Drury. Under Drury's influence, Abbot decided to travel to North America; and in 1773, having received sponsorship from the Royal Society and from Drury and Thomas Martyn (*fl.* 1760–1816), Abbot sailed to Virginia, where he began shipping specimens to his British patrons. In December 1775 he moved to the lower Savannah River area of Georgia, where he lived for the rest of his life, residing at various times in Savannah and in Bulloch, Burke, and Screven counties.

Abbot apparently supported himself almost entirely by providing specimens and watercolour drawings of insects, spiders, and birds to buyers in America and to his correspondents in Britain and Europe, including William Swainson, Heinrich Escher (1776–1853), John Francillon (1744–1816), Baron Frédéric de Lafresnaye (1783–1861), Edward Smith Stanley, thirteenth earl of Derby, and John Latham. During much of his lifetime, Abbot was the most prolific and talented illustrator of birds and insects in America; and Swainson noted that Abbot's insect specimens were 'certainly the finest that have ever been transmitted as articles of commerce to this country' (Simpson, *North Carolina Historical Review*).

Because Abbot never published any works under his own name, the extent of his contributions to ornithology and entomology remained largely unrecognized until the latter half of the twentieth century. Although he may have viewed his work as mostly commercial, his data and illustrations were of considerable significance to a number of major scientific publications. He remains best-known for providing data and the 104 illustrations to the earliest extensive monograph devoted entirely to North American entomology, Sir James Edward Smith's *Natural History of the Rarer Lepidopterous Insects of Georgia* (1797). Abbot made an additional 103 drawings intended as a second volume; these were sent to Swainson but remained unpublished until after being rediscovered in the 1980s in New Zealand. Abbot's specimens from Georgia were used for illustrations in Thomas Martyn's *Psyche: Figures of Nondescript Lepidopterous Insects* (1797); in Jean A. Boisduval's and John L. Le Conte's *Histoire générale et iconographie des Lépidoptères et des Chenilles de l'Amérique septentrionale* (1829–33); and in Charles A. Walckenaer's *Histoire naturelle des insectes: Aptères* (1837, 1841). Some of Abbot's observations on wasps were used by Charles Darwin in his *Journal of Researches during the Voyage of HMS Beagle* (1845). Although Abbot's bird illustrations were not reproduced during his lifetime, he provided extensive data for John Latham's second supplement to his *General Synopsis of Birds* (1801), for Latham's multi-volume *General History of Birds* (1821–8), and for Alexander Wilson's *American Ornithology* (1808–14). Thousands of Abbot's original watercolour drawings of insects, spiders, and birds survived in public and private collections in the United States and in Britain.

In creating his illustrations, Abbot used graphite to sketch the outline of the subject on paper and then completed the drawing using watercolours. His entomological drawings demonstrate an extraordinary attention to detail, with individual scales and fine texture shown accurately. His style was heavily influenced by Eleazar Albin's *Natural History of English Insects* (1720, 1749), which portrayed the metamorphosis of Lepidoptera by showing a dominant food plant, with feeding larvae, pupae, and adult. Abbot's early use of this format suggests that he may have learned to rear Lepidoptera from larvae while he was still in London. In most of his drawings, Abbot arranged the insects in tabular and geometric patterns radiating around a central point, thus resembling specimens placed in collection boxes or drawers. His ornithological illustrations are remarkable for their detail of morphology and plumage, particularly in recognizing sexual and age differences. These drawings are in the old style, now known as 'stump and magpie' or 'bonsai', in which the bird is perched on a small, stunted tree trunk, which is usually gnarled and twisted toward one side and adorned with generalized moss, lichens, or other embellishments. Abbot probably learned this style from his set of Edwards's *Natural History of Uncommon Birds*, from at least twenty plates of which he copied the outline figures, as the basis for more than sixty of his own drawings. Abbot also borrowed outlines and plates from Latham's *General Synopsis of Birds* (1781–1801) and from Wilson's *American Ornithology* (1808–14). He probably used a sketchbook or master set to produce many of his bird drawings, as there is extensive duplication of illustrations among his many surviving collections, which contain more than 1400 plates showing more than 210 species.

Correspondence indicates that Abbot was married and had a son, but no details have been confirmed, and both apparently died before Abbot. He is believed to have died in 1840, but the date is not definitively established. He was buried on the plantation of his friend William McElveen in Bulloch county, Georgia.

MARCUS B. SIMPSON JUN.

Sources R. S. Wilkinson, 'John Abbot's London years', *Entomologist's Record*, 96 (1984), 110–23, 165–76, 222–9, 273–85 · M. B. Simpson, 'Artistic sources for John Abbot's watercolor drawings of American birds', *Archives of Natural History*, 20 (1993), 197–212 · M. B. Simpson jun., 'The artist–naturalist John Abbot (1751–*ca* 1840): contributing to the ornithology of the southeastern United States', *North Carolina Historical Review*, 61 (1984), 347–90 · M. J. Largen and V. Rogers-Price, 'John Abbot, an early naturalist-artist in North America', *Archives of Natural History*, 12 (1985), 231–52 · E. G. Allen, 'The history of American ornithology before Audubon', *Transactions of the American Philosophical Society*, new ser., 41/3 (1951), 387–591 · J. Abbot, 'Notes on my life', *Lepidopterists' News*, 2 (1948), 28–30
Archives Chetham's Library, Manchester · Georgia University, Athens, Georgia · Harvard U., Houghton L. · NHM · Smithsonian Institution, Washington, DC | BL, Egerton MSS · Carnegie Museum, Pittsburgh, Andrei Avinoff collection · Cornell University, Ithaca, New York, Elsa G. Allen MSS · Merseyside County Museum, Liverpool, zoology collection
Likenesses J. Abbot?, self-portrait, watercolour, NHM

Abbot, Sir Maurice (1565–1642), merchant and politician, was born on 2 November 1565 and baptized three days later at Holy Trinity Church, Guildford, the fifth of the six sons of Maurice Abbot (1519/20–1606), a merchant, and his wife, Alice Marsh or March (1525/6–1606). The elder Maurice was an illiterate clothworker who manufactured fine kerseys, and is said to have been persecuted for protestantism under Mary. He proved sufficiently prosperous to send at least three of his sons, including Maurice, to Guildford's grammar school, but whereas Maurice's elder brothers George *Abbot (1562–1633) and Robert *Abbot (1559/60–1618) went on to university and pursued glittering careers in the church, Maurice himself, as befitted a younger son, was apprenticed to the London draper William Garway some time during the 1580s. After joining the newly formed Levant Company in 1588, he travelled to Aleppo, where, in 1592, he lent the English ambassador to Constantinople 4600 ducats, a sum which suggests that he had already begun to make his fortune.

Marriages and early career with the East India Company Abbot completed his apprenticeship and was admitted to the Drapers' Company in 1596. In the following year he suffered the loss of his first wife, Joan, the eldest daughter of George Austen, deputy chamberlain of the exchequer and successively Guildford's town clerk and mayor. However, eight months later, on 27 May 1598, he married Margaret (d. 1630), the eighteen-year-old daughter of the London alderman and mercer Bartholomew Barnes, a match which reflected his rising status as a merchant. Unlike his earlier marriage, which proved childless, this second union was blessed with children—five sons and five daughters in all, of whom seven were still alive when Abbot died in 1642. The newly wed couple may have spent their first few years together at Abbot's property in the parish of St Michael Bassishaw, but by 1602 they had moved to Coleman Street, having leased a house from the Drapers' Company, for which they paid an entry fine of £200. This was to remain Abbot's permanent residence for the rest of his life, and, despite the other demands on his time, he soon became active in running the affairs of his local church, St Stephen's, helping to audit parish accounts from 1605 and serving on the vestry from at least 1622. As a vestryman he took a leading role in appointing the puritan preacher John Davenport in 1624, despite the fact that the rival candidate was a chaplain to Abbot's own brother, George, then archbishop of Canterbury.

A founder member of the East India Company in 1600, Abbot was slow to pay in his contribution of £240 to the company's first joint stock, but quick to climb the ladder of promotion, obtaining a seat on the board in 1607. However, it was in the Levant Company that he seems first to have achieved a measure of real authority, with his appointment as the company's husband, the officer who authorized bills of lading and presided over routine administration. In July 1608 the Levant merchant and traveller John Sanderson advised the English agent at Constantinople that

> If master Morris Abbot offer you kindness in any thing that may concern you of the company's, accept it; and be sure to

hold fast master [Nicholas] Leate. For those two do now lead all the Company, especially master Abbot. The governor his words are of little weight amongst them.

By 1611 Abbot occupied a seat on the board of directors, but his ascendancy proved short-lived, for in 1613 he resigned from office, 'he having many other present business[es] of his own' to attend to. Members of the company's rank and file remained anxious to retain his services in some capacity, however, and for two years running (1614–16) they elected him treasurer.

Civic and political duties In addition to his membership of the Levant and East India companies, Abbot gained entry to the Muscovy Company (also known as the Russia Company) and the Company of Merchant Adventurers, joined the newly formed French (1611) and North-West Passage (1612) companies, and was a member of the board of the ill-fated Virginia Company from 1610. His increasing stature in the merchant community was inevitably accompanied with the burden of civic duties. By 1612 he appears to have been serving as a deputy alderman, and between 1615 and 1618 he twice held office as the City's auditor. In January 1615 his energy and diplomatic skills—Sanderson judged him 'a good discerner of differences and an undoubted impartial man'—led the East India Company to dispatch him to The Hague with two other commissioners to help ambassador Sir Henry Wotton negotiate a settlement with the Dutch over the growing number of trade disputes between the two nations in the Far East. English unwillingness to join the Dutch in expelling the Spaniards from the East Indies meant that Abbot and his colleagues proved unsuccessful, but this setback did no harm to Abbot's career in the company, as two months after his return to England he was elected deputy governor. He was again appointed a commissioner to negotiate with a visiting Dutch delegation in 1619, when he and his colleagues extracted concessions from them, but the English soon accused the Dutch of breaking the agreement, and in November 1620 Abbot, together with Sir Dudley Digges, returned to The Hague. There they learned that a Dutch East Indiaman had been seized at Plymouth, an action which they disowned but which stymied their proceedings. On returning to England in February 1621 they reported to the king, but the vague assurances they had received from the Dutch led to complaints from fellow merchants and 'some great ones', so that they were forced to explain themselves before James and the privy council in the following month.

During his absence in the Netherlands, Abbot was elected MP for Hull at the request of Archbishop Abbot, the town's high steward. Although he arrived only after the start of the parliament, Abbot nevertheless played a prominent role in the debates on trade, fiercely attacking the Dutch, whom he accused of undercutting English merchants in the Baltic and threatening the existence of both the Eastland and Muscovy companies. However, he was probably too busy securing his admission to the Great Farm of the Customs later that year to attend the winter sitting of the 1621 parliament, for he took no known part in its business. During the course of the following year he

and Digges wrote a 'memorial' to the English ambassador at The Hague, Sir Dudley Carleton, in which they urged that attempts be made to secure the restoration of goods seized by the Dutch from English merchants in the Far East. At about the same time Abbot was summoned before the council board for failing to contribute to the benevolence raised by the government to help James I's son-in-law, the deposed Elector Frederick V, recover the Palatinate, where he was persuaded to donate £50.

On East India Company business During the elections for the 1624 parliament, Archbishop Abbot again wrote to the electors of Hull on behalf of his brother, but though his letter of nomination arrived only after the freemen had cast their votes, the townsmen were evidently satisfied with his brother's performance in the previous parliament and again returned him to serve as their burgess. Unlike his role in the 1621 parliament, where Abbot had addressed matters that affected Hull's trade, in 1624 he acted almost exclusively as a spokesman of the East India Company, an organization in whose affairs Hull's merchants had little interest. Answering complaints from Sir Edward Seymour on 1 March that the company was stripping the country bare of the ships and mariners that it would need in the forthcoming war with Spain, Abbot pointed out that its vessels in the Thames which were being prepared for sea were not as heavily manned as Seymour supposed, and that they were needed to defend English interests in the Far East against the Spaniards. Five days later Abbot rallied to the defence of a fellow East India Company merchant, Robert Bateman, MP for London, after Bateman endeavoured to parry the charge levelled by Sir Thomas Estcourt that the cargo of the company's ships included forty chests of bullion. Bateman's attempt to allay fears that the company was contributing to the shortage of coin by pointing out that the sum involved amounted to less than £40,000 failed to convince his listeners, who called for the company's books to be inspected. As the debate grew louder and more angry, Abbot rose to speak. Explaining that he was now effectively the head of the East India Company, following the recent death of the governor, Sir William Halliday, he repeated Bateman's assurances, denied that the company exceeded the sum it was permitted by patent to export each year, and offered to present the company's accounts to the house as proof. Turning in an altogether more robust performance than Bateman, he went on to assert that the company was actually a net importer of specie, for, while its annual bullion exports amounted to less than £100,000, it imported commodities worth £400,000.

The parliamentary complaints against the East India Company, which prompted the Lords to order a stay of its ships in the Thames, concealed an attempt by the lord high admiral, the duke of Buckingham, to extract money from the company. In 1622 company ships had seized goods belonging to the Portuguese at Hormoz valued at £100,000. If the company had acted legitimately, then it owed the duke a share of the spoils in the form of admiralty tenths; if it had behaved piratically then it deserved to be fined. Following the outburst by Seymour (an ally of the duke's and the former vice-admiral of Devon), Abbot and a number of other senior company officials petitioned Buckingham for the release of their ships, but were threatened with prosecution and imprisonment if they failed to compound. On 23 March it was later recorded, 'considering that they should lose more than was demanded by unloading their ships, besides their voyage, they resolved to give the duke ten thousand pounds'. Their decision to come to terms led to the immediate lifting of the order restraining the company's ships from departure.

Governor of the East India Company Abbot was formally elected as governor of the East India Company in mid-April, though only after contesting the post with Sir William Cockayne, and was re-elected in July during the annual round of elections of senior company officials. His bullish defence of the company's interests in parliament, which had included maintaining the company's reputation against the complaints levelled by the widow of one of its former employees, Sir Thomas Dale, undoubtedly help to explain his rise to the top, though Abbot himself considered that reaction to the news of the Amboyna massacre of ten English settlers by Dutchmen, which reached England in May 1624, lay behind his reappointment in July. Long experience in dealing with the Dutch over the Far East must have made him the natural choice for many of the company's members. Apart from resigning from the board of the Levant Company, one of his first acts as governor was to advise the king 'that all the treaties with the Dutch are but so many treacheries', but despite the confidence reposed in him by the company's rank and file he was ultimately powerless to obtain reparation.

Further political career Abbot achieved the distinction of being the first man to be knighted by Charles I following the latter's accession in 1625, to whom shortly after he sold a cut diamond for £8000. During the first Caroline parliament (1625) he again represented Hull, but appears to have played no part in its proceedings. In August he was elected master of the Drapers' Company, having earlier occupied its other senior offices. Four months later he lost his lucrative position in the Great Farm of the Customs when the syndicate to which he belonged made too low a bid. In 1626 he was returned to parliament for both Hull and London, and chose to sit for the latter. Once in the Commons he again demonstrated a keen concern for matters of trade. When, for instance, the committee of trade debated the French seizure of the wine fleet at Bordeaux, Abbot drew on his own bitter experience to warn that English merchants could expect no redress. A ship in which he had owned a half-share, the *Tiger* of London, had been seized in Tunis Road with a cargo worth £10,000 twelve years earlier, but despite spending £700 or £800 in prosecuting the case in France he had never succeeded in recovering his goods. Abbot's principal service to the parliament, however, probably concerned Buckingham's 'extortion' of £10,000 from the East India Company two

years earlier, for it seems likely that it was he who furnished the details which formed article 6 of the impeachment charges drawn up against the duke. Abbot's hostility towards Buckingham is suggested by his appointment to the committee to consider a proposal for creating a joint stock company to pay for a naval war against Spain in the West Indies. The author of the project was Sir Dudley Digges, with whom Abbot had been associated during the recent struggle for control of the Virginia Company. Digges's patron was Abbot's brother the archbishop, who was now one of Buckingham's leading enemies. It was probably because he had been drawn into the anti-Buckingham lobby that Abbot was among those singled out for payment of a punitive privy seal loan following the collapse of the 1626 parliament.

Abbot was finally admitted to London's aldermanic bench in December 1626. Towards the end of 1627 he was pricked as sheriff, which meant that he was prevented from standing for election to the 1628 parliament. Nevertheless, as governor of the East India Company he was summoned to the House of Lords in June to answer the complaint of the earl of Warwick, who demanded £28,000 in compensation from the company for seizing two of his ships at Surat some years earlier. After negotiating with the Lords' committee appointed to investigate the matter, Abbot and his fellow delegates agreed to pay the earl £4000. Later that year Abbot was one of twelve London merchants who broke into London's customs house and removed currants belonging to them which had been confiscated after they had refused to pay a newly imposed duty. This action had the effect of encouraging other merchants to refuse to pay tonnage and poundage, but Abbot cautioned the East India Company from following suit for fear of antagonizing the king and so jeopardizing their trade with Persia.

Abbot became a widower for a second time in 1630. In 1633 he joined the newly formed Society of the Fishery of Great Britain and Ireland, a company which sought to create a fishing fleet to rival that of the Dutch, but it was so undercapitalized that he withheld his subscription. As governor of the East India Company he came under increasing attack during the 1630s from members unhappy at the company's growing losses. In 1632 one member contrasted the terms of the company's charter, which allowed the governor to remain in office for one year only, with Abbot's unbroken tenure of the governorship since 1624. Another member, Lord Saye and Sele, questioned whether it was wise to permit one man to become a 'perpetual dictator', even if the charter did allow for the possibility of re-election. Nevertheless, Abbot appears to have enjoyed the confidence of the majority of the company's members, for a motion to unseat him was defeated in July 1636. It remains unclear why Abbot eventually stepped down in 1638, but his advancing years—he was now aged seventy-three—and the fact that he had been elected lord mayor probably explain his departure rather than the machinations of his enemies. Indeed, he was replaced by his long-term ally, the deputy governor Sir Christopher Clitherow.

City politics Abbot's mayoralty was marked by difficulties in persuading London's citizens to contribute towards the king's naval and military costs. On one occasion he was forced to borrow £1000 on the City's behalf after its citizens refused to pay for the hire of a ship for the fifth ship money fleet. He subsequently laboured hard to recover his costs and committed three citizens to Newgate after they refused to enter into bond to appear before the privy council to explain their non-payment. During the king's absence in the north he and his fellow aldermen were granted a commission of lieutenancy with the power to exercise martial law. These powers attracted the attention of the imprisoned radical protestant John Lilburne, who in June 1639 wrote a pamphlet urging Abbot and his colleagues to use their new-found authority to release him from the Fleet, and inciting London's apprentices to storm the prison if they did not. Abbot and the aldermanry acted swiftly to suppress this seditious pamphlet, an act which earned them the council's commendation. However, the council was rather less pleased with Abbot and a number of other aldermen for refusing to lend money to the king that same month.

Abbot served a second term as master of the Drapers' Company in 1638–9. In November 1640 he contributed £400 towards the City's loan to the king of £50,000, its share of the cost of paying off the armies in the north. He retired from the board of the East India Company in the following July. His final months were marred by the bankruptcy of his eldest son, Edward, for whose losses of £3000 he appears to have been liable as sole surviving surety. After drawing up his will in November 1642, he died in early December (and not on 10 June 1640, as one contemporary recorded) and was buried on 7 December at St Stephen, Coleman Street.   ANDREW THRUSH

Sources A. Thrush, HoP, Commons · CSP col. · E. B. Sainsbury, ed., A calendar of the court minutes … of the East India Company, 11 vols. (1907–38) · T. W. King, 'Remarks on a brass plate formerly in the church of Holy Trinity at Guildford and now remaining in the hospital there', Surrey Archaeological Collections, 3 (1865), 254–66, esp. 266 [Abbot family tree] · The travels of John Sanderson in the Levant, 1584–1602, ed. W. Foster, Hakluyt Society, 2nd ser., 67 (1931), 252 · courts of assistants' minute book, 1603–40, Drapers' Hall, London · Levant Company minute books, PRO, SP 105/147 · Levant Company minute books, PRO, SP 105/148 · CSP dom. · APC, 1542–1631 · JHC, 1 (1547–1628) · W. Notestein, F. H. Relf, and H. Simpson, eds., Commons debates, 1621, 7 vols. (1935) · parliamentary diaries, 1624, Yale U., Yale Center for Parliamentary History · W. B. Bidwell and M. Jansson, eds., Proceedings in parliament, 1626, 1: House of Lords (1991), 467–8 [article 6 of the impeachment charges against Buckingham] · A. B. Beaven, ed., The aldermen of the City of London, temp. Henry III–[1912], 2 vols. (1908–13) · S. M. Kingsbury, ed., The records of the Virginia Company of London, 4 vols. (1906–35) · C. T. Carr, ed., Select charters of trading companies, AD 1530–1707, SeldS, 28 (1913) · churchwarden's accounts, St Stephen Coleman Street, GL, MS 4457/2 · vestry minutes, St Stephen Coleman Street, GL, MS 4458/1 · parish register, London, St Stephen Coleman Street, GL, MS 4449/2, fol. 122 · letters by Archbishop Abbot to Hull's corporation, Hull RO, L166, L167, L204 · newsletters, BL, Add. MS 11405 · BL, Add. MS 12497, fol. 324 · N&Q, 4th ser., 10 (1872), 326 [notes by Sir James Bagg on the parliament of 1626] · R. Ashton, The crown and the money market, 1603–1640 (1960) · V. Pearl, London and the outbreak of the puritan revolution: city government and national politics, 1625–1643 (1961); repr.

with corrections (1972) · R. Brenner, Merchants and revolution: commercial change, political conflict, and London's overseas traders, 1550–1653 (1993) · H. Stevens, ed., The dawn of British trade to the East Indies as recorded in the court minutes of the East India Company, 1599–1603 (1886); facs. edn (1967) · VCH Surrey, vols. 2–3 · PRO, E 401/2586, p. 404 [Privy Seal loan demanded, 1626] · PRO, SP 14/127/48; SP 14/156/14 [1622 benevolence] · accounts by Robert Bateman, PRO, SP 28/162 · CUL, MS Dd.xii.71 · J. L. Chester and G. J. Armytage, eds., Allegations for marriage licences issued by the bishop of London, 1, Harleian Society, 25 (1887), 250 · C. R. Webb, The international genealogical index: parishes and periods in the 1988 edition for Surrey (1989) · A. Hughes, List of sheriffs for England and Wales: from the earliest times to AD 1831, PRO (1898) · W. A. Shaw, The knights of England, 2 (1906), 188 · will, PRO, PROB 11/192, sig. 5

Archives BL, official corresp., Egerton MS 2086 · Drapers' Hall, London | GL, St Stephen Coleman Street records · PRO, Levant Company MSS, SP 105

Wealth at death small bequests

Abbot, Robert (1559/60–1618), bishop of Salisbury, was born at Guildford, Surrey, 'in a house now an ale-house bearing the sign of the three mariners, by the river side, near to the bridge, on the north side of the street, in St Nicholas's parish' (Wood, Ath. Oxon., 2.224). He was the third of six sons of Maurice Abbot (1519/20–1606), clothworker or shearman, and his wife, Alice, née Marsh or March (1525/6–1606); George *Abbot (1562–1633) and Maurice *Abbot (1565–1642) were his younger brothers. Like George and Maurice, Robert was schooled at Edward VI's foundation at Guildford. He matriculated at Balliol College, Oxford, aged seventeen, in December 1577, although he apparently first went into residence the year before. A controversial opponent later sneered that he ('a meane tanner's sonne') 'was at his first coming to Oxford but a poor scholler, gladde to sweepe and dresse up chambers' and to 'play the drudge for a slender pittance' (W. Bishop, A Reproofe of M. Doct[o]r Abbots Defence, 1608, 124–5). Being dispensed from five terms' residence, he graduated BA in 1579. He became a fellow in 1581 and proceeded MA in 1583. He supplicated for a preaching licence from Oxford University in January 1587 and shortly thereafter acted as lecturer at St Martin's, Oxford, at Abingdon, Berkshire, and then in Worcester. A much cited comparison between the Abbot brothers was: 'George was the more plausible preacher, Robert the greater scholar; George the abler statesman, Robert the deeper divine; gravity did frown in George, and smile in Robert' (Fuller, Worthies, 2.360). It seems clear, however, that Robert was also well thought of among his contemporaries as a preacher. He had 'thronged auditories at Oxford, Abington, Worcester, Bingham' (Featley, 551) and himself regarded preaching as 'the very aire by which we take the breath of the spirit' (The Exaltation of the Kingdome and Priesthood of Christ, 1601, 22).

Daniel Featley gave as instance of his predicatory powers Abbot's first sermon at Worcester. Apparently already resident in the city, in January 1589 he was presented by the crown at the instance of Archbishop John Whitgift to All Saints' rectory; only at this point did he resign his Balliol fellowship. On 8 February 1589 he married Margaret Baker (d. 1596) at All Saints; they had a son, Thomas (1594–1621/2). Abbot also had a daughter, Martha (d.

Robert Abbot (1559/60–1618), by unknown artist, 1615–18

1650/51)—who later married Sir Nathanael Brent—either with Margaret or, more probably, with his second wife (the first mentioned by biographers), Martha Dighton (*d.* 1617), daughter of the Worcester alderman Christopher Dighton. He married Martha on 30 August 1597. Abbot's career as published theologian had already begun. In Lent 1590 he was drawn into controversy by a Marian priest, Paul Spence, then 'prisoner in the castle of Worcester'; to supersede rumour, he was encouraged by Bishop Edmund Freake (*c.*1516–1591), 'for the citie of Worcester and others thereabout, for their satisfaction in this cause', to publish their debates, and these appeared (possibly improved) as *The Mirrour of Popish Subtilties* (1594). It was, however, dedicated not only to Freake's successor as bishop, Richard Fletcher, but also to Archbishop John Whitgift; not unexpectedly, it attracted a wider audience.

From a BTh (1594), in 1597 Abbot proceeded DTh at Oxford, being dispensed from attendance at lectures owing to other duties. Oxford proposed him that year to initiate the Gresham divinity lectures in London, but Anthony Wotton of Cambridge was preferred. For the doctorate Abbot maintained ostentatiously Calvinist articles derived, despite their lack of official sanction, from Archbishop Whitgift's Lambeth articles—directly from the first, and tangentially from the sixth and ninth: 'By the eternal predestination of God some are ordained to life and others to death. The salvation of the elect is most certain. The elect cannot in this life fulfil the law of God' (*Reg. Oxf.*, 2/1. 119).

When Bishop Gervase Babington induced him to publish as *The Exaltation of the Kingdome and Priesthood of Christ*

(1601) his Worcester Cathedral sermons of Christmas 1596, Abbot remembered Worcester as 'that citie wherein I have bestowed the greatest service in my life' (sig. A3r). However, when in 1598 John Stanhope, impressed by a Paul's Cross sermon, presented him to the rectory of Bingham, Nottinghamshire, Abbot was glad to move. He later thanked Stanhope for this gift 'onely for the worke's sake which I performed, being myselfe wholy strange and unknowne to you'. It served, he said:

> to free mee of that incessant labour wherein I had beene imployed before … and to setle mee in a place, where I might freely dispose of myselfe … [and] in some part to bestow my time to the common benefit of the whole Church. (*A Wedding Sermon Preached at Bentley in Darbyshire*, 1608, sigs. A2v–A3r)

Abbot's career was boosted in 1603 by the accession of James I. He was appointed a royal chaplain and a member of the York ecclesiastical commission, presumably as a prominent Nottinghamshire clergyman, although he is unlikely to have been active. He also published *Antichristi demonstratio* (repr. 1608), on a subject so dear to the king's heart that he condescended to include a dissertation of his own. It was a work firmly in the Elizabethan tradition associated with John Foxe, seeing the true church as consisting in allegedly heretical minorities rather than in an 'apostolic succession' corrupted by the papal Antichrist. The *Demonstratio* even tended to justify resistance to Roman Catholic monarchs, an idea less welcome to James.

A more monumental, and safer, work was Abbot's *The Defence of the 'Reformed Catholicke' of M. William Perkins* (1606) against the attacks of William Bishop and other Catholics. By implication, Abbot stepped into the shoes of the late great English Calvinist theologian. The first part of the work inevitably exploited the Gunpowder Plot, although Abbot confessed to having been sent Bishop's book by Archbishop Richard Bancroft 'in Januarie last a full yeere since' when he was 'under a surgeon's hands for a grievous infirmitie in mine eies' (sig. A2r). In *The Second Part of The Defence of the 'Reformed Catholicke'* (1607), Abbot ascribed his whole undertaking to 'your majestie's appointment' and wished that James's 'sacred bloude' might escape shedding by 'them who account it a martyrdome to die … for murthering of Christian princes' (sigs. A2, A3v–A4r). A new branch of this controversy was his *Antilogia adversus Apologiam Andreae Eudaemon-Joannis Jesuitae pro Henrico Garneto Jesuita proditore* (1613), a vindication of the condemnation of Garnet in 1606. Catholics, now as then, have condemned its resort to cheap defamation; if Abbot impugned Garnet's chastity, however, he was retorting to Catholic attempts to resurrect the tired canard of Henry VIII's being Anne Boleyn's incestuous father, and Abbot's use of Gunpowder Plot papers has been acknowledged as more reliable than that of his controversial colleague Lancelot Andrewes.

In 1611, the year his brother became archbishop of Canterbury, Abbot dedicated *The True Ancient Roman Catholicke*, a follow-up against Bishop, to Prince Henry, the new hope for international Calvinist activism, but that was dashed by Henry's death the next year, as also was any prospect of the prince's 'helping hand upon the next voydance to lift him higher in the Church' (Featley, 545–6). However, in 1610 Abbot had gained the mastership of Balliol, a promotion he ascribed to Bancroft 'without my expectation or seeking' (The Old Waye, 1610, dedication). He was reportedly strict, never missing evening prayers and always alert for evaders, having long complained of popular preference 'in time of holy exercise to sit at cards by a warme fire then to sit with God in a colde church' (The Exaltation of the Kingdome and Priesthood of Christ, 1601, 40). Moreover, 'he every weeke viewed the buttery booke, and if he found lavish expence upon any man's name he would punish him severely for it' (Featley, 544). None the less, he fed the visiting scholar Isaac Casaubon sumptuously in 1613. His mastership showed some recovery in undergraduate numbers—there were at least sixty-five throughout, from a low point of forty-one in 1608, and as many as eighty-nine in 1616. But he and his brother George failed ultimately to secure for Balliol the legacy of Thomas Tisdale, which went to Pembroke College.

Abbot's theological status was underlined when in May 1610 he became a fellow of the new Chelsea College, unusually for one not concerned with the King James Bible. He also gained Normanton, a prebend of Southwell, Nottinghamshire, to go with Bingham. He was made preacher at Gray's Inn in early 1612, and later that year was induced, allegedly with difficulty, to accept the regius chair of divinity at Oxford. Besides his duties at the university church and Balliol, however, he still took 'great paynes in often preaching soe voluntarely at Carfax', that is, his old post of St Martin's, for which the city council voted him a present of plate in 1615 (Salter, 246). He lost the bishopric of Lincoln to Richard Neile in 1614, however, when the promise of it for him failed to induce his brother George to fall in with the royal wish to have Frances Howard's first marriage annulled.

A simultaneous problem for both Abbot brothers was that perceived relaxation in the imminence of the Roman Catholic threat was encouraging impugners of Calvinistic doctrine within the Church of England, specifically at Oxford. Robert Abbot had taken the lead from 1612 in suspecting John Howson of Christ Church of the laxer approach to the problems of divine predestination and human free will associated with the Dutch theologian Jacobus Arminius. Howson complained of being 'censured shamefully without any article exhibited against mee' (Cranfield and Fincham, 328). Abbot reportedly argued, 'whatt will men thinke butt thatt there weare division in theire Churche', and Roman Catholics were indeed encouraged to hear of the dispute (Questier, 191). In a sermon of Lent 1615 William Laud of St John's criticized Abbot's doctrine; after Easter Laud 'was fain to sit patiently and hear myself abused almost an hour together, being pointed at as I sat' as Abbot demanded whether he were 'Romish or English? Papist or Protestant? … a mungrel or compound of both …' (Heylyn, 68).

These attacks on what Abbot believed to be English Arminianism did not go well. Howson appeared before the king but was exculpated. Neile, Abbot's successful rival for Lincoln, supported Laud, reporting that Archbishop Abbot 'him selfe acknowledged his brothers error in it, and Dr Abotts him selfe asked pardon for it' (Cranfield and Fincham, 323). The failures against Howson and Laud decisively 'strengthened the confidence of the anti-Calvinists' (Holland, 261–2). Robert Abbot persevered with an anti-Arminian treatise, De gratia et perseverantia sanctorum, but died before publication. So topical and eagerly awaited was the work that 'the printer John Bill was prepared to send partially incomplete copies to the United Provinces within a week of the author's death', and Abbot's brother hastily sent complete ones to the ambassador there (ibid., 233).

There is no obvious basis for Heylyn's allegation that Abbot attacked Laud as a diversion from his own Calvinistic deficiencies, having 'incurred the high displeasure of the supralapsarians' (Heylyn, 66), although his rejection of Theodore Beza's view of predestination as preceding creation was later misrepresented by Laud's ally Francis White as an attack on Calvin himself. Nor was it so much that Abbot was a 'manifest' 'sublapsarian' (Tyacke, 'Anglican attitudes', 151), as that he used an expedient metaphysical bypass:

> These counsels and purposes we understand to be without difference of time with Him who at one sight beholdeth all things from beginning to end … it is absurd to thinke that God would decree what to doe with man before He had decreed to create man. (Third Part of the Defence of the 'Reformed Catholike', 1609, 59)

Nominating Abbot to succeed Henry Cotton as bishop of Salisbury, James is alleged to have said, 'Abbot, I have had very much to do to make thee a bishop; but I know no reason for it, unless it were because thou writest against one [that is, William Bishop]' (Featley, 544). This was just a pretext for a royal pun—the obstacle had been James's own resentments over the Howard nullity, less of an issue by 1615. John Chamberlain wrote not of opposition to the appointment but 'great meanes used' for it, presumably to James by George Abbot, mentioned as 'on foot again' (Chamberlain, 1.598, 610). Richard Field, who considered Robert Abbot 'too positive' in matters of theological 'extreme difficultie', told his son that James was to have made him [Field] bishop of Salisbury, 'but the sollicitation of some great ones prevailed with him for … Dr Abbots' (Field, 22, 15–16).

Abbot was consecrated by his brother on 3 December 1615. An anonymous sermon on the occasion noted that 'an older brother is to be consecrated by a younger, as Aaron was by Moses' and recalled John Jewel, the last theologian of international stature to hold the see: 'it seemeth the flocke … promise themselves in you to find their Jewell againe' (Corpus Christi College, Oxford, MS 288, fol. 111v). For the first six months Abbot performed his duties at Balliol and at his old preaching centre of Abingdon, just within his diocese. He lived at Salisbury from June 1616.

Still preaching actively, he was also praised for his hospitality and charity, and he shamed the Salisbury chapter into disgorging £500 towards belated cathedral repairs.

In November 1617 Abbot's second wife died. Two months later he married Bridget (d. 1635x46), widow of John Cheynell, an Oxford physician, and daughter of John Egioke of Worcestershire. Chamberlain reported that the archbishop 'was nothing plesed with that when he heard that, nor I thincke nobody els that wisht him well' (Chamberlain, 2.140). The hostile Peter Heylyn elaborated that George Abbot wrote Robert 'such a sharp and bitter letter … that not being able to bear the burthen of so great an insolency, he presently died' (Heylyn, 68). Heylyn claimed that the archbishop opposed episcopal remarriage in principle, but as it seems Robert had already married twice, lack of a decent interval was more probably the objection.

Abbot did die within two months of the marriage. With possible artistic licence derived from his brother's famous wish to die in the pulpit, Featley wrote that Robert Abbot fell ill of kidney stone after preaching in his cathedral on John 14: 16—'I will pray the father and he shall give you another comforter that he may abide with you for ever' (Featley, 549). He lasted overnight before dying at Salisbury on 2 March 1618 and was buried in the cathedral three days later. Abbot's nuncupative will, made on the day of his death, 'in greate extremitie of sicknes', requested a funeral 'without any manner of charge'. Not only, he alleged, had his second wife had an expensive 'long sicknes' but, 'havinge enjoyed his bishopricke but a little while', he was 'scarcely able to paye unto his majestie his first fruites and tenthes'. While his third instalment of first fruits was due the month before Abbot died, his estate was forgiven it as well as the last. Abbot divided what he had equally between his wife and his children, Thomas, now a fellow of All Souls College, Oxford, and Martha. Thomas edited *De suprema potestate regis* (1619), the regius professor's defence of the royal supremacy. However, Abbot's 'Praeelectiones sacrae in Epistolam … ad Romanos' (Bodl. Oxf., MSS e Musaeo 10–13), running to 3692 pages, remained unpublished; his preface 'to the listeners', not 'readers', probably indicates a similar origin in professorial lectures.

Distinguished in James I's early controversy with the Roman Catholics, Robert Abbot's views later became less fashionable high in the church—although he was a favourite authority for William Prynne to cite against the Laudians. By his death his brother lost a valued ally, and his party a respected voice; a year later, the anti-Arminian Synod of Dort asked whether the Thirty-Nine Articles saw saving grace as applied universally or restrictively and Walter Balcanqual appealed to 'my late lord of Salisbury … who was thought to understand the meaning of our confession as well as any man' (Hales, 2.103). Yet only three out of five British delegates upheld Abbot's view, and the Church of England would not approve the synod.

JULIAN LOCK

Sources D. Featley, 'Dr Robert Abbot', in T. Fuller, *Abel redevivus, or, The dead yet speaking: the lives and deaths of modern divines* (1651), 538–58 · S. M. Holland, 'Archbishop George Abbot: a study in ecclesiastical statesmanship', PhD diss., U. Lond., 1991, 9ff., 28ff., 39–40, 220, 233ff., 260ff., 273ff. · P. A. Welsby, *George Abbot: the unwanted archbishop, 1562–1633* (1962) · W. Oldys, *Life of Dr George Abbot … to which are added lives of his brothers Dr Robert Abbot … and Sir Morris Abbot* (1777) · T. W. King, 'Remarks on a brass plate formerly in the church of Holy Trinity at Guildford and now remaining in the hospital there', *Surrey Archaeological Collections*, 3 (1865), 254–66 · S. H. Cassan, *Lives and memoirs of the bishops of Sherborne and Salisbury, from the year 705 to 1824*, 3 pts (1824) · Fuller, *Worthies* (1811), 2.359–60 · P. Heylyn, *Cyprianus Anglicus, or, The history of the life and death of … William … archbishop of Canterbury* (1668), 66–71 · Wood, *Ath. Oxon.*, new edn, 2.224–7 · *Reg. Oxf.*, 2/1.119, 2/2.73, 2/3.82 · 'John Howson's answer to Archbishop Abbot's accusations at his "trial" before James I', ed. N. W. S. Cranfield and K. Fincham, *Camden miscellany, XXIX*, CS, 4th ser., 34 (1987) · *The letters of John Chamberlain*, ed. N. E. McClure, 2 vols. (1939) · K. Fincham, *Prelate as pastor: the episcopate of James I* (1990) · N. Tyacke, 'Religious controversy', *Hist. U. Oxf.* 4: *17th-cent. Oxf.*, 569–620 · K. Fincham, 'Oxford and the early Stuart polity', *Hist. U. Oxf.* 4: *17th-cent. Oxf.*, 179–210 · N. Tyacke, *Anti-Calvinists: the rise of English Arminianism, c.1590–1640* (1987) · K. Fincham and P. Lake, 'The ecclesiastical policy of King James I', *Journal of British Studies*, 24 (1985), 169–207 · N. Tyacke, 'Anglican attitudes: some recent writings on English religious history from the Reformation to the civil war', *Journal of British Studies*, 35 (1996), 139–67 · A. Milton, *Catholic and Reformed: the Roman and protestant churches in English protestant thought, 1600–1640* (1995) · P. White, *Predestination, policy and polemic: conflict and consensus in the English church from the Reformation to the civil war* (1992) · K. Firth, *The apocalyptic tradition in Reformation Britain, 1530–1645* (1979) · J. P. Sommerville, 'Jacobean political thought and the controversy over the oath of allegiance', PhD diss., U. Cam., 1981, 64–5, 87, 123, 163, 306, 316 · J. P. Sommerville, *Royalists and patriots: politics and ideology in England, 1603–1640*, 2nd edn (1999) · J. Brodrick, *The life and work of Blessed Robert Francis Cardinal Bellarmine, S.J., 1542–1621*, 2 vols. (1928) · M. Pattison, *Isaac Casaubon, 1559–1614* (1875), 353–4, 400–01, 403, 409 · N. Field, *Some short memorials concerning the life of … Dr Richard Field*, ed. J. Le Neve (1717), 15–16, 22 · W. Prynne, *Anti-Arminianisme, or, The Church of England's old antithesis to new Arminianisme* (1630) · J. Hales, *The golden remains of the ever-memorable Mr John Hales of Eton College: letters from the synod of Dort*, 2nd edn (1673), [pt 2], p. 103 · M. C. Questier, *Newsletters from the archpresbyterate of George Birkhead*, CS, 5th ser., 12 (1998), 191–2 · H. Savage, *Balliofergus, or, A commentary upon the foundation, founders, and affaires of Balliol College* (1668), 113–14 · J. Jones, *Balliol College: a history*, 2nd edn (1997) · A. Clark, transcripts from Balliol College archives, Bodl. Oxf., MSS Top. Oxon. e. 123–124 · H. E. Salter, ed., *Oxford council acts, 1583–1626*, OHS, 87 (1928), 246 · D. E. Kennedy, 'King James I's college of controversial divinity at Chelsea', *Grounds of controversy: three studies in late sixteenth and early seventeenth century English polemics*, ed. D. E. Kennedy (1989), 91–126 · J. Ward, *The lives of the professors of Gresham College* (1740), 36 · PRO, exchequer, first fruits office, composition books, E334/10–12, 15 · PRO, exchequer, first fruits office, plea rolls, E337/15, nos. 6, 52 · J. Britton, *History and antiquities of the cathedral church of Salisbury* (1814), 48 · Salisbury espiscopal register, Wilts. & Swindon RO, D1/2/19 · register of Archbishop Whitgift, LPL, vol. 1, fols. 378–9 · register of Edmund Freke, bishop of Worcester, Worcs. RO, BA 2648/10 (i), fol. 64v · parish registers, Worcester, All Saints and Worcester, St Swithins, Worcs. RO · *VCH Surrey*, 2.169, 3.548–9 · *Calendar of the manuscripts of the most hon. the marquis of Salisbury*, 24 vols., HMC, 9 (1883–1976), vol. 9, p. 394; vol. 24, p. 236 · J. Foster, *The register of admissions to Gray's Inn, 1521–1889, together with the register of marriages in Gray's Inn chapel, 1695–1754* (privately printed, London, 1889), 129 · will, PRO, PROB 11/131, fol. 48

Archives BL, corresp. with Isaac Casaubon, Burney MS 363 · Wilts. & Swindon RO, Salisbury episcopal register, D1/2/19

Likenesses portrait, 1615–18, Maidstone Museum and Art Gallery [see illus.] · F. Delaram, line engraving, c.1618, BM, NPG ·

engraving, 1620 (after portrait, Salisbury Cathedral School), repro. in A. M. Hind, *Engraving in England in the sixteenth and seventeenth centuries* (1955), pl. 83 • F. Delaram, portrait (after portrait, 1615–18), repro. in A. M. Hind, *Engraving in England in the sixteenth and seventeenth centuries* (1955), pl. 119 • W. and M. van de Passe, line engraving, BM; repro. in H. Holland, *Herōologia* (1620) • fresco (after portrait, Salisbury Cathedral School?), Bodl. Oxf. • portrait, Salisbury Cathedral School; copy, Christ Church Oxf.

Wealth at death estate divided equally between wife, son, and daughter: will, PRO, PROB 11/131, fol. 48

Abbot, Robert (*fl. c.*1589–1652), Church of England clergyman and religious writer, was most probably the Robert Abbot who graduated BA from Peterhouse, Cambridge, in 1605 and was incorporated MA at Oxford on 14 July 1607. Nothing is known of his family background and early life, but in 1639 he wrote 'I have lived now by God's gratious dispensation above fifty years' (R. Abbot, *A Triall of our Church-Forsakers*, 1639, epistle to the reader). After serving as curate to a Mr Haiward at St Mary Woolchurch in London, Abbot was presented in 1616 to the Kentish wealden living of Cranbrook in the gift of the archbishop of Canterbury, George Abbot, whom he thanked fulsomely in one of his later publications. There is, however, no evidence of any family link between the two men. By 1617 he had married, but his wife's name is unknown.

At Cranbrook there was a tradition of puritanism going back to the mid-1570s, but Abbot's early publications suggest that he was more concerned by the threat to the established church from Catholicism. In 1623 Abbot published a series of visitation, assize, and other sermons under the title *A Hand of Fellowship to Helpe Keepe out Sinne and Antichrist*, which were dedicated to members of 'mine owne circle' and in which he tried to counter the 'adversaries of … The Church of England', who were busy to 'gaine appetites and affections to Rome' (Abbot, *A Hand of Fellowship*, A1v, A2v). Abbot's circle included the Kentish gentlemen Sir Thomas Roberds, Sir Henry Baker, Sir Thomas Hendley, Mr Walter Roberts, and Mr Peter Curthope and their wives. In this publication Abbot also mentioned his gratitude to the archbishop of Canterbury, from whom 'I have received all my worldly maintenance' (ibid., A1r). In 1625 Abbot followed this with the publication of a visitation sermon entitled *The Danger of Popery*, which was dedicated to the archdeacon of Canterbury, William Kingsley. In 1626 Abbot published a sermon preached at Cranbrook on a day of thanksgiving for London's deliverance from the plague, which illustrated the importance that he continued to attach to his 'friends, kindred and acquaintance[s]' in the City (Abbot, *Bee Thankfull London and her Sisters, or, A Sermon of Thankfulnesse*, A2r). Abbot also assiduously cultivated his local contacts and in 1638 published a sermon preached at the consecration of Sir John Baker's chapel at Sissinghurst. In 1639 he published four more sermons with a dedication to Walter Curll, bishop of Winchester, who until 1616 had been a fellow of Peterhouse. Abbot thanked the bishop for his 'favour to myself' and for his encouragements to Abbot's eldest son while he was at Oxford and for 'your exhibition

to my youngest sonne' in Cambridge (Abbot, *Foure Sermons*, leaf A4r). Robert Abbot the younger had matriculated from Merton College, Oxford, in 1634, aged seventeen, and graduated BA in 1637, before proceeding MA in 1639 from Emmanuel College, Cambridge. Peter Abbot, almost certainly his brother, was admitted as a pensioner to Emmanuel on 20 February 1637, and graduated BA early in 1641.

By the late 1630s Abbot was experiencing problems with his puritan parishioners. He outlined his own conformist stance in *A triall of our church-forsakers, or, A meditation tending to still the passions of unquiet brownists* published in 1639 with the intention of refuting separatist opinions. Abbot argued that the Church of England was a true church with a true ministry and true worship, and throughout he emphasized his own compliance with authority. Thus on the puritan rejection of kneeling at communion Abbot argued that 'they must kneel', because kneeling was 'neither commanded nor forbidden by God, but commanded by the King and Church'. In 1641 Abbot reported the activities of the Cranbrook separatists to Sir Edward Dering, as MP for Kent. He complained that 'they would have the votes about every matter of jurisdiction, in choice, admission of members, and ministers, excommunication and absolution to be drawn up from the whole body of the Church in common, both men and women'. Abbot was alarmed that the separatists also opposed the use of the Book of Common Prayer and episcopacy. Although Abbot confessed to Dering that he would like to see some reform of ceremonies and of the prayer book, he also maintained that 'episcopacy is lawfull, and a better way to governe the church then any other that I knowe' (BL, Stowe MS 184, fol. 28r). In another letter to Dering, dated November 1641, Abbot argued that it was not within the power of the House of Commons to convene a national synod, which lay in the 'native prerogative' of the king (BL, Add. MS 26785, fol. 49r).

In 1643 the tensions between Abbot and the Cranbrook radicals probably prompted him to move before 9 March, when his successor was admitted, to the living of Southwick, Hampshire, under the patronage of Honoria, Lady Norton. In 1646 Abbot published a children's catechism along with three sermons dedicated to Lady Norton's daughters. By 1652 Abbot was minister at St Augustine's, Watling Street, London, and in that year he published *A Christian Family Builded by God*, a conduct book for governors of families. In the dedication of this book to his parishioners Abbot described himself as 'aged' and afflicted by 'the burthen of impotent age' (Abbot, *A Christian Family*, A2r, A3r), a theme he expanded in the reissue of *The Young Mans Warning-Piece* in the same year, when he complained of grey hairs and dim eyes, and that 'the dayes are come wherein I have little pleasure in them' (Abbot, *The Young Mans Warning-Piece*, epistle dedicatory). He was not readmitted to the Cranbrook living following the Restoration in 1660, but his date of death is unknown.

JACQUELINE EALES

Sources BL, Stowe MSS 184, fols. 27, 35, 43, 47; 744, fol. 15 • BL, Add. MS 26785, fol. 49 • Foster, *Alum. Oxon.* • Venn, *Alum. Cant.* • R. J.

Acheson, 'The development of religious separatism in the diocese of Canterbury, 1590–1660', PhD diss., University of Kent, 1983 · P. Collinson, 'Cranbrook and the Fletchers: popular and unpopular religion in the Kentish weald', *Godly people: essays on English protestantism and puritanism* (1983), 399–428 · *Walker rev.*, 209 **Archives** BL, letters to Sir Edward Dering, Stowe MSS 184, fols. 27, 35, 43, 47; 744, fol. 15; Add. MS 26785, fol. 49

Abbot, William (1790–1843),

actor, was born at Chelsea, London, on 12 June 1790. He made his stage début in 1806 at Bath, and remained a member of the Bath company for some seasons. He appeared at the Haymarket in London in the summer of 1808, on the occasion of the benefit of the tragedian Charles Young, and reappeared there in 1810. At Covent Garden in 1812 he became successful as a performer of light comedy, melodrama, and juvenile tragedy. He was the first to play Lothair in Pocock's *The Miller and his Men*, and took the parts of Appius Claudius and Modus in Sheridan Knowles's plays *Virginius* and *The Hunchback*. He played Pylades to W. C. Macready's Orestes in Ambrose Philips's *The Distressed Mother* on the latter's first appearance at Covent Garden in 1816. 'Mr. Abbot never acts ill', wrote Hazlitt the same year. The critics applauded both the spirit of his acting and his 'acute sense of propriety of emphasis'.

In 1827 Abbot was engaged, at a weekly salary of 20 napoleons, as stage manager of the English company visiting Paris, with Harriet Smithson as their 'leading lady'. He played Charles Surface among other parts, but *The School for Scandal* was little admired at the Salle Favart. After the season in Paris, Abbot, with others of the company, attempted a tour of English performances in the French provinces, but the experiment was wholly unsuccessful. Significant roles in Abbot's later career included that of Romeo to the Juliet of Fanny Kemble in 1830 at her Covent Garden début. Leigh Hunt wrote of this performance: 'Mr Abbot has taken it in his head that noise is tragedy, and a tremendous noise he accordingly makes. It is Stentor with a trumpet. … We hear he is a pleasant person everywhere but on the stage, and such a man may be reasonably at a disadvantage with his neighbours somewhere.' Abbot adapted from the French two melodramas, *The Youthful Days of Frederick the Great* and *Swedish Patriotism, or, The Signal Fire*, produced at Covent Garden in 1817 and 1819 respectively.

Abbot left England in 1835 to try his fortune in America, where he played Hamlet in 1836 in Philadelphia. From 1837 to 1841 he was manager of the New Charleston Theatre, Charleston, to which he attracted stars such as Ellen Tree. He maintained an excellent resident company there but met with limited success. In 1843 he married Mrs Elizabeth Bradshaw, *née* Buloid, an actress, but died on 1 June 1843, probably in New York, although some sources give Baltimore.   E. D. COOK, rev. KATHARINE COCKIN

Sources Adams, *Drama* · *Who was who in America: historical volume, 1607–1896* (1963) · *The biography of the British stage, being correct narratives of the lives of all the principal actors and actresses* (1824) · T. A. Brown, *History of the American stage* (1870) · Hall, *Dramatic ports.* · Genest, *Eng. stage* · W. Donaldson, *Recollections of an actor* (1865) **Likenesses** mezzotint (after unknown artist), BM, NPG · prints, BM, NPG · prints, Harvard TC

Abbotshall. For this title name *see* Ramsay, Sir Andrew, of Abbotshall and Waughton, first baronet, Lord Abbotshall (1620?–1688).

Abbott, Augustus (1804–1867),

army officer in the East India Company, the eldest of five sons of Henry Alexius Abbott of Blackheath, Kent, a retired Calcutta merchant, and his wife, Margaret, daughter of William Welsh of Edinburgh, writer to the signet, was born in London on 7 January 1804. He was the elder brother of Sir Frederick *Abbott and Sir James *Abbott.

Augustus Abbott was educated at Warfield, Berkshire, under Dr Faithfull, at Winchester College, and at the East India Company's military college at Addiscombe from 1818 to 1819. He went to India, commissioned second lieutenant in the Bengal artillery in April 1819. His first active service was at the fort of Bakhara in Malwa in December 1822. At the siege of Bharatpur in December 1825 and January 1826 he successfully commanded a small battery and gained the favourable notice of Lord Combermere, the commander-in-chief, who in October 1827 appointed him adjutant of the Karnal division of artillery. In 1833–4 he served against the forts of Shekawati, returning afterwards to Karnal. He was promoted brevet captain in April 1834 and captain in May 1835.

From 1838 to 1842 Abbott served in the First Anglo-Afghan War, which the British fought to install as their client ruler Shah Shuja. In August 1838 he was given command of a light field battery, whose 9-pounder guns, as an experiment, were drawn by camels. He joined the army of the Indus under Sir John Keane for the invasion of Afghanistan. He served with his battery at the capture of Ghazni on 23 July 1839, and at the occupation of Kabul on 7 August; the battery camels having died or been stolen— in what he called 'this land of thieves' (Low, *Afghan War*, 93)—Abbott replaced them with local horses. In January 1840 he and his battery were part of the punitive force under Lieutenant-Colonel Orchard, which captured the fort at Pashat, north-east of Jalalabad. Abbott was commended in Orchard's dispatch, but privately considered it a 'dirty little Expedition' (Low, *Afghan War*, 115). He took part in the expedition into Kohistan, north of Kabul, under Brigadier-General Robert Sale, who attributed his capture on 29 September 1840 of Tutamdara, at the entrance of the Gohraband Pass, to Abbott's guns. On 3 October Abbott distinguished himself at the unsuccessful attack on Jalgah. On 2 November Dost Muhammad was brought to bay at Parwandara, where the infantry, supported by Abbott's battery, successfully cleared the pass and valley of Parwan; Abbott repeatedly requested, but was not sent, 18-pounder guns.

In September 1841 Abbott served in Colonel Oliver's punitive expedition into Zurmat, then returned to Kabul on 19 October in time to join Sale's brigade on their march towards Jalalabad, to withdraw to India after finishing their tour of duty in Afghanistan. In November many Afghan groups rose against Shah Shuja and the British, and Sale's brigade had to fight its way through. Abbott commanded the artillery in the actions at Tezin and in the

Jagdalak Pass, where he led the advance guard. On 13 November Sale's brigade occupied the town of Jalalabad and its dilapidated defences. From late November they were besieged by a larger Afghan force, in 1842 commanded by Muhammad Akbar Khan. The situation in Afghanistan was uncertain and dangerous. From Dr William Brydon, who reached Jalalabad on 13 January 1842, the garrison learned of the massacre of the British force retreating from Kabul. In January Sale called a council of war on the crucial decision whether to withdraw, as ordered by Pottinger and Shah Shuja, or to stay and fight. Sale and Captain G. H. Macgregor, the political agent, favoured negotiated withdrawal. Captain George Broadfoot and Captain C. Oldfield, the cavalry commander, backed by Captain Henry Havelock, strongly opposed this, but Abbott and other officers did not support them. Only later were Abbott and others convinced, and so at the reconvened council of war they supported Broadfoot. Sale acquiesced and the garrison fought on—despite shortages of food and ammunition, and an earthquake on 19 February—and made several successful sorties.

As artillery commander Abbott played a key role in the defence. He mounted guns on the defences, constructed carriages for captured ordnance, and, short of ammunition, improvised 'pebble-grape' from stones. Apparently 'the life and soul of the garrison in their worst times' (Low, *Afghan War*, 309), he helped to maintain morale. His artillery supported the sorties, and in March he was slightly wounded. He wrote privately: 'We have no confidence in Sale, who is a very good fellow, but a very inefficient General' (Low, *Afghan War*, 294). In April, after false news that Pollock's relief force advancing from India had been defeated in the Khyber, the 'fiery spirits' Abbott, Broadfoot, and Oldfield urged Sale that to save itself the garrison must attack and defeat its besiegers. Sale refused. Abbott then urged the other officers to disobey Sale and attack, but most would not. However, Sale changed his mind and ordered an offensive. On 7 April the garrison sallied out and, with Abbott's artillery playing a major role, decisively defeated the Afghans and ended the siege.

On 16 April Pollock's army arrived and the 'illustrious garrison'—as Lord Ellenborough, the governor-general, later called the defenders of Jalalabad—joined it. Abbott, who had already been appointed Pollock's commandant of artillery, in July accompanied Brigadier-General Monteath's punitive column against the Shinwaris, and his guns decided the victory at Mazina. He again distinguished himself in actions in August and early September and at the battles of Tezin and the Haft Kotal on 12 and 13 September, when Akbar Khan was finally defeated. Abbott returned to India with the army, and as one of the 'illustrious garrison' was welcomed by Lord Ellenborough at Ferozepore on 17 December. During the war he had repeatedly been mentioned in dispatches. He was promoted brevet major, and made a CB in October 1842 and honorary aide-de-camp to the governor-general, a distinction conferred on him by three successive governors-general. Ellenborough appointed him to the well-paid post of gun-

carriage agent at Fatehgarh, which he held from 1843 to 1847.

Abbott married in 1843 Sophia Frances, daughter of Captain John Garstin (66th and 88th regiments); they had four daughters and three sons. All the sons had military careers: the eldest, Augustus Keith (b. 1844), was major, Indian Staff Corps; the second, William Henry (b. 1845), major-general, commanded the Munster fusiliers; and the youngest, Henry Alexius (b. 1849), became a colonel, Indian Staff Corps, and CB, and commanded Malakand brigade.

In July 1845 Abbott was promoted major. From 1845 to 1855 he was principal commissary of ordnance. He was promoted inspector-general of ordnance in 1855 and in 1858 colonel-commandant of the Bengal artillery. He advised the government on artillery and related matters, and was a member of the committee on the defences of Ferozepore. Ill health compelled him to return home in 1859. In December of that year he was promoted major-general. He died at his home, 4 Paragon Buildings, Bath Road, Cheltenham, on 25 February 1867.

Abbott was a brave and expert professional artilleryman, who enjoyed an adventurous and distinguished career. Pollock praised him as 'the finest artillery officer in India' (Low, *Afghan War*, 54), and Ellenborough included him among those to whom his Indian administration was especially indebted. His most important active service was in Afghanistan, where he repeatedly distinguished himself in battle. At the siege of Jalalabad his not initially supporting Broadfoot at the council of war might have had disastrous results, but his role was nevertheless crucial in the defence and subsequent victory.

The fourth of his brothers, **Saunders Alexius Abbott** (1811–1894), army officer in the East India Company, was born on 9 July 1811. Educated privately and at Addiscombe (1826–8), he joined the Bengal infantry in 1828. In 1836 he was appointed assistant in the revenue survey under Henry Lawrence, and he held survey charges from 1838 to 1842. At the beginning of the First Anglo-Sikh War (1845–6) he was crucial in expediting supplies to Lord Harding's army before the battle of Mudki, and in force-marching reinforcements, including elephant-drawn artillery, before the battle of Ferozeshahr. He participated in both battles and at the latter, on Harding's staff, was severely wounded. He was mentioned in dispatches and promoted brevet major. He served in civil government appointments in the Punjab and Oudh, and was honorary aide-de-camp to the governor-general from 1846 to 1863. During the mutiny he kept his district of Hoshiarpur tranquil and sent supplies to the army before Delhi. From 1858 to 1863 he was commissioner of the Lucknow district. He was promoted colonel in 1861 and major-general in 1865. He was married (his wife's name was Harriot Margaret). In 1864 Abbott retired and became manager at Lahore of the Sind, Punjab, and Delhi Railway. He returned to England in 1872 and from then until his death was a director of the railway. He lived in South Kensington and died at 2 Grand Avenue Mansions, Brighton, on 7 February 1894.

The youngest brother, **Keith Edward Abbott** (*d.* 1873), was consul-general at Tabriz in Persia, and afterwards at Odessa, where he died on 28 April 1873.

R. H. VETCH, *rev.* ROGER T. STEARN

Sources *The Afghan war, 1838–42: from the journal and correspondence of the late Major-General Augustus Abbott*, ed. C. R. Low (1879) • J. W. Kaye, *History of the war in Afghanistan*, 2 vols. (1851) • C. R. Low, *The life and correspondence of Field-Marshal Sir George Pollock* (1873) • *The Times* (13 Feb 1894) • H. M. Durand, *The First Afghan War and its causes* (1879) • H. M. Vibart, *Addiscombe: its heroes and men of note* (1894) • J. A. Norris, *The First Afghan War, 1838–1842* (1967) • *Annual Register* (1842) • F. W. Stubbs, *History of the … Bengal artillery*, 2 (1877) • G. R. Gleig, *Sale's brigade in Afghanistan: with an account of the seisure and defence of Jellalabad* (1846) • P. Macrory, *Signal catastrophe: the story of a disastrous retreat from Kabul, 1842* (1966) • T. A. Heathcote, *The Afghan wars, 1839–1919* (1980) • H. H. Dodwell, ed., *British India, 1497–1858* (1929), vol. 4 of *The Cambridge history of the British empire* (1929–59) • Boase, *Mod. Eng. biog.* • C. E. Buckland, *Dictionary of Indian biography* (1906) [Saunders Alexius Abbott] • *CGPLA Eng. & Wales* (1873); (1894) [grants of probate of Keith Edward Abbott and Saunders Alexius Abbott]

Wealth at death under £800: probate, 11 March 1867, *CGPLA Eng. & Wales*

Abbott, Charles, first Baron Tenterden (1762–1832), judge, was born in Canterbury on 7 October 1762, the second son of John Abbott (*d.* 1785), a hairdresser, with a shop opposite the western portal of the cathedral, and his wife, Alice, *née* Bunce (*d.* 1793). After learning to read at a dame-school, Abbott was admitted on the foundation to King's School, Canterbury. He was an industrious and steady student, and became captain of the school at the age of seventeen. Although his father intended him to be apprenticed to a hairdresser, the trustees of the school paid for him to go to Oxford. He matriculated at Corpus Christi College on 21 March 1781, immediately obtaining a vacant scholarship. He won the chancellor's medal for Latin composition in 1784, and, having taken the degree of BA in 1784, won the chancellor's medal for English composition in 1786 with an essay entitled 'On the use and abuse of satire'. After the death of his father in 1785 Abbott turned down the chance to go to Virginia as a tutor, intending instead to enter the church. However, his plans changed after he became the private tutor to Mr Yarde, the son of Sir Francis Buller, justice of the king's bench, who advised him to pursue a career at the bar. Abbott was admitted a student of the Middle Temple on 16 November 1787, moving to the Inner Temple in May 1793. On Buller's advice he spent several months in the office of the attorneys Sandys & Co., and followed this by becoming a pupil of the special pleader George Wood. By dint of hard work he qualified himself for practice very quickly. Ever anxious about his financial prospects, he decided to practise as a special pleader below the bar, while at the same time taking pupils. As a special pleader he was able to earn up to £1000 a year, and was sufficiently prosperous to marry Mary (*d.* 1832), the eldest daughter of John Lagier Lamotte, a gentleman of Basildon in Berkshire, on 13 July 1795. They had two sons and two daughters: John Henry (1796–1870), Mary (*d.* 1858), Catherine Alice (*d.* 1879), who later married Sir John Rowland *Smyth, and Charles (1803–1838).

Charles Abbott, first Baron Tenterden (1762–1832), by Samuel William Reynolds senior, 1820 (after William Owen, exh. RA 1819)

The bar and the bench After his call to the bar in Hilary term 1796, Abbott practised on the Oxford circuit, where he was soon in great demand as a junior counsel for his learning and ability to master abstruse technicalities. He was appointed junior counsel to the Treasury—or 'Treasury devil'—by the solicitor-general, Sir Vicary Gibbs, and drew up indictments and opened pleadings in a number of state prosecutions in the 1790s, including the treason trials of R. T. Crossfield, James O'Coigley, and Arthur O'Connor, and the libel trial of John Reeves. In 1801 he was appointed recorder of Oxford. However, he had less success in attracting the lucrative commercial briefs which were argued at Guildhall, and it was on the advice of John Scott, first Baron Eldon, that he published, in 1802, his *Law Relative to Merchant Ships and Seamen*. The book won the praise of both judges and city attorneys and attracted great business for Abbott, who was henceforth employed in most of the great charter party and mercantile cases at Guildhall. He became standing counsel for several corporations and chartered companies, as well as the Bank of England, on whose behalf he conducted forgery prosecutions at the Old Bailey. By 1807 his annual earnings had grown to £8026 5*s.* Nevertheless, while he was the leading chamber counsel, he never took silk and was never successful as a *nisi prius* advocate. As a lawyer his style of arguing was clear without being brilliant, his opinions were learned without being profound, his advice was safe without being bold.

In 1808 Abbott turned down a seat on the king's bench, in place of Sir Soulden Lawrence, since it would involve a significant drop in his income. Five years later he was bypassed for the solicitor-generalship, Edward Law, first Baron Ellenborough, taking the view that 'he has many disadvantages in the want of personal consequence, appearance, and rank in professional and popular estimation' (BL, Add. MS 38255, fol. 90v). By 1815 Abbott was tiring of his work at the bar and, with his eyesight fading, thought of retiring altogether. However, on the death of John Heath in 1816, a vacancy appeared in the common pleas, and Abbott was appointed to it in February. He was made a serjeant-at-law on 12 February, giving rings with the characteristic motto *labore*. His promotion irritated some of the other serjeants, who looked dimly on the appointment of a king's bench lawyer with a moderate *nisi prius* practice. However, there were few common pleas lawyers who were his equal in skill and learning. In May 1816 the death of Sir Simon Le Blanc opened a vacancy in the king's bench, and Abbott was transferred to that court. He initially refused, being unwilling to exchange the agreeably light caseload of the common pleas for the much higher one in king's bench, but was persuaded to accept by Ellenborough and Gibbs, the two chief justices. He was knighted on 25 May 1816. Two years later, in September 1818, when the ailing Ellenborough resigned as chief justice, Abbott was appointed in his place without a peerage. James Scarlett later observed that Abbott's elevation was 'owing to the supposed unfitness at that time of the lawyers, official or connected with the Ministry, for that place' (Scarlett, 84). In fact, the post had been refused by both the attorney-general, Sir Samuel Shepherd (who was deaf), and the solicitor-general, Sir Robert Gifford (who felt unqualified for it). Abbott felt that he did not have a sufficient fortune to sustain a peerage, but when Sir Robert Gifford was raised to the peerage in 1824 (to enable him to hear appeals in the Lords), Abbott took the view that he should also have been ennobled, given that his office was superior to Gifford's at the rolls. In the event, he was raised to the peerage only in 1827, after Canning's rise to power, on the suggestion of James Scarlett. He took the title Baron Tenterden of Hendon, which was immediately derided as ridiculous in the *Gentleman's Magazine*, which observed that 'to style a town "of" a village is past endurance' (*GM*, 1st ser., 98/1, 1828, 5).

Abbott as judge Abbott brought to the bench the habits of a chamber counsel. He felt that an address to a jury could be framed like a special plea, and he disliked the passionate and rhetorical mode of argument often found at *nisi prius*. Abbott also proved to be a much slower judge than his predecessors as chief justice, a problem exacerbated both by the fact that the caseload was higher than it had previously been, and by the increase in the number of leading barristers handling commercial cases. At first he tried to counter this by sitting later, and by resuming his sittings after the circuit, but both proved unpopular with the bar. Nevertheless, after five or six years on the bench, lawyers began to acknowledge him to be an efficient judge, and he was praised for his skill in being able to sum up even the most difficult cases in a clear and cogent way

for the jury. His greatest fault was his bad temper. Ballantine thought of him as 'a sour old man with the manners of a pedagogue' (Ballantine, 2.111), while Serjeant Robinson described him as 'morose, surly, and uniformly ill-tempered' (Robinson, 153). He was caustic with counsel who resorted to high rhetoric, curt with advocates who sought to test evidence by repeated cross-examination, and impatient of any vanity, self-importance, or evasiveness, whether in a barrister or a witness. Moreover, 'his dislike to an attorney amounted almost to aversion' (Polson, 1.359).

Abbott's irritability did not extend, however, to his treatment of defendants in criminal cases, and he was regarded as notably more temperate in handling political cases than his predecessor. Indeed, Abbott handled William Hone's first trial for blasphemous libel in 1817 with such forbearance that Ellenborough insisted on taking over in the second two trials, in the (unfulfilled) hope of securing convictions. Abbott was similarly temperate in his handling of Richard Carlile's 1819 trial for blasphemy for republishing Thomas Paine's *Age of Reason*, later reflecting 'I have often doubted whether I did not in that case permit too much to be done; but I thought then that it was better to err on the side of forbearance' (*R. v. Davison*, 1821, *Reports of State Trials*, new ser., 1.1367).

If his treatment of defendants was polite, Abbott nevertheless sought to defend the established church and state when expounding the law in the political trials over which he presided. These included the trial in 1820 of the Cato Street conspirators. He also presided over several blasphemy cases, showing himself determined to defend religion from calumny. He refused to let Carlile comment on passages from the Bible, and to call witnesses to testify to the nature of Christianity. In a case later brought against Mary Carlile for publishing a report of her husband's trial, he held that it was unlawful to publish even a correct account of a trial if it contained blasphemous matter (3 B. & Ald. 167), and in *R. v. Davison* (1821), he confirmed the judge's right to fine and gaol a defendant who attempted to revile religion in the course of his defence. His handling of juries in political cases, however, was sometimes controversial. At the end of Thomas Jonathan Wooler's trial in 1817, when the foreman stated that the jury had found the defendant guilty, but that three jurymen wanted to state special grounds, Abbott recorded the verdict as guilty, in spite of angry protestations from the defendant. Sir Francis Burdett later told the Commons that any judge wishing to entrap a jury into a verdict would do just what Abbott had done, and the verdict was subsequently overturned. Abbott encountered Wooler judicially again in the case of *R. v. the Benchers of Lincoln's Inn* (1825), when he ruled that the court had no power to grant a mandamus to an inn of court, to compel it to admit an individual, so that he could qualify for the bar. Abbott's treatment of the law in political cases could also be controversial, as in Burdett's trial for seditious libel in 1820. Burdett was tried in Leicestershire, where his article was composed, rather than in London, where it was sent for publication. Abbott ruled in the king's bench that the publication of a libel did not require the actual communication of its contents, and drew a questionable analogy with the law of treason, where a treasonable paper not delivered was none the less acceptable as evidence of an overt act. The result was to allow a trial in Leicestershire, rather than before a Middlesex jury.

When it came to civil litigation Abbott consistently sought to protect private property and was cautious of commercial speculation. In a number of cases he sought to put commercial risks onto the shoulders of traders rather than of customers. In *Montague* v. *Benedict* (1825), for instance, he ruled that a husband was not liable for the debts of his wife in purchasing jewels if they were not necessary to her station and if there was no evidence of his assent. The decision, he felt, would have the beneficial effect of making traders more cautious. In *Hall* v. *Fuller* (1826), he held that it was the bank, rather than the customer, who should bear the risk if a cheque was fraudulently altered by the holder, while in *Gill* v. *Cubitt* (1824), he overruled a decision by Lord Kenyon, by holding that a broker could not recover on a stolen bill of exchange unless he had exercised reasonable caution to make sure the holder was legitimate. Abbott felt that Kenyon's decision had merely encouraged the theft of such securities; but he was himself later overturned on this point.

In *Josephs* v. *Pebrer* (1825), decided during a speculative boom in company formations, Abbott held that an unincorporated company with transferable shares was illegal since it violated the Bubble Act. In this case Abbott observed that shares were being traded at higher premiums than at any time since the passing of that act, which he felt encouraged ruinous speculation. 'In such transactions', he said, 'one cannot gain unless another loses, whereas in fair mercantile transactions each party, in the ordinary course of things, reaps a profit in his turn' (3 B. & C. 644). However, in a number of later cases, such as *Vice* v. *Lady Anson* (1827) and *Dickinson* v. *Valpy* (1829), he sought to protect shareholders from the debts of the company. Similarly, in *Bourne* v. *Freeth* (1829), he held that a man who subscribed his name to a prospectus and who encouraged others at a meeting to take certain premises was not liable as a partner for work later done.

Abbott's desire to protect the individual property holder is also reflected in some of his decisions in other areas. In *Blundell* v. *Catterall* (1821), he ruled that there was no common-law right to bathe in the sea, and hence a commercial operator had no right to transport customers across the sea-shore on another's land. 'Public convenience', he said, 'is, in all cases, to be viewed with a due regard to private property, the protection whereof is one of the distinguishing characteristics of the law of England' (5 B. & Ald. 268). More controversially, he ruled in *Ilott* v. *Wilkes* (1820) that a trespasser who knew that there were spring guns set in a wood could not maintain an action for injury against the landowner. While admitting the inhumanity of the practice, he observed 'that repeated and increasing acts of aggression to property may perhaps reasonably call for increased means of defence and protection' (3 B. & Ald. 304). The decision was later overturned by a statute (7 & 8 G. IV c. 18).

On the bench Abbott was a great friend and defender of those in authority, especially of the unpaid magistracy. In *R.* v. *Borron* (1820), he dismissed a case where a criminal information was sought against a Lancashire magistrate who had refused to investigate a charge against other magistrates in the county. 'To punish as criminal any person, who, in the gratuitous exercise of a public trust, may have fallen into error or mistake', he ruled, 'belongs only to the despotic ruler of an enslaved people, and is wholly abhorrent from the jurisprudence of this kingdom' (3 B. & Ald. 434). This attitude led him on occasion to shield magistrates from criticism.

Tenterden in the Lords Tenterden was a high tory in politics, and in the Lords resolutely opposed the repeal of the Test and Corporation Acts in 1828, unsuccessfully moving an amendment to the bill to require the chief magistrate of all corporate towns to be an Anglican. In the following year he opposed Catholic emancipation, which he felt would lead to the overthrow of the Church of England. In his view the bill would settle nothing, and any calm which followed would be 'delusive and temporary' (*Hansard 2*, 1828, 308). Indeed, he told George IV that such a concession to the Catholics would be a breach of his coronation oath. He was equally a determined opponent of the Reform Bill, which he felt would vest all the power of the state in the House of Commons, and give the power of returning a majority of that house 'to a class of persons far below the middle class of society' (*Hansard 3*, 1832, 398). He said that, as chief justice, he was 'peculiarly bound to uphold the chartered rights of the people' (*Hansard 3*, 1831, 302) which he argued were being treated with contempt by the bill, and he warned that passing the bill would establish a precedent for the annihilation of all other rights. Tenterden ended his contribution to the Reform Bill debates by declaring, 'Never shall I enter the doors of this House, after it has become the phantom of its departed greatness' (*Hansard 3*, 1832, 400).

Tenterden also resisted legislation to reform the criminal code. In 1830 he opposed the Forgeries Punishment Bill, which sought to remove the death penalty for forgeries of stock or negotiable instruments. Tenterden's view was that prosecutors were not deterred by the harshness of the penalty, and that the severity of the law was necessary for the protection of property. In the following year he spoke against a petition of the grand jurors of Middlesex on capital punishment, arguing that judges always 'felt the utmost anxiety and solicitude to discover any circumstances which could lead them to recommend a mitigation of punishment' through the exercise of the royal prerogative of mercy (*Hansard 3*, 1831, 1181). None the less, he was noted for his severity as a judge, and for his reluctance to recommend mercy.

Tenterden was, however, not an enemy to law reform. In the mid-1820s he helped Peel in drafting his bills to consolidate the criminal law. In 1830 he agreed to become a member of the ecclesiastical courts commission, having earlier advised Peel on appointments to the common-law and real property commissions. He drew up and piloted a number of bills which sought to shorten and simplify proceedings and to save expense. He was responsible for the act known as Lord Tenterden's Act (9 Geo IV c. 14), concerning contract law, which amended James I's Statute of Limitations and extended some provisions of the Statute of Frauds. He further prepared the Mandamus and Prohibition Acts (1 W IV c. 3 and 1 W IV c. 21), the Interrogatories Act (1 W IV c. 22), the Interpleader Act (1 & 2 W IV c. 58), and the Uniformity of Process Act (2 & 3 W IV c. 39) which grew out of the recommendations of the common-law commissioners. He also piloted the Prescription Act (2 & 3 W IV c. 71), which, while seeking to introduce certainty and simplicity into this area of law, was drafted in a complex way and turned out to create numerous problems. Indeed, it has been described as 'one of the worst drafted Acts on the Statute Book' ('Law reform committee: fourteenth report', *Parl. papers*, 1966–7, 39, Cmnd 3100, para. 40).

Tenterden enjoyed a happy and modest family life. As Charles Greville put it, 'his manners were remarkably plain and unpolished, though not vulgar' (*Greville Memoirs*, 2.330). This was reflected in his desire in his will to be buried 'in the least ostentatious and most frugal manner possible' (PROB 11/1808/730). A private man, he was said to have associated less with his fellow lawyers than any man of his day. Indeed, Denis Le Merchant observed after his death, 'Prejudiced and selfish, he had few friends in private, and his hostility to liberty caused him to have none in public' (Aspinall, 281). He remained hard-working to the last. In declining health, he presided at the trial of the mayor of Bristol, Charles Pinney, for misconduct and neglect of duty during the riots there. On the third day of the trial he was confined to his sickbed, and he died on 4 November 1832 at his London home, 28 Russell Square. His last words, sitting up in bed, and making a motion as if dipping his pen in an inkstand, were, 'Gentlemen of the Jury, you are discharged' (Polson, 1.360). At his own request, Tenterden was buried at the Foundling Hospital, London, of which he was a governor, on 10 November 1832.   MICHAEL LOBBAN

Sources J. Campbell, *Lives of the lord chancellors*, 4th edn, 10 vols. (1856–7), vol. 3 · 'Life of Lord Tenterden', *Law Magazine*, 26 (1841), 51–87 · H. Brougham, *Historical sketches of statesmen who flourished in the time of George III*, 3rd ser., 2 (1845), 19–29 · *GM*, 1st ser., 102/2 (1832), 568 · A. Polson, *Law and lawyers, or, Sketches and illustrations of legal history and biography*, 2 vols. (1840), 1.354–60 · J. Grant, *The bench and the bar. By the author of 'Random recollections of the Lords and Commons', 'The great metropolis', etc*, 2 vols. (1837), 1.81–5 · *Legal Observer*, 5 (1832–3), 19 · Holdsworth, *Eng. law*, 13.516–28 · W. C. Townsend, *The lives of twelve eminent judges* (1846), 2.234–78 · E. Brydges, *The autobiography, times, opinions, and contemporaries of Sir Egerton Brydges*, 1 (1834), 401–24 · Foss, *Judges*, 9.68–73 · W. H. Wickwar, *The struggle for the freedom of the press, 1819–1832* (1928) · J. A. Epstein, *Radical expression: political language, ritual and symbol in England, 1790–1850* (1994) · P. C. Scarlett, *A memoir of the Right Honourable James, first Lord Abinger, chief baron of her majesty's court of exchequer* (1877) · *The Greville memoirs, 1814–1860*, ed. L. Strachey and R. Fulford, 8 vols. (1938) · W. Ballantine, *Some experiences of a barrister's life*, 2nd–5th edns (1882) · B. C. Robinson, *Bench and bar: reminiscences of one of the last of an ancient race*, 2nd edn (1889) · A. Aspinall, ed., *Three early nineteenth-century diaries* (1952) [extracts from Le Marchant, E. J. Littleton, Baron Hatherton, and E. Law, earl of Ellenborough] · *The Times* (5 Nov 1832) · *The Times* (8 Nov 1832) · *The Times* (12 Nov 1832) · *The journal of Mrs Arbuthnot, 1820–1832*, ed. F. Bamford and the duke of Wellington [G. Wellesley], 2 (1950), 246–7 · *Reports of state trials*, new ser., 8 vols. (1888–98) · *Barnewall and Alderson's King's bench reports* [B. & Ald.] · *Barnewall and Cresswell's King's bench reports* [B. & C.] · Burke, *Peerage* (1924) · IGI

Archives BL, corresp. with Sir Robert Peel, Add. MSS 40353–40430 · Devon RO, corresp. with Lord Sidmouth

Likenesses C. Picart, stipple, pubd 1804 (after J. Northcote), NPG · W. Owen, oils, 1818, CCC Oxf. · S. W. Reynolds senior, engraving, 1820 (after W. Owen, exh. RA 1819), NPG [*see illus.*] · J. Wood, oils, 1824, Middle Temple, London · J. W. Wright, watercolour drawing, 1830, Inner Temple, London · P. W. Sarti, marble bust, 1883, Middle Temple, London · H. R. Cook, stipple (after S. H. Gimber), BM, NPG · J. Hollins, oils (after W. Owen), Royal Courts of Justice, London · H. Meyer, stipple (after C. Penny), BM, NPG

Wealth at death under £120,000: GEC, *Peerage*, 12 (1953); GM

Abbott, Charles Stuart Aubrey, third Baron Tenterden (1834–1882), diplomatist, was the son of the Hon. Charles Abbott (1803–1838), brother of John Henry, second Baron Tenterden, and of Emily Frances, née Stuart (d. 1886). He was born in Dean Street, Park Lane, London, on 26 December 1834, and was educated at Eton College (1848–53). In 1854 he entered the Foreign Office, one of the last three clerks, the other two being Lord Currie and Sir Percy Anderson, to be appointed purely by the patronage of the foreign secretary, Lord Clarendon, before the introduction of examinations in 1855.

Abbott was first employed on the affair of the *Cagliari* in Naples in 1858, work for which it might be said he had a natural affinity, since his grandfather had published a definitive work, *The Law Relative to Merchant Ships and Seamen* in 1802; and, as a junior in the American department, he was given the task of preparing the papers for the *Alabama* arbitration proceedings with the USA. Abbott, although officially précis writer (1866–8) to Lord Stanley, was actually employed successively on the royal commission on the neutrality laws (February 1867–May 1868); as secretary to the royal commission into the laws of naturalization and allegiance (May 1868–January 1869); as secretary to the joint high commission between the USA and Great Britain considering the *Alabama* and other American Civil War issues, in Washington (February–May 1871); and finally as British agent at the general arbitration of the *Alabama* claims (November 1871–June 1872). The successful outcome of these proceedings owed much to Abbott's good sense in moderating the xenophobic tendencies of the commissioners. His reward came almost immediately, for when Edmund Hammond retired in 1873, Lord Tenterden (as Abbott had become in 1870 in succession to his uncle) was appointed permanent undersecretary, Lord Derby preferring him to the more experienced Sir Robert Morier, who was thought to be too much in earnest. As permanent under-secretary, Tenterden did little materially to alter the system of work established by Edmund Hammond. The office continued to advise and recommend, hence Disraeli's recommendation to Lord Salisbury on his way to Constantinople in 1876 to trust to his own convictions and not to the promptings of

'"Tenterdenism", which is a dusty affair and not suited to the times' (Cecil, 2.95). Tenterden's physical appearance was commented upon by Sir Charles Dilke, who wrote: 'I have seen two men both in the Foreign Office service that looked like bears—Lord Tenterden a little black graminivorous European bear; old White a polar bear, if ever I saw one' (Gwynn and Tuckwell, 1.266).

In 1878 Tenterden was a royal commissioner at the Paris Exhibition, and the same year he was promoted to the rank of KCB. He was a distinguished freemason, and was installed provincial grand master of Essex on 2 July 1879. He was twice married: first, on 2 August 1859, to his cousin Penelope Smyth (d. 1879), with whom he had four children; and second, on 13 January 1880, to Emma, née Bailey (d. 1928), widow of Henry Rowcliffe QC. Tenterden was taken suddenly ill at Nelson Cottage, Lynmouth, and died there of cerebral haemorrhage on 22 September 1882. He was buried in Brendon, Devon.   R. A. JONES

Sources FO List (1883), 190–91 · The Times (23 Sept 1882) · J. M. Collinge, ed., Office-holders in modern Britain, 8: Foreign office officials, 1782–1870 (1979) · R. Jones, The nineteenth-century foreign office: an administrative history (1971) · Foreign Office, diplomatic and consular sketches: reprinted from Vanity Fair (1883), 25–30 · J. Tilley and S. Gaselee, The foreign office (1933), 110–11 · Burke, Peerage (1914) · GEC, Peerage, new edn, vol. 12/1 · G. Cecil, Life of Robert, marquis of Salisbury, 4 vols. (1921–32) · S. Gwynn and G. M. Tuckwell, The life of the Rt. Hon. Sir Charles W. Dilke, 2 vols. (1917) · Gladstone, Diaries
Archives BL, letters and diplomatic memoranda, Add. MS 64796 · PRO, corresp., FO 363 | BL, corresp. with Sir Charles Dilke, Add. MSS 43878–43884 · BL, corresp. with W. E. Gladstone, Add. MSS 44182–44678 · BL, corresp. with Sir Ansters Lanyard, Add. MSS 39124–39140 · BL, corresp. with Lord Ripon, Add. MS 43528 · Bodl. Oxf., letters to Benjamin Disraeli · Bodl. Oxf., letters to Sir William Harcourt · CUL, letters to Lord Hardinge · Lpool RO, corresp. with Lord Derby · NRA, priv. coll., letters to Lord Hammond · PRO, corresp. with second Earl Granville, PRO 30/29 · PRO, letters to Odo Russell, FO 918 · PRO, letters to Sir William White, FO 364/1
Likenesses Ape [C. Pellegrini], caricature, chromolithograph, NPG; repro. in VF (17 Aug 1878)
Wealth at death £1394 9s. 10d.: probate, 7 Nov 1882, CGPLA Eng. & Wales

Abbott, Edwin (1808–1882), headmaster, was born in London on 12 May 1808, the son of Edward Abbott, an oilman and Italian warehouseman, of St Martin's Lane, London, and his wife, Charlotte. The Abbott family were descended from George Abbot, archbishop of Canterbury; later generations were farmers from Dorset and Somerset.

After his family fell on hard times Abbott entered the Philological Society of Marylebone, Middlesex, in 1818, which had been established as a library in 1792, and became a charity school under influential Anglican patronage in 1797. Admission was limited to 'necessitous' sons of the middle classes 'reduced by accident or misfortune'. During his time as a pupil, and, later, as monitor and junior assistant, the school experimented with the Pestalozzi system and ceased corporal punishment. He left the school in June 1822, but returned as master pro tempore late in 1826. He was confirmed as headmaster of the renamed Philological School of General Instruction in 1827 with a salary of £100 a year, which rose to £500 before his retirement in 1872.

Abbott greatly increased the reputation and prosperity of the school, which in 1857 was rebuilt along Gothic lines at New Road, Marylebone. He expanded the curriculum to include English, German (from 1840), and science (electricity 1854; chemistry 1870). In 1834 the school established ties with the newly founded King's College, London, and became a feeder for the City of London School. Abbott's letters reveal a firm but humane disciplinarian. His rule was 'a child's first duty is obedience to those who are in authority over him; and if he does not learn this, everything which he does learn is more likely to do him harm than good' (to Mr Chapman, 7 July 1859, headmaster's letter book, 2, Westminster Archives).

With D. Walther, printer, Abbott in 1841 published a translation of volume 3 of J. H. Merle D'Aubigné's History of the Great Reformation (3 vols., 1838–41). He also published A Second Latin Book (1858). Ahead of his time in teaching English, he wrote A Handbook of English Grammar (1845; 3rd edn, 1877), and A Concordance to Pope (1875), edited by his son Edwin Abbott *Abbott. The groundwork for the latter's famous work Flatland (1884) was laid by his father's Handbook of Arithmetic and First Steps in Algebra (7th edn, 1876).

Abbott married his first cousin Jane Abbott (1806–1882) about 1830. They had eight children: Jane (1832–1859); Elizabeth (1834–1880); Charlotte (1835–1884); Anne (b. 1837); Edwin Abbott (1838–1926); Edward (1840–1859); Alice (c.1841–c.1892); and Sydney (1844–1887). Elizabeth married, in 1857, John Humffreys *Parry, serjeant-at-law, a sympathizer with the moral-force Chartists, and a former pupil and close friend of Abbott. The latter was moved by the 'condition of England' question and maintained friendships with leading Christian socialists. As churchwarden of Christ Church, Marylebone, Abbott supported the appointment of John Llewelyn Davies to the rectory. Abbott's daughter Alice married Davies's curate, Richard Haworth Hart (1830–1888).

Abbott died at 18 Palace Square, Upper Norwood, Surrey, on 27 May 1882, shortly after the death of his wife on 22 April. They were both buried in Kensal Green cemetery, Abbott on 31 May. Described by The Times (31 May 1882) as 'a most efficient and popular member of the educational profession', his influence over the St Marylebone High School for Boys (as the school was renamed in 1901) extended long after his death; two succeeding headmasters, William Moore and Charles Houseman, were brought up as master and boy under him.

JAMES M. BORG

Sources The Times (31 May 1882) · The Times (13 Oct 1926) · E. McNeal, The Philological School, 1792–1954, 2 vols. (1939) · E. Parry, My own way: an autobiography (1932) · private information (2004) [T. Banchoff] · d. cert. · CGPLA Eng. & Wales (1882) · DNB
Archives City Westm. AC, letters as headmaster
Likenesses portrait, c.1845, 38 New Road, Marylebone, London; formerly at St Marylebone School · C. Armytage, c.1872, 38 New Road, Marylebone, London; formerly at St Marylebone School
Wealth at death £748 10s. 7d.: probate, 27 June 1882, CGPLA Eng. & Wales

Abbott, Edwin Abbott (1838–1926), headmaster and writer, was born at 38 Gloucester Place, Marylebone, Middlesex, on 20 December 1838, the eldest son of Edwin *Abbott (1808–1882), headmaster of the Philological School, Marylebone, and his wife, Jane Abbott (1806–1882), a first cousin. Educated at the City of London School under Dr G. F. W. Mortimer, he entered St John's College, Cambridge, as a scholar in 1857, became senior classic and senior chancellor's medallist in 1861, and was elected to a fellowship at his college in 1862. He resigned this position in 1863 on account of his marriage with Mary Elizabeth (1843/4–1919), daughter of Henry Rangeley, landed proprietor and coal owner, of Unstone, Derbyshire. They had one son and one daughter. Abbott was ordained deacon in 1862 and priest in 1863.

Having held teaching appointments at King Edward's School, Birmingham, and Clifton College, Abbott was elected in 1865, at the early age of twenty-six, to the headmastership of the City of London School, which he held until his retirement in 1889. The school had already risen greatly in reputation under Abbott's predecessor and teacher, Dr Mortimer; but it was owing to Abbott's inspiration that it won the distinction of providing the highest intellectual training. His greatness as an educator derived partly from his organization of new methods of instruction, partly from his initiation of many innovations in the school curriculum, and partly from what can only be called his genius for teaching. Having a reverence for physical science not often found among the classical scholars of his day, he made an elementary knowledge of chemistry compulsory throughout the upper school. As regards classical instruction, he instilled in his pupils the greatest respect for severe standards of formal scholarship; but he breathed new life into it, being among the first, for instance, to adopt the reformed pronunciation of Latin. Having caught the enthusiasm then prevalent at Cambridge for the study of comparative philology, Abbott provided advanced teaching in the subject for the members of his sixth form, where he introduced his keenest pupils to the study of Sanskrit. More than one of them—notably Professor Cecil Bendall—became eminent Sanskrit scholars.

Abbott's most fruitful innovation in the traditional curriculum was the introduction of English literature as an integral part of form-teaching throughout the school. Every term his sixth form studied a play of Shakespeare as they studied a Greek play, in the hope that the language and soul of one great world would help to interpret the other. His own enthusiasm for great literature inspired the careers of such pupils as Arthur Henry Bullen, Sidney Lee, and others who won fame as English scholars and men of letters. Of all the capacities that he strove to evoke in his pupils, Abbott valued most highly that of the clear expression of serious thought, which he conceived to be the chief result of the Oxford Greats training; and of all his pupils he was perhaps proudest of H. H. Asquith, whom he regarded as its best representative.

A great moral and religious teacher, Abbott had the mark of the spiritual leader in that he could impart to others something of his own inspiration. Without driving or overtaxing his pupils, he made intellectual effort a kind of religion for them; his deep reprobation of intellectual slackness and unveracity was such a spur to them that his sixth form became a most stimulating training ground for eager and receptive spirits. In spite of a frail and delicate physique, Abbott could keep discipline without effort. He was an impressive preacher: in the pulpit he was a bold and original exponent of advanced broad church doctrines. His own university elected him Hulsean lecturer in 1876, and Oxford invited him to be select preacher in 1877. But, next to teaching, Abbott's vocation lay in writing; and it was probably the attraction of complete leisure for literary work, as well as his weariness of administration, which prompted his retirement at the zenith of his reputation and at the comparatively early age of fifty in 1889.

During the active period of his life Abbott produced much. He began to publish in 1870, and his important works include *Shakespearean Grammar*, in 1870; *English Lessons, for English People*, in 1871 (written with J. R. Seeley); and *How to Write Clearly*, in 1872. The English classical author on whom Abbott laboured most was Francis Bacon. In 1877 he published *Bacon and Essex* to correct the partial judgement of James Spedding of Bacon's action on the occasion of the trial of the earl of Essex. The introduction which accompanied his seventh edition of Bacon's *Essays* (1886) contains an original and masterly study of Bacon's varied activities and complex character.

More numerous and perhaps more weighty than Abbott's works of secular scholarship are his theological writings. Their range is wide, for they include treatises of textual criticism, showing the most minute and laborious attention to statistical details and to linguistic interpretation (*Johannine Vocabulary*, 1905; *Johannine Grammar*, 1906), as well as works of high religious imagination and bold constructive power, such as *Philochristus* (1878), *Onesimus: Memoirs of a Disciple of Paul* (1882), and *Silanus the Christian* (1906). These are striking expositions of the broad church point of view; the first is dedicated to J. R. Seeley. His broad church sympathies also inspired *Philomythus* (1891), a critique of J. H. Newman's 'Essay on miracles', and *The Anglican Career of Cardinal Newman* (2 vols., 1892). However, he is most remembered as the author of *Flatland, or, A Romance of many Dimensions*, published under the pseudonym of A Square in 1884. At once a lesson in higher dimensional geometry, a social satire, and an expression of religious principle, this work gives lasting testimony to Abbott's genius as a teacher and to his literary and moral imagination.

Abbott died of influenza at his home, Wellside, Well Walk, Hampstead, London, on 12 October 1926, and was buried in Hampstead cemetery.

L. R. FARNELL, rev. ROSEMARY JANN

Sources *The Times* (13 Oct 1926) • Venn, *Alum. Cant.* • A. E. Douglas-Smith, *The City of London School* (1937) • T. F. Banchoff, 'From *Flatland* to hypergraphics: interacting with higher dimensions', *Interdisciplinary Science Reviews*, 15 (1990), 364–72 • R. Jann, 'Abbott's *Flatland*: scientific imagination and "natural Christianity"', *Victorian Studies*, 28 (1985), 473–90 • J. Smith, L. I. Berkove, and G. A. Baker, 'A grammar of dissent: *Flatland*, Newman, and the theology of probability',

Victorian Studies, 39 (1996), 129–50 · private information (1937) · personal knowledge (1937) · b. cert. · m. cert. · d. cert. · *CGPLA Eng. & Wales* (1926)

Archives St John Cam., corresp., notebooks, and papers | BL, corresp. with Macmillans, Add. MS 55114 · King's AC Cam., letters to Oscar Browning

Likenesses W. & D. Downey, woodburytype photograph, NPG; repro. in W. Downey and D. Downey, *The cabinet portrait gallery* (1891), vol. 2 · H. von Herkomer, oils, City of London School · J. Russell & Sons, photograph, NPG

Wealth at death £17,436 14*s*. 10*d*.: probate, 1 Dec 1926, *CGPLA Eng. & Wales*

Eric Symes Abbott (1906–1983), by Walter Bird, 1966

Abbott, Eric Symes (1906–1983), dean of Westminster, was born on 26 May 1906 at Nottingham, the younger son and second of three children of William Henry Abbott, schoolteacher, and his wife, Mary Symes, also a teacher. A Dame Agnes Mellor scholar at Nottingham high school, he won a further scholarship to Jesus College, Cambridge (of which he became an honorary fellow in 1966), to read classics. A second class in part two (1928) following a first in part one (1927) was probably to be accounted for by many hours on the river coxing the college first eight, winning a trial cap, and being president of the university branch of the Student Christian Movement. In 1928 he crossed Jesus Lane to Westcott House and there came under the single most formative influence in his life: B. K. Cunningham. He obtained a third class in part one of the theological tripos in 1929.

Ordained in St Paul's Cathedral to serve at St John's, Smith Square (1930–32), Abbott was then requested by King's College, London, to become chaplain. So began the twenty-five years in which he was to give all his care and almost all of himself to students who were being prepared for ordination. He was also chaplain to Lincoln's Inn in 1935–6. In 1936, at the age of thirty, he accepted the wardenship of Lincoln Theological College with a staff that included a future archbishop of Canterbury. Here he shared his Anglican perception of priesthood with his students, opening up for them a way of interior faith, prayer, and self-discipline appropriate for the demands of parochial pastoral ministry. He was also canon and prebendary of Lincoln Cathedral (1940–60).

The Second World War was coming to an end when Abbott was invited back to King's College as dean (1945–55). This unique position as dean of the whole college in harness with a lay principal, as well as being head of the department and faculty of theology and warden of the hostel for theological students in Vincent Square, enabled him to influence the post-war revival of the college as a whole, to build up the staff in theology, and to create a postgraduate one-year college at Warminster for the immediate preordination spiritual and pastoral training (Lincoln style) of King's ordinands.

The total burden of this complex responsibility would have been more than enough; but to this public work was added private work of an exacting kind, a seemingly endless sequence of individuals drawn to him by his preaching and personality to seek spiritual guidance. This led to a vast correspondence (the 'apostolate of the post', as he called it). Even on holiday he would spend most mornings and evenings writing letters and the 'famous' postcards. It is not surprising that latent heart trouble which was to dog his later years was aggravated by his years in London. The invitation in 1956 to become the sixth warden of Keble College, Oxford (but the first to be elected by the fellows under a new set of statutes), undoubtedly prolonged his working life. He was made an honorary fellow in 1960.

A colleague writing about the bracing effect of Abbott's four years at Keble commented: 'His main achievement was to give the college confidence in itself. He consolidated the college both in its internal and external relations. Though not an academic he understood and encouraged academic excellence' (private information). His swift intelligence, acute perception, and subtle wit, together with his accessibility, drew senior and junior members alike to consult him. An annual Eric Abbott lecture was later established at Keble in his memory.

In 1959 came the invitation to be dean of Westminster. Abbott's vision of the abbey was of a great church in which all questing men and women, irrespective of faith and race, would 'see Jesus'. The theme for the celebration in 1965–6 of the 900th anniversary of the founding of the abbey was 'One People'. Events were planned to relate the abbey to the needs and aspirations of the modern world. The dean was present at almost all.

Throughout his years as dean Abbott influenced the form and preparation of services for weddings, memorials, and celebrations of national independence. Three royal weddings prepared and conducted by him further deepened his pastoral relationship with the royal family. His presence, prayer, and preaching, his care for art, music, literature, and drama, enhanced the worship and work of the abbey during fifteen years—years which for him included episodes of debilitating ill health. He became a freeman of the city of Westminster in 1973. In 1974 he accepted the need to retire, but continued his ministry to individuals from his home in Vincent Square.

In 1966 he was appointed KCVO and made an honorary DD of London University. He was unmarried. He died at Haslemere on 6 June 1983. The stone that marks his grave in the abbey carries the inscription: 'Friend and counsellor of many, he loved the Church of England, striving to make this House of Kings a place of pilgrimage and prayer for all peoples. *Pastor Pastorum*'.   SYDNEY EVANS, *rev.*

Sources *The Times* (7 June 1983) · *WWW* · *CGPLA Eng. & Wales* (1983) · *Eric Symes Abbott: a portrait* (1983) · private information (1990)
Archives King's Lond., corresp. and papers | FILM BFI NFTVA, current affairs footage | SOUND BL NSA, sound recording
Likenesses W. Bird, photograph, 1966, NPG [*see illus.*]
Wealth at death £48,517: probate, 19 July 1983, *CGPLA Eng. & Wales*

Abbott, Evelyn (1843–1901), classical scholar, was born at Epperstone, Nottinghamshire, on 10 March 1843, the third of the five sons of Evelyn Abbott, a farmer and landowner, and his wife, Mary Lambe. Educated first at Lincoln grammar school and afterwards at the Somersetshire College, Bath, Abbott was elected in 1862 to an open exhibition at Balliol College, Oxford. He gained a high academic reputation and was also a good athlete. In 1864 he won the Gaisford prize for Greek verse and a first class in classical moderations. In the Easter vacation of 1866, just before he entered for his final examination, he fell in a hurdle race and injured his spine. Unfortunately, unused to illness as he was, he did not recognize the serious nature of the accident, and continued his exertions, both at his books and at cricket, as if nothing had happened. In the summer he obtained a first class in *literae humaniores*. In the following autumn, when the damage became obvious, it was too late for a cure; he became hopelessly paralysed in the legs, and never walked again. For thirty-five years, thanks to a very strong natural constitution and great courage and patience, he managed to overcome this handicap. He soon began to take private pupils, sometimes near his birthplace in Sherwood Forest, sometimes at Filey. In 1870 he was appointed sixth-form master at Clifton College by John Percival. In 1873 Benjamin Jowett, master of Balliol, invited him to return to Oxford, and until 1875 he took work at Corpus as well as at Balliol. In 1873 he graduated BA and MA. In 1874 he was elected a fellow and tutor of Balliol. From that time until his resignation, only a few days before his death, he was a mainstay of the administration and teaching of his college. At first he taught mainly Latin and Greek literature; in his later years Greek history was his principal subject. He became Jowett lecturer in Greek in 1895, was librarian of the college from 1881 to 1897, and in 1882 served as junior bursar.

Throughout his life Abbott was constantly engaged in writing in addition to his college work. He was well versed in German, and besides Curtius's *Elucidations of the Students' Greek Grammar* (1870) he published *History of Antiquity* (6 vols., 1877–81), a translation of the work by Max Duncker. He also assisted Sarah Francis Alleyne (*d.* 1885) in English versions of Duncker's history of Greece (2 vols., 1883–6) and *Outlines of Greek Philosophy* (1885), a translation of the work by Zeller. He was editor of *Hellenica* (1880; 2nd edn, 1898), a collection of essays on Greek themes, and was general editor of the 'Heroes of the Nations' series, to which he contributed a life of Pericles (1891). Other works were *Elements of Greek Accidence* (1874) and an index to Jowett's translation of Plato (1875). With Lewis Campbell he wrote a biography of Benjamin Jowett, master of Balliol and his lifelong friend (1897). His most important literary work was his *History of Greece* in three volumes (1888–1900), admirable alike for its learning, sound judgement, and simple and lucid style. The sceptical view of the *Iliad* and *Odyssey*, which regards them as purely works of poetical imagination, had not previously been so ably presented, and it demonstrated Abbott's independent method in treating historical problems.

Abbott, who was made LLD of St Andrews in 1879, maintained his activities until a few weeks before his death at Knotsford Lodge, Great Malvern, on 3 September 1901. He was buried at Redlands cemetery, near Cardiff.

     J. L. STRACHAN-DAVIDSON, *rev.* M. C. CURTHOYS

Sources personal knowledge (1912) · J. Foster, *Oxford men and their colleges* (1893) · G. Faber, *Jowett* (1957) · *The Times* (6 Sept 1901) · d. cert.
Archives Bodl. Oxf., letters to George and Richard Bentley
Likenesses pencil drawing, Balliol Oxf.
Wealth at death £1763 13*s.*: resworn probate, July 1902, *CGPLA Eng. & Wales* (1901)

Abbott, Sir Frederick (1805–1892), army officer in the East India Company, was the second son of Henry Alexius Abbott of Blackheath, Kent, a retired Calcutta merchant, and his wife, Margaret, daughter of William Welsh of Edinburgh, writer to the signet. He was the brother of Augustus *Abbott and Sir James *Abbott. He was born on 13 June 1805 at Littlecourt, near Buntingford, Hertfordshire. Educated at Warfield, Berkshire, under Dr Faithfull, and at Addiscombe College from 1820 to 1822, he was commissioned into the Bengal Engineers in 1823.

After the usual professional training at Chatham, Abbott arrived in India in December 1823. He was posted to the sappers and miners in February 1824 and promoted lieutenant in May. In the First Anglo-Burmese War he was assistant field engineer under Captain John Cheape in the force under Sir Archibald Campbell. He was adjutant to the sappers and miners from November 1825 until April 1826. He went through the whole campaign, and distinguished himself in the capture of the heights of Napadi, near Prome, on 2 December 1825, when he led storming parties in the assaults on three stockades, was wounded and was mentioned in dispatches.

After the war Abbott was employed in the public works

department at Burdwan, Cawnpore, Karnal, and elsewhere. He was promoted captain in July 1832. On 14 February 1835 he married Frances, widow of Lieutenant-Colonel H. De Burgh and daughter of Lieutenant-Colonel Cox, Royal Artillery; his wife and daughter (later Mrs St George Tucker) predeceased him. He went home on furlough in 1838. Returning in 1840 he was shipwrecked at Mauritius. He arrived at Calcutta in December 1840, and in June 1841 became garrison engineer and barrack master at Fort William, and civil architect at the presidency.

During the First Anglo-Afghan War, in February 1842, he was appointed chief engineer of the 'army of retribution' under Major-General George Pollock, sent to relieve the garrison of Jalalabad, where Abbott's brother Augustus commanded the artillery, and to restore British prestige in Afghanistan after the humiliating capitulation and subsequent annihilation of Major-General William Elphinstone's army on its retreat from Kabul. Abbott took part in forcing the Khyber Pass on 5 April, but by the time Pollock arrived at Jalalabad the garrison had saved itself by a victory on 7 April over Akbar Khan. Abbott participated in actions in August and September, and in the occupation of Kabul on 15 September, and was mentioned in dispatches. The mutilated corpse of the treacherously murdered British envoy Sir William Macnaghten had been hung from a meat-hook and 'exposed to the insults of the populace' (*Annual Register*, 1842, 238) in Kabul's celebrated grand bazaar. Pollock in retribution ordered Abbott to destroy the bazaar and mosque. Abbott, though personally regretting this, superintended their demolition by gunpowder. For his services he received in December 1842 a brevet majority.

Abbott resumed his post of superintending engineer of the North-Western Provinces in December 1842. In the First Anglo-Sikh War in 1846 he served in the army of the Sutlej. He commanded the bridging establishment and acted also as aide-de-camp to Sir Henry Hardinge, the governor-general. He took part in the battle of Sobraon (10 February), for which he was mentioned most favourably in dispatches. In June 1846 he was promoted brevet lieutenant-colonel, and made a companion in the Order of the Bath. He retired from the active list in December 1847. His reports on public works continued to be used as textbooks for subsequent operations.

In 1851 Abbott succeeded Major-General Sir Ephraim Stannus as lieutenant-governor (principal) of the military college at Addiscombe. He was initially unpopular with the cadets who disliked his manner, reforms, and punishments, and his wife's support of Catherine Marsh's revivalism among the cadets aroused some resentment. Nevertheless he ran the college competently and was twice reappointed to his post. He was knighted in 1854. On the amalgamation of the East India and royal services in 1861 the college was closed. In 1859 he was appointed a member of the royal commission on the defences of the United Kingdom presided over by Sir Harry Jones, which recommended a massive and expensive programme of fortifications, resulting in 'Palmerston's follies'. In 1866 he was a member of a committee to inquire into the Royal

Engineer Establishment at Chatham. He was also a member of the council of military education, but resigned in 1868. His hobbies were microscopy and the study of polarization of light. He died at his home, Goshen, The Avenue, Branksome Park West, Bournemouth, on 4 November 1892, and was buried in Bournemouth cemetery, Wimborne Road, on 8 November. In his long career Abbott was successful as a civil engineer in India; as a combat engineer in the Anglo-Burmese, Anglo-Afghan, and Anglo-Sikh wars; and, more controversially, as a military educator at Addiscombe. R. H. VETCH, *rev.* ROGER T. STEARN

Sources *Royal Engineers Journal*, 23 (1893) · *The Times* (7 Nov 1892) · H. M. Vibart, *Addiscombe: its heroes and men of note* (1894) · J. W. Kaye, *History of the war in Afghanistan*, 2 vols. (1851) · C. R. Low, *The life and correspondence of Field-Marshal Sir George Pollock* (1873) · G. R. Gleig, *Sale's brigade in Afghanistan: with an account of the seisure and defence of Jellalabad* (1846) · W. Porter, *History of the corps of royal engineers*, 2 vols. (1889) · W. Broadfoot, 'Addiscombe: the East India Company's military college', *Blackwood*, 153 (1893), 647–57 · *Annual Register* (1842) · E. W. C. Sandes, *The Indian sappers and miners* (1948) · C. R. Low, *The Afghan war, 1838–1842* (1879) · J. A. Norris, *The First Afghan War, 1838–1842* (1967) · P. Macrory, *Signal catastrophe: the story of a disastrous retreat from Kabul, 1842* (1966); repr. as *Kabul catastrophe* (1986) · d. cert.
Likenesses cartoon, repro. in Vibart, *Addiscombe*, 311 · photograph, repro. in Vibart, *Addiscombe*, 191
Wealth at death £21,245 7s. 2d.: resworn probate, Jan 1893, *CGPLA Eng. & Wales* (1892)

Abbott, George (1604–1649), writer and politician, was born in 1604 and baptized on 13 March at St Mary Bishophill Junior, York, the son of George Abbott (*d.* 1607) of York and Joan, the daughter of Aleyn Penkeston. Both Abbott's father and grandfather Penkeston were counted minor gentry in the city, but neither was a freeman. Abbott's grandfather, another George Abbott, was a yeoman farmer, of Featherstone, near Pontefract, and members of the Abbott family remained there throughout this subject's lifetime, to provide jurors for the West Riding quarter sessions. On his father's side Abbott was related to the Pickering family, settled in various places in Yorkshire, and there was a modest family estate of the Penkestons at Sheriff Hutton in the North Riding. Thus both the Abbotts and Penkestons were recently arrived in York from elsewhere in Yorkshire and their claim to gentility was somewhat tenuous. George Abbott's father died in November 1607 and Abbott himself moved south, to Caldecote in north Warwickshire, soon after January 1609, when his mother married William *Purefoy (*c.*1580–1659), who owned the manor there.

There is no evidence that Abbott attended either Oxford or Cambridge universities, and it is likely that he lived a comparatively secluded life at Caldecote with his mother and stepfather, free to pursue independent studies. If these intellectual interests were at first unfocused, they were given a new purpose with the appointment by Purefoy to the living of Caldecote of Richard Vines, a forceful puritan minister. From his arrival in 1630 Vines became Abbott's spiritual and academic mentor, and under his guidance Abbott published his first book, *The Whole Booke of Job Paraphrased*, in 1640. It provided by means of parallel texts—the book in the Authorized Version and Abbott's summary of it—an accessible introduction to a difficult work of scripture, and was motivated by Abbott's desire to evangelize through publishing.

Abbott was elected MP for Tamworth, not far from his stepfather's home, in the Short Parliament of April 1640. The inhabitants resented the election by the civic oligarchy of an outsider, and he did not represent the borough when parliament reassembled in November. His next book, *Vindiciae sabbathi* (1641), was more topical than the first, and Abbott took advantage of the times to denounce what he considered Laudian disregard for sabbath observance. On the outbreak of civil war Abbott's stepfather was among the most active of Warwickshire parliamentarians, and on 28 August 1642 Abbott found himself, in the absence of any other menfolk, defending Caldecote House, his mother, and her servants, against eighteen troops of horse under the command of Prince Rupert. Heroic, not to say traumatic, though it was, this incident was his only involvement in military action, but he settled down to become a prominent local committeeman on behalf of parliament over the next few years. He was rewarded for his diligence by a seat in the House of Commons, once again for Tamworth, from 2 October 1645. His contribution to the proceedings of the house during 1646 was modest, his most significant service signalled by his appointment to the committee for plundered ministers and as a commissioner for regulating access to the Lord's supper, both appointments which recognized his authority in matters ecclesiastical and theological.

In November 1646 Abbott fell sick and was given leave to retire to the country. He never recovered, and died on 21 February 1649 at Caldecote, where he was buried. His last book, *The Whole Book of Psalms Paraphrased* (1650), was a companion volume to his first, and appeared after his death. He never married, and the tomb erected for him by his mother recorded his defence of Caldecote and his scholarly distinction.   STEPHEN K. ROBERTS

Sources HoP, *Commons, 1640–60* [draft] · W. Dugdale, *The antiquities of Warwickshire illustrated*, rev. W. Thomas, 2nd edn, 2 (1730), 1099 · will, PRO, PROB 11/207, fol. 405*v* · will of George Abbott of York, proved, 30 Jan 1608, Borth. Inst. · will of George Abbott of Whitewood in Featherstone, proved, 29 July 1619, Borth. Inst. · A. Hughes, *Politics, society and civil war in Warwickshire, 1620–1660* (1987) · parish register, York, St Mary Bishophill Junior [baptism], 13/3/1604 · parish register, York, St Martin Coney Street · parish register, York, St Michael le Belfry · memorial, Caldecote Church, Warwickshire

Wealth at death house and lands at Baddesley, Ensor, Warwickshire; houses at York and Cornborough, Sheriff Hutton, Yorkshire: PRO, PROB 11/207, fol. 405*v*

Abbott, Sir James (1807–1896), army officer, third son of Henry Alexius Abbott of Blackheath, Kent, a retired Calcutta merchant, and his wife, Margaret, daughter of William Welsh, writer to the signet, of Edinburgh, was born on 12 March 1807. He was the brother of Augustus *Abbott and Frederick *Abbott. He was educated at a school in Elliott Place, Blackheath, kept by John Potticany, an Independent minister, and one of his schoolfellows was Benjamin Disraeli. Abbott was trained at Addiscombe College,

near Croydon, from 1821 to 1823, and was commissioned second lieutenant in the Bengal artillery in June 1823.

Abbott arrived in India in December 1823. His first active service was at the second siege of Bharatpur, under Lord Combermere, in December 1825 and January 1826, when he served under his brother Augustus with the artillery, and took part in the assault and capture of the fortress on 18 January. For twelve years after the siege the Bengal artillery had no war service. Abbott was promoted lieutenant and appointed adjutant of the Sirhind division of artillery in September 1827. From October 1835 he was employed in the revenue survey of Gorakhpur until August 1836, when he was placed in charge of that of Bareilly, and was officially commended. In June 1838 he was promoted brevet captain.

In November 1838 Abbott joined the army of the Indus, under Sir John Keane, which invaded Afghanistan. He reached Kandahar in April 1839. In July he accompanied his friend Major Elliott D'Arcy Todd as assistant political officer on his mission to Herat. This resulted in Abbott's involvement in the difficult and dangerous 'Great Game', the struggle for influence and intelligence in central Asia between Russian and British agents, far from British seapower. British policy was to attempt to limit Russian expansion, in order to safeguard India. In 1839, partly in response to the British intervention in Afghanistan, Russia sent a military expedition against the khanate of Khiva, in Turkestan, ostensibly to free Russian slaves and end raids on caravans, but in fact to bring Khiva under Russian control. The ruler of Khiva, Allah Quli Khan, wrote to Todd requesting British artillerymen to help fight the Russians. Todd, because of the urgency of the situation and the slowness of communication with his superiors, had to act on his own initiative. Cautiously, he refused military aid and in December 1839 sent Abbott on a mission to Khiva to advise the khan to remove the pretext for Russian intervention by freeing the Russian slaves, and if there were already war between Russia and Khiva to offer mediation. In fact the Russian expedition failed disastrously in the exceptionally cold winter, and in February 1840 withdrew before reaching Khiva.

Abbott's task was not easy. He lacked diplomatic experience and knowledge of Khiva. He wrote that he went 'to a Court, of the language and manners of which I am utterly ignorant, and to accomplish that of which the most sanguine have no hope' (Kaye, *History of the War*, 1.519) and that he 'did not start upon his tour primed and prefaced' (Abbott, 1.xi). He rode to Khiva where the Khivans, who had never seen an Englishman, initially suspected he might be a Russian agent. He wrote back recommending more British intervention in Turkestan, including military aid to Khiva. He failed to persuade the khan to free the Russian slaves. Exceeding his authority, he was persuaded by the khan to agree to a treaty providing for the establishment of a British agent at Khiva and British mediation between Khiva and Russia. Abbott decided to go to Russia to negotiate this mediation. He acted on his own initiative and forged documents to justify his journey to Russia. In

March 1840 he left Khiva. In April his party was attacked and kidnapped by Kazakhs. His right hand was injured by a sword cut and he lost several fingers. Later, fearing retribution, the kidnappers freed him and his party. He reached Russian territory on the Caspian, and ultimately St Petersburg. His reception was cool and suspicious, and the Khivan terms he brought were rejected. He returned to England in August and received the thanks of Palmerston, the foreign secretary, for his conduct of the mission. In August 1841 he was promoted captain, and in 1843 was awarded a pension of £50 per annum for his injuries.

Despite his courage and initiative, Abbott's mission had failed. It was his successor at Khiva, Lieutenant Richmond Shakespear, who achieved the freeing of the slaves. Abbott, however, believed that his own mission had succeeded. In 1843 he published his version in his two-volume *Narrative of a Journey from Heraut to Khiva, Moscow and St Petersburgh*; in 1856 he published an enlarged edition. He claimed that his efforts had been crowned with the most signal success and that he had negotiated the release of the slaves, ending Russia's pretext for taking Khiva and so advancing closer to India. He also criticized central Asian slavery and debauchery and Russian militarism, and warned of future Russian aggression against India.

Abbott returned to India in September 1841, and was appointed second in command of the Merwara local battalion and assistant to Captain Dixon, the superintendent of Merwara. In 1842 he was appointed assistant to the resident at Indore, with charge of Nimar. In February 1844 he married Margaret Anne Harriet (d. 1845), daughter of John Hutchison Fergusson of Trochraigne, Ayrshire, and they had a daughter, Margaret H. A. Fergusson-Abbott. In 1845 he was appointed commissioner of Hazara. During his rule Hazara rose from desolation to prosperity. Abbott raised the whole population, and after many small actions retained control of the district and nearly all the forts. He trained the raw levies of the mountaineers, and though for several months cut off from communication with British troops, he occupied the Marquella Pass and held off superior Sikh and Afghan forces until the war ended in February 1849. He received the thanks of the governor-general and of both houses of parliament and was promoted brevet major in June 1849.

Abbott continued to rule in Hazara. In December 1852 he planned the operation and commanded a column of the successful Black Mountain expedition to punish the Hasanzais for the murder of two British tax officials. He left Hazara in 1853. Abbottabad, named after him, is a memorial of his achievement.

Abbott was promoted lieutenant-colonel in July 1857, then successively promoted, finally attaining the rank of general in October 1877, when he retired from the active list. On 24 October 1868 he married Anna Matilda (d. 1870), youngest daughter of Major Reymond de Montmorency of the Indian army, and they had a son, James Reymond de Montmorency Abbott. He was made a companion in the Order of the Bath in May 1873 and knighted (KCB) in May 1894. He died at Ellerslie in Ryde, Isle of Wight, on 6 October 1896.

Abbott was a brave soldier, a successful administrator, a pious evangelical, and an imaginative writer of romantic verse. Sir Henry Lawrence described him as 'of the stuff of the true knight-errant' (Vibart, 372).

R. H. VETCH, rev. ROGER T. STEARN

Sources *The Times* (8 Oct 1896) • C. R. Low, *The Afghan war, 1838–1842* (1879) • J. Abbott, *Narrative of a journey from Heraut to Khiva, Moscow and St Petersburgh*, 2nd edn, 2 vols. (1856) • M. E. Yapp, *Strategies of British India: Britain, Iran and Afghanistan, 1798–1850* (1980) • F. W. Stubbs, ed., *History of the organization, equipment, and war services of the regiment of Bengal artillery*, 1 (1877) • H. M. Vibart, *Addiscombe: its heroes and men of note* (1894) • J. W. Kaye, *History of the war in Afghanistan*, 1 (1851) • J. W. Kaye, *Lives of Indian officers*, 2 (1867) • P. Hopkirk, *The great game: on secret service in high Asia* (1990) • m. cert. • d. cert.
Archives BL OIOC, corresp. and papers, MS Eur. F 171, MS Eur. C 210 225, MS Eur. E 277
Likenesses B. Baldwin, watercolour drawing, 1841, NPG
Wealth at death £2245 11s. 7d.: probate, 17 Dec 1896, *CGPLA Eng. & Wales*

Abbott, Sir John Joseph Caldwell (1821–1893), prime minister of Canada, was born on 12 March 1821 at St Andrews, Argenteuil county, Lower Canada, the eldest son of the Revd Joseph *Abbott (*bap.* 1790, *d.* 1862) and Harriet Bradford.

John Joseph Abbott was educated privately at St Andrews, then at McGill College (1843–7). He maintained a close connection with the university: he began lecturing in law in 1853, and from 1855 to 1880 he was professor and dean of the faculty; in 1854 he was made BCL and in 1867 DCL; and in 1881 he was appointed to the board of governors. Abbott was admitted to the bar of Lower Canada in October 1847 as a specialist in commercial law, and his clients included the Hudson's Bay Company, Bell Telephone, Canadian Pacific Railway, the Séminaire de St Sulpice, the Bank of Montreal, and the Standard Life Assurance Company. In 1862 he was named queen's counsel.

Although Abbott claimed to loathe politicians, he is best remembered for his contribution to public life. It began somewhat ominously when he signed the annexation manifesto in 1849, calling for the union of Canada with the United States. His recruitment of 300 men, called the Argenteuil rangers, in 1861 during the *Trent* affair was designed to demonstrate his loyalty. He was afterwards commissioned lieutenant-colonel and made commanding officer of the regiment.

In 1857 Abbott contested the constituency of his native county of Argenteuil. Although he lost the election he challenged the results, and after a two-year investigation he obtained the seat, which he held until 1874. In 1860 he published the investigation's proceedings under the title *The Argenteuil Election Case*, a vivid account of electoral practices at the time. In 1862 he entered the moderate Reform government of John Sandfield Macdonald and Louis Victor Sicotte, an administration which adopted the 'double majority'. This meant that no ministry could be satisfied with the confidence merely of the whole house; it must command a majority from both Lower Canada and Upper Canada. This unworkable device led to the ministry's defeat in 1863, within a year of its formation. In the reconstituted house the double majority was abandoned, a change which brought about the retirement both of Sicotte, the French-Canadian leader, and of Abbott, the ministry's solicitor-general, who was the ministerial representative for the English of Lower Canada.

Short as was his term of office, Abbott introduced a number of legislative measures, including the use of stamps in the payment of judicial and registration fees in Lower Canada, a consolidation and remodelling of the jury law, and the drafting of an act respecting insolvency, which became the foundation of Canadian jurisprudence on that subject. In drafting this legislation, Abbott based his work on the leading principles of English, French, and Scottish law. The following year he published *The Insolvent Act of 1864*, with notes on the rules of practice and the fees prevailing in Lower Canada.

After his departure from the Macdonald–Sicotte ministry Abbott remained unaffiliated to any party for several years before joining the Conservatives after confederation, a cause he supported only reluctantly, fearing that it would reduce the political influence of the English minority in Lower Canada. He was elected to the House of Commons for Argenteuil in 1867 and 1872, and in 1873 his name figured largely in the Pacific scandal. The previous year he had become fellow director with Sir Hugh Allan in a project to build a Canadian Pacific Railway. Allan advanced more than £25,000 to the Conservative leaders during the elections and disbursed the money through Abbott, then his confidential adviser. After the elections the Liberals obtained copies of correspondence and vouchers regarding the money transactions from a clerk in Abbott's office. The public outcry, debate, and recriminations in the house obliged the Conservative government to resign, and in the election in 1874 they were routed. Abbott was returned for his old constituency, but was unseated following a petition. Four years later he was defeated, but in 1880 he won a by-election, only to have the result set aside owing to bribery by one of his agents. He was re-elected in a by-election in 1881 and in the general election the same year; he held this seat until 1887, when he was called to the senate, where he served as house leader. Although not a cabinet member during his years in the house, he served the government in several ways: a chairman of the house committee on banking, he was also sent to London to secure the Colonial Office's support for his government's dismissal of the lieutenant-governor of Quebec, Luc Letellier de Saint-Just, as well as to negotiate trade issues.

A polished, well-mannered man of broad interests, Abbott played a prominent role in the social and cultural life of Montreal, where he lived with his wife, Mary Martha Bethune, whom he had married on 26 July 1849 and with whom he had four sons and four daughters. He was a founder of the Art Association of Montreal, the Fraser Institute, a free library, museum, and art gallery, which he served as life president, and the Protestant Institution for Deaf-Mutes and the Blind. He was twice elected mayor of Montreal (1887, 1888), and in 1887 he secured a charter for the Royal Victoria Hospital; as its first chairman he presided over the construction of its large, well-appointed building.

In the senate Abbott represented the Quebec division of Inkerman. At the same time he was sworn of the Canadian privy council, and became a member of the cabinet of Sir John Alexander Macdonald, without portfolio, acting as government spokesman in the upper house. On Macdonald's death in 1891 Abbott became prime minister and president of the council, the other cabinet members retaining their portfolios. Although he inherited a divided cabinet and was in ill health, Abbott was more than a caretaker. He expedited a backlog of legislative and administrative business, including a reform of the criminal code, negotiations with Washington, and an attempt to deal with the corruption in his party. Despite his efforts, his declining health precipitated his resignation on 5 December 1892; he had been nominated KCMG in May 1892. He died at Montreal on 30 October 1893.

CARMAN MILLER

Sources NA Canada, John Abbott MSS • C. Miller, 'Abbott, John Joseph Caldwell', *DCB*, vol. 12 • M. Ogilvy, 'Sir J. J. C. Abbott', *Men of the day: a Canadian portrait gallery*, ed. L.-H. Taché (1890–94) • P. B. Waite, *The man from Halifax: Sir John Thompson, prime minister* (1985) • A. W. P. Buchanan, *The bench and bar of Lower Canada down to 1850* (1925) • D. S. Lewis, *Royal Victoria Hospital, 1887–1947* (1969) • C. Miller, 'Abbott, Joseph', *DCB*, vol. 9
Archives NA Canada

Abbott, Joseph (*bap.* 1790, *d.* 1862), Church of England clergyman, the son of Joseph Abbott and his wife, Isabella, was baptized on 10 June 1790 at Little Strickland, Westmorland; his date of birth is not known. He attended Bampton School, Bampton, Westmorland, and from 1808 to 1812 Marischal College, Aberdeen; after graduating MA he was ordained in the Church of England.

Abbott was typical of a group of serious-minded younger clergymen who were entering the church during the first decades of the nineteenth century. By his own account his decision to take holy orders resulted from a circumstance 'involving in its consequences so much of sorrow and misery', which induced him 'to form a more true and correct estimate of the comparative value of the things of heaven and of earth' (Abbott, 4). Appointed to the curacy of Long Stratton, Norfolk, he threw himself energetically into the duties of a parish priest. Although not 'without a fair and reasonable prospect of preferment', Joseph Abbott and his younger brother, William, sought employment as missionaries with the Society for the Propagation of the Gospel in Foreign Parts, and in 1818 Joseph left England to take up his appointment as priest at St Andrews, seigneury of Argenteuil, Lower Canada. His motive in emigrating was not so much the result of a 'zealous and devoted missionary spirit' as of an ambition to be 'placed in a much wider and more extensive sphere of usefulness' (ibid., 6).

Abbott's first charge in Lower Canada was a disappointment. Many of his difficulties can be traced to an unbending high-church theology, which interpreted the sacrament of communion as the 'mystical body of Christ's Holy Catholic Church' (Abbott, 20), and the Church of England as 'the principal if not the only bond of union between these North American colonies and the mother-country' (ibid., 125) and the sole guarantee of a conservative and monarchical constitution. At a more practical level Abbott dismissed dissenters, who comprised the majority of his parish, as dupes of 'unauthorized teachers' (ibid., 42) whose sole motives he believed to be envy and fanaticism. With his own congregation he insisted on a rigid separation between communicants and non-communicants, a demand which would have alienated many church members attracted by the more latitudinarian ways of his predecessor, the Revd Richard Bradford.

Despite Abbott's marriage to Bradford's daughter, Harriet, on 10 August 1820, his energy in opening mission stations in remote parts of the district, and ministering to the British garrison at Grenville Station—activities which secured him the appointment as the first rector of St Andrews by Bishop Jacob Mountain in 1822—his congregation comprised only 21 of the 156 families resident in the parish. Indeed, as he reported to the Society for the Propagation of the Gospel in 1819, 'this is an American settlement' and 'those very people that profess to be real Churchmen have requested me to dispense with reading the Litany the Lords prayer the prayer for the King & royal family & to model the Liturgy after their own fancy' (Abbot to sec., 26 April 1819, SPG MS C, box 4/29). In 1825 he exchanged churches with his brother William and moved to a new mission near Yamaska Mountain, Lower Canada. He returned to the Argenteuil seigneury in 1830 to take charge of the Church of England mission at Grenville.

It was at Grenville that Abbott enjoyed his greatest influence, as a leading promoter of the Royal Institution for the Advancement of Learning, which sought to create a network of parish schools in Lower Canada. Between 1843 and 1852 he occupied a variety of positions at McGill University, Montreal, including the offices of chaplain and vice-principal, though his association with Principal John Bethune's design to turn the college into an Anglican institution was widely resented. However, it was during these years that Abbott established a literary reputation through works such as *Philip Musgrave* (1846), a fictionalized biography of a Church of England clergyman drawn from his own journals; and *Memoranda of a Settler in Lower Canada, or, The Emigrant in North America* (1842).

Abbott died at Montreal on 10 January 1862 and is remembered as a leader in the planting of the Church of England in Lower Canada. Of his and Harriet's seven children, one, John Joseph Caldwell *Abbott (1821–1893), became the third prime minister of Canada in 1891.

MICHAEL GAUVREAU

Sources C. Miller, 'Abbott, Joseph', *DCB*, vol. 9 · J. Abbott, *Philip Musgrave, or, Memoirs of a Church of England missionary in the North American colonies* (1846) · NA Canada, Society for the Propagation of the Gospel, 'C' MSS, Canada, Dio Quebec, Reel A-199, Box IV/29

Archives McGill University, Montreal, minutes of board of governors · NA Canada, Society for the Propagation of the Gospel

Abbott, Keith Edward (d. 1873). *See under* Abbott, Augustus (1804–1867).

Abbott, Lemuel (d. 1776), Church of England clergyman and poet, whose family background is obscure, became curate of Ansty, Leicestershire, in 1756, and vicar of Thornton, in the same county, in 1773. He published *Poems on Various Subjects, whereto is Prefixed a Short Essay on the Structure of English Verse* (1765). Abbott and his wife, Mary, were probably the parents of the artist Lemuel Francis *Abbott (1760/61–1802). Lemuel Abbott died in April 1776.

THOMPSON COOPER, *rev.* MICHAEL BEVAN

Sources J. Nichols, *The history and antiquities of the county of Leicester*, 4/2 (1811), 984 · S. F. Creswell, *Collections towards the history of printing in Nottinghamshire* (1863), 34
Likenesses V. Green, mezzotint, pubd 1800 (after L. F. Abbott), BM, NPG

Abbott, Lemuel Francis [Samuel] (1760/61–1802), portrait painter, was the elder son of a clergyman in Leicestershire—probably the Revd Lemuel *Abbott (d. 1776), curate of Anstey, later vicar of Thornton, and his wife, Mary. In 1775, at the age of fourteen, he was apprenticed to Francis Hayman, after whose death in the following year he returned to his parents and apparently continued to study portrait painting independently. About 1780 he settled in London, and resided for many years in Caroline Street, Bloomsbury. On 16 November 1786 he married Anna Maria Magdalen Tracey at St George the Martyr, Queen Square, London. Their son Edward Francis Abbott was born on 20 December 1787. Between 1788, when he was a candidate for election as an associate of the Royal Academy, and 1800 he showed fifteen male portraits at the Royal Academy and seems to have specialized in painting portraits of diplomatists, colonial governors, and senior naval officers. The heads of his male portraits were accurate likenesses, particularly his naval portraits, examples of which are in the National Maritime Museum, London, notably the half-length of Nelson (who sat to him several times), shown at the Royal Academy in 1800, and the whole-length of Sir Peter Parker. Several commentators have noted the weakness of his whole-length poses. His portraits of the poet William Cowper (1792) and the sculptor Joseph Nollekens are in the National Portrait Gallery, London. His portraits were engraved by Valentine Green, Joseph Skelton, and William Walker among others. Although it was said that his parsimonious disposition led him to engage no assistants, with the result that he was overwhelmed with commissions he could not fulfil, it is known that the sporting painter Ben Marshall was apprenticed to him for three years in 1791.

By July 1798 Abbott was certified insane. It has been supposed that insanity was due to an 'ill-assorted marriage' (Redgrave, *Artists*, 1), though Abbott referred in his will of October 1800 to his 'dear wife', who was his executrix and beneficiary. He last exhibited at the Royal Academy in 1800. Abbott died at his home in Penton Street, Clerkenwell, London, on about 5 December 1802. Waterhouse noted that his unfinished works were completed by a 'less sensitive hand' (Waterhouse, *18c painters*, 21). Farington noted in his diary on 25 January 1803 that Abbott died 'about six weeks ago' 'in a State of Insanity. A commission of Lunacy had been taken out & it then proved that He was not possessed of more than 3 or 400 pounds a year' (Farington, *Diary*, 5.1966). On 17 August Farington noted that during a visit to Nollekens:

> a boy near 16 years of age was drawing upon a Slate from a Plaister figure. Nollekens told me He was the only son of the late Mr. Abbot, Portrait Painter. His mother is a Roman Catholic & a Bigot. She insists upon Her Son becoming a Romish Priest, which He refuses, & she will in consequence scarcely see him.   (ibid., 6.2109)

A. NISBET

Sources A. C. Sewter, 'Some new facts about Lemuel Francis Abbott', *The Connoisseur*, 135 (1955), 178–83 • E. Edwards, *Anecdotes of painters* (1808); facs. edn (1970) • Waterhouse, *18c painters* • Redgrave, *Artists* • Graves, *RA exhibitors* • *IGI* • K. K. Yung, *National Portrait Gallery: complete illustrated catalogue, 1856–1979*, ed. M. Pettman (1981) • Bryan, *Painters* • will, PROB 11/1385, fols. 13v–14r • J. D. Champlin and C. C. Perkins, eds., *Cyclopedia of painters and paintings*, 4 vols. (1888) • B. Stewart and M. Cutten, *The dictionary of portrait painters in Britain up to 1920* (1997) • Farington, *Diary*, 3.1082; 5.1966; 6.2190; vol. 17
Likenesses V. Green, mezzotint, pubd 1800 (after L. Abbott), BM, NPG
Wealth at death under £5000: Sewter, 'Some new facts'

Abbott, Saunders Alexius (1811–1894). *See under* Abbott, Augustus (1804–1867).

Abbott, Thomas Eastoe (1786/7–1854), poet, was born at East Dereham, Norfolk. He was descended from a Suffolk family, and resided for many years at Darlington. For his services in connection with the Royal Free Grammar School, he was presented with a valuable testimonial by the inhabitants of that town. Abbott's published poetical works included *Peace, a Lyric Poem* (1814); *The Triumph of Christianity* (1819); and *The Soldier's Friend* (1828). He died at Rose Villa, Darlington, on 18 February 1854, aged sixty-seven.   THOMPSON COOPER, *rev.* MEGAN A. STEPHAN

Sources J. Latimer, *Local records, or, Historical register of remarkable events which have occurred in Northumberland and Durham … 1832–57* (1857), 338 • Watt, *Bibl. Brit.* • Boase, *Mod. Eng. biog.* • T. Cooper, *A new biographical dictionary: containing concise notices of eminent persons of all ages and countries* (1873) • *GM*, 2nd ser., 41 (1854), 443 • d. cert.

Abdullah ibn Hussein [ʿAbd Allāh ibn al-Ḥusayn] (1882–1951), emir of Transjordan and founder of the Hashemite kingdom of Jordan, was born in February 1882 in Mecca in the Ottoman province of Hejaz. He was the second of three sons of Hussein ibn Ali (1853–1931) and Abdiyya bint Abdullah (*d.* 1886). His parents, who were first cousins, both held the title sherif, denoting their descent from the prophet Muhammad. Their income derived from waqfs (pious endowments in the form of property) and an allowance from the ruling grand sherif of Mecca, Abdullah's great-uncle.

Abdullah's mother died when he was four and his paternal great-grandmother subsequently cared for him. Private tutors taught him tribal lore, poetry, history, calligraphy, and recitation of the Koran. This life was disrupted in 1891 when his father was effectively exiled to Constantinople by order of the Ottoman sultan, Abdul Hamid II, owing to a familial dispute with the grand sharif. Abdullah and his two brothers, Ali (1879–1935) and *Feisal (1886–1933), joined him a few months later. Their social circle in Constantinople was confined to the Turkish élite and persons of a similar religious standing. In 1902 he married his first cousin Misbah bint Nasser, and a son and heir, Talal, was born in 1909 (*d.* 1972). They also had a daughter, Haya.

Abdullah's first decisive political intervention occurred in 1908 when he persuaded his father to stand for the vacant position of grand sherif of Mecca. Amid the turmoil of the Young Turk revolution, Hussein's candidature proved successful, helped by the tacit backing of Britain. Abdullah promptly returned to Mecca in December after sixteen years away. In 1909 he became a deputy for Mecca in the parliament established by the Young Turks, requiring him to return to Constantinople for the winter months. This effectively made him Hussein's go-between with the Ottoman government until the outbreak of war in 1914. He took, polygamously, a second wife, Suzdil Hanum, in 1912 and had three more children, Naif, Munira, and Maqbula.

During the First World War Abdullah became involved in discussions with British officials over the future of Hejaz and in 1915 encouraged his father to negotiate with Britain's high commissioner to Egypt, Henry McMahon, about Arab independence from Turkish rule. Abdullah subsequently became the political driving force behind the Arab revolt and was a vigorous advocate of the British connection. The reward came in 1916 when his father was granted the title king of Hejaz. Yet it was his brother Feisal who emerged from the revolt as Britain's main Arab mediator owing to his successful military campaigns with T. E. Lawrence. Feisal acquired control over Syria but French forces, upholding the Sykes–Picot agreement of 1916, expelled him in July 1920.

This ejection provided Abdullah with an opportunity to advance his own political ambitions in northern Arabia, after he had been thwarted in the south on the battlefield against Ibn Saʿud in May 1919. In early 1921 Abdullah entered Transjordan (then part of the Palestine mandate) with a view to marching on Damascus. At the insistence of Winston Churchill, Britain's colonial secretary, Abdullah was allowed to stay in Amman provided that he curbed anti-Zionist activities in the area and ceased his hostility to the French in Syria. Feisal, meanwhile, was offered the throne of Iraq, a lasting source of jealousy to his competitive brother. Abdullah's position in Transjordan became more secure in September 1922 when the League of Nations accepted Britain's decision to separate it from Palestine. The emirate of Transjordan formally came into being on 25 May 1923.

Abdullah's immediate task as emir was to consolidate his rule over the native sedentary and nomadic tribes. In this nation-building process he was dependent on the armed 'reserve force' formed in 1921 by Lieutenant-Colonel Frederick Peake, seconded from the Palestine police. Renamed the Arab Legion in May 1923, it was led by Glubb Pasha (Sir John Glubb) between 1930 and 1956. As well as maintaining internal order, the Arab Legion—which was trained and paid for by the British—was responsible for protecting Transjordan's borders. The main threat came from Ibn Sa'ud, who overthrew Abdullah's father as king of Hejaz in 1924, creating in due course Saudi Arabia. This military dependence on Britain was reinforced by the appointment of a succession of political advisers, notably St John Philby between 1921 and 1924 and Alec Kirkbride from 1927. A legislative council was created in 1928 but its relations with the emir were mainly advisory and he was essentially an autocrat.

By the end of the decade Abdullah was firmly established in Transjordan but, as a contemporary noted, this was akin to a falcon being trapped in a canary's cage. His great ambition was to rule the historic 'fertile crescent' which encompassed Syria, Lebanon, Palestine, and Transjordan. In pursuit of this goal he floated a variety of federation schemes with neighbouring states and keenly advocated Arab unity when it suited his purposes. Fellow Arab rulers, protective of their own positions, came to mistrust him, while Arab nationalists increasingly condemned him as a British puppet. His cultivation of contacts with Zionist leaders in Palestine, based on a pragmatic and realistic view of Jewish nationalism, also incurred their hostility. By the mid-1930s Abdullah recognized that Britain would always block his greater Syria plans and so he narrowed his immediate focus to Palestine.

During the Second World War Abdullah proved to be Britain's most faithful ally in the Middle East. He zealously maintained internal order in Transjordan and gave full support to Britain's suppression of pro-axis nationalists in Iraq in 1941. The only friction occurred in the negotiations leading to the creation of the Arab League, Abdullah favouring a version of his fertile-crescent ambitions rather than the Egyptian-led anti-Hashemite bloc that eventually emerged in March 1945. In recognition of Abdullah's wartime loyalty Britain granted formal independence to Transjordan in March 1946 (the 'Trans' prefix was dropped in 1947), while veiling the continuing defence relationship under a treaty of alliance. Abdullah's title changed from emir to king in May 1946. The impression remained, however, that he was a British stooge. Officials in the British Foreign Office referred to him as 'Mr Bevin's little king'.

In 1947, as Palestine descended into civil war, Abdullah intensified his contacts with Jewish leaders. The upshot was a loose—and much debated—understanding based on Jordan's seizing the Arab-designated parts of Palestine under the United Nations partition plan, leaving the rest for the new state of Israel. Britain's foreign secretary, Ernest Bevin, encouraged this as he preferred an enlarged Jordan to a Palestinian state led by the pro-Nazi ex-mufti of Jerusalem, Hajj Amin al-Huseini. A few days before the outbreak of the Arab–Israeli War on 15 May 1948, however, the Arab League appointed Abdullah the commander-in-chief of its armies. It would appear that

the plan was either to lock him into the official Arab policy of opposing partition or, failing that, to make him the scapegoat for the expected military defeat.

Unhindered by his new collective responsibilities Abdullah ordered the Arab Legion to seize Palestinian territory west of the River Jordan. The armistice of 1949 left the West Bank under his control, much to the anger of other Arab governments who wanted the area to form the basis of a Palestinian state. To the Palestinian refugees Abdullah was the great betrayer of their cause. His formal annexation of the West Bank in May 1950—adding 900,000 Palestinians to the existing population of 450,000—prompted a crisis in the Arab League. A compromise agreed in June permitted Jordan to hold on to the territory until a final settlement of the Palestine question. Meanwhile Abdullah's attempts to reach a peace treaty with Israel earned him yet more vilification in the Arab world.

On 20 July 1951, while Abdullah was attending Friday prayer at the Al-Aqsa mosque in Jerusalem, a 21-year-old tailor's apprentice named Mustafa Ashu emerged from behind the entrance and shot him dead with a bullet in the head. The assassin, who was immediately killed by the royal bodyguard, allegedly had links with Hajj Amin al-Huseini. Abdullah's body was flown back to Amman that day for burial in the Royal Tombs at the Royal Court on 23 July.

A son of the Arabian peninsula, Abdullah was an Arab traditionalist and devout Muslim all his life. He was particularly attached to the simplicity of tribal values and loved the accompanying poetry and storytelling. But he was also a product of Constantinople's *belle époque* with its ethnic and religious diversity, and from this he acquired a deep understanding of nationality issues. At the time of his death (and indeed for a long time afterwards) his realism and moderation towards Zionism were unique among Arab leaders. To Britain, Abdullah was the loyal client whose small but stable country was considered a strategic asset and therefore worth its stipend. Although his British advisers thought him well schooled in 'Ottoman intrigue', they nevertheless warmed to his charm and impish personality. Kirkbride, who knew him best of all, described him as the 'king with a twinkle in his eye'. While he enjoyed pomp and ceremony, his official expenses were in keeping with Jordan's size. He wrote two volumes of memoirs, *Mudhakkarati* in 1945 and *Al Takimilah* in 1951. From the First World War onwards his abiding concern was to create an Arab homeland based upon natural, historic frontiers rather than Anglo-French imperial constructs. The pursuit of this goal, however, brought him the enmity of neighbouring Arabs and, in the end, his death at the hands of a stateless Palestinian. Ironically his legacy was a stable and modern Hashemite dynasty over a country famously created by a stroke of Churchill's pen.

MICHAEL T. THORNHILL

Sources M. C. Wilson, *King Abdullah, Britain and the making of Jordan* (1990) · A. Shlaim, *The politics of partition* (1990) · T. E. Lawrence, *Seven pillars of wisdom* (1935) · R. Storrs, *Orientations* (1939) · B. Westrate, *The Arab bureau* (1992) · M. T. Thornhill, 'Britain and the politics of the Arab League, 1943–50', *Demise of the British empire in the Middle East*, ed. M. J. Cohen and M. Kolinsky (1998) · A. Kirkbride, *From the wings: Amman memoirs, 1947–1951* (1976) · J. Glubb, *A soldier with the Arabs* (1957) · P. R. Graves, ed., *Memoirs of King Abdullah* (1950) · King Abdullah of Jordan, *My memoirs completed* (1978) · www.kinghussein.gov.jo/hashemites.html, 1 Aug 2001

Archives PRO, Amman embassy files on partition of Palestine, FO 816/111, FO 816/115, FO 816/116 · Royal Engineers, Brompton barracks, Chatham, Kent, J. Glubb diaries · St Ant. Oxf., J. Glubb collection · St Ant. Oxf., H. St John Philby papers | FILM BFI NFTVA, 'Trans-Jordan proclaims emir king', British News, 10 June 1946 · BFI NFTVA, news footage · British Movietone News archives, newsreel footage

Likenesses photographs, repro. in Wilson, *King Abdullah* · photographs, St Ant. Oxf. · photographs, L. Cong., Matson collection · photographs, IWM · portrait, repro. in King Abdullah of Jordan, *My memoirs*

Abdul Rahman, Tunku (1902–1990), prime minister of Malaysia, was born in Alor Setar, Kedah (a Malay state then under British 'protection'), on 8 February 1902, the seventh son of Abdul Hamid Halim Shah, sultan of Kedah (*fl.* 1882–1943), and his Thai wife, Makche Menjelara. Abdul Rahman, known as the Tunku (prince), was educated in Alor Setar, in Bangkok, at the Penang Free School, and at St Catharine's College, Cambridge (1922–5), where he acquired the reputation of a playboy and failed to take a degree. In 1931 he entered the Kedah government service. In 1938 he started legal training at the Inner Temple but returned to Malaya on the outbreak of war. When the Japanese invaded in December 1941, he prevented the retreating British from taking his father with them, on the ground that the ruler should remain with his people. During the occupation Japan restored Kedah to Siam, and the Tunku continued in state administration.

The aftermath of war was a turbulent period for Malaya. The upheaval of the Japanese occupation was exacerbated by rice shortages, racial conflict, and a crisis in Anglo-Malay relations over the Malayan Union constitution, whose provisions to reduce the sultan's authority and to offer citizenship to non-Malays provoked unprecedented opposition from Malays, who feared being overwhelmed by the Chinese. Led by Dato Onn bin Jaafar, they formed the United Malays National Organization (UMNO) and forced the British to replace the union with a federation (February 1948), which safeguarded the Malays' political position. Although Abdul Rahman participated in the struggle against the Malayan Union, he resumed legal studies at the Inner Temple in 1947. Having been called to the bar, in 1949 he joined the Kedah legal department, later transferring to the federal legal department as a deputy public prosecutor.

Shortly after the resolution of the crisis in Anglo-Malay relations the Chinese-dominated Malayan Communist Party launched an armed struggle. The consequent emergency (1948–60) aggravated the polarization of Malays and the Chinese, and when Dato Onn proposed to bring them together by opening UMNO to non-Malays he was forced out of the party. Somewhat surprisingly, the Tunku emerged as his successor and resigned his government appointment. A Malay prince, the Tunku could be relied

Tunku Abdul Rahman (1902–1990), by unknown photographer, pubd 1959

upon to preserve the communal identity of UMNO; English-educated and experienced in government, he was equipped to champion Malay interests in negotiations with the British. Like Dato Onn, however, the Tunku recognized the need to reach an accommodation with non-Malays. His approach was far less precipitate than Onn's: he worked for the formation of what became known as the Alliance, a coalition between UMNO and the non-communist Malayan Chinese Association and Malayan Indian Congress.

The British at first dismissed the Tunku as lightweight, and were concerned that his Alliance would institutionalize rather than bridge communal divisions. The first federal elections of July 1955, when the Alliance won fifty-one of the fifty-two elected seats, established the Tunku's nationalist credentials. He was appointed chief minister, and, after he had refused to compromise with the Communist leader Chin Peng during the Baling talks (December 1955), the British accepted the Alliance demand for independence by 31 August 1957 at the London conference in January–February 1956. The elaborate independence constitution, drafted by a commission of Commonwealth jurists chaired by Lord Reid, attempted to strike a balance between the rights of all Malayan citizens on the one hand and the special privileges of the Malays on the other. In effect it confirmed Malay control of government and Chinese economic dominance. As prime minister of independent Malaya, Abdul Rahman retained close links with Britain through the sterling area, the Commonwealth, and the Anglo-Malayan defence arrangement. In 1963 Malaya merged with the former British colonies of Singapore, Sarawak, and North Borneo (renamed Sabah) to form Malaysia, with the Tunku as head of government.

Tunku Abdul Rahman was robustly anti-communist, genuinely committed to non-communalism, and unashamedly reliant on his loyal deputy, Tun Abdul Razak. Although he presented himself as the happy prince presiding over a multiracial society, the security of the country, race relations, and eventually his own political position were subjected to immense strain. In 1963 Indonesia launched a three-year but unsuccessful armed 'confrontation' against Malaysia. Then Lee Kuan Yew's political ambitions and vigorous campaign for a 'Malaysian Malaysia' proved too much for Alliance leaders, who forced the secession of Singapore in August 1965. Third, radical Malays criticized the Tunku's compromises with the Chinese, who for their part complained that they were relegated to the status of second-class citizens. Following general elections in May 1969, communal tensions erupted in violence, which effectively ended the Tunku's political career. In September 1970 he was succeeded as prime minister and party leader by Tun Abdul Razak. From 1970 to 1973 the Tunku served as secretary-general of the Islamic Secretariat in Jiddah. Having retired to Penang, he took up journalism with the *Star*, and, although he had not been noticeably squeamish about detaining opponents when prime minister, in old age he was an outspoken but inviolable critic of the authoritarianism of Dr Mahathir (prime minister from 1981). He died in Kuala Lumpur on 6 December 1990. Abdul Rahman was thrice married and his children included four whom he adopted. His third wife, whom he married in 1939, was Sharifah Rodziah binti Saiyid Alwi Barakbah (d. 2000). Among his many honours and titles were the awards of Companion of Honour (1961) and an honorary doctorate of law from Cambridge (1960).

The relatively smooth transfer of colonial power to the Alliance convinced some that Abdul Rahman was a British stooge. This taunt misses the mark, for, although he did not acquire the accolade of a 'prison graduate' or bear the scars of a freedom fighter, and while he lacked the charisma of Sukarno and the drive and administrative capacity of Lee Kuan Yew, the Tunku pursued his own political goals, which were shaped by a shrewd assessment of the needs of Malaysia's multiracial society. Indeed, Tunku Abdul Rahman flourished as a consensus politician whose relaxed style and genuine humanity—which more than compensated for an exasperating disinclination to master a brief—helped him steer his country into the post-colonial world.   A. J. STOCKWELL

Sources H. Miller, *Prince and premier: a biography of Tunku Abdul Rahman Putra Al-Haj, first prime minister of the Federation of Malaya* (1959) • A. J. Stockwell, ed., *Malaya*, 3 vols. (1995), ser. B/3 of *British documents on the end of empire* • Tunku Abdul Rahman, *Looking back: Monday musings and memories* (1977) • *The Times* (7 Dec 1990)
Archives Arkib Negara (national archives), Malaysia, UMNO papers | FILM 'End of Empire Malaya', Granada TV (1985)

Likenesses photograph, repro. in Miller, *Prince and premier*, frontispiece [*see illus.*] • photographs, Hult. Arch.

Abdurahman, Abdullah (1872–1940), political leader and physician, was born on 18 December 1872 in Wellington, a country town in south-western Cape Colony, the eldest son of the nine children of Abdul Arraman (also known as Rahman), small trader and civic figure, who was a patron of Cape Muslim welfare and burial societies, and his only wife, Kadija Dollie, seamstress. His parents were Cape Muslims or Cape Malays, and his grandparents were imported Dutch East India Company slaves Abdul and Betsy Jemalee, who had managed to buy their freedom and also, following the British occupation, benefited from the friendship and generosity of Lady Duff Gordon.

Abdurahman was educated at a small Calvinist mission school in Wellington (1877–80), at the Catholic Marist Brothers College, Cape Town (1881–4), and at the South African College, Cape Town (1884–7), where he was the first 'Cape coloured' pupil. Born into a house filled with the optimism of education and belief in the value of British culture, in 1888 he was sent to study medicine at the University of Glasgow, qualifying as a doctor (MB, CM) in 1893. After practical training in London, in 1895 he returned to South Africa, where he established and ran until the late 1930s a flourishing multiracial private medical practice in Cape Town. He was a particularly wealthy member of the tiny urban coloured élite which he embodied so well, his income enabling him to accumulate a large house, expensive cars, a yacht, and a holiday cottage. Abdurahman was a fine vindication of those who believed in the assimilation of respectable, English-speaking coloured people into a common middle-class society, thereby diluting a white-dominated South Africa.

Abdurahman was made richer by his marriages. The first, on 22 May 1894, to the British Helen (Nellie) Potter James (1877–1953), whom he met when a student in Glasgow, produced two daughters before ending in divorce on 17 August 1923. Their younger daughter, Zainunissa (Cissy) Abdurahman (1890–1963), married a Cape Town Indian doctor, A. H. Gool, and became an imposing political figure, devoting most of her life to fighting racial discrimination and poverty as a municipal councillor in Cape Town. Abdurahman's second marriage, on 16 November 1925, was to Margaret May Stansfield; they had two daughters and a son. His widow, like some other coloureds, emigrated to Canada in the 1960s to escape apartheid.

Abdurahman, the gentleman professional, came to public prominence in September 1904 when he was elected the first non-European Cape Town city councillor, a position he held (except for two years, 1913–15) until he died. He rapidly acquired a reputation as a lucid orator and watchful administrator, and became influential in local government through chairing public health, public works, streets and drainage, and numerous other council committees between 1923 and 1937. His exceptional political reach in municipal affairs not only gave him a steady grip on his personal coloured electorate but assured him of attention from white councillors, particularly those from wards with a substantial proportion of coloured voters. Throughout his tenure he pushed for various forms of municipal improvement and welfare intervention to improve living conditions for the Cape Town poor. His expansive legislative presence was buttressed further when, in March 1914, he became the first coloured man elected to the Cape provincial council, a position which he held until his death. In provincial politics he devoted himself to the advocacy of coloured needs in health provision and, especially, schooling.

The importance of education was central to Abdurahman's thinking and to much of his public work because he believed that improving school facilities and standards would enable coloured people to improve their economic and social circumstances in a segregationist order. He worked with Dr A. H. Gool to launch the first secular schooling for Muslim children, and was instrumental in setting up the first two coloured secondary schools in Cape Town, Trafalgar High School in 1911, and Livingstone High School in 1934. Concerned to nourish a political environment of community improvement, in 1913 he spearheaded the formation of the professional Teachers' League of South Africa to mobilize coloured teachers behind a low-key but dogged campaign to reform the segregated education system. While this accomplished little, if anything, Abdurahman's legacy of educational activity was both large and enduring.

Abdurahman's greatest political mark by far came through his involvement in the coloured political organization the African Political (later, Peoples') Organisation (APO), founded in September 1902 in the mood of post-war disillusionment to oppose racial segregation and press Britain to safeguard non-European rights in South Africa after its victory in the Second South African War. Joining the APO in 1903, Abdurahman was elected president in April 1905, unifying its factions around his forceful personality and dominating the organization during his thirty-five-year presidency. While the APO grew into a national body with thousands of members and hundreds of branches, Abdurahman's reputation was such that it became popularly known as Abdurahman's Political Organisation.

The APO was a coloured pressure group, and Abdurahman and the APO initially differentiated between coloureds and Africans: Abdurahman on occasion referred to 'barbarous natives' (Odendaal, 98). In 1906, with the new British Liberal government preparing to grant 'Europeans only' responsible government to the Transvaal and Orange River Colony, Abdurahman campaigned to enfranchise coloureds there. In 1906 he led a delegation to London and argued, against the Liberal ministers' insistence that they were bound by article 8 of the treaty of Vereeniging, that its term 'native' did not apply to coloureds. Their mission failed. From the Queenstown conference (November 1907) Abdurahman co-operated to varying degrees with African politicians. The British Liberal government, continuing its policy of conciliating the Boers, prepared to establish a self-governing union of South Africa, and the national convention (1908–9) there drafted a constitution which the colonial parliaments

approved (June 1909). Although the Cape's non-racial franchise was entrenched, the draft constitution contained crucial colour-bar restrictions. From the start Abdurahman and the APO—in co-operation with William Philip Schreiner and other Cape liberals and with African politicians—campaigned against it. Abdurahman denounced it as 'unjust [and] un-British' (Thompson, 326). Having failed in South Africa, they attempted to persuade the British government and parliament. Abdurahman and other APO leaders joined the 'Coloured and Native Delegation'—called the 'nigger deputation' in the hostile South African press—led by Schreiner which arrived in England in July 1909. They were supported by Sir Charles Dilke and by Labour Party leaders, the London Missionary Society, and the Aborigines Protection Society, but failed to persuade the government. Abdurahman was active in the lobbying and propaganda, and warned, rightly, that the provisions for changing the constitution would lead to the disfranchisement of Cape non-Europeans. The delegates attended the parliamentary debates on the bill: Abdurahman wrote that the archbishop of Canterbury's speech was 'the most hypocritical piece of humbug I ever listened to' (Odendaal, 221). In South Africa the agitation against the proposed legislation rallied many more to the APO. From May 1909 it published a fortnightly paper, *A.P.O.*, edited, partly written, and latterly subsidized by Abdurahman.

Abdurahman's British education, cultured manner, and liberal beliefs in merit and equality of citizenship for all within modern Western civilization lay at the centre of communal coloured political organization for decades, while his patronage of clubs and musical and debating societies helped to mesh the common interests of English- and Afrikaans-speaking Muslim, Christian, and Indian élites. Under his direction the APO ventured beyond ethnic coloured mobilization against segregation, between 1927 and 1934 attempting to negotiate a united black political front in collaboration with African leaders such as Davison Don Tengo Jabavu. This came to nothing, and Abdurahman ended as he had started, a sectional leader obliged by circumstances to press for the advancement of his subordinated community. Although he was not the only coloured leader—his rivals included John Tobin—Abdurahman's reputation with the coloured electorate—significant in Cape politics—enabled him to attempt to influence the main political parties, though he never became a member of any of them. In 1904 he was supported by the Afrikaner Bond, but in 1908 he supported the Progressive Party, and after union the Unionist Party and its successors, the South African and United parties.

Abdurahman's moderate tactics of bargaining, compromise, and negotiation with sympathetic white liberal interests brought derisory political dividends, and by the later 1930s a younger generation of radicals in groups such as the left-wing National Liberation League were denouncing him for favouring middle-class coloured rights at the expense of working-class struggle and black unity. But he retained his personal popularity among his coloured constituency, and it was only after his sudden death that the APO went into serious decline.

Abdurahman died of cardiac arrest at his home, 60 Lower Kloof Street, Cape Town, on 2 February 1940, and was buried on 3 February at Maitland cemetery, Cape Town. His funeral attracted over 30,000 mourners, with Cape Town city council providing a guard of honour. He remains the single most prominent personality in coloured South African politics, a stature underlined in 1999 when President Nelson Mandela awarded him a posthumous order for meritorious service, class 1 (gold), for his contribution to the struggle against racial oppression.

BILL NASSON

Sources DSAB · M. Adhikari, 'Abdullah Abdurahman', *They shaped our century: the most influential South Africans of the twentieth century* (1999), 437–41 · G. Lewis, *Between the wire and the wall: a history of South African 'coloured' politics* (1987) · I. Goldin, *Making race: the politics and economics of coloured identity in South Africa* (1987) · A. Odendaal, *Vukani Bantu! The beginnings of black protest politics in South Africa to 1912* (1984) · R. E. van der Ross, *The rise and decline of apartheid: a study of political movements among the coloured people of South Africa, 1880–1985* (1986) · G. M. Gerhart and T. Karis, eds., *From protest to challenge: a documentary history of African politics in South Africa, 4: Political profiles, 1882–1964* (1977) · S. Trapido, 'The origin and development of the African Political Organisation', *The societies of southern Africa in the 19th and 20th centuries*, 1 (1970), 89–111 · *Cape Times* (20 Feb 1940) · *Cape Argus* (20 Feb 1940) · *Die Burger* (21 Feb 1940) · *The Sun* [Cape Town] (23 Feb 1940) · *Indian Opinion* (23 Feb 1940) · *Cape Standard* (27 Feb 1940) · *South African Medical Journal* (9 March 1940) · W. I. Addison, *A roll of graduates of the University of Glasgow from 31st December 1727 to 31st December 1897* (1898) · J. H. Raynard, 'Dr Abdullah Abdurahman: the man and his work', *The Sun* [Cape Town] (1 March–21 June 1940) [ser. of sixteen articles] · L. M. Thompson, *The unification of South Africa, 1902–1910* (1960) · R. Hyam, *Elgin and Churchill at the colonial office, 1905–1908* (1968) **Archives** priv. coll., papers · U. Lond., Institute of Commonwealth Studies, corresp. and papers · University of South Africa, Pretoria, Documentation Centre for African Studies, family papers | University of Cape Town, Waradia Abdurahman's collection, papers **Likenesses** C. Marston, oils, 1910, Trafalgar High School, Roeland Street, Cape Town, South Africa

Abdy, Edward Strutt (1791–1846), campaigner against slavery and racism, was the fifth and youngest son of Thomas Abdy Abdy, born Thomas Abdy Rutherford (1755–1798), Church of England clergyman of Albyns, Essex, and his wife, Mary, daughter of James Hayes of Holyport, Buckinghamshire, a bencher of the Middle Temple. He was probably born in Essex. He was educated at Felsted School and Jesus College, Cambridge, from where he graduated BA in 1813 and proceeded MA in 1817. He was elected to a fellowship there. Admitted to the Middle Temple on 19 June 1813, he did not practise law because of his poor health.

Nothing is known of Abdy's life between 1817 and 1833. By the latter date he was well enough known in progressive circles to be part of the delegation led by William Crawford of the Society for the Improvement of Prison Discipline and the Reformation of Juvenile Offenders which visited the United States of America between April 1833 and October 1834 to examine two American prison systems which might provide a model for prison reform at home. Abdy's main personal interest, however, was in the

condition of the black population of the USA ('Africo-Americans' as he called them) and the relations between blacks and whites. His *Journal of a Residence and Tour* (1835), which he published in three volumes on his return, is the principal source of information for his life and an important source for the history of slavery and racism in the USA because of his firsthand observations of anti-black and anti-abolitionist riots and of attitudes of whites to blacks. He writes with deep feeling about the treatment of blacks in the USA, particularly in non-slave-holding states where the delegation was conducting its investigations and where he was appalled at the systematic racism he encountered. He was convinced of the importance of free trade to the fight against slavery and was a member of the Anti-Corn Law League until he resigned in 1845 after the league had made alliances with anti-tariff slave owners from the southern United States. He made his resignation public in one of a number of letters he published on the subject of slavery in *The Liberator* and the *National Anti-Slavery Standard*, both American publications. He had close contact with prominent abolitionists in the USA including Maria Weston Chapman and her sisters Anne and Deborah, and seems to have influenced the views on slavery of William Ellery Chapman and Lydia Maria Child. He played a part in the formation of the (American) Anti-Slavery League.

It is not known where Abdy settled on his return to England or how he spent his later years, though he kept his interest in abolition and the treatment of free black people, publishing a pamphlet entitled *American Whites and Blacks: in Reply to a German Orthodermist* (1842) in which he argued for the mixing of the races. His published letters on abolition were sent from the University Club, London, but he died in Bath on 12 October 1846. He was probably in Bath to take the waters: he had been in poor health for much of his life and had become interested in the subject of cures, publishing in 1842 *The Water Cure*, a translation of a pamphlet by Rudolf von Falkenstein. In his will he left £500 to Maria Weston Chapman to promote work against slavery. He was unmarried.

ELIZABETH BAIGENT

Sources E. Abdy, *Journal of a residence and tour in the United States of North America*, 3 vols. (1835) · private information (2004) [H. Morris] · M. Weston Chapman, 'Edward Abdy', *Liberty Bell* (1847) · H. Morris, ed., 'Channing in a bad light', www. EarlyRepublic.net/jmisc [*Jacksonian Miscellanies*, 88], 19 Oct 1999 · Venn, *Alum. Cant.* · *DNB* · T. F. Harwood, 'Prejudice and anti-slavery: the colloquy between William Ellery Channing and Edward Strutt Abdy, 1834', *American Quarterly*, 18 (1966), 697–700 · C. Taylor, *British and American abolitionists* (1974) · C. Taylor, *Women of the anti-slavery movement: the Weston sisters* (1994) · J. Hutchinson, ed., *A catalogue of notable Middle Templars: with brief biographical notices* (1902)

Abdy [*née* Smith], **Maria** (*c*.1800–1867), poet, was the daughter of Richard Smith, a solicitor, and his wife, Maria, *née* Smith (1773–1828/9), who was the daughter of a solicitor and sister of James *Smith (1775–1839) and Horatio (Horace) *Smith (1779–1849), joint authors of the famous poetic parodies *Rejected Addresses* (1812). Very little is known about her life, apart from the fact that her first years were spent in the neighbourhood of Russell Square,

London. Although from a dissenting family on her mother's side, in 1821 she married J. Channing Abdy, a curate who two years later took over from his father, the Revd W. J. Abdy (*d.* 1823), as rector of St John's, Southwark. At least one of her hymns was written for his church, on the occasion of the centenary of its consecration. This was published in her first volume, modestly entitled *Poetry* (1834) and signed Mrs Abdy. Seven further volumes followed between 1838 and 1862, each with identical title-pages except for the date and number series (second series, third series, and so on), published for private circulation by a local printer. They are not, as has sometimes been supposed, reprints of each other, although a few poems do make more than one appearance. A voracious reader in her youth (see 'The Last New Book', *Poetry*, 3rd ser. 1842), and the recipient of comic poems from her uncle Horace, Maria Abdy had begun her own writing at an early age, and was apparently encouraged into publication by her husband, no doubt in the service of the church. Yet not all of her poems deal with pious subjects: she contributed to a number of periodicals (the *New Monthly* and the *Metropolitan* magazines) and annuals such as *The Keepsake* and the *Book of Beauty*. While some poems undertake serious social criticism of the working conditions of young single women ('The Dressmaker', for example, and a number of poems on the plight of the governess), others in a lighter vein display a shrewd sense of humour. 'The Chaperon's Complaint' (*Poetry*, 6th ser., 1854) is one such example of her gift for social satire. She had at least one child, Albert Channing, born in 1828, who later became an Anglican priest. Widowed in 1845, Maria Abdy died at 7 Marine Terrace, Margate, Kent, on 19 July 1867 and was buried at St Peter's churchyard, Isle of Thanet.

VIRGINIA H. BLAIN

Sources A. H. Beavan, *James and Horace Smith: a family narrative* (1899) · *DNB* · Blain, Clements & Grundy, *Feminist comp.* · *GM*, 4th ser., 4 (1867) · *CGPLA Eng. & Wales* (1867)

Wealth at death under £10,000: probate, 9 Aug 1867, *CGPLA Eng. & Wales*

À Beckett, Arthur William (1844–1909), humorist and journalist, the third son of Gilbert Abbott *À Beckett (1811–1856) and Mary Anne Glossop (1817–1863), was born at Portland House, North End, Fulham, on 25 October 1844. He was educated at Honiton, then at Felsted School (1858–9). His eldest brother was Gilbert Arthur *À Beckett (1837–1891). Like so many contemporary journalists, including both his brothers, his first journalism was in part supported by a clerkship, in Arthur's case, at the War Office. From there he migrated to the Post Office, but left the civil service altogether after only three years in 1865. Journalism was always his first vocation, but at various times he took other employment. From 1871 to 1874 he was private secretary to the fifteenth duke of Norfolk. He resigned in the same year that he, like his close friend, Francis Cowley Burnand, converted to Roman Catholicism. In 1877 he joined Gray's Inn and was called to the bar in 1882, but never practised; in 1887, however, he served as Master of the Revels at his inn of court.

From 1865 to 1868 À Beckett assisted Burnand with a

Arthur William À Beckett (1844–1909), by Lafayette, pubd 1907

penny evening humorous paper, the *Glow-Worm*; and from 1868 to 1870 edited the magazine *Britannia*. Although he did not consider it important at the time, his most significant editorship was of the short-lived weekly *Tomahawk*, which combined satire, informed rumour, and social intelligence. It owed something to contemporary Parisian models, but was designed for a very specific English readership. *Tomahawk* was the inspiration for and progenitor of Gibson Bowles's later enormously successful *Vanity Fair*. A prolific, facile writer, À Beckett engaged tirelessly, but with little distinction, in a multitude of literary tasks. He was by turn, and often simultaneously, novelist, dramatist, versifier, humorist, and editor. During the Franco-Prussian War of 1870–71 he acted as special correspondent to the *Globe* and the *Standard*. This experience kindled an enthusiasm for 'amateur soldiering' which he indulged as a militia captain commanding a company of the 4th battalion of the Cheshire regiment. For a year, in 1896, he edited the *Naval and Military Magazine*.

À Beckett's longest, most significant, literary connection was with *Punch*. The title of one of his volumes of recollections, *The À Becketts of Punch* (1903), reveals that he thought of the magazine almost as a family property. He claimed, incorrectly, that his father was one of its founders. To his chagrin his earliest contributions to *Punch* were refused. But in May 1874 he was asked to contribute, and in August of the following year he was made a member of the staff. *Punch* never had a more ardent devotee. In

1880 Burnand became editor and, after a short, initial period of reforming activity, he appointed À Beckett as his deputy. Known by everyone in the literary world, popular, cheerful, self-assured, and careless, À Beckett presided over *Punch*'s decline into decrepitude. He would have nothing changed; all new blood was excluded. What at first had been gay, spontaneous, novel, became by repetition dull, predictable, and mechanical. Eventually, in 1902, the long-suffering proprietors were obliged to act: À Beckett, confidently expecting to be made editor, was instead asked to resign. His amazement, outrage, wounded ambition, and injured pride at this unexpected outcome were thoroughly indulged in a rambling, autobiographical fragment, *Recollections of a Humorist* (1907).

From 1893 to 1895 À Beckett also served as working editor of the *Sunday Times*. With such a double burden, even his irrepressible energy could guarantee neither accuracy nor originality. Yet egotism and naivety were so balanced in his character that he could as little appreciate his faulty work at the *Sunday Times*, or understand why Cardinal Manning was not anxious to purchase a loss-making sporting sheet on his recommendation, as comprehend why he had been dismissed from *Punch*. He had little real talent as a journalist. His geniality, abundant charm, and kindliness best explain how he managed for so many years to keep a number of demanding and important jobs. He was a good committee man, serving the Society of Authors from 1891 until 1903, and was an office holder and president of the Newspaper Society (1893–4) and the Institute of Journalists (1900–01).

On 17 February 1876, À Beckett married Susannah Frances, only daughter of Forbes Winslow MD; they had two sons. Susannah was an occasional contributor to various magazines, and a vice-president of the Society of Women Journalists. À Beckett died of post-operative shock on 14 January 1909, after the amputation of a leg; he was buried in Mortlake Catholic cemetery.   A. J. A. MORRIS

Sources A. À Beckett, *The À Becketts of Punch: memories of father and sons* (1903) • A. W. À Beckett, *Recollections of a humorist* (1907) • A. W. À Beckett, *Green-room recollections* (1896) • *The Times* (19 Jan 1909), 12–15 • *ILN* (23 Jan 1909) • R. G. G. Price, *A history of Punch* (1957) • M. H. Spielmann, *The history of 'Punch'* (1895) • *WW*
Likenesses H. Furniss, pen and pencil sketch, NPG • Lafayette, photograph, repro. in À Beckett, *Recollections of a humorist [see illus.]* • portrait, repro. in *ILN* (18 Jan 1909)

À Beckett, Gilbert Abbott (1811–1856), comic writer and police magistrate, was born at The Grange, Hampstead, Middlesex, on 17 February 1811, the third son of William A'Beckett (1777–1855), a reform solicitor, and his wife, Sarah Abbott. His forebears were an ancient Wiltshire family, who traced their ancestry back to the fourteenth century and claimed descent from St Thomas a Becket. He entered Westminster School on 10 January 1820, and remained there until August 1828. At this time, according to his son Arthur William *À Beckett (À Beckett, 15), À Beckett quarrelled with his father and did not see him thereafter for more than two decades. On leaving school, he and his older brothers William *A'Beckett (1806–1869), who went on to become chief justice in Australia, and

Gilbert Abbott À Beckett (1811–1856), attrib. Charles Couzens, 1855

Thomas, who also later emigrated to Australia, founded *The Censor*, a youthfully ebullient journal of ephemera, gossip, tales, and theatre notices. Appearing bi-weekly from 6 September 1828 to 4 April 1829, *The Censor* was the first of a series of short-lived periodicals of which À Beckett was proprietor and editor, including the *Literary Beacon* (1831), the *Evangelical Penny Magazine* (1832), *The Thief* (1833), and *The Wag* (1837). According to his enemy Alfred Bunn, who later attacked him as Sleekhead, À Beckett founded thirteen papers, 'all total failures' (Bunn, 6).

With *Figaro in London*, however, À Beckett developed a formula (modelled on the Paris prototype) which proved both successful and influential. Embellished by the cartoons of Robert Seymour, *Figaro* was dominated by gossip, humorous squibs, and above all circumstantial, opinionated, often scurrilous theatre reviews. Walter Jerrold referred to it as a journal of 'ready fun and … the daring of youth' (Jerrold, *Douglas Jerrold*, 4), and by the time À Beckett handed the editorship over to his friend Henry Mayhew, three years after its first number had appeared on 10 December 1831, the weekly penny magazine had a circulation of 70,000 and was reputed to have brought its editor an income of more than £1000 a year. Its popularity fed directly into the far greater and longer-lasting success of *Punch*, for which À Beckett was the most prolific contributor from its first appearance in 1841 until the time of his death fifteen years later: Spielmann later wrote that in column inches, his copy must have neared the height of the Eiffel Tower (Altick, 44). He was also a leader writer for

The Times and the Morning Herald, and as The Perambulating Philosopher he contributed regularly to the Illustrated London News.

During these years À Beckett was vigorously pursuing his interest in the theatre, not only as a reviewer but as a playwright: as house writer for the Coburg Theatre and as lessee of the Fitzroy. Some forty plays by his hand (several written in collaboration with Mark Lemon, first editor of Punch) were published, and a further twenty have been traced in the lord chamberlain's collection or in contemporary playbills. The earliest was The King Incog, performed at the Fitzroy on 9 January 1834; the last Sardanapalus, or, The 'Fast' King of Assyria, performed at the Adelphi on 20 July 1853. Others included The Revolt of the Work-House (Fitzroy, 24 February 1834); The Man with the Carpet Bag (Strand, 19 January 1835); The Chimes, adapted by À Beckett and Lemon from Dickens's Christmas book and performed at the Adelphi on 19 December 1844; and Timour, or, The Cream of Tartar, adapted from Monk Lewis's Timour the Tartar (Princess, 24 March 1845). À Beckett's characteristic mode was theatrical burlesque, and he is recognized as a 'mainstay' of that form in its heyday (Adams, 33). He also wrote Scenes from the Rejected Comedies (1844), a volume of parodies of plays by his contemporaries, including James Sheridan Knowles, Douglas Jerrold, Thomas Noon Talfourd, and Edward Bulwer-Lytton.

Working in collaboration with his associates on Punch, À Beckett wrote a number of volumes of burlesque prose, including The Comic Blackstone (1844), illustrated by George Cruikshank, which had originally appeared in Punch, The Comic History of England (1847), and The Comic History of Rome (1851), both illustrated by John Leech. Each of these was frequently reprinted throughout the rest of the century. He edited George Cruikshank's Table Book (1845), and along with Thackeray, Albert Smith, and the Mayhew brothers À Beckett was a contributor to The Comic Almanack (1835–53). Under the pseudonym Poz he wrote imitations of Dickens, Oliver Twiss, the Workhouse Boy (four weekly parts, 1838) and Posthumous Papers of the Wonderful Discovery Club (1838), a children's book illustrated by Leech, Hop o' my Thumb (1844), and a book of humour also illustrated by Leech, The Fiddle Faddle Fashion Book (no date).

At the same time as he was engaged in these literary and theatrical activities, À Beckett was building a legal career. He entered Gray's Inn on 25 April 1828 and was called to the bar on 27 January 1841, soon earning a reputation as an 'excellent and upright lawyer' (The Times, 3 Sept 1856). He worked for a time with the poor-law commission, writing well-received reports on the laws of settlement and removal and on the Andover workhouse scandal. On the strength of these reports he was appointed in 1849 as a Metropolitan Police magistrate, first for Greenwich and latterly for Southwark, where he was noted for his benevolence in distributing funds from the poor box to the deserving poor, and for his 'acuteness, humanity and impartiality' in rendering justice; 'one of the best' magistrates of his day, was the verdict of The Times in its obituary notice (ibid.).

À Beckett was a member of the Reform Club from 1841,

and of the Garrick Club from 1842. On 21 January 1835 he married Mary Anne (1817–1863), daughter of Joseph Glossop, the builder of the Coburg Theatre. They had four sons, including Gilbert Arthur *À Beckett (1837–1891), and two daughters. From 1845 to 1847 they lived at Portland House, Fulham, Middlesex, and from 1848 until his death in 1856 their address was 10 Hyde Park Gate South, Kensington Gore, London. Their style of living seems to have been beyond their means, because a number of surviving letters in the Punch archives are pleas to his publisher, Frederick Evans, for advances on wages due to him, and three years after his death his widow successfully petitioned the Royal Literary Fund for financial assistance, and was granted £60.

On 30 August 1856, while on holiday with his family in France, À Beckett died suddenly and unexpectedly of typhus at Boulogne, predeceased by one of his sons from the same fever. Expressions of admiration for his 'great ability' and grief at his death are to be found in the letters of Dickens (Letters of Charles Dickens, 4.137; 8.179–82) and of Jerrold (Jerrold, Douglas Jerrold, 2.636–42), whom À Beckett was visiting in Boulogne at the time. His remains were later removed to Highgate cemetery, where a monument was erected to his memory. Its inscription (reproduced in Illustrated London News, 13 June 1857) repeats Jerrold's praise in the Punch obituary (13 September 1856) of À Beckett as 'a genial manly spirit; singularly gifted with the subtlest powers of wit and humour; faculties ever exercised by their possessor to the healthiest and most innocent purpose'.   PAUL SCHLICKE

Sources A. À Beckett, The À Becketts of Punch: memories of father and sons (1903) • M. H. Spielmann, The history of 'Punch' (1895) • A. Bunn, A word with Punch (1847) • The Times (3 Sept 1856) • The Critic (15 Sept 1856), 436–7 • ILN (6 Sept 1856), 248 • ILN (13 June 1857), 570 • H. Vizetelly, Glances back through seventy years: autobiographical and other reminiscences, 2 vols. (1893) • D. Jerrold, Punch, 31 (1856), 101 • The letters of Charles Dickens, ed. M. House, G. Storey, and others, 12 vols. (1965–2002) • W. Jerrold, Douglas Jerrold, dramatist and wit, 2 vols. [1914] • W. B. Jerrold, Jerrold's Punch (1910) • Old Westminsters, vols. 1–2 • W. D. Adams, A book of burlesque (1891) • F. C. Burnand, 'Mr Punch: his predecessors and competitors', Pall Mall Magazine, 29 (Jan–April 1903), 390–97 • R. D. Altick, 'Punch': the lively youth of a British institution, 1841–1851 (1997)
Archives Wilts. & Swindon RO, family tree of À Becketts | Punch offices, London, archives • PRO, poor-law reports
Likenesses attrib. C. Couzens, watercolour miniature, 1855, NPG [see illus.] • J. Leech, engraving, repro. in Punch (9 Jan 1847) • engraving, repro. in À Beckett, À Becketts of Punch • miniature, priv. coll.

À Beckett, Gilbert Arthur (1837–1891), playwright and satirist, born at Portland House, Fulham, Middlesex, on 7 April 1837, was the eldest son of Gilbert Abbott *À Beckett (1811–1856), journalist and Metropolitan Police magistrate, and his wife, Mary Anne (1817–1863), composer, daughter of Joseph Glossop, clerk of the cheque to the Honourable Corps of Gentlemen-at-Arms. He entered Westminster School on 6 June 1849, became a queen's scholar in 1851, was elected to Christ Church, Oxford, in 1855, and graduated BA in 1860. On 15 October 1857 he entered Lincoln's Inn, but was never called to the bar. Instead, in 1858 he took a clerkship at the Treasury, until June 1862, when he became a clerk in the office of the

Gilbert Arthur À Beckett (1837–1891), by Bassano

examiners of criminal law accounts. In 1865 he gave up this appointment to concentrate on journalism. For the next three years he contributed to *The Glowworm* and other journals and began to send occasional contributions to *Punch*.

À Beckett turned his attention to writing for the stage in 1867, and on 4 March 1867 his first play, *Diamonds and Hearts*, a comedy, was performed at the Haymarket, with moderate success. Three more of his comedies were produced within a six-month period: *Glitter* (St James's Theatre, 26 December 1868); *Red Hands* (St James's, 30 January 1869); and *Face to Face* (Prince of Wales, Liverpool, 29 March 1869). *Red Hands* was the best received of these plays, with *The Times* noting that 'The good folks are thoroughly good, the bad are villains of the deepest dye, and the best dressed man in the story is, according to established precedent, the greatest rascal of them all' (*The Times*, 2 Feb 1869).

À Beckett married Emily, eldest daughter of William Hunt JP of Bath; they had a son and a daughter. In 1873 he edited twenty-four numbers of the weekly magazine *Junius*. During this year his play *In the Clouds: an Extravaganza* was performed at the Alexandra on 3 December. Meanwhile, throughout 1873 and 1874 he collaborated with W. S. Gilbert on *The Happy Land*, a burlesque version of *The Wicked World*, and with Herman Merivale on the tragedy *The White Pilgrim*. *The Happy Land*, first performed at the Court Theatre on 3 March 1873, attracted controversy with its caricatures of the three statesmen Gladstone, Lowe, and Ayrton. À Beckett's satire provoked a question in the House of Commons, and the actors were forced to change their make-up and costumes after an official visit to the theatre by the lord chamberlain.

In 1879 À Beckett was invited by Tom Taylor, the editor of *Punch*, to join À Beckett's younger brother Arthur on the permanent staff of the magazine. Three years later he was 'appointed to the Table' and dined at the weekly *Punch* dinners until his death. He never became a known popular favourite, but he made the 'How we advertise now' column his speciality. He also wrote an acclaimed parody of a boy's sensational shocker (March 1882), and he provided

the idea for one of Sir John Tenniel's best cartoons for *Punch*, entitled *Dropping the Pilot*, depicting Bismarck's resignation in 1889.

À Beckett not only participated in his family's journalistic tradition but, like his mother, was also an accomplished musician, and during the early 1880s he wrote songs and music for the German Reeds' entertainment. In 1883 he published, with his brother Arthur William *À Beckett, *The Comic Guide to the Royal Academy*, which sold well and ran to three editions. In the following year he wrote the librettos for Charles Villiers Stanford's operas *The Canterbury Pilgrims*, produced at Hamburg on 18 April 1884, and *Savonarola*, produced at Covent Garden on 9 July of the same year. In his last years he wrote the lyrics for the operetta *La cigale*, which at the time of his death was nearing its 400th performance at the Lyric Theatre.

In 1889 À Beckett suffered a great shock from the death by drowning of his only son. Some years earlier he himself had fallen down the steps of Gower Street Station, which had left him partially paralysed in both legs and in delicate health. He died at his home, 12 Michael's Grove, South Kensington, London, on 15 October 1891 and was buried in Mortlake Catholic cemetery. *Punch* devoted some appreciative stanzas to his memory, bearing the epigraph 'Wearing the white flower of a blameless life' (24 Oct 1891). He was survived by his wife, and his only daughter, Minna, who in 1896 married Hugh Clifford (*d.* 1907) CMG, governor of Labuan and British North Borneo.

KATHERINE MULLIN

Sources M. H. Spielmann, *The history of 'Punch'* (1895), 381–4 • *ILN* (24 Oct 1891), 531 • *The Athenaeum* (24 Oct 1891), 558 • *The Era* (24 Oct 1891) • Foster, *Alum. Oxon.* • Boase, *Mod. Eng. biog.* • *The Times* (2 Feb 1869) • *The Times* (19 Oct 1891) • *The Gazette* (21 March 1821) • *Old Westminsters*, vols. 1–2 • *DNB* • *BL cat.*

Archives BL

Likenesses Bassano, photograph, NPG [*see illus.*] • R. T., pencil sketch, NPG; repro. in *ILN* • R. T., wood-engraving (after photograph by A. Bassano), NPG; repro. in *ILN*

Wealth at death £48: probate, 12 Nov 1891, *CGPLA Eng. & Wales*

A'Beckett, Sir William (1806–1869), judge, was born on 28 July 1806 in London, the eldest son of William A'Beckett (1777–1855), solicitor, and his wife, Sarah, *née* Abbott. After attending Westminster School and serving articles with his father, he determined on the bar and was called at Lincoln's Inn on 30 June 1829. A relatively briefless barrister, he wrote biographical sketches for publication. On 1 October 1832 at St Pancras, he married his cousin Emily, daughter of Edward Hayley. She died in June 1841; he married her younger sister, Matilda, at Melbourne on 30 October 1849. (The UK act of 1835, rendering void marriages within the prohibited degrees celebrated subsequently, did not extend to New South Wales.) Four sons and a daughter were born of the first marriage; the second was childless.

A'Beckett went to Sydney in 1836 and practised at the bar. He was appointed solicitor-general of New South Wales in March 1841 and acting judge of the supreme court in July 1844. On 3 February 1846 he became resident judge of that court for the district of Port Phillip (as Victoria was called before its separation from New South Wales) and moved to Melbourne. On the establishment of the supreme court of Victoria, following separation in 1851, A'Beckett was made chief justice (19 January 1852). His knighthood (24 November 1852) had been sought through his brother, Gilbert Abbott *À Beckett.

In 1852 A'Beckett published, under the name Colonus, a pamphlet *Does the discovery of gold in Victoria … deserve to be considered a national blessing, or a national curse?* He thought the latter. He published a manual for magistrates (1852), a travel book, *Out of Harness* (1854), and volumes of poetry in 1824, 1829, and 1863. His poems are favourably discussed by Clifford Pannam; his judicial decisions by E. G. Coppel, who described him as 'a sound lawyer'.

A'Beckett had suffered from paralysis in the legs since the late 1840s. He retired in February 1857 and remained in Melbourne until 1863 when he returned to England. He died at his residence in Church Road, Upper Norwood, Surrey, on 27 June 1869.   PETER BALMFORD

Sources E. G. Coppel, 'The first chief justice of Victoria', *Australian Law Journal*, 27 (1953), 209–22 · P. de Serville, *Pounds and pedigrees: the upper class in Victoria, 1850–80* (1991) · C. Pannam, *Sir William's muse: the literary works of the first chief justice of Victoria, Sir William a'Beckett* (1992) · G. Serle, *The golden age: a history of the colony of Victoria, 1851–1861* (1963) · *Melbourne Monthly Magazine*, 2 (1855), 29–30 · *AusDB* · *The Times* (1 July 1869), 10e · J. M. Bennett, *Sir William a'Beckett: first chief justice of Victoria, 1852–1857* (2001)

Likenesses attrib. H. Moseley, oils, *c.*1867, Library of the Supreme Court of Victoria, Melbourne, Australia · T. a'Beckett, portrait, repro. in B. Niall, *Martin Boyd: a life*, rev. edn (1990), facing p. 34 · T. Chuck, photograph, State Library of Victoria, Australia · T. Chuck, photograph (part of composite *Supreme Court Bench, 1852–94*), State Library of Victoria, Australia · H. S. Sadd, engraving (after drawing by E. Dalton), State Library of Victoria, Australia

Abel (*fl.* 744–747), suffragan bishop of Rheims, first appears in the acts of the Council of Soissons in March 744, which record the elevation of himself and one Hartbert to the status of archbishops, although the acts mention no specific sees. Historians have considered these appointments as a restoration of the lapsed ancient Gallic provincial organization under the inspiration of St Boniface, by whose initiative the synod had been convened. In June of the same year Pope Zacharias wrote and sent pallia at Boniface's request to confirm the latter's appointment of Abel to the see of Rheims, along with Hartbert to Sens and Grimo to Rouen, and to acknowledge their professions of faith. Zacharias was therefore surprised to receive another letter from Boniface written that August which requested a pallium only for Grimo, and he wrote back to ask why Boniface had omitted mention of Abel and Hartbert this time. If a reply was forthcoming, it has not survived. Abel seems never to have been confirmed as archbishop. His next and final appearance is as one of five 'co-bishops' who, along with Boniface, addressed a letter in 746 or 747 to Æthelbald, king of Mercia, castigating the king for his adultery.

Before his promotion at Soissons, Abel may have been a monk in the monastery of Lobbes (canton Hainault) under Abbot-Bishop Ermino (*d.* 737). However, this information is given only by the late tenth-century writer Folcuin, who also claimed that Abel was Irish, contradicting the contemporary evidence of a letter of Boniface to the Mercian priest Herefrid describing the co-authors of the letter to Æthelbald as all Anglo-Saxon born and bred. Given the known contacts between Anglo-Saxon monastic figures and Ireland in this period, the possibility that Abel had spent some time in Ireland (as did, for example, Ecgberht (639–729)) is a plausible explanation for Folcuin's statement. The identification of the bishop with the monk was rejected by Levison, but accepted by Ewig.

The elevation of Abel and Hartbert to metropolitan status at the Council of Soissons was clearly intended to end the exploitation of high ecclesiastical offices by lay magnates like Milo, who had control of the see of Rheims, in conjunction with that of Trier, from *c.*722. It is likely that Milo was not a consecrated bishop, but enjoyed the temporalities of these dioceses while the three men, including Abel, who bore the title of bishop at Rheims in this period were suffragans who performed the liturgical and pastoral duties of the episcopal office. Despite the explicit involvement of Pippin III, mayor of the palace and *de facto* ruler of the west Frankish kingdom, in the decrees of the council, it is clear from Pope Zacharias's second letter of 744 and the absence of any further references to Abel as archbishop that this attempt at institutional reform of the west Frankish church failed. Boniface complained again of these abuses to Zacharias in 751.

Some historians, following the report of Hincmar, the ninth-century archbishop of Rheims, have thought that Abel was ejected from his see by Milo in 748 to make way for his successor, Tilpin. However, Milo's death and Tilpin's accession have now been placed more correctly in 762 or 763. With this change to a later date for the end of Milo's control of Rheims there is no longer any secure date for the end of Abel's episcopacy. Although he fades from view entirely after his participation in the letter to Æthelbald in 746 or 747, his title of 'co-bishop' there suggests that a *modus vivendi* had been achieved in Rheims. While naturally drawing on the support of Boniface as a fellow ecclesiastic with an Anglo-Saxon outlook, Abel was more willing to adapt to the circumstances which he found on the continent, and to compromise with the aristocratic families who governed the Frankish church.   MARIOS COSTAMBEYS

Sources A. Werminghoff, ed., *Concilia aevi Karolini*, 2 vols., MGH Concilia, 2 (Hanover, 1906–8); repr. (1979), vol. 2 · M. Tangl, ed., *Die Briefe des heiligen Bonifatius und Lullus*, MGH Epistolae Selectae, 1 (Berlin, 1916); repr. (Munich, 1989), nos. 57–8, 73–4, 87 · Fulcuinus, 'Gesta abbatum Lobiensium', [*Annales, chronica et historiae aevi Carolini et Saxonici*], ed. G. H. Pertz, MGH Scriptores [folio], 4 (1841); repr. (1982) · Hincmar, 'Vita Remigii episcopi Remensis', *Passiones vitaeque sanctorum aevi Merovingici*, ed. B. Krusch, MGH Scriptores Rerum Merovingicarum, 3 (Hanover, 1896); repr. (1977) · E. Ewig, 'Milo et eiusmodi similes', *Spätantikes und fränkisches Gallien: gesammelte Schriften*, ed. H. Atsma, 2 (Munich, 1979), 189–219, esp. 193–4 · E. Ewig, 'Saint Chrodegang et la réforme de l'église franque', *Spätantikes und fränkisches Gallien: gesammelte Schriften*, ed. H. Atsma, 2 (Munich, 1979), 232–59, esp. 238 · W. Levison, *England and the continent in the eighth century* (1946)

Abel, Clarke (*c.***1780–1826**), naturalist and surgeon, was educated for the medical profession and served as a surgeon in Norwich. He is sometimes styled MD but it is not clear if he qualified as such. He accompanied Lord Amherst's embassy to China in 1816 as its chief medical officer. This embassy, which went further into the interior of China than was normally possible, had something of the character of an expedition, and (through the influence of Sir Joseph Banks) Abel acted as its naturalist. He made his reputation with his *Narrative of a Journey in the Interior of China … in the Years 1816 and 1817* (1818).

Abel gathered an extensive collection of botanical and mineralogical specimens in China. On the way back to England these (together with several other collections entrusted to his care) were all lost on 16 February 1817, when the embassy's frigate, HMS *Alceste*, sank in the straits of Gaspar. The only items to escape the disaster were a small collection of plants that he had given to Sir George Staunton, who was based in China and returned to England separately, and some rocks that he gave to Captain Basil Hall, whose gunship was not attached to the returning party. The plants brought back by Staunton were described by Banks's librarian, Robert Brown, in a botanical appendix to Abel's *Narrative*, in which several new species were identified. Brown also defined a genus of shrub within the honeysuckle family, based on material from China, which he named *Abelia* in Abel's honour.

Abel's *Narrative* contains descriptions of the orang-utan and the boa, as well as observations on the geology of the Cape of Good Hope which have been highly praised for their detail and accuracy. He had frequent periods of poor health, including much of the voyage to China. He was elected a fellow of the Royal Society in 1819 with the support of Staunton and Brown among others, and was also a member of the Linnean, Geological, and Asiatic societies, and of the Medical and Physical Society of Calcutta. He was highly esteemed by his colleagues, both for his enthusiasm for natural history and for his agreeable manner. Appointed surgeon to Lord Amherst when the latter became governor general in India, he spent his last years travelling that country. He died at Cawnpore, India, on 24 November 1826. B. D. JACKSON, *rev.* P. E. KELL

Sources C. Abel, *Narrative of a journey in the interior of China* (1818) · *GM*, 1st ser., 97/2 (1827), 644 · *Asiatic Journal*, 23 (1827), 669–70 · *GM*, 1st ser., 88/2 (1818), 518–20 · *Catalogue of scientific papers*, Royal Society, 1 (1867), 4 · Desmond, *Botanists*, rev. edn · *The record of the Royal Society of London*, 4th edn (1940) · G. Long, ed., *The biographical dictionary of the Society for the Diffusion of Useful Knowledge*, 4 vols. in 7 (1842–4)
Likenesses P. W. Wilkins, engravings (after drawings on stone by M. Gauci), RS · portrait, Carnegie Mellon University, Pittsburgh, Hunt Institute · portrait, repro. in A. M. Coats, *The quest for plants* (1969), 94–5

Abel, Sir Frederick Augustus, first baronet (1827–1902), chemist and explosives expert, was born on 17 July 1827 at Woolwich, the eldest son of Johann Leopold Abel (1795–1871), a music master in Kennington, and his wife, Louisa (*d.* 1864), daughter of Martin Hopkins of Walworth. His paternal grandfather, August Christian Andreas Abel (*b.* 1751), was court miniature painter to the grand duke of Mecklenburg-Schwerin.

Abel was attracted to a scientific career by a visit at the

Sir Frederick Augustus Abel, first baronet (1827–1902), by Frank Bramley, 1900

age of fourteen to an uncle in Hamburg, A. J. Abel, a mineralogist and pupil of Berzelius. After a course of chemistry under Dr Ryan at the Royal Polytechnic Institution, he entered the Royal College of Chemistry, founded in October 1845 under A. W. Hofmann, as one of the twenty-six original students. Next year he became an assistant, holding the position for five years. In 1851 he was appointed demonstrator of chemistry at St Bartholomew's Hospital to Dr John Stenhouse, and in March 1852 lecturer on chemistry at the Royal Military Academy at Woolwich in succession to Faraday. With Charles Loudon Bloxam (*d.* 1887), his assistant and successor there, he published a useful *Handbook of Chemistry, Theoretical, Practical, and Technical* (1854; 2nd edn, 1858).

Abel married Sarah Selina (1854–1888), daughter of James Blanch of Bristol. They had no children. He became ordnance chemist at Woolwich on 24 July 1854, and was made chemist to the war department there in January 1856. He retired from Woolwich in 1888. His first wife died in the same year, and on 31 December 1888 he married Guilietta La Feuillade (1853–1892).

At Woolwich, Abel was the chief official authority on all matters connected with explosives. The transformation of arms and ammunition which took place during his tenure necessarily occupied the greater part of his scientific career, though almost every branch of technical science was enriched by his labours. The supersession of black by 'smokeless' powder was due to his researches on gun cotton, founded on the attempts of Baron von Lenk to utilize this explosive in 1862. He developed the process of reducing gun cotton to a fine pulp, which enabled it to be worked and stored without danger; the results were published as *Gun Cotton, a Lecture* (1874) and *The Modern History of Gunpowder* (1879). Another important research, undertaken jointly with Andrew Noble, determined the nature of the chemical changes produced on firing explosives. This work, carried out at great personal risk, threw new light on the theory of explosives. The conclusions were published in various papers and lectures from 1871 to 1880: *On Explosive Agents* (1871), and *Researches on Explosives with Capt. Noble* (1875, 1880).

The explosion in Seaham colliery in 1881 led to the appointment of a royal commission on accidents in coal mines on which Abel served. This in turn prompted his researches on dangerous dusts (1882), in which he investigated the part played by dust in bringing about an explosion. In other directions he reached equally important results. As an expert in petroleum he devised the Abel open-test, with a flashpoint of 100 °F, legalized in 1868, which was superseded in 1879 by the Abel close-test, with a flashpoint of 73 °F. He also carried out many researches into the composition of alloyed metals with reference to their physical properties.

Abel's last piece of work, carried out with James Dewar, was the invention of cordite in 1889. The use of high explosives abroad forced the British government to search for a better material than gun cotton, and a committee was appointed in 1888, under Abel's presidency, to examine all the modern high explosives. None of them was exactly suitable to service requirements, and their inventors would not make the necessary modifications. Abel and Dewar therefore devised and patented a compound of gun cotton and nitroglycerine and assigned it to the secretary of war in 1890. The wording of the patent application was crucial, for it allowed them to circumvent other patents held in the fields of nitroglycerine and nitrocotton explosives, principally those of Alfred Nobel and his company. The selection of gun cotton rather than soluble nitrocellulose seemed to many to have been made purposely to take advantage of a gap left in Nobel's earlier patent for ballistite. Nobel decided to sue when he learned that Abel and Dewar had, early in 1889, seen full specifications of his invention in their capacity as members of the government's explosives committee. The cordite case lasted three years (1892–5); Nobel lost, having no case in law, but many believed that he had been harshly treated.

Abel contributed over sixty-five papers to scientific publications, and some important articles to the ninth edition of the *Encyclopaedia Britannica*. His remarkable powers of organization and his official position as scientific adviser to the government gave him a prominent role in the scientific world. He was elected FRS in 1860, and received the royal medal in 1887. He was successively president of the Chemical Society (1875–7), the Institute of Chemistry (1881–2), the Society of Chemical Industry (1883), and the Institution of Electrical Engineers. He was president of the Iron and Steel Institute in 1891, and was awarded the Bessemer gold medal in 1897. He acted as chairman of the Society of Arts (1883–4) and received the Albert medal in 1891. The Telford medal was bestowed on him by the Institution of Civil Engineers in 1879.

He presided over the chemistry section of the British Association in 1877, and as president of the association in 1890 he gave an address on recent practical applications of science. When the foundation of the Imperial Institute was decided on in 1887, Abel was appointed organizing secretary, remaining its honorary secretary and director from its opening in 1893 until it was transferred to the Board of Trade in 1901. He was made CB in 1877, was knighted in 1883, became KCB in 1891, a baronet in 1893, and GCVO in 1901; he received honorary degrees of DCL (Oxford, 1883) and DSc (Cambridge, 1888). He combined with his scientific capacity high accomplishments as a musician. Abel died of cardiac failure at his residence, 2 Whitehall Court, London, on 6 September 1902 and was buried at Nunhead cemetery on 11 September.

ROBERT STEELE, rev. K. D. WATSON

Sources *JCS*, 87 (1905), 565–70 · *Nature*, 66 (1902), 492–3 · *The Times* (8 Sept 1902) · *The Times* (12 Sept 1902) · F. D. Miles, *A history of research in the Nobel division of ICI* (1955) · m. cert., 1888 · d. cert.
Archives BL OIOC, letters to Sir George Birdwood, MS Eur. F 216 · CKS, letters to Edward Stanhope · CUL, letters to Sir George Stokes · ICL, corresp. with Henry Edward Armstrong · Royal Institution of Great Britain, London, Dewar MSS · Royal Society of Chemistry, London · RS · Wellcome L., corresp. with John Spiller
Likenesses photograph, 1860, RS · M. Thomas, oils, 1877, Inst. EE · F. Bramley, oils, 1900, NPG [*see illus.*] · W. & D. Downey, woodburytype photograph, NPG; repro. in W. Downey and D. Downey, *The cabinet portrait gallery* (1890), vol. 1 · H. J. Whitlock, carte-de-visite (as a young man), NPG · four sepia photographs, RS · photograph, RS · two prints, Chemical Society, London
Wealth at death £21,082 4s. 3d.: probate, 2 Dec 1902, CGPLA Eng. & Wales

Abel, John (1578/9–1675), master carpenter, was probably born and lived at Sarnesfield, Herefordshire. A Catholic recusant, he was brought before a church court in 1618 for contracting a secret marriage with his wife, Johanna. She was still alive in 1640, when she appeared in a list of recusants with her husband. Few other facts are known about Abel's private life. Very little of Abel's work, too, can be firmly documented; by the late eighteenth century he was already a legend and many attributions were made which can no longer be sustained. His name was regularly connected, for instance, with the Hereford market hall (dem. 1862), which was certainly built before he was born. It seems it was the local antiquary John Price who first made this connection in 1796; in 1846 John Clayton, author of *A Collection of Ancient Timber Edifices*, added several more attributions.

Abel's first documented commission was at Kington in 1625, when he signed a contract to build a school according to the terms of the will of Lady Margaret Hawkins: he supplied all the materials and was paid £240. Only a window and some ceiling beams of this building now survive and, being of stone, it was not typical of his later work in timber. In March 1633 he signed another contract 'for the rebuilding and repairing' of Dore Abbey church in Herefordshire (Gregory, 7); here his patron was John, first Viscount Scudamore, a close friend of Archbishop Laud. The work included re-roofing the church, flooring the tower, creating a new bell-frame, and, probably, carving the robust classical screen. The work was completed for the reconsecration service in March 1634 and, apart from some minor reorganization in the nineteenth century, Dore Abbey remains one of the most complete Laudian settings in England. Eighteen years were to pass before 'John Abell of Sarnesfield, carpenter', signed another contract for a 'new building' at Tyberton Court in March 1652, for which he was to be paid £30. A plan of 'The modell of ye New Building' still exists among the Tyberton Court papers—possibly in Abel's hand—which shows the ground floor of a modest house with two rooms, 19 feet and 14 feet respectively, served by a central chimney-stack. The parlour has a large mullioned bay window (Herefs. RO, A81/394).

Three other buildings can be added with some confidence to this list from the collections for the history of Herefordshire made by Thomas Blount of Orleton about 1675. At Sarnesfield, Blount noticed Abel's monument in the churchyard and added that 'he built the several market Houses of Brecnoc, Kington and Lemster' (*History of Herefordshire*, 56). Brecon was built in 1624 (dem. nineteenth century) and Leominster was completed by March 1634. It originally stood in Broad Street, but in 1835 was rebuilt by John Arkwright of Hampton Court, Herefordshire, as the Grange Court, next to the priory church, where it remains, now serving as offices. The building is decidedly Renaissance and 'prodigiously decorated' (Pevsner, 228) with grotesque masks, pilasters, and caryatid figures; it is regarded as Abel's finest work. The Kington market hall was built in 1654 and demolished in 1820; no visual record remains. These market halls were built in timber and had lengthy inscriptions of a pious nature, parts of which have been traced to St Jerome and Cato the elder. Elements of these inscriptions also occur on the screen at Dore Abbey, and also on a fragment of a domestic screen at Monnington Court on the Wye and a tablet in the chancel of Vowchurch church, which was provided with a sturdy new roof in 1613. Thus, two more works may be tentatively added to Abel's *œuvre*. One of the contributors to the restoration of Vowchurch in 1613 was Rowland Vaughan of the New Court in the Golden Valley. Vaughan's book on the 'drowning' of meadows, published in 1610, refers to a 'joyner' and 'levellour … my man John' (Vaughan, 87–8) with whom the squire fell out because he wished to take the credit for Vaughan's waterworks. This seems likely to be John Abel, whose work as a millwright is referred to in the Scudamore correspondence relating to Dore Abbey in 1632.

Thomas Blount also describes an episode in 1645 during the civil war when Abel

> being in Hereford City when the Scots besieged it … made a sort of Mills to grind corn which were of great use to the besieged … for which King Charles the first did afterwards honor him with the Title of one of his Master Carpenters. (*History of Herefordshire*, 56)

The royalist governor of Hereford, Sir Barnabus Scudamore, also wrote about 'an expert carpenter, the only man in all the country to make mills, without whom we had

been much disfurnisht of meanes to make Powder (after our Powder-mill was burnt) or grind corne' (Webb, 388). Quoting another contemporary source, John Webb refers to a siege engine called 'the Sow' which Abel built for Scudamore to deploy against the parliamentary garrison at Canon Frome in October 1645.

John Abel died in January 1675 and was buried in Sarnesfield churchyard on 31 January; he was in his ninety-seventh year. His tombstone refers to two wives, but nothing is known of his second wife. Blount records the original form of the inscription on his monument, which was later modified slightly when recut during the Victorian era:

> This craggy Stone covering is for an Architector's Bed
> That lofty Buildings raised high, yet now lyes low His Head
> His line and Rule, So Death concludes, are locked up in Store
> Build they that [who] list, or they that wist, for He can Build
>   no More
> His House of Clay could Hold no Longer
> May Heavens joy frame (build) Him a Stronger
> Vive ut vivas in vitam aeternam.
> (*History of Herefordshire*, 56)

Abel left a son, John, who is recorded as a churchwarden of Sarnesfield in 1699.   DAVID WHITEHEAD

Sources Colvin, *Archs.* · *The 1675 Thomas Blount manuscript history of Herefordshire*, ed. R. Botzum and C. Botzum (1996) · D. L. Gregory, *John Abel of Sarnesfield* (1980) · H. M. Colvin, 'The restoration of Abbey Dore church in 1633–4', *Transactions of the Woolhope Naturalists' Field Club*, 32 (1946–8), 235–7 · J. Clayton, *A collection of ancient timber edifices* (1846) · Herefs. RO, LC Deeds 880 · Herefs. RO, Tyberton Court MSS, 3471; A81/394 · *Herefordshire*, Pevsner (1963) · J. Webb, *Memorials of the civil war … as it affected Herefordshire*, ed. T. W. Webb, 2 vols. (1879) · S. R. Jones and J. T. Smith, 'The houses of Breconshire', *Brycheiniog*, 11 (1965), 114–17 · R. Vaughan, *His booke*, ed. E. B. Wood (1897)

Archives Herefs. RO, LC Deed 880 · Herefs. RO, Tyberton Court MSS

Abel, Karl Friedrich (1723–1787), composer and concert impresario, was born on 22 December 1723 in Cöthen, Saxony, one of six children. His father, Christian Ferdinand Abel (*c*.1683–1737), served as violinist for Johann Sebastian Bach, under whom Karl Friedrich may have studied at the Thomasschule in Leipzig. By 1743 Abel had joined Johann Adolf Hasse's opera orchestra in Dresden. On 5 April 1759 he gave his first public concert in London, playing mostly his own compositions; soon the patronage of Edward, duke of York, brother of George III, and the encouragement of the tenor Thomas Linley led to appearances in Bath. In 1763 Abel helped J. S. Bach's youngest son, Johann Christian Bach, to establish himself in London, and the two soon shared lodgings, first in Meard's Street and later at Teresa Cornelys's establishment, Carlisle House, Soho Square. Both men were named as chamber musicians to Queen Charlotte in 1764. They befriended the Mozarts during their visit to London, starting that same year; one of Abel's symphonies was copied by the young Wolfgang Amadeus, which led to the work's misattribution for a time as Mozart's K18.

On 23 January 1765 Cornelys hosted the first of the 'Bach–Abel' concerts. Subscribers paid 5 guineas to attend a series of concerts, which were directed by Bach and Abel

Karl Friedrich Abel (1723–1787), by Thomas Gainsborough, exh. RA 1777

in alternate weeks. The series gained a reputation for its socially elevated clientele as well as for the quality and range of the performances, and for the 1768 season the composers broke with Cornelys and moved to William Almack's New Rooms in King Street. Bach undertook the financial arrangements but they continued to direct the concerts alternately, and both were involved in attracting musicians. In 1774 they returned the series to Carlisle House, following Cornelys's disgrace, but the next year they moved to their new room in Hanover Square, built in association with the dancing-master and stage-manager Giovanni Gallini.

Abel was the last great virtuoso on the viola da gamba, and he won special praise for his depth of expression. While most of his compositions stress refinement and lightness of touch, some suggest the emotional power of his performances: the C minor andante of the symphony in E♭, op. 7 no. 6, is indeed moving enough to be Mozart's. Abel produced sonatas not only for his favourite instrument but also for flute and continuo. Abel's œuvre, widely published in his lifetime, includes 45 symphonies, 15 solo concertos, 18 string quartets, 24 trios, and over 50 sonatas. He gave both instrumental and vocal instruction.

Abel's circle of friends included artists as well as musicians. Thomas Gainsborough exchanged paintings and sketches with him in return for music and instruments; he produced two portraits of him. He never married. His gregariousness involved over-indulgence in food and drink, which contributed to illness in later life. He was notably witty in his adopted language: on being told that forgery merited hanging, Abel expressed mock concern, since any composer was 'a notorious forger of notes' (Angelo, 1.458). Famed for his generosity, he organized and participated in many benefit concerts throughout his career.

Commenting on Abel as taste-maker, Burney describes him as 'the umpire in all musical controversy' and 'an infallible oracle' (Burney, *Hist. mus.*, 2.1019). Abel and Bach introduced British audiences to composers such as Joseph Haydn and performers such as Johann Christian Fischer and Wilhelm Cramer. They chose never to publish their programmes or the names of the performers, instead relying on their reputation as impresarios alone. They faced increased competition after the Pantheon in Oxford Street opened in 1774, damaging their authority and their financial security, and in 1776 they sold their shares in the Hanover Square rooms to Gallini. Abel managed the 1782 series alone following Bach's death, but for the next year handed the management of the concerts over to Willoughby Bertie, fourth earl of Abingdon, Gallini's brother-in-law. He returned to the continent in 1782, visiting his brother, the musician Leopold August Abel, but by 1785 he had resettled in Hanover Square, London. He made his last concert appearance on 21 May 1787.

Abel died in Hanover Square, London, on 20 June 1787. Gainsborough expressed deep sorrow that he would never see 'Poor Abel' again (Williamson, 195). The *Morning Post* of 22 June opined that the viola da gamba would 'probably die with him' (Burney, *Hist. mus.*, 2.1020). Beginning in the late twentieth century, however, the full range of Abel's works has enjoyed revival and re-examination. Critics once considered him a holdout against the classical style, but later assessments frequently coincide with the opinion of his contemporaries that 'Abel belongs to the good innovators' (Abel, 27).

STEPHEN M. BUHLER

Sources *New Grove*, 2nd edn · W. Knape, *Karl Friedrich Abel: Leben und Werk eines frühklassischen Komponisten* (1973) · Burney, *Hist. mus.*, new edn · M. Charters, 'Abel in London', *MT*, 114 (1973), 1224–6 · G. Beechey, 'Carl Friedrich Abel's six symphonies, op. 14', *Music and Letters*, 51 (1970), 279–85 · M. Cyr, 'Carl Friedrich Abel's solos: a musical offering to Gainsborough?', *MT*, 128 (1987), 317–21 · S. McVeigh, *Concert life in London from Mozart to Haydn* (1993) · [K. F. Abel], *27 pieces for the viola da gamba*, ed. W. Knape (1993) · C. S. Terry, *John Christian Bach*, 2nd edn (1967) · G. Williamson, *The ingenious Mr Gainsborough* (1972) · M. Rosenthal, *The art of Thomas Gainsborough* (1999) · H. Angelo, *Reminiscences*, 2 vols. (1828–30) · *GM*, 1st ser., 57 (1787), 549–50 · H. Gärtner, *Johann Christian Bach: Mozarts Freund und Lehrmeister* (1989)

Likenesses T. Gainsborough, oils, *c*.1760–1769, NPG · T. Gainsborough, chalk drawing, *c*.1763, NPG · T. Gainsborough, oils, exh. RA 1777, Hunt. L. [*see illus.*] · C. J. Robineau, oils, 1780, Royal Collection · W. N. Gardiner, caricature, 1787, repro. in J. Mee, *The oldest music room in Europe* (1911), facing p. 32 · J. Nixon, caricature, ink wash over chalk, 1787, NPG · J. Nixon, etching, pubd 1787 (after W. N. Gardiner), BM, NPG · T. Rowlandson, pen-and-ink caricature, repro. in Cyr, 'Carl Friedrich Abel's solos', 319 · attrib. Teeds, oils, U. Oxf., faculty of music

Abel, Robert [Bobby] (1857–1936), cricketer, was born at 18 Commercial Street, Rotherhithe, London, on 30 November 1857, the son of Thomas Abel (b. c.1815), a lamplighter, and his wife, Elizabeth Highland (b. 1816). After attending school in Southwark and playing cricket for Southwark Park, he began his illustrious career as a professional cricketer at the Oval. He played 514 matches for Surrey, but it was a slow beginning. He was twenty-three before making his début in 1881, and it was 1886 before he was firmly established in the Surrey side. Thereafter he became one of England's most productive batsmen. An opening bat of phlegmatic certainty, his compact efficiency was such that in eight successive summers (1895–1902) he exceeded 2000 runs, including the then first-class record of 3309 in 1901. This dauntless consistency eventually earned him the grand total of 33,124 first-class runs, at an average of 35.46 and with seventy-four centuries. His best innings was 357 not out, for Surrey against Somerset at the Oval in 1899, at that time the second highest score in county championship cricket. In the same year he shared a stand of 447 with Tom Hayward for Surrey against Yorkshire at the Oval, which stood as a world fourth-wicket record until 1943–4. Rightly regarded as a most adept slip fielder, he took no fewer than 586 catches.

Abel played thirteen times for England between 1888 and 1902, and, along with four other professionals, he was involved in the abortive claim for extra money for the Oval test of 1896. However, in an era of mercurial amateur 'cracks', he never became an international star. Rather was it his pleasant fate to be the most popular Surrey 'pro' when that county played successfully to crowded houses. His sobriquets—the 'Cock Sparrow', the 'Mighty Atom', the 'Little 'Un', and, indisputably the most quoted, the 'Guv'nor'—bear testimony to that renown. Bobby Abel was the classic case of the little man triumphing over larger foes and thereby deserving the plaudits of the ordinary onlooker. He waddled with duck-like gait to open the innings, a curiously gnomic figure who could not have been more unlike, in stature and style, the magnificent ones of that golden age. Less than 5 feet 8 inches in height, 'he has', wrote C. B. Fry, 'a curious manner of standing at the wicket (wrapping, as it were, his left leg round the front of his right)' (Lemmon, 76–7), from which strange position he then carefully demonstrated what H. S. Altham called 'that inexhaustible talent for run-making' (Altham, 174). It seems somehow fitting that, down the road from the Oval in 1889, when Bobby Abel was reaching his peak, Charlie Chaplin, personification of the sorely tried little fellow and masterly exponent of the ten-to-three shuffle, was born.

An eye infection which, in 1893, had briefly threatened to end Abel's career, recurred in the early 1900s, and, although glasses helped a little, he had to give up the game. He played his last first-class match in 1904, and, like many professional cricketers, became involved in sports shops and in coaching. Married to Sarah Reffell (1861–1923) at St Martin-in-the-Fields, London, on 31 January 1881, Abel was as prodigious in domestic as in professional life, fathering no fewer than eleven children. Two,

Thomas Ernest and William John, played first-class cricket. Abel died at his home, 43 Handforth Road, Stockwell, London, on 10 December 1936.

ERIC MIDWINTER

Sources P. Bailey, P. Thorn, and P. Wynne-Thomas, *Who's who of cricketers* (1984) · B. Green, ed., *The Wisden book of obituaries* (1986) · D. Lemmon, *The official history of Surrey county cricket club* (1989) · H. S. Altham, *A history of cricket* (1926) · private information (2004) · b. cert. · d. cert. · *CGPLA Eng. & Wales* (1937)
Likenesses photographs, Surrey county cricket club, Oval, Kennington, London
Wealth at death £864 9s. 7d.: probate, 11 Nov 1937, *CGPLA Eng. & Wales*

Abell, Adam (1475×80?–1537?), Franciscan friar and chronicler, was born in Salt Preston, Haddingtonshire, but the names and occupations of his parents are not recorded and details of his early life are scant. What little is known is derived largely from his chronicle, *The Roit or Quheill of Tyme*, which records that he spent his childhood in the Augustinian abbey of Holyrood beside Edinburgh, where a kinsman, Robert Bellentyne, was abbot. It was at Holyrood that he probably received most of his education, either in the abbey itself or possibly at the grammar school in the Canongate which was under the abbey's control. There is no concrete evidence that he studied at a university, though his knowledge of canon law does suggest some higher education.

In 1495 Abell was professed as an Augustinian canon regular at Inchaffray Abbey in Perthshire. He subsequently became dissatisfied with the state of religious discipline there and, perhaps inspired by the example of Bellentyne, who resigned the abbacy of Holyrood and retired to the stricter Carthusian house in Perth, applied to transfer to another religious house. A Vatican penitentiary act of 16 June 1508 preserves his request to transfer either to another Augustinian establishment or to an Observant Franciscan house. However, Abell was still at Inchaffray two years later, when he signed a petition, dated 20 June 1510, from the convent to Lord Oliphant concerning the annual rents of Pitcairns. Although the precise date is unknown Abell did, however, eventually leave Inchaffray for the Observant Franciscan friary of Jedburgh, traditionally believed to have been founded in 1513 but recorded in the Scottish treasurer's accounts in 1505.

Abell's only surviving work is *The Roit or Quheill of Tyme*, a chronicle in Scots composed after his transfer to the Franciscans of Jedburgh, and preserved in a unique manuscript in the National Library of Scotland (MS 1746). In the introduction to the chronicle Abell refers to an earlier Latin version of the work which is now lost. The precise dates of composition are unknown, but the chronicle may be dated on internal evidence to the late 1520s and 1530s; the colophon to the main part of the text and the short preamble to its continuation indicate that the body of the chronicle was complete by 1533, and the continuation added when the translation was made shortly thereafter. The continuation ends abruptly in 1537, as though interrupted.

The *Roit* belongs to the genre of universal chronicle, a form characteristic of medieval historical writing. It opens with a brief account of creation and carries on through biblical, classical, medieval European, papal, and Scottish history, both real and legendary, and thus reflects the medieval vision of history as the progressive unfolding of the divine plan for the world and its creatures. For his material Abell relied heavily on such works as Eusebius's *Chronicon*, Peter Comestor's *Historia scholastica*, Walter Bower's *Scotichronicon*, and Hector Boece's *Scotorum historiae*, but he did not follow any author slavishly and frequently discarded his sources' opinions in favour of his own interpretation.

Abell's chronicle is historically significant for a variety of reasons. As one of a very limited number of chronicles of known Franciscan authorship anywhere in Europe it is an international rarity. Within a Scottish context it is unique. Aside from its distinction as the last surviving chronicle from pre-Reformation Scotland, it addresses material which other Scottish historical writings of the time do not. For example, neither Boece nor his contemporary translators deal with the reigns of James II, III, IV, or V, choosing to end, as Bower did, with the assassination of James I in 1437. Abell, however, continues his chronicle up to 1537, providing an eyewitness perspective on the reigns of James III, IV, and V, and provides the only chronicle accounts of those reigns to be written before the Reformation. Equally interesting are his views on contemporary ecclesiastical issues, including the *commendam* system and plurality of benefice, both of which he attacks with vigour. He is particularly critical of seekers of church offices, noting that unworthy candidates are led 'nocht to the cheptur but to the king's chalmer' (NL Scot., MS 1746, fol. 85v; Thorson, 171). His grievance against them was not caused by material damage arising from greed or financial mismanagement, but rather by the spiritual harm caused by the poor moral example given by absentee curates and lay abbots; in this his assessment is supported by Mark Dilworth's findings that Scottish monasteries were not hurt by greedy commendators as contemporary monasteries in France were.

The date and place of Abell's death are not recorded in surviving sources. There are two indications that he did not live to finish his work and probably died in 1537, the date of the latest material in the chronicle. One is the abrupt end of the continuation of the *Roit*, which cuts off in the middle of a sentence, with some events still unresolved; and the other is the phrasing of the short introduction to the continuation, which reads in part: 'heir he begynnis quhair he lewit in þe ȝere of God 1534 ȝeris and sa procedand for his schort tyme' (NL Scot., MS 1746, fol. 119v; Thorson, 241). The place of Abell's burial is also unrecorded, but the excavation of the Jedburgh friary conducted between 1983 and 1985 revealed several graves in the church and cloister, and it is likely that he was buried there.   STEPHANIE M. THORSON

Sources A. Abell, 'The roit or quheill of tyme', NL Scot., MS 1746 · S. Thorson, 'Adam Abell's *The roit or quheill of tyme*: an edition', PhD diss., U. St Andr., 1998 · J. Durkan, 'The Observant Franciscan province in Scotland', *Innes Review*, 35 (1984), 51–7 · J. Anderson, *The Oliphants in Scotland* (1879) · A. M. Stewart, 'Adam Abell's *Roit or quheill of tyme*', *Aberdeen University Review*, 44 (1971–2), 386–93 · A. M. Stewart, 'The final folios of Adam Abell's *Roit or quheill of tyme*: an Observantine friar's reflections on the 1520s and 30s', *Stewart style, 1513–1542: essays on the court of James V*, ed. J. H. Williams (1996), 227–53 · J. B. Paul, ed., *Compota thesaurariorum regum Scotorum / Accounts of the lord high treasurer of Scotland*, 3 (1901), 58 · J. Todd, 'Jedburgh friary', *Discovery and excavation in Scotland* (1985), 2 · M. Dilworth, 'The commendator system in Scotland', *Innes Review*, 37 (1986), 51–72 · M. Dilworth, *Scottish monasteries in the late middle ages* (1995), 14–16, 18–23, 58
Archives NL Scot., MS 1746

Abell, Sir George Edmond Brackenbury (1904–1989), administrator in India, was born on 22 June 1904 in Sanderstead, Surrey, the eldest in the family of two sons and two daughters of George Foster Abell, director of Lloyds Bank, and his wife, Jessie Elizabeth Brackenbury. His brother, Sir Anthony Abell, became governor of Sarawak. He was a scholar and senior prefect of Marlborough College, and scholar of Corpus Christi College, Oxford, where he obtained a first class in classical honour moderations (1925) and a second in *literae humaniores* (1927). A triple blue, in rugby, cricket, and hockey, he captained the Oxford rugby fifteen in 1926, and played cricket for Worcestershire. In 1928 he married Susan (*d.* 1992), daughter of Frank Norman-Butler, inspector of schools, and they were close companions throughout the rest of his life. They had two sons and a daughter.

Abell joined the Indian Civil Service as a district officer in the Punjab in 1928, becoming deputy registrar of co-operative societies and a settlement officer. He enjoyed the work, and coped effectively with crises, quelling a riot in Dera Ghazi Khan gaol by walking into the middle of it while the warders were taking refuge on the roof. In 1941 the governor of the Punjab appointed him as his private secretary, and in 1943 he was promoted deputy secretary to the viceroy, the second marquess of Linlithgow. In 1945 he took over as private secretary to the viceroy, by then Viscount Wavell, and he continued to hold this post under Louis Mountbatten until the end of the raj, thereafter serving as Mountbatten's secretary when he became governor-general of India.

Abell's role in government during the critical years leading up to the partition and transfer of power in India was of central importance. Although the Hindus regarded his Punjab background with suspicion, Wavell, whom he liked and admired, used him to coax M. K. Gandhi, describing him as 'diplomatic and persuasive'. He wrote the first draft of the handover scheme to be presented to the new Labour government, and he was on the small committee used by Wavell to work out the details of his 'breakdown plan'. He tended to moderate Wavell's tougher telegrams but respected his soldierly directness. However, he came to feel that the British position in India was untenable, that partition was inevitable, and that the British should extricate themselves quickly. Although less comfortable with Mountbatten's personality, he therefore worked happily to implement his policy. He drafted the partition

Sir George Edmond Brackenbury Abell (1904–1989), by Walter Bird, 1964

plan for the viceroy with General Hastings Ismay, and he helped to keep him from some of the mistakes inevitably made in the rush to meet the deadline. 'The Lord needs George or Ismay to steady him', commented a diarist close to the scene.

On his return to England in 1948 Abell joined the Bank of England as an adviser, serving as a director from 1952 until 1964. He was responsible for all matters connected with staff, and for the buildings. He developed the new graduate entry, organizing a career structure which made proper use of graduates' talents. He also ended the old division between men and women, and integrated them into one staff. He had directorial responsibility for three major new Bank of England buildings, including the New Change office block at the top of Cheapside.

Abell was first civil service commissioner from 1964 until 1967, chairman of the Rhodes trustees from 1969 until 1974 (having been a trustee from 1949), and chairman of the governors of Marlborough College from 1974 until 1977. He was also president of the council of Reading University between 1970 and 1974. This was at a time of rapidly increasing numbers and general student restlessness. That Reading did not suffer the disruption of many other universities had much to do with the confidence which Abell engendered in dons and students. They respected his mind, and his sense of humour defused many difficult situations.

Abell enjoyed the outdoor life, shot well, and tied his own fishing flies. He remained the all-rounder throughout his life, and he brought his common sense and his clear mind to a wide range of problems. He retained the discretion of the civil servant, and his response to biographers and journalists who wanted to get behind the scenes of the closing years of the raj was that he continued to regard his role as that of a private secretary.

Abell was appointed OBE (1943), CIE (1946), and KCIE (1947). He received an honorary LLD from Aberdeen University in 1947, and became an honorary fellow of Corpus Christi College in 1971. He died at his home, Whittonditch House, Ramsbury, near Marlborough, Wiltshire, on 11 January 1989 and was buried at Ramsbury church.

ROGER ELLIS, *rev.*

Sources P. Ziegler, *Mountbatten: the official biography* (1985) · *Wavell: the viceroy's journal*, ed. P. Moon (1973) · *CGPLA Eng. & Wales* (1989) · personal knowledge (1996) · private information (1996)
Likenesses W. Bird, photograph, 1964, NPG [*see illus.*]
Wealth at death £731,594: probate, 16 Dec 1989, *CGPLA Eng. & Wales*

Abell, John (*b.* 1653, *d.* in or after 1716), singer and composer, was born in Aberdeenshire and was admitted as a 'gentleman of his majesty's chapel extraordinary' on 1 May 1679, about which time he is listed among the musicians of the king's private music, as singer, lutenist, and violinist. Charles II proposed to send him to Venice 'in order to show the Italians what good voices were produced in England' (Hawkins, 4.445) but by 1682 he had returned to England, when John Evelyn recorded of him in his diary (27 January 1682): 'After supper, came in the famous treble, Mr. Abel, newly returned from Italy; I never heard a more excellent voice; one would have sworn it had been a woman's, it was so high, and so well and skilfully managed' (*Diary and Correspondence*, 2.163). Between 1679 and 1688 he received from the crown large sums of 'bounty money', ostensibly for the purposes of study, though Hawkins cites Thomas Brown's intimations that 'Abell was a man of intrigue' (Hawkins, 4.446). He graduated MusB from Cambridge in 1684, and was married the following year, on 29 December 1685, to Lady Frances Knollys. At the revolution he was discharged from the Chapel Royal as a papist, and went to the Netherlands and Germany, where he supported himself by his talents as a singer and player on the lute. In the course of his travels he went as far as Warsaw, where it is said that he refused a request of the king of Poland to sing before the court. The day after this refusal he was ordered to appear at the palace:

> Upon his arrival he was seated in a chair in the middle of a spacious hall, and immediately drawn up to a great height: presently the king with his attendants appeared in a gallery opposite to him, and at the same instant a number of wild bears were turned in; the king bad him then chuse him whether he would sing, or be let down among the bears; Abell chose the former, and declared afterwards that he had never sung so well in his life. (Hawkins, 4.446)

In 1696 overtures were made to Abell through Daniel Purcell to return to England and sing on the stage at a salary of £500 per annum, but in 1698 he was still abroad (at Aix-la-Chapelle), though he offered to return and sing at the opera in English, Italian, Spanish, or Latin, for £400 per annum, provided his debts were paid. In 1698 and 1699 he occupied the post of intendant at Kassel; but he seems soon after to have returned to England, for Congreve heard him sing in 1700, and in 1701 he published *A Collection of Songs, in English* and *A Collection of Songs, in Several Languages*, the latter being 'distinguished more for patriotic fervour than musical excellence' (Spink, 257). In 1703 he published *A Choice Collection of Italian Ayres* and an ode for Queen Anne's birthday, *Hark, Britain, Hark*, the music for which does not appear to have survived. The date of his death is unknown, but in his later years he is said to have been at Cambridge, and in 1716 he gave a concert at Stationers' Hall. Mattheson says that Abell possessed some secret by which he preserved his pure alto voice unimpaired until old age; his extreme carefulness in matters of diet is recorded by the same author.

W. B. SQUIRE, *rev.* NICHOLAS SALWEY

Sources J. Hawkins, *A general history of the science and practice of music*, 4 (1776), 445–6 · *Tom Brown's letters from the dead to the living*, 4th edn (1707), vol. 2, p. 36 · *Diary and correspondence of John Evelyn*, ed. W. Bray, new edn, ed. [J. Forster], 4 vols. (1850–52), vol. 2, p. 725 · I. Spink, 'Abell, John', *New Grove* · I. Spink, *English song: Dowland to Purcell* (1974), 257–8 · R. McGuinness, *English court odes, 1660–1820* (1971), 25 · H. G. Farmer, 'John Abell', *Hinrichsen's Musical Year Book*, 7 (1952), 445 · J. Mattheson, *Der vollkommene Capellmeister* (1739), 95 · *IGI* · E. F. Rimbault, ed., *The old cheque-book, or book of remembrance, of the Chapel Royal, from 1561 to 1744*, CS, new ser., 3 (1872), 17, 129

Abell, Thomas (d. 1540), Roman Catholic priest and martyr, is of obscure origins. He was in priest's orders by May 1513. Nothing else is known about his early life beyond his studies at Oxford, where he determined as a BA in 1514, and proceeded MA in 1518. In 1522 he was admitted to the rectory of Great Berkhamsted, Hertfordshire, which was vacant by 1530.

A chaplain to the queen by 1528, Abell became a participant in the political intrigues and theological debates surrounding the annulment of the king's marriage. In 1529 Abell travelled to Spain ostensibly to retrieve a legal document for use in the divorce trial in England. This document, a brief of dispensation, had been discovered by the Spanish only in 1528, and Queen Katherine possessed a copy of it prior to Abell's trip. The brief supplemented the 1503 bull issued by Pope Julius II that had dispensed Henry and Katherine from the impediment of affinity that would have existed if Katherine's first marriage to Arthur, prince of Wales, had been consummated. Yet while the papal bull employed some odd language, referring to the first marriage as 'perhaps consummated' (*forsan consummatum*), the brief of dispensation in Spain did not. In fact the brief appeared to derail the king's argument for the annulment of the marriage.

Suspecting a forgery the king's supporters demanded the original document be sent to England. Under pressure from both Henry VIII and Thomas Wolsey, Katherine wrote a letter to Charles V requesting that the original brief be sent to England. The first man chosen for the conveyance of Katherine's letter had his arm broken in the French town of Abbeville while *en route* for Spain; rumours blamed agents of Wolsey. The second man chosen to carry Katherine's letter and retrieve the brief was Thomas Abell, who travelled to the court of Charles V

in Spain in 1529. A long-time servant of the queen, Juan de Montoya, accompanied Abell as a guide and interpreter. The presence of Montoya has led some to suggest that Katherine did not truly trust Thomas Abell, but there is no direct evidence of mistrust. Abell apparently presented Katherine's original letter to the emperor along with a second one authored by himself that urged Charles to act in five ways: 1. to keep the brief in Spain for safe keeping; 2. to urge the papacy to put a halt to the trial in England, allowing it to proceed only in Rome; 3. to instruct the imperial ambassadors to complain to the pope that he had been too eager to please Henry at the expense of Katherine's interests; 4. to send an expert in canon law as an ambassador to England; 5. to have experts study the issue and provide information to Katherine. Charles agreed and produced a copy of the brief for the English, even allowing the English ambassadors to read and compare the copy and the original in a meeting at Valladolid during which Abell was present.

Upon returning to England from Spain, Abell received as a reward from Katherine the rectory of Bradwell by the Sea, in Essex, and was instituted on 23 June 1530. He continued to be a strong and vocal advocate of the queen. When a questionable plebiscite at the University of Paris voted to support the king's case for annulment, the vote was represented as unanimous to Henry by the French ambassador. It was Abell who presented the king's council with a list of forty-four doctors who supported the validity of the marriage. The king banished Abell from court.

In response to the government-inspired *Censurae academiarum* (1531), translated in the same year as *The Determinations of the Universities*, Abell wrote in support of the validity of Katherine's marriage the *Invicta veritas*, with an erroneous place of publication and date—Lunenberg, 1532—on the title-page. Drawing on Old Testament and New Testament texts as well as several church fathers Abell argued against the position of the king with biblical citations and logical construction. Abell's work seemed to promote political ripples even in the House of Commons. Imprisoned in 1532, Abell concelebrated mass at least once in the presence of the lieutenant of the Tower, but was released in early 1533.

Abell then continued to address and refer to Katherine as queen, instead of princess dowager, in contradiction to the law. In December 1533 during the duke of Suffolk's failed attempt to move Katherine and her household to Fotheringhay Castle, Abell was arrested again. He was charged along with John Fisher, bishop of Rochester, and Thomas More with misprision of treason for concealing knowledge of the treasonous prophecies of Elizabeth Barton, known as the Nun of Kent, in November 1533. A letter apparently written by Abell during his imprisonment offering spiritual encouragement to a fellow prisoner is probably the invention of the Franciscan martyrologist Thomas Bourchier.

After six years of imprisonment Abell was hanged, drawn, and quartered, along with Edward Powell and Richard Fetherston on 30 July 1540. The crime for all three men was treason, since they refused to acknowledge the

Act of Supremacy. His execution was part of a calculated policy by the government since on the same day three reformers—Robert Barnes, Thomas Garrett, and William Jerome—were burnt for heresy at Smithfield. The execution of papists and heretics on the same day demonstrated the determination of the Henrician government to be seen to be steering an independent course between the Roman and protestant camps on the continent.

The image of a bell with the letter 'A' on it, and the name Thomas above, remains carved on the wall of Abell's prison cell in the Beauchamp Tower. He was beatified by Pope Leo XIII on 29 December 1886.   GARY G. GIBBS

Sources J. J. Scarisbrick, *Henry VIII* (1968) · J. E. Paul, *Catherine of Aragon* (1966) · Wood, *Ath. Oxon.*, new edn · *CSP Spain*, 1535–40 · *LP Henry VIII*, vols. 4–5, 16 · Emden, *Oxf.*, vol. 4

Abell, Sir Westcott Stile (1877–1961), naval architect and surveyor, was born on 16 January 1877 at Littleham in Devon, the first of the four sons of Thomas Abell, house painter and, later, builder and member of Exmouth council for over fifty years, and of his wife, Mary Ann Stile. He also had a half-sister. He was educated at West Buckland and Devon County schools and the Royal Naval Engineering College, Keyham (1892–7), before proceeding in 1897 to the Royal Naval College, Greenwich. At the age of twenty he lost his right hand and suffered serious throat injuries while lighting fireworks to celebrate the diamond jubilee. Despite this handicap, he taught himself to write with his left hand and recovered to such good purpose that he passed out head of his year (1900) at Greenwich with a level of marks unsurpassed for many years.

Abell entered the Royal Corps of Naval Constructors in 1900, was attached to the staff of the chief constructor at Devonport Dockyard, and was shortly afterwards transferred temporarily to the Admiralty to assist at the inquiry into the stability of the royal yacht *Victoria and Albert*. After a further short spell at Devonport, he was posted to the Admiralty, and from 1904 to 1907 he was professional private secretary to Sir Philip Watts, director of naval construction. During this period he was closely involved with the committee on designs which had been appointed by Sir John Fisher. In 1902 Abell married Beatrice Gertrude (*d.* 1953), daughter of Joseph Wyld Davenport, dentist, of Devonport. They had one son, T. W. D. Abell, who adopted his father's profession, and three daughters, one of whom married the scientist D. W. W. Henderson.

In 1907 Abell became junior lecturer on naval architecture at the Royal Naval College until his selection in December 1909 to be professor of naval architecture in the newly founded chair at Liverpool. In 1909 he also became a member of the Institution of Naval Architects. In 1913 he was appointed a member of the committee of the Board of Trade to examine the application of the Merchant Shipping Act to the internationalization of load lines. It was for this work that he was awarded the James Watt gold medal in 1919. He was chairman of the technical subcommittee, and his lifelong interest and association with the solution of the problems of safety of life at sea

probably dated from this period. His outstanding contributions to the Institution of Naval Architects on these subjects must certainly have earned him recognition by the committee of Lloyd's register of shipping, and in 1914 he was invited to fill the post of chief ship surveyor, a position which he occupied with distinction for the next fourteen years. On vacating the chair at Liverpool, he was succeeded by his brother Thomas Bertrand Abell.

During the First World War, Abell made a significant contribution in the field of merchant shipbuilding and was also closely associated with the Admiralty in the construction of great numbers of naval auxiliary craft. He also served on a special Admiralty committee to determine the feasibility of submarine merchant vessels to thwart the growing U-boat menace, and in 1917 was also appointed technical adviser to the controller of shipping. Among his many other commitments he was a member of a war committee on the distribution of steel and of the advisory committee on the merchant shipbuilding programme.

In recognition of his outstanding services Abell was created KBE in 1920, and now turned his attention to the peacetime problems of ship classification and safety. Fully aware that the war had stimulated technological advance, he directed a complete revision of the structural requirements of Lloyd's rules and effected major amendments to their philosophy, which resulted in an increase of structural efficiency and, as a corollary, the reduction of steel weights. For the first time longitudinal framing was recognized as a valid form of construction. He also recruited many young graduates of attainment who were later to rise to eminence in the service of Lloyd's.

Abell served on the Board of Trade load-line committee in 1927, but in 1928 he resigned his appointment with Lloyd's register to take up the chair of naval architecture at the Armstrong College of Durham University at Newcastle upon Tyne; and, shortly after his return to academic affairs, he was a British delegate at the international Safety of Life at Sea Conference in 1929. It was he who designed the channel train ferry, for which special docks had to be built at Dover and Dunkirk. Three ships were built, one of which was launched by Abell's wife. They were used for mine-laying during the Second World War.

Abell made many important contributions to technical institutions. His publications included *The Ship and her Work* (1932), *The Safe Sea* (1932), and *The Shipwright's Trade* (1948), the last of which exhibited a profound understanding of ships and shipbuilding. It was he who was responsible for getting the *Cutty Sark* dry-docked at Greenwich, and his worry about the condition of the *Victory* at Portsmouth caused Lord Louis Mountbatten to get the woodwork restored.

Abell was a member of the executive committee of the National Physical Laboratory and chairman of the Froude ship research subcommittee of the ship division of the laboratory. It was in large measure due to his resource and initiative that the new ship hydrodynamics laboratory at Feltham was completed in 1959.

Abell was a source of help and encouragement to the younger men of his profession, particularly during his tenure of office in the Worshipful Company of Shipwrights. On public occasions his experience, shrewd understanding, and wit were inestimable assets.

Abell was president of the Institute of Marine Engineers (1924–5), master of the Worshipful Company of Shipwrights (1931–2), and president of the Smeatonian Society of Civil Engineers (1941). At the time of his death he was senior honorary vice-president of the Royal Institution of Naval Architects. Both he and his wife held the freedom of the City of London. He did much for the Institute of Marine Engineers and Shipbuilders in Newcastle, which awarded him a gold medal and placed a gilt plaque in his honour in Bolbec Hall, Newcastle. Abell died on 29 July 1961 at his home, 95 Kenton Road, Gosforth, Newcastle upon Tyne. J. McCallum, rev.

Sources *The Times* (31 July 1961) · personal knowledge (1981) · *WWW* · *CGPLA Eng. & Wales* (1961)
Likenesses F. Humphris, crayon drawing, 1945, priv. coll.; in family possession in 1981
Wealth at death £5741 17s. 1d.: probate, 6 Nov 1961, *CGPLA Eng. & Wales*

Abell, William (d. 1474), manuscript artist, is associated by documentary evidence only with the consolidation charter of Eton College of March 1446, for which he was paid £1 6s. 8d. But a number of other works can be attributed to him on stylistic grounds, including the similarly illuminated charter for Henry VI's twin foundation of King's College, Cambridge. In addition to work for Henry VI and his queen, Margaret of Anjou, Abell illuminated a variety of liturgical, religious, and secular texts, including a book of hours (New York, Pierpont Morgan Library, MS 893), which probably belonged to Henry Beauchamp, duke of Warwick (d. 1446), and the missal of Thomas Ashenden, abbot of Abingdon, dated 1461 (Bodl. Oxf., MS Digby 227). He is named in various contemporary documents, which show that he was resident in London from before 1448, when he was already a member of the Stationers' Company, until his death in 1474. Among other works attributable to him are the cartulary of St Bartholomew's, Smithfield, from the period 1456–68, and a grant of arms to the Tallow Chandlers' Company of 1456.

On the surviving evidence, Abell is the most important native illuminator to have been working in the mid-fifteenth century. He reacts to the elegance of the international Gothic style seen in the work of early fifteenth-century illuminators, such as Siferwas and Johannes, with more angular forms, harsher colours, and exaggerated, sometimes grotesque, facial types. Using French and Flemish models, some of which he copies directly—as in a manuscript of Christine de Pisan's *Épître d'Othée*—he deepens exterior and interior spaces, though he never uses aerial or vanishing-point perspective with the sophistication of his continental counterparts. Indeed, at this date luxury illuminated manuscripts were already being imported in quantity from the Low Countries, and his work cannot compare in quality or inventiveness with that of contemporary artists working in Ghent and Bruges. J. J. G. Alexander

Sources J. J. G. Alexander, 'William Abell "lymnour" and 15th-century English illumination', *Kunsthistorische Forschungen: Otto Pächt zu seinem 70. Geburtstag*, ed. A. Rosenauer and G. Weber (1972), 166–70 · R. Marks and N. Morgan, *The golden age of English manuscript painting, 1200–1500* (1981), 30–31, fig. 21, pls. 38–40 · C. P. Christianson, *A directory of London stationers and book artisans, 1300–1500* (1990), 59–60 · K. L. Scott, *Later Gothic manuscripts, 1390–1490*, 2 vols. (1996)
Archives Bodl. Oxf., MS Digby 227 · Eton · Morgan L., MS 893

Abell, William (b. c.1584, d. in or after 1655), vintner and local politician, was the son of Thomas Abell of Oundle, Northamptonshire, and his wife, Suzanna Barker. He was probably born at Oundle, where his grandfather William Abell had endowed Oundle School in the 1560s. In March 1598 he was bound apprentice in the London Vintners' Company, gaining his freedom in 1602 or shortly thereafter. He married at an unknown date Isabel, daughter of Thomas Launders (d. 1593), draper and alderman of Beverley, Yorkshire. The couple had two sons, William (d. 1661) and Richard (b. 1609?), who worked as 'servants and officers' for Sir John Lenthall in 1652 (PRO, SP 16/24/16), and two daughters, Susanna, who later married Henry Field, and Mary.

Abell, who owned The Ship tavern off Old Fish Street, was raised to the livery in the Vintners' Company in 1614 and became an assistant in 1628. Elected deputy alderman for Queenhithe ward in 1634, he rose to be alderman for Bread Street ward in 1636, and was pricked for sheriff in 1637–8, having also been elected master of the Vintners' Company in 1637. In February that year Abell, as sheriff of London, arrested the puritan minister Henry Burton, who following the publication of two anti-episcopal sermons had been suspended from the ministry and ordered to be apprehended. Abell broke into Burton's barricaded home and carried off his prisoner with some violence, an act which generated much personal hostility towards him from London's puritan community.

Abell's unpopularity was further increased by his involvement with the disputed wine monopoly. This dispute had arisen some years previously in response to the king's demands for money and his attempt to force the Vintners to raise the duty on wine from £3 to £4 per tun. They in return sought various concessions, only some of which were granted: they were forbidden to sell victuals and tobacco, but granted the monopoly of retailing wine, thus excluding the Coopers, who had previously shared the privilege. At this stage two of the king's agents, the lawyer Richard *Kilvert and James, third marquess of Hamilton, threatened prosecution of all retailers and merchants selling wine contrary to price and condition. The Vintners named Abell and others to negotiate, and secured advantageous terms, agreeing to a 40s. payment in exchange for a retail monopoly and the farm of the licence fee. Further discussion on whether to farm the payment of duties led to Abell and Kilvert apparently offering to handle the matter. Arguments turned on whether Abell and Kilvert planned to make a profit for themselves, but Abell signed the indenture in June 1638, some months before his term as master expired. The bad feeling engendered within the wine trade and against

William Abell (*b. c.*1584, *d.* **in or after 1655**), by unknown engraver, 1641 [*The Copie of a Letter Sent from the Roaring Boyes in Elizium*]

monopolies more generally led to a torrent of pamphlets. Satirists had a field day declaiming against the unlikely trio of Kilvert (an ecclesiastical lawyer), Hamilton (a courtier), and Abell (an alderman). Moreover Abell and his family were accused of having grown rich by illegal means, as he had been provided with a spacious house in Aldermanbury to use as his office and an annual salary of £500.

At the meeting of the Short Parliament in 1640 complaints about the wine monopoly were made to Abell but he was saved by its dissolution. When the Long Parliament met later that year MPs and the Vintners' Company accused him of having contrived the monopoly for his personal profit. Abell found himself arraigned as a delinquent and summoned to appear before the parliamentary committee of grievances; by January 1641 he was in custody, having been refused bail. In March parliament resolved that the 40s. impost was illegal, as were the orders which prohibited the Coopers from buying and selling wine, and the Vintners from dressing and selling meat. Isaac Penington, MP for the City, spoke on behalf of Abell, accusing Kilvert as mainly responsible, and Abell himself was the likely author of *A True Discovery of the Projectors of the Wine Project* (1641), which presented him as having acted with the company's consent and solely out of concern for the company's welfare. This tract was answered by *A true relation of the proposing, threatening and persuading the vintners to yield to the imposition upon wines* which accused Abell of having forced the generality of retailers into an unprofitable contract with the king. How

much Abell profited personally from the wine licences is unknown; while he claimed that he gained nothing opponents alleged that he made £57,000. By an order of the House of Commons of 1641 this sum was raised on his lands and estates to be employed to the public use.

On 1 September 1641 Abell was released on bail of £20,000. In April 1642, having been branded a delinquent, he was granted a pardon for £2000, and in June following was discharged from the aldermanic bench on account of his absence. He was once again taken into custody in 1644 for non-payment of the parliamentary assessment tax. Abell then disappears from the historical record until 1652, when he was living at Hatfield, Hertfordshire, and was briefly imprisoned 'concerning dangerous words against the public peace lately spoken by him in Northall Woods, near Hatfield' (PRO, SP 16/24/14). He was granted a passport to the Netherlands in 1655 after which no more is heard of him. It seems unlikely that he was the William Abell of All Hallows, London Wall, whose widow, Elizabeth, was granted administration of her husband's estate in 1656.　　　　　　　　　　　　　　　　　DAGMAR FREIST

Sources V. Pearl, *London and the outbreak of the puritan revolution* (1961) · [W. Abell?], *A true discovery of the projectors of the wine project, out of the Vintners' owne orders made at their commonhall* (1641) · Vintners' Company court minutes, GL, MSS 15201/3, 15201/4 · *An exact legendary compendiously containing the whole life of alderman Abel* (1641) · *A true relation of the proposing, threatening and persuading the vintners to yield to the imposition upon wines* (1641) · A. Crawford, *History of the Vintners' Company* (1977) · repertories of the court of aldermen, CLRO, vols. 51–5 · *JHC*, 2 (1640–42) · 'Boyd's Inhabitants of London', Society of Genealogists, London · Vintners' Company membership, 1428–1602, GL, MS 15211/1, p. 232a; 1602–60, MS 15211/2 · *The Ancestor*, 1 (1902), 274 · state papers, Charles I, PRO, SP 16

Likenesses woodcut, 1641 (*The copie of a letter sent from the Roaring Boyes in Elizium*), BM, NPG [*see illus.*] · W. Hollar, etching, BM

Abendana, Isaac (*d.* **1699**), Hebraist and book collector, was born in Spain and was taken at an early age to Hamburg, Germany. By 1660 he had completed rabbinical studies and by his own account sought the 'wisdom of medicine' (Katz, 'The Abendana brothers', 36) at the University of Leiden in the Netherlands. Isaac and his brother Jacob *Abendana clubbed together to produce Hebrew books for the Christian market, and they thereby became acquainted with some of the most eminent Christian Hebraists of the day. Having been approached by Adam Boreel—who with John Dury and Samuel Hartlib in England hoped to persuade a learned Jew to translate the Mishnah, the Hebraic core of the Talmud, into Latin—Isaac Abendana arrived in Oxford on 3 June 1662 and presented himself to Edward Pococke and other prominent Hebraists there. Yet it was John Lightfoot, Christian Hebraist at Cambridge, who secured an academic position for Abendana, and from 1663 until 1667 he was on the payroll of Trinity College, Cambridge, working on his translation of the Mishnah. He seems to have left Trinity in less than friendly circumstances, possibly because his bookselling came to overwhelm his scholarly duties, but by 1669 he was once again with a proper position, this time as an employee of the university itself. By the time of his final payment in 1676 Isaac Abendana had completed translating the Mishnah into Latin, nearly thirty years after the project first began to be discussed in the Hartlib circle, although his labours were never published.

Accordingly Abendana left Cambridge and moved to Oxford, spending much of the period between 1681 and 1685 in London, where his brother Jacob was leader of the Sephardi community. From 1689 Isaac served as lecturer in Hebrew at Magdalen College, Oxford, a position he held until his death ten years later. During his Oxford years Isaac Abendana became known as a resident authority on all matters Jewish and as the chief purveyor of Hebrew books, a situation he consolidated by inventing the Oxford diary, which in its original form included not only information relevant to university men but also a yearly essay on some aspect of Jewish religion and culture. These essays made the almanacs widely sought after even when their immediate practical use had passed, and they were later published in book form.

Isaac Abendana died on 17 July 1699 while visiting his friend Arthur Charlett, master of University College, Oxford, who informed the antiquary Thomas Tanner that 'Old Abendana rising at 4 to see me, having lighted his Pipe, fell down dead' (Katz, 'The Abendana brothers', 46). A merchant Jew passing through the town conveyed Abendana's body to London for burial, putting an end to a thirty-seven-year Oxbridge career, during which time he had a virtual monopoly on Hebrew studies at the two universities. DAVID S. KATZ, rev.

Sources D. S. Katz, 'The Abendana brothers and the Christian Hebraists of seventeenth-century England', *Journal of Ecclesiastical History*, 40 (1989), 28–52 · I. Abrahams, 'Isaac Abendana's Cambridge Mishnah and Oxford calendars', *Transactions of the Jewish Historical Society of England*, 8 (1915–17), 98–121

Abendana, Jacob (c.1630–1685), leader of the Sephardi Jewish community in London, was born in Spain and was taken with his brother Isaac *Abendana to Hamburg, Germany, as a child. Jacob studied at the Yeshiva de los Pintos at Rotterdam, and at the age of twenty-five he was already a rabbi in Amsterdam. As early as 1660 or 1661 he was in contact with Adam Boreel, the continental Christian Hebraist of the circle dominated by John Dury and Samuel Hartlib, who commissioned him to translate the Mishnah, the Hebrew part of the Talmud, into Spanish. After finishing this task Jacob collaborated with his brother Isaac to put out in 1662 an edition of the *Mikhlal yofi*, Solomon ibn Melik's thirteenth-century commentary on the Bible, with Rabbi Jacob's own supercommentary. The work was published with the approbations of Christian scholars, including the celebrated Jean Buxtorf the younger, which was a new departure for Jewish authors of a Hebrew book. Jacob Abendana followed up this success with a Spanish translation of Judah HaLevi's twelfth-century *Kuzari*, which was published in 1663 and was dedicated to Sir William Davidson, the English resident in Holland.

By the beginning of 1668 Jacob had joined his brother Isaac in England, and with him he set about selling Hebrew books to a devoted clientele that included Henry Oldenburg, Robert Boyle, and Thomas Barlow of the Bodleian Library. During this visit to London the Jewish community there gave Abendana a gift equivalent to the yearly salary of the congregation's rabbi, perhaps in the hope that he would stay. In fact he returned to Amsterdam, but in 1681 he agreed to serve as leader of the English Sephardi community, which had been so generous to him years before. In that year he was host to the Princess Anne, who came to the synagogue during passover, the first occasion on which a member of the royal family visited the Jews at prayer.

Jacob Abendana died in London in 1685; he had no children. Although his Spanish translation of the Mishnah was never published, and indeed is now lost, when Surenhusius began publishing his own Latin version at Amsterdam in 1698 he paid tribute to Abendana's work.

DAVID S. KATZ, rev.

Sources D. S. Katz, 'The Abendana brothers and the Christian Hebraists of seventeenth-century England', *Journal of Ecclesiastical History*, 40 (1989), 28–52

Abenon, d', family (*per.* 1086–*c*.1400), gentry, were a knightly family holding lands from 1086 onwards. They gradually extended their estates and became prominent in the county community in Surrey without ever participating notably in national affairs.

Roger d'Abenon (*d.* before 1100), the first identified member of the family, held an estate at Abenon (now La Folletière-Abanon) in central Normandy, near the *caput* at Orbec of his lord Richard fitz Gilbert, ancestor of the Clares, earls of Hertford. An important tenant in England, Roger was one of only two holding estates both in fitz Gilbert's East Anglian block, at Freston, Suffolk, and in his south-eastern block, at Albury and West Molesey, Surrey.

Roger's descendant (perhaps nephew) **Enguerrand** [i] **d'Abenon** (*fl. c.*1113–1130) proved a generous monastic benefactor, granting tithes and churches to the Benedictine priory of Stoke by Clare, Suffolk, founded by Gilbert de Clare (*d.* 1117); land to the newly founded Cistercian abbey at Waverley, Surrey; and the whole of his Molesey manor to the Augustinian priory of Merton, Surrey, choices presumably dictated by a mixture of tenurial loyalties and ties of neighbourhood. The family was already focusing its interests on Surrey, where they acquired more Clare tenancies, including the estate at Stoke D'Abernon to which they gave their name and with which they came to be most closely associated.

Enguerrand's connections were not merely local, however; he witnessed two of Henry I's charters, and his Merton grant was made for the soul of the king 'qui me nutrivit' ('who brought me up'), pointing to a period in early life spent at court. Nothing is known of Enguerrand [i]'s nephew, Enguerrand [ii]. The latter's son, **Enguerrand** [iii] **d'Abenon** (*d.* before 1194), was a major Clare tenant in 1166, with four fees which may have already included Fetcham, just south of Stoke D'Abernon (where the family is known to have held land in the following century of the Clares and of the Warenne earls of Surrey). Enguerrand [iii] had probably also acquired another Clare manor at Pavenham, Bedfordshire, by 1176, these further Clare enfeoffments and Enguerrand's attest-ation of a Clare charter bearing witness to the continuing vitality of tenurial ties. Enguerrand was probably the second husband of Maud de Camoys, widow of another Clare tenant with Surrey lands.

None the less, like many substantial subtenants the d'Abenons had by now established other ties. Enguerrand held half a fee of Robert, the younger bastard son of Henry I, at Drewsteignton and Bradford D'Abernon, Devon, the result perhaps of friendships forged during Enguerrand [i]'s stay at court. Because of their remoteness from the Surrey estates, Drewsteignton was used for dower, and Bradford D'Abernon was soon given to a cadet branch and did not descend with the Surrey estates.

Enguerrand [iii] and his son Roger [see below] also had personal ties with William Marshal, who spent his honeymoon at Stoke D'Abernon in 1189. Both witnessed William's charters and in 1200 William exchanged Roger's ancestral Norman estate for a small manor at Duxford and rents in Cambridgeshire. The exchange must have been to the financial disadvantage of Roger, but it meant he did not suffer confiscation when Normandy was lost in 1204. Duxford, like the Devon estates, was also used to provide for widows and younger sons.

During the lifetime of Enguerrand [iii]'s son **Sir Roger d'Abenon** (*d*. before 1210) the d'Abenons were involved in one of their few major lawsuits, brought in 1200 and concerning an estate at Lasham, Hampshire, granted to Enguerrand [iii] by the widow of Roger de Clere (a major Warenne tenant in Surrey and elsewhere). It was finally resolved in 1207 with a partition between Ralph de Clere (*d*. 1232x43) and Walter, one of Enguerrand's brothers. This **Walter d'Abenon** (*d*. before 1219/20) succeeded to the family lands on Roger's death, but, on following the Clares into rebellion against John in 1215, forfeited his estates, valued at £40 per annum, for a time.

On the death of Walter's son, Enguerrand [iv] (*d*. 1234), the crown briefly assumed control. In 1235, however, Enguerrand [iv]'s uncle **Gilbert d'Abenon** (*d*. 1236), youngest brother of Enguerrand [iii] and Walter, secured the release of the claims of his nephew Jordan, the son of an elder brother, William, in exchange for Gilbert's land at Duxford. Gilbert, unlike his nephew, was an active knight who served on knightly juries and commissions from 1220 onwards. He did not enjoy his estates for long, however, and died leaving as heir a minor. None the less, the family's aggrandizement continued, for Gilbert's marriage to a neighbouring child heiress, Maud de la Lote, brought lands at Headley, close to Fetcham, and he may have acquired the Clare estate at Walton-on-Thames, north-west of Stoke D'Abernon, with which he dowered Enguerrand's widow.

Gilbert's son **John [i] d'Abenon** (1223–1277) married Avelina, probably a member of the *Chaworth family, whose interests in Derbyshire and Nottinghamshire were the subject of successful litigation in 1248, although whether the d'Abenons retained lands here very long seems doubtful. This marriage, unusual for a family which normally looked to the neighbouring gentry for brides, may have been arranged by John's guardian, John of Gatesden, who had interests in Nottinghamshire. John's more parochial concerns are reflected in a dispute with the neighbouring Chertsey Abbey, and the acquisition of an abbey rent at Great Bookham.

In 1253 John [i] was granted free warren in several manors and an exemption from jury service and office holding. As one of Surrey's foremost knights he was appointed by the Oxford parliament in 1258 to inquire into misgovernment in the county, and after the baronial victory at Lewes in 1264 was entrusted with Guildford Castle and lands in Surrey and Sussex of several royalists, including John de Warenne, earl of Surrey (*d*. 1304). He was also sheriff of the two counties from 1264–5. In 1266 John played his part in the process of settlement after the barons' wars when he was appointed to inquire into Clare and Warenne rights in particular manors.

John [i]'s son and heir, **John [ii] d'Abenon** (*d*. 1327), took up knighthood after distraint proceedings in 1278. Although summoned to serve in the French and Scottish wars John's main contribution seems to have been administrative. He served as conservator of the peace, tax assessor and collector, and on *ad hoc* commissions, mainly but not exclusively in Surrey, from 1279 until the early 1320s. He was also an MP for Surrey on five occasions.

Apart from a grant of turfs at Stoke D'Abernon to Waverley in 1282, little is known about John [ii]'s land exploitation in Surrey, but in Duxford he was busily extending his holdings through such means as purchases from freeholders. The fact that his Clare fees were valued at £80 in 1314 (double the 1215 figure) suggests that, even allowing for inflation, the d'Abenons managed all their resources with care. John [ii]'s wife, Constance, with rights in South Lambeth, appears in the Guildford Dominican friary's obituary list. Two Johns, probably John [ii] and John [iii], are also listed. Dominicans had executed Enguerrand [iv]'s will, so the d'Abenons clearly had a number of connections with this order.

John [ii]'s main claim to fame is the monumental brass in Stoke D'Abernon church. Long celebrated as the earliest military brass in England, dated to the late thirteenth century and identified as John [i], scholarship has now redated it to *c*.1327 and to John [ii]. A work of high-quality craftsmanship, it is thought to be one of a group of brasses produced at this time by a London workshop with clients in the south-east and midlands.

John [iii] d'Abenon (1267?–1344/5), son of John [ii], attended the Dunstable tournament in 1307 and fought at Boroughbridge in 1322. He was commissioner of array several times and in 1325 was instructed to go to Guyenne with John de Warenne, earl of Surrey (*d*. 1347); Gilbert, the last Clare earl, had died in 1314. After his father's death, John took a similarly active role in local affairs, including stints as MP and sheriff. Another brass in Stoke D'Abernon church, redated to the 1340s and of perhaps inferior but more elaborate workmanship, is now identified as John [iii]. The brass belongs to the 'mass end' of a London workshop's output, stylistically part of a group produced for clients all over England between *c*.1333 and 1350.

John [iii] died at a considerable age, his son John [iv] having predeceased him. The inheritance passed to his grandson **William d'Abenon** (d. 1358), MP three times and active participant in Surrey administration until exempted from juries and office holding in 1354. He had two daughters, but the younger, Margaret, predeceased him and the whole inheritance passed to **Elizabeth d'Abenon** (b. 1340, d. after 1394) and to her children with her first husband, William Croyser, a Bedfordshire neighbour and a royal official.

The family arms were azure, a chevron or.

ANNE POLDEN

Sources C. A. F. Meekings, 'Notes on the de Abernon family before 1236', *Surrey Archaeological Collections*, 72 (1980), 157–73 • C. S. Perceval, 'Some account of the family of Abernon, of Albury and Stoke D'Abernon', *Surrey Archaeological Collections*, 5 (1871), 53–74 • C. A. F. Meekings and D. Crook, eds., *The 1235 Surrey eyre*, 1, Surrey RS, 31 (1979) • *VCH Surrey*, vols. 2–3 • *VCH Cambridgeshire and the Isle of Ely*, vol. 6 • P. Binski, 'The stylistic sequence of London figure brasses', *The earliest English brasses: patronage, style, workshops, 1270–1350*, ed. J. Coates (1987) • J. Blair, 'English monumental brasses before 1350: types, patterns and workshops', *The earliest English brasses: patronage, style, workshops, 1270–1350*, ed. J. Coates (1987) • L. C. Loyd, *The origins of some Anglo-Norman families*, ed. C. T. Clay and D. C. Douglas, Harleian Society, 103 (1951) • R. Mortimer, 'The beginnings of the honour of Clare', *Anglo-Norman Studies*, 3 (1980), 119–41 • R. Mortimer, 'Land and service: the tenants of the honour of Clare', *Anglo-Norman Studies*, 8 (1985), 177–97 • D. Crouch, *William Marshal: court, career, and chivalry in the Angevin empire, 1147–1219* (1990) • M. Bassett, *Knights of the shire for Bedfordshire during the middle ages*, Publications of the Bedfordshire Historical Society, 29 (1949) • F. B. Lewis, ed., *Pedes finium, or, Fines relating to the county of Surrey* (1894) • J. S. Purvis, 'Obituary calendar of the Dominican friary of Guildford', *Surrey Archaeological Collections*, 42 (1934), 90–99 • *Members of parliament: return to two orders of the honorable the House of Commons*, House of Commons, 1 (1878), pt 1 • *Chancery records*

Likenesses brass (John [ii] d'Abenon), Stoke D'Abernon church • brass (John [iii] d'Abenon), Stoke D'Abernon church • brasses, repro. in Coates, ed., *Earliest English brasses*, pp. 93, 109 • equestrian seals (Roger d'Abenon, Enguerrand [iv] d'Abenon), repro. in *BM Catalogue of seals*, vol. 2, p. 235

Abenon, Elizabeth d' (b. 1340, d. after 1394). *See under* Abenon, d', family (*per.* 1086–c.1400).

Abenon, Enguerrand d' (fl. c.1113–1130). *See under* Abenon, d', family (*per.* 1086–c.1400).

Abenon, Enguerrand d' (d. before 1194). *See under* Abenon, d', family (*per.* 1086–c.1400).

Abenon, Gilbert d' (d. 1236). *See under* Abenon, d', family (*per.* 1086–c.1400).

Abenon, John d' (1223–1277). *See under* Abenon, d', family (*per.* 1086–c.1400).

Abenon, John d' (1267?–1344/5). *See under* Abenon, d', family (*per.* 1086–c.1400).

Abenon, John d' (d. 1327). *See under* Abenon, d', family (*per.* 1086–c.1400).

Abenon, Roger d' (d. before 1100). *See under* Abenon, d', family (*per.* 1086–c.1400).

Abenon, Sir Roger d' (d. before 1210). *See under* Abenon, d', family (*per.* 1086–c.1400).

Abenon, Walter d' (d. before 1219/20). *See under* Abenon, d', family (*per.* 1086–c.1400).

Abenon, William d' (d. 1358). *See under* Abenon, d', family (*per.* 1086–c.1400).

Aberconway. For this title name *see* McLaren, Charles Benjamin Bright, first Baron Aberconway (1850–1934); McLaren, Laura Elizabeth, Lady Aberconway (1854–1933); McLaren, Henry Duncan, second Baron Aberconway (1879–1953).

Abercorn. For this title name *see* Hamilton, James, first earl of Abercorn (1575–1618); Hamilton, James, sixth earl of Abercorn (c.1661–1734); Hamilton, James, eighth earl of Abercorn (1712–1789); Hamilton, James, first duke of Abercorn (1811–1885); Hamilton, James, second duke of Abercorn (1838–1913).

Abercrombie, David (1909–1992), phonetician, was born in Birkenhead on 19 December 1909, the eldest of the three sons and a daughter of the poet and critic Lascelles *Abercrombie (1881–1938) and Catherine, *née* Gwatkin (b. 1881/2). One of his brothers was the biologist Michael *Abercrombie (1912–1979). His early years were spent in Ryton, Gloucestershire, in a comfortable home often visited by two family friends of his parents, Robert Frost and Rupert Brooke.

On the outbreak of the First World War the family returned to Merseyside, where Abercrombie was educated at Liverpool College. From 1922 to 1929 his father occupied the chair of English literature at Leeds University, and Abercrombie became a student at Leeds in his father's department. It was here that Eric Gordon lectured on Old Norse, and Abercrombie was thanked in print by him for his 'illuminating comments on the description of Old Norse sounds' (E. V. Gordon, *An Introduction to Old Norse*, 1927); Abercrombie was just seventeen. He graduated BA in English in 1930 with third-class honours. Immediately he began an MA at Leeds on the phonetic basis of i-mutation. It was never completed, but it carried forward his undergraduate interest in the pronunciation of Old Norse, and foreshadowed a later one, namely prosodic phonology.

Through his father, who was a member of the BBC's advisory committee on spoken English, Abercrombie met Daniel Jones, professor of phonetics at University College, London. An unexpected consequence was that he was able to spend two years, from 1931 to 1933, as a teaching *assistant* at the Lycée Louis-le-Grand in Paris, at the same time as learning French, attending classes in phonetics at the Institut de Phonétique at the Sorbonne (the University of Paris), and sitting the examination of the International Phonetic Association. From 1933 to 1937 he was back in England as an assistant lecturer in English to non-native speakers of English, and also contributing to the teaching of French, at the London School of Economics (LSE).

From 1938 to 1940 Abercrombie worked for the British Council in Athens as director of studies at the Institute of English Studies. From 1940 to 1945 he lectured on English at Cairo University, also acting as an assistant censor in control headquarters of Anglo-Egyptian censorship. His compatriots in Cairo included the novelists Lawrence Durrell and Olivia Manning, and the cookery writer Elizabeth David. In 1944 he married Mary Henderson *née* Marble (*d.* 1998), of Illinois and California, the mother of Mortimer Henderson and Mary Brown (*née* Henderson).

After the Second World War, Abercrombie returned to the LSE for two years until his appointment to a lectureship in phonetics at the University of Leeds (1947–8). In the following year he moved to Edinburgh University, where he established not only a department of phonetics with a distinctively different approach to the subject, but also his own reputation as one of the twentieth century's leading phoneticians. Up until then phonetics had often been regarded as a practical, ancillary discipline in the study of modern languages, which had as its aim the teaching of a native-like reproduction of the sounds of a language. Abercrombie, drawing on his knowledge of the work of particular phoneticians from the seventeenth century onwards, held that the role of phonetics in an undergraduate curriculum was to determine and exemplify a general theory of speech production, with its properties and possibilities. Speech as a worldwide phenomenon, not the speech of a particular language or group of languages, should be the salient characteristic of phonetics at the undergraduate level. With the help of a small group of colleagues, including J. C. (Ian) Catford, he made this a guiding principle in his development of courses at Edinburgh. He is rightly credited with establishing phonetics as an autonomous discipline in the British university system. He was promoted to senior lecturer in 1951, to reader in 1957, and to a personal professorship in 1964; the established chair was created for him in 1967. He was elected a fellow of the British Academy in 1991. Abercrombie's published work ranges over not only questions of general phonetics, but also aspects of the history of phonetics, of writing systems (particularly shorthand), and the contributions of phonetics to the teaching of English as a foreign language.

Lascelles Abercrombie inspired in his son a love of poetry but also a curiosity about the mechanics of poetry, particularly rhythm—see Lascelles Abercrombie's *Principles of English Prosody* (1923). This led David to investigate the relationships between rhythm in poetry and the far more complex forms of rhythm in speech. Again thanks to his father he came to know Robert Bridges, for whom he devised a reformed system of English spelling used in the publication of Bridges' collected essays. He also devised the phonetic script used by C. K. Ogden in his *General Basic Dictionary* (1942).

Abercrombie was an inspired and inspiring teacher. He was as lucid in speaking about phonetics as in writing about it. He asked high standards of his students, but in return the hospitality and sociability that he and his wife, Mary, extended to them, as well as to colleagues and visitors, was legendary. At heart he was a wise and gentle person. Abercrombie died on 4 July 1992 in Edinburgh. Mary died in London on 28 April 1998.

M. K. C. MacMahon

Sources A. J. Aitken and E. Uldall, 'Obituary. Prof David Abercrombie: distinguished phonetician', *The Scotsman* (9 July 1992) · P. Ladefoged, 'David Abercrombie, 1909–1992', *PBA*, 90 (1996), 239–48 · J. Laver and R. E. Asher, *The Independent* (11 July 1992) · *The Times* (28 Aug 1992) · *WW* (1992) · L. J. Windsor, 'David Abercrombie: minding our language', *The Guardian* (21 Aug 1992) · personal knowledge (2004) · private information (2004) [Dr Mark Shipway, Leeds University Archive; Mrs Elizabeth Uldall, U. Edin.] · *CCI* (1992)
Archives U. Leeds, Brotherton L.
Wealth at death £150,985.53: confirmation, 10 Sept 1992, *CCI*

Abercrombie, John (1726–1806), horticulturist and writer, was born in Prestonpans, near Edinburgh, the son of a market gardener. He was educated at a grammar school, and at the age of fourteen began to work under his father. He went to London about 1751, and was employed first in the Royal Botanic Gardens at Kew, and next at Leicester House; he then worked for nearly twenty years as a gardener for several noblemen and gentlemen, including the botanist William Munro. In the 1750s he married a woman employed in the household of Sir James Douglas, for whom he was working, and they had two sons and sixteen daughters. Abercrombie survived them all except for one son.

About 1770 Abercrombie established a market garden near Hackney, and also leased a public house near Mile End, which he turned into the 'Artichoke Tea Garden'. He later sold the lease and set up a nursery and market garden at Tottenham. His first work on practical gardening, *Every Man his Own Gardener*, appeared in 1767 under the title of *Mawe's Gardener's Calendar*. Abercrombie had written to Thomas Mawe, head gardener to the duke of Leeds, offering £20 in return for permission to use his name as author. The book was a great success, and eventually, in 1776, Abercrombie added his own name on the title page as joint author with Mawe. The book continued to be issued, in revised editions, until 1879. Abercrombie did not meet Mawe until after the publication of the second edition, when Mawe invited him to Yorkshire. They remained friends, and collaborated on *The Universal Gardener and Botanist* (1778).

In 1779 Abercrombie published his first book solely under his own name, *The British Fruit Gardener and Art of Pruning*. In the 1780s he published a number of books on practical gardening. One of the most popular of his works was the *Gardener's Pocket Journal and Daily Assistant* (1790), which by 1857 had reached a thirty-fifth edition. Among his more specialized works were *The Complete Forcing Gardener* (1781); *The Complete Wall Tree Pruner* (1783); *The Propagation and Botanical Arrangement of Plants and Trees, Useful and Ornamental* (1784); and *The Hot House Gardener, or, The General Culture of the Pineapple and Method of Pruning Early Grapes* (1789); a German translation of this appeared at Vienna in 1792. Abercrombie was also invited to Russia to superintend the gardens of Catherine the Great, but he panicked at the last minute and did not go, sending a copy of *Every Man his Own Gardener* instead.

In 1796 Abercrombie moved to Somers Town in central London, and worked on *The Practical Gardener* and on revising his earlier works. Despite the success of his manuals, he became impoverished at the end of his life, and was supported by his friend James Donn, curator of the Cambridge Botanic Garden, who brought out *Practical Gardening* in 1813. Abercrombie died on 15 April or on 2 May 1806 at his house in Chalton Street, Somers Town, London, after falling down some steps and breaking his hip.

FRANCIS ESPINASSE, *rev.* ANNE PIMLOTT BAKER

Sources F. M. G. Cardew, 'John Abercrombie', *Journal of the Royal Horticultural Society*, 72 (1947), 245–8 · Desmond, *Botanists* · *A new catalogue of living English authors: with complete lists of their publications, and biographical and critical memoirs* (1799) · *The practical gardener*, 2nd edn (1817) [James Mean's memoir]
Likenesses line engraving, BM, NPG; repro. in J. Abercrombie, *Every man his own gardener*, 16th edn (1800)

Abercrombie, John (1780–1844), physician, eldest of four sons of the Revd George Abercrombie and his second wife, Barbara Morice, was born on 10 October 1780 in Aberdeen, where his father was parish minister of East Church, and exerted a powerful influence on his religious and moral upbringing. Abercrombie attended the local grammar school and then Marischal College, Aberdeen. In 1800 he went to Edinburgh University to study medicine, and took his degree in June 1803. His thesis, 'De fatuitate alpina', reflected a general interest in the student population for studies on mental medicine. He was very diligent and admired by other students for his indefatigable energy and the deep, practical, and unobtrusive piety which regulated his subsequent life. He then spent a further six months at St George's Hospital in London and on his return became FRCS Edinburgh, producing a probationary essay, 'On paralysis of the lower extremities from diseased spine'.

Almost immediately Abercrombie took a house in Nicholson Street and went into general practice. He rapidly became a popular figure in Edinburgh, but despite a burgeoning private practice gave much of his time to the poor, acting as one of the medical officers at the Royal Public Dispensary. In this role he subdivided the poorer areas of Edinburgh into districts and allotted them different students, supervising their work himself. He was also appointed public vaccinator along with Drs Gillespie and Bryce, and together they introduced Jenner's discovery to the city. On 22 October 1808 he married a very wealthy woman, Agnes, daughter of David Wardlaw, a manufacturer, of Netherbeath, and they had seven daughters. This wealth enabled him to keep a carriage, and reduced the necessity for him to obtain a full-time academic or medical post. He was noted for the close attention he paid patients, visiting up to three or four times a day. His popularity created many rivals but his disarming and inoffensive personality helped him avoid conflict. His private means also provided the opportunity to pursue academic interests. From 1816 to 1824 Abercrombie contributed a series of papers on pathological subjects to the *Edinburgh Medical and Surgical Journal*. These led to the publication of his two chief works in 1828, *Pathological and Practical Researches on Diseases of the Brain and Spinal Cord* and *Diseases of the Stomach, Intestinal Canal, the Liver and the other Viscera of the Abdomen*, both of which went through several editions.

Considering his limited access to anatomy facilities it is surprising that he was able to produce these, and although there was little original material in them, they did establish his name.

Abercrombie did from time to time attempt to secure a more permanent post. On the death of Professor James Gregory in 1821 he applied for the chair in the practice of medicine but owing to town council opposition was unsuccessful. At that time posts were often considered the sole property of one or other of the two colleges, and Abercrombie subsequently became a licentiate of the College of Physicians in 1823, and a fellow in 1824. In 1825 Lizars canvassed his support for the creation of a new infirmary, proposing posts for himself, Robert Liston, and Alexander Morison among others, but nothing came of this. In 1828 on the death of Professor Duncan, Abercrombie applied for the post of king's physician for Scotland and was appointed.

Following his move to membership of the College of Physicians, Abercrombie gradually established himself as the leading physician in Edinburgh. He had an extensive private practice and his services were in demand throughout Scotland. He was very generous to professional colleagues, helping them find work and in several cases acting as their family physician.

The monographs for which Abercrombie is best known concerned the intellectual and moral nature of man. In 1830 he published *The Intellectual Powers and the Investigation of Truth*, which went into numerous editions and in 1860 was introduced as a textbook at Calcutta University. This was followed by *The Philosophy of Moral Feelings* in 1835, and although the books reflected the influence of Reid, Brown, and Dugald Stewart, neither demonstrated any original thinking. Lord Cockburn rather scathingly commented that his 'fame might have stood higher had he published fewer books'. That year he also became DCL at Oxford.

In the last decade of his life Abercrombie wrote a number of essays on subjects of everyday usefulness, which were collected into a volume called *Elements of Sacred Truth* which sold 20,000–30,000 copies. On his election as lord rector of Marischal College, Aberdeen, in November 1835 he addressed the students on the great principle of self-government, of calling oneself to account, and the habit of self-inspection so beloved of evangelicals. Gradually he immersed himself in Bible study and revealed religion, and finally, in 1840, took the painful decision to leave the established church.

Abercrombie was an extremely generous man, and donated widely to Edinburgh charities and benevolent societies. He also lent his support to the Medical Missionary Society in China, which was attracted by his devotion to learning and to man as an intellectual and moral being. Abercrombie was not especially clubbable, and could be very taciturn, but he was a regular member of the College of Physicians, an honorary member of the Provincial Medical and Surgical Association, and a vice-president of the Royal Society of Edinburgh. In 1841 he suffered a stroke but made a good recovery. He subsequently suffered another stroke as he was getting into his carriage, and died suddenly on 14 November 1844 at his home, 19 York Place, Edinburgh, of a burst coronary artery; he was buried in West Church, Edinburgh. NICK HERVEY

Sources Chambers, *Scots.* (1835) · *IGI* · *Provincial Medical and Surgical Journal* (Feb 1844), 267–8 · Morison diaries, Royal College of Physicians of Edinburgh · P. Parker, *Statements respecting hospitals in China preceded by a letter to John Abercrombie M.D.* (1842) · m. reg. Scot · J. Grant, *Cassell's old and new Edinburgh*, 3 vols. [1880–83], vol. 2, p. 187 · *DNB*
Archives Royal College of Physicians of Edinburgh, corresp. and papers | U. Edin., New Coll. L., letters to Thomas Chalmers
Likenesses F. Croll, line engraving, medallion, NPG; repro. in *Hogg's Instructor*, 3.145 · woodcut (after medallion on monument, Edinburgh), repro. in Anderson, *Scot. nat.*

Abercrombie, Lascelles (1881–1938), writer and university teacher, was born at Manor House, Ashton upon Mersey, Cheshire, on 9 January 1881, the fifth son, and the eighth of nine children, of William Abercrombie (*d.* before 1909), stockbroker, of Ashton upon Mersey, and his wife, Sarah Anne, *née* Heron (*d. c.*1916). One of his brothers was (Leslie) Patrick *Abercrombie, the town planner. From boyhood Abercrombie was devoted to music and literature; his taste was fostered at a preparatory school, and also at Malvern College, where he read Greek and Latin eagerly. From 1900 to 1902 he studied science at the Victoria University of Manchester, but then turned to journalism for a living, and to poetry for his vocation. He reviewed much in the Liverpool daily press; his first poem, 'Blind', appeared in 1907 and his first volume of verse, *Interludes and Poems*, in 1908. On 23 January 1909 he married Catherine (*b.* 1881/2), daughter of Owen Gwatkin, surgeon, of Grange-over-Sands; they had one daughter and three sons, the eldest of whom, David *Abercrombie, became a phonetician, and the youngest, Michael *Abercrombie (1912–1979), a biologist. After a stay of more than a year in Birkenhead he and his wife migrated first to Herefordshire and then in 1911 to Gloucestershire, where, inspired by happiness and by the noble scenery, he published some of his best verse. It included *Mary and the Bramble* (1910), *The Sale of St. Thomas*, act I (1911), and also some poetic plays in *New Numbers*, 1–4 (1914), a periodical privately issued in partnership with Rupert Brooke, John Drinkwater, and Wilfrid Gibson.

Abercrombie now came to be recognized as a leading poet of the new generation, distinguished for his lyrical power and speculative daring. He was praised by Robert Bridges for his lucid exposition of difficult themes, and Yeats was to devote eight pages of the *Oxford Book of Modern Verse* (1936) to Abercrombie's poetry. He responded profoundly to natural beauty; his love poetry was ardent and exalted; and the mystical and metaphysical strain was ever present. It is heard again in the prose of *Speculative Dialogues* (1913), with its musings on life and love and on the last things; and also in several dramatic poems, such as *Deborah* (1912), which were not designed for the stage. But several were acted; of these the most notable is *The End of the World* (published in *New Numbers*), in which some homely folk are terrified by a false alarm that doomsday

has arrived. His appreciative study of Thomas Hardy, published in 1912, gives some insight into his own poetic development.

Abercrombie was still to write his best verse, but his richest period of poetic production was over. The First World War came as a grievous interruption. Although a keen patriot, he was not strong enough for military service, and laboured in Liverpool as an examiner of munitions. After the war he took up a lecturership in poetry at Liverpool University; this appointment, which he held from 1919 to 1922, was an event that was to affect his whole career. He spoke upon his own craft; he held public audiences, not least by his rare gift for reading aloud; and he taught small classes the outlines of literary criticism and of its history. Abercrombie published many critical studies, often based on the public lectures which he gave at Cambridge, at Baltimore, to the British Academy, and elsewhere. They include *An Essay towards a Theory of Art* (1922), *Principles of English Prosody* (1924), and *Romanticism* (1926). In 1930 Oxford University Press published (in the Oxford Poets) Abercrombie's collected *Poems*, all but one, the richest and maturest of all, the completed *Sale of St. Thomas* (1931). Here, in a style which often rises to grandeur, he proclaims his faith in an omnipresent divine spirit embodying the law of ideal beauty. Abercrombie deepened and ennobled English metaphysical poetry. He charged it anew with his passionate feeling for the essential beauty of nature and of human nature. *Poetry, its Music and Meaning* (1932) ably states the artistic and critical convictions upon which his work was based.

A very active professor, Abercrombie rose quickly in the academic world. He occupied the chair of English literature at Leeds University from 1922 to 1929 and was Hildred Carlile professor of English literature in London University, at Bedford College for Women, from 1929 to 1935. In 1935 he became Goldsmiths' reader in English at Oxford and a fellow of Merton College. He received honorary degrees from the universities of Cambridge, Manchester, and Belfast, held several special lecturerships, including the Clark lecturership at Trinity College, Cambridge, in 1923, and was elected a fellow of the British Academy in 1937. But his health declined, and he died of diabetes at the Hospital of St John and St Elizabeth, St John's Wood, London, on 27 October 1938; he was survived by his wife. A final volume of his work, *Lyrics and Unfinished Poems*, appeared in 1940. OLIVER ELTON, *rev.*

Sources *The Times* (28 Oct 1938) · O. Elton, 'Lascelles Abercrombie, 1881–1938', *PBA*, 25 (1939), 394–421 · W. Gibson, *English*, 2 (1939) · personal knowledge (1949) · private information (1949) · b. cert. · m. cert. · d. cert. · E. S. Fisher, 'Lascelles Abercrombie: a biographical essay', *English Literature in Transition, 1880–1920*, 25 (1982), 28–49 · *CGPLA Eng. & Wales* (1939)
Archives Bodl. Oxf., corresp.; literary papers · Indiana University, Bloomington, Lilly Library, letters and writings · State University of New York, Buffalo, E. H. Butler Library, literary papers · U. Leeds, Brotherton L., corresp. and papers, incl. literary MSS | BL, corresp. with Society of Authors, Add. MS 63206 · Bodl. Oxf., letters to Walter de la Mare · Bodl. Oxf., corresp. with Sidgwick and Jackson · JRL, letters to the *Manchester Guardian* · JRL, letters to Allan Monkhouse · LUL, letters to Thomas Sturge Moore · NL Scot., letters to John Dover Wilson · Ransom HRC, corresp. with John

Lane • Somerville College, Oxford, letters to Percy Withers and family • Trinity Cam., letters to R. C. Trevelyan and Mrs E. Trevelyan • U. Leeds, Brotherton L., letters to Arthur Ransome
Likenesses W. Stoneman, photograph, 1937, NPG
Wealth at death £2425 7s. 8d.: probate, 30 Jan 1939, CGPLA Eng. & Wales

Abercrombie, Michael (1912–1979), biologist, was born at The Gallows, Ryton, Dymock, Gloucestershire, on 14 August 1912, the third son in the family of three sons and a daughter of Lascelles *Abercrombie (1881–1938), poet and critic, and his wife, Catherine (b. 1881/2), daughter of Owen Gwatkin, surgeon, of Grange-over-Sands. The Abercrombies were a distinguished family for, in addition to Lascelles, Michael counted among his uncles Sir (Leslie) Patrick *Abercrombie, a pioneer of town planning, Rudolph (Rody), physician and field naturalist, and Charles, a businessman. Michael's brother David *Abercrombie became a professor of phonetics in the University of Edinburgh.

Abercrombie attended Liverpool College, and then from 1922 went to Leeds grammar school, proceeding as top Hastings scholar to Queen's College, Oxford, in 1931. At Oxford he read zoology under the tuition of Gavin de Beer. De Beer arranged for him to work for a period at the Strangeways Research Laboratory in Cambridge under C. H. Waddington with whom he began to study the early development of the domestic chicken by experimental methods, giving particular attention to the signals involved in laying down the body plan. He completed this work at the school of pathology in Oxford, where he shared a room with his friend and contemporary Peter Medawar. The work gained him a first-class honours degree in 1934. He could have extended his studies for a PhD but, at the time, it was not fashionable in Oxford to do so. During this period Abercrombie took an active part in the extensive programme of research on the degeneration of peripheral nerves then in progress in the zoology laboratories under the direction of J. Z. Young.

In 1938 Abercrombie lectured in the zoology department at Birmingham University, while concurrently holding a research fellowship at Queen's College, Oxford. Here he met and (on 17 July 1939) married Minnie Louie (Jane) Johnson (b. 1909/10), a fellow zoology lecturer three years his senior. She was the daughter of Stanley Johnson, an electrical engineer. He moved to Birmingham on a Beit memorial fellowship in 1940 and then became a lecturer in 1945. His most important enterprise at this time was to inaugurate a series of biological texts entitled New Biology, published by Penguin Books, aimed at bringing advanced biology in an intelligible form to sixth formers and first-year biology students. Unfortunately both Abercrombies quarrelled, as had many others, with Lancelot Hogben, Birmingham's head of zoology. Thus in 1946 Abercrombie took a lectureship in the department of anatomy in University College, London, working under his old tutor, Gavin de Beer, the head of the embryology sub-department. He was reader in embryology from 1950 to 1959.

It was here that Abercrombie began the research which made his international reputation, for it was his belief (not shared by de Beer) that embryological problems could be studied in the processes of wound repair, as they might occur in adult animals. His interest in wound healing led him to study cell movement. He was a pioneer in the study of the cellular interactions and cell movement in tissue culture, making particular use of time-lapse cinematography which enabled the visualization of the cells' activities to be greatly speeded up. He juxtaposed two actively growing cultures of fibroblasts—connective tissue cells—which showed that, when the cells migrating outwards from them came into contact with cells from the neighbouring piece of tissue, cell movement ceased. The discovery of this phenomenon, contact inhibition—much less pronounced in cancerous cells than in normal—led to his election to the Royal Society in 1958. It was the basis of his claim to become, first, titular professor of embryology at University College (1959–62) and then Jodrell professor of zoology and comparative anatomy (1962–70). In 1962 he also spent eight months in the Carnegie Institute of Embryology in Washington.

Abercrombie had strongly left-wing opinions. He joined the Communist Party in 1932, but in due course the same humanity and sense of justice that had caused him to join the party caused him to leave it. His last appointment (1970–79) was to succeed Dame Honor B. Fell as the head of the Strangeways Research Laboratory in Cambridge, an appointment whose administrative obligations he coped with as well as a man could who derived no pleasure whatsoever from the exercise of power. He was firm, though, and looked after the interests of his staff. At the same time he was a fellow of Clare Hall.

When the verdict of the market place brought 'new biology' to an end Abercrombie and his wife wrote and published a Dictionary of Biology (with C. J. Hickman, 1950), a fine example of concision and clear writing. Abercrombie's work on contact inhibition continued and provided important insights on the control of cell movement. He was awarded an honorary doctorate by Uppsala University and won the Ernst Bertner award for cancer research. He died at his home, 2 Bridge Lane, Little Shelford, Cambridge, on 28 May 1979.

PETER MEDAWAR, rev. L. WOLPERT

Sources P. Medawar, Memoirs FRS, 26 (1980), 1–16 • personal knowledge (1986) • b. cert. • m. cert. • d. cert. • WWW
Archives Wellcome L., MSS | UCL, corresp. with J. Z. Young
Likenesses photograph, repro. in Trends in Cell Biology, 8 (1998), 124–6

Abercrombie, Sir (Leslie) Patrick (1879–1957), town planner, was born on 6 June 1879 at Green Bank, Sale, Altrincham, one of a family of nine. His father, William Abercrombie (d. before 1909), came from Fife and was a Manchester stockbroker and businessman, with literary and artistic interests; his mother, Sarah Anne Heron (d. c.1916), was from Yorkshire. Among his siblings was Lascelles *Abercrombie (1881–1938), the poet. In 1887 Lynngarth, a new family home, was built in Brooklands Road, Ashton. It was designed by a Leicester architect, Joseph Goddard,

Sir (Leslie) Patrick Abercrombie (1879–1957), by Howard Coster, 1944

and decorated with the advice of J. Aldam Heaton, who frequently worked with Richard Norman Shaw. The arts and crafts interiors left a strong impression on the young Patrick Abercrombie, and inculcated a love of architecture. With his two younger brothers, he was educated at Locker's Park preparatory school, Hemel Hempstead, Hertfordshire (1891–3), before attending Uppingham School, Leicestershire (1893–6), and the Realschule, Lucerne, Switzerland (1896–7).

Training and early career On 11 May 1897 Abercrombie was articled to a Manchester architect, Charles Henry Heathcote, for four years, at a premium of £300; at the same time he also attended evening classes at Manchester School of Art. On completion of his articles he worked for three years in the Liverpool office of Sir Arnold Thornely. His Liverpool post prompted his move to Birkenhead, on the Wirral, which he described as 'a complete break, possibly the most complete in my life' (Abercrombie, pt I, chap. 2, 1). The area remained his home until 1936. In 1906 he worked for the Chester architect Philip Lockwood for a year, but was disappointed in his hopes of a partnership. However, the historic walled town—then under transformation by the Grosvenors, the major landholders—left a lasting impression upon him. In 1907 C. H. Reilly, head of the Liverpool University school of architecture, offered him an appointment as junior lecturer and studio instructor. This was a defining moment in Abercrombie's career, and began his long involvement with civic design and town planning.

When W. H. Lever (subsequently the first Lord Leverhulme) endowed the chair of civic design at Liverpool University in 1909, initially filled by Stanley Davenport Adshead, he also provided sufficient resources to fund a research fellowship and the publication of *Town Planning Review*, the first journal to be devoted to this subject in Great Britain. Abercrombie was appointed by Adshead to fill the fellowship and to edit the *Review*: his literary inclinations and growing knowledge of town planning, a subject which commanded increasing public attention, and which had become a local government function under the Housing and Town Planning Act of 1909, made him the obvious choice as editor. With Adshead, he was the chief contributor to the early volumes, providing many suggestions for the development of Merseyside, chronicling the contemporary growth of the garden city movement, and publishing articles on planning and civic design in continental cities. Abercrombie's fellowship took him abroad every year, and he visited Rome, Florence, Paris, Vienna, Brussels, and Berlin. His breadth of vision was influenced by, and matched, that of Patrick Geddes, in emphasizing the symbiotic cultural and social interdependence of the city–region. This underlay his subsequent writing, teaching, and practice. Following Adshead's resignation in 1915, Abercrombie was appointed his successor as Lever professor of civic design, a post he held for twenty years.

Initially, Abercrombie's practice involved modest projects including housing schemes at Chester and Mouldsworth, built before 1914. Although his early architectural education was influenced by the arts and crafts movement, he developed a simplified Georgian style, which was reflected in his subsequent planning work, particularly at Dormanstown. This rational style represented the English equivalent of emergent modernism in architecture, and became widely influential through its use by Louis de Soissons at Welwyn Garden City from the early 1920s. In 1914, in association with Sydney and Arthur Kelly, Abercrombie entered the Dublin town planning competition, at the prompting of Patrick Geddes. Owing to the outbreak of the First World War, the assessors (who included Geddes) were unable to confer. Announcement of the award of the first prize to Abercrombie and the Kellys was deferred until 1916, and the plan was not published in full until 1922. Nevertheless, it established Abercrombie's international reputation. In 1914 he collaborated with Sydney Kelly and Manning Robertson on a sketch development plan for Dublin county borough. In 1920, in conjunction with Adshead and Stanley Ramsey, Abercrombie designed Dormanstown, an industrial village to house the employees of Dorman Long, the Middlesbrough steel-founders. The same year he was appointed, with Henry Johnson, to prepare a regional planning scheme for 169 square miles around Doncaster, centre of the expanding south Yorkshire coalfield. Approved in 1922, this was the first plan of its type to be published in Britain, and included proposals for ten satellite communities, separated from each other and Doncaster by a green belt, with a 120 foot reservation for the improved A1 road, the major highway from London to the north.

The inter-war years Abercrombie was a leading consultant throughout the inter-war period, and worked prolifically. In 1923 he and his brother Lascelles were asked to report on the preservation of Stratford upon Avon. He produced the Sheffield civic survey (1924), the east Kent regional planning scheme (1925, with John Archibald), the Bristol and Bath regional planning scheme (1930, with B. F. Brueton), the Cumbrian regional report (1932), the east Suffolk regional planning scheme (1935), and the Gloucestershire rural development scheme (all with Sydney Kelly). In many of his plans preservation of rural amenity and landscape was a common thread. In 1929, with the earl of Mayo and Adshead, he prepared a report on the Thames valley, from Cricklade to Staines, presenting a survey of the existing situation, and suggestions for preservation. Regrettably, the scope of many of his plans of the 1920s lay beyond the narrow confines of statutory town planning, which was largely concerned with the regulation of suburban development. Abercrombie was a leading advocate of the broader perspective, reflected to a degree in the 1932 Town and Country Planning Act. In 1933 his book *Town and Country Planning*, published in the Home University Library, brought the subject to a growing middle-class readership.

Abercrombie's love of the traditional English landscapes and historic country towns found a broader expression in the 1920s. In May 1926 his article 'The preservation of rural England' in the *Town Planning Review* acted as catalyst for the foundation of the Council for the Preservation of Rural England; Abercrombie was also co-founder with Clough Williams-Ellis of the council's Welsh equivalent. As chairman of the executive committee of the council, Abercrombie undertook much advisory work on their behalf. In 1935 he succeeded Adshead as professor of town planning at University College, London, which post he held until 1946. From 1936 he was also consultant architect to the Department of Health for Scotland.

In 1937 Abercrombie was appointed a member of the royal commission on the distribution of the industrial population, chaired by Sir Montagu Barlow. This sought to analyse the causes of concentration of population in London and the industrial conurbations, and to recommend possible changes to redress regional imbalance. Abercrombie set out a critique of planning under the 1932 act in his 'Dissentient memorandum', which appeared in the *Report*, published in 1940, a few months after the outbreak of the Second World War. He called for national strategic policy guidance and the interlocking of plans at regional and local level. As a consultant, he had long been concerned by the lack of consistency between advisory regional plans and the statutory local authority plans, where individual councils were motivated by local self-interest, rather than a broader perspective. As Lord Holford wrote, 'if any one man had a truly synoptic view of the physical planning problems of the British Isles, that man was Abercrombie' (*DNB*). In May 1940 Abercrombie travelled to Ceylon, where, with A. Clifford Holliday, his former student, he planned a new site and buildings for the University of Ceylon at Peradinya. The blitz bombing of London and other cities in 1940 revealed the urgency of planning for reconstruction, promoted by Lord Reith, minister-designate of works. Upon his return to Britain, Abercrombie became involved with two major plans for London.

Plans for London and other cities The London plans were probably Abercrombie's greatest achievement. The *County of London Plan*, published in 1943, covered inner London—the area administered by the London county council with the exception of the City. It was prepared in collaboration with J. H. Forshaw, architect to the council. Wesley Dougill, who had been senior lecturer at Liverpool, made a significant contribution to the preparation of the plan, but died a few months before its publication. Abercrombie also brought in Arthur Ling, who prepared a functional analysis of land uses and open spaces. The key problems addressed were traffic congestion, poor housing, inadequate and haphazardly distributed open space, and conflicting land uses. Redevelopment of slum neighbourhoods would entail mixed development, which also included some high-rise housing, set in open space: an English reworking of Le Corbusier's 'radiant city' of the 1920s, which shaped the post-war housing response by the London county council and the London boroughs. Influenced by the contemporary 'precinct theory' of the traffic expert and theorist Alker Tripp, Abercrombie proposed traffic-free areas for the university area in Bloomsbury, around St Paul's, and the Temple. In addition to the technical innovation of the proposals, the plan also strongly emphasized the need to preserve and underpin the traditional character of each locality, based on the peripheral market towns and villages which had been absorbed into the metropolis. Abercrombie's recurrent preoccupation with the human side of his profession—his concept of a town as primarily the setting for human life, rather than a mere pattern of roads and land uses—was updated from Geddes; however, it tended to be overlooked by those responsible for implementation in the post-war political arena. In his 1933 book *Town and Country Planning* Abercrombie commended the comprehensive analytical approach found in the privately funded *Regional Plan for New York and its Environs* (1929), for which Thomas Adams had been consultant. American analytical methods and techniques such as height-zoning were advocated in the plan.

The *Greater London Plan, 1944*, which covered the outer area of London and parts of the home counties, was commissioned by the standing conference on London regional planning, at the request of the minister for town and country planning. Its preparation overlapped with, and was complementary to, the county of London plan. With Abercrombie, Gordon Stephenson and Peter Shepheard also worked on the plan. Its context recognized the spreading influence of the capital city beyond its immediate local government unit. Abercrombie drew four rings, beginning with consolidation of the urban core of the county, through the suburban ring, the green belt, and an outer country ring. The green belt was intended to curb the further spread of suburbs; codified as the metropolitan green belt in 1955, it effectively halted London at its 1939 limits. Within the green belt, new development unrelated to agriculture was to be strictly controlled. The county of London plan had suggested the necessity for planned decentralization of more than a million people and associated industry, and this was to be accommodated in a ring of new towns beyond the green belt. The eight 'first generation' new towns were commenced, following legislation in 1946, by state-created development corporations: although only two were built on the sites proposed by Abercrombie, they have been recognized as a major planning achievement. The road plan, of major motorway radials and rings, was implemented only in modified form, and not completed until the mid-1980s, with the M25. Abercrombie saw London continuing as a world port and manufacturing centre, and failed to anticipate the startling expansion of the service sector and office employment. Nevertheless, his strategy guided the planning of London and the home counties for a half-century after its publication in 1945, despite the lack of a regional executive to co-ordinate the constituent local authorities.

Another important plan by Abercrombie, for Plymouth, was commissioned in the autumn of 1941 by Viscount Astor, lord mayor of the city, which had been intensively bombed, virtually obliterating the city centre. In the plan for Plymouth (1943) comprehensive replanning created a traffic-free shopping centre, based on Tripp's precincts, with a grand central axis—Armada Way—sweeping from the railway station, across Royal Parade, where the guildhall and rebuilt civic centre were located, and onwards to the hoe. Unfortunately the architecture failed to match the boldness of the concept, with Abercrombie opting for the safety of the stripped Georgian style, which was carried through with little imagination or flair. In the broader context of the plan, as usual, Abercrombie declined to be constrained by administrative boundaries, but the adjoining authorities failed to participate actively in the plan, and the proposed regional dimension was lost. He subsequently collaborated with Edwin Lutyens on the plan for Kingston upon Hull, published in 1945, but little of it was implemented.

Before the war's end Abercrombie began work on a major regional plan for the Clyde valley, with Robert Matthew. This was published in 1946, and was followed by a west midlands plan in 1948, and a plan for Edinburgh in 1949. The 1947 Town and Country Planning Act placed emphasis on statutory development planning by local authorities, but Abercrombie took no direct role in statutory planning (nor in the implementation of his Greater London proposals through the 1946 New Towns Act). The post-war period witnessed the expansion of his consultancy work, with no diminution of his energy or enthusiasm in his sixties and seventies. He travelled widely, to Addis Ababa, Hong Kong, and Cyprus. As late as 1956 he returned to Addis Ababa, to spend six weeks putting the finishing touches to his plan for that city.

Conclusion Abercrombie was knighted in 1945, and was also an officer of the order of the crown of Belgium, and of the Légion d'honneur of France. Among professional honours he received were the Ebenezer Howard memorial medal (1943), the royal gold medal for architecture (1946), the gold medal of the American Institute of Architects (1949), and the gold medal of the Town Planning Institute (1955). He had been president of the Town Planning Institute in 1925, and vice-president of the Royal Institute of British Architects in 1937–9. He was a member of the Royal Fine Arts Commission and of the royal commission on the location of industry. After retirement from London University in 1946, Abercrombie gave much time to the Union Internationale des Architectes, established following conferences in London and Brussels in 1947 and 1948. He served as the union's president from 1951 to 1956, and gained the support of the USSR, the United States, and South American republics, in addition to western European countries. He received honorary degrees from the universities of London, Liverpool, and Melbourne.

Abercrombie's written style was elegant, and he was a meticulous draughtsman. His interests were wide-ranging, and he had a close-clipped manner of speech and a ready wit. Patrician in appearance, with sharp features, and wearing a monocle (having lost the sight of his left eye in his youth), he enjoyed the finer things of life. In 1944, after an air raid had seriously damaged the offices in which the Greater London plan was under preparation, Abercrombie braved the wrath of the wardens to retrieve a case of vintage claret from the cellar, which he opened there and then to boost the morale of his staff before getting down to the task of sorting through the debris. A great believer in co-operation, he invariably acknowledged the contribution of partners and collaborators. He was a sympathetic mentor to several generations of students, some of whom collaborated with him later in their careers.

On 5 August 1908 Abercrombie married (Emilia) Maud (1885/6–1942), daughter of Robert Gordon, a corn merchant; the couple had a son and a daughter. The death of his wife in 1942 was a grievous loss for Abercrombie. He himself died at his Berkshire home, the Red House at Aston, on 23 March 1957. He had retained a summer home, Penrhos Bach, Holy Island, Anglesey, and he was buried on 27 March at Rhoscolyn, Anglesey. A memorial service was held at St Martin-in-the-Fields, London, on 24 April 1957, when the address was given by Clough Williams-Ellis. He stated, 'I feel that one of Patrick's great services was that he gave wings to planning, never letting its ultimate end—more happiness for more people—be obscured by its solemn technical processes' (C. Williams-Ellis, 'Address … at the memorial service for Sir Patrick Abercrombie', RIBA BAL, biography file, 1). Abercrombie's embracing vision was predicated upon acceptance of the planner as an expert, a characteristic rejected by the community participation movement of the 1960s, and scarcely possible under the statutory process of the late twentieth century.   MERVYN MILLER

Sources G. Dix, 'Patrick Abercrombie', *Pioneers in British planning*, ed. G. E. Cherry (1981), 103–25 · G. Dix, 'Patrick Abercrombie: pioneer of planning', *ArchR*, 166 (1979), 130–32 · *DNB* · 'Leslie Patrick

Abercrombie: a centenary note', *Town Planning Review*, 50/3 (1979), 257–64 • P. Abercrombie, autobiography, c.1940, U. Lpool L., special collections and archives • F. J. O. [F. J. Osborn], 'Sir Patrick Abercrombie', *Town and Country Planning*, 25/5 (May 1957), 199 • C. Williams-Ellis, 'A genial wizard: an appreciation of Sir Patrick Abercrombie', *The Listener* (8 Aug 1957), 199–200 • P. Shepheard, 'Memories of Abercrombie', *New Towns Record, 1946–1996*, ed. A. Burton and J. Hartley (1996) [CD-Rom (1996)] • 'Presentation of the T. P. I. gold medal to Sir Patrick Abercrombie', *Journal of the Town Planning Institute*, 41 (1955), 229–34 • G. Pepler, 'Patrick Abercrombie: an appreciation', *Journal of the Town Planning Institute*, 43 (1957), 130–32 • A. Manno, *Patrick Abercrombie: a chronological bibliography with annotations and biographical material*, Leeds Planning Research Paper, 19 (1980) • *Liverpool Post* (25 March 1957) • *The Guardian* (25 March 1951) • *The Times* (25 March 1957) • *Western Morning News* (25 March 1957) • b. cert. • m. cert. • d. cert. • private information (2004) [G. Dix]

Archives Church of England Record Centre, London, plans relating to ecclesiastical commissioners' estates • King's School, Canterbury, letters relating to plan for Sturry Court • PRO, corresp. and papers relating to Greater London Plan, HLG85 • RIBA • U. Lpool L., corresp. and papers incl. MSS autobiography | BL, corresp. with Sir Sydney Cockerell, Add. MS 52703 • NL Scot., letters to Patrick Geddes • PRO, corresp. with colonial secretary, CO967, 959 • University of Strathclyde, corresp. with G. L. Pepler • Welwyn Garden City Central Library, corresp. with Sir Frederick Osborn | FILM BFI NFTVA, documentary footage

Likenesses E. Chambre Hardman, photograph, c.1925, U. Lpool, archives • photograph, 1925, Royal Town Planning Institute • H. Coster, photograph, 1944, NPG [*see illus.*] • H. Coster, photographs, NPG

Wealth at death £22,506 0s. 9d.: probate, 27 Aug 1957, CGPLA Eng. & Wales

Abercromby, Alexander, Lord Abercromby (1745–1795), judge and essayist, was born on 15 October 1745, probably at Menstrie, Clackmannanshire, the fourth and youngest son of George Abercromby of Tullibody, Clackmannanshire (1705–1800), who had trained as an advocate, and his wife, Mary (d. 1767), daughter of Ralph Dundas of Manour, Perthshire. His brothers included Sir Ralph *Abercromby of Tullibody (1734–1801) and Sir Robert *Abercromby (1740?–1827), both army officers. He was educated at the University of Edinburgh, where he was remembered for his good looks and engaging personality, and was admitted a member of the Faculty of Advocates on 13 December 1766. Soon afterwards he was appointed sheriff-depute of Stirlingshire. He campaigned from this position to have the duties on spirits lowered in order to help reduce smuggling. In the early part of his career he was better known in Edinburgh for his participation in social life, and was a member of the Feast of Tabernacles, a club which grew up around Henry Dundas. In the late 1770s he came to concentrate more on advancement in the legal profession. His appearance in the case of *Wilson* and *Maclean*, on behalf of a claimant whose receipt from a dead shipmaster was alleged to be a forgery, brought his skills as a pleader to attention, and in 1780 Dundas, by then lord advocate, appointed him advocate-depute alongside Robert Blair and William Craig. Abercromby then resigned his post in Stirlingshire.

Abercromby was a founder of the *Mirror Club, a literary society which emerged from the Feast of Tabernacles

in the late 1770s. He had been a close friend of Henry Mackenzie since university, and was closely associated with Mackenzie in the editing of *The Mirror*, for which he wrote eleven essays during 1779 and 1780, including one on the manners of women which warned them to protect their 'certain delicacy of sentiment and of manners' (Dwyer, 129) and thus their reputations, and reminded them that they held the power 'to form and correct the manners of men' (ibid.). He also contributed nine papers to *The Mirror*'s successor, *The Lounger*, in 1785 and 1786. Mackenzie wrote that Abercromby's articles were 'distinguished by an ease and gentlemanlike turn of expression, by a delicate and polished irony, by a strain of manly, honourable and virtuous sentiment' (Mackenzie, 'Account', 6–7). Between 1780 and 1783 he was a curator of the library of the Faculty of Advocates, and was one of the signatories of the protest against the application by the Society of Antiquaries for a royal charter, in which they challenged the position of the Advocates' Library as the repository of choice for ancient Scottish manuscripts.

On 30 May 1792 Abercromby was appointed to the bench of the court of session, where he took the title of Lord Abercromby, and a few months afterwards, following the death of Sir David Dalrymple, Lord Hailes, was appointed a lord commissioner of justiciary. Like Mackenzie, he regarded the French Revolution 'with horror and indignation' (Mackenzie, 'Account', 14) and as a judge took part in the sedition trials of the 1790s. He had no sympathy for political reformers. He once justified his interpretation of a patriotic statement as treasonous with the words 'We all know … new manners necessarily give birth to new crimes' (Dwyer, 37). His fierce opposition to the cause of reform led to a breach with another of his oldest friends, the philosopher Dugald Stewart. He was taken ill with a chest complaint while on the northern circuit in spring 1795; his condition deteriorated, and in late summer he travelled to Exmouth, Devon, where he died, probably of a disease of the lungs or heart, on 17 November 1795.

J. B. PAUL, rev. MATTHEW KILBURN

Sources H. Mackenzie, 'Account of the life of Lord Abercromby', *Transactions of the Royal Society of Edinburgh*, 4/1 (1798), appx 1–15 • J. Dwyer, *Virtuous discourse: sensibility and community in late eighteenth-century Scotland* (1987) • *Literature and literati: the literary correspondence and notebooks of Henry Mackenzie*, ed. H. W. Drescher, 1: *Letters* (1989) • A. Stewart, ed., *The minute book of the Faculty of Advocates*, 3: *1751–1783*, Stair Society, 46 (1999) • *The anecdotes and egotisms of Henry Mackenzie, 1745–1831*, ed. H. Thompson (1927); facs. repr. (1996) • M. Fry, *The Dundas despotism* (1992) • G. Brunton and D. Haig, *An historical account of the senators of the college of justice, from its institution in MDXXXII* (1832) • IGI

Likenesses H. Raeburn, oils, 1788–9, Faculty of Advocates, Parliament House, Edinburgh • J. Tassie, paste medallion, 1791, Scot. NPG

Abercromby, Alexander (1784–1853), army officer, born on 4 March 1784, was the youngest son of General Sir Ralph *Abercromby (1734–1801) and his wife, Mary Anne (d. 1821), daughter of John Menzies of Ferntower, Crieff, Perth. James *Abercromby, speaker of the House of Commons, was his elder brother. He entered the army at an early age, and served as a volunteer with the 92nd regiment in the expedition to The Helder in 1799. He soon obtained his commission; he was with several regiments, and served in Egypt. He was appointed aide-de-camp to his father's former lieutenant and friend, Sir John Moore, during his command in Sicily in 1806, but was not with him in Spain. Like his elder brother, Sir John *Abercromby, he was rapidly promoted, and in 1808, when only twenty-four, became lieutenant-colonel of the 28th regiment.

Abercromby accompanied his regiment to Portugal to reinforce Wellington after the battle of Talavera. He commanded it at the battle of Busaco and in the lines of Torres Vedras, and as senior colonel commanded his brigade at the battle of Albuera. His services there were conspicuous, and his brigade was later praised by Napier. He was soon superseded, but commanded his regiment at the surprise of Arroyo Molinos and the storming of the forts at Almaraz. In 1812 he joined the staff of the army, and was present as assistant quartermaster-general at the battles of Vitoria, the Pyrenees, and Orthez. He served in the same capacity in 1815, and was present at Quatre-Bras, Waterloo, and the storming of Péronne. He was promoted to a colonelcy in the 2nd (Coldstream) guards, and made a CB (June 1815) and a knight of the order of Maria Theresa of Austria, of the Tower and Sword of Portugal, and of St George of Russia.

After the death of his elder brother John, Abercromby was elected in April 1817 MP for the county of Clackmannan, to maintain the family interest. A whig, he neither spoke nor opposed the government, and voted variously. He retired from parliament in 1818. He was in command of the 2nd guards, but retired on half pay when there seemed no likelihood of another war, and died unmarried at his country seat in Clackmannanshire on 27 August 1853. He was a competent regimental and staff officer, but the long peace after Waterloo gave him no opportunity to show whether he had his father's ability to command an army. H. M. STEPHENS, rev. JAMES LUNT

Sources J. Philippart, ed., *The royal military calendar*, 3rd edn, 5 vols. (1820), vol. 4 · W. F. P. Napier, *History of the war in the Peninsula and in the south of France*, 6 vols. (1850) · *The dispatches of … the duke of Wellington … from 1799 to 1818*, ed. J. Gurwood, 13 vols. in 12 (1834–9) · C. Oman, *Sir John Moore* (1953) · Boase, *Mod. Eng. biog.* · Burke, *Gen. GB* · Burke, *Peerage* · HoP, *Commons*
Archives NA Scot., corresp. with Lord Seafield

Abercromby, David (d. 1701?), physician and philosopher, most probably belonged to the Abercrombys of Seaton in the north-east of Scotland where he is believed to have been born. It is not known if Abercromby married or had children, although what survives of his biography makes marriage unlikely. Nothing is known of his parentage.

By his own account Abercromby's family were, 'and ever were, for the most part, zealous Romanists' (DNB) who ensured that his education involved instruction in that faith. Abercromby's early commitment to Catholicism and his aptitude in Catholic theology are measured by the fact that he subsequently joined the Jesuit order in France, although the reasons for his move to France are

not known. During his time with the French Jesuits Abercromby graduated MD and became a practising physician—a profession which he maintained for the rest of his life with considerable success. His medical expertise is reflected in some of his later publications, the first of which, *Tuta, ac efficax luis venereae, saepe absque salivatione mercuriali, curandae methodus*, a treatise on syphilis, published at London in 1684, was subsequently translated into French, Dutch, and German. In the following year Abercromby published a work on the pulse, *De variatione, ac varietate pulsus observationes*, which was also published in French at Paris, and *Nova medicinae tum practicae, tum speculativae clavis, sive, Ars explorandi medicas plantarum, ac corporum quorumcumque facultates ex solo sapore*. His medical works are not insignificant and have been described as earning him 'a place of honour' in Albrecht von Haller's *Bibliotheca medicinae practicae* of 1779 (DNB).

After some twenty years abroad Abercromby returned from France to Scotland, a move motivated by deepening spiritual and intellectual uncertainty. On his immediate return, however, he accepted an invitation from the Jesuit order to challenge the defence of protestantism proposed by John Menzies (or Menzeis; 1624–1684), professor of divinity at Marischal College in Aberdeen. To that end Abercromby composed the first of his religious works, *Scolding no scholarship in the abyss. Groundless grounds of the protestant religion, as holden out by M. Menzeis in his brawlings against M. Dempster* (1669). Menzies' response was published at London in 1675 as *Roma mendax, or, The falshood of Rome's high pretences to infallibility and antiquity evicted. In confutation of an anonymous pamphlet undertaking the defence of Mr Dempster Jesuit*. The 'anonymous pamphlet' is Abercromby's *Scolding No Scholarship*. While *Scolding No Scholarship* gives neither place of publication nor publisher, the date of publication suggests that Abercromby returned to Scotland that year or shortly before. The poor reception of the work by both protestant and Catholic camps may have crystallized ongoing spiritual doubts. Abercromby's departure from Scotland, and that of his family, for London two years later was certainly the result of his renouncing Catholicism and embracing protestantism, a conversion exemplified in the second of his religious works, *Protestancy to be embrac'd, or, A new and infallible method to reduce Romanists from popery to protestancy, a treatise of great use to all his majestie's subjects, and necessary to prevent errors and popery*, first published at London in 1682. This work was republished in 1686 as *Protestancy Proved Safer than Popery*. A similar work on a similar theme, *Reasons why a Protestant should not Turn Papist*, published anonymously at London the following year, had been attributed to Robert Boyle (1627–1691) until Edward B. Davis suggested that the true author was Abercromby (Davis, 611–29). Given the subject of the work, the date of publication, and Boyle's patronage of Abercromby, Davis's thesis has considerable plausibility.

During his time with the Jesuits, Abercromby also gained a reputation as a philosopher and divine, teaching grammar, mathematics, and philosophy 'in the most renowned universities of Europe' (DNB). His proficiency in philosophy is clear in three substantial philosophical works: *A Discourse of Wit*, first published in 1685 (2nd edn, 1686), the *Academia scientarium* (1687), a philosophical–scientific dictionary with Latin facing English entries arranged alphabetically from 'Algebra' to 'Rectiline trigonometry', and *A Moral Discourse of the Power of Interest* (1690). The *Moral Discourse* is dedicated to Boyle, who is praised throughout Abercromby's works; typically, as 'The English Philosopher' and 'The Chief Pillar of the Royal Society'. The *Academia scientarium* concludes with a five-page appendix devoted to Boyle and the corpuscularian philosophy. Abercromby was a member of Boyle's circle, a principal recipient of Boyle's patronage during the 1680s, and, at the author's own request, translated several of Boyle's works into Latin (although Abercromby's name does not appear in these texts, the translator's prefaces are initialled 'D. A. M.D.').

Despite his familiarity with the corpuscularian philosophy of his patron, and his competence in scholastic philosophy, historians have largely ignored Abercromby's philosophical works. An exception to this rule is A. B. Grosart who claimed that within *A Discourse of Wit* 'Dr Thomas Reid's philosophy of common sense … is distinctly taught'—a century before Reid's works were published (*DNB*). While Abercromby does appeal to 'common sense', the *Discourse* contains nothing analogous to the reflective consideration given to the concept by the third earl of Shaftesbury (1671–1713) in *Sensus communis: an Essay on the Freedom of Wit and Humour*. As one commentator has pointed out, the sceptical character of much of Abercromby's philosophy frequently contradicts that of the school of common sense and allies Abercromby more closely to David Hume rather than Reid (Tomassi). Abercromby's epistemology is, however, ultimately distinguished from Humean scepticism in so far as it is clearly underwritten by revelation, and a firm commitment to teleological arguments for the existence of God, many of which are constructed from medical and chemical examples.

Abercromby is believed to have continued as a practising physician in London and, subsequently, in the Netherlands (probably in Amsterdam). The exact duration of Abercromby's stay there is not known, nor are the place and date of his death; he is believed to have died in 1701.

PAUL TOMASSI

Sources D. Abercromby, *A discourse of wit*, 2nd edn (1686) · D. Abercromby, *Academia scientarium, or, The academy of sciences* (1687) · D. Abercromby, *Scolding no scholarship in the abyss* (1669) · D. Abercromby, *A moral discourse of the power of interest* (1690) · E. B. Davis, 'The anonymous works of Robert Boyle and the *Reasons why a protestant should not turn papist* (1687)', *Journal of the History of Ideas*, 55 (1994), 611–29 · *DNB* · P. Tomassi, 'David Abercromby (d. 1702?), Thomas Reid and the Scottish philosophy', *Reid Studies: an International Review of Scottish Philosophy*, 4/1 (autumn 2000), 53–68

Abercromby, James (1706–1781), army officer and politician, was born in Glassaugh, Banffshire, the son of Alexander Abercromby (1677–1728), laird of Glassaugh, politician and army officer, and his wife, Helen Meldrum. With his father's assistance he became commissioner of supply

James Abercromby (1706–1781), by unknown artist

and justice of the peace in Banffshire. In 1734 he entered parliament as MP for Banffshire, and held the seat for the next twenty years. Other appointments were the governorship of Stirling Castle and the post of king's painter in Scotland. He married Mary Duff, a third cousin; they had two children. Having entered the British army, he rose steadily through the officers' ranks. In 1746 he was promoted lieutenant-colonel of the 1st battalion of the Royal regiment of foot, the Royal Scots, with the rank of colonel. That same year he was quartermaster-general in James St Clair's expedition against Lorient, and in 1747 he was wounded at Hulst. Corpulent, lethargic, and unambitious, he avoided responsibility in all these duties. Nevertheless, he was guaranteed a secure future in the army by his friendship with, and patronage of, the duke of Newcastle and the earl of Loudoun.

In 1756, during the Seven Years' War, Abercromby's political connections paid off. That year Loudoun was appointed commander of British forces in North America. At Newcastle's behest he chose Abercromby as his second in command, with the ranks of colonel of the 44th regiment and major-general in America. In the summer Abercromby proceeded to Albany, New York, and arrived a month before Loudoun. There he prepared for a summer campaign against Fort Crown Point, but when Loudoun arrived in July he found conditions so chaotic that he abandoned offensive plans. In 1757 Loudoun and Abercromby contemplated an assault on Louisbourg. However, they rejected the idea, and for the remainder of the year Abercromby commanded at Albany while Loudoun abortively plotted an attack against Fort Ticonderoga. As Loudoun's subordinate, Abercromby stolidly performed all the duties assigned him, but evinced little initiative of his own.

In March 1758 William Pitt recalled Loudoun, and appointed Abercromby commander in America and colonel of the 60th, or Royal American, regiment, ordering him to advance against Fort Ticonderoga. To assist Abercromby as his second in command, Pitt appointed George Augustus, Lord Howe, the promising young commander of the 55th regiment in New York. On 6 July Howe was killed in a French ambush, and Abercromby, bereft of his subordinate's wise counsel, was unsure how to proceed. He rejected what was possibly the wisest course: to mount cannon on Mount Defiance, which dominated the fort, and thus compel a French surrender. Instead he ordered a frontal assault against enemy fortifications on 8 July that resulted in a bloody slaughter. Compelled to retreat, and with his army's confidence in him destroyed, he was recalled by Pitt. Despite his incompetence, in 1758 he was promoted lieutenant-general and in 1772 general. He returned to parliament, where he supported coercive policies against the colonies. His son, James, was killed on 24 June 1775 at Bunker Hill. Abercromby spent his last years in Glassaugh and died there on 23 April 1781. His daughter, Jane, inherited his property. PAUL DAVID NELSON

Sources P. D. Nelson, 'Abercromby, James', *ANB* • *Correspondence of William Pitt, when secretary of state, with colonial governors and military and naval commissioners in America*, ed. G. S. Kimball, 2 vols. (1906) • S. Pargellis, ed., *Military affairs in North America, 1748–1765: selected documents from the Cumberland papers in Windsor Castle* (1936) • *Writings of General John Forbes relating to his service in North America*, ed. A. P. James (1938) • J. Grant, ed., *Records of the county of Banff, 1660–1760* (1922) • R. R. Sedgwick, 'Abercromby, James', HoP, *Commons, 1715–54* • F. Anderson, *Crucible of war: the Seven Years' War and the fate of empire in British North America, 1754–1766* (2000) • L. H. Gipson, *The British empire before the American revolution*, 6–7 (1946–9) • D. E. Leach, *Arms for empire: a military history of the British colonies in North America, 1607–1763* (1973) • H. H. Peckham, *The colonial wars, 1689–1762* (1964)
Archives Hunt. L., corresp. and papers • PRO, corresp. as commander-in-chief in North America, WO34 • Virginia State Library, Richmond, letter-book | BL, corresp. with Frederick Haldimand, Add. MS 21666 • Hunt. L., Loudoun papers
Likenesses drawing, NPG [*see illus.*] • oils, New Brunswick Museum, Webster collection

Abercromby, James (1707–1775), colonial agent and politician, was baptized on 24 August 1708 at Alloa, Clackmannanshire, the third son of Alexander Abercromby (*d.* 1753), MP for Clackmannanshire in the Scottish parliament, and Mary (*b. c.*1680), daughter of Alexander Duff of Braco. He was educated at Westminster School (which he entered in 1720) and the University of Leiden (1724–5), studied at Lincoln's Inn (1726), and was called to the bar in 1738.

At twenty-four Abercromby travelled to America, having been commissioned as attorney-general for South Carolina. There he settled for thirteen years, acquiring 6980 acres of land. Between 1739 and 1745 Abercromby was a member of the colony's assembly. He returned from America in May 1744 but soon re-established his connection. Abercromby spent the rest of his working life in the nebulous role of colonial agent. As a colony's 'liaison officer' (Lonn, 358) it was Abercromby's job to look after its

affairs in Britain, lobbying parliament to advance its interests. His twenty-six years in the service of first North Carolina and then Virginia made him one of America's longest-serving agents.

Abercromby's long association with America gave him ample scope for reflection on its relationship with Britain. He crystallized these musings into two treatises: *An Examination of the Acts of Parliament relative to the Trade and the Government of our American Colonies* (1752); and *An Inquiry into the Nature, and the Rights of Colonies, Ancient, and Modern* (1774). Abercromby set out a plan for Britain to deal with America more effectively. He realized that the logical outcome of the existing relationship was independence. However, for Abercromby, as for most of his contemporaries, this was unthinkable. He urged that a clear and simple line of command should replace the hotchpotch of laws, taxes, and administrative authorities. Abercromby was in no doubt about the hierarchy of this structure: 'The first principle of colony government, whether amongst ancient or modern nations, has ever been to make the colonies subservient to the interests of the principal state' (*Magna Charta*, 45). According to Abercromby, colonists should not have the same rights of representation as subjects in Britain. Britain should rule decisively and, if need be, mercilessly.

Abercromby also sat for Clackmannanshire from 1761 to 1768, one of the very few MPs to have sat in a colonial assembly. He consistently voted in accordance with his principles on America, and at odds with colonial opinion. He supported Grenville and his Stamp Act, opposing its repeal in 1766. Abercromby lost his seat in 1768, as his constituency alternated in representation with Kinross-shire.

Despite his avowed views and parliamentary stance, Abercromby always represented his colonial employers' cause professionally. He enthusiastically pursued their claims, once even earning a reprimand from the privy council. Certainly he profited from his determined efforts. He earned £400 per annum by the 1760s, drew further fees from personal work for governors, and charged up to 2.5 per cent commission on any funds he wrested from government. But dedication to his clients was the hallmark of his career. As he declared, 'I aim at no more than serving those who employ me to the utmost of my power' (*Letterbook*, 334).

Abercromby was deputy auditor-general of plantations from 1757 to 1765. From about 1758 he lived on his Brucefield estate in Clackmannanshire until his death, which occurred before November in 1775. Abercromby was unmarried, and his estate passed to his brother George.

IAN K. R. ARCHER

Sources *Letterbook of James Abercromby, colonial agent, 1751–1773*, ed. J. C. Van Horne and G. Reese (1991) • E. Lonn, *The colonial agents of the southern colonies* (1945) • W. B. Edgar, N. L. Bailey, and A. Moore, eds., *Biographical directory of the South Carolina house of representatives*, 5 vols. (1974–92) • *Magna charta for America: James Abercromby's 'An examination of the acts of parliament relative to the trade and the government of our American colonies' (1752) and 'De jure et gubernatione coloniarum, or, An inquiry into the nature, and the rights of colonies, ancient, and modern' (1774)*, ed. J. P. Greene, C. F. Mullett, and E. C.

Papenfuse (1986) • E. Haden-Guest, 'Abercromby, James', HoP, *Commons, 1754–90* • J. M. Simpson, 'Abercromby, Alexander', HoP, *Commons, 1715–54* • M. G. Kammen, *A rope of sand: the colonial agents, British politics, and the American revolution* (1968) • P. D. G. Thomas, *British politics and the Stamp Act crisis: the first phase of the American revolution, 1763–1767* (1975) • P. Lawson, *George Grenville: a political life* (1984) • B. Donoghue, *British politics and the American revolution: the path to war, 1773–75* (1964) • IGI • Old Westminsters

Archives Hunt. L., corresp. and papers • North Carolina State Archives, Raleigh, letter-book • Pennsylvania State Archives, Harrisburg, collection • PRO, corresp. as commander-in-chief in North America, WO 34 • Virginia State Library, Richmond, letter-book | BL, Grenville MSS • BL, corresp. with Frederick Haldimand, Add. MS 21666 • Hunt. L., Stowe and Grenville MSS • Library of Virginia, Richmond, Virginia colonial records • South Carolina Historical Society, Charleston, Robert Pringle letter-book • University of Virginia, Charlottesville, headquarter papers of Brigadier-General John Forbes • West Virginia State Archives, Charleston, war records collection

Wealth at death substantial landholdings in South Carolina; left Scottish estate to brother: *Letterbook*, ed. Van Horne and Reese; Haden-Guest, 'Abercromby, James'

Abercromby, James, first Baron Dunfermline (1776–1858), speaker of the House of Commons, the third son of General Sir Ralph *Abercromby (1734–1801), and his wife, Mary Anne, *née* Menzies, was born on 7 November 1776. Sir John *Abercromby and Alexander *Abercromby, both army officers, were his brothers. James Abercromby was educated at Edinburgh high school and Christ Church, Oxford, and was called to the bar at Lincoln's Inn in 1800. In 1801 he obtained a commissionership of bankruptcy, and subsequently he became auditor to the estates of the duke of Devonshire. He broke with family tradition in becoming a whig, and was MP for Midhurst, 1807–12, and for Calne, 1812–30.

Without special claims for promotion as a politician, Abercromby owed his success chiefly to his power of clear and judicious statement, and the prudent use he made of opportunities. His career was also influenced to a considerable extent by the prominent part which he took in the discussion of Scottish business. In 1824 and 1826 he brought forward a motion for a bill to amend the representation of the city of Edinburgh; but although on both occasions he received large support, the power of election remained until 1832 in the hands of the self-elected council of thirty-three. Abercromby served as judge-advocate-general in the brief Canning and Goderich governments, 1827–8. In 1830 he became chief baron of the exchequer of Scotland, and when in 1832 the office was abolished, he received a pension of £2000 p.a. He was chosen along with Francis Jeffrey (and with expenses paid) to represent Edinburgh in the first reformed parliament, having been cautious about parliamentary reform. Grey thought him a 'perfect humbug'. As on various questions of privilege he had shown a special knowledge of the forms of the house, his claims for the speakership were considered by his party in 1833, but Edward John Littleton, afterwards Lord Hatherton, was ultimately chosen to oppose Manners Sutton, who was elected. At the end of the Grey government he was in the cabinet (July–December 1834) as master of the mint. At the opening of the new parliament in 1835 the condition of the political atmosphere was in some respects so uncertain, that the choice of a speaker awakened exceptional interest as a touchstone of party strength; and amid much excitement Abercromby—who stood only on the insistence of Melbourne—was chosen over Manners Sutton by 316 votes to 306, a triumph for the whigs and the occasion for the Lichfield House compact. Abercromby's term of office was marked by the introduction of several important reforms in the management of private bills, tending to simplify the arrangements and minimize the opportunities for jobbery. He was the first Scot to be speaker. In spite of failing health he retained office until May 1839, his capacity to control the house declining. On retiring, with a pension of £4000 p.a., he was created Baron Dunfermline of Dunfermline in the county of Fife.

Dunfermline continued to interest himself in public affairs connected with Edinburgh, and was one of the originators of the United Industrial Schools for the support and training of destitute children. He wrote a life of his father, Sir Ralph Abercromby, which was published posthumously in 1861. He married Mary Anne, daughter of Egerton Leigh of Cheshire, in 1802. His son Ralph (1803–1865) was a diplomatist and a Liberal. Dunfermline died at his home, Colinton House, Midlothian, on 17 April 1858, his widow dying there on 2 August 1874, aged ninety-six.

T. F. HENDERSON, rev. H. C. G. MATTHEW

Sources GEC, *Peerage* • J. A. Manning, *The lives of the speakers of the House of Commons* (1850) • J. Anderson, *A history of Edinburgh* (1856) • A. D. Macintyre, *The Liberator: Daniel O'Connell and the Irish party, 1830–1847* (1965) • GM, 3rd ser., 4 (1858), 547–51 • HoP, *Commons* • P. A. C. Laundy, *The office of speaker* (1964) • M. Brock, *The Great Reform Act* (1973)

Archives NL Scot., corresp. and papers • NL Scot., political memorandum book | BL, corresp. with John Allen, Add. MS 52182 • BL, corresp. with Lord Holland, Add. MSS 51574–51575 • BL, corresp. with Sir Robert Peel, Add. MSS 40364–40506 • Chatsworth House, Derbyshire, letters to sixth duke of Devonshire • NA Scot., letters to James Loch • NA Scot., letters to Lord Panmure • NL Scot., letters to Anne, Lady Baird • NL Scot., letters to John Burton • NL Scot., corresp. with George Combe • NL Scot., letters to second Baron Dunfermline • NL Scot., corresp. with Edward Ellice • NL Scot., corresp. with the Haldane family • NL Scot., corresp. with Lord Jeffrey • NL Scot., letters to second earl of Minto • NL Scot., letters to Andrew Rutherford • NRA, priv. coll., corresp. with T. F. Kennedy • PRO, corresp. with Lord Russell, PRO 30/22 • UCL, letters to James Brougham

Likenesses stipple, pubd 1838 (after J. Hayter), BM, NPG • W. Brodie, marble bust, 1858, Scot. NPG • H. Cook, line engraving (after J. Stewart), BM, NPG • G. Hayter, group portrait, oils (*The House of Commons, 1833*), NPG • J. Jackson, oils, Hardwick Hall, Derbyshire • T. Lupton, mezzotint (after C. Smith), BM, NPG • J. Watson-Gordon, oils, Scot. NPG • D. Wilkie, group portrait, oils (*The first council of Queen Victoria, 1837*), Royal Collection • portrait, repro. in Burke, *Gen. GB* (1838)

Wealth at death £20,180 17s. 6d.: confirmation, 8 Oct 1858, NA Scot., SC 70/1/102/34 • £6950 4s. 6d.: additional estate in Wiltshire, 8 Oct 1858, NA Scot., SC 70/1/102/98 • £5281 2s. 10d.: additional inventory, 13 Oct 1859, NA Scot., SC 70/1/102/895

Abercromby, John (supp. *fl.* 1561), Benedictine monk, is recorded only in Thomas Dempster's *Historia ecclesiastica*, a lengthy compilation of short biographies which sometimes have a substratum of fact, but more often no factual basis whatever. Dempster's few lines on Abercromby are vague. He adds 'I think' (*ut puto*) to his being a Benedictine, and gives 1561 merely for his being alive. The account of his death is bland and totally lacking in detail: Abercromby resisted heresy, upheld the purity of religion, and also suffered death for Christ. Tanner, whose only source was Dempster, makes Abercromby a Benedictine without qualification. To describe him as having been condemned to death and executed about 1561 is to go beyond even these frail sources.

Abercromby has not come to light in recent scholarly work, nor is he found in the published records. There were ten Benedictine monasteries with communities in sixteenth-century Scotland: four of traditional black monks, four formerly Tironensian, and two Cluniac. No Abercromby is found in any of them in the period 1540–80. There were Abercrombies at Scone (Augustinian) and perhaps other monasteries, but none was involved in Reformation controversy. Abercromby's two alleged works, 'Veritatis defensio' and 'Haereseos confusio', likewise lack any authentication. The only possible conclusion is that John Abercromby is a figment, a 'ghost' fabricated by Thomas Dempster. MARK DILWORTH

Sources *Thomae Dempsteri Historia ecclesiastica gentis Scotorum, sive, De scriptoribus Scotis*, ed. D. Irving, rev. edn, 2 vols., Bannatyne Club, 21 (1829) · Tanner, *Bibl. Brit.-Hib.*, 1–2

Abercromby, Sir John (1772–1817), army officer, was the second son of the famous General Sir Ralph *Abercromby (1734–1801) and his wife, Mary Anne (d. 1821), daughter of Captain John Menzies. His brothers included James *Abercromby and Alexander *Abercromby. He was born on 2 April 1772 at Tullibody, Alloa, Clackmannanshire. He entered the army in 1786 aged fourteen, as an ensign in the 75th regiment. He became lieutenant in 1787 and captain in 1792. He first saw service as aide-de-camp to his father during the campaigns in Flanders in 1793–4. His father's military reputation and dependence on his services assured his rapid rise, with promotion to major of the 94th regiment in May 1794 and then, in July, when aged only twenty-two, to lieutenant-colonel in the 112th regiment.

In 1795 Abercromby transferred into the 53rd, and accompanied his father to the West Indies in 1796–7, to Ireland in 1798, and in the expedition to The Helder in 1799 as military secretary. This was a post of more than usual importance on the staff of Sir Ralph, who was extremely short-sighted, and so was heavily dependent upon his personal staff during battle. Abercromby junior excelled in this capacity, with his father owing much of his success to his son's ability to assess a military situation, particularly during the attack on Morne Fortuné in St Lucia.

Abercromby was promoted to colonel on 1 January 1800, becoming a deputy adjutant-general in the army under his father's command in the Mediterranean, attached to General Hutchinson's division. In Egypt he distinguished himself, twice being publicly thanked by Hutchinson.

Abercromby's presence in France at the time of the rupture of the peace of Amiens in 1803 led to his being imprisoned at Verdun. He was held in captivity for five years, during which time he was promoted to major-general in 1805, and made colonel of his former regiment, the 53rd, in 1807. After the battle of Vimeiro in 1808 Abercromby was released in exchange for General Brennier. He returned to England, and was appointed commander-in-chief at Bombay in 1809. He played a major role in Lord Minto's expedition from India to capture Mauritius, an important French base lying on the route between England and India. Initial surveys suggested that any attack on the island by a large force would meet failure. However, subsequent reconnaissance had proven this assumption to be erroneous. During the journey the *Ceylon*, on which Abercromby and his staff were sailing, was captured by the French frigate *Venus* only to be recaptured by Captain Rowley's *Boadicea*. On 22 November Abercromby left the island of Rodriguez with the Madras and Bombay divisions, being joined close to Mauritius by the Bengal division. As the senior general present, he assumed overall command, disembarking on 29 November with 6300 European soldiers, 2000 sailors, and 3000 sepoys. After an unsuccessful skirmish on 30 November, General Decaen realized that further resistance would be futile and so surrendered possession of the island on 2 December. This campaign earned Abercromby the thanks of parliament.

Abercromby soon returned to Bombay, continuing to command the forces there until 1812 when he was appointed commander-in-chief and temporary governor of Madras. The previous incumbent, Sir George Barlow, had been released from his duties as a result of the so-called 'white mutiny' by the Madras officers. However, the quiet manner and affable nature of General Abercromby brought matters under control. Having vacated the governorship in May 1813, Abercromby was forced to return home the following December owing to the adverse effects of the climate upon his health.

On his return Abercromby was well received; he had been promoted lieutenant-general in 1812, and was now, in 1815, made a KCB and GCB. During the same year his brother George resigned the seat of Clackmannan to make way for him. However, his poor health precluded his playing any active part in politics. He died on 14 February 1817, while convalescing at Marseilles, where he was buried with full military honours. He was unmarried. Sir John undoubtedly possessed the military abilities of his family, but circumstances ensured that he had little opportunity to display these, except as military secretary to his father, and during the relatively straightforward capture of Mauritius. H. M. STEPHENS, rev. S. KINROSS

Sources HoP, *Commons* · J. Thomas, *Universal pronouncing dictionary of biography and mythology*, 5th edn (1930) · J. Foster, *Members of parliament, Scotland ... 1357–1882*, 2nd edn (privately printed, London, 1882) · J. Haydn, *The book of dignities: containing rolls of the official personages of the British empire* (1851) · Fortescue, *Brit. army*, vol. 7 · E. C. Joslin, A. R. Litherland, B. T. Simpkin, and others, eds., *British battles and medals*, 6th edn (1988) · Lord Dunfermline [J. Abercromby], *Lieutenant-General Sir Ralph Abercromby KB, 1793–1801: a memoir* (1861) · T. N. Dupuy, C. Johnson, and D. L. Bongard, *The encyclopedia of military biography* (1992) · D. Chandler and I. Beckett, eds., *The Oxford illustrated history of the British army* (1994) · b. cert.

Archives NA Scot., letters to Sir Alexander Hope · NL Scot., corresp. with first earl of Minto

Abercromby, Patrick (*b.* **1656**, *d.* in or after **1716**), antiquary, was born at Forfar, the third son of Alexander Abercromby of Fetterneir and his wife, Jean Seton. The family was a branch of the Abercrombys of Birkenbog in Banffshire, which in turn descended from the Abercromby of Abercromby line in Fife. As the family appears to have been Catholic, Abercromby would not have attended the local parish school, and seems to have been educated privately and at Catholic institutions on the continent. The *Records of the Scots Colleges* (p. 58) states that 'Patritius Abercromby', the son of Alexander Abercromby of Fetterneir, entered the college at Douai at the age of fourteen, but it is not known how long he stayed there. He may also have studied in Paris. He returned to Scotland some time before 1685, and took the degree of MD at St Andrews University in that year.

In July 1685 Abercromby's elder brother Francis was created Lord Glassford by James VII and II on the occasion of his marriage to Baroness Sempill. Possibly in connection with this, Abercromby himself was appointed physician to the king in the same year, and went to England to take up the post. Some writers (Anderson, *Scot. nat.*, 3–4; Chambers, *Scots.*, 1.3) have suggested that he only converted to Catholicism in 1685, in order to obtain this post from the Catholic king; however, his attendance at Douai would counter this, and Chalmers stated that the whole family was Catholic (Chalmers, 58).

Abercromby naturally lost his post at the revolution in 1688. He then seems to have spent some time abroad, returning to Scotland during the reign of Queen Anne. He settled in Edinburgh, and devoted himself to the study of Scottish history and antiquities.

A confirmed Jacobite, Abercromby naturally opposed the Union of 1707, which, by entrenching the Hanoverian succession, officially precluded any chance of a Stuart restoration. He produced two pamphlets on the subject in 1707. The first was called *Advantage of the Act of Security Compared with those of the Intended Union*, and the second entitled *A Vindication of the same Against Mr De Foe*. As the title implies, this pamphlet took issue with the propaganda of Daniel Defoe, who was one of the most prominent of the English pro-Union pamphleteers. Also in 1707, he produced a translation of Beaugué's *L'histoire de la guerre d'Écosse* (1556), an account of the conflicts of the Scots and their French allies with the English in the mid-sixteenth century.

Abercromby's most important work was his *Martial Atchievements of the Scots Nation*, which covered Scottish history from the earliest times to the fifteenth century. The first volume was published in Edinburgh in 1711 by Robert Freebairn, and the second in 1715 by Freebairn and Thomas Ruddiman, also in Edinburgh. Much of the early 'history' in the first volume is now regarded, in the light of more recent scholarship, as purely mythical. However, the work also contained evidence of genuine biographical and historical research, in which he was seconded by other prominent Scottish antiquaries of the day, including Ruddiman and Alexander Nisbet. Abercromby's Jacobitism naturally led him to take a markedly royalist view of history, and the work is unavoidably biased. It sees the monarchy as the most enduring and admirable feature of Scottish history, takes a very severe view of the Scottish nobility for their frequent opposition to royal authority, and treats favourably of royal attempts to control noble power. Abercromby also wrote some 'Memoirs of the Abercrombys', which were never published; the manuscript seems to have disappeared. Another work attributed to him, the *Discourse of Wit* (1685), was in fact written by Dr David Abercromby, a contemporary but no relation.

Abercromby's last years were apparently marked by poverty, and Ruddiman never received any payment from him for printing the second volume of the *Atchievements*. The year of his death is uncertain. He was definitely alive in 1716, because George Crawfurd, in his *Peerage* of that year, referred to him as 'my worthy friend' (p. 167). He probably died in or soon after 1716, but other years have been suggested, including 1720 and 1726. Ruddiman's account books still listed him as a debtor in the 1730s, although this does not necessarily mean that he was still alive. He appears to have left a widow in severe poverty, about whom nothing at all is known.

ALEXANDER DU TOIT

Sources C. D. Abercromby, *The family of Abercromby* (1927), 105–6 · Chambers, *Scots.* (1855), 1.2–4 · W. Anderson, *The Scottish nation*, 1 (1868), 3–4 · *Encyclopaedia Britannica*, 9th edn (1875–89), vol. 1, pp. 37–8 · G. Chalmers, *The life of Thomas Ruddiman* (1794), 58–9 · C. Kidd, *Subverting Scotland's past: Scottish whig historians and the creation of an Anglo-British identity, 1689–c.1830* (1993), 74–5, 80–81, 168–9 · G. Crawfurd, *The peerage of Scotland: containing an historical and genealogical account of the nobility of that kingdom* (privately printed, Edinburgh, 1716), 167 · P. J. Anderson, ed., *Records of the Scots colleges at Douai, Rome, Madrid, Valladolid and Ratisbon*, New Spalding Club, 30 (1906), 58
Archives U. Edin., Laing collection
Wealth at death died in poverty: *Encyclopaedia Britannica*; Chalmers, *Life of Thomas Ruddiman*; Chambers, *Scots.*; Anderson, *Scot. nat.*

Abercromby, Sir Ralph, of Tullibody (1734–1801), army officer, was born in October 1734 at Menstrie, Clackmannanshire, and baptized on 26 October at Logie, Perthshire. He was the second but eldest surviving son of George Abercromby (1705–1800), a lawyer by training and a descendant of the Abercromby family of Birkenbog, Aberdeenshire, and his wife, Mary (*d.* 1767), daughter of Ralph Dundas of Manour, Perthshire. His younger brothers were Sir Robert *Abercromby and Alexander *Abercromby. He was reared at his parents' principal home, Tullibody House, near Alloa. Having been taught by a private tutor, the Revd James Syme, and at a school in Alloa headed by a Mr Muir, he entered Rugby School on 12 June 1748, and there he remained until 1752. It had long been expected that he would follow in his father's footsteps and he duly studied law, first at Edinburgh University from 1752 to 1753, then at Leipzig in autumn 1754.

Sir Ralph Abercromby of Tullibody (1734–1801), by John Hoppner, c.1797–8

Early career Abercromby's interest in the legal profession faded and on his return to Britain he told his father of his plans for a military career. Though somewhat disappointed his father helped him to make a start by purchasing him a cornetcy in the 3rd dragoon guards in March 1756. The Seven Years' War began a few months later, and in 1758 Abercromby accompanied his regiment on active service to Germany. Acting as an aide to General Sir William Pitt he was soon introduced to the realities of eighteenth-century European warfare and, like so many of his contemporaries, he became fascinated by the military machine of Frederick the Great. He was particularly struck by its approach to discipline and to the care of the rank and file: the former could be brutal in the extreme and was designed to make the men fear their officers more than the enemy; the latter emphasized keeping the troops fit for service through rudimentary hygiene programmes, providing basic shelter where possible—be it in buildings or tents—and issuing appropriate clothing and adequate rations. This blending of expediency with strict paternalism held a natural appeal for the likes of the young Abercromby. A staunch Christian—he was made an elder of Clackmannan parish on 5 July 1768—with a well-developed sense of justice and *noblesse oblige*, his interest in moral and political philosophy had been strong enough to attract him to lectures on these subjects while still a university student. Influenced by, among other things, his faith and Enlightenment reasoning, throughout his life he evinced a humanitarian concern for the underdog that did not always find universal admiration. If his decision, as laird, to sponsor the establishment of a school for the poor in Tullibody (at some time after 1768 and before 1783)

was well received his sympathy for American and—initially at least—French revolutionaries, as well as for Ireland's indigent, downtrodden peasantry, proved more controversial.

In February 1760 Abercromby was made a lieutenant and by 1762 he was able to purchase a captaincy. The end of the Seven Years' War saw him posted to Ireland, where he enjoyed further promotions: he became a major in 1770, a lieutenant-colonel in 1773, and brevet colonel in 1780, and was commander of the 103rd foot, King's Irish, from 1781 until its disbandment two years later. On 17 November 1767 at Ferntower, Perthshire, he married Mary Anne (d. 1821), second daughter of John Menzies of Ferntower. They had seven children: Anne (1768–1844), who married Donald Cameron of Lochiel; George, later second Baron Abercromby (1770–1843); the army officer Sir John *Abercromby (1772–1817); Mary (1773–1825); James *Abercromby, later speaker of the House of Commons and first Baron Dunfermline (1776–1858); Katharine (1780–1841), who married Thomas Buchanan; and Alexander *Abercromby (1784–1853), also an army officer.

Abercromby's involvement in politics very nearly brought his respectable if as yet unglamorous military career to a premature end. In 1774 he stood for election to parliament as a ministerial candidate for Clackmannanshire, a county which his uncle James *Abercromby (1707–1775) had represented from 1761 to 1768. The election proved a bitter affair. His opponent was Colonel James Francis Erskine, who was backed by several families with Jacobite histories and a loathing for the management of Scottish politics by Sir Lawrence Dundas. When Erskine impugned the honour of Robert Bruce, Lord Kennet, whose wife, Helen, was Abercromby's sister, Abercromby fought a pistol duel in Kennet's defence. Neither man was injured however and Abercromby went on to secure the seat. Effectively a placeman, he had little enthusiasm or liking for his role in the Commons. His insistence on voting in accordance with his own conscience soon alienated his powerful sponsors and, together with his views of the American War of Independence, damaged his chances of professional advancement. Not only did he openly express admiration for George Washington but also, like many Britons at the time, he opined that the conflict with the rebellious colonists was essentially a civil war that had been provoked by an inept monarch and his ministers. Much as he longed to lead his regiment into action he declined to serve in America, even though two of his brothers did so; James was killed at Brooklyn, while Robert—later General Sir Robert Abercromby—returned with a distinguished record. Clackmannanshire's representation alternated with that of Kinross-shire, and Abercromby did not seek election in 1780. He unsuccessfully contested the seat as an ally of Henry Dundas and William Pitt the younger in 1784. He had been placed on half-pay in 1783, when his regiment was disbanded, and was promoted to major-general in 1787 but his military career now seemed to be in the doldrums. The next year he chose not to stand for Clackmannanshire in a by-election and supported instead his brother Burnet, who had made a fortune in India. He retired to Edinburgh to devote time to his family.

The French Revolutionary Wars Abercromby initially supported the French Revolution, hoping, like many disciples of the Enlightenment, that it would engender greater freedom in Europe. He felt that the revolutionaries had some legitimate grievances and he advocated mediation between them and the British government until war was declared. Once war had begun he seized the opportunity to revive his military career. His martial skill and parliamentary connections soon secured him a posting. As a brigade commander in the ill-fated Flanders campaign of Frederick, duke of York, he played a prominent part in the fighting, notably in July 1793 at Valenciennes, where he directed the storming parties, and in September 1794 at Boxtel, where a young lieutenant-colonel, Arthur Wellesley, later duke of Wellington, underwent his baptism of fire while covering the withdrawal of Abercromby's forces. By this time, however, the French were in the ascendancy and York, recalled to Britain, ceded command of his army to Lieutenant-General Sir William Harcourt, a cavalry veteran of the American war. He was soon pressed into retreat by the advancing foe and by the growing demoralization and indiscipline among his own forces. Like Wellesley, Abercromby, whose units often formed the rearguard during the withdrawal to the River Ems, further enhanced his own reputation during this otherwise ignominious operation and, on his return to England early in 1795, he was hailed as Britain's greatest general. He was created knight of the Bath on 22 July 1795.

In November 1795 Abercromby was appointed to lead an expedition against the French possessions in the West Indies. Having arrived at Jamaica early in 1796 he first took St Lucia, entrusting it to his ablest subordinate, Colonel (later General Sir) John Moore, and then Demerara. He also relieved St Vincent and reorganized the defences of both that island and of Grenada. Sir Charles Grey's operations in 1794 had highlighted the perils that the Caribbean climate held for European troops, and Abercromby did his best to improve and maintain his soldiers' health; he established sanatoria, forbade parades and exercises during the hottest times of the day, and modified the troops' uniforms to make them more appropriate to the prevailing atmospheric and topographical conditions. He also strove to bolster the morale of officers and men alike. Even when not recommended by the authorities some of the former were given staff and governmental positions, while the latter occasionally enjoyed pecuniary rewards—which were presumably similar to the prize money distributions made to Royal Navy crews during this period—and were even entrusted with some minor civil offices. Abercromby went home for the summer but returned at the end of 1796, captured Trinidad, and appointed Colonel (later Lieutenant-General Sir Thomas) Picton its governor.

An attempt to take Puerto Rico failed for want of sufficient forces. Abercromby had moreover fallen ill and now resigned his command. In December 1797 he returned to duty as commander-in-chief of the troops in Ireland, a country with which he was familiar and which was troubled by the United Irishmen's rising and by related French invasion scares. Much of the garrison comprised protestant Irish yeomanry and English and Scottish militia units, most of the latter being volunteers who could demand to be returned home. Given that they lacked the discipline of regular troops Abercromby believed them to be more of a liability than an asset at a time of serious civil unrest, and on 26 February 1798 he issued a general order containing comments to that effect. This so enraged the authorities, notably John Jeffreys Pratt, second Earl Camden, lord lieutenant of Ireland, that Abercromby tendered his resignation.

These events notwithstanding Abercromby was appointed head of the garrisons in Scotland, a position he retained for some eighteen months before being sent to the Netherlands in command of a division in the Helder campaign. On 10 September 1799 his men helped to beat off a limited attack by elements of General Guillaume Brune's Franco-Batavian forces. Shortly afterwards Russian troops arrived to support the duke of York's army, and together they struck at Brune's heavily outnumbered men at Bergen (Alkmaar) on 16 September. The Russo-British forces failed to orchestrate their efforts effectively; repulsed, they did not advance again until 2 October. The second assault on Bergen was also marred by poor co-ordination, though Abercromby, who had two horses killed under him during the fighting, achieved all his objectives. Seeking to exploit his advantage York pushed on but, checked by Brune at Castricum, concluded the convention of Alkmaar on 18 October, whereby he agreed to release all prisoners and evacuate his forces, provided that they were not molested. The campaign's principal objective had been to capture what remained of the Dutch fleet. This had been accomplished at the outset; nevertheless the operation was widely seen as a shameful failure, not least by Abercromby, who accordingly declined his grateful government's offer of a peerage.

Mediterranean command and Abu Qir Bay After spending a few months quietly in Scotland, Abercromby was appointed to succeed Sir Charles Stuart as commander of Britain's troops in the Mediterranean. He reached Minorca in June 1800. Judging that, in the light of Napoleon's victory at Marengo, his original orders—to mount an expedition to Italy—were impracticable, he spent many weeks awaiting fresh instructions. When these finally arrived they directed him first to Gibraltar, where his army was to absorb a force under General Sir James Murray-Pulteney, and then to Cadiz, which he was to attack, assisted by the fleet of Vice-Admiral George Keith Elphinstone, first Baron Keith. This proved easier said than done, however; Keith thought the anchorage unsafe and Abercromby was loath to venture ashore without close naval support. On 5 October an attempt was made to disembark his troops but the landing operation proceeded too slowly for comfort. Rather than risk being left with a small portion of his force exposed to attack on the beachhead Abercromby, with Keith's agreement, decided to retire altogether.

On 24 October new orders arrived, directing Abercromby to Malta, from where he was to land in Egypt and expel or capture its French garrison. He spent the opening weeks of 1801 at Marmorice Bay, north of Rhodes, integrating some reinforcements from Britain into his army and trying—through John Moore, who approached the local vizier at Jaffa—to secure some tangible assistance from the Turkish authorities in the form of fresh water supplies, provisions, and landing craft. Little was proffered, while Moore reported that the available Turkish troops were a wild, plague-ridden mob. In the interim Abercromby had his own soldiers practise disembarking by boat so that the forthcoming landing might proceed more smoothly than that at Cadiz. On 21 February the fleet sailed for Abu Qir Bay, arriving there early on 2 March. Because of adverse weather, however, it was as late as 8 March before the amphibious assault could commence.

Once started this ran like clockwork. All of 5 miles of shallow water separated the transport ships' anchorage from the beach yet all Abercromby's 14,000 infantry, 1000 cavalry, and 600 gunners were ferried ashore in a single day. Nevertheless all chance of achieving surprise had been lost. Besides mounting some resistance at the water's edge the French had been granted time in which to concentrate their forces for a counterstroke. While General Jacques-François de Boussay, baron de Menou, brought up reinforcements from Cairo and Upper Egypt, General Louis Friant's soldiers blocked the isthmus along which the British now advanced towards Alexandria. After a fierce skirmish on 13 March, the latter pulled back to a defensive position that was assailed by Menou's 12,000 troops shortly before dawn on 21 March. The fighting was confused and heavy but after four hours the French were driven back into their fortified lines. They had sustained some 3000 casualties, the British 1376.

Among the latter was Abercromby. Either because of his not inconsiderable courage, his severe short-sightedness, or both he had strayed dangerously close to the enemy. In the poor light he only narrowly escaped capture by a French dragoon and, not long afterwards, was struck by a musket ball in the thigh and was evacuated to the fleet's flagship, HMS *Foudroyant*. Even then his concern for the well-being and efficiency of the rank and file shone forth; he insisted that a soldier's blanket that had been fashioned into a pillow for him by an aide should be returned to its rightful owner at once. After rallying a little he faltered, and finally succumbed to septicaemia at 11 p.m. on 28 March 1801. He was buried on Malta, where a simple monument was erected to his memory. Others were raised in St Paul's Cathedral, London (by parliamentary grant), and at St Giles's, Edinburgh. On 28 May 1801 his widow was created Baroness Abercromby of Aboukir and Tullibody and was voted a pension of £2000 by parliament. Lady Abercromby died on 11 February 1821 at Charlotte Square, Edinburgh. A biography of Abercromby was published by his son James in 1861.

Abercromby was a popular, well-known commander who became something of a father figure within the British army. His heroic death, like that of his most famous subordinate, John Moore, who fell at Corunna in 1809, caught the British public's imagination and inspired many an artist. Coming after a long period of reverses and disappointments his triumph at Abu Qir, which rendered France's foothold in Egypt quite untenable, restored the army's reputation and testifies to his considerable abilities as a general. The mere prospect of defeat there was evidently sufficient to intensify French efforts to negotiate an end to the revolutionary war. If the treaty of Amiens truncated the political effects of Abercromby's victory its military significance lingered. Indeed it proved the first of the many victories that the British army secured in its lengthy struggle with Napoleonic France.

DAVID GATES

Sources Lord Dunfermline [J. Abercromby], *Lieutenant-General Sir Ralph Abercromby KB, 1793–1801: a memoir* (1861) · T. C. Gordon, *Four notable Scots* (1960) · *The diary of Sir John Moore*, ed. J. F. Maurice, 2 vols. (1904) · B. Edwards, *The history, civil and commercial, of the British colonies in the West Indies*, 3rd edn, 3 vols. (1801) · T. C. Gordon, *A history of Clackmannan* (1936), 171 · E. Haden-Guest, 'Abercromby, Ralph', HoP, *Commons, 1754–90* · D. G. Henry, 'Abercromby, Sir Ralph', HoP, *Commons, 1790–1820* · E. Haden-Guest, 'Clackmannanshire', HoP, *Commons, 1754–90*, 1.475 · R. G. Thorne, 'Clackmannanshire', HoP, *Commons, 1790–1820*, 2.527–8 · GEC, *Peerage*, new edn · IGI
Archives NAM, orderly book | Broomhall, Dunfermline, corresp. with Lord Elgin · CKS, corresp. with first Marquess Camden · NA Scot., corresp. with Henry Dundas; letters to Sir Alexander Hope · NAM, letters to Frederick Maitland · NRA Scotland, priv. coll., letters to Sir David Dundas and Colonel Brownrigg
Likenesses J. Hoppner, oils, *c.*1797–1798, Scot. NPG [*see illus.*] · C. Kay, caricatures, etchings, 1801, NPG · G. F. Pidgeon, silver medal, 1801 (after B. West), Scot. NPG · S. W. Reynolds, mezzotint, pubd 1801 (after J. Hoppner), BM, NPG · copper medal, 1801, Scot. NPG · S. Arnold, oils, 1802 (*Death of Sir Ralph Abercromby*), NAM · P. de Loutherbourg, group portrait, oils, 1802 (*Battle of Alexandria, 21 March 1801*), Scot. NPG · P. de Loutherbourg, group portrait, oils, 1802 (*The landing of British troops at Aboukir, 8 March 1801*), Scot. NPG · J. Northcote, oils, 1802 (*Death of Sir Ralph Abercromby*), Scot. NPG; version, NPG · H. Bone, enamel miniature, 1808 (after J. Hoppner), Scot. NPG · bronze medal, 1897, Scot. NPG · C. Smith, oils (after J. Hoppner), Scot. NPG · T. Stothard, group portrait, oils (*Sir Ralph Abercromby at the Battle of Alexandria, 1801*), Royal Collection · R. Westmacott, equestrian figure on monument, St Paul's Cathedral, London · prints, BM, NPG

Abercromby, Robert (1536–1613), Jesuit, was born at Murthly, in the parish of Little Dunkeld, Perthshire, a kinsman of Richard Abercromby, last abbot of Inchcolm (d. 1549). He matriculated at St Mary's College at the University of St Andrews in 1551, and graduated in humanities from St Salvator's College in 1558. In September 1562 he was one of a group of Roman Catholic graduates who left Scotland in the company of the Jesuit Edmund Hay.

After a short stay at Louvain in the Southern Netherlands, Abercromby entered the Society of Jesus at Rome in August 1563. The following year he was recommended by Juan Polanco, secretary to the father general, for the pioneer Jesuit foundation at Braunsberg on the Baltic coast. This college, the first on Polish soil, was intended by Cardinal Hosius, the bishop of Warmia, as the base for a Roman Catholic counter-offensive in northern Poland

and Scandinavia. Abercromby taught at its secondary school, opened in 1565, and in 1569 was appointed novice master, responsible for the training of the first generation of native-born Polish Jesuits. He also pursued an active apostolate among Scottish and English emigrés along the Baltic coast.

In 1580 Abercromby returned to Scotland and spent six weeks on a fact-finding mission, in the course of which he had three audiences with the young James VI. His report on this mission is as revealing of his character as of the contemporary state of Scottish Catholicism. Abercromby was over-sanguine in his hopes of converting the king and of turning the tide against the Calvinist reformers, and was over-reliant on the good faith of the nobility.

In 1582 Abercromby was seconded for a year as adviser to Hieronim Rozdrażewski, the newly appointed bishop of Włocławek, who set about reforming his diocese on Tridentine lines. He acted as the bishop's representative in Danzig, where he laid the foundations for a Catholic recovery, undertaking the reform of decayed religious houses and appointing German-speaking clergy. When the Braunsberg novitiate was moved to Cracow in 1586, Abercromby went with it, but the following year he was replaced by a native Polish Jesuit and left for the Scottish mission.

Abercromby's nineteen-year apostolate in Scotland coincided with a rapid decline in the fortunes of the Catholic community there. Abercromby was willing to countenance attendance at the kirk, but his policy of accommodation proved unacceptable to Rome. In 1592 he became implicated in the affair of the Spanish blanks, being alleged to have collected signatures from prominent Catholic nobles to blank letters which were intended to be pledges of support for a Spanish landing in Scotland. In spite of pressure from the kirk, James VI was indulgent to Abercromby and his fellow Jesuits. In 1599, with the king's apparent connivance, he was allowed access to Holyroodhouse, where, as he later reported, he received the queen, Anne of Denmark, into the Roman church, even though she did not openly acknowledge her change of religion. Abercromby was by now disillusioned with James, whose overtures to Rome he regarded as merely a political move to secure papal support for his claim to the throne of England.

For the last five years of his mission (1601–6) Abercromby was a fugitive, forced to take refuge in the northeast under the protection of the marquess of Huntly. Now aged and ill, he returned to Braunsberg in the summer of 1606. His last years were clouded by the furore which followed the publication at Braunsberg in 1611 of an anonymous libel on King James purporting to be the work of one Bartholus Pacenius and carrying a false imprint. Copies of the work, a reply to the king's apology for the oath of allegiance, were seized at Danzig. The scurrilous tone of the libel was out of keeping with Abercromby's character, and he vehemently and convincingly denied authorship. He died at Braunsberg on 19 August 1613, and was buried there.

G. MARTIN MURPHY

Sources M. Murphy, 'Robert Abercromby, SJ (1536–1613) and the Baltic Counter-Reformation', *Innes Review*, 50 (1999), 58–75 • W. J. Anderson, 'Narratives of the Scottish Reformation, pt 1: report of Father Robert Abercromby, S.J., in the year 1580', *Innes Review*, 7 (1956), 27–59 • A. Loomie, 'King James's Catholic consort', *Huntington Library Quarterly*, 34 (1970–71), 303–16 • L. Grzebień, *Encyklopedia wiedzy o jezuitach na ziemiach Polski i Litwy, 1564–1995* (Krakow, 1996) • A. Bellesheim, *History of the Catholic Church in Scotland*, ed. and trans. D. O. H. Blair, 3 (1889), 451–4 • P. Czaplewski, ed., *Korespondencja Hieronima Rozdrażewskiego*, 2 vols. (Torun, 1937) • W. Forbes-Leith, ed., *Narratives of Scottish Catholics under Mary Stuart and James VI* (1885) • F. Shearman, 'The Spanish blanks', *Innes Review*, 3 (1952), 81–103 • J. H. Pollen, ed., *Papal negotiations with Mary queen of Scots during her reign in Scotland, 1561–1567*, Scottish History Society, 37 (1901) • J. M. Anderson, ed., *Early records of the University of St Andrews*, Scottish History Society, 3rd ser., 8 (1926), 156, 255

Archives Archivum Romanum Societatis Iesu, Rome, corresp. with Rome, Anglia 42 [copies, Jesuit House, Farm Street, London]

Abercromby, Sir Robert (1740?–1827), army officer and administrator in India, son of George Abercromby (1705–1800) of Tullibody and his wife, Mary, *née* Dundas (d. 1767), was baptized at his family's Scottish estate, Menstrie, near Tullibody, in Clackmannanshire, on 13 October 1740, which was possibly also the day of his birth. He came from one of those Scottish landed families that were to play an important role in British military and imperial history over the next two centuries. Robert's army service was entirely in imperial settings. Having enlisted as a volunteer at the outbreak of the Seven Years' War, he won a commission by battlefield gallantry in North America, displayed during General Sir James Abercromby's vain and costly frontal assault on the French at Fort Ticonderoga, New York, on 8 July 1758. War's end found him a captain, and a decade of half-pay followed. When the American War of Independence broke out, he returned to active service, unlike his brother Ralph, who had reservations about the conflict. Lieutenant-Colonel Robert Abercromby served throughout the American war (during which another of his brothers was killed in action). His youngest brother was the judge Alexander *Abercromby. The connection that would shape the last decade of his military career was made during the closing stages of that war. Abercromby took part in the southern campaign that ended in Yorktown. Lord Cornwallis, under whom he served, and who had a good eye for dependable subordinates, would thereafter push his career forward.

Promoted colonel in 1782, Abercromby left for India (where Cornwallis had become governor-general and commander-in-chief in 1786) with his regiment, the 75th foot, in 1788. Major changes were taking shape in the governance of the East India Company's recently acquired empire. Controlling, and revamping, the company civil administration and military service were both priorities in London. Cornwallis's appointment had signalled the government's intention to push this agenda vigorously. In collaboration with Henry Dundas, who managed Indian affairs for the younger Pitt (and assiduously forwarded the careers of Scots in India), Cornwallis had elaborated a scheme of using British army officers as presidency governors (and commanders-in-chief). As a mechanism for asserting metropolitan control, it had much to recommend it. Its thinly veiled distrust of the company's military officers, however, set Cornwallis and Dundas on a collision course with them. One of the casualties of that collision would be Robert Abercromby.

After two years in India, Abercromby, now promoted major-general, duly became lieutenant-governor and commander-in-chief at Bombay. Cornwallis, who often proved very shrewd about his subordinates' limitations, had warned Dundas that Bombay was probably the limit of Abercromby's abilities. The next few years bore out his judgement. Initially, however, Abercromby proved successful. He managed the Bombay army's part in the Third Anglo-Mysore War (1790–92) competently, if not brilliantly, and upon its conclusion was knighted. The following year, however, Cornwallis returned home and his duties were divided. Abercromby now found himself commander-in-chief, India, while one of Cornwallis's most talented civilians, Sir John Shore, became governor-general. Part of Cornwallis's legacy to Shore and Abercromby, however, was a plan for the future of the company's army that quickly brought Abercromby face to face with the spectre of a 'white mutiny' by the company's officers.

Dundas and Cornwallis believed a separate army in India was anomalous, and dangerous. Cornwallis and other British officers also believed it was professionally inferior, a belief they took few pains to conceal. The plan for army reorganization on which Cornwallis worked during his last months in India and finalized in London in 1794 reflected these views. It amalgamated the company's army with the regular British establishment, reorganizing it and sweeping away many of its officers' cherished financial perquisites in the process. Since its independent status and considerable perquisites were what made Indian military service attractive to many company officers to begin with, it was a measure bound to provoke stiff opposition, especially in the large and powerful Bengal army, whose officers were in fact organizing their resistance even before Cornwallis left. This was the situation Abercromby inherited.

Several factors then combined to make Abercromby's task an impossible one. Cornwallis, despite his own doubts, had promoted him a step too far. Long delays in shaping the arrangements in London gave the Bengal officers ample time to organize both a vigorous London lobby and a resistance plan in India. Shore had been told to avoid territorial expansion, so no war, or preparation for one, distracted the officers from their grievances. Abercromby, to make matters worse, was intermittently ill. Moreover, he validated Cornwallis's doubts, and weakened his own position, by mismanaging a punitive expedition against the company's client state of Rampur. Decisive victory when the army took the field was necessary to sustain the mystique of British invincibility, which was the most important item in the company's arsenal. In October–November 1794 Abercromby barely won a costly, inconclusive engagement, and then granted generous terms rather than face another. His standing with the Bengal army, never firm, plummeted. When, therefore, it became clear, in the winter of 1795–6, that there was an active conspiracy among the officers to defeat any changes of which they disapproved, there was little Abercromby, with only one under-strength British regiment available to back him, could do. Indeed, what he did, in concert with Shore, was to manage the inevitable concessions as adroitly as possible, averting an officers' coup that might have threatened the stability of the company's rule. Abercromby may not have been a great battlefield tactician, but he showed himself a shrewd political realist. He toured the cantonments of the Bengal army promising both concessions and amnesty. When orders from London, based on Cornwallis's plan, at length arrived in the spring of 1796, they were, therefore, already a dead letter. The concessions Shore and Abercromby made to a body of officers equally irreplaceable and indispensable were largely confirmed by London and gave the Bengal army the shape it retained until it was destroyed by the mutiny of 1857. While the home government had to accept what had happened, both Shore and Abercromby were speedily replaced. Abercromby, his eyesight failing, left India in 1797 with what Shore referred to as a 'very moderate fortune', a relatively uncommon situation for someone who had commanded two presidency armies. Although promoted lieutenant-general in 1797, he was never again on active service. He succeeded his more famous brother Sir Ralph *Abercromby as MP for Clackmannan in 1798. However, he resigned the seat in 1802 because of increasing blindness. In the same year he was promoted general. At the time of his death, in November 1827, at Airthrey, near Stirling, he was the British army's most senior general and had played a significant, if inadvertent, role in the consolidation of the British empire's 'other army'.

RAYMOND CALLAHAN

Sources BL OIOC, Home misc. • PRO, Cornwallis MSS • Harvard U., Melville MSS • University of Minnesota, Ames Library of South Asia, Hobart MSS • R. Callahan, *The East India Company and army reform, 1783–1798* (1972) • *DNB* • bap. reg. Scot.
Archives BL OIOC, Home misc. series, corresp. relating to India • Harvard U., Houghton L., corresp. relating to India | Bible Society, Swindon, letters to Lord Teignmouth • NA Scot., corresp. with Henry Dundas • NA Scot., letters to Sir Alexander Hope • PRO, corresp. with Lord Cornwallis, PRO 30/11

Aberdare. For this title name *see* Bruce, Henry Austin, first Baron Aberdare (1815–1895); Bruce, Clarence Napier, third Baron Aberdare (1885–1957).

Aberdeen. For this title name *see* Gordon, George, first earl of Aberdeen (1637–1720); Gordon, George Hamilton-, fourth earl of Aberdeen (1784–1860).

Aberdeen and Temair. For this title name *see* Gordon, John Campbell, first marquess of Aberdeen and Temair (1847–1934); Gordon, Ishbel Maria, marchioness of Aberdeen and Temair (1857–1939) [*see under* Gordon, John Campbell, first marquess of Aberdeen and Temair (1847–1934)].

Abergavenny. For this title name *see* Nevill, William, first marquess of Abergavenny (1826–1915).

Aberhart, William (1878–1943), politician and evangelist in Canada, was born in Hibbert township, near Seaforth, Perth county, Ontario, on 30 December 1878, the son of William Aberhart (who as a child had been brought from Germany) and his wife, Louisa Pepper, the daughter of an Englishman. He was educated at schools in Ontario and at a business college at Chatham, Ontario, and he graduated from a correspondence programme of Queen's University, Kingston, as BA in 1906. He married in 1902 Jessie, daughter of George Flatt, of Galt, Ontario, with whom he had two daughters.

Aberhart took up school teaching and became principal of a school at Brantford. In 1910 he moved to Alberta, then an agricultural region recently established as a province, and in 1915 became principal of Crescent Heights high school, Calgary, a post which he held until he entered the provincial government in 1935. As an active lay preacher he formed in 1918 an institute for the study of the Bible. He began broadcasting in 1924 and funds from his audience quickly enabled the institute to build premises for its classes in 1927 and to extend its broadcasting. It was known as the Calgary Prophetic Bible Institute.

The universal collapse of wheat prices after 1929 caused profound distress among the wheat farmers, and to them, as to the urban unemployed in the years of depression, Aberhart's vigorous broadcasts at once brought the comforts of evangelical preaching and the hope of economic relief through the issue of a free, popular currency known as social credit. His monetary theories, which he began to broadcast after 1932, were adopted from those of Major Clifford Hugh Douglas, of Fearnan, Perthshire, who visited Canada several times and whose views had already been made familiar by the United Farmers Party of Alberta, which had formed the Alberta government since 1921 and was also represented in the House of Commons at Ottawa. In 1933 Aberhart published a pamphlet, *The Douglas System of Economics*, which found a wide sale.

Aberhart's advocacy of social credit drew increasing attention to his broadcasts and led to the formation of listening or study groups throughout Alberta, which were later organized as the Alberta Social Credit League. This league at first had no intention of challenging the provincial government, but it adopted political tactics in pressing its policies upon the government by petitions, delegations, and extensive activity by the local study groups, to which the government replied by appointing Douglas as one of its advisers. In the elections of August 1935 Social Credit candidates, approved by Aberhart and the party leaders, won fifty-six out of the sixty-three seats in the provincial legislature, and Aberhart, who later was returned for Okotoks–High River by acclamation, was called upon to form a government. He became premier and minister of education.

Aberhart was a man of robust physique and mercurial temperament, who won respect for his energy and fervour. In office, as in education, he proved a sound administrator and organizer. His electoral success, in the critical economic situation of the time, flowed from his popular influence as a Bible teacher and an advocate of social credit, one of the aspects of which was an election promise to distribute a 'social dividend' of £25 a month to every adult in the province. More significantly, his power with the public was due to his championship of the debtors against their creditors, whom he described as eastern Canadian and international bankers and financiers. In its early, more radical years, the Social Credit Party resembled earlier farm debtors' movements in western America, such as that for 'free silver'. But the movement's leadership was primarily urban-based and party support in the 1935 provincial election reflected a split between better-off Albertans and those struggling to make it through the depression, rather than an urban–rural split. Provincial legislation to control banks and cancel debts, public or private, was, however, found *ultra vires* by the courts and disallowed. Attempts to control the press were also ineffective. The government had to be content with establishing a parallel provincial banking system of so-called treasury branches.

Aberhart's outlook remained greatly influenced by the Douglas social crediter, L. D. Byrne, the technical adviser to the Alberta Social Credit Board. But, for the most part, after his re-election in 1940 Aberhart's policies reflected an acceptance of the limitations on a provincial government in the area of credit and banking. During its first term in office the Social Credit government passed legislation of benefit to farmers and workers, and alienated most of the business community. In its second term, although the government was active in social welfare, labour questions, and the field of education, it moved away from radical experimentation, turning towards both cautious administration and opposition to the state activity in business advocated by socialists. Aberhart died in Vancouver on 30 May 1943, while still in office. He was survived by his wife.   GRAHAM SPRY, *rev.* ALVIN FINKEL

Sources D. R. Elliott and I. Miller, *Bible Bill: a biography of William Aberhart* (1987) · A. Finkel, *The social credit phenomenon in Alberta* (1989) · R. Hesketh, *Major Douglas and Alberta social credit* (1997) · E. Bell, *Social classes and social credit in Alberta* (1993) · C. B. Macpherson, *Democracy in Alberta* (1953) · L. Hannant, 'The Calgary working class and the social credit movement in Alberta', *Labour/Le Travail*, 16 (1985), 97–116 · J. A. Irving, *The social credit movement in Alberta* (1959) · J. R. Mallory, *Social credit and the federal power in Canada* (1954) · H. Schaltz, 'Portrait of a premier: William Aberhart', *Canadian Historical Review*, 45 (1964), 185–211 · private information (1959) · personal knowledge (1959)
Archives Provincial Archives of Alberta

Abernethy family (*per. c.*1260–*c.*1465), landowners, is of obscure origins, but was certainly a native Scottish family rather than of Norman descent. Orm of Abernethy was a grandson of Gillemichael, earl of Fife in the early twelfth century, and in the 1170s he received confirmation from William the Lion of the lay abbacy of the Culdee monastery of Abernethy in south-east Perthshire, although Orm's son, Laurence, was the last to use the abbatial title. **Hugh of Abernethy** (d. 1291), Laurence's son, came to prominence as a loyal supporter of the Comyns, whose patronage helped him to secure the office of sheriff of Roxburgh by 1264, and he appears as a regular witness to royal documents throughout the 1260s and 1270s. However, following the death of Alexander III in 1286 the precarious political stability was further threatened by the murder outside Brechin in September 1289 of Duncan, earl of Fife, by his own kinsmen Patrick and William of Abernethy, who, according to Fordun, acted with the advice and consent of Hugh of Abernethy. No explanation is offered in contemporary records, although the Lanercost chronicle ventures the conventional charges of excessive greed and cruelty on the part of the earl. The perpetrators were dealt with, and Hugh died, possibly in prison, in 1291. He was succeeded by his son, **Alexander Abernethy** (d. in or before 1315), who swore fealty to Edward I in 1291; his rewards between 1301 and 1303 included the office of warden of Scotland between the Forth and the Mounth. While he was deprived of office in King Edward's final ordinances of 1305 and consequently took part in the national struggle, his loyalties were firmly for Balliol's claims over Bruce's. He was absent from Robert I's first parliament in 1309, received Clackmannan in Stirlingshire from Edward II in 1310, and led an unsuccessful defence of Dundee against Edward Bruce in 1312. In 1314, Abernethy having been forfeited and settled on the earl of Angus, Alexander went to England, and he was dead by 1315.

The Abernethy line was continued in the person of William Abernethy of Saltoun, Haddingtonshire, from another branch of the family; the exact line of inheritance is obscure and did not include the forfeited barony of Abernethy itself. He subscribed the Declaration of Arbroath in 1320 and witnessed a charter of King Robert in 1322, but otherwise little is known of his life until his forfeiture following the battle of Halidon Hill in 1333. He was among the knights at the court of David II, however, from whom he received a grant of Rothiemay in Banffshire in 1345. He died in 1346, probably at the battle of Nevilles Cross, and was succeeded by his son, George Abernethy of Saltoun and Rothiemay, who suffered imprisonment in the Tower of London after his own capture at Nevilles Cross. George Abernethy appears as a witness to a marriage contract in 1370, but died the following year, when he was succeeded by his elder son, George (d. before 1400). His second son, John, went to the Holy Land, where he had died by 1381. The younger George Abernethy was succeeded by his son, William, who served as a hostage for the ransom of James I, his estates being valued at 500 marks sterling. When he died, without heirs, before 1428, he was succeeded by his brother, Laurence.

Laurence Abernethy (c.1400–1463) was created a lord of parliament as Laurence, Lord Saltoun of Abernethy, on 28 June 1445. His elevation at this date suggests he was regarded as a supporter of the Douglases, who were then dominant in government. But he appears as a frequent royal charter witness in April and May 1452, offering support to the king in the crucial period following the murder of William, eighth earl of Douglas. As justiciar, he held a justice court at Lochmaben in 1454, where some of his judgments may have antagonized the already beleaguered Douglases, for his lands were harried and burnt by

the ninth earl of Douglas in 1455. He was dead before 7 December 1463, when his son William appears as a royal charter witness as Lord Abernethy; confirmation of his title was given on 28 January 1464. The importance of the family as substantial landowners at that time is demonstrated by the enumeration of its possessions, which included Saltoun in Haddingtonshire, Rothiemay in Banffshire, Redie in Angus, Dalgety in Fife, Glencorse in Edinburghshire, and other lands in Lauderdale and Roxburgh. C. A. McGLADDERY

Sources G. W. S. Barrow, *Robert Bruce and the community of the realm of Scotland*, 3rd edn (1988) · N. H. Reid, ed., *Scotland in the reign of Alexander III, 1249–1286* (1990) · *Scots peerage*, 7.396–407 · J. M. Thomson and others, eds., *Registrum magni sigilli regum Scotorum / The register of the great seal of Scotland*, 11 vols. (1882–1914), vol. 2 · G. Burnett and others, eds., *The exchequer rolls of Scotland*, 6 (1883) · A. Grant, 'The development of the Scottish peerage', *SHR*, 57 (1978), 1–27 · GEC, *Peerage*, new edn, vol. 11

Abernethy, Alexander (d. in or before 1315). See under Abernethy family (per. c.1260–c.1465).

Abernethy, John (1680–1740), Presbyterian minister, was born on 19 October 1680, the son of John Abernethy (d. 1703), minister at Brigh, co. Tyrone, and his wife, a member of the family of Walkinshaw, of Walkinshaw, Renfrewshire. His father, who had settled in Ireland during the Commonwealth and had been ejected from his church living at Minterburn in 1661, accompanied Patrick Adair to London to represent the Irish dissenting interest to William III in 1689. His mother took refuge in Derry, losing all her children but John during the Jacobite siege; he was with relatives at Ballymena, who transported him for safety to Scotland. After attending grammar school in Renfrewshire until 1692 he rejoined his parents, by then settled at Coleraine, and completed his schooling there. In 1693 he entered Glasgow University in the first year of the philosophy course, graduating MA c.1696. Information on his performance is entirely lacking, but his regent was John Tran, an unregenerate scholastic. Abandoning plans for a medical career, he next studied divinity at Edinburgh University, under the orthodox George Campbell. Attempts to trace his later independence of mind to anything positive in his Scottish education are baseless. His family environment is the likeliest influence on his lifelong love of learning and in the development of his superior intellectual and social skills.

Abernethy was entered on trials by the Route presbytery over the winter of 1701–2 and was licensed to preach on 3 March. After supply preaching at Coleraine he visited and preached in Dublin during the tensions following the deposition of Thomas Emlyn, and chose not to stay. By January 1703 he was 'a probationer in the presbytery of Antrim' (Route presbytery minutes, 19 Jan 1703). He received calls to both Antrim and Coleraine, the latter as assistant to his ailing father, who died on 14 November 1703. The General Synod of Ulster determined in favour of Antrim, where he was ordained in August 1703. He married Susannah Jordan (d. 1712), with whom he had one son and three daughters. In 1713 Abernethy began keeping a spiritual diary, six volumes of which were available to his

John Abernethy (1680–1740), by John Brooks (after James Latham)

obituarist, James Duchal, in the 1740s. In this he recalled a time when he was 'a child in religion (that is, beginning to be serious)', subject to 'a warm imagination, laying too great stress upon what I accounted divine impressions, upon fervours and raptures in religion' (Duchal, preface, xviii). He early resolved that religion must be a rational exercise, although it was the preacher's role also to engage the heart. About 1705 he initiated a regular meeting for ministers and ministerial candidates to study biblical exegesis, circulate recent scholarship, explore the grounds of dissent, and pool ideas on pastoral practice. Their reading was not solely doctrinal or narrowly sectarian. Belfast became their regular meeting place and they were subsequently called the Belfast Society.

Abernethy's first published sermon, marking the accession of George I, was a call for moral reform; it also argued for a consent theory of monarchical authority and was the first of his pieces defending a protestant conception of liberty. He was moderator of the general synod in 1715–16, concluding his term with an added urgency in the moral message, since he shared the prevailing apprehensions that 'Antichrist's fall, and the commencement of the millennium' were imminent; he also thought, however, that such calculations were less certain than 'the essential doctrines of faith, the Deity of our Saviour, and the Redemption of the Elect by his death' (J. Abernethy, *Sermon Recommending the Study of Scripture-Prophecie*, 1716, 11). The same synod debated the conversion of the Irish. Abernethy was enthusiastic about this enterprise: Duchal indicates that from this date it took over much of his diary. Though never on the synod's list of Irish speakers he must have developed sufficient fluency. He began to visit the Irish community alongside Lough Neagh with some regularity,

preaching in public and conversing in private. The number of long-term converts was probably small but when there were attempts to move him to another congregation, in 1717–18, an Irish-speaking deputation lobbied the meetings of the synod.

Benjamin Hoadly's famous sermon before the king in March 1717 on the text 'My Kingdom is not of this World' changed Abernethy's view of the authority of church judicatories, confessions, and doctrinal declarations. Later that year he received a call to Usher's Quay, Dublin, which was resisted by his congregation and rejected by the synod. It was repeated in 1718, with a competing call from Belfast; both were again opposed by Antrim. After a three-way contest in the synod there was a second adjudication between the two leading contenders. The vote favoured Dublin—with doubtful legality, since Dublin was beyond their jurisdiction—and Abernethy was involuntarily released from connection with the synod at the same time as they gave him three months to leave. The Antrim presbytery protested, his congregation refused to concur, and the matter went into abeyance. Abernethy told the following year's synod that he could not in conscience accept a ruling that would destroy his principal usefulness. The synod approved a compromise requiring him to move for a trial period without obligation. The presbytery protested:

> that as the former proceedings of this Synod in this affair have been offensive, injurious, and tending to subvert the Constitution of this Presbyterian Church, and the most Essential Rights of Presbyteries and their members, so this last resolution is arbitrary, opposing mere authority to reason, and in contempt of the plain fundamental liberties of the members of a Christian Society. (*Records of the General Synod of Ulster*, 1.506)

Even conservative members of the presbytery backed Abernethy at this stage, while several of his allies in the Belfast Society were recruited for the other side and probably led the compromise. Abernethy went to Dublin for three months but returned, confiding in his diary that the argument for his removal 'depends upon servile notions of ecclesiastical power, which are attended with confusion and fear, but without light, and they destroy a rational choice' (Duchal, preface, xliii).

Abernethy's opposition to central regulation had, by the end of 1719, extended to regulation in belief, when his sermon *Religious Obedience Founded on Personal Persuasion* followed closely upon the Salters' Hall debate in London. By emphasizing the fallibility of human assemblies and reserving to all believers the right to search scripture for themselves he saw himself as the authentic upholder of the Reformation. The cogency of his argument that opposition to human religious conventions in public life required a questioning of the dissenters' own autocratic controls was lost on his orthodox brethren, who adopted a narrowly doctrinaire reading of the Westminster confession and consistently misrepresented Abernethy's strictly bibliocentric position as a believers' free-for-all. After Samuel Haliday's controversial installation at Belfast in 1720 a seven-year struggle for the soul of the synod ensued. Conservative members of the Belfast Society withdrew and it became associated narrowly with the non-subscription movement. Initially—and perhaps throughout—a majority of ministers sought an accommodation in the interests of unity, but a minority of vocal heresy hunters raised enough fears among the laity to ensure a split. In 1725 the Antrim presbytery was reconstituted to embrace non-subscribing ministers and their congregations without regard to geographical boundaries but a year later they were suspended indefinitely from association with the synod, and Abernethy lost some congregational support. There is no evidence that the non-subscribers did harbour heresy at the time. Abernethy's piety, integrity, and pastoral diligence were exemplary but ecclesiastical historians have argued that his idealism blinded him to the imminent reality of the threat to doctrine. This is almost certainly false. He was one of the finest minds and had the greatest reformist vision of anyone in eighteenth-century Irish dissent. He undoubtedly understood the situation in England, where non-subscription was opening the way to doctrinal diversity, but he regarded freedom of conscience as less evil in its consequences than inquisition.

With the death of Joseph Boyse in 1729 Abernethy alone had the stature to assume Boyse's political mantle in the campaign for the religious and political liberties of the dissenters. In 1730 he accepted a call to be Boyse's successor at Wood Street, Dublin. This congregation was English Presbyterian in orientation and home to the leading intellectuals in Irish dissent; the charge that he had previously declined had been an orthodox congregation with whom he could expect little rapport. Once established in Dublin, however, he vigorously represented the interests of the estranged subscribers as much as non-subscribers. Within a year he published *The Nature and Consequences of the Sacramental Test Considered*, adopting a natural-law defence of dissenters' rights to civil and military office: the sacrament is for spiritual, not civil, ends, and people may read scripture for themselves in judging how they will receive it. Swift honoured him with a scurrilous response, which Abernethy countered in a series of five able pamphlets, *Reasons for the Repeal of the Sacramental Test* (1733), written jointly with the prominent bookseller William Bruce.

Abernethy now turned to more philosophical writing. Two volumes of discourses on the being and attributes of God began as sermon series, but for a sophisticated public. The first, *Discourses Concerning the Being and Natural Perfections of God*, was published before his death in 1740; the second, *Discourses concerning the Perfections of God; in which his Holiness, Goodness, and other Moral Attributes, are Explained and Proved*, posthumously in 1742. The two works together were reissued throughout the century as a set, with no common title, and with London, Glasgow, and Aberdeen imprints. They were commended by Archbishop Thomas Herring and other Anglicans, and read in the dissenting academies and in the Scottish universities. The distinction between natural and moral attributes had been given currency by Samuel Clarke but Abernethy's exposition deploys the philosophy of Francis Hutcheson. Hutcheson had sent Bruce the manuscript of his own *System of Moral Philosophy* to secure Abernethy's comments in 1737, though there is no hard evidence that Abernethy saw it. However, his aesthetic argument for the natural perfections makes innovative use of Hutcheson's earlier account of the constituents of beauty, arguing that the 'variety' in nature is inconsistent with its being the work of necessity and that its 'uniformity' is inconsistent with its being the work of chance. The account of the moral attributes of deity reflects a Hutchesonian ethic, while the problem of evil is resolved through a theory of rational choice. Religion is seen as a relationship with deity grounded in intelligence, that leads to reverence, love, and trust; it should not be based on fear, which caters to the passions and induces superstition.

Abernethy changed his preaching style for Dublin, not only becoming more philosophical but adopting a written text. The four volumes of posthumously published *Sermons on Various Subjects* (1748–51) therefore belong largely to this period. The manuscripts had passed to Abernethy's son, Jack (later a London merchant). Duchal, as editor, had access to them for six years before the first volume appeared; his conception of the project, which he discussed in detail with Bruce, evolved over the interval. He was disinclined to print 'some passages pretty amazing' from Abernethy's diary, on incidents for which there was no other corroboration, and wished to avoid setting down information that risked being contested (Hincks, 78–9). Duchal identified most with the practical moralist in Abernethy, and selected discourses to project this character. What is plain, nevertheless, is that Abernethy had repudiated Calvinism. His emphasis throughout is on the freedom of reason and the rational control of passion and action; human sin is acknowledged but attributed to a corrigible failing in self-control.

In Dublin, Abernethy had remarried. His second wife was a daughter of John Boyd, of Rathmore, co. Antrim. No further children are recorded. Abernethy died intestate, of gout, at his home in Whitefriar Street, Dublin, on 1 December 1740. He was buried in St Bride's churchyard on 3 December; remains from this graveyard were subsequently removed to Mount Jerome. His son obtained administration of his estate on 15 December 1741.

M. A. STEWART

Sources J. Duchal, preface, in J. Abernethy, *Sermons on various subjects*, 4 vols. (1748–51), vol. 1 · *Records of the General Synod of Ulster, from 1691 to 1820*, 3 vols. (1890–98), vols. 1, 2 · Route presbytery minutes, 1701–6, Presbyterian Historical Society of Ireland, Belfast · T. D. Hincks, 'Notices of William Bruce, and of his contemporaries and friends, Hutcheson, Abernethy, Duchal, and others', *Christian Teacher*, new ser., 5 (1843), 72–92 · F. J. Bigger, *The two Abernethys* (privately printed, Belfast, 1919) · C. Innes, ed., *Munimenta alme Universitatis Glasguensis / Records of the University of Glasgow from its foundation till 1727*, 3, Maitland Club, 72 (1854), 154–5 · J. McConnell and others, eds., *Fasti of the Irish Presbyterian church, 1613–1840*, rev. S. G. McConnell, 2 vols. in 12 pts (1935–51) · A. W. G. Brown, 'John Abernethy, 1680–1740: scholar and ecclesiast', *Nine Ulster lives*, ed. G. O'Brien and P. Roebuck (1992), 127–47 · J. Duchal, *Sermon on occasion of the much lamented death of the late Reverend Mr John Abernethy* (1741) · J. Mears, *Sermon on the occasion of the much lamented death of the Revd. Mr John Abernethy* (1741)

Likenesses engraving, 18th cent. (after portrait), repro. in *Universal Magazine* · portrait, 18th cent. · J. Brooks, mezzotint (after J. Latham), BM, NPG [*see illus.*]

Abernethy, John (1764–1831), surgeon, born in Coleman Street, London, on 3 April 1764, was one of the five children of John Abernethy, a merchant, and his wife, Elizabeth Weir from Antrim in Ireland. Abernethy's early education took place at Wolverhampton grammar school, and at the age of fifteen he was apprenticed to Charles Blicke, surgeon to St Bartholomew's Hospital, London. He was to remain at Bart's for the remainder of his career.

Abernethy initially followed the surgical practice of the hospital and attended the courses of lectures offered there and at other London medical schools. William Blizard appointed Abernethy his prosector in anatomy, encouraging his interest in that subject. In 1787 he was appointed assistant surgeon at Bart's, a post he held for twenty-eight years before promotion to full surgeon. During the 1790s Abernethy published several papers on a variety of anatomical topics. On the strength of these contributions he was in 1796 elected a fellow of the Royal Society. Between 1814 and 1817 he served as professor of anatomy and surgery at the Royal College of Surgeons.

Abernethy also offered private lectures in anatomy in a house in Bartholomew Close, near to the hospital. These were so successful that the governors of Bart's were persuaded to build a lecture theatre within the hospital to accommodate his classes. His popularity as a teacher was in large part due to the robust humour and extravagant histrionics which he brought to the classroom. However, in 1824 Thomas Wakley, editor of the newly established journal *The Lancet*, published Abernethy's lectures without his permission. This action was part of Wakley's campaign against what he saw as the corrupt élite that dominated the medical profession. It was, in particular, designed to undermine this group's exclusive control of the dissemination of medical knowledge. Abernethy sought an injunction to prevent this piracy but was rebuffed by the court of chancery. He remained resentful at this affront, complaining in 1830, 'who would labour in this manner [lecturing], under the persuasion that the fruits of his exertions might be surreptitiously taken from him?' (Abernethy, 3.iii).

Abernethy had himself attended the lectures of John Hunter, with whom he was also personally acquainted. In later life Abernethy emphasized the importance of Hunter's personal and intellectual influence on the development of his own ideas, and after Hunter's death he professed himself to be the spokesman for Hunter's physiological and pathological views. He took the opportunity of his lectures to promote the merits of the Hunterian Museum and to propound his own interpretation of Hunter's theory of life.

Abernethy's lectures were the occasion of a notorious controversy between Abernethy and his erstwhile pupil, William Lawrence. During his lectures at the Royal College of Surgeons Abernethy took every opportunity to insist that life does not depend on organization—a view

John Abernethy (1764–1831), by Sir Thomas Lawrence, 1819–20

he attributed to John Hunter (Abernethy, 4.53). This was, *prima facie*, simply a physiological theory which could be supported by various kinds of empirical evidence. At the same time, however, Abernethy was anxious to draw attention to what he saw as the wider implications of his doctrine of vitality.

Abernethy argued that if philosophers 'once saw reason to believe that life was something of an invisible and active nature superadded to organisation, they would then see equal reason to believe that mind might be superadded to life as life is to structure'. Thus, 'even physiological researches enforce the belief … that, in addition to his bodily frame, [humankind] possesses a sensitive, intelligent mind'. This was an opinion which, moreover, tended 'in an eminent degree, to produce virtuous, honourable, and useful actions' (Abernethy, 4.95). In short, Hunter's theory of life possessed metaphysical, theological, and ethical, as well as scientific, implications. In the period of social and political unrest in Britain following the French Revolution there was a widespread sentiment that all available resources should be employed to bolster the religious and moral foundations of society.

Lawrence, however, in his 1816 lectures on comparative anatomy at the Royal College of Surgeons, poured scorn both on Abernethy's theory of vitality and on the cultural significance ascribed to it. Abernethy responded in his own lectures given at the college in 1817. He did not refer to Lawrence by name, directing his attacks instead at the party of 'modern sceptics', whom he saw as the principal opponents of the Hunterian doctrine of vitality. He repeated his claim that 'the belief of the distinct and independent nature of mind incites us to act rightly from principle … regardless of our own personal feelings and interests' (Abernethy, 4.156).

He implied that 'sceptics' resented this notion because it might compromise their personal liberty. Abernethy appealed to the nationalistic prejudices of his audience—as well as to their fears about social stability—by suggesting that scepticism was a typically French philosophy, which had helped to prepare the way for the revolution. The British medical profession should, he urged, strenuously resist 'opinions tending to subvert morality, benevolence, and the social interests of mankind' (ibid., 157–8).

Abernethy also suggested that British physiologists were morally superior to those on the continent because they were less inclined to resort to animal experimentation in their investigations. He maintained that most such experiments were gratuitously cruel and added nothing to scientific knowledge. He was especially critical of the enquiries on animal reproduction conducted by the Abbé Spallanzani who was, in Abernethy's view, 'a filthy-minded fellow' (Abernethy, 4.233).

Abernethy was not noted for his skill as an operative surgeon. He did, however, publish many papers on the management of surgical cases, notably those involving injury of the head. He also published an essay on the classification of tumours. His most notable contribution to the practice of medicine lay, however, in his attempts to emphasize the non-surgical aspects of the conditions that he and his colleagues encountered.

In his Hunterian oration of 1819 Abernethy maintained that the distinction that had evolved between physic and surgery was largely arbitrary: 'Medicine is one and indivisible … The physician must understand surgery, and the surgeon the medical treatment of disease' (Abernethy, 4.23). In particular he believed that the distinction between 'local' and 'constitutional' diseases, upon which the division of labour between physician and surgeon was predicated, was misleading. It was well known, he claimed, that local diseases could lead to general disorders such as fever; moreover, in his 'Essay on the constitutional origin, and treatment of disease' he wrote: 'My observations have led me to believe that most local diseases are preceded by general indisposition, of which the disordered state of the digestive organs is an evidence, and may have been a cause' (ibid., 1.196). A close attention to the workings of the digestive system was consequently 'indispensably necessary, even in the common practice of the surgeon' (ibid., 1.206). Abernethy's position cannot be described as either localist or generalist. His tendency was, however, to emphasize constitutional over local causes of illness. In some ways his system is comparable to that of his French contemporary, F. J. V. Broussais: both were systematists and both emphasized the intestine as the source of illness. Given Abernethy's prejudice against the French, he was not inclined to dwell on this similarity.

In his lifetime Abernethy was, however, best-known not as a lecturer or writer, but as a medical practitioner. He enjoyed a large and lucrative private practice in London, drawing his patients from the wealthier sections of society. Patients were known to travel from as far away as Scotland to consult him. Abernethy's success as a practitioner is the more remarkable in view of his notorious brusqueness with patients as well as with colleagues. He was capable of being egregiously rude even to aristocratic patients. Contrary to the conventions of the polite medicine of the time, Abernethy also tended to disregard the peculiarities of the particular case and to refer every ailment to the disorders of the digestion that he saw as at the root of all disease. It was his custom to refer every patient to 'the 1st part of my surgical Observations page 72' (Jacyna, 260). An obituarist claimed that such 'routinism' was 'generally ludicrous, but sometimes tragical'; he claimed to know of cases where a patient's life had been lost because of Abernethy's 'blind perseverance in one system of treatment totally inapplicable to the existing disease' (Medico-Chirurgical Review, new ser., 15, 1831, 286).

Some patients certainly were repelled by this eccentricity and instead sought the services of other practitioners such as Astley Cooper. Many, however, remained loyal to Abernethy despite the indelicate language and, on occasion, rough physical handling they might receive from him. According to his biographer he had 'an amount of practice to which neither he nor any other man could do full justice' (Macilwain, 161). In a usually sycophantic society a reputation for plain speaking could apparently enhance rather than damage a medical reputation. Indeed, one contemporary was of the opinion that Abernethy's 'roughness of manner' was cultivated 'from inclination—habit—or perhaps DESIGN' (Jacyna, 261).

On 9 January 1800 Abernethy married Anne Threlfall of Edmonton, Middlesex, with whom he had a number of children. His youngest daughter, Elinor, married Sir George Burrows (1801–1887). Abernethy and his family lived at various addresses in London, including St Mildred's Court and 14 Bedford Row.

Abernethy retired from his post of surgeon at Bart's on 24 July 1827. He continued to lecture, however, for a further year. He resigned his seat on the court of examiners at the Royal College of Surgeons in 1829. He was by this time infirm and had difficulty in walking, and he retired to Enfield, where, after a protracted illness, he died on 28 April 1831. He was buried at Enfield parish church, and was survived by his wife.   L. S. JACYNA

Sources J. Abernethy, *The surgical and physiological works* (1830) · G. Macilwain, *Memoirs of John Abernethy*, 3rd edn (1856) · A. Desmond, *The politics of evolution: morphology, medicine and reform in radical London* (1989) · L. S. Jacyna, 'Mr Scott's case: a view of London medicine in 1825', *The popularization of medicine, 1650–1850*, ed. R. Porter (1992), 252–86 · *GM*, 1st ser., 70 (1800), 587 · private information (1997)

Archives CUL, lectures on anatomy · RCP Lond., notes of lectures · RCS Eng., notes of surgical lectures · RS, anatomical papers · U. Birm. L., lectures on surgery · U. Edin. L., notes on the cranium · Wellcome L., lecture notes

Likenesses G. Dance, pencil drawing, 1793, NPG · T. Lawrence, oils, 1819–20, St Bartholomew's Hospital, London [*see illus.*] · R. Cooper, stipple, pubd 1825 (after C. Penny), BM · W. Bromley, line engraving, pubd 1827 (after T. Lawrence), BM · C. W. Pegler, oils, 1828, St Bartholomew's Hospital, London · R. W. Sievier, marble bust, 1828, St Bartholomew's Hospital, London · F. Chantrey, marble bust, 1833, RCS Eng. · W. Groves, marble bust, 1837, St Bartholomew's Hospital, London · E. McInnes, mezzotint, 1842 (after T. Lawrence), Wellcome L. · J. Cochran, stipple (after T. Lawrence), Wellcome L. · W. Daniell, soft-ground etching (after G. Dance), Wellcome L. · J. Thomson, stipple (after J. Partridge), BM, NPG; repro. in *European Magazine* (1819) · C. Turner, mezzotint (after C. W. Pegler), Wellcome L.

Abernethy, Laurence, **Lord Saltoun of Abernethy** (*c*.1400–1463). *See under* Abernethy family (*per. c*.1260–*c*.1465).

Abernon, Pierre d'. *See* Fetcham, Peter of (*fl.* 1267–1276).

Abershaw, Louis Jeremiah [Jerry] (*c*.1773–1795), highwayman, operated for many years on the roads between London, Kingston, and Wimbledon, and had his headquarters at the Bald-Faced Stag inn near Kingston. When in hiding he frequented the 'old house in West Street', in Clerkenwell, London, which was noted for its dark closets, trapdoors, and sliding panels, and was said to have once been an asylum for Jonathan Wild and Jack Sheppard (Pinks, 355). Prone to violence, Jerry Abershaw, as he was known, gained a reputation as a dangerous and much feared criminal. On one November night, after several hours spent upon the road, he was taken ill at the Bald-Faced Stag, and a doctor, William Roots, was sent for from Kingston. Abershaw entreated the doctor, who was in ignorance of his patient's name, to travel back under the protection of one of his own men, but the gentleman refused, declaring that he feared no one, even should he meet with Abershaw himself. The story was said to be frequently repeated by the highwayman, as a testimony to the eminence he had gained in his profession.

On 13 January 1795 Abershaw shot dead David Price, a Union Hall officer who had been sent to arrest him, in the Two Brewers public house in Maid Lane, Southwark. He also attempted to shoot a second officer, Barnard Turner. For these crimes he was brought to trial at the Surrey assizes in Croydon on the 30 July. Although a legal flaw in the indictment invalidated the case of murder against him, he was convicted and sentenced to death on the second charge of felonious shooting. Abershaw is reported to have received his sentence with extraordinary sang-froid, putting on his own hat at the same moment as the judge assumed the black cap, and 'observing him with contemptuous looks' while he pronounced judgment. During the few days that intervened between his conviction and execution he spent his time sketching with black cherries scenes from his exploits on the walls of his cell.

On 3 August 1795 Abershaw was hanged on Kennington Common, and his body afterwards set on a gallows on Putney Common. While being driven to the gallows he

appeared entirely unconcerned, had a flower in his mouth … and he kept up an incessant conversation with the persons who rode beside the cart, frequently laughing and nodding to others of his acquaintances whom he perceived in the crowd, which was immense. (*Oracle and Public Advertiser*, 4 Aug 1795)

However, according to *The Times*, 'previous to being turned off, he threw a Prayer Book which was offered him among the crowd; and afterwards his hat and shoes. … He seemed to struggle much in dying'. A pamphlet on his career, entitled *Hardened Villany Displayed*, published soon after his death, described him as 'a good-looking young man, only 22 years of age'. The coolness with which Abershaw met his death prolonged his notoriety, and his name was commonly used as a synonym for a daring thief in the early nineteenth century.

SIDNEY LEE, *rev.* HEATHER SHORE

Sources J. Timbs, *English eccentrics and eccentricities* (1875), 546 · A. F., *The criminal recorder, or, Biographical sketches of notorious public characters*, 1 (1804), 28–32 · A. Knapp and W. Baldwin, *The Newgate calendar, comprising interesting memoirs of the most notorious characters*, ed. E. V. Mitchell (New York, 1926); repr. (1928), 223–7 · *The Times* (25 June 1795) · *The Times* (31 July 1795) · *The Times* (4 Aug 1795) · G. W. Thornbury and E. Walford, *Old and new London: a narrative of its history, its people, and its places*, 6 vols. (1873–8), vol. 6, pp. 335, 497 · W. J. Pinks, *The history of Clerkenwell*, ed. E. J. Wood, 2nd edn (1881), 355 · G. F. Berkeley, *My life and recollections*, 1 (1865), 198 · E. W. Brayley, J. Britton, and E. W. Brayley, jun., *A topographical history of Surrey*, 3 (1844), 56–7 · H. D. Miles, *Jerry Abershaw, or, The mother's curse* (1847–8) · E. Kilmurray, *Dictionary of British portraiture*, 2 (1979) · A. Griffiths, *The chronicles of Newgate*, 2 vols. (1884); repr. (New York, 1987)
Likenesses J. Chapman, stipple, pubd 1804, NPG

Abetot, Urse d' (*c*.1040–1108), administrator, derived his name from St Jean d'Abbetot, near Tancarville (Seine Inférieure) where he was probably born. He appears in Domesday Book as a tenant-in-chief in the counties of Hereford, Gloucester, Warwick, and Worcester, and as a subtenant in Dorset, Oxfordshire, and Wiltshire. He is styled 'Urso de Wirecestre' from his position as sheriff of Worcestershire, an office which he held from shortly after the Norman conquest. William of Malmesbury, describing him as *vicecomes Wigorniae a rege constitutus* ('appointed sheriff of Worcester by the king'), tells the story of his encroaching on the cemetery of Worcester Cathedral priory to make the ditch around his castle, and being sternly rebuked by Archbishop Ealdred (*d.* 1069): 'Hattest thu Urs, haue thu Godes kurs' (*De gestis pontificum*, 253). Urse earned a reputation in Worcestershire as a predator on monastic lands, especially those of the monks of Worcester: in one case he seized a manor as a marriage portion for his daughter, and Evesham Abbey, too, suffered at his hands. However, he was a benefactor of Great Malvern Priory, which, during a fourteenth-century lawsuit, claimed him as its founder. On the revolt of the earl of Hereford in 1075 he joined Bishop Wulfstan of Worcester and Abbot Æthelwig of Evesham in defeating the earl's forces.

In the reign of William II, d'Abetot was a prominent official in the royal administration. He remained sheriff of Worcestershire for life, and died in the course of 1108, when he was succeeded in his lands and office by his son Roger, who was banished *c*.1110 after killing an officer of Henry I. Roger d'Abetot was in turn succeeded as sheriff of Worcestershire by Osbert d'Abetot, who held office until a date between 1113 and 1116. Osbert was probably a brother of Urse and the ancestor of the d'Abetots who were prominent in Worcestershire in the twelfth and thirteenth centuries, and who gave their name to the places Croome d'Abitot and Redmarley d'Abitot. Urse's daughter was probably named Emmeline; Dugdale identified her from a register of the dean and chapter of Worcester—presumably register II (now lost), since she is not named either in register I or in the rental of 1240. She married Walter (I) de Beauchamp (d. c.1133), who acquired the estates of Urse. The cognizance of the bear, borne by their descendants, the Beauchamp earls of Warwick, signified descent from Urse (ursus, Latin 'the bear'). Urse was also survived by a widow, Alice. His brother, Robert Dispenser (surnamed from his office in the royal household), had died about 1097, and some, at least, of his estates were acquired by Urse, but were subsequently divided between the Beauchamp and Marmion families, suggesting that Robert was survived by a daughter, married to Robert Marmion.

J. H. ROUND, rev. EMMA MASON

Sources E. Mason, ed., *The Beauchamp cartulary: charters, 1100–1268*, PRSoc., new ser., 43 (1980) · *Hemingi chartularium ecclesiæ Wigorniensis*, ed. T. Hearne, 2 vols. (1723) · *Willelmi Malmesbiriensis monachi de gestis pontificum Anglorum libri quinque*, ed. N. E. S. A. Hamilton, Rolls Series, 52 (1870) · R. R. Darlington, ed., 'Winchcombe annals, 1049–1181', *A medieval miscellany for Doris Mary Stenton*, ed. P. M. Barnes and C. F. Slade, PRSoc., new ser., 36 (1962), 111–37, 122 · *Florentii Wigorniensis monachi chronicon ex chronicis*, ed. B. Thorpe, 2, EHS, 10 (1849), 11 · Dugdale, *Monasticon*, 3.447 · T. Habington, *A survey of Worcestershire*, ed. J. Amphlett, 2 vols., Worcestershire Historical Society (1895–9), vol. 2, pp. 178, 263 · F. West, *The justiciarship in England, 1066–1232* (1966), 10–12 · I. J. Sanders, *English baronies: a study of their origin and descent, 1086–1327* (1960) · R. R. Darlington, ed., *The cartulary of Worcester Cathedral Priory (register I)*, PRSoc., 76, new ser., 38 (1968), no. 41 · R. R. Darlington, 'Aethelwig, abbot of Evesham', *EngHR*, 48 (1933), 177–98 · W. Dugdale, *The baronage of England*, 2 vols. (1675–6), vol. 1, p. 225
Archives BL, the Beauchamp cartulary, Add. MS 28024

Abingdon. For this title name *see* Bertie, Willoughby, fourth earl of Abingdon (1740–1799).

Abingdon, Alexander (*fl.* 1291–1316), sculptor, also known as 'Imaginator' or 'le Imagineur', is of unknown origins, though it has been conjectured that he trained in the masons' yard of Abingdon Abbey. He was a citizen of London at least from 1305, when his name appears in city records, but he was working in London by 1291 and he probably lived there for most of his life, associated with one of the workshops producing monumental effigies. His occupational names probably indicate that he was a specialist in carving fine figurework, able to turn his hand to a range of techniques. He was one among a group of craftsmen who collaborated on the monuments to Queen Eleanor ordered by Edward I between 1291 and 1294. These commissions were highly prestigious and Alexander's involvement indicates that he was considered to be at the forefront of his profession.

After Eleanor of Castile's sudden death from a fever at Harby in Lincolnshire on 28 November 1290, Edward I commissioned twelve crosses in her memory to be erected along the route of her funeral cortège from Lincoln to Westminster. Three tombs were also made, one for her viscera at Lincoln Cathedral, one for her bones at Westminster Abbey, and one for her heart at the London Blackfriars Church. Payments to craftsmen were made for many of these monuments between 1291 and 1294, and it is from the surviving accounts that we learn that Abingdon worked on two out of the three costliest crosses, those at Waltham, Essex, and Charing Cross, London, and on two of the tombs, at Lincoln and at Blackfriars.

For the Waltham and Charing crosses, Abingdon supplied stone statues, the monuments themselves having been built respectively by Roger and Richard of Crundale and by Richard of Crundale and Nicholas Dymenge. Only his statues from the Waltham cross survive: three standing figures of the queen herself. At Lincoln he collaborated with the mason Nicholas Dymenge in making the marble tomb-chest. For both Lincoln and for the Blackfriars' heart-tomb he made some 'cerae', which were probably wax models, likely to have been for lost-wax castings by William of Suffolk, who was paid for making small metal images. It has been suggested that he might also have supplied the wax models for the bronze effigies of Eleanor, cast by William Torel for the Lincoln and Westminster tombs, for some scholars have noted a marked resemblance between his figures and Torel's surviving London effigy.

Abingdon's only other documented commission was of unknown extent—a piece of work for which in 1312 he was under contract to William Estone, parson of Stanwell, Middlesex. Nevertheless, on the basis of stylistic comparisons with his three surviving statues, numerous other important works associated with royal and other leading patrons of the period have been attributed to him. There is general consensus that the effigy of Aveline, countess of Lancaster (d. 1273), in Westminster Abbey is by Alexander, and that the weepers on the adjacent tomb of her husband, Earl Edmund Crouchback (d. 1296), and possibly the effigy as well, are also by him. That these works can also be closely associated with other master masons in the king's service indicates how the creation of important monuments continued to be a collaborative enterprise between craftsmen. The designs of Aveline's and Edmund's tombs have been attributed to successive principal royal master masons: Richard of Crundale, with whom Alexander worked on the Waltham and Charing crosses, and Michael of Canterbury. It is likely that Alexander and Michael of Canterbury also worked together at Ely on the tomb of Bishop William of Louth (d. 1298), Alexander again being responsible for the effigy. The names of the two men appear together in London records for 1316 when, in Abingdon's last documented appearance, they stood surety for three masons accused of breach of contract concerning a boundary wall at Eltham Palace, Kent. Also included in Alexander's putative œuvre have been the wooden effigy of Archbishop John Pecham (d. 1292) at Canterbury Cathedral, the tomb of Bishop William March (d. 1302) at Wells Cathedral, and a female effigy of a member of the Beche family at Aldworth, Berkshire (c.1300).

VERONICA SEKULES

Sources PRO, exchequer, king's remembrancer, accounts various, E 101/352/27; E 101/353/1, 9, 19 · [B. Botfield and T. H. Turner?], eds., *Manners and household expenses of England in the thirteenth and fifteenth centuries, illustrated by original records*, Roxburghe Club, 57

(1841), 95–139 • R. Brown, H. M. Colvin, and A. J. Taylor, eds., *The history of the king's works*, 1 (1963), 479–86 • M. J. H. Liversidge, 'Alexander of Abingdon', *Abingdon essays: studies in local history*, ed. W. J. H. Liversidge and M. J. H. Liversidge (1989), 89–111 • J. Alexander and P. Binski, eds., *Age of chivalry: art in Plantagenet England, 1200–1400* (1987), 361–6 [exhibition catalogue, RA] • P. G. Lindley, *Gothic to Renaissance: essays on sculpture in England* (1995), 11–12 • W. R. Lethaby, *Westminster Abbey and the king's craftsmen* (1906), 177–8, 245–7 • A. Gardner, *A handbook of English medieval sculpture* (1935), 14, 197–202 • R. R. Sharpe, ed., *Calendar of letter-books preserved in the archives of the corporation of the City of London*, [12 vols.] (1899–1912), vol. B, pp. 156, 160, 179; vol. D, p. 289 • P. Biver, 'Tombs of the school of London at the beginning of the fourteenth century', *Archaeological Journal*, 67 (1910), 51–65 • L. Stone, *Sculpture in Britain: the middle ages*, 2nd edn (1972), 143–7, 155, 164, 167 • J. Hunter, 'On the death of Eleanor of Castile, consort of King Edward the First and the honours paid to her memory', *Archaeologia*, 29 (1842), 167–91 • P. Williamson, *Gothic sculpture, 1140–1300* (1995), 217–18 • J. Harvey and A. Oswald, *English mediaeval architects: a biographical dictionary down to 1550*, 2nd edn (1984); pbk edn (1987), 1 • E. A. Wendebourg, *Westminster Abbey als königliche Grablege zwischen 1250 und 1400* (1986), 100–01 • C. Wilson, 'The medieval monuments', *A history of Canterbury Cathedral, 598–1982*, ed. P. Collinson and others (1995), 451–510, esp. 462–3 • P. Binski, *Westminster Abbey and the Plantagenets: kingship and the representation of power, 1200–1400* (1995), 108, 109

Abingdon, Edmund of

Abingdon, Edmund of [St Edmund of Abingdon, Edmund Rich] (*c*.1174–1240), archbishop of Canterbury, was one of the earliest known teachers of arts in the nascent University of Oxford and the first Oxford master to be raised to the altars of the church.

Youth and education Edmund was born at Abingdon, the eldest son of Reginald, called Rich (Dives), and Mabel of Abingdon. He had three, possibly four brothers, one of whom, Robert of *Abingdon, was to follow him in an ecclesiastical career. There is no medieval authority for the use of the name Rich as a patronymic by either Edmund or Robert. In medieval sources they are always designated by their birthplace. Edmund also had two sisters, Margaret and Alice, whom, after the death of the parents, he placed as postulants in the small Northamptonshire nunnery of Catesby. As a master at Oxford, he donated his father's house in West Street, Abingdon, in free alms to the hospital of St John the Baptist outside the east gate of Oxford. His father's occupation is unknown. The statement in some sources that Reginald obtained his wife's consent to retire to the abbey of Eynsham is not supported by other sources and appears to rest on a confusion. Possibly he was engaged in the wool trade or in retailing cloth. He seems to have died when the children were still young, and the task of bringing them up fell to the mother, a devout and strong-minded woman, who trained her sons in the habit of prayer and inculcated her own ascetic practices. Edmund recalled that when he and his brother Robert were students at Paris, she sent them parcels of linen in which she enclosed hair shirts for their use. It was evidently under her powerful influence that they embarked on a clerical career.

Edmund gained his early schooling in grammar at Oxford. It is to this period of his life that are attached the gracious legends of his encounter with an apparition of the Christ Child in the meadows outside the town and the story of his youthful vow of perpetual celibacy, ratified by his espousal with a ring of the statue of the Blessed Virgin. As teenagers, he and Robert were sent to the schools at Paris to hear lectures on the liberal arts. In due course, Edmund incepted as a master. He then returned to Oxford and taught for a period of six years. Roger Bacon, himself a younger contemporary, asserted that Edmund was the first teacher to expound Aristotle's *Sophistici elenchi* ('Problems of the sophists') at Oxford; his regency in arts was thus a milestone in the reception of the new logic by the Oxford schools. Unfortunately the chronology of his academic career is unclear. One of his pupils was Walter de Gray, subsequently royal chancellor and archbishop of York, who testified that he had heard Edmund's lectures in arts. Gray paid a fine for the chancery on 21 October 1205, and this indicates that Edmund's regency must have begun well before 1200; in fact, it may be hypothetically assigned to the years 1196 to 1202.

Among those who wrote to postulate Edmund's canonization, the University of Oxford testified to his devout and ascetic life during the period of his regency in arts. Relying upon information supplied by his former pupil and colleague, the Dominican Robert Bacon, the masters referred to his custom, then unusual among the artists, of assisting at mass daily before he lectured, and to the fact that, although he had not yet obtained a benefice, he used his lecture fees to build a chapel dedicated to the Blessed Virgin Mary, in the parish where he resided. It was said that at this period he adopted a practice, which he later made permanent, of restricting his sleep to a few hours every night and sleeping fully clothed, not in his bed but propped against it, and devoting the rest of the night to prayer. Bacon also supplied the story of Edmund's decision to abandon the arts and return to Paris for the study of theology. His formidable mother, now dead, appeared to him in a dream and questioned him reproachfully about the strange geometric figures he was demonstrating in the schools. His stammered explanations were brushed aside. She grasped his hand and drew in it three circles in which she wrote the words 'Father, Son, Holy Spirit'. 'My dear son', she said, 'henceforth apply yourself to no figures other than these' (Lawrence, 229–30). The anecdote is testimony to the powerful impact of Mabel of Abingdon upon her son's imagination, as well as to the enduring tradition of monastic theology, which regarded the secular sciences as merely introductory to the study of theology.

Paris and Salisbury The dating of Edmund's second Paris residence and his return to Oxford to teach theology is problematic. Robert Bacon, who was already teaching theology at Oxford in 1219, described himself as Edmund's special pupil and auditor of his lectures, which provides a pointer to the date of Edmund's inception as a doctor of theology. The Oxford schools were in abeyance from 1209 until July 1214 owing to a quarrel with the town authorities over the summary hanging of two clerks. As none of the sources for Edmund's academic life mentions this episode or refers to any interruption of his teaching, it is probable that he incepted after it. A letter of postulation from the Augustinian priory of Merton in Surrey alludes to the fact that he resided at the priory for a year or more before assuming the magistral chair as a theologian. Matthew Paris says that he stayed at the priory 'desiring to lecture', implying an enforced postponement. This suggests that his brief retirement was forced on him by the suspension of the Oxford schools and that he incepted in 1214 after the return of the university to Oxford had been negotiated by the papal legate.

There are indications that, like many advanced students, Edmund interrupted his theological studies in the Paris schools and took a benefice for a period in order to finance himself for the course. Matthew Paris observes that he had been presented to livings, but that he resigned them when he returned to the schools. At some time after 1214 he was instituted to a living by his old pupil, Walter de Gray, archbishop of York, but its whereabouts has not been traced. The first preferment of which there is record is his appointment to the treasurership of Salisbury Cathedral by Bishop Richard Poore at some time between January and August 1222. He held this office, with the annexed prebend of Calne, until he was elected archbishop of Canterbury in 1233. Possibly while he was treasurer he continued to teach in the cathedral school of Salisbury, which had a fine scholastic tradition. It was during this period, too, probably in the year 1226–7, that he was one of those selected by a mandate from Pope Honorius III to preach the crusade. He was evidently assigned a circuit that included Oxford and the west of England. The hagiographers report the miraculous forbearance of the rain clouds that allowed him to preach in the open air at Oxford, Gloucester, Worcester, Leominster, and Hereford.

Those who knew Edmund during his time at Salisbury testified to his eloquence as a lecturer and preacher, his great personal austerities, and his generosity to the poor. They also reported that he found administrative business distasteful and that he could hardly be induced to examine the accounts or to attend chapter meetings. As a result of his generosity and indifference to money matters, he was often impoverished and tided over the year as a guest of an old pupil of his Oxford days, Stephen of Lexinton, the Cistercian abbot of Stanley. When Abbot Stephen urged him to cut his prodigal alms-giving, Edmund retorted that it was best to err on the side of generosity, since theologians had an unsavoury reputation for avarice. An ascetic by training and by instinct a scholar and a recluse, he retreated at intervals to Merton Priory and Reading Abbey, where he impressed the monks by the frugality of his diet and his meticulous observance of the monastic regime. He was happiest in his study or quietly ministering to his parishioners in his rectory at Calne. He was, in fact, in his study at Calne when monks arrived from Canterbury Cathedral priory towards the end of September 1233 to inform him that he had been elected archbishop. His reluctance to accept the appointment was genuine and prolonged.

Archbishop of Canterbury Edmund was the fourth candidate to be elected, after the see of Canterbury had been vacant for two years following the death of Archbishop Richard Grant in August 1231. Three previous candidates—Ralph Neville, the royal chancellor and bishop of Chichester, John of Sittingbourne, the prior of Christ Church, Canterbury, and Master John Blund, a scholar and canon of Chichester—had all been quashed by Pope Gregory IX on the advice of the archdeacon of Canterbury, Simon Langton, who was present at the curia. It was probably Langton who suggested Edmund to the pope, who in turn instructed the Canterbury monks to elect him. This they did on 20 September. The king's assent was given on 10 October, and the pallium was collected from the tomb of St Peter in Rome by a delegation from Canterbury on 3 February 1234. Edmund was consecrated archbishop in Canterbury Cathedral on Laetare Sunday, 2 April 1234, by the bishop of London, Roger Niger, in the presence of Henry III and the court and the suffragans of the Canterbury province.

As a schoolman-bishop devoted to pastoral care and the reform of the church, Edmund was in the tradition of Stephen Langton, whose biblical classes he may well have attended at Paris. He gathered round himself an administrative *familia* of learned clerks and *magistri*, which included such notable men as Thomas of Freckenham, formerly Langton's official, Elias of Dereham, the canon and architect of Salisbury who had also served Langton, Nicholas of Burford, Edmund's own official, Geoffrey of Ferring, afterwards dean of St Paul's, and Richard de Wyche, the future bishop of Chichester and saint, whom Edmund appointed his chancellor. One of the most conspicuous in this corps of helpers was Edmund's own brother, Robert of Abingdon, whom he installed in the rich rectory of Wingham, Kent, and used as his adviser throughout his episcopate, entrusting Robert during his absence abroad with his powers of ecclesiastical patronage. It was not thought inappropriate for high-minded bishops to employ their relatives in this way. Langton had provided a precedent by appointing his brother, Simon Langton, to the archdeaconry of Canterbury.

Edmund entered on the primacy at a time of political crisis. Following the fall of the justiciar, Hubert de Burgh, in August 1232, the young king Henry III had assumed the reins of personal government, acting through the officers of the royal household. This, and a general resumption of lapsed royal rights, had aroused baronial fears. Richard Marshal, earl of Pembroke, leader of the baronial opposition to these changes, was raising war against the king in the Welsh marches, and a strong lead from the church was needed if civil war on a wider scale was to be averted. Edmund, who had not yet been consecrated archbishop, immediately set to work to bring the situation under control. He dispatched intermediaries to negotiate peace between the king and the earl, and a truce was concluded at Brockton in Shropshire on 6 March 1234. In April, following his consecration, Edmund successfully pressed on the king a demand for the dismissal of his unpopular councillors, Peter des Roches, the bishop of Winchester, and his nephew Peter des Rivaux, who had been the agent of the administrative changes. From May to July the archbishop busied himself in the marches, reconciling the rebels, and after the death of Earl Richard in Ireland, he persuaded the king to release the Marshal estates to Gilbert, the heir, and to issue a general amnesty. Edmund personally escorted Gilbert Marshal and Hubert de Burgh with other leaders of the rebel party to the king's presence at Gloucester to receive the royal pardon. By his bold leadership he had averted civil war and forced on the king a reconstruction of his council, and his pacification was to be long remembered by loyalists and rebels alike.

There is evidence that in the midst of these secular preoccupations Archbishop Edmund endeavoured to make a visitation of some parts of his ecclesiastical province. He obtained a papal rescript, dated 8 May 1237, authorizing him to use spiritual sanctions against certain unnamed prelates and heads of religious houses who were impeding his visitation. Unfortunately the record of his movements is too patchy to allow the identification of the prelates or places involved. There is, however, evidence that he was planning to visit the cathedral priory of Worcester in July 1236, and later, in 1239, his claim to make a metropolitan visitation of the monastic houses of London encountered opposition from the bishop of London, Roger Niger. As yet, regular and systematic visitation was far from being common practice in England.

Conflicts of jurisdiction One of the problems that demanded Edmund's attention was the encroachment of the royal courts upon ecclesiastical jurisdiction. A conflict arose over the different treatment of bastardy in the secular courts and those of the church, which claimed exclusive jurisdiction over matrimonial matters. Since the time of Pope Alexander III, canon law decreed that a child born out of wedlock was legitimized by the subsequent marriage of its parents; but the secular courts refused to accept this doctrine, which had important consequences for the inheritance of land. In 1234 Archbishop Edmund secured the king's agreement that the royal judges would ask the bishop for the facts when a question of bastardy arose, but this left the matter of subsequent legitimization untouched. Under pressure from Robert Grosseteste, bishop of Lincoln, Edmund raised the matter again in 1236 before a council at Merton and sought to have the English common law brought into line with canon law on this point, but his request was refused by the magnates with the famous words 'We do not wish to change the laws of England, which are customary and well tried' (Lawrence, 160).

Some of the pressure was taken off Edmund by the arrival in July 1237 of Cardinal Otto di Monteferrato, a legate *a latere*, who came at the king's request. Edmund and his suffragans submitted to him a list of clerical grievances that they desired him to raise with the king. Among these were several concerning the encroachment of the royal courts on the jurisdiction of the church. It was complained that benefit of clergy was being disregarded in personal actions and that writs of prohibition were being issued to stop actions over tithes and advowsons from being pursued in the ecclesiastical courts. The belief that the legate's presence was a source of annoyance to Edmund rests upon the biased allegations of Matthew

Paris, whose prejudices on the subject of foreigners and agents of Rome are well known. It is evident that the cardinal enjoyed the archbishop's confidence. Although the legate took precedence over the archbishop and presided over the assembly of prelates summoned to London in November 1237, the important series of canons promulgated by the council, which displayed a detailed grasp of English problems and constituted an enduring body of English church law, clearly reflected the advice and concerns of Archbishop Edmund.

The oath Edmund had taken as a metropolitan required him to make an *ad limina* visit to Rome every three years. Besides this, he had pressing matters to pursue at the papal curia. He was engaged in a law suit with the cathedral chapter of Rochester, which had in 1235 elected Richard Wendene as bishop, ignoring the fact that patronage of the see belonged to the archbishops of Canterbury; consequently Edmund had refused to consecrate Wendene. He was also anxious to obtain a judgment against the validity of the marriage of the king's sister Eleanor, who had taken a vow of perpetual chastity in the archbishop's presence after the death of her first husband. Edmund left England for Rome in late December 1237, returning home in August of the following year, having failed to secure judgment in his favour on either count.

The dispute with the cathedral priory The last months of Edmund's episcopate were clouded by a prolonged conflict with the monks of his cathedral chapter. In 1238 he had revived an old project, attempted and abandoned by two of his predecessors, of founding a college of secular canons in the diocese, to provide for the clerks employed in his administration. The place chosen was Maidstone, and a plan was drawn up by Elias of Dereham for a great collegiate church with fifty prebends, to be endowed out of the lands of the archbishopric. The monks of Christ Church fiercely resisted the plan, fearing it might encroach on their properties and lead to a transfer of their electoral rights, and even the see itself, to the new foundation. Having sued the archbishop in the papal curia and lost their appeal, they sought the intervention of the crown, and in November 1239 they obtained a writ to halt the building operations at Maidstone, in effect terminating the plan.

The breach between Edmund and the cathedral priory was deepened and personalized by a conflict over his claim to appoint the officers of the monastery. During his absence abroad, the prior had been deposed by the legate on account of his part in the forgery of the privilege of St Thomas of Canterbury, and on his return Edmund also deposed the sub-prior. The monks refused to accept his judgment and in January 1239 they aggravated their rebellion by electing themselves a new prior without the archbishop's consent. Edmund responded to these acts of defiance by excommunicating those responsible and then by placing the cathedral monastery under an interdict, which was not to be lifted until after his death.

On 9 August 1240 Pope Gregory IX issued a summons to a general council, to meet at the following Easter. In response to the summons and moved by a determination to prosecute his case against the monks at the curia, Edmund set out for Rome late in the autumn of 1240. He took with him his chancellor, his chaplain, and his domestic staff. Unfortunately the precise date of his departure is uncertain, but the evidence points to mid-October. He broke his journey at the Cistercian abbey of Pontigny, where he sought the privilege of confraternity, but while there he was taken ill. The party turned back, but on reaching the village of Soisy, Edmund was too weak to proceed further and he died there in a small Augustinian priory on 16 November. His body was claimed by the abbot of Pontigny and was borne back to the abbey for burial amid popular approval. The implausible story that he had withdrawn from England into voluntary exile is unsupported by any of the numerous letters written within two years of his death to postulate his canonization or by contemporary chroniclers, other than Matthew Paris. The notion of exile was inserted into the hagiographical tradition by Edmund's chaplain, Eustace of Faversham, a Canterbury monk, who wished to liken his master to St Thomas of Canterbury.

Writings, reputation, and canonization Edmund's literary legacy was small but significant. The work by which he was chiefly known in the middle ages was his treatise on the spiritual life entitled *Speculum ecclesie* or, as it was called in the Anglo-Norman version, *Le merure de seinte eglise*. In its original form it was a Latin treatise for the instruction of people who had embraced the religious life and it was probably written by Edmund early in his academic career as a theologian; possibly it was the fruit of his enforced year of leisure at Merton Priory about 1213–14. The work was translated into Anglo-Norman and Middle English and later a second expanded Latin version was translated from the Anglo-Norman. The large number of surviving manuscripts indicate that it was widely read in the late thirteenth, and the fourteenth, centuries. It is not a very original work. Edmund's account of the spiritual life advances from basic doctrinal instruction to teaching about the higher reaches of contemplative prayer. It shows familiarity with the masters of the contemplative life from Gregory the Great to St Bernard, but it is chiefly indebted to the writings of Hugh of St Victor. Apart from a stray sermon of his, the only identified product of Edmund's university teaching is his *Moralities on the Psalms*, which survives in a single thirteenth-century manuscript. This is a type of gloss, comprising a 'spiritual' exegesis of scripture with a practical moral bias, that was common in the early decades of the thirteenth century.

The initiative in postulating the pope for Edmund's canonization was taken by the Cistercian general chapter of 1241, and in the following year letters of postulation were collected from the University of Oxford, several English monasteries, and the prelates of England and France. Pope Innocent IV issued commissions of inquiry on 23 April 1244, and after examining the evidence, he pronounced St Edmund to be enrolled in the calendar of the saints on 16 December 1246 at Lyons Cathedral. A ceremony of translation took place at Pontigny in the following summer, attended by Louis IX and many French nobles

and prelates. The records of the canonization process, many of which survived and are deposited in the museum at Sens, provided the material for the authors of six different but interdependent lives of St Edmund, which were composed in the decade following his death. His shrine at Pontigny was visited by Henry III and continued to attract a steady flow of English pilgrims until the close of the thirteenth century.

Later judgements on Edmund have been coloured by the story that he fled in the face of opposition in order to end his days at Pontigny. He was strongly attracted by the religious life, and several of his pupils were moved by his teaching to become monks; but he was not a man to desert his post. He was a conscientious and zealous pastor, resolute in defending the prerogatives of his see, and capable of bold leadership, as was shown in his handling of the political crisis of 1233–4. Some of his difficulties, in particular his conflicts with the chapters of Rochester and Canterbury, were the consequence not of indecision but of failings that often beset the intellectual and the ascetic in politics—an unwillingness to compromise and an inability to understand the anxieties and motives of men more worldly than himself.   C. H. LAWRENCE

Sources C. H. Lawrence, *St Edmund of Abingdon: a study of hagiography and history* (1960) • *The life of St Edmund by Matthew Paris*, ed. and trans. C. H. Lawrence (1996) • E. Martène and U. Durand, *Thesaurus novus anecdotorum*, 5 vols. (1717), vol. 3 • W. Wallace, *St Edmund of Canterbury* (1893) • *Paris, Chron.* • *Matthaei Parisiensis, monachi Sancti Albani, Historia Anglorum, sive … Historia minor*, ed. F. Madden, 3 vols., Rolls Series, 44 (1886–9) • *The historical works of Gervase of Canterbury*, ed. W. Stubbs, 2 vols., Rolls Series, 73 (1879–80) • *Ann. mon.* • C. F. Slade and G. Lambrick, eds., *Two cartularies of Abingdon Abbey*, 2 vols., OHS, new ser., 32–3 (1990–92) • *Chancery records* • *Les registres d'Innocent IV*, ed. E. Berger, 4 vols. (Paris, 1884–1921) • D. A. Callus, 'Introduction of Aristotelian learning to Oxford', *PBA*, 29 (1943), 229–81 • A. B. Emden, *An Oxford hall in medieval times: being the early history of St Edmund Hall* (1927) • Edmund of Abingdon, *Speculum religiosorum and Speculum ecclesie*, ed. H. P. Forshaw (1973) • A. D. Wilshere, ed., *Edmundi Abingdonensis Mirour de Seinte Eglyse*, Anglo-Norman Text Society (1982) • H. P. Forshaw, 'St Edmund's *Speculum*: a classic of Victorine spirituality', *Archives d'Histoire Doctrinale et Littéraire du Moyen Âge*, 39 (1972), 7–40 • dean and chapter library, Worcester, MS Q67 [text of Edmund's *Moralitates in psalmos*]
Archives Musée de Sens, records of canonization process • Worcester Cathedral, dean and chapter library, MS Q67
Likenesses M. Paris, drawing, repro. in Lawrence, *St Edmund of Abingdon*, frontispiece • seal, BL; Birch, *Seals*, 203

Abingdon, Henry (d. 1437), ecclesiastic and college head, probably came from Abingdon in Berkshire. He was first elected a fellow of Merton in 1390 and spent most of his later career either there or fulfilling his residential duties as a canon of Wells, where from 1410 he held first the prebend of Wedmore Quarta, followed speedily by Wedmore Quinta. He held the latter at least until October 1419, when he obtained Combe Undecima, which he held until his death. Until 1427 he may have retained Wedmore Quinta also. In addition he had two parish churches in succession: Weston Zoyland, Somerset, from 1403 to 1436, and Monkton, Somerset, from 1436 until his death, with licence to be absent for study. In 1399 he was ordained priest and by 1410 was a doctor of theology. One trace remains of his disputations (Oxford, Corpus Christi College, MS 280, fol. 123v, a reply to him).

Elected a delegate of the university to the Council of Constance, Abingdon defended there the university's claim to precedence over Salamanca, and the priority of England over Spain. On 27 October 1417 he also preached a notable sermon (*Sitis repleti fructu justitie*), against exemptions and simony (published by Walch; manuscripts in Vienna, Österreichische Nationalbibliothek, MS 4958, fols. 419–27v, and Stuttgart, MS Theol. Q 366). In it he quoted a passage on exemptions from the reform programme drawn up by Oxford University for the council, and emphasized the need for bishops who were true pastors, and instructed the people in correct doctrine rather than greedily hunting for revenues; he was particularly critical of exemptions as upsetting the right order in the church and undermining the position of the bishop, and advocated a wholesale revocation of exemptions. In 1421 he was elected warden of Merton College, a post he retained until his death. Under him the north transept of the college chapel was completed and work on the tower progressed; he contributed £20 to a new peal of bells. He preached before convocation of Canterbury in July 1422 when the main business was discussion of the forthcoming Council of Pavia. In December 1432 Abingdon was chosen to attend the Council of Basel as a representative of the English clergy. He can be traced there until July 1435, when he was also appointed their proctor by the bishop of Bath and the chapter of Wells. By late 1437 he was dead. He owned a library and gave a book to Merton College (Oxford, Merton College, MS M.3.4.).

MARGARET HARVEY

Sources Emden, *Oxf.*, 1.7–8 · A. N. E. D. Schofield, 'The first English delegation to the Council of Basel', *Journal of Ecclesiastical History*, 12 (1961), 167–96 · A. N. E. D. Schofield, 'The second English delegation to the Council of Basel', *Journal of Ecclesiastical History*, 17 (1966), 29–64 · C. W. F. Walch, ed., *Monimenta medii aevi*, 1/2 (1757), 183–205 · F. M. Powicke, *The medieval books of Merton College* (1931), 76, 194 · H. Finke and J. Hollnsteiner, eds., *Acta Concilii Constanciensis*, 2 (1923), 423

Archives Österreichische Nationalbibliothek, Vienna, MS 4958, fols. 419–427v · CCC Oxf., MS 280, fol. 123v · Stuttgart, MS Theol. Q 366

Abingdon [Abyndon], **Richard** (*d.* in or before **1322**), administrator, was probably a native of Abingdon in Berkshire, and possibly a relation both of Stephen Abingdon, who became butler of the royal household under Edward II, and of the Stephen Abingdon who was a London alderman. He was a master of arts, probably of Oxford, and became a clerk in the exchequer. On 22 March 1284 he was appointed as chamberlain of north Wales, an office he held until January 1286. Later in 1284 he was sent to Dublin to collect the revenues of the vacant archbishopric, and on 23 March 1285 was presented by Edward I to a moiety of the prebend of Lusk in St Patrick's Cathedral, Dublin. In June he was ordered to send the revenue from duties on wool and wool-fells in Ireland to assist in fortifying new towns in north Wales. In October 1294 he was sent to take charge of the archbishopric of Dublin, vacant following the death of John of Sandford. He remained there until

November 1296, when he was ordered to restore the temporalities to the new archbishop, William of Hothum. In 1297 he was in Cumberland raising money for the defence of England against Scottish raids.

On 23 September 1299 Abingdon was appointed a baron of the exchequer in place of John Lisle. In the winter and following spring he was employed on the border, with powers to fine all who disobeyed the king's lieutenant, and to victual any castles that might be captured from the Scots. Early in 1302 he was given custody of the temporalities of the diocese of Ely, *sede vacante*, and in April that year was presented by Edward I to the rectory of Willingham, Cambridgeshire, in the same diocese. He was appointed as an attorney for the treasurer, Walter Langton, bishop of Coventry and Lichfield, in January 1303, when the latter went to Rome. In December 1304 Abingdon became a canon of Lichfield and prebendary of Wellington, Shropshire, and in October 1305 a canon of Salisbury and prebendary of the Minor Pars Altaris. He was cited to appear before the pope in January 1306 for unlawfully retaining another preferment, as a canon of Wells and prebendary of Yatton. In March 1309 he exchanged his earlier appointment in Salisbury for the prebend of Horton, and in April 1309 was given papal dispensation to retain this and his other canonries, prebends, and livings.

Abingdon was not reappointed as a baron of the exchequer at the very beginning of the reign of Edward II, probably because of his associations with the disgraced treasurer, Walter Langton, but on 20 January 1308 he was restored to office, with the same status he had previously held. He was also summoned to the coronation in February 1308. For the rest of his active career he was prominent both in the business of the exchequer and as a member of numerous royal commissions. In March 1308, for example, he was appointed to levy a tenth and fifteenth in the city of London and its suburbs, and in April 1310 he was ordered to assess and levy the twenty-fifth imposed upon London in aid of the Scottish war.

In June 1313 Abingdon was sent to Bristol, with other royal commissioners, to assess the tallage which the burgesses were refusing to pay. During the hearing at the Bristol Guildhall a riot broke out, many were killed, and for a time Abingdon was held prisoner. In 1316 he held the manor of Horton, Gloucestershire, and also held property in Wiltshire and Berkshire, probably at Abingdon. In that year Abingdon again levied a fifteenth in London, but soon afterwards became incapacitated, and on 18 June 1317 was replaced as baron of the exchequer. He was dead before March 1322, and in 1327 two secular chaplains were endowed to say daily mass for his soul in the abbey church at Abingdon.

J. R. S. PHILLIPS

Sources Emden, *Oxf.*, 1.4–5 · G. A. Williams, *Medieval London: from commune to capital* (1963) · H. J. Lawlor, *The fasti of St Patrick's, Dublin* (1930) · T. F. Tout, *The place of the reign of Edward II in English history: based upon the Ford lectures delivered in the University of Oxford in 1913*, rev. H. Johnstone, 2nd edn (1936) · J. C. Davies, *The baronial opposition to Edward II* (1918); repr. (1967) · A. Beardwood, ed., *Records of the trial of Walter Langeton, bishop of Coventry and Lichfield, 1307–1312*, CS, 4th ser., 6 (1969) · E. A. Fuller, 'The tallage of 6 Edward II and the

Bristol rebellion', *Transactions of the Bristol and Gloucestershire Archaeological Society*, 19 (1894–5), 172–278 • *Chancery records* • *CPR, 1327–30*
Wealth at death held at least eight canonries and other ecclesiastical livings; also other property

Abingdon, Robert of [Robert Rich] (*d.* 1243), ecclesiastic and supposed hagiographer, was the younger brother of Edmund of *Abingdon and his assistant in the administration of the diocese and province of Canterbury. He was the second son of Reginald the Rich and Mabel of Abingdon, but neither he nor his brother ever used the name Rich as a patronymic. Both were sent as boys (*c.*1190–95) to the schools of Paris to study the arts. Robert in due course incepted as a master, but it does not seem that he proceeded to a higher faculty. He was in England in 1214, and he evidently played an active part in the political troubles of 1216–17 which won him the approval of the papal legate, Cardinal Guala, and for this he was rewarded with a licence to hold an additional benefice in plurality. He was rector of Bocking in 1225, but had relinquished this living by November 1232, probably on being presented to the more important rectory of Wingham. Both these churches were in the archbishop's patronage. A letter from the Franciscan Adam Marsh shows that he was also holding the rectory of Risborough at the time of his death. He evidently died in 1243 before 27 September, when Wingham was declared vacant. Matthew Paris reports miracles at his tomb in the annal for 1244. During his brother's years as archbishop (1234–40), Robert held a position of eminence in the archiepiscopal household and was entrusted by his brother with important responsibilities. During Edmund's absence abroad in 1238 he was authorized to exercise the archbishop's ecclesiastical patronage and shared with the official the power to visit religious houses in the Canterbury diocese.

There is no contemporary evidence for the claim that Robert wrote a life of St Edmund. The assertion of Wilfrid Wallace, in *St Edmund of Canterbury* (1893), that Robert was the author of the conventional and derivative life that he printed from BL, Faustina MS B.i was a guess without any basis in textual criticism. The only evidence for a possible contribution by Robert to the hagiographical tradition is contained in a rubricated subtitle to the A text of the life by Eustace of Faversham, Edmund's chaplain and his earliest biographer. This subtitle, written in the same thirteenth-century hand as the rest of the text, runs as follows:

> Here begins the Life of the glorious confessor Edmund, archbishop of the church of Canterbury, set forth [*edita*] at Pontigny and dispatched [*transmissa*] to Master Robert of Abingdon, so that his labour may illuminate what is obscure, temper what is superfluous, fill in gaps and supplement what is lacking. (BL, Royal MS 2 D.vi, fol. 151)

In other words, Robert was invited to inspect, and from his personal knowledge to amend, the life compiled by Eustace. It is impossible to identify any material in this life that Robert might have supplied. It was not compiled until 1242–3, and possibly he was dead before it reached him.   C. H. LAWRENCE

Sources C. H. Lawrence, *St Edmund of Abingdon* (1960) • *CEPR letters*, vol. 1 • *Curia regis rolls preserved in the Public Record Office* (1922–), vol. 7 • *CPR, 1232–47* • Paris, *Chron.*, vol. 4 • *The historical works of Gervase of Canterbury*, ed. W. Stubbs, 2: *The minor works comprising the Gesta regum with its continuation, the Actus pontificum and the Mappa mundi*, Rolls Series, 73 (1880) • K. Major, ed., *Acta Stephani Langton*, CYS, 50 (1950) • A. M. Woodcock, ed., *Cartulary of the Priory of St Gregory, Canterbury*, CS, 3rd ser., 88 (1956) • Canterbury Cathedral, dean and chapter muniments, Register A • Life of St Edmund by Eustace of Faversham, BL, Royal MS 2 D.vi
Archives BL, Royal MS 2 D.vi, fol. 151 • Canterbury Cathedral, dean and chapter muniments, Register A

Abinger. For this title name *see* Scarlett, James, first Baron Abinger (1769–1844).

Abington, Edward (*c.*1553–1586). *See under* Babington, Anthony (1561–1586).

Abington [*née* Barton], **Frances** [Fanny] (1737–1815), actress, was born in lowly circumstances and grew up in the slums around Drury Lane. Her mother died when she was fourteen; her father, who according to some accounts was the son of Christopher Barton of Norton, Derbyshire, was discharged as a private soldier in the king's guards and opened a cobbler's stall in Vinegar Yard, near Drury Lane Theatre. Her brother was an ostler in Hanway Yard.

Fanny Barton sold flowers and sang in the streets of Covent Garden from an early age, and acquired the nickname 'Nosegay Fan'. The story was told that 'the gay girl used to get on the tables of Covent Garden taverns, and recite bits of Shakespeare; being rewarded with a trifling collection' (Matthews and Hutton, 1.191). She became the servant of a French milliner in Cockspur Street, from whom she acquired her taste in dress and a knowledge of French, and afterwards served as a kitchenmaid under the cook Robert Baddeley, who later became a famous comedian. Various accounts of her early life hint at prostitution in St James's Park and Leicester Fields; they also emphasize her determination to educate herself and to make a career on the stage. As well as the French she had learned from the milliner, she could converse in Italian.

In the summer of 1755 Theophilus Cibber, manager of the Haymarket Theatre, secured a company of young novices to present Susannah Centlivre's *The Busy Body* on 21 August. The playbills announced 'the character of Miranda by Miss Barton, being her first essay'. During this short season she went on to act a number of parts, including Desdemona and Sylvia in George Farquhar's *The Recruiting Officer*. She was then engaged by Edward Shuter for minor roles for one season at Bath and the summer theatre at Richmond, Yorkshire. On 29 October 1756 Fanny Barton appeared as Lady Pliant in Congreve's *The Double Dealer* as a member of the Drury Lane company, having been engaged at the recommendation of Samuel Foote. During this, her first full season, she performed a few secondary characters, but finished the season as Lucy in John Gay's *The Beggar's Opera*. Her career advanced slowly, because the principal parts went to Hannah Pritchard and Kitty Clive. On 21 June 1759, at the church of St Martin-in-the-Fields, she married James Abington (*d.* 1806), one of the king's trumpeters; he also played at

Frances Abington (1737–1815), by Sir Joshua Reynolds, 1771 [as Miss Prue in *Love for Love* by William Congreve]

Drury Lane, and was her own music master. She was thereafter billed as Mrs Abington. The Abingtons left Drury Lane after a disagreement with the management, and went to Ireland in November to join Brown's Dublin company.

Mrs Abington's first performance in Dublin, as Mrs Sullen in Farquhar's *The Beaux' Stratagem*, at Smock Alley on 11 December 1759, brought her immediate success. She was rapidly taken up by fashionable Dublin society, and her dress was widely imitated: the cap she wore in James Townley's *High Life below Stairs* became the prevailing fashion of the day, known as the 'Abington cap', one milliner adding, 'for those who need 'em' (Matthews and Hutton, 1.192). This was a sly reference to her affair with the Irish MP, Mr Needham, whose mistress she had become. Her marriage was an unhappy one, and the Abingtons soon separated; Frances paid her husband an annual allowance on condition that he leave her alone. Her professional success in Dublin, especially as Lady Townly in Colley Cibber's *The Provoked Husband* and Lucinda in Samuel Foote's *The Englishman in Paris*, was enormous. On 22 May 1760 she appeared at the Crow Street Theatre, and from then on alternated her services between the two theatres, bargaining for the best contract.

In 1765, after five years in Ireland, Mrs Abington returned to England with Mr Needham; he died at Bath that summer, leaving her generously provided for in his will. At David Garrick's invitation she rejoined the Drury Lane company, and appeared on 27 November as Widow Belmour in Arthur Murphy's comedy *The Way to Keep Him*, which Murphy later dedicated to her in a new edition. In

the following seventeen seasons Mrs Abington established herself as one of the leading comedy actresses of her generation, her notable parts including Lady Betty Modish in Cibber's *The Careless Husband*, Beatrice in *Much Ado about Nothing*, and Millamant in Congreve's *The Way of the World*. She played Miss Walsingham in Hugh Kelly's *The School for Wives* (1774), and the author enthused: 'With respect to Mrs Abington, enough can never be said … she is called the first priestess of the comic muse in this country' (Bell, 7.vi).

Celebrated as she had become, Mrs Abington was not an easy employee: she had 'that irritability of disposition and inclination to give trouble to her employers' (*Life of Mrs Abington*, 56). A lengthy and fractious correspondence between her and Garrick reveals frequent quarrels about his assigning roles in favour of Jane Pope and accusations that he was plotting her ruin. On 5 May 1775 they signed an agreement, granting her a weekly salary of £12 and an annual clothing allowance of £60, but Garrick retired the following year and Mrs Abington resumed her unsettled life. Garrick had complained of her in 1772 that 'I never yet saw Mrs Abington theatrically happy for a week together' (*Letters*, 2.830), and on 7 March 1776 he counselled her against following him into retirement. She seems to have lost conviction in the purposes of acting, which was perhaps restored with what became her most celebrated part, Lady Teazle in Sheridan's *The School for Scandal* (1777), written especially for her.

On 29 November 1782 Mrs Abington acted Lady Flutter in Frances Sheridan's *The Discovery* at Covent Garden, and she played various parts in the seasons of 1784–8. She returned there for the 1789–90 season, but retired suddenly on 12 February 1790, without a farewell benefit. Her admirer Horace Walpole wrote:

Scarce had our tears forgot to flow,
By Garrick's loss inspired,
When Fame, to mortalize the blow,
Said Abington's retired.
(Matthews and Hutton, 1.190)

Apart from a few performances in Ireland in July 1793, Mrs Abington did not appear again until 14 June 1797 at a benefit performance at Covent Garden. She returned to act Beatrice in *Much Ado about Nothing* on 6 October 1797, on which occasion she was described in *The Monthly Visitor* as 'too big and heavy to give any effect to the more gay and sprightly scenes' (Highfill, Burnim & Langhans, *BDA*). Her last appearance was on 12 April 1799, as Lady Racket in Arthur Murphy's farce *Three Weeks after Marriage*.

Mrs Abington's reputation as an excellent actress was based on her performances in comedies of manners. The public disliked her as the comic servant Scrub in Farquhar's *The Beaux' Stratagem* (1786), as they did not wish to see her degraded. She recognized her own limitations, and wrote to Garrick of 'such light and easy characters of comedy as my talents confine me to' (*Life*, 73). She became a dictator of tasteful fashion, making the figure taller by wearing the ziggurat headdress, or wearing red powder in her hair. She was regularly consulted by ladies on the newest styles of dress, and was admired by people of rank and status such as Dr Johnson, the duke of Dorset, General Paoli, Oliver Goldsmith, and Walpole. Sir Joshua Reynolds was also an admirer; he purchased twelve tickets for her benefit in 1772 and he painted several portraits of her—as Miss Prue in *Love for Love*, Roxalana in Isaac Bickerstaff's *The Sultan*, and, most importantly, as *The Comic Muse*, the companion piece to his portrait of Sarah Siddons as *The Tragic Muse*.

Mrs Abington is presumed to have retired on a comfortable income, having been the mistress of William Petty, first marquess of Lansdowne (1737–1805) (they appeared together in the *Town and Country Magazine tête-à-tête* portraits in 1777); she is said to have lost a great deal of money at cards, and John Taylor, in his *Records of my Life*, claims to have seen her 'attired in a common red cloak, and with the air and demeanour of the wife of an inferior tradesman' (*DNB*). Frances Abington died at her Pall Mall home on 4 March 1815, and was buried in St James's, Piccadilly. According to one obituarist she was 'liberal and generous', which left her far from affluent, but her will reveals that she was by no means destitute, and among her legacies were donations to the theatrical funds of Drury Lane and Covent Garden. The same writer says: 'for a long series of years she was the unrivalled female ornament of the British stage in Comedy, and in the general range of sprightly characters, particularly in the higher walks of fashionable life' (*GM*, 284).   ALISON ODDEY

Sources Highfill, Burnim & Langhans, *BDA* · *The life of Mrs Abington—formerly Miss Barton—celebrated comic actress* (1888) · J. B. Matthews and L. Hutton, eds., *Actors and actresses of Great Britain and the United States from the days of David Garrick to the present time*, 5 vols. (1886) · T. Wilkinson, *The wandering patentee, or, A history of the Yorkshire theatres from 1770 to the present time*, 4 vols. (1795) · C. B. Hogan, ed., *An index to 'The wandering patentee' by Tate Wilkinson* (1973) · S. Richards, *The rise of the English actress* (1993) · P. Fitzgerald, *Samuel Foote: a biography* (1910) · J. Hampden, *An eighteenth-century journal, being a record of the years 1774–1776* (1940) · A. S. Turberville, ed., *Johnson's England*, 2 vols. (1933) · J. Bell, ed., *Bell's British theatre*, 7 (1797) · B. Joseph, *The tragic actor* (1959) · W. Macqueen-Pope, *Ladies first* (1952) · *The letters of David Garrick*, ed. D. M. Little and G. M. Kahrl, 3 vols. (1963) · S. West, *The image of the actor* (1991) · *IGI* · *GM*, 1st ser., 85/1 (1815), 284 · *DNB*

Likenesses J. Reynolds, oils, 1764–5, Waddesdon Manor, Buckinghamshire · J. Zoffany, oils, 1768, Petworth House, West Sussex · J. Watson, mezzotint, pubd 1769 (after J. Reynolds), BM, NPG · J. Reynolds, oils, white domino, 1771, Yale U. CBA, Paul Mellon collection [*see illus.*] · T. Hickey, oils, 1775, Garr. Club · F. Bartolozzi, stipple, pubd 1783 (after R. Cosway), BM, NPG · J. Sayers, caricature, etching, pubd 1786, NPG · J. Sayers, etching, pubd 15 Feb 1786 (after his portrait), BM, NPG · J. Thornthwaite, line engraving, pubd 1792 (after I. Taylor), BM, NPG · S. W. Reynolds, mezzotint, pubd 1835 (after J. Reynolds), BM, NPG · E. Judkins, mezzotint, pubd 1876 (after J. Reynolds), BM, NPG · R. B. Parkes, mezzotint, pubd 1876 (after J. Reynolds), BM, NPG · R. Cosway, portrait (as Thalia) · J. Reynolds, white domino (as Roxalana in *The sultan*) · J. Roberts, drawings, BM · J. Roberts, watercolour on vellum, repro. in J. Bell, *Bell's edition of Shakespeare's plays*, 9 vols. (1773–4) [facs. edn (1969)] · R. West, chalk drawing, Garr. Club · Delftware wall tile, Man. City Gall. · mezzotint (after Reynolds), NPG · portrait, repro. in *The life of Mrs Abington*, inside cover · portrait, repro. in Macqueen-Pope, *Ladies first*, 144 · portraits, repro. in Highfill, Burnim & Langhans, *BDA* · prints, BM, NPG

Wealth at death will left with various bequests: Highfill, Burnim & Langhans, *BDA*

Ablett, Noah (1883–1935), miners' leader and adult educator, was born on 4 October 1883 in Ynys-hir, near Porth, Rhondda, Glamorgan, the tenth of eleven children of John Ablett, miner, and his wife, Jane, *née* Williams. Educated at Ferndale higher grade school, he was a boy preacher. He followed his father and elder brothers and started work in the Standard colliery, Ynys-hir, when he was twelve, studying meanwhile for the excise branch of the civil service. When a pit accident interrupted his studies, however, he was told he would be unable to enter the civil service, and subsequently continued working in the mines.

A member of the Independent Labour Party (ILP), Ablett was self-educated, reading Karl Marx and other socialist writers. In 1907 he attended Ruskin College, Oxford, on a correspondence course scholarship, and later on a scholarship from the Rhondda no. 1 district of the South Wales Miners' Federation (SWMF). He quickly made his mark on educational thinking at Ruskin, and organized classes in Marxian economics and history as an alternative to the traditional liberal curriculum. Representing the college's Marxian Society he expressed his suspicions of the university's desire to help the education of working people, believing instead in independent working-class education (IWCE). He became influenced by the thinking of Daniel De Leon, the theorist of the Socialist Labor Party of the USA: De Leon believed that workers should form industrial unions to overthrow capitalism, which would in turn provide forms of industrial democracy within a socialist society. Strike action, especially the general strike, held a central place in industrial unionist philosophy.

Shortly after returning to south Wales in 1909, Ablett was elected checkweighman at Maerdy colliery. He established Marxist educational classes and promoted industrial unionism with the intention of linking working-class education and class struggle in south Wales. Although he initially founded a branch of the British Advocates of Industrial Unionism, with whom he had contact in Oxford, he quickly focused on bringing change to and through the SWMF. His views were well suited to the structures of the south Wales coalfield, its union, and its society, and were spread across the coalfield by networks of activists, many associated with the Plebs' League. The Cambrian combine dispute of 1910–11 highlighted Ablett's revolutionary politics for many others in the coalfield. He joined the SWMF executive committee in January 1911, at the same time as three other new members from the Rhondda, and they made a considerable impact as a new generation of leaders committed to greater militancy. He was hostile to the way that the majority in the executive committee were conciliatory to the coal owners over the Cambrian dispute.

As a consequence of the strike, Ablett helped form the Unofficial Reform Committee and was a joint author in 1912 of the pamphlet entitled *The Miners' Next Step* which had much influence on advanced thinking both within and outside the SWMF, but was met with particular hostility in the press. It demanded rank-and-file control of a centralized and industrial union, called for antagonistic relations with employers, and rejected nationalization of the mines in favour of encroaching workers' control. Its contents determined the agenda of the left in south Wales for the next decade and more. This hardline socialist stance caused Ablett to break with the more moderate ILP in 1910.

Ablett's intellect and personality made him a leading proponent of IWCE nationally, opposed to links with universities which he saw as capitalist institutions. He contributed an influential article on IWCE to the first issue of *Plebs* in February 1909. In March 1909 differences over the direction of the college resulted in a students' strike in support of the principal, Dennis Hird, who had been forced to resign. As chairman of the south Wales branch of the Plebs' League, established in January 1909, Ablett was influential (along with another ex-student, Ted Gill) in promoting the idea within the SWMF of an alternative to Ruskin. He saw the need for a residential college as a cadre training school for the labour movement. The Central Labour College (CLC) was established later that year, following the principles of IWCE and on a Marxian basis. Ablett was a member of its provisional committee representing the Plebs' League from 1909 to 1911, and the college's early survival was probably due in large part to his dedication. He served on the board of management representing the Rhondda no. 1 district from 1911 to 1915, subsequently representing the SWMF, which with the National Union of Railwaymen took over responsibility for the college. He was chair of the board of governors and was its strongest advocate. His book *An Easy Outline of Economics*, published by the Plebs' League, became a basic text for understanding Marxist economics, and was very popular in the labour movement.

Ablett was the only member of the SWMF executive committee prepared to take strike action to try to stop the impending First World War, as a part of an international movement, and he gained some notoriety for his role in the south Wales miners' strike of 1915. He supported the Russian Revolution in 1917 and attended the Leeds convention representing the south Wales miners.

In 1912 Ablett married Annie Howells; they had a son and a daughter. Elected as miners' agent for Merthyr in 1918, Ablett gave up his post of checkweighman at Maerdy colliery. From 1921 to 1926 he was a member of the executive committee of the Miners' Federation of Great Britain (MFGB). He twice sought the SWMF nomination for the post of general secretary of the MFGB: he was beaten in 1918 by Frank Hodges, while in 1924 his transferred votes were decisive in ensuring victory for A. J. Cook over W. H. Mainwaring.

When the south Wales coalfield's fortunes changed in the 1920s, the Merthyr district suffered earlier, deeper, and longer than most others. The lock-outs of 1921 and 1926 exacerbated the problems, and the district went into steep economic decline. Ablett's role as visionary for the

south Wales coalfield diminished, and a new generation of leaders came to the fore. In November 1926, towards the end of the miners' lock-out, he arranged a local settlement for Hill's Plymouth collieries, to prevent these pits from being shut permanently. In the ensuing row he assumed responsibility for the agreement even though he had the secret approval of Tom Richards, the general secretary of the SWMF. He was suspended from the executive committee of the SWMF and lost his seat on that of the MFGB. He was also removed as chairman of the governors of the CLC, which had suffered a series of recent scandals. He considered that he had sacrificed his career for the people of Merthyr, although excessive drinking over a long period had already become a major contributory factor in his decline.

High unemployment undermined the SWMF in Merthyr, as did the opening of Taff Merthyr colliery, a stronghold of the rival South Wales Miners' Industrial Union. During the last years of his life Ablett tried to shore up the SWMF, which he had worked so hard to shape. He was the most outstanding organic intellectual to emerge from the south Wales coalfield, and his thinking shaped a generation of miner activists. He remained militant throughout his life. He died of cancer on 31 October 1935 at his home, Rock Villa, Dyke Street, Merthyr Tudful, just a few weeks after the successful 'stay down' strikes which marked the saving of the SWMF. He was survived by his wife.

HYWEL FRANCIS

Sources J. Atkins, *Neither crumbs nor condescension: the Central Labour College, 1909–1915* (1981) · J. Bellamy and J. Saville, 'Ablett, Noah', *DLB*, vol. 3 · W. W. Craik, *The Central Labour College, 1909–1929: a chapter in the history of working-class education* (1964) · P. Davies, *A. J. Cook* (1987) · D. Egan, 'The unofficial reform committee and the miners' next step', *Llafur*, 2/3 (1978), 64–80 · D. Egan, 'Noah Ablett, 1883–1935', *Llafur*, 4/3 (1985), 19–30 · H. Francis and D. Smith, *The Fed: a history of the south Wales miners in the twentieth century* (1980) · R. Lewis, 'The South Wales miners and the Ruskin strike of 1909', *Llafur*, 2/1 (1976) · R. Lewis, *Leaders and teachers* (1993) · R. P. Arnot, *South Wales miners / Glowyr de Cymru: a history of the South Wales Miners' Federation*, [1–2] (1967–75) · *CGPLA Eng. & Wales* (1935) · m. cert.
Archives NL Wales, Mainwaring MSS
Wealth at death £230 19s. 3d.: administration, 12 Dec 1935, *CGPLA Eng. & Wales*

Abney, Sir Thomas (1639/40–1722), merchant and mayor of London, was born at Willesley, Derbyshire, the youngest of four sons of James Abney, landowner, and Jane Mainwaring (*d.* after 1640). The Abney family had owned land at Willesley for several centuries, and James Abney served as high sheriff of Derbyshire in 1656. After the early death of his mother Thomas Abney was sent to Loughborough, Leicestershire, to live with his mother's sister, the widow of Sir Edward Bromley, a baron of the exchequer under James I and Charles I. He was educated at a school in Loughborough before being sent to London to pursue a career in trade. His elder brother Sir Edward Abney (1631–1728) became a noted civil lawyer and served as MP for the borough of Leicester from 1690 to 1698.

By 1668 Thomas Abney was a freeman of the London Fishmongers' Company and a resident of the parish of All

Hallows, London Wall. On 24 August of that year he married Sarah (d. 1698), daughter of Joseph *Caryl, an Independent divine. His marriage reflected the puritan values he had absorbed in his upbringing, and he became a member of the presbyterian meeting ministered to by the Revd Thomas Jacombe. A linen draper by trade, Abney eventually relocated to St Peter Cornhill, where he was a neighbour of draper Samuel *Shute, his relation by marriage and a whig sheriff of London and Middlesex in 1681–2. Although he signed one of the exclusion-era London petitions calling for parliament to sit, Abney remained relatively uninvolved in political affairs until after 1688.

Abney contributed to a civic loan to the prince of Orange during the revolution that year and became a regular contributor to London loans to William III thereafter. He was elected to the London common council in 1690 and 1692 before being chosen alderman for Vintry ward in December 1692. In June 1693 Abney and Sir William Hedges (a moderate tory) were elected sheriffs of London and Middlesex in preference to Sir William Gore, a staunch churchman, recommended to the electors by Lord Mayor Sir John Fleet. Abney was knighted by William in November 1693 upon the king's return from the continental campaign of that year; and he joined the London lieutenancy commission in February 1694, when it was enlarged to favour the City whigs. When the subscription for the Bank of England was launched later that year Abney purchased shares worth £4000 and was chosen one of the bank's directors, a position to which he was annually re-elected until his death almost thirty years later. At some point he and his partner Henry Kelsey also became involved in the re-export of Indian cloth.

In September 1700 Abney was promoted by the whigs, together with Sir William Hedges, for the mayoralty of London. Abney was the whig choice, but they coupled his candidacy with that of the moderate Hedges in hopes of blocking the election of Sir Charles Duncombe, a popular tory alderman. The whig sheriffs declared the Common Hall majority to have fallen on Abney and Hedges. Despite Duncombe's commanding lead in a subsequent poll, the whig-dominated court of aldermen elected Abney over the objections of their tory colleagues. Such disagreements seem not to have spoiled either the civic show on the day of Abney's installation or the accompanying banquet, which was attended by leading whig courtiers, noblemen, and parliamentary politicians. But Abney's whig friends were disappointed in May 1701 when, coming under court pressure, he joined civic tories in stopping a corporation petition intended to embarrass William's tory ministry. Later in the year, however, when Louis XIV recognized James Stuart, the Pretender, on the death of James II, Abney was instrumental in securing a corporation address to William that condemned this 'great indignity and affront' (common council journal, 53, fol. 123). When William dissolved parliament at this juncture and turned to the whigs for leadership of his government Abney and three other whig Bank of England directors were successfully promoted for the City's seats in the House of Commons. Abney's Westminster service was,

however, cut short by William's death, he and two of his fellow whig City MPs being defeated by three tories put up for Queen Anne's first parliament in 1702.

By the time of his mayoralty and parliamentary service Abney was also among the most visible of London's nonconformist leaders. He had been chosen a manager of the Common Fund for the support of Independent and Presbyterian clergy in 1691, and, upon the collapse of that venture, he became a manager in 1694 of the similar Presbyterian Fund. By 1698 he was serving as a member of the New England Company, which sponsored nonconformist missionaries to Native Americans. Abney's occasional conformity for the sake of office-holding was attacked during his mayoralty by Anglicans and by the dissenting Daniel Defoe in his Enquiry into the Occasional Conformity of Dissenters (1701). John Howe, who was Abney's pastor at the time, replied with a defence of the practice but Abney was much less active in the City thereafter. He continued to serve as alderman, moving to Bridge Without as senior alderman in 1716, and to serve on the London lieutenancy commission. He was prime warden of the Fishmongers' Company in 1704–6, and he was president of St Thomas's Hospital from 1707 until his death.

Abney's first wife followed six of their seven children to the grave in 1698, and was buried on 18 March, and his surviving son, Edward, died in 1704. On 21 August 1700 Abney married Mary (d. 1750), daughter of Presbyterian merchant John Gunston. They had three daughters. Upon the death of her brother, Mary became the heir to the Gunstons' Stoke Newington mansion, which eventually became Abney House. Abney and his wife spent the last twenty years of his life there and at a summer home in Theobalds, Hertfordshire. After 1712 they were joined by Dr Isaac Watts, who became their chaplain and tutor to their daughters in a household noted for its piety. Abney apparently contemplated resignation from his London offices in response to the Occasional Conformity Act of 1711 but, at the urging of the Hanoverian ambassador, he ceased his attendance at public nonconformist meetings instead. He died at Theobalds on 6 February 1722 in the eighty-third year of his age and was buried on 16 February at St Peter Cornhill, London, with his first family. Isaac Watts remained with Abney's second family until his death in 1748. Abney's widow, who died on 25 January 1750, succeeded him as a notable nonconformist benefactor, and his nephew Thomas *Abney (1690/91–1750), the youngest son of his brother Edward, took his place as a nonconformist leader.   GARY S. DE KREY

Sources N. Luttrell, *A brief historical relation of state affairs from September 1678 to April 1714*, 6 vols. (1857), vol. 2, pp. 630, 634; vol. 3, pp. 117, 123, 131, 218; vol. 4, pp. 566, 689, 692, 694–5; vol. 5, pp. 110–14, 193, 198; vol. 6, p. 202 · A. P. Davis, *Isaac Watts: his life and works* (1943), 31–9, 67–8 · G. S. De Krey, 'Trade, religion, and politics in London in the reign of William III', PhD diss., Princeton University, 1978, 314, 393–4, 402–3, 409, 430n., 528, 623 · G. S. De Krey, *A fractured society: the politics of London in the first age of party, 1688–1715* (1985), 92, 200, 201 · A. Gordon, ed., *Freedom after ejection: a review (1690–1692) of presbyterian and congregational nonconformity in England and Wales* (1917), 198 · E. Calamy, *An historical account of my own life, with some reflections on the times I have lived in, 1671–1731*, ed. J. T. Rutt, 1

(1829), 435–6; 2 (1829), 245–6 · N. H. Keeble, *The literary culture of non-conformity in later seventeenth-century England* (1987), 37 · journals, CLRO, court of common council, vol. 51, fols. 144–5, 150, 168; vol. 53, fol. 123 · CLRO, MSS 40/34–36 · CLRO, Alchin 33/15 · *London Post*, 207 (30 Sept–2 Oct 1700); 219 (28–30 Oct 1700) · M. Henry, letter to P. Henry, 27 June 1693, Bodl. Oxf., MS Eng. lett. e. 29., f. 154 · Newdigate newsletter, 24 June 1693, Folger, L.c. 2190 · *English Post* (28–30 Oct 1700) · *CSP dom.*, 1694–5, p. 21; 1697, pp. 69, 543 · W. A. Shaw, ed., *Calendar of treasury books*, 8, PRO (1923), 1972–9; 10 (1935), 1152–3, 1158; 16 (1938), 271, 308; 23 (1949), 1709, 77 · G. W. G. Leveson Gower, ed., *A register of … the parish of St Peeters upon Cornhill*, 2, Harleian Society, register section, 4 (1879) · *DNB* · repertories of the court of aldermen, CLRO, 105.551, 555 · GL, MS 4069/2, fols. 384–5, 394 [Cornhill inquest minutes] · Presbyterian Fund board minutes, DWL [vol. 1 (1694–1722)] · will, PRO, PROB 11/584, sig. 46 · [D. Defoe], *An enquiry into the occasional conformity of dissenters*, [another edn] (1701) · J. Howe, *Some considerations of a preface to an enquiry* (1701) · J. Smith, *The magistrate and the Christian* (1722) · W. M. Acres, 'Directors of the Bank of England', *N&Q*, 179 (1940), 39 · N. C. Hunt, *Two early political associations* (1961), 117n., 168, 203–4 · W. D. Jeremy, *The Presbyterian Fund and Dr Daniel Williams's Trust* (1885), 122 · W. Kellaway, *The New England Company, 1649–1776* (1961), 220, 289

Likenesses oils (as young man), Bank of England, London · oils, Bank of England, London

Wealth at death £10,000 in visible wealth: will, PRO, PROB 11/584, sig. 46

Abney, Sir Thomas (1690/91–1750), judge, was baptized on 3 April 1691 at Willesley, Derbyshire, the second son of Sir Edward Abney of Willesley and his second wife, Judith, daughter and coheir of Peter Barr, a London merchant. His father was member of parliament for Leicester in 1690 and 1695, and his uncle Sir Thomas *Abney (1639/40–1722) was sometime lord mayor of London. At the age of sixteen, in November 1707, he was admitted both to Wadham College, Oxford, and to the Inner Temple, and in 1713 he was called to the bar. He seems to have settled in the London region, and in 1731 was elected chairman of the Middlesex sessions at Hick's Hall. He came to prominence in 1733 when he was appointed attorney-general of the duchy of Lancaster and king's counsel, and was thereupon elected a bencher of his inn. Two years later he became judge of the palace court of Marshalsea, and was knighted. In 1738 he lobbied Lord Hardwicke, the lord chancellor, unsuccessfully for the chief justiceship of Chester, claiming to have been 'longer in the king's service than any gentleman in Westminster Hall' (BL, Add. MS 35586, fol. 95) except for Robert Pauncefort, and offering to resign the Marshalsea; but the position went to Matthew Skinner. The next year he sought a place in the court of exchequer on the death of Mr Baron Thompson, but had to give way to Martin Wright and await two more vacancies. In 1740 he was made a baron of the exchequer in succession to Wright, and in 1743 he was translated to the common pleas, where he remained as a puisne judge until his death from 'gaol fever' on 19 May 1750. The work of an assize judge was made hazardous by the unhealthy state both of the gaols and of crowded courtrooms, and in 1741 Abney had consulted Hardwicke as to whether he might be excused from visiting Exeter, which was rumoured to be contagious, and again in 1746 he wrote of

'very great apprehensions on account of the gaol distemper among the rebel prisoners' (BL, Add. MS 35588, fol. 205) in the north. Hardwicke recommended some precautions and Abney survived, only to fall prey to a fatal outbreak of disease at the Old Bailey, which also claimed Mr Baron Clarke, the lord mayor, and several others. Even after these 'black sessions' Hardwicke was sceptical about the cause of the fatalities, and refused to accept that conditions in the gaols were to blame.

Sir Michael Foster wrote of Abney in 1792 that:

> he was through an openness of temper, or a pride of virtue habitual to him, incapable of recommending himself to that kind of low assiduous craft, by which we have known some unworthy men make their way to the favour of the great … In his judicial capacity he constantly paid a religious regard to the merits of the question … and his judgment very seldom misled him. In short when he died, the world lost a very valuable man, his majesty an excellent subject, the public a faithful able servant. (Foster, 75)

Abney's reports of cases in the central courts have never been published, but were sometimes cited in court and remain in manuscript for the years 1737 to 1744; they contain some lively obituary comments on his brethren. He was clearly a man of great learning, and there is evidence that this extended beyond the legal field. Recent scholarship has indicated that in the 1720s Abney made substantial additions to the text of William Woolley's manuscript history of Derbyshire. 'The bias of the additional material towards the hundred of Repton & Gresley, in which Willesley lay, as well as the legalistic tone of much of the new material, is also strong circumstantial evidence that it is the work of Abney' (Derbyshire RS, 6.xlvi).

Abney married Frances (d. 1761), daughter of Joshua Burton of Brackley, Northamptonshire, and they had a son. The family seat, Willesley Hall, which had become Sir Thomas's country residence, descended to the son's only daughter, who married General Sir Charles Hastings, bt; and their descendants, assuming the surname Abney-Hastings, remained there until recent times.

J. H. BAKER

Sources Baker, *Serjeants* · Inner Temple, London · Sainty, *King's counsel* · Sainty, *Judges* · Foster, *Alum. Oxon.* · W. Musgrave, *Obituary prior to 1800*, ed. G. J. Armytage, 1, Harleian Society, 44 (1899) · R. Somerville, *Office-holders in the duchy and county palatine of Lancaster from 1603* (1972) · U. Lond., MS IHR 976 · G. Harris, *The life of Lord Chancellor Hardwicke*, 3 vols. (1847) · M. Foster, *A report of some proceedings on the commission for the trial of the rebels in the year 1746* (1792) · Foss, *Judges* · *Reports of adjudicated cases in the court of common pleas during the time Lord Chief Justice Willes presided in the court* (1799) [1737–58] · IGI · DNB · *Derbyshire Record Society*, 6 (1981)

Archives Bodl. Oxf., notes on parliamentary proceedings · Inner Temple, London, papers | BL, letters to Lord Hardwicke, Add. MSS 35586–35588, *passim*

Likenesses E. Seman, oils, Harvard U., law school

Abney, Sir William de Wiveleslie (1843–1920), civil servant and photographic scientist, was born at Derby on 24 July 1843, the eldest son of Edward Henry Abney (*bap.* 1811, *d.* 1892), vicar of St Alkmund's, Derby, afterwards prebendary of Lichfield, and Catharina, daughter of Jedediah Strutt of Greenhall, Belper. Through his mother, he was the great-great-grandson of Jedediah Strutt (1726–1797), the inventor and partner of Richard Arkwright. He married Agnes Mathilda, daughter of Edward William Smith of Tickton Hall, near Beverley in the East Riding of Yorkshire, on 4 August 1864. They had one son and two daughters. After Agnes's death in 1888, he married Mary Louisa, daughter of the Revd Eward Nathaniel Mead, of East Barnet, Hertfordshire, on 3 December 1889. They had a daughter.

Abney was educated at Rossall School in Lancashire and the Royal Military Academy at Woolwich. In 1861 he was commissioned as a lieutenant in the Royal Engineers, and he served in the sappers and miners at Bombay before being transferred to the public works department in 1865. Two years later he returned to England and was stationed at Chatham, where he developed the Abney level, a surveying instrument for use during military reconnaissance, which was cheaper and more versatile than its predecessors. In 1871 Abney was appointed assistant to the instructor in telegraphy at the School of Military Engineering, and shortly afterwards he was given a small chemical laboratory and photographic darkroom in the electrical school. He published *Instruction in Photography for Use at the School of Military Engineering, Chatham* in the same year and also became an active member of the Royal Photographic Society of London (later the Royal Photographic Society). *Instruction in Photography* was very popular and the eleventh edition was published in 1905. He was promoted to captain in 1873, and was always called Captain Abney until 1900, when he was knighted. His work demonstrated the importance of photography to the armed forces for surveying and reconnaissance and it was removed from the supervision of the instructor in electricity to form part of a new school of chemistry and photography in 1874. Abney became an assistant instructor in this new department, and in the same year was also listed as an assistant instructor in surveying. He was chosen to organize the photographic observation in Egypt of the transit of Venus in 1874. Afterwards, as a result of his Egyptian trip, he wrote *Thebes and its Five Great Temples* (1876).

Although Abney did not formally retire from the army until 1881, he left Chatham in 1877 to become an inspector of science schools of the Department of Science and Art at South Kensington. He was highly regarded by his new employers and he was promoted assistant director for science in 1884 and director for science in 1893. When the Department of Science and Art was replaced by the Board of Education in 1899 he was made a principal assistant secretary. Abney retired in 1903, following the changes brought about by Balfour's Education Act. He then became an adviser to the science department of the Board of Education and a member of the advisory council for education to the War Office. He was also appointed lecturer on colour vision at the Imperial College of Science and Technology in South Kensington in 1909.

The middle of the nineteenth century saw several high-powered commissions set up to investigate the state of science education in England. The Taunton Commission of 1868 had allowed government to make grants for building school laboratories, and the Devonshire Commission of 1872 strongly supported secondary science education. Abney himself gave evidence to the Samuelson Commission of 1881–4. One of Abney's major tasks was to approve grants for setting up and fitting out school laboratories. At Chatham he had become convinced of the importance of practical work in scientific education and at the Department of Science and Art he considered the establishment of new school laboratories as his particular mission. At first he sought to lay down a standard plan for these laboratories, based on his experience at Chatham, but eventually practically any plan was accepted if it met the 'absolute necessities of instruction'. His approach was later criticized for creating an excessive uniformity, but the numbers speak for themselves. When Abney joined the department only a handful of school laboratories existed, but in 1903, when he retired, 1165 laboratories were recognized by the Board of Education.

Abney also pursued photographic research in a darkroom, which was entered from the galleries of the South Kensington Museum (on the site of the Victoria and Albert Museum), but may have actually been in the neighbouring Royal College of Science (later Imperial College). It was described in 1883 as a cold and draughty backstairs lumber room. His studies were thorough and precise rather than inspired, and he must have found it difficult to balance his scientific work with his administrative duties. As early as 1873, at Chatham, he had developed the papyrotype photolithographic process which used paper coated with bichromated gelatin to create the initial image, and in his early years at South Kensington he concentrated on improving photographic emulsions, the development of prints, and photographic printing paper—then in its infancy. He introduced hydroquinone as a developer in 1880 and the gelatino-citrochloride emulsion printing process in 1881, which became the basis of POP (Printing Out Paper), which was very popular with amateur photographers at the end of the nineteenth century. In this period Abney published *Emulsion Processes in Photography* (1878), later retitled *Photography with Emulsions*, the third edition appearing in 1885, and the popular *Treatise on Photography* (1878) which reached its tenth edition in 1905.

As a result of this work Abney developed a photographic emulsion that was sensitive in the infrared region of the electromagnetic spectrum. William Herschel had discovered that the sun radiated energy beyond the red end of the visible spectrum in 1800, but no permanent visible record of the infrared spectrum of the sun was possible until Abney used his new emulsion for this purpose. More importantly, with his colleague Major-General Edward Robert Festing FRS he studied the infrared absorption spectra of numerous organic and inorganic chemical compounds. They established in 1881 that the absorption bands were associated with groups of atoms in the molecules rather than the molecule as a whole, and tentatively correlated different bands to specific groupings, for instance the nitro group in nitrobenzene. In the hands of later physicists and chemists, infrared spectroscopy became an important method of identifying such groups.

Abney was also interested in the development of colour photography, and saw the need to clarify the whole field of colour analysis and colour vision beforehand. He developed a colour photometer in 1885, and carried out a wide range of colour measurements with Festing. He also investigated the sensitivity of the eye to light and colour. On the basis of his research he introduced his own system of colour photography in 1905. It employed three separate lenses and colour separation positives, but was not a commercial success. Abney published *Trichromatic Theory of Colour* (1914) on the basis of his research, and he tested the colour vision of a merchant seaman as his last official act in the summer of 1920 in his colour vision laboratory at Imperial College. Appropriately for someone engaged in the administration of science education, Abney was an enthusiastic lecturer and gave several series of popular lectures on 'the chemical action of light' and on the subject of light and colour.

Abney was elected a fellow of the Royal Society in 1876 at the relatively early age of thirty-three, and was awarded the society's Rumford medal for his work on spectrum analysis in 1882. For his work at the Department of Science and Art, he was made CB in 1888 and KCB in 1900. Abney was prominent in the London-based scientific societies—serving as president of the Royal Photographic Society in 1892–4, 1896, 1903, and 1905; president of the Royal Astronomical Society in 1893–5; and president of the Physical Society in 1895–7. He was also chairman of the Royal Society of Arts in 1903–5, and was elected a vice-president of the Royal Institution in 1905 and a member of the council of the Chemical Society in 1882–4. A keen traveller, he often visited the Swiss and Italian Alps and published *The Pioneers of the Alps* (1887) with Carus Dunlop Cunningham. He listed painting, golf, and shooting as his interests in *Who's Who*. Abney also helped to establish a national collection of photographic history at the Science Museum in South Kensington, now transferred to the National Museum of Photography, Film, and Television at Bradford.

Abney lived for many years at Rathbone Lodge, South Bolton Gardens, not far from his office in South Kensington, and at a country residence at Measham Hall in Leicestershire. He went to Folkestone in autumn 1920 because of his failing health, and died there, at 12 Grimstone Avenue, of kidney failure and bronchitis on 2 December 1920.

PETER J. T. MORRIS

Sources C. Jones, 'Sir William de Wiveslie Abney', *Photographic Journal*, new ser., 45 (1921), 296–310 [incl. selective bibliography] · E. H. G-H., *PRS*, 99A (1921), i–v · B. Ferguson, *Photographic Journal*, new ser., 45 (1921), 44–6 · C. J. [C. Jones], *JCS*, 119 (1921), 529–32 · E. H. G.-H., 'Sir W. de W. Abney', *Royal Engineers Journal*, new ser., 33 (1921), 92–5 · J. M. Eder, *History of photography*, trans. E. Epstean (1945) · H. Baden Pritchard, *The photographic studios of Europe* (1883), 55–9 · Y. M. Rabkin, 'The adoption of infrared spectroscopy by chemists', *Isis*, 78 (1987), 31–54 · W. Abney, 'Presidential address', *Report of the British Association for the Advancement of Science* (1903), 865–75 · D. B. Thomas, *The Science Museum photography collections* (1969) · E. W. Jenkins, *From Armstrong to Nuffield: studies in twentieth century science education in England and Wales* (1979), chap. 7 · b. cert. · m. cert. [Agnes Smith] · m. cert. [Mary Louisa Mead] · d. cert.

Archives Sci. Mus., photography, optics, and surveying collections, artefacts | CUL, letters to Sir George Stokes · RA, letters to Royal Astronomical Society
Likenesses E. Lanteri, bronze bust, c.1903, RS · J. Russell & Sons, photograph, NPG · photograph, repro. in *Photographic Journal* (1921), frontispiece · photograph, RS
Wealth at death £27,534 19s. 6d.: probate, 24 Jan 1921, CGPLA Eng. & Wales

Aboyne. For this title name *see* Gordon, James, second Viscount Aboyne (d. 1649); Gordon, Charles, first earl of Aboyne (d. 1681).

Abraham, Ashley Perry (1876–1951). *See under* Abraham, George Dixon (1871–1965).

Abraham, Charles John (1814–1903), bishop of Wellington, New Zealand, born on 17 June 1814 at the Royal Military College, Sandhurst, was the second son of Captain Thomas Abraham of the 16th regiment, who was on the staff there, and Louisa Susannah, daughter of Edward Carter of Portsmouth. After attending Dr Thomas Arnold's school at Laleham, he went in 1826 to Eton College as an oppidan, but to save expenses he soon went into college, then half empty. He reached the sixth form, and played in the school cricket eleven. In 1833 Abraham went as a scholar to King's College, Cambridge, which then gave its own degrees without university examination in a tripos. Abraham was a good and accurate scholar, with a special memory for Horace and Homer, which he retained through life. He graduated BA in 1837 and succeeded to a fellowship at King's, which he held until 1849. He proceeded MA in 1840 and DD in 1859, and took the *ad eundem* degree of MA at Oxford on 14 June 1849.

Abraham was ordained deacon in 1838 and priest in 1839, and after entering on parochial work as curate of Headley Down, Hampshire, he returned to Eton in 1840 as a master. For nine years he threw himself heart and soul into Eton life. There were few masters and the classes were large and unwieldy; Abraham had more than ninety boys in his division. With George Augustus Selwyn, who was private tutor to the earl of Powis's sons at Eton and curate of Windsor, Abraham now began the friendship which determined his career. When in 1841 Selwyn became bishop of New Zealand, Abraham was anxious to follow him, but for the present the calls of Eton kept him at home. In the interests of the reform of the school he resigned the lucrative post of housemaster to become assistant master in college, in 1846, and was largely responsible for the rapid improvement in the moral tone of the King's scholars. He helped to modify the system of fagging, and repressed the old college songs. He widened the range of the curriculum, combining the teaching of history and geography and stimulating the boys' interest in history and literature. During this time he published several works, including *The Unity of History* (1845). The collegers regarded him as a kind adviser and friend, and in 1850 gave a font and cover to the college chapel as a tribute of their regard. His pupils included Edward Henry Stanley, fifteenth earl of Derby, to whom for a time he was private tutor at Knowsley, and Lord Robert Arthur Talbot Gascoyne Cecil, later third marquess of Salisbury and prime

Charles John Abraham (1814–1903), by Francis Holl (after George Richmond)

minister, who visited him in New Zealand in 1852. In 1848 Abraham was appointed divinity lecturer of St George's Chapel, Windsor, and the following year, when he became BD at Cambridge, he published his *Festival and Lenten Lectures*.

Abraham left Eton at Christmas 1849 to join Bishop Selwyn in New Zealand. On 17 January 1850 he married Caroline Harriet (*d.* 1877), daughter of Sir Charles Thomas Palmer, bt, of Wanlip, Leicestershire. They arrived in Auckland harbour in July 1850. Selwyn at once put Abraham in charge, as chaplain and principal, of St John's College, Auckland, a small training college for Maori and English youths. In 1853 he was made archdeacon of Waitemata, with the oversight of a large district. He supported church and Maori rights against the settler interest.

Abraham visited England in 1857 for surgical treatment of an arm broken in a fall from his horse. While he was in England the new dioceses of Wellington and Nelson were constituted: Abraham was consecrated bishop of Wellington at Lambeth Palace on 29 September 1858, and his friend Edmund Hobhouse became bishop of Nelson. After returning to New Zealand, for twelve years Abraham was fully occupied in creating the machinery of his new diocese, the chief town in which had just been made the seat of government. He continued to take the Maori side and was a member of the 'missionary party', opposing settler attitudes and lobbying for the replacement of governor T. Gore Brown. He promoted Maori education and attempted to encourage Maori participation in church government.

In 1870 Abraham returned to England with Selwyn, who was appointed to the see of Lichfield, and owing to Selwyn's temporary failure of health became coadjutor-bishop. In 1872 he was collated to the prebendal stall of Bobenhall in Lichfield Cathedral, and in 1876 he was made a canon residentiary and precentor. He assisted in the revision of the medieval statutes of the cathedral, taught in the theological college, and was responsible for the fabric of the cathedral and improving the music. In 1875–6 Abraham was also non-resident rector of Tatenhill, in Needwood Forest. A total abstainer, he was long a frequent speaker at meetings of the United Kingdom Alliance.

After Selwyn's death in April 1878, Abraham, with Bishop Edmund Hobhouse and Sir William Martin, organized, by way of memorial, Selwyn College, Cambridge, which was opened in October 1882 and of which he was a chief benefactor. Abraham worked with William Dalrymple Maclagan, Selwyn's successor at Lichfield, until 1890, when he resigned his canonry, thenceforth living with his only son, the Revd Charles Thomas Abraham (later bishop of Derby), first at Christ Church, Lichfield, until 1897, and afterwards at Bakewell, Derbyshire. He died on 4 February 1903 at Bakewell vicarage, and was buried at Over Haddon churchyard. A memorial was placed in Eton College chapel. W. G. D. FLETCHER, rev. H. C. G. MATTHEW

Sources *Selwyn College Calendar* (1903–6) [articles by A. L. Brown and C. T. Abraham] · *The Times* (5 Feb 1903) · *The Times* (9 Feb 1903) · *The Times* (13 Feb 1903) · C. J. Abraham, *Journal of a walk with the bishop of New Zealand* (1856) · W. E. Limbrick, ed., *Bishop Selwyn in New Zealand, 1841–68* (1983) · H. W. Tucker, *Memoir of the life and episcopate of George Augustus Selwyn*, 2 vols. (1879) · A. K. Davidson, 'Abraham, Charles John', *DNZB*, vol. 1
Archives NL NZ, Turnbull L., corresp. and papers | Auckland Public Library, letters to Sir George Grey · BL, letters to E. W. Gladstone, Add. MSS 44369–44786 · Selwyn College, Cambridge, letters to E. Coleridge
Likenesses F. Holl, stipple (after G. Richmond), NPG [see illus.] · wood-engraving, NPG; repro. in *ILN* (1859)
Wealth at death £1037 11s. 1d.: probate, 12 May 1903, *CGPLA Eng. & Wales*

Abraham, Sir Edward Penley (1913–1999), biochemist, was born at 47 Southview Road, Southampton, on 10 June 1913, the son of Albert Penley Abraham, a customs and excise officer, and his wife, Mary Abraham, *née* Hearne. Educated at King Edward VI School, Southampton, and Queen's College, Oxford, he graduated with first-class honours in chemistry in 1935. After joining Sir Robert Robinson's natural products group at the Dyson Perrins Laboratories, Abraham worked with Ernst Chain, a biochemist who joined the Sir William Dunn School of Pathology in 1935 under Howard Florey. Chain was investigating the chemistry of lysozyme, a bacteriolytic enzyme discovered in nasal secretion by Sir Alexander Fleming in 1922 and later found in many animal tissues. Abraham obtained a crystalline sample of lysozyme in 1937, gained his doctorate in the following year, and won a Rockefeller Foundation travelling scholarship which enabled him to spend a year at the Hans von Euler Institute, Stockholm. In 1939 he married Norwegian-born Asbjörg Harung. They had one son.

Investigation of penicillin After returning to Oxford in November 1939 Abraham joined the Dunn School of Pathology in January 1940 with a Medical Research Council grant to work on Florey's wound shock programme. Chain, whose work on lysozyme had stimulated his interest in antibacterial substances produced by microorganisms, persuaded Florey to join him in a survey of these products. One of the first to be investigated was penicillin and Abraham, as a member of the research team, played a crucial role. Florey, with Norman Heatley, studied its clinical use as an antibiotic. As the available supplies of penicillin were very impure Chain and Abraham set out to obtain pure penicillin and determine its chemical structure. The barium salt dissolved in amyl acetate was repeatedly extracted with water and Abraham used chromatography on a column of powdered alumina. The active fraction was treated with aluminium amalgam and chromatographic separation was repeated until the alumina appeared homogeneous. A substantial degree of purification was thus achieved. From the purified sample Abraham obtained crystals of the sodium salt for X-ray analysis.

Hope of producing sufficient penicillin to supply the armed forces resulted in a major Anglo-American effort in 1941. Chemical synthesis was not then possible and the traditional fermentation methods remained the only certain way to manufacture penicillin in large quantities. In 1943 sulphur was found in the penicillin molecule and in October Abraham proposed a molecular structure which included a cyclic formation containing three carbon atoms and one nitrogen atom, the β-lactam ring, not then known in natural products. This structure was not immediately published due to the restrictions of wartime secrecy. When it was made public it was strongly disputed until finally confirmed in 1945 by Dorothy Crowfoot Hodgkin using X-ray analysis. In the same year Florey, Chain, and Sir Alexander Fleming shared the Nobel prize in physiology or medicine for the discovery. Recognizing its potential commercial value Florey proposed that the drug should be patented, but the Medical Research Council declined. Chain and Abraham found four types of penicillin, all with the same molecular structure but each differing in certain elemental constituents. In use, bacterial resistance to penicillin was soon observed and it was found that by introducing synthetic modifications of substituents in the β-lactam ring the problem could be overcome. A new generation of semisynthetic penicillins followed, but total chemical synthesis of the drug was not achieved until 1959.

Florey secured an endowment from Lord Nuffield for three research fellowships at Lincoln College, Oxford, and Abraham received one of these in 1948. He and his colleagues continued to investigate the chemistry and biology of antibiotic substances and his laboratory soon gained an international reputation for work in this field. Abraham's main interest was in theoretical studies of the chemical structures and modes of action of antibacterial substances, but his work was often of great practical importance. Thus Chain suspected that the resistance of some bacteria to penicillin was due to their ability to produce an enzyme and Abraham confirmed this, discovering an enzyme which they called penicillinase in extracts of E. coli and other cultures. Further studies indicated that penicillinase was one, though not the only, cause of bacterial resistance. The discovery was crucial for the success of clinical trials on penicillin.

This work was interrupted in the early 1950s when Florey received some specimens of a new organism found near the outfall from a Sardinian sewer by Professor Giuseppe Brotzu, rector of the University of Cagliari. This organism, when grown in culture, produced a substance with antibacterial properties similar to penicillin and Florey asked Abraham to investigate it. The fungus producing this substance was identified as a species of *cephalosporium* and under the aegis of Glaxo more than 40,000 strains of this micro-organism were tested. With Guy Newton, Abraham found that the effective antibacterial agent was penicillin N, but other weaker antibacterial substances were also present. One of these, labelled cephalosporin C, attracted Abraham's attention because it was not destroyed by penicillinase. With Newton he succeeded in isolating this unstable water soluble antibacterial compound and determined its structure by classical degradative methods. He was at first reluctant to publish his results as the ultraviolet spectrum appeared incompatible with his proposed molecular structure which, like the penicillins, had a β-lactam ring in the molecule. However, when he was asked to speak about cephalosporin C at an international conference in 1961 it became clear that he could not describe the degradative evidence without revealing his conclusions about the structure. Dorothy Hodgkin later confirmed Abraham's proposed structure by X-ray crystallography.

Commercial production of antibiotics In 1949 the government, realizing that the failure to patent the penicillin discoveries had resulted in a massive loss of potential revenue, established the National Research Development Corporation (NRDC). This organization had provided some financial support for the work on cephalosporin C and wished to make the most of the results. The weak antibacterial activity made commercial development unattractive but it was suggested that if the side chain attached to the β-lactam ring could be replaced by other substituents the antibiotic activity of the molecule might be increased. This was realized when the phenacetyl derivative of 7-amino-cephalosporanic acid showed a 200-fold increase in antibacterial activity. Based on this observation a new group of antibiotics was developed using 7-amino-cephalosporanic acid as the key intermediate. It was also found that the cephalosporin C molecule had a second site which could be substituted with various groups and a huge variety of cephalosporins became possible. Many of these were manufactured under patents and licences by British, American, and Japanese pharmaceutical companies and some soon became established in clinical medicine. They all have low toxicity and act against a much wider range of bacteria than penicillin. They provide an alternative for the treatment of patients who show penicillin hypersensitivity and can be used to treat infections caused by penicillin-resistant organisms.

Cephalosporin patents yielded massive royalties which, for twenty years, accounted for much of the income of the NRDC. Royalties were also received by Abraham and Newton personally and they both founded charitable trusts to support medical, biological, and chemical research in Oxford. By the end of the twentieth century the E. P. Abraham Research Fund had donated more than £30 million to Oxford University, mainly to the Sir William Dunn School of Pathology and to Lincoln College, where Abraham held a fellowship from 1948 until his retirement in 1980. The Edward Abraham research building on South Parks Road, Oxford, opened in 2000, received about £5.5 million from Abraham's Research Fund. King Edward's School, Southampton, also benefited, as did many individuals whom Abraham helped privately.

Abraham received many honours, including several honorary degrees and the fellowship of the Royal Society in 1958. He was appointed CBE in 1973 and was knighted in 1980. After retirement he continued his research, collaborating with Professor Sir Jack Baldwin on the biosynthesis of the penicillins and cephalosporins. He also took a personal interest in the running of the trust funds. For the Royal Society, Abraham provided biographical memoirs of Florey (1971) and Chain (1979), in both of which his own significant contributions are lightly treated as part of the teamwork for which he always gives the major credit to his subjects.

Abraham was a modest man of conservative habits, and despite his growing wealth and his many honours his lifestyle did not change. He worked daily in his laboratory, eating a frugal lunch in his room. In the evening he would return to his home at Boars Hill as to a haven. He was devoted to his wife, Asbjörg, and seldom travelled without her. They took long summer holidays at their mountain chalet in Norway where they would walk and ski. Abraham had few hobbies, but he and his wife were both enthusiastic gardeners and delighted in showing people round their extensive and immaculate garden. Following a stroke Abraham died at St Luke's Nursing Home, Oxford, on 9 May 1999. He was survived by his wife.

N. G. COLEY

Sources W. H. Brock, *Biographical dictionary of scientists*, ed. T. I. Williams, 4th edn (1994) • T. I. Williams, *Howard Florey: penicillin and after* (1984) • G. MacFarlane, *Howard Florey: the making of a great scientist* (1979) • *The Times* (12 May 1999) • *Daily Telegraph* (12 May 1999) • *The Independent* (13 May 1999) • E. P. Abraham, 'Howard Walter Florey', *Memoirs FRS*, 17 (1971), 255–302 • H. W. Florey and E. P. Abraham, 'The work on penicillin at Oxford', *Journal of the History of Medicine and Allied Sciences*, 6 (1951), 302–17 • J. M. T. Hamilton-Miller, 'Sir Edward Abraham's contribution to the development of the cephalosporins, a reassessment', *International Journal of Antimicrobial Agents*, 15 (2000), 179–84 [portrait] • b. cert. • d. cert. • WW

Archives CUL, corresp. with Peter Mitchell • Wellcome L., corresp. with Sir Ernst Chain

Likenesses W. Suschitzky, photograph, 1944, NPG; *see illus. in* Robinson, Sir Robert (1886–1975) • B. Organ, pencil drawing, Sir William Dunn School of Pathology, Oxford • R. Young, bust, Sir William Dunn School of Pathology, Oxford

Abraham, George Dixon (1871–1965), photographer and rock-climber, was born at Derwent Street, Keswick, Cumberland, on 7 October 1871, the eldest son of George Perry Abraham (1844–1923), photographer, and his wife, Mary, *née* Dixon. G. P. Abraham had moved from London to Keswick, where he established a very successful photographic business and was for fifteen years a councillor. George Dixon Abraham was educated at Manchester grammar school and Manchester School of Art; his brother **Ashley Perry Abraham** (1876–1951), born at Derwent Terrace, Keswick, on 20 February 1876, went to Blackman's School. Both subsequently worked in their father's shop, helping to develop its worldwide reputation as the Lake District's leading supplier of photographs.

The Abraham brothers, including in due course the youngest brother, John Abraham (*b.* 1889), were also enthusiastic rock-climbers. George and Ashley were pioneers of Lakeland rock exploration. They usually climbed together, George—bandy-legged but with strong hands—in the lead; he was the more patient, working out the sequence of his moves. He was punctilious about the nailing of his boots and could place the edge nails into the smallest wrinkle in the rock. He climbed for fifty years without there being any record of his falling. Both brothers continued to climb in nailed boots after other climbers adopted rubber soles. George was 'a good friend … unselfish in mountaineering as in life and possessed of a sense of humour which made climbs done with him seem easier than they really were' (Somervell, 360). Ashley was 'agile and quick—tall, broad and powerful, with great Cumberland legs and a southern high colour, fire and enterprise' (Young, 404).

In the 1890s the Abrahams produced the first photographs of climbers in action, which were soon in demand for illustrations for books and guides. Owen Glynne Jones's *Rock Climbing in the English Lake District* (1897) had thirty full-page photographs, mostly taken by Ashley. After Jones's death in 1899 the Abrahams began producing guides to rock climbs, following Jones's grading of climbs and thus saving many young climbers from exceeding their capabilities. Around 1900 the brothers planned to produce a guide to Snowdonia but here they ran into obstructive secrecy and resentment over their intrusion into the area from the leisured classes who made up the majority of climbers in Snowdonia and looked down on the Abrahams, who were in trade. Nevertheless, *Rock Climbing in North Wales* was published in 1906.

George Abraham married at Gospel Oak Congregational Chapel, London, on 16 October 1900, Winifred Ellen (1870/71–1939), daughter of David Davies, a sculptor, and raised two daughters. After her death he married on 18 April 1940, at the register office, Cockermouth, Cumberland, Clara (*b.* 1899), the daughter of Thomas Young, a haulage contractor of Keswick; she survived him. Ashley Abraham married on 21 October 1902 Lucy Barlow (*b.* 1877), daughter of George Kennedy, Congregational minister, with whom he had three sons and a daughter.

When the Fell and Rock Club of the English Lake District was founded in 1906 Ashley Abraham was the first president. Climbing in the Lake District was notably democratic, attracting many young men from the factories of industrial Lancashire to enjoy the challenge of the Lakeland crags. The Fell and Rock Club welcomed women into its ranks, and Ashley's wife, Lucy, was among the early female members. George Abraham's travels to Scotland and the Alps provided material for more climbing books and as a pioneer of motoring he wrote *Motorways in Lakeland* (1913) and *Motorways at Home and Abroad* (1928) to satisfy a growing market, while Ashley toured England giving lantern-slide talks. In the early 1920s he made a five-minute travelogue for Pathé about climbing Napes Needle. Both brothers became directors of G. P. Abraham Ltd, which was carried on by Ashley's sons.

Ashley Abraham died at the Royal Infirmary, Edinburgh, on 9 October 1951. He was never a member of the Alpine Club, although it did honour him with an obituary. George Abraham was admitted to membership in 1954, when he was over eighty; he died at his home, Idwal, Chestnut Hill, Keswick, on 4 March 1965.

ANITA MCCONNELL

Sources T. H. Somervell, *Alpine Club Journal*, 70 (Nov 1965), 359–60 · G. W. Young, *Alpine Club Journal*, 58 (May 1962), 404 · *WWW* · *The Times* (6 March 1965), 12a · *The Times* (8 Oct 1996), 7 · *British Journal of Photography*, 98 (1951), 644 · A. Hankinson, *A century on the crags: the story of rock climbing in the Lake District* (1988) · b. cert. · m. certs. · d. cert. · b. cert. [Ashley Perry Abraham] · m. cert. [Ashley Perry Abraham] · *CGPLA Eng. & Wales* (1951) [Ashley Perry Abraham]

Likenesses double portrait, photograph (with Ashley Abraham), repro. in *The Times* (8 Oct 1996), 7

Wealth at death £32,085: probate, 1965, *CGPLA Eng. & Wales* · £24,494 8s. 8d.—Ashley Abraham: probate, 1951, *CGPLA Eng. & Wales*

Abraham, Gerald Ernest Heal (1904–1988), musicologist, was born on 9 March 1904 in Newport, Isle of Wight, the only child of Ernest Abraham, manufacturer, and his wife, Dorothy Mary Heal, a jeweller's daughter. In spite of his strong musical interests, he planned a naval career, attending a naval crammer in Portsmouth. Ill health forced him to abandon this, though he retained a lifelong interest in naval history, and after studying for a year in Cologne he published his first book on music, a study of Aleksandr Borodin (1927), an autodidact like himself. Apart from some piano lessons in early life, he was self-taught, but during the following years he contributed widely to musical periodicals and also published monographs on Nietzsche (1933), Tolstoy (1935), and Dostoyevsky (1936), as well as an introduction to contemporary music, *This Modern Stuff* (1933; renamed *This Modern Music* in later reprints). He taught himself Russian and published two collections of his primarily analytical essays, *Studies in Russian Music* (1935) and *On Russian Music* (1939). In collaboration with M. D. Calvocoressi, he wrote *Masters of Russian Music* (1936). In 1935 he joined the BBC as assistant editor of *Radio Times* and subsequently served as deputy editor of *The Listener* (1939–42), remaining its music editor until 1962. In 1936 he married (Isobel) Patsy, daughter of

Stanley John Robinson, a pharmacist; they had one daughter.

During the Second World War, when interest in Russian music was at fever pitch, he published *Eight Soviet Composers* (1943) and made a valuable behind-the-scenes contribution to broadcasting as director of gramophone programmes (1942–7), helping to lay the foundations of the Third Programme in 1946. He returned to the BBC in 1962, as assistant controller of music, after having spent the intervening years (1947–62) as the first professor of music at Liverpool University. He spent a further year as chief music critic of the *Daily Telegraph* (1967–8) before becoming the Ernest Bloch professor of music at the University of California at Berkeley (1968–9). His lectures there were subsequently published under the title *The Tradition of Western Music* (1974). Although the public tended to associate him with Slavonic and Romantic music, his scholarship was of quite unusual breadth and depth. He edited symposia on Tchaikovsky (1945), Schubert (1946), Sibelius (1947), Grieg (1948), Schumann (1952), and Handel (1954). He set in motion *The History of Music in Sound* (gramophone records and handbooks) and the *New Oxford History of Music*. The latter occupied him for the best part of three decades; he edited three of its ten volumes personally—the third, *Ars nova and the Renaissance, 1300–1450*, in collaboration with Dom Anselm Hughes (1960); the fourth, *The Age of Humanism, 1540–1630* (1968); and the eighth, *The Age of Beethoven, 1790–1830* (1982). During this time he also brought out his magisterial, synoptic overview of western music, *The Concise Oxford History of Music* (1979). He was closely involved in *The New Grove Dictionary of Music and Musicians* (1980). His selfless work as an editor is nowhere better exemplified than in his completion of Calvocoressi's Master Musicians study of Mussorgsky (1946) and his work on seeing Calvocoressi's larger study through the press in 1955 (published in 1956).

Abraham was of medium height, with a genial and warm personality. His writings are exceptional in the field of musicology not only for their scholarship, which was always worn lightly, but also for their freshness, originality, and readability. He had the rare ability to stimulate the interest and engage the sympathies of the less informed as well as the specialist reader, and he commanded a ready wit with the gift for a felicitous and memorable phrase. Although he wrote widely on Russian music and literature, he was also the author of *Chopin's Musical Style* (1939), a penetrating study which was a model of lucidity, economy, and good style. Always a Wagnerian, Abraham long planned a book on Wagner's musical language. In the 1940s he even made a conjectural reconstruction of a quartet movement that was published by Oxford University Press. He also made a conjectural completion of Schubert's 'Unfinished' symphony in 1971.

Abraham held honorary doctorates from the universities of Durham, Liverpool, and Southampton, and Berkeley, and was a fellow of the British Academy (1972), and president of the Royal Musical Association (1969–74). He was appointed CBE in 1974. From 1973 to 1980 he was chairman of the British Academy's early English church music committee. Some of his finest and most absorbing writing is to be found in *Slavonic and Romantic Music: Essays and Studies* (1968). Whether as a lecturer or broadcaster, his erudition was always tempered by a keen sense of humour. The publication of *Slavonic and Western Music: Essays for Gerald Abraham* (1985), edited by Malcolm Hamrick Brown and Roland John Wiley, paid him fitting and timely tribute. Abraham had an abiding love of the English countryside and the music of Sir Edward Elgar, and from the early 1960s he lived in the Old School House, Ebernoe, near Petworth, Sussex, until his death at the King Edward VII Hospital, Midhurst, on 18 March 1988.

ROBERT LAYTON, *rev.*

Sources M. H. Brown and R. J. Wiley, eds., *Slavonic and Western music: essays for Gerald Abraham* (1985) · J. Westrup, ed., 'A birthday greeting to Gerald Abraham', *Music and Letters*, 55 (1974), 131–5 · personal knowledge (1996)
Wealth at death £160,541: probate, 22 June 1988, *CGPLA Eng. & Wales*

Abraham, Robert (1775–1850), architect, was born in the parish of St Pancras, London, on 12 February 1775, the son of John Abraham, builder, and his wife, Mary, *née* Mottershead. He became a pupil under the surveyor James Bowen, and began his professional life as a London building surveyor when his extensive practice brought him into contact with 'some of the chief Roman Catholic families in England'. Eliza Brown (1777/8–1818), whom he married, was the daughter of the botanical artist Peter Brown. An accomplished flower painter, Eliza Abraham exhibited one of her flower pieces at the Royal Academy in 1814. She died in 1818 at their home in Keppel Street, near Russell Square, London, at the early age of forty, leaving Abraham with the responsibility of bringing up their ten children.

It was not until after the Napoleonic Wars, when Nash's projected plans for improving London generated a lively interest in architecture, that, in middle age, Abraham was able to establish a successful architectural practice. Many of his most important commissions resulted from the patronage of the twelfth duke of Norfolk, though perhaps his best-known work was the county fire office (1819; dem. 1924), at the top of Lower Regent Street. In designing his famous Quadrant, Nash used the county fire office as the *point de vue* to which the line from Carlton House ran. In his volume on the cities of London and Westminster in his series The Buildings of England, Pevsner noted that 'it was eminently characteristic that by that time an office building could be designed in imitation of Inigo Jones's range at old Somerset House and could hold the balance against Carlton House' (*London and Westminster*, 560).

Abraham's considerable practical knowledge was passed on to a number of pupils, including his son H. R. Abraham (1803/4–1877), who was given the commission for the Middle Temple Library, following the marriage in 1824 of his sister Eleanor Mary (Ellen) to Richard Bethell, Baron Westbury, lord chancellor (1861–5). In 1842 several of Abraham's other pupils—who included G. Alexander, H. Flower, J. Lockyer, Thomas Little, T. Mackintosh, R. E.

Phillips, M. J. Stutely, C. Verelst, and J. Woolley—presented him with a gold box, an indication of the respect and affection in which he was held as a master of his profession. Together with the successfully maintained duties of his architectural practice and sole responsibility for his family, this gesture by his pupils suggests a more than customary token of acknowledgement. Colvin describes Abraham as 'a competent practitioner in the diverse styles expected of an English architect in the early nineteenth century, but his reputation rested on reliability rather than originality as a designer' (Colvin, *Archs.*, 47).

Abraham was a fellow of the Society of Antiquaries. He died at 32 York Terrace, Marylebone, Middlesex, on 11 December 1850, and was buried in the extension of Hampstead churchyard.

ANNETTE PEACH

Sources Colvin, *Archs.* · *The Builder*, 8 (1850), 598, 602 · parish register, St Pancras Old Church · *GM*, 1st ser., 88/2 (1818), 644 · *IGI* · Graves, *RA exhibitors* · T. A. Nash, *The life of Richard, Lord Westbury*, 2 vols. (1888), vol. 1, pp. 44, 49; vol. 2, p. 13 · *London 1: the cities of London and Westminster* (1957), 560 · J. S. Curl, *Georgian architecture* (1993), 143, 176 · H. Hobhouse, *Lost London* (1971), 90 · *DNB* · d. cert.
Archives RIBA BAL, MSS collection · RIBA BAL, drawings collection · RIBA BAL, biography file

Abraham, Roy Clive (1890–1963), scholar of African languages and colonial administrator, was born on 16 December 1890 in Melbourne, Australia. From a Jewish background, he studied at University College, London, preparatory school, at Clifton College, Bristol, and also at various establishments in Germany. From 1923 to 1924 he was a Brassey scholar (in Italian) at Balliol College, Oxford, where he was awarded a first-class honours degree in oriental languages (Arabic and Persian); he was prepared to be examined in Ethiopic (his proficiency stemming from a study period at Leipzig University in 1920) but no examiner could be found. In 1927 Abraham took a certificate in anthropology from University College, London, and a diploma in (classical) Arabic from the School of Oriental Studies, University of London, in 1930.

During the First World War and its aftermath (1914–23), Abraham saw British army service in Arabia and on the north-western frontier with the Indian army, where he acquired a working knowledge of Hindustani. His first experience of sub-Saharan Africa was in 1925, when he entered the administrative service of the northern provinces of Nigeria; he continued in the service until 1944, working initially as an administrative officer and (acting) government anthropological officer. His wife, Sadie, lived with him in Nigeria, and they had one son, Donald.

Sometimes difficult and temperamental, Abraham's relations with colleagues, then and later, often proved to be turbulent. Nevertheless, he was almost immediately seconded on a six-year language research project to Bauchi province in north-eastern Nigeria, and it was there, in 1926, that he conducted his first independent linguistic study of an African language, working on Bole (Bolanci), a west Chadic (Afro-Asian) language. He then assisted G. P. *Bargery in the compilation of the latter's monumental and authoritative *Hausa-English Dictionary*

(1934). Abraham learned about the role of contrastive tone in west African languages from Bargery, and in his *Principles of Hausa* (1934) he simplified Bargery's six-tone system to the correct three-tone system for Hausa.

This was an especially productive period for Abraham, and he published yet more pedagogically-motivated works, including *The Grammar of Tiv* (1933) and *The Principles of Idoma* (1935), the first detailed linguistic description of an eastern Kwa language. Although the quality of his prolific output varied, and was sometimes abstruse, Abraham's grammars and dictionaries represented major descriptive and analytical contributions to the study of African languages. In 1941–2, during the Second World War, he taught Hausa to soldiers in the Royal West African frontier force, after which he served in Ethiopia, teaching Amharic and Somali. Later in the war he was based in Kenya, South Africa, France, and Italy, and with the British military mission in Moscow, completing his military career with the rank of major.

In 1945 Abraham was awarded a Leverhulme research fellowship to research the Semitic languages of Ethiopia and Eritrea (including Amharic and Ge'ez). In 1946 he was frustrated in his attempt to succeed Bargery as lecturer in Hausa at the School of Oriental and African Studies (SOAS), London. His relationship with Bargery had become increasingly strained since their collaboration on Bargery's 1934 Hausa dictionary, and Abraham was of the opinion that Bargery had actively hindered his appointment. Relations were at such a low ebb that Abraham felt compelled to complain to the director of SOAS about Bargery's presence on the selection board, at the same time apologizing for his behaviour. Subsequently appointed to a new lectureship in Amharic, Abraham held the post from 1948 until he retired in 1951. During this same period he also taught Tigrinya and began research into Berber, Oromo, and Somali. In 1949 he was awarded the degree of DLitt by the University of Oxford on the basis of three of his published works on Tiv.

Further works by Abraham included his *Dictionary of the Hausa Language* (with Mai Kano), which was published in 1949; and in 1951 *The Principles of Somali* (with Solomon Warsama) appeared in mimeograph form. In 1952, Abraham embarked on a study of Yoruba, having made his own way to Ibadan, Nigeria. This led to his *Dictionary of Modern Yoruba* (1958). Beset by diabetes and ill health in the later stages of his life, Abraham's dogged determination and intellectual curiosity drove him to do further research on Igbo, and he was close to completing a dictionary and grammar when he died from a coronary thrombosis and stroke at his home, 11 West View, Hendon, on 22 June 1963 at the age of seventy-two. He was survived by his wife and son. A key figure in African language scholarship during the twentieth century, Abraham worked for over thirty years on a wide range of disparate languages in the Afro-Asian family, as well as in Niger-Congo. A commemorative volume in honour of his outstanding contribution to the understanding of African languages was published in 1992.   PHILIP J. JAGGAR

Sources R. G. Armstrong, 'Roy Clive Abraham, 1890–1963', *Journal of West African Languages*, 1/1 (1964), 49–53 • P. E. H. Hair, 'A bibliography of R. C. Abraham—linguist and lexicographer', *Journal of West African Languages*, 2/1 (1965), 63–6 • P. J. Jaggar, ed., *Papers in honour of R. C. Abraham (1890–1963)* (1992) [esp. P. J. Jagger, 'Roy Clive Abraham: a biographical profile and list of writings', 1–4; J. E. Lavers, 'R. C. Abraham: the Bolewa and Bolanci', 29–35] • d. cert. • *CGPLA Eng. & Wales* (1963) • handlist of the papers of Roy Clive Abraham, SOAS, MS 193280

Archives SOAS, notes and papers

Wealth at death £5035 12s. od.: probate, 22 Aug 1963, *CGPLA Eng. & Wales*

Abraham, William [*pseud.* Mabon] (1842–1922), trade unionist and politician, was born at Cwmafon, near Port Talbot, Glamorgan, on 14 June 1842, the fourth son of Thomas and Mary Abraham. His father, a coalminer and copper smelter, soon died, leaving his mother to raise a large family. Mabon, as he was generally known, ended his formal education at the national school, Cwmafon, at the age of ten, when he started work underground as a door boy. On 18 August 1860 he married Sarah Williams (*bap.* 1842, *d.* 1900), daughter of David Williams, the local blacksmith. They had twelve children, of whom eight survived infancy. Sarah died suddenly on 13 July 1900.

After an abortive trip to Chile in search of work in 1864–5, Mabon worked at Cwmafon spelter works and a tinplate works near Swansea, before returning to coalmining at Caercynydd pit, near Gowerton. The rest of his life was bound up with coal and coalminers. In 1871 he addressed his first union meeting, speaking for the Amalgamated Association of Miners (AAM), which was newly recruiting in south Wales, and set up an AAM lodge at Waunarlwydd. In 1872 he was elected treasurer of Loughor district and to the national executive. His attendance at the executive's Manchester meetings led to dismissal as a collier: in December 1872 he worked his last shift as a miner and became paid agent of the Loughor district of the AAM.

In the underdeveloped state of trade unionism in south Wales, Mabon's meteoric rise was perhaps unexceptional: what was remarkable was the extent to which he then dominated mining unionism there for nearly forty years. After the AAM rapidly withered amid the depression and defeats of 1874–5, he became the main figure, charged with keeping the idea of trade unionism alive. As part of the settlement of the five-month lock-out of 1875 (the third major stoppage in five years), the coal owners had determined on a system whereby wage rates would be 'automatically' adjusted to the market price of coal. Part of the mechanism for this scheme was a joint sliding scale committee: in July Mabon became the first chairman of the workers' side, a position he held until the sliding scale was abandoned in 1902. He was president of the South Wales Miners' Federation (SWMF) from its inception in 1898 until he resigned in 1912, making way for more aggressive leaders.

The eventual demand for a different leadership style largely explains why Mabon's reputation slumped for a long period after his death. He was charged with presiding over and preserving an innocuous form of trade unionism. Apart from supporting the sliding scale, there was

William Abraham [Mabon] (1842–1922), by Sir Benjamin Stone, 1901

the ambiguity of union finances, including the pay of agents such as Mabon, which was dependent on employers making deductions from pay. It was also felt that at his death Mabon left more money (£32,777 net) than was proper for a union leader. Against all this, Mabon's career must be seen in the context of the near total collapse of unionism by the mid-1870s. After his original base at Loughor disappeared, he moved to the Rhondda in 1877 to become the agent for the Cambrian Miners' Association, the largest of several district-based organizations which kept the notion of unionism alive. Mabon's role was indispensable: he was a compelling orator in both languages and won general acceptance as the legitimate, responsible voice of labour. His status as a major public figure was exemplified by the fact that manufacturers of tobacco and sauces sought his endorsement. Above all, the later recriminations in a different industrial climate ignored the robust claims he had advanced for the rights of labour.

The first challenge to his dominance came with the formation in 1888 of the Miners' Federation of Great Britain (MFGB), which totally opposed sliding scale systems. A small branch was set up in Monmouthshire under the able leadership of William Brace, but Mabon comfortably saw off this threat. But the harder line adopted by coal owners gradually undermined his advocacy of conciliation. In 1896 they disdainfully rejected his proposals for raising prices by restricting output. In 1898 they imposed a deliberately humiliating settlement after a bitter six-month stoppage. In response the miners immediately formed the

SWMF, and installed Mabon as president. At the next MFGB conference, Mabon attended as one of 'three penitent Welshmen' who renounced sliding scales.

The 1898 settlement had signalled the limits of conciliation: a decade later the Mines Eight Hour Act, which had its greatest effect in south Wales, effectively made the policy completely unworkable. It simultaneously reduced miners' piece-work earnings while raising owners' costs. The result was especially poignant since Mabon, the apostle of conciliation, had also championed the eight-hour day. Faced with lower living standards and worsened working conditions, miners looked to younger, more aggressive leaders. The turbulence of the coalfield in the year-long Cambrian combine strike of 1910–11 over abnormal places, and the national 1912 struggle for a minimum wage, was not the world which Mabon, now nearly seventy, had hoped to create. He stepped down as SWMF president, but still served the industry through the International Miners' Congress and as MFGB treasurer.

Alongside his central concern with miners' unionism, William Abraham was elected to parliament for Rhondda in 1885. He thus became the first Welsh miners' MP, defeating the official Liberal candidate, a local coal owner, and held the seat (Rhondda up to 1918, then West Rhondda) until he retired in 1920. Essentially a Liberal, he reluctantly renounced the label when the MFGB joined the Labour Party in 1909. He made no great mark in the House of Commons as an orator, but served on three royal commissions (mining royalties, 1889; labour, 1891; and mines, 1906). He was appointed JP in 1887, was sworn of the privy council in 1916, and received an LLD from the University of Wales in 1918. Mabon was a lifelong Calvinistic Methodist, a lay preacher, Band of Hope activist, and a renowned choir conductor, with a rich tenor voice of his own. In person he was very striking and wore a substantial black beard. Keir Hardie described him in 1888 as being 'five feet by four feet, correct measurement, so that he is not as broad as he is long, though I should say he soon will be' (W. J. Stewart, *Keir Hardie*, 1821, 45). He died at his home, Brynybedw, in Pentre, Glamorgan, on 14 May 1922, and was buried on 18 May at Treorci cemetery. His funeral effectively closed the entire valley with its mixed throng of populace and personages.   JOHN WILLIAMS

Sources E. W. Evans, *Mabon (William Abraham, 1842–1922): a study in trade union leadership* (1959) · *Western Mail* [Cardiff] (15 May 1922) · *Western Mail* [Cardiff] (3 Oct 1922) · *South Wales News* (15 May 1922) · *The Times* (15 May 1922) · *DLB* · *DNB* · L. J. Williams, 'The first Welsh labour M.P.', *Morgannwg*, 6 (1962), 78–94 · C. Williams, *Democratic Rhondda: politics and society, 1885–1951* (1996), 31–45 · K. O. Morgan, 'The new liberalism and the challenge of labour: the Welsh experience, 1885–1829', *Welsh History Review / Cylchgrawn Hanes Cymru*, 6 (1972–3), 288–312 · L. J. Williams, 'The strike of 1898', *Morgannwg*, 9 (1965), 61–79 · R. P. Arnot, *South Wales miners / Glowyr de Cymru: a history of the South Wales Miners' Federation*, [1] (1967) · *South Wales Daily News* (1880) · *Tarian y Gweithiwr* (1875–97) · m. cert. · d. cert.

Archives NL Wales, autograph sermons, MSS 8159–8160 · NL Wales, testimonial minute book, MSS 12520 | NL Wales, records of Monmouthshire and South Wales Coalowners' Association

Likenesses B. Stone, two photographs, 1901, NPG [see illus.] · photograph, 1918, NL Wales · Elliott & Fry, postcard photograph,

NL Wales · J. Owen, photograph, NL Wales · photograph, NL Wales · woodcut, NPG

Wealth at death £33,315 10s. 7d.: probate, 28 Sept 1922, *CGPLA Eng. & Wales*

Abrahams, Abraham. *See* Tang, Abraham ben Naphtali (d. 1792).

Abrahams, Barnett (1831–1863), college head, was born in Warsaw, Poland, eldest child of Abraham Susman (c.1801–1880), known as Abraham Abrahams, and his second wife, Esther Reisel. His father, a leading authority on Jewish religious slaughter, settled in England in 1839 and was joined by his wife and son two years later. Two further sons were born in 1843 and 1844.

Abrahams received his early rabbinical instruction from his father and later from the chief rabbi himself, Nathan Marcus Adler. In 1849 Abrahams was admitted to the Spanish and Portuguese congregation's theological college. The elders defrayed the cost of his education at the City of London School and University College, from which he graduated BA. Abrahams married on 7 June 1854 Jane (1834–1895), daughter of Abraham Rodrigues Brandon. There were six children of this marriage. Two of his sons, Joseph and Moses, became Jewish ministers, and Israel an author and teacher.

In 1851 Barnett was invited to preach at Bevis Marks, the main synagogue of the Spanish and Portuguese community, and made a favourable impression. He became assistant *dayan* in 1854, although there was no full *dayan* at that time, and in 1856 was elected chief of the ecclesiastical court. His duties included the position of acting head of the community. He was the youngest man to act as *dayan* in the London Jewish community and the first English Jewish minister to hold a British university degree. In 1858, on the resignation of Dr Loewe as headmaster of Jews' College, London, the Jewish theological seminary, Barnett was elected his successor and became principal of the college; he continued to carry out his religious duties.

Barnett's chief interest was the education of the young, and he was the founder, in 1860, of the Association for the Diffusion of Religious Knowledge, the precursor of the Jewish Religious Education Board. This society provided a free sabbath school for Jewish children and distributed pamphlets on religion and history. Its first tract, entitled *The Lamp, the Light, and the Way of Life* (n.d.), was written by him.

Barnett Abrahams died unexpectedly, at Finsbury Square, London, on Sunday 15 November 1863, of acute rheumatism after an illness of a few days, and was buried the next day at the cemetery of the Spanish and Portuguese congregation, Mile End. The mourners were led by the chief rabbi. A daughter was born posthumously to Abrahams and his widow survived until 1895. Immediately after his death a memorial fund was opened for the benefit of his widow and children; it closed in May 1864, after just over £2000 had been raised. In December 1864 a tablet was erected in his memory by the Jewish infant school, Commercial Street, by the working classes of the Jewish faith.

On 21 November 1863 a discourse on their founder was delivered by G. J. Emanuel to the Association for the Diffusion of Religious Knowledge. In a special service held in his memory on 22 November 1863 by A. P. Mendes on behalf of the Spanish and Portuguese congregation, it was said that as a teacher of men Abrahams was remarkable for his burning zeal. As a teacher of youth, he was patient, kind, and gentle. However, in an article published in the *Transactions of the Jewish Historical Society* in 1968, Barnett's granddaughter maintained that he suffered from a violent temper and that his wife kept crockery available for him to smash to relieve his feelings.

DOREEN BERGER

Sources *Jewish Chronicle* (1862–4) · *Jewish Chronicle* (1880) · P. Abrahams, 'Abraham Sussman—from Berdichew to Bevis Marks', *Transactions of the Jewish Historical Society of England*, 21 (1962–7), 243–60 · A. M. Hyamson, *Jews' College, London, 1855–1955* (1955), 27–8 · I. Harris, *Jews' College jubilee volume* (1906), xviii–xix · I. Singer and others, eds., *The Jewish encyclopedia*, new edn, 12 vols. (1925) · G. H. Whitehill, ed., *Bevis Marks records*, 3: *Abstracts of the Ketubot or marriage-contracts and of the civil marriage registers of the Spanish and Portuguese Jews' Congregation for the period 1837–1901* (1973) · A. P. Mendes, 'The influence of a good name', 22 Nov 1863, Jews' College Library, London · S. Sebag, 'Lines written on the death of the late, lamented Rev. Barnett Abrahams, B.A.', 1864, Jews' College Library, London · *CGPLA Eng. & Wales* (1863) · private information [archivist of the Spanish and Portuguese Synagogue, London]

Wealth at death under £450: administration, 21 May 1864, *CGPLA Eng. & Wales*

Abrahams, Doris Caroline [*pseud.* Caryl Brahms] (1901–1982), writer and songwriter, was born at 28 Morland Road, Croydon, Surrey, on 8 December 1901, the only child of Henry Clarence Abrahams, a wholesale jeweller, and his wife, Pearl, one of the twenty-one children of Moses and Sultana Levi, who had arrived in England from Constantinople about 1873. She was educated privately, at Minerva College in Stonygate, near Leicester, and at the Royal Academy of Music, where she failed her LRAM. At the academy, already an embryo critic, she did not care to listen to the noise she made when playing the piano. She began to write light verse for a student magazine and then for the *Evening Standard*. At this time she adopted her pseudonym so that her parents, who envisaged a more domestic future for her, would be unaware of her literary activities; she became generally known as Caryl Brahms.

Ballet class as a child and her later exposure to the Diaghilev Ballet in the south of France encouraged Brahms to apply to Viscountess Rhondda to write ballet criticism for *Time and Tide*. She also wrote on opera and the theatre for the same newspaper, the *Daily Telegraph*, and many others. In 1930 Gollancz published her volume of children's verse, *The Moon on my Left*.

At this time Brahms met S. J. Simon (Secha Jascha Skidelsky), a White Russian student of agriculture, an international bridge player, and an inspired humorist. In the early thirties they contributed captions for 'Musso, the home page dog' cartoons by David Low in the *Evening Standard*. In 1936, during which Brahms also edited a popular primer, *Footnotes to the Ballet*, they collaborated on a novel, *A Bullet in the Ballet* (1937), their classic comedy thriller which introduced the Stroganoff Ballet Company.

Another Stroganoff novel, *Casino for Sale*, followed in 1938. *The Elephant is White* (1939) again deployed a cast of eccentric Russian *émigrés*. In 1940 they hit on a new and original vein of wild, anachronistic, historical humour with *Don't, Mr Disraeli!* (1940), a novel set, 'not in the Victorian Age but in its literature'. They brought a similar approach to the Elizabethan age in *No Bed for Bacon* (1941). Their other novels were *No Nightingales* (1944), *Six Curtains for Stroganova* (1945), *Titania has a Mother* (1944), and *Trottie True* (1946). A stage version of *A Bullet in the Ballet*, starring Léonide Massine and Irina Baronova, foundered in Blackpool.

In 1948 Brahms and Simon had just begun their last collaboration, *You Were There* (1950), when Simon died suddenly. Brahms finished the book alone, continued to write fiction, and increased her criticism of theatre and opera as well as ballet. Her collected book of theatre notices, *The Rest of the Evening's my Own*, was published in 1964. She followed it with *Gilbert and Sullivan* (1975) and with *Reflections in a Lake* (1976), a study of Chekhov's four great plays.

In 1954 Brahms had met Ned Sherrin, who asked permission to adapt *No Bed for Bacon* as a stage musical. Seeing that he challenged no comparisons with Simon, she suggested a collaboration. The production of the musical at the Bristol Old Vic was not a success but it laid the foundation of a partnership which over the next twenty-eight years produced seven books, many radio and television scripts, and several plays and musicals for the theatre including *I Gotta Shoe* (1962–3), *Sing a Rude Song* (1970), *Liberty Ranch* (1972), *Nickleby and me* (1975), *The Spoils of Poynton* (1968, from Henry James), and latterly *Beecham* (1980) and *The Mitford Girls* (1981), both of which had respectable West End runs.

In her sixties, Brahms's enthusiasm for ballet waned. She became a devotee of show-jumping and the All-England course at Hickstead took the place of Covent Garden in her life as she argued that the horses moved more gracefully than contemporary ballerinas. She also began to write songs for the BBC television programme *That Was The Week That Was* (1962) and, as a lyric writer, she won an Ivor Novello award (1966) for the title song of *Not So Much a Programme More a Way of Life*. Her song compilations were a feature of *Side by Side by Sondheim* (1976) and the television series *Song by Song* (1979–80). The latter also became a book (1984). In 1978 she was appointed a governor of the National Theatre.

Physically Brahms's aspect seemed not to change for the last three decades of her life, until a noticeable enfeeblement in the last two years. She was dark, tiny, with a very prominent nose on which she permanently perched large dark, forbidding spectacles. Her pouter-pigeon figure and thrust-forward chin matched her combative approach to life. She sparred energetically with colleagues and bank managers and conscientiously encouraged young artistes. Her work with Simon will surely survive as an example of the most sensitive and innovative comic fiction during the middle years of the twentieth century. She died of heart failure on 5 December 1982 at her home, 3 Cambridge Gate, Regent's Park, London. She was unmarried.

NED SHERRIN, *rev.*

Sources *The Times* (6 Dec 1982) · C. Brahms and N. Sherrin, *Too dirty for the windmill: a memoir* (1986) · C. Brahms, 'Palookas in peril', diary, priv. coll. · personal knowledge (1990) · b. cert. · d. cert.
Archives IWM, diary
Wealth at death £47,765: probate, 25 May 1984, *CGPLA Eng. & Wales*

Abrahams, Harold Maurice (1899–1978), athlete and civil servant, was born at 30 Rutland Road, Bedford, on 15 December 1899, the youngest in the family of two daughters and four sons of Isaac Klonimus (1850–1921) of Vladislavovka in Russian-occupied Poland and his wife, Esther Isaacs, of Merthyr Tudful. Klonimus, who proclaimed himself a Lithuanian Jew, escaped to Britain and by 1880 had changed his name to Abrahams, in recognition of his father, Abraham Klonimus (*b.* 1810).

Though Isaac Abrahams never mastered the script (and barely the speech) of his host country, he set up the Bedfordshire Loan Company in 1885 and was naturalized in 1902. In the county town, in addition to moneylending, he dealt as a certificated pedlar in jewellery, gold, and silver plate. Despite their tempestuous marriage Esther and he raised four remarkable sons. Adolphe, the eldest, after gaining firsts at Emmanuel College, Cambridge, became a consultant physician at Westminster Hospital and was knighted in 1939. Sir Sidney Solomon (Solly) Abrahams, who competed for Britain at both the Olympic celebrations at Athens (1906) and Stockholm (1912), was sworn of the privy council after serving as chief justice of Tanganyika and Ceylon. The third son, Lionel, became senior partner of his firm of solicitors and was coroner for Huntingdonshire.

Harold Abrahams was sent to Bedford School, briefly to St Paul's, and afterwards to Repton, where he won the public schools' 100 yards and long-jump championships in 1918. His imagination had been fired in the summer of 1908, when he watched his brother compete in the fourth Olympic games at the White City stadium, London. He served briefly as a second lieutenant in 1919 and then went up to Gonville and Caius College, Cambridge, to read law. If the road to popularity at university lies in never inculcating a sense of inferiority into one's contemporaries, Abrahams stood little chance of being popular. Athletically he swept all before him with three wins in the freshmen's sports at Fenners and was immediately selected for the sixth Olympic games in Antwerp. He stood 6ft ½in. and had a spare but muscular frame. He won a unique eight victories at the 100 yards, 440 yards, and long jump in the annual Oxford versus Cambridge sports. His election to the Hawks club was opposed due to a contribution by him to *The Times*, which the committee regarded as immodest. *Chariots of Fire*, a highly successful film on the life of Abrahams, stressed an antisemitic undertone of his time at Cambridge. Though he did not live to see the film, Abrahams, on his own testimony, would certainly have regarded such a portrayal as over-fanciful.

Before the next Olympic games, held in the stade de Colombes in Paris in 1924, Abrahams trained assiduously with his north-country coach Sam Mussabini, a French

Harold Maurice Abrahams (1899–1978), by A. R. Coster, 1924 [after winning the 100 yards at the AAA championship at Stamford Bridge, London, on 21 June 1924]

Arab. For nine months they worked on the theory of perfecting the start, on arm action, control of the stride pattern, and a then-unique 'drop' finish of the torso on to the tape. As a stickler for accuracy, Abrahams would have regarded the portrayal of Mussabini in the stade de Colombes (whereas he remained anxiously in Britain) as an excess of cinematic licence. At the 1924 Amateur Athletics Association (AAA) championship Abrahams won the 100 yards in 9.9 seconds but was still a fifth of a second outside the British record set the previous year by the great Scottish rugby and athletic hero and 440-yard champion Eric Liddell. In Paris the twenty-three eliminating heats to bring the seventy-five starters down to twelve semi-finalists were to be staged on Sunday 6 July and Liddell, a strong sabbatarian, felt impelled to confine himself to the 200 and 400 metres, in which he took the bronze medal in the shorter event and the gold medal for 400 metres in a time which gave him the metric world record. Abrahams equalled the Olympic record in the 100 metres in the second round with 10.6 seconds and next day, despite being badly 'left' in a poor start in the semi-final, came through (again in 10.6 seconds) to beat by inches the world record holder, Charles Paddock, from the USA. Abrahams later said that the next three-and-three-quarter hours were the worst in his life because now he knew he could win. At 7.05 p.m. he came out with the four Americans, Paddock, Scholz, Murchison, and Bowman, and the Oxford Rhodes scholar Arthur Porritt, from New Zealand.

Abrahams was drawn in lane four and got a perfect start. He showed fractionally ahead at half-way and dropped on to the tape 2 feet clear of Scholz, with Porritt beating Bowman for third. His winning time of 10.52 seconds would under later rules have been returned as 10.5 but was rounded up to 10.6. Abrahams thus set three Olympic record-equalling performances in the space of twenty-six hours. In Paris there were no flag-raising victory ceremonies. His gold medal, sadly later stolen, was sent to him by post. In May 1925 Abrahams severely injured a leg when attempting to improve on his English native long-jump record of 24 feet 2½ inches (7.38 metres), which had been set at Woolwich and which survived for more than thirty years.

His athletic career ended, Abrahams applied his analytical mind to the bar, to which he had been called at the Inner Temple in 1924, and where he practised until 1940. He also engaged in athletics administration and journalism with the *Sunday Times* (1925–67), and was a consummate radio broadcaster with the BBC for fifty years (1924–74). Against the stolid petty opposition of senior office-holders in various governing bodies, often athletes *manqués*, he managed by sheer force of personality and with very few allies to raise athletics from a minor to a major national sport. His innovative mind and drafting ability enabled him to rewrite the AAA rules of competition which themselves transformed the rules of the International Amateur Athletic Federation. He was possessed of a fresh resonant voice, while his clear diction and wide vocabulary were models for any English speaker.

Abrahams served as honorary treasurer (1948–68) and chairman (1948–75) of the British Amateur Athletic Board. In November 1976 he was elected president of the AAA. He was an unrivalled compiler of athletics statistics and was founder president of both the world and British associations in this field, the Association of Track and Field Statisticians (instituted in 1950) and the National Union of Track Statisticians (instituted in 1956). His *Oxford versus Cambridge, 1827–1930* (compiled with J. Bruce-Kerr, 1931), which listed all the 7489 blues, inevitably resulted in the exposure of a number of self-appointed blues in the bars and clubs of the world. During the Second World War he was with the Ministry of Economic Warfare (1939–44) and then with the new Ministry of Town and Country Planning until 1963. He was secretary of the National Parks Commission (1950–63). He was appointed CBE in 1957.

In 1936 Abrahams married Sybil Marjorie, daughter of Claude Pilington Evers, assistant master at Rugby School. She was a D'Oyly Carte singer and producer of light opera and died suddenly in 1963. During his fourteen years as a widower, Abrahams always carried a gold medallion bearing her effigy in profile. This he privately referred to as 'my real gold medal'. They had an adopted daughter and an adopted son. Abrahams died on 14 January 1978 at Chase Farm Hospital, Enfield, London.

NORRIS MCWHIRTER

Sources private information (2004) · personal knowledge (2004) · *The Times* (16 Jan 1978) · *The Times* (24 Jan 1978) [obit. of the marquess of Exeter] · M. Watman, 'The legendary Harold Abrahams', *Athletics Weekly* (28 Jan 1978), 16–17, 20–21 · P. Lovesey, *The official centenary history of the Amateur Athletics Association* (1979) · CGPLA Eng. & Wales (1978)

Archives U. Birm. L., papers | FILM BFI NFTVA, sports footage | SOUND BL NSA, performance recording

Likenesses photographs, 1923–9, Hult. Arch. · A. R. Coster, photograph, 1924, Hult. Arch. [see illus.] · photograph, 1924, CUL; repro. in Lovesey, *Official centenary history*, 77

Wealth at death £27,425: probate, 2 June 1978, CGPLA Eng. & Wales

Abrahams, Sir **Lionel Barnett** (1869–1919), economist and civil servant, was born in London on 9 December 1869, the only son of Mordecai Abrahams, secretary to the Initiation Society. Educated at the City of London School and Balliol College, Oxford, where he was an exhibitioner between 1892 and 1896 and won the Arnold historical essay prize in 1894, he headed the civil service list in 1893, electing to join the India Office. Marriage to Lucy, daughter of N. S. Joseph, followed in 1896. They had one son. In 1898 Abrahams became secretary to the Indian currency committee, an appointment which brought him into close contact with Indian currency affairs during an eventful period of their history and with which he remained closely associated during the next two decades as assistant financial secretary at the India Office (1901), financial secretary (1902–11), and assistant under-secretary of state for India (1911–17). He also served on departmental committees on Indian railway administration and finance (1907–8) and west African finance (1912), and was a member of the Indian wheat committee (1915).

Known to have been John Maynard Keynes's mentor on Indian finance, Abrahams is rarely spoken of outside the context of the economist's early career. Even the recognition accorded to him by the editor of Keynes's *Collected Writings* as the 'moulder and manipulator of India's involved but efficient financial system' (p. 38) does inadequate justice to the wider significance of his contribution. Although the idea derived from David Ricardo, Abrahams was among the first consciously to implement the gold exchange standard, which enabled countries to settle their external accounts in major currencies, helping thereby to reduce their dependence on gold and expand world trade. India became a pioneer of this new system when the rupee was placed on it at the turn of the century, and during the next few years Abrahams perfected the type of management and intervention the gold exchange standard required to make its working mimic the gold standard. According to R. S. Sayers his contributions were also of 'high importance in the development of ideas on central banking', of which he was an early, if somewhat unconventional, exponent. Nor was he loath to advance unorthodox policies such as floating the rupee exchange rate to mitigate the impact of an unstable global environment on the Indian economy. Floating exchange rates too had few supporters when he proposed them in 1919. But both this idea and the gold exchange standard were adopted widely in later years.

Sayers recalls Keynes going 'out of his way', while lecturing in Cambridge in 1928, 'to pay tribute to the perception and originality' of Lionel Abrahams. Others, including officials of the government he served with rare ability and imagination during a quarter-century spent at the India Office, and posterity, have however been less generous. His relative anonymity among historians of India too is a puzzle. An answer to this may lie partly in the somewhat technical nature of his achievements and the erroneous view that by the time of his death a few days before his fiftieth birthday they had been undone by the economic shocks of the First World War.

Abrahams was created Companion of the Bath in 1908 and made Knight Commander of the Bath in 1915. The history and social and religious life of his community also engaged his interest. A member at one time of the Jewish Board of Guardians, he contributed to the *Jewish Quarterly Review* and was the author of *The Expulsion of the Jews from England in 1290*. He also wrote articles entitled 'The economic position and influence of Jews in England' and 'The exchequer of the Jews' for the *Palgrave Dictionary of Political Economy*. He died at his home, 18 Porchester Terrace, Hyde Park, London, on 30 November 1919.

G. BALACHANDRAN

Sources G. Balachandran, *John Bullion's empire: Britain's gold problem and India between the wars* (1996) · *The collected writings of John Maynard Keynes*, ed. D. Moggridge and E. Johnson, 15 (1971) · R. S. Sayers, 'The young Keynes', *Economic Journal*, 82 (1972), 591–9 · *The Times* (2 Dec 1919) · d. cert.
Archives BL OIOC | CUL, Hardinge MSS
Wealth at death £9963 18s. 5d.: probate, 16 March 1920, CGPLA Eng. & Wales

Abrahams, **Louis Barnett** (1839–1918), headmaster, was born on 3 October 1839 at Swansea, the son of Barnett Abrahams (1785–1868) and his second wife, Hannah (*fl.* 1820–1868), the daughter of Locabel Levy of Lissa, Poland. There was also one daughter of this marriage. His father took the position of *chazan*, or synagogue cantor, in the Jewish congregation of Manchester in 1845.

Abrahams received his early education at the Hebrew School of the Manchester congregation, but suffered a breakdown in health and was sent to live with his uncle, Rabbi Aaron, a rabbinic judge (*dayan*) of the London Ashkenazi community. He entered the Jews' Free School, situated in Bell Lane, Whitechapel, as a pupil, and was taken on probation in 1854 as a pupil teacher by the headmaster, Moses Angel. Awarded the degree of BA by the University of London in 1863, he qualified by 1864 as a certified assistant teacher. He was singled out by being given charge of the seventh standard, which he taught for the next twenty years. Abrahams married on 11 February 1869 Fannie Rosetta (*b.* 1848), eldest daughter of Ephraim Mosely. A son and daughter were born in 1870 and 1871 respectively at 77 Tavistock Crescent, London.

In 1869 the committee of the council on education raised his teacher's certificate, unusually, from the fourth degree to the first class of the third degree. By 1870 he was head of English at the Jews' Free School. In 1874, after graduating with honours from the Tonic Sol-Fa College, he was appointed superintendent of musical studies, and introduced the teaching of singing into the school. Abrahams was elected vice-master in 1884 with the practical management of the school in his hands. In 1897 he became headmaster on the retirement of Moses Angel, under the rules of the London county council, into whose control the school had passed.

From 1884 onwards the effects were felt at the school of the influx of Russian Jews. Most of the children were unable to speak English. Although endeavouring to preserve a Jewish atmosphere at the school, Abrahams was opposed to the use of Yiddish, feeling it was a barrier to integration. The Anglicization of the pupils became in his eyes even more important as a bulwark against anti-semitism. Abrahams instituted the first uniformed cadet corps to be introduced inside an elementary school and established a corps of the Jewish Lads' Brigade. A gymnasium was erected, swimming baths were started, and sports organized. With the erection of the Rothschild wing in 1897, he was able to supervise a technical school.

Abrahams required all his pupil teachers to enter training college. His difficulties increased after the passing of the Education Acts of 1902–3, as these involved a loss of independence and an increasing reliance on government funding. He also had to deal with a group of trade-union-orientated teachers. Despite his administrative duties, he nevertheless found time to compile a manual of scripture history for school use. As well as translating a Jewish prayer book into English, he composed a chronological history of England for his pupils.

Louis Barnett Abrahams retired in 1907, having served the Jews' Free School for nearly fifty-four years and seen it grow into the largest elementary school in the country. He was presented with his portrait, which still hangs in the school. As well as his pioneering work at the school he acted as the first editor of the *Jewish Record* in 1868. He also served as honorary secretary of the Jewish Religious Education Board at its foundation, treasurer of the Jewish branch of the Happy Evening Society, vice-president of the League of Mercy, and as a member of the Maccabean Physical Training Committee. Abrahams retired to Westcliff-on-Sea and became honorary president of the synagogue, finally settling at The Retreat, Portland Road, Hove, where he died on 3 June 1918, survived by his wife.

DOREEN BERGER

Sources *Jewish Chronicle* (8 June 1918) · G. Black, *JFS: the history of the Jews' Free School, London, since 1732* (1998) · I. Singer and others, eds., *The Jewish encyclopedia*, 12 vols. (1901–6) · Great Synagogue Marriage Records, Mormons (Church of Latter Day Saints) [microfilm] · *Jewish Record* (Dec 1868) · *CGPLA Eng. & Wales* (1918)
Likenesses S. J. Solomon, portrait, 1908, Jews' Free School, London
Wealth at death £5316 6s. 8d.: probate, 10 Sept 1918, *CGPLA Eng. & Wales*

Abram, Annie (1869–1930), historian, was born at 45 Myddelton Square, Clerkenwell, London, on 26 May 1869, the younger daughter and fourth child of George Abram (1833–1897?), law stationer, and his first wife, Ann Arding (1835–1869), who died a month later. Her name was originally registered as Edith Mary, but was altered to Annie, presumably after her mother's death. Educated at home and in a private school, in 1902, aged thirty-three, she entered Girton College, Cambridge, to read for the historical tripos; how she had spent the intervening years is unknown. Spurred on by teachers such as William Cunningham, a pioneer of economic history, and his ally Ellen McArthur, armed with good classes in the tripos (a first in part one in 1904, a second in part two in 1905), and taking her BA from Trinity College, Dublin, in 1906 (Cambridge degrees being still closed to women), she enrolled as a postgraduate student at the London School of Economics.

Other Girtonians had already taken this route, most recently Alice Murray (Radice), whose paper—'exceedingly interesting and in many places highly amusing' (*Girton Review*, May 1903, 2)—to the college History Club, 'The social state of England during the Wars of the Roses', may first have attracted her to the period and topics she would make her own. In 1909 she was awarded the London degree of DSc for her dissertation, 'Social England in the fifteenth century: a study of the effects of economic conditions', which was published the same year; it was followed in 1913 by *English Life and Manners in the Later Middle Ages*, broader in scope than its predecessor and enriched by numerous illustrations of her own choosing, which she dedicated 'to the memory of my father'. Articles she published subsequently (there were no more books) included 'Women traders in medieval London' (*Economic Journal*) and 'Military service in a Flemish commune: Bruges, 1288–1480' (*History*), both 1916; the latter seems to represent her only excursion, historically speaking, across the channel.

Abram's evocative accounts of everyday life in late medieval England are based on an impressively wide array of primary sources, ranging from the early Chancery proceedings through customs accounts, wills, and private correspondence to cookery books, jewellery, and common artefacts; and although towns tend to predominate, the countryside is not neglected. Her habit of weighing medieval practices and attitudes against what she regarded as their modern equivalents, while it irritated one reviewer, in retrospect provides a telling commentary on conditions in her own day. Elected as a fellow of the Royal Historical Society in 1911, she long continued to be regarded as an authority in her field.

Annie Abram remained single and left no personal papers. From 1905 to 1907 she held part-time teaching appointments at both Girton and Westfield colleges. While there is no record of other paid employment, she may conceivably have played a part in the family business, Abram & Son, whose premises in Middle Temple Gateway were conveniently close to the Public Record Office. From about 1902 she made her home in Hampstead, initially with her brother Ernest and from 1911, still close to friends and family, in a series of lodgings or private apartments. She died at 12 Mansfield Road, Aldrington, Hove, Sussex, from enteritis on 17 October 1930, leaving an estate of well over £10,000. She bequeathed £200 and her clothes to the Church Army and £50 to the Sailors' Orphan Girls' School and Home in Hampstead.

JANET SONDHEIMER

Sources K. T. Butler and H. I. McMorran, eds., *Girton College register, 1869–1946* (1948) · *Girton Review* (1902–31) · census returns, 1861, 1881 · *TRHS* (1911–30) · *The Times* (18 Dec 1930) · b. cert. · d. cert. · index of deaths, June–Sept 1897, General Register Office for England
Wealth at death £10,408 2s.: probate, 12 Dec 1930, *CGPLA Eng. & Wales*

Abrams, Harriett (*c*.1758–1821), singer and composer, was, according to her niece's husband, Thomas Adolphus Trollope, the daughter of a man who came to England 'in the suite of some Hanoverian minister, in what capacity I never heard' (Trollope, 151). She was described by William Thomas Parke as a pupil of Thomas Augustine Arne, but this is not apparent from Arne's reference to her in a letter to David Garrick in September 1775. A soprano, she made her début on 28 October 1775 at Drury Lane Theatre, London, as the Little Gypsy in *May Day*, an afterpiece written for her by Garrick with music by Arne. William Hopkins, the company's prompter, noted in his diary:

> Miss Abrams (a Jew) about 17 Years old. She is very Small a Swarthy Complexion, has a very Sweet Voice & a fine Shake, but not quite power enough yet—both the Piece & the Young Lady were receiv'd with great Applause.   (Stein, 155)

She sang for five seasons at Drury Lane in musical afterpieces and plays, notably as an Italian Girl in Sheridan's *The Critic* on 30 October 1779, and then became a concert singer. From 1781 until the end of the decade Miss Abrams was a leading London soloist, appearing in the Concerts of Antient Music, the Academy of Ancient Music, and concert series organized by Venanzio Rauzzini and Johann Peter Salomon. She sang at Salisbury, Cambridge, Winchester, Oxford, and Birmingham, at the Three Choirs meetings of 1781 and 1782, and in the Handel commemoration concerts at Westminster Abbey of 1784–7 and 1790. Charles Burney, writing of the 1784 Handel performances, praised the sweetness, taste, and expression of her singing and noted that although her voice was not regarded as theatrical she was audible in every part of the abbey.

Harriett's sister, Miss G. Abrams, who took child roles at Drury Lane during Harriett's last two seasons there, was probably the Miss Abrams junior who sang with her sister in concerts in 1781–2. Nothing more is known of her. Jane Abrams (*c*.1766–1813/14) made her first appearance when she sang at Harriett's benefit concert in 1782, and a third sister, the contralto Theodosia [*see below*], joined Miss Abrams and Miss Abrams junior in the Concerts of Antient Music in 1783. Jane appears to have withdrawn from public performance, while Harriett and Theodosia continued to appear as soloists and became particularly admired as a duo, the Miss Abrams. They sang together in public concerts and increasingly at private entertainments in the houses of the aristocracy. Harriett also organized concerts, including a series at the home of George Venables-Vernon, second Baron Vernon, in winter 1791–2 when the oboist William Thomas Parke was one of the musicians she engaged. After 1791 the sisters' only advertised appearances were in Harriett's annual benefits, at which Joseph Haydn presided at the pianoforte in 1792, 1794, and 1795. Eliza (*c*.1776–1831), the youngest of the Abrams sisters, played piano concertos in Harriett's 1788 and 1789 benefits and from 1790 also sang in vocal ensembles with her sisters. Two brothers, the violinist William and the cellist Charles, worked as professional musicians and, according to Doane's *Musical Directory* (1794), shared a house with their sisters. Flora Abrams, who played the violin at minor venues between 1776 and 1782, may have been a relative.

Harriett Abrams was a successful composer of songs, duets, and trios. She published two sets of Italian and English canzonets, a collection of sixteen Scottish songs harmonized for two and three voices, and, in 1803, a book of twelve songs dedicated 'with Her Majesty's most Gracious Permission' to Queen Charlotte. There are also about a dozen separately published songs, several of which quickly appeared in editions in the USA. Her most frequently republished piece was *Crazy Jane* (1799), a setting of a poem by Matthew 'Monk' Lewis, whose first biographer wrote: 'the ballad has been wedded to music by several composers; but the original and most popular melody was by the celebrated Miss Abrams, who introduced and sung it herself at fashionable parties' (Baron-Wilson, 189).

On 2 June 1791 Harriett was baptized at St George's, Hanover Square, together with Jane, Theodosia, Eliza, and their elder sister Charlotte, who married a few days later. In 1799 John Philip Kemble supped with the unmarried Abrams sisters at their London home, met them at the house of the earl and countess of Mount Edgcumbe, and dined with them at Broadstairs, Kent, in August. After Theodosia's marriage in 1804, the sisters retired to Devon to 'enjoy the well earned emoluments of their profession' (Lysons, 215). When Harriett made her will in 1819, she had £5770 in stocks, the lease of a house in Montague Square, St Marylebone, and a small estate at Englefield Green, near Egham, Surrey. She died at Theodosia's home, The Braddons, South-Hill, Torquay, Devon, on 8 March 1821 and was buried at St Saviour, Tormoham, Devon, on 12 March 1821. According to Mount Edgcumbe, Harriett, Theodosia, and Eliza, 'who were unrivalled in their line, and whose united voices formed the very perfection of harmony' (Edgcumbe, 1824, 142), continued to sing together to the delight of their friends until shortly before Harriett's death.

Theodosia Abrams [*married names* Fisher, Garrow] (*c*.1769–1849), singer, seems to have made her début in the Concerts of Antient Music in 1783, and she was the youngest of the principal vocal performers listed for the 1784 Handel commemoration concerts. She then appeared in almost every concert and private entertainment in which Harriett performed, singing as a soloist as well as in ensembles. On 6 August 1804, at Plympton St Maurice, Devon, she married the 21-year-old Thomas Fisher (1782–1810), a captain in the North Devon militia, who died in May or June 1810, leaving her with two children, Charles and Harriett. On 17 March 1812, at St Margaret's, Westminster, she married Joseph Garrow (1789–1857), the clever, musical, and artistic son of a Scottish father and Indian mother, who had trained as a lawyer but never practised. Their only child, Theodosia [*see* Trollope, Theodosia], was born on 28 November 1816. The Garrows lived in Torquay, where Joseph became the friend and correspondent of Walter Savage Landor and where the poet Elizabeth Barrett found him 'a sensible intelligent man & an active magistrate' (*Letters of Elizabeth Barrett Browning*, 1.316). On a continental tour with her parents, the younger Theodosia met Thomas Adolphus *Trollope, elder brother of the novelist Anthony Trollope, and they married in April 1848. Tom Trollope remembered his mother-in-law as still vigorous, 'a very fierce old lady' with 'brilliant and fierce black eyes' (Trollope, 156). He relates how the composer and pianist John Baptist Cramer had told him admiringly that she had been able to pick out a false note played by a single instrument in a large orchestra. Mount Edgcumbe described Theodosia's voice as the most beautiful contralto he had ever heard, and found it still unimpaired in 1834. Her health declined after the death of her daughter Harriett in Florence on 12 November 1848 and the Garrows returned to England the following June. She died at her home, The Braddons, South-Hill, Torquay, Devon, on 4 November 1849. Her death was attributed on her death certificate to deranged digestion, abscess, and exhaustion. She was buried at St Saviour, Tormoham, Devon, on 8 November 1849.

OLIVE BALDWIN and THELMA WILSON

Sources G. W. Stone, ed., *The London stage, 1660–1800*, pt 4: *1747–1776* (1962) · C. B. Hogan, ed., *The London stage, 1660–1800*, pt 5: *1776–1800* (1968) · S. McVeigh, 'Calendar of London Concerts, 1750–1800', Goldsmiths College, London [restricted-access database] · summary account book of Drury Lane Theatre, BL, Add. MS 29709 · *The letters of David Garrick*, ed. D. M. Little and G. M. Kahrl, 1 (1963) · E. P. Stein, *David Garrick, dramatist* (1938) · D. J. Reid, 'Some festival programmes of the eighteenth and nineteenth centuries [pts 1–2]', *Royal Musical Association Research Chronicle*, 5 (1965), 51–79; 6 (1966), 3–23 · B. Pritchard and D. J. Reid, 'Some festival programmes of the eighteenth and nineteenth centuries [pt 4]', *Royal Musical Association Research Chronicle*, 8 (1970), 1–22 · D. Lysons, *History of the origins and proceedings of the meeting of the Three Choirs* (1812) · C. Burney, *An account of the musical performances … in commemoration of Handel* (1785) · *Concerts of Antient Music as performed at the New Rooms, Tottenham Street* (1781–6) [programme bks] · *Concerts of Antient Music as performed at the New Rooms, Tottenham Street* (1788–9) [programme bks] · R. Edgcumbe, *Musical reminiscences of an old amateur* (1824) · R. Edgcumbe, *Musical reminiscences, containing an account of the Italian opera in England from 1773*, 4th edn (1834) · W. T. Parke, *Musical memoirs*, 1 (1830) · H. C. Robbins Landon, *Haydn in England: 1791–1795* (1976), vol. 3 of *Haydn: chronicle and works* · S. McVeigh, *Concert life in London from Mozart to Haydn* (1993) · professional memoranda of John Philip Kemble, BL, Add. MS 31973 · M. Baron-Wilson, *The life and correspondence of M. G. Lewis*, 1 (1839) · 'Abrams, Harriett', *The catalogue of printed music at the British Library to 1980*, ed. L. Baillie, 1 (1981) · B. G. Jackson, *A guide to surviving music by women from the 16th through the 18th century* (1994) · J. Doane, *A musical directory for the year 1794* (1794) · *GM*, 1st ser., 80 (1810), 597 · *GM*, 1st ser., 82/1 (1812), 386 · T. A. Trollope, *What I remember*, 2 (1887) · *The letters of Elizabeth Barrett Browning to Mary Russell Mitford*, ed. M. B. Raymond and M. R. Sullivan (1983) · *Torquay and Tor Directory and General Advertiser for the South of Devon* (29 Nov 1848) · *Torquay and Tor Directory and General Advertiser for the South of Devon* (20 June 1849) · *Torquay and Tor Directory and General Advertiser for the South of Devon* (4 July 1849) · *Torquay and Tor Directory and General Advertiser for the South of Devon* (7 Nov 1849) · parish register, Westminster, St George's, Hanover Square, 2 June 1791 [baptisms] · parish register, Devon, Plympton St Maurice, 6 Aug 1804 [marriage: Theodosia Abrams and Thomas Fisher] · parish register, Westminster, St Margaret's, 17 March 1812 [marriage: Theodosia Abrams and Joseph Garrow] · parish register, Devon, Tormoham, St Saviour, 12 March 1821, burial: Harriett Abrams · parish register, Devon, Tormoham, St Saviour, 8 Nov 1849 [burial: Theodosia Garrow] · will, PRO, PROB 11/1642, fol. 247 · will of Eliza Abrams, PRO, PROB 11/1791A, fol. 556 · administration of goods of Jane Abrams, PRO, PROB 6/190, fol. 179

Likenesses print, pubd 1778 (as Sylvia in *Cymon*), repro. in *The Vocal Magazine* (1778) · J. Nixon, engraving, 1788 (*A duett at the Hanover Square concert*; after his watercolour caricature, 1788) · J. Nixon, watercolour caricature, 1788 (*Harrison's concert, Hanover Sqr., duett Miss Abram's*), V&A

Wealth at death £5770 in bonds and stocks, plus house in Montague Square, and small estate at Englefield Green, near Egham, Surrey: will, PRO, PROB 11/1642, fol. 247

Abrams, Mark Alexander [*formerly* Max Alexander Abramowitz] (1906–1994), social scientist, was born at 57 Balfour Road, Edmonton, London, on 27 April 1906, one of eight children born to Abraham (Abram) Abramowitz, also known as Abramovich or Abrams, and his wife, Annie (Hannah), *née* Issercorwitz. His father was a journeyman bootmaker and later a shopowner and house agent, and, according to Abrams, a 'philosophical anarchist'. His parents were immigrants of Latvian and Lithuanian Jewish stock. Abrams had some early interest in the rabbinate, but in the event, after Latymer School, Edmonton, he decided to study economics at the London School of Economics. On 20 June 1931 he married Una Strugnell (1906–1981), schoolteacher, daughter of Leonard Strugnell, insurance clerk. They had one son and one daughter.

Abrams was a fellow at the Brookings Institute in Washington, DC, from 1931 to 1933, and then returned to England to join the research department of the London Press Exchange (LPE), at that time one of Britain's leading advertising agencies. During the mid- to late 1930s he undertook the pioneering work in social investigation which was to make him influential in establishing and developing elements of sociology, in social and market research, and in opinion polling. Large-scale surveys of newspaper and magazine readership, and of consumer behaviour, established his authority in both developing and evaluating mass communications—an authority he was to retain for decades. During the same period he established contacts with like-minded scientists abroad. He did much to help refugees escape from Nazi Europe, and was one of Sigmund Freud's helpers in his final move to England in 1939.

During the Second World War, Abrams worked first with the overseas department of the BBC, from 1939 to 1941, then with the psychological warfare board, and then at Supreme Headquarters Allied Expeditionary Force (SHAEF). In these latter positions he undertook further pioneering survey work, at the psychological warfare board investigating, among other things, the impact of bombing on civilian morale. His work on food consumption during the war was a turning point in government data collection. The National Food Survey, a large-scale investigation into the nature and extent of national food consumption, ran, in one form or another, for the next sixty years. Indeed, Abrams's work was instrumental in establishing the widespread use of survey research to monitor the population's experience, needs, and beliefs, and set a pattern which survived and grew into the twenty-first century.

During the late 1940s the market and social research industries underwent major expansion. In 1946 Abrams founded Research Services Ltd, which developed into one of the UK's largest and most influential survey research companies. He also established the Market Research Society, the professional association for Britain's research business. He remained managing director, and then chairman, of Research Services Ltd until 1970. His first marriage having been dissolved in 1951, on 20 March 1953 he married Jean Bird (*b.* 1917), journalist, daughter of Frederick Lucien Bird, municipal research director. They had one daughter.

In the 1950s and 1960s Abrams had strong links with the Labour Party and undertook many private polls for them. He was a member of the Metrication Board from 1969 to 1979. In 1970 he left Research Services Ltd to become director of the Survey Research Unit at the Social Science Research Council. Then, in 1976—at the age of seventy—he became research director at Age Concern. During this same period he was an adviser to the Consumers' Association and, from 1978 until his death, was a vice-president of the Policy Studies Institute. Also, though less formally, he encouraged the careers of a number of young researchers.

In 1981 Abrams's son Philip Abrams, at the time professor of sociology at Durham University, died suddenly. This was a difficult period but he drew strength from his wife, his daughters, his studies, and his love of music. He died at the Royal Sussex County Hospital, Brighton, on 25 September 1994; he was survived by his wife and daughters.

Abrams was one of the founding fathers of structured social investigation, and his work on its techniques, utilization, and evaluation had a major impact on the post-1945 growth in the use of survey research by commerce and government. A small but vivacious and humorous man, with twinkling eyes and a love of argument (he retained his enthusiasms well into his eighties), he was a courageous, experimental, and occasionally idiosyncratic researcher who believed that the views of all members of society should be assessed and taken into account in policy formulation. He was accepted and respected both in academia and in the commercial sector, and, unusually for the period, managed to bridge the gap between the two. He believed in research not only as a means of describing society, but as an instrument to help improve it. He was a skilled raconteur and debater, with a profound belief in democracy.   MICHAEL WARREN

Sources *The Guardian* (27 Sept 1994) · *The Times* (29 Sept 1994) · *The Independent* (24 Oct 1994) · WWW, 1991–5 · b. cert. · m. certs. · d. cert. · personal knowledge (2004) · private information (2004) [family]
Archives CAC Cam., research papers incuding those relating to BBC Propaganda Research | SOUND BL NSA, oral history interview
Likenesses photograph, repro. in *The Times* · photograph, repro. in *The Independent*

Abrams, Theodosia (*c.*1769–1849). *See under* Abrams, Harriett (*c.*1758–1821).

Abramsky, Yehezkel (1886–1976), rabbinic scholar and Orthodox Jewish leader, was born on or about 7 February 1886 in Dashkovtsy, near Most and Grodno, Lithuania, the third child and eldest son of Mordecai Zalman Abramsky, a local timber merchant, and his wife, Freydel Goldin of Grodno. As a markedly promising Talmudic student he began while a boy the then usual peripatetic training at the *yeshivoth* (seminaries) of Telz, Mir, Slobodka, and particularly at Brisk under Hayyim Soloveitchik, the teacher and mentor he always venerated: and he earned his certification as a rabbi before he was eighteen. He married in 1909 Reizel (*d.* 1965), daughter of Israel Jonathan Jerusalimsky, head of the Jewish court at Iehumen, Russia. They had four sons.

Abramsky's ability as a jurisconsult was quickly recognized in Russia, and he was successively rabbi of Smolyan, Smolevich, and Slutzk. With the Bolshevik revolution and increasing attempts to repress traditional Jewish observance and culture, Abramsky exerted himself to encourage its continuation—for example, by surreptitious (albeit legal) arrangement for circumcisions. For the same purpose he was co-founder in 1928 of a Hebrew periodical—the last in Russia—*Yagdil Torah*, which after two issues was proscribed. The Soviet government understood well Abramsky's standing in Russian Jewry; and, partly concerned for its own reputation abroad, in 1926 and again in 1928 it refused him permission to leave and take up the rabbinate of Petah Tikvah in Palestine. Worse followed. Herbert Hoover, as president of the United States, sent an interfaith commission to investigate religious freedom in Russia as a prerequisite to establishing closer relations with the USSR. Abramsky, when interviewed, had said nothing; his silence was construed by the authorities as defamation of the Soviet Union, and he spent months eluding arrest. He was apprehended in 1929 and the death sentence demanded, but he was condemned (without trial) to five years' hard labour in Siberia.

Worldwide Jewish concern elicited diplomatic intervention, and in 1931, in exchange for six communists held by Chancellor Brüning's government in Germany, Abramsky was given a month to leave Russia. Two of his sons were retained as hostages, and to avoid endangering them Abramsky in 1935 declined to succeed A. I. Kook as Ashkenazi chief rabbi of Palestine. Anthony Eden, the British foreign secretary, personally intervened to secure their release in 1937, Abramsky having come to London in 1932 as rabbi of the right-wing Orthodox community (Mahzikey Ha-dath). He was naturalized a British subject in 1937.

The United Synagogue, whose dominance within the Orthodox community was secured by act of parliament, invited Abramsky to head its ecclesiastical court. After undertakings that there would be no lay pressure for unacceptable relaxations of the law, he accepted and discharged his duties with exemplary conscientiousness until his retirement to Jerusalem in 1951. Notably, he tightened up the standards of kosher slaughtering; and he stood firm against conversions to Judaism of dubious sincerity for matrimonial purposes.

Abramsky's clarity of exposition drew large audiences for his London discourses (delivered in Yiddish) on aspects of Jewish law: even more well attended were his twice-weekly lectures in Jerusalem *yeshivoth*, maintained until a few years before his death. As president of the Council of *Yeshivoth*, the Private Education League, and other national bodies he was no mere figurehead, and whenever he made representations to the Israeli government regarding the protection of religious interests, he was heard with unfailing respect.

Abramsky's scholarly work followed traditional rabbinic methodology, ignoring external influences and parallels in, for example, Roman law. It was prodigious and fruitful. A memorial volume, published in Hebrew in Jerusalem in 1978, collected his Talmudic *novellae* and *responsa*, but his major monument was the 24-volume *Hazon Yehezkel*, a commentary on the Tosefta or 'supplementary' digest of Jewish law compiled *c*.200 CE. Planned during the First World War, its approach was quite different from Lieberman's work which paralleled it in publication. The first volume appeared in 1925, the last in 1975; Abramsky had continued work on it in Siberia, smuggling it out on cigarette paper. In 1955 he was the first recipient of the Israel prize for literature; and he was the first commentator whose notes to the Talmud were printed alongside the classical commentaries in his own lifetime.

More significant than Abramsky's appointments and honours were his influence, his transparent saintliness, and his personal magnetism. Sir Robert Waley Cohen, lay leader of the United Synagogue and of an upper-class English background, recognized his sincerity and responded to it. And once, when an assimilated Jew, applying for a religious divorce, sneered at the 'medievalism' of Abramsky's court, he met with a dignified rebuke that elicited apology. His leadership in England partly stimulated more intense observance and wider familiarity with rabbinic sources in segments of the United Synagogue, but conversely it accentuated Orthodox disregard for the analogously reinvigorated Reform community. Besides his world stature in rabbinical scholarship, Abramsky was respected in Israel as the last outstanding representative of a Jewish cultural life that had for 400 years shaped the Jewries of Russia and Poland: and the crowd (estimated at perhaps 40,000) attending his funeral made it the largest ever seen in Jerusalem, where he had died on 19 September 1976.   RAPHAEL LOEWE, *rev.*

Sources *The Times* (20 Sept 1976) · *Jerusalem Post* (20 Sept 1976) · *Jewish Chronicle* (24 Sept 1976) · *Jewish Chronicle* (1 Oct 1976) · *Jewish Chronicle* (8 Oct 1976) · private information (1986) [family; C. Abramsky]
Archives priv. coll.
Likenesses portrait, repro. in *Encyclopaedia Judaica* (1971), vol. 2, p. 171

Abu al-Hasan [Abū'l-Ḥasan; *known as* Mirza Abu al-Hasan Shirazi] (**1776–1846**), diplomatist for Persia, was born in Shiraz, the second son of Mirza Muhammad Ali, a high-ranking Persian court official. His mother was also closely connected with the court through her brother, Hadji Ibrahim Khan, the powerful prime minister of Agha Muhammad Shah, who reigned from 1787 to 1797; his fall from grace early in the next reign caused members of the family, including Abu al-Hasan, then governor of Shustar and married to Ibrahim Khan's daughter, to flee for their lives. After making the Mecca pilgrimage Abu al-Hasan sought refuge in India. Pardoned by the shah after more than two years there, he returned to Persia and served as assistant

to his brother-in-law, the shah's second minister. In Tehran he came to the attention of the British minister Harford Jones, who suggested to the shah that Abu al-Hasan should accompany James Morier to London to secure the finalization of the Anglo-Persian preliminary treaty of friendship and alliance, signed in Tehran in March 1809.

Abu al-Hasan was the first Persian envoy to London since 1626. Though he spent less than eight months in England (November 1809–July 1810) he quickly made a remarkable impression. The British government, anxious for Persian friendship, paid him exceptional attention; high society, and especially women, lionized him. He was the first Persian to become a freemason in England. He quickly learnt passable English, and owed his social success to personality, wit, and intelligence, combined with engaging manners and a fine presence—his tall, handsome figure enhanced by a flowing black beard and exotic dress.

For Abu al-Hasan's services in London the shah appointed him a khan, while the East India Company, on the advice of Gore Ouseley, awarded him a life pension, which damaged his reputation among his fellow countrymen but not his career. He took part in peace negotiations with the Russians, signing the treaties of Gulestan (1813) and Turkmanchai (1828), and went as ambassador to St Petersburg (1814–16) in an unsuccessful attempt to secure the return of Georgia. Although his second and last mission to England (May 1819–March 1820) was politically disappointing, the British government having lost interest in Persia and being unwilling to support its claims against Russia, he again attracted great attention, this time mainly on account of a mysterious 'fair Circassian' woman who arrived with him but left before his departure. He paid brief visits to Edinburgh and Dublin before returning to Tehran, where he was foreign minister from 1824 to 1834 and again from 1840 until his death in 1846. He played a helpful role in the negotiation of the Anglo-Persian commercial treaty of 1841. Abu al-Hasan justifiably resented his friend Morier's ill-disguised portrayal of him as Mirza Firouz in his two *Hajji Baba of Ispahan* novels.

DENIS WRIGHT

Sources D. Wright, *The Persians among the English* (1985), 53–69 · J. Morier, *A journey through Persia, Armenia and Asia Minor to Constantinople in the years 1808 and 1809* (1812) · J. Morier, *A second journey through Persia, Armenia and Asia Minor to Constantinople between the years 1810 and 1816* (1818) · Radstock, 'A slight sketch of the character, person etc. of Abul Hasan, envoy extraordinary from the king of Persia to the court of Great Britain from the years 1809 and 1810', *GM*, 1st ser., 90/1 (1820), 119–22 · Philoxenus Secundus [S. Weston], *Persian recreations, or, Oriental stories* (1812) · J. Kay, *A series of original portraits and caricature etchings … with biographical sketches and illustrative anecdotes*, ed. [H. Paton and others], 2 (1838), 300–09 · 'Sketches of society: memoir of the Persian ambassador', *Literary Gazette* (8 May 1819), 299–300 · I. M. Abu al-Hasan, *A Persian at the court of King George, 1809–10: the journal of Mirza Abul Hassan Khan*, ed. and trans. M. M. Cloake (1988) · C. W. Millard, 'A diplomatic portrait: Lawrence's *The Persian ambassador*', *Apollo*, 85 (1967), 115–21 · H. Javadi, 'Abu'l Hasan Khan Ilci, mirza', *Encyclopaedia Iranica* (1985), 3.308–10 · J. B. Fraser, *Narrative of a journey into Khorasan in the years 1821 and 1822* (1825), 149–51 · I. Ra'in, *Mirza Abul Hasan Khan Ilchi* (1978) · PRO, FO 60/142

Archives BL, Hayrat Nameh (Book of wonders), abridged, Add. MS 23546 · Majles Library, Tehran, Hayrat Nameh (Book of wonders) | Balliol Oxf., Morier MSS · BL, Jones Brydges MSS, Add. MS 41768 · BL, Morier MSS, Add. MSS 33839–33844 · BL, Wellesley MSS, Add. MS 37285 · BL OIOC, East India Company MSS, L/PS/3/3, L/PS/5/541 · Bodl. Oxf., Gore Ouseley diaries · Hereford County Library, Kentchurch Court MSS · PRO, Foreign Office papers, FO 60 60/2, 4, 6, 11, 15, 19, 24, 68, 118 · PRO, Foreign Office papers, FO 248/47
Likenesses J. Bacon, two busts, 1810 · W. Beechey, oils, 1810, BL · T. Lawrence, oils, 1810, Fogg Museum, Cambridge, Massachusetts · M. Gauci, lithograph, 1819, BM · J. Lucas, mezzotint (after T. Lawrence), BM

Abudacnus, Josephus (*fl.* 1595–1643), scholar of oriental languages, was born in Cairo. His parents were Copts, his father probably connected with the Ottoman administration. His Arabic name, Yusuf ibn Abu Dhaqn, was Latinized as Josephus Abudacnus (or Barbatus). In 1595, after a rudimentary education in Cairo and already popular in ecclesiastical circles, he was entrusted with a letter from the Coptic patriarch Gabriel VIII to the pope, Clement VIII, who hoped to effect a union between the churches of Alexandria and Rome. On his arrival in Rome, Abudacnus converted to Catholicism and joined the Discalced Carmelites, changing his name to Brother Macarios but never actually professing. In Rome he acquired his knowledge of languages. To Turkish, Arabic, and Greek, which he had learnt in Egypt, he added Latin, Syriac, Aramaic, Hebrew, and above all Italian. By 1608 he had left the Carmelites and had moved to Paris, where he was employed as interpreter at the French court and gave some tuition in Arabic, even if he had little command of the classical language.

In Paris, Abudacnus met the Arabists at the Collège Royal and the Huguenot scholar Isaac Casaubon. His pupils included Casaubon's young friend Thomas Erpenius, the future professor of Arabic at Leiden. From Erpenius he acquired a letter of introduction to William Bedwell and, in the summer of 1610, set out for England. Benefiting from the Western interest in Eastern Christians, he approached, and was welcomed by, bishops and scholars, obtaining a letter from Richard Bancroft, archbishop of Canterbury, for John King, bishop of London and vice-chancellor of Oxford, and one from Thomas Bodley for his librarian Thomas James. Bodley was evidently charmed by the Egyptian visitor who 'speaketh French and Italian very readily; also Latin well enough, to explicat his minde: being likewise, as I ghesse, of a kind and honest disposition … I would be glad to understand', he continued, 'that he might be provided of a competent intertainment, to keep him in Oxon, lest Cambridge should endevour, as I make account they would, to draw him unto them' (*Letters of Sir Thomas Bodley*, 193–4).

Abudacnus arrived at Oxford in mid-August 1610 and lodged at St Mary Hall. At the university he gave some instruction in Arabic—we know neither how much nor to whom—and contributed a poem in Aramaic, Syriac, Arabic, and Turkish to the *Eidyllia* lamenting the death of Henry, prince of Wales (1612). He spent much time in London, where he dined with Bedwell and Lancelot Andrewes (then bishop of Ely), took part in the marriage festivities arranged for the king's daughter Elizabeth, and taught some basic Arabic to Miles Smith, the future bishop of Gloucester. He also encountered Ferdinand de Boisschot, the ambassador of the archdukes of the Spanish Netherlands, and, furnished with his letters, left England for Antwerp in the autumn of 1613.

In the Spanish Netherlands, Abudacnus, who now presented himself as former professor of Arabic at Oxford, claimed to teach 'all oriental languages'. He lectured to prospective missionaries in Antwerp, and then, after serving the Archduke Albert as Turkish interpreter, was appointed reader at the University of Louvain with the support, and at the expense, of the ruler. In Louvain, where he arrived in October 1615, he published a brief and derivative work on Hebrew grammar, the *Speculum Hebraicum* (1615), and compiled an Arabic grammar which remained in manuscript (Vienna, Österreichische Nationalbibliothek, MS 15161). His insistence on lecturing in Hebrew, however, infuriated the full professor in the subject, and led to his enforced resignation. In the late summer of 1618 he set out for the court of Maximilian of Bavaria in Munich, where he assisted the ducal librarian in cataloguing oriental manuscripts.

In the spring of 1622 Abudacnus made for the imperial court in Vienna. On his way he stopped in Linz to meet the astronomer Johann Kepler, who was as beguiled by him as Bodley had been and accorded him a letter for the imperial librarian Sebastian Tengnagel. During his short stay in Vienna, Abudacnus received his final appointment, as interpreter to the imperial envoys in Constantinople.

It was probably in Constantinople (where he arrived in 1623), rather than in Oxford, that Abudacnus completed the little work on which his reputation rests, his history of the Copts, the *Historia Jacobitarum*, a superficial account of the organization, ceremonies, and sacraments of the Church of Alexandria. The Oxford orientalist Humphrey Prideaux justifiably described it as 'pidleing' (Madan, 3.309). Yet it was the only study of the Copts written by a Copt to be known in Europe at the time, and was sometimes preferred to far better informed books by European scholars.

How the manuscript made its way to Oxford is a mystery, but it might have been taken back by the professor of Arabic, Edward Pococke, who was in Constantinople from 1637 to 1640. It was first published in Latin, presumably by Thomas Marshall, in 1675. In 1692 and 1693 it appeared in the English translation of Sir Edwin Sadlier, while the Latin version was reprinted in Lübeck in 1733 and in Leiden in 1740.

Abudacnus was dismissed from imperial service, and his name ceases to be mentioned, after the imperial resident Johann Rudolf Schmid was recalled to Vienna in 1643. Whatever his shortcomings as a scholar, he was one of the small number of Copts to travel in the West, and one of the very few to write anything between 1500 and 1700.

ALASTAIR HAMILTON

Sources A. Hamilton, 'An Egyptian traveller in the republic of letters: Josephus Barbatus or Abudacnus the Copt', *Journal of the Warburg and Courtauld Institutes*, 57 (1994), 123–50 · J. R. Jones, 'Learning

Arabic in Renaissance Europe (1505–1624)', PhD diss., SOAS, 1988 · G. Graf, *Geschichte der christlichen arabischen Literatur*, 4 (1951) · L. Scherman, 'Abudacnus (Barbatus), ein koptischer Orientalist aus dem siebzehnten Jahrhundert, und seine Beziehungen zu München', *Jahrbuch für Münchener Geschichte*, 2 (1888), 341–54 · H. de Vocht, 'Oriental languages in Louvain in the XVIIth century: Abudacnus and le Wyt de Luysant', *Le Muséon*, 59 (1946), 671–88 · *Letters of Sir Thomas Bodley to Thomas James, first keeper of the Bodleian Library*, ed. G. W. Wheeler (1926) · P. Meienberger, *Johann Rudolf Schmid zum Schwarzenhorn als kaiserlicher Resident in Konstantinopel in den Jahren 1629–1643* (1973) · V. Buri, *L'unione della chiesa copta con Roma sotto Clemente VIII* (1931) · F. Madan, *Oxford literature, 1651–1680* (1931), vol. 3 of *Oxford books: a bibliography of printed works* (1895–1931); repr. (1964)

Archives Österreichische Nationalbibliothek, Vienna, Arabic grammar, MS 15161 · Österreichische Nationalbibliothek, Vienna, letters to Tengnagel, MS 9737

Acca [St Acca] (*d.* **740**), bishop of Hexham, is best known as the disciple of Wilfrid and patron of Bede. He became a monk at an unknown date and joined the household of Bishop Bosa of York after 678; but he seems to have attached himself to Wilfrid after the latter's reinstatement in the reduced see of York in 686. He remained thereafter in Wilfrid's service until 709 or 710, when Wilfrid died, probably following him into exile in 691 and certainly accompanying him on his second journey to Rome in 703, when he was entertained by Archbishop Willibrord in Frisia. By then he seems to have become one of Wilfrid's closest associates: when Wilfrid recovered consciousness after suffering a near-fatal stroke at Meaux as he was returning from Rome, it was for Acca that he asked and to Acca whom he related the vision of St Michael that he had just experienced.

Although Wilfrid's kinsman, the priest Tatberht, seems to have been regarded, in Ripon at least, as Wilfrid's principal heir, it was Acca who in 709, in accordance with Wilfrid's dying wishes, succeeded to the bishopric and abbey of Hexham. As joint heir, therefore, he took an active part in the sponsoring of Wilfrid's cult, and together with Tatberht commissioned Stephen of Ripon's life. He was also active in sponsoring the cult of King Oswald of Northumbria, the site of whose victory at 'Maserfelth' was in the care of the Hexham community. Himself a notable scholar and leader of the chant (*cantor*), at Hexham, Acca continued his predecessor's policy of enrichment: he completed, it seems, churches which Wilfrid had begun late in life, and ornamented the abbatial church of St Andrew with fresh works of art, with sacred vessels, lamps, and treasures made of gold and precious stones, and with altar frontals made of silk. He also followed Wilfrid in promoting church music, taught in Hexham for twelve years by Maban, a singer trained in Kent, and in collecting relics of the apostles and martyrs which he installed in newly created chapels within the abbatial church. In addition, he built up the library, collecting works of theology and acts of the martyrs.

Perhaps Acca's most crucial role was as patron of Bede, whose diocesan he was and whose abbots (of Wearmouth-Jarrow) he customarily confirmed in office. Acca seems to have prompted Bede to write many of his biblical commentaries, in particular those on the gospels of Luke and Mark. The bishop's only surviving composition, a letter to Bede (addressed as 'most beloved'), suggests that he was both learned and persuasive. The letter, which records Acca's longstanding and oft-expressed desire that Bede should write about Luke, was expressly intended to preface that work. Studded with allusions to the Fathers, it argues that there was a need for someone as skilled as Bede to distil the difficult higher learning of the earlier commentary by Ambrose into something more digestible for the less accomplished readers of their own times.

Bede in return seems to have held Acca in high regard. He met and corresponded with his diocesan frequently, especially in the early years of his episcopate, and dedicated many of his biblical commentaries to him, referring to him in the warmest of terms as 'dearest' or 'most beloved of all bishops on earth' (*carissime, amantissime*, and 'dilectissime ac desiderantissime omnium qui in terris morantur antistitum'). His poem on the day of judgment concludes with an invocation of Acca, his father, whom he enjoins to live a fortunate life and to pray for him, Bede. He also accorded Acca a highly affectionate and laudatory notice in the *Historia ecclesiastica gentis Anglorum*.

Acca was still bishop of Hexham when Bede completed his *Historia* in 731, but was driven from his see in that year, or shortly afterwards, and was never restored. According to an unsupported post-conquest Hexham tradition, he became bishop of Whithorn. The reasons for Acca's downfall are obscure, but almost certainly they are bound up with contemporary dissension within the Northumbrian royal house which culminated in the temporary deposition and enforced tonsuring of King Ceolwulf in 731. Bede's lengthy jeremiad on the 'adversities which befall us', in the preface to *De templo*, written only a little before 731, perhaps alludes to these events.

Acca died in 740 and, although still unrestored, was buried in the cemetery at Hexham. His grave was marked by two grandly ornamented crosses, one apparently bearing his epitaph and now often identified with an inscribed stone finely carved with oval medallions of plant-scroll and preserved at Hexham Priory church. In the mid-eleventh century Acca became the object of a cult. His remains were translated to a feretory inside the church, where they became the focus of miracles, and the vestments in which he had been buried, together with other gravecloths, were removed and treated as relics. In 1154 there was a second translation, in which the bishop's remains, identified by a label, were enclosed in a casket, together with those of three of his successors, and placed on a carved feretory (*tabula*) next to the high altar. By the thirteenth century Durham Cathedral and the abbeys of Hyde and Peterborough claimed to possess relics of Acca. The saint's main feast was 20 October, the day of his death.   ALAN THACKER

Sources Bede, *Hist. eccl.* · Bede, 'In Lucae evangelium expositio', ed. D. Hurst, in *Bedae venerabilis opera: pars 1, opera exegetica* (1960) · E. Stephanus, *The life of Bishop Wilfrid*, ed. and trans. B. Colgrave (1927) · J. Raine, ed., *The priory of Hexham*, 1, SurtS, 44 (1864) · Symeon of Durham, *Opera* · D. P. Kirby, ed., *Saint Wilfrid at Hexham* (1974) · Bede, 'De templo', *Bedae venerabilis opera: pars 2, opera exegetica*, ed. D. Hurst, 2a (1969), 140–234

Accum, Friedrich Christian (1769–1838), chemist, was born on 29 March 1769 at Bückeburg, Westphalia, the sixth of the seven children of Christian Accum (*b.* 1727), a soap maker, and his wife, Judith Susanne Marthe, *née* Le Motte (*b.* 1732). His father, named Herz Marcus at birth, was born to a Jewish family from Włotho on the Weser but converted to Christianity while serving in the local infantry of Schaumburg-Lippe. His mother was the daughter of a hat and stocking maker of Huguenot descent.

Accum was educated at the local *Gymnasium* and also had private tuition in French and English. On leaving school he was apprenticed to the Brande family pharmacy at Hanover. A royal appointment as apothecary to George III was held by this business and it was in this connection that Accum transferred to the London pharmacy in Arlington Street in 1793. His residence at this time was at 17 Haymarket. During his early London years he attended the School of Anatomy (founded by William Hunter) in Windmill Street, Soho, where his enthusiasm was noticed by the physician Anthony Carlisle. Later, when Carlisle's colleague, the chemist William Nicholson, founded the *Journal of Natural Philosophy, Chemistry and the Arts*, Accum supported the venture through written contributions.

In 1800, Accum set up business independently at 11 Old Compton Street, Soho, from where he supplied chemicals and apparatus and lived throughout his remaining twenty years in England. For a short while, between 1801 and 1803, he was assistant chemical operator at the Royal Institution, perhaps serving William Thomas Brande, the son of his former employer. Emulating his peers, Humphry Davy and Brande, Accum began some popular presentations of chemistry, from his own premises in 1802 and later at Dr Hooper's Medical Theatre in nearby Cork Street. From 1809, he gave lecture courses at the Blackfriars Surrey Institution. His income from lecturing was supplemented by that subscribed by pupils who, for 160 guineas per annum (or 260 guineas if resident), could acquire laboratory skills as well as chemical knowledge. This was the route taken by Alexander Garden, an early tutee, who formed a partnership with his master for about ten years before setting up on his own account in Oxford Street.

Following some demonstrations on gas lighting given by a fellow German, F. A. Winsor, at the Lyric Theatre in 1803–4 Accum developed a certain expertise in the subject and represented Winsor's patents interests before a committee of the House of Commons in May 1809. In 1810 a bill was passed which permitted the incorporation of Winsor's London chartered Gas Light and Coke Company, of which Accum became a director. In this connection, he also became associated with Rudolph Ackermann, publisher of the *Repository of Arts and Manufactures*, who lit up his Strand residence by gas in 1811. From the *Annals of Philosophy* for 1815, and elsewhere, it is clear that Accum was a skilful propagandist; certainly, by 1815, the streets of Westminster were lit by coal gas. However, the work which helped to promote gas lighting generally was his *Practical Treatise on the Gas Light* (1815; 3rd edn, 1816) which

was also well received abroad (Paris, 1816; Berlin, 1816; Weimar, 1819).

Accum's first book, *A Theoretical and Practical Chemistry* (1803), was privately published and dedicated to the managers of the Royal Institution. This work was one of the earliest chemical texts to be based on Lavoisier's principles. Between 1800 and 1818 he published a number of practical texts on chemistry and analytical mineralogy, and, for the more affluent clientele attending his lectures, he provided *Chemical Amusements* (1817), designed to accompany the chemical chests available from his Soho shop. This book achieved great popularity, and went through multiple editions in Britain and overseas. He also wrote tracts on the arts of brewing, baking, and winemaking, evidently intended for a popular audience.

Accum's training in pharmacy gave him a lifelong interest in food adulteration and poisons. As early as 1798, he contributed a paper, 'Genuineness and purity of drugs and medical preparations', to Nicholson's *Journal*. Some twenty years later he made a vehement attack on merchants whom he exposed for their dubious methods and fraudulent claims. One thousand copies of the *Treatise on Adulterations of Food and Culinary Poisons* (1820; 4th edn, 1822) were sold in the first month after its appearance. The impact of this topic is attested by the appearance of two foreign editions (Philadelphia, 1820, and Leipzig, 1822) as well as part reprints in Ackermann's *Repository*. Not until 1860, however, was Accum's crusade vindicated when a food adulteration act was passed by parliament.

Despite all his hard-earned success, it was Accum's misfortune to lose all within a month. His downfall came towards the end of 1820 after he was seen (through a peephole) tearing leaves from texts in the Royal Institution library. Following a warrant to search Accum's residence, the librarian identified a further thirty stray pages. In consequence, he was arrested and first charged with robbery, and then, when this charge was dismissed, with the 'mutilation' of library books. As a result of this action by the managers of the Royal Institution he became an object of ridicule, though his friend Anthony Carlisle stood by him, publicly asking them to withdraw their case (*The Times*, 10 Jan 1821). Nevertheless the case was called on 5 April 1821; the defendant failed to appear, having departed for Germany, where he remained for the rest of his life.

After the unfortunate publicity had subsided, and in the author's absence, Accum's friend Ackermann published a remaining manuscript, *Culinary Chemistry* (1821). Accum's later works were published either anonymously or under the pseudonym Mucca. The authoritative yet anonymous *Dictionary of Apparatus and Instruments Employed in Operative and Experimental Chemistry* (1824), an elaborate illustrated text describing over 200 laboratory items, may be attributed to him.

At the age of fifty-two, after nearly thirty years in London, Accum had to begin life afresh in Germany, away from his enemies. For a short while he joined Gottlieb Nathusius, who had set up an industrial complex at Alt-Haldensleben for the purpose of conducting technical and economic experiments on the production of food-stuffs and building materials. In 1822, he accepted the dual position of professor of technical chemistry and mineralogy at the Royal Industrial Institute, and professor of physics, chemistry, and mineralogy at the Royal Academy of Construction, in Berlin. His principal and final work from this period was *Physische und chemische Beschaffenheit der Baumaterialen deren Wahl, Verhalten und zweckmässige Anwendung* (1826), a text on the chemical and physical properties of building materials, written for architects, masons, and carpenters in training.

Accum never made any significant contributions to pure chemistry, but those he made to technical and industrial chemistry were important; likewise, his activities as lecturer and author played a significant part in the diffusion of chemical practice. Apart from his membership of the Royal Institution, he corresponded with the Royal Irish Academy, the Linnean Society, and the Royal Academy of Sciences of Berlin. His final years in Berlin were more passive, although he retained a consultative position until his death. He died on 28 June 1838 aged sixty-nine.   BRIAN GEE

Sources C. A. Browne, 'The life and chemical services of Frederick Accum', *Journal of Chemical Education*, 2 (1925), 1–27 • R. J. Cole, 'Friedrich Accum (1769–1838): a biographical study', *Annals of Science*, 7 (1951), 128–43 • B. Gee, 'Amusement chests and portable laboratories: practical alternatives to the regular laboratory', *The development of the laboratory*, ed. F. A. J. L. James (1989), 37–59 • DNB • manager's minutes, 9 Feb 1801, Royal Institution of Great Britain, London, 2,124 • manager's minutes, 3 Oct 1803, Royal Institution of Great Britain, London, 3,152 • E. W. Steib, *Drug adulteration and control in 19th century Britain* (1966), 160–69
Likenesses T. Rowlandson, pen, pencil and watercolour caricature, 1809, Museum of London • S. Drummond, engraving, repro. in Browne, 'Life and chemical services of Frederick Accum' • J. Thomson, stipple (after S. Drummond), BM, NPG; repro. in *European Magazine* (1820)

Achard of St Victor. *See* St Victor, Achard of (*c*.1100–1171).

Acherley, Roger (*bap*. 1662?, *d*. **1740**), political writer and lawyer, was the son of John Acherley of Stanwardine, in the parish of Baschurch, Shropshire; he may have been Roger Atcherley, son of John and Mary Atcherley, who was baptized at Baschurch on 23 December 1662. He entered the Inner Temple on 6 March 1686. On 3 April 1689, describing himself as 'a young Student of the Temple' (BL, Egerton MS 3346, fol. 15), Acherley wrote to Thomas Osborne, earl of Danby, lord president of the council, with an essay, 'An expedientt to secure the certaine meeting and sitting of parliaments'. This suggested that it should become illegal for the crown to collect revenues granted to the monarch by parliament if parliaments were neither called regularly nor allowed to sit. No answer from Danby survives. Acherley was called to the bar on 21 June 1691, and it may have been about this time that he married Elizabeth, daughter of Richard Vernon, of Hanbury, Worcestershire, and sister of the barrister and law reporter Thomas *Vernon (1654–1721). They had a daughter, Letitia. Acherley's practice as a barrister included five cases before the House of Lords between 1704 and 1716. He may

also have been involved in mining in Shropshire at this period, as a Roger Atcherley leased part of a copper mine at Clive in 1711, the other part of which belonged to a Vernon.

Acherley's politics were strongly whig. In the latter years of Queen Anne's reign he suspected the queen and the ministry of Robert Harley, earl of Oxford, of planning the accession of James Francis Edward Stuart, the Old Pretender, on Anne's death. According to his own account, in 1712 he wrote to the court of Hanover that they should insist that the elector or another prince of the electoral family have a house and revenue attached to them in England as a condition of the peace at the end of the War of the Spanish Succession. In subsequent correspondence, mainly with Gottfried Wilhelm von Leibniz and with Johann Kaspar von Bothmer, Acherley urged that the Hanoverians assert forcefully their right to the succession. In a letter of October 1713 Acherley proposed that a writ of summons be demanded for the electoral prince of Hanover, George Augustus (later George II), so that the prince could sit in the House of Lords as duke of Cambridge. Acherley's alarmist letters concerning the danger to the succession expressed widespread fears among whigs that Anne and the tories intended a return to arbitrary government, and may have encouraged Georg von Schutz, the Hanoverian envoy to England, to demand a writ of summons for George Augustus from Lord Chancellor Harcourt on 12 April 1714. Schutz's action spurred Anne to allow the writ to be issued, but the elector (who had probably at first approved the request) then repudiated Schutz, presumably in order to avoid further offence to Anne and moderate political opinion in Britain. Acherley's prospects also suffered. Following the accession of George I, in August 1714, he did not receive a government appointment—contrary to his expectations; his bitterness over this perceived ingratitude affected much of his later writing.

Following the death of his brother-in-law Thomas Vernon, in 1721, Acherley challenged a codicil to Vernon's will. This excluded Acherley's wife, Elizabeth, from succeeding to the Hanbury estate, which instead was left to Vernon's widow and then to his cousin Bowater Vernon. It also increased a legacy left to Acherley's daughter, Letitia, from £1000 to £6000, providing that neither she nor her mother challenged the settlement, and removed Acherley as a trustee of the estate. The case was brought before chancery in 1722; Lord Chancellor Macclesfield ruled the codicil valid in a hearing on 20 November 1723, and his judgment was upheld by the House of Lords in 1725. Acherley also claimed Vernon's unpublished law reports, but these were confiscated by the court on Macclesfield's instructions and subsequently edited for publication by William Melmoth and William Peere Williams.

Acherley's most important publication was *The Britannic Constitution*, published in 1727. Described as 'a lengthy argument designed to prove the legality and justice of the Revolution Settlement in State and Church' that defends the revolution of 1688 'by means of the arguments used by those who had made it' (Holdsworth, *Eng. law*, 12.341),

Acherley in fact regretted that there had been no summary of the British constitution as established at the revolution. The book defended the contractual basis of the constitution with 'vehemence' (Gunn, 160). In the first part of the work he hypothesized a constitutional convention, held not long after the biblical flood, when the island of Britain was first settled. To Acherley the crown was an estate of the realm rather than a supreme power over the estates. His prehistoric assembly had devised the original contract between the monarch and the people; the monarch ruled according to laws prescribed by parliament, consisting of mutually independent king, lords, and commons. Subjects and king were bound by a reciprocal oath of allegiance to uphold that contract. A king who violated that contract vacated the throne. In the second part of the book Acherley argued proofs of the constitution from recorded history and demonstrated violations.

Acherley returned to similar ground with his work of 1731 *Free Parliaments*, which reiterated the independence of the Commons and called for the Pension Bill to be passed, by which members of the Commons would have to declare to the Commons the pensions that they held or risk a fine. In its historical survey he also alleged that the real purpose of the treaty of Utrecht had been to allow Anne to reintroduce arbitrary monarchical government and bring in the Pretender. An appendix printed the correspondence between Acherley and the Hanoverian court between 1712 and 1714. Among Acherley's other published works were *The Jurisdiction of the Chancery as a Court of Equity Researched*, published in 1736 and including a discussion of the constitutional role of the Lords, and *Reasons for Uniformity in the State*, which appeared both separately and as a supplement to a reissue of *The Britannic Constitution* in 1741. Acherley died 'in an advanced age, at his house in Greenwich' (*London Daily Post*) on 16 April 1740.

MATTHEW KILBURN

Sources [R. Acherley], 'A narrative of Mr R. A.: correspondence with the house of Hanover, 1712–14', BL, Add. MS 38507, fols. 88–110 · R. Acherley, letter to the earl of Danby, 1689, BL, Egerton MS 3346, fol. 15 · R. Acherley, 'An expedientt to secure the certaine meeting and sitting of parliaments', 1689, BL, Egerton MS 3346, fols. 16–17 · R. Acherley, *The Britannic constitution, or, The fundamental form of government in Britain* (1727) · R. Acherley, *Free parliaments, or, An argument on their constitution, proving some of their powers to be independent* (1731) · J. A. W. Gunn, *Beyond liberty and property: the process of self-recognition in eighteenth-century thought* (1983) · Holdsworth, *Eng. law*, 12.339–41 · *DNB* · P. Yorke, *Acherley v. Vernon*, 1722, BL, Add. MS 36148, fols. 89–90v [manuscript notes] · *The manuscripts of the House of Lords*, new ser., 12 vols. (1900–77), vol. 6, pp. 49–51; vol. 7, p. 338; vol. 10, p. 191; vol. 12, pp. 212, 312, 314 · F. A. Inderwick and R. A. Roberts, eds., *A calendar of the Inner Temple records*, 3 (1901), 274, 346, 438 · F. A. Inderwick and R. A. Roberts, eds., *A calendar of the Inner Temple records*, 4 (1933), 2 · 'Clive mine', www.ap.pwp.blueyonder.co.uk/clive.htm, 21 March 2002 · *IGI* · E. Gregg, *Queen Anne* (1980) · R. Hatton, *George I: elector and king* (1978) · *London Daily Post and General Advertiser* (21 March 1741)

Archives BL, corresp. with J. K. von Bothmer, G. W. von Leibniz, and others, Add. MS 38507, fols. 88–110 [copies]

Acheson, Archibald, second earl of Gosford (1776–1849), governor-in-chief of British North America, was born on 1 August 1776, the eldest son of Arthur Acheson, first earl of

Gosford, and his wife, Millicent, the daughter of Lieutenant-General Edward Pole, of Radbourne in Derbyshire. He entered Christ Church, Oxford, and received his BA on 22 January 1796 and an MA on 26 October 1797. During the Irish uprising of 1798 he served as lieutenant-colonel in the Armagh militia. In 1807 he became colonel. On 20 July 1805 he married Mary (14 April 1777–30 June 1841), the only daughter of Robert Sparrow, of Worlingham Hall in Beccles, Suffolk, and they had a son, Archibald, third earl of Gosford (1806–1864), and four daughters, of whom Millicent married Henry Bence Jones.

On 9 January 1798 Acheson was elected to the Irish House of Commons as a member for Armagh. He voted against union on 20 January 1800, although his father supported the measure in the Irish House of Lords and was rewarded with an earldom. By the terms of the Union Act Acheson became a member of the British House of Commons in 1801, and he was returned for Armagh at the general elections of 1802 and 1806. On 14 January 1807 he succeeded his father as second earl of Gosford and in 1811 was chosen as a representative peer for Ireland. While he seldom intervened in debate he gave a general support to the whig party. In 1832 he was gazetted lord lieutenant and *custos rotulorum* of Armagh, offices he held for life, and on 3 September 1834 he was nominated captain of the yeomen of the guard and was called to the privy council.

Although born into the protestant establishment, Gosford favoured power sharing with the Catholics in Ireland. In 1825 he opposed a bill to outlaw the Catholic Association, led by Daniel O'Connell, and in 1829 voted for Catholic emancipation. He was an outspoken opponent of the Orange lodge and in June 1835, in his capacity as lord lieutenant, presented a conciliatory report on riots in Armagh. A resolution censuring his report was defeated in the Commons and Joseph Hume proposed a motion eulogizing his conduct. The motion was supported by O'Connell and his followers and by the radicals.

On 13 June 1835 Gosford was created a peer of the United Kingdom, adopting the title Baron Worlingham from an estate that came to him through his wife, and on 1 July 1835 he was appointed governor of Lower Canada and governor-in-chief of British North America. He was also placed at the head of a commission of inquiry with Sir Charles Edward Grey and Sir George Gipps to examine the grievances of the Lower Canadian assembly. Gosford's appointment was based on the assumption that there was a close analogy between Ireland and Lower Canada and that the whig policy of conciliation might be applied to Lower Canada as well as Ireland. Indeed, Gosford's instructions emphasized that his priority was to conciliate the assembly of Lower Canada and that the duty of the commission was to submit a comprehensive proposal to resolve the disputes between the executive and the assembly. Unfortunately Gosford's instructions were less conciliatory than originally intended because William IV refused to agree to the original draft, and he warned Gosford to 'Mind what you are about in Canada.'

On arriving in Quebec on 24 August 1835, Gosford distanced himself from the policies of his predecessor, Lord

Aylmer, who had become identified with the English or constitutionalist party, and he set about the hopeless task of conciliating Louis-Joseph Papineau and the members of the *parti patriote*, who dominated the assembly. Although Gosford was sufficiently popular to persuade the assembly, which met on 27 October 1835, not to disband, he was unable to persuade it to grant supplies. He did manage to co-opt the support of a number of moderate *patriotes* but he also incurred the hostility of the constitutionalists, particularly after he refused to condone their decision to organize a rifle corps. Gosford's efforts at conciliation were hindered by the release of the text of his instructions, which showed the limitations placed upon his freedom of action. When it became clear that the Gosford commission could neither recommend an elected legislative council nor surrender the crown's revenues without a civil list, a number of the moderate *patriotes* so assiduously wooed by Gosford drifted back into Papineau's fold. The *patriotes* withdrew from the assembly and Gosford was forced to prorogue it on 21 March 1836.

Gosford persisted in the policy of conciliation. He appealed to the Melbourne ministry to allow him to reconstruct both the executive and the legislative council, but he was prohibited from making any changes until the Gosford commission had completed its inquiries. On 15 November 1836 the commissioners presented their final report, which recommended that the imperial parliament reject the extreme demands of the assembly and provide the executive with the funds it would need for carrying on the government without the assembly's support. On 6 March 1837 Lord John Russell introduced into the House of Commons ten resolutions which generally embodied the recommendations of the Gosford commission and included a measure appropriating £142,000 of revenues raised in Lower Canada for payment of arrears owed to the colony's civil servants. The Russell resolutions meant that Gosford's policy of co-opting moderates no longer had any chance of success. When the assembly met on 25 August 1837 the members appeared in homespun as a protest against using British imports and refused supplies. The legislature was dissolved, never to meet again, and the *patriotes* moved towards a confrontation with the government. In September Gosford dismissed a number of militia officers and magistrates for attending public meetings advocating civil disobedience and the following month he recommended suspending the constitution. In November he reluctantly issued warrants for the arrest of Papineau and the leading *patriotes*. Admitting that he was increasingly isolated and that his unpopularity with the English party would be a liability in the event of a rebellion, he submitted his resignation. During the rebellion he sought to restrain Major-General Sir John Colborne, the commander-in-chief of the British forces, and in December he even freed 112 rebels as an act of clemency. Early in 1838 he learned his resignation had been accepted, and he departed on 27 February 1838, handing over control of the administration to Colborne. By this time Gosford was an isolated and somewhat pathetic figure. Historians have been equally unkind to him and have

usually dismissed him as a well-meaning incompetent. This judgement is unfair. Although handicapped by the vacillation of the Melbourne ministry, he had sincerely sought to conciliate moderate French-Canadian opinion. He failed but his failure was probably inevitable, and his efforts at conciliation were not entirely unsuccessful and probably limited the severity of the rebellion.

Gosford received the thanks of the ministry and was awarded the GCB (civil division) on 19 July 1838. Initially he approved of Lord Durham's appointment to Canada but he blamed the second rebellion in the autumn of 1838 on Durham's stupidity. He opposed the union of Upper and Lower Canada and criticized the Union Bill of 1840 in the House of Lords. During the 1840s his interests again focused on Ireland, where he split with O'Connell over the issue of repeal. Thereafter, while serving as lord lieutenant and vice-admiral of the coast of the province of Ulster, he devoted his attention to his estates, to the development of the linen industry in Ireland, and to the promotion of agriculture. He died at his residence at Market Hill on 27 March 1849, and was buried on 18 April 1849 at Mullaghbrack.

T. B. BROWNING, rev. PHILLIP BUCKNER

Sources *DCB*, vol. 7 · P. A. Buckner, *The transition to responsible government: British policy in British North America, 1815–1850* (1985) · GEC, *Peerage* · E. Lodge, *Peerage, baronetage, knightage and companionage of the British empire*, 81st edn, 3 vols. (1912) · HoP, *Commons* · Foster, *Alum. Oxon.*
Archives PRO NIre., corresp. and papers relating to Canada · PRO NIre., corresp. and papers relating to Ireland | Lpool RO, letters to E. G. Stanley · NRA, priv. coll., dispatches to Sir John Colborne
Likenesses R. J. Lane, lithograph, 1828 (after T. Phillips, 1826), BM, NPG · G. Hayter, group portrait, oils (*The trial of Queen Caroline*, 1820), NPG

Achilli, (Giovanni) Giacinto (*b. c.*1803), Dominican priest, anti-Catholic polemicist, and seducer, was born in the village of Celleno, 18 miles from Viterbo, then in the Papal States. He joined the Dominican order in 1819, studied at the convent of the Minerva in Rome, and was ordained a priest at Lucca in 1825. In 1826 he was appointed lecturer at the Dominican convent of Gradi in Viterbo and professor in the local seminary, but was immediately deprived of the faculty to teach for an unnamed fault and spent a year at the convent of La Quercia, also in Viterbo. He returned as *lector philosophiae* in the seminary in Viterbo in 1827. In 1831 he allegedly seduced the eighteen-year-old Elena Valente, and in 1833, in the sacristy of the church of Gradi, the 28-year-old Rosa di Alessandris. His other supposed victims included Vincenza Guerra in 1835 at Montefiascone.

On 1 September 1833 the episcopal court convicted Achilli of the seduction of Alessandris; he was fined 50 scudi, which were given to the victim's father, and was relieved of his priestly faculties. Achilli claimed to his later protestant followers that he had voluntarily relinquished his post in Viterbo on being offered professorships in the Minerva and the Sapienza University in Rome and at Macerata, and that he had held the posts of visitor to the Dominican houses in the Papal States and Tuscany and of vicar of the master of the Sacred Apostolic Palace. It

(**Giovanni**) **Giacinto Achilli** (*b. c.*1803), by unknown engraver, pubd 1850

is possible that the Dominican provincial and visitor Father Brocchetti took Achilli with him on visitation to demonstrate Brocchetti's belief in Achilli's repentance. Achilli was also to claim that Cardinal Serra had asked him to preach the Lenten sermons in 1835 in the cathedral at Capua (where he is said to have committed further offences against women), and that he had received papal permission for his secularization in 1835, but made it effective only in 1839, when he ceased to be a Dominican and became a secular priest. In 1837 he was appointed prior of the convent of San Pietro Martyro in Naples, where he was accused by a fifteen-year-old girl, Sophia Maria Principe, of raping her in the sacristy on Good Friday 1840. He was twice expelled by the police from the city, on 8 September 1840 and on 21 February 1841.

On 16 June 1841 the Roman Inquisition permanently suspended Achilli *a divinis* from his priestly faculties and sentenced him to a penance of three years in a remote Dominican house at Nazzaro. In 1842 he travelled as the servant of Signor Pietro Boccaciampi to Corfu, then a British protectorate, where he assumed the title of *cavaliere*, or knight, declaring himself a political refugee and escapee from the fortress of Ancona. The papal consul asked for his extradition. Fraser, the secretary of the high commissioner, at first approved the request, but then refused it on discovering that Achilli had become a protestant, while the first of Achilli's two public letters to Pope Gregory XVI attacking Catholicism was printed by the government press. He is also said to have commissioned an obscene statue of the pope. He was taken under the protection of Isaac Lowndes, the Scottish presbyterian secretary of the Bible Society, and founded an 'Italian church'. He had an affair with Marianna Crisaffi, the wife of Nicolo Garamoni, a tailor, but deserted her for Albina Coriboni, the wife of a chorus singer, with whom he travelled to Zante,

where he employed her husband as a protestant clerk in his chapel. He formed close links with liberal Italian nationalists in exile, among them Flaminio Lolli, who later denounced him, implicating him in the fatal expedition to Cosenza against the kingdom of Naples of the Bandiera brothers, whose personal effects he was alleged to have misappropriated after their execution.

Achilli moved to Malta in 1846, where he opened an Italian church and contributed to a religious journal, the *Indicatore maltese*. In May 1847 he went to London and was appointed professor at the Protestant College of St Julian's on Malta, which had the aim of propagating protestantism in Italy. His colleagues included Pietro Leononi Pignotti, a former Carmelite, Fortunato Saccares, a former Capuchin, and the former parish priest of the church of the Maddalena in Rome, Luigi de Sanctis. While in London, Achilli claimed to have discovered an English translation of the lost sixteenth-century Italian Calvinist treatise, *Del beneficio di Cristo*, and to have translated it back into Italian. During his absence from Malta another former priest in the college, the Armenian Giovanni Keosse, brought charges of fornication against Saccares and Leononi before the college principal, Dr George Horatio Hadfield, and the London committee of the college, declaring that Achilli had encouraged them in their misbehaviour.

Achilli returned to Malta in December 1847, but he sent Saccares to Sicily to remove him from the inquiry, and in May 1848 was dismissed with his confrères. In June he returned to London. His supporters in England included Sir Culling Eardley Eardley, the president of the Evangelical Alliance, established in 1846 to denounce Roman Catholicism. In January 1849 Achilli left for Rome, then in the hands of the revolutionary government, joined the revolutionary club the Circolo Popolare, and circulated his own writings *La chiave di San Pietro* and *La sedia di San Pietro* and Giovanni Diodati's translation of the Bible. He was married in Rome on 24 June 1849 by Saccares to Josephine Hely, the youngest daughter of Captain James Hely, whose family he had befriended when in England. After the fall of the Roman Republic he was imprisoned in the Castel Sant'Angelo, where the great Oratorian Father Augustine Theiner, later prefect of the Vatican archives, tried to reconcile him to the church. The secretaries to the protestant Committee of the London Society for the Religious Improvement of Italy and Italians, one of them Lewis H. Tonna, sent a memorial of 4 October 1849 asking for his release by the French government, its troops having occupied Rome.

The request was granted and Achilli was brought to England to function at an Italian chapel and to lecture against the Catholic church under the auspices of the Evangelical Alliance by Eardley, who claimed him as a victim of the Inquisition and a martyr for protestantism in *The imprisonment and deliverance of Dr. Giacinto Achilli, with some account of his previous history and labours* (1850). The English Catholic Cardinal Nicholas Wiseman reviewed this work and the anonymous *Brief Sketch of the Life of Giacinto Achilli* (1850) in the *Dublin Review* in July 1850, accusing Achilli of numerous sexual offences and of lying about his own history.

Lewis Tonna wrote *The Real Dr Achilli* (1850) in reply to Wiseman. While in London Achilli is said to have raped or molested four of his domestic servants, Catherine Gorman, Harriet Harris, Jane Legge, Sarah Wood, and also a Mlle Fortay.

Achilli responded to Wiseman's attack with his *Dealings with the Inquisition, or, Papal Rome, her priests, and her Jesuits, with important disclosures* (1851). This controversy fed the flames of the popular uproar over the restoration of the English Catholic hierarchy in November 1850, and J. H. Newman repeated Wiseman's charges that Achilli was guilty of sexual immorality and lying about his past on 28 July 1851 in the fifth of his *Lectures on the Present Position of Catholics in England* (1851). In August Newman heard that the Evangelical Alliance intended to support Achilli in a libel action against him, and sent two of his fellow Oratorians, Joseph Gordon and Nicholas Darnell, to Italy to collect evidence to corroborate his accusations. Because Wiseman had lost the papers from the Roman and Neapolitan authorities on which his assertions had been based, the rule bringing Newman to trial was made absolute in November, and Newman's lawyer, James Harting, and his old friend Maria Rosina Giberne also went to Italy to seek testimony from Achilli's victims. Elena Giustini, *née* Valente, who came with her husband, and Sophia Maria Balisano, *née* Principe, accompanied by her mother, gave evidence against Achilli at Newman's trial, as did some of the London servants whom he had assaulted, with Hadfield and the seventh earl of Shaftesbury, others for the Malta College, and witnesses from Viterbo, Corfu, Zante, and Malta. The presiding judge, John Campbell, was, however, an aggressively anti-Catholic protestant who appealed to the jury's prejudice, though he was the first to admit, albeit with disparaging remarks, a document of the Roman Inquisition (testifying to Achilli's suspension) into the proceedings of a modern English court. Newman was convicted of libel in June 1852 but, when sentenced on 31 January 1853, was fined the relatively small sum of £100 and not imprisoned. His expenses of £12,000 were borne by a subscription from Catholics in England, France, Ireland, Germany, and North and South America; some of the surplus was spent on building the university church in Dublin. The second edition of *The Present Position of Catholics* replaced the pages about Achilli with an appeal in Latin to the judgment of posterity.

Despite his victory in the courts Achilli was discredited by the trial, and in 1853 he went with a party of Swedenborgians to the United States, where the American Bible Union published his translation of the Greek New Testament into Italian in 1854. He sent his wife back to Italy, and in December 1859, sporting a splendid white beard, appeared before a JP in Jersey City accused of adultery with a Miss Bogue. In March 1860 he left Miss Bogue and his eldest son, aged eight, to the care of the Oneida community, with a note implying that he would commit suicide and that spirits would carry him off to see the Lord. The date and circumstances of his death are not known.

Achilli was a man of some ability with knowledge of both ancient and modern languages. It is not clear that he was simply a hypocrite; given his insistence to his colleagues and his victims that they were doing nothing wrong, and his scornful refusal at times to answer the charges against him in court, he possibly became an enthusiast of the Calvinist antinomian type satirized by James Hogg in *The Confessions of a Justified Sinner* (1824), whose religious assurance carries him straight into disregard for the moral law. SHERIDAN GILLEY

Sources W. F. Finlason, *Report of the trial and preliminary proceedings in the case of the queen on the prosecution of G. Achilli v. Dr Newman* (1852), 202 • N. P. Wiseman, *Dr Achilli: authentic 'Brief sketch of the life of Dr Giacinto Achilli'* (1851) [expanded from *Dublin Review*, 56 (1850)] • G. Achilli, *Dealings with the Inquisition, or, Papal Rome, her priests, and her Jesuits, with important disclosures* (1851) • *The letters and diaries of John Henry Newman*, ed. C. S. Dessain and others, [31 vols.] (1961–), vols. 14–15 • M. C. Mirow, 'Roman Catholicism on trial in Victorian England: the libel case of John Henry Newman and Dr. Achilli', *Catholic Lawyer*, 36 (1995–6), 401–53 • D. Cantimori, 'Achilli, Giacinto', *Dizionario biografico degli Italiani*, ed. A. M. Ghisalberti, 1 (Rome, 1960), 144
Likenesses engraving, pubd 1850, NPG [*see illus.*]

Achurch, Janet (1864?–1916), actress, is a figure about whose birth and parentage little is known. Her mother died in giving birth to her, possibly on 17 January 1864. Educated privately, she sometimes had Achurch as a surname, at other times Sharp. She was descended, she herself claimed, from a long line of actors. According to *Who was Who in the Theatre* her great-grandparents James and Mary Achurch Ward had been managers of the Theatre Royal, Manchester, and friends of the Kemble family in the late eighteenth century and it was apparently assumed from the start that this striking-looking young woman would follow the family tradition. In 1881 she was sent to Sarah Thorne's actor-training school in Margate (where, a few years later, Harley Granville Barker received his first training for the stage). She made her first appearance on the stage in a farce called *Betsy Baker* at the Olympic Theatre, London, in January 1883. During the latter part of 1883 and in 1884 she toured the English provinces in a variety of plays, including C. H. Hazelwood's *Lady Audley's Secret* (dramatized from Mary Elizabeth Braddon's melodramatic novel) and *The New Magdalen* (Wilkie Collins). Of her performance in the latter, Bernard Shaw wrote in the *Saturday Review* that it showed her to be 'the only tragic actress of genius we now possess' (Shaw, *Dramatic Opinions*, 221).

In 1884 Achurch married St Aubyn Miller but the marriage proved a disaster and was dissolved after only a few months. In 1885 she joined the Frank Benson company, contracted to play leading parts, on tour, in Bulwer Lytton's *The Lady of Lyons*, Dion Boucicault's *The Corsican Brothers*, and three Shakespeare parts—Gertrude, Desdemona, and Lady Macbeth. She stayed with the company for only one season. Early in 1886 she married Charles Charrington (d. 1926), an actor in the Benson company at that time. During 1887 and 1888 she alternated between playing in London and touring nationally with various companies. Her London appearances included Lady Teazle with the Farren-Conway company at the Strand Theatre in

Janet Achurch (1864?–1916), by Barraud, 1887

July 1887 and a season with Herbert Beerbohm Tree at the Haymarket Theatre in January 1888. In 1889, when she was still only twenty-three, she undertook the management of the Novelty Theatre, London, where on 7 June she appeared as Nora in the first English production of Ibsen's *A Doll's House*. This was a turning point both in her career and in English critical appreciation of Ibsen. Granville Barker thought it the most dramatic theatrical event of the decade. Charles Charrington, her husband, appeared with her in this production, playing the part of Dr Rank and, immediately after its limited run was over, on 5 July 1889 they left London for a two-year theatre tour of Australia. The tour was successful and they extended it to include New Zealand, Tasmania, India, and Egypt. However, while in Cairo Janet Achurch almost lost her life in childbirth. The child was stillborn and, though she continued with her stage performances, she was able to do so only with increasingly large doses of morphia, which the doctor had prescribed. She already had a tendency towards alcoholism; to this was now added morphine addiction.

In spite of physical debility and depression, immediately on her return to London in 1892 Achurch plunged into a heavy and continuous programme of work. At the Avenue Theatre she repeated her success as Nora in a new production of *A Doll's House* and subsequently, during 1893 and 1894, was continuously engaged, although playing in several undistinguished pieces. In November 1896, in spite of being pregnant again, she undertook the challenging and exacting role of Rita in Ibsen's *Little Eyolf*. The cast of this production also included Mrs Patrick Campbell and Elizabeth Robins. Shaw praised her performance:

> She played with all her old originality and success, and with more than her old authority over her audience … For the first time one clearly saw the superfluity of power and the vehemence of intelligence which make her often so reckless as to the beauty of her methods of expression. (Shaw, *Dramatic Criticism*, 197)

For just such qualities of the actor's craft Shaw, on another occasion, compared Janet Achurch—and favourably—with Eleonora Duse, whose work he much admired.

The following year Achurch played the lead in the first production of Shaw's *Candida*, the play that he had written in 1894 with her very much in mind and which he had in 1895 offered to the American actor Richard Mansfield, on condition that he cast Janet Achurch as the eponymous heroine. When Mansfield refused to do as he wished Shaw withdrew his offer of the play, which remained unperformed. Achurch finally played the part at Her Majesty's Theatre, Aberdeen, on 30 July 1897 at the start of a provincial tour and, later, at the Strand Theatre, London, on 1 July 1900 under the auspices of the Stage Society. At the same theatre, and again for the Stage Society, on 16 December 1900 she played the leading role of Lady Cicely Waynflete in the first production of Shaw's *Captain Brassbound's Conversion*. About her performance in this Shaw, in a splendid letter to her, said: 'Lady Cicely is the first sign you have given of reaching the wise age of comedy and being able to play the fiddle as well as the trombones and drums' (Shaw, *Letters*, 2.208).

Achurch appeared in Ibsen twice more before her career closed, though in both cases the play had been seen in England before: in 1902 in *The Lady from the Sea* and in 1911 in *A Doll's House* (in which she no longer played Nora but the lesser part of Mrs Linde). On 15 May 1903 she played the part of Leila Daintree in the first (and only) production of *Mrs Daintree's Daughter*, a piece which is interesting for its history and its associations rather than for any intrinsic merit. It was written by Janet Achurch herself in 1897–8, based on Guy de Maupassant's novel *Yvette*, at the encouragement of Shaw.

Janet Achurch's last appearance on the London stage was in October 1913, as Merete Beyer in John Masefield's version of *The Witch*, a Norwegian play by Wiers-Jenssen; she had played the part two years before in an earlier production of the play. Exhausted and ill, she announced her official retirement immediately after the play closed. She died, aged fifty-two, at 4 Devonshire Terrace, Ventnor, Isle of Wight, on 11 September 1916. The cause of death was morphine poisoning. She was survived by one daughter, Nora, and by her husband, Charles Charrington, who died in 1926.

ERIC SALMON

Sources I. Herbert, ed., *Who's who in the theatre*, 17th edn, 2 vols. (1981) · G. B. Shaw, *Our theatre in the nineties*, 3 vols. (1931) · G. B. Shaw, *Dramatic opinions and essays* (1909) · W. de la Mare, ed., *The eighteen-eighties: essays by members of the Royal Society of Literature* (1930) · M. Holroyd, *Bernard Shaw*, 1 (1988) · *Shaw's dramatic criticism: a selection*, ed. J. F. Matthews (1959) · *Collected letters: Bernard Shaw*, ed. D. H. Laurence, 4 vols. (1965–88), vol. 2 · *The Oxford Ibsen*, ed. J. W. McFarlane, 7 (1966) · *The Bodley Head Bernard Shaw: collected plays with their prefaces*, 1 (1970) · d. cert. · C. Archer, *William Archer* (1931)

Likenesses Barraud, photograph, 1887, NPG [*see illus.*] · photograph, 1899, repro. in D. H. Laurence, ed., *Collected letters: Bernard Shaw*, vol. 1

Ackerley, Joe Randolph (1896–1967), writer and literary editor, was born on 4 November 1896 at 4 Warmington Road, Herne Hill, south London, the younger son and second of the three children of Alfred Roger Ackerley (1863–1929), fruit importer, of London, and his mistress, Janetta Katherine Aylward (1864–1946), an actress. His parents married in 1919. He was educated at Rossall School, Fleetwood, Lancashire, and at Magdalene College, Cambridge, where he obtained a third class in English in 1921, having abandoned law after a short time. His education had been interrupted by the First World War, in which he served on the western front as an officer in the 8th battalion of the East Surrey regiment. Twice wounded, he was captured in May 1917 and subsequently exchanged into internment at Mürren in Switzerland. These experiences, and the death in action of his elder brother, Peter, resulted in a pronounced strain of melancholy in his character.

In 1922 Ackerley received an appreciative letter from E. M. Forster about his long meditative poem 'Ghosts'. This led to an enduring friendship, the closest of Ackerley's life. It was at Forster's suggestion that Ackerley spent five months in India as companion-secretary to the eccentric maharaja of Chhatarpur.

The anthology *Poems by Four Authors* (1923) contained ten poems Ackerley had written while an undergraduate, and in 1925 the play based upon his experiences as an internee, *The Prisoners of War*, was produced in London. Its 'difficult' themes (the war and homosexuality) made it a *succès d'estime*, but although he was hailed as a coming dramatist, he never completed another play.

In 1928 Ackerley became an assistant producer in the talks department of the BBC. Through Forster he had acquired a wide circle of literary acquaintances, many of whom he recruited to make broadcasts on the radio. In 1932 he edited *Escapers All*, derived from a series of talks given by men who had escaped from prisoner-of-war camps. That same year he also published *Hindoo Holiday*, based on his Indian diaries. In spite of many excisions on the grounds of libel and obscenity, the book's sly humour and brilliant character-drawing ensured excellent sales and consolidated his reputation.

In 1935 Ackerley became literary editor of *The Listener*, a post he held for twenty-four years. He wanted the magazine to be 'in the vanguard of contemporary thought, the forefront of the battle' and commissioned reviews, articles, stories, and poems which reflected this. 'I think that people *ought* to be upset', he wrote; 'I think that life is so important and, in its workings, so upsetting that nobody should be spared' (*Letters*, 115). This was a policy which led to many disagreements with his timid employers, and he waged a vigorous guerrilla campaign against the prudery and philistinism of the BBC hierarchy. His integrity, charm, tact, and an insistence upon the highest standards led to his being widely considered the finest literary editor of his generation.

Ackerley flouted convention both in and out of the office. Strikingly good-looking and energetically homosexual, he conducted a long but conspicuously unsuccessful search among working-class men for 'the Ideal Friend'. His father's life had also been sexually unorthodox, for he had kept a second mistress and fathered three daughters whose existence was discovered by Ackerley only after his father's death. Ackerley's crusade to tell the truth, however uncomfortable and inconvenient that might be, arose from his belief that his relationship with his father had been compromised by their inability to confide in each other.

In 1956 Ackerley published *My Dog Tulip*, a shockingly frank and funny portrait of his Alsatian bitch, Queenie. The story of how he acquired her from a petty criminal and gradually transferred his love from man to dog is told in his novel *We Think the World of You* (1960), which won the W. H. Smith award. Although unconsummated, this relationship was undoubtedly the most satisfactory of his life and resulted in his passionate advocacy of animal rights.

In retirement Ackerley revised what was to be his masterpiece, a 'family memoir' begun in the 1930s which was eventually published as *My Father and Myself* (1968). He lived in considerable squalor and acrimony in a small flat at 17 Star and Garter Mansions, 6 Lower Richmond Road, Putney, London, with his 'three bitches': Queenie, his ageing Aunt Bunny, and his emotionally unstable sister, Nancy. After the death of Queenie in 1961 he became increasingly morose. Although disenchanted with the human world, he turned his misanthropic gloom to good account in witty and self-deprecatory letters. He died from a coronary thrombosis on 4 June 1967 at his home in Putney and was cremated at Putney Vale crematorium.

PETER PARKER

Sources P. Parker, *Ackerley* (1989) · *The letters of J. R. Ackerley*, ed. N. Braybrooke (1975) · F. King, ed., *My sister and myself* (1982) · *The Times* (6 June 1967) · b. cert. · d. cert.
Archives Georgetown University, Lauinger Library, corresp. with Sir Arnold Lunn · King's AC Cam., letters to W. J. H. Spratt · NYPL, Henry W. and Albert A. Berg collection of English and American Literature · Ransom HRC · Tate collection, corresp. with Lord Clark
Likenesses H. Coster, photograph, c.1939, NPG · D. Bachardy, pencil, ink, and wash, 1961, NPG · photographs, priv. coll. · photographs, repro. in Parker, *Ackerley*
Wealth at death £13,360: probate, 18 Dec 1967, CGPLA Eng. & Wales

Ackermann, George (1803–1891), publisher and artist, was born in London on 29 January 1803, the second surviving son of Rudolph *Ackermann (1764–1834) and Martha, née Massey (1769–1811). By nature quiet, gentle, and something of a dreamer, he was nevertheless an obedient son and began a long and active business career by joining his father's business as publisher of books and prints at 101 Strand in London. Shortly after his twenty-third birthday he was sent to Mexico City where he established an outlet for the sale of Ackermann publications in Spanish. Two of his watercolour views of the city were published as aquatints in 1826. He travelled to Guatemala where he opened another outlet, and it was here that he fell in love in 1828 with Jeanette (Netty) Haefkins (1812–1899), the sixteen-year-old daughter of the Dutch consul. Together they climbed the 13,000 foot Volcán de Agua, where Ackermann carved Netty's name on the summit. When, however, he was summoned home in 1829 because of his father's poor health, Netty's father refused them permission to exchange letters. On her return to Europe in 1832 they met again, and they were married in Leerdam, the Netherlands, in 1835. They had seven children, and their family homes in the London area were at various times in Camberwell, Brixton, and Paddington.

In the meantime, upon his return from Guatemala, Ackermann had brought with him an important collection of plants which he presented to the botanic garden in Sloane Street, Chelsea, one new specimen being named by the Royal Botanic Gardens at Kew *Epiphyllum Ackermanii*. On his father's retirement in 1832 he formed a partnership with two of his younger brothers at 96 Strand. Ackermann & Co. published prints of the early railways, botanical and sporting subjects, games, embossed maps, panoramas, travel books with lithographed illustrations, drawing books, and the popular annual *Forget-me-Not*. The company received the royal appointment as 'Book and Printsellers to HM Queen Victoria and HRH Prince Albert'. In 1839 it published the first manual of photography, *Ackermann's Photogenic Drawing Apparatus*; in 1841 the classic *Art of Engraving* by T. H. Fielding; and in 1843 two prints of a remarkable prototype 'ariel carriage' designed by the pioneers of flight Henson and Stringfellow. A short-lived financial crisis in 1843, however, required the planned publication of the magnificent *Orchidaceae of Mexico and Guatemala*, which contained several of Ackermann's drawings, to be brought out by another publisher. Ackermann & Co. later published two hundred marine prints and two important colour-plate books of costume: *Travels in North America* (1843–4), portraying Native American tribal clothing, and *The Clans of Scotland* (1845–7), fixing the tartan image of the clans. In 1851 Ackermann & Co. took a stand at the Great Exhibition in Hyde Park, London, and published what have become the definitive views of the Crystal Palace after Brannon and McNevin. In 1855, however, the brothers agreed to end their partnership, though George continued to trade as Ackermann & Co. at 106 Strand until 1861.

In 1862, at the age of fifty-nine, Ackermann emigrated to North America with Netty and their four youngest children. Initially bound for Portland, Maine, their ship was driven by a storm up the St Lawrence River and the family disembarked at Quebec. Ackermann bought a small homestead in the pioneer settlement of Madoc in Upper Canada (Ontario), though he quickly abandoned farming to teach drawing in a succession of small towns in Ontario, including Belleville where he developed a special concern for the hearing impaired. Soon after his arrival in Canada he set himself the task of illustrating a classification of the wild flowers of Upper Canada, drawn up by the Harvard botanist Asa Gray. In search of new specimens he left the Great Lakes to move to the Atlantic maritime province of Prince Edward Island in 1876. In all, he painted over four hundred botanical studies and, in addition,

twenty topographical views of early Canadian townships which have proved to be of historical interest. These Canadian paintings came to light only in 1994 in Saskatchewan. Ackermann left Prince Edward Island in 1887 to live with his son in Chicago and it was there he died, on 22 August 1891, at the Marine Hospital, Lake View. He was survived by his wife and five children. JOHN FORD

Sources family MSS, priv. coll. · J. A. Ford and E. Fraser, *Brave new worlds: George Ackermann in the Americas* (1998) · J. Ford, *Ackermann, 1783–1983: the business of art* (1983) · J. A. Ford, 'Rudolph Ackermann: culture and commerce in Latin America', *Andres Bello: the London years*, ed. J. Lynch (1982), 137–52 · J. Haefkins, *Centraal Amerika* (1832) · G. Ackermann, *The Times* (6 May 1859) · *GM*, 2nd ser., 31 (1849) · *GM*, 3rd ser., 6 (1859) · *The Art Journal illustrated catalogue: the industry of all nations, 1851* [1851] · *Curtis's Botanical Magazine*, new ser., 11 (1837) · *The life and adventures of George Augustus Sala*, 2 vols. (1895) · T. Faulkner, *An historical and topographical description of Chelsea and its environs*, [new edn], 2 vols. (1829) · H. Gernsheim and A. Gernsheim, *The history of photography* (1955) · J. E. Hodgson, *The history of aeronautics in Great Britain, from the earliest times to the latter half of the nineteenth century* (1924)
Archives NRA, priv. coll., family papers
Likenesses M. Cosway, pencil drawing, 1811, priv. coll. · oils, 1835, priv. coll. · D. Dingman, photograph, c.1869, priv. coll. · Clark & Bowness, photograph, c.1880, priv. coll. · Clark & Bowness, photograph, c.1885, priv. coll.

Ackermann, Rudolph (1764–1834), publisher, was born on 20 April 1764 at Stollberg, near Leipzig, in Saxony, the sixth child of Barthel Ackermann (1723–1798), a saddler, and his wife, Justina Scharschmidt (1732–1808). He was educated at the Latin school at Stollberg and then at Schneeberg, where his family had moved in 1775. At the age of fifteen Ackermann was apprenticed to his elder brother Friedrich, a saddler; it was during this period that he also learned to draw and engrave. In 1782 he left Schneeberg to train as a carriage designer, first in Dresden and then at Hueningen, in Switzerland. In 1784 he travelled to Paris where he was employed for six months by the celebrated carriage maker Antoine Carassi. He worked for the carriage making firm of Simons in Brussels in 1785–6 before arriving in England in 1787, aged twenty-three. His model of a state coach for the carriage maker Goodall led to his first important commission, the design of a state coach for the lord lieutenant of Ireland in 1790; he was also employed to decorate the existing coach of the lord mayor of Dublin. He designed a state coach for George Washington in America, and an innovative security mail coach which ran between Charing Cross and Greenwich. Between 1791 and 1820 he published thirteen books of designs for carriages. In 1792 he married Martha Massey (1769–1811), an Englishwoman, and set up house at 7 Little Russell Street, Covent Garden.

Ackermann formed close connections with other émigrés from Saxony, most significantly for his own future career with the Facius brothers and with J. C. Stadler, all then employed as engravers by the leading print publisher John Boydell. In 1795 he moved to 96 Strand and opened a drawing school which he ran for ten years. In 1796 he published the first of many drawing books and

Rudolph Ackermann (1764–1834), attrib. François Nicholas Mouchet, 1810–14

also medallions and the first transparency prints, anticipating rival claimants by some three years. In 1797 he moved to larger premises at 101 Strand (known as 'The Repository of Arts' from 1798) and published many decorative hand-coloured prints, including over 100 political and social caricatures by and after Thomas Rowlandson. Ackermann also sold old master paintings and artists' and fancy papers, and in 1799 began to manufacture watercolour paints. The expansion of his business was in part financed by Prince Philipp von Lichstenstein, an Austrian then resident in London.

In 1801 Ackermann had taken out a patent for the waterproofing of paper and cloth; he opened a manufactory in Chelsea, but closed the business after the dishonesty of one of his partners cost him the sum of £1000. In 1804 a carriage of his design carried the pope to the self-coronation of Napoleon Bonaparte in Paris, and at the end of the following year he was commissioned to design the elaborate funeral carriage and the emblematic designs on the coffin of Admiral Lord Nelson. In 1806, using false papers, Ackermann travelled to Saxony, then under Napoleonic blockade: he visited Hamburg and Leipzig, escaping French troops by disguising himself as a coachman, and travelled to Vienna before returning to England. A more substantial contribution to the war effort followed: in 1807 the War Office conducted trials on Ackermann's design for a paper distributor to be carried in an air balloon for the purpose of distributing propaganda over continental Europe. On 24 March 1809 he was naturalized as a citizen of the United Kingdom.

The years 1808 and 1809 saw the first issue of two publications which secured Ackermann's reputation as a publisher of the finest colour plate books: *The Microcosm of London*, which appeared from 1808 in parts, completing publication in 1810, contained 104 large folio hand-coloured aquatints. The *Repository of Arts*, a monthly magazine, begun in 1809, featuring fashion and social and literary news, continued for twenty years, during which time 1432 hand-coloured plates appeared in it. It remains an important sourcebook for Regency style and fashions. Ackermann employed not only the architectural draughtsman Augustus Pugin, but also a figure drawer of genius, Thomas Rowlandson, who filled the interior views of London's landmark buildings with convincing life. Other fine topographical books followed, all with aquatint plates and all originally issued in parts. They included *Westminster Abbey* (1811–12), *Oxford* (1813–14), *Cambridge* (1814–15), and *The Public Schools* (1816). The author of the texts was William Combe, whom Ackermann paired with Rowlandson in another series of colour plate books of a different style. The three *Tours of Dr Syntax* (1812, 1820, and 1821), featuring the picaresque adventures of a naïve skin-and-bone clergyman, became runaway best-sellers.

Ackermann was an enthusiastic promoter of artists of the English watercolour school and at various times employed W. H. Pyne, Thomas Heaphy, and John Gendall at 101 Strand. From 1813 his weekly 'conversazioni', held during the London season in his gas-lit 'Great Room', served to introduce artists to patrons. His wife Martha, who bore him nine children, had died in 1811, but with his eldest daughter Angelica at his side he was also a regular and considerate host at his home in Camberwell Grove from 1815, and then at Ivy Cottage, Fulham, from 1825. There are many testimonies to his private generosity and also to his fondness for food and Moselle wine.

Ackermann continued to maintain extensive German connections, and in 1814 he became active in fund-raising activities for the widows and orphans of Germany. As secretary of two distinct London committees, and with powerful royal and church support, he distributed over £200,000 to more than 100 districts in Germany. He escorted Prince Blücher to the charity concert at the Chapel Royal, and his role as a benefactor was recognized by awards from both the king of Saxony and the king of Prussia. In 1816, as a result of a close friendship with Antonin Schlichtegroll of Munich, himself the friend of the inventor Alois Senefelder, Ackermann established the first significant lithographic press in England and played an important part in popularizing lithography by publishing Senefelder's *Treatise* in 1818. In 1817 Ackermann patented the moveable axle invented by a servant of the king of Bavaria, and in 1822 he introduced to England the German 'gift book'. This first annual, *Forget-me-Not*, proved an unprecedented commercial success, 20,000 copies a year being published.

Ackermann was among the first to recognize the commercial possibilities of the emerging independence movement throughout the Spanish colonies of South and Central America. He had first met Lopez Mendez, Bolívar's

London representative, in 1819, and paid for supplies for Bolívar's campaign of liberation. In 1822 he was chosen to print the bond certificates for the first Colombia loan. In the next five years he invested in government bonds and in mining stock in South America. Sending his son George *Ackermann (1803–1891) to Mexico and Guatemala, he opened shops in both countries and in Colombia, Argentina, and Peru, and published over 100 books in Spanish, including textbooks which played an important part in the education of the newly independent republics.

In 1825 Ackermann established his eldest son, Rudolph, in a print shop at 191 Regent Street. He continued to publish decorative books and colour plate books, including the most lavish of all, John Nash's *Royal Pavilion*, in 1826, and in 1827 opened a new and extended 'Repository of Arts' at a cost of between £7000 and £8000 at 96 Strand. In the same year, at the age of sixty-three, he remarried. The following year he wrote that he was working from 6 a.m. to midnight every day; at this time large losses on the South American investments were confirmed, as well as piracy of his Spanish publications. Overwork and worry affected his health and in 1830 he had a serious stroke, followed by paralysis. He formally handed over his business (Ackermann & Co.) to his younger sons in October 1832. He had a second stroke in November 1833 and died on 30 March 1834 at his home at Cold Harbour, Finchley. Though brought up a Lutheran protestant, Ackermann had later worshipped in the Church of England, and he was buried in the Portugal Street burial-ground of St Clement Danes on 7 April. He was survived by his wife, Hannah, and by six of the nine children of his first marriage.

A portrait of about 1814 shows Ackermann as a powerfully built man, with a rather reserved expression. A loyal friend and an affectionate—if overbearing—parent, he was most relaxed in the company of women. Though a passionate Anglophile, Ackermann retained a strong German accent until his death and both anticipated and contributed to the influence of German culture in the mid-Victorian art world. As a publisher he was both creative and efficient, bringing to the commercial production of colour plate books innovative techniques and an uncompromising attention to detail which ensured uniform high quality. His fine sensitivity to art was not complemented by unerring literary taste, and he published much second-rate letterpress, poetry, and history. While the partnership of Ackermann & Co. was dissolved in 1855, the print business which Ackermann had established for his eldest son, Rudolph, survived, becoming Arthur Ackermann & Son and closing down as recently as 1992.

JOHN FORD

Sources J. Ford, *Ackermann, 1783–1983: the business of art* (1983) · J. A. Ford, 'Rudolph Ackermann: publisher to Latin America', *Bello y Londres*, ed. O. S. Urdaneta, 1 (1980), 197–224 · J. A. Ford, 'Rudolph Ackermann: culture and commerce in Latin America', *Andres Bello: the London years*, ed. J. Lynch (1982), 137–52 · J. A. Ford, 'Ackermann imprints and publications', *Maps and prints: aspects of the English booktrade*, ed. R. Myers and M. Harris (1984), 109–24 · *GM*, 2nd ser., 1 (1834), 560–61 · *New Sporting Magazine*, 7 (1834) · 'Rudolph Ackermann: eine säcular Erinnerung', *Didaskalia*, 104 (14 April 1864) · W. P. [W. Papworth], 'Rudolph Ackermann of the Strand, publisher [2 pts]', *N&Q*, 4th ser., 4 (1869), 109–12, 129–31 · C. Niedner, 'Rudolph Ackermann und die englischen Hilfsaktionen 1807 und 1813 ff', *Neues Archiv für Sächsische Geschichte und Altertumskunde* (1921), 242–55 · *Genealogisches Handbuch Burgerlicher Familien Deutsches Geschlechterbuch* (1889–1919) · R. Wolfram, *Männer des Verdienstes um Volkswohl im biographischen Skizzen* (Zwickau, 1866) · F. Schulze, *Geschichte der Familien Ackermann aus gödern in Altenburgischen Ostkreise, 1560–1913* (1913)

Archives American Society of Antiquities, Worcester, Massachusetts, corresp. · BL, corresp., Add. MSS 35130, 35133, 36594–36595, Egerton MSS 2247–2248 · BM, corresp. · Bodl. Oxf., corresp. · Coutts Bank, London, bank accounts · Free Library of Philadelphia, corresp. · LPL, papers as joint secretary of Westminster Association · NL Scot., corresp. · Rothschilds Bank, London, corresp. · U. Edin. L., corresp. · U. Lpool L., corresp. | BL, Combe MSS · Sheff. Arch., letters to James Montgomery

Likenesses attrib. F. N. Mouchet, oils, 1810–14, NPG [*see illus.*]

Wealth at death portrait by Mouchet; Meissen figures; order of merit; enamelled parrot; diamond ring: will

Ackland, Mary Kathleen Macrory- [*pseud.* Valentine Ackland] **(1906–1969)**, poet, was born on 20 May 1906 at 54 Brook Street, Mayfair, London, the younger daughter of Robert Craig Ackland, a West End dental surgeon, and his wife, Ruth Kathleen, *née* Macrory (d. 1961). She attended Queen's College in Harley Street and a finishing school in Paris, and came out as a débutante in 1923, the year that her father died from cancer. Her privileged upbringing and genteel education (of whose limitations she was painfully aware) prepared her for no career other than marriage, and Ackland's youth was an unhappy one, marked by sexual and religious confusion, melancholia, and alcohol addiction, all recorded with forensic self-absorption in her confessional memoir, *For Sylvia: an Honest Account*, published posthumously in 1985. After converting from the Anglican faith to Roman Catholicism, on 9 July 1925 she made a hasty and brief marriage to (Alan) Richard Turpin, (b. 1902/3), a stamp dealer and later a minor novelist. Within months she had left him (they were divorced on grounds of nullity in 1927) and had gone to live in East Chaldon, Dorset, where she became friends with the writer T. F. Powys and his family. Here she widened her circle of artistic acquaintance—which already included Augustus John and Eric Gill—to include the sculptors Stephen Tomlin and Betty Muntz. At almost 6 feet tall, with close-cropped hair, Ackland's striking physical appearance made her an attractive model to Gill and others; at the same period her adoption of Valentine as her name and pseudonym and almost exclusive conversion to masculine clothing emphasized the lesbian side of her (then) bisexual nature.

When in 1930 Ackland fell in love with the well-known novelist and poet Sylvia Townsend *Warner (1893–1978), the two women set up home together in Chaldon, later living briefly in Norfolk and then back in Dorset (in Maiden Newton from 1937) for the rest of their thirty-eight-year 'marriage'. The relationship has been thoroughly documented, in Warner's *Diaries* (1994), *Letters* (1982), and the lovers' voluminous correspondence, published as *I'll Stand By You* (1998), which bears witness to the essential contentment of their domestic life, despite Ackland's infidelities and chronic melancholia. Much of the latter was connected with the failure, in worldly terms, of her poetry. Very little of her work was published during her lifetime other than in periodicals (including *Life and Letters Today*, the *London Mercury*, the *New Statesman*, *Left Review*, and *Our Time*). Early in their relationship Warner had promoted Ackland's work vigorously; the only substantial result was a joint collection, *Whether a Dove or Seagull*, published in 1934, which did little to launch Valentine's career though it constituted an interesting experiment in presentation, along the lines of Wordsworth's and Coleridge's jointly published *Lyrical Ballads*. In the melding together of the two writers' work (the poems were unattributed in the text), Warner and Ackland made a gesture against 'the frame of mind which judges a poem by looking to see who wrote it' (S. T. Warner and V. Ackland, 'Note to the reader', *Whether a Dove or Seagull*, 1934). At the same time anonymity afforded them considerable licence, and the collection is remarkable for its love poems, many of which were so sexually explicit as to pass contemporary reviewers without comment.

Ackland's growing interest in social issues and left-wing politics led her to join the Communist Party in 1935. She became a regular contributor to Edgell Rickword's *Left Review*, *The Countryman*, and the *Daily Worker* and in 1936 published a study of rural poverty based on her polemical journalism entitled *Country Conditions*. During the Spanish Civil War in 1936 she and Warner worked with the Red Cross in Barcelona and in the following year they were both delegates at the International Writers' Conference in Madrid. During the Second World War she worked as a civil defence clerk and as a doctor's dispenser. By 1953 Ackland had become disillusioned with the Communist Party and resigned. Three years later she rejoined the Catholic church (having lapsed quickly the first time) and remained in that faith until the late 1960s, when she became a Quaker.

Ackland's meditative lyric voice is most at home describing the natural world (which she does in an exaltedly scientific spirit) and has much more in common with the past writers she admired, particularly John Clare, William Cowper, Thomas Traherne, and George Crabbe, than with her contemporaries. An intuition that she was in many ways out of step with her time contributed to her ambivalence about appearing in print. Her habit of revising poems was symptomatic of a feeling that her work was always, as it were, 'in progress'; significantly her most frequent theme is transience and the equivocal nature of 'the moment'. The poet Wendy Mulford has characterized Ackland's poetry as 'wrestling with the paradox of feeling' (Mulford, 208), a struggle which is visible in both content and form. Written mostly in free verse, all Ackland's work contains strong undercurrents of the traditional forms from which she is deviating.

At her death in 1969, Ackland had only one publication to her name apart from *Whether a Dove or Seagull*, a privately printed booklet *Twenty-Eight Poems* (1957). *Later Poems* appeared in 1970, *Further Poems* in 1978, and a substantial selection entitled *The Nature of the Moment* in 1973.

The attention her poetry has attracted posthumously seems to derive some of its energy from the neglect she suffered during her lifetime; Ackland's obscure (and personally disappointing) career is regarded by some critics as constituting a reproach to an earlier generation of canon-mongers (see Jane Dowson's comments on Valentine Ackland in *Women's Poetry of the 1930s: a Critical Anthology*, 1996). Though none of her books is currently in print, selections from Ackland's work (generally the more polemical parts of it) are included in many recent anthologies of left-wing, lesbian, and thirties' poetry. The increasing interest in Ackland both as a writer and as a minor lesbian icon is reflected in her inclusion in the Writer's Gallery at Dorset County Museum, which opened in 1997.

Valentine Ackland died from breast cancer on 9 November 1969 at her home, Lower Frome Vauchurch, Maiden Newton, and was buried at St Nicholas's Church, East Chaldon, on 22 November.   CLAIRE HARMAN

Sources V. Ackland, *For Sylvia: an honest account* (1985) · C. Harman, *Sylvia Townsend Warner* (1989) · W. Mulford, *This narrow place: Sylvia Townsend Warner and Valentine Ackland: life, letters and politics, 1930–1951* (1988) · S. Pinney, ed., *I'll stand by you: selected letters of Sylvia Townsend Warner and Valentine Ackland* (1998) · *The diaries of Sylvia Townsend Warner*, ed. C. Harman (1994) · b. cert. · m. cert. · d. cert.

Archives Dorset County Museum, Dorchester, Sylvia Townsend Warner and Valentine Ackland collection, corresp. and papers | U. Reading L., Chatto and Windus archive · U. Reading L., letters to Joyce Finzi · U. Reading L., letters to Helen Thomas

Likenesses J. Finzi, drawing, U. Reading, Finzi Room · E. Gill, study, Dorset County Museum, Dorchester, Dorset · photograph, Dorset County Museum, Dorchester, Dorset, Sylvia Townsend Warner and Valentine Ackland collection, photographic collection; repro. in Harman, *Sylvia Townsend Warner*, pl. 12

Ackland, Rodney (1908–1991), playwright, was born Norman Ackland Bernstein on 18 May 1908, at 5 Palmeira Gardens, Southend, Essex, the only son of Nathan Bernstein, a Jewish mantle manufacturer originally from Warsaw, and his wife, Emily Diana Lock (*c*.1874–1959), a former musical comedy artiste specializing in pantomime boys under the stage name Ada Rodney. Nathan Bernstein made a fortune out of jewellery in the East End of London, and lost it again when his business went bankrupt in 1914. Young Norman and his two sisters grew up under the spell of their mother, who sold stockings from door to door to support the household while attempting to revive her stage career, with enthusiastic support from her small son.

Ackland was, by his own account, educated at the cinema, putting in time at Balham grammar school until he was old enough, at fourteen, to leave and set about becoming an actor himself. He took a day job as a shop boy at Swan and Edgar, and almost immediately embarked on a lifelong affair with the Russian theatre by landing the part of Medvediev in Maksim Gorky's *The Lower Depths* at London's tiny, experimental Gate Theatre. In 1926 he saw the first English production of Anton Chekhov's *Three Sisters* (with the young John Gielgud as Tusenbach) in Theodore Komisarjevsky's seminal season at Barnes. Ackland always said it turned him into a playwright.

He was nineteen when he wrote his first play, *Improper*

People, performed at the Arts Theatre in 1929. His acting career (which included stints with J. B. Fagan's Oxford Players and the Masque Theatre in Edinburgh) reached its peak the same year when he starred in a touring production of John van Druten's *Young Woodley*. He had his first success as a playwright with *Strange Orchestra*, directed in 1931 by Gielgud in the West End. Mrs Patrick Campbell emerged from retirement only to retreat into it again when she realized that the star part was a cheerful, disorderly single mother (Laura Cowie took over the role, with Jean Forbes Robertson and Hugh Williams).

Ackland's raffish early plays had a gaiety and exuberance that distracted attention from their subversive content. But, as his imagination deepened and his technical reach grew bolder, his work increasingly dismayed audiences accustomed to the artificially restricted emotional, social, and intellectual range of drawing-room comedy. Ackland produced his own characteristic variation on the form in *Birthday* (1934), which dissects standard middle-class assumptions and behaviour with a sombre ferocity and wit that come closer to John Vanbrugh or William Wycherley than to Ackland's more popular contemporaries, such as Dodie Smith, Terence Rattigan, and Noël Coward.

After October in 1936 was the nearest Ackland came to a West End hit ('Mr Ackland's theme is gloom,' wrote James Agate, 'but I came out dog tired from laughing' (*Sunday Times*, 1936)). It was followed by *The Dark River*, a strange, musical, unsettling play, by turns painful and wildly funny, that remains one of the most powerful evocations in any medium of England on the brink of the Second World War. Peggy Ashcroft shone as the heroine but, by the time the play reached the West End in 1941 with air-raid sirens interrupting the first night, the last thing London audiences wanted was a serious attempt to come to grips on stage with a frightening present and a still more uncertain future.

Ackland's professional career spanned the 1930s, 1940s, and early 1950s when, in Kenneth Tynan's memorable phrase, straight plays in the West End seldom strayed far outside 'a country house in what used to be called Loamshire but is now, as a heroic tribute to realism, sometimes called Berkshire' (K. Tynan, *Curtains: a Critic's View of Plays, Players and Theatrical Events, 1950–1960*, 1961, 86). Ackland's world is harsher, seedier, invincibly urban, sexually louche, emotionally unstable, and morally far from reassuring. He dealt with precisely the kind of realities the Loamshire play was designed to exclude. After the war, in an age of austerity when audiences craved glamour, frivolity, and escape, Ackland's unheroic view of the period in *The Pink Room* (1952), set in a drinking club on the eve of the 1945 general election, was rejected as morally degenerate by reviewers. Their onslaught effectively put a stop to his career as a playwright.

Ackland was the forerunner and should have been the natural ally of the theatrical generation that came to power with the upheavals sparked off by John Osborne's *Look Back in Anger* in 1956. But, by a characteristically Acklandesque irony, the new wave of angry young iconoclasts made no distinction between Ackland's work and the stylized sentimentality of the well-made West End play which he had himself long and stubbornly resisted. For most of the second half of his life, his plays remained unperformed and out of print.

Ackland found consolation, to the astonishment of friends who had always known him as frankly and flamboyantly homosexual, in a serenely happy marriage to Mab Lonsdale, herself an accomplished writer, wit, and daughter of the playwright Frederick (Freddy) *Lonsdale. Married in 1952, the two were inseparable until her death in 1972. Ackland's life reflected to a startling degree the inconsistencies, reversals, and ambiguities of an imaginative world so powerful that people he met frequently started behaving as shambolically as characters in an Ackland play.

Ackland was championed by independent directors such as Frith Banbury and Tyrone Guthrie. Actors—from Edith Evans, Flora Robson, Peter Ustinov, and Paul Scofield to Judi Dench and Alex Jennings—responded to his work with unfailing relish. His memoirs remained unfinished except for *The Celluloid Mistress* (1954), devoted to his largely unrequited passion for the cinema. He left a string of brilliantly theatrical adaptations of other people's work, ranging from Hugh Walpole's *The Old Ladies* (1935) to Bulgakov's *The White Guard* (1934), Ostrovsky's *Diary of a Scoundrel* (1942), and Dostoyevsky's *Crime and Punishment* (1946). He came to see himself with a certain gloomy relish as the British theatre's invisible man. 'I can't keep from my mind the bitter reflection that, when I was 15, my career started in *The Lower Depths*,' he wrote in 1986, 'and now, when I'm 78, it's in the lower depths that I'm finishing.' He lived just long enough to see the start of a widespread revival of his reputation, helped in part by his award-winning adaptation of Ostrovsky's *Diary of a Scoundrel* as *Too Clever by Half* in 1988.

Ackland died of leukaemia at home in Richmond on 6 December 1991, and was cremated at Mortlake later that month. *The Pink Room*, revised and retitled *Absolute Hell*, made a triumphant return to the National Theatre in 1995. Ackland was Chekhovian in his structural command of rhythm and pattern, in his ability to write orchestrally for a large cast, and in his effect on audiences who saw themselves and their world reflected too clearly for comfort in the mirror of his work. More than any other playwright of his generation, he operated alongside poets such as Auden and MacNeice, and novelists such as Powell, Greene, and Waugh, at the cutting edge of contemporary writing between and just after the two world wars.

HILARY SPURLING

Sources personal knowledge (2004) · private information (2004) · J. Spurling, *Contemporary dramatists*, ed. J. Vinson (1973) · C. Duff, *The lost summer* (1995) · *The Times* (7 Dec 1991) · *Daily Telegraph* (7 Dec 1991) · *The Independent* (7 Dec 1991) · N. Dromgoole, introduction, in R. Ackland, *Absolute hell* (1990) · H. Spurling, 'Rodney Ackland', *The Spectator* (22 Nov 1968) · H. Spurling, 'Neglected master of the English style', *Daily Telegraph* (22 March 1988)

Archives priv. coll., playscripts, MSS, theatre programmes, letters, interviews, recollections, etc.
Likenesses photograph, 1930, Hult. Arch. · photograph, repro. in theatre programme (May 1997) [*After October*, Chichester Theatre] · photograph (in youth), priv. coll. · photograph, repro. in *The Times* · photograph, repro. in *Daily Telegraph* (7 Dec 1991) · photograph, repro. in *The Independent* · photographs, repro. in theatre programmes (1992–5) [*Absolute hell*, National Theatre, London, and Staatstheater, Stuttgart]

Ackland, Thomas Gilbank (1791–1844), Church of England clergyman, the son of Thomas Ackland, chaplain to the Fishmongers' Company, was educated at Charterhouse School and St John's College, Cambridge. He became BA in 1811 (the year in which he married Mary Hopkinson), and MA in 1814. He was ordained deacon in 1813 and priest in 1814; in 1818 he was appointed rector of St Mildred's, Bread Street, a post which he held until his death, at Wadworth, on 20 February 1844. Apart from holding the curacy of St Bartholomew by the Exchange, he was also domestic chaplain to the duke of York, and lecturer at two other churches in the City. His published works include *Miscellaneous Poems* (1812) and several sermons. [ANON.], rev. SARAH BROLLY

Sources *GM*, 2nd ser., 21 (1844), 659 · Venn, *Alum. Cant.* · [J. Watkins and F. Shoberl], *A biographical dictionary of the living authors of Great Britain and Ireland* (1816)

Ackland, Valentine. *See* Ackland, Mary Kathleen Macrory- (1906–1969).

Ackroyd, Dame (Dorothy) Elizabeth [Betty] (1910–1987), civil servant and consumer rights campaigner, was born at Hydrastin House, Wilpshire, Lancashire, on 13 August 1910, the daughter of Major Charles Harris Ackroyd MC, an army officer, and his wife, Dorothy Margaret Baynes. After being educated privately, she entered St Hugh's College, Oxford, in 1930, where her studies were interrupted by ill health. She read philosophy, politics, and economics, taking a second in 1934. She then embarked on postgraduate research, writing a thesis under the supervision of G. D. H. Cole on the economic policy of trade unions since the First World War, and qualified for a BLitt degree in 1936. For a while she was research assistant on a survey of social services in Oxford and adjacent areas organized by Barnett House.

Betty Ackroyd, as she was known, remained unmarried and chose to pursue a career. In 1940 she joined the Ministry of Supply as a principal, rising to under-secretary by 1952. Over the next three decades she had a wide experience in a number of exacting fields. She was director of the steel and power division of the Economic Commission for Europe in 1950–51 and a member of the United Kingdom delegation to the high authority of the European Coal and Steel Community in 1952–5. Her choice of specialization within the civil service was deliberate. She confided to a friend that she had chosen to acquire a reputation as an expert in heavy industry because this was the best way to overcome the difficulties encountered by women in the pursuit of a career in Whitehall. While she would not have called herself a feminist, she did not accept any notion of a subordinate role for women. Her quick mind and toughness enabled her to surpass the obstacles of her gender; 'men of the type who were accustomed to waffling on committees found her disconcerting, and she did not suffer their ramblings gladly' (*The Times*).

When the Consumer Council was set up by the Conservative government in 1963 to review and, where appropriate, resolve problems experienced by consumers, Betty Ackroyd was appointed its first director. She brought her formidable powers to her work there, acquiring the affectionate title of public protector no. 1. Yet ultimately even she admitted that her success was limited. The council was large and unwieldy and did not meet often enough to address the many problems she wanted tackled. British industry was slow to respond to its initiatives and she felt that the British public acquiesced too readily in low standards. She counted among her greatest defeats her failure to stop banks closing on Saturdays; the failure of the government to establish regional Consumer Council offices, especially one in much-neglected Scotland; and the failure to get 10s. not £1 accepted as the basis for the new decimalized currency.

The year 1970 was one of mixed achievement. Ackroyd was made a dame of the British empire but she was unable to prevent first a reduction in the grant for the Consumer Council, and then, in 1971, its abolition by the incoming Conservative government of Edward Heath. When the government later set up the Office of Fair Trading she was disappointed not to be appointed to a post there. She always felt that her straight speaking was not popular with politicians. This, however, was not the end of her contribution to consumer affairs. Michael Young sought her advice when he became the first chair of the National Consumer Council, and she was vice-president of the Consumers' Association from 1970 to 1986 and remained on its executive committee until her death.

After her retirement in 1971 Ackroyd remained actively involved in public life. From 1971 to 1978 she was president, and from 1978 to her death chairman, of the Patients Association, an independent pressure group committed to representing and defending patients' interests, especially in relation to the National Health Service. From 1980 she was on the executive of the National Council for Voluntary Organizations. She was a member of the Post Office Users' National Council, and of the executive of the Pedestrians' Association for Road Safety; she was also active on the Westminster police consultation committee. At various times she chaired the South-Eastern Electricity Consumer Council and the Cinematograph Films Council. She had a succession of horses in training at Newmarket. (One, sired by Derby winner Morston, she named Moron for amusement, with the horse duly living up to its name.) In her membership of the Horserace Totalisator Board (1975–84) and Bloodstock and Racehorse Industries Confederation Ltd (1977–8) she was able to combine both her leisure interest and her professional expertise.

A friend and colleague noted that Ackroyd always liked to say that she looked forward to a day when she had 'absolutely nothing to do'. But that time never came. Despite or perhaps because of her active public career she was considered a very private person. She died on 28 June 1987 at the Royal Marsden Hospital, Chelsea, London.

MARGARET JONES

Sources *The Times* (30 June 1987) · *The Independent* (2 July 1987) · *WWW*, 1981–90 · private information (2004) [J. Mitchell; Lord Young of Dartington; R. McRobert] · Oxf. UA · b. cert. · d. cert. · *CGPLA Eng. & Wales* (1988)
Wealth at death £536,709: probate, 28 Jan 1988, *CGPLA Eng. & Wales*

Acland [*née* Cunningham], **Alice Sophia**, Lady Acland (1849–1935), co-operative movement activist and advocate of women's advancement, was born on 3 February 1849 at Heath Lodge, Petersfield, Hampshire, the eldest daughter of the Revd Francis Macaulay Cunningham (1815/16–1899) and his wife, *née* Alice Charlotte Poore. Alice was educated at the local church school, and work as a district visitor, following her father's appointment as rector of Witney, Oxfordshire, fostered her concern for the poor. Her interests were shared with the Oxford don Arthur Herbert Dyke *Acland (1847–1926), whom she married on 14 June 1873. They had two sons and a daughter.

The Aclands' circle included Christian socialists and co-operators, particularly E. V. Neale and Thomas Hughes. However, Alice Acland attributed her interest in co-operation to contact with working people of the northern industrial centres, whom she met while accompanying her husband on speaking tours from the mid-1870s onwards. Her admiration for the working-class women that she met was reflected in her sketches 'Women's lives', published in the *Co-operative News*. Struck by the lack of opportunities for women beyond the domestic sphere, Acland participated in discussion of increased female involvement in co-operation during the movement's 1882 congress. Her friendship with Samuel Bamford, editor of the *Co-operative News*, enabled her to overcome initial opposition and establish a weekly 'Women's corner' in the paper from January 1883. She advocated greater female participation in co-operation through women's meetings and discussion groups, and intended the 'Corner' as a link between women throughout Britain. Conscious of male resistance, Acland called not overtly for women's rights, but for a greater sense of self-worth:

> We trade too much on our weakness as compared to men. … We cause our womanhood to be despised—not to be respected. It is our own fault, and men have not, perhaps, been unwilling that it should be so. … England can never be all it might, when more than one-half of the nation hangs behind the other part. (*Co-operative News*, 6 Jan 1883, 25)

The suggestion of co-operative women's meetings stimulated several responses, most significantly Mary Lawrenson's plan for a Women's League for the Spread of Co-operation—later the Women's Co-operative Guild. Acland agreed to lead the guild, inviting prospective members to write to her, but she resisted more active propagandism, particularly platform speaking, in her concern not to offend male sensibilities. The guild was not immediately successful, and only three local branches were established during 1883. The year also saw the first

national meeting of the guild at the Co-operative Congress, which confirmed Acland as organizing secretary.

Acland's health was, however, failing. Illness hampered her work for the guild, and her editorial duties on the 'Women's corner' were deputed to her assistant, Amy Sharp. In 1884 Acland retired as guild secretary and her tenure as national president (1884–6) was similarly curtailed. She also resigned as editor of the 'Women's corner' in 1886. She retained a limited involvement with the guild, chairing a meeting at the 1892 Manchester Festival. However, for the remainder of her life Alice's poor health precluded an active public role.

Alice became Lady Acland in 1919 when her husband succeeded as thirteenth baronet. The title passed to her eldest son, Francis, when Sir Arthur died in 1926. Lady Acland was a complete invalid for the last twelve years of her life, but she retained the affection of co-operative women who granted her the freedom of the guild in 1931. She died on 5 July 1935 at home at 85 Onslow Square, London, survived by one son and her daughter. She was cremated at Golders Green on 8 July and her ashes interred with those of her husband at the Columb John Chapel, on the family estate at Killerton, Devon, on 10 July. A memorial service was held at St Martin-in-the-Fields, London, on 11 July.

Alice Acland worked for greater equality between men and women; her vision was apolitical and consistent with nineteenth-century notions of distinctions between male and female traits. She contended that women's lack of business knowledge militated against their participation in co-operative management; rather, female spirituality and gentleness should be applied to the moral salvation of both the co-operative movement and national life. Drawing strength of purpose from her own Christian convictions she insisted that quietness need not make women ineffectual: 'There are moments when speaking up is needed, and these we must not miss' (*Co-operative News*, 9 June 1883, 532–3).

MARTIN PURVIS

Sources 'Women's corner', *Co-operative News* (6 Jan 1883) · 'Women's corner', *Co-operative News* (20 Jan 1883) · 'Women's corner', *Co-operative News* (17 Feb 1883) · 'Women's corner', *Co-operative News* (10 March 1883) · 'Women's corner', *Co-operative News* (31 March 1883) · 'Women's corner', *Co-operative News* (14 April 1883) · 'Women's corner', *Co-operative News* (12 May 1883) · 'Women's corner', *Co-operative News* (26 May 1883) · 'Women's corner', *Co-operative News* (9 June 1883) · 'Women's corner', *Co-operative News* (20 July 1935) · *Women's Outlook* (3 Aug 1935) · C. Webb, *The woman with the basket: the history of the Women's Co-operative Guild, 1883–1927* (1927) · M. L. Davies, *The Women's Co-operative Guild, 1883–1904* (1904) · *The Times* (9 July 1935) · 'A chat with Lady Acland', *Women's Outlook*, 3/26 (1921), 35–6 · J. Bellamy and H. F. Bing, 'Acland, Alice Sophia', *DLB*, vol. 1 · b. cert. · m. cert. · d. cert. · Venn, *Alum. Cant.*
Archives Devon RO, family MSS
Likenesses photograph, *c.*1880–1885, repro. in Davies, *Women's Co-operative Guild 1883–1904*, 15 · photograph, 1910–1920?, repro. in Webb, *Woman with the basket*, between pp. 16 and 17 · photograph, 1933, repro. in *Women's Outlook*, 16/345, 617
Wealth at death £403 9s. 7d.: administration, 5 Oct 1935, *CGPLA Eng. & Wales*

Acland, Sir Arthur Herbert Dyke, thirteenth baronet (1847–1926), politician and educational reformer, was

Sir Arthur Herbert Dyke Acland, thirteenth baronet (1847–1926), by W. & D. Downey, pubd 1894

born at Holnicote, near Porlock, Somerset, on 13 October 1847, the third son of Sir Thomas Dyke *Acland, eleventh baronet (1809–1898), and his first wife, Mary (d. 1851), daughter of Sir Charles Mordaunt, eighth baronet, of Massingham, Norfolk. The Aclands, leading landowners in the west of England, were well established, both at the University of Oxford and in wider political circles. Sir Thomas Acland was an educational reformer and Arthur recalled growing up among his father's reports for the Taunton commission. He entered Rugby School in 1861 and matriculated from Christ Church, Oxford, in 1866. He obtained a second class in classical moderations (1868) and also in the final school of law and modern history (1870), graduating BA in 1870 and MA in 1873.

In 1871 Acland was appointed lecturer, and in 1872 tutor, at Keble College, then newly founded. As the third son, however, Acland was educated to enter the church, being known from birth in the family as 'the little clergyman'. In 1872 he was ordained deacon and after his marriage on 14 June 1873 to Alice Sophia (1849–1935), daughter of Francis Macaulay Cunningham, the vicar of Witney [see Acland, Alice Sophia], the young couple were expected to take up the family living at Luccombe, Somerset. Beset by doubts as to the validity of Anglican dogma, Acland suffered a nervous collapse. He later told R. B. Haldane in a letter in

1898: 'I knocked up my brain early in life and have overstrained it ever since' (Matthew, 9). His curacy under Mandell Creighton in Embleton, Northumberland, did nothing to reassure him. A tour of the industrial north in 1875 and, in particular, to the working men's club in Rochdale, however, suddenly provided invigoration and a growing political awareness. It also confirmed his decision to resign holy orders, and he took advantage of the Clerical Disabilities Act in 1879.

Acland's time as principal of the new Oxford Military College from 1875 to 1877 proved unhappy. In 1879 he was appointed steward of Christ Church and was a senior student there in 1884–5. He was the first treasurer of Somerville College. In 1884 he was appointed senior bursar of Balliol College and was made an honorary fellow in 1888. While at Oxford he gathered around him a group of young fellows and undergraduates, including Herbert Llewellyn Smith, J. A. Spender, L. T. Hobhouse, and Michael Sadler, known as the Inner Ring, who met at his home to discuss political and social questions. Acland remained a mentor for many of them. He urged Spender to investigate old age pensions and sickness insurance and wrote the introduction to the findings in *The State and Pensions in Old Age* (1892).

Extramural teaching and Liberal politics In 1878 Acland was appointed secretary responsible for 'the provision of Lectures and Teaching in the large towns of England and Wales', a new initiative of the University of Oxford delegacy of local examinations (which had been founded by his father in 1857). The chairman was his close friend T. H. Green, the Balliol idealist philosopher, and it was his teaching which Acland now began to translate into a programme of 'education for citizenship'. Significantly, it was the industrial north of England, with its growing political strength, to which Acland directed his efforts. His great success as a lecturer, often to audiences of more than seven hundred, and the rapport he established with working men, and especially co-operators, laid the foundation for the unique contribution of Oxford University extension. In 1882 he brought the Co-operative Congress to Oxford and in meetings in the Sheldonian Theatre and Balliol College leading co-operators and sympathetic university dons forged relationships which were to result eventually in the creation of the Workers' Educational Association and the joint tutorial classes. Acland not only lectured but provided syllabuses and texts for classes. In 1882, with Professor Cyril Ransome, he produced *A Handbook of the Political History of England*, which had considerable popularity as a book of reference and reached a new edition in 1913. In 1883 he published *The Education of Citizens* and in 1884, with Benjamin Jones, *Working Men Co-Operators*, an account of the artisans' co-operative movement in Great Britain. University extension did much to emphasize the gaps in educational provision, particularly between elementary and higher education, and it was to a campaign for the provision of greater educational opportunity, which he felt would underpin a democratic society, that Acland was to devote the rest of his life.

In December 1885 Acland was elected as Liberal MP for the newly formed Rotherham division of the West Riding of Yorkshire with a majority which was one of the largest in the country. In a series of painstakingly researched speeches on education, land reform, and local government reform he established a reputation in parliament as a leading exponent of a new positioning of Liberalism, based on links with the working classes. His earnestly democratic stance and his zeal for social justice won him a following among a group of young Liberal MPs including Haldane, Grey (well known to Acland since Embleton days), Asquith, Atherley-Jones, and particularly Tom Ellis, the Welsh member for Merioneth.

Welsh education and technical instruction Since 1881 Acland had kept a home at Clynnog Fawr, Caernarvonshire. Buoyed by the deep friendship he had formed with Ellis, Acland began discreetly to orchestrate the campaign for Welsh education. He injected his advanced democratic ideals into the proposals for the reorganization of secondary schooling, ensuring better access for both girls and boys, as well as providing guidelines for an enhanced common curriculum. He pointed out what might be achieved through the use of county councils as educational authorities. He guided the passage of the Welsh Intermediate Education Bill. He chaired a series of meetings of the joint committees of the Welsh counties at Shrewsbury in 1890, and, with great political skill, achieved unanimity of purpose throughout Wales. As alderman of Caernarfon, he submitted the first scheme for approval under the Welsh Intermediate Act of 1889, providing a model for the other Welsh county councils and anticipating the reform of English secondary education. In government Acland helped to crown the new system by assisting with the creation of a linked University of Wales.

In 1887, with Henry Roscoe, Acland founded the National Association for Technical Education to persuade the government to organize and supervise secondary and technical education. He furthered the passing of the Technical Instruction Acts of 1889 and 1891 and, by diverting revenue from liquor duties ('whisky money') to county councils for the benefit of education, allowed what was virtually a secondary education system to grow up. With the assistance of H. Llewellyn Smith, he edited a comprehensive review, with guidelines for reconstruction, of secondary education, published as *Studies in Secondary Education* (1892).

In government 1892–1895 In August 1892 Acland was appointed vice-president of the committee of council on education in Gladstone's fourth ministry, Gladstone overruling Harcourt's attempt to make him chief whip. Morley recalled that to admit 'the son of the oldest of all the surviving friends of his youth' (J. Morley, *Life of Gladstone*, 3.494–5) gave personal gratification to Gladstone. Morley dubbed Acland and his earnest friends, Asquith, Haldane, and Grey, the 'Brethren'. With his uncompromising and ardent nature, Acland could be a demanding colleague but Haldane wrote admiringly, 'I would rather be like Arthur Acland, with all his fanaticisms, than anyone I

know just now' (D. Sommer, *Haldane of Cloan: his Life and Times, 1856–1928*, 1960, 90) and Morley recorded that he was one of the 'inner ring' in the cabinet.

By taking advantage of his considerable administrative freedom Acland made substantial gains. He exploited the 1891 act rapidly to extend the number of children with free places and he publicized the right to free education by urging parents to make 'representations' about 'deficiencies'. In his codes of 1893 and 1895, he ended payment by results and liberalized the curriculum in elementary schools. In 1893 the age for compulsory attendance at school was raised from ten to eleven. Acland's syllabus for the evening school code, 'The life and duties of a citizen', reiterated his belief in the democratic power of adult education, and evening school education spread at an unprecedented rate once work of the highest possible level could be attempted and age restrictions were removed. Fresh appointments invigorated the inspectorate but when grants were refused to schools deemed inefficient, Acland was accused of being the enemy of voluntary schools. In particular his circular on the sanitary and hygienic requirements of the department, including the provision of playgrounds, was felt by hard-up church schools to impose onerous obligations on them. For some churchmen he was 'a bitter little Radical' and taunts of apostasy wounded him (Acland, journal, 3 Sept 1893).

At Acland's prompting request, a national conference on secondary education held in Oxford in 1893 resulted in a memorial to the prime minister from the convocation of the university calling for a royal commission. The resulting commission of 1894, chaired by James Bryce, had among its members many close to Acland—H. Llewellyn Smith, Harry Reichel, Roscoe, T. H. Warren, and Sadler—and the recommendations laid the foundation of Balfour's 1902 Education Act. In 1895 Acland appointed Michael Sadler to be director of the newly created department of special inquiries with the hope that such information would help to maintain the momentum of reform when he left office. He instituted a new departmental committee with the Charity Commissioners and the Department of Science and Art, foreshadowing a single central authority for education. Asquith described him as 'the success of the Government' but by the time of the Liberals' fall from power in 1895 he was feeling 'squeezed out'. He was a formidable opponent of Conservative educational measures but in 1899 he resigned his seat, fearing a breakdown in health. His father's death in 1898 had resulted in a period of personal crisis. As the unrecognized heir to his childless elder brother, he sublimated his unhappiness by writing a loving memoir of his father, *Sir Thomas Acland: Memoir and Letters* (1902).

Educational administration and policy In 1900 Acland was called on to lead the Liberal attack on the proposed new Education Act. Once passed, however, he decided to 'work it to the best of our ability' (Acland, journal, 4 Feb 1903). For seven years he guided his local West Riding of Yorkshire county council in implementing a system of secondary education, taking a particular interest in Pickering grammar school where he was chairman of governors. He also assisted the Yorkshire College at Leeds to receive its charter as a university in 1904. As chairman of Bedford College (1903–15) and Imperial College (1907–25) he ensured an important period of growth.

Acland's influence remained strong at national level. From 1906 he chaired the consultative committee of the Board of Education and, with the help of members who had long been close to him, such as Reichel, T. H. Warren, Mansbridge, and Sadler, produced a series of wide-ranging and far-sighted reports which kept up the pressure for further reform. Successive education ministers, Birrell, Haldane, and Trevelyan, turned to him for coaching and direction. He continued to champion the case for greater democratic representation in the management of schools, the provision of better teacher training, pay, and pensions. In his lengthy evidence to the royal commission on the civil service in 1912 he took the opportunity to air his dissatisfaction. The changes he advocated anticipated those of many later educational reformers: a wider curriculum, a revised examination system, supplemented by both teacher assessment and school inspection.

Liberalism and Labour Acland continued to exert influence on the political fortunes of the Liberal Party, persuading Grey and Haldane to join the cabinet in December 1905. He became president of the National Liberal Federation in 1906 but he resigned in 1907, feeling out of sympathy with 'official Liberalism'. When Asquith offered him a peerage in 1908 he refused it as 'inconsistent with all we care most about in life on the democratic side' (Acland, journal, 9 Aug 1908).

In 1912 Acland chaired an inquiry, linked to Lloyd George's campaign for land reform, into 'the facts of Land in town and country and Rural conditions generally'. The report, published in 1913, with an introduction by Acland, was very favourably received in progressive circles, despite recommendations for a ministry of land, a legal minimum wage for farm workers, and compulsory power to acquire land for allotments. Acland began to raise money and work on a number of the Webbs' research projects, such as mother and infant welfare, and conditions for women in industrial work, and he chaired a committee set up to investigate the feasibility of forming an institute in London to further such research. For Beatrice Webb, he was the most enlightened and far-seeing of all the liberal politicians of the last decade of the nineteenth century and the first decade of the twentieth (Webb, 77n). He maintained his friendship with Lloyd George but judged that his influence had been 'overall degrading to public life' (Acland, journal, 23 April 1920). In the 1922 general election he helped to finance young Labour candidates, among them Hugh Dalton, and rejoiced when Labour almost doubled its membership. He gave £600 a year for three years to the rental of the Parliamentary Labour Club, close to the House of Commons, for members and their wives.

On 18 February 1919 Acland succeeded his brother Sir Charles Thomas Dyke Acland, as thirteenth baronet. 'We shrug our shoulders and make the best of the "Sir Arthur" and "Your ladyship"', he commented (Acland, journal, March 1919). He received the honorary degree of LLD from the universities of Leeds (1904) and Bristol (1912). He died at his London home, 85 Onslow Square, on 9 October 1926 and was cremated at Golders Green. His ashes were interred at Columb John Chapel in the Killerton estate, Devon. He was succeeded as fourteenth baronet by his elder son, Francis Dyke Acland (1874–1939), also a Liberal MP. He left £10,000 to found four scholarships, two for the Labour Party and two for the central co-operative board, to allow young men and women to travel abroad and do research of value to either organization. The trust, the Acland Memorial Fund, still continues.

ANNE OCKWELL

Sources Acland journals, 'Sprydon', Broadclyst, Devon · Devon RO, Acland family papers · Duke U., Perkins L., Acland family MSS · *The Times* (11 Oct 1926) · J. Morley, *Recollections*, 2 vols. (1917) · B. Webb, *Our partnership*, ed. B. Drake and M. I. Cole (1948) · H. H. Asquith, *Memories and reflections, 1852–1927*, ed. A. Mackintosh, 2 vols. (1928) · Gladstone, *Diaries* · G. M. Holmes, 'The parliamentary and ministerial career of A. H. D. Acland, 1886–97', *Durham Research Review*, 4, no. 15 (Sept 1964), 128–39 · J. Bellamy and H. F. Bing, 'Acland, Arthur Herbert Dyke', *DLB*, vol. 1 · R. T. Stearn, *Oxford Military College, 1876–1896* (1996) · G. Sutherland, *Policy-making in elementary education, 1870–1895* (1973) · P. Clarke, *Liberals and social democrats* (1978) · J. A. Spender, *The life of the Right Hon. Sir Henry Campbell-Bannerman*, 2 vols. (1923) · H. C. G. Matthew, *The liberal imperialists: the ideas and politics of a post-Gladstonian élite* (1973)

Archives Bodl. Oxf., family corresp. · Bodl. Oxf., letters to his father · Devon RO, family corresp. · Duke U., Perkins L., letters to his father · NL Scot., notes · priv. coll., journals | BL, letters to Campbell-Bannerman, Add. MSS 41234–41239 · BL, corresp. with Lord Gladstone, Add. MSS 46054–46063 · BL, corresp. with W. E. Gladstone, Add. MSS 44499–44789, *passim* · BL, corresp. with Lord Ripon, Add. MSS 43637–43639 · BL, letters to J. A. Spender, Add. MSS 46391–46393 · Bodl. Oxf., letters to Herbert Asquith · Bodl. Oxf., corresp. with Lord Bryce · Bodl. Oxf., corresp. with Sir William Harcourt · Bodl. Oxf., corresp. with Lord Kimberley · Bodl. Oxf., Rewley House MSS · Bodl. Oxf., Sadler MSS · King's AC Cam., letters to Oscar Browning · LMA, corresp. relating to Toynbee Hall · NL Scot., corresp. with Lord Rosebery · NL Wales, letters to D. R. Daniel · NL Wales, letters to T. E. Ellis · NL Wales, Rendel MSS · U. Newcastle, Robinson L., corresp. with Walter Runciman · U. Newcastle, Robinson L., corresp. with C. P. Trevelyan

Likenesses W. & D. Downey, woodburytype photograph, NPG; repro. in W. Downey and D. Downey, *The cabinet portrait gallery*, 5 (1894) [see illus.]

Wealth at death £23,749 3s. 8d.: probate, 12 Jan 1927, CGPLA Eng. & Wales · £175,800: further grant, 22 Feb 1927, CGPLA Eng. & Wales

Acland [*née* Fox, Fox-Strangways], **Lady Christian Henrietta Caroline** [Harriet] (**1750–1815**), diarist, was born at Kilmington, Somerset, on 3 January 1750 and baptized on 16 January at St James's, Piccadilly, London. She was the third surviving daughter of Stephen Fox, later first earl of Ilchester (1704–1776), a landowner, and his wife, Elizabeth Strangways-Horner (c.1722–c.1793). Her father took the additional surname of Strangways in 1758. Lady Harriet was married on 7 January 1771 by special licence at Redlynch Park in Somerset to John Dyke *Acland (1747–1778), a colonel in the Devon militia, whose father, Sir Thomas Acland, gave the couple the two Somerset estates of Pixton in Dulverton and Tetton near Taunton.

In 1776 Acland was serving as a major in the 20th foot when his regiment was sent with Burgoyne's army to

North America, for which campaign he was accompanied by his wife, valet, lady's maid, and dog. During the expedition Lady Harriet kept a journal which covers the period from 1 March 1776 until 2 January 1778, when she and her husband arrived at New York on their way home on parole. It was written jointly by herself and an unknown writer who was probably Major Acland's valet. As a record of military events it adds little to other published accounts of the time; more informative are its comments on the seven-week sea voyage to North America and the reactions of Lady Harriet's entourage to their first sight of American landscapes, villages, and native customs. There is a very laconic reference to the incident at Dovegot (modern Coveville) on 15 September 1776, when the Aclands' dog, Jack, knocked over a candle and set fire to their tent, from which Lady Harriet only just escaped in time. Such anecdotes as this were described in more detail in the memoirs later published by Lady Harriet's great admirer Thomas Anburey, a volunteer with the 29th foot, in which he makes frequent reference to her social grace, cheerful fortitude, and devotion to her husband.

On 9 October 1777, two nights after Acland had been wounded and taken prisoner at the second battle of Saratoga (Bemis Heights), Lady Harriet—herself several months pregnant—crossed the Hudson River in an open boat, accompanied by her maid, a military chaplain, and Acland's valet, to join him in captivity and nurse him back to health. They travelled under a white flag of truce, and Lady Harriet also carried a *laissez-passer* from Burgoyne to the American general Horatio Gates. Accounts of that night differ, but all agree that she was treated with great courtesy by General Gates, who described her as 'the most amiable, delicate little piece of Quality you ever beheld' (J. Wilkinson, *Memoirs of my Own Times*, 1816, 1.274). This dramatic episode, immortalized in Robert Pollard's painting of the Hudson River crossing, which was published in an engraving in the mid-1780s, captured the public's imagination in Britain, and Lady Harriet was celebrated for her outstanding heroism and loyalty to her husband. The Aclands were allowed to return to England in January 1778, and it seems likely that their son, John, was born during the voyage, for he was baptized at Broadclyst church on 21 March 1778, shortly after their arrival home.

Lady Harriet was left a widow in November 1778 and outlived both her surviving children: John, who died on 23 April 1785, and Elizabeth Kitty, who died on 5 March 1813. She had continued to live at Pixton until 1796, when the estate passed to the earls of Carnarvon on her daughter's marriage to Henry, Lord Porchester, later second earl of Carnarvon. Thereafter Lady Harriet resided at Tetton House. She was, however, a frequent visitor to the Carnarvon residence at Highclere in Hampshire, and it may have been during one of these visits that she gave her journal to her daughter and grandchildren. The *Gentleman's Magazine* and other periodicals published highly inaccurate obituaries of her after her death, from cancer, at Tetton House on 21 July 1815. She was buried at Broadclyst church on 28 July.   JENNIFER THORP

Sources *The Acland journal: Lady Harriet Acland and the American War*, ed. J. D. Thorp (1993) · T. Anburey, *Travels through the interior parts of America, 1776–1781*, 2 vols. (1789) · parish records, Broadclyst, Devon RO · Hants. RO, Carnavon of Highclere papers · Som. ARS, Herbert papers · A. Acland, *A Devon family: the story of the Aclands* (1981), 29–44 · W. L. Stone, 'Lady and Major Acland', *Magazine of American History* (Jan 1880) · 'Reminiscences of Lady Harriet Acland', *Magazine of American History* (Aug 1886) · J. Burgoyne, *A state of the expedition from Canada* (1780) · C. Hibbert, *Redcoats and rebels: the war for America, 1770–1781* (1990) · *GM*, 1st ser., 85/2 (1815), 186–7 · Burke, *Peerage* (1970) · *DNB* · *IGI*
Archives Devon RO, journal · Devon RO, Broadclyst parish records, 1148M · Hants. RO, MSS, 103M91 [photocopies] · Highclere Castle, Hampshire, journal · priv. coll., MSS | Hants. RO, Carnavon MSS, 75M91 · Highclere Castle, Hampshire, Herbert MSS
Likenesses J. Reynolds, oils, 1771, priv. coll. · R. Pollard, oils, 1777, Killerton, Devon · R. Pollard, engraving, 1785, priv. coll. · J. Chapman, stipple, pubd 1796, NPG · Ridley, stipple, pubd 1800 (after Rivers), NPG · S. W. Reynolds, mezzotint, pubd 1820 (after J. Reynolds), BM, NPG

Acland, Sir Henry Wentworth, first baronet (1815–1900), physician, was the fifth of the nine children and the fourth son of Sir Thomas Dyke *Acland, tenth baronet (1787–1871), and Lydia Elizabeth Hoare (d. 1856). Born at the family home of Killerton, at Broadclyst in Devon, on 23 August 1815, he was educated first at a private school in Mitcham, Surrey, and then, from 1828 until 1832, at Harrow School. He was never happy at Harrow, but by the time he left (prematurely because of concern about his health) he had shown himself to be a notable rackets player and become a monitor. Contact with the physician who treated him for his weak heart fostered his ambition for a medical career, but on the advice of Sir Benjamin Brodie his entry to professional study was postponed. For the next two years, during which he studied as a private pupil of the Revd Thomas Fisher in Cornwall, he read widely and developed his modest musical talents, before matriculating at Christ Church, Oxford, in 1834.

University education and early career At Christ Church Acland followed his father and two of his elder brothers, Thomas Dyke *Acland (1809–1898) and Arthur Acland. He did so without distinction, however, taking a pass degree to graduate BA in 1840, after an undergraduate career that was seriously interrupted by a recurrence of the illness he had suffered at Harrow and by long periods spent sailing in the Mediterranean (a pursuit that he continued to enjoy into his eighties). Despite his fragile health he was far from idle in these years. Three visits to the Troas in 1838 inspired his first publication, *The Plains of Troy* (1838), a short book, illustrating a 7 foot long panoramic drawing, in which he speculated, learnedly though not always convincingly, on the location of Troy and on the sites of events described in Homer's *Iliad*. Acland worked hard at Oxford and mixed easily with the more serious undergraduates, but his interests extended beyond the predominantly classical curriculum of the time to include attendance at the geological lectures of the Revd William Buckland and the striking up of numerous friendships, most notably with John Ruskin, who entered Christ Church as a fellow-commoner in January 1837 and was later to speak

Sir Henry Wentworth Acland, first baronet (1815–1900), by Julia Margaret Cameron, 1867

warmly of Acland in the first volume of his *Praeterita* (chapter II).

Although Acland did not attempt an honours degree (few undergraduates at Christ Church did at this time), his abilities were recognized. In this, two particular attachments were important: his respectful association with the dean of Christ Church and regius professor of Greek, Thomas Gaisford, and his much warmer relationship with his tutor Henry Liddell (which lasted through Liddell's own long reign as dean between 1855 and 1891); these helped to make the prospect of a fellowship of All Souls a realistic possibility. Even more significant, however, were the favour traditionally shown to families of the antiquity and distinction of the Aclands and the fact that Henry's elder brother Thomas had been a fellow of the college from 1831 to 1839. The examination that Acland took in October 1840 was a perfunctory affair, and he was duly elected. The fellowship, which did not require his residence in Oxford, gave him the freedom to study medicine at St George's Hospital, London. In the three and a half years that he spent as a student in London, he found the coarseness of his peers uncongenial and instead strengthened his ties with older scientific and medical friends, including Sir Benjamin Brodie, the anatomist Richard Owen, William Frederick Chambers, who had treated him in his earlier illnesses, and George Gisbourne Babington, a physician and cousin of Lord Macaulay whom he regarded as 'far the most superior man about St George's'. Both Acland's health and his commitment to his medical studies were at times precarious, but a period of mainly clinical training at the university and at the Royal Infirmary in

Edinburgh and the careful attentions of Brodie and Chambers saw him through.

Acland was marked profoundly by his experiences in Edinburgh, in particular by his contacts with William Pulteney Alison, professor of the practice of medicine, with whom he lived, and John Goodsir, the curator of the university's museum, who was soon to become professor of anatomy. After eighteen months in which he learned methods involving the use of the microscope and stethoscope that were significantly in advance of those taught at St George's, he began to look forward to the prospect of a lucrative practice in London. But in 1845 Benjamin Kidd resigned unexpectedly from the Dr Lee's readership in anatomy at Christ Church, and Gaisford, as dean, offered the post to Acland. Although the readership carried a stipend of only £200 a year, the prospect of a return to Oxford was attractive, and in accepting the position Acland sealed a bond with the university that lasted until his death. He completed his medical examinations in 1846, first in Oxford, where he took his BM (in preparation for the DM degree that he took in 1848), and then in London for the licentiateship of the Royal College of Physicians (he became a fellow in 1850), and he succeeded Dr Wootton in what was to become over the next quarter of a century a thriving and time-consuming practice extending far beyond the boundaries of the city. On 14 July 1846, with his future assured (and subsequently to be strengthened still further by his appointment as physician to the Radcliffe Infirmary), Acland married Sarah Cotton (*d.* 1878), the sister of two Christ Church friends, William and Henry Cotton, and the daughter of the philanthropist and governor of the Bank of England William *Cotton (1786–1866). In the following year they settled in Wootton's house in Broad Street, where they lived for the rest of their lives. They had seven sons and one daughter.

Role in the development of scientific and medical education at Oxford By the mid-1840s the case for a reform of science in Oxford was already being articulated by a small but vociferous group led by Charles Daubeny, who at the time held simultaneously the chairs of chemistry, rural economy, and botany. On his appointment to Christ Church, Acland immediately joined Daubeny and the reader in experimental philosophy, the Revd Robert Walker, in advocating the creation of the new honour school of natural science that was introduced in 1850 and in working to secure proper premises for the university's dispersed and poorly housed scientific collections (including the extensive anatomical collection that Acland controlled, catalogued, and over the years improved, at Christ Church). The meeting of the British Association for the Advancement of Science in Oxford in 1847, for which Acland served as local secretary, gave strength to both causes, as did the alliances that he was able to deploy beyond the dozen or so professors and readers in scientific, mathematical, and medical posts, notably with Liddell and Edward Bouverie Pusey, with whom he had family connections. In the face of a body of conservative Oxford opinion that saw science as a costly, even morally threatening, addition to the undergraduate curriculum, Acland's gentle charm and manifest piety provided essential reassurance.

The conception of the syllabus for the honour school that Acland articulated in his *Remarks on the Extension of Education in the University of Oxford* (1848) owed much to Daubeny: in particular, the requirement that candidates in the school should study all three of the 'primary' sciences—natural philosophy, chemistry, and physiology (essentially biology)—was one that Daubeny had advocated before Acland took up the cause. Nevertheless, Acland's belief in the value of a broad grounding in science and in the dangers of premature specialization was profound and, along with his principle that the aim of the Oxford syllabus in science was not the training of 'professed' scientists but the disciplining of the mind, it remained the enduring bedrock of his educational thinking. In 1857 he succeeded the elderly and conservative James Adey Ogle as regius professor of medicine and as clinical professor at the Radcliffe Infirmary, and his beliefs assumed a new importance in the views he was called upon to formulate on the future of medical education in Oxford. Arguing from a conviction that an exposure to the full range of primary sciences was an essential foundation for physicians and surgeons, he resolutely opposed the establishment of clinical training in the university. Such training, in his view, could only be pursued effectively in London or some other big city, after the student had undergone the general education and experienced the interaction with students bent on other careers that Oxford provided.

Through the 1850s Acland's convictions bore visible fruit in the evolving plan for the new University Museum. With a characteristic mixture of tenacity and emollience and from a position of growing influence, reinforced by his appointment as Radcliffe librarian in 1851, Acland did more than anyone to guide the plan through the often acrimonious debates in convocation. In this he was greatly helped from the mid-1850s by the crucial alliance he forged with a newcomer to Oxford, the quietly effective John Phillips, deputy reader (later reader and then professor) in geology, whose ideas squared entirely with his own. It was essential to Acland's, and Phillips's, conception that the museum should house all the sciences under a single roof: in this way the various disciplines would be able to stimulate one another, and the bonds between them would be reinforced. The result was the handsome building, erected on land taken from the parks, that was opened for public use in 1860, on the occasion of another meeting of the British Association for the Advancement of Science. In accordance with the guidelines that had been elaborated for the design, the areas devoted to the various sciences—not only the three primary sciences but also geology, mineralogy, anatomy, and zoology—and to the Radcliffe Library (the rich scientific holdings of which were moved to the museum from the Radcliffe Camera) were arranged around a central glass-covered court; except for the observatory, which was housed in a small free-standing building, only the chemistry laboratory stood slightly apart, though it was still connected to the main structure by a short corridor.

Other aspects of the University Museum's design, besides its general disposition, bore the stamp of Acland's engagement. The choice of the Rhenish Gothic style submitted by the Dublin architects Deane and Woodward, in preference to the Palladianism of the most likely alternative (by E. M. Barry), pleased Acland, who campaigned discreetly in its favour. In this he was influenced by his association with Ruskin, whose two letters on the museum were published with an extensive description of the building, an account of its construction by Acland, and a letter from Phillips, in *The Oxford Museum* (1859). The fine carvings of flowers and animals on the windows and on the capitals of the pillars around the central court also reflected Acland's taste, though again it was a taste moulded by Ruskin. The aesthetic qualities of the museum, which was the first major public building in the Gothic style, aroused generally favourable comment. But soon its impracticality became apparent. Leaks in the glass roof over the court were common; heating was expensive; and the cost of lighting (by gas) was so high that the use of the building after dark had to be limited. More seriously for the reputation of Oxford science, the facilities for the individual sciences came quickly to be regarded as cramped and, by the standards of the laboratories that began to be erected in many German universities and even elsewhere in Britain from the 1870s, inadequate.

Acknowledgement of the University Museum's shortcomings was reflected in Robert Clifton's campaign for a separate building for experimental philosophy, which was opened in 1870 as the Clarendon Laboratory, and in additions to the original plan that continued to be made until the First World War. At the same time, criticism of Acland's conception of the essential unity of the sciences was manifested by the gradual erosion of his ideal of a single coherent syllabus that discouraged specialization and, most woundingly for a man who always preferred compromise to confrontation, by attacks on his views on medical education. One of these came in the form of a letter headed 'A lost medical school', which appeared in the *British Medical Journal* in January 1878. '[M]edical education at Oxford, it was alleged, had practically ceased in the previous twenty-five years. There were no lectures in medicine, anatomy or physiology, and under Acland the Regius chair had been turned into a sinecure' (Robb-Smith, 577). It is a mark of Acland's discretion and courtesy that even in the last twenty years of his life, when his opinions were most vehemently contested, he maintained good relations with younger colleagues of a very different persuasion, such as Edwin Ray Lankester, and Arthur Thomson, whose arrival as university lecturer in anatomy in 1885 and subsequent involvement in the promotion of professional medical studies in Oxford signalled the rejection of Acland's vision. The final, essentially unchanged statement of this vision, in *Oxford and Modern Medicine*—a long letter to the physician to St Bartholomew's Hospital, James Andrew, that he printed for private circulation in 1890 and published in 1896—was read with as much respect as ever. But it represented a conception of medical training that most contemporaries by then regarded as outdated.

'An effective man of business' Inevitably, Acland was drawn into similar debates outside the university as well. As Oxford's representative on the newly formed General Council of Medical Education and Registration from 1858 and as president of the council from 1874 until his retirement in 1887, he promoted the unification of the profession and the restructuring of the hitherto chaotic system of qualifications administered by twenty-one different licensing bodies with very diverse standards and objectives. He also championed improved procedures for the removal of incompetent members of the profession and spoke consistently in favour of the suitability of women for medical study and practice, commending them especially for work in India.

Acland's services during the cholera epidemic that affected Oxford in 1854 from early August until late October enhanced his reputation as a selfless physician and stimulated his lifelong concern with public health and sanitation. Drawing on his observation of the less severe epidemic of 1849, he instituted emergency procedures for the distribution of medicines, the cleansing and destruction of clothing, and the nursing of the sick. Although 116 of the 199 confirmed cases of cholera proved fatal, the measures he took (once he assumed a leading role as consulting physician to the local board of health in early September) did much to control an outbreak that at its height threatened many more lives. Acland's account of the epidemic and of the conditions that fostered its spread, published as a richly informative *Memoir on the cholera at Oxford in the year 1854, with considerations suggested by the epidemic* (1856), helped to ensure that Oxford never again suffered a significant recurrence of the disease. While Acland recognized the role of the particular meteorological conditions that prevailed in the late summer and early autumn of 1854, he identified the root cause of the epidemic as the inadequacy of much of the city's drainage and the dangers of the large quantities of sewage that poured into the Isis and Cherwell rivers. His subsequent support for causes related to public health made its mark in numerous addresses and publications. But it also took a more practical form in his work for the royal sanitary commission, on which he served from 1869 to 1872, and in his relentless promotion of the improvement of the water supply and sanitation of Oxford and the surrounding villages, most notably in Marsh Gibbon, a community for which, as master of the almshouse at Ewelme (a position he held *ex officio* as regius professor), he had a special responsibility.

Acland was not immune to the attractions of elegant, cultivated society or of the celebrity that his career brought him. He derived much satisfaction from his appointment as medical adviser to the prince of Wales during the prince's residence as a nobleman at Christ Church in 1859 and from the invitation in the following year to attend the prince during his visit to Canada and the United States. Thereafter he maintained a close affection

for the royal family, serving them once again when he became physician and unofficial mentor to the sickly Prince Leopold, a student in Oxford from 1872 to 1876. His attachment did not go unrecognized: he was made CB in 1883 and KCB in 1884, and in 1890 Queen Victoria created him a baronet. These, however, were only the most notable of many honours, which included his election as a fellow of the Royal Society in 1847, appointment by the emperor of Brazil as knight officer of the imperial order of the Rose, honorary degrees at Cambridge, Dublin, Durham, and Edinburgh, and memberships of academies and societies throughout the world.

Despite his high reputation and the influence he exercised, Acland was not an original thinker. He was above all an effective man of business who used his charm and conciliatory powers in pursuit of the causes to which he remained consistently loyal. In this aspect of his life, he drew strength from his unblemished integrity. This was bred of a religious faith that led him to constant observance, a closeness to Pusey and Newman, and, in the debate on evolution by natural selection, a sympathy for Owen against Darwin and Huxley (though characteristically he did not commit himself in public). Another essential support was his energy. His visits to America in 1879 (undertaken while grieving his wife's death in the previous year), the eastern Mediterranean in 1886, and America again in 1888 were strenuous, time on each of them being devoted to his constant preoccupations with education and public health. Despite the removal of an eye in 1888, increasing deafness, and other signs of advancing years, he maintained his zest for travel and public appearances into the 1890s. Although he had resigned the clinical professorship in 1880, when the post was laid down in order to create lectureships in medicine and surgery, he remained as regius professor until 1894 and as Radcliffe librarian until 1900. By the late 1890s, however, his failing health and the grief caused by the deaths of several of his closest friends were at last getting the better of him. A gradual but never unhappy decline ended with his death, at his home in Broad Street, Oxford, on 16 October 1900. He was buried three days later, in Holywell cemetery, Oxford.   ROBERT FOX

Sources J. B. Atlay, *Sir Henry Wentworth Acland,… regius professor of medicine in the University of Oxford: a memoir* (1903) · *BMJ* (27 Oct 1900), 1281–7 · *The Lancet* (20 Oct 1900), 1158–60 · J. B. S. [J. B. Sanderson], *PRS*, 75 (1905), 169–74 · *The Times* (17 Oct 1900) · A. Robb-Smith, 'Medical education', *Hist. U. Oxf. 6: 19th-cent. Oxf.*, 563–82 · R. Fox, 'The University Museum and Oxford science, 1850–1880', *Hist. U. Oxf. 6: 19th-cent. Oxf.*, 641–91 · J. Howarth, 'Oxford for arts: the natural sciences, 1880–1914', *Hist. U. Oxf. 7: 19th-cent. Oxf. pt 2*, 457–97 · H. C. Harley, 'Sir Henry Acland and his circle', *Oxford Medical School Gazette*, 18 (1966), 9–22

Archives Bodl. Oxf., Radcliffe Science Library, corresp. and papers · Bodl. Oxf., corresp. and papers · Devon RO, family corresp. · Oxf. U. Mus. NH, corresp. and papers relating to the founding of the University Museum; corresp. relating to Oxford science departments · RCP Lond., letters | All Souls Oxf., letters to Sir William Anson · BL, corresp. with W. E. Gladstone, Add. MS 44091 · BL, corresp. with Florence Nightingale, Add. MS 45786 · BL, letters to Sir Richard Owen, Add. MS 39954 · Bodl. Oxf., letters to George Richmond · CUL, letters to Sir George Stokes · Devon RO, letters to Arthur Acland · NL Scot., corresp. with Lord Rosebery ·

Oxf. U. Mus. NH, letters to Sir E. B. Poulton · U. Newcastle, Robinson L., letters to Sir Walter Trevelyan

Likenesses J. E. Millais, pencil and watercolour drawing, 1853, Ruskin Galleries, Bembridge School, Education Trust Ltd · A. Munro, plaster bust, c.1857, Bodl. Oxf. · D. J. Pound, stipple and line engraving, 1859 (after photograph by Maull and Polyblank), NPG, Wellcome L. · J. M. Cameron, photograph, 1867, National Museum of Photography, Film and Television, Bradford [see illus.] · E. Edwards, photograph, 1867, Wellcome L. · W. W. Ouless, oils, exh. RA 1886 · J. E. Boehm, bronze bust, 1887, Oxf. U. Mus. NH · H. von Herkomer, oils, 1888, AM Oxf. · Taunt & Co., cabinet photograph, c.1890 (with Dr Benjamin Jowett), NPG · G. B. Black, lithograph, Wellcome L. · W. Holl, stipple engraving ('Grillion's Club' series; after G. Richmond), BM, NPG · G. Richmond, crayon drawing, repro. in Atlay, *Sir Henry Wentworth Acland*, facing p. 104 · photographs, repro. in Atlay, *Sir Henry Wentworth Acland* · photographs, repro. in *The Lancet* · photographs, repro. in *BMJ* · photographs, repro. in Harley, 'Sir Henry Acland and his circle'

Wealth at death £56,606: probate, 21 Dec 1900, *CGPLA Eng. & Wales*

Acland, James (1799–1876). *See under* McCalmont, Frederick Haynes (1846–1880).

Acland, Sir John (c.1552–1620), politician and benefactor, was the younger son of John Acland (d. 1553) of Acland Barton in the parish of Landkey, north Devon, and Margaret, daughter and coheir of Hugh Radcliff of Stepney and the Middle Temple. He was born into an established gentry family which already bore heraldic arms and owned lands in five other Devon parishes. He was educated at Lincoln's Inn and abroad and, earlier, possibly at Exeter College, Oxford. Acland inherited lands in London from his mother and gained further wealth from his two marriages: the first was to Elizabeth, daughter of George Rolle of Stevenstone and widow of Robert Mallet of Woolleigh, and the second, in 1605, was to Margery, daughter of Henry Portman of Orchard Portman, Somerset, and widow of Sir Gabriel Hawley of Buckland, Somerset.

After his first marriage John lived at Woolleigh, part of the marriage jointure of his first wife until the marriage of his stepdaughter in 1590 to Arthur Acland, son and heir of his brother, Hugh. By then John Acland had moved into his newly built house on the estate purchased at Columbjohn in east Devon. Acland served as a JP from 1583, and his elder brother, Hugh, was also on the commission of the peace. From 1592 the survival of the quarter session records shows him active taking recognizances in the east division and usually attending quarter sessions two or three times a year. In 1600 and 1601 Acland was among those who received orders from the privy council to organize the embarkation of troops to serve in Ireland. He also received instructions to intervene in several trade disputes. Acland was MP for Saltash in 1584 and was elected knight of the shire in January 1607 in place of Sir Thomas Ridgeway, who had been appointed treasurer for Ireland. He had been knighted on 14 March 1604.

Acland left a permanent impact on the county of Devon with his numerous benefactions. While he was a member of parliament he promoted an act in 1609 to provide for his gift of £540 to bind 200 apprentices in Devon for seven years. This was outlined in a record of some of his gifts which Acland later required the mayor and corporation of Exeter to keep to ensure their permanence. These included his grant of the proceeds of the rectory and church of Churchstowe with the chapel of Kingsbridge to the mayor and corporation of Exeter so that they could provide £20 quarterly in perpetuity to purchase bread for the poorest in six Exeter parishes and in other specified towns and parishes. These payments were to start on Lady day 1617, presumably the date of this record of gifts, which was repeated in his will. The towns and parishes he specified for these grants were areas where Acland owned lands. Another endowment concerned the maintenance of the chapel he had had repaired and rededicated at Columbjohn, together with the stipend for a minister to preach every sabbath and hold divine service there every day. He also built a school for Broadclyst, of which this minister would be the schoolmaster. Acland's interest in his home area of Broadclyst extended to being one of the founder members of the Eight Men of Broadclyst, which met each month to consider the affairs of the parish. His one major benefaction outside Devon was £800 to build the new hall with cellars under it at Exeter College, Oxford. He also provided £16 per annum to support two scholars at that college from the high school in Exeter.

Acland constructed the memorial to himself and his two wives in the church of St John at Broadclyst (where he was eventually buried) in 1613, well in advance of his death at Columbjohn on 14 February 1620. He portrays himself as devout, holding a Bible. He had no children and was briefly succeeded by his brother, Hugh, and then by Hugh's grandson, John, later the first baronet, who inherited the lands of both branches of the Acland family and established Killerton, which adjoined Columbjohn, as his principal residence.   MARY WOLFFE

Sources Devon RO, D1/140/1–5 · HoP, *Commons, 1558–1603* · *Report of the commissioners concerning charities containing that part which relates to the city of Exeter* (1825) · PRO, PROB 11/136 · A. Acland, *A Devon family: the story of the Aclands* (1981) · *Report on records of the city of Exeter*, HMC, 73 (1916) · APC, 1615–16, 17, 25, 31, 32 · J. Prince, *Danmonii orientales illustres, or, The worthies of Devon* (1701) · Devon RO, QSOB 1–5; QS Rolls 1 & 2 · list of Acland leases, Devon RO · agreement entailing land on Arthur Acland on his marriage to Eleanor Mallet, Devon RO, 1148M/box 1 (7) · inquisition post mortem, abstract, West Country Studies Library · C. W. Boase, ed., *Registrum Collegii Exoniensis*, new edn, OHS, 27 (1894), 318

Acland, John (1699–1796), Church of England clergyman and writer on social issues, was the second son of John Acland (d. 1703), of Beerford, Devon, and his wife, Elizabeth, daughter of Richard Acland of Fremington, Devon. His father was MP for Callington, Cornwall, and his older brother was Sir Hugh Acland, sixth baronet, of Columb-John, Devon. He matriculated from Exeter College, Oxford, in 1718, receiving his BA in 1721 and MA in 1725. He was instituted to the vicarage or rectory of Broadclyst, Devon, on his own petition in 1753 and also served as a JP.

In 1786 Acland published *A Plan for Rendering the Poor Independent of Public Contributions, Founded on the Basis of the Friendly Societies, Commonly called Clubs*. To this was added a letter from Dr Richard *Price (1723–1791), who commended the scheme, and wished it more success than his own had 'met with some years ago' (Thomas, 59). It is clear that Acland had been prompted by the failure of previous legislation for the encouragement of friendly societies in Devon. This had ensured that the funds of friendly societies might be supplemented by grants in aid from the proceeds of the poor rate. It provided, among other things, for the payment of sums of money on the marriage of members and the birth of their children; however, owing to the burden this put on the ratepayers, the schemes proved unworkable.

Acland suggested a modified application of this idea. He proposed that there should be established throughout the country, by the authority of parliament, a general club or society for the support of the poor in sickness, in old age, and when out of work. With certain exceptions, every adult male or female receiving a certain wage was to be compelled to contribute to this fund, and a similar obligation was imposed on the bulk of the community. In this way pauperism was gradually to be extinguished, and the recipients of aid from the fund might regard themselves as members of a state friendly society.

The proposal excited considerable attention at a time when the increase of the poor rate was causing general anxiety. A pamphlet by John Howlett, responding to Acland's, appeared in 1788. A bill based on Acland's ideas about poor relief and the settlement of illegitimate children was introduced into the House of Commons in December 1787, with an actuarial table by Richard Price, but came to nothing. Although it was discussed in Sir Frederick Eden's The State of the Poor (1797), it was judged to have fundamental defects. A second pamphlet by Acland, outlining a refutation of Edward King's attempt to prove the public utility of the national debt, and to explain the cause of the high price of provisions, was published at Exeter in 1796. It was given a brief and approving notice in the Gentleman's Magazine for November 1796.

Acland died in 1796. Although a country priest, he made an important contribution to poor-law reform, envisaging far-reaching policies which went beyond the then accepted framework of the old parish-based poor law. He did this via the principles of insurance and self-help. While in the short term his ideas did not have much practical influence, beyond small reforms affecting friendly societies, they nevertheless expanded the terms of reference of debates before 1834. In the longer term such ideas (propagated in various forms by later authors) were to prove highly influential in the history of social policy and administration.

FRANCIS ESPINASSE, rev. K. D. M. SNELL

Sources H. R. T., 'Acland, Rev. John', Dictionary of political economy, ed. H. R. I. Palgrave (1894–9) · G. Long, ed., The biographical dictionary of the Society for the Diffusion of Useful Knowledge, 4 vols. in 7 (1842–4) · J. R. Poynter, Society and pauperism: English ideas on poor relief, 1795–1834 (1969) · J. Wilson, The imperial gazetteer, 2 vols. (1872) · R. Polwhele, The history of Devonshire, 3 vols. (1793–1806) · R. Thomas, Richard Price: philosopher and apostle of liberty (1924) · G. B. Cone, Torchbearer of freedom: the influence of Richard Price on eighteenth-century thought (1952) · Burke, Peerage · GM, 1st ser., 66 (1796), 944–5 · Foster, Alum. Oxon. · J. S. Crossette, 'Acland, Sir Hugh', HoP, Commons

Acland, John Dyke (1747–1778), army officer and politician, was born on 18 February 1747 and baptized the following day at North Petherton, Somerset, the elder of the two sons of Sir Thomas Acland, seventh baronet (1722–1785), a landowner and politician, and his wife, Elizabeth, the daughter and heir of Thomas Dyke of Tetton, Somerset. He was educated at Eton College (1763–4) and University College, Oxford, whence he matriculated on 1 April 1765. He left London on 7 October 1766 for the grand tour accompanied by Thomas Vivien, travelled to Florence and Venice, and arrived in Paris in May 1767. It has been incorrectly stated that his travelling companion was Thomas Townshend, later Viscount Sydney, with whom he was painted by Joshua Reynolds in the portrait Young Archers. On 7 January 1771 he was married by special licence to Lady Christian Henrietta Caroline Fox-Strangways (1750–1815), diarist [see Acland, Lady Christian Henrietta Caroline]. More commonly known as Harriet, his wife was one of the daughters of Stephen Fox, first earl of Ilchester (1704–1776), of Redlynch, Somerset, and Elizabeth Strangways-Horner (c.1722–c.1793). Acland's father settled the estates of Pixton, Devon, and Tetton on the couple and their heirs. Their first child, Elizabeth Kitty, was born on 13 December 1772.

In October 1774 Acland was elected MP for the Cornish borough of Callington on Lady Orford's interest. He quickly added his voice to the call for tough measures against the American colonies and urged the prime minister, Lord North, not to concede the right of taxation to the colonies. He had purchased his entry into the 33rd foot as ensign in March 1774, advancing to captain in 1775, and was eager for the king to raise new regiments. Already colonel of the Devon militia, he pestered the king and North into allowing him to purchase a company. He again aired his warmongering views to the Commons when he moved the address on 26 October 1775, declaring that MPs had to choose between acquiescing in the independence of America and going to war. Accompanied by his wife, he sailed for America from Ireland in April 1776, having bought a major's commission in the 20th foot.

Acland proved to be a valiant soldier and was wounded at Hubbardton on 7 July 1777. He was in the advance party in General Burgoyne's attack on the American forces at Bemis Heights on the Hudson River when he was wounded in the legs and captured on 7 October 1777. In one of the most romantic episodes of the war, Lady Harriet crossed the Hudson at night and successfully petitioned General Gates to allow her to nurse Acland back to health. The couple remained in American captivity until early 1778, when Acland was released on parole; they returned to England, where their second child, John, was baptized on 21 March. Warmly praised for his actions by George III at a personal audience, Acland spent the next few months recuperating at his estate at Pixton. A quarrel with Lieutenant Lloyd provoked Acland into challenging Lloyd to a duel, which was fought on Bampton Down. Neither was injured, but Acland caught a chill and died from the resulting fever on 22 November 1778 at Pixton Park. He was buried on 28 November at Broadclyst, Devon, and was survived by his wife and children. His son, who was briefly eighth baronet, died in 1785, and his daughter, who married Henry George Herbert, second earl of Carnarvon, died on 5 March 1813.

W. P. COURTNEY, rev. S. J. SKEDD

Sources The Acland journal: Lady Harriet Acland and the American war, ed. J. D. Thorp (1993) · J. Brooke, 'Acland, John Dyke', HoP, Commons, 1754–90 · GEC, Baronetage · GEC, Peerage · J. Ingamells, ed., A dictionary of British and Irish travellers in Italy, 1701–1800 (1997)
Likenesses S. W. Reynolds, mezzotint, pubd 1820 (after J. Reynolds), BM, NPG

Acland, Sir Richard Thomas Dyke, fifteenth baronet (1906–1990), politician and benefactor, was born on 26 November 1906 at Broadclyst, Devon, his ancestral home, the eldest in the family of three sons and one daughter of Sir Francis Dyke Acland, fourteenth baronet (1874–1939), landowner and liberal politician, and his wife, Eleanor Margaret, the outspoken anti-war daughter of Charles James Cropper, of Ellergreen, Westmorland, landowner and grandee. He was educated at Rugby School and at Balliol College, Oxford, where he received a second class in philosophy, politics, and economics in 1927. His career epitomized a family tradition of reformist public service, both nationally and in the west country.

Acland stood unsuccessfully as a Liberal for Torquay in 1929 and Barnstaple in 1931, capturing the latter seat in 1935. Radical by temperament, he became involved in the efforts of the Left Book Club to create a progressive alliance, and by the beginning of the Second World War he had moved from conventional, secular Liberalism towards a Christian socialist concern for the transformation of the privileged world in which he grew up. His Penguin best-seller of 1940, *Unser Kampf*, eloquently summed up the aspirations of many who saw the war as an opportunity to escape from the disillusionments of the 1920s and 1930s and establish a more egalitarian, less class-ridden society. This message was repeated in *The Forward March* (1941) and *What it will be like* (1942), and then elaborated, after the proposals of the social reformer Sir William Beveridge, in *How it can be done* (1943). Acland married, in 1936, the architect Anne Stella Alford, daughter of Robert Greenwood Alford, of Cheyne Walk, London. They had four sons, the youngest of whom died in 1945 when he was five days old. In 1939 Acland succeeded his father in the baronetcy upon the latter's death.

Having served briefly as a lieutenant in the Royal North Devon yeomanry, initially as a ranker, Acland returned to politics and brought together Forward March, a loose alliance of the discontented but hopeful, and the dissident intellectuals of the 1941 Committee under the writer J. B. Priestley, to found the Common Wealth Party in July 1942. Sheltered by the electoral truce between the major parties, the Common Wealth Party was active in wartime by-elections, and by 1945 had four MPs. Its appeal was essentially to the more modest, professional middle classes, notably in London and on Merseyside; although its membership was never more than 15,000, the party

Sir Richard Thomas Dyke Acland, fifteenth baronet (1906–1990), by Howard Coster, 1939

was organized with panache by R. W. G. Mackay, and the evangelistic Acland proved himself a master of electioneering tactics. For funding they could also rely upon sympathetic businessmen such as Alan Good and Denis Kendall.

In the general election of 1945 the Common Wealth Party lost all its MPs and the deposits of every candidate, as politics reverted to the familiar two-party pattern. Nevertheless, Acland's creation had helped to prepare the way for Labour's victory, and in this he was the crucial element. Rarely effective in the House of Commons, he was an inspired and tireless propagandist who packed wartime meetings across the country; tall, gangling, and intense, with hawklike features, and always putting his case in a rasping voice in simple, moralistic terms but with a socialist slant, he was seen by many as the true prophet of a better future. As an earnest of his personal commitment to common ownership, he made over his family's vast Killerton estates in Devon to the National Trust in 1943 and always lived frugally if generously. But Labour's first attainment of full power meant that his moment of historical importance had passed.

Acland returned to the House of Commons in 1947 as MP for Gravesend in Kent under the sponsorship of the Labour politician Herbert Morrison, and he remained committed to Labour for the rest of his life. Increasingly a maverick, divorced from mainstream politics, he resigned his seat in 1955 in protest against the development of the H-bomb and never returned to parliament. More and more his interests had become one-dimensional. A devout Anglican since 1940, he served as a church estates commissioner in 1950–51 and maintained his friendship with left-wing bishops thereafter; but his attention came to centre upon education, a traditional concern of both his father and his grandfather Sir A. H. D. *Acland. Abandoning Westminster, he was senior lecturer at St Luke's College of Education, Exeter, from 1959 to 1974.

In retirement Acland wrote freely on educational matters, the problems of securing world peace, and, in his last years, the difficulties facing the 'third world'. Now that he was a figure of the past, having outlived his period of influence during the Second World War, he had few readers. He continued to cherish his beloved Devon countryside and protect its traditions, including—somewhat surprisingly—stag-hunting. Acland died at his home, Broadclyst, on 24 November 1990 and was succeeded in the baronetcy by his eldest son, John Dyke Acland (b. 1939). A. F. THOMPSON, rev.

Sources R. Acland, *Unser Kampf* (1940) · R. Acland, *The forward march* (1941) · R. Acland, *What it will be like* (1942) · R. Acland, *How it can be done* (1943) · P. Addisen, *The road to 1945* (1975) · A. Calder, *The people's war: Britain, 1939–1945* (1969) · *WWW* · *Dod's Parliamentary Companion*
Archives Borth. Inst., letters relating to War on Want · Devon RO, diaries, incl. his wife's diaries · U. Sussex, corresp., diaries, papers | BL, corresp. with Marie Stopes, Add. MS 58557 · HLRO, letters to David Lloyd George · King's Lond., Liddell Hart C., corresp. with Basil Liddell Hart · U. Warwick Mod. RC, corresp. with Sir Victor Gollancz
Likenesses H. Coster, photograph, 1939, NPG [*see illus.*] · H. Magee, group photograph, 6 Feb 1943 (*Commonwealth Leaders*), Hult. Arch.
Wealth at death £258,619: 1992, *CGPLA Eng. & Wales*

Acland, Sir Thomas Dyke, tenth baronet (1787–1871), politician and philanthropist, the eldest son of Sir Thomas Dyke Acland, ninth baronet (d. 1794), and Henrietta Anne (d. 1841), the only daughter of Sir Richard Hoare, was born in London on 29 March 1787. He became heir to the family estates when his father died on 17 May 1794. He was educated at Harrow School and Christ Church, Oxford, where he graduated BA on 23 March 1808, and MA 16 June 1814. On 15 June 1831 he received the honorary degree of DCL. While at Oxford he helped to found Grillion's Club (1812), which attracted many eminent politicians.

In October 1812 Sir Thomas was elected MP for Devon, as a tory, but lost his seat in 1818, when the yeomanry brought forward Hugh *Fortescue, Lord Ebrington, as their champion, and remained out of parliament until he was again returned for Devon in 1820. When the duke of Wellington declared himself in favour of Catholic emancipation, he found in Acland an energetic supporter. This offended Acland's former friends, but drew to his side in the election of 1830 the whigs of Devon, who split their votes between him and his old antagonist, Lord Ebrington. By this time Acland had spent, it was believed, over £80,000 in his parliamentary contests; it is perhaps worth noting that his wealth at death was less than £70,000. His new friends were displeased at his vote for General Gascoyne's motion, which caused the rejection of the first Reform Bill, and the loss of his seat was the penalty which he paid for his conduct. From 1831 to 1837 he was without a seat in parliament; but from the latter year until 1857 he represented North Devon as a Conservative. He stood by protection until 1840, but voted with Peel for free trade, though never a thorough-going Peelite.

On 7 April 1808 Acland married, at Mitcham, Lydia Elizabeth (d. 1856), only daughter of Henry Hoare, of Mitcham Grove, head partner in the banking firm of Messrs Hoare, and an active supporter of all church work at home and in the colonies. In the house of his father-in-law he passed many happy days, and there he met many zealous churchmen. His interest in religious progress is shown by the references in the first volume of Bishop Wilberforce's life and by a passage in Sir Walter Scott's diary for 1828, where Acland is styled 'the head of the religious party in the House of Commons'. Alexander Knox and Bishop Jebb were also numbered among his friends, and he is frequently mentioned (as 'Sir T. A.') in their thirty years' correspondence. Lady Acland died in 1856, and in the next year her husband withdrew into retirement. Contemporaries saw Acland as an independent politician and a thorough gentleman, and in 1861 a statue of him by Stephens was erected in Northernhay, Exeter, as a 'tribute of affectionate respect for private worth and public integrity'. His death occurred suddenly at his home at Killerton, Broad Clyst, on 22 July 1871. His children included Sir Thomas Dyke *Acland (1809–1898), who succeeded to the title, and Sir Henry Wentworth *Acland (1815–1900), the noted physician. W. P. COURTNEY, rev. H. C. G. MATTHEW

Sources Boase, *Mod. Eng. biog.* · J. B. Conacher, *The Peelites and the party system* (1972) · *The journal of Sir Walter Scott*, ed. W. E. K. Anderson (1972) · J. B. Sweet, *A memoir of the late Henry Hoare* (1869) · HoP, *Commons* · Burke, *Peerage*
Archives Bodl. Oxf., family corresp. · Devon RO, chronicles, accounts, and letters; corresp. and papers; corresp., mainly family, and related papers; letters to his brother Arthur | BL, corresp. with Sir S. H. Northcote, Add. MSS 50036–50037, *passim* · Bodl. Oxf., corresp. with Sir H. W. Acland
Likenesses F. Chantrey, pencil drawing, NPG · R. Cooper, stipple and line engraving (after W. Owen), NPG · Hill & Saunders, carte-de-visite, NPG · F. C. Lewis, stipple (after J. Slater), BM, NPG · F. C. Lewis, stipple (after G. Richmond), NPG · J. Ramsay, oils, Ugbrooke Park, Devon · S. W. Reynolds, mezzotint (after W. Owen), BM, NPG · G. Richmond, drawing, repro. in J. Slater and G. Richmond, *Portraits of members of Grillion's Club*, 2 (1864) · E. B. Stephens, statue, Northernhay, Exeter · print (after H. T. Wells), NPG
Wealth at death under £70,000: probate, 5 Sept 1871, *CGPLA Eng. & Wales*

Acland, Sir Thomas Dyke, eleventh baronet (1809–1898), politician and educational reformer, born at Killerton, Devon, on 25 May 1809, was the eldest son of Sir Thomas Dyke *Acland (1787–1871), politician and philanthropist, and his wife, Lydia Elizabeth (d. 1856), only daughter of Henry Hoare of Mitcham Grove, head partner in the banking firm of Messrs Hoare. Sir Henry Wentworth *Acland was his younger brother. Like his father, Acland was educated at Harrow School—where in 1826 he won the Peel prize with a dissertation published in the same year as *Oratio numismate Peeliano dignata et in Scholæ Harroviensis auditorio recitata die Iun. 1 A.D. mdcccxxvi*—and at Christ Church, Oxford, where he matriculated on 28 June 1827, and graduated BA with a double first (1831) and MA (1835). His tutor was Thomas Vowler Short, and among his friends were W. E. Gladstone, Francis Doyle, Frederic Rogers, and Frederick Denison Maurice, whom he met at

Sir Thomas Dyke Acland, eleventh baronet (1809–1898), by Hills & Saunders

the W. E. G. Essay Society. From 1831 to 1840 he was fellow of All Souls, and in 1837 he was returned to parliament as Conservative member for West Somerset. At the general election of 1841 he declined to identify himself with the protectionists, and though he showed leanings towards the Young England party during that parliament, he followed Peel on his conversion to free trade, and did not seek re-election to parliament in 1847. In 1845 he was a founder of 'the Engagement', the secret lay religious group of which Gladstone was also a member. He was also a prominent member of Grillion's Club, whose history he wrote (1864).

From the first Acland interested himself in educational matters; his early efforts were devoted to the maintenance and defence of church schools, and to the establishment of diocesan theological colleges, but later on he became an advocate of more liberal educational projects. In 1857–8 he took the leading part in the establishment of the Oxford local examinations system, and in 1858 published *Some Account of the Origin and Objects of the New Oxford Examinations*, which reached a second edition in the same year. On 14 June 1858 he was created DCL of Oxford University. He had equally at heart the improvement of English agriculture and the promotion of technical education

for the benefit of practical farmers, and much of the success of the Bath and West of England Agricultural Society (the *Journal* of which he conducted for seven years) was due to his efforts. He was a founder of the Royal Agricultural College in 1845. In 1851 he published *The Farming of Somersetshire*, and forty years later he wrote an *Introduction to the Chemistry of Farming, Specially Prepared for Practical Farmers* (1891).

Acland also took an active part in the volunteer movement; he raised five corps of mounted rifles, was lieutenant-colonel of the 3rd Devonshire volunteer rifles from 1860 to 1881, major of the 1st Devonshire yeomanry cavalry from 1872, and published *Mounted Rifles* (1860) and *Principles and Practice of Volunteer Discipline* (1868). Acland was at the same time a discriminating patron of art, and was one of the early admirers of Millais. Another of his friends was Ruskin, and in 1871 Acland and William Francis Cowper (afterwards Baron Mount-Temple) were the original trustees of Ruskin's Guild of St George.

In 1859 Acland unsuccessfully contested Birmingham as a moderate Liberal against John Bright, but in 1865 he was returned as a Liberal for North Devon, the representation of which he shared with Sir Stafford Northcote (afterwards earl of Iddesleigh) for twenty years. He served on the schools commission in 1864–7, and took an unusually active part in the debates in committee on W. E. Forster's Education Bill in 1870–71. He succeeded his father as eleventh baronet on 22 July 1871, and was sworn of the privy council in 1883. In November 1885 he was returned to parliament for West Somerset. In the following June he voted in favour of Gladstone's first Home Rule Bill, and, as a consequence, was defeated by Charles Isaac Elton in July 1886. This closed his political career.

Acland married, first, on 14 March 1841, Mary, the eldest daughter of Sir Charles Mordaunt, baronet, with whom he had two daughters and three sons, namely Sir Charles Thomas Dyke Acland, twelfth baronet, Francis Gilbert (d. 1874), and Arthur Herbert Dyke *Acland. His first wife died on 11 June 1851, and on 8 June 1856 Acland married Mary, the only surviving child of John Erskine, and niece of the second earl of Rosslyn; she died on 14 May 1892.

Acland died at the family home, Killerton, Broad Clyst, Devon, on 29 May 1898, ten days after his friend Gladstone, who was seven months his junior; he was buried in the family vault at Culm St John on 3 June. A memorial tablet in recognition of Acland's services to the cause of education was placed by his friends in the Examination Schools at Oxford. He was an excellent example of the Liberal county member, independent but ultimately loyal. With Gladstone, he epitomized the development from Christ Church Conservatism to Liberalism.

A. F. Pollard, rev. H. C. G. Matthew

Sources Boase, *Mod. Eng. biog.* · *Memoir and letters of … Sir Thomas Dyke Acland*, ed. A. H. D. Acland (privately printed, London, 1902) · Gladstone, *Diaries* · J. G. Millais, *Life of Millais*, 1 (1899) · Burke, *Peerage*
Archives Bodl. Oxf., corresp. · Devon RO, corresp. and papers · Duke U., Perkins L., corresp. and papers | Balliol Oxf., letters to David Morier · BL, corresp. with Lord Carnarvon, Add. MS 61024 · BL, corresp. with W. E. Gladstone, Add. MS 44092 · Bodl. Oxf.,

corresp. with Sir Henry Wentworth Acland · Bodl. Oxf., letters to W. E. Gladstone · LPL, letters to A. C. Tait relating to bishop of Natal · Pusey Oxf., letters to E. B. Pusey · St Deiniol's Library, Hawarden, letters to W. E. Gladstone

Likenesses Hills & Saunders, photograph, NPG [*see illus.*] · J. Slater, drawing, repro. in J. Slater and G. Richmond, *Portraits of members of Grillion's Club*, 1 (1864)

Wealth at death £74,141 15s. 5d.: probate, 5 July 1898, CGPLA Eng. & Wales

Acland, Sir Wroth Palmer (1770–1816), army officer, was the son of Arthur Palmer Acland of Fairfield, and nephew of Sir Thomas Acland bt. He entered the army in 1787 as ensign in the 17th regiment, becoming a lieutenant in 1790 and captain in 1791 before being placed on half pay until the outbreak of war with France. Acland was appointed to the 3rd regiment (the Buffs) in May 1793, serving in Flanders under the duke of York. In 1795 he was promoted major, and purchased the lieutenant-colonelcy of the 19th regiment. In 1796 he accompanied his regiment to Ceylon, and in 1799 became by exchange captain and lieutenant-colonel in the 2nd (Coldstream) guards, with which he served in Egypt. He became colonel in 1803, and, after serving at the battle of Maida in 1806, was appointed brigadier-general and ordered to take command of a brigade being assembled at Harwich for Portugal in 1808.

Acland's brigade sailed together with that of Brigadier-General Anstruther in May, and on reaching the Douro received orders from Sir Arthur Wellesley to proceed to Maceira Bay. There Wellesley covered the dangerous disembarkation of Acland's brigade before drawing up the two newly arrived brigades with the rest of his army in a strong position at Vimeiro. Acland's brigade was stationed on the left of the churchyard forming the key to the British position. This would have been endangered had it not been for Wellesley's realization that Junot intended to turn the British left. He therefore transferred his brigades from the right flank to bolster Acland on the left. Acland's major contribution was to cover Anstruther's drive, which forced back the main French column of advance.

Ill health ensured that Acland had to leave Portugal soon after the battle, and deprived him of the glory of serving under Sir John Moore, as Anstruther was to do. In 1810 Acland was promoted major-general, and commanded a division in the abortive expedition to the Scheldt. In 1814 he was promoted lieutenant-general; in 1815 he became one of the first KCBs and he was made colonel of the 1st battalion of the 60th regiment. He died on 8 March 1816 from a recurrence of the fever that had threatened his life in Portugal.

H. M. STEPHENS, *rev.* S. KINROSS

Sources Fortescue, *Brit. army*, vols. 5–6, 8 · W. F. P. Napier, *History of the war in the Peninsula and in the south of France*, 2 (1829) · C. W. C. Oman, *A history of the Peninsular War*, 1 (1902) · E. C. Joslin, A. R. Litherland, B. T. Simpkin, and others, eds., *British battles and medals*, 6th edn (1988) · J. Haydn, *The book of dignities: containing rolls of the official personages of the British empire* (1851)

Aconcio, Jacopo [Jacobus Acontius] (*c.*1520–1566/7?), theologian and military engineer, was perhaps born at Ossana, in the Val di Sole, not far from Trento in Italy, the son of Gerolamo Aconcio and his wife, Oliana. After studying law

Aconcio was admitted to the Collegio dei Notai of Trento in 1548, and the next year entered the service of Count Francesco Landriano, a prominent figure at the court of the emperor Charles V, then at Vienna. Aconcio remained with Landriano until 1556, when he became secretary to Cardinal Madruzzo, the imperial governor in Milan. According to Aconcio's own recollection, he had already become attracted to the ideas of the Reformation while still with Landriano, views confirmed in Milan. Since he could not openly express such thoughts in Italy, he decided to choose a career by which he could earn a living in exile, and settled on military engineering. He claims to have taught himself through conversations with Landriano and other military men and through careful observation of existing fortifications. While at Milan he sought the guidance of Giovanni Maria Olgiati, a leading expert, who was full of helpful advice.

By 1556 it was evidently unsafe for Aconcio to stay any longer; he fled to Basel, and then to Zürich. In Basel he probably met Bernardino Ochino and other Italian reformers, and could have become acquainted with their radical doctrines. There he wrote his first works: *Dialogue di Silvio e Mutio*, which purports to reveal the arguments of the Lutherans in order that they be refuted, but really supports them and their criticisms of the Roman Catholic church; and a *Summa de Christiana religione*, which presents his own concept of basic religion, freed from all the contentious points that divided Christendom. Both were published in 1558. On a more secular note, he published a little treatise, *De methodo*, in which he argues that the method of intellectual enquiry must be logical, proceeding by analysis, as in mathematics, from a few basic principles to certain conclusions.

From Switzerland, Aconcio moved to Strasbourg where he wrote to urge Maximilian, then king of Bohemia, and later emperor, to become a protestant (as some of the reformers hoped), suggesting that Elizabeth, the new queen of England, would then be a good match for him, as she would only marry a protestant. Aconcio had met some of the Marian exiles in Switzerland and by 1559 was contemplating a move to England, having great hopes of the new regime. Sir William Cecil, the secretary of state, for his part was interested in recruiting Italian experts in the new style of fortification. Thus by September Aconcio was in England. Within a few months of his arrival he applied for a patent for a number of mechanical inventions as well as novel types of furnace for use in brewing and dyeing. This would appear to be among the earliest English requests for a patent on grounds of original invention. Although a patent was not awarded on this occasion, a later application in September 1565 for machines for grinding, crushing, and cutting wood was indeed granted. Aconcio's applications refer to innovative windmills, and watermills operated from a small pool or even a well, perhaps intending some kind of perpetual motion device. Without further detail it is not clear how his inventions may have differed from similar collections, mainly Italian, which were in circulation at that time. In any case he was awarded a substantial royal pension in 1561, and was subsequently naturalized.

Soon after his arrival in England, Aconcio distributed a book that he had composed on the fortification of cities, presumably to assist his search for employment. No copies survive, and there is no trace of a supposed publication of this treatise in 1582. He put forward a scheme for draining marshland along the south bank of the Thames between Erith and Plumstead. Work was begun with some success, but bad weather damaged what he had managed to complete, and he was obliged to hand over control of the project to his compatriot Castiglione and other partners. Finally in 1564 he was at last engaged as a military engineer, at Berwick, where Sir Richard Lee's plans had been criticized by the government's chief Italian expert, Giovanni Portinari. Aconcio went to Berwick to help draw up a joint report. He made his own suggestions, some of which were carried out; a sketch map of his grander scheme is preserved at Hatfield House.

Meanwhile Aconcio had been busy developing his religious views, which were much more radical than his engineering. From 1560 he had become involved in a dispute which had split the Strangers' Church—the Dutch church, which he joined after the Spanish reformers' church had been disbanded. The minister had been severely attacked for allowing Anabaptist refugees to join the church. Indeed loyal Calvinists had already been enquiring about Aconcio's past, as if he had always been suspect. When Bishop Grindal took the side of the objectors, Aconcio wrote to him to defend the minister and himself. This may have been the spur for him to publish his major work, the *Stratagematum Satanae* (1565), a military metaphor appropriate for a military engineer. The book was published in Basel, which required at least one, perhaps two, long visits to Switzerland.

In this book Aconcio turns the persecution of heresy upside down; instead of the heretics being seduced by the devil, it is the wish to persecute which is diabolical, for it is the means whereby the devil injures true Christianity. Given the fallibility of human judgement, and men's love of their own opinions, it can never be certain that any particular doctrine is totally erroneous. Satan moreover seeks to persuade men to ignore the bidding of their own consciences by surrendering their judgement to another (meaning all priests and ministers), while he encourages those with influence to exert their authority over the consciences of others. Curses, denunciations, and cruel punishments will only reinforce sectarian resistance. In effect persecution is wrong but also ineffective, having led to the present multiplication of opinions, all passionately defended. For Aconcio there are only a very few fundamental teachings in Christianity, derived directly from the plain meaning of the New Testament; everything else can be accepted or rejected so that any disagreement should be conducted mildly, acknowledging that either or indeed both sides may have a case—or may be wrong.

A short treatise in Italian, *Una essortatione al timor di Dio* ('An exhortation to the fear of God'), Aconcio's true confession of faith, was published (1580?) after his death by Giovanni Battista Castiglione, who was his executor. A treatise on the writing of history survives in manuscript, but was utilized, as he acknowledges, by Thomas Blundeville in his own work, the first essay in English on the proper study of history. In this treatise Aconcio does maintain that history should be studied to learn of God's providence. However he mainly adopts a more secular standpoint, to seek examples of prudence and foresight, whether public or private, and to investigate the actual relation of actions to their consequences.

After 1566 nothing more is heard of Aconcio, so the date and place of his death are uncertain; he probably died in 1566 or 1567, perhaps in London. His writings suffer from prolixity and a tendency to repeat similar arguments in an overgeneralized manner. Nevertheless, the *Stratagematum Satanae* in particular had considerable influence, notably in Britain and in the Netherlands, among those who feared persecution for dissenting beliefs and those who stressed the rights of all members of the church, not only the clergy, to express their opinions freely. Several editions appeared during the seventeenth century, with French, Dutch, and German translations: an English translation of the first part of the book appeared just after the civil war, in 1648. If he aimed primarily at toleration among protestants, Aconcio's pioneering exposition lent itself to a wider scope, and was later taken up by those who sought a general toleration and freedom of religious expression.

A. G. KELLER

Sources C. D. O'Malley, *Jacopo Aconcio* (Rome, 1955) · A. G. Kinder, *Jacobus Acontius*, Bibliotheca Dissidentium, 16 (Baden-Baden, 1994) · L. White, 'Jacopo Aconcio as an engineer', *American Historical Review*, 72 (1966–7), 425–44 · D. Cantimori, 'Aconcio, Jacopo', *Dizionario biografico degli Italiani*, ed. A. M. Ghisalberti, 1 (Rome, 1960), 481–95 · E. R. Briggs, 'An apostle of the incomplete Reformation, Jacopo Aconcio', *Proceedings of the Huguenot Society*, 22 (1970–76), 481–95

Archives Hatfield House, Hertfordshire, Cecil papers, maps II/29

Likenesses line engraving, BM

A'Court, William, first Baron Heytesbury (1779–1860), diplomatist, was the eldest son of Sir William Pierce Ashe A'Court, first baronet (1747–1817), MP for Aylesbury, and his second wife, Letitia (d. 1821), daughter of Henry Wyndham of Salisbury. He was born in the cathedral close at Salisbury on 11 July 1779 and educated at Eton College. He was secretary of legation at Palermo and Naples (1801–7), and chargé d'affaires there (1801–2 and 1803). In 1807, soon after Napoleon had occupied Naples, but not Sicily, A'Court was sent as secretary to the earl of Pembroke's special mission to Vienna. He married Maria Rebecca (1783–1844), second daughter of the Hon. William Henry Bouverie, son of the earl of Radnor, on 3 October 1808. In 1812 he became first commissioner for affairs in Malta and was concerned with the establishment of a permanent system of civil government there.

In April 1813 A'Court received his credentials as envoy-extraordinary to the Barbary states (Algiers, Morocco, Tripoli, and Tunis), to which he travelled in the summer and autumn of 1813. The most pressing problem was that of piracy, although he was also instructed to obtain supplies for the British army in Spain. He returned to Naples as minister-plenipotentiary in 1814. A conservative, he was sent to modify the sympathy of his predecessor, William Bentinck, for liberal reform. His conduct during the Neapolitan revolution of 1820 was approved by the foreign secretary, Lord Castlereagh, although A'Court tempered disapproval with compassion and signed passports to aid the escape of leading rebels from Austrian vengeance. In 1822 he became envoy-extraordinary to Spain and, in 1824, ambassador to Portugal.

A'Court had succeeded his father as second baronet in 1817, the same year he became a privy councillor. In 1819 he was made GCB and in 1828 created Baron Heytesbury of Heytesbury, Wiltshire. He was ambassador to Russia from 1828 to 1832. He arrived there soon after the outbreak of the Russo-Turkish War of 1828–9, and proceeded to the tsar's headquarters at Odessa. Modern research has vindicated Heytesbury's conclusion that the tsar did not desire the disintegration of the Ottoman empire, believing that it provided a safe buffer state for Russia's southern flank, but it earned him a reprimand from the prime minister, the duke of Wellington, who was convinced of Russia's aggressive intentions.

In 1835 Sir Robert Peel invited Heytesbury to become governor-general of India but, because of the change of ministry, he did not take up the appointment. In the second Peel administration, he was lord lieutenant of Ireland from 1844 to 1846, where, it has been concluded, 'With no controversial record in domestic politics to prejudice him … he faced his task in Ireland with calm, objectivity and a practised talent for administration' (Gash, 427). He was conciliatory in religious matters but his administration was overtaken by the horrors of the Irish famine. Although petitioners in Ireland sometimes found him cold, he was one of the first to warn the government of the magnitude of the problem and co-operated with Peel in scientific inquiries into the cause of the potato blight and its possible remedy. He left office with Peel. From 1841 to 1857 he held the honorific post of governor of the Isle of Wight. He died at home at Heytesbury House, Wiltshire, on 31 May 1860. Heytesbury was one of the ablest diplomats of his time, but little known to the public and generally under-rated. He also dabbled in literature, and published *Montalto: a Tragedy in Five Acts, with other Poems* in 1840. He was succeeded in the barony by the elder of his two sons, William Henry Ashe A'Court. He also had a daughter.   MURIEL E. CHAMBERLAIN

Sources *GM*, 3rd ser., 9 (1860), 90 · BL, Heytesbury MSS · *FO List* (1861) · S. T. Bindoff and others, eds., *British diplomatic representatives, 1789–1852*, CS, 3rd ser., 50 (1934) · M. E. Chamberlain, *Lord Aberdeen: a political biography* (1983) · R. J. Kerner, 'Russia's new policy in the Near East after the peace of Adrianople', *Cambridge Historical Journal*, 5 (1935–7), 280–90 · N. Gash, *Sir Robert Peel: the life of Sir Robert Peel after 1830* (1972) · C. K. Webster, *The foreign policy of Castlereagh*, 2 vols. (1925–31) · H. Temperley, *The foreign policy of Canning, 1822–1827*, 2nd edn (1966) · Burke, *Peerage* (1939) · *Annual Register* (1860) · GEC, *Peerage* · *The Times* (2 June 1860)

Archives BL, corresp. and papers, Add. MSS 41511–41563 · PRO, Foreign Office MSS · Wilts. & Swindon RO, corresp. and papers | BL, corresp. with Lord Aberdeen, Add. MSS 43089, 43114–43115 · BL, corresp. with Lord Melbourne, Add. MSS 60440–60442 · BL, corresp. with Sir Robert Peel, Add. MS 40479 · Durham RO, corresp. with Lord Castlereagh · NL Scot., corresp. with Robert Liston · PRO, corresp. with Stratford Canning, FO352 · PRO, corresp. with Lord Ellenborough, PRO30/12 · PRO NIre., corresp. with Lord Castlereagh · U. Nott. L., corresp. with Lord Bentinck · U. Southampton L., corresp. with Lord Palmerston

Likenesses E. U. Eddis, oils, 1844, NG Ire.

Wealth at death under £60,000: probate, 24 July 1860, *CGPLA Eng. & Wales*

Acton, Charles Januarius Edward (1803–1847), cardinal, was born at Naples on 6 March 1803, the second son of Sir John Francis Edward *Acton, sixth baronet (1736–1811), of Aldenham Hall, near Bridgnorth, Shropshire. Sir John was commander-in-chief of the land and sea forces of the kingdom of Naples and prime minister; he married, by papal dispensation, Mary Ann (1786–1873), daughter of his brother, Joseph Edward Acton, a lieutenant-general in the service of the Two Sicilies, and governor of Gaeta. These Italian connections proved significant for Charles Acton's later career. Having received some rudimentary instruction from the bishop of Marseilles, he and his elder brother Richard were sent to England to be educated after their father's death in 1811. Initially, they were placed at a school kept by the Abbé Quegné at Parsons Green, near London. Presently, they were transferred to a protestant school at Isleworth, and then to Westminster School; their departure from this establishment was due to the pressure which was (unsuccessfully) placed on them to convert. After Acton and his brother had spent a period as private pupils of a protestant clergyman called Jones, Charles Acton was admitted to Magdalene College, Cambridge, in July 1819. Here he completed his secular education, undisturbed despite his faith, as his tutor, Neville, did not require attendance at chapel. This was, as Wiseman observed, 'a very unusual preparation for the Roman purple' (Wiseman, 476). However, young Acton, having a strong religious vocation, entered the Accademia Ecclesiastica in Rome, where he was ordained priest. Leo XII made him one of his chamberlains, and in 1828 appointed him secretary to Monsignor (afterwards Cardinal) Lambruschini, the papal nuncio at Paris. Shortly afterwards he was nominated vice-legate or governor of Bologna by Pius VIII. He left the city before revolution broke out there and in the neighbouring provinces after the death of Pius VIII.

Acton was in England in 1829, in which year he performed the marriage of his only sister, Elizabeth, to Robert Throckmorton. On the accession of Gregory XVI in 1831 he was made secretary to the *disciplina regolare*, the congregation which dealt with violations or relaxations of discipline in religious communities. He was also appointed assistant judge to the civil courts of Rome. Next he was nominated auditor of the apostolic chamber, or first judge of the Roman civil courts. This appointment led naturally to his election to the Sacred College, where he replaced Cardinal Weld: on 24 January 1842 he was proclaimed cardinal-priest of the title of Santa Maria della Pace. He also became protector of the English College at Rome.

Cardinal Acton was the interpreter and only witness of the important interview that took place in 1845 between Gregory XVI and Tsar Nicholas I of Russia. At the pope's request, Acton wrote a precise account of this conference, but he never allowed it to be seen. His extensive legal knowledge and ability to manage ecclesiastical affairs, as well as his influential connections, assured his prominence at the centre of Vatican business. Every matter of consequence relating to England and its dependencies was referred by the pope to Acton, and it was mainly due to his enthusiasm that England was, in 1840, divided into eight Roman Catholic districts or vicariates-apostolic. (Previously there had been only four vicariates, created by Innocent XI in 1688.) The 1840 division was the prelude to the eventual restoration of the Roman Catholic hierarchy granted by Pius IX in 1850, to which Acton was opposed: when, in 1840, a hierarchy was sanctioned for Australia, Acton was hostile, and his opposition undoubtedly helped to prevent the restoration in England until after his death. Cardinal Acton's health, never very strong, began to decline in the late 1840s. He retired to Palermo and then to Naples, where he died in the Jesuit convent on 23 June 1847. THOMPSON COOPER, rev. ROSEMARY MITCHELL

Sources Burke, *Peerage* · Gillow, *Lit. biog. hist.* · H. E. Wiseman, *Recollections of the last four popes and of Rome in their time* (1858) · F. J. Cwiekowski, *The English bishops and the First Vatican Council* (1971) · E. R. Norman, *The English Catholic church in the nineteenth century* (1984)
Archives Archivio Vaticano, Vatican City, corresp. and papers · CUL, corresp. · Venerable English College, Rome, speech | Magd. Cam., letters to Acton family · University of Notre Dame, Indiana, university archives, letters to his mother and sister, Lady Throckmorton · Warks. CRO, letters to his family and sister, Lady Throckmorton · Westminster Archdiocesan Archives, London, letters to his mother and brother, F. R. E. Acton
Likenesses V. Moroni, oils, 1844, Coughton Court, Warwickshire · G. A. Periam, line engraving (aged twenty-seven; after T. Uwins), BM · line engraving, NPG · oils (as a boy), Coughton Court, Warwickshire · portrait, repro. in *Catholic Directory* (1843)

Acton, Edward (d. 1707), naval officer, was the son of Mary Acton, and was related to the Acton family of Shropshire. He entered the navy as a volunteer on the *Diamond* in September 1691, was lieutenant on the *Advice* in May 1693, and succeeded as captain on 7 October 1694 following his predecessor's death. The ship was docked in England in May 1695 for repairs, and on 25 June he made out his will, naming his widowed mother, Mary Acton of St Paul's, Covent Garden, his agent and executor. He probably did not marry, and his mother duly proved his will. He served at Kinsale in September 1695, and in December his was one of five ships sent to the East Indies. On his return in November 1697 he and two other captains were suspended for alleged victualling irregularities, but he was reinstated on 11 January 1700. Having learned that two ships were to be fitted out for the West Indies, he asked for one of the commands, noting, 'I do humbly hope in regard of what I have suffered these Three years past and that I have declined all employment, relying only on his Majesties Service' (PRO, ADM 1/4135). He was appointed successively to the fifth rates *Dolphin* and *Lynn* and given command of the fourth rate *Bristol* in May 1701. Seriously ill with 'a fit of the Rhumatism' he was unable to sail, again to the West Indies, until 1702.

In 1703 Acton returned to England with captains Richard Kirkby and Cooper Wade, both sentenced to death for failure to support Vice-Admiral Edward Benbow. Acton witnessed Kirkby's will and sat up with him the night before his execution, on the *Bristol* on 16 April 1703. Service in the West Indies appears to have affected his health, leaving him frequently ill and weak, perhaps with recurring bouts of fever. After the execution he sought leave to go to Bath, 'being well assured by the doctors of this Country and when at Jamaica the same that it was impossible to gain my lost health but by that means …'. His hopes of an early return did not take place, and in January 1704 he successfully sought to be considered for command of the *Kingston*, 'I having bin a long time out of command' (PRO, ADM 1/1436). He took part in the capture of Gibraltar in July 1704. At the battle of Malaga on 13 August 1704 the *Kingston*, having expended all of its ammunition, drew out of the line and 'got without shot of the enemy' (PRO, ADM 52/200/14), resulting in Acton's trial, but acquittal, by court martial in January 1705. Appointed to the *Bedford* in December 1704, he was sent again to the Mediterranean, and was present at the annihilation of the French fleet at Marbella in March, and the relief of Gibraltar and capture of Barcelona in October. He moved to the *Grafton* in January 1706 and returned with the fleet to Lisbon to refit, where he fell ill. He rejoined the fleet in June and took part in the capture of Alicante in July. Present at Ibiza and Minorca in September, he was sent ashore as a hostage during negotiations at Majorca. He returned to England with Admiral Leake in October 1706.

The *Grafton*, refitted, was one of three ships which sailed from the Downs on 1 May 1707 with the Lisbon and West Indies trade in convoy. The same day they met a French squadron under Forbin off Dungeness, with nine ships of the line and several privateers. Battle began at noon, with the *Grafton*, in the rear of the line, exchanging fire with one of the French ships. Two other French ships came up and boarded the *Grafton*, joined by the first attacker. In half an hour the *Grafton* was overpowered, her colours struck, and Acton killed.

J. K. LAUGHTON, rev. PETER LE FEVRE

Sources paybook, *Diamond*, PRO, ADM 33/155 · log of *Advice* kept by Edward Acton, PRO, ADM 51/13/3–6 · captain's letters A, 1698–1707, PRO, ADM 1/1435, 1436 · S. Martin-Leake, *The life of Sir John Leake*, ed. G. Callender, 2 vols., Navy RS, 52, 53 (1920) · *Life of Captain Stephen Martin, 1666–1740*, ed. C. R. Markham, Navy RS, 5 (1895) · master's log, *Prince George*, PRO, ADM 52/181/3 · lieutenant's log, *Grafton*, PRO, ADM 51/4201/6 · master's log, *Kingston*, PRO, ADM 52/200/14 · *CSP dom.*, 1699–1700, 317, 352 · *The manuscripts of the House of Lords*, new ser., 12 vols. (1900–77), vol. 6, pp. 187–9 · J. H. Owen, *War at sea under Queen Anne, 1702–1708* (1938) · PRO, PROB 11/500, fols. 271v–272 · captain's log, *Royal Oak*, PRO, ADM 51/4139/4

Acton, Sir Edward (1865–1945), judge, was born at Stretford in Lancashire on 6 November 1865, the son of Henry Morell *Acton (1828–1907) [see under Acton, Henry], one of the editors of the *Manchester Guardian*, and his wife, Anne Shaw, daughter of Nathaniel Williamson, sharebroker, of Manchester. He was educated at Uppingham School, where he was an exhibitioner, and Wadham College,

Oxford, where he held a classical scholarship and the Hody Greek exhibition. He was at Oxford from 1884 to 1888 and thus was a precursor rather than a member of that remarkable group of Wadham lawyers which included Frederick Edwin Smith (the future earl of Birkenhead), Alexander Adair Roche (later Lord Roche), and John Allsebrook Simon (later Viscount Simon). After gaining a first in classical moderations (1886) and a second in *literae humaniores* (1888), Acton joined the Inner Temple, where he was awarded a foundation scholarship in 1890; he was called to the bar in 1891 and later became a bencher of his inn.

Acton joined the northern circuit and practised in Manchester and Liverpool, where he soon built up an extensive practice. On 12 August 1903 he married Edith Nina, daughter of Conrad William Alexander Tulloch, a chartered accountant, of London. Acton and his wife were devoted to each other; there were no children of the marriage. In 1913 Acton became a lecturer in the law of evidence and procedure at the University of Manchester. In 1918, when he might have been expected to be thinking of taking silk, he surprised those who knew him by accepting appointment as a county court judge. For the next two years he worked on circuit 18 at Nottingham.

In 1920 arrears of work in the King's Bench Division made it necessary to appoint two additional judges and Acton was chosen to fill one of these posts by Birkenhead, the lord chancellor, himself an old member of the northern circuit. Such a promotion from the county court to the High Court had never been made before. The experiment was successful, however, and the precedent created in Acton's case has since been followed on a number of occasions. Acton received the customary knighthood on his appointment to the bench in 1920. In 1934 ill health compelled him to retire and he lived quietly, a semi-invalid, at his home, The Hatch, Churt, Surrey, where he died on 17 November 1945. He was survived by his wife.

At the bar Acton had a large and solid practice; as an advocate he was sound and accurate but not spectacular. These qualities he displayed on the bench. In his judgments he was content to deal closely with the case in hand without feeling it necessary to elaborate on the surrounding legal field or to strive after the distinction of creating precedents for quotation in the books. Although he was so modest, his decisions satisfactorily stood the test of appeal.

Acton was interested in the theatre and music, though as an auditor rather than a performer. A portrait by John St Helier Lander is in Wadham College, of which he was elected an honorary fellow in 1923. The artist's attempt to overcome the belittling effect on the face which the wearing of a full-bottomed wig can have has not been entirely successful, and the picture gives the impression that Acton was of larger proportions than was the fact.

W. O. HART, rev. ALEC SAMUELS

Sources *The Times* (19 Nov 1945) · private information (1959) · Burke, *Peerage* (1939)
Likenesses J. St H. Lander, oils, Wadham College, Oxford
Wealth at death £45,259 15s. 8d.: probate, 1946

Acton, Eliza (1799–1859), writer on cookery and poet, was born at Battle, Sussex, on 17 April 1799, the eldest of the five children of John Acton and his wife, Elizabeth, *née* Mercer. The Actons were a Suffolk family, and returned there soon after Eliza was born. The rest of the children, three more daughters and a son, were all born in Ipswich, where they lived at St Peter's. John Acton was a brewer and a partner in the firm of Halliday, Studd, and Acton.

At the age of seventeen Eliza Acton and a Miss Nicholson opened a school for girls in Claydon, near Ipswich. This lasted until Eliza Acton left in 1820, when it soon closed down. She was said to be delicate, and spent some time in France for her health. It has been suggested that while there she had an unhappy love affair with a French army officer, after which she returned home, and the *Poems* that she published in 1826 were mostly about unrequited love. This volume had a modest success, being reprinted within a few weeks, and she also wrote two longer poems, 'The Chronicles of Castel Framlingham' which appeared in the *Sudbury Chronicle* of 1838, and 'The Voice of the North' to commemorate the first visit of Queen Victoria to Scotland in 1842.

In 1837 Eliza Acton was living in Tonbridge, Kent, at 1 Bordyke, near to the school with which she had some connection. Her publishers, Longmans, suggested she should write something more practical than poetry so, for the next few years, she applied herself to meticulous research for the work by which she is best known: *Modern Cookery for Private Families*, first published in 1845. This was an immediate and lasting success running into several editions, and was the standard work on the subject until the end of the century, establishing Eliza Acton as the first of the modern cookery writers. She wrote with great charm and clarity, but what marked the book as innovative was her original plan of listing, very exactly, the ingredients, the time taken, and possible pitfalls for the inexperienced cook. This was a completely new format, all other books on the subject being far less exact in their instructions.

This became the standard way of writing cookery books, except that Eliza Acton's summary of ingredients followed the recipe, whereas it is now more usually at the beginning. Typical of her style of writing was her recipe for 'China chilo':

Mince a pound of undressed loin or leg of mutton, with or without a portion of its fat; mix with it two or three young lettuces shred small, a pint of young peas, a teaspoonful of salt, half as much pepper, four tablespoonsful of water, from two to three ounces of good butter, and, if the flavour be liked, a few green onions minced. Keep the whole well stirred with a fork over a clear and gentle fire until it is quite hot, then place it closely covered by the side of the stove, or on a high trivet, that it may stew as softly as possible for a couple of hours. One or even two half-grown cucumbers, cut small by scoring the ends deeply as they are sliced, or a quarter of a pint of minced mushrooms may be added with good effect; or a dessertspoonful of currie-powder and a large chopped onion. A dish of boiled rice should be sent to table with it.

Mutton, 1 pint; green peas, 1 pint, young lettuces, 2; salt 1 teaspoonful; pepper ½ teaspoonful; water, 4 tablespoonsful; butter, 2 to 3 oz: 2 hours. Varieties: cucumbers, 2; or mushrooms minced, ¼ pint; or currie-powder, 1 dessertspoonful, and 1 large onion.   (Acton, *Modern Cookery*, 241–2)

The descriptions and asides in the writing show clearly that she knew her subject well, and she wrote that the recipes 'were all proved under our own roof, and under our own personal supervision' (Acton, *Modern Cookery*, preface, x).

Some time after the publication of *Modern Cookery* Eliza Acton went to live in London, at Snowden House, John Street, Hampstead, where she worked on her next book. This was *The English Bread Book*, published in 1857. A serious and scholarly account of the history of bread and its making, with a severe attack on the malpractices of bakers and millers in adulterating the product, this also contained recipes for the home bread maker. It was not reprinted until 1990 and did not make the impact of her earlier work.

In character Eliza Acton seems to have been like a kindly schoolteacher, showing great humour and understanding. She was a well-established middle-class spinster, with a wide and varied circle of friends, several of whom she quotes as the source of some of her recipes. Judging from an etching made from a portrait by Sir William Beechey, she was also elegant, gentle, and thoughtful. Eliza Acton suffered from ill health a good deal of her life and died at home, of premature old age, on 13 February 1859. She was buried in Hampstead churchyard on 17 February.

ELIZABETH RAY

Sources parish register (births), Ipswich, Suffolk, Suffolk RO, Ipswich, 1816–1820 · *Ipswich Journal* (13 March 1816) · *Ipswich Journal* (18 Jan 1820) · *Ipswich Journal* (21 Oct 1826) · *Ipswich Journal* (19 Feb 1859) · census returns for Tonbridge, Kent, 1841, PRO, J 409 9B · parish register, Battle, 1799, E. Sussex RO · parish register (burials), St John's, Hampstead, London, 17 Feb 1859 · *DNB* · *Fraser's Magazine*, 31 (1845), 465–74 · letter from Eliza Acton's doctor, LMA, Q/WIL/479 · E. David, preface, in *The best of Eliza Acton*, ed. E. Ray (1968) · M. Aylett and O. Orlish, *First catch your hare: a history of the recipe-makers* (1965) · E. Acton, *Modern cookery for private families*, new edn (1874) · E. Acton, *The English bread book* (1857) · d. cert.
Likenesses I. G. Spurgeon, etching (after W. Beechey), NPG

Acton, Eugenia de. *See* Lewis, Alethea (1749–1827).

Acton, Sir Harold Mario Mitchell (1904–1994), aesthete and author, was born at his parents' magnificent villa at La Pietra, a mile north of Florence, on 5 July 1904, the son of Arthur Mario Acton (*d.* 1953) and his wife, Hortense Mitchell (*d.* 1962). His father was a cosmopolitan artist, interior designer, and dealer in art and antiques, who acted as adviser to and agent for the American architect Stanford White. (He was a witness to White's murder on the roof of Madison Square Garden in 1906.) Although Arthur Acton was ostensibly descended from the minister of state to the king and queen of Naples, Sir John Acton (grandfather of the historian Lord Acton), cosmopolitan gossips such as Mabel Dodge, then resident at the nearby Villa Curonia, thought him illegitimate—which no doubt he was, though a godson of the future Cardinal Manning, then

Sir Harold Mario Mitchell Acton (1904–1994), by John Ward, 1985

archbishop of Westminster (diary of M. D. Luhan and information from Dialta Alliata di Montereale, who believes that Arthur may have been the son of his ostensible father's brother, Harold). Arthur studied painting in Paris where, through Stanford White, he met and befriended the gay bachelor Guy Mitchell and his sister Hortense, children of the Chicago-based founder of the Illinois Trust and Savings Bank. Thanks to his marriage to Hortense Mitchell, Arthur was able to confirm his acquisition of La Pietra and the adjacent villas, filling what had been rented properties with pictures and *objets d'art* on a scale that surpassed the more specialized efforts of rival collectors resident in early-twentieth-century Florence, Charles Loeser, Herbert Horne, and Bernard Berenson (with whom he occasionally collaborated). Beyond his achievement in turning La Pietra itself into a veritable museum was the creation of its neo-Renaissance garden, done with the professional assistance of White and Charles Platt (who are acknowledged on an obscurely placed plaque), and Paul Chalfin, who is not (Lord, 5).

Eton and Oxford After a private education in Florence; Wixenford, near Wokingham in Berkshire; Château Lancy, near Geneva; and a school which he remembered as Lawnwood (Acton, *Memoirs*, 66–7) but which was in fact Ashlawn, near Benenden in Kent, in May 1918 Harold Acton was sent to Eton College; his younger brother, Chicago-born William, joined him there a year later. Here Harold rose to precocious prominence as an aesthete, a term he remained proud to use until the day he died. He and his wealthy homosexual friend Brian Howard competed with each other to shock and impress. During vacations from Eton, Harold and his brother stayed with a 'Miss C.' in Evelyn Gardens, exploring London through the eyes of Whistler, whose prints they acquired in the Caledonian Market and Charing Cross Road. It was Whistler's pictures, he later realized, that encouraged his taste for the oriental. Miss C. took the brothers to meet Sargent (who was also born in Florence) and Wilson Steer in their respective studios. They also visited their mother's relations in America. Between seeing the collections of their father's friends and associates in Florence (including both Loeser's Cézannes and Berenson's primitives), the great London collections, and now those of Frick, Mellon, Bache, and Isabella Gardner (in large part formed on the advice of Berenson and Joseph Duveen), the Acton brothers were becoming connoisseurs in their own right.

Although Harold Acton also painted at Eton, it was William who took up art as a profession, encouraged by praise from Roger Fry and Leon Bakst. Harold was instead increasingly drawn towards literature. While still at Eton he helped Howard to edit a literary magazine, the *Eton Candle*, his own contributions to which were praised by Edith Sitwell. When he went up to Christ Church, Oxford, in 1922, Acton was thus already a published poet who had been entertained by Ottoline Morrell at Garsington, both of which achievements encouraged *The Spectator* to accept his Eliot-influenced 'Cathedral interior' for publication during his first term. Having moved into Christ Church's Venetian-Gothic Meadow Buildings, he painted his rooms 'lemon yellow and filled them with Victorian bric-a-brac', inventing for himself a specifically mid-nineteenth-century look, consisting of grey bowler-hat, side-whiskers, stock, jacket with wide lapels, and broad, pleated trousers which became known as Oxford bags. In April 1923 Duckworth published a volume of this first-year undergraduate's verse, *Aquarium*, issued in the same format and in the same month as Edith Sitwell's *Bucolic Comedies*. Meanwhile, his literary criticism inspired awe among contemporaries such as Graham Greene, who in 1925 wrote that 'Although I wouldn't admit it to anyone else, his attack in *The Cherwell* was the best and most awful criticism I've ever had, and my alterations I try to make in my stuff are founded on it' (N. Sherry, *The Life of Graham Greene*, vol. 1, 1989, p. 170).

In partnership with an American Quaker relation of Mary Berenson called Alfred Nicholson, Acton founded a paper called the *Oxford Broom*, intended to sweep away '*fin de siècle* cobwebs'. His rejection of the 1890s twilight was quite distinct from Bloomsbury's Frenchified reaction against Victorian culture. He promoted good-humoured, 'large-limbed, high coloured' mid-Victorianism to the extent of buying a Wilkie drawing of Daniel O'Connell with his allowance (letter to his mother, 20 Oct. 1924, Acton MSS). He proposed an 'Early Victorian Exhibition', accompanied by an illustrated catalogue for which Lytton Strachey would write the introduction.

To promote our campaign I read papers to the Newman and other societies about the British genre painters, Wilkie,

Frith, Augustus Egg and Martineau, and tried to revive an interest in the flesh-tints of Etty and the cataclysms of Martin the Mezzotinter. (Acton, *Memoirs*, 128)

Acton's battle cry of 'back to mahogany' was facetiously at odds with the serious-minded pseudo-ethnicity (and sub-modernism) of Roger Fry's Omega workshop. Acton's friend Robert Byron agreed that 'never had Britain been more resplendent than between 1846 and 1865' (Acton, *Memoirs*, 119), while Evelyn Waugh devoted himself to writing a monograph on the by then unfashionable Rossetti.

Although there was a decidedly decadent side to a social circle that included Brian Howard, Desmond Harmsworth, Robert Byron, Peter Quennell, and John Sutro, and a provocatively modernist side to the student who recited Eliot's *Waste Land* to ever-provincial Oxonians through a megaphone, and invited Gertrude Stein to speak to the Ordinary Society, Acton had already begun to develop a more earnest curiosity about a wider range of cultural achievement. Though the seeds of his later enthusiasm for (and expertise in) Chinese culture had already been sown, at this stage he was more overtly interested in the ancient culture of the west. Accustomed to learning from, and in several instances befriending, distinguished visitors to La Pietra of his parents' generation, he now formed a friendship with the Oxford scholar John Davidson Beazley, world expert on Greek vases, and his exotic wife, Marie. During his first long vacation, instead of returning to Italy (partly because there he ran the risk of being called up for military service), he accompanied Beazley and his wife to Madrid; there he further enlarged his cosmopolitan education, both in the Prado and in the concert halls. In a later letter to his mother he referred to Maurice Bowra as 'very brilliant and a fine Greek scholar—quite a god at Oxford without being aloof like Beazley' (5 Sept 1932, Acton MSS).

Poetry, fiction, and the Medici Throughout this period Acton regarded himself as, above all, a poet. In February 1925 Thomas Balston of Duckworth was apparently pleased enough with *Aquarium* to publish the twenty-year-old undergraduate's second volume of verse, *An Indian Ass*, in an edition of 1000 copies. The jazzy effects of *Aquarium* were here overlaid by a rather lush vocabulary which, while still redolent of Eliot's influence, was perhaps too celebratory to secure truly fashionable status. After graduating in 1926 with a fourth in French, Acton lingered in Oxford and then established himself in an apartment at 29 quai de Bourbon on the Île St Louis. The following year his parents set up him and his brother William, recently down from Oxford, at 108 Lancaster Gate, London. Here they socialized intensively but also maintained the house as a showcase for their father's *objets d'art*, some of which, their friends duly noted, were for sale. In Paris Harold consolidated a friendship with Gertrude Stein about whose 'Function in Modern Literature' he wrote in the *Oxford Outlook*. He was also in touch with Norman Douglas, who suggested the theme of saints for the title of his third and longest collection of poems, *Five Saints and an Appendix* (1927). Acton described his energetic approach as the poetic equivalent to Luca Giordano, covering ceilings with baroque frescoes.

Unfortunately, the publisher Robert Holden went out of business simultaneously with publishing *Five Saints* and the collection made little impact. Disappointed by the reception of his 'still-born' book, with Gertrude Stein's encouragement Acton now wrote and published a short novel, entitled *Cornelian* and featuring a cubist title-page designed by McKnight Kauffer. Acton was already hard at work on a much longer novel when this appeared in March 1928. Though in his own later account this 'turned sour in the writing' because of assuming 'a bright modern manner' foreign to his nature, *Humdrum* was published by Chatto and Windus in October 1928 (Ritchie, 25). Unfortunately it appeared more or less simultaneously with Evelyn Waugh's *Decline and Fall*. Cyril Connolly reviewed both novels in the *New Statesman*, and not only compared Acton's writing talents unfavourably with Waugh's, but concluded by expressing surprise that Waugh could have dedicated his novel 'in homage and affection' to the incompetent scribbler of *Humdrum*.

Greatly disappointed by the reception of his writings in both creative genres, Acton now turned to non-fiction, albeit of an imaginative kind. Having pioneered the revival of interest in Victoriana (which sustained others such as John Betjeman for an entire lifetime), he now turned to the similarly abandoned late Medici. *The Last of the Medici* (1930) was an eccentric publication, consisting of Acton's translation of a scurrilous eighteenth-century account of the Grand Duke Gian Gastone's bizarre private life, which the publisher Pino Orioli asked his friend Norman Douglas to introduce. Acton's fourth and last book of poems, *This Chaos*, was published in an edition of 150 copies in Paris in the winter of 1930–31 by Nancy Cunard, at whose house at La Chapelle-Réanville near Paris Acton was staying. Having abandoned his Chinese servant Chong Sung in London and holidayed in Corsica, he returned to La Pietra in September 1931, though he spent the next six months in England.

By the time *This Chaos* appeared, however, Acton was already at work on *The Last Medici*. Published by Faber in 1932, after they had insisted on his cutting 30,000 words from the typescript, *The Last Medici* was not very well received, Waugh dismissing it in his diary as dull and consisting of 'long citations from Reresby, Evelyn and contemporary travellers. Also endless descriptions of fêtes and processions' (pp. 311–12). It is just these now fashionable ingredients which have in recent years made this one of Acton's most appreciated books.

China and Naples Apparently not required in Europe, Acton—after a tour of America, Hawaii, and the Far East in 1932 funded by his 'generous uncle' Guy Mitchell—settled in China, where he might have remained had war not intervened. He taught English at Peking (Beijing) University, translated Chinese poetry and plays, and wrote what is probably his best novel, *Peonies and Ponies*, published in 1941. This and his *Memoirs of an Aesthete* (1948) reveal his profound love of *ancien régime* China, while a fascinating series of letters from China to his mother and uncle Guy covering the six years he spent there contains accounts of visiting friends from Osbert Sitwell and Robert Byron to Michael and Anne Rosse and Bryan Guinness and his second wife (Acton MSS). Having moved into a new, much larger 'palace' enthusiastically described in a letter to his mother (13 May 1936, Acton MSS), apart from a visit to Italy (for Christmas), Britain, Ireland, and France, from December 1936 to the spring of 1937, he remained in China until 1939 after the Japanese invasion, when he left most of his possessions in Peking, fully intending to return. He never saw them again.

In Peking, on 6 October 1938, Acton had written in a letter: 'It is a pity Winston Churchill is so erratic; so far he had been the only man with a gift of prophecy and almost a touch of genius though nobody pays any attention to him' (Acton MSS). During the Second World War, after lecturing in Italy on a British Council tour in 1940 and returning to London (1940–41), Acton served in RAF intelligence in India. He was indignant that Foreign Office suspicion of his previous lifestyle meant that no use was made of his knowledge of China. Shortly before he was demobilized, after a spell in Paris in late 1944, he heard of his brother's tragic death in Italy. Judging by his reception at La Pietra, which had been occupied by the Germans, he felt that his parents would have preferred that he rather than William had died. While his father concentrated on gathering together those pictures and antiques that had been dispersed during the war, Acton wrote and published his *Memoirs of an Aesthete* which he dedicated to the memory of his brother. He then travelled extensively in Mexico and North America, where at Berkeley he collaborated with his close friend and former pupil Chen Shih-hsiang in translating the beautiful, late Ming play *The Peach Blossom Fan* (published in 1976).

Acton was tempted to return to China or to become an American citizen, but despite his parents' relative coolness towards him he felt he could not abandon them entirely. He had meanwhile written the ironical Neapolitan novella *Prince Isidore* (1950), and now decided to compromise by renting a seaside villa at via Posillipo 37 in Naples and embarking upon his great two-volume history of the Bourbon rulers of that city. Arthur Acton died on 22 March 1953 but Harold remained based in Naples for most of the decade. He wrote to Waugh of his 'tempestuous' relationship with his father—'How little others knew of his violent temperament'—and of his sense that he had always disappointed him. He wrote that the villa, its gardens, and its collection would be bequeathed to the city of Florence 'after my death' despite his father's 'major concern that they would never be mine' (Acton to Waugh, 30 May 1953, BL, Add. MSS, Waugh correspondence). The absence of a will remains something of a mystery, though properties had been settled on Arthur's mistress, Ersilia Beacci, who died in the following year, from as early as 1917. Though he continued to aspire to financial independence by means of his writing, Harold remained essentially dependent on parental support. Friends who visited him at La Pietra commented on his lack of either car or latchkey even in late middle age.

As a historian of and apologist for the Bourbons of Naples, Acton was a revisionist *avant la lettre*, maintaining a position very different from his liberal relation Lord Acton, who had deeply disapproved of their Anglo-Neapolitan ancestor, Sir John Acton. But the context for his narrative was a rich and thoroughly researched tapestry of the social and cultural life of what had been one of the greatest cities in the world. Osbert Sitwell wrote an enthusiastic puff for the dust jacket of the first volume but published reviews were critical, one by Raymond Mortimer causing particular hurt to the author. This period of hard work culminated in *The Last Bourbons* (1962). The Duveen-inspired novel about fakes and frauds, *Old Lamps for New* (1965), also failed to receive enthusiastic reviews, and this no doubt encouraged Acton to return to autobiography and writing about his famous friends in *More Memoirs of an Aesthete* (1970).

Florence Acton's widowed mother died in 1962, and as the only legitimate heir Harold inherited La Pietra, the other villas and farms, and property in Florence which included the Palazzo Lanfredini, home of the British Institute Library. Although the negotiations continued into the 1990s, it was not long after he came into possession of this substantial legacy, the custodianship of which he took extremely seriously, that he decided to bequeath the bulk of his estate to New York University, Oxford and Christ Church having failed to respond to his offers. He featured La Pietra in his next major publication, *Tuscan Villas* (1973), illustrated with photographs by his young German companion of more than a decade, Alexander Zielcke. In the following year his support for the British Institute and his hosting of distinguished guests—including, on a regular basis, Princess Margaret—had earned him a knighthood (he had been appointed CBE in 1965). In 1975 he published his 'biographical memoir of a dear friend', *Nancy Mitford*, which was criticized for being too discreet about her poignant love life (just as he was to criticize Selina Hastings for categorizing him as homosexual in her more detailed biography of Mitford). *The Pazzi Conspiracy* (1979) was a slighter and less original study than *Tuscan Villas* but sound enough in its judgements to outlast many more academic studies of fifteenth-century Florence. *Three Extraordinary Ambassadors* (1983) covered the Anglo-Italian ingredients in the lives of Henry Wotton, Horace Mann, and William Hamilton in a way that is both readable and informative. On 4 July 1984, his eightieth birthday, Acton was presented with a Festschrift at the British Institute in Florence. The following year the commune of Florence made him an honorary citizen. Apart from introductions to exhibition catalogues devoted to Florentine and Neapolitan baroque art, his last serious piece of historical writing was the introduction to an anthology, *Florence: a Travellers' Companion*, which he asked Edward Chaney to compile and edit (1986; reissued 2002 as *A Traveller's Companion to Florence*). Though now in his eighties, Acton produced a cultural history of Florence which covered the required range with extraordinary skill and in a style worthy of Gibbon (a cousin of the eighteenth-century Actons).

Acton's last years were largely devoted to hosting lunch, tea, and dinner parties, though he continued to write short stories, articles, and reviews. He would take a siesta after lunch and then re-emerge, tall, bald, slightly stooped, but with a springy walk and immaculate in three-piece suit, to resume entertaining both residents (mostly English or American) and/or more or less grand tourists for Punt e Mes or whisky, usually until dinner. Though some considered Acton a snob, he was essentially meritocratic, a master at entertaining such a variety of interesting people that he managed to make Florence seem as cosmopolitan as it had been during the Renaissance. His conversation was culturally wide-ranging, even if it erred on the side of often mischievous gossip rather than introspection. But when his health began to decline, he became concerned about maintaining his reputation as a great raconteur and allowed Zielcke to limit the number of guests. Once the servants were instructed to refer all calls to Zielcke, however, the reduction in visitor numbers became somewhat indiscriminate and old friends found it as difficult to get through as did tourists trying their luck. Eventually telephone messages and letters failed to reach him, and during his long final illness it became impossible for anyone other than doctors and lawyers to see or speak to him. It was during this period that Sir John Pope-Hennessey's secretary, Michael Mallon, replaced Edward Chaney as Acton's nominated literary executor.

Il Barone, as his servants called him, died at La Pietra on 27 February 1994, and was laid out like a grand duke in the hall of the villa to which he had devoted so much of his life. He was buried in the Gli Allori cemetery south of Florence. In 1993 a British will was superseded by an American and Italian one, the latter leaving most of the estate, in the form of an almost $1 billion trust, to New York University. Harold Acton should be remembered as a writer of impressive range and talent, as well as one of the greatest hosts and conversationalists of his century.

EDWARD CHANEY

Sources H. Acton, *Memoirs of an aesthete* (1948) · H. Acton, *More memoirs of an aesthete* (1970) · Villa La Pietra, Florence, Acton MSS · E. Chaney, 'Sir Harold Acton', *The evolution of the grand tour: Anglo-Italian cultural relations since the Renaissance* (1998); rev. edn (2000) · E. Chaney and N. Ritchie, eds., *Oxford, China and Italy: writings in honour of Sir Harold Acton* (1994) · J. Lord, *Some remarkable men: further memoirs* (1996) · N. Ritchie, *Harold Acton: a bibliography* (1984) · *The diaries of Evelyn Waugh*, ed. M. Davie (1976) · private information (2004) [Dialta Alliata di Montereale; Mark Roberts] · P. Gunn, *The Actons* (1978)

Archives New York University, Villa La Pietra, Florence, corresp. | Birr Castle archives, Offaly, Republic of Ireland, papers and corresp. with Lord Rosse and Lady Rosse · BL, letters to Lady Aberconway, Add. MS 70836, fols. 89, 104, 118 · BL, Add. MS 71181, fols. 1–46v · BL, Add. MS 71609, fols. 1, 5–26v · BL, letters to Sir Roy Forbes Harrod and Lady Harrod, Add. MS 72766, fol. 22 · Georgetown University, Washington, DC, letters to Christopher Sykes · Harvard University, Florence, Italy, Center for Italian Renaissance Studies, letters to Bernard Berenson | SOUND BL NSA, 'Hunting the philistines', T2706KBD1 · BL NSA, performance recordings · priv. coll., performance recordings

Likenesses J. Banting, carbon ink and pencil, c.1930, NPG · J. Ward, pencil and watercolour, 1985, NPG [*see illus.*] · L. Guarnieri, watercolour, repro. in Chaney and Ritchie, eds., *Oxford, China and*

Italy, limited edn (1994) · D. Hill, portrait, oils, Villa La Pietra, Florence, Italy · photographs, Villa La Pietra, Florence, Italy · slides, priv. coll.

Wealth at death approx. $500,000,000; total trust estimated as high as $1 billion: 1994, *New York Times*

Acton, Henry (1797–1843), Unitarian minister, was born on 10 March 1797, at Lewes, Sussex, the third of four sons of William Acton, a labourer, and his wife, Mary. Apprenticed at sixteen to a printer, Acton was led by biblical study from Anglicanism to Unitarianism and to the General Baptist chapel in Eastport Lane, Southover. So evident was his promise in a small discussion group there, as well as in a similar group of fellow working men, that when his apprenticeship was ended by agreement in 1818, members of Westgate Chapel, the Unitarian congregation in Lewes, offered to subsidize his attendance at the school in Hove kept by Dr John Morell (1775–1840), the Unitarian minister at Brighton.

Earlier the same year, with William Browne, a fellow apprentice, Acton had begun to supply the pulpit at the Old Meeting-House in nearby Ditchling, alternating services there with Eastport Lane. When his schooling ended in 1821, he became minister at Walthamstow and two years later was made co-pastor with James Manning (1754–1831) at George's Meeting, Exeter. There, for a time, he was second master at a school at Mount Radford. In 1833–7, with a member of his congregation, the physician and classicist Thomas Foster Barham (1794–1869), he conducted a periodical, the *Gospel Advocate*. Shortly after his settlement he married Mary Curtis (d. 1868); they had three sons and three daughters.

On Manning's death in 1831 Acton wanted to be made sole pastor, but the congregation, despite its declining state, chose to appoint a second minister, probably reflecting Acton's disinclination to pastoral work. Strangers sometimes found him haughty, and his talent at raillery gave some offence, but his extraordinary skill at extempore preaching—a formidable memory made even prepared sermons seem spontaneous—was greatly appreciated. His lectures in 1835 defending Unitarianism against an Anglican challenger, Dr Daniel Bagot, led a grateful congregation to vote him £100; a year earlier he had taken on Henry Phillpotts (1778–1869), bishop of Exeter, and in a series of lectures in 1840 attacked the then much-canvassed doctrine of apostolic succession. His published works are listed in the volume of selected sermons that appeared in 1846.

Acton was also active in civil rights and liberal causes; his last appearance at a public meeting was to protest the education clauses of Sir James Graham's factory bill of 1843. He died of apoplexy at Exeter, on 22 August 1843; an appeal to assist his widow and children brought wide support.

Roger Curtis Acton (1827–1906), eldest son and second child of the above, was born in Exeter and trained there as a journalist under Thomas Latimer, the crusading editor of the radical *Western Times*. He later joined the staff of the *Illustrated London News*. Loyal to his inherited liberalism, in 1860 Acton published (and dedicated to Lord John Russell)

a translation of a work by Conte Terenzio Mamiani della Rovere, entitled *Rights of Nations, or, The New Law of European States*, which set out a clear doctrine of national sovereignty. Acton's contributions to the *Illustrated London News* cannot be traced, but his general area of responsibility is suggested by subsequent publications. In 1869 he provided the narrative history for an account, separately published by the *Illustrated London News*, of the British Abyssinian expedition of 1868 and the life and reign of King Theodore which it ended. An early member of the Royal Colonial Institute (later the Royal Empire Society), he published a descriptive sketch of British possessions in *Our Colonial Empire* (1881), and in 1899 produced *The Transvaal Boer Speaking for Himself*, an abridged translation of a history of the southern African republic by C. N. J. du Plessis (1836–1928). Acton died in Hale, Cheshire, on 2 March 1906 of broncho-pneumonia and heart failure.

Henry Morell Acton (1828–1907), journalist, was born in Exeter in 1827, third child and second son of Henry Acton. From the Presbyterian college, Carmarthen, he entered Manchester New College in 1845, but uncertainty about the ministry led him to resign in 1848. He was recruited by Jeremiah Garnett (1793–1870) to the *Manchester Guardian*, where he became a leader writer. His 'tact and delicacy' were called upon notably in 1871 to make amends when the new editor, C. P. Scott (1846–1932), incautiously appealed to wealthy Mancunians to support physical science at Oxford just as Owens College, in Manchester, was struggling into existence. On 29 July 1863 Acton married Anne Shaw Williamson, daughter of Nathaniel Williamson, sharebroker, of Whalley Range, Lancashire; they had a daughter and a son, Edward *Acton, who achieved prominence as a judge.

In 1844 Acton was forced into retirement, with a handsome (and unusual) pension, to make way for William Thomas Arnold, whom Scott thought essential to his own future political career. The newspaper's historian sees Acton's departure as marking the end of an era, as whiggism was abandoned for Gladstonian Liberalism (Ayerst, 237–8), but it also signals a shift from an earlier reliance on a notably Unitarian provincial culture to recruiting from the older universities. Acton was deeply involved in Manchester literary and theatrical life. Suffering from 'senile decay', he died on 21 February 1907 at Glendale, Ashley Road, Hale, Cheshire.

JENNETT HUMPHREYS, rev. R. K. WEBB

Sources W. James and J. R. Wreford, eds., *Sermons…with a memoir of his life* (1846) · *Christian Reformer, or, Unitarian Magazine and Review*, 10 (1843), 604 · W. James, 'Memoir of the late Rev. Henry Acton', *Christian Reformer, or, Unitarian Magazine and Review*, 10 (1843), 755–70 · J. M. Connell, *The story of an old meeting house* (1916) · George's Meeting, Exeter, trustees' minute book, 1818–80 · George's Meeting, Exeter, annual general meeting minute book, 13 Sept 1835 · George's Meeting, Exeter, annual general meeting minute book, 20 Sept 1835 · George's Meeting, Exeter, annual general meeting minute book, 9–23 June 1839 · parish register (birth), St John the Baptist, Southover, Lewes, Sussex, 10 March 1797 · census returns for Exeter, 1841 · d. cert. · *The Inquirer* (7 Nov 1868) · *Manchester Guardian* (22 Feb 1907) [obit. of H. M. Acton] · D. Ayerst, *Guardian: biography of a newspaper* (1971) [H. M. Acton] · J. L. Hammond, *C. P.*

Scott of the Manchester Guardian (1934) [H. M. Acton] · J. B. Atkins, Incidents and reflections (1947) [H. M. Acton] · H. M. Acton to the Executive Committee, Manchester New College, 18 May 1848 and undated reply from R. B. Aspland, Harris Man. Oxf., Wood papers, ff 60–3 · d. cert. [H. M. Acton] · d. cert. [Roger Curtis Acton] · R. Acton, trans., preface, in T. M. della Rovere, Rights of nations, ed. and trans. R. Acton (1860) · [R. Acton], 'Reminiscences of Mr. Latimer', Western Times (13 Jan 1888) · IGI

Wealth at death £5035 19s.—Henry Morell Acton: will, 1907

Acton, Henry Morell (1828–1907). See under Acton, Henry (1797–1843).

Acton, John Adams- (1830–1910), sculptor, was born on 11 December 1830 at Acton Hill, Middlesex, one of the two surviving sons and three daughters of William Adams, an artist, and his wife, Helen Elizabeth Humphreys. His sister Clarissa was also an artist, and exhibited at the Royal Academy. He added Acton to his surname in 1869 to avoid confusion with other artists called John Adams.

Adams was educated at Ealing Grove School (founded by Lady Byron, wife of the poet Lord Byron), and then trained with the sculptors Timothy Butler and Matthew Noble before attending the Royal Academy Schools from 1853 to 1858. After winning early medals in the antique and life classes, he went on to win a gold medal for an allegorical sculpture group, *Eve Supplicating Forgiveness at the Feet of Adam* (1855). In 1858 he won the Royal Academy's travelling studentship and went to Rome, where he stayed until 1865. While there he became known to John Gibson, the most significant British sculptor in Rome. Gibson acknowledged Adams's talent for portraiture, and subsequently sent many distinguished visitors to his studio, including Gladstone, who became his patron and close friend. Throughout his stay in Rome, Adams executed numerous significant portrait commissions as a result of Gibson's recommendations. Many of these patrons affirmed his talent as a portrait sculptor when they returned to London, thereby ensuring his reputation and future commissions. Adams-Acton married on 15 April 1875, at St Mark's Church, Hamilton Terrace, London, Marion (1846–1928) [see Acton, Marion Jean Catherine Adams-], adopted daughter of George Edwards *Hering, artist, born Marion Hamilton of the Isle of Arran, a novelist writing under the name of Jeanie Hering. They had three daughters and four sons, two of whom later became sculptors.

After an eight-month sojourn in India, where Adams-Acton endeavoured to secure further important contacts and commissions, they returned to settle in London. From 1880 they lived at 103 Marylebone Road, his studio being located in Salisbury Mews, until he could find a freehold with sufficient land to build a large studio adjacent to his house. This he found at 8 Langford Place where he lived and worked from 1882 to 1906; he then moved to 17 Abbey Road for the last years of his working life. These residences were all in St John's Wood, a district favoured by many artists in the nineteenth century. Each summer the Adams-Acton family stayed in Mrs Adams-Acton's house at Brodick on the Isle of Arran.

Adams-Acton was popular as a portrait sculptor mainly

John Adams-Acton (1830–1910), by Samuel Alexander Walker, pubd 1893

working in marble. His ability to produce a natural likeness was in great demand. He was also sought after to undertake allegorical, classical, and heroic work. Important commissions included the monument to Bishop Waldegrave (1869; Carlisle Cathedral), the Cruikshank memorial (c.1871; St Paul's Cathedral, London), the Wesley memorial (c.1875; Westminster Abbey), and the memorial to Cardinal Manning (1908; Westminster Cathedral). He also executed a colossal statue of Titus Salt for Bradford (1874); statues of Queen Victoria for Kingston, Jamaica, and the Bahamas; and *W. E. Gladstone* for Liverpool and Blackburn. Edward VII, as prince of Wales, sat to him on many occasions.

A number of Adams-Acton's portrait busts are in the National Portrait Gallery, London. He exhibited regularly at the Royal Academy until 1892, sending statues or busts of Gladstone, Lord Brougham, John Bright, Charles Dickens, Charles Spurgeon, Earl Russell, Archbishop Manning, Disraeli, and Pope Leo XIII. Notable sitters included Lord Shaftesbury, Lord Roberts, and Sir Edwin Landseer. Considered the best of his ideal works were *The First Sacrifice*, *The Lady of the Lake*, *Pharaoh's Daughter*, *Zenobia*, and *The Millennium*. Adams-Acton's last, unfinished work was a small figure of *The Angel of Peace*. He died at his wife's home on the Isle of Arran on 28 October 1910.

S. E. FRYER, rev. ANNE MACPHEE

Sources B. Read, *Victorian sculpture* (1982) · A. M. W. Stirling, *Victorian sidelights* (1954) · E. Morris and F. Milner, *And when did you last see your father?* (1992) [exhibition catalogue, Walker Art Gallery, Liverpool, 13 Nov 1992 – 10 Jan 1993] · P. Curtis, ed., *Patronage and practice: sculpture on Merseyside* (1989) · m. cert.

Archives BL, letters to W. E. Gladstone, Add. MSS 44480–44522
Likenesses S. A. Walker, photograph, pubd 1893, NPG [see illus.]

Acton, John Emerich Edward Dalberg, first Baron Acton (1834–1902), historian and moralist, was born at Naples on 10 January 1834, the only child of Sir Ferdinand Richard Edward Acton, seventh baronet (1801–1837), and

John Emerich Edward Dalberg Acton, first Baron Acton (1834–1902), by Eveleen Myers, 1890s

Marie Louise Pelline de Dalberg (1812–1860), the French-bred heir of Emeric Joseph, duc de Dalberg, the last survivor of an eminent German noble family with its seat at Herrnsheim. After his father's early death in Paris, his mother took him to England where she married (2 July 1840) Granville George Leveson-Gower, Lord Leveson, later second Earl Granville, the Liberal statesman. The Acton family had long been settled at Aldenham in Shropshire, receiving a baronetcy in 1643 for loyalty to Charles I. Acton was descended from a Roman Catholic cadet branch of the family which had settled in France. The baronetcy passed in 1791 to the eldest of that line, Sir John Francis Edward Acton (1736–1811), who had entered the Neapolitan naval service, reorganized it and the army, and eventually became prime minister of Naples. Because of his harsh repression of rebels, it is said, his grandson refused the income from his Italian estates. In 1799 General Acton married his brother's daughter by papal dispensation. Their younger son, Charles Januarius Edward Acton (1803–1847), became a cardinal.

Education and early career Cosmopolitan by birth and breeding, speaking several languages and related to the nobilities of south Germany, France, and Italy, Acton was only in part an Englishman. His education was similarly varied. In 1842 he was sent to a school in Paris under Félix Dupanloup, passing in 1843 to Oscott College, then under the future cardinal Nicholas Wiseman, who made Oscott a centre of the Roman Catholic revival in England. In 1848 he went to Edinburgh for two rather unsatisfactory years under the tutelage of Dr Henry Logan. Then, in 1850, he

found the master who formed his mind: he went to Munich for six years of private study under Professor Ignaz von Döllinger, living in his house. Döllinger was the foremost Roman Catholic church historian in Germany, a major figure in the scientific school of historians of whom Ranke was the leader. Under Döllinger's training Acton became a scientific and critical historian, particularly critical in dealing with the history of his church. Döllinger also initiated him in Burkean liberalism, cultivating a hatred of all forms of absolutism whether in church or state. The ethical effect of Döllinger's teaching was a deep commitment to the value of truth, especially in historiography, and to the sovereignty and freedom of conscience. Finally, Döllinger introduced Acton to the liberal Catholic movement of the continent, particularly on his annual visits with him to France, where Acton met the leading figures such as Montalembert and Broglie. Introduced early to eminent men, Acton had little opportunity to interact with his contemporaries.

In 1853 Acton accompanied Lord Ellesmere, commissioner to an industrial exhibition, to the United States, meeting many eminent figures. In 1856 he was attached to the mission of Lord Granville to the coronation of Tsar Alexander II of Russia. In 1857 he travelled with Döllinger to Italy, where he had connections, particularly Marco Minghetti, later premier, a relative and correspondent. Most important was his visit to Rome, where he was introduced to Pope Pius IX. From this Roman visit Döllinger dated his own disillusionment with the papacy. Acton was merely cool; personally devout, he was unimpressed by Roman institutions.

Returning to England in 1857, Acton settled at Aldenham, where he built his great library; but he did not have the tastes of a country squire. He sought to enter politics, and a seat was found for him in the whig interest at Carlow, where he was elected without making a personal appearance in 1859. He was not a suitable representative for this unruly Irish constituency, and he turned to his neighbouring borough of Bridgnorth in the 1865 election. He was elected by a majority of one but unseated in 1866 on a scrutiny. A second candidacy at Bridgnorth in 1868 was a failure. Acton was unsuited for competitive political life. He spoke only three times in the House of Commons, and when made a peer he appeared infrequently in the House of Lords. A failure as a practical politician, he was to achieve success as the confidant and adviser of William Ewart Gladstone.

On her deathbed in 1860, Acton's mother arranged a marriage between her son and his cousin, Countess Maria (Marie) Anna Ludomilla Euphrosina (1841–1923), second daughter of Count Johann Maximilian von Arco-Valley and his wife, Anna Margareta Maria Juliana Pelina, Countess Marescalchi; she viewed it as a dynastic alliance of two noble houses. Acton wooed his bride through her mother, of whom he was very fond. Considered too young to marry in 1860, she eventually became attached to another suitor, who was however disqualified by epilepsy. The engagement with Acton was once broken off, but later resumed after intervention by Döllinger. The couple were married on 1 August 1865 at St Martin in Austria, and despite the adverse circumstances of the union, it does not seem to have been initially unhappy. Acton's letters to his bride in 1865 and his pregnant wife in 1870 were full of tenderness. But the pair proved to be intellectually incompatible: Acton was unsuccessful in using his letters to Marie as a means of testing out his thoughts on serious questions, as he later did with Mary Gladstone. But it was in the intellectual sphere that Acton's true career lay.

Liberal Catholicism and The Rambler One of Acton's objectives on his return to England was to develop an active intellectual life among English Catholics, introducing them to the critical scholarship he had learned on the continent. For this purpose he needed a periodical organ, which he found in 1858 when he acquired a principal share in the proprietorship of *The Rambler*, a monthly founded in 1848 by an Oxford convert, John Moore Capes, which had originally served as an organ for the converts, better educated than their 'old Catholic' co-religionists. Already, especially under the editorship of Richard Simpson, *The Rambler* had moved to a liberal Catholic position, supporting freedom of scholarship and philosophic speculation and coming into conflict with Cardinal Wiseman and his organ, the *Dublin Review*. In 1859 the bishops forced Simpson's resignation as editor. He was succeeded by John Henry Newman, who himself was forced to resign after two numbers. Acton then took the editorship, consolidating *The Rambler's* position as the organ of the liberal Catholic movement in England. He contributed several articles, some of which have been republished, and numerous reviews. The conflict with the ultramontanism of Wiseman, Henry Edward Manning, and William George Ward intensified. Partly to avert episcopal censure, the journal was transformed into the quarterly *Home and Foreign Review* in 1862; but the review was itself censured by Wiseman and William Bernard Ullathorne, bishop of Birmingham. None the less, the *Home and Foreign Review* established itself not only as the rival of Ward's *Dublin Review* but as one of the great periodicals of the age, notable for its learning and its European rather than insular character, winning the praise of Matthew Arnold for its knowledge and play of mind. Its excellence was especially displayed in numerous short notices of books in many languages, many of them written by Acton, a voracious reader and knowledgeable critic.

In late 1863 Acton attended a congress of Catholic scholars at Munich, where Döllinger gave an address urging a progressive historical rather than scholastic theology and demanding freedom of Catholic scholarship. Acton hailed this enthusiastically in the *Home and Foreign Review* (Jan 1864). But it aroused the direct hostility of Roman authority, and a papal brief to the archbishop of Munich asserted that Roman Catholic thought was bound by the decisions of Roman congregations. This was an explicit rejection of the fundamental principles of the review, denying any distinction between fixed dogma and theological opinion. Acton, knowing that a direct confrontation with Rome could only lead to a condemnation

by an authority higher than English bishops, chose to 'sacrifice the existence of the *Review* to the defence of its principles, in order that I may combine the obedience which is due to legitimate ecclesiastical authority, with an equally conscientious maintenance of the rightful and necessary liberty of thought'. This statement, reasserting both his principle of freedom of thought and his loyalty to the authority of Rome, appeared in an article entitled 'Conflicts with Rome' in the final issue of the *Home and Foreign Review* in April 1864. This was the end of the liberal Catholic movement in England. The movement was decisively condemned in December 1864 by the encyclical *Quanta cura* and its appended *Syllabus of Errors*, the pope's refusal to 'come to terms with progress, liberalism, and modern civilization'. Acton could not endorse the *Syllabus* and spoke in 1865 of belonging 'rather to the soul than the body of the Roman Catholic Church'. His sacramental piety was not impaired, but his hopes for explicitly Catholic intellectual activity were dashed.

Acton turned to pure historical research, making several tours of archives throughout Europe between 1864 and 1868 for a variety of projects, none actually published. It was in the course of these archival tours that he became indignantly aware of the mendacity regularly practised by Roman Catholic historians to further the interests of their church. Also during this time he developed his hatred for religious persecution, which he regarded as nothing other than murder. These two concerns raised his opposition to Rome from the ecclesiastical to the ethical plane, leading to the rigorous moralism of his later years.

The liberal Catholics were able to return to literary endeavours, though not as a religious movement, when they founded a weekly journal, *The Chronicle*, in 1867, underwritten by Sir Rowland Blennerhassett and edited by T. F. Wetherell, Acton's former sub-editor. Acton served as Roman correspondent for *The Chronicle* and wrote several articles. The journal, too liberal for Catholics and too Catholic for liberals, lasted only a year. In 1869 the Acton circle, again with Wetherell as editor, took over the former organ of the Scottish Free Church, the *North British Review*, keeping it going until 1871. Acton contributed weighty articles, notably 'The massacre of St Bartholomew' (October 1869), where his scholarship was marred by his sharp anti-papal bias. Both these periodicals were secular rather than religious in character, devoted primarily to Gladstonian Liberalism. Acton was also able to express his thoughts on recent history with lectures delivered to the Bridgnorth Literary and Scientific Institution on the American Civil War in 1866 and on the Mexican empire in 1868.

Acton, Gladstone, and the First Vatican Council During these years Acton's friendship with Gladstone became one of intimacy and mutual admiration. Acton, much younger, treated Gladstone with the respect due his seniority, but the younger man had the greater influence upon the elder. Gladstone shared his moralism and respected his learning and wisdom. Acton influenced Gladstone more than any other man, on subjects ranging from his support of the South during the American Civil War to his eventual conversion to home rule. Their friendship grew steadily from 1866, when they were in Rome together. On 11 December 1869, Acton was created a peer, on Gladstone's recommendation, as Baron Acton of Aldenham, one of the first two Roman Catholic peers created since emancipation. There were political reasons: he and his fellow, Lord Howard of Glossop, had recently lost seats, and more Liberal peers were needed in the Lords. But Gladstone, aside from wishing to compliment his friend, had the additional motive of seeking to strengthen Acton's position at Rome, where he was already working to organize opposition to the impending definition of papal infallibility at the First Vatican Council.

Acton played a remarkable role for a layman during the council. He was Gladstone's personal agent and observer, and he urged him to have Britain join other powers in diplomatic action to prevent the definition. This was foiled not, as has been alleged, because of Manning's influence on Odo Russell, the British diplomatic agent, but because Gladstone found resistance in the cabinet led by the foreign secretary, Lord Clarendon. Acton also sought to influence European public opinion by writing detailed accounts of the council to Döllinger at Munich, who combined them with others in a series published in the Augsburg *Allgemeine Zeitung* under the name of Quirinus. They were published as a book at Munich and translated into English as *Letters from Rome on the Council* (1870). Acton was responsible only for fifteen of the letters, and he differed from Döllinger on some of the others, Döllinger opposing infallibility as untrue and Acton because it was immoral, the symbol of papal absolutism and the ultramontane system of untruthfulness and justification of persecution. Acton's most important activity was within the council itself, where, although not a member, he organized the minority of opposition bishops, urging them to hold together in resistance, and in general functioning as a sort of minority whip. His ability was recognized by all, but most of the opposition bishops were unreliable for his purpose, opposing the definition only on the ground of its being inopportune. Expecting defeat, the minority withdrew from Rome, allowing the dogma to be adopted in July 1870. Acton had already left.

From Tegernsee, his wife's family home, Acton issued his *Sendschreiben an einen deutschen Bischof des vaticanischen Concils* (1870), quoting from anti-infallibilist statements and asking whether the bishops still maintained their resistance. They did not; within a year all the bishops had submitted. This was a grave moral crisis for Acton but in a way it eventually made it easier for him to live with the newly defined dogma. He could argue, as his correspondent Archbishop Kenrick of St Louis did, that the consent of the church at large remedied any defects in the council itself and that he need not give internal assent to the dogma; he could trust, as a believer in the development of doctrine, that in time infallibility could be acceptably incorporated into the body of Roman Catholic dogma. So he did not leave the church. Döllinger, whose quarrel was with the dogma itself rather than the existing system

which it represented, could not submit and was excommunicated; and other opponents formed a small secessionist 'Old Catholic' communion.

Acton's position was unchallenged until 1874, when Gladstone published his pamphlet on *The Vatican Decrees in their Bearing on Civil Allegiance*, inspired in part by Acton's letters to him during the council. Acton had advised against publication, and he responded to Gladstone in letters to *The Times*, vindicating the loyalty of British Catholics by showing that they had disregarded papal instructions in the past and that the practical power of the papacy was not increased by the decrees. He struck a final blow at ultramontanism, showing by historical examples that church authorities had for centuries committed political crimes without the aid of the dogma of infallibility. This was a defence of Catholics at the expense of the church as an institution, and when reproached for this Acton asserted the duty of uttering historical truth, which might disgrace churchmen but could never tarnish the holiness of the church. Archbishop Manning, by now an enemy, demanded an explanation (November 1874); Acton evaded an outright acceptance of infallibility, saying only that he submitted to the acts of the council, relying on God's providence in the government of the church. Manning was dissatisfied and referred the matter to Rome. But Acton had satisfied his diocesan bishop as to his orthodoxy; he was a layman and a peer; and Rome took no action. For months, however, Acton expected to be excommunicated, a fate especially dreadful to one whose simple devotion was centred on the sacraments. When he said that communion with Rome was dearer than life, the emphasis should be placed on 'communion'. Retaining that, he withdrew from religious controversy.

Historical writings Acton turned to the study of history, for which he had built a library of some 60,000 volumes. In 1863 he had published a tract, *Human Sacrifice*, and an edition of *Les matinées royales*, alleged memoirs of Frederick the Great which he later found to be spurious. He edited Nicholas Harpsfield's *Narrative of the Divorce* and *Letters of James II to the Abbot of La Trappe* for the Philobiblon Society (1872–6). But his original publications were few. He would not write until he had read all the sources, a rule which was fatal in the era of the opening of archives. The spur of journalism was no longer available to him. He published an article in the *Quarterly Review*, 'Wolsey and the divorce of Henry VIII' (January 1877), and a review of Sir Erskine May's *Democracy in Europe* (January 1878) which displayed his learning, and a substantial article on George Eliot in the *Nineteenth Century* (March 1885). In 1886 he was one of the founders of the *English Historical Review*, contributing to the first number a massively learned article, 'German schools of history' (German trans. 1887), part of his programme of introducing German scholarship to England, and later publishing some substantial reviews. He also served the cause of learning as a trustee of the British Museum and a member of the Historical Manuscripts Commission. But he published no book, though he formulated several book projects. The greatest of these was a 'History of liberty', which occupied him from 1877 to 1883.

The only result, aside from a mass of notes, was a pair of lectures at Bridgnorth in 1877 on the 'History of freedom' in antiquity and in Christianity, published in French translation in Paris in 1878. Of his other projects, a biography of Döllinger yielded an article, 'Döllinger's historical works', in the *English Historical Review* (1890). Acton was a natural essayist, of the monographic sort, with a somewhat difficult and allusive style and a flair for aphorisms.

Another reason why Acton wrote no book was his sense of isolation. He was not isolated from intellectual society; he was a member of Grillion's, the Club, and the Athenaeum among other clubs, met the best intellectual society and corresponded copiously. But he was isolated in his intellectual position by his rigorous moralism. He insisted on an absolute moral standard in history, the basic test being murder, with the historian as judge condemning not only the murderer but even more those who encouraged or justified the murder; this required him to condemn the leaders of his own church most of all for their justification of persecution. In 1879 he discovered that Döllinger, for all his opposition to infallibility, did not share this fundamental criticism of the pre-1870 church, and a painful correspondence of several years ended in their intellectual separation. The shock left Acton's creative faculties almost paralysed for a time. He was indeed isolated, as he found later when he wrote a severe review of Mandell Creighton's *History of the Popes* (1887), faulting him for being insufficiently condemnatory of medieval popes. In the ensuing correspondence, in which Creighton made the better case, Acton uttered his best-known aphorism, 'power tends to corrupt, and absolute power corrupts absolutely' (Acton to Creighton, 3 April 1887, cited in L. Creighton, *Life … of Mandell Creighton*, 1904, 1, chap. 13). The standard of morality was not always compatible with his other standard of impartiality, and in practice Acton did not always adhere to either, having a whig bias toward seeing history as progress to liberty.

Although publishing little and isolated in his fundamental principles, Acton was known and appreciated in the intellectual world for his erudition, which he freely shared. An American visitor called him the nearest approach to omniscience he had met. Honours came to him: in 1872 the University of Munich gave him an honorary doctorate of philosophy, and he became an FSA in 1876. In 1888 he was made an honorary LLD at Cambridge, in 1889 an honorary DCL at Oxford. In 1891, at Gladstone's suggestion, he received an honorary fellowship of All Souls.

Finances and lordship-in-waiting Acton suffered financial troubles during these years. Although the Aldenham estate of some 6000 acres had a nominal rental of about £7500, it was heavily encumbered; Acton paid little attention to management, and the 1870s were years of agricultural depression. In 1879 he had to sell his house at Herrnsheim and let that at Aldenham, taking out a large loan as well. Henceforth he lived mostly abroad, at Tegernsee and Cannes. In the late 1870s and 1880s, his marriage seems to have suffered too: there are definite signs of unhappiness, even estrangement. His financial situation was finally eased in 1890 when, at Gladstone's suggestion, Andrew Carnegie purchased his great library, allowing Acton to keep it for his lifetime. (After Acton's death, Carnegie gave the library to John Morley, who gave it to Cambridge University Library, where it is separately housed.) It is unclear, however, how long-lived Acton's marital difficulties were.

When forming his fourth ministry in 1892, Gladstone wished to include Acton, who avidly sought a place; but no place could be found for him more consequential than lord-in-waiting. His political role was to speak for the government on Irish issues in the Lords. As a courtier, he won the favour of Queen Victoria, whose German interests he shared. She made him a KCVO in 1897.

Regius professor and the Cambridge Modern History Acton was destined to achieve eminence neither as politician nor as courtier, but as a scholar. In 1895 Lord Rosebery, whom Acton had helped to bring into the 1892 cabinet, nominated him to become regius professor of modern history at Cambridge. He was immediately elected a professorial fellow of Trinity College, where he took up residence. On 11 June 1895 he delivered an impressive inaugural lecture on the study of history, urging his favourite themes, the unity of modern history as the progress of liberty, the importance of the critical scientific method of research, and the duty of the historian to uphold the moral standard in history. The lecture was published with Germanic footnotes of extensive quotations; it was translated into German in 1897.

Acton entered fully into Cambridge life and professorial work, and his Cambridge years were the happiest of his life. His pleasure in his college rooms, bachelor digs, may have been connected to his marital problems. He gave a course of lectures on the French Revolution, followed a few years later by a course on modern history, both published after his death. The lectures were well attended by dons, students, and the public. Their impressiveness was enhanced by Acton's striking dignity, his flowing beard, and the deep voice in which he read from his text. But his work at Cambridge was not limited to lecturing. He revitalized the history school, stagnant under his predecessors Charles Kingsley and Sir John Seeley. He entertained his colleagues and gave freely of his wisdom to don and undergraduate alike.

In 1896 the syndics of the Cambridge University Press approached Acton with a proposal for a collaborative work which became the Cambridge Modern History. He accepted the editorship, drew up the plan of chapters for the twelve volumes, and began to solicit contributors. That part of the work was the hardest, as he had to deal with collaborators none of whom shared his historical moralism and many of whom opposed each other on other issues; all he could do was exhort them to be impartial. The strain broke him down; characteristically, none of his own chapters was completed. Yet the first volume was in type before he died; and the plan of work is his monument.

Death and reputation Acton suffered a paralytic stroke in 1901 and withdrew to Tegernsee, where he died, after receiving the sacraments of his church, on 19 June 1902, and where he was buried. He was survived by his widow, three daughters, and a son, Richard Maximilian (1870–1924), who succeeded him as the second Baron Acton. The cosmopolitan character of the Acton family is illustrated by the fact that the second lord, a British diplomat, found it advisable to obtain a private act of naturalization in 1911.

Aside from periodical articles, Acton published in his lifetime only scattered lectures and edited works. After his death, the extent of his writings was revealed by the publication of his two courses of lectures (1906, 1910) and two volumes of collected essays (1907), all edited by J. N. Figgis and R. V. Laurence, who also edited his selected correspondence (1917). Two other volumes of letters appeared shortly after Acton's death, and several further volumes both of essays and letters have subsequently been published (the greatest compilation is the three-volume *Selected Writings* edited by J. Rufus Fears, 1986–8). A bibliography of Acton's writings was edited by W. A. Shaw for the Royal Historical Society in 1903, but there is still no truly complete and accurate bibliography. Acton's notes, in Cambridge University Library, are a mine of aphorisms.

Acton's reputation was revived after the Second World War, when his defence of liberty against absolutism was perceived as a prophetic warning against totalitarianism. This aspect of the Acton revival has been misappropriated by neo-conservative ideologues; but it produced Gertrude Himmelfarb's biography (1952). There was also a renewed interest in Acton as a historian, under the auspices of Herbert Butterfield. A third aspect of the Acton revival has come from interest in his liberal Catholicism. There has been some reaction against this revived study of one whose life was largely a failure. But others may feel that failure is especially worthy of study when it reveals the fierce integrity of Acton's devotion to conscience, to truth, and to liberty. JOSEF L. ALTHOLZ

Sources G. Himmelfarb, *Lord Acton: a study in conscience and politics* (1952) • R. Hill, *Lord Acton* (2000) • *Briefwechsel [von] Ignaz von Döllinger*, ed. V. Conzemius, 1–3 (Munich, 1963–71) • *The correspondence of Lord Acton and Richard Simpson*, ed. J. L. Altholz, D. McElrath, and J. C. Holland, 3 vols. (1971–5) • *Letters of Lord Acton to Mary Gladstone*, ed. H. Paul (1904) • J. L. Altholz, *The liberal Catholic movement in England: the 'Rambler' and its contributors, 1848–1864* [1962] • D. McElrath and others, *Lord Acton: the decisive decade, 1864–1874* (1970) • H. Tulloch, *Acton* (1988) • R. L. Schuettinger, 'Bibliography of the works of Lord Acton', *Lord Acton: historian of liberty* (1976), 191–35 • Charlotte, Lady Blennerhassett, 'The late Lord Acton', *EdinR*, 197 (1903), 501–34 • H. Butterfield, *Lord Acton* (1948) [Historical Association pamphlet G9] • O. Chadwick, *Acton and History* (1998) • O. Chadwick, *Acton and Gladstone* (1998) • G. Watson, *Lord Acton's History of Liberty* (1994) • Gladstone, *Diaries* • GEC, *Peerage*

Archives CUL, corresp. and papers • CUL, draft proposal and letters relating to Cambridge Modern History • Downside Abbey, near Bath, letters to Richard Simpson • Shrops. RRC, corresp., mainly relating to historical and religious interests | Birmingham Oratory, letters to J. H. Newman • BL, letters to Lord Gladstone, Add. MSS 46044–46055, *passim* • BL, letters to Mary Gladstone, Add. MS 46239 • BL, corresp. with W. E. Gladstone, Add. MSS 44093–44094 • BL OIOC, letters to Sir Mountstuart Grant Duff, MS Eur. F 234 • Bodl. Oxf., letters to Lord Bryce • Bodl. Oxf., letters to H. A. L. Fisher • CUL, Blennerhassett MSS • King's AC Cam., letters to Oscar Browning • NL Ire., letters to Alice Stopford Green • NL Scot., corresp. with Lord Rosebery • Pembroke College, Oxford, corresp. with Sir Peter Renouf • PRO, corresp. with Lord Granville, PRO30/29 • PRO, letters to Odo Russell, FO918 • Trinity Cam., letters to Lord Houghton • Trinity Cam., letters to Henry Sidgwick • U. St Andr. L., letters to Wilfrid Ward

Likenesses F. S. von Lenbach, oils, *c.*1879, NPG; copy by L. Arco-Vallery, Trinity Cam. • E. Myers, photograph, 1890–99, NPG [*see illus.*] • F. Sargent, pencil, NPG • photograph, repro. in Abbot Gasquet, *Lord Acton and his circle* (1906), frontispiece • photograph, Bettmann archive, New York • photograph, CUL

Acton, Sir John Francis Edward, sixth baronet (1736–1811), naval officer and administrator in the Neapolitan service, descended from the Actons of Aldenham Hall, Shropshire, was born in Besançon, Franche Comté, France, in 1736 (baptized 3 June). His father, Dr Edward Acton (1709–1775), had settled there and married a local girl, Anna Catherine Loys (*d.* 1767), daughter of Francis Loys de Gray: to do so he converted to Roman Catholicism, and his sons were brought up as Catholics. John Acton's two younger brothers, Joseph (1737–1808) and Richard, entered the French service in Fitzjames's horse, but, after attending the Jesuit college at Besançon, at the age of fourteen John opted for the Tuscan service under his uncle, Commodore John Acton. There he soon made his mark and in 1762, when he was simultaneously a naval lieutenant and an army captain, he was described by Edward Gibbon, the historian and a distant relative, as 'a very pretty sensible young man' (*Journal*, 121–2).

Although the Tuscan navy was very much an auxiliary service, it was the one in which Acton made his mark, and he was responsible for introducing a class of light shallow-draught craft, which proved invaluable during an unsuccessful joint expedition with the Spaniards against Algiers in 1775. The Spaniards, led by a General O'Reilly, were ambushed after landing, and a total disaster was only averted when Acton took a squadron of his shallow-draught boats close inshore to bring them off again. He thus came highly recommended when Grand Duke Leopold of Tuscany was asked by his sister, Queen Maria Caroline of Naples, for an officer who could reorganize the near moribund Neapolitan navy. After arriving in Naples on 4 August 1778 Acton immediately impressed both the queen and the British ambassador, Sir William Hamilton, who reported him to be 'a very sensible man, and has the character of an excellent sea officer', adding that 'I can perceive him to be still an Englishman at heart' (Acton, 182).

Once Acton's plan for reorganizing the Neapolitan navy had been approved by the king, Ferdinand IV, he was appointed *pro tempore* secretary of state for the Neapolitan marine with the rank of lieutenant-general. On 1 January 1779 he was given the position of minister of war as well. The elevation of a foreigner, and particularly an Englishman, aroused considerable hostility, not only in Naples but also in Spain. Nevertheless, the overt hostility of

Sir John Francis Edward Acton, sixth baronet (1736–1811), by Peter Eduard Ströhling, c.1793

Charles III of Spain only served to consolidate Acton's position, since the queen was determined to assert Naples's independence and not to give way to her father-in-law. Indeed, as Hamilton reported in November 1780,

> General Acton's favour augments daily, he has become in a manner for some time past prime minister, and made such alterations, particularly in the administration of the finances, as must in a short time be productive of the most happy effects for this country. He is sensible, steady and honest. (Acton, 189)

The dockyard at Castellammare was modernized and within six years the strength of the navy had been increased to 150 ships, while under their protection the merchant fleet also increased proportionally and with it foreign trade. Acton similarly did his best to reform the army by increasing its size and engaging a number of foreign professionals to command it. Unsurprisingly this was again unpopular and, probably because he lacked personal experience and expertise in soldiering, here he was rather less successful. In fact, when presented with a proposal for changing his soldiers' uniform, King Ferdinand is, perhaps apocryphally, reputed to have grumbled that Acton could dress them in any colour he liked but they would still run away. Following the death of his cousin Sir Richard Acton, fifth baronet, on 20 November 1791, Acton became the sixth baronet.

Acton's unpopularity among the nobility prompted a pro-Spanish faction, led by the titular prime minister, the marchese della Sambuca, to plot against him, but their correspondence was intercepted and, with enough evidence to convict him of treason if need be, Sambuca was dismissed in 1786 (replaced by Caracciolo, prime minister 1786–9) and exiled to Palermo. Acton's addition of the foreign ministry to his portfolio in 1789 consolidated his position as *de facto* prime minister. Another dangerous rival, Prince Caramanico, had to be dealt with more circumspectly as he was a favourite of the queen. However, Acton succeeded in shuffling him off as an ambassador first to London and then to Paris, before finally getting rid of him by having him appointed viceroy of Sicily, where he died so suddenly in January 1795 as to give rise to rumours that Acton had had him poisoned.

In 1793 Acton's English sympathies led Naples to join the alliance against revolutionary France and send a contingent to take part in the defence of Toulon. In 1798, however, an offensive against the French forces in northern Italy ended in disaster and necessitated the flight of Acton and the royal family to Palermo. A Jacobin faction then seized control of Naples and in December 1798 proclaimed the Parthenopean republic, which lasted five months before being overthrown by counter-revolutionary insurgents led by Cardinal Ruffo and the intervention of Nelson and the British navy. Acton once again revealed his ruthlessness in the white terror that followed. He then astonished everyone by marrying, with papal dispensation, on 2 February 1800 his thirteen-year-old niece Mary Ann (1786–1873), the elder daughter of General Joseph Edward Acton (1737–1808), apparently to keep their accumulated wealth in the family. In 1801, as the price of peace, the French initially demanded Acton's dismissal, but although this was refused he was eventually compelled, under French pressure, to resign in 1804 and retire to Palermo. He returned briefly to power in Sicily in 1806 before dying at Palermo on 12 August 1811, leaving a daughter and two sons; the elder, Ferdinand Richard Edward, became seventh baronet and was the father of the historian John, Lord Acton. The younger son, Charles Januarius Edward *Acton, became a cardinal. Sir John was buried in Palermo.   STUART REID

Sources H. Acton, *The Bourbons of Naples* (1956) · Sir William Hamilton's reports, PRO, FO 70 · *The dispatches and letters of Vice-Admiral Lord Viscount Nelson*, ed. N. H. Nicolas, 7 vols. (1844–6) · *Journal*, ed. D. M. Low (1929) · R. Hill, *Lord Acton* (2000) · Burke, *Peerage* (1967) **Archives** CUL, corresp. | BL, corresp. with Sir W. Hamilton, Egerton MSS 2639–2640 · BL, letters to Lord Nelson, etc., Add. MSS 34903–34946 · BL, corresp. with Sir A. Paget, Add. MS 48398 · NL Scot., letters to Hugh Elliot · NL Scot., corresp. with Sir F. Graham · NMM, corresp. with Sir W. Hamilton; letters to Lord Nelson **Likenesses** P. E. Ströhling, miniature, c.1793, NPG [*see illus.*] · F. Bartolozzi, stipple (after C. Marsili), NPG; repro. in Acton, *Bourbons*, facing p. 238 · G. M. Griffoni, oils, Coughton Court, Warwickshire

Acton, Marion Jean Catherine [Jeanie] **Adams-** [*formerly* Jeanie Hering] (1846–1928), writer, was born Marion Hamilton on 21 June 1846, in Brodick, Isle of Arran, Scotland, the daughter of Edith Hamilton and an unidentified Scottish nobleman. Before the age of four she was adopted by George Edwards *Hering (1805–1879), a landscape painter born in London of a German baronial family, and his wife, Catherine (*née* Bromley), an artist. Her mother agreed to the adoption because it afforded her daughter better material and social circumstances. Henceforth known as Jeanie Hering, she moved to London and resided in St John's Wood, which was noted for its artistic community. She attended a day school in Finchley Road, London, from the age of six and finished her education with two years at school in Münster, Westphalia, Germany, between 1862 and 1864.

Having modelled for many painters of the St John's Wood school and joined in the group's amateur performances, Hering initially wanted to become an actress, but her adoptive parents disapproved of the theatre as a career. She turned to writing, and four years after leaving school published *Garry, a Holiday Story* (1868), a novel about a girl and her dog on holiday. A succession of other children's books followed, often drawing heavily on her own experiences: *Golden Days* (1873) tells of life at a girls' boarding-school in Germany; *Through the Mist* (1874) narrates the romances of twin young women from Brodick, where the Herings had a summer home; *Elf* (1887) describes the early childhood of a Scottish girl. A clear moral or religious lesson distinguishes many of her stories, among them *Truth will Out* (1873) and *Honour is my Guide* (1886). She published over a dozen commercially successful novels between 1868 and 1894, many with George Routledge & Sons, a leading children's book publisher of the period, and she also wrote picture books, magazine stories, and plays.

In 1874 Hering met John Adams-*Acton (1830–1910), a prizewinning sculptor, and they married on 15 April 1875 at St Mark's Church, Hamilton Terrace, London. After visiting India for eight months, they settled in St John's Wood and spent summers at the family home in Brodick. They had four sons and three daughters.

Through commissions and artistic friendships, Adams-Acton, as she became known, and her husband met many famous figures of the time, including William Gladstone, George Eliot, Robert Browning, and Cardinal Manning, and she became a noted hostess. Known also for her independent and sometimes impetuous personality, in 1887 she walked from London to Brodick—a seven-week 500 mile journey—with two nursemaids and her children, one of whom was pushed the entire way in a perambulator. A spirit of adventure, and perhaps a desire to gather raw material for her stories, inspired this journey to her birthplace. She had already written stories about the travels of perambulators, and she published her account of this journey as *The Adventures of a Perambulator* in 1894. She was fascinated by spiritualism and the occult, and she often consulted astrologers, attended séances, and collected folk stories. In later life she began to write and dictate her reminiscences, though only sporadically. From these fragments A. M. W. Stirling created a posthumous memoir combining Adams-Acton's own words with third-person narrative, which was published as *Victorian Sidelights* in 1954. Adams-Acton died on 10 October 1928 at her home, 99 Clifton Hill, St John's Wood, Middlesex, and was buried in Brodick. SIOBHAN PEIFFER

Sources A. M. W. Stirling, *Victorian sidelights: from the papers of the late Mrs. Adams-Acton* (1954) • *The Times* (22 Dec 1954) • *The Times* (12 Oct 1928) • *The Times* (31 Oct 1910) • *CGPLA Eng. & Wales* (1928)
Likenesses P. Calderon, oils, repro. in Stirling, *Victorian sidelights*, facing p. 32 • J. S. Sant, portrait (aged three), repro. in Stirling, *Victorian sidelights*, frontispiece
Wealth at death £145 15s. 0d.: probate, 4 Dec 1928, *CGPLA Eng. & Wales*

Acton, Ralph (*supp. fl.* after **1179**), supposed preacher and compiler of sermons, is said to have composed various series on the Sunday gospels and epistles, and on the gospels and epistles for saints' days, which are listed by Bale, with incipits, from three manuscripts no longer extant. Tanner identified the Sunday sermons in three surviving manuscripts in Oxford, two of which in fact contain the entire cycle of sermons; one of these is termed at the end 'the book called Acton', while the preface refers to the author as Radulfus. Presumably Bale reconstructed the author's identity from these separate pieces of evidence. The collection of sermons on the gospels and epistles for saints' days has also come to light in a Manchester manuscript, which has been used by at least one modern scholar as evidence of late medieval preaching. However all the sermons whose incipits are given by Bale are by Radulphus Ardens, a master of Paris who became archdeacon of Poitiers in 1179; the preface, though it occurs in some English manuscripts only, is evidently also by Ardens, as it gives his name, Radulfus. The name Acton, associated with the book rather than the author, may only be that of the scribe of the exemplar; another manuscript, instead of the formula naming Acton, ends with the name Sutton. Ralph Acton, therefore, appears to be a literary ghost.

JEREMY CATTO

Sources sermons, Bodl. Oxf., MS e. Museo. 5 • Lincoln College, Oxford, MSS lat. 112 and 116 [sermons] • JRL, MS lat. 367 [sermons] • Bale, *Index*, 326 • Tanner, *Bibl. Brit.-Hib.*, 4 • Radulphus Ardens, 'Homiliarum', *Patrologia Latina*, 155 (1854) • G. R. Owst, *Literature and pulpit in medieval England*, 2nd edn (1966) • J. B. Schneyer, *Repertorium der lateinischen Sermones des Mittelalters: für die Zeit von 1150–1350*, 5 (Münster, 1974) • Emden, *Oxf.*

Acton, Roger Curtis (1827–1906). *See under* Acton, Henry (1797–1843).

Acton, William John (1812/13–1875), surgeon specializing in genito-urinary disorders, was baptized at Shillingstone, Dorset, on 12 May 1814, the second son of Edward Acton (1785/6–1875), curate of the parish, and his wife, Elizabeth (*c*.1788–1817). He had two brothers, John (who also went into the church) and Henry, and at least one sister. Acton's early education is not known, but in 1830 he was under the care of Dr Mant, and in 1831 he became an articled pupil of Charles Wheeler, apothecary to St Bartholomew's Hospital, London. In 1836 Acton went to Paris, the European centre for this subject, to study venereology as an *externe* at the female venereal hospital under the famous American-born venereologist, Philippe Ricord, whom Acton was always to revere. In 1839 Acton became secretary of the Parisian medical society, but in 1840 he returned to London. He obtained membership of the College of Surgeons in the same year and set up as a consulting surgeon at 5 George Street, Hanover Square, London, publishing the first edition of *A Practical Treatise on Diseases of the Urinary and Generative Organs* in 1841. In 1842 he was elected to fellowship of the Royal Medical and Chirurgical Society. He moved to 46 Queen Anne Street, London, in 1843. At about that time he was appointed surgeon to the Islington Dispensary. Throughout the 1840s he contributed to the medical press and introduced a number of innovations in the treatment of venereal diseases.

By 1851 Acton was a successful consulting surgeon, residing at 46 Queen Anne Street with Robert Tubbs, a 47-year-old widower, magistrate for the cities of London and Westminster. On 6 March 1852 he married Sarah Jane Tabberer (*b.* 1821/2, *d.* 21 March 1875), daughter of Alexander Tabberer, a merchant, and moved to 17 Queen Anne Street. They had at least four children: William John (1853), Emma (1854), Gertrude Jane (1857), and Arthur Henry (1861). Acton's practice was apparently exclusively confined to the disorders of the urinary and generative organs. Although this area was often associated with unscrupulous and commercially minded quacks, Acton's reputation among his fellows was high. Sir James Paget, in a generous obituary tribute to the Royal Medical and Chirurgical Society, claimed that Acton was 'careful and safe in practice, and had much technical skill' (Paget, 76). Paget attributed Acton's failure to inquire into outstanding questions of the pathology of syphilis to his devotion to the teachings of Ricord. Above all, Paget concluded,

> let it be remembered to his honour, that he practised honourably in the most dangerous of specialities; that he wrote decently on subjects not usually decent; and that he never used the opportunities which his practice offered for quackery or extortion … [He] was always clearly on the side of morality.   (ibid.)

Acton was not concerned only with technical aspects of the treatment of venereal diseases but with the wider social issues with which these diseases were intricately connected. During the 1850s he became increasingly involved in writing about and taking action on these wider questions. Besides publishing articles and letters to the press on venereal diseases in the army and navy, prostitution, and illegitimacy, he was active in the Society for the Suppression of Vice, and in prosecuting quacks under the Medical Act 1858. During the 1860s he was a great supporter of the regulation of prostitution through the Contagious Diseases Acts and an advocate for their extension from garrison and port towns to the general populace.

In 1857 Acton published the two works for which he is best remembered: *The functions and disorders of the reproductive orders in youth, in adult age, and in advanced life: considered in their physiological, social, and psychological relations* and *Prostitution, considered in its moral, social, and sanitary aspects, in London and other large cities: with proposals for the mitigation and prevention of its attendant evils*, both of which went into several editions. The latter book expanded his 1851 pamphlet on *Prostitution in Relation to Public Health*, previously a chapter in his *Practical Treatise* (1841). In *Prostitution* he addressed social problems and made recommendations for dealing with them, while *Functions and Disorders* addressed problems of the individual. There is a certain disjunction between the message of *Prostitution*—that prostitution was ineradicable and regulatory measures were required to obviate its worst social effects—and that of *Functions and Disorders*, which advocated, presumably with some expectation of the prescription being followed, a stringent degree of male continence both before and within marriage. Although this work contains Acton's most quoted statement, that 'the majority of women … are not very much troubled with sexual feeling of any kind' and submitted to their husbands principally from the desire for maternity (4th edn, 1865, 112–13), it is addressed to, and almost exclusively about, the male. His views on prostitution are, several writers have commented, unusually realistic and humane for the period.

About 1862 Acton purchased Fern Acres, a country property in the parish of Fulmer, Buckinghamshire, where he subsequently spent much of his time in the enjoyment of farming and other country pursuits, while retaining his flourishing London practice. In 1875 he was subjected to the double blow of his father's death and his wife's dying from breast cancer. Acton was discovered dead in his bathroom at 17 Harley Street on 7 December, the cause being fatty degeneration of the heart. The officiousness of the coroner for central Middlesex in ordering an inquest was rebuked by the *British Medical Journal*, which pointed out that Acton had recently been examined by eminent physicians and that his death was quite consistent with their diagnoses.

LESLEY A. HALL

Sources BMJ (11 Dec 1875), 740 · J. Paget, *Proceedings of the Royal Medical and Chirurgical Society*, 8 (1875–80), 74–6 · *Medical Times and Gazette* (18 Dec 1875), 697 · *Medical Directory* (1875) · Boase, *Mod. Eng. biog.* · M. J. Peterson, 'Dr Acton's enemy: medicine, sex, and society in Victorian England', *Victorian Studies*, 29 (1985–6), 569–90 · W. Acton, *Prostitution in relation to public health*, ed. P. Fryer (1968) · S. Marcus, *The other Victorians* (1966) · census returns, 1851 · m. cert. · d. cert. · d. cert. [Sarah Acton] · Foster, *Alum. Oxon.*, 1715–1886 [Edward Acton] · *CGPLA Eng. & Wales* (1876)

Archives Women's Library, London

Likenesses portrait, repro. in Peterson, 'Dr Acton's enemy'

Wealth at death under £25,000: probate, 8 Jan 1876, *CGPLA Eng. & Wales*

Acworth, George (1534–1581×6), administrator and scholar, was born in London in 1534, the son of Thomas Acworth, a merchant taylor of London, and his wife, Anne. Thomas came from Bedfordshire, where his father, also named George, had been elected knight of the shire for that county in 1529. During his youth George Acworth showed both an aptitude and a love for learning which his father recognized by deciding to send him to university. He matriculated at Peterhouse, Cambridge, during Michaelmas 1548 and received his BA degree in 1552. He graduated MA in 1555, at which ceremony he subscribed to the Marian articles of religion. Peterhouse elected him in 1554 to a fellowship, which he held until 1562. After receiving his MA degree he went overseas to study the civil law, first at Louvain, then at Paris, and finally at Padua where he was made DCL in 1558. His departure from England during the era of the Marian exiles was coincidental and purely for educational purposes.

Hoping to use his newly acquired education to secure

employment in the English church, Acworth wrote a predictably fawning letter to Archbishop Reginald Pole on 1 December 1558 requesting a prebend, unaware that both Pole and Mary I had died. He quickly discovered that Elizabeth was now queen and, having travelled to Venice, wrote to her on 13 December 1558 proclaiming the loyalty of the English students and scholars at Padua while expressing negative judgements of the Marian regime. Soon afterwards he returned to England, where he obtained the coveted position of public orator of Cambridge University on 16 May 1559, an office which he resigned some time after 30 June 1560. On 14 February 1561 Cambridge conferred the degree of LLD on him, and shortly thereafter he took up the position of chancellor and vicar-general of the diocese of Winchester under Bishop Robert *Horne. Horne and Acworth appear to have got along well, as the new chancellor married the bishop's daughter Elizabeth on 24 December 1564. The couple ultimately produced a son and three daughters.

Between 1561 and 1567 Acworth conducted numerous visitations of the various Oxford colleges under the supervision of the bishop of Winchester. During these visitations he took action against both crypto-Catholics and radical protestants, although he was apparently more tolerant of popish survivals than was Bishop Horne. Some sources identify Acworth as the MP for Hinden, Wiltshire, for 1563 although it is more likely that this was his cousin of the same name. In July 1568 he participated in a visitation of Corpus Christi College, Cambridge, for Archbishop Matthew Parker, the first strong connection between the two men. However, Acworth's relations with Horne had soured to the point that on 21 January 1569 the bishop requested that Acworth be removed from the Hampshire commission of the peace as he had 'becomen an unmeet man' (Hatfield House, Cecil MS 202/73–4) while mentioning that Acworth was no longer his chancellor.

Acworth next joined the household of Archbishop Parker, mostly working on the archbishop's research projects into early British church history. He wrote part of Parker's *De antiquitate Britannicae ecclesiae* (1572), and assisted in its publication. At Parker's request he published *De visibili Rom'anarchia* (1573) in response to Nicholas Sander. Parker's death in 1575 left Acworth without a position and on 25 October 1575 he wrote to William Cecil, Lord Burghley, requesting employment. A position came by late 1575, but it was in the troubled protestant ecclesiastical establishment in Ireland as the vicar-general of Adam Loftus, archbishop of Dublin. There he engaged in the various ultimately futile efforts to make Ireland protestant. During his years with Loftus, Acworth served to the archbishop's complete satisfaction in spite of vague (and probably unfounded) rumours that he was sent to Ireland only as a punishment for immoral behaviour. He died some time after 26 April 1581 but no later than 1586; his wife survived him.   RONALD H. FRITZE

Sources DNB · L. G. H. Horton-Smith, *George Acworth* (1953) · HoP, *Commons, 1558–1603* · M. McKisack, *Medieval history in the Tudor age* (1971) · C. M. Dent, *Protestant reformers in Elizabethan Oxford* (1983) · C. H. Garrett, *The Marian exiles: a study in the origins of Elizabethan puritanism* (1938) · Venn, *Alum. Cant.* · Hatfield House, Cecil MS 202

Acworth, Sir Jacob (c.1668–1749), shipbuilder, about whom details of parentage and early life are unknown, began his apprenticeship as a carpenter about 1682. He was probably a relative of William Acworth (1615–1672) who served as storekeeper of Woolwich Dockyard from 1637 until his death. Jacob Acworth served in the *Hope* (70 guns) in 1685–7, and as carpenter in several other ships until 1696. Two years later he became master mastmaker and then second assistant master shipwright at Chatham. It was probably about this time that he married Elizabeth Sliter, whose father was the master ropemaker and a teacher of navigation at Chatham. Her mother was connected to the Pett family, who still had some influence in the dockyards at that time. In 1705 Acworth became master shipwright in the small yard at Harwich. In 1708, while master shipwright at Sheerness, he was temporarily suspended from duty for negligence. He became master shipwright at Woolwich in 1714.

In November 1714 the post of assistant surveyor of the navy was revived for Acworth and in 1715, on the death of Daniel Furzer, he became surveyor. He was the only carpenter to reach such a rank in the eighteenth century, for other surveyors had spent their careers in the dockyards rather than at sea. Soon after he was appointed Acworth was given the task of examining and approving the plans and models of new ships being built or rebuilt in the dockyards. He was critical of Joseph Allin's design for the three-decker *Victory* of 1737 with three rows of open stern galleries, and considered Royal Navy ships to be 'too heavy, too loose and too high without these additional encumbrances, which I am sure cannot add beauty, but must be in every respect disagreeable' (PRO, ADM 91/2). The ship was lost in 1744 with all hands. In other cases Acworth was much more diplomatic. In 1739, for example, he wrote to the master shipwright at Plymouth in these terms:

> … as to the draught you design for the *Exeter*, though the body is not strictly agreeable to my sentiments, it may do very well, but had the ship more rake afore the body would have less resistance, sheer better and look much pleasanter to the eye. … I only mention it for your consideration. (Lavery, 2.164)

The long Acworth era coincided with an ultra-conservative period in British warship design, caused by many factors including a lack of real competition from the French and Spanish between 1715 and 1730, and an underlying belief that ship design, enshrined in the 'establishments of dimensions', could not be improved. Unsuccessful types, such as three-deckers of 80 guns, were replaced in service by similar ships. By the early 1730s it was clear that the French were beginning to develop new types of ship. The first attempt to reappraise British design was made in 1732, when the Admiralty attempted to bypass Acworth and ordered that the master shipwrights should propose new dimensions. This led to disagreement among them and in 1733 it was Acworth himself who broke the deadlock by proposing a slight increase in the size of each class. The outbreak of war with

Spain in 1739 caused another reappraisal, the result being that Acworth proposed a further slight increase in size in 1741.

However, these alterations did not protect him from criticism. In 1744 Admiral Vernon attacked Acworth as 'a half-experienced and half-judicious surveyor' who had 'half ruined the navy' (*Memorial*, 77). By the mid-1740s, as the Admiralty came under the influence of George Anson, Acworth came to symbolize all the faults of ship design. His position was not improved by his autocratic manner. Acworth was said by Henry Legge, one of the lords of the Admiralty, 'to have so much of the nature of Pompey the Great in him that he cannot bear an equal' (H. Legge to duke of Bedford, 6 March 1746, Baugh, 89–90). It was said that the Navy Board was 'determined to be led by the nose by a brute of a shipwright, who never did any good in his life, but to his own creatures' (ibid., 48).

Acworth's tendency to reminisce about the distant past was equally unappealing to an administration seeking reform. In 1744 he and his colleagues on the Navy Board answered his critics with a statement which throws interesting light on the way in which they regarded their role. The Admiralty:

> were invested with the power of *directing* the building of ships ... but the *execution* of this power is necessarily placed in the navy board. It is a trust reposed in us by the Crown from an opinion we ... were competent judges in such matters.   (PRO, ADM 106/2182)

Another new establishment of dimensions was proposed by the Admiralty in 1745, but a committee of sea officers set up under Sir John Norris was almost as conservative as the surveyor. It retained the 80-gun ships and allowed another modest increase in dimensions. By 1746 the members of the Admiralty board were determined to secure Acworth's retirement. Their attempts proved unsuccessful and the Admiralty was forced to appoint his professional rival, Joseph Allin, as joint surveyor in 1747. Acworth died in 1749.   BRIAN LAVERY

Sources D. A. Baugh, *British naval administration in the age of Walpole* (1965) · B. Lavery, *The ship of the line*, 2 vols. (1983–4) · C. Knight, '"Carpenter" master shipwrights', *Mariner's Mirror*, 18 (1932), 411–22 · J. M. Collinge, *Navy Board officials, 1660–1832* (1978) · PRO, ADM 91/2 · PRO, ADM 106/2182

Acworth, Sir William Mitchell (1850–1925), railway economist, was born at Rothley, Leicestershire, on 22 November 1850, the third son of the Revd William Acworth, vicar of Rothley, and his wife, Margaret Dundas, daughter of Andrew Mitchell of Maulside, Beath, and Blythswood Place, Glasgow. He was educated at Uppingham and at Christ Church, Oxford, where he matriculated on 13 May 1871. After taking a degree in history in 1872, for eighteen months he tutored the two sons of Crown Prince Frederick of Germany, William (afterwards Kaiser Wilhelm II) and Henry. On returning to Britain he was appointed in 1875 an assistant master at Dulwich College, where he remained until 1885. In 1878 he married Elizabeth Louisa Oswald (*d.* 1904), eldest daughter of James Brown, of Orangefield, Ayrshire. In 1886 he was elected a member, later chairman, of the Metropolitan Asylums Board. He

served on the London county council from 1889 to 1892, and in 1890 was called to the bar at the Inner Temple.

Having begun to specialize in railway affairs, in 1889 and 1890 Acworth published his first books, descriptive accounts of the railways in England and Scotland respectively. In 1891 he turned his attention to the economic and statistical aspects of his topic, and the principles that governed the fixing of railway rates. After visiting the United States to learn about statistical methods used in American railroads, he severely criticized British railway accounts in *The Railways and the Traders*, published that year. These criticisms led to accounting procedures being overhauled by the UK railways in 1911.

Soon after its foundation in 1895, Acworth began lectures for railway students at the London School of Economics. In 1905 he published his best work, *The Elements of Railway Economics*, a pioneer textbook that was widely translated. A revised edition, co-authored by W. Tetley Stephenson, appeared in 1925. He wrote many articles on railway economics for technical and other periodicals in Britain, and also in the United States, where his work was highly esteemed. His knowledge of such matters earned him membership of the royal commission on railway accidents in 1899, on the viceregal commission on Irish railways in 1906, and on the Board of Trade committee on railway accounts and statistics the same year. He became a director of the Underground Electric Railways of London Ltd and of the Midland and South-Western Junction Railway.

Acworth gained political experience as a Unionist candidate for the Yorkshire constituency of Keighley in the general elections of 1906, 1910, and 1911. In the First World War he served for a time in the Red Cross, until in 1916 he was made a member of the royal commission of inquiry into the Canadian railways. A year later he gave evidence in the US congress before the joint committee on interstate and foreign commerce; his testimony was revised and published in 1920 as *A Historical Sketch of State Railway Ownership*, in which Acworth gave his reasons for preferring private enterprise. During that year the British authorities required railway accounts to be expressed in terms of ton-miles and passenger miles.

In 1921 Acworth received a knighthood and was appointed chairman of the committee on Indian railway policy and administration. After the committee had concluded its work a year later, he was created KCSI. In 1923 he married Elizabeth Learmonth, younger daughter of Thomas Wotherspoon, of Hundleshope, Peeblesshire. There were no children of either marriage. That year the council of the League of Nations invited him to undertake an investigation of the Austrian railways. In 1924 the reparations commission, set up to implement the Dawes plan, asked him to draw up a scheme for reorganizing the German railways. Fluent in French and German, and with a barrister's training in addition to his unparalleled railway expertise, he dominated the inquiry, which recommended a public corporation to supersede the former government department. That task proved so exacting for a man in his seventies that Acworth suffered a breakdown and died at A8 the Albany, Piccadilly, London, on 2 April 1925, shortly before he was due to depart for a similar investigation in Romania. His unique collection of transport literature was bequeathed to the London School of Economics.

A supporter of private enterprise, Acworth was, in some instances, led to recommend measures of state control owing to chaotic post-war conditions; but he always strongly emphasized the necessity of separate railway budgets and of adequate safeguards against political interference. A man of concentrated energy, he undertook much journalistic work for *The Times*. He served on the councils of the Royal Economic Society and the Royal Statistical Society, having presided over the economics section of the British Association in 1908. Not surprisingly, his entry in *Who's Who* listed no recreations. He was noted for his moral courage, fair-mindedness, hospitality, and sense of humour. Widely read, he often lamented (as did some economists) that he knew so little economic theory, although he had great skill in unravelling quantitative data. Although practical railway officers often charged him with being too theoretical, they turned up in droves to his lectures, and some helped to supervise the teaching curriculum. No recognition gave him so much satisfaction as this acceptance by his own country's railway industry.

C. E. R. SHERRINGTON, *rev.* T. A. B. CORLEY

Sources *The Times* (3 April 1925) · *The Times* (4 April 1925) · *The Times* (7 April 1925) · *The Times* (8 April 1925) · *The Times* (13 April 1925) · W. T. Stephenson, *Economic Journal*, 35 (1925), 327–9 · L. Macassey, review, *Economic Journal*, 35 (1925), 590–94 · H. G. Fenelon, *Railway economics* (1932) · *WWW*, 1916–28 · private information (1937) · b. cert. · d. cert.
Archives BLPES, corresp. and papers relating to railways
Likenesses W. Stoneman, photograph, 1925, NPG
Wealth at death £26,874 15s. 10d.: resworn probate, 25 June 1925, *CGPLA Eng. & Wales*

Ada [*née* Ada de Warenne], **countess of Northumberland** (*c*.1123–1178), consort of Prince Henry of Scotland, was one of the family of three sons and two daughters of William (II) de *Warenne, earl of Surrey (*d*. 1138), and his wife, Isabel (Elizabeth) de Vermandois (*d*. 1147), widow of Robert de Beaumont, count of Meulan and earl of Leicester (*d*. 1118), daughter of Hugues le Grand, count of Vermandois, and granddaughter of Henri I of France. Her eldest brother, William (III) de *Warenne, had succeeded as earl of Surrey by 1138 and her sister Gundreda married as her first husband *Roger, earl of Warwick (*d*. 1153). Ada's wider family included the eight children of her mother's first marriage, most notably the mighty Beaumont twins, her half-brothers *Robert, earl of Leicester, and *Waleran, count of Meulan and earl of Worcester. Her marriage to Prince *Henry (*c*.1115–1152), the only surviving son of *David I, king of Scots, was celebrated in England soon after the second treaty of Durham of 9 April 1139, when King Stephen had sought peace with the Scots by confirming Henry's rights to the earldom of Huntingdon, and in addition granting him the earldom of Northumberland.

Although Orderic Vitalis speaks of a love match, the marriage was almost certainly arranged at Stephen's command; and possibly one of the Durham treaty's terms (its text is lost) had specifically provided for it in order to bind Henry more effectively to Stephen's cause, in the support of which the Beaumont twins were then at the forefront.

While Ada's marriage failed to settle relations between the kingdoms, her contribution to Scottish history was profound. Her public role as first lady of the Scottish court (there was no queen of Scotland from 1131 to 1186) was originally limited by her numerous pregnancies; but her fecundity averted a catastrophe when Henry, the expected successor to the kingship, died prematurely in 1152. During her widowhood she enjoyed in full measure the respect and status to which she was entitled as mother of two successive Scots kings, *Malcolm IV and *William the Lion. After Malcolm's enthronement as a boy of twelve in 1153, she figured prominently in his counsels and was keenly aware of her responsibilities. According to the well-informed William of Newburgh, Malcolm's celibacy dismayed her, and she endeavoured, albeit fruitlessly, to sharpen his dynastic instincts by placing a beautiful maiden in his bed. She was less frequently at William the Lion's court from 1165, no doubt because of the periodic illnesses that obliged her to turn to St Cuthbert for a cure. Her chief dower estates were the burghs and shires of Haddington and Crail, and Haddington possibly became her main residence. She also had lands in Tynedale at Whitfield, near Hexham, and in the honour of Huntingdon at Harringworth and Kempston.

Ada's cosmopolitan tastes and connections reinforced the identification of Scottish élite society with European values and norms. Reginald of Durham regarded her piety as exemplary, and she played a notable role in the expansion of the reformed continental religious orders in Scotland. If she had a preference, it was for female monasticism, and by 1159 she had founded a priory for Cistercian nuns at Haddington, apparently at the instigation of Abbot Waldef of Melrose (*d*. 1159). Her household attracted Anglo-Norman adventurers, and she personally settled in Scotland knights from Northumberland and from the great Warenne honours in England and Normandy. Ela, the wife of Duncan (II), earl of Fife (*d*. 1204), was probably one of Ada's Warenne nieces, and her great-nephew *Roger (*d*. 1202) became chancellor of Scotland and bishop of St Andrews. Two of Ada's three sons became kings of Scots; *David, the youngest, was the fifth Scottish earl of Huntingdon. She and Henry also had three daughters: Ada (*c*.1142–1205), who married Florence (III), count of Holland; Margaret (*c*.1145–1201), who married first *Conan (IV), duke of Brittany (*c*.1135–1171), and second Humphrey (III) de *Bohun of Trowbridge (*d*. 1181); and Maud, or Matilda, who died in infancy in 1152. Ada outlived Henry by twenty-six years and died in 1178.

KEITH STRINGER

Sources V. Chandler, 'Ada de Warenne, queen mother of Scotland (*c*.1123–1178)', *SHR*, 60 (1981), 119–39 · A. O. Anderson, ed., *Scottish annals from English chroniclers, AD 500 to 1286* (1908); repr. (1991) · *Reginaldi monachi Dunelmensis libellus de admirandis beati*

Cuthberti virtutibus, ed. [J. Raine], SurtS, 1 (1835) • Jocelin of Furness, 'Vita sancti Waldeni', *Acta sanctorum: Augustus*, 1 (Antwerp, 1733), 241–77 • K. J. Stringer, *Earl David of Huntingdon, 1152–1219: a study in Anglo-Scottish history* (1985) • D. Crouch, *The Beaumont twins: the roots and branches of power in the twelfth century*, Cambridge Studies in Medieval Life and Thought, 4th ser., 1 (1986) • A. O. Anderson and M. O. Anderson, eds., *The chronicle of Melrose* (1936)

Ada, Sister. *See* Vachell, Ada Marian (1866–1923).

Adair, Archibald (*d.* 1647), Church of Ireland bishop of Waterford and Lismore, was the fourth son of Ninian Adair (*fl.* 1588), laird of Kinhilt in Galloway, and Catherine Agnew of Lochnaw, also in Galloway. He matriculated at St Andrews University in 1593 and graduated MA in 1596. He appears to have been presented to the vicarage of Torkington, near Stoneykirk (or Stephenkirk), on 8 June 1585. A pamphlet entitled *Response à l'outrecuidance de l'apostat Cayer* by Archibald Adair 'escossays' was published in Paris in 1603.

In a blistering account of a meeting of Church of Ireland bishops in Dublin in July 1611, Bishop Andrew Knox of the Isles and Raphoe mentioned that he had brought with him Adair, his new dean of Raphoe, to assist in preaching and in controversy with Catholics. Adair was one of about a dozen Scots imported by Knox to serve in his Irish diocese. The 1622 visitation described him as 'an eloquent scholar and a good preacher of God's word, given to hospitality and good conversation' (TCD, MS 550, p. 212). He was resident and found graduate clergy to serve the parishes annexed to the deanery. Such dutifulness certainly made a good impression in Armagh, because when Archbishop Ussher canvassed the bishopric of Clogher for him in 1629 he also enclosed a testimony written by the previous primate, Christopher Hampton. In November 1629 Adair was nominated to the bishopric of Killala and Achonry, with a direction to the lords justices that they assist the bishop in recovery of see lands (he was consecrated in May 1630). In October 1633 Charles I, on the bishop's petition, set up a special commission to investigate all cases relating to the temporalities. By 1636 much land had been recovered and Adair was consulted on arrangements for church lands for the projected plantation of Connaught.

Adair's steady career fell victim to the political turbulence created by the Scottish national covenant. In July 1639 John Corbet, a refugee Scottish minister and author of two anti-Presbyterian tracts, arrived in Killala to take up a benefice arranged for him by the lord deputy. About 4 miles from Killala, Corbet, according to his own deposition, met some other clergy. One of them told him that, while dining, Adair had remarked that the new man 'was an impure corbie [raven] thrust out of God's ark' (PRO, SP 63/257/28). When Corbet and Adair finally met a row broke out over tithes, during which it was alleged that the bishop maintained that he would sooner have subscribed to the covenant than left wife and children behind him. Further derogatory remarks followed and the whole matter rapidly came to the attention of Dublin Castle.

Corbet made a sworn statement on 10 August 1639. On 20 February 1640 Adair appeared before all the members of the high commission court in Dublin. As it was fewer than forty days to parliament he tried to claim privilege in the hope of benefiting from the forthcoming general pardon. In fact the Irish privy council had already decided to retransmit the pardon specifically exempting Adair and to stop his writ of summons. The commissioners more cautiously indicated they would proceed to a conditional hearing and sentencing subject to a final decision from the House of Lords, when they met, on denial of the writ. Despite the plea by Bishop Bedell of Kilmore that there was no spiritual or doctrinal offence at issue, Adair was sentenced to degradation by his metropolitan, a £2000 fine, and imprisonment. On 31 March the Lords unanimously found him unfit to have any summons to parliament. He was formally deposed *ab officio et beneficio* by Richard Boyle, archbishop of Tuam, in St Patrick's Cathedral on 18 June. While this affair attracted much attention it was rapidly overtaken by the scandal of accusations of sodomy against John Atherton, bishop of Waterford and Lismore.

In October 1640 Killala and Achonry were granted to another Scottish refugee, Bishop John Maxwell of Ross. Sir Robert Stewart, MP for Londonderry and a long-standing patron of Adair, now worked hard for his rehabilitation. On 7 June 1641 the king ordered the 'false charges' erased from the record and restored him to his rank and bishopric. He was simultaneously translated to the now vacant bishopric of Waterford and Lismore. At an unknown date he married a Mistress McDowall of Garthland. Like many clergy he left Ireland after the rebellion, and he died in Bristol in 1647.

JOHN MCCAFFERTY

Sources H. Cotton, *Fasti ecclesiae Hibernicae*, 6 vols. (1845–78) • John Corbet's deposition, PRO, SP 63/257/28 • A. Mackenzie, *William Adair and his kirk* (1933) • *CSP Ire., 1611–47* • *Journals of the House of Lords of the kingdom of Ireland*, 1 (1779) • A. F. S. Pearson, 'Alumni of St. Andrews and the settlement of Ulster', *Ulster Journal of Archaeology*, 3rd ser., 14 (1951), 7–14 • *Fasti Scot.*, new edn, vol. 6 • J. Ware, 'Diary of events', Pearse Street Library, Dublin, Gilbert Collection, MS 169 • A. Adair, *Response à l'outrecuidance de l'apostat Cayer* (Paris, 1603) • E. S. Shuckburgh, ed., *Two biographies of William Bedell, bishop of Kilmore, with a selection of his letters and an unpublished treatise* (1902) • A. Clarke, 'The Atherton file', *Decies: Journal of the Old Waterford Society*, 11 (1979), 45–55 • visitation records, 1622, TCD, MS 550 • T. W. Moody and others, eds., *A new history of Ireland, 9: Maps, genealogies, lists* (1984)

Adair, Gilbert Smithson (1896–1979), physiologist, was born on 21 September 1896 in Whitehaven, the elder child and only son of Harold Adair, manager of an iron ore mine in Cumberland, and his wife, Anna Mary Jackson, from Garstang. The family later moved to nearby Egremont. Adair was educated privately at home for several years and, encouraged by both parents, became absorbed in the area and its natural history, particularly at the sea-shore. A room in the house was set up as a laboratory, equipped with a microscope. In his early teens Adair was sent to Bootham, the Quaker school in York. There he found life spartan, even for his simple tastes. The school recognized his talents in biology and chemistry, and he successfully took the entrance scholarship examination at King's College, Cambridge, in 1914. He entered that college in 1915, obtaining a first class in part one of the natural sciences tripos in 1917.

With his defective eyesight, Adair failed in his attempt to join the Friends' Ambulance Unit. He entered the Food Investigation Board to inquire into the then important problem of preventing wastage of imported food on cargo ships. He returned to King's College, Cambridge, as a research student in 1920 and joined the physiological laboratory, though he retained links with the Food Investigation Board which proved to be useful when a Refrigeration Research Station (later the Low Temperature Research Station) was established in Cambridge in 1922. Adair was granted cold-room facilities which he continued to use until his death. In 1923 he was elected to a research fellowship at King's College and published several major papers during his tenure, so that in 1928 the college made him an official fellow for five years, allowing him to concentrate on research. From 1931 to 1945 he was assistant director of research in the physiological laboratory, from 1945 to 1963 reader in biophysics, and from 1963 honorary fellow of King's College. In 1939 he was elected fellow of the Royal Society.

After early work on the diffusion of electrolytes in gels, Adair entered on what was to be his major field, the physical chemistry of haemoglobin and its interactions with simple gases. His work between 1924 and 1930 was the first to show that haemoglobin was a well-defined material with highly specific structure, unique molecular weight, and the capability of reacting stoichiometrically and reproducibly. In particular he is remembered for perfecting and simplifying the osmotic pressure method of measuring molecular weight, which was subsequently widely used by himself and by others throughout the world. By 1940 he had published some forty-five papers on the application of osmotic and membrane potential measurements to a variety of protein systems. From 1940 to 1977, although the volume of his output fell somewhat, he was in great demand from visiting scientists and PhD students, to whom he was always willing to demonstrate patiently and fully his latest developments. He was an excellent teacher. Many of his later papers were written in collaboration with visitors from all parts of the world. His last paper (with K. Imai from Japan) returned to his favourite subject, haemoglobin.

In July 1931 Adair married Muriel Elaine (c.1900–1975), one of the three daughters of George Hardinge Robinson, a stockbroker from Southport. Muriel entered Girton College in 1918, and went on to obtain a research fellowship at Newnham, and a staff fellowship at Girton. At one stage she worked with Sir Frederick Gowland Hopkins but eventually she turned to proteins and collaborated with Adair in many papers from 1930 onwards. She also accompanied him on climbing expeditions. They had no children.

Although quiet and retiring, Adair made many friends. Climbing in the Lake District, in the Dolomites, and in Colorado, as well as around the university and college buildings in Cambridge in the earlier part of his life, was later replaced by an interest in his garden. Here he and his wife spent much time, encouraging nearly all forms of wild life (ducks and rooks excluded). Muriel died on 2 January 1975; Adair on 22 June 1979, in Cambridge.

PALEY JOHNSON, *rev.*

Sources P. Johnson and M. F. Perutz, *Memoirs FRS*, 27 (1981), 1–27 · personal knowledge (1986) · private information (1986) · *CGPLA Eng. & Wales* (1979)
Archives CUL, corresp. with U. R. Evans
Wealth at death £218,461: probate, 20 Aug 1979, *CGPLA Eng. & Wales*

Adair, James (*fl.* 1736–1775), trader and author in America, was probably born in Ireland but his place of birth and parentage have been the subject of much conjecture. He lived most of his life in the upcountry South, above the fall line in what was to become South Carolina and Georgia, a territory between the orbits of the English, French, and Spanish coastal colonies and the interior domains of the large American Indian nations—the Chickasaw, Choctaw, Cherokee, and Catawba. His name first appears in 1736 among the Cherokee people in the southern Appalachian mountains.

Over decades in this region Adair wrote *The history of the American Indians … containing an account of their origin, language, manners … and other particulars, sufficient to render it a complete Indian system … with a new map of the country*. His *History* was unique on literary and scholarly merits in the colonial South and was the only first-hand portrait of the evanescent world of mixed white, red, and black inhabitants he often called home. The book pioneered the practice of comparing cultures now standard in ethnohistory. 'One great advantage my readers will here have,' he wrote in his preface; 'I sat down to draw the Indians on the spot … and lived with them as a friend and brother.' Published in 1775 in London and reprinted in Germany in 1782, the *History* influenced many contemporary and nineteenth-century authors in its scholarly 'proof' of the descent of American Indians from the lost tribes of Israel. The work became an encyclopaedic source for generations of scholars. Autobiography as well as history, the book reveals much about the temperament and politics of the author but few details of his life. It was written in stages, and is best read in reverse, from end to beginning, from the final powerful political appeal to the elaborate proof of the Jewish lineage of American Indians that dominates most of the text.

Five years after his advent in the Cherokee towns Adair was living among the Chickasaws, near the Mississippi River (he would later call himself an English Chickasaw); appeared again stirring up civil war among the Choctaw in Mississippi for the purpose of speculative trading profit; and entered the records once more as an English ally and commander of a Chickasaw force during the British and American war against the Cherokees during 1759–62. He made his last appearance seeking sponsorship and endorsements for the publication of his book during the late 1760s and early 1770s. In 1774 he was briefly visible and aligned with land speculators seeking to create Georgiana, a new colony, out of ceded American Indian lands. At this moment an unlikely common cause emerged: loyalist landowners and Scottish traders, wealthy métis families, tribal leaders, and Adair all sought accommodation rather than revolution.

During the revolutionary era Adair undertook a final revision of his book, and found a new expression of purpose. The *History* ends with a plea for a new society in which American Indians, acknowledged as 'freemen and equals', live side by side with their colonial neighbours in 'happy settlement of the land around them' (Williams, 222). Adair hoped for such a union and summoned for native America a connection to Jewish history, ancestral even to European traditions, to give standing to the cause of the Native American during the revolutionary period. Adair's voice and message were drowned out by war, just as his book was published. Its negative reception in Britain, where accounts featuring American Indians usually fared well, only aided its passage into obscurity. Unmoored from the political urgency of its time, the *History* and Adair's career have been largely forgotten, except by some historians, who still draw on the work as an example of European views of American Indians. As a result, both the book and its writer have been reduced to a strange and perplexing footnote to 'frontier' history. The last clear record of his life is the publication of his book in 1775 in London, where some sources place him. Whether he died in England, or returned to the southern United States mountains (as local family traditions claim), is unknown, as is the place of his burial. There has been speculation that he left children, both white and Indian.

TOM HATLEY

Sources *Adair's history of the American Indians*, ed. S. C. Williams (Johnson City, TN, 1930); repr. (New York, 1973) • T. Hatley, *The dividing paths: Cherokees and South Carolinians through the era of revolution* (1993) • J. Adair, *History of the American Indians* (1775)

Adair, James (1743?–1798), judge and serjeant-at-law, whose place of birth remains unknown and whose date of birth is unconfirmed, was the first son of James Adair, a Belfast merchant, and Margaret Maxwell of co. Down where the younger Adair later inherited estates. While his early years remain somewhat obscure it is known that Adair received a good education, spending seven years at Eton College (1753–9) and being admitted at the age of sixteen to Peterhouse, Cambridge, where he obtained a BA in 1764, proceeding MA in 1767. About a year before obtaining his second degree Adair married Elizabeth Spencer, with whom he had one son, James, and a daughter, Mary Ann. From an early stage Adair was an opponent to the court; this found expression in his *Thoughts on the Dismission of Officers, Civil and Military, for their Conduct in Parliament* (1764) and *Observations on the Power of Alienation in the Crown* (1768). He was admitted to Lincoln's Inn on 24 February 1761 and was called to the bar in 1767.

By 1770 Adair had begun to distinguish himself in his profession and to take an active interest in the politics of the time. In that year he became embroiled in a dispute with John Horne Tooke as an advocate of John Wilkes. Tooke publicly attacked Adair and maintained a long-term resentment, once claiming that: 'I would rather at any time lose a cause than be condemned to hear Adair gain it for me' (Rogers, 139). Tooke's invective at the time, however, merely served to raise the public profile of Adair and, as the *Gentleman's Magazine* pointed out: 'To this trifling circumstance Mr Adair was essentially indebted for much of his subsequent importance in life' (*GM*, 721). In 1771 Adair was prominent as one of the defence counsel in the proceedings against the publishers of Junius's letters; in subsequent years he continued to enhance his professional reputation and was appointed serjeant-at-law on 28 April 1774. While not considered by some contemporaries 'as a striking example of forensic eloquence' as a barrister, Adair 'was very much esteemed and consulted on account of his profound legal knowledge' (ibid.). He also had strong political aspirations which saw him serve as MP for Cockermouth between 1775 and 1780 where he voted with the Rockingham whigs; while in September 1782 he unsuccessfully contested Southwark as an ally of Charles James Fox. In parliament Adair was outspoken against the North administration, was an advocate of reform measures, and strongly opposed the American war. He was also reputedly a Unitarian by faith, but supported a bill introduced in 1778 to relieve Catholics from the penalties imposed by the act of 1699 whereby priests could be prosecuted for keeping schools.

In October 1779 Adair succeeded John Glynn as recorder of London, being paid £600 per annum until 1785 when his salary was increased to £1000. He resigned from the position on 24 June 1789 upon which occasion the court of aldermen voted him thanks and conferred on him the freedom of the City in recognition of his able and diligent service. While the *Gentleman's Magazine* suggests that Adair's resignation was due to the somewhat snobbish attitude of considering common council business 'a drudgery … [that was] beneath him' (*GM*, 721), it is more likely that he resigned on account of his increasing professional commitments and in the interest of his own health. Politics may also have played a part in his decision, with the members of the London corporation transferring their political allegiance during Adair's term of office from his party, the Foxite whigs, to the administration of the younger Pitt.

During the 1780s Adair maintained a balance between his professional endeavours, which included his appointment in 1782 as king's serjeant and being ascribed as author of *Discussions of the Law of Libels* (1785), and his political interests, including his membership of the whig club which dated from 24 June 1784. Through the whig club Adair became known to Charles James Fox but with the progress of the French Revolution during the 1790s he distanced himself from the Foxite cause and became a firm supporter of the war against France. On 3 August 1793 Adair was offered by William, fourth Earl Fitzwilliam, the borough of Higham Ferrers, which he served until his death. A memorandum issued for the members of parliament by Adair in May 1794 highlighted his continuing support for the war against France and his advocacy of government measures to suppress those who sought to 'overturn the constitution … by giving any new power to the body of the people, or asserting any rights in them, inconsistent with the just prerogative of the crown and the rights and privileges of the nobles' (BL, Add. MS 53804, fol. 169). When the duke of Portland joined the ministry in July 1794, Adair had ambitions of becoming lord chancellor of Ireland. Edmund Burke thought 'so scandalous an appointment' would outrage the Irish bar: 'Adair is a mungrel in respect of the policy—not Irishman enough to be known on that side of the Water, not enough of a Stranger to be reputed English' (*Correspondence*, 8.68–9). Three years later Adair maintained hopes of being appointed Irish chancellor, again drawing the wrath of Burke who referred to Adair as 'that low, intriguing, and perfidious tool' (*Correspondence*, 9.355).

Throughout the 1790s Adair saw himself as compelled 'to support an administration I dislike' (Thorne, 22). To the Pitt government he conferred only 'a *general* support' and felt 'it a duty to oppose them in some instances' (ibid., 23). While his allegiance to the government was somewhat inconsistent, he was an advocate in parliament for the abolition of the slave trade and relief of dissenters. With the threat of jacobinism looming large in the wake of the French Revolution, however, Adair was ambiguous and contradictory in his stance on radicalism and reform. While he opposed the prosecution of the Scottish radicals in 1793–4 and successfully served as defence counsel with Thomas Erskine at the trial for high treason of William Stone in 1796, he was as king's serjeant involved in the prosecution of Thomas Hardy and Tooke in 1794 for treason and on 5 January 1795 denounced the activities of radicals in a speech to the Commons. Later in 1795 Adair supported the bills against sedition which he retrospectively observed were of 'utmost service to the country' (ibid., 24), yet he was, ironically, in favour of a petition against the legislation being presented in parliament. In 1796 he became chief justice of Chester and in June 1798 joined the London and Westminster light horse volunteers at a time when Britain faced the prospect of invasion from France. As a public figure Adair's manner drew diverse assessments from his contemporaries over the years. Burke thought him to be 'the dullest and most unpleasant of Men' (*Correspondence*, 8.69) and the *Public Ledger* described him as 'rather tedious in speaking' (Drummond, 6). Yet even the critical *City Biography*, which stated that 'his action was awkward, and his voice better suited to a rookery than a Senate', could not deny that 'his talents … were strong, improved by labour and sharpened by practice; he was a correct, methodical, and plausible speaker' (ibid.). Adair died in London on 21 July 1798 of a stroke while returning from a shooting exercise with the light horse volunteers. He was buried six days later at Bunhill Fields cemetery near his parents' graves.

MICHAEL T. DAVIS

Sources S. Rogers, *Recollections* (1859) · *GM*, 1st ser., 68 (1798), 720–21 · *DNB* · will, PRO, PROB 11/1314, fols. 231r–232 · R. G. Thorne, 'Adair, James', HoP, *Commons, 1790–1820* · M. M. Drummond, 'Adair, James', HoP, *Commons, 1754–90* · *The correspondence of Edmund Burke*, ed. T. W. Copeland and others, 10 vols. (1958–78), vols. 8–9 · R. A. Austen-Leigh, ed., *The Eton College register, 1753–1790* (1921) · BL, Add. MS 53804 · H. W. Woolrych, *Lives of eminent serjeants-at-law of the English bar*, 2 vols. (1869)

Archives BL, corresp. and papers, Add. MSS 50829–50830, 53800–53808, 53815 | U. Nott. L., letters to duke of Portland, PWF 12–31

Likenesses C. H. Hodges, mezzotint, pubd 1789 (after G. Romney), BM, NPG

Wealth at death see will, PRO, PROB 11/1314, fols. 231r–232

Adair, James Makittrick (1728–1801), physician, originally surnamed Makittrick, was the son of James Makittrik, a physician in Ayr, and Miss Adair (*b.* 1700), the daughter of Miss Dunbar and Robert Adair of Maryport Farm, Kirkmaiden, Mull of Galloway. His brother John practised medicine in Winchester. James assumed the name of Adair about 1783. He studied in Geneva and took the degree of MD at Edinburgh in 1766. He practised before and after that date in Antigua, and he later defended the island's slave owners in his *Unanswerable Arguments Against the Abolition of the Slave Trade* (1790). His medical writings enjoyed a considerable reputation in continental Europe; his degree thesis on the yellow fever of the West Indies was reprinted in E. G. Baldinger's collection of medical treatises (1776), and his *Philosophical and Medical Sketch of the Natural History of Human Body and Mind* (1787), which was aimed at the lay person, was also translated abroad. Adair married Anne Barter and they had (at least) a daughter, Anne, and a son, James.

After returning from Antigua Adair practised at Andover, Guildford, and Bath, and wrote, for the benefit of those visiting the latter place, a volume entitled *Medical Cautions for the Consideration of Invalids* (1786). Adair became friendly with the poet Robert Burns, to whom he was introduced by the Revd Dr Lawrie, whose son Archibald married Adair's sister, Anne. Adair accompanied Burns on his tour of Stirlingshire during the autumn of 1787, and on 16 November 1789 he married Charlotte Hamilton, half-sister of Burns's friend Gavin Hamilton (1753–1805).

Adair could provoke animosity. At one time he was in Winchester gaol for sending a challenge to a duel; at another time he engaged in controversy with Dr Freeman and Philip Thicknesse. Thicknesse published an angry letter to him in 1787, and Adair replied with an abusive dedication in his *Essays on Fashionable Diseases* (1790?). When Thicknesse wrote his *Memoirs and Anecdotes* (1788–91), his opponent replied with a list, entitled *Facts and Anecdotes* (1790), which he pretended that Thicknesse had omitted. Thicknesse asserted that Adair had stolen his adopted surname from a physician at Spa. Adair died at Ayr in 1801.

W. P. COURTNEY, rev. MICHAEL BEVAN

Sources J. Adair, *Essays on fashionable diseases* (1790?) · *GM*, 1st ser., 72 (1802), 475, 582 · private information (2004) [A. Silver] · J. A. Mackay, *R. B.: a biography of Robert Burns* (1992) · I. McIntyre, *Dirt & deity: a life of Robert Burns* (1995)

Adair, John (1660–1718), geographer and cartographer, was born on 2 September 1660 in Leith, Scotland. Nothing is known of his parents or his early education. The first firm reference to Adair dates from May 1681, when he was granted a licence by the privy council to survey Scotland and produce maps. Adair that month signalled his intentions and requested assistance in his 'Advertisement anent surveying all of the Shires of Scotland and making new Mapps of it'. Adair's first known work, a map of Clackmannanshire, dates from 1681. By 1682 Adair had established connections with Moses Pitt, produced manuscript plans of the Roman camp at Ardoch, and been commissioned by the geographer royal, Sir Robert Sibbald, who termed Adair 'mathematician and skilful mechanick', to undertake the maps for his intended description of Scotland ancient and modern (*An Account of the Scottish Atlas*, 4). Adair's antiquarian interests centred on Roman Scotland: in addition to his plan of Ardoch manuscript sketches by him survive of Roman statuary. His natural history interests were more varied: his shell collection in particular was commented upon by contemporaries, and he sketched Scotland's birds and whales and collected mineralogical specimens. On 14 June 1686, by act of parliament, Adair's mapping was to be funded from an annual tonnage levy of 1*s*. (Scots) on native ships over 8 tons, and 2*s*. for foreign ships, to be paid annually for five years. His mapping is important because it represents the first survey-based mapping of Scotland since Timothy Pont's work of the late sixteenth century (work which, through the offices of Robert Gordon and others, formed the basis of Blaeu's 1654 *Atlas* of Scotland). Some time before September 1687 Adair married Jean Oliphant. No formal records exist either of the marriage or of the birth of known children: James (the eldest son), Patrick, a divinity student, and two daughters, Jean and Anna.

Adair presented a paper on the capercaillie, and showed his maps to the Royal Society in November 1687. He was elected a fellow on 30 November 1688. By the early 1690s Adair's work was being hindered by lack of money and by disputes with Sibbald. By August 1692 the privy council noted that he had completed ten sea maps, for which he had received £120 Scots from the tonnage levy although the work had cost him twice as much, and ten county maps, for which he had received less than £50. By August 1694 Adair's expenses sustained in producing maps of Scotland were nearly three times as much as he had received from the tonnage levy and other sources. He undertook commissions to survey private estates, including Sir William Bruce's formal garden at Craigiehall near Edinburgh. His interests in Scotland's natural history and antiquities are apparent in his sketch of a black-winged stilt in Sibbald's *Scotia illustrata* (1684), in his sketch of a whale, and in his circulated list of queries of 1694 concerning the description of Scotland. These queries, fourteen in total, asked for information about what virtuoso contemporaries understood as 'curious' facts about Scotland's natural productions and people. Such distributed queries, designed to elicit facts about natural and civil history, were an important means of securing reliable natural knowledge in the later seventeenth century. Adair should not be seen as just a Scottish map maker. He had connections with the Low Countries and London, and practised several of the ways—mapping, reporting, and querying—by which nations could know themselves.

The tonnage levy in support of Adair's mapping was increased fourfold on 16 July 1695. In the summer of 1696

representations were made to the privy council from the countess of Wemyss that the increased levy was proving prejudicial to the export of coal and salt on foreign ships. Her request that the imposition be delayed was agreed, despite Adair's counter-claim that accurate maps were an incentive to foreign trade and that a shortfall in funds would restrict his work. In October 1696 the privy council reduced the tonnage levy for foreign ships to 8*s*. per ton. Adair's work was also hindered by another claim upon the tonnage levy as a funding source. John Slezer, from 1671 chief engineer with the army in Scotland, had published his pictorial account of Scotland, *Theatrum Scotiae*, in 1693, and he intended a further work, 'Of ancient Scotland, and its ancient people'. The Scottish parliament, in approving Slezer's work, added his name to the beneficiaries of the 1695 Tonnage Act. Privy council records for August 1697 show tonnage funds being given to Slezer and much smaller sums to Adair.

Adair was again involved with the wider scientific networks of London's Royal Society in 1697, being invited by Hans Sloane and Charles Preston to correspond over the north-west highlands and outer isles. Adair set out for the Western Isles, via the Orkneys, in May 1698 on board the *Mary* of Leith under the command of John Whyte. He was accompanied by Martin Martin, a Skye-born man then establishing himself as a correspondent for the Royal Society. Adair's letter of 20 December 1698 to Hans Sloane records his intentions to publish a description of the area together with maps. Adair's publication plans received a setback with Martin's publication in 1698 of *A Late Voyage to St Kilda*. A testament of 2 August 1699 from Thomas Whyte, ship's captain and son of the skipper of Adair's 1698 voyage, notes that Adair owed £480 for that earlier voyage. Adair worked by triangulation. He spent considerable sums on the latest available instruments, some purchased in Holland in 1687. A manuscript of 1696 notes his purchase of 'a large Azimuth Compass for navigating the Isles' and a 'telescope 16 foot long'. His survey methods were shared by others, but his work is of interest in being a relatively unusual combination of terrestrial survey and ship-based coastal measurement.

Adair's *Description of the Sea Coasts and Islands of Scotland*, which concentrates upon Scotland's east coast, was published in 1703. An intended second part was never published, although records from 1704 show further maps in preparation. The 1703 *Description* shows Adair capable of first-class work: the high-quality engraving was by James Clark of Edinburgh. It represents an important contribution to Scottish, and, even, to British map making and it is unfortunate that the companion volume was never produced.

A further tonnage imposition in support of Adair's work was ratified by act of parliament on 25 August 1704. In 1707 Adair produced, in manuscript, a 'Short account of the kingdome of Scotland' with special reference to its coasts and fishing. From 1708 to 1712 he was active in plans for new docks at Bo'ness, discussing the ports of south-west Scotland and undertaking further private commissions. A list dated 2 June 1713 enumerates nineteen maps not yet printed, mostly of Scotland's west coast. By late 1715 Adair's work was curtailed through gout, although he was active in the summer of 1716 in reviewing schemes to control flooding in Perth. He died at home in the Canongate on 15 May 1718.

In a disposition of 16 May 1698 Adair had sought to provide for his wife upon his death. Records of July 1718 reveal considerable debts, however, and from early 1719 his wife sought redress from debtors. She secured an annual pension of £40 in 1722, back-dated to Adair's death, and sums were forthcoming from the dukes of Queensberry and Argyll and the sale of Adair's instruments. Relatively few manuscript sea charts by Adair have survived. A fire in the exchequer office in 1811 is thought to have destroyed Adair's papers, and certainly by 1836 no trace of his documents could be found.

It would be fair to describe Adair as an under-achiever, despite extensive fieldwork and first-class finished maps. His various titles—the king's geographer, hydrographer royal, her majestie's geographer/the queen's geographer—indicate considerable contemporary esteem. He was also made a burgess of Stirling (in 1685), of Canongate (1699), and of Aberdeen (1706). Yet too much was left in manuscript, and, in consequence, Adair's importance has been diminished. Difficulties over funding and disputes with Sibbald, Slezer, and Martin certainly did not help his cause. If he is remembered principally for his mapping, his interest in antiquities, natural history, and utilitarian natural philosophy also mark him as representative of the period. CHARLES W. J. WITHERS

Sources P. Vasey, 'John Adair geographer and surveyor: a source list', ed. I. Hill, typescript, 1998, NA Scot. · MSS, NA Scot., RD 14/11, RD 13/17/82, RH 14/84, RD 4/55, RD 3/76, RD 12/24, RH 14/203 (vol. 3), E 7/4, RD 2/68, RD 12/38/172, GD 277/Box 7/Bundle 2, RD 12/28/377, RD 12/30/847 · *Reg. PCS*, 3rd ser. · NL Scot., Adv. MSS 33.515, 15.1.1, 6.1.14, 6.282(31) · *APS*, 1124–1707 · T. Birch, *The history of the Royal Society of London*, 4 vols. (1756–7), vol. 4, pp. 551–2 · letterbooks, RS · bap. register · NA Scot., MSS SC 39/37/6
Wealth at death see NA Scot., MS SC 39/37/6 (4 July 1718)

Adair, Patrick (1624?–1693/4), Presbyterian minister and historian, was the son of John Adair of Genoch in Galloway. His family were prominently involved in the Scottish migration to Ulster in the seventeenth century, and he was the nephew of Sir Robert Adair, a major Scots colonizer in mid-Antrim, and of the Revd William Adair, who in 1644 administered the solemn league and covenant in Ulster. As a boy Patrick was present in St Giles's Cathedral, Edinburgh, in 1637 when the use of a new Scottish prayer book provoked the riot traditionally associated with Jenny Geddes. He graduated MA from St Andrews University in 1642 and went on to study divinity at Glasgow. On 7 May 1646 he was ordained and installed in Cairncastle, co. Antrim, by a presbytery formed at Carrickfergus in 1642 by chaplains and elders of the Scots army sent to Ulster in response to the Irish rising. His settlement in Cairncastle has been attributed to the patronage of Scottish colonist and church elder James Shaw, whose castle at Ballygally remains a landmark on the co. Antrim coast.

In 1648 Adair and Shaw were members of a committee appointed by the presbytery to correspond with George Monck and Sir Charles Coote, the parliamentary commanders in Ulster, on matters of Presbyterian concern. This was the first of many occasions when Adair acted as spokesman and negotiator for the Ulster Presbyterians in their fluctuating fortunes in the seventeenth century. The presbytery's condemnation in 1649 of the execution of Charles I and the ecclesiastical policies of the Westminster parliament ended hopes of amicable relations with the new regime. Adair and others continued a covert ministry, 'taking what opportunities they could to preach in the fields or in barns and glens' (Adair, 181). About 1650 he married Margaret, daughter of the Revd Robert Cunningham of Holywood, co. Down, and their first child, William, was born in 1651. Adair was involved in a public discussion with Independent and Baptist ministers in Antrim in 1652. Later that year and in January 1653 he also participated in negotiations with the government over Presbyterian unwillingness, on grounds of conscience, to take an engagement oath of loyalty to the Commonwealth and abjure monarchy. His forthright defence of the Presbyterian position while disavowing any insurrectionary intention earned his co-religionists and himself no relief, and subsequently his home was raided by soldiers who took away papers critical of the regime's policies and actions, in particular the execution of the king. These might have proved incriminating, had not an alert and courageous maidservant retrieved them from the soldiers' baggage when they spent the night in nearby Larne. A plan to transplant the Ulster Scots to Munster was not implemented, and the position of Presbyterian ministers improved, welcomed by Adair as 'a great calm after the storms they had endured' (ibid., 202). Official recognition brought state salaries for ministers, but not at first the tithes for which Adair argued. He received £50 in 1655 and £100 in 1656. With the Presbyterian cause advanced, the original Ulster presbytery became five meetings of presbytery—Antrim, Down, Route, Laggan, and Tyrone—and arrangements were adopted for ministerial training.

Adair was one of eight ecclesiastical advisers in the Dublin Restoration convention in 1660, but the Restoration church settlement brought ejection and outlawry for Presbyterian ministers. Their position was exacerbated by the Blood plot of 1663 when protestants planned to seize Dublin Castle and kidnap Ormond. As a consequence a number of Presbyterian ministers were arrested, and Adair was briefly imprisoned before being released through the intervention of Lord Massereene, on condition that he live peaceably. This he and his brethren did; in his words, 'the few ministers took every opportunity … to creep up by degrees to the exercise of their ministry' (Adair, 283). A meeting-house was built in Cairncastle by 1669 and the hearth money roll for the parish in that year records Patr Adare as living in Ballyhackett townland. His house there was still standing when Classon Porter included Adair in his *Brief Biographical Sketches* in 1884. After the death of his first wife Adair married his cousin Jean (d. 1673/5), daughter of Sir Robert Adair of Ballymena. The couple had three sons, Archibald, Alexander, and Patrick, and one daughter, Ellen. Negotiations with the government—in which Adair was involved—led to the *regium donum* grant for Presbyterian ministers in 1672, and in 1674 he was called to Belfast to succeed the Revd William Keyes, called in turn to the Bull Alley congregation in Dublin where Adair had mediated in a dispute in 1671 and 1672. A widower once more, in Belfast Adair married his third wife, Elizabeth Anderson, *née* Martin, who survived him.

As a representative of the Ulster Presbyterians Adair welcomed William III to England in 1689 and to Ireland in 1690. He and his son William, minister in Ballyeaston, were among the first trustees of a new and increased *regium donum* fund. He did not long survive the Williamite revolution, however. He is recorded as attending the synod of Ulster in 1691 and 1692 (there are no minutes for 1693), and in 1694 he is recorded as 'being now dead'. In his will, dated 26 January 1693, he requested that his body should be buried in Belfast, but the location of his grave is unknown. His permanent contribution to Irish Presbyterianism was his 'True narrative of the rise and progress of the Presbyterian government in the north of Ireland', covering the period 1623–70. His original manuscript was lost for many years, but was recovered in the nineteenth century and used by James Seaton Reid in his *History of the Presbyterian Church in Ireland* before being edited and published by W. D. Killen in 1866 as *A True Narrative of the Rise and Progress of the Presbyterian Church in Ireland*. For Adair the Scottish migration to Ulster in the seventeenth century was providential, 'to make way for a more full planting of the gospel' and 'a more full reformation' in Ireland, 'the land being overgrown with idolatry and barbarousness' (Adair, 91), and 'the first means God used for this end was the sending over of the Scotch army' (ibid., 92).

FINLAY HOLMES

Sources DNB · P. Adair, *A true narrative of the rise and progress of the Presbyterian church in Ireland (1623–1670)*, ed. W. D. Killen (1866) · T. Witherow, *Historical and literary memorials of presbyterianism in Ireland, 1623–1731* (1879) · J. McConnell and others, eds., *Fasti of the Irish Presbyterian church, 1613–1840*, rev. S. G. McConnell, 2 vols. in 12 pts (1935–51) · J. Classon Porter, *Ulster biographical sketches* (1884) · *Irish Presbyterian*, 14 (Feb 1908) · *Irish Presbyterian*, 29 (June 1923) · *Christian Unitarian*, 4 (1865) · J. S. Reid and W. D. Killen, *History of the Presbyterian church in Ireland*, new edn, 1 (1867) · S. O Saothai, 'Patrick Adair of Cairncastle (1624–1694)', *The Glynns: Journal of the Glens of Antrim Historical Society*, 2 (1984), 18–28 · P. Kilroy, *Protestant dissent and controversy, 1660–1714* (1994) · St John D. Seymour, *The puritans in Ireland (1647–1661)* (1921) · T. C. Barnard, *Cromwellian Ireland* (1975) · A. F. S. Pearson, *Origins of Irish Presbyterianism* [n.d.] [also typescript in Union Theological College Library, A. F. S. Pearson, 'Scottish and puritan settlements in Ireland, 1560–1640] · *Fasti Scot.* · will, Presbyterian Historical Society, Belfast

Wealth at death £400: will, Presbyterian Historical Society, Belfast

Adair, Sir Robert (1763–1855), politician and diplomatist, was the son of Robert Adair, sergeant-surgeon to George III, and Lady Caroline Keppel. He was born on 24 May 1763, and was sent to Westminster School in 1773, and thence to the University of Göttingen, where George Canning, who styled him 'bawba-dara-adul-phoolah' and many other names, satirized him as falling in love with 'sweet Matilda

Sir Robert Adair (1763–1855), by Thomas Gainsborough, mid-1780s

Pottingen'. He attended Lincoln's Inn in 1780, and was called to the bar in 1785, but barely practised. Before he was twenty he was ranked among the intimate friends of Charles James Fox, and, had the whig minister gained the seals of the Foreign Office in 1788, Bob Adair would have been his under-secretary. When the French Revolution broke out, he visited Berlin, Vienna, and St Petersburg, to study its effects on foreign states, and to qualify himself for diplomatic office. He arrived in St Petersburg in June 1791. Some of his political opponents believed that he had been dispatched by Fox to Russia to thwart the policy of William Pitt, and the accusation was reproduced in 1821 in G. P. Tomline's *Memoirs of … Pitt*, which brought about an angry exchange of pamphlets between Tomline and Adair. He sat in parliament for the whig boroughs of Appleby (1799–1802) and Camelford (1802–12). He remained a loyal Foxite, drawing up a manifesto of loyalty in February 1793 and writing in the press on Fox's behalf. He became the butt of much Pittite satire.

On 7 July 1805 Adair made a disastrous marriage, to Angélique Gabrielle, daughter of the marquis de l'Escuyer d'Hazincourt. This French connection—his wife was known as 'Talleyrand's spy'—kept him out of office when the whigs returned in 1806. Fox sent him instead, without instructions, to Vienna—in fact, according to Lady Bessborough, 'pour être quitte de sa femme' (quoted in HoP, *Commons*). Adair separated from his wife and in 1809 was moved by Canning to the Constantinople embassy, from which he returned in 1810. He published memoirs of these negotiations in *Historical Memoir … of Vienna in 1806* (1844) and *The Negotiations for the Peace of the Dardanelles in 1808–9* (2 vols., 1845). He was given a pension of £2000 p.a. in 1811.

In 1828 Adair's diplomatic services were recognized by his admission to the privy council. From 3 August 1831 to July 1835 he was engaged on a special mission to the newly crowned king of the Belgians (his exertions helped to prevent a general war between the Flemish and the Dutch troops), and he visited Prussia in 1835–6. He was appointed GCB (civil) in 1831, and the success of his mission was further rewarded by the grant of the highest pension which could be awarded him. Among his other writings are reprints in 1802 and 1853 of Fox's *Letter to the Electors of Westminster in 1793*, with an application of its principle to subsequent events, and a sketch of the character of the duke of Devonshire (1811). His ability to reminisce about diplomatic and political life made him a frequent guest at the chief whig houses of London until the end of his long life, and his role as the last living Foxite came to gain him respect and applause very different from the contempt in which he had been held in his heyday. He died at 11 Chesterfield Street, Mayfair, London, on 3 October 1855, aged ninety-two. W. P. COURTNEY, rev. H. C. G. MATTHEW

Sources GM, 2nd ser., 44 (1855), 535 · HoP, Commons · Lord John Russell, *The life and times of Charles James Fox*, 3 vols. (1859–66)
Archives Bedford Office, London · BL, corresp., Add. MSS 47565, 47594, 48398–48399 · BL, corresp., Dep 3989 · PRO, accounts, FO 95/503/4 | BL, corresp. with Charles James Fox, Add. MS 51459 · BL, corresp. with Lord and Lady Holland, Add. MSS 51607–51611, 52003 · Cumbria AS, corresp. with Sir Charles Bagot · Herefs. RO, letters to Sir Harford Jones · Herts. ALS, letters to William Martin Leake · NL Scot., corresp. with second earl of Minto · PRO, corresp. with Stratford Canning, FO 352 · PRO, corresp. with Lord Granville, PRO 30/29 · U. Durham L., corresp. with second Earl Grey · U. Southampton L., corresp. with Lord Palmerston · U. Southampton L., letters to duke of Wellington · Woburn Abbey, Bedfordshire, corresp. with sixth duke of Bedford
Likenesses T. Gainsborough, oils, 1783–7, Baltimore Museum of Fine Art [*see illus.*] · G. Hayter, pen-and-ink drawing, BM

Adalbert [St Adalbert, Adalbert Levita] (*supp. fl.* **early 8th cent.**), missionary, is associated with Willibrord and venerated at Egmont, near Alkmaar in the Netherlands. He makes his earliest appearance in a life written between 978 and 993 by monks of the monastery of Mettlach near Saarbrücken. The life gives few concrete details of Adalbert, saying only that he was of English origin, a disciple of St Ecgberht and a companion of Willibrord on his mission beginning in 690 to convert the heathen Frisians. His identity is highly dubious, since there is no contemporary or near contemporary record of him.

Adalbert's life gives as much information about the family of the first counts of Holland as it does about the saint himself. They promoted his cult in order to identify themselves with a holy figure, in a way which raises the suspicion that Adalbert was not a genuine historical personality. The work tells that Dietrich I (Theodericus) founded a monastery at Egmont in 922 to which he translated the relics of the saint. His son, Dietrich II, rebuilt the church there in stone and this latter's son Egbert, the archbishop of Trier, sponsored the hagiography itself. The name Adalbert was extremely common in early medieval northern Germany and the Low Countries, and there are a number of well-attested figures who could represent the prototype for the invention of a saintly Adalbert. Most notable among these are Willibrord's successor as abbot of Echternach, called variously Albertus or Adalbertus, who is probably the 'Adalbertus abbas' who subscribed a charter of the Frankish mayor of the palace Pippin II in 714, and the Englishman Aldbercht who, with one Tyccea, addressed a letter to Lull, archbishop of Mainz, between 755 and 786. There is, however, no direct evidence connecting either figure with the Adalbert whose remains were interred at Egmont around 922.

After its initiation by the early counts of Holland, Adalbert's cult did take hold in the region of Egmont. In the twelfth century a monk of Egmont attached an account of further miracles to the tenth-century life. The story of Adalbert seems to have grown in the telling and later medieval accounts embellish the meagre details of the earliest life. At the end of the fifteenth century, Johannes de Leydis included an account of Adalbert in his *Chronicon Egmundanum*, based on the works of the fourteenth-century Egmont monk Leo and the fifteenth-century chronicler Johannes de Beka. The traditions they recorded had probably passed into oral memory at Egmont and told that Adalbert was appointed first archdeacon of Utrecht by Willibrord after his consecration in 695, that he was then dispatched to preach the gospel in 'Kennemaria' (the North Sea coastland of the Low Countries between Haarlem and Alkmaar), and that he built a church there, at Egmont. These sources also give the date of his death as 25 June, a date still celebrated as the feast day of their patron saint by the inhabitants of the region in 1709, prompting its acceptance by Henschen and Papebroch in the Bollandist *Acta sanctorum*. The idea that Adalbert was the grandson of Oswald, king of Deira, was drawn from the *Vita sancti Swiberti* by pseudo-Marcellinus, long known as a forgery. None of these late medieval traditions can be shown to antedate the foundation of the abbey of Egmont which, until its destruction by the Spanish in 1573, fostered the cult of the saint. By then Adalbert had become a part of the religious fabric of the region.

Uncertainties concerning Adalbert's identity were perpetuated by Thomas Tanner, who unjustifiably attributed some extant letters to him in his *Bibliotheca Britannico-Hibernica* (1748), and by William Smith and Henry Wace, who were misled into entering the name twice in their *Dictionary of Christian Biography* (1877) because Mabillon had listed the name under the year 740, his date for Willibrord's death. MARIOS COSTAMBEYS

Sources 'Vita Adalberti', *Acta sanctorum: Junius*, 4, 94–110 · C. Wampach, *Urkunden und Quellenbuch zur Geschichte der altluxemburgischen Territorien*, 2 (Luxembourg, 1936), no. 24 · M. Tangl, ed., *Die Briefe des heiligen Bonifatius und Lullus*, MGH Epistolae Selectae, 1 (Berlin, 1916), no. 129 · J. de Leydis, *Chronicon Egmundanum, seu, Annales regalium Abbatum Egmundensium*, ed. A. Matthaeus (1692) · pseudo-Marcellinus, *Vita sancti Swiberti, De probatis sanctorum historiis*, ed. L. Surius, 2 (Cologne, 1571), chaps. 6, 14 · W. Wattenbach, W. Levison, and H. Löwe, *Deutschlands Geschichtsquellen im Mittelalter: Vorzeit und Karolinger*, 2 (Weimar, 1953) [on the falsity of 'Marcellinus'] · Tanner, *Bibl. Brit.-Hib.* · W. Smith and H. Wace, eds., *A dictionary of Christian biography*, 1 (1877) · J. Mabillon, ed., *Annales ordinis sancti Benedicti*, 2 (1704), bk 12, chap. 65

Adalbert of Spalding. *See* Spalding, Adalbert of (*fl.* *c.*1160).

Adam [Adam the Welshman] (*c.*1130–1181), theologian and bishop of St Asaph, has on the authority of Du Boulay's *Historia universitatis Parisiensis* (1665), and of Thomas Tanner's *Bibliotheca Britannico-Hibernica* (1748), been confused with a fictitious Adam Anglicana and, even in the most recent histories of the Paris schools, with Adam of *Balsham. Yet contemporary writers, such as Walter of St Victor and Roger of Howden, who refer to him as Adam the Welshman (Walensis), leave no doubt as to his identity and to his Welsh origins.

The date of Adam's move from Wales to Paris is unknown. According to his own statement, he was provost of the schools of Peter Lombard, the most famous teacher of theology of the mid-twelfth century, to whose doctrines he adhered throughout his life. He would have begun his studies at the cathedral of Notre-Dame a few years before 1160, the year of Lombard's death; this suggests that Adam was born in the early 1130s. Gerald of Wales states that he and Adam had been good comrades and fellow scholars in Paris 'when they were rather poor and private persons' (*Gir. Camb. opera*, 1.38), without any official position. Gerald (*b.* 1146) cannot have been a Paris scholar before 1163—or, probably, a year or two later. They must have been associated for a few years after Gerald's arrival, before Adam rose in the hierarchy of the schools. His promotion to provost was followed by his nomination as a canon of the cathedral.

Some years later Adam is heard of again, in a different context. Serious trouble had broken out in the Welsh cathedral of St Asaph. In keeping with the practice of Norman kings of filling Welsh bishoprics with clergy of Norman descent, one Godfrey had been appointed bishop. According to Roger of Howden, the hostility of the Welshmen forced Godfrey to abandon his bishopric and to solicit the help of Henry II. However, Archbishop Richard of Canterbury decreed that he should return to his see or resign. Hoping in vain to be rewarded with an abbey, Godfrey resigned; whereupon, at the Council of Westminster, on 18 May 1175, the king nominated Adam as bishop of St Asaph. On 13 October 1175, 'Adam, canon of Paris' was consecrated at Westminster by the archbishop of Canterbury.

Adam's tenure was far from peaceful. Soon, in 1176, he was embroiled in a bitter fight with Gerald of Wales, then archdeacon of St David's, who in his autobiography gives a vivid account of his having to resist the bishop of St Asaph, who was trespassing on the rights of St David's by attempting to dedicate the church of Ceri, on the boundary between the two sees, but—according to Gerald— belonging of old to his own jurisdiction; the dedication was to serve Adam as pretext to seize it and the whole region between Wye and Severn. Persuasion and appeals to their companionship at Paris having failed, the dispute became more and more heated until each, at the top of his voice, excommunicated the other's party. At this stage

Gerald ordered all the bells to be rung at triple intervals and—according to his colourful account—'since the Welsh greatly dread such ringing of bells when they are rung against themselves, the bishop and his men at once broke off their sentence of excommunication and, mounting their horses, made off as fast as they could' (*Gir. Camb. opera*, 1.37). Afterwards Adam is alleged to have declared that 'he had no wish to do anything against the archdeacon who had of old been his good comrade and friend' and praised him 'because he was quick to defend the rights of his church to the best of his power'. Gerald in turn sent him some presents, 'enhancing his gift with fair words' and with an offer to welcome him in his own house and 'entertain him honourably'. This did not prevent Gerald from 'going with all speed to the king' at Northampton, to tell him 'how the bishop of Llanelwy [St Asaph] sought to seize a parish of the church of St David which was in the king's own hand during the vacancy of the see'; Gerald asked the king 'to restrain the bishop from such presumption by royal letters and messengers'. In a lighter vein he added that 'as the laity and people of Wales were thieves and ravishers of other things, so their bishops were thieves and ravishers of churches', which was greeted by laughter. Some of the listeners would have relished the fact that the man who made this remark against Adam— the Welshman—was, at least from his father's side, partly of Welsh extraction. Then the king, praising Gerald and blaming Adam, told his dignitaries the full story of their quarrel, which had reached him even before Gerald's speedy arrival. When they heard how the bishop and the archdeacon mutually excommunicated each other by name, all the courtiers 'laughed long and loud', obviously not only at Adam's expense (*Gir. Camb. opera*, 1.38–9).

There is no indication that the king complied with Gerald's request that Adam be reprimanded; on the contrary, in the following year Adam appeared on various occasions in the entourage of the king: he took part in the important meeting of the council at which Henry II acted as arbiter of the conflicting territorial claims of the kings of Castile and Navarre (March 1177), and he signed as a witness. He testified again as a witness when the king granted a new charter to Christ Church, Canterbury (April 1177), and he accompanied King Henry on his visits to Windsor and other places in May 1177.

In 1179 Adam went to Rome, with the archbishop of Canterbury and three other bishops from England, to attend the Third Lateran Council. Pope Alexander III, who convened it, had repeatedly pronounced himself against the Christological doctrine of Adam's former master, Peter Lombard, and had formally condemned it. Walter, prior of St Victor of Paris, had savagely attacked it as heretical and 'diabolic'. Adam's hope that the council would afford an opportunity of explaining Lombard's teaching, of putting it into context, proved futile. The heavy programme of administrative and political issues prevented any discussion of doctrinal matters. Certain cardinals insisted that there were more important subjects to be treated. When the pope insisted that questions of faith and of heresy be dealt with, they departed. The pope had, shortly before, in 1177, reiterated his condemnation of Lombard's Christology; Adam, realizing that a discussion was impossible, left the council, but not without boldly confronting Alexander III and declaring: 'My Lord Pope, I, once a clerk and provost of Peter Lombard's schools, shall defend the *Sentences* of the master' (Mansi, 22, col. 248). One generation later, his Paris master's doctrine of the Trinity was, in 1215, explicitly defended by the Fourth Lateran Council; and for many centuries Lombard's *Sentences* became in the teaching of the universities the most commented-upon textbook of ecclesiastical doctrine.

As several contemporary chroniclers report, Adam died in 1181 at the abbey of Osney, close to Oxford. What brought him there, far from his see, is not known. Adam is described by Gerald of Wales as haughty, headlong in his actions, garrulous, verbose, and presumptuous. Since the quality of Gerald's style is not matched by the objectivity of his judgement, little reliance can be placed on his description of an adversary. Adam's lifelong attachment to his master, and his standing up for him in dangerous circumstances, are evidence of his steadfastness and his courage. RAYMOND KLIBANSKY

Sources C. E. Du Boulay, *Historia universitatis Parisiensis*, 2 (Paris, 1665) · Tanner, *Bibl. Brit.-Hib.* · Gauthier de St Victor, 'Le *Contra quatuor labyrinthos Franciae*', ed. P. Glorieux, *Archives d'Histoire Doctrinale et Littéraire du Moyen Âge*, 19 (1952), 187–335 · P. Glorieux, 'Mauvaise action et mauvais travail', *Recherches de Théologie Ancienne et Médiévale*, 21 (1954), 179–93 · H. Denifle, 'Abaelards *Sentenzen* und die Bearbeitungen seiner Theologie', *Archiv für Litteratur- und Kirchengeschichte des Mittelalters*, 1 (1885), 407 · *Chronica magistri Rogeri de Hovedene*, ed. W. Stubbs, 2, Rolls Series, 51 (1869), 78 · *Gir. Camb. opera*, vol. 1 · *The autobiography of Giraldus Cambrensis*, ed. and trans. H. E. Butler (1937) · *Radulfi de Diceto … opera historica*, ed. W. Stubbs, 1: 1148–79, Rolls Series, 68 (1876) · *The historical works of Gervase of Canterbury*, ed. W. Stubbs, 2 vols., Rolls Series, 73 (1879–80) · J. D. Mansi, *Sacrorum conciliorum nova, et amplissima collectio*, 22 (Florence, 1778), cols. 208–17 · *Ann. mon.*, vol. 4

Adam [Adam of Caithness] (d. 1222), abbot of Melrose and bishop of Caithness, is variously described as having been a foundling and as having originated in Cumberland. He was elected bishop on 5 August 1213 when he was abbot of Melrose, the third bishop to be appointed to Scotland's most northerly diocese in the Scottish kings' long-running campaign to draw the province of Caithness more firmly under their authority. The tension which arose during the episcopacy of his predecessor, John, between the bishop and Earl Harald Maddadson over financial payments (which resulted in Bishop John's maiming), continued into Adam's episcopate and resulted in his death. On this occasion resentment was aroused by the bishop's demand for increased tithes, probably bringing traditional dues into line with Scottish practice. *Orkneyinga Saga* says he raised the teinds (tithes) of butter from one *spann* for every twenty cows, to one for every fifteen, and then to one for every ten, and it was the farmers who objected most. The annals of Dunstable, however, mention Earl John's resentment at increased demands for

hay, concerning which the bishop and earl 'had made promise to the king of Scotland' (Anderson, *Scottish Annals*, 337). The blame for the ensuing fracas was laid by the saga writer on the farmers, who led an attack on the bishop and burnt him to death in his house at Halkirk on 11 September 1222. The Dunstable annalist, however, depicts the earl as the prime mover, if not the actual murderer of the bishop, and certainly the slayer of the bishop's chaplain (named Serlo, a monk of Newbattle). Earl John bore some responsibility and had to submit, forfeiting half his earldom, while King Alexander II, on a retaliatory expedition, visited dreadful retribution on the farmers, maiming and outlawing many and confiscating their lands. Adam was first buried in the 'baptismal church' at Skinnet, but in 1239 his remains were translated to the new cathedral built at Dornoch in Sutherland by his successor Bishop Gilbert, when 'no few miracles were performed', according to the Melrose chronicles. There appears, however, to have been no move to have Adam canonized.

BARBARA E. CRAWFORD

Sources J. Anderson, ed., *The Orkneyinga saga*, trans. J. A. Hjaltalin and G. Goudie (1873) · A. O. Anderson, ed., *Scottish annals from English chroniclers, AD 500 to 1286* (1908) · D. E. R. Watt, ed., *Fasti ecclesiae Scoticanae medii aevi ad annum 1638*, [2nd edn], Scottish RS, new ser., 1 (1969) · B. E. Crawford, 'The earldom of Caithness and the kingdom of Scotland, 1150–1266', *Essays on the nobility of medieval Scotland*, ed. K. J. Stringer (1984), 25–43 · B. E. Crawford, 'Norse earls and Scottish bishops in Caithness', *The Viking age in Caithness, Orkney, and the North Atlantic*, ed. C. Batey, J. Jesch, and C. D. Morris (1993), 129–47 [Papers from the 11th Viking Congress] · W. Bower, *Scotichronicon*, ed. D. E. R. Watt and others, new edn, 9 vols. (1987–98), vol. 5 · B. E. Crawford, 'Catanensis ecclesia (Caithness)', *Series episcoporum ecclesiae Catholicae occidentalis*, ed. O. Engels and others, 6th ser., 1, ed. D. E. R. Watt (1991) · A. O. Anderson and M. O. Anderson, eds., *The chronicle of Melrose* (1936) · J. Stevenson, ed., *Chronicon de Lanercost, 1201–1346*, Bannatyne Club, 65 (1839)

Adam Anglicus (supp. *fl.* **14th cent.**), supposed theologian, is described in a treatise on the immaculate conception of the Virgin by the fifteenth-century Dominican Vincentius Bandellus as one of the notable theologians of the past, a doctor of Paris who in a commentary on the *Sentences* declared that the Virgin had been conceived in original sin. Though he avowedly draws on Bandellus, Bale prefers to call Adam 'Scholasticus' and implies, wrongly, that his source has described him as a Dominican; he also attributes to him a volume of *quaestiones* and much else, unspecified, but declares himself unable to say when Adam lived. Pits amalgamates Bale's accounts of Adam Scholasticus and Adam Wodeham and Quétif states that the two men are one and the same, while Tanner adds a further degree of confusion by identifying Bale's Adam Scholasticus with Adam of Balsham and dating him to the reign of Henry II. Commentaries on the *Sentences* by Wodeham survive in various recensions, but do not appear to contain any discussion of the immaculate conception; as a Franciscan he is in any case very unlikely to have held the views attributed to Adam Anglicus by Bandellus. The same may be said of Adam of Ely, who lectured on the *Sentences* to the Norwich Franciscans in 1337 and was known as

Adam junior to distinguish him from Wodeham. Two possibilities remain. Either Adam was an otherwise unrecorded Paris theologian, or Bandellus mistakenly attributed the forename Adam to one of the other Englishmen who taught in the Paris schools.   HENRY SUMMERSON

Sources V. Bandellus, *Tractatus de singulari puritate & praerogativa conceptionis salvatoris nostri Jesu Christi* (1481) • Bale, *Cat.*, 2.81–2 • J. Pits, *Relationum historicarum de rebus Anglicis*, ed. [W. Bishop] (Paris, 1619); repr. (1969) • Tanner, *Bibl. Brit.-Hib.* • J. Quétif and J. Echard, *Scriptores ordinis praedicatorum recensiti*, 1 (Paris, 1719), 739–40 • Emden, *Oxf.*, 3.2082 • Emden, *Cam.*, 211

Adam of Barking. *See* Barking, Adam of (*fl. c.*1176–*c.*1200).

Adam of Domerham. *See* Damerham, Adam of (*d.* in or after 1291?).

Adam of Evesham. *See* Senlis, Adam de (*d.* 1189).

Adam of Orlton. *See* Orleton, Adam (*c.*1275–1345).

Adam of Usk. *See* Usk, Adam (*c.*1350–1430).

Adam Scotus. *See* Dryburgh, Adam of (*c.*1140–1212?).

Adam the Carthusian (*supp. fl.* **1340**), supposed religious writer, appears to be the creation of John Bale (*d.* 1563), who gave a distinct and false identity to one of the names under which Adam of *Dryburgh (*d.* 1212?) was known. Of the six works that Bale attributed to Adam the Carthusian, five are now known to have been written by others. The sixth, *Speculum spiritualium*, an anonymous early fifteenth-century devotional and mystical miscellany associated with the Bridgettines and Carthusians, is found, in different forms, in at least eleven manuscripts as well as in an early edition printed in Paris and published in London in 1510. It has been attributed to Adam, a Carthusian monk, on the basis of an ambiguous entry in the contemporary index to the early sixteenth-century catalogue of the brothers' library of the Bridgettine abbey of Syon. But it seems more likely that this indicates only that Adam the Carthusian (that is, Adam of Dryburgh) is one of the authors cited in it.   W. N. M. BECKETT

Sources Bale, *Cat.* • Tanner, *Bibl. Brit.-Hib.* • J. Bullock, *Adam of Dryburgh* (1958) • A. I. Doyle and V. Gillespie, eds., *Catalogue of the library of Syon Monastery, Isleworth* [forthcoming] • N. R. Ker, ed., *Medieval libraries of Great Britain: a list of surviving books*, 2nd edn, Royal Historical Society Guides and Handbooks, 3 (1964) • A. G. Watson, ed., *Medieval libraries of Great Britain: a list of surviving books … supplement to the second edition*, Royal Historical Society Guides and Handbooks, 15 (1987) • N. R. Ker and A. J. Piper, eds., *Medieval manuscripts in British libraries*, 4 vols. (1969–92) • A. I. Doyle, 'Books connected with the Vere family and Barking Abbey', *Transactions of the Essex Archaeological Society*, new ser., 25 (1955–60), 222–43 • A. I. Doyle, 'Publication by members of the religious orders', *Book production and publishing in Britain, 1375–1475*, ed. J. Griffiths and D. Pearsall (1989), 109–23 • C. B. Rowntree, 'Studies in Carthusian history in later medieval England, with special reference to the order's relations with secular society', DPhil diss., University of York, 1981 • devotional miscellany, Bodl. Oxf., MS Douce 322 • devotional miscellany, BL, MS Harley 1706 • *Speculum spiritualium* (Wolfgang Hopylius, Paris, 1510)

Archives BL, MS Harley 1706 • Bodl. Oxf., MS Douce 322

Adam, Alexander (1741–1809), schoolmaster and classical scholar, was born on 24 June 1741 at Coats of Burgie, a

Alexander Adam (1741–1809), by Sir Henry Raeburn, *c.*1805

small farm in the parish of Rafford, Moray, the youngest child of the large family of John Adam (*d.* 1758), tenant farmer, and Christian Watson. He was taught to read in a local dame-school before attending the parochial school in Rafford, where he was taught Latin by the schoolmaster George Fiddes. He usually studied in the early morning by the light of splinters of bogwood while his mother and her maids spun wool. Before he was fifteen he taught briefly at Edinkillie School, and in the winter of 1756–7 he stood in for the master at the school at Alves, who was studying at Aberdeen University. Despite his failure to win a bursary from Aberdeen University in 1757 and his family's worsening finances he was encouraged to persist with his studies, and early in 1758 he walked to Edinburgh, where his mother's relative James Watson, minister of Canongate, arranged free admission to the university logic class. He lived very frugally on an income of 4 guineas a year, which he made from teaching a few private pupils, until spring 1760, when he was appointed headmaster of George Watson's Hospital. He re-established discipline in the school but reluctantly left in November 1763 because he wanted more time for his own studies. He became tutor in the family of the printer Alexander Kincaid, later lord provost of Edinburgh.

In April 1765 Adam was invited to take Mr Matheson's class at Edinburgh high school on account of the rector's ill health. He continued to assist Matheson after he returned to the school, and in the summer of 1767 was appointed joint-rector with him, having passed several gruelling examinations. In the following year he was appointed rector, following Matheson's retirement, but he continued to give half his salary to Matheson, who returned in 1769 to give private tuition and remained at the school until his death, in April 1799.

Adam successfully managed a school of some 400 boys by devising a methodical two-year-long curriculum that he and his four assistant masters taught. His own class averaged over 100 pupils yet he appears to have maintained discipline with a light hand. He was extremely conscientious as a teacher and devoted long hours of study in preparing for his lessons. Among his pupils were Walter Scott, Thomas and Charles Dundas, Francis Jeffrey, Henry Brougham, and Francis Horner. Another of his more illustrious pupils, Henry Cockburn (later Lord Cockburn), wrote of Adam's skill as a master:

> Never was a man more fortunate in the choice of a vocation. He was born to teach Latin, some Greek, and all virtue. In doing so he was generally patient, though not, when intolerably provoked, without due fits of gentle wrath; inspiring to his boys, especially the timid and backward; enthusiastically delighted with every appearance of talent or goodness; a warm encourager by praise, play and kindness; and constantly under the strongest sense of duty.
> (Memorials … by Henry Cockburn, 5)

Adam's headship, however, was not without controversy. His introduction of Greek into the curriculum brought him into conflict with the Edinburgh University authorities, who argued that he was infringing the privileges of the professor of Greek, at that time Robert Hunter but soon afterwards Andrew Dalzel. A more serious dispute erupted when Adam started using his own Latin grammar in the school. He had written *The Principles of Latin and English Grammar* after observing how grammar was taught abroad on a trip to France in 1771; unlike previous grammars—such as Thomas Ruddiman's, which was in use in the school—Adam's was in English rather than in Latin. The town magistrates, many of whom were closely connected with the university, refused to approve Adam's grammar, and his masters continued to use Ruddiman's. A compromise was reached in 1785 whereby both grammars were accepted for use in the school. In spite of these battles Edinburgh University awarded Adam the degree of LLD on 9 August 1780. His grammar was republished many times, in both British and American editions, as *The Rudiments of Latin and English Grammar*.

On 26 August 1775 Adam married Agnes (Nansie) Munro at Kinloss, where her father was minister. They had three children, the eldest of whom, Alexander, died young. In 1780, following Nansie's death, Adam married Jane (*b*. 1751), the daughter of Walter Cosser, the controller of excise in Edinburgh, and his wife Agnes Wilson; they had two daughters and one son. To provide for his growing family Adam taught private pupils; he never allowed himself holidays and devoted his free time to his own studies. In 1791 he published *Roman Antiquities, or, A Description of the Manners and Customs of the Romans*, a compendium intended for students of Latin literature. He was paid £600 for the copyright and the work was translated into German, French, and Italian. He published other educational works: a volume of classical biography, a Latin dictionary,

and *A Summary of Geography and History, both Ancient and Modern* (1794; 6th edn, 1824).

Adam was an energetic man who rose early, took brisk walks up Arthur's Seat, and was economical in his habits; characteristically he wore a shabby brown jacket when teaching. He was a thoroughgoing whig in politics and attracted criticism in the 1790s for lecturing his pupils on the principles of liberty, democracy, and republicanism. His school continued to thrive, and in his final term there were 167 boys in his class. On 13 December 1809, four days after the death of his son James Adam, he was seized by an apoplectic fit while teaching his class; he died five days later at his house in George Square. His dying words were addressed to an imaginary class: 'But it grows dark, boys—you may go; we must put off the rest till tomorrow' (Henderson, 166). He was buried at St Cuthbert's on 29 December 1809 after a public funeral at the school.

J. B. PAUL, *rev.* S. J. SKEDD

Sources A. Henderson, *An account of the life and character of Alexander Adam* (1810) · W. Steven, *The history of the high school of Edinburgh* (1849) · *Memorials of his time, by Henry Cockburn* (1856) · will, NA Scot., 70/1/2, 394–404 · IGI
Archives NRA Scotland, priv. coll., corresp. and MSS
Likenesses H. Raeburn, oils, *c*.1805, Scot. NPG [*see illus.*] · C. Turner, mezzotint, pubd 1808 (after H. Raeburn), BM, NPG
Wealth at death approx. £11,500

Adam, Sir Charles (1780–1853), naval officer, was the second son of William *Adam (1751–1839), of Blairadam, Kinross, and of Eleanora (1749–1808), daughter of the tenth Lord Elphinstone, and sister of Captain Elphinstone, afterwards Admiral Lord Keith. John *Adam (1779–1825), administrator, and Frederick William *Adam, army officer, were two of his siblings. He was born on 6 October 1780, and entered the navy at an early age, under the patronage of his uncle, with whom he continued to serve in the Mediterranean and at the capture of the Cape of Good Hope. In 1795 Keith sent him to the *Victorious* (74 guns) as acting lieutenant and he remained on the East India station until 1802. In June 1799 he was made captain, and appointed to the frigate *Sybille*, in which, on 19 August 1801, in difficult circumstances and with intricate navigation, he captured the French frigate *Chiffonne* in Mahé roads, in the Seychelles. He was appointed in May 1803 to command the *Chiffonne*, and served in her under Lord Keith in the North Sea, taking part in the blockade of Boulogne and the north coast of France through the summer of 1805. In 1811–13 he commanded the *Invincible* (74 guns) in operations on the coast of Spain.

After the peace Adam was appointed captain of the royal yacht, a post which reflected his father's service in the household of the prince of Wales. He left this post in May 1825, when he was promoted rear-admiral; he became vice-admiral in 1837 and admiral in 1848. In August 1835 he was made KCB. Adam sat as MP for Kinross in 1831–2 and for Clackmannan and Kinross from 1833 to 1841. He was married to Elizabeth (*d*. 1871), daughter of Patrick *Brydone; among their children was William Patrick *Adam, politician and Indian administrator.

Adam served for seven years as first naval lord—in

November–December 1834, between April 1835 and September 1841, and finally from July 1846 to July 1847. He worked closely with his brother-in-law Gilbert Elliot, earl of Minto, and his friend Henry Eden, Lord Auckland. Modern accounts of his period in office have been heavily influenced by the memoirs of Sir John Briggs, then a junior Admiralty official, which were more concerned with the picturesque and eccentric aspects of senior naval officers than their abilities. Yet even Briggs observed that Adam was a man of sound judgement. Moreover, he was a trusted colleague of the foreign secretary, Palmerston, with whom he formed a good working relationship. Adam presided with tact and judgement over a half-decade in which the naval estimates reached their lowest point in the nineteenth century, and the brief but spectacular Syrian campaign of 1840. Although the Minto Admiralty board of 1835–41 was entirely whig in politics, and largely dominated by the Elliot faction, it functioned well and was responsible for Sir William Symonds's improved battleship designs, the construction of significant numbers of powerful steam warships, and the critical decision to adopt Francis Pettit Smith's screw propeller. Between August 1841 and May 1845 Adam was commander-in-chief in the West Indies. His return to the Admiralty in 1846 was a sop to Minto, who had been excluded from office by Lord Lansdowne's faction, and reflected a severe shortage of competent senior admirals of whig politics. It ended when Adam took his reward with the prestigious retirement post of governor of the Royal Naval Hospital, Greenwich. He died there on 16 September 1853.

Adam was a noteworthy senior naval lord. If his party loyalties precluded serious opposition to the low estimates of the era, themselves more a feature of the failure of whig economic policy than political choice, he made good use of those funds that were available. As the Syrian campaign of 1840 demonstrated the Royal Navy remained unequalled as a force for upholding British interests after half a decade of his professional stewardship.

J. K. LAUGHTON, rev. ANDREW LAMBERT

Sources NMM, Minto MSS · NL Scot., Minto MSS · The Keith papers, 1, ed. W. G. Perrin, Navy RS, 62 (1927) · The Keith papers, 2–3, ed. C. Lloyd, Navy RS, 90, 96 (1950–55) · Selections from the correspondence of Admiral John Markham, ed. C. Markham, Navy RS, 28 (1904) · A. D. Lambert, The last sailing battlefleet: maintaining naval mastery, 1815–1850 (1991) · J. H. Briggs, Naval administrations, 1827 to 1892: the experience of 65 years, ed. Lady Briggs (1897) · W. James, The naval history of Great Britain, from the declaration of war by France, in February 1793, to the accession of George IV in January 1820, 5 vols. (1822–4) · C. N. Parkinson, War in the eastern seas, 1793–1815 (1954) · O'Byrne, Naval biog. dict. · GM, 2nd ser., 40 (1853), 528

Archives NRA Scotland, priv. coll., corresp. and papers | BL, letters to Lord Wellesley, Add. MS 13760 · NA Scot., letters to James Loch · NL Scot., letters to Lord Minto · NMM, letters to Lord Minto

Likenesses bust, 1885; originally in Painted Hall, Greenwich Royal Naval Hospital · G. Hayter, group portrait, oils (The House of Commons, 1833), NPG

Adam, Sir Frederick William (1784–1853), army officer, was born on 17 June 1784, the fourth son of the Rt Hon. William *Adam (1751–1839), privy councillor, lawyer, and lord lieutenant of Kinross, from Blair Adam, and his wife, the Hon. Eleanora Elphinstone (1749–1808) from Elphinstone Tower, near Stirling, second daughter of Charles Elphinstone, tenth Lord Elphinstone. Adam had a sister, Clementina, and four brothers: John Elphinstone [see Adam, John (1779–1825)], Charles [see Adam, Sir Charles (1780–1853)], William George (1781–1839), and Francis. On 5 November 1794 he joined John and William as a boarder at Charterhouse School, London. He appears in the Army List as an ensign in the 26th foot (4 November 1795), then lieutenant (2 February 1796); and he served, on attachment, with the 27th foot for the expedition to The Helder, fighting in actions on 27 August, 19 September, and 2 October 1799, and securing a captaincy in the 9th foot on 30 August. Having transferred to the Coldstream Guards as lieutenant and captain on 8 December 1799, he went with Lieutenant-General Sir Ralph Abercromby's 1801 expedition to Egypt, taking part in the opposed landing on the 8th, the skirmish on the 13th, and the battle of Alexandria on 21 March. On his return from Egypt he spent a year studying German in Dresden. He became a major in the 5th battalion of reserve (9 July 1803) and brevet lieutenant-colonel (28 August 1804), then joined the 21st foot as one of three lieutenant-colonels (5 January 1805).

On 27 July 1806 Adam landed in Sicily in command of the regiment's 1st battalion, which subsequently joined Major-General Alexander Mackenzie's unsuccessful attempt to seize Alexandria during the summer of 1807. The following year he commanded the battalion during an abortive British attack on the mainland castle of Scylla. In the night of 17–18 September 1810, 4000 French troops began landing on Sicily, south of Messina. At dawn, with the 21st, men of the German legion, and two field guns, Adam drove the invaders back to their boats and overwhelmed an isolated detachment, capturing 850 prisoners and a French colour. Lieutenant-General Sir John Stuart, the commander-in-chief, expressed his 'sincere thanks for your conduct … for your attack on the enemy and the gallant manner in which you made them surrender' (Buchan, 156). Adam became aide-de-camp to the prince regent on 8 February 1811, and went on leave for most of that year, in which he married Amelia, only daughter of Stephen Thompson. His wife died in 1812 at Messina, however, shortly after giving birth to their daughter, also Amelia (d. 1839).

On advancing to colonel, on 20 February 1812, and being appointed deputy adjutant-general in Sicily, Adam relinquished command of his battalion. A few months later he led a brigade under Lieutenant-General Sir John Murray against the French in Alicante, eastern Spain. Faced by overwhelming enemy forces at Biar on 12 April 1813, Adam was wounded in a stubborn rear-guard action, but successfully fell back to Castalla, where next day he helped to drive off persistent French assaults. Following the capture of Tarragona, Lieutenant-General Lord William Bentinck, now in command, deployed Adam in advance of the main body at the pass of Ordal. There his unsupported brigade was overrun on 12 September 1813, with Adam suffering a broken left arm and shattered left hand, 'ever after mutilated and powerless' (Reumont, 20), which caused him to be invalided home. Promoted major-general (4 June 1814), Adam led the 3rd brigade in Lieutenant-General Sir Henry Clinton's division, comprising battalions of the 52nd, 71st, and 95th regiments at Waterloo. In the early stages of the battle his brigade was positioned on Wellington's right flank to discourage an enemy outflanking movement. At 11 a.m., he wrote prophetically to his father: 'It is believed we shall have a general action this afternoon' (NRA, 9954). Towards 5 p.m. the brigade did move forward to high ground north-east of Hougoumont, where it came under spasmodic attack from skirmishers, cavalry, and field artillery. When the imperial guard launched Napoleon's final assault against the Mont St Jean-Ridge in the evening, Adam's brigade, spearheaded by the 52nd, decisively struck the French columns from the flank as they wavered in the face of frontal fire from the brigade of guards. At about 8.30 p.m., with pursuit of the retreating enemy under way, Wellington pointed to French artillery dangerously positioned on a low ridge ahead: 'Adam, you must dislodge those fellows' (Pakenham, 578). His brigade duly obliged, though not before its commander had been severely wounded. In Wellington's subsequent dispatch, he 'particularly' mentioned Adam 'for His Royal Highness's approbation' (Siborne, 831).

In 1815 Adam was appointed KCB, and became a knight of the Austrian order of Maria Theresa and the Russian order of St Anne, both first class. Two years later he took command of all troops stationed in the Mediterranean (excluding Gibraltar). During the spring and early summer of 1818 he visited archaeological sites in and around Athens, travelling also to Morea and Albania. On 23 June 1820 he married, secondly, Diamantina Palatino (d. 1 June 1844), former wife of Count Souffis, on Corfu, where he served as lord high commissioner of the Ionian Islands from 1824 to 1832. In office he maintained neutrality during Greece's struggle for independence from Turkey, deploring 'acts of positive and unquestioned piracy in our own Channel' by Greek privateers and ordering troops to protect a shipwrecked Turkish crew from molestation by the pro-Greek inhabitants of Zante. On 22 February 1831 he admitted to Charles, though, that 'my recent occupation has been an irksome and a laborious one' (NRA, 9954). In May 1832 Adam also wrote unenthusiastically on his appointment as governor of Madras: 'Indeed, papa, you cannot do otherwise than accept, for if you do not you will not have the offer of anything else'; and his pessimism was soon confirmed. Within a year, he declared 'how little I like either the country or the duties of my office' (ibid.), but he remained in Madras until 1837, despite suffering the 'first attacks of the malady which terminated his life' (Reumont, 52). After leaving India, Adam lived in Rome until Diamantina's death. Initially holding the local rank in the Ionian Islands from 10 February 1824, Adam advanced to substantive lieutenant-general on 22 July 1830. The following year he became a privy councillor and in 1833 received the GCMG. Meanwhile, appointed colonel of the 73rd foot (22 May 1829), he moved in the same

capacity to the 57th (4 December 1835), and to his old regiment, the 21st (31 May 1843). Adam was nominated GCB on 20 June 1840, and promoted general on 9 November 1846. On 24 July 1851 Adam married his third wife, Anne Lindsay (d. 1904), daughter of John Maberley (d. c.1840)—army contractor, manufacturer, banker, and MP for Rye (1816–18) and Abingdon (1818–32)—and the following year their son Charles Fox Frederick was born. Returning from a visit to his brother Admiral Sir Charles, governor of Greenwich Hospital, Adam died suddenly of apoplexy on Greenwich railway station on 17 August 1853. At the time of his death he was serving on the board of general officers with overall responsibility for the administration of army clothing.

The duke of York, when commander-in-chief of the army, described Adam as 'an intelligent and distinguished officer' (Fortescue, Brit. army, 10.240); and, in his history of the Royal Scots Fusiliers, John Buchan concluded that 'Adam may well rank as one of the most distinguished sons of the regiment' (Buchan, 196). Sir William Napier's stricture 'that whoever relies on the capacity of Sir Frederick Adam either in peace or war will be disappointed' (Fortescue, Brit. army, 9.381) was evidently coloured by a clash between Adam and the historian's brother Charles in the Ionian Islands. Of striking appearance, upright, with 'snow-white' hair from an early age, clear blue eyes, and 'the most pleasing smile', socially Adam had 'the utmost courtesy, the kindest manner, the most amiable gentleness in conversation' (Reumont, 55). He was, nevertheless, a strict military disciplinarian.

JOHN SWEETMAN

Sources Army List · A. von Reumont, Sir Frederick Adam: a sketch (1855) · report no. 9954, NRA, priv. coll. · J. Buchan, The history of the royal Scots fusiliers, 1678–1918 (1925) · E. Longford [E. H. Pakenham, countess of Longford], Wellington, 2 vols. (1969–72); pbk edn (1971–5) · W. Siborne, The Waterloo campaign, 1815 (1895) · W. S. Moorsom, ed., Historical record of the fifty-second regiment (Oxfordshire light infantry), from the year 1755 to the year 1858 (1860) · W. J. P. Aggett, The bloody eleventh, 2 (1994) · Fortescue, Brit. army, vols. 9–10 · E. A. Brett-James, The 100 days (1964) · C. Dalton, The Waterloo roll call, 2nd edn (1904); repr. (1971) · R. L. Arrowsmith, ed., Charterhouse register, 1769–1872 (1974) · HoP, Commons · GEC, Peerage · Boase, Mod. Eng. biog. · Burke, Peerage (1967)

Archives BL, corresp., Add. MSS 49112–49113, 49120, passim · NA Scot., journals, accounts, letters · NRA Scotland, priv. coll., corresp. and papers · Bykelty, Fife, Blair-Adam MSS | BL, corresp. with Sir William A'Court, Add. MSS 41535–41536 · BL, corresp. with Lord Bathurst, loan 57 · NL Scot., letters to Lord Melville · NMM, letters to Sir Edward Codrington · PRO, corresp. with Stratford Canning, FO352 · U. Nott. L., corresp. with Lord William Bentinck

Likenesses P. Proselendis, bronze statue, c.1835, Corfu · W. Salter, group portrait, oils, 1836, Wellington Museum, Apsley House, London · W. Salter, oils, NPG · G. F. Watts, crayon drawing, repro. in Buchan, History of the royal Scots fusiliers, 156 · photograph, Blair-Adam MSS · photograph, repro. in Belgium News and Continental Advertiser (17 June 1893)

Adam, George (fl. 1826–1828), journeyman carpenter and trade unionist, is a figure about whose personal life nothing is known. He became one of the leaders of a group of radical artisan trade unionists in London who campaigned for political reform, workers' education, and legislation in the interests of labour over strikes, wages, machinery, and free trade. The chief episode which brought them together was the agitation led by John *Gast (c.1772–1837) in 1825, opposing the reimposition of penal legislation against trade unions; the delegate organization formed in the course of it went on to found the *Trades' Newspaper*, the world's first trade union newspaper.

By the mid-1820s Adam was secretary of the First Society of Carpenters, and in 1827 was one of the chief architects of the new Friendly Society of Operative Carpenters and Joiners, usually known as the General Union of Carpenters, the first national union in that trade. Late in 1826 he was elected to the committee of the London Mechanics' Institute, where he led the criticism of the steady exclusion of working men from an effective say in its management. At the same time he was elected on to the committee of management of the *Trades' Newspaper*, of which he became the leading figure until, as the *Trades' Free Press*, it was sold in December 1827. In 1827 he was also secretary of the Mechanics' Anti-Bread Tax Association campaigning against the corn laws, and took a leading part in meetings organized by John Gast in favour of a tax on machinery to slow down the pace of mechanization and provide funds to relieve those thrown out of work by it.

From these activities emerged the General Association, in which Adam was active in 1828 in favour of a general union of the artisan trades and in organizing support for the striking Kidderminster carpet weavers. With Gast he was also active on a committee of delegates of the London benefit societies which campaigned successfully against a bill introduced into parliament to restrict and control their activities. He was subsequently a member of the twelve-man committee that proceeded to draw up a bill of its own, which was passed into law in 1829.

IORWERTH PROTHERO

Sources I. J. Prothero, *Artisans and politics in early nineteenth-century London: John Gast and his times* (1979)

Adam, James (1732–1794). *See under* Adam, Robert (1728–1792).

Adam, James (1860–1907), classical scholar and philosopher, born on 7 April 1860 at Kinmuck in the parish of Keithhall near Inverurie in Aberdeenshire, was second child and only son of James Adam and his wife, Barbara Anderson. The father owned the general store and tailor's shop which served the neighbouring countryside; he died of typhoid fever when his son was only eight. His mother by her own energy carried on the business, and brought up her six children. He made rapid progress at the parish school of Keithhall under George Kemp MA, and having spent some months at the grammar school of Old Aberdeen won the third bursary at Aberdeen University in October 1876. Though chiefly interested in Greek, Adam took a good place in most of the classes of the arts course. His devotion to Greek was fostered by the professor, William Geddes. In 1880 he graduated with first-class honours in classics and carried off the chief classical prizes and the Ferguson scholarship. Meanwhile in spring 1880 he had

been elected classical scholar at Gonville and Caius College, Cambridge. In summer 1882 he was placed in division one of the first class in the classical tripos, part one. In 1883 he just missed the Craven scholarship, but in 1884 was awarded the first chancellor's medal and obtained a specially brilliant first class (only once equalled) in part two of the classical tripos with distinction in classics, ancient philosophy, and comparative philology.

In December 1884 Adam was elected a junior fellow and was soon appointed classical lecturer of Emmanuel College, where he settled down at once to his life's work as a teacher. During his undergraduate career at Cambridge he had concentrated with increasing enthusiasm on the study of Plato, and for the rest of his life some work of Plato (most frequently the *Phaedo* or some books of the *Republic*) was usually the subject for one of the two courses of intercollegiate lectures. Aristotle's *Ethics*, Lucretius, Cicero's *De finibus*, and above all the Greek lyric poets were also frequent subjects. His lectures were full of wit as well as learning, and however mystical some might consider his philosophical views, there was no lack of precision in his scholarship.

Throughout his teaching career Adam took classes with rare intermissions at Girton College, and was a keen supporter of the claims of women to degrees, when the question came before the senate of the university in 1897. He married, on 22 July 1890, one of his Girton pupils, Adela Marion (1866–1944), youngest daughter of Arthur Kensington, formerly fellow and tutor of Trinity College, Oxford. They had two sons and a daughter. Adela Adam taught classics at Girton and Newnham colleges and became a research fellow of Girton (1920–23).

Adam regarded a knowledge of Greek as an essential part of university education, and he resolutely opposed all attempts to make Greek an optional subject of study. At Easter 1890 he visited Greece. In the same year he was appointed joint tutor of his college with William Napier Shaw, and in 1900, the number of tutors having been mean time increased, he succeeded Shaw as senior tutor. His relations with pupils and colleagues were kindly and affectionate, while his efficiency as a lecturer proved of great benefit to the college. The changes in the classical tripos, which came into force in 1903, emphasized the importance of ancient philosophy, and the college hall was barely able to hold the numbers that flocked to Adam's lectures on Plato and Aristotle.

In 1887, inspired probably by his closest friend, Robert Alexander Neil, Adam published his first edition of a Platonic dialogue, the *Apology*. This was followed by the *Crito* in 1888, the *Euthyphro* in 1890, and (in conjunction with his wife) the *Protagoras* in 1893. In 1890 he had announced an intention of preparing an edition of the *Republic*. In 1897 he published a revised text. This, however, differed in many passages from the large edition in two volumes which appeared after many years of labour in 1902, and immediately took its place as the standard edition. Adam's notes and excursuses, which are very concise considering the difficulty of the subject, represent a judgement based upon a thorough knowledge of the vast work of his many predecessors. The outstanding quality of his translations and notes is reflected in the longevity of his scholarly work: a second edition of his *Republic* was published in 1962 and of his *Protagoras* in 1971.

In textual matters Adam became steadily more conservative, believing that the tradition of the Platonic text was in the main quite sound. An investigation preliminary to his edition of the *Republic* was a discussion in his *Platonic Number* (1891). His interpretation was confirmed by Professor Hilprecht's discovery of the Babylonian perfect number. At Christmas 1902 he was nominated Gifford lecturer at Aberdeen, choosing for his subject 'The religious teachers of Greece', and delivering the lectures in 1904 and 1905.

In spring 1907, Adam, who, amid his unceasing work, retained his youthful appearance in middle age, was attacked by illness. He died on 30 August 1907 at 5 Albyn Place, Aberdeen, after an operation, and was buried at Woking.

The Gifford lectures, which were left complete but not finally revised for publication, were edited with a short memoir by Adam's widow and published in 1908 (2nd edn, 1909). A collection of his essays and lectures, *The Vitality of Platonism, and other Essays*, was edited by his widow in 1911. These collected papers best illustrate the bent of Adam's mind in later life. For many years he had been deeply interested in the relationship between Greek philosophy and the New Testament. Though he would not have said with Westcott that 'the final cause of Greek was the New Testament', he certainly tended to regard Greek philosophy pre-eminently as a 'Praeparatio evangelica', and his occasional lectures on such semi-religious topics at summer meetings in Cambridge found large and appreciative audiences. Witty and paradoxical in conversation, though with a vein of melancholy in his nature, Adam found fullest scope for his abilities as a teacher, and to education in the highest sense all his work as lecturer and writer was devoted.   PETER GILES, *rev.* MARK J. SCHOFIELD

Sources J. Adam, *The religious teachers of Greece*, ed. A. M. Adam (1908) [ed. with a memoir by A. M. Adam]; 2nd edn (1909) · personal knowledge (1912) · private information (1912) [family] · Venn, *Alum. Cant.* · m. cert. · K. T. Butler and H. I. McMorran, eds., *Girton College register, 1869–1946* (1948)
Archives King's AC Cam., letters to Oscar Browning
Likenesses photograph, Emmanuel College, Cambridge
Wealth at death £10,920 3s. 7d.: probate, 8 Oct 1907, *CGPLA Eng. & Wales*

Adam [Adams], **Jean** (1704–1765), poet, was born on 28 April 1704 in Cartsdyke, near Greenock, Renfrewshire, one of five children of John Adam, a mariner, and his wife, Jean Eddie, reportedly a woman of little common sense. Jean Adam's scanty education comprised reading, writing, and sewing, but after her father's death when she was still young she entered domestic service with the minister of West Kirk, Greenock, where she was encouraged to read—not only religious works, from which she acquired a reputation for piety and the knowledge of Calvinist theology manifest in her verse, but also Milton's poems and translations of the classics.

Later Adam kept a day school, reputedly at the quay head at Cartsdyke (36 Main Street), where she is said to have lived in the family home bequeathed to her and her sister Ann by her grandfather William Adam, a shipmaster. According to a former pupil, Mrs Fullarton, whose reported recollections of Jean Adam provide the principal source of information, she 'treated her pupils with great tenderness, and was much beloved by all of them'. She often sang her own songs, and once read *Othello* to them 'with uncommon pathos', finding the ending so affecting that she fainted away. Another time she announced that she was going to walk to London to pay her respects to Samuel Richardson out of admiration for *Clarissa*; she is said to have completed the journey there and back in six weeks. She was inspired to write poetry while eking out her income by 'assisting at needlework' in the house of Mr Dennistoun of Colgrain in Dunbartonshire; there she discovered and became 'intoxicated' by Sidney's *Arcadia*, which 'roused her latent powers of rhyme into activity' (Williamson, 265).

Adam's *Miscellany Poems* was published in 1734, with the aid of a Mr Drummond, collector of customs and excise in Greenock, who retrieved her scattered manuscripts and helped raise a subscription. Customs officers figure numerously among the 123 subscribers, others include the laird of Cartsburn, Thomas Crauford (to whom the book is dedicated), wig makers, a coppersmith, and other artisans. The volume contains eighty poems, mainly on religious and moral subjects, two of them ('The Happy Pair' and 'The Pinnacle of Diana's Temple') showing traces of Sidney's influence. Her name is given on the title-page in the Anglicized form Jane Adams, and the text is in strict English. She defends the plain diction of her poems by saying they 'had Truth enough, to Compensate for the Want of Ornament' (*Miscellany Poems*, sig. A2v). At their best they are vigorously expressed and display a fervent imagination, but not the realism or vivacity of the vernacular song, 'There's nae luck about the house', for which Jean Adam is best known. This piece, described by Burns as 'one of the most beautiful songs in the Scots, or any other language' (Cromek, 1.67), is attributed to her by local tradition, corroborated by Mrs Fullarton, who frequently heard her recite it and claim it as her own. It has also been ascribed to W. J. Mickle on circumstantial evidence and his widow's testimony, but after exhaustive consideration of all the factors, Alexander Rodger argues compellingly that the language and content of the song weigh strongly in support of Jean Adam's claim.

Adam's later career was unprosperous. *Miscellany Poems* failed commercially, and she squandered her savings by shipping a large consignment of copies to Boston, Massachusetts, where they remained unsold. She gave up her school some time after 1751, and made a precarious living as itinerant needlewoman and domestic worker, on one occasion after 1760 arriving destitute at Mrs Fullarton's house. She died in Glasgow's Town's Hospital (a workhouse) on 3 April 1765, having been admitted the previous day on the recommendation of baillies at Greenock as 'a poor woman, a stranger in distress' who 'for some time has been wandering about' (Cromek, 1.195); she suffered the final humiliation of a pauper's burial.

KARINA WILLIAMSON

Sources parish register, Greenock West, Renfrewshire, 1704 [baptism] · R. H. Cromek, ed., *Select Scotish songs, ancient and modern*, 2 vols. (1810), 1.67–70, 189–99 · A. Rodger, *Jean Adam of Cartsdyke: her authorship of the ballad 'There's nae luck about the house', vindicated* (1866) · S. Tytler and J. L. Watson, *The songstresses of Scotland*, 1 (1871), 21–48 · G. Williamson, *Old Greenock from the earliest times to the early part of the nineteenth century* (1886), 143–4, 264–6 · *Miscellany poems. By Mrs Jane Adams in Crawfordsdyke* (1734), sigs. A–A2v · *The visitor, or, Literary miscellany*, 2 vols. (1818), 2.263–74, 293–308 · [W. Motherwell], *The harp of Renfrewshire* (1819), xxi–xxv · J. Donald, *Old Greenock characters* (1920), 192–3 · G. Stronach, 'Who wrote "There's nae luck aboot the hoose"?', *The Dunedin Magazine* [4 page offprint] (Nov 1913) · A. Cunningham, ed., *The songs of Scotland, ancient and modern*, 3 (1825), 303–4 · G. F. Graham, ed., *The songs of Scotland*, 3 vols. (1848), 2.159–60 · A. Brown, *The early annals of Greenock* (1905), 46
Wealth at death see Cromek, ed., *Select Scotish songs*

Adam, John (1721–1792), architect, was born in Edinburgh. He was the eldest of the four sons of the entrepreneur and architect William *Adam (*bap.* 1689, *d.* 1748) and his wife, Mary Robertson (1699–1761). He attended Dalkeith grammar school. His father's sudden death in 1748 propelled him into the main stream of Scottish life during the Edinburgh Enlightenment. Like his father, he was a strong supporter of the Union and the immediate advancement of his career owed much to the patronage of the duke of Argyll and his political associates. He succeeded William Adam as master mason to the Board of Ordnance and from that position undertook the building and rebuilding of the highland forts after the Jacobite rising of 1745. It was a lucrative business and the profits, especially from Fort George, Inverness (1748–69), paid for the grand tours of his brothers Robert *Adam and James *Adam [*see under* Adam, Robert].

Adam took over several commissions and clients from his father, notably work at Hopetoun House, Linlithgowshire (1750–54), and he reworked the paternal designs for Dumfries House, Ayrshire (1754–9), Yester, Haddingtonshire (1758–61), and Arniston, Edinburghshire (1754–8). His construction in Edinburgh of the royal exchange (1756–61) was perhaps his most notable achievement as a public architect. In all of these he refined and tamed his father's baroque style and at Dumfries House produced an almost textbook example of the Palladian villa, repeated confidently and independently at Moffat House (1761–3). His imagination also extended to the Gothic and he worked in both manners at Inveraray for the duke of Argyll (1751–60) and more strikingly at the vast, symmetrical castle built, but not finished, for the duke of Douglas at Douglas (1757–61). He engraved these and other designs by his father and brothers for a book that appeared posthumously as *Vitruvius Scoticus* in 1811. Behind all such work was considerable learning and interest in architectural theory, both of which were apparent in the large library he put together at Blair Adam, Kinross-shire, the family home. It was here that he indulged his enthusiasm for landscape gardening by laying out in the 1760s The Hill and The Glen in the informal style with a ruined castle,

John Adam (1721–1792), by James Tassie, 1791

decayed bridge, and Gothic towers. However, his increasing financial difficulties after the failure of Fairholme's Bank in 1764 and the troubles of William Adam & Co., in which he was a partner, at the Adelphi put an end to such ambitious schemes. These led directly to the attempted sale of the Blair Adam estate as well as his Edinburgh villa at North Merchiston.

Adam more or less gave up his practice at the end of the 1760s, though he continued with his business interest in the Carron ironworks of Falkirk and with property development in Edinburgh, especially at the eponymous Adam Square (1763–4), and elsewhere. He died on 25 June 1792 and was buried in the Adam mausoleum in Greyfriars churchyard, Edinburgh: 'Firm in adversity, not elated in prosperity'. He left a widow, Jean, *née* Ramsay (1721–1795), daughter of John Ramsay, merchant of Woodstone, Kincardineshire, with whom he had a son, the politician William *Adam (1751–1839).

A. A. TAIT

Sources Colvin, *Archs.* · W. Adam, *Blair Adam*, 5 parts (1834) · [A. A. Tait], *Robert Adam at home, 1728–1978: drawings from the collection at Blair Adam* (1978) [exhibition catalogue, West Register House, Edinburgh] · A. A. Tait, *The landscape garden in Scotland* (1980) · J. Fleming, *Robert Adam and his circle: in Edinburgh and Rome* (1962) · W. Adam, *Vitruvius Scoticus*, ed. J. Simpson (1980) · D. King, *The complete works of Robert and James Adam* (1991); repr. (2001), appx C ['Works done by John Adam on his own'] · *Catalogue of the library at Blair Adam* (1883)
Archives Mount Stuart Trust, Isle of Bute, corresp. and papers relating to Dumfries House · NA Scot., papers · NA Scot., plans and papers relating to house at Balnagown · NRA, priv. coll., corresp. and papers · Blair Adam, Kinross-shire, family archives | BL, corresp. with G. Loch, Add. MS 40865
Likenesses J. Tassie, medallion, 1791, NPG [*see illus.*] · F. Cotes, portrait, Blair Adam, Fife

Adam, John (1779–1825), administrator in India, was the eldest son of William *Adam (1751–1839) and Eleanora Elphinstone (1749–1808), second daughter of Charles, tenth Baron Elphinstone. His brothers included Charles *Adam, naval officer, and Frederick William *Adam, who served in the army. He was born in Edinburgh on 4 May 1779, was educated at Charterhouse School and, following his nomination to a writership in Bengal in 1794, spent a year at Edinburgh University. He arrived in Calcutta in 1796 and subsequently spent the greater part of his career there in military and political administration. He was private as well as political secretary to the marquess of Hastings, whom he accompanied in the field during the Anglo-Maratha War of 1817–18.

In 1819 Adam took up a seat on the governor-general's council and from January to August 1823 he served as acting governor-general during the interregnum between the administrations of Lord Hastings and Lord Amherst. His seven months in power were active ones. He added four regiments to the Bengal army, enlarged the judicial establishment, assigned an annual grant of 100,000 rupees to Indian education, and appropriated Calcutta's town duties for public works in the city. He also withdrew official support from the banking firm of Palmer which had exerted a destabilizing influence over the nizam of Hyderabad. Adam's administration achieved notoriety, however, for deporting to England James Silk Buckingham, publisher of the satirical *Calcutta Journal*, and for introducing legislation restricting criticism of government measures by the press. Buckingham, afterwards an MP and founder of *The Athenaeum*, failed to win immediate redress but in later life was awarded a pension by the East India Company in recognition of its shabby treatment of him.

Adam's health had long been poor, but he delayed his departure for England to see Amherst settled into office. He sailed in March 1825 but died on 4 June off the coast of Madagascar. His reputation for charitable and principled behaviour had won him much respect in Calcutta. His portrait was painted by George Chinnery for the Calcutta town hall and a monument to his memory in St John's Church, Calcutta, was raised by public subscription.

KATHERINE PRIOR

Robert Adam (1728–1792), attrib. George Willison, *c*.1770–74

Sources J. J. Higginbotham, *Men whom India has known: biographies of eminent Indian characters*, 2nd edn (1874) · *The Bengal obituary, or, A record to perpetuate the memory of departed worth*, Holmes & Co. (1848) · C. Lushington, *A short notice of the official career and private character of the late J. Adam, Esq.* (1825) · East India Company documents, BL OIOC, Haileybury MSS · A. T. Pringle and others, *List of the private secretaries to the governors-general and viceroys from 1774 to 1908* (1908)
Archives BL OIOC, Home misc. series, corresp. relating to India, corresp. and papers · Cleveland Public Library, Ohio, letters · JRL, corresp. relating to Pindaree War · NAM, corresp. · NRA, priv. coll., corresp., journals, and papers | BL, Wellesley MSS · BL OIOC, letters to Lord Amherst, MS Eur. F 140 · BL OIOC, corresp. with Mountstuart Elphinstone, MS Eur. F 87–89 · BL OIOC, letters to Sir T. Monro, MS Eur. F 151 · Bodl. Oxf., corresp. with Sir Henry Russell · U. Leeds, university archives, earl of Harewood MSS · University of Keele Library, Raymond Richards MSS
Likenesses C. Turner, mezzotint, 1829 (after T. Lawrence), BL OIOC · G. Chinnery, oils; originally in Calcutta town hall · T. Lawrence, portrait; originally in Government House, Calcutta
Wealth at death small, as 'barely to yield him a competencey': *Bengal obituary*, 25–7

Adam, Robert (1728–1792), architect, was born at Kirkcaldy in Fife on 3 July 1728, the second son of William

*Adam (*bap.* 1689, *d.* 1748), architect, and his wife, Mary Robertson (1699–1761), the daughter of William Robertson of Gladney. He was educated at the high school of Edinburgh and in 1743 matriculated at Edinburgh University, which he left in 1745–6 to join his father's architectural office. His younger brother, **James Adam** (1732–1794), architect, was born at North Merchiston, Edinburgh, on 21 July 1732, and was also educated at Edinburgh University, where he matriculated in the autumn of 1751, and was part of the firm by 1754. He died, unmarried, at 13 Albemarle Street, London. His elder brother, John *Adam (1721–1792), also an architect, is noticed separately.

Scotland Robert Adam and his brother James were notable products of the great eighteenth-century force of the Scottish Enlightenment, an intellectual fraternity which included the historian William Robertson, David Hume, and Adam Smith, all of whom moved in the close Adam circle. Its characteristics of logic and common sense, independence, curiosity, and pragmatism were mixed in Adam's case with less cerebral emotions and a strong visual sense. During his time at the university Adam probably attended one of the local drawing schools, for he then had ambitions to be a painter. This was balanced by the influence of his father's extensive library which had been assembled at the family home of Blair Adam in Fife. Apart from the conventional histories and classical texts, there was a working collection of illustrated architectural books in English, French, and Italian, and a series of manuals on architectural draughtsmanship. Possibly the most visually stimulating part of the library was a small collection of prints, mostly Dutch and many of landscapes:

these encouraged Adam in his more sophisticated experiments in composition and perspective. Several of his copies after Gaspar Dughet and Marco Ricci were made in the 1750s and remain in volume 56 of the Adam volumes in Sir John Soane's Museum, London.

On William Adam's death in 1748 Robert Adam went into partnership with his elder brother, John, undertaking the building and rebuilding of the highland forts after the conclusion of the Jacobite rising of 1745. These projects brought to Scotland a team of draughtsmen from the Board of Ordnance which included the brothers Paul and Thomas Sandby. Though the board was concerned principally with the repair and expansion of the existing system of forts such as forts William and Augustus, it was professionally connected with the Adam family; they as royal master masons, were the contractors for the building of the ambitious Fort George, outside Inverness. Mapping and recording such installations was part of the programme and Paul Sandby's composite sheet of plans and views of Duart Castle, of 1748, exploited the Picturesque qualities of the castle and its setting. This Picturesque style greatly influenced Adam: the Sandbys taught him the artistic potential of the ruin and also the drawing and wash technique necessary to transfer it successfully to paper. This aesthetic education was balanced by his more practical experience at Fort George, where paper drawings were swiftly turned into masonry and joinery work. Moreover as an eighteenth-century fort, it was the culmination of a military tradition stretching to antiquity and offered the imaginative Adam a visual overview of the history of forms and functionalism. His castle apprenticeship gave Adam an insight into the origins and survival of such archaic forms as the battlement and turret and the adaptability of others, such as the fosse, which had evolved into the ha-ha of garden architecture. Much of this consciousness of tradition appeared in the small pen drawings he made around 1752, probably while he was at Fort George; the conservative cast of these designs fits well with the character of the major architectural work undertaken by the brothers at Hopetoun House, near Edinburgh, where they continued to work in the style introduced by their father when he gained the commission in 1725.

Italy The next critical stage in the development of Adam and his brother James was their Italian tours of 1755–7 and 1760–63 respectively. Robert departed for Italy in 1754 to undertake a modified and idiosyncratic form of the grand tour, and reached Rome in 1755; it was in every way a period of intense professional training during which the skills learned in Scotland were tested and given an international gloss by the Roman circle in which he now moved. The intellectual centre of this new world was the French Academy in the Palazzo Mancini on the Corso. This Francophone group was dominated by Charles-Louis Clérisseau, pensionnaire until 1754, who provided Adam with associates such as Jean-Baptiste Lallemand, Laurent-Benoit Dewez, and the architect–engraver G. B. Piranesi. In more practical terms Clérisseau was the visual force behind Adam's travel book *The Ruins of the Palace of the Emperor Diocletian at Spalatro* (1764), in which the style of the architectural views was very much of his making. For the more formal aspects of his training, especially for figure drawing, Robert Adam took lessons in one of the Roman drawing academies, that of Pompeo Batoni, a portrait painter with a large British clientele (he later painted James Adam in 1763). In following such an individualistic training—more that of the talented dilettante than the professional artist—both Adam and, later, his brother James were careful to be seen as amateurs who collected, saw the sights, and took professional drawing lessons. Robert wrote candidly to his family in Scotland that he was certain that 'my being an artist if I am discovered to be such may do me hurt' (Clerk of Penicuik MSS, GD 18/4806), and he was prepared to invent a family history and role to support gentlemanly pretensions—'A good lye well timed does well' (ibid., GD 18/4807). Such dilettantism was reinforced in his tour to Naples and the adjoining antique sites, which he and Clérisseau made in the April of 1755. It was Clérisseau, as the traditional cicerone, who established the itinerary and the sites to be sketched, and each day he and Adam produced at least three acceptable views, often of the same scene, despite the hot and humid weather. The same route was again followed visually and factually in 1761, when Clérisseau took James Adam to the area. The sites visited and drawn were largely those by Clérisseau that appeared in the later engravings of the Abbé de Saint Non, *Le antichiti di Pozzuoli, Baja e Cuma*, in 1769. James Adam's own rather dull account of the tour was published anonymously in *The Library of the Fine Arts*, in 1831.

In the composition of architectural scenery Robert Adam was in the hands of Lallemand. Instruction seems to have been by imitation and variation, after using Lallemand's chalk drawings as source material. His crumbling terraces and overgrown villa gardens, often filled with fragments of antiquity, were copied and collected by Adam throughout his Roman period. His association with Lallemand was complemented by time spent with Dewez, studying basic architectural composition. Three years Adam's junior and probably 'much attached' to the circle around the Roman office of the architect Luigi Vanvitelli, Dewez proved to be such an able and agreeable companion that Adam took him to London with him in 1758. His method of teaching seems to have been based on theme and variation: a simple geometric shape was chosen and developed by both men with as much attention paid to technique as to composition. A run of such compositions remains in the Soane Museum, notably in Adam volume 55. Much of this work suggests a meeting of like minds rather than a conventional pupillage arrangement in which copying the classical orders and their details was the rule. A third and rather less professional member of this loose group was Piranesi, who powerfully influenced Adam's vision of the past. His ideas, later expressed in his *Parere su l'architettura* (1765), on the importance of the freedom of the unfettered imagination were ones which Adam shared, though the drawings he made alongside Piranesi fell short of the latter's brilliant invention.

London During these two Roman years Adam succeeded in transforming himself from a provincial and rather green Scottish architect into a cosmopolitan figure, ready indeed to put into effect 'the Antique, the Noble & Stupendous' (Clerk of Penicuik MSS, GD 18/4764). There was no question of a return to the Scottish practice of John Adam in Edinburgh and he settled down in London, arranging around himself his collection of pictures and antique fragments which advertised his taste and judgement and through them the Adam style. The practice itself was housed in Lower Grosvenor Street and remained there until its removal in 1772 to Royal Terrace in the great Adam development besides the Thames, the Adelphi. The opening years of the office, that is the period until James Adam returned from Rome in 1763 and became a partner in the practice, set a pace and style which lasted into the mid-1770s. The new, post-Roman style was reflected in the drawings of the period: here the rococo classicism, seen in the interiors of his work at Hatchlands, Surrey (1758–61), and Shardeloes, Buckinghamshire (1759–63), of the early 1760s, quickly gave way to a more complex and obviously antique manner as Adam's often imported draughtsmen watered down the style demanded by the brothers. Of these émigré figures Giuseppe Manocchi was possibly the most significant: although his association with it was short (1765–6), he decisively introduced stronger and bolder colours to the London office. The use of dark backgrounds for Adam's Etruscan style in the interiors of Derby House, London, Osterley Park, Middlesex, and Home House, London, may be traced back to him. Such enthusiasm for colour elevated it to an essential element in the Adam interior, where it assumed a role as vital as that of the pilaster or cornice. Indeed, the fusion of such elements was continued on the exterior of his buildings, where the delicate relief sculpture echoed (if it did not repeat) the interior. In certain instances, as at Harewood House, Yorkshire, and Kenwood House, Hampstead, Adam managed by this continuity of decoration to bind together buildings where his contribution was not the only one. This hallmark of the Adam style became one of the major targets of critics of the brothers' work.

The Works in Architecture of Robert and James Adam *The Works in Architecture of Robert and James Adam* appeared in several sections between 1773 and 1778 and were reissued as two volumes in 1786 with a third, posthumous, volume in 1822. The book marked a decisive watershed in the Adam practice and the brothers' careers. The comparative failure of their speculative building venture at the Adelphi and the adverse attention it attracted made it necessary for the brothers to rehabilitate their reputation and reassess their future. This was the role of *The Works*, setting out what had been achieved and planning what was to come. The Adelphi, begun in 1768, was a huge speculative scheme to build an elevated terrace of twenty-two private houses, with the space below let as warehouses, adjacent to the north bank of the Thames. The national credit crisis of 1772 led to its abandonment and to near financial ruin for Adam. The period of the 1770s was difficult: as Adam candidly admitted in April 1780, 'For some time past

the very particular state of affairs in this country, has prevented the expensive Art of Architecture from being cultivated as it was formerly. So that my brother and I have for many months found ourselves far from being fully employed' (Clerk of Penicuik MSS, GD 248/3395/1). *The Works* had to an extent anticipated such a situation and was published to encourage the expansion of the practice and to set out new directions to be followed. The plates themselves broke new ground: they showed individually a mixture of furniture, chimney-pieces, and decorative details set out in the form of a balanced composition, and this novel form was strengthened by the changing sequence of the prints themselves, from flat elevation to deep perspective. There could be no more effective advertisement for the Adam style, where movement, variety, and irregularity of plan and elevation were all subsumed in the evocative spirit of the Picturesque. Such a spirit was to characterize the later Adam practice, where a distinction was made between what Adam termed the architectonic (basic architecture) and the wider-ranging, more associative style of the Picturesque.

Architectural work Adam's work in the thirty years of the practice after 1760 was more or less evenly divided between his roles as a country house and a town architect. Apart from the different settings, the grand town house and the country house shared much the same purpose as a centre for the display of wealth and conspicuous consumption: Norfolk House, Northumberland House, and Devonshire House were not unlike some country mansion come to town, though they all presented a strong contrast with the more humdrum terrace house found in the smaller London squares. However, even the dullest terrace block could in Adam's hands be transformed into some Parisian palace quarter, as was demonstrated in Charlotte Square, Edinburgh, or in his more complex schemes for Portland Place, London. It was with them in mind that the arch Georgian revivalist Sir Albert Richardson wrote that 'Robert Adam became a master of elevational design: he could make several frontages look like a single palace and could produce the effect of a dominant idea when called upon to design a house in the midst of others' (Richardson, 86). It was in them that Adam effected the most brilliant part of his revolution, fully publicized in *The Works*.

The town house Adam's most brilliant exercise in manipulating the internal space of the terrace house was Derby House in Grosvenor Square. Built in 1728 (dem. 1861) and acquired by Edward Stanley, eleventh earl of Derby, in 1750, it was a typical town house; it had a parlour–drawing room downstairs with a first and second front room and drawing-room above. Little of this could be changed, so Adam was faced in 1773 with remodelling a narrow building, a task which required imagination and ingenuity in equal parts. The original two front rooms were probably bedrooms, as in most houses in the square; Adam moved them to the rear, arranged on two floors. These became the private apartments of Lord and Lady Derby, one above the other, connected by their own stair and with Adam's mezzanine for a servant between them. Here he was reworking his designs for Wynn House in St James's Square of two years earlier (extended 1936). In such arrangements, as Adam freely admitted, he was adapting the grander system of the contemporary French *petits appartements*, where a distinction was made between private and public rooms and the intimate and formal. He combined the French concept of the *enfilade* (succession of rooms) with the traditional English circuit, popular since the 1730s, where the staircase led to an interconnected group of reception rooms. Because of the narrowness of Wynn House and Derby House as terrace constructions, the Adam circuit was irregular and asymmetrical and produced what may be termed a Picturesque plan.

In several ways the plans of Derby House and Wynn House followed from Adam's earlier commission at Lansdowne (originally Shelburne) House, where he and James Adam had collaborated from 1762 until about 1771. Begun for John Stuart, third earl of Bute, who sold it before completion to William Petty, second earl of Shelburne, it represented the alternative to the terrace house in its scale and almost rural setting at the bottom of Berkeley Square. It was further distinguished as a building in that Adam had started it from scratch. His design was for a large villa with short, contracted wings, a three-bay Greek Ionic centrepiece and with the principal rooms, including the huge library (never finished), all on the ground floor with bedrooms above in the true villa tradition. The arrangement of the bedrooms of Lord and Lady Lansdowne, one above the other, was repeated on a more intimate scale at Wynn House and Derby House.

In terms of their contribution to eighteenth-century architecture there can be little doubt that Derby House and Wynn House and the interiors of Home House (1773) in Portman Square set a new standard of brilliance, movement, and informality. The relatively small sites of such buildings made demands upon Adam's ingenuity and capacity to create a space which satisfied the same fastidious society which crossed the more ample threshold of Lansdowne House. His very success in devising such interiors ensured his damnation in the nineteenth century. As early as 1821 the classical architect C. R. Cockerell dismissed Adam as 'not an artist of any force nor of very sound judgemt', whose

> plans are a labyrinth. He did not acknowledge the effect of the vista nor the good sense of it. In the obvious & palpable disposition of the house your way is never direct sometimes sideways like a crab, sometimes thro' alcove or corner you come into a magnificent room you know not how.
> (D. Watkin, *C. R. Cockerell*, 1974, 60)

Country houses Robert Adam's country house practice was large and varied. He worked in England, in Scotland, and in Ireland at Headford (1772–5) and Castle Upton (1788–90). But for all his energy and ambition, he failed to build the great country house of his Roman dreams. His early commissions for Osterley, Harewood House, Yorkshire, and Kedleston Hall, Derbyshire—however grand—were all for remodelling or adapting the works of others: at Harewood, John Carr of York, at Kedleston, James Paine

and Matthew Brettingham. At Witham Park, Somerset, work on a new house came to an end with the sudden death of William Beckford, lord mayor of London, and even at Syon House, Middlesex, Adam's thorough reconstruction of the courtyarded interior was radically curtailed. Perhaps his grandest house was Luton Hoo of 1766 for the prime minister, the third earl of Bute. Here Adam incorporated what remained of an earlier building into his uncompromisingly neo-classical design. Yet even this prize eluded his grasp and the house was never fully completed. Instead, a late work, Gosford House, East Lothian (begun in 1791; now much altered), remains as virtually the best example of a large and original country house by Robert Adam.

In the most typical of Adam's early country houses of the 1760s there was a strong expression of the orthodox Palladian villa, popular in the opening decades of the century and exemplified by Lord Burlington's Chiswick House, London. Mersham-le-Hatch, Kent, and Witham Park, both begun in 1762, showed contrasting solutions to the form of block and flanking wings, derived from Palladio in the 1630s and revived by the early eighteenth-century Palladian architects. Mersham reflected this type in perhaps its starkest form, underscoring the more self-conscious academicism of the double pediments and Diocletian windows of the much grander Witham Park. Such compositions make a dramatic contrast with both Adam's early villa designs of the 1750s, where such restrained classicism was absent, and his villa compositions towards the end of his career. His triangular-plan villa at Walkinshaw, Glasgow, of 1791 (dem. 1927) was typical of these and perhaps came closest to the European neo-classicism of Claude-Nicholas Ledoux, Friedrich Gilly, and Gianantonio Selva. Walkinshaw was based on the small design which Adam had produced in 1789 for a guard house to his Register House (1774) in Edinburgh: the source for both plans probably lay in the geometric designs in Jean François de Neufforge's *Recueil élémentaire d'architecture* (1757–77), one of several French treatises that Adam owned.

The importance of patronage from the earl of Bute for Adam's early career is often overlooked; Adam relied throughout his life on his Scottish connections and remained loyal to them. At a time when Bute was bitterly unpopular Adam bravely publicized in *The Works* his gratitude for the earl's protection and friendship. As well he might: Bute had provided Adam with the key commission for Lansdowne House in 1762, as well as Highcliffe Castle, Hampshire (1773), improvements at South Audley Street, London, and of course Luton Hoo. He had also ensured that Adam was appointed, with Sir William Chambers, as royal architect in 1761, and it was to Bute that James Adam looked to realize his scheme for the rebuilding of the Houses of Parliament, on which he had laboriously worked in Rome in 1762–3. In much of this the Adam brothers were disappointed and in 1774 Luton was still incomplete, although this was disguised in *The Works*. The plates there showed none of the existing house and instead set out, especially in elevation, a building almost aggressive in its severity and simplicity and considerably more advanced stylistically than Kedleston or Harewood. The disappearance of much of Adam's house after the fires of 1821 and 1843 and its rebuilding in the twentieth century virtually eliminated one of Adam's most important buildings and much of his standing as a neo-classical architect.

Picturesque style The change of direction in the Adam practice during the mid-1770s stemmed partly from Adam's enthusiasm for the Picturesque. During the 1770s and the following decade he explored—through his countless wash and watercolours—how this literary and visual movement could find an effective architectural expression. This interest he shared with James Adam, who had succeeded his brother as architect of the king's works in 1769. He also developed an interest in agriculture, acquiring an estate in Essex in the 1770s and publishing the prosaic and down-to-earth *Practical Essays on Agriculture* in 1789, with a further edition in 1794. Robert Adam began to experiment more ambitiously with the complicated relationship between a building, its setting, and a sense of history. Typical of this was his scheme for an office court at Brampton Bryan in Herefordshire (1777), cast as an abandoned and decayed Roman camp, and the equally extraordinary office court proposed for Kirkdale, Kirkcudbrightshire, in 1789. Even though such drawings do not always relate to an identifiable commission, they illuminate Adam's visual thinking and give the source for his cottage and lodge designs, and the hybrid and revival styles of his country houses. Possibly the most extreme creation of this Picturesque phase was Adam's clifftop castle at Culzean in Ayrshire (1777). It stands isolated on a promontory, reached only by a causeway viaduct, in a ruined castle style, which served as a viewing platform for the surrounding informal landscape. The asymmetrical form and the mixture of classical and Gothic details on the castle's exterior reflected similar ideas to those with which Adam had experimented in his designs for The Oaks in Surrey (1777). In theoretical terms such buildings belonged to Richard Payne Knight's 'mixed style', explained in his later *An Analytical Inquiry into the Principles of Taste*. Adam's interiors at Culzean were classical and of these the oval double staircase and circular drawing-room, with its seaward views, were a remarkable expression of the Picturesque ideal. None of the other seaside castles, such as Highcliffe or Seaton, East Lothian (1790), matched this marriage between setting, plan, and elevation.

It is essential to appreciate both the discipline and the range of Adam's mature Picturesque style. It left behind the Chinese and various extravagances associated with the rococo, and offered instead a sustained meditation on the fundamental themes of Western architecture, represented for Adam in the classical and Gothic styles, which he saw as integral parts of the same continuous tradition rather than as conflicting forces. His vision of classicism extended from the Antique to the Renaissance and the cinquecento, and he grasped the often subtle evolution of the style. He sought a common ground between his designs in the style of Michelangelo for Luton, his grotesque work after Raphael's Vatican Loggie, and the newly discovered forms at Herculaneum. The same flexibility was apparent in his Gothic, which developed from classical military forms into the Romanesque and the Scottish vernacular. Whether he worked in a medieval or a classical idiom, Adam tempered his archaeological learning to achieve a stylistic originality: no one confused his south front of Kedleston with a Roman triumphal arch and no one was expected to confuse Culzean with a Welsh castle such as Harlech. At Alnwick Castle, Northumberland, in the 1770s, where he replaced James Paine, a clear and unmistakable distinction was drawn between his work in a late Gothic style and the surviving medieval work.

Public architecture In his introduction in 1764 to *The Ruins of the Palace of the Emperor Diocletian* Adam wrote that 'Public buildings are the most splendid monuments of a great and opulent people.' He felt too that such commissions were a judgement on an architect's career, and his own comparative lack of success was a source of bitter disappointment. Matters had opened well enough for him with his joint appointment with Chambers as architect of the king's works in 1761. This should have led to greater things but, apart from minor works on the royal palaces, his most important commission was the Admiralty screen of 1760 and the remodelling of the paymaster-general's house (1771), both in Whitehall. He was effectively excluded by Chambers from work at the royal palaces at Richmond and Windsor; the plum official commission at Somerset House went to Chambers as well. To fill this vacuum Adam resorted to speculative building and to the expansion of his Scottish practice. His work in Edinburgh on the Register House of 1774, and later at the university (1789), Bridewell prison (1791), and the South Bridges scheme (1790), and in Glasgow on the infirmary and university (1790s), all came towards the end of his career and were completed by James Adam after 1792. In the speculative field, his ambitious rebuilding of whole quarters of London, at the Adelphi (1768–72), Portland Place (1776–90), and Fitzroy Square (1790–94), and in Scotland at Charlotte Square, Edinburgh (1791), all showed what Adam could achieve independent of 'princely patronage'. In his bid for extending King's College, Cambridge, and the adjoining university library (1788) he attempted to manipulate the college's finances so that his scheme—'one of the best & most simple of my inventions'—might be undertaken (A. Doig, *The Architectural Drawings Collection of King's College, Cambridge*, 1979, 31).

Adam's virtual exclusion from official patronage had less to do with the failure of influence than with his reputation as a poor administrator, especially weak in the area of finance. The repercussions of the relative failure of their enterprise at the Adelphi, where Adam was saved by an act of parliament promoting a lottery—using unfairly, it was thought, his position as member of parliament for Kinross-shire (1768–74)—the further unattractive lawsuit over the Liardet patent (for the composition of stucco) of 1774 turned such influential figures as his patron Lord

Lansdowne against him. There was the growing acceptance in professional circles that he lacked sound financial judgement, indicated by the sales from the Adam collections of 1773 and 1785. Earlier his client at Harewood had ominously warned that everything should be done properly 'mais pas trop'; at Brasted, Kent, in 1788, the villa cost £9500, instead of the agreed maximum of £5000. As Adam candidly admitted, he had 'an abhorrence of all manner of calculations' (Innes and Clerk MS 3070, Guildhall Library, London).

Churches and theatres Church architecture was a further branch of public building; unfortunately, the scale and number of commissions offered in Britain was significantly less than in other major European (and Catholic) countries. Here again Adam's patronage was limited and the most eye-catching—and quite deliberately so—of his churches was at Mistley in Essex (1776). Like all Adam's ecclesiastical buildings, it was conceived more for its scenographic impact than for its effectiveness as a religious building. The interior of the rectangular structure of 1735 was taken over and little changed by Adam, apart from galleries added to take an increased congregation from the expanded resort. The addition of the twin towers to the east and west, and twin porticoes at the north and south, were all designed for the external spectator rather than the devout. The church was to mark the centre of the new spa town, to catch the eye from the sea and country, and provide a dramatic silhouette from the windows of the remodelled house of his client Richard Rigby. The same emphasis on the church as a landmark was evident in his larger but incomplete scheme for the Edinburgh church of St George's in Charlotte Square. The church was planned to close the vista down George Street in much the same fashion as his Register House terminated a similar view from the university, on the edge of the Old Town. In all of them, and as at Mistley, he used the theme of a Pantheon-style dome and campanile, though much of the vigour of his design for St George's (1791) was lost in the adapted scheme of 1811. When the church was opened three years later, the *Scots Magazine* unhelpfully remarked that 'It is certainly a pity that the Adam design was not used' (J. Gifford, *Buildings of Scotland: Edinburgh*, 1984, 291).

The same scenographic element was strongly and appropriately present in Adam's work as a theatre architect. His scheme for the Haymarket Opera House, London, of around 1789 was perhaps the most ambitious and complex of his later public buildings. No design showed better his mastery of space, his sense of movement, and his capacity for variety than this projected building. Adam quite deliberately contrasted, in the surviving drawings in the Soane Museum, the different public spaces. The green room and the tavern were domestic in comparison with the scale of the assembly room and public auditorium. Such an expression of variety was continued in the long façade to the Haymarket, in which five palace fronts moved restlessly back and forward to emphasize the asymmetry of the composition. In some ways the sheer invention of these designs was a return to Adam's Roman

studies of the 1750s and a studied contrast with the subdued monumental elevation of his Lincoln's Inn scheme of 1772. Adam was reviving here his youthful boast to build 'such a palace as Inigo [Jones] would stare at with amazement: make Palladio look blanc, & make the Nation wonder' (Clerk of Penicuik MSS, GD 18/4815). If Lincoln's Inn evoked legal gravitas, the opera house, in the liveliness of its decoration and the rapidity of movement, reflected the theatre.

The opera house was Adam's swansong as an architect of public buildings in London. That it was never realized can hardly have cheered him in his final years. His disappointment was perhaps tempered by public works in Glasgow and Edinburgh, where something of his grandeur of temperament was stamped on the neo-classical enclaves he gave to both cities. He wrote of his Edinburgh University commission that 'Though the Money is no indifferent object to me, I am conscious I have been infinitely more activated by the motive of leaving behind me a monument of my talents, such as they are, than by any hope of gain whatever' (A. G. Fraser, *The Building of Old College*, 1989, 96).

Office In all of the Adam brothers' work little could have been achieved without the effective support of a well-organized office. Such an office turned projects into buildings, trained future draughtsmen and architects, such as Joseph Bonomi and George Richardson, and housed the reference collection of drawings which is now in the Soane Museum. Located in Lower Grosvenor Street, the office was established immediately after Robert Adam's return from Rome in 1758; he was joined there by James Adam in 1764. The years of 1758–9 were critical. Adam had originally intended to bring Clérisseau back with him from Rome '& give him the Inspection of our Drawing Room, & so put things in perspective & make views of all the principal places in England & get him to oversee anything one intends to publish' (Clerk of Penicuik MSS, GD 18/48 11). This did not happen, and instead Adam had to make do with Agostino Brunias and Laurent-Benoit Dewez, who were a far cry from his Roman establishment, where he had 'three or four lads constantly working for me'. With Dewez's defection from the office in 1759, Adam had only one experienced draughtsman at his disposal. The difficulties of the situation were candidly discussed in a letter of November 1758 to James Adam, where an employee imported from John Adam's office in Edinburgh was seen as lacking the 'least fire or ambition to become equal to his Neighbours as he never touched a pen but in the Drawing room where he was quite awkward & insufferably slow' (Clerk of Penicuik MSS, GD 18/4853). The situation changed for the better by about 1767, when there were between ten and twelve clerks at least in the office, under the direction of Robert Morison, one of Adam's experienced draughtsmen. Such an office was not a cheap concern, for any reasonable draughtsman was paid about £40 per year, with boarding running to an additional £40. Both Bonomi and Richardson, Adam's right-hand men, were paid between £40 and £60 p.a. during their period in the office in the 1760s and 1770s. To put these sums in perspective, Adam paid his copyist in Rome a shilling a day.

Two of Adam's most distinguished Italian imports to the office were Antonio Zucchi, who returned with James Adam, and Giuseppe Manocchi, another James Adam protégé, who appeared on the payroll in 1765. Both were decorative artists and each had a quite specific influence on both the office and the Adam style. Manocchi was the important colourist, Zucchi a figure artist whose sphere of work extended from arabesque to the iconographical figures in Adam's roundels and panels, and even the frontispiece of *The Works in Architecture* itself. Of the decorative painters employed by the office, G. B. Cipriani had an early involvement with both Adam and Chambers, Peter Borgnis with the later Adam office, and Biagio Rebecca with James Wyatt and Henry Holland as well as Adam. The speculative building element of the Adam practice involved Daniel Robertson, Robert Morison, and John Robertson, the office clerk during its final years in 13 Albemarle Street. In all aspects of drawing Adam demanded a recognizable degree of uniformity from his assistants, and encouraged them to develop within the strict confines of the Adam style. The brothers were proprietorial about their designs: all office drawings were Adam property and office drawings were signed as such. It was this collection, magnificent in its range and intimacy, which appeared privately on the market after the suicide of William Adam (1738–1822), the youngest brother of Robert and James.

The Adam collection of drawings The idea of disposing of the drawings collection surfaced in 1802 and sales from it were made in the more general Adam auctions of 1818 and 1821. The death of William Adam left the entire collection in the hands of Adam's niece Miss Clerk. Some time between her arrival in London to act as a housekeeper for William Adam in 1810 and his death in 1822 the collection was catalogued and insensitively arranged according to type in at least fifty-four volumes, although two of them, volumes 7 and 26, contained specifically drawings by and collected for James Adam. The whole was offered for sale to the British Museum in 1822 and turned down. At this point the collection was described by Miss Clerk as comprising fifty-four large folios, 'a great number of them beautifully finished & coloured'. She added perceptively:

> But what is reckoned more valuable than any of the furnished drawings, is an infinite number of sketches of all the different kinds of buildings, decoration & furniture. I have mentioned a great number of them in black chalk & though evidently hastily done, they show in a still greater degree the fertility & variety of Mr Adam's genius. (Tait, 'The sale', 453)

The significance of the sketches was again emphasized in the correspondence about the Edinburgh sale of 1833, where it was stressed that the collection was notable for 'sketches of first ideas—working plans of various designs—& drawings of innumerable Chimney Pieces, Ceilings & ornaments of all sorts—many of which are coloured in the way they were to be executed' (ibid.). Sir John Soane was approached in early 1832 to buy the collection

but declined, largely because he had not fully established his architectural museum in Lincoln's Inn. After he did so in 1833 with a private act of parliament, there was a rapid expansion of his collecting activities, which included the purchase of the Adam collection: there was at the time considerable fear that the collection would be acquired by a bookseller who 'we believe intended to break up & disperse the collection for profit' (I. G. Brown, 'Robert Adam's Drawings', *Book of the Old Edinburgh Club*, 1992, 31). In preserving the collection Soane showed the same understanding of architectural drawing and the complementary nature of the collection at which Miss Clerk had hinted. Such an understanding was not universal: as late as 1912 Reginald Blomfield wrote in his *Architectural Drawing and Draughtsmen* that the drawings were not 'particularly stimulating, nor are they suggestive. Nothing is left to the imagination; everything is finished with laborious completeness, and the effect is depressing and even paralysing' (Blomfield, 79–80).

Last decade Adam's principal London enterprise during the last decade of his career was the development of Fitzroy Square (1790–94); he built little of significance in England beyond London after his work at Mistley in Essex in the 1780s. His energies were mainly directed towards Scotland, where he enjoyed a healthy country-house practice as well as several public commissions in both Glasgow and Edinburgh. Not only did his country-house practice bloom there in the 1780s, but his visual imagination too was clearly drawn back to his Scottish roots, as his Picturesque compositions hauntingly demonstrate. The scenery and castles which he had sketched with the Sandby brothers some thirty years earlier were revived and reinvented in these watercolours. In the same spirit, the conceptual grandeur of the Adelphi scheme was repeated in his urban developments in Glasgow and Edinburgh, compensating for the lost opportunities of the Haymarket Opera House, London, of about 1789, and at Lincoln's Inn, where Sir Robert Taylor was preferred for the expansion of 1774–80.

Adam's account book for the year 1791–2 has survived in the National Archives of Scotland, Edinburgh. It demonstrates the energy he showed in directing buildings virtually across the breadth of Scotland, while his base remained in Albemarle Street in London. It was virtually a one-man operation, for James Adam had little to do with the practice in the 1780s, a situation summed up by his sister in 1792, when she wrote 'about the different articles of business which Jamie is a stranger to as he lived so much in the country & had not an opportunity of knowing much of what was doing in the architecture part of the business' (Clerk of Penicuik MSS, GD 18/4961). A price was paid: Robert Adam had been ill in 1787 and in 1789, suffering from 'the complaint in his stummach, which has been so long a tiresome complaint to him' (ibid.). It proved fatal three years later, on 3 March 1792. William Adam wrote to the family in Scotland from 13 Albemarle Street, where Robert died, describing the death scene straightforwardly:

> he sleeped very composedly the first part of the night but all at once the vein opened up again. Then at 4 oclock this

morning when he threw up a vast quantity of blood that weakened him to that degree he appeared then to be quite gone, his pulse being totally gone, he however recovered again but in so low & exhausted a state that he only struggled for life in very great Pain till 2 oclock when he became quiet & went off very easily.   (Clerk of Penicuik MSS, GD 18/4972)

Adam, who was unmarried, was buried privately in the south side of Westminster Abbey: his pall-bearers—the duke of Buccleuch, earl of Coventry, earl of Lauderdale, Viscount Stormont, Lord Frederick Campbell, and Mr Pultene—testify to Adam's patronage and gift for friendship.

It can be accepted that Robert Adam was a man of great charm and ability, both of which were sufficiently deep to inspire loyalty and respect in all circumstances. His leading draughtsman, Joseph Bonomi, spoke kindly of him when perhaps he had little reason to do so, his contemporaries compared him favourably with the pompous Chambers. Nothing could possibly be more in his favour than a letter written by one of his clients (at Brasted in Surrey) in 1788, when he had received a bill for virtually double the estimated cost for his modest country house. The client, Dr John Turton, wrote that:

I have ever admired you as an ingenious, I have ever esteemed you as an honest man. You have been woefully mistaken in your calculations. You have led me into difficulties, but it never hath, or I trust will shake my good opinion of you—I shall ever follow you with my good wishes & rejoice in every good that may happen to you.   (Innes and Clerk MS 3070, Guildhall Library, London)

Eighteenth-century criticism Turton's generous view of Robert Adam was not generally held: success and self-confidence had bred instant and often implacable enemies. Criticism of the Adam style began early and indeed was well advanced before his death. The pamphlet *The Exhibition* (*c*.1779), purporting to be by a Roger Shanhagan but in reality by William Porden and the elder Robert Smirke, set the tone. Cast in the form of notes to a fictitious academy exhibition and ironically pre-empting that of the Royal Academy in Somerset House of 1780, it described three Adam schemes: 'A Temple for Northern Patriotism', one of 'Virtue', and a 'Section of a Lady's Dressing Room'. All three were jibes at Adam buildings and his patrons. 'Northern Patriotism', according to Shanhagan's commentary, was 'very like the building opposite the Admiralty', that is to say, the paymaster-general's office rebuilt in 1771 during Lord North's premiership and seen as a piece of cronyism; that of 'Virtue' was almost a copy 'of Lord Stormont's house in Portland Place', and referred to Kenwood, rebuilt for the lord chancellor, Lord Mansfield (Stormont), who had found for Adam in the Liardet stucco case of 1778 in a judgment that was widely held as favouritism—hence the ironic 'virtue'. The 'Lady's Dressing Room' represented Drury Lane Theatre and its dressing-rooms, of 1776, conspicuous for the extravagance associated with the Adam style. These were used to mount a superficial and unsubtle attack on Adam. The prefaces to *The Works in Architecture* were also criticized as arrogant and lacking in humility or diffidence—'no writer ever there was so arrogant as the Adams' (Shanhagan, 28–30)—and the architect was also blamed for his conspicuous failure to distinguish between decoration appropriate to the interior and exterior.

James Peacock followed Shanhagan's assault in 1785. In his small book *Nutshells* he attacked the Adam style of decoration as, 'this adamantine fetter', and speculated where 'our great buildings may escape being debauched, and having their magnificence eclipsed by the superlative nicities of modern proportion and modern decoration'. Peacock also disliked the perspective drawing that Adam had made very much his own, as *The Works in Architecture* showed. He asserted that 'the artist, indeed, who should have occasion to build a palace in an alley, may very rationally have recourse to perspective illustrations, in case a spectator, once or twice in a century, should be invited to take a break-neck view' (Peacock, 72). In the face of such negative criticism Soane's opinion of 1810 was much more understanding. As he saw it, such supposed failings had little to do with Adam's standing as an architect of imagination and versatility who had banished from interior decoration what Soane termed 'the heavy architectural conceits which prevailed in all buildings before this time'. However, Soane added that he may have 'sometimes indulged in the extreme of fancy and lightness' (Lees-Milne, 154). In fact, Soane went as far as to admire the interior of Drury Lane as showing

what the architecture of the interior of a theatre should be; and what it could be, when directed by the mind of genius. The decoration displayed a lively, rich fancy, and correct application of that lightness and variety so peculiarly adapted to theatrical architecture, which distinguished every part of the work.   (D. Watkin, *Sir John Soane, Enlightenment Thought and the Royal Academy Lectures*, 1996, 87)

It was, of course, exactly the opposite opinion to that expressed in Shanhagan's fictional catalogue entry.

Later criticism A similar sympathetic understanding of Adam was apparent in the review of Allan Cunningham's *Lives of the most Eminent British Architects* that appeared in *The Library of the Fine Arts* in 1831. The anonymous reviewer had taken exception to Cunningham's omission of Adam from the *Lives* and set out his own lengthy analysis of Adam and the Adam style. As it set much of the mood of nineteenth-century criticism, it is worth quoting at some length. The reviewer maintained that:

there are, nevertheless, numerous redeeming points in his style; and—though almost invariably neutralised by his own infelicity, many real excellencies. Invention he certainly possessed; and his designs abound with ideas capable of furnishing far more beautiful compositions than any of his own: this is surely some merit.   (Leigh, 1.99)

The review continued:

his external architecture was, we grant, generally pretty: he seems to have depended by far too much on merely adscititious embellishment, covering even his architraves with carving, while the windows are altogether naked. His forte lay in the arrangement and decoration of interiors: nor is it too much to affirm, that it is to him we are indebted for much of that comfort combined with elegance, which is so peculiarly the characteristic of an English house.   (ibid.)

Such an interpretation was altogether fairer and more sophisticated than the description of Adam's works as the 'depraved composition of a corrupt eye' which appeared in George Gwilt's *Encyclopaedia of Architecture* of 1842.

The interpretation of Adam as a sort of flawed genius remained for most of the nineteenth century and was reflected in the Adam revival in the 1870s. It followed the thinking of *The Library of the Fine Arts* that the fault of Adam 'exuberance' could easily be corrected 'by paring away his redundancies and omitting his superfluities' (Leigh, 1.99), a process that called into being several lifeless and repetitive interiors. In a sense, the Adam style remained popular as a caricature during the century, where the terraced houses of London, Dublin, and Edinburgh all contained 'a single "Adam" fanlight or a portico, with inside an "Adam" stairway, an "Adam" grate, or just an "Adam" frieze' (Lees-Milne, 169). There was also the snobbish antiquarian attitude to architecture which encouraged a neglect of the immediate past. Such an attitude became less tenable with the publication in two folio volumes of *The Architecture of Robert and James Adam* by Arthur Bolton in 1922. As curator of the Soane Museum, Bolton used the Adam drawings to establish a new and scholarly interpretation of both Adam and his buildings, and one which has largely stood the test of time. Bolton rightly concluded his preface with the unequivocal statement:

> Comparatively few people have ever seen a really first class Adam building inside and out, and their ideas of Adam work are too apt to be based on the exterior of the much altered Adelphi, the incomplete designs of Portland Place, Fitzroy Square, and possibly the Coffee Room of some hotel 'in the Adam style'. To such it is hoped that this work will be a revelation of the personality of a great architect, a stylist and decorative artist of the first order. (Bolton, 1.viii)

A. A. TAIT

Sources NA Scot., Clerk of Penicuik MSS · Sir John Soane's Museum, London, Sir John Soane's MSS · R. Adam, *The ruins of the palace of the Emperor Diocletian at Spalatro in Dalmatia* (1764) · R. Adam and J. Adam, *The works in architecture of Robert and James Adam / Les ouvrages d'architecture de Robert et Jaques Adam*, 2 vols. (1773–8) · R. Shanhagan, [W. Porden, and R. Smirke], *The exhibition* (1779) · Jose Mac Packe [J. Peacock], *Nutshells* (1785) · J. M. Leigh, ed., *The library of the fine arts*, 3 vols. (1831) · W. Young, *Town and country mansions and suburban houses* (1874) · R. Blomfield, *Architectural drawing and draughtsmen* (1912) · J. Swarbrick, *Robert Adam and his brothers* (1915) · A. T. Bolton, *The architecture of Robert and James Adam*, 2 vols. (1922) · J. Summerson, *Georgian London* (1945) · J. Lees-Milne, *The age of Adam* (1947) · J. Fleming, *Robert Adam and his circle* (1962) · A. Richardson, *An introduction to Georgian architecture* (1949) · D. Stillman, *The decorative work of Robert Adam* (1966) · D. Stillman, *English neoclassical architecture*, 2 vols. (1988) · E. Harris, *The furniture of Robert Adam* (1963) · E. Harris and N. Savage, *British architectural books and writers, 1556–1785* (1990) · A. Rowan, *Robert Adam: catalogue of architectural drawings in the Victoria and Albert Museum* (1988) · D. King, *The complete works of Robert and James Adam* (1991) · A. A. Tait, *Robert Adam: drawings and imagination* (1993) · Colvin, *Archs.* · J. Harris, *Headford House and Robert Adam* (1973) · J. Harris, *Sir William Chambers* (1970) · T. McCormick, *Charles-Louis Clérisseau* (1990) · J. Wilton-Ely, *The mind and art of Giovanni Battista Piranesi* (1978) · J. Fleming, 'A retrospective view by John Clerk of Eldin', *Concerning architecture*, ed. J. Summerson (1968) · A. A. Tait, 'The sale of Robert Adam's drawings', *Burlington Magazine*, 120/904 (July 1978), 451–4 · M. H. B. Sanderson, 'Robert Adam's last visit to Scotland, 1791', *Architectural History*, 25 (1982) · M. H. B. Sanderson, *Robert Adam and Scotland* (1992) · A. Rowan, *Designs for castles and country villas by Robert and James Adam* (1985) · E. Harris, *The genius of Robert Adam* (2001)

Archives Blair Adam, Fife, MSS | CKS, letters and accounts to Sir Edward Knatchbull · Essex RO, Chelmsford, accounts, day books, etc., relating to Audley End · GL, letters relating to business affairs of Adam brothers · NA Scot., Clerk of Penicuik MSS · NA Scot., family corresp.; papers relating to Monymusk House · Northumbd RO, Newcastle upon Tyne, accounts for work for Sir J. H. Delaval · NRA Scotland, priv. coll., corresp. and papers relating to the Adam brothers
Likenesses A. Ramsay, portrait, *c.*1754 (James Adam) · M. Ramsay, portrait, *c.*1754 · L. Pecheux, miniature, *c.*1755, Blair Adam, Fife · P. Batoni, portrait, 1763, priv. coll. · P. Batoni, portrait, *c.*1763 (James Adam) · attrib. G. Willison, oils, *c.*1770–1774, NPG [*see illus.*] · J. Tassie, paste medallion, 1792, Scot. NPG · J. Adam, portrait · R. Adam, self-portrait · F. Cotes, portrait (James Adam) · attrib. D. Martin, portrait, NPG
Wealth at death sale of collection and possessions (1818 and 1821): Bolton, *Architecture*, vol. 2, pp. 338–9

Adam, Robert Moyes (1885–1967), photographer and botanist, was born on 1 January 1885 at the Evangelical Union manse, Carluke, Lanarkshire, Scotland, the son of John Adam (1841–*c.*1916), minister in the Evangelical Union church, and Isabella Adam (*née* Moyes). He was to become a botanist at the Royal Botanic Garden in Edinburgh but was best-known as one of the foremost landscape photographers in Scotland. He combined natural artistic ability with a meticulous approach to the technical quality of his photographs and a lifelong love of the wilderness. The resulting distinctive style made him an obvious choice for the illustration of numerous calendars, books, and articles about the highlands and islands from the 1930s to the 1950s.

Adam lived for most of his childhood in Brunswick Street, Edinburgh, after his father became minister of the Kirk Memorial, Abbeymount, in 1891, and it was here that he began to explore his interest in photography and wildlife, purchasing his first quarter-plate camera at the age of fourteen. After leaving school, he studied science at Heriot-Watt College in Edinburgh and drawing at the Edinburgh College of Art. In 1901 he began to keep a register of his photographs which grew to nine volumes, spanning fifty-five years and containing details of around 15,000 glass negatives.

In 1903 Adam started work at the Royal Botanic Garden in Edinburgh, preparing lecture illustrations for the professor of botany, Isaac Bayley Balfour, and by 1906 he had begun to use photography to record the plants. During the first ten years of his post he attended classes in botany at the University of Edinburgh and in 1914 he was made a permanent member of staff at the gardens with the title assistant in charge of the studio. In 1915 he was regraded to botanist and remained in this post until his retirement. About this time he also moved to 17 West Brighton Crescent, Portobello, Edinburgh, where he lived with his wife, Ann (*née* Stewart), and their two children. In 1949 he retired to Kingussie, Inverness-shire. A heart attack in 1956 brought an end to his strenuous photographic expeditions. He made a full recovery and lived a further eleven years; he died in Edinburgh on 13 November 1967, aged eighty-two.

Among the books that Adam illustrated perhaps the best-known was a collaborative venture with the writer

Hugh Quigley, *The Highlands of Scotland*, published in 1936. His pictures were also published regularly throughout the 1940s and 1950s in the *Scots Magazine*, *Scotland's Magazine*, *The Scotsman*, and *Picture Post*. As well as his commercial success he was undoubtedly aware of the potential impact of his images and he made direct use of them in an environmental campaign against the 1929 proposal for a hydro-electric scheme in Glen Affric. He sent four hand-printed photographs of the glen to each Scottish MP and to the national newspapers and the ensuing public interest resulted in substantial modifications to the scheme. In the late twentieth century his mountain photographs have provided conservationists and landscape historians with a reliable record of the Scottish landscape in the first half of the century and his photographs of rural life provide a rich source for historians. For example, his photographs from an early bird-watching trip to the tiny Hebridean island of Mingulay in 1905 unwittingly captured a dying community. Within seven years the last inhabitants had left the island forever.

Adam's spare-time photography eventually encroached on his professional life and in his latter years at the botanic garden he was known to be developing and printing his own work in the studio. He could be a rather surly character who kept himself to himself, but in his capacity as official artist to the Botanical Society of Edinburgh and as a regular lecturer at the Alpine Botanical Club he was noted for his enthusiasm. Until the end of his career he used his 1908 half-plate camera with 6½ x 4¾ in. glass plates and wooden tripod. The weight, estimated at 30 lbs, and the inflexibility of this system meant that he left little to chance and many photographs were planned months in advance. He printed all his photographs himself with great precision and as a result his unmistakable printing style is very difficult to replicate today.

Robert Moyes Adam was a modest, private man whose physical strength was essential to the pursuit of his art. He gave up photography in 1956 after his heart attack forced him to stop mountaineering. In 1958 he sold his negatives to the Dundee publishing firm D. C. Thomson, home of the *Scots Magazine* and they passed the collection to the St Andrews University Library in 1987. Although he published widely, and sold his work privately, few of his own prints are in public photographic collections and despite his technical precision and evident abilities as an artist he was never recognized as a 'professional' photographer.

S. K. HILLHOUSE

Sources H. Gilbert, 'Scotland's photographer', *Scotland's S.M.T. Magazine*, 39 (March 1947), 26–30 · [R. Daw], 'Photograph by Robert M. Adam [pt 1]', *Scots Magazine*, 61 (1954), 433–48 · [R. Daw], 'Photograph by Robert M. Adam [pt 2]', *Scots Magazine*, 62 (1954–5), 29–44 · [R. Daw], 'In solitary places, a second selection of the work of Robert M. Adam introduced by the editor', *Scots Magazine*, 88 (1967–8), 520–29 · [R. Daw], 'A great photographer, a tribute to Robert M. Adam who, for half a century, recorded the Scottish scene with artistry and devotion', *Scots Magazine*, 88 (1967–8), 420–31 · G. Oliver and O. Onions, *Robert Moyes Adam, photographer, 1885–1967* (1969) [exhibition catalogue, Peebles Art Gallery, 16–30 Aug 1969] · private information (2004) · H. R. Fletcher and W. H. Brown, *The Royal Botanic Garden, Edinburgh, 1670–1970* (1970) · H. Quigley and R. M. Adam, *The highlands of Scotland* (1936) · b. cert. · *CCI* (1967)

Archives U. St Andr. L., collection

Likenesses photograph, repro. in 'Photograph by Robert M. Adam [pt 1]', 6 (9), p. 434 · photograph, repro. in Gilbert, 'Scotland's photographer', p. 26

Wealth at death £9493 12s.: confirmation, 22 Dec 1967, *CCI*

Adam, Sir Ronald Forbes, second baronet (1885–1982), army officer, was born on 30 October 1885 in Bombay, the eldest son of Sir Frank Forbes Adam, first baronet (1846–1926), a Scot who was a well-known industrialist in Lancashire and Bombay, and his wife, Rose Frances Kemball (1863–1944), daughter of C. G. Kemball, former judge, high court, Bombay. Adam was educated at Fonthill, East Grinstead, Sussex; Eton College; and the Royal Military Academy, Woolwich. He was commissioned into the Royal Artillery in July 1905. Posted to India in May 1911, he was serving with N battery (eagle troop) Royal Horse Artillery (RHA) at Secunderabad when the First World War broke out.

During the war Adam served in France and Flanders as a battery officer and, from July to October 1915, as adjutant of 3rd brigade, Royal Field Artillery (RFA), 28th division. On 1 July 1916 he was serving with 58th battery RFA and witnessed the attack of the 20th Manchesters near Fricourt. In November 1917 he went to Italy with the British forces and, as GSO2 Royal Artillery 14th corps, he saw the battle of Vittorio Veneto and the final collapse of the Austro-Hungarian armies. He was mentioned three times in dispatches and appointed DSO in June 1918 and OBE in June 1919. On 7 January 1915 he married Anna Dorothy Pitman (1892–1972), daughter of Frederick Islay Pitman, the celebrated Cambridge oarsman and city financier. They had four daughters: Barbara, Margot, Bridget, and Isobel.

In 1919 Adam was made brigade major, Royal Artillery, Bordon; in 1920 he was admitted to the Staff College, Camberley; and in 1922 he went to the War Office as GSO3. He became an instructor at the Staff College in 1923, before returning to the War Office as GSO2 in 1927. In 1926 he succeeded his father as baronet. In 1931 he passed through the Imperial Defence College and in 1932 he was sent back to the Staff College as GSO1 in charge of the senior division. He returned once more to the War Office in 1935 as GSO1 in the directorate of military operations and intelligence, and became deputy director of military operations on the reorganization of the directorate in 1936. In autumn 1936 he left the War Office to become commander Royal Artillery, 1st division, at Aldershot. The division was sent to Shanghai but the artillery remained behind. In September 1937 he was made commandant of the Staff College with the rank of major-general: a meteoric rise at a time of relative stagnation in the promotion system.

It was not long, however, before Adam was recalled to the War Office. Following the so-called 'purge' of the army council by Leslie Hore-Belisha (secretary of state for war) in December 1937, which saw Lord Gort succeed Sir Cyril Deverell as chief of the Imperial General Staff (CIGS), the post of deputy chief of the Imperial General Staff (DCIGS) was revived. In January 1938 Adam was appointed to it. Regarded as a 'thinker' who would complement Gort's 'drive', Adam instituted a number of reforms during his time as DCIGS. These included the establishment of a combined operations centre at Eastney; the merging of the Royal Military College, Sandhurst, and the Royal Military Academy, Woolwich; and the reorganization of both the infantry battalions and the armoured division. He was also responsible for making arrangements for the dispatch of the British expeditionary force (BEF) to France in the event of war. Moreover, when personal relations broke down between Hore-Belisha and Gort, Adam, who got on well with both men, acted as a 'go-between' and was the mainstay of the general staff during this period.

Shortly after the outbreak of war Adam, who had been promoted lieutenant-general while DCIGS, was appointed commander of 3rd army corps. Early in 1940 he travelled to France with 51st Highland division headquarters (a division which was to form part of his corps) and in April 3rd corps took over a section of the BEF's line to the left of 2nd corps. Adam recalled that he, along with the other British corps commanders, was concerned about the planned allied advance into Belgium in the event of a German attack in the west. He considered that the French had placed their worst divisions in the gap between the Maginot line and the forces which were to advance into Belgium, and that this could leave British troops exposed in the event of a German attack in the area. However, General Sir Edmund Ironside (the new CIGS) had agreed to the plans and Adam thought that Gort (commander of the BEF) was too loyal to question orders. During the early months of 1940 British formations were attached to the French army in front of the Maginot line for short periods in order to gain operational experience. At the beginning of May 51st Highland division took over part of the French line. Adam considered that this would be an honour for an excellent Territorial Army division. He was later saddened that he had ordered the fate of the division: in the German onslaught it was cut off from the rest of the BEF and eventually forced to surrender at St Valéry.

On 10 May 1940 the Germans attacked the Low Countries and the BEF duly advanced into Belgium, 3rd corps being retained in depth in the area of the River Scheldt. As a result of the swift German advance through the Ardennes the BEF was forced to withdraw to the French frontier. On 24 May plans were made for 3rd corps to counter-attack south against the flank of the German penetration. The plans were cancelled, however, and on 26 May Adam was ordered to hand over his corps and go back to Dunkirk to organize the bridgehead and the embarkation of the BEF, a task accomplished with great success. On 30 May Adam himself was ordered to embark and in the afternoon he went down to the beach. There he met Brigadier Frederick Lawson (who had been lent from 48th division to assist Adam) and they rowed out to a waiting destroyer in a canvas boat which they found in the dunes. On the voyage home Adam shared a cabin with Lieutenant-General Sir Alan Brooke (commander of 2nd corps) who had paddled out to the same destroyer. Brooke was an old friend who had been a brother subaltern in eagle troop RHA before the First World War and a fellow instructor at the Staff College in the mid-1920s.

At the beginning of June 1940 Adam was appointed general officer commanding-in-chief, northern command. His command stretched from the Scottish borders in the north, to Derbyshire in the west, and to Leicestershire in the south. During the summer Adam inspected the coast defences, toured units, and visited lord mayors in order to reassure them that the civilian population could count on the army's help in an emergency. During his time at northern command Adam demonstrated an unusual degree of concern for the psychological welfare of his men. He concluded that measures needed to be taken to improve the morale and efficiency of the army, the vast majority of which was based in Britain and taking little active part in the war effort.

In May 1941 Adam (nicknamed Bill by his old army friends) was appointed adjutant-general with responsibility for personnel matters in the army. A tall, burly, strong-jawed figure in moulded tunic and gleaming leatherwork, Adam appeared every inch the traditional senior army officer: 'the kind of man', observed one commentator, 'who is probably a good change bowler and certainly a welcome guest for a week-end's shooting' (Adam papers, xiii/i). Realizing, however, that the wartime conscript army required different handling to the peacetime regular army if its willing co-operation was to be maintained, and that the string of defeats which the army suffered in the early period of the war compelled new methods and techniques, Adam oversaw a range of initiatives to improve morale and efficiency. New personnel selection methods were introduced, most notably War Office selection boards which incorporated psychiatrists into the officer selection process. Special training units were established to reform delinquent young soldiers. Efforts were made to improve relations between officers and men by encouraging better man-management practices on the part of junior officers, and instituting weekly 'request hours' during which men could approach their officers informally over any issue that was troubling them. Some of the rituals of the service were modified, instructions being issued that elaborate inspections of troops by senior officers should be kept to a minimum and that standards of 'spit and polish' should be suited to the occasion and observed in a manner that the troops could understand and respect.

A vast Army Welfare Service was built up which included the establishment of a broadcasting section to liaise with the BBC over wireless programmes for the troops, a newspaper section to oversee the production of army newspapers, and a legal aid scheme under which soldiers were offered free legal advice on a range of civil matters. An impressive array of education schemes was laid on for the troops and included the organization of weekly current affairs discussions under the auspices of the Army Bureau of Current Affairs (ABCA). These discussions, which were to be conducted by junior officers in training time, were intended to inspire some crusading fervour among the soldiers by persuading them of the objectives for which Britain was fighting. Underpinning these wartime developments army morale reports were compiled every quarter, drawing on the views of commanders and censorship returns of soldiers' letters, and a morale committee was set up in the War Office to monitor the reports and co-ordinate action on the basis of the assessments. Adam was also closely concerned with the demobilization of the army and the establishment of civil resettlement units to help repatriated prisoners-of-war in their transition to civilian life.

The fact that Adam, who was promoted full general in 1942, was prepared to employ a variety of new, and sometimes radical, techniques inevitably led to some criticism from traditionalist elements within government and the army. Churchill, for instance, was thoroughly suspicious of Adam's innovations and tried to put a stop to the ABCA scheme which some Conservative MPs viewed with considerable political distrust. General Sir Bernard Paget (commander-in-chief home forces) went as far as describing Adam as 'a serious menace both to morale and discipline' (MacKenzie, 120). Adam, however, enjoyed the backing of Sir James Grigg (secretary of state for war) and General Sir Alan Brooke (who became CIGS in December 1941 and lunched with Adam every week when they were both in London). Moreover, once he was persuaded that a project was desirable and practicable he was not easily deflected from his task and applied all his energy and tactical sense to its fulfilment. Some of Adam's wartime initiatives were not applied as effectively as he had intended, and in several respects the clock was turned back in the post-war army. Nevertheless they made an important contribution to morale and efficiency and represented a significant advance in terms of the army's development as a social institution. One contemporary commentator christened Adam the army's 'number one democrat' (Sullivan, 3). Adam was made a CB in 1939, a KCB in 1941, and a GCB in 1946.

In July 1946 Adam retired from the army. He continued to hold a number of honorary appointments, serving as colonel commandant of the Royal Artillery (1940–50), the Royal Army Educational Corps (1940–50), and the Royal Army Dental Corps (1945–51). He was also president of the MCC (1946–7), cricket, fishing, and gardening being his spare-time passions. Adam's progressive record as adjutant-general, however, made him much sought after by various civilian organizations, particularly in the field of adult education, and ensured that his post-war career would be an unusual one for a retired regular soldier. He served as chairman or president of such bodies as the linoleum working party (1946), the National Institute of Industrial Psychology (1947–52), the council of the Institute of Education, University of London (1948–67), the Library Association (1949), and the National Institute of Adult Education (1949–64). He was also a member of the council of the Tavistock Clinic (1945–53), the Miners' Welfare Commission (1946–52), and the governing body of Birkbeck College (1949–67). In addition Adam became chairman and director-general of the British Council (1946–54), member and subsequently chairman of the executive board of UNESCO (1950–4), and principal of the working men's college (1956–61). In 1960 he published (with Charles Judd) *Assault at Arms: a Policy for Disarmament*, a short book produced in association with the United Nations Association of Great Britain and Northern Ireland (of which Adam was chairman in 1957–60). Adam was awarded an honorary LLD degree by the University of Aberdeen (1945), and made an honorary fellow of Worcester College, Oxford (1946). He died peacefully at his home in Faygate, Sussex, on 26 December 1982, aged ninety-seven, and was buried at St Mary Magdalene churchyard, Rusper, near Horsham, Sussex, on 5 January 1983.

Although Adam was said to have no intellectual pretensions, he had an alert pragmatic mind and a marked ability to get to the heart of any problem that confronted him. 'He was fundamentally a good man', noted one observer, 'animated by a passionate desire to extend the benefits of knowledge and social progress as widely as possible.' He also possessed 'a warm and generous heart, a notable gift of fellowship and, above all, complete integrity' (*The Times*, 5 Jan 1983, page 12). Adam's achievements as adjutant-general during the Second World War have, perhaps understandably, been overshadowed by those of other senior officers more directly involved in the planning and conduct of operations. He deserves to be remembered, however, as a key architect of the wartime citizen army and among the most notable army reformers of his generation. He has been described as one of the most enlightened soldiers ever to have held the post of adjutant-general (Dixon, 13).

JEREMY A. CRANG

Sources King's Lond., Liddell Hart C., Adam MSS · PRO, war office MSS · WW · *The Times* (5 Jan 1983) · *Journal of the Royal Artillery*, 110 (1983) · *Gunner*, 148 (March 1983) · *Army List* · J. A. Crang, *The British army and the people's war, 1939–1945* (2000) · J. A. Crang, 'The defence of the Dunkirk perimeter', *The battle for France and Flanders, 1940: sixty years on*, ed. B. Bond and M. D. Taylor (2001) · *Chief of staff: the diaries of Lieutenant-General Sir Henry Pownall*, ed. B. Bond, 1 (1972) · B. Bond, *France and Belgium, 1939–1940* (1975) · B. Bond, *British military policy between the two world wars* (1980) · H. V. Dicks, *Fifty years of the Tavistock Clinic* (1970) · N. F. Dixon, *On the psychology of military incompetence* (1976) · L. F. Ellis, *The war in France and Flanders, 1939–1940* (1953) · D. Fraser, *Alanbrooke* (1982) · B. H. Liddell Hart, *The memoirs of Captain Liddell Hart*, 2 (1965) · E. Linklater, *The highland division* (1942) · S. P. MacKenzie, *Politics and military morale: current affairs and citizenship education in the British army, 1914–1950* (1992) · V. Sullivan, 'Army's no 1 democrat', *Leicester Evening News* (27 April 1946) · private information (2004) · Burke, *Peerage* (1980) · m. cert.
Archives King's Lond., Liddell Hart C., corresp., diaries, and papers · Royal Artillery Institution, Woolwich, London, photograph albums | FILM BFI NFTVA, news footage · BFI NFTVA, propaganda footage (Ministry of Information) · IWM FVA, actuality footage · IWM FVA, news footage | SOUND IWM SA, oral history interview · IWM SA, recorded talk
Likenesses S. Morse-Brown, drawing, 1947, IWM · Bassano & Vandyk Studios, photograph, repro. in Liddell Hart, *Memoirs of Captain Liddell Hart*
Wealth at death £327,000: private information

Adam [*née* King], **Ruth Augusta** (1907–1977), writer and feminist, was born on 14 December 1907 at the vicarage in Arnold, a mining parish in Nottinghamshire, the second of the four children of the Revd Rupert William King (1874–1955), a Church of England vicar, and Annie Margaret, *née* Wearing (1878–1945). She was educated from 1920 to 1925 at St Elphin's, Darley Dale, Derbyshire, a girls' boarding-school, and she then taught for five years in poverty-stricken elementary schools in the mining area of Nottinghamshire. On 24 May 1932 she married Kenneth Adam (1908–1978), a journalist on the *Manchester Guardian* who later became the first director of BBC television.

Ruth Adam's best novel, *I'm Not Complaining*, a tartly anti-Lawrentian view of women's lives in the depression, narrated by an unmarried woman teacher, was published in 1938 and was reissued as a Virago Modern Classic in 1983. Between 1937 and 1947 Ruth Adam had four children but she also managed to work for the Ministry of Information during the war and to write several novels of social reportage, a child's history of America, many radio scripts, including radio plays and broadcasts for the BBC's *Woman's Hour*, as well as the first of her *Church of England Newspaper* women's pages. Between 1944 and 1976 Ruth Adam wrote more than 2000 of these weekly 'pages' in which she was free to articulate her position as a Christian socialist feminist for a sometimes startled readership composed mainly of church wives. She raised such issues as paid work for married women, the necessity for good childcare, and the social usefulness of older women in the community, and she also discussed the wider issues of the need for peace and justice and for an enlightened penal policy towards juvenile offenders, the plight of refugees, and the historical significance of Sylvia Pankhurst and the suffragettes. Her standpoint was that of a commonsensical 'social feminist' who insisted on the value of the work done by mothers in the home as well as on the contribution of women in careers.

In 1955 Ruth Adam, with her friend the London county councillor Peggy Jay, co-founded the Fisher Group, a think-tank on social policy and the family which gave evidence to government committees of inquiry and contributed to such legislative reforms as the 1963 and 1969 Children and Young Persons Acts and the Local Authority Social Service Act of 1970. Arising out of this concern Ruth Adam wrote her disturbing novels *Fetch Her Away* (1954) and *Look Who's Talking* (1960) about girls in care, which are rare in their sympathetic depiction of women social workers. A stark contrast is her novel *A House in the Country* (1957), which gives a comic account of her own family's attempt at living in a commune. In 1966 and 1967 she published books on G. B. Shaw and on Beatrice Webb. Perhaps Ruth Adam's most unusual achievement was her writing, at the very end of her life, of *A Woman's Place, 1910–1975*, a succinct, witty, and trenchant social history of British women in the twentieth century that pulled the many interests of her own life together. Ruth Adam remained intellectually alert and alive to new ideas and events and this last book testifies to her thoughtful analysis of the gains and losses for British women up to and including the women's liberation movement. That she has been overlooked in the history of British feminist writing is largely due to her choice of a non-feminist readership—teenage girls for her comic strip *Susan: a Girl Nurse* in *Girl*; harassed vicars' wives in draughty, impoverished parsonages for her women's page in the *Church of England Newspaper*; and

overworked women in the caring professions for her booklets and fiction on children in need. Moreover she was never an extremist, and hence escaped citation by both friends and foes of the women's movement. Ruth Adam's whole life testified to her kind of optimistic, gradualist feminism. Her marriage was a partnership of genuine equals and she regarded the children as the first job in hand for herself and her husband. But she was rarely seen without a book or a writing-pad, whether by the kitchen stove or in a hospital bed. Ruth Adam died at the Hospital of St John and St Elizabeth, Marylebone, London, on 3 February 1977. SYBIL OLDFIELD

Sources Blain, Clements & Grundy, *Feminist comp.* • S. Tsai, 'The life and work of Ruth Adam', DPhil diss., U. Sussex, 1998 • J. Morgan, Introduction, in R. Adam, *I'm not complaining* (1983) • R. Adam, women's page, *Church of England Newspaper* (1944–76) • R. Adam, family page, *Church of England Newspaper* (1944–76) • *The Times* (7 Feb 1977) • *Church of England Newspaper* (Feb 1977) • private information (2004) [C. Adam] • m. cert. • *CGPLA Eng. & Wales* (1977) • d. cert.
Archives BBC WAC, radio scripts and corresp. with the BBC
Likenesses M. F. King, photographs, 1915–50, priv. coll. • C. Adam, photographs, in or after 1950–1959, priv. coll.
Wealth at death £4879: probate, 26 May 1977, *CGPLA Eng. & Wales*

Adam, Thomas (1701–1784), Church of England clergyman, was born at Leeds in the West Riding of Yorkshire on 25 February 1701, the third of the six children of Henry Adam, solicitor and town clerk of Leeds corporation, and his wife, Elizabeth Blythman, daughter of Jasper Blythman, a distinguished recorder of Leeds and grandson of Sir John Stanhope. He received his education firstly at the grammar school at Leeds, under Thomas Barnard, and then at Queen Elizabeth's School at Wakefield. After two years, from 1720 to 1722, at Christ's College, Cambridge, where his tutor was Matthew Hutton, future archbishop of York and of Canterbury, he moved to Hart Hall, Oxford, where Dr Richard Newton was principal. He took the degree of BA in 1724 and left Oxford with lasting scruples over clerical pluralism after reading Newton's book on the subject. In 1724 he was presented, through the interest of an uncle, to the living of Wintringham in Lincolnshire; being under age ecclesiastically, it was 'held' for a year for him. Here he remained for fifty-eight years, never wishing to change and repeatedly resisting pressure put upon him to look higher. His income rarely exceeded £200 per annum. In 1730 he married Susanna Cooke (d. 1760), daughter of the neighbouring vicar of Roxby; they had only one daughter, who died young.

Adam would later think of the early years of his ministry as merely 'formal'. Reading William Law in 1736 pricked his conscience and precipitated more than ten years of spiritual anxiety. About 1748 he experienced evangelical conversion in the midst of prayer and the close study of Romans, and this was confirmed by his reading of Luther. In the 1750s he began corresponding with Samuel Walker of Truro and was drawn into a growing network of evangelical clergy. Like Walker, he was strict about church order, and on this point he clashed with John Wesley repeatedly. Although he drew large crowds to his church, he never saw large numbers converted. His lasting influence would be as a spiritual director—he was consulted by the evangelical Lord Dartmouth and the merchant banker John Thornton—and as a devotional writer. From 1759 he suffered ill health, which included recurring pain from kidney stones. In August 1760 his wife died; his diary left evidence of his resignation in the midst of suffering. He died on 31 March 1784 and was buried in his own churchyard.

Adam's popular *Lectures on the Church Catechism* (1753) stressed the urgency of personal, inward conversion and profoundly influenced William Romaine. Besides his published sermons and biblical commentaries, his *Works* were collected posthumously in three volumes (1786). His most important posthumous publication was *Private Thoughts on Religion* (3rd edn, 1803). These entries from his diary have an aphoristic quality and were organized by his editors, in the manner of Pascal's *Pensées*, under various headings. The book remained in print in Great Britain and America throughout the nineteenth century and was translated into several foreign languages. Such diverse men as Samuel Taylor Coleridge, Reginald Heber, Thomas Chalmers, and John Stuart Mill paid tribute to the searching power of Adam's 'thoughts'.

A. B. GROSART, rev. D. BRUCE HINDMARSH

Sources J. Stillingfleet, 'Life and character of the author', in T. Adam, *Private thoughts*, 3rd edn (1803) [prefixed to] · G. C. B. Davies, *The early Cornish evangelicals, 1735–60* (1951) · L. E. Elliott-Binns, *The early evangelicals: a religious and social study* (1953) · J. D. Walsh, 'The Yorkshire evangelicals in the eighteenth century', PhD diss., U. Cam., 1956 · P. Lineham, 'Adam, Thomas', *The Blackwell dictionary of evangelical biography, 1730–1860*, ed. D. M. Lewis (1995) · Venn, *Alum. Cant.* · Foster, *Alum. Oxon.* · C. Hole, *Memoir of the Rev. T. Adam* (1895) · A. Westoby, 'Memoir of Thomas Adam', in *Exposition of the four gospels … by the Rev. Thomas Adam*, ed. A. Westoby, 1 (1837)

Adam, William (*bap.* **1689**, *d.* **1748**), builder and architect, was baptized on 24 October 1689 at Abbotshall church, Kirkcaldy, Fife. He was the only surviving child of John Adam, builder and merchant, and of his wife, Helen, daughter of the third Lord Cranstoun. Descended from a minor landed family in Forfarshire, William Adam's father had set up in business in Kirkcaldy, 'which thence forward became the limited scene of his architectural abilities' (NA Scot., GD18/4981). Of William Adam's early education nothing is known except that he was, in his own words, 'Bred a Mason and served his time as Such' (NA Scot., CS230/A2/1). On 30 May 1716 William Adam married Mary Robertson (1699–1761), daughter of William Robertson of Gladney, minister of Greyfriars Church, Edinburgh. Of their children four sons and six daughters survived to adulthood. The sons were John *Adam (1721–1792), who married Jean Ramsay, the daughter of an Edinburgh merchant, Robert *Adam (1728–1792), James *Adam (1732–1794) [see under Adam, Robert], and William Adam (1738–1822). Of the daughters, Jean married Thomas Kennedy of Dunure, MP for Ayrshire, Susannah married John Clerk of Eldin, and Mary married John Drysdale, clerk to the general assembly of the Church of Scotland.

In time Adam inherited and expanded his father's business interests. Sir John Clerk of Penicuik, first baronet, on

a jaunt to Fife in 1728, visited Kirkcaldy, where he inspected 'a Brick work belonging to Mr. Adam Architect' as well as '20 several projects' including 'Barley mills, Timber mills, coalwork, salt pans, marble works, highways, Farms, Houses of his come a building and Houses belonging to others not a few' (NA Scot., GD18/2108). Others made use of Adam's expertise. The third duke of Hamilton was charged £200 for 'going frequently to Bo'ness during the Course of Six years Superintending the fitting of the Coal and Salt Work and erecting the fire Engine' (NL Scot., MS 8265). On occasion Adam took industrial works into his own hands. Thus he acquired the lease of the Craigleith quarry near Edinburgh to guarantee continuity in the supply of stone for the numerous building projects for which he acted as contractor. As Adam's affairs prospered, he could afford in 1731 to purchase the estate of Blair Crambeth (renamed Blairadam) in Kinross-shire.

Adam journeyed to the Low Countries and he is credited with introducing 'a Modle of Barley Miln from Holland … and also the making of Dutch Pantiles in Scotland' (NA Scot., GD18/4981), presumably at the 'Brick work' in Kirkcaldy. He travelled to England in 1727 at the behest of the second earl of Stair. At Stamford they were joined by Sir John Clerk. When in London, Adam had his portrait painted by William Aikman, a cousin of Clerk. Adam may have met James Gibbs, for he is listed as a subscriber to Gibbs's *A Book of Architecture*, published in 1728. Adam's own intended publication was *Vitruvius Scoticus*. Modelled on Colen Campbell's *Vitruvius Britannicus*, it was to contain plates of work by Adam and his immediate predecessors in Scotland. Although there were some subscribers, the volume did not appear until long after Adam's death, in 1811, when it was published by his grandson William. While in London, Lord Stair procured the grant of a baronetcy for Adam but it lapsed with the death of George I. In 1728 Adam settled with his growing family in Edinburgh, which henceforward became the centre for his expanding architectural commissions. Adam's status was recognized in 1728, when he was elected a burgess and guild brother in Edinburgh. In that same year he secured a government appointment as clerk and storekeeper of the works in Scotland; two years later he became mason to the Board of Ordnance in Scotland (North Britain), an office which fell to John Adam on his father's death.

Adam first appeared as an architect in 1721, when he began to be employed by John Ker, first duke of Roxburghe, at Floors Castle, Roxburghshire, and by Charles Hope, first earl of Hopetoun, at Hopetoun House, Linlithgowshire. Although paid as a mason at Floors, Adam laid claim in *Vitruvius Scoticus* to be the designer. Floors was a rectangle of eleven bays with square angle towers. According to Bishop Pococke, 'The whole is built of rough stone, but with window cases of hewn stone. It is strange so large a house should not afford one good room' (*Tours in Scotland*, 330). In the room ratios, the pedimented towers, and the union of pavilions with the centre there is a debt to the principles of the Venetian architect Andrea Palladio as codified by Colen Campbell in the first two volumes of *Vitruvius Britannicus*, published in 1715 and 1717. That

Floors was outclassed by Hopetoun may be owing to Lord Hopetoun, a subscriber to *Vitruvius Britannicus*, which featured the mansion begun in 1698 to the design of Sir William Bruce, which in its French origins was out of countenance with the new Italian pedagogy. Adam was paid £21 'To Takeing down of old house' (Hopetoun MSS, bundle 636) and thereafter he and his sons were continuously employed at Hopetoun House until the mid-1750s. The extended showfront which masks Bruce's truncated mansion owes much of its detailing to the richly textured Castle Howard, Yorkshire, by Sir John Vanbrugh. Despite the omission of the intended tetrastyle portico, Hopetoun can still be rated as the finest classical country house in Scotland.

How such prestigious commissions came Adam's way is not known. Perhaps it was through the patronage of Sir John Clerk or of Adam's 'great friend' the second earl of Stair (Adam, *Blair Adam*, 73). In 1723 the latter was 'making a Canal and several very grand Improvements' at Newliston, Linlithgowshire (Macky, 325), doubtless by Adam, who also designed landscapes at Hopetoun and at Arniston, Edinburghshire, for Robert Dundas, later Lord Arniston. Lord Stair could never afford to build his intended mansion, which would have had a conventional hall and saloon plan but interrupted by a tribune flanked by staircases.

Adam was more fortunate with Sir John Clerk, who wrote, 'In May 1723 I not only finished my design for the House of Mavisbank, under the correction of one Mr. Adams, but laid the foundation of the House' (*Memoirs*, 114–15). Mavisbank, Edinburghshire, was a villa, an occasional residence when Sir John was fulfilling official duties in Edinburgh. Yet with its awkward proportions, banded pilasters, and excess of carving, Mavisbank is apart from contemporary English villas. The overall rustication of The Drum (originally Somerville House), Edinburghshire, for James, Lord Somerville, and the chaste essay from Gibbs's *A Book of Architecture* that is Arniston, Edinburghshire, demonstrate the width of Adam's pragmatism, as does the ornateness of Duff House, Banffshire (1735–40), where the cost of the profusion of carved stonework led to a protracted lawsuit between the client, William, Lord Braco, and the architect. Adam's last major country house was Inveraray Castle, Argyll, begun in 1745 for the third duke of Argyll and when completed the first major manifestation of the Gothic revival. Adam was the executant architect since the design was provided by the English architect Roger Morris, who as master carpenter to the Board of Ordnance went to Scotland, where he and Adam met. After the failure of the Jacobite rising of 1745 there was much work on strengthening government fortifications and the building of Fort George, Inverness-shire, which would be completed by his sons. As the Hanoverian peace and ensuing prosperity settled across Scotland, Adam was called upon to provide a series of public buildings, including Robert Gordon's Hospital, Aberdeen (1730–32), Dundee Town House (1732–4; dem.), Glasgow University Library (1732–45; dem.), and in Edinburgh the Orphans' Hospital (1734–5), George Watson's Hospital

(1738–41), and the Royal Infirmary (1738–48). His sole ecclesiastical commission, Hamilton Church, Lanarkshire (1731–4), was modelled on James Gibbs's discarded design for St Martin-in-the-Fields, London.

Adam, Old Stone and Lime, as his children called him, died in Edinburgh on 24 June 1748 'from a severe cold, which fell upon his kidneys' (Adam, *Blair Adam*, 93). He was buried in the family mausoleum in Greyfriars churchyard, Edinburgh. John Clerk of Eldin described his father-in-law as 'a man of a vigorous and enterprising genius who, at an early period of his life, had established himself the universal architect of his country' (NA Scot., GD18/4981). His business enterprises were continued in Scotland by his eldest son, John. Robert and James would extend the family influence further afield once they set up in practice in London.   JAMES MACAULAY

Sources NA Scot., Clerk of Penicuik MSS, GD18 · Colvin, *Archs.* · J. Gifford, *William Adam, 1689–1748* (1989) · W. Adam, *Vitruvius Scoticus*, ed. J. Simpson (1980) · 'William Adam', *Architectural Heritage*, 1 (1990) [whole issue] · J. Fleming, *Robert Adam and his circle in Edinburgh and Rome* (1962) · W. Adam, *Blair Adam from 1733 to 1834* (1834) · J. Macaulay, *The classical country-house in Scotland, 1660–1800* (1987) · J. Macaulay, *The Gothic revival, 1745–1845* (1975) · *Memoirs of the life of Sir John Clerk of Penicuik*, ed. J. M. Gray, Scottish History Society, 13 (1892) · building accounts for Duff House, Banffshire, 1743, NA Scot., CS 230/A2/1 · Hopetoun House, South Queensferry, Hopetoun MSS · J. Macky, *A journey through Scotland* (1723) · *Tours in Scotland, 1747, 1750, 1760 by Richard Pococke*, ed. D. W. Kemp, Scottish History Society, 1 (1887) · J. T. Davidson, *The link town of Abbotshall* (1951) · bap. reg. Scot. · m. reg. Scot. · Adam family memorial, Greyfriars churchyard, Edinburgh

Archives NRA, priv. coll., family papers | Hopetoun House, South Queensferry, West Lothian, Hopetoun MSS · NA Scot., letters to Sir John Clerk · NA Scot., letters to Sir A. Grant and receipt book · NRA, priv. coll., letters to duke of Hamilton · NRA, priv. coll., accounts for work at Hopetoun House

Likenesses W. Aikman, oils, 1727, Blairadam, Kinross-shire · marble bust, Scot. NPG; copy, priv. coll. · marble bust (after marble bust, Scot. NPG), Greyfriars churchyard, Edinburgh

Adam, William (1751–1839), politician and advocate, was born on 2 August 1751, the son of John *Adam (1721–1792), architect, of Blair Adam, Kinross-shire, and Jean (1721–1795), daughter of John Ramsay of Woodstone, Kincardineshire; he was the nephew of the architects Robert and James *Adam [see under Adam, Robert]. After attending Edinburgh University he went up to Christ Church, Oxford, in 1769, and subsequently may have gone on a grand tour. He became an advocate in Scotland in 1773 and was called to the English bar in 1782. On 7 May 1777 he married Eleanora (1749–1808), daughter of Charles Elphinstone, tenth Lord Elphinstone (1711–1781), and Clementina Fleming (1719–1799), with whom he had a daughter and five sons, among them Sir Frederick William *Adam.

Early career, 1774–1788 Adam abandoned his Scottish legal practice in 1774, when elected to parliament for the pocket borough of Gatton, in Surrey, with the assistance of a family friend, Sir William Mayne. He initially made his mark as an independent member but gradually shifted towards government, declaring his support for Lord North on 25 November 1779. For this change of heart

William Adam (1751–1839), by Sir Henry Raeburn

Adam was ridiculed by Charles James Fox, whom he challenged to a duel. This was fought in Hyde Park on 29 November and Fox was slightly wounded, his survival being jokingly attributed to Adam's reliance on government powder. No bitterness ensued from this dispute; rather it became the starting point of an enduring friendship.

At the 1780 general election Adam transferred to Wigtown burghs, and in September was appointed treasurer of the ordnance. On 26 March 1781 he gave an explanation of his recent political conduct, stating that he had 'opposed the minister as long as he thought the American war was pursued for unjust purposes' but had changed his opinion once it became a question of preventing American independence. He insisted that office had been 'bestowed upon him unasked' and that he would have no compunction in voting against the government if necessary (J. Debrett, *The Parliamentary Register*, 45 vols., 1781–96, 2.335–40). Adam remained loyal to North to the end and, after losing his place under Rockingham in 1782, was re-instated by the Fox–North ministry in April 1783. This was a reward for his role as a go-between in the formation of the coalition. Adam, who was by now North's intimate friend, had initially suggested a rapprochement with Lord Shelburne but was incensed at the humiliating terms on offer. He therefore advocated coalition with Fox as the best means of preventing the destruction of North's political influence. Now a thorough convert to coalition, he soon added the duke of Portland to his friends and admirers in the whig leadership. In the wake of the India Bill crisis in December 1783 Adam was dismissed and also

forced to change seats at the subsequent general election, being returned for Elgin burghs in 1784. He joined the Whig Club in 1785 and continued to take an active role in debate, but his family's financial difficulties forced him to devote a great deal of time to legal work in order to gain money.

Party manager, 1788–1794 During the regency crisis of 1788–9 Adam acted as secretary-in-waiting to Portland as prospective first lord of the Treasury. Although the king's recovery meant that Adam never gained the actual appointment, he fulfilled equivalent functions for the whig opposition during and after the crisis. He had responsibility for managing party finances and co-ordinating electoral activity. Under the direction of Portland and Adam the party was even able to contest seats where there had been no recent opposition interest. Impressive as this electoral organization was in comparison to earlier opposition efforts, it remained far from nationwide in scope and was still heavily dependent on direct contacts with electoral patrons. In the 1790 general election Adam may be credited, nevertheless, with helping to prevent a repetition of the disasters of 1784. He made himself particularly useful in adding a Scottish dimension to opposition organization. This was partly coincidental, however, and derived much of its impetus from resentment at the growing hegemony of Henry Dundas.

In 1790 Adam was returned for Ross-shire with the support of his friend Francis Mackenzie of Seaforth. He acted as one of the unofficial whips of the whig opposition and was prominent in this capacity in the attacks on Pitt's foreign policy in 1791–2. The defection of Edmund Burke and the disintegration of opposition in the wake of the French Revolution caused Adam a great deal of unhappiness. He disapproved of the extreme responses of both alarmists and reformers within the party and tried unsuccessfully to bring about concerted action by Fox and Portland to hold the party together. Indeed Adam was on good terms with MPs of all shades of opinion and was involved not only in organizing party finances, but also in managing the debts of leading figures such as Fox and Lord Robert Spencer, as well as those of the royal princes, the duke of York and the prince of Wales. He therefore had a stake in the party's united survival. He even aspired at one stage to the management of the finances of the dukes of Bedford, Devonshire, and Portland, believing that this would bring 'wealth power and occupation' for himself and security for his children; but this scheme failed to materialize (Blair Adam MSS, William Adam to John Adam, 29 Nov 1791).

Adam generally voted with Fox but refused to endorse the Society of the Friends of the People. In a debate on 25 May 1792 he denounced the recent royal proclamation against sedition, despite Portland's known approval of it, but also made clear his hostility to parliamentary reform. In the debates of 13–15 December, when Fox declared his commitment to reform and proposed recognition of the French republic, Adam made it clear that he would remain loyal to Fox, notwithstanding reservations about some of his views. In early 1793 he spoke out strongly against the war and took a leading role in opposing the government's traitorous correspondence bill, marshalling a wealth of legal and historical precedents in his arguments. On 7 May he opposed Charles Grey's motion for parliamentary reform, while Fox marked his refusal to compromise with the followers of Portland by voting with Grey. Although Adam was not in favour of parliamentary reform (except in so far as supporting minor adjustments to Scottish electoral procedures) he had continued to support Fox rather than his fellow opponents of reform, who were pressurizing Portland into splitting the party.

Adam's management skills were sorely tested at this time. There were recurrent complaints from the aristocratic leadership of the party over the misuse of party funds to subsidize extremist propaganda. Adam had been notified by Portland and Fitzwilliam in 1791 that 'not another shilling' would be subscribed unless the whig press was shut to the doctrines of '[Richard] Price, etc. and his school' (Sheffield Archives, WWM F115/54, Portland to Fitzwilliam, 21 April 1791). In the aftermath of Fox's intransigent conduct in the spring of 1793 Portland and Fitzwilliam suspended all subscriptions beyond the present year and only agreed to pay anything on condition that no new money should be given towards newspapers. Alarmed by the disintegration of the party's organizational framework Adam exerted himself to bring about a reconciliation between the party leaders. He did not directly apprise Fox of his soundings, hoping instead to play upon Fitzwilliam's friendship with Fox since boyhood and Portland's long-suffering tolerance of Fox's public outbursts. Adam also expressed indignation at the way in which some politicians were blatantly using the party's disintegration as 'a golden bridge to pass to places, pensions, contracts, honours and titles, without that loss of character which ought to attend such conduct' (Northants. RO, Fitzwilliam (Milton) MS 45, Adam to Fitzwilliam, 31 Oct 1793). But neither the entreaty to preserve old friendships nor the appeal to political integrity succeeded in swaying the grandees. Fitzwilliam refused to countenance Adam's suggestion that the party should reunite to criticize the conduct of the war, and Portland made it clear that 'after *all that had passed*, it is not for *us to seek* an explanation' (ibid., Portland to Fitzwilliam, 11 Nov 1793). But Adam did succeed in persuading them to help with the payment of Fox's debts, not only through personal contributions, but also by endorsing a public subscription to this end. Adam succeeded in collecting over £61,000, which cleared Fox's debts and established a permanent annuity of £2000 a year.

In parliament Adam was active in defence of the radicals Muir and Palmer, who had been convicted in Scotland of sedition and subjected to harsh sentences of transportation; they possessed no right under Scottish law to appeal to the House of Lords. Late in 1793 Adam had introduced a bill to remove this anomaly, and in the light of their subsequent convictions he planned to move a retrospective clause that would grant them right of appeal. This tactic was defeated on 4 February 1794, as was his

motion on 10 March for an account of their trial. He also gave a speech lasting more than three hours, on 25 March, calling for a committee of inquiry into the Scottish criminal law, but this too was rejected.

Out of parliament, 1794–1806 Adam's political conduct had placed him in an awkward situation with his electoral patron in Ross-shire, who supported the war. Having surrendered any further claim to the seat he had hoped to transfer to Banbury, on the interest of Lord Guilford, son of his old friend Lord North. But owing to resistance from Banbury corporation Guilford was unable to make good his offer, and Adam found himself out of parliament between 1794 and 1806. He retired in April 1794, before the junction of the Portland whigs with Pitt's ministry, but wrote to the duke on 7 July, formally severing their connection. He continued to maintain contact with the Foxite opposition and even acted as electoral manager in 1796 and 1802, albeit on a much reduced scale and largely on Scottish business. During his time out of parliament he sought to advance his legal career, taking silk in 1796. He developed a lucrative practice, specializing at the bar of the Commons and also the Lords. His need for money was considerable because of inherited debts from his father, who died in 1792, and the bankruptcy in 1801 of an uncle who owed him £25,000. In 1802 he gained several prestigious and financially rewarding posts: auditor to the sixth duke of Bedford, counsel to the East India Company, and solicitor-general (from 1805 attorney-general) to the prince of Wales.

Later career, 1806–1839 With the return to power of the Foxites in 1806 Adam expected to be offered a place in government, though he was not sure whether he should surrender his legal practice for the uncertainties of political office. In the event nothing substantial was proposed and he was fobbed off with promises for the future. In the meantime he was promoted within the prince's establishment to the chancellorship of the duchy of Cornwall. His services as an electoral manager for Scotland were again utilized, and he strongly urged Lord Grenville (Fox's coalition partner) to strike at the continuing power of Lord Melville (the former Henry Dundas). Although a longstanding political opponent of Melville, he bore him no personal animosity, and even served as his defence counsel in his pending impeachment. Melville's acquittal in June 1806 gave rise to a degree of political embarrassment, as Adam's health was toasted by his political enemies at celebratory dinners.

Adam decided to return to parliament, notwithstanding the anticipated loss in income of £1500 a year that would result from giving up his legal work in both houses. 'The effect', he informed Bedford on 13 October 1806, 'may possibly be good … A person so much connected with Fox … cannot after so long a secession from parliament come back without some observation' (Blair Adam MSS). In particular he thought it would help to demonstrate Foxite confidence in the Grenvillites, their coalition partners. He was elected without opposition for Kincardine, though only after lengthy negotiations. On behalf of the ministry he conducted some frenetic, though rather belated, electoral activity in Scotland, gaining some successes but falling far short of eliminating the Melville interest.

During the short-lived 'ministry of all the Talents' of 1806–7 Adam did not succeed in his aim of gaining a place in the reformed Scottish judiciary. Instead he was forced by the government's fall and the snap dissolution to contest Kincardine in 1807, winning what he regarded as a personal victory over Melville. He had been distressed by the defection of the prince of Wales over the Catholic question, and in parliament was once more prominent in debate for the opposition. He did not support, however, the attacks on the duke of York in 1809 for alleged abuse of army patronage. Indeed he made an ill-judged assertion of the duke's innocence, which prompted the unfounded accusation that Adam's own son had gained his army commission by corrupt means. In 1810 Adam gave strong support to Speaker Charles Abbot, who had vigorously exerted parliamentary privilege by issuing a warrant on 6 April for the arrest of the radical member Sir Francis Burdett for publishing an inflammatory speech and address. Adam believed that the defence of privilege was more important than party rivalry, and was disappointed by the tame response of ministers. But his suggestion that the opposition should therefore promote a declaratory bill to protect MPs' privileges was vetoed.

Adam continued to be plagued with financial difficulties. In 1808 he was forced to borrow money to pay the debts of his eldest son, John *Adam (1779–1825), in India and he also planned to sell his Kincardineshire estate. Two years later, with a temporary loan of £10,000 from his aristocratic whig friends, he hoped to make investments that would set him up for retirement. His final significant contribution to party politics was the advice that he gave during the regency crisis of 1810–11, when his knowledge of events and arguments from 1788–9 proved extremely useful. It was therefore slightly embarrassing that it was partly at Adam's instigation that the prince of Wales was reconciled to making no immediate ministerial changes. Adam suggested a face-saving formula by which Spencer Perceval's administration was to consider itself merely as a caretaker ministry until the regency restrictions expired. It became apparent, however, by mid-1811 that the prince would probably not bring in the whig opposition, even when free to do so. Partly to avoid inevitable embarrassment Adam decided to resign his seat at the earliest opportunity. This decision was taken by some observers as a clear indication that no ministerial changes would be made by the prince regent. But personal financial difficulties, not least the destruction of his salmon fishery by flooding, also prompted Adam to retire. He spoke in parliament for the last time on 27 January 1812, having stayed on so long only out of loyalty to the prince, in order to oversee the financial arrangements for an unrestricted regency.

In 1815 Adam finally obtained Scottish legal office, being appointed lord chief commissioner of the newly created jury court; at the same time he was sworn of the privy council. In some quarters his appointment was denounced as a mere job, but he proved eminently suitable. Although his career was never distinguished by high office in government it warrants praise for his contribution as a political manager. A more ambitious man of the same talents might have risen higher but Adam chose consistency over expediency. Loyal to friends and never vindictive towards enemies, he received in his final years a thoroughly merited reward. He died, at the age of eighty-seven, on 17 February 1839.   DAVID WILKINSON

Sources D. E. Ginter, ed., *Whig organization in the general election of 1790: selections from the Blair Adam papers* (1967) • D. E. Ginter, 'The financing of the whig party organization, 1783–1793', *American Historical Review*, 71 (1965–6), 421–40 • F. O'Gorman, *The whig party and the French Revolution* (1967) • D. Wilkinson, 'The political career of William Henry Cavendish-Bentinck, third duke of Portland, 1738–1809', PhD diss., U. Wales, Aberystwyth, 1997 • E. Haden-Guest, 'Adam, William', HoP, *Commons, 1754–90* • D. R. Fisher, 'Adam, William', HoP, *Commons, 1790–1820* • *DNB* • Blair Adam MSS, priv. coll. • Fitzwilliam (Milton) MSS, Northants. RO
Archives BL OIOC, corresp. and MSS relating to India, home misc. series • Bodl. Oxf., MSS relating to Westminster election returns • NRA Scotland, priv. coll., Blair Adam MSS | Beds. & Luton ARS, letters to S. Whitbread • BL, corresp. with C. J. Fox, Add. MSS 47561, 47568, 47569 • BL, corresp. with Lord Grenville, Add. MS 58973 • BL, corresp. with Lord Holland, Add. MS 51595 • BL, corresp. with earls of Liverpool, Add. MSS 38214–38471, *passim* • BL, corresp. with R. Peel, Add. MSS 40317–40381 • BL, corresp. with S. Perceval, Add. MS 49175, *passim* • BL OIOC, letters to W. F. Elphinstone, MSS Eur. F 87–89 • NA Scot., corresp. with J. Loch • NA Scot., letters to Lord Melville, GD51 • NL Scot., corresp. with F. Graham; corresp. with R. Liston; letters to J. G. Lockhart; corresp. with Robertson-Macdonald family • NL Scot., corresp. with W. Scott, MSS 3886–3919, *passim* • Northants. RO, Fitzwilliam (Milton) MSS, corresp. with E. Burke • NRA Scotland, priv. coll., corresp. with J. Skene • U. Durham L., Grey of Howick collection, letters to second Earl Grey • U. Nott. L., letters to duke of Portland, PwF36–47
Likenesses S. W. Reynolds, mezzotint, pubd 1804 (after J. Opie), BM, NPG • J. P. Quilley, mezzotint, pubd 1833 (after C. Smith), NPG • H. Raeburn, oils [*see illus.*] • C. Smith, oils, Kinross County Council • bust, Abbotsford House, Borders region

Adam, William (1828–1898), carpet manufacturer, was born on 10 June 1828 in Paisley, the eldest of five children and the only son of Peter Adam (*c*.1798–1861), hand-loom weaver, and his wife, Elisa.

Adam began his career in Paisley, working as a hand-loom cotton weaver and later as a warehouseman. On 16 June 1854 he married Agnes, daughter of John Thomson of Paisley, moving soon afterwards to Glasgow where two of their sons and a daughter were born. He was employed as a foreman in James Templeton's carpet manufacturing business where he gained a thorough understanding of the chenille Axminster hand-loom weaving process which his employer had patented in 1839.

In the late 1850s Adam left Scotland for Kidderminster where he introduced the chenille Axminster process to Brinton and Lewis, a leading Kidderminster firm which made Brussels carpeting. Less than a year later, however, he went into partnership with George Race, a cashier of the firm, and together they founded their own chenille

Axminster rug manufacturing business. The partnership was dissolved in September 1862 and Adam then became manager of the rug making business of H. R. Willis of Kidderminster.

In 1869 Adam made the decision which was to transform his future, entering into a partnership with Michael Tomkinson (1841–1921) to found the Kidderminster firm that later played a major role in the British carpet industry and helped to make Axminster carpeting a familiar object in middle-class homes. Tomkinson supplied the leadership and commercial acumen, but Adam's contribution in technical and production aspects was no less vital.

In 1878 when Tomkinson took a major new initiative by purchasing in the USA the United Kingdom rights to Halcyon Skinner's spool Axminster loom, it was Adam who ensured that spool Axminster looms were speedily installed and fully operational. However, his biggest achievement was the invention of a successful setting power-loom for weaving chenille Axminster carpeting, patented in 1880–82. Licences to use the invention were granted to three other firms including James Templeton & Co. which had developed a less efficient loom. Meanwhile Tomkinson and Adam were busy installing eighty looms of their own.

Adam's wife, who had borne three more children, died at their residence, Elderslie House, Leswell, Kidderminster, on 14 January 1878. On 1 July 1879 in Derby Adam married Emma (d. 1903), daughter of Edward Grigg, veterinary surgeon; they had two sons.

The firm of Tomkinson and Adam continued to expand. It was one of the two leading producers of Axminster carpeting in the UK and was to become the fourth largest firm in the carpet industry by the early years of the twentieth century. Adam solved the practical problems involved in the expansion and patented further improvements to chenille and Axminster power-looms. He underwent major surgery in 1893, however, and was less active during the last five years of his life, as his health declined. His eldest sons, Peter and William, had become partners in the firm some years earlier.

Adam was a staunch Liberal, but seldom appeared on public platforms. He was a strong supporter of the temperance movement and a vice-president of the Midland Temperance League. In later life he served as a JP for Kidderminster. A devout nonconformist, he attended the countess of Huntingdon's chapel in Kidderminster, and then for the last twenty-five years of his life the Old Meeting-House, later known as Baxter Congregational Church. Adam was made a deacon in 1876, and served on the executive of the Worcestershire Union of Congregational Churches. He made numerous charitable donations privately and supported various congregational churches in Worcestershire. The largest public gift was £1250 towards the cost of Baxter Church, erected in 1884. However, in the year before he died he bought a country estate of over 2000 acres at Buckland, Gloucestershire, for £50,000.

Adam died of apoplexy on 13 December 1898 at Elderslie House, Leswell, Kidderminster, where he had lived for many years since leaving Scotland. The funeral was at Baxter Church and he was buried in Kidderminster cemetery on 17 December 1898.   JAMES NEVILLE BARTLETT

Sources J. N. Bartlett, *Carpeting the millions: the growth of Britain's carpet industry* (1978) · *Kidderminster Shuttle* (17 Dec 1898) · *Kidderminster Shuttle* (25 Sept 1897) · *Kidderminster Shuttle* (10 Nov 1900) · F. H. Young, *A century of carpet marking, 1839–1939* (1943) · census returns, 1851, 1861 · Tomkinson & Adam price list, Oct 1869, Hereford and Worcester County Museum, Hartlebury · m. cert. · d. cert. [Agnes Adam] · d. cert. · d. cert. [Emma Adam]
Likenesses photograph, repro. in *Kidderminster Shuttle* (17 Dec 1898), suppl.
Wealth at death £211,291 9s. 2d.: resworn probate, July 1899, CGPLA Eng. & Wales

Adam, William Patrick (1823–1881), politician and administrator in India, was the elder son of Admiral Sir Charles *Adam (1780–1853) of Blairadam, Kinross. His mother was Elizabeth (d. 1871), daughter of Patrick *Brydone, FRS. Born at Ancrum, Roxburghshire, on 14 September 1823, Adam was educated at Rugby School, where he was said to have been a model for Scud East in *Tom Brown's School Days*, and at Trinity College, Cambridge, where he took his degree of BA in 1846. Three years later he was called to the bar by the Inner Temple, and in 1851 unsuccessfully contested, as a Liberal, Clackmannan and Kinross, the family seat. From 1853 to 1858 Adam was in India as private secretary to Lord Elphinstone, governor of Bombay. He married, on 23 February 1856, Emily Eliza, daughter of General Sir William *Wyllie. In 1859, after his return to Britain, he contested Clackmannan and Kinross for a second time, and on this occasion with success. For the succeeding twenty-one years he continued to represent this constituency. In 1865 he became a junior whip in Lord Palmerston's government, and was reappointed to that post when Gladstone became prime minister in 1868. In 1873 he was appointed first commissioner of public works, and sworn of the privy council.

Appointed chief whip on the resignation of A. W. Peel in 1874, Adam rendered valuable services to his party. His advice was constantly sought, not only by his leaders, but by Liberal supporters throughout the country, and his energy (as well as money from his own pocket) greatly contributed to the success of the Liberals in the election of 1880, a success that he confidently foretold amid many apparently discouraging omens. With Lord Rosebery he took the initiative in May 1878 in suggesting that Gladstone stand for Midlothian. In Gladstone's ministry of 1880 Adam, to his disappointment, was offered no more than his former post of first commissioner of works; but before the end of the year he accepted the governorship of Madras. On 27 November 1880, after being entertained by his political friends at complimentary dinners in Edinburgh and London, Adam left for India; but a few months after he had entered on his duties at Madras he was seized with an illness, from which he had suffered at earlier periods of his life, and died at Ootacamund on 24 May 1881. There, two days later, he was buried. On 20 May 1882

William Patrick Adam (1823–1881), by John Moffat

Adam's eldest son, Charles Elphinstone Adam, was created a baronet in recognition of his father's public services, while his widow was given the precedence of a baronet's wife.

Adam owed the successes of his political life to his solid administrative capacity and his universally popular manner. He was no brilliant speaker, however, and, although often invited, rarely took part in public meetings, which would have made him familiar to the general public. He was the author of a pamphlet, *Thoughts on the policy of retaliation and its probable effect on the consumer, producer, and shipowner* (1852).   SIDNEY LEE, *rev.* H. C. G. MATTHEW

Sources Boase, *Mod. Eng. biog.* · Venn, *Alum. Cant.* · Burke, *Peerage* · Gladstone, *Diaries* · H. J. Hanham, *Elections and party management: politics in the time of Disraeli and Gladstone* (1959)
Archives NRA, priv. coll., corresp. and papers | BL, corresp. with W. E. Gladstone, Add. MS 44095
Likenesses Ape [C. Pellegrini], lithograph, repro. in *VF* (27 June 1874), 176 · Barraud, photograph, NPG · J. Moffat, photograph, NPG [*see illus.*] · portrait, repro. in *ILN*, 77 (1880), 564 · portrait, repro. in *The Graphic*, 23 (1881), 589
Wealth at death £54,014 7s. 3d.: confirmation, 17 Oct 1881, *CCI*

Adami, John George (1862–1926), pathologist, was born on 12 January 1862 in the Albion Hotel, Piccadilly, Manchester. He was the second son of five sons and four daughters of John George Adami, hotel proprietor, and his wife, Sarah Ann Ellis, daughter of Thomas Leech of Urmston, Lancashire. His mother was the sister of Daniel John Leech (1840–1900), professor of materia medica and therapeutics in the Victoria University and physician to the Manchester Royal Infirmary. The Adami name came from an Italian ancestor who migrated to Bavaria and became

protestant in the sixteenth century. Both Adami's parents had many doctors in their families.

Adami was baptized in Manchester Cathedral, and at the age of ten he went to Old Trafford School. After matriculating, he moved to Owens College, Manchester, and passed the first part of the London BSc. In 1880 he entered Christ's College, Cambridge. At Cambridge he was greatly influenced by, and later became a friend of, Sir Michael Foster. Even as a student Adami showed a broad interest in the place of science in the community, and delivered a paper to the exclusive Natural Science Club: 'The medical degree with special reference to the new Medical Act'. He gained a first class in both parts of the natural science tripos (1882, 1884), and then worked for eight months at Breslau under Rudolf Heidenhain. From 1885 to 1887 he was house physician at the Royal Infirmary, Manchester. In 1888 he returned to Cambridge as university demonstrator in pathology. In 1889 Adami was exposed to rabies, and received anti-rabies immunization from the Pasteur Institute in Paris. He returned to the Pasteur Institute the following year and worked under the key French immunologists and bacteriologists Pierre Roux, Ilya Mechnikov, and Louis Pasteur. In March 1891 Adami was elected to a fellowship at Jesus College, Cambridge.

An old friend from Owens College drew Adami's attention to the new chair in pathology and bacteriology at McGill University, Montreal, and Adami was appointed in 1892. He found a young university and a department badly hampered by lack of funds, buildings, and equipment. These material needs were met by the generosity of J. H. R. Molson and Lord Strathcona, who endowed the chair of pathology and financed the pathology wing in the university and the Royal Victoria Hospital. Under Adami the hospital had an autopsy rate of 80 per cent. Adami was a good teacher with an original mind in research. He considered that the department of pathology should be of value to the community at large, and in 1894 he became bacteriologist to the department of agriculture. Montreal had great poverty, and was divided into French and British parts. Adami became involved in the campaign against pulmonary tuberculosis, and was the English president of the City Improvement League, which was concerned with city planning, water supplies, clean streets and rented accommodation. He was also the English president of the Child Welfare Exhibition of 1912, which made the public aware of increasing infant mortality, and chairman of a representative committee on venereal disease. Adami married Mary Stuart, daughter of James Alexander Cantlie, of Montreal, in 1894; they had a son and a daughter. His wife was intimately connected through her mother with Lord Strathcona and Lord Mountstephen, two great benefactors of McGill University. She died in 1916.

Adami contributed an important chapter on inflammation to Sir Clifford Allbutt's *System of Medicine* (1896), which attracted particular attention. In 1899 he was invited to apply for the chair of pathology at Cambridge; although tempted, he eventually declined the offer. He was elected FRS in 1905. Adami finished *The Principles of Pathology* during a sabbatical in 1906, while collaborating with Ludwig

Aschoff in Marburg. It was an important teaching text, but somewhat too long for students. The book emphasized the role of functional as well as structural changes in disease. In 1911 Adami was elected president of the Canadian Association for the Prevention of Tuberculosis, and in 1912 he became president of the Association of American Physicians and the Royal Society of Canada. However, he realized that the idea that intestinal derangements (stasis and absorption of toxins) caused many diseases made its adherents appear obsessed, and in 1914 he wrote that '[for the last fourteen years] I have largely permitted this particular field to lie fallow' (Adami, *BMJ*, 24 Jan 1914). In the same year Adami wrote to Sir William Osler, regius professor of medicine at Oxford University, and formerly of McGill, indicating the desire of doctors for a medical history of the war. In due course Adami became assistant director of medical services (in charge of records) to the Canadian expeditionary force, and wrote *The War Story of the Canadian Army Medical Corps* (1918).

In 1919, with the support of William Osler and Sir Clifford Allbutt, Adami was appointed vice-chancellor of the University of Liverpool. He was made CBE in the same year. The university was then in the throes of post-war expansion, its numbers having grown from under 900 in August 1914 to 2600 by 1919. Adami's chief service was to raise by appeal the large sum of £360,000 for new buildings and equipment, and the endowment of new chairs and additional lectureships. Adami placed a high value on the contribution that the university could make to the then great commercial city of Liverpool. He strengthened the links between business and academic life and maintained the interest of the districts around the city. This made fund-raising easier. In particular, he raised money for a multidisciplinary approach to cancer research. He was an untiring and witty public speaker, accessible, genial, and energetic; he had a lively and well-stocked mind and a broad range of interests. His scientific judgement was good and his reputation in the university and city was high.

Adami developed a lymphoma about 1918 and suffered from great tiredness for two years. However, he remained active. He married, on 4 April 1922, Marie, elder daughter of the Revd Thomas Wilkinson, of Litherland, near Liverpool. They had no children. Adami received treatment for his lymphoma from Dr W. B. Coley in America, who was treating tumours with bacterial toxins. He died in Ruthin Castle, a private hospital in Ruthin, Denbighshire, on 29 August 1926. His funeral was four days later at Liverpool Cathedral and he was buried at Allerton cemetery. A memorial service for the University of Liverpool was held in the cathedral in October. He was survived by his wife.

Adami's chief service to pathology was to link it more closely with clinical medicine, stressing always the importance of preventive medicine. Before the First World War he fought a campaign in Canada for public health and in particular child welfare and measures against tuberculosis. As chairman of the Medical Research Committee in 1917 on standardization of routine pathological methods, he was influential in the standardization of the Wassermann test for syphilis in British laboratories, and spoke out fearlessly on venereal disease in an address to the Royal Institute of Public Health, under the title 'The policy of the ostrich' which was published in the *Canadian Medical Association Journal* in 1919. Adami also championed the use of immunization with BCG (attenuated bovine tubercle bacillus) for the prophylaxis of tuberculosis at a time when this approach was neglected in Great Britain.

H. B. GRIMSDITCH, *rev.* GEOFFREY L. ASHERSON

Sources M. Adami, *J. George Adami: a memoir* (1930) [introduction by Sir Humphry Rolleston] · H. Rolleston, 'John George Adami', *BMJ* (11 Sept 1926), 507–9 · *The Lancet* (4 Sept 1926), 522–4 · *Journal of Pathology and Bacteriology*, 30 (1927), 151–67 · E. H. Bensley, 'McGill medical luminaries', *Nature*, 118 (1926), 453–4 · b. cert. · m. cert. · d. cert. · *CGPLA Eng. & Wales* (1926)
Archives Medical Research Council, London, corresp. · U. Lpool L., letters · Wellcome L., papers | NL Wales, letters to John Glyn Davies
Likenesses W. Stoneman, photograph, 1917, NPG · J. Bacon & Sons, photograph, Wellcome L. · F. T. Copnall, oils, U. Lpool · portrait, McGill University, Montreal, Quebec, Canada, Assembly Hall, Strathcona Anatomy and Dentistry Building
Wealth at death £21,267 9s. 7d.: probate, 1 Dec 1926, *CGPLA Eng. & Wales*

Adams family (*per.* 1734–1817), makers of scientific instruments and globes, came to prominence through **George Adams senior** (*bap.* 1709, *d.* 1772), who was baptized on 17 April 1709 in the parish of St Bride's, Fleet Street, London, the eldest surviving son of Morris Adams (*d.* 1725) and his wife, Mary (*d.* 1732). His father was a liveryman of the Loriners' Company, but was a cook by trade, with his own business in Shoe Lane. In 1724 George was apprenticed in the Grocers' Company to James Parker, mathematical instrument maker, on whose death in 1726 he was turned over to Thomas Heath for the remainder of his term. By the time he became free of the Grocers' Company in 1733, both his parents were dead. In 1734 he started his own business as a maker of mathematical instruments in Fleet Street, 'near the Castle Tavern', a few doors from Shoe Lane, adopting the sign of Tycho Brahe's Head. The business continued at various addresses in Fleet Street for eighty-three years.

Adams's early products included navigational quadrants and orreries (astronomical models). In 1738 he moved to larger premises on the corner of Racquet Court, taking his shop sign with him. His first major publication from there, *Micrographia illustrata* (1746), was attacked by Henry Baker FRS, who accused him of plagiarism, but it served to publicize his entry into the field with a new form of portable microscope, several examples of which survive. In 1748 he succeeded William Deane as mathematical instrument maker to the Office of Ordnance, a post which he held until his death in 1772. He also succeeded Deane as instrument maker to the Royal Mathematical School at Christ's Hospital. The former appointment brought many government orders, for drawing, gunnery, and surveying instruments, for the use of the artillery and engineers, and for demonstrational equipment for the Royal Military Academy, Woolwich.

During his residence in St Bride's parish Adams served his turn in most of the parish offices, becoming senior churchwarden in 1748. However, in February 1757 a fire in adjoining premises obliged him to move, and his subsequent address near Water Lane, on the other side of the street, was in the parish of St Dunstan-in-the-West. This became no. 60 when Fleet Street was numbered in July 1766. The Adams business remained there until its demise in 1817.

About Christmas 1756, just before the fire, Adams was appointed mathematical instrument maker to the prince of Wales (the future George III). New forms of instrument dating from this period include a trunnion-mounted microscope and an architectonic sector. Following the death of George II in 1760, Adams became mathematical instrument maker to George III, which, although unsalaried, was the most prestigious appointment available in this field. Many of the extant instruments in the King George III collection at the London Science Museum are from his workshop. In mid-1766 he launched new 18 in. and 12 in. globes, with a *Treatise* describing their construction and use. The dedication to the king was contributed by Dr Samuel Johnson. The unusual form of mounting and relatively high price of Adams's globes drew scathing comments from Benjamin Martin, proprietor of the long-established Senex's globes, but they proved popular and many examples survive.

George Adams was a liveryman of the Grocers' Company and served twice as a warden. He was twice married and had at least thirteen children, but many died in infancy. Two daughters survived from his first marriage to Ann (*d.* 1747), whose surname is unknown. The elder, Sarah (1738–1812), married Robert Blunt of Charing Cross, linen draper, in 1759, and had a large family. Adams's second marriage, to Ann Dudley (1721/2–1809?), took place at St Martin-in-the-Fields in 1748. It produced six daughters and three sons, two of whom survived to maturity— George and Dudley. As well as his London property, George Adams senior owned an estate at Langley Marish, Buckinghamshire. He died suddenly on 17 October 1772, aged sixty-three, and was buried in St Bride's churchyard.

After Adams's death the Fleet Street business was continued in all its aspects, initially by his widow, Ann, and **George Adams junior** (1750–1795). The latter, who had been apprenticed to his father in 1765, became free of the Grocers' Company in November 1772 and a liveryman in 1773. In July 1774 he married Hannah Marsham, at St Dunstan-in-the-West, Fleet Street. The ordnance appointment was lost to Jeremiah Sisson on George Adams senior's death, but the appointment to the king continued, and in 1787 George junior became optician to the prince of Wales (the future George IV) as well. Before then, about 1780, he began to receive ordnance orders as a result of Jeremiah Sisson's bankruptcy. A substantial ordnance trade developed in the build-up to the Napoleonic wars but, unlike his father, George junior did not have a monopoly in this area. Between 1785 and 1792 he supplied numerous instruments to Martinus van Marum for Teyler's Foundation at Haarlem in the Netherlands, most of

which survive, and other continental institutions including the University of Coimbra, in Portugal.

In the 1780s George junior began to write and publish a number of illustrated textbooks dealing with the physical sciences, in particular *Essay on Electricity* (1784), *Essays on the Microscope* (1787), *Astronomical and Geographical Essays* (1789), *Geometrical and Graphical Essays* (1791), and *Lectures on Natural and Experimental Philosophy* (5 vols., 1794). The last work had a strong religious theme, and was undertaken, Adams said, specifically to counter the atheistic approach to the subject then prevalent on the continent. Failing health caused him to move to Southampton, where he died on 14 August 1795, aged forty-five. He and Hannah had no children.

George Adams senior's widow, Ann, was still alive when her son George died, leading to uncertainty about the ownership of the business. At first Hannah Adams tried to carry it on in both its bookselling and instrument-making aspects, and a barometer signed by her is known. She managed to secure the appointment of mathematical instrument maker to his majesty for herself, but she lost the important ordnance trade to her brother-in-law Dudley and after less than a year was obliged to give up. The stocks and copyrights of George junior's books were sold to W. and S. Jones of Holborn, who continued to publish edited and updated editions until 1813. The stock-in-trade at 60 Fleet Street was sold by auction in June 1796. Hannah retired to Clapham, Surrey, where she died in 1810 leaving an estate of about £20,000, almost all of which went to her own blood relations.

Dudley Adams (1762–1830), the youngest child of George senior and his second wife, was not quite ten years old when his father died. In 1777 he was apprenticed to his brother George to train as a mathematical instrument maker. Ten years later he married a widow, Margaret Sophia de Langlade, at St Marylebone parish church. To enable him to establish a separate business his mother gave him the globe plates and tools that had belonged to his father, and in mid-1788 he opened a shop at 53 Charing Cross. Here he concentrated on globe making but also sold all types of mathematical instruments. In 1794, possibly as a result of supplying some 28 in. globes for Lord Macartney's mission to China, he was appointed globe maker to George III.

On the death of his brother in August 1795 Dudley immediately secured the ordnance appointment for himself. In July 1796, having ousted Hannah from 60 Fleet Street, he moved there. He seems to have been a poor businessman: in 1806 he lost the ordnance trade to Matthew Berge, Jesse Ramsden's successor. In 1810 he reissued his father's obsolete *Treatise on the Globes*, absurdly calling it the '30th' edition. In May 1817 he was adjudged bankrupt, and the Adams instrument business, founded in 1734, came to an end.

Dudley's assets were dispersed in a series of auction sales between July and September 1817. They included the freehold premises at 60 Fleet Street and a country estate called Nutting Grove in Buckinghamshire. The sale particulars suggest that he had been living well beyond his means. By 1820 he had purchased the 'medico-electrical therapeutics' business of the late Francis Lowndes in St Paul's Churchyard, located from 1822 at 22 Ludgate Street. He continued this until 1827 or later, publishing several tracts on the subject, such as *Electricity is the Fountain, the Great Vivifying Principle of Nature* (1820), against considerable opposition from the orthodox medical faculty. His tracts and minimal surviving correspondence indicate that during the 1820s his mental state gradually deteriorated, and it is probable that he died insane. He was buried in St Bride's churchyard, Fleet Street, on 20 March 1830, aged sixty-seven.

Dudley's wife died in 1801. Guild records reveal that they had a son George, apprenticed in 1811, but as no further trace of him has been found it is presumed that he died before completing his apprenticeship. Lack of an heir may have been what caused Dudley to neglect his business, leading to his bankruptcy. A portrait of him by Ramsay Reinagle is mentioned in the will of his elder sister Isabella but has not been traced. Isabella died shortly after Dudley in 1830, when the surname Adams in this particular dynasty died out.   JOHN R. MILLBURN

Sources GM, 1st ser., 65 (1795), 708–9 [George Adams jun.] · J. Brown, *Mathematical instrument-makers in the Grocers' Company, 1688–1800* (1979) · J. R. Millburn, 'The office of ordnance and the instrument-making trade in the mid-18th century', *Annals of Science*, 45 (1988), 221–93 · A. Q. Morton and J. A. Wess, *Public and private science: the King George III collection* (1993) · St Bride's, Fleet Street, registers, vestry minutes, and churchwardens' accounts, GL · parish register, vestry minutes, and churchwardens' accounts, St Dunstan-in-the-West, Fleet Street, GL · letters, Dudley Adams to earl of Liverpool, BL, Add. MS 38281, fols. 27, 29, 72–3 · letters, Dudley Adams to Robert Peel, BL, Add. MSS 40375, fols. 275–6; 40383, fols. 207–8 · will, PRO, PROB 11/981, sig. 348 [George Adams sen.] · will, PRO, PROB 11/1265, sig. 531 [George Adams jun.] · will, PRO, PROB 11/1515 [k], sig. 486 [Hannah Adams] · J. R. Millburn, *Adams of Fleet Street, instrument makers to King George III* (2000) [incl. Adams catalogues and trade cards] · parish register, London, St Bride's, Fleet Street [baptism, George Adams sen.], 17/4/1709 · parish register, London, St Martin-in-the-Fields [marriage, George Adams sen. to Ann Dudley], 6/7/1748 · parish register, London, St Bride's, Fleet Street [burial, George Adams sen.], 24/10/1772 · parish register, London, St Bride's, Fleet Street [baptism, George Adams jun.], 25/6/1750 · parish register, London, St Dunstan-in-the-West [marriage, George Adams jun.], 3/7/1774 · parish register, London, St Dunstan-in-the-West [baptism, Dudley Adams], 5/12/1762 · parish register, London, St Marylebone [marriage, Dudley Adams], 11/2/1787 · parish register, London, St Bride's, Fleet Street [burial, Dudley Adams], 20/3/1830
Archives BL, earl of Liverpool and Robert Peel, letters, MSS [Dudley Adams] · Sci. Mus., King George III collection [George Adams sen.] · Teylers Foundation, Haarlem, Holland, van Marum corresp. [George Adams jun.]
Likenesses R. Reinagle, portrait (Dudley Adams)
Wealth at death left £800 specific legacies; also owned the business, two freehold properties; George Adams sen.: PRO, PROB 11/981, sig. 348 · left £4000 specific legacies; plus land in Essex and Surrey; book copyrights; George Adams jun.: PRO, PROB 11/1265, sig. 531; PRO, PROB 11/1515, sig. 486 [Hannah Adams] · probably nil; Dudley Adams

Adams, Andrew Leith (1827–1882), army surgeon and naturalist, born on 21 March 1827, was the son of Francis *Adams (1796–1861), surgeon, and his wife, Elspeth Shaw (*d.* 1845). Appointed army surgeon in 1848, Adams joined the 22nd (Cheshire) regiment and was posted to India. Between 1849 and 1854 he served in Dagshai, Rawalpindi, and Peshawar. In 1861 he was posted to Malta, to which he returned in 1868 after serving two years in New Brunswick.

A naturalist in the best Victorian tradition, who readily accepted the ideas of Charles Darwin, Adams made interesting observations in zoology, geology, and anthropology; he also reported on the Maltese cholera epidemic of 1865. While in India he was a keen ornithologist: he studied birds in the Siwalik hills around Dagshai and was the first naturalist to explore the interior of Ladakh. His observations were detailed in his papers 'The birds of Cashmere and Ladakh' and 'Notes on the habits, haunts, etc. of some of the birds of India' (*Proceedings of the Zoological Society of London*, 1858, 169–90 and 466–512), and in his book *Wanderings of a Naturalist in India, the Western Himalayas and Cashmere* (1867). He collected the type specimens of the orange bullfinch *Pyrrhula aurantiaca* and the black-winged (Tibet, Adams's) snowfinch *Montifringilla adamsi*, and was the first to discover the breeding site of the brown-headed gull *Larus brunnicephalus* on the lakes of the Tibetan plateau. He also differentiated the Kashmir race of the house martin *Delichon urbica cashmeriensis*.

All his observations have the stamp of a lively mind and a keen observer. Like most of his colleagues he devoted much time to hunting; he bagged eleven brown bears on one trip in Kashmir. While in Malta he studied the dwarf palaeofauna of Pleistocene cave deposits, which resulted in his *On the Natural History and Archaeology of the Nile Valley and the Maltese Islands* (1870). In New Brunswick his interests ranged from the customs and myths of the native peoples to the Pleistocene geology of the region, as detailed in the narrative of his explorations, *Field and Forest Rambles, with Notes and Observations on the Natural History of Eastern Canada* (1873). In later life he devoted much time to palaeontology, and produced a monograph on British fossil elephants (1877).

After retirement in 1873 Adams returned to England, and was then appointed professor of zoology at the College of Sciences, Dublin; in 1878 he became professor of natural history at Queen's College, Cork. He was elected FGS in 1870 and FRS in 1872. He married on 26 October 1859 at Manchester Cathedral Bertha Jane Grundy [*see* Adams, Bertha Jane Leith]. He died from a pulmonary haemorrhage on 29 July 1882, at Rushbrook Villa, Queenstown, Cork. He was survived by his wife, who achieved prominence as a novelist, who travelled with Adams to Malta, New Brunswick, Guernsey, and Ireland, and their son, the writer Francis William Lauderdale *Adams (1862–1893).   ANTHONY J. GASTON

Sources A. L. Adams, *Wanderings of a naturalist in India, the western Himalayas and Cashmere* (1867) · A. L. Adams, 'The birds of Cashmere and Ladakh', *Proceedings of the Zoological Society of London* (1858), 169–90 · A. L. Adams, 'Notes on the habits, haunts, etc. of some of the birds of India', *Proceedings of the Zoological Society of London* (1858), 466–512 · J. Gould, 'Descriptions of two new species of the family Hirundinidae', *Proceedings of the Zoological Society of London* (1858), 355–6 · A. L. Adams, *On the natural history and archaeology of the Nile valley and the Maltese Islands* (1870) · A. Leith Adams, *Field and forest* *rambles, with notes and observations on the natural history of eastern Canada* (1873) • *Nature*, 26 (1882), 337 • *CGPLA Ire.* (1882) • d. cert.

Wealth at death £856 4s.: probate, 21 Aug 1882, *CGPLA Ire.* • £53 in England: English probate sealed in Ireland, 13 Feb 1883, *CGPLA Ire.*

Adams [*née* Grundy; *other married name* de Courcy Laffan], **Bertha Jane Leith** (1837–1912), novelist, was born on 24 August 1837 at Moss-side, Lancashire, the eldest daughter of Frederick Grundy, solicitor, and Jane, *née* Beardoe. She married an army surgeon, Andrew Leith *Adams (1827–1882), son of Francis *Adams, physician and classical scholar, on 26 October 1859, moving with him to Malta, where the first of their two sons, Francis William Lauderdale *Adams, was born. She nursed the sick and dying in Malta's cholera epidemic of 1865, organizing the soldiers' wives to assist. Adams joined her husband in subsequent postings in New Brunswick, Guernsey, and London, and, after his retirement from the army in 1873, in Dublin and Cork, where he became professor of zoology and natural history.

Adams's first published story, 'Keane Malcombe's Pupil', appeared in 1876 in *All the Year Round*. In 1877 she published *Winstowe* (3 vols.), the first of her thirteen novels, and in 1879 she edited the short-lived monthly magazine, *Kensington*. She joined the staff of *All the Year Round*, where she published a number of short stories and serialized three novels.

On 1 September 1893, nine years after her husband's death, Adams married the Revd Robert Stuart de Courcy Laffan (1853–1927), son of Sir Robert Michael *Laffan (1819–1882), governor of Bermuda. She attempted to use her new name professionally, publishing *Louis Draycott* (2 vols., 1889) as Mrs R. S. de Courcy Laffan, but she soon resumed writing as Mrs Leith Adams (or Leith-Adams). She aided her husband in his work as headmaster of King Edward's School, Stratford upon Avon (1885–95), as principal of Cheltenham College, Cheltenham (1895–9), and as rector of St Stephen Walbrook, London (1899–1927). Her sons' illnesses and early deaths also made writing difficult. The younger died of tuberculosis in Queensland in 1892. Depressed by his brother's death and his own incurable lung disease, Francis Adams, the aesthetic novelist and poet, committed suicide in Margate in September 1893.

Adams's novels frequently used her varied experiences: the cholera epidemic in *Madelon Lemoine* (3 vols., 1879), New Brunswick rural life in *Aunt Hepsy's Foundling* (3 vols., 1881), and army life in *A Garrison Romance* (3 vols., 1892). Though often melodramatic, sentimental, and didactic, her novels were quick-paced and readable. Consistently praised for their vivid descriptions and for keeping the reader's interest, many went through multiple editions. Among her most popular were *Geoffrey Stirling* (3 vols., 1883), a tale of a widow's revenge for her husband's death; *Bonnie Kate* (3 vols., 1891), a new-woman novel of marital strife; and *Colour Sergeant, No. 1 Company* (2 vols., 1894), a romance between a major's niece and a disguised nobleman during the Fenian scare. She also published eight short-story collections and two volumes of poetry.

Starting with *A Song of Jubilee* (1887), Adams increasingly turned from fiction to poetry, drama, and lectures. In 'Fictional literature as a calling for women', she advised her hearers to use Field and Tuer's 'Author's hairless paper pad' (Laffan, 175–6) and to read Shakespeare, Meredith, Hardy, both Carlyles, and George Eliot (ibid., 164–7). Most important, she insisted that they 'do *nothing* without being paid' for otherwise they were '*wronging some unknown sister worker*' (ibid., 164). In addition to her literary abilities, Adams was an accomplished pianist and a lover of dogs. She died at her home, 119 St George's Road, Eccleston Square, London, on 5 September 1912 after a long illness, and was buried at Brookwood.

ELLEN MILLER CASEY

Sources Blain, Clements & Grundy, *Feminist comp.* • J. Sutherland, 'Adams, Mrs [Bertha Jane] Leith', *The Stanford companion to Victorian fiction* (1989) • *The Times* (10 Aug 1882) • *The Times* (7 Sept 1912) • *The Times* (18 Jan 1927) • D. C. Laffan, *Dreams made verity: stories, essays and memories* (1910) • H. C. Black, 'Mrs Leith Adams', *Notable women authors of the day* (1893), 284–98 • 'Laffan, Mrs Bertha', Allibone, *Dict.* • J. Sutherland, 'Adams, Francis [William Lauderdale]', *The Stanford companion to Victorian fiction* (1989) • Boase, *Mod. Eng. biog.* • 'Laffan, Rev. Robert Stuart de Courcy', Allibone, *Dict.*, suppl. • 'Adams, Andrew Leith', Allibone, *Dict.*, suppl. • 'Adams, Andrew Leith', *DNB*

Likenesses photograph, repro. in Black, 'Mrs Leith Adams'

Wealth at death £445: administration, 1913

Adams, Clement (*c.*1519–1587), schoolmaster and map engraver, was born at Buckington, Warwickshire. He was educated at Eton between 1530 and 1536, and subsequently at the King's Hall, Cambridge. From 17 August 1536 he was tutored in classics, mathematics, and geometry at Cambridge by John Cheke; he graduated BA in 1540–41 and MA in 1544. In 1548 he joined the London circle around Sebastian Cabot interested in applying mathematics to navigation and discovery. The basis for Clement Adams's fame is that about 1549 he re-engraved Sebastian Cabot's world chart as printed in 1544 in Nuremberg. The only surviving copy of that 1544 world chart is one assembled from four sheets at the Bibliothèque Nationale, Paris (cartes et plans, rès ge. AA 582). When republished in London with the changes introduced by Clement Adams it presented some of the problems of the north-west passage, but by further detailing the zone marked in 1544 as 'Terra Incognita' focused English attention on the north-east passage.

In reward, on 3 May 1552 Adams was appointed for life as schoolmaster to the king's henchmen (namely, the young courtly companions of Edward VI) at a salary of £40 per annum. Teaching these children at Greenwich put him in regular contact both with those preparing maps and plans of fortifications and the king's works there, and also with the University of Cambridge, where in 1564 he was criticized for invalidly wearing the gown of his office over the boys. In 1571 he exchanged his office for one with the same pay but without formal teaching obligations, and used the income to acquire the manor and advowson of White Waltham, Berkshire. It is not known when Adams married, but he had seven surviving children, one of whom was the architect Robert *Adams (d. 1595). On 2 March

1582 Robert transferred his workplace to Greenwich from Baynard's Castle, where at the same salary he would take forward his father's work as one distinguished in 'the excellent rules of Geometrical observations'.

Clement Adams had set down in 1554 a Latin account, *Anglorum navigatio ad Muscovitas*, describing his involvement with Sebastian Cabot in planning the voyage of 1553–4 made by Richard Chancellor and the ill-fated Sir Hugh Willoughby. As translated by Hakluyt, Adams explained that

> certaine grave Citizens of London, and men of great wisdome … resolved upon a new and strange Navigation. And whereas at the same time one Sebastia Cabota, a man in those dayes very renowned, happened to be in London, they began first of all to deale and consult diligently with him … to open a way and passage for our men for travaile to newe and unknowen kingdomes.   (Hakluyt, 1598, 1.243)

In addition to this translation first made for Hakluyt's *Divers Voyages* (1582), the dedicatory preface refers to 'the mappe of Sebastian Cabot, cut by Clement Adams … which is to be seene in her maiesties privie galerie at Westminster, and in many other ancient merchant's houses'. Elsewhere, Hakluyt explains that Cabot's discovery of the West Indies provided the subject of the map which Adams engraved. In 1576–7 Richard Willes, then studying at Oxford for his MA, noted in his *History of Travayle* that one of Adams's maps was kept at Chenies, Buckinghamshire. Clement Adams died on 9 January 1587. He was buried at St Alfege, Greenwich, as was his son Robert in 1595. His text was re-edited by Marnius and Aubrius as *Rerum Moscoviticarum …*, published in Frankfurt in 1600.

R. C. D. BALDWIN

Sources R. Hakluyt, *The principall navigations, voiages and discoveries of the English nation* (1589), 270–79 · R. Hakluyt, *The principal navigations, voyages, traffiques and discoveries of the English nation*, 1 (1598), 243–55; 3 (1600), 6 · R. Eden, ed., *Decades of the new world* (1555), 256 · CPR, PRO, C66/846m27; C66/1076m21; C66/1197m11; C66/1202m3; C66/1207m33; C66/1222m7 · BL, Cotton MS Julius IX, fol. 46 · BL, Harley MS 7033, fol. 96 · W. Sterry, ed., *The Eton College register, 1441–1698* (1943), 1 · Venn, *Alum. Cant.* · R. W. Shirley, *The mapping of the world: early printed world maps, 1472–1700* (1983), 92–3 · C. Marnius and J. Aubrius, eds., *Rerum Moscoviticarum auctiores varii* (Frankfurt am Main, 1600) · *Republica Muscoviae et urbes* (Leiden, 1630), 311–64 · E. G. R. Taylor, *The mathematical practitioners of Tudor and Stuart England* (1954); repr. (1970), 169
Archives BL, Cotton MSS · BL, Harley MSS

Adams, Dudley (1762–1830). *See under* Adams family (*per.* 1734–1817).

Adams, Fanny (1859–1867), murder victim and source of a colloquial expression, was born on 30 April 1859 in Tanhouse Lane, Alton, Hampshire, the fourth of seven children of George Adams (*b.* 1830), a labourer, later a bricklayer, and his wife, Harriet Mills (*b.* 1830).

Few people who use the expression 'sweet Fanny Adams' know of its origin. However there was a time when it would have been instantly recognized, when the name Fanny Adams made sensational headlines, creating a wave of horror, revulsion, and pity. The story is simple but horrific. On the afternoon of Saturday 24 August 1867 eight-year-old Fanny, her younger sister, Lizzie, aged five

and a half, and their near neighbour Minnie Warner, also eight years old, were playing near their Tanhouse Lane home in the country market town of Alton. They were approached by a man who offered them money for sweets. Fanny was abducted and taken to a nearby hop garden where she met her death. It appears that the murderer, a solicitor's clerk named Frederick Baker, later returned to the scene and dismembered the body.

When Fanny failed to return home by 7 p.m. a search was conducted by neighbours and parts of her body were found. So savage was the butchery that other body parts were recovered only after extensive searches lasting for several days. The suspect, to whom the child's concerned mother spoke during the afternoon following the abduction, was apprehended the same evening. An inquest was held a few days later and a jury returned a verdict of 'wilful murder against Frederick Baker'. This fact was recorded on the child's death certificate and was noted in the margin of the parish burial register (she was buried in the town cemetery on 28 August).

Following a formal committal hearing, the prisoner was taken to Winchester prison to await trial at the county assizes, where after a two-day hearing early in December, Frederick Baker was convicted by the jury fifteen minutes after retiring, and was sentenced to death by Mr Justice Mellor. Baker was hanged before some 5000 people at 8 a.m. on Christmas eve 1867. The local newspaper recorded that a large proportion of the crowd consisted of women. It was one of the last public executions held at Winchester.

A headstone for Fanny Adams was erected by public subscription in 1874 in the Alton cemetery on the Old Odiham Road, within a short distance of the murder scene. This might have been the only reminder of this tragic affair had it not been for the macabre humour of British sailors in the naval port of Portsmouth some 30 miles away. Served with tins of mutton as the latest shipboard convenience food in 1869, they gloomily declared that the contents were all chopped up and unrecognizable—just like sweet Fanny Adams.

'Sweet F. A.' was gradually accepted throughout the armed services as a euphemism for 'sweet nothing' and has passed into common (and vulgar) usage. As an aside, the large tins in which the meat was originally packed for the Royal Navy were also used as mess tins, and a century later navy mess tins were still colloquially known as 'fannys'.

TONY CROSS

Sources *Hampshire Chronicle* (1867) [various dates] · *Illustrated Police News* (1867) · b. cert. · d. cert. · register, Alton [baptism] · headstone · T. Cross, 'The story of sweet Fanny Adams', 1992, Hampshire County Council Museums Service [leaflet] · census returns for Alton, 1861, 1871

Adams [*formerly* Adam], **Francis** (1796–1861), physician and classical scholar, was born on 13 March 1796 at Auchinhove, Lumphanan, Aberdeenshire, the son of James Adam, a small farmer and builder, and his wife, Elspet Black. He was educated at the parish school, winning a bursary to King's College, Aberdeen, in 1809. He found himself 'shamefully mistaught' in classics, and with extraordinary energy devoted, in his own words, 'seventeen hours a day to the study of Virgil and Horace' (Adam, 53), reading each of these authors six or seven times in succession, before passing on to Greek. He graduated MA in 1813, and afterwards studied medicine at Edinburgh before becoming a member of the Royal College of Surgeons of London, on 1 December 1815. He returned to Scotland and settled in 1819 as a medical practitioner in the small village of Banchory-Ternan, Aberdeenshire, where he spent the remainder of his life. Shortly after moving to Banchory he married Elspeth (d. 1845), daughter of William Shaw, a local landowner, with whom he had seven children. His second son was Andrew Leith *Adams (1827–1882), later professor of natural history at Dublin and Cork.

Adams combined in a remarkable manner the character of a busy country doctor and an indefatigable scholar, sleeping for only three or four out of twenty-four hours, and often working throughout the night. Throughout the whole of his life his fondness for classical and especially Greek literature amounted to a passion. Although unceasingly engaged in his profession, he found time to read 'almost every Greek work which has come down to us from antiquity, with the exception of the ecclesiastical writers' (Adam, 53). In pure classics his chief works, *Hermes philologus*, on the difference between the Greek and Latin syntax (1826), and his papers on Greek prosody in the *Classical Journal*, are outdated; but they were regarded highly enough in his day and he was offered, but declined, the chair of Greek at Aberdeen. His appendix to George Dunbar's *Greek Lexicon*, however, contains valuable explanations of the Greek names of animals and plants, as might be expected from an enthusiastic botanist and naturalist. Adams also published *Arundines Devae, or, Poetical Translations on a New Principle*, 'by a Scotch physician' (1853); and a translation of *Hero and Leander* from the Greek of Musaeus, with other poems (1820), but these do not rise above the pedestrian.

Adams's most important labours were in the subject of Greek medicine, in which he effected more than any British scholar for nearly a century and a half, since John Freind. His attention was first drawn to the subject by a Dr George Kerr of Aberdeen, whose library, after his death, Adams acquired and made the foundation of his studies. In 1834 he published the first volume of a translation of Paul of Aegina, the author of a medical encyclopaedia written in Greek about AD 610, but the publication was interrupted as the project was losing money. The scheme was afterwards taken up by the Sydenham Society of London, and the complete translation was published in three volumes (*The Seven Books of Paulus Aegineta, Translated from the Greek, with a Commentary*, 1844–7). The translation is sound and retains its value as the only English one of the writer, whose Greek text is not easy of access even in a modern library. The chief value of the work resides in the substantial commentary, which shows wide and accurate learning and gives the fullest account of Greek and Roman therapeutics (and to some extent Arabic) in any modern language. Considering that Adams was writing in

isolation, remote from great libraries and immersed in professional work, it was a remarkable performance.

Adams later prepared, also for the Sydenham Society, an English translation of some of the writings in the Hippocratic corpus, the supposed 'genuine' works (*The Genuine Works of Hippocrates, Translated from the Greek*, 2 vols., 1849). An accurate version, though based on a poor Greek original text, it nevertheless implied an insistence on the superiority of the so-called genuine texts over others contained within the Hippocratic corpus. It therefore distracted attention for over a century from texts of equal importance in the study of ancient Greek medicine in the fifth and fourth centuries BC. Adams further brought out, under the auspices of the same society, an edition of Aretaeus of Cappadocia (*fl.* AD 150) containing the revised Greek text with an English translation (*The Extant Works of Aretaeus the Cappadocian*, 1856). Although the edition of the Greek has long been superseded, the English version has not, and it remains a useful starting point for investigating this ancient author, whose descriptions of disease are among the best to survive from antiquity. This work, involving reference to important libraries, brought Adams into communication with many English and foreign scholars, and procured for him an honorary MD from Aberdeen in 1856. He had already received an honorary LLD degree from the University of Glasgow, in 1846.

Adams was regarded as a good practitioner and skilful surgeon, frequently visiting the surgical wards of the Aberdeen Royal Infirmary, and he had an extensive and time-consuming obstetric practice. His medical writings consisted of papers on a variety of subjects, including burns, adder bites, arsenic poisoning, club-foot, uterine haemorrhage, and surgery of the knee. They show, along with much learning, a strong tendency to hold outmoded views. For example, Adams obstinately refused to believe that the sounds of the foetal heart could be heard by auscultation. He was an excellent naturalist, being well-versed in the botany and ornithology of Scotland, especially of Deeside, and he presented a paper to the British Association.

Adams died from bronchitis at Bellfield, Banchory-Ternan, on 26 February 1861. A monument to his memory was erected at Banchory by public subscription. It is a granite obelisk, bearing a Latin inscription by Professor Geddes of Aberdeen.

Adams's reputation in his own special field of scholarship remains high. His translations are good and generally accurate, though not brilliant or always elegant, but he was working from texts that were both difficult to understand and badly transmitted over the centuries. His notes are less valuable for their critical insight than for their richness in accessory learning, and they represent almost the last era in which ancient medical texts were cited and used for their value in modern medicine. Adams's choice of Paul and Aretaeus was determined at least as much for their clinical value as for their antiquity. His assessment of the authors and their works was traditional, however, and Adams stands a little apart from contemporary medical historians like W. A. Greenhill, and Charles Daremberg, of

France, who sought to reinterpret ancient medicine from a more strictly historical perspective. Adams's *Hippocrates* continued to be regarded as the standard English version into the 1970s.   VIVIAN NUTTON

Sources *Aberdeen Herald and General Advertiser* (2 March 1861) · *The Scotsman* (27 Feb 1861); repr. in 'Dr Adams of Banchory', *Medical Times and Gazette* (16 March 1861), 292–3 · *The Scotsman* (9 March 1861); repr. in 'Dr Adams of Banchory', *Medical Times and Gazette* (16 March 1861), 292–3 · J. Brown, *Horae subsecivae*, 3 vols. (1885–9), vol. 1, pp. 245–76 · C. Singer, 'A great country doctor: Francis Adams of Banchory (1796–1861)', *Bulletin of the History of Medicine*, 12 (1942), 1–17 · J. Craig, 'Francis Adams (1796–1861)', *Aberdeen University Review*, 39 (1961–2); pubd separately (1961) [repr. *The Lancet*, 25/2/1961] · A. Adam, 'Dr Francis Adams of Banchory (1796–1861), "doctissimus medicus Britannorum"', *Scottish Medical Journal*, 42 (1997), 53–4 · parish register (baptism), Lumphanan, 19/3/1796 · d. cert.

Likenesses W. Brodie, bust, U. Aberdeen L. · Drummond, photograph (after Brodie), Wellcome L.

Wealth at death £3010 13s. 6d.: confirmation, 7 Aug 1861, NA Scot., SC 5/41/17/428-49

Adams, Francis William Lauderdale (1862–1893), writer, was born on 27 September 1862 at Valletta in Malta. The grandson of the Scottish classicist and medical scholar Francis *Adams (1796–1861), he was the first of two sons born to Andrew Leith *Adams (1827–1882), army surgeon and natural historian, and his wife, Bertha Jane Leith *Adams, *née* Grundy (1837–1912), editor of the *Kensington* magazine, writer for *All the Year Round*, and popular novelist. After a peripatetic childhood in Malta, England, New Brunswick, and Ireland, Adams was educated at several schools in the midlands, and matriculated with a strong grounding in ancient classics from Shrewsbury School in 1879. He spent some time as an attaché to the British embassy in Paris, where he drank in contemporary European thought and culture and started writing his first novel, *Leicester, an Autobiography*, before taking up a position as assistant master at Ventnor College on the Isle of Wight. After two years his health broke down and he gave up teaching to pursue a literary career.

On 31 July 1884 Adams married Helen Elizabeth Uttley (1857–1886). In the same year his first book of verse, *Henry and other Tales*, was published. In 1883 or 1884, he joined H. M. Hyndman's Democratic Federation in London, and embarked for Australia in search of a climate that would better suit him, both physically and politically. He hoped that Australia would embody the best aspects of British society, without what he perceived to be the corruption and decadence of the Old World. Despite this political optimism, he became notorious for writing that 'to treat of "Culture" and "Society" in Australia, in the sense that one does of the greater European capitals, would be like treating of the snakes in Iceland' (*The Australians*, 1893, 39). Adams published literary essays in Melbourne journals and worked as tutor on a pastoral property in Jerilderie, New South Wales, where he was joined by his wife, Helen. After a short period in Sydney he moved north to Queensland, where he worked as a journalist and became involved in local politics; he continued to write poetry, fiction, drama, and literary essays. In 1885 *Leicester, an Autobiography*, was published in London. His other published

works of this time include: *Madeline Brown's Murderer* (Melbourne, 1886), *Australian Essays* (London and Melbourne, 1886), *Poetical Works* (London and Brisbane, 1887), and *Songs of the Army of the Night* (Sydney, 1888), the last of which was so popular in socialist circles as to be reprinted in London in 1890, 1891, 1894, and 1910. Adams's personal charisma and revolutionary zeal influenced other radicals in Australia, such as Mary Gilmore and William Lane, and a wider circle of writers and journalists who were impressed by his mixture of intellect and political commitment. After the death of his wife and their infant son in 1886, in 1887 Adams may have married (Ella) Edith Goldstone (*b.* 1865, *d.* in or after 1913), a nurse who may have been an actress and bookshop assistant. There were no surviving children, and after Edith remarried in 1896 she remained childless.

In March 1890, suffering severely from tuberculosis and a growth in his throat, Adams returned to England to pursue his literary career. Several works were published in the final years of his life: *John Webb's End* (London, 1891), *The Melbournians* (London and Sydney, 1892), *Australian Life* (London, 1892), and *The Australians: a Social Sketch* (London, 1893). *The Australians* is best remembered for its pithy analysis of Australian society and culture, particularly in the context of relations between Britain and Australia during the last years of colonial rule. Adams died on 4 September 1893, in a boarding-house at 9 Gordon Road, Margate, shortly before his thirty-first birthday, of a self-inflicted gunshot wound during a massive haemorrhage. The suicide caused a sensation, and the widow's statement at the inquest that she had assisted her husband's death by removing his false teeth made her the subject of some speculation. The jury reached a charitable but misleading verdict of temporary insanity, and expressed regret that his wife had not prevented the fatal act. The Sydney *Bulletin* expressed the more common view:

> To those who knew Francis Adams well, the news of his death by his own hand, and with the connivance of his pitying, devoted wife, will come with no shock of surprise. He was a man to whom the idea of suicide was familiar. (*Bulletin*, 16 Sept 1893, 7)

He was buried at the new cemetery in Margate on 9 September, under a broken column.

Francis Adams had begun to establish a reputation in England as a gifted but erratic writer when he died. Several of his books were published posthumously, including his analysis of British foreign relations in *The New Egypt: a Social Sketch* (1894); a play, *Tiberius*, which was edited and introduced by W. M. Rossetti; a 'new woman' novel, [Agnes Farrell], *Lady Lovan* (1895); and *Essays in Modernity* (1899).   MEG TASKER

Sources M. Tasker, *Struggle and storm: the life and death of Francis Adams* (2001) · C. Turnbull, *These tears of fire: the story of Francis Adams* (1949) · University of British Columbia, Angeli-Dennis MSS · I. M. Britain, 'Francis Adams: the Arnoldian as socialist', *Historical Studies* [Melbourne], 15 (1971–3), 401–23 · I. M. Britain, 'Adams, Francis', *DLB*, vol. 5 · S. Murray-Smith, 'Adams, Francis', *AusDB*, vol. 3 · *DNB* · G. A. Cevasco, ed., *The 1890s: an encyclopedia of British literature, art, and culture* (1993) · M. Tasker, *Francis Adams: a research guide* (1996) · *Daily Chronicle* [London] (5–7 Sept 1893) · 'Distressing suicide of an author', *Keble's Margate and Ramsgate Gazette* (9 Sept 1893) · *The Bulletin* [Sydney, NSW] (16 Sept 1893) · *Westminster Gazette* (5 Sept 1893) · *Pall Mall Gazette* (6 Sept 1893) · *ILN* (9 Sept 1893) · *Commonweal* (16 Sept 1893) · H. S. Salt, *Seventy years among savages* (1951), 83 · E. Jones, 'Francis Adams, 1862–1893: a forgotten child of his age', *Essays and Studies by Members of the English Association*, new ser., 20 (1967), 76–103 · V. Palmer, 'Life and death of Francis Adams', *Southerly* [Sydney], 15/2 (1954), 102–4 · F. Harris, *Frank Harris, his life and adventures: an autobiography*, ed. G. Richards (1947) · m. cert. · d. cert. · d. cert. [H. Uttley] · parish register, Margate, St John the Baptist [burial] · War Office records, WO 76211, form 360 (Andrew Leith Adams) · Shrewsbury School register, 1798–1898 · *CGPLA Eng. & Wales* (1893)

Archives FM Cam., letters to Wilfrid Scawen Blunt · Mitchell L., NSW, Stephens MSS · NL Aus., Miller MSS; Palmer MSS · Richmond Local Studies Library, London, letters to D. B. W. Sladen · University of British Columbia, Vancouver, Angeli-Dennis MSS **Likenesses** F. W. L. Adams, photograph, repro. in F. W. L. Adams, *Tiberius: a drama*, ed. W. M. Rossetti (1894) · F. W. L. Adams, photograph, State Library of Victoria, Melbourne; repro. in Tasker, *Struggle and storm* · photograph, University of British Columbia, Angeli-Dennis MSS · photograph, repro. in *The Bulletin* [Sydney] (8 March 1890) · photograph, repro. in *The Bulletin* [Sydney] (14 Oct 1893) **Wealth at death** £193 6s. 9d.: probate, 18 Sept 1893, *CGPLA Eng. & Wales*

Adams, (John) Frank (1930–1989), mathematician, was born on 5 November 1930 in Woolwich, London, the elder son (there were no daughters) of William Frank Adams, civil engineer, and his wife, Jean Mary Baines, biologist, both of London. He was educated at Bedford School and then spent the years 1948 and 1949 doing national service in the Royal Engineers. He went to Trinity College, Cambridge, where he was a wrangler in part two (1951) and gained special credit in part three (1952) of the mathematical tripos. He continued at Cambridge as a research student, first under A. S. Besicovitch and then, more significantly, under Shaun Wylie. His PhD dissertation (1955) was on algebraic topology, which remained his main research interest for the rest of his life. Adams spent the year 1954 at Oxford, as a junior lecturer, where he came under the influence of J. H. C. Whitehead, then the leading topologist in the country. In 1953 he married Grace Rhoda, daughter of Charles Benjamin Carty, time and motion engineer. Soon after their marriage she became a minister in the Congregational church. They had a son and three daughters (one adopted). Family life was extremely important to Adams, though he preferred to keep it separate from his professional life. The family used to do many things together, especially fell-walking in the Lake District.

Adams returned to Cambridge in 1956 as a research fellow at Trinity College and developed the spectral sequence which bears his name, linking the cohomology of a topological space to its stable homotopy groups. In 1957–8 he was a Commonwealth fellow at the University of Chicago, where he proved a famous conjecture about the existence of H-structures on spheres, using the same ideas. On his return from the United States he became fellow, lecturer, and director of studies at Trinity Hall, Cambridge. There, in 1961, he confirmed his already high international reputation by solving another famous problem, concerning vector fields on spheres. For this he invented

some operations in K-theory, which later bore his name, and these proved to be of fundamental importance.

In 1962 Adams left Cambridge for Manchester University, where in 1964 he became Fielden professor in succession to M. H. A. Newman and was elected a fellow of the Royal Society at the early age of thirty-four. At Manchester he took much further the powerful methods he had originated at Cambridge in a celebrated series of papers 'On the groups J(X)', which opened up a new era in homotopy theory. In the first of these he made a bold conjecture about the relation between the classification of vector bundles by stable isomorphism and their classification by stable homotopy equivalence of the associated sphere-bundles. Reformulated in various ways this Adams conjecture (later a theorem) became one of the key results in homotopy theory.

By 1970 Adams was the undisputed leader in his field and his reputation was such that he was seen as the obvious person to succeed Sir William Hodge as Lowndean professor of astronomy and geometry at Cambridge. He was delighted to return to Trinity, his old college, though he never became very active in its affairs. Among his various research interests in this later phase of his career three subjects predominated: finite H-spaces, equivariant homotopy theory, and the homotopy properties of classifying spaces of topological groups. Although he published important papers on these and other subjects throughout this period he also began to publish more expository work, notably his lecture notes on *Stable Homotopy and Generalised Homology* (1974) and his monograph, *Infinite Loop Spaces* (1978), based on the Hermann Weyl lectures he gave at Princeton University. The latter, especially, gives a good idea of his magisterial expository style and particular brand of humour.

Adams was an awe-inspiring teacher who expected a great deal of his research students and whose criticism of work which did not impress him could be withering. For those who were stimulated rather than intimidated by this treatment, he was generous with his help. The competitive instinct in Adams was highly developed, for example in his attitude to research. Priority of discovery mattered a great deal to him and he was known to argue such questions not just as to the day but as to the time of day. In a subject where 'show and tell' is customary he was extraordinarily secretive about research in progress.

Although Adams enjoyed excellent physical health he suffered a serious episode of depressive illness in 1965 and there were further episodes of depression later. To what extent his professional work was adversely affected by the nature of the treatments he received to help control the condition is not clear, but certainly his contributions to research in later years were not as innovative as those of his youth. Moreover, he never played the prominent role in the academic and scientific world to which his professional standing would have entitled him. Even so, his influence was great; those who turned to him for an opinion were seldom left in any doubt as to his views.

Adams's great contributions to mathematics were recognized by the awards of the junior Berwick (1963) and senior Whitehead (1974) prizes of the London Mathematical Society and the Sylvester medal (1982) of the Royal Society. He received the degree of ScD from Cambridge in 1982. He was elected a foreign associate of the National Academy of Sciences of Washington, DC (1985), and an honorary member of the Royal Danish Academy of Sciences (1988), and was made an honorary ScD at the University of Heidelberg in 1986. His collected works were published in 1992. He acted as treasurer of the local branch of the Labour Party and might be described as an intellectual Fabian in outlook. Adams died immediately following a night-time accident in the car he was driving on the A1 near Brampton, Huntingdonshire, on 7 January 1989.

I. M. JAMES, rev.

Sources I. M. James, *Memoirs FRS*, 36 (1990), 1–16 · *CGPLA Eng. & Wales* (1989)
Archives Trinity Cam., corresp. and papers
Likenesses bronze head, priv. coll. · photograph, repro. in James, *Memoirs FRS* · photograph, repro. in N. Ray and G. Walker, eds., *Adams memorial symposium on algebraic topology*, 2 vols. (1992)
Wealth at death £154,180: probate, 7 March 1989, *CGPLA Eng. & Wales*

Adams, George (*b.* 1697/8), translator and writer, was the son of George Adams (*d.* 1724?), clergyman (probably rector of Upton, Huntingdonshire, 1703–24). He was educated at Peterborough School and at St John's College, Cambridge, where he was admitted, aged eighteen, as a sizar on 23 May 1716 and graduated BA in 1720 and MA in 1735; in 1729 he became a fellow of the college. He was ordained deacon in Lincoln on 13 March 1720 and priest on 3 September 1722. Little else is known of his life and works. His name is primarily associated with the first complete English prose translation of the non-fragmentary seven plays of Sophocles, *The tragedies of Sophocles, translated from the Greek, with notes historical, moral, and critical* (2 vols., 1729). The plain English rendering, while meeting Adams's own unpretentious terms ('that by that means it might be helpful to the learners of the Greek language'; preface), displeased some: the much acclaimed translator George Colman remarked that 'the beauties of Sophocles lay buried in Adams's prose' (*The Comedies of Terence*, 2nd edn, 1768, vol. 1). The long preface included an essay entitled 'A defence of tragick poetry'; the warm dedication to William Montagu, fifth earl and second duke of Manchester, contains indications of the author's residence in the neighbourhood of Kimbolton Castle and of his loyalty to the Hanoverian succession. Fifteen years later he published *The Heathen Martyr, or, The Death of Socrates, an Historical Tragedy* (1746), advertised in the *Gentleman's Magazine* with the title 'The life of Socrates … by G. Adams M.A.' (*GM*).

Adams has also been credited with the production of theological works, the tenor of which is indeed consistent with the loyal Anglican attitude displayed in the dedicatory note prefixed to the *Sophocles*; authorship, however, is controversial. The earliest of such volumes, *Vera fides: a Poetical Essay, in Three Cantos* (1731), outlined the mysteries of divine providence and human redemption, for the benefit of 'our modern atheists, deists and infidels' (subtitle); similarly polemic mood inspired *The deist confuted. Wherein his principal objections against revealed religion, especially against Christianity are briefly stated and answered* (1734) and *An exposition of some articles of religion, which strike at the tenets of the arians and socinians. Likewise at the infidels, Romanists, Lutherans and Calvinists. In several sermons and dissertations* (1752). An edition of select theological writings completes the list of works in his name (*A system of divinity, ecclesiastical history and morality; collected from the writings of authors of various nations and languages … designed also to teach the reader a perfect skill in Hebrew, Greek and Latin* (1768)). The single autobiographical reference to be found is offered in the Latin dedication of the *Exposition*, in which Adams, addressing Thomas Sherlock, bishop of London, states that he has been serving in the diocese of London for twenty years ('per viginti, et quod excurrit annos, in tua hac Diocesi sacro munere perfunctus sim'; fol. 1r).

Such evidence rules out the possibility of identifying the author of the theological works with the Revd George Adams who held the rectory of Sibsey, Lincolnshire, from 1731 to 1779, and who featured among the subscribers of *A Collection of Sermons … on Various Subjects* by G. Harvest MA, fellow of Magdalene College, Cambridge (1754). Other suggested identifications have been put forward to no avail: the Revd. George Adams of King's College (MA, 1733), prebendary of Seaford and Wightring in the diocese of Chichester (1736–50), was dead by 26 September 1750; a junior George Adams of St John's (1717–1783), rector of Widdington, Essex (1757–83), did not obtain his MA degree until 1772. The question, first raised in the pages of *Notes & Queries* for 1855 and 1860, as to whether the religious writer and the translator were in fact the same person is a puzzle as yet unsolved.

ANNA CHAHOUD

Sources *DNB* · D. Bank and others, eds., *British biographical archive* (1984–98) [microfiche; with index, 2nd edn, 1998] · Venn, *Alum. Cant.* · *Graduati Cantabrigienses: sive catalogus … ab anno 1659 usq. … 1823, … e libris subscriptionum desumptus* (1823), 2 · G. Adams, dedication, *The tragedies of Sophocles, translated from the Greek … by G. Adams, A.B.* (1729) · G. Adams, dedication, *An exposition of some articles of religion … in several sermons and dissertations … by G. Adams, M.A.* (1752) · *N&Q*, 11 (1855), 367 · *N&Q*, 2nd ser., 9 (1860), 162 · *GM*, 1st ser., 16 (1746), 560 · S. Gillespie, *Poets on the classics: an anthology of English poets' writings on the classical poets and dramatists from Chaucer to the present* (1988), 202 · *Fasti Angl., 1541–1857*, [Chichester], 48, 61 · L. M. Brüggeman, *A view of the English editions, translations and illustrations from the ancient Greek and Latin authors* (1797), 1.103

Adams, George, senior (*bap.* 1709, *d.* 1772). *See under* Adams family (*per.* 1734–1817).

Adams, George, junior (1750–1795). *See under* Adams family (*per.* 1734–1817).

Adams, Gladstone (1880–1966), motorist and inventor of a windscreen wiper, was born on 16 May 1880 at 4 St Ann's Row, Newcastle upon Tyne, son of John Adams, metal merchant, and his wife, Agnes, *née* M'Gregor, and was educated at Rutherford College, Newcastle. He lived all the rest of his life in Whitley Bay, Northumberland, where he had a photographic business in Station Road, which was later transferred to his home in Beverley Park, Monkseaton. He joined the Northumberland yeomanry, a territorial horse regiment, in 1900, and served for ten years. On 27 January 1914 he married Laura Annie (b. 1885/6), daughter of Joseph Dixon Clark, an artist, of Whickham, near Gateshead. They had one son. At the outbreak of the First World War Adams joined the army, transferring to the Royal Flying Corps, and reaching the rank of captain by the end of the war. As acting adjutant for 15th wing he helped to arrange the funeral of Baron Manfred von Richthofen (the Red Baron).

Adams had the idea for a windscreen wiper after he had driven from Newcastle to London for the FA cup final at Crystal Palace on 25 April 1908, when Newcastle United were beaten 3–1 by Wolverhampton Wanderers. It began to snow, and he had to fold down his windscreen in order to improve his vision. In itself, the journey from Newcastle, in a Darracq car, was such an achievement that the car was later displayed in a shop window in Oxford Street.

Adams took out a patent for a windscreen wiper in 1911. The patent provided for a 'moving squeegee'—a horizontal bar with a rubber strip pressing against the outside of the windscreen—operated either by the hand or foot of the driver by means of cords, pulleys, and springs, or automatically at intervals by the power used to propel the car. But the patent was never published and was later abandoned, although Adams wrote in a letter of 1964 that his patent had been stolen by a Newcastle man called Capstaff, who took out a patent in the USA, and later made a fortune running a shipyard. He presented a demonstration model to the Newcastle Museum of Science and Engineering in 1951. There are others who have claims to have been the inventor of the windscreen wiper. It is usually attributed to Prince Henry of Prussia, who fitted a hand-operated rubber wiper to the Benz car in which he set off from Hamburg to London on 5 July 1911, but hand-operated wipers appeared in France as early as 1907.

Adams served as president of the Photographic Dealers Association and the Professional Photographic Association. A member of the Northumberland county council for many years, he was also a Whitley Bay councillor almost continuously from 1937 to 1963, and was chairman of the Whitley Bay council 1947–8. Adams died on 28 July 1966 at Wooley Hospital, Slaley, near Hexham, Northumberland, survived by his wife.   ANNE PIMLOTT BAKER

Sources P. Robertson, *The new Shell book of firsts* (1994) • *The Journal* [Newcastle upon Tyne] (4 Aug 1966) • *The Journal* [Newcastle upon Tyne] (23 March 1980) • *Shields News* (5 Aug 1966) • *Local heroes*, BBC 2, 1997, www.bbc.co.uk/local-heroes/prog4/htm • b. cert. • m. cert. • d. cert. • CGPLA Eng. & Wales (1966)
Likenesses photograph, repro. in *Shields News* (14 March 1949)
Wealth at death £4630: administration, 22 Sept 1966, CGPLA Eng. & Wales

Adams, Sir Grantley Herbert (1898–1971), prime minister of the Federation of the West Indies, was born on 28 April 1898 in Bridgetown, Barbados, the second of six sons (there was also a daughter) of Fitzherbert Adams, a primary school headmaster, and his wife, Rosa Frances Turner. Education mattered in his family and Adams won a scholarship to Harrison College and then the coveted Barbados scholarship. He entered St Catherine's Society, Oxford, in 1918, took part in undergraduate Liberal politics, played much cricket, and was president of the junior common room. He obtained third classes in classical honour moderations in 1921 and jurisprudence in 1923.

After being called to the bar (Gray's Inn) in 1923, Adams returned home where he built a reputation as a shrewd, forceful barrister. He was also a leader writer for the conservative *Agricultural Reporter*, but as the West Indies sank ever deeper into the depression of the 1930s, his politics became more radical as he took up the cause of the Barbadian working man. In 1934 he was elected a member of the house of assembly for St Joseph, surprisingly beating a white planter; he soon proved to be as adept at politics as he was at the bar. After serious riots in July 1937, the radicals sent Adams to London to press for a royal commission to examine West Indian conditions. In 1939 the Moyne commission went to the Caribbean.

This London visit had important consequences for Adams. He became friends with Labour Party members who were interested in the colonies, such as Sir R. Stafford Cripps, Arthur Creech Jones, and Rita Hinden; his vague but deeply felt radicalism was channelled into Fabian socialism. He also saw the need for a political party backed by a trade union. On his return he helped to found the Barbados Progressive League in 1938, from which were soon to spring the Barbados Workers' Union and the Barbados Labour Party which was led by Adams.

Adams was appointed by the governor to the executive committee in 1942, and made leader of the house of assembly when the Barbados Labour Party won nine seats, a bare majority, in 1946. In 1954 Adams, who had become QC (Barbados) in 1953 and who was by then a respected Caribbean statesman, became premier. Yet when Barbados became independent in 1966, Adams and his party were in opposition after a defeat by the Democratic Labour Party.

Despite his Barbadian preoccupations, Adams played his part in the wider world of cold war diplomacy in the immediate post-war years, the most successful of his life. He was in the British delegation at the first meeting of the United Nations in 1948 when he eloquently defended the British colonial record; he was appointed to the committee of experts of the International Labour Organization in 1949; he was president of the Caribbean Labour Congress and vice-chairman of the International Confederation of Free Trade Unions when these bodies were fighting against communist domination.

Even before the war Adams believed that the solution to the problems of the Caribbean colonies lay in a federation. After the war he played a leading part in the planning conferences at Montego Bay in 1947 and London in 1953 and 1956. He became leader of the new Federal Labour Party and the first and, as it turned out, the only prime minister of the Federation of the West Indies in 1958. For various reasons Jamaica and Trinidad, the most powerful members, dropped out, leaving behind the fatally weakened rump of the small islands and Barbados. The federation staggered on until 1962, and a frustrated and bitterly disappointed Adams returned to the parochial world of leading the opposition in Barbados. After increasing illness he resigned his seat in 1970.

Adams belonged to that generation of English-educated nationalist politicians such as Norman Manley of Jamaica and Eric Williams of Trinidad who led their countries towards independence and ensured that they followed the Westminster model afterwards. In Barbados he broke the planter domination of society, encouraged economic diversification, and laid the foundations for a welfare state.

In private life Adams was amiable and witty and he delighted in the post-war flowering of West Indian cricket. He married Grace Thorne, who was from a white planter family, in 1929; this was in itself a portent of social change. Their only child, Tom (1931–1985) [see Adams, John Michael Geoffrey Manningham], was a prime minister of Barbados in the 1970s.

Adams was appointed CMG in 1952 and knighted in 1957. In 1958 he received an honorary DLitt from Mount Allison. He died at Bridgetown on 28 November 1971.

DONALD WOOD, rev.

Sources F. A. Hoyos, *Grantley Adams and the social revolution* (1974) · *The Times* (29 Nov 1971) · *The Times* (3 Dec 1971) · private information (1986)
Archives Bodl. RH, papers relating to West Indies Settlement Commission | Bodl. RH, corresp. with Arthur Creech Jones

Adams, Henry (1713–1805), shipbuilder, was born in Deptford, the son of Anthony Adams, a shipwright at the town's royal dockyard. In 1726 he began his apprenticeship to Benjamin Slade, the foreman of the yard. Adams moved to Hampshire in 1744 and was appointed naval overseer for the building of the *Surprise* (24 guns) in James Wyatt and Major's yard at Buckler's Hard, near Beaulieu, Hampshire. The yard was then in difficult times and, following the departure of three successive builders, Adams took it over in March 1748, with support from the duke of Montagu. In 1747 Adams had married Elizabeth Smith (d. 1759) of Beaulieu; they had two children, who died in childhood.

Adams's first ship, the *Mermaid* (24 guns), was launched in 1749, a year after the end of the War of the Austrian Succession. Naval work dried up, and Adams built some herring busses for the British Fisheries Society; however, in 1754, upon the threat of another war with France, he signed a contract for another 24-gun ship, and this soon led to further orders for small warships. His work on the *Coventry* (28 guns) was criticized in 1756 and it was recommended that the naval overseer, Mr Snooks, should not be employed again. Nevertheless, Adams was awarded the contract for a frigate, the *Thames* (32 guns), in 1757. In 1760, a year after his first wife's death, Adams married Anne Warner (c.1738–1827), daughter of the steward of the manor of Beaulieu; they had seven children.

Early in 1762 Adams signed the contract to build the *Europe* (64 guns), his first ship of the line. Because of doubts about the site at Buckler's Hard, the Navy Board insisted that it be built at Lepe, near the mouth of the Beaulieu River. In 1763 he entered a partnership with William Dudman and William Barnard, who ran a private shipyard at Deptford. Naval work came to an end after the peace in 1763 and the Buckler's Hard site was for several years used mainly as a timber yard. In 1771 Adams was contracted to build a 74-gun ship at Deptford, followed by three smaller ships at Buckler's Hard. By the end of the year the Navy Board had accepted that the site was suitable for larger ships after some improvements and Adams was contracted for the *Vigilant* (64 guns). Following the outbreak of the American War of Independence in 1775 Adams flourished as a naval contractor. Many frigates and smaller ships were built, but the most famous product of the yard was the *Agamemnon* (64 guns), begun in 1779 and launched in April 1781. At the end of that year Adams was contracted to build an even larger ship, the *Illustrious* (74 guns), which was not completed until 1789.

In 1792 Adams lost a lawsuit against his former partners in Deptford and his family were forced to depend on Buckler's Hard as their sole source of income. In 1793, at the age of eighty, he retired and left the running of the business to his sons Balthazar and Edward. Adams died at Buckler's Hard in 1805, and was buried in Beaulieu church on 3 November. The yard went bankrupt in 1811.

Adams was typical of dozens of private shipbuilders who worked for the Royal Navy in the age of sail. His name is remembered partly because the rural site at Buckler's Hard survived intact and was opened as a museum in 1963. His reputation is perhaps exaggerated because he built the *Agamemnon*, which was highly praised by Nelson when he commanded her, after five years on half pay, from 1793 to 1796. Yet Adams did not design the *Agamemnon*, but merely constructed her to a plan originally drawn by Sir Thomas Slade.

BRIAN LAVERY

Sources A. J. Holland, *Buckler's Hard, a rural shipbuilding centre* (1985) · P. Banbury, *Shipbuilders of the Thames and Medway* (1971) · J. E. Barnard, *Building Britain's wooden walls: the Barnard dynasty, c.1697–1851* (1997)
Likenesses portrait, Buckler's Hard Museum, Hampshire

Adams, Henry Cadwallader (1817–1899), Church of England clergyman and author, was born on 4 November 1817 at 6 Great James Street, Holborn, London, the third son of John Adams, of St Pancras, an assistant judge, and his second wife, Jane, daughter of Thomas Martin of Nottingham. He was educated at Westminster School and Winchester College and at Balliol College, Oxford, and then at Magdalen College, where he graduated BA in 1840 (second class honours in *literae humaniores*) and proceeded MA in 1842. In June 1843 he was appointed an examiner in the responsive schools and then in July he was elected a probationer-fellow of Magdalen. He was appointed master of Magdalen College School on 22 March 1844 but resigned a month later to take up an appointment as master at Winchester College, a post he retained until 1851. He was ordained a deacon on 20 December 1846 and a priest in 1852 by the bishop of Oxford. He was appointed curate of Greinton, Somerset, in 1852. Upon his marriage to Esther Pell Edmonds, the second daughter of Richard

Edmonds, rector of Woodleigh, Devon, on 6 July 1852, Adams resigned his Magdalen fellowship. He became chaplain to Bromley College, Kent, in 1855, a post he held until 1867 when he resigned to become vicar of Dry Sandford with Cothill, Berkshire, where he remained until 1878. On 15 July of that year he was installed by the bishop of Chichester as vicar of Old Shoreham, Sussex, where he stayed until 1896.

Adams was a prolific writer (in Allibone's supplement forty-seven works are listed), his works dividing into four principal categories: religious commentaries, Greek and Latin grammars, school stories, and historical tales such as *The Boy Cavaliers, or, The Siege of Clidesford* (1868), *Friend or Foe: a Tale of Sedgemoor* (1870), or *Tales of the Prophets* and *Tales of the Kings* (both 1872). Adams's forte, however, was as a writer of boys' school stories. He extolled the monitorial system, and he was one of the first of the Victorians to treat this subject seriously with such stories as *Tales of Charlton School* (1851) or *Schoolboy Honour* (1861). In the *Saturday Review* his history of Winchester College, *Wykehamica* (1878), is praised partly as a collection of school stories that will be popular among boys but 'its higher value, as the author perceives, lies in its record of the birth and development of the English system of public schools' (*Saturday Review*, 47/1214, 1 Feb 1879, 148). Adams was also a passable poet. He died at his home, West Uplands, Portsmouth Road, Guildford, Surrey, on 17 October 1899.

GUY ARNOLD

Sources W. D. Macray, *A register of the members of St Mary Magdalen College, Oxford*, 8 vols. (1894–1915), vol. 6 · J. R. Bloxam, *A register of the presidents, fellows … of Saint Mary Magdalen College*, 8 vols. (1853–85), vol. 4 · J. B. Wainewright, ed., *Winchester College, 1836–1906: a register* (1907) · Allibone, *Dict.* · Foster, *Alum. Oxon.* · Crockford (1899) · m. cert. · d. cert.
Archives BM · Magd. Oxf.
Wealth at death £8523 17s. 7d.: probate, 27 Dec 1899, *CGPLA Eng. & Wales*

Adams, James (1737–1802), Jesuit and philologist, was born on 3 November 1737 to William Adams and Anne or Sarah Spencer; he refers to Bury St Edmunds as his 'native town' (*Euphonologia Linguae Anglicanae*, 1794, 7). He was educated at the Jesuit college in St Omer (1746–55) and the Scots College at Douai (1755–6), and entered the Society of Jesus at Watten on 7 September 1756. After his noviciate he was the professor of languages at the college at St Omer until its closure by the French government in 1762, when the members of the college fled to Bruges; Adams was at the college there in 1763–4. In 1767 he completed a theology degree at Liège and was ordained, thereafter completing his tertianship at Ghent. He was a missioner in Lancashire (1768) and Staffordshire (from 1769 until the suppression of the Jesuits in 1773). Early biographers state that he remained at St Omer and fled from France to Edinburgh upon the outbreak of the French Revolution (Watkins and Shoberl), but he left France well before that time; further, his philological works show a particular interest in the pronunciation of English in Scotland.

Between 1792 and 1799, while living in London, Adams

published several works, primarily on English pronunciation. His principal work, the *Euphonologia Linguae Anglicanae* (in Latin and French, 1794; substantially revised and published in English as *The Pronunciation of the English Language*, 1799), attempts to demonstrate that the pronunciation of English is regular and not capricious (in part to correct the impression left by the many 'exceptions' to rules given in textbooks of English intended for those learning it as a second language), as well as contributing to a debate on the relative merits of English and French as a lingua franca for Europe. There is a good deal of anti-French sentiment and satire in the *Euphonologia*—for instance, the French are said to have ruined their own country, and should be hindered from doing damage in the rest of Europe (p. 14)—which is somewhat tempered in the *Pronunciation*. His minor works include an *Oratio academica* in Latin and English (an advertisement for his *Euphonologia*), a translation with commentary of 'Rule Britannia' into Latin verse, an English translation of a French introduction to portraiture, and a sermon which he preached in Soho on 7 March 1798. The preface to his *Pronunciation of the English Language* proposes a second part to that work, on the rules of 'accidents, syntax, &c.' (p. 5), but this was never published. Further, a letter in 1801 to his Edinburgh publisher, John Moir, indicates that Adams had in hand a new 'Tour through the Hebrides' to counter that of Dr Johnson, whom he describes as an 'ungrateful depreciating cynic' (Oliver). In August 1802 he retired to Dublin, where he died on 6 December.

STEPHEN R. REIMER

Sources G. Holt, *The English Jesuits, 1650–1829: a biographical dictionary*, Catholic RS, 70 (1984) · H. Foley, ed., *Records of the English province of the Society of Jesus*, 7 vols. in 8 (1875–83) · E. F. Sutcliffe, *Bibliography of the English province of the Society of Jesus, 1773–1953* (1957) · *DNB* · G. Oliver, *Collections towards illustrating the biographies of the Scotch, English and Irish members of the Society of Jesus*, 2nd edn (1845) · [J. Watkins and F. Shoberl], *A biographical dictionary of the living authors of Great Britain and Ireland* (1816)

Adams, James Williams (1839–1903), army chaplain, born on 24 November 1839 in Cork, was the only son of James O'Brien Adams, magistrate of Cork (d. 1854), and his wife, Elizabeth Williams. Educated at Hamlin and Porter's School, on the South Mall, Cork, he went to Trinity College, Dublin (BA 1861). He excelled in athletics, and was regarded as the strongest man in Ireland, vying with his friend Frederick Burnaby in gymnastic feats. He was ordained deacon 1863 and priest 1864 and served curacies at Hyde, Hampshire (1863–5), and at Shottesbrooke, Berkshire (1865–6).

In October 1866 Adams became a chaplain on the Bengal establishment under Bishop Robert Milman at Calcutta. There he had a severe attack of fever, and after sick leave in Ceylon was appointed to Peshawar. He was tireless in visiting the outstations Nowshera and Kohat; he restored and beautified the church and cemetery at Peshawar, and received the thanks of government for his exertions in the cholera camps during two outbreaks. Except for some months at Allahabad (March to December 1870) he remained at Peshawar until December 1872. He was then stationed at the camp of exercise at Hassan-Abdal army

James Williams Adams (1839–1903), by unknown photographer, in or after 1881

headquarters until March 1873, and in 1874 he was sent to Kashmir on special duty. There he built, largely with his own hands, a church of pine logs, where services were frequently held for the numerous visitors to Gulmarg and Sonamarg; it was later accidentally burnt down. In January 1876 he was appointed to Meerut, and in December took charge of the cavalry and artillery camp for the Delhi durbar on the visit of the prince of Wales.

Subsequently Adams experienced much active service. In November 1878 he joined the Kurram field force under Sir Frederick (afterwards Earl) Roberts, and was at all the operations in the advance on Kabul. At Killa Kazi on 11 December 1879 he risked his life in rescuing several injured men of the 9th lancers, who were in danger of drowning in a watercourse while under Afghan fire. Lord Roberts witnessed Adams's exploit and recommended him for the Victoria Cross, which he received from the queen on 4 August 1881. He also took part in Roberts's march from Kabul to Kandahar in August 1880, and was at the battle of Kandahar on 1 September 1880. While in England on furlough he married on 16 August 1881 Alice Mary, daughter of General Sir Thomas *Willshire. She survived him with their only daughter, Edith Juliet Mary.

On returning to India later in 1881 Adams spent a year at Lucknow, then three years (1883–5) at Naini Tal. In 1885 he accompanied the field force under Roberts to Burma, and took part in the operations there.

Through twenty years' service in India 'Padre Adams' was highly regarded by the soldiers. In 1886 he settled in England, and from 1887 to 1894 he held the rectory of Postwick near Norwich. After two years' rest in Jersey he became in 1896 vicar of Stow Bardolph with Wimbotsham near Downham Market. He was appointed in 1900 honorary chaplain to Queen Victoria, and King Edward made him chaplain-in-ordinary in 1901. In 1902 he left Stow for the small living of Ashwell, near Oakham, Rutland. There, at the rectory, he died on 20 October 1903.

H. M. VIBART, rev. JAMES FALKNER

Sources Army List · The Times (Oct 1903) · LondG (26 Aug 1881) · H. B. Hanna, The Second Afghan War, 3 vols. (1899–1910) · Lord Roberts [F. S. Roberts], Forty-one years in India, 2 vols. (1897) · T. E. Toomey, Heroes of the Victoria Cross (1895) · m. cert. · d. cert.

Likenesses Elliott & Fry, photograph, in or after 1881, NAM · photograph, in or after 1881, NPG [see illus.] · Shrubside, photograph, repro. in Toomey, Heroes of the Victoria Cross, 209 · photograph, Royal Library [album, 1879]

Adams, John (1662–1720), college head, was born in London, the son of a Lisbon merchant in the City. He was educated at Eton College and at King's College, Cambridge, where he matriculated in Lent 1680 and was elected fellow in 1682. He graduated BA (1683), MA (1686), and DD (1705). He then travelled in France, Italy, Spain, and Ireland, and became an accomplished linguist. He was presented by Lord Chancellor Jeffreys to the parish of Higham, in Leicestershire, in 1687. In 1694 he was appointed rector of St Alban, Wood Street (in the gift of Eton College), and was presented to the rectory of St Bartholomew, London, by Lord Chancellor Harcourt. He was made prebendary of Canterbury in 1703 and canon of Windsor in 1708. He served as chaplain to William III and also to Queen Anne, with whom he was a great favourite. According to Jonathan Swift, who dined with Adams at Windsor, he was 'very obliging' (J. Swift, Journal to Stella, 12 Aug, 16 and 20 Sept 1711). Adams was licensed to marry Mary Reynolds of Wingham, Kent, on 19 September 1710. They had at least two sons: Edward (d. 1755), who became a fellow of King's, like his father, and George, who was prebend of Chichester from 1736 to 1752.

In 1711 Adams was made rector of Hornsey, in Middlesex. In the following year he was elected provost of King's College, whereupon he resigned the lectureship of St Clement Danes. His principal achievement at King's was to initiate the building fund that financed James Gibbs's Founders' Building, completed in 1749. He was vice-chancellor of Cambridge University in 1712–13; he had been Boyle lecturer in 1703 but his lectures were never published. He was an eloquent preacher, and fifteen of his sermons were printed. He died of apoplexy on 29 January 1720.
[ANON.], rev. S. J. SKEDD

Sources Venn, Alum. Cant. · A. Chalmers, ed., The general biographical dictionary, new edn, 1 (1812) · R. A. Austen-Leigh, ed., The Eton College register, 1698–1752 (1927) · P. Searby, A history of the University of Cambridge, 3: 1750–1870, ed. C. N. L. Brooke and others (1997), 13–14

Adams, John (b. before 1670, d. 1738), cartographer, came originally from Shropshire. He attended Shrewsbury School, and later lived at Tanfield Court, Inner Temple, London, where he was a barrister. He is best known as a surveyor and map maker, in which capacity he worked with his brother William Adams (*fl.* 1671–1702). In 1677 he engraved on copper a map of England and Wales 'full six feet square' (177 cm × 176 cm) on which the distance of each town from its nearest neighbours was 'entered in figures in computed and measured miles' (that is, with and without compensation for slope). This map was not based on a new survey but rather on pre-existing maps. In its first state no rivers were shown, but these had been added by 1680. In that year he published the *Index villaris, or, An alphabetical table of all cities, market-towns, parishes, villages, private seats in England and Wales* (reprinted with elaborate additions in 1690 and 1700). The index was compiled from such sources as hearth tax returns, navigational works, and works to aid land travellers, notably those of John Ogilby. It was designed to be used in conjunction with the map and refers some 24,000 places to a graticule using geographical co-ordinates.

Realizing the inadequacies of his map and with the support of the Royal Society, Adams proposed a geodetic survey of the whole of England and Wales. The *Dictionary of National Biography* states that he completed this survey, but there seems little evidence for this view. A smaller map by Adams, possibly from 1685, is obviously drawn from his earlier map, but the position of some places is improved. This has led Heawood to speculate that these might be early results of his survey. Some surveying did indeed take place. A base-line was measured in Somerset in 1681 and Adams worked in the field with John Caswell, later professor of astronomy at Oxford. He received advice on instruments from John Flamsteed and appears to have designed some instruments himself. However, no maps are thought to have resulted from this survey, though new versions of his map, some entirely re-engraved, continued to be offered by rival map makers for many years.

Adams has been identified, on inadequate grounds, with a 'Joannes Adamus Transylvanus', the author of a Latin poem describing the city of London, which was translated into English verse about 1675 and is reprinted in the *Harleian Miscellany*, volume 10. Adams died in 1738.

ELIZABETH BAIGENT

Sources F. W. Steer and others, *Dictionary of land surveyors and local map-makers of Great Britain and Ireland, 1530–1850*, ed. P. Eden, 2nd edn, ed. S. Bendall, 2 vols. (1997) · W. L. D. Ravenhill, 'John Adams, his map of England, its projection and his *Index villaris* of 1680', *GJ*, 144 (1978), 424–37, pl. ii, iii · E. Heawood, 'John Adams and his map of England', *GJ*, 79 (1932), 37–44 · E. G. R. Taylor, *The mathematical practitioners of Tudor and Stuart England* (1954)
Archives Cumbria AS, Kendal, letters to Sir Daniel Fleming

Adams, John (1735–1826), president of the United States of America, was born on 19 October 1735, in the north parish (in 1792 named Quincy) of Braintree, Suffolk county, Massachusetts, the eldest child of 'Deacon' John Adams (1692–1761), a local farmer, shoemaker, and office-holder, and his wife, Susanna, *née* Boylston (1709–1797), whose extended family was prominent in medicine and trade in Boston. Through both parents Adams was descended from early seventeenth-century English emigrants to Massachusetts.

John Adams (1735–1826), by Gilbert Stuart, *c.*1800–15

Education and the law, 1740s–1774 In his youth John Adams loved outdoor pursuits and wanted only to be a farmer, but his father, hoping that his son would become a minister, placed him with a series of Braintree schoolmasters. The last of these finally ignited Adams's ardour for learning, and he entered Harvard College in 1751, excelled in mathematics, natural philosophy, and debating, and graduated in 1755. During his college years a rancorous dispute between Braintree's minister and his parishioners confirmed Adams's growing conviction that the pulpit was not for him, and in 1756 he began reading law with a Worcester attorney. In 1758 he returned to Braintree and was admitted to the county bar. After a faltering beginning, Adams made rapid progress and was admitted a barrister before the Massachusetts superior court in 1762.

Buoyed by his growing success and the inheritance of a house from his father, Adams wed Abigail Smith (1744–1818) of Weymouth on 25 October 1764. Marriage to this bright and spirited daughter of the Revd William Smith of Weymouth and Elizabeth Quincy, a member of Braintree's leading family, enhanced Adams's social status, but Abigail's great contributions to John's career were her willingness to endure long separations, her unshaken belief in his abilities, and her perceptive advice on people and events. The Adamses raised four children: Abigail (1765–1813), who married William Stephens Smith; John Quincy (1767–1848), who became America's leading diplomat and sixth president; Charles (1770–1800); and Thomas Boylston (1772–1832).

Like most eighteenth-century New England lawyers, Adams practised every kind of law that came his way, in courts from Cape Cod to the Maine frontier. Unlike most colonial lawyers he soon became a widely read and profound legal scholar. He felt that his progress was slow and painful, but within a dozen years he was regarded as the most learned and successful attorney in Massachusetts, a position confirmed by his brilliant defence of the British soldiers charged with the Boston massacre.

From his early twenties John Adams felt a keen hunger for fame. 'Reputation', he confessed to his diary in 1759, 'ought to be the perpetual subject of my Thoughts, and the Aim of my Behavior'. Unlike many colonial lawyers, however, Adams sought renown largely within and through his profession, and did not regard the law as an avenue to public office, particularly elective office. He served for only two years as a Braintree selectman, and for just a single year in the Massachusetts legislature. Yet Adams was intensely involved in public life, from his drafting of Braintree's protest against the Stamp Act (1765) to his legal defence of John Hancock in the *Liberty* smuggling case (1768), of the British soldiers in the massacre trials (1770), and of the constitutional position of the Massachusetts legislature in its controversy with Governor Thomas Hutchinson (1773).

Adams also wrote many pseudonymous newspaper essays that sought to counter political faction and keep Massachusetts independent of the control of what he saw as a succession of corrupt British ministries. Some of these pieces, notably his 'Dissertation on the canon and feudal law' (1765) and 'Independence of the judges' (1773), made a rather limited case for colonial autonomy within the British empire. But the logic of his argument eventually drove Adams, as author of the Massachusetts house of representatives' replies to Governor Hutchinson, to declare well in advance of other colonial spokesmen that the British parliament had no absolute authority over Massachusetts whatsoever.

Convinced now of the gravity of the imperial crisis, the heretofore politically cautious John Adams welcomed the Boston Tea Party: 'This Destruction of the Tea is so bold, so daring, so firm, intrepid and inflexible, … that I cant but consider it as an Epocha in History' (*Diary*, 17 Dec 1773). Britain's parliament promptly responded by closing the port of Boston and altering Massachusetts's revered charter of 1692. To meet the crisis the Massachusetts house, in June 1774, named John Adams and four others to meet leaders from other colonies in the first continental congress in Philadelphia.

Congress and independence, 1774–1777 Adams's career as a lawyer and political theorist was already quite exceptional, but from his entering congress in September 1774 to his final departure in 1777 he displayed a level of energy, creativity, and political sensitivity that he had never shown before. Congress's task was difficult: to persuade or force the British parliament to rescind its Boston Port, Massachusetts Government, and other 'intolerable' acts, and reach a new accommodation with all the colonies over imperial taxation. Adams was mildly disappointed that congress even bothered to petition both George III and the British public, but was pleased with the measures in which he had a hand: a bold declaration of rights and its coercive companion, the non-importation Continental Association (October 1774). No member of congress took its work more seriously, as evidenced by the fact that Adams's diary and correspondence are the only contemporary record of many of that body's important deliberations.

Upon his return to Massachusetts in November, Adams found a vigorous patriot government controlling every town except Boston, home to General Thomas Gage's army. But loyalists were beginning to speak out, and when Daniel Leonard, as Massachusettensis, assaulted the work of congress, John Adams, as Novanglus (January–April 1775), replied in a series of learned essays that justified congressional resistance to a tyrannical ministry. Only a 'republican' government, he declared, could protect the people's liberties, and, in an argument unique among America's patriot leaders, he explained that such a government could be either a scrupulously constitutional hereditary monarchy—as he believed Britain's government had been before 1763—or a state dependent directly upon the authority of the people.

In April 1775 open warfare broke out at Lexington and Concord. Adams returned to congress, and in June led Massachusetts's delegates to propose that their forces, then besieging General Gage in Boston, become a continental army under congress's control and that George Washington be named its commander-in-chief. In congress's autumn session Adams threw himself into incessant committee work to supply the army and take the first steps toward establishing a navy, a venture to which he would return a quarter-century later when, as president, he initiated the establishment of the department of the navy (1798). By the spring of 1776 Adams, always a key member of congress, had become its single most important, and overworked, member.

Adams's first challenge in the new year, however, came from outside congress. Thomas Paine's *Common Sense* appeared in January and swept the colonies with its enthusiasm for independence, which Adams admired, and its preference for weak or non-existent executives, which he deplored. Several congressmen whose provinces were restructuring their governments turned to Adams for advice, and he responded with the most influential pamphlet of his career, *Thoughts on Government* (April 1776). Adams succinctly considered the role of the people, lower legislative houses, councils, executives, and qualifications for voting and office-holding, and, explicitly allowing for considerable variation from colony to colony, recommended a balance between two legislative chambers and a strong executive, a formula that would soon characterize most of America's new state governments. He then wrote congress's recommendation that every colony establish a government under which 'every kind of authority under the [crown] should be totally suppressed, and all the powers of government exerted, under the authority of the people' (*Journals of the Continental Congress*, May 1776, 4.358).

Adams now assumed the central role in each of

congress's major decisions. Having been appointed in June to the committee to draft the Declaration of Independence, he assisted Thomas Jefferson in that endeavour, and on 1–2 July led the debate to approve independence itself. From June to September he laboured to produce congress's plan of treaties, America's first blueprint for its foreign policy. And again in June, he assumed the presidency of the board of war, the most demanding post in congress. Adams held this position until his departure from congress in November 1777.

Republican diplomacy, 1778–1788 Upon his return to Braintree, Adams believed that his national career, sustained at considerable financial and emotional cost to his family and himself, was well over, and he immediately resumed his law practice. Congress had other ideas, and in November 1777 appointed him to join its envoys Benjamin Franklin and Arthur Lee in Paris. Recognizing both congress's urgent need to bring order to its factious diplomatic commission and the signal honour it had given him, Adams promptly accepted, and in 1778 he set sail with his young son John Quincy Adams.

Having landed at Bordeaux in April, Adams learned that the commission had secured its first objective, a treaty of alliance with France, on 6 February, a week before he had left Boston. But there was still much to do, and over the next ten months he organized the commission's business, persuaded his colleagues to seek more French naval aid (in vain), and tried to steer a neutral course between the feuding Franklin and Lee. As a friend and ally of Virginia congressman Richard Henry Lee, Adams was widely expected to side with Lee's brother; however, Adams soon concluded that Arthur Lee was no diplomat, and that Franklin was the only envoy America needed in Paris. He discreetly suggested this measure to friends in congress, but the full body had already reached the same conclusion and, without formally dissolving the commission and recalling Adams and Lee, it named Franklin sole minister to Versailles.

Receiving the news in February 1779, Adams felt humiliated at this cavalier treatment, but was delighted to return home and resume his private career. This time his neighbours had other plans. In August he was elected to Massachusetts's constitutional convention. That body's drafting committee chose him to compose the constitution, and in the early autumn John Adams drafted an intricate, detailed, and remarkably clear organic law which, with modest changes in convention, became the Massachusetts constitution of 1780. This work, Adams's finest constitutional achievement, is the world's oldest written constitution still in operation.

But Adams had no time to admire his creation. In September congress named him sole minister-plenipotentiary to negotiate peace with Britain. Even Adams thought the appointment premature: the North ministry was in no mood to concede American independence. Moreover, Adams was posted to Paris, where congress directed him to co-ordinate his initiatives with America's only European ally. By early summer 1780, with little pressing work to do, Adams was drawn into quarrels with the French foreign minister, the comte de Vergennes (who wanted Adams to do nothing), over American currency devaluation, the level of French commitment to the naval war, and the public status of his own appointment.

John Adams was too enterprising to endure this confinement for long. His first initiative was to write several anonymous essays espousing peace with America, including *A Translation of the Memorial to the Sovereigns of Europe upon the Present State of Affairs between the Old and New World* [by Thomas Pownall] into *Common Sense and Intelligible English*, published in 1781, and *Letters from a Distinguished American*, published in 1782, both in London. These works, while making at best a modest contribution to concluding peace with Great Britain, powerfully explain Adams's distinctive view of international relations.

In July 1780 Adams took more direct action, moving to Holland even before receiving a commission to the Netherlands. There, in two years of lobbying, propaganda, and negotiation, he secured recognition of the United States (April 1782), America's first Dutch loan (June), and a treaty of amity and commerce (October). Congress, meanwhile, had revoked his appointment as sole peace-negotiator in favour of his heading a commission, which it directed to consult with France in all its negotiations. But Adams promptly followed his triumph in the Netherlands by returning to Paris: there he allied with John Jay to convince fellow commissioner Benjamin Franklin to ignore the comte de Vergennes and conclude the preliminary treaty (November 1782) that became the definitive treaty of peace with Britain (September 1783).

Adams's remaining years abroad were anticlimactic, but had their rewards. In October 1783 he first visited England with his son John Quincy, and in 1784 his wife and daughter joined him in Europe. His appointment as America's first minister to the court of St James's (1785–8) proved less fruitful than his joint commission of 1784–5 with Franklin and Jefferson to negotiate commercial treaties. Their collaboration, however, yielded only one treaty, with Prussia in 1785 (a second, with Morocco in 1786, followed Franklin's return to America). But a visit with Abigail to the Netherlands, where they witnessed the brief triumph of the republican patriot party over the prince of Orange (August–September 1786), stimulated Adams to begin his longest work, *A Defence of the Constitutions of Government of the United States* (London, 1787–8). This three-volume historical treatise, a defence of America's state constitutions, particularly Adams's Massachusetts constitution of 1780, propounded a separation and balance of powers between a two-house legislature, a powerful executive, and an independent judiciary. Although the *Defence* was of no help to the Dutch patriots, who were overwhelmed by the invading Prussian army before its completion, its first volume may have given some ammunition to the delegates in Philadelphia framing America's new federal constitution. As he was completing the work, Adams, who could not persuade the Pitt ministry to negotiate a commercial treaty with America, resigned his commissions to Britain and the Netherlands and returned to Massachusetts in the spring of 1788.

Federal executive, 1789–1801 Again Adams thought his public career might be at an end, but he did covet the potential in one new office, vice-president in the new federal government. It appeared to be the logical place from which to succeed the president apparent, George Washington. In the first federal elections his countrymen ratified Adams's ambition, but hardly with the unanimity they bestowed on the general.

His two-term vice-presidency (April 1789 – March 1797) keenly disappointed John Adams. His only duty was to preside over the US senate without speaking his opinion on any issue. His occasional inability to observe this rule and his support for quasi-monarchical titles for the presidency drew instant criticism from many senators. Adams was able to assist Washington by casting the greatest number of tie-breaking votes in the senate by any vice-president, but his unpopularity in the southern states and a distant relationship with Washington effectively locked him out of the president's informal counsels. He compounded his isolation by writing a series of newspaper essays, the *Discourses on Davila* (1790–91), that attacked the principles of the French Revolution while praising the virtues of powerful executives, and even of monarchs.

When Washington issued his farewell address (September 1796), Adams was still the logical if not inspiring choice for the general's federalist supporters. In a close election he defeated his old friend and new rival, Thomas Jefferson, leader of the opposition republicans. John Adams's one-term presidency (March 1797 – March 1801) was almost completely occupied with concerns over America's deteriorating relations with France, and the attendant division of most Americans into fiercely anti-French (federalist) and pro-French (republican) factions. His great achievement as president was to prevent full-scale war and conclude his term with a lasting peace with France.

The 'quasi-war' began with the French directory's decision to attack American neutral shipping that it saw as aiding its arch-enemy, Great Britain. Adams sent a peace mission to Paris, but the directory and its foreign minister, Tallyrand, demanded humiliating terms and a secret bribe, to agents labelled X, Y, and Z, before negotiations could begin. In 1798 Adams revealed the bribe offer and called for raising an army and creating a permanent navy. Congress concurred and, in measures that later generations of Americans would find the most unfortunate of Adams's presidency, it enacted an Alien Act to expel recent French and French-sympathizing immigrants and a Sedition Act to silence republican newspapers that libelled the president and his war policy. In July, at the height of his popularity, Adams signed both measures.

Almost immediately France signalled a reassessment of its policy, and in December 1798 Adams named new peace commissioners, to be dispatched when the time was ripe. When that time came, in October 1799, he faced fierce criticism both from congress and his own cabinet. By May 1800 the opposition of Alexander Hamilton's Anglophile and Francophobe high federalists had become intolerable, and Adams forced secretary of war James McHenry

and secretary of state Timothy Pickering from office. America's negotiators concluded a lasting peace with France by the convention of Mortefontaine in October, but the widening split in federalist ranks had become irreparable with the appearance of Alexander Hamilton's savage *Letter … Concerning the Public Conduct and Character of John Adams* (September 1800), and Adams lost his bid for re-election to Thomas Jefferson.

John Adams's last months in office were dismal. His second son, Charles, whose profligacy had alienated Adams, died of acute alcoholism in November 1800, just as the president occupied the still uncompleted executive mansion in Washington. He did exert a continuing federalist influence on the government by his appointment of several new judges, notably Chief Justice John Marshall. But his estrangement from Jefferson prompted him to leave Washington early on inauguration day (4 March 1801), without seeing his successor take the oath of office.

Retirement and retrospective, 1801–1826 Upon his retirement Adams felt rejected and misunderstood, especially by those who had once been friends and allies. He crossed swords with his one-time friend and now republican critic Mercy Otis Warren, and sought to justify his career privately in his incomplete autobiography (1802–7) and publicly in his letters published in the *Boston Patriot* (1809–12). Then, in 1812, at the urging of his friend Benjamin Rush, Adams renewed his correspondence with Thomas Jefferson. This remarkably charitable and even-tempered exchange of views on a wide range of subjects, continuing to the eve of their deaths in 1826, characterized Adams's last years. He still faced severe blows: the harshest were the deaths of his two Abigails, his daughter in 1813 and his wife in 1818. But America's growing pride in national union, following the Anglo-American War of 1812–14, and the course of John Quincy Adams's brilliant career gave Adams real pleasure, and assured him that America's grand experiment was not disintegrating so rapidly as he had once feared. At Quincy, Norfolk county, the end came, fittingly, on 4 July 1826, the fiftieth anniversary of the Declaration of Independence. Adams's last recorded words were: 'Thomas Jefferson survives' (Ellis, 210). But Jefferson died several hours before Adams, on this same bright day.

John Adams was a remarkable public figure from several perspectives. He was probably the most learned of America's 'founding fathers' in the fields of history, political theory, and the law, and his was an eminently practical learning. Called the Atlas of Independence in congress, he was America's foremost civilian leader, its master constitutional architect in the 1770s, and its most effective diplomatic negotiator in the 1780s. Yet Adams was seldom a popular leader and was never popular for long, even in New England. He often worked effectively with others, but his natural style was to think, write, and act on his own, often in isolation, not only in Europe, but as chief executive. His presidency was effective in defending America's basic national interests, but it was the least popular and possibly the least important of his major contributions to his nation. For his energy, integrity, and devotion to his country John Adams has always enjoyed a solid reputation, but his appeal to both scholars and laymen has waxed and waned repeatedly. As of this writing, however, both his political thought and his public career are attracting new admirers.

The man behind this exceptional career was equally distinctive. Socially and constitutionally conservative, and viewed by his opponents as nearly a monarchist, Adams was always a moderate and a pragmatist in his politics. In his strong cultural, intellectual, and scientific interests he was a progressive son of the Enlightenment, despite his dislike of the French *philosophes*. His Arminian and then Unitarian religious convictions placed him somewhere between orthodox Christianity and the deism of Franklin and Jefferson, a position that was not uncommon among his fellow parishioners in Braintree/Quincy. Above all, Adams believed that the great value of organized religion, like that of sound government, was in curbing the excesses of all men, including himself. Although he could display a fierce temper, he was at heart a warm and charitable man. Adams was never close to most of his colleagues on the national stage, but in a long and often contentious public career he seems to have taken deep personal offence to just two men, Benjamin Franklin and Alexander Hamilton.

In appearance Adams was somewhat below average height, stocky, and, as he aged, rather portly. Through much of his career he suffered from occasional severe fevers, persistent inflammation of the eyes, and several lesser ailments, possibly all of a chronic nature, but he reached his late eighties with all his faculties intact and able to walk 3 miles. He apparently died of simple heart failure at ninety years and eight months. Adams was buried in the first parish cemetery in Quincy, but his remains, with those of Abigail, were later removed to a crypt beneath the (Unitarian) First Church in that city.

RICHARD ALAN RYERSON

Sources *Adams papers, 1639–1889* (1954–9) [microfilm] · *Diary and autobiography of John Adams*, ed. L. H. Butterfield and others, 1–4 (1961) · *Papers of John Adams*, ed. R. J. Taylor and others, 10 vols. (1977–96) · L. H. Butterfield and others, eds., *Adams family correspondence*, [6 vols.] (1963–) · *The works of John Adams, second president of the United States*, ed. C. F. Adams, 10 vols. (1850–56) · *Legal papers of John Adams*, ed. L. K. Wroth and H. B. Zobel, 3 vols. (1965) · *The Adams–Jefferson letters*, ed. L. J. Cappon, 2 vols. (1959) · A. Oliver, ed., *Portraits of John and Abigail Adams* (1967) · J. Ferling, *John Adams, a life* (1992) · P. Smith, *John Adams*, 2 vols. (1962) · P. Shaw, *The character of John Adams* (1976) · J. J. Ellis, *Passionate sage: the character and legacy of John Adams* (1993) · Z. Haraszti, *John Adams and the prophets of progress* (1952) · C. B. Thompson, *John Adams and the spirit of liberty* (1998) · J. R. Howe, *The changing political thought of John Adams* (1966) · R. B. Morris, *The peacemakers: the great powers and American independence* (1965) · G. S. Wood, *The creation of the American republic* (1969) · J. W. S. Nordholt, *The Dutch republic and American independence* (1982) · M. Dauer, *The Adams federalists* (1953) · A. De Conde, *The quasi-war: the politics and diplomacy of the undeclared war with France* (1966) · *Records of the town of Braintree, 1640 to 1793*, ed. S. A. Bates (1886)

Archives Archives Centrales de la Marine, Paris · Bibliothèque Nationale, Paris · L. Cong. · Mass. Hist. Soc., diaries, letters, letterbooks, and papers · PRO · Paris, diplomatic archives · The Hague, diplomatic archives | National Archives and Records Administration, Washington, DC, papers of the Continental Congress; records of the senate; executive department records

Likenesses B. Blyth, pastel drawing, 1766, Mass. Hist. Soc. · J. S. Copley, oils, 1783, Harvard U. · M. Brown, oils, 1788, Boston Athenaeum · J. Trumbull, oils, 1793, Harvard U. · G. Stuart, oils, *c*.1800–1815, National Gallery of Art, Washington, DC [*see illus.*] · J. B. Binon, marble bust, 1818, City of Boston (Faneuil Hall) · G. Stuart, oils, 1823, priv. coll. · J. Browere, plaster life mask, 1825, New York State Historical Association · C. Ferret de Saint-Mémin, crayon physiognotrace, Metropolitan Museum of Art, New York

Wealth at death $43,089 incl. 240 acres of land in Quincy, valued at $18,665; $21,000 in public and private securities: inventory, 1826, probate court, Dedham, Massachusetts

Adams, John (1750?–1814), schoolmaster and educational writer, was born in Aberdeen. He was educated at Aberdeen University and may have been the John Adams who graduated MA from King's College in 1768. After obtaining a preaching licence he travelled to London, where he was appointed minister of the Scottish church in Hatton Garden. He subsequently opened an academy in Putney, which proved very successful. He published a large quantity of educational works, most of which passed through numerous editions. Designed for use in schools, his books provided both teacher and pupil with concise and useful introductions to reading, Latin composition, ancient and modern history (both British and European), geography, and travel literature. He published an abridged version of Edward Gibbon's *History of the Decline and Fall of the Roman Empire* in 1789 and a volume of sermons on theological subjects in 1805, which he dedicated to Lord Grantham. Adams died in Putney in 1814.

SIDNEY LEE, *rev.* S. J. SKEDD

Sources J. G. Gorton, *Appendix to Gorton's biographical dictionary* (1834) · *The biographical dictionary of the Society for the Diffusion of Useful Knowledge*, 4 vols. (1842–4) · P. J. Anderson, ed., *Officers and graduates of University and King's College, Aberdeen, MVD–MDCCCLX*, New Spalding Club, 11 (1893)

Adams, John [*alias* Alexander Smith] (1768?–1829), seaman, mutineer, and settler, was born in London probably in 1768 and was serving under the name of Smith as an able seaman on HMS *Bounty* at the time of the mutiny on 28 April 1789 [*see* Bligh, William]. He took a prominent part, guarding Bligh before he was turned adrift. When the ship returned to Tahiti, where several of the ship's company determined to stay, Smith, with eight others, under Fletcher Christian, believed it would be too dangerous to stay there. They accordingly sailed in the *Bounty*, taking with them from the island the women they had kidnapped, half a dozen men as servants, and some youths. Despite the search for them, nothing was heard of them for nearly twenty years. In 1808 a Mr Folger, commanding an American merchant ship, accidentally landed at Pitcairn Island, and found there a mixed population of thirty-five persons, speaking English, and governed by an Alexander Smith, who made no secret of being one of the mutineers of the *Bounty*. According to his story, they had reached this island after leaving Tahiti, and, having resolved to settle there, ran the ship on shore, took out of her all they could, and set her on fire; but one night four years later the Tahitian men, disgusted at their

John Adams (1768?–1829), attrib. Richard Beechey, 1825

treatment, and short of women, murdered the British; Smith alone escaped, albeit severely wounded. In revenge, the women, also at night, killed the murderers, Smith being thus left the one man on the island, with some eight or nine women and several children. In this account Smith avoided any involvement in the slaughter. The story was reported to the Admiralty by the senior officers at Valparaiso and Rio de Janeiro, but no steps were taken to verify it; and it either was not known or had been forgotten when, on 17 September 1814, Sir Thomas Staines and Captain Pipon in the frigates *Briton* and *Tagus*, on their way from the Marquesas to Valparaiso, touched at the same island, not knowing exactly what it was, as their chart was erroneous. To their surprise they found this unknown island inhabited by English-speaking people, descended, they were told, from the *Bounty* mutineers, and educated in the precepts of Christianity by Smith, who now called himself Adams. He was described as being then (1814) a man of venerable appearance, and about sixty years old. At first he naturally supposed the warships had come to seize him and send him to England, but he was reassured by his visitors, who seem to have considered the lapse of time and the good government of the island as expiating the offence of which he had been guilty. Staines praised his conduct and his care of the settlement, and especially his religious training of the population.

In 1825 the island was visited by Captain Beechey in HMS *Blossom*. He described Adams as an old man, in his sixty-fifth year. Beechey obtained from him a detailed narrative of the course of events since he came to the island;

but, comparing it with what he had formerly told Sir Thomas Staines, the conclusion is that little or no reliance is to be placed on it. A certain part of the story of the settlement of Pitcairn Island is thus necessarily lost; for Adams, as the only white survivor, was the only witness questioned. No one seems to have thought that anything could be gained by questioning the old women who had come to the island with him. Indeed, Adams was always very anxious to avoid their being interviewed. It appears probable that Adams was the instigator and perpetrator of much of the violence that occurred in 1793 and 1795. His subsequent conduct may well be explained by guilt and remorse.

Adams died on Pitcairn Island in 1829. His later life is often referred to as an example of a sincere and practical repentance following on a career of crime. It would be easy to overrate its value as such. Of Adams's antecedents nothing is known; but he must have been, in many respects, an exceptional man, for the average able seaman of 1789 was certainly not qualified to train young children in the principles of morality or religion, or to teach them to speak the correct English which these islanders had learned. It may therefore be assumed that he had received an education unusual for his rank in life. This may explain why a man of twenty should already feel the need for an alias in signing on to the *Bounty*.

J. K. LAUGHTON, rev. ANDREW LAMBERT

Sources G. Kennedy, *Captain Bligh: the man and his mutinies* (1989) · J. Marshall, *Royal naval biography*, 4 vols. (1823–35) [with 4 suppls.]
Likenesses attrib. R. Beechey, drawing, 1825; Bonhams, 20 March 1996, lot 2 [see *illus.*] · R. Beechey, pencil sketch, repro. in Kennedy, *Captain Bligh* · J. A. Vinter, lithograph (after R. Beechey), BM · portrait, repro. in F. W. Beechey, *Narrative of a voyage to the Pacific and the Behring's Strait* (1831)

Adams, Sir John (1857–1934), educationist, was born at Glasgow on 2 July 1857, the third son of Charles Adams, a master blacksmith in the Trongate, Glasgow, and his wife, Barbara McCallum. After attending St David's School he became a pupil teacher at Old Wynd School (later Oatlands School). There he received encouragement from the headmaster, Mr Liddell, and won a queen's scholarship, entering the Glasgow Free Church Training College and the University of Glasgow (1875), where he graduated with a first class in mental and moral science. He taught in the Aberdeen Free Church Training College Demonstration School, 1879–81, returning as a lecturer in 1883. He then became headmaster of the Jean Street School, Port Glasgow, and afterwards rector of Campbeltown grammar school. This experience of school practice formed a sound basis for his subsequent work as a trainer of teachers and a university lecturer in education. In 1890 he was appointed principal of the Free Church Training College, Aberdeen. He married in 1893 Agnes Anne, youngest daughter of John Cook, a shipowner, of Ashley, Aberdeen.

In 1898 Adams became rector of the Free Church Training College, Glasgow. Here his connection with university teaching began, for he then held the lectureship in education in the University of Glasgow. He had already achieved the local distinction of being president (from

1896) of the Educational Institute of Scotland, and had gained wider fame by the publication of a provocative little book, the forbidding title of which, *Herbartian Psychology Applied to Education*, belied the sprightliness of its contents.

In 1902 Adams visited Canada and published an account of the protestant schools of the province of Quebec. He was appointed principal of the London Day Training College, and became the first professor of education in the University of London, also in 1902. He was pre-eminently the teacher of London teachers—not only teachers in training, but also teachers at work—for he lectured abundantly in the evenings as well as in the daytime. After he had, in 1922, retired from training-college work and become emeritus professor, he travelled overseas, and by the delivery of series of lectures in the USA, South Africa, Australia, and New Zealand he became an international figure in the world of education. He settled in Los Angeles, and lectured at the University of California between 1923 and 1934.

Adams published more than 160 books and articles, the most important of which, in addition to *Herbartian Psychology*, are *Exposition and Illustration in Teaching* (1909), *The Evolution of Educational Theory* (1912), *The Student's Guide* (1917), and *Everyman's Psychology* (1929). All these works, like his lectures, are characterized by an easy style, a shrewd wisdom, and a 'pawky' humour. In addition he wrote books for boys under the pseudonym Skelton Kuppord. In 1925 he was knighted for his services to education, and the honorary degree of LLD was conferred upon him by St Andrews University.

As a lecturer Adams was a memorable figure. His impressive bald head, his Scottish accent, his clear, incisive style, and particularly his sly humour, rendered him attractive to audiences all over the English-speaking world. He died suddenly, as the result of a stroke, at Los Angeles on 30 September 1934. He had no children.

P. B. BALLARD, *rev.* M. C. CURTHOYS

Sources *The Times* (2 Oct 1934) · *Times Educational Supplement* (6 Oct 1934) · M. Sadler, *John Adams: a lecture in his memory, being the second John Adams lecture* (1935) · R. R. Rusk, 'Sir John Adams, 1857–1934', *British Journal of Educational Studies*, 10 (1961–2), 49–57 · WWW · CGPLA Eng. & Wales (1934)
Archives Bodl. Oxf., corresp. with Sidgwick & Jackson · King's AC Cam., letters to Oscar Browning · NL Scot., corresp. with publishers

Adams, Sir John Bertram (1920–1984), physicist and scientific administrator, was born on 24 May 1920 at 105 Canbury Park Road, Kingston, Surrey, the only son and younger child of John Albert Adams (*c*.1890–*c*.1964) and his wife, Sarah Ethel Emily Searles (1890–*c*.1970). He had a sister, Marjorie, who was eight years his senior. Their father had a good job working for Paquin's, a high-class London couturier, until the First World War but he never fully recovered from being badly gassed in action and after the war he was unemployed for long periods. Between 1931 and 1936 Adams attended Eltham College as a day boy, having won an entrance scholarship, but because of financial hardship in the family he left early

and went to work at the Siemens laboratories in Woolwich. He continued his studies at the South-East London Technical Institute and obtained a higher national certificate in 1939.

During the Second World War Adams worked at the Telecommunications Research Establishment, first at Swanage and then at Malvern. His particular responsibility was the development of microwave radar systems, and it was through this that his outstanding engineering skills first came to be recognized.

On 23 January 1943 he married Renie, daughter of Joseph Warburton, engineer. She was at that time a flight officer in the Women's Auxiliary Air Force; they had one son and two daughters. In 1945 Adams moved to the Atomic Energy Research Establishment at Harwell where his exceptional ability again became quickly evident and in 1953 the director, Sir John Cockcroft, arranged for him to go to the newly formed high energy physics laboratory at the Conseil Européen de Recherches Nucléaires (CERN), in Geneva. He went as a junior member of the team formed to build the world's largest elementary particle accelerator and before he left in 1961 he had served as director-general for a year. At Cockcroft's request Adams then left CERN to take charge of the development of Britain's controlled thermonuclear fusion programme. This again involved building a new laboratory, this time on a green-field site at Culham in Oxfordshire. Once again he created a splendidly effective research organization.

Adams was appointed controller at the Ministry of Technology in the first Labour government of Harold Wilson, although he remained director of Culham. In 1966 he became member for research of the UK Atomic Energy Authority. Neither of these two appointments suited his talents particularly well and in April 1969 he chose to return to CERN to take charge of a project whose future, to say the least, was very uncertain. The proposal was to build a new giant accelerator on a completely new site somewhere in Europe. The British government initially refused to join this project. In less than two years Adams, in conjunction with Bernard Gregory, the then director-general of CERN, transformed the plan so that the accelerator could be built on the Geneva site and at a fraction of the originally estimated cost. Britain then joined the revised project and it went ahead. The accelerator was completed in just over five years from approval and within the originally estimated cost. In 1976 Adams became executive director-general of a unified CERN laboratory serving in harness with Leon van Hove who acted as director-general for research. The period from 1976 to 1981 was one of remarkable accelerator development at CERN. Completion of the world's first proton–antiproton collider in 1981 led ultimately to the award of the Nobel prize for physics to Rubbia and van der Meer in 1994 for the discovery of the intermediate vector boson. The large electron–positron project (LEP) was also approved by the CERN council in June 1981. When Adams's term of office as director-general ended in December 1981 he remained at CERN but ceased to play any significant role in its affairs. His experience and knowledge were, however, much sought after outside the organization both in Europe and in the United States.

Adams's record both as an administrator and as an engineer is remarkable, especially considering the complexity of the work at Culham and Geneva. That this was done by one who did not have a university education is salutary. His achievements were recognized through the award of many honours and distinctions. They include honorary doctorates from the universities of Geneva (1960), Birmingham (1961), Surrey (1966), Strathclyde (1978), and Milan (1980); the Röntgen prize of the University of Giessen (1960); the Duddell medal of the Physical Society (1961); the Royal Society's Leverhulme and royal medals (1972 and 1977); and the Faraday medal from the Institution of Electrical Engineers (1977). He was elected FRS in 1963 and a foreign member of the USSR Academy of Sciences in 1982. He was appointed CMG in 1962 and knighted in 1981. He was a fellow of Wolfson College, Oxford (1966), the Manchester College of Technology, the Institution of Electrical Engineers, and the Institute of Physics.

Adams died from lung cancer on 3 March 1984 at the Hôpital Cantonal Universitaire, Geneva, near his home at Founex in the Swiss canton of Vaud, close to the mountains where he loved to walk and ski. He was cremated at Geneva on 8 March, and was survived by his wife.

G. H. STAFFORD

Sources G. H. Stafford, *Memoirs FRS*, 32 (1986), 3–34 · private information (1996) · personal knowledge (2004) · M. C. Crowley-Milling, *John Bertram Adams, engineer extraordinary* (1993) · b. cert. · m. cert. · d. cert.
Likenesses photograph, repro. in *Memoirs FRS*, 11 · photograph, repro. in *Memoirs FRS*, 24 · photograph, repro. in *Memoirs FRS*, facing p. 3

Adams, John Bodkin (1899–1983), general practitioner and forger, was born on 20 January 1899 in Randalstown, co. Antrim, the elder son of Samuel Adams, watchmaker, and his wife, Ellen Bodkin (*d.* 1943), formerly of Desertmartin, co. Tyrone. The younger son was born in 1903 and died of pneumonia in 1916. Shortly after John was born the family moved to Ballinderry Bridge, co. Tyrone, where he attended a Methodist day school. The family were strictly religious and worshipped regularly at a Plymouth Brethren meeting-place where the father frequently preached. In 1911 the family moved to Coleraine, mainly to permit Adams to study at a local academy. He qualified in 1917 for Queen's College, Belfast, and graduated in 1921.

Adams became an ophthalmic house surgeon and casualty officer in Bristol Royal Infirmary, and then, responding to an advertisement for a 'Christian doctor assistant', joined an Eastbourne general practice. By relieving his partners of all night calls Adams was soon able to rent a modest house in Upperton Road and invite his mother to join him. The family reunion brought a revival of the religious pattern—family prayers in the home and the advent of a Bible class for the Young Crusaders. When his partners retired Adams was able to slot into the 'good life' of Eastbourne. He looked for a more suitable residence, and

in 1930 for £5000 he acquired Kent Lodge, a Victorian villa later to be valued in the doctor's estates at £100,000.

The charm and ebullience of the soft-spoken, loquacious, teetotal bachelor quickly led Adams into the homes of the wealthy. By 1955 he had established himself in hunting and fishing circles. Yet he did not ignore his poor patients. On the other hand signs of his avaricious nature were beginning to appear, and rumours began. In 1935 Mrs Matilda Whitton, a 72-year-old patient, had left Adams £3000. Relatives disputed the will but it was upheld by the courts. The rumours were revived between 1944 and 1955 during which period Adams received fourteen legacies totalling £21,600 from octogenarian patients.

In July 1956 Mrs Gertrude Hullett, another of Adams's patients, died aged fifty. Heartbroken at the recent death of her husband, Mrs Hullett had often spoken to her solicitor and friends of her intention to take her own life. Adams was not present when she died and an autopsy established that she had swallowed a massive dose of barbiturates. The inquest jury found that she had committed suicide 'of her own free will', but in winding up the proceedings the coroner announced that the chief constable 'had invoked the aid of Scotland Yard to investigate certain deaths in the neighbourhood'. Mrs Hullett's will disclosed that she had left Adams a Rolls-Royce car and had previously given him a cheque for £1000 which he had 'specially cleared'.

On 24 November 1956 Adams was arrested on a series of minor charges. Soon a further charge was added: 'That he did in November 1950 feloniously and with malice aforethought murder Edith Alice Morrell.' Refused bail, Adams spent the next 111 days in prison. Meanwhile, the bodies of two other patients were exhumed but only one of them was in good enough condition to decide the cause of death, cerebral thrombosis, which was that given by Adams on the death certificate. At the committal proceedings the crown maintained it was essential that evidence regarding the deaths of Mr and Mrs Hullett should be given and despite defence objections the magistrates agreed—a decision which in 1967 led to a change in the law.

Physically Adams seemed strong enough to withstand the trial but his facial appearance was against him. In good humour and smiling he resembled a genial Mr Pickwick but in sombre, grim moments he tended to appear quite capable of the crimes soon to be laid at his door. The trial was opened at the Old Bailey by the attorney-general, Sir Reginald Manningham-Buller. He first called four nurses who gave their version from memory of the treatment of Mrs Morrell six years earlier. Then the defence, conducted by F. Geoffrey Lawrence, produced a trump card: the nurses' actual notebooks, which gave a very different version. The seams of the crown's case had started to come apart, and worse was to follow.

The chief medical witness, Arthur Henry Douthwaite, senior physician at Guy's Hospital, London, revised his theories in the witness box after admitting he had not seen the reports of three other doctors in Cheshire who had started Mrs Morrell on a course of heroin and morphia before she came under the care of Adams. Another expert, in answer to the judge, Patrick Devlin, said, 'I do not think it is possible absolutely to rule out a sudden catastrophic intervention by some natural cause'. The defence, perhaps wisely, decided not to put the talkative Adams into the witness box. In his summing up Devlin told the jury that the case for the defence was manifestly a strong one. The jury found Adams not guilty.

On 26 July 1957 Adams appeared at Lewes assizes to answer the minor charges which remained on the calendar. Adams was charged with making a false statement on three cremation forms, drug offences, and forgery. He pleaded guilty and was fined £2400. As a consequence he was struck off the medical register, but four years later his name was restored and he returned to a flock of private patients. He died on 4 July 1983 in Eastbourne General Hospital of heart failure, after breaking a leg. He left an estate of £408,305, a sum which included substantial libel damages and the sale of Kent Lodge.

PERCY HOSKINS, rev. MICHAEL BEVAN

Sources P. Devlin, *Easing the passing* (1985) · P. Hoskins, *Two were acquitted* (1984) · R. Hallworth and M. Williams, *Where there's a will* (1983) · S. Bedford, *The best we can do* (1958) · private information (2004) · personal knowledge (2004)
Likenesses photographs, repro. in Hoskins, *Two were acquitted*
Wealth at death £408,305: probate, 29 Sept 1983, *CGPLA Eng. & Wales*

Adams, John Couch (1819–1892), by Sir Hubert von Herkomer, 1888

Adams, John Couch (1819–1892), astronomer, was born on 5 June 1819 at Lidcot, a farm near Launceston, Cornwall, the eldest of the seven children of Thomas Adams (1788–1859), a poor tenant farmer, and his wife, Tabitha Knill Grylls (1796–1866), a farmer's daughter who had received some education from her uncle John Couch. She inherited Couch's library, including a few astronomy books, which engaged John in boyhood. Of his brothers, Thomas became a missionary, George a farmer, and the third, William Grylls *Adams FRS (1836–1915), professor of natural philosophy and astronomy at King's College, London. Adams was brought up in a close Wesleyan family and had his mother's good ear and love of music. From the nearby village school at Laneast, where he learned Greek and algebra, at the age of twelve he moved to the private school at Devonport (later at Saltash and Landulph) run by his cousin the Revd John Couch Grylls. There he learned classics and largely taught himself mathematics. Astronomy was his passion; in the Devonport Mechanics' Institute he studied astronomy articles in Rees's *Cyclopaedia*, and Vince's *Fluxions* introduced him to higher mathematics. In 1835 at Landulph he observed Halley's comet, and in 1836 he calculated and observed an annular eclipse and planetary conjunctions. The following year he became a private tutor. A small inheritance left to his mother in 1836 enabled the family to make the further sacrifices involved in sending Adams to university; he won a scholarship and entered St John's College, Cambridge, as a sizar in October 1839. He won the first prize in Greek testament every year, and in 1843 graduated as senior wrangler and first Smith's prizeman, and was elected a fellow of his college.

Adams achieved lasting fame as the co-discoverer of the giant planet Neptune by mathematical calculation. He is remembered for two other major achievements: his memoir on the secular acceleration of the moon's mean motion and his determination of the orbit of the Leonid meteorids. These resulted from 'a great deal of intricate and elaborate mathematical investigation' carried out with great skill and accuracy on 'specific, well-expressed problems', rather than by someone exploring 'completely new fields and making startling discoveries' (private information). Adams modestly and rightly regarded himself as a celestial mechanician in the strong line of J. L. Lagrange, P.-S. Laplace, C. Delaunay, C. F. Gauss, and P. A. Hansen.

Adams's long career may be seen as having three principal elements: his work between 1841 and 1846 which, when he was only twenty-seven, led to his co-discovery of Neptune; his subsequent career as a mathematical astronomer, which included thirty-three years as a professor at Cambridge (from 1859 until his death); and his concurrent direction of the Cambridge observatory (from 1861 to 1892).

Neptune By the 1820s it was known that the planet Uranus was not following the orbit predicted since its discovery in 1781. Adams rejected various hypotheses because they were incapable of being tested by exact calculation; he realized that the amount of observed deviation could not be caused by the perturbations due to the masses of Jupiter and Saturn alone. Either Newton's laws of gravitation were wrong or there must be an unknown planet beyond Uranus. Because he had complete faith that Newton was not in error, and because the physical quantities of Uranus's mass and the extent of deviation were known, Adams's great inspiration was to believe that he could break all precedent and work from known perturbations to deduce the orbit, position, and mass of the body that must be exerting a gravitational attraction upon Uranus. On 3 July 1841 he recorded his determination to investigate the problem. It was later hailed as one of the grandest intellectual problems ever tackled. After finals, in the summer of 1843 he calculated the first of six solutions of ever-increasing accuracy. He tutored undergraduates in order to send money to contribute to his brothers' education, and even made time to teach his bedmaker, Mrs Ireland, to read. In September 1845 he gave the elements and position of the new planet to James Challis (1803–1882), director of the Cambridge observatory, who gave him a letter of introduction to the astronomer royal at Greenwich, G. B. Airy (1801–1892). In October, without prior appointment, Adams twice called at Greenwich and left his derived elements. Airy responded with what he considered a fundamental question; Adams thought it trivial and neglected to reply.

In the summer of 1845, unaware of Adams's work, U. J. J. Le Verrier in Paris investigated the problem. Adams's diffidence deterred him from publishing results until they were checked very carefully. Le Verrier published papers on his own method and progress, then in June 1846 a first predicted position which Airy saw was very close to that given by Adams in October 1845. Convinced, Airy pressed Challis to use the Cambridge 11.25 inch telescope, 'in the hope of rescuing the matter from a state which is ... almost desperate' (Smart, 1947, 59). There were three ways of finding a predicted planet: noticing that a 'stellar' object was a disc, not a point source; noticing that in a specific region there was a 'star' not recorded on accurate star maps which included faint stars; and noticing that a particular 'star' had moved. Having no star charts, on 29 July Challis commenced an unavoidably laborious search, relying on the third method. Since Paris had no suitable telescope, Le Verrier sent his own prediction to J. G. Galle at the Berlin observatory. There H. C. D'Arrest found that one corner of a newly available star chart covered the predicted position. This was very important, because Neptune was too small to be recognized as a disc when using the magnification appropriate for a planet search. The planet was duly found on the first night's search, 23 September, only 2° 27' from the position Adams had given—a marvellous prediction. It was found because Le Verrier had published his prediction and then energetically pressed a search. French triumph was spoiled when Sir John Herschel and then Richard Sheepshanks, foreign secretary of the Royal Astronomical Society (RAS), insisted on having Adams's prior solution recognized.

Adams had not given Airy or Challis the details of his work or method which might have persuaded them. Then he took 'for granted' that Airy would have 'communicated my results among his correspondents' (Glaisher, 'Biographical notice', xxviii). J. W. L. Glaisher, who knew all three men, excused Adams on the grounds of youth and extreme modesty. He concluded that Challis: 'As professor in the University ... should not have allowed a young Senior Wrangler, through modesty or diffidence or inexperience, to do such injustice to himself' (ibid., xxvi). Challis admitted his failures. Airy's explanation that such a search was not the business of the national observatory has been upheld by his biographers. But contemporaries found it inexplicable that Airy, even when his doubts were removed, did nothing to urge Adams to publish or adequately to affirm his work when lavishing praise on Le Verrier. Hence the Royal Society was led to blunder by awarding the Copley medal to Le Verrier in 1846 without mentioning Adams. This was remedied only when they awarded the Copley to him in 1848 and elected him FRS in 1849. Adams's work on comets had secured his election to the RAS in 1845; the society awarded no medal for Neptune. In 1847 Adams declined a knighthood because he could not afford the social consequences. However, in 1848 his college established an Adams prize in his honour and the government awarded him a pension. Adams was lionized in his university, perceived as having the most imaginative English mathematical mind and power of calculation since Newton. He never uttered a word against Challis or Airy, and that reticence and his genial nature endeared him to many.

Celestial mechanician Adams continued as a tutor at St John's until his fellowship expired in 1852. A congenial career post eluded him for more than a decade. He was extraordinarily uncompetitive, reluctant to publish imperfect work to stimulate debate or claim priority, averse to correspondence about it, and forgetful in practical matters. The pension, then additional stipends, enabled him to work in his own way.

When he was elected president of the RAS for 1851–3, Adams urged the need to reinvestigate the lunar and planetary theories and prepare new tables. This led him to his second major achievement. By 1851 he had started work on several problems contributing to the three body problem of the interactions between earth, sun, and moon, known as the lunar theory. Edmond Halley had discovered a fundamental problem, the acceleration of the moon. In 1787 Laplace had discovered the cause, the action of the sun upon the moon and the decrease of the eccentricity of the earth's orbit. In a paper to the Royal Society on the secular acceleration of the moon's mean motion (1853) Adams showed that Laplace's supposed definitive work had omitted some terms from the equations and accounted for only half the observed change in longitude of nearly 12 arc seconds per century. Calculating for additional tangential force, Adams's residual discrepancy of 5.7 arc seconds, very close to modern values, is now known to be due to the moon's tidal drag leading to a slowing down of the rate of rotation of the earth, and thus an increase in the length of the day. His paper caused great controversy among French astronomers, but he simply disproved each objection as it arose.

Adams continued with work on the fine detail of variables in the moon's orbit—lunar parallax and perigee. By rigorous comparison he traced errors, and in 1852 produced valuable new tables of the moon's parallax and in 1856 added corrections for the values given in the *Nautical Almanac*. He was anxious to obtain the superintendence of the *Nautical Almanac* office which became available in 1853, but he had displayed no organizational ability, and the Admiralty selected John Hind (1823–1895). In February 1853 Adams was elected a fellow of Pembroke College, which enabled him to continue tutoring. In autumn 1857 he was elected professor of mathematics at the University of St Andrews, but shortly afterwards the Lowndean chair of astronomy and geometry became vacant at Cambridge. His appointment in March 1859 was a formality; the university publicly recognized his achievements by bestowing a prestigious post and stipend which allowed him to remain among friends.

Director, Cambridge observatory The commonly perceived inefficiency at the Cambridge observatory during the search for Neptune had been due not least to a lack of funds for employing and retaining sufficient assistants. In 1858 Challis was ill and had a huge backlog of observations to reduce and publish. Airy was fully aware of this. By December 1858 he had negotiated Anne Sheepshanks's donation of a fund for the observatory in memory of her brother. In November 1860 she was persuaded to add £2000 for a new instrument; in December Challis asked to be relieved. By February 1861 he and Adams's close friend G. G. Stokes, the Lucasian professor, had persuaded Adams to accept the superintendence for £250, conditional upon his not having to observe or process reductions or publications, and that if these interfered with his research he could resign. These extraordinary terms were acceptable only because the Sheepshanks fund would enable him to retain an experienced senior assistant.

Thus Adams chose, and at the age of forty-two was appointed to, one of the most prestigious and important astronomical posts in Britain. He moved to the observatory beyond the city in September 1861. In October 1862 he met Elizabeth (Eliza; 1827–1919), the 34-year-old daughter of Halliday Bruce of Dublin. She was a guest and friend of Stokes's wife, herself a daughter of T. R. Robinson, the director of Armagh observatory. Probably on Robinson's recommendation Adams visited Ireland in December to engage Andrew Graham (1815–1908), director of Markree observatory, to become his chief assistant at Cambridge. While he was staying with Robinson at Armagh, Eliza, also a guest there, agreed to marry him. They were married on 2 May 1863; they had no children.

Adams loved his university, his science, and the academic life. He fulfilled his primary duty from 1860 to 1889 by diligently lecturing in one term of each year. His course was on the lunar theory, which illustrated geometrically the analytical process so important to advanced mathematicians. Every year he rewrote several lectures.

Adams's second responsibility was the observatory. Cost precluded replacing the Northumberland refractor. Graham's expertise and interest lay in continuing to catalogue and chart accurate star positions for zones along the ecliptic, the great circle of the earth's orbit intersecting the celestial sphere. This was useful for precise determination of planetary orbits, and therefore of real utility. Adams's policy was to limit use of the Northumberland refractor to special observations. A new 8 inch transit circle by Troughton and Simms was ordered in 1867 and installed in December 1870. The Astronomische Gesellschaft (the German astronomical society) asked Adams to deploy the powerful new instrument on their last available zone, which happened to extend Graham's Markree ecliptic zone. Observations commenced in 1871 and were mainly completed by 1886, and the zone was published in 1897. Beyond Adams's initial help evaluating instrument errors, everything was delegated to Graham. The single programme for twenty-six years, continuity of staff, and funds for computing prevented stress. Yet by 1872 Airy complained that, with nothing published since 1859, 'Cambridge is beginning to lose place' (letter from Airy to G. H. Richards, 13 Sept 1872, CUL, RGO 6 150/158). The observations for 1861–5 were not published until 1879. In 1882 Adams helped the ageing and widowed Graham by allowing the keenest of the computers, Anne Walker (*b. c.*1864), to move into the observatory and to be remunerated and work effectively as his third assistant. Even so the observations for 1866–9 were published only in 1890.

The Leonids Adams's third major achievement resulted from H. A. Newton of Yale's having analysed historical observations to predict correctly in 1864 a meteor shower that would occur in November 1866 from a radiant point in Leo. Newton asserted that the longitude of that node (intersection of the orbit with the celestial equator) was increasing. This presented a difficult but attractive problem of celestial mechanics. The leading astronomers of Europe made various contributions, but it was Adams who by March 1867 calculated the effect of planetary perturbations upon the advance of the node and derived 'a definitive orbit' for the Leonids which coincided with that of Tempel's comet, thus establishing 'the close relation between comets and meteors' (Dreyer and Turner, 162). Some experts considered this a more difficult work than lunar acceleration.

Because of his pre-eminent expertise on the lunar theory, Adams often received queries from the *Nautical Almanac* office when revising the ephemerides for their tables, which were so essential to navigators; he always responded promptly. In 1881 he contributed refined ephemeris tables of the positions of the Galilean satellites of Jupiter.

Adams neither did much research in nor searched for new mathematical principles, and he played no major role in the mathematical societies of his day. From eleven published papers on pure mathematics he is remembered for the somewhat eccentric calculation of Euler's constant, which is used in integration and calculation, to 236 decimal places. Although few observations emerged from Cambridge, Adams's work was admired for reaffirming Newton's laws, eliminating errors, and refining fundamental theory. Altogether he published sixty-two scientific papers in various journals (only three with the Royal Society), nearly fifty of them with the RAS. He wrote seventeen of them while a tutor at St John's, only four in his first decade as director of the observatory, and only two after 1884 as his health failed. For work on lunar perigee and acceleration he was awarded the RAS gold medal in 1866.

Adams's mass of unpublished work was edited by his brother William and R. A. Sampson (1896 and 1900). From 1849 Adams attempted to work towards a theory of terrestrial magnetism and determination of the Gaussian magnetic constants for any part of the globe. William published: 'The numerous tables … calculated with the utmost care under Professor Adams' minute supervision and instruction … by Mr Graham, who has done a great part of the work, and by Mr Todd [the second assistant] and other assistants' (*Papers*, 2.xxvii–xxviii). Global maps with contour lines of equal magnetic variation were attached. But a major constraint had been the lack of observational data for the southern hemisphere, where there were only three stations.

By accepting directorship of a leading scientific institution, Adams not only assumed a responsibility for the scientific output of the observatory but raised expectations for his potential influence in matters of patronage upon which the community of observers completely depended. His office made him a visitor to the Royal Greenwich Observatory and ensured a place on the RAS council, which he served from 1854 to 1892. His lack of engagement with the politics of the discipline may be inferred from his attendance at the dinners of the RAS Club, which preceded the eight RAS meetings each year. The club was the élite policy-forming coterie to which he was elected 'by acclamation' in 1851 (Turner, xxxiv) and which in 1876 elected him vice-president (he served until 1887), and later an honorary life member. While council member and society president from November 1851 to June 1853 he attended five of sixteen dinners. From 1866 to 1873, years notable for the endowment for solar research debate which split the RAS in 1872, he attended less than once a year; as president again from November 1874 to June 1876 he was absent six times.

Adams's correspondence shows that he was prompt to help with information but avoided controversy, and he usually did not reply to appeals for intervention or patronage. The exceptions were his unselfish proposal of Hencke and Hind for the 1848 RAS medal, soliciting a government pension for Hind in 1851, and in 1879 moving with uncharacteristic speed to ensure that Hind was elected RAS president despite Airy's mooted intervention. Adams's generosity and love of truth are exemplified by his securing Cambridge's honorary LLD for Le Verrier in 1874 and, when president, the RAS gold medal for him in 1876. On Airy's retirement in 1881 Adams was offered the post of astronomer royal, but surprised nobody when he declined.

When Isaac Newton's mathematical papers were left to Cambridge University in 1872 Adams was perceived as 'so penetrated with Newton's style and thought that he was peculiarly fitted to be his interpreter' (Glaisher, 'Biographical notice', xlv), and he gave immense time and care to the catalogue which was published in 1888. From 1869 he was an early and active supporter of the provision of higher education for women in Cambridge: from 1873 until Newnham College was incorporated in 1880 he was the first president of the association which lobbied for such provision, and he was one of the first Cambridge professors to admit women to his lectures.

Adams necessarily worked alone. He was a consummate master of all the refined and delicate methods in the highest and most complicated and difficult field of astronomy, as well as of the detailed processes by which theory and observation are connected. From analysis of Adams's diary and dated work, Glaisher summarized that 'For forty-five years [1843–88] his [powerful] mind was constantly directed to mathematical research relating principally to astronomy' but that, owing to an 'innate craving for perfection', he published only a fraction of what he accomplished (Glaisher, 'Biographical notice', xlii–xliii), and thereby limited his contribution to the discipline. Adams and his contemporaries used classical methods of computing which involved an iteration of successive approximations for each perturbation. Such analytical methods have been replaced by methods of numerical integration. But although much of Adams's work was therefore superseded, fifty years later an astronomical professor declared it impossible to do justice to his 'multifarious researches' on celestial mechanics (Smart, 1947, 85).

Adams was happily married, profoundly devout, and enjoyed social visits, house guests, entertaining, music, dancing, parties, long daily walks, croquet, bowls, and whist. He shared contemporary interests in mesmerism and the occult. A bibliophile, when not socializing in the evenings he read. He attended the weekly meetings of The Family, a university dining club, at least from 1860 to 1889. He was much involved in college and university business. He did not shirk the public exposure of accepting honorary degrees from Oxford, Dublin, Edinburgh, and Bologna; he was a correspondent of the Académie Royale des Sciences and of the academy at St Petersburg.

Adams became seriously ill in October 1889 and had a stomach haemorrhage. Partial recovery was followed several times by relapses, the last of which in June 1891 left no hope. He died at the observatory on 21 January 1892. The queen wished him buried in Westminster Abbey, but following a funeral service at Pembroke College he was buried five days later in St Giles's cemetery, close to the observatory. Memorials were erected in both Truro and Westminster cathedrals. In 1919 Eliza Adams died in Cambridge of influenza, aged ninety-one. In her husband's memory she left a bequest to augment the stipend of a John Couch Adams astronomer, who was not to be a professor.

ROGER HUTCHINS

Sources W. M. Smart, 'John Couch Adams and the discovery of Neptune', *Occasional Notes of the Royal Astronomical Society*, 2 (1947), 33–88 · M. Grosser, 'Adams, John Couch', *DSB* · D. W. Hughes, 'J. C. Adams, Cambridge and Neptune', *Notes and Records of the Royal Society*, 50 (1996), 245–8 · *The scientific papers of John Couch Adams*, ed. W. G. Adams and others, 2 vols. (1896–1900) · J. W. L. Glaisher, 'Biographical notice', in *The scientific papers of John Couch Adams*, ed. W. G. Adams and others, 1 (1896), xv–xlviii · *History of the Royal Astronomical Society*, [1]: *1820–1920*, ed. J. L. E. Dreyer and H. H. Turner (1923); repr. (1987), 161–2 · H. H. Turner, ed., *Records of the RAS Club* (1904) · F. J. M. Stratton, 'The history of the Cambridge observatories', *Annals of the Solar Physics Observatory, Cambridge*, 1 (1949), 1–26 · private information (2004) [D. W. Hughes] · A. Chapman, 'Private research and public duty: G. B. Airy and the search for Neptune', *Journal for the History of Astronomy*, 19 (1988), 121–39 · H. M. Harrison, *Voyager in time and space: the life of John Couch Adams, Cambridge astronomer* (1994) · L. E. Doggett, 'Celestial mechanics', *History of astronomy, an encyclopedia*, ed. J. Lankford (1997), 131–40 · G. B. Airy, letter to G. H. Richards, 13 Sept 1872, CUL, Royal Greenwich Observatory papers, RGO 6 150/158 · A. J. Meadows, *Greenwich observatory: the story of Britain's oldest scientific institution*, 2: *Recent history (1836–1975)* (1975) · *Catalogue of scientific papers*, Royal Society, 19 vols. (1867–1925) · G. B. Airy, *Autobiography of Sir George Biddell Airy*, ed. W. Airy (1896) · J. W. L. G. [J. W. L. Glaisher], 'James Challis', *Monthly Notices of the Royal Astronomical Society*, 43 (1882–3), 160–79 · R. Sheepshanks, letter to G. B. Airy, 15 Dec 1846, CUL, Royal Greenwich Observatory papers, RGO 6, 229, 63 · [J. W. L. Glaisher], *Monthly Notices of the Royal Astronomical Society*, 53 (1892–3), 184–209 · *DNB* · *Journal of the British Astronomical Association*, 2 (1891–2), 196–7 · 'The collected papers of Prof. Adams', *Journal of the British Astronomical Association*, 7 (1896–7), 486 · I. B. Cohen, 'Newton, Isaac', *DSB* · J. W. L. Glaisher, *The Observatory*, 15 (1892), 173 · W. M. Smart, 'John Couch Adams and the discovery of Neptune', *Nature*, 158 (1946), 648–52 · H. S. Jones, 'G. B. Airy and the discovery of Neptune', *Nature*, 158 (1946), 829–30 · St John Cam., Adams MSS · CUL, Royal Greenwich Observatory papers · RAS, letters · RAS, Sheepshanks MSS

Archives Cornwall RO, awards, corresp., and papers · St John Cam., corresp., diaries, and papers | CUL, Royal Greenwich Observatory papers, corresp. with Sir George Airy, RGO/6 941–53 RGO/6 · CUL, letters to Sir George Stokes, Add. 7342 and 7656 · RAS, letters to the Royal Astronomical Society · RAS, letters to Richard Sheepshanks · RS, corresp. with Sir J. F. W. Herschel · RS, letters to Sir John Lubbock, A38–A64

Likenesses photograph, *c.*1846–1856, repro. in Smart, 'John Couch Adams', facing pp. 62, 63 · N. N. Burnard, marble bust, exh. RA 1849, RAS · S. Cousins, mezzotint, pubd 1851 (after T. Mogford), BM, NPG · T. Mogford, oils, 1851, St John Cam. · L. E. Barker, drawing, 1869, St John Cam. · cartoon, pen, 1872, St John Cam. · A. B. Joy, marble bust, exh. RA 1873?, St John Cam. · H. von Herkomer, oils, 1888, Pembroke Cam. [*see illus.*] · H. C. Fehr, marble bust, 1903, Launceston Library, Cornwall · A. G. Dew Smith, photograph (as an old man), St John Cam. · Fawks, drawing, St John Cam. · H. von Herkomer, oils, replica, NPG · A. B. Joy, medallion, Westminster Abbey, London · F. W. H. Myers, photograph, repro. in Glaisher, *The Observatory*, facing p. 173 · Stodart, portrait (after steel engraving from photograph by Mayall), in Adams, ed., *Collected scientific papers*, vol. 1, frontispiece · drawing, St John Cam. · plaster bust, St John Cam. · stained-glass window, St John Cam.

Wealth at death £32,433 12s. 8d.: probate, 2 March 1892, CGPLA Eng. & Wales

Adams, John Michael Geoffrey Manningham [Tom] (**1931–1985**), prime minister of Barbados, was born on 24 September 1931 in St Michael, Barbados, the only child of Sir Grantley Herbert *Adams (1898–1971), later prime minister of the Federation of the West Indies, and his wife, Grace, only daughter of Alexander Thorne, shipping agent, and his wife, Millicent. He was educated at the Ursuline convent, and at Harrison College in Barbados, and then at Magdalen College, Oxford, to which he was admitted after winning the Barbados scholarship in 1951. He obtained third-class honours in philosophy, politics, and economics in 1954.

In 1954 Adams began to study law at Gray's Inn; he was called to the bar in 1959. While a law student, he worked as a producer in the overseas service of the BBC where he met Genevieve Turner, who was employed as a secretary. They were married in 1962. Genevieve was the daughter of Philip Turner, principal assistant solicitor (later solicitor) to the Post Office. There were two sons of the marriage.

Adams worked for six months in the Gray's Inn chambers of Dingle Foot and then returned to Barbados in January 1963. After settling his family and setting himself up as a barrister in chambers he began his political career. He was secretary of the Barbados Labour Party from 1965 to 1969. He won a seat in the house in 1966 and was leader of the opposition from 1971 to 1976. He became prime minister and finance minister of Barbados in September 1976 and remained in that office until his death in 1985.

Adams had a formidable task before him when he entered public life. He had to function under the shadow of his illustrious father's name and, in addition, he was faced with a redoubtable opponent, Errol Barrow, who led the Democratic Labour Party and was then prime minister of Barbados. But at the BBC he had developed the talents that made him the island's most skilful communicator. His oratory was such that he attracted large audiences to meetings of the assembly. And, while he excelled in parliamentary debate, he soon showed he was no mean opponent on the political platform. In addition, what helped him to win three by-elections and two general elections was his flair for organization.

One of Adams's ambitions was to bring to reality his father's dream of a West Indies united and self-governing. He was actively involved in the Caribbean Community which sought to attain some of the late federation's objectives. He was in every sense a Caribbean man. He promptly sent military assistance to St Vincent when the premier, Milton Cato, asked for help in 1979 against a revolt in the Grenadines. And when the premier of Grenada, Maurice Bishop, was killed in 1983 and that island was threatened with a Marxist take-over, Adams joined with the leaders of the Organization of Eastern Caribbean States and persuaded President Ronald Reagan of the USA to assist them in a rescue mission. Adams regretted the decline of British influence.

Adams was tall and handsome and possessed the common touch. He was fond of gardening and philately, bridge, and poker. He loved dancing and merrymaking, even to the extent of embarrassing his entourage. He drove himself hard at both work and play and slept only four hours a night. In due course his many-sided activities began to take a toll on his health. He made light of the first signs that should have warned him that his heart was beginning to feel the strain. Later he consulted a Harley Street specialist, who advised open-heart surgery late in 1984. Adams decided to postpone any such operation until he had completed pressing business abroad that would help him in the unceasing tasks of social reform and financial stability. However, he collapsed on the afternoon of 11 March 1985, at Ilaro Court, the official residence of the prime minister, and a medical certificate confirmed that his death that day was due to cardiac failure.

ALEXANDER HOYOS

Sources F. A. Hoyos, *Tom Adams* (1988) · private information (1990) · *WWW* · *The Times* (13 March 1985)
Likenesses photograph, repro. in *The Times*

Adams, Joseph (1755×7–1818), physician, was the youngest of the three sons of Joseph Adams (1725?–1783), an apothecary in Basinghall Street, London. He was educated to succeed his father, studying in London under David Pitcairn and Percivall Pott at St Bartholomew's Hospital and Guy's Hospital; most importantly, he attended the lectures of John Hunter at St George's Hospital. Hunter became a lifelong influence for Adams, who showed him 'a partiality bordering on enthusiasm' (Uwins, 168). Adams worked in London as an apothecary, probably taking apprentices. In 1795 appeared what he and his contemporaries considered his most important work, *Observations on Morbid Poisons* (2nd rev. edn 1807). He divided poisons into two categories: those that were harmless to the host (for example, the venom of a snake) and those that were 'morbid' and carried a disease. In 1796 he bought an Aberdeen MD and in the same year was elected an extra-licentiate of the Royal College of Physicians, London. He was elected licentiate in 1809.

About 1796, at the suggestion of Dr Saunders (probably William Saunders), Adams and his wife, who had no children, travelled to Madeira, an island popular with consumptives. Adams practised there for eight years. While in Madeira he wrote on cancer of the breast (1801), and an account of leprosy and the lazaretto (1806), as well as more than one article or pamphlet about Madeira, presumably intended to attract patients. From 1801 until his death there is hardly a volume of the *Medical and Physical Journal* (*London Medical and Physical Journal* from 1815) that does not have a contribution from Adams. He obviously enjoyed writing: his style is clear, his meaning precise. Writing was also a way of bringing himself to the attention of his medical colleagues.

By 1805 Adams had returned to London. He was elected physician to the Smallpox Hospital as successor to William Woodville. He was also physician at the New Finsbury or Central Dispensary, an editor of the *Medical and Physical Journal* from 1808 to 1809, president of the Medical Society of London and the London Philosophical Society, and a fellow of the Linnean Society. Adams built up a substantial private practice and gave lectures, which included lectures on heredity, from his house in Hatton Garden. He never stopped writing, publishing articles and works on cowpox (1807), inoculation and vaccination (1807), Madeira (1808), epidemics (1809), and a memoir of John Hunter (1817, 2nd edn 1818). He divided diseases into endemic (those arising in secluded communities), epidemic (such as influenza), infectious (arising from confined air, or poverty), and contagious (such as smallpox,

scarlet fever, and measles). Adams was in favour of vaccination rather than inoculation against smallpox. He concluded that plague and yellow fever were not contagious, because they were not invariably caught by those who came into contact with them.

Adams's *A Treatise on the Supposed Hereditary Properties of Diseases* (1814; 2nd edn with different title, 1815), the theoretical part of which attracted little contemporary attention, is now regarded as perhaps the first work setting out modern principles of genetic inheritance. A. G. Motulsky was the first (1959), followed by A. E. H. Emery (1989), to notice Adams's importance to genetics in that he distinguished between hereditary (dominant) and familial (recessive) disease, and defined congenital illness, both hereditary and non-hereditary. Emery wrote that Adams 'emphasised the role of inbreeding in producing clustering of certain inherited disorders' (founder effect), 'the occasional appearance of a disorder in only certain members of a family while others, who have affected descendants, remain healthy', and 'variable age at onset'; he also 'emphasised the importance of environmental factors in precipitating disease in certain genetic disorders; and finally, recommended the establishment of registers for the purpose of preventing genetic disease' (Emery, 116, 117). Adams's work was the result of reading, observation, and clinical experience, rather than scientific experiment. Adams himself said that heredity does 'not admit of experiment' (Adams, 10). He discussed earlier work at length, but made no reference to P. L. M. de Maupertuis, who in 1745 and 1752 had demonstrated the inheritance in one family of polydactyly (extra fingers or toes). Adams's reading was wide: he appeared to be at home with both Latin and Greek, and was familiar with contemporary medical writing. Among those who consulted Adams were Samuel Taylor Coleridge and Joanna Southcott.

Adams died at his home, 17 Hatton Garden, London, on 20 June 1818. He had broken his leg about two weeks before, was recovering well, but died suddenly from what was probably a pulmonary embolus; there was said to be a history of sudden death in his family. Writing a long and affectionate obituary, his good friend David Uwins clearly thought highly of Adams, but did notice his concern for reputation and dislike of criticism. Adams was buried at Bunhill Fields, London, with the motto *Vir justus et bonus* ('A just and good man') on his grave. JEAN LOUDON

Sources D. Uwins, *London Medical Repository*, 10 (1818), 167–70 · A. E. H. Emery, 'Joseph Adams (1756–1818)', *Journal of Medical Genetics*, 26 (1989), 116–18 · A. G. Motulsky, 'Joseph Adams (1756–1818)', *AMA Archives of Internal Medicine*, 104 (1959), 490–96 · GM, 1st ser., 88/1 (1818), 638–9 · Munk, *Roll* · J. Adams, *A treatise on the supposed hereditary properties of diseases* (1814) · B. Glass, 'Maupertuis and the beginnings of genetics', *Quarterly Review of Biology*, 22 (1947), 196–210 · *Monthly Gazette of Health*, 3 (1818), 966–8 · *London Medical Journal*, 4 (1784), 213 [obit. of father] · P. J. Wallis and R. V. Wallis, *Eighteenth century medics*, 2nd edn (1988)
Likenesses engraving, RCS Eng.; repro. in Emery, 'Joseph Adams', 116

Adams, Katharine (1862–1952), bookbinder, was born on 25 November 1862 at Bracknell in Berkshire, the second daughter among the three children of the Revd William

Fulford Adams (d. 1912) and his wife, Catherine Mary Horton (bap. 1830, d. 1912). As a child she lived at Little Faringdon, Oxfordshire, where her friends included William Morris's daughters, May and Jennie, and where she made some early experiments in bookbinding in cobbler's leather and in needlework. The connection with the Morris family proved useful when she began binding professionally during the 1890s. After a short period of training with Sarah Prideaux (1853–1933) and T. J. Cobden-Sanderson (1840–1922) in London in 1897, she set up a workshop in Lechlade, where her first commission came from Janey Morris. In 1901 she established the Eadburgh Bindery in Broadway, Gloucestershire. Adams initially worked alone, but was later able to employ two women assistants, whom she herself trained. For several years during this period she taught binding to the nuns at Stanbrook Abbey, although she was never quite reconciled either to the restrictions imposed upon the nuns or to the practical difficulty of teaching through a grille. She remained at Broadway until after her marriage to Edmund James Webb (1853–1945), an independent scholar, on 25 November 1913. Late in 1915 she and her husband moved into Oxfordshire, living at Noke and Islip before returning to Gloucestershire in the 1930s. She continued to bind under her maiden name of Adams throughout this period; her last binding was completed only a few years before her death.

Adams's bindings were acclaimed from an early stage in her career, and (unlike many arts and crafts style bindings of the time) are still admired for their technical competence (Lewis, 33). She took first prize in bookbinding at the Oxford arts and crafts exhibition of 1898, and was soon receiving regular commissions from the engraver and typographer Emery Walker (1851–1933), St John Hornby (1867–1946), and the bibliophile Sydney Cockerell (1867–1962), who became a close friend. In the early years of the twentieth century she regularly exhibited both in London and abroad, showing her work not only in Belgium, France, and Germany, but as far afield as St Louis, Missouri, and Cape Town, South Africa, and winning several awards. She became the second president of the Women's Guild of Art, and in 1938 a fellow of the Royal Society of Arts. Important commissions included Queen Mary's psalter and *The Buildings of the British Museum*, presented to Queen Mary and George V respectively, the Ashendene Press *Tutte le opere di Dante Alighieri*, which has been described as 'possibly her finest binding' (Tidcombe, 139), and the Doves Press Bible, of which she and Cobden-Sanderson bound the only two copies printed on vellum. She was a highly accomplished gold finisher, described as a 'markedly individual' designer, and 'one of the few binders of any date or country who made a success of pictorial designs in gold on leather' (Nixon, *Broxbourne Library*, 224). Intricate *pointillé* work was a particular feature of her style, and her attention to detail is apparent from a letter in which she wrote of one of her bindings:

The effect of the dotted background was quite intentional. The effect of light on the gold can be varied by the angle at which the tool is used. That background was worked with

the book upside down—if you turn it, you will see the difference. (Lewis, 35)

She designed many of her own finishing tools, including her signature tool: the initials KA in sanserif, separated by a catherine wheel. They are now in the British Library bindery, London.

Although Adams described herself as someone who 'felt rather keenly the ups and downs of life' (Tidcombe, 137), her letters give consistent evidence of the 'great charm and keen sense of humour' mentioned in her obituary (Cockerell). A photograph of Katharine Adams taken c.1930 (repr. Tidcombe), when she was aged about seventy, shows her with long grey hair swept back from her face, a broad forehead and high cheekbones, dark eyes, a steady gaze, and a firm but kind mouth. A less distinct photograph (repr. Tidcombe) taken c.1905 shows her in profile, revealing a fairly short, perhaps slightly turned up nose, and a rather large chin. Her hair in the earlier photograph is dark, and caught up in a large coil at the back of her head. She died a widow at her home, The Cherries, St Briavels, Gloucestershire, on 15 October 1952, at the age of eighty-nine.

JANE GRIFFITHS

Sources M. Tidcombe, *Women bookbinders, 1880–1920* (1996) · J. R. Abbey, *English bindings, 1490–1940, in the library of J. R. Abbey*, ed. G. D. Hobson (privately printed, London, 1940) · R. H. Lewis, *Fine bookbinding in the twentieth century* (1984) · H. M. Nixon, *Broxbourne library: styles and designs of bookbindings from the twelfth to the twentieth century* (1956) · H. M. Nixon, *Five centuries of English bookbinding* (1978) · letters to and from Sydney Cockerell and Katharine Adams, BL, Add. MS 71213 · V. Meynell, ed., *The best of friends: further letters to Sydney Carlyle Cockerell* (1956) · S. Cockerell, *The Times* (20 Oct 1952) · S. Prideaux, *Modern bookbindings: their design and decoration* (1906) · IGI · m. cert. · d. cert.

Archives Bodl. Oxf. | BL, Add. MSS 45300–45304, 45307, 45330, 43694, 50002, 50004, 54231 · J. P. Getty Library, Wormsley · Southern Methodist University, Dallas, Bridwell Library · U. Cal., Berkeley, Bancroft Library

Likenesses photograph, c.1905, repro. in Tidcombe, *Women bookbinders* · photograph, c.1930, repro. in Tidcombe, *Women bookbinders*

Wealth at death £22,846 5s. 7d.: probate, 23 Jan 1953, CGPLA Eng. & Wales

Adams, Mary (supp. *fl.* 1652), self-proclaimed virgin mother, is a fiction whose existence rests in the creation of one pamphlet formed around her alleged misdeeds and blasphemies. This work is called *The Ranters Monster* and was printed in London for George Horton in March 1652. *The Ranters Monster* relates how one Mary Adams of Tillingham, Essex, named herself the Virgin Mary, claiming that 'she was conceived with child of the Holy Ghost'. Furthermore, it was reported how she denied the teachings of the gospel and wickedly declared that 'Christ was not yet come in the flesh; but she was to bring forth the Savior of the World, and that all those that did not believe in him were damn'd'. For these blasphemies it was ordered by the local minister that Adams be imprisoned until the time of her delivery. After a protracted labour of eight days, she gave birth on the ninth day to a stillborn, ugly, misshapen monster. This loathsome creature was said to have neither hands nor feet, but claws like a toad. Adams herself became consumed by disease, rotting away, her body disfigured by blotches, boils, and putrid scabs. To compound her sins she refused to repent, and committed the terrible crime of suicide. This 'true Relation' was confirmed by a group of village notables, among them the minister, churchwardens, and parish constable, their names appended to the end of the text (*The Ranters Monster*, 3–5). The account in *The Ranters Monster* was reproduced in some contemporary newsbooks, and later in a broadside enumerating the great blasphemers of the times. It may also have come to the attention of John Reeve and Lodowick Muggleton, who were to denounce the false Christs, false prophets, and 'counterfeit Virgin Mary's' of the world (Reeve, 5).

No one by the name Adams nor any one of the witnesses named in *The Ranters Monster* occurs in any of the records of the parish of Tillingham, Essex. It can only be concluded that the pamphlet is fictitious. The supposed profusion of 'false Virgin Maries' in the minds of Reeve and Muggleton hint at the genesis of the tale (Muggleton, 157). For the story of Mary Adams bears a strong resemblance to the case of Joan Robins, the supposed spouse of John Robins, whose disciples were said to believe that in July 1651 she would give birth to 'the Saviour of all that shall be saved in this world' (E. H., 3). Moreover, *The Ranters Monster* can also be seen as forming part of an older tradition, that of the genre of monstrous births. Monstrous births could be interpreted as providential signs warning against private and public sin, and their appearance was chronicled with great care. There are several examples of this type of literature in the period, among them *A Declaration of a Strange and Wonderfull Monster* (1646), from which the woodcut illustration on the title-page of *The Ranters Monster* was taken. In this earlier work the alleged begetter of a monstrous child is stigmatized as a papist, this association of the deliverance of evil into the world by a sinful creature being a recurring theme in works of this kind. Indeed the character of Mary Adams can be seen as serving a particular function in *The Ranters Monster*: as a warning against the licentiousness of the Ranters. Constructed as a devout, godly woman, Adams becomes victim to the familiar slippage through various forms of religious belief, becoming successively a Baptist, a member of the Family of Love, and finally a Ranter. As a Ranter she is said to maintain diabolical tenets: the denial of God, heaven, and hell, and the opinion that a woman may have sexual relations with any man—regardless of his marital status. As such *The Ranters Monster* is instructive both for its fictive, yet evidently believable, account of a woman claiming to be the new Virgin Mary, soon to be delivered of a Christ child, and for its construction of assumed Ranter beliefs. ARIEL HESSAYON

Sources *The Ranters monster: being a true relation of one Mary Adams* (1652) · J. Reeve, *A remonstrance from the eternall God* (1653), 5 · L. Muggleton, *A true interpretation of the eleventh chapter of the Revelation* (1662), 157 · parish register, Tillingham, Essex, Essex RO, Chelmsford, D/P 237/1/5 · E. H., *All the proceedings of the sessions of the peace holden at Westminster* (1651), 3 · *A declaration of a strange and wonderfull monster* (1646) · *A list of some of the grand blasphemers* (1654) · *Faithful Scout*, 60 (5–12 March 1652), 455 [printed in J. Raymond, ed., *Making the news: an anthology of the newsbooks of revolutionary England, 1641–1660* (1993), 185] · *Weekly Intelligencer* (16–23 March 1652), 394–5 · *French Intelligencer* (23–30 March 1652), 144 · parliamentary survey of Tillingham manor, Essex, 1649, GL, MS 25,631, fols.178–87 · *Dutch Spy*, 2 (24–31 March 1652), 11–12

Adams [*née* Campin], **Mary Grace Agnes** (1898–1984), television producer and programme director, was born on 10 March 1898 at Well House Farm, Hermitage, Berkshire, the elder of two daughters (her sister died aged three) and second of four children of Edward Bloxham Campin, farmer, of Hermitage, and his wife, Catherine Elizabeth Mary (*d.* 1938), daughter of Edwin Gunter, farmer, of Alveston. Mary's mother brought up the three surviving children in Penarth, Wales, under conditions of great hardship; Mary's father died of consumption in 1910. A scholarship to Godolphin School, Salisbury, led to University College, Cardiff, where Mary Adams gained first-class honours in botany (1921). She then became a research scholar and Bathurst student at Newnham College, Cambridge (1921–5), and published papers on cytology.

Mary Adams held tutorial and lectureship posts at Cambridge for extramural and board of civil service studies (1925–30). In 1928 she broadcast a series (published as *Six Talks on Heredity*, 1929), which proved a transition point. Gripped by the educational possibilities of the BBC, she joined its staff in 1930 as adult education officer. Her inspiring flair for teaching, especially the young, and organizational skills had a new outlet. She stayed in sound broadcasting until 1936: under the exactitudes of Sir John Reith, director-general of the BBC, she combined information with informality in obligatorily scripted programmes. She was appointed to the newly established television service in 1936, becoming the first woman television producer. An atmosphere of history-in-the-making, experimentation, and excitement prevailed, though the budget was minuscule. The headquarters was at Alexandra Palace, north London, and Mary Adams was in charge of education, political material, talks, and culture. She persuaded the eminent—for example, C. E. M. Joad, S. Gordon Russell, Julian Huxley, and John Betjeman—to appear on this alarming new medium, but with the outbreak of the Second World War in 1939 the service was shut down.

From 1939 to 1941 Mary Adams was director of home intelligence in the Ministry of Information and the years 1942–5 were spent working in North American service broadcasting, where she produced morale-boosting programmes—for example, *Transatlantic Quiz*. Returning to BBC TV in 1946, she was ever breaking new ground, bubbling with ideas, enlisting the services of the distinguished in arts and science for programmes, and cutting red tape. She was head of television talks (1948–54) and assistant to the controller of television programmes (1954–8). She stimulated others to achieve, and could spot and harness enthusiasm and talent. For example, in the early 1950s, the young zoology graduate David Attenborough (who at this stage had never seen television) realized, after a revelatory five-minute conversation with Mary Adams, the potential force of television for the future, joined the staff at Alexandra Palace, and went on to create and produce numerous ground-breaking wildlife series. Mary Adams herself promoted and produced many programmes (always with a purpose): cooking; gardening; art; intellectual quizzes, for example *Animal, Vegetable, Mineral?* (1952–9, 1971); material for children, such as *Muffin the Mule* (1946–55) and *Andy Pandy* (1950–69, 1970–76); science, for example *Eye on Research* (1957–61); and world celebrations, such as *The Restless Sphere* with the duke of Edinburgh in International Geophysical Year (1957). The first to make medicine accessible to the public, she shook the medical profession out of its secretive complacency with such series as *A Matter of Life and Death* (1949–51, 1952), *Matters of Medicine* (1952–3, 1960), *The Hurt Mind* (1957), and *Your Life in their Hands* (1958–64). There were many repeats and revivals of her programmes. Her productive years from 1942 to 1958 could not have been so successful without her working relationship and friendship with Nora Wood, who skilfully manipulated an often chaotic environment to combine cheerful progress with a singular and telling output.

When Mary Adams retired in 1958 she began a new career. The Consumers' Association, which had been established in 1957, resulted from her deliberations with Julian Huxley in 1937. She was its deputy chairman from 1958 to 1970, and induced a nervous *Which?* magazine to produce the first comparative tests of contraceptives and a reluctant BBC to produce the first consumer programmes giving brand ratings. Simultaneously, she advised the BBC (and was, contrastingly, a member of the Independent Television Authority, from 1965 to 1970), wrote for *Punch*, and played far-sighted roles in organizations concerned with Anglo-Chinese understanding, the unmarried mother and her child, British railway design, British Medical Association planning, mental health, women's groups, telephone users, and eugenics.

With science, as with the arts, she made people sit up, with ideas that were daring, in support of what was new, often with a strong feminist slant, and expressed with animation, even provocation. Spurning notes for public speaking, she arrived well informed, sensed the atmosphere, then, in a style that teased and delighted, injected serious and original proposals. She was a creative persuader at work, yet paradoxically indecisive at home. She was appointed OBE (1953), an associate of Newnham College, Cambridge (1956–69), and a fellow of University College, Cardiff (1983).

Mary Adams married on 23 February 1925 (Samuel) Vyvyan (Trerice) Adams (1900–1951), the younger son of Samuel Trerice Adams, canon of Ely and rural dean of Cambridge. Her husband was Conservative MP for West Leeds (1931–45), an early determined anti-Nazi, and a radical reformer. He was adopted for the Conservative seat of Darwen in 1951, and earmarked for cabinet rank by Winston Churchill, but his untimely drowning on 13 August of that year denied this political resurgence. One daughter, Sally, was born of the marriage in 1936.

In appearance Mary Adams was small, birdlike, always well dressed, with bright blue eyes and, in public, a knowing confidence. Her character, though full of contradictions, was magnetic. She was a socialist, a romantic communist, and could charm with her charisma, spontaneity, and quick informed intelligence. She was a fervent atheist and advocate of humanism and common sense, accepting her stance without subjecting it to analysis. These qualities ensured she was the centre of attention in a social setting, and she involved herself with all the right people. Yet a streak within compelled her to dread, then court, loneliness and it decreed that her marriage was to be less than happy: she could not live in harmony with herself, nor be truly supportive to those close to her who needed help. She had an unexpected, dry put-down humour. A stroke in 1980 affected her memory; when flummoxed and cornered by a social worker's banal and routine questions, she wriggled out of it with, 'If you want the details, you can always look me up in *Who's Who*'. She died in University College Hospital, London, on 15 May 1984, and was cremated at Highgate crematorium, London.

SALLY ADAMS

Sources *The Times* (18 May 1984) · private information (1990) [N. Wood, C. Campin, I. Hughes-Stanton, A. Armit] · personal knowledge (2004) · *WWW* · *WWBMP*, vol. 3
Archives BBC WAC, corresp. and papers · U. Sussex Library
Likenesses D. Salmon, oils
Wealth at death £152,931: probate, 28 Sept 1984, *CGPLA Eng. & Wales*

Adams, Mary Jane Bridges- [*née* Mary Jane Daltry] (1854–1939), socialist and educationist, was born on 19 October 1854 at Maesycwmer, Bedwas, Monmouthshire, south Wales, the daughter of William Daltry, an engine fitter, and his wife, Margaret Jones. She was born into a family of civil engineers, and her father later held an appointment at the Elswick works, Newcastle. Mary began life as a pupil teacher, but achieved success in the University of London matriculation examination, where she was placed in the first division in 1881; a year later, in June 1882, she passed the University of London's intermediate examination in arts. Mary attended classes in English language and literature, English history, French, Latin, and Greek, and passed through Bedford College with distinction in Greek and mathematics. Eventually she became headmistress in a board school, and afterwards a teacher in Birmingham and London.

On 22 October 1887 Mary married Walter Bridges Adams (d. 1902), a tutor, the son of William Bridges *Adams, civil engineer and radical, and his third wife, Ellen Rendall. Marriage reinforced existing personal and political networks. Mary moved in the same progressive political circles as Peter Kropotkin and William Morris; Walter's sister, Hope, married the Bavarian socialist Dr Lehmann.

In 1894 Mary Bridges-Adams unsuccessfully contested the Greenwich division of the London school board, supported by the Royal Arsenal Co-operative Society, sixty trade organizations, and the London Nonconformist Council. On that occasion her campaign was swamped by the interdenominational controversy over religious teaching in the board schools, and she came fifth in the poll to elect four members, receiving 16,638 votes. She was elected in 1897 and held the seat as the sole Labour member until the 1903 London Education Act abolished the board, transferring its responsibilities to the London county council (LCC). Her chief demands were for free, compulsory education, for a secular curriculum, and for equal educational opportunity. Adding a concern for free school meals and medical care she joined Lyulph Stanley and Stewart Headlam in supporting the development of the higher grade and evening continuation schools.

In November 1901 Mary Bridges-Adams initiated the foundation of the National Labour Education League, which sought to give effect to the views of trade unions to strengthen and develop the educational side of the labour movement. She was active in the campaign against the Conservative Education Acts of 1902–3, arguing that working people should be ready not merely with a negative policy of opposition but a positive education programme based on the scheme outlined by John Richardson in his book *How It Can Be Done, or, Constructive Socialism* (1895). On 21 March 1903 the executive (including Ben Cooper, W. D. Steadman, and H. R. Taylor of the LCC) lobbied Lord Londonderry, president of the Board of Education, to save the school board for London, the league's last recorded political action.

Mary Bridges-Adams was one of the few early Labour figures to be involved with the Froebel movement, and she supported what is generally recognized as the first free kindergarten in England, which opened at Woolwich in 1900. A member of the Woolwich branch of the Women's Co-operative Guild throughout the 1890s and warden of a women's settlement in Greenwich in 1897, she campaigned locally for improved housing and sanitation for the working classes, as well as the provision of such cultural facilities as public concerts, a municipal picture gallery, and free library. She was an honorary member of an association of trade union officials to facilitate the exchange of information on the legal position of trade unions; its council of management included Mona Wilson and Margaret Bondfield.

Mary Bridges-Adams continued the fight for free school meals and in February 1905 organized a motor tour with Frances, countess of Warwick, John Clynes, Sir John Gorst, and Will Thorne to publicize the cause. As Lady Warwick's secretary and collaborator she ran a London-based office and discussion centre, visitors to which included Gorst, Thorne, and Winston Churchill. One of her lasting achievements was the establishment of the first Open Air School for Recovery in Bostall Woods, owned by the Royal Arsenal Co-operative Society. At her request in May 1907 the society offered its land to enable the London county council to investigate the therapeutic effects of open air and regular meals on debilitated children. The countess of Warwick was the main speaker at an inaugural meeting arranged by the co-operators, and the day school opened on 22 July 1907. It continued until 19 October 1907, during which time forty-nine boys and sixty-four girls benefited from the scheme. The experiment was judged a success and in June 1908 the school

reopened on Shooter's Hill. Both sites predate the pioneering work of Margaret McMillan at the school clinic and open-air centre in Deptford.

In 1909 adult education became a key focus of Mary Bridges-Adams's work. She was a fierce critic of the Workers' Educational Association, supporting the Marxist tradition of the Plebs League and the Central Labour College from a commitment to self-governing working-class adult education. Early in 1912 she began a campaign to establish a working women's labour college, and a year later established a Working Women's Movement. She installed herself as resident principal of the first of these colleges, Bebel House, and continued to live at this address, 96 Lexham Gardens, Kensington, until her death.

In 1914 Mary Bridges-Adams's political activism gained an added dimension when she fought to preserve the right of asylum enjoyed by refugees from tsarist Russia, among them Georgy Chicherin, a future Soviet foreign minister. Her main allies in parliament were two Liberals: Joseph King and Lord Sheffield (formerly the Hon. Edward Lyulph Stanley), an old colleague from the London school board and close personal friend. Her obituary in *The Times*, written from close personal knowledge, stated that this last crusade exhausted her. It also attested to her skills both as a public speaker and as 'an inveterate flutterer of dovecotes': in March 1917 Lord Derby, the secretary of state for war, speaking in the House of Lords, denounced her activities as dangerous.

Mary Bridges-Adams's feminist credentials are less clear. The obituary notice refers to her belief in universal adult suffrage and dismissal of Votes for Women as a small 'bourgeois' affair. She did belong to the Women's Local Government Society, but the suggestion that she was a militant suffragette is based on unreliable evidence. Speaking from the hustings in 1894 she herself said she disapproved of young mothers being school-board teachers and believed home was the best place for them. Six years later she reiterated the point, though she did not support the operation of a marriage bar. She died at Princess Beatrice Hospital, London, on 14 January 1939, and was cremated at Golders Green crematorium four days later. She was survived by a son, William Bridges-*Adams, the theatrical producer.　　　　JANE MARTIN

Sources *The Times* (16 Jan 1939) · *DLB* · E. F. E. Jefferson, *The Woolwich story, 1890–1965* (1970) · T. Gautrey, 'Lux mihi laus': school board memories (1937) · W. T. Davis and W. B. Neville, eds., *The history of the Royal Arsenal Co-operative Society Ltd, 1868–1918* (1922) · J. Attfield, *With light of knowledge: a hundred years of education in the Royal Arsenal Co-operative Society, 1877–1977* (1981) · *Labour Leader* (20 July 1901) · *Labour Leader* (21 Feb 1901) · *Labour Leader* (5 Nov 1902) · *Labour Leader* (22 Nov 1902) · *School Board Chronicle* (1897–1904) · *The young Rebecca: writings of Rebecca West, 1911–17*, ed. J. Marcus (1982) · M. Blunden, *The countess of Warwick* (1967) · *Blackheath Gazette* (19 Oct 1894) · *Blackheath Gazette* (26 Oct 1894) · A. Mansbridge, *The trodden road* (1940) · *Justice* (6 July 1907)

Archives Co-operative Wholesale Society, London, archives of the south-east retail group [spec. archive of the Royal Arsenal Co-operative Society Ltd] · LMA, London county council records, report on the first LCC Open-air School of Recovery, Bostall Road, Plumstead, 22.53 LCC

Adams, Maurice (1850–1935), socialist and moral philosopher, was the youngest child of John Botroele Adams, a general agent who specialized in building and insurance work. His elder sister Mary had been born nine years earlier in Birmingham. After leaving school, Adams qualified as a chartered insurance broker and joined his father's firm, which became John B. Adams & Son, Incorporated Insurance Brokers, of Moorgate, London. He remained in business as an insurance broker until retirement. On 10 June 1880 he was married in the parish church of Lambeth to Ada Clementina Barnett, four years his junior, and the daughter of John Barnett, a microscope maker. He and his wife spent the rest of their lives near Croydon, Surrey, first at Norbury Cottage, Beulah Road, Thornton Heath, and then, from about 1900, at Fairdeen Cottage, 52 Downs Road, Coulsdon. They had one son, John, born in 1881, who later joined the family firm. Some time in the 1880s Adams's sister Mary, a spinster, moved in with them.

In the late 1870s Adams became profoundly dissatisfied with the religion of his family, and began to seek an alternative. He met William Jupp, a Congregationalist minister who was having problems accepting the discipline of church membership, and who later founded a free religious movement in the Croydon area. The two men became lifelong friends, both of them living for a while in Beulah Road. They went on long walks together, during which Adams pursued his amateur interest in botany. When Thomas Davidson, a peripatetic philosopher, returned briefly to England from 1882 to 1884, Adams and Jupp were part of the small group which collected around him to discuss religion, ethics, and social reform. A difference of opinion within the group led to those who emphasized the importance of economic and social reform departing to form the Fabian Society, while those who remained continued as the Fellowship of the New Life, emphasizing the importance of reforming the spiritual and moral basis of society. Adams joined both organizations, but his main concerns and activities were those of the fellowship. He resigned from the Fabian Society together with Ramsay MacDonald, Mrs Pankhurst, and Henry Salt on 20 April 1900 in protest at the society's failure to adopt a clear stance in opposition to the Second South African War.

Adams edited the newspaper of the fellowship, the *Sower* (renamed *Seedtime* after the first issue), from its inception in July 1889 until the final issue of February 1898. He also wrote articles on subjects such as 'Equality', 'Labour in America', and 'Domestic servitude'. He edited, with an introduction, Thomas More's *Utopia* (1890), and he wrote short works on *The Ethics of Social Reform* (1887) and *Giordano Bruno* (1905). All of his writing reflected the socialism of the fellowship; a socialism which owed more to Emerson and Wordsworth than to Marx, more to the utopian visions of Thomas More and Giordano Bruno than the schemes for municipalization taking shape with the Fabian Society. The members set out to promote the spiritual ethic they believed would inspire people to transform their own lives, and thereby rid society of abuses such as sweated labour. Although the fellowship had little direct impact on British politics, it was the fountainhead for much of the peculiarly ethical socialism which spread throughout the country at the turn of the century. This was something Adams foresaw when he wrote, in the last issue of *Seedtime*, upon the disbanding of the fellowship, 'it is not to its meetings that the Fellowship must look for the spread of its teaching, but to the lives of those who have received the Fellowship ideal'.

Adams himself carried the fellowship ideal into several other groups. He lectured on topics such as 'The self and the moral life' to organizations such as the Christo-Theosophical Society. He was a member of the Humanitarian Society, which published his lecture on 'The sweating system' as a tract in December 1896. From 1902 to 1922 he was a member of the Rainbow Circle, a progressive discussion group, speaking on 'The basis of ethics' in October 1908, and again on 'William James' in December 1911. Most importantly, when the fellowship disbanded, he led some of the members into the Croydon Ethical and Religious Fellowship as part of the British Ethical Movement. In April 1898 he was one of the ethical thinkers Stanton Coit brought together in the Society of Ethical Propagandists, a group of men who could not take holy orders because their consciences kept them out of the churches but who were to act as quasi-religious teachers. All this time his fundamental concern remained the same: to use evolutionary theory to buttress a science of ethics highlighting the growth of co-operation, and inspiring a higher individualism centred on self-realization through the good of others. Adams died at his home in Coulsdon, Surrey, on 3 December 1935; his wife survived him.

MARK BEVIR

Sources *Seedtime* (1889–98) • W. Jupp, *Wayfarings* (1918) • Yale U., Davidson papers • Nuffield Oxf., Fabian Society MSS • *Coulsdon & Purley Times and Surrey County Mail* (6 Dec 1935) • M. Freeden, ed., *Minutes of the Rainbow Circle, 1894–1924* (1989) • I. D. Mackillop, *The British ethical societies* (1986) • register of births, deaths, and marriages • census returns • d. cert. • *CGPLA Eng. & Wales* (1935)

Adams, Orion (1717?–1797), printer, baptized in Manchester Cathedral on 17 April 1720, was born in Manchester, probably in 1717, the son of Roger *Adams (1681?–1741), printer of the *Manchester Weekly Journal* from 1719 to at least 1725 and from 1732 of the Chester newspaper *Adams's Weekly Courant*, and his wife, Elizabeth (d. 1771/2), daughter of John Buckley. Orion Adams's 'instability and eccentricities' (*GM*) meant that it was Elizabeth Adams and not he who succeeded to the paper in 1742 and Adams embarked on a life which was 'a lamentable scene of chequered events' (ibid.).

In the 1740s Adams was active as a master printer in Northgate Street, Chester, where a chapbook entitled *The Suffolk Garland* is recorded from his press in 1747. On 18 November 1750 he married Ann Holliwell at Frodsham. By 1752 Adams was in Manchester, where he started a short-lived newspaper, *Orion Adams's Weekly Journal*, and an equally ephemeral fortnightly periodical, modestly entitled *The Humorist, or, The Magazine of Magazines*.

Undaunted by his failure in Manchester, Adams was in Plymouth by 1758, where he sought to establish *The Plymouth Magazine*, a venture which proved as abortive as a newspaper, probably entitled *The Plymouth Gazette*, which was discontinued by 14 January 1760 and of which no issues survive. He stayed in Plymouth until 1763, when he printed Thomas Alcock's *Observations on that part of a late act of parliament which lays an additional duty on cyder and perry*. In 1766 Adams was incarcerated for debt in the king's bench prison in London and applied for relief under act of parliament in the *London Gazette* of 16 August. Later that year he was in Dublin as a partner of T. Ryder, a relative of the actor Thomas Ryder (1735–1791), with whom he published plays by Isaac Bickerstaff, David Garrick, and Thomas King in 1766 and 1767. In 1768 he was a partner in Birmingham with Nicholas Boden, with whom he produced a family Bible in 150 parts. Claims by the partners that it was superior to John Baskerville's work provoked the latter into producing a rival publication in 130 parts. At the Shakespeare festival of 1769 Adams cut a splendid figure, arriving from Birmingham in his own carriage, but he left the partnership with Boden in April that year and a few months later he was apparently reduced to distributing playbills for an itinerant company. He had many connections with the stage, knowing Spranger Barry (*d.* 1777), Henry Mossop (*d.* 1774), and other leading actors. Between his periods as a master printer he eked out a living in many London and provincial offices as a journeyman.

In 1775 Adams reappeared in Devon, marrying Susanna Baker by licence at St George's, Exeter, on 6 August and printing for Miss Jenny Hawtin in Totnes the tenth edition of *The Fatal Curiosity*, a work of which he was the proprietor. He was in Clare Market, London, in 1788 when *Proceedings on the Trial of Warren Hastings* was printed for him. Adams stands as a representative of the many obscure and wandering printers who helped to establish printing in the provincial towns of England in the eighteenth century and was described by Daniel Prince in a letter to John Nichols dated 8 October 1795 as 'an old itinerant type' (Nichols). When in his seventies he would frequently walk from London to Chester and back 'with a heart as light as his pocket; for, under all adversities his temper was cheerful, obliging and friendly' (*GM*). During April 1797 he died in poverty in a lodging near Chester.   IAN MAXTED

Sources *GM*, 1st ser., 67 (1797), 445 · Nichols, *Lit. anecdotes*, 3.708, 9.572 · C. H. Timperley, *Encyclopaedia of literary and typographical anecdote*, 2nd edn (1842), 795 · I. Maxted, *The Devon book trades: a biographical dictionary* (1991), 164 · F. E. Pardoe, *John Baskerville of Birmingham: letter founder and printer* (1975), 97–112 · R. M. Wiles, *Freshest advice: early provincial newspapers in England* (1965), 336, 449, 480 · *ESTC* · H. R. Plomer and others, *A dictionary of the printers and booksellers who were at work in England, Scotland, and Ireland from 1726 to 1775* (1932), 2 · J. I. Dredge, *Devon booksellers and printers in the 17th and 18th centuries* (1885–91), 36

Adams, Richard (*bap.* 1620, *d.* 1661), poet, was baptized at St Leonard Eastcheap in London on 8 January 1620, the second son of Sir Thomas *Adams, first baronet (*bap.* 1586, *d.* 1668), and his wife, Ann (1592–1642), daughter of Humphrey Maptide (*d.* 1594) of Frinton, Essex. He was admitted as fellow-commoner at St Catharine's College, Cambridge, on 28 April 1635, but did not matriculate. In the following year he contributed a Latin epigram to the congratulatory verses issued by the university on the birth of the Princess Anne (*Synodia*, sig. L3v). He left without taking a degree and enrolled at Gray's Inn on 23 July 1639, after which his career is obscure. Adams died on 13 June 1661 and was buried six days later as 'Richard Adams de London armiger' in Lancaster Priory church, where he is commemorated by a modest wall tablet in the chancel (Roper, 695).

Adams's presence in the area at the time of his death may be explained by his connection with the family of Bindloss of Borwick Hall in north Lancashire. Some lines 'To the most Accomplish'd Lady Madame Binlosse', subscribed 'From your most humble servant & most admirer R. Adams', were probably dedicated to Dorothy, wife of Sir Robert Bindloss (*d.* 1688) who served as MP for Lancaster from 1646 until Pride's Purge in December 1648. They survive in British Library MS Harley 3889, an anthology of some two dozen royalist pieces composed between 1647 and 1655 that includes work by Davenant, Montrose, Alexander Brome, Thomas Jordan, and Henry Hughes MD. Seven additional pieces are signed with the initials 'R. A.', of which one is addressed to a brother of the writer and four are poems and elegies on Charles I. Adams himself was not the copyist, and some doubt is thrown on the accuracy of the attributions by the fact that the poem beginning 'Let Turkey boast of empire' (fol. 34v), though subscribed 'RA', was published in George Wither's *Vaticinium votivum* of 1649.   W. H. KELLIHER

Sources Venn, *Alum. Cant.*, 1/1 · *Synodia*, Cambridge University (1637) · *N&Q*, 3rd ser., 5 (1864), 42–3 · W. O. Roper, ed., *Materials for the history of the church of Lancaster*, 4, Chetham Society, 59 (1906) · H. Brierley, ed., *The registers of the parish church of Lancaster* (1908) · GEC, *Peerage*, new edn · HoP, *Commons, 1660–90* · *VCH Lancashire*, vol. 8 · BL, MS Harley 3889 · *DNB*

Adams, Richard (1626/7–1698), clergyman and ejected minister, was the son of Charles Adams, clerk, of Woodchurch in the Wirral, Cheshire, and his wife, Isabel, daughter of Thomas Bennet of Barnston in the same county. One of his brothers was Thomas *Adams (1631/2–1670). The Adams family had held the advowson at Woodchurch since about 1540 and Charles Adams was probably the rector. Having for several terms attended Cambridge University, Richard Adams was admitted on 24 March 1647 to Brasenose College, Oxford; he was aged twenty at his matriculation on 3 June. He graduated BA on 3 November 1648 and MA on 29 May 1651, and was incorporated at Cambridge in that degree in the following year. He served Brasenose as junior bursar for two years, 1651–3, and as senior bursar in 1654–5. A fellow of Brasenose from 30 May 1649, he resigned after his admission on 25 July 1655 to the rectory of St Mildred, Bread Street, London.

Adams held this living until his ejection for nonconformity in 1662, his successor being instituted on 23 February 1664. He married twice. Nothing is known of his first wife, but by a licence of 7 September 1678, when he was at least fifty-one, he married Ann Wadsworth (*b.*

1651/2) of St Olave's, Southwark, a widow aged twenty-six. Of Adams's brothers, Thomas is perhaps the most interesting. He too attended Brasenose, becoming a fellow in June 1652, Greek lecturer in 1655, and junior bursar for the year 1658–9, but in 1662 he was removed for nonconformity; his book *The Main Principles of the Christian Religion* was issued after his death in 1670, having been prepared for the press by Richard Adams.

In the 1660s Adams took up the pastorate of a small congregation in Southwark. On 1 May 1672 he was licensed as a presbyterian at the house in Cheapside of another brother, John. But he did not forget Woodchurch, where in 1655 a free school had been founded. In 1676 he donated to it an escritoire and 344 books, adding a further fifty-four volumes in 1681. Adams and Edward Beale contributed joint commendatory prefaces to two books by Stephen Charnock, *A Discourse upon the Existence of God* (1682) and *A Discourse of Divine Providence* (1684). Adams was a firm believer in fortitude in the face of suffering. In a sermon on the question of 'How may child bearing women be most encouraged, and supported against, in, and under the hazard of their travail', he was sure that 'if her life be holy, though her throws and pangs be grievous, yet she shall have surpassing joy that if a child is born; and if she dies in child bearing, her soul will be eternally happy' (Annesley, 634). His second wife, however, survived both childbirth and the death of her husband. Richard Adams died on 7 February 1698 in the parish of St Olave, Southwark, and was buried in the chancel of his old church, St Mildred, Bread Street, on 16 February. At his funeral the sermon was preached by a friend of fifty years, John Howe. By his will, proved on 18 May 1698, Adams left property in Kent; the financial arrangements were designed chiefly for the education and maintenance of John, the elder, and Peter, the two sons of his second marriage, both minors.

STEPHEN WRIGHT

Sources Calamy rev. · [C. B. Heberden], ed., *Brasenose College register, 1509–1909*, 2 vols., OHS, 55 (1909) · Venn, *Alum. Cant.* · F. Gastrell, *Notitia Cestrienses, or, Historical notices of the diocese of Chester*, ed. F. R. Raines, 1, Chetham Society, 8 (1845), 181 · S. Annesley, ed., *A continuation of morning exercise questions* (1683), 633–63 · J. Howe, *A sermon on the much lamented death of … Richard Adams* (1698) · will, PRO, PROB 11/445, sig. 112, fol. 157r–157v
Wealth at death property in Kent: will, PRO, PROB 11/445, sig. 112, fol. 157r–157v

Adams, Sir Richard (1709/10–1774), judge, was the son and heir of John Adams of the parish of St Olave, Southwark. He was admitted to the Inner Temple on 23 October 1727. Called to the bar in 1736, Adams practised as one of the common pleaders of London until 1748, when he was elected recorder of that city, after a close contest, by the casting vote of the lord mayor. The Inner Temple shortly afterwards elected him a bencher. He was knighted in 1752, while still recorder of London, and it is said that George II was so impressed by one of his speeches in that office that he personally selected him for the bench. The appointment came in 1753, when he was made one of the barons of the exchequer in succession to Edward Clive, and he sat in the court of exchequer for nearly twenty

years, declining the opportunity to move to the common pleas in 1754.

Adams married a daughter (d. 1755) of James Molinier and they had at least two sons. He died on circuit at either Bedford or Huntingdon, from gaol fever believed to have been caught at the Old Bailey; the date is variously given as 14, 15, 16, or 18 March 1774. Sir John Wilmot, who knew him intimately for forty years, said: 'I never saw him out of temper in my life' (Wilmot, 199–200). J. H. BAKER

Sources Baker, *Serjeants* · Sainty, *Judges* · Foss, *Judges* · BL, Hardwicke correspondence, Add. MS 35592, fol. 329 · Inner Temple, London · *Annual Register* (1774), 191 · *GM*, 1st ser., 44 (1774), 142 · *IGI* · will, PRO, PROB 11/995, fols. 256r–256v · J. E. Wilmot, *Memoirs of the life of the Right Honourable Sir John Eardley Wilmot*, 2nd edn (1811) · W. Musgrave, *Obituary prior to 1800*, ed. G. J. Armytage, 1, Harleian Society, 44 (1899)
Wealth at death at least £3830: will, PRO, PROB 11/995, fols. 256r–256v

Adams, Robert (d. 1595), architect, was one of seven surviving children of Clement *Adams (c.1519–1587), schoolmaster to the royal pages of honour (1552–87) and a designer and engraver of some reputation, who wrote a Latin account of Richard Chancellor's expedition of 1553–4 to Russia. Nothing is known of his early life, but he first came to prominence in the building world with a design for the house at Dogmersfield, Hampshire, which was under construction in 1581 for Henry Wriothesley, second earl of Southampton, 'according to the forme … and modell made by Adams of Grenewch' (Wriothesley's will). In 1581–2, together with Humphrey Coole, an instrument maker, he was responsible for 'new making the Dial in the Great Garden at Whitehall' (PRO, E 351/3216). His associated talent as a cartographer is evident from a number of maps which survive at Hatfield House and in the British Library, including a plan of Flushing (dated 1585), a map of the Thames showing the queen's progress from Tilbury to London (1588), and a plan of Drake's island, Plymouth (1592). He also drew a series of scenes of the defeat of the armada which were engraved by Augustine Ryther and published in 1590.

In 1592 Adams advised on the fortification of Plymouth and in the following year he designed and supervised the construction of Star Castle on St Mary's in the Isles of Scilly. He left the island with the works still in progress to take up the post of surveyor of the royal works, which was granted to him on 31 August 1594. His appointment to the leading position in the works must, at least in part, have been based on his reputation as a designer: in this respect it represented a break with the previous tradition of giving the post to a working craftsman or an administrator and provided a foretaste of the increasing architectural significance of the role. However, his impact on the organization can only have been slight, as he died at Greenwich within twelve months of taking up the office. He was buried in the north aisle of Greenwich church, close to his father, and was commemorated by a monument erected by his servant Simon Basil, who was himself to become surveyor in 1606; on it he was described as 'Architecturae peretissimo' (Stow, 804). In his lifetime Adams enjoyed the particular favour of the queen and was granted a pension of £40 a year in 1582 'for good causes and considerations' (patent roll, PRO, C 66/1222). After his death she expressed her personal sorrow and the desire that his plans should be preserved.   MALCOLM AIRS

Sources H. M. Colvin and others, eds., *The history of the king's works*, 6 vols. (1963–82), vol. 3, pp. 94–5; vol. 4, pp. 591–3 • J. Summerson, 'Three Elizabethan architects', *Bulletin of the John Rylands University Library*, 40 (1957–8), 202–28, esp. 204–9 • J. Stow, *The survey of London*, ed. A. M. [A. Munday] and others, rev. edn (1633), 804 • will of Henry Wriothesley, second earl of Southampton, PRO, PROB 11/65, sig. 45 • R. A. Skelton and J. Summerson, *A description of maps and architectural drawings in the collection made by William Cecil, first Baron Burghley*, Roxburghe Club (1971), 43, 65–6 • PRO, works accounts, E 351/3216 • PRO, patent roll, C 66/1222 • map of Thames, BL, Add. MS 44839 • A. M. Hind, *Engraving in England in the sixteenth and seventeenth centuries*, 1 (1952), 144–5 • *Calendar of the manuscripts of the most hon. the marquis of Salisbury*, 5, HMC, 9 (1894), 378–9 • Catalogue of plans and models in Adams's hands, 1595, PRO, SP 12/253, no. 167 **Archives** BL, Add. MSS • Hatfield House, Hertfordshire, Hatfield collection • PRO, state papers

Adams, Robert (1794/5–1875), surgeon, was born in Dublin, the son of Samuel Adams, a solicitor, and his wife, Elizabeth, *née* Filgate. He entered Trinity College, Dublin, on 6 November 1809, at the age of fourteen, and graduated BA in 1814 and MA in 1832; he became MB and MD in 1842. He began the study of medicine by apprenticeship to William Hartigan from 20 February 1810, and he became licentiate of the Royal College of Surgeons in Ireland in 1815; he was elected member (equivalent to the later fellow) in 1818.

After spending some time on the continent to increase his professional knowledge, Adams returned to Dublin to practise, and was elected surgeon successively to the Jervis Street Hospital and the Richmond Hospital. It is related that he applied for the latter post against a candidate of equal ability, John McDonnell. The dilemma was resolved by the generous gesture of Richard Carmichael, who said that the hospital could not afford to lose either applicant and who resigned his own post to create a second vacancy. Adams took part in founding the Richmond (afterwards the Carmichael) school of medicine, and lectured there on surgery for some years. He was three times elected president of the Royal College of Surgeons in Ireland (1840, 1860–61, and 1867–8), and in 1861 he was appointed surgeon to the queen in Ireland and regius professor of surgery at the University of Dublin.

Adams had a high reputation as a surgeon and pathological anatomist. He was celebrated in his lifetime for his *Treatise on Rheumatic Gout, or Chronic Rheumatic Arthritis of All the Joints* (1857); today, however, he is remembered mainly for his description of heart block (Stokes-Adams syndrome). This work, though describing a disease known for centuries, contained much new and important research. A long article by Adams in the *Dublin Hospital Reports* describes how in May 1819 he was called to see a 68-year-old man who was recovering from what appeared to be an apoplectic attack. 'What attracted my attention', Adams wrote, 'was the irregularity of his breathing and remarkable slowness of the pulse which generally ranged at the rate of 30 per minute' (Adams, 396). Frederick Willius and

Thomas Keys included this early case of heart block in their *Cardiac Classics* (1941). Eoin O'Brien has commented further on 'the range of cardiac pathology presented and the depth of reasoning applied by Adams to explain the disorders of cardiac function' (O'Brien, 127).

Adams resided at 22 St Stephen's Green, north Dublin. His first wife (*née* Lebas) was of French extraction. On 8 June 1841 he married Mary, daughter of Major Alexander Nixon Montgomery of Bessington Park, co. Monaghan. A contemporary described Adams as a short, stout man with a chubby face; he was the best of company, possessed of a fund of stories, and was never known to repeat himself. He died on 13 January 1875 at his home, 22 St Stephen's Green, north Dublin, and was buried in Mount Jerome cemetery.   J. F. PAYNE, *rev.* J. B. LYONS

Sources C. A. Cameron, *History of the Royal College of Surgeons in Ireland*, 2nd edn (1916) • E. T. O'Brien, 'Robert Adams', *Journal of the Irish Colleges of Physicians and Surgeons*, 3 (1973–4), 127–9 • Burtchaell & Sadleir, *Alum. Dubl.* • F. A. Willius and T. E. Keys, *Cardiac classics* (1941) • R. Adams, 'Cases of diseases of the heart, accompanied with pathological observations', *Dublin Hospital Reports*, 4 (1827), 353–453 • *The Lancet* (23 Jan 1875), 145 • *BMJ* (6 Feb 1875), 194 • *Medical Press and Circular* (27 Jan 1875), 86 **Likenesses** J. H. Lynch, lithograph (after S. C. Smith), Royal College of Physicians of Ireland, Dublin **Wealth at death** under £3000: probate, 2 March 1875, *CGPLA Ire.*

Adams, (Wilfred) Robert (*c.*1900–1965), actor, was born in Georgetown, British Guiana, the son of Robert Adams, boat builder. He was educated at St Stephen's Scots School, later St Joseph's Intermediate. In 1920 he won a government scholarship to be trained as a teacher at Jamaica's Mico Teachers' Training College, from which he graduated with honours. While teaching in British Guiana he produced and acted in amateur stage productions. After his arrival in Britain in the 1920s he was forced to earn a living in low-paid jobs, such as labouring, before a sports promoter encouraged him to become a professional wrestler. Consequently Adams became well known in British and European wrestling circles as the Black Eagle, and achieved the distinction of becoming heavyweight champion of the British empire. Away from the sporting world, he was a founder member of Dr Harold Moody's League of Coloured Peoples in 1931.

Adams started appearing as a supporting player in films in 1934. After playing the Nubian slave in Gabriel Pascal's 1945 screen version of George Bernard Shaw's *Caesar and Cleopatra*, he found himself elevated to movie stardom when he was cast in a leading role in the melodrama *Men of Two Worlds*. He played Kisenga, a composer and concert pianist who, after spending fifteen years touring Europe, agrees to return to his village in Tanganyika to assist the district commissioner in persuading the villagers—including his family—to leave the area to avoid a sleeping sickness epidemic. In spite of Thorold Dickinson's sensitive documentary-style direction, which at times gave the film great emotional power, *Men of Two Worlds* failed because of its condescending view of Africans. Nevertheless, at the time of the film's release in 1946, most critics

(Wilfred) **Robert Adams** (c.1900–1965), by Frank Lilley, 1949

considered this 'ground-breaking' film a sincere attempt to explore themes concerning the battle of science against superstition, and of modern medicine against the power and influence of the African witch doctors. Adams himself said in an interview in 1947:

> If all my screen parts were as dignified, human and moving as the one in *Men of Two Worlds*, then one might soon be able to influence cinemagoers in the right direction. And if they see Negroes playing cultured, intelligent people often enough, they will begin to realise that the coloured man is not necessarily a superstitious, hymn-singing buffoon. Out of the suffering of the last war, people have learned to have a measure of understanding; and we wish earnestly that this spirit of co-operation and helpfulness will persist. (*Film Quarterly*)

Adams began his stage career in 1935 and three years later he played the lead in Eugene O'Neill's *The Emperor Jones* at Cambridge's Arts Theatre. In 1939 he gave an impressive performance as the Caribbean strike leader in *Colony* for the left-wing Unity Theatre. Towards the end of the war he founded the Negro Arts Theatre and, with the support of the Colchester Repertory Theatre, staged Eugene O'Neill's *All God's Chillun' Got Wings*. In interviews Adams spoke of his plans to stage works by black writers, as well as ballet and dance. He planned to extend their work by touring the USA and the British empire under the auspices of the British Council, but his venture was short-lived. Britain was not ready to accept—or support—a black theatre company. However, in 1946, the Unity Repertory Company did invite Adams to appear in another production of *All God's Chillun' Got Wings* and in 1948 he

played Bigger Thomas in a repertory production of Richard Wright's *Native Son* (1948) at London's Boltons Theatre.

Before the war Adams became the first black actor to appear on British television when he performed in several productions broadcast live by the BBC from Alexandra Palace. These included John Webster's *The Duchess of Malfi* (1938) and the lead in Eugene O'Neill's *The Emperor Jones* (1938). When the BBC resumed its television service after the war, he appeared in several plays, including *All God's Chillun' Got Wings* (1946) and *The Merchant of Venice* (1947). As the prince of Morocco in the latter he became the first black actor to play a Shakespearian role on television. However, in spite of his success, by the 1950s Adams's acting career was in decline. He had already considered law as an alternative career, and qualified as a barrister in September 1948.

After a long break from acting, in 1958 Adams returned to London's West End stage in Eugene O'Neill's *The Iceman Cometh*. He also made a number of appearances on television, including *The Green Pastures* (1958) and Errol John's *Moon on a Rainbow Shawl* (1960). His final screen appearance was a far cry from his starring role in *Men of Two Worlds*. For Joseph Losey's *The Criminal* (1960) he received a screen credit for his role as a prison inmate called Judas, but he was little more than a glorified extra, appearing just long enough for the audience to observe a sad, disillusioned, tired old man. According to his friend Peter Noble, he was 'disheartened by not having any follow-ups to *Men of Two Worlds*' (private information), and he returned to British Guiana, where he took a job as headmaster of a school, and also worked in the government's information department. He died in British Guiana in 1965.

STEPHEN BOURNE

Sources S. Bourne, 'Robert Adams: in two worlds', *Black in the British frame: black people in British film and television, 1896–1996* (1998), 84–91 · J. Richards, 'Filming emergent Africa: "Men of two worlds"', *Thorold Dickinson: the man and his films* (1986), 109–36 · *Film Quarterly* (spring 1947), 16–18 · *Daily Argosy* [British Guiana] (15 Sept 1949) · *Daily Chronicle* [Georgetown, British Guiana] (30 Dec 1949) · private information (2004) [Peter Noble]

Likenesses F. Lilley, photograph, 1949, Hult. Arch. [*see illus.*] · photographs, repro. in Bourne, 'Robert Adams: in two worlds', following p. 116 · photographs, Hult. Arch.

Adams, Robert (1917–1984), sculptor and designer, was born on 5 October 1917 at Far Cotton, Northamptonshire, the youngest of the three children of Arthur and Emily Adams. From about 1930 to 1951 he lived in Hardingstone, near Northampton. He left school at the age of fourteen and did manual work but probably between 1937 and 1946 attended evening classes, part-time, in life drawing and painting at the Northampton School of Art. He was a conscientious objector during the Second World War, serving instead in civil defence. By that time he had started to sculpt and he showed his first carvings in the exhibitions of the civil defence artists at the Cooling Galleries, London, in 1942–4.

From 1946 Adams devoted himself full-time to sculpture, soon establishing a reputation both in London and abroad. He carved in wood, working in series. His first important series was a group of abstract works resembling unfurling buds. These sculptures, together with another series of abstracted figures, were shown at his first one-man exhibition in November 1947 – January 1948 at Gimpel Fils, London. This avant-garde, Francophile gallery continued to support him by holding one-man exhibitions of his work approximately every two years until his death. In 1948 and 1949 he visited Paris, where he became a close friend of the sculptor Maxime Adam-Tessier who took him to the studios of Henri Laurens and Constantin Brancusi. In June 1949 Adams held a one-man exhibition at the Galerie Jeanne-Bucher in Paris.

In 1949 Adams was elected to the London Group and took up a part-time teaching post at the Central School of Arts and Crafts, London, which he held until 1961. The school provided him with facilities for welding and printmaking. There he joined a colleague, Victor Pasmore, in forming a small group, which included Anthony Hill, Kenneth and Mary Martin, and Adrian Heath, devoted to rigorously constructed abstract art. Adams showed in the group's exhibitions in the early 1950s, as well as in exhibitions organized by official institutions, notably the Arts Council and the British Council, both of which continued to support him in his later years. He was one of the first British artists to become aware of the vital post-war art of the United States. In April 1950 he had an exhibition at the Passedoit Gallery in New York and he spent from September to December in the city. Among the American artists he met were Alexander Calder, Herbert Ferber, Day Schnabel, and Robert Motherwell. While there he also met Patricia Devine (d. c.1988), an Irish Roman Catholic, whom he married in 1951, converting from Anglicanism to Catholicism. On his marriage he settled in London, where he remained until 1971.

By 1951 Adams was regarded as one of the most promising of young British sculptors. In that year a large construction in wood, *Apocalyptic Figure*, was commissioned by the Arts Council for the Festival of Britain. In the following year he showed abstracted figures in wood and brass rod in the important exhibition, 'New aspects of British sculpture', at the twenty-sixth Venice Biennale; these won him international acclaim. His sculptures soon became entirely abstract, built up of geometric forms of wood, brass, or bronze. Some were illustrated, with an accompanying statement by him, in the book *Nine Abstract Artists*, devoted to the artists gathered around him and Pasmore, which was edited by Lawrence Alloway in 1954. By then Adams had also become friendly with the abstract artists working in St Ives, Cornwall, notably Wilhelmina Barns-Graham, David Lewis, and the assistants to Barbara Hepworth, Terry Frost and Denis Mitchell. While most of his work of the 1950s is on a small scale, he contributed large works to architectural commissions and to outdoor exhibitions of sculpture, such as the 'Third London county council international exhibition of sculpture in the open air' at Holland Park in 1954. Among his architectural works was the pavilion, with Colin St John Wilson and others, for the exhibition 'This is to-morrow' at the Whitechapel Gallery, London, in 1956, and a massive relief in reinforced concrete (1957–9) for the city theatre in Gelsenkirchen, Germany. In the next two decades he continued to execute large-scale architectural works, but in materials such as bronzed steel or stainless steel.

Adams began to construct with welded iron rod and steel sheet in 1956. Again, he expressed the qualities of these materials, so his forms changed radically. There is more emphasis on silhouette, and forms are drawn in space to suggest movement, or stability and rest. The metal is either left in its natural state or coated in a bronze finish and then patinated to a deep brown—almost black. While some of his metal sculpture is built up in the round, he developed, from 1960, a series of flatter *Screen Forms* made from rectangular plates which he cut and drilled so that light penetrates them.

In 1961 a retrospective exhibition of Adams's sculpture was held at the Ferens Art Gallery, Hull, and the Hatton Gallery, University of Newcastle upon Tyne. In the following year he had a one-man exhibition at the thirty-first Venice Biennale. As well as the *Screen Forms* he showed works with large rectangular or curved metal planes, held in orthogonal supports, which resemble the forms in Pasmore's paintings done at that time. There were also sculptures built up from myriads of triangular and rectangular steel segments, their formations resembling patterns of leaves, or rock strata. Works from the biennale were sent on tour to European cities in 1963 and in that year Adams also had an exhibition in New York, at the Bertha Schaefer Gallery. For the second time he visited the United States, where he had major patrons. In 1968 he had a further exhibition there of his largest, and most minimal, works in welded steel sheet. In 1971 he had a final retrospective exhibition which toured to Northampton and elsewhere before ending at the Camden Arts Centre, London. In the same year he left London and moved to Great Maplestead, Essex. His technique again changed remarkably and he returned to carving, first a series of marbles and then wood patterns which he cast in bronze in sand moulds. He continued to produce bronzes for the next decade. They are solid, small-scale, and sometimes fully rounded but often almost flat, with subtle depressions and varied surface finishes. Although still abstract, some are inspired by landscape, and others by sea waves.

Robert Adams died at Great Maplestead on 5 April 1984; he was survived by his wife and a daughter, Mary (b. 1963). From 1950 to 1980 he was one of the foremost abstract sculptors working in Britain. Although his techniques changed radically during this time, all his work is characterized by an asymmetric balance and a full exploitation of the particular qualities of materials. Examples of his work may be found in the Tate collection; the museums of modern art in New York, Rome, and Turin; the Museu de Arte Moderna, São Paulo, Brazil; Heathrow airport, London; and on the P. & O. liner *Canberra*.

ALASTAIR GRIEVE

Sources A. Grieve, *The sculpture of Robert Adams* (1992) · A. Grieve, *Robert Adams, 1917–1984: a sculptor's record* (1992)
Archives Tate collection, photographs, sketchbooks, and letters

Likenesses R. Adams, self-portrait, oil sketch, c.1946, Tate collection

Adams, Roger (1681?–1741), printer and publisher, is thought to have been born at Chester, and may have served an apprenticeship to a member of the Chester Company of Painters, Glaziers, Embroiderers and Stationers, although there is no entry of his name in the minute books of that company. He did, however, become a freeman of the city of Chester, by purchase, on 20 February 1714. It is possible that he may have worked for Edward Ince, who was the first commercial printer in Chester from 1710 until 1718, but this has not been verified. Adams married Elizabeth Buckley (d. 1771/2), daughter of John Buckley, apothecary of Chester, at St Oswald's Church, Chester, on 28 May 1713. They had at least eight children of whom four are known to have reached adulthood: John (bap. 1714, d. 1757), William (bap. 1719, d. after 1741), Orion *Adams (1717?–1797), and Dorothy (1717?–1757?), his twin sister.

Adams had his first printing office in Manchester, 'At the lower end of Smithy Door' (near the collegiate church). Two books are known to have come from his Manchester press in 1716 and 1719. It was from this address that he also printed and published the *Manchester News-Letter*, later renamed the *Manchester Weekly Journal*, from December 1718 or January 1719.

The paper sold at 1d.; only thirty-five copies are known to survive, and these cover only twenty-nine issues. The largest number of these, twenty-three copies, are in the library of All Souls College, Oxford, and are for the five-month period from 6 August 1724 to 31 December 1724. The date of its demise was probably 1728, the year in which Roger Adams may have set up presses in Shrewsbury and Eastgate Street, Chester. One work (undated but assigned to 1728), *Tair o Gerddi Newyddion* ('Three new ballads'), has the imprint 'Argraphwyd gan Roger Adams ... Mwythig' ('Printed by Roger Adams, Shrewsbury'), while Thomas Badeslade's *Some Short and Plain Considerations* (also c.1728) bears the imprint 'Chester: Printed by Roger Adams in Eastgate Street'.

Adams also published a newspaper, the *Weekly Courant*, in Chester, although this was not the town's first paper. William Cooke, Chester's second commercial printer, had issued his *Chester Weekly Journal* from 1721 until 1733. This was briefly replaced by the *Industrious Bee* in 1733 and then by the *Chester Weekly Tatler* in the following year. If Roger Adams did move from Manchester to Chester in 1728, then he did so in competition with the established printer, William Cooke. However, Cooke may have been in financial difficulties about this time, as he was made to pay £25 by the Stationers' Company in 1727 (for his admittance) and in 1734 he was fined £10 for having sold an unstamped newspaper. From the numbering on surviving copies of Adams's *Courant*, it would appear to have been started in November 1732, although it has been claimed to date from 1730. The earliest known copy, number 51, is for Wednesday 7 to Wednesday 14 November 1733, and bears the imprint: 'CHERTER [sic]: Printed by Roger Adams, Where Advertisements are taken In. Where any Person may have

any small Parcels carried by the News-Men, thro' the Nine Counties they Travel, with great Care and Diligence'. Adams's first dated book was Peter Nourse's *Athrawiaeth yr eglwys* ('Doctrine of the church') (Chester, 1731), although several undated, but datable, books survive from about 1724. One of these, *A Sermon Preach'd at St. Hilary's Chapel Denbigh, in 1728* (1730), carries the address in the imprint as 'Roger Adams in Fleshmonger Lane'. Another work, *A Catalogue of the Lords, Knights and Gentlemen who Compounded for their Estates* (1733), uses the same typefaces as were employed by William Cooke, thus suggesting that, about 1732–3, Adams had taken over the printing office which had been used for the *Chester Weekly Journal*.

The last known book to come from Roger Adams's press was *The Raree Show, or, The Foxtrapt* (1740). The precise date of his death is unknown; according to the parish register of St John's, Chester, he was buried on 14 November 1741. Following his death the *Courant* and the general printing business were taken over by his widow, Elizabeth, and his son John. Roger's will was proved at Chester in 1748. His son Orion had his own printing business and in July 1750 returned to Manchester where, in 1752, he resumed publication of *Adams' Weekly Journal* from the same address as that at which his father had printed the original *Weekly Journal*. Orion's twin sister, Dorothy, married William Monk, who had been her father's apprentice, and their son, John Monk, took over the running of the printing and publishing business in January 1772 following the death of Elizabeth Adams. The newspaper, under the title of *Chester Courant*, continued to be published weekly until its final issue dated 7 September 1982. **D. NUTTALL**

Sources D. Nuttall, *A history of printing in Chester* (1969) · J. Black, 'Manchester's first newspaper: the *Manchester Weekly Journal*', *Transactions of the Historic Society of Lancashire and Cheshire*, 130 (1980), 61–72 · *The book trade in Cheshire to 1850: a directory* (1992) · H. R. Plomer and others, *A dictionary of the printers and booksellers who were at work in England, Scotland, and Ireland from 1668 to 1725* (1922) · H. R. Plomer and others, *A dictionary of the printers and booksellers who were at work in England, Scotland, and Ireland from 1726 to 1775* (1932) · G. R. Axon, 'Roger and Orion Adams, printers', *Transactions of the Lancashire and Cheshire Antiquarian Society*, 39 (1921), 108–24 · J. H. E. Bennet, ed., *The rolls of the freemen of the city of Chester*, 2, Lancashire and Cheshire RS, 55 (1908) · parish register (burial), St John's, Chester, 14 Nov 1741

Adams, Samuel (1722–1803), revolutionary politician in America, was born on 27 September 1722, one of three children (who survived to adulthood) of Samuel Adams (1689–1748) of Boston and his wife, Mary, *née* Fifield (d. after 1748). Adams inherited his political activism from his father, a brewer and member of the Massachusetts house of representatives. The elder Adams, who lost significant funds when the British parliament outlawed the Massachusetts land bank of 1740–41 at the behest of Governor William Shirley, was active in the 'Boston Caucus', the town's leading opposition political organization. Meanwhile young Samuel was attending Harvard College, from which he graduated BA in 1740. He obtained his MA in 1743, arguing in the affirmative a thesis that set the agenda for the rest of his life: whether it was 'lawful to

Samuel Adams (1722–1803), by John Singleton Copley, *c*.1772

resist the Supreme Magistrate, if the Commonwealth cannot otherwise be preserved'.

After failing in business, the younger Adams became involved with the opponents of Governor Shirley's vigorous prosecution of King George's War (1744–8) against the French in Canada. He was among the founders of the *Independent Advertiser*, a short-lived (1748–9) newspaper that was the American colonists' first anti-war periodical. Here he was among those who defended a crowd that protested against naval impressment as 'an Assembly of the People' rather than 'a low-lived Mob' (8 Feb 1748) on the grounds that their 'liberty, property, and to some extent their lives' had been threatened by the navy's action. This was the first use of John Locke's *Second Treatise of Government* to justify violent resistance to authority in the American colonies. Adams now also sought political office for himself. He served in a variety of Boston town offices, including that of scavenger (refuse collector), eventually becoming a tax collector. His extremely lax execution of this job may account for his popularity among the middling and lower sort. By 1764 his account was £8000 in arrears and the largest town meeting in Boston's history assembled to consider his fate. Adams, however, had become friends with John Hancock (1737–1793), whose uncle Thomas had died that year, leaving his nephew sole heir to the largest fortune in Massachusetts. Hancock paid off Adams's debts and the two men first took their seats in the Massachusetts assembly in 1765. Their election, following the announcement of parliament's passage of the Stamp Act, demonstrated how firmly the people of Boston and Massachusetts repudiated the party of Lieutenant-Governor

Thomas Hutchinson, who favoured milder, written protests against the new imperial regulations and, in the last analysis, submission if these proved futile.

From 1765 to 1775 Adams was among the principal leaders of the Boston resistance, though his own destruction or loss of many of his papers makes it nearly impossible to determine his true role in various proceedings. As clerk of the assembly, he certainly signed, even if he did not necessarily write, its protests to the governor and crown. Friends and enemies both placed him at the centre of the 'caucus', the political machine which exerted great control over town meetings and public assemblies. He also wrote numerous pamphlets under pseudonyms such as Vindex and Candidus urging his fellows to defend their liberties from what he considered the illegal incursions of the crown and parliament. Two principles encapsulate Adams's writings in this period: government cannot abridge man's 'natural' rights to life, liberty, and property without his consent by representation; and only a morally virtuous people that repudiated luxury and sloth would be inclined to stand up for these rights.

Historians argue about Adams's connection to the rioting that plagued Boston from the Stamp Act protests of August 1765 to the Tea Party of 16 December 1773. While loyalists believed him to be heavily implicated, there is no convincing evidence in his writings or elsewhere that he urged anything other than written protests and the boycott of British imports. He persuaded Governor Hutchinson to evacuate the British troops after the Boston massacre of 5 March 1770, perhaps hinting that these 600-odd men were in mortal danger from an incensed populace, but no hard evidence links him with a conspiracy to drive the soldiers from the town. In 1772 he was principally responsible for organizing the committees of correspondence, which kept the American people informed about the condition of Boston and Massachusetts as they struggled against new impositions. Adams's role in the Boston Tea Party is again disputed: some sources say he (and Hancock) participated in disguise, and that having chaired the town meeting which tried in vain to have the tea sent back, he signalled the 'party' by announcing: 'This meeting can do nothing further to save this country'. However, another account states that he and the town leaders tried to prevent the town from taking this extreme measure and so further provoking the British.

In any event the British government—like scholars who take the charges of leading loyalists such as Hutchinson at face value—believed Adams to be the ringleader of revolt. According to the Impartial Administration of Justice Act, one of the so-called Intolerable Acts of 1774, people could be tried in Britain for crimes they committed in America. When General Thomas Gage arrived with a large army that year to implement these laws, rumours circulated that Adams and John Hancock were to be sent to Britain and tried for treason. In February 1775 both men fled Boston, and were present at Concord when the American War of Independence broke out that April. 'What a glorious morning this is', Adams is believed, but not proven, to have said once hostilities commenced. That the troops which marched on Concord had hoped to seize Adams and Hancock appears likely given that Gage exempted them from a general amnesty he offered all the rebels that June.

While Adams is best known for his role in beginning the revolution, his contribution did not end there. Between 1775 and 1781 he served in the continental congress, signed the Declaration of Independence, and played an important role in Massachusetts from the 1780s until his death. Consistently for him, although paradoxically for others, he urged that those who protested against Massachusetts state taxes in Shays's rebellion (1786) ought to be hanged rather than accommodated: he reasoned that in monarchical governments people did not have the option of electing new representatives who could tax them as they pleased, which people in republics certainly did. (Hancock, elected governor in 1787, pardoned almost all the rebels who were not involved in random violence.) Although initially opposed to the United States constitution, Adams was persuaded by federalists who in 1788 orchestrated a demonstration of the Boston populace to change his mind and spoke powerfully in favour of ratification in Massachusetts.

Adams was a stern moralist who throughout his career mourned the moral degeneracy of his fellows. He hoped the new republic would institute a 'Christian Sparta', but was disappointed. He served as lieutenant-governor of Massachusetts from 1788 until Hancock, the perennial governor, died in 1793, and then as governor until he retired in 1797. But Adams, who joined the Jeffersonian democratic republicans, had little power in this predominantly federalist state: as it had Hancock, the populace continued to elect him as a symbol of the democratic revolution. When his fellow anti-federalist Thomas Jefferson was elected president in 1801, Adams rejoiced that the nation might now secure its free institutions and establish the moral rectitude to guarantee them: in one of his final letters he wrote to Jefferson that there is 'reason to believe, that the principles of Democratic Republicanism are already better understood than they were before', and they would extend internationally until 'the proud oppressors over the Earth shall be totally broken down and those classes of Men who have hitherto been victims of their rage and cruelty shall perpetually enjoy perfect Peace and Safety till time shall be no more' (*Writings*, 4.410).

Adams was twice married: first in 1749 to Elizabeth Checkley (1725–1757), with whom he had two children, and second, in 1765, to Elizabeth Welles (1733–1808). He died on 2 October 1803 at Boston and, most fittingly, was buried in a simple grave in Boston's Granary burialground, behind the Park Street Church. The men killed in the Boston massacre surround him, much as the inhabitants of Boston had during the revolutionary era. Like Thomas Paine, never interested in business or acquiring more wealth than he needed to live on, Adams made resistance, then revolution, and finally reform his lifework.

To this day historians debate whether Adams was a master incendiary (C. K. Shipton and J. C. Miller) or a sincere defender of liberty who reluctantly (P. Maier) or eagerly (W. M. Fowler) moved the United States towards revolution. All agree he was an essential figure in Boston from 1765 to 1775; however, given the paucity of his unpublished papers, and the ongoing historical debates over the cause he supported, Adams's true motivation will always remain elusive.   WILLIAM PENCAK

Sources W. V. Welles, *The life and public services of Samuel Adams*, 3 vols. (Boston, 1865) · W. M. Fowler, *Samuel Adams: radical puritan* (1998) · J. C. Miller, *Sam Adams: pioneer in propaganda* (1936) · C. K. Shipton, 'Samuel Adams', *Sibley's Harvard graduates: biographical sketches of those who attended Harvard College*, 10 (1958), 420–64 · P. Maier, *The old revolutionaries: political lives in the age of Samuel Adams* (1980), 3–50 · *The writings of Samuel Adams*, ed. H. A. Cushing (1908)
Archives NYPL, MSS | Mass. Hist. Soc., Warren-Adams letters
Likenesses J. S. Copley, oils, *c.*1772, Museum of Fine Arts, Boston [*see illus.*]
Wealth at death $16,000 real estate; $665 personal property: Shipton, 'Samuel Adams', 464

Adams, Sarah Flower (1805–1848), poet, was born on 22 February 1805 at Great Harlow, Essex, the daughter of Benjamin *Flower (1755–1829), nonconformist editor of the radical *Cambridge Intelligencer*, and Eliza Gould (1770–1810), a Devon schoolteacher. Her father was famous for going to prison in defence of his right to freedom of expression in 1799, while her mother had been forced out of her school for refusing on principle to cancel her subscription to his *Intelligencer*; they married in 1800. Her elder sister Eliza *Flower (1803–1846) was a talented musician and composer, who later set many of Sarah's hymns to music. Their mother died in 1810 when Sarah was five; their father sporadically taught the girls himself with occasional help from village schoolmasters.

By 1820 the family had moved to Dalston, near Hackney. Harriet Martineau met them, and was so struck with the sisters that she later modelled the Ibbotson girls in her novel *Deerbrook* (1839) on them. In 1823 the family travelled to the highlands of Scotland with a party of friends of the Revd W. J. Fox, and on 8 September Sarah easily broke the female record with her swift ascent of Ben Lomond. On their return they became friends with the young Robert Browning, the 'poet boy', as they called him; he discussed his religious doubts with Sarah, unsettling her beliefs, and supposedly modelled 'Pauline' on Eliza.

After their father's death in 1829, Sarah fell ill with what became tuberculosis. While recuperating on the Isle of Wight she composed her long poem *The Royal Progress* (published in 1845), on the last queen of the Isle, Isabella, who in 1293 had abdicated in favour of the English king Edward I. The sisters were left in the care of Fox, wellknown South Place Unitarian preacher and editor of the *Monthly Repository*, to which Sarah (as 'S. Y.') contributed essays, poems, and stories from 1834 to 1836. She met a fellow contributor, the widower William Bridges *Adams (1797–1872), engineer and inventor, at the house of her friend the feminist writer Harriet Taylor and they married

Sarah Flower Adams (1805–1848), after Margaret Gillies

on 24 September 1834. With his encouragement she pursued a career on the stage, which she believed to be a vocation of high moral power, and was initially successful (as Lady Macbeth at Richmond in 1837; then Portia and Lady Teazle), with praise by Macready leading to an engagement for the Bath Theatre, traditionally a springboard to London. But her health broke down again and she was forced to reorient her ambition towards literature, publishing her finest long poem, *Vivia perpetua: a Dramatic Poem in Five Acts*, in February 1841. In it the Christian martyr Vivia is put to death, refusing compromise, with her baby at her breast; issues of women's freedom from male control are canvassed throughout the poem:

> Never yet
> Found I true dignity in any one
> Who let the world's opinion cripple thought.

Sarah Flower Adams also contributed poetry reviews (including one of Elizabeth Barrett) to the *Westminster Review*. Described by Fox's daughter as 'tall and singularly beautiful' (Bridell-Fox, v), she described herself (in May 1837) as 'very thin, very deaf (making me very stupid), and five feet two and a-half' (ibid., x). Her deafness (as an adult) was inherited from her father. Her best-known hymn, 'Nearer, my God, to Thee', composed in 1840 and expressive of her struggle with religious doubt, was first published in 1841 with twelve more of her hymns in a collection edited by W. J. Fox. It was altered by later editors into more orthodox shape, and is reported to have been played by the band as the ocean liner *Titanic* went down in 1912 (Stephenson, 62). Sarah Flower Adams was a strong supporter of all human rights, especially those of women, but also those of the working classes. She wrote a number of political poems, some for the Anti-Corn Law League (excerpts were printed in Fox, vol. 4), and in 1845 a non-preachy verse catechism for factory schools, *The Flock at the Fountain*. She died, probably of cancer, at 1 Adam Street, Middlesex, on 14 August 1848, two years after her sister, and was buried with Eliza and her parents in the family plot at Harlow on 21 August, her own hymns sung at her funeral.   Virginia H. Blain

Sources H. W. Stephenson, *The author of 'Nearer, my God, to Thee'* (*Sarah Flower Adams*) (1922) · E. F. Bridell-Fox, preface, in S. F. Adams, *Vivia perpetua*, new edn (1893) · R. Garnett and E. Garnett, *The life of W. J. Fox, public teacher and social reformer, 1786–1864* (1910) [Actually begun by Fox's daughter, Mrs Bridell Fox, and completed by R. G.'s son Edward Garnett] · W. J. Fox, 'Miss Barrett and Mrs Adams', *Lectures addressed chiefly to the working classes*, 4 vols. (1845–9), vol. 4 · J. Julian, *Nearer, my God, to Thee: the original autograph MS together with biographical, historical, and critical notes* (1911) · M. D. Conway, *Centenary history of the South Place Society* (1894) · *Westminster Review*, 50 (1849), 540–42 · E. Taylor, *Memories of some contemporary poets: with selections from their writings* (1868)
Likenesses photograph touched with chalk (after drawing by M. Gillies), NPG [*see illus.*]

Adams, Stephen. *See* Maybrick, Michael (1841–1913).

Adams, Thomas (*b*. in or before **1566**, *d*. **1620**), printer, son of Thomas Adams, yeoman, of Neen Savage, Shropshire, was apprenticed to Oliver Wilkes, stationer, on 29 September 1582 for seven years, and turned over to George Bishop on 14 October 1583 for the same period. He was admitted a freeman of the Stationers' Company on 15 October 1590, and admitted to the livery on 1 July 1598. He appears to have commenced business by having the books and ballads printed by Robert Walley assigned to him on 12 October 1591. Thereafter, until 1614, he registered numerous books in all classes; some were issued jointly with John Oxenbridge and John Newbery. He also printed music books, among others pieces by John Dowland, the lutenist, and Thomas Ravenscroft.

On 14 March 1611 Adams purchased the rights of Bishop, his former master, including the remainders of sixty important works. He was elected under-warden of the Stationers' Company in 1610 and upper warden in 1614 and 1616. Adams died in London in 1620, some time between 2 March and 4 May, leaving to the Stationers' Company the sum of £100. He was survived by his wife, Elizabeth (*d*. 1638), who in 1625 sold his rights to their former apprentice Andrew Hebb.

H. R. Tedder, *rev.* Anita McConnell

Sources Arber, *Regs. Stationers*, vols. 3–4 · J. Ames, *Typographical antiquities, or, An historical account of the origin and progress of printing in Great Britain and Ireland*, ed. W. Herbert, 3 vols. (1785–90), vol. 2, p. 1305 · C. H. Timperley, *A dictionary of printers and printing* (1839), 467 · will, PRO, PROB 11/135, sig. 37 · W. W. Greg, ed., *A companion to Arber* (1967), 58 · Nichols, *Lit. anecdotes*, 3.593

Adams, Thomas (1583–1652), Church of England clergyman, matriculated from Trinity College, Cambridge, in the Lent term of 1598 and graduated BA in 1602 and proceeded MA in 1606 from Clare College; he was ordained deacon and priest in Lincoln diocese on 23 September 1604. He served as curate of Northill, Bedfordshire, from

1605 to 1611, when he was sacked by its new patron. However, his Northill parishioners signed a petition stating that Adams had 'behaved himselfe soberly in his conversation, painfully in his calling, lovingly amongst his neighbours, conformable to the orders of the Church, and in all respects befittingly to his vocation' (Maltby, 78), and this testimony may have aided his appointment in 1612 as vicar of Willington, Bedfordshire, by its patron, Thomas Egerton, Baron Ellesmere. Ellesmere advanced him on 21 December 1614 to the vicarage of Wingrave, Buckinghamshire, but by 1619 Adams was in London, where he remained for the rest of his life. The dean and chapter of St Paul's in 1619 collated him to two rectories, St Benet Paul's Wharf (on 15 June) and the small church of St Benet Sherehog (on 6 July). From 1618 to 1623 he also preached at St Gregory by Paul's. He served as chaplain to Henry Montagu, first earl of Manchester and chief justice of king's bench, and the dedicatees of his numerous published sermons included such influential men as Ellesmere, Montagu, Donne, and William Herbert, third earl of Pembroke. Pembroke and Manchester also received the dedication of Adams's *Works* (1629), and his extensive *Commentary* (1633) on the second epistle of Peter was dedicated to the eminent civil lawyer and judge Sir Henry Marten.

Adams 'was esteemed an Excellent Preacher' by his contemporaries (Walker, 2.164), and a modern assessment holds that he is 'one of the more considerable buried literary talents of the seventeenth century' (Chandos, 156). Sermon titles such as *Mystical Bedlam* (1615), *The White Devil* (1614), *The Devil's Banquet* (1614), and *The Gallant's Burden* (1612) exemplify his lively style. Although Adams was described by Robert Southey as 'the prose Shakespeare of puritan theologians … scarcely inferior to Fuller in wit or to Taylor in fancy' (*DNB*), he was a Calvinist episcopalian rather than a puritan. Like puritans he craved careful observation of the sabbath and was deeply hostile to Rome, the Jesuits, and the papacy, as well as to idleness, over-indulgence in worldly pleasures, and conspicuous consumption in all its forms. His sermons abound in statements that puritans would have admired. For example, at Paul's Cross in 1623 he thundered against London's:

> innumerable swarmes of … men and women, whose whole imployment is, to goe from their beds to the Tap-house, then to the Play-house, where they make a match for the Brothel-house, and from thence to bed againe … What an armie of these might bee mustred out of our Suburbs? (*The Barren Tree*, 1623, 48–9)

When James I sought a Spanish marriage for Prince Charles, Adams denounced 'the Romish Idols' and Solomon's disastrous love of 'idolatrous women'; he concluded that 'when Religion and Superstition meet in one bed, they commonly produce a mungrell generation' (*The Temple*, 1624, 34–5). Unlike puritans, however, he endorsed kneeling to receive communion and castigated the 'fond scrupulositie' of those who demanded such a rigid 'conformitie to the primitive times, as if the Spouse of Christ might not weare a lace or a border, for which she could not plead prescription'. For Adams the outcome of

the abolition of episcopacy that some puritans sought would have been a nightmarish 'Anabaptisticall ataxie or confusion' (*Works*, 931, 933).

From the 1610s through the mid-1620s Adams was highly visible in print, but for reasons which are unclear he spent the latter part of his career in obscurity, publishing nothing after 1633. Although two of Adams's powerful patrons, Pembroke and Ellesmere, were gone from the scene before 1630 Manchester remained a potent figure in the 1630s, but the connection yielded no obvious further advantage. Adams held the rectory of St Benet Paul's Wharf until sequestered during the civil wars, but thereafter continued to live in the rectory house. In a posthumously published work, *God's Anger and Man's Comfort* (1653), he referred to his 'neccessitous and decrepit old age'. In his will, dated 12 April 1651, he stated his desire to be buried in the churchyard with few friends attending and 'without any Funerall Service' (*Walker rev.*, 42). The small bequests to several grandchildren (the highest 10 shillings) are the only evidence that he had married; the fact that the grandchildren had two other surnames indicate that he had at least two daughters. He died in 1652, and was buried on 26 November.　　　　J. SEARS McGEE

Sources J. S. McGee, 'On misidentifying puritans: the case of Thomas Adams', *Albion*, 30 (1998), 402–18 · *Walker rev.* · J. Walker, *An attempt towards recovering an account of the numbers and sufferings of the clergy of the Church of England*, 2 pts in 1 (1714) · Venn, *Alum. Cant.* · J. Angus, 'Memoir of Adams', in *The works of Thomas Adams*, 3 (1862) · R. Newcourt, *Repertorium ecclesiasticum parochiale Londinense*, 1 (1708) · G. Hennessy, *Novum repertorium ecclesiasticum parochiale Londinense, or, London diocesan clergy succession from the earliest time to the year 1898* (1898) · J. Maltby, *Prayer book and people in Elizabethan and early Stuart England* (1998) · T. Cogswell, *The blessed revolution: English politics and the coming of war, 1621–1624* (1989) · J. Chandos, *In God's name* (1971) · L. Hedges, 'Thomas Adams and the ministry of moderation', PhD diss., U. Cal., Riverside, 1974 · G. Lipscomb, *The history and antiquities of the county of Buckingham*, 4 vols. (1831–47) · [Chestlin], *Persecutio undecima: the churches eleventh persecution* (1648) · C. W. Foster, ed., *The state of the church in the reigns of Elizabeth and James I*, Lincoln RS, 23 (1926) · *DNB*

Adams, Sir Thomas, first baronet (*bap.* 1586, *d.* 1668), local politician, was born at Wem, Shropshire, where he was baptized on 6 December 1586, the second son of Thomas Adams (*bap.* 1559, *d.* 1607) of Wem, yeoman, and his wife, Margaret, daughter of John Erpe of Shrewsbury. He married Ann (1592–1642), daughter of Humphrey Maptide (or Mapstead) of Trenton, Essex; they had three sons, among them the poet Richard *Adams (*bap.* 1620, *d.* 1661), and three daughters, and three other children who died in infancy.

Possibly with a view to becoming a clergyman, Adams was admitted into Sidney Sussex College, Cambridge, in 1600 and graduated BA in 1606. However, most unusually, he had also been bound apprentice to the Drapers' Company in 1604; he gained his freedom in 1612, entered the livery in 1624, joined its governing body in 1639, and served as master in 1640–41. From relatively modest origins, he had risen by 1640 to become a wealthy London woollen draper with substantial premises on Gracechurch Street. He had also become an assistant of the Massachusetts Bay Company in 1629 and was made free of the East India Company in 1641. There was a parallel rise up the civic hierarchy: a common councillor for Bridge Within in 1639, sheriff in 1639–40, alderman in 1639–49, and lord mayor in 1645–6. Civic pre-eminence was confirmed by his appointment as colonel of the Blue regiment of the City's militia in 1642–5 and as president of St Thomas's Hospital in 1643–50.

Adams's political and religious instincts and convictions were a blend of pragmatic conservatism and solid principle. Previously in trouble for opposing the collection of ship money in London, he was prepared by 1640 to join the majority of aldermen in making returns of inhabitants in their respective wards who would be able to contribute to a royal loan. He also served on the committee for a City banquet to celebrate the king's return from Scotland in November 1641. January 1642 brought personal tragedy with the sudden death of his wife, allegedly from fright at the rumour of an attack on the City by royalist ultras. Shortly afterwards he joined fellow aldermen in protesting to the Lords against the proposed radical change in control over the London militia. In July Adams visited the pro-royalist Mayor Gurney in the Tower during his trial, and he was one of the aldermen who refused to obey parliament's order to appoint a deputy mayor.

After the outbreak of civil war Adams did not accompany his militia company onto the battlefield. However, he did play an active role in schemes to raise money for parliament's war effort and was one of the moderates on the aldermanic bench. In 1643 he played a prominent part in bringing the radical militia subcommittee at Salters' Hall under the control of the more moderate London militia committee. In the following year he gave evidence against Archbishop Laud at his trial. By the time of his election in 1645 as lord mayor Adams had emerged as a leading political presbyterian, and one of his earliest actions was to cancel, ostensibly on grounds of public order, a public discussion between Baptists and presbyterians. His own religious convictions were described in his funeral sermon as emphatically Anglican; a regular communicant at the pro-royalist St Dionis Backchurch, he befriended its minister, Dr Nathaniel Hardy. Yet he was also prepared to serve as a trustee for the sale of bishops' lands in 1646–7. During his mayoralty Adams was rightly suspected of pro-royalist leanings and in April 1646 he was aroused from his bed at midnight for questioning about a report (false as it happened) that he was hiding the recently escaped king in London.

Adams was a leading figure in London's attempted counter-revolution in the summer of 1647. He was appointed to the presbyterian-dominated London militia committee in May, after it had been purged of leading Independents, and was implicated in the force on both houses of 26 July, when a presbyterian crowd invaded parliament. After the army's consequent march on London, his impeachment was ordered by the Commons and he was imprisoned in the Tower. When finally summoned before the Lords in April 1648, he adopted a defiant stance and earned a £500 fine and recommittal to the Tower. Yet in the changed political climate of the summer of 1648 the impeachment charges against him were dropped.

The political revolution of 1648–9 saw Adams purged from the aldermanic bench and during the 1650s he was suspected of providing large sums of money for royalist plots and the exiled Charles II. Elected an MP for London in 1654 and again in 1656, his reputation earned him the distinction of being the only member to be excluded from both protectorate parliaments. At the Restoration he was one of the City's commissioners sent to Charles II at The Hague, where he was knighted in May; the next month he became a baronet. He was soon restored to his aldermanry and the presidency of St Thomas's Hospital, and in 1662 was appointed governor of the Irish Society.

Adams died in London at his house in Ironmonger Lane on 24 February 1668, following a fall from his coach. After his death a giant kidney stone was removed from his body and exhibited at the Royal Society: 'bigger I think then my fist, and weighs above 25 ounces,' Samuel Pepys observed when he was shown it, 'and which is very miraculous, never in all his life had any fit of it, but lived to a great age without pain' (Pepys, 9.136). A congregation of over a thousand civic dignatories attended Adams's funeral sermon at St Katharine Cree, London, on 10 March, after which he was buried at Sprowston in Norfolk, whose manor he had purchased in 1661. His will, made two and a half weeks before his death, included several charitable bequests including the endowment of an Arabic lectureship at Cambridge and a school at Wem. Sir William Adams (1634–1687), his only surviving son, succeeded to his substantial properties and estates in London, Shropshire, Essex, and Norfolk.   KEITH LINDLEY

Sources will, PRO, PROB 11/326, sig. 39 · A. B. Beaven, ed., *The aldermen of the City of London, temp. Henry III–[1912]*, 2 (1913), 64, 181 · HoP, *Commons, 1640–60* [draft] · J. R. Woodhead, *The rulers of London, 1660–1689* (1965), 15 · GEC, *Baronetage*, 3.37–8 · *The journal of Thomas Juxon*, ed. K. Lindley and D. Scott, CS, 5th ser., 13 (1999), 113–14, 123, 151, 164 · J. Wilford, *Memorials and characters, together with lives, of divers eminent and worthy persons* (1741), 86–90; appx, 27–8 · V. Pearl, *London and the outbreak of the puritan revolution* (1964), 292–3 · IGI · 'Boyd's Inhabitants of London', Society of Genealogists, London, 9006 · Pepys, *Diary*, 9.136 · BL, Lansdowne MS 255, fol. 358 · Venn, *Alum. Cant.*, 1/1.6 · A. W. Hughes Clarke and A. Campling, eds., *The visitation of Norfolk … 1664, made by Sir Edward Bysshe*, 1, Harleian Society, 85 (1933) · parish register, All Hallows Staining, 1668, GL, MS 17824 [burial]
Archives CUL, letters to Abraham Wheelock
Wealth at death £30 in annuities; £5170 in bequests; lands in Essex, Norfolk, Shropshire; properties in London: will, PRO, PROB 11/326, sig. 39 · endowed Arabic lectureship at Cambridge; founded a school at Wem, Shropshire

Adams, Thomas (1631/2–1670), ejected minister and writer on Christian doctrine, was born at Woodchurch parsonage, Cheshire, one of at least three sons of Charles Adams and his wife, Isabel Bennet 'the daughter of a worthy gentleman'—Thomas Bennet, from the same parish (Adams, 1). His father and grandfather were successively both owners of the advowson and incumbent of the parish. Adams was admitted to Brasenose College, Oxford, at the age of seventeen on 14 July 1649, having matriculated in April of that year. He was made a fellow on 2 June

1652 and graduated BA on 8 February 1653, proceeding MA on 28 June 1655. During 1658–9 he was a junior bursar. Edmund Calamy wrote that 'he performed all his exercises with applause' and was 'generally beloved for his learning, piety, good humour, and diligence' (Calamy, *Abridgement*, 2.66).

After a distinguished career at college Adams was ejected from his fellowship for nonconformity in 1662. He spent the remainder of his life as a chaplain in private families, first with that of Sir Samuel Jones of Shropshire, and later Northamptonshire and Oxfordshire. Following that he was chaplain to Elizabeth Vere, the dowager duchess of Clare so that he might join his brothers John and Richard *Adams (1626/7–1698) in London. Calamy recorded that his services to the family, 'by his catechising and weekly preaching were very acceptable' (Calamy, *Abridgement*, 2.67). Adams wrote *The Main Principles of Christian Religion* (1675), an explanation of Christian doctrine which examined the creed, the ten commandments, the sacraments, and the Lord's prayer. It was prefaced by his younger brother, Richard, the ejected minister of St Mildred, Bread Street, who described his elder sibling as being of 'so sweet and peaceful temper that his moderation was known unto all' (Adams). Adams died on 11 December 1670.

CAROLINE L. LEACHMAN

Sources R. Adams, foreword, in T. Adams, *The main principles of Christian religion* (1675) · E. Calamy, ed., *An abridgement of Mr. Baxter's history of his life and times, with an account of the ministers, &c., who were ejected after the Restauration of King Charles II*, 2nd edn, 2 vols. (1713), vol. 2, pp. 66–7 · *Calamy rev.* · Wood, *Ath. Oxon.*, new edn, 4.604 · Wood, *Ath. Oxon.: Fasti* (1820), 170, 187 · G. Ormerod, *The history of the county palatine and city of Chester*, 2nd edn, ed. T. Helsby, 2 (1882), 524 · [C. B. Heberden], ed., *Brasenose College register, 1509–1909*, 2 vols., OHS, 55 (1909)

Archives BL, Harley MSS 2153, 2140, 2178

Adams, Thomas (1730?–1764), army officer, remains of unknown birth and parentage. He commenced his military service in 1747 as a volunteer with the army under the command of the duke of Cumberland in the Netherlands. On 25 June of the same year he obtained a commission as ensign in the 37th foot, in which regiment he rose to the rank of captain nine years later. He was subsequently transferred to the 84th foot, and was serving as a major in that regiment in India, when, in 1762, five years after the battle of Plassey, he was appointed to the command of the united forces of the crown and of the East India Company in Bengal.

It was a very critical period in British Indian history. Since 1749 the company had been fighting a prolonged war with the French for control of the Carnatic in southern India, ending with Eyre Coote's capture of Pondicherry, in January 1761. In Bengal, Clive's victory at Plassey (1757) against the local Mughal nawab Siraj ud-Daula, had allowed the company to become the preponderant influence in that province through the new nawab they installed, Mir Jafar. However, Mir Jafar, perhaps because of his close association with the company, was unable to establish his authority or an effective administration. So

Clive's successors at Calcutta organized a palace coup at Murshidabad, the nawab's capital, in October 1761, replacing him with his more able and energetic son-in-law, Mir Kasim. Alarmingly for the British, Mir Kasim proved to be too independent, reforming the armed forces he inherited along European lines and putting the artillery and some of the infantry under mercenary European officers. An inevitable tension born of jealousy and suspicion grew between Mir Kasim and Calcutta, making what was unofficially called a dual government impossible to sustain. The situation was exacerbated by some unscrupulous councillors who, for their own private commercial advantage, flagrantly abused the favourable terms under which the company traded, to the detriment of the Mughal treasury.

War eventually broke out between the company and Mir Kasim in 1763 when William Ellis, in control of the company's business at Patna in Bihar, perceiving the nawab's warlike preparations, took it upon himself on 25 June to seize the city by surprise, but could not hold on to it against Mir Kasim's troops. The British garrison was captured and a sizeable proportion (300 Europeans and 2500 sepoys, one-quarter of the forces available in Bengal) was lost to the company as casualties or prisoners of war. The European elements among the latter were subsequently murdered by Mir Kasim. War was declared by Calcutta on 7 July and Major Adams was ordered by the council to take the field with what remained of the company's army to reinstate Mir Jafar at Murshidabad and to attack Mir Kasim wherever he should be in the province. The campaign, conducted at first during the monsoon, was the hardest in combat terms that the British experienced in the early years of the raj. Adams had about 5000 Indian and European troops, largely infantry with artillery support; Mir Kasim faced him with up to 40,000, over half of whom were trained in modern European methods but also including a large force of irregular cavalry. Adams's logistical problems were considerably eased by his access to the Ganges River system, which enabled him to bring his supplies and artillery up in boats behind his marching troops.

The campaign opened on 17 July, when a British convoy of supplies and treasure for the army, guarded by a battalion of Sepoys (600 men) and six guns, was attacked by one of Mir Kasim's generals with a large force of cavalry (reckoned by contemporaries to number 17,000), but without supporting infantry or artillery. A fierce fight ensued, with the company's force losing its guns and treasure no fewer than three times before Mir Kasim's troops finally withdrew, baffled. The losses on both sides were severe; but the British commander, Lieutenant Glenn, with his attenuated detachment, was able to join Adams the next day at Katwa (100 miles north of Calcutta) not far from Plassey. Adams's further progress towards Murshidabad was now barred by another numerically superior enemy force, under one of Mir Kasim's best generals, Muhammad Taki Khan. On 19 July, Adams's advance guard was thrown back by enemy rocket men and effective musket fire which emboldened Muhammad Taki Khan to attack the main force with his élite cavalry corps of Afghans, Persians, and Rohillas. The battle swayed back and forth, finally favouring Adams when a cavalry charge, at his right flank led by Muhammad Taki Khan himself, was ambushed by a hidden force of Sepoys perspicaciously placed there by Adams. Muhammad Ali Khan was killed at the head of his troops, who, disheartened, retreated precipitating a general enemy withdrawal. Both sides had again lost heavily, but resistance to Adams's further advance after three days' rest was brushed aside, and Murshidabad was entered on the 25 July, where Mir Jafar was reinstalled as nawab.

With the first part of his mission accomplished, on 27 July Adams, with an enhanced but still relatively small army, set out to hunt down the remainder of Mir Kasim's still formidable forces, including as they did his European-trained and led infantry corps. He came upon them on the plains of Gheria 37 miles from Murshidabad. Mir Kasim himself was still not, nor would he ever be, personally in the field; undoubtedly, this was a grave error because his ultimate defeat was due partly to disunion among his military leaders. On 2 August Adams, though facing odds of six to one, boldly placed himself (as Clive had done at Plassey and the future duke of Wellington was to do at Assaye) in a perilous strategic position between the converging courses of two rivers, thus giving him physical cover on his flanks but facing chaotic compression should he be forced to retreat. The enemy occupied an entrenched line from which it would have been difficult to dislodge them. However, perhaps emboldened by their greater numbers, their well-drilled élite infantry, the need to find a role for their 10,000 cavalry, and the opportunity to destroy totally the company's field army, they accepted Adams's challenge for a battle in the open field. After an opening exchange of artillery fire, a spirited Mughal cavalry charge broke through Adams's left wing and attacked the rear of his main body, already holding off a strong attack from Mir Kasim's European-trained infantry and rocket men in front. Adams shored up his battered left with his reserve, but had the enemy attacked his right with the same vigour as their other troops had, Adams's little army could well have been enveloped. But the attack from that direction was feeble, so Adams left a small masking force to face it and threw more men into the centre and with its momentum threw back the enemy. Undoubtedly Mir Kasim's forces had suffered from a disunited command and the decision of the European mercenary officers at this point to withdraw their crucial units when they believed the battle was lost. Adams's coolness and adroit timing, and the superior discipline of his Indian and European troops under extreme stress and danger, also help to account for his victory, though again it was bought dearly with many lives.

Adams followed the retreating enemy forces until, after a week, on 11 August, he came up against their last and very formidable line of field defences at the foot of the Oondwa Nullah Pass through the Rajmahal Mountains leading towards Mir Kasim's capital at Monghyr. The enemy occupied ground nearly a mile wide between the Ganges and some country slashed by ravines and anchored on a solitary hill topped by a fortification. In front of them was a rampart 60 feet thick and 10 feet high mounted with artillery, fronted by a ditch 60 feet wide and 12 feet deep. In front of this lay a deep natural morass broken only by one stretch of dry land, 200 yards long, along which a road ran up to a gate in the rampart. This time, the enemy did not come out of its defences and Adams was forced to try to batter a breach through the wall close to the gate. This took a month and the breach proved to be very narrow (one man's width). Then, a stroke of luck (a European deserter from Mir Kasim's forces formerly in the company's army) gave Adams knowledge of a treacherous ford through the morass to the fortified hill on his left. This enabled him to devise a more sophisticated plan of attack than the predictable one of a single assault on the breach. Three hours before dawn on 4 September a 1000-man column was sent through the swamp to attack the hill while the main body of the army advanced towards the breach. The garrison on the hill, thinking themselves impregnable, were taken by surprise and by bayonet. A signal flare announcing this success launched the main attack which succeeded, owing to the distraction to the west where the diversionary column was advancing within the ramparts and soon joined the main force pouring through the now opened main gate. Panic set in among the defenders, who were slaughtered not only by the advancing company forces but also by their own rear guard under orders to prevent a flight; others perished by falling down the precipitous banks of the river in flood to the rear. This time the defeat was virtually decisive; thousands of Mir Kassim's troops had died, the demoralized remainder had fled in chaos. The cost to the company's army was just over 500 killed and wounded.

Adams relentlessly pursued the survivors of the defeated army. He bought his way into Monghyr a 100 miles further on after breaching the wall. Mir Kasim had fled. The only citadel now left to him, a formidable one, was Patna, the chief city of Bihar. Patna was invested late in October. This time an assault had to be made, during the night of 6 November, on two breaches which had been made by Adams's siege guns. The fighting was severe, with many casualties on both sides, but Patna eventually fell to the company. Mir Kasim still had 30,000 troops left but neither he nor they had the will to face Adams again. The displaced nawab finally fled into Oudh where Adams could not follow, to be defeated with the nawab wazir Shuja ud-Daula and the heir apparent to the Mughal throne the following year at the famous battle of Buxar by Colonel Hector Munro, Adams's eventual successor.

Adams, meanwhile, had returned to Calcutta, his health broken. He died, on the eve of leaving for Britain, on 16 January 1764, without learning that he had been made up to brigadier-general in London in recognition of his exploits. His achievement had indeed been remarkable.

He had driven a relentless and continually victorious campaign at the wrong time of the year, against superior numbers. The fortitude of his Indian and European troops was a credit to his leadership and the superior discipline the British had instilled into their Bengal army. He was a man of great resource and coolness who prevailed in two desperate battles, conceived and executed a daring night attack on an apparently impregnable fortification, and conducted a successful formal siege against a strong and resolutely defended fortified city. His expenditure of his last drop of energy in fulfilling his duty was exemplary, yet compared with the better known military exploits of Clive, Coote, and Munro, his achievement has gone largely unrecognized—a curiosity difficult to explain.

G. J. BRYANT

Sources G. B. Malleson, *The decisive battles of India: from 1746 to 1849 inclusive* (1885) · Fortescue, *Brit. army*, vol. 3
Archives BL, order book, Add. MS 6049

Adams, Thomas (1807–1873), lace merchant and manufacturer, was born on 5 February 1807 at Worksop, Nottinghamshire, the son of Thomas Adams, a maltster, and his second wife, Catharine, *née* Smith, of Sutton-cum-Lound, Nottinghamshire. The elder Adams moved his family to Ware, Hertfordshire, but died while Thomas was still a child. His widow took her children to Sheffield, where Thomas received a modest education before being apprenticed at the age of fourteen to a draper at Newark, Nottinghamshire. Afterwards he worked for a short time in the London warehouse of Bodens, the Derby-based lace manufacturers. He was also in France for a time. In 1830 he returned to Nottingham, where he established his own business, buying plain and decorated nets from some of the 1200 or so artisans active in the district, which he then finished and sold on to wholesalers and retailers. In 1832 he began a long partnership with James Page and other small manufacturers, trading as Adams, Page & Co. at St Mary's Gate. Adams and Page discarded the lesser capitalists in 1856 but incorporated in 1862, the foundation capital being £112,000.

On 2 September 1830 Adams married Lucy Cullen, the daughter of a Nottingham draper; they had ten children over the next twenty years. The completion of a railway line between London and Nottingham brought increased trade and prosperity for Adams. Wholesalers and exporters now travelled directly to Nottingham to buy their nets and laces, the quality and design of which had improved steadily over the previous thirty years. A few other manufacturers opened their own warehouses, but, unlike Adams, such men lacked the necessary commercial experience and capital. The *Nottingham Daily Guardian* (19 May 1873) reported: 'We have heard it stated that he was a hard and sharp man of business, not exactly that he would do anything dishonest—that we do not believe—but one who would make a good bargain.' Adams seems to have concentrated on the home market but may also have been selling to Mediterranean countries.

In the years following the Nottingham Enclosure Act of 1845 the old commercial heart of the town was rebuilt as the Lace Market, and in 1855 Adams proudly opened his new palatial warehouse at its centre in Stoney Street, though it was criticized by some as too grand for commercial purposes. Before long it employed 600 people, 500 of them women, who enjoyed the amenities of a library, a schoolroom, rest rooms, a canteen, and, probably the most important to Adams, a chapel where the employees could begin their working hours by attending a daily service at his expense. During these years Adams emerged as the leading evangelical layman in Nottingham. He gave generously towards the cost of building new churches in the growing city and he promoted missionary societies and Sunday schools. He sat as a JP on both town and county benches, was elected to Nottingham corporation in 1836, and was a member of the Poor Law Board for many years, but he seldom attended these last two bodies, admitting that he found it easier to make money than to make speeches. The whig majority on the corporation denied him the opportunity of becoming alderman or mayor.

Adams's health began to fail about 1870, and he died at his home, Lenton Firs, Lenton, Nottingham, on 16 May 1873. He was buried on 19 May in the Church cemetery at Forest Road, memorials being placed to him in Lenton parish church and St Mary's, Nottingham. His wife survived him, but his sons Samuel and John, whom he hoped would succeed him in business, both died young. The firm continued for another two generations, largely because of Adams's policy of promoting senior clerks to the board.

GEOFFREY OLDFIELD

Sources W. Milton, *Religion and business: memorials of Thomas Adams J.P. of Nottingham* (1874) · *Nottingham Daily Guardian* (19 May 1873) · R. Mellors, *Men of Nottingham and Nottinghamshire* (1924), 216 · *Nottingham Review* (12 July 1855) · F. A. Barnes, *Priory demesne to university campus* (1993), 256–60 · *Nottingham Journal* (13 July 1855) · parish register, Worksop, priory church, 1807 [baptism] · parish register, Nottingham, St Mary's, 2 Sept 1830 [marriage] · d. cert.
Archives Bank of England, London, Samuel Dobree's diary [21 Aug 1857] · Notts. Arch., deposits relating to Thomas Adams & Co. Ltd, M10689–10751, M19675–19745
Likenesses photograph, repro. in Barnes, *Priory demesne to university campus*, 253 · portrait, Cooper and Keywood Ltd, 11 St Mary's Gate, Nottingham
Wealth at death under £90,000: probate, 12 July 1873, CGPLA Eng. & Wales

Adams, Thomas (1871–1940), town and country planner, was born on 10 September 1871 at Meadow House Farm, Corstorphine, Edinburgh, the eldest of the four children of James Adams (1841/2–1888), dairyman, and his wife, Margaret, *née* Johnstone (1847/8–1899), housekeeper. Educated at Daniel Stewart's College in Edinburgh (1884–c.1887), he ran the farm after his father's death and from 1893 farmed in the Pentland hills. Adams was a tall, lithe, attractive man with a ruddy complexion. He married Caroline Bertha Weierter (1875–1965) on 22 December 1897; of their five children, the eldest two (James and Frederick) became leading planners in, respectively, Britain and America. A utilitarian, Adams became a Liberal election agent and a journalist but in 1900 moved to London to pursue a literary career. His interest in 'the land question' led to his appointment as the first paid secretary of Ebenezer Howard's Garden City Association in 1901. In 1904 he became the first manager of Letchworth Garden City, energetically promoting the co-operative commonwealth, which, he argued, combined the advantages of town and country while having none of their disadvantages. Adams's flair for administration and public relations gave Letchworth a sound start. His devotion to a rural renaissance led to his first book, *The Garden City and Agriculture* (1905). From October 1906 he became the first planning consultant in Britain, designing several garden suburbs; while lacking the inventiveness of those planned by Parker and Unwin, these demonstrated Adams's fine eye for landscape. His abilities and experience led to his appointment in 1910 as town planning assistant to the Local Government Board (in effect, the first planning inspector), with responsibility for implementing the 1909 planning legislation. Adams investigated over a hundred proposals and argued for regional planning in London and elsewhere. He also qualified as a surveyor. Recognizing the need for professional education and status, he was chiefly responsible for the foundation of the Town Planning Institute in 1913–14; 'It was a foregone conclusion' that he should be the inaugural president, wrote Patrick Abercrombie, as he was 'justly looked up to as the head of the profession in this country' (*Town Planning Review*, October 1914, 243–4, 248–9).

In October 1914 Adams became town planning adviser to the Canadian commission of conservation. In Canada, a *laissez-faire* society, he promoted planning through education, lobbying, propaganda, legislation, garden suburbs, advice, research, and professionalism. By 1919 he had inspired a civic improvement league, university courses, model communities, post-war reconstruction, provincial planning acts, the Town Planning Institute of Canada (of which he was the first president), and the journal *Town Planning and the Conservation of Life*. His most notable achievements were the replanning of Halifax, Nova Scotia, after an explosion, and the comprehensive monograph *Rural Planning and Development* (1917). However, Canada returned to *laissez-faire* ways and Adams's system collapsed; he left in 1923, though later he made plans for several towns.

Adams formed a partnership in 1922 with Francis Longstreth Thompson, an engineer, joined later by the architect Maxwell Fry. They undertook a score of regional, industrial village and town plans in Britain but Adams was preoccupied with the regional plan of New York, where he was general director of plans and surveys from 1923 to 1929. A respected and regular visitor to the USA since 1911, Adams's planning philosophy, meliorist rather than radical, voluntarist rather than collectivist, suited the American milieu. The regional plan (5000 square miles), encompassing eight *Regional Survey* volumes (1927–31) and two volumes of the *Regional Plan* (1929–31), recommended decentralization of population and industry, satellite towns, orbital highways, parkways connecting country

parks, and zoning. It eschewed public housing and coercive measures and favoured privatism and the motorized middle class. While the plan earned the approbation of the establishment, the radical Lewis Mumford, spokesman for the collectivist Regional Planning Association of America, attacked its timidity, superficiality, and capitalist ethos in his articles on 'The plan of New York' in the *New Republic* of 15 and 22 June 1932. Adams's reply of 6 July stressed its practicality; most of its major recommendations were carried out by 1940.

In 1930 Harvard appointed Adams part-time director of research in planning; he had been a visiting professor at the Massachusetts Institute of Technology since 1921. He produced *The Neighborhoods of Small Homes* (1931, with Robert Whitten), *Recent Advances in Town Planning* (1932), *The Design of Residential Areas* (1934), and *The Outline of Town and City Planning* (1935), all lucid, broadly historical, well-researched works, distilling his experience and demonstrating his capacity for harmonizing elements of the environmental professions. He was made an honorary DEng by New York University (1932) and a fellow of the Royal Institute of British Architects (1934). After a heart attack in 1934, Adams did little planning but was an influential elder statesman, sponsoring the town and country planning summer schools (1933), stimulating the National Housing and Town Planning Council, and transforming the fledgeling Institute of Landscape Architects, of which he was president from 1937 to 1939, broadcasting, and adding to his hundreds of articles. In 1930 he settled at Yew Tree Cottage, Henlys Down, Battle, Sussex, where he died, aged sixty-eight, on 24 March 1940. Adams was a great planning pioneer, with a string of 'firsts'. He bestrode the British, Canadian, and American planning scenes between 1910 and 1940; none matched his tireless and skilful advocacy of planning, his organizing ability, his shrewd and practical professionalism, and his grasp of regional planning. He was a man of integrity, unfailing good humour, sense of fun, and conciliatory nature. While his faith in 'associated individualism' limited the scope and effectiveness of his planning, he left numerous monuments to his ability to integrate town and country, ascribable to his perceptive distillation of his formative years in and around Auld Reekie.   MICHAEL SIMPSON

Sources U. Lpool L., special collections and archives, Adams family MSS • b. cert. • m. cert. • d. cert. • *Town Planning Review* (1910–40) • *The Garden City* [and successor journals] (1904–40) • Royal Town Planning Institute, London • Town and Country Planning Association, London, archives of Garden City Association • Letchworth Museum, archives of First Garden City Ltd • Harvard U., School of Design MSS • Massachusetts Institute of Technology, USA, Department of City Planning MSS • Cornell University, USA, Regional Plan of New York archive • NA Canada, Commission of Conservation MSS • papers, Canadian Institute of Planners, Ottawa • London, Landscape Institute MSS • London, National Housing and Town Planning Council MSS

Archives Landscape Institute, London • National Housing and Town Planning Council, London • Royal Town Planning Institute, London • Town and Country Planning Association, London • U. Lpool L., papers of and about him, collected by his biographer | Welwyn Garden City Central Library, corresp. with Frederic Osborn

Wealth at death £5621 17s. 0d.: probate, 25 March 1940, *CGPLA Eng. & Wales*

Adams, Sir Walter (1906–1975), university administrator, was born on 16 December 1906 at Brighton, the son of Walter Adams, a builder's clerk, and his wife, Margaret Evans. He was educated at Brighton, Hove, and Sussex grammar school and at University College, London, where he read history, being awarded the BA degree with first-class honours in 1928, and where he was subsequently appointed to a lectureship in history. He married in 1933 Tatiana (*d.* October 1975), daughter of Alexander Makaroff, lawyer; they had three sons and one daughter.

In 1933 Adams resigned his lectureship in order to become general secretary of the Academic Assistance Council (later the Society for the Protection of Science and Learning), a body formed under the presidency of Lord Rutherford of Nelson to assist university teachers displaced on account of race, religion, or political opinion. The work gave Adams wide administrative experience as it involved the raising and administration of a fund of approximately £70,000, the establishment of local committees in nearly all British universities, and the making of contracts with government departments, national and international educational organizations, and universities all over the world, in order to help academic refugees to find posts. In this he was notably successful, and many refugee scholars later expressed their personal gratitude to him for his sympathy and practical help. In 1937–8 he served as secretary to a survey of the refugee question undertaken under the auspices of the Royal Institute of International Affairs and the Rockefeller Foundation.

In 1938 Adams was appointed secretary of the London School of Economics (LSE) and after the outbreak of war had to cope with the problems of evacuating the school to Cambridge. In 1941 he was granted leave of absence to take up an appointment with the political intelligence department of the Foreign Office. From 1942 to 1944 he was in America as deputy head of the British Political Warfare Mission to the United States. In 1945 he returned to London as assistant deputy director-general of the political intelligence department, a post which he gave up the following year; he devoted the rest of his career to university administration.

In 1946 Adams became the secretary of the newly formed Inter-University Council for Higher Education Overseas, and he was involved in the foundation of universities and university colleges throughout the British Commonwealth. This experience led naturally to his appointment in 1955 as principal of the newly established University College of Rhodesia and Nyasaland. This was to prove the most taxing assignment of his career, as the running of a multiracial university in Rhodesia in the 1960s became increasingly difficult, especially after the unilateral declaration of Rhodesian independence in 1965. Adams was caught between the desire to maintain the college as a multiracial institution and his belief that it was essential to maintain academic standards, even if this meant fewer black students. At the same time, he believed

Sir Walter Adams (1906–1975), by Godfrey Argent, 1970

that the future of the college depended on remaining on good terms with the Rhodesian government. As a result he was criticized both by those who accused him of discriminating against black students and compromising with the government and by those who were against any kind of multiracial education at all.

Adams was always a man who preferred compromise to confrontation and it was unfortunate for him that, when he left Rhodesia on appointment as director of the LSE in 1967, he was faced with some hostility among a section of the LSE students on account of his position in Rhodesia. This added to the student unrest characteristic of universities all over the world in 1967–9. Adams showed considerable dignity in the face of personal attacks and uninformed criticism and was also supported by the sympathy of several of the refugee scholars whom he had helped thirty years earlier and who were outraged at the suggestion that he was in any sense a racist. These disturbances, which were on a very small scale compared with those in many universities in Europe and the USA, soon died down, and Adams was able to resume the task for which he was most suited, of being an efficient and humane administrator, dedicated to scholarly values and academic independence.

Adams published in collaboration with H. W. Robinson a scholarly edition of *The Diary of Robert Hooke, 1672–80* (1935). He was appointed OBE in 1945 and CMG in 1952, and was knighted in 1970. He retired in 1974 and died suddenly on 21 May 1975 while on a visit to Salisbury,

Rhodesia, where he had gone to receive an honorary doctorate from the university of which he had once been head. He also had honorary degrees from Malta and Melbourne.   JAMES JOLL, rev.

Sources *The Times* (22 May 1975) · private information (1986) · personal knowledge (1986) · *CGPLA Eng. & Wales* (1975)
Archives BLPES, papers · U. Leeds, Brotherton L., letters to Esther Simpson | Bodl. Oxf., corresp. relating to Society for the Protection of Science and Learning · Bodl. RH, corresp. with Margery Perham
Likenesses G. Argent, photograph, 1970, NPG [*see illus.*] · R. Buhler, oils, 1974, London School of Economics
Wealth at death £21,070: probate, 4 Nov 1975, *CGPLA Eng. & Wales*

Adams, William (1564–1620), navigator, was born in Gillingham, Kent, the son of John Adams. His mother and the precise date of his birth are unknown, but he was baptized on 24 September 1564 at St Mary Magdalen, Gillingham. He had at least one brother, Thomas.

Early life Details of his early life are sketchy and are derived largely from his own letters written in Japan. From the age of twelve until he turned twenty-four he was an apprentice in Limehouse to Nicholas Diggens, a well-established shipbuilder who later contracted with the East India Company to repair its ships. The end of his apprenticeship coincided with the coming of the Spanish Armada, and Adams served in the conflict as master of the *Richard Dyffylde*, a supply ship of 120 tons. Soon thereafter he joined the Barbary Company (established in 1585), which traded with Morocco, serving as pilot and master. This he did for ten years. According to Jesuit sources written after his arrival in Japan, he served on various Dutch voyages in quest of a north-west passage, but he himself makes no mention of such activity and it is highly unlikely that he did so.

Voyage to Japan In 1598 Adams joined one of the Dutch East India voyages which preceded the establishment of the Dutch East India Company (VOC), the so-called *voorcompagnie* voyages. He was one of a number of experienced English seafarers recruited by the Dutch; another was John Davis. He joined a fleet of five ships financed by a Rotterdam partnership headed by Pieter van der Haegen and Johan van der Veken and was appointed pilot of the admiral's ship the *Hoop* (250 tons, 130 men), commanded by Jacques Mahu. Other Britons employed on the voyage included Adams's brother Thomas. The goal of the voyage was to sail to the East Indies by way of the Strait of Magellan to procure spices and other Asian goods and, following Drake's example, to assault Spanish settlements in South America.

The ships left Rotterdam on 27 June 1598, sailed down the west African coast, where the Portuguese settlement on Annobón was attacked, moved out across the Atlantic, touched the coast of Brazil on 2 January 1599, and reached the strait on 6 April. The onset of winter made passage impossible. Finally, on 3 September, their crews depleted, the ships cleared the strait, intending to rendezvous off the Chilean coast. Inevitably in these treacherous waters the ships became separated and only two ships—the *Hoop*

and the *Liefde*, to which Adams had transferred—met on 9 November, off the island of St Mary. (Of the other ships, one made it across the Pacific to the spice islands, one returned home, and the other was captured by the Spanish.) The crews of both ships had been further reduced by Indian attacks when they had attempted to land on the mainland to secure provisions. In one such skirmish Adams's brother perished. Wisely, plans to attack the Spanish in Peru were dropped, and a decision was taken to sail for Japan, where, according to information provided by one of the original members of the voyage, Dirck Gerritsz, a veteran of Portuguese voyages thither, who was on the ship which returned to Rotterdam, they would find a market for their cloth. The voyage across the Pacific proved no less perilous than the hardships that had gone before. More men were lost in an engagement with native people in the Hawaiian Islands, and during a terrific storm in late February 1600 the ships became separated. The *Hoop* perished. Only the *Liefde* made it to Japan, arriving about 19 April off the coast of Bungo, in present-day Oita prefecture, with about two dozen survivors, all sick or exhausted. It was the first non-Iberian European vessel to reach Japan, and Adams was the first recorded Englishman to arrive there.

Adams in Japan Adams had arrived at a major historical turning point in Japanese history. The civil wars which had ravaged the country since the late fifteenth century were in abeyance. Peace had been achieved with ruthless efficiency thanks to the military campaigns of Oda Nobunaga and Toyotomi Hideyoshi, and the latter had successfully devised and imposed policies which laid the foundations for lasting political stability. Hideyoshi intended that his young son Hideyori should succeed him, and created a council of regents to guarantee the succession. One of the regents, however, Tokugawa Ieyasu, made a bid for power and defeated his opponents at the battle of Sekigahara on 21 October 1600. It was Ieyasu whom Adams, the fittest among the *Liefde*'s surviving crew, was brought before in Osaka in May 1600 to answer questions about the provenance of the recently arrived ship, and it was his good fortune that he got on well with the man who would soon become overlord, then shogun, of Japan, founder of the Tokugawa dynasty, which ruled Japan until 1867.

Ieyasu and his entourage quizzed Adams thoroughly, and the Englishman provided the Japanese with information about a Europe divided along political and confessional lines, thus breaking the monopoly of information about Europe held by the Catholic missionaries, notably the Jesuits, who had first reached Japan in 1549, and the more recently arrived mendicants. His debriefing convinced Ieyasu that the new arrivals were not the 'theeves and robbers of all nations' (Farrington, 69) that the Jesuits and Portuguese in Nagasaki had portrayed them as, and that the *Liefde* had indeed come to Japan for trade. This prospect was highly attractive to Ieyasu, who intended to promote yet another of Hideyoshi's legacies, increased overseas trade.

Shortly after Adams's meetings with Ieyasu, the lot of the remaining survivors of the *Liefde* improved, although relations among them proved contentious. The vessel itself was destroyed in a storm as it was being brought up from Kyushu to Edo for closer examination. Adams claimed that for the first few years of his stay he wanted to leave Japan and return home, where he had a wife, Mary (née Hyn), whom he had married on 20 August 1589, and two children, one of whom, Deliverance, survived him, but that his requests, and those of other survivors, were rejected. Their maritime skills were precisely those which Ieyasu could draw upon to improve Japanese deep-sea expertise. Adams, in particular, supervised the construction of two ships, one of which was given to Rodrigo de Vivero y Velasco, a former governor of the Philippines whose ship was wrecked off the Japanese coast in 1609 *en route* for New Spain, where he was to become interim governor.

The restriction against the *Liefde*'s crew leaving Japan was relaxed gradually, but not for Adams. In 1605 his request to sail to Patani in Siam to contact the VOC and encourage it to come to Japan was turned down (the *Liefde*'s captain and another crew member went instead and delivered the invitation). But his resolve to leave weakened anyway as he began to prosper in Japan. He became one of Ieyasu's informal advisers, giving the shogun knowledge about foreign countries as well as recreational instruction in mathematics and geometry. His services were rewarded generously. Ieyasu made him a *hatamoto*, or banner man, with a small estate of about 100 households generating an income of 150 or 250 *koku* of rice (1 *koku* = 180.4 litres) at Hemi on the Miura peninsula, not far from the growing Tokugawa stronghold of Edo. It is from the location of this estate that his modern Japanese name, Miura Anjin (Miura pilot), is derived, although when alive, and in historical documents, he was known simply as *anji*, pilot. Richard Cocks, the head of the East India Company's factory in Japan during its ten-year existence (1613–23), visited the estate in 1615 and, impressed, noted that Adams 'hath power of life & death over [the inhabitants], they being his slaves & he as absolute authorete over them as any *tono* [lord] … in Japon' (*Diary of Richard Cocks*, 1.311). He also had a residence in Edo in a district which bears his or a namesake's cognomen today, Anjin-cho (pilot block), near Nihonbashi.

Another reason for not leaving Japan was Adams's marriage to an unknown Japanese woman, sometimes said to be the daughter of Magome Kagayu, the official in charge of the *tenmasho* (pack- or post-horse office) in Edo, although there is no evidence to support this contention. They had two children, and she was a woman with her own business skills. According to English law (1 Jas 1 c11) Adams was free to remarry as he had lived abroad continuously for over seven years, but, unlike many such individuals at home, he did not abandon his English family but provided for them financially, sending money through the English and Dutch companies.

News of the arrival of the *Liefde* in Japan reached Rotterdam in August 1601, when Oliver van Noort successfully completed his circumnavigation, and was published soon thereafter. Over the next few years both the East India Company and VOC (founded in 1600 and 1602 respectively) considered establishing direct trade with Japan. In letters to both companies' servants in south-east Asia Adams encouraged their employers to come to Japan. But it was not until 1609 that the Dutch took up the invitation they had received in Patani in 1605 and sent two ships to Japan, and not until 1613 that an English ship, part of the company's eighth voyage, under the command of John Saris, arrived. The Dutch requested and were given permission to trade. Adams was highly regarded by the Dutch, and in 1611, on their second visit to Ieyasu, when they secured a *shuinjo* (vermilion seal letter) from the shogun giving them trade privileges in Japan, he acted as interpreter. In a letter to the English company's agent in Bantam on Java urging the company to come to Japan, he greatly overstated his influence with the authorities and what he had achieved on behalf of the Dutch. The Japanese were interested in expanding foreign trade at this juncture and new foreigners were welcome. Moreover, Japanese sources make it clear that he acted as interpreter, not negotiator. He repeated this service for the English in 1613.

Both companies set up trading factories in Hirado, a small island domain off the north-west coast of Kyushu, and Adams entered the English company's service despite Saris's misgivings that he was more Japanese than English and too close to the Dutch, and Adams's umbrage at Saris's behaviour towards him. He had finally been given permission to leave Japan, but because of his sour relations with Saris, and a desire to make money, he turned down the offer of a passage home. In truth, life in Japan was agreeable and full of opportunity; in England the future was too uncertain. He remained on the company's payroll until 1616, with a salary of £100 per annum, a part of which the directors paid to his wife in England. For the English company he undertook two voyages to Siam, in 1614 and 1615, the first of which was aborted at Naha in the Ryukyu kingdom. He made two voyages on his own account, one in 1617 to Faifo in Cochin-China, the other in 1619 to Tongking, and one in 1618 as master of a junk owned by a Chinese based in Nagasaki destined for Faifo which was also aborted.

Influence and reputation Adams died in Hirado after a long illness on 16 May 1620 and was buried there. His will was drawn up on the day of his death with Richard Cocks and William Eaton as overseers and executors, and his estate was valued at approximately £493. Save for some small bequests, half the estate was left to his wife and surviving child, Deliverance, in England and half to his son, Joseph, and daughter, Susanna, in Japan. On 8 October 1621 probate was granted to Mary Adams, who was made administrator of the will. The estate in England was valued at £165 9s. 10d. Deliverance, then married to one Goodchild, petitioned the company in August 1624 for release of part of the estate sent back from Japan, her mother having already died. As was their wont in such cases, the directors demurred and the final settlement is unknown. Writing to the company in 1620, Cocks, disregarding the frequent mistrust, acrimony, and strained relations over the previous years, paid generous tribute to Adams, mourned his loss, and noted that he had been 'in such favour w'th two Emperours [shoguns] of Japon as never was any Christian in these p'tes … & might freely have entred & had speech w'th th'Emperours when many Japon kings [*daimyo*] stood w'thout & could not be p'mitted' (Farrington, 824). Cocks was overestimating his influence. He had enjoyed favour with the first two shoguns and special privileges, notably unrestricted trade in Japan after 1616, when the trading privileges of the English and Dutch were circumscribed, but he had no influence on policy. His services, especially his linguistic ones in official negotiations, were valuable but not indispensable to either the English or the Dutch. Cocks proved himself a shrewd lobbyist for his employers, and the Dutch—and occasionally the English—could draw upon the assistance of another survivor of the *Liefde*, Jan Joosten Lodensteyn, like Adams a *hatamoto*, who had similarly prospered in Japan and who had equally good contacts with the first two shoguns until his choleric temperament made him unwelcome at court.

As for his relations with European Catholics in Japan, Adams claimed that these were even-handed, despite the efforts of the Jesuits and Portuguese to brand the crew of the *Liefde* as pirates. This is true of his relations with Portuguese and Spanish traders but not of those with the missionaries. The Jesuits believed he was a manipulative schemer who prejudiced Ieyasu against them, and held him responsible for encouraging the shogunate to expel all missionaries in 1614. This was not the case and accepts too easily Adams's inflated sense of his own importance to the first two Tokugawa rulers. The causes of the banning of Christianity in Japan are highly complex. Neither the long-term nor the proximate reasons for the outcome have anything to do with Adams's opinions on either Roman Catholicism or the missionaries' activities in Japan.

After Adams's death Joseph inherited his father's estate, and the familiar name, Anjin. He became an established merchant in his own right, trading overseas until the 1630s, when such direct participation in foreign trade by Japanese was banned. Although not mentioned in the will (they were estranged by the time of his death), Adams's Japanese wife survived him and may have died in 1634. Neither the year of Joseph's nor his sister's death are recorded. Besides Joseph and Susanna, Adams had another child, born to his consort in Hirado. About the mother and child nothing significant is known.

After his death Adams was largely forgotten in England until the second half of the nineteenth century, when, after Commodore Matthew Perry's visit in 1853, Japan was forced to open itself to increased Western contact and trade, although Samuel Purchas published material about him in his *Purchas his Pilgrimes* (1625) and Thomas Fuller mentioned him in his *Worthies of England* (1662). In Japan his memory is said to have been kept alive during the Edo period. The residents of Anjin-cho are reported to have made a donation to Jodoji temple in Hemi after his death. If so, this was a payment for Buddhist prayers for the repose of his soul, although in his will Adams himself made it clear that he remained a Christian. Two stone lanterns, allegedly paid for by the Anjin-cho residents in 1798, were erected beside what were later said to be the tombs of Adams and his Japanese wife, the so-called *anjin-tsuka*, or pilot tumuli, near Jodoji. The documentary evidence purporting to confirm the link between Anjin-cho and Jodoji is no longer extant.

In 1872 the tombs were found by an expatriate Englishman, James Walters, who claimed, unilaterally, that an inscription on one of the two stelae beside the tumuli gave a date which corresponds to 1634, since taken to be the year Adams's Japanese wife died. Walters also promoted the story of a link between Anjin-cho and Jodoji. An excavation in 1905 showed that the tomb alleged to be Adams's contained no human remains. It is possible that the artefacts Walters found are connected to Joseph rather than William Adams. It is equally possible, indeed more likely, that there is no connection with either.

With Walters's 'discovery' the making of the modern myth of William Adams began. In the late nineteenth and early twentieth centuries he was more familiar in Britain than in Japan, where he was championed mainly by expatriates. At a time when the origins of the British empire were being located in an imagined golden age of heroic Elizabethan seafaring, his story had an obvious attraction at home and a contemporary ring for expatriate Britons in Japan, many of whom saw themselves as teachers, instructing the Japanese in Western knowledge, as they believed Adams had done before them.

In Britain his fame ebbed and flowed according to the state of Anglo-Japanese relations. In 1885 he made it into the *Dictionary of National Biography*, and in the years immediately following the signing of the Anglo-Japanese naval alliance in 1902 a number of publications appeared. In 1934, after years of lobbying, and at a time of Anglo-Japanese alienation, a memorial clock was erected in Gillingham to a native son who was said to have discovered Japan. The inspiration for this monument came from Japan, where, after a successful subscription by Japanese and British benefactors, patronized by Prince Arisugawa Takehito and Prince Arthur of Connaught, the *anjin-tsuka* were restored and officially dedicated by the British ambassador on 30 May 1918. Another memorial, to the memory of the company's factory in Hirado on which Adams's name and those of the other Englishmen who had served the company in Japan were inscribed, was unveiled in Hirado on 29 May 1927.

During the war one book about Adams was published in Japan. After 1945 his fame in Japan grew but receded in Britain. He again became useful diplomatically, this time in the quest to restore friendly Anglo-Japanese relations. In August 1947 yet another memorial was dedicated, in Ito on the Izu peninsula, where he reportedly supervised the building of the two ships for Ieyasu. This was unveiled by the commander-in-chief of the British Commonwealth forces of occupation in Japan. A whimsical poem was added the following year by Edmund Blunden. Since then an annual festival has been held to commemorate Adams, and there is an official memorial service at the *anjin-tsuka*, now in Tsukayama Park in Yokosuka city.

By the end of the twentieth century Adams, or rather his legend, had become more renowned in Japan than in Britain. In addition to the Ito festival and a few others elsewhere, he had become a 'fact' in Japanese school history textbooks which the proverbial schoolboy is expected to remember. Biographies about him continue to appear, but none add to the existing stock of knowledge.

DEREK MASSARELLA

Sources A. Farrington, *The English factory in Japan, 1613–1623*, 2 vols. (1991) • F. C. Wieder, ed., *De Reis van Mahu en de Cordes door de Straat van Magalhães*, 3 vols., Linschoten Society, 21–2, 24 (1923–5) • M. E. van Opstall, *De Reis van de Vloot van Pieter Willemsz Verhoeff naar Azië, 1607–1612*, 2 vols., Linschoten Society, 73–4 (1972) • P. Pratt, *History of Japan: compiled from the records of the English East India Company*, ed. M. Paske-Smith (1972) • M. B. T. P. Smith, ed., *A glympse of the 'English house' and English life at Hirado, 1613–1623* (1927) • *The Far East*, 3 (1872) • K. Morishige, 'Gaiban tsūsho', *Kondo Seisai zenshū*, 1 (Tokyo, 1905) • A. Hayashi, ed., *Tsūkō ichiran*, 6 (Tokyo, 1913) • *Kokushi daijiten* (Tokyo, 1979) • E. M. Satow, ed., *The voyage of Captain John Saris to Japan, 1613*, Hakluyt Society, 2nd ser., 5 (1900) • C. J. Purnell, 'The log book of William Adams, 1614–19', *Transactions of the Japan Society, London*, 13/2 (1916) • *Diary of Richard Cocks, 1615–1622: diary kept by the head of the English factory in Japan*, ed. Historiographical Institute, University of Tokyo, 3 vols. (1978–80) • G. Milton, *Samurai William: the adventurer who unlocked Japan* (2002)
Archives BL OIOC, letters, information • Bodl. Oxf., logbook of four voyages to Japan, Siam, and Cochin-China
Wealth at death 1972 tael, 2 mas, 4 condrin in Japan [approx. £493]: Farrington, *The English factory in Japan* • £165 9s. 10d. in England: Pratt, *History of Japan*

Adams, William (1706–1789), Church of England clergyman and college head, was born at Shrewsbury on 17 August 1706, the son of John Adams, mayor of Shrewsbury in 1726, and his wife, Elizabeth Jorden. Adams entered Pembroke College, Oxford, on 6 August 1720, graduated MA in 1727, became fellow of his college and, in 1734, tutor in place of William Jorden, his cousin. Samuel Johnson (1709–1784) had been one of Jorden's pupils, and during his short university career (1728–9) began a lifelong friendship with Adams. 'I was his nominal tutor, but he was above my mark', Adams later recalled (Macleane, 339).

In 1730 Adams accepted the curacy of St Chad's in Shrewsbury. In 1747 he was made prebendary of Gaia Major in Lichfield Cathedral, and in 1749 prebendary of Llandaff, where he became precentor in 1750. In 1755 he became rector of Counde in Shropshire, and in 1756 proceeded BD and DD at Oxford. He was elected to the mastership of Pembroke, to which was attached a prebend of Gloucester, in 1775, and resigned St Chad's. He was made archdeacon of Llandaff in 1777 and retained these offices and the rectory of Counde until his death.

As archdeacon he was head of chapter and in spite of his mastership of Pembroke he did not neglect his Llandaff duties; although non-resident he attended every chapter meeting for thirty years. He married Sarah Hunt, and they had a daughter, who in 1788 married B. Hyatt of Painswick in Gloucestershire.

Adams's friendship with Johnson was commemorated by James Boswell in his *Life of Samuel Johnson* (1791), and

Adams provided invaluable information about the great man. Adams attended the first performance of Johnson's *Irene* in 1749. He tried to reconcile Johnson to the earl of Chesterfield's incivility in 1754, though at the same time taking a message from Bishop William Warburton to Johnson approving of his 'manly behaviour'. In June 1784 Johnson, accompanied by Boswell, paid a visit to Adams at Oxford. Johnson stayed at Pembroke lodge for a fortnight, and appreciated the attentions of Adams and his daughter.

Adams published some occasional sermons, one of which, *A Test of True and False Doctrine* (1770), preached at St Chad's on 4 September 1769 and directed against the Methodist doctrines of W. Romaine, led to some controversy, in which neither of the principals took part. His chief work, entitled *An Essay on Mr Hume's Essay on Miracles* (1752), was probably the first major response to David Hume's 1748 publication, and was a temperate statement of the argument for the credibility of Gospel miracles. Johnson wrote that Adams had 'lately commended himself to the best part of mankind by his confutation of Hume on miracles' (Redford, 1.80). A poetic tribute praised

Candid Adams, by whom David fell
Who ancient miracles sustained so well.
(Macleane, 394)

The master of Pembroke later accepted David Hume's invitation to dine, and at least one account records that the Scottish philosopher told Adams, 'You have treated me much better than I deserved' (Long).

On a number of occasions Adams and Johnson had serious discussions about religion. It was Adams who first suggested Johnson should produce a book of prayers for daily use—a plea to which Johnson eventually responded with *Prayers and Meditations* (1785); and shortly before Johnson's death Adams tried to bring him to belief in a merciful God. Adams later wrote that 'we had much serious talk together for which I ought to be better as long as I live' (Boswell, 2.553).

William Adams died at his prebendal house in Gloucester on 13 January 1789. Generous tributes in the *Gentleman's Magazine* described him as 'a mild and excellent man; a governor of his college; careful to promote the interests of his young men'. His sentiments in religion were said to be 'liberal' (GM, 176).

LESLIE STEPHEN, rev. PAT BANCROFT

Sources D. Macleane, *A history of Pembroke College, Oxford*, OHS, 33 (1897) • Foster, *Alum. Oxon.* • A. Chalmers, ed., *The general biographical dictionary*, new edn, 32 vols. (1812–17) • G. Long, ed., *The biographical dictionary of the Society for the Diffusion of Useful Knowledge*, 4 vols. in 7 (1842–4) • J. Boswell, *The life of Samuel Johnson*, 2 vols. (1791) • *The letters of Samuel Johnson*, ed. B. Redford, 5 vols. (1992–4) • private information (1885) • *GM*, 1st ser., 59 (1789), 176, 214 • Nichols, *Illustrations* • chapter act books, Lichfield Cathedral archives, Lichfield, no. 7 • *Fasti Angl.* (Hardy) • J. H. Burton, *Life and correspondence of David Hume*, 2 vols. (1846) • J. L. Clifford, *Dictionary Johnson* (1979) • H. E. Forrest, *Old houses of Shrewsbury* (1912)
Archives Glos. RO, corresp. and papers
Likenesses oils (after J. Opie), Pembroke College, Oxford

Adams, William (*bap.* **1746**, *d.* **1805**), potter, was baptized on 15 June 1746 in Tunstall, Staffordshire, the posthumous son of Edward Adams (*d.* 1745/6), potter, and Martha, daughter of Joseph and Elizabeth Adams. There were three William Adamses who were potters in north Staffordshire in the later eighteenth century, so care is needed in attributing their work correctly. This William Adams was the most distinguished of the three. He was brought up by his grandfather and apprenticed to the potter John Brindley, brother of the canal builder James Brindley. In 1771 he married Mary (*d.* 1805), daughter of John Cole of Tunstall, and founded the Greengates Pottery, where his jasper ware was of such a high quality and sophisticated design that it was assumed wrongly that he had worked with Josiah Wedgwood. He stamped his wares 'Adams & Co.', and nearly 300 examples have been identified. He also made fine underglaze blue printed ware, with the help, from 1785, of the Swiss Adam Monglott.

Adams, his elder son, and his wife all died in 1805, Adams himself in January in Staffordshire, leaving only his younger son, Benjamin, to carry on the family business. The works were closed in 1820, after having given up the production of jasper ware and having latterly produced mainly utilitarian wares. The reputation of Adams has been overshadowed by that of Wedgwood, and knowledge of his work has been largely the subject of the ceramic specialist. ALISON KELLY

Sources Wedgwood Museum, Barlaston, Staffordshire · W. Turner, *William Adams, an old English potter* (1904) · R. Nicholls, *Ten generations of a potting family* [1931] [compiler] · D. Peel, *A pride of potters* (1957) · G. Godden, *Staffordshire porcelain* (1983) · P. W. L. Adams, *A history of the Adams family of north Staffordshire* (1914) · E. Meteyard, *The life of Josiah Wedgwood, from his private correspondence and family papers*, 2 vols. (1865–6)
Likenesses bronze bas-relief (posthumous), Whitworth Art Gallery
Wealth at death younger son inherited prosperous works

Adams, William (**1772–1851**), lawyer and diplomatist, the youngest son of Patience Thomas Adams, filazer of the court of king's bench, and Martha, daughter of Thomas Marsh, was born at 39 Hatton Garden, London, on 13 January 1772. On his father's side he was connected with an old Essex family, and his mother was descended from William Wykeham. He was educated at Tonbridge School, and in 1787 entered Trinity Hall, Cambridge, of which he later became a fellow. At the age of twenty-five he began to attend the courts at Doctors' Commons. In 1799 he took the degree of LLD, and in November of the same year he was admitted into the College of Advocates.

Obtaining a high reputation for business capacity and mastery of legal details, Adams served on several important commissions, including that appointed in 1811 to regulate the practice of the vice-admiralty courts abroad, and the commission of 1815–24 inquiring into the duties, offices, and salaries of the courts of justice and the ecclesiastical courts of England. His chief claim to distinction, however, was the part he took in the negotiations for a treaty with the United States in 1814 after the capture of Washington; he was one of the three commissioners sent to represent England, and was entrusted with the sole preparation of the dispatches relating to maritime law, the most delicate and important part of the negotiation. In 1815 he was also named one of the three plenipotentiaries sent to conclude a convention of commerce between Great Britain and the United States, which was signed on 3 July.

Adams was twice married, first to Sarah Scott from 1803 until her death in 1806 and second, in 1811, to the Hon. Mary-Anne Cockayne (*d.* 1873), with whom he had four sons, including George Edward *Cokayne, and four daughters.

In 1820 Adams was named as one of the counsel for the bill of divorce against Queen Caroline. The hard work he put into this task had serious effects on his health, and in 1825 he was compelled on this account to retire from professional life. He spent his last years at Thorpe in Surrey, where he died on 11 June 1851 and was buried six days later in Thorpe churchyard. He was survived by his second wife. T. F. HENDERSON, *rev.* JONATHAN HARRIS

Sources *GM*, 2nd ser., 36 (1851), 197–200 · *Annual Register* (1851), 297
Likenesses G. Hayter, group portrait, oils (*The trial of Queen Caroline*, 1820), NPG · G. Hayter, portrait (study for *The trial of Queen Caroline*, 1820), NPG

Adams [*later* Rawson], **Sir William** (**1783–1827**), oculist, was born at Stanbury, Morwenstow, Cornwall, on 5 December 1783, the youngest son of Henry Adams (*d.* 1811) and his wife, Demaris (1736/7–1788), daughter of Simon and Anne Cottle. He bore the name Adams throughout his professional life until, shortly before his death, he took his wife's surname of Rawson. Adams began his medical training as assistant to John Hill, a surgeon at Barnstaple, and about 1805 went to London to complete his education at St Thomas's and Guy's hospitals. The London Infirmary in Charterhouse Square for curing diseases of the eye had recently been established by John Cunningham Saunders, the demonstrator in anatomy at St Thomas's; Adams attended his demonstrations and assisted him in the surgical operations at the infirmary. In 1807 he was elected MRCS and shortly afterwards moved to Exeter. There he helped to establish the West of England Infirmary for curing eye disease on the lines of the institution at which he had been trained in London, and practised as the surgeon there. From 1807 to 1810 he lived and worked for the most part in Exeter and Bath, but he claimed to have operated successfully also in Dublin and Edinburgh. In 1810 he returned to London to establish a practice there. His subsequent career seems to have been extraordinarily active both in his profession of oculist and in other, sometimes surprising, fields. But often his actions provoked controversy, and he had enemies.

At this time Egyptian ophthalmia (a conjunctival disease, principally trachoma) was a serious and widespread problem in Europe, following Napoleon's Egyptian campaign: many soldiers had been dismissed from the army as blind from this cause, and the disease spread rapidly to the civilian population throughout Europe. Although the London Infirmary already existed to treat the ophthalmia,

Adams proposed the founding of another similar institution exclusively for the treatment of the military pensioners. In 1813 he encouraged the belief that he had discovered a cure for the complaint, although his enemies claimed that the discovery had been made by John Vetch. Adams performed several operations in the hospital for seamen at Greenwich, and controversy raged for several years over whether they had been successful, and on the originality of his treatment. Other operations by him, well publicized at the time, are reported to have been helpful or harmful in about equal measure.

Nevertheless Adams was successful in his profession at this time, being made surgeon and oculist-extraordinary to the prince regent and to the dukes of Kent and Sussex, and he was knighted in 1814. In 1817 an ophthalmic institution was established for him in part of the York Hospital at Chelsea, but was found to be inconvenient for the purpose. Instead, from 1817 to 1821 he gave free treatments at Regent's Park (in a building then used as a hospital, although he had himself originally built it for the manufacture of steam guns). Adams pressed a claim for public money to support this institution, being strongly supported in this by Lord Palmerston, and following a report by a select committee parliament voted him £4000. The post of ophthalmic surgeon to the army was created for him, at a salary of £1500, which greatly offended the military surgeons.

Adams married Jane Eliza, fourth daughter and coheir of Colonel George Rawson, MP for Armagh; they had five children. In 1825 Adams inherited a considerable sum of money from his wife's family, and in compliance with the will of Colonel Rawson's widow, changed his name by royal licence to Rawson. He invested much of this money in silver mines in Mexico and other South American mines, encouraging his family and friends to do likewise. Many Mexican mines had lain derelict since the years of revolution after 1810, and needed investment to bring them back into production. When he lost heavily on these ventures Rawson published two pamphlets on the state of mining in the region, one with a letter to the directors of the Anglo-Mexican Mine Association, complaining that share prices fluctuated in response to inaccurate statements put out regarding the likely yields from these mines, the other a letter to George Canning. He died at his house, Upper Gloucester Place, Dorset Square, London, on 4 February 1827 and was buried in St John's Wood cemetery five days later.   W. P. COURTNEY, rev. J. M. TIFFANY

Sources S. Duke-Elder, *System of ophthalmology*, 8/1 (1965), 260–61 · E. T. Collins, *The history and traditions of the Moorfields Eye Hospital: one hundred years of ophthalmic discovery and development*, 1 (1929); facs. edn (1974), 30 · G. Cantrell, *A history of the Exeter Eye Infirmary* (1985) · G. Gorin, *History of ophthalmology* (1982), 73–4 · J. Hirschberg, *The history of ophthalmology*, trans. F. C. Blodi, 8a (1987), 92–106 · *GM*, 1st ser., 97/1 (1827), 187 · W. Rawson, *The present operations … of the Mexican Mine Associations analysed* (1825) · W. Rawson, *The actual state of the Mexican mines and the reasonable expectations of the shareholders of the Anglo-Mexican Mine Association* (1825)
Archives Suffolk RO, Ipswich, letters to Mrs English

Adams, William (1814–1848), Church of England clergyman and author, born in January 1814, was the second son

of Serjeant John Adams of St Pancras, London, assistant judge at the Middlesex sessions, and Eliza Nation (d. January 1814), only child of William Nation, banker, of Exeter. Adams attended Eton College from 1826, before matriculating at Merton College, Oxford, in 1832. He took a double-first degree in 1836, and became a fellow and tutor at Merton in 1837. He was presented to the college living of St Peter-in-the-East, Oxford, in 1838, proceeding MA in 1839. Since his income from St Peter's was less than he gave to charity, Adams combined his work as vicar and tutor.

Over Easter 1842 Adams delivered some exceptional parish lectures entitled 'Warnings of Holy Week'. Later that year he went to Eton as examiner for the Newcastle scholarship; here a light-hearted swim brought on a severe cold which affected his lungs. During that summer he wrote his first allegory, *The Shadow of the Cross* (1842), a work intended for children, and made notes for a boys' school story, *The Cherry Stones*. On medical advice he spent the winter in Madeira, but returned to England too ill for his duties at St Peter's, and instantly resigned. He moved to Bonchurch, Isle of Wight, which had been recently praised by Dr G. A. Martin for its mild climate, and rented a house sheltered by the famous Undercliff and adjacent to the little Gothic church of St Boniface.

Here Adams was befriended by Elizabeth Sewell (1815–1906), the novelist and educationist, and by Captain Swinburne, his wife, Lady Jane, and their small son, Algernon Charles Swinburne (1837–1909). The Sewells were influenced by the Oxford Movement, which also attracted Adams. On his good days he would walk or ride horseback, enjoying the scenery. The villagers called him 'the good gentleman' and the Revd Erskine Neale wrote of 'his own loving spirit' (Neale, 162). His friends appreciated his sense of humour, his lively conversation, and his stories.

Adams's next allegory, *The Distant Hills* (1844), showed children learning to lead a Christian life. *The Fall of Croesus* (1846), taken from Herodotus and also addressed to children, taught that wealth does not bring happiness. It ended with his personal reflection that sometimes an 'early and peaceful death' might be better than remaining 'longer amidst the trials and temptations of the world' (p. 128). His best story, *The Old Man's Home* (1846), captivated a wide audience, including William Wordsworth. Interpreted allegorically, the conversation of the old man, hovering between sanity and madness, was full of religious truths. Finally the old man died, thus reaching 'home', the churchyard where his wife and children were buried. So compelling was Adams's presentation that many readers believed it to be a true story and made pilgrimages to St Boniface's churchyard, searching for the old man's grave; later editions stressed that the story was entirely fictitious.

By 1847 Adams knew he was dying. He swiftly revised his Holy Week lectures for publication, dedicating them to his St Peter's parishioners, and then, in collaboration with Elizabeth Sewell and her brother, the Revd William Sewell (1804–1900), wrote one of three stories in *The Sketches*, proceeds of which helped to establish a village school. On 24 June 1847 he laid the foundation-stone of a larger church for the village. He finished *The King's Messengers*, a powerful Eastern tale illustrating the right and the wrong way to use wealth. It ended with the customary section for children's questions and discussion. It was Adams's last piece of work. He weakened markedly during Christmas, and died on 17 January 1848 at his home, Winterbourne, Bonchurch. He was buried on 27 January in the old churchyard there, with a stone cross laid horizontally above his grave so as to cast a shadow. His father sold his books to the publisher and donated the money to Adams's favourite charities. *The Cherry Stones*, finished by one of his half-brothers, was published in 1852. Adams's books were reprinted for many years; several were translated into Swedish, and in Calcutta in 1849 *The King's Messengers* was published in English and Bengali.

BRENDA COLLOMS

Sources 'Memoir', W. Adams, *Sacred allegories* (1864) · E. Neale, *The earthly resting-places of the just* (1851) · J. White, *Bonchurch* (1849) · E. M. Sewell, *The autobiography of Elizabeth M. Sewell*, ed. E. L. Sewell (1907) · H. R. Holloway, *A remembrance of Bonchurch* (1849) · G. A. Martin, *The Undercliff of the Isle of Wight* (1849) · Foster, *Alum. Oxon.* · private information (2004)
Archives NL Scot., corresp. with J. R. Hope-Scott
Likenesses J. H. Lynch, lithograph, V&A · W. H. Mote, stipple (after G. Richmond), BM, NPG; repro. in White, *Bonchurch* · G. or T. Richmond, portrait (in his academic gown, seated)

Adams, William (1820–1900), surgeon, was born on 1 February 1820, the eldest son of James Adams, surgeon, of 39 Finsbury Square, London. He was educated at W. Simpson's private school in Hackney and then at King's College School, London, from 1835 to 1837. He trained at St Thomas's Hospital between 1838 and 1842 under Joseph Henry Green. Training as a surgeon when anaesthesia and antiseptic methods were undeveloped Adams gained an exceptionally thorough grasp of anatomy and a meticulous operating technique, described as 'careful but slow'. He shared the contemporary view that post-operative infection was caused by excessive exposure of the wound to the air; consequently he favoured subcutaneous surgery with minimum excision of the skin, and was slow to adopt Lister's techniques of antisepsis.

Adams was admitted MRCS in 1842, the year that he was appointed curator of the museum and demonstrator of morbid anatomy at St Thomas's Hospital, posts that he held until 1854. The hospital had just purchased Grainger's Medical School and a member of the latter's staff who had been a leading body snatcher in the 1820s became Adams's 'chief dead-house assistant' and provided him with numerous gruesome anecdotes. In 1850 Adams married Mary Anne Mills, daughter of John Mills, who predeceased him. There were two sons of the marriage.

Adams was admitted FRCS in 1851. During the same year he became assistant surgeon to the Royal Orthopaedic Hospital and in 1857 was promoted joint senior surgeon. His resignation in 1872 followed a confrontation with the hospital committee. This arose from criticisms of the two senior surgeons in the annual report on the hospital. When it was put to the vote that these criticisms be

deleted since they were fallacious, the motion was defeated. It was later revealed that an assistant surgeon, B. E. Brodhurst, had rigged the vote by paying the membership fee of 1 guinea each for thirty-two new governors to vote against Adams and his colleague. Brodhurst subsequently accepted the post of senior surgeon, despite general condemnation of his conduct. The *British Medical Journal* commented: 'The services of the two senior surgeons, who have chiefly made the hospital distinguished through a long series of years, have been lost, and their long career of brilliant and gratuitous exertions rewarded with insult and crowned with ingratitude' (Plarr).

After his appointment as lecturer on surgery and medical practice at the Grosvenor Place medical school in 1854 Adams elected to specialize in orthopaedic surgery. However, it was while acting as surgeon to the Great Northern Hospital, London, from 1855 to 1891 that he established his reputation as the leading orthopaedic surgeon in England. There he devised the operation, subsequently known by his name, of osteotomy of the neck of the femur within the capsule of the hip-joint to relieve ankylosis of the joint, for which he invented a special knife that he called 'my little thaw'. As surgeon to the National Hospital for the Paralysed and Epileptic, 1874 to 1891, he performed much general surgery.

Adams was elected vice-president of the Pathological Society of London, 1867; president of the Harveian Society, 1873; and president of the Medical Society of London, 1876, in which year he travelled to the USA as the society's representative at the International Medical Congress. He was the author of some fifteen medical books and papers, the best known being his Lettsomian lecture of 1869 on diseases of the joints and his Jacksonian prize essay on club foot, later praised as 'a classic, for it is an epitome of the knowledge of the time' (Plarr).

Adams devoted most of his time and energy to hospital work but established a private practice at 5 Henrietta Street, Cavendish Square, between 1853 and 1896. In 1896 he moved to 7 Loudoun Road, St John's Wood, where he died on 3 February 1900. Adams was regarded by his colleagues with a mixture of affection and irritation. 'He was a good but prolix talker, with a soft voice and a pronounced lisp' (Plarr). Sir James Paget complained that 'he never finished his sentences' (ibid.). The museum curator at St Bartholomew's Hospital recalled that 'he would often come in later days and waste two or three hours of valuable time, having nothing to do' (ibid.). But his reminiscences of the old body-snatching days were enthralling, and a contemporary described him as 'a most genial and humorous man, hospitable, exceedingly kind and a voluminous talker' (*The Lancet*, 812).

F. R. MILES

Sources V. G. Plarr, *Plarr's Lives of the fellows of the Royal College of Surgeons of England*, rev. D'A. Power, 2 vols. (1930) · *The Lancet* (17 March 1900), 812 · *BMJ* (10 Feb 1900), 359 · King's College School archive, King's College School, Wimbledon Common, London · S. S. Sprigge, *The life and times of Thomas Wakley* (1897)
Likenesses photograph, *c.*1870, King's College School archive · Mayall, photograph (of William Adams, 1820–1900?), Wellcome L.
Wealth at death £270: probate, 21 Feb 1900, *CGPLA Eng. & Wales*

Adams, William (1823–1904), engineer, was born in Limehouse, London, on 15 October 1823, the second son and third child in the family of three sons and two daughters of John Samuel Adams, clerk of works to the East India Dock Company, and his wife, Jean Walker. He was educated privately in Margate.

In 1841 Adams was apprenticed as a machinery fitter with Miller and Ravenhill, shipbuilders at Orchard Wharf, Blackwall, London. In 1846 he joined the firm of Charles Blacker Vignoles (1793–1875) as a draughtsman and, two years later, Philip Taylor, shipbuilder, in Marseilles and Genoa, working as a marine engineer there and in ships of the Royal Sardinian Navy. Adams married Isabella, daughter of Charles Park, mechanical engineer, at Genoa in 1852. They had seven sons and three daughters.

Adams returned to Britain later in 1852 and planned the North London Railway's Bow locomotive and carriage works, becoming locomotive and carriage superintendent in 1854. To deal with its rapidly increasing commuter traffic, in 1855 Adams introduced new high-capacity suburban trains with continuous brakes, probably the first in Britain. He was also first to use coal gas for train lighting in 1862. New passenger locomotives of greater power, of 4–4-0 tank type, from 1865 embodied his patent two-axle guiding bogie with lateral movement controlled by springs. This greatly improved their smoothness of travel over curves and allowed higher speeds without risk of derailment. It was one of the major developments in locomotive design and was adopted worldwide.

In 1873 Adams took up a similar appointment with the Great Eastern Railway. He modernized their Stratford works, using largely American labour-saving machines and equipment which, in many cases, enabled process costs to be reduced five- to tenfold. In 1878 he pioneered the introduction of 2–6-0 type freight locomotives in Britain and, as consultant to the London, Tilbury, and Southend Railway, 4–4-2 passenger tank locomotives, which were highly successful and were built in enlarged form over the next fifty years.

On becoming locomotive superintendent of the London and South Western Railway in 1878, Adams rapidly introduced urgently needed, more powerful, and reliable locomotives for passenger, suburban, and freight traffic, which were robust in construction and elegant in outline, especially the outside-cylindered 4–4-0 express type. A major development, patented by Adams and his nephew Henry in 1885, was the Vortex steam exhaust system which increased combustion efficiency and locomotive power. It was applied to over 500 locomotives in Britain, France, and Austria. Adams retired because of ill health in 1895.

Adams was a kindly man who took a keen interest in his staff and his fellow men. He was musically talented, with a fine bass voice like his father. While with the North London Railway he persuaded its directors to provide suitable accommodation for concerts and evening classes at the Bow and Bromley Institute. He was a member of the Institutions of Civil and Mechanical Engineers and a founder member of the Association of Railway Locomotive Engineers. Adams died on 7 August 1904 at Hillrise, Amersham Road, Putney, London. GEORGE W. CARPENTER, rev.

Sources E. H. Wilson, 'William Adams, 1823–1904', *Transactions* [Newcomen Society], 57 (1985–6), 125–48 · *CGPLA Eng. & Wales* (1904) · d. cert.
Wealth at death £63,672 13s. 3d.: probate, 2 Sept 1904, *CGPLA Eng. & Wales*

Adams, William Bridges (1797–1872), railway engineer, was born in Madeley, Staffordshire, the son of a coachbuilder, and showed an early aptitude for engineering. As a young man he was sent to the Americas because of ill health, and during the early 1820s lived in Chile, working as an assistant to Lord Cochrane, the commander of the Chilean navy. On his return home he became a partner in his father's London coach-building business, and was for a time pupil to the engineer John Farey, before opening his own factory in 1843 at the Fairfield Works, Bow, east London, where he manufactured railway vehicles. His interest in reducing the weight and improving the stability and quality of ride of railway rolling-stock led him to produce some innovative designs; he was one of the earliest British engineers to experiment with multi-axle vehicles and swivelling bogies on the American pattern, and in 1863 he introduced the first successful radial axle-box for railway locomotives, which eased movement around curves by allowing the axle and wheels a degree of lateral movement. The invention with which he is most associated, however, is the fish-plate joint for railway track, patented in 1847, which solved one of the besetting problems of early railways—that of contriving a strong but flexible device for joining the ends of the rails. The basic design of Adams's fish-plate is still in use today.

Despite his inventiveness, Adams was unsuccessful alike in his commercial enterprises and in his inventions. His works failed, and he gained little profit from his many patents; even that for the fish-plate joint brought him very little, and soon passed out of his hands. He took out no fewer than thirty-two patents; besides those connected with railways, he patented improvements in road carriages, in ship propulsion, guns, wood-carving, and other machines. He was the author of several books, the most technically important being *The Varieties of Permanent Way* (1857) and *Roads and Rails* (1862), and of numerous memoirs and articles. He read several papers to the Society of Arts and the Institution of Civil Engineers, and made many contributions to the journal of the former society, as well as to many scientific and technical periodicals. He was also the author of several radical political pamphlets of the 1830s, published under the pseudonym of Junius Redivivus.

Adams was married three times. His second wife, whom he married on 24 September 1834, was the poet Sarah Flower *Adams (1805–1848). His third wife, Ellen, outlived him. He died on 23 July 1872 at Cuthbert House, Broadstairs, Kent, and was buried at St Peter's Church in the town. H. T. WOOD, rev. RALPH HARRINGTON

Sources *Engineering* (26 July 1872) · *The Engineer* (26 July 1872) · C. H. Ellis, *Twenty locomotive men* (1958) · J. Marshall, *A biographical*

dictionary of railway engineers (1978) · *Journal of the Society of Arts*, 20 (1871–2), 763–4 · W. B. Adams, *English pleasure carriages* (1837); facs. edn with introduction by J. Simmons (1971) · register of deaths
Archives UCL, corresp. with Sir Edwin Chadwick
Wealth at death under £1000: administration with will, 21 Nov 1872, *CGPLA Eng. & Wales*

Adams, William Bridges- (1889–1965), theatre producer, was born on 1 March 1889 at 8 Marlborough Villas, Wealdstone, Harrow, the only son of Walter Bridges Adams (*d.* 1902), tutor, and his wife, Mary Jane Daltry (1854–1939) [*see* Adams, Mary Jane Bridges-]. Nothing in his background suggested a theatrical career, and he remained to the end of his days a quite untheatrical person. But he was brought up on Shakespeare, Dickens, and Wagner—and this helped to counteract the seriously, although not smugly, socialist ambience of his home. He was educated at Bedales School and he matriculated as a non-collegiate student at Oxford in January 1908, migrating later that year to Worcester College. He played Leontes in *The Winter's Tale* and Prospero in *The Tempest* for the Oxford University Dramatic Society. At the same time he had friends in Cambridge, and he was associated with the production of Marlowe's *Dr Faustus* by the Cambridge Amateur Dramatic Club in 1907. At Oxford he staged two operas for Hugh Allen, and he directed the Oxford millenary pageant. His visual sense, always very acute, was quickened by the Post-Impressionists and by personal contacts with Charles Ricketts and Charles Shannon. On leaving Oxford, without taking a degree, he assisted Nugent Monck in the stage-management of William Poel's production of *The Two Gentlemen of Verona* for Sir Herbert Beerbohm Tree at His Majesty's Theatre. He admired the character and, to some extent, the genius of Poel, but kept his distance from what he liked to call 'Elizabethan Methodism'. After further experience in Shakespeare repertory, with Lena Ashwell and with the Stage Society, Bridges-Adams appeared in 1916 with Sir George Alexander at the St James's, learning the difference between what Oscar Wilde had described as Alexander's 'behaviour' and the 'throw it away' school of naturalism. His next move was to Liverpool where in 1916–17 he directed in repertory at the Playhouse, giving it the name by which it became well known.

In 1919 the control of the annual Shakespeare Festival at Stratford upon Avon passed into the hands of the Stratford governors and London's Shakespeare Memorial National Theatre committee. Bridges-Adams was appointed to direct the festivals, inheriting a number of players who had previously worked with Sir Frank Benson, as well as a certain local disappointment that Benson was no longer there to direct them himself. The Memorial Theatre was not well adapted to the methods of production advocated by Harley Granville-Barker and Poel, and Bridges-Adams himself hankered a little after the romanticism of Irving's Lyceum, of which he knew only by hearsay. But his own productions—which he designed himself—were scenically effective in their simple way, and he secured swift and clear performances of six plays

rehearsed in only five weeks. They were given virtually unabridged (except for his removal of Christopher Sly in *The Taming of the Shrew*, for whom he had conceived an irrational dislike), and this earned him the sobriquet of Mr Unabridges-Adams. He was not afraid of sensible innovation, putting Richard II into black armour inherited from the black prince, interpreting the apparitions in *Macbeth* as the sovereigns of the Stuart dynasty, and making Banquo's ghost re-enter as the murdered Duncan. In contrast to Poel's archaism and Barker's hygienic tidiness, there was a sense of bustling 'boot and saddle' about these early productions. He preserved the footlights and the live musicians in the well of the orchestra.

On 6 March 1926 the Memorial Theatre was burnt down, greatly to the relief of G. B. Shaw. Within hours of the mysterious conflagration Bridges-Adams was on the spot, tracing in the mud with his umbrella the plan for an enlarged stage. The spring festival went forward in the local cinema, with costumes lent from America by Julia Marlowe and E. H. Sothern; and American generosity, activated by three American tours, made it possible for the new Memorial Theatre, designed by Elisabeth Scott, to be opened by the prince of Wales on 23 April 1932. Bridges-Adams was happily at home at the drawing-board, and although he wrote that if he had been given 'a free hand with the whole building … we should have had a better and cheaper theatre' (Beauman, 111), the stage was very much as he had planned it. He had insisted on 'absolute flexibility—a box of tricks out of which the childlike mind of the producer may create whatever shape it pleases' (Speaight, 20). This disappointed the 'Elizabethan Methodists', but not the guest directors—Tyrone Guthrie and Theodore Komisarjevsky—or the guest designers—Aubrey Hammond and Norman Wilkinson—who were now invited to use it. Stratford seemed in a fair way of becoming the British Bayreuth of Bridges-Adams's dreams. The governors, however, were still content with more limited horizons. They were unwilling to pay the larger salaries that would attract a stronger company, although players such as Randle Ayrton, George Hayes, and Fabia Drake continued to give exemplary performances. In 1934 Bridges-Adams resigned—'not without due thought', as he told the governors, 'and not without reluctance'. He wanted an easier schedule of rehearsals and opening nights, and a closer liaison with other bodies working in the same field, giving him larger resources in personnel, for which he was prepared to forgo a certain degree of independence. He wanted an international status for the theatre and more guest directors of international repute. When he found little backing for these policies, he felt that it was time for him to go. He declined the offer of a governorship.

Bridges-Adams had directed at Stratford twenty-nine out of the thirty-six plays in Shakespeare's first folio, as well as *The Merry Wives of Windsor* at the Lyric, Hammersmith, in 1923, and *Much Ado about Nothing* at the New Theatre in 1926. But he was not an ambitious man, and he was among the few who had not begrudged Granville-Barker his early retirement. He had married on 13 September 1929 Marguerite Doris (1899–1963), formerly the wife of Colin Reith Coote and the daughter of the late William Henry Wellsted, architect. She had comfortable private means and he now settled down with her at Badingham in Suffolk; they had one son, Nicholas (1930–1998), who became a distinguished barrister and recorder of the crown court. His earlier marriage, on 10 August 1915, to the actress Muriel Edith Amy, daughter of William Dymock Pratt, architect, had been annulled. Together they had directed the Bristol and Liverpool repertory theatres. In 1936 he directed *Oedipus Rex* at Covent Garden, and he was appointed to the council of the Royal Academy of Dramatic Art and to the building advisory committee for the National Theatre. In 1937 he became honorary dramatic adviser for the British Council, with special responsibility for their foreign tours; from 1939 to 1944 he worked as a full-time member of their staff. After the war he moved with his wife to Ireland and built a house to his own design at Castletownbere in co. Cork. There he completed the first volume of *The Irresistible Theatre* (1957), which promised to be a classic of its kind, and he contributed the chapter on the Edwardian theatre to Simon Nowell-Smith's symposium *Edwardian England* (1964). He maintained, at the same time, a close and fascinating correspondence with his friends. A selection of letters—many of them addressed to the American scholar Arthur Colby Sprague, along with three broadcast talks—was edited with a memoir by Robert Speaight (1971). They demonstrate the depth of his concern with the history of the theatre.

Bridges-Adams was at once sociable and solitary. At Stratford he had kept somewhat aloof from his company, but he delighted in his membership of the Garrick and Savile clubs. A brilliant conversationalist, for he could listen as well as talk, he was free with illuminating comment on the theatre, which he had never ceased to love, although he had left it when he was still so young. He was appointed CBE in 1960, a welcome, if belated, recognition of the foundations he had laid, on which others were to build with the means that had been denied him. No one since Granville-Barker had shown a surer grasp of Shakespearian stagecraft, or a clearer mind on the essential content of the plays. His wife died, very suddenly, in 1963; Bridges-Adams died on 17 August 1965 at his home in Bantry, co. Cork, after recovering gradually a little of his former zest for a life that he had endured, at need, as a stoic and had otherwise enjoyed as an epicurean. He was buried at the abbey cemetery in Bantry.

ROBERT SPEAIGHT, *rev.* STANLEY WELLS

Sources b. cert. · m. cert. · personal knowledge (1981) · private information (1981, 2004) · R. Speaight, ed., *A Bridges-Adams letter book* (1971) · S. Beauman, *The Royal Shakespeare Company* (1982) · S. Brock and M. J. Pringle, *The Shakespeare Memorial Theatre, 1919–1945* (1984)
Archives University of Calgary Library, corresp., press clippings, photographs, working documents, scripts, proofs, etc. | Harvard U., Houghton L., letters to Arthur Sprague

Likenesses G. R. Schelderup, chalk drawing, 1959, Royal Shakespeare Theatre, Stratford-upon-Avon, Gallery
Wealth at death £1324: probate, 18 Jan 1966, *CGPLA Éire*

Adams, William Davenport (1851–1904), journalist and compiler of reference works, was born at Park Terrace, New Park Road, Brixton, on 28 December 1851, the elder surviving son of William Henry Davenport *Adams (1828–1891), then a private tutor, and his wife, Sarah Esther, *née* Morgan. He entered Merchant Taylors' School in January 1863, and proceeded to Glasgow Academy and Edinburgh University, where poor health prevented him from getting a good degree. Becoming a journalist, he was appointed in 1875 as leader writer and literary and drama critic for the *Glasgow Daily News*; later he edited the evening and weekly editions. On 19 October 1875 he married Caroline Estelle, the daughter of John Körner, a Polish exile of a noble family. From 1878 to 1880 he was the editor of the *Greenock Advertiser*, from 1880 to 1882 the acting editor of the *Nottingham Guardian*, from 1882 to 1885 the editor of the *Derby Mercury*, and from 1885 until his death the literary editor and drama critic of the London *Globe*. In addition to his many newspaper and journal articles, Adams published: *A Dictionary of English Literature, being a Comprehensive Guide to English Authors and their Works* (1878), *By-Ways in Book-Land* (1888), *A Book of Burlesque* (1891), and *With Poet and Player* (1891).

Adams's main interest was drama, and he spent twenty years compiling his *A Dictionary of the Drama*, which was to be 'a guide to the plays, playwrights, players, and playhouses of the United Kingdom and America, from the earliest times to the present day'. Only the first of the two projected volumes (A–G) was completed when he died, on 26 July 1904 at 17 Burstock Road, Putney. He was buried at Putney Vale cemetery.

LEWIS MELVILLE, *rev.* NILANJANA BANERJI

Sources *The Times* (28 July 1904) · C. J. Robinson, ed., *A register of the scholars admitted into Merchant Taylors' School, from AD 1562 to 1874*, 2 (1883) · W. D. Adams, 'Apologia pro vita mea', *The Theatre*, 4th ser., 23 (1894), 70–75 · W. D. Adams, 'Criticism in advance', *The Theatre*, 4th ser., 24 (1894), 107–11 · W. D. Adams, 'The silence of Mr Gilbert', *The Theatre*, 4th ser., 24 (1894), 286–91 · b. cert. · d. cert.
Likenesses A. Ellis, woodburytype photograph, *c.*1894, NPG · photograph, repro. in Adams, 'Apologia pro vita mea'

Adams, William Edwin [*pseuds.* Caractacus, Ironside, Uncle Toby] (1832–1906), radical and journalist, was born in humble circumstances in Cheltenham, Gloucestershire, on 11 February 1832, the son of John Adams, a tramping plasterer, and his wife, Sarah, *née* Wells. He was raised by his widowed maternal grandmother, Anne Wells, and her three unmarried daughters, all of a radical political persuasion, at 250 High Street, from which dwelling they worked as washerwomen to Cheltenham's wealthy residents. He was educated briefly and intermittently at a dame-school, a private seminary (Gardner's academy) paid for by doing laundry work, and then, towards the end of 1844, at a Wesleyan day and Sunday school in Cheltenham; he was not religious later in life. In adult years he attended evening classes of the London and Manchester branches of the Working Men's College.

Adams started work as a bookseller's errand boy, but in 1846 was apprenticed for seven years as a printer to the proprietor of the *Cheltenham Journal*. Before completing his indentures, he was chairing branch meetings of the National Charter Association, the Fraternal Democrats, and the People's Institute, a literary and debating society that he founded. Apart from the works of Thomas Paine, the greatest political influence on him was the republican internationalism of Giuseppi Mazzini, whom he long afterwards spoke of as 'the greatest teacher since Christ'. In 1851 he founded the Cheltenham Republican Association, came into close contact with the leading English disciple of Mazzini, the Chartist W. J. Linton, and raised funds to assist European refugees.

In 1854 Adams went to work as a printer on the production of Linton's *English Republic* at Brantwood, a mansion beside Lake Coniston and future home of John Ruskin. When that journal ceased in 1855, he tramped to London, where he found work on the *Illustrated London News* and became active in Chartist–radical circles and debating clubs; here he participated in discussions that formed the basis of his pamphlet *Tyrannicide: is it Justifiable?*, which appeared on 13 February 1858. A spirited defence of Felice Orsini's vain attempt to assassinate Napoleon III a month earlier, the pamphlet contributed to the hostile political climate that led to the fall of Palmerston's government on 19 February 1858. The prosecution of the publisher of the pamphlet, Edward Truelove, caused a controversy about the extent of freedom of political discussion. John Stuart Mill, one of Adams's supporters, made the affair the subject of a note in his second chapter of *On Liberty* in 1859.

Adams's talents were recognized both by the secularist Charles Bradlaugh, for whose *National Reformer* he wrote radical–republican and anti-slavery articles between 1861 and 1863 under the pseudonym Caractacus, and then by Joseph Cowen jun., the Tyneside radical, industrialist, and newspaper proprietor, who employed him as editor of the *Newcastle Weekly Chronicle* from 1864 until his retirement in 1900. Under Adams's editorship the *Weekly Chronicle* was transformed. Politically, the paper's advanced radicalism, support for trade union rights, co-operatives, 'Lib-Labism' and internationalism, exemplified by Adams's series of articles signed Ironside, earned it a reputation as the 'Pitmen's bible'. More generally, Adams succeeded in creating a family newspaper and magazine in one by including a range of special interests such as a 'literary supplement', antiquarian features, a 'ladies' column', and a very large 'children's corner' run by Adams himself as the avuncular Uncle Toby and centred on the 'Dicky Bird Society'. Adams married Elizabeth Jane Owen Smith in London on 25 May 1858; they had two sons and five daughters.

As a lifelong radical and Mazzinian internationalist who laid stress on duties rather than rights, Adams came to deplore the emergence of socialism in the 1880s. Following serious illness and a tour of the north-east USA, the experiences of which were serialized in the *Weekly Chronicle* and then published as a travelogue entitled *Our*

American Cousins (1883; repr. 1992), Adams largely abandoned politics. Instead, he used his editorial power to concentrate on a range of local cultural concerns and conservation interests. He was a founder member of the Newcastle Tree Planting Society, a campaigner for the spread of bowling greens for working men and parks for the people, a committee member and benefactor of the Newcastle Free Library (1880), and a tireless supporter of the preservation and collection of north-east folk music and literature. In June 1893, at a public ceremony in recognition of his public-spiritedness, Novocastrians presented him with a cheque for 450 guineas. Bad health forced him during the English winters to the warmer climes of Funchal, Madeira, where he wrote his *Memoirs of a Social Atom* (1903). He died at the Bella Vista Hotel, Funchal, Madeira, on 13 May 1906 and was buried there. On the first anniversary of his death a marble bust was unveiled in Newcastle Public Library by the miners' leader Thomas Burt MP.

OWEN R. ASHTON

Sources W. E. Adams, *Memoirs of a social atom*, 2 vols. (1903); repr. with introduction by J. Saville (1968) · O. R. Ashton, *W. E. Adams: chartist, radical and journalist, 1832–1906* (1991) · N. Todd, *The militant democracy: Joseph Cowen and Victorian radicalism* (1991) · M. Milne, *Newspapers of Northumberland and Durham* (1971) · *Newcastle Daily Chronicle* (15 May 1906) · *Newcastle Weekly Chronicle* (19 May 1906) · b. cert. · parish register (baptisms), Cheltenham, Gloucestershire, St Mary, 18 March 1832

Archives Bishopsgate Institute, London, Howell collection · Co-operative Union, Holyoake House, Manchester, Holyoake MSS · Harvard U., Houghton L., Linton MSS · Newcastle Central Library, Cowen MSS

Likenesses C. Neuper, marble bust, Newcastle upon Tyne Central Library · lithograph, repro. in *Winter's Magazine*, 5 (1893), 236

Wealth at death £1222 12s. 5d.: probate, 26 Oct 1906, CGPLA Eng. & Wales

Adams, William George Stewart (1874–1966), university professor and college head, was born on 8 November 1874 at Hamilton, Lanarkshire, the second son and youngest of the four children of John Adams, headmaster of St John's Grammar School, Hamilton, with Aberdonian farming ancestors, and his wife, Margaret, of Appin, daughter of John Stewart of Glasgow, cotton manufacturer. Often recalling his happy childhood in later years, Adams went to his father's school and to Glasgow University. There he won a first class in classics in 1897 and was awarded a Snell exhibition to Balliol College, Oxford, where he gained a second class in classical moderations (1898) and firsts in Greats (1900) and modern history (1901).

Adams became a tutor at Borough Road Training College, Isleworth, Middlesex (1901–2), and in 1902 went as lecturer in economics to the University of Chicago, the start of his lifelong interest in America, which he often revisited. In 1903 he became lecturer in economics and secretary of university extension at Manchester University. In his early career the two major influences upon him were Samuel Augustus Barnett and Arthur Lionel Smith, but in 1905 he became superintendent of statistics and intelligence at the Irish department of agriculture and technical instruction in Dublin under Sir Horace Plunkett, who then became the dominant influence upon him, especially with his belief in rural smallholdings; in later years Plunkett's name often featured in Adams's speeches and casual remarks. In 1908 Adams married Muriel, daughter of William Lane, a Treasury solicitor, of Stonehurst, Killiney, co. Dublin; they had one son. In 1910 Adams was appointed lecturer in political science at Oxford, and his career prospered with the rapid growth in Oxford's politics teaching under the twin influences of the Rhodes scholars and the students of Ruskin College. His post became a readership later in the year, and in 1912 he became Gladstone professor. His chair was held at All Souls, and he continued in the post until elected the college's warden in 1933.

In 1911 Adams's Irish expertise led to his joining the committee advising the cabinet on Irish finance, and both then and later he promoted a federalism that still seemed the feasible and peaceful route towards an Irish settlement. 1914 must have been a busy year for him because in that year he launched three large projects. First, he published two businesslike and severely empirical chapters—on trade and public administration—in the British volume of the six-volume *Oxford Survey of the British Empire*, edited by A. J. Herbertson and O. J. R. Howarth. Second, he comprehensively surveyed United Kingdom library services for the Carnegie United Kingdom Trust, whose publishable parts, again factual in approach and without comment, appeared in 1915 with a wealth of statistics largely designed to expose patchy regional library provision. Third, he founded and edited the *Political Quarterly*, whose eight issues before its demise in 1916 drew together practical and academic concerns in politics. It included articles by distinguished authors (Lindsay, Lewis Namier, and Arnold Toynbee), updates on current developments in government and international relations, and reviews of relevant books. Harold Laski in his inaugural lecture of 1926 still felt the need for such a journal, a need acknowledged when the new *Political Quarterly* was launched in 1931.

Adams's first two editorials sympathetically discussed Irish home rule, but his third (later published as a pamphlet) portrayed the war as 'first and foremost a struggle of freedom against militarism', with liberty as the source of peace and the unifying principle of the British empire. The war also prompted Adams's public commitment as editor to the advance of internationalism, and his editorial in May 1915 argued strongly for an all-party coalition, claiming that 'the danger of our type of constitution is the excess of party government'. In the same year Adams joined the Ministry of Munitions, and through the influence of Thomas Jones was invited in December 1916 to join Lloyd George's personal secretariat, editing the reports of the war cabinet and serving until 1918 as one of the private secretaries to Lloyd George, whose courage and decisiveness he admired. At the general election of 1918 Adams turned down the chance of a couponed seat in the House of Commons, and in 1919 he returned to Oxford.

There, with his carefully prepared and lucid lectures, he did much to establish Oxford's new degree in politics,

philosophy, and economics. He joined the royal commission on the universities of Oxford and Cambridge, and played a full part in the university's life as a member of its hebdomadal council from 1912 to 1924 and as pro-vice-chancellor in 1939–45. In 1919 he was prominent among the founders of the National Council of Social Service (now the National Council for Voluntary Organizations), and chaired it from 1920 to 1949. He was very active in the Oxford Preservation Trust, and for some years owned and ran a farm on Boars Hill which was progressive in its methods. He tried to keep alive Plunkett's spirit of co-operation, and was prominent among the founders of the National Federation of Young Farmers' Clubs, chairing it from 1928 to 1946. He was keen to encourage village halls, women's institutes, and rural crafts and industries. George Haynes, a close colleague in the National Council, recalled 'the noble head on robust shoulders, the deep melodious voice ringing across the conference hall, the firm friendly handshake for friends and strangers alike, the strong, kindly gaze both compelling and reassuring' (*Social Service Quarterly*, 136), and spoke of Adams's lifelong enthusiasm and taste for human idiosyncrasy which led him to 'discover' people wherever he went.

In 1933 Adams was elected warden of All Souls. In that role he was personally modest but showed a firm grasp of practical issues requiring decision, and encouraged groups to meet in the college to discuss public issues. Among the most important of these was the 'All Souls group', which from June 1941 brought together experts on educational matters. Adams was appointed Companion of Honour in 1936. On retiring from All Souls in 1945 Adams and his wife went to live in Donegal, where he took an active interest in Magee University College, Londonderry. His wife died in 1956 and Adams died at Fahan House, co. Donegal, on 30 January 1966.

Contemporaries often remarked upon Adams's impartiality, public spirit, optimism, and friendliness—qualities which equipped him to draw people together for shared purposes but which left posterity with a somewhat colourless image, especially as his few publications are not self-revealing. Yet Adams was widely trusted in high circles, and there is a fourfold context in which it is possible to comprehend a career now no longer feasible: the unashamed dominance of liberal-minded and rational debate within an intellectual élite with close links to Whitehall and Westminster; the vitality of a Liberal Party whose yoking of intellectuals, subordinate nationalities, and organized labour created a powerful progressive machine; the widespread belief in 'citizenship' as a set of voluntarist and rationalistic attitudes transitional between an individualist religious idealism and a secular and collectivist professionalism; and an academic world where respect was won from colleagues less through prolific publication than through displaying wisdom in informal debate. As George Haynes (who had reason to know) pointed out, Adams's 'most natural medium of communication was through the spoken word, and that is perhaps why so many persons, eminent or unknown, came to him for help and advice' (*DNB*).

BRIAN HARRISON

Sources DNB · J. Turner, *Lloyd George's secretariat* (1980) · G. Haynes, 'Dr W. G. S. Adams, CH 1874–1966', *Social Service Quarterly*, 39/4 (March–May 1966), 135–6 · J. Turner, *British politics and the Great War: coalition and conflict, 1915–1918* (1992) · E. L. Ellis, *T. J.: a life of Dr Thomas Jones* (1992) · T. Jones, *Whitehall diary*, ed. K. Middlemas, 3 vols. (1969–71)
Archives BL, corresp. with Sir William Ashley, Add. MS 42256 · BL, letters to Albert Mansbridge, Add. MSS 65257A–65258 · Bodl. Oxf., corresp. with L. G. Curtis · King's Lond., Liddell Hart C., corresp. with Sir B. H. Liddell Hart · NL Wales, corresp. with Thomas Jones
Likenesses A. Christie, portrait, 1942, All Souls Oxf. · A. Christie, portrait, 1942, National Council for Voluntary Organizations

Adams, William Grylls (1836–1915), scientist and university teacher, was born on 10 February 1836 at Lidcot, Laneast, Cornwall, the youngest son of the four sons and three daughters of Thomas Adams (1788–1859), small estate owner and farmer, and his wife, Tabitha Knill Grylls (1796–1866). The eldest son, John Couch *Adams (1819–1892), was an astronomer and the discoverer of the planet Neptune. Adams was educated at a private school in Birkenhead and then entered St John's College, Cambridge, to study mathematics in 1855, graduating twelfth wrangler in 1859. He received the ScD degree in 1889. He was a fellow of St John's College from 1865 to 1869 and it was at Cambridge that he attended the experimental science lectures of George Stokes.

In 1859 Adams was appointed vice-principal of Peterborough Training College. In the following year he moved to Marlborough College as mathematics master, where he remained until 1863 when he was appointed lecturer in natural philosophy at King's College, London, under James Clerk Maxwell. In 1865 Maxwell moved to Cambridge and Adams, who was said to be a better disciplinarian than Maxwell, replaced the latter as professor of natural philosophy, a post he held until his retirement in 1905. In 1864–5 he also taught at Highgate School. On 24 August 1869 he married Mary Dingle, daughter of Richard Dingle, a farmer, at Lewannick in Cornwall.

While at King's College Adams was in the forefront of the development of science education. Many of the students at King's would enter manufacturing or engineering. With this in mind, Adams introduced a substantial practical element into the physics course with a strong emphasis upon measurement and the application of mechanics to practical engineering situations. Eventually his practical regime was extended to all branches of physics taught there. He was also successful in improving laboratory accommodation at the college and this helped to bring in money partly via the Whitworth scholarship scheme. While in London he attended John Tyndall's lectures at the Royal Institution and he was a member of a committee intended to increase college autonomy over teaching and examining.

Adams undertook a number of educational roles outside King's College. He was an examiner in physics for the Department of Science and Art from 1879 until 1892 and for the universities of London and Cambridge. He played an active role in the formation of the Physical Society in 1874 and was its president from 1878 until 1880. In 1880 he was president of Section A of the British Association for the Advancement of Science and gave an address to the association's annual meeting outlining recent developments in physics. He was a member of its council in 1878–83. In 1884 Adams was president of the Society of Telegraph Engineers and Electricians (later to become the Institution of Electrical Engineers). He gave a presidential address in which he outlined some measurements made on the efficiency of dynamos used at an electrical exhibition at the Crystal Palace in 1882. This was a period of very rapid growth in the technology of electrical power generation and transmission and Adams was at the vanguard of this new technology.

Adams had a variety of research interests of which one was magnetism. He studied the change in resistance produced by magnetization in iron and steel (1875). He compared magnetograph curves recorded at the observatories of Kew, Stonyhurst, Lisbon, Coimbra, Vienna, and St Petersburg (1880), and examined magnetic disturbances produced simultaneously at a number of locations (1893). He studied the polarization of light (1871), and in the late 1870s developed new forms of the polariscope, an instrument for studying the polarization of light. His particular instrument was used for determining the optical axes of biaxial crystals. In addition he studied the action of light on selenium (1875, 1877) and on selenium and tellurium (1876). Adams also determined lines of flow curves and equipotential surfaces in both two- and three-dimensional objects. This was the subject of his Bakerian lecture to the Royal Society in 1875. He had been elected to a fellowship of the Royal Society in 1872 and was a member of the Kew observatory committee of the society as well as being on the board of visitors of the Royal Observatory, Greenwich. His interest in astronomy took him to Sicily in 1871 to study eclipses. He was a much travelled man and in his earlier years he had been a proficient mountaineer and a member of an alpine mountaineering club.

Adams had a great interest in lighthouse illumination and in 1885 he conducted work for Trinity House on a comparison of oil and electric lights for this purpose. In 1883 he gave a series of public lectures (the Cantor lectures) on electrical lighting. He edited two sets of volumes of the scientific papers of his brother John in 1896 and 1901. Those who knew Adams spoke of him as a very approachable colleague and teacher, and a man of great geniality. He retired from King's College, London, in 1905. A year later he went to live at Heathfield in Broadstone, Dorset, where he died on 10 April 1915. He was survived by his wife, two sons, and a daughter. GRAHAM I. BIRLEY

Sources W. G. Adams, 'Presidential address to section A', *Report of the British Association for the Advancement of Science*, 50 (1880), 447 · G. C. F. [G. C. Foster], *PRS*, 91A (1915), lxiii–lxiv · *Nature*, 95 (1915), 180 · D. S. L. Cardwell, *The organisation of science in England*, rev. edn (1972) · Venn, *Alum. Cant.* · F. J. C. Hearnshaw, *The centenary history of King's College, London, 1828–1928* (1929) · G. J. N. Gooday, 'Precision measurement and the genesis of physics teaching laboratories in Victorian Britain', PhD diss., University of Kent at Canterbury, 1989 · m. cert. · d. cert.

Archives Cornwall RO, diaries, corresp., and family papers | CUL, letters to Sir George Stokes
Wealth at death £13,224 1s. 1d.: probate, 26 Aug 1915, *CGPLA Eng. & Wales*

Adams, William Henry Davenport (1828–1891), journalist and author, was born in London on 5 May 1828, the grandson of Captain Adams RN (d. 1806), and the only son of Samuel Adams (1798–1853), born in Ashburton, Devon, an Inland Revenue officer, and his wife, Elizabeth Mary, *née* Snell. He was christened William Henry, and assumed the additional name of Davenport at the wish of his great-uncle, Major Davenport. Educated privately under George Dawson, Adams soon became a voracious reader. On 26 December 1850 he married Sarah Esther, the daughter of Timothy Morgan, a shoemaker. They had six children, two of whom died in infancy, leaving two daughters and two sons.

After some experience as a family tutor in the Isle of Wight, Adams entered his career as a journalist by editing a provincial newspaper in the Isle of Wight. As a young man he began to be known in London newspaper circles through his work for the *Literary Gazette*, the *London Journal*, and *London Society*. He also began to establish a reputation for himself as a popular science writer, a writer for boys, a translator, and a lexicographer. Among his early writings, about 140 works in total, were his guides to the Isle of Wight: *The Garden Isle* and *Guide to the Isle of Wight*. In 1870 Adams founded the Episcopalian newspaper the *Scottish Guardian*, which he edited until 1878, and subsequently he launched and edited a series of volumes called The Whitefriars Library of Wit and Humour.

Adams's best-known works, which ranged from military history to guides to Shakespeare, included *Memorable Battles in English History* (1862, 1868, and 1878), *Famous Ships of the British Navy* (1868), *The Arctic World: its Plants, Animals, and Natural Phenomena* (1876), *English Party Leaders* (2 vols., 1878), *The Merry Monarch* (1885), and *Good Queen Anne* (1886). He also brought out *A Concordance to the Plays of Shakespeare* and a single-volume annotated edition of Shakespeare's *Plays* in 1886, as well as publishing translations from the French of works by L. Figuier, J. C. F. Hoefer, A. Manguin, Jules Michelet, and B. H. Revoil. Adams supervised a new edition of Mackenzie's *National Cyclopedia*, and did a large amount of reading and writing for Messrs Black (for whom he wrote guides to Kent and Surrey), for Blackie & Son of Glasgow, and Nelson & Sons, Edinburgh, under whose auspices he wrote several books for children, many anonymously, including *The Land of the Nile* and *Venice Past and Present*. Adams died at 46 Alexandra Road, Wimbledon, on 30 December 1891, and was buried at Kensal Green cemetery, London. His eldest son, William Davenport *Adams, was the author of the *Dictionary of English Literature*.   THOMAS SECCOMBE, *rev.* JOANNE POTIER

Sources *Biograph and Review*, 2 (1879), 185–8 · *The Times* (31 Dec 1891), 10 · *Annual Register* (1891), 212 · *Daily Graphic* (2 Jan 1892) · Boase, *Mod. Eng. biog.* · m. cert. · d. cert.
Archives BL, corresp., loan 96; Add. MSS 42577, fol. 241, 44416, fol. 333 · U. Birm. L., notebooks of poems | LUL, letters to Austin Dobson

Likenesses portrait, repro. in *Daily Graphic*, 12 · portrait, repro. in *London Figaro* (6 Jan 1892), 11

Adamson, Sir (William Owen) Campbell (1922–2000), industrialist, was born on 26 June 1922 at 17 Hamilton Drive, Glasgow, the only son of John Adamson, chartered accountant, who became senior partner of Arthur Young (later Ernst and Young), a leading accountancy firm, and his wife, Elsie Glendinning. He was educated at Rugby School and Corpus Christi College, Cambridge, where he read economics, a subject much dominated at that time by the teachings of John Maynard Keynes, whose influence never left him.

Adamson had hereditary night-blindness, which meant that when he moved around at night he had to be guided. As a result he was rejected by the armed forces, in spite of strenuous efforts to join up. He had a brief wartime stint at the Royal Institute of International Affairs, but then, refusing to be an accountant like his father, went into the steel industry. He started in 1945 as a management trainee with Baldwins, in south Wales, and went on to work in the merged Richard Thomas and Bicaldwins (RTB), where his father was a director. By the age of thirty-six he was in charge of the construction and operations division of RTB's huge Spencer works at Llan-wern. Through no fault of his the new Llan-wern works was less efficient than it might have been, since it was only half the appropriate size, owing to a decision by the Macmillan government to build another half-sized work at Ravenscraig in Scotland. On 26 May 1945 Adamson married (Ada) Gilvray Allan (1921/2–1998), a sociologist, with whom he had two sons and two daughters.

Before the nationalization of steel in 1947 RTB became part of the Steel Company of Wales (SCOW), where Adamson was in charge of labour relations. He made his mark for the humanity of his management, and first came to wider notice as a flexible and sensible negotiator when he formulated an equitable settlement for the bricklayers, who had the unpleasant job at that time of repairing blast furnaces when they were still red-hot.

Adamson's distinguished record in the steel industry drew him to the attention of Harold Wilson's second Labour government, and he was invited in 1967 (the year that the steel industry was nationalized for the second time) to join the comparatively new Department of Economic Affairs as deputy under-secretary. Adamson's role was that of senior industrial adviser, in charge of co-ordinating all the other industrial advisers. This was at a time when the department was losing its struggle with the Treasury over the direction of economic policy, and after two years Adamson was glad to leave. Technically, he was still attached to SCOW, and the first chairman of the nationalized British Steel, Lord Melchett, wanted to appoint him to a senior managerial post. But Adamson wanted a holiday between leaving Whitehall and deciding on a new job. With his wife, Gilvray, he planned a safari drive across the Sahara—a long-cherished ambition. As they were about to depart, John Davies, the founder director-general of the Confederation of British Industry (CBI), following its initial four years, rang to suggest that

Adamson might be interested in the CBI job, which he was leaving. The Adamsons duly left for their holiday, and received on their return to Cairo the somewhat surprising news that Adamson had been appointed to the job.

As director-general of the CBI at a turbulent time in industrial relations and in economic affairs, Adamson rapidly became a well-known and respected national figure. He believed that industry should play a leading role in industrial affairs, in collaboration with government and trade unions, and that confrontation with the unions was a fruitless policy. On this basis he rapidly brought the fledgeling CBI to the forefront of national affairs, and influenced both the government and the unions to co-operate more closely, in collaboration with the CBI. He also tried to persuade his members of the benefits of metrification and of joining the Common Market, of which he was a keen supporter. He was one of the first British industrialists to be convinced of the need to link Britain with Europe, and his leadership was crucial in influencing Britain's largest companies to support Edward Heath's pro-European policies. Another notable achievement was to get 900 of the CBI's member firms to agree in 1971 to limit their price rises to 5 per cent. Without this, Heath's pay and prices policy would never have taken off, although it eventually failed because the trade unions were not prepared to limit their wage demands. It was, however, recognized that Adamson was no soft touch, in spite of his friendliness with the unions, and he was known both to ministers and union leaders as Campbell Adamant.

In 1974 Adamson was involved in the widely publicized 'Heath episode'. He had never been a strong supporter of Heath's Industrial Relations Act (1971). Two days before the general election of February 1974, which Heath lost, Adamson made a speech to the Industrial Relations Society at what he thought was a private meeting. Asked what the Conservatives should do with the Industrial Relations Act if they won the election, he replied: 'If I were them I would try to get close to the unions and hammer out something better' (*The Times*). This comment speedily became public, to Adamson's great embarrassment, and his view (which was in fact widely shared) had to be repudiated by the CBI. The unlikely claim was made by Heath that Adamson had cost him the election by his remarks. Adamson tendered his resignation, which was refused, partly on account of strong support from his staff, but his reputation undoubtedly suffered from this episode. He stayed at the CBI until 1976, when he was knighted.

Adamson was, however, still widely respected, and accepted several part-time board appointments. Then in 1978 he was appointed chairman of the Abbey National Building Society. Here he led a revolution. He was convinced that the building society movement needed to modernize itself, and he set about changing the status of the Abbey National from mutual ownership to a public company. There followed a long debate, both internally and in public, during which the potential problems of the Abbey National competing with established banks were much discussed. Eventually, however, Adamson obtained the unanimous approval of the board to put the proposal to the members of the society, from whom he obtained 90 per cent approval. Accordingly, in 1989 Abbey National was the first building society to become a bank. It was followed by many other building societies, and later by several mutual insurance companies. Adamson retired from the Abbey National in 1991, having seen the new company make a prosperous start.

Adamson served on the boards of several other public companies, including Renold Chains, the Imperial Group, Yule Catto, Tarmac, Revertex Chemicals, and Lazards. He was vice-chairman of the National Savings committee from 1975 to 1977, and he served on the advisory committee of the BBC and on the Design Council, as well as on the boards of many charities, among them Sane, the National Council for Voluntary Organizations, and Changing Faces. He was also a governor of Rugby School (1979–83). In 1984 he founded the Family Policy Studies Centre, of which he became chairman, and appointed Malcolm Wicks, later a Labour MP, as its first director. Adamson's first marriage was dissolved in 1984, and on 22 September 1984 he married Josephine Logan (Mimi) Lloyd-Chandler, *née* Lloyd (*b.* 1932/3), who survived him. Adamson died on 21 August 2000. A memorial service was held for him on 6 October at St Mary's Church, Battersea, where he had been a regular worshipper.

Adamson was one of the outstanding industrialists of his era. His liberal and humane instincts were evident in everything he did, while at the same time he was a bold innovator in all his public roles. This was true in the steel industry, at the CBI, and, above all, at the Abbey National. He had a strong social conscience and ethical principles, and he worked tirelessly for the public good.

AUBREY SILBERSTON

Sources *The Guardian* (23 Aug 2000) · *The Independent* (29 Aug 2000) · *Daily Telegraph* (24 Aug 2000) · *The Times* (26 Aug 2000) · *The Scotsman* (31 Aug 2000) · *WW* (2000) · b. cert. · m. certs.
Archives U. Warwick Mod. RC, corresp. and papers rel. to the CBI
Wealth at death £1,089,930—gross: probate, 9 Feb 2001, *CGPLA Eng. & Wales* · £1,070,631—net: probate, 9 Feb 2001, *CGPLA Eng. & Wales*

Adamson, Daniel (1820–1890), engineer and entrepreneur, was born on 30 April 1820 at Shildon, co. Durham. He was the thirteenth of fifteen children, seven sons and eight daughters, born to Daniel Adamson, landlord of the Grey Horse at Shildon, and his wife, Ann. It was the nearest house to the site of the Shildon locomotive works, the first railway locomotive works in the world, built by the Stockton and Darlington Railway. From this house his father operated a horse-drawn passenger coach service, the *Perseverance*, on the Stockton and Darlington Railway.

Adamson was educated at Edward Walton Quaker school, Old Shildon, and showed a strong aptitude for mathematics. On his thirteenth birthday he left school to become an apprentice to Timothy Hackworth, engineer to the Stockton and Darlington Railway, and had risen to be general manager of the Stockton engine works by about

1850, when he moved to become manager of Heaton foundry in Stockport. Soon after this he established his ironworks at Newton Moor, Dukinfield, 6 miles from Manchester, which exported boilers and much else all over the world. He also established the Newton Moor Spinning Company in 1862, and the Yorkshire Steel and Iron Works at Penistone, West Riding of Yorkshire, in 1863. These were the first works in the country to depend wholly upon the large-scale manufacture of steel according to the inventor Henry Bessemer's patent. He also set up the North Lincolnshire Iron Company at Frodingham in 1864–5. It was a pioneer contribution to the development of the Lincolnshire iron field.

Between 1852 and 1888, Adamson took out nineteen patents, all connected with engineering or metallurgy. He read papers to the Iron and Steel Institute, three of which were published. He received the Bessemer gold medal from Bessemer himself for his achievements. His reputation was such that in 1889 he was invited by the Italian government to report on the potential of the iron mines in Elba; but, above all, Adamson was the man who made the Manchester Ship Canal happen. He called the crucial public meeting at his house, The Towers, Didsbury, Manchester, on 27 January 1882, inviting the mayors of Manchester and surrounding towns, along with leaders of trade and industry, and of co-operative and labour movements. The engineering and commercial arguments were put forward. The cost was estimated at £4.5 million. Adamson became chairman of the provisional committee and on 6 August 1885 had the thrill of seeing the Canal Act passed. Optimistically, he declared that in five years the canal shares would have doubled in value and that the canal would save £1 million a year to the trade of the district. However, there was still inadequate financial backing. Adamson had hoped that through such arrangements as the Co-operative Share Distribution Company, which enabled shares to be acquired by weekly instalments, working men would provide much of the capital, but Rothschilds were brought in. It was recommended that the board be reconstituted so Adamson resigned on 10 February 1887, in favour of Lord Egerton of Tatton; he continued to support the project actively, but died before the canal was opened.

Adamson received wide recognition. He became vice-president of the Institution of Mechanical Engineers and president of the Iron and Steel Institute. He was also a member of the Institution of Civil Engineers, the Geological Society, the British Iron Trades Association, and many others. Active in public life, he was a director of the Manchester chamber of commerce, JP for Cheshire and Manchester, and chairman of Dukinfield local board; he also contested Heaton Norris for Lancashire county council as a Liberal.

Adamson was a firm disciplinarian, but generally popular with his workmen. He approved of trade unions, but as a constructive force working with management towards greater efficiency. He professed broad Anglican allegiance. He died on 13 January 1890 at The Towers, Didsbury, of an infection contracted in Italy, and was buried in the southern cemetery, Withington, Manchester, on the 16th. He left a widow, Mary, and two daughters: Alice Ann, the wife of Joseph Leigh, one-time mayor of and MP for Stockport, later knighted for his work as a director of the canal; and Lavinia, the wife of William J. Parkyn, Adamson's partner and manager of the Dukinfield works.

J. GORDON READ

Sources J. G. Read, 'Adamson, Daniel', *DBB* · 'Manchester Ship Canal bills', *Parl. papers* (1882–5) · memoir, *Institution of Mechanical Engineers: Proceedings* (1890), 161–71 · *Ashton-under-Lyne Reporter* (18 Jan 1890) · *The Engineer* (17 Jan 1890) · *Manchester Guardian* (14 Jan 1890) · *Auckland Chronicle* (29 April 1876) · *A memorial to Daniel Adamson* (1935) · B. T. Leech, *History of the Manchester Ship Canal*, 1 (1907) · D. A. Farnie, *The Manchester Ship Canal and the rise of the port of Manchester, 1894–1975* (1980) · private information (2004) · CGPLA Eng. & Wales (1890)

Archives Greater Manchester County RO, Manchester, family and business papers | Greater Manchester County RO, Manchester, Manchester Ship Canal archives · Lancs. RO, D. A. Parkyn MSS, DDX/101

Likenesses bust, Manchester Ship Canal Company, Quay West, Trafford Wharf Road, Manchester · oils, probably Man. City Gall.

Wealth at death £54,168 10s. 10d.: probate, 17 Nov 1890, CGPLA Eng. & Wales

Adamson, Henry (*bap.* 1581, *d.* 1637), poet and historian, was baptized in Perth on 11 November 1581, the son of the merchant James Adamson (*d.* after 1617), who served as dean of guild in 1600 and provost between 1609 and 1612, and Margaret Anderson, the sister of Henry Anderson who became a magistrate of Perth in 1611. The minutes of Perth town council dated March 1618 record Adamson's appointment as precentor and singing master of the Sang School; on 3 May 1620 he was appointed reader of the kirk of Perth. In 1620 he married Katherine, daughter of William and Helen Buchanan. By March 1626 he had been appointed clerk of the presbytery of Perth.

Adamson's elegy on the death of John Gall, a Perth merchant who had died of consumption, was composed as early as 1620 but remained unpublished in his lifetime. It was printed at Edinburgh as *The Muses Threnodie, or, Mirthfull mournings on the death of Master Gall … with the most remarkable antiquities of Scotland, especially at Perth* (1638). The elegy is preceded by an 'Inventarie' in rhymed octosyllables of the curiosities in the cabinet of George Ruthven, a Perth physician, which, as the preface explains, 'by a Catachrestick name, he usually calleth *Gabions*'. This is followed by several short elegies in Latin and English on the early death of Adamson himself; one of these was written by Thomas Crawford, headmaster of Edinburgh high school. The main elegy takes the form of a dialogue between Gall and his friend and mourner Ruthven, who was about ninety-two years old when the poem was published. The poem is divided into nine parts, or 'muses'; besides elegizing Gall, Adamson chronicles the history of the city of Perth and its neighbourhood, and includes a fanciful account of the arrival of the Romans.

Adamson sent a manuscript copy of *The Muses Threnodie* to William Drummond of Hawthornden; in a letter from Edinburgh dated 12 July 1637, Drummond urged him to publish. However, Adamson had died earlier the same year and publication was eventually undertaken by his brother, John *Adamson (1576–1651?), principal of the University of Edinburgh. Drummond's letter is printed in *The Muses Threnodie* in the form of a preface. The book was dedicated 'To his native Town of Perth: the Lord Provost, Baillies, and Counsel thereof, his worthie patrons'; the minutes of Perth town council dated 12 February 1638 record an order for the production of thirty copies.

KATHARINE A. CRAIK

Sources D. C. Smith, *The historians of Perth and other local and topographical writers, up to the end of the nineteenth century* (1906) · parish register, Perth, A. K. Bell Library, Perth [baptism] · minutes of Perth town council, A. K. Bell Library, Perth · T. H. Marshall, *The history of Perth, from the earliest period to the present time* (1849) · Anderson, *Scot. nat.* · A. Campbell, *An introduction to the history of poetry in Scotland*, 2 pts in 1 (1798–9) · H. Adamson, *The muses threnodie, or, Mirthful mournings on the death of Mr Gall*, ed. J. Cant (1774)

Wealth at death see will, NA Scot.

Adamson [née Johnston], **Janet Laurel** (1882–1962), labour movement activist and politician, was born at Kilmarnock on 9 May 1882, one of the six children of Thomas Johnston, a railway porter, and Elizabeth, née Denton. Her father died young and her mother had to become a dressmaker to support the family. As Jennie, as Janet was known, recalled many years later in parliament, 'my mother was left a widow with six young children and the impressions left on me by my young life have never been removed by the passage of time' (*Hansard 5C*, 17 June 1942, 1578). She attended secondary school, but also had to take up dressmaking to help her mother; however, she also managed to gain some employment as a schoolteacher. In 1902 she married William Murdoch Adamson (1881–1945), a pattern maker and trade union activist; they had two daughters and two sons.

In 1908 Jennie Adamson joined the Labour Party, and in 1912 the Workers' Union, in which her husband was already achieving prominence. His union duties required them to move from Scotland, initially to Manchester, where Jennie Adamson became involved in the women's suffrage movement, but more conspicuously in trade union activity, especially during the Black Country strike of 1913. In 1915 her husband was moved to Belfast, where Jennie Adamson continued her trade union work. In 1921 they moved to Lincoln, following William's appointment as head of the Workers' Union's east midland division. There Jennie immediately became involved with the Lincoln co-operative society, and from 1922 to 1925 she was a poor-law guardian, working especially for child welfare. She created a stir with her Boots for Bairns campaign, which she launched with a procession of the unemployed together with their barefoot children, headed by a booted elephant borrowed from a local circus, marching uphill to the workhouse.

In 1923 William Adamson was elected Labour member of parliament for Cannock Chase, and the family moved to London, where Jennie Adamson found increased scope for her political activity. She was on the women's national strike committee supporting the general strike, and in 1927 she was elected to the London Labour Party's executive committee. In 1928 she became chairman of the Standing Joint Committee of Industrial Women's Organisations; in 1929 she was also chairman of the Labour Women's National Conference, as well as the London Labour women's national advisory committee. From 1928 to 1931 she was on the London county council; from 1927 to 1947 she was on the Labour Party's national executive committee, and was party chairman in 1935–6. She chaired women's international conferences in Vienna and Paris in 1931 and 1933 respectively, as well as representing British women at socialist conferences in Belgium, Czechoslovakia, Germany, and Switzerland.

In 1933 Jennie Adamson was selected to contest the parliamentary constituency of Stockport; however, in the general election of 1935 she stood for Dartford, but was unsuccessful. In 1938 the Conservative member for Dartford died, and at the ensuing by-election in November 1938 she was returned with a majority of 4238; her vociferous opposition to the recently concluded Munich agreement seems to have played a part in her victory. She and her husband were then the only married couple each with seats in the House of Commons. Opposing the Military Training Bill on 8 May 1939, she asked 'When we have got conscription what is the difference between Fascism and democracy?' (*Hansard 5C*, 8 May 1939, 104). Soon after the outbreak of war in 1939 she became active in the parliamentary campaign for equal compensation for war injuries (originally women's compensation was set at a lower rate than that for men, and excluded women not in employment), which was eventually successful in 1943. She emphasized that she was not an 'extreme feminist'. In parliament on 20 March 1941 she expressed impatience with feminists who said that in preference to unequal compensation for war injury they would prefer to have no compensation at all (*Hansard 5C*, 20 March 1941, 395). Still, she supported many feminist causes, notably the campaign for family allowances to be paid to the mother; however, she was restrained from being too vocal in this respect by the fact that from 1941 she was additional parliamentary private secretary to Sir Walter Womersley, the minister for pensions and national insurance. None the less in June 1943 she did introduce a Commons motion to provide for proxy marriage for pregnant girls. She remained with the ministry as parliamentary secretary until 1946, with special responsibility for war orphans. In the general election of 1945 she was returned as Labour and Co-operative MP for Bexley; however, she applied for the Chiltern Hundreds in 1946.

By this time Jennie Adamson had undergone a double bereavement. In 1944 her younger son had died on active service with the Royal Air Force, and her husband had died in October 1945. After leaving the House of Commons she became deputy chairman of the National Assistance Board, a post that she held until 1953, when she retired. She died of pneumonia at 18 Blyth Road, Bromley, on 25 April 1962, and was survived by her elder son and both daughters. She was cremated at Honor Oak crematorium, south-east London.

DAVID DOUGHAN

Sources *DLB*, vol. 5 · O. Banks, *The biographical dictionary of British feminists*, 2 (1990) · *WWW*, 1971–80 · *Daily Herald* (5 Dec 1936) · *Stockport Express* (21 Dec 1933) · *Dartford Chronicle and Kentish Times* (4 Nov 1938) · *Dartford Chronicle and Kentish Times* (11 Nov 1938) · *Labour party conference report* (1962) · *CGPLA Eng. & Wales* (1962) · b. cert. · d. cert. · *Dartford Chronicle and Kentish Times* (11 Nov 1938), p. 5
Likenesses portrait, repro. in *Dartford Chronicle and Kentish Times* (4 Nov 1938), 5, 11 · portrait, repro. in *Dartford Chronicle and Kentish Times* (11 Nov 1938), 5 · portrait, repro. in *Stockport Express*, 12 · portrait, repro. in *Daily Herald* (20 July 1936), 15
Wealth at death £7023 14s. 0d.: probate, 14 Sept 1962, *CGPLA Eng. & Wales*

Adamson, John (1576–1651?), university principal and writer, was the son of James Adamson (*d.* after 1617), provost of Perth. His younger brother was Henry *Adamson, poet and historian. He graduated MA from the University of Edinburgh on 30 July 1597. The following year he was made regent of philosophy at Edinburgh after a public disputation to succeed George Robertson. He retained this post until his presentation by Sir John Home on 19 April 1604 to the ministry of North Berwick in Haddington presbytery.

On 2 May 1606 Adamson was contracted to marry Marion (*d.* 1651), daughter of Thomas Auchmoutie, burgess and merchant of Edinburgh, the marriage being registered in Edinburgh on 2 July 1606. Two children, David and Marie, were baptized in Edinburgh in 1608 and 1611 respectively. On 20 March 1609 Adamson was admitted to Liberton in Edinburgh presbytery, following presentation by James VI. This move was the result of Adamson being 'injuriously used' (Craufurd, 97) by Home, who had apparently hit the minister on the sabbath and was keen to avoid an inquiry into the matter. In 1616 Adamson was a member of the Aberdeen Assembly, to which he and John Hall presented a confession of faith. Hall, Patrick Galloway, and Adamson were then named to a committee to draw up a form of liturgy and a catechism for the church. In 1617 Adamson presided over the public disputation at Stirling Castle before James VI to commemorate his return to Scotland. Subsequently, he collected and arranged the poems and verses delivered on this occasion, including his own, which he published in 1618 under the title *The Muses Welcome to the High and Mighty Prince James*. He probably collected the Latin poems of Andrew Melville, which were published in 1620 under the title *Viri clarissimi A. Melvini mvsae*.

On 21 November 1623 Adamson succeeded Robert Boyd as principal of Edinburgh University, apparently with the express approval of Archbishop John Spottiswoode. That year he also published *The Ark*. In 1629 he was given charge of the son of the earl of Angus in order to assist in his religious education. He was ordered by the Scottish privy council to examine several Latin grammars in the early 1630s, and in June 1633 was instrumental in preparing the pageant and speeches which celebrated Charles I's entry into Edinburgh. In 1637 he published *Dioptra gloriae divinae* and a Latin catechism for students, *Eloquiorum Dei, sive methodus religionis Christianae catechetica*. He preached in February the following year in favour of 'the renewing of the old covenant' (*Letters and Journals of Robert Baillie*, 1.52),

and called it 'papal, antichristian, tyrannical to any bishops to do anything in God's matters without consent of the whole church' (Johnston, 306). In the 1640s Adamson regularly represented Edinburgh University at general assemblies of the kirk, at meetings of the commissions appointed by general assemblies, and at meetings of the commissioners from the universities. He may have been sympathetic to the engagement in 1648. His date of death is unknown; he was alive in May 1651, but probably died later in the year. However, his successor as principal was not chosen until January 1653.

STUART HANDLEY

Sources *Fasti Scot.*, new edn, 1.170, 380; 7.381; 8.32 · T. Craufurd, *History of the University of Edinburgh from 1580 to 1646* (1808) · A. Dalzel, *History of the University of Edinburgh from its foundation*, 2 vols. (1862) · A. Grant, *The story of the University of Edinburgh during its first three hundred years*, 2 vols. (1884) · T. Corser, *Collectanea Anglo-poetica, or, A ... catalogue of a ... collection of early English poetry*, 1, Chetham Society, 52 (1860), 12–15 · D. Calderwood, *The history of the Kirk of Scotland*, ed. T. Thomson and D. Laing, 8 vols., Wodrow Society, 7 (1842–9) · *The letters and journals of Robert Baillie*, ed. D. Laing, 3 vols., Bannatyne Club, 73 (1841–2) · *Diary of Sir Archibald Johnston of Wariston*, 1, ed. G. M. Paul, Scottish History Society, 61 (1911), 301, 306 · T. M'Crie, *The life of Andrew Melville*, 2 (1819), 456, 511 · H. Paton, ed., *The register of marriages for the parish of Edinburgh, 1595–1700*, Scottish RS, old ser., 27 (1905), 5 · *Reg. PCS*, 2nd ser., vols. 3–4 · T. Murray, *The life of Samuel Rutherford* (1828), 344–5 · W. Makey, *The church of the covenant, 1637–1651* (1979)

Adamson, John (1787–1855), antiquary and Portuguese scholar, the last surviving son of Lieutenant Cuthbert Adamson RN and his second wife, Mary Huthwaite, was born on 13 September 1787 at his father's house in Gateshead. After education at the Royal Grammar School, Newcastle upon Tyne, he entered, in 1803, the counting-house of his elder brother Blythman, a merchant in Lisbon. The anticipation of the French invasion of 1807 caused him to leave that country, but he was already full of the devotion to Portugal which was to shape his literary career. While at Lisbon he studied the language and collected a few books, among them being the tragedy of *Dona Ignez de Castro* by Nicola Luiz, which was translated and printed by Adamson in 1808 as his first attempt in authorship. On his return to Britain he became articled to Thomas Davidson, a Newcastle solicitor and clerk of the peace for Northumberland, to whom he later dedicated his *Memoirs ... of Camoens* (1820). In 1810 Adamson printed a small collection of sonnets, chiefly translations from the minor works of Luis de Camoëns. The following year he was appointed under-sheriff of Newcastle, and he retained the office until the passing of the Municipal Corporation Act in 1835. He became a member of the Newcastle Literary and Philosophical Society about this time, and was one of its secretaries from 1825 until his death. On 3 December 1812 he married his cousin Elizabeth Huthwaite, with whom he had four sons and three daughters. He was one of the founders of the Newcastle Antiquarian Society in 1813, and was appointed co-secretary with the Revd John Hodgson. He was responsible for production three years later of a printed catalogue of the society's library, which was followed by supplements.

Newcastle during the early part of the nineteenth century numbered many notable antiquaries and book collectors among its inhabitants. With John Fenwick, J. Trotter Brockett, and the Revd J. Hodgson, Adamson was one of the chief founders of the Newcastle Typographical Society, which was to consist of only thirty members. The books published by this body were well and uniformly printed in crown octavo, illustrated with vignettes of the arms and devices of the respective editors, cut in wood by Thomas Bewick and his pupils. Editions were usually limited, and in most instances were for private circulation only. The first in the series was *Cheviot: a Poetical Fragment*, edited in 1817 by Adamson, under whose supervision ten other volumes of verse were issued between then and 1831. His own publications, with the exception of the *Memoirs ... of Camoens*, published by Longman, were also published by the society. They all exhibit his device by Bewick on the title-page, overshadowed by a ruined Gothic church within trees.

In 1820 Adamson's *Memoirs of the Life and Writings of Luis de Camoens* was published: it established his name as a scholar of Portuguese and, as an exhaustive account of its subject, still remains of some value. It was well received, being warmly praised by Robert Southey in the *Quarterly Review* in April 1822. The two volumes included a life of the poet, notices concerning the *rimas* or smaller poems, a translation of an essay by Dom Joze Maria de Souza, an account of the translations and translators of the *Lusiad*, a critique of the editions of Camoëns, and reviews of his commentators and apologists.

Portuguese literature was not, however, Adamson's sole pursuit. Attentive to his professional duties, he also interested himself in local affairs, and served as secretary to the Newcastle and Carlisle Railway Company. He was also a skilled numismatist, and devoted much attention to conchology. His *Conchological Tables* (1823) were a useful guide for amateurs; his private cabinet comprehended 3000 different species, and he had two dedicated to him— *Conus adamsonii* and *Porphyrobaphe adamsonii*. He also collected fossils and minerals; the former remain in the Hancock Museum, University of Newcastle upon Tyne, while the latter were given to the University of Durham, their present whereabouts being unknown. In 1836 he printed a catalogue of his Portuguese library under the name of *Bibliotheca Lusitana*. It was a remarkable collection, brought together by the labour of twenty-five years and at great expense. Unfortunately, a large part of the library was destroyed by a fire on 16 April 1849.

Adamson's love for the sonnet form prompted him to bring out, in 1842, the first part of a collection entitled *Lusitania illustrata*, consisting of rather austere translations from Portuguese sonneteers with biographical notices. It was followed, in 1846, by a second part devoted to ballads, which was dedicated to Almeida Garrett, the distinguished Portuguese writer. Adamson was in regular correspondence with Garrett, who was particularly interested in the collection and study of ballads as popularized by Sir Walter Scott. In 1845 Adamson printed another small volume of original and translated sonnets.

As a reward for his services in publicizing the literature of her country in Britain, the queen of Portugal conferred upon Adamson the knighthoods of Christ and of the Tower and Sword in 1841. He was also diligent in bringing English literature to the attention of the Portuguese. He was a fellow of the Society of Antiquaries of London, and a member of many British and continental philosophical and antiquarian bodies. His last work, which appeared in 1853, was an edition of the first five cantos of the *Lusiad*, translated by his deceased friend Edward Quillinan. In spite of failing health Adamson continued working to within three days of his death, which took place in Newcastle on 27 September 1855. He was buried on 29 or 30 September at Jesmond cemetery, Newcastle.

H. R. TEDDER, rev. C. M. FRASER

Sources G. Pallister, *John Adamson, 1787–1855: an eminent Novocastrian* (1982) · R. Welford, *Men of mark 'twixt Tyne and Tweed*, 1 (1895), 11–15 · C. E. Adamson, 'John Adamson', *Archaeologia Aeliana*, 3rd ser., 10 (1913), 110–12 · L. N. Rodrigues Correia Raitt, *Garrett and the English muse* (1983), 9–10 · P. Davis and C. Brewer, eds., *A catalogue of natural science collections in north-east England* (1986), 8, 168
Archives Bodl. Oxf., letters to Mark Noble · Bodl. Oxf., letters to Sir Thomas Phillipps · U. Newcastle, Robinson L., letters to Sir Walter Trevelyan
Likenesses lithograph, repro. in Adamson, 'John Adamson', 110–11

Adamson, Sir John Ernest (1867–1950), educationist, was born at Westgate Common, Wakefield, Yorkshire, on 11 January 1867, the son of Tom Adamson, engine fitter, and his wife, Eliza Stokoe. He attended St Michael's elementary school, Wakefield, and went on to St Mark's College, Chelsea (1889–91), where he trained as a teacher. He was subsequently appointed to the staff of the St Mark's College Training School. In 1891 he became a tutor and lecturer in the theory and method of teaching at South Wales Training College, Carmarthen, while studying for a BA at London University, which he obtained in 1894. He subsequently gained an MA in philosophy (1901). On 23 April 1897 he married Gwendolyn Mary (b. 1872/3), daughter of John Howell Thomas, of Starling Park, Carmarthen.

In 1902 Adamson moved to South Africa where he was to play a major role in the shaping of educational policy in the reconstruction era. On the recommendation of Sir Michael Sadler he was appointed principal of the new Normal College in Pretoria which was to provide teachers for the new Transvaal Colony, and in 1905 he became director of education for Transvaal, a post which he occupied with distinction until 1924. He first worked under Viscount Milner's military regime with Patrick Duncan as minister of education. He very effectively brokered an agreement which brought the Christian national schools of the post-war era into the ambit of state education.

When the Transvaal achieved responsible government in 1907, Adamson worked closely with the new minister of education, J. C. Smuts, to lay the foundations of a new education system which found expression in the Transvaal Education Act of 1907. The new system was designed to promote reconciliation and to balance the rights and demands of the Dutch and English sections of the population in the highly volatile political context of the time.

The fact that he learned Dutch and Afrikaans and showed great sympathy with the cause of his former enemies was of great assistance in these delicate negotiations.

Adamson's role in the development of educational policy in Transvaal can be seen in the context of the growth of a new form of educational administration that sought to link schooling with a systematic approach to social reconstruction. His outstanding achievements were the introduction in 1916 of compulsory schooling for all white children between the ages of seven and fifteen and the successful accommodation of both sections of the white population to the new state educational system with his sympathetic treatment of language and religious issues. His annual reports as director of education from 1906, and the reports of the council of education (an advisory body on educational policy chaired by Adamson from 1913) provide invaluable sources for the study of education in Transvaal from the end of the Second South African War to the early years of union. After 1910 he served under three successive administrators of Transvaal: Johan Rissik (1910–15), A. G. Robertson (1915–24), and J. H. Hofmeyr (1924–9), retiring from his post after the defeat of the South African Party in 1924.

As director for nineteen years Adamson was active in all fields of educational policy development—provision, governance, legislation, finances, curriculum development (especially post-1916), medium of instruction and language issues, inspection and supervision, teacher training, teaching methods, teachers' conditions of service, non-sectarian religious teaching, and high-school selection. He paid a great deal of attention to the issue of equal educational provision for all white inhabitants of the province, with special attention to the demand for adequate schooling in the countryside and the provision of appropriate vocational education. With hindsight he can perhaps be criticized for showing too little concern for the education of the indigenous people where he advocated a policy of 'proceeding cautiously', despite the lively debate that surrounded this issue at the time. Yet he was to note in 1920 that 'neither from the missionary side nor from the side of the Government is responsibility towards native education recognised and accepted as it should be'.

Adamson's major academic work was *The Individual and the Environment: some Aspects of the Theory of Education as Adjustment* (1921) for which he received a DLitt from London University in 1920. It represents a rather dense summary of contemporary British educational philosophy focused around the notion of education as an 'adjustment' to 'the world of nature', 'the world of civilization', and 'the world of morality'. Perhaps the most striking aspect of the work to the modern reader is its extremely abstract and general nature and the absence of any significant reference to his South African experience in nearly 400 pages of text, perhaps reflecting the gulf between the formal study of philosophy of education at that time and the everyday world of policy development and educational practice in colonial South Africa. Other writings include *The Theory of Education in Plato's 'Republic'* (1903), The

Teacher's Logic (1904), *Externals and Essentials* (a collection of essays, 1933), 'Education for a brave new world' (1941 unpublished), a book of poetry, *Songs of the South* (1915), and numerous articles and presentations on educational topics.

Adamson was appointed CMG in 1923 for his exceptional service, and was knighted in 1924. He was a member of the councils of the University of the Cape of Good Hope (1906–17) and the University of South Africa (1918–24), and was vice-chancellor of the latter from 1922 to 1926. Following his retirement as director of education for Transvaal, he was principal and professor of education at Rhodes University College (1924–30).

In 1935, while Sir Percy Nunn was on leave of absence, Adamson undertook most of his teaching duties at the London Institute of Education for six months. During the latter part of his career he also chaired a South African union government committee of inquiry into subsidies to universities, university colleges, and technical colleges (its report was published in 1933) and another into the position of languages in the South African education system (it reported in 1941). Much of our knowledge of his life comes from the biography by G. P. van Rooyen in the form of a PhD dissertation (University of Potchefstroom, 1951) which emphasizes his role as a pioneer educational planner and a friend of the Afrikaner. Adamson, who was a talented musician and an ardent golfer until his eightieth year, died on 25 April 1950 at Muizenberg, near Cape Town, South Africa. His wife predeceased him; they had no children.

PETER KALLAWAY

Sources First report of the (Transvaal) council of education, 1913, Archives of the Transvaal, TP 7 · Second report of the (Transvaal) council of education, 1914, Archives of the Transvaal, TP 4 · G. P. van Rooyen, 'Sir John E. Adamson', PhD diss., University of Potchefstroom, 1951 · E. G. Macherbe, *Education in South Africa* (1925), vol. 1 · A. K. Bot, *Honderd jaar onderwys in Transvaal* (Pretoria, 1936) · J. C. Coetzee, *Onderwys in Transvaal, 1838–1937* (1941) · Reports of the director of education, 1906–24, Archives of the Transvaal · *DNB* · b. cert. · m. cert.

Archives National Archives of South Africa, Pretoria, Transvaal archives depot | FILM BFI NFTVA, current affairs footage

Adamson, Joy [*née* Friederike Viktoria Gessner] (1910–1980), conservationist and artist, was born on 20 January 1910 in Troppau, Silesia, the second of the three children of Viktor Gessner (d. 1933/4), civil servant, and his wife, Traute Greipel (1888?–1973). Her mother's family was well off, owning lands and paper factories. After her parents were divorced in 1922 she was brought up by her maternal grandmother in Vienna. She attended a boarding-school for four years and then took a variety of courses, mainly in art and music. At twenty, volatile and troubled, she eloped with the son of a wealthy banker; the affair ended in 1932 leaving her with serious psychological damage, which was not alleviated by periods of psychoanalysis. On 17 January 1944, after two short-lived marriages, between which she emigrated to Kenya, she took as her third husband George Adamson (1906–1989), assistant warden with the Kenya game department.

Joy Adamson's first major undertaking, begun about 1937, was a pioneering project painting east African plants. After initial instruction from her second husband, Peter Bally (b. 1895), a botanist at the Coryndon Museum, Nairobi, she completed a classic series of about 500 scientifically accurate colour paintings, many exceptional for their freshness and vigour. The Royal Horticultural Society in London recognized the outstanding quality of the work, awarding her their Grenfell gold medal in 1947. While accompanying George Adamson on his safaris she became impressed with the urgency of recording the rapidly vanishing rituals and regalia of the peoples of Kenya. Starting in 1948, and always under-funded, although supported for a time by a government commission, she painted about 580 watercolour portraits. Authentic and admirably representative of Kenya's native peoples, these constitute a veritable 'Bayeux tapestry', capturing the 'arresting and lasting images' of ways of life now gone (House, 182). Many are housed in the National Museums of Kenya, Nairobi; some are reproduced in her book *The Peoples of Kenya* (1967).

Joy Adamson became famous, however, as the author of the best-selling trilogy *Born Free*, *Living Free*, and *Forever Free* (1960–62), the wonderful story of Elsa the lioness, further popularized in Columbia Film Studio's box-office success, *Born Free* (1966). Beginning in 1956 George and Joy Adamson reared the cub Elsa until she reached maturity, successfully released her to the wild, and retained her affection and trust even after she had mated and borne cubs—a unique achievement for the time. Although not scientific in the formal sense, the Adamsons' work was a significant contribution to animal psychology, demonstrating that lions are capable of a far wider range of behaviour than previously assumed. From the broader perspective, *Born Free* (books and film) brought a new public awareness of African wildlife and was one of the factors in the rise of the conservation movement. Royalties (£250,000 by the mid-1960s) and funds raised by Joy Adamson's worldwide promotional tours were largely funnelled into the Elsa Conservation Trust, which concentrates especially on conservation in Kenya. In 1977 Joy Adamson was awarded the Austrian cross of honour for science and the arts. She undertook two additional animal studies, successfully rearing and re-establishing in the wild first a cheetah and then a leopard (described in books published in 1969, 1972, and 1980).

Temperamental, restless, autocratic, and so difficult to work with that sooner or later she broke with almost all her close associates, Joy Adamson was nevertheless a vibrant, magnetic personality, handsome in her youth with blond hair and striking blue eyes. She brought energy, tenacity, courage, and vision to her many undertakings. She died at Isiolo, Kenya, on 3 January 1980, of stab wounds inflicted during an altercation with a disgruntled former employee. Her body was cremated at Nairobi crematorium and her ashes were placed on the graves of Elsa the lioness and Pippa the cheetah in Meru National Park, Kenya. MARY R. S. CREESE

Sources A. House, *The great safari: the lives of George and Joy Adamson* (1993) · G. Adamson, *My pride and Joy* (1986) · J. Adamson, *The searching spirit* (1978) · *WW* (1969–80) · B. A. Ogot, *Historical dictionary of Kenya* (1981) · G. Adamson, *Bwana game: the life story of George Adamson* (1968) · J. Adamson, *Born free* (1960) · J. Adamson, *Living free* (1961) · J. Adamson, *Forever free* (1962) · *Biographical dictionary of botanists represented in the Hunt Institute portrait collection*, Hunt Institute for Botanical Documentation (1972) · *The Times* (5 Jan 1980) · *The Times* (6 Jan 1980)

Archives Trustees of Elsa Conservation Trust, Cheltenham, papers, paintings, and photographs · Trustees of Elsa Conservation Trust, Elsamere, Naivasha, Kenya, papers, paintings, and photographs | Rice University, Houston, Texas, Woodson Research Center, corresp. with Julian Huxley

Likenesses photograph, 12 Sept 1969, Hult. Arch. · Dumont, photographs, 12 Jan 1971, Hult. Arch. · photograph, repro. in House, *The great safari*, facing p. 338 · photographs, Elsa Conservation Trust · photographs, repro. in Adamson, *The searching spirit* · photographs, repro. in Adamson, *My pride and Joy*

Adamson [Constantine], **Patrick** (1537–1592), archbishop of St Andrews, was born, probably in Perth, in March 1537. He was said to have been the son of a baker, but his grandfather Dionysius Adamson or Constantine was town clerk of Perth in the late fifteenth century, while his father, Patrick (d. 1570), the only son of Dionysius, was a merchant who served as bailie and dean of gild there. The elder Patrick Adamson and his wife, who is unknown, had three sons—Patrick, Henry, killed in Perth on 16 April 1598, and James, later provost of the burgh—and a daughter, Violet, who married Andrew Simson, master of Perth grammar school.

Early career and travels After attending Perth grammar school the younger Patrick proceeded to St Andrews University, enrolling in St Mary's College in 1554. As a determinant in 1556 he was described as 'pauper'. He graduated MA in 1558, adhered to the Reformation, and in December 1560 was considered apt by the general assembly for 'ministering and teaching' in the reformed church. In December 1562 the assembly deemed him appropriate for the ministry in Aberdeen if he were not chosen for Perth, but by 1563 he had become minister of Ceres in Fife and acted as the assembly's commissioner for establishing churches in north-east Scotland. Despite the misgivings of the assembly (which had refused him licence to leave his congregation in 1564), he left the parish ministry for France by 1566 as tutor to the eldest son of James MacGill of Nether Rankeillour, recently dismissed from the office of clerk register.

Having been imprisoned for six months in Paris for publishing a work naming James, the newly born son and heir of Mary, queen of Scots, as prince of Scotland, England, France, and Ireland, Adamson travelled to Padua and then Geneva, where he met Calvin's successor Theodore Beza, and studied law at Bourges. On returning home he was encouraged by the assembly in August 1571 to re-enter the ministry; he preached first at court in 1570 before serving at Paisley from 1572 and acting as chaplain to the regent, Morton. In March 1575 he responded to the assembly's complaint that he had not been sufficiently active as its commissioner for Galloway by indicating that he had received no stipend for visitation. In August 1575 he was identified in the assembly as a non-resident minister who wasted his patrimony. As minister to the regent's household, however, he received an annual pension on 15 June

PENSO80 · DÁV TRVI · · ATATIS ·33· AN · 1569 ·

Patrick Adamson (1537–1592), by unknown artist, 1569

without the advyse of the Generall Assemblie', proved disingenuous (Melville, 57). A royal licence to elect, with no name mentioned, had been issued on 10 March 1575, though confirmation of Adamson's election and a mandate to consecrate him were forthcoming only on 21 December 1576; he gained the temporalities on the 31st.

As his appointment coincided with the general assembly's resolution to dispense with diocesan episcopacy, Adamson found himself at odds with the assembly's plans. He was repeatedly rebuked for declining to submit to the assembly's jurisdiction, for usurping the office of visitor, for granting collation to benefices, for voting in parliament without the assembly's approval, and for failing to undertake a congregational ministry. In October 1578 the assembly threatened him with excommunication. He had been obliged by 1581 to assent to the *Second Book of Discipline* of 1578, with its presbyterian strategy, doing so over dinner in the presence of Andrew Melville, Alexander Arbuthnot, and others. At the same time he secretly encouraged the duke of Lennox, who headed James's government, to persevere in his efforts to install Robert Montgomery to the vacant archbishopric of Glasgow. In 1582 he was the intended victim of assassination by Patrick Lermonth, a son of the laird of Dairsie. In the parliament of October 1582 he associated himself with the ultra-protestant Ruthven raiders, who had seized power in August and were sympathetic to the presbyterians.

So long as the presbyterians controlled the assembly, Adamson's cause looked forlorn. But with the rise to power in 1583 of James Stewart, earl of Arran, whose hostility to the presbyterians was undisguised, Adamson returned to prominence as an apologist for episcopacy *iure divino* and for the crown's supremacy over the church. In the winter of 1583–4, on a visit to Lambeth Palace in London, he sought support for his ecclesiastical policies from John Whitgift, newly installed as archbishop of Canterbury. Ostensibly his reason for leaving Scotland was to visit the continent on grounds of ill health; but he was anxious to escape from impending excommunication by the general assembly (which had suspended him in October 1583); and he saw that an episcopally governed Scottish church would foster Anglo-Scottish friendship and prepare the way for James VI's accession to the English throne. The debate between presbyterianism and episcopacy had intensified in England as in Scotland, and Adamson hoped that a united strategy might emerge for curbing co-operation between their ecclesiastical opponents in the two kingdoms. His mission was plainly a diplomatic one. Whitgift, however, remained guarded, stressing that nothing could be achieved without the English government's approval, but presented him with a copy of his book against the presbyterian Thomas Cartwright. Adamson also met the archbishop of York and bishop of London, from whom he borrowed but failed to repay, and sought permission to visit Oxford and Cambridge.

Advocate of episcopacy In a series of articles submitted to Whitgift and also addressed to the churches of Geneva and Zürich, and to the French church in London (to which

1575 of £300 Scots for life or until such time as he gained a benefice. There were attempts, too, to secure for him an academic post. As minister of Paisley, Adamson chose to live in Glasgow, where he became, as 'a man of notable ingyne [ability], letters and eloquence', a 'grait frind and companion' of the university principal, Andrew Melville (Melville, 53). His candidature for academic office was actively canvassed when George Buchanan decided in 1570 to resign the principalship of St Leonard's College, St Andrews. Indeed, Buchanan himself had recommended Adamson as his successor. He had met Adamson in Paris during his residence there in the winter of 1565–6 when Adamson had contributed liminary verse to the first edition of the *Franciscanus*. Despite Buchanan's patronage and a presentation from the privy council, Adamson did not fill the principalship, presumably because he was not satisfied with the conditions attached.

Archbishop of St Andrews In 1572, as minister of Paisley, Adamson preached against John Douglas's appointment to the archbishopric of St Andrews in a discourse on three sorts of bishop: 'my lord bishop' or papal prelate, 'my lord's bishop' or court bishop, and 'the Lord's bishop' or minister of the gospel. Yet he was already the client of Morton and James MacGill, now reinstated as clerk register, and showed no reluctance to accept the archbishopric on Douglas's death, when offered it by the regent. His assurances to the general assembly in October 1576, that 'he wald receave na office judgit unlawfull be the Kirk; and as to that bischoprik, he wald na wayes accept of it

Andrew Melville responded), Adamson denounced presbyterian theories, expounding an ecclesiology which was deferential to monarchy, Erastian in outlook, episcopal in form, and conformed essentially to the Elizabethan model of church government. He began by asserting that it lay within the prince's power to appoint a form of church polity, for the prince under Christ was chief head of church and commonwealth alike: in both his judgment was sovereign. Such a theory contrasted sharply with the views of John Knox and Andrew Melville, who denied the crown's supremacy over the church. For Adamson, government of the church, under the king, ought to be committed wholly to diocesan bishops who alone had power to conduct ordinations and chair synods. Such rigid views were at variance with the reformers' flexible proposals: in particular, the exclusive right to ordain or inaugurate ministers which he attributed to bishops had never been characteristic of the activities of superintendents, and Knox himself, as a parish minister, had inaugurated his successor in St Giles's.

By reasserting the traditional right of the pre-Reformation bishops to a seat in parliament—a topic on which even the convention of Leith in 1572 had remained silent—Adamson was at a stroke reverting to a practice which negated reformed thought on the separate jurisdictions of church and state. Even so he inadvertently came close to advocating a 'two kingdoms' theory of his own, in that his claim for the scriptural and apostolic origin of episcopacy stood at odds with his suggestion that bishops were delegates of the crown: for if bishops derived their authority immediately from the apostles and through them from Christ, the king in establishing episcopacy was approving that which he could not withhold. Bishops, Adamson maintained, possessed an exclusive power of oversight and visitation, though he allowed that they might delegate authority to others. Here again his ideas introduced an inflexible and dogmatic approach quite contrary to the character of the Scottish polity, where the church, or more usually the general assembly, commissioned individuals to undertake for a spell necessary supervisory duties. Reliance on an exclusive form of episcopal oversight, even after the convention of Leith, was not a feature of the governing order of the church.

Adamson's thoughts on the assembly, as one who had refused to submit to its authority and jurisdiction, were predictably stimulating: in effect, his proposals left no room for a regularly constituted general assembly as a champion of ecclesiastical independence, which he was intent on subverting. The autonomy and representative nature of the assembly, presided over by an elected moderator, where decisions were reached by the votes of the majority, had thwarted unimpeded episcopal rule. Adamson therefore proposed to abolish the office of an elected moderator and to reduce the assembly's status by having it meet only 'upon a great and weightie occasion' (Calderwood, 4.54), under licence from the prince, and by prohibiting it from formulating enactments without the prince's approval. What he seemed intent on doing, as was made explicit in 1584, was to replace the assembly, which hitherto had represented the Christian community, with an exclusive 'conventioun generall of clergie', an 'assemblie of bishops or clerks' (ibid., 145–6), subservient to the king in parliament. His whole train of thought seemed to exclude the wider community from a place on church courts.

The participation of lairds and barons in presbyteries was condemned by Adamson as introducing 'a great confusion in the kirk, and an occasion of continuall seditioun' (Calderwood, 4.54). Even more provocative were his views on the nature of the eldership, which Knox and the first reformers had justified as an order which, 'O Lord, thou of thy mercie hes now restoired unto us agane efter that the publict face of the Kirk hes bene deformed by the tyrany of that Romane Antichrist' (Knox, 2.153). Challenging from the outset, Adamson insisted that 'seniors, or elders of the laick sort, are not agreeable with the Scriptures, nor ancient puritie of the primitive kirk' (Calderwood, 4.54). In all of this there was little which would have startled Whitgift, Bancroft, or Bilson in England, but his novel views ran counter to established practice in the kirk. Even Arran, who was prepared to prohibit presbyteries from meeting, was not persuaded to adopt Adamson's ideas on abolishing elders and instead issued a proclamation allowing kirk sessions to function as they had done in the past. Though condemning lay elders, Adamson was ready to recognize the office of doctor or teacher; but according to his own definition doctors should have no voice in governing the church, nor 'power to preache, but by the appointment of bishops' (ibid.). Here was the archbishop's reply to Andrew Melville, who, as theology professor, held the office of doctor. No less revealing were Adamson's thoughts on the church's patrimony. With a reverence for statute law and constitutional procedure, he believed that it was no business of a reformed church to claim for itself the wealth of the Roman church. Instead, he argued that the kirk should be content to accept what the laws of the land allowed; and he strongly supported patronage and the ancient system of benefices in its entirety. All this was one aspect of a many-sided conservative reaction which had set in with Arran's rise to power.

In so far as Adamson's proposals were founded on a recognition of the royal supremacy and upon an uncompromising form of episcopacy, and in so far as they rested on a repudiation of the eldership and a rejection of ecclesiastical independence and of the assembly's traditional role, his theories ran counter to the main stream of Scottish reformed thought. His object, according to James Melville, was 'to practise the alteration of the haill esteat and discipline of the Kirk' and during his English stay he 'practised with the Bischopes for Conformitie, and gaiff tham *dextra societatis*' (Melville, 141). Nor does Melville's verdict differ materially from that of another contemporary, who, displaying no apparent presbyterian bias, disclosed how:

the king directit Patrick Archebishop of Sanctandrois to Ingland, to tak sure cognitioun of the ecclesiasticall policie of that cuntrie, and to report the same to his Majestie at his return, that he mycht frayme the kirk of Scotland conforme; bot this tuik na gude succes, for albeit this Bishop was a man of rare learnyng, and of excellent doctrine in the kirk, yit his actions and proceidings in lyff and conversatioun war nawayis correspondent; and the baneist Ministers of Scotland had certefeit sum of the counsall and prelatis of Ingland heirof, sa that the man was the les regairdit in his negociatioun.   (Thomson, *James the Sext*, 205)

Return to Scotland: further controversies   When his opponents sought to discredit Adamson, spreading rumours that he favoured a restoration of Romanism, he felt obliged to expound his protestant faith in a series of sermons in which he praised King James so fulsomely that Elizabeth deemed it necessary to command him to desist and to reserve for private occasions his advocacy of James's claims to the English crown. But if his mission to England proved a failure, when Adamson returned home, by May 1584, he found his ideas vindicated when parliament overthrew presbyteries, asserted the supremacy of the crown over the church, and entrusted oversight to bishops and other royal commissioners in ecclesiastical causes. On gaining access to the registers of the general assembly he mutilated them by removing sections of the minutes inimical to bishops. He also produced a manifesto defending the legislation of 1584 in the form of *A declaration of the king's majesty's intention and meaning concerning the late acts of parliament*. Printed in 1585, it was used as ammunition by Richard Bancroft, later bishop of London and archbishop of Canterbury, in his own campaign against presbyterianism.

In the declaration Adamson explained that the first act of the legislation in 1584 on the liberty of preaching and administration of the sacraments was designed to promote the work of the reformed church by a prince who was 'a theologue and his heart replenished with the knowledge of the heavenlie philosophie'; the second act affirming the king's authority over all estates, spiritual and temporal, was not an assertion of headship, which alone was Christ's, but a recognition of the king's duty as 'the cheefe and principall member appointed by the law of God to see God glorified, vice punished and vertue mainteanned within his realme'; the third act discharging all ecclesiastical courts not authorized by the king in parliament was aimed at prohibiting presbyteries, whose proceedings tended to 'disquietnesse, seditioun and trouble', and general assemblies, which sought 'to prescrive the law to the king'; and the twentieth act approving diocesan episcopacy was consistent with ancient practice and beneficial to the king, who was 'a bishop of bishops and universall bishop within his realme'. Just as James opposed the 'popular confusioun' which stemmed from a parity among ministers, so too did he eschew lordly rule and recognize that a bishop's authority should be limited and circumscribed by a council of thirteen ministers selected from the synod (Calderwood, 4.254–67).

The presbyterians in turn produced 'An answere to the declaration', as claim and counter-claim became increasingly acrimonious. During 1584 Adamson had occupied the pulpit in Edinburgh after the flight to England of its

presbyterian ministers. From the safety of Berwick upon Tweed, James Lawson and Walter Balcanqual wrote to their parishioners in Edinburgh and to the town council and kirk session explaining their flight, to which Adamson responded by accusing them of inflaming 'the hearts of the subject against their prince'. Not only did the ministers rebut Adamson's attack, but their very literate wives, Janet Guthrie and Margaret Marjoribanks, who remained in Edinburgh, penned a lengthy and learned refutation of Adamson's 'calumnious and blasphemous answere', in which as 'two simple women' lacking 'the suggarred eloquence of Cicero or Demosthenes' they denied that their husbands were implicated in the Ruthven raid (while noting that Adamson himself had once approved it), upbraided him for introducing 'in the kirk your new devised Popedome', and argued the case for 'equalitie in jurisdictiouns and authoritie in the kirk' as 'the verie true order left by the Spirit of God for the best forme to governe his kirk and preserve it frome the tyrannical pride and ambitioun of your prelates' (Calderwood, 4.126–41).

Death, works, and assessment   With Arran's downfall at the close of 1585 and the return of the presbyterian lords and ministers from exile in England, Adamson found himself on the defensive once again. He was censured in the synod of Fife in 1586, but declined to acknowledge its jurisdiction over him. Excommunicated by the synod, he responded by excommunicating some presbyterian leaders, including Andrew and James Melville. The assembly held in May 1586, which King James VI attended, attempted to reconcile the irreconcilable by combining bishops with presbyteries, and Adamson submitted and was absolved. Further accusations against him led to his suspension from the ministry in 1587, his deposition by 1589, and his further excommunication, which was lifted with his recantation in 1591. He died in poverty on 10 February 1592, probably in St Andrews.

Adamson and his wife, Elizabeth, daughter of William Arthur of Kernis, had two sons, James and Patrick, and a daughter who married Thomas Wilson, an advocate. In 1620 Wilson published his father-in-law's collected works (most of which had been printed during his lifetime) under the title *Reverendissimi in Christo patris Patricii Adamsoni, Sancti-Andreæ in Scotia archiepiscopi dignissimi ac doctissimi, Poemata sacra, cum aliis opusculis*, and he also prepared for publication Adamson's *De sacro pastoris munere tractatus* (1619) and *Refutatio libelli de regimine ecclesiae Scoticanae* (1620). Adamson wrote another work, 'Psyllus', apparently not published, against presbyterian discipline.

A gifted scholar and elegant Latin poet, Adamson seemed happier outside his see, whose patrimony he dilapidated. His skills as a courtier outweighed those he showed as a pastor. Thus Archbishop John Spottiswoode, who notes how some of Adamson's writings were suppressed, regarded him as a man 'of great learning, and a most persuasive preacher, but an ill administrator of the Church patrimony' (Spottiswoode, 2.415). Another assessment was more critical. James Melville, while recognizing

Adamson's 'manie grait giftes' and how he 'specialie excellit in the toung and pen', considered him 'a maist dangerus enemie, wha, if he haid bein endowit bot withe a comoun civill piece of honestie in his delling and conversatioun, he haid ma meanes to haiff wrought mischeiff in a kirk or countrey nor [than] anie I haiff knawin or hard of in our yland' (Melville, 293).

JAMES KIRK

Sources D. Calderwood, *The history of the Kirk of Scotland*, ed. T. Thomson and D. Laing, 8 vols., Wodrow Society, 7 (1842–9) · J. Spottiswoode, *History of the Church of Scotland*, ed. M. Napier and M. Russell, 3 vols., Spottiswoode Society, 6 (1847–51) · *The autobiography and diary of Mr James Melvill*, ed. R. Pitcairn, Wodrow Society (1842) · T. Thomson, ed., *Acts and proceedings of the general assemblies of the Kirk of Scotland*, 3 pts, Bannatyne Club, 81 (1839–45) · *CSP Scot.*, 1547–93 · M. Livingstone, D. Hay Fleming, and others, eds., *Registrum secreti sigilli regum Scotorum / The register of the privy seal of Scotland*, 8 vols. (1908–82) · R. Bannatyne, *Memoriales of transactions in Scotland, 1569–1573*, ed. [R. Pitcairn], Bannatyne Club, 51 (1836) · D. Moysie, *Memoirs of the affairs of Scotland, 1577–1603*, ed. J. Dennistoun, Bannatyne Club, 39 (1830) · J. Knox, *History*, ed. D. Laing (1846–64) · [T. Thomson], ed., *The historie and life of King James the Sext*, Bannatyne Club, 13 (1825) · G. Donaldson, ed., *Accounts of the collectors of thirds of benefices*, Scottish History Society, 3rd ser., 42 (1949) · J. Kirk, *The Second Book of Discipline* (1980) · M. I. Stavert, *Perth guildry book, 1452–1601* (1993) · A. I. Dunlop, ed., *Acta facultatis artium universitatis Sanctiandree, 1413–1588*, 2 vols., Scottish History Society, 3rd ser., 54–5 (1964) · I. D. McFarlane, *Buchanan* (1981) · J. M. Anderson, ed., *Early records of the University of St Andrews*, Scottish History Society, 3rd ser., 8 (1926), 154, 156, 259 · T. M'Crie, *The life of Andrew Melville*, 2 vols. (1819) · *Viri clarissimi A. Melvini Musae et P. Adamsoni vita* (1620) · J. Kirk, *Patterns of reform: continuity and change in the Reformation kirk* (1989) · G. Donaldson, *Scottish church history* (1985)
Archives LPL, corresp. with Archbishop Whitgift and others
Likenesses oils, 1569, Scot. NPG [*see illus.*]

Adamson, Robert (1821–1848). *See under* Hill, David Octavius (1802–1870).

Adamson, Robert (1852–1902), philosopher, was born at Edinburgh on 19 January 1852, fifth of the six children of Robert Adamson (*d.* 1855), solicitor, and Mary Agnes Buist, daughter of Matthew Buist, factor to the earl of Haddington. His father died when Adamson was three years old, and his mother—whose own father had been ejected for heresy from the Society of Friends—was at pains to ensure her children's education and to share their studies. The boy passed from Daniel Stewart's Hospital, Edinburgh, to Edinburgh University in November 1866, and, after obtaining first prizes in metaphysics and in English literature, graduated in 1871 with first-class honours in philosophy and with a scholarship awarded to the best graduate in that subject. He spent the summer of 1871 at Heidelberg, and acted as assistant the following winter to Henry Calderwood, professor of moral philosophy at Edinburgh, and in 1872–4 to A. Campbell Fraser, professor of logic and metaphysics. During these years he read omnivorously in the Signet Library and elsewhere, and gained other postgraduate scholarships or fellowships, including the Ferguson scholarship and the Shaw fellowship, both open to graduates of any Scottish university. In 1874 he was appointed additional examiner in philosophy in the university, and joined the editorial staff of the *Encyclopaedia Britannica* (9th edn). He contributed a large number of articles on subjects of general literature, and in the third volume began a series of important philosophical articles, including those on Francis Bacon, Hume, Kant, Fichte, and Schelling, and an article on 'Logic', which, along with a book on Kant (1879) and one on Fichte (1881), expressed the idealism of his earlier thought.

In the summer of 1876 Adamson was appointed professor of philosophy and political economy at Owens College, Manchester, in succession to W. Stanley Jevons. After six years economics was established as a separate chair, but he greatly extended the philosophical teaching, especially after 1880, when the creation of the Victoria University gave him freedom to plan the work in accordance with his own views. He also gave popular lectures in Manchester, for example on 'The restoration of Germany'. On 6 September 1881 he married Margaret (*b.* 1858/9), daughter of David Duncan, a Manchester linen merchant, who survived him with two sons and four daughters, the eldest of whom, Mary (1882–1966), became labour MP for Blackburn [*see* Hamilton, Mary Agnes]. He was made an honorary LLD of Glasgow in 1883.

In 1893 Adamson was appointed professor of logic at the University of Aberdeen. He moved to Glasgow in 1895 on his election to the professorship of logic and rhetoric there. Between 1885 and 1901 he acted on six occasions as examiner for the moral science tripos at Cambridge. For five years (1887–91) he was one of the examiners in mental and moral science in the University of London. He was also the first external examiner in philosophy (1896–9) to the newly founded University of Wales.

Adamson took an active part in academic business. At Manchester he warmly supported the admission of women students to college and university on equal terms with men; he also supported the enfranchisement of women. He threw himself zealously into the movement for an independent university, and when the Victoria University was created in 1880 he took a prominent part in its organization. He acted as temporary registrar, was first secretary and afterwards chairman of the new board of studies, and gave important assistance to the institution of the university department for training elementary teachers. At Glasgow he served on the court as well as on the senatus, and took a leading part in the early stages of the movement which afterwards resulted in substituting a three-term system for the unbroken session of the Scottish universities. He was also a keen politician, and gave active support to the advanced liberal party.

After the early 1880s Adamson's publications became fewer, partly because of the pressures of teaching and university business, partly because of his active, practical nature. He was a friendly man who radiated happiness. He took up climbing and tennis and found 'time for everything—except to write' (Sorley, xliii). The gradual change in his philosophical views also made it hard for him to commit them to print. Aside from a period as a student when the works of John Stuart Mill appealed to him, he was strongly influenced throughout his career by Kant. But his project of bringing Kant's critical method into constant discourse with new knowledge supplied by science generated a continual evolution of his thought away from idealism and towards a version of realism. During his period at Owens College his approach to Kant was broadly Hegelian, but by the mid-1890s he was arguing that the antitheses and abstractions of Kant's thought were to be resolved in a unity supplied not by speculative philosophy or metaphysics but by a return to concrete experience. He held that, contrary to the subjectivist character of Kant's theory of knowledge, the reality that precedes mind's activity is not a turmoil of unconnected sensations. It has an integrity which can be rediscovered by the systematic exclusion of the divisions imposed by the mind. Mind is not, however, less essential than, or inferior to, nature; each is a partial manifestation of reality. An outline of a theory of knowledge on these lines is given in the concluding part of Adamson's posthumously published *Development of Modern Philosophy* (1903), a work which was derived by its editor, W. R. Sorley, from notes on Adamson's lectures. Two other works were also published posthumously, *The Development of Greek Philosophy* (1908) and *A Short History of Logic* (1911). But Adamson's mature thought was never worked out by him in detail, nor subjected to the same thorough criticism as idealistic philosophies received at his hands.

Both in his earlier and in his later period Adamson's own views are developed by means of a critical study of the history of thought. Following the biological analogy of 'recapitulation' he found in the history of philosophy a treatment, only more elaborate and leisurely, of the same questions as those which face the individual enquirer. In general his work is distinguished by extensive and exact learning, by keen perception of the essential points in a problem, by great power of clear and sustained reasoning, by complete impartiality, and by rigid exclusion of metaphor and the imaginative factor. More than thirty years after his death he was described as 'since Sir William Hamilton … undoubtedly the greatest philosophical scholar whom the British nation has produced' (Metz, 495). On 5 February 1902 he died of enteric fever at Glasgow; his body was cremated at the Western Necropolis. In 1904 the Adamson lecture was founded in his memory at the University of Manchester. His philosophical books, numbering about 4387 volumes, were presented to Manchester University by his wife.

W. R. SORLEY, rev. C. A. CREFFIELD

Sources W. R. Sorley, preface, in R. Adamson, *The development of modern philosophy*, ed. W. R. Sorley, 1 (1903) · H. J. Jones, *Mind*, new ser., 11 (1902) · *Manchester Guardian* (4 June 1904) · R. Metz, *A hundred years of British philosophy*, ed. J. H. Muirhead, trans. J. W. Harvey (1938) [Ger. orig., *Die philophischen Strömungen der Gegenwart in Grossbritannien* (1935)] · private information (1912) · m. cert. · *CGPLA Eng. & Wales* (1902)
Archives JRL, papers | NL Scot., letters to Alexander Campbell Fraser · NL Scot., corresp. with Haldane family
Likenesses G. Bayes, medallion, 1903–4, U. Glas.; replica, University of Manchester
Wealth at death £3323 7s. 2d.: confirmation, 10 April 1902, CCI

Adamson, Thomas (*fl.* **1680**), military writer, was the author of *England's Defence: a Treatise Concerning Invasion*, published in 1680, in which he was described as master gunner of His Majesty's Train of Artillery. His background is unknown.

England's Defence consists principally of a text by Thomas Digges submitted to the earl of Leicester before the Spanish Armada in 1588, which contributed to the debate on the most effectual method of resisting an invading force. The possibility of a French invasion prompted Adamson to publish this text, adding information regarding the strength of the British forces and the requirements for a train of field artillery, a field magazine, and the defence of a fort. He also included lists of the governors of the thirty-one garrisons in England and the lords lieutenant and high sheriffs of the coastal counties.

Adamson's preface examined the danger of a French invasion, which he feared would be supported by Roman Catholics in England, with the aim of imposing Catholicism. He advocated a spontaneous and spirited defence if an invasion occurred, and regarded passive obedience, by which it would be opposed only by special order, as treachery, promoted by the Jesuits and Catholic clergy. While insisting that his aim was to secure the government and not to stir up rebellion, he nevertheless included the potentially inflammatory comment that if the governor of any place proved to be a traitor, the people and soldiers were justified in killing him. In Adamson's opinion, 'the end of Government is to preserve the People' (Adamson, preface).

STEPHEN PORTER

Sources T. Adamson, *England's defence: a treatise concerning invasion* (1680) · *DNB*

Adamson, William [Willie] (**1863–1936**), politician and trade unionist, was born at Halbeath, near Dunfermline in Fife, on 2 April 1863, the son of James Armstrong Adamson, a coalminer, and Flora Cunningham. He attended a dame-school run by the wife of a mining engineer, and left at the age of eleven to work in the mining industry, where he was employed for the next twenty-seven years. He married, on 25 February 1887, Christine Marshall (*d.* 1935), a winder in a damask factory, with whom he had two sons and two daughters.

The 1870s were a decade of vigorous trade-union activity in the Scottish coalfields, but, with the exception of Fife, union organization proved brittle. The Fife and Kinross Miners' Association survived some difficult periods, not least because the coal owners, sensitive to the pressures of the export trade, preferred negotiation to conflict. Adamson first became active in the union as a branch delegate; he became vice-president in 1894, assistant secretary in 1902, and general secretary, the senior post, in 1908. Through amalgamation his organization became in 1917 the Fife, Kinross, and Clackmannanshire Miners' Association. Moreover from the 1890s mining trade unionism became more effective in other Scottish coalfields. The various unions came together in 1894 to form the Scottish Miners' Federation—the National Union of Scottish Mineworkers from 1914—and this body in turn affiliated to the Miners' Federation of Great Britain.

William Adamson (1863–1936), by Bassano, 1920

Adamson was in many respects typical of the leaders who dominated British and Scottish miners' conferences before 1914. He was an active Baptist, a total abstainer, an admirer of Robert Burns, and, as a young man, involved in a mutual improvement society. His acquisition of the skills appropriate for a respectable miners' official went along with a conciliatory attitude to industrial relations. Politically Adamson was initially a Liberal, but the prominence of the Fife union had led by the late 1880s to demands that the West Fife constituency have a miners' representative. The reluctance of local Liberals and the emergence of independent Labour organization led in January 1910 to a three-cornered contest with Adamson, who had been a Labour member of Dunfermline council since 1905, standing as a Labour candidate. Unsuccessful in his first attempt, he defeated the Liberal in a straight fight in December 1910 to become the first Scottish miners' Labour MP. He was helped by the relative absence of ethnic and religious divisions among Fife miners, compared with the situation in Lanarkshire.

Adamson's electoral success was founded on modest claims for the Labour Party. 'The Labour Party was the workers' own party' (*Dunfermline Press*, 3 Dec 1910), but he also emphasized that the pre-war Labour Party was not a socialist party. He was a strong supporter of Britain's involvement in the First World War (his elder son was killed in the conflict) although he was at first unhappy about military conscription and voted against the second reading of the Military Service Bill in January 1916. The involvement of key Labour figures in the Lloyd George coalition and the marginalization of critics of the government combined to elevate Adamson to the chairmanship of the Parliamentary Labour Party, in succession to Arthur Henderson, in October 1917. He retained the post until 1921 when he was replaced by J. R. Clynes. He was appointed a privy councillor in 1918. His experience as effectively party leader in the Commons was unhappy. Many felt that he lacked the necessary qualities. 'He has neither wit, fervour nor intellect; he is most decidedly not a leader, not even like Henderson, a manager of men' was Beatrice Webb's characteristically acerbic judgment (*Diaries*, 330, 14 Jan 1919). Yet the weakness of the parliamentary party after 1918 was not simply the consequence of its leader's limitations. Comprising only a small contingent of MPs, mostly trade unionists, it seemed ill-equipped to cope with the challenges of post-war politics. Adamson's style reflected the pre-war party's status as a pressure group, but with an expanded electorate and a divided Liberal Party, Labour's ambitions had been transformed.

Throughout the 1920s Adamson remained a senior figure within the Parliamentary Labour Party. He headed the Scottish Office in both the 1924 and the 1929 governments. On the second occasion, Ramsay MacDonald proposed that Adamson move to the Lords, leaving the junior minister, Tom Johnston, to answer for the Scottish Office in the Commons. The plan was abandoned when MacDonald discovered that Adamson had a son; the premier was opposed to appointing peers with heirs. Nevertheless Johnston often functioned as the effective secretary of state with Adamson as ceremonial head (Johnston, 100–102). This arrangement could give sustenance to the claim that Adamson's ministerial appointments simply reflected his place in the Labour Party hierarchy. 'There are so many considerations which have nothing to do with merit. The Labour Party has its "Dukes"—in its 18th century meaning of the term—the great trade unions have to be represented—viz Adamson!' (Beatrice Webb to Arthur Ponsonby, undated, Ponsonby papers, 671). Yet such representation in a Labour cabinet made an impact in the crisis of August 1931: Adamson voted with the minority who opposed any cut in unemployment benefit. Tom Johnston recalled Adamson's response to the proposed reduction. 'I've never voted against the poor yet, and I can't now' (*Political Diary of Hugh Dalton*, 198–9, 15 March 1936).

From this perspective Adamson's political career culminated in a principled stand. Whatever his caution and flexibility he revealed himself to be a stalwart defender of the labour interest in the face of orthodox financial pressures. Yet alongside his political seniority, Adamson's post-war trade union position became increasingly beleaguered, and this carried political consequences. During the First World War, a critical left-wing current had developed within the Fife miners' union. These radicals emphasized Adamson's responsiveness to coal owners' demands, the implications of mechanization for skilled colliers, and the lack of democracy within the union. Following the miners' defeat in the 1921 lock-out, criticism focused on the democracy issue. The culmination was a split at the end of 1922 with the formation of a separate

Reform Union among the Fife miners under Philip Hodge of the Independent Labour Party.

When a general election was called late in 1923, the Reform Union decided to run Hodge as a parliamentary candidate against Adamson in the West Fife constituency. Hodge had tried to secure the official Labour nomination, but having failed ran as a Reform candidate. In a straight fight he polled 6459 votes (over 34 per cent), an indication of many miners' disillusion with Adamson. The enmities meant that reunification of the two unions was achieved only in 1927. Several influential members of the Fife left were now in the Communist Party and that body favoured reunion. The lengthy dispute of 1926 placed a premium on solidarity, but the reunited union had to deal with the consequences of a thorough defeat. Reunification meant new elections both for posts in Fife and for the coalfield's representatives on the Scottish executive. The left made a significant advance and Adamson and his allies endeavoured by creative use of the rule book to evade the consequences. Mining unionism in Fife, and Lanarkshire, descended into chaos. The Fife county board suspended Adamson as secretary on the ground that he had broken his mandate, whereupon he resigned and set up a new union, the Fife, Clackmannan, and Kinross Miners' Union. Significantly this new body became the official Fife union within the National Union of Scottish Mineworkers and therefore within the Miners' Federation of Great Britain. The lack of constitutional procedure involved in creating the new union counted for little against a broad agreement among miners' union officials that communist growth must be blocked at all costs. The shambles was intensified as communists moved towards their sectarian 'class against class' policy, which produced yet another union, the United Mineworkers of Scotland. Yet to radicals in Fife, a separate 'red' miners' union could seem the only credible response to Adamson's contempt for union decisions.

The imbroglio damaged the veteran leader's position in West Fife. In the 1929 election the Communist candidate, Willie Gallacher, polled over 6000 votes, and two years later he increased this to nearly 7000. Gallacher's intervention effectively cost Adamson his seat in 1931: the Conservative margin of victory was under 2000. Much worse faced him when he contested the seat again in November 1935. Several villages were now communist strongholds. A twelve-week dispute at the Valleyfield colliery saw members of Adamson's union ignoring his pleas to return to work; instead his members co-operated with the 'red' United Mineworkers of Scotland. The issue intensified long-standing criticism about his industrial policy. Recently widowed and ageing, he was no match for Gallacher and the Fife communists. He was defeated by 593 votes and died soon afterwards in a nursing home near Dunfermline on 23 February 1936.

Adamson's reputation was damaged by the divisions within Fife mining unionism in the 1920s. Most accounts of him have been provided by left critics and have emphasized his autocracy and caution. In several respects he was characteristic of a generation of miners' leaders, but his world in Fife disintegrated and he faced talented opponents. A more nuanced portrait was offered by Tom Johnston:

> he was the soul of loyalty and good comradeship … caution personified with a capital P; he carried on for years a relentless warfare with the communists in his county, and his motto in that warfare as I once told him was the Covenanters' banner at Tippermuir 'Jesus and No Quarter'. (*Memories*, 101)

DAVID HOWELL

Sources W. Knox, ed., *Scottish labour leaders, 1918–39: a biographical dictionary* (1984) • W. Knox and J. Saville, 'Adamson, William', *DLB*, vol. 7 • A. Campbell, *The Scottish miners, 1874–1939*, 2 vols. (2000) • S. Macintyre, *Little Moscows: communism and working-class militancy in inter-war Britain* (1980) • T. MacDougall, ed., *Militant miners* (1981) • R. Martin, *Communism and the British trade unions, 1924–1933* (1969) • G. Pottinger, *The secretaries of state for Scotland, 1926–1976* (1979) • T. Johnston, *Memories* (1952) • G. Walker, *Thomas Johnston* (1989) • *Beatrice Webb's diaries, 1912–1924*, ed. M. I. Cole (1952) • *Dunfermline Press* (22 Jan 1910) • *Dunfermline Press* (29 Jan 1910) • *Dunfermline Press* (3 Dec 1910) • G. A. Hutt, 'Democracy in the Scottish miners' unions', *Labour Monthly* (June 1928), 348–56 • W. Allan, 'The position of the Scottish miners', *Labour Monthly* (May 1929), 278–84 • S. V. Bracher, *The Herald book of labour members* (1924) [profile] • *The political diary of Hugh Dalton, 1918–1940, 1945–1960*, ed. B. Pimlott (1986) • Ponsonby papers, Bodl. Oxf. • m. cert. • *Cowdenbeath and Lochgelly Times* (30 Nov 1910) • *Cowdenbeath and Lochgelly Times* (7 Dec 1910) • *Cowdenbeath and Lochgelly Times* (21 Nov 1923) • *Cowdenbeath and Lochgelly Times* (28 Nov 1923) • *Cowdenbeath and Lochgelly Times* (5 Dec 1923) • *Cowdenbeath and Lochgelly Times* (12 Dec 1923) • *Cowdenbeath and Lochgelly Times* (28 Sept 1931) • *Cowdenbeath and Lochgelly Times* (21 Oct 1931) • *Cowdenbeath and Lochgelly Times* (28 Oct 1931) • D. Howell, *MacDonald's party: Labour identities and crisis, 1922–1931* (2002)

Archives Methil Public Library, Methil, Fife, Proudfoot MSS • NA Scot. • NL Scot., Records of Fife Miners' Unions and Scottish Miners' Federation • NUM, Hilden Street, Leigh, Lancashire area offices, records of Miners' Federation of Great Britain • People's History Museum, Manchester, Parliamentary Labour Party records

Likenesses Bassano, photograph, 1920, NPG [*see illus.*] • T. Curr, portrait, St Andrews House, Edinburgh

Wealth at death £9805 0s. 4d.: confirmation, 29 May 1936, *CCI*

Adcock, Sir Frank Ezra (1886–1968), historian of Greece and Rome, was born on 15 April 1886 at Desford, Leicestershire, the fourth of the five children of Thomas Draper Adcock, schoolmaster, head of the Desford Industrial School, and his wife, Mary Esther Coltman. He was educated at the Wyggeston grammar school, Leicester, and as a scholar of King's College, Cambridge, where he obtained first-class honours in both parts of the classical tripos (1908–9) and won the Craven scholarship (1908), a chancellor's medal (1909), and the Craven studentship (1910). As was then the custom at the beginning of a professional career in classical studies, he attended the seminars of Wilamowitz in Berlin and Eduard Meyer in Munich from 1910 to 1911. He was elected a fellow of his college and appointed to a university lectureship in classics in 1911; his early research and first publications concerned the problems of source-criticism relating to the statesman Solon. From 1913 to 1919 he was lay dean of King's.

Adcock's service in the First World War was armchair

but distinguished: he went into the intelligence division of the Admiralty as an interpreter of codes and ciphers, and in 1917 was appointed OBE. The crucial determinant of his academic career was that as soon as the war was over J. B. Bury decided to launch the previously projected *Cambridge Ancient History*, and chose Adcock to join himself and S. A. Cook in the editorship. Volume 1 was published in 1923; from the death of Bury in 1927 Adcock was in effect chief editor of the great undertaking, of which the last volume, thanks to his energy and constancy, came out in the nick of time in 1939. In 1925 he was promoted to the chair of ancient history at Cambridge. From 1929 to 1931 he was president of the Roman Society; and already in 1929 academic honours began to accrue to him, with an honorary degree of DLitt of Durham University, followed in 1936 by fellowship of the British Academy.

In 1939 Adcock reverted to wartime duties in a branch of the Foreign Office, and stayed until 1943, when he was released to his college and his chair. From 1947 to 1948 he was president of the Classical Association. He retired from his chair in 1951, and served as vice-provost of King's from 1951 to 1955. In 1954 he was knighted, and further academic distinctions followed: the honorary degrees of LittD of Dublin and of Manchester (both in 1955) and of DLitt of Leicester (1961).

Adcock was a small round man, who lost his hair early; he had a rosy colour, twinkling, intent eyes that peered from behind strong spectacles, a Leicestershire accent, and an 'r'-lisp. Having been brought up a Methodist, he remained sympathetic and helpful to Methodism all his life. He was a very competitive golfer and a cricket enthusiast, but he had no gift for the arts, and indeed, although very clever and learned, was not an intellectual. Nevertheless, Cambridge accepted him as one of the notable personalities of his age, celebrated for his wit in conversation and in lectures. He was perhaps the last of the studied wits: his sallies were strategically prepared, and part of the fun of his famous lectures in the flat-accented, high-pitched, maiden-auntish voice was to detect the build-up of forces, feel the imminence of the punch-line, observe the dawning of the tiny smirk on the bland face, and savour the release of tension when the *bon mot* came.

The writings of Adcock apart from his contributions to the *Cambridge Ancient History* are not extensive: eight or nine good papers mostly related to the *Cambridge Ancient History* chapters, and the short books and brochures which arose from his visiting lectures—*The Roman Art of War under the Republic* (1940, the Martin classical lectures, Oberlin); *The Greek and Macedonian Art of War* (1957, the Sather classical lectures, California); and *Roman Political Ideas and Practice* (1959, the Jerome lectures, Michigan). The Raleigh lecture to the British Academy (1953) was entitled 'Greek and Macedonian kingship', the Todd memorial lecture (Sydney, 1961), 'The character of the Romans'. In addition, three independent short books were published at Cambridge: *Caesar as Man of Letters* (1956), *Thucydides and his History* (1963), and *Marcus Crassus, Millionaire* (1966). But essentially Adcock's monument is

the *Cambridge Ancient History*, and in two ways—in his vigorous and determined editorship that brought it to fruition (and as part of a scholar's monument that achievement must not be underestimated), and in his own chapters. There are ten in all, and in them he made the central periods of both Greek and Roman political history his own: the archaic age and the Thucydidean age of Athens, and the late Roman republic, with Julius Caesar and, as a summing up, the achievement of Augustus. What they contain is political history entirely (with war as an extension of policy)—a conception against which the fashion of Adcock's age was turning, but which faithfully reflected his own ideal of history. It was a Thucydidean ideal, both in being political and in being magisterial: the historian tells the reader what he thinks is fit for the reader to know. It was also a tribute to Clio as a muse, for Adcock wrote with a poise and style which never lapsed into idiosyncrasy, and had the rare gift of being able to transfer the twinkle in the eye to the printed page.

Adcock was still musing and writing about the Greek and Roman political past to the end of his life. To King's, as undergraduate and bachelor don, he had been devoted (not short of partisanship) for sixty years; and he gave a paper to the King's College Classical Society only three days before his death, which came peacefully, at King's College, on 22 February 1968. J. A. CROOK, *rev.*

Sources A. H. McDonald, *Journal of Roman Studies*, 56 (1966) [incl. bibliography] · L. P. Wilkinson, *Frank Ezra Adcock … a memoir* (privately printed, Cambridge, 1969) · N. G. L. Hammond, 'Frank Ezra Adcock, 1886–1968', *PBA*, 54 (1968), 425–34 · personal knowledge (1981) · private information (1981)

Archives Bodl. Oxf., corresp. with Society for Protection of Science and Learning

Likenesses Ramsey and Muspratt, photograph, Cambridge; repro. in Hammond, 'Frank Ezra Adcock', facing p. 425

Wealth at death £50,932: probate, 19 June 1968, *CGPLA Eng. & Wales*

Adda (*d.* **565**?). *See under* Ida (*d.* 559/60).

Addedomarus (*fl.* **35 BC**). *See under* Roman Britain, British leaders in (*act.* 55 BC–AD 84).

Addenbrooke, John (*bap.* **1681**, *d.* **1719**), physician and benefactor, was born at Kingswinford in Staffordshire, and baptized on 13 June 1681 at the parish church in West Bromwich, the only son of Samuel Addenbrooke, vicar of West Bromwich, and Matilda Porry of Wolverhampton. His was a family of small landowners in the west midlands whose motto was *Nec temere nec timide* ('Neither rashly nor timidly'). Little is known about Addenbrooke until his admission, through his family connections, to St Catharine's College, Cambridge, as a pensioner, in December 1697. He graduated BA in 1702, held scholarships of 30s. per quarter in subsequent years, and was elected a fellow in 1704. He proceeded MA in 1705 and ML in 1708.

Addenbrooke probably intended to enter the church like other members of his family, but instead was to be the first to enter medicine. His tutor was John Leng (1665–1727), later bishop of Norwich, who delivered the Boyle lectures in 1717 and 1718, entitled 'Natural obligations to believe the principles of religion and divine revelation'. It is likely that Addenbrooke was part of a group of medical students who were largely self-educated, undertaking botanical rambles, dissecting a variety of animals, watching the chemistry experiments of Richard Waller and the physiological experiments of Stephen Hales, and, probably, attending Richard Mead's ward rounds at St Thomas's Hospital, London. He taught materia medica at Cambridge from 1705 but had only seven pupils, two of whom were relatives. He was bursar of St Catharine's for one year from November 1709, lending money for the building of the new chapel, but he did not proceed to MD until 1712. His teaching was based on his own collection of drugs and chemicals, and he accumulated a considerable library on anatomy and materia medica (presented by him to St Catharine's). On 8 September 1706 he was admitted as an extra-licentiate of the Royal College of Physicians, London, allowing him to practise medicine outside a 7 mile radius.

Addenbrooke appears to have left Cambridge after Michaelmas 1711, having married Susan Fisher (d. 1720), niece of Sir William Dawes, master of St Catharine's College. Dawes had been elected in 1697 after Susan's father, Peter Fisher, rector of Bennington, resigned before he himself was admitted as master. There were no children of the marriage. Addenbrooke practised medicine in London until at least August 1716 and published in 1714 his only book, *A Short Essay upon Free Thinking*, an obscurely written defence of orthodox Anglican Christianity, equating opposition to free thinking with anti-clericalism. Ill health forced his retirement to Littlecourt, Buntingford, Hertfordshire, where he died on 7 June 1719; he was buried in the chapel at St Catharine's (his wife died a little more than six months later, in London).

A servant at Buntingford described Addenbrooke as being tall and thin and of studious bearing. He had many oddities and, at times, was supposed to be insane. He left a modest fortune after debts and legacies: £4067 2s. 1¼d. 'to hire, fit-up, purchase or erect a building fit for a small physicall hospital for poor people'—an intention only disclosed in his will (Rook and Martin, 177). The master and fellows of St Catharine's were given responsibility as trustees but the hospital was not completed until October 1766. The dilatoriness of the trustees ensured that it was not the first voluntary general hospital in the provinces: Winchester County Hospital opened in 1736, and at least a dozen opened before Addenbrooke's Hospital in Cambridge (Woodward, appx 1). In summary:

> During his short life … he made no contribution to medical science and his career as a teacher and physician was not notably successful; had he not founded the hospital at Cambridge it is unlikely that he would have found his place, modest though it is, in the history of medicine. (Rook, Carlton, and Cannon, 12)

JOHN WOODWARD

Sources A. W. Langford, 'John Addenbrooke, pensioner, fellow, lecturer and bursar of Catharine's Hall and doctor of medicine', *St Catharine's Society Magazine* (Sept 1935), 43–51 · A. W. Langford, 'John Addenbrooke, pensioner, fellow, lecturer and bursar of Catharine's Hall and doctor of medicine', *St Catharine's Society Magazine* (Sept 1936), 36–45 · A. W. Langford, 'John Addenbrooke, pensioner, fellow, lecturer and bursar of Catharine's Hall and doctor of medicine', *St Catharine's Society Magazine* (Sept 1937), 61–6 · A. Rook and L. Martin, 'John Addenbrooke, 1680–1719', *Medical History*, 26 (1982), 169–78 · A. Rook, M. Carlton, and W. G. Cannon, *The history of Addenbrooke's Hospital, Cambridge* (1991) · J. Woodward, *I do the sick no harm: a study of the British voluntary hospital system to 1875* (1974) · Venn, *Alum. Cant.*

Archives St Catharine's College, Cambridge, deposit of books · St Catharine's College, Cambridge, medicine chest (containing materia medica collection)

Wealth at death approx. £4500: will, PRO, C11/2206/5; Rook and Martin, 'John Addenbrooke'

Addenbrooke, John (1759–1827). *See under* Homfray family (*per.* 1702–1833).

Adderley, Charles Bowyer, first Baron Norton (1814–1905), politician, born at Knighton House, Leicestershire, on 2 August 1814, was the eldest son of Charles Clement Adderley (1780–1818) and his wife, Anna Maria (d. 1827), daughter of Sir Edmund Burney Cradock-Hartopp, first baronet, a descendant of Oliver Cromwell. On the death without issue of his great-uncle, Charles Bowyer Adderley of Hams Hall, Warwickshire, on 12 April 1826, Charles succeeded to the great family estates round Birmingham, elsewhere in Warwickshire, and in Staffordshire. He was subsequently taken from school at Redland near Bristol, and placed under a clerical tutor of low-church views, who deepened the evangelical convictions with which his parents had imbued him. In 1832 he became a gentleman commoner at Christ Church, Oxford, where he maintained his piety and acquired a knowledge of music and art, and a love of tobacco and horse-back riding—he rode daily until he was eighty-eight, and hunted for many years. At Christ Church he began, too, a lifelong friendship with John Robert Godley, who greatly influenced him. He took a pass degree in 1835.

From 1836 to 1841 Adderley mainly spent his time in travel, study, and the management of his estates. He sought to develop his property on enlightened principles. When he came of age in 1835 the estate at Saltley near Birmingham supported a population of 400, which grew to 27,000 in his lifetime. He planned the streets of the town in 1837 so as to avoid the possibility of slums, and hence may be called the father of town planning. In providing, endowing, and supporting places of worship in Saltley he spent £70,000. He gave Adderley Park to Birmingham; in 1847 he promoted the foundation of the Saltley Church Training College (in which he maintained a lifelong interest) and in 1852 he founded the Saltley Reformatory on the model of that at Mettray, near Tours, in France.

The family residence at Hams Hall was not far from the home of Sir Robert Peel at Drayton Manor, Tamworth. Peel urged Adderley to enter parliament and in June 1841 he was elected as a tory for Staffordshire North. He held the seat through eight elections, retiring in 1878. Adderley opposed Peel's free trade policy of 1846, although he formally abandoned protection at the general election of

Charles Bowyer Adderley, first Baron Norton (1814–1905), by William Holl (after George Richmond, c.1857)

1852. At first he took little part in debate, but wrote occasionally—on general topics in the *Morning Chronicle* in 1848 and on colonial subjects in *The Spectator* in 1854.

Colonial questions Gradually colonial questions roused Adderley's enthusiasm, and he soon gave important services to the cause of colonial development. In 1849 he was involved with his friends Godley, Edward Gibbon Wakefield, Gladstone, and George William, fourth Baron Lyttelton, in the Church of England colony of Canterbury in New Zealand. In the same year he strenuously resisted Lord Grey's proposal to transport convicts to the Cape, and elaborated his argument in a pamphlet, *Transportation not Necessary* (1851). To Adderley's advocacy the Cape colonists assigned the government's abandonment of its threat to send Irish political convicts among them, and by way of gratitude they named Adderley Street after him. Penal colonial settlements were abrogated in 1852, partly owing to Adderley's activity.

Meanwhile in 1849 Adderley helped Wakefield to found the Colonial Reform Society for promoting colonial self-government, and he became its secretary. In *The Australian Colonies Bill Discussed* (1849) he urged complete delegation of powers to the colony while throwing on it the cost of any imperial assistance. The independent constitution of New Zealand was drafted at Hams Hall in 1850 and the constitution of the other colonies followed this precedent. In *Some Reflections on the Speech of Lord John Russell on Colonial Policy* (1850) Adderley declared that principles of self-government could alone yield 'thriving colonies, heartily and inseparably and usefully attached to England'. He powerfully developed his views in *The Statement of the Present Cape Case* (1851); in his *Remarks on Mr. Godley's Speech on Self-Government for New Zealand* (1857); in his letter to Disraeli on *The Present Relation of England with her Colonies* (1861;

2nd edn 1862); and finally in his *Review of 'The colonial policy of Lord John Russell's administration,' by Earl Grey* [1853], *and of subsequent colonial history* (3 pts, 1869), a comprehensive survey of the progress of colonial freedom. At the age of ninety, in his *Imperial Fellowship of Self-Governed British Colonies* (1903), he enunciated anew his lifelong conviction that 'colonial self-administration and imperial fellowship' are 'co-ordinate elements' in 'true colonial relationship'.

Service in Conservative governments In Lord Derby's first administration of 1852 Adderley, having moved the motion on the Cape which led to the fall of Russell's government, refused the secretaryship of the Board of Control, and continued to advocate as a private member of the House of Commons social and educational as well as colonial reforms with a political independence which earned him the epithet of liberal conservative. In 1852 he introduced a reformatory schools bill, for bringing refractory children or young criminals under educational control. In 1853 he opposed with great foresight the abandonment of the Orange River sovereignty. In 1854 he was responsible for the Young Offenders Act (a part of his 'reformatory' policy), and he introduced the Manchester and Salford Education Bill, in which a local education rate was first proposed. In *Punishment is not Education* (1856) and in his *Tract on Tickets of Leave* (1857) he pushed further his plea that education might cure crime more effectively than punishment.

On the formation of Lord Derby's second ministry in February 1858 Adderley was appointed vice-president of the education committee of the privy council. His office also constituted him president of the Board of Health, and a charity commissioner. The educational situation was peculiarly interesting. On 21 June 1858 Adderley, in moving the education vote, gave the first official estimate of the cost of a national system of elementary education: he put the amount at a million pounds per annum. At the same time he pointed out that that was the first day on which the University of Oxford was conducting its middle-class examinations throughout the country, and was thereby inaugurating a new correlation of the universities to national life. Next day the first royal commission on elementary education was announced.

During his brief term of office Adderley consolidated the accumulated minutes of the council on education, prepared the way for the revised code, passed a Reformatory Act amending that of 1854, and (faithful to the principle of devolution) passed a first Local Government Act, the term 'local government' being his own invention.

In March 1859 Derby's ministry was defeated on a second reading of its Reform Bill. A dissolution followed, leaving the Conservatives in a minority. In the event Lord Palmerston became prime minister. The outbreak of war in New Zealand in 1860 moved Adderley deeply, but he advised the colonists to provide an army of their own, while urging that all parts of the empire should give mutual help in case of need. In the same year he introduced without success an education bill which aimed at making education compulsory. In Derby's third administration of 1866 Adderley became under-secretary for the colonies, and was immediately confronted by the difficult case of Governor Edward John Eyre whom he controversially defended from the attacks of John Stuart Mill and others. In the same session he carried through the House of Commons the British North America Act (1867), which created the dominion of Canada. Amid his parliamentary occupations, Adderley published *Europe Incapable of American Democracy* (1867), in which he sought to reconcile his Conservative faith with advanced ideas of social freedom and progress.

Adderley continued in office when Disraeli succeeded Derby as prime minister. He resigned with his colleagues in December 1868, and was made KCMG the next year by Gladstone, the new prime minister, who was a personal friend. 'I am glad our opponents decorate our bench,' remarked Disraeli. Adderley was made chairman of the sanitary commission which reported in 1871 and led to the passing of the Public Health Acts of 1872 and 1875. He took a prominent part in opposing Irish disestablishment.

When Disraeli returned to office in February 1874, Adderley became president of the Board of Trade, but owing to his frank independence, which the prime minister feared, he was not admitted to the cabinet. 'Single-heartedness, unfailing temper, and unwearied zeal' characterized his departmental work. The amendment of the merchant shipping law was his first official concern in the House of Commons, and he was brought into painful conflict with Samuel Plimsoll. Adderley's bill of 1875 was assailed by Plimsoll and withdrawn. In 1876 another bill which legalized a 'loadline' usually named after Plimsoll, although Adderley claimed it as his own, was introduced and passed. On 8 March 1878 Adderley retired from office with a peerage, taking the title of Baron Norton. In the same year he presided at the Cheltenham meeting of the Social Science Congress, and he was a frequent speaker in the House of Lords on education and colonial and social questions. In 1880 he refused an offer of the governorship of Bombay. In his speech in the upper house on the education code of May 1882 (reprinted as a pamphlet) he practically advocated free education and protested against the complexity of the code with its detailed system of payment by results. He sat on the reformatory and industrial schools commission (1883) and on the education commissions of 1883–4 and 1887. In 1884 he played some part in effecting a compromise between the two houses on the Liberal government's Reform Bill.

Religious views Norton had long played an active part in religious affairs. As early as 1849 he had published a devotional *Essay on Human Happiness* (rev. edn 1854). In his *Reflections on the Rev. Dr. Hook's Sermon on 'the Lord's Day'* (1856) he dwelt on the need for popular parks, gardens, and reading-rooms for Sunday recreation and religious contemplation. A strong churchman, he nevertheless advocated in 1889 a union between the Church of England and the Wesleyans, and he developed an aspiration to heal protestant schism and stay controversy in *High and Low*

Church (1892, 2nd edn 1893). His hope of reconciling apparently opposing social as well as religious forces found expression in his *Socialism* (1895), in which respect for manual labour and zeal in social service and social reform were shown to harmonize with Conservative and Christian feeling. In his *Reflections on the Course from the Goal* (1898, 2nd edn 1899) he discussed the formation of character. His religious views kept him in touch with all classes of thinkers, and neither doctrinal nor political differences affected his private friendship. With Gladstone especially he was long on cordial terms. Cobden and Bright were among his political friends, and he reckoned Archbishop Benson, Cardinal Manning, Dr Dale, and Edward King, bishop of Lincoln, among his intimate acquaintances. To the end of his life Norton wrote long letters to *The Times* on his favourite themes of social reform, education, and colonial affairs. He was not a brilliant writer or speaker, and was reckoned by political colleagues to be tenacious and outspoken to the verge of obstinacy and bluntness, but his views were enlightened, generous, and far-seeing, and they influenced the progress of public opinion. He was in addition a skilled musician and a competent art critic.

Adderley married on 28 July 1842 Julia Anne Eliza (*d*. 1887), daughter of Chandos Leigh, first Baron Leigh of Stoneleigh. There were ten children—five sons and five daughters. He was succeeded, as second Baron Norton, by his eldest son, Charles Leigh Adderley. His youngest son, James Granville *Adderley (1861–1942), became vicar of Saltley in 1904. Lady Norton died on 8 May 1887. Norton died at his home, Hams Hall, on 28 March 1905, and was buried in the family vault in Lea Marston church, Warwickshire. The Norton Memorial Hall at Saltley was erected in his memory.

J. E. G. DE MONTMORENCY, rev. H. C. G. MATTHEW

Sources W. S. Childe-Pemberton, *Life of Lord Norton* (1909) · B. Semmel, *The Governor Eyre controversy* (1962) · A. Jones, *1884: the politics of reform* (1972) · Gladstone, *Diaries* · W. P. Morrell, *British colonial policy in the age of Peel and Russell* (1930) · W. P. Morrell, *British colonial policy in the mid-Victorian age* (1969) · P. Smith, *Disraelian Conservatism and social reform* (1967) · GEC, *Peerage*

Archives Birm. CA, corresp. and papers · NRA, priv. coll., diaries and letters | BL, corresp. with W. E. Gladstone, Add. MSS 44361–44523 · BL, corresp. with Sir Robert Peel, Add. MSS 40498–44603 · Bodl. Oxf., corresp. with Benjamin Disraeli · Bodl. Oxf., letters to Sir William Harcourt · Bodl. Oxf., corresp. with Lord Kimberley · Lpool RO, letters to fourteenth earl of Derby · Lpool RO, letters to Lord Stanley · NL Ire., letters to George Monck

Likenesses W. Holl, stipple, *c*.1857 (after drawing by G. Richmond, *c*.1857), BM, NPG; repro. in J. Slater and G. Richmond, *Portraits of members of Grillion's Club* (1864), vol. 2 [*see illus.*] · J. Hood, painting, 1890 · Spy [L. Ward], cartoon, NPG; repro. in *VF* (17 Sept 1892) · H. Weigall, oils, Birmingham Museums and Art Gallery · carte-de-visite, NPG

Wealth at death £49,036 4*s*. 2*d*.: probate, 2 May 1905, CGPLA Eng. & Wales

Adderley, Humphrey (1512–1598), courtier, was born at Blake Hall, the family home, near Cheadle, Staffordshire, the fourth of seven children of Thomas Adderley (*c*.1480–1538), gentleman and landowner, and his wife, Joan, daughter of John and Elizabeth Thirkill of Smallwood,

Cheshire. The Adderley family was of considerable importance and antiquity in Staffordshire; it is through this connection that he probably became a groom of the wardrobe of the robes, and later a yeoman of the wardrobe of the robes from about 1530 to about 1570. The royal court had no permanent base and periodically moved on a circuit encompassing Whitehall, Nonsuch, Woodstock, St James's, Somerset Place, Oatlands, Richmond, Greenwich, Hampton Court, and Windsor. This was a journey of some 220 miles (excluding various progresses), and involved dedicated and meticulous planning, for which only a few people were intellectually suited. Adderley's service through the reigns of four monarchs illustrates his exceptional personal qualities which engendered long-lasting trust and discretion.

On 4 April 1562 Queen Elizabeth presented Henry, earl of Huntingdon, John Cholmeley, and Humphrey Adderley with Weddington Manor, Warwickshire, valued at £30 19s. 4d. (previously owned by Henry, duke of Suffolk), and the advowson of the rectory at Weddington. This was supplemented with Packington Heath Manor, Leicestershire, valued at £20 6s. 4d. and its capital messuage. By 1566 Adderley had become the sole owner of Weddington and its rectory and no longer held any rights at Packington. About 1566 he had Weddington Hall constructed in brick and local Attleborough sandstone. It was situated on a low ridge overlooking the River Anker flood plain and had uninterrupted views of the geologically unique and beautiful Oldbury–Hartshill Ridge until the hall's demolition in 1928. This ridge featured numerous halls and granges, notably Dugdale's Merevale Hall; the views from the ridge were immortalized in Drayton's 'Polyolbion'. Adderley's lands, which extended over 800 acres, were farmed by a mixture of arable and pasture. In addition he leased a parcel of land at nearby Higham on the Hill, Leicestershire, from the queen, who also gave him a black gown.

In 1571 Adderley married Anne North of Northampton. This union produced a daughter, Anne (bap. 20 May 1578), who married William Wightman of Wykin, Leicestershire. It is possible that his first wife died during or shortly after the birth of Anne. On 7 May 1581 he married Elizabeth, daughter of Richard Capel of Rudgwick, Sussex. They had three children, including a son, Humphrey (b. 1583), who married Jane, daughter of Thomas Ward of Nunthorpe, Yorkshire; Jane (b. 2 Feb 1589) married the local antiquarian William Burton of Lindley; the youngest child was Katherine (b. 10 Jan 1594), who married Harvey Bagot of Blithefield, Staffordshire.

On 29 July 1598 Adderley died at Weddington Hall; he was buried in the churchyard of St James's Church, Weddington. His estate was perhaps £2000 or £3000 in value as deduced from the numerous bequests in his will. His legatees included Sir John Harington, a confidant of Elizabeth. The fourteenth-century vicar's vestry at St James's contains an alabaster plaque on the north wall summarizing his status in the royal household. His descendants are the barons Norton of Norton in the Moors, Staffordshire.

ALAN F. COOK

Sources will, PRO, PROB 11/92, sig. 64 · *CPR, 1560–63* · catalogue of Norton MSS, no. 1220, 21 year lease at Higham, 1564, Birm. CL · catalogue of Norton MSS, no. 1753, schedules of 528 deeds and plans relating to the Adderley estates in Staffordshire and Warwickshire, sixteenth to nineteenth centuries, no. 1773, Birm. CL · additional printed pedigrees (undated), William Salt Library, Stafford, D538/C/26/14 · additional wills and papers, c.1638, Staffs. RO, D1721/3/227 · J. Arnold, ed., *Queen Elizabeth's wardrobe unlock'd* (1988) · J. Arnold, *Lost from her majestie's back* (1980) · *VCH Warwickshire*, vol. 4 · W. Dugdale, *The antiquities of Warwickshire illustrated*, rev. W. Thomas, 2nd edn, 2 vols. (1730) · W. Camden, *The visitation of the county of Warwick in the year 1619*, ed. J. Fetherston, Harleian Society, 12 (1877) · W. H. Rylands, ed., *The visitation of the county of Warwick … 1682 … 1683*, Harleian Society, 62 (1911) · F. W. Kittermaster, *Warwickshire arms and lineages compiled from 'The herald's visitation' and ancient manuscripts* (1866) · Burke, *Gen. GB* (1835) · Burke, *Peerage* (1840) · *Debrett's Peerage* (1840) · Walford, *County families* (1864) · G. J. Armytage and W. H. Rylands, eds., *Staffordshire pedigrees*, Harleian Society, 63 (1912), 2–3

Wealth at death approx. £2000–£3000—manor of Weddington: will, PRO, PROB 11/92, sig. 64

Adderley, James Granville (1861–1942), Church of England clergyman and Christian socialist, was born on 1 July 1861 at Hams Hall, Warwickshire, the fifth and youngest son of Charles Bowyer *Adderley, first Baron Norton (1814–1905), and his wife, Julia Anne Eliza (d. 1887), eldest daughter of Lord Leigh. He was educated at Eton College, and Christ Church, Oxford (1879–84), where in spite of a student ban on theatricals Adderley founded the Philothespian Society. Summoned before Benjamin Jowett as vice-chancellor, he persuaded the latter to lift the ban and was an original member of the Oxford University Dramatic Society. Jimmie Adderley was both a comic and a tragic actor. Throughout his life he maintained strong links with the stage, and as a priest pioneered ritualistic services, plays, and pageants.

A layman until 1887, Adderley became an 'evangelical catholic', working in poor parishes in London. From the union leader Ben Tillett, and especially through living at Oxford House Settlement, Bethnal Green, he learnt about the miseries of working-class life. As the first head (1885–6) of the settlement Adderley influenced such future bishops as Hensley Henson, his successor, and Cosmo Gordon Lang, then a presbyterian law student. Ordained in 1887 as 'a rolling stone', he became the active head of the Christ Church Mission, Poplar (1888–93), raising funds to build St Frideswide's Church and for the creation of the Central London cemetery. As elsewhere in the future, he organized light-hearted festivities, often playing the piano for his flock. Viewing the Church of England as 'a sort of tame pet' of the upper classes (Adderley, 251), he determined to identify himself with the workers, collecting £800 for the striking dockers (1889) and becoming a very popular open-air orator. He joined Stewart Headlam's controversial Church and Stage Guild (1889) and the Christian socialist Guild of St Matthew (1890).

Although disapproving of Headlam's aid to Oscar Wilde (1895), Adderley yet visited him just before his release from prison (1897). He was a prolific and militant writer of articles, pamphlets, and novels in the Christian socialist

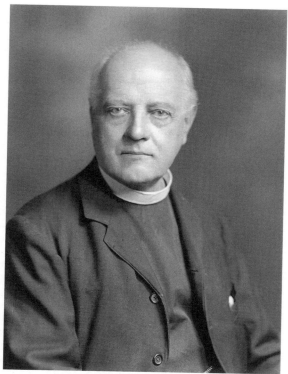

James Granville Adderley (1861–1942), by Lafayette, 1932

cause. For example, he demanded the nationalization of slum property, a living wage, the abolition of the 'caste' system of the public schools and the closed shop. He assisted the Independent Labour Party candidates Will Crooks and Keir Hardie, whom he greatly admired, in their electoral contests.

With his mentors, Charles Gore and Henry Scott Holland, Adderley helped found the Christian Social Union (1889) and obtained financial support from G. H. Davis for its influential monthly *The Commonwealth* (1896). Most of his own articles appeared in the more popular *Goodwill*, an 'insert' for parish magazines which he edited (1894–1909). In 1908 he joined the breakaway Christian Socialist League which demanded that the community should own both land and capital. The emergence of guild socialism, syndicalism, and distributism caused him to become an eclectic socialist, uncertain of some of his earlier views.

Adderley's first novel, *Stephen Remarx* (1893), was rejected by twenty publishers but had reached twelve editions by 1904. Its admirers included Gladstone, who wrote to Adderley's father about it (Adderley, 171). Imitating its hero and influenced by the example of St Francis of Assisi, of whom he wrote a biography (1900), Adderley was one of the founders of the Society of the Divine Compassion in the slums of Plaistow (1894–7). On 20 January 1894 Adderley, Henry Chappel, and Henry Hardy (Father Andrew) took their first vows. The 'communist' brothers did their own cooking and housework. Adderley slept on a plank bed. As a roaming missioner he decided he lacked a

monastic vocation and under a milder rule became the incumbent of Berkeley Chapel, Mayfair (1897–1900), where he produced a special catechism for the children of the rich. His friend Percy Dearmer was his 'curate' (ibid., 80).

As vicar of the poorer St Mark's, Marylebone (1901–4), Adderley became something of a modernist, inviting controversial lecturers to his church, a practice he continued in his subsequent livings. Among these were to be the Oxford biblical scholars S. R. Driver and William Sanday, as well as Oliver Lodge, Arthur Balfour, George Lansbury, Maude Royden, G. K. Chesterton, and the spiritualist Vale Owen. Adderley was also much influenced by Roman Catholic 'modernists', especially George Tyrrell. From 1904 to 1913 he accepted his father's livings in Birmingham—St Saviour's, Saltley, and from 1913 to 1918 the poorer St Gabriel's, Deritend, which he turned from evangelical to high Anglican Christian socialist parishes, whence he became an honorary cathedral canon (1913–18). While there he founded the Sisterhood of the Incarnation of the Eternal Son, led by Mother Gertrude. Though, as elsewhere, immersed in public activities he never neglected individuals, being particularly solicitous of the sick and the difficult.

A strong supporter of Britain's entry into the First World War, Adderley in his perceptive *In Slums and Society* (1916) lamented over his break with pacifist socialist friends such as Keir Hardie and George Lansbury. He succeeded the popular Dick Sheppard, with whom he made friends, as padre to an Australian field hospital. From 1918 to 1923, 'appointed by a Duke' (Stevens, 60) he was vicar of St Paul's, Covent Garden, where he was able to call on actors to assist him. He joined the Modern Churchman's Union, but, invited to address one of its conferences, as an Anglo-Catholic, he criticized its liberal protestant ethos and was never asked to do so again (ibid., 69). Yet he objected to Bishop Gore's episcopal edict that 'You may go as far as I do but no further' (ibid., 60). They remained friends, however, with shared socialistic political views. He kept an open mind on the ministry of women.

After a rather unhappy spell as incumbent at St Anne's, in class-conscious Highgate (1923–9) he was appointed by Ramsay MacDonald to succeed his wartime friend, G. A. Studdert Kennedy (Woodbine Willie) at St Edmund, King and Martyr, Lombard Street (1929–37). The church had no rectory and he found a house in Bethnal Green, where he had discovered his vocation. He took in poorer ordinands studying at King's College, London. Possessing adequate means and always lavish in his charities, he charged them little or nothing. In 1930 he became a member of the general committee of the SOS Society which provided shelter for the homeless. In 1935 he was made prebendary of Hoxton, in St Paul's Cathedral.

Adderley died on 1 June 1942 in the County Hospital, Bedford (in which town his sister lived). His ashes were laid in East London cemetery. His lack of resentment, his sense of humour, his genuine piety, and his sacrificial life impressed even his critics. Admitting his dislike of

Adderley's socialism, Bishop Hensley Henson nevertheless in an obituary noted that he was whimsical, impulsive, daring, and affectionate; a man of fundamental goodness and of moral courage.   N. C. MASTERMAN

Sources J. G. Adderley, *In slums and society: reminiscences of old friends* (1916) • T. P. Stevens, *Father Adderley* (1943) • P. D'A. Jones, *The Christian socialist revival, 1877–1914* (1968) • N. Dearmer, *The life of Percy Dearmer* (1940) • K. S. Inglis, *Churches and the working classes in Victorian England* (1963) • *CGPLA Eng. & Wales* (1942) • A. Wilkinson, *Christian socialism: Scott Holland to Tony Blair* (1998) • W. Paget, *In my tower*, 2 vols. (1924)
Likenesses Lafayette, photograph, 1932, NPG [*see illus.*] • photograph, repro. in Stevens, *Father Adderley*, frontispiece • photographs, repro. in Adderley, *In slums and society*
Wealth at death £8910 4s. 11d.: probate, 28 Aug 1942, *CGPLA Eng. & Wales*

Addington. For this title name *see* Hubbard, John Gellibrand, first Baron Addington (1805–1889).

Addington, Anthony (1713–1790), physician, born on 13 December 1713, was the youngest son of Henry Addington (1659–1729), gentleman, of Twyford, Oxfordshire, and his second wife, Elizabeth (*c*.1670–1746), eldest daughter of Anthony and Joanna Watts of Sulgrave, Northamptonshire. He was sent as a scholar to Winchester College, and was thence elected to Trinity College, Oxford. He graduated BA in 1739 and MA in 1740, and having decided on medicine as his profession he graduated MB in 1741 and MD in 1744. After settling as a physician at Reading, he married, in 1745, Mary (*d*. 1778), the daughter of the Revd Haviland John Hiley, headmaster of the town's grammar school. Their son Henry *Addington was later to become prime minister.

Addington obtained a good general practice, and a reputation for the treatment of mental illness. He built a house adjoining his own for the reception of his insane patients. In 1753 Addington published, with a dedication to the lords of the Admiralty, *An Essay on the Sea Scurvy*. The essay displayed considerable reading, but was of little practical value. The method proposed for preserving the freshness of water at sea was the addition to it of muriatic acid (hydrochloric acid). In 1754 Addington left Reading for London. In 1755 he was a candidate of the College of Physicians, in 1756 a fellow, and being censor in 1757 he also delivered the Goulstonian lecture for that year. For twenty years Addington practised in London with great success.

Among Addington's patients was William *Pitt, first earl of Chatham, his professional connection with whom ripened into friendship. In *Chatham Correspondence* (1840) there are several letters from the statesman indicating a warm personal interest in Addington and his family. During his severe illness in 1767 Chatham declined George III's suggestion that another physician should be called in to assist Addington. The opposition saw in this confidence a proof that Chatham's disease could only be insanity. This gossip, with damaging reflections on Addington's professional capability, was reproduced in one of Horace Walpole's letters, in which Addington is referred to as 'originally a mad doctor' and as 'a kind of empiric' (*Letters of Horace Walpole*, 45). Chatham, in a grateful letter to Addington, attributed his recovery to his physician's 'judicious sagacity and kind care'. Four years before, Addington had restored to health Chatham's second son, William Pitt, by a course of treatment which included the seductive remedy of port wine.

Chatham seems sometimes to have used Addington as his mouthpiece in society, and in communicating to him a striking memorandum about his views on the future of the struggle with the American colonists in the July of 1776, Chatham strictly commanded him, when repeating these views in conversation with others, to employ 'the very words' of the written paper. Addington's excessive zeal was perhaps a factor in the misunderstanding between Chatham and Bute in the winter of early 1778. Sir James Wright, a friend of Lord Bute, told Addington, who was his physician, that Bute wanted Chatham recalled to office. Addington communicated this statement to Chatham, adding that Bute desired a coalition ministry, of which Chatham should be the head and he himself a member. Chatham was indignant at the idea, which Bute then disowned. But some months after Chatham's death in the same year a report spread—originating from Bute, according to Horace Walpole (*Last Journals*, 275)—that the overtures had been made by Chatham to Bute. To disprove this insinuation a statement was drawn up and issued, probably by Lady Chatham and William Pitt; it was certainly not by Addington, who was generally believed to have been the author, for evidence proves the contrary. Entitled *An authentic account of the part taken by the late earl of Chatham in a transaction which passed in the beginning of the year 1778* (1778), it consisted of letters from and to Addington, Sir James Wright, and Chatham, and included 'Dr Addington's narrative of the transaction'. The statement and the controversial correspondence to which it gave rise were reprinted in the *Annual Register* for 1778.

In 1780 Addington was able to retire and buy the estate of Upottery in Devon. His last years were spent at Reading, where he attended the poor without payment. He was called in by the prince of Wales to attend George III in 1788, and was examined before parliamentary committees with regard to the king's condition. He predicted the early recovery which actually took place, on the grounds that he had never known a case of insanity not preceded by melancholy that had not been cured within twelve months.

Addington died at Reading on 22 March 1790 and was buried at Fringford, near Twyford, Oxfordshire.

FRANCIS ESPINASSE, *rev.* CLAIRE L. NUTT

Sources Munk, *Roll* • G. Pellew, *The life and correspondence of … Henry Addington, first Viscount Sidmouth*, 3 vols. (1847) • *Correspondence of William Pitt, earl of Chatham*, ed. W. S. Taylor and J. H. Pringle, 4 vols. (1838–40), vol. 4 • Cobbett, *Parl. hist.*, 27.692 • *The letters of Horace Walpole, earl of Orford*, ed. P. Cunningham, 5 (1857), 45 • H. Walpole, *Memoirs of the reign of King George the Third*, ed. D. Le Marchant, 2 (1845), 450 • Lord P. Stanhope, *Life of Pitt*, 2nd edn, 1 (1862), 12 • H. Walpole, *Journal of the reign of King George the Third*, ed. Dr Doran, 2 (1859), 275 • E. M. G. Belfied, *Annals of the Addington family* (privately printed, [1954])
Archives Devon RO, corresp. with family, library catalogue, papers relating to his treatment of scurvy

Likenesses J. Rowell of Reading, oils, *c.*1750, RCP Lond. • T. Banks, marble bust, 1791, V&A; related bust, RCP Lond.

Addington, Henry, first Viscount Sidmouth (1757–1844), prime minister, was born on 30 May 1757, the fourth child and eldest son of Anthony *Addington (1713–1790), physician, and his wife, Mary (*d.* 1778), daughter and heir of the Revd Haviland John Hiley, headmaster of Reading grammar school. The Addingtons belonged to the minor gentry of Oxfordshire, but Anthony Addington, having practised successfully in Reading, shifted in 1754 to London, where he soon acquired a high-ranking clientele.

Early years Dr Addington was ambitious for his sons to build on his social success. Five-year-old Henry was sent to Dr William Gilpin's highly regarded school at Cheam (1762–9), and later to Winchester College (1769–73). When he left Winchester over some incident in which 'vicious boys' attacked him, his father sent him to Dr Goodenough's school at Ealing. Brasenose, the Oxford college which he entered in 1774, had the best reputation for serious learning, which suited Addington, who had all along found study congenial. His name had been put down for Lincoln's Inn in 1771 while he was still at Winchester.

Addington took his degree in February 1778, though he stayed on at Oxford and did not begin his legal studies in London until 1780. His marriage the next year, on 19 September 1781, signalled his family's rising status, for his bride, Ursula Mary (1760–1811), was the daughter and coheir of Leonard Hammond of Cheam, who belonged to the armigerous gentry. They were to have six children, two sons and four daughters. Thanks to James Sutton, Addington's brother-in-law, the young couple were able to set up in London in a house in Southampton Street, off the Strand. How seriously Addington read law is impossible to determine, since to become a barrister, as he did in 1784, the only formal requirement was to eat dinners in hall. But in later life he often recalled his legal training as most valuable, and it would have been out of character for him to have wasted the opportunity. Furthermore, his chances of election to parliament diminished in 1780 when Devizes, where Sutton was influential, acquired two new representatives.

Addington's most famous contemporary at Lincoln's Inn was William Pitt. Their acquaintance had begun in boyhood when Dr Addington had been Lord Chatham's physician and confidant. However, soon married, not a Cambridge friend, and not yet in parliament, Addington remained outside Pitt's inner circle. Pitt summoned him when he became prime minister in December 1783, probably because he was having difficulty filling up the minor offices in his wild-card administration and wished to encourage Addington's parliamentary ambitions.

Member of parliament The general election in April 1784 saw Addington returned for Devizes, a corporation borough run by wealthy local clothiers. The sitting member, whom Addington displaced without a contest, seems to have caused offence during his short tenure and Sutton took the opportunity to push forward his young brother-in-law. Sutton's influence in the borough was secured the

Henry Addington, first Viscount Sidmouth (1757–1844), by Sir William Beechey, in or before 1803

same year by Addington's election as recorder. Addington continued to represent Devizes until he accepted a peerage in 1805.

Once in the House of Commons, Addington remained silent until his third session and then spoke only at Pitt's particular request that he second the address (24 January 1786). According to Cobbett's *Parliamentary History* he spoke only seven times in the 1784–90 parliament up to his election as speaker. As the opposition pointed out on that occasion, his candidature was the weaker from his being little known to the house. Parliamentary speaking was never Addington's forte. As a back-bencher in his first parliament his few contributions were short but sensible expositions of some key point. For example, on the Regency Bill (10 February 1789), opposing the opposition's demand that the prince of Wales sit on the council of regency, he drew attention to the parallel case of private families where the heir was denied the management of a lunatic's affairs as a matter of principle.

Addington became speaker on 8 June 1789. Pitt's majority, of course, ensured his election, but Pitt chose him in the first instance because he was loyal and capable. Addington, typically, had made himself well informed about parliamentary procedure. The limited evidence of division lists shows him to have been a regular attender. Addington had also sat on several Commons committees, including that given the important task of estimating public income and expenditure in support of Pitt's sinking fund scheme (1786). Above all Addington was generally liked; handsome in appearance, dignified, sociable, amiable to political friends and foes alike, young in a house which consistently had a high proportion of members in their twenties and thirties.

Speaker, 1789–1801 Addington was being acclaimed for his performance as speaker on completing his first full session, winning 'the esteem even of the opposition' (Thorne, 3.39). In 1796 and 1801 he was re-elected unanimously. He handled sittings of the house with good sense in a period when partisan feelings might easily have got out of hand. One instance of his impartiality was in 1790, when he ruled that the dissolution earlier that year did not terminate the impeachment proceedings against Warren Hastings, a case being ardently pursued by Edmund Burke and other opposition members. He argued knowledgeably and intelligently in defence of this decision when Hastings's friends brought it to debate. On two occasions when a vote was tied, he similarly enunciated the principle that the speaker should vote for rather than against further discussion when the measure itself was not at stake. There were rulings, too, against members voting on matters in which they had a pecuniary interest. His was the traditional yet accepted view of the Commons, that it existed primarily not to legislate but to voice grievances and restrain the executive as the 'grand inquest of the nation'. However, Addington left the house to cope as best it could with a rapidly increasing workload.

Addington's great achievement as speaker was to restore the prestige of the office, which had suffered since Speaker Onslow's time. A speaker's reputation was largely founded on his management of the house during debates. Addington possessed the personal authority, impartiality, and parliamentary knowledge to keep good order and direct members on matters of procedure and practice. He was also healthy enough to endure the increasing number of sittings into the morning hours. On first coming to the chair he seems to have refused an official sinecure, though this was the usual way in which speakers covered the heavy hospitality expenses of the office and Addington certainly could not have afforded to do without the extra income. Instead he was granted a fixed salary of £6000. The speaker's status was further enhanced in 1795, when an official residence was created for him in Palace Yard. Addington initiated the collection of portraits in Speaker's House.

Addington's relationship, both personal and political, with Pitt was never closer than during his speakership. Pitt confided in him over his fumbling, suddenly ended courtship of Eleanor Eden, Lord Auckland's daughter. Pitt, too, specially asked to see Addington before he fought his duel with George Tierney in May 1798, and Addington went to Putney Heath to watch from afar, perhaps guilt-stricken that the quarrel had originated in the Commons during debate. When Pitt's health broke down in 1800 he retired to Woodley, Addington's small estate near Reading, to recuperate.

The friendship was one of very different personalities: Addington placid, placatory, and genial; Pitt emotional, assertive, and prickly. There was a difference of social rank as well. The two paired well probably because Addington did not expect total familiarity and because Pitt genuinely liked Addington's helpful, undemanding ways. Pitt clearly thought highly of Addington's political abilities; as early as 1793 he contemplated making him secretary of state to relieve Henry Dundas, who was overworked managing both the war and domestic affairs. After debates the prime minister often retired with his closest lieutenants to Speaker's House to talk politics. Pitt particularly valued Addington's financial expertise. The 'voluntary contribution' of 1798 was Addington's idea. Addington's contribution to financial policy must have helped Pitt to look on him as his successor, for finance was accepted as the key business of the state, overriding even war and diplomacy.

Pitt thought of resigning in favour of Addington in 1797, probably in February after the failure of peace negotiations. The king was ready to accept Addington. Pitt's idea was that the other ministers and his supporters would remain in office and that he would 'direct' from the sidelines while Addington, as a new face endorsed by the king and already popular in the Commons, would rebuild support. When Pitt resigned in 1801 he envisaged Addington in exactly the same caretaker role.

None of the principals—George III, Pitt, and Addington—involved in the crisis of January 1801 seriously considered any alternative to Addington as prime minister. The king called in Addington in the hope that he could persuade Pitt to drop Catholic emancipation, but when negotiation proved fruitless both insisted that he take office. Both, indeed, played on his loyalty and highly developed sense of duty. 'Lay your hand upon your heart,' said the king, 'and ask yourself where I am to turn for support if *you* do not stand by me.' 'I see nothing but ruin, Addington, if you hesitate', Pitt replied with equal grandiloquence (Ziegler, 93).

Five of Pitt's cabinet resigned with him, and some lesser office-holders, a result neither Pitt nor Addington expected or wanted. When finally established Addington's cabinet consisted of ten ministers, four of whom continued from Pitt's but with the most important posts—the Treasury and the three secretaryships—in new hands. Government making showed Addington that politicians could feel a stronger loyalty to Pitt than to an administration approved by both Pitt and the king, so many left or refused office though they had not been involved in the contretemps with George III or made any public commitment in favour of Catholic emancipation. Early on he signalled that his administration was not to be regarded merely as a continuation of Pitt's without Pitt. Even before he took office on 14 March—a delay of several weeks occurred because George III suffered another bout of insanity—Addington resisted Pittite pressure to stand down in favour of Pitt, who now was ready to drop emancipation during the king's lifetime.

Prime minister, 1801–1804 The first verdict on Addington's government was that it would struggle in parliament because of the prime minister's deficiencies as a Westminster orator. However, Pitt thought the administration could keep on having the last say in the division lobbies 'as Mr Pelham's had done' (Thorne, 3.41). Addington, himself capable in public business, had in Lord Hobart and Lord Pelham secretaries of state who had cut their teeth in the powerful and demanding Irish secretaryship. Addington's foreign secretary, Lord Hawkesbury, a future long-serving prime minister, was likewise a well-prepared 'office man'. This was not the 'Goose Administration' of Canning's spite. Its parliamentary position was also secured by its 'general principles': a pragmatic, *now* was *not* the time' approach to Catholic emancipation; hostility to 'jacobinism'; and the necessity of peace to avert the effects of Britain's renewed isolation in Europe and economic problems at home.

Addington in his first speech as prime minister, on 25 March 1801, announced that his government would try for peace. This was by unanimous decision of the cabinet, conveyed to George III not, as would have been usual, by the foreign secretary but by Addington himself. The peace policy was above all his, though he was also strongly backed by Pitt. As the negotiations over the preliminaries took place in London, he was able to give them constant oversight, checking and overruling Hawkesbury on some matters. Once agreement had been reached on 1 October, he wrote to a number of leading politicians to explain the government's position. Economic difficulties and their predicted effect on state finances had particularly impressed Addington. He and Pitt went over the figures and concluded that war for any effective purpose was unaffordable.

As important in the context of Britain's critical position in 1801 were the parallel negotiations conducted with Russia. Addington and Hawkesbury understood better than Pitt and Grenville that Britain could not afford Russia's hostility because of her influence over the other Baltic powers; the League of Armed Neutrality of 1800, if it had lasted, would have seriously damaged Britain's trade, naval resources, and international position. Furthermore Russia was potentially Britain's most powerful ally against France. Addington's government quickly achieved rapprochement with Russia: diplomatic contact was resumed in late March, and an Anglo-Russian convention was signed on 17 June.

The peace with France which followed was a political triumph. The preliminaries were carried without a division in the Commons, and the eventual treaty of Amiens by huge majorities in both houses. Such a triumph increased Addington's independence from Pitt. Pitt does not seem to have been consulted on the final treaty proposals. For several months from October 1801 Addington was talking with George Tierney about bringing in a few of the opposition. Meanwhile the king offered ostentatious support to '*His* Chancellor of the Exchequer'. George III always liked Addington's respectful yet friendly and businesslike attitude to him, and Addington, from the start, insisted on most matters going to the king only through him. Within months of Addington becoming prime minister the king granted him possession of White Lodge in Richmond Park.

Addington was under no illusions that peace would be lasting. The policy of preparedness faltered only with respect to the navy, where Lord St Vincent's independent pursuit of reform proved seriously disruptive. The army's strength was kept up to about 60 per cent of its wartime numbers. Moreover, ministers as early as February 1802 were devising a balloted army of reserve. This was part of a comprehensive attempt to reorganize the home defences during the 'Amiens interlude'. Addington and his ministers disliked the huge volunteer force that had emerged during the French Revolutionary Wars as too localized and too outside the control of the gentry and military. They preferred instead a 'large' militia mostly stationed in the counties, which would restore gentry interest and reassert the principle of personal service among the general population. As a result the volunteers, with the exception of the yeomanry cavalry, were totally disbanded. Militia reform was embodied in the 1802 Militia Act, which was also a consolidating measure.

Addington produced two peacetime budgets, in April and December 1802. The key problem was the heavy expense of the army and outstanding war costs as the armed forces were slowly reduced. Nor could Addington ignore the public expectation that taxation would be lowered, especially the income tax. With the income tax gone, Addington had to raise an even larger loan to cover expenditure in 1802. For 1803 Addington again proposed to borrow to cover the deficit, but also declared himself satisfied that existing taxes would be sufficient to service this new loan. Pitt, however, took strong exception to this second budget and was conspicuous by his absence when it was presented. He feared that borrowing on such a scale would produce a repetition of the slow strangling of the 'system of credit' that had occurred in 1793–7. Addington had more faith in the expansionary effects of peace and, indeed, greater confidence in Britain's overall economic strength.

Yet Addington observed thoroughly Pittite financial principles. Loans were covered by sufficient taxation to defray interest and amortize the debt, the famous sinking fund policy of 1786. Reform to minimize evasion and fraud and reduce the costs of revenue collection went on steadily; Addington, for example, increased the yield of the lottery by 20 per cent. Public confidence in the financial operations of government further required administrative rationalization and adequate information. Addington consolidated the sinking funds and the indirect taxes, removed the public service expenses, such as public buildings and colonial and diplomatic establishments, from the civil list, and paid off the king's and the prince of Wales's debts. Above all he can claim to have made the first 'budget speech', in April 1802.

The last months of 1802 can be regarded as the high point of Addington's administration, with notable achievements in foreign policy, finance, and national defence to its credit. Yet important matters continued to be referred to Pitt, and in January 1803, in three meetings with him, Addington tried to establish whether he would offer support in the coming session. Pitt again eschewed opposition, indicating that he would return to office only with the agreement of the king and cabinet. But when parliament did meet he stayed away altogether, well aware of the continued impregnability of Addington's government.

Addington must have been very confident of his situation because in March 1803 he attempted the master stroke of bringing in Pitt and Dundas (now Lord Melville) without Grenville, who had declared open opposition. The proposal was for Addington and Pitt to act as equals under Lord Chatham as prime minister. Pitt's hostile reception of these terms, his threat to move into opposition even, changed the game immediately. The great object became getting Pitt into office away from increasingly unbenevolent neutrality, while keeping a strong Addingtonian presence in government and the Grenvilles out altogether. The office Addington envisaged for himself was secretary of state with a peerage. On a second try, therefore, Pitt was offered the premiership with the request that a substantial number of existing ministers and office-holders remain.

This second overture showed the extent to which Pitt had distanced himself from Addington's government. Pitt responded to Addington's offer by requiring him and his colleagues to retire to minor offices, Addington to the speakership of the House of Lords, a position, Pitt said, which had once existed. The ministers supposed that the Grenvilles were behind this attempt to 'new-model' the government and, rejecting it, made a spirited declaration of collective loyalty. These exchanges ended on 18 April. Pitt returned to parliament on 23 May and on 3 June, when the ministers were under attack for the breakdown of negotiations with France, he signalled his disaffection by moving the orders of the day. Pitt's denial of public support was a turning point for Addington's administration, suddenly threatening what had been an invincible parliamentary position. In June and July the conciliation of Pitt became so urgent that the cabinet for the first time began to defer to his ideas and thus to lose confidence in the government's right to continue.

The government's decline and fall The attempted censure of the government's foreign policy on 3 June was defeated by massive majorities. Addington and Hawkesbury took an increasingly tough line with Napoleon from late in 1802. In view of Napoleon's aggressive diplomacy the only issues that could be posed were tactical ones of whether enough had been done to constrain him. When war was declared by Britain on 18 May, parliament and public opinion were generally satisfied that the government had been left no option.

Once war had been embarked on, Addington's administration also proved largely invulnerable to criticism over its diplomacy and strategy. While it never managed to create a new coalition of powers to resist France, this was hardly cause for surprise in view of the general exhaustion of Europe after a decade of war. Behind the scenes, in fact, the ministers continued to cultivate Russian goodwill, thus laying the foundations of the Third Coalition. The conduct of the war was necessarily defensive, though

Napoleon's miscalculation that Britain would not declare war when it did meant that he was not ready for invasion, nor in a position to challenge Britain's naval superiority.

The government's and the public's preoccupation, however, was, understandably, with home defence. Again the ministers took timely action. In March the militia had been called out and new regulations for volunteers published. As the major counter-invasion force, the army in 1803 doubled its effective strength in Britain and Ireland to about 90,000, to which could be added an army of 30,000 reserve men. Out of this expansion came plans in 1804 to form a 'disposable force' for offensive operations. The navy was somewhat slower to get on a war footing, after the upheaval of St Vincent's reforms. Nevertheless, the French navy was even worse prepared, so that, concentrated in home waters, the British from the start of the war enjoyed a comfortable superiority.

Despite the government's more than adequate defence preparations, a crisis over national defence developed rapidly from the time of the declaration of war. In the end these issues were to undermine the cabinet's solidarity and its parliamentary support to the point of collapse. These anxieties turned politicians towards Pitt. Pittite belittlement of Addington as 'the Doctor' (begun by Canning in 1802) became particularly telling in this context. Addington's own folly had been to turn up in the Commons wearing uniform to announce the declaration of war. It was in 1803 that Canning wrote his famous couplet:

> Pitt is to Addington
> As London is to Paddington.

The need to keep Pitt from outright opposition while maintaining the government's independence produced some striking volte-face. In June 1803 Addington, reviving the income tax, put a well-conceived measure before parliament, in particular applying the principle of taxation at source which would make evasion more difficult than Pitt's tax had done. A further feature of the proposal was the exemption allowed for the first £150 of earned as opposed to unearned income. Under attack from Pitt on 13 July, Addington first carried the exemption on a vote, then next day conceded its extension to unearned income. He also gave ground on his key principle by permitting the bank to pay fundholders without deducting tax.

The cabinet's worst surrender by far was to succumb to Pitt's demand, backed by a threat of independent parliamentary action, for unlimited volunteering. A Levy En Masse Act was passed on 27 July. The armed population the ministers had always disliked as dangerous and unserviceable now came into existence. The numbers involved were beyond effective regulation; but such difficulties were quickly turned into allegations of ministerial ineptitude.

When the new parliamentary session commenced Pitt prolonged Addington's agony by declining 'systematic opposition' while reserving the right to support or oppose measures according to their merits. The major business was the bill clarifying and consolidating the volunteer laws. The five weeks it took to get through the Commons and further delays in the Lords raised questions about the government's competence to manage parliament. Signs that Pitt was developing into a committed adversary—on 15 March he made a slashing attack on the state of the navy—further indicated Addington's increasing isolation and his removal as only a matter of time.

The critical erosion of support occurred in both houses in April. The last battles were again fought out on issues of national defence, though specifically relating to the Irish militia. On 13 April, in a large house, Addington's majority slumped to fifty-eight. On 19 April the Lords divided seventy-seven to forty-eight and on 24 April ninety-four to sixty-one, the largest minorities seen there since the regency debates in 1789.

By this time Addington and his cabinet were frantically seeking salvation. They continued to make strenuous efforts to rally support in the Lords before the state of the nation was debated on 30 April. They considered a dissolution. They also made another approach to Pitt, using Lord Eldon, in the hope that he would want to stay independent of the Fox–Grenville 'co-operation'. Pitt's response was that he would talk only with the king. Indeed, on 23 April, on Fox's motion for an inquiry into the defence of the country, he moved into outright opposition, demanding the government's resignation. This attack was repeated on 25 April on the Army of Reserve Suspension Bill. Addington's majority in a well-attended house slipped from fifty-two to thirty-seven. It was the end. Addington told the king the cause was hopeless, and on 29 April, after calculating that they would have no more than a majority of ten in the Lords the next day, the cabinet finally resolved to go. The prime minister's last task was to present his budget on 30 April. He gave up the exchequer seals on 10 May.

That Addington's ministers stuck by him to the bitter end was a tribute to his personal and political skills in dealing with them. Addington governed through his cabinet, valuing and building up a collective loyalty—which explains the sharp rebuke he administered to Eldon at one of the last meetings on discovering an unauthorized approach to Pitt in March 1804. Addington, too, always got on well with the king, a political asset he was able to trade off for years to come. On his resignation the king immediately offered him an earldom and a pension of £4000 for his wife. When Addington declined these rewards he was prevailed on to accept the life tenancy of White Lodge and the gift of a Sir William Beechey royal portrait.

However, these were strengths that counted for less in the wider political world. Addington appears to have misused his dispensation of patronage, characteristically preferring personal loyalty to political advantage. George Huntingford, his old Winchester tutor, was made bishop of Gloucester, and Dr Goodenough dean of Rochester, rich prizes indeed. Many were surprised when Charles Bragge, his brother-in-law, assumed the important office of secretary at war. Politicians who were in a position to judge, together with the king himself, concluded that Addington was 'not equal to the government of the country' (Rose, 2.156). He did not dominate his cabinet when that was

called for; his tactical sense was lacking, especially when it came to the management of parliament. Above all he never shone in debate, which became a fatal inadequacy once a perception of national crisis had developed and his majority came under pressure. A temperate man, the final onslaught against his government saw him drinking 'perhaps twenty glasses of wine at dinner to invigorate himself for debate' (Thorne, 3.45). Yet on the whole his government's record on finance, foreign policy, and national defence was a good one.

Opposition and office, 1804–1805 Once in opposition Addington played the same game as Pitt had done: 'I will not be the stalking-horse or cat's paw of Opposition nor will I be extinguished by Mr Pitt' (Ziegler, 227). He revealed this hand in June in opposing, in concert with Fox and Grenville, Pitt's Additional Force Bill when the government's majorities were as weak as Addington's had been in April.

Pitt's managers calculated Addington's following in the Commons at forty-one, enough to hold the balance. When the overture came in December 1804 Addington skilfully put the negotiation on the ground of a reconciliation, which then enabled him to press for the strong representation of his friends in the cabinet and outside. He asked for two cabinet places (for St Vincent and Hobart, now Lord Buckinghamshire); but in declining a position for himself he also surely knew that Pitt would be bound to insist on his coming in. This bid for two places paid off. Addington became lord president of the council and Buckinghamshire chancellor of the duchy of Lancaster. Otherwise Pitt's goodwill was less than apparent. Addington's elevation to the Lords as Viscount Sidmouth (12 January 1805) was at Pitt's behest; he himself would rather have sat in the Commons alongside Pitt as a mark of his political importance.

Sidmouth was sworn lord president on 14 January 1805. Six months later he and Buckinghamshire were out. Tension arose first over Lord Melville's case, Sidmouth threatening resignation if the allegations against Melville's administration of the navy were not submitted to the Commons for inquiry. Sidmouth felt strongly that the credit of his government was at stake; for it had not only launched the investigation into the state of the navy but had also endured much criticism over St Vincent's reforms. On 8 April, in the famous tied division, most of Sidmouth's followers voted for Melville's censure. As to the next stage of legal process Sidmouth took the hard line of favouring criminal prosecution rather than impeachment.

Matters came to a head when Sir Charles Middleton was appointed to the Admiralty as Lord Barham on Melville's resignation. Sidmouth complained that Pitt had not only passed over an opportunity to advance Buckinghamshire and bring Bragge into the cabinet but had also given the vacant place to a friend of Melville's and opponent of St Vincent's. Though his connection had brought votes to the government, it had not been given the offices promised to show that it was a genuine coalition. Sidmouth finally surrendered his office on 5 July. Nevertheless his personal relations with Pitt survived his accusations of 'injustice' and 'arrogance'. Pitt paid a friendly visit to White Lodge in September, and Sidmouth called at the house of the dying Pitt in January 1806 in order 'to show, not merely attention, but the affection that has never been extinguished' (Ziegler, 248).

The 'ministry of all the talents', 1806–1807 Grenville's commission to form a government on Pitt's death soon brought him to Sidmouth's door. Grenville wanted a union of parties and believed such a broad-based administration to be possible given that the war had overriding importance. Sidmouth could only agree. All politicians also had to accept that as George III had relinquished the principle of exclusion by admitting Fox to office, so they could not be too sensitive about old animosities. That said, Sidmouth's way back to office was smoothed by Grenville's readiness to leave the previous Pittite ministers outside his administration, if only for the time being. The only stipulation about policy Sidmouth felt it necessary to make was that he would not support Catholic emancipation. On this occasion there was no cause for complaint about the distribution of offices. Sidmouth sat in the cabinet as lord privy seal with Lord Ellenborough, lord chief justice. Five junior posts went to his closest followers.

During most of 1806 'all the talents' worked together better than the participants had a right to expect. Grenville held regular cabinet meetings and freely consulted Fox and, to a lesser extent, Sidmouth. There were no serious disputes over policy. Grenville's developing preference for a maritime war and Fox's peace negotiations were hardly an issue for Sidmouth, since Britain's continental alliances had collapsed. In the reshuffle following Fox's death in September, Bragge was given office and Sidmouth again became lord president of the council.

At this point, however, Grenville began to dominate policy. Sidmouth, particularly, feared his influence was declining, perhaps because his connection had lost about one-third of its strength in the 1806 election. It annoyed Sidmouth that he was not consulted on Grenville's plan for financing the war long term. Neither did Grenville tell him of his bill to abolish the slave trade which, though not a government measure, was bound to discomfort Sidmouth as a confirmed 'gradualist'.

The crisis that developed over the admission of Catholics to all military offices was the last straw. Sidmouth did his duty by the cabinet in getting the king to accept that in Britain, as in Ireland, Catholics should be able to hold up to colonel's rank, but he then discovered that pro-Catholic ministers were offering the more generous concession. Sidmouth flatly refused to force the king's conscience, declared his own opposition and told the king that his ministers were manipulating and deceiving him. Worse followed when Grenville's overtures to Canning during these same weeks came to light. Sidmouth, who regarded Canning as his chief political adversary and the man who had poisoned his relations with Pitt, now said he would not sit in a cabinet with Canning and resigned.

Opposition, 1807–1812 In March 1807 Sidmouth began his longest period out of office before his retirement from politics in 1824. George III's dismissal of the talents had the effect of consolidating the Grenville–Grey (Foxite) alliance. Once the opposition had taken up Catholic emancipation and the king's role in politics as issues of principle, there was little hope of reproducing the grand coalition of 1806–7. Sidmouth's affinities were with the Pittites; but here the main stumbling block was Canning who had long denigrated Sidmouth. Sidmouth's other major consideration after the experiences of 1806–7 was to take office only if effective power and influence could be exercised within the government, preferably as secretary of state. An important reason for Sidmouth's refusal to serve with Canning was that he believed, with Pitt removed, that Canning would dominate Hawkesbury and Castlereagh, the other Pittite leaders—who anyway had shown little loyalty to Sidmouth in 1804 and 1805. On the other hand, a government of himself and these two without Canning would be more like a genuine triumvirate.

Isolated between government and opposition, Sidmouth defined his politics as a right to oppose ministers only so far as there was no chance of the opposition forcing themselves on the king. He used this independence in 1807 to attack the Copenhagen expedition and in 1808 the orders in council, both issues to do with Britain's relations with neutrals and which, in Sidmouth's mind, harked back to the armed neutrality of 1801 and the danger of provoking its revival. Such a stand also accorded with his consistent support of a war strategy based on continental alliances. He never opposed the Peninsular intervention, though in April 1809 he joined in the search for scapegoats following the evacuation of Sir John Moore's army. On all three occasions Sidmouth, no doubt, was stimulated into opposition by the embarrassment each caused Canning as foreign secretary.

Canning and Castlereagh's departure from the government in September 1809 allowed Sidmouth to think again of office. However, when the offer came from Spencer Perceval, the new prime minister, Sidmouth found that he himself was excluded for the time being; 'our Friends of the old Pitt connection', explained Perceval, were still prejudiced against him (Gray, 262). This attitude left Sidmouth much where he had been, and in the ensuing session he and his little band (eight MPs on the opposition's count) gave steady support for an inquiry into the Walcheren fiasco. So hard was the government run on this issue that two attempts were made in 1810 to win back Canning, Castlereagh, and Sidmouth. However, while the latter two were eager to see a reunion of Pittites, they would not contemplate sharing office with Canning. Sidmouth's opportunity finally came in April 1812 when Lord Wellesley, Canning's champion in the cabinet, resigned. Perceval promptly recruited Castlereagh and then conducted a reshuffle to bring in Sidmouth, Buckinghamshire, and Bragge Bathurst—Sidmouth as lord president.

Home secretary, 1812–1822 Perceval's assassination on 11 May and the eventual formation of a government headed by Lord Liverpool gave Sidmouth an even stronger position in the cabinet. Returning to his colleagues with the prince regent's commission in his pocket, Liverpool began by asking Sidmouth to take the Home Office—'it will mean everything to me' (Pellew, 3.78). This was the kind of high office Sidmouth had wanted all along, especially after being driven into the political wilderness in 1807: 'I would not be a Noun adjective to any Government' (Ziegler, 274). Sidmouth remained very conscious of his standing as a former prime minister, one, moreover, whose sense of 'public duty' could not be questioned since he had served at the monarch's express command. To him was due a 'situation of perfect and unqualified responsibility' (ibid., 274), the heading of one of the great departments of state. In 1812 his satisfaction was the greater because Vansittart, Bragge Bathurst, and Buckinghamshire all joined him in office, which made a further point of the influence he still commanded.

Sidmouth obviously felt secure because in July he supported Liverpool in another attempt to recruit Canning. He still hoped to see Pitt's party rebuilt, and the price of Canning's inclusion was not too great if Canning would serve under Liverpool and Castlereagh and as Sidmouth's equal. In the event Canning held out for higher rank. Sidmouth later made him pay for his presumption by blocking the reshuffle that would have given him the Admiralty in 1813, and doing the same in 1816 so that he got only the cabinet place that was vacant, the comparatively junior post of president of the Board of Control. Canning, in fact, was made to suffer to the very end of Sidmouth's political career. In preparing for his retirement in 1821 Sidmouth intrigued with other ministers to prevent Canning's return to office (especially to the Home Office), with the result that Canning accepted the governor-generalship of India. The next year Castlereagh's suicide suddenly delivered the 'whole inheritance' of the Foreign Office and leadership of the Commons into Canning's hands, but Sidmouth—this time without support from his colleagues—still tried to persuade George IV against it. Unsuccessful, he resigned the cause and encouraged Bragge Bathurst to leave the cabinet, and Vansittart to move from the exchequer to a lesser post.

Sidmouth relinquished the Home Office on 17 January 1822 after more than nine years in the position. In a period of social unrest and resurgent popular politics the administration of law and order imposed a heavy workload by the standards of the day on Sidmouth and his tiny bureaucracy at Whitehall. Irish business, also the responsibility of the home secretary, added to the pressure. Sidmouth feelingly complained at the end of his tenure that 'the whole strength of the establishment has been insufficient to carry on the current business of the office' (N. Gash, *Mr Secretary Peel*, 1961, 298). Yet he rose above such difficulties by attending assiduously and finding satisfaction in the routine of administration. More than a few ministers of his day did not. What Sidmouth lacked was what made his successor, Robert Peel, a great home secretary—a commitment to reform at a time when the pressures in favour of reform were mounting inexorably. During Sidmouth's

tenure the reform of police, gaols, and the system of justice was largely left in the hands of whigs and humanitarians acting through parliament.

Sidmouth, along with Castlereagh, was regarded by popular radicals as the architect of repression. Though more alarmist than some of his colleagues, he never imagined any far-reaching review of the powers of the state to contain and weaken popular radicalism. He would regulate popular rights of assembly, association, and free speech only as far as these were, in his words, becoming 'wrongs'—being used to promote violence and insurrection. The ultimate step he seems to have contemplated was to apply 'Irish' measures in England where in proclaimed districts the magistrates would have been able to act outside the normal constraints of the law, though always only under parliamentary authority.

In the post-war crisis of order Sidmouth's response was thoroughly traditionalist. The increasing scale of disorder was met with increasing military force; after the Peterloo massacre Sidmouth asked for and got reinforcements. The anti-radical legislation Sidmouth secured from an initially reluctant cabinet in 1817, and again in 1819, mainly aimed at the popular press, popular meetings, and supposed radical military activity, was largely an *ad hoc* response to recent events, emphasized by the time limitation on some of the acts. They can also be described as declaratory rather than effective, as they were mostly intended to rally the magistrates and well-affected public in the localities on whom policing and order mainly depended. Sidmouth told one correspondent that he wanted to be remembered as 'the country gentlemen's secretary of state' (Thorne, 3.46). He pushed hard for an early meeting of parliament (which also meant legislation) both in 1817 and in 1819 because as home secretary his alarmism had been fed by the amount of information he received, which led him to imagine a threat of national proportions. His colleagues, having a more localized view of distress and radical activity, tended to be more sceptical and conceded the point reluctantly.

Sidmouth's hostility to parliamentary reform was typical of the conventional views he held on the great issues of the day. In defending the political power of property he was unexceptional in seeing himself as defending 'the Constitution as established at the Revolution [of 1688]'. His rejection of 'party' and 'formed opposition' and his respect for the royal veto on policy or ministerial appointments also accorded with prevailing constitutional principles. He was against a free trade in corn on the grounds that the corn laws existed to protect landed property, the foundation of social order. He believed wages should be left to find their own level and capital its most profitable operation, *laissez-faire* views of impeccable orthodoxy. His opposition to Catholic emancipation and continued hope for the protestantization of Ireland were based on the traditional protestant position that Catholic beliefs were incompatible with 'liberty'. Piously Anglican, he was also doggedly traditionalist in upholding a church establishment as the best security for religious, and therefore social, order. In 1811 he even attempted to restrict by legislation the activities of itinerant preachers, who were often Methodists. Addington's religious politics, together with his royalism, particularly separated him from the whigs. They anathematized such views, reviving the old whig–tory antithesis; Addington might thus be said to have made a negative contribution to the rise of party.

On his retirement from the Home Office, Sidmouth, by request of the king, stayed on in the cabinet as minister without portfolio. George IV, like his father before him, had found Sidmouth businesslike and agreeable in the closet, never more so than in 1820–21 when he was under pressure from the cabinet to make a settlement with the queen and, later, to restore Canning to office. At this time he often served Liverpool as a go-between. Sidmouth, since he was always sensitive to being written off as a nonentity, no doubt welcomed the king's insistence that he continue in the cabinet; a royal pension of £3000 made the same point. Liverpool reluctantly agreed to both honours in order to facilitate the larger reconstruction of his government. However, Sidmouth was never comfortable in a cabinet increasingly dominated by Canning. He seized the opportunity finally to go in November 1824 over the issue of Britain's recognition of the new republics formed out of the ruins of Spain's American empire.

Assessment and last years In 1833 George Richmond made a watercolour drawing of Sidmouth, full length, in statesmanlike pose; it is now in the National Portrait Gallery. It immediately evokes Samuel Bamford's description on the occasion of his appearance before the privy council in 1817:

> The person who addressed me was a tall, square, and bony figure, upwards of fifty years of age, I should suppose, and with thin, and rather grey hair: his forehead was broad and prominent, and from their cavernous orbits looked mild and intelligent eyes. His manner was affable, and much more encouraging to freedom of speech than I had expected.
> (S. Bamford, *Passages in the Life of a Radical*, 1840–44, 2.95)

Earlier portraits show Sidmouth as fine-featured and darkly handsome, with the same air of intelligent engagement with the world. His face was discoloured by a severe attack of erysipelas in 1807, but in general he was robustly healthy.

As a person Sidmouth made few enemies. But he was too bland in his personality to inspire the devotion accorded to Pitt or Canning. Temperamentally unsuited to politics as a personal contest, he welcomed nothing more than the handshake that reconciled him with old adversaries whatever political differences remained. Canning was surprised with such an interview in August 1812. Sidmouth equally valued loyalty and friendship; Pitt hurt him deeply by his shift of political allegiance in 1803–4; Canning he distrusted as letting little stand in the way of his ambition. In retirement he destroyed all the papers which he considered might reflect badly on Pitt. Fellow politicians most commonly accused Sidmouth of vanity, in that he remained acutely sensitive to criticism of his administration long afterwards, and inflated the importance of himself and his party. This self-importance was probably deep-seated. It was the response of the first of the minor gentry to hold the office of prime minister and who throughout his subsequent career was victimized as 'the Doctor'.

On leaving Liverpool's government Sidmouth spent the remaining twenty years of his life mostly at Richmond and at his estate at Upottery in Devon, which he had inherited from his father. He attended the House of Lords infrequently, hardly at all after the 1832 Reform Act passed, which he opposed to the end. Wellington's earlier concession of Catholic emancipation had similarly appalled him. His first wife had died in June 1811, and he remarried on 29 July 1823. His second wife, Mary Anne, was the widow of Thomas Townshend of Hovington, Warwickshire, and only daughter and heir of William Scott, first Baron Stowell, and his first wife, Anna Maria Bagnall. Nearly thirty years younger than Sidmouth, she predeceased him, aged fifty-nine, in April 1842. Mary Anne, his eldest child, who never married, nursed him through his final illness. Sidmouth died, probably of pneumonia, on 15 February 1844 at White Lodge, Richmond Park. He was buried at Mortlake on 23 February. His heir was his second son, William. His eldest son, Harry, a severe depressive and invalid all his adult life, had died in 1823.

Addington's reputation has long languished in the shade of the younger Pitt. Canning's brilliant sarcasms at Addington's expense set the tone of the first historical treatments from which even recent studies are directly descended. Victorian Liberals disliked his toryism. Victorian tories despised his mediocrity—'without Pitt nothing could be strong' (Croker, 514). George Pellew's biography (1847) could not turn this tide; it indeed strengthened Addington's fate because it was dismissed as an act of family piety and because the author suppressed documents that would have depicted the relationship with Pitt as more combative. Pitt's standing as great statesman and war minister soared to new heights from the late nineteenth century as Britain's world position came under increasing threat. In the same hands—Fortescue (1909), Holland Rose (1911)—Addington was accused of bungling his country's diplomacy and national defence at a time when it never stood in greater peril. Addington continued to get a rough ride from the military historians such as Glover (1963). The growing interest of historians in popular movements focused attention on Sidmouth at the Home Office. This work, led by Thompson (1963), reiterated the view that he was an unimaginative reactionary. Ziegler (1965) produced the first properly researched biography, which can be said to have inaugurated the reassessment of Addington by portraying him as a politician of skill and substance who deserved better than to be regarded as Pitt's 'shadow'. The 1990s saw the beginnings of a strong revisionist current, at least with respect to Addington's administration. Its foreign policy and conduct of the war were usefully defended by Fedorak (1991), Hall (1988), and Cookson (1997).   J. E. COOKSON

Sources G. Pellew, *The life and correspondence of … Henry Addington, first Viscount Sidmouth*, 3 vols. (1847) · P. Ziegler, *Addington: a life of Henry Addington, first Viscount Sidmouth* (1965) · R. G. Thorne,

'Addington, Henry', HoP, *Commons, 1790–1820* · C. D. Hall, 'Addington at war: unspectacular but not unsuccessful', *Historical Research*, 61 (1988), 306–15 · C. J. Fedorak, 'In search of a necessary ally: Addington, Hawkesbury, and Russia, 1801–1804', *International History Review*, 13 (1991), 221–45 · J. E. Cookson, *Lord Liverpool's administration: the crucial years, 1815–1822* (1975) · J. E. Cookson, *The British armed nation, 1793–1815* (1997) · J. Ehrman, *The younger Pitt*, 3: *The consuming struggle* (1996) · P. Jupp, *Lord Grenville, 1759–1834* (1985) · D. Gray, *Spencer Perceval: the evangelical prime minister, 1762–1812* (1963) · N. Gash, *Lord Liverpool* (1984) · M. W. McCahill, 'The House of Lords and the collapse of Henry Addington's administration', *Parliamentary History*, 6 (1987), 69–94 · P. D. G. Thomas, *The House of Commons in the eighteenth century* (1971) · Cobbett, *Parl. hist.*, vols. 26, 36 · *The diary and correspondence of Charles Abbot, Lord Colchester*, ed. Charles, Lord Colchester, 3 vols. (1861) · *The diary of Henry Hobhouse, 1820–1827*, ed. A. Aspinall (1947) · *The later correspondence of George III*, ed. A. Aspinall, 5 vols. (1962–70) · *Diaries and correspondence of James Harris, first earl of Malmesbury*, ed. third earl of Malmesbury [J. H. Harris], 4 vols. (1844) · *The diaries and correspondence of the Right Hon. George Rose*, ed. L. V. V. Harcourt, 2 vols. (1860) · Earl Stanhope [P. H. Stanhope], *Life of the Right Honourable William Pitt*, 4 vols. (1861–2) · [J. W. Croker], review of Pellew's *Life of Sidmouth*, QR, 79 (1846–7), 484–558 · G. C. Lewis, 'The Addington, Pitt and Grenville administrations', *Essays on the administration of Great Britain from 1783 to 1830* (1864) · J. H. Rose, *William Pitt and the great war* (1911) · R. Glover, *Peninsular preparation: the reform of the British army, 1795–1809* (1963) · E. P. Thompson, *The making of the English working class* (1963) · GEC, *Peerage*

Archives Devon RO, corresp. and papers · Glos. RO, corresp. | BL, corresp. with third Earl Bathurst, loan 57 · BL, corresp. with second earl of Chichester, Add. MSS 33107–33111 · BL, corresp. with Lord Grenville, Add. MS 58928 · BL, corresp. with third earl of Hardwicke, Add. MSS 25707–25710, 35349–36278 · BL, corresp. with second earl of Liverpool, Add. MSS 38241–38575, *passim* · BL, letters to Viscount Nelson and Earl Nelson, Add. MSS 34908, 34918, 34931, 34992 · BL, letters to Sir Robert Peel, Add. MSS 40181–40617 · BL, corresp. with Lord Wellesley, Add. MSS 13712, 37282–37313, 37416, *passim* · BL, letters to Thomas Willis, Add. MS 41694 · BL, corresp. with William Windham, Add. MSS 37876–37888, *passim* · BL, corresp. with C. P. Yorke, Add. MSS 35706, 45036 · Bucks. RLSS, corresp. with Lord Hobart · CKS, letters to William Pitt · CKS, letters to Lord Whitworth · CUL, letters to Sir R. J. Burton · CUL, corresp. with Spencer Perceval · Dorset RO, letters to Nathaniel Bond · Durham RO, letters to William Pitt · Glos. RO, Bragge Bathurst MSS · Glos. RO, corresp. with Estcourt family · Glos. RO, letters to Lord Redesdale · Hants. RO, corresp. with William Wickham · Mitchell L., Glas., Glasgow City Archives, corresp. with Henry Monteith · NA Scot., corresp. with Lord Melville · NL Scot., corresp. with Archibald Campbell Colquhoun · NRA Scotland, priv. coll., corresp. with William Adam · NRA Scotland, priv. coll., corresp. with duke of Hamilton · priv. coll., letters to Lord Eldon · PRO, Chatham MSS, PRO 30/8/101–60 · Royal Arch., letters to George III · Sheff. Arch., corresp. with Edmund Burke · Sheff. Arch., letters to Earl Fitzwilliam · Suffolk RO, Bury St Edmunds, corresp. with marquess of Bristol · U. Nott. L., corresp. with duke of Newcastle · U. Nott. L., letters to fourth duke of Portland · W. Yorks. AS, Leeds, corresp. with Joseph Radcliffe relating to Luddite disturbances in West Riding

Likenesses silhouette, 1774 (as schoolboy in mortar board), repro. in Ziegler, *Addington*, 72 · F. Wheatley, oils, c.1785–1786, Yale U. CBA · K. A. Hickel, group portrait, oils, 1793–4 (*The House of Commons, 1793–4*), NPG · K. A. Hickel, oils, 1794, Lincoln's Inn, London · J. S. Copley, oils, 1797, City Art Museum, St Louis, Missouri · J. S. Copley, oils, 1797–8, repro. in J. D. Prown, *John Singleton Copley*, 2 vols. (1966), pl. 615 · W. Beechey, oils, in or before 1803, NPG [*see illus.*] · J. Parker, line engraving, pubd 1803 (after W. Beechey), BM · medal, 1803, BM · J. S. Copley, oils, 1809, repro. in Prown, *John Singleton Copley*, pl. 616 · R. Westmacott, bronze bust, c.1810, Somerset House, London · E. Bird, two oil paintings, 1814 (*Louis XVIII*

embarking at Dover, 1814* and *Louis XVIII landing at Calais 1814*) · G. Hayter, group painting, oils, 1820 (*The trial of Queen Caroline, 1820*), NPG · T. C. Thompson, oils, c.1822, repro. in R. Walker, *Regency portraits*, 2 vols. (1985), pl. 1096 [mezzotint] · S. W. Reynolds and S. Cousins, mezzotint, pubd 1823 (after T. C. Thompson), BM, NPG · W. Behnes, bust, marble, 1831, NPG · G. Richmond, watercolour drawing, 1833, NPG · C. Smith, drawing, c.1835, repro. in Pellew, *Life and correspondence* · J. Doyle, caricatures, BM · T. Phillips, oils (after J. S. Copley), Palace of Westminster, Speaker's House

Addington, Henry Unwin (1790–1870), diplomatist and civil servant, the second son of John Hiley Addington MP (d. 1818) and Mary (d. 1833), the daughter of Henry Unwin, and the nephew of Henry Addington, first Lord Sidmouth, was born on 24 March 1790. He was educated at Winchester College and entered the Foreign Office in January 1807. He was an attaché in Sicily, Madrid, Berlin, and Stockholm before being appointed secretary of legation, first in Switzerland (1814–18) under Stratford Canning and then in Denmark (1821–2). In both postings he was chargé d'affaires for extended periods. He then became secretary of legation in Washington (1822–6) and was chargé d'affaires there during the important period from June 1823 to August 1825, when the Monroe doctrine was promulgated. Addington's reports suggest that President Monroe himself would have agreed to the British proposal of co-operation to prevent European intervention in Latin America and that it was his secretary of state, John Quincy Adams, who insisted on unilateral action. Addington's dispatches on this were considered so sensitive that they were reclassified as private letters, which would prevent future publication in a blue book (Temperley, 122, 488–9).

Addington was particularly charged to negotiate a treaty for the suppression of the slave trade. He attributed the failure of the negotiations partly to the American reluctance to concede on the right of search issue and partly to 'party spirit', that is, the strength of the southern states in the senate. On his return to Britain in 1826, he was named plenipotentiary, with William Huskisson, to conduct the Oregon boundary negotiations with the American minister Albert Gallatin. An American historian has accused him of being unduly influenced by Sir George Simpson, the governor of the Hudson's Bay Company, and of deliberately concealing details of the 1826 negotiations from his then political chief, Lord Aberdeen, at the time of the Ashburton–Webster negotiations on the same subject in 1842 (Merk, 197–204); Addington, however, could have defended his actions in 1842 on the grounds that Aberdeen had specifically opted for a completely new approach.

Addington owed his appointment as minister-plenipotentiary to Spain (1829–33) to the duke of Wellington, and after the change of ministry he found himself out of sympathy with Lord Palmerston's liberal policy in the Iberian peninsula. Addington believed that the conservative pretenders, Don Carlos in Spain and Don Miguel in Portugal, were preferable to the young queens, Isabella and María, and did not scruple to press his point. Palmerston secured his recall in 1833. On 10 November 1836

Addington married Eleanor Anne (*d.* 1877), eldest daughter of Thomas Grimston Bucknell-Estcourt, MP for Oxford University; they had no children.

Addington remained unemployed until Lord Aberdeen appointed him under-secretary at the Foreign Office in 1842, a post he retained until 1854. The work of the Foreign Office was increasing at an enormous rate and by 1848 it was clear that new arrangements were necessary. The Foreign Office wanted a simple increase in staff, but the Treasury was in favour of a radical overhaul. The main battle took place under Addington's successor, Edmund Hammond, but Addington was concerned with the early stages. A Treasury inquiry into the Foreign Office was undertaken in 1850 and in 1854 Addington was invited to comment on the famous Northcote–Trevelyan report on the civil service in general. Throughout, Addington took the line that the Foreign Office was unique because of its special responsibilities and need for confidentiality. Even though young clerks were necessarily employed as mere copyists, the proposed distinction between 'intellectual' and 'mechanical' employment was not sustainable there. He deployed similar arguments against entry by competitive examination, preferring the old system of 'nomination', although he conceded that clerks should be recruited within certain age limits and subjected to probation.

In this, as in everything else, Addington (nicknamed Pumpy in the Foreign Office) was a thorough-going conservative. Kenneth Bourne concluded, mainly on the evidence of Palmerston's opinion of him in the 1830s, that he was also irredeemably stupid (Bourne, 410, 460, 473), but Addington's career as a whole suggests obstinacy rather than stupidity. Despite his experience in the field—unusual at the time—he was a less effective permanent under-secretary than either his predecessor, John Backhouse, or his successor, Edmund Hammond. He once boasted to Aberdeen that he had managed to slip away from the office without anyone's noticing, to receive the dry reply 'Scarcely very flattering to you, Mr Addington!' (*Cambridge History of British Foreign Policy*, 3.585). He was sworn of the privy council in 1854 and died at his London residence, 78 Eaton Place, on 6 March 1870.

MURIEL E. CHAMBERLAIN

Sources FO List (1870), 51 · The Times (9 March 1870) · 'Report and papers relating to the re-organisation of the permanent civil service', Parl. papers (1854–5), 20.346–58, no. 1870 · PRO, FO 366/449 · R. Jones, The nineteenth-century foreign office: an administrative history (1971) · H. Temperley, The foreign policy of Canning, 1822–1827, 2nd edn (1966) · K. Bourne, Palmerston: the early years, 1784–1841 (1982) · A. W. Ward, The Cambridge history of British foreign policy, 1783–1919, ed. A. W. Ward and G. P. Gooch, 3 vols. (1922–3) · F. Merk, The Oregon question (1967) · E. Hertslet, Recollections of the old foreign office (1901) · Burke, Peerage
Archives Devon RO, diaries, journals, and papers | All Souls Oxf., corresp. with Charles Vaughan · BL, corresp. with Lord Aberdeen, Add. MSS 43231–43255 · BL OIOC, letter to Lady Amherst, MS Eur. F 140 · Glos. RO, corresp. relating to North American boundary commission · Norfolk RO, corresp. with Sir Henry Lytton Bulwer · PRO, corresp. with Lord Granville, PRO 30/29 · PRO, FO 366/449, 166–189; FO 5/177, 184–186, 197–198; FO 72/366–369, 378–381, 390–395, 405–411 · U. Southampton L., corresp. with Lord Palmerston · Woburn Abbey, Bedfordshire, corresp. with Lord George William Russell
Wealth at death under £35,000: probate, 4 April 1870, CGPLA Eng. & Wales

Addington, Stephen (1729–1796), Independent minister and tutor, was born at Northampton on 9 June 1729, the seventh son of Samuel Addington, who was either a hatter or a glover, and his wife, Mary. He was a student at Philip Doddridge's academy at Northampton from 1746 to 1750, after which he became minister at the Independent chapel at Spaldwick, Huntingdonshire. On 13 February 1752 he married Agnes Reymes, the daughter of Robert Reymes of Norwich, and moved to a congregation at Market Harborough. From 1758 he also ran a successful boarding-school in the neighbouring village of Kibworth and wrote several school textbooks, including works on arithmetic, geography, and Greek grammar.

In 1781 Addington moved to London to become minister to a congregation in Miles's Lane, Cannon Street, and in 1783 became also tutor at the evangelical academy in Mile End, later to become Hoxton Independent Academy. In theology he belonged to the conservative section of dissent. He was a prolific writer and author of twenty works, which, in addition to his school textbooks, included several sermons, a collection of psalm tunes, and various learned treatises on religious and moral themes. His interests extended also to social and political issues and in 1772 he published *An Inquiry in to the Reasons for and Against Inclosing Open Fields*, in which he displayed a keen understanding of the hardships enclosure could bring to the rural poor.

In later life Addington suffered from several paralytic strokes, which caused him to relinquish his tutorship at the end of 1790 and his pastorship in June 1795. He died from a stroke on 6 February 1796 at the Minories, Mile End, and was buried in Bunhill Fields.

ALEXANDER GORDON, *rev.* M. J. MERCER

Sources C. Surman, index of dissenting ministers, DWL · W. Wilson, The history and antiquities of the dissenting churches and meeting houses in London, Westminster and Southwark, 4 vols. (1808–14), vol. 1, pp. 499–511 · J. Nichols, The history and antiquities of the county of Leicester, 2/2 (1798), 504 · H. McLachlan, English education under the Test Acts: being the history of the nonconformist academies, 1662–1820 (1931), 237–8 · J. A. Jones, ed., Bunhill memorials (1849), 5 · J. C. Davies, Georgian Harborough: a picture of Market Harborough during the reigns of the first four Georges (1969), 86–9 · Allibone, Dict. · GM, 1st ser., 66 (1796), 255, 348 · Evangelical Magazine, 4 (1796), 124 · list of students at Doddridge's academy, drawn up by Noah Jones, DWL, New College archives, L54/3/42
Archives DWL, New College archives, essays written while a student at Northampton Academy, L62/1–9
Likenesses engraving, 1796, DWL, New College archives, in bound volume, L64/2/95 · engraving, BM, NPG; repro. in Protestant Dissenting Magazine (1796), 80 · two engravings, DWL, New College archives, in bound volume, L64/2/17, 18

Addinsell, Richard Stewart (1904–1977), composer and pianist, was born at 31 Woburn Square, London, on 13 January 1904, the younger of the two sons of William Arthur Addinsell, chartered accountant, and his wife, Annie Beatrice Richards. His adoring mother arranged for him to be educated at home, and this seemingly made him allergic to institutions thereafter. He went to Hertford College, Oxford, in 1922 to study law, but was there for only eighteen months and failed to take a degree. His thoughts were by now on music, and he enrolled at the Royal College of Music in 1925, but lasted there only two terms. In 1926 he made his West End début as a composer with his songs for *Charlot's Revue*, which were followed by contributions to a further Charlot revue, *Jumbles*, in 1927. The following year saw the start of a collaboration with Clemence Dane on *Adam's Opera* for the Old Vic, and in 1929 he began a journey around Europe, visiting Berlin, Vienna, and other major theatrical and musical centres.

The 1930s brought songs for further West End plays. These included dramatizations of J. B. Priestley's *The Good Companions* (1931) and Lewis Carroll's *Alice in Wonderland* (1932), as well as various works by Clemence Dane—*Come of Age* (1933), *Moonlight is Silver* (1934), *L'Aiglon* (also 1934), and *The Happy Hypocrite* (1936)—and Shakespeare's *The Taming of the Shrew* (1937). He later collaborated with Dane on her religious play cycle for radio, *The Saviours*, and in 1943 on a new version of *Alice in Wonderland*, incorporating *Alice through the Looking Glass*. Addinsell wrote music for many other BBC productions, as well as for Emlyn Williams's plays *The Light of Heart* (1940) and *Trespass* (1947) and also for Christopher Fry's theatre adaptation of *Ring Around the Moon* (1950).

By then, however, Addinsell was associated more particularly with films. In 1933 he had visited Hollywood for an aborted project involving the Czech-born actor Francis Lederer, but in 1936 his association with Dane and Douglas Fairbanks junior (co-star of *Moonlight is Silver*) led to him composing music for the film *The Amateur Gentleman*. There followed a long succession of film scores, notably for *Fire over England* (1937), *The Lion has Wings* and *Goodbye Mr Chips* (both 1939), and *Dangerous Moonlight* and *Gaslight* (both 1940). The pseudo-Rakhmaninov 'Warsaw' concerto in *Dangerous Moonlight*, played on screen by Anton Wallbrook and on the soundtrack by Louis Kentner, enjoyed a sensational international success. This had been produced in conjunction with Addinsell's arranger and orchestrator from 1937 to 1942, Roy Douglas, Addinsell's method of working being to compose at the piano and hand the result to his assistant. Besides Douglas, other collaborators included Leonard Isaacs (between 1936 and 1948) and Douglas Gamley (from 1957 to 1965).

Addinsell proved one of the most inventive of all British composers of the period. His further film scores included *Love on the Dole* (1941), *The Day will Dawn* (1942), *Blithe Spirit* (1945), *Diary for Timothy* (1946), *The Passionate Friends* (1948), *Scrooge* (1951), *Tom Brown's Schooldays* (1951), *Sea Devils* (1953), *Beau Brummel* (1954), *The Prince and the Showgirl* (1957), *The Admirable Crichton* (1957), *A Tale of Two Cities* (1958), *The Roman Spring of Mrs Stone* (1961), *The Greengage Summer* (1961; released in America as *Loss of Innocence*), *Waltz of the Toreadors* (1962), and finally *Life at the Top* (1965).

Addinsell also composed concert works, which included a miniature piano concerto, *The Smokey Mountains*

(1950). In addition he worked for many years as accompanist and composer for the actress Joyce Grenfell, whom he met in 1942. His post-war theatre work included music for revues such as *The Lyric Revue* (1951), *Penny Plain* (1951), *Airs on a Shoestring* (1953), and various one-woman shows given by Joyce Grenfell until 1965, when failing health prevented him from playing the piano and led to his retirement from film composition. Addinsell was a quiet and introverted man, but one who could be generous to his close circle and who came alive at the piano. In retirement at his home at 1 Carlyle Mansions, Cheyne Walk, Chelsea, he helped his partner, Victor Stiebel (*b.* 1907), the couturier, through the ravages of muscular sclerosis. Stiebel died in 1976, and Addinsell himself died from bronchopneumonia and osteoporosis at 1 Carlyle Mansions on 14 November 1977.   ANDREW LAMB

Sources J. Huntley, *British film music* (1947) · J. Grenfell, *Requests the pleasure* (1976) · J. Parker, ed., *Who's who in the theatre*, 9th to 13th edns (1939–61) · b. cert. · d. cert. · P. Lane, disc notes, in *British light music: Richard Addinsell*, BBC Concert Orchestra, conducted by Kenneth Alwyn (1999) [Marco Polo 8.223732] · P. Lane, disc notes, *Richard Addinsell* (1997) [ASV CD WHL 2108] · P. Lane, disc notes, *Richard Addinsell—film music* (1999) [ASV CD WHL 2115]

Likenesses A. Buckley, photograph, repro. in Grenfell, *Requests the pleasure*, p. 166 · V. Stiebel, photograph, repro. in Grenfell, *Requests the pleasure*, p. 171

Wealth at death £284,623: probate, 17 Jan 1978, CGPLA Eng. & Wales

Addis, Sir **Charles Stewart** (1861–1945), banker and government adviser, was born on 23 November 1861 in Edinburgh, the youngest of twelve children of the Revd Thomas Addis (1813–1899), a Free Church of Scotland minister, and his wife, Robina, daughter of a tea merchant in South Leith. He had five brothers and six sisters. Addis entered the Edinburgh Academy at the age of eleven, where he worked hard and did well. Yet, made deeply unhappy by his stern father's demands to excel, he left school at fifteen to become an apprentice at Peter Dowie & Co., general importers. In 1880 he obtained a clerkship with the Hongkong and Shanghai Banking Corporation (HSBC) in London, a move which shaped the rest of his career, for after only three years he was appointed to the bank's eastern staff.

Between 1880 and 1905 Addis held many assignments, including Hong Kong, Peking (Beijing), Shanghai, Calcutta, and Korea, positions that provided the young banker with the knowledge of international finance, as well as the social and diplomatic training, which ultimately led to his advancement to the top ranks of international banking and government counsel. The years in Peking (1886–8) were particularly important, since here, as an attractive young bachelor, Addis became part of the small and intimate diplomatic community, establishing lifelong friendships and gaining confidence and prestige. He continued to study Chinese, and began writing articles for the local English-language newspaper, the *Chinese Times*. Addis was ambitious and level-headed, determined to advance in the world.

In January 1894, while home on leave, Addis met and fell in love with Eba (Elizabeth) McIsaac, the daughter of the provost of Saltcoats, and within six months they were married. They then returned to Shanghai, where Addis had been appointed sub-manager of the HSBC branch. A son, Thomas, was born in 1895, the first of their thirteen children. Another son, John, was destined half a century later to become the first British ambassador to the People's Republic of China.

While in Shanghai in the late 1890s, Addis observed China's decline as an empire and participated in the establishment of the system of financial controls which transformed the Middle Kingdom into a semi-colonial outpost of Britain and its imperial rivals. Following his return to London in 1905 as junior manager of the London office of the HSBC, and his subsequent appointment in 1911 as senior manager, Addis worked closely with the world's leading bankers and businessmen, as well as Foreign Office and Treasury officials. He was knighted in 1913 for his role in creating the Six Power China Consortium. In 1921 he was created KCMG for helping to create the second China consortium.

With the outbreak of the First World War, Addis's financial expertise attracted the attention of government leaders who were seeking ways to finance the huge, growing debt to America. At the same time, Addis gained national attention through his advocacy of free trade in such leading academic journals as *The Economist* and the *Economic Journal*. He was appointed to the Cunliffe currency committee in 1917, and in May 1918 he was elected to the court of the Bank of England where he subsequently became a close friend and adviser of its governor, Montagu Norman. Throughout the 1920s Addis and Norman defended the bank's independence from government control and succeeded in achieving Britain's return to the gold standard in 1925.

In addition to his role as central banker and as a government adviser on China policy, Addis also participated in the post-war settlements in Europe, helping to shape the Dawes plan (1924), and the Young plan (1929), which created the Bank for International Settlements. All of these efforts, which aimed at satisfying the American demand for payment of the war debts and the Europeans' insistence that German reparations provide sufficient funds for such payment, ultimately failed.

Although Addis preached Anglo-American co-operation as the key to world peace, he also defended the HSBC's dominant role in China, and successfully obstructed American post-war ambitions to supplant British influence. In the 1930s, after failing to convince the American Hoover administration to support free trade, Addis gave his support to the British imperial policy of protection and abandonment of the gold standard. His hopes to achieve permanent peace had proved unattainable as Europe moved inexorably towards war.

During the last decade of his life Addis was finally able to devote time to his family and his country estate, Woodside, at Frant, in Sussex. The decision he had made in China to pursue success in business had displaced his interest in music, literature, and nature, but had never eclipsed his dedication to his wife and family: in his daily diary he always noted small items of family news alongside major international issues. His family life was not without tragedy: his youngest son, Dick, was killed in air combat in the early years of the Second World War, leaving behind a wife and an unborn son.

Throughout his life Addis found refuge in the religious teachings of his early training, maintaining his belief in the ultimate triumph of righteousness, despite wars and personal tragedies. His distinguished career was built on a reputation for personal integrity. Perhaps his most significant insight was that international financial stability is a prerequisite for world peace. Addis died of cancer at his home on 14 December 1945 and was buried at the village church at Frant, Sussex.   ROBERTA ALLBERT DAYER

Sources R. A. Dayer, *Finance and empire: Sir Charles Addis, 1861–1945* (1988) · R. A. Dayer, *Bankers and diplomats in China, 1917–1925: the Anglo-American relationship* (1981) · R. G. Hawtrey, *Economic Journal*, 56 (1946), 507–10 · F. H. H. King and others, *The history of the Hongkong and Shanghai Banking Corporation*, 4 vols. (1987–91) · D. E. Moggridge, *British monetary policy, 1924–1931: the Norman conquest of $4.86* (1972) · B. J. C. McKercher, ed., *Anglo-American relations in the 1920s: the struggle for supremacy* (1991) · R. S. Sayers, *The Bank of England, 1891–1944*, 3 vols. (1976) · M. H. Williams, *Catalogue of the papers of Sir Charles Addis* (1986)
Archives Bank of England, London, corresp. and papers · SOAS, corresp., diaries, and papers | Bank of England, London, Addis MSS, committee of treasury minutes MSS, ADM 16 · Bank of England, London, Montagu Norman MSS · GL, Morgan Grenfell MSS · Harvard U., Baker Library, Thomas W. Lamont MSS · Hongkong and Shanghai Banking Corporation, London, archives · ING Barings, London, Lord Revelstoke MSS · PRO, Cab 23, Cab 58, Cab 27.PREM 1, FO 371, FO 800, T160, T172 · U. Cam., Marshall Library of Economics, committee on the currency and Bank of England and note issues hearings, 28 Jan 1925 · Cunliffe committee MSS, committee on the currency and foreign exchanges after the war, T185
Likenesses Vandyk?, photograph, 1922, NPG · A. K. Lawrence, mural, 1928, Bank of England · Derso, cartoon, 1929, priv. coll. · portrait, 1930, NPG · group portraits, photographs, Hongkong and Shanghai Banking Corporation, London, archives · photographs, SOAS
Wealth at death £114,299 1s. 6d.: probate, 16 March 1946, CGPLA Eng. & Wales

Addison, Charles Greenstreet (*bap.* 1812, *d.* 1866), barrister and legal writer, was baptized on 1 April 1812, the youngest son of William Dering Addison of Newark House, Maidstone, the descendant of an old Kentish family, and his wife, Susan Whiting. Addison was called to the bar at the Inner Temple on 10 June 1842, and practised thereafter on the home circuit. He subsequently became revising barrister for East Kent and also for West Kent, and attained a good practice and reputation.

As a young man, Addison travelled widely, and in 1838 he published *Damascus and Palmyra: a Journey to the East* (reprinted in 1973). This work described a tour through the Near East from Greece to Syria, and was interspersed with comments on the social and political conditions of the areas visited. It benefited from revisions and illustrations by William Makepeace Thackeray, and was published in both London and Philadelphia; it proved to be a success, and was referred to by John Stuart Mill in one of his essays. Addison was also inspired by the restoration of the Temple Church to write two other books: in 1842 he brought out a *History of the Knights Templars* (which reached a third edition in 1852), and its success motivated him to bring out a shorter book in 1843, *The Temple Church*.

Addison's legal fame rests on his two extensive works, the *Treatise on the Law of Contracts* (1845), which reached an eleventh edition in 1911, and *Wrongs and their Remedies* (1860), which reached an eighth edition in 1906. These books were considered essential for lawyers, for they treated their subjects more extensively than any previous English treatise had done. However, their treatment of the subjects was not perfect. Despite the fact that Addison commented at the outset of his treatise on contracts that the law was founded on universal, immutable, and eternal principles of right and wrong, in the body of his work he eschewed theoretical or jurisprudential explanations. He rather plunged the reader into the details of legal practice. Similarly, in his work on torts, Addison failed to extract clear general principles from his large range of cases. This approach was typical of that of the dedicated but unphilosophical practitioners of common law in the mid-nineteenth century; but for that reason Addison's books did not provide a foundation for later editors to build on in the way that Joseph Chitty's work on contracts did.

In November 1848 Addison married Frances Octavia, the twelfth child of James Wolfe Murray, Lord Cringletie, a senator of the college of justice in Scotland. Addison died suddenly of a stroke on 19 February 1866 at his home at 29 Alfred Place, Thurloe Square, London, and was survived by his wife and seven children.   MICHAEL LOBBAN

Sources *Law Times* (10 March 1866), 308 · *ILN* (10 March 1866), 243 · Boase, *Mod. Eng. biog.* · Holdsworth, *Eng. law*, 15.300, 348 · *IGI* · d. cert.

Wealth at death under £7000: administration, 31 March 1866, *CGPLA Eng. & Wales*

Addison, Charlotte (*bap.* 1680, *d.* **1731**). See under Addison, Joseph (1672–1719).

Addison, Christopher, first Viscount Addison (1869–1951), politician, was born at the Willows Farm, Hogsthorpe, Lincolnshire, on 19 June 1869. His father, Robert Addison (1838–1899), who came from a long line of yeoman farmers, grazed cattle in Lindsey, east Lincolnshire. Later he moved to a much larger farm of 200 acres at Stallingborough, near Grimsby. In 1861 Robert Addison married Susan (*d.* 1913), daughter of Charles Fanthorpe, a customs official in Lincolnshire. Seven of their twelve children survived. Christopher was the youngest of three boys. He retained the outlook and style of a countryman all his life; he was instinctively an agrarian radical, rooted in the peasantry of the Danelaw.

Medicine, marriage, and radical politics Addison was sent off to Trinity College, Harrogate, at the age of thirteen. Thereafter he went to Sheffield medical school and, despite much financial stringency, on to St Bartholomew's Hospital, where he graduated with honours. He proved to be an exceptionally able medical student, especially in the field of human anatomy. In 1893 he was appointed demonstrator, later lecturer, in the Sheffield medical school, and

Christopher Addison, first Viscount Addison (1869–1951), by Howard Coster, 1945

in 1897, at the age of twenty-eight, became the first holder of the Arthur Jackson chair of anatomy. In 1893 he had gained his doctorate from the University of London. In 1901 he delivered the prestigious Hunterian lectures at the Royal College of Surgeons and then moved to Charing Cross Hospital, where he later became dean. His research as a physiologist and anatomist, especially in relation to the abdominal organs, was most distinguished. His name was given to Addison's plane, a method of identifying the shape and position of the pancreas. In 1904–6 he served as secretary of the Anatomical Society of Great Britain.

From his childhood, however, Addison had a compelling interest in politics. His early radicalism startled his Conservative father. While at Charing Cross, he developed a lifelong concern with health and social deprivation in London's East End. He also backed land nationalization. He thus campaigned actively for the Liberals in the 1906 general election. Another radical impulse came from his marriage, on 25 March 1902, to Isobel Mackinnon Gray (1875/6–1934), the daughter of Archibald Gray, a wealthy shipping man active in Indian trade. She was a passionate Christian socialist. In an exceptionally happy marriage, they were to have three sons (one of whom died in early childhood) and two daughters. In addition, his wife's wealth enabled him to think of a political career, and in 1907 he was adopted as Liberal candidate for the Hoxton division of Shoreditch, an East End constituency that had somewhat surprisingly remained Unionist in 1906.

Lloyd George's lieutenant: national health insurance and munitions In the general election of January 1910, Addison captured Hoxton with a 338 majority; at the age of forty, therefore, he left medicine for the uncertain fortunes of politics. In the following general election that December he increased his majority to 694. In both contests he campaigned strongly as a vehement supporter of Lloyd George's People's Budget and social reform programme, and of the government's Parliament Bill to curb the power of the Lords. It proved to be Lloyd George who was largely responsible for his political breakthrough. The chancellor's massive National Insurance Bill of 1911 ran into opposition both from the industrial assurance companies and from the doctors. Addison emerged as a member of the British Medical Association advisory committee on the bill, but one who strongly backed Lloyd George's measure. He persuaded Lloyd George to frame concessions to the medical profession on the make-up of the new health committees, the terms of service under the new act, and the levels of remuneration. His campaigning did much to persuade the doctors to come to terms with Lloyd George's measure. From that time onwards, Lloyd George regarded the unassuming Dr Addison with high respect for his administrative skills and also his moral courage. They worked closely together in 1912–14 on behalf of a range of radical causes, health and housing, a new Medical Research Council, women's suffrage, Ireland, and the land taxes included in Lloyd George's budget of April 1914. Together, Addison recorded, they 'dreamed dreams but based them on existing realities'. On 8 August 1914 Asquith made him parliamentary secretary to the Board of Education.

But by now Addison, like all other politicians, saw his world engulfed by world war. He had been a member of the radical foreign affairs group, critics of Grey's foreign policy. But he was no Little Englander and no pacifist. Like Lloyd George, he accepted the necessity to declare war on Germany after the invasion of Belgium. His fortunes became ever more closely entwined with those of Lloyd George now. When the political crisis of May 1915 saw Asquith's Liberal government transformed into a coalition including the Unionists and Labour, Addison found himself moved as under-secretary to Lloyd George's new office as minister of munitions. His political role now moved on to a higher plane. He was an essential lieutenant as Lloyd George used munitions' production to transform the war economy. He was most active in costing contracts and in negotiations with arms manufacturers and the unions. Here he had to handle delicate issues over dilution of skilled labour and the use of women workers. There was a prolonged crisis on the Clyde where the Clyde Workers' Committee called for strikes; Addison was centrally involved in trying to provide a solution through the use of trade cards and 'de-badging' procedures, and with some success. He became, therefore, a major practitioner of 'war socialism'. Also he became much involved in the political manoeuvres that led to the triumph of Lloyd George. He was among those Liberals who strongly backed Lloyd George in the cabinet wrangles on military

conscription. The latter's success in April 1916 severely damaged the authority of Asquith and encouraged many Liberals to think of him as a replacement at 10 Downing Street. To this end, Addison showed Lloyd George a list he had drawn up with David Davies and F. G. Kellaway of Liberals who would back Lloyd George as premier. It retained its relevance that summer and autumn as the war went increasingly badly with heavy defeat on the Somme, failure in Gallipoli, the Grand Fleet mauled at Jutland, the surrender of Romania, and Asquith's ineffective handling of Ireland after the Easter rising.

In the crucial events of 1–9 December 1916, days central to the collapse of British Liberalism, it was the relatively little-known Dr Addison who was among the kingmakers. When Asquith rejected the idea of a war committee that Lloyd George, Bonar Law, and Carson had put to him, Addison and Kellaway 'on our own account' drew up a list of Liberal MPs prepared to support a Lloyd George government. It emerged that forty-nine would do so without equivocation and that another 126—making well over half the Liberals in the house—would do so if one were formed. Lloyd George's position as the possible head of an all-party coalition was much strengthened. Addison also made contact with key Labour leaders. Lloyd George duly became prime minister on 7 December. Two days later, Addison (who had turned down the position of chief whip) became minister of munitions. He had been central to a palace revolution that transformed both his own career and the long-term future of British party politics.

Addison remained at munitions until July 1917. He developed the established strategies for enhanced arms production, including the shipping and tank-building programmes, and the new aeroplanes. He was also again embroiled in difficulties with labour. The continuing problems with dilution led to a three-week strike of over 200,000 engineering workers in May 1917 and meant a temporary falling out with Lloyd George over the press coverage that resulted. However, Addison's reputation for executive competence survived, while he also remained a crucial Liberal ally for the beleaguered prime minister. When in July 1917 Lloyd George sought to remodel his government, notably by bringing in Churchill to munitions, Addison moved to the new Ministry of Reconstruction, concerned with post-war social and economic planning. Here he took on a wide remit including health, housing, the poor law, agriculture, and resettlement. His role here led to some criticism that the reconstruction programme was confused and ill-focused. Addison, however, had at least one considerable achievement to his credit, victory over the Local Government Board in proposing a new Ministry of Health. His work gave the coalition much of its domestic manifesto henceforth. He was also pivotal to Lloyd George's dominance within the coalition. Addison's was a crucial voice in creating the Coalition Liberals, to give Lloyd George a power base in negotiating a post-war alliance with the Unionists. In the 'coupon' general election in December 1918, Addison was a key Liberal figure in the coalition. Its massive election victory, with 526 government supporters returned, as against 57 Labour and about 24 Asquithians, appeared to be a triumph for the British right. Addison, however, saw the coalition as radical, designed to promote social reform and a land fit for heroes. Post-war tensions resulted from this conflict.

Post-war reconstruction: health and housing In January 1919 Addison became president of the Local Government Board, charged with giving substance to the government's pledges of post-war reform. His immediate task was setting up a new Ministry of Health, and indeed he took over this new office that June. Even more momentous a reform was his Housing and Town Planning Act (the Addison Act) which launched a massive new programme of house building by the local authorities, with the quite new principle of a Treasury subsidy to cover the difference between the capital costs and the income earned through rents from working-class tenants, over and above a penny rate levied by the local authorities. This was amended at the end of 1919 to include a £150 subsidy to private builders. Controversy dogged the housing programme from the start. Progress in house building was slow, the private enterprise building industry was fragmented, the building unions were reluctant to admit unskilled workers, the local authorities could hardly cope with their massive new responsibilities, and Treasury policy overall was unhelpful. In addition, the costs of the Treasury subsidy began to soar, with uncontrolled prices of raw materials leading to apparently open-ended subventions from the state. Addison thus became a prime target for the right-wing 'anti-waste' campaign. For the left, the 'homes for heroes' were simply not being built. However, Addison could ultimately claim that, in spite of all difficulties, 210,000 high-quality houses were built for working people, and that an important new social principle of housing as a social service had been enacted.

The real problem with Addison, though, was that in a coalition government lurching to the right he was a constant radical gadfly, on foreign affairs, India, and Ireland as well as domestic reform, in meeting the challenge from Labour. Lloyd George, long impatient with the soaring costs of state housing, thus transferred Addison from health in March 1921 to the anomalous post of minister without portfolio. His standing in the government rapidly collapsed. There was public humiliation in the enforced cutting of his ministerial salary. As the economy deteriorated and 'anti-waste' pressure mounted, Addison was a target for all those who felt the government was being both incompetent and socialistic. The reversal of coalition social reform policies led to the halting of the housing programme, the effective end of the Treasury subsidy, and the phasing down of slum clearance. The Geddes 'axe' soon followed, and on 14 July Addison resigned. In an angry, incoherent speech in the Commons, he denounced the government for its broken promises on social reform. Later, he wrote a fierce pamphlet, *The Betrayal of the Slums* (1922). There was a violent and highly public falling out with his old ally Lloyd George. Addison now seemed a marginalized figure in the wilderness, destroyed by the all-powerful prime minister. In reality, it was Lloyd George who was now almost finished, Addison whose career had thirty years still to run.

Labour Party and agriculture When the Lloyd George coalition unexpectedly fell in October 1922, Addison ran at the subsequent general election a month later as an independent Liberal at Shoreditch. In fact, he enjoyed the support of neither Asquithian nor Lloyd Georgian Liberals in the constituency, and found himself having to finance both rival Liberal associations there simultaneously. His agent mismanaged his funds, and the debts he faced left him close to bankruptcy. Almost inevitably, he was defeated at Shoreditch in 1922, finishing a poor third in the poll to Labour. However his determination to remain in politics on the left remained intense. He now spoke for Labour candidates and became close to Ramsay MacDonald and other Labour leaders. At the end of 1923 he joined the Labour Party. Where Churchill, Mond, Guest, Greenwood, and Grigg among the Coalition Liberals were to move to the right, Addison was unique in joining Labour. In the 1924 general election, called after the resignation of the first Labour government, he stood as a Labour candidate at Hammersmith South, but was unsuccessful. He now spent much time in writing, notably in producing two-volume reminiscences, *Politics from Within* (1924), and *Practical Socialism* (1926). But his main priority lay in working on agriculture, a quite new priority for Labour with its traditional roots in urban, industrial areas. He emphasized the need for guaranteed prices for wheat farmers and minimum wages for farm labourers. His chosen mechanism was that of marketing boards for key foodstuffs, an idea which was very much his own and which proved prophetic. He was particularly anxious to improve Labour prospects in rural areas in view of Lloyd George's new campaigns through the 'green book'. Addison also advocated the nationalization of land. In the 1929 general election he returned to the house as Labour MP for Swindon, and became parliamentary secretary for agriculture under MacDonald.

As a senior politician, Addison was from the first a major figure in the second Labour administration, even in a minor post. He rapidly began to dominate Noel Buxton, his minister, and to take the initiative in putting forward proposals for the marketing of home food produce and advocating the idea of an empire marketing board. He also showed a zeal to support home agriculture, including through quotas for production, that led some ministers to fear protectionist tendencies. In June 1930 he succeeded Noel Buxton as minister for agriculture within the cabinet, and was able to press his various policies with the more force. He was also an important figure politically since he formed a link of a kind between the minority MacDonald government and his old leader, Lloyd George, with whom relations had been somewhat repaired. Ideas on agriculture became the basis for suggestions of a wider Lib–Lab collaboration, including on policies to combat unemployment. There seemed a prospect of the pre-war progressive alliance being re-established, this time with Labour as the dominant partner.

Addison launched in cabinet a series of plans to remedy

the long depression in agriculture and food production generally. He pressed for import boards for cereal growers, quotas for production, and new powers for local authorities to take over land for cultivation. The most important of his proposals, however, was his Agricultural Marketing Bill of 1931. This measure, by raising the price for the producer, lowering it for the consumer, and fostering an overall expansion of agriculture through guaranteed prices and regular price reviews, was to inaugurate a long-term revolution in policy. It was to be extended under the National Government and the wartime coalition into the marketing of milk, potatoes, cheese, cereals, livestock, and fruit, and to form much of the basis of the post-war Labour government's programme. It was a remarkable instance of Addison's executive skill and flair in obtaining all-party co-operation. However, everything changed in the financial crisis of August 1931. When, following the May report, MacDonald called for massive cuts in public spending including in unemployment benefit, Addison led the opposition. He denounced a policy introduced to placate foreign bankers that would seriously erode standards of public health and education, and was the first to urge that Britain leave the gold standard. He was the one middle-class member of the nine members of MacDonald's government who opposed cuts in social spending. The government fell and a new National Government under MacDonald now emerged. Addison was bitterly opposed to it. He was among the plethora of former Labour ministers who lost their seats in the October 1931 general election, being defeated at Swindon by a Conservative.

Labour peer Although now in his early sixties, Addison retained all his zest for politics. He was an active figure in Labour policy making in the thirties, especially in the New Fabian Research Bureau (of which he was chairman 1933–7) and the 'XYZ group' to discuss economic policy. He remained active in crusading on Labour's behalf in rural areas and wrote an influential work, *A Policy for British Agriculture*, in 1939. He also continued to collaborate with politicians in other parties, retaining his links with Lloyd George (and even, surprisingly, being invited to become a trustee of the 'Lloyd George Fund'—which he declined after some thought). He also maintained close relations with the agriculture minister, the Conservative Walter Elliot, who pressed on with the policy of marketing boards. In 1934 he got back into the house in a by-election in his old seat at Swindon, but in the 1935 election he was unexpectedly defeated again, by the Conservative candidate, the rugby player Wavell Wakefield. Addison's career took a new turn, however, on 22 May 1937 when he went to the Lords as Baron Addison—as it happened, the only Labour peer to be created by Neville Chamberlain, an old adversary. Addison also took a major part in the discussion of foreign affairs, especially in attacking the appeasement policies towards the European dictators. He was a fierce critic during the Italo-Abyssinian War and condemned the policy of non-intervention during the Spanish Civil War. As a distinguished medical man, he was chairman of the Spanish Medical Aid Committee: he was

also prominent in the Socialist Medical Association. He also kept in touch with his old ministerial colleague Winston Churchill in providing information on the failures of defence policy, especially in the air.

During the Second World War Addison took no significant role, other than serving as chairman of the Buckinghamshire War Agricultural Executive Committee. His personal life had now changed considerably. His first wife, Isobel, had died in 1934, and on 4 November 1937 Addison had married a second time. His new wife was (Beatrice) Dorothy Low (1895/6–1982), the daughter of a solicitor, (Frederick) Percy Low, who was also a Conservative agent. The new Lady Addison manifestly did not share Addison's radicalism. However, as a poised and supportive wife she sustained his morale and enduring ambition. They lived in the village of Radnage, in Buckinghamshire, quite near Chequers. Addison remained prominent in public debate during the war, speaking out on land issues and on post-war reconstruction. Of particular importance was the close relationship he struck up with his Buckinghamshire neighbour, the Labour leader, Clement Attlee. The latter enormously valued Addison's judgement and long experience in a variety of public offices, and their relationship became particularly close. When Labour won a landslide election victory in 1945, Attlee became prime minister. One of his first decisions was to make Addison (from 2 July 1945 Viscount Addison of Stallingborough) secretary to the dominions and leader of the House of Lords.

Attlee's cabinet Addison began his important role at the age of seventy-six. He remained, however, an active and highly influential politician and was in the cabinet right down to the fall of the government in October 1951, by which time he was eighty-two. He was an important figure in cabinet, where members deferred to his experience (Harold Wilson called Addison 'a wise old man') and Attlee gave him particular latitude in debate. He took a particular interest, as befitted his record, in social welfare, and gave Aneurin Bevan crucial backing in the debate on the nationalization of hospitals. Housing and agriculture were other pet subjects that claimed his attention. As dominions secretary he was a leading figure in meetings of Commonwealth heads of government, and struck up an unexpectedly close friendship with the Canadian prime minister, Mackenzie King. He and his wife went on a cross-continental tour of Canada in the autumn of 1946. He was also closely involved with Field Marshal Smuts, who had served with him in government under Lloyd George in 1917. In October 1947, in a cabinet reshuffle, he left Commonwealth relations to become lord privy seal, while continuing to lead the Lords. One ominous concern of his proved to be British policy towards nuclear weapons. He was a member of the six-man top secret committee known as GEN 163, which took in January 1947 the momentous decision that Britain should continue secretly to develop the atomic bomb. He had few doubts that Britain should retain her own nuclear deterrent.

Addison played a major unseen role as chairman of key cabinet committees and member of the future legislation committee. But his most important role in the Attlee years was leading the House of Lords. That body had a huge majority of hereditary tory peers at a time of a massive Labour majority in the Commons, and it required all Addison's statesmanship and emollient qualities to ensure that a constitutional crisis was averted. He made the small band of (mainly elderly) Labour peers a surprisingly effective fighting force. But in addition, through his personal ascendancy over the Lords and his good relationship with Lord Cranborne (later Lord Salisbury), the tory leader, he managed to get a vast body of legislation through a hostile chamber largely unscathed. Measures of nationalization, planning, and state intervention on an unprecedented scale were put on the statute book with little difficulty. When a real crisis emerged in the summer of 1947 over iron and steel nationalization (a measure over which he himself was not enthusiastic), Addison had to call on all his powers of diplomacy. In the end, steel nationalization passed through the Lords at the end of 1949, but there was also the passage of a parliamentary act to reduce the delaying powers of the upper house to one year only. All in all, his leadership of the Lords was one of the most distinguished phases of his long career.

Even after the general election of February 1950, when Attlee clung onto office by only six votes, Addison remained a member of his cabinet. He remained active in Commonwealth affairs, including the crisis surrounding Seretse Khama in Bechuanaland. He was among those who tried to persuade Bevan not to resign from the government over health service charges in the spring of 1951. He was one of eight cabinet ministers present on 19 September 1951 when Attlee unexpectedly told them that he was going to call another general election. Labour now lost office, and the Conservatives returned under Winston Churchill, another important figure in Addison's long career. By now, however, he was a dying man, stricken by cancer. He died at his home, Neighbours, at Radnage, on 11 December 1951, and is buried in the churchyard of St Mary's Church there. A memorial service was held in Westminster Abbey on 30 January 1952, attended by Attlee and many others. He left two sons and two daughters.

Christopher Addison, a quiet, uncharismatic man and a dull speaker, had an astonishing career. A distinguished professor of medicine, he turned politician in middle age and remained a major figure in public life for a further forty years. He illustrates the continuities of the progressive tradition in British politics. He was a leading 'new Liberal' before 1914 and a natural convert to Labour after 1918. However, whereas many Liberals who joined Labour did so in reaction against the war, Addison embraced the wartime experience and saw it as a major argument for constructive democratic socialism. He was the one significant Coalition Liberal who moved left after the fall of Lloyd George. He was also a generally effective minister, the only one to serve in both post-war governments. His record at munitions was rather mixed, and his achievement at reconstruction hard to assess. However, he was a pioneer minister of health whose controversial housing policy was a major new departure. At agriculture under Labour in 1930–31 he was remarkably innovative in promoting marketing boards. As leader of the Lords under Attlee he was a major success, showing himself again an idealistic radical who could use power. Finally, he was a crucial figure at pivotal moments in party politics, helping to build up Lloyd George prior to 1916, breaking with him in 1921, leading the revolt against MacDonald in 1931, and emerging as remarkably influential under Attlee in his final years. The most notable doctor ever to be involved in British politics, he played a much underestimated part, in two periods of war and reconstruction, in making Britain a welfare democracy and a more humane society.

KENNETH O. MORGAN

Sources Bodl. Oxf., MSS Addison · HLRO, Lloyd George papers · HLRO, Bonar Law papers · PRO, public records CAB, HLG, MUN, DO · PRO, MacDonald MSS · HLRO, Stansgate papers · Bodl. Oxf., MSS H. A. L. Fisher · NL Wales, Lloyd George papers · NL Wales, Thomas Jones papers · BLPES, Dalton MSS · Trinity Cam., Montagu MSS · C. Addison, *Politics from within*, 2 vols. (1924) · C. Addison, *Four and a half years*, 2 vols. (1934) · K. Morgan and J. Morgan, *Portrait of a progressive* (1980) · m. certs. · d. cert.

Archives Bodl. Oxf., family, personal, and political corresp. and papers · JRL, Labour History Archive and Study Centre, corresp. relating to Co-op milk prices · PRO, public records CAB, HLG, MUN, DO | BLPES, Dalton MSS · Bodl. Oxf., letters to Clement Attlee · Bodl. Oxf., MSS H. A. L. Fisher · HLRO, corresp. with Lord Beaverbrook · HLRO, corresp. with J. C. C. Davidson · HLRO, Bonar Law papers, letters to Andrew Bonar Law · HLRO, Lloyd George papers, corresp. with David Lloyd George · HLRO, letters to Herbert Samuel · HLRO, Stansgate papers · NL Wales, Lloyd George papers · NL Wales, Thomas Jones papers · PRO, MacDonald MSS · PRO NIre., corresp. with Edward Carson · Trinity Cam., Montagu MSS | FILM BFI NFTVA, documentary footage · BFI NFTVA, news footage

Likenesses W. Stoneman, photograph, 1937, NPG · H. Coster, photograph, 1945, NPG [*see illus.*] · P. Shepherd, portrait, 1946–9, priv. coll. · H. Coster, photographs, NPG · photographs (with C. Attlee, M. King, and others), priv. coll.

Wealth at death £16,220 1s. 0d.: probate, 21 Feb 1952, *CGPLA Eng. & Wales*

Addison, Henry Robert (1805–1876), playwright and army officer, was born of Irish parentage in 1805 at Calcutta, and spent his early life in India. He acquired on 12 July 1827 a commission in the cavalry as cornet in the 2nd dragoon guards, and progressed to lieutenant on 15 March 1831. Part of his army service was spent in western Ireland during the period of Daniel O'Connell's election in co. Clare in 1828. On 10 December 1828 he married at Limerick Mary, daughter of Thomas Phillips Vokes; they had at least one son and one daughter.

In June 1833 Addison went on half pay. His first extant plays were melodramas with songs or operettas specially written for Mrs Waylett: *Lo Zingaro*, *Jessie, the Flower of Dumblaine*, and *The Butterfly's Ball* (all performed at the Adelphi, 1833). Addison was adept at catching the public mood: all his early plays were successful and many were printed. During the 1835–6 season several were performed at Drury Lane and Covent Garden, and about this time he joined the Dramatic Authors' Society, of which most leading playwrights were members. In August 1836 he leased the Queen's Theatre, Fitzroy Square, with Mrs Waylett again as his star, but this excursion into management failed to last the season.

As recommended in his guidebook for the English resident, *Belgium as she is* (1838), Addison in 1837 settled temporarily in Bruges, where it was possible to live more cheaply than in Britain while retaining contact through a largish expatriate community. Here he attempted his first fictional writing with *Diary of a Judge* (1838)—six 'strictly original' tales of crime and justice in Napoleon's time— and also met Charles Lever, whom he pestered for space in his *Dublin University Magazine*. The lively series of 'Dramatic doings' (1840–41) which resulted drew partly on his experience as a raw recruit to play writing, and included surprisingly frank portraits of prominent contemporaries such as Bunn, Fitzball, Planché, and Moncrieff. Lever described Addison in 1841 as a portly, flamboyant *bon viveur* with well-waxed moustache, disposed to tall stories. He is fictionalized as the comic Captain Bubbleton in Lever's picaresque novel of the Napoleonic period, *Tom Burke of 'Ours'* (1844), where his extravagant boasting is redeemed by his loyalty to the hero. Addison's discursive, casual style was well suited to his inventive anecdotal versions of his Indian experiences for *Bentley's Miscellany* (1841–5) and *Ainsworth's Magazine* (1848). At the same time he resumed his dramatic career in London, principally writing successful farces such as *Sophie's Supper* (1849), *No. 117 Arundel Street, Strand* (1860), and *Locked in with a Lady* (1863). Three of his plays—he is said to have written more than sixty—were still in print, in Dicks's Standard Plays, at the end of the century. In 1849–50 he edited the first *Who's Who*, then an almanac and lists of public officials.

In 1865 Addison published *Behind the Curtain*, a moderately successful three-volume sensational novel featuring sibling rivalry, baby substitution, abduction, madness, and attempted murder, and ending with the hero's restoration to his inheritance. His *Recollections of an Irish Police Magistrate* (1862) drew on his own experiences, as well as chronicling the detective work of his father-in-law, Thomas Phillips Vokes, Limerick's magistrate during the troubles of the late 1820s and early 1830s. On a lower level was *'All at Sea': Recollections of a Half-Pay Officer* (1863), a loosely connected series of tales told by, or to, a would-be missionary *en route* for Africa. Addison knew Paris well as a sometime resident—he was a reporter for the London papers at the 1867 Paris Universal Exhibition—and his last work was a brief, though graphic, account of a visit to Paris after the 1870 commune, when mutilated bodies still littered the streets. He died aged seventy-one at his home, 32 Albion Street, Hyde Park, London, on 24 June 1876.

JOHN RUSSELL STEPHENS

Sources 'Our portrait gallery, no. XXIII: Henry R. Addison, esquire', *Dublin University Magazine*, 18 (1841), 505–8 · Boase, *Mod. Eng. biog.* · *Era Almanack and Annual* (1868), 17 · J. Shattock, ed., *The Cambridge bibliography of English literature*, 3rd edn, 4 (1999) · *Era Almanack and Annual* (1874), 4 · A. Nicoll, *Early nineteenth century drama, 1800–1850*, 2nd edn (1955), vol. 4 of *A history of English drama, 1660–1900* (1952–9), 251, 567 · A. Nicoll, *Late nineteenth century drama, 1850–1900*, 2nd edn (1959), vol. 5 of *A history of English drama, 1660–1900* (1952–9) · *CGPLA Eng. & Wales* (1876) · parish register (marriage), Limerick, 10 Dec 1828

Likenesses sketch, repro. in *Dublin University Magazine*, 18 (1841), facing p. 505

Wealth at death under £450: resworn probate, Nov 1878, *CGPLA Eng. & Wales*

Addison, John (d. 1540), clergyman, was born in York diocese and studied at Cambridge, where he graduated BA in 1506, subsequently proceeding MA (1509), BD (1515), and DD (1523). A fellow of Pembroke College from 1505 to 1522, on which title he was ordained priest at York in 1506, he was appointed a university preacher in 1513. He left Cambridge to become chaplain to Bishop John Fisher of Rochester (who appointed him vicar of St Nicholas's, Rochester, in May 1522, a post he resigned in 1524). In this capacity he supervised the publication of Fisher's *Assertionis Lutheranae confutatio*, published in Antwerp in 1523, and carried messages between his patron and Katherine of Aragon during the latter's divorce case. Fisher promoted him successively to the rectories of Snodland (1524; resigned in 1530), Woldham (resigned by February 1534), and Bromley (1530), but Addison forfeited his preferments by attainder in 1534, when, with Fisher, he was convicted of misprision of the treason of Elizabeth Barton. In his will he refers to this as 'the tyme of my trowbles', the period 'when I lost my goodes' (PRO, PROB 11/28/106). However, he redeemed himself by prompt conformity to the royal supremacy, and by 1536 had received the plum rectory of Loughborough, worth over £40 a year, from the earl of Huntingdon (perhaps at royal instigation). He preached obedience to God and king across northern England in the wake of the Pilgrimage of Grace, and wrote a treatise (now lost) against the papacy. With Cromwell's backing he was appointed in 1537 to the rectory of Caldbeck as, in effect, the only learned preacher in Carlisle diocese—his will refers to 'my Quares of sermons written' (ibid.). He died at Caldbeck in summer 1540. His will (made on 30 July, and proved on 20 October), which suggests that he also maintained a residence in London, bequeathed numerous books of scholastic theology, as well as 'the bishops boke callyd the Institution of a Christen man' (ibid.) and an English New Testament.

RICHARD REX

Sources M. Bateson, ed., *Grace book B*, 2 vols. (1903–5) · W. G. Searle, ed., *Grace book Γ* (1908) · will, PRO, PROB 11/28, sig. 14 · *LP Henry VIII*, 12/2, no. 268; 13/1, nos. 547, 695(2); 14/1, no. 190 · act of attainder, 25 Henry VIII c. 12 · register, Pembroke Cam., fol. 64v · Venn, *Alum. Cant.*, 1/1.8 · J. Fisher, *Assertionis Lutheranae confutatio* (1523), title page, *verso* · John Fisher to Hermann Lethmaet, Gemeentelijke Archiefdienst, Gouda, MS 959 · W. G. D. Fletcher, *The rectors of Loughborough* (1892)

Addison, John (*fl.* 1735–1736), translator, evidently received a good education, though nothing is known about his family or his life other than the fact that he published in London two books of translation from the classics. The first, *The works of Anacreon translated into English verse, with notes explanatory and poetical, to which are added the odes, fragments, and epigrams of Sappho, with the original Greek* *plac'd opposite to the translation* (1735), was advertised in the *Gentleman's Magazine* without the translator's name, but with the comment that it included 'the Heads of Anacreon and Sapho curiously engrav'd'. Addison lists the contents in both Greek and English; he also gives a 'Life of Anacreon' and a 'Life of Sappho', both in English. The engraving of Sappho is described as 'taken from a Busto in the Possession of the Earl of Pembroke at Wilton House'.

In his preface Addison reviews several earlier English versions of Anacreon's poems, but, while praising those of Cowley and Pilkington, he concludes: 'I know of none that can so properly be call'd a Translation as those which Mr. Stanley publish'd, whose Writings are an Honour to his Country'. Addison himself translates into couplets and heavily annotates every page. Ode 11, titled 'On Himself', is a typical example of his verse:

> I'm often by the Women told,
> Alas! Anacreon, thou growst old:
> Here, in this glass thyself survey,
> Fall'n is thy Hair, quite fall'n away!
> No Ringlets wanton o'er thy Brow,
> It's all a Field of Baldness now.
>
> But whether still soft-curls my Hair,
> Or, flying hence, has left me bare,
> I know not; this indeed I know,
> If, as they tell me, old I grow,
> It's time to snatch short Joys from Fate,
> And haste to live ere it's too late.
> (p. 49)

Near the end of the following century A. H. Bullen comments in his introduction to an edition of *Anacreon*: 'In the eighteenth century, the translations of John Addison, Thomas Fawkes, etc. were highly esteemed, but it must be confessed that they are dull, uninspired, mechanical performances' (*Anacreon*, xiii–xiv). From Sappho, Addison gives the odes 'An Hymn to Venus' and 'On a young maid whom she lov'd', in addition to fragments and epigrams.

Addison next published *The works of Petronius Arbiter in prose and verse, translated from the original Latin, … to which are prefix'd the life of Petronius, done from the Latin, and a character of his writings by Monsieur St. Evremont* (1736). This work is heavily annotated in English, and it includes 'A key to the principal characters'. Justifying his interest in Petronius, Addison states in a preface: 'There is no Part of Nature, no Profession, which Petronius does not admirably paint; He is a Poet, an Orator, and a Philosopher, at his Pleasure.' A title-page illustration, from an engraving by Gerard Vandergucht (1698–1777), depicts a writer about to record the story of Rome's fall, as a satyr points toward the flames engulfing the distant city. This is accompanied by the following epigraph:

> When gay Petronius, to correct the Age,
> Gave way of old to his Satirick Rage,
> With just Resentment fir'd, he meant to shew
> How far Licentiousness at last might go:
> Blushing we read the loose, the flagrant Tale,
> And loath the Vice thus shewn without a Veil.

JOYCE FULLARD

Sources BL cat., 2.296; 7.348 · T. Clayton, *The English print, 1688–1802* (1997) · *GM*, 1st ser., 5 (1735), 740 · *Anacreon: with Thomas Stanley's translation*, ed. A. H. Bullen (1893)

Addison, John (*c.*1766–1844), double bass player and composer, was born in London, the son of a village mechanic. As a child he showed considerable musical ability, learning to play a variety of instruments, including the flageolet, flute, bassoon, and violin. He was also self-taught in composition, and his early works include a set of *Six Sonatas or Duets* for two violins or recorders, op. 1 (1772). He became a member of the Royal Society of Musicians on 7 October 1793, and in the same year married Elizabeth Willems (*d.* 1840), an orphan and the ward of his parents, who was a niece of the bass singer F. C. Reinhold. After her marriage she sang with success at Vauxhall Gardens, where Addison was a cellist, and at other places in London; she made a notable appearance at Covent Garden as Rosetta in *Love in a Village* on 17 September 1796. She then obtained an engagement in Liverpool, where her husband played first cello and then double bass in the orchestra. In 1797 they went to Bath, where Mrs Addison studied under Rauzzini, and then to Dublin; Addison became director of the amateur orchestra of a private theatre there, and, having to arrange the music, improved himself in composition. After three years they moved to Manchester where Addison abandoned music for a time and embarked on cotton manufacture, which resulted in the loss of a considerable sum.

Resuming his original career in London, Addison played the double bass for many years at the Italian Opera, the Concerts of Ancient Music, and the Vocal Concerts. He also shared with Michael Kelly the management of a music business and produced most of his own theatrical music, making himself known through several popular operas for Covent Garden and the English Opera House at the Lyceum. The most successful of his dramas were *The Sleeping Beauty* (6 December 1805, Drury Lane) and *The Russian Impostor* (22 July 1809, Lyceum). Another important work is his sacred drama *Elijah*, first performed at the Drury Lane Lenten oratorios on 3 March 1815. Addison also composed many songs and glees and achieved some success as a teacher of singing, instructing Alex Lee and Pearman, among others; he wrote a singing method in 1836 entitled *Singing Practically Treated, in a Series of Instructions*. He died at Camden Town on 30 January 1844.

W. B. SQUIRE, rev. DAVID J. GOLBY

Sources W. H. Husk and A. Loewenberg, 'Addison, John', *New Grove* · *Musical Examiner* (10 Feb 1844), 414–15 · [J. S. Sainsbury], ed., *A dictionary of musicians*, 2 vols. (1824) · *GM*, 2nd ser., 21 (1844), 328 · J. P. Wearing, *American and British theatrical biography* (1979)
Likenesses R. Cooper, stipple, pubd 1819 (after J. Slater), BM, NPG

Addison, Joseph (1672–1719), writer and politician, was born on 1 May 1672 at the rectory, Milston, a hamlet north of Amesbury in Wiltshire, the son of Lancelot *Addison (1632–1703) and his wife, Jane, *née* Gulston (*c.*1635?–1684). His father was at that time vicar of Milston, and Joseph is said to have been baptized on the same day, indicating

Joseph Addison (1672–1719), by Sir Godfrey Kneller, c.1703–12

that there were doubts about the baby's survival. His mother came like his father from a clerical and royalist background; her brother William Gulston had held the living at Milston prior to Lancelot, and became bishop of Bristol in 1679. Joseph was the oldest child in the family to survive infancy. His sister Dorothy, born in 1674, was twice married, while his two brothers achieved minor note in the world. Gulston (1673–1709) entered the service of the East India Company and was briefly governor of Fort St George (Madras) prior to his sudden death, and Lancelot (1680–1710), a fellow of Magdalen College, Oxford, followed him to India in 1710.

The young Addison spent his first eleven years at Milston, although he may have received some private schooling at Amesbury and Salisbury. In June 1683 his father was elected dean of Lichfield, and the family moved to a substantial deanery in the cathedral close there. Joseph attended the ancient Lichfield grammar school, where Samuel Johnson studied a generation later. Although Addison's father soon received preferment as archdeacon of Coventry and gained increasing renown as an author of theological books, he was evidently a poor financial manager and the family enjoyed no great prosperity.

Despite the loss of Jane Addison, the Addisons seem to have been a close-knit and harmonious group according to Richard Steele, who made holiday visits to them at the deanery. The celebrated friendship of Addison and Steele began when Joseph was sent to the Charterhouse School in London at thirteen. From 1685 the boys were under the direction of a new master of the Charterhouse, the speculative and unorthodox Thomas Burnet. Steele was the older of the two by just seven weeks. Both young men were bound for Oxford at the end of their schooldays.

Oxford On 18 May 1687 Addison matriculated at Queen's College, his father's alma mater. Two years later, as Steele was entering Christ Church, Addison moved to Magdalen College, having been elected to a demyship on 30 July 1689 thanks to the efforts of one of the tutors at Queen's, William Lancaster. This mark of recognition came because of the young man's attainments in classical learning, and above all for his skill in composing Latin verse. Lancaster had seen a poem entitled *Tityrus et Mopsus* in a collection published by the university to welcome the new king, William III; against the grain of his ancestry, Addison had taken sides in opposition to the Stuart cause. Also admitted to Magdalen on the same election were three individuals who would later achieve prominence in the church. Two of them, with orthodox and whiggish views, would achieve bishoprics: these were Hugh Boulter, a future dean of Christ Church and archbishop of Armagh, and Richard Smalbroke. The third was the notorious high-church preacher Henry Sacheverell, who never progressed beyond an opulent living which his tory friends found for him, but who served as the lightning rod around which politics and religion flashed during the second decade of the eighteenth century. Sacheverell was Addison's closest ally in this group, and the two men may have been room-mates at Magdalen. Little is known of the young Joseph's days as an undergraduate, except that he evidently prospered as a student under his tutor William Cradock, and that he acquired the habit of strolling in the huge park surrounding the college. A riverside path named Addison's Walk still commemorates his fondness for solitude among the scenes of well-manicured nature. Nor is there any evidence of contacts between Addison and his old friend Steele, who left the university in 1692 without a degree and joined the army.

By this time Addison was already taking the first steps to academic success and so potentially towards clerical eminence. On 6 May 1691 he became bachelor of arts; on 14 February 1693 he proceeded to the master's degree; and on 30 July 1697 he was made a probationer fellow. Finally, exactly one year later, he became a full fellow of the college. All this indicated high talent and a measure of social adroitness. He had kept the support of important figures such as Lancaster, and he was on sufficiently good terms with the authorities to be allowed to retain his fellowship without entering on holy orders, as was normally required. Here he may have had the assistance of the college president, John Hough, who had been installed by the fellows in defiance of James II, and who moved on in 1699 to Lancelot Addison's diocese of Lichfield as bishop. Joseph cemented his good relations in the university when he assembled a collection of Latin poems, *Musarum Anglicanarum analecta* (1699), mostly contributed by members of Magdalen and Christ Church. Eight of the editor's own works appeared in this anthology.

Moreover, the young man had made astute contacts outside Oxford. Addison's main coup came when he attracted the interest of John Dryden, still the greatest man of letters in the nation despite a loss of court patronage following the revolution of 1688. Addison's first step was to write a congratulatory poem, laying special emphasis on Dryden's skills as a translator—one side of the poet's work comparatively unappreciated until the latter part of the twentieth century. This poem appeared in Dryden's miscellany *Examen poeticum* in June 1693. Soon afterwards Addison made the acquaintance of the great publisher Jacob Tonson senior, who had issued the miscellany. Next year the fourth volume of Tonson's series contained four items by Addison, including versions of Ovid and Virgil. There were also two English poems, the more notable being 'An Account of the Greatest English Poets', dedicated to Sacheverell. In the manner of the age, this work finds most writing previous to the seventeenth century crude and artless, with the highest praise reserved for John Milton, Abraham Cowley, and Dryden. There followed negotiations with Tonson concerning a translation of Ovid, and subsequently plans for a version of Herodotus, neither of which came to fruition. However, in 1697 Addison resumed his links with Dryden when he supplied an essay on the *Georgics* to the great translation of Virgil; this was anonymous, but in a postscript Dryden paid tribute to the contribution of 'the most Ingenious Mr. *Addison of Oxford*'.

As a writer Addison did his long-term prospects no harm when he established contact with Dryden and Tonson. In the process, too, he got to know the ablest among their younger associates: this was William Congreve, already a well-respected poet and translator, as well as the brightest star in the dramatic firmament. From a worldly point of view Addison scored two direct hits of even greater significance. He managed to attract the support of the greatest patrons of the age, men who occupied at the same time a major position in the world of politics. One was John, Baron Somers, at this time lord keeper: in 1695 Addison composed a 'Poem to his Majesty', to which he sensibly added a dedicatory letter to Somers, and thus laid the basis for a long-lasting intimacy with one of the pillars of the post-revolution establishment. The other was Charles Montagu, later Lord Halifax, who had made a name for his poems: now, as chancellor of the exchequer, he was spearheading an overhaul of Treasury affairs which gave rise to the financial revolution. In 1697 Addison dedicated to Montagu his most admired Latin poem, *Pax Gulielmi auspiciis Europeae reddita*, that is 'Peace restored to Europe under the guidance of William'. The king could have made little of this effusion, celebrating the recently signed peace of Rijswijk, but it proved effective in gaining Montagu's support.

As a result, Montagu arranged a Treasury grant of £200 allowing Addison to make an extended stay on the continent. The idea was that he should take advantage of his travel abroad to learn languages and equip himself for a diplomatic career. In addition he required leave of absence from his fellowship at Magdalen, and on 17 August the college granted permission for him not to take holy orders during the time he was away. According to

Steele's later account, this was helped by a letter from Montagu to the outgoing college president, John Hough, in which he emphasized that he had no desire to do the church any injury 'other than keeping Mr. Addison out of it' (Smithers, 43).

Travels Armed with his stipend, as well as copies of the collection of Latin verse to distribute on his journeys, Addison made his way from Dover to Calais in August 1699. He had been briefed in the office of the secretary of state by Abraham Stanyan, a near contemporary who had already begun to make his mark as a diplomat. Stanyan was to remain an important contact in the political world; he could easily give the untravelled Addison a better sense of power struggles which were threatening the fragile peace achieved in 1697. Once in Paris, Addison tasted a careful selection of the pleasures of the town, including opera, and wrote dutiful letters to his patrons Halifax and Somers. At Versailles he noted a picture of Louis XIV represented as Jupiter blasting the Danube and Rhine with thunderbolts, an image which seems a few years later to have inspired his best-known line, in the poem on Blenheim. However, he still had very little command of spoken French, and by December he had moved to Blois, in order to acquire what was regarded as the purest spoken form of the language. A series of masters since the sixteenth century had made the town a centre for teaching the renowned Tourangeau accent. This meant that the place, lying low on the Loire, was 'very much infested with fogs & German Counts', as Addison informed Stanyan (*Letters*). According to a story told by a priest many years later, Addison lived a retired and austere existence during almost a year at Blois: 'He had his masters generally at supper with him, kept very little company beside, and had no amour whilst here that I know of—and I should have known if he had had any' (Spence, 1.331). There was however time for a brief tour of central France with a new acquaintance, Edward Wortley Montagu. Wortley is now known almost entirely as the husband of the formidable Lady Mary, but in his youth he seemed to hold promise as a diplomat and whig politician, besides being the heir to a great business fortune. Both Wortley and his wife remained loyal friends to Addison.

By late summer 1700 Addison, now more fluent in conversation, had returned to Paris and was able to see more of Stanyan, who had been appointed secretary at the embassy there. Interviews were arranged with leading figures in French culture, notably the philosopher Nicolas Malebranche and the poet Boileau, then at the peak of his influence throughout the western world as a living embodiment of all that was classical and therefore best. Though Boileau was sixty-four, considered elderly in those days, and somewhat deaf, he impressed his visitor with his comments on literature, including a preference for Homer's unselfconscious manner of narrative over the preachy manner of his fashionable imitator Fénelon—a valuation of showing rather than telling, in modern terms. Addison was grateful for the advice and his later criticism shows how much he learned from Boileau's precepts and example.

Soon it was time to move on again: the ideology of the grand tour discouraged lingering too long. After travelling south to Marseilles Addison took ship for Italy on 12 December 1700, but was driven back by a storm. In the end he reached Genoa by land, and then proceeded through Pavia to Milan and then Venice, after which he followed the accustomed route south, choosing to go via San Marino and Loreto as he journeyed briefly to Rome and then on to Naples. He climbed Vesuvius, sailed round Capri, and sailed back up the coast to Rome. Here he passed a more extended sojourn, visiting churches, annotating architecture and antiquities, and undertaking trips out to literary shrines such as Tivoli and Frascati. There were poetic echoes on almost every corner for a man as deeply imbued in the ancient corpus as Addison, and he was to coin the phrase 'classic ground' to express a pervading atmosphere of ageless accomplishment, as the familiar texts sprang unbidden into his mind.

At length Addison was obliged to leave these congenial scenes, and journeyed via Siena to Florence. As the war with France intensified and the manoeuvres of the French and imperial armies came closer, the pace of his journey quickened. He crossed the Alps by Mount Cenis in December 1701, working on the poem 'A Letter from Italy', which he would dedicate to Montagu (now Lord Halifax) and which would prove one of his most popular works. In the safety of Geneva, he paused for some time, going on expeditions round the lake while anticipating his nomination as secretary to Prince Eugène, the imperial commander. Then came the unexpected news of the death of King William on 8 March 1702. Halifax, Somers, and other whig patrons were dismissed from office, and Addison's prospects suddenly looked bleak, after he had enjoyed a decade of steady ascent. He decided to continue his travels, and in the autumn journeyed through Switzerland and the Tyrol to Vienna. At the end of the year he proceeded on another snowbound journey to Dresden (much of the entire tour was carried out in winter), and thence to Hamburg, where he may have met the youthful Handel. The final stages of his odyssey took him through Leiden and Amsterdam. While in Holland he belatedly learned of the death of his father, which had occurred more than a year before. On hearing the news he wrote a letter to Bishop Hough, not without a certain eye for his own self-interest as he reminded the bishop of his 'just sense of duty and gratitude' (*Letters*). While he hovered uncertainly in the Dutch cities, Jacob Tonson concocted a plan to have him act as tutor to a son of the proud duke of Somerset. But Addison's acceptance was not couched in sufficiently humble terms, and the chance was lost. Finally, he was forced to return to England early in 1704, with no job lined up and no obvious career path beckoning.

Public office During Addison's absence on his travels the whigs had lost political control, at least for a short time. But their leaders had not given up all the levers of cultural power. One of the sites in which they continued to exert influence was the Kit-Cat Club, formed at the beginning of the century with Tonson as its secretary. This was a group of aristocrats, socialites, writers, and intellectuals, whose official business ran to little more than inscribing fanciful toasts to the reigning beauties of the town, but whose sphere of patronage extended very widely. Somers and Halifax were among the founding figures, along with their junto colleague Lord Wharton, the duke of Somerset, and the earl of Carlisle. Literature and drama were represented by Congreve, John Vanbrugh, William Walsh, and Samuel Garth. Other younger aspirants to the fame and fortune which admission to the society conferred were Abraham Stanyan and Richard Steele, who had stolen a march on his old schoolfriend by establishing his career as a dramatist. It was within this circle that Addison now attempted to make his presence felt.

Addison's chance came after he had been back in England for a few months. The *Letter from Italy* was published in this year, and made safe the interest of Halifax. Through another Kit-Cat member, Henry Boyle, now chancellor of the exchequer, it was arranged that Addison should be appointed a commissioner of appeal in excise, on condition that he wrote a poem to celebrate the battle of Blenheim, where in August Marlborough had enjoyed his greatest triumph of the entire war. The appointment was gazetted early in November, and a month later the verses were ready. On 14 December 1704 Tonson published *The Campaign, a Poem, to His Grace the Duke of Marlborough. By Mr. Addison* in a folio of twenty-four pages. It was a defining moment in the author's career: second and third editions were soon required, and even the notorious jealousies of the literary world were suspended as he basked in praise from all quarters. As time went on, the tories felt a need to set up a rival hero such as the mediocre Admiral George Rooke, and John Philips tried to put a different spin on events with a poem addressed to Robert Harley. But it was to no avail: Addison had seized his great opportunity.

Though Addison's shapely couplets have come to seem bland to later generations, they caught the right note at this juncture. One image above all struck the imagination of the public, when the general is likened to an angel, 'calm and serene' in the midst of tumult, who 'rides in the whirlwind, and directs the storm'. The line recalls the picture Addison had seen at Versailles, but he managed to give the idea an immediately topical ring, with a reference to 'rising tempests' shaking 'a guilty land'. Everyone knew what this referred to—the great storm which had flattened much of southern England just a year before, on 26–7 November 1703. Unlike most of his readers, Addison had not been on hand to witness the destruction; but he knew how easily this natural disaster could serve as an emblem of national decline, which must be halted by the quasi-divine intervention of the duke and his allies. Queen Anne, by comparison, receives only half-hearted plaudits.

Gradually during 1705 the political climate changed. Somers and Halifax were back in the privy council, high-church tories like the earl of Nottingham and Sir Edward Seymour were ousted from government, and the whigs did well in a general election. All this brightened the prospects for Addison, and in July he was appointed undersecretary in the office of the secretary of state for the southern department, Sir Charles Hedges. It was an administrative as much as a political position, but it confirmed Addison, still in his early thirties, as a coming man. He retained his job when Marlborough's son-in-law the earl of Sunderland took over as secretary in early December 1706. By that time Addison had embarked on a more momentous task, when he accompanied Halifax to Hanover in summer 1706. The declared purpose of the mission was to invest the young electoral prince with the Order of the Garter, but the real business on hand was to keep the Hanoverian court apprised of what was happening about the succession to the English throne—an issue which constantly lay behind the day-to-day manoeuvres of domestic politics.

All this time Addison had not neglected his career as a man of letters. His *Remarks on Several Parts of Italy*, based on his grand tour experience and larded with poetic allusions, reached the public in November 1705, with a dedication to Somers. By the standards of modern travel writing, this is deficient in picturesque human detail: a reader would hardly know that Addison was serving as a bear leader, conducting on their passage to manhood two youths, one of them the nephew of Charles Montagu. But the book is often eloquent on art, history, and literature. After this Addison turned to the musical theatre, with one of the first attempts to produce a full-blown English opera. His libretto for *Rosamond* was set by Thomas Clayton, who had recently enjoyed some success with *Arsinoë*. It was based on the legend of fair Rosamond Clifford, the mistress of Henry II. Addison chose this subject because the plot was laid around Woodstock Park, where Blenheim Palace had just begun to take shape, so that the narrative could use features of the landscape such as Rosamond's Bower. The opera proved a failure on its first performance at Drury Lane on 4 March 1707, and has never entered the repertory in Clayton's setting. Nevertheless Tonson published Addison's words in a quarto of thirty-six pages, with the text 'humbly inscribed' to Sarah Churchill, duchess of Marlborough. The opera was reprinted once or twice, but not staged again until the youthful Thomas Arne produced a new musical setting at Lincoln's Inn Fields in 1733. It is unfortunate that little of the music survives, since it enjoyed considerable success in its own time.

Addison's personal qualities enabled him to achieve a central position in the literary world quite early in his career. He had made friends with Jonathan Swift, he came to know Thomas Tickell and Ambrose Philips, and he retained the esteem of Congreve and Steele. At this stage none seems to have resented his seemingly irresistible rise, which is a tribute to his talents for good fellowship. He assisted other writers, as when he supplied a prologue for a tragedy *Phaedra and Hippolytus*, composed by Edmund Smith, an old friend from Oxford days, in 1706. Further help was given to Steele, in revising a play *The tender husband* (1705), and more concrete aid when he loaned Steele the large sum of £1000 a year later. Perhaps in an effort to limit the need for further hand-outs, Steele was made editor of the government newspaper the *London Gazette* on 1

May 1707. Most of the information this staid organ relayed would have come from the office of the secretaries of state, and it is virtually certain that his old schoolfriend played some part in gaining the appointment for Steele.

Meanwhile, Addison's own star continued to rise. He wrote a pamphlet entitled *The present state of the war and the necessity of an augmentation considered*, which came out late in 1707. This set out the standard whig objectives in pursuing the war against France, and the reasons for driving it on to a decisive conclusion, thus preventing a solid French and Spanish alliance against British trading interests. In March 1708 the ministry had its hand strengthened by successful measures against a planned invasion by the Pretender, and soon afterwards the whigs gained a resounding victory in the general election. The moderate tory Robert Harley was squeezed out of office, and in due course Somers and Wharton regained a major role in affairs. This was naturally good for Addison, described by a contemporary about this time as 'really a very great man with the juncto' (Smithers, 150). He was himself elected to parliament for the small Cornish borough of Lostwithiel, having gained enough of the two dozen or so voters to satisfy the mayor, who was a far from impartial returning officer. Eventually, on petition, the Commons decided through its committee of privileges that he had not been duly elected. It took little time to find another pliable constituency, and in March 1710 the thirteen accommodating voters of Malmesbury in Wiltshire (a town where Wharton held a strong interest) sent Addison back to Westminster. He remained member for the borough until his death. When re-elected in 1710, he was so popular that according to Swift 'if he had a mind to be chosen king he would hardly be refused' (Swift, *Journal to Stella*, 1.52).

By this time Addison had made further progress in the world of politics. In December 1708 he was appointed secretary to the new lord lieutenant of Ireland, who happened to be Wharton, at a salary of about £2000 per year. Along with this job came appointment to the Irish privy council, and when the new team arrived at Dublin in April 1709 Addison shared in a grand ceremony of welcome. He was soon elected to the Irish House of Commons as member for Cavan, and took a large role in the business of state for the next few months. Despite parliamentary quarrels, government measures were forced through in the ensuing session, until parliament was prorogued at the end of August. Addison now had time to visit the site of the battle of the Boyne and also to drop in briefly on his friend Swift at Laracor, near Belfast Lough. In May 1710 he came back with the lord lieutenant for a further session of parliament, but by this time the political tide was turning, and both Wharton and Addison could see that their hold on office was fragile. For his part Addison tried to insure his future by obtaining the patent for a post as keeper of the records in Bermingham's Tower, in effect curator of the Irish public records. Later, when estranged, Swift claimed that Addison had been forced to purchase 'an old obscure Place … of Ten Pounds a Year, and to get a salary of £400 annexed to it, though all the Records there are not worth Half a Crown, either for Curiosity or Use' (*Prose*

Works, 10.58). In fact Addison paid £230 to his predecessor in May 1710 to gain the patent, and in return he was promised £400 annually from the royal establishment.

When Addison returned to London in August 1710 he entered a world of politics which had been completely transformed. The whigs and the Marlborough faction were in retreat, with Harley and more uncompromising tories installed in government. Wharton was about to be dismissed, which meant that Addison too would be out of a job. Following the deaths of two brothers in India, he had expected a sizeable inheritance; but legal disputes and the neglect of the trustees meant that Gulston Addison's considerable fortune was whittled down by the time it belatedly reached Joseph. To cap these things, he had resigned his Oxford fellowship. Soon he would be writing glumly to Wortley Montagu, 'I have within this twelvemonth lost a place of £2000 per ann. An estate in the Indies of £14,000, and what is worse than all the rest, my mistress' (*Letters*). Nothing is known of the mistress, but Addison faced a bleaker prospect on the political front than he had known since he first entered public life. Fortunately, his literary career had taken off in the most spectacular fashion.

The Tatler, The Spectator, and Cato It was chiefly through Richard Steele that Addison was able to devote himself to periodical literature, the department of writing on which his fame has subsequently rested. Steele had founded *The Tatler* on 12 April 1709; it ran for 271 issues, appearing every Tuesday, Thursday, and Saturday until 2 January 1711. Presented as the work of 'Isaac Bickerstaff Esq.', it occupied two sides of a folio sheet, printed in two columns, with news stories as well as advertisements diversifying the contents at first. Gradually the focus of the paper became a single long essay, which might deal in social satire, dramatic criticism, or moral reflection. Mildly reformist in outlook, the journal directed its attacks mainly against affectation, vanity, and complacence in the world of politics and society. *The Tatler* quickly gained a following, and after a year was selling in the region of 3000 copies per issue. Addison contributed his first essay on 20 May 1709, and in all wrote almost fifty papers unaided, as well as more than twenty in collaboration with Steele. From the start his manner is slightly more polished and urbane than that of his friend, and even in his humorous pieces Addison brings a dignified port alien to Steele.

After the closure of *The Tatler*, a yawning gap in the market must have been as obvious to Addison and Steele as it was to the reading public at large. They responded by initiating *The Spectator* on 1 March 1711, thus embarking on one of the most triumphant literary projects of the age. Before the paper closed on 6 December 1712, it had gone through 555 issues, had regularly sold up to 4000 copies (indeed even larger figures for a few numbers), and had transformed periodical writing in English. *The Spectator* came out six days a week, Monday to Saturday. This time the work was more equally shared, with both Addison and Steele contributing about 250 essays each. Their main assistant was Eustace Budgell, who wrote about thirty papers. As with *The Tatler*, collected volumes of papers

were published to mop up demand in subsequent months and years, and these too sold well. Even the imposition of a government stamp tax on journals in August 1712 could do no more than temporarily slow down the irresistible rise in *The Spectator*'s cultural and commercial fortunes. From this time onwards the title became one of the most famous in the annals of publishing: hundreds of editions appeared over the next two centuries, there were selections and translations into several languages, and its pages were dotted with familiar sayings which found their way into every dictionary of quotations.

In the case of *The Tatler*, Steele had taken the initiative, and his relaxed satire of coffee-house concerns had defined the tone of the journal as that of a knowing man about town. Little use was made of the ostensible author, Isaac Bickerstaff (an elderly astrologer). With *The Spectator*, the guiding hand is generally agreed to have been that of Addison. It was he who wrote the opening number, introducing readers to the 'Spectator'—an observant and well-travelled individual, whose detached viewpoint and shrewd reflections on life inform the journalistic discourse throughout the paper's run. He may also have invented the club of friends and associates frequented by the Spectator, although Steele composed the second paper in which the members first appear. Among this group the most regular figures included the whig merchant Sir Andrew Freeport and the superannuated beau Will Honeycomb, with a great knowledge of the 'gallantries and pleasures of the age'—which appear to date back to the Restoration in their content and manner. However, the most popular character by far was the bluff tory squire Sir Roger de Coverly, up from the Worcestershire country to enjoy the social round in London. He became a byword for traditional rural virtues, with his combination of naïvety, honesty, and benevolence.

As well as creating this enduring group of men, Addison achieved an even greater success by his innovatory use of the journal to publish some of the most important literary criticism in English before the time of Samuel Johnson. In a daring coup, he ventured to write extended series of papers, stretched over a number of issues, on serious themes such as tragedy and *Paradise Lost*; and then, most audaciously of all, on a topic of large aesthetic import throughout the eighteenth century, the pleasures of the imagination. In other critical papers, Addison wrote influential discussions of true and false wit; of the attraction of old ballads like 'Chevy Chase'; and of the absurdities, as they were then seen, of Italian opera. Another vein lay in allegorical visions and dreamscapes, where Addison dramatized the glamour and danger of commerce and credit. Perhaps his most characteristic piece occurs in *Spectator* no. 69, in which he portrays the royal exchange as a theatre of global trade, and the mercantile community as a beneficent fraternity who 'knit Mankind together in a mutual Intercourse of good Offices'.

The last years of Queen Anne, though unpropitious for Addison in his political capacity, saw him prominent in society. He dominated the gatherings at a coffee house near Covent Garden where he had set up in business a former servant, Daniel Button. This was both a meeting place for the literary crowd, and the office of Steele's periodical *The Guardian*. Here Addison's 'little senate' congregated, with the regular clientele including Ambrose Philips, Thomas Tickell, Eustace Budgell, Samuel Garth, and of course Addison and Steele themselves. Alexander Pope sometimes visited the coffee house, but he was soon estranged by the resolutely whiggish tone of the place. These years also had one more triumph in store for Addison as a writer. It came unexpectedly in the field of drama, where his talents had hitherto scarcely appeared to lie. In fact his surprise hit *Cato* may have been first drafted at Oxford, and revised during his grand tour; it is thought to have undergone surgery at the hands of such distinguished play-doctors as Dryden, Colley Cibber, and Swift. Only four acts had been completed, however, until the success of Ambrose Philips's play *Distrest Mother* in 1712 apparently convinced Addison that his own work easily matched this stiff recension of Racine's *Andromaque*. He wrote the final act quickly and friends such as George Berkeley began to puff the forthcoming dramatic attraction. The rising poet Pope was consulted and gave muted encouragement. Steele remained determined to see the play staged, and took an 'officious' role in promoting its success.

Cato was premièred at Drury Lane on 14 April 1713, a first night which has gone down in theatrical history with a notoriety scarcely matched until the opening of *The rite of spring* two centuries later. Both whigs and tories were keen to appropriate to their cause the sententious lines of lofty political declamation: rival claques set up a chorus of cheers and jeers at every key moment in the drama. After the final curtain, Lord Bolingbroke called the leading actor Barton Booth to his box and presented him with 50 guineas for 'defending the cause of liberty so well against a *perpetuall dictator*' (A. Pope, *Correspondence*, ed. G. Sherburn, 5 vols., 1956, 1.175). On this tory reading, Caesar represented the duke of Marlborough. The play ran for twenty nights and could have held the stage longer, but the star actress, Anne Oldfield, who played the rather vapid role of Cato's daughter, seems to have become pregnant. The managers were able to clear £1350 each by the end of the year, and there were equally crowded audiences to witness performances at Oxford. Before June was out seven editions had appeared, with piracies and a translation into French not far behind. Orange women hawked the work to grand personages driving through the park, and the prologue and epilogue (by Pope and Samuel Garth respectively) were peddled in the streets. Even the queen, it appeared, would have been glad to receive the dedication, but Addison with his habitual caution baulked at such a gesture of commitment.

It was a prudent move. Similarly, the fifty-two papers which Addison contributed to a new journal, *The Guardian*, which Steele began in March 1713, mixed bland satire in the old vein with essays on social reform. He managed to avoid the scabrous political conflicts in which Steele had become involved, even when a general election was called

and he had to spend a short time in what passed for electioneering at Malmesbury. But it was impossible to remain always on the sidelines in this moment of fierce partisan strife: the commercial clauses attached to the treaty of Utrecht aroused opposition in the City of London from whigs and tory merchants alike. Addison weighed into the attack on Bolingbroke, the architect of the treaty, with a pamphlet entitled *The trial and conviction of Count Tariff*, allegorizing the debate over international trade which the clauses had provoked. He also wrote several papers for a revival of *The Spectator* which began a short run in June 1714. This suffered the fate of most sequels: not even some lively contributions by Addison and his colleague, Budgell, could breathe life into this project, and it failed to capture the market which its predecessor had won over so easily. In any case, when Addison wrote his last essay for the series on 29 September 1714, such amiable diversions had come to seem irrelevant to the great matters in hand.

A new era On 1 August 1714 the queen died. Less than a week before this, Harley had been forced to relinquish power, and the other members of his administration were too shell-shocked by these sudden turns of events to react effectively. The elector of Hanover was duly proclaimed as George I, and made a triumphal entry into London a few weeks later. Tories of every persuasion lost their posts at court and in the government; military and ecclesiastical promotions were now reserved for loyal whigs. A general election in the following January confirmed the new political realities. In 1715–16 came the ill-managed rising of the Old Pretender, which left Jacobites in a still more marginal and exposed position, one they would continue to hold so long as the Stuart cause maintained its tottering existence. Addison was perfectly placed to reap the benefit of this situation, as an experienced administrator and a Hanoverian of unquestioned fidelity.

As early as 3 August Addison was appointed as secretary to the lords justices, a body of regents set up to handle the change of regime. His first duties included supervising the arrangements for the queen's funeral and the new king's arrival. There was a general expectation that he would become a secretary of state, especially as his patron Halifax took a leading role in the affairs of the justices. However, when the monarch was settled in England and the interim group disbanded, the new council of state included only grandees such as Halifax, Somers, and Wharton. The earl of Sunderland was appointed lord lieutenant of Ireland, and Addison had to go back to his former post as secretary in this department. It must have seemed like a comedown. He had no success in efforts to obtain some more senior role in government, such as a place on the Board of Trade, despite vigorous solicitations he had directed to Halifax. His prospects, which had appeared so bright when the whigs' day dawned, now grew dim once more. In quick succession Wharton and Halifax died; although Somers lingered for another year, he was no longer an active force. In August 1715 Sunderland moved on and Addison lost office with him. Paradoxically, he seemed for a time to be almost as sharply cut off from political patronage as he had been under the rule of the tories.

More resilient as he aged, Addison kept himself in the public eye with a new journal, *The Freeholder*, which ran twice weekly between December 1715 and June 1716. The period coincided with the collapse of the Jacobite rising and the trial of the rebel lords; naturally such matters dominated the contents of *The Freeholder*. Addison's fortunes moved back into the ascendant: in January 1716 he became a commissioner of trade and plantations, although as this was a place of profit he had the inconvenience of taking a trip to Malmesbury to get himself re-elected to parliament. Meanwhile, his stalled dramatic career resumed with the production of a comedy, *The drummer*, put on by Steele, now manager at Drury Lane, on 10 March 1716. Despite a good cast and extensive lobbying on its behalf by the author's loyal friends at Button's Coffee House, the play enjoyed only moderate success at the box office.

Addison's private life was now blossoming. In 1713 he had been able to buy for £8000 an estate just outside what was then the small town of Rugby named Bilton Hall. This comprised a stone house with Tudor origins and 1000 acres of land, permitting Addison to launch himself as a lord of the manor, country gentleman, and improver of the landscape, even though he had previously been a resolute townee. A relative named Edward Addison, a half-pay officer, looked after the planting of trees and the stocking of fish ponds in the absence of the owner. The estate bordered on Dunsmore Heath and its poor soil created problems for the inexperienced gardener. Another more significant leap into the unknown came when, in middle age, Addison married Charlotte Rich, *née* Myddleton, countess of Warwick [**Charlotte Addison** (*bap.* 1680, *d.* 1731)]. The wedding took place in the City of London on 9 August 1716; the groom was forty-four and the bride thirty-six. The couple had known each other since at least 1705, when Thomas Hearne reported a rumour that they were to be married. Lady Warwick had been left a widow at twenty-one, on the death of her first husband, Edward Rich, earl of Warwick (1673–1701), with a son aged three who was to become a protégé of Addison. Eighteen months after the remarriage of his mother, the young earl would attain his majority and enter the House of Lords; after some rakish moments he gave promise of settling down into a man of promise. Sadly he did not get the chance to repay Addison for all the kindness shown to him in his youth, for his stepfather had only a short time to live.

It appears that Addison was reasonably happy in his marriage (though some gossips alleged he was treated disdainfully by his wife) and in his role as a landowner. However, he faced occasional set-backs in his private life. The estate of his brother Gulston in India was finally settled, but not much if anything remained for Joseph. There were also unpleasant exchanges with old friends. He was now estranged from Pope, with whom relations had been strained since Addison's protégé Tickell embarked on a rival translation of the *Iliad* in 1714. Although this version did not proceed beyond the first book of the epic, Addison seems to have led the chorus of Buttonians in expressing a preference for Tickell's translation over Pope's. An immediate result was that Pope drafted a devastating portrait of Addison as the time-serving 'Atticus', first undertaken in 1715 and sent to the subject of the lines in the following year, apparently as a kind of warning to be held over the head of Addison. Much later the lines squirmed into print and became the basis for a famous passage in Pope's 'Epistle to Arbuthnot' (1735). The two men were never fully reconciled, although Pope wrote an appreciative epistle in verse, 'To Mr. Addison, Occasioned by his Dialogues on Medals'. This work was first published in 1720, and went into the posthumous collection of Addison's *Works* in the following year. It concerns dialogues on the study of ancient coins which Addison had written at the time of his continental tour in 1702. Pope had seen these in manuscript, but they appeared in print only after Addison's death as a portion of his *Works*.

Last years At this time Addison still had in store his highest political attainment, but also a rapid decline in health and a bitter struggle with his lifelong friend Steele. Currently the dominant whig party was split between two factions, led respectively by Sunderland and James Stanhope, and by Viscount Townshend and Robert Walpole. Addison naturally sided with his former chief Sunderland, who was trying to convince the king that his rivals were unreliable. When this faction came to the fore early in 1717 Addison was rewarded with the post of secretary of state for the southern department. He took the oaths on 6 April. His responsibilities included southern and Catholic Europe, as well as large areas of the wider world. Addison took his duties seriously, but he suffered from the fact that he had never shone as a public speaker, as well as from his lack of a parliamentary following or interest group, excluding a few unimportant individuals such as his under-secretary Tickell. In addition there were excruciating moments caused by rifts in the royal family, which came to a head when the king became embroiled in an absurd quarrel with the prince and princess of Wales over the birth of their son in October 1717. It is understandable that Addison, elderly in his ways at forty-five, had little stomach for such hostilities. In December he appears to have suffered a slight stroke. By early 1718 the leaders of the Stanhope faction wished to ease their leader back into the management of foreign affairs and Addison had to sacrifice his position as secretary of state to achieve this end. With his health severely impaired by his brief spell at the head of government, he was happy to accept a pension of £1600 per year. He left office on 13 March 1718.

Sadly, Addison's retirement was neither long-lasting nor free from trouble. Sunderland had introduced a controversial bill to limit the creation of peers in future, except where an old peerage was extinguished by death. Steele attacked this measure in the first issue of a paper named *The Plebeian* on 14 March 1719. Addison felt obliged to come to the aid of his leader in two essays called the *Old Whig*, on 19 March and 2 April, even though he may have recognized that the measure had much to do with the king's desire to block the avenues of power for the prince of Wales when he came to the throne. The outcome was a sharp volley of angry words in which the two old friends traded unpleasant personal slurs. By now the decline in Addison's health was even more apparent. He made his will on 14 May, leaving most of his possessions to his wife, expressing the hope that she would take good care of their infant daughter Charlotte, who had been born on 30 January. He had tried Bath, but the waters proved unavailing for what may have been a failure of the heart and lungs. Two weeks before he died, according to a story told by Pope, Addison asked his stepson Lord Warwick to summon John Gay, so that he could apologize for some mysterious injury he had once done to Gay; but this remains unexplained. On his deathbed he is said to have sent for Warwick, and said to the young man in a low voice, 'See in what peace a Christian can die' (Smithers, 460). He died at Holland House, Kensington, the home his wife had brought to him, on 17 June 1719. His body was taken to lie in state at the Jerusalem Chapel at Westminster Abbey, where he was buried on the evening of 26 June.

The earl of Warwick did not long survive his stepfather; he died in 1721, aged twenty-three, allegedly worn out by his excesses. The countess lived until 1731, while her daughter Charlotte lasted to the age of seventy-eight, dying in 1797. Charlotte, who never married, suffered from deafness and other ailments; the suggestion that she was feeble-minded seems to be unwarranted.

Addison enjoyed an immense contemporary reputation, and it was augmented when Tickell's edition of his *Works* came out in four volumes (1721). Although his term at the highest echelons of power was brief and undistinguished, his hold on literary fame was much more secure. Despite the barbs of the 'Epistle to Arbuthnot', he came to be regarded as one of the most eminent writers in the language; Pope himself acknowledged that 'No whiter page than Addison remains'. Macaulay actually considered him about the most admirable single figure in recent British history. Such views rested mainly on the enduring currency of *The Tatler* and, especially, *The Spectator*, for *Cato* had gradually disappeared from view. Until the end of the nineteenth century the periodical essays were among the most widely read documents in the language, with an immense influence at home and abroad (witness the debt which Benjamin Franklin admitted to these works). The papers were liked for their mildly whiggish, progressive tone, but even more for their humour, warmth, and empirical good sense. Not for nothing had Addison claimed in *Spectator* no. 10 that he had 'brought Philosophy out of Closets and Libraries, schools and Colleges, to dwell in Clubs and Assemblies, at Tea-Tables and in Coffee-Houses'. In the twentieth century Addison rapidly lost ground after he was discovered to be the first Victorian. His belief in trade as an agent of progress has been found complacent, his appeals to women readers have seemed patronizing, and his comic episodes have been regarded as facetious by-play. However, his stock has risen a little in recent decades, as his criticism has been reassessed for its innovative role in developing approaches through the psychology of literary response and through popular culture. He will never again loom as large as once he did, but he possesses qualities as a writer which will ensure his survival, above all his spare, precise, and equable prose style. PAT ROGERS

Sources P. Smithers, *The life of Joseph Addison*, 2nd edn (1968) · *The letters of Joseph Addison*, ed. W. Graham (1941) · L. Aikin, *The life of Joseph Addison*, 2 vols. (1843) · *The correspondence of Richard Steele*, ed. R. Blanchard, 2nd edn (1968) · J. Swift, *Journal to Stella*, ed. H. Williams, 2 vols. (1948) · J. Spence, *Observations, anecdotes, and characters, of books and men*, ed. J. M. Osborn, new edn, 2 vols. (1966) · *The prose works of Jonathan Swift*, ed. H. Davis and others, 16 vols. (1939–74) · J. Sutherland, *Background for Queen Anne* (1939) · N. Ault, 'Pope and Addison', *New light on Pope* (1949), 101–27 · GEC, *Peerage*
Archives BL, corresp., Add. MSS 61101–61710 · BL, corresp., literary MSS, and papers, Add. MSS 3540, 7058, 7121, 9828, 12113, 21110, 22908, 33441, 36193, 36201, 36772, 37349, 37364, 38728 · BL, corresp., literary MSS, and papers, Stowe MSS 227, 241–242; Harley MS 6944; Sloane MS 34075 · BL, family letters and papers · Bodl. Oxf., literary MSS and papers; letters and papers · Magdalen College, Oxford, letters and papers · PRO, corresp., SP 35/1 & 3, SP 78/161/48–183 | BL, letters to George Bubb, Egerton MSS 2174–2175 · NA Scot., letters to John Dalrymple, first earl of Stair · TCD, corresp. with William King
Likenesses G. Kneller, oils, c.1703–1712, NPG [*see illus.*] · C. Jervas, oils, 1714, Knole, Kent · G. Kneller, oils, 1716, Yale U. · M. Dahl, oils, 1719, NPG · J. Simon, mezzotint, 1719 (after M. Dahl), BM, NPG · J. Faber junior, mezzotint, 1733 (after G. Kneller), BM, NPG · J. Houbraken, line engraving, 1748 (after G. Kneller), BM, NPG · G. Kneller, oils, second version, Bodl. Oxf. · J. Richardson, oils, Althorp, Northamptonshire · mezzotint (after G. Kneller), NPG · pencil drawing, NPG
Wealth at death most property left to wife and swallowed up in her larger property: will

Addison, Lancelot (1632–1703), dean of Lichfield, was born at Meaburn Town Head, Maulds Meaburn, in the parish of Crosby Ravensworth in Westmorland, where the family had been resident since the days of Henry III. He was baptized at Crosby Ravensworth on 4 March 1632. His father, Lancelot Addison, was the local parson, and had at least one other son, John, who subsequently emigrated to Maryland.

Education Lancelot was first educated at Appleby grammar school. He matriculated as a servitor at Queen's College, Oxford, on 27 February 1651, graduated BA as a taberdar on 25 January 1655 and proceeded MA on 4 July 1657. While he was at Oxford he developed a lasting friendship with Joseph Williamson, a distant relative from Cumberland, after whom he is supposed to have named his eldest son. In 1657 Addison was selected to deliver a speech as *terrae filius*, a traditional academic pantomime in which the speaker was allowed considerable freedom to exercise his wit in criticizing the church, the state, and the university. Addison, however, went too far. Displaying the impetuousness and tactlessness which were to impair his career on more than one occasion he made a violent attack on the puritanism of the day. He was consequently made to retract his speech in convocation on his knees. Addison then left Oxford. Having taken orders he ministered privately to royalist and episcopalian families near Petworth in Sussex. His courage at Oxford and his subsequent integrity bore fruit, and while he was in Sussex he enjoyed the patronage of Henry King, who was living in retirement before resuming his office as bishop of Chichester.

Tangier In 1660, with the Restoration and probably thanks to Joseph Williamson, Addison received his first official appointment, as chaplain to the English garrison in Dunkirk, and in December 1662 he was presented to the vicarage of Hilmarton in Wiltshire (where he never lived). In October of that year the fortress of Dunkirk was sold back to France, and in spring 1663 the governor, Andrew, Lord Rutherford, earl of Teviot, transferred the English garrison to Tangier, which had been acquired by Charles II's marriage treaty with Portugal signed in January 1661. Addison accompanied what became the Tangier regiment, and served a garrison which would number between about 1200 and 1500 men, a part of whom were Irish Catholics. His appointment had to be approved by the bishop of London (first Gilbert Sheldon and then, from September 1663, Humphrey Henchman), and he was paid a salary of 6s. 8d. a day, which was raised to 10s. in 1668. Within a year of his arrival, on 3 May 1664, Teviot was killed in an ambush by the Moroccan forces. Addison, who wrote a brief account of the military events at Tangier in that year, later expressed his deep admiration for a man who, had he lived, 'would have made Tanger as famous an English Colony as it was once a Roman' (L. Addison, *The Moores Baffled: being a Discourse Concerning Tangier, Especially when it was under the Earl of Teviot*, 1681, 25–6).

Addison remained in Tangier for some seven years. He was in constant correspondence with Joseph Williamson and served under Teviot's successors, Lord Belasyse and John, earl of Middleton. His stay in Tangier enabled him to assemble the information he would publish in his later works on Morocco and Islam. In his approach Addison was remarkably open minded, meeting and obtaining information from numerous Muslims, including the Moroccan emissaries to the English ambassador, Lord Howard, in 1669, and various European converts to Islam. Above all, however, he depended on the man he called 'my best help', Josef Messias, the Jewish secretary of Tetuan (L. Addison, *West Barbary*, 1671, sig. a4v).

In 1670 Addison returned to England on leave. He never went back to Tangier, but, on 11 June, married Jane Gulston (*c*.1635?–1684), the daughter of Nathaniel Gulston and sister of William Gulston, who became bishop of Bristol in 1679. They had six children: Jane, who died in infancy in 1671; his most illustrious son, Joseph *Addison, born on 1 May 1672, followed by Gulston (1673), Dorothy (1674), Anne (1676), and Lancelot (1680).

On his marriage Addison was appointed by Sir Frederick Hyde, the patron of the living, to succeed William Gulston as rector of Milston in Wiltshire. He thus obtained a house with an income of £120 per year. To the Hyde family Addison was to remain attached, dedicating his *Introduction to the Sacrament* (1682) to Robert Hyde, 'my Truly Worthy and much Honored Patron'. One of Addison's first gestures was to raise a collection in Milston for the redemption of English captives in Barbary. Shortly after obtaining the living at Milston he was appointed chaplain-in-ordinary to the king.

Scholarly writings At the rectory of Milston, Addison could devote himself to scholarship. His most important works, which he dedicated to Williamson, who was knighted in 1672 and appointed secretary of state in 1673, were the result of his experiences in Morocco. In 1671 he published *West Barbary, or, A Short Narrative of the Revolutions of the Kingdoms of Fez and Morocco*. Besides giving a brief history of Morocco from the early sixteenth century to his own day Addison described the country, the local customs, and the people. Despite his generally anti-Islamic tone Addison was sympathetic to his subject, maintaining that 'this Unlick'd, Uncultivated People agree with the wisest Nations, in making the care of Religion and Justice to suppress Vice and encourage Virtue, as the only method to make a State happy', stressing that 'what is commonly call'd Barbarous is but a different Mode of Civility', and commending the religious devoutness and the liberality of the Moroccans (Addison, *West Barbary*, sigs. a2r–v).

While *West Barbary* was one of a number of works on Morocco to appear in the second half of the seventeenth century, Addison's next book, *The Present State of the Jews* (1675), which ran through four editions in ten years, was unique in its kind, possibly the first study of Moroccan Jewry and certainly one of the few to appear before the twentieth century. In contrast to the official English diffidence towards the Jews, suspected of passing information to the Moroccans, Addison was far from hostile to the Jewish community. He deplored their treatment and their insecurity in a Muslim country and praised their patience, good humour, sobriety, and temperance.

Addison's *First State of Mahumedism* came out in 1678, to be reissued the following year under the title *The Life and Death of Mahumed*. On the face of it the work was in an ancient tradition of anti-Islamic propaganda, a biography of 'the onely great Impostor, that ever continued so long prosperous in the World', its purpose was to 'justly awake all Christian Magistrates into a timely suppression of False Teachers … lest … they second Heresies with Force and propagate Enthusiasm with Conquest' (Addison, *First State*, iii–iv). There were indeed notes of hostility, especially when it came to discussing the Prophet's polygamy. Yet Addison endeavoured to be objective. He dismissed the 'many ridiculous but usual Stories' about the Prophet which had been exploded by Arabists such as Edward Pococke, and proposed to base himself on Arab sources. 'I have kept myself to the Orientals in this account', he wrote, 'and am induced to believe they are the fittest to be our informers, as dealing in their own story' (ibid., 99). But, despite the Arabic word list at the end of the book, Addison's Arabic is unlikely to have been good enough to read his sources in the original, and his lengthy quotations from Arab writers such as al-Bayawi are taken from J. H. Hottinger's *Historia orientalis* (1651). By 1697 Addison's work had been superseded by Humphrey Prideaux's highly successful *True Nature of Imposture Fully Display'd in* the *Life of Mahomet*, in which Addison was not so much as mentioned.

In 1675 Addison was created BD and DD at Oxford, and in 1678 was made a prebendary of Salisbury. By then he was becoming one of the spokesmen of the Anglican church. In 1677 he had published *A Modest Plea for the Clergy*, a defence of the dignity of priesthood in the face of the discredit into which it had lapsed after the Restoration. He argued at length for its antiquity and attributed the contempt with which it was treated partly to an increasing lack of discipline and partly to the poverty of so many of its members. He also expressed his admiration for Chaucer.

Dean of Lichfield In 1681 the rectory of Milston was destroyed by fire, and Addison's precarious financial situation was aggravated by having to rebuild it. Two years later he was appointed dean of Lichfield. The royal mandate was dated 25 May 1683; the election and instalment took place on 8 June; and on 4 October, Addison took the oaths of supremacy and allegiance. The appointment to the deanery was accompanied by the prebends of Brewood and Adbaston. In 1684 he was made archdeacon of Coventry and held the office *in commendam* with Milston and Lichfield. But for all his promotions Addison remained in debt, owing money for his son Joseph's education and for the repair of the rectory in Milston. On 30 June 1684 his wife, Jane, died. He married Dorothy Hacket, *née* Danvers, the widow of Philip Hacket, esquire, and youngest daughter of John Danvers of Shackerstone in Leicestershire, and his financial situation improved.

Addison appears to have been an energetic, albeit somewhat autocratic, dean of Lichfield. He supervised the rebuilding of the bishop's palace. To his duties at the cathedral he added that of preaching every second Sunday at the church of St Michael. He regularly visited his archdeaconry of Coventry, inspected schools to ensure that the catechism was being taught correctly, and, often with schoolchildren in mind, continued to produce devotional works. These were immensely popular. His *Introduction to the Sacrament* (1682), which had the advantage of being a duodecimo pocket edition, was, according to the bookseller William Crooke, 'so well liked by a great many Ministers, that they gave them by dozens at a time to their poor Parishioners' (L. Addison, *Introduction to the Sacrament*, 1686, sig. A4v). It was included, together with Addison's catechism, in *The Christian's Manual*, which first appeared in 1691 and went through six editions by 1724. In 1696 Addison published a short history of Arianism, *Christos Autotheos, or, An Historical Account of the Heresie Denying the Godhead of Christ*, an indication that he was engaged in the anti-Arian campaign which had grown in reaction to the views of the unitarians and the writings of Locke and Toland, and would reach its peak in the eighteenth century.

Until his death Addison saw himself as a custodian of Anglican orthodoxy. In 1684 he reported to William Sancroft, archbishop of Canterbury, 'I have in the city of Lichfield so throwly punished the Dissenters, as to bring them all to the Holy Communion, except three or four Anabaptists, and one Quaker. And as to the careless in Religion, I am endeavouring, throw God, to bring them to a better mind' (Bodl. Oxf., MS Tanner 131, fol. 89). He was always ready to act against nonconformist preachers, even in areas outside his jurisdiction. His sympathies and his integrity sometimes made him quarrelsome. He disliked his first bishop of Lichfield, Thomas Wood—but then the 'refractory' Wood, who mocked Addison's poverty, was widely disliked. When Addison attended the lower house of convocation at Westminster on 4 December 1689 his opposition to the policy of comprehension which would have broadened the spectrum of the Church of England destroyed his chances of preferment under the new king and lost him his chaplaincy-in-ordinary. He made matters worse by quarrelling with his chapter and thus with William Lloyd, appointed bishop of Lichfield in 1692. In 1699 Lloyd was succeeded by John Hough, a man who was generous to Addison and his family, adding a further benefice to the deanery, but in the last months of his life Addison was engaged in quarrelling with him too.

Addison's more diplomatic son Joseph wrote to Hough 'to vindicate one of the best of Fathers' soon after the dean's death. From his letter there emerges the portrait of a man who, though high principled and quarrelsome, was affectionate and emotional (*Letters*, 45). The impression is confirmed by Steele in *The Tatler*, who described Lancelot Addison as the only man 'whom I thought to live with his Children with Equanimity and a good Grace', a model father who regarded as his greatest defect his inability to hide his preference for his eldest son, Joseph (Aitken, 4.204–5), and who clearly lived up to the high standards which he set for the clergy in his devotional works.

By September 1702 Addison is reported to have been confined to his deanery, and, on 20 April 1703, he died. He was buried three days later in the churchyard of Lichfield Cathedral. In 1719 Joseph had a monument erected to his memory inside the west wall of the cathedral building. His second wife survived him, and died in 1719. His second son, Gulston, served in the East India Company at Fort St George and was appointed its governor shortly before his death in 1709. His second daughter, Dorothy, married first James Sartre, a prebendary of Westminster of French origin, and then, after his death in September 1713, Daniel Combes. She herself died in 1750. His youngest son, Lancelot, finally, gained a high reputation as a classical scholar at Oxford but died in 1710 after visiting his brother in India.

ALASTAIR HAMILTON

Sources P. Smithers, *The life of Joseph Addison* (1968) · E. M. G. Routh, *Tangier: England's lost Atlantic outpost, 1661–1684* (1912) · Foster, *Alum. Oxon.* · *DNB* · *The life of Joseph Addison: to which is prefixed the life of Dr. Lancelot Addison* (1733) · H. E. Savage, *Lichfield Cathedral: the last quarter of the seventeenth century* (1932) · T. Harwood, *The history and antiquities of the city of Lichfield* (1806) · *VCH Wiltshire* · J. Spurr, *The Restoration Church of England, 1646–1689* (1991) · G. A. Aitken, ed., *The Tatler*, 4 vols. (1898–9) · *The letters of Joseph Addison*, ed. W. Graham (1941) · J. L. Chester and G. J. Armytage, eds., *Allegations for marriage licences issued by the dean and chapter of Westminster, 1558 to 1699; also, for those issued by the vicar-general of the archbishop of Canterbury, 1660 to 1679*, Harleian Society, 23 (1886) · *IGI*

Archives Bodl. Oxf., corresp. with Sancroft, Tanner MSS 29–35, 131

Likenesses line engraving, NPG · oils, Lichfield Cathedral; repro. in Savage, *Lichfield Cathedral*

Wealth at death £1927 7s. 6d.: will, proved 7 June 1703, Smithers, *Life of Joseph Addison*, 88

Addison [*née* Wilmshurst], **Laura** (1822–1852), actress, the daughter of Thomas Wilmshurst, a grocer, was born at Colchester, Essex, on 15 November 1822. Despite family opposition, her lack of training, and the absence of any patronage, she made her stage début in Norwich, under the name Miss Addison, as Elvira in Sheridan's *Pizarro*, and in November 1843 took the part of Lady Townly in Vanbrugh's *The Provoked Husband* at the Worcester theatre. She then went to Glasgow, where she played Desdemona to W. C. Macready's Othello, in which role she met with the approval of that tragedian. After she had some success in both Dublin and Edinburgh, Macready was instrumental in ensuring her engagement by Samuel Phelps for Sadler's Wells, and she made her first London appearance in August 1846 as Lady Mabel in Westland Marston's *The Patrician's Daughter*. She remained at Sadler's Wells for three seasons portraying Shakespearian heroines, including Julia, Portia, Isabella, and Lady Macbeth. She also appeared as Panthea in a revival of Beaumont and Fletcher's *A King and No King*, and as the first Margaret Randolph in *Feudal Times* and Lilian Saville in *John Saville of Haysted*, both by James White. In 1849 she moved to the Haymarket with the Keans, and in 1850 transferred to James Robertson Anderson's Drury Lane, where her roles included Bianca in Dean Milman's *Fazio* and Leonora in an English version of Schiller's *Fiesco*. In 1851 she went to New York, where she appeared at the Broadway Theatre in September as Lady Teazle. She also performed in Philadelphia, but died suddenly on 3 September 1852 from 'a congestion of the brain' on board the steamer *Oregon* on a journey from Albany to New York. She was buried in the Second Avenue cemetery in New York.

E. D. COOK, rev. J. GILLILAND

Sources Adams, *Drama* · Boase, *Mod. Eng. biog.* · S. D'Amico, ed., *Enciclopedia dello spettacolo*, 11 vols. (Rome, 1954–68) · Hall, *Dramatic ports.* · *Dictionary of the drama*, vol. 5 · J. Tallis, *Tallis's drawing room table book of theatrical portraits, memoirs and anecdotes* (1851)

Likenesses Hollis, stipple and line engraving (as Queen Mary in Schiller's *Mary Stuart*; after daguerreotype by Mayall), BM, NPG; repro. in *Tallis's drawing room table book* · W. Hollis?, stipple and line engraving (after daguerreotype by Paine), BM, NPG; repro. in *Tallis's drawing room table book* [*see illus.*] · Mayall, daguerreotype, BM · five prints, Harvard TC · portrait, repro. in *Theatres of London*, vol. 6 · print, repro. in *Theatrical Times*, 1 (1847), 185

Addison, Thomas (1795–1860), physician, was born in April 1795 at Long Benton, near Newcastle upon Tyne, the younger son of Joseph Addison (1756–1823), a grocer and flour dealer, and his wife, Sarah, *née* Shaw (1761–1841). Educated privately and at Newcastle grammar school, Addison became fluent in Latin. In 1812 he entered Edinburgh University as a medical student and graduated MD in 1815 with an inaugural dissertation entitled *De syphilide et hydrargyro*. He went to London where he was appointed house surgeon at the Lock Hospital treating syphilitic cases, a disease on which he became an authority. In

Laura Addison (1822–1852), by W.? Hollis, pubd 1851 (after Paine) [as Imogen in *Cymbeline*]

December 1817 Addison entered Guy's Hospital medical school as a pupil. He became a licentiate of the Royal College of Physicians on 22 December 1819, took a house in Hatton Garden, and began private practice. He also joined the Public Dispensary, Carey Street, under Thomas Bateman the dermatologist. When Bateman retired in 1821 Addison took charge for about eight years.

At Guy's, Addison's knowledge of skin diseases led the physicians to consult him in difficult cases and he was appointed demonstrator of cutaneous diseases. His expertise was unknown outside the hospital, but his wide practical knowledge of medicine attracted the attention of Guy's treasurer, Benjamin Harrison, who secured Addison's appointment as assistant physician in January 1824. Addison was one of the first to use Laënnec's stethoscope and was distinguished for accurate diagnoses of chest affections. His clear perceptions of disease were backed by an ability to impart information to others and in 1827 he was appointed lecturer on materia medica. His reputation as a teacher grew and in 1837 he was appointed lecturer on the practice of medicine, jointly with Richard Bright, and physician to the hospital. In 1838 he became a fellow of the Royal College of Physicians and in the following year he gave an accurate account of appendicitis. Bright ceased to lecture on medicine in 1840, leaving Addison as sole lecturer until 1854/5. On 14 September 1847 at Lanercost church, Cumberland, he married Elizabeth Catherine Hanxwell (1800–1872), a widow with a son and a daughter from her first marriage.

Addison was president of the Royal Medico-Chirurgical

Thomas Addison (1795–1860), by Alfred Hone, 1838

Society in 1849–50. He was the first to observe that the inflammatory exudation in pneumonia and phthisis takes place in the air-cells of the lungs in opposition to the accepted view that phthisis was due to small granular tumours in the lung tissues, as in tuberculosis. This was an important observation, but the work for which he is best known began on 15 March 1849 when he described a peculiar idiopathic anaemia, later named Addison's anaemia. Its symptoms were increasing debility, without wasting of the general frame. In some cases Addison noticed that the suprarenal capsules (adrenal cortex) were diseased or destroyed and he described this condition in 1855 in *On the Constitutional and Local Effects of Disease of the Suprarenal Capsules,* illustrated with coloured lithographs. He did not clearly distinguish this as a separate disease at first, but following further observations he recognized the diseased suprarenal capsules as the direct cause of a specific anaemic condition, with gross discoloration of the skin, later called Addison's disease. His accounts of both these diseases were as complete as the resources available to him allowed. His discoveries revealed the importance of the ductless glands and initiated the important science of endocrinology.

Addison was an eloquent and powerful lecturer, yet he was always uncomfortable when speaking in public, even to his pupils. Although appearing outwardly confident he was extremely sensitive and diffident and this led to his being thought haughty and distant by those who did not understand the effort required to conceal his nervousness. He spent most of his time in the hospital where his professional interests lay and his reputation stood high. He was one of those who gave to Guy's medical school the prominence it achieved in the nineteenth century, yet outside the hospital he remained almost unknown, neither seeking nor receiving public recognition. Addison's private practice was small, due largely to his manner. He would spend an inordinate time over diagnosis, but once he had identified the cause of an illness he was satisfied and did not display the same diligence in alleviating or curing the condition. He believed in the healing powers of nature and generally prescribed very lightly or not at all when he did not know of any beneficial drug. He was apt to regard all diseases as serious and was seldom content until he could ascribe the symptoms to a specific organic malfunction. This was perhaps due to his constant work at the hospital where only the most serious cases were seen, and to the hours he spent almost daily in the post-mortem room. One of the finest pathologists of his day, he was thoroughly conversant with morbid appearances in the tissues and organs. His knowledge of serious diseases may also have led to an increased sensitivity about his own health and when, about 1859, he suffered an attack of jaundice followed by gallstones, from which he was slow to recover, he decided to resign from Guy's Hospital. He moved from Berkeley Square to Brighton where, after Christmas 1859, his health began to fail and his resignation was accepted on 28 March 1860. He grew increasingly depressed, making several attempts to end his own life, in the last of which he was successful. He died in Brighton at his home, 15 Wellington Villas, on 29 June 1860 and was buried in the north-east corner of Lanercost Abbey churchyard, Cumberland, on 5 July.   N. G. COLEY

Sources W. Hale-White, *Guy's Hospital Reports,* 4th ser., 6 (1926), 253–79 · G. Pallister, *Thomas Addison, MD, FRCP, (1795–1860)* (c.1975) [privately printed, Newcastle upon Tyne] · S. Wilks and G. T. Bettany, *A biographical history of Guy's Hospital* (1892), 221–34 · *Munk, Roll,* 3.205–11 · *Medical Times and Gazette* (7 July 1860), 20–21 · H. Dale, 'Thomas Addison, pioneer of endocrinology', *BMJ* (13 Aug 1949), 347–52 · S. Wilks and T. Daldy, *A collection of the published writings of Thomas Addison,* New Sydenham Society (1868) · E. A. Underwood, 'Addison, Joseph', *Biographical dictionary of scientists,* ed. T. Williams, 4th edn (1994) · E. R. Long, 'Addison and his discovery of idiopathic anaemia', *Annals of Medical History,* new ser., 7 (1935), 130–32 · K. D. Keele, 'Addison on the "Supra-renal capsules": an essay review', *Medical History,* 13 (1969), 195–202 · *DSB,* 1.59–60 · H. Lonsdale, *The worthies of Cumberland,* 4 (1873), 241 · *Boase, Mod. Eng. biog.,* vol. 1 · P. M. F. Bishop, 'Dr Addison and his work', *Guy's Hospital Reports,* 4th ser., 34 (1955), 275–94 · d. cert.

Likenesses A. Hone, marble bust, 1838, RCP Lond. [*see illus.*] · J. Towne, marble bust, 1852, Guy's Hospital, London; repro. in D. Power, *British masters of medicine* (1936), 84 · W. Bewick?, oils (as a young man), Guy's Hospital, London · sepia photograph? (as an older man)

Wealth at death under £30,000: probate, 4 Oct 1860, *CGPLA Eng. & Wales*

Addy, William (*bap.* **1618**?, *d.* **1695**?), stenographer and writing-master, has been plausibly, although on entirely circumstantial evidence, identified as the William Addy who was baptized in Wath upon Dearne, West Riding of Yorkshire, on 13 September 1618, the third son of John

Addy (d. 1645), tanner and parish clerk, and Margaret Hanson.

In 1684 Addy published *Stenographia, or, The art of short-writing compleated in a far more compendious method than any yet extant*, a shorthand system which was, as Addy himself acknowledged, heavily dependent upon that of Jeremiah Rich. It was engraved throughout by John Sturt, and included a portrait engraved by Sturt after S. Barker. Four further editions of *Stenographia* appeared between about 1688 and about 1725.

In 1687 Addy produced the earliest complete Bible to be printed in shorthand. It included the metrical psalms of Sterngold and Hopkins and its popularity led to two further issues in the same year. Like *Stenographia*, it was engraved throughout by John Sturt, but featured a new portrait of Addy both drawn and engraved by Sturt. The second edition of Addy's shorthand Bible (1689?) virtually replicated the first, apart from a minor alteration made to accommodate a dedication to William III (proclaimed king on 13 February 1689). A third edition appeared in 1695.

According to Musgrave's *Obituary* (Armytage, 1.11), Addy's death took place in 1695; if this is correct, his name is included in error in Samuel Pepys's 'Alphabetical list of surviving maister pen-men of England' of 1699.

FRANCES HENDERSON

Sources W. Addy, *Stenographia* (1684) · W. J. Carlton, *Bibliotheca Pepysiana*, 4: *Shorthand books* (1940), 104–9 · S. O. Addy, 'The Addy family of Darton and elsewhere in the West Riding', *Yorkshire Archaeological Journal*, 27 (1923–4), 166–96 · R. C. Alston, *A bibliography of the English language from the invention of printing to the year 1800*, rev. edn, 8: *Treatises on shorthand* (1974), 29–30 · W. Musgrave, *Obituary prior to 1800*, ed. G. J. Armytage, 1, Harleian Society, 44 (1899) · S. Pepys, 'Alphabetical list of surviving maister pen-men of England', 1699, Magd. Cam., pl. 2983 · Wing, *STC*

Likenesses J. Sturt, engraving, 1684 (after portrait by S. Barker), NPG; repro. in Addy, *Stenographia* · J. Sturt, engraving, 1687 (after his own portrait), NPG; repro. in W. Addy, *The holy Bible … in shorthand* (1687)

Adeane, Michael Edward, Baron Adeane (1910–1984), courtier, was born on 30 September 1910 in London, the only son of Captain Henry Robert Augustus Adeane of the Coldstream Guards, who was killed in action in 1914, and his wife, Victoria Eugenie (d. 1969), daughter of Arthur John *Bigge (later Lord Stamfordham). He was educated at Eton College (1923–8) and at Magdalene College, Cambridge, where he achieved a second class (first division) in part one of the history tripos (1930) and a first class (second division) in part two (1931). The college made him an honorary fellow in 1971.

Adeane then joined the Coldstream Guards, and from 1934 to 1936 was aide-de-camp to two successive governors-general of Canada, the earl of Bessborough and Lord Tweedsmuir. In 1937 he was appointed equerry and assistant private secretary to George VI, and accompanied the king and queen on their visit to Canada and the United States in the summer of 1939. On 10 January 1939 he married Helen (c.1920–c.1995), elder daughter of Richard Chetwynd-Stapleton, stockbroker, of Headlands, Berkhamsted. They had a daughter and a son. On the outbreak

Michael Edward Adeane, Baron Adeane (1910–1984), by Godfrey Argent, 1969

of the Second World War he rejoined his regiment, being promoted to major in 1941. From 1942 to 1943 he was a member of the joint staff mission in Washington with the acting rank of lieutenant-colonel. From 1943 to 1945 he served with the 5th battalion Coldstream Guards as company commander and second-in-command. In the battle of Normandy he had to take over command of the battalion, was wounded in the stomach, and mentioned in dispatches. In 1945 he returned to Buckingham Palace and for the remainder of the reign served as assistant private secretary to George VI. In 1947 he was a member of the royal party on their visit to South Africa, and in 1952, having been seconded to the staff of Princess Elizabeth, was with her in Kenya at the time of her father's death. The new queen decreed that he should continue as one of her assistant private secretaries, which he did until, on the retirement of Sir Alan Lascelles on 1 January 1954, he became her principal private secretary, retaining this office until his retirement in 1972. He was also keeper of the queen's archives (1953–72).

The three main duties of the queen's private secretary are to be the link between the monarch and her ministers, especially her prime ministers, to make the arrangements for her public engagements and for the numerous speeches which she is called upon to make, and to deal with her massive correspondence.

The first twenty years of the reign were marked by demands for an ever expanding programme of public engagements at home and abroad, and by an intrusive, and not always charitable, scrutiny of the queen and her family by the media. It was largely due to Adeane that the monarchy was able to adjust to these pressures, while retaining its essential dignity and mystery. Although some judged his advice to be unduly cautious and the speeches which he drafted for the queen to be lacking in imagination, he was able to avoid the controversies to which a more adventurous private secretary might have exposed a constitutional sovereign. In his dealings with the queen he was by no means sycophantic, but was not prepared to pressure her to do things which she did not want to, unless they were constitutionally necessary. Thus, although it was suggested that it would be appropriate in India if she adopted the customary national form of greeting with clasped hands, Adeane did not press the queen to do something which did not come naturally to her. In relations with governments he adhered rigidly to the principle that the sovereign must accept ministerial advice, especially from the prime minister. This may have deterred him from contemplating advising her to express a contrary view to Sir Anthony Eden at the time of the Suez crisis, or from resisting ministerial advice to keep Sir Anthony Blunt in his appointment as surveyor of the queen's pictures after his treachery as a spy had been unmasked.

Adeane had to deal with six British prime ministers and with many more from Commonwealth countries as well as with their governors-general. He treated all with equal courtesy and respect and was invariably well briefed on their personalities and policies. These qualities showed to particular advantage during overseas tours. During these years the queen visited almost every country in the Commonwealth, several of them more than once, and many foreign countries, including most of those in western Europe. Adeane was responsible for the arrangements for all these visits. He also performed a notable service to the royal family by his compelling evidence to the select committee of the House of Commons on the civil list in 1971 outlining the queen's workload and commitments. He gave a vivid description of the volume of this workload and, in particular, of its relentless regularity. Adeane listed the formidable number of audiences, investitures, privy councils, and garden parties held during each year—including the weekly audiences with the prime minister of the day and the numerous provincial visits to every county in the United Kingdom. He estimated that the queen had to set aside up to three hours a day reading cabinet papers, Foreign Office dispatches, and telegrams as well as communications from Commonwealth countries, as well as many personal letters. But above all he emphasized that, unlike ministers or indeed any one of her subjects, she could not look forward to a period of retirement. Her commitment to her job was lifelong and unremitting. This led later to the civil list's being reviewed annually and submitted to parliament in the same way as a departmental budget.

Professor Harold Laski wrote in 1942:

> The Secretary to the Monarch occupies to the Crown much the same position that the Crown itself in our system occupies to the Government; he must advise and encourage and warn. … The Royal Secretary walks on a tight-rope below which he is never unaware that an abyss is yawning. … A bad Private Secretary, who was rash or indiscreet or untrustworthy might easily make the system of constitutional monarchy unworkable. (*Fortnightly Review*, 158, July–Dec 1942)

By these criteria, Adeane was highly successful.

In his style of work Adeane closely resembled his grandfather Lord Stamfordham, of whom it was said that he was 'a man of persistent industry, making it his practice to finish the day's work within the day' (*DNB*). Like him too, he was 'regarded by his colleagues with a love which perhaps never wholly cast out fear'. His wisdom, sense of humour, and discretion endeared him to other members of the royal family and their households, to whom his advice was always available. But he could also be severe on any lack of tact or competence. He was a popular member of several dining clubs, having an acute, but subtle, sense of humour; and although he enjoyed conversation, he would never gossip about the royal family. A totally concentrated listener, he rarely came away from such occasions without useful information which he stored in a capacious and accurate memory.

Adeane was at heart a countryman, a fine but unassuming shot and a skilful fisherman, though his opportunities for indulging in either sport were limited. He was an enthusiastic gardener, on the roof of his house in Windsor Castle and in the small gardens of the house in Chelsea and the cottage in Aberdeenshire which he made his homes in his retirement. He also painted in watercolours and was a voracious reader of biography, history, and Victorian novels, especially those of Anthony Trollope. Modest, even spartan in his personal life, he nevertheless appreciated good food and wine and liked to smoke a good cigar. He was entirely free from social, religious, and racial prejudice. In appearance he was not impressive, being little over 5 feet 6 inches tall and having lost most of his hair in his twenties. Although he was apt to suffer from hay fever in the summer, his sturdy, compact frame withstood other complaints and he was rarely absent from his desk. A house on the south Spanish coast at Moacar gave him a week or two's relaxation during the August holiday period.

On his retirement in 1972 Adeane acquired several directorships, including those of Phoenix Assurance, the Diners Club, the Banque Belge, and the Royal Bank of Canada. He was also appointed chairman of the Royal Commission on Historical Monuments and served as the queen's representative on the board of the British Library. He was a fellow of the Society of Antiquaries and a governor of Wellington College. His honours came in a steady progression after the war until his retirement. He was appointed MVO in 1946, CB in 1947, KCVO in 1951, KCB in 1955, GCVO in 1962, GCB in 1968, and on his retirement in 1972 received the Royal Victorian Chain. He was sworn of the privy council in 1953 and made a life peer in 1972. As a member of the House of Lords he sat on the cross-benches but spoke rarely. His son, Edward, was private secretary to the prince of Wales (1979–85), the third member of the

Bigge family to serve the royal family in this most intimate appointment. Adeane died in Aberdeen on 30 April 1984 of heart failure after enjoying two days' fishing on the Dee. He was cremated at Golders Green crematorium. It was characteristic of his modesty that, by his special request, no thanksgiving service was held in his memory.

EDWARD FORD

Sources B. Pimlott, *The queen* (1996) · S. Bradford, *Elizabeth II* (1996) · E. Longford, *Elizabeth R: a biography* (1983) · *The Times* (2 May 1984) · personal knowledge (2004) · Burke, *Peerage* (1967) · *WWW*
Archives Royal Arch., MSS | CUL, corresp. with Sir Samuel Hoare · NL Scot., letters to Lord Ballantrae · U. Birm. L., corresp. with Lord Avon
Likenesses G. Argent, photograph, 1969, NPG [*see illus.*] · D. Poole, oils, Royal Collection
Wealth at death £517,460: probate, 10 Aug 1984, *CGPLA Eng. & Wales*

Adela, countess of Blois (c.1067–1137), princess, was in all probability the youngest daughter of *William I, the Conqueror (1027/8–1087), and his queen, *Matilda of Flanders (d. 1083). Adela's birth date is usually calculated as c.1060–62, but panegyric poetry written for her during adulthood suggests that her father was a crowned king at the time of her birth. It is most likely that Adela was born between the Norman conquest and the birth of her youngest brother, Henry, the future *Henry I, in late 1068 or 1069. Her later literacy and patronage of poets indicate that she was carefully educated, either in a monastic setting or by private tutors. Later sources claim that, as a child, she was promised in marriage to Simon Crispin, count of Amiens, the son and prospective heir of Étienne, count of Valois and Mantes, but that in 1077 Crispin elected to take monastic rather than marriage vows. Some time later Adela was affianced to Étienne-Henri, son of Theobald, count of Blois and Chartres. Orderic Vitalis, a contemporary chronicler, describes a formal betrothal ceremony in Bourgueil, after which Adela and Étienne-Henri were married in a lavish ceremony that took place in Chartres, the chief town of Theobald's family. The date of the wedding may have been considerably later than the 1080 or 1081 dates that are often cited. It seems that the marriage negotiations, which began as early as 1080, were quite protracted, and the first firmly datable document in which Adela appears as Étienne-Henri's wife is a charter of 1085. In panegyric poetry composed about the time of the marriage Adela is described as valorous, learned, and generous, a worthy daughter of the Anglo-Norman royal family. Adela's two oldest sons were probably born before the death of her father-in-law in 1090, when Étienne-Henri and Adela succeeded as count and countess of Blois.

As countess, Adela participated in many of her husband's charitable donations, appearing either as a co-donor or mentioned as a family member consenting to alienations of land. Her name was also associated with her husband's in several of his early judicial *acta*. On occasion Adela appears as the instigator of donations to religious institutions, and it seems to have been she who initiated a friendship with Bishop Ivo of Chartres, the local diocesan. Despite a few issues that led to conflict, countess and bishop generally worked together quite effectively as lay

and ecclesiastical authorities to maintain peace and order in the county. Adela bore another son, or perhaps two, between 1090 and her husband's departure on the first crusade in 1095. While he was away, she acted as head of the family and served as her husband's regent. Surviving documents show Adela to have been in full control of the comital courts. Several letters from the count to Adela hint at an affectionate and trusting relationship, and also attest to Adela's control of the family finances. However, Adela is also reported to have been quite critical when her husband returned to the county before she considered the terms of his crusader's vows fulfilled. With her approval Étienne-Henri returned to the Holy Land with a group of other French nobles in 1101; he died there in combat at the siege of Ramallah in May 1102.

The widowed Adela, by now the mother of five sons, assumed rule of the county on behalf of her under-age children. Of her daughters, only one, Matilda, is securely attested in contemporary sources, although Adela may have borne as many as three other girls. Her eldest son, Guillaume, originally designated heir to the county, had been set aside in favour of his younger brother Theobald by the time the latter was knighted in 1107. Surviving sources show Adela involved in settling many disputes among monasteries, and between monastic and lay lords, even after Theobald came of age. In fact mother and son continued to act jointly until Adela's retirement in 1120, and Adela made several tours throughout the family's holdings during her active years.

As a daughter of the English royal family and head of an important French family, Adela maintained ties with both the Anglo-Norman and Capetian kings. She seems to have been particularly close to her brother Henry, who became king of England in 1100, and she supported his interests over the claims of their brother *Robert, duke of Normandy, and Robert's son William Clito. Several times between 1103 and 1105 England's exiled archbishop, Anselm of Canterbury (d. 1109), stayed with Adela as her guest. In 1105, when Pope Paschal II (r. 1099–1118) was on the brink of excommunicating Henry for his failure to come to terms on the question of lay investiture, Adela helped to arrange a meeting in Normandy that led to a temporary truce between archbishop and king. Anselm later wrote to the pope praising her skill as a negotiator and peacemaker, and described her as an ardent supporter of the papal reform movement.

Pope Paschal II spent a great deal of time in Adela's domains during his tour of the French kingdom in 1107, and she also received Archbishop Thurstan of York (d. 1140) when he passed through her lands. She maintained friendships with many other leading ecclesiastical figures in England and France who bolstered both her family's prestige and their real power. Her correspondents included the poet–prelates Hildebert, bishop of Le Mans, and Abbot Baudri of Bourgueil, who became, perhaps with Adela's support, bishop of Dol. Hildebert's surviving works include four letters to Adela and at least two poems written for her, while Baudri wrote, among other works, a poem of some 1368 lines dedicated to Adela. This poem, which is Baudri's masterpiece, contains an extended, probably imagined, description of Adela's bedchamber. In return for the poems, the liberal Adela gave valuable gifts to both men, including elaborate liturgical garments that they both mention in their writings. Hugh of Fleury also dedicated his *Ecclesiastical History together with the Deeds of the Romans and the Franks* to her.

Adela, like other French nobles, was faced with the task of maintaining or extending her family's influence and holdings in the face of the increasingly powerful French monarchy. Relations with the Capetians had been good throughout the eleventh century. In 1101 Adela sent a contingent of knights to aid Philippe I's son Louis as he battled against rebel castellans north of Paris, but by 1107 her newly knighted son Theobald had joined other young nobles in a revolt against the prince. Four years later relations deteriorated to the point of open warfare which culminated in 1113 with the defeat of a Capetian–Angevin force by the armies of Henry I, Adela and Theobald, and their allies. The peace agreement of 1113 left the status of Normandy open, and this issue led to war again by 1118. Once more Adela used her wealth and diplomatic skills for the benefit of all her kindred. In 1120 Adela retired to the Cluniac priory of Marcigny where she continued to be active in political affairs although she ceased to style herself countess. She lived to see her fourth son, *Stephen, crowned king of England in 1135 before her own death in 1137, perhaps on 8 March. A later tradition based on a misidentification purports that she was buried beside her mother and sisters at Holy Trinity, Caen, but contemporary evidence places her tomb site at Marcigny.

Adela's children benefited from her successful tenure as head of the important comital family. After a youthful misadventure involving an armed attack on the canons at Chartres, Adela's son Guillaume married the heiress of Sully and consolidated the family's position in northern Berry. He seems to have been content there and dropped out of family records by about 1108. Theobald enjoyed a successful career as count of Blois, and eventually became the maternal grandfather of Philip Augustus of France (r. 1180–1223) through his daughter Adela, the second wife of Louis VII (r. 1137–80). A third son, Odo, died young. Stephen's career as king of England is well known, as is that of Adela's youngest son, Henry de *Blois, who became a Cluniac monk and later bishop of Winchester. Her daughter Matilda married Richard, earl of Chester, and drowned with her husband in the wreck of the *White Ship* in 1120, leaving no children.

LOIS L. HUNEYCUTT

Sources K. A. LoPrete, 'A female ruler in feudal society: Adela of Blois (c.1067– c.1137)', PhD diss., 2 vols., University of Chicago, 1992 • K. A. LoPrete, 'The Anglo-Norman card of Adela of Blois', *Albion*, 22 (1990), 569–89 • K. A. LoPrete, 'Adela of Blois and Ivo of Chartres: piety, politics and the peace in the diocese of Chartres', *Anglo-Norman Studies*, 14 (1991), 131–52 • K. A. LoPrete, 'Adela of Blois as mother and countess', *Medieval mothering*, ed. J. C. Parsons and B. Wheeler (1996), 313–34 • *S. Anselmi Cantuariensis archiepiscopi opera omnia*, ed. F. S. Schmitt, 6 vols. (1938–61); repr. with *Prolegomena, seu, Ratio editionis* (1968) • *Eadmeri Historia novorum in Anglia*, ed. M. Rule, Rolls Series, 81 (1884) • Ordericus Vitalis, *Eccl. hist.* • Baudri of Bourgueil, *Les oeuvres poétiques de Baudri de Bourgueil (1046–1130)*, ed. P. Abrahams (1926) • 'Epistolae', *Patrologia Latina*, 162 (1854), 11–290 • Guibert of Nogent, 'Historia quae dictur gesta Dei per Francos', *Recueil des historiens des croisades: historiens occidentaux*, 4 (Paris, 1879), 117–263 • *Hugh the Chanter: the history of the church of York, 1066–1127*, ed. and trans. C. Johnson (1961) • Suger, abbot of St Denis, *Vie de Louis VI le Gros*, ed. and trans. H. Waquet (Paris, 1929) • *The Gesta Normannorum ducum of William of Jumièges, Orderic Vitalis, and Robert of Torigni*, ed. and trans. E. M. C. van Houts, 2 vols., OMT (1992–5) • Hildebertus Cenomanensis, *Patrologia Latina*, 171 (1854) • M. A. E. Green, 'Adela of Blois', *Lives of the princesses of England*, 1 (1849), 34–71 • E. M. C. van Houts, 'Latin poetry and the Anglo-Norman court, 1066–1135: the *Carmen de Hastingae proelio*', *Journal of Medieval History*, 15 (1989), 39–62 • *The letters of Peter the Venerable*, ed. G. Constable, 2 vols. (1967)

Adelaide [Princess Adelaide of Saxe-Meiningen] **(1792–1849)**, queen of the United Kingdom of Great Britain and Ireland, consort of William IV, was the eldest child of George Frederick Charles, duke of Saxe-Meiningen (d. 1803), and Louisa Eleanora (d. 1837), daughter of Christian Albert, prince of Hohenlohe-Langenburg. She was born on 13 August 1792 in Meiningen, and named Adelaide Louisa Theresa Caroline Amelia (Adelheid Luise Therese Caroline Amalie). In 1818 she became engaged to William, duke of Clarence (1765–1837) [see William IV], the third son of George III and Queen Charlotte. The crisis in the royal family occasioned by the death of Princess Charlotte had created an urgent need for Clarence and his brothers to provide legitimate heirs to the throne, and to find suitable wives to bear them. Princess Adelaide had never met Clarence when she accepted the proposal of marriage made by his proxy, the duke of Cambridge. A temporary difficulty was caused by the refusal of parliament to raise the duke's allowance by the £10,000 he demanded, but Adelaide and her mother arrived in London on 4 July 1818. Her first meeting with Clarence took place at Grillon's Hotel, Albemarle Street, and was an immediate success. The marriage took place at Kew, simultaneously with that of the duke of Kent, on 11 July (not 13 July as has frequently been asserted) after a delay of two days, occasioned by the ill health of Queen Charlotte. Adelaide, who was personable rather than attractive, brought to the marriage an amiable disposition, an inclination towards domesticity, and a willingness to accept the ten illegitimate children of her husband's liaison with Dorothy Jordan. The marriage proved a happy one, despite the disparity in years (the bride was in her twenty-sixth, the bridegroom in his fifty-third year) and the absence of any preliminary courtship.

The duke and duchess of Clarence passed the first year of their marriage in Hanover, where, in 1819, a daughter was born to them. She was hurriedly named Charlotte Augusta Louisa, but lived only a few hours. Their second child, the Princess Elizabeth Georgina Adelaide, born on 10 December 1820, died in the following year. On two occasions the duchess miscarried, in 1819 and in 1822, on the latter occasion losing twins; although there were later reports of pregnancies, none was confirmed, and the Clarences remained childless.

The principal English residence of the duke and duchess was Bushey Park, Middlesex, where they lived in comparative retirement until the accession of William to the

Adelaide (1792–1849), by Sir William Beechey, c.1831

Her own health suffered, and for the rest of her life she was an invalid, travelling in the Mediterranean region in search of a favourable climate. She died from the rupture of a blood vessel in the chest at Bentley Priory, near Stanmore, Middlesex, on 2 December 1849. Her written requests that she should be buried simply, and her remains borne to the grave by sailors, were complied with at her interment at Windsor on 13 December. On her death she was widely mourned, not least by Queen Victoria, who had a lasting affection for her aunt, and recorded that 'All parties, all classes, join in doing her justice' (Letters of Queen Victoria, 2.273).

E. M. CLERKE, rev. A. W. PURDUE

Sources M. Hopkirk, Queen Adelaide (1946) · P. Ziegler, King William IV (1971) · M. F. Sandars, The life and times of Queen Adelaide (1915) · The letters of Queen Victoria, ed. A. C. Benson and Lord Esher [R. B. Brett], 3 vols., 1st ser. (1907), vol. 2 · J. Doran, Memoir of Queen Adelaide (1861) · J. Dewhurst, Royal confinements (1980)

Archives Royal Arch. | BL, corresp. with Princess Lieven, Add. MS 47347 · Flintshire RO, Hawarden, letters to duchess of Northumberland · LPL, letters to William Howley and Mrs Howley · Niedersächsisches Hauptstaatsarchiv Hannover, Hanover, letters to duke of Cumberland · NRA Scotland, priv. coll., letters to Lady Catherine Sinclair · unknown location, letters to Lady Sheffield · W. Yorks. AS, Leeds, Yorkshire Archaeological Society, letters to Lady Wellesley · Warks. CRO, letters to earl and countess of Denbigh · Warks. CRO, letters to Sir J. W. Waller

Likenesses Mrs J. Green, miniature, c.1821, Royal Collection · W. Beechey, oils, c.1831, NPG [see illus.] · W. Beechey, oils, exh. RA 1831, Trinity House, London · J. Simpson, oils, c.1832, Brighton Art Gallery · S. W. Reynolds, mezzotint, pubd 1833 (after A. Grahl), BM · D. Wilkie, double portrait, watercolour study, c.1833 (with William IV), Tate collection · D. Wilkie, oils, c.1833, Scot. NPG · D. Wilkie, oils, c.1835–1838, Examination Schools, Oxford · H. Room, group portrait, oils, 1837 (Queen Adelaide receiving Malagissy ambassadors), Queen's Palace Museum, Madagascar · M. A. Shee, oils, exh. RA 1837, Royal Collection · G. Hayter, group portrait, oils, 1840 (Marriage of Queen Victoria and Prince Albert), Royal Collection · C. R. Leslie, group portrait, oils, 1841 (Christening of the princess royal), Royal Collection · J. Lucas, pencil drawing, 1844, BM · W. C. Ross, miniature, 1844, Royal Collection · J. Thomson, stipples, pubd 1845 (after J. Lucas and G. Richmond), BM, NPG · F. X. Winterhalter, oils, 1849, Royal Collection · G. Boul, marble bust, Royal Collection · F. Chantrey, stone medallion, AM Oxf. · caricatures, BM, NPG · prints, BM, NPG

throne on the death of George IV, 26 June 1830. By a bill passed in the following November, the queen was nominated as regent, in case a child of hers should survive the king. The modest style of the new monarch and his court was typified by the frugal coronation, or 'Half Crownation' as some critics termed it, on 8 September 1831. The queen gave respectability to the court and exercised a calming influence on her excitable and eccentric husband; she also attempted, without success, to improve the relations between the king and the duchess of Kent, mother of the heir presumptive, Princess Victoria.

Queen Adelaide was strongly opposed to political change and her supposed interference in politics made her very unpopular during and after the reform agitation. Her carriage was once attacked in the streets by an angry mob, who were beaten off by the canes of her footmen. On the dismissal of Melbourne's ministry in 1834, the words used in The Times, 'The queen has done it all,' were placarded over London although there is little evidence of her political influence over the king. The dismissal of her tory chamberlain, Lord Howe, for voting against the ministry, caused her much annoyance, and she refused to accept anyone in his place, which he continued to fill unofficially, thus fuelling speculation about the nature of their relationship.

In the spring of 1837, Queen Adelaide was summoned to Germany to her mother's deathbed; shortly after her return, the king became ill. He died in her arms on 20 June, and when he was buried at Windsor on 8 July, the queen, contrary to precedent, attended the funeral.

Adelard of Bath. See Bath, Adelard of (b. in or before 1080?, d. in or after 1150).

Adelida [Adeliza] (d. before 1113), princess, was probably the eldest of the daughters of *William I, the Conqueror (1027/8–1087), and *Matilda of Flanders (d. 1083). As Adelida she heads most lists of the names of the Conqueror's daughters, including the one in the mortuary roll of Abbess Matilda of Ste Trinité at Caen, which is authoritative, since it was compiled under the guidance of Adelida's sister Cecily, who became Abbess Matilda's successor. She had either four or five sisters: Cecily, Constance, Matilda, *Adela, and perhaps Agatha; and four brothers: *Robert Curthose, William Rufus [see William II], Richard, and *Henry I.

There are two traditions about Adelida's career: one claims that she was betrothed to Harold Godwineson [see Harold II], and the other that she became a nun. Orderic

Vitalis in his interpolations of the *Gesta Normannorum ducum* says that Adeliza (*sic*) had been contracted to Earl Harold before the Norman conquest of England. For this information he relied on the work of William of Poitiers, the contemporary biographer of William the Conqueror. Unfortunately, William of Poitiers does not name the girl involved, nor does he say whether she was the same as the daughter(s) involved in the two other marriage alliances which he describes, respectively with Herbert II, count of Maine, and with two rivalling kings in Spain. Robert de Torigni repeats Orderic's assumption that Adeliza was Harold's betrothed, but calls her Adelida, while other Anglo-Norman historians like William of Malmesbury and Eadmer refer to the betrothal without naming the daughter. In his later ecclesiastical history Orderic Vitalis, however, introduces the name of another daughter, Agatha (who is not otherwise known), to whom he attributes the betrothal to Earl Harold and King 'Amfurcius' of Spain, and adds that she died as a virgin at Bayeux. Moreover, in the same passage, Orderic explains that Adeliza was a virgin under the protection of Roger de Beaumont. This presumably means that she was a nun of St Léger at Préaux. If so, she may tentatively be identified with either Prioress Adelina or the nun Adeliza of that nunnery mentioned in the St Léger section of Abbess Matilda's mortuary roll. She almost certainly is the dedicatee of the prayers and meditations of Anselm of Canterbury, who addresses her as Adelida 'venerable lady of royal nobility'. The two traditions about Adelida (or Adeliza) are not mutually exclusive. She may have been betrothed several times to different suitors and since none of the schemes resulted in marriage, she probably took the veil. Whether as a nun or as a lay princess, her appearance in Abbess Matilda's mortuary roll means that she died before 1113.

ELISABETH VAN HOUTS

Sources F. Barlow, *William Rufus* (1983), 441–5 · L. Delisle, ed., *Rouleaux des morts du IXe au XVe siècle* (1866), 182, 207, 285, 289 · *The Gesta Normannorum ducum of William of Jumièges, Orderic Vitalis, and Robert of Torigni*, ed. and trans. E. M. C. van Houts, 2, OMT (1995), 160–61, 262–3 · Ordericus Vitalis, *Eccl. hist.*, 3.113–14 · Guillaume de Poitiers [Gulielmus Pictaviensis], *Histoire de Guillaume le Conquérant / Gesta Gulielmus ducis Normannorum et regis Anglorum*, ed. R. Foreville (Paris, 1952), 88–9, 142–3, 230–31 · *S. Anselmi Cantuariensis archiepiscopi opera omnia*, ed. F. S. Schmitt, 6 vols. (1938–61), vol. 3, pp. 113–14 · R. W. Southern, *Saint Anselm: a portrait in a landscape* (1990), 91–3, 103–5

Adeliza [Adeliza of Louvain] (*c*.1103–1151), queen of England, second consort of Henry I, was a daughter of Godfrey, count of Lower Lorraine and duke of Brabant (*d.* 1139), and his first wife, Ide, daughter of Henri (III), count of Namur. Adeliza's birth date is unknown, but the often cited approximate date of 1103 cannot be far wrong, since chroniclers refer to her as *puella* (a girl) at the time of her marriage to *Henry I (1068/9–1135) in 1121, and she bore seven children after 1135. Charlemagne was an ancestor of both her parents, a fact that was celebrated by Adeliza's descendants but unknown or irrelevant to contemporaries.

Nothing is known of Adeliza's education, but her later patronage of French poetry suggests early exposure to literature. King Henry, whose first wife had died in 1118, married her soon after his only legitimate son was drowned in 1120, when he stood in urgent need of a male heir. Eadmer of Canterbury reports that Henry's advisers agreed that she had the necessary beauty, morals, and character to become queen of England. In addition to giving Henry the possibility of fathering more children, the marriage strengthened England's existing diplomatic alliances within the German empire.

The chronicler John of Worcester states that Adeliza was chosen queen before her wedding and formal coronation, which took place in Windsor on 24 and 25 January 1121. Henry's decision to have the ceremonies performed by the diocesan bishop, Roger of Salisbury (*d.* 1139), led to a dispute with the archbishop of Canterbury, culminating in the articulation of the archbishop's right to serve as the royal chaplain anywhere in England. In marked contrast to her predecessor, Queen Matilda, Adeliza took little part in governing the realm. Although she attested a few of her husband's charters, and accompanied Henry to Normandy in 1125, 1129, and probably 1131, she never served as a regent, and does not appear as part of the king's curia. Personal inclination probably contributed to her absence from the public sphere, as did the diminishing need for day-to-day administrative involvement by members of the royal family as Henry's government developed. Adeliza did receive and administer substantial dower properties, including the county of Shropshire. Several of these properties, such as Queenhithe in London and the custody of Barking and Waltham abbeys, both in Essex, had been held by Henry's first wife and were claimed by subsequent queens consort as belonging to them by right of office. Adeliza maintained her own household, bringing several staff members from Lorraine. Her first two chancellors were promoted to bishoprics during Henry's reign, Godfrey to Bath in 1123, and Simon to Worcester two years later. She retained ties to her natal family, giving wedding gifts of land to both a brother and a cousin.

The chronicler Henry of Huntingdon quotes a Latin poem written to celebrate Adeliza's beauty, but she is perhaps best remembered as a patron of French literature. She sponsored Philip de Thaon's *Bestiaire*, and the Anglo-Norman version of the *Voyage of St Brendan* was rededicated to her. Geoffrey Gaimar implies that she commissioned a lost verse biography of Henry I from the poet David. But her most significant contribution to the Anglo-Norman realm into which she had married was a negative one: although there is no reason to doubt the fertility of either husband or wife, Adeliza failed to bear the looked-for son to Henry I.

After Henry's death in 1135, and probably after 1137, Adeliza married William d'*Aubigny (Pincerna), Henry's butler (*d.* 1176). William took the title of earl of Arundel after property belonging to the dowager queen. They had seven children who survived to adulthood. In 1139 Henry's daughter, the Empress Matilda (*d.* 1166) landed in Sussex to claim the English throne. William of Malmesbury reports that Adeliza had sent messengers to Normandy guaranteeing the empress's safety, but after receiving her at Arundel Castle, she surrendered her to King Stephen when threatened with an army. Adeliza did, however, negotiate a safe conduct allowing Matilda to join her half-brother, Robert, earl of Gloucester (d. 1147), in Bristol. Throughout the rest of the civil war Adeliza and her husband remained loyal to King Stephen.

Like most other aristocratic women of the era, Adeliza patronized a number of religious houses. Among the recipients of her charity were Boxgrove Priory, Sussex, the cathedral church at Chichester, Henry's monastic foundation of Reading, her own foundation of the Augustinian priory of Pynham, Sussex, and several leper houses. The date of Adeliza's death is reported in continental sources as 24 March 1151. Her last datable charter was issued in 1150, at which time she had retired to the continental monastery of Affligham in Flanders, which had been founded by her father and uncle. The annals of Margam claim that the queen is buried in Affligham, but a charter issued by Adeliza's half-brother Jocelyn in favour of Reading Abbey states that she was buried there, presumably next to her first husband.   LOIS L. HUNEYCUTT

Sources L. Wertheimer, 'Adeliza of Louvain and Anglo-Norman queenship', *Haskins Society Journal*, 7 (1995), 101–15 · *Reg. RAN*, vol. 2 · B. R. Kemp, ed., *Reading Abbey cartularies*, 2 vols., CS, 4th ser., 31, 33 (1986–7) · *Eadmeri Historia novorum in Anglia*, ed. M. Rule, Rolls Series, 81 (1884) · William of Malmesbury, *The Historia novella*, ed. and trans. K. R. Potter (1955) · 'Arundel', GEC, *Peerage* · A. Strickland and [E. Strickland], *Lives of the queens of England*, new edn, 1 (1902) · E. M. C. van Houts, 'Latin poetry and the Anglo-Norman court, 1066–1135: the *Carmen de Hastingae proelio*', *Journal of Medieval History*, 15 (1989), 39–62 · *The Anglo-Norman voyage of St Brendan by Benedeit*, ed. E. G. R. Waters (1928) · *Ann. mon.*, vol. 1
Archives priv. coll., charter
Likenesses seal (after a seal of Queen Matilda I and Queen Matilda II), priv. coll.
Wealth at death Honour of Arundel and other properties

Adelmare, Cesare (d. **1569**). *See under* Caesar, Sir Julius (*bap.* 1558, d. 1636).

Adelsdorfer, Elisabeth Johanna de Boys. *See* Frazer, Lilly, Lady Frazer (1854/5–1941).

Adelstein, Abraham Manie [Abe] (**1916–1992**), occupational physician and medical statistician, was born on 28 March 1916 at Trichard, eastern Transvaal, South Africa, the fourth of five children (four boys and one girl) of Nathan Adelstein, miller in Trichard, and Rosie Cohen, both Jewish immigrants from Latvia. Educated at the Marist Brothers College in Johannesburg, where he became head prefect, he studied medicine at the University of Witwatersrand and qualified MB BS in 1940. After a brief spell as intern at the Johannesburg General Hospital he volunteered for the South African Medical Corps as a medical officer and served in South Africa until 1945. In 1942 he married Cynthia Gladys Miller (b. 1921) of Ladybird, also a former Witwatersrand student, who subsequently obtained an MSc in psychology at Cape Town and worked as a psychologist.

On demobilization Abe (as he was always known to his friends) returned to Witwatersrand for postgraduate studies in public health and obtained a DPH in 1947 before joining South Africa Railways as health officer for Transvaal province later that year. In 1951 he was seconded to work in Professor Austin Bradford Hill's department of medical statistics at the London School of Hygiene and Tropical Medicine. While there he published what became a classic paper showing that 'accident proneness' in the railways was a product of the conditions of work rather than a characteristic of the individual. On returning to South Africa he became director of medical research and statistics in South Africa Railways, but his antipathy to apartheid made him anxious to leave the country, and in 1961 he accepted a post as senior lecturer in medical statistics in the department of social and preventive medicine in the University of Manchester.

Adelstein's years at Manchester were marred by recurrent illness, but he published useful papers on the mortality from coronary disease in South African railway workers—which showed the striking difference between the high rate in white people (then the highest in the world) and the low rate in black people—and (with Zena Stein and Mervyn Susser) on the incidence of mental disease in the general population, a category of disease that was just beginning to be studied epidemiologically. It was, however, in his subsequent post as chief medical statistician in the General Register Office (1967–81), a government department later subsumed into the office of population censuses and surveys and then the office of national statistics, that he made his mark on British medicine. Ever since the days of William Farr the registrar-general's medical publications had provided mortality data of prime importance to public health, which highlighted the geographical, socio-economic, and temporal differences in mortality by sex and age. These had pointed to potential causes of disease and had monitored the health effects of national policies, whether active in the control of infectious disease or *laissez-faire* in relation to economic development, and the practice had grown up of collaborating with selected research workers in providing unpublished data for their use and analysis.

During Adelstein's tenure of the post, the information available in the registrar's office was made available to all bona fide research workers and the chief medical statistician was at their service to help them decide what material would be most useful and how it could be analysed most effectively. Within the department he recognized the need for establishing a cohort based on a random sample of the population, defined at a national census, and for following its members up within the department; for by law the personal information obtained at a census was confidential to the department and it was only by analysis within that department that the information could be made of medical use. He consequently initiated the longitudinal study of a 1 per cent sample of the population which began to bear fruit only after his death.

With his background in South Africa, Adelstein could be especially helpful to the World Health Organization, with which he worked extensively in developing health-information systems in developing countries. These were important in enabling comparisons to be made between countries with different cultures, health-care systems, and facilities for recording information and hence for assessing their relative needs.

After formal retirement Adelstein became an honorary professor at the London School of Hygiene and Tropical Medicine, where he continued to undertake research into the role of social factors in disease. From 1956 on he was plagued by a series of disabling and life-threatening diseases, which necessitated multiple operations, but he never allowed this to distort his outward tranquillity. He combined throughout, according to Alwyn Smith, a Manchester colleague, 'a sometimes breathtaking honesty with a gentle kindness and an ability to recognise the good points of others. He never appeared even to think unkindly of anyone, and a gentle smile was never far away, whatever the folly or obtuseness of those around him' (*The Independent*). He died at his home, 21 Dunstan Road, Golders Green, London, on 18 October 1992, survived by his wife, son, and daughter.   RICHARD DOLL

Sources J. Fox, *BMJ* (28 Nov 1992), 1358 · M. Marmot, *The Lancet*, 340 (1992), 1463 · A. Smith, *The Independent* (3 Nov 1992), 11a–d · *WWW* · *CGPLA Eng. & Wales* (1993) · d. cert.
Likenesses photograph, repro. in Fox, *BMJ*
Wealth at death £67,687: probate, 1993

Adgar [William] (*fl.* 1150×1200), Anglo-Norman translator, was baptized Adgar but reveals that he was more commonly known as William; Trouvère (roughly meaning 'poet') is a later and inauthentic epithet. As the author of the first vernacular rendering of the miracles of the Virgin Mary, he is sometimes identified with a William who was chaplain and perpetual vicar of St Mary Magdalen, Milk Street, London (1162–1200), who held his living from St Paul's Cathedral (he does not appear to have been a canon). His collection of forty-nine miracles of the Virgin, entitled *Gracial* (found in BL, Egerton MS 612, BL, Add. MS 38664, and a fragment, Dulwich College, MS 22), was written for a friend called Gregory and dedicated to one Maud, 'dame Mahaut', most likely the abbess of Barking (*c*.1175–95) who was a natural daughter of Henry II. The collection seems to exist in a number of redactions which stem from Adgar himself. The whole surviving text runs to 8786 lines of octosyllables. The source, which Adgar allegedly found in the book cupboard (*almarie*) at St Paul's, seems to have been provided by a canon of the cathedral (1148–62) called Alberic ('mestre Albri'), who compiled a collection of miracles from William of Malmesbury, Anselm, abbot of Bury, and Prior Dominic of Evesham. Adgar's vernacular compilation, from the second half of the twelfth century, was revised in the thirteenth century by Everard of Gateley, a monk of Bury.   TONY HUNT

Sources *Adgar: 'Le gracial'*, ed. P. Kunstmann (1982) · M. D. Legge, *Anglo-Norman literature and its background* (1963), 187–91
Archives BL, Add. MS 38664; Egerton MS 612 · Dulwich College, MS 22

Adie, Alexander James (1775–1858), maker of scientific instruments, was born on 7 January 1775, and baptized at Greyfriars parish church, Edinburgh, the posthumous second son of John Adie and his wife, Elizabeth, *née* Miller.

His father was a printer, one of the proprietors of the *Edinburgh Evening Courant*, and was said to have contributed articles to the *Scots Magazine*. He died about three months before Alexander was born, and although his widow remarried she too died shortly thereafter, and the boy was adopted by his maternal uncle, John Miller (1746–1815), with whom he lived until Miller's death.

At the age of twelve Adie was apprenticed to a stocking maker, but on the death a short time later of his elder brother, John, he was apprenticed as his replacement to their uncle, an optician. In later life, he regretted the curtailed education of his youth, and attended lectures and sought out private tuition. He became a partner with his uncle from 1803, and continued to trade under the name Miller and Adie until 1822, when the firm became Alexander Adie. On 22 October 1804 he married Marion Ritchie, with whom he had four sons and seven daughters. Three of his sons became successful scientific instrument makers: the eldest, John *Adie (1805–1857), subsequently went into partnership with his father; the third, Richard (1810–1881), started a business in Liverpool; and the youngest, Patrick (1821–1886), began one in London.

Although the firm's products were aimed at satisfying the expanding demand for surveying instruments, both the University of St Andrews and Anderson's Institution of Glasgow are known to have purchased Adie's demonstration apparatus for their natural philosophy classrooms. His mechanical skills soon attracted the attention of a number of inventive patrons, among whom was the Edinburgh-based natural philosopher, David Brewster (1781–1868), who commissioned a number of newly designed instruments from Adie for his research work in optics. As a scientific journalist and editor, Brewster publicized Adie's skills by promoting his own work, particularly in connection with his experiments with jewel lenses for microscope optics during the 1820s. Another early patron was Sir James Hall (1761–1832) of Dunglass, who undertook a series of experiments between 1798 and 1805 which ultimately confirmed James Hutton's (1726–1797) argument for the igneous origin of basalt and other types of rock. Adie also manufactured a series of differential thermometers used in the pioneering work on the nature of heat by Sir John Leslie (1766–1832), professor of mathematics at the University of Edinburgh; these were advertised in Leslie's publications between 1808 and 1820. A further patron was the civil engineer Robert Stevenson (1772–1850), whose improvements in lighthouse optics called upon Adie's practical mechanical skills. The construction of an improved form of the pantograph, called the eidograph, was produced by Adie in 1821 for its designer, William Wallace, professor of mathematics at the University of Edinburgh.

Adie was interested in the science of meteorology from an early date, and began a register with barometer, thermometer, and wind and rain gauges, all constructed himself. His records ran from 1795 to 1805, and again between 1821 and 1850, and were later used in discussion by James David Forbes (1809–1868), professor of natural philosophy at the University of Edinburgh, and also a patron of Adie during the 1830s. Adie's interest in weather led him to design, and subsequently patent, in December 1818, his sympiesometer or 'new air barometer'. This instrument used oil as its hydrostatic fluid, together with a column of gas. It was particularly useful as a marine barometer, as its sensitivity provided early warning of weather changes at sea, and its construction meant that it was less likely to break in storms. Until the invention of the aneroid barometer in 1861 the sympiesometer appears to have sold in reasonable numbers.

An active member of the Wernerian Natural History Society, Adie was elected to the Royal Society of Edinburgh in 1819 and was a founder member of Brewster's Society for the Encouragement of the Useful Arts in Scotland (later the Royal Scottish Society of Arts), instituted in 1821. In the same year, Brewster introduced Adie to the young J. D. Forbes, whose interests in geology and the nature of heat led to a project funded by the British Association for the Advancement of Science to investigate heat flow in soil and bedrock. Three sites around Edinburgh were chosen, for which Adie constructed four remarkable thermometers, of 3, 6, 12, and 24 ft in length, during 1836–7. This appears to have been his final special commission.

Alexander's eldest son, John, joined him in the workshop about 1826. The business traded as Adie & Son from 1835 until 1881, long after both had died. It is not known when Alexander ceased work altogether, but from about 1840 he suffered poor health. He spent much of his retirement experimenting with horticulture. John committed suicide in early 1857, and by that time Adie was becoming senile. After a severe illness followed by a bad cold, he died at his home, Canaan Cottage, Newington, Edinburgh, on 4 December 1858, aged eighty-three. He was buried at Greyfriars churchyard. A. D. MORRISON-LOW

Sources T. N. Clarke, A. D. Morrison-Low, and A. D. C. Simpson, *Brass and glass: scientific instrument making workshops in Scotland* (1989), 25–74 · A. D. C. Simpson, 'An Edinburgh intrigue: Brewster's Society of Arts and the pantograph dispute', *Book of the Old Edinburgh Club*, new ser., 1 (1991), 47–73 · Accounts, legal papers and correspondence relating to the trust of Alexander James Adie, scientific instrument maker in Edinburgh, 1819–68, Edinburgh City Archives · d. cert. · b. cert. · m. cert. · Old parochial register 685 1/36 (baptism)
Archives NA Scot., Henderson MSS, GD 76/464 · National Museums of Scotland, Edinburgh, Arthur Frank MSS
Wealth at death £13,216 19s. 7½d.: SC 70/1/101, p. 10

Adie, John (1805–1857), maker of scientific instruments, was born on 27 September 1805 in Edinburgh, the eldest of four sons of Alexander James *Adie (1775–1858), scientific instrument maker, and his wife, Marion, née Ritchie. Although his early years remain obscure, it can be assumed that he served his apprenticeship in Edinburgh, probably under his father or another master optician or brass-founder. On 24 September 1840 he married Elizabeth Barron, from an Aberdeenshire family; his own sister Elizabeth married a lawyer, George Barron, writer to the signet, from the same family. John's marriage was childless; his wife died in the 1850s.

Adie's expertise lay in his mechanical and scientific ability, which was attracting patronage by his early twenties.

He was sent to London to the firm of Troughton and Simms, to familiarize himself with the setting up of a complex instrument, the mural circle, ordered for the Edinburgh Astronomical Institution in 1827 and finally installed in the Calton Hill observatory in 1834. By the late 1820s John was undertaking commissions, previously fulfilled by his father, for special devices for Sir John Leslie (1766–1832). He was, like his father, attracted to meteorological work, in particular for the Edinburgh mathematics teacher William Galbraith, and also for Professor J. D. Forbes (1809–1868). The firm exhibited at the Paris Exhibition of 1855, though not at the 1851 Great Exhibition in London. John's business connections perhaps spread over an even greater area than those of his father, encompassing commissions for William Swan (1818–1894), an experimenter in optics who subsequently became professor of natural philosophy at the University of St Andrews. Among these were special thermometers, a collimating magnet, optical instruments, including the selaometer, a device for measuring the luminous impressions on the eye. Other commissions came from the civil engineer Alan Stevenson (1807–1865), son of the lighthouse builder Robert Stevenson and, like him, engineer to the Northern Lighthouse Board. Adie also realized various practical improvements to surveying instruments, proposed by John Sang, Thomas Stevenson, and J. D. Forbes, and others.

Family papers reveal that Adie set up house after 1838 in Edinburgh's fashionable New Town. From the retirement of his father at some point during the early 1840s, he ran the Edinburgh business until his own death in early 1857, after which it was taken over by his younger brother Richard (1810–1881), who had started up a similar enterprise in Liverpool in 1835. Adie was somewhat overweight, preferring to drive rather than to walk; he was also, evidently, fairly musical. Not enough information survives to say where his political sympathies lay. After his wife's death, he seems to have resumed his earlier bachelor existence, while throwing himself into his work. However, he seems to have been prone to fits of despondency, and on the evening of 5 January 1857, he shot himself in his own house at 50 Northumberland Street. He was buried in Greyfriars churchyard, Edinburgh. A. D. MORRISON-LOW

Sources T. N. Clarke, A. D. Morrison-Low, and A. D. C. Simpson, *Brass and glass: scientific instrument making workshops in Scotland* (1989), 25–74 · A. McConnell, *Instrument makers to the world: a history of Cooke, Troughton & Simms* (1992), 27 · b. cert. · m. cert. · d. cert.
Archives National Museums of Scotland, Edinburgh, History of Science section, scientific instruments | NA Scot., Henderson MSS, GD 76/464 · National Museums of Scotland, Edinburgh, Arthur Frank collection
Wealth at death £2194 2s. 5d.: 7 May 1860, NA Scot., SC 70/1/104, pp. 568–80

Adis, Henry (fl. 1641/2–1663), General Baptist leader and writer, was in 1648 a prisoner in the Tower Chamber of the Fleet prison, 'in the seventh year of the Author's Oppression, being the 8th year of this Parliament's Reformation' (Adis, *A Spie*, title-page). Before his imprisonment, he had been an 'Upholdster' in Covent Garden, repairing and cleaning cloth and fabric (ibid., sig. Cv), and after his imprisonment he seems to have returned there, giving his address as Princes Street in 1660. Nothing is known of Adis's parents, but by 1648 it seems that he was married with 'three small children' (ibid.).

In 1648 Adis published *A Spie, Sent out of the Tower-Chamber in the Fleet* and *A Cup for the Citie*, in which he criticized the tyrannical and arbitrary nature of the parliamentarian regime and prophesied doom following the overthrow of Charles I. In *A Spie, Sent out* Adis explicitly condemned the 'unsavory' William Lenthall, speaker of the House of Commons, for denying him both his freedom and the means of supporting a family (Adis, *A Spie*, sigs. B2, Cv). Indeed, Adis's early political stance may have stemmed from his own experience of the injustices of the legal system for which he held Lenthall, as a commissioner of the great seal and master of the rolls, directly responsible. From his reference to his having 'suffer'd in a Court of Equity', and the possibility that he was a gaoled debtor, it seems that his imprisonment may have been as much the cause as the result of his engagement in religious and political controversy (ibid., sig. Bv). At this time, Adis also penned *The Symptoms of Ruin, or, The Sword and Famine, the Attendants of Oppression*, a work no longer extant.

Adis's most prolific period of publishing came in the early years of the Restoration. In 1659 he co-authored (with Richard Pilgrim, William Cox, and Abel Hutchins) *A declaration of a small society of baptized believers, undergoing the name of Free-Willers, about the City of London*. This tract sought to distinguish the commitments of Adis and his fellow Free-Willers from the doctrines and the violent radicalism associated with certain other Baptists. The *Declaration* advocated complete religious toleration and promised obedience to magistrates in all but spiritual matters, along with patient and peaceful sufferance of persecution. Central to it was staunch opposition to taking oaths which, Adis believed, had been instrumental in causing the civil wars.

Adis's other writings elaborate these same issues. He frequently (and idiosyncratically) styled himself a 'Fannatick' at this time to signal clearly his status as a Dissenter infamously persecuted and vilified as such. From 1660 his tracts generally bear the same words on their title-page, 'By Henry Adis, a baptized believer, undergoing the name of a Free-Willer; and also most ignominiously by the tongue of infamy, called a *Fannatick*, or a *mad man*'. In *A Fannatick's Mite* (1660) Adis declared his loyalty to Charles II while refusing none the less to vow allegiance to him. He also urged the monarch to shun debauchery, reform the nation, and offer liberty of conscience to all. Unsurprisingly, Adis was soon forced to write *A Fannatick's Letter Sent out of the Dungeon of the Gate-House Prison of Westminster* (1661?), proclaiming his peaceable principles after being arrested and imprisoned, possibly for publishing his '*good advice to the King*' (p. 24), but more probably for being a Baptist, and therefore seen as a potential danger at the time of the Venner rising (6 January 1661). Having spent many weeks in gaol, Adis was finally released on 25

March 1661: the king himself, allegedly, had 'sent fifty pound' to discharge him and others '*unjustly imprisoned in his Name*' (Adis, *Fannatick's Alarm*, 9–10).

Adis capitalized on such royal interest, subsequently publishing *A Fannatick's Alarm* (1661), a vitriolic attack on Sir Richard Browne, lord mayor of London, whom Adis charged with tyrannizing 'the *Kings Friends*' (p. 29). To reinforce his innocence 'about the late Insurrection' and to declare obedience and loyalty to the monarch once more, Adis also composed *A Fannaticks Addresse, Humbly Presented to the King and his Peers* (1661). In addition he engaged in further controversy at this time by producing *A Fannatick's Testimony Against Swearing* (1661) in answer to those Baptists (John Tombes, Henry Den, Jeremiah Ives, and Theophilus Brabourne) who asserted the lawfulness of taking the king's oath.

In June 1662, following the Quaker Act and other legislation penalizing Dissenters, Adis petitioned the king for his own and six other families (including that of Richard Adis, presumably Henry's son) to be transported to Surinam. Gaining free pass and royal protection from Charles II, they arrived in 1663, Adis describing in *A Letter Sent from Syrranam*, dated 10 December 1663 and published in 1664, how he and his family enjoyed there 'the freedom of our Liberties in the service of our God', despite the need for 'Reformation' among the colony's other Christians (Adis, *A Letter*, 4–6). Before he emigrated, Henry Adis also compiled *A Fannatick's Primmer* (1660?), a manual to help instruct children to read the scriptures. Nothing more is known of him; it may be presumed he did not return from Surinam.
                                       MICHAEL DAVIES

Sources Greaves & Zaller, *BDBR* · H. Adis, *A spie, sent out of the Tower-Chamber in the Fleet* (1648) · H. Adis, *A fannatick's alarm, given to the mayor in his quarters, by one of the sons of Sion, become Boanerges* (1661) · H. Adis, 'A fannaticks addresse, humbly presented to the king and his peers' [1661], *A collection of scarce and valuable tracts … Lord Somers*, 2 (1751), 220–31 · H. Adis, *A letter from Syrranam, to his excellency, the Lord Willoughby of Parham* (1664) · *CSP col.*, 5.92–3, no. 310 [8 June 1662] · W. T. Whitley, ed., *A Baptist bibliography*, 2 vols. (1916–22) · W. T. Whitley, ed., *Minutes of the general assembly of the General Baptist churches in England*, 1: 1654–1728 (1909), xv, xxxv · T. Crosby, *The history of the English Baptists, from the Reformation to the beginning of the reign of King George I*, 4 vols. (1738–40), vol. 3, appx v, pp. 91–110 · A. C. Underwood, *A history of the English Baptists* (1947), 91–2 · R. L. Greaves, *Deliver us from evil: the radical underground in Britain, 1660–1663* (1986), 26 · L. F. Brown, *The political activities of the Baptists and Fifth Monarchy men in England during the interregnum* (1912), 8, n. 15 · B. R. White, *The English Baptists of the seventeenth century* (1983), 97–8 · J. H. Wood, *A condensed history of the General Baptists of the New Connexion* (1847), 152 · Watt, *Bibl. Brit.*, 4.18, col. b · *BL cat.* · T. Harris, *London crowds in the reign of Charles II* (1987), 76

Adkins, Robert. *See* Atkins, Robert (1628/9–1685).

Adler, Henrietta [Nettie] (1868–1950), social worker and Jewish political activist, was born in London on 1 December 1868, the elder daughter of Rabbi Dr Hermann *Adler (1839–1911) and his wife, Rachel Joseph (d. 1912). Her father was the son of Dr Nathan Marcus *Adler, chief rabbi of the United Hebrew Congregations of the British Empire. From 1879 Hermann was delegate chief rabbi, acting for his father in the many duties for which the office called, and in 1891, following Nathan's death the previous year,

Hermann became chief rabbi in his own right. Nettie Adler thus grew up in an Orthodox Jewish milieu; she remained loyal to this upbringing throughout her life. However, her relationship with her father was rarely happy. Educated privately, Nettie rebelled against Hermann's attempts to dictate to her the terms on which her life was to be led. In 1894 she fell in love with Isaac Friedner, a synagogue official in Liverpool. Hermann considered Friedner to be unworthy of his daughter, forbade the match, and intercepted their correspondence. Nettie never married. In politics Hermann was a staunch tory. Nettie identified with the Liberal Party, a move which Hermann viewed as nothing less than an act of familial treachery. During the London county council (LCC) elections of March 1904, when Nettie (as a good Liberal) campaigned against state aid for denominational schools, Hermann let it be known publicly that she was working without his authority or consent.

In common with many middle-class women in Victorian England, Nettie Adler was drawn into social and educational work among the poor, specifically, in her case, among the Jewish and non-Jewish slum-dwellers of London's East End. More or less automatically she joined the visiting committee of the Jewish Board of Guardians and the Jewish religious education board. But her belief that charity would not by itself alleviate the consequences of poverty drew her also to the world of local government in the capital. She joined the Progressive Party—in effect the liberal party in London municipal politics—and quickly rose in its ranks, becoming a school manager under the auspices of the London school board, and from 1905 until 1910 serving as a co-opted member of the LCC's education committee.

At its inception (1889) women had not been expressly excluded from membership of the LCC; the prohibition came about as a result of subsequent legal action, which was reversed by the Liberal government in 1908. Nettie was at once adopted by the Progressives in the LCC's Central Hackney division. At the LCC elections of March 1910 she brought into the division a glittering array of Liberal personalities, including the Jews Herbert Samuel and Rufus Isaacs and the non-Jews Sidney Webb and Sir J. W. Benn, the leader of the Progressives at county hall. Nettie made no secret of her Jewish identity, refusing to campaign on the Saturday of the poll, the Jewish sabbath. She won a comfortable majority, thus becoming one of the first two women (the other was Susan Lawrence, a Municipal Reformer) to sit as of right on the LCC, of which she was deputy chairman in 1922–3.

Nettie's tenure of the Central Hackney division provided the springboard for a remarkable career focused not merely on London government but also on the more general problems of poverty, especially among children and young people. As a justice of the peace attached to juvenile courts she became an internationally acknowledged authority on juvenile delinquency. She accepted membership of a number of important inquiries into aspects of child poverty in the inter-war period, and served on the committee on wage-earning children, of which she was joint honorary secretary from 1899 until 1946, the departmental committee on charity collections (1925–7), and the advisory committee of the Board of Trade on juvenile labour exchanges. The high regard in which she was held in Whitehall was reflected in her appointment as a commander in the Order of the British Empire in 1934.

Nettie's political career was, however, blighted in three respects. As a Progressive she suffered as a result of the decline in Liberal fortunes after 1918. As a Jewess she was a victim of the resurgence of antisemitism in Britain after the First World War. She also suffered from poor health. In 1925, as a protest against the anti-Jewish prejudices of the Municipal Reformers (that is, the Conservatives) on the LCC, she declined to continue the arrangement by which she had 'shared' the Central Hackney division with a member of that party, and lost the seat. In 1928 she won it back in spite of a Municipal Reform campaign in which her Jewish identity was made into a major issue at the polls. In 1931 she announced that she would not fight the seat again.

A member of the governing bodies of numerous Jewish and non-Jewish charities and educational institutions, Nettie Adler was also a prolific writer on social themes, publishing many articles and pamphlets on children as wage earners, working women, the treatment of young offenders, and the juvenile court system. She wrote for the *Times Literary Supplement* and contributed the chapter entitled 'Jewish life and labour in east London' to the *New Survey of London Life and Labour*, edited by Hubert Llewellyn Smith and published in 1934. She died of heart failure at Glazbury Nursing Home, 20 Glazbury Road, London, on 15 April 1950. GEOFFREY ALDERMAN

Sources G. Alderman, *London Jewry and London politics, 1889–1986* (1989) · G. Alderman, *Modern British Jewry* (1992) · *Jewish Chronicle* (21 April 1950), 16 · *The Times* (17 April 1950), 7 · *WWW* · d. cert.
Archives Board of Deputies of British Jews, London, archives, MSS · LMA, London county council archives, MSS
Likenesses photograph, repro. in *Jewish Chronicle*
Wealth at death £6939 17s. 4d.: probate, 14 Nov 1950, CGPLA Eng. & Wales

Adler, Hermann (1839–1911), chief rabbi, was born in Hanover on 30 May 1839, the second son of two sons and three daughters of Nathan Marcus *Adler (1803–1890), then chief rabbi of Hanover, and his first wife, Henrietta Worms (d. 1854). In June 1845 the family moved to London, where Nathan Adler was installed as chief rabbi of the United Hebrew Congregations. Hermann attended University College School and University College, London, graduating BA in 1854. He determined to follow his father into the rabbinate, and carried out a range of ecclesiastical duties while pursuing private study. In 1860 his father sent him to Prague, where two years later he received rabbinical ordination from S. J. Rapoport, chief rabbi there. In December 1862 he obtained from the University of Leipzig the degree of PhD for a thesis on druidism.

In practice Adler acted henceforth as secretary and assistant to his father, who was clearly grooming him to

Hermann Adler (1839–1911), by Solomon Joseph Solomon, exh. RA 1906

succeed to his office. In 1863 Adler was appointed temporary principal of Jews' College, London, where he taught until 1879 and to the chairmanship of which he ultimately succeeded in 1887. In February 1864 he became first minister at the fashionable Bayswater synagogue. On 3 September 1867 he married Rachel (d. 1912), elder daughter of Solomon Joseph, a well-to-do businessman. They had two daughters and a son. Adler took a particular interest in Jewish education, establishing schools in Bayswater and making arrangements for Jewish religious instruction at schools of the London school board in the East End. It was during these two decades—the 1860s and 1870s—that Adler perfected his skills as a preacher; it is doubtful whether the Anglo-Jewish sermon has ever reached greater heights as an art form.

It was also in this period that Adler met and made friends with a wide range of non-Jews occupying positions of authority and influence in government and society. In time he came to move in the very highest social circles. Well spoken, dignified, and cultured, Adler came to be regarded by them as the respectable face of Jewish Orthodoxy, conforming to Orthodox norms but eschewing extremes. When his father practically retired from office in 1879, it was a foregone conclusion that he would become 'delegate' chief rabbi. And it was regarded as inevitable that he should succeed to the office following his father's death, as he did in 1891.

Adler moved easily and with grace in the world of high society, and he deliberately used this status to bolster and reinforce his authority within the Jewish world. He saw himself as, and wished others to think of himself as, the Jewish equivalent of the archbishop of Canterbury. He wore gaiters and 'canonicals'. He styled himself 'the very reverend', a term unknown in the Jewish canon. His name was a byword for patriotism. He was also an avowed tory, preaching in favour of the Second South African War even though he must have known how controversial that conflict was within British politics. He became a good friend of the future Edward VII, who enjoyed his company (the king is said to have referred to him as 'my Chief Rabbi') and appointed him a commander in the Royal Victorian Order, an honour conferred for personal services rendered to the monarch or to members of the royal family.

Yet as Adler's stature increased within the non-Jewish world, it fell within the Jewish. Adler, unlike his father, was no Talmudic scholar. Unlike his father, he was latitudinarian in his religious outlook. Although, in a famous incident in 1892, he vetoed the appointment of Morris Joseph as minister of the newly constructed Hampstead synagogue on account of Joseph's Reformist leanings, Adler was himself prepared to sanction practices which were at variance with the strictest interpretations of Jewish Orthodoxy—for instance, the introduction of verbal consents by the bride and bridegroom in the marriage service. In mid-Victorian Britain, where the moneyed and interrelated 'cousinhood' ruled Anglo-Jewry, Adler's interpretation of Orthodoxy fitted perfectly. But as the pace of immigration to Britain of Jews from Russia and Poland increased during the 1880s and 1890s, his position became increasingly fraught.

Between 1880 and 1906 a 'native' Anglo-Jewry of some 60,000 souls was swamped by at least twice as many Jewish immigrants. Adler's chief rabbinate was deeply scarred by a series of conflicts with this immigrant body. His right-wing, anti-socialist, and anti-trade-unionist views were not welcomed in the slums of Whitechapel, Leeds, or Manchester into which the immigrant Jewish poor settled in large numbers. It is true that he identified himself with a number of public protests against the persecution of Jews in tsarist Russia. It is equally true that he used his influence to try to stem the refugee tide, and that he refused to condemn the passage of the Aliens Act of 1905, passed in response to a wave of 'anti-alien' sentiment. Among the immigrants Zionism was a popular creed. Adler (along with almost all the Anglo-Jewish establishment) viewed the idea of a separate Jewish nationality as anathema and likely to jeopardize emancipation. Addressing the Anglo-Jewish Association in July 1897, he condemned the forthcoming First Zionist Congress (summoned in Basel by Theodor Herzl) as 'an egregious blunder', and for good measure he denounced the very idea of a Jewish state as 'contrary to Jewish principles' (Jewish Chronicle, 16 July 1897, 13). Adler distinguished himself as the only western European rabbi to contribute to a collection of anti-Zionist essays published in Warsaw in 1900.

Of all the disputes Adler entered into with the immigrants, none was more bitter, or more bitterly fought, than those which stemmed from his interpretation of Jewish religious law. He permitted mixed-sex choirs in synagogues under his control. He turned a blind eye to palpable infringements of Orthodox practice regarding the preparation and sale of kosher meat and poultry, with the result that in London's East End, and in Liverpool and Manchester, his religious authority in these matters was openly defied. In eastern Europe every Jewish community had its own rabbi. Adler's insistence on being recognized as a unique rabbinical authority, not even subject to the rulings of his own *beth din* (ecclesiastical court), brought him into ridicule. Worse still, it threatened to bring schism into Anglo-Jewry. Adler's authority was only restored, in 1905, through the efforts of Samuel Montagu, first Baron Swaythling, the staunchly Orthodox Liberal politician and founder (1887) of the Federation of Synagogues.

Adler continued for the remainder of his life to be dogged by conflict and confrontation with immigrant rabbis, whose refusal to acknowledge his suzerainty he regarded with the deepest anger. Though clever, up to a point, he was not a wise man. He understood the limitations neither of his own intellect nor, in changing circumstances, those of his own office. In seeking to reinforce the legitimacy of that office through the support of the non-Jewish world Adler scored a dazzling but short-term victory. His death was mourned, but he himself was unloved by the Yiddish-speaking poor who now formed the majority of Anglo-Jewry.

Adler died of heart failure on 18 July 1911 at his residence, 6 Craven Hill, London, and was buried in the Willesden cemetery of the United Synagogue. His elder daughter, Henrietta (Nettie) *Adler (1868–1950), became one of the first women to sit on the London county council. A son, Alfred, entered the Jewish ministry but predeceased his father. GEOFFREY ALDERMAN

Sources G. Alderman, *Modern British Jewry* (1992) · G. Alderman, *The Jewish community in British politics* (1983) · G. Alderman, 'The British chief rabbinate: a most peculiar practice', *European Judaism*, 23 (1990), 45–58 · *CGPLA Eng. & Wales* (1911) · d. cert. · m. cert. · *DNB*
Archives Jewish Theological Seminary, New York, corresp. and papers · LMA, Archives of the Chief Rabbinate, corresp. and papers · U. Southampton L., account book | NRA, papers · U. Southampton L., corresp. with J. H. Hertz
Likenesses H. S. Mendelssohn, cabinet photograph, 1890, NPG · S. J. Solomon, portrait, exh. RA 1906, London College of Jewish Studies [*see illus.*] · W. and D. Downey, woodburytype photograph, NPG; repro. in W. Downey and D. Downey, *The cabinet portrait gallery*, 3 (1892) · Spy [L. Ward], caricatures, chromolithographs, repro. in *VF* (31 March 1904) · photographs, United Synagogue, London · photographs, London College of Jewish Studies · portraits, United Synagogue, London · portraits, London College of Jewish Studies
Wealth at death £13,528 11s. 4d.: probate, 10 Aug 1911, *CGPLA Eng. & Wales*

Adler, Jacob (1855–1926), actor, was born on 1 January 1855 in Odessa, Ukraine, the son of Feivl Abramovich, an Orthodox Jewish wheat merchant, and his wife, Hesye. Of the twelve children of Hesye and Feivl (she had one son with her first husband, whom she divorced), only Jacob and a younger sister, Sarah, survived infancy.

Jacob's parents had ambitious plans for him, hoping that with his quick mind he would become a doctor. Schooling did not agree with him, however, and he eventually left to earn his own living. With abundant charisma and beautiful handwriting, he advanced rapidly through a series of clerical and civil-service positions, culminating in a prestigious job as municipal overseer of weights and measures. His solid income allowed him to live the life of the bon vivant; he dressed like a dandy, caroused until the wee hours, and frequently attended the Russian theatre. There he became the leader of a claque that supported a popular local actress, and was bitten hard by the theatrical bug.

When Adler learned that a Yiddish company led by Avrom Goldfaden was active in Bucharest, he extended an invitation to them to visit Odessa, and in 1879 they did so. Adler became an extra in the company and travelled with them to Kherson, thereby staying away from his office job so long that he was fired. Intentionally or not, he virtually forced himself into becoming a professional actor.

Adler toured extensively with the Yiddish troupe, soon making his way to more important roles in such plays as Goldfaden's *Brayndele kozak* and *Shmendrik*. During one of these early tours, in Yekaterinoslav, he met and married Sofia (Sonya) Oberlender. In 1882 Adler joined the throng of Jews fleeing Russia in the wake of worsening conditions after the assassination of Tsar Alexander II. Adler settled for several years in London, where he and Sonya were among the pioneers who established Yiddish theatre in the East End. Sonya died in 1885. They had two children: Rivke, who died at age three, and Abe, who, like many of the Adler children by four different mothers, became an actor himself. At about the same time, another child was born to Adler out of wedlock, when Jenny Kaiser gave birth to a son named Charlie, who took his father's last name.

Shortly after Sonya's premature death, Jacob married an actress named Dina Stettin, who became an international star, primarily as Dina Feinman, after her divorce from Adler a few years later and her marriage to leading man Sigmund Feinman. Adler and Dina had one daughter, Celia, who also became a major star.

Adler was part of the original troupe at the Prince's Club Theatre in London, where in 1887 a false fire alarm created a stampede, leading to the deaths of seventeen in the audience. At least partly in response to the tragedy, Adler soon left London for the United States. Initially bypassing New York, the hub of the American Yiddish theatre, he worked for a short time in Chicago, then returned to Europe, where he spent two years performing in Warsaw. In 1889 he passed through London again before being invited to perform in New York, where he spent most of the rest of his career.

Adler formed his two most lasting partnerships shortly after arriving in New York. He had fallen in love with actress Sara Heimovich-Heine (c.1858–1953), who was married at the time to actor Maurice Heine. In 1891 he and Sara both obtained divorces in order to marry each other. As a couple and as individuals they became theatrical royalty, and most of their children became professional actors as well. Frances and Julia had successful careers on the Yiddish stage; Stella and Luther crossed over into the American (English-language) stage with great success; and Stella made an indelible impact on American acting with her actor training programme.

The other crucial partnership in Adler's career—a symbiotic professional relationship that transformed the development of the Yiddish theatre—was his involvement with playwright Jacob Gordin. Missing from Adler's many talents as a performer was a good singing voice, which often seriously limited a repertoire dominated by operettas and musical comedies. Adler's salvation as a leading man came in the form of Gordin, a Russian intellectual who, shortly after immigrating to New York in 1891, met Adler and other Yiddish actors and was inspired to write plays for the first time. Gordin's first effort, later that same year, was *Siberia* (1891), which audiences reportedly resisted until Adler won them over through sheer force of personality. Gordin went on to write several more leading roles that became among Adler's best-known creations, including the title characters *Der yidisher kenig Lir* ('The Jewish King Lear') and *Der vilder mentsh* ('The Wild Man'), and *Elisha Ben Abuye*. So effective was Adler as Dovid Moysheles, the contemporary Russian Jewish version of King Lear, that he was deluged with letters from parents thanking him for making their Shloymes and Moyshes better children.

The late 1890s and beginning of the 1900s brought Adler's creative peak, with talented playwrights like Gordin, Leon Kobrin, and David Pinski writing for him. He also attracted attention outside the Jewish quarter with his portrayal in 1901 of Shylock, modelled closely on Henry Irving's sympathetic reading of the role. The production attracted, among others, prominent producers like Daniel Frohman, who mounted a Broadway production two years later with Adler playing Shylock in Yiddish, and an English-speaking supporting cast. The production was a critical as well as a commercial success, and Adler reprised the role on Broadway in 1905.

An aged and feeble Adler gave his last performance in 1925, and died of a stroke on 31 March 1926 in New York city. The following day tens of thousands of onlookers lined the streets of New York to pay their last respects as his body was carried to its final resting place in Mount Carmel cemetery.

JOEL BERKOWITZ

Sources C. Adler, *Tsili Adler dertseylt* [Celia Adler tells], 2 vols. (1959) · J. Adler, *My life on the stage*, trans. L. Rosenfeld Adler (1999) · L. Rosenfeld Adler, *Bright star of exile: Jacob Adler and the Yiddish theatre* (1977) · M. Mayer, *Idish teater in London, 1902–1942 / Yiddish theatre in London, 1902–1942* [1943] · Z. Zylbercweig, ed., *Leksikon fun yidishn teater*, 1 (New York, 1931), 13–32

Archives YIVO Institute for Jewish Research, New York, YIVO Archives

Likenesses photographs, YIVO Photo Archives, New York

Adler, Jakub [Jankel] (1895–1949), painter, was born on 26 July 1895 in Tuszyn, near Łódź, Poland, the eighth of the twelve children of Eliasz Adler, a timber and coal dealer, and his wife, Hana Laja, *née* Fiter. Adler grew up in Łódź in the world of Hasidic Jewry, which had a lasting influence on his subject matter. After training as a goldsmith in Belgrade, he moved to Barmen, Germany, in 1913. He stayed there until the end of the First World War, studying at the Kunstgewerbeschule in Barmen (under Gustav Wiethüchter) and at the Akademie der Künste in Düsseldorf. In 1918 he returned to Łódź, where he co-founded the Jewish artistic association Ing Idisz ('Young Yiddish').

After lengthy visits to Warsaw, Paris, and Berlin, Adler lived in Düsseldorf from 1922 to 1933. Throughout this period he was active in the artistic life of both the Rhineland and Berlin, participating in various exhibitions, among them a show with Franz W. Seiwert at the Barmen Museum in 1928, the Internationale Ausstellung revolutionärer Künstler held in Berlin in 1922, and several exhibitions of the Novembergruppe, the latter demonstrating his left-wing attitudes. In 1923 he became a member of the Rheingruppe, and in 1932 joined the Selection e. V., a Berlin-based artists' association to which, among others, Wassily Kandinsky and Lyonel Feininger belonged. In the 1920s Adler won his first prizes, including a gold medal for *Katzen* (1927, Cologne, Museum Ludwig). His paintings of this period are dominated by static human figures and heavy facial features and limbs derived from expressionism and cubism.

In the 1930s Adler's works grew more objective. He also produced abstract paintings, for example, *Composition* (1933, priv. coll., Tel Aviv). This development may have been influenced by Paul Klee, with whom he worked from 1931 in the Akademie der Künste in Düsseldorf, where they both had studios. Their time together is the basis of an article later published by Adler: 'Memories of Paul Klee' (*Horizon*, 6, 1942, 264–7). In 1933 he participated in a show of the Collective Artists' Association, held at the Rockefeller Center in New York. In the same year he signed, with other left-wing artists and intellectuals, the Urgent Appeal against the newly elected Nazi government. Because he was Jewish, his works were included in the exhibition Kulturbolschewistische Bilder, held in Mannheim in 1933 and labelled 'degenerate'. As a result of further discrimination, he left Germany.

From 1933 to 1940 Adler lived in France, in Paris, Argelès-sur-Mer, and Cagnes-sur-Mer, except for a two-year stay in Poland (1935–7) during which he was reunited with his wife, Betty Kohlhaas (1899–1971), a drawing teacher, and his daughter, Nina (b. 1927). His works were shown in the Exhibition of German-Jewish Artists' Work held in the Parsons' Galleries, London, in 1934. This was organized by Carl Braunschweig in order to draw attention to the Nazis' infamous art policy, but it did not prevent the notorious Entartete Kunst ('Degenerate art') exhibition in Munich in 1937, where Adler's paintings hung under the slogan 'Offenbarung der jüdischen Rassenseele' ('Revelation of the Jewish racial soul').

In 1940 Adler left France with the Polish foreign army, in

which he was a volunteer, and went to Scotland, where he was soon demobilized on health grounds. Except for a brief visit to the artists' colony in Kirkcudbright, he stayed in Glasgow from 1941 to 1943. He soon showed his works in one-man exhibitions, at the studio of the sculptor Benno Schotz, who introduced him to his supporters, Moray Glasser and Fred Nettler, and at the Annan Gallery, Glasgow. Together with his fellow countryman, the painter Josef Herman, whom he had met in Poland in 1936, he became one of the early members of the Glasgow New Art Club, founded by John Duncan Fergusson in 1940.

In 1943 Adler moved to London, where he eventually settled in one of the studios at 77 Bedford Gardens. There he met the poet Michael Hamburger (who dedicated a poem to him entitled 'Flowering cactus: in memoriam Jankel Adler') and the three painters Robert Colquhoun, Robert MacBryde, and John Minton, who were his neighbours. Although all of them were affected by Adler, it was Colquhoun who most reflected his influence. As well as giving stylistic advice (regarding surface patterning and treatment of form), he encouraged Colquhoun to study his Celtic roots. At the same time, Adler's own paintings grew more expressive and the shapes of the objects more angular. Further, in addition to Jewish subject matter, the fate of mankind became significant, as in *The Mutilated* (1942, Tate collection). Besides his contacts with British artists he also met fellow refugee painters, including Martin Bloch and Ludwig Meidner, in the Ohel, a club run by the brothers Alexander and Benjamin Margulies in 1943–4. In 1945 he moved to Aldbourne, Wiltshire, where he died at his home, Whitley Cottage, of a heart attack on 25 April 1949; he was buried in Aldbourne. His death occurred just after his application for British citizenship had been rejected because of his contacts with anarchist groups.

Since the end of the Second World War Adler's works have been shown in one-man exhibitions held at home and abroad, including a memorial show organized by the Arts Council in 1951 and a touring exhibition in Germany organized by the Wuppertal Art and Museum Association in 1955. The largest exhibition of his work, including over 150 paintings and drawings, was held in Düsseldorf, Tel Aviv, and Łódź in 1985–6. Examples of Adler's work are in the Tate collection, the Tel Aviv Museum of Art, Israel, the Museum Ludwig, Cologne, and the Kunstmuseum im Ehrenhof, Düsseldorf.   JUTTA VINZENT

Sources J. Adler, 'Memories of Paul Klee', *Horizon*, 6 (1942), 264–7 · J. Adler, 'Der Veg von Yiddishen Künstler', *Issachar Baer Ryback: sein Leben und Shaffen* (1937) [partly trans. and pubd as 'The thorny path of the Jewish artist', *Jewish Quarterly*, 3 (1975), 24–5] · *Jankel Adler, 1895–1949* (1985) [exhibition catalogue, Städtische Kunsthalle, Düsseldorf, Tel Aviv Museum of Art, and Muzeum Sztuki, Łódź] · D. Farr, 'Art and artists in wartime Glasgow', *Apollo*, 88 (1968), 120–24 · M. Hamburger, 'Flowering cactus: in memoriam Jankel Adler', *Flowering cactus: poems, 1942–49* (1950) · *Robert Colquhoun* (1981) [exhibition catalogue, Glasgow Art Gallery, Aberdeen Art Gallery, 1981] · P. Kort, 'Jankel Adler', *'Degenerate art': the fate of the avant-garde in Nazi Germany*, ed. S. Barron (1991), 194–6 [exhibition catalogue, Los Angeles County Museum of Art, 17 Feb – 12 May 1991] · S. W. Hayter, *Jankel Adler* (1948) · *New painting in Glasgow,*

1940–6 (1968) [exhibition catalogue, NG Scot.] · *CGPLA Eng. & Wales* (1949)
Archives Tate collection | FILM Bayrisches Rundfunk, Munich, Germany, 'Jankel Adler, Maler der Juden', documentary film | SOUND Ossietzky-Lesesaal, Hamburg, Germany
Likenesses O. Dix, oils, 1926, repro. in *Jankel Adler, 1895–1949*; priv. coll. · A. Sander, photograph, 1928, Museum Folkwang, Essen, Germany, photographic collection
Wealth at death £1876 11s. 2d.—with will (limited): administration, 12 Aug 1949, *CGPLA Eng. & Wales*

Adler, Nathan Marcus (1803–1890), chief rabbi, was born on 15 January 1803 in Hanover, the third son of Mordecai Baer Adler, the unofficial chief rabbi in Hanover. His mother's name remains unknown. Adler's education, a synthesis of strict Orthodox Judaism and the world of secular scholarship, typified the modern outlook of 'Torah-true' Judaism fashioned in the wake of the Enlightenment. Adler attended in succession the universities of Göttingen, Erlangen, Würzburg, and Heidelberg; he obtained the degree of PhD from Erlangen in 1828. At the same time he studied for the rabbinate, and on 27 March 1828 received rabbinical ordination from Abraham Bing, chief rabbi of Würzburg. The following year he obtained appointment as *Landesrabbiner* (chief rabbi) of Oldenburg, from which, later the same year, he accepted an invitation to become the first official chief rabbi of Hanover. Adler married first Henrietta Worms (d. 1854) of Frankfurt, with whom he had two sons and three daughters. He and his second wife, Celeste Lehfeldt, had one son and two daughters.

His early career moves distinguished Adler as a man of ambition as well as intellect. Hanover was then still under British rule, and it was to the prize of the British chief rabbinate that Adler's attention was inevitably drawn. During the eighteenth century this office had evolved from the rabbinate of the Great Synagogue, Duke's Place, Aldgate, in the City of London, the oldest Ashkenazi synagogue in Britain, founded in 1690 by central European Jews following the German and Polish rituals. Provincial communities, as well as lesser London Ashkenazi congregations, came by stages to regard the rabbi of Duke's Place as the supreme religious authority of Ashkenazi Jews throughout Britain, and indeed throughout the British empire. David Tevele Schiff, rabbi at Duke's Place from 1765 to 1791 (and Adler's great-uncle), styled himself 'rabbi of London and the provinces', and his successor, Solomon Hirschell, was generally known as 'chief rabbi of the German and Polish Jews in England'. Hirschell's death in 1842 created the vacancy that Adler determined to fill. On 13 October 1844 he was, by an overwhelming majority, elected to succeed Hirschell, and on 9 July 1845 was installed at the Great Synagogue.

In contrast to his predecessors at Duke's Place, Adler was a rabbinical scholar of international repute, most famous for his work *Netinah laGer* (1875), a Hebrew commentary on the Aramaic translation of the Hebrew Bible known as the Targum Onkelos. As chief rabbi he could claim an allegiance which his predecessors could not, for his was the first election in which provincial communities as well as the major London Ashkenazi congregations had

Nathan Marcus Adler (1803–1890), by Barraud, pubd 1889

claims were not idle boasts: he could in practice veto the recognition—and therefore the establishment—of all new Ashkenazi congregations throughout the British empire.

Adler attempted to use his authority and his own personal charisma to refashion, over time, the entire religious topography of Anglo-Jewry. He was obsessed with the need to maintain the status of his office. He set his face against the right of any Orthodox congregation anywhere in the empire to appoint its own rabbinical authority without his approval; he refused even to permit the members of his *beth din* (ecclesiastical court) to be 'called' to the reading of the Torah scroll by their rabbinical titles. Ashkenazi synagogues within the City of London had to seek his approval before inviting speakers to address them. But he did recognize the importance of educational reform. He was a tireless campaigner for more Jewish day schools, and it was on his initiative in 1855 that Jews' College was established in London, under his authority, to train Jewish 'reverends' (not rabbis) who could minister to the congregations over whom he alone presided in a rabbinical capacity. The culmination of these efforts was his seminal role in the negotiations which resulted, in 1870, in the union of the major Ashkenazi congregations in London into one United Synagogue (established by private act of parliament), of which he was the supreme religious authority.

Adler's reforms were only a qualified success. The standard of religious education undoubtedly improved, but Jews' College failed to attract more than a handful of candidates for the ministry; most of these came from poor families, and as ministerial salaries remained low, there resulted a high turnover in the tenure of ministerial positions. Adler was lukewarm towards the campaign for Jewish political emancipation; he supported it in principle, but did not himself give it a very high priority. He fully supported the policy of his predecessor in refusing absolutely to recognize the legitimacy of the West London Reform Synagogue. In Manchester, however, he succeeded in defending the authority of his office against Reformers only by acquiescing in the establishment of Britain's second Reform congregation. The promoters of the United Synagogue Act had wanted the position of chief rabbi recognized by law; but Gladstone's government, which had so recently disestablished the Anglican church in Ireland, objected to the legislative underpinning of ecclesiastical jurisdiction, and the private bill had to be modified to meet this objection. Adler did not therefore become, by the authority of British statute law, the chief rabbi, but merely chief rabbi of congregations agreeing to recognize him as such.

Adler failed to raise synagogue attendances, which during the 1880s seem not to have risen above 15 per cent on sabbath mornings. Belonging to the United Synagogue was deemed to be more important than attending it, and, in any case, most members regarded synagogue attendance as a social rather than a religious obligation. The establishment of the United Synagogue was followed by

taken part. Practically his first act on assuming office was to address a questionnaire to all the congregations throughout the British empire acknowledging his authority. This unique survey revealed a collection of communities in which observance of Orthodox practice was lax, and synagogal attendance and educational facilities poor. These findings seem to have reinforced Adler's own personal view: that the Orthodox structure in Britain was too weak to permit the existence of self-governing Jewish communities, as were commonly found in central and eastern Europe, and that what was needed was a highly centralized set of religious institutions. This view coincided exactly with that of Sir Moses Montefiore, whose presidency of the Board of Deputies of British Jews spanned, with gaps, the period 1835–74. In Montefiore Adler found a willing ally (albeit a Sephardi one), ever ready to support his policy of command and control.

In 1847 Adler published his *Laws and Regulations for All the Synagogues in the United Kingdom*. Through these he claimed to have the authority to regulate religious observance in all the Ashkenazi synagogues in the United Kingdom, and even to sanction the formation of new congregations and the construction of new synagogues. The Registration Act of 1836 had recognized the president of the Board of Deputies as the sole authority competent to certify to the registrar-general the names of marriage secretaries of synagogues 'of Persons professing the Jewish Religion'. Montefiore made it clear that in the case of Ashkenazi synagogues he would provide this certification only if so authorized by the Ashkenazi chief rabbi. Thus Adler's growing pressure for liturgical reform and for the removal of prayers deemed to be superfluous or objectionable (for instance, those asking for the blood of Jewish martyrs to be avenged or for the intercession of angels). Adler made some concessions, but he found the process personally distasteful. In 1880 he went into virtual retirement in Brighton; his second son, Hermann *Adler (1839–1911), was appointed 'delegate' chief rabbi to carry out the major duties of the office. Nathan Marcus Adler died at his home, 36 First Avenue, Hove, on 21 January 1890 and was buried two days later at the Willesden cemetery of the United Synagogue, London.   GEOFFREY ALDERMAN

Sources G. Alderman, *Modern British Jewry* (1992) · V. D. Lipman, *A history of the Jews in Britain since 1858* (1990) · *CGPLA Eng. & Wales* (1890) · d. cert. · *DNB*
Archives Jewish Theological Seminary, New York, Archives, corresp. and papers · LMA, Archives of Chief Rabbinate, corresp. and papers
Likenesses Barraud, photograph, 1889, NPG; repro. in *Men and Women of the Day*, 2 (1889) [see illus.] · oils, Adler House, London · photographs, United Synagogue, London · portraits, United Synagogue, London
Wealth at death £5571 0s. 1d.: resworn probate, Dec 1890, *CGPLA Eng. & Wales*

Adminius (*fl. c.*AD **40**). See under Roman Britain, British leaders in (*act.* 55 BC–AD 84).

Adolph, Anton von Freenthal [Joseph Antony] (*b.* **1721**), painter, was born on 6 July 1721 in Nikolsburg, Austria, the son of Josef Franz Adolf (1671–1749), painter and brother of Carl Josef Adolph (*d.* 1771), painter. He studied with his father and at the Academy of Painting, Sculpture and Architecture in Vienna. In 1745 he was in Paris, and in 1750 he was in London. Very little is known of his stay or stays in Britain apart from his work. His best-known portrait produced in Britain is that of the future George III, *Prince of Wales on Horseback* (date unknown), which was engraved and published in 1755 by Bernard Baron, and later engraved in mezzotint by Gerhard Bockman. Adolph also painted life-size portraits of the fourth marquess of Lothian with his wife and children (*c*.1750, marquess of Lothian collection), and two civic portraits, *Benjamin Hancock* and *Elisha de Hague* for St Andrew's Hall, Norwich, in 1764 (Civic collections, Norwich). Portraits of Mary Gurdon and Brampton Gurdon (who appears not to be related to Brampton Gurdon, Boyle lecturer in 1721), painted in Suffolk, are signed and dated 'Adolphus 1765' (Lord Cranworth collection). His work of this period shows a development in his arrangement of poses, from the stiff conventionality of the *Fourth Marquess of Lothian* to the fluent gesticulation of *Elisha de Hague Sr.*

The date of, and reason for, Adolph's return to the continent are not known. He worked in the residence of the archbishops of Ölmuz at Kremsier, Austria, painting decorative schemes in the great hall of the castle, as well as portraits, from about 1769 to 1772. Two equestrian portraits by Adolph are in the emperor's rooms at Klosterneuburg, and three altar paintings by him are in the collegiate church at Nikolsburg. Adolph's later work was appreciated by contemporaries for its warm colours and skilful composition. Neither his marital status nor the date of his death is known.

                    W. C. MONKHOUSE, *rev.* NICHOLAS GRINDLE

Sources G. Meissner, ed., *Allgemeines Künstlerlexikon: die bildenden Künstler aller Zeiten und Völker*, [new edn, 34 vols.] (Leipzig and Munich, 1983–) · Waterhouse, *18c painters* · archive material, Courtauld Inst., Witt Library · *Engraved Brit. ports.*
Archives Courtauld Inst., Witt Library

Adolphus Frederick, Prince, first duke of Cambridge (**1774–1850**), tenth child and seventh son of *George III and Queen *Charlotte, was born at the Queen's Palace (now Buckingham Palace), St James's Park, London, in the evening of 24 February 1774. On 2 June 1776 he was made a knight of the Garter, with three of his elder brothers. Having received his earlier education at Kew under Dr Hughes and Mr Cookson, he was sent, with his brothers *Ernest and *Augustus (the later dukes of Cumberland and Sussex) to Göttingen, entering the university there on 6 July 1786. At the age of twelve he was too young to profit widely from a traditional university education but he worked assiduously at classical studies, history, moral philosophy, mathematics, and theology until 1790, when he travelled to Berlin to improve his knowledge of military tactics. When Britain went to war with revolutionary France, Prince Adolphus was appointed colonel in the Hanoverian army. In the summer of 1793 he fought in Flanders, under the command of his brother *Frederick, duke of York. He was wounded in the shoulder and briefly held captive, until rescued in a raid by British infantrymen. He recuperated at Kew and Windsor over the following winter, his good looks, courteous manners, and sensitivity to music and the arts ensuring his popularity at court. He became, and remained, the king's and queen's favourite son. Unlike his brothers, he was never entangled with debtors, nor was there any scandal in his private life.

Prince Adolphus served in the campaign of 1794–5 as colonel and major-general in General Walmoden's corps, retreating northwards across Holland in a bitterly cold winter campaign. He remained with his father's Hanoverian troops for more than six years and was in residence in the city of Hanover when, early in 1801, the electorate was occupied by the Prussians, allegedly to forestall a French invasion. Prince Adolphus protested in person to King Frederick William III, who assured him that Prussia had no intention of annexing his father's lands. Later in the year the prince returned to England.

Peerages fell comparatively late to the younger sons of George III, and were conferred simultaneously on the princes Augustus (whose principal creation was that of duke of Sussex) and Adolphus on 24 November 1801, when the latter was created baron of Culloden, earl of Tipperary, and duke of Cambridge. On 3 February 1802 he was sworn of the privy council, and took his place at the board on the left hand of the king.

After the withdrawal of Prussian troops from the electorate in March 1802, the duke returned to Hanover. He

Prince Adolphus Frederick, first duke of Cambridge (1774–1850), by Sir Thomas Lawrence, begun 1818

could not, however, persuade his father's German subjects to offer a strong resistance to the French when, at the end of May 1803, the young General Mortier invaded Hanover, and the duke was fortunate to escape to England. Subsequently he was appointed colonel-in-chief of the King's German Legion, a force in British pay which in 1805 was destined for the relief of Hanover as part of Pitt's grand strategic design for the third coalition. Although the duke of Cambridge crossed briefly to northern Germany, the project was abandoned without any thrust being made into Hanover. Thereafter, for eight years, the duke remained in England, with apartments at St James's Palace and at Windsor Castle. He took no part in politics and, although he was nominal military commander of the home district and colonel-in-chief of the Coldstream Guards, he saw no active service. On 26 November 1813 he was promoted, with his brother, the duke of Cumberland, to be field marshal in the British army.

The duke of Cambridge again took the command in the electorate of Hanover on the recovery of its independence in 1813 and served as governor-general. After the elevation of the electorate into a kingdom, he was, in November 1816, appointed to the viceroyalty. In this capacity, on 7 October 1821, he was host to his brother, *George IV, on the only occasion in the twenty-three years of dual kingship when the sovereign went (for a month) into residence in Hanover. The administration of Hanoverian affairs by the duke of Cambridge was characterized by wisdom, mildness, and discretion, and by the introduction of timely and conciliatory reforms. He successively weathered the storms, both political and academic, of the revolutionary period of 1831, and his prudent management of affairs was said to have gone 'a great way to preserve the Hanoverian crown for his family'. The duke's long residence in Hanover ended in July 1837, when the death of *William IV severed the dynastic link with the United Kingdom, since by Salic law no woman could accede to the Hanoverian crown. The new ruler of Hanover was not the duke of Cambridge's niece, who became Queen Victoria, but his eldest surviving brother, the duke of Cumberland.

Cambridge returned sadly to England and, for the last thirteen years of his life, interested himself in charitable causes. He had married at Kassel on 7 May 1818, and at London on 1 June, the Princess Augusta Wilhelmina Louisa (1797–1889), third daughter of Frederick, landgrave of Hesse-Cassel, and his wife, Caroline Polyxena of Nassau-Usingen. Three children were born during their parents' residence in Hanover: *George William Frederick Charles, second duke of Cambridge (1819–1904); Augusta Caroline (1822–1916), who married the grand duke of Mecklenburg-Strelitz in 1843 and maintained a lively correspondence with her niece, George V's consort, Queen Mary, even after the coming of war in 1914; and *Mary Adelaide (1833–1897), who was Queen Mary's mother.

In middle age the first duke of Cambridge became amiably eccentric, enjoying musical parties so much that he sometimes became a spontaneous participant, either at the top of his voice or on his violin. He was president of at least six hospitals, and the patron or vice-patron of more than a score of other beneficent corporations. In both Hanover and London the duke of Cambridge always showed a particular sympathy and interest towards the Jewish people, their institutions and cultural traditions. He was not an orator, either in the House of Lords or in any other place; but his earnestness and sincerity won from his audience the tribute of attention and respect. He died at Cambridge House, Piccadilly, on the evening of Monday 8 July 1850, and was buried at Kew on 17 July, amid the scenes of his childhood, and near his favourite suburban retreat.   ALAN PALMER

Sources R. Fulford, *Royal dukes* (1933) · A. Palmer, *Crowned cousins: the Anglo-German royal connection* (1985) · C. Hibbert, *George IV*, new edn, 2: *Regent and king* (1975) · J. H. Jesse, *Memoirs of the life and reign of King George the Third*, 2nd edn, 3 vols. (1867) · *The Times* (9 July 1850) · *United Services Gazette* (13 July 1850)

Archives Bodl. Oxf., letters | BL, corresp. with Lord Aberdeen, Add. MS 43051 · BL, corresp. with Sir John Willoughby Gordon, Add. MS 49471, *passim* · BL, corresp. with second earl of Liverpool, Add. MSS 38190–38564, *passim* · BL, corresp. with Sir Robert Peel, Add. MSS 40401–40585, *passim* · Bucks. RLSS, letters to Sir W. H. Fremantle · Dorset RO, letters to Fanny Williams · Niedersächsisches Hauptstaatsarchiv, Hannover, letters to duke of Cumberland · NL Scot., letters to Lord Lynedoch · priv. coll., letters to Lord Conyngham · priv. coll., letters to Andrew Robert Drummond · priv. coll., letters to Lord Leconfield · Royal Arch., letters to George III · U. Southampton L., letters to duke of Wellington · W. Sussex

RO, letters to duke of Richmond · Warks. CRO, letters to Sir J. A. Waller · Warks. CRO, letters, incl. to Sir Alexander George Woodford

Likenesses B. West, group portrait, oils, 1778, Royal Collection · T. Gainsborough, oils, 1782, Royal Collection · stipple, pubd 1806, BM, NPG · W. Skelton, line engraving, pubd 1808 (after W. Beechey), BM · J. Godby, stipple, pubd 1814 (after F. Rehberg), BM, NPG · T. Lawrence, oils, begun 1818, Royal Collection [*see illus.*] · E. E. Girardot, oils, 1845–7, Army and Navy Club, London · L. Macdonald, marble bust, 1846, Royal Collection · G. G. Adams, marble bust, 1866, Royal Collection · D. Chodowiecki, etching (aged six), BM; repro. in *Lauenburg calendar* (1782) · J. Doyle, pencil caricature, BM · H. Edridge, drawing, Royal Collection · G. James, group portrait, oils (*The banquet at the coronation of George IV*, 1821), Royal Collection · W. C. Ross, miniature, Royal Collection · B. West, three group portraits, oils, Royal Collection · portrait, Royal Collection

Wealth at death widow left under £160,000: GEC, *Peerage*

Adolphus, John (1768–1845), barrister and historian, was born in London on 7 August 1768; he was of German-Jewish descent. His grandfather was domestic physician to Frederick the Great, and wrote a French romance, *Histoire des diables modernes* (1763), which is sometimes wrongly ascribed to Adolphus.

Adolphus was brought up by a wealthy great-uncle, who paid for his education, and sent him at the age of fifteen to be placed in the office of his agent for some estates in St Kitts. Adolphus's chief occupation was attendance at the sittings of the one law court of the island, and after little more than a year he returned to London. His great-uncle was dead, having left him a sum which would not support him while studying for the law, but which enabled him to be articled to an attorney. He was admitted as an attorney in 1790, and in 1793 he married Martha Elizabeth (d. 1843), daughter of the Revd Ralph Leycester of White Place, Berkshire; they had two children, John Leycester *Adolphus and Emily Adolphus, later Henderson, poet and author of a biography of her father.

Adolphus soon abandoned his profession as an attorney in order to write, and was fortunate enough to gain the friendship of Archdeacon William Coxe whom he helped with his *Memoirs of Sir Robert Walpole*. In 1799 Adolphus published his first acknowledged work, *Biographical Memoirs of the French Revolution*, strongly anti-Jacobin in tone, and in this, as in other points, differing widely from the *Biographical Anecdotes of the Founders of the French Republic* published anonymously in 1797, and often but erroneously ascribed to Adolphus. He also wrote the memoirs which appear in the 'British cabinet' (1799), a series of portraits of more or less distinguished English men and women.

In 1802 Adolphus published his chief work, the *History of England from the Accession of George III to the Conclusion of Peace in 1783*. It was based on thorough research, and though avowedly written from a conservative standpoint, was praised for its impartiality in the second number of the *Edinburgh Review*. The papers of George Bubb Dodington, Lord Melcombe, were placed at Adolphus's disposal in the preparation of this work, and they enabled him to throw light on the conduct of Lord Bute, and on the political events of the earlier years of the reign of George III, who,

in conversation, expressed his surprise at the accuracy with which some of the first measures taken after his accession had been described.

The success of the history and the friendly offices of Coxe brought Adolphus into close connection with Henry Addington, then prime minister, who employed him for a number of political services, including electioneering and occasional pamphleteering. In 1803 Adolphus published a pamphlet entitled *Reflections on the Causes of the Present Rupture with France* in vindication of the policy of the British government. He is also believed to have written *A Letter to Robert Ward, Esq., M.P.* (1804), a defence of Addington after William Pitt the younger had gone into opposition.

Adolphus had meanwhile entered himself at the Inner Temple, and in 1807 he was called to the bar. He joined the home circuit, and concentrated on criminal cases. At the Old Bailey he worked his way to the leadership, which he retained for many years. The first of his more notable successes was his very able defence in 1820 of Arthur Thistlewood and the other Cato Street conspirators. Among the cases in which he subsequently distinguished himself were the trials of John Thurtell, James Greenacre, and François Courvoisier.

At the same time Adolphus continued to write and publish, producing a number of books between 1818 and 1832, including a memoir of John Barrister, comedian, and a personal friend of his. He contributed to the *Annual Register*, *Law Magazine*, and the *British Critic*. He wrote a report of the trial of Queen Caroline. The anonymous *Memoirs of Queen Caroline* (1824) has also been ascribed to him.

Adolphus's *History* had gone through four editions when, at the age of seventy, he began the task of continuing it to the death of George III. Adolphus was working on the eighth volume when he died at his son's house in Montague Street, Russell Square, on 16 July 1845.

FRANCIS ESPINASSE, rev. JONATHAN HARRIS

Sources E. Henderson, *Recollections of the public career and private life of the late John Adolphus* (1871) · *GM*, 2nd ser., 24 (1845), 314–15 · *Law Magazine*, 35 (1846), 54–67 · *The diaries and correspondence of the Right Hon. George Rose*, ed. L. V. V. Harcourt, 2 vols. (1860), vol. 2, p. 189 · *N&Q*, 5th ser., 4 (1875), 233–4 · *Fraser's Magazine*, 66 (July 1862)

Likenesses V. Green, mezzotint, pubd 1804 (after T. Walker), BM, NPG · W. Ridley, stipple (after Allingham), BM, NPG; repro. in *Monthly Mirror* (1803) · portrait, repro. in Henderson, *Recollections*, frontispiece

Adolphus, John Leycester (bap. 1794, d. 1862), barrister and writer, was baptized on 28 August 1794 at St Martin-in-the-Fields, Westminster, London, the son of John *Adolphus (1768–1845), barrister and historian, and Martha Elizabeth, née Leycester (d. 1843). He had a sister, Emily, later Henderson, poet and biographer of their father. He was educated at Merchant Taylors' School, London, and, as head monitor, was elected a scholar of St John's College, Oxford, in 1811. In 1814 he gained the Newdigate prize for English verse on the subject of Niobe; in 1816 Adolphus took a second class in classics, and in 1818 was awarded the chancellor's prize for an English essay on biography, in which he took special care to justify curiosity regarding the lives of authors. His anonymous *Letters to*

Richard Heber, esq., containing critical remarks on the series of novels beginning with 'Waverley', and an attempt to ascertain their author was published in 1821. In it he demonstrated Walter Scott's authorship of the Waverley novels through analysis of coincidences of style, treatment, and sentiment in Scott's acknowledged poetry and prose, at a time when the Waverley novels were still unacknowledged by Scott. Such coincidences had been noted previously by Southey and Sydney Smith, but never with such thoroughness nor wit. Adolphus adopted a format familiar at that time from works such as Malcolm Laing's edition of the Ossian poems (1805), which juxtaposed passages from Homer, Milton, and James Macpherson, in order to demonstrate that Macpherson himself had not just translated but, *pace* his own claims, written these works. However, unlike Laing's, Adolphus's work was celebratory and tactful, rather than hostile. This, combined with an almost definitive marshalling of what he himself called 'circumstantial evidence' (Adolphus, 3), a form of proof then at the height of its prestige in legal and literary circles alike, was much praised by Scott in private and others in public. The *Letters* remains 'the one important book on Scott in his own time' (Hillhouse, 107).

The publication of the *Letters* led to a friendship between Adolphus and Scott, who wrote to Richard Heber, addressee of the *Letters*, speculating that they were by Heber's brother Reginald, afterwards bishop of Calcutta. On learning Adolphus's identity, Scott invited him to his home, Abbotsford, though without admitting the truth of Adolphus's inferences. The introduction to Scott's *The Fortunes of Nigel* (1822) is similarly elusive, mentioning the *Letters* with praise, but also noting that circumstantial evidence is never final. A year later, in 1823, Adolphus visited Scott at Abbotsford and thereafter the two saw each other a number of times in both London and Scotland. After Scott's death in 1832 his son-in-law and biographer John Lockhart solicited from Adolphus a reminiscence of these occasions. Adolphus's vivid memoir is quoted generously in Lockhart's *Life*, where it occupies a place of honour.

In 1822 Adolphus was called to the bar at the Inner Temple. He at once joined the northern circuit, and became solicitor-general of the then county palatine of Durham in 1855. He was made judge of the Marylebone county court by Lord St Leonards, and in conjunction with R. V. Barnewall and T. F. Ellis produced reports of the cases tried in the king's and queen's bench from 1834 to 1852. He was a bencher of the Inner Temple and shortly before his death was appointed legal adviser of his old Oxford college, St John's. For years Adolphus was an active member of the general literature committee of the Christian Knowledge Society. He travelled widely on the continent, a practice first encouraged, in his youth, by his father. In 1858 he published his *Letters from Spain in 1856 and 1857*. He also wrote many metrical *jeux d'esprit*; Thomas Macaulay praised one of these, 'The Circuiteers, an Eclogue', parodying the forensic style of two eccentric barristers on the northern circuit, as 'the best imitation he ever read' (*DNB*).

At the time of his death Adolphus was engaged in completing his father's *History of England under George III*. He died on 24 December 1862 at his home at 12 Hyde Park Square, London. His wife, Clara, survived him.

FRANCIS ESPINASSE, rev. RICHARD MAXWELL

Sources [J. L. Adolphus], *Letters to Richard Heber, esq.* (1821) • 'A law pastoral', *N&Q*, 3rd ser., 5 (1864), 6–7 • 'J. L. Adolphus', *GM*, 3rd ser., 14 (1863), 246–7 • D. C. L., 'The late Mr. J. L. Adolphus', *The Times* (30 Dec 1862) • W. B. Todd and A. Bowden, *Sir Walter Scott: a bibliographical history* (1999), p. 477 • J. C. Carson, *A bibliography of Sir Walter Scott, 1797–1940* (1943) • J. T. Hillhouse, *The Waverley novels and their critics* (1936) • J. Lockhart, *Memoirs of Sir Walter Scott*, ed. A. W. Pollard (1914) • *IGI*
Archives NL Scot., corresp.
Wealth at death £8000: probate, 13 Jan 1863, *CGPLA Eng. & Wales*

Adomnán [St Adomnán] (627/8?–704), abbot of Iona and writer, who became known to history as the ninth abbot of Iona and the outstanding Irish churchman of his day, was born of the royal line of Cenél Conaill, a dynasty which formed part of the over-kingdom of the northern Uí Néill and which occupied most of what is now co. Donegal. Given his importance, it is not surprising that both his paternal and maternal lines of descent are documented. His father, Rónán, son of Tinne, belonged to the Síl Sétnai branch of Cenél Conaill. His mother, Rónnat, daughter of Ségíne, was of the Cenél nÉndai who occupied territory corresponding roughly to the modern barony of Raphoe, south of the Inishowen peninsula. Síl Sétnai territory was north-west and south-west of this, in the modern baronies of Kilmacrenan and Tirhugh respectively; Adomnán's paternal kin were associated with Kilmacrenan.

Adomnán died on 23 September 704. According to the annals of Ulster, he was in his seventy-seventh year at the time. This points to his having been born between 24 September 627 and 23 September 628 but, in fact, his birth is entered in the annals of Ulster under the year 624. However, as his birth date was undoubtedly entered retrospectively, it should probably be given less weight than the information in his obit.

Early career The works and deeds on which Adomnán's fame in later centuries rests all date to the time when he was abbot of Iona, although he did not come to this office until 679, when he was already in his fifties. Of his pre-abbatial career nothing can be said with certainty. It is not known, for example, where he received his early education or in which monastery he was ordained priest; but in order to have acquired the kind of reputation which led to his election to the prestigious office of abbot of Iona and head of that monastery's vast *paruchia* (federation of churches), he must surely have had a long association with some Columban house or houses. It is clear from his life of Columba that he was personally acquainted with his immediate predecessor in the abbacy, Faílbe (669–79). As there is no indication that he was similarly acquainted with any of his other predecessors, it might be supposed that he first joined the community on Iona at some time during Faílbe's abbacy. However, this must remain in doubt: as Faílbe had spent the years 673–6 in Ireland, it is possible that the exchanges with him described by Adomnán in the life of Columba may have taken place in Ireland during that time. Nevertheless, as there is no hard evidence to the contrary, one should not dismiss the possibility that Adomnán had been part of the community of Iona for a considerable length of time before he became abbot, perhaps since his youth. His election entailed a departure from established practice in that the descendants of Columba's uncle, Ninnid, had dominated the abbacy for almost eighty years, whereas Adomnán was a fifth-generation descendant from another uncle, Sétnae, whose line had not previously held the abbacy. However, he came to office with one advantage of which he made full use during his term as abbot: his familiarity with the workings of royal power; the descendants of Sétnae had been the ruling dynasty of Cenél Conaill since the late sixth century, and seven of them had been over-kings of the northern Uí Néill.

Abbot of Iona Only four events in Adomnán's abbatial career are securely dated, and the first of these shows him acting as a royal envoy. In 687, according to the Irish annals, he conducted sixty captives back to Ireland. These captives had been taken in a raid dispatched in 684 by Ecgfrith, king of Northumbria, on Brega, in southern Uí Néill territory, and brought back to Northumbria. One year later, a Pictish–Irish alliance defeated and killed Ecgfrith at 'Nechtansmere'. It has been argued convincingly that the Uí Néill, Adomnán's kinsmen, took part in the alliance that revolted against Ecgfrith in order to support the claim of his half-brother Aldfrith to the Northumbrian kingship, and that the raid on Brega in southern Uí Néill territory in the preceding year should therefore be regarded as a pre-emptive strike by Ecgfrith against his rival's allies. Ecgfrith died at 'Nechtansmere' and Aldfrith succeeded him as king.

Aldfrith was the child of a union between Oswiu (Ecgfrith's father and predecessor as king) and the daughter of a northern Uí Néill king. Before 685 he had lived on Iona, perhaps also in Ireland, and had acquired a reputation as a notable scholar. Adomnán seems to have held him in very high esteem: he refers to him as *amicum* in the life of Columba and his expectation that Aldfrith would appreciate his scholarship was justified for, as Bede relates, when Adomnán presented the king with his *De locis sanctis*, Aldfrith saw to it that many copies of the work were made and distributed. It is likely that mutual sympathy based on personal acquaintance existed before Adomnán visited Aldfrith's Northumbrian court in 687, in which case he must have stood out as an ambassador whom the Uí Néill might very reasonably expect to receive a favourable hearing from Aldfrith on the question of the return of the captives.

In the life of Columba, Adomnán states that he paid a second visit to Northumbria two years after the first, in 689, but he does not give its purpose. The third and fourth firm dates are found in the Irish annals: for the year 692, these offer the bald statement that he visited Ireland and, for the year 697, the more detailed statement that he visited Ireland and gave his *Lex innocentium* ('Law of the

innocents'), known in Irish as *Cáin Adomnáin* ('The law of Adomnán'), to the people.

Dating and course of career The four firmly dated events of 687, 689, 692, and 697 have been used to deduce approximate dates for the completion of Adomnán's two major works, *De locis sanctis* and the life of Columba (*Vita Columbae*). *De locis sanctis* is Adomnán's account of the description given to him by a Frankish bishop, Arculf, of the holy places of Palestine, the Near East, and the Mediterranean, which he had visited. On the basis of references within the text, Arculf's pilgrimage is thought to have taken place during the years 679–82; the earliest possible date for his arrival at Iona is put at 683. As noted already, Bede relates that Adomnán presented a copy of *De locis sanctis* to King Aldfrith when he visited Northumbria, but without specifying any date for this event. If the visit in question was that which resulted in the return of the captives taken from Brega, *De locis sanctis* must have been completed by 687. However, Adomnán's reference to a second visit in 689 means that this date is an alternative *terminus ad quem*. As this reference to Adomnán's second visit occurs in the life of Columba, it is certain that that work was not completed before 689, but a date closer to 700 is suggested by the fact that Adomnán speaks of one miracle wrought by Columba as having occurred after the meeting of the Irish synod: the meeting in question is very likely to have been that at which the *Lex innocentium* was promulgated, in 697.

Scholars in earlier times relied primarily on Bede's account of Adomnán, but it is now recognized that the Irish sources provide fuller and more accurate information. The most significant event of Adomnán's career, as described by Bede, was his conversion to the observances of the Roman church, in particular in regard to the date of the Easter celebration. This occurred, according to Bede, on the single visit to Northumbria which he credits to Adomnán. He relates that Adomnán was chastised by the Northumbrian clergy for adhering to the Celtic dating, submitted to their superior learning, and thereafter adopted the Roman custom with enthusiasm. On returning home, he tried to persuade the community of Iona and its subject houses to follow suit, but failed. He then left Iona for Ireland, where he succeeded in inducing almost all of the churches which were not under the jurisdiction of Iona to accept the Roman Easter. He did not return to Iona until the last year of his life when, once again, he urged conformity on his own community, but to no avail.

Advocacy of the orthodoxy of the Roman cause and celebration of the role played by the English race in bringing the whole of the island of Britain into conformity with it is an evident bias in Bede's *Historia ecclesiastica*. It is accepted that this bias also colours his presentation of the activities of the Irish. Bede assumed that Christian peoples were obliged to preach the gospel to their neighbours and, conscious of the debt of the English church to Irish missionaries before the time of the Synod of Whitby, he portrayed the conversion by the English of some of the Irish who persisted in the Celtic customs after that date as due requital of this debt. He fits Adomnán into this context by figuring him as the exemplary Irish Romanist who spent the last years of his life trying to bring the Columban community and other churches into conformity. The community on Iona was finally converted to the Roman Easter in the year 716 by the English bishop, Ecgberht, an event which Bede portrays as bringing Adomnán's earlier endeavours to fruition.

In forming his assessment of Adomnán, Bede is very likely to have had access only to Northumbrian, and perhaps to Pictish, sources and informants; in any case, his account is not supported by the Irish evidence. First, as the annals state that Adomnán visited Ireland in the years 692 and 697, he cannot have been resident there throughout the period in question. There is no supporting evidence for a serious breach in relations between Adomnán and his community. Neither is it apparent that conformity with Roman custom was Adomnán's priority during this time, and it is noteworthy that he himself offers only one passing reference to the Easter controversy in his writings. Far from showing him to have devoted all his energies to promoting conformity, and as undermined by the lack of it, the Irish sources portray him as exercising strong leadership over the Columban church in Scotland and Ireland from his power base on Iona.

Adomnán the lawgiver Adomnán's most ambitious undertaking in this period was the promulgation of the *Lex innocentium* at the great synod held in 697 at Birr, in present-day Offaly. According to this law's provisions, three categories of persons were henceforth under the special protection of Adomnán, and of his successors in the abbacy of Iona. These were women, clerics, and children, the 'innocents' of the law's title, so called because they were exempt from the duty to take up arms in times of war. Severe penalties are prescribed for a range of offences against all three categories, committed in times of war or peace, but the most severe and detailed prescriptions relate to offences against women.

This enactment shows that Adomnán was willing and able to use his position as head of the Columban *familia* to rally the highest clerical and secular powers to a humanitarian cause. The law claimed an unprecedented jurisdiction: it was to be effective over the whole island of Ireland and over those areas of Scottish and Pictish territory in which the Columban church had influence. The list of ninety-one ecclesiastical and secular guarantors which forms part of the law's text includes one representative or more for every major kingship, over-kingship, and monastic centre in the country. The list of secular guarantors is headed by Loingsech mac Óenguso, king of Tara and Adomnán's kinsman. That of the ecclesiastical guarantors is headed by Fland Febla, bishop-abbot of Armagh, and also includes Coeddi, bishop of Iona. *Pace* Bede, this list shows that, towards the end of the seventh century, Adomnán's standing was such that he was able to transcend any controversies within his own *familia*, and the sectional interests of lesser ecclesiastical and secular federations, uniting them all in common support of his law. An edition of the law (under the title *Cáin Adamnáin*), based on the two extant copies, in Oxford, Bodleian Library, MS

Rawlinson B 512, and in Brussels, Bibliothèque Royale, MS 2324-40, was published by Kuno Meyer in 1905.

The life of Columba Adomnán's life of Columba, one of the best sources for the history of the early Irish church, is also a biography of considerable literary merit. Adomnán's conviction of the saintly attributes of his predecessor, Columba (521–597), shines through it. To Iona's ample record of Columba's sanctity, Adomnán added the fruit of his own enquiries on both sides of the Irish sea, blending the whole with recognizable hagiographical references which emphasized the common bond between Columba and all the saints of Christendom. By writing a new life of Columba, he proved that his recent acceptance of the Roman observance did not diminish in any respect his devotion to Iona's founder who, in his own day, had adhered to Celtic custom. Thus he made an implicit appeal to the Irish churches which were divided on the Easter question—including Iona, no doubt—to abandon their embattled positions, and to sublimate their differences in respect for a saintliness which far surpassed mere orthodoxy. His life also reminded the Northumbrian church of its debt to the saint and his followers.

Adomnán's organization of the subject matter into three books dealing with the saint's prophecies, miracles, and angelic visitations finds no direct parallel in Latin hagiography, but it seems that Gregory the Great's life of St Benedict (book 2 of the *Dialogues*) provides the closest. An analysis of the sources he used has shown that a large part of the life of Columba's material derives from oral and written traditions about Columba which originated on Iona and were passed on there until Adomnán's day. Adomnán drew on an account of the saint's *virtutes*, compiled by his predecessor, Cumméne, very probably during the abbacy of Ségéne (623–52); this possibly was his most important source of information about Columba. The narratives deriving from Iona contain a wealth of circumstantial, onomastic, and genealogical detail and the thaumaturgic element in them is muted. In these respects they differ from the narratives of unknown provenance which describe events in various places in Ireland and Scotland, far removed from Iona; some of these have biblical or hagiographical prototypes while others probably derive from oral tradition, and show the popular dissemination of Columba's cult. In them, the well-defined character which emerges from the Iona-derived narratives tends to be blurred to a conventional hagiographical figure.

Adomnán's canon and its fate The copy of the life of Columba closest in date to the original is in a codex now in Schaffhausen Public Library, the scribe of which was Dorbéne, almost certainly the abbot of Iona who died in 713. Three further manuscripts descend from an equally early sister-copy, and a fifth manuscript, perhaps written at Rheims, dates from the ninth century. The standard modern edition, which is based on the Schaffhausen text, is that of A. O. and M. O. Anderson, *Adomnan's Life of Columba* (2nd edn, 1991). The copious notes in an earlier edition by William Reeves, *The Life of St Columba* (1857), are still very useful.

In medieval times, it seems that the fame of *De locis sanctis* outshone that of the life of Columba. Adomnán, meticulous in his treatment of the information supplied by Arculf, points out that his account was given in response to his own careful enquiries, and he supplements this account by drawing on a range of exegetical authors, particularly Jerome. Thus he did far more than redact a pilgrim's itinerary: he made an important contribution to the study of places and place names mentioned in the scriptures as a means of elucidating manifold meanings and resolving apparent problems of interpretation. By presenting it to King Aldfrith, Adomnán ensured that it became known in Anglo-Saxon circles at an early date. Bede praised the work very highly in his *Historia ecclesiastica*, where he cited abridged excerpts from it, and he also reworked much of the content in his own *De locis sanctis*, written in the early years of the eighth century. The many extant medieval copies on the continent attest to its popularity there. The text earned Adomnán a place in the series of catalogues of illustrious Christian writers, the model for which was Jerome's *De viris illustribus*. Four continental copies date from the ninth century, and it is on these that modern editions are based; a number of fragments survive from the same period. The first modern critical edition was that by P. Geyer, published in 1898. A more recent edition, essentially a reworking of Geyer's but with many useful notes, is that by L. Bieler, published, for the second time, in 1965.

The attribution of two further texts to Adomnán has yet to be properly tested. The first of these is the *Canones Adomnani*, published by L. Bieler in 1963. One reason to treat the attribution seriously is that a citation from this text also appears in a recension of *Collectio canonum Hibernensis*, where it is attributed to Adomnán. An Old Irish poem in praise of Columba is also attributed to Adomnán. Columba aside, Adomnán is the only abbot of Iona who is known to have been made the subject of a biography. This life, written in Irish, is supposed to have been composed at Kells between 961 and 964. It has been edited by M. Herbert and P. Ó Riain, as *Betha Adamnáin: the Irish life of Adamnán* (1988).

Adomnán died on Iona in 704 and was buried there. In 727 his relics were taken to Ireland, on which occasion his law was renewed; the relics were returned to Iona three years later. It is clear that he was revered as a saint within a few decades of his death.

MÁIRÍN NÍ DHONNCHADHA

Sources *Adomnán's Life of Columba*, ed. and trans. A. O. Anderson and M. O. Anderson, rev. edn, rev. M. O. Anderson, OMT (1991), xv–lxxii · Adomnán of Iona, *Life of St Columba*, ed. and trans. R. Sharpe (1995) · M. Herbert, *Iona, Kells, and Derry: the history and hagiography of the monastic familia of Columba* (1988), 9–35, 47–56, 129–50 · H. Moisl, 'The Bernician royal dynasty and the Irish in the seventh century', *Peritia*, 2 (1983), 103–26 · J.-M. Picard, 'The purpose of Adomnán's *Vita Columbae*', *Peritia*, 1 (1982), 160–77 · J.-M. Picard, 'Bede, Adomnán, and the writing of history', *Peritia*, 3 (1984), 50–70 · *Adamnan's De locis sanctis*, ed. D. Meehan, Scriptores Latini Hiberniae, 3 (1958), 1–34 · T. O'Loughlin, 'The exegetical purpose of Adomnán's *De locis sanctis*', *Cambridge Medieval Celtic Studies*, 24 (1992), 37–53 · T. O'Loughlin, 'Adomnán the Illustrious', *Innes Review*, 46 (1995), 1–14 · M. Ní Dhonnchadha, 'The guarantor list of Cáin Adomnáin, 697', *Peritia*, 1 (1982), 178–215 · M. Ní Dhonnchadha, 'The *Lex innocentium*: Adomnán's law for women, clerics and youths, 697 AD', *Chattel, servant or citizen: women's status in church, state and society*, ed. M. O'Dowd and S. Wichert (1995), 58–69 · M. Herbert and P. Ó Riain, eds. and trans., *Betha Adamnáin: the Irish life of Adomnán*, ITS, 54 (1988), 1–44 · T. M. Charles-Edwards, 'The new edition of Adomnán's *Life of Columba*', *Cambrian Medieval Celtic Studies*, 26 (1993), 65–73 · M. W. Pepperdene, 'Bede's *Historia ecclesiastica*: a new perspective', *Celtica*, 4 (1958), 253–62 · T. M. Charles-Edwards, 'Bede, the Irish and the Britons', *Celtica*, 15 (1983), 45–52 · D. A. Bullough, 'Columba, Adomnan and the achievement of Iona', *SHR*, 43 (1964), 111–30; 44 (1965), 17–33 · A. A. M. Duncan, 'Bede, Iona and the Picts', *The writing of history in the middle ages: essays presented to Richard William Southern*, ed. R. H. C. Davis and J. M. Wallace-Hadrill (1981), 1–42 · T. O'Loughlin, 'The Latin version of the scriptures in use in Iona', *Peritia*, 8 (1994), 18–26 · T. O'Loughlin, 'The library of Iona in the late seventh century: the evidence from Adomnán's *De locis sanctis*', *Ériu*, 45 (1994), 33–52 · *Cáin Adamnáin: an old-Irish treatise on the law of Adamnan*, ed. and trans. K. Meyer (1905) · W. Reeves, *The life of St Columba* (1857) · L. Bieler, *The Irish penitentials* (1963) [incl. *Canones Adomnani*, pp. 176–81] · J. H. Bernard and R. Atkinson, eds. and trans., *The Irish Liber hymnorum*, 2 vols., HBS, 13–14 (1898), vol. 1, p. 184 [incl. poem attributed to Adomnán] · F. Wasserschleben, *Collectio canonum Hibernensis*, 2nd edn (1885)

Archives Bodl. Oxf., MS Rawl. B.512 · Royal Library of Belgium, Brussels, MSS 2324–2340

Adrain, Robert (1775–1843), mathematician and university teacher, was born on 30 September 1775 in Carrickfergus, Ireland, the eldest of five children. His father, a teacher and maker of mathematical instruments, had emigrated from France, and his mother was of Scottish descent. Both of Adrain's parents died when he was fifteen and in order to support himself and his siblings he opened a school at Ballycarry. The school was a success, and led to a lucrative position as a private tutor. About 1795 he married Ann Pollock (*d.* in or after 1834); they had one daughter, Margaret, before political events intruded. In the Irish uprising of 1798 Adrain took up arms as an officer with the insurgent forces, and his employer, an officer of the crown, offered a price for Adrain's capture. Not long afterwards, Adrain was shot in the back by one of his own men, and was widely rumoured to be dead. Although severely wounded he survived, and with great difficulty escaped with his wife and infant daughter to New York.

Upon his arrival in America Adrain travelled to Princeton, New Jersey, to avoid the yellow fever then prevalent in New York. He taught at a Princeton academy for two years before moving on to a principalship in York, Pennsylvania, and then to a succession of other teaching positions. In 1805 he became principal of an academy in Reading, Pennsylvania, in 1809 a professor at Queen's College, New Brunswick, New Jersey, in 1813 a professor at Columbia College, New York city, and then in 1826, after a brief return to Queen's College, he moved to the University of Pennsylvania, Philadelphia, where he remained until 1834, becoming vice-provost in 1828. One of his students at Columbia remembered him as genial '"Old Bobbie" … an Irish gentleman, of large size, broad beaming face, and silvery voice' (*Harper's*, 414, 1884, 820), but his career as a teacher was not without blemish. In 1834, he was forced to resign because of his inability to deal with noisy disorder in his classes, a contagion that became intolerable when it threatened to spread to other classes. By this time he had a total of seven children, and he moved his family back to New Brunswick. Then, from 1836 to 1840, he left his family to take up yet another teaching position at the Columbia College grammar school. He returned to New Brunswick in 1840. One of his sons, Garnett Bowditch Adrain (1815–1878), served as a member of the US congress in 1857–61.

Adrain has two claims to fame in the history of mathematics; one is as the editor of a series of mathematical periodicals that served as an impetus to serious mathematical research in America, the other is as the author of a short article in one of his journals that is recognized as one of the earliest original contributions to theoretical statistics. As early as 1804 Adrain was contributing to the first mathematical journal in America, the *Mathematical Correspondent*, and four years later in 1808 he founded his own, *The Analyst, or, Mathematical Museum*. Unlike most Americans Adrain was familiar with European research work, and his contributions to these and other periodicals that followed were at a higher level than those of others, introducing deeper problems and attempts at solutions in areas including Diophantine algebra, geometry, and elliptic integrals.

In the fourth number of the first (and only) volume of *The Analyst*, Adrain contributed a solution to a problem in surveying that was remarkable for the time, leading to his being frequently described as an independent co-discoverer (with C. F. Gauss and A. M. Legendre) of the method of least squares, a method for combining astronomical or geodetic observations so as to reduce the effect of unavoidable observational errors in determining theoretical constants. There is evidence that Adrain had read Legendre's 1805 treatment of least squares at the time, but Adrain's method of attack, starting with two derivations of the normal distribution for errors, was surely original with him and independent of both Legendre and Gauss. Adrain's manuscript, now lost, was apparently dated 1808, although the issue containing his result probably appeared in 1809, the same year as Gauss's publication of his version of the method. Adrain's work on this received no published notice until 1871 when it was rediscovered by Cleveland Abbe.

In other work Adrain published two articles on the figure of the earth in 1818 in the *Transactions of the American Philosophical Society*, and from 1811 onwards edited several American editions of C. Hutton's *Course in Mathematics*. He was elected to the American Philosophical Society in 1812 and the American Academy of Arts and Sciences in 1813. He died at New Brunswick on 10 August 1843.

STEPHEN M. STIGLER

Sources S. M. Stigler, 'Mathematical statistics in the early states', *Annals of Statistics*, 6 (1978), 239–65 • S. M. Stigler, ed., *American contributions to mathematical statistics in the nineteenth century*, 2 vols. (1980) • J. L. Coolidge, 'Robert Adrain and the beginnings of American mathematics', *American Mathematical Monthly*, 33 (1926), 61–76 • C. Abbe, 'Historical note on the method of least squares', *American Journal of Science*, 3rd ser., 1 (1871), 411–15 • M. J. Babb, 'Robert Adrain: man and mathematician', *General Magazine and Historical Chronicle*, 28 (1926), 272–84 • J. Dutka, 'Robert Adrain and the method of least squares', *Archive for History of Exact Sciences*, 41 (1990–91), 171–84 • G. B. Adrain, 'Robert Adrain, LLD', *United States Magazine and Democratic Review*, 14 (1844), 646–52 • E. R. Hogan, 'Robert Adrain: American mathematician', *Historia Mathematica*, 4 (1977), 157–72 • 'Columbia College', *Harper's New Monthly Magazine*, 69 (1884), 813–31, esp. 820 • D. J. Struik, 'Adrain, Robert', *DSB*

Archives University of Pennsylvania, Philadelphia, Van Pelt Library

Likenesses Verlynden, oils, 1822, Col. U.

Adrian IV [*real name* Nicholas Breakspear] (d. **1159**), pope, was the first and, so far, only Englishman to be elected pope. As such, a web of myth surrounds his origins, and no doubt much is later tradition woven at the great abbey of St Albans. But the following facts seem reliable. He was born in or near St Albans (Matthew Paris says he came from Abbots Langley) and was given the name of Nicholas. His father was Richard, as is certainly stated in a contemporary calendar of obits, not Robert (de Camera) as Matthew Paris says; allegedly and probably a priest, Richard later became a monk of St Albans. He may have been a married priest, for during the course of Pope Adrian IV's struggle against the emperor Frederick Barbarossa, it was widely proclaimed by imperial propagandists that this was so. Nicholas had a brother, Ranulf or Randulf, clerk of Feering, Essex, a church in the patronage of the abbot and convent of Westminster, who alleged that Ranulf retained it after he had become an Augustinian canon at Missenden. And Ranulf's son, N. [?Nicholas], pledged the fee that he held of the abbot of St Albans, not to lay claim to his father's church. The story about the future pope's rejection for the noviciate by the abbot of St Albans cannot be checked (it originates with Matthew Paris): it became the seed of what was probably the additional fantasy that Pope Adrian laughingly rejected certain presents offered to him by the abbot of St Albans, although he accepted mitres and sandals which had been made by Christina of Markyate, a local recluse. But certainly St Albans fed upon the story of the local boy who had made good. His surname Breakspear seems to occur first in Matthew Paris. R. L. Poole argued that Nicholas became an Augustinian canon at Merton, Surrey, on the seemingly incontrovertible evidence of the last sentence in one of John of Salisbury's letters, but this might be taken to mean no more than that there was a connection by reciprocal prayer between the Augustinian abbeys of Merton and St Ruf.

The next certain step in Nicholas's career is his arrival in Arles, where he spent some time in the schools and then became a canon regular, and later abbot, of St Ruf near Avignon. As such he came to the notice of Pope Eugenius III who, in 1149, created him cardinal-bishop of Albano. In this capacity he was sent as legate to Scandinavia. Such was the success of his mission that he was later seen as the apostle of Scandinavia. In August and September 1152 he presided over a council of the Norwegian church at Nidaros (now Trondheim), which promulgated reforming canons, and he set up an ecclesiastical province there. In Sweden he called a council at Linköping. He reorganized the Swedish church under the primacy of the Danish archbishopric of Lund and severed the Scandinavian church from its previous German dependence. He also introduced, with royal assent, the annual payment of Peter's pence. It appears that he travelled through England on his way to Norway and that he may have taken with him advisers who knew Norway from trading contacts.

Eugenius III's successor, Anastasius IV, died on 3 December 1154. By this time the legate was back in Rome and on 4 December he was chosen as pope, taking the name of Adrian. On Sunday 5 December he was enthroned and crowned at St Peter's. Within the city of Rome itself, the pope's position was precarious, due to the machinations of the heretic, Arnold of Brescia, who had the support of the senators. The commune was hostile, and the pope therefore left shortly after Easter 1155 for Viterbo. His primary task was to control the emperor, Frederick Barbarossa, whose aid he needed within the city and in the papal patrimony. Frederick, for his part, as the newly elected emperor, was eager to secure his coronation by the pope. Pope met emperor at Nepi on 7 June 1155 in what turned out to be a spectacular contest between the two to gain propagandist supremacy. It was on this occasion that Frederick refused to perform the ceremonial duty of leading the pope's horse and aiding him to dismount. Adrian replied by refusing Frederick the kiss of peace. But the emperor still required crowning by the pope, and after the consultation and examination of certain documents by the imperial party, the ceremony was performed, by Frederick leading the pope's horse in full view of the emperor's army. Frederick's coronation took place at St Peter's on 18 June, in a ceremony which, it has been argued, was a reformed one, symbolically highlighting the difference between the anointing of a mere layman and that of a priest. The emperor was not anointed on the head, as befitted a priest, but between the shoulders and on the right arm, and the investing of him with a sword drew attention to the emperor's role as defender of the faith and 'protector' of the pope.

But Frederick did not come to the assistance of Adrian by driving back the king of Sicily, William I (1151–66), who was threatening the papal lands, or by quelling the Romans. He returned north, leaving the pope in virtual exile at Tivoli. The pope now appeared to be wedged between a recalcitrant emperor and a ravaging and advancing king of Sicily. It was at this juncture that Adrian received overtures from the Byzantine emperor, Manuel I, and from the barons of Apulia, eager to take advantage of King William's excommunication by the pope. William treated for peace, which Adrian at first refused, but after William had successfully defeated both the Greeks and the Apulians, in June 1156, the pope invested William with Sicily, Apulia, and Capua at the concordat of Benevento. In return William performed homage, and promised his loyalty and the payment of an annual census.

The papal alliance with Sicily brought about a worsening of relations with the emperor. In the course of diplomatic discussions, Adrian's message to Frederick at Besançon in 1157 proved inflammatory. On this occasion the pope used the term *beneficium* in his letter to the emperor which the imperial chancellor, Rainald von Dassel, sought to translate as fief (rather than as benefice), thereby making the pope say that the empire was a fief of the papacy. Relations between pope and emperor did not improve. Frederick had ambitions in northern Italy and he bitterly resented the pope's alliance with the Sicilians. In his relations with the eastern emperor, Manuel, and the eastern church, Pope Adrian showed himself a true son of the reforming papacy. He could not accept any power for the emperor that was not dependent on the pope. Although Manuel's troops had entered Italy, subdued the Balkans, and pacified Hungary, Adrian was not impressed by Manuel's suggestion that the secular sword was his, while the pope's sword was simply a spiritual one. In a letter to the archbishop of Thessaloníki, he clarified his line of thought: St Peter was the governor of *all* the faithful. The pope, as his vicar, did not share this authority with others; and a letter to the patriarch of Grado, about the church of Constantinople, reiterated the theme that the eastern church was subject to the West.

Adrian IV was not unmindful of the interests and well-being of his English homeland. He was generous with privileges to St Albans Abbey, and he confirmed the archbishop of York both in the latter's metropolitan authority over the Scottish bishops, and in his freedom from that of Canterbury. But of longer-lasting significance was the bull *Laudabiliter*, whereby he granted Ireland to Henry II as a hereditary fee, on the grounds that all islands converted to Christianity belonged to the Holy See according to the donation of Constantine, and in return for an annual payment of 1d. Matthew Paris, who provides the text of *Laudabiliter*, spoke of the vast solitude of Ireland, describing it as 'a kind of limbo' and of its 'bestial men' who were to be brought to the faith. This grant is associated with a visit to the pope by John of Salisbury, on behalf of the king. While the text of *Laudabiliter* is open to question, it cannot be doubted that there was papal approval of some kind for the Irish mission. The pope was keenly interested in the advancement of a centralized papacy. He played what was probably no small part in the realization of the notion that his court was the final court of Christendom. Appeals were encouraged to the papal court. Adrian IV died at Anagni on 1 September 1159. His final act, the nomination of a successor, Cardinal Bernard, bishop of Porto, a candidate acceptable to the pro-imperial party, might have been his master stroke, had it been accepted, and might have saved the church from the impending schism. He was buried on 4 September in an ancient red granite tomb in St Peter's, near the body of Pope Eugenius III, according to Boso, in front of the main altar in the oratory of the Virgin which had been constructed by Pope Gregory III: the tomb was later moved to the Vatican grottoes.

Adrian's biographer and chamberlain, Boso, described him as mild and kindly in bearing, of high character and learning, famous as a preacher, and renowned for his fine voice. Something of his character emerges, too, from the account of John of Salisbury whom he had favoured with his friendship and whom he had asked to tell him what people thought of the Roman church. The pope was apparently deeply aware of the crushing responsibilities of his office, which he described in some graphic detail— the pallium was full of thorns and the burnished mitre seared his head. He would have preferred to have remained a simple canon of St Ruf, he said. Nevertheless, his pontificate was extremely formative. There are echoes of his activities among the reforming popes of the thirteenth century. He attempted the implementation of canon law in Scandinavia as legate. He formulated an aggressive policy towards the papal patrimony in central Italy, under the hand of his chamberlain, Boso, using feudal rights to assert his lordship. He sought to curtail and control the powers of the emperor. The archives of his pontificate are not extensive, but the picture emerges of an assiduous administrator, a man of strange vision and singular purpose, though of balanced judgement, who became something of a role model for later popes.

JANE E. SAYERS

Sources L. Duchesne, ed., *Le Liber pontificalis*, 2nd edn, 2 (Paris, 1955), 388–97 • R. Howlett, ed., *Chronicles of the reigns of Stephen, Henry II, and Richard I*, 1, Rolls Series, 82 (1884), 109–12 • *Gesta abbatum monasterii Sancti Albani, a Thoma Walsingham*, ed. H. T. Riley, 3 vols., pt 4 of *Chronica monasterii S. Albani*, Rolls Series, 28 (1867–9), vol. 1, pp. 112–13, 124–9 • *The letters of John of Salisbury*, ed. and trans. H. E. Butler and W. J. Millor, rev. C. N. L. Brooke, 2 vols., OMT (1979–86), vol. 1, pp. 87–8, no. 50; vol. 2, pp. 9–10, no. 6 [Lat. orig. with parallel Eng. text] • John of Salisbury, *Policraticus*, ed. and trans. C. J. Nederman (1990), 132–6, 173, 224–5 • *Ioannis Saresberiensis episcopi Carnotensis Metalogicon libri IIII*, ed. C. C. I. Webb (1929), bk 4, chap. 42 • *Ottonis et Rahewini gesta Friderici I. imperatoris*, ed. O. Waitz and B. von Simson, 3rd edn, MGH Scriptores Rerum Germanicarum, [46] (Hanover, 1912) • W. Ullmann, 'The pontificate of Adrian IV', *Cambridge Historical Journal*, 11 (1953–5), 233–52 • Pope Adrian IV, 'Epistolae et privilegia', *Patrologia Latina*, 188 (1855), 1361 • *Matthaei Parisiensis, monachi Sancti Albani, Historia Anglorum, sive … Historia minor*, ed. F. Madden, 3 vols., Rolls Series, 44 (1886–9), 1.299, 304–6, 310; 3.192–4 • *Paris, Chron.*, 2.210–11 • *Letters and charters of Gilbert Foliot*, ed. A. Morey and others (1967), 465–6 • R. W. Southern, *Medieval humanism and other studies* (1970), 234–52 • R. L. Poole, 'The early lives of Robert Pullen and Nicholas Brakespeare', *Studies in chronology and history* (1934), 287–97

Adrian de Castello. *See* Castellesi, Adriano (*c.*1461–1521).

Adrian, Edgar Douglas, first Baron Adrian (1889–1977), physiologist, was born in London on 30 November 1889, the youngest of the three sons (there were no daughters) of Alfred Douglas Adrian, civil servant, and his wife, Flora Lavinia, daughter of Charles Howard Barton. His eldest brother lived for only a few days, while the other, Harold, who showed great promise, died at the age of twenty-two. In 1903 Adrian went as a day boy and king's scholar to Westminster School. He started in classics, but moved to the modern side in 1906. He entered Trinity College, Cambridge in 1908 as a major scholar in natural sciences, and was placed in the first class in part one of the natural sciences tripos (1910) and in part two (1911). While at Cambridge, he became known for his skill in roof climbing

Edgar Douglas Adrian, first Baron Adrian (1889–1977), by Walter Stoneman, 1932

and obtained a half-blue in fencing. He also acquired a taste for hill walking and mountaineering which remained with him all his life.

On the academic side, Adrian was most influenced by his Trinity supervisor, Keith Lucas, a young physiologist of great distinction. Adrian first collaborated with Lucas and then continued on his own in a study of the nerve impulse, which won him a fellowship at Trinity College in 1913. At that time the Cambridge school of physiology was at the height of its fame, but housed deplorably. In a memoir on Lucas, Adrian has left an amusing account of the way in which Lucas, F. G. Hopkins, A. V. Hill, J. Barcroft, W. M. Fletcher, W. B. Hardy, G. R. Mines, and other distinguished scientists were crowded together into cellar rooms, which flooded so easily that the inhabitants had to walk about on duckboards. In addition,

A side door led to a dark chamber in which all the frogs were kept and beyond this was the centrifuge driven by a large gas engine of obsolete design which shook the building and added the smell of warm oil and half-burnt gas to that of frog and rat.   (*Memoirs FRS*, 25, 1979, 12)

Some months before the First World War, Adrian decided to abandon research for a few years in order to complete his medical degree. He began clinical training at Addenbrooke's Hospital, Cambridge, in the summer of 1914 and started in earnest at St Bartholomew's Hospital, London, in July 1914. After acquiring a medical degree he worked on nerve injuries and shell-shock, first at the National Hospital, Queen Square, and later at the Connaught Military Hospital in Aldershot, where he remained until the end of the war, in spite of strenuous efforts to get to France. Later, Adrian wrote that he owed his interest in clinical neurology to Sir Francis Walshe and to Sir Adolph Abrahams.

In 1919 Adrian returned to Cambridge to work in the physiological laboratory and to Trinity College, where he looked after the medical students, as well as lecturing and demonstrating in the university. For a time he continued with analytical electrophysiology of the kind which he had started with Lucas. These researches led to some excellent papers, but Adrian was clearly dissatisfied with this line of work, as he referred later to getting bogged down in somewhat unprofitable experiments. In 1925 he started to use a valve amplifier built to the design of the American H. S. Gasser, who with Erlanger was the first to record nerve impulses with a cathode ray oscilloscope and valve amplifier. The cathode ray tubes that existed in those days had such low actinic power that they would have been useless for Adrian's purposes, but he got by initially with home-made capillary electrometers, and later made good use of the excellent mechanical oscilloscope devised by his young colleague, Bryan H. C. Matthews. With these relatively inexpensive instruments Adrian and his colleagues produced a series of outstanding papers. The initial breakthrough was made by Adrian working on his own, perhaps with some help from Sybil Cooper, but he was joined later in 1925 by Yngve Zotterman from Sweden, with whom he subsequently wrote three distinguished papers. Other important collaborations were those with Rachel Matthews on the eye, with Detlev W. Bronk on motor impulses, with Bryan Matthews on electrical waves from the sensory cortex (Berger rhythm), and much later with G. Moruzzi on the motor cortex and pyramidal tracts. The main conclusions are summarized in three short books, all written versions of lectures: *The Basis of Sensation* (1928), *The Mechanism of Nervous Action* (1932), and *The Physical Background of Perception* (1946).

Adrian's work with Zotterman (1925–6) established beyond doubt that the nerve impulse is invariant, and that the intensity of sensation is conveyed by the frequency of impulses and the quality by the type of nerve fibre in action. There are subtle qualifications to this last principle, but it still stands as a broad generalization. Another very important conclusion is that adaptation to a steady stimulus generally takes place peripherally and that some sense organs, like those concerned with touch, adapt rapidly, whereas others, like muscle spindles, adapt very slowly, or not at all.

In 1927–8 Adrian and Bronk showed that there is only one kind of impulse in a motor nerve fibre as well as in a sensory one, and that the force of muscular contraction, like the intensity of sensation, is graded by varying the frequency of nerve impulses and the number of nerve fibres in action.

During the early 1930s Adrian became increasingly interested in the way in which the nervous system might generate electrical rhythms and this interest led to the well-known papers, written with Matthews and Yamagiwa, which consolidated the initial work of Hans Berger and helped to found the important clinical subject of electroencephalography. During the Second World War, Adrian did important experimental work on vestibular receptors, the cerebellum, and the motor and sensory cortex. His last studies on the sense of smell (1937–59) rank as an important contribution to a fascinating problem.

Adrian received many honours, including the Nobel prize, shared with C. S. Sherrington, in 1932, the OM in 1942, and a peerage in 1955. He was professor of physiology at Cambridge from 1937 to 1951, master of Trinity College from 1951 to 1965, foreign secretary of the Royal Society (1946–50), president of the Royal Society (1950–55), chancellor of the University of Leicester (1957–71), and vice-chancellor (1957–9) and chancellor (1968–75) of the University of Cambridge. He was president of the British Association in 1954 and of the Royal Society of Medicine in 1960–61. Adrian's tenure of all these offices is particularly remembered for the magnificent speeches that he made at important ceremonial occasions. He attended the House of Lords as regularly as his many academic commitments allowed, sitting on the crossbenches and speaking mainly on medical and scientific problems or university affairs. Adrian received honorary degrees from twenty-nine universities, and was an honorary or foreign member of an even larger number of academies and scientific societies.

In 1923 Adrian married Hester Agnes Pinsent (1899–1966) [see Adrian, Hester Agnes, Lady Adrian], daughter of Hume Chancellor Pinsent, a solicitor in Birmingham, and Dame Ellen Frances *Pinsent, distinguished for her work on mental health, an interest later shared by her daughter. They had two daughters and a son, the physiologist Richard Hume *Adrian, second Baron Adrian (1927–1995). After his wife's death, Adrian returned to live in Trinity College. He died in the Evelyn Nursing Home in Cambridge on 4 August 1977.   A. L. Hodgkin, rev.

Sources A. Hodgkin, *Memoirs FRS*, 25 (1979), 1–74
Archives Medical Research Council, London, corresp. and papers · Trinity Cam., corresp., working papers, literary MSS, speeches as master of Trinity College | CAC Cam., corresp. with A. V. Hill · CUL, corresp. with Francis John Worsley Roughton · Nuffield Oxf., corresp. with Lord Cherwell · Rice University, Houston, Texas, Woodson Research Center, corresp. with Sir Julian Huxley · Trinity Cam., letters to Sir Geoffrey Taylor
Likenesses W. Stoneman, photograph, 1932, NPG [see illus.] · R. Moynihan, pencil, 1950, Trinity Cam. · R. Spear, oils, 1953, Trinity Cam. · R. Tollast, drawing, c.1964, CAC Cam. · G. Argent, photograph, 1969, NPG · L. Gowing, oils, University of Leicester · E. Halliday, drawing, Royal Society of Medicine, London · F. McWilliam, bronze bust, Trinity Cam. · A. R. Middleton Todd, RS · R. H. Rushton, watercolour drawing, Royal Society of Medicine, London · photograph, repro. in *Memoirs FRS*

Adrian [*née* Pinsent], **Hester Agnes**, **Lady Adrian** (1899–1966), penal reformer, was born at Lordswood House, Harborne, Birmingham, on 16 September 1899, the only daughter and youngest child of Hume Chancellor Pinsent (d. 1920), a solicitor, and his wife, Ellen Frances Parker

(1866–1949) [*see* Pinsent, Dame Ellen Frances], the social reformer and novelist. Both her brothers were killed in the First World War. It is possible that her strong sense of public service owed something to the desire to serve as her parents had done, but also to contribute as her brothers would have done had they lived. She attended a small girls' school, Crofton Grange, near Orpington, Kent, before entering Somerville College, Oxford, in 1919. After graduating in 1922 with second-class honours in modern history, she intended to follow her mother's vocation as a psychiatric worker, and visited Cambridge for the purpose. There she met Edgar Douglas *Adrian (1889–1977), a fellow of Trinity College, Cambridge, whom she married on 14 June 1923; they had a son, Richard Hume *Adrian, second Baron Adrian, and two daughters. Her husband, who became professor of physiology at Cambridge and master of Trinity College, was raised to the peerage in 1955.

After settling in Cambridge, Hester Adrian immediately became active in voluntary organizations, and in 1936 she was appointed to her first official position, as a JP for the city of Cambridge. As a billeting officer of the Women's Voluntary Service in Cambridge, she helped to organize accommodation for evacuees during the Second World War, and through her involvement in the evacuation survey of Margaret Cole and Susan Isaacs she gained valuable insights into the lives of urban children. She chaired the juvenile panel of the Cambridge magistrates' courts from 1949 to 1958 and chaired the Cambridge bench as a whole from 1955 to 1958. From 1947 she sat on the council of the Magistrates' Association. Her experience as a magistrate was recognized by the major figure in Cambridge criminology, Sir Leon Radzinowicz, who in 1960 invited her to join the management committee of the new Cambridge Institute of Criminology. In 1959 she was president of the Howard League for Penal Reform.

Apart from the penal system, Hester Adrian's main interest was in mental health, both in the area in which her mother had been active—mental handicap or mental deficiency, as it was then called—and in mental illness. She started her life's work in this field just after her marriage when she became honorary secretary of the Cambridgeshire Mental Welfare Association in 1924, an office which she held until 1934. Her career of voluntary work as a committee woman included the chairmanship of Cambridge special schools from 1935 to 1964, of united Cambridge hospitals from 1960, and of the training committee for teachers of mentally handicapped people from 1963. She was on the management committee of the old fever hospital which operated as the local mental hospital at Fulbourn from 1947, and later chaired it from 1951 to 1957.

From the 1950s Lady Adrian was particularly active as a member of national bodies, including the royal commission on the law relating to mental illness and mental deficiency (1954–7) and the Home Office marriage guidance training board. She served on the Home Office departmental committee on the law relating to children and young persons (1959–60), chaired by Lord Ingleby, and then on

the royal commission on the penal system in England and Wales from 1964 to 1966. Here she made a vital contribution, as Radzinowicz recorded in his *Adventures in Criminology* (1999, 333–52), when she resigned with five other members, insisting that the penal system needed full research by experts, and that an advisory council should ensure that changes to the system were informed by the results of proper inquiry. In particular she pointed out that the government had published a white paper on young offenders which showed that they had not been communicating their intentions to the royal commission for scrutiny at all. This acuteness of observation and readiness to accept disfavour was typical, as was her insistence on research and the need for practicality of reform. She was made DBE in 1965.

Hester Adrian's achievements are all the more remarkable when it is recognized that she was also running a large house in Cambridge and, from 1951 to 1965, the master's lodge at Trinity College. She helped to make the lodge 'a delightful centre of hospitality' (*The Times*, 23 May 1966) during her husband's period of office as master of Trinity and vice-chancellor of the university. She was always active, enjoying holidays in Cornwall and climbing in the Lake District until an accident in 1942 crushed her leg above the knee and she had to have it amputated. She continued to ride a bicycle with a wooden leg and although she had to give up dancing, an activity which she had much enjoyed as a young woman, she remained extremely active until her early and sudden death at her home, Burrells End, 58A Grange Road, Cambridge, on 20 May 1966.

Obituaries record Hester Adrian's wisdom and good sense and her calm pursuit of collective responsibility in the many public bodies which she joined, and on which she always made a sensible, quiet contribution. The only major controversy which lingers is the extent of her commitment to her mother's great concern, eugenics. Before the Second World War both Hester and her husband, along with many other progressives and academics, supported the Eugenics Society. They belonged to the reform eugenicists who wished to remove the social inhibitions against encouraging hereditary talent. Hester Adrian is commemorated by a special school and a research unit into mental handicap named after her. D. THOM

Sources *The Times* (23 May 1966) · *WWW* · *Somerville College register, 1879–1971* [1972] · b. cert. · m. cert. · d. cert.
Wealth at death £57,859: probate, 13 July 1966, *CGPLA Eng. & Wales*

Adrian, Max [*real name* Max Bor] (1903–1973), actor, was born on 1 November 1903 in northern Ireland, the son of Edward Norman Cavendish Bor and his wife, Mabel Lloyd, *née* Thornton. He was educated at Portora Royal School, Enniskillen, renowned for its teaching of English, whose past pupils included Samuel Beckett. Adrian described himself as being 'one third Irish, one third English and one third German', whose supposed national attributes he considered were reflected in his acting. He had an Irish love of words and an English restraint, often combined with a penchant for the sardonic *double entendres* of a night-club compère from the Weimar republic. Despite this distinctive style, he was a versatile and accomplished actor, equally at home in classical drama, intimate revue, and the theatre of the absurd. He also appeared with distinction in films, television, and one-man shows.

Adrian began his stage career as a chorus boy on the lowest rung of the theatrical business, performing in a chorus line while the reels were being changed at a silent moving-picture house. He graduated to the Gaiety Theatre at Douglas in the Isle of Man, before touring in George Gershwin's *Lady be Good* (1927) and receiving his first West End walk-on part at the Globe Theatre during the run of *The Squall* (1927). He decided to become an actor rather than a dancer and gained experience in weekly repertory in Northampton, where he took on about forty leading roles a year (1930–32). 'They're extraordinary people in Northampton', he later recalled, 'they hold nothing against you. I still have friends there' (interview with Barry Norman, *The Times*, 4 Sept 1972).

Adrian's first big opportunity came when he appeared as Albert Arnold in an early Terence Rattigan comedy, *First Episode* (1934), which started out at a theatre club, Q, transferred to the Comedy Theatre in the West End and to New York under another title, *College Sinners*. But the play was less successful than expected and he returned to smaller roles and provincial appearances before appearing for the first time in a classical repertory company in London, playing Shakespeare and George Bernard Shaw. His performance as Pandarus in a modern-dress *Troilus and Cressida* at the Westminster Theatre (1938) was further developed in a Royal Shakespeare Company production in 1960, and transformed for a generation the understanding of this lascivious, brooding character in Shakespeare's powerfully ambiguous, anti-war play.

Adrian joined the Old Vic company in 1939, playing the Dauphin in Shaw's *Saint Joan*, and joined John Gielgud's company at the Haymarket (1944–5) as Puck in *A Midsummer Night's Dream* and Osric in *Hamlet*. During the Second World War, exempted from military service, he discovered his talents in intimate revue, playing in Herbert Farjeon's *Light and Shade* (1942) at the Ambassadors. This genre, rarely seen today, gave him the chance to sing, dance, take part in short sketches, and explore his gift for timing pointed witticisms. He appeared in *Tuppence Coloured* (1947), *Oranges and Lemons* (1948), *Penny Plain* (1951), and *Airs on a Shoestring* (1953), which ran for almost two years at the Royal Court Theatre in London and subsequently toured. Its contributors included Michael Flanders, Donald Swann, and Joyce Grenfell, while the producer was Laurier Lister, who became Adrian's lifelong partner.

'A pleasant and genial revue', wrote Ivor Brown in *The Observer* in 1953, in which 'Max Adrian carries out most of the men's jobs', but the days of such light-hearted entertainment were coming to an end. The mood of British theatre was changing with John Osborne's *Look Back in Anger* (1956) and the arrival of the Angry Young Men. The English Stage Company took over at the Royal Court Theatre, where Lister had his successes. A new generation of satire

approached with *Beyond the Fringe* (1959). Adrian appeared in two less successful revues, *From Here to There* (1955) and *Fresh Airs* (1956), which he co-directed, but in December 1956 he went to New York to play Dr Pangloss in *Candide* at the Martin Beck Theater. He stayed in the US to join summer stock companies and in 1958, appeared in a double bill, *The Lesson* and *The Chairs*, by the French-Romanian absurdist writer Eugene Ionesco, at the Phoenix Theater. The *New York Times* critic, Brookes Atkinson, wrote that his 'elaborate politesse, giving way gradually to fanaticism and ghastly exuberance, is funny and grisly at the same time' (obituary in *New York Times*, 20 Jan 1973, quoting from a review published in 1958).

In Britain there were vigorous attempts to transform repertory theatre into a system which more closely resembled the continental models. The first came with the establishment of the Royal Shakespeare Company (RSC) from its origins in the Shakespeare Memorial Theatre at Stratford upon Avon. Its leader was the director Peter Hall, and the company was hired on long-term contracts to play in repertory in Stratford and London. Adrian was invited to join Hall's company with such actors as Peggy Ashcroft, Peter O'Toole, and Diana Rigg, a time which he recalled as the happiest in his life. 'There was a magic about that company' (interview with Barry Norman, *The Times*, 4 Sept 1972).

At the RSC actors were encouraged to extend their acting ranges by taking on roles for which they might not usually have been cast. Adrian played Feste in *Twelfth Night*, Jacques in *As You Like It*, Father Barré in John Whiting's *The Devils*, and a range of smaller parts. His abilities as a team member brought him to the attention of Sir Laurence Olivier, who invited him to join the first National Theatre company in 1963. He played Polonius in the opening production of *Hamlet*, Serebryakov in Chekhov's *Uncle Vanya*, and the Inquisitor in Shaw's *Saint Joan*. After leaving the National Theatre, he played in West End and regional theatres, before devising (with Lister) his first one-man show, *An Evening with G. B. S.* (George Bernard Shaw). With this and another one-man show, *Gilbert and Sullivan*, he toured the British Isles, the United States and (under the auspices of the British Council) many commonwealth countries.

Adrian's screen career began with *The Primrose Path* (1933) and continued through many distinguished British films, such as Olivier's *Henry V* (1944). He usually provided memorable cameos rather than centre-screen performances, but under the director Ken Russell his sardonic and detached presence pervaded such films as *The Music Lovers* (1970) and *The Devils* (1970, from Whiting's play). He also appeared in lighter screen roles, in *The Boy Friend* (1971), or as Frankie Howerd's stooge in the television series *Up Pompeii*; but his most haunting performance perhaps came in Ken Russell's film made for television, *Song of Summer*, about the relationship between the infirm and partly paralysed composer, Delius, and his intuitive secretary, Eric Fenby. As Delius, Adrian's gestures were minimal, but he evoked the composer's fastidious and haunted sensibility.

Adrian died from a heart attack on 19 January 1973 at his home, Smarkham Orchard, Shamley Green, near Guildford, Surrey, after returning from the television studios where he had been recording Bertolt Brecht's *The Caucasian Chalk Circle* (1973) for the BBC. At his memorial service, the great names of British theatre at the time paid tribute to his style and professionalism. The lessons were read by Alec Guinness and Laurence Olivier, the tribute paid by Joyce Grenfell. He was survived by his partner, Laurier Lister, with whom he lived at Shamley Green.

JOHN ELSOM

Sources I. Herbert, ed., *Who's who in the theatre*, concise 16th edn (1978) · *The Times* (20 Jan 1973) · *The Times* (23 Jan 1973) · *Daily Telegraph* (20 Jan 1973) · *The Guardian* (20 Jan 1973) · *The Stage* (8 Feb 1973) · *New York Times* (20 Jan 1973) · interview with Barry Norman, *The Times* (4 July 1972) · *Sunday Telegraph* (10 Oct 1973) · *The Observer* (April 1953) · private information (2004) [Patrick Garland] · d. cert. · *CGPLA Eng. & Wales* (1973)

Wealth at death £14,163: probate, 12 March 1973, *CGPLA Eng. & Wales*

Adrian, Richard Hume, second Baron Adrian (1927–1995), physiologist, was born on 16 October 1927 in Grange Road, Cambridge, the only son and youngest of the three children of Edgar Douglas *Adrian, first Baron Adrian (1889–1977), physiologist, and his wife, Hester Agnes *Adrian, daughter of Hume Chancellor Pinsent, a solicitor in Birmingham, and his wife Ellen Frances *Pinsent. On his father's side he was descended from an earlier Richard Adrian, a Huguenot refugee who had fled to England after the massacre of St Bartholomew in 1572; the line of descent also includes a surgeon who attended Sir Philip Sidney after the battle of Zutphen, clerics, a silk weaver, and three generations of civil servants. Hester Pinsent's family was related on her father's side to the philosopher David Hume; both she and her mother were created DBE for their work on mental health.

Early life and education At the age of eight Adrian went to King's College School, Cambridge, but early in the Second World War he and his twin sister, Jennet, were sent to the USA to live with the family of Detlev Bronk, who had worked with Adrian's father in Cambridge and who was at that time director of the Johnson Foundation in Philadelphia. There Adrian spent three years at Swarthmore high school. He was, though, anxious to return to England as soon as possible and, after graduating from high school and spending one semester at Swarthmore College, he went home in late 1943 to join Westminster School, still evacuated to Herefordshire. In January 1945 he entered Cambridge as an undergraduate at Trinity College, reading for the natural sciences tripos and choosing subjects appropriate for medicine.

As an undergraduate Adrian was greatly influenced by Alan Hodgkin, who had just returned from his wartime work on radar and, with Andrew Huxley, was resuming work on the mechanism of message transmission along nerves—work which had been halted at a most promising stage by Hitler's invasion of Poland in 1939. In his third year Adrian took the advanced course in physiology, completed his double first, and decided that he wanted to be a

Richard Hume Adrian, second Baron Adrian (1927–1995), by Ian Fleming, 1992

physiologist. At that time it was still conventional for physiologists to be medically qualified, and in 1948 he went to University College Hospital, London, to take the clinical course. He said later that he was glad to have done so, and that it taught him many things, especially about people, that he would not otherwise have learned. One of these things was that he did not enjoy clinical work; he completed his medical qualifications without the full year of house jobs that later became a prerequisite for registration. By this time the war had been over for six years, but having been exempt from military service during his medical training Adrian was now drafted into the Royal Army Medical Corps and sent to the chemical defence experimental establishment at Porton Down. There he worked on protective measures against mustard gas and nerve gases, and on more theoretically interesting questions about the actions of nerve gases particularly at synapses.

Released from the army early in 1954, Adrian spent four months 'in an extended journey in the Middle East (Turkey, Iraq, Jordan, Syria, the Lebanon) mostly with an archaeological interest—inevitably with a growing interest in the unsettled politics of the region' (Adrian, 1993). This was the start of an important facet of his life. At archaeological digs he seems to have been a useful visitor. The archaeologist David Oates described the impression that Adrian made on a party of visiting German archaeologists by his skill with an esoteric piece of surveying equipment with which the visitors were unfamiliar—a skill he had acquired the previous day.

Research into muscle behaviour In the autumn of 1954 Adrian returned to Cambridge to begin work as a research student in the physiological laboratory, under the supervision of Alan Hodgkin. Within two years he had discovered a major source of error in the standard method of using microelectrodes to determine the voltage difference across cell membranes, and had shown how such errors could be avoided. The fundamental problem that he was preparing to tackle, and to whose solution over the next thirty years he was to make a massive contribution, is called by physiologists the problem of excitation-contraction coupling. It is to understand how the spread of excitation along the surface of a muscle fibre activates the contractile machinery that forms the bulk of the fibre. By the mid-1950s Hodgkin and Huxley had shown that transmission along nerve fibres is fully explained by sequential changes in the selective permeability of the surface membrane to sodium ions and potassium ions—changes caused by the peculiar responses of the relevant ion channels to changes in voltage. There was good evidence that spread of excitation along a muscle fibre was essentially similar.

The mid-1950s also led to major advances in understanding of the contractile machinery. In muscle the two main proteins form interdigitating sliding rods, whose overlap increases in the presence of adenosine triphosphate and calcium ions. Since adenosine triphosphate is always present but the concentration of calcium ions is very low in the resting fibre, it seemed likely that excitation-contraction coupling involved the release of calcium ions deep within the fibre. The crucial question was: how do the changes at the surface membrane trigger this release?

The work of microscopists had shown that the fibres of skeletal muscle possess two systems of tubules—transverse tubules, running at right angles to the fibre surface and opening onto that surface, and longitudinal tubules forming a closed network within the fibre, and expanding into little 'cisterns' where they abut on the transverse tubules. The fluid in the cisterns is rich in calcium ions, and one possibility was that passive spread of electrical current from the surface of the fibre down the transverse tubules somehow released calcium from the cisterns. By a long series of ingenious experiments and careful mathematical analysis, however, Adrian and his colleagues showed that passive spread of current could not explain the observed behaviour, and that a mechanism very similar to that responsible for the conduction of an impulse along the surface of the fibre must be responsible for conducting an impulse along the membranes of the transverse tubules into the depths of the fibre. They also found evidence for the movements of charged particles at the junction between the transverse and longitudinal tubules—movements that they suspected were involved in triggering the release of calcium ions. Later work has confirmed their suspicions and suggests that molecules of two kinds interact. One acts as a sensor that changes shape in response to a change of voltage across the membrane of the transverse tubule; the other forms a channel in the membrane of the adjacent cistern—a channel that is opened by the change in shape of the sensor.

Although most of Adrian's work was concerned with the behaviour of normal muscle, he and his colleagues were also interested in the rare inherited disease myotonia congenita, first described in humans more than a century ago but also found in goats. The characteristic feature of this disease is that contraction of a muscle tends to persist after the cessation of voluntary effort. A human patient cannot relax his grip; a startled goat tends to fall over. Four myotonic goats were dispatched from Cincinnati, and the work nearly foundered at an early stage when they arrived at London airport without any papers. It was, the customs man explained on the telephone, against the rule for animals to be disembarked without proper papers, and the goats would have to be shot. Eventually, however, Adrian persuaded him that though the goats could not properly be disembarked there could be no objection to their being 'disemplaned'. A detailed analysis of the electrical properties of the muscles of these goats showed that the accumulation of potassium ions in the transverse tubules, coupled with the (known) abnormally low chloride permeability of the surface membrane of the muscle fibres, could account for the continued excitation of the muscle after excitation through the nerve had stopped. It became reasonable to assume that a similar explanation accounted for the symptoms in human patients.

Cambridge career Adrian was elected to a research fellowship at Corpus Christi College, Cambridge, in 1955, and to a teaching fellowship and university demonstratorship in the following year. A university lectureship followed in 1961, a readership (in experimental biophysics) in 1968, and (following Adrian's election to the fellowship of the Royal Society in 1977) an *ad hominem* professorship in cell physiology in 1978, the year he was also awarded the Cambridge MD degree on the basis of published work; he had been given an honorary doctorate by the University of Poitiers in the previous year.

Adrian enjoyed his time at Corpus Christi and made lasting friendships there. It was at a dinner given by the master, the physicist Sir George Thomson, that he met a striking young Newnham research student, Lucy Caroe (*b.* 1935), daughter of the architect Alban Douglas Rendall Caroe and granddaughter of Sir William Bragg, and on 1 April 1967 she became his wife. The college still reflected some of the conservatism of the twenty-five-year reign of the previous master, Sir William Spens. During a period as dean of college Adrian sometimes found it necessary to protect lively undergraduates from crusty dons, and it was probably this that later gave him the reputation of having been something of a 'young Turk'. In 1961 he accepted an invitation to become tutor for natural sciences at the newly founded Churchill College, Cambridge, and he remained a fellow of Churchill for the next twenty years, becoming an honorary fellow in 1985.

In 1981 Adrian was elected master of Pembroke College—an unusual appointment, for he was not a Pembroke man. A contentious problem needing urgent attention was the admission of women, and it is a measure of Adrian's skill as master that by June 1982 the college had agreed to their admission, and that this agreement had been reached with only seven votes cast against and with no ill feeling. During the eleven years of Adrian's mastership the academic standing of the college rose, the number of graduate students doubled, undergraduate accommodation was increased, stonework was cleaned, and for two years the boat club even went 'head of the river'. The college continued to be a very friendly society; the master, though an agnostic, willingly and admirably performed his duties in chapel; and Lucy Adrian was an excellent hostess in the master's lodge while continuing her work as a fellow of Newnham.

At the time Adrian was master of Pembroke, the vice-chancellor of the university held office for only two years and was chosen from among the heads of the colleges. In 1985 Adrian was an obvious choice. He had succeeded his father in the House of Lords in 1977, like him choosing to sit on the cross-benches. In 1979 he became a founder member of the House of Lords select committee on science and technology, and by 1985 he was also a member of the Home Office committee on animal experiments, a trustee of the British Museum and of the Natural History Museum, a member of the British Library board, chairman of the governing body of the Agricultural and Food Research Council's Animal Virus Research Institute, and a member of the governing bodies of Imperial College and of Westminster School. He had also been an extremely influential member of the House of Lords select committee on the Laboratory Animals Protection Bill, had served on the council of the Royal Society and on the Medical Research Council's neurosciences board, and had represented Cambridge University on the General Medical Council.

As vice-chancellor Adrian was independent, conscientious, and well-informed. He was an excellent chairman, invariably courteous and fair, saying rather little but always effectively, and ready to oppose pressure groups if he felt they were not pursuing useful policies. His main anxieties were eloquently summarized in his annual addresses, which he wrote himself, being one of the last vice-chancellors to do so. His first concern was the financial stringency caused by the decrease in real terms of the government grant; and his second was the increasingly dirigiste attitude to individual universities of the government, the University Grants Committee (UGC), and the Committee of Vice-Chancellors and Principals: 'It used to be said that the UGC was a characteristic British device for insulating universities from Government. We delude ourselves if we continue in that belief' (Adrian, 1986). Adrian felt strongly that universities would remain independent only if they could raise a much greater fraction of their funds from non-government sources, and while he was vice-chancellor two major steps were taken towards this aim. A development office was set up, and a company was created through which the university could profit from commercial developments arising from research in its various departments. In addition, five new professorships were established, four of them with the help of new benefactions, and the first interdisciplinary research centre (in

superconductivity) was started. The administrative machinery at the core of the university was also strengthened: the comatose long-term planning committee was reconstituted under the chairmanship of the vice-chancellor, and a small vice-chancellor's advisory group was formed. Adrian's main contribution to opposing the government's dirigiste tendency, though, came not during his vice-chancellorship but two years later, during the House of Lords' discussion of the Education Reform Act of 1988, when he played an important part in limiting the government's powers to interfere in the academic work of the universities.

Final years and character During his period as vice-chancellor Adrian sometimes expressed hopes of getting back to work in the laboratory. Instead, however, his administrative roles multiplied: he was president of the Research Defence Society, trustee of the Daiwa Anglo-Japanese Foundation, member of the council of management of the Baring Foundation, British representative on the Council of Scientists' Human Frontier Science Program Organization. In 1990 he took a year's sabbatical leave from the university to become prime warden of the Goldsmiths' Company, and in 1992, approaching the age of sixty-five, he retired from both his professorship and the mastership of Pembroke. In 1993 he was appointed deputy lieutenant of Cambridgeshire. In that year he and Lucy were to visit Melbourne, where he had been invited to lecture, but he became ill with an abdominal cancer, from which he died at the Evelyn Hospital, Cambridge, on 4 April 1995. He was buried on 11 April in the churchyard of St Margaret's Church, Cley-next-the-Sea, Norfolk. A memorial service was held at the church of Great St Mary, Cambridge, on 24 June 1995. There were no children of his marriage, and the peerage became extinct on his death.

It is easier to say what Adrian achieved than what sort of person he was. The portrait by Daphne Todd in the hall at Pembroke is a good likeness but it portrays him as austere and patrician, and he was rarely either. Tall, handsome, and distinguished-looking, with an invariably courteous manner and wide general interests ranging from archaeology and Middle Eastern politics to joinery and English silver, he was genuinely diffident about his own remarkable achievements. And though he confessed to having enjoyed climbing, sailing, skiing, and 'driving fast cars fast', he insisted that 'in none of these was I any better than average' (Adrian, 1981). He was an entertaining companion, with an excellent dry sense of humour. Speaking as prime warden in the gilded magnificence of the newly refurbished Goldsmiths' Hall, he explained to the decorated diners how glad the company was to be back in its own premises: 'Be it ever so humble, there's no place like home'. And going through old correspondence, he found copies of a letter written by his father to Lucy's parents at the time of her engagement to Richard. 'There were', he said, 'three drafts, each warmer and more spontaneous than the last'. The strength of Adrian's character is perhaps most clearly shown in a long letter to a friend and former colleague, written as he lay dying of cancer. It is devoid of self-pity, concerned for Lucy, detachedly accurate in the clinical aspects, and gently amusing in discussing day-to-day events.   IAN GLYNN

Sources A. F. Huxley, *Memoirs FRS*, 43 (1997), 13–30 · R. H. Adrian, annual address as vice-chancellor, *Cambridge University Reporter* (8 Oct 1986), 28–31 · R. H. Adrian, annual address as vice-chancellor, *Cambridge University Reporter* (7 Oct 1987), 18–24 · R. H. Adrian, draft of lecture to be given as Scott visiting fellow at Osmond College, Melbourne, 1993 · B. Till, address at Richard Adrian's memorial service, *Gazette* [Pembroke College Cambridge Society] (1995), 43–9 · *Gazette* [Pembroke College Cambridge Society] (1992), 5–7 · R. H. Adrian, *curriculum vitae* prepared for Pembroke College, 1981 · *The Times* (8 April 1995) · *The Independent* (8 April 1995) · *WWW*, 1991–5 · Burke, *Peerage* · m. cert. · d. cert. · personal knowledge (2004) · private information (2004)
Likenesses D. Todd, oils, 1987, Pembroke Cam. · I. Fleming, photograph, 1992, priv. coll. [*see illus.*] · P. Nathan, effigy on medal, 1992, Goldsmiths' Hall, London · photograph, repro. in *The Times*
Wealth at death £693,202: probate, 2 Aug 1995, CGPLA Eng. & Wales

Adshead, (Sylvia) Mary (1904–1995), mural painter and designer, was born on 15 February 1904 at 46 Great Russell Street, Bloomsbury, London, the only child of Stanley Davenport *Adshead (1868–1946), architect and academic, and Mary Annie (1874–1960), *née* Blackie, teacher and housewife, who both had considerable influence on her career and early success. A delicate child, she was educated initially at home by her mother. From 1910 until 1913 the family spent part of each year in Liverpool, where her father was professor of town planning. In 1914 they moved to Mortlake and she attended Putney high school from 1916 to 1919, after which she spent six months at a Paris *lycée*. Her father's position as a professor at London University enabled her to receive a concessionary place at the Slade School of Fine Art at the early age of sixteen; there she caught the final years of Henry Tonks's famously misogynist regime. Unusually, he took a particular interest in her work, allowing her to pursue what he called her 'tapestry style', a witty blend of sophistication and naïvety, and turn her back on the strict academic approach, then *de rigueur* in art schools. Her ability to marshal elegant designs on a grand scale made her a natural mural painter. In 1924 Tonks was responsible for arranging her first mural commission, *The Joys of the Country*, in collaboration with a fellow student, Rex Whistler, for the memorial hall of the Highways Boys' Club in Shadwell. It attracted the attention of architects and led to many further commissions for her, including a large mural, *The Housing of the People*, at the British Empire Exhibition in 1924 at Wembley and a mural on desert island life for the dining-room of Charles Reilly, professor of architecture at Liverpool University, which was exhibited at the Royal Institute of British Architects when she was just twenty-two. (It is now owned by Liverpool University Art Gallery.)

Occasionally commissions for the cultivated rich went awry. In 1928 Mary Adshead executed a series of panels for Lord Beaverbrook's dining-room at Newmarket evoking the spirit of the town's fair and horse races and peopling them with likenesses of his friends. The project foundered when Lady Diana Cooper, a fashionable beauty depicted in one of the panels, persuaded him that, given his quarrelsome nature, it was unwise to immortalize a group of people with whom he was bound to fall out. Beaverbrook returned the panels with a two-thirds rejection fee. (The work was reassembled for exhibition at Peter Jones department store in 1930 before being rolled up and stored. Later all but three panels were destroyed by fire.)

On 30 April 1929 Mary married Stephen *Bone (1904–1958), son of the artist Sir Muirhead Bone, and in that year she moved from her parents' house at 2 Chester Gate to 9 Knightsbridge, London. Although they had been students together at the Slade, they hardly knew each other until later. Both unusually tall, they made a striking couple. In the early years of their marriage they made tours through Europe, sketching and painting. In 1930 she had her first solo exhibition at the Goupil Gallery and was elected to the New English Art Club. Commissions for murals and designs flowed in, but the birth of the first of their three children, Quentin, in 1931 inevitably brought distractions. In that year they moved to 43 Haverstock Hill, Hampstead. She was an immensely practical woman and a stalwart in the marriage. In 1933 another son, Sylvester, was born, and in 1937 a daughter, Christina. Also in 1937 she exhibited at the Redfern Gallery, London, and they moved up the hill to no. 140. At the outbreak of war she moved the family to The Barn, Downton, Hampshire, and in 1940 to 26 Portland Place, Leamington Spa, where Stephen was in the camouflage organization. After the war they moved back to 140 Haverstock Hill, where she lived for the rest of her life. She worked on three illustrated children's books with Stephen (1936, 1942, and 1953) and illustrated *Bonfires and Broomsticks* by Mary Norton in 1948; from 1949 she also designed stamps. However, her career was underpinned by a constant flow of mural commissions. In 1953 she became the secretary of the Society of Mural Painters.

Stephen's tragic premature death from cancer in 1958 in some ways released a new wave of energy in Mary. She travelled in the United States and Europe and studied mosaic decoration in Ravenna and Sicily. Though she had three further solo exhibitions in 1971, 1979, and 1986 (a retrospective at Sally Hunter Fine Art, London), she also exhibited with Stephen's work in 1974, 1980, and 1989. Lameness caused by painting off ladders hampered her work and life in later years but she remained purposefully active to the end. She died at home of heart failure on 3 September 1995 and was cremated at Golders Green crematorium on 11 September.   SALLY HUNTER

Sources *The Times* (9 Sept 1995) · *The Guardian* (7 Sept 1995) · family archives, priv. coll. · gallery archives, Sally Hunter Fine Art, 54 Clarendon Road, London W11 · b. cert. · m. cert. · d. cert. · private information (2004) [family]
Archives priv. coll., works and papers
Likenesses M. Adshead, self-portrait, 1931, Graves Art Gallery, Sheffield; repro. in *The Independent* (7 Sept 1995) · photograph, repro. in *The Times*
Wealth at death £1,107,833: probate, 1996, CGPLA Eng. & Wales

Adshead, Stanley Davenport (1868–1946), architect and town planner, was born at Bowden Vale, Bowden, Cheshire, on 8 March 1868. He was the second of eight children and eldest son of Joseph Adshead, an artist, and his wife, Eliza Davies. He was educated at Buxton, and on leaving school at sixteen was articled to the architect J. Medland Taylor in Manchester. Adshead described him as 'a relic of the Dickens era' (Powers, 106). He moved on to the office of Salomon and Eli in Manchester and later described the revelatory effect of his first visit to London during these years, when Bloomsbury appeared as 'something strange, fresh and pacifying' in contrast to Manchester (ibid., 109). He was determined to move, and in 1890 got a job with George Sherrin, where he learned from other assistants, notably H. V. Lanchester and E. A. Rickards. He followed Rickards into the office of Dunn and Watson and thence to Howard Ince, who was building a studio house in Maida Vale for the sculptor Alfred Gilbert. Several more moves ensued, with Adshead rising up an artistic scale to finish in the office of William Flockhart, which involved him in a four-year spell as clerk of works at Rosehaugh, Argyll, a vast eclectic mansion on the Black Isle. There he met his future wife, Mary Annie (1874–1960), daughter of Andrew Blackie of Strathpeffer. They were married on 24 October 1900.

On his return to London in 1898 Adshead found a new occupation as a freelance perspective artist, drawing the schemes of other architects for competition and exhibition. His style for this work was atmospheric in a limpid way, avoiding the tricks then common in this important art of architectural persuasion. In 1900 he made the perspectives for five out of six of the entries in the competition for the new central criminal courts. In 1904 he finally won a competition in his own name for a library and technical school at Ramsgate, from which followed a pavilion in the same town, in which Adshead began to explore the late eighteenth-century revival style with which his architecture is largely associated. His practice failed to thrive, however, and he was happy to be offered the newly created chair of civic design at the University of Liverpool in 1909. This proposal came from the professor of architecture, C. H. Reilly, one of Adshead's associates in London at the turn of the century, who wanted to add town planning in a grand artistic style to the existing architectural curriculum. Adshead thus acquired a new career as a result of Reilly's insight and the sponsorship of William Hesketh Lever (later the first Lord Leverhulme), although there was a secondary motive in the hope that he would teach Liverpool students to make fine presentation drawings. Adshead and Reilly shared a mission to purify Edwardian classicism, which implied a greater sympathy with neoclassicism, including its grand urban schemes and attacks on late projects by Norman Shaw, who described them as 'tin-pot professors'. Adshead was secretary of an evanescent 'Classical Society' around 1907.

Adshead's subject became newly fashionable in the wake of the first Town Planning Act in 1909, and he was the first editor of the *Town Planning Review*, which promoted formal design in place of garden city vernacular. He broadened Reilly's propagandist thrust with sensitivity to places and their evolution, awakened in him by one of his colleagues, Ramsay Muir. Reilly's student and successor (in both his university chairs), Sir Patrick Abercrombie, believed that Adshead's synthesized and balanced approach, which combined the monumental, statistical, and legalistic aspects of the years before 1914, was the foundation on which the planning profession in Britain was based: 'He might appear contradictory or confusing in his verbal approach, but the final verdict showed an unerring logical and artistic sense' (quoted in Powers, 122). In 1914 Adshead left his half-time position in Liverpool for a new chair in civic design at University College, London, where he remained until retirement in 1935, becoming a colleague of Professor A. E. Richardson, whose architectural office was for a time housed below Adshead's London office and residence at 46 Great Russell Street.

Adshead's practice, in partnership with Stanley Ramsey (the author of the *Dictionary of National Biography* entry on Adshead), was commissioned in 1911 to design extensive new buildings to replace existing slums on the duchy of Cornwall estate, Kennington, London, in an initiative by Sir Walter Peacock, secretary to the prince's council. As Ramsey characterized their work:

> From the outset, Adshead insisted that it was to be a Royal Estate and he it was who laid down the broad principles of development. There remained, and do remain to this day, many fine examples of late eighteenth century and Regency buildings in the neighbourhood, and we decided that the architectural expression for the new buildings should be a modern transcript of these styles.   (S. Ramsey, 'Our work together', MS, family papers)

The main development consisted of terraces of two-storey houses in yellow London stock brick, some of which formed Courtenay Square, and a quadrangle of old people's dwellings. Additional sections, increasingly in flats, were inserted in the existing streetscapes until the end of the 1920s, and a new church of St Anselm was planned in 1914 and completed in modified form in 1933. It cannot be claimed that the Kennington work was influential as an alternative to the tenement type dwellings which constituted the majority model for slum clearance projects between the wars, but it was widely admired.

In 1917 Adshead was commissioned to build a workers' settlement for Dorman Long steel works at Redcar, called Dormanstown. Conventional in external appearance, the paired Georgian houses were in fact based on a steel frame, and a formal layout was proposed. Adshead and Ramsey also designed a number of smaller housing projects under the Housing Act of 1919, in Totnes, Brighton, and elsewhere. In the 1920s he continued to produce a small number of buildings similar in approach to the Kennington estate; the only exception, at the end of his career, was Scurr House, Stepney, in 1932, a tenement block with emphatic horizontal balconies which are modernist in style.

During the 1920s Adshead produced a number of published planning surveys of different parts of England, including south Tees-side, the Thames valley, west Essex, Scarborough, Teignmouth, and York, which were distinguished by his line drawings of landscape and towns. In

1930 he visited Northern Rhodesia to select and plan a site for the capital, Lusaka. Adshead's book *Town Planning and Town Development* (1923) was his major statement of the subject, and covered issues of regional planning, street layout, and the impact of the motor car and mobile leisure, illustrated with photographs of good and bad practice. In 1941 his book *A New England: Planning for the Future* proposed a nationwide rationalization of land use and transport; it was followed by *New Towns for Old* (1943).

Adshead and his wife had one child, (Sylvia) Mary *Adshead (1904–1995). She studied painting at the Slade School of Art and became well known as a mural painter with a strong, slightly naïve style who executed a number of commissions for her father's buildings, and those of his contemporaries and pupils. Adshead, who was very tall, was described as 'rather of the dreamy and slow-moving type' (W. A. Downe, 'Some memories', *Sir Albert Richardson, 1880–1964*, ed. A. Powers, S. Houfe, and J. Wilton-Ely, 1999). C. H. Reilly recognized Adshead's qualities when he wrote, 'The classical backbone of his thought has never prevented his appreciating the romantic interest of accidental things' (Reilly, 26). Adshead died at Chapel Cottage, Lower Ashley, New Milton, Hampshire, on 11 April 1946 of stomach cancer. His wife survived him.

ALAN POWERS

Sources priv. coll., family papers · biography file, RIBA BAL · A. Powers, 'Architects I have known', *Architectural History*, 24 (1981), 103–23 · C. H. Reilly, *Representative British architects of the present day* (1931) · S. D. Adshead, *New towns for old* (1943) · *The Times* (13 April 1946) · *RIBA Journal*, 53 (1945–6), 309 · *Town Planning Review*, 19 (summer 1947), 120–22 · *The Builder*, 170 (1946), 385 · *DNB* · b. cert. · m. cert. · d. cert. · *CGPLA Eng. & Wales* (1946)

Wealth at death £6892 13s. 2d.: probate, 5 Sept 1946, *CGPLA Eng. & Wales*

Adson, John (*bap.* 1587?, *d.* 1640), musician and composer, may have been the Johannes Adson baptized at Watford, Northamptonshire, on 24 January 1587. Nothing else is known of his origins. By 1604, well before the usual age to finish an apprenticeship (which was about twenty-four), he was employed as a cornetto player at the court of Duke Charles III of Lorraine, having been recruited in England by the French cornetto player Jean Presse. When the duke died in 1608, an engraving of his funeral showed players of five cornettos, two sackbuts, and two bass shawms alongside a group of singers. By 1613 Adson had returned to England. On 23 May 1614 he was appointed to the London waits and paid for serving from the previous Christmas. He kept this place until his death.

In 1621 Adson published *Courtly Masking Ayres for Violins, Consorts and Cornetts*, which contains twenty-one anonymous pieces in five parts and ten in six parts, largely taken from the court masque repertory. The music for masques was often provided by composers outside the court, so it is not surprising that a wait like Adson had access to it. His collection was dedicated to George Villiers, marquess of Buckingham (the unpopular favourite of James I and Charles I), who was a frequent participant in masques and may have sponsored the publication. A few pieces of Adson's own have survived in manuscript.

On 4 November 1633 Adson was sworn into a court place as a musician 'for the flute and cornet' (Ashbee, 73), being paid from the previous Michaelmas. A warrant dated 13 January 1636 to pay Adson 'for a treble cornett and a treble recorder by him provided and bought for his Majesty's service' (ibid., 85) shows that he was required to play the recorder and perhaps other wind instruments beyond those that his nominal place warranted.

Adson had ten children with at least two wives: on 26 February 1614 he was licensed to marry Jane Lanerie, and by 1629, after her death, he had taken his second wife, Anne. It was presumably on behalf of his eldest son, Islay or Islip (*bap.* 1615), that he petitioned the City of London's court of aldermen on 15 September 1634 'in regard of his charge in breeding up a son to perfection in voice, song and music for the City's service' (repertories of the court of aldermen, fol. 235) and was granted the proceeds of making someone a freeman of the city by redemption (£2 6s. 8d.). Another son, Roger (*bap.* 1621), was apprenticed to Ambrose Beeland, a fellow London wait and later a fellow royal musician.

Soon after he joined the court Adson ran into a conflict of loyalties. Many of the royal musicians and some independent musicians took part in James Shirley's masque *The Triumph of Peace*, presented jointly by the inns of court on 3 February 1634 at Whitehall and ten days later at Merchant Taylors' Hall. For the second performance Bulstrode Whitelocke, in overall charge of the music, chose the wind musicians ('loud music') from the Blackfriars and Cockpit theatres to fill two chariots for processions before and after the masque. The Blackfriars musicians consisted of six of the London waits, including Adson. In a letter to Whitelocke dated 12 February, the younger Nicholas Lanier, the master of the king's musick, claimed that the royal musicians had been excluded at the suggestion of Adson, whom he dubbed 'an unworthy fellow' (Sabol, 18–19). Whitelocke replied that he had 'thought the service was too mean' for the royal musicians and begged Lanier to 'take no dislike to Mr Adson upon this occasion'. In the event, Adson was one of the twelve court wind musicians who played in the processions.

Adson's association with the King's Company, who played at both the Blackfriars Theatre and the Globe Theatre, is confirmed by two references to him in the company's plays. He took the minor role of an invisible spirit in *The Late Lancashire Witches* by Thomas Heywood and Richard Brome (1634); and his music is referred to, in a playfully derogatory manner, in William Cavendish's *The Country Captain* (1639–40).

Adson died in London on 29 June 1640 and was buried the following day at St Giles Cripplegate, London, the church of the parish in which he had lived (on Redcross Street) since about 1615. He was survived by his second wife.

DAVID LASOCKI

Sources A. Ashbee, ed., *Records of English court music*, 3 (1988) · D. Lasocki, 'Professional recorder players in England, 1540–1740', PhD diss., University of Iowa, 1983 · repertories of the court of aldermen, CLRO, 48 · A. Sabol, 'New documents on Shirley's masque *The triumph of peace*', *Music and Letters*, 47 (1966), 10–26 · *IGI* ·

parish register, London, St Giles Cripplegate, 30 June 1640, GL [burial] · marriage licence, bishop of London marriage allegations, 26 Feb 1614, GL, MS 10, 105/5 [unnumbered fol.]

Archives Bodl. Oxf., MS Mus. sch D. 220 · FM Cam., MS MU 734, US-NH Filmer 3

Ady, Cecilia Mary (1881–1958), historian, was born on 28 November 1881 at Edgcote, Northamptonshire, the only child of the Revd (William) Henry Ady (d. 1915), rector of Edgcote and later of Charing, Kent, and Ockham, Surrey, and his wife, Julia Mary *Cartwright (1851–1924), who was a brilliant amateur historian who enjoyed a reputation as an art critic and biographer of such historical figures as Beatrice d'Este and Castiglione. Ady was privately educated at home at the rectory of Charing, under the tutelage of her mother, before entering Oxford in 1900 as a scholar at what was then St Hugh's Hall. She obtained a first in the honours school of modern history in 1903. At Oxford she was a pupil of Edward Armstrong, who fostered her interests in Italian studies and included her first book, *History of Milan under the Sforza* (1907), in his series, The States of Italy.

After travel in Italy and an interval at home, Ady became tutor in modern history at St Hugh's in 1909. From the beginning she took an active role in the governance of her college, being elected to the council for the first time in 1913 and becoming vice-principal for a term of three years in 1915. Her rise to positions of authority in her college derived, in part, from her position as protégée and confidante of its principal, Eleanor Jourdain, who addressed her in private letters with such terms of endearment as 'Baby Don' and 'mia cara Cecilia'. Ady's popularity with her pupils and leadership in the senior common room eventually led Miss Jourdain to perceive her as a rival. The clash of these two strong and ambitious personalities resulted in a 'row', that led to Ady's being dismissed from her tutorship in November 1923 with less than a week's notice. The prestige of St Hugh's was badly shaken by this dispute, which was the subject of an inquiry by Lord Curzon, the university chancellor. Ady was vindicated and subsequent constitutional changes brought self-government to the women's colleges at Oxford, placing women tutors in a position of independence comparable to that of their male counterparts. Refusing an offer from the University of Birmingham in 1924 Ady accepted the post of tutor to the Society of Home Students, returning to her college as research fellow in 1929. On her retirement in 1951 she was elected to an honorary fellowship. Her portrait, on the viewer's far right, in Henry Lamb's 'Conversation Piece', an oil of six St Hugh's fellows painted in 1936, captures at once Ady's commanding presence and her famous affability.

Throughout her long career at Oxford, Ady remained devoted to the study of the personalities and politics of the Italian Renaissance. The second book, *Pius II (Aeneas Silvius Piccolomini): the Humanist Pope* (1913), dedicated to 'My Mother', was a standard 'life and times' account which emulated her mother's method in its complete mastery of and copious quotation from literary sources. Ady's skill at broad synthesis was evidenced in 'Italy, 1250–1527', her chapter in the collection of essays, mainly by women history dons, *Italy, Mediaeval and Modern* (1917). In 1929 she published *A History of Modern Italy, 1871–1915*, a translation of the work by Benedetto Croce, and, ever loyal to her friend and mentor, edited a posthumous collection of Edward Armstrong's *Italian Studies* (1934). Her capacity for clear summary was shown in the chapter entitled 'Florence and north Italy, 1414–1492', in volume 8 of the *Cambridge Medieval History* (1936). During the early 1930s Ady spent much of her leisure time conducting archival and manuscript research in Italy, especially Bologna, which resulted in her only solid historical monograph, *The Bentivoglio of Bologna: a Study in Despotism* (1937). The publication of this distinguished work caused Oxford University to confer on her the degree of DLitt in 1938. Perhaps most revealing of her approach to the Italian Renaissance was her Annual Italian Lecture read before the British Academy, 'Morals and manners of the Quattrocento', which celebrated the great 'opportunity for self-expression' of the Italian ruling families as comparable to England's country gentry before the first Reform Bill (see *PBA*, 28, 1942, 179).

After leaving St Hugh's College in 1923, Ady established her home in Oxford at 40 St Margaret's Road, where she kept an open door for friends, fellow dons, and old pupils. The product of a devout home, she was a moderate Anglo-Catholic churchwoman, took an active role in the affairs of her diocese, and wrote on the role of women in the church as well as historical studies on church organization. In post-war Oxford she regularly offered 'The Italian Renaissance' as a special subject, while she continued her work of popularization with *Lorenzo Dei Medici and Renaissance Italy* (1955), published in the Teach Yourself History series. In her mature years she supervised the theses of a number of postgraduates, men and women, several of whom became leading historians of the Italian Renaissance in the second half of the twentieth century. These pupils, along with fellow dons, contributed a brilliant collection of essays, *Italian Renaissance Studies* (1960), which had been planned in her honour and was dedicated to her memory after her death at St Luke's Nursing Home, 20 Linton Road, Oxford, on 27 March 1958. Her most immediate legacy was a bequest of £10,000 for the salary of the chaplain at St Hugh's. But her larger influence was as one of the founders of the school of Italian Renaissance studies that flourished in the United Kingdom in the decades after her death. BENJAMIN G. KOHL

Sources P. Griffin, ed., *St Hugh's: one hundred years of women's education in Oxford* (1986) · 'Cecilia Ady', *Oxford Magazine* (1 May 1958), 392, 394 · J. R. Hale, 'Biographical note', *Italian Renaissance studies: a tribute to the late Cecilia M. Ady*, ed. E. F. Jacob (1960), 484–7 · V. M. Brittain, *The women at Oxford: a fragment of history* (1960) · A. Emanuel, 'Cecilia Mary Ady', *An encyclopedia of British women writers* (1988), 1–2 · *The Times* (28 March 1958) · *The Times* (3 April 1958) · *The Times* (7 April 1958) · J. R. Hale, 'In memoriam: Cecilia M. Ady', *Italian Studies*, 14 (1959), 105 · J. M. C. Ady, *A bright remembrance: the diaries of Julia Cartwright*, ed. A. Emanuel (1989) · b. cert. · will, 17 Aug 1954 · CGPLA Eng. & Wales (1958) · B. G. Kohl, 'Cecilia M. Ady, the Edwardian education of an historian of Renaissance Italy', *The Victorian and Edwardian response to the Italian Renaissance*, ed. J. E. Law and L. Ostermark-Johansen [forthcoming]

Archives Northants. RO, Delapre Abbey, diaries · St Hugh's College, Oxford, archives | Northants. RO, Cartwright of Edgcote papers

Likenesses H. Lamb, group portrait, oils, 1936 (*Conversation piece*), St Hugh's College, Oxford · H. A. Freeth, charcoal sketches, c.1940, St Hugh's College, Oxford · photographs, St Hugh's College, Oxford; repr. in Griffin, ed., *St Hugh's*

Wealth at death £68,210 1s. 0d.: probate, 21 May 1958, *CGPLA Eng. & Wales*

Ady, Joseph (1775/6–1852), fraudster, was the son of John Ady (1743/4–1812), a recording clerk for the Society of Friends. He was a hatter, hosier, and accountant at various times, in premises at 11 The Circus, Minories, London, and 6 Charlotte Street, Wapping. Failing in business, he devised a means of extracting money from the credulous. He would look up the lists of unclaimed inheritances, dividends, and bequests, and then write, without stamping his letters, to any people of those names that he could find, offering to produce 'something to their advantage' on payment of 20s. Specimens of his letters are given in Boase, *Modern English Biography* (1892). In 1833 the lord mayor of London issued a general warning about his activities, and the court of aldermen directed that measures be taken against him; but it was difficult to identify a specific crime. An amendment to the Post Office Act ruled that unstamped letters must be returned to sender, but Ady circumvented the ruling by devising a system of marking the envelopes to make it appear that the stamps had come off in the post. On 7 February 1835 he was sentenced to seven years' transportation, later commuted to one year in a house of correction, for obtaining money (a sovereign) under false pretences. In 1851 he was again imprisoned for a similar offence, but was released early on grounds of failing health. He died at his brother's house, 89 Fenchurch Street, London, on 17 July 1852, and was buried on 23 July in the Quaker burial-ground in Whitechapel.

THOMPSON COOPER, rev. J. GILLILAND

Sources GM, 2nd ser., 38 (1852), 437 · T. De Quincey, *De Quincey's works*, 14 vols. (1854–60), vol. 6, pp. 258, 327 · Boase, *Mod. Eng. biog.* · H. Buckler, *Central criminal court minutes of evidence* (1835), 1.646–52

Archives W. Sussex RO, letters to duke of Richmond

Adye, James Pattison (1783–1831). *See under* Adye, Stephen Payne (d. 1794).

Adye, Sir John Miller (1819–1900), army officer, was born at Sevenoaks, Kent, on 1 November 1819, the son of Major James Pattison Adye, Royal Artillery, and Jane, daughter of J. Mortimer Kelson of Sevenoaks. His grandfather Major Stephen Payne *Adye, Royal Artillery, had three sons in the regiment. John Adye entered the Royal Military Academy, Woolwich, in February 1834. He passed out at the head of his batch, and was commissioned second lieutenant in the Royal Artillery on 13 December 1836. Serving successively in Malta, Ireland, and England, he was promoted first lieutenant in July 1839, second captain in July 1846, and captain in April 1852. He commanded the artillery at the Tower of London during the 1848 Chartist threat.

In May 1854, on the outbreak of the Crimean War, Adye

Sir John Miller Adye (1819–1900), by Maclure & Macdonald, pubd 1882 (after Fradelle)

went to Turkey as brigade major of artillery. He was made a brevet major on 22 September, and became assistant adjutant-general of artillery. He was present with the headquarter staff at Alma, Balaklava, and Inkerman, and served throughout the siege of Sevastopol, remaining in the Crimea until June 1856. He was mentioned in dispatches, and made brevet lieutenant-colonel on 12 December 1854 and CB on 5 July 1855. He received the Mejidiye (fourth class) and the Légion d'honneur (third class). Adye married in 1856 Mary Cordelia, daughter of Admiral Sir Montague Stopford. They had several children; their eldest son, John, became a Royal Artillery colonel.

In July 1857, during the Indian mutiny, Adye was sent to India as assistant adjutant-general of artillery. He arrived at Cawnpore on 21 November to find that Sir Colin Campbell had already left for the relief of Lucknow, and that the Gwalior contingent was advancing upon Cawnpore. He took part in the actions fought there by Major-General Charles Ash Windham on the 26th and following days, and afterwards wrote *The Defence of Cawnpore* (1858). He was present at the battle of 6 December, in which the Gwalior contingent was routed by Sir Colin Campbell after his return from Lucknow. His administrative duties then compelled Adye to return to Calcutta, and he saw no more fighting during the mutiny. He was mentioned in dispatches, and became regimental lieutenant-colonel on 29 August 1857 and brevet colonel on 19 May 1860.

From May 1859 Adye commanded the artillery in the Madras presidency. He was deputy adjutant-general of artillery in India from March 1863 until 1868, and implemented the amalgamation of the three East India Company regiments of artillery with the Royal Artillery, which required patience and tact. In November 1863 he joined the commander-in-chief, Sir Hugh Rose, at Lahore, and was sent by him to the Ambela valley, where the progress of General Chamberlain's expedition against the Sitana fanatics was blocked. Adye, accompanied by Major F. S. Roberts, was to report on the situation. He was present at the action of 15 December which finally dispersed the Sitana warriors, and at the burning of Mulka a week later. He was mentioned in dispatches.

After nine years of Indian service Adye returned to England. He had formed strong views, which he frequently expressed, on the importance of trusting the people of India and admitting them to high office, civil and military. He believed in a frontier policy of conciliation and subsidies. He became regimental colonel on 6 July 1867.

On 1 April 1870 Adye was appointed director of artillery and stores, and has been blamed for the failure of the British artillery to match foreign artillery improvements. He believed in wrought-iron muzzle-loaders and succeeded in retaining them while he held office. However, he supported Cardwell's reforms, and when they were criticized by John Holms, Liberal MP for Hackney, Adye replied in a pamphlet, *The British Army in 1875* (1876).

In autumn 1872, with Colonel Charles George Gordon, Adye reported on the British cemeteries in the Crimea. He was made KCB on 24 May 1873, and promoted major-general on 17 November 1875 and lieutenant-general in 1879.

On 1 August 1875 Adye became governor of the Royal Military Academy, Woolwich. He participated in the public controversy over Russian expansion towards India and British relations with Afghanistan. He minimized the Russian threat, and advocated the conciliation of Afghanistan while opposing frontier changes. He replied (in October 1878) to Sir James Fitzjames Stephen's letters in *The Times* in support of the forward policy, and in December printed for private circulation a pamphlet entitled *England, Russia, and Afghanistan*.

When Gladstone returned to office in 1880, Adye was appointed (1 June) surveyor-general of the ordnance. Gladstone wrote of the military members of the Commons that Adye was 'better than any now there' (Gladstone, 9.549). Nevertheless Adye failed to find a seat in parliament. In August 1882 he accompanied Wolseley to Egypt as chief of the staff, with the temporary rank of general, and contributed to the success of the campaign. He was mentioned in dispatches (*London Gazette*, 8 Sept and 6 Oct 1882), and received the thanks of parliament, the GCB, and the grand cross of the Mejidiye.

Adye returned to the War Office in October 1882, but left at the end of the year to become governor of Gibraltar. There he tried to reconcile the dual interests of a fortress and a commercial city, relaxed some of the military restrictions on trade, and provided recreation rooms for the garrison. He remained there nearly four years, and retired on 1 November 1886. He published at various dates

several pamphlets and books, including *Recollections of a Military Life* (1895), which contained autobiographical reminiscences illustrated by his own sketches, Adye being an excellent artist. He became general on 20 November 1884, and a colonel-commandant in the Royal Artillery on 4 November 1881. He was also honorary colonel, from 6 May 1870, of the 3rd Kent artillery volunteers and the 3rd volunteer battalion, Royal West Kent regiment. Adye died on 26 August 1900 at Cragside, Rothbury, Northumberland, while on a visit to his son-in-law, Lord Armstrong.

E. M. LLOYD, rev. JAMES LUNT

Sources J. M. Adye, *Recollections of a military life* (1895) · J. M. Adye, *The defeat of Cawnpore* (1858) · J. M. Adye, *Review of the Crimean war to the winter of 1854–55* (1860) · J. Adye, *Sitana: a mountain campaign on the borders of Afghanistan in 1863* (1867) · *The Times* (27 Aug 1900) · *Hart's Army List* (1897) · Gladstone, *Diaries* · d. cert.
Archives Royal Artillery Institution, Woolwich, London, papers | Balliol Oxf., letters to Sir Robert Morier · BL, memoranda and corresp. with W. E. Gladstone, Add. MSS 44129–44500 · BL, corresp. with G. D. Ramsay, Add. MS 46448
Likenesses photograph, 1880–89, The Convent, Gibraltar · Maclure & Macdonald, print, pubd 1882 (after photograph by Fradelle), NPG [*see illus.*]
Wealth at death £12,458 19s. 5d.: probate, 24 Oct 1900, *CGPLA Eng. & Wales*

Adye, Ralph Willett (*bap.* 1764, *d.* 1804). See under Adye, Stephen Payne (*d.* 1794).

Adye, Stephen Galway (1773–1838). See under Adye, Stephen Payne (*d.* 1794).

Adye, Stephen Payne (*d.* 1794), army officer and writer on military justice, entered the Royal Military Academy, Woolwich, as a cadet in June 1757, and was appointed second lieutenant in the Royal Artillery in September 1762; he was promoted first lieutenant in May 1766, captain lieutenant in March 1773, and captain in June 1780. After the Seven Years' War he was on the staff of James Pattison in Portugal. He had married by 1764; no details of his wife are known other than that her first name was Elizabeth.

During the 1760s Adye served as deputy judge-advocate-general in North America, where he prepared a *Treatise on Courts-Martial, to which is Added an Essay on Military Punishments and Rewards*, published in New York and then in London in 1769. It went through several editions and, modified by later editors, became the standard work for military judicial practice in the late eighteenth and early nineteenth centuries, although John Williamson's *Elements of Military Arrangement* (1782) is held to be more informative regarding contemporary procedure. Adye was more interested in precedent and the evolution of military law than current practice in military trials. He compared military justice favourably with that in civilian courts, pointing out that a soldier convicted of a petty crime was more likely to receive corporal than capital punishment. He stressed the advantages a general court martial had over a jury trial, emphasizing the time restrictions under which juries suffered, whereas a general court martial endured no limitations on their deliberations and could convict or acquit by majority verdict. For Adye, all soldiers, whether officers or rank and file, were equal, and a court martial could be compared to a trial of a peer in the House of Lords.

Adye was a brigade-major of artillery during the American War of Independence. He was aide-de-camp to General Pattison when in command of the Royal Artillery in New York, and a 'most able and energetic staff officer' (Duncan, 1.326). Adye retired in May 1790 and in January 1793 was appointed to command a company of invalid artillery on Jersey, where he died on 24 March 1794.

Adye's family was distinguished in the Royal Artillery for more than a century. He had three sons in the regiment. The eldest, **Ralph Willett Adye** (bap. 1764, d. 1804), was baptized on 5 December 1764 at St Mary the Virgin at the Walls, Colchester, Essex. He was commissioned second lieutenant in January 1781 and promoted captain in April 1801, and wrote *The Bombardier and Pocket Gunner* (1798 and many editions), a standard work. He died at Gibraltar on 22 October 1804. The second son was **Stephen Galway Adye** (1773–1838), who joined the Royal Artillery as a cadet in August 1788, was promoted second lieutenant in April 1793, captain in May 1803, and lieutenant-colonel in December 1814. He served in Egypt in 1801, on the 1809 Walcheren expedition, and in the Peninsular War, and commanded the artillery of the first division at Waterloo. He was promoted colonel in July 1825 and major-general in January 1837, and was made a CB. In August 1825 he was appointed a member of the ordnance select committee. From June 1835 he was director of the Royal Laboratory, Woolwich, and he supervised the London firework display for the 1838 coronation. He died at his Woolwich residence on 13 September 1838, survived by his wife.

The third son, **James Pattison Adye** (1783–1831), joined the Royal Artillery as a cadet in March 1797, and proceeded second lieutenant in August 1799, captain in December 1814, and brevet major in August 1819. On 16 June 1817 he married Jane Kelson at Sevenoaks, Kent. He died near Naples on 26 October 1831. One of his surviving sons was Sir John Miller *Adye (1819–1900).

H. M. CHICHESTER, rev. ROGER T. STEARN

Sources J. Kane, *List of officers of the royal regiment of artillery from the year 1716 to the year 1899*, rev. W. H. Askwith, 4th edn (1900) · F. Duncan, *History of the royal regiment of artillery*, 2 vols. (1879) · O. F. J. Hogg, *The royal arsenal: its background, origin, and subsequent history*, 2 vols. (1963) · R. Muir, *Tactics and the experience of battle in the age of Napoleon* (1998) · H. Strachan, *From Waterloo to Balaclava: tactics, technology and the British army, 1815–1854* (1985) · A. J. Guy, ed., *The road to Waterloo: the British army and the struggle against revolutionary and Napoleonic France, 1793–1815* (1990) · *GM*, 2nd ser., 10 (1838), 659 · A. N. Gilbert, 'British military law, discipline and the conduct of regimental courts martial in the later eighteenth century', *EngHR*, 102 (1987), 859–86 · A. N. Gilbert, 'Military and civilian justice in eighteenth-century England: an assessment', *Journal of British Studies*, 17 (1978), 41–65 · *IGI*

Æbbe [St Æbbe, Ebba] (d. **683**?), abbess of Coldingham, was the daughter of Acha, queen of Northumbria, and uterine sister of kings *Oswald and *Oswiu. According to late and unverifiable traditions preserved mainly in a life ascribed to the twelfth-century hagiographer Reginald of Durham, after a period of exile in Scotland she received the veil from Bishop Finan of Lindisfarne (d. 661). Bede relates in his *Historia ecclesiastica* that she was abbess of the double monastery of 'Urbs Coludi' (identified as Coldingham in Berwickshire) by c.672, when Æthelthryth, her nephew King Ecgfrith's queen, took the veil there at the hands of the Northumbrian bishop Wilfrid. Like her niece, Abbess Ælfflæd, of Whitby, Æbbe was a friend of Cuthbert, who visited her at Coldingham when he was prior of Melrose. Unlike Ælfflæd, however, she was then also on good terms with Wilfrid, who, according to his biographer Stephen of Ripon (Eddius Stephanus), was released from his imprisonment on his return from Rome c.681 at her request.

The double monastery of Coldingham, although undoubtedly an important royal foundation, had acquired an unsavoury reputation by the 730s. According to Bede, during the rule of Æbbe its inmates, with the single exception of an austere Irishman called Adomnán, were given over to the worldly pleasures of feasting and drinking, gossip, fine clothing, and sexual indulgence. Adomnán, who had been told in a vision that the monastery would be destroyed by fire as a punishment for these lapses, eventually transmitted the warning to Æbbe herself, who apparently enforced a more penitential regime while she was abbess. After her death, however, the inmates returned to their old ways and the monastery was duly burnt and apparently abandoned. The date of these events is uncertain, but clearly they happened well before the 730s when Bede was writing, since they were related to him by a priest who had been an inmate of Coldingham long before. According to Reginald's life, Æbbe died in 683, and the positioning of the Coldingham material in Bede's *Historia ecclesiastica* is compatible with such a date.

It is not clear when or where Æbbe's cult began. Although the aftermath of her rule would seem unpropitious to its development, it should be remembered that Bede's standards were not necessarily those of his contemporaries, and that the way of life which he condemned at Coldingham may have been far from unusual in royal proprietary houses. At all events the cult was sufficiently established and sufficiently early to give the abbess's name to St Abb's Head at Coldingham, where Kirk Hill has been identified as the site of Urbs Coludi, and to Ebchester (in what is now co. Durham), where Reginald claimed Æbbe also established a community. In the earlier eleventh century Alfred, son of Westou, guardian of St Cuthbert's shrine, claimed to have brought relics of St Æbbe to Durham, where they were reputed to rest with the body of St Cuthbert.

According to Reginald's life, long after her death Æbbe's relics were discovered by shepherds at the ancient site of 'Urbs Coludi', and translated to a stone sarcophagus on the south side of the altar of the church of St Mary at Coldingham. These events apparently postdated the establishment there of monks from Durham in the early twelfth century. Later, perhaps in an attempt to revive interest in the cult, the monks opened the tomb and translated the remains to a new shrine on the altar. From 1188, however, the cult became centred on an oratory built at 'Urbs Coludi', the construction of which the saint herself had ordered in a vision to a simple layman.

Æbbe's feast day, 25 August, occurs only in some post-conquest calendars, including one from Durham, to which it was added in a thirteenth-century hand. The **Ebba** (*supp. fl.* 870) whom Roger Wendover and Matthew Paris named as abbess of Coldingham when the house was sacked by vikings about 870 is entirely unhistorical.

ALAN THACKER

Sources Bede, *Hist. eccl.*, 4.19, 25 · E. Stephanus, *The life of Bishop Wilfrid*, ed. and trans. B. Colgrave (1927) · B. Colgrave, ed. and trans., *Two lives of Saint Cuthbert* (1940) · 'De sancta Ebba virgine et abbatissa', *Nova legenda Anglie, as collected by John of Tynemouth, J. Capgrave, and others*, ed. C. Horstman, 1 (1901), 303–8 · Symeon of Durham, *Opera*, vol. 1 · F. Wormald, ed., *English Benedictine kalendars after AD 1100*, 1, HBS, 77 (1939) · W. Blew, ed., *Breviarium Aberdonense*, 2 vols., Maitland Club, 70 (1854) · Bodl. Oxf., MS Fairfax 6
Archives Bodl. Oxf., MS Fairfax 6

Áed Allán mac Fergaile (d. **743**), high-king of Ireland, perhaps ruled Cenél nEógain from the death of his father, *Fergal mac Máele Dúin, in 722 until his own death in 743; he was high-king from 734 until his death, in succession to his northern rival, Flaithbertach mac Loingsig of Cenél Conaill (d. 765). Áed Allán's mother is said to have been a daughter of Ernán (or Ernaine) of Cenél Conaill; his son, Máel Dúin, was also king of Cenél nEógain, but not high-king of Ireland.

Áed Allán was principally responsible for establishing Cenél nEógain as the leading Uí Néill dynasty of north-western Ireland just as Clann Cholmáin was emerging as the main Uí Néill power in the midlands. From his reign until the tenth century the high-kingship alternated between Cenél nEógain in the north-west and Clann Cholmáin in the midlands. The shift in the balance of power in the north-west was mainly achieved by the conquest, at the expense of Cenél Conaill, of a sub-kingdom known as Mag nÍtha, now the valley of the River Finn in Donegal. This expansion was achieved by hard fighting during the 730s; it made it much more difficult for Cenél Conaill to maintain good communications between its main territory around the modern town of Donegal (Tír nÁeda) and its lands lying along the north coast of Donegal as far east as Lough Swilly. A corollary of the conquest of Mag nÍtha was that the Uí Néill sub-kingdom of Cenél nÉndai, in the area around Raphoe (Donegal), shifted from Cenél Conaill to Cenél nEógain overlordship.

Once Áed Allán was high-king he reinforced the ability of a northern Uí Néill overlord to strike at midland rivals within the Uí Néill and at traditional enemies in Leinster by winning a decisive battle in 735 at Faughart (co. Louth), against Áed Rón, king of the Ulstermen, and the latter's ally and neighbour, Conchad mac Cuanach, king of Mag Coba (western Down). This battle detached the Conailli Muirthemne of what is now co. Louth from the province of Ulster and gave Cenél nEógain a territorial foothold on the east coast at the north-eastern corner of the midland plain. As a result, the Airgialla people of the modern counties of Armagh, Monaghan, Londonderry, and Tyrone came to be dominated mainly by Cenél nEógain, and with them came the alliance between Cenél nEógain and the church of Armagh. For the next two centuries Cenél

nEógain's fortunes and those of the heirs of Patrick of Armagh were closely intertwined. The first major illustration of this connection is the successive record in the annals of two events in 737: first, a meeting between Áed Allán and Cathal mac Finguini, king of Munster (d. 742), at the monastery of Terryglass (Tír dá Glas), close to the frontier between Munster and the Uí Néill; and second the proclamation of the law of Patrick throughout Ireland. In the next year, 738, Áed Allán's victory at the battle of Áth Senaig was to avenge his father's death in 722 at the hands of the Leinstermen; the annals of Ulster, in a fit of eloquence unique for the period, declared that 'in that battle more died than we have discovered to have been laid low in past ages in a single attack and fallen in ferocious conflict'. This was the culmination of Áed Allán's achievement. He was killed five years later, in 743, by the king of Clann Cholmáin, Domnall mac Murchada, who thereby became high-king of Ireland. The battle is placed by some annals in what is now co. Longford, which suggests that Áed Allán was attacking Uí Néill neighbours, and probable allies, of Clann Cholmáin.   T. M. CHARLES-EDWARDS

Sources W. Stokes, ed., 'The annals of Tigernach [8 pts]', *Revue Celtique*, 16 (1895), 374–419; 17 (1896), 6–33, 119–263, 337–420; 18 (1897), 9–59, 150–97, 267–303, 374–91; pubd sep. (1993) · *Ann. Ulster* · M. C. Dobbs, ed. and trans., 'The Ban-shenchus [3 pts]', *Revue Celtique*, 47 (1930), 283–339; 48 (1931), 163–234; 49 (1932), 437–89 · W. M. Hennessy, ed. and trans., *Chronicum Scotorum: a chronicle of Irish affairs*, Rolls Series, 46 (1866) · M. A. O'Brien, ed., *Corpus genealogiarum Hiberniae* (Dublin, 1962) · K. Meyer, ed., 'The Laud genealogies and tribal histories', *Zeitschrift für Celtische Philologie*, 8 (1910–12), 291–338 · F. J. Byrne, *Irish kings and high-kings* (1973)

Aed Find (d. **778**). See under Dál Riata, kings of (act. c.500–c.850).

Áed mac Bricc (d. **589**). See under Meath, saints of (act. c.400–c.900).

Áed mac Caírthinn. See Mac Caírthinn mac Cainnig (d. 506) under Ulster, saints of (act. c.400–c.650).

Áed mac Néill [Áed Findliath mac Néill] (d. **879**), high-king of Ireland, was the son of *Niall mac Áeda (d. 846), king of Ailech and high-king of Ireland, and Gormflaith (d. 861), daughter of Donnchad mac Domnaill, king of Meath and high-king of Ireland. Áed was a dynast of Cenél nEógain, of the Uí Néill confederation, and resided both at his ancestral fortress of Ailech and at Armagh. Although famous in later ages for his piety, he was an astute player of the political games of his time.

The earliest notice of Áed is in the year 855 (by which time he was already king of Ailech) when he and his brother Flaithbertach raided the Ulaid kingdoms, on the north-east coast. The following year he faced an invasion of his own lands by a band of Gallgoídil (Norse-Irish), which he defeated with heavy losses at Glenelly (Tyrone). His growing power alarmed the high-king Máel Sechnaill mac Máele Ruanaid who made a show of strength in 860 by leading an expedition to Áed's lands with troops drawn from the four quarters of Ireland, camping at Mag nDumai, near Armagh. A night raid on the high-king's forces by Áed and his nephew Flann mac Conaing of Síl nÁeda Sláine failed to force Máel Sechnaill to withdraw. In retaliation Áed raided Máel Sechnaill's lands in 861 and 862 with the support of his viking son-in-law *Olaf the White of Dublin.

After the death of Máel Sechnaill, in 862 or 863, Áed gained the high-kingship. He demonstrated his ability to protect his supporters in 864 by blinding a neighbouring prince in punishment for an attack on the lands of his nephew Flann. That same year, to ensure recognition of his supremacy throughout the north, he attacked and defeated his old enemies the Ulaid at Uriel (Louth). By 866 Áed's alliance with the vikings had ended and the hostilities erupted into open warfare when he destroyed all the viking settlements in the north, from Donegal to Antrim. In 868 another alliance ended tragically in the battle of Killineer (near Drogheda, Louth) when Áed put down a revolt by his kinsman Flann mac Conaing, who died in the fighting. Flann had been aided by troops from Dublin and Leinster, which led Áed to begin the campaigns in the south-east that would occupy him in the last decade of his reign. He now had a new ally, Cerball mac Dúnlainge, the king of Osraige and the brother of Áed's queen, Land. In 870 the brothers-in-law raided Leinster from Dublin as far as Gowran (Kilkenny); and in 874 Áed devastated Killashee (near Naas). A legend claims that Áed practised political assassination on the expedition of 870, when he was the host of a banquet at Dublin for the viking chieftains, during which they were slain.

The last years of Áed's life were troubled by increasing dissatisfaction among his subjects. To forestall rebellion among the Ulaid in 871 the *lethrí* ('joint king') Cathalán was slain on Áed's orders. There was disquiet among the Uí Néill themselves, and the Óenach Tailten (fair of Teltown, Meath), over which the high-king presided by right of his office, was not celebrated in 873, 876, or 878. Áed died on 20 November 879 at Dromiskin (Louth) and he was buried at Armagh. He had two known wives: Máel Muire (*d*. 913), the daughter of the Scottish king Cináed mac Alpín [*see* Kenneth I], whose son was the high-king *Niall mac Áeda (Niall Glúndub); and Land, daughter of Dúngal mac Fergaile of Osraige. His son Máel Duin, who ruled Ailech on his father's behalf, died in 867. His daughter Eithne (*d*. 917) became the queen of *Flann Sinna, Áed's successor as high-king, and was also married to Máel Ciaráin mac Rónáin and Flannacán mac Cellaig of Brega. Two other sons were Domnall, who became king of Ailech and died in religious retirement in 915, and Máel Dub who was revered as a saint.   BENJAMIN T. HUDSON

Sources Ann. Ulster · J. N. Radner, ed., *Fragmentary annals of Ireland* (1978) · M. C. Dobbs, ed. and trans., 'The Ban-shenchus [3 pts]', *Revue Celtique*, 47 (1930), 283–339; 48 (1931), 163–234; 49 (1932), 437–89 · J. H. Todd, ed. and trans., *Cogadh Gaedhel re Gallaibh / The war of the Gaedhil with the Gaill*, Rolls Series, 48 (1867) · K. Meyer, 'Das Ende von Baile in Scáil', *Zeitschrift für Celtische Philologie*, 12 (1918), 232–8 · M. A. O'Brien, ed., *Corpus genealogiarum Hiberniae* (Dublin, 1962) · E. Hogan, *Onomasticon Goedelicum* (1910) · S. Mac Airt, ed. and trans., *The annals of Inisfallen* (1951) · W. M. Hennessy, ed. and trans., *Chronicum Scotorum: a chronicle of Irish affairs*, Rolls Series, 46 (1866) · AFM · F. J. Byrne, *Irish kings and high-kings* (1987) · D. Ó Corráin, *Ireland before the Normans* (1972) · T. W. Moody and others, eds., *A new history of Ireland, 9: Maps, genealogies, lists* (1984)

Áed Oirdnide mac Néill (*d*. 819), high-king of Ireland, was the son of *Niall Frossach (*d*. 778); he was king of Cenél nEogain and subsequently the last king of Tara (high-king) before the viking attacks began to accelerate. In his rule can be seen a further development of the military power of the Uí Néill already visible in the reign of his predecessor and rival, *Donnchad mac Domnaill of Cland Cholmáin.

Donnchad mac Domnaill, father of Áed's queen Euginis, died in 797, probably early in the year. His authority, at its height in the 780s, was beginning to decline when Áed Oirdnide made his first attempt to assert his military prestige further south. In 794 he attacked the minor kingdom of Mugdorna Maigen, around Domnach Maigen (now Donaghmoyne to the north of Carrickmacross, co. Monaghan). If he could establish his power in this area, he would find it easier to influence the church of Armagh, by now a traditional ally of his lineage. In 789 Dub dá Leithe, abbot of Armagh, had brought some of the most precious relics of his church to an assembly, probably that of Tailtiu; Donnchad mac Domnaill, an ally of the *familia* of Columba, rather than that of Armagh's Patrick, publicly dishonoured both abbot and relics at Ráith Airthir, the royal fort nearby. Some years later, Áed Oirdnide would work closely with Dub dá Leithe's son, Condmach, when he, in turn, became abbot of Armagh. Donnchad's death in 797 was rapidly followed by Áed's victory over his sons and their allies in a battle in Brega, just to the south of Tailtiu and within a mile or two of the place where Dub dá Leithe and the relics of Armagh were dishonoured. Later the same year Áed ravaged Mide, the heartland of Cland Cholmáin power, and the annals of Ulster date his reign as high-king of Ireland from that second expedition, not from his victory earlier in the year. The principal rival dynasty from among the Uí Néill had first to be compelled to submit.

The strength of Áed Oirdnide's authority as high-king is illustrated by two very different achievements. The first was the absence of any major viking attacks on Ireland during his reign after 798; the second was his ability to divide and rule. In 802, immediately after the death of Donnchad mac Domnaill's brother, Muiredach, king of Mide, Áed led an army into Mide and divided it between two sons of Donnchad, Ailill and Conchobor. In 804 Áed harried Leinster; military aggression was followed in the same year by a demonstration of ecclesiastical power: the synods of the Uí Néill met at Dún Cuair, a fort just to the north of the Leinster frontier under the presidency of Condmach, son of Dub dá Leithe. The activities of 804 were followed the next year by Áed's division of Leinster between two rivals, both from within the ruling Uí Dúnlainge.

The scale of Áed Oirdnide's military achievements were signalled by an unprecedented reaction. In 808 Conchobor mac Donnchada, by now established as the king of Mide, brought an army of the Connachta, led by their king Muirgus mac Tommaltaig, to challenge the authority of the high-king. The Connachta had not intervened within the territory of the Uí Néill since the sixth century. The annalist, unusually, shows his sympathy when he records that 'after three nights they fled in haste, and Áed son of Niall moved to meet them, and he burnt the borderlands of Mide, and their flight was compared with that of goats and kids' (*Ann. Ulster*, s.a. 808).

There were no more challenges to Áed Oirdnide's secular authority. Opposition was, however, voiced by two influential monastic communities. The first was the notably ascetic monastery of Tallaght in northern Leinster. In 811 the community of Tallaght prevented the holding of the assembly and fair of Tailtiu, 'so that there arrived neither horse nor chariot on the part of Áed mac Néill' (*Ann. Ulster*, s.a. 811); the precinct of Tallaght had been invaded by the Uí Néill, and it required many gifts to undo the insult.

Áed Oirdnide also fell foul of the Columban federation. In 817 the annals of Ulster have two entries, formally independent but presumably parts of a single transaction. In the first they record the killing of the head of Raphoe, a church next door to the home kingdom of Áed Oirdnide, but which looked to Adomnán, abbot of Iona and member of the Cenél Conaill, as its founder, and thus part of the community of Columba. That community, therefore, 'went to Tara to excommunicate Áed'. An offence committed in the north-west, the home of both offender and victim, was penalized by an excommunication pronounced at Tara, symbol of a secular overkingship, in the eastern midlands and more than 100 miles from Raphoe.

These episodes do not imply a consistent pattern by which relations with churches other than Armagh were cool if not hostile. If sources of uncertain date and authority are to be believed, Áed Oirdnide freed the churches of Ireland from military service, perhaps on the occasion of the meeting of the synods at Dún Cuair in 804. He is said to have done this at the request of 'Fothad of the Scriptures', a renowned exegete. There is also the matter of Áed's own by-name, Oirdnide. The obvious translation, 'ordained', may give a misleading impression. The term 'ordain' was used for any act by which a person's status was enhanced, whether that was a secular or a religious act, such as a blessing or an anointing. Áed was given this by-name in the king-lists, but it does not occur in the contemporary entries in the annals of Ulster. On the other hand, Áed Oirdnide was the contemporary of Charlemagne, there were contacts both ecclesiastical and secular between Francia and Ireland, and innovation in forms of royal or imperial inauguration was the order of the day. Moreover, a king of Munster of the same period may have had some form of ecclesiastical inauguration.

Áed Oirdnide mac Néill died in 819, reputedly at Áth dá Ferta in Conailli Muirthemne (modern co. Louth); there is no record of his burial place. His wife Euginis had died in 802.   T. M. CHARLES-EDWARDS

Sources W. Stokes, ed., 'The annals of Tigernach [8 pts]', *Revue Celtique*, 16 (1895), 374–419; 17 (1896), 6–33, 119–263, 337–420; 18 (1897), 9–59, 150–97, 267–303, 374–91; pubd sep. (1993) • *Ann. Ulster* • M. C. Dobbs, ed. and trans., 'The Ban-shenchus [3 pts]', *Revue Celtique*, 47 (1930), 283–339; 48 (1931), 163–234; 49 (1932), 437–89 • R. I. Best and others, eds., *The Book of Leinster, formerly Lebar na Núachongbála*, 6 vols. (1954–83), vol. 3, pp. 613–21 • W. M. Hennessy, ed. and trans., *Chronicum Scotorum: a chronicle of Irish affairs*, Rolls Series, 46 (1866) • M. A. O'Brien, ed., *Corpus genealogiarum Hiberniae* (Dublin, 1962) • K. Meyer, ed., 'The Laud genealogies and tribal histories', *Zeitschrift für Celtische Philologie*, 8 (1912), 291–338 • F. J. Byrne, *Irish kings and high-kings* (1973)

Áed Sláine mac Diarmata (*d.* 604), joint high-king of Ireland, was the son of *Diarmait mac Cerbaill (*d.* 565), high-king of Ireland, and of Mugain, daughter of Conchrad (or Conrí) mac Duach. His epithet means 'of Slane' (in Meath, on the River Boyne above Newgrange). He was the eponymous ancestor of Síl nÁeda Sláine ('the seed of Áed Sláine'), a dynasty based around Knowth and Lagore. For a few generations Síl nÁeda Sláine was regularly in a position of overlordship among the Uí Néill dynasties, but by the mid-eighth century it had been eclipsed by its southern Uí Néill rivals, Clann Cholmáin, which traced its lineage to Áed Sláine's brother, Colmán Mór (*d.* 555 or 558). In both of the chronicle entries referring to Áed Sláine he is seen in conflict with this brother's progeny. A third brother, Colmán Bec (*d.* 587), gave rise to a less prominent dynasty.

A medieval tale sympathetic to Síl nÁeda Sláine (though set down centuries after Áed's time) describes his birth. His mother became pregnant through drinking holy water. She bore a lamb, and then, falling pregnant again the same way, a fish (both are symbols of Christ). On the third occasion, she bore Áed Sláine. Of him St Finnian prophesied, 'he will surpass his brethren and more kings will come from him than from the sons of others' (Rayner).

The life of St Columba, written by Adomnán about 700, tells of a prophecy made by Columba: he warned that Áed should never commit the crime of kin slaying, lest he lose the prerogative of the kingship of all Ireland which had been predestined for him by God; rather, he would rule only part of the realm of his father, and that for only a short time. In spite of this injunction, Áed killed his nephew Suibne, the son of Colmán Mór. While the saint's warning is commonplace hagiographical hindsight, the killing is almost certainly authentic, for it is also reported in the annals of Ulster under the year 600. In an annal four years later, this chronicle tells of the deaths of Áed Sláine and Colmán Rímid (a member of the Cenél nÉogain dynasty), and adds that 'they ruled Tara at the same time with equal power' (*Ann. Ulster*, 604.2). Adomnán seems to have understood the joint reign to have begun with the death of Suibne, for he says that Áed, in fulfilment of Columba's prophecy, ruled his part of the kingdom for only four years and three months. The king-lists, uncomfortable with the concept of an interregnum, generally allow him and Colmán Rímid a joint reign of six or seven years, evidently beginning it at the death of the previous king of Tara (high-king of Ireland), Áed mac Ainmerech.

Joint reigns of Tara were frequent in the sixth and seventh centuries, but on all the other occasions the co-rulers were members of a single dynasty, while Áed Sláine and Colmán Rímid were not only of different dynasties, but of dynasties in opposite corners of the territories ruled by the Uí Néill. The earliest list of the kings of Tara, *Baile Chuinn Chétchathaig*, which is approximately contemporary with the life of St Columba, may not acknowledge the reign of either Áed Sláine or Colmán Rímid (its 'Áed, glorious champion' may refer to their predecessor, Áed mac Ainmerech, or their successor, Áed Allán). However, this text is notably reluctant to admit any joint reigns into its scheme. Although Adomnán seems to have viewed the period 600–04 as a division of territory rather than a sharing of authority, the concept of a joint kingship is supported by the chronicle entry of 604 and by the testimony of later king-lists, and Áed Sláine may justifiably be regarded as a king of Tara.

His killing in 604, at Lough Sunderlin, Westmeath, was undertaken by (or on behalf of) Conall mac Suibni, the son of the Suibne whom Áed Sláine had killed in 600. While there was doubtless an element of revenge, his death was a consequence of the wider struggle for supremacy in the area of Meath, for on the same day there also fell the king of the Leinster dynasty of Uí Fhailgi, which was presumably in alliance with Áed Sláine against the kindred of Colmán Mór.

Áed Sláine's sons included Conall (*d*. 612), Ailill and Congal (both *d*. 634), Dúnchad (*d*. 659), Diarmait (*d*. 665), *Bláimac mac Áeda (*d*. 665), and Máel Odor, and he had a daughter, Rontud. He was married to Ethne ingen Brenaind Daill.   PHILIP IRWIN

Sources *Ann. Ulster* · *Adomnán's Life of Columba*, ed. and trans. A. O. Anderson and M. O. Anderson, rev. edn, rev. M. O. Anderson, OMT (1991), 39 · A. P. Smyth, 'Húi Failgi relations with the Húi Néill, in the century after the loss of the plain of Mide', *Études Celtiques*, 14 (1974–5), 503–23 · L. J. Rayner, ed. and trans., 'The birth of Áed Sláine', *Legends of the kings of Ireland* (1988), 13–17 · F. J. Byrne, *Irish kings and high-kings* (1973) · G. Murphy, 'On the dates of two sources used in Thurneysen's *Heldensage*: 1. *Baile Chuind* and the date of *Cin Dromma Snechtai*', *Ériu*, 16 (1952), 145–56 · M. C. Dobbs, ed. and trans., 'The Ban-shenchus [pt 2]', *Revue Celtique*, 48 (1931), 163–234, esp. 217, 219

Áed Uaridnach mac Domnaill [Áed Allán mac Domnaill] (*d*. 612), high-king of Ireland, was the son of Domnall mac Muirchertaig; his mother is said to have been Bríg, daughter of Archa (or Orcha) mac Caírthind. A partner of Áed Uaridnach, the mother of his son Máel Fithrich (*d*. 630 or 636), was Damnat, daughter of Murchad from Mag Luirg (in the north of Roscommon); he also had a son named Dáire. The name Uaridnach, which has been interpreted as 'of the shivering disease' or, most plausibly, 'cold his spear', seems to be a later designation intended to distinguish him from his celebrated descendant and namesake, Áed Allán mac Fergaile (*d*. 743).

Áed Uaridnach belonged to the Cenél nEogain branch of the Uí Néill, which gave its name to the Inishowen (Inis Eóghain) peninsula in Donegal and to Tyrone (Tír Eoghain). At this period its territories lay in Inishowen and in parts of the Foyle basin; Tyrone was only conquered later. Given the peripheral position of Cenél nEogain's lands in the north-west, Áed Uaridnach's acquisition of the high-kingship of Ireland after the death of his predecessors, Áed Sláine and Colmán Rímid in 604, was only

possible because of intermittent collaboration between Cenél nEogain and Cenél Conaill, its Uí Néill neighbour to the west, and between the Uí Néill of the north and those of the midlands. Such collaboration against others did not preclude much infighting between rival branches of the proliferating Uí Néill kindred. Even within Cenél nEogain there was a rivalry, and soon a feud, between the descendants of Áed Uaridnach's grandfather, Mac Ercae, and those of the latter's brother Feradach. In the later sixth century and until Áed Uaridnach's death in 612, Cenél Maic Ercae was dominant within Cenél nEogain; after 612 Cenél Feradaig came to the fore and remained there for nearly a century, until the accession of Áed Uaridnach's great-grandson, *Fergal mac Máele Dúin, to the kingship of Cenél nEogain shortly after 700.

At the beginning of Áed Uaridnach's reign as king of Cenél nEogain after the death in 604 of his first cousin, Colmán Rímid, the hegemony of the Uí Néill was under severe threat from the attacks on Brega mounted by the king of Leinster, Brandub mac Echach. This threat was made more grave by a feud between the Uí Néill of Brega and those of Mide. In 604 both the joint kings of Tara, Colmán Rímid of Cenél nEogain and Áed Sláine, the ruler of Brega, were killed by other Uí Néill. In 605, however, the annals record the defeat of Brandub at the hands of the Uí Néill, an entry exceptional for its reference to the Uí Néill as a cohesive force. According to the Clonmacnoise annals, Áed Uaridnach's reign as high-king began after this battle; Áed Uaridnach had presumably been the leader of the Uí Néill armies. The antiquity of this entry is uncertain, but it is quite likely to reflect reality, especially because it does not date Áed's reign from the deaths of his predecessors in 604: the recognition of an interregnum is a symptom of authenticity. The rest of Áed Uaridnach's reign appears to have been uneventful, even though he was remembered in a late seventh-century regnal list of Tara (cast as a prophecy, the *Baile Chuinn*, 'The frenzy of Conn') as 'supremely noble Áed who shall smite a smiting'. He died, apparently in his bed, in 612.   T. M. CHARLES-EDWARDS

Sources *Ann. Ulster* · F. J. Byrne, *Irish kings and high-kings* (1973) · M. C. Dobbs, ed. and trans., 'The Ban-shenchus [pt 2]', *Revue Celtique*, 48 (1931), 163–234, esp. 221 · G. Murphy, 'On the dates of two sources used in Thurneysen's *Heldensage*: 1. *Baile Chuind* and the date of *Cin Dromma Snechtai*', *Ériu*, 16 (1952), 145–56 · M. O'Daly, ed. and trans., 'A poem on the Airgialla', *Ériu*, 16 (1952), 179–88 · W. Stokes, ed., 'The annals of Tigernach [8 pts]', *Revue Celtique*, 16 (1895), 374–419; 17 (1896), 6–33, 119–263, 337–420; 18 (1897), 9–59, 150–97, 267–303, 374–91; pubd sep. (1993) · W. M. Hennessy, ed. and trans., *Chronicum Scotorum: a chronicle of Irish affairs*, Rolls Series, 46 (1866) · M. A. O'Brien, ed., *Corpus genealogiarum Hiberniae* (Dublin, 1962)

Áedán [St Áedán, Aidan] (*d*. 651), missionary and bishop, was an Irish monk of Iona. All that is known about him comes from Bede's *Historia ecclesiastica*, completed in 731. King Oswald of the Northumbrians (*r*. 634–42) converted to Christianity while in exile from Northumbria among the Irish, applied to Iona under Abbot Ségéne for a bishop, and, having first received a man too austere for the English, acquired Áedán, who had expressed the view that his predecessor ought to have first given them 'the milk of easier doctrines' before going on to more perfect and sublime teachings. Áedán (Bede gives his name in the Anglicized form Aidan) thus proved his own discretion, 'the mother of virtues' (Bede, *Hist. eccl.*, 3.5). Oswald gave him the island of Lindisfarne for his monastic centre; it was not then an episcopal seat, for there Áedán, albeit a bishop, lived in the Ionan custom, in obedience to the abbot (not named in Áedán's time). He did not partake of the fast living at Oswald's court; he rarely dined there, and if he did, he and his company of clerics quickly withdrew to read or pray. But he could not do without court contact; like Cuthbert later, he needed aristocratic connections to make his missionary trudging effective, and in his early Northumbrian days, when he did not know the English language perfectly (there are signs that he achieved fluency in English later on), he relied on Oswald himself as interpreter. Dinner at Oswald's court one Easter Sunday was the context for a famous story. A silver dish of delicacies had been brought in, but, aware of the poor begging outside, Oswald ordered the food to be distributed to them and the dish to be broken up and divided among them. Whereupon the bishop grasped the king's right hand, saying 'may this hand never grow old' (Bede, *Hist. eccl.*, 3.6).

Amid Áedán's missionary involvements, he frequently retreated to Farne Island, near Lindisfarne, to lead a solitary life of prayer. Even here, however, he was close to, and could support, the king, for the island was across barely 2 miles of sea from Bamburgh Castle, an important royal centre. Once, whether under Oswald or his son Oswin is not clear, Bamburgh was attacked and set on fire by King Penda of the Mercians, but on Áedán's prayer (he could see what was happening) the wind suddenly changed and blew the flames back onto the Mercians. Another famous story is told of Áedán and Oswine, king after Oswald's death in Deira, the southern part of Northumbria, while Oswin ruled in Bernicia, the northern part. Oswine had given Áedán a royal horse with splendid trappings for his missionary journeys, and Áedán gave it to the first beggar he encountered. When the king remonstrated, Áedán replied, 'What, O king, is this son of a mare dearer to you than this son of God?' The king prostrated himself remorsefully before his bishop, and Áedán prophesied that he would not live long, 'for never before have I seen a humble king' (Bede, *Hist. eccl.*, 3.14). Bede includes a little cluster of miracle narratives concerning Áedán to highlight his sanctity. At one point Bede criticizes Áedán strongly; he observed not the Roman discipline of calculating the date of Easter, but the Ionan way. Some have thought this Romanist bigotry on Bede's part; but it is likely that Bede's concern, in holding up Áedán as a model Christian and churchman, was to avoid possible criticism of himself on the Easter issue.

How did Bede know what he knew about Áedán? The obvious source would have been Lindisfarne, but there the cult of St Cuthbert appears to have all but obliterated the memory of the earlier Áedán, and no written life survived. Hence Bede had to piece together fragments of information from various sources. The story of Oswald and the hand probably came from the church at Bamburgh, where it would explain their relic of St Oswald's arm. Bede was shown Áedán's place of solitude on Farne by the people of Bamburgh. The story of Oswine and the horse probably came from Whitby Abbey, whither the ladies of the Deiran court, who would know the tradition, retired. Áedán had helped to initiate Hild (d. 680), Whitby's abbess, into a monastic career and had ordained Heiu, the founder of Hartlepool monastery, which Hild ruled before moving to Whitby, and at which, according to Bede, Áedán often visited her. An account of one of Áedán's miracles came from Gateshead, a monastery a few miles up the Tyne from Bede's Jarrow. It required perceptiveness, therefore, to see how this material (and several of the stories are centred on kings rather than on Áedán) could serve Bede's moral idealism in recreating a historical figure who could easily have been lost to posterity. St Botwulf, clearly a great figure in the Christianization of East Anglia, *has* been virtually lost, for there was no East Anglian Bede to recreate him. Much is lost that might have been known about Áedán. For instance, Oswin of Bernicia and Oswine of Deira were at daggers drawn, and Áedán, bishop of all Northumbria, was bishop to both. How did he cope with this diplomatic challenge?

Áedán is thought of as a bishop in the Irish tradition, and so he was in some ways, with his wanderings in Northumbria, his obedience to an abbot, and his eschewing of horse travel—at the last following St Martin of Tours, the fourth-century monk-bishop for whom the Irish had great veneration. Although he records that some of these practices were continued by Áedán's disciple, Ceadda (Chad), Bede (through whose eyes Áedán is now seen) imposed on this supposedly Celtic churchman a largely Roman image and ideal, derived from Pope Gregory the Great's writings which he knew well. Áedán's retreats to Farne Island reflect Gregory's insistence that a pastor must combine the contemplative with the active life. Among his virtues Áedán had due priestly authority which enabled him to reprove the powerful; likewise Gregory would not see bishops depreciate themselves unduly, lest they were unable to discipline the lives of their subjects. The virtue of *mansuetudo*, or serenity, which Bede attributes to Áedán, was also highly valued by Gregory, who believed too that discretion was the mother of virtues. The picture of this Irish bishop owes much to the Roman Gregory. It is a warning against dividing the story of the English conversion too much into separate Roman and Celtic elements. Áedán died on 31 August 651, leaning against a church on a royal estate near Bamburgh, a final indication of how vital royal support was in his mission. He was probably buried at Lindisfarne.

HENRY MAYR-HARTING

Sources Bede, *Hist. eccl.*, vol. 3 · D. P. Kirby, 'Bede's native sources for the *Historia ecclesiastica*', *Bulletin of the John Rylands University Library*, 48 (1965–6), 341–71 · H. Mayr-Harting, preface, *The coming of Christianity to Anglo-Saxon England*, 3rd edn (1991), 6 · A. Thacker, 'Bede's ideal of reform', *Ideal and reality in Frankish and Anglo-Saxon society*, ed. P. Wormald, D. Bullough, and R. Collins (1983), 130–53

Aedán [Áedan, Aidan] **mac Gabrán** (c.535–609?), king of Dál Riata, was overking of the Dál Riata in Argyll and Antrim from 574 until, probably, 608 or 609 [see Dál Riata, kings of]. *Gabrán, who died c.558, was succeeded by his nephew Conall mac Comgall; Aedán was said to have been 'ordained' as king by Columba only after Conall's death in 574. His status in Britain was apparently that of an independent Irish provincial king. In northern Ireland he accepted the overlordship of Áed, Ainmire's son, head of the Cenél Conaill, and the relationship was formally acknowledged at Druim Cete in Derry in 575, bypassing claims to overlordship made by the king of the Ulaid of north-east Ireland, Báetán, son of Cairell.

Legend credited Aedán with many battles, and with a campaign in Orkney c.580. Some alleged warfare against Picts perhaps confounds him with his descendant Kenneth (or Cinaed) I, Alpin's son. A battle of Man or Manau, won by Aedán c.582, must have been fought either in Man or near the Forth. If the latter, it could have been his victory over the Miathi in which two of his sons were lost. His catastrophic defeat by 'Saxons' was the battle of 'Degsastan' which Bede dated in 603; apparently a failed attempt to halt the northward expansion of the Northumbrian Angles under Æthelfrith.

Aedán died on 17 April, probably in 609; he was said to have been in the seventy-fourth year of his age. Fordun reports that he was buried at Kilkerran in Kintyre, a statement of uncertain value. Although he may have abdicated the kingship in the previous year, he was succeeded by one of his younger sons, *Eochaid Buide (d. c.629) [see under Dál Riata, kings of (act. c.500–c.850)]. At least six other sons are known, four of whom died before him, killed in battle.   MARJORIE O. ANDERSON

Sources Ann. Ulster · M. O. Anderson, Kings and kingship in early Scotland, rev. edn (1980), 253, 264, 270, 281, 286, 290 · Adomnán's Life of Columba, ed. and trans. A. O. Anderson and M. O. Anderson, rev. edn, rev. M. O. Anderson, OMT (1991) · Bede, Hist. eccl. · A. O. Anderson, ed. and trans., Early sources of Scottish history, AD 500 to 1286, 1 (1922); repr. with corrections (1990), 26, 75–7, 125–6 · J. Bannerman, Studies in the history of Dalriada (1974) · G. Mac Niocaill, Ireland before the vikings (1972), 76–9 · Johannis de Fordun Chronica gentis Scotorum / John of Fordun's Chronicle of the Scottish nation, ed. W. F. Skene, trans. F. J. H. Skene, 2 vols. (1871–2)

Ælberht (d. 779/80), archbishop of York, was the teacher of Alcuin, whose Versus de patribus regibus et sanctis Euboricensis ecclesiae ('Verses on the Fathers, Kings and Saints of the Church of York') constitute the principal source for his career (Alcuin, ll. 1397–1596). Some details are recorded in the early northern annals preserved in the Historia regum and the Anglo-Saxon Chronicle: the dates of his archiepiscopate; that he received the pallium from Pope Hadrian in 773; that he died at 'Ceastre' (possibly Chester-le-Street, co. Durham); and that Eanbald (I) had been elected as his successor before his death—Alcuin gives information placing the date as July 778, although 777 is also possible, and explains that Eanbald functioned as his 'associate bishop' (Alcuin, ll. 1565, 1518). He may also have corresponded with Lul, archbishop of Mainz, if (as seems probable) he is the latter's English correspondent who appears in two letters under the name Coena, presumed to be a nickname.

This person is described as 'adorned with the insignia of the highest pontificate' so was evidently an archbishop, and, since Lul was asking for works of Bede, almost certainly an archbishop of York (Tangl, nos. 124–5).

Alcuin provides further details of Ælberht's career. A relative and boon companion of Archbishop Ecgberht, himself the brother of King Eadberht of the Northumbrians, he was placed in a monastery in childhood by his family (Alcuin, ll. 1415–29); he was apparently educated at the school of York Minster. Alcuin's account of his work as archbishop is panegyrical in style, a trait given further emphasis because Alcuin seems to have regarded Ælberht as a model for later archbishops; but it is clear, nevertheless, that he had a major impact on the development of the church of York in three respects. First, he was responsible for assembling the library, travelling abroad, including to Rome, to collect books for it. By Alcuin's account, it contained a wide range of Latin writers and also Greek writers in Latin translation, and it was certainly of major importance, as is apparent in Alcuin's own training, and in demands for its books made by the continental missionaries Boniface and Lul. Second, Ælberht was a teacher of the so-called seven liberal arts, not only the trivium (grammar, rhetoric, dialectic), but also the quadrivium (music, astronomy, geometry, and arithmetic), which led to studies of Holy Scripture; and he also taught compute (the study of fixing the festivals of the church) and natural history. Third, Ælberht was a patron of art and architecture at York. According to Alcuin, he endowed the church of St Peter (York Minster) with two altars. The first was dedicated to St Paul and stood on the site of the baptism of the first Christian king of Northumbria, Eadwine. That it was very costly is indicated by Alcuin's describing it as 'covered with gold, silver, and jewels', lit by a chandelier which 'held three great vessels, each of nine tiers', and having on it a cross covered 'entirely with precious metals', the whole weighing 'many pounds in pure silver'. The second altar, dedicated to the martyrs and Holy Cross, was apparently just as rich, and had on it a cruet 'made in pure gold and of great weight' (Alcuin, ll. 1490–1520). Ælberht's archiepiscopate also saw the construction and consecration in York of the church of the Beneficent Wisdom (Alma Sophia), which was built under his orders by Eanbald (the future Archbishop Eanbald (I)) and Alcuin. This church is now lost, but, to judge from Alcuin's description, it was an imposing structure comprising many chapels and thirty altars. The dedication is an unusual one and may suggest the influence on Ælberht of churches of the Holy Wisdom at Constantinople or Benevento. He was clearly an ambitious prelate, and the choice for his consecration in 767 of 24 April, the feast day of that most ambitious of York ecclesiastics, Wilfrid, may have been a deliberate one in the context of Ælberht's aspirations. A reference in one of Alcuin's letters to how the predecessors of Archbishop Eanbald (II) faced hostility from kings and princes (Dümmler, no. 232) probably encompasses Ælberht. If so, the reasons for this hostility are not known, although Alcuin's observation elsewhere that he 'in justice … did not spare evil kings and nobles'

(Alcuin, l. 1479) suggests that it may have been condemnation of royal morals which led to the archbishop's difficulties. His archiepiscopate coincided in any case with a turbulent period of Northumbrian history, encompassing the expulsion of King Alhred in 774 and possibly also that of King Æthelred in 779. Ælberht died on 8 November, in either 779 or 780.

DAVID ROLLASON

Sources Symeon of Durham, *Opera* · Alcuin, *The bishops, kings, and saints of York*, ed. and trans. P. Godman, OMT (1982) · J. Earle, ed., *Two of the Saxon chronicles parallel with supplementary extracts from the others*, rev. C. Plummer, 2 vols. (1892–9) · E. Dümmler, ed., *Epistolae Karolini aevi*, MGH Epistolae [quarto], 4 (Berlin, 1895) · M. Tangl, ed., *Die Briefe des heiligen Bonifatius und Lullus*, MGH Epistolae Selectae, 1 (Berlin, 1916) · D. A. Bullough, 'Albinus deliciosus Karoli regis: Alcuin of York and the shaping of the Carolingian court', *Institutionen, Kultur und Gesellschaft im Mittelalter*, ed. L. Fenske, W. Rosener, and T. Zotz (1984), 73–92

Ælfflæd [St Ælfflæd, Elfleda] (654–714), abbess of Strensall–Whitby, was the daughter of *Oswiu, king of Northumbria (d. 670), and his wife, *Eanflæd. She was dedicated to religion when scarcely a year old, in fulfilment of a vow made by her father before his victory at the battle of the Winwæd, and placed in the care of her maternal relative *Hild, first at the monastery of Hartlepool and two years later at the new foundation 'Streanæshalch', which has been plausibly linked with both Strensall near York and Whitby, and which may have had communities in both places.

Strensall–Whitby, a double monastery ruled by an abbess and comprising a group of high-born nuns served by a group of male chaplains, achieved great eminence under Hild, as a royal proprietary community and a nursery of bishops. That tradition was maintained by Ælfflæd, who succeeded Hild as abbess in 680, initially in conjunction with her mother, Eanflæd. Like Hild, Ælfflæd played an important role in the political and ecclesiastical life of Northumbria. In 684 she summoned the celebrated hermit Cuthbert to meet her on Coquet Island for a consultation about her brother King Ecgfrith's plans to make him a bishop, and about the future of Ecgfrith himself. The exalted nature of her authority as abbess is indicated by the fact that after 685 she maintained under her command at Strensall–Whitby an episcopal adviser, the unfortunate Trumwine, former bishop of the Picts, expelled from his see after Ecgfrith's defeat and death at 'Nechtansmere'.

Ælfflæd's opinions mattered. She probably inherited from Hild a hostility to Wilfrid, the bishop of the Northumbrians expelled in 678, and maintained friendly relations with his intruded successors, who included the Whitby-trained Bosa at York. She also continued her friendship with Cuthbert after he became bishop of Lindisfarne in 685, and in 687 probably had a hand in promoting Hild's pupil John of Beverley to the bishopric based at Wilfrid's great foundation of Hexham. In 686, therefore, when Archbishop Theodore of Canterbury sought to make peace between Wilfrid and the Northumbrian king, Ælfflæd's half-brother Aldfrith, he found it prudent to write to both king and abbess. Twenty years later, at the final settlement of Wilfrid's affairs, Ælfflæd was among the senior ecclesiastics consulted by Theodore's successor Berhtwald and those ruling in the name of the young king Osred. By then she was clearly more favourably disposed towards Wilfrid and testified to Aldfrith's deathbed intention to seek accommodation with the bishop, earning thereby the commendation of Wilfrid's biographer: 'ever the comforter and best counsellor of the whole kingdom' (Eddius Stephanus, 133). Her speech at the council was presented as decisive: Ælfflæd, it seems, could make and unmake bishops. Significantly, in the rearrangements consequent upon Wilfrid's partial restoration, John of Beverley, who had been trained at Whitby and Canterbury, received the crucial see of York.

Ælfflæd's ecclesiastical activities also included the promotion of saints' cults. She was clearly active in establishing that of her friend Cuthbert, whose girdle she possessed and claimed to have wonder-working properties. More importantly, between 680 and 704, while Eanflæd was still alive, she was responsible for the translation of her grandfather Eadwine's remains from Hatfield Chase, where he had fallen in battle in 633, to a place of honour on the south side of the altar in her conventual church. The move, when coupled with the fact that the church was already the burial place of Oswiu and Hild, made the monastery a shrine to the union of the two Northumbrian kingdoms, that of her father's Bernicia and her mother and grandfather's Deira. As an adjunct to those activities, Ælfflæd also played a key role in promoting the cult of Pope Gregory the Great as apostle of England; Whitby tradition sought to emphasize the link between the king and the pope whose emissary Paulinus had been responsible for his baptism. In this, as in other matters, Ælfflæd seems to have co-operated closely with Archbishop Theodore.

Ælfflæd was clearly a learned woman. Bede terms her *magistra* and *doctrix*, epithets which suggests that like Hild she acted as a teacher and spiritual guide at Strensall–Whitby. Her international contacts are indicated by a surviving letter, written about 700, commending an unknown pupil (also an abbess), on pilgrimage to Rome, to Adolana, abbess of Pfalzel, near Trier. The letter is written in competent, if florid, Latin, which may owe more to contact with the school of Canterbury than with the Northumbrian cultural centres of Wearmouth and Jarrow. Other literary productions of Ælfflæd's community include a life of Gregory the Great (a less accomplished work) and perhaps a life of Abbess Hild.

Ælfflæd died aged about sixty in 714 and was buried at Strensall–Whitby. Her cult was late, and she was not commemorated in any pre-conquest calendars. According to William of Malmesbury, her remains, together with those of Trumwine and King Oswiu, were discovered and elevated shortly before 1125. Glastonbury, Durham, and Salisbury claimed to possess relics. Her feast day is 8 February.

ALAN THACKER

Sources M. Tangl, ed., *Die Briefe des heiligen Bonifatius und Lullus*, MGH Epistolae Selectae, 1 (Berlin, 1916) · Bede, *Hist. eccl.*, 3.24; 4.26 · E. Stephanus, *The life of Bishop Wilfrid*, ed. and trans. B. Colgrave (1927) · B. Colgrave, ed. and trans., *The earliest life of Gregory the*

Great ... by an anonymous monk of Whitby (1968) • B. Colgrave, ed. and trans., *Two lives of Saint Cuthbert* (1940) • *Willelmi Malmesbiriensis monachi de gestis pontificum Anglorum libri quinque*, ed. N. E. S. A. Hamilton, Rolls Series, 52 (1870), 254 • P. H. Blair, 'Whitby as a centre of learning in the seventh century', *Learning and literature in Anglo-Saxon England: studies presented to Peter Clemoes on the occasion of his sixty-fifth birthday*, ed. M. Lapidge and H. Gneuss (1985), 3–32 • *Venerabilis Baedae opera historica*, ed. C. Plummer, 2 vols. (1896) • P. S. Barnwell, L. A. S. Butler, and C. J. Dunn, 'The confusion of conversion: Streanæshalch, Strensall and Whitby and the Northumbrian church', *The cross goes north: processes of conversion in northern Europe, AD 300–1300*, ed. M. Carver (2003), 311–26

Ælfgar, earl of Mercia (d. 1062?), magnate, was the son of *Leofric, earl of Mercia, and *Godgifu (Godiva). He married, perhaps in the late 1020s, Ælfgifu, probably a kinswoman of Cnut's first wife, *Ælfgifu of Northampton. Her known lands lay in the east midlands and East Anglia, and in the 1040s Ælfgar attested an East Anglian will at the head of the Essex witnesses (*AS chart.*, S 1531). These connections perhaps explain why he was given the earldom of East Anglia, first during the exile of Harold Godwineson in 1051–2, and again after Harold succeeded to Wessex in 1053. In 1055 he was outlawed for treason; the E text of the Anglo-Saxon Chronicle alleges his guilt but the other texts regard him as at most mildly culpable. Perhaps Ælfgar was alarmed at the appointment of Tostig Godwineson, rather than Waltheof, Earl Siward's heir, as earl of Northumbria, and feared that he too might be displaced when his father died. He raised troops in Ireland, and, in alliance with the Welsh king, *Gruffudd ap Llywelyn, attacked Hereford. The local levies were overwhelmed and the city sacked, and Earl Harold had to collect a force from 'very nearly all England' (*ASC*, s.a. 1055, text C) to drive the invaders back into Wales. A peace was concluded on terms noticeably favourable to Ælfgar, who was reinstated. In 1057 he succeeded to Mercia on his father's death; East Anglia passed to Harold's brother Gyrth. Ælfgar's second exile, in 1058, must be seen against the continuing rise of the Godwinesons, for by now Harold had received not only Wessex but Hereford too, after the death of Earl Ralph in 1057. Ælfgar again allied with Gruffudd, now husband of his daughter *Ealdgyth (their daughter Nest later married *Osbern fitz Richard [see under Richard Scrob] and was reinstated once more. In 1062 he supported the election of Wulfstan (c.1008–1095) as bishop of Worcester, but is not heard of thereafter. He was probably dead before Harold launched his successful campaign against Gruffudd in 1063, for he would surely have tried to help his son-in-law had he been living.

Eadwine [Edwin], earl of Mercia (d. 1071), magnate, Ælfgar's son, succeeded to his father's earldom. His widowed sister Ealdgyth married Earl Harold and in 1065 Harold supported the election of Eadwine's brother *Morcar as earl of Northumbria, against his own brother Tostig. Eadwine and the Mercians in turn supported Harold's election as king the following year, though the Northumbrians had to be won over by the advocacy of Bishop Wulfstan. Tostig attempted to regain his earldom with the help of Harald Hardrada, king of Norway. They

defeated a force led by Eadwine and Morcar at Gate Fulford, on 20 September, only to be killed five days later at Stamford Bridge. Losses among the northern levies probably account for the absence of Eadwine and Morcar from the battle of Hastings on 14 October. After Duke William's victory, they initially supported the election of Edgar Ætheling, but later submitted to William at Little Berkhamsted, and accompanied the king to Normandy in 1067. Both were confirmed in office, but the appointment of Roger de Montgomery as earl of Shrewsbury, probably in 1068, undermined Eadwine's position. He sought help from Bleddyn ap Cynfyn of Gwynedd, but a show of power by King William brought him to heel, and the brothers played no part in the English uprising of 1069–70. The merciless crushing of the revolt must, however, have affected their followers, and Eadwine's authority was further reduced by the establishment of the earldom of Chester in 1069–70. In 1071, Eadwine and Morcar 'fled away and travelled aimlessly in woods and moors' (*ASC*, s.a. 1071, texts D, E). Eadwine was betrayed by three of his men, and killed, with twenty faithful knights, 'all fighting desperately to the last' (Ordericus Vitalis, *Eccl. hist.*, 2.258–9). Morcar joined other English dissidents at Ely and was captured when the isle fell; he spent the rest of his life as a prisoner in the custody of Roger de Beaumont. Neither Eadwine nor Morcar left descendants, but Godric of Corby, another Ely insurgent, may have been a son of their brother Burgheard, who died at Rheims in 1061.

ANN WILLIAMS

Sources *ASC*, s.a. 1064, 1065, 1066, 1071, 1072 [texts C, D, E] • Ordericus Vitalis, *Eccl. hist.*, vol. 2 • *AS chart.*, S 1027–8, 1031, 1033–4, 1036, 1055, 1478, 1531 [Ælfgar]; S 1026, 1030, 1041–3 [Eadwine] • P. H. Sawyer, ed., *Charters of Burton Abbey*, Anglo-Saxon Charters, 2 (1979) • F. Barlow, *Edward the Confessor* (1970) • K. L. Maund, 'The Welsh alliances of Earl Ælfgar of Mercia and his family in the mid-eleventh century', *Anglo-Norman Studies*, 11 (1988), 181–90 • P. A. Clarke, *The English nobility under Edward the Confessor* (1994) • A. Williams, *The English and the Norman conquest* (1995) • F. Barlow, ed. and trans., *The life of King Edward who rests at Westminster* (1962) • A. Farley, ed., *Domesday Book*, 2 vols. (1783), 1.134v, 222, 222v, 231v, 247v, 252, 280v; 2.286v, 287, 373v, 374 • *The Vita Wulfstani of William of Malmesbury*, ed. R. R. Darlington, CS, 3rd ser., 40 (1928) • F. E. Harmer, ed., *Anglo-Saxon writs* (1952) • C. P. Lewis, 'An introduction to the Cheshire Domesday', *The Cheshire Domesday*, ed. A. Williams and R. W. H. Erskine (1991) • C. P. Lewis, 'The early earls of Norman England', *Anglo-Norman Studies*, 13 (1990), 207–23

Ælfgifu (fl. 956–966), consort of King Eadwig, was possibly a descendant of Ealdorman Æthelfrith of Mercia (fl. c.900) and of his wife, Æthelgyth, who may have been niece of Ealhswith, wife of King Alfred, and thus of Mercian royal blood. She was certainly a blood relative of King *Eadwig (d. 959), from whom she was separated in 958 because they were too closely related.

This enigmatic woman achieved notoriety through the portrayals of her in the late tenth-century lives of saints Dunstan and Oswald. From the former comes the famous story of Eadwig deserting his coronation feast in 956 to disport himself with Ælfgifu and her mother, before being forcibly returned to his royal duties by Dunstan, an action which earned the bishop Ælfgifu's hatred. Subsequent lives develop her evil reputation, labelling her as a Jezebel for her opposition to Dunstan and her malign influence over the king. These stories may give some indication of her importance, but little of her biography. They form part of a posthumous vilification of Eadwig's reign and a sanctification of the two bishops through a portrayal of them as wronged prophets facing a latter-day Jezebel. The mid-tenth-century context of Ælfgifu was both more political and less colourful.

Eadwig's marriage to Ælfgifu, at an unknown date, was of considerable importance in his manoeuvring for advantage in the succession dispute after 955; if she were a woman of royal Mercian descent it may have been critically important in his attempts to establish himself there. It seems to have been her maternal ancestry which was particularly significant; her mother is associated with her in the stories and in the only surviving contemporary documents which mention Ælfgifu. In the factions which formed before and after 955, Ælfgifu and her mother found themselves opposed to Dunstan, Archbishop Oda, and the dowager queen, Eadgifu, widow of Edward the Elder. Dunstan was exiled, but Oda was the man who separated the king and his wife in 958 as the balance began to shift decisively against Eadwig after Edgar was accepted as king of Mercia; the separation should be seen as a part of these shifts. It is another measure of Ælfgifu's significance that she was apparently exiled. If her association with Æthelfrith's family is correct, she was related to Ealdorman Æthelstan Half-King and his sons, who played key roles in the unfolding of events in these years. The marriage does not seem to have held this family to Eadwig's allegiance, a warning against overemphasizing the success of marriage alliances in overriding other interests, against seeing families as monolithic interest groups, and about the need to read faction carefully. The importance of her family led to Ælfgifu's prominence; it did not necessarily protect her in the changing circumstances of the 950s.

In the longer term it may have ensured Ælfgifu some sort of survival. By the mid-960s she was back in England and sufficiently restored in fortune to be receiving charters from King Edgar; she is also presumed to have made a will (AS chart., S 1484). Her new situation is as enigmatic as her origins. It is unclear whether Edgar was granting her land, restoring her fortunes in a gesture of conciliation, or reluctantly accepting the reinstatement of a woman of important connections. After his third marriage, c.965, to Ælfthryth, Edgar seems to have taken a number of steps to organize the land holding of the female members of his family, and perhaps to assert family unity. Any reconciliation which occurred should perhaps be seen in this context. Ælfgifu seems to have paid a heavy price for reinstatement: most of her land was given to the king and royal family and her heriot, or death duty, recorded in her presumed will, is the largest in any surviving tenth-century document. It is difficult to be certain whether she was restoring old West Saxon dower land to the royal family, or whether the lands she left the king, queen, and prince were her own. If the latter, then her marriage to Eadwig was responsible for the crown's acquisition of a sizeable proportion of its important lands to the north of the Thames valley.

Among the lands Ælfgifu left was Wing, in Buckinghamshire, and the substantial remodelling of the chancel of the surviving church there should possibly be associated with her local residence in dowagerhood, though she arranged for burial in Winchester near her royal husband. The last mention of Ælfgifu is in the New Minster charter of 966. The problems in the reconstruction of her biography are a warning of how far the winners of Edgar's reign rewrote the history of the mid-tenth century and of how much of its politics, particularly its family politics, are lost.   PAULINE STAFFORD

Sources W. Stubbs, ed., *Memorials of St Dunstan, archbishop of Canterbury*, Rolls Series, 63 (1874) · [Byrhtferth of Ramsey], 'Vita sancti Oswaldi auctore anonymo', *The historians of the church of York and its archbishops*, ed. J. Raine, 1, Rolls Series, 71 (1879), 399–475 · C. Hart, *The Danelaw* (1992), 455–65, 569–604 · N. Brooks, 'Arms, status, and warfare in late Saxon England', *Ethelred the Unready: papers from the millenary conference* [Oxford 1978], 81–103 · H. M. Taylor and J. Taylor, *Anglo-Saxon architecture*, 2 (1965) · M. A. Meyer, 'The queen's "demesne" in later Anglo-Saxon England', *The culture of Christendom* (1993), 75–113 · P. Stafford, *Unification and conquest* (1989) · P. Stafford, 'The portrayal of royal women in England, midtenth to mid-twelfth centuries', *Medieval queenship*, ed. J. C. Parsons, new edn (1994), 143–67 · D. Whitelock, ed. and trans., *Anglo-Saxon wills* (1930) · *AS chart.*, S 745, 1484 · charter, New Minster (966)

Ælfgifu [Ælfgifu of Northampton] (*fl.* **1006–1036**), first consort of King Cnut, was the daughter of Ælfhelm, ealdorman of southern Northumbria (*d.* 1006), and of Wulfrune. She belonged to a great midlands family important throughout the tenth and early eleventh centuries, and the epithet attached to her name by the late eleventh century probably reflects landholding in this area. Wulfric Spot, the founder of Burton Abbey (*d. c.*1005), was the brother of her father or mother; her grandmother was Wulfrune, patron of the religious community at Wolverhampton. In 1006 her father fell from power and was murdered, apparently at the command of King Æthelred, while her brothers Ufegeat and Wulfheah were blinded. Although the family remained powerful, it again fell under suspicion of treachery during the attack of the Danish king, *Swein Forkbeard in 1013–14, when more members were put to death. At some date between 1013 and 1016 Ælfgifu was married to Swein's son, *Cnut. The marriage was a significant part of the process by which Swein established himself first in the north midlands. She had two sons with Cnut, Swein and Harold Harefoot [see Harold I (*d.* 1040)].

After his conquest of England, Cnut married King Æthelred's widow, Emma (Ælfgifu). There is, however, no indication that Ælfgifu was repudiated. In 1030 she was sent with her son Swein to rule Norway after the defeat of Óláf Haraldsson at the battle of Stiklestad. Cnut was attempting to rule Norway directly, rather than relying on loose overlordship and the friendship of the *jarls* (earls) of Hlathir as his father and grandfather had done. In 1034 Ælfgifu and Swein were driven out. He went to Denmark, where he soon died; but by 1036, after the death of Cnut, Ælfgifu was back in England successfully working to secure the throne for her son Harold Harefoot; Harold's strong backing north of the Thames probably owed something to her family connections. Harold's reign is poorly documented, and apart from one possible reference to her as the 'lady', or queen, she disappears.

In the bitter struggle for the throne after Cnut's death Ælfgifu of Northampton was called a concubine, and considerable doubt was cast over the birth of her sons, doubt which later flowered into stories that their respective fathers were a shoemaker and a priest. Such accusations are typical of the propaganda surrounding succession disputes and a poor guide to the relative status of Cnut's two marriages. Ælfgifu's sons were named after Cnut's father and grandfather, which suggests at least a claim on family lands, as does their assignment to rule Norway, and possibly England, respectively. Neither English nor Danish royal practice ruled out the repudiation of wives, but Ælfgifu's continued importance after the second marriage is unusual. In Scandinavian history her regency in Norway was remembered as 'Alviva's time', and became a byword for oppressive rule; Scandinavian legend makes her concubine of Óláf Haraldsson as well as Cnut. Her later reputations demonstrate how readily opprobrium attaches to the name of ruling women and the vulnerability of women to attack in dynastic politics.

PAULINE STAFFORD

Sources M. W. Campbell, 'Queen Emma and Ælfgifu of Northampton: Canute the Great's women', *Medieval Scandinavia*, 4 (1971), 60–79 · P. H. Sawyer, ed., *Charters of Burton Abbey*, Anglo-Saxon Charters, 2 (1979), xxxviii–xliii · W. H. Stevenson, 'An alleged son of King Harold Harefoot', *EngHR*, 28 (1913), 112–17 · P. Sawyer, 'Cnut's Scandinavian empire', *The reign of Cnut*, ed. A. R. Rumble (1994), 10–22 · A. Campbell, ed. and trans., *Encomium Emmae reginae*, CS, 3rd ser., 72 (1949), xxiii, 39–40, 83 · *Florentii Wigorniensis monachi chronicon ex chronicis*, ed. B. Thorpe, 1, EHS, 10 (1848), 190 · M. K. Lawson, *Cnut: the Danes in England in the early eleventh century* (1993)
Likenesses portrait, *c*.1016–1020, BL, Stowe MS 944, fol. 6

Ælfgifu. *See* Emma (*d.* 1052).

Ælfheah (*d.* **971**). *See under* Ælfhere (*d.* 983).

Ælfheah [St Ælfheah, Elphege, Alphege] (*d.* **1012**), archbishop of Canterbury, owes his fame to the circumstances of his death—he was murdered in 1012 at viking hands. This makes it difficult to know whether recorded details of his early life were invented to suit later hagiographic needs or whether they are in fact accurate. As abbot of Bath he attests charters from *c*.970, but he may also have been instrumental in the refounding of Bath, living there first as a hermit after an initial spell with a community at Deerhurst. It is also possible, as claimed by William of Malmesbury, that he was at some stage monk and prior of Glastonbury. Whether this is accepted or not, it is at least clear that he was a protégé of St Dunstan, a former abbot of Glastonbury, for it was Dunstan, as archbishop of Canterbury, who recommended to the king that he appoint Ælfheah to the see of Winchester; on 19 October 984 Ælfheah was duly consecrated bishop.

As bishop of Winchester Ælfheah was heir to the plans and ambitions of his predecessor, the reformer Æthelwold (*d.* 984). Æthelwold had redesigned his cathedral,

giving pride of place to the relics of St Swithun. Ælfheah completed Æthelwold's building, furthering not only the cult of St Swithun but also that of Æthelwold himself. A new high altar was surmounted by a five-staged tower 115 feet high, topped by a golden weathercock. The finished cathedral was dedicated in 993 or 994. In 996 Ælfheah oversaw the translation of Æthelwold's body from the crypt to a new tomb within the choir of the church. Such occasions were made all the more memorable by the sound of Æthelwold's organ, stupendously enlarged by Ælfheah. According to Wulfstan Cantor's life of St Swithun: 'the sound makes so much clamour … that men stop their ears with their hands … and the melody of the pipes is heard all over the city' (Yorke, 158).

Ælfheah's episcopate at Winchester coincided with the renewal of viking attacks. In 994, a force led by Olaf Tryggvason harried the south of England. Danegeld, first paid to Olaf in 991, was again offered to him, but this time it was followed up by negotiations that led to Olaf's confirmation as a Christian and a promise that he would never again attack England. Entries in the Anglo-Saxon Chronicle suggest that Ælfheah not only officiated at Olaf's confirmation at Andover but may also have taken a share in the making of the peace treaty.

In 1006, after the death of Ælfric, Ælfheah became archbishop of Canterbury, the fourth of the five monk-bishops appointed to the see by Æthelred II. From Winchester Ælfheah brought with him St Swithun's head to put on Canterbury's high altar, as well, it seems, as a number of liturgical and artistic practices. Thus the change over reflected in the Arundel psalter of the early eleventh century from a Glastonbury to a Winchester calendar can most reasonably be attributed to Ælfheah's influence, as can the adoption at about this time of the acanthus frame, characteristic of the Winchester style, in Canterbury's scriptorium. As Ælfheah had at Winchester furthered the cult of Æthelwold, now at Canterbury he patronized that of Dunstan, commissioning Adelard of Ghent to write a life in the form of a series of readings for his feast day.

No evidence has survived to throw light on whether Ælfheah was or was not active as a reformer within his province. It is, however, clear that he was in regular attendance at Æthelred's court and that *c*.1008, together with Wulfstan, archbishop of York, he encouraged the king to hold a national council at Enham in Hampshire. This meeting, opening as it did at Pentecost with solemn abjurations of heathenism and declarations of peace and friendship, had something in common with continental peace assemblies of the same period. As a way of combating the vikings it cannot, however, be said to have been effective.

In September 1011 vikings were at the gates of Canterbury; after a fortnight's siege they were let in, according to the Anglo-Saxon Chronicle (*ASC*, text E, s.a. 1011) through the treachery of a certain Ælfmær 'whose life Archbishop Ælfheah had saved' (how is not recorded). The city was ransacked and Ælfheah taken prisoner. The vikings now demanded £48,000 to be paid by the following Easter, 13 April. The money was duly found, whereupon a further sum was requested as ransom for Ælfheah. Ælfheah refused to allow this to be collected. On 19 April 1012, during a drunken viking feast, anger against Ælfheah erupted, the archbishop was seized and:

> shamefully put to death: they [the vikings] pelted him with bones and ox-heads, and one of them struck him on the head with the back of an axe, so that he sank down with the blow, and his holy blood fell on the ground, and so he sent his holy soul to God's kingdom.   (ASC, text E, s.a. 1012)

On the following day Ælfheah was buried in London at St Paul's.

In the eyes of his contemporaries Ælfheah's death made him a martyr; only after the Norman conquest was the question raised, by the then archbishop of Canterbury, Lanfranc, as to whether Ælfheah deserved the status since he had died over the matter of a ransom rather than for Christ. The argument was rebutted by Anselm, abbot of Bec, on a visit to Canterbury, on the grounds that Ælfheah had died for justice and therefore truth. At the time of his death such theological niceties were not at issue; not only does the Anglo-Saxon Chronicle call Ælfheah a martyr, so too did the German chronicler Thietmar of Merseburg (c.975–1018) even though, in Thietmar's version of the event, Ælfheah would have paid up had he had the necessary cash. According to Thietmar, the viking leader Thorkell stood out against the treatment meted to Ælfheah and it has been conjectured that this may explain his defection later in the year to Æthelred.

With the accession to the English throne in 1016 of the Danish Cnut, the cult of Ælfheah threatened to become something of an embarrassment. Cnut's solution was to become Ælfheah's most fervent patron. In 1023 he ordered the removal of the relics from London to Canterbury where they were placed on the north side of the high altar. Only a finger (or so it was later claimed) stayed behind in London, a gift of Cnut to Westminster Abbey.

Ælfheah's claim to sanctity, as with a number of other Anglo-Saxon saints, was not seen to require the validation of a life until after the Norman conquest, when Archbishop Lanfranc, once he had been persuaded of Ælfheah's merits, commissioned his precentor Osbern (himself of Anglo-Saxon birth) to produce the kind of documentation then thought necessary. Osbern accordingly wrote a translation, life, and passion. The nature of Osbern's achievements as Ælfheah's hagiographer is a matter of some controversy. He has much to say that is not in the Anglo-Saxon Chronicle, not least about the translation of 1023 which, he claims, took place not with 'the happy jubilation' recorded in the chronicle but as an undercover operation requiring both stealth and the deployment of an impressive number of housecarls to ensure that the body could be moved without causing a riot. Osbern is, however, famed as a prolific rather than a factually accurate writer. Whenever possible he relies on biblical parallels; in this case Ælfheah becomes a second St Stephen at the moment of his death, while Osbern likens the translation of 1023 to the fetching of the Ark of the Covenant by David. None the less, it is still not impossible that some historical veracity may lie behind Osbern's imputation of the Londoners' attachment to Ælfheah's relics.

At Canterbury, throughout the middle ages, Ælfheah's reputation remained high. Together with Dunstan he occupied a key position in the community's consciousness of its Anglo-Saxon past. In the rivalry that was developing between St Augustine's, Canterbury, and the cathedral, these two saints had a special place as being exclusively cathedral property. After the rebuilding of the cathedral following the fire of 1174, both Ælfheah and Dunstan were returned to their honoured positions north and south of the high altar, with new stained-glass windows illustrating scenes of their lives. It is perhaps a mark of Ælfheah's standing that, when faced with martyrdom, Thomas Becket is said to have commended his cause to him.

HENRIETTA LEYSER

Sources *ASC*, s.a. 984, 993, 1006 [text A]; s.a. 1023 [text D]; 994, 1006, 1011–12, 1023 [text E] · *Die Chronik des Bischofs Thietmar von Merseburg*, ed. R. Holtzmann, 2nd edn (Berlin, 1955) · Osberno, 'Vita s. Alphegi archiepiscopi Cantuariensis', *Anglia sacra*, ed. [H. Wharton], 2 (1691), 122–48 · Osbern, 'Translatio Sancti Aelfegi Cantuariensis archiepiscopi et martiris', *The reign of Cnut*, ed. A. R. Rumble (1994), 283–315 · N. Brooks, *The early history of the church of Canterbury: Christ Church from 597 to 1066* (1984) · M. K. Lawson, *Cnut: the Danes in England in the early eleventh century* (1993) · J. Crook, ed., *Winchester Cathedral: nine hundred years, 1093–1993* (1993) · B. Yorke, ed., *Bishop Æthelwold: his career and influence* (1988) · N. Ramsay, M. Sparks, and T. Tatton Brown, eds., *St Dunstan: his life, times and cult* (1992) · Eadmer, *The life of St Anselm, Archbishop of Canterbury*, ed. and trans. R. W. Southern (1962) · P. Wormald, *How do we know so much about Anglo-Saxon Deerhurst?* (1993)

Ælfhere (d. 983), magnate, was the son of Ealhhelm, ealdorman of central Mercia (what is now Worcestershire and Gloucestershire) from 940 to 951. Ælfhere and his brothers are greeted as kinsmen by successive kings, though the degree of relationship is unknown. They were particularly close to Eadwig (d. 959), who appointed Ælfhere ealdorman in 956. When, in 957, Eadwig's brother Edgar (d. 975) took over the lands north of the Thames, Ælfhere attests his charters as premier ealdorman, a position which he retained when Edgar became king of all England on his brother's death. He appears as ealdorman of Mercia in the leases issued by Oswald, bishop of Worcester, from 962 onwards, and Byrhtferth of Ramsey describes him as 'prince of the Mercian people' (Byrhtferth of Ramsey, 1.443). Edgar's fourth law code implies an equality of status among the three leading ealdormen, Ælfhere, Æthelwine of East Anglia (d. 992), and Oslac of Northumbria (d. 975), who outranked all other lay officials; and the other ealdormen in Mercia—Æthelmund (940–65) in the north-west and Æthelstan (nicknamed *rota*; 955–70) in the south-east—were probably subject to Ælfhere's overall control. He may also have administered central Wessex after the death of his brother Ælfheah [see below] in 971 until the appointment of Æthelmær in 977.

Ælfhere's rise coincided with a reduction in the authority of Æthelwine's family and the rivalry between them surfaced during the succession crisis after Edgar's death in 975. Ælfhere supported Queen Ælfthryth in asserting the claims of her son Æthelred, as did Æthelwold, bishop of

Winchester, whereas Æthelwine, with Archbishop Dunstan and Oswald of Worcester, upheld the rights of Edward the Martyr, Edgar's son with his first wife. The coronation of Edward averted a civil war, but did not end the disturbances. Edward's reign has been seen as a period of reaction against the growing power of the reformed monasteries, initiated by Ælfhere and opposed by Æthelwine, but this is both simplistic and misleading. Ælfhere is said to have disbanded houses established by Æthelwold (*ASC*, s.a. 975, text E), yet is also presented as defending Æthelwold's foundation at Ely against the oppression of Æthelwine (*Liber Eliensis*, 79–80); and he was a benefactor of Abingdon (*AS chart.*, S 1216), founded by Æthelwold, and Glastonbury, reformed by Æthelwold's teacher, Dunstan. The only named house destroyed at this time is Winchcombe, Gloucestershire, founded by Oswald, bishop of Worcester, though the monks of Evesham and of Pershore later claimed that Ælfhere had seized lands belonging to them. Ælfhere may well have resented the appointment of Oswald, a close friend of Æthelwine, to the bishopric of Worcester: although the Worcestershire triple hundred of Oswaldslow, controlled by the bishop, can no longer be regarded as a liberty from which the ealdorman was excluded, Oswald was as much a royal officer as Ælfhere himself and their spheres of authority overlapped. It is also clear that the wealth of the reformed monasteries was sometimes acquired by dubious means and many disputes involved attempts by the 'donors' to obtain a better price for their lands than they originally received (*AS chart.*, S 792).

King Edward was murdered at Corfe, Dorset, in 978. No contemporary source implicates Ælfhere, who in 979 oversaw the translation of Edward's body from Wareham to Shaftesbury, where his cult was quickly established. Under Æthelred II, Ælfhere continued to hold the preeminence he had enjoyed under Edgar, until his death on 22 October 983. His wife may have been the Eadflæd from whom his successor Ælfric Cild [*see below*] abstracted land in Gloucestershire, but no children are recorded; Ælfric, sometimes styled Ælfhere's son, was actually his brother-in-law and *Odda of Deerhurst, who has also in the past been described as Ælfhere's son, was probably not related to him at all. Ælfhere was buried at Glastonbury Abbey, where he was long remembered as a generous benefactor.

Ælfric Cild (*fl.* 975–985), magnate, was the brother-in-law (not son, as the twelfth-century chronicler at Abingdon calls him) of Ælfhere. His wife may have been Æthelflæd, Ealhhelm's daughter, recorded *c.*950 (*AS chart.*, S 1539); his son Ælfwine, killed at Maldon in 991, was remembered in the will of his uncle, Ælfheah, who died in 971, and also, as Ealhhelm's grandson, in the Old English poem, *The Battle of Maldon*. Ælfric Cild (literally 'child', but probably meaning 'nobleman' in this context), came from the east midlands; he had lands in Huntingdonshire and is associated with Bishop Æthelwold in the foundation both of Peterborough and of Thorney. After the death of Edgar in 975 he is found visiting Ely in company with Queen Ælfthryth and her son, the future Æthelred II. He succeeded

as ealdorman of Mercia in 983 and held his position until early in 985, when he was banished by a council held at Cirencester; the charge was treason. No details are given, though he is accused of seizing land in Gloucestershire belonging to Eadflæd, possibly Ælfhere's widow (*AS chart.*, S 896, 937). The date of his death is not recorded. Henry of Huntingdon seems to regard his banishment as unjust; and the twelfth-century Abingdon chronicle says he fled to Denmark, later returning to England with a band of viking raiders. Both sources, however, conflate Ælfric Cild with his namesake, *Ælfric of Hampshire, who died in 1016.

Ælfheah (*d.* 971), magnate, was probably the eldest of Ealhhelm's sons, since he was married by 940 to Ælfswith. She was a kinswoman of King Eadwig (*AS chart.*, S 662), who made Ælfheah his seneschal and in 959 appointed him ealdorman of central Wessex. Ælfsige, bishop of Winchester, addressed Ælfheah as 'my beloved friend' (*AS chart.*, S 1491) and made him guardian of his son Godwine (*d.* 1001); Brihthelm, Ælfsige's successor, was also a kinsman of Ælfheah (*AS chart.*, S 615). Ælfheah was connected with *Ælfthryth, who married Edgar in 964 or 965 and he may have been godfather to one of her sons; in his will (*AS chart.*, S 1485) he made bequests to both athelings and to their mother. Ælfheah's will, when compared with the royal charters in his favour, allows some estimate to be made of his wealth: about 700 hides of land in seven shires. The will also mentions his brothers, but names only Ælfhere; the others were Eadric (*AS chart.*, S 1292), who probably predeceased him, and Ælfwine, who became a monk of Glastonbury and was living in 975 (*AS chart.*, S 802, 1276). Ælfheah also made a bequest to his sister's son Ælfwine, son of Ælfric Cild. He died on 18 April 971 and was buried at Glastonbury Abbey, of which he and his wife were benefactors; he also gave lands to Abingdon, Bath, the Old Minster, Winchester, and Malmesbury. He left two sons, Ælfweard and Godric; the latter is perhaps the earldorman of Lindsey killed at the battle of 'Assandun' in 1016.

ANN WILLIAMS

Sources *ASC*, s.a. 975, 979 [texts D, E]; s.a. 983, 985, 1016 [texts C, D, E]; s.a. 1001 [text A] · *AS chart.*, S 411, 462, 564, 585–6, 597, 615, 639, 662, 702, 747, 775, 796, 802, 866, 896, 937, 1216, 1276, 1292, 1447, 1485, 1491, 1539 · John of Worcester, *Chron.* · [Byrhtferth of Ramsey], 'Vita sancti Oswaldi auctore anonymo', *The historians of the church of York and its archbishops*, ed. J. Raine, 1, Rolls Series, 71 (1879), 399–475, esp. 443–55 · E. O. Blake, ed., *Liber Eliensis*, CS, 3rd ser., 92 (1962) · W. D. Macray, ed., *Chronicon abbatiae de Evesham, ad annum 1418*, Rolls Series, 29 (1863) · J. Stevenson, ed., *Chronicon monasterii de Abingdon*, 2 vols., Rolls Series, 2 (1858) · W. D. Macray, ed., *Chronicon abbatiae Rameseiensis a saec. x usque ad an. circiter 1200*, Rolls Series, 83 (1886) · *The early history of Glastonbury: an edition, translation, and study of William of Malmesbury's De antiquitate Glastonie ecclesie*, ed. J. Scott (1981) · D. Scragg, ed., *The battle of Maldon, AD 991* (1991) · A. J. Robertson, ed. and trans., *Anglo-Saxon charters*, 2nd edn (1956) · Henry, archdeacon of Huntingdon, *Historia Anglorum*, ed. D. E. Greenway, OMT (1996) · D. Whitelock, ed. and trans., *Anglo-Saxon wills* (1930) · A. Williams, 'Princeps Merciorum gentis': the family, career and connections of Ælfhere, ealdorman of Mercia, 956–983', *Anglo-Saxon England*, 10 (1982), 143–72 · S. Keynes, *The diplomas of King Æthelred 'The Unready' (978–1016): a study in their use as historical evidence*, Cambridge Studies in Medieval Life and Thought, 3rd ser., 13 (1980) · M. Blows, 'A Glastonbury obit-list', *The archaeology and* history of Glastonbury Abbey: essays in honour of the ninetieth birthday of C. A. Ralegh Radford, ed. L. Abrams and J. P. Carley (1991), 257–69, esp. 263–7 • M. Locherbie-Cameron, 'The men named in the poem', The battle of Maldon, AD 991, ed. D. Scragg (1991), 241–2 • B. Yorke, 'Æthelwold and the politics of the tenth century', Bishop Æthelwold: his career and influence, ed. B. Yorke (1988), 65–88 • C. R. Hart, The early charters of eastern England (1966) • John of Glastonbury, Cronica, sive, Antiquitates Glastoniensis ecclesie, ed. J. P. Carley (1978), 36

Ælfred. See Alfred (848/9–899).

Ælfric (d. 1005), archbishop of Canterbury, was perhaps a monk of Abingdon in his earlier years. He is recorded in its chronicle as abbot, although the abbatial lists do not leave room for him. The statement that he was abbot receives corroboration from the fact that the magnate Wulfric Spot gave to Archbishop Ælfric (as he then was) the Kentish vill of Dumbleton, which his predecessors had taken unjustly from the church of Abingdon. King Æthelred confirmed this vill to Ælfric for life, with reversion to Abingdon, and it was duly restored under the terms of the archbishop's will.

Ælfric became the first abbot of St Albans from its refoundation, holding office from c.969. His activities at St Albans were formerly confused with those of his brother and successor, Leofric, whose term of office can be firmly dated only from c.995. It may be that Ælfric continued to hold St Albans for a time after he attained episcopal rank. The confusion about their activities, though, can be traced to Matthew Paris. In his autograph manuscript of the Gesta abbatum, the names of Ælfric and Leofric have been transposed in the headings to the sections on their respective abbacies. Paris did not suspect the error of transposition and his efforts to amend the material on Ælfric in the light of what he himself knew of him further confused the issue. He stated that Leofric was first elected archbishop of Canterbury, but declined the office, saying that Ælfric was more worthy of it. Rival claims by St Albans and by Ely to the relics of St Alban were enhanced by stories of heroic attempts to save them from marauders, and Ælfric was erroneously implicated in the accounts of these efforts.

About 992 Ælfric was elected bishop of Ramsbury, and retained this office for life, even though he was translated to Canterbury in 995. He went to Rome for his pallium in 997. The English author of the life of St Dunstan, composed at the very end of the tenth century, dedicated his work to Archbishop Ælfric. The archbishop's brother Leofric was said to be the son of 'the earl of Kent' (Gesta abbatum, 1.28), and Ælfric, during his years in Canterbury, perhaps enjoyed the support of a powerful kin-group in the south-east.

Some indication of Ælfric's personal wealth, both in goods and in lands, is given in his will. While Abingdon was now repossessed of its alienated vill of Dumbleton, Christ Church, Canterbury, also received a tenurial bequest, and several properties were granted to St Albans, together with all his books. Further bequests of land included one to his sisters and their sons. His best ship was bequeathed to his lord (King Æthelred), together with sixty helmets and sixty breastplates. One ship was bequeathed to the people of Kent, and another to the

people of Wiltshire whose bishop (of Ramsbury) he was. These bequests are a reminder of the steadily worsening political situation, in the face of Danish attacks. Personal bequests included a philactery; and a ring and a codex of the psalter to Archbishop Wulfstan of York, who was one of Ælfric's executors (Abbot Leofric, the brother of Ælfric, was the other). A cross was bequeathed in Ælfric's memory to Bishop Ælfheah of Winchester, his successor at Canterbury. Slaves were to be freed, and debts annulled. Ælfric died on 16 November 1005. He was buried at Abingdon, but in the reign of Cnut (r. 1016–35) his remains were translated to Canterbury.

EMMA MASON

Sources D. Knowles, C. N. L. Brooke, and V. C. M. London, eds., The heads of religious houses, England and Wales, 1: 940–1216 (1972) • R. Vaughan, Matthew Paris, Cambridge Studies in Medieval Life and Thought, new ser., 6 (1958); repr. (1979) • J. Stevenson, ed., Chronicon monasterii de Abingdon, 2 vols., Rolls Series, 2 (1858), vol. 1 • W. Stubbs, ed., Memorials of St Dunstan, archbishop of Canterbury, Rolls Series, 63 (1874) • E. B. Fryde and others, eds., Handbook of British chronology, 3rd edn, Royal Historical Society Guides and Handbooks, 2 (1986) • Gesta abbatum monasterii Sancti Albani, a Thoma Walsingham, ed. H. T. Riley, 3 vols., pt 4 of Chronica monasterii S. Albani, Rolls Series, 28 (1867–9), vol. 1

Ælfric (d. 1016), magnate, must be distinguished from his contemporary *Ælfric Cild [see under Ælfhere (d. 983)], who was ealdorman of Mercia from 983 to 985. In 982 he succeeded Ealdorman Æthelmær (977–82) in a command which included Hampshire (AS chart., S 891, 946) and Wiltshire (ASC, s.a. 1003). Ælfric was one of the new men of Æthelred II (d. 1016), later to be blamed for leading the young king astray. In a charter of 993 (AS chart., S 876) he is censured for buying the abbacy of Abingdon for his brother Eadwine and encouraging the king to alienate the abbey's lands to laymen, among whom his son Ælfgar should probably be numbered (see below). Nevertheless, Ælfric continued to rise through the hierarchy of ealdormen; between 993 and 998 he was second only to Æthelweard and after the latter's death was premier ealdorman until ousted by Eadric Streona (d. 1017) about 1009. He was later described as 'one of those in whom the king trusted most' (ASC, s.a. 992, text F) and was remembered at Abingdon as the controller of the king's household (maior domus regie), though the force of this is somewhat lessened by the fact that he is confused with his namesake, Ælfric Cild. Whether he is the ealdorman Ælfric reproved in a papal letter for despoiling the abbey of Glastonbury is uncertain; the addressee might be Ælfric Cild.

Ælfric's appointment coincided with the renewal of viking raids on England. In 991 an English army commanded by Ealdorman Byrhtnoth was defeated at Maldon, Essex, by a host which continued to campaign in England until 994. In 992 a fleet was assembled at London, to 'entrap the Danish army anywhere at sea' (ASC, s.a. 992), and Ælfric was one of those chosen to lead it. The Anglo-Saxon Chronicle alleges that Ælfric not only warned the Danes of the English approach, but absconded from the fleet the night before the battle; in one version, he is even said to have fled to the Danes. It must be remembered, however, that the chronicler of Æthelred's reign, who was probably a Londoner, is noticeably hostile to the king's West Saxon and Mercian commanders. Abingdon Abbey preserved a tradition that when Ælfric Cild was exiled in 985 he fled to Denmark and later returned with a viking army, and if this has any basis, Ælfric Cild's activities may have been confused with those of his namesake. It is also possible that Ælfric had been in legitimate communication with the viking army. The surviving treaty between Æthelred II and the viking leaders, probably concluded in 994, refers back to earlier, local agreements, establishing a general truce 'in accordance with the terms which Archbishop Sigeric [of Canterbury] and Ealdorman Æthelweard [of the western shires] and Ealdorman Ælfric made, when they obtained permission from the king to purchase peace for the districts which they had rule over, under the king' (*English Historical Documents*, 1.401). John of Worcester says that Æthelweard and Ælfric, as well as Archbishop Sigeric, had advised the payment of tribute after the disaster at Maldon in 991.

In 1003, according to the Anglo-Saxon Chronicle, Ælfric disgraced himself again. A viking force led by Swein Forkbeard, king of Denmark, had stormed Exeter and moved into Wiltshire. The men of Wiltshire and Hampshire advanced to meet it, led by Ealdorman Ælfric, but:

> he was up to his old tricks. As soon as they were so close that each army looked on the other, he feigned him sick, and began retching to vomit, and said that he was taken ill, and thus betrayed the people whom he should have led. As the saying goes: 'When the leader gives way, the whole army will be much hindered' (*ASC*, s.a. 1003)

Despite these strictures, Ælfric remained in office, though the chronicler loses interest in his career and after 1007 transfers his attack to Eadric Streona, ealdorman of Mercia. Ælfric himself was killed on 18 October 1016, fighting for King Edmund Ironside at the battle of 'Assandun'.

Ælfric's wife was perhaps the lady Wulfgifu, commemorated in the *Liber vitae* of the New Minster at Winchester, who, like Ælfric, had a son called Ælfgar. Ælfric's son can be identified with the thegn who attested royal charters between 982 and 990, and who in 986 received an estate in Wiltshire belonging to the Old Minster at Winchester. He must also have been the king's reeve who received lands in Wiltshire belonging to Abingdon Abbey in the time of Ælfric's brother, Abbot Eadwine (985–90). In 993, for unspecified reasons, the king had him blinded and he probably died soon afterwards; his Wiltshire land was restored to the Old Minster in 997. His widow, Ælfgifu (also commemorated in the New Minster *Liber vitae*), married Wulfgeat, Leofeca's son, who, in 1006, forfeited his lands, including those belonging to Abingdon, for unspecified crimes. ANN WILLIAMS

Sources ASC, s.a. 992 [texts E, F]; s.a. 993 [text E]; s.a. 1003 [texts E, F]; s.a. 1016 [texts D, E, F] · John of Worcester, *Chron.*, vol. 2 · J. Stevenson, ed., *Chronicon monasterii de Abingdon*, 2 vols., Rolls Series, 2 (1858) · P. Stafford, 'The reign of Æthelred II: a study in the limitations on royal policy and action', *Ethelred the Unready: papers from the millenary conference* [Oxford 1978], ed. D. Hill (1978), 15–46 · S. Keynes, *The diplomas of Æthelred II, 'the Unready', 978–1016* (1980) · S. Keynes, 'The historical context of the battle of Maldon', *The battle of Maldon, AD 991*, ed. D. Scragg (1991), 81–113 · W. Stubbs, ed., *Memorials of St Dunstan, archbishop of Canterbury*, Rolls Series, 63 (1874) · S. Keynes, ed., *The Liber vitae of the New Minster and Hyde Abbey, Winchester* (Copenhagen, 1996) · C. R. Hart, *The early charters of northern England and the north midlands* (1975) · A. J. Robertson, ed. and trans., *Anglo-Saxon charters*, 2nd edn (1956) · F. E. Harmer, ed., *Anglo-Saxon writs* (1952) · AS chart., S 861, 876, 891, 918, 946 · *English historical documents*, 1, ed. D. Whitelock (1955)

Ælfric [Ælfric Puttoc] (*d.* **1051**), archbishop of York, first appears as provost of New Minster, Winchester. He was consecrated to the see of York in 1023 by Archbishop Æthelnoth of Canterbury. Ælfric was a benefactor to the secular canons of Beverley, and translated the body of St John of Beverley with great magnificence. In 1026 he went to Rome, and obtained his pallium from Pope John XIX, the first archbishop of York to do so.

A grant by King Cnut to Ælfric of land at Patrington, Yorkshire, suggests that he was a close adherent of Cnut. Similarly, the letter quoted by William of Malmesbury and the Worcester chronicle, which Cnut sent to his English subjects from Rome in 1027, was addressed to Ælfric as well as to Æthelnoth of Canterbury.

Ælfric may have been opposed to the accession of Harold I. Certainly, on the accession of Harthacnut, he was among those sent by the king to disinter the body of his brother Harold and throw it into a sewer. In 1040, Ælfric, with others, accused Earl Godwin and Bishop Lyfing of Worcester of the murder of the atheling Alfred, the king's half-brother. Harthacnut took away the bishopric of Worcester from Lyfing and gave it to Ælfric, but returned it the next year. William of Malmesbury took an unsympathetic view of these events, attributing them to Ælfric's initiative. However, since the Worcester chronicle is silent on the motives behind them, and the 'D' text of the Anglo-Saxon Chronicle, whose section for these years was written in the west midlands, calls him 'very venerable and wise', Malmesbury's damning assessment might be put down to the prejudice of a monk against a patron of the secular clergy.

In 1043 Ælfric assisted at the coronation of Edward the Confessor. He died, probably at Southwell, Nottinghamshire, on 22 January 1051, and was buried at Peterborough. Ælfric's byname 'Puttoc' probably means 'kite'. Since it is first recorded in the Worcester chronicle, but does not appear in the closely related chronicle attributed to Symeon of Durham, it has been suggested that 'Puttoc' was an opprobrious Worcester invention, denigrating the man who had attempted to unite Worcester with York in 1040. WILLIAM HUNT, *rev.* MARIOS COSTAMBEYS

Sources ASC, s.a. 1040, 1041, 1051, 1052 [texts C, D] · AS chart., S 968 · John of Worcester, *Chron.*, s.a. 1040, 1041, 1051 · *Willelmi Malmesbiriensis monachi de gestis pontificum Anglorum libri quinque*, ed. N. E. S. A. Hamilton, Rolls Series, 52 (1870) · J. Raine, ed., *The historians of the church of York and its archbishops*, 2, Rolls Series, 71 (1886) · J. M. Cooper, *The last four Anglo-Saxon archbishops of York*, Borthwick Papers, 38 (1970) · F. Barlow, *The English church, 1000–1066: a history of the later Anglo-Saxon church*, 2nd edn (1979)

Ælfric. See Ælric (*fl.* 1050–1051).

Ælfric (II) (*supp. fl.* **1070**), supposed abbot of St Albans, appears among the mid-eleventh-century abbots of St Albans in the *Gesta abbatum* as begun *c.*1250 by Matthew

Paris, who apparently used an 'ancient roll' of Bartholomew the clerk, servant of the twelfth-century Adam the cellarer; this stated that Ælfric (II) died in office at St Albans. But the record of the abbots between the abbey's refoundation c.970 and the succession in 1077 of Abbot Paul is confused and obscure. In the *Gesta* Ælfric (II) is the brother and successor of Abbot Leofric, who was in fact the brother and successor of Ælfric (I) (abbot from c.969 to 990?), later bishop of Ramsbury and archbishop of Canterbury; some confusion between the two Ælfrics seems likely. Moreover, the name Ælfric also appears apropos the contest between Ely and St Albans about which possessed the genuine relics of St Alban. According to the *Liber Eliensis*, when the fugitive Stigand, archbishop of Canterbury (d. 1072) came to Ely, evidently in 1070, he summoned from St Albans an Abbot Ecgfrith, whom he had appointed but about whom the *Gesta* is silent. Ecgfrith brought, as well as treasure, the genuine relics; he died at Ely after 1077. A variant of this story, taken by John Tynemouth (*fl.* 1350) from a twelfth-century Ely source, gives the fugitive abbot's name as Ælfric (Alfricus, Alfridus) (Horstman, 1.36). At St Albans, the truth about Ælfric (II) (or Ecgfrith) may have been suppressed and the legendary account of the *Gesta* substituted. In any case, the dates, deeds, and even historicity of Ælfric (II) are uncertain.

H. E. J. COWDREY

Sources *Gesta abbatum monasterii Sancti Albani, a Thoma Walsingham*, ed. H. T. Riley, 3 vols., pt 4 of *Chronica monasterii S. Albani*, Rolls Series, 28 (1867–9), vol. 1, pp. 31–8 • E. O. Blake, ed., *Liber Eliensis*, CS, 3rd ser., 92 (1962) • C. Horstman, ed., *Nova legenda Anglie, as collected by John of Tynemouth, J. Capgrave, and others*, 2 vols. (1901) • D. Knowles, C. N. L. Brooke, and V. C. M. London, eds., *The heads of religious houses, England and Wales*, 1: *940–1216* (1972), 65–6 • R. Vaughan, *Matthew Paris*, Cambridge Studies in Medieval Life and Thought, new ser., 6 (1958)

Ælfric Bata (*fl. c.*1010). *See under* Ælfric of Eynsham (*c.*950–*c.*1010).

Ælfric Cild (*fl.* 975–985). *See under* Ælfhere (*d.* 983).

Ælfric of Eynsham [Ælfric Grammaticus, Ælfric the Homilist] (*c.*950–*c.*1010), Benedictine abbot of Eynsham and scholar, is of unknown origins, though his language suggests he came from Wessex. He was educated under Æthelwold in the monastic school at Winchester, and after becoming a monk and priest was sent about 987 to the abbey of Cerne Abbas, Dorset, newly founded (or refounded) by the thegn Æthelmær, son of Ealdorman Æthelweard, where he was probably in charge of the school. There he apparently remained, producing a stream of books, until 1005, when Æthelmær, now an ealdorman, founded the abbey of Eynsham and Ælfric became the first abbot: Æthelmær himself lived for a time with the new community, possibly under compulsion after falling out of favour at court, but was back in an active role a few years later. Internal allusions suggest that Ælfric had at some stage in his life travelled in the north of England and in Italy, and that he may have been taught by Dunstan as well as by Æthelwold.

It is because of his writings that Ælfric of Eynsham is also known as Ælfric Grammaticus and Ælfric the Homilist. His earliest known works are the *Sermones Catholici* produced between 990 and 995, comprising two series of forty homilies on the gospels, the saints, and doctrinal themes, arranged according to the church year. Although he presented them primarily as preaching texts for the unlearned, the prefaces and incidental notes show that Ælfric anticipated readers as well as listeners, including learned laity and clergy. The project was evidently encouraged, if not commissioned, by Sigeric, archbishop of Canterbury, and by Ealdorman Æthelweard and the homilies were widely circulated, probably through the resources of Canterbury: some thirty manuscripts drawing on the collection are still extant, ranging from the late tenth century to the early thirteenth; the earliest is a copy of the first series with annotations in Ælfric's own hand (BL, Royal MS 7 C.xii). Over the next decade or so Ælfric built on this project, revising the collection, adding about forty new homilies and organizing them into different collections and selections. The original impetus for his work, which Ælfric identified in his first preface, was the coming reign of Antichrist, and the consequent need for orthodox teaching in the vernacular to replace erroneous teachings which were circulating widely in England. While the idea of the approaching millennium came to figure less in his writings as time went by, to be replaced in part by the new crisis posed by the vikings, the importance of knowledge and orthodoxy remained central. He made extensive use of Augustine, Gregory the Great, Jerome, Bede, and the Carolingians Haimo of Auxerre and Smaragdus of St Mihiel (as well as a range of anonymous saints' lives), and frequently cited them as authorities; but although he presented his work as translation it was rather a process of selection, adaptation, and independent argument. He also showed a detailed knowledge of the vernacular translations associated with King Alfred and wrote of them approvingly. The erroneous or heretical teachings which he aimed to supplant seem to have included apocryphal legends of the saints, aspects of doctrine, and superstitious practices such as prognostics. His homilies mostly take the form of either close interpretation of the Bible, often using allegory, or narratives of saints; but they also discuss a range of topics such as fatalism and free will, auguries, the Trinity, the resurrection of the body, the origin of the soul, clerical marriage, medicinal magic, and the belief in the devil as a creator.

These two collections were closely followed by a third, devoted mainly to the lives and passions of saints. Although the saints are mainly those honoured by the monks rather than the laity, the collection was made at the request of Ealdorman Æthelweard and his son Æthelmær, and was apparently designed for reading rather than preaching. Ælfric generally abridged and simplified his sources to concentrate on narrative, but the choice of subjects and appended discussions show a particular interest in such topics as the doctrine of the just war, royal and military saints, the history of English monasticism, the problem of the vikings, the interpretation of dreams, the careers and fates of Old Testament kings, and the gods of classical and Danish paganism. At about the same time (c.998) Ælfric produced a grammar of Latin (written in English and partially designed to explain the vernacular too), a Latin colloquy on trades and occupations, and the first of a succession of Old Testament translations and paraphrases, written in part for the use of the more learned laity: these were subsequently combined with the work of another translator to produce an illustrated copy of the Hexateuch. His role as an authority on church practice and canon law is evident in the pastoral letters commissioned from him by Wulfsige, bishop of Sherborne, and Wulfstan, bishop of Worcester and archbishop of York, for circulation to their clergy; and his importance as an adviser to the king and his counsellors is suggested by a text, perhaps part of a letter, in which he cites the biblical and classical precedents for a king delegating leadership of the army to others.

Ælfric probably died about 1010 (no date is recorded and the name is so common in the period that he is hard to identify in the records). As a scholar, he was the leading product of the tenth-century monastic reform, reflecting that movement's characteristic concerns with learning and monastic ideals, and also its close relations with the leading laity. If he surpassed most of his contemporaries in the range of his reading, he may also have differed from them in the rigour of his views: his conservative position on the cult of the Virgin was evidently not shared even at Winchester; his resistance to apocryphal and unorthodox teachings did not prevent his own work being mingled with such texts in contemporary manuscripts; and his strict views on clerical celibacy seem not to have been widely shared—in one letter to a landowner he bitterly remarks that 'you told me that your anchorite at home advised you' that celibacy was unnecessary (Assmann, 13). His works were in great demand and copied and read for the next two centuries and more, but often heavily adapted and selected by others. That process continued in early modern times. His works were prominent among the Anglo-Saxon manuscripts collected by Matthew Parker, archbishop of Canterbury from 1559 to 1575, and his associates, and were cited in support of protestant doctrines and vernacular versions of the scriptures. His discussion of eucharistic theory became the first Old English text to be printed when it was issued by Parker in 1566 and it was cited repeatedly in religious controversy down to the nineteenth century; but Parker rejected as an interpolation the two miracle stories with which Ælfric had carefully balanced his more figurative view of the eucharist.

As a writer Ælfric perfected a form of Old English which has become the model for modern analysis of the language and the manuscripts testify to his care in the use of grammar and vocabulary. He was a conscious stylist, but explicitly rejected the obscure vocabulary and convoluted syntax which was fashionable in contemporary Anglo-Saxon Latin writings and even in the vernacular, and created instead an elegant and balanced prose, using simpler vocabulary and structures. In his later writings he developed a style of writing modelled in part on verse, using rhythm and alliteration and occasional poetic language, though in a form that remained firmly prose and preserved the balance and lucidity of the earlier style. He left a few works in Latin and was a very competent Latinist, but chose to devote his energies almost entirely to writing in English.

Ælfric Bata (*fl. c.*1010), Benedictine monk and author, was a pupil of Ælfric of Eynsham. He is known only for a set of Latin colloquies in Oxford, St John's College, MS 154, one of which is an expansion of that by his teacher.

MALCOLM GODDEN

Sources B. Thorpe, ed., *The homilies of the Anglo-Saxon church: the first part, containing the 'Sermones Catholici', or, Homilies of Ælfric*, 2 vols. (1844–6) • *Ælfric's Catholic homilies: the second series, text*, ed. M. Godden, EETS, supplementary ser., 5 (1979) • *Homilies of Ælfric: a supplementary collection*, ed. J. A. Pope, EETS, original ser., 259, 260 (1967–8) • *Ælfric's Lives of saints*, ed. W. W. Skeat, 2 vols. in 4, EETS, 76, 82, 94, 114 (1881–1900); repr. (1966) • *The Old English version of the Heptateuch: Ælfric's treatise on the Old and New Testament, and his preface to Genesis*, ed. S. J. Crawford, EETS, orig. ser., 160 (1922); repr. with two additional manuscripts (1969) • *Ælfric's prefaces*, ed. J. Wilcox (1994) • *Ælfrics Grammatik und Glossar*, ed. J. Zupitza (Berlin, 1880); repr. with preface by H. Gneuss (1966) • *Ælfric's colloquy*, ed. G. N. Garmonsway (1939) • *Die Hirtenbriefe Ælfrics*, ed. B. Fehr (Hamburg, 1914); repr. with an introduction by P. Clemoes (Darmstadt, 1966) • B. Assmann, ed., *Angelsächsische Homilien und Heiligenleben* (Göttingen, 1889) • K. Barker, ed., *The Cerne Abbey millennium lectures* (1988) • M. McC. Gatch, *Preaching and theology in Anglo-Saxon England* (1977) • P. Szarmach and B. Huppe, eds., *The Old English homily and its backgrounds* (1968)

Archives BL, Royal MS 7 C.xii | St John's College, Oxford, MS 154 [Ælfric Bata]

ÆLFSIGE (d. 959), archbishop of Canterbury, was appointed bishop of Winchester in 951. From that date he regularly witnessed charters of kings Eadred and Eadwig, his name appearing at the head of the attesting bishops, until 958 when he was translated to Canterbury on the death of Archbishop Oda or Odo. He set out towards the end of that year to obtain his pallium from Pope John XII, but met his death from intense cold when he got into difficulties crossing the Alps and was buried there. His will suggests that Ælfsige was married and the Anglo-Saxon Chronicle records that his son, Godwine of Worthy, died fighting against the vikings in 1001. Under the terms of the will, mother and son were placed under the protection of Ælfheah, ealdorman of central Wessex. That and other entries in the will suggest that Ælfsige was well connected among the aristocracy of Wessex and in control of a substantial amount of land, though some of the named estates seem to have been endowments of the Old and New minsters in Winchester. Ælfsige exemplifies some of the aspects of the secular clergy to which the monastic reformers most objected and it is not surprising to find he had a bad reputation with post-conquest historians who claimed that he obtained his archbishopric through simony and showed disrespect to Odo's tomb.

BARBARA YORKE

Sources W. Stubbs, ed., *Memorials of St Dunstan, archbishop of Canterbury*, Rolls Series, 63 (1874), 37–8 • D. Whitelock, ed. and trans., *Anglo-Saxon wills* (1930), nos. 4, 16, 17, 114–16 • *Willelmi Malmesbiriensis monachi de gestis pontificum Anglorum libri quinque*, ed. N. E. S. A.

Hamilton, Rolls Series, 52 (1870), 25–6, 165 • N. Brooks, *The early history of the church of Canterbury: Christ Church from 597 to 1066* (1984), 237–8 • *ASC*

Ælfstan of Boscombe (*fl.* **1043–1065**), nobleman, is identified by Domesday Book as a substantial landholder, with an estate of some 237 hides of land, scattered over eight shires, making him the fifth richest of the recorded preconquest thegns below the rank of earl. Most of this land was probably his inheritance, but the charter whereby King Edward gave him Sevington, Wiltshire, is still extant (*AS chart.*, S 999). Clearly he was an important magnate; and he is probably the Ælfstan who attests royal charters between 1043 and 1065, latterly as *princeps*, an appellation suggesting high rank. His largest concentration of land (just over 70 hides) was in Wiltshire; this included two minor estates held as a tenant of the abbot of Malmesbury and the bishop of Sherborne respectively.

Ælfstan also had a respectable holding (just over 50 hides) in Bedfordshire and Hertfordshire. In these shires he is described as a thegn of King Edward, which suggests that he was a royal servant. If he is identical with Ælfstan *wicgerefa* ('portreeve') who, between 1053 and 1066, attests a private grant of land in Bedfordshire to St Albans (*AS chart.*, S 1235), he may have been reeve of Bedford; another St Albans memorandum is attested by Godwine, portreeve of Oxford (*AS chart.*, S 1425). He may also be identical with the Ælfstan the Staller, who attests a Kentish document of *c*.1045 (*AS chart.*, S 1471), for stallers are sometimes found well outside their own areas as agents for the king's interests. The name is not uncommon, however, and unless Ælfstan is given the distinctive toponym of his estate at Boscombe, Wiltshire, his identity cannot be established with certainty without other indications.

Ælfstan may have died in or before 1066, for he attests no documents of the Conqueror's reign. The bulk of his estate, with some inconsiderable exceptions, passed first to Ralph de Limesey, who was perhaps sheriff of Hampshire early in William I's reign, and thence to the 1086 holder, William, count of Eu. ANN WILLIAMS

Sources A. Farley, ed., *Domesday Book*, 2 vols. (1783), 1.47, 61, 67, 71v, 80v, 96v, 138v, 139, 166v, 167, 169, 211v, 212 • P. A. Clarke, *The English nobility under Edward the Confessor* (1994) • S. Keynes, *An atlas of attestations in Anglo-Saxon charters, c.670–1066* (privately printed, Cambridge, 1993) • R. Abels, 'An introduction to the Bedfordshire Domesday', *The Bedfordshire Domesday*, ed. A. Williams (1991) • S. Keynes, 'A lost cartulary of St Albans Abbey', *Anglo-Saxon England*, 22 (1993), 253–79 • J. A. Green, *English sheriffs to 1154* (1990) • *AS chart.*, S 999, 1235, 1425, 1471

Ælfthryth (d. **929**), princess, was the youngest of three daughters of King *Alfred (d. 899) and Queen *Ealhswith, daughter of Æthelred Mucel, ealdorman of the 'Gaini'. She also had two brothers. According to her father's biographer Asser, she was educated with her brother Edward at the royal court, where 'under the solicitous care of tutors and nurses … they have attentively learned the Psalms, and books in English and especially English poems, and they frequently make use of books' (Keynes and Lapidge, 90–91). Between 893 and 899 she married Baudouin (II), count of Flanders (d. 918), with whom she

had two sons, Arnulf (I) of Flanders (d. 965) and Adelulf of Boulogne and Ternois (d. 933) as well as two daughters, Ealhswith and Eormenthryth, whose existence is mentioned exclusively by the chronicler Æthelweard. By her father's will she received Wellow, on the Isle of Wight, Ashton (perhaps Ashton Keynes in modern Wiltshire), Chippenham, and £100. From the mid-eleventh century, in the *Liber traditionum* and a spurious charter, the monks of St Peter at Ghent claimed that in 918 she gave them land at Lewisham, Greenwich, and Woolwich. Count Baudouin died on 2 January 918 and was buried in the abbey of St Peter at Ghent, at the explicit request of Ælfthryth who wished to be buried beside him, and thus not like his father in St Bertin at St Omer, which was closed to women. There is no contemporary evidence for the year and date of Ælfthryth's death: the eleventh-century annals of St Peter at Ghent are the only source for its having occurred in the year 929, while her epitaph, written *c*.1000, gives 7 June as her obit. ELISABETH VAN HOUTS

Sources *Alfred the Great: Asser's Life of King Alfred and other contemporary sources*, ed. and trans. S. Keynes and M. Lapidge (1983), 90–91, 177 • *The chronicle of Æthelweard*, ed. and trans. A. Campbell (1962), 2 • Folcuin [Folcwin], 'Gesta Abbatum Sithiensium', ed. O. Holder-Egger, [*Supplementa tomorum I–XII, pars I*], ed. G. Waitz, MGH Scriptores [folio], 13 (Hanover, 1881), 607–35, 627 • P. Grierson, ed., *Les annales de Saint-Pierre de Gand et de Saint-Amand* (1937), 17 • J. Dhondt, 'La donation d'Elftrude à Saint-Pierre de Gand', *Académie Royale de Belgique: Bulletin de la Commission Royale d'Histoire*, 105 (1940), 117–64 • S. Keynes, 'The æthelings in Normandy', *Anglo-Norman Studies*, 13 (1990), 173–205 • L. C. Bethmann, 'Witgeri Genealogia Arnulfi comitis', [*Chronica et annales aevi Salici*], ed. G. H. Pertz, MGH Scriptores [folio], 9 (Stuttgart, 1851), 302–4, esp. 303 • K. Strecker and others, eds., *Die Ottonenzeit*, 3 vols., 5 (Leipzig, 1937–79), 298, no. 32 • *AS chart.*, S 1205a • A. Fayen, ed., *Liber traditionum sancti Petri Blandiniensis* (Ghent, 1906), 52–3, no. 60
Archives state archives, Ghent, Belgium • University of Ghent, Belgium

Ælfthryth (d. **999×1001**), queen of England, consort of King Edgar, was the daughter of *Ordgar (d. 971), a powerful magnate of south-west England, and of a royally descended mother of unknown name; her brother Ordulf was founder of Tavistock Abbey. She married first, *c*.956, Æthelwold, ealdorman of East Anglia, son of *Æthelstan Half-King; after his death in 962 she became the third wife of King *Edgar in 964. With Edgar she had two sons, Edmund, who died in childhood in 971, and Æthelred (d. 1016), who became king as *Æthelred II, the Unready, after the murder of his stepbrother in 978.

Ælfthryth is a controversial figure. Later legend makes her an enemy of St Dunstan, who accused her and her husband of adultery and won her undying hatred, and associates her with the death of an abbot of Ely, with witchcraft, with the seizure and depredation of Barking nunnery, with the death of her first husband, Æthelwold, with the seduction of King Edgar during the lifetime of her first husband, and, most famously, with the murder of her stepson *Edward (c.962–978) so that her own son might rule. Some of this reflects the hagiographical development of Dunstan, pitted against a series of Jezebels, and the growth of the cult of Edward the Martyr. Stories of her legendary beauty and seduction are probably romantic additions, though hints of Edgar's involvement in the death of Æthelwold may echo contemporary gossip. Her reputation possibly suffered from the vilification of her son Æthelred after the conquest of Cnut. Most of the stories can be dismissed as later stereotyped accretions, typically gathering around the name of a politically active and important woman, and particularly around that of a stepmother faced with the rival claims of older stepsons. But her involvement in the death of Edward the Martyr raises serious questions. The court and family politics in which she was involved bred such accusations, but at the same time produced precisely such action.

Birth and family connections determined the choice of Ælfthryth as a wife, first for the eldest son of the most important English magnate of the mid-tenth century, and then by King Edgar. Her royal marriage was accompanied by her father's appointment as ealdorman in the south-west. The legitimacy of her union with Edgar was stressed and she was certainly crowned and anointed as queen in 973, apparently against some opposition, though with considerable display; a near contemporary account pictures her feasting after the coronation with abbots and abbesses in a silken gown sewn with pearls and precious stones. Such emphasis on her status was important to the claims of her two sons Edmund and Æthelred, who faced an older brother from one of Edgar's earlier marriages. When Edgar died in 975, that eldest son, Edward, became king, but Ælfthryth's younger son, Æthelred, had his supporters; the ensuing debate is another potential source of Ælfthryth's later reputation, since candidates for succession were besmirched through their mothers. Edward was murdered three years later by Ælfthryth's own followers as he arrived to visit her and his young brother Æthelred at Corfe. Although the earliest accounts do not implicate the queen directly, and the details of the planning will never be known, it is difficult to exonerate her from all blame.

Murderess or not, Ælfthryth was one of the most important tenth-century queens. Although based in her roles as royal wife and mother, her power was exercised widely. She was remembered as a benefactress at Peterborough and Ely, and the rule of life for English monks and nuns promulgated c.970 gave her general responsibility for nunneries. But, as so often in the early middle ages, the political and the pious marched together. Ælfthryth's dower lands in Rutland, if not in east Suffolk, formed a basis for her interests in East Anglia and the fenlands and made her an integral part of the extension of West Saxon rule there. Her alliance with Æthelwold, bishop of Winchester, in these foundations linked her to monastic reform, but also to a bishop who was virtually court chaplain; it has a context in court and family politics, as does her interest in nunneries. Control of nunneries was an important part of the manoeuvring of tenth-century royal women. Ælfthryth took over Wherwell, if not Amesbury, in Wessex and Barking in Essex. The abbess whom Ælfthryth ousted at Barking was a cousin of Edgar's second wife, Wulfthryth, herself abbess of the great royal nunnery at Wilton.

Ælfthryth's most active roles, typically, came after her husband's death. She may have acted as virtual regent, perhaps alongside Bishop Æthelwold, during Æthelred's minority. His majority put an end to her greatest power, though she remained dowager queen. Æthelred's first wife was totally eclipsed by her and she had responsibility for the rearing of the heirs to the throne. When they and their household emerged in the 990s, she enjoyed a renewed status and it was then that her brother Ordulf became one of her son's closest advisers. But it was a twilight role. By c.1000, if not before, she was spending much time in her nunnery foundation of Wherwell, where her granddaughter would later be abbess. It was there that she died, on 17 November, in 999, 1000, or 1001, and there that she was buried.

PAULINE STAFFORD

Sources C. Hart, 'Two queens of England', *Ampleforth Journal*, 82 (1977), 10–15, 54 · A. Campbell, ed. and trans., *Encomium Emmae reginae*, CS, 3rd ser., 72 (1949), 62–5 · W. Stubbs, ed., *Memorials of St Dunstan, archbishop of Canterbury*, Rolls Series, 63 (1874) [esp. lives by 'B.', Adelard, Osbern, and Eadmer] · [Byrhtferth of Ramsey], 'Vita sancti Oswaldi auctore anonymo', *The historians of the church of York and its archbishops*, ed. J. Raine, 1, Rolls Series, 71 (1879), 399–475 · C. Hart, *The Danelaw* (1992), 569–604 · M. A. Meyer, 'The queen's "demesne" in later Anglo-Saxon England', *The culture of Christendom* (1993), 75–113 · P. Stafford, *Unification and conquest* (1989) · P. Stafford, 'The portrayal of royal women in England, mid-tenth to mid-twelfth centuries', *Medieval queenship*, ed. J. C. Parsons, new edn (1994), 143–67 · M. A. Meyer, 'Women and the tenth century English monastic reform', *Revue Bénédictine*, 87 (1977), 34–61 · P. A. Stafford, 'The king's wife in Wessex, 800–1066', *Past and Present*, 91 (1981), 3–27 · *The life of St Æthelwold / Wulfstan of Winchester*, ed. M. Lapidge and M. Winterbottom, OMT (1991) · *The chronicle of Hugh Candidus, a monk of Peterborough*, ed. W. T. Mellows (1949) · A. Bell, 'Gaimar and the Edgar–Ælfthryth story', *Modern Language Review*, 21 (1926), 278–87 · E. A. Freeman, 'The mythical and romantic elements in English history', *Historical essays* (1875), 1–39 · C. E. Wright, *The cultivation of saga in Anglo-Saxon England* (1939) · C. Fell, ed., *Edward, king and martyr* (1971) · *L'estoire des Engleis by Geffrei Gaimar*, ed. A. Bell, Anglo-Norman Texts, 14–16 (1960) · T. Symons, ed. and trans., *Regularis concordia Anglicae nationis monachorum sanctimonialiumque / The monastic agreement of the monks and nuns of the English nation* (1953) · 'La vie de Sainte Wulfhilde par Goscelin de Cantorbéry', ed. M. Esposito, *Analecta Bollandiana*, 32 (1913), 10–26 · E. O. Blake, ed., *Liber Eliensis*, CS, 3rd ser., 92 (1962) · S. Keynes, *The diplomas of King Æthelred 'The Unready' (978–1016): a study in their use as historical evidence*, Cambridge Studies in Medieval Life and Thought, 3rd ser., 13 (1980) · J. L. Nelson, 'The second English ordo', *Politics and ritual in early medieval Europe* (1986), 361–74

Ælfwald (*fl. c.*760). *See under* South Saxons, kings of the (*act.* 477–772).

Ælfwald I (d. 788). *See under* Oswulf (d. 759).

Ælfweard (d. 1044), abbot of Evesham and bishop of London, is said by the chronicle of Evesham to have been a relative of Cnut, presumably through Cnut's first, English, wife, Ælfgifu of Northampton. He was a monk of Ramsey and was made abbot of Evesham by King Æthelred in 1014. With the king's help Ælfweard managed to recover the property of the abbey from Godwine, ealdorman of Lindsey, and Evesham was placed under the personal protection of Cnut's second wife, and queen, Emma. He also successfully resisted the claim of the bishop of Worcester over the abbey. He was made bishop of London in 1035, but retained his position as abbot. After the death of Harold I in 1040, he may have been among those sent on an embassy to Harthacnut, who was then at Bruges, to invite him to take the throne.

Ælfweard was liberal in his benefactions to Evesham, transferring religious and secular books there from London, rebuilding the shrine of St Ecgwine, and adding a guest house to the abbey complex. He purchased the relics of the Flemish saint, Odulf, which had been stolen by vikings and brought to London, and had them installed at Evesham. He also removed the relics of St Osgyth from Chich, Essex, to St Paul's in London and the Evesham chronicler believed that it was as a divine punishment for this act that Ælfweard contracted leprosy. As the disease took hold of him, he retired from his bishopric and abbacy, but the monks of Evesham refused to admit him. In anger at this rejection, he removed all the books and ornaments with which he had enriched the abbey and took them with him to Ramsey Abbey, where he died on 27 July 1044, and where he was buried.

WILLIAM HUNT, *rev.* MARIOS COSTAMBEYS

Sources ASC, s. a. 1044 [text D] · W. D. Macray, ed., *Chronicon abbatiae de Evesham, ad annum 1418*, Rolls Series, 29 (1863) · W. D. Macray, ed., *Chronicon abbatiae Rameseiensis a saec. x usque ad an. circiter 1200*, Rolls Series, 83 (1886) · John of Worcester, *Chron.*, s. a. 1044 · AS chart., S 1423 · F. Barlow, *The English church, 1000–1066: a history of the later Anglo-Saxon church*, 2nd edn (1979) · D. Whitelock, *Some Anglo-Saxon bishops of London* (1975)

Ælfwig (d. 1066), abbot of New Minster, Winchester, is reliably evident only in the *Liber vitae* of New Minster (later Hyde Abbey). This work gives the probable year of his appointment as 1063, and the information that he was killed in the battle of Hastings on 14 October 1066 (*abbas ... occisus in Bello*; Birch). It is clear that William the Conqueror punished the abbey severely for the part which it had taken in resisting his invasion. The later tradition that made Ælfwig Harold's uncle and Godwine's brother is confused and doubtful.

WILLIAM HUNT, *rev.* MARIOS COSTAMBEYS

Sources W. de G. Birch, ed., *Liber vitae: register and martyrology of New Minster and Hyde Abbey, Winchester*, Hampshire RS, 5 (1892) · D. Knowles, C. N. L. Brooke, and V. C. M. London, eds., *The heads of religious houses, England and Wales, 1: 940–1216* (1972) · Dugdale, *Monasticon*, vol. 2

Ælfwine (d. 1047), bishop of Winchester, was formerly a royal priest in the service of King Cnut. According to Goscelin, Ælfwine helped Ælfstan, abbot of St Augustine's, Canterbury, to persuade Cnut to permit the relics of St Mildrith to be translated there. Ælfwine's influence with the king is indicated by his election to the rich see of Winchester in 1032. He was supportive of the nuns of the city, notably Ælfgiva, 'abbess of Cologne', and daughter of Earl Æthelwold. The break in tradition which brought a secular priest to be bishop in the monastic cathedral prompted resentment which underlies a later Winchester story in which Ælfwine was depicted as the lover of the dowager Queen Emma. It was related that both were imprisoned when their alleged plotting against the king became known, but the less stringently guarded Emma contrived to write to the other diocesan bishops, asking them to persuade her son King Edward to permit her to clear her own name, and also that of Ælfwine, by undergoing the ordeal of the hot iron. In a ritual in Winchester Cathedral, she walked unscathed over nine heated ploughshares, and a solemn reconciliation followed. A ballad based on this apocryphal story was sung before Bishop Adam Orleton during celebrations in Winchester, probably in 1334. Ælfwine died on 29 August 1047.

EMMA MASON

Sources *Ann. mon.*, vol. 2 · *Polychronicon Ranulphi Higden monachi Cestrensis*, ed. C. Babington and J. R. Lumby, 9 vols., Rolls Series, 41 (1865–86), vol. 7 · R. M. Haines, *The church and politics in fourteenth-century England: the career of Adam Orleton, c. 1275–1345*, Cambridge Studies in Medieval Life and Thought, 3rd ser., 10 (1978) · F. Barlow, *The English church, 1000–1066: a history of the later Anglo-Saxon church*, 2nd edn (1979) · S. J. Ridyard, *The royal saints of Anglo-Saxon England*, Cambridge Studies in Medieval Life and Thought, 4th ser., 9 (1988) · E. B. Fryde and others, eds., *Handbook of British chronology*, 3rd edn, Royal Historical Society Guides and Handbooks, 2 (1986) · P. Stafford, *Queen Emma and Queen Edith* (1997)

Ælla. *See* Ælle (*fl.* late 5th cent.); Ælle (d. 867).

Ælla (d. in or after 597?), king of Deira, was the son of Iffa. His existence is firmly documented, although the dates of his floruit are disputed. There is archaeological evidence for the settlement of Germanic people in what is now eastern Yorkshire by the late fifth century, and, according to the *Historia Brittonum*, Ælla's ancestor Soemil (*fl. c.*450) first separated Deira from Bernicia, thus suggesting that the kingdom of the Anglian Deirans came into being at about that time. But Deira's rulers before Ælla are ciphers and he may be the first of a new line. The common text of the Anglo-Saxon Chronicle records that Ælla 'succeeded to the Northumbrian throne' in 560 (s.a. 560) and that he died in 588. The northern recension of the chronicle adds that he reigned for thirty years. But the validity of the chronicle's Deiran dates has been questioned; its evidence contradicts Bede's statement that Ælla was one of the kings reigning at the time of Augustine's arrival in England in 597, so that alternative regnal dates from the late 560s to about the end of the century are possible.

According to a picturesque tradition, Pope Gregory the Great was moved to send Augustine as a missionary to the Anglo-Saxons by the sight of Anglian slave boys in Rome. Enquiring of their origin he was told they were from Deira and punned on the Latin meaning, saying that they must therefore be delivered from wrath (*de ira*) and, on learning that the name of their king was Ælla, added 'Alleluia should be sung in that land' (Bede, *Hist. eccl.*, 2.1). It was left to Ælla's son, *Eadwine, to introduce Christianity to Northumbria. After Ælla's death the Bernician Æthelric reigned in Deira and Eadwine and his other children fled into exile. If this was in 588, Eadwine would have been only three years old. Ælla's daughter Acha married the Bernician king *Æthelfrith, and under one of her sons, Oswald, the two Northumbrian kingdoms were united.

ROSEMARY CRAMP

Sources Bede, *Hist. eccl.*, 2.1 · B. Colgrave, ed. and trans., *The earliest life of Gregory the Great ... by an anonymous monk of Whitby* (1968) ·

ASC, s.a. 560, 588 [texts A, C] • D. N. Dumville, 'The Anglian collection of royal genealogies and regnal lists', *Anglo-Saxon England*, 5 (1976), 23–50 • M. Miller, 'The dates of Deira', *Anglo-Saxon England*, 8 (1979), 35–61 • D. P. Kirby, *The earliest English kings* (1991)

Ælle [Ælla] (*fl.* **late 5th cent.**), king of the South Saxons, is said by the Anglo-Saxon Chronicle to have arrived in Britain in 477 with his three sons, Cymen, Wlencing, and Cissa. Their traditional landing place was at Cymenesora, a place on the Sussex coastline near Selsey Bill which has since been lost to erosion; here they killed many Britons and forced others to flee into the weald. The chronicle notes two subsequent engagements: in 485 a battle with the British near a stream called 'Mearcredesburna'; and in 491 an assault by Ælle and Cissa on Andredesceaster (the Roman fort at Anderida, near Pevensey), with the subsequent massacre of all the British defenders. The dates are more likely than not artificial, representing abstruse calculations by the ninth-century compilers of the chronicle, and it is clear that some legendary elements are involved: Ælle and his sons arrive in the conventional three ships, and the place name Cymenesora (Cymen's bank or shore) has an obvious connection with the name of the first son. But it may be the case that authentic early traditions underlie some of the detail. Ælle was evidently a notable figure, whose activities may well have been remembered for generations; he is mentioned by Bede as the first of seven kings who held *imperium* ('dominion') over all the kingdoms south of the Humber and who are called by the Anglo-Saxon Chronicle *bretwaldas* (literally, perhaps, 'wide rulers'). It is difficult to decide what these terms would have meant in a fifth-century context; perhaps Ælle was recognized as the pre-eminent war leader of the Germanic invaders of southern England, or came to be so in retrospect. Nothing is known about the date of his death (indeed, the chronicle dates provide only an uncertain basis for determining his floruit and nothing is known of his descendants); he may have been the founder of a South Saxon dynasty, but there is no firm evidence linking him with later South Saxon rulers [*see* South Saxons, kings of the].

S. E. KELLY

Sources *ASC*, s.a. 477, 485, 491 • Bede, *Hist. eccl.*, 2.5 • F. M. Stenton, *Anglo-Saxon England*, 3rd edn (1971), 17–19 • M. Welch, 'The kingdom of the South Saxons: the origins', *The origins of Anglo-Saxon kingdoms*, ed. S. Bassett (1989), 74–83, 254–6 • M. Welch, *Early Anglo-Saxon Sussex*, 2 vols. (1983), 253–9 • J. Campbell, ed., *The Anglo-Saxons* (1982), 26, 38, 53 • S. E. Kelly, ed., *Charters of Selsey*, Anglo-Saxon Charters, 6 (1998) • P. Wormald, 'Bede, the "Bretwaldas" and the origins of the "gens Anglorum"', *Ideal and reality in Frankish and Anglo-Saxon society*, ed. P. Wormald, D. Bullough, and R. Collins (1983), 99–129 • S. Keynes, 'Rædwald the Bretwalda', *Voyage to the other world: the legacy of Sutton Hoo*, ed. C. B. Kendall and P. S. Wells (1992), 103–23 • S. Fanning, 'Bede, *Imperium* and the Bretwaldas', *Speculum*, 66 (1991), 1–26

Ælle [Ælla] (*d.* **867**), king of Northumbria, is an extremely obscure figure, owing to the lack of contemporary annals for ninth-century Northumbria. Only Symeon of Durham's *Libellus de exordio … Dunelmensis ecclesie* gives an implied date of 862 for his accession, stating that 867 was the fifth year of his reign. Although there are no coins in Ælle's name, numismatic evidence relating to the reign of his predecessor Osberht strongly suggests that Ælle may have become king in 866, on the eve of the viking attack on York. According to the Anglo-Saxon Chronicle and Asser, the Northumbrians had at that time expelled Osberht and replaced him with Ælle, who was a 'tyrant' and not of the royal blood. This information may be defective, however, for the *Historia de sancto Cuthberto*, written probably in eleventh-century Durham but with access to early northern sources, describes Osberht as Ælle's brother. At all events, the two men combined to retake York after the vikings had captured it on 1 November 866, but were killed when the vikings stormed it again on 21 March 867. The *Historia de sancto Cuthberto* implies that Ælle's fate derived from his guilt in seizing from the community of St Cuthbert the vills of Cliffe, Wycliffe, and Crayke in what is now Yorkshire. Scandinavian sources (possibly originating in the northern Danelaw), and the early thirteenth-century writing of Saxo Grammaticus, give a more colourful explanation, according to which the leaders of the viking army, Hálfdan and Ivarr, were the sons of a certain Ragnar Loðbrok, whom Ælle had previously defeated and put to death in a snake-pit. The sons' attack on York was represented as vengeance for the death of their father, and in certain sources as taking the form specifically of their putting Ælle to death by means of the bloodthirsty blood-eagle ritual. The late date of the sources in question and their quasi-legendary character make it very unlikely that this account of the deaths of Ragnar and Ælle had any basis in reality, although it remains the basis of the only popular modern image of Ælle, in the film *The Vikings* (1958). Equally unlikely is an English tradition, similar to one associated with King Osberht, that Ælle's rape of the wife of a merchant called Arnulf led the latter to call in the vikings by way of revenge.

DAVID ROLLASON

Sources Symeon of Durham, *Libellus de exordio atque procursu istius, hoc est Dunhelmensis, ecclesie / Tract on the origins and progress of this the church of Durham*, ed. and trans. D. W. Rollason, OMT (2000) • *ASC*, s.a. 867 • *Asser's Life of King Alfred: together with the 'Annals of Saint Neots' erroneously ascribed to Asser*, ed. W. H. Stevenson (1904) • Symeon of Durham, *Opera* • *L'estoire des Engleis by Geffrei Gaimar*, ed. A. Bell, Anglo-Norman Texts, 14–16 (1960) • A. P. Smyth, *Scandinavian kings in the British Isles, 850–880* (1977)

Ælnoth. *See* Ailnoth (*fl. c.*1085–*c.*1122).

Ælric (*fl.* **1050–1051**), archbishop-elect of Canterbury, was probably a kinsman of Earl Godwine and had been brought up in the monastery of Christ Church at Canterbury from early youth. The only reliable information about him appears in the earliest life of Edward the Confessor, a text which clearly favours Godwine's family. His name is given there as Ælricus, which 'is as likely to represent Ægelric [Æthelric] as to be a misspelling of Ælfric' (Brooks, 303, n. 146). The life states that the monks of Christ Church elected Ælric archbishop following the death of Archbishop Eadsige in October 1050, and that they then persuaded Earl Godwine to support their choice. However, at a time of factional struggles at court between the native earls, especially Godwine and his sons, and the court clerks and foreigners whom King Edward preferred to appoint to bishoprics, it is likely that it was Godwine who orchestrated the election of his kinsman. Edward's rejection of the candidature of Ælric and appointment instead of the Norman bishop of London, Robert of Jumièges, as archbishop at a council meeting in mid-Lent 1051, was a major factor leading to the rebellion and exile of Godwine later that year.

WILLIAM HUNT, *rev.* MARIOS COSTAMBEYS

Sources F. Barlow, ed. and trans., *The life of King Edward who rests at Westminster*, 2nd edn, OMT (1992) · N. Brooks, *The early history of the church of Canterbury: Christ Church from 597 to 1066* (1984) · F. Barlow, *The English church, 1000–1066: a history of the later Anglo-Saxon church*, 2nd edn (1979) · F. Barlow, *Edward the Confessor* (1970)

Aelsinus (*fl. c.*1023–*c.*1031), Benedictine monk and scribe of New Minster, Winchester, is known only because, unusually, he identified himself in one of his own productions. In a cryptic colophon in British Library, MS Cotton Titus D.xxvii, fol. 13*v*, he used the common code of replacing every vowel with the consonant that follows it. Decoded, the first section of the note reads: 'Frater humillimus et monachus Aelsinus me scripsit/sit illi longa salus. Amen.' ('The most humble brother and monk Aelsinus wrote me; may long-lasting health be his. Amen.') The note proceeds to identify the owner of the manuscript (and here Aelsinus made several grammatical mistakes which he subsequently corrected). Decoded, the corrected version reads: 'Aelfwinus monachus aeque decanus me possidet' ('Aelfwinus monk and dean owns me').

Aelsinus was the first scribe of Aelfwinus's prayer book, for which he copied calendrical and computistical material, Ælfric's *De temporibus anni*, St John's account of the passion, and some prayers (BL, Cotton MS Titus D.xxvii, fols. 2*r*–21*v*, 30*r*–55*r*, 57*r*–64*v*, line 8; with Cotton MS Titus D.xxvi, fols. 68*r*, line 11–75*v*, and 80*r*–*v*). He drew arches and diagrams as the setting for some of the computistical texts (BL, MS Cotton Titus D.xxvii, fols. 10*v*–13*r*).

Aelsinus's distinctive hand appears in two other books. He wrote the great majority of the New Minster *Liber vitae* (BL, Stowe MS 944), and also the calendar and *computistica*, Cambridge, Trinity College, MS R.15.32, 13–36. All three of Aelsinus's books are datable, providing some chronology for his career. The prayer book dates from 1023–9, the *Liber vitae* from *c.*1031, and the calendar probably from *c.*1025. Two of his three books contain drawings by the same highly talented artist, but there is no reason to identify these with Aelsinus.

The New Minster *Liber vitae* includes three Ælfsiges (the Old English equivalent of the name Aelsinus) apart from the abbot of that name, among the early entries for members of the New Minster (BL, Stowe MS 944, fol. 20*v*, no. vii; fol. 21*v*, nos. v and xi). The first (who is probably too early) is described as *cantor*; the second and third as *sacerdos* (priest) and *levita* (deacon) respectively. An obit added to Aelfwinus's prayer book refers to an 'Aelfsinus sacerdos', suggesting that this is our man and recording that he died on 13 July (year unstated).

Aelsinus wrote both Latin and Old English texts. His hand is fluid and untidy, and this is particularly pronounced in the *Liber vitae*, where the script is larger (and where one would have expected neater work). His letter forms are rectilinear in general aspect, quite angular in detail, and his writing had a perceptible slope to the right. Minims and ascenders and descenders alike vary in size; and this, along with the sometimes exaggerated size of 'st' and 'ct' ligatures and the high back of the 'a', gives the writing a variable aspect. In Latin texts he tended to use rustic capitals for rubric and sentence capitals; while Stowe 944 includes monumental coloured display capitals to accentuate incipits. The square elements of his writing look rather outmoded for the 1020s and 1030s, and in general his hand was better suited to Old English than to English Caroline script. Aelsinus is an uninspiring witness to the quality of English Caroline script being practised at the New Minster in the second quarter of the eleventh century.

RICHARD GAMESON

Sources BL, MS Cotton Titus D.xxvii; xxvi · BL, MS Stowe 944 · N. R. Ker, ed., *Catalogue of manuscripts containing Anglo-Saxon* (1957) · *Ælfwine's prayerbook*, ed. B. Günzel, HBS, 108 (1993) · S. Keynes, ed., *The Liber vitae of the New Minster and Hyde Abbey, Winchester* (Copenhagen, 1996)

Archives BL, MS Stowe 944 · BL, MS Cotton Titus D.xxvii; xxvi · Trinity Cam., MS R.15.32, 13–36

Æsc (*d.* 512?). *See under* Kent, kings of (*act. c.*450–*c.*590).

Æthelbald (*d.* 757), king of the Mercians, was the son of Alweo and the grandson of Eowa (*d.* 642), brother and possible co-ruler with the celebrated King *Penda. His descent gave him a strong claim to the kingship of the Mercians, and this no doubt explains why he was forced to spend years in miserable exile before his succession; he is said to have been persecuted in particular by his cousin *Ceolred (*d.* 716), Penda's grandson. During his period of exile he formed a close relationship with and frequently visited the hermit *Guthlac, who was living on an island in the Cambridgeshire fens; the latter was by origin a Mercian nobleman of royal stock, and was probably Æthelbald's close kinsman. From Guthlac he is supposed to have received consolation in the form of a prophecy that he would eventually succeed to the Mercian kingship and become a great ruler, a prophecy which was confirmed by a vision when Æthelbald rushed to mourn over Guthlac's body when he died in 715. After he became king, Æthelbald erected a splendid shrine over Guthlac's remains. Although later sources, especially the mid-fifteenth-century forgery known as Pseudo-Ingulf, state that he founded the monastery of Crowland on the site, these traditions from Crowland are notoriously unreliable and the 'foundation-charter' in Æthelbald's name is an obvious fake (*AS chart.*, S 82).

Rise to power over southern England Ceolred died young in 716, supposedly after suffering divine affliction for his evil ways, and Æthelbald assumed the kingship with apparent ease. Within fifteen years he had become the most powerful king in England south of the Humber. Bede, describing the situation in England in 731, states explicitly that all the southern kingdoms were subject to Æthelbald at that time: he mentions particularly Kent, the East Saxons, the

East Angles, the West Saxons, the Mercians, 'the people who dwell to the west of the river Severn', the Hwicce (living in part of modern Gloucestershire, Worcestershire, and Warwickshire), Lindsey (modern Lincolnshire), the people of the Isle of Wight, and the South Saxons. Modern scholars have sometimes been sceptical about Bede's authority for this definitive statement; there has been, for instance, a suggestion that the Canterbury sources on which Bede relied for so much of his information about southern England may have had their own reasons for inflating Æthelbald's position. But it seems unlikely that Bede could have been to any significant degree misled about the contemporary political situation. Certainly it would appear that in the 730s Æthelbald was disposed to make some very extravagant claims about his status. In the text of a celebrated charter of 736 Æthelbald is styled 'king not only of the Mercians but also of all the provinces which are known as the *Sutangli*' (where the last word is usually translated 'South English'), while in the witness list he appears as *Rex Britanniae*, 'king of Britain' (*AS chart.*, S 89). The longer of these titles recurs in variant forms in other charters in Æthelbald's name (*AS chart.*, S 94, 96); the shorter and more ambitious is not found in any other surviving document. It has been debated whether the use of the style *Rex Britanniae* had any political implications, or whether it was simply a grandiose but empty posture. Notoriously, Bede does not mention any Mercians in his celebrated list of seven kings who held *imperium* over England south of the Humber, although Æthelbald and his predecessors Penda and Wulfhere certainly had some claims to be included in that select company. When the Anglo-Saxon Chronicle later extended Bede's list with an eighth name, that of the West Saxon king Ecgberht (*d.* 839), it used a term *Bretwealda*, or *Brytenwealda*, which might possibly translate 'ruler of Britain'. The evidence is very tenuous, but the style applied to Æthelbald in the charter of 736 could perhaps have some connection with his political ambitions.

Æthelbald probably owed his dominant position in the 730s at least in part to the recent removal of two powerful and long-established rivals: the Kentish king Wihtred died in 725, leaving his kingdom to be divided between his sons, and his West Saxon counterpart, Ine, resigned in the following year. Military success no doubt had an important role to play in the establishment of widespread overlordship. In 733 Æthelbald occupied the West Saxon royal centre at Somerton, in what is now Somerset, and he would certainly seem at some stage to have been in control of the border territory of the upper Thames valley which was regularly disputed between the Mercian and West Saxon rulers: for he was in a position to give the minster at Cookham (in modern Berkshire) to the cathedral church in Canterbury (*AS chart.*, S 1258). Cuthred, who succeeded to the West Saxon kingdom in 740, seems to have chafed under Mercian overlordship. The Anglo-Saxon Chronicle (a West Saxon source and thus not unprejudiced) celebrates his accession with the statement that he 'fought stoutly against King Æthelbald' and mentions an episode in 752 when he met the Mercian king in battle at

an unidentified 'Beorhford'; some later manuscripts of the chronicle add the claim that Cuthred triumphantly put Æthelbald to flight. This picture of valiant resistance against Mercian domination is supported by some brief annals added to a manuscript of Bede's history: here it is noted that in 750 Cuthred of Wessex rose against Æthelbald and 'Angus' (Oengus, king of the Picts). Yet it is also possible that the Mercian ruler and his West Saxon counterpart sometimes co-operated against a common enemy. Under the year 743 the Anglo-Saxon Chronicle records that Æthelbald and Cuthred fought against the British (*Walas*). If this was indeed a joint expedition (and the evidence is admittedly slight), then it may perhaps have a connection with a reference in a document in the Welsh Book of Llandaff to what seems to have been a devastating Mercian assault or series of assaults on Wales, particularly in the Wye valley in the area of Hereford. Cuthred's death in 756 was followed by civil war in Wessex, which probably allowed Æthelbald to re-establish any influence over the kingdom which had been lost as the result of Cuthred's intransigence: when Cynewulf became king of the West Saxons in 757 one of his first actions seems to have been to witness a conveyance by Æthelbald of land in what is now Wiltshire (*AS chart.*, S 96). Possibly this reflects an occasion when the two rulers met in border territory.

The alliance between Æthelbald and the Pictish ruler Oengus, mentioned in connection with Cuthred's rebellion, seems likely to have developed in response to Æthelbald's ambitions with regard to Northumbria, which he is said to have ravaged in 737 and to have treacherously invaded in 740 while the Northumbrian king Eadberht was engaged in fighting against the Picts. Nothing is known about the political or other consequences of these incursions.

The exercise of overlordship The nature of Æthelbald's overlordship of southern England is likely to have varied from kingdom to kingdom, according to the relative size and strength of each: major tribes such as the West Saxons, the East Angles, and the men of Kent may have paid tribute and been technically subject, but smaller peoples probably saw much more direct interference in their affairs. Æthelbald evidently dominated the formerly independent kingdom of the Hwicce, freely disposing of land within its territory; its native rulers sometimes abjectly confirm the records of these donations, lucky to be given the status of *subreguli* or under-kings. The Mercian king also granted away land in Middle Saxon territory (modern Middlesex), which would seem previously to have been part of the East Saxon kingdom (*AS chart.*, S 100). Most importantly, he controlled the great trading emporium at London, where his agents collected tolls from merchants and ships. As a special favour he occasionally granted certain religious houses a permanent exemption from the tolls due on their trading ships when they arrived in London. A major recipient of this bounty was the Kentish double-monastery known as Minster in Thanet, which seems to have owned a small fleet of ships plying up the Thames to London; its abbess in the 730s, later celebrated as St Mildrith, may have been distantly related to him, which perhaps explains his patronage of her house. The bishop of Rochester and the brethren of the Kentish minster of Reculver are also known to have benefited from similar toll-exemptions, as did the bishops of London and Worcester. The granting of such privileges to Kentish ecclesiastics did not amount to direct interference in Kentish affairs, as has sometimes been suggested; but it could well represent a judicious exercise of patronage designed to enhance Æthelbald's position with respect to Kent, a wealthy and strategically located territory which dominated the crucial trade routes between London and the continent. Kent was also important as the location of the seat of the southern primate, the archbishop of Canterbury. There is reason to think that Æthelbald may have had some hand in the appointment of two, or possibly three, archbishops: Tatwine (731–4), Nothhelm (735–9), and perhaps Cuthbert (740–60); the first two were clerics from houses in territories under Æthelbald's direct control and there is an outside chance that Cuthbert had been bishop of the Mercian-controlled see of Hereford. A degree of influence over the Canterbury primate would almost certainly have proved an important factor in the maintenance of Æthelbald's domination over southern England.

Relations with the church One major ecclesiastical figure of the period was deeply suspicious of Æthelbald's attitude towards the church. In 746 or 747 Boniface, in association with eight other missionary bishops, wrote a letter of admonition to the Mercian king. He began with praise of the positive aspects of Æthelbald's rule: he was a generous donor of alms; he kept a strong hand on the kingdom, preserving law and order and maintaining peace; and he was known as a defender of widows and the poor. On the debit side, Boniface was deeply disturbed by the bad example of Æthelbald's refusal to take a single lawful wife in matrimony; from which it can be deduced that the Mercian king was probably an unapologetic polygamist, with a harem of concubines. Boniface goes on to accuse Æthelbald of committing fornication with holy nuns and virgins in monasteries (evidently a favourite sport of Anglo-Saxon kings to judge from the frequency of such accusations): it may be that some of the women in question were the daughters of important magnates, who had been removed from the marriage market for tactical reasons. It seems probable that Boniface felt rather more strongly about the next failings with which he taxes Æthelbald, that he had violated many of the privileges of churches and monasteries, that he had stolen ecclesiastical revenues, and that he had allowed his noblemen to oppress monks and priests to a greater extent than earlier Christian kings; here Boniface makes great play of the miserable end of Æthelbald's predecessor Ceolred, who is supposed to have committed the same errors. Boniface's letter represents a bold gamble, that he would be able to shame the Mercian king into changing his policies towards the church in his realm, but it was a gamble that seems to have paid off: in 747 a synod of southern bishops assembled at 'Clofesho' under Æthelbald's auspices to discuss strategies for reforming and strengthening the Southumbrian church; and in 749 the Mercian king issued a privilege for the Mercian churches and minsters, promising that they would be exempt from all taxes and other burdens, apart from the common obligations to maintain bridges and provide for defence against an enemy (AS chart., S 92).

Character and murder The evidence for Æthelbald's reign is tantalizingly meagre. He was clearly a tough and vigorous king, who successfully imposed order on his subjects and dominated his neighbours; the alliance with Oengus of the Picts and his possible co-operation with Cuthred of Wessex against the Welsh may hint at statesman-like qualities. He would seem to have had a strong pious streak, as demonstrated by his friendship with Guthlac and the extensive patronage of the church which is suggested by his surviving charters. Against this must be set the hints of a more intransigent and turbulent character, echoes of the uncompromising nature of his great-uncle Penda. His refusal to adapt to Christian monogamy may be one aspect of this. Perhaps he was a violent man: he is said to have paid compensation to an abbess of Gloucester for smiting her kinsman, a detail mentioned in a way which indicates that this was not a regular killing in war but a more ambiguous action (AS chart., S 1782). He does not seem to have been loved by his closest associates, for in 757 he was murdered at Seckington in what is now Warwickshire, apparently by members of his bodyguard who treacherously attacked him at night (presumably while he slept). An anonymous visionary later claimed to have seen him suffering in Hell. Æthelbald's body was buried in the minster at Repton (modern Derbyshire), where Guthlac had begun his ecclesiastical career. There is some suggestion that a carved stone discovered near Repton church in 1979 may be a fragment of a cross erected by King Offa as a memorial to his predecessor; indeed, it has been conjectured that the carving of a mounted warrior (flamboyantly moustached) on one side of the stone may perhaps be intended as a representation of Æthelbald.

S. E. KELLY

Sources ASC, s.a. 716, 733, 737 (texts D, E); 740, 743, 752, 757 • Bede, Hist. eccl., 5.25 • Bede, Hist. eccl., continuations • Felix's life of Saint Guthlac, ed. B. Colgrave (1956), 124, 139, 148–50, 152, 164–5 • AS chart., S 82–103, 1257–8, 1679, 1778, 1782, 1823–7 • M. Tangl, ed., Die Briefe des heiligen Bonifatius und Lullus, MGH Epistolae Selectae, 1 (Berlin, 1916), nos. 55, 73, 92 • The letters of Saint Boniface, trans. E. Emerton (1940), 123–30, 190 • English historical documents, 1, ed. D. Whitelock (1955), no. 177 • P. Sims-Williams, Religion and literature in western England, 600–800 (1990), 35–6, 48, 52, 119, 123, 135, 145–7, 338 • S. Kelly, 'Trading privileges from eighth-century England', Early Medieval Europe, 1 (1992), 3–28 • M. Biddle and B. Kjølbye-Biddle, 'The Repton stone', Anglo-Saxon England, 14 (1985), 233–92 • F. M. Stenton, 'The supremacy of the Mercian kings', Preparatory to 'Anglo-Saxon England': being the collected papers of Frank Merry Stenton, ed. D. M. Stenton (1970), 48–66 • F. M. Stenton, Anglo-Saxon England, 3rd edn (1971), 203–6 • J. G. Evans and J. Rhys, eds., The text of the Book of Llan Dâv reproduced from the Gwysaney manuscript (1893), 192 • A. Thacker, 'Kings, saints and monasteries in pre-viking Mercia', Midland History, 10 (1985), 1–25
Likenesses carved stone, probably Repton church, Derbyshire

Æthelbald (d. 860), king of the West Saxons, was the second of the five sons of *Æthelwulf (d. 858), king of the

West Saxons, and his first wife, *Osburh (*fl.* 839), the daughter of one of Æthelwulf's officials and herself descended from the West Saxon royal line. Starting in the 840s, Æthelbald attested his father's charters as a king's son and in 850 he received the rank of ealdorman. In 855, when Æthelwulf went to Rome, Æthelbald was left in charge of the West Saxons, while his younger brother *Æthelberht was appointed king of Kent and the southeast.

Æthelwulf was gone for over twelve months, returning in 856 with a new bride, *Judith (*b.* after 843, *d.* *c.*870) [*see under* Æthelwulf], daughter of the Frankish king Charles the Bald. Asser reports that in Æthelwulf's absence there was a plot to prevent his return hatched in the west of Wessex, either by Æthelbald, or by Ealhstan, bishop of Sherborne, and Eanwulf, ealdorman of Somerset, or by all three. But, since the annals of St Bertin relate that the king of the Franks took steps to ensure the safety of his daughter, it seems improbable that he would have allowed her to be taken to a country in civil war. It is more likely that Æthelbald revolted after hearing of his father's marriage to Judith, who had her own royal lineage and might produce heirs more throne-worthy than he. Asser notes that to avoid civil war Æthelwulf divided the previously united kingdom, assigning the western parts to Æthelbald and keeping the eastern parts for himself. It has been thought this meant that Æthelbald kept Wessex, while Æthelwulf displaced Æthelberht as king of Kent. But Wessex and its south-eastern extensions were hardly a 'previously united' kingdom and, given that Æthelbald's co-conspirators were from the west of Wessex and that Asser and other sources suggest that Æthelwulf returned to rule his own kingdom, it is more likely that Æthelwulf kept central and eastern Wessex, allowing Æthelbald to rule western Wessex. The absence of coins in Æthelbald's name may also suggest that West Saxon coinage was in Æthelwulf's name until his death.

Whatever the situation between Æthelwulf's return in 856 and his death in 858, after Æthelwulf's death Æthelbald became sole king of the West Saxons, with his younger brother remaining as king of Kent. Æthelbald also married Judith, his father's widow: there were political precedents, though Asser reports the move with horror. Very little is known of the rest of Æthelbald's reign: a solitary surviving charter issued in his name (*AS chart.*, S 326) is attested by King Æthelbald, King Æthelberht, Judith, and others, suggesting that he remained on good terms with his younger brother. Æthelbald died in 860 and was buried at Sherborne.   SEAN MILLER

Sources *ASC*, s.a. 855, 860 · *Alfred the Great: Asser's Life of King Alfred and other contemporary sources*, ed. and trans. S. Keynes and M. Lapidge (1983) · J. L. Nelson, ed. and trans., *The annals of St Bertin* (1991) · *AS chart.*, S 326 · S. Keynes, 'The West Saxon charters of King Æthelwulf and his sons', *EngHR*, 109 (1994), 1109–49 · P. Stafford, 'Charles the Bald, Judith and England', *Charles the Bald: court and kingdom*, ed. M. T. Gibson and J. L. Nelson, 2nd rev. edn (1990), 139–53 · D. P. Kirby, *The earliest English kings* (1991) · P. Grierson and M. Blackburn, *Medieval European coinage: with a catalogue of the coins in the Fitzwilliam Museum, Cambridge*, 1: *The early middle ages (5th–10th centuries)* (1986), 308

Æthelberht (*fl.* 733–747?). *See under* South Saxons, kings of the (*act.* 477–772).

Æthelberht [St Æthelberht, Ethelbert] (779/80–794), king of the East Angles, was the son of King Æthelred of the East Angles and was executed in 794 by order of King Offa of Mercia, as a result of which he came to be regarded as a royal martyr. His cult, which probably started life as a focus for resistance to Offa's oppressive rule, flourished in medieval England: sixteen churches were dedicated to him, including Hereford Cathedral, and for a time Hereford was second only to Canterbury as a magnet for English pilgrims. His feast day was 20 March. Beyond this little can be said for certain about one of the more obscure of Anglo-Saxon kings. The only pre-conquest reference to Æthelberht is found in the Anglo-Saxon Chronicle, whose compiler records that 'Offa, king of the Mercians, had Æthelberht beheaded' (*ASC*, s.a. 792). However, the paucity of pre-conquest source material is offset by a relative glut of post-conquest information, which affords the opportunity to reconstruct some kind of context for the assassination.

Three separate lives of St Æthelberht were written in the twelfth century by authors with connections to Hereford Cathedral (including Gerald of Wales and Osbert de Clare); and in the thirteenth century the story was told by the St Albans monks Roger of Wendover and Matthew Paris. It would seem that Æthelberht was the son of King Æthelred and his wife, Queen Leofruna. The history of Offa's dealings with the East Anglian kings before 794 is extremely hazy, but the fact that coins bearing his name were minted in East Anglia in the early 790s suggests that he exercised some sort of overlordship in that region in the time of Æthelred and Æthelberht. They may have been native East Angles whose position as sub-kings was imposed upon them after military defeat by the Mercians, or they may have been Mercian appointees, perhaps even with Mercian royal blood: Matthew Paris and Gerald of Wales both claimed that Æthelberht ruled the East Angles because he was Offa's kinsman.

The post-conquest sources are agreed that Æthelberht succeeded his father as a young man. In the Hereford version of events he was fourteen years old when he came to the throne, which, given that he seems to have been murdered soon afterwards, gives a date of 779 or 780 for his birth. The compiler of the Anglo-Saxon Chronicle does not explain why Offa felt the need to dispose of the young Æthelberht, but it was presumably because he was perceived as some kind of threat. The St Albans view that Offa was blameless and that the crime was perpetrated by his evil consort, Cynethryth (or Cwenthryth), can be written off as special pleading by monastic authors who were not only prejudiced against women, especially those in positions of power, but also eager to clear the name of their founder and benefactor, Offa, who had established and endowed St Albans Abbey in 793. Nevertheless Cynethryth may have had *some* involvement in the affair. The Hereford lives make her co-conspirator with Offa, which is by no means unlikely, as there is evidence that she was

Æthelberht [St Æthelberht] (779/80–794), coin

and there is the same implication in the pages of the St Albans writers, who agree that the martyr's relics were conveyed to Hereford Cathedral after his murder, where they worked various miracles in later times.

ANDY TODD

Sources M. R. James, 'Two lives of St Ethelbert, king and martyr', *EngHR*, 32 (1917), 214–44 · Paris, *Chron.* · W. Wats, ed., *Vitae duorum Offarum* (1639) · *ASC*, s.a. 792 [texts A, E, F] · *Ricardi de Cirencestria speculum historiale de gestis regum Angliae*, ed. J. E. B. Mayor, 2 vols., Rolls Series, 30 (1863–9) · W. B. MacCabe, *The legend of St Ethelbert, king of the East Angles* (1848) · D. W. Rollason, 'The cults of murdered royal saints in Anglo-Saxon England', *Anglo-Saxon England*, 11 (1983), 1–22 · A. Thacker, 'Kings, saints and monasteries in pre-viking Mercia', *Midland History*, 10 (1985), 1–25 · F. Wormald, ed., *English kalendars before AD 1100*, 1, HBS, 72 (1934) · Osbert of Clare, 'Life of Æthelberht', Landesbibliothek, Gotha, MS I.81 · A. T. Bannister, *The cathedral church of Hereford* (1924) · P. Sims-Williams, *Religion and literature in western England, 600–800* (1990)
Likenesses coin, BM [*see illus.*]

Æthelberht (d. 865), king of the West Saxons, was the third of the five sons of *Æthelwulf (d. 858), king of the West Saxons, and his first wife, *Osburh (fl. 839), herself descended from the West Saxon royal line. Shortly before Æthelwulf went to Rome in 855, Æthelberht was appointed sub-king of Kent (really modern Kent with Essex, Surrey, and Sussex), a position he kept until 860. On Æthelwulf's return in 856, the eldest surviving son, *Æthelbald, was able to rule the western part of Wessex and Æthelwulf himself took the eastern part; Æthelberht was allowed to retain his position in Kent. Æthelwulf seems to have intended Æthelberht to establish a cadet branch of West Saxon kings in Kent. However, when Æthelbald died in 860 the kingship of the West Saxons passed to Æthelberht, presumably because his brothers *Æthelred and *Alfred were considered too young to lead a country facing viking attacks (Alfred was only eleven).

It was under Æthelberht that Wessex and its south-eastern extension became a united kingdom. Unlike his predecessors, Æthelberht did not appoint another member of his family as sub-king of Kent. Further, a charter (*AS chart.*, S 327) issued in the first year of Æthelberht's reign reflects an extraordinary new kind of assembly: it was the first charter of a West Saxon king to include a full complement both of West Saxon and of Kentish witnesses.

The Anglo-Saxon Chronicle describes Æthelberht's reign as one of good harmony and great peace. Although this was true of internal affairs, the vikings remained a threat, unsuccessfully storming Winchester and ravaging all eastern Kent. Æthelberht died in the autumn of 865 and was buried at Sherborne beside his brother Æthelbald.

SEAN MILLER

Sources *ASC*, s.a. 860 · *Alfred the Great: Asser's Life of King Alfred and other contemporary sources*, ed. and trans. S. Keynes and M. Lapidge (1983) · *AS chart.*, S 266, 327–33 · M. L. R. Beaven, 'The beginning of the year in the Alfredian Chronicle', *EngHR*, 33 (1918), 328–42 · S. Keynes, 'The West Saxon charters of King Æthelwulf and his sons', *EngHR*, 109 (1994), 1109–49 · S. Keynes, 'The control of Kent in the ninth century', *Early Medieval Europe*, 2 (1993), 111–32 · P. Grierson and M. Blackburn, *Medieval European coinage: with a catalogue of the coins in the Fitzwilliam Museum, Cambridge*, 1: *The early middle ages (5th–10th centuries)* (1986), 309–10 · H. Pagan, 'Coinage in southern England, 796–874', *Anglo-Saxon monetary history: essays in*

an important political figure in her own right, upon whom Offa relied for counsel. There are signs that Æthelberht stood in some way for East Anglian independence from Mercia, for he began to issue coins bearing his own name, a luxury which Offa allowed to none of his dependent kings. It is feasible, therefore, that his execution represents an attempt by Offa to stop an incipient rebellion in its tracks by depriving the East Angles of their figurehead, who died heirless. Alternatively, if Mercian royal blood flowed in Æthelberht's veins, then this would have weighed heavily against him, for Offa was eager to secure the uncontested succession of his son Ecgfrith as king of Mercia, and, as his contemporary Alcuin observed, he pursued a ruthless policy of eliminating possible rivals, chief among whom would have been a sub-king with Mercian royal blood.

The sources differ widely on the method of Æthelberht's assassination. In Matthew Paris's version he sits on a booby-trapped chair which falls down into a pit, where he is smothered with drapes and then beheaded; while Gerald of Wales describes how he was ambushed and decapitated by an assassin named Gwinbert, who delivered his head to Offa. The fact that Æthelberht lost his head in all versions of the story strengthens the possibility that he was perceived by Offa as an obstacle to Ecgfrith's succession, since decapitation was the traditional punishment in literature and in fact for usurpers or would-be usurpers. There is also consensus among the post-conquest sources that the occasion of Æthelberht's murder was a visit to Offa's court to receive the hand of his daughter, who is named by various authors as Ælfthryth, Ælfrida, Etheldritha, and Ælfflæda. Thus it would seem that Offa used his daughter as bait with which to draw Æthelberht out of East Anglia so that he could be disposed of more easily. The Hereford branch of the tradition maintained that when Æthelberht came to visit him Offa was holding court near Hereford, at the royal estate of Sutton,

Æthelberht (*d.* 865), coin

memory of Michael Dolley, ed. M. A. S. Blackburn (1986), 45–65 · C. Blunt, 'A Burgred-type coin with, apparently, the name of King Æthilbearht of Wessex', *British Numismatic Journal*, 3rd ser., 7 (1952–4), 54–6
Likenesses coin?, *c.*865, FM Cam.; repro. in *British Numismatic Journal*, 27/1 (1952), pl. VII.8 · coins, BM; repro. in Pagan, 'Coinage in southern England', pl. 4.1, nos. 17–18 [*see illus.*]

Æthelberht I (*d.* **616**?), king of Kent, was the successor of his father, King *Eormenric (*fl.* 550x600) [*see under* Kent, kings of], and a member of the Kentish royal dynasty, the Oiscingas, said to have been founded by *Æsc [*see under* Kent, kings of], son of Hengist.

Chronology of the reign It has generally been assumed that Æthelberht became king in 560 or 561, on the basis of Bede's information that he ruled for fifty-six years and died on 24 February 616. This would have been a reign of quite exceptional length (no other Anglo-Saxon king is known to have ruled for so long), and there has been some suspicion that Bede's figures may not be entirely reliable; for instance, it has been suggested that fifty-six years properly applied to Æthelberht's age at death, and not the length of his reign. Some reliance has been placed on two brief comments by Gregory of Tours in relation to the marriage between Æthelberht and *Bertha (*b. c.*565, *d.* in or after 601), daughter of the Merovingian Frankish king Charibert, which is unlikely to have taken place before the mid-570s. In the first instance (which occurs in a part of Gregory's *Libri historiarum* probably written in 581 or before) Gregory says simply that Bertha married a certain Kentishman; in the second (composed *c.*589) he states that her husband was 'the son of a certain king in Kent' (*History of the Franks*, 9.26). The implication would seem to be that Æthelberht was not yet king when he married Bertha (apparently between the mid-570s and 581) and that he may not have succeeded his father until after 589.

It is difficult to know how much weight to give to Gregory's comments. He was a contemporary, and he was a close associate of Bertha's mother; on the other hand, he clearly had little or no interest in Anglo-Saxon matters and may have been mistaken about Æthelberht's status. The English sources (which may not be entirely independent of Bede) agree in giving Æthelberht a very long reign. One version of the Anglo-Saxon Chronicle mentions Æthelberht's accession under the year 565 and states that he ruled for fifty-three years (*liii* is conceivably a scribal error for *lvi*). The annal for 568 in the Anglo-Saxon Chronicle mentions an incident in which the West Saxon rulers Ceawlin and Cutha fought against Æthelberht and drove him into Kent. This may have been another man, perhaps a recalcitrant West Saxon princeling; but if it was the more celebrated Æthelberht, then it would appear that already in 568 he was in a position to lead an army into a neighbouring kingdom. A possible explanation for the discrepancy between Gregory and the English sources is that Æthelberht was appointed co-ruler or sub-king during his father's lifetime, but did not have full power until Eormenric's death; but this seems incapable of proof.

Conversion to Christianity The most important episode in Æthelberht's reign was the arrival in Kent in 597 (or possibly late 596) of a party of missionaries sent from Rome by Pope Gregory the Great. The king had already been exposed to Christianity for some years; his marriage to Bertha had been approved only on condition that she was permitted freely to practise her faith, and she had brought with her from her homeland a bishop named Liudhard (and presumably also a Christian retinue). Bede's account of the meeting between Æthelberht and the missionaries stresses the king's suspicion of the new arrivals and indicates that he was still a committed pagan; but it is difficult to believe that the mission would have gone ahead without some kind of prior consent or request from Æthelberht. He may have been bowing to pressure from his Frankish connections; certain letters of Pope Gregory hint at some Merovingian involvement in the decision to attempt the conversion of Kent (and the fact that the Franks had sent a bishop to Kent as Bertha's chaplain rather than a simple priest may indicate that they had already made some plans to evangelize the area). Certainly Æthelberht received Augustine and his companions most graciously and very quickly agreed to be baptized. The exact date of his conversion remains uncertain; Bede at one stage says that it took place twenty-one years before Æthelberht died (which would seem to be *before* Augustine's arrival in Kent). Certainly there is good reason to suppose that Æthelberht was Christian by the end of 597, for in a letter of July 598 Pope Gregory boasts that up to Christmas of the previous year Augustine had made ten thousand English converts; such mass conversions are unlikely to have taken place until after the king had accepted Christianity.

Overlordship Already at the time of Augustine's arrival Æthelberht seems to have been to some degree acknowledged as overlord of all the English kingdoms south of the Humber. According to Bede, he was the third Anglo-Saxon ruler to enjoy such recognition; his predecessors had been Ælle of the South Saxons, who probably lived in the fifth century, and Ceawlin of the West Saxons, who died about 593. The exact nature of Æthelberht's overlordship is very unclear (it was probably in the main a question of military leadership), but certain episodes in Bede's narrative do indicate that he had some authority outside the boundaries of Kent. It was apparently with Æthelberht's help that Augustine summoned the bishops of the Britons for a conference at 'Augustine's Oak', which appears to have been located somewhere on the border between the modern counties of Gloucestershire and Wiltshire or Somerset (possibly Æthelberht did no more than provide a safe conduct or an escort). Æthelberht appears to have dominated the kingdom of the East Saxons, ruled in the early seventh century by his nephew *Sæberht (d. 616/17), son of his sister Ricule; he superintended the conversion of the East Saxons and built the church of St Paul's in London as an episcopal seat for Mellitus. Æthelberht's relations with Rædwald of East Anglia are more difficult to define. Bede identifies Rædwald as the fourth of the Southumbrian overlords, and adds an obscure comment which has been translated as indicating that Rædwald began to enjoy this position before Æthelberht died; a preferable interpretation may be that during Æthelberht's lifetime Rædwald retained the military leadership of the East Angles, which would normally have devolved upon the Southumbrian overlord. It seems probable that Rædwald was first introduced to Christianity while in attendance at Æthelberht's court.

Kingship on the Frankish model In Kent itself Æthelberht was responsible for a number of important innovations. Perhaps as early as 602–3 he compiled with his advisers a written law-code, which gave the fledgeling Kentish church a secure position within the kingdom but which was also concerned with a wide range of secular issues. As far as is known, the use of writing was effectively introduced into England by the Roman missionaries in 597; and so it is interesting that Æthelberht's code was in English rather than Latin, since it implies that an almost immediate effort had been made to transform the native language from an oral to a written form. Presumably the vernacular was chosen for reasons of practicality and in order to stress continuity; Æthelberht's written code was probably an extension of oral pronouncements previously made in assembly by himself and his predecessors. Bede says that Æthelberht was here influenced by Roman example, but the real parallels for his legislation lie in the law-codes issued by the Germanic kings on the continent, including the Franks.

Another possible innovation on the part of Æthelberht was the creation of a royal capital city at Canterbury. When Augustine arrived in 597 Æthelberht gave him a dwelling-place in the city, which Bede describes as the *metropolis* or chief city of his realm and elsewhere as a 'royal city'. To grasp the unusual nature of this statement it must be realized that in sixth-century England there is almost no evidence of any continuing urban life in the old Roman cities; virtually the whole population lived on the land, and the kings followed suit, making an itinerant progress from one royal estate to another. Canterbury itself would appear to have been essentially deserted for a long period during the fifth century, and population levels during the sixth are likely to have been very low. The idea that a sixth-century Anglo-Saxon kingdom might have a royal 'capital' is certainly remarkable.

A third area where Æthelberht seems to have made an important change which reflected on the nature of kingship in Kent is in the establishment of a royal burial church on the outskirts of Canterbury, St Peter and St Paul (which was to develop into St Augustine's Abbey); this was intended to provide a dynastic burial place for the kings of Kent, who were interred in a chapel dedicated to St Martin, and also to cater for the archbishops of Canterbury. This innovation marked a very significant break with the past, and underlined Æthelberht's commitment to the new religion; it also seems to reflect an imitation of the burial practices of the Frankish royal dynasty (the connection is emphasized by the dedication of the royal burial chapel, for the cult of St Martin was closely associated with the Merovingians). It seems likely that in this instance Æthelberht was influenced by the wishes and expectations of his Frankish queen, but there may well be a deeper level of aspiration involved. In accepting Christianity, perhaps establishing a capital, issuing a law-code, and creating a dynastic burial church, Æthelberht was following in the footsteps of the Frankish king Clovis, who had effectively founded the fortunes of the Merovingians. Whether Æthelberht saw himself as the English Clovis it is impossible to say, but it does seem likely that he was very influenced by Frankish ideas of kingship. His marriage to Bertha was not an isolated episode of cross-channel contact. Kent was an important Frankish trading partner, and the sixth-century Kentish cemeteries have yielded a profusion of Frankish and Frankish-style luxury grave-goods. And Æthelberht's marriage may not have been the first alliance between the Merovingians and the Oiscingas; his father Eormenric had a name of distinctively Frankish type. There is a controversial hypothesis that Kent and other kingdoms of southern England were in fact under Merovingian overlordship during parts of the sixth and seventh centuries. Certainly there are hints that the Frankish kings did like to think that they should enjoy some kind of hegemony over their neighbours, but it is debatable whether this was ever translated into reality in southern England. It is particularly hard to credit in the case of Æthelberht, whose power over his own neighbours seems incompatible with subordination to the Merovingians.

Death, burial, and succession Bede's date for Æthelberht's death (24 February 616) is probably correct, although it has been pointed out that some early annals give an obit in 618 (presumably this is to be connected with the information behind the later annal in text E of the Anglo-Saxon Chronicle which gives an accession date in 565 and a reign length of fifty-six years). Æthelberht was buried in the new royal mausoleum at Canterbury; an unofficial cult seems to have developed and from the thirteenth century his name appears in calendars. According to later sources at St Augustine's, Bertha (who appears to have taken the Anglo-Saxon name Æthelburh after her arrival in England) died before her husband, and before the new burial church was consecrated; she was buried outside and later transferred into the royal burial chapel. Æthelberht appears to have married again (at a very venerable age, if the traditional date for his accession is correct) or to have had a concubine, for after his death his son *Eadbald (d. 640) married his father's widow (that is, his stepmother), to the consternation of the Roman missionaries. Æthelberht's known offspring are Eadbald, who succeeded him, and a daughter, Æthelburh (also known as Tate), who married King *Eadwine of the Northumbrians in 625. Some Kentish sources also credit him with another daughter named Eadburh, said to have been buried in the minster at Lyminge (but there may be confusion here with a later Abbess Eadburh of Minster in Thanet).

There are five surviving charters in Æthelberht's name, three from St Augustine's and one each from the episcopal archives at St Paul's in London and Rochester. None is authentic, or has any genuine basis.   S. E. KELLY

Sources Bede, *Hist. eccl.*, 1.24–6, 32–3; 2.2–3, 5 • *ASC*, s.a. 568, 616; s.a. 565 [text E] • *Gregorii Turonensis opera*, ed. B. Krusch and W. Levison, MGH Scriptores Rerum Merovingicarum, 1/1 (Hanover, 1937–52) • Gregory of Tours, *The history of the Franks*, ed. and trans. L. Thorpe (1974) • F. Liebermann, ed., *Die Gesetze der Angelsachsen*, 1 (Halle, 1898), 3–8 • N. Brooks, 'The creation and early structure of the kingdom of Kent', *The origins of Anglo-Saxon kingdoms*, ed. S. Bassett (1989), 55–74 • N. Brooks, *The early history of the church of Canterbury: Christ Church from 597 to 1066* (1984), 5–7, 63–4 • I. Wood, *The Merovingian kingdoms, 450–751* (1994) • *Gregorii I papae registrum epistolarum*, ed. P. Ewald and L. M. Hartmann, MGH Epistolae [quarto], 2 (Berlin, 1892–9), 30 • *English historical documents*, 1, ed. D. Whitelock (1955), nos. 29, 163 • S. E. Kelly, ed., *Charters of St Augustine's Abbey, Canterbury, and Minster-in-Thanet*, Anglo-Saxon Charters, 4 (1995), nos. 1, 2, 3 • K. H. Krüger, *Königsgrabkirchen der Franken, Angelsachsen, und Langobarden* (Munich, 1971), 264–87 • K. Blockley and others, *Excavations in the Marlowe car park and surrounding areas*, The Archaeology of Canterbury, 5 (1995) • D. W. Rollason, *The Mildrith legend: a study in early medieval hagiography in England* (1982) • J. M. Wallace-Hadrill, *Bede's Ecclesiastical history of the English people: a historical commentary*, OMT (1988)

Æthelberht II (d. 762), joint king of Kent, succeeded to the kingdom of Kent with his brother **Eadberht I** (d. 748) in 725 after the long reign of their father, *Wihtred (d. 725), who had re-established the kingdom's independence after the foreign invasions of the late 680s. Their half-brother Alric is said by Bede to have been coheir, but there is no trace of him after 725 and it is possible that he was denied power. Understanding of this period has been obscured by the incorrect chronological framework proposed by the twelfth-century chronicler William of Malmesbury, who gave the three brothers consecutive reigns: Eadberht from 725 to 748; Æthelberht from 748 until 762; and Alric from 762 until 796. The issue was further confused by radical emendation in the later middle ages of the muniments of St Augustine's Abbey and of Christ Church, Canterbury, intended to bring them into line with Malmesbury's chronology. In fact, Æthelberht and Eadberht seem to have ruled jointly from 725. The

kingdom may have been divided between them, with Æthelberht based in the east and Eadberht in the west; Æthelberht was apparently regarded as the senior ruler. Eadberht died in 748 and was buried in Reculver Minster; his position in west Kent was inherited by his son **Eardwulf** (d. in or before 762). Æthelberht survived until 762, and chose to be buried in the monastery of St Peter and St Paul (later St Augustine's Abbey) in Canterbury.

By 731 Kent, along with the other kingdoms south of the Humber, appears to have acknowledged the overlordship of Æthelbald, king of the Mercians. It is impossible to say whether this degree of domination lasted until Æthelbald's death in 757. None of the Kentish charters issued by Æthelberht, Eadberht I, or Eardwulf has any reference to Mercian overlordship, but this does not prove that Kent was independent; in his dealings with the rulers of major kingdoms such as Kent, Æthelbald may simply have required the payment of tribute and some measure of deference, rather than control over routine land transactions. Eadberht at least is known to have attended Æthelbald's court, for he attests a charter of the Mercian king that was issued in London in 748 (*AS chart.*, S 91).

The death of Æthelberht II in 762 precipitated a succession crisis in Kent. Over the next few years an unusually large number of charters were issued, making it possible to identify no fewer than five kings of Kent, evidently jockeying for power and attempting to win support through land-grants. In east Kent Æthelberht was succeeded by **Eadberht II** (*fl.* 762–763), probably his son; but within two years Eadberht had been replaced by a certain **Eanmund** (*fl.* 763–764), who was in turn supplanted by **Heahberht** (*fl.* 764). In west Kent Eardwulf does not seem to have survived 762; in his place there appeared a King **Sigered** (*fl.* 762–765), who in one charter is explicitly called 'king of half Kent' and whose name suggests that he may have had some connection with the East Saxon royal dynasty. By 765 Sigered had also been swept away, and west Kent was in the hands of King **Ecgberht II** (*fl.* 765–779), who was destined to cling to power for very much longer than his immediate predecessors.

Meanwhile, the new king of the Mercians, Offa, had taken advantage of the political turmoil to impose his overlordship on Kent; in 765 he issued a charter directly concerning land in Kent which was effectively a confirmation of a charter of Sigered (*AS chart.*, S 105). But Offa's growing control over the kingdom seems to have received a sudden check in 776. The Anglo-Saxon Chronicle records that in that year a battle took place at Otford in Kent between the Mercians and the men of Kent, but does not mention the outcome. Most later medieval historians assumed that Offa was victorious, but it has been pointed out that there is no evidence for Mercian overlordship in Kent in the years immediately after that battle; instead, there are charters issued by King Ecgberht II in 778 and 779 and by a King **Ealhmund** (*fl.* 784) in 784 which make no reference at all to Offa. There is now general agreement that the men of Kent, probably led by King Ecgberht, rebelled against Mercian rule in 776 and succeeded in winning independence from Offa for almost a decade.

Ecgberht seems to have become king of the whole of Kent (the fate of Heahberht is uncertain); there survive about a dozen coins in his name, probably struck at Canterbury, which are some of the earliest examples of a new silver coinage based on Carolingian weights (the dating of these coins is uncertain and they may belong to the period before the battle of Otford; there is a single example in the name of Heahberht). Ealhmund was probably Ecgberht's successor (and apparently the father of the future King *Ecgberht who was to rule Wessex from 802 until his death in 839). But Offa's power could not be withstood for much longer, and by 785 he had reimposed his control on the kingdom. In that year he issued the first of a series of charters making direct grants of land in Kent, without reference to any native ruler; it is to be assumed that Ealhmund had been killed or driven out. From 785 until the 820s Kent was treated as a province of the Mercian kingdom; only in 796–8 was there a brief resurgence of Kentish independence, when *Eadberht Præn (perhaps a descendant of the ancient Kentish dynasty) ruled for a short time as king of Kent.

S. E. KELLY

Sources AS chart., S 23–38, 86–8, 91, 105, 110–11, 123, 125, 128–31, 134, 143 · ASC, s.a. 748, 762, 778 · F. M. Stenton, 'The supremacy of the Mercian kings', EngHR, 33 (1918), 433–52; repr. in D. M. Stenton, ed., Preparatory to 'Anglo-Saxon England': the collected papers of Frank Merry Stenton (1970), 48–66 · Bede, Hist. eccl., 5.24 · Willelmi Malmesbiriensis monachi de gestis regum Anglorum, ed. W. Stubbs, 2 vols., Rolls Series (1887–9), vol. 1, pp. 17–18 · S. E. Kelly, ed., Charters of St Augustine's Abbey, Canterbury, and Minster-in-Thanet, Anglo-Saxon Charters, 4 (1995), esp. appx 3, 'The kings of Kent' · P. Grierson and M. Blackburn, Medieval European coinage: with a catalogue of the coins in the Fitzwilliam Museum, Cambridge, 1: The early middle ages (5th–10th centuries) (1986), 280–81 · K. H. Krüger, Königsgrabkirchen der Franken, Angelsachsen, und Langobarden (Munich, 1971), 264–87

Æthelburh [St Æthelburh, Ethelburga] (fl. 664), abbess of Barking, was the sister of *Earconwald (d. 693), abbot of Chertsey and bishop of London. Nothing certain is known of her family background, though she may have originated among the Kentish aristocracy: Æthelburh shares her name with the Kentish princess who became queen of the Northumbrians and a saint, and her brother's name contains the same Earcon- prefix as members of the Kentish royal dynasty (for example, Earconberht). Probably at some point between about 664 and 675, Earconwald founded a monastery at Barking, Essex, for his sister. It was a double community, housing both monks and nuns, of a type familiar in seventh-century Francia. Bede's source for his description of it in his Historia ecclesiastica gentis Anglorum may have been modelled on an account of the abbey of Faremoutiers-en-Brie, which was led for a time by another Æthelburh, one of the daughters of Anna, king of the East Angles (d. 654), with whom Barking's Æthelburh should not be confused. Bede had at his disposal a libellus (a 'little book') of the miracles of Æthelburh, now lost, probably composed at Barking, and perhaps conveyed to him by his friend, the London priest (and future archbishop of Canterbury) Nothhelm. From this source Bede drew the report that the plague of 664–5 wrought heavy casualties in the monastery, so that a new cemetery had to be laid out. Among other miracles, Bede recounts

that Æthelburh's imminent death was revealed in a vision to one of the nuns, whose own death was later foretold by an apparition of the abbess.

Barking seems quickly to have acquired extensive property. Æthelburh was the recipient of a charter, of which an authentic copy survives, issued by one Hodilred (Æthelred), a kinsman of the East Saxon king, which enlarges the abbey's estates; this serves partially to validate otherwise questionable documents in which Earconwald himself reviews Barking's endowment by a series of East Saxon, West Saxon, and Mercian kings, and claims that he had received papal protection for the whole on his visit to Rome in 677 or 678 (though extant papal charters for Earconwald's minsters of St Paul's and Chertsey are certainly bogus).

The twelfth-century chronicle of John of Worcester records that Æthelburh's death took place in 664 and, under 675, that she was succeeded by Hildelith. Neither year is likely to be accurate, though the day given for her death, 11 October, is also that under which she is commemorated in six pre-conquest calendars. Her burial at Barking is attested by an early eleventh-century list of saints' resting-places. Barking later celebrated translation feasts on 7 March, 4 May, and 23 September.

The translation of Earconwald in 1148 prompted the writing of his life and an account of his miracles, which formed the basis of accounts of the saint by John Tynemouth (fl. 1350; now printed in the Nova legenda Anglie) and by the Bollandists. It is these sources that offer the fictional information that Æthelburh and her brother were born at 'Stallington' in Lindsey; that they were the children of the local king, Offa; that Æthelburh converted her father but left home to avoid marriage; and that Earconwald brought Hildelith from 'across the sea' to instruct Æthelburh in the monastic life.

MARIOS COSTAMBEYS

Sources Bede, Hist. eccl., 3.19; 4.7–10 · AS chart., S 1171, 1246, 1248 · A. W. Haddan and W. Stubbs, eds., Councils and ecclesiastical documents relating to Great Britain and Ireland, 3 (1871), 161–3 · J. M. Wallace-Hadrill, Bede's Ecclesiastical history of the English people: a historical commentary, OMT (1988) · John of Worcester, Chron. · F. Wormald, ed., English kalendars before AD 1100, 1, HBS, 72 (1934) · C. Horstman, ed., Nova legenda Anglie, as collected by John of Tynemouth, J. Capgrave, and others, 2 vols. (1901) · J. B. L. Tolhurst, ed., The ordinale and customary of the Benedictine nuns of Barking Abbey, 2 vols., HBS, 65–6 (1927–8) · B. A. E. Yorke, Kings and kingdoms of early Anglo-Saxon England (1990) · D. Whitelock, 'Bede and his teachers and friends', Famulus Christi: essays in commemoration of the thirteenth centenary of the birth of the Venerable Bede, ed. G. Bonner (1976), 19–39 · D. W. Rollason, 'Lists of saints' resting-places in Anglo-Saxon England', Anglo-Saxon England, 7 (1978), 61–93

Æthelflæd [Ethelfleda] (d. 918), ruler of the Mercians, was the daughter and first-born child of *Alfred (d. 899), king of the West Saxons and later of the Anglo-Saxons, and his wife, *Ealhswith (d. 902), daughter of Æthelred, ealdorman of the 'Gaini', and Eadburh who, according to Alfred's biographer Asser, was a member of the Mercian royal house. Æthelflæd was born probably in the early 870s. By the time Asser had begun writing his life of Alfred in 893, and perhaps as early as 887, she had married the

Mercian ealdorman and ruler *Æthelred, who was certainly older, perhaps much older, than her. In the two or three years after the disappearance from the scene of Ceolwulf II in 879, Æthelred had come to rule over the English half of the Mercian kingdom that had been dismembered by the vikings, submitting to Alfred's overlordship. His marriage to Æthelflæd cemented a close bond, which renewed viking attacks in the 890s only strengthened. After Æthelred fell ill at some time in the decade 899–909 the sources accord leadership of the Mercians to *Edward the Elder or to his sister Æthelflæd. The West Saxon version of the Anglo-Saxon Chronicle records Edward sending a Mercian army against the vikings in 909 and 910. In the latter year Æthelflæd is credited with the building of a fortification at 'Bremesburh' (the location of which is now unknown), by the so-called Mercian register (embedded in texts B, C, and D of the chronicle). It may be this chronicle that is referred to by an early twelfth-century Durham catalogue as 'Elfledes Boc' (perhaps 'Æthelflæd's book'). She also seems to have had a particular association with Gloucester. The royal hall just outside the town at Kingsholm was used for a great council in 896, the mint was striking coins in the name of Alfred at the end of the ninth century, and the street pattern is strikingly similar to that of some of Alfred's burhs in Wessex. Æthelflæd was responsible for the foundation of a new minster at Gloucester, originally dedicated to St Peter (and not to be confused with the old minster of St Peter, on the site of the modern cathedral). The church was a variation on an insular theme: a rectangular structure with a western apse, an unusual feature in England that must have owed something to Carolingian architecture.

On Æthelred's death in 911, Æthelflæd was accepted as ruler by the Mercians: thereafter, the Mercian register describes her as Myrcna hlæfdige, 'Lady of the Mercians', the precise equivalent of Æthelred's habitual title of Myrcna hlaford, 'Lord of the Mercians'. Æthelflæd's direct replacement of her husband seems to have encouraged her brother Edward to attempt to establish his family's control of Mercia. He had already sent his son *Æthelstan to be brought up by his sister and her husband. On the latter's death he assumed direct jurisdiction over London and Oxford, two towns which Alfred had earlier put under Æthelred's control and which were vital to the make-up of the kingdom of the Anglo-Saxons.

As the Mercian register makes clear, Æthelflæd shared in her brother's effort to reconquer the Danelaw. The first attack came in 909, when the Anglo-Saxon Chronicle records that Edward sent a combined army of West Saxons and Mercians into the territory of the northern Danish army. It must have been this force that brought back to English Mercia the relics of the seventh-century Northumbrian royal saint Oswald from their resting-place at Bardney in Lincolnshire. Æthelflæd had them translated to her new minster at Gloucester, which afterwards took that saint's name. The essential precursor to systematic reconquest was the extension into Mercia of the system of fortified sites—burhs—which Alfred had begun to construct in Wessex. These served the dual purpose of consolidating the defence of English territory and providing bases for attacks on viking-occupied areas. Sometimes two were built in one location, to dominate both banks of a river. While Æthelred was still alive, in addition to 'Bremesburh', Worcester (between 887 and 899) and Chester (907) had been fortified. Thereafter, brother and sister seem to have co-ordinated their construction programme. In 912, at Bridgnorth and perhaps at the unlocated 'Scergeat', Æthelflæd had burhs built to prevent crossings of the Severn, which viking armies had accomplished twice in living memory. Edward constructed two at Hertford to defend the southern part of Mercia which he controlled and, having moved into Essex, one at Witham. In 913 Æthelflæd responded to viking raids into Edward's territory by fortifying Tamworth and Stafford. The gap between Tamworth and Hertford was plugged in 914, when Edward had two burhs built at Buckingham, and Æthelflæd one at Warwick, while she also strengthened her northern defences with a burh at Eddisbury and, in 915, those of the Wirral with one at Runcorn. The burh at Chirbury, and perhaps that at the unlocated 'Weardburh', shored up the frontier with Wales in the same year, and Edward fortified Bedford, having received the submission of its viking army. In 916 he protected Essex from sea-borne attack with a burh at Maldon. Æthelflæd must also have rebuilt the defences of Gloucester and Hereford during this period.

This activity provided the bases for the successes of 917. In that year, after Edward had ordered the occupation and fortification of Towcester, three separate viking forces attacked English territory, but were rolled back. Before the end of the year, all the Scandinavian armies of East Anglia had submitted to Edward and offered him their allegiance. In the meantime Æthelflæd sent an army that attacked and captured Derby and the area of which it was the centre, the first of the viking 'Five Boroughs' of the north-east midlands to fall. She lost 'four of her thegns, who were dear to her' there (ASC, s.a. 912, recte 917). In the following year, a co-ordinated campaign to capture the remaining four viking strongholds took Edward to Stamford, while Æthelflæd entered Leicester without opposition. She died, however, at Tamworth on 12 June 918, not sharing with her brother the completion of the reconquest of the southern Danelaw.

In the period of these campaigns, Æthelflæd also had other concerns that she seems to have tackled independently from Edward. There may be a kernel of truth behind the report of the Irish 'fragmentary annals'—a late source, heavily embroidered with legendary accretions—that she led a combined army against the viking Ragnall (d. 920/21) at the second battle of Corbridge in 918: she may at least have sent a Mercian force to bolster that of Ragnall's northern opponents. She may even, as the 'fragmentary annals' go on to suggest, have made an agreement with the Picts and the Scots for co-ordinated action against recently arrived Norse aggressors in Northumbria. Her prominence in the north is indicated by the Mercian register, which states that in 918 the men of York offered her their submission and allegiance. She can therefore be seen as laying the foundations for Edward's (temporary) pacification of the north in 920. Relations with the Welsh are harder to fathom, the only recorded event being an expedition in 916 which captured the wife of the king of Brycheiniog as punishment for the murder of the Mercian abbot Ecgberht and his companions.

Æthelflæd was buried alongside her husband in the east *porticus* of her minster at Gloucester. Following her death, Edward initially allowed her daughter Ælfwynn, who must have been nearly thirty but was still unmarried, to hold a nominal rulership over the Mercians. After six months, however, she was 'deprived of all authority in Mercia' and carried off to Wessex (*ASC*, s.a. 919, texts B, C, D). At about the same time, the West Saxon version of the chronicle reports that all the people of Mercia, Danes and English, submitted to Edward. This act may have been premeditated: Edward's dispatch of his eldest son, Æthelstan, to be brought up among the Mercian aristocracy suggests as much. The bringing together of two (or, with the Danes, three) peoples under one rule did not amount to the creation of a single state, at least initially, but it does seem to have provoked some resentment among the Mercians, which lay behind a rebellion at Chester in 924. It is not known whether Æthelflæd herself approved of her brother's moves towards single rulership. In this context it is notable that her career emerges largely from the Mercian register, while the West Saxon version of the chronicle (text A), written within a few years, minimizes her significance. The latter text does not, however, obscure Æthelflæd's achievement, by dint of her high birth, her marriage, the political situation, and, it seems sure, her own ability, of a distinctively prominent role for a woman of her era. It made an impression on later generations. Writing *c.*1130, Henry of Huntingdon declared her 'to have been so powerful that in praise and exaltation of her wonderful gifts, some call her not only lady, or queen, but even king' and follows this with a poem describing her as 'worthy of a man's name' and 'more illustrious than Caesar' (Henry, Archdeacon of Huntingdon, 309). Behind this twelfth-century rhetorical gloss lies recognition of the vital role that Æthelflæd played in the creation of the English kingdom.   MARIOS COSTAMBEYS

Sources F. T. Wainwright, 'Æthelflæd, lady of the Mercians', *Scandinavian England* (1975), 305–24 • F. M. Stenton, *Anglo-Saxon England*, 3rd edn (1971) • *ASC*, s.a. 910, 912–18 [texts B, C, D] • *ASC*, s.a. 918 [texts A, E] • *AS chart.*, S 221, 223–5, 367, 1280 • S. Keynes, 'King Alfred and the Mercians', *Kings, currency and alliances: history and coinage of southern England in the ninth century*, ed. M. A. S. Blackburn and D. N. Dumville (1998), 1–46 • J. N. Radner, ed., *The fragmentary annals of Ireland* (1978) • Henry, archdeacon of Huntingdon, *Historia Anglorum*, ed. D. E. Greenway, OMT (1996) • C. M. Heighway, 'Anglo-Saxon Gloucester to AD 1000', *Studies in late Anglo-Saxon settlement*, ed. M. L. Faull (1984), 105–26 • P. R. Szarmach, 'Æðelflæd of Mercia, mise en page', *Words and works: studies in medieval English language and literature in honour of Fred C. Robinson*, ed. P. S. Baker and N. Howe (1998), 105–26

Æthelfrith (d. *c.*616), king of Northumbria, was the son of Æthelric. He succeeded to the throne of Bernicia in 592, and in 604 to the joint Northumbrian kingdom of Deira and Bernicia which he ruled until 616. His first wife was Bebba, who is traditionally said to have given her name to the royal site of Bebbanburh, or Bamburgh. But it was his marriage to his second wife, Acha, princess of Deira, which cemented Æthelfrith's claim to Deira. He is the first historically attested ruler of Northumbria, and, in his relatively long reign, established that kingdom as a major political force in Britain.

Æthelfrith is described by Bede in the early eighth century as a heroic war leader almost in the terms of epic poetry:

> a very brave king and most eager for glory. He ravaged the Britons more extensively than any other English ruler. … For no ruler or king had subjected more land to the English race or settled it, having first either exterminated or conquered the natives. (Bede, *Hist. eccl.*, 1.34)

This land taking and settlement can perhaps be seen reflected in the scattered late sixth-century pagan burial-grounds of co. Durham and Northumberland, and certainly his name was well known in British sources where he was called Flesaur—the Artful. By *c.*602 Æthelfrith's conquests threatened the Irish immigrants living in Dalriada (modern Argyll) and their formidable king, Aedan, son of Gabran, marched against him with a very strong army. At a place known as Degsastan (plausibly Addinston, Berwickshire), Æthelfrith defeated him, so that Aedan's army was 'cut to pieces' and he fled with a handful of survivors (Bede, *Hist. eccl.*, 1.34). After this defeat, according to Bede, the Irish in Britain were discouraged from warring against the English until his day.

Having made safe his northern frontiers, Æthelfrith turned his attention to the Britons of Wales in an attempt to secure territory in the west and to cut off the Welsh from the British peoples in the north. He assembled a great army and attacked the Britons, led by the king of Powys, Selyf Sarffgadau, at Chester, some time between 613 and 616. Æthelfrith, who was a heathen, observed a large group of clerics standing apart from the British army, surrounded by guards, and asked who they were and for what purpose they had gathered there. On hearing that they were monks from the monastery of Bangor Is-coed who had come to pray for the British troops, he ruthlessly said, 'If they are praying to their God against us, even if they do not bear arms, they are fighting against us, assailing us as they do with prayers for our defeat' (Bede, *Hist. eccl.*, 2.2). So he ordered them to be attacked first, killing, according to Bede, 1200 of them. He then won the battle, although not without heavy losses.

By that time Æthelfrith was the dominant ruler in north Britain, while south of the Humber the most powerful ruler was Rædwald, king of the East Angles, at whose court Eadwine, the exiled heir of the Deiran throne, had taken refuge. Æthelfrith sent messengers with large sums of money demanding that Eadwine should be killed, and later, further messengers with larger bribes threatening to make war on Rædwald if he did not kill or surrender Eadwine. The East Anglian king was almost ready to give in to the demands, but his wife persuaded him that no honourable man would betray his guest for bribes; no doubt Rædwald also felt that to surrender to Æthelfrith's threats would be to give up his own pre-eminent position in southern England. As soon as the messengers had gone, Rædwald gathered a large army and marched against Æthelfrith, who did not have time to assemble a comparable force. At a battle by the River Idle, on the border between Mercia and Northumbria, c.616, Æthelfrith was defeated and killed, and the victorious Rædwald established Eadwine as king of Northumbria.

Æthelfrith's seven sons and many of his young nobles fled into exile among the Dalriadan Irish and the Picts. The northern recension of the Anglo-Saxon Chronicle preserves the names of his sons as Eanfrith, *Oswald, *Oswiu, Oslac, Oswudu, Oslaf, and Offa. In the longer term, it was Æthelfrith's lineage which prevailed in Northumbria and three of his sons, Eanfrith, Oswald, and Oswiu, succeeded Eadwine, followed by his grandson *Ecgfrith. ROSEMARY CRAMP

Sources Bede, *Hist. eccl.*, 1.34; 2.2; 3.1 · Nennius, 'British history' and 'The Welsh annals', ed. and trans. J. Morris (1980) · ASC, s.a. 593, 603, 605, 616, 617 [text E (northern recension)] · D. N. Dumville, 'The Anglian collection of royal genealogies and regnal lists', *Anglo-Saxon England*, 5 (1976), 23–50

Æthelgar (d. 990), archbishop of Canterbury, was a monk of Glastonbury under Dunstan (later archbishop of Canterbury) and of Abingdon under Æthelwold (later bishop of Winchester). In 964 Bishop Æthelwold expelled the secular clergy from New Minster, Winchester, in favour of monks and he appointed Æthelgar as abbot. According to New Minster tradition, Æthelgar was a generous benefactor, enlarging the abbey and enhancing its prestige through the translation of the relics of St Swithun. On 2 May 980 he was consecrated bishop of Selsey, the South Saxon see, but he did not dispossess the canons of this church. He appears to have retained the abbacy of New Minster throughout his episcopate. Æthelgar succeeded Dunstan as archbishop of Canterbury about the middle of 988, apparently relinquishing control of New Minster, and went to Rome for his pallium in that or the next year. He visited the abbey of St Bertin, near St Omer, on his way both to and from Rome, and his gifts to this monastery were so large that the abbot considered him its patron, and attributed its restoration to him. Æthelgar died on 13 February 990, after a pontificate of one year and three months. WILLIAM HUNT, rev. MARY FRANCES SMITH

Sources C. R. Hart, *The early charters of northern England and the north midlands* (1975) · ASC, s. a. 963, 964, 980, 988 [texts A, C, E] · W. de G. Birch, ed., *Liber vitae: register and martyrology of New Minster and Hyde Abbey, Winchester*, Hampshire RS, 5 (1892) · W. Stubbs, ed., *Memorials of St Dunstan, archbishop of Canterbury*, Rolls Series, 63 (1874) · John of Worcester, *Chron.* · *Willelmi Malmesbiriensis monachi de gestis pontificum Anglorum libri quinque*, ed. N. E. S. A. Hamilton, Rolls Series, 52 (1870) · William of Malmesbury, *Gesta regum Anglorum / The history of the English kings*, ed. and trans. R. A. B. Mynors, R. M. Thomson, and M. Winterbottom, 2 vols., OMT (1998–9)

Æthelheard (d. 740), king of the West Saxons, became king in 726 after his predecessor, Ine, retired to Rome. The succession was disputed, but Æthelheard defeated the other claimant, an atheling named Oswald. Æthelheard's name does not appear in any extant genealogy of the West Saxon kings, and there is no direct evidence for his ancestry or connections. However, the inference, sometimes drawn, that he was an outsider, may not be correct. Since Ine had a long reign with a planned ending, it is likely that he designated his successor, and the most obvious person to have been so named is Æthelheard. It is quite possible that he was Ine's son, and that this was why no one thought it worthwhile to draw up a separate genealogy for him.

Æthelheard married a woman named Frithugyth. Again there is no direct evidence for her antecedents, but it has been suggested that she was related to Frithuwold of Surrey, Frithuswith (St Frideswide of Oxford), and others of similar names active at this period. She appears to have enjoyed a position of some power and importance during Æthelheard's reign. She witnessed all of her husband's surviving charters, made grants of land both jointly with the king and independently, and travelled to Rome with Bishop Forthere in 739.

Æthelheard and Frithugyth are recorded as making grants of land in Somerset and Devon to the monastery at Glastonbury. Two such grants were probably made in 729; others cannot be dated precisely. In 739 Æthelheard gave land at Crediton, near Exeter, to Forthere, bishop of Sherborne, for the foundation of a monastery. Apparently the West Saxons controlled at least part of Devon at this time, but wars against the Cornish were a feature of West Saxon history down to the tenth century, and it may be that the monastery at Crediton was intended to consolidate West Saxon power in a precariously held border area.

During the later, if not the earlier, years of his reign, Æthelheard may have been subject to some sort of overlordship by Æthelbald, king of the Mercians. In his *Historia ecclesiastica*, Bede states that all the English kingdoms south of the Humber were subject to Æthelbald in 731, and the Mercian king's charters of the 730s make similar claims. In 733 Æthelbald occupied Somerton in Somerset, and charters furnish evidence for his continuing power in that area during the 740s. A reference (which may itself be authentic although surviving in a dubious charter) to Æthelheard crossing the Severn on an expedition against the Welsh suggests that the West Saxons were assisting the Mercians, though it is unclear whether they were subject to, or in alliance with, the Mercian king on this occasion. However, there are obvious motives for hyperbole in the Mercian sources, and the Crediton grant shows that Æthelheard continued to act as an independent king in at least some respects. Æthelheard died in Wessex in 740 and was succeeded by *Cuthred, who was probably his designated successor and may have been his son.

HEATHER EDWARDS

Sources ASC, s.a. 726, 728, 733, 737, 739, 740, 741 · AS chart., S 93, 253, 254, 255, 1676, 1679 · Bede, *Hist. eccl.*, 5.23 · S. Keynes, 'England, 700–900', *The new Cambridge medieval history*, 2, ed. R. McKitterick (1995), 18–42 · F. M. Stenton, 'The supremacy of the Mercian kings', *Preparatory to 'Anglo-Saxon England': being the collected papers of Frank Merry Stenton*, ed. D. M. Stenton (1970), 48–66 · F. M. Stenton, *Anglo-Saxon England*, 3rd edn (1971) · P. Wormald, 'Bede, the "Bretwaldas" and the origins of the "gens Anglorum"', *Ideal and reality in Frankish and Anglo-Saxon society*, ed. P. Wormald, D. Bullough, and R. Collins (1983), 99–129 · H. Edwards, *The charters of the early West Saxon kingdom* (1988) · S. Bassett, ed., *The origins of Anglo-Saxon kingdoms* (1989)

Æthelheard [Ethelhard] (*d.* **805**), archbishop of Canterbury, was abbot of Louth in Lindsey before his elevation to the archbishopric of Canterbury on the death of Jænberht on 12 August 792. Nothing is known of his antecedents, but he can be assumed to be of Mercian extraction. He certainly owed his appointment to Offa, king of the Mercians, who had previously persuaded the papacy to divide Jænberht's province of Canterbury and elevate the Mercian see of Lichfield to an archbishopric. Æthelheard thus received only the Kentish, West Saxon, and South Saxon bishoprics, while those of the Mercians and East Angles remained in the hands of Hygeberht of Lichfield. Æthelheard was consecrated by Hygeberht on 21 July 793, and during the lifetime of Offa (and for a while afterwards) attested royal charters in a subordinate position to him, following the custom of distinguishing seniority between equals in rank by the date of consecration.

On Offa's death in 796, the Kentishmen rose in rebellion against Mercian dominance. They were led by Eadberht Præn, an exile in Offa's reign, who now became king. Æthelheard, as a Mercian and an adherent of Offa, was presumably unacceptable to the new regime, and fled to the protection of Offa's son and successor, Ecgfrith, who gave him a minster at 'Pectanege' (possibly Patney, Wiltshire) as a residence (*AS chart.*, S 1258). In 797 Alcuin wrote to the Kentish people, urging them to recall their archbishop and warning against any attempt to replace him. He also wrote to Æthelheard personally, censuring him for abandoning his see, but recognizing that it was the archbishop's own clergy who counselled flight. Whether Æthelheard felt physically threatened by the new Kentish regime is uncertain, but it is possible that the episcopal church was attacked and damaged during his absence; no archives have survived from the period before 798, though there is plentiful documentation thereafter.

Ecgfrith himself died on 16 December 796, to be succeeded by a distant kinsman, Cenwulf. The new king opened negotiations with the papacy for the reunification of the southern province, but the difficulties were multiplied by the continuing hostility of the Kentishmen to Mercian overlordship. It was perhaps to counter this that Cenwulf attempted to have the archiepiscopal see moved from Canterbury to London, then a Mercian city; the see was vacant after the departure of Bishop Eadbald, who had fled abroad, for reasons which are now irrecoverable, in 796. Two missions were sent to Pope Leo III, one in 797, which miscarried, and another in 798. Pope Leo refused to countenance the removal of the archiepiscopal see from Canterbury, but did excommunicate Eadberht Præn, and within the year Cenwulf's forces overran Kent, captured and mutilated Eadberht, and restored Æthelheard to Canterbury.

The problem of the archbishopric of Lichfield remained. The objection had always been to the division of the southern province, not to Hygeberht personally.

Alcuin, in his letter to Æthelheard cited above, urged restoration of 'the unity of the Church', but recommended that Hygeberht should retain his pallium for life as a personal dignity, while relinquishing the right to ordain bishops. This compromise seems to have been implemented in the late 790s; Hygeberht retained his archiepiscopal title until at least 799 (*AS chart.*, S 155) but it was Æthelheard who received professions of obedience from Eadwulf of Lindsey and Tidferth of 'Domnoc' in 799, Deneberht of Worcester between 798 and 800, and Wulfheard of Hereford in 801.

In 801 Æthelheard himself journeyed to Rome, accompanied by Cyneberht, bishop of Winchester, and two laymen, the Mercian thegn Ceolmund, formerly in the service of King Offa, and the Northumbrian Torhtmund, who had served the murdered King Æthelred. He was helped on his way by Alcuin, who sent him a saddle horse and wrote to Charlemagne on his behalf. Æthelheard delivered further letters from his king to the pope, and, on 18 January 802, received a papal letter permitting the restoration of the southern province. The separation was ended at the Council of 'Clofesho' on 12 October 803 (*AS chart.*, S 1431a). Hygeberht had already resigned both his title and his see: Ealdwulf, his successor as bishop of Lichfield, was already in office in 800 or 801 (*AS chart.*, S 106, 158) and Hygeberht attests the 'Clofesho' decrees as a simple abbot, in the following of Bishop Ealdwulf (*AS chart.*, S 1431b).

Despite the problems he faced, Æthelheard's episcopate saw a greater frequency of synodal councils than those of his immediate predecessors. At least eleven synods are recorded for his time: at 'Clofesho' in 792, at Chelsea in 793, at 'Clofesho' again in 794, at London in 795, at Chelsea again in 796, at 'Clofesho' in 798, at Tamworth in 799, at Chelsea yet again in 800 and 801, at 'Clofesho' in 803, and at 'Aclea' in 804. In addition to these, there may have been a synod at Bath in 796. In the earlier synods, Hygeberht and Æthelheard seem to have presided jointly (*AS chart.*, S 136, 137, 139). It is possible that Æthelheard presided alone at London in 795 and Chelsea in 796, but the texts of the diplomas which record these meetings are later and may have been emended after the abolition of the archbishopric of Lichfield (*AS chart.*, S 132, 150, 151). Both archbishops were present at 'Clofesho' in 798 and at Tamworth in 799 (*AS chart.*, S 153, 155); the charter recording the latter is Hygeberht's last attestation as archbishop. Both men attest a charter from the Synod of Chelsea in 801 (*AS chart.*, S 158), but Hygeberht, though his name appears first, is styled only 'bishop' (*episcopus*). The frequency of synodal meetings is presumably connected with the contemporary movement for reform of the church; that of 792 saw the issue of Offa's privilege to the Kentish churches (*AS chart.*, S 134), while the council of 803 prohibited the election of laymen or seculars as lords of monasteries (*AS chart.*, S 1431b).

Æthelheard's closeness to Offa is demonstrated by the letter from Charlemagne addressed to him and to Bishop Ceolwulf of Lindsey, asking them to intercede with the Mercian king on behalf of some Mercian exiles in Francia who wished to return home. The king's favour did not, however, extend to returning the minster of Cookham, in what is now Berkshire, given to Christ Church by Offa's predecessor King Æthelbald, but seized first by Cynewulf of Wessex and subsequently by Offa himself (*AS chart.*, S 1258). It was not until the synod at 'Clofesho' in 798 that Æthelheard finally came to an agreement with Offa's widow, Cynethryth: she kept Cookham, and received in addition the minster at 'Pectanege' given to Æthelheard by her son Ecgfrith, but in return she granted the archbishop 110 hides (sulungs) of land in Kent, at North Fleet, Teynham, and 'the source of the Cray'. In 799 Æthelheard made an even better deal with King Cenwulf (*AS chart.*, S 155, 1259), recovering the church's estates at Charing, Great Chart, and Bishopsbourne, jointly assessed at 44 sulungs of land, for no more than 100 mancuses (£12 10s.). In all, Æthelheard appears as an effective and energetic archbishop, concerned both to preserve the integrity and endowment of his see and to ensure the health and discipline of the English church. He died on 12 May 805 and was buried at Christ Church, Canterbury; his successor was his archdeacon Wulfred.   ANN WILLIAMS

Sources N. Brooks, *The early history of the church of Canterbury: Christ Church from 597 to 1066* (1984) · S. Keynes, *The councils of Clofesho* (1994) · *ASC*, s.a. 791, 799 · *English historical documents*, 1, ed. D. Whitelock (1955) · A. W. Haddan and W. Stubbs, eds., *Councils and ecclesiastical documents relating to Great Britain and Ireland*, 3 (1871) · S. E. Kelly, ed., *Charters of Selsey*, Anglo-Saxon Charters, 6 (1998)

Æthelmund (d. before 746). *See under* Hwicce, kings of the (act. *c.*670–*c.*780).

Æthelnoth (d. 1038), archbishop of Canterbury, was a son of Æthelmær, ealdorman of the western shires, and grandson of Ealdorman *Æthelweard, the chronicler. A Glastonbury story relates that, at his baptism by Dunstan, the infant held up his hand in the manner of a bishop blessing the people, whereupon Dunstan prophesied that he would become an archbishop. Æthelnoth became a monk of Glastonbury, and in later years, besides enlisting Cnut's support for Glastonbury, he donated to it a copy of Hrabanus Maurus's *De laudibus sanctae crucis*, and also a prayer book illuminated in gold. According to Osbern, Æthelnoth enjoyed Cnut's favour because he had given holy chrism to the king, implying his participation either in a ceremony of confirmation at Southampton in 1016, or else in Cnut's coronation by Archbishop Lyfing in 1017. Æthelnoth's brother Æthelweard was executed by Cnut in 1017, while a brother-in-law, also called Æthelweard, was banished in 1020.

Æthelnoth was dean of Christ Church, Canterbury, when, in 1020, he was elected archbishop, an elevation which may denote a reconciliation between the king and the survivors of Æthelmær's family. Archbishop Wulfstan of York notified King Cnut and Queen Emma that he had consecrated Æthelnoth according to the king's mandate, and urged that Æthelnoth should be entitled to the same rights and honours as Dunstan and his other predecessors in office. The consecration took place on 13 November 1020. In 1022, Æthelnoth travelled to Rome and received

his pallium from Pope Benedict VIII, who is said, in three versions of the Anglo-Saxon Chronicle, to have consecrated and blessed him with great solemnity on 7 October. On the pope's instructions, Æthelnoth immediately celebrated mass, wearing the pallium, and afterwards they dined together in state. The D text of the chronicle adds that Æthelnoth afterwards took a pallium from the altar before leaving Rome. The archbishop returned to England with an arm of St Augustine of Hippo in an ornate reliquary, which he gave to Coventry; it cost him 100 talents of silver and one of gold.

In 1023 King Cnut gave permission for the translation of the remains of the murdered Archbishop Ælfheah (Alphege) to Canterbury. The cortège set out on 8 June, and the account in the chronicle (text D) indicates the dignified and public nature of the journey. Osbern, however, reports that the relics were strongly guarded and followed by Æthelnoth with a rearguard, in order to thwart any intervention by hostile citizens of London. The procession entered Christ Church, Canterbury, on 11 June, and four days later Æthelnoth, together with Bishop Ælfsige of Winchester and Bishop Brihtwine of Wells, reinterred Ælfheah's body. The archbishop encouraged Cnut to send money to foreign churches, including Chartres, and restrained him when he spoke disparagingly of St Edith while visiting Wilton. Æthelnoth was politically useful to Cnut in consecrating Bishop Gerbrand of Roskilde, and in acting with Cnut to strengthen the position of Bishop Joseph of Llandaff; he was also a co-recipient of the letter sent by Cnut to his English subjects following his visit to Rome. Cnut issued several writs in favour of the archbishop and his church. The *Encomium Emmae Reginae* relates that, following Cnut's death, his son Harold Harefoot summoned Æthelnoth, 'a man endowed with great courage and wisdom', requiring the archbishop to consecrate him king, and to hand over the crown and sceptre, but the archbishop refused to consecrate anyone other than a son of Emma, and forbade all the bishops from participating in a consecration. The implied date of this story is 1036, at which time there was a possibility that Harthacnut would return to England. Harold was elected king in 1037, and Gervase reports that Æthelnoth crowned him in London. In Æthelnoth's last years, some of his duties were taken over by the royal priest Eadsige. Æthelnoth 'the Good' (as the chronicle calls him) died on 28 or 29 October, or else on 1 November, 1038, and was buried in Christ Church, Canterbury. Æthelric, bishop of Sussex is said to have prayed that he would not long survive 'his dearly beloved father' Æthelnoth, and he himself duly died a week later.   EMMA MASON

Sources *ASC*, s. a. 1020, 1022, 1023, 1038 [texts D, E] · *The historical works of Gervase of Canterbury*, ed. W. Stubbs, 2 vols., Rolls Series, 73 (1879–80) · *Willelmi Malmesbiriensis monachi de gestis pontificum Anglorum libri quinque*, ed. N. E. S. A. Hamilton, Rolls Series, 52 (1870) · F. E. Harmer, ed., *Anglo-Saxon writs*, 2nd edn (1989) · A. Campbell, ed. and trans., *Encomium Emmae reginae*, CS, 3rd ser., 72 (1949) · John of Worcester, *Chron.*, vol. 2 · *The early history of Glastonbury: an edition, translation, and study of William of Malmesbury's De antiquitate Glastonie ecclesie*, ed. J. Scott (1981) · M. K. Lawson, *Cnut: the Danes in England in the early eleventh century* (1993) · William of

Malmesbury, *Gesta regum Anglorum / The history of the English kings*, ed. and trans. R. A. B. Mynors, R. M. Thomson, and M. Winterbottom, 2 vols., OMT (1998–9), vol. 1

Æthelred (*d.* after **704**), king of the Mercians, was the son of *Penda (*d.* 655). He succeeded his brother *Wulfhere as king of the Mercians, just after the latter's disastrous defeat by *Ecgfrith of Northumbria *c.*674. This seriously diminished Mercian hegemony over the kingdoms of southern England and Æthelred's first task was to restore the situation. Control in the south-east was established in 676 by a punitive raid into Kent, in which Rochester was sacked. Æthelred was married to Ecgfrith's sister *Osthryth, but this did not prevent him from inflicting a decisive defeat on his brother-in-law, at the battle of the Trent, in 679. He thereby recovered control of Lindsey, signalled by his patronage of the monastery at Bardney, whither Osthryth translated the remains of her uncle St Oswald. Æthelred also asserted his lordship over the kings of the Hwicce and may have been instrumental in founding the monastery of St Peter's, Gloucester, about 681. It was perhaps his sister-in-law Æthelflæd, Osthryth's sister, who had, a little earlier, founded the short-lived monastery at Fladbury, in modern Worcestershire; the house was later in the hands of Queen Osthryth. Æthelred also kept up Mercian pressure on the West Saxon kingdom; his nephew Berhtwald administered a territory on the borders of the Hwicce and the West Saxons, and was able to dispose of land in what is now Wiltshire (*AS chart.*, S 1169).

Mercian relations with Northumbria remained poor. In 681, 'to flatter King Ecgfrith' (Eddius Stephanus, chap. 40), Æthelred prevented Berhtwald from assisting the exiled Northumbrian Bishop Wilfrid, but matters changed after Ecgfrith's death in 685; when Wilfrid quarrelled with his successor, King Aldfrith (*c.*692), Æthelred received him in Mercia and gave him the bishopric of the Middle Angles. Deteriorating relations with Northumbria are suggested by the murder in 697 of Queen Osthryth, 'by her own Mercian nobles' (Bede, *Hist. eccl.*, 5.24); it may be that her personal household was implicated but no further details are given. She was buried at Bardney. Soon afterwards Æthelred gave Fladbury to the bishopric of Worcester 'for the forgiveness of my sins and those of my late wife Osthryth' (*AS chart.*, S 76). He may have married again, for a late source alleges that his son *Ceolred was not a child of Osthryth (Macray, 73). In 704, however, he abdicated and retired as abbot to Bardney, whence he continued to advise his successor, *Coenred, son of Wulfhere, and uphold the cause of Bishop Wilfrid. The date of his death is unknown; he was buried at Bardney, where both he and his murdered wife were venerated as saints.

ANN WILLIAMS

Sources Bede, *Hist. eccl.* · E. Stephanus, *The life of Bishop Wilfrid*, ed. and trans. B. Colgrave (1927) · B. Yorke, *Kings and kingdoms of early Anglo-Saxon England* (1990) · D. P. Kirby, *The earliest English kings* (1991) · P. Sims-Williams, *Religion and literature in western England, 600–800* (1990) · D. W. Rollason, 'Lists of saints' resting-places in Anglo-Saxon England', *Anglo-Saxon England*, 7 (1978), 61–93 · W. D.

Macray, ed., *Chronicon abbatiae de Evesham, ad annum 1418*, Rolls Series, 29 (1863)

Æthelred (*d.* **888**), archbishop of Canterbury, was archbishop from 870 until his death on 30 June 888, during the height of the viking wars. The statement in the F version of the Anglo-Saxon Chronicle that he was the bishop of Wiltshire before his translation to Canterbury in 870 was derived from the life of Archbishop Ælfric a century later, and cannot be accepted. Pope John VIII instructed Æthelred to encourage English churchmen to give up their short-cut tunics and to follow continental practice in wearing full ankle-length habits, but the archbishop's main concern was dealing with the viking threat. Evidence from a coin hoard, which suggests that a viking force may have occupied the great archiepiscopal manor of Croydon in Surrey at some time between 869 and 872, or soon after this, helps to indicate the seriousness of this threat. The manor was assessed at 80 hides in 1066, so its loss deprived either the archbishopric or its lessee of valuable revenues. There was also a deterioration in the literacy of the cathedral community at Canterbury, reaching such a stage that its scribes could not translate documents from Latin into English. In addition there was a disagreement between Archbishop Æthelred and King Alfred as to the extent of the royal lordship over ecclesiastics, and it is possible that authority over the Kentish monasteries was in dispute. During Æthelred's period as archbishop there was, however, one important gain for the see. The 'golden gospels' were donated to Canterbury by Ealdorman Alfred who had bought them from a heathen army for a sum of pure gold. Æthelred made attempts to overcome the threats posed by the vikings and the West Saxon monarchy and he established important links with a wealthy patron, but during his pontificate, as a result of its scribes' poor literacy, Canterbury was no longer able to fulfil its metropolitan role in providing bishops-elect with professions of faith.

A. F. WAREHAM

Sources N. Brooks, *The early history of the church of Canterbury: Christ Church from 597 to 1066* (1984) · F. E. Harmer, ed., *Select English historical documents of the ninth and tenth centuries* (1914) · *ASC*, s.a. 888 · BL, MS Arundel 68, fol. 32

Æthelred (*d.* **911**), ruler of the Mercians, took over the government of that portion of Mercia left to the English after the vikings had dismembered the kingdom in 877 and King Ceolwulf II had disappeared from the scene two years later. Nothing certain is known of how Æthelred attained leadership of the Mercians, nor of his family background. He first appears in 883, by which time he had recognized the overlordship of the West Saxon king, *Alfred: he made a grant to Berkeley Abbey in that year with Alfred's assent. Although the chronicler Æthelweard (*d.* 998), who used sources independent of the extant versions of the Anglo-Saxon Chronicle, calls Æthelred 'king', the title accorded to him by the latter texts is 'ealdorman'. He certainly seems to have remained in some form of submission to the West Saxon kings for the rest of his life. His allegiance predates the occupation of London in 886 by Alfred, to whom 'all the English people that were not under subjection to the Danes' submitted (*ASC*, s.a. 886).

Alfred's immediate concession to Æthelred of control over London, which had been in Mercian hands earlier in the century, perhaps reflects the king's need to maintain unity among those English peoples who remained outside viking territory. Even more important for cementing the bond between the West Saxon and Mercian rulers was Æthelred's marriage to Alfred's daughter and eldest child, *Æthelflæd, which had happened by the time Asser was writing his life of the king in 893, and perhaps took place as early as 888. Æthelred was probably older than his wife, perhaps considerably so.

The year 892 brought new viking invaders to England, and Æthelred took part in a concerted effort to oppose them. After the initial defeat of one viking leader, Hæsten, he stood godfather to one of Hæsten's two sons, while Alfred sponsored the other. In 893 Æthelred took reinforcements from London to join Alfred's eldest son, *Edward (870s?–924), in pinning down one force at Thorney in Buckinghamshire. Finding themselves insufficiently strong to assault the army directly, Æthelred and Edward allowed it to leave English territory. Later in the year, a reinforced viking army set out on a raid up the Thames valley, and then up the Severn. Æthelred followed it, with a force that included the ealdormen of Wiltshire and Somerset, contingents drawn from every fortified settlement in English Mercia and Wessex east of the Parret, and a detachment sent by the Welsh princes. The raiding army was besieged on the Severn at Buttington near Welshpool, but eventually cut its way out and limped back to its base at Shoebury, Essex. The presence of Welshmen in Æthelred's force indicates the seriousness of the threat posed by the viking army. The relationship between the Welsh princes and the Mercian ruler was usually more hostile: Asser records that individual Welsh princes submitted to Alfred in order to obtain protection against Æthelred.

Æthelred's role in the ensuing campaign is nowhere made explicit, though it is highly likely that he co-ordinated the Mercian response to further raids. Late in 893 part of the viking force in Essex, joined by men from East Anglia and Northumbria, established itself at Chester but was starved out and moved to Wales, which it devastated for nearly a year; on its return east it avoided Wessex and Mercia altogether. In 895 an English army was obliged to shadow a viking party across the midlands to the Severn, where the vikings over-wintered. The dispersal of this force marked the end of serious viking assaults during Alfred's reign.

The construction of the defensive system of fortified sites (burhs) which Alfred began was chiefly continued by Edward and Æthelflæd after Æthelred's death. Nevertheless, Æthelred and Æthelflæd were approached by Werferth, bishop of Worcester, to fortify that town for the defence of the people and the security of the cathedral. Of even more importance to the Mercian rulers, perhaps, was Gloucester, where there is evidence for a royal palace and mint and where the street pattern is strikingly similar to that of some of Alfred's burhs in Wessex. Æthelflæd

founded a new minster there, to which relics of the Northumbrian royal saint Oswald were translated in 909, and where, according to Æthelweard, both she and her husband were buried.

At some time in the decade after Alfred's death in 899 Æthelred seems to have fallen ill. Leadership of the Mercians is then accorded to Edward the Elder or to Æthelflæd: the West Saxon version of the Anglo-Saxon Chronicle credits Edward with sending the Mercian army against the vikings in 909 and 910, and the so-called 'Mercian Register' (embedded in texts B, C, and D of the chronicle) records that Æthelflæd built a fortified settlement at 'Bremesburh' in 910. Æthelred died in 911—the precise date is unknown. Æthelflæd was subsequently able to assume rulership of the Mercians herself. The title by which she was known, *Myrcna hlæfdige*, 'Lady of the Mercians', was an adaptation of Æthelred's habitual title of *Myrcna hlaford*, 'Lord of the Mercians'. Her brother Edward, however, 'succeeded to London and Oxford and to all the lands which belonged to them' (*ASC*, s.a. 911).

MARIOS COSTAMBEYS

Sources F. M. Stenton, *Anglo-Saxon England*, 3rd edn (1971) · *ASC*, s.a. 886, 893, 911 · *AS chart.*, S 217–23, 346, 371, 1280 · *The chronicle of Æthelweard*, ed. and trans. A. Campbell (1962) · S. Keynes, 'King Alfred and the Mercians', *Kings, currency and alliances: history and coinage of southern England in the ninth century*, ed. M. A. S. Blackburn and D. N. Dumville (1998), 1–46 · C. M. Heighway, 'Anglo-Saxon Gloucester to AD 1000', *Studies in late Anglo-Saxon settlement*, ed. M. L. Faull (1984), 35–54 · J. N. Radner, ed., *Fragmentary annals of Ireland* (1978)

Æthelred I (d. 796). See under Oswulf (d. 759).

Æthelred I [Ethelred I] (d. 871), king of the West Saxons, was the fourth of the five sons of *Æthelwulf (d. 858), king of the West Saxons, and his first wife, *Osburh (fl. 839), herself descended from the West Saxon royal line. Æthelred first attested his father's charters in 854 as a king's son, a title he retained through the reigns of his brothers *Æthelbald and *Æthelberht, until he himself became king in 865.

The elevation of Æthelred, and even more so the elevation of his younger brother, *Alfred, would have seemed unlikely in the 850s. In the arrangements Æthelwulf made after his return from Rome in 856, Wessex and its south-eastern extensions were divided between Æthelred's elder brothers Æthelbald and Æthelberht. On Æthelwulf's death in 858, Æthelbald took over Wessex, married *Judith [see under Æthelwulf], his stepmother and an anointed queen of the Frankish royal line, and doubtless expected to produce heirs.

After Æthelbald's childless death in 860, Æthelberht joined Wessex to his existing kingship of Kent. It seems likely that Æthelred would have been expected to gain Wessex: a note in the historical preamble to King Alfred's will that part of Æthelwulf's inheritance was meant to descend among Æthelbald, Æthelred, and Alfred suggests that Æthelberht was expected to set up his own cadet branch of the family in Kent, and so no longer to need estates in Wessex. However, on Æthelbald's death Æthelred and Alfred gave up their part of that inheritance to

Æthelberht, on condition that he return it to them on his death. The likeliest explanation is that Æthelberht received the kingship of Wessex, and also the inheritance intended to descend to Æthelred and Alfred, because his younger brothers were considered too young to lead a country facing viking attack in 860: Alfred was only eleven, Æthelred perhaps a year or so older. This explanation would accord with the fact that twice, in 862 and 863 (and presumably once he had come of age), Æthelred issued charters as king of the West Saxons (*AS chart.*, S 335 and 336). He must have done so as Æthelberht's deputy or in his absence, as there is no record of conflict between the brothers and Æthelred continued witnessing Æthelberht's charters as a king's son in 864.

After Æthelberht's death in 865, Æthelred became sole king of the West Saxons. In the same year, what the Anglo-Saxon Chronicle calls the 'great heathen army' arrived in England and completely changed the scale of the viking attacks: within five years, these vikings had conquered and installed their own rulers over Northumbria and East Anglia. In 868, when they took Nottingham in Mercia, the Mercian king *Burgred, Æthelred's brother-in-law, asked for West Saxon help. Æthelred and Alfred led the West Saxons to Nottingham and besieged the vikings: there was no decisive battle, but the Mercians were able to make peace with (presumably buy off) the vikings, who returned to York.

The vikings turned their attention to Wessex late in 870, setting up base at Reading. Æthelred and Alfred led the West Saxons against the vikings there, resulting in a large battle with great slaughter which the West Saxons lost. Four days later Æthelred and Alfred again fought against the vikings, at Ashdown (in what are now called the Berkshire Downs), and this time were victorious. A fortnight later they were defeated by the vikings at Basing and two months afterwards, at 'Meretun', they again fought and again lost; to make matters worse, after this battle another viking army (the 'great summer army') sailed up the Thames and landed at Reading.

Æthelred died shortly after Easter in 871 and was buried at Wimborne Minster. He had two sons, Æthelhelm and Æthelwald. The latter rebelled against Alfred's son Edward in 899 and was killed at the battle of the Holme in 902. The only other known descendant of Æthelred is Æthelweard, ealdorman of the western provinces in the late tenth century, who notes his descent from Æthelred in his chronicle.   SEAN MILLER

Sources ASC, s.a. 865–871 • John of Worcester, *Chron.* • *Alfred the Great: Asser's Life of King Alfred and other contemporary sources*, ed. and trans. S. Keynes and M. Lapidge (1983) • *The chronicle of Æthelweard*, ed. and trans. A. Campbell (1962) • S. Keynes, 'The West Saxon charters of King Æthelwulf and his sons', *EngHR*, 109 (1994), 1109–49 • A. Williams, 'Some notes and considerations on problems connected with the English royal succession, 860–1066', *Anglo-Norman Studies*, 1 (1978), 144–67, 225–33 • P. Grierson and M. Blackburn, *Medieval European coinage: with a catalogue of the coins in the Fitzwilliam Museum, Cambridge*, 1: *The early middle ages (5th–10th centuries)* (1986), 311

Likenesses four-line lunette type coin, *c*.866, repro. in Grierson and Blackburn, *Medieval European coinage*, pl. 58, no. 1341 [FM Cam. coin 1341] • lunette type coin, *c*.866–871, repro. in Grierson and

Blackburn, *Medieval European coinage*, plate 58, nos. 1342–4 [FM Cam. coin 1342–4] • brass effigy, Wimborne Minster, Dorset

Æthelred II (*fl. c*.854–*c*.862). *See under* Eardwulf (*fl.* 796–*c*.830).

Æthelred II [Ethelred; *known as* Ethelred the Unready] (*c*.966x8–1016), king of England, was the younger son of King *Edgar (*r.* 959–75) and his wife, *Ælfthryth (*d.* 999x1001), daughter of Ealdorman *Ordgar. The separate elements of his name (*Æthel-ræd*) mean 'noble' and 'counsel'; and although the name was in common usage, contemporaries might well have been more than usually conscious of its literal significance when applied to a king. Æthelred's record was, however, such that already in the twelfth century (if not before) his name was associated by wits and critics with the noun *un-ræd*, denoting an ill-advised course of action and implying criticism of his conduct of the warfare against the Danes. The noun *unræd* was later transformed into the adjective *unredi*, with a very different kind of pejorative import, and it was as the outcome of this process that the king came to be known to posterity as Æthelred 'the Unready'. Æthelred's posthumous reputation has rendered him synonymous with bad rulership and left him a figure of fun; yet while there is no mistaking the ultimate defeat of the English, a rather different impression of the king emerges when the attempt is made to understand the course of the viking invasions in relation to all other aspects of his long and complex reign.

Æthelred's family Æthelred had an elder half-brother *Edward, born *c*.962, and an elder half-sister *Edith (St Edith of Wilton), born between 961 and 964. King Edgar married Ælfthryth in 964; their eldest son, Edmund, was born *c*.965, and Æthelred himself was probably born not earlier than 966 and not later, or much later, than 968. The paternity of Æthelred's half-siblings is not in question, but there seems to have been some confusion about the identity of Edward's mother and some doubt about the legitimacy of Edith's birth. Edward was described by Osbern of Canterbury as Edgar's son from an illicit union with a nun of Wilton Abbey, and by Eadmer of Canterbury (and John of Worcester) as born to Edgar's first wife, Æthelflæd the Fair; Edith is said to have been Edgar's daughter from an illicit union with Wulfthryth, who later became abbess of Wilton. It is possible, against this background, that the marriage of Edgar and Ælfthryth in 964 was intended not least to resolve a situation which had given cause in high places for some embarrassment and concern; and it may well have been regarded, at the time, as a significant moment in Edgar's reign. Interestingly, it was in 964 that King Edgar took decisive action in driving clerks from the old and the new minsters at Winchester, and replacing them with monks from Abingdon. In a charter issued just two years after the king's marriage, in 966, Edmund was accorded precedence over his elder half-brother, Edward, and was perhaps pointedly styled *clito legitimus* ('legitimate prince'); no less pointedly, Edmund's mother, Ælfthryth, was styled *legitima coniunx* ('legitimate

Æthelred II (*c*.966×8–1016), silver penny

wife'). The charter in question, which is extant in its original form (*AS chart.*, S 745), was drafted by none other than Æthelwold, bishop of Winchester, and symbolized the king's confirmation of privileges to the New Minster, which had been reformed two years before. It was patently not a product of the royal writing office, and may not in that sense have represented an 'official' point of view; but it lay on the high altar of the New Minster at Winchester for the rest of King Edgar's reign, within reach of the community and in full sight of God.

Æthelred the atheling It is not known where Æthelred was born, and it is only possible to guess how he might have spent the earliest years of his life. The prevailing impression of the 960s, and especially the later 960s, is of a period when Edgar was engaged in the consolidation of a realm reunited in 959, and when his enthusiastic support for the monastic reform movement was beginning to make a significant impression on the course of affairs. The atheling Edmund died in 971, and it seems likely that whatever recognition he had enjoyed as King Edgar's legitimate heir was accorded henceforth to his younger brother. Yet it was beyond anyone's power effectively to determine the succession in advance; and when Edgar died, on 8 July 975, those left in positions of power would have had to make their choice between the king's eldest surviving son, Edward (aged about thirteen), and his youngest son, Æthelred (aged at most about nine and perhaps only six or seven). Queen Ælfthryth would naturally have promoted the cause of her son Æthelred, and might in this respect have enjoyed the support of Bishop Æthelwold; others would no less naturally have preferred Edward, as the elder son, and would presumably have been prepared to set aside any lingering doubts about his parentage.

In the event, Edward was 'elected' king, on 17 July 975; Æthelred, perhaps by way of compensation, was assigned the use of those estates which pertained to kings' sons.

The evidence of charters and coinage suggests that the business of royal government continued as usual, yet there seem to have been many who tried to take advantage of the situation, in their own interests, by seeking to undo whatever had been done during Edgar's reign. Three estates (Bedwyn and Burbage, in Wiltshire, and Hurstbourne, in Hampshire) which King Edgar had previously given to Abingdon Abbey, even though they properly belonged to kings' sons, were withdrawn from the abbey and reassigned to Æthelred 'by the decree and order of all the leading men' (*AS chart.*, S 937; *English Historical Documents*, 1, no. 123); so it would appear that King Edward's councillors were concerned to ensure that Æthelred's interests were respected. Æthelred is said to have visited Ely Abbey during Edward's reign, perhaps significantly in the company of Bishop Æthelwold; but little else is known of his activities at this time.

Less than three years after his accession, King Edward fell foul of an opposing faction among the secular nobility. On 18 March 978 he came to visit his 'much-loved brother' Æthelred, who was staying with his mother, Queen Ælfthryth, at Corfe in Dorset; and although Edward is said to have been intent upon 'the consolation of brotherly love', he was soon surrounded by Æthelred's thegns and treacherously killed (Byrhtferth, 4.18). Æthelred and Ælfthryth benefited most directly from Edward's death, but there is no need to presume that they had organized it themselves. Edward was probably murdered by men acting on their own initiative and in their own interests, who hoped they would prosper under Æthelred; however, it was Queen Ælfthryth who as the wicked stepmother later attracted the blame and who is said (by William of Malmesbury) to have founded religious houses at Amesbury and at Wherwell in expiation for her part in the crime.

The young king, 978–991 It must be assumed that soon after King Edward's death a meeting was convened at which the atheling Æthelred was chosen as king in his place. Æthelred was at most about twelve and perhaps only nine or ten years old. The conduct of the kingdom's affairs would at this stage have been in the hands of a group of the king's councillors, presumably including Queen Ælfthryth herself, as well as Dunstan, archbishop of Canterbury, Æthelwold, bishop of Winchester, and Ælfhere, ealdorman of Mercia. The most pressing issue in the opening months of the new reign was doubtless the identification and punishment of those responsible for Edward's murder (an obscure and contentious issue), and appropriate obsequies for the late king's body would also need to be performed for the matter ever to be allowed to rest. Almost a year elapsed before the discovery of Edward's supposed remains, their burial at Wareham on 13 February 979, and their ceremonial translation from Wareham to Shaftesbury five days later. Within three months of the ceremony at Shaftesbury, Æthelred was anointed king at Kingston, Surrey, on 4 May 979. According to one chronicler, the event took place 'with much rejoicing by the councillors of the English people' (*ASC*, texts D, E). Byrhtferth of Ramsey states similarly that when Æthelred was consecrated king, by Archbishop Dunstan and Archbishop Oswald, 'there was great joy at his consecration', and describes the king in this connection as 'a young man in respect of years, elegant in his manners, with an attractive face and handsome appearance' (Byrhtferth, 5.4). Another important event was the completion of Bishop Æthelwold's building works at the Old Minster, Winchester, marked by the rededication of the church of St Peter, in the presence of the king, on 20 October 980. Bishop Æthelwold brought a great throng of bishops, abbots, ealdormen, and thegns to Winchester, from a meeting of the king and his councillors at Andover, and entertained them lavishly; and 'all who had previously seemed his enemies, standing in God's path, were suddenly made, as it were, sheep instead of wolves' (Wulfstan of Winchester, *Life of St Æthelwold*, chap. 40).

Viking raids on England resumed in 980, after a lull of nearly a hundred years. Initially, the raids were sporadic, and probably amounted to little more than local irritation: Southampton, Thanet in Kent, and Cheshire were ravaged in 980; St Petroc's Monastery, at Padstow, Cornwall, was sacked in 981, and great damage was done along the coast in the south-west; three ships of vikings ravaged Portland, Dorset, in 982; Watchet, in Somerset, was ravaged in 988, and Goda, 'the Devonshire thegn', was killed. The more significant factors at play in the 980s were probably personal and domestic, as the king, now in his teens, broke free from the influence of those who had controlled events in his boyhood. It might be supposed that there was a formal occasion when Æthelred came of age, at which stage he would have gained greater independence of action; but while distinctions between infancy, boyhood, adolescence, manhood, and old age are commonplace in the literature, there is no clear indication that the passage from boyhood (*pueritia*) into adolescence (*adolescentia*), at the age of fourteen, need have made much difference in itself.

The significant turning point at this stage in Æthelred's reign seems to have been the death of Æthelwold, bishop of Winchester, on 1 August 984. By this date the king would have been at most about eighteen years old and perhaps only fifteen or sixteen, but in either case fully capable of making his own way in the world. The immediate consequences of Æthelwold's death are indicated in a charter drawn up in summer 993 (*AS chart.*, S 876), whereby the king restored privileges to Abingdon Abbey. The event had deprived the country of one 'whose industry and pastoral care administered not only to my interest but also to that of all inhabitants of the country', and had ushered in a period of wrongdoing, when the king was under the influence of councillors who in their greed had led him astray. The wrongdoing would appear to have involved the abuse of church privileges, though not all of the king's men were implicated, and the wrongdoing was not necessarily widespread. Following the death of Ælfhere, ealdorman of Mercia, on 22 October 983, the principal ealdormen during the 980s were Æthelwine of East Anglia, Byrhtnoth of the East Saxons, and Æthelweard of

the western provinces. Æthelwine and Byrhtnoth were committed to the protection and promotion of the interests of religious houses at (respectively) Ramsey and Ely, and the credentials of Æthelweard, the chronicler, are equally impeccable. Yet not all religious houses could rely upon the same level of support in high places. Abingdon Abbey, which had done so well in the 960s and early 970s, was a case in point. There the death of Abbot Osgar in May 984, compounded by Bishop Æthelwold's death soon afterwards, exposed the abbey to the danger of exploitation by unscrupulous men. The king was persuaded to reduce the abbey to servitude by Wulfgar, bishop of Ramsbury and a certain Ealdorman Ælfric. The latter was almost certainly the ealdorman of Hampshire, eager to take advantage of an opportunity for advancing the career of his brother Eadwine, for whom he was able to purchase the abbacy. A different kind of local difficulty arose at Rochester. A bald statement in the Anglo-Saxon Chronicle, to the effect that in 986 'the king laid waste the diocese of Rochester' (*ASC*, texts C, D, E), seems at one level to exemplify the king's supposed violent streak, but analysis of the king's charters reveals that it represents the expression of more deep-rooted factors. Æthelred had fallen out with Ælfstan, bishop of Rochester, in 984, and had then been persuaded by Æthelsige, a royal household thegn, into giving him some of the church's land. In short, it looks as if in 984 unscrupulous men took advantage of the loss of firm direction in order to advance their own interests, just as others had done in 975, following the death of King Edgar. The development was one of which Æthelred came to be ashamed, and to regret.

It must have been during this period (*c*.985) that Æthelred married for the first time. According to material compiled *c*.1100 at Worcester, his first wife was called Ælfgifu, daughter of a nobleman (*comes*) called Æthelberht, who is otherwise unknown; William of Malmesbury does not give her name, and seems to have presumed that she was a woman of low birth; while the north-country monk Ailred of Rievaulx, writing in the early 1150s, identifies her (without naming her) as the daughter of a *comes* called Thored (Thorth). In his youth Ailred had served as chief steward in the household of David I, king of Scots (*r*. 1124– 53), who through his mother, Margaret, was a great-great-grandson of King Æthelred and his first wife; Ailred was thus in a good position to know about David's maternal forebears. Combining his evidence with that from Worcester makes it possible to say that Æthelred's first wife, Ælfgifu, was the daughter of Thored who held office as earl of Northumbria from *c*.975 to *c*.992, attesting Æthelred's charters quite regularly in the 980s; he also gave land in Yorkshire to the church of St Cuthbert at Chester-le-Street (*AS chart.*, S 1660). The marriage must have served to strengthen Æthelred's position in a region where a king of the West Saxon line always needed friends; and although the names chosen for their sons (*Æthelstan, Ecgberht, *Edmund, Eadred, Eadwig, and Edgar) suggest that Æthelred and Ælfgifu had decided from the outset to commemorate the king's own predecessors, it is important to bear in mind that the sons had some natural affinity, through their mother, with the nobility of the northern Danelaw. Æthelred also had at least three daughters from his first marriage, called Edith, Ælfgifu, and Wulfhild. It is striking, however, that Queen Ælfgifu left no trace of her own position in the king's household or at court. She did not attest any of her husband's charters in the later 980s or 990s; and there is reason to believe that at least some of her children (including Æthelstan) were brought up by a foster-mother and by their paternal grandmother, Queen Ælfthryth.

There is evidence that King Æthelred was engaged in at least some diplomatic activity in the late 980s. In 990 Pope John XV (r. 985–96) dispatched Leo, bishop of Trevi, to England, in an attempt to make peace between Æthelred, 'king of the West Saxons', and Richard 'the marquis' (count of Rouen). Nothing is known of the cause of the dispute, though it is a reasonable presumption that it had to do with Norman readiness to give shelter and sustenance to viking raiders. Æthelred sent his own envoys to Normandy, and on 1 March 991 Leo issued a letter at Rouen on the pope's behalf addressed 'to all the faithful', declaring that peace between the king and the marquis 'should remain ever unshaken' (English Historical Documents, 1, no. 230). Unfortunately for all concerned, the effectiveness of the treaty depended largely upon the quiescence of those who were not themselves party to it.

The viking army in England, 991–1005 The direction of events in Æthelred's reign was affected in the 990s by a dramatic increase in the scale and incidence of viking activity. The circumstances of this development are hard to elucidate. The raiders of the 980s had doubtless told tempting tales of rich pickings in England, and might well have represented the English as vulnerable to attack; but it seems unlikely that such reports reflected on the competence or otherwise of the government carried on in Æthelred's name. For the viking leaders of the 990s, the furtherance of their ambitions back home was probably their chief purpose, with the acquisition of English gold and silver, rather than the conquest of territory, their prime objective. Understanding of their impact on the English in these years depends largely upon the answer to a simple question: were the English faced with a succession of separate raiding armies, which returned home for the winter only to come back the following summer, or were they dealing with a single force which after its first arrival maintained a threatening presence in England for well over a decade? Although the question will always remain open to discussion, a close reading of the annals in the Anglo-Saxon Chronicle suggests that the bulk of the viking force was based in England throughout the years 991 to 1005.

In late summer 991 a large viking fleet arrived off Folkestone, in Kent, and made its way around the south-east coast and up the Blackwater estuary. The viking force was opposed at Northey Island, near Maldon, by an English army led by Ealdorman Byrhtnoth, as told in the famous Old English poem, *The Battle of Maldon*. It was decided in the aftermath of Ealdorman Byrhtnoth's death, and the defeat of his army, that 'tribute' (gafol) should be paid to

the vikings, 'because of the great terror they were causing along the coast' (ASC, texts C, D, E); and on this first occasion, the payment was of 10,000 pounds. There is no indication that the victorious viking fleet returned whence it came; indeed, it would appear that the fleet was active along the east coast in 992 (when the king's father-in-law, Earl Thored, was one of those entrusted with the leadership of the English fleet) and again in 993 (when 'a very large English army' was collected, the leaders of which 'first started the flight' (ASC, texts C, D, E), and that it was essentially the same fleet, now led by Olaf Tryggvason and Swein Forkbeard, which came up the Thames estuary, towards London, in 994.

At this point the king and his councillors came to terms with the vikings. The army received another payment of gafol, said to be '16,000 pounds in money' according to the chronicler (ASC, texts C, D, E), or '22,000 pounds in gold and silver' according to a treaty drawn up at about this time (II Æthelred, chap. 7.2). The leaders of the viking force are identified in the treaty as Olaf, Jostein, and Guthmund, son of Steita, without mention of Swein Forkbeard; so it may be that Swein had gone his own way—he is reported to have been active in the Irish Sea in 995 before leaving to reassert his position as king of Denmark. Olaf Tryggvason, on the other hand, was in 994 received into the Christian faith in a ceremony at Andover, with King Æthelred standing sponsor to him; he received gifts from the king, promised 'that he would never come back to England in hostility' (ASC, texts C, D, E), and seems then to have returned to Norway, where he set about establishing himself as king in his own land. Other component parts of the viking force appear to have decided to stay in England, for it is apparent from the treaty that some had chosen to enter into King Æthelred's service as mercenaries, based presumably on the Isle of Wight.

For some three years following (994–7) the mercenary force seems to have had little to do, and to have remained at peace; but although the circumstances are unrecorded, the vikings eventually resumed hostile activities. In 997 'the Danish army went round Devon into the mouth of the Severn', ravaging extensively in Wales and the south-west; in 998, 'the army turned back east', ravaging first in Dorset and operating thereafter from the Isle of Wight; and in 999 'the army came again round into the Thames', ravaging in Kent (ASC, texts C, D, E). There is no suggestion that this was a new fleet or army, and presumably the mercenary force created in 994 from the residue of the raiding army of 991 had turned on those whom it had been hired to protect. Nor is it suggested that these 'Danes' received gafol during the years 997–1000, and it may have been in despair or desperation that in the summer of 1000 the viking fleet went to Normandy; if it received shelter there from Duke Richard II, any pact which had hitherto existed between England and Normandy must have been broken.

It was probably much the same force which returned to England in May 1001, ravaging first in Hampshire and then further west in Devon, before returning to its base on the Isle of Wight. The king and his councillors determined to make 'peace' (*frith*) with the fleet 'on condition that they should cease their evil-doing', and in the opening months of 1002 the vikings received a payment of 24,000 pounds (*ASC*, texts C, D, E). In 1003 the Danish army was active in the west country, and it emerges from the Anglo-Saxon Chronicle that the army was now under the command of Swein Forkbeard, suggesting that he had decided to resume operations in England. It is doubtless significant that in the coinage introduced at about this time the king was portrayed neither crowned nor bareheaded but wearing a helmet, capturing the spirit of a kingdom under sustained attack from a foreign power. In 1004 Swein and his fleet were in East Anglia, where they met fierce opposition from Ulfcytel. But although there does not appear to have been any further payment of *gafol*, in the end it was not a feat of arms which drove the Danes from England but an act of God. The effects of the great famine of 1005 were felt widely on the continent, and in the British Isles. The Anglo-Saxon chronicler, enjoying the inestimable advantage of hindsight, comments wryly that the army 'let little time elapse before it came back' (*ASC*, texts C, D, E).

English responses It is within this context that Æthelred's response to the viking threat in the 990s and early 1000s must be assessed, and the impact of the viking raids on the course of his reign judged. The king himself has acquired particular notoriety for his policy of paying large sums of gold and silver to the vikings, in the hope thereby of inducing them to go away; but this policy must take its place as just one among a number of measures adopted in the 990s for the defence of the kingdom. Present knowledge of the military response—and indeed of such matters as the quality of leadership displayed by the king and his commanders in the field, and of the degree of loyalty shown by others towards the king—depends largely upon the word of an anonymous chronicler conducting the nation's post-mortem soon after its conquest by a foreign power. It is almost impossible not to be affected by his compelling account of disaster precipitated by treachery, compounded by incompetence, and relieved only by defeat, though by no means does he tell the whole story. The payments of *gafol* appear at first sight to be a poor substitute for military action, and hardly seem calculated to achieve any purpose other than to encourage the raiders to come back for more. Yet the policy had been adopted in the past by Alfred the Great, Charles the Bald, and many others, and in certain circumstances may have seemed the best available way of protecting the people against loss of life, shelter, livestock, and crops. Though undeniably burdensome, it constituted a measure for which the king could rely on widespread support. It is an irony of Æthelred's reign, however, that the coinage thus accumulated by those whose business was terrorism and extortion, and carried back to Scandinavia by them, now supplies the bulk of the evidence for the effective operation of the monetary system of England in the late tenth and early eleventh centuries.

The English response to viking raids gained an additional dimension in 994, when for the first time the king

was able to deal directly with their leaders. Olaf Tryggvason had not been defeated in battle; but by receiving him 'at the bishop's hands', Æthelred took advantage of the power of the Christian faith to bind sponsor and subject together, and at the same time to bring the subject into a new political order, just as Alfred and many others had done before him. No less significant is the inception, at least in the context of Æthelred's reign, of the decision to employ vikings as mercenaries, charged with defending the kingdom against other viking raiders. The policy appears to have had some effect in 994–7, but the arrangement seems then to have been abandoned, to be followed by the renewed outbreak of hostilities in 997–1001, and the further payment of *gafol* in 1002. The so-called massacre of St Brice's day, when Æthelred ordered the killing of 'all the Danish men who were in England' (*ASC*, texts C, D, E), implemented on 13 November 1002, is another of the king's counter-measures which has attracted strong disapproval; yet judged in its immediate context, and shorn of later accretions, the 'massacre' should be seen as the reaction of people exasperated by the behaviour of the vikings in their midst, after a decade of slaughter, pillage, and extortion, directed not at the inhabitants of the Danelaw but at precisely those 'Danes' who had so recently been employed as mercenaries and then turned against their employers.

Another counter-measure, adopted in 1000–01, in the immediate aftermath of the sheltering of the viking army in Normandy, was the renewal of the Anglo-Norman alliance. This probably came immediately after Æthelred's dispatching of a fleet to Normandy, for the express, but in the event frustrated, purpose of conquering the duchy and capturing Duke Richard; unsurprisingly, the story, as told by the Norman chronicler William of Jumièges, does not redound to the king's credit. It was at about the same time (*c*.1000) that Æthelred's first wife died, and, perhaps no less significantly, that his mother, Queen Ælfthryth, died. The king entered into negotiations with Richard II, and as a result secured the hand of his sister *Emma (d. 1052), daughter of Richard I, who in the spring of 1002 came to England and on her marriage to the king was accorded a new name (Ælfgifu) and full dignity at the king's court.

To judge from the witness lists in the king's charters, Æthelred's sons from his first marriage had from 993 onwards been accorded a place of honour at court, and it is significant that they retained this status after their mother's death and after their father's marriage to Emma. Æthelred and his new wife soon had a family of their own. The eldest son *Edward (King Edward the Confessor), was born between 1003 and 1005, followed by at least two further children, Gode and *Alfred. A later commentator, blessed with the advantage of hindsight, stated that just before Edward's birth all the men of the country took an oath that if a boy should come forth he would rule over them (Barlow, i.1), and a Norman source states that in his youth Edward was 'anointed and consecrated as king' (*Inventio et miracula S. Wulfrani*, chap. 18). The truth is likely to have been different. His parents are said to have been at

Ely *c*.1005, when they presented their eldest son, Edward, at the holy altar, and entrusted him to the community for upbringing with the boys there. Æthelstan, eldest son of the king's first marriage, evidently remained the prospective heir, and the charters show that Edward had to take his place behind his elder half-brothers.

Law, culture, and government The arrival of the viking army in England in 991, and its threatening presence thenceforth until its departure in 1005, no doubt significantly affected domestic affairs in the kingdom throughout this extended period. The invasion of 991 would have been regarded, in accordance with a rationale reaching back through Alfred to Alcuin, and ultimately to the Old Testament, as divine punishment for the sins of the English people, prompting many to reflect on whatever might have been the underlying cause. So, in addition to the various forms of response directed at the vikings themselves, other forms of response are encountered, aimed, in effect, at appeasing the Almighty.

By summer 993, when the viking force was active north and south of the Humber estuary, Æthelred had seen the errors of his ways and was beginning to break free from the influence of the men who had led him astray in the later 980s. A different group of councillors now had the king's ear, and a period of wrongdoing gave way to one of reflection and reform. The great triumvirate of monastic reformers—Bishop Æthelwold and archbishops Dunstan and Oswald—had been succeeded in court circles by those trained during the golden age of Edgar's reign, including Sigeric and Ælfric, successive archbishops of Canterbury from 990 to 1005, Ælfheah, bishop of Winchester, Wulfstan, bishop of London, Ælfweard, abbot of Glastonbury, Wulfgar, abbot of Abingdon, and Ælfsige, abbot of the New Minster, Winchester. Prominent among the king's lay advisers during this period were his kinsman Ealdorman Æthelweard, his maternal uncle Ordwulf, and Æthelweard's son Æthelmær. Yet the witness lists in the king's charters which allow detection of these changes in the composition of the king's council suggest that by the end of this period some of those in high places had had enough. Æthelmær founded a monastery at Eynsham, in Oxfordshire, and to judge from the charter confirming its foundation, issued in 1005 (*AS chart.*, S 911), chose this moment to retire from the secular life. Ordwulf also disappears from the witness lists in 1005, and seems to have withdrawn to the monastery which he had founded at Tavistock, in Devon. Perhaps the departure of the viking force in 1005 encouraged Æthelmær and Ordwulf to think that the time had come for them to seek a quieter life; if so, their optimism proved sadly mistaken.

It is difficult to detect particular instances where these men influenced the course of affairs in the 990s, though Archbishop Sigeric is credited with devising the policy of paying *gafol*, and Abbot Ælfsige and the thegns Æthelmær and Ordwulf are specifically mentioned in an important charter of 993 in favour of Abingdon Abbey (*AS chart.*, S 876), and may be presumed, with Abbot Wulfgar, to have

persuaded the king to set off in a new direction. Yet what is so striking about the years from 991 to 1005, when the vikings were at large and men such as these were in control of the nation's affairs, is that the period witnessed some of the most intense activity in the proper ordering of Christian society among the English. Whether it was fear of the impending millennium which concentrated the collective mind, or simply fear of the vikings, is a moot point; but the evidence of all this activity does much to compensate for the very incomplete record of events in the Anglo-Saxon Chronicle.

The king's charters reveal that several estates which had been taken from churches in the later 980s were in the mid- and later 990s restored to their rightful owners. Yet there was far more to it than that. This was a period for church building, for recruitment into the religious life, and for the furnishing of churches with relics, privileges, books, treasures, and estates, and so for the increase of their revenues. The dedication of Bishop Æthelgar's multi-storeyed tower at the New Minster, Winchester, in the mid-980s, was matched by Bishop Ælfheah's further building works at the Old Minster, including additional crypts (each with its own altar and relics), a more powerful organ, and a new tower (surmounted by a golden weathercock) dedicated some time between summer 993 and late October 994. Between 995 and 1002 there seems to have been a veritable outburst of enthusiasm for the translation of the relics of saints from one resting-place to another, suggestive of a determination to secure their intercession as well as to ensure the safety of their remains: Cuthbert at Durham in 995; Æthelwold at Winchester on 10 September 996; Edith at Wilton on 3 November 997; Edward at Shaftesbury on 20 June 1001; Oswald at Worcester on 15 April 1002; Ivo at Ramsey on 10 June 1002; and several others who appear to have been translated at about the same time.

Following his charter of 993 for Abingdon, in 994 Æthelred confirmed Ealdred, bishop of St Germans (in the exposed south-eastern corner of Cornwall), in his control of St Petroc's Minster, Bodmin, which lay inland and further west (*AS chart.*, S 880). A monastery at Cholsey in Berkshire was founded *c*.994 in honour of Æthelred's half-brother Edward. In 998 the king authorized Wulfsige, bishop of Sherborne, to convert his community to the Benedictine rule (S 895). The relics of Edward had been translated at Shaftesbury in the midst of intense viking activity in Wessex, and later in the same year Æthelred granted the minster of Bradford-on-Avon, Wiltshire, to the nuns of Shaftesbury, for use as a refuge 'against the inroads of the barbarians' (*adversus barbarorum insidias*), by a charter which shows that the abbey had become the centre of a flourishing cult (S 899). Other religious houses to benefit from royal support during this period include Wherwell, Hampshire, which received a charter in 1002 (S 904), Burton, Staffordshire, which received a charter in 1004 (S 906), and Eynsham, Oxfordshire, which received its charter in 1005 (S 911).

It is the concentration of all this activity in a relatively short period of time that makes it so impressive, and creates a context for intense productivity of other kinds. The fine arts, represented by sculpture, manuscript decoration, and metalwork, would appear to have flourished. The need for books, extending from essential service books to works of learning and literature, was matched by the availability of the resources and expertise necessary to produce them. Scholars of the calibre of Wulfstan of Winchester, Byrhtferth of Ramsey, and Ælfric of Cerne (later of Eynsham) produced a remarkable variety of works, in Latin and in the vernacular. Wulfstan followed his *Narratio metrica de S. Swithuno*, composed in the mid-990s, with his life of St Æthelwold, composed *c.*1000. Byrhtferth's life of St Oswald was composed at about the same time. A person known only by his initial B produced a life of St Dunstan, also *c.*1000. The greater part of Ælfric's output was generated within this period, and reflects his own response to the worsening events. When Ælfric had completed his 'First series' of homilies *c.*990, followed by his 'Second series' *c.*992, he was still based at Cerne, in Dorset, some distance removed from the dangers which at that time afflicted the people of the south-east, London, and East Anglia; so it is not surprising that the viking raids did not at that stage loom large in his consciousness. By the mid-990s, when he was writing his *Lives of Saints* on behalf of Ealdorman Æthelweard and his son Æthelmær, the need for prayer against the heathen was made more explicit. He subsequently translated the book of Judith into English, expressly for the instruction of laymen charged with the defence of their land 'against the invading army' (Crawford, 48). Perhaps it is paradoxical that so much activity could take place when the country was under viking attack, or perhaps the reign of Alfred shows that this is precisely what should be expected. At all events, there is no mistaking the determination of the English to have God on their side.

The measures taken in direct response to the viking raids, and the other activities of a kind intended to be pleasing in the sight of God, were matched by administrative reforms which reflect some credit on the institutions and practices of royal government at a time of great stress. The two law-codes known to modern scholarship as I Æthelred and III Æthelred appear to have been intended to complement each other. The former, promulgated at Woodstock in Oxfordshire, was 'for the promotion of peace [*frith*] for all the people', in accordance with English law; the latter, promulgated at Wantage in Berkshire, was similarly 'for the promotion of peace [*frith*]', but was directed towards the five boroughs of the Danelaw. The codes are not dated, but were produced probably in the mid-990s, perhaps in 997, when a meeting was convened at Wantage 'for dealing with matters of various kinds' (*AS chart.*, S 891); and together they represent an attempt to codify aspects of the different practices which had arisen in different parts of Æthelred's kingdom. Like other kings before and after him, Æthelred did not find it easy to deal effectively with the entrenched power of his ealdormen, though by building on administrative arrangements established earlier in the tenth century he encouraged the emergence of the shire-reeve (sheriff) as the king's representative in the localities. There is otherwise every indication that the business of royal government continued to be conducted in the normal way, at periodic meetings of the king's council held on royal estates at various places in southern England, and no doubt also in darker corners as the king and his household moved from one place to another.

The renewal of viking attacks, 1006–1009 It is Æthelred's misfortune, however, that he has come to be judged, not altogether unreasonably, on the basis of the last decade of his reign, when matters went progressively from bad to worse to calamitous. The period from 1006 to 1012 witnessed two of the most devastating of all viking raids on England, which had the cumulative effect of undermining the ability of the English to resist any further attack. It is no coincidence that these years also witnessed the meteoric rise of *Eadric Streona, ealdorman of the Mercians, who in 1015–16 came to play a major role in the downfall of the English, while in the same period Archbishop Wulfstan of York came to the fore as one of the king's leading statesmen, writing law-codes and homilies which reflect not so much the inability of an enfeebled government to respond in a crisis, as the desperation of a battered people praying for deliverance from their enemies.

The annal in the Anglo-Saxon Chronicle for 1006 reports dissension among the king's councillors in its usual inscrutable way: 'In the same year Wulfgeat was deprived of all his property, and Wulfheah and Ufegeat were blinded and Ealdorman Ælfhelm killed' (*ASC*, texts C, D, E). But what at first sight reads like a series of punishments inflicted on certain laymen for their respective misdemeanours, proves when taken together with charter and other evidence to represent nothing less than a palace revolution, as remaining members of the old guard, now without the protection of the king's kinsmen Æthelmær and Ordwulf, succumbed to a plot engineered by Eadric Streona. Wulfgeat was a prominent thegn and leading member of the king's household; so his forfeiture, for unspecified reasons, has all the makings of political intrigue. Ælfhelm, ealdorman of Northumbria, was a member of a prominent Mercian family, while Wulfheah and Ufegeat were his sons. The evidence implicating Eadric Streona is relatively late, but charter witness-lists suggest that he and his brothers were conspicuous at court in 1005–6, and were at the core of the party which benefited most noticeably from the passing of the old order. It so happened that Malcolm II, king of Scots (*r.* 1005–34), penetrated deep into Northumbria in 1006, until repulsed at Durham by Uhtred, son of Earl Waltheof, who as a reward for his good services received the earldom of the whole of Northumbria. Malcolm may have been taking advantage of trouble in the south, or acting on his own initiative at the outset of his reign; in any event, the fact that Malcolm's attack is not registered in the Anglo-Saxon Chronicle is a salutary reminder that the horizons of a chronicler writing in southern England were somewhat restricted.

Some time after midsummer in 1006, continues the chronicler, a force described as 'the great fleet' arrived at Sandwich, 'and did just as they were accustomed, ravaged, burnt, and slew as they went'. That the leader of the viking force was probably a certain Tostig was of no consequence to the annalist, who simply reports the devastating impact of the vikings as they passed through Hampshire and Berkshire and back to their base on the Isle of Wight, leaving their mark 'on every shire of Wessex'. The king and his councillors were driven against their inclinations to make another payment of *gafol* to the viking army. The sum of 36,000 pounds was collected and paid over to the vikings in 1007, whereupon the 'great fleet' presumably returned to Scandinavia. The only other recorded event in 1007 seems in an unexplained way to have arisen from the agonies of the previous year, and marks the next stage in the rise of Eadric Streona—he was now made ealdorman of Mercia. At least the payment of *gafol* brought temporary respite for the English, who used the time well. In 1008 'the king ordered that ships should be built unremittingly over all England, namely a warship from 310 hides, and a helmet and corselet from eight hides' (*ASC*, texts C, D, E); and in the same year, at Pentecost (16 May), a meeting was convened at (King's) Enham in Hampshire, at which Archbishop Wulfstan produced the first of the codes of law (represented by the texts known as V and VI Æthelred) in which he set out to reform English society in ways calculated to earn God's support in the struggle against the vikings. In 1009 the newly built ships were brought to Sandwich, 'and were to stay there and protect this country from every invading army'. Unfortunately, the ambitious Brihtric, brother of Eadric Streona, chose this moment to make an accusation against Wulfnoth 'the South Saxon' (probably the father of Godwine, later earl of Wessex), leading to the destruction of many of the ships and the dispersal of the ship-levy; 'and no better than this was the victory which all the English people had expected' (*ASC*, texts C, D, E).

The immediate sequel must have seemed inevitable. The chronicler continues, 'When this ship-levy had ended thus, there came at once after Lammas [1 August] the immense raiding army, which we called Thorkell's army, to Sandwich'. The king and his councillors were at Bath, and their immediate response was the promulgation of a law-code (VII Æthelred) which laid down an elaborate programme of public prayer to be implemented on the Monday, Tuesday, and Wednesday preceding Michaelmas, which in 1009 fell on Thursday 29 September. On these three days, all the nation was enjoined to fast on bread and herbs and water; priests were instructed to lead their people barefoot to church, carrying relics and invoking Christ; religious communities were to sing their psalters; and mass-priests were to say mass 'for our lord and for all his people'. Among other measures, one penny (or the value of a penny) was to be paid from each hide of land, and brought to church, where all the money would be divided up into three and distributed 'for God's sake'. Perhaps it was in specific connection with the programme of prayer that the authorities decided to issue a special type

of silver penny, without parallel before or after, bearing on one side not a stylized image of the king but an image of the Lamb of God, and on the other side not a standard cruciform device but an image of the dove, symbol of the Holy Spirit. The extraordinarily distinctive and highly charged *Agnus Dei* coinage was current for only a short period, in the autumn of 1009; and it may be significant that the design which had presumably been chosen in 1009 to serve as the next substantive issue, after *Helmet*, was a reversion to the *Small Cross* type introduced by and perhaps therefore associated with King Edgar, at his moment of glory in 973.

The impact of Thorkell the Tall, 1009–1012 Some impression of the course and impact of 'Thorkell's army', as it ravaged large parts of southern England in 1009 and 1010, can be gained from reading the Anglo-Saxon Chronicle for those years; it explains how, when Æthelred and his councillors sued for peace in 1011, they were clearly a broken regime. 'All those disasters befell us through bad policy [*unrædas*], in that they were never offered tribute [*gafol*] in time nor fought against; but when they had done most to our injury, peace and truce were made with them; and for all this truce and tribute [*gafol*] they journeyed none the less in bands everywhere, and harried our wretched people, and plundered and killed them' (*ASC*, texts C, D, E). The final outrage took place after the 'peace and truce' had been agreed. Some time between 8 and 29 September 1011 the vikings besieged Canterbury, captured Archbishop Ælfheah and several others, ransacked the whole borough, and then took the archbishop back with them to their ships. The chronicler goes on to record how in early April 1012, 'Ealdorman Eadric and all the chief councillors of England' were at London, apparently in order to supervise the payment of *gafol*, amounting to 48,000 pounds. The payment was made soon after Easter (13 April), and at Greenwich, on the following Saturday (19 April), the vikings, in a drunken stupor, pelted the defiant archbishop with bones and ox-heads, until one of their number struck him down with the back of an axe and killed him. The viking army then dispersed 'as widely as it had been collected'.

The failure of the English to withstand the onslaught of the viking army in 1009–10 testifies to the success of Thorkell's own tactics, always on the move and creating terror wherever he went, as much as it proclaims the incompetence and irresolution of those responsible for organizing the kingdom's defence. A charter of Æthelred's granting land in Derbyshire to his thegn Morcar, issued in late December 1009 (*AS chart.*, S 922), is enough to show that business was then continuing as usual, in the aftermath of Thorkell's invasion, but no charter survives for the *annus horribilis* of 1010, and only abbreviated texts of two charters issued in 1011; consequently little is known of the continued operation of royal government in those years. It is apparent, however, that a major development took place while Thorkell's army was at large in Æthelred's kingdom. Charters issued in 1012 show that Eadric Streona had by then gained significant promotion in the order of precedence so carefully observed among the king's ealdormen. Ealdorman Ælfric had occupied the prime position for the previous ten years, from the death of Ealdorman Æthelweard (probably in 998) until the charter of late 1009; but some time during the period 1010–12 Eadric overtook the two ealdormen senior to him, and he must have gained this promotion at the expense of Ælfric, who continued to attest charters until his death in 1016.

Eadric's new position finds due reflection in the Anglo-Saxon Chronicle for 1012, and it was perhaps later in the same year that Eadric found a pretext or opportunity for ravaging St David's in south-west Wales. Interestingly, all three of Æthelred's known daughters from his first marriage are said to have been given in marriage to earls who came into prominence during the latter years of the reign: Eadgyth (Edith) married Eadric Streona of Mercia; Ælfgifu married Uhtred of Northumbria; and Wulfhild married Ulfcytel of East Anglia. Marriage within the English nobility represented a departure from earlier practice, when kings' daughters were sent overseas or hidden away in nunneries; and it may be that the policy, if it can be dignified as such, was itself an indication of Æthelred's determination to bind the kingdom together in any way that he could.

After the dispersal of the viking force in 1012, forty-five ships from the Danish army 'came over to the king, and they promised him to defend this country, and he was to feed and clothe them' (*ASC*, texts C, D, E). It transpires that it was Thorkell himself who thus entered into King Æthelred's service, as leader of a mercenary army based at Greenwich; and it was in this connection that Æthelred instituted the annual land-tax known as the *heregeld* or 'army-tax', later known as 'danegeld' because it was paid to the Danish mercenaries (the term was later still mistakenly applied to the *gafol* levied to pay off invaders). A chronicler reporting on the abolition (in fact only the temporary suspension) of the tax in 1051, remarks how oppressive it had been, and how it 'always came before other taxes' (*ASC*, text D); yet it was one of the earliest and (from the king's point of view) most effective systems of public taxation in medieval Europe, and the basis of much that would follow.

The invasions of Swein Forkbeard and Cnut, 1013–1016 The raids of 1006–7 and 1009–12 all but destroyed the capacity of the English to offer any further resistance to the Danes. The point was probably not lost on Swein Forkbeard, king of Denmark, who took the earliest opportunity to launch an invasion, bent on conquest rather than merely on extortion. He arrived with his fleet at Sandwich in the summer of 1013, whereupon he made his way northwards up the coast to the Humber, and from there came south through the east midlands, receiving submission wherever he went. King Æthelred and Thorkell held out against him at London, so Swein went westwards via Wallingford to Bath, and there received the submission of Ealdorman Æthelmær (who had evidently come out of his retirement at Eynsham) and all the western thegns, before returning to his ships; 'and all the nation regarded him as full king' (*ASC*, texts C, D, E). The citizens of London also submitted;

whereupon Swein demanded full payment and provisions for his army over the winter, and Thorkell demanded the same for the mercenary force at Greenwich. Æthelred stayed initially with Thorkell's mercenaries, then, after Queen Emma and the athelings Edward and Alfred had crossed the sea to seek refuge in Normandy, he moved to the Isle of Wight for the Christmas festival, before joining his family in Normandy.

Swein Forkbeard died on 3 February 1014. The Danish force elected his son Cnut as king, but the councillors of the English people 'determined to send for King Æthelred, and they said that no lord was dearer to them than their natural lord if he would govern them more justly than he did before' (*ASC*, texts C, D, E). Æthelred sent his son Edward back to England, with messengers, and undertook 'that he [Æthelred] would be a gracious lord to them, and reform all the things which they all hated'; moreover, everything said and done against the king would be forgiven, 'on condition that they all unanimously turned to him without treachery'. Æthelred came home to his people in the spring, 'and he was gladly received by them all'. Soon afterwards Æthelred took decisive action, bringing his full force to Lindsey and driving Cnut from the kingdom. It was at about this same time that Archbishop Wulfstan first preached his *Sermo ad Anglos* ('Sermon to the English'), commenting at length on the decline which had set in since the days of King Edgar and had aroused the displeasure of God, and calling upon the English to mend their ways. Also in 1014 Wulfstan drafted further legislation for the king, including a code dealing with ecclesiastical matters (VIII Æthelred), probably complemented by a code focusing on secular matters (now lost, except for parts incorporated in II Cnut, chaps. 69–76), which may have enacted some of the promised reforms.

Æthelred's return to England in the spring of 1014 raised the profile of Æthelstan, his eldest son from his first marriage, as his most obvious prospective successor. A glimpse of the circles in which Æthelstan moved is provided by his will (*AS chart.*, S 1503; *English Historical Documents*, 1, 129), which suggests that the atheling enjoyed good relations with his father, with his brothers Edmund and Eadwig, and with a number of prominent thegns, including Sigeferth and his brother Morcar. Æthelstan died, however, on 25 June 1014, and henceforth his younger brother Edmund must have been regarded as their father's likely successor. Although it is difficult on the available evidence to understand the full complexity of domestic politics in the last years of Æthelred's reign, it is apparent that matters came to a head in 1015, at a 'great assembly' convened at Oxford. According to the chronicler, Eadric Streona 'betrayed Sigeferth and Morcar, the chief thegns belonging to the Seven Boroughs: he enticed them into his chamber, and they were basely killed inside it' (*ASC*, texts C, D, E). The king seized their property, and held Sigeferth's widow at Malmesbury; whereupon the atheling Edmund took her against Æthelred's will, married her, went to the east midlands, and took possession of all Sigeferth's estates, and Morcar's, 'and all the people submitted to him'. At first sight, it looks as if Edmund was taking a stand against his father; but beneath the surface it was perhaps more a matter of Edmund taking a stand against the machinations of Eadric Streona, who was himself the driving force behind the king's actions at this time. Eadric had been the dominant voice in the king's council for at least three years, and it may be that his actions at Oxford had left Edmund with no choice but to take drastic action.

After his death in 1014 Swein Forkbeard had been succeeded as king of Denmark by his son Harald, whose younger brother Cnut not unnaturally sought to make a kingdom for himself in England. It was Cnut's good fortune that when he invaded England, in the late summer of 1015, he came in the midst of this major domestic crisis, and was soon able to benefit from it. Upon arrival at Sandwich, he went south round the coast and then west into Wessex, so perhaps intending to leave Eadric Streona and Edmund temporarily to their own devices. Edmund's challenge had effectively denied Eadric any further prospect of advancement, and may even have helped to bring the king and Edmund back together; if so, it was under these circumstances that Eadric deserted from the English side, taking the Danish mercenary fleet with him into Cnut's service. The West Saxons submitted to Cnut, who stayed in the south-west until Christmas. In the opening months of 1016 Cnut and Eadric were active in Mercia, while Edmund and Æthelred attempted without much success to organize resistance. Edmund then joined forces in Northumbria with his brother-in-law Earl Uhtred, and went on the offensive into Eadric's home territory; but they were outmanoeuvred by Cnut, who was soon threatening York. Uhtred returned to Northumbria, where he submitted 'out of necessity' to Cnut and was then killed on the orders of Eadric Streona. For his part, Edmund rejoined his father in London. After Easter (1 April) Cnut turned with all his ships towards London, but his adversary died just as the campaign was drawing to its climax. In the words of the chronicler: 'He [Æthelred] ended his days on St George's Day [23 April], and he had held his kingdom with great toil and difficulties as long as his life lasted' (*ASC*, texts C, D, E).

Æthelred was succeeded as king by his eldest surviving son, Edmund Ironside, who after some spirited resistance was eventually defeated by Cnut at the battle of Ashingdon on 18 October 1016. For a few weeks the kingdom was divided between Edmund, in Wessex, and Cnut, in Mercia and Northumbria; then, after Edmund's death on 30 November 1016, Cnut succeeded to the whole kingdom. Æthelred's only remaining son from his first marriage, Eadwig, styled king of the *Ceorls*, was soon killed on Cnut's orders. He was also survived by the three children of his second marriage: Edward, Alfred, and Gode (who married first Dreux, count of the French Vexin, and then Eustace (II), count of Boulogne). All three took refuge in Normandy. In 1017 Cnut married their mother, Emma, hoping thereby to undermine their position, to gain her support for himself, and to provide for the succession with a son of his own. Æthelred's grandson through Edmund Ironside was Edward the Exile (*d.* 1057), whose children included

Margaret, wife of Malcolm III, king of Scots. Through her, the descendants of Æthelred came to include several kings of Scotland; and through Margaret's daughter Matilda, wife of Henry I, the blood of the West Saxon kings was passed on from Æthelred to the Plantagenet kings of England.

According to Goscelin of St Bertin, Queen Emma moved Æthelred's body from London to Wilton Abbey, so that he could rest beside the body of his half-sister, St Edith; but all the indications are that he was buried at St Paul's. During the middle ages Æthelred's mortal remains lay entombed beside those of Sæbbi, king of the East Saxons, in the north wall of the choir of Old St Paul's Cathedral. An inscription placed on a tablet on the wall above Æthelred's tomb (shown in an engraving by Wenceslaus Hollar published in Dugdale's *History of St Paul's Cathedral*, 1658), tells the tale of St Dunstan's prophecy on the day of the king's coronation, and of the unhappy outcome of the king's reign. The tombs of both kings were destroyed when fire engulfed Old St Paul's in September 1666.

Assessments of King Æthelred Æthelred has gained notoriety as a king whose acts of cruelty, cowardice, and incompetence were equalled only by the treachery, guile, and greed of those around him, and in this process he has come to be regarded as the personification of an age of national degeneracy. The major source of information is the account of the reign in the Anglo-Saxon Chronicle, which deals largely with the viking invasions; it was put together in its received form soon after the Danish conquest in 1016, so only when the chronicle is read in conjunction with and in relation to the king's charters, lawcodes, coinage, and other forms of evidence, does a properly balanced picture of the reign begin to emerge. Yet Æthelred made enough of an impression, for better or worse, to ensure that he would always capture the historical imagination. The stories about Archbishop Dunstan's prophetic powers, displayed first on the occasion of Æthelred's baptism (when the boy urinated in the font) and again on the occasion of his coronation in 979, appear to have originated in the successive lives of St Dunstan by Adelard, Osbern, and Eadmer; they were picked up thereafter by the Anglo-Norman historians writing in the first half of the twelfth century, and thus entered the mainstream of English historical tradition. The story of the king's lifelong hatred of candles, because his mother had beaten him with them as a boy when he was so upset about his half-brother's death, originated in the *Passio S. Eadwardi*.

The more general presentation of Æthelred's reign, as a period when the people suffered under a king of singular incompetence, was developed by William of Malmesbury on the basis of his own reading of the Anglo-Saxon Chronicle, though it was Henry, archdeacon of Huntingdon, who propounded the notion that Æthelred's marriage to Emma of Normandy set in motion a train of events leading to the Norman conquest, and who took the view that the payments of tribute represented the origins of the oppressive taxation of his own day. It is also instructive to see how tales of the so-called 'massacre of St Brice's day' became steadily worse as they were told and retold in the twelfth and thirteenth centuries.

It is perhaps not surprising that the principal Æthelredian subjects found among the paintings, prints, and other illustrations of English history in the late eighteenth and early nineteenth centuries are the murder of Edward the Martyr and the massacre of St Brice's day; there was nothing that was uplifting, and precious little that was romantic. Among modern historians, the prime example was set by Sharon Turner, whose influential *History of the Anglo-Saxons* was first published between 1799 and 1805. Turner made little attempt to assess the quality of the evidence or to consider dimensions of the subject beyond the tale of military catastrophe related in the Anglo-Saxon Chronicle. To his credit he made some use of the poem on the battle of Maldon, and found in Archbishop Wulfstan's *Sermo ad Anglos* 'a contemporary picture of the internal state of England during this reign'. Yet Æthelred is made personally responsible for the outcome of events, and when the time comes is dismissed with utter contempt: 'At this crisis, the death of Ethelred released England from its greatest enemy' (Turner, 1.277). For E. A. Freeman, writing in the 1860s, Æthelred 'is the only ruler of the male line of Ecgberht whom we can unhesitatingly set down as a bad man and a bad King' (Freeman, 1.258–9), and few of his readers would have missed the resonances of a formulation adapted from the Book of Common Prayer: 'Under Æthelred nothing was done; or, more truly, throughout his whole reign he left undone those things which he ought to have done, and he did those things which he ought not to have done' (ibid., 1.297).

In the early 1940s Sir Frank Stenton wrote of 'national degeneracy', and regarded Æthelred himself as 'a king of singular incompetence' (Stenton, 394–5). There has since been some attempt at rehabilitation, based on a deeper understanding of the problems that confronted the king, on a more critical assessment of the literary sources which form the basis of the traditional account of his reign, and on the integration of evidence derived from Æthelred's charters, law-codes, and coins. It remains difficult, however, for modern historians of the revisionist persuasion to have much effect on such a deeply rooted tradition. Indeed, it will long remain Æthelred's fate to be ridiculed among the very worst of English kings, as for example in the American composer Richard Wilson's one-act comic opera, *Aethelred the Unready*, which received its world première in New York on 13 May 2001.

Æthelred the Unready undoubtedly deserves better. It is clear that much lay beneath the surface of recorded events, just as it is self-evident that a reign of thirty-eight years, in which so much took place, cannot be reduced to a simple matter of good or bad kingship. In the final analysis it is as difficult to decide what credit, if any, Æthelred can take for the positive aspects of his reign as it is to apportion blame for its manifestly disastrous outcome. It is enough, however, to suggest in this way that there was more to Æthelred than the familiar tale of viking invasions, exacerbated by incompetence, treachery, and

intrigue in high places: unequal to the challenge that confronted him, and unfortunate in the circumstances that engulfed him, but always more interesting than merely unready.   SIMON KEYNES

Sources ASC · AS chart. · *English historical documents*, 1, ed. D. Whitelock (1955) · law codes I–X Æthelred, *Die Gesetze der Angelsachsen*, ed. F. Liebermann, 3 vols. (1903–16), 1.216–70 · 'law codes I–X Æthelred', *The laws of the kings of England from Edmund to Henry I*, ed. A. J. Robertson (1925), 47–133 · J. J. North, *English hammered coinage*, 3rd edn, 2 vols. (1994), vol. 1 · William of Malmesbury, *Gesta regum Anglorum / The history of the English kings*, ed. and trans. R. A. B. Mynors, R. M. Thomson, and M. Winterbottom, 2 vols., OMT (1998–9), vol. 1, pp. 268–314 · John of Worcester, *Chron.*, vol. 1; 2.430–84 · Henry, archdeacon of Huntingdon, *Historia Anglorum*, ed. D. E. Greenway, OMT (1996), 326–56 · *The life of St Æthelwold / Wulfstan of Winchester*, ed. M. Lapidge and M. Winterbottom, OMT (1991) · Wulfstan of Winchester, *Narratio metrica de Sancto Swithuno*, *Frithegodi monachi breviloquium vitae beati Wilfridi et Wulfstani Cantoris narratio metrica de Sancto Swithuno*, ed. A. Campbell (1950), 65–177; M. Lapidge, *The cult of St Swithin* [forthcoming] · *The Gesta Normannorum ducum of William of Jumièges, Orderic Vitalis, and Robert of Torigni*, ed. and trans. E. M. C. van Houts, 2 vols., OMT (1992–5), 2.10–22 · Ailred of Rievaulx, *De genealogia regum Anglorum*, *Rerum Anglicarum scriptores X*, ed. R. Twysden (1652), 1.347–70 · *Ælfric's Lives of saints*, ed. W. W. Skeat, 2 vols. in 4, EETS, 76, 82, 94, 114 (1881–1900); repr. (1966) · *The Old English version of the Heptateuch: Ælfric's treatise on the Old and New Testament, and his preface to Genesis*, ed. S. J. Crawford, EETS, orig. ser., 160 (1922); repr. with two additional mansucripts (1969) · F. Barlow, ed. and trans., *The life of King Edward who rests at Westminster* (1962) · J. Williams ab Ithel, ed., *Annales Cambriae*, Rolls Series, 20 (1860) · *Inventio et miracula S. Wulfrani*, *The Normans in Europe*, ed. E. van Houts, Manchester Medieval Sources (2000), chap. 18 · [Byrhtferth?], 'Extracts from the anonymous Life of St Oswald', *English historical documents*, 1, ed. D. Whitelock (1955), 839–43, no. 236 · S. Turner, *The history of the Anglo-Saxons*, 4 vols. (1799–1805); 7th edn, 3 vols. (1852) · E. A. Freeman, *The history of the Norman conquest of England, its causes and its results*, 6 vols. (1867–79); 2nd edn, vols. 1–4 (1870–76); 3rd edn, vols. 1–2 (1877) · F. M. Stenton, *Anglo-Saxon England*, 3rd edn (1971), 373–90 · D. Hill, ed., *Ethelred the Unready: papers from the millenary conference* [Oxford 1978] (1978) · S. Keynes, 'The declining reputation of King Æthelred the Unready', *Anglo-Saxon history: basic readings*, ed. D. A. E. Pelteret (2000), 157–90 · S. Keynes, *The diplomas of King Æthelred 'the Unready', 978–1016: a study in their use as historical evidence* (1980) · D. Scragg, ed., *The battle of Maldon, AD 991* (1991) · S. Keynes, 'The vikings in England, c.790–1016', *The Oxford illustrated history of the vikings*, ed. P. Sawyer (1997), 48–82 · S. Keynes, 'England, 900–1016', *The new Cambridge medieval history*, 3, ed. T. Reuter (1999), 456–84 · P. Wormald, *The making of English law: King Alfred to the twelfth century*, 1: *Legislation and its limits* (1999) · S. Keynes, *An atlas of attestations in Anglo-Saxon charters, c.670–1066* (2002)
Likenesses silver penny, BM [see illus.]

Æthelric (*fl. c.*693–736). See under Hwicce, kings of the (*act.* c.670–c.780).

Æthelric (d. 1034), bishop of Dorchester, was a former monk of Ramsey and a generous patron of his monastery. His election to the see of Dorchester in 1016 perhaps owed something to his family connections, although these are unknown. Given the extent and geographical location of this large see, it was perhaps believed that a local man would prove to be the most effective bishop. During his early years at the monastic school in Ramsey, Æthelric and three more 'noble youths' once climbed up among the bells, and accidentally cracked one. Abbot Eadnoth (993–

1006) refused to expel them, arguing that in later years they might be in a position to assist the monastery.

Bishop Æthelric was concerned that good disciplinary standards should be maintained at Ramsey. When the unpopular Abbot Withman complained of the monks' lack of discipline, Æthelric paid a visit in disguise, and saw for himself that the monks were well-behaved. He censured the abbot for making false allegations about them, but at the same time ordered the monks to be obedient towards Withman. On another occasion, abbot and monks alike were proved to be negligent, but when they humbly submitted to Æthelric's criticisms he granted them some land. Having decided to acquire for Ramsey the relics of St Felix, which were located in the royal manor of Soham, Æthelric obtained the permission of King Cnut for the transfer, and prompted Æthelstan, the abbot of Ramsey, to send a party to Soham by boat, to seize the body. The Ramsey chronicle tells of a miraculous mist which prevented the hostile intervention of a group of monks from Ely.

Æthelric's episcopate coincided with a wave of Danish settlement in the wake of Cnut's invasion. He brought a court case against the powerful Danish magnate Thorkell the Tall, then regent in England during Cnut's absence, accusing his wife of the murder of her stepson. Only after Cnut's return to England was Thorkell brought to court, where his attempt to clear his wife by swearing on his beard failed when the beard came away in his hand. The stepson's grave was discovered and the wife convicted of murder. Thorkell was judged guilty of perjury, and of flouting the bishop's jurisdiction, and in compensation gave land to Æthelric, who granted it to Ramsey. Rather more apocryphal is a story of Æthelric winning an estate in a bet with a drunken Dane. Æthelric died in 1034 and was buried at Ramsey Abbey.   EMMA MASON

Sources W. D. Macray, ed., *Chronicon abbatiae Rameseiensis a saec. x usque ad an. circiter 1200*, Rolls Series, 83 (1886) · M. K. Lawson, *Cnut: the Danes in England in the early eleventh century* (1993) · F. Barlow, *The English church, 1000–1066: a history of the later Anglo-Saxon church*, 2nd edn (1979) · *ASC*, s. a. 1034 [texts C, E] · John of Worcester, *Chron.*, vol. 2

Æthelstan (*fl.* 714?). *See under* South Saxons, kings of the (*act.* 477–772).

Æthelstan [Athelstan] (**893/4–939**), king of England, was the eldest son of King *Edward the Elder (870s?–924), with his first wife, Ecgwynn.

Family and early life Information about Æthelstan's youth is found only in the twelfth-century *Gesta regum Anglorum* by William of Malmesbury; this long account of the king's life may at least in part be based on pre-conquest sources, although its precise evidential value is questionable. If Æthelstan was indeed aged thirty on his accession to the throne in 924, he must have been born to King Edward in 893 or 894, while his grandfather King *Alfred was still ruling. Little is known about the future king's mother, whose name is not given in any pre-conquest English sources. The verse account by Hrotsvitha of Gandersheim of the marriage of Otto I of Saxony to Eadgyth,

Æthelstan (893/4–939), manuscript illumination [with St Cuthbert]

Æthelstan's half-sister, which implies that Æthelstan's mother was socially inferior to Eadgyth's, may reflect rivalry among the offspring of Edward the Elder's different liaisons, rather than being intended to represent Æthelstan as illegitimate, though William of Malmesbury would later represent him as such.

According to William, King Alfred honoured his grandson as a child, investing him with the gift of a scarlet cloak, a belt set with gems, and a Saxon sword with a gilded scabbard; Æthelstan can have been no more than five or six years old at the time, for Alfred died in 899. The story presents problems, but does not lack corroboration. A short acrostic poem bearing the legends ADALSTAN/ IOHANNES, surviving in a single manuscript in Oxford (Bodl. Oxf., MS Rawl. C.697, fol. 78v), which praises the prince as 'abundantly endowed with the holy eminence of learning', and prays that he will fulfil the promise implied by the 'noble rock' of his name (Lapidge, 72–81), was apparently written to commemorate the ceremony of Æthelstan's investiture. William of Malmesbury reports further that Alfred had Æthelstan educated and trained for rulership at the court of his daughter, *Æthelflæd, and her husband, *Æthelred, ealdorman of the Mercians; if so, the young man would have gained his military experience in the Mercian campaigns to conquer the Danelaw, indeed Æthelstan may have represented his father's interests in Mercia after his aunt's death in 918.

Æthelstan himself appears never to have married, for what reason one can only speculate. Having four younger brothers, he may have been trying to prevent conflict over the succession to the West Saxon throne, conceivably influenced in this by the prevalence of rumour about the legitimacy of his own birth; alternatively—or additionally—this could have been a decision inspired by a religious vocation to chastity. The allusion in the twelfth-century *Liber Eliensis* to an otherwise unattested daughter of Æthelstan's—'Æðida filia regis Æðelstani'—who supposedly made a gift to Ely (*Liber Eliensis*, 292) must remain unexplained, unless it is assumed that the Ely author mistook one of the king's many sisters for his daughter.

Accession Considerable confusion surrounds the accession of Æthelstan following the death of his father, Edward the Elder, on 17 July 924. During his reign Edward had taken direct control of Mercia, creating a single 'Anglo-Saxon' kingdom, but it is not clear that his composite realm would have been inherited as a single entity by his heirs. The Mercian register (a set of early tenth-century annals incorporated in the Anglo-Saxon Chronicle) reports that on Edward's death Æthelstan was chosen king by the Mercians and consecrated at Kingston upon Thames, Surrey. But his coronation did not take place until 4 September 925, a delay apparently to be accounted for by Edward's realm being divided on his death, with Æthelstan being chosen as king in Mercia, and his half-brother Ælfweard, born to Edward's second wife, Ælfflæd, succeeding to Wessex. However, the Mercian register notes that Ælfweard died 'very soon' after his father—only sixteen days after, according to the D version of the chronicle. Æthelstan would have succeeded to the combined kingdom only after his half-brother's premature death and possibly not without opposition; this may be the correct reading of the sequence of events reported in the Mercian register.

Some political difficulties apparently surrounded the start of Æthelstan's reign in Wessex. In a charter of 925 (from the part of the year when Æthelstan's authority seems to have been recognized only in Mercia), Æthelstan was termed 'supervisor of the Christian household of the whole region well-nigh in the whirlpools of cataclysms' (*AS chart.*, S 395). William of Malmesbury reports particular opposition to Æthelstan's rule at Winchester, the place of Ælfweard's burial; a certain Alfred was said to have organized a plot to blind Æthelstan, supposedly on account of his illegitimacy, and Ælfweard's younger brother Eadwine was allegedly complicit in this enterprise. It is notable that the bishop of Winchester did not apparently attend the king's coronation in 925, nor does he appear among the witnesses to royal charters during 926. It may be appropriate to see Æthelstan as something of an outsider at the West Saxon court even after his accession there; King Edward's widow, *Eadgifu, seems to have been marginalized on her stepson's accession, since she did not attest any of his charters.

That the tensions within royal circles persisted beyond 925 may be suggested by the suspicious death of the atheling Eadwine (Ælfweard's brother) in 933. The E manuscript of the Anglo-Saxon Chronicle records laconically for 933: 'In this year the ætheling Eadwine was drowned at sea'. The twelfth-century historians Symeon of Durham and William of Malmesbury attribute this event to conspiracy and violence in which Æthelstan himself was involved. The details can be safely ignored, but that there was indeed a background of political unease to Eadwine's death is suggested by the account given by Folcwin the Deacon in his *Gesta abbatum S Bertini* (chap. 107), written before 962 at St Bertin, where Eadwine was buried. According to Folcwin, 'King' Eadwine left England following 'some disturbance in his kingdom', but was shipwrecked and washed ashore in Flanders, where he was buried with honour; Æthelstan subsequently sent several gifts of alms to St Bertin on his brother's behalf. Perhaps the chronicler knew more than he was prepared to say. But it is more likely that Folcwin was confused over Eadwine's royal status than that the latter was co-ruler with Æthelstan. In the one diploma that Eadwine witnessed (*AS chart.*, S 1417), he attested next after the king as *cliton*, atheling.

Wars Æthelstan's posthumous reputation rests largely on his prowess in war, notably his famous victory over the combined forces of the kings of Dublin, Scots, and Strathclyde at 'Brunanburh' in 937. But although this victory consolidated Æthelstan's position as sole king of England, it might properly be seen as the final phase of a process begun much earlier in his reign. Once he came into possession of all of his father's kingdom, Æthelstan found himself heir to a wider realm than that inherited by any previous West Saxon (or indeed Anglo-Saxon) king. Apart perhaps from the ruler of English Bernicia at Bamburgh, Ealdred, son of Eadwulf, he was the sole native English ruler in England. The kingdom of the Northumbrians was ruled by the Danish king, *Sihtric Cáech (formerly king in Dublin). In 926 Æthelstan and Sihtric met at Tamworth, the old Mercian capital, where they made an alliance sealed by Sihtric's marriage to a sister of Æthelstan. That the treaty involved at the very least a commitment on both sides not to invade the territory of the other, nor to support the other's enemies, seems plausible; where the boundary between their respective territories lay is not entirely clear, since it may be that Sihtric was minting coins in Lincoln as well as in York.

When Sihtric died, the year after this marriage treaty was agreed, Æthelstan took control of his kingdom. The report in the northern version of the Anglo-Saxon Chronicle in using the standard phraseology of royal succession—'Æþelstan cyning feng to Norðhymbra rice'—seems to imply that this was in some sense a legitimate accession to a territory to which Æthelstan had some claim. Similarly, William of Malmesbury asserts that on Sihtric's death Northumbria became Æthelstan's lawfully, belonging to him both by ancient right and by reason of the recent marriage alliance. Æthelstan may at the same time have driven out the one remaining claimant to Northumbrian power, representative of the house of Bamburgh. Two other texts presented Æthelstan's acquisition of Northumbria rather as the conquest it more plausibly was. The northern annals incorporated into the *Historia regum* attributed to Symeon of Durham state that Æthelstan added Sihtric's dominion (*imperium*) to his own, driving out the latter's son (*recte* brother) Guthfrith. Æthelstan's acquisition of Northumbria in 927 is also described in military terms in a poem, 'Carta dirige gressus', written in that year by Petrus, probably a clerk in the king's retinue: 'He [Æthelstan], with Sihtric having died, in such circumstances arms for battle [*armat tum in prelio*] the army of the English throughout all Britain' (Lapidge, 89).

The acquisition of Northumbria made Æthelstan the first West Saxon ruler to have a border with the Scots. Seeking recognition of his new position over the English kingdoms, and wary of the potential support his new neighbours might offer to the exiled Scandinavians, Æthelstan gathered the other kings in the island to Eamont, near Penrith. There on 12 July 927 Hywel of the West Welsh, Constantine, king of the Scots, Owain, king of the people of Gwent, and Ealdred, son of Eadwulf, from Bamburgh, all 'established peace with pledge and oaths in the place which is called Eamont and renounced all idolatry and afterwards departed in peace' (*ASC*, s.a. 927, text D). Constantine's submission is also reported in the poem 'Carta dirige gressus', which celebrated 'this England now made whole' (*ista perfecta Saxonia*; Lapidge, 89–90). The Owain present at Eamont was in fact probably Owain of Strathclyde, on the border of whose territory the meeting took place; the submission of Owain of Gwent is more plausibly placed by William of Malmesbury later in the same year at Hereford. William also reports (uniquely, and so unverifiably) that the Scottish king was baptized as Æthelstan's godson at Eamont, and that although an attempt to secure Guthfrith's person failed, Æthelstan nevertheless took the opportunity to raze to the ground a fortress that the Danes had built at York, 'in order to leave disloyalty no place of refuge' (Malmesbury, *Gesta regum*, 214–15).

Other matters occupied Æthelstan south of the Humber in the next few years, but the Scottish peace did not prove permanent and in 934 the king found himself (perhaps driven by some offensive move from the north) obliged to plan a new campaign. According to the Anglo-Saxon Chronicle, in that year 'King Æthelstan went into Scotland with both a land force and a naval force, and ravaged much of it' (*ASC*, s.a. 934, text C). Something of the preparation for this enterprise can be seen from the witness lists to Æthelstan's charters in this period; on 28 May the king was at Winchester, where he made a grant witnessed by a number of his English thegns, three of the Welsh kings, and five earls of Scandinavian origin (*AS chart.*, S 425), while a broadly similar group witnessed a charter granted at Nottingham on 7 June (*AS chart.*, S 407). The fullest account of the expedition is that given among the northern annals incorporated into Symeon of Durham's *Historia regum*: on his way north the king stopped at the then resting-place of the community of St Cuthbert, Chester-le-Street, and having commended himself and his expedition to the saint's protection, 'he then subdued his enemies, laid waste Scotland as far as Dunnottar and

Wertermorum with a land force, and ravaged with a naval force as far as Caithness' (Symeon of Durham, *Opera*, 2.124). That the attack was made as far north as Caithness (part of the Norse kingdom of Orkney) hints at the beginning of the alliance between Scots and Norsemen that was to find full expression in their attempted joint invasion of England in 937; it also demonstrates the strategic advantages to a West Saxon king of the acquisition of the kingdom of York. The success of Æthelstan's 934 expedition is noted also by John of Worcester, who blames Constantine for provoking the war by violating the peace between him and Æthelstan, and reports that the Scots king was forced to give up his son as a hostage after his defeat.

'Brunanburh' Individually Æthelstan's northern neighbours lacked the strength to counter the wealth and military capability of the enlarged English kingdom; together, however, they might have hoped to check Wessex's northward expansion, if not reverse some of its more recent gains. The most celebrated of the military engagements of Æthelstan's reign was the occasion on which he inflicted a crushing defeat on a combined army led by Constantine, king of the Scots, Olaf Guthfrithson, king in Dublin, and Owain, king of Strathclyde, at a place called 'Brunanburh'. To the annalist of Ulster, this was a 'great victory' for Æthelstan, a 'great, lamentable and horrible battle' in which several thousand Norsemen died as well as a large number of Saxons (*Ann. Ulster*, 384–7). According to the contemporaneous Old English poem recorded in the Anglo-Saxon Chronicle under the year 937, 'Æthelstan, lord of nobles, dispenser of treasure to men, and his brother also, Edmund ætheling, won by the sword's edge undying glory in battle round *Brunanburh*'. On the field died five kings and seven earls from Ireland, as well as the son of the king of the Scots; the combined West Saxon and Mercian force suffered heavy losses but achieved a decisive victory. Well might the chronicle exult that:

> Never yet in this island before this by what books tell us and our ancient sages, was a greater slaughter of a host made by the edge of the sword, since the Angles and Saxons came hither from the east, invading Britain over the broad seas, and the proud assailants, warriors eager for glory, overcame the Britons and won a country. (*ASC*, s.a. 937, text C)

The site of this battle remains a subject of controversy among historians. It has been customary to suppose that it occurred somewhere on the Scottish border, but it has also been argued that it was more plausibly on the frontier established by Edward between English and viking Mercia, that is on Watling Street, possibly even as far south as Northampton. The Old English poem implies that wherever the battle occurred it was near enough to the coast (or to an estuary or a river deep enough for ships to get far inland) for the defeated Norsemen to return swiftly to Dublin by sea. It is also known from the poem that the battle occurred outside Wessex and beyond Constantine's own territory.

For the remaining two years of his life Æthelstan retained his control over the north, although the fragility of that hold is suggested by the speed with which his brother *Edmund lost it on his succession in 939.

Æthelstan's claim to a kingship of Britain was based on more, however, than his conquest of Northumbria and effective subjugation of the Scots. He had expansionist interests also in western Britain, as William of Malmesbury suggests, in his account of the submission by Welsh princes to the king at Hereford in 927. Supposedly the River Wye was agreed on this occasion as the boundary between the English and the Welsh, and an implausibly vast annual tribute imposed. The chronicler had named Hywel, king of the West Welsh, and Owain, king of Gwent, among those who submitted at Eamont; the charter evidence suggests that Idwal, king of Gwynedd, should be included with these in the Hereford submission. Hywel, Idwal, and Guriat (son of Rhodri) attested a charter issued at a meeting in Exeter in April 928, in which they are all described as *subreguli* (*AS chart.*, S 400). This meeting of the king's council probably coincided with Æthelstan's driving the Cornish out of Exeter and the fixing of the boundary of their province at the Tamar; the king supposedly reinforced that city's defences on this occasion, memory of his building-works there surviving into the twelfth century. The legal tract known as the ordinance of the Dunsæte, a short agreement for the settlement of disputes between the Welsh and English on both sides of the River Wye, may date from the period after the agreement between Æthelstan and the Welsh in 927.

The reluctance with which the Welsh kings accepted Æthelstan's overlordship is hinted at by William of Malmesbury; the fear that they would conspire against him may have prompted the West Saxon king to demand their regular attendance at his court. Several Welsh *subreguli* attest the king's charters in the 930s, and three of them appear to have accompanied Æthelstan on his Scottish expedition of 934. The subject Welsh clearly resented their subordinate status, reinforced as it may have been by the payment of frequent gifts, if not of regular tribute. An apparently contemporary poem, *Armes Prydein vawr* ('The great prophecy of Britain'), looks forward to the day when the British will rise up against their oppressors and drive them back to the sea.

Kingship As the early eleventh-century author of the Old English list of the relics which the king had given to the church of Exeter reminded his audience, by grace of God Æthelstan 'ruled England singly, which prior to him many kings had shared between them' (Bodl. Oxf., MS Auct. D.2.16, fol. 8r). Furthermore, he achieved by force of arms (and surely also of personality) the submission of other rulers within the British Isles, the Welsh, the Scots, and the Norse claimants to the kingdom of York. In these circumstances one might expect to find some sophistication in the articulation of Æthelstan's dignity and status, both through the royal styles adopted in his charters, and also in the language and imagery of his charters and coins alike. At the beginning of his reign Æthelstan had himself described in his charters as 'king of the Anglo-Saxons' (*AS chart.*, S 396–7, 394), continuing the style first adopted by his grandfather Alfred and used by his father, Edward the Elder. This title reflected his rule over a combined West Saxon and Mercian polity, but was arguably inadequate to represent his military and political achievement of creating an English monarchy. After 927 Æthelstan's diplomas affect more grandiose regnal styles, making the king *rex Anglorum* ('king of the English'; *AS chart.*, S 399–400, 403, 412, 416), *rex totius Britanniae* ('king of the whole of Britain'; *AS chart.*, S 431, 437, 445–6), or 'nodante dei gratia basileos Anglorum et eque totius Brittannie orbis curagulus' ('by grace of God king of the English and equally guardian of the whole country of Britain'; *AS chart.*, S 429–31, 438, 446). On his coins Æthelstan chose also to be represented as *rex totius Britanniae*.

Whether Æthelstan, or the members of his immediate circle, indeed desired to portray the king's rule in quasi-imperial terms, in emulation of his Saxon contemporaries or Carolingian predecessors, is uncertain. Æthelstan's expression of his hegemony, including his use of *imperator* (*AS chart.*, S 392), and his claim to rule not just the English but all the peoples round about (*AS chart.*, S 441–2), can be paralleled in earlier English contexts which may offer more plausible models. Beyond the rhetoric, however, the sheer practical difficulties of administering so large a realm demanded innovative solutions. After the documentary silence of the later years of his father's reign, Æthelstan's resumption of the issuing of royal diplomas in 925 testifies to a reinvigorated monarchy, and the years of his rule represent a formative period in the creation of the late Anglo-Saxon state. The charters issued in the king's name between 928 and 935 are all the work of a single, apparently royal, scribe, known to modern historians as Æthelstan A. The texts of this scribe's charters are remarkable as much for their literary qualities (testimony to the intellectual environment of the royal court) as for their diplomatic structure and formulation. The witness lists with which they are supplied are of particular interest, recording the presence of the Welsh and occasionally Scottish sub-kings, large numbers of ecclesiastics (abbots as well as bishops), and ealdormen from the Danelaw areas of England. Furthermore, it is possible from these charters to establish the king's itinerary around his expanded realm, since they record the day and place of issue more precisely than earlier diplomas. In centralizing charter production in a royal chancery, the king was taking an unprecedented degree of control over this important area of royal activity; beyond 935 the king's diplomas were still apparently centrally produced in a royal writing office, but by more than one scribe, none with the flamboyance of Æthelstan A.

The scale of Æthelstan's councils—the number of participants, the breadth of the geographical area from which they were drawn, and the frequency with which they were held—marked for Stenton an important change in the character of royal councils; for him these were 'national assemblies, in which every local interest was represented, and they did much to break down the provincial separatism which was the chief obstacle to the political unification of England' (Stenton, 352). These changes may have been the result of pragmatism rather than deliberate innovation, no previous king having needed to devise systems for governing both sides of the Humber, and for uniting all the separate Anglo-Saxon kingdoms into a single polity. The regularity of the gatherings may have assisted with the process of cultural assimilation, as surely will have the gradual conversion of the Danelaw population to Christianity; yet the speed with which the kingdom of York recovered its autonomy after Æthelstan's death should be a reminder of the fragility of Wessex's hold, and its abhorrence to many of the king's reluctant subjects. Problems with the preservation of the peace are evident in Æthelstan's legislation, the vitality of which is one of the most impressive features of his government. In total six law codes survive from this reign, together with a short ordinance on almsgiving: four of the codes are official royal productions, including two general proclamations of laws from the king, one issued at Grately, the second at Exeter following continued violations of the earlier code (II Æthelstan and V Æthelstan); two other codes represent reports to the king about the keeping of his peace by the men of Kent and by the bishops and reeves of the London district (III Æthelstan and VI Æthelstan). The law codes reveal Æthelstan's concern to fulfil his obligation to govern his people effectively, while at the same time illustrating the difficulties of controlling so diverse a population.

Æthelstan's coins shed further light on his perceptions of his kingship. His willingness to exploit the new political circumstances he had created is evident not just from the adoption of the legend proclaiming him king of Britain, but by the imposition of his coinage over his whole realm, enforced in law: 'there is to be one coinage over all the king's dominion and no one is to mint money except in a town' (II Æthelstan, chap. 14). Rather than meaning that there was to be only one type of coin in circulation, this provision may have been intended to ensure that only the coins of the West Saxon king were to be accepted currency within his realm; the hoard evidence certainly indicates that non-English types were kept out quite successfully, as well as demonstrating that old types were not removed from circulation as soon as new ones were introduced. The sites of mints, and the numbers of moneyers at each of them, were similarly tightly controlled by law; yet it is clear that coinage was still, in fact, organized on a local basis. Another innovation lay in the pictorial representation on Æthelstan's coins; in the 'crowned bust' type, issued from c.933, the king was depicted wearing a crown, a simple band with three stalks, each surmounted by a globule. The significance of this imagery is hard to determine, but it is difficult to resist the conclusion that this was a further symbolic promotion of Æthelstan's status and a reflection of his own conception of his kingship. It is unlikely to be coincidental that the inclusion of a crown (as opposed to a helmet) among the kingly regalia conferred at inauguration is first attested in the second Anglo-Saxon coronation ordo, which dates from the first half of the tenth century and may plausibly be dated to Æthelstan's reign. The rite was intended for one who

would be king over the Saxons, Mercians, and Northumbrians, a king elected *in regnum Albionis*, who was to be honoured before all the kings of Britain. Similarly, in both the known manuscript depictions of the king Æthelstan is pictured wearing a crown, and in one he is also holding a sceptre. In these spheres Æthelstan and his circle appear to have been searching for outward signs and symbols to mark the unprecedented nature of his rule.

Foreign contacts Æthelstan is the first Anglo-Saxon king who might genuinely be thought to have pursued a 'foreign policy', in the shape of the marriage alliances and fostering arrangements he negotiated strategically with his continental neighbours, and the refuge he offered at his court to exiles from abroad, as well as the more conventional overtures of friendship he made to foreign, especially German and Breton, religious houses. William of Malmesbury makes much of this aspect of Æthelstan's rule, reporting that 'the whole of Europe sang his praises and extolled his merits to the sky; kings of other nations, not without reason, thought themselves fortunate if they could buy his friendship either by family alliances or by gifts' (Malmesbury, *Gesta regum*, 216–17).

One of Æthelstan's sisters, Eadgifu, had already been given in marriage to Charles the Simple, king of the Franks, during her father's lifetime. When Charles was deprived of power and Robert, count of Paris, made king in 922, Eadgifu returned to England with Charles's son and heir, Louis, taking shelter at her father's court and remaining there after Æthelstan's accession. Æthelstan's defence of his nephew's interests is clear from his receipt of the Frankish embassy that sought the return of Louis d'Outremer (so named from his sojourn in England) as king in 936; the king demanded oaths of goodwill from the legates and arranged for an English escort to accompany the young king back to Francia. But it was expediency rather than sentiment that governed Æthelstan's diplomatic policy. Despite his obvious support for the Carolingian line in West Francia, the king married another of his sisters into the rival Robertian family; the marriage of Eadhild in 926 to Hugh, duke of the Franks and son of Count Robert, is reported in both English and Frankish sources from the tenth century. William of Malmesbury provides an elaborate account of the embassy that came to the English court at Abingdon to promote Hugh's suit; the magnificent gifts supposedly brought to the West Saxon king included the sword of Constantine the Great, its scabbard decorated with a nail from the crucifixion, Charlemagne's famous lance (allegedly that with which the centurion Longinus had pierced Christ's side on the cross), and the standard of St Maurice, as well as pieces of the true cross and the crown of thorns enclosed in crystal (Malmesbury, *Gesta regum*, 218–21). It is difficult to determine how much credence should be given to this story, but the Malmesbury community claimed that Æthelstan had bequeathed them the relics of Christ's passion, and it may be that there were other traditions of the house by which the king's acquisition of such valuable relics was recollected.

The most celebrated, and arguably most prestigious, of

the marriages negotiated by Æthelstan was that contracted with the Liudolfing house, recently elevated to the kingship in Saxony, even though it was the historic and saintly lineage of the West Saxon house that made its daughters eligible brides for the young Otto, rather than the particular achievements of the girls' half-brother. English and German sources agree that Æthelstan sent two of his sisters to Saxony for the young prince to choose whom he preferred. The girls were escorted to Germany in the autumn of 929 by Cenwald, bishop of Worcester, bearing lavish gifts for their Saxon hosts. Otto's choice fell to the elder of the two girls, Eadgyth; the fate of her younger sister, Ælfgifu, has puzzled historians since the late tenth century. Contemporary sources disagree on her name, as well as on the identity of her husband, but it seems likely that she married Louis, brother of Rudolf II, king of Burgundy, with whom she had the son named 'Henricus filius Ludowici' who appears in Burgundian sources between 943 and 961. Although this marriage obviously enhanced Æthelstan's European connections, it was surely contracted on Ælfgifu's behalf by her new in-laws, the arrangement serving the immediate purpose of sealing Ottonian influence in the Rhône valley and the area between the Jura and the Alps.

Beyond the liaisons contracted through these marriages, Æthelstan further promoted English interests in foreign affairs by other means. Having helped Louis d'Outremer to return to West Francia in 936, Æthelstan appears to have continued to support his nephew after his accession to the throne, sending a fleet to help him by attacking the Flemish coast at Thérouanne in 939. Æthelstan's dealings with the count of Flanders were more complicated. Earlier in 939, when Count Arnulf captured Montreuil-sur-Mer he had sent the wife and sons of the captured Count Herlouin of Ponthieu to Æthelstan's court for safe keeping; yet the English raid on the Flemish coast in 939 seems to have led to an abrupt change in Flemish tactics and to have ended friendly relations between the courts of England and Flanders.

Other foreign exiles found refuge with the English king in this period. According to the chronicle of Nantes (written in the mid-eleventh century on the basis of earlier annals) a number of Bretons fled their land for fear of the Danes and sought refuge at the court of King Æthelstan; among these was a certain Mathuedoi, count of Poher, who took with him his son Alain, afterwards known as Crooked Beard. The English king is said to have stood as Alain's godfather at his baptism and to have fostered him at his own court; when in 936 Alain returned to his native Brittany he did so with Æthelstan's support. Hákon, son of the Norwegian king Harald Fairhair, was reputedly fostered at Æthelstan's court; his nickname in Scandinavian sources is Aðalsteinsfóstri ('Æthelstan's fosterling'), and he is reported (admittedly only in texts dating from the twelfth and thirteenth centuries) to have reclaimed his kingdom with military help from his foster father. The story is not implausible, although Hákon's presence in England is not recorded in any contemporary English sources. William of Malmesbury does, however, report

Æthelstan's reception at York of an embassy from King Harald of Norway, who sent him a magnificently furnished viking long ship. The extent and breadth of Æthelstan's connections within the British Isles and beyond is remarkable and unprecedented.

Religion and learning Æthelstan was a king noted for his piety, even in an age when pious devotion was a recognized attribute of the good monarch. He founded two new religious houses, at Milton Abbas in Dorset and at Muchelney in Somerset, and reputedly made substantial grants of land to existing houses, notably Malmesbury. The king's fervour is evident both from his efforts to attract ecclesiastics to his court, and from his interest in religious manuscripts and particularly in the collection of relics. He may have inherited some relics from his grandfather, King Alfred (*AS chart.*, S 1043); he certainly already had a substantial collection of saints' relics by his accession; the text of a manumission granted by the king on the day of his coronation referred to oaths sworn on the king's *haligdom* (BL, Royal MS 1 B. vii, fol. 15*v*). In his *Gesta pontificum* William of Malmesbury reports that he had found in a shrine at Milton Abbas in Dorset a letter from Radbod, prior of St Samson's at Dol in Brittany, addressed to Æthelstan and sent with a gift of relics 'which we know to be dearer to you than all earthly substance' (Malmesbury, *De gestis pontificum*, 399–400). In the prelude to a list of relics supposedly given to Exeter by King Æthelstan it was said that the king had sent men overseas to buy relics for him. The churches of Westminster and Glastonbury, and the New Minster at Winchester, also laid claim to relics given by Æthelstan. The church of Abingdon even claimed to have received some of the relics that Æthelstan had been given by Hugh, duke of the Franks.

'There was scarcely any ancient house in all England that he did not adorn with buildings or ornaments, books or estates', recalled William of Malmesbury (Malmesbury, *Gesta regum*, 206–7). Æthelstan's generosity as a donor of manuscripts is apparent from surviving manuscript inscriptions that record the king's gift of books to Christ Church and St Augustine's at Canterbury (BL, Cotton MS Tiberius A.ii, and LPL, MS 1370; BL, Royal MS 1 A.xviii), to the minster at Bath (BL, Cotton MS Claudius B.v), and to the community of St Cuthbert, then at Chester-le-Street (BL, Cotton MS Otho B.ix, and Cambridge, Corpus Christi College, MS 183). A number of these manuscripts are gospel books, of which one is worth singling out for special mention: Tiberius A.ii. Written perhaps at Lobbes in Belgium in the late ninth or early tenth century, this manuscript has inscriptions associating it with Otto, the German king who married Æthelstan's sister Eadgyth, and with Æthelstan himself. Two inscriptions on folio 15 record Æthelstan's gift of this manuscript to Christ Church, Canterbury; the first, in prose, describes the king as 'Anglorum basyleos et curagulus totius Bryttaniae'— terms reminiscent of the royal styles used in his charters between 935 and 939, implying that the inscription dates from the last years of the king's reign. The second is a poem, beginning 'Rex pius Æðelstan', that celebrates

Æthelstan's achievements; written in the present tense, it would also seem to date from the end of his reign.

Of these manuscripts, only Cambridge, Corpus Christi College, MS 183 (whose contents include a collection of texts celebrating the life of St Cuthbert) was wholly written in England during Æthelstan's reign, and this appears to have been specially commissioned for presentation to the community of the saint at Chester-le-Street. The reverse side of the first folio of the first quire of the manuscript carries a splendid picture of a king presenting a book to a saint; the king, wearing a crown, stands holding a book in both hands; the saint, standing in front of his church, has a halo above his head and gives a blessing with his right hand while holding a book in his left. Although the figures are not labelled, there can be no doubt that the two are Æthelstan and St Cuthbert. Similar in style was a portrait in the other manuscript given by the king to Chester-le-Street (burnt in the Cotton Library fire of 1731 but known from various antiquarian descriptions of the undamaged manuscript); this was a gospel book written probably in Brittany in the late ninth or early tenth century. In the Otho B.ix picture the king, again crowned, and holding a sceptre in his left hand, knelt to offer a book to St Cuthbert with his right hand; this picture bore an inscription: 'Æthelstan, the pious king of the English, gives this gospel book to St Cuthbert, the bishop' (Keynes, 'Athelstan's books', 173–4). One further manuscript may have been intended for the king to give to Chester-le-Street: a de luxe copy of Aldhelm's prose *De virginitate* (BL, Royal MS 7 D.xxiv) made by the scribe of Cambridge, Corpus Christi College, MS 183. The text and illustrations are, however, incomplete and the gift, if planned, was seemingly abandoned (Gretsch, 359–67). According to the *Historia de sancto Cuthberto* Æthelstan visited the shrine of St Cuthbert on his way north to Scotland in 934, and while there drew up a *testamentum*, which he placed beside Cuthbert's head, recording his gifts to the saint; these included vestments and other sacred texts, together with a substantial estate at Wearmouth, as well as 'this gospel book'. The vestments may have been the embroideries found in the coffin of St Cuthbert in 1827; from the inscriptions on the maniple and stole it is clear that these had originally been made for Frithestan (bishop of Winchester 909–31), on the orders of Edward's queen, Ælfflæd.

Beyond his generosity as a patron of religious houses, Æthelstan should be remembered for his promotion of learning at his court. In this he was certainly assisted by his reception of scholars from abroad, as well as of continental princes and nobles, thereby helping to foster an intellectually vibrant environment. The learned men who attended his court included Bretons (notably Israel the Grammarian), Franks, Germans, Irish, Italians, and possibly even the Icelander Egill Skallagrímson, fragments of whose verses in praise of the king survive. Bishop Cenwald, travelling round German monasteries in 929, may have hoped to collect books and possibly relics, to gain some insights into German monasticism, and conceivably to recruit German ecclesiastics for the English church. During and beyond Æthelstan's reign there were men with German names among the clerical communities at the New Minster, Winchester (it is not clear, however, whether they were members of that community, or of the royal household), and at London, and there may have been a German priest at Abingdon. Some of the king's moneyers, too, had German names.

Æthelstan's reign also represented a crucial period in the background to the monastic revolution that reached its climax in the reign of King Edgar. Many of the leading ecclesiastics of that later movement had spent time in their youth at the court of King Æthelstan, and thereby had the opportunity of contact with the ideas and new manuscript books circulating around the king. Some of the bishops in Æthelstan's circle identified themselves in charters as *monachi*, including Cenwald of Worcester, Ælfheah of Winchester, Oda of Ramsbury, and Theodred of London; although it is possible that these men had taken individual professions of monastic vows, it may be that they styled themselves monks to mark their confraternity with continental religious houses. Cenwald visited a number of German monasteries and Oda had spent time at Fleury. The reign of Æthelstan saw the continuation of the revival of ecclesiastical Latin learning for which Alfred had laid the foundations, together with a developing interest in Old English prose and in the production of scholarly glosses, notably to explain the Latin writings of Aldhelm (Gretsch, 332–83). The same period witnessed the gradual restructuring of religious provision for the laity and an expansion in aristocratic lay devotion. Æthelstan's personal piety thus helped to sponsor a religious revival that extended far beyond the collection and commissioning of luxury manuscripts or the esoteric pursuit of relics.

Death Æthelstan died at Gloucester on 27 October 939 and was buried, not with his father and elder brother at the New Minster in Winchester, but rather in Malmesbury Abbey, perhaps a further indication of his distance from the West Saxon establishment. William of Malmesbury provides an account of Æthelstan's funeral, reporting that many gifts in gold and silver were carried before the body, as well as 'many relics of saints, bought in Brittany, for such were the objects on which he expended the treasure accumulated and left untouched by his father' (Malmesbury, *Gesta regum*, 228–9). The chronicler's particular interest in this king is clearly at least in part explained by the presence of Æthelstan's tomb at his own abbey; it was on the basis of his own observation that he describes the king as not above the average height, slim in build with fair hair 'as I have seen for myself in his remains, beautifully intertwined with golden threads' (Malmesbury, *Gesta regum*, 214–15).

Historical significance and reputation Æthelstan's importance as the first king of all England cannot be doubted. Yet there are few contemporary or near-contemporary narrative accounts of his reign, the Anglo-Saxon Chronicle being particularly sparse in this period; historians have had perforce to turn to the account of William of Malmesbury in their attempt to build a fuller picture of the king and his achievements. William may well have had access to sources no longer extant, but that these included an extended verse narrative dating from the tenth century, as was once suggested, now seems unlikely. In spite of these difficulties, it is clear that Æthelstan's historical significance was already recognized in his own time, and remarked beyond his death. The poem *Rex pius Aðelstan*, entered in a continental hand in manuscript Tiberius A.ii, the gospel book presented by Otto the Great, gives an idea of the lavish praise heaped upon Æthelstan by panegyrists during his lifetime; it opens with the lines:

> Holy King Æthelstan, renowned through the wide world,
> whose esteem flourishes and whose honour endures
>   everywhere.
> (Lapidge, 95–6)

In noting that Æthelstan died 'an untroubled death', the annalist of Ulster describes the West Saxon king as 'pillar of the dignity of the western world' (*Ann. Ulster*, 386–7). Ealdorman Æthelweard's *Chronicon* illustrates the king's reputation at the end of the tenth century, calling Æthelstan 'rex robustissimus' and 'rex venerandus', and dwelling on the consequences of his victory at 'Brunanburh' and the submission of the Scots and the Picts. In a discussion of the nature of kingship which forms the epilogue to his translation of the Old Testament book of Judges, Æthelweard's contemporary Ælfric, monk of Cerne and later abbot of Eynsham, draws attention to English kings 'victorious because of God', including Æthelstan 'who fought against Anlaf and slaughtered his army and put him to flight, and afterwards with his people dwelt in peace' (*Heptateuch*, ed. Crawford, 416–17).

Modern accounts of the reign attempting to integrate the full range of available sources for Æthelstan begin with Armitage Robinson's account in his 1922 Ford Lectures, *The Times of St Dunstan* (1923); however, although Robinson did much to demonstrate Æthelstan's significance as a collector of books and relics, and to sketch his foreign contacts, he presented the reign essentially as a prelude to the later tenth-century monastic revolution. Stenton's discussion in his *Anglo-Saxon England* (1943, third edition 1971) focused especially on the role of Æthelstan in promoting the formation of the English state, while Kirby (1976) and Loyn (1980–81, repr. 1992) demonstrated the significance of his relations with the Welsh kings. Michael Lapidge's critical analysis of the poems about Æthelstan (1981), questioning the reliability of William of Malmesbury, has had a considerable impact on perceptions of the king. An attempt to restore the credibility of William's account has recently been made by Michael Wood (Wood, 149–68). Other recent studies have dealt with cultural aspects of the reign, for instance the king's manuscript collection and his foreign connections, and attention has also been given to the Celtic dimension at Æthelstan's court (Sharp).

Beyond his undoubted military achievements, and the administrative and governmental advances made notably in the centralization of charter production and the tighter royal control of the coinage, Æthelstan stands out most remarkably for the extent of European diplomatic activity promoted through his court, to which the marriage alliances and the intellectual energy of his circle both bear witness. Although the sources of his information cannot all be verified, William of Malmesbury's account offers the most comprehensive view of Æthelstan; in the words of the twelfth-century poet whom he quoted (and with whose opinion he patently concurred) this was indeed a great king, glory of his native land: 'magnus Adelstanus, patriae decus' (Malmesbury, *Gesta regum*, 210).

SARAH FOOT

Sources ASC · *The chronicle of Æthelweard*, ed. and trans. A. Campbell (1962) · *The battle of Brunanburh*, ed. A. Campbell (1938) · William of Malmesbury, *Gesta regum Anglorum / The history of the English kings*, ed. and trans. R. A. B. Mynors, R. M. Thomson, and M. Winterbottom, 2 vols., OMT (1998–9) · Hrotsvitha, 'Gesta Ottonis', in *Hrotsvithae opera*, ed. H. Homeyer (Munich, 1970) · Hrotsvitha, *Gesta Ottonis / Deeds of Otto I*, trans. B. H. Hill, *Medieval monarchy in action: the German empire from Henry I to Henry IV*, ed. and trans. B. H. Hill (1972), 118–37 · AS chart., S 392, 394–7, 399, 400, 403, 407, 412, 416–17, 425, 429–31, 437–8, 441–2, 445–6, 1043, 1417 · C. E. Blunt, 'The coinage of Æthelstan', *British Numismatic Journal*, 42 (1974), 35–160 · F. Liebermann, ed., *Die Gesetze der Angelsachsen*, 3 vols. (Halle, 1903–16) · 'Historia regum', Symeon of Durham, *Opera*, 2.3–135 · 'Historia de sancto Cuthberto', Symeon of Durham, *Opera*, 1.192–214 · *Les annales de Flodoard*, ed. P. Lauer (1905) · Richer of Saint-Rémy, *Histoire de France, 888–995*, ed. and trans. R. Latouche, 2 vols. (Paris, 1930–37) · *La chronique de Nantes*, ed. R. Merlet (1896) · Folcuin [Folcwinus], 'Gesta Abbatum Sithiensium', ed. O. Holder-Egger, [*Supplementa tomorum I–XII, pars I*], ed. G. Waitz, MGH Scriptores [folio], 13 (Hanover, 1881), 607–35, 600–35 · John of Worcester, *Chron.* · Taliesin, *Armes Prydein / The prophecy of Britain*, ed. I. Williams, trans. R. Bromwich (1972) · S. Keynes, ed., *The Liber vitae of the New Minster and Hyde Abbey, Winchester* (Copenhagen, 1996) · *Willelmi Malmesbiriensis monachi de gestis pontificum Anglorum libri quinque*, ed. N. E. S. A. Hamilton, Rolls Series, 52 (1870), 399–400 · *Ann. Ulster* · *The Old English version of the Heptateuch: Ælfric's treatise on the Old and New Testament, and his preface to Genesis*, ed. S. J. Crawford, EETS, orig. ser., 160 (1922); repr. with two additional manuscripts (1969), 416–17 · E. O. Blake, ed., *Liber Eliensis*, CS, 3rd ser., 92 (1962) · M. Förster, ed., 'Exeter relic list (Bod. MS Auct. D.2.16, fol. 8r)', *Zur Geschichte des Reliquienkultus in Altengland* (Munich, 1943), 63–114 · M. Swanton, ed. and trans., 'Exeter relic list (Bod. MS Auct. D.2.16, fol. 8r)', *Anglo-Saxon prose*, 2nd edn (1993), 19–24 · D. N. Dumville, 'Between Alfred the Great and Edgar the Peaceable: Æthelstan, first king of England', *Wessex and England from Alfred to Edgar* (1992), 141–72 · S. Keynes, 'King Athelstan's books', *Learning and literature in Anglo-Saxon England: studies presented to Peter Clemoes on the occasion of his sixty-fifth birthday*, ed. M. Lapidge and H. Gneuss (1985), 143–201 · J. A. Robinson, *The times of St Dunstan* (1923) · M. Lapidge, 'Some Latin poems as evidence for the reign of King Athelstan', *Anglo-Saxon England*, 9 (1981), 61–98 · R. I. Page, 'The audience of *Beowulf* and the vikings', *The dating of Beowulf*, ed. C. Chase (1981), 113–22 · F. M. Stenton, *Anglo-Saxon England*, 3rd edn (1971) · M. Wood, 'The making of King Æthelstan's empire: an English Charlemagne?', *Ideal and reality in Frankish and Anglo-Saxon society*, ed. P. Wormald, D. Bullough, and R. Collins (1983), 250–72 · H. R. Loyn, 'Wales and England in the tenth century: the context of the Æthelstan charters', *Society and peoples: studies in the history of England and Wales, c.600–1200* (1992), 173–99 · D. P. Kirby, 'Hywel Dda: Anglophil?', *Welsh History Review / Cylchgrawn Hanes Cymru*, 8 (1976–7), 1–13 · K. Leyser, 'The Ottonians and Wessex', *Communications and power in medieval Europe: the Carolingian and Ottonian centuries*, ed. T. Reuter (1994), 73–104 · D. N. Dumville, 'Brittany and "Armes Prydein Vawr"', *Études Celtiques*, 20 (1983), 145–59 · P. Grierson, 'The relations between England and Flanders before the Norman conquest', *TRHS*, 4th ser., 23 (1941), 71–112 · C. F. Battiscombe, ed., *The* relics of St Cuthbert (1956) · C. Brett, 'A Breton pilgrim in England in the reign of King Æthelstan', France and the British Isles in the middle ages and Renaissance, ed. G. Jondorf and D. N. Dumville (1991), 43–70 · K. Harrison, 'A note on the battle of Brunanburh', Durham Archaeological Journal, 3 (1984), 63–5 · A. P. Smyth, Scandinavian York and Dublin: the history of two related Viking kingdoms, 2 vols. (1975–9) · D. Rollason, 'St Cuthbert and Wessex: the evidence of Cambridge, Corpus Christi College, MS 183', St Cuthbert: his cult and his community, ed. G. Bonner, D. Rollason, and C. Stancliffe (1989), 413–24 · R. L. Poole, 'The Alpine son-in-law of Edward the Elder', Studies in chronology and history, ed. A. L. Poole (1934), 115–22 · L. H. Loomis, 'The holy relics of Charlemagne and King Æthelstan: the lances of Longinus and St Mauricius', Speculum, 25 (1950), 437–56 · English historical documents, 1, ed. D. Whitelock (1955), nos. 24, 25, 26, 228, 239 (I) · M. Gretsch, The intellectual foundations of the English Benedictine reform (1999) · S. M. Sharp, 'England, Europe and the Celtic world: King Æthelstan's foreign policy', Bulletin of the John Rylands University Library, 79 (1997), 197–220 · M. Wood, In search of England: journeys into the English past (2000)

Archives BL, Psalter, MS Cotton Galba A.xviii
Likenesses manuscript drawing, BL, Cotton MS Otho B.ix · manuscript illumination (with St Cuthbert), CCC Cam., MS 183, fol. 1v [see illus.]

Æthelstan [Ethelstan, Æthelstan Half-King] (fl. 932–956), magnate, was the second of four sons of Ealdorman Æthelfrith, who ruled the southern and eastern territories of Mercia. Æthelfrith was descended from the West Saxon royal family and held extensive estates in Somerset and Devon. His wife, Æthelgyth, Æthelstan's mother, came from a wealthy family with estates in Buckinghamshire. Æthelfrith survived until about 915. Three years later the West Saxon royal house took over direct control of Mercia and under the new regime all of Æthelfrith's four sons became ealdormen in the second quarter of the tenth century. Ælfstan, the eldest, received his father's ealdordom but died in 934. Æthelstan, created ealdorman in 932, took over the ancient kingdom of the East Angles, which had been ruled directly for forty years by the Danish king Guthrum and his successors until it came under the control of King Edward the Elder in 917–18. Besides Norfolk and Suffolk, Æthelstan's area of jurisdiction extended to practically the whole of the eastern Danelaw, from the Thames to the River Welland. It included Huntingdonshire, Cambridgeshire, and Northamptonshire, plus the fenland territory that was later known as the Holland division of Lincolnshire. Bedfordshire and Hertfordshire may also have been under his control. In addition to all this—a territory as large as Normandy—Æthelstan held extensive family estates outside his ealdordom, in Wessex and Mercia. His younger brother Æthelwold was made ealdorman in 940 and held jurisdiction in Kent and the adjacent shires; he died in 946. Æthelstan's youngest brother, Eadric, held the neighbouring ealdordom of central Wessex from 942 until his death in 949. By the mid-940s the three surviving brothers wielded immense power; between them they controlled well over half the extensive territories of the West Saxon kingdom. From 943 onwards Æthelstan habitually witnessed first, and his brother Æthelwold second among the duces ('ealdormen') subscribing to royal charters; Eadric signed in third to

sixth place until Æthelwold's death, after which he was second only to Æthelstan.

For the whole of his brief reign (939–46), the young king Edmund remained strongly under the influence of his mother, Eadgifu, and of Æthelstan, who between them must have decided much of royal policy. Nor was the position much changed when Edmund's brother Eadred succeeded, for Eadred's adult years were clouded by chronic illness and the responsibilities of Æthelstan continued unabated. Moreover, from 944 onwards Æthelstan and his wife, Ælfwyn (d. 986), had fostered in their own household the infant atheling Edgar, a future king of England. In 949 Æthelstan added to his responsibilities that of the governance of south-east Mercia, and from the end of 951 onwards that of central Mercia too. These territories, like all the other areas under his control, must have been governed by suffragans. He was also prominent in military affairs, helping King Æthelstan and his successors gradually to secure control of territories under Danish occupation as far north as Strathclyde. Such deeds were remembered for a long time and in his eulogy on Æthelstan over two centuries later a chronicler at Ramsey Abbey praised him because 'apud hostes patriae non nullam virtus bellica invidiam generavit' ('his warlike virtue aroused great dread among the enemies of the country'; Chronicon abbatiae Rameseiensis, 11). The power exercised by Æthelstan and his family can be compared only with that of Godwine's family a century later; it is no wonder that he was remembered in later years as the 'Half-King'.

It is a measure of the Half-King's achievement that the eastern Danelaw remained in subjection to the West Saxon royal line, its inhabitants loyal and quiescent, throughout the period of his government. There is no mention of revolts, of collaboration with the Danes of northern England in subversive movements, or of encouragement of viking raiders along the eastern coastline. He brought the administration of the eastern Danelaw into line with the system operating in Wessex, English Mercia, and the south-east. In conformity with the rest of the kingdom, East Anglia was hidated and divided into hundreds, units of local government that persist to the present day. In matters of local interest, law, and custom the Danes were allowed a considerable measure of autonomy; but in national affairs, such as the control of the mints, the raising of the geld, and the provision of military service, the area was no less effectively governed than the rest of the territories subject to the English crown. In this Æthelstan was helped by a group of subordinate Danish earls and English ealdormen scattered throughout his province. The beginning of East Anglian prosperity, so evident a century and a half later in Little Domesday Book, may fairly be credited to Æthelstan's rule. Development of continental trade led to significant steps in the growth of Ipswich, Thetford, and Norwich.

Æthelstan Half-King was a constant and powerful friend of the English church, both nationally and within his own ealdordom, where the conversion of the Danes was zealously consolidated, church building and endowment by landowners encouraged, and a diocesan framework reconstituted. His wife, Ælfwyn, whom he must have married soon after receiving his ealdordom, was of undistinguished birth; she appears to have come from a Huntingdonshire family whose estates were destined to form the nucleus of the large endowment of Ramsey Abbey. It is probable that Æthelstan's household, where Edgar was fostered, was centred somewhere in the neighbourhood. Perhaps it was at Upwood, on the edge of the fens, which is known to have been the home of his son and eventual successor, *Æthelwine.

The death of King Eadred on 23 November 955 led to a profound change in the circumstances, if not the fortunes, of the Half-King and his family. The new monarch, Eadwig, a youth of fifteen who appears to have been brought up in Wessex, commenced his reign inauspiciously by a major confrontation with Dunstan, then bishop of London and Worcester and a close friend of Æthelstan. Eadwig disappeared from his coronation banquet and Dunstan found him, crown cast to one side, in a compromising situation with a lady named Ælfgifu and her mother, Æthelgifu, who were Eadwig's close relatives. Moreover, Æthelgifu (whose husband has not been identified) was almost certainly Æthelstan's sister. Dunstan remonstrated with the young Eadwig and brought him back forcibly to the banqueting hall. Shocked and humiliated by these developments, Æthelstan supported Dunstan's action. Eadwig never forgave them. Dunstan was banished and the estates of Queen Eadgifu, Eadwig's grandmother and close associate of Æthelstan, were confiscated. Æthelstan himself, his power base shattered, resigned his ealdordom to his eldest son, Æthelwold, in 956 or 957 and became a monk at Glastonbury, a house he had already endowed heavily with his family's west country estates while Dunstan had been abbot there. It is not known when Æthelstan died. The fortunes of the family of the Half-King received only a temporary setback; the ealdordom passed from Æthelwold to his brother Æthelwine.   CYRIL HART

Sources C. Hart, *The Danelaw* (1992), 569–604 • W. D. Macray, ed., *Chronicon abbatiae Rameseiensis a saec. x usque ad an. circiter 1200*, Rolls Series, 83 (1886) • [Byrhtferth of Ramsey], 'Vita sancti Oswaldi auctore anonymo', *The historians of the church of York and its archbishops*, ed. J. Raine, 1, Rolls Series, 71 (1879), 399–475 • E. O. Blake, ed., *Liber Eliensis*, CS, 3rd ser., 92 (1962) • *AS chart.*, S 442, 480, 481, 498, 545, 1711
Wealth at death relatively wealthy

Æthelstan Ætheling [Athelstan the Atheling] (d. **1014**), prince, was the eldest son of *Æthelred II (c.966x8–1016), king of England, and of Æthelred's first wife, Ælfgifu, daughter of Thored (Thorth), who held office as earl of Northumbria from c.975 to c.992. Æthelstan was born probably in the early or mid-980s, and made his first appearance as a witness in a charter of King Æthelred for Abingdon Abbey issued in 993. Little is known of his childhood and youth, though there is reason to believe that he may have spent some part of it on a royal estate at Æthelingadene (Dean 'of the athelings', identified as Dean

in west Sussex), and that his paternal grandmother, *Ælfthryth, may have played a significant part in his upbringing. Æthelstan continued to attest charters in the later 990s and in the early years of the eleventh century, invariably positioned ahead of his younger brothers; his last appearance is in a charter dated 1013. King Æthelred's marriage to *Emma of Normandy, in 1002, does not appear to have affected Æthelstan's position as his father's prospective successor, and it must be assumed that sooner or later Æthelstan became a significant political force in the kingdom. He would have witnessed the increasing influence at court of Ealdorman Eadric Streona, and may well not have approved; he seems also to have formed a friendship with Sigeferth and Morcar, two of the leading thegns of the 'Five Boroughs' in the east midlands. In 1013 King Æthelred was forced into temporary exile in Normandy; and while it is not known for certain what became of Æthelstan and of his surviving younger brothers, *Edmund (Ironside) and Eadwig, during the reign of King Swein Forkbeard (1013–14), it seems likely that they remained somewhere in England.

Æthelred returned from exile in the spring of 1014, whereupon Æthelstan would have resumed his position as his father's prospective successor. It would appear, however, that Æthelstan fell ill during the early summer of that year. He received his father's permission to draw up his will on 25 June 1014, and died later on the same day. It emerges from the will (copies of which were preserved in the archives of Christ Church, Canterbury, and the Old Minster, Winchester) that Æthelstan held land in at least ten counties of south-eastern England, and that he took special interest not only in the religious houses at Winchester and Canterbury, but also in those at Shaftesbury and Ely. His personal possessions included no fewer than eleven swords (one of which had belonged to Offa, king of the Mercians), a coat of mail (which had been lent to Morcar), two shields, a drinking-horn, a silver-coated trumpet, and a string of fine horses. Æthelstan was buried at the Old Minster, Winchester. His untimely death meant that his younger brother, Edmund Ironside, entered the political arena as King Æthelred's prospective successor. Edmund was soon forced, in effect, to take a stand against the regime personified by his ailing father but controlled by Eadric Streona, prompting Eadric to transfer his allegiance to Cnut, and leading ultimately to the defeat of the English at the battle of Ashingdon in 1016.

SIMON KEYNES

Sources D. Whitelock, ed. and trans., *Anglo-Saxon wills* (1930), 56–63 • *AS chart.*, S 1503 • *English historical documents*, 1, ed. D. Whitelock (1955) • S. Keynes, 'Queen Emma and the *Encomium Emmae reginae*', *Encomium Emmae reginae*, ed. and trans. A. Campbell, CS, Classic Reprints, 4 (1998), xiii–lxxxvii • N. J. Higham, *The death of Anglo-Saxon England* (1997)

Æthelthryth [St Æthelthryth, Etheldreda, Audrey] (d. **679**), queen in Northumbria, consort of King Ecgfrith, and abbess of Ely, was the daughter of *Anna, king of the East Angles (d. 654?). Her immediate kindred was dominated by women in religion, later venerated as saints, including three sisters, *Seaxburh, Æthelburh, and Wihtburh, a half-sister, Sæthryth, and two nieces, Eormenhild and Eorcongota. Two of these were abbesses and one was a nun at the important Frankish monastery of Faremoutiers-en-Brie, a connection that was to prove significant for Æthelthryth's own reputation as a saint.

Virgin Queen According to a local twelfth-century source, the *Liber Eliensis*, Æthelthryth was born in Exning, in west Suffolk. In 652, probably while still very young, she married Tondberht, ealdorman or prince of the Middle Anglian province of the South Gyrwe. The *Liber Eliensis*, following a lost text, alleged that Tondberht thereupon gave her the Isle of Ely as dower (*dos*), a statement which conflicts with the evidence of Æthelthryth's near contemporary, Bede, who believed that the great estate (*regio*) of Ely, assessed at 600 hides, had come to her from the East Angles. There are some indications that Bede was right. If, as an early source suggests, the whole of Tondberht's own territory of the South Gyrwe was assessed at only 600 hides, he can scarcely have offered land of exactly that value as dower. Æthelthryth's probable birth on a royal estate nearby and the continuing association of Ely itself with Anna's kin also suggest that the area was East Anglian royal land. Whether, however, that land was bestowed upon Æthelthryth at her first marriage, or granted to her later after the collapse of her second must remain uncertain.

Tondberht died after three years of wedlock, his wife, it seems, still a virgin. Æthelthryth continued a widow for a further five years before marrying *Ecgfrith (645/6–685), son of King Oswiu of Northumbria, in 660. It is unclear how far she herself had any say in this second union. If, however, she was as devoted to her virgin status as contemporaries came to believe, she is unlikely actively to have sought it out. More probably, recent upheavals in local Middle Anglian politics provided the immediate stimulus. Oswiu's expulsion from Mercia in 658, after three years of direct rule, seems to have left the kingdom's eastern border, including the province of the South Gyrwe, increasingly under the influence of Æthelthryth's paternal uncle, the East Anglian king. He may well have had diplomatic reasons for putting pressure upon his niece to contract the union with Ecgfrith. The East Anglian royal house already had strong dynastic links with that of Northumbria, through the marriage of another of Æthelthryth's paternal uncles with the Deiran princess Hereswith. Hereswith, the mother of Aldwulf, soon (*c*.664) to succeed his uncle as king of the East Angles, was the cousin of Oswiu's queen, Eanflæd, and sister of Hild, by the late 650s abbess of Whitby and an influential figure in Northumbria.

Æthelthryth's relationship with her new husband, who in 660 was about fifteen—somewhat younger than she— was not very successful. By 670, when Ecgfrith succeeded his father as king of Northumbria, he and his wife had fallen under the influence of the kingdom's forceful and ambitious bishop, Wilfrid, whom Ecgfrith may well have known since the late 650s. Wilfrid, who obtained his see in controversial circumstances in 668, was then at the height of his career. As he himself told Bede, despite all Ecgfrith's blandishments, he used his influence with the queen at that time to strengthen her resolve to remain a virgin. Thereafter events developed rapidly. About 672, after twelve years as Ecgfrith's wife, Æthelthryth was consecrated a nun by Wilfrid and entered the ill-fated monastery of Coldingham, where her husband's aunt Æbbe was abbess. A year later she left Northumbria to found a monastery on her great estate at Ely. By 678, Ecgfrith had divorced her and Iurminburg had replaced her as his consort. Before that date, while already a nun and still queen, she had taken the momentous step of giving to Wilfrid the large estate on which he founded his great new monastery of Hexham.

Little is known of Æthelthryth's household while she was in Northumbria. In her early years, it was presided over by the East Anglian Owine, who came north with her in 660, but later became a monk at Ceadda's monastery of Lastingham and by 672 was a member of the bishop's community at Lichfield. Of her other dependants, only the Northumbrian thegn Imma is known; he had entered the service of Ecgfrith's brother Ælfwine before 679, but seems to have retained links with Æthelthryth's kindred. Captured and enslaved in London after Ælfwine's death at the battle of Trent in 679, he successfully appealed to the queen's nephew, King Hlothere of Kent, to ransom him.

Abbess and saint Æthelthryth ruled her new foundation at Ely for some seven years before dying of plague on 23 June 679. Bede described her way of life there in terms intended to indicate that she strictly espoused monastic values, as promoted by Pope Gregory the Great. Æthelthryth, he claimed, wore only woollen garments, seldom bathed except before the greater feasts, ate generally once a day, and was assiduous in the office and in prayer. Her monastic humility was apparent in the simple arrangements she decreed for her burial: she was to be interred in a wooden coffin amid her departed nuns. Some alleged that she showed powers of prophecy before her death.

Æthelthryth was clearly a remarkable woman, with sufficient force of character to preserve her virginity through two marriages, to abandon the second of these despite her royal husband's opposition, and to set up, apparently on her own initiative, a successful dynastic community, which she handed on to her sister Seaxburh. The crucial factor in the establishment of her reputation, however, was a major posthumous miracle: at the translation organized by Abbess Seaxburh to seal her sister's status as a saint sixteen years after her death, in 695, her body was found incorrupt. At this carefully orchestrated ceremony, attended by Bishop Wilfrid, a tent was erected over the grave in the outdoor cemetery of the nuns, and Æthelthryth's body, still fresh and undecayed, was lifted from its resting place, washed, and clothed in new robes. It was then brought within the abbatial church and placed in a marble sarcophagus, almost certainly situated next to the principal altar, the position it still occupied in the late tenth century. The occasion was marked by further wonders and was clearly shaped by similar translations of Æthelthryth's and Seaxburh's relatives at Faremoutiers-en-Brie, which had also been marked by the great sign of incorruption.

Incorruption had featured in one of Ambrose's translations in late fourth-century Milan and in several such ceremonies in sixth-century Gaul. In England, while Oswald's arm preserved at Bamburgh was already held to be imperishable, Æthelthryth's was the first instance of an entire body (her example was to be followed shortly by that of Cuthbert in 698). The impact of the miracle on the clerical élite was immense. Both Bede and Wilfrid's biographer Stephen of Ripon expressly mention it as incontrovertible evidence that Æthelthryth had died a virgin. The impression made upon Bede in particular is evidenced by his poem in praise of Æthelthryth's virginity, published in the *Historia ecclesiastica gentis Anglorum*; by her commemoration, together with Cuthbert, in the world chronicle which he attached to his great treatise on time published in 725; and by the fact that, uniquely among English saints, she received a full historical notice in his martyrology.

The pre-conquest cult Æthelthryth's cult was fostered in eighth-century Ely, where in addition to the imperishable body, the original grave clothes and coffin also worked wonders. The monastery seems to have been drawn firmly into the orbit of Mercia by the end of the seventh century, when Seaxburh's daughter, Eormenhild, who had married the Mercian king Wulfhere, in widowhood succeeded her mother at Ely. It was probably during this period that Æthelthryth's cult was first promoted in the ancient province of Lindsey, where the *Liber Eliensis* associates it with the foundation of two churches and where indeed there are two churches with early dedications to the saint. Possibly Eormenhild's daughter, Werburh (*d.* 709), who in later tradition is said to have been given charge of Mercian monasteries by her uncle King Æthelred and who is strongly associated with both Ely and with monastic foundations in Lindsey, may have fostered the cult in the area.

Æthelthryth features in Alcuin's late eighth-century poem on York and in the ninth-century Old English martyrology, although neither account adds anything to that of Bede. At Ely, her community apparently enjoyed some form of continuous existence for about two centuries after its foundation. According to a narrative compiled in the later tenth century by one of its former members, the priest Ælfhelm, it still comprised a mixed community of priests and nuns when the Danes attacked and dispersed it in the late ninth century. Despite the reported violence, the Danish attack made little impact on the cult. Members of the community seem soon to have returned to Ely, and the shrine itself evidently survived the Danes' attempts to loot it. By the 940s a community of married priests was again actively promoting Æthelthryth.

Bishop Æthelwold of Winchester's refoundation of Ely *c.*970 involved a fresh sponsorship of Æthelthryth's cult, part of his enlisting of the seventh-century church, as idealized by Bede, in the service of reform. The existing guardians, excoriated for their unchastity, were replaced by Benedictine monks, who recorded the saint's recent miracles, above all her punishment of their polluted predecessors. Under Æthelwold's guidance they gave due honour to Æthelthryth's shrine beside the high altar, placing next to it the newly translated remains of the saint's sister Seaxburh and niece Eormenhild, together with those of another sister, Wihtburh, forcibly removed from Dereham in Norfolk. Images of all four saints stood on either side of the high altar. These activities publicized the cult very effectively. St Æthelthryth was widely commemorated in later Anglo-Saxon calendars not only on the day of her deposition (23 June) but also—especially in communities in East Anglia or under the influence of Winchester—on the day of her translation (17 October). About 1000 Ælfric included an account of her, derived wholly from Bede, in his lives of the saints.

Post-conquest developments The continuing vitality of her cult is demonstrated by the role assigned to Æthelthryth in the English revolt against the Normans of 1070–71, in which her community was heavily involved. She was viewed as the special patron and protectress of the rebels, who swore an oath of loyalty on her relics. Despite these affiliations, the Norman abbots continued to promote St Æthelthryth, and the late eleventh and early twelfth centuries saw the production of a considerable amount of new material relating to the cult. Goscelin of Canterbury allegedly produced a text termed a *prosa*, no longer identifiable, and new miracles were recorded. In 1106 the relics of St Æthelthryth, together with those of Sts Seaxburh, Wihtburh, and Eormenhild were translated to new shrines in the reconstructed choir of the abbey church, Æthelthryth being placed in the position of honour east of the high altar. New lives in prose and verse, including fresh miracles, were produced thereafter, in the time of the first bishop, Hervey (1109–31).

St Æthelthryth's cult, from the thirteenth century magnificently accommodated in Bishop Northwold's extension of the choir, continued to be promoted at Ely throughout the middle ages. The fair held there in association with her feast day (23 June) was a major event at which ribbons that had touched the shrine were in great demand; the quality of the items sold there was, however, such that it gave rise to the adjective 'tawdry', derived from St Audrey, the name by which the saint was then known. Besides Ely, some dozen medieval churches were dedicated to the saint. By the later middle ages her relics were widely distributed among English churches, including Glastonbury, St Albans, Salisbury, Thetford, and Waltham. Durham claimed to possess a stole she had given to St Wilfrid and in 1536 an East Anglian religious foundation allegedly held various personal items including a wimple and a comb. The shrine itself, in the cathedral monastery, was destroyed at the dissolution, but since the late nineteenth century the cult has been promoted at St Etheldreda's, Ely Place, the former chapel of the London palace of the bishops of Ely, returned to Catholic worship in 1874.

ALAN THACKER

Sources Bede, *Hist. eccl.*, 4.3, 19–20, 22 • Bede, 'Chronica majora', *Opera didascalia*, ed. C. W. Jones, 2 (1977) • H. Quentin, *Les* *martyrologes historiques du haut moyen âge* (Paris, 1908) · Eddius Stephanus, 'Vita sancti Wilfridi', *Passiones vitaeque sanctorum aevi Merovingici*, ed. B. Krusch and W. Levison, MGH Scriptores Rerum Merovingicarum, 6 (Hanover, 1913), chaps. 19, 22 · E. O. Blake, ed., *Liber Eliensis*, CS, 3rd ser., 92 (1962) · S. Ridyard, *The royal saints of Anglo-Saxon England* (1988) · A. Thacker, 'The making of a local saint', *Local saints and local churches in the early medieval west*, ed. A. Thacker and R. Sharpe (2002), 45–74 · *VCH Cambridgeshire and the Isle of Ely*, vol. 4 · I. G. Thomas, 'The cult of saints in medieval England', PhD diss., U. Lond., 1975 · *LP Henry VIII*, 10.143 · Goscelin of St Bertin, *The female saints of Ely*, OMT [forthcoming] · CCC Cam., MS 393

Æthelwealh (*d. c.*685). *See under* South Saxons, kings of the (*act.* 477–772).

Æthelweard [Ethelwerd] (*d.* 998?), chronicler and magnate, was ealdorman of south-western England. He styled himself 'Patricius Consul Fabius Quaestor', a latinization of 'Æthel-/ealdorman/Fabius/-weard'. He was the father of Æthelmær, grandfather of one Æthelweard and grandfather-in-law of another: all also ealdormen, and two of the same south-western ealdormanry as Æthelweard himself. He is important for his family's status as outlying members of the royal dynasty, and as holders over three generations of a key post in Anglo-Saxon government; but more important for the culture that made him and his son patrons of the homilist Ælfric of Eynsham, and that led him to produce a remarkable Latin version of the Anglo-Saxon Chronicle (down to 975). This was written for Abbess Matilda of Essen, who was descended from King Alfred; Æthelweard's prefatory letter to her claims descent from Æthelred I, Alfred's elder brother, and he later says that Æthelred was his *atavus* (great-grandfather, great-great-grandfather, great-great-great-grandfather, or merely ancestor).

More light may be shed on Æthelweard's family by the charter whereby his son Æthelmær founded Eynsham Abbey (1005). It records the acquisition by Æthelweard and Æthelmær of lands from (among others) 'kinsmen' named Godwine and Bishop Brihthelm. In a will of *c.*970 Ælfgifu made a bequest to an Æthelweard who was probably her brother, and Ealdorman Ælfheah's will of much the same date left land to a 'kinsman' Æthelweard. Ælfgifu may be the lady whose marriage to King Eadwig was dissolved because of consanguinity. Ealdorman Ælfhere, Ælfheah's brother, is said by an early charter of Eadwig to be 'of the king's kin'; he or Ælfheah had a son named Godwine. Eadwig also promoted his 'dear relative', Brihthelm, to a bishopric. Æthelweard may thus have been Eadwig's brother-in-law and have belonged to a branch of the dynasty that came to new prominence under his rule; he does give one of the few positive verdicts on Eadwig. But there is no proof that the will's Ælfgifu was the former queen, and some reason to think that the Æthelweard it favours was a thegn of increasing seniority in Edgar's councils, who remained a thegn when the chronicler became an ealdorman (probably 976, or *c.*973). If his kin were in one sense a casualty as much as a beneficiary of the success of Alfred's line, there is no hint of his own disaffection. His book simply rejoiced in his royal pedigree. As ealdorman

he consistently witnessed the charters of Edward the Martyr and Æthelred II; third or fourth in ranking until 990, top from then to 998, when he evidently died. In one of his last appearances, he is *occidentalium provinciarum dux* ('ealdorman of the western provinces'). He was an architect of the peace (linked to payment of danegeld) made by Æthelred and Olaf Tryggvason (994?). His son led the 'western thegns' in submission to the victorious Swein (1013). But Cnut's purge in effect destroyed the family: the homonymous grandson was killed in 1017, the grandson-in-law outlawed in 1020.

Although intended for an overseas reader, Æthelweard's work survives only in one English manuscript. This was largely burnt in the Cottonian fire of 1731, but had been printed by Henry Savile in 1596. The only medieval author to use it was William of Malmesbury, and the manuscript could be the copy he saw. Aspects of the chronicle usually singled out are its eccentric Latin (which William set the fashion in deploring), and the impression it gives of access to a text of the Anglo-Saxon Chronicle better in various ways than any now extant. Neither point may do justice to its author. His Latin, like his chronological and geographical excursions, is learned. He not merely knew Aldhelm; he could imitate his pursuit of exhibitionist neologism, literary variation, and poetic cadence. It is as if he were striving for a style suited to secular narrative, as Einhard had, but with Aldhelm, not Cicero and Suetonius, as his guide. The book is annalistic in structure, but is ordered in four books that make sense in terms of the story told. Many of its deviations from the Anglo-Saxon Chronicle arise from misreadings. But the written sources which must underlie such extra information as his unique and important account of the 890s need not have been restricted to an unusually well-stocked chronicle. He could be an independent (if not very detailed) source for the half-century before his own time; why should he not have researched further details for earlier centuries from whichever sources? What he omits (episcopal succession, other kingdoms, the apostasy of the second Christian West Saxon king) fits his professed intention to exalt his and Matilda's family. His is therefore a work not just of translation but of history, and it exhibits a pronounced intelligence.

Æthelweard's exceptional literary commitment is confirmed by his regular appearance as patron of Ælfric's *Homilies, Lives of Saints*, and biblical renditions. Æthelmær, co-dedicatee of *Lives of Saints*, founded both Ælfric's abbeys of Cerne and Eynsham, making him abbot of the latter. Ælfric wrote for other laymen but for none so much. An intriguing speculation arises from a gift by Æthelmær's son-in-law to an abbey that may be identified as his own foundation of Buckfast. It was a copy of Bede's *Apocalypse* and Augustine's *Adulterous Unions* (each a topical concern in England *c.*1000), and its later-tenth-century scribe also wrote the Exeter book of Old English verse. Æthelweard can well be envisaged as the kind of man to relish literary celebration of aristocratic values in the era of *The Battle of Maldon*. In his family the cultures of scribe and warrior met. He may therefore be perceived in ways that have become familiar to Carolingian scholarship but have yet to strike chords in study of the Anglo-Saxons. His counterparts were the Carolingian nobles who were close (even related) to royalty and its ideologists, cultivated and devout, ministerially active, loyal at least until their position became intolerable, and victims as much as they were movers in the age's seismic politics.

PATRICK WORMALD

Sources *The chronicle of Æthelweard*, ed. and trans. A. Campbell (1962) • *AS chart.*, S 582, 615, 1484, 1485, 751, 830, 832, 876, 891, 895, 911 • F. Liebermann, ed., *Die Gesetze der Angelsachsen*, 1 (Halle, 1898), 220–25 • *ASC*, s. a. 994, 1013, 1017, 1020 [text E] • *Ælfric's prefaces*, ed. J. Wilcox, Durham Medieval Texts, 9 (1994), 1b, 4, 5a, b, d, p. 42 • K. Leyser, 'The Ottonians and Wessex', *Communications and power in medieval Europe: the Carolingian and Ottonian centuries*, ed. T. Reuter (1994), 73–104, esp. 74, 84–5, 98–9 • B. Yorke, 'Æthelwold and the politics of the tenth century', *Bishop Æthelwold: his career and influence*, ed. B. Yorke (1988), 65–88 • S. Keynes, *The diplomas of King Æthelred 'The Unready' (978–1016): a study in their use as historical evidence*, Cambridge Studies in Medieval Life and Thought, 3rd ser., 13 (1980), 186–208 • S. Keynes, 'Cnut's earls', *The reign of Cnut*, ed. A. R. Rumble (1994), 43–88, esp. 67–70 • J. Bately, *The Anglo-Saxon Chronicle: texts and textual relationships* (1991), 41–53 • M. Winterbottom, 'The style of Æthelweard', *Medium Ævum*, 36 (1967), 109–18 • J. Campbell, 'England, *c.* 991', *The battle of Maldon: fiction and fact*, ed. J. Cooper (1993), 1–17 • A. Williams, *Land, power and politics: the family and career of Odda of Deerhurst* (privately printed, Deerhurst, 1997), 4–6

Archives BL, Cotton MS Otho A.x

Æthelwine [Ethelwine, Æthelwine Dei Amicus] (*d.* **992**), magnate and founder of Ramsey Abbey, Huntingdonshire, was the fourth and youngest son of *Æthelstan, known as the Half-King (*fl.* 932–956), and his wife, Ælfwyn (*d.* 986). He was a few years older than the atheling *Edgar, who was king from 959 to 975 and who had been reared as his foster brother in the same household. Æthelwine succeeded to the ealdordom of East Anglia in 962 after the death of his eldest brother Æthelwold and held it until his own death on 24 April 992. It is not known why Æthelwine, rather than one of his two surviving older brothers, inherited the ealdordom; perhaps it was because King Edgar knew him best. Æthelwold's ealdordom had probably included southern Northumbria within its remit, but responsibility for that province was taken over by Oslac. The remainder of the ealdordom included Cambridgeshire, the southern part of Lincolnshire, and possibly Bedfordshire, all of which were given to Æthelwine. From 984 to 990 he probably also had charge of central and northwest Mercia. During his early years of office Æthelwine was fourth in precedence of the ealdormen witnessing royal diplomas; from 966 onwards he witnessed fifth, from 971 second, and from 983 until his death he headed the lists, with Byrhtnoth in second place.

The politics of Edgar's reign revolved to a large extent around the power struggle that had developed between the East Anglian and Mercian ealdordoms, with rivalry between Æthelwine's family on the one hand and the two brothers Ælfhere, ealdorman of Mercia, and Ælfheah, ealdorman of Wessex, on the other. Both families had ties of kinship with the royal house of Wessex. Æthelwine was the principal lay patron of Benedictine monasticism in

England, whence his nickname, Dei Amicus ('Friend of God'). He found a strong supporter in Byrhtnoth, ealdorman of Essex, who also held Huntingdonshire and Northamptonshire and may have exercised a general supervision of the Five Boroughs and Northumbria during part of this period. Altogether Ælfhere's influence was dominant in the early years, though differences with Æthelwine sharpened during the 'anti-monastic' reaction which followed the death of King Edgar in 975. But Ælfhere died in 983 and his brother-in-law Ælfric Cild (the last important adherent to Ælfhere's party) was banished two years later. Shorn of this opposition, Æthelwine and Byrhtnoth were able to work closely together during the next eight years.

Within his own ealdordom, as in national affairs, Æthelwine exercised his great power no less effectively than his father had done before him. In the pages of the *Liber Eliensis*, and to a lesser extent the house chronicle of Ramsey Abbey, it is possible to watch him go about his duties; no other ealdorman had his official acts recorded in such detail for posterity. In Cambridgeshire he presided over meetings of the whole shire, of groups of hundreds, and even of a single hundred. Sometimes he sat with the royal reeve, but only once (in spite of what might be expected from the laws) with the diocesan bishop. According to the chronicles, Æthelwine had his hall and kept his court at Upwood near Ramsey. This court would have been concerned with the administration of his family estates rather than with his duties as ealdorman. He held also, on lease from Ely, the lordship of the five and a half hundreds of Wicklaw in Suffolk, probably the greatest franchise then in lay hands.

As might be expected, Ealdorman Æthelwine was a considerable landowner in his own right. Details of most of his properties have not survived, but he and his family laid claims in Cambridgeshire and Northamptonshire, and there were large estates in Huntingdonshire, Cambridgeshire, Norfolk, and Suffolk. With these lands Æthelwine, his three wives—successively Æthelflæd (*d.* 977), Æthelgifu (*d.* 985), and Wulfgifu (*d.* 994)—his brother Ælfwold, and his sister-in-law Ælfhild, endowed his foundation at Ramsey.

The monastery owed its origins to the miraculous cure of a bad attack of gout which Æthelwine suffered about 963, a cure which he ascribed to St Benedict. In return he built a tiny wooden church on the Isle of Ramsey in the southern fenlands, near his home at Upwood; here he placed a simple community of three men who aspired to become monks. Shortly afterwards Æthelwine met Oswald, bishop of Worcester, at a funeral at Glastonbury (a foundation strongly supported by Æthelwine's family and where his father had ended his days as a monk). He offered Oswald the site at Ramsey for the building of a major monastery and Oswald sent monks from his own small community at Westbury-on-Trym, near Bristol. A larger wooden chapel was built, then a stone church with a central and a western tower, which was consecrated in 974. This proved to have inadequate foundations and a second stone church was erected, with conventual out-buildings, and consecrated in 991. This rebuilding, as well as the initial foundation, were handsomely furnished by Æthelwine, who decorated the high altar and installed a magnificent organ, a novelty in England at that time. Soon afterwards, Abbo of Fleury, the greatest scholar of the age, came to instruct the monks in the new learning, which was then transmitted from Ramsey to other reformed English abbeys. For many years Ealdorman Æthelwine and Bishop Oswald met annually at Ramsey to discuss its affairs and foster the quality of its learning.

After a long illness, during which he was cared for by the community, Æthelwine died at Ramsey on 24 April 992 and was buried there. Byrhtferth of Ramsey, in his life of Oswald written two decades later, included a flowery obituary of Æthelwine. A century and a half later, another tribute was paid by an anonymous monk of Ramsey, compiler of the house chronicle. Æthelwine is said to have been handsome, cheerful, and, though illiterate, endowed with every virtue. A brass effigy was placed on his tomb at the end of the thirteenth century. In addition to Ramsey, Æthelwine was patron of satellite foundations at St Neots and Crowland. His three sons with his first wife, Æthelflæd (Leofwine, Eadwine, and Æthelweard), were local thegns who did not achieve an eminence comparable to that of their father. Æthelweard was killed at the battle of 'Assandun' in 1016. CYRIL HART

Sources W. D. Macray, ed., *Chronicon abbatiae Rameseiensis a saec. x usque ad an. circiter 1200*, Rolls Series, 83 (1886) • [Byrhtferth of Ramsey], 'Vita sancti Oswaldi auctore anonymo', *The historians of the church of York and its archbishops*, ed. J. Raine, 1, Rolls Series, 71 (1879), 399–475 • E. O. Blake, ed., *Liber Eliensis*, CS, 3rd ser., 92 (1962) • C. Hart, *The Danelaw* (1992), 591–8 • C. R. Hart, *The early charters of eastern England* (1966) • C. R. Hart, 'The foundation of Ramsey Abbey', *Revue Bénédictine*, 104 (1994)

Wealth at death certainly wealthy: Ramsey chronicle

Æthelwold [St Æthelwold, Ethelwold] (904×9–984), abbot of Abingdon and bishop of Winchester, was a leading figure in the tenth-century church reform movement. He was born in Winchester to noble parents during the reign of Edward the Elder, probably between 904 and 909.

Early career and training As a youth Æthelwold spent a period in the royal household of King Æthelstan and may be the 'Æthelwold' who appears in the witness lists of royal charters in 932 and 934 (*AS chart.*, S 417 and 425). After a period of royal service Æthelstan arranged for him to be ordained by Bishop Ælfheah I of Winchester and he became a priest on the same day as Dunstan. After a period in the late 930s studying with Ælfheah in Winchester, Æthelwold moved to Glastonbury where Dunstan had been made abbot. At Glastonbury he studied grammar, metrics, and patristics and, following Dunstan's example and teaching, took his vows as a monk; subsequently he was appointed dean. During the reign of King Eadred (r. 946–55), Æthelwold wished to travel to Europe to receive a more thorough grounding in the monastic way of life, presumably at one of the reformed Benedictine houses such as Fleury. On the advice of his mother, Eadgifu, the king refused Æthelwold permission to leave the country, and

instead granted him the former monastic site at Abingdon, which at that time was served by a small body of secular priests. Æthelwold set about transforming Abingdon into a model Benedictine community, of which he became abbot. He was joined by clerics from Glastonbury, Winchester, and London who took vows as monks and one of them, Osgar, was subsequently sent to Fleury to study the observance of the Benedictine rule there. Eadgifu and Eadred were generous patrons and the king granted the 100-hide royal estate based on Abingdon to the new community before his death in 955. Work was begun on a new church, though it was not completed until the reign of King Edgar.

Bishop of Winchester and church reformer The appointment of Edgar as king of all England in 959 gave Æthelwold the opportunity to initiate reform in the church on a much wider scale. He was already an intimate of the young king, having acted as his tutor. Æthelwold has been identified as the scribe known as 'Edgar A' who wrote a large number of the original charters to have survived from the period 960–63, and the implication is that he was in the personal service of the king during that time. In 963 Edgar appointed Æthelwold to the vacant see of Winchester and he was consecrated bishop on 29 November. In the following year, with the connivance of the king and with the support of an armed force led by a royal official, Æthelwold had the clerics of the Old and New Minsters expelled and replaced by monks from Abingdon; Chertsey and Milton Abbas were also reorganized as monasteries in the same year. Plans for the expulsion had been carefully laid as the king had sought permission from the pope the previous autumn. Further support from the king enabled Æthelwold to reintroduce monasticism in East Anglia, and between 964 and 971 he refounded monasteries at Peterborough, Ely, and Thorney. Nunnaminster in Winchester and probably other nunneries in the Winchester diocese were also affected by Æthelwold's zeal; Nunnaminster and Wilton were both enclosed by walls at this time.

A synod held in Winchester some time between 970 and 973 agreed that a common rule should be followed by all the monastic communities in England. The customary which was adopted is known as the *Regularis concordia* and was written by Æthelwold himself. His pupil Ælfric identifies Æthelwold as the author in a composition he wrote for his own monks at Eynsham and there are also verbal links with other works attributed to Æthelwold. The basis of the customary is the rule of St Benedict, but some customs were also adopted from continental reformed houses and the advice of monks from Fleury and Ghent is acknowledged. Customs not paralleled on the continent probably indicate the retention of native practices and the emphasis on prayers for the royal house no doubt reflects the close relationship between King Edgar and Æthelwold. Æthelwold also encouraged close study of the Benedictine rule itself and was commissioned by King Edgar and Queen Ælfthryth to provide a translation of it into Old English. Eight manuscripts or fragments survive suggesting a widespread circulation of the work.

Æthelwold has emerged from modern scholarship as the driving force behind the movement to reintroduce monasticism into Anglo-Saxon England in the late tenth century. Some further idea of his overall aims comes from an anonymous document known as 'an old English account of King Edgar's establishment of the monasteries' of which Æthelwold is believed to be the author; it may have been composed to form a preface to his translation of the rule of St Benedict. The text suggests that Æthelwold's ideal was a return to the time of Bede, when the church was dominated by monks. His interest in and respect for that period can also be seen in his revival of the cults of seventh-century saints in his foundations, including those of St Æthelthryth and her saintly kinswomen at Ely and of St Birinus at Winchester. However, Æthelwold's historical vision seems to have led him to an espousal of monasticism that was more extreme than that of Dunstan and Oswald, the other great English monastic leaders in the reign of Edgar. Both Dunstan and Oswald followed the practice of many continental bishops in maintaining both secular priests and monks in their households and did not follow Æthelwold in his dramatic expulsion of secular clerks and their replacement by monks for all diocesan duties. Æthelwold's determination to achieve what he considered right also comes through from the zeal with which he obtained estates for his monasteries. It was not only the king who had to surrender lands to provide support for these foundations. The archives of Winchester and the *Libellus Æthelwoldi* from Ely show that many small landowners were obliged to give up estates apparently on the grounds that the lands had once been granted to the religious communities, but had been alienated subsequently. Compensation was given, but does not seem to have been overgenerous and there were attempts to reclaim estates or renegotiate terms after the deaths of King Edgar and Æthelwold. If necessary, charters were forged to prove claims to title for which appropriate documentation had not survived or had never existed. Æthelwold in his various compositions shows himself to have been acutely aware of the pressures on monasteries and nunneries which might lead to church estates falling into secular hands and one of his priorities seems to have been to try to ensure that foundations were able to retain their wealth and independence.

Patron and scholar Some of the wealth accumulated by Æthelwold was used to rebuild churches and to furnish them in an appropriate manner, for he was also a major patron of ecclesiastical art and architecture; unfortunately only written accounts remain. His gifts to Abingdon are said to have included an altar table or retable, made of gold and silver and decorated with sculptured figures of the apostles, which cost £300. In addition to many other fittings he gave a gold chalice of immense weight, three gold and silver crosses which were 4 feet in length, and a golden-plated wheel which supported twelve lamps from which hung numerous small bells. Æthelwold's magnificent commissions might be matched by gifts from the royal house. King Edgar provided Old Minster, Winchester, with a gold and silver shrine for St Swithun,

which was decorated with jewels and scenes showing the passion, resurrection, and ascension of Christ. These costly pieces have not survived the passage of time, but some of the manuscripts decorated at Winchester or other foundations associated with Æthelwold do still exist and are testimony to the high standards of craftsmanship which he encouraged. Foremost among these is the *Benedictional of St Æthelwold* produced for Æthelwold's own use by his chaplain Godeman, whom he later appointed abbot of Thorney. The manuscript is lavishly decorated with gold and with full-page figural scenes in elaborate acanthus-leaved borders. Many scenes draw on continental prototypes, but others, including one of a bishop pronouncing benediction in a church, which may be intended as a portrayal of Æthelwold in Old Minster, seem to be original compositions. The artistic workshops established by Æthelwold continued to be influential after his death, both at home and abroad.

None of the churches commissioned by Æthelwold survive. The one for which there is most information is Old Minster in Winchester, which has received substantial excavation, but is also described in some detail in the accounts of the miracles of St Swithun, who was translated there in 971. Æthelwold sponsored a major replanning of the west end of the church so that the original seventh-century building was extended to incorporate the first burial place of St Swithun and a free-standing tower of St Martin, which became the centre point of a massive western entrance or westwork, comparable to similar structures in France and Germany. The rebuilding was completed in 980 and the dedication was a major ceremonial occasion attended by the young King Æthelred II (d. 1016), who had recently ascended the throne, and all the court. Evidence for some of the fixtures and fittings was also revealed by the excavations, including finds of window glass, glazed floor-tiles, and bell-pits. The rebuilding of the Old Minster was accompanied by a broader replanning of its physical surroundings. The south-eastern quarter of the town was reorganized so that Old Minster, New Minster, and Nunnaminster each had its own precinct, separated by walls from each other and from the activities of the town. Streams were diverted to serve the monastic buildings of Old Minster, which presumably were newly built at this time. Æthelwold also founded an episcopal palace at Wolvesey in the extreme south-eastern corner of the city.

Larger churches were required at Æthelwold's foundations to allow the performance of the full Benedictine liturgy laid down in the *Regularis concordia*, which required numerous altars, processions, and provision for several choirs. Æthelwold drew upon the best of continental practice, but also seems to have been responsible for some imaginative innovations such as the re-enactment of the visitation to the tomb on Easter day, which has been seen as of prime importance in the development of liturgical drama. Monks from Fleury and Corbie were brought over to instruct the monks of Abingdon in the performance of plainchant, and the surviving 'Winchester tropers' enable some reconstruction of musical practice in Winchester which included development of forms of harmony. Æthelwold in the *Regularis concordia* decreed that monks should hear mass each day and at Winchester he instituted private supplementary offices for his monks, which can be partly reconstructed from surviving manuscripts. But what has been seen as the most original and influential of his liturgical reforms was the production of a new form of benedictional represented in the texts of his own benedictional and the so-called 'Ramsey Benedictional' which was also produced at Winchester. The new benedictional involved a skilful blend of the two main forms in use in contemporary Europe and may be the work of Æthelwold himself or, if not, was certainly commissioned by him. Like the *Regularis concordia*, the Winchester benedictionals also took account of traditional English practices and incorporated benedictions for St Swithun and St Æthelthryth, two saints whose cults Æthelwold had specially promoted. All later English benedictionals were influenced by the new tradition established at Winchester.

In addition to his other activities Æthelwold personally taught the older pupils at Winchester and their works suggest that they regarded him with much respect and affection. Wulfstan Cantor wrote: 'It was always agreeable to him to teach young men and mature students, translating Latin texts into English for them, passing on the rules of grammar and metric, and encouraging them to do better by cheerful words' (*Life*, chap. 31). The surviving writings in both Old English and Latin which can be attributed to Æthelwold provide independent support for his reputation as a great scholar. His translation of the rule of St Benedict into Old English suggests that he had a nearly faultless command of Latin grammar. The *Regularis concordia* is written in clear, straightforward Latin, but he also seems to have favoured a more rhetorical and flamboyant style with much use of Greek words, which shows the influence of Aldhelm. His pupil Wulfstan Cantor refers to his skill in the composition of Latin verse as well, but only two lines survive in a charter which can be attributed to him with any certainty (*AS chart.*, S 745). Æthelwold also promoted the use of written Old English to enable essential texts to reach a wider body of people. His vernacular writings show a concern with clarity and with defining a precise Old English vocabulary which is believed to have played an important role in the development of Standard Old English.

The work of Æthelwold's pupils can also be interpreted as testimony to his own scholarship and saw his ideals carried into the next generation. These pupils included Ælfric, subsequently abbot of Eynsham, who was the most prolific author in Old English in the late Saxon period. He continued Æthelwold's concern with grammatical correctness in Old English and with the translation of Latin texts into the vernacular. Another pupil, Wulfstan Cantor, was a leading writer in Latin, both in prose and verse, and as an expert in musical theory continued Æthelwold's interest in the development of the liturgy. Æthelwold also

commissioned new works from his entourage at Winchester, of which the most significant were connected with the promotion of the cult of St Swithun. Lantfred, a foreign scholar who had joined the community at Old Minster, produced the detailed *Translatio et miracula S. Swithuni* which Wulfstan Cantor used as the basis for his own *Narratio metrica de sancto Swithuno* written in hexameters. Æthelwold also had much patronage to bestow on those who followed him loyally and many of his monks became abbots or bishops.

Political rule Although Æthelwold is primarily remembered for his contribution to the late Anglo-Saxon church, it must not be forgotten that he also played a political role. Some facets of church reform had ramifications that went beyond the ecclesiastical sphere. Æthelwold's refoundation of the fenland monasteries and recovery of large tracts of land in East Anglia may have had the subsidiary motive of creating an alternative power base to that of the ealdormanic families of the area. The emphasis on prayers for the royal house in the *Regularis concordia* not only recognized the importance of their patronage, but also helped to stress the sanctity of kingship and the distance between the king and his greatest nobles. Æthelwold's involvement in contemporary politics emerges most clearly in his support for Edgar's third wife, Ælfthryth, and their son Æthelred. Towards the end of the reign of Edgar it seems to have become an issue whether he should be succeeded by Æthelred or by Edward, the son of his first wife. Dunstan and Oswald appear to have supported Edward as the elder son, but Æthelwold backed Æthelred. Documents produced at Winchester towards the end of Edgar's reign stress the priority of Æthelred's claim over that of Edward, who is described as being of lesser status, apparently on the grounds that his mother, unlike Ælfthryth, was not a consecrated queen. Ælfthryth's status was further enhanced when she was given a supervisory role over the nunneries in the *Regularis concordia*. The queen was a major patron of Æthelwold. A tradition preserved at Peterborough described her hiding in his closet so that she could find out how best to help him; when she heard him praying to be allowed to refound Peterborough, she leapt out and promised her support. Gifts of land from the queen are recorded, as is her help in reacquiring alienated possessions. However, Æthelwold's espousal of her cause may have more complex roots, stretching back to the obligations and allegiances he may have inherited as a member of a noble family based in Winchester. After Edward was murdered in 978, Æthelwold seems to have played a major advisory role during Æthelred's minority. It is significant that it was only after Æthelwold's death that Æthelred began to rule in his own right and marked his independence by acting against the interests of some of the reformed monastic houses.

Death, cult, and subsequent reputation Æthelwold died on 1 August 984 at Beddington in Surrey, an Old Minster estate. His body was moved to Winchester on 3 August for burial in the crypt of Old Minster, as he had previously arranged with Wulfstan Cantor. Twelve years later, in 996, Æthelwold appeared to Ælfhelm, a citizen of Wallingford, and instructed him to visit his tomb to be cured of blindness and to report the matter to Wulfstan. The miracle was taken as the necessary sign which preceded the formal recognition of Æthelwold as a saint and his body was translated soon after, on 10 September 996, from the crypt to the choir of Old Minster. The rebuilding of the east end of the church had recently been completed under the supervision of Æthelwold's successor Ælfheah II, possibly in preparation for the translation. Wulfstan seems to have played the leading role in the promotion of Æthelwold's cult, including the composition of a life, which Ælfric subsequently abridged in Latin and Old English. Wulfstan's life is the main source for Æthelwold's early years and contains accounts of miraculous signs from the time he was in his mother's womb onwards. Many of these details are likely to have come from Æthelwold himself and suggest that he may have laid plans for his eventual cult before his death. Wulfstan also seems to have been in charge of the liturgical development of the cult and has been identified as the author of the necessary hymns, collects, tropes, and mass sets which have survived.

In spite of Wulfstan's dedication Æthelwold's cult seems never to have achieved great popularity and was rarely celebrated beyond the foundations which had some personal link with the saint. There is no record of the type of apocryphal stories which are a feature of Dunstan's cult, and even in Winchester he did not have either the following or the miracle-working reputation enjoyed by his own protégé Swithun. The Æthelwold of Wulfstan's life inspires respect rather than devotion. Wulfstan stresses Æthelwold's personal piety and strict adherence to Benedictine practice, but his saint is an often formidable authoritarian who, for instance, commands a monk to show his devotion by plunging his hand into a boiling pot of stew, while another monk who had the presumption to watch Æthelwold while he was reading at night was punished with temporary blindness.

Wulfstan's portrayal shows the influence of tenth-century continental saints' lives and the expected characteristics of the new breed of Benedictine saints, but there also seems little doubt that Æthelwold was a controversial figure in his own lifetime. He may have inspired great devotion from his pupils, but it would appear he also had many enemies among those he dispossessed of land and position and such enmities may have been exacerbated by his involvement in contemporary politics. Wulfstan records Æthelwold's triumph over his enemies at the dedication of the west end of Old Minster in 980, when the supporters of Æthelred and of the murdered Edward the Martyr came to be reconciled:

> God in his love gave such grace to the holy bishop that those high lay dignitaries, ealdormen, potentates and judges, and all who had previously seemed his enemies, standing in God's path, were suddenly made, as it were, sheep instead of wolves: they revered him with extraordinary affection and lowering their necks to his knee and humbly kissing his hand, commended themselves in all things to the prayers of the man of god. (*Life*, chap. 40)

After Æthelwold's death his enemies attempted revenge on his foundations, and his cult and lives may have been in part an attempt to recreate by other means the protection he had so effectively provided during his lifetime.

The way Wulfstan chose to present Æthelwold has influenced, of course, the way he has been viewed by later historians, who have tended to stress the stern authoritarian rather than the affectionate 'father' of monks who encouraged his pupils with cheerful words. David Knowles wrote of his 'austere and intransigent temper' (Knowles, 39) and Frank Stenton of 'the crude strength of his somewhat unattractive personality' (Stenton, 452). Events such as the forceful expulsion of the secular clerks at Old Minster have left a bitter taste and have given him a reputation for ruthless insensitivity which is not shared by the other tenth-century monastic reformers. His importance to the tenth-century reform movement has always been acknowledged, but appreciation of the range of his contributions and of his scholarship has only come in more recent years. Of particular importance has been the identification of his authorship of various key works of the tenth-century reform period, and his stock has risen with the close examination of these texts and others associated with him. There has also been a fuller appreciation of the fact that Æthelwold cannot be seen just as a monastic reformer; his career must also be viewed in a broader ecclesiastical context and in terms of contemporary politics in which he was a major player. The Æthelwold who has emerged is not necessarily more likeable, but commands greater admiration for his learning, depth of vision, and ability to carry through his policies. However, one of the clearest recognitions of his importance comes in a charter of King Æthelred issued some nine years after Æthelwold's death, which acknowledges how his passing 'deprived the country of one whose industry and pastoral care ministered not only to my interest but also to that of all the inhabitants of the country, the common people as well as the leading men' (*AS chart.*, S 876).

BARBARA YORKE

Sources *The life of St Æthelwold / Wulfstan of Winchester*, ed. M. Lapidge and M. Winterbottom, OMT (1991) • B. Yorke, ed., *Bishop Æthelwold: his career and influence* (1988) • T. Symons, ed. and trans., *Regularis concordia Anglicae nationis monachorum sanctimonialiumque / The monastic agreement of the monks and nuns of the English nation* (1953) • D. Whitelock, M. Brett, and C. N. L. Brooke, eds., *Councils and synods with other documents relating to the English church, 871–1204*, 2 vols. (1981) • D. Whitelock, 'The authorship of the account of King Edgar's establishment of monasteries', *Philological essays: studies in Old and Middle English language and literature in honour of Herbert Dean Meritt*, ed. J. L. Rosier (1970), 125–36 • H. Gneuss, 'The origin of standard Old English and Æthelwold's school at Winchester', *Anglo-Saxon England*, 1 (1972), 63–84 • M. Korhammer and others, eds., *Words, texts and manuscripts: studies in Anglo-Saxon culture presented to Helmut Gneuss on the occasion of his sixty-fifth birthday* (1992) • D. Parsons, ed., *Tenth-century studies* (1975) • *The benedictional of St Æthelwold: a masterpiece of Anglo-Saxon art*, ed. A. Prescott (2002) • R. Deshman, *The benedictional of St Æthelwold* (1995) • E. O. Blake, ed., *Liber Eliensis*, CS, 3rd ser., 92 (1962) • *The chronicle of Hugh Candidus, a monk of Peterborough*, ed. W. T. Mellows (1949) • E. John, *Orbis Britanniae and other studies* (1966) • D. J. Sheerin, 'The dedication of the Old Minster, Winchester, in 980', *Revue Bénédictine*, 88 (1978), 261–

73 · S. Keynes, *The diplomas of King Æthelred 'The Unready' (978–1016): a study in their use as historical evidence*, Cambridge Studies in Medieval Life and Thought, 3rd ser., 13 (1980) · A. E. Planchart, *The repertory of tropes at Winchester*, 2 vols. (1977) · *AS chart.*, S 417, 425, 745, 876 · S. Keynes, *An atlas of attestations in Anglo-Saxon charters, c.670–1066*, rev. (privately printed, Cambridge, 1996) · J. A. Robinson, *The times of St Dunstan* (1923) · D. Knowles, *The monastic order in England*, 2nd edn (1963) · F. M. Stenton, *Anglo-Saxon England*, 3rd edn (1971) **Likenesses** manuscript drawing, BL, Cotton MS Tiberius A.iii, fol. 2v; *see illus. in* Edgar (943/4–975) · portrait?, repro. in Deshman, *Benedictional of St Æthelwold*

Æthelwold Moll (*fl.* 759–765). *See under* Oswulf (*d.* 759).

Æthelwulf (*d.* 858), king of the West Saxons, was the son of *Ecgberht (*d.* 839), king of the West Saxons. His mother's identity is unknown; no siblings are recorded. He was sent by his father to take control of Kent in 825. In 838 Ecgberht held an assembly at Kingston, Surrey: Æthelwulf was acknowledged as Ecgberht's heir, and perhaps (the evidence is oblique) received royal consecration from episcopal hands, in return for concessions to Canterbury and other churches. When Ecgberht died in 839, Æthelwulf succeeded, giving his eldest (and perhaps adult) son, Æthelstan, 'the kingdom of Kent, of Essex, of Surrey and of Sussex' (*ASC*, s.a. 836). Æthelwulf's wife was *Osburh (*fl.* 839), who as far as is known bore all his recorded offspring. Her ancestry was traced back to 'Goths and Jutes', who had received control of the Isle of Wight from their royal Cerdicing kinsmen. Æthelwulf married Osburh well before 839—their second son, Æthelbald, subscribed charters from c.840. Their daughter Æthelswith married the Mercian king *Burgred in 853. Four of their five sons successively became kings of Wessex: *Æthelbald (858–60), *Æthelberht (860–65), *Æthelred (865–71), and *Alfred (871–99). In 856 Æthelwulf married Judith [*see below*], daughter of the Carolingian king Charles the Bald (823–877) of West Francia and his queen, Ermentrude (*d.* 869); whether Osburh had died or been repudiated is uncertain. Æthelwulf and Judith had no offspring and Æthelwulf died on 13 January 858.

Æthelwulf's reign has been relatively under-appreciated in modern scholarship. Yet he laid the foundations for Alfred's success. To the perennial problems of husbanding the kingdom's resources, containing conflicts within the royal family, and managing relations with neighbouring kingdoms, Æthelwulf found new as well as traditional answers. He consolidated old Wessex, and extended his reach over what is now Devon and Cornwall. He ruled Kent, working with the grain of its political community. He borrowed ideological props for his kingship from Mercians and Franks alike, and went to Rome, not to die there, like his predecessor Ine (as recalled in the Anglo-Saxon Chronicle's account of Æthelwulf's genealogy), but to return, as Charlemagne had, with enhanced prestige. Æthelwulf coped more effectively with Scandinavian attacks than did most contemporary rulers.

Æthelwulf and Kent and Mercia Possibly himself descended from the kings of Kent, Æthelwulf oversaw the evolving

Æthelwulf (*d.* 858), coin

association of Kent with Wessex rather than, as had formerly been the case, with Mercia. His sub-kingship of Kent is well documented in charters: in some, Ecgberht acted in Kent with his son's permission. The Rochester mint may have worked for son as well as father. Æthelwulf in turn established his son Æthelstan as sub-king of Kent, but exercised a more direct control over the sub-kingdom than Ecgberht had. Æthelstan, who attested as 'king' his father's charters for Kentish beneficiaries, apparently never issued charters or coins of his own. Æthelwulf visited Kent on several occasions: taking only a small retinue of West Saxons, he drew local Kentish nobles into his presence, and had them attest his Kentish charters. Æthelwulf, like Ecgberht, but unlike Kent's earlier Mercian overlords, had indigenous Kentish nobles as loyal ealdormen. For instance, Ealdorman Alhhere benefited directly from Æthelwulf's largess and also requested Æthelwulf's grant to a Kentish thegn of property at Canterbury. Already in 838, Kentish minster communities had chosen Æthelwulf 'for protection and lordship', and he had promised them freedom to elect their heads without interference from 'any other party': they were exchanging the archbishop of Canterbury's 'protection' for Æthelwulf's. Æthelwulf ran a Carolingian-style family firm of plural realms, held together by his own authority as father-king, and by the consent of the distinct élites. Increasingly heavy Scandinavian attacks convinced Kentishmen in halls and minsters, in countryside and town, that their best hope of security lay in West Saxon royal power. In Kent as elsewhere, local ealdormen had born the brunt, but in 850, says the Anglo-Saxon Chronicle, 'King Athelstan and Ealdorman Alhhere destroyed a great host at Sandwich in Kent, captured nine ships and drove off the rest' (*ASC*, s.a. 851). (Æthelstan may have died soon after this, his last recorded action.) Hardly coincidentally, Alhhere and Æthelstan came also in 850 to Wilton (in modern Wiltshire) and Æthelwulf granted the ealdorman a vast estate in Kent. Archbishops of Canterbury now remained firmly within the West Saxon orbit; and Canterbury housed the main mint for Æthelwulf's whole kingdom.

From the 820s, Mercian dominance south of the Thames had weakened. In 840 Ashdown, in the west of what is now Berkshire, was already under West Saxon control and the birth of Æthelwulf's youngest son, Alfred, at Wantage in 848 or 849 suggests West Saxon control there then. By 858 the whole shire was in West Saxon hands. King Berhtwulf of Mercia (r. 840–52) was Æthelwulf's close ally. Their moneyers co-operated. In 853 Æthelwulf was asked by Berhtwulf's successor Burgred (r. 852–74) and his witan 'to help them bring the Welsh back into subjection' (ASC, s.a. 854): a joint campaign was successful. That same year, Æthelwulf gave his daughter in marriage to Burgred, perhaps claiming a certain superiority over the new Mercian king. This kind of alliance was to continue under Æthelwulf's sons.

Æthelwulf in Wessex Wessex remained the heart of Æthelwulf's kingdom: charters show him staying at, or summoning assemblies to, Wilton, Southampton (Hamtun), Edington, Dorchester, and Winchester. Æthelwulf's interest in Winchester, where his father was buried, and where Bishop Swithun was his appointee in 852–3, represented a shift of focus, only partially balanced by generous grants of a new shrine for St Aldhelm at Malmesbury and of land in what is now Somerset to his *princeps* Ealdorman Eanwulf. This area was to become the power base of Æthelwulf's second son, Æthelbald, as, later, of his youngest son, Alfred. Æthelwulf's grant to himself, dated 26 December 846, of the large estate at South Hams, in the west of modern Devon, reveals a clear strategy: as 'bookland', it would be available for him 'to leave eternally to anyone whatever as it may be pleasing to me' (AS chart., S 298). Æthelwulf would thence reward loyal followers and fund the establishment of West Saxon control in this frontier zone. The Hams charter, surviving as an original, was subscribed by 'Æthelbald, king's son', perhaps already endowed in Somerset. In a Kentish charter dating to 855, and attested by his third son, Æthelberht as 'king', Æthelwulf granted land near Rochester to his thegn Dunn 'on account of the tithing of lands which … I have decided to do for some of my thegns' (AS chart., S 315). This grant, dated in relation to Æthelwulf's 'proceeding to Rome', referred back to the 'decimation' mentioned by the Anglo-Saxon Chronicle under 855 (apparently correct for Kent, though West Saxon charters suggest 854): 'King Æthelwulf booked the tenth part of all his land throughout all his kingdom'. Although much of the charter evidence is shaky, this 'decimation' certainly occurred (unlike an alleged earlier one in 844). Æthelwulf apparently released from secular burdens one tenth of all land in lay hands hitherto subject to them, thus enabling the owners to make grants to churches: a royal act of exceptional piety, and also of exceptional astuteness, designed to win the king secular as well as ecclesiastical friends, since laymen were keen to endow churches under their own patronage; but designed, too, to ensure a constant supply of the prayers believed to bring victory.

The papacy and the Franks The consecration of Offa of Mercia's son Ecgfrith as king in 787 may have inspired whatever Ecgberht arranged for Æthelwulf in 838. Carolingian precedent was probably more influential still. The Kingston assembly took place only months after the 837 Christmas assembly at Aachen, when Louis the Pious granted his son Charles (the Bald) a kingdom. Early in 839 Ecgberht was in touch with Louis about the Scandinavian threat to Franks and English and the need for repentance to avert divine punishment. Ecgberht sought permission to travel through Francia on pilgrimage to Rome, but died before he could accomplish it. In 855 Æthelwulf made a similar request to Charles the Bald, and this time the journey was made. Continental contemporaries registered its impact. Charles gave 'the king of the Anglo-Saxons … all the supplies a king might need, and … an escort, with all the courtesies due to a king' (Annals of St Bertin, s.a. 855). The biographer of Pope Benedict III recorded Æthelwulf's arrival at Rome 'with a multitude of people', and carefully noted Æthelwulf's gifts to St Peter: 'a fine gold crown weighing 4 lb., … one sword bound with fine gold; four silver-gilt Saxon bowls; one all-silk white shirt with roundels, with gold-studding; and two large gold-interwoven veils', as well as lavish donations of gold and silver to 'the clergy, leading men, and people of Rome' (Davis, 187). On the way home in 856, Æthelwulf enjoyed Charles's hospitality for three months, perhaps joining him in a successful campaign against Scandinavians west of the Seine. Lupus, abbot of Ferrières, Charles's confidant, had written to Æthelwulf c.852 to felicitate him on a recent victory against pagans and to solicit, in return for prayers, a gift of lead for the monastery roof (the request implies appreciation of Æthelwulf's access to the resources of the Mendip Hills). In July 856 Æthelwulf was betrothed to Charles's daughter **Judith** (b. after 843, d. c.870); on 1 October the marriage was solemnized and Judith was consecrated in an elaborate ceremony, while her husband 'conferred on her the title of queen: something not customary before then to him or his people' (Annals of St Bertin, s.a. 856). Charles, constructing a network of quasi-imperial alliances, and perhaps anxious to concert operations against the vikings, evidently thought Æthelwulf a useful son-in-law. Æthelwulf wanted a share of Carolingian charisma, emphasizing his own status through Judith's. His Frankish connection, insistently recalled by the compilers of the Anglo-Saxon Chronicle in the early 890s, continued Ecgberht's, and was as politically significant. Already, in the 840s, a Frank named Felix 'was responsible for Æthelwulf's letters': Lupus, who thought Felix wielded much influence over the king, referred in similar wording to Felix's job and to that of Charles's arch-chancellor. The influence of Carolingian diplomacy is undetectable in the texts of Æthelwulf's charters, yet Æthelwulf may have had a little chancery and Felix may have headed it. In Wessex, as in Francia, the drafting of charters was the work of notaries (such as, in Æthelwulf's entourage, the deacon Eadberht), but a Carolingian's arch-chancellor might oversee added enactment clauses: perhaps Felix was behind Carolingian-style references in 'decimation' charters of 854 to their production *in palatio nostro*. Felix's appointment indicates substantial similarities of form and substance, as well as high-level contacts, between West Saxon and Frankish regimes.

Judith Judith's consecration may have restored, even enhanced, the status of queenship in Wessex: within two generations, a queen's rite complemented the king's in Anglo-Saxon liturgical books. The prestige she herself conferred explains why, when Æthelwulf died, her stepson Æthelbald 'against God's prohibition and Christian dignity, and also contrary to the practice of all pagans … married Judith, daughter of Charles king of the Franks'. Asser's further comment about 'great disgrace' (*Life of Alfred*, chap. 17) was not echoed in the Frankish record of the event. Although Asser's claim about its being contrary to pagan practice had been anticipated by Bede, who cited St Paul to the same effect, none the less Augustine of Canterbury had found it necessary to consult Pope Gregory about the lawfulness of stepmother marriage and Eadbald of Kent had married his father's widow in 616. Similar cases are attested among early medieval peoples in the British Isles and on the continent. A dowager queen seems to have been regarded as in some sense embodying her late husband's realm, hence to marry her conferred, or strengthened, a claim to rule.

Æthelbald's death in 860 left Judith little future in Wessex. She was no older than seventeen, and still childless. 'Selling up the possessions she had acquired' there (*Annals of St Bertin*, s.a. 860), she returned to her father who kept her 'under episcopal guardianship, and with all the honour due to a queen' (ibid.), in his stronghold of Senlis. Thence, early in 862, she fled with Baldwin, count of Flanders, at his instigation, and married him. The couple sought diplomatic support from King Lothar II and Pope Nicholas I, and apparently an offer of refuge from Roric, the viking lord of Frisia. Charles the Bald, initially furious, soon forgave his daughter, who settled down in Flanders and produced two sons. Baldwin died in 879. Some time between 893 and 899, their son Count Baldwin (II) married Alfred's daughter Ælfthryth. If Judith was still alive, she probably helped negotiate this match. If not, the advantages of cross-channel alliance behind her own successive West Saxon marriages were not lost on her son. Perhaps she brought him up on stories of her youthful career. In the mid-tenth century Judith was remembered by the genealogist of the counts of Flanders as 'most wise, and beautiful', the transmitter of Carolingian blood to the comital dynasty, while any scandals were forgotten. Six generations after Judith, her descendant and namesake, the daughter of Count Baldwin (IV), remade an English connection through her marriage to Tostig Godwineson.

Dealing with Scandinavians From the early 840s the Anglo-Saxon Chronicle reports Scandinavian raids as increasingly frequent, and, in 850–51, a viking force as overwintering 'for the first time'. Æthelwulf's efforts at resistance are reported too: he fought unsuccessfully against thirty-five ships' companies of Danes at Carhampton in what is now Somerset in 843; in 851, after Danes had stormed Canterbury and London, and put the Mercians to flight, 'Æthelwulf and his [second] son Æthelbald with the West Saxon levies fought against them at *Acleah* and there made the greatest slaughter of a heathen host that we have heard tell of up to this present day' (*ASC*, s.a. 851). News of this important success reached West Francia. Notable in the chronicle's coverage of Æthelwulf's reign are repeated references to victories won by ealdormen with the men of their shires. Derived from contemporary records, and contrasting with the emphasis in the 870s on royal command, these entries present a more consensual leadership style in Æthelwulf's reign than in the earlier part of Alfred's.

Family politics Vikings were not Æthelwulf's only problem in the 850s. For him in his later years, as for Alfred and several ninth-century Carolingians, tensions revealed in other sources, between the ageing father and adult sons, and between older and younger sons, are suppressed in the main annalistic record. According to the Anglo-Saxon Chronicle for 853, Æthelwulf sent Alfred to Rome, where Pope Leo IV 'consecrated him king and stood sponsor to him at confirmation'. A fragment of a letter from Leo to Æthelwulf reports Alfred's reception and investiture 'with the belt of consulship' (*English Historical Documents*, 1, no. 219). Mid-ninth-century entries in the *Liber vitae* of San Salvatore, Brescia, indicate that Æthelred accompanied Alfred to Italy (he too may have been given an honorific reception at Rome, though neither the chronicle compilers nor the eleventh-century excerptor of Leo's letter were interested in recording that) and also suggest that Alfred went to Rome a second time, with his father. The terms of Æthelwulf's will, as described in Alfred's will (made between 879 and 888), indicate a considerable age gap between his two older surviving (after 851) sons and the two younger. These terms bear out charter evidence that Æthelwulf meant Æthelbald to inherit Wessex, and Æthelberht Kent. In sending his two younger sons to Rome (as Charlemagne had sent his, in 781), he affirmed their throneworthiness and hoped to secure them against the fate that threatened some little Carolingian contemporaries, of being tonsured (and hence excluded from the succession) by elder brothers. There was no better way to provide such security, and underwrite paternal arrangements, than to invoke papal authority (as Charlemagne sent his projected *divisio regni* of 806 to the pope for 'approval'). If Æthelwulf intended Æthelred and Alfred to remain in the running, he may have thought Sussex, Essex, or even Surrey, capable of being reconstituted as separate kingdoms. He was also providing against one or both the elder sons dying heirless.

One provision of Æthelwulf's will (mentioned in Alfred's will), concerned a particular part of his personal inheritance (*yrfe*), as distinct from the royal lands that sustained the kingship: evidently a rich estate (or cluster of estates) situated in old Wessex. The two younger sons were to have shares in this along with their eldest brother, Æthelbald, on condition that 'whichever of us should live longest was to succeed to the whole [estate]' (*English Historical Documents*, 1, no. 96). *Pace* some modern historians, this provision had nothing to do with the kingdom of Wessex, and introduced no new principles of fraternal succession or the realm's indivisibility. When Æthelbald died in 860, Æthelberht took over Wessex and became, at his younger brothers' request, temporary trustee for their shares of the *yrfe*. Asser in his *Life of Alfred* (written in 893) clarifies Æthelwulf's last years, without conflicting with the other, fragmentary, evidence. Asser states that Alfred went to Rome in 853, and again, with Æthelwulf, in 855. Then, 'while King Æthelwulf was returning from Rome, his son Æthelbald with all his councillors [Asser names Ealhstan bishop of Sherborne and Eanwulf ealdorman of Somerset as chief conspirators] tried to perpetrate a terrible crime: expelling the king from his kingdom'. News of Æthelwulf's impending Carolingian marriage had evidently provoked the rebellion, as Æthelbald reacted to the threat of displacement by higher-born (half-)brothers. Father and son negotiated a peace, whereby Æthelwulf received his kingdom's 'eastern districts', Æthelbald the western. Asser disapproved, 'because the western part of the Saxon land has always been more important than the eastern' (*Life of Alfred*, chap. 12). Although this agreement has usually been read as severing Wessex again from the acquired lands to the east, Asser perhaps described a division of Wessex itself between parts west and east of Selwood: if so, Æthelwulf's West Saxon reign continued until 858, as implied by the Anglo-Saxon Chronicle's assigning him a reign length of eighteen and a half years. It is hard to see why Asser should have invented the story of the rebellion (though the chronicle understandably suppressed it).

In, or soon after, late 856 Æthelwulf made a will, says Asser, 'so that his sons should not quarrel unnecessarily among themselves after his death'. He prospectively 'divided his kingdom between his two eldest sons', while 'his personal inheritance was split between his sons, daughter and kinsmen' (*Life of Alfred*, chap. 16). Æthelwulf's planned division of his recently constructed composite kingdom has been judged retrograde by some historians—a judgement coloured by teleology. Throughout the middle ages, dynastic thinking impelled the accumulation of plural realms in order to provide, through redistribution, for plural sons. Æthelwulf had long foreseen separate futures for Wessex and Kent. Yet Wessex itself was not to be divided (as perhaps in 856), and nor was any acquired realm. Æthelwulf's two younger sons, not yet of age, were designated to no kingdom. Within Wessex, Æthelwulf distinguished, significantly, between kingdom and personal inheritance. His moveable wealth (recall his resources in gold, silver, and lead) was to be split, in terms reminiscent of Charlemagne's will, between 'children, nobles, and the needs of the king's soul' for which last 'a great sum of money should be taken every year to Rome'. Judith remained childless, yet may well have cared for her young stepchildren, as Carolingian stepmothers did theirs. Æthelwulf's death early in 858 may have been unexpected. His body was buried at Steyning, Sussex, and only later transferred to Winchester. As the will stipulated,

Wessex went to Æthelbald, the 'eastern districts' to Æthelberht.

The Anglo-Saxon Chronicle, especially its record of Æthelwulf's military effort against vikings, its stress on his Carolingian marriage, and its 855–8 entry with his lengthy genealogy, shows why his remembered reign had such importance for Alfred's court. Charter evidence shows the living Æthelwulf hard at work maintaining the support of aristocrats, West Saxon and Kentish, and especially of his thegns. A token, still extant, of that bond is the gold ring, about an inch across, richly decorated with religious symbols, and inscribed 'Ethelwulf Rex'. Found at Laverstock, Wiltshire, in 1780, it was surely made to be a gift from this royal lord to a brawny follower: the sign of successful ninth-century kingship.   JANET L. NELSON

Sources ASC, s.a. 823, 836, 851, 853, 854, 855 • *Alfred the Great: Asser's Life of King Alfred and other contemporary sources*, ed. and trans. S. Keynes and M. Lapidge (1983) • *English historical documents*, 1, ed. and trans. D. Whitelock (1955), nos. 88, 89, 96, 217, 218, 219 • J. L. Nelson, ed. and trans., *The annals of St Bertin* (1991) • R. Davis, ed. and trans., *The lives of the ninth-century popes* (Liber pontificalis): the ancient biographies of ten popes from AD 817–891 (1995) • AS chart., S 202, 288, 290, 292, 294, 298, 300, 301, 302, 303, 304, 305, 307, 308, 314, 315, 320, 322, 326, 334, 1438, 1860, 1862 • S. Keynes, 'The West Saxon charters of King Æthelwulf and his sons', *EngHR*, 109 (1994), 1109–49 • B. Yorke, *Wessex in the early middle ages* (1995) • P. Wormald, 'The ninth century', *The Anglo-Saxons*, ed. J. Campbell (1982), 132–57 • J. L. Nelson, 'Reconstructing a royal family: reflections on Alfred, from Asser', *People and places in northern Europe, 500–1600: essays in honour of Peter Hayes Sawyer*, ed. I. Wood and N. Lund, [another edn] (1991), 47–66 • S. Keynes, 'The control of Kent in the ninth century', *Early Medieval Europe*, 2 (1993), 111–32 • D. P. Kirby, *The earliest English kings* (1991) • J. L. Nelson, 'The Franks and the English in the ninth century reconsidered', *The preservation and transmission of Anglo-Saxon culture*, ed. J. Rosenthal and P. Szarmach (1997), 190–208 • P. A. Stafford, 'The king's wife in Wessex, 800–1066', *Past and Present*, 91 (1981), 3–27 • N. Brooks, *The early history of the church of Canterbury: Christ Church from 597 to 1066* (1984) • P. Stafford, 'Charles the Bald, Judith and England', *Charles the Bald: court and kingdom*, ed. M. T. Gibson and J. L. Nelson, 2nd rev. edn (1990), 139–53 • J. L. Nelson, *Charles the Bald* (1992) • A. Scharer, 'The writing at King Alfred's court', *Early Medieval Europe*, 5 (1996), 177–206 • S. Keynes, 'Anglo-Saxon entries in the *Liber vitae* of Brescia', *Alfred the Wise: studies in honour of Janet Bately*, ed. J. Roberts and J. L. Nelson (1997), 99–119 • L. Webster and J. Backhouse, eds., *The making of England: Anglo-Saxon art and culture, AD 600–900* (1991), 268–9 • A. P. Smyth, *King Alfred the Great* (1995) • R. McKitterick, *The Frankish kingdoms under the Carolingians, 751–987* (1983) • *Asser's Life of King Alfred: together with the 'Annals of Saint Neots' erroneously ascribed to Asser*, ed. W. H. Stevenson (1904) • John of Worcester, *Chron.*

Likenesses coin, BM [*see illus.*]

Affleck, Sir Edmund, baronet (1725–1788), naval officer, ninth son of the eighteen children of Gilbert Affleck (1684?–1764), politician, of Dalham Hall, Suffolk, and Anna Dolben, was born on 19 April 1725. He became a lieutenant in the Royal Navy in July 1745, commander in May 1756, and captain on 23 March 1757; and he served throughout the Seven Years' War, first in the *Mercury* (20 guns) and afterwards in the *Launceston* (40 guns). He remained in employment during the subsequent years of peace and in 1778 was appointed to the *Bedford* (74 guns), and sailed for North America with Vice-Admiral John Byron.

The *Bedford* returned after being damaged in a gale; and

she was next employed in the channel with Sir Charles Hardy in the campaign of 1779, and afterwards formed part of the force with which Sir George Rodney was sent out to relieve Gibraltar. When Rodney's force fell in with the Spanish squadron off Cape St Vincent on 16 January 1780 the *Bedford*, with Affleck still in command, was foremost in attacking the retiring enemy.

After returning to England the *Bedford* was again sent out to North America, where she reinforced the squadron with Admiral Marriot Arbuthnot in Gardiner's Bay. In the action of 16 March 1781 the *Bedford* was in the rear of the British line but took no effective part. Throughout the following summer Affleck was employed as commissioner of the port of New York; he resumed command of the *Bedford* in the autumn, and on 12 November sailed with Sir Samuel Hood for the West Indies. Flying the pennant of commodore, Affleck played an important role in the repulse of the French at St Kitts on 26 January 1782. Later Hood's squadron joined Sir George Rodney, and formed part of the fleet which fought to leeward of Dominica on 9 and 12 April 1782; Affleck took a leading part in both actions, especially the second one, during which the *Bedford* passed through a gap in the enemy's line at almost the same moment that Rodney, unseen in the smoke, passed through another. For this service Affleck was made a baronet on 10 July 1782 and on his return to England in 1784 was promoted rear-admiral of the blue. He was married, first, to Esther (*d.* 1787), daughter of John Ruth and widow of Peter Creffield of Ardleigh Hall, near Colchester. On 14 May 1788 he married Margaret (*née* Burgess), widow of Revd William Smithers, of Colchester.

A supporter of William Pitt, Affleck was elected MP for Colchester in March 1782 and spoke twice on naval matters before his death in Colchester on 19 November 1788.

J. K. LAUGHTON, *rev.* ROGER MORRISS

Sources J. Brooke, 'Affleck, Edmund', HoP, *Commons*

Affleck, Philip (*b.* after 1725?, *d.* 1799), naval officer, was one of the eighteen children of Gilbert Affleck (1684?–1764), politician, of Dalham Hall, Suffolk, and Anna Dolben. He was the younger brother of Edmund *Affleck, also a naval officer, who was born in April 1725. He first went to sea in the service of the East India Company, and, having entered the navy, was made a lieutenant by Admiral Edward Boscawen in 1755 in order to replace one of the casualties in the fleet in Nova Scotia waters. According to his passing certificate he was then upwards of thirty-four years old, although this would appear incorrect given his relation to his brother Edmund. On 1 August 1758 he was promoted commander; he accompanied Edward Boscawen in the sloop *Grammont* to the Mediterranean the following year; and two days after the defeat of De la Clue, on 18 August 1759, he was again promoted by Boscawen. After a short period in command of Boscawen's flagship, the *Namur* (90 guns), he was appointed to the *Panther* (60 guns) and sent to India, where, for the next two years, he served under the orders of admirals Charles Steevens and Samuel Cornish. In the hurricane of 1 January 1761 Affleck was one of those who helped to save their

ship by cutting away her masts as she rode to anchor on a lee shore. In May he exchanged ships with William Newsom; he thus took command of the store ship *Southsea Castle*, but resigned from her before the 1762 Manila campaign. In 1779 he was appointed to the *Triumph* (74 guns) in the Channel Fleet under Sir Charles Hardy. When he suggested in November that the *Triumph* be refitted at Portsmouth, rather than Plymouth, the earl of Sandwich remarked that he liked to accommodate the personal convenience of officers like the two Affleck brothers whom he characterized as both 'very respectable and thoroughly right headed'.

Affleck was sent to the West Indies to reinforce Sir George Rodney in the spring of 1780, and was with him in the engagements with the comte de Guichen on 15 and 19 May, in his visit to New York in September, and at the capture of St Eustatius in the following February; he returned with Rodney to England as a passenger in August 1781. In the following year he was involved in the battle of the Saints and later criticized Rodney for not pursuing the beaten enemy (Mulgrave Castle Archives, Box VI:II/153). Subsequently he was reappointed to the *Triumph* which, following the cessation of hostilities, was commissioned as a guardship. He obtained his flag on 24 September 1787, and in 1790 went to the Jamaica station as commander-in-chief, where he was relieved in 1792 by Commodore John Ford. On his return home he was promoted vice-admiral of the blue (1 February 1793), and on 26 April he was appointed one of the lords of the Admiralty under the earl of Chatham. Towards the end of 1793 he was elected vice-president of the marine society, and he continued at the Admiralty until 1796, when he retired into private life. He had attained the rank of admiral of the white when he died at Bath on 21 December 1799.

NICHOLAS TRACY

Sources 'Memoir of the public services of the late Philip Affleck', *Naval Chronicle*, 21 (1809), 445–51 • D. Syrett and R. L. DiNardo, *The commissioned sea officers of the Royal Navy, 1660–1815*, rev. edn, Occasional Publications of the Navy RS, 1 (1994) • J. Charnock, ed., *Biographia navalis*, 6 (1798), 346–7 • W. E. May, 'The *Panther* affair', *Mariner's Mirror*, 55 (1969), 401–10 • Mulgrave Castle Archives, Box VI:11/153 • IGI • HoP, *Commons*

Archives PRO, ADM1/382; ADM 107/4, P. 301

Likenesses E. Penny, oils, 1767–71, NMM • L. F. Abbott, oils, NPG • oils (after a portrait, *c.*1793–1795), NMM

Africanus, Scipio (*c.*1702–1720), servant, was born of an African family that most likely came from west Africa, where many Bristol merchants bought or captured black men and women for transport to the American colonies. He became the servant of Charles William Howard, seventh earl of Suffolk and second and last earl of Bindon, who in 1715 had married Arabella, daughter and coheir of Sir Samuel Astry and his wife, Elizabeth Morse. The Morse family occupied the Great House in Henbury, Gloucestershire, near Bristol. Whether Scipio was acquired after the marriage or inherited from the family who previously occupied the house is unknown. He died at Henbury on 21 December 1720, closely followed by his master, in February 1722, and his mistress only four months later.

Scipio's elaborate gravestone remains in the churchyard of St Mary's, Henbury, with its black cherubs and distinctive epitaph, perhaps a tribute to the regard in which his employers held him, in contrast to the general anonymity of servants at that date and the virtual invisibility of black people and their stories in the official records of society. His name implies some knowledge of classical history and literature by those who gave it to him. Polybius's account of his namesake's capture of Carthage by the Romans in the third century BC suggests that black slaves might expect freedom from servitude if they exhibited goodwill towards their conquerors. The words of the epitaph reinforce this attitude, recording the victory of Christianity over paganism: 'I who was Born a PAGAN and a SLAVE now sweetly sleep a CHRISTIAN in my Grave'. While aspects of Scipio's life remain unrecorded the status that he was accorded on his death is a monument to attitudes on race and colour in the colonial era; his is one of the very few marked burial places of the 10,000 black slaves and servants present in British society in the early eighteenth century.

TIM MACQUIBAN

Sources A guide to Henbury (1958) · J. Walvin, England: slaves and freedom, 1776–1838 (1986) · B. Hill, Servants (1996) · P. Fryer, Aspects of British black history (1995) · Burke, Peerage (1999) · J. P. Rodriguez, ed., The historical encyclopedia of world slavery (1997) · gravestone, St Mary's Church, Henbury, Gloucestershire

Aga Khan III [Mohammed Shah] (1877–1957), leader of the Ismailis, was born in Karachi on 2 November 1877, a member of the ruling Kajar dynasty in Persia, the son of Aga Ali Shah, Aga Khan II (d. 1885), and Shams al-Muluk, known as Lady Ali Shah (c.1850–1938), a former Persian princess, and a woman of character and vision, who was alive to the importance of the role, political and religious, which her son, named Mohammed Shah, would have to fill, and brought him up with a care, skill, and judgement for which he always remained grateful. He succeeded his father as the third Aga Khan (a title bestowed on his grandfather by the British government) and as forty-eighth head of the Ismaili sect of the Shi'i Muslim community.

The Aga Khan assumed the active administration of the imamate in 1893, in his sixteenth year. His 11–12 million followers, scattered over India, Burma, the Middle East, and Africa, looked to him not only as their spiritual leader but for the resolution of their temporal problems. On taking over the imamate he instructed his followers in Bombay to keep out of communal rioting, and in 1901 he applied spiritual sanctions to Ismailis who had made murderous attacks on Sunnis. He consistently urged his followers to identify themselves, in manners, language, and customs, with the countries in which they lived. There were occasions when his liberal and moderate attitude failed to carry his community with him, as in 1901, when the Ithna Ashari sect broke away, and again during the Balkan wars (1912–13) and the Khilafat agitation (1919–24). But his was a restraining influence, and broadly speaking the community responded to his lead over political issues. His spiritual influence remained unshaken, even after old age and ill health had reduced his political importance.

The Aga Khan was chosen in 1897 by the Muslims of

Aga Khan III (1877–1957), by Dorothy Wilding, c.1953

western India to convey to the viceroy their greetings to the queen empress on her diamond jubilee. In 1898 he began a lifelong series of visits to Europe, Africa, Asia, and America, and was received at Windsor by Queen Victoria. In 1902 Lord Curzon nominated him to the viceroy's legislative council, on which he served for two years, declining a second term. He used the opportunity to urge the claims of a Muslim university at Aligarh, to which he had lent substantial financial support.

The Aga Khan was married in 1896 to a cousin in her teens, Shahzadi Begum. There was no issue, and the marriage was dissolved in 1907. In 1908 he married, in Cairo, by Muslim rites, an Italian lady, the artist and dancer Theresa Magliano (1889–1926), with whom he had a son who died in infancy, and Aly Khan.

The Aga Khan had maintained the friendliest of relations with the Indian Congress leaders, and particularly with G. K. Gokhale. He had spared no pains to maintain communal unity, to integrate Muslim political feeling with the Congress Party, and so to present a united front, with constitutional advance as its objective, to the British government. He had, too, done his best to reduce the communal antagonisms which derived from the partition of Bengal of 1905. But by 1906, now established as a political force, and as the recognized leader and spokesman of the Indian Muslims as a whole, he began to conclude that Congress would prove incapable of representing Indian Muslim feeling: 'already that artificial unity which the British Raj had imposed from without was cracking'; 'our only hope lay along the lines of independent organization and action'.

In that year the Aga Khan led a delegation to Lord Minto

which urged the case for the increased participation of Muslims in the political life of the country and pressed that they should be regarded as a nation within a nation, with rights and obligations safeguarded by statute, with adequate and separate representations both in local bodies and on legislative councils, and with a separate communal franchise and electoral roll. Lord Minto's reply was reassuring.

Later in 1906 the All-India Muslim League was founded, and the Aga Khan was elected its first president, an office which he held until 1912. He lent his active support to the Morley–Minto Council reforms of 1909, but intercommunal feeling continued to grow, despite the cancellation of the partition of Bengal.

On the outbreak of war in 1914 the Aga Khan, who had exercised a restraining influence on Indian Muslim opinion during the Balkan wars of 1912–13, was in Zanzibar. He at once volunteered his services and instructed his followers to render all possible support. He was advised that he could help best in the diplomatic field. His endeavours to promote Turkish neutrality failed, but when Turkey joined the central powers and, by declaring a *jihad* or holy war, created a difficult situation for Indian and other Muslims, he unhesitatingly and successfully urged on them full co-operation with the allies. In 1915 he was entrusted with a mission of major importance to Egypt, the effect of which was to reassure Egyptian opinion and to secure the internal stability of the country, with the invaluable consequent assistance to the allies of a strategically placed and dependable base.

On his return to England in September 1914 the Aga Khan had again met Gokhale, and with him strove to compose a memorandum on Indian constitutional progress representing their joint views on the establishment of federation in India as a step towards self-government. Early in 1915 Gokhale died, addressing his political testament to the Aga Khan, and not to M. K. Gandhi or any Hindu leader, for publication two years later, by when he hoped the war would be over and India capable of working out her own destiny. The testament was duly published, with a further plea by the Aga Khan that after the war east Africa might be reserved for Indian colonization in recognition of India's services. But it was overtaken by events which led to the Montagu–Chelmsford Council reforms of 1919.

Ill health prevented the Aga Khan from taking the part he would have wished in these developments. But his enforced leisure resulted in 1918 in his *India in Transition*, dedicated to his mother, a thoughtful and closely argued study which attracted much attention. He reminded the British of their grant of full self-government to South Africa, and urged the case for the sharing of power in India and for a widely based South Asian Federation, of which an India ultimately self-governing must be the centre and pivot.

After the war the Aga Khan was active in pressing on the allies the long-term importance of the question of the caliphate, and of a policy towards Turkey which should be practical as well as temperate, just, and equitable.

Strongly as his own sympathies lay with Turkey, he was a realist and a restraining influence on Muslims in India, and as such sharply criticized by many members of his community during the Khilafat agitation, the leaders of which, Muhammad and Shaukat Ali, had the active support of Gandhi and the Congress.

By 1924 difficulties in Kenya between the British settlers on the one hand, and the British government and the local Indian interests on the other, resulted in a committee of inquiry under John Hope Simpson. The Aga Khan, who had declined the chairmanship, was a member, and the committee's report proposed compromises, more particularly over Indian immigration into east Africa, and the reservation of certain districts in the coastal lowlands which were of much importance to India.

From 1924 to 1928 the Aga Khan spent 'a period devoted almost exclusively to my own personal and private life' (Aga Khan, 168). At the end of 1928 an All-Indian Muslim Conference met at Delhi under his chairmanship to formulate Muslim opinion in view of the commission under Sir John Simon on India's constitutional future. Its unanimous conclusions, the more significant in that they had the support of M. A. Jinnah, remained the guiding light for the Muslim community in all subsequent discussions. They contemplated a federal system with complete autonomy and residuary powers vested in the constituent states; took note that the right of Muslims to elect their representatives in the various Indian legislatures was now the law of the land, of which they could not be deprived without their consent; and stipulated that in the provinces in which Muslims constituted a minority they should have a representation in no case less than that already enjoyed, and that they must have their due share in the central and provincial cabinets.

The Simon report of 1930 was followed by the three round-table conferences of 1930–32. The Aga Khan was elected chairman of the British-India delegation and throughout played a material part in the discussions. At all times alive to the importance of compromise, and of adapting communal claims to the interests of India as a whole, he made an important contribution to securing a unanimous report from the joint select committee (1933–4) presided over by Lord Linlithgow which resulted in the Government of India Act of 1935. But he failed to secure Congress acceptance of a joint memorandum, with the drafting of which he was closely concerned, embodying a united demand on behalf of all communities covering almost every important political point at issue, which sought to ensure continuity in the process of the further transfer of responsibility, and which, in his judgement, would have immensely simplified all future constitutional progress.

With the passing of the Government of India Act the Aga Khan ceased for the time actively to concern himself with Indian constitutional advance. But his high standing, religious and political, his extensive travels and wide contacts, his fluency in the principal European languages, and his independence of outlook had made him increasingly a figure not merely of Indian and Commonwealth but of international importance, and from 1932 he was for some years prominent in the League of Nations. He was a representative of India at the world disarmament conference at Geneva in 1932, was leader of the Indian delegation to the League of Nations assembly in 1932 and 1934–7, and in 1937 president of the assembly. It was while president that he visited Hitler. He subsequently lent his fullest support to the Munich settlement, suggesting in a much criticized article in *The Times* that Hitler should be taken at his word, and questioning whether he had really meant what he had said in *Mein Kampf*.

On the outbreak of war in 1939 the Aga Khan was in Europe. He at once issued a manifesto urging his followers to give the fullest support to Britain. In the winter of 1939–40 he visited India, when he persistently restated British war aims, and endeavoured to act as an intermediary with Reza Shah of Persia. He led a deputation to the viceroy on behalf of Indians in South Africa, and endeavoured, unsuccessfully, by discussion with the nawab of Bhopal and Gandhi, to bring about mutual understanding between the Indian parties for the prosecution of the war. He returned to Europe in April 1940, and on the fall of France withdrew to Switzerland, where he remained under medical treatment, barred from political activity, until the end of the war. The criticism which his inactivity provoked took perhaps insufficient account of his serious and continued ill health. In 1929 he had married Andrée Carron (*b. c.*1898), with whom he had one son, Sadruddin. This union having been dissolved by divorce in the Geneva civil courts in 1943 (the Aga Khan being awarded custody of the son), he married in 1944 the former Miss France, Yvette Larbousse (1906–2000), who survived him, and to whose devoted care in old age and illness he owed much.

The Aga Khan returned to India in 1946 to find that, while his influence remained unshaken with his own community, which celebrated his diamond jubilee in India and east Africa in 1946, the Muslim political leadership had passed decisively to Jinnah, to whom he was to pay a generous tribute in his *Memoirs*. After partition in 1947 the Aga Khan ceased to be an active participant in Indian politics.

Ill health in his later years greatly reduced the Aga Khan's activity, but he maintained the closest touch with the Ismaili community, and continued to travel extensively. In 1949 he took up Persian citizenship, while remaining a British subject. His platinum jubilee was celebrated in Karachi in February 1954. In that year he published his *Memoirs*.

Throughout his life the Aga Khan was keenly interested in horse-racing, and his scientific concern with bloodstock and breeding methods had a material effect on English horse-breeding. On coming to the English turf after 1918, he won the Queen Mary Stakes at Ascot in 1922 (Cos) and had thereafter a record of outstanding distinction, winning, in addition to many minor successes, the Derby in 1930 (Blenheim); the Two Thousand Guineas, Derby, and St Leger (the triple crown) with Bahram in 1935; and the Derby again in 1936 (Mahmoud), 1948 (My Love), and 1952 (Tulyar). In 1954 he finally disposed of his studs.

Shrewd, active, a connoisseur of the arts, a good scholar, a citizen of the world, an experienced and courageous politician, a hardworking religious leader alive to the importance of the education and physical fitness of his community, with great material resources, the Aga Khan was for long a major figure in Indian politics, and in his time, helped by his broad-minded and constructive approach and his instinct for compromise, he gave service of great value to his community and to the Commonwealth.

In 1898 Queen Victoria had personally invested the Aga Khan with the KCIE. He was appointed GCIE (1902), GCSI (1911), GCVO (1923), and GCMG (1955), thus receiving his last decoration from Elizabeth II. He held also the Brilliant Star of Zanzibar (first class, 1900), and (1901) the royal Prussian order of the Crown (first class, which he returned on the outbreak of war in 1914). In 1934 he was sworn of the privy council, the first Indian, other than members of the judicial committee, to receive this honour. He was an honorary LLD of Cambridge (1911). In 1916 George V gave him an honour which he particularly valued, a salute of eleven guns, and the rank and precedence for life of a first-class ruling chief of the Bombay presidency.

The Aga Khan died at Versoix, near Geneva, on 11 July 1957, and was buried at Aswan. He nominated as his successor as Aga Khan IV his grandson Karim (*b.* 1936), elder son of Aly Khan.

GILBERT LAITHWAITE, *rev.* FRANCIS ROBINSON

Sources Aga Khan, *The memoirs of Aga Khan: world enough and time* (1954) · S. Jackson, *The Aga Khan: prince, prophet and sportsman* (1952) · Sirdar Ikbal Ali Shah, *The Prince Aga Khan: an authentic life story* (1933) · F. Daftary, *The Isma'ilis: their history and doctrines* (1990) · H. J. Greenwell, *The Aga Khan* (1952) · M. Bose, *The Aga Khans* (1984) · A. Edwards, *Throne of gold: the lives of the Aga Khans* (1995)
Archives Royal Institute of International Affairs, Chatham House, London | BL OIOC, letters to W. R. Lawrence, Eur. MSS F 143 | FILM BFI NFTVA, actuality footage · BFI NFTVA, news footage | SOUND BL NSA, current affairs recording · BL NSA, recorded talk
Likenesses black and white photographs, 1923–c.1960, Hult. Arch. · D. Wilding, photograph, c.1953, NPG [*see illus.*] · J. Berwick, portrait, priv. coll. · O. Birley, portrait, priv. coll. · E. Souza, portrait, priv. coll. · Van Dongen, portraits, priv. coll.

Agar, Augustus Willington Shelton (1890–1968), naval officer, was born in Kandy, Ceylon, on 4 January 1890, the son of John Shelton Agar, an Irish tea planter from co. Kerry. He was the youngest of thirteen children, and his Austrian mother, whose maiden name was Cruwell, died shortly after his birth. He was sent to England when he was eight years old. He was educated at Framlingham College, Suffolk, and at Eastman's naval academy, Southsea, Hampshire, and entered the training ship *Britannia* as a cadet in May 1905.

In September 1906 Agar was appointed midshipman to the battleship *Prince of Wales*, with the Mediterranean Fleet. Successive appointments as midshipman to battleships followed. In January 1910 he was promoted sublieutenant, and he continued training and examinations at Portsmouth and at the Royal Naval College, Greenwich. In April 1911 he joined the destroyer *Ruby*, with the Home

Fleet. In June 1912 he was promoted lieutenant, and in April 1913 he attended the Central Flying School at Upavon, where he gained his pilot's licence.

In August 1913 Agar was appointed to the battleship *Hibernia*, which formed part of the 3rd battle squadron, the Grand Fleet, at the outbreak of war in August 1914. In 1915 *Hibernia* was deployed to the Dardanelles, and ultimately covered the Gallipoli evacuations in January 1916. In December of that year Agar joined the old cruiser *Iphigenia*, which had been converted into a headquarters and repair ship for minesweeping trawlers covering the approaches and supply routes to Murmansk and Archangel in north Russia. *Iphigenia* arrived at Busta Voe in late February 1917, remained on station for a year, and returned to Chatham in February 1918.

By May 1918 Agar was operating from Osea Island, Essex, with a flotilla of light coastal motor boats (CMBs), armed with torpedoes or mines and capable of nearly 40 knots. After the armistice he was employed by the Admiralty, in conjunction with the Foreign Office and MI5, on intelligence duties against Bolshevik Russia. Operating as agent ST 34 he contacted other British agents in Helsinki. Communications were maintained by two 40 foot CMBs based at Terrioki, near the Finnish border and 25 miles by sea from St Petersburg. Agar's CMBs ran a courier service to and from St Petersburg, linking with British agents who included ST 25, Paul Dukes, who became famous after he published a book about his experiences.

Agar participated in more orthodox naval operations with units of the Baltic fleet commanded by Rear-Admiral Sir Walter Cowan. On the night of 17 June 1919 Agar penetrated Kronstadt harbour in CMB 4 and sank the 6650 ton Bolshevik cruiser *Oleg* with a single torpedo. The CMB's three-man crew were decorated, Agar himself being awarded the Victoria Cross. He resumed his courier duties but also, on the night of 18 August 1919, participated in operation RK, the raid by eight CMBs on Kronstadt. This brilliant but hazardous action resulted in the sinking of two Bolshevik battleships and a submarine depot ship. All the CMB crews were decorated; two VCs were awarded and Agar received the DSO.

In September 1919 Agar returned to England, and in January 1920 he was again posted to Osea Island. On 20 July 1920 he married Mary Frances Katherine Petre, seventeenth Baroness Furnivall (1900–1968), daughter of Bernard Henry Philip Petre, fourteenth Baron Petre. In September he was appointed to the cruiser HMS *Chatham*, New Zealand station, and promoted lieutenant-commander. In December 1923, after his return to England, he was appointed to the royal yacht *Victoria and Albert* for two years, and promoted commander in December 1925. In April 1926 he was appointed to the destroyer *Witch*, division leader of the third destroyer flotilla, Mediterranean Fleet, commanded by Admiral Sir Roger Keyes. In September 1927 he attended the Royal Naval Staff College, Greenwich, followed by a course at the Army Staff College, Camberley. He also separated from his wife, who initiated divorce proceedings. The couple were formally divorced in 1931. In January 1930 he was selected as naval

adviser to the high commissioner for New Zealand, who was attending the London naval conference, and in September he was appointed to command the new sloop *Scarborough* on the North American and West Indies station, for a three-year commission. In February 1932 he married Ina Margaret Lindner in Bermuda.

Agar returned to England in 1933, and in October attended the senior officers' war course at Greenwich. Having been promoted captain in December 1933 he undertook a short course at the tactical school at Portsmouth, and then studied at the Imperial Defence College for a year. His next seagoing appointment was to the anti-aircraft cruiser *Curlew*, in January 1936. The following January he was appointed to the cruiser *Emerald*, his favourite ship, which sailed in June from Chatham to the East India station, and returned in July 1938. The ship was prepared for the Reserve Fleet, a process briefly interrupted by the Munich crisis in September 1938. Agar remained on *Emerald* for six months, and was next appointed captain of the Royal Naval College, Greenwich.

In July 1939 Agar was reappointed to *Emerald*, joining the Home Fleet at Scapa Flow in August. After the outbreak of the Second World War, on 3 September, the ship was assigned to the northern patrol, to carry out blockade duties against Nazi Germany. In October, with her sister ship *Enterprise*, she transported 5 tons of gold bullion from England to Nova Scotia, to pay for war materials. She was subsequently deployed on gruelling Atlantic convoy duties during the harsh winter of 1939–40. In June 1940 Agar was appointed to command the sixteenth destroyer flotilla at Harwich, escorting coastal convoys. A succession of shore appointments followed, culminating in his appointment as chief staff officer, coastal forces.

In August 1941 Agar was made captain of the cruiser *Dorsetshire*, which was deployed to the south Atlantic on search and escort duties. After Japan's invasion of Malaya on 8 December *Dorsetshire* was engaged in various duties, including escorting the last convoys from doomed Singapore and Rangoon (which fell on 15 February and 8 March 1942 respectively). On 5 April she and the cruiser *Cornwall*, ordered to rendezvous with Admiral Sir James Somerville's Eastern Fleet, were caught and sunk in the Indian Ocean by a powerful force of Japanese naval dive-bombers. This was Agar's last seagoing command; in 1943 he was declared unfit for further active sea service. Placed on the retired list, he was offered, as commodore, the combined office of president and captain of the Royal Naval College, Greenwich, a position that he held until 1946. In retirement he took up farming at Alton, Hampshire.

Agar never achieved flag rank. He states in his biography, *Footprints in the Sea* (1959), that he was not driven by ambition, and his divorce may have led to prejudice in certain quarters. Yet he epitomized the 'sea dog' of British naval tradition: honourable, extremely brave, and totally dedicated to king, country, and the Royal Navy. He was appointed a younger brother of Trinity House (1936) and vice-president of the Sailors' Home and Red Ensign Club (1957); his clubs included the Athenaeum and the Royal

Yacht Squadron (naval member). He died at his home, Anstey Park House, Alton, on 30 December 1968. He had at least one stepdaughter, who registered his death.

JOHN R. BULLEN

Sources A. W. S. Agar, *Footprints in the sea* (1959) · *The Times* (1 Jan 1969) · *WWW* · P. Dukes, *The story of ST 25* (1938) · S. W. Roskill, *The war at sea, 1939–1945*, 3 vols. in 4 (1954–61) · C. Andrew, *Secret service: the making of the British intelligence community* (1985) · *CGPLA Eng. & Wales* (1969) · m. cert. [Mary Frances Katherine Petre] · d. cert. · Burke, *Peerage* (2000)
Archives SOUND IWM SA, 'British RNVR officer serving from 1919…', BBC, 13 Dec 1967, 71772 [Agar discusses aspects of his military career] · IWM SA, oral history interview
Wealth at death £9580: probate, 28 March 1969, *CGPLA Eng. & Wales*

Agar, Charles, first earl of Normanton (1736–1809), Church of Ireland archbishop of Dublin, the third son of Henry Agar, MP for Gowran, co. Kilkenny, Ireland, and Anne Ellis, daughter of Welbore *Ellis (1661/2–1734), bishop of Meath, and Diana Briscoe, was born on 22 December 1736 at Gowran Castle, co. Kilkenny. He was educated at Westminster School (1747–1755?) and Christ Church, Oxford, where he graduated BA in 1759, MA in 1762, and DCL in 1765. In 1763 he was appointed chaplain to the duke of Northumberland, lord lieutenant of Ireland. This was a sure path to preferment and Agar became rector of Ballymagarvey and Skryne, in the diocese of Meath, in the same year. He was successively rector of Annagh, in the diocese of Kilmore (1765–6), and dean of Kilmore (1765–8), and was consecrated bishop of Cloyne in 1768. In 1774 he wondered why, in view of his consistent support for the administration, he had not been offered the archbishopric of Tuam, although he candidly admitted that it was not his preference. Four years later he assured the viceroy, Buckinghamshire, of his devotion to his majesty's business in Ireland and clearly hoped to succeed the dying archbishop of Dublin. He was disappointed in this, partly, in his view, because of bad relations with the archbishop of Armagh, and was given the archbishopric of Cashel, to the considerable dissatisfaction of his family and connections. On 22 November 1776 he married Jane Benson (1751/2–1826), eldest daughter of William Benson of co. Down and Frances Macartney-Porteous. They had three sons and one daughter.

In late eighteenth-century Ireland, when patronage and political connections counted for much, and government management of Irish affairs called for considerable skill, Agar was well placed to receive recognition, and he relentlessly pursued his political and ecclesiastical ambitions. He was described by one contemporary as 'very active in business, a good speaker, and very ambitious of being employed by government as minister in the house of lords' (G. O. Sayles, ed., 'Contemporary sketches of the members of the Irish parliament of 1782', *Proceedings of the Royal Irish Academy*, 56/ 3c, 1954, 273). Through family and other connections (his brother James, Viscount Clifden, alone controlled four borough seats), he was a power to be reckoned with, and when Edmund Sexten Pery, speaker of the Irish Commons and one of his family connections, sought Agar's support in obtaining a bishopric in 1780

(secured in 1781) for his brother William Cecil he was solemnly assured that his and the candidate's dependability as 'the sincere and steady friend of administration' was crucial (*Buckinghamshire MSS*, 160–62). Yet Agar himself was forced briefly into opposition during the regency crisis mainly because of the English whig connections of his maternal uncle and mentor Welbore Ellis (later first Lord Mendip). He soon returned to his allegiance, being described by one modern historian as 'one of the fastest movers throughout the crisis' (McDowell, 342). Although never a major political figure such as Boulter or Stone, he was a prominent member of the 'Irish cabinet' of the 1780s and 1790s, and was a formidable draftsman of legislation and parliamentary speaker. His standing in the House of Lords was such that he was able both to carry and defeat measures there, occasionally against the wishes of government, and came nearly top of the ballots for the secret committees of 1793, 1797, and 1798, set up to inquire into the United Irishmen and the causes of the unrest that foreshadowed the rising in 1798.

Agar's experience of agrarian agitation in the Munster dioceses of Cloyne and Cashel, particularly the Rightboy resistance to the payment of tithes to the established Church of Ireland, convinced him of the vulnerability of that church, which played a vital role in maintaining the constitution, and informed his opposition to Catholic relief, which he believed would undermine the principle of protestant ascendancy. His opposition to concessions to Catholics and dissenters was strongly felt, yet not expressed to the point of defeating government relief measures. In 1780 he protested against the bill to relieve dissenters of the sacramental test as making a material alteration in the constitution, but his most trenchant criticism was reserved for the Catholic relief bills of 1782, 1792, and 1793. The Catholic promoters of relief understandably regarded Agar as adamantly opposed to their cause, given his uncharacteristically tactless and ill-considered reference to Catholicism as 'a religion for knaves and fools' (*Report … on the Roman Catholic Bill*, 245), a remark that drew a rebuke from Lord Donoughmore. Despite commenting that the 1793 bill, by extending the parliamentary franchise to Catholics, would concede too much, Agar reluctantly voted for the measure because it had been framed by 'his majesty's ministers in this country' (*A Full and Accurate Report*, 384–5). His loyalty was rewarded by his creation in 1795 as Baron Somerton.

Agar's temperament responded freely to the rebellion of 1798, and in the face of those politicians and others who advocated a degree of leniency towards the insurgents and their leaders—for example, through their preference for transportation rather than execution—he pressed for the death penalty as a surer deterrent. In the matter of the proposed union of Ireland with Great Britain in the aftermath of the rebellion he showed himself more open to negotiation, and his behaviour during the immediate pre-union period provides an example of his capacity to extract the maximum reward from government for his services. The distribution of honours that paved the way for the passing of the Act of Union presented him with a fresh opportunity for promotion in the church. He had misgivings about the measure, partly because he believed that the position of the established Church of Ireland was not secured thereby; he was proved right in this, for disestablishment came within seventy years. He also criticized the provision whereby the Irish spiritual peers would be represented at Westminster by one archbishop and three bishops, the archbishops taking their turn. In Agar's view the four archbishops alone would have provided the appropriate representation. He gave way, persuaded by his advancement from baron to Viscount Somerton in 1800, and his election as one of the original twenty-eight Irish representative peers, which secured him a seat for life, as well as by confirmation from government that the archbishopric of Dublin might soon come his way, which it did in the following year. His ambitions for Armagh were not given official encouragement as the crown had since 1701 passed over Irish-born prelates for that office. Nor did his ambitions end there, and in 1806 he received the earldom of Normanton. Not, as his wife explained, that he 'is a flight of stairs above it in his own person already' but 'for his dear son's advantage' (M. MacDonagh, *The Viceroy's Post-Bag*, 1904, 207–8).

Agar was a friend of the equally career-conscious John Hely-Hutchinson, provost of Trinity College, Dublin, who had strong views on the improvement of Irish education, and some correspondence between them would suggest that Agar held thoughtful views on the subject, such as raising the age of entry to the college, and bringing masters from leading English schools to enhance those in Ireland. He served on a government commission of inquiry into Irish education, established in 1806, but to judge from the minutes he neither attended nor contributed much. More notable was the great wealth that he accumulated, partly, it was incorrectly claimed by his critics, by a tendency to treat episcopal property as his own. His fortune was divided between the English and Irish Funds, and he had cash in the Bank of Ireland (often called the National Bank) and some bank stock.

Agar died on 14 July 1809 at his home in Great Cumberland Place, London, and was buried on 21 July in Westminster Abbey, where an immodest but accurate inscription on his monument credits him with the building of at least seventeen churches and twenty-two glebe houses, and with the framing of eighteen acts of parliament for regulating and supporting the Church of Ireland. He is also credited with instigating the completion (apart from the spire) of the new cathedral at Cashel which had been founded in the 1750s to replace the medieval edifice on the Rock and had languished ever since. He paid part of the cost of building it out of his own personal resources, and donated to it what was then one of the best organs that money could buy. To him was also attributed the high standard of music at the cathedral and in the metropolitical province of Cashel generally. His widow died on 25 October 1826, aged seventy-four, at 13 Montague Square, and was buried with him in Westminster Abbey.

KENNETH MILNE

Sources *Correspondence of Charles, first Marquis Cornwallis*, ed. C. Ross, 3 vols. (1859) · *Memoirs and correspondence of Viscount Castlereagh, second marquess of Londonderry*, ed. C. Vane, marquess of Londonderry, 12 vols. (1848–53) · A. P. W. Malcomson, *John Foster: the politics of the Anglo-Irish ascendancy* (1978) · *A report of the debates in both houses of the parliament of Ireland on the Roman Catholic Bill* (1792) · *A full and accurate report of the debates in the parliament of Ireland in the session 1793 on the bill for the relief of his majesty's Catholic subjects* (1793) · A. P. W. Malcomson, *Archbishop Charles Agar: churchmanship and politics in eighteenth-century Ireland, 1760–1810* (Dublin, 2002) · R. B. McDowell, *Ireland in the age of imperialism and revolution, 1760–1801* (1979) · T. Bartlett, *The fall and rise of the Irish nation: the Catholic question, 1690–1830* (1992) · E. M. Johnston, 'The state of the Irish House of Commons in 1791', *Proceedings of the Royal Irish Academy*, 59C (1957–9), 1–56 · E. M. Johnston, 'Members of the Irish parliament, 1784–7', *Proceedings of the Royal Irish Academy*, 71C (1971), 139–246 · H. Cotton, *Fasti ecclesiae Hibernicae*, 6 vols. (1845–78) · *Journals of the House of Lords of the kingdom of Ireland*, 8 vols. (1783–1800) · GEC, *Peerage* · *The Times* (17 July 1809) · G. C. Bolton, *The passing of the Irish Act of Union: a study in parliamentary politics* (1966) · *The manuscripts of the earl of Buckinghamshire, the earl of Lindsey … and James Round*, HMC, 38 (1895)
Archives Beds. & Luton ARS, Stuart MSS · Hants. RO, corresp. and papers | BL, corresp. with Lord Hardwicke, Add. MSS 35728–35758, *passim* · NL Ire., letters to bishop of Limerick
Likenesses W. Say, mezzotint, pubd 1803 (after oil painting by G. C. Stuart, 1783–93), NG Ire. · portrait, Christ Church Oxf.
Wealth at death £400,000: GEC, *Peerage*, 642

Agar, Eileen Forrester (1899–1991), artist, was born on 1 December 1899 at Quinta la Lila, Flores, a suburb of Buenos Aires, Argentina, the second of three daughters of James Senior Agar (1860–1925), businessman, and his wife, Mary (Mamie), *née* Bagley (1875–1943), whose family came from Maine, New England. The Agars were one of the many Scottish families who emigrated to Argentina to make their fortunes, a feat James Agar achieved by becoming head of the family firm of Agar Cross. Agar was brought up in considerable style and comfort first in Argentina and then in England, to which the family repaired after her father's retirement in 1911. Showing an early aptitude for art, she was encouraged at school by Lucy Kemp-Welch. Her formal training began in 1918 when she attended weekly classes at the Byam Shaw School of Drawing and Painting. After a period at the sculptor Leon Underwood's Brook Green School at Hammersmith, London (1920–21), where she met Henry Moore, Gertrude Hermes, and Rodney Thomas, she studied part-time at the Slade School of Fine Art (1921–4) under Henry Tonks.

Striking out on her own, Agar set up home and studio in Chelsea, but destroyed most of her early work. A woman of considerable beauty, she was never short of admirers. On 4 November 1925 she married her fellow Slade student Robert Arthur (Robin) Bartlett (1900–1976) and lived for periods in France. The relationship was not a success. Agar dated what she called her emotional nativity to 1926 when she met the man who was to be her companion for fifty years and who eventually became her second husband, on 29 February 1940. This was Joseph Bard (1892–1975), a Hungarian writer then married to the American journalist Dorothy Thompson. Agar and Bard took a flat together in London, where Agar painted *Self-Portrait* (1927), which she considered her first successful work. Over the next three

Eileen Forrester Agar (1899–1991), self-portrait, 1927

years the pair travelled much abroad, living for a time in Portofino, Italy, where Ezra Pound befriended them, and Paris, where Agar studied under the Czech cubist Frantisek Foltyn. In 1930 Agar and Bard settled in a pair of flats in the same London block, which was to remain their base until 1958. Their friend Rodney Thomas, the architect, designed innovatively curving furniture for both studio and flats. In 1931 Bard, in collaboration with Leon Underwood, launched a quarterly arts magazine called *The Island*, which lasted for only four numbers but published contributions from Henry Moore, Naomi Mitchison, and C. R. W. Nevinson. Agar wrote a seminal piece in the fourth number (December 1931) entitled 'Religion and the artistic imagination', in which she expounded her theory of 'womb-magic', stressing the creative importance of the unconscious and the feminine imagination.

Agar's own work was developing rapidly and in 1933 she mounted her first solo exhibition, at the Bloomsbury Gallery in London. A retrospective of seven years' work, it included her early realist portraits, her Foltyn-influenced abstracts, and her latest imaginative paintings which attempted to combine the two in a new way. She began experimenting seriously with collage and sculpture, particularly after meeting the artist Paul Nash at Swanage in 1935. Nash was to play a crucial role in Agar's life until his death in 1946, both as lover and as artistic mentor. In 1936, somewhat to her surprise, Agar was selected to exhibit in the International Surrealist Exhibition in London, showing three oils and five objects. Her brand of lyrical and imaginative painting was in fact quite independent of surrealism, but Agar thoroughly enjoyed being part of a movement with which she had so much in common, and which was also taking Europe by storm. She remained loyal to surrealism even when it went out of fashion in the post-war years, but she lived long enough to see its popularity return fifty years later in the mid-1980s.

Agar's principal artistic output was as draughtsman, painter, collagist, and maker of objects. She was an infrequent printmaker but enjoyed a very active period of taking photographs in the 1930s, which resulted in a number of telling images. Her first serious photos were taken of the rocks at Ploumanach in Brittany when on holiday there in 1936; subsequent snapshots record a magical holiday in 1937 at Mougins in the south of France with Picasso, Éluard (with whom she had a brief affair), and Man Ray. Meanwhile Agar exhibited with the surrealists in England and New York.

The Second World War disrupted Agar's life and art. Although she continued to exhibit and painted a number of watercolour landscapes in the Lake District, she felt her work was to some extent on hold. Only when she travelled to Tenerife to stay with friends in the early 1950s was her imagination fully released once more. So began a middle period of consistent productivity, of highly coloured, imaginative, and lyrical paintings mixing myth and nature, that became even brighter when she turned to acrylic paints in 1965. In 1971 she was given a retrospective exhibition at the Commonwealth Institute in London. Although she continued to paint until 1986, when she completed a series of paintings of the Ploumanach Rocks she had photographed half a century before, and after that concentrated on collages, much of her time in the late 1970s and early 1980s was taken up with a book to commemorate her second husband, who died in 1975. This eventually metamorphosed into her autobiography, entitled *A Look at my Life*, published in 1988. Two highly successful commercial exhibitions, a host of surrealist group shows, and a television documentary, *Five Women Painters* (Channel 4, 1989), rendered her last years triumphant. She died at her home, Flat E, 47 Melbury Road, London, of heart failure, on 17 November 1991, and was buried with her second husband, Joseph Bard, in Gunnersbury cemetery, London, on 26 November. She had no children. Examples of her work are in the Tate.

ANDREW LAMBIRTH

Sources E. Agar and A. Lambirth, *A look at my life* (1988) • A. Lambirth, *Eileen Agar: a retrospective* (1987) [exhibition catalogue, Birch and Conran, London, 8 July–7 Aug 1987] • T. Grimes, J. Collins, and O. Baddeley, *Five women painters* (1989) • A. Simpson, D. Gascoyne, and A. Lambirth, *Eileen Agar* (1999) [exhibition catalogue, NG Scot., 1 Dec 1999–27 Feb 2000 and Leeds City Art Gallery, Leeds, 9 March–30 April 2000] • *The Independent* (19 Nov 1991) • *The Times* (20 Nov 1991) • personal knowledge (2004) • private information (2004)
Archives Tate collection, corresp., notebooks, diaries, and draft autobiography | FILM BFI NFTVA, *Omnibus*, BBC1, 20 Nov 1983 • BFI NFTVA, 'Five women painters', Channel 4, 7 Oct 1989 • BFI NFTVA, documentary footage | SOUND BL NSA, National Life Story Collection, 'Artists' lives', 18 April 1990, C466/01/1–4
Likenesses E. F. Agar, self-portrait, oils, 1927, NPG [*see illus.*] • group portrait, photograph, 1936, Hult. Arch. • photographs, *c*.1936–1948, repro. in Agar and Lambirth, *A look at my life* • J. Bard, photograph, 1937, repro. in Agar and Lambirth, *A look at my life* • C. Beaton, photograph, 1937, repro. in Agar and Lambirth, *A look at my life* • Snowdon, photograph, *c*.1986, repro. in Agar and Lambirth, *A look at my life* • O. Eliason, photograph, *c*.1988, repro. in

Agar and Lambirth, *A look at my life*, cover · J. Weaver, photograph, repro. in *The Independent*

Agard, Arthur (1535/6–1615), archivist and antiquary, was born at Foston, Derbyshire, the second of the three sons of Clement Agard of Foston and his wife, Eleanor, daughter of Thomas Middlemore of Edgbaston. He matriculated from Queens' College, Cambridge, at Michaelmas 1553, but nothing further is known of his education, and there is no doubt that the greater part of his learning came by his study of the records of which he had charge. His knowledge of the common law may have been acquired first in one of the inns of court. Anthony Wood records that Agard was made deputy chamberlain of the exchequer as early as 1570 by Sir Nicholas Throckmorton, and although there is no official record of the nomination, Wood's claim is borne out by Agard's own statement, appended to his will on his deathbed, that he had been deputy chamberlain under Throckmorton and his six successors, 'sub quibus militavi 45 annis' ('under whom I served for forty-five years'; PRO, PROB 11/126, fol. 95v). Perhaps like other gentlemen of no particular fortune he began by studying the law, but unlike most others found himself drawn to study its history through its incomparable records, and secured congenial employment at the exchequer by Throckmorton through friendship or patronage. Only in 1603, however, is he known to have received a formal appointment.

The formal stages of Agard's career are thinly documented, but there is abundant evidence of his activities. He combined great energy with a strong critical sense, and concerned himself as much with the safe keeping and good order of the records as with their contents. At the same time his mind ranged over those contents, over changes in handwriting, over the origin and meaning of technical terms that had fallen into disuse, and over the history of the government of England before and since the conquest. Those interests led him to make inventories and abstracts of records, and to seek to impose order in their keeping. He graphically described the principal enemies of archives as fire, water, rats, and mice, and, in some respects the most troublesome of all, misplacement. Fire could be avoided by forbidding the use of naked lights, though lanterns might be permitted; protection against damage by water required careful maintenance and regular inspection; rats and mice might be frustrated by strong boxes. Misplacement, however, was of two kinds. There was the ever-present risk of returning records to the wrong shelf or strongroom, but there was also the danger that records removed for reference elsewhere, even by duly attested warrant, might never be returned. Records can be at risk from their custodians' colleagues.

Those were the precepts that informed the inventory that Agard and his colleagues compiled of the four treasuries at Westminster. The treasuries were then the principal strongrooms in which the records of the crown—the archive now known as the public records—were stored. They comprised the treasury of the receipt, the treasury over the little gatehouse of the New Palace, that in the

chapter house of the abbey, and the treasury built in the cloisters. It appears from Agard's comments on the treasuries, and from some of the many annotations that he made on the records themselves, that he was himself responsible for some recent rearrangements. It is also interesting, in the light of his comments on the importance of keeping the records in their proper places, that Domesday Book, which he and others recognized as a jewel of the collection, was then kept apart in his own office. It was later lodged in the chapter house, which in Agard's day contained plea rolls and the great collection of feet of fines, a unique record of titles to land running continuously from the late twelfth century and now extending to Victoria's reign. The plea rolls had been a particular object of Agard's attention, for he was substantially responsible for the celebrated compilation of cases known as the *Abbreviatio placitorum* (published by the Record Commission in 1811), which has served as a guide to the rolls over many centuries. In its present form the *Abbreviatio* is the work of various hands, but Agard's own contributions, notably in the abstracts of the rolls of Edward I and Edward II, are distinctive and notably competent.

By the time the inventories were completed in 1610, Agard had been at work on the records for at least forty years. His annotations and transcripts show that he had ranged widely, both among the public records and in cartularies and chronicles, and that he was at all times as much aware of the uses to which historical documents could be put as he was of the need to keep them securely and in good condition. The archive was in daily use as an administrative resource, but its integrity and gradual development over some 500 years gave it an exceptional historical value. Despite the conservatism to which the records attested, however, the changes of the sixteenth century had interrupted tradition, most obviously in religious observances, but in practice in much else. The middle ages therefore became an object of study, and needed interpretation. The first antiquarian society in England assembled in the later years of Elizabeth I's reign, and Agard was prominent among its members.

The meetings of the Elizabethan Society of *Antiquaries are not closely documented, but a list dating from *c*.1592, in Agard's own hand, shows a settled membership of about twenty-four. The meetings continued with some regularity until 1607, and over those years explored such topics as the origins of titles of nobility, the antiquity of the common law, castles, parliaments, and measurements of land. Agard's contributions were of particular cogency. He drew on various occasions on a study of Domesday Book which was the first of its kind, and the precursor of many scholarly discussions. It had led him to examine the text known as the *Dialogus de Scaccario*, a unique account of the administration of the kingdom in the twelfth century, which he identified and attributed (correctly) to Richard fitz Nigel, Henry II's treasurer.

Upon the death of his wife, Margaret Butler, in 1611 Agard raised a monument to her in the cloister of Westminster Abbey, near the door of the chapter house. He died between 22 and 24 August 1615 in his eightieth year, and was also buried in the abbey, with an inscription which describes him justly as a diligent examiner of the records in his care. By his will, dated 16 January 1615 but concluded on 22 August following, he made bequests of money, plate, and clothing to various members of his family, particularly to the children of his deceased brother Geoffrey. Of them, William Agard, presumably the eldest son, was appointed his executor and residuary legatee, receiving lands that Agard had bought in Staffordshire. To Sir Robert Cotton, a colleague and associate of many years whom he described as 'a moste faithefull and deere freind', he bequeathed twenty 'manuscripts of antiquitie' of Cotton's own choosing (PRO, PROB 11/126, fol. 95r). The will is accompanied by a schedule of the papers, original and manuscript, which Agard willed to the treasurer and chancellor of the exchequer to deposit with the other records of the department.

In his constructive concern for the records Agard is recognizably the first of a long line of such custodians. His work on Domesday Book places him with Abraham Farley and many later learned commentators. Agard's indexes have been gratefully used by many students before and since the opening of the Public Record Office, and their usefulness has not been exhausted in the twenty-first century.   G. H. MARTIN

Sources will, PRO, PROB 11/126, fols. 94v–95v • BL, Stowe MSS, 527–531 • F. Palgrave, ed., *The antient kalendars and inventories of the treasury of his majesty's exchequer*, RC, 2 (1836) • *A collection of curious discourses written by eminent antiquarians*, ed. T. Hearne, rev. T. Aylotte, 2 vols. (1771) • *The visitation of Derbyshire … by William Dugdale*, ed. G. D. Squibb, Harleian Society, new ser., 8 (1989) • G. O. Sayles, ed., *Select cases in the court of king's bench*, 7 vols., SeldS, 55, 57–8, 74, 76, 82, 88 (1936–71), vol. 2 • Wood, *Ath. Oxon.*, new edn, 2.427–8 • M. McKisack, *Medieval history in the Tudor age* (1971) • D. C. Douglas, *English scholars, 1660–1730*, 2nd edn (1951) • *Guide*, PRO (HMSO, 1963?) • Venn, *Alum. Cant.*, 1/1.9 • J. L. Chester, ed., *Westminster Abbey register* (1876)

Archives BL, collectanea, Stowe MSS 527–531 • PRO, indexes, 1 class INDI

Wealth at death see will, PRO, PROB 11/126, fols. 94v–95v

Agas [Agus], **Benjamin** (*bap.* 1622, *d.* 1689), clergyman and ejected minister, was born in Wymondham, Norfolk, the son of Edward Agas, the vicar of Wymondham, where he was baptized on 5 September 1622. In 1639 he entered Corpus Christi College, Cambridge, graduating BA in 1643 (incorporated at Oxford in 1653, as Haggas) and proceeding MA in 1657. If the Edward Agas who in 1645 was one of five ministers nominated to the Staindrop classis, Durham, was his father, as seems likely, then it was probably from him that Agas learned his presbyterian principles.

Agas became rector of Chenies, Buckinghamshire, on 30 November 1648. A sermon he preached at the instigation of one Abraham Chambers before the lord mayor, Sir Christopher Pack, and aldermen of the City of London at St Paul's on 9 September 1655 was published as *The Male of the Flock* (1655) with a dedication to William Russell, fifth earl of Bedford. When, shortly before the Act of Uniformity came into force on Black Bartholomew day 1662, Agas was asked his intentions, he replied that 'such things were

required and enjoyed, as I could not swallow, and therefore should be necessitated to march off, and sound a Retreat' (Agas, *Antidote*, 6). Three years after his ejection he was still living at Chenies. In August 1665 he became chaplain to Arthur Annesley, first earl of Anglesey, a position he held until at least 1674.

Calamy attributes to Agas the anonymous *Gospel Conversation* (1667), recommending it as 'well worthy the Perusal of pious Christians' (Calamy, *Continuation*, 1.143), and also an unnamed 'handsome Sheet in Vindication of Nonconformity' (Calamy, *Abridgement*, 2.107). This was *A Letter from a Minister to a Person of Quality, Shewing some Reasons for his Non-Conformity*, an undated folded folio sheet addressed to an unidentified lady and signed A. B. It justifies as the chief grounds for nonconformity unwillingness to repudiate the solemn league and covenant and inability to subscribe unfeigned assent and consent to all in the Book of Common Prayer: 'A man might well think that this Book … dropped immediately out of Heaven, and … is nothing else but a continual Oracle from first to last' (p. 1). The *Letter* was defended from the animadversions of Edward Stillingfleet's *The Unreasonableness of Separation* (1681) by the anonymous *Antidote Against Dr. E. Stillingfleet's 'Unreasonableness of Separation'* (1681). This Calamy attributes to Agas (Calamy, *Continuation*, 1.143); and the author of the *Antidote* incidentally identifies himself as the writer of the *Letter*.

That Agas's churchmanship and theology set him in the moderate wing of nonconformity is suggested by his being one of the fifteen presbyterian ministers who in 1681 subscribed the *Judgement of Non-Conformists, of the Interest of Reason, in Matters of Religion* of which Richard Baxter was the compiler (other signatories included, besides Baxter himself, Thomas Manton and William Bates). At the Middlesex sessions, 1682, Agas was found guilty of repeatedly holding conventicles from July to November at either his home or an unspecified meeting-place in the London parish of St Giles-in-the-Fields and was fined £840. On 30 April 1687 he accompanied the nonconformist ministers Vincent Alsop and Daniel Burgess the younger in a delegation which presented an address of thanks to James II for his declaration of indulgence (Alsop's speech on the occasion was published anonymously as *The Humble Address of the Presbyterians*, 1687).

Agas died some time during May 1689. Under 30 May the New England judge Samuel Sewall, then on a visit to England, wrote in his diary:

> went to the Funeral of Mr. Agust, Non-conf. Minister, who used to preach on the Sabbath where Mr. Alsop keeps his Lecture. Hath left some Thousands to a little Daughter of 2 or 3 years old. Buried at St. Giles' Church from the 3 Compasses, Kirby Street, Hatten Garden, Dr. [Thomas] Gilbert principal Bearer. (Sewall, 1.217–8)

This entry suggests that towards the end of his life Agas preached either to the presbyterian church meeting in Tothill Street, Westminster, of which Vincent Alsop became pastor in 1677, or at Pinners' Hall, where Alsop was a lecturer from 1685. Agas's will, signed on 21 May 1689 as of St Andrew's parish, Holborn, shows him to have been a man of means, with property in St Giles' parish, London, in Helpstone, Northamptonshire, Hockley, Essex, and elsewhere. The will makes no mention of his wife, who presumably predeceased him, but it confirms Sewall's statement about his daughter, Philips; Agas left his entire estate to her, with the proviso that if she were to die childless it should pass to Corpus Christi College, Cambridge, to establish fellowships for two scholars from Wymondham, to found a school at Wymondham (the schoolmaster to be paid £50 per annum if learned in Greek and Hebrew), and to provide £10 apiece to ten scholars from the Wymondham school sent to Cambridge, 'being perfect Hebricians'. N. H. KEEBLE

Sources B. Agas, *The male of the flock* (1655) · [B. Agas], *Gospel conversation* (1667) · A. B. [B. Agas], *A letter from a minister to a person of quality, shewing some reasons for his non-conformity* [n.d., 1679/80] · [R. Baxter], *The judgement of non-conformists, of the interest of reason, in matters of religion* (1681) · [B. Agas], *An antidote against Dr E. Stillingfleet's 'Unreasonableness of separation'* (1681) · S. Sewall, *The diary … 1674–1729*, ed. M. Hasley Thomas, 2 vols. (New York, 1973) · E. Calamy, ed., *An abridgement of Mr. Baxter's history of his life and times, with an account of the ministers, &c., who were ejected after the Restauration of King Charles II*, 2nd edn, 2 vols. (1713) · E. Calamy, *A continuation of the account of the ministers … who were ejected and silenced after the Restoration in 1660*, 2 vols. (1727) · Calamy rev. · Venn, *Alum. Cant.* · W. A. Shaw, *A history of the English church during the civil wars and under the Commonwealth, 1640–1660*, 2 vols. (1900) · *Reliquiae Baxterianae, or, Mr Richard Baxter's narrative of the most memorable passages of his life and times*, ed. M. Sylvester, 1 vol. in 3 pts (1696) · W. Kennett, *A register and chronicle ecclesiastical and civil* (1728) · DNB

Agas, Radulph [Ralph] (*c.*1540–1621), land surveyor, was probably a native of Stoke by Nayland in Suffolk. His parents are not known, but it is likely he was a relative of Edward *Aggas, son of Robert Aggas of Stoke by Nayland. Radulph (or Ralph) was physically disabled and appears to have been based at Stoke throughout his life; his wife's identity is unknown but he had at least three sons and two daughters.

Agas's own statements in 1596 and 1606 suggest that he started practising as a surveyor about 1566. The earliest work that can be attributed to him is a map of land at West Lexham, Norfolk, in 1575, one of the first known estate maps drawn to scale. Agas was one of the leaders of the emerging body of skilled land surveyors. Many of his subsequent surveys and maps of estates were of lands in Bedfordshire, Essex, Norfolk, and Suffolk, and he also worked further afield: he surveyed land at Carlton-cum-Willingham in Cambridgeshire; in 1583 he surveyed estates of Corpus Christi College, Oxford, in Berkshire, Gloucestershire, and Oxfordshire as well as in Bedfordshire; in 1597 he surveyed land in the fens; and in the following year he worked at Cobham in Surrey. He was also an early maker of town maps, mapping Oxford in 1578 as if seen by a bird flying over it; this plan was engraved on eight plates and published ten years later. He mapped Dunwich town and haven in Suffolk in 1587. A map of Cambridge dated 1592, formerly attributed to Agas, is now thought more likely to have been by John Hamond; nor is Agas now believed to have been the author of the map of London with which he was previously credited. In 1600 he was marshal of Covenham in Lincolnshire. His latest

known professional appearance dates from 1606, when he gave an opinion to commissioners inquiring into concealed lands belonging to the crown.

Agas deplored contemporary practices by untrained surveyors, and in 1596 published *A Preparative to Platting of Landes*, a pamphlet in which he advertised his methods and experience. By recommending—and using—the theodolite, he placed himself among those mathematical practitioners who were promoting geometrical methods of land measurement. In a later advertisement, of 1606, Agas claimed wide-ranging skills, such as reading old documents and restoring any that were unclear, finding weights and measures of solid bodies, writing in a minute script, and replanting trees; he also announced a recipe for the preservation of the eye. During his visits to London he lodged at various inns: at the Flower de Luce, over against the Sun without Fleetbridge in 1596, and at the sign of the Helmet in Holborn at the end of Fetter Lane ten years later.

It seems that Agas enjoyed occasional support from Lord Burghley and Robert Cecil and this stood him in good stead in some of his legal controversies. Between 1578 and 1583 Agas was rector of Gressenhall, Norfolk, and during these years he complained to the privy council of a parish campaign of persecution against him which brought him into discredit with his bishop. In 1581 his enemies were reprimanded, but when he tried to further the causes of protestantism and justice in 1589 and later, and accused Sir William Waldegrave (the chief landowner of Stoke by Nayland), Lady Waldegrave, and others of offences which included sedition and recusancy, he had a harder time. Agas was convicted of slander by the court of king's bench and imprisoned, but he presented another petition to the privy council, perhaps through his contacts with the Cecils, and was released in March 1591. He was back before the courts in 1595, this time in Star Chamber, accused of issuing seditious pamphlets. In 1598 he was there again, when his efforts to obtain for the crown its rights from the wardship of the estates of a neighbour, John Payne, met with severe opposition. Agas and his two elder sons, Robert and Thomas, were described as lewd, perverse, and quarrelsome, but Thomas Browne, the royal farmer of Payne's lands, wrote to Cecil on Agas's behalf and the surveyor escaped perpetual imprisonment. Agas died on 26 November 1621 at Stoke by Nayland and was buried there the next day. SARAH BENDALL

Sources D. MacCulloch, 'Radulph Agas: virtue unrewarded', *Proceedings of the Suffolk Institute of Archaeology*, 33 (1973–5), 275–84 · I. Darlington and J. Howgego, *Printed maps of London, circa 1553–1850* (1964) · R. Agas, *A preparative to platting of landes and tenements for surveigh* (1596) · F. W. Steer and others, *Dictionary of land surveyors and local map-makers of Great Britain and Ireland, 1530–1850*, ed. P. Eden, 2nd edn, ed. S. Bendall, 2 vols. (1997) · H. Hurst, *Oxford topography: an essay*, OHS, 39 (1899) · *Proceedings of the Society of Antiquaries of London*, 2nd ser., 6 (1873–6), 81–99 · E. G. R. Taylor, 'The surveyor', *Economic History Review*, 17 (1947), 121–33 · T. Gardner, *An historical account of Dunwich* (1754) · *GM*, 2nd ser., 35 (1851), 468–9 · A. S. Mason, 'A measure of Essex cartography', *Essex 'full of profitable thinges'*, ed. K. Neale (1996), 253–68 · P. D. A. Harvey, *Maps in Tudor England* (1993) · R. Parker, *Men of Dunwich* (1980) · *Winthrop papers*, 1 (Boston, 1925), 237 · H. G. Aldis and others, *A dictionary of printers* *and booksellers in England, Scotland and Ireland, and of foreign printers of English books, 1557–1640*, ed. R. B. McKerrow (1910) · BL, Lansdowne MSS 73.29, 84.32, 165.4 · parish registers, Stoke by Nayland, 27 Nov 1621 [burial]

Archives Bodl. Oxf., maps and surveys · Cambs. AS, maps and surveys · CCC Oxf., maps and surveys · Essex RO, maps and surveys · Holkham Hall, Norfolk, maps and surveys · Norfolk RO, maps and surveys · Suffolk RO, Bury St Edmunds, maps and surveys · Surrey HC, maps and surveys | BL, Add. MSS, Egerton MSS, Lansdowne MSS, Sloane MSS

Agasse, Jacques-Laurent (1767–1849), painter, was born on 24 March 1767 at Geneva, and baptized there at the Temple Neuf on 21 April, the son of Philippe Agasse (1739–1827), merchant, and his wife, Catherine Audeoud (1737–1818). His family were merchants of Huguenot origin who had been established in Geneva since the early seventeenth century. Political unrest, an aristocratic sponsor, and the importance of the British school of sporting painting encouraged Agasse to spend most of his working career in Britain, where he died. He showed an early interest in studying horses, dogs, and farm animals at the family's country house in Crévin, Savoy, and drew from nature from the age of seven. In 1782 his father sent him to the École du Calabri, the state drawing school. Here he made friends with Firmin Massot (1766–1849) and Adam-Wolfgang Töpffer (1766–1847). The three were to form a distinct Genevese school of painting, although all were influenced by their visits to England. Even after Agasse had moved permanently to London, they continued to collaborate on paintings. Since the drawing school was weak in the fine arts, Agasse travelled to Paris in 1786 to further his training. Here he studied in the studio of the history painter Jacques-Louis David. At the same time he studied anatomy, dissection, and osteology at the Musée d'Histoire Naturelle.

Forced to return to Geneva by the French Revolution in 1789, Agasse there met the Hon. George Pitt (later second Baron Rivers) about 1790. Pitt invited him to England, where animal and sporting art was flourishing. His visit was brief; when the revolution ruined his parents financially, Agasse returned to Geneva, where he now had to paint for a living. Between 1794 and 1796 Agasse took refuge in Lausanne but in 1798 he became an associate of the drawing committee of the Société des Arts, now run by the state. He showed four paintings at its third exhibition: *Tumble from a Phaeton*, *Picture of Animals*, *Portrait of a Man with a Horse*, and *Dog*. Such subjects were to remain the backbone of his *œuvre*.

Following a brief stay in Paris, Agasse arrived in London in autumn 1800. He planned to obtain commissions from Lord Rivers's sporting friends, to sell via public exhibitions, and to publish prints. Six months after his arrival he exhibited two paintings at the Royal Academy: *A Disagreeable Situation* (priv. coll.) and *Portrait of a Horse, the Property of J. Abbot Esq.*. In 1801 he was commissioned to paint a portrait of *Gaylass*, a black mare owned by the prince of Wales's racing manager, which he exhibited at the Royal Academy the following year. Commissions for other portraits of thoroughbreds followed.

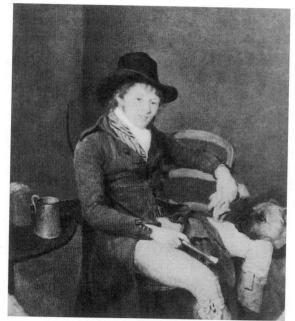

Jacques-Laurent Agasse (1767–1849), by Firmin Massot and Jacques-Laurent Agasse

Agasse continued to exhibit at the Royal Academy (until 1845), the British Institution (1807–11 and 1831–2), and various provincial exhibitions, but when Töpffer visited in 1816 he found his painting room stacked with unsold canvases and commented that 'He has never found homes for his exhibited pictures' (*Agasse*, 33). Agasse's collaboration with the engraver Charles Turner, established in 1802, may have been more financially successful. Together they published sporting prints, sold through a network of printsellers and by subscription. The arrangement lasted until about 1818 and Agasse went on to work with other print publishers, including Ackermann, Colnaghi, and Francis Moon.

Lord Rivers remained Agasse's principal patron. Agasse worked often at his house, Stratfield Saye, Hampshire, as well as his other estates. His portraits of Lord Rivers pursuing his coursing and racing interests are among Agasse's most outstanding works and include *Portrait of Lord Rivers Coursing at Newmarket with his Friends* (1818; Musée d'Art et d'Histoire, Geneva), and *Lord Rivers' Groom Leading a Chestnut Hunter towards a Coursing Party in Hampshire* (1807; Tate collection). Another patron was Francis Augustus Eliott, second Baron Heathfield; he appears in the painting *Gentleman on Horseback (Lord Heathfield)* (exh. RA, 1811; Musée d'Art et d'Histoire, Geneva). Heathfield was vice-president of the Royal Veterinary College and was able to gain access for Agasse to its dissection room and other facilities. The college commissioned six pictures showing the results of Lord Morton's experiments at cross-breeding a quagga (a South African equine quadruped, related to the zebra) and a 7/8 Arabian chestnut mare (1821; Royal College of Surgeons of England).

Better known today are Agasse's paintings of exotic animals, such as the life-sized *Two Leopards* (1808; priv. coll.), *Two Tigers* (1808), and *Two Lions* (1808; both priv. coll.), all bought by Rivers. The animals formed part of Polito's menagerie at Exeter 'Change, the Strand, London, where Agasse started to paint in 1803. Polito's son-in-law Edward Cross, who later took over the menagerie, was to become a lifelong friend. Probably through Cross's influence, George IV commissioned Agasse to paint his own exotic animals, the *Nubian Giraffe* (1827) and the *White-Tailed Gnus* (1828; both Royal Collection).

Agasse first lived in London with the Chalon family of painters—themselves of Swiss origin—at 8 Church Lane, Kensington. A few moves later he settled at 4 Newman Street, near Oxford Circus, at the time a centre of artistic life. Agasse broadened his *œuvre*, producing Thames river views such as *Landing at Westminster Bridge* (1818; Museum Stiftung Oskar Reinhart, Winterthur) and, using his landlord George Booth's children as models, some sensitively painted childhood genre scenes, for example, *The Pleasure Ground* (1830; Musée d'Art et d'Histoire, Geneva) and *An Important Secret* (1833; priv. coll.). Despite living in such an artistic honeypot, Agasse seems to have been isolated and unbending. Töpffer reported with concern in 1816, 'He is still the same man, quite out of place in this corrupt world with his rather starchy honesty and boundless candour' (*Agasse*, 21). His sister Louise Étiennette in a letter of 16 August 1819 reported that 'He has never been able to understand … that you cannot change people and that you cannot go blithely along pretending you have nothing to do with them and following your own brilliant notions and inspiration' (ibid., 22).

Agasse's great patron Rivers died in 1828; the area around Newman Street began to decline and so did Agasse's career. He still produced animal and childhood subjects but came to rely on potboiler portraits, mostly of members of his immediate circle such as the Cross family and the Swiss Huguenot community. In 1838 he moved near to Fitzroy Square, and in 1842, after an absence of almost a decade, exhibited at the Royal Academy *A Fishmonger's Shop* (1840; priv. coll.). He exhibited again in 1843, in 1844, and for the last time in 1845. He continued to paint unremarkable works until two months before his death in London on 27 December 1849. He was apparently unmarried.

Agasse's work has perhaps been underestimated. Less anthropomorphic than that of Landseer, it may lack the animal vitality of Stubbs, but has the same understanding of anatomy and sense of absolute accuracy. It shows the influence of the neo-classical and Romantic movements, with the freshness of working from nature. There is evidence that he was also responsible for the horses in the works of others. At the height of his career he was able to command prices of £300 for *Lord Rivers' Stud Farm* (1806–7; Yale U. CBA), and the number of copies commissioned of works such as *Miss Cazenove on a Grey Horse* (exh. RA, 1808), *Lord Heathfield* (exh. RA, 1811), and *Gaylass* indicate his reputation. Later portraits seem to have been commissioned out of sympathy and after his death his remaining works

were sold at Christies for a mere £21 15s. 6d. to pay for his funeral and burial at St John's Wood Chapel. Agasse's reputation was re-examined in 1989 with an exhibition at the Tate Gallery, London, jointly organized by the Musée d'Art et d'Histoire, Geneva, which has a large collection of his work. It was stated in the exhibition catalogue that Agasse showed 'a technique and sensitivity that made him second only to George Stubbs as a sporting artist and painter of animals' (p. 9).   H. J. BRACEGIRDLE

Sources *Jacques-Laurent Agasse, 1767–1849* (1988) [exhibition catalogue, Musée d'Art et d'Histoire, Geneva, and Tate Gallery, London, Nov 1988 – April 1989; incl. essays by R. Loche, D. Buyssens, and C. Sanger, and bibliography] • **Archives** Bibliothèque Publique et Universitaire, Geneva, Musée d'Art et d'Histoire, MS catalogue autographe de son œuvre, inv. no. 1906-I • **Likenesses** F. Massot, portrait, repro. in *Jacques-Laurent Agasse, 1767–1849*; priv. coll. • F. Massot and J.-L. Agasse, portrait, Museum Stiftung Oskar Reinhart, Winterthur [*see illus.*] • **Wealth at death** £21 15s. 6d.—paintings sold to cover funeral expenses: *Jacques-Laurent Agasse*

Agate, James Evershed (1877–1947), drama critic, was born at Pendleton, Lancashire, on 9 September 1877, the eldest of the five sons and one daughter of Charles James Agate (1832–1909), cotton manufacturer's agent, and his wife, Eulalie Julia Young, daughter of a widowed piano teacher. Although generally regarded during his lifetime as the writer from Manchester who had conquered London in the 'man from the provinces' manner of Arnold Bennett and J. B. Priestley, Agate was not of Lancashire ancestry. His father came originally from Horsham, Sussex, and his mother was a Yorkshirewoman who had been educated in Paris and Heidelberg and studied the piano under a pupil of Chopin. The young Agates were taught to speak French fluently and to appreciate the fine points of music and the arts. Their father was chairman of the committee of the Unitarian chapel which the family attended; James in his teens was its secretary. Charles Agate was also a keen theatregoer who had once run away from home to see Macready. He encouraged his children to visit good plays and took James to see Sarah Bernhardt perform; she became for the child the model of theatrical performance ever after; 'Her acting on that evening' he said later, 'unveiled for me the ecstasy of the body and the torture of the mind' (Harding, 19). His only sister, May, later studied under her in Paris.

Agate was educated at Giggleswick, where he topped his class in English, Latin, history, and French, and at Manchester grammar school. Oxford or Cambridge would have suited him perfectly but he left school in 1896 to enter into his father's business, learned to weave, and sold grey cloth for seventeen years. Although his mind was more concerned with the arts than with the cotton trade, he was described as 'a fascinating mixture of the intellectual and the philistine' (Hobson, Knightley, and Russell, 88). From boyhood Agate had been a 'cricket fanatic' (Harding, 7); he later liked to live in Derbyshire, to dress like a sporting farmer, and to own and to exhibit show

James Evershed Agate (1877–1947), by Howard Coster, 1934

the chair of dramatic criticism on the *Saturday Review*, a covetable post once held by G. B. Shaw, whose contributions had first fired in Agate the ambition to become a drama critic. The talent that he displayed won him, in 1923, the theatre critic's post on the *Sunday Times*, which he held until his death. He was also drama critic for the British Broadcasting Corporation from 1925 to 1932.

Although his fiction was unsuccessful, Agate set his hand to writing about himself, and aspired to be the diarist of his epoch. In twelve years from 1935 he wrote nine volumes under the title *Ego*, the last appearing posthumously. They record chiefly the books, plays, personalities, club talk, and bohemian life of the time. But Agate had no interest in politics or social problems and this limited what might have been a wonderful landscape of London life.

Agate never lost his sense of himself as a character bestriding his own stage. Unashamedly the egoist, he played the part with a nice mixture of humour and panache. He had a 'feverish love of a daily crisis' (Hobson, Knightley, and Russell, 143). Editors generally were tolerant of his extravagance and exhibitionist nature, although doubts crept in as his reputation as 'another Oscar Wilde' spread (ibid., 150). In 1945 Lord Kemsley, proprietor of the *Sunday Times*, threatened to replace him with a 'married man' when he learned, belatedly, of his homosexuality (ibid., 276).

Agate was an 'immensely prolific' (*The Times*, 7 June 1947, 6) and at times inspired critic, writing with passion and scholarship. His *Sunday Times* articles were described as being in themselves 'wonderful performances' (Hobson, Knightley, and Russell, 146). He was a hedonist in the best sense, seeking pleasure of the senses to the end; but his hedonism was mitigated by discernment. He died at his home at Queen Alexandra Mansions, Grape Street, Holborn, London, on 6 June 1947 and was buried at Hendon Park cemetery, Mill Hill, on 11 June.

IVOR BROWN, *rev.* MARC BRODIE

Sources personal knowledge (1959) · *The Times* (7 June 1947) · J. Harding, *Agate* (1986) · H. Hobson, P. Knightley, and L. Russell, *The pearl of days: an intimate memoir of the Sunday Times, 1822–1972* (1972) · D. Ayerst, *Guardian: biography of a newspaper* (1971) · *WWW* · *CGPLA Eng. & Wales* (1947) · *The Times* (9 June 1947)
Archives Bodl. Oxf., corresp. with Sidgwick & Jackson · JRL, letters to Allan Monkhouse · Man. CL, Manchester Archives and Local Studies, MSS |FILM BFI NFTVA, news footage |SOUND BL NSA, P1197W C1 · BL NSA, performance recordings
Likenesses E. J. Burra, ink caricature, 1932, NPG · H. Coster, photographs, c.1933–1934, NPG [*see illus.*] · F. Mann, photograph, 1939, NPG · A. McBean, print, 1940–49, NPG · photograph, repro. in Hobson, Knightley, and Russell, *Pearl of days* · photograph, NPG · photographs, repro. in Harding, *Agate*
Wealth at death £2522 17s. 1d.: probate, 1 July 1947, *CGPLA Eng. & Wales*

hackneys, a pastime which he continued for much of his life.

A passionate theatregoer, Agate in January 1906 wrote a letter on the subject to the *Daily Dispatch* in Manchester. The editor printed it and asked for more, resulting in a weekly drama criticism column. After a year he joined the *Manchester Guardian* team of critics which included C. E. Montague and Allan Monkhouse, and under their guidance he 'quickly mastered the tricks of the trade' of journalism (Harding, 37).

During the First World War, with his experience of horses, Agate was sent as a captain in the Army Service Corps to buy hay in the south of France. This duty gave some leisure for writing. His first book, in the form of letters, *L. of C.* (*Lines of Communication*), came out in 1917 and was followed by a book of essays on the theatre, *Buzz, Buzz!* (1918). In his early twenties he had written a play called *The After Years* which was less than successfully realized, as was his later fictional output of another play and three novels, which have been described as 'of small import' (Harding, 25).

Agate married in France in 1918 Sidonie Joséphine Edmée Mourret-Castillon, daughter of a rich landowner from Salon. The marriage lasted only a short time. From then Agate was openly homosexual in his relationships.

After his return to London, Agate bought, with characteristic caprice, a general store in South Lambeth Road, a business venture which rapidly failed. But he was finding success as a critic. In 1921 Filson Young appointed him to

Aggas, Edward (*b.* in or before **1549**, *d.* **1625**?), bookseller and publisher, was the son of Robert Aggas (*d.* in or before 1564), of Stoke by Nayland, Suffolk, and probably related to Radulph *Agas, who was a native of the same place. He was apprenticed to the London stationer Humphrey Toy for nine years from Easter 1564, and probably took his freedom of the Stationers' Company about the period covered by the break in the records. He never rose above the rank of yeoman within the company.

From 1576 to at least 1595 Aggas worked at the sign of the Red Dragon at the west end of Paul's Churchyard, London; in 1603 he was in Long Lane, London, at the sign of the Oak Tree. He published many theological works and translations from the French; he probably translated some of the latter texts himself. His device, a wyvern rising out of a ducal coronet (illustrated by McKerrow, no. 199), is believed by some commentators to be merely a printer's ornament. A son, Elmore, was apprenticed to the London stationer Gregory Seton in November 1603.

Aggas buried one wife, Alice, in the parish of St Vedast, Foster Lane, in 1581 and another, Phoebe, in the parish of St James's, Clerkenwell, in 1607; he left a widow, Katherine, probably in early January 1625. His undated will, in which he asked to be buried in St Sepulchre's Church, was proved in January 1625; he left one surviving son, Samuel, upon whom, 'in regarde I accounte that he hath had a very sufficient some out of my labours, vizt, above forty poundes, together with the bringinge uppe of his three children, I cannot be perswaded to cast awaie any more' (PRO, PROB 11/145, fol. 72).   H. R. TEDDER, *rev.* I. GADD

Sources Arber, *Regs. Stationers* · *STC, 1475–1640* · W. A. Littledale, ed., *The registers of St Vedast, Foster Lane, and of St Michael le Quern, London*, 2, Harleian Society, register section, 30 (1903), 132 · R. Hovenden, ed., *A true register of all the christenings, mariages, and burialles in the parishe of St James, Clerkenwell, from … 1551 (to 1754)*, 4, Harleian Society, register section, 17 (1891), 96 [burials, 1551–1665] · W. A. Jackson, ed., *Records of the court of the Stationers' Company, 1602 to 1640* (1957) · R. B. McKerrow, *Printers' and publishers' devices in England and Scotland, 1485–1640* (1949) · will, PRO, PROB 11/145, fols. 71v–72r

Aggas, Robert (*c.*1620–*c.*1682), landscape and scene painter, was the son of Samuel Agas of St Andrew's parish, Holborn. The family was originally from Stoke by Nayland in Suffolk. Samuel Agas was the son of Edward *Aggas, a bookseller and printer, and relative of Radulph or Ralph Agas, a land surveyor and mapmaker. In 1635 Samuel was chosen for the livery and to serve as a steward of the Painter–Stainers' Company. He paid a fine rather than serve as warden in 1647, but was upper warden in 1653–4. He died at West Ham in April 1669.

Robert Aggas was considered a good landscape painter, both in oil and in distemper, and skilful in introducing architecture into his compositions. Buckeridge wrote in 1706 that he was 'reckoned among the best of our English landskip Painters; and became eminent, not so much by his labour and industry, as through the bent of his natural genius' (de Piles, 354–5). Robert was apprenticed to his father and made free of the Painter–Stainers' Company in 1646. In 1679 he presented the company with his only extant work, a landscape at sunset, which still hangs in the Painters' Hall. He was employed by Charles II as a scene painter for 'the theatre in Covent Garden', presumably the Theatre Royal, Drury Lane, but thought by Walpole to refer to the Dorset Garden Theatre (Walpole, 169). Redgrave said that he was also employed at the Blackfriars

(dem. 1655) and Phoenix (formerly the Cockpit) theatres. In 1677 he and another scene painter, Samuel Towers, petitioned the lord chamberlain against the King's Company for work done at the Theatre Royal. It was thought that Robert Aggas died in 1679, but he may still have been alive in 1682, when he and Towers were named in a petition for payment against the United Company of the King's Company and the Duke's Company of the Dorset Garden Theatre.   W. C. MONKHOUSE, *rev.* ARIANNE BURNETTE

Sources M. Edmond, 'Limners and picturemakers', *Walpole Society*, 47 (1978–80), 60–242 · W. A. D. Englefield, *The history of the Painter–Stainers' Company of London* (1950) · Highfill, Burnim & Langhans, *BDA*, vol. 1 · [B. Buckeridge], 'An essay towards an English school of painting', in R. de Piles, *The art of painting, with the lives and characters of above 300 of the most eminent painters*, 3rd edn (1754), 354–439 · H. Walpole, *Anecdotes of painting in England … collected by the late George Vertue, and now digested and published*, 2nd edn, 1 (1765) · E. K. Waterhouse, *The dictionary of British 16th and 17th century painters* (1988) · A. Nicoll, *A history of Restoration drama, 1660–1700*, 3rd edn (1940) · Redgrave, *Artists* · *A catalogue of the pictures, prints, drawings, etc., in the possession of the Worshipful Company of Painter–Stainers at Painters' Hall* (1908) · Vertue, *Note books*, vol. 2 · B. Weinreb and C. Hibbert, eds., *The London encyclopaedia*, rev. edn (1993)
Archives GL, MS 5667/1 (211, 219) · PRO, LC 5/190–191

Aggrey, James Emman Kwegyir (1875–1927), pastor and educationist, was born at Anomabu, Gold Coast, on 18 October 1875, the son of Kodwo Kwegyir Aggrey, a gold assayer and official at the court of the Fanti chiefdom of Anomabu, and his wife, Abena Andua. Neither parent was Christian, but in 1883 they had him baptized and sent him to the Methodist school in Cape Coast. In 1891, after a probationary year in charge of a nearby village school, he became a teacher in the school and in 1898 headmaster. In 1898 a bishop of the black American African Methodist Episcopal Zion (AMEZ) church arrived to recruit Africans for training in the United States as missionaries. Aggrey volunteered and was sent to Livingstone College, an AMEZ college in Salisbury, North Carolina. He did well in his studies, and graduated BA in 1902. But instead of returning as a missionary he stayed at Livingstone as a teacher and studied for AM and DD degrees, both conferred in 1912. He also took summer courses at Columbia University, New York, and was awarded an MA in 1922. On 8 November 1905 he married Rosebud Rudolf Douglass, a black American. They had four children.

From 1914 Aggrey was also pastor of two black congregations near Salisbury. Horrified by the squalor and degradation in which these mostly illiterate victims of white exploitation lived, he dropped his college-trained preaching for the pastoral mission of encouraging enterprise and self-respect. He advised them to use their plots of land to grow vegetables and raise chickens for sale, and to co-operate to build decent houses and buy fertilizer. His confident but unassertive manner, coupled with the rapid practical success of his efforts, impressed many local whites, who came to welcome the people's improved living conditions. This experience underpinned two of Aggrey's firm beliefs: that agriculture can be educational, and that black and white should live together in harmony.

In 1919 an American foundation, the Phelps-Stokes Fund, financed a commission to investigate education in Africa. Its inquiry was related to the controversy raging in America over whether 'the Negro' should not be given industrial and agricultural training rather than a literary education. To give the commission more weight by including an African among its otherwise white American and British membership, Aggrey was appointed a member. They toured most of sub-Saharan Africa, covering west and southern Africa in 1920–22, and eastern and, again, southern Africa in 1924. Aggrey was the star. Welcomed with amazed enthusiasm by Africans, his disconcertingly effortless self-confidence won over Europeans. The occasional racist insults he was ready to laugh off. In South Africa, where within three months he made 150 speeches, he also won official approval by denouncing Marcus Garvey's 'Back to Africa' message, which offended against racial harmony. Though uncompromisingly Christian, he was undogmatic and non-sectarian. He delighted his audiences with riddles and parables. His image of racial harmony was the piano keyboard, with its black and white keys, and he urged black people not to accept the status of chickens assigned to them but to stretch their wings and fly like eagles.

On Aggrey's visit to the Gold Coast he made friends with the governor, Sir Gordon Guggisberg (1869–1930), an unconventional colonial administrator who initiated far-reaching development projects. In 1924 Aggrey returned home and helped Guggisberg found Achimota College, an institute of higher education, where he was appointed assistant vice-principal. But he longed to return to Columbia to complete work for a doctorate. In 1927 he went on leave to New York, where, quite suddenly, on 30 July at St Nicholas Avenue, he died of meningitis. He was buried in Salisbury, North Carolina, the following month.

Somehow Aggrey always seems to have diffused the racial harmony he preached. He could win over white Kenya settlers as well as black American intellectuals (suspicious of his advocacy of agriculture), with whom, unknown to his white friends, he kept close contact. His own career, his relentless pursuit of academic qualifications, and his work for Achimota all showed that he would only be satisfied with the best for African education. Aggrey's indirect influence was also to shape the political history of Africa. After hearing him as a schoolboy, Nnamdi Azikiwe, first president of Nigeria, was inspired to go to the United States for education, as was Kwame Nkrumah, first president of Ghana, whom Aggrey taught briefly at Achimota. CHRISTOPHER FYFE

Sources E. W. Smith, *Aggrey of Africa: a study in black and white* (1929) · T. J. Jones, *Education in Africa* (1922) · T. J. Jones, *Education in east Africa* (1925) · K. J. King, *Pan-Africanism and education* (1971) · R. E. Wraith, *Guggisberg* (1967) · K. Nkrumah, *Ghana: the autobiography of Kwame Nkrumah* (1957) · K. A. B. Jones-Quartey, *A life of Azikiwe* (1965)

Archives NYPL, Schomberg collection, J. E. Bruce papers · Union Theological College, New York, C. H. Fahs papers

Likenesses photograph, repro. in Smith, *Aggrey of Africa*

A'Ghobhainn, Iain Mac. *See* Smith, Iain Crichton (1928–1998).

Agilbert (*d.* 679x90), bishop of the West Saxons, was from a leading Frankish family, certainly connected with the family of St Audoin (St Ouen), who died in 684, and probably with the royal Merovingian family itself. He was the second bishop of the West Saxons and, later, bishop of Paris. According to Bede (*Hist. eccl.*, 3.7), some time after Cenwalh had been restored as leader of the West Saxons in 646, Agilbert arrived in his kingdom. He was a 'Gaul' or Frank, who was already a bishop when he arrived, having been ordained in Francia, presumably without a see. Before his arrival in England he had been studying in Ireland. Cenwalh invited Agilbert to stay among the West Saxons as their bishop, in the see established by Birinus at Dorchester-on-Thames. This position Agilbert held 'for some years' until Cenwalh tired of his 'barbarous speech', which presumably means that the bishop never properly mastered the language of his hosts. The West Saxon kingdom was then divided into two sees, one being given to Bishop Wine. Agilbert, it is said, was deeply offended and left the kingdom. He then seems to have headed north to the court of the Northumbrian kings Oswiu and Aldfrith, for the life of St Wilfrid states that Agilbert ordained Wilfrid priest at Ripon at the king's command; this happened in 663 or 664. In 664 Agilbert appeared alongside Wilfrid and with his priest Agatho at the famous Synod of Whitby, where he championed the Romanist cause. It was, however, Wilfrid who spoke 'in his own tongue' for their side in the dispute, which again hints at Agilbert's poor command of English. Shortly after the synod, Agilbert was back in Francia where, along with eleven other bishops, he took part in Wilfrid's consecration as bishop at Compiègne; this also took place in 664. Although Bede refers to Agilbert in this context as bishop of Paris, he cannot have been appointed to that city until 666 or 667, for there is a charter of that date attested by Importunus, his predecessor as bishop there. Agilbert must have become bishop by 668, however, since in that year he entertained Theodore in Paris as the latter made his way from Rome to Canterbury to take up the archbishopric.

Agilbert's fortunes in England seem to have been governed by the tide of Mercian expansion, rather than to have been the result of his inability to speak English properly. He left southern England around the time the Mercians acquired control of the area to the south of the Thames valley, but at a later point (*c.*670), when Mercian influence in Wessex was on the wane, Cenwalh invited him back to become bishop of Winchester. Now bishop of Paris, Agilbert declined the offer and sent his nephew Leuthere in his place. He died some time between 679 and 690, and he was buried in the crypt which he had built at the double monastery of Jouarre, east of Paris, over which his sister Theodechild had presided as abbess.

Agilbert's career serves to emphasize the strong links between the Frankish and the English ruling élites in the mid-seventh century. His very name was the Frankish form of Æthelberht, which may suggest that he had some family relationship with the Kentish royal house, and it was at this time, according to Bede (*Hist. eccl.*, 3.8), that Earcongota (daughter of Eanbald, king of Kent) and several other Anglo-Saxon princesses joined Frankish monasteries, perhaps through the agency of Agilbert. At the same time that the bishop first appeared in England, the all-powerful mayor of the palace in northern Francia was Erchinoald. The mayor had acquired the Anglo-Saxon Balthild, whom, about 648, he provided as a wife for the Frankish king, Clovis II. On the latter's death in 657, Balthild emerged as a powerful dowager queen. Interestingly, Agilbert's departure from Francia to Ireland was probably at the time that Balthild first became queen, and his return to his homeland coincided with her fall from power in 663 or 664. Once back in Francia, Agilbert was clearly a supporter of Erchinoald's successor as mayor, the notorious Ebroin, whose most influential ally was Audoin, with whom Agilbert was also linked. It was no doubt at Ebroin's behest that Agilbert entertained Theodore in 668, for Bede tells of how the mayor monitored the archbishop's every move through Francia. The last that is heard of Agilbert is on another (and this time plainly disreputable) mission for Ebroin, some time between 676 and 679. It is therefore reasonable to speculate that Agilbert's stay in England was as an exile in retreat from the ruling faction of Erchinoald and, later, of Balthild—an exile which came to an end when Ebroin and Audoin got the upper hand in Francia. His sojourn in Ireland may likewise have had a dimension in Frankish politics, for it may have been he who prepared the way for the exile of the young king, Dagobert II, who was sent there some time between 651 and 657. Agilbert may also have played a part in Dagobert's return from Ireland in 676, which was arranged through the bishop's old friend, Wilfrid. His career in Ireland, England, and upon the continent invites speculation at every turn, but the overall impression is clear enough: Agilbert was a figure of international importance through whom Frankish influence on the development of the church in southern England was maintained. PAUL FOURACRE

Sources Bede, *Hist. eccl.* · E. Stephanus, *The life of Bishop Wilfrid*, ed. and trans. B. Colgrave (1927) · H. P. R. Finberg, *The early charters of Wessex* (1964) · J. Guerot, 'Les Origines et le premier siècle de l'abbaye', *L'Abbaye royale de Notre-Dame de Jouarre*, ed. Dom Y. Chaussy and others (1961) · A. Lohaus, *Die Merowinger und England*, Münchener Beiträge zur Mediävistik und Renaissance Forschung, 19 (1974) · P. Fouracre and R. Gerberding, *Later Merovingian France* (1996)

Aglen, **Sir Francis Arthur** (1869–1932), official in the Chinese service, was born at Mulgrave House in Scarborough on 17 October 1869, the son of Archdeacon Anthony Stocker Aglen, later rector of St Ninian's, Alyth, Perthshire, and his wife, Margaret Elizabeth, eldest daughter of Stephen Mackenzie, surgeon. He was educated at Marlborough College, and in 1888, on the advice of Sir Robert Hart, he joined the Chinese maritime customs service of which Hart was the head. That service played an important part in the economy of China, providing the government with its most reliable source of revenue, and underwriting the large foreign loans upon which it was dependent.

Between 1888 and 1900 Aglen served in a number of posts in Peking (Beijing), Amoy (Xiamen), Canton (Guangzhou), and Tientsin (Tianjin); in 1897 he was appointed to the rank of commissioner. Shortly after the Boxer uprising broke out in 1900 he was posted to Shanghai as officiating inspector-general while Hart was a refugee in the British legation under siege in Peking. In 1906 Aglen married Senga Marion, daughter of Professor Sir Isaac Bayley *Balfour, regius keeper of the Royal Botanic Garden, Edinburgh. They had three sons and two daughters; she died at sea in 1925.

Between 1901 and 1910 Aglen served as commissioner in Nanking (Nanjing) and Hankow (Hankou) and as chief secretary at the inspectorate-general, Peking. After a dispute with the Chinese authorities Hart left China on leave in 1908 and never returned, although he remained titular head of the customs service until his death in 1911. In 1910 Aglen became officiating inspector-general, and on Hart's death was appointed head of the service by the Chinese government.

During Hart's time the responsibilities of the customs had been concerned only with collecting duties and preventing smuggling; Chinese officials were responsible for banking the revenue and for using it to service loans and other financial obligations to foreign governments for which it was security. However, Aglen's appointment as inspector-general coincided with the anti-Manchu revolution of 1911–12, which caused the administrative arrangements of the Chinese to break down. Faced by these unprecedented difficulties, Aglen arranged for the safety and integrity of customs revenue by placing it in foreign banks in his own name. This was intended to be a temporary measure, but it was so successful that the Chinese authorities gave it formal recognition for the whole of Aglen's term as inspector-general (1911–27). In fact, in 1914 he was entrusted with the task of servicing loans guaranteed by customs revenue earmarked for that purpose. He was appointed KBE in 1918.

As political conditions in China became increasingly chaotic during the 1920s Aglen found his responsibilities becoming not only more onerous but also more difficult to carry out without coming into conflict with one or other of the Chinese factions making demands upon him as custodian of revenues of which he was in sole charge. His problems came to a head in 1927 when he was instructed by the Chinese government to collect surtaxes on foreign trade to which the treaty powers had not agreed, although the charges had been approved in principle during the Peking tariff conference of 1925–6. Aglen refused to allow his officers to collect these duties until they had been formally approved. In consequence, despite protests from the diplomatic corps, the Chinese government dismissed him from his office on 31 January 1927. In that year he became GCMG. Aglen also received many honours both from China and from other countries, including Japan, France, Italy, Denmark, Belgium, and Norway. On 2 July 1927 he married Anna Moore (*b.* 1883/4), daughter of Murray Pringle Ritchie, a shipping agent, of Santiago, Chile. Aglen died at Meigle Hospital, Meigle, Perthshire, on 26 May 1932. He was survived by his second wife.   H. F. OXBURY, *rev.*

Sources *The Times* (27 May 1932) · *WWW* · private information (1993) · *CGPLA Eng. & Wales* (1932) · b. cert. · m. cert. · S. F. Wright, *Hart and the Chinese customs* (1950)
Archives Mitchell L., NSW, letters to G. E. Morrison · SOAS, corresp. with C. A. V. Bowra and G. F. H. Acheson
Wealth at death £57,608 11s. 5d.: probate, 16 July 1932, *CGPLA Eng. & Wales*

Aglio, Augustine Maria [*formerly* Agostino Maria] (1777–1857), painter and lithographer, was born on 15 December 1777 in Cremona, Italy, one of several children of Gaetano Aglio, a notary, and Marianna Mondini. He moved with his family in 1787 to Milan, where he was educated at the Collegio dei Barnabiti. Having been admitted to the Accademia di Brera in Milan, he was taught painting by Andrea Appiani and ornamental drawing and design by Giocondo Albertolli.

Aglio served as a volunteer in the Legione della Repúbblica Cisalpina and fought in the battle of Faenza in 1797, then went to Rome for two years. There he entered the studio of the landscape painter Luigi Campovecchio. He was recommended by Canova to the architect William Wilkins, who in 1799 offered him employment as a draughtsman on his antiquarian expedition to Sicily, Greece, and Egypt. Aglio provided drawings for the aquatints to Wilkins's *The Antiquities of Magna Graecia* (1807). He returned to Rome in 1802. In 1803 Wilkins offered him the post of drawing-master at Caius College, Cambridge. Aglio accepted, but soon quarrelled with Wilkins, and went to London as a drawing-master. He married Laetitia Clarke, the daughter of a merchant, at St Anne's Church, Soho, on 16 March 1805.

In 1804 Aglio decorated the boxes in the King's Theatre, Haymarket, with Gaetano Marinari, and in 1808 he succeeded the latter there as a scene-painter. Other theatre commissions followed, notably from Drury Lane Theatre. In 1807 Aglio worked at Ackworth Park and painted frescoes at Woolley Hall in Yorkshire (and probably at Bretton Hall nearby). He also painted frescoes for the duke of Bedford at Woburn, Bedfordshire (*c.*1808). This was followed in 1810 by a commission to paint the lakes of Killarney, which he also reproduced as a set of lithographs. Other interior decorations of Aglio's in London included the Pantheon in Oxford Street (1811), the ceiling and the apse of the Roman Catholic chapel, Moorfields (1819), the Roman Catholic chapel in Duncan Terrace, Islington (1837), the pavilion in the gardens of Buckingham Palace (1843–5), and the Olympic Theatre (1849). Among other works were frescoes in the old Manchester town hall (1831). From 1807 to 1846 Aglio exhibited mainly landscapes at the Royal Academy and biblical subjects at the Society of British Artists. He normally signed his work 'A. Aglio'.

In 1809 Aglio made his first lithographs. This new autographic process suited his rapid drawing style, and he produced work in this medium for the rest of his career. His subjects included landscapes, portraits of the famous, the coronation of Queen Victoria, miscellaneous reproductive prints after other artists' work, and a set of 100 plates entitled *Architectural Ornaments* (1820–21). These provided useful examples of advanced French neo-classical design for silversmiths and others.

Aglio used lithography to advertise himself and illustrate his own works. The frontispiece to his book *Sketches of the Decorations in Woolley Hall, Yorkshire* (1821) is a lithographed self-portrait in the form of an idealized neo-classical bust, and precedes illustrations he made of his own frescoes.

The biggest print-making project Aglio undertook was *Antiquities of Mexico* (9 vols., 1830–48), which he illustrated with lithographs reproducing ancient Mexican hieroglyphics preserved in the royal libraries of Europe. Edward King, Viscount Kingsborough, had financed the project, but died bankrupt in 1837, plunging Aglio into financial difficulty as well. Unremitting work had always been Aglio's only solution, but in 1850 he suffered a stroke which partially paralysed him. Although he managed to complete some works, aided by his son, also Augustine Aglio, he was never to recover. He died in his son's house in Camberwell, London, surrounded by his family, on 30 January 1857, and was buried in Highgate cemetery. Examples of his prints and drawings are in the Print Rooms of the Victoria and Albert Museum and the British Museum.   CHARLES NEWTON

Sources F. Sacchi, *Cenni sulla vita e le opere di Agostino Aglio* (1868) · E. Croft-Murray, *Decorative painting in England, 1537–1837*, 2 (1970) · J. Elkan, ed., *Catalogue of the Searight collection of paintings* (1990) [microfiche]
Likenesses etching, repro. in Sacchi, *Cenni sulla vita* · lithograph (after self-portrait by A. Aglio), repro. in A. Aglio, *To Godfrey Wentworth junr esqre this series of sketches of the interior and temporary decorations in Woolley Hall, Yorkshire* (1821)

Aglionby, Edward (1520–1591?), member of parliament, was born at Carlisle, the son of Richard Aglionby, and was at Eton College about 1532. In 1536 he was admitted to a scholarship at King's College, Cambridge, where he was a fellow from 1539 to 1548. Here he graduated BA in 1540–41, and MA in 1544, being incorporated in that degree at Oxford much later, in 1566. In 1547 Aglionby became member of parliament for Carlisle. He had already made an important connection with the powerful Dudley family, writing to William Cecil in 1547 or 1548 of his service to John Dudley, Viscount Lisle. Following the death of Thomas Dalston, Aglionby was returned by January 1552 for Carlisle in a by-election, serving the city again in March 1553 and possibly in 1559. As a member for Carlisle he followed another Edward Aglionby (*d.* 1553), assistant deputy warden of the west marches and captain of Carlisle Castle, and Hugh Aglionby, clerk of the council to Katherine Parr, but the family relationships are obscure.

It is unclear whether Aglionby was implicated in Dudley's attempt to prevent Mary's accession, but in June 1554 he sued for a pardon for unspecified offences. By this time, however, he had begun to sink new roots in the west midlands. Aglionby's settling in Warwickshire was closely connected with his first marriage, about 1553, to Katherine, daughter of Roger Wigston (*d.* 1542) of Wolston, Warwickshire. Katherine was the widow of both Thomas Warren and Giles Forrester, and she brought property at Balsall to the marriage. Her new husband soon made this estate, called Temple Balsall, his home. The Dudley connection was strengthened by the union, since from July 1553 the earls of Warwick were lords of the manor of Temple Balsall. Aglionby accumulated extensive properties in Warwickshire, as well as parcels of land in Staffordshire and Northamptonshire.

Aglionby translated a work by Matteo Gribalde of Padua, with a preface by Calvin, which was published in 1550, but the end of Edward's reign rendered such books as dangerous as his political connections. The subsequent eclipse of the Dudleys probably explains his absence from public life until Elizabeth's accession. In December 1569 the treasure for the supply of the army sent to suppress the northern uprising was committed to Aglionby's charge. Though delayed by bad weather and lack of horses, it was reported on new year's day that he had arrived safely at Berwick with £10,000. In 1571–2 his public career blossomed through the influence of the Dudleys, who effectively controlled the government of the town of Warwick. At a meeting at the Burgess Hall on 26 March 1571 a letter was read out from Ambrose Dudley, earl of Warwick, in the favour of 'my friend Mr Edward Aglionby's sufficiency' to represent the town in the House of Commons, and the assembled company duly chose Aglionby and John Fisher as their two burgesses (Kemp, 26–9). Early in the parliamentary session, on 9 April, Aglionby spoke in the debate on the Bill for Church Attendance, arguing that private chapels of gentlemen should not be exempt from its provisions: there should be 'equality between the prince and the poor men' (Hartley, 205). In a second speech on 20 April he argued that the bill should be supported, since church attendance was a matter of 'outward show', of vital concern to the magistrate, but it should not be extended to the receiving of the sacrament, in which private conscience must have the decisive voice: 'The conscience of man is eternal, invisible, and not in the power of the greatest monarchy in the world, in any limits to be straitened, in any bounds to be contained' (ibid., 240). Aglionby's speeches contained several scholarly references to eminent authorities and were well received. He sat on the committee charged to consider this issue, and was also named to another concerned with the licences and dispensations granted by the archbishop of Canterbury.

The corporation of Warwick elected Aglionby as the town's recorder, in succession to his brother-in-law, Sir William Wigston, on 12 August 1572. On that date Warwick received a visit from Queen Elizabeth. The event was recorded in great detail in the town's black book, and includes an account of the long speech with which the new recorder welcomed the Queen. He noted the presence in the streets of a 'populous concourse of this multitude, the ways and streets filled with company of all ages, desirous to have fruition of your divine countenance'. But in his comments on the status and ambitions of Warwick, Aglionby seems to have struggled to reconcile the protocols of gender with those of monarchy. The queen's reply set him straight:

> Her majesty called him to her, gave her hand to kiss, and withal smiling said, 'Come hither little recorder. It was told me that you would be afraid to look upon me, or to speak boldly; but you were not as afraid of me as I was of you, and I now thank you for putting me in mind of my duty, and that should be in me.' (Kemp, 87–91)

From 1574 Aglionby acted in Warwick as a loyal local servant of the state, reporting to the privy council on unresolved property disputes and on activities deemed to be seditious. By 1561 he was on the commission of the peace in Warwickshire. In August 1581 he and the other justices were instructed to examine Sir William Catesby and to search his premises following the examination of the Jesuit Edmund Campion, with a view to exposing activities prejudicial to the state. About 1577 he was appointed the first recorder of Stratford upon Avon. In 1580 he succeeded John Throckmorton as recorder of Coventry. In August 1588, the year of the Armada, he was listed as one of the sixty Warwickshire gentlemen who contributed 100 horse from the county. By this time Aglionby's public career was coming to a close. On 29 September 1587 he had been replaced as recorder of Warwick, being 'content and desirous to leave the said room and office', 'because of his great age and impotency to travel and failing of sight' (Kemp, 382). Soon afterwards he was succeeded in the recordership of Coventry by Sir John Harington.

About 1572 Aglionby had bought lands at Barnacle, near Coventry, and it seems likely that here, having disgorged the bulk of his far-flung properties, he spent the years of his retirement from public life. The will of an Edward Aglionby of Barnacle, Warwickshire, was proved on 14 October 1591, but it makes no mention of the recorder's wife, Katherine, or their children: the widow, and executor, is named as Mary. If this testator is the same Edward Aglionby who was born in Carlisle in 1520, he had married again, and the children of his first marriage had perhaps died. Though the possibility of confusion certainly exists, the Barnacle connection, and the fact that Katherine is believed to have died soon after 1587, may suggest that the testator was in fact the Edward Aglionby here noticed.

STEPHEN WRIGHT

Sources HoP, *Commons, 1509–58* · HoP, *Commons, 1558–1603* · W. Dugdale, *The antiquities of Warwickshire illustrated*, rev. W. Thomas, 2nd edn, 2 vols. (1730) · T. Kemp, ed., *The Black Book of Warwick* [1898] · *VCH Warwickshire*, vols. 2–4, 8 · W. Sterry, ed., *The Eton College register, 1441–1698* (1943) · J. Nichols, *The progresses and public processions of Queen Elizabeth*, 3 vols. (1788–1805) · A. L. Beier, 'The social problems of an Elizabethan country town: Warwick, 1580–90', *Country towns in pre-industrial England*, ed. P. Clark (1981), 46–85 · T. E. Hartley, ed., *Proceedings in the parliaments of Elizabeth I*, 3 vols. (1981–95)

Wealth at death landed property at Barnacle, Warwickshire: value unknown

Aglionby, John (1566/7–1610). *See under* Authorized Version of the Bible, translators of the (*act.* 1604–1611).

Agnes (*fl.* 1410). *See under* Women in trade and industry in York (*act. c.*1300–*c.*1500).

Agnew family (*per.* 1817–1986), art dealers, maintained the firm established by **Thomas** [i] **Agnew** (1794–1871) in Market Street, Manchester, in 1817. Thomas Agnew was born in Liverpool on 16 December 1794, the posthumous son of John Agnew of Culhorn, Wigtownshire, and his wife, Jane Glover. His father was descended from the Sheuchan branch of the Agnew of Lochnaw family. After studying drawing and modelling in Liverpool, Thomas Agnew moved to Manchester, where he was apprenticed in 1810 to Vittore Zanetti, an Italian printseller and dealer in clocks and optical instruments. He became Zanetti's partner in September 1817; Zanetti retired in 1828, and Thomas became sole proprietor in 1835. Under his direction, Zanetti and Agnew increasingly dealt in works of art, print publishing, and picture frame carving and gilding.

On 19 February 1823 Thomas Agnew married Jane Garnet Lockett (*d.* 1864), daughter and coheir of William Lockett (*d.* 1856), a wealthy businessman and first mayor of Salford. Their son **Sir William Agnew**, first baronet (1825–1910), born on 20 October 1825 in Salford, established Agnews as a leading international firm. A second son, Thomas [ii], born in 1827, was followed by two more sons and four daughters. The elder Thomas, an ardent Swedenborgian, sent his sons William and Thomas to the Revd J. H. Smithson's Swedenborgian school in Salford; adhering to their father's faith, with its emphasis on good works, they absorbed its mixture of scientific, pantheistic, and theosophic doctrines.

After an apprenticeship to his father in 1840, William and his brother Thomas became his partners in 1850; the firm traded as Thos. Agnew & Sons from Exchange Street from 1826 until the Manchester branch closed in 1932, when it became a limited company. Surviving records show that stock was valued at £27,000 in 1851, of which £5700 was in pictures, £700 in watercolours, with £16,000 owed the firm; this compares with £7000 of stock held in 1824. The firm traded chiefly in British contemporary artists such as Daniel Maclise, J. R. Herbert, and Clarkson Stanfield; J. M. W. Turner's *View from Barnes Terrace* (National Gallery of Art, Washington, DC) was listed at £252, and was the first of many Turners to pass through Agnews; works by William Etty, T. S. Cooper, Sir Edwin Landseer, J. B. Pyne, and William Westall also feature. Agnews catered primarily for the newly wealthy self-made northern and midland industrialists such as Joseph Gillott, T. Horrocks Miller, Sir William Armstrong, George Holt, and John Graham of Glasgow.

A London branch was opened at 5 Waterloo Place in 1860. Stock held in June 1861 totalled £61,000, comprising £14,000 in pictures, £6300 in watercolours, with engravings and money owed making up the balance. Agnews began bidding at Christies on a considerable scale; in one month (May 1861), for example, they spent £2400 at the auction room. Thomas [ii] may have initiated the London move, but he lacked his elder brother's wider interests, preferring to concentrate on money-making, and left over £500,000 on his death in 1883, much of it made outside picture dealing. In 1875 the firm moved to 39 (now 43) Old Bond Street, formerly an old coaching yard, where it built its present spacious galleries.

After the elder Thomas's retirement in 1861 (he died on 24 March 1871 at his home, Fairhope, Eccles Old Road, Pendleton, Salford), William Agnew became the guiding force of the firm. Sir Geoffrey Agnew described his great-grandfather's exuberant vitality, immense ambition, strong will, occasional ruthlessness, and highest probity. An imposing man, William Agnew was a born actor (he always bid at auction in a top hat) and a most persuasive salesman; he was decisive and often bought ahead of the taste of his day. His business acumen was tempered by a personal charm and simplicity that endeared him to many, including the artists, musicians, politicians, and clients whom he frequently entertained either at Summer Hill, Salford, or at Great Stanhope Street, London.

Among William Agnew's coups was the purchase in 1884 from the Leigh Court sale of Hogarth's *Shrimp Girl* and *Miss Fenton* for the National Gallery. Earlier, on 6 May 1876, he had bought from the Wynn Ellis sale Gainsborough's *Duchess of Devonshire* (1783) for £10,505. Stolen later that month, it was not recovered until March 1901, when it was purchased by J. Pierpont Morgan. Holman Hunt benefited from William's purchase in 1873 of *The Shadow of Death* for £10,500, including the engraving rights (which recouped much of the initial outlay from sales of the engraving); in 1883 Agnew presented it to Manchester City Art Gallery. He discovered the young Fred Walker in 1864, and presented *The Harbour of Refuge* (1872) to the Tate Gallery in 1893, in memory of his wife, Mary Kenworthy, whom he had married on 25 March 1851; she died on 2 September 1892. John Millais, Frederic Leighton, and Edward Burne-Jones he treated in an avuncular style, and he encouraged his client Henry Tate to found the Tate Gallery.

William and Mary Agnew had four sons and two daughters. Their eldest son, George William (1852–1941), and their second son, **(Charles) Morland Agnew** (1855–1931), born in Salford on 14 December 1855, joined the firm in 1874 and 1878 respectively; a nephew, **(William) Lockett Agnew** (1858–1918), son of Thomas [ii] and his wife, Anne Kenworthy, born on 20 April 1858 at Hope, Eccles Road, Pendleton, Salford, joined in 1881. Between 1880 and his retirement in 1895 William formed two great collections: those of Sir Charles Tennant and Sir Edward Guinness (later first earl of Iveagh). The most famous of the Tennant pictures, Constable's *The Opening of Waterloo Bridge* (1832), bought from Agnew in 1891, entered the Tate Gallery in 1987. Lord Iveagh began collecting in June 1887, and by April 1891 had bought from Agnews some 223 pictures and drawings. Sixty-two of the choice collection he left to the nation with his beautiful Adam house at Kenwood had come from Agnews.

In 1870 William Agnew and his two brothers Thomas [ii]

and John Henry joined their brother-in-law William Bradbury (who had married William's sister Laura) in the London printing firm of Bradbury and Evans (the proprietors of *Punch*), now renamed Bradbury and Agnew. William Agnew became chairman in 1890 and took a keen interest in *Punch* and its illustrators.

A staunch Liberal and close friend of Gladstone, William Agnew became MP for South-East Lancashire in 1880–85, and for the Stretford division of Lancashire in 1885–6. In 1885 he spoke in the House of Commons in support of the purchase for the nation at £83,250 of Raphael's *Ansidei Madonna* and Van Dyck's portrait of Charles I from the duke of Marlborough's collection. He supported Gladstone's Home Rule Bill in the spring of 1886 and was defeated at the general election held that summer. He unsuccessfully contested the Prestwich division in 1892. Deeply involved in philanthropic enterprises, especially in Manchester, he was also a music patron. On Lord Rosebery's recommendation he was created a baronet on 2 September 1895; he died at his London home, 11 Great Stanhope Street, Mayfair, on 31 October 1910, and his body was cremated at Golders Green. His son George William succeeded him in the baronetcy; he became Liberal MP for Salford, and was an expert on eighteenth-century English mezzotints.

Morland and Lockett Agnew, assisted by Sir George's second son, (George) Colin Agnew (1882–1975), who, after Sir George's retirement in 1902, joined in 1906, continued the business successfully until the outbreak of war in 1914. Morland (who retired in 1913) and Colin were connoisseurs, Lockett, who was highly sociable, the superb salesman. Agnews had become internationally known, and many of the leading American collectors were among its clients. Morland's son (Charles) Gerald (1882–1954) joined in 1904, and was put in charge of the Manchester branch until 1914. In addition to a Paris branch, Colin opened a branch in Berlin in 1908. A New York branch, opened in 1925, was closed in 1932. One of Morland's coups was the purchase in 1905 of Velázquez's 'Rokeby Venus' (its beauty hidden under grime), which he sold for £45,000 to the National Gallery. Hugh Ladas (Tim) Agnew (1894–1975), Gerald's younger brother, who joined in 1920, reorganized the finances and administration of the firm. Lockett died at his home, 10 Chesterfield Street, Mayfair, on 15 February 1918; Morland died on 23 May 1931 at his home, Durrants, Croxley Green, Rickmansworth.

The 1920s boom years were followed by the severe slump of the early 1930s, and in October 1931 **Sir Geoffrey William Gerald Agnew** (1908–1986) became first a salesman, then a partner, at a most unpropitious time. Geoffrey, born on 11 July 1908 at Knutsford, Cheshire, was the elder son of Gerald Agnew (1882–1954) and his wife, Olive Mary (*d.* 1946), daughter of William Danks, a canon of Canterbury. Educated at Eton College, where he was an oppidan scholar in 1923, he read history at Trinity College, Cambridge, graduating in 1930. As a fifth generation member of Agnews, he was proud of the family tradition; on 25 April 1934 he married art historian the Hon. Doreen Maud (1908/9–1990), younger daughter of Herbert Merton

Jessel, first Baron Jessel; they had two sons and a daughter, and the younger son, Julian (*b.* 1943), eventually succeeded his father as chairman. In his *Agnew's, 1817–1967* (1967) Sir Geoffrey recalled the difficulties of selling even the top-quality pictures; Agnews was overstocked, and only staved off bankruptcy by making several important, highly profitable, private sales in the late 1930s. He became managing director in 1937, and revived the practice of exhibiting works by contemporary British artists, although keeping more to the safely established and orthodox rather than the avant-garde.

Unfit for military service during the Second World War, Geoffrey Agnew returned to Eton as a memorable history master and OTC company commander. A man of great energy, and bluff, commanding presence, his booming voice and showmanship masked an innate taste and sensibility, which, combined with wide knowledge, a formidable memory, and great perseverance, made him a dynamic leader and masterly negotiator. Returning to Agnews, he was chairman from 1965 to 1982, and quickly re-established its international pre-eminence, winning the confidence equally of museum directors and wealthy collectors, some of whom, like his best client, Paul Mellon, became personal friends. He sold Mellon in 1966 Turner's *Dort or Dordrecht: the Dort Packet-Boat from Rotterdam Becalmed* (1818), one of the finest earlier works still privately owned. Turner was an artist of whom he spoke with great warmth and understanding. He became founder chairman of the Friends of the Courtauld Institute in 1970, chairman of the Society of London Art Dealers in 1970–74, an adviser to the trustees of Chequers, and was involved in many charities. Knighted in 1973, he died at his home, Flat 3, 6 Onslow Square, London, on 22 November 1986, and his body was cremated at Putney. The firm still flourishes and remains an essentially family concern: it has played a major role in the English art world for nearly two centuries.

DENNIS FARR

Sources G. Agnew, *Agnew's, 1817–1967* (1967) • 'Agnew, Sir William', *DNB* • *The Times* (25 Nov 1986) [Sir Geoffrey William Gerald Agnew] • private information (2004) • personal knowledge (2004) • E. Joll, ed., *Agnew's, 1982–92* (1992) • J. Agnew, ed., *A dealer's record: Agnew's, 1967–81* (1981) • Burke, *Peerage* (1949) • Burke, *Peerage* (1970) • *WWW, 1916–28* • *WW* (1972); (1982); (1996) • *Debrett's Peerage* (1995) • b. cert. [Charles Morland Agnew, 1855–1931] • d. cert. [Charles Morland Agnew, 1855–1931] • b. cert. [Geoffrey William Gerald Agnew, 1908–1986] • m. cert. [Geoffrey William Gerald Agnew, 1908–1986 and Doreen Maud Jessel] • b. cert. [William Lockett Agnew, 1858–1918] • d. cert. [William Lockett Agnew, 1858–1918] • d. cert. [Thomas Agnew, 1794–1871] • *CGPLA Eng. & Wales* (1871) [Thomas Agnew (1794–1871)] • *CGPLA Eng. & Wales* (1911) [William Agnew (1825–1910)] • *CGPLA Eng. & Wales* (1918) [William Lockett Agnew (1858–1918)] • *CGPLA Eng. & Wales* (1931) [Charles Morland Agnew (1855–1931)] • *CGPLA Eng. & Wales* (1987) [Geoffrey William Gerald Agnew (1908–1986)]

Archives Agnews, London, family and business archive | BL, letters to W. E. Gladstone, Add. MSS 44443–44785, *passim* [Sir William Agnew] • Harvard University, near Florence, Italy, Center for Italian Renaissance Studies, letters to Bernard Berenson [Geoffrey W. G. Agnew]

Likenesses S. W. Reynolds, oils, *c.*1825 (Thomas Agnew) • M. Noble, marble bust, 1853 • H. E. Furniss, pen-and-ink caricature, *c.*1880–1910 (William Agnew), NPG; repro. in *Punch* • F. Holl, oils,

1883 (William Agnew) • L. Fildes, oils, 1898 (Lockett Agnew) • photograph, *c*.1900 (Sir William Agnew), Hult. Arch. • G. Agnew, photograph, *c*.1910 • M. Agnew, photograph, *c*.1910 • Snowdon, group portrait, photograph, 1963 (*The managing directors of Agnew's*) • J. Ward, pen and wash drawing, 1972 (Geoffrey Agnew) • H. J. Brooks, group portrait, oils (*Private view of the old masters exhibition, 1888*), NPG • oils (William Agnew), Manchester Reform Club • stipple and line engraving (Thomas Agnew), NPG

Wealth at death under £80,000—Thomas Agnew: probate, 24 May 1871, *CGPLA Eng. & Wales* • £337,457 5*s*. 4*d*.—Charles Morland Agnew: probate, 1931, *CGPLA Eng. & Wales* • £600,000—William Lockett Agnew: probate, 1918, *CGPLA Eng. & Wales* • £1,353,592 10*s*. 8*d*.—Sir William Agnew: probate, 1911, *CGPLA Eng. & Wales* • £487,376—Geoffrey William Gerald Agnew: probate, 10 June 1987, *CGPLA Eng. & Wales*

Agnew, Sir Andrew, of Lochnaw, fifth baronet (1687–1771), army officer, was born on 21 December 1687 at Innermessan Castle, Wigtownshire, the eldest son of the twenty-one children of Sir James Agnew, fourth baronet (*c*.1660–1735), and his wife, Mary (*c*.1652–1742), daughter of Alexander Montgomerie, eighth earl of Eglinton.

Agnew joined Marlborough's army immediately after the battle of Blenheim, and on 11 May 1705 was commissioned as cornet in Major Andrew Agnew's troop of Lord John Hay's Royal Scottish dragoons (Scots Greys). He saw action at Ramillies, Oudenarde, and Malplaquet. On 9 December 1709 he was promoted captain in Lord Strathnaver's regiment of foot. In 1711 he was serving in Portugal. Following the peace of Utrecht when his regiment was disbanded he was reduced as a captain on half pay. In London he eloped with Eleanor (*c*.1698–1785), daughter and eventual heir of a kinsman, Captain Thomas Agnew, of Creoch, and Richmond, Surrey, and they were married on 12 May 1714 at St Benet Paul's Wharf. They had seven sons and eleven daughters. Although Agnew's father disapproved of the match and felt that Thomas Agnew had been 'very indifferently used by my son' (Agnew, 2.227), he was reconciled to his son by the efforts of John Dalrymple, second earl of Stair, and eventually a post-nuptial agreement was signed on 22 April 1719.

During the Jacobite rising of 1715 Agnew served in Colonel Pocock's regiment, which was disbanded in Ireland in 1718, when he was moved to the 21st Royal Scots Fusiliers. In 1724 Agnew's father assigned to him his hereditary sheriffdom of Galloway and henceforth he combined the duties of this office with his military career, his regiment being quartered in Ireland between 1728 and 1737. He was promoted major on 16 January 1737 and lieutenant-colonel on 2 November 1739. He commanded the regiment at Dettingen, and held brigade commands under William Augustus, duke of Cumberland, in Flanders at Bruges, Ghent, and Ostend. During the 1745–6 Jacobite rising he defended Blair Castle, Perthshire, when it was besieged by rebel forces in March 1746. After Culloden he was promoted on 15 August 1746 to the colonelcy of the 10th marines. This regiment was disbanded in 1748. With the abolition of heritable offices in 1747, Agnew received £4000 compensation. In 1750 he was appointed governor of Tynemouth Castle, and was promoted major-general

on 3 February 1756 and lieutenant-general on 3 April 1759. Agnew died in Lochnaw in 1771, probably on 14 August, and was succeeded by his fifth son, Sir Stair Agnew, as sixth baronet.   STUART HANDLEY

Sources A. Agnew, *The hereditary sheriffs of Galloway*, 2 vols. (1893), vol. 2, pp. 145–387 • GEC, *Baronetage* • W. A. Littledale, ed., *The registers of St Bene't and St Peter, Paul's Wharf, London*, 2, Harleian Society, register section, 39 (1910), 122 • B. Lenman, *The Jacobite risings in Britain, 1689–1746* (1980), 31, 280 • *Scots Magazine*, 47 (1785), 312 • C. Dalton, *George the First's army, 1714–1727*, 1 (1910), 180–81 • *Annual Register* (1771) • *Annual Register* (1803), 180 • *Calendar of the manuscripts of the marquess of Ormonde*, new ser., 8 vols., HMC, 36 (1902–20), vol. 8, pp. 334–5 • Chambers, *Scots.* (1868–70), 1.21–3
Archives NA Scot., military papers

Agnew, Sir Andrew, seventh baronet (1793–1849), promoter of Sabbatarian legislation, was born at Kinsale, Ireland, on 21 March 1793, into an ancient and distinguished family in Wigtownshire. He was a posthumous son, his father, Andrew Agnew, an army officer, having died on 11 September 1792. His mother, Martha, was the eldest daughter of John de Courcey, twentieth Lord Kingsale, premier baron of Ireland. He was schooled chiefly by private tutors, but partly at the University of Edinburgh; and his religious education made a deep impression on him. Succeeding his grandfather, Sir Stair Agnew, when only sixteen, Agnew spent his early years chiefly in the improvement of his ancestral castle and estate, and in 1830 he was elected unopposed as MP for Wigtownshire, as 'a moderate reformer'. He sat for the county until 1837. His marriage on 11 June 1816 to Madeline (*d*. 1858), daughter of Sir James Carnegie and his wife, Agnes Murray, *née* Elliot, brought them nine children.

It was after Agnew's third election, in 1832, that the sabbath movement began to attract public attention, mainly through the efforts of an English association, the Lord's Day Society. When it was resolved to secure parliamentary support for the protection of the Lord's day, Agnew in 1832 took charge of the movement. A committee of the House of Commons was appointed to procure information on the facts of the case, and a bill introduced to achieve the desired ends. Agnew's bill prohibited all open labour on Sunday, excepting works of necessity and mercy. He encountered intense and varied opposition on account of the thoroughgoing nature of his bill, but he firmly refused to modify it. The bill was introduced on four occasions, eventually being read a second time in 1837. The clauses were about to be discussed in committee when William IV's death caused a dissolution of parliament. Agnew was defeated in Wigton burghs in 1837 and no further attempt was made to pursue the movement in parliament.

In a private capacity Agnew continued to advocate the cause in many ways, and not without success, and he was an energetic philanthropist. Though a strong anti-Catholic, he was esteemed by his circle. An attack of scarlet fever ended Agnew's life, at the age of fifty-six, on Thursday 28 April 1849. His widow died on 21 January 1858.   W. G. BLAIKIE, *rev.* H. C. G. MATTHEW

Sources T. McCrie, jun., *Memoirs of Sir Andrew Agnew* (1850) · Boase, *Mod. Eng. biog.* · J. Wolffe, *The protestant crusade in Great Britain, 1829–1860* (1991) · Burke, *Peerage*
Archives NA Scot., corresp. | U. Edin., New Coll. L., letters to Thomas Chalmers
Likenesses G. Hayter, group portrait, oils (*The House of Commons, 1833*), NPG · J. T. Smyth, line engraving (after J. Watson-Gordon, 1850), NPG

Agnew, Sir Andrew (1882–1955)

Agnew, Sir Andrew (1882–1955), oil industrialist, was born on 28 February 1882 at 30 Roxburgh Street, Greenock, the son of Andrew Agnew, grocer, and his wife, Margaret. He was educated at Holmscroft School in Greenock. In 1912 he married Belle McKissock, daughter of James McClymont of Girvan; they had two sons.

Agnew's career in the oil industry began in 1903 when he went to the Far East as a member of the staff of Messrs Syme & Co., agents for marketing Shell oil in the Straits Settlements. After two years he was promoted to take charge of their petroleum agency work. When Asiatic Petroleum, Royal Dutch Shell's marketing company, opened its own office in Singapore in 1908, Agnew transferred to their staff and in 1911 was appointed manager and Shell's representative in the Singapore area. During his time in Singapore, Agnew was very active in the local community, being a member of the legislative council of the Straits Settlements and a justice of the peace. He also held positions on the Singapore Harbour Board and the Singapore chamber of commerce. In the First World War Agnew remained in the Far East, where he was commandant of the Singapore civil guard and chairman of the Mesopotamian river craft committee, which was responsible for dispatching workers and supplies to Mesopotamia. In 1918 he was made a CBE for this work, and was one of the first to be awarded this new distinction.

In 1919 Agnew returned to London, where he remained for the rest of his career. He was appointed manager of the Anglo-Saxon Petroleum Company, a subsidiary of Shell, in 1920. Two years later he was made a director of Shell Transport and Trading (one of the Shell group's two parent companies), as well as of Asiatic Petroleum and Anglo-Saxon Petroleum. In 1924 he was appointed to the board of N. V. de Bataafsche Petroleum Maatschappij, Shell's Dutch company. In 1935 Agnew became managing director of Shell Transport and Trading, a position he held until ill health forced him to retire in 1953. His style of leadership was very personal. He was in constant correspondence with Shell offices throughout the world. All staff returning to London on leave were interviewed very thoroughly by him to ascertain detailed facts about their areas of business. He was also in close contact with the other Shell managing directors, especially with Frederick Godber, managing director from 1929 and chairman from 1946, with whom he had a family connection, as one of his sons married one of Godber's daughters. Agnew was energetic in his work, and a man of action rather than of long-term planning. He was described by a colleague as 'the very picture of a rugged Scot, and his actions did not belie his appearance' (Oriel, 215). His interests lay in dealing with immediate market shares and pricing, and negotiations with governments, especially during the difficult trading conditions of the depression. He played a key role, along with Sir John Cadman, chairman of the Anglo-Persian Oil Company, in the organization of the so-called 'As-Is' oil cartel, agreed at Achnacarry Castle, Scotland, in 1928, and this largely determined the strategies of the major oil companies in the 1930s (Ferrier, 463).

Agnew's interests and influence extended beyond Shell to the wider petroleum industry. In 1923 the UK government proposed a petroleum bill, much of which was unacceptable to the industry. Agnew was chosen by the oil companies as one of two representatives to conduct their negotiations, which were ultimately successful. During the Second World War Agnew was chairman of the Petroleum Board, being unanimously nominated for the position by the British oil companies. The board ensured that competition between the oil companies was suspended in order to provide adequate supplies of oil. The success of this endeavour was due largely to Agnew's extensive knowledge of the oil industry and the respect that he commanded within it. He was elected to serve as president of the Institute of Petroleum, the industry's trade body, from 1946 to 1948.

Agnew received many honours in addition to being made a CBE. He was knighted in 1938, was created a Commander of the order of Orange Nassau in 1939 and a chevalier of the Légion d'honneur, and was awarded the United States medal of freedom with silver palm. He died of a cerebral thrombosis on 4 March 1955 at his home at Glenlee Park, Kells, Kirkcudbrightshire, having suffered from ill health for the previous few years, and was buried two days later in Kells cemetery. He was survived by his wife.

ANGELA KENNY

Sources company papers, Shell Group, London, archives · b. cert. · d. cert. · Kirkcudbright parks and burials department records · J. A. Oriel, *Journal of the Institute of Petroleum*, 16 (1955), 215 [obituary] · D. Yergin, *The prize: the epic quest for oil, money and power* (1991) · J. H. Bamberg, *The history of the British Petroleum Company*, 2: *The Anglo-Iranian years, 1928–1954* (1994) · WWW · R. W. Ferrier, *The history of the British Petroleum Company*, 1: *The developing years, 1901–1932* (1982)
Archives Shell Group, London, archives · U. Warwick Mod. RC, BP archives
Likenesses photographs (family portraits)
Wealth at death £205,375 6s. 4d.: confirmation, 26 July 1955, *CCI*

Agnew, Sir Geoffrey William Gerald (1908–1986). *See under* Agnew family (*per.* 1817–1986).

Agnew, Sir James Willson (1815–1901)

Agnew, Sir James Willson (1815–1901), medical practitioner and politician in Tasmania, born at Ballyclare, co. Antrim, Ireland, on 2 October 1815, was the son of James William Agnew, a physician, and Ellen Stewart, of Larne, co. Antrim. Educated for the medical profession at University College, London, at Paris, and at Glasgow, he qualified as MRCS in 1838 and graduated MD from Glasgow in 1839. That September he sailed for Sydney, Australia, on the *Wilmot*, arriving on 26 January 1840. He spent a few months practising in Sydney, and planned to take up land at Port Phillip, but accepted an invitation to become private secretary to Sir John Franklin, then governor of Van Diemen's Land. When he reached Hobart Town the post had been filled, but on 24 December 1841 he was appointed assistant surgeon on the agricultural establishment; in July 1842 he moved to Saltwater Creek on the Tasman peninsula as assistant surgeon. On 28 February 1845 he was transferred to be assistant surgeon (and later colonial surgeon) at Hobart Town, with charge of the general hospital. Concurrently he established a wide private practice, which laid the foundation of his influence among the people of Hobart Town. On 27 April 1846 he married Louisa Mary (d. 1868), the daughter of Major J. Fraser of the 78th highlanders. Of their six children, two sons and a daughter survived.

Agnew was one of the founders of the Tasmanian (Royal) Society, was elected to its council in 1851, and was honorary secretary from 1861 to 1881 and again from 1884 to 1894. He also served on the boards of the Tasmanian Museum and Art Gallery and the Hobart Public Library, as president of the racing club, and as chairman of the botanical garden.

In 1877 Agnew gave up his practice, and at the general election of July that year entered the legislative council as member for Hobart. He served in three short ministries led by P. O. Fysh, and under W. R. Giblin between August 1877 and February 1880, when he resigned in order to visit Melbourne and then England. His first wife had died on 10 March 1868, and on 19 November 1878 he married Blanche, the daughter of William Legge, of Tipperary, the widow of Revd Dr Parsons of Hobart Town; they had no children, and she died on 16 December 1891.

After returning from England in 1881, Agnew re-entered the legislative council in 1884. From 8 March 1886 to 29 March 1887 he was premier; he was also chief secretary until 1 March. His tenure of office was marked by educational reform, in which, as a member of the council of education and of the university, he was particularly interested. In 1891 he left the colony for a long visit to England; on his return to Tasmania in 1894 he was made KCMG. In 1899 he was disabled by illness, and he died at his home in Hobart Town on 8 November 1901. He was accorded a public funeral and buried at the Cornelian Bay cemetery, Hobart Town. Known as Good Doctor Agnew, he made material contributions to the cultural and social as well as the political life of Tasmania.

C. A. HARRIS, rev. ELIZABETH BAIGENT

Sources AusDB · Mail [Tasmania] (9 Nov 1901) · Mail [Tasmania] (16 Nov 1901) · B. Burke, A genealogical and heraldic history of the colonial gentry, 2 vols. (1891–5) · E. L. Piesse, The foundation and early work of the society: with some account of other institutions of early Hobart (1913) [on the Royal Society of Van Diemen's Land]
Likenesses T. Cole, portrait, Tasmanian Club, Hobart · portrait, repro. in Mail [Tasmania] (16 Nov 1901)

Agnew, (William) Lockett (1858–1918). See under Agnew family (per. 1817–1986).

Agnew, (Charles) Morland (1855–1931). See under Agnew family (per. 1817–1986).

Agnew, Patrick Alexander Vans (1822–1848), East India Company servant, was born at Raipur in Chhattisgarh in central India on 21 April 1822, the second son of Patrick

Vans Agnew (1783–1842), lieutenant-colonel in the Madras army and afterwards a director of the East India Company, and his wife, Catherine, née Fraser (d. 1879). Agnew was educated privately before entering the East India College, Haileybury, in 1838 to take up a writership in the Bengal civil service. He went out to Bengal in 1841 and in the following year was posted to Delhi as an assistant to the commissioner. In 1845 he was appointed assistant to Major Broadfoot, superintendent of the Cis-Sutlej states. He was present at the battle of Sobraon early in 1846 and was afterwards employed in defining the borders of Kashmir. In 1847, as assistant to the governor-general's agent on the north-west frontier, he embarked on a mission to Gilgit. His diaries from this mission reveal him as a dutiful but politically unimaginative officer who was often frustrated by the atmosphere of intrigue that shrouded frontier politics.

In the spring of 1848 the new resident at Lahore, Frederick Currie, charged Agnew with overseeing the transfer of the government of Multan from the outgoing diwan, Mul Raj, to a new Sikh official, Sirdar Khan Singh Man. The job was a delicate one, perhaps beyond Agnew's diplomatic skills. Mul Raj was a competent governor who had made it clear that he was resigning only because of British encroachments on his independence. Neither his troops, fearful of unemployment, nor the population at large looked favourably upon his replacement by a British puppet. Agnew, accompanied by Lieutenant William Anderson of the 1st Bombay fusiliers and an escort of about 2500 Sikhs and Gurkhas, arrived at Multan on 18 April 1848 and encamped in an idgah near the fort. At a first meeting with Mul Raj, Agnew asked, somewhat precipitately, to see the state's revenue accounts. On the 19th he again erred in accepting control of the fort before Mul Raj had emptied it of his own men. As he and Anderson attempted to leave the fort they were attacked by a Multani sentry and in the ensuing scuffle both sustained severe sword cuts. With difficulty they retreated to the safety of the idgah but during the night their escort was won over to the Multanis, who were now committed to revolt against the British. On the morning of the 20th an angry crowd burst into the idgah and murdered them.

The killing of two such young and pitifully vulnerable men sent shock waves throughout British India and hastened the Second Anglo-Sikh War and the British annexation of the Punjab. In the following January, when Britain had wreaked its revenge on Multan, the mutilated bodies of Agnew and Anderson were dug up from outside the idgah and buried with military honours in the Multan Fort. For some years, until overtaken by the cataclysm of 1857, the fate of 'poor Agnew' was frequently invoked in Anglo-Indian memoirs as a symbol of the inextinguishable nobility of British endeavour in India.

KATHERINE PRIOR

Sources M. Irving, A list of inscriptions on Christian tombs or monuments in the Punjab, North-West Frontier Province, Kashmir, and Afghanistan, ed. G. W. de Rhé-Philipe, 2 (1912) · H. B. Edwardes, A year on the Punjab frontier in 1848–49, 2 vols. (1851) · [A. Rayner], ed., Political diaries, 1847–49 (1915) [from Punjab government records] · BL

OIOC, Haileybury MSS · Fauja Singh, *After Ranjit Singh* (1982) · Burke, *Gen. GB* (1914)
Archives NA Scot., Vans Agnew MSS

Agnew, Thomas (1794–1871). *See under* Agnew family (*per.* 1817–1986).

Agnew, Sir William, first baronet (1825–1910). *See under* Agnew family (*per.* 1817–1986).

Agnew, Sir William Gladstone (1898–1960), naval officer, was born in London on 2 December 1898, the fifth son of the six children of (Charles) Morland *Agnew (1855–1931) [*see under* Agnew family], art dealer, and his wife, Evelyn Mary (d. 1932), daughter of William Naylor, of Paddington Green, London. He was the grandson of Sir William Agnew, first baronet. He joined the Royal Navy in September 1911 and was at Dartmouth when war broke out in 1914. He was sent to sea as a midshipman, serving in the battleships *Glory* and *Royal Oak* and in the destroyer *Skilful*. After the war his appointments included the royal yacht and in 1924 he went to the *Excellent*, the gunnery school at Portsmouth, to qualify as a specialist in gunnery. During these years he played rugby football regularly for the navy as well as cricket, hockey, and tennis. On 24 April 1930 he married Patricia Caroline (d. 1977), younger daughter of Colonel Alfred William Bewley CMG of Campanella, Alverstoke, Hampshire. They had no children.

Agnew's first ship as a specialist officer was the cruiser *Durban* and in 1931 he was appointed gunnery officer of the battleship *Queen Elizabeth*, flagship of the Mediterranean Fleet. He was promoted commander in 1932 and captain in 1937.

On the outbreak of war in 1939 Agnew was given command of the armed merchant cruiser *Corfu* and in October 1940 was transferred to the cruiser *Aurora*. Over the next year and a half Agnew's name and that of his ship were to become famous as part of the 'short but brilliant career' of force K (Roskill, 173). After the *Aurora* had a share in the sinking of a German cruiser, a destroyer, and two supply ships, in the summer of 1941, Agnew was sent to the Mediterranean as the senior officer of a group consisting of the *Aurora*, her sister ship the *Penelope*, and the destroyers *Lance* and *Lively*—force K. This move was quickly justified. On the night of 8 November force K intercepted a strongly escorted enemy supply convoy of seven ships bound for north Africa. Agnew had made carefully thought-out plans for just such an encounter and had discussed his tactics in detail with the other commanding officers. As a result he was able to stalk the convoy undetected and took the enemy completely by surprise. All the supply ships and one of their escorting destroyers were sunk without damage to force K. As he left his ship on return to harbour Agnew was spontaneously cheered by the officers and men of the *Penelope*—a rare tribute. A great leader, he was also remembered by colleagues for his friendly and modest manner. For his services in this action he was appointed CB in 1941.

Further sorties by force K led to the sinking of three fuel tankers. All these successes created a critical fuel situation for the German air force in north Africa and had an important effect on axis plans. In December the *Aurora* struck a mine but Agnew got her safely back to England after temporary repairs in Malta. Although force K was not reformed, at the end of 1942 the *Aurora* formed part of the naval force in operation Torch, the allied invasion of north Africa, and from then on was constantly in action. It was a tribute to Agnew and the *Aurora* that the ship was chosen to carry George VI from Tripoli to Malta for the royal visit to the island in June 1943. For this service the king appointed Agnew CVO.

The *Aurora* played a full part in the allied invasions of Italy and Sicily, carrying out a great many bombardments in support of the landings. In October, however, she was severely damaged in an air attack in the eastern Mediterranean. Agnew took his damaged ship into Alexandria and was ordered home to take command of the *Excellent*. He had been appointed DSO in April 1943 and subsequently received a bar (1944).

After the war, in March 1946, Agnew was appointed to command the battleship *Vanguard*. He was promoted rear-admiral in January 1947 and remained in command for the royal visit to South Africa. On conclusion of the tour he was promoted KCVO. In August 1947 Agnew was appointed director of personal services at the Admiralty, where he remained until October 1949. He notably complained while in this position that the developing welfare state in Britain made life in the services less attractive. Civilian life had become 'a free and easy Tom Tiddler's ground on which he (i.e. the sailor) would be advised to stake a claim at the earliest possible moment' (Grove, 45). In January 1950 he retired from the navy at his own request, and later in the year was promoted vice-admiral on the retired list.

For the next three years Agnew was the general secretary of the National Playing Fields Association and re-established this organization after its hiatus during the war. He became involved in local government and the Christian stewardship campaign in his local parish. He died at his home, Glentinion, Palmerston Way, Alverstoke, Gosport, Hampshire, on 12 July 1960. His funeral was held at Alverstoke on 16 July.

A. D. NICHOLL, rev. MARC BRODIE

Sources *The Times* (13 July 1960) · Burke, *Peerage* · S. Roskill, *The navy at war, 1939–45* (1960) · E. J. Grove, *Vanguard to Trident: British naval policy since World War II* (1987) · *WWW* · *CGPLA Eng. & Wales* (1960) · personal knowledge (1971) · private information (1971)
Archives IWM, MSS relating to naval service | FILM BFI NFTVA, news footage · IWM FVA, news footage
Likenesses W. Stoneman, photograph, 1946, NPG
Wealth at death £64,061 11s. 8d.: probate, 3 Oct 1960, *CGPLA Eng. & Wales*

Agricola. *See* Julius Agricola, Gnaeus (AD 40–93).

Aguilar, Grace (1816–1847), writer on Jewish history and religion and novelist, was born on 2 June 1816 in Hackney, Middlesex, the eldest of the three children of Emanuel Aguilar (1787–1845), merchant, and his wife, Sarah (d. 1854), daughter of Jacob Dias Fernandez of London. Her parents were Sephardic Jews and her father was a prominent member of the Spanish and Portuguese Jewish congregation in London. She was educated at home, and began writing poetry and drama as a child. In 1828 her father's ill health led to the family's removal for several years to Teignmouth, Devon, where Grace Aguilar mixed in Christian society and often attended chapel. In a theological essay from this time she wrote: 'There is nothing, in my opinion, that enlarges an unprejudiced mind more than joining with those of another faith in their religious ceremonies' (Aguilar, 'On a lecture', 1). During the 1830s she also wrote several novels and stories, some of which were published over ten years later. When her family returned to London, she ran a school for Jewish boys with her mother at their home in Hackney.

Grace Aguilar's first major published works were on Jewish subjects. At a time when British Jews were under increasing pressure to convert to Christianity, she produced three works of apologia on behalf of Judaism: a translation of Baltasar Orobio de Castro's *Israel Defended* (1838); *The Spirit of Judaism* (1842), an explanation of Jewish beliefs and practices which was published in America; and *The Jewish Faith: its Spiritual Consolation, Moral Guidance, and Immortal Hope* (1846), which took the form of letters addressed to a Jewish girl encouraging her to remain loyal to her faith. She also addressed a female readership in *The Women of Israel* (1845), a book of essays on Old Testament heroines. Grace Aguilar was one of the few Victorian writers for a popular readership who attempted to defend Judaism and argue for religious tolerance. Her first published work of fiction, *Records of Israel* (1844), related the stories of Jews fleeing persecution in fifteenth-century Spain and Portugal. Her 'History of the Jews in England', published anonymously in 1847 in *Chambers' Miscellany*, declared support for Jewish political and civil equality, and argued that 'the disabilities under which the Jews of Great Britain labour are the last relic of religious intolerance' (Aguilar, 'History of the Jews in England', 16). Although one contemporary Jewish newspaper questioned her authority on theological matters, Grace Aguilar's work was well received among British and American Jews. In 1847, in recognition of her efforts to reassess the role of women in Judaism, she was presented with a tribute by a group of young Jewish women. 'Until you arose', they wrote, 'it has in modern times never been the case that a woman in Israel should stand forth the public advocate of the faith of Israel' (Abrahams, 146). But despite her wish to contest the arguments of Christian missionaries, Grace Aguilar's work on Jewish themes was undoubtedly influenced by the evangelical climate of her time; indeed, her work was much praised by the protestant press for its high moral tone.

Grace Aguilar was best-known in the Victorian period, however, for her popular domestic and historical novels which celebrated the role of the middle-class mother in teaching and maintaining standards of charity, obedience, and piety. She also contributed to the periodicals *The Keepsake* and *La Belle Assemblée*. After its publication in 1847, her novel *Home Influence: a Tale for Mothers and Daughters*

went through nearly thirty editions. The sequel, *The Mother's Recompense* (1851), and *Woman's Friendship* (1850) were published posthumously under the editorship of Sarah Aguilar, as well as two historical romances, *The Days of Bruce: a Story from Scottish History* (1852) and *The Vale of Cedars* (1850), a tragic tale of Jewish heroism set during the Spanish Inquisition, which became one of her most successful works. With the publication of this novel, Grace Aguilar's mission to promote religious tolerance in Victorian England finally reached a wide readership. The pious and didactic quality of her writing led to a decline in its popularity in the twentieth century, but more recently her importance as the first successful Anglo-Jewish novelist has been re-evaluated.

Grace Aguilar was described by a friend as being 'tall and slight; her manner gentle and persuasive; but when she spoke she was remarkably earnest, and when she became excited, her full dark eyes were dazzling in their brightness' (*Art Union*, 378). She is said to have been charitable to both Jews and Gentiles despite not being wealthy herself (ibid.). In June 1847 she left England for Frankfurt am Main, Germany, to visit her brother and to seek a cure for her declining health. Some weeks after arriving she became weaker and died of a spinal disease on 16 September 1847 in Frankfurt, where she was buried in the Jewish section of the cemetery.

NADIA VALMAN

Sources UCL, Aguilar MSS, MS Add. 378 [on loan from the Jewish Museum] · *Art Union*, 9 (1847), 378 · N. D. Valman, 'Jews and gender in British literature, 1815–1865', PhD diss., Queen Mary College, London, 1996 · B.-Z. L. Abrahams, 'Grace Aguilar: a centenary tribute', *Transactions of the Jewish Historical Society of England*, 16 (1945–51), 137–48 · G. Aguilar, 'On a lecture on the twenty-second Psalm, by the Rev. R. S. Anderson, 9th Nov 1836', *Sabbath thoughts and sacred communings* (1836) · [G. Aguilar], 'History of the Jews in England', *Chambers' miscellany of useful and entertaining tracts*, 18 (1847), 1–32 · [C. E. Tonna], 'Jewish literature', *Christian Lady's Magazine*, 20 (1843), 221–30 · M. Galinsky, *The origin of the modern Jewish woman writer: romance and reform in Victorian England* (1996) · P. E. Hyman, *Gender and assimilation in modern Jewish history: the roles and representations of women* (1995) · G. Aguilar, preface, *Home influence: a tale for mothers and daughters*, 2 vols. (1847) · [S. Aguilar], 'Memoir of Grace Aguilar', in G. Aguilar, *Home influence: a tale for mothers and daughters*, another edn (1892), ix–xiv · C. Scheinberg, 'Miriam's daughters: women's poetry and religious identity in Victorian England', PhD diss., Rutgers University, 1992

Archives priv. coll. · UCL, notebooks, corresp., and papers | Bodl. Oxf., letters to Isaac Disraeli · University of North Carolina Library, Chapel Hill, Cohen MSS

Likenesses J. Cochran, stipple and line engraving, NPG · portrait, repro. in G. Aguilar, *The mother's recompense: a sequel to 'Home influence'* (1851)

Agus, Benjamin. *See* Agas, Benjamin (*bap.* 1622, *d.* 1689).

Agutter, William (1758–1835), Church of England clergyman, was born on 8 October 1758, the eldest son of Guy Agutter (1729–1768), a wool-stapler, and his wife, Dinah, both of the parish of All Saints, Northampton. He was baptized on 10 October 1758 at All Saints' Church, thereby continuing a long family connection with the parish. He matriculated at Lincoln College, Oxford, on 18 March 1777, aged eighteen. In 1780 he obtained a demyship at Magdalen College, Oxford, and retained it until 1793. Agutter graduated as BA in 1781 and MA in 1784. During this time he was ordained into Anglican orders and gained some reputation in the pulpit. He was much influenced by the high-churchmanship of the president of Magdalen, George Horne, and other members of the college. At St Mary's Church, Oxford, on 23 July 1786 he preached before the university and used the example of the deathbeds of Johnson and Hume to drive home 'the difference between the death of the righteous and the wicked' (Agutter, *Difference*, 11). Agutter was at pains to emphasize that 'the confidence or the tranquillity of the infidel are no arguments in his favour' (ibid.). At Oxford he was a friend of the Revd John Henderson, an eccentric prodigy of learning, and when Henderson died in 1788, aged only thirty-one, Agutter accompanied the corpse to Kingswood near Bristol and preached the funeral sermon. It is a learned, whimsical narrative that still reads well.

Agutter finally left Oxford in 1793 when, on 29 May of that year, he married Anne Broughton of Canonbury Place, Islington, London, a daughter of the Revd Thomas Broughton. During the 1790s, though holding no parochial cure, he preached on a regular basis, facing up to the challenges of the decade in a distinctively Christian manner. Many of Agutter's sermons were printed by request. He was a strong loyalist for whom republicanism was the 'lowest and worst' of all forms of government, as he put it in *Christian Politics* (p. 9). Agutter bemoaned the spread of false principles in the world, which had 'sapped the foundations of morality and religion, and threatens the existence of happiness and peace' (Agutter, *Sermon*, 6). His political conservatism was tempered by a strong humanitarian streak and a lifetime's commitment to the abolition of the slave trade. In a sermon preached before the corporation of Oxford as early as 1788 he observed that 'this unrighteous traffick in human blood is not more destructive to those concerned in it, than disgraceful to the religion they profess, and to the nation which tolerates their crimes' (Agutter, *Abolition of the Slave Trade*, 22). Such trenchant views were at one with Agutter's conviction that 'The life of every one from helpless infancy to infirm old age, is sacred, and ought to be regarded as such' (Agutter, *The Origin and Importance of Life*, 25). It was extremely appropriate that in 1797 he was appointed to the post of chaplain and secretary to the Asylum for Female Orphans in Lambeth, originally founded in 1758. After the French revolutionary wars he appears to have lived in retirement. Agutter died on 26 March 1835 in Upper Gower Street, London.   NIGEL ASTON

Sources GM, 1st ser., 58 (1788), 1031 · GM, 1st ser., 63 (1793), 479 · GM, 2nd ser., 4 (1835), 98 · Foster, *Alum. Oxon.* · J. C. Cox and C. A. Markham, eds., *The records of the borough of Northampton*, 1, ed. C. A. Markham (1898) · J. R. Bloxam, *A register of the presidents, fellows ... of Saint Mary Magdalen College*, 8 vols. (1853–85) · Nichols, *Illustrations*, 7.316 · R. M. Sarjeantson, *A history of the church of All Saints', Northampton* (1901) · N&Q, 6th ser., 3 (9 April 1881) · W. Agutter, *The difference between the deaths of the righteous and the wicked, illustrated in the instance of Dr Samuel Johnson and David Hume, Esq.: a sermon preached before the University of Oxford, at St Mary's Church, on Sunday, July 23, 1786* (1800) · W. Agutter, *The abolition of the slave trade considered in a religious point of view, a sermon preached before the corporation of Oxford,* at St Martin's Church, Oxford (1788) · W. Agutter, *The origin and importance of life, preached at St Giles's, Northampton, 13 Sept. 1789, and later at Carshalton* (1789) · W. Agutter, *A sermon preached on the day of general thanksgiving, 19 December 1797, in the chapel of the Asylum for Female Orphans* (1798) · pedigree of Agutter family of Northampton, Northants. RO
Likenesses J. Clover, portrait, exh. RA 1834

Aguzzi, Elizabeth Clarice [Lizzie] (1856–1938), equestrian performer, was born at 3 Felix Street, Lambeth, London, on 4 February 1856, the daughter of Antoni Aguzzi, an equestrian performer, and his wife Helen, *née* Smith. Her circus performances, as a bareback and trick act rider, were first noted in the 1870s. Playbills for her performances at Hengler's circus in London for the 1873–4 season advertised her engagements in Paris, Madrid, and Lisbon, as well as at Carl Hagenbeck's circus in Germany. She later rode with Barnum and Bailey's and with Sanger's circus.

Lizzie Aguzzi married William François (Billy) Harvey (1833–1889), an equestrian clown, with whom she had two sons, Erno and Will, who achieved some popularity in the 1890s, under the name the Aguzzi Brothers, as equestrian performers and wire-walkers. Lizzie Aguzzi appeared with William Holland's Grand International Cirque at the Theatre Royal, Covent Garden, during the 1884–5 season in a graceful double act with her husband. She was with Hengler's at Birmingham in 1886, and again at the Covent Garden circus in 1889, in which year her husband died. The last record of her performing is with Alfred Whitmee's short-lived circus at Oxford in 1893. She died on 10 May 1938 in Tooting Bec Hospital, London.

JOHN M. TURNER

Sources *World's Fair* (21 Feb 1914) · *World's Fair* (8 July 1939), p. 19, col. 2 · *The Times* (6 Dec 1873) · *Birmingham Daily Post* (3 March 1886) · b. cert. · d. cert.
Archives Circus Friends Association, Blackburn, archives

Aherne, (William) Brian de Lacy (1902–1986), actor, was born on 2 May 1902 at The Pleasaunce, King's Norton, Worcestershire, the son of William Lacy Ahern (d. 1946) (who later amended his name to Willoughby de Lacy Aherne), architect, and his wife, Louise Thomas (d. c.1940), an amateur actress who was among the co-founders of the Birmingham Repertory Theatre. Having made his acting début in Sir Barry Jackson's pantomime *Finfinella* in 1909, he enrolled in the Italia Conti Drama School, where he appeared, as a creature of the woods, alongside Noël Coward in the school's Christmas production, *Where the Rainbow Ends*, at the Garrick in 1913.

Aherne completed his schooling at Edgbaston School, Birmingham, and Malvern College, but abandoned his subsequent training as an architect to accept a clerking post in a shipping office in Liverpool. In his spare time he starred in such Green Room Club presentations as A. A. Milne's *The Romantic Age*. In December 1923 he returned south for the Savoy Theatre's revival of *Paddy, the Next Best Thing*, by W. Gayer-Mackay and Robert Ord, which resulted the following year in his first West End success—as Langford in Leon Gordon's *White Cargo* at the Playhouse. He also made his screen bow in 1924, in *The Eleventh Commandment*. But despite headlining such acclaimed Anthony

469

AHMAD KHAN, SAIYID

Asquith pictures as *Shooting Stars* (1928) and *Underground* (1929), he always adopted a slightly dismissive attitude towards the medium.

Aherne went on tour in Australia with Dion Boucicault's company, and on his return to London in 1927 landed the lead in Sidney Howard's *The Silver Cord* at the St Martin's Theatre, only to begin an affair with the playwright's wife, Clare Eames. In his autobiography, *A Proper Job* (1969), Aherne confessed that it took him twenty years to recover fully from her sudden death in November 1930. By this time he had moved into talkies, with *The W Plan* (1930), and scored stage successes in Oliver Goldsmith's *She Stoops to Conquer* (Lyric, Hammersmith, 1928) and George Farquhar's *The Beaux' Stratagem* (Royalty, 1930), as well as playing a pivotal part in the foundation of British Actors' Equity in 1928.

Still in mourning, Aherne decided to try his luck in America. But rather than accept a contract offer from Twentieth Century Fox he joined Katherine Cornell in Rudolf Besier's *The Barretts of Wimpole Street* at the Empire on Broadway in February 1931. (Eventually they played Elizabeth Barrett and Robert Browning some 1000 times in various revivals, as well as before US troops stationed in Italy, France, and the Netherlands during the latter days of the Second World War.) Rejecting Irving G. Thalberg's invitation to sign for MGM and Douglas Fairbanks's suggestion to front remakes of his swashbuckling silents, Aherne teamed with Cornell again in such plays as *Lucrèce* (1932), *Romeo and Juliet* (1934), and George Bernard Shaw's *Saint Joan* (1936). But the impact of the depression on Broadway finally forced him to consider Hollywood entreaties, although he preferred to remain freelance, thus enabling him to co-star with Marlene Dietrich in Paramount's *The Song of Songs* (1933), Joan Crawford in MGM's *I Live my Life* (1935), and Katharine Hepburn in RKO's *Sylvia Scarlett* (both 1935).

However, Aherne never fully established himself in the front rank, losing both *A Tale of Two Cities* and *Lost Horizon* to fellow exile Ronald Colman. Yet this allowed him to accept more challenging character parts, most notably donning the huge handlebar moustache of a robust French peasant in *The Lady in Question* (1940), one of four films he made for director Charles Vidor, and concealing himself beneath several layers of old-age make-up in *Smilin' through* (1941). Openly indifferent to Hollywood hype, he was thought to embody an aloof brand of Englishness that fitted him for such film ventures as *Beloved Enemy* (1936) and *The Great Garrick* (1937). Yet his greatest success came playing the Austrian-born Emperor Maximilian in the Warner Bros. biopic, *Juarez* (1939), for which he earned an Oscar nomination for best supporting actor.

In 1937 Aherne told *Film Weekly*, 'I don't want the brief fame of a film star' (20 March 1937), which was just as well, as his fortunes began to dip sharply after the war. He did, however, star with Rosalind Russell in *Hired Wife* (1940), *My Sister Eileen* (1942), and *What a Woman* (1943). His marriage to actress Joan Fontaine proved short-lived (1939–44) and he was rejected for active service on account of his sinuses, despite holding a pilot's licence. Instead, he divided his energies between his vineyard in La Quinta, California, and raising funds for the British War Relief Association and the Hollywood Victory Committee, before entertaining troops in liberated Europe with Katherine Cornell. In 1946 Aherne married Eleanor de Liagne Labrot.

Five years passed between *Smart Woman* (1948) and minor supports as Montgomery Clift's attorney in Alfred Hitchcock's *I confess* and the Captain in Jean Negulesco's *Titanic* (both 1953). Stage assignments were equally scarce, although he drew praise for his work as Professor Higgins in a touring production of the George Bernard Shaw-inspired *My Fair Lady* (1958) and as Shaw himself in Jerome Kilty's *Dear Liar* (adapted from Shaw's correspondence with Mrs Patrick Campbell) at the Billy Rose Theatre in March 1960, which marked his last collaboration with Katherine Cornell. Having played King Arthur in *Lancelot and Guinevere* (1962), Aherne returned to the London stage for the first time in three decades, opposite Edith Evans in Enid Bagnold's *The Chinese Prime Minister* (1965). Following *Rosie* (1968), another pairing with Rosalind Russell, he retired, with his second wife, to a house on the shores of Lake Geneva. Brian Aherne died of heart failure in Venice, Florida, on 10 February 1986.   DAVID PARKINSON

Sources B. Aherne, *A proper job: the autobiography of an actor's actor* (Boston, 1969) · J. Vinson, ed., *The international dictionary of films and filmmakers: actors and actresses* · *Variety* (12 Feb 1986) · *The Times* (12 Feb 1986) · *Daily Telegraph* (12 Feb 1986) · RKO press release, BFI [microfiche] · Universal press release, BFI [microfiche] · *Films Weekly* (17 March 1933) · *Films Weekly* (20 March 1937) · *Picturegoer* (10 Jan 1942)
Archives Syracuse University, New York | FILM BFI NFTVA
Likenesses portrait, Huntley Archive, London · portrait, Ronald Grant Archive, London · portrait, Kobal Collection, London

Ahmad Khan, Sir Saiyid [Syed Ahmed Khan] (1817–1898), Muslim leader in India, was born on 17 October 1817 in Khwaja Farid's *haveli* (mansion) near the Tiraha Bahram Khan in Delhi, the youngest of the three children (two boys and one girl) of Saiyid Muttaqi (d. 1838), a Mughal noble, and his wife Aziz-un-Nisa Begam, daughter of Khwaja Fariduddin Ahmad (1747–1828), envoy of the East India Company to Persia and Burma and prime minister of the Mughal emperor, Akbar II. His father's family were Husaini Saiyids, who had migrated to India from Herat in the time of Akbar; his mother's family, who claimed descent from the Sufi saint Sheikh Yusuf Hamadani (d. 1140), had in the early eighteenth century settled in Delhi as traders from Kashmir.

Saiyid Ahmad was educated in Persian and Arabic but when young was noted neither for ability nor for self-discipline. After his father's death, and against his family's wishes, he began to work in the judicial branch of the East India Company's administration, serving in Agra, Mainpuri, Fatehpur Sikri, and, from 1846, in Delhi. In 1855 he was promoted to assistant magistrate of Bijnor, where in the mutiny of 1857 he rescued the British population of the district. From 1858 he was magistrate in Moradabad, Ghazipur, and Aligarh, and then in 1867 was promoted to judge of the small-cause court in Benares, which he served until his retirement in 1876. From 1878 to 1882 he was on the central legislative council. He gave evidence to the education commission of 1882 and served on the public service commission of 1887. In 1888 he was made KCSI.

There were three transforming experiences in Saiyid Ahmad's life, the cumulative impact of which made him the outstanding Indian Muslim leader of his day. The first was the death of his elder brother in 1845. Up to this time he had pursued carnal and aesthetic pleasures; thenceforward he devoted himself to serious matters, growing a beard and attending Delhi's Madrasa Rahimiya to repair gaps in his education. The second formative experience was the mutiny uprising of 1857. It was a personal tragedy—many of his relatives and friends were killed—and a great human and cultural tragedy, in which tens of thousands died or were displaced, and Delhi was destroyed as a focus of Muslim culture. For a moment Saiyid Ahmad considered leaving India for good, but decided to stay and devote himself to his people. His third transforming experience was his seventeen-month visit to Britain in 1869 and 1870: it was here that he studied the sources of European ascendancy, and his ideas for Indian education crystallized.

After the mutiny it was evident to Saiyid Ahmad that education was essential to building a bridge between the north Indian élites and the government. His ideas about how to achieve this evolved gradually. One was the importance of using the medium of Indian languages: to this end he founded at Ghazipur the Scientific Society, the major activity of which was the translation into Urdu of European texts, on subjects ranging from mechanics and modern farming to mathematics and history. Another objective was the establishment of sympathetic educational environments for Indians, such as the schools he founded in Moradabad and Ghazipur in 1858 and 1864. These ideas came together in Saiyid Ahmad's unsuccessful proposal to the government in 1867 to found a vernacular university. It was only after visiting Britain and consulting fellow Muslims that he produced a plan that succeeded: it was to establish a college which was independent of government, adopted the residential model of Oxford and Cambridge, and taught English literature, oriental languages, and European science through the medium of Urdu. In 1877 the Muhammadan Anglo-Oriental College was founded at Aligarh (though market forces soon forced it to teach through the medium of English alone). In 1886 Saiyid Ahmad established the Muhammadan Educational Conference to take the message of Aligarh to the rest of India. Two points should be noted about his achievement: although the college would not have been founded without his energetic fund-raising efforts, it did benefit from government patronage; and although Saiyid Ahmad's early endeavours were for both Hindus and Muslims, and Hindu students were welcome at Aligarh, he came increasingly to work for Muslims alone after Hindus tried to replace the Persian script with the Devanagari, and Urdu with Hindi, as the government language in the late 1860s.

Successful educational reform required attention to custom and belief. One concern was countering the perceived threat of Christian missionaries. Saiyid Ahmad strove to alleviate fears through his commentary on the Bible (1862–87), which aimed to remove the suspicions of Christians about Islam, to refute the arguments of Muslims that the text of the Bible was corrupt, and to demonstrate how Muslims and Christians held beliefs in common. When necessary he went on the attack, publishing his *Khutbat-i-Ahmadiya* (1870) to refute the derogatory picture of the prophet in the *Life of Mahomet* by William Muir, the lieutenant-governor of his province. A second concern was to overcome Muslim religious prejudices which hampered progress. This was answered by the foundation in December 1870 of a new periodical, the *Mohammedan Social Reformer*, in which he and his supporters attacked injurious customs and beliefs. (The only chinks in his liberal credentials were his opposition to English education for women and his support for purdah.) A third concern was to foster an understanding of Islam which would not be troubled by European science. In order to answer this concern, Saiyid Ahmad developed a new Islamic theology, which he set out in his Koran commentary published over the years 1880 to 1904. Echoing the Christian natural theologians, whose work he knew, he began from the position that the work of God (nature) and the word of God (Koranic revelation) must be in harmony. He distinguished between the essence of the Koran and what belonged to the time in which it was revealed, and showed that this essence could flourish in the modern world without fear of scientific discoveries or social change. Many found Saiyid Ahmad's views too advanced, and he was bitterly attacked; he succeeded, however, in laying the foundations of Islamic modernism.

Saiyid Ahmad was a keen historian; his first notable work was *Asar-i-Sanadid* (1847), in which he recorded the inscriptions and buildings of Delhi and the lives of notable inhabitants. For this research he received an honorary fellowship of the Royal Asiatic Society; the book was also translated into French. Subsequently, he edited Barani's *Tarikh-i-Firoz Shahi* (1862), Abu'l-Fazl's *A'in-i-Akbari*, and the *Tuzuk-i-Jahangiri* (1864), and wrote a history of Bijnor (lost in the mutiny) and a *History of the Revolt in Bijnor* (1858). A strong historical understanding underpinned his Islamic modernism.

Saiyid Ahmad had considerable influence over the style and content of Urdu literature. He championed the development of a simple and clear prose style over the florid forms of the day, aiming to fashion the language into an effective medium for serious ideas. He also encouraged Urdu poets to adopt the 'natural poetry' of the Victorian British, paving the way for verse to convey social, moral, and political messages. Thus he gave direction to the work of Hali, Shibli, Nazir Ahmad, and many others, who came to form the 'Aligarh school' in Urdu literature.

Such a man was bound to play a major political role. In 1858 Saiyid Ahmad launched himself in public life by publishing *The Causes of the Indian Revolt*, in which he demonstrated that the mutiny was not the outcome of a conspiracy, as many British thought, but of a breakdown of trust between society and government; what was needed, he felt, was education for Indians, and their representation on the central legislative council. Two years later, in order to demonstrate Muslim support for the British, he started his journal, the *Loyal Muhammadans of India*. In 1866 he founded the British Indian Association to improve the efficacy of British Indian government. He was a noted speaker in the central legislative council, and was the first Indian to propose a bill (for smallpox vaccination) of his own. Most significant was his opposition to the Indian National Congress: he objected in particular to its demand for elections to the legislative council, on the grounds that Muslims and the Hindu landed gentry of northern India were not ready for it. Saiyid Ahmad's opposition led to a generation of Muslims not joining the Indian nationalist movement.

Little is known of Saiyid Ahmad's wife, whom he married about 1835 and who died in 1861, leaving him a daughter and two sons, the younger of whom, Saiyid Mahmood, was to gain great distinction as a lawyer. On 27 March 1898 Sir Saiyid Ahmad Khan died in Aligarh from the effects of a stricture of the urethra; he was buried next to the mosque at his college in Aligarh. Physically, he was most impressive: 'a herculean frame, with broad and pensive forehead, compassionate but thoughtful eyes, leonine jaw and a white flowing beard, when he walked his majestic gait gave the impression of a "ship in motion"' (Nizami, 156). Indian and Briton acknowledged him as a natural leader—sincere, magnanimous, persevering, and courageous, as well as unusually energetic, buoyant, and humorous; his was a noble but, in his later years, somewhat autocratic temperament. Although he believed that Hindus and Muslims in India should form one nation, he laid the foundations of institutions and understandings which were to underpin the growth of Muslim separatism. FRANCIS ROBINSON

Sources A. H. Hali, *Hayat-i Javed*, trans. K. H. Qadiri and D. J. Matthews (1979) · K. A. Nizami, *Sayyid Ahmad Khan* (1966) · F. Robinson, *Separatism among Indian Muslims: the politics of the United Provinces' Muslims, 1860–1923* (1974) · C. W. Troll, *Sayyid Ahmad Khan: a reinterpretation of Muslim theology* (1978) · D. Lelyveld, *Aligarh's first generation: Muslim solidarity in British India* (1978) · G. F. I. Graham, *The life and work of Sir Syed Ahmad Khan KCSI* (1909) · H. Malik, *Sir Sayyid Ahmad Khan and Muslim modernisation in India and Pakistan* (1980) · C. Shackel, 'English translation of Sir Sayyid Ahmad Khan's "Sirat-e-Faridiya"', *Islamic Culture*, 46 (Oct 1972), 307–36 · K. A. Nizami, *Sir Syed album* [1983]
Archives Aligarh Muslim University, India, Maulana Azad Library
Likenesses Lala Deen Dayal, photograph, priv. coll. · cartoon, repro. in *Oudh Punch* (4 Aug 1881) · photograph, priv. coll.

Aickin, Francis (*c.*1735–1812), actor, was born in Dublin. After a brief period of work in his father's weaving business, in 1754 he followed his younger brother James *Aickin into the theatre, and over the next ten years performed in most of Ireland's theatres. His reputation for reliability encouraged Garrick to employ him at Drury Lane, where he made his début as Dick in Vanbrugh's *The Confederacy* on 17 May 1765. He remained a stalwart of Garrick's company for ten years, usually in secondary roles

such as Banquo, Tybalt, or Edmund in *King Lear*, but also as a stage Irishman in comedy. His finest role, one to which he laid claim for most of his long career, was that of Pierre in Otway's *Venice Preserv'd*. Garrick's sudden dismissal of Aickin at the end of the 1773–4 season 'for behaviour apparently nagging and unpleasing to the prompter' (Stone and Kahrl, 593) ended a professional friendship of great significance to Aickin, but he was immediately offered work at the rival playhouse of Covent Garden, with a small increase in salary over the £7 per week Garrick had paid him. He remained a regular in the Covent Garden company until 1792, and made his last London appearance as Jaques in *As You Like It* on 9 November 1792.

Aickin and his first wife, an Irish singer variously recorded as Catherine, Margaret, or Mary Tipper, had established a hosiery business in London, and the income from that helped to sustain them and their five children. Mrs Aickin died on 25 September 1786, and Aickin had disposed of the business by March 1788 when he married a widow named Lowe, who brought him £800 per year. But the theatre was Aickin's life. Each summer, when Drury Lane and Covent Garden were closed, he spent the season at the Haymarket or in Bristol, Richmond, or Cork. It was at Liverpool that he first entered into management, from 1789 to 1796 jointly with John Philip Kemble and from 1796 to 1803 alone. The playhouse in Williamson Square was notoriously unruly, and Aickin's conscientious efforts to enhance it were only partially successful. He had already entered into partnership with John Jackson at the Theatre Royal, Edinburgh, when his Liverpool lease ran out, and he retained his financial interest in Edinburgh until his death.

With rare exceptions, Aickin was liked and respected by his fellows. As he grew older his acting lost its subtlety, and his harshly rhetorical performance of villainous characters earned him the nickname of 'Tyrant Aickin', although his own temperament was anything but tyrannical. He was living modestly in Edgware at the time of his death on 8 November 1812. He was buried at Stanmore church, Middlesex. In his will, dated 25 April 1811, he left £200 together with his gold watch and gold buttons to his surviving son and everything else to his surviving daughter. In a codicil, dated 11 February 1812, he recorded that 'it pleased God to add two hundred a year to my Income on the Edinburgh Theatre'. Aickin divided the bonus equally between his son and his daughter. His other children and his second wife had predeceased him. PETER THOMSON

Sources Highfill, Burnim & Langhans, *BDA* · G. W. Stone, ed., *The London stage, 1660–1800*, pt 4: *1747–1776* (1962) · C. B. Hogan, ed., *The London stage, 1660–1800*, pt 5: *1776–1800* (1968) · G. W. Stone and G. M. Kahrl, *David Garrick: a critical biography* (1979) · J. Boaden, *Memoirs of Mrs Siddons*, 2 vols. (1827) · J. C. Dibdin, *The annals of the Edinburgh stage* (1888)
Likenesses P. Dighton, watercolour tinted drawing, before 1776 (as Bolingbroke), BM · C. Grignion, print, 1776 (after R. Dighton), BM, NPG; repro. in J. Bell, ed., *Bell's edition of Shakespeare's plays*, 9 vols. (1773–4) · W. Walker, engraving, 1777 (after portrait as Phocion by Dodd) · J. Heath, engraving (after bust by A. Davis), Harvard

TC • W. Loftis, watercolour (as Henry IV), Folger • engraving (as Zanga), Harvard TC

Wealth at death £200, gold watch, chain, and seals, gold buttons bequeathed to son; residue incl. money in funds, bonds, household furniture to daughter; codicil records additional income of £200 p.a.: will, Highfill, Burnim & Langhans, BDA

Aickin, James (c.1736–1803), actor, was born in Dublin, the younger son of a weaver. While still under the age of twenty he joined an Irish theatre company, thus setting a precedent which his older brother Francis *Aickin would soon follow. Aickin made a sufficient impression to earn himself a place at the Smock Alley playhouse in Dublin, where he performed from 1756 to 1759. He was then engaged by the manager of the Canongate Theatre in Edinburgh, who had just dispensed with the services of West Digges and was in urgent need of an actor to replace him. Though never a great actor, Aickin was, like his brother, a reliable one. James Boaden thought his voice 'among the sweetest that ever met the ear' (Boaden, 2.60), and Samuel Foote considered him an excellent actor. He was sufficiently versatile in these early days to play Scandal in Congreve's *Love for Love*, Peachum in *The Beggar's Opera*, and Lord Randolph in Home's *Douglas*.

While at Edinburgh, or perhaps before his arrival there, Aickin married an actress who was in the Canongate company with him. They are not known to have had children before her sudden death in 1762. The young widower remained in Edinburgh until 1767, when a managerial decision not to employ a flamboyant local favourite called George Stayley provoked a destructive riot, fomented by students from the university. As the first signatory of a defiant letter, Aickin was at particular risk when, on 24 January 1767, Stayley's supporters set about gutting the interior of the theatre. In the circumstances, his engagement at Garrick's Drury Lane from November 1767 was a desperately needed salvation. He remained at Drury Lane for the rest of his active life, evidently unaffected by his brother's unexpected dismissal in 1774. Except in benefit performances he rarely played the lead, and towards the end of his career his increasing weight (he was nicknamed 'Belly') tended to confine him to elderly roles. In his heyday, though, he was a competent Macduff, Horatio in *Hamlet*, and Edgar in *King Lear*. The *St James's Chronicle* of 3–5 March 1772 found his Rosencrantz in that year's Drury Lane revival of *Hamlet* both well dressed and well bred. His status in the company was recognized by his appointment to the committee that set up the Drury Lane Actors' Fund in 1776 and above all by his appointment as acting manager under Sheridan after John Philip Kemble's disgruntled departure from Drury Lane in 1796.

The quarrel that had led Aickin to challenge Kemble to a duel in 1792 was the most sensational event in Aickin's generally quiet life. The duel took place on 1 March in Marylebone Field, with Charles Bannister acting as second to both men. Aickin having fired first, and missed, Kemble declined to fire back, and the two men were formally reconciled. The arrangement whereby, from 1783 onwards, Aickin took £60 per annum in lieu of benefit was not interrupted. From about 1789 Aickin's health deteriorated. He seems to have suffered a mild stroke in late 1799, returned to the stage on 7 January 1800, played his last part, as Las Casas in Sheridan's *Pizarro*, on 14 February 1800, and shortly afterwards suffered a second, more serious stroke. He died on 17 March 1803, and his funeral at St Anne's Church in Soho was attended by the Drury Lane company. PETER THOMSON

Sources Highfill, Burnim & Langhans, BDA • J. C. Dibdin, *The annals of the Edinburgh stage* (1888) • G. W. Stone, ed., *The London stage, 1660–1800*, pt 4: 1747–1776 (1962) • C. B. Hogan, ed., *The London stage, 1660–1800*, pt 5: 1776–1800 (1968) • J. Boaden, *Memoirs of the life of John Philip Kemble*, 2 vols. (1825) • K. A. Burnim, *David Garrick, director* [1961]

Likenesses W. Walker, engraving, 1776 (as Horatio; after drawing by D. Dodd) • J. Heath, 1800 (after portrait by A. Davis) • attrib. S. De Wilde, oils, Garr. Club • W. Loftis, watercolour (as Guyomar), Folger • gouache drawing, Garr. Club • theatrical prints, BM, NPG

Aickin, Joseph (fl. 1693–1705?), grammarian, was, according to the title-page of his *English Grammar* (1693), a 'Schoolmaster in Fisher-street, near Red Lion Square in Holborn and lately one of the Masters of the Free-School of London-Derry'. An indication of his philosophy appears from the preface statement that English teachers cannot be more respected and better paid 'till it be found that the English Tongue is copious enough of itself, to express every thing and notion' and 'till people do see that it may be perfectly acquired, without being beholden to the Latine' (sig. A3r).

The *English Grammar* was intended for children to learn their mother tongue. Aickin, aware of Comenius's *Orbis sensualium pictus* (1658), recognized some of its pedagogical implications and used pictures to illustrate words that children should be able to learn by associating word with picture and not have to remember the names of the letters. One example is his symbolical alphabet, where, for instance, 'r' appears beside an animal head illustration as 'How doth the Dog grin?' (Aickin, *Grammar*, pt 1, insert between pp. 16 and 17). Aickin mentions that he intended to produce a version of Comenius 'adapted to the English Tongue' (ibid., pt 1, p. 66), evidently a monolingual version given the presence of Hoole's 1659 bilingual edition, but this project was never realized.

One further contribution Aickin makes to teaching English is the first explicit expression of the identity between the active verb and the transitive verb which has 'always the Oblique or Accusative word after it' (Aickin, *Grammar*, pt 2, p. 17).

Twentieth-century commentators have, however, usually castigated Aickin not only for plagiarizing the seventeenth-century grammarian Christopher Cooper and, through him, John Wallis, but also for misinterpreting them. Dobson, for example, reports him as being 'original only in the nature of his mistakes' (Dobson, 355). Aickin had read widely in his field and, I think, felt he was presenting the undeniable laws of grammar. This may help to explain why, for him, plagiarism was not an issue and why he seems to have a knack for recognizing recent insights, publishing them, and then demonstrating that he has entirely missed the point. Two instances will suffice. Firstly, in thinking about pronunciation, Aickin is unable to ignore spelling as, in denying that 'baal' is pronounced 'bawl', he says 'baal' has 'not the least sound of *w* in it' (Aickin, *Grammar*, sig. A5v). Secondly, in the grammar section, while discussing verbal tense, he says 'We have only two times, present and preterit … and all the rest of the tenses are supplied by auxilary Verbs' (ibid., pt 2, p. 10), thereby failing to recognize that auxiliary verbs can also only have present or past tense as Wallis had done.

Aickin appears to have moved to Dublin by the end of the decade. In 1698 a Joseph Aickin produced a short *Address to the Magistrates, Clergy, and Learned Gentlemen of the City of Dublin*, presenting, according to the title-page, 'a rational and expeditious method of teaching the English, Latin and Greek tongues'. The following year a long poem, *Londerias*, commemorating the siege of Londonderry of ten years earlier, was also published in Dublin over the name of Joseph Aickin; its imprint described the author's school as being 'near Essex-Bridge' in the city. He may also have been the Joseph Aickin who wrote a short treatise entitled *The Mysteries of the Counterfeiting of the Coin of the Nation* (1696) and who delivered a sermon about 1697 which was published in Dublin in 1705. Nothing further is known about him.   R. D. SMITH

Sources I. Michael, *The teaching of English from the sixteenth century to 1870* (1987) • I. Michael, *English grammatical categories and the tradition to 1800* (1970) • E. J. Dobson, *English pronunciation, 1500–1700*, 2nd edn, 1 (1968) • J. A. Comenius, *Orbis sensualium pictus* (1658) • E. Vorlat, *The development of English grammatical theory, 1586–1737, with special reference to the theory of parts of speech* (1975) • A. P. R. Howatt, *A history of English language teaching* (1984) • *ESTC*

Aickman, Robert Fordyce (1914–1981), writer and campaigner for inland waterways, was born on 27 June 1914 at 77 Fellows Road, Hampstead, London, the only child of William Arthur Aickman (d. 1941), an architect, and his wife, Mabel Violet (c.1890–1943), daughter of Richard Marsh, born Bernard Heldmann, the prolific Victorian author of popular fiction. Robert Aickman's father was a man of unknown origin and age, though he was perhaps in his mid-fifties when his son was born, and the surname is believed to be Scottish. His mother's family was originally German, deriving from a certain Heldmann who had fled from Bavaria to Nottingham in 1848 and made a fortune from textiles. Richard Marsh met William Arthur Aickman in the gentlemen's lavatory of a grand hotel in Edwardian Eastbourne, and was soon to encourage his marriage to his younger daughter, thirty years William Arthur Aickman's junior. The marriage, and Aickman's childhood, was predictably unhappy, though the family lived in a substantial house, Langton Lodge, at Stanmore, Middlesex. Aickman attended Highgate School and began to be interested in writing there, but he did not then go up to Oxford or Cambridge, as might have been hoped. He entered a period of youthful drifting, writing some theatre reviews for the periodical *The Nineteenth Century and After*, but eventually finding himself alone at Langton Lodge after his mother left his father, who then fell terminally ill and ended his life in a nursing home.

Aickman was eventually rescued from the severe depression this isolation caused when he began to attend

Robert Fordyce Aickman (1914–1981), by Ida Kar, late 1950s

the queue for tickets at London's Covent Garden Opera, and acquired a series of female friends and lovers. The outbreak of the Second World War brought this lifestyle to an end, but he declared himself a conscientious objector and won total exemption from war service. On 5 September 1941 he married (Edith) Ray Gregorson (1913/14–1983), a secretary whom he had met through the opera queue, but more from sympathy than love. They set up a literary agency together, and moved to 11 Gower Street in Bloomsbury, which was to be Aickman's home for much of his life. They divorced in 1957, and she later became an Anglican nun.

In 1946 Robert and Ray Aickman, with Tom (L. T. C.) Rolt and Rolt's wife, Angela, set up the Inland Waterways Association, to preserve and enhance the canals of Britain, which were at that time in such a state of neglect as seemed likely to end in their ultimate disappearance. Aickman was chairman and Rolt secretary, and the organization quickly gained momentum and influence, becoming in many ways a model for the many campaigning pressure groups of post-war Britain. Aickman remained active and superbly energetic in the waterways campaign until 1964, and although his autocratic style of leadership provoked much dissension, it is nevertheless agreed that the salvation of Britain's canals owes more to him than to any other person.

In 1951 Aickman and Elizabeth Jane Howard published *We are for the Dark*, a volume of six ghost stories, where each contributed three, but did not identify who had written which. Aickman was eventually to publish eleven more volumes of what he called 'strange stories', and he succeeded in giving new life to what had been classically an Edwardian genre. Barry Humphries describes his quality:

> To all his uncanny tales he brings his peculiar erudition; his elegant elliptical style. Some of his most disturbing stories are not without flashes of humour and a sly, morbid

eroticism. Above all, he can evoke in a few lines of concentrated prose the tenebrous and oppressive atmosphere of a very bad and inescapable dream. (Humphries, 10)

Between 1964 and 1972 Aickman edited the first eight volumes of *The Fontana Book of Great Ghost Stories*, to all but the sixth of which he contributed learned and stimulating introductions. His other published works included two fantasy novels and two volumes of autobiography, and many stories and plays remained unpublished. He was an inveterate leader and joiner of organizations relating to his interests in transport, theatre, orchestral music, opera, and ballet.

Aickman was a shy man, who blossomed in public life: constitutionally solitary, he derived lifelong solace from relationships with women. He died at the Homeopathic Hospital, Camden, London, on 26 February 1981, of cancer, showing great courage in the face of death, and was cremated at Putney Vale. At odds with the modern world, he left a permanent mark on it through his two disparate but oddly linked fields of endeavour.   C. A. R. HILLS

Sources D. Bolton, *Race against time* (1990) · R. Aickman, *The attempted rescue* (1966) · V. Colby, ed., *World authors, 1980–1985* (1991) · R. Aickman, *The river runs uphill* (1986) · B. Humphries, 'Foreword', in R. Aickman, *Night voices* (1985) · personal knowledge (2004) · private information (2004) [E. J. Howard; J. Sutherland; A. Sutherland] · b. cert. · m. cert. · d. cert.
Archives Boat Museum, Ellesmere Port, collection of canal images · Bowling Green State University, Ohio, corresp., literary MSS, and papers · PRO, corresp.; papers relating to inland waterways, PRO 30/82 | CUL, corresp. with Sir Peter Markham Scott
Likenesses P. Scott, pencil drawing, 1949, repro. in Aickman, *The river runs uphill* · I. Kar, photograph, 1956–9, NPG [*see illus.*] · drawing (as a boy), repro. in Aickman, *Attempted rescue*, frontispiece · photograph (in later life), repro. in Colby, ed., *World authors*
Wealth at death £55,904: probate, 18 May 1981, *CGPLA Eng. & Wales*

Aidan. *See* Aedán mac Gabrán (*c.*535–609?); Áedán (*d.* 651).

Aidan mac Gabrán. *See* Aedán mac Gabrán (*c.*535–609?).

Aidé, (Charles) Hamilton (1826–1906), novelist and poet, born in the rue St Honoré, Paris, on 4 November 1826, was the younger son of George Aïdá (*d.* 1830), a diplomatist and the son of an Armenian merchant settled in Constantinople, and his wife, Georgina Collier (*d.* 1875), second daughter of Admiral Sir George *Collier. Aidé's youth was marked by the deaths of his cosmopolitan father in a duel in Paris, when Aidé was only four years old, and of his brother Frederick (1823–31), killed in an accident in Boulogne the following year.

Taken by his mother to England, Aidé was educated privately at East Sheen and Greenwich until the age of sixteen, when he was sent to the University of Bonn. In 1846 he obtained a commission in the British army, serving with the 85th light infantry until 1853, when he retired with the rank of captain. After a period of foreign travel he settled in England, living chiefly at Lyndhurst in the New Forest with his mother until her death at Southsea, Hampshire, on 12 October 1875. He then took rooms in

Queen Anne's Gate, London, where he entertained prominent figures in the British and French social and artistic worlds.

Aidé, who spoke and wrote French as easily as English, devoted himself to society, music, art, and literature. In 1856 he published his first volume of poems, *Eleanore, and other Poems*. His first novel, *Rita*, also appeared in 1856 and enjoyed greater popularity than his poetry, running to four editions within nine years and being translated into French in 1862. Aidé capitalized on his success, producing *Confidences: by the Author of 'Rita'* in 1859, which also sold well. His novels were light romances set in fashionable society and were simply written, under an obvious French influence. His frequent use of first-person female narrators led some early reviewers to believe that he was a woman. In 1868 he serialized a novel, *The Marstons*, in *Fraser's Magazine*, and he was to write a further fifteen novels over the next forty years, including *Penruddock* (1873), an autobiographical novel containing revealing sections on the protagonist's 'vexed relation with his mother' (Sutherland, 13) and his experiences in the army. Also of interest is *A Voyage of Discovery* (1892), which contains a depiction of American society that angered many transatlantic readers.

The *Biograph and Review* observed that 'Certainly the combination of poet, novelist, dramatist and musical composer is an unusual one, and exhibits Mr Aidé as a man of exceptional powers and accomplishments'. In the 1870s Aidé had turned his attention to the stage, and *Philip*, a romantic drama in four acts, was produced by Henry Irving at the Lyceum in London in February 1874, Irving taking the title role. A year later, *A Nine Days' Wonder*, adapted from Aidé's simultaneously published novel for copyright reasons, was staged at the Court Theatre by John Hare. It was compared to French drama and praised for its 'neatness of construction rare in English art' (Knight, 46).

Meanwhile, Aidé continued to write novels and poetry. *Poet and Peer* (1880) and *Introduced to Society* (1884) confirmed his reputation as a writer of light popular fiction. In 1882 he produced a collection of poetry, *Songs without Music: Rhymes and Recitations*, which was enlarged in 1889. Many poems appeared in popular Victorian anthologies, and he set many to music. 'The Danube River', 'The Spanish Boat Song', and 'Brown Eyes and Blue Eyes' were among his best-known songs. A collection of seven one-act plays entitled *We are Seven: Half Hours on the Stage, Grave and Gay* appeared in 1902, and his final collection of poems, *Past and Present*, in 1903.

Aidé died, unmarried, at 28 Half Moon Street, Piccadilly, London, on 13 December 1906 and was buried in the churchyard of All Souls, South Ascot, Berkshire. A novel, *The Chivalry of Harold*, was published posthumously in 1907.   KATHERINE MULLIN

Sources J. Knight, *Theatrical notes* (1893), 44–7 · A. T. C. Pratt, ed., *People of the period: being a collection of the biographies of upwards of six thousand living celebrities*, 2 vols. (1897) · R. S. Gower, *Old diaries, 1881–1901* (1902) · *Biograph and Review*, 3 (1880), 171–2 · *WWW, 1897–1915* · J. Sutherland, *The Longman companion to Victorian fiction* (1988), 12–13 · *The Times* (17–21 Dec 1906) · G. Vapereau, ed., 'Aidé (Hamilton)', *Dictionnaire universel des contemporains*, 6th edn (Paris, 1893), 14 · J. D.

Brown, *Biographical dictionary of musicians: with a bibliography of English writings on music* (1886), 9 • *Biographical Magazine*, 9 (1887), 56–66 • R. Gower, *My reminiscences*, 2 vols. (1883) • *William Allingham: a diary*, ed. H. Allingham and D. Radford (1907) • *CGPLA Eng. & Wales* (1907) • *DNB*

Archives NRA, corresp. and literary papers • West Glamorgan Archive Service, Swansea, account book | Trinity Cam., letters to F. H. W. Myers • Yale U., Beinecke L., letters to Frederick Locker-Lampson

Likenesses S. Della Rovera, oils

Wealth at death £43,562 9s. 3d.: resworn probate, 15 Feb 1907, *CGPLA Eng. & Wales*

Aigle, Richer de l' (c.1095–1176), baron, the eldest son of Gilbert de l'Aigle and Juliana, daughter of Geoffroi, count of Mortagne, was a member of a family with a tradition of service to the Norman dukes. His great-grandfather, Engenulf, had been killed at Hastings and his grandfather Richer during a Norman campaign in Maine. His father was a leading member of Henry I's military household and had received lands around Pevensey in Sussex which had been forfeited to the crown by Guillaume, count of Mortain, in 1106. On the death of his father about 1117 Richer sought from King Henry, in addition to the family property on the southern Norman marches, his father's English lands. When Henry refused on the grounds that the English lands should go to his younger brothers, Geoffroi and Engenulf, Richer carried out his threat to change allegiance to the king of France, Louis VI. The timely intervention of his mother's brother, Rotrou, count of Perche, secured the English lands for him, though he was probably estranged from the king for the best part of a year.

In 1131 Richer was in possession of the Sussex lands and it must have been at about this period that his acquaintance with the Becket family led to a friendship with the young Thomas Becket. In 1136 when Normandy waited for the arrival of King Stephen, with Geoffrey Plantagenet, count of Anjou, poised to assert the claims of his wife, the Empress Matilda, Richer was again involved in disorder on the Norman frontier. In 1137 he and his uncle Rotrou agreed to support King Stephen, and he was granted the castle at Bonsmoulins as a reward for his services. He was in England at the royal court in 1139, and in September 1140, while leading a company of knights to England, he was captured by agents of the earl of Leicester and imprisoned until his uncle Rotrou secured his release. In the early 1150s he seems to have established good relations with the new duke of Normandy, the young Henry Plantagenet, whose charter of liberties for Rouen he witnessed, but in 1152 he was involved in further lawlessness and Henry burned his castle at Bonsmoulins. It comes as no surprise therefore that in the 1153 settlement between King Stephen and Henry the de l'Aigle family lands in Sussex were assigned to Stephen's younger son, William, and in 1158 Richer was forced to surrender Bonsmoulins to Henry II. In the late 1150s his foundation of a Fontevraudine priory at La Chaise du Theil, near l'Aigle, received a royal confirmation from King Henry, which may indicate a return to favour. By the mid-1160s Richer had regained his Sussex lands and in 1166 made a return

dealing with their knight service, although his returns to the Norman inquiry in the 1170s were incomplete.

Richer was a benefactor of the monasteries of Lyre, La Trappe, and Thiron, as well as the priories of Wilmington in Sussex, Notre Dame du Désert, and St Sulpice-de-Lisle in Normandy. He married Beatrix, whose parentage is unknown, and was the father of Richer, Roger, Engenulph, and a daughter, Juliana, wife of Gilbert of Tillières. Richer died in 1176, probably on 24 August, and was buried in the priory of St Sulpice-sur-Risle. He was a cross-channel magnate of the second rank, whose family fortunes in England were founded on the breakup of the great honours of William the Conqueror's companions. His landed interests in England, which may well have been greater than the family's original Norman estates, were finally resumed by the crown in 1231 when his grandson Gilbert died without direct heirs.

KATHLEEN THOMPSON

Sources Ordericus Vitalis, *Eccl. hist.*, esp. vol. 6 • Cartulaire du prieuré de Saint-Sulpice-sur-Risle, Archives Départementales du Loiret, D668 • *Chronique de Robert de Torigni*, ed. L. Delisle, 2 (Rouen, 1873), vol. 2 • *Materials for the history of Thomas Becket, archbishop of Canterbury*, 4, ed. J.C. Robertson, Rolls Series, 67 (1879), 6 • K. Thompson, 'The lords of Laigle: ambition and insecurity on the borders of Normandy', *Anglo-Norman Studies*, 18 (1995), 177–99 • K. Thompson, 'Lords, castellans, constables and dowagers: the rape of Pevensey from the 11th to the 13th century', *Sussex Archaeological Collections*, 135 (1997), 209–20

Aigueblanche, Peter d' [Peter de Aqua Blanca] (d. 1268), bishop of Hereford and royal counsellor, was descended from the family of Briançon, holders of the lordship of Aigueblanche (Savoie) in the Tarentaise or valley of the upper Isère, dependants of the counts of Savoy.

Early career in England, 1237–1244 The names of Aigueblanche's father and mother are unknown, and he himself is unrecorded before his appearance in 1237 as a clerk, possibly the treasurer of William of Savoy, bishop-elect of Valence and uncle of Queen Eleanor of Provence. In March 1238 he was presented by the king to the church of St Michael-on-Wyre in Lancashire, and following the death of his patron, William of Savoy, in 1239, he took up permanent residence in England. In April 1240 he was in receipt of an annual fee from the king of £20, and from July he served as keeper of the king's wardrobe.

Having in July 1240 been granted a prebend at Hereford, on 24 August Aigueblanche was elected bishop, a promotion at Hereford due entirely to royal favour. However, since Hereford was not a wealthy see, later that year the king attempted unsuccessfully to have him elected to the far richer bishopric of Durham. On 23 December 1240 he was consecrated bishop of Hereford at St Paul's Cathedral in London, by the archbishop of York and the bishop of Worcester acting in the presence of the papal legate Otto. The king supplied him with many precious gifts, including use of the archbishop of Canterbury's house at Lambeth for the feast of his consecration, a jewelled mitre valued at £82, venison and victuals for his feast, game and rabbits with which to stock his episcopal estates, and a loan of £300. Over the next few months, moreover, Bishop

Peter d' Aigueblanche (d. 1268), tomb effigy

with the duty of delivering the archbishop's pallium and with receiving Boniface's oath of fealty.

Servant of king and archbishop, 1244–1253 Throughout this period Aigueblanche was frequently commissioned by Pope Innocent IV to grant benefices to favoured alien and royal clerks, and to act as papal spokesman to the king. As a result he became embroiled in a long-standing dispute between the pope and Henry III over the king's harsh treatment of William of Raleigh, bishop of Winchester. At Reading in the spring of 1244, and again at Westminster, he is said to have delivered stern rebukes to Henry, demanding a reconciliation with Raleigh, and threatening a sentence of interdict against the king's private chapel. In the summer of 1245 he attended the general council held by Innocent IV at Lyons, while by the early months of 1246 he was in Savoy, acting as an agent of Henry III in the process by which Count Amadeus was persuaded to render homage to the king for various of his alpine lordships. Thereafter he returned to England, where he had been charged by the pope with a commission to collect the first fruits of vacant churches on behalf of the financially embarrassed archbishop, an unprecedented tax which stirred up resentment against both Boniface and Peter. Until Boniface's return to England in 1249 Peter continued to serve as his principal deputy, with a supervisory role over the Canterbury estates.

For much of 1246 Aigueblanche was active in the diocese of Hereford, securing the return of manors and churches alienated by his predecessors, serving as papal commissioner in the collection of subsidies for the forthcoming crusade, and issuing a series of statutes enforcing residence upon the clergy of prebendal churches. In September 1247, and again in November 1249, he went on missions to France, and on the latter occasion he travelled on to the papal court, to serve as royal proctor in matters touching the crusade. Aigueblanche himself took the cross at about this time, probably early in 1250. He appears to have spent much of the next two years with the pope or in affairs overseas, including a prolonged series of hearings, completed at Sens in 1251, intended to clarify the circumstances of Henry III's marriage to Eleanor of Provence, by proving the irregularity of an earlier contract of marriage which had been negotiated but not finalized between Henry and Jeanne, the heir of Ponthieu, before 1236. Since Jeanne had later married Alfonso, king of Castile, it may well be that these hearings were intended to ease the way for a marriage between Henry's and Eleanor's son Edward, and a Castilian princess, duly negotiated by Aigueblanche at Toledo in a series of embassies between 1253 and the spring of 1254.

In his absences overseas Aigueblanche appointed proctors to administer the diocese of Hereford, including an alien named Bernard, prior of Campagne in Gascony. This foreign domination of his see appears to have been bitterly resented, and in the course of a long-standing dispute between the bishop and chapter of Hereford over their respective temporalities, eventually settled in the chapter's favour, the summer of 1252 witnessed a serious

Peter received a series of royal charters, awarding him market privileges, rights of free warren, and timber within the king's forests. Although he had relinquished his position as keeper of the king's wardrobe, he remained active in royal service, and in August 1241 accompanied the court to Shrewsbury, where he participated in a peace settlement with the Welsh. That autumn the king failed once again to have him translated to a richer see, this time that of London.

In November 1241 Aigueblanche was involved as papal judge-delegate in the king's dispute with the bishop of Bath and Wells over the patronage of Glastonbury Abbey, and in March 1242 he was sent overseas, at first to Poitou, to prepare for the king's proposed expedition there, and then to Provence, where in July 1242, at Tarascon, he sealed the marriage treaty for an alliance between Richard of Cornwall, Henry III's brother, and Sanchia, a daughter of the count of Provence and sister of Queen Eleanor. By August he was once again in Poitou with the king. As a Savoyard he was inevitably brought into contact with the king's uncle, Boniface of Savoy, elected archbishop of Canterbury in February 1241, but absent and unconsecrated for several years thereafter. By 1243 Aigueblanche was acting as chief agent of the absentee archbishop-elect. At Easter 1244 he was summoned to Dover to greet Boniface on his arrival in England, charged by the pope outbreak of violence in Herefordshire, in which Aigueblanche's own life was threatened, his and his supporters' barns were burned, and Prior Bernard was murdered before the high altar of Hereford Cathedral. In February 1253, to protect him from further attacks, Aigueblanche was promised access to the royal castle at Hereford whenever he should ask for it. In the same year he was among the bishops and magnates who sealed a solemn sentence upholding Magna Carta, and at much the same time is said to have unsuccessfully petitioned the English clergy to grant an aid to the king.

'The Sicilian business', 1253–1258 In June 1253 Aigueblanche accompanied Henry III's expedition to Gascony, and from there headed embassies to Castile to arrange for the marriage of the future king, Edward I. In October 1253 it was Peter who solemnly held the king's hand as Henry III swore an oath to confer Gascony upon his eldest son. In the following month he received royal letters of safe conduct as envoy to the papal court, and he seems to have remained with the new pope, Alexander IV, at Naples, for much of the spring of 1255. There he negotiated a notorious arrangement whereby the pope confirmed a grant of the kingdom of Sicily to Henry III, originally made by Innocent IV in 1254, to serve as an apanage for Henry's younger son Edmund. In return, Henry was not only to conquer Sicily and to eject its ruler, King Manfred, but also to repay all the expenses already incurred by the papacy in warfare against Manfred, estimated at the huge sum of 135,000 marks of silver.

To cover the costs of his embassy, and to begin the payment of the enormous debt now owed to the pope, Aigueblanche raised loans at the papal curia from the merchants of Florence and Siena, against which, as security for repayment, he pledged the future proceeds of a tax of a tenth imposed by the pope upon the English church since 1252. In so doing, and to the great outrage of the English clergy, he employed a series of blank schedules that had been sealed by the clergy and handed to him to use in his negotiations with the pope, but whose contents were left to Peter to complete according to his own discretion. Monastic chroniclers are unanimous in their assertion that the signatories to these letters had received no warning that their letters would be used to raise loans, let alone to raise loans for such a doomed venture as the conquest of Sicily. This, more than anything, was to mark out Peter as the most hated alien bishop in England. Something of the extravagance of his arrangements can be gauged from a bond, issued at Naples in April 1255, by which the merchants of Siena accepted 10,000 marks of gold from Peter in return for their surrender of a crown, regalia, and various jewels previously pawned to them by Frederick II. All told, 'the Sicilian business', was to bankrupt Henry III, and to stir up a storm of protest from his English subjects.

Aigueblanche must take at least part of the blame for this fiasco, although it should be noted that he was acting merely as an agent of the king, that the bishops and clergy had freely agreed to seal the blank charters that he was later accused of misusing, and that his pledging of future

tax revenues merely imitated an arrangement of September 1254, whereby the king had financed Peter's own expenses at the papal court by raising loans from the merchants of Florence secured against the proceeds of the clerical tenth within the sees of Hereford and Worcester. On his return to England in 1255 he found himself an object of hatred among bishops and barons alike. Despite his own attempts and those of the papal envoy Rostand to collect the tenth in England and Ireland, resistance was widespread and impassioned. Aigueblanche returned to the papal court as the king's envoy in November 1255, and in September 1256 was once again sent to Gascony. There, in April 1257, he was empowered to conduct negotiations over breaches of the Anglo-French truce. When the archbishop of Bordeaux fell ill that same year, Aigueblanche is said to have made no secret of his desire to succeed him, but, like an earlier request from the king in 1254 that Peter be translated from Hereford to Lincoln, this came to nothing. By 1257 Aigueblanche was suffering severe discomfort from a polypus in his nose, for the treatment of which he is said to have travelled to Montpellier, home to a major medical school.

Enemy of the barons, 1258–1267 With the outbreak of baronial rebellion, in the early summer of 1258, Aigueblanche's manor of Ledbury was attacked by the bailiffs of John (II) Fitzalan of Clun. As chief author of 'the Sicilian business', he was not surprisingly excluded from royal counsels, and between July and November 1258 was summoned to render accounts for his receipts from the papal tax. Pleading illness, he failed to cross to England, but he had returned to England by June 1259, and in that month and again in November was engaged in peace negotiations with the Welsh. In November 1261, with the resurgence in the king's personal power, he was appointed one of three royalist representatives set to adjudicate on the baronial programme of reform, and in the following year, together with Leonardo, precentor of Messina, he was appointed by the pope to resume the collection of money still owing from the Sicilian affair.

With the drift towards civil war Aigueblanche was singled out as a target for baronial reprisals. His houses, parks, and warrens were attacked before February 1262, and for a time he was himself barricaded within the city walls of Hereford. In the same year he was active against the Welsh, and wrote to the king of his inability to prevent attacks. In February 1263 he was asked to surrender Hereford Castle to a new royalist constable. In the same month he was expected to attend Henry III in Paris. On 7 June 1263 he was forcibly seized in Hereford Cathedral by Roger of Leybourne, Roger de Clifford, John Giffard, and other marcher lords. From there he was carried off, with various of his canons and clergy, to imprisonment at Walter de Baskerville's castle of Eardisley. The temporalities of his see were plundered by the barons. The date of his capture was later accepted at court as the official commencement of civil war. Aigueblanche himself was released following representations to the parliament of September 1263, although not until Archbishop Boniface had absolved the barons from any guilt in the affair.

In September, Aigueblanche crossed with Henry III to Amiens, where he is said to have been instrumental in stirring up French indignation against the barons, and where in January 1264 he witnessed the judgment issued by Louis IX, entirely quashing the baronial programme of reform. Thereafter he remained overseas throughout the period of civil war. His lands remained in baronial hands, and in June 1265 he was sent a fierce rebuke, no doubt dictated by the barons, demanding that he return to his diocese on pain of the sequestration of his temporalities. In August, following the royalist victory at Evesham, he and his canons received letters of protection, and he was subsequently promised the repayment of money seized by the previous custodians of his lands. None the less, various of his manors, including Bishops Castle and Ledbury North, continued to be withheld by the royalist John Fitzalan, while others were effectively detached by the Welsh. In February 1267 he received further letters of protection, presumably to go overseas to Savoy, where he is found at Aiguebelle in April.

Death and legacy The final months of Aigueblanche's life are shrouded in obscurity, but his will, drawn up at Sugwas in Herefordshire on 26 November 1268, demonstrates that his death, on 27 November, took place in England. Despite the terms of his will, requesting burial at Aiguebelle in Savoy, the bishop's body was buried in Hereford Cathedral, beneath a magnificent carved tomb and effigy, perhaps of foreign workmanship, from which it was exhumed in 1925. The canons of Aiguebelle later exhibited a rival tomb, with a fifteenth-century bronze effigy which was destroyed at the Revolution. But there can be little doubt that this monument was the result of later wishful thinking. His will, which survives, assigns most of his estate to the collegiate church at Aiguebelle which he had founded in the 1250s, and to which, on 21 April 1267, he had granted statutes modelled upon those of Hereford Cathedral. It also reveals the extent of his property holding in France. Until 1254 he had held the small Cluniac priory of Innimont in the diocese of Belley, perhaps through the influence of Archbishop Boniface. In 1254 Aigueblanche had exchanged Innimont for the priory of Ste Hélène-du-Lac in his native Tarentaise, augmented by Boniface in September 1255 with an assignment of the castle and lordship of Ste Hélène-des-Millères. In 1267 these secular rights were willed to Peter's nephew and namesake, the lord of Briançon. In addition Aigueblanche disposed of houses in Lyons and Paris, and willed property and money in France to various hospitals and monasteries in the Tarentaise. His glossed Bible was to be sold to clothe the poor, while his obituary was celebrated as far afield as Geneva.

During Aigueblanche's lifetime, as early as 1252, he had assigned the Hereford churches of All Saints and St Martin to the hospital of St Anthony at Vienne near Lyons. Many of his nephews and kinsmen had already obtained prebends and offices within Hereford Cathedral, where they continued to form an identifiable Savoyard faction as late as the 1290s. Matthew Paris, one of his sternest critics, accuses Aigueblanche of 'fox-like cunning', claiming that

'his memory exudes a sulphurous stench' (Paris, *Chron.*, 5.510). In reality, despite his supposed inability to speak the English language, Peter was a reasonably conscientious bishop and diocesan, who rebuilt and enriched the temporalities of his see, confirmed churches to the religious, and enforced residence upon the canons of his cathedral. His gifts to the chapter included part of the manor of Holme Lacy and the church of Bockleton, while throughout his episcopate he obtained regular gifts of timber from the king, used in an ambitious programme of new building at Hereford Cathedral, in the completion of the presbytery and a new north transept. Neither his property disputes with his chapter, nor his nepotistic advancement of his own kinsmen were in any way exceptional by the standards of the time. Less defensible is Aigueblanche's political career, where he undoubtedly played a part in widening the breach between king and barons, and where his negotiations over Sicily can be regarded as at best foolhardy and at worst thoroughly dishonest.

NICHOLAS VINCENT

Sources Chancery records · Paris, *Chron.*, vols. 4–5 · *CEPR letters*, vol. 1 · C. E. Woodruff, ed., 'The will of Peter de Aqua Blanca, bishop of Hereford, 1268', Camden miscellany, XIV, CS, 3rd ser., 37 (1926) · R. G. Griffiths and W. W. Capes, eds., *Registrum Thome de Cantilupo, episcopi Herefordensis*, CYS, 2 (1907) · W. W. Capes, ed., *Charters and records of Hereford Cathedral*, Cantilupe Society (1908) · J. Webb, ed., *A roll of the household expenses of Richard de Swinfield, bishop of Hereford, during part of the years 1289 and 1290*, CS, 59, 62 (1853–5) · *Ann. mon.* · T. Stapleton, ed., *De antiquis legibus liber: cronica majorum et vicecomitum Londoniarum*, CS, 34 (1846) · P. Chaplais, ed., *Diplomatic documents preserved in the Public Record Office*, 1 (1964) · J. N. Dalton, ed., *The manuscripts of St George's Chapel, Windsor Castle* (1957) · BL, Cotton MS Cleopatra E.i, fols. 194r–195r · Canterbury Cathedral Library, chartae antiquae MSS B.393, M.364 · J. L. Wurstemberger, *Peter der Zweite, Graf von Savoyen, sein Haus und seine Lande*, 4 vols. (1856–8) · E. L. Cox, *The eagles of Savoy: the house of Savoy in thirteenth-century Europe* (1974) · F. Mugnier, 'Les Savoyards en Angleterre au XIIIe siècle', *Mémoires et documents publiés par la Société Savoisienne*, 29 (1890) · L. Vercoutère, 'À propos de la découverte d'une colonne féodale du XIIIe siècle aux Avanchers (Savoie): les seigneurs de Briançon et d'Aigueblanche en Tarentaise du Xe au XIVe siècles', *Recueil des mémoires et documents de l'Académie de la Val d'Isère*, new ser., 8/pt 2 (1936) · L. Ménabréa, *Des origines féodales dans les Alpes occidentales* (1865) · J.-P. Chapuisat, 'A propos des relations entre la Savoie et l'Angleterre au XIIIe siècle', *Bulletin Philologique et Historique* (1960) · F. M. Powicke, *King Henry III and the Lord Edward: the community of the realm in the thirteenth century*, 2 vols. (1947) · J. R. Maddicott, *Simon de Montfort* (1994) · H. M. Colvin, 'Holme Lacy: an episcopal manor and its tenants in the twelfth and thirteenth centuries', *Medieval studies presented to Rose Graham*, ed. V. Ruffer and A. J. Taylor (1950), 15–40 · W. N. Yates, 'Bishop Peter de Aquablanca (1240–1268): a reconsideration', *Journal of Ecclesiastical History*, 22 (1971), 303–17
Likenesses tomb effigy, Hereford Cathedral [see illus.]

Aiken, Francis Thomas [Frank] (1898–1983), Irish revolutionary and politician, was born on 13 February 1898 at Carrickbracken, Camlough, co. Armagh, into a well-to-do farming family. He was the son of a James Aiken and his wife, Mary McGeeney. As well as being a farmer, his father was also a builder, responsible for many churches in south Armagh, and was a county councillor and the first nationalist chairman of the local board of guardians. Frank Aiken was educated by the Christian Brothers in Newry, before leaving school at sixteen to manage the family farm. He joined the Irish Volunteers in 1913, belonged to the Gaelic Athletic Association, and in 1914 became secretary to the local branch of the Gaelic League. In 1917 he became chairman of the Co-operative Flax-scutching Society in co. Armagh.

In June 1918 Aiken was elected commandant of the Camlough battalion of the volunteers (soon to be known as the IRA). He organized the Dáil loan in Armagh in 1919–20, and was elected to the county council in 1920 and to the Dáil in 1921. During the War of Independence he distinguished himself as a fighter, most notably through a train derailment in June 1921 which killed forty British soldiers. By the time of the July 1921 truce he was commandant of the 4th northern division. He supported de Valera in opposing the 1921 Anglo-Irish treaty, but strove to avoid what he felt would be the catastrophe of an IRA split and civil war. When fighting broke out in Dublin in June 1922, Aiken held back from precipitate action in hopes of a quick truce. Imprisoned by government forces lest he change his mind, he led a daring mass escape from Dundalk prison in July 1922 and joined the civil war. When the irreconcilable IRA leader Liam Lynch was killed in April 1923, Aiken, who had survived the fatal engagement, succeeded him as chief of staff. On 28 May he issued the 'dump arms' order which ended the conflict while preserving republican *amour propre* by avoiding a surrender of weapons. He won a Dáil seat in co. Louth as an abstentionist in the general election of August 1923, and held it until his retirement in 1973. Comfortably off through inheritance, he was able to devote himself largely to politics.

Aiken's political life was marked by his unswerving loyalty to de Valera, by his personal integrity, and by his dogged pursuit of pet projects while in office. He supported de Valera in the split with republican purists which produced Fianna Fáil in 1926, and he took his Dáil seat in 1927, when the party abandoned abstention. When Fianna Fáil won power in 1932, de Valera gave him the sensitive post of minister for defence, where, contrary to expectations, he quickly won the confidence of his former military enemies and ensured that the army remained a docile, if emaciated, instrument of the state. An early advocate of turf development, he was vindicated by the eventual emergence of a successful indigenous industry. He married, on 3 October 1934, Mary Maud Davin, director of the Dublin Municipal School of Music, the daughter of John Davin, hotel proprietor. They had two sons and a daughter.

As minister for the co-ordination of defensive measures between 1939 and 1945, Frank Aiken is remembered for a rigid and pedantic media censorship, and for his spring 1941 mission to the United States seeking food, weapons, and shipping. The Roosevelt administration was hostile to Irish neutrality, and Aiken's difficult experience at their hands influenced his attitude to post-war world politics. From 1945 to 1948 he was an unexceptional minister for finance, but he found his true niche as minister for external affairs from 1951 to 1954, and from 1957 to 1969 (from 1965 to 1969 he was also tánaiste, or deputy prime minister). He believed that because of its history Ireland could identify with and assist the new African and Asian states emerging through decolonization, so he was an enthusiast for the United Nations once Ireland was admitted in 1955. The policy he pursued there consequently exhibited an independence of thought on issues such as decolonization, the admission of China, disarmament, and nuclear non-proliferation; this often irritated the United States, but undoubtedly enhanced the country's standing in the international community. Closer to home, his Armagh upbringing left him fatalistic rather than fanatical about partition, and he was always a moderating influence within Fianna Fáil. This was particularly important when nationalist feeling ran high during the first years of the modern northern troubles.

Frank Aiken was an austere figure, tall, reserved, and immune either to intimidation or to flattery. A friend wrote that he was indifferent to the opinions of his political friends, his opponents, or indeed of anyone except de Valera. Yet he was a man of quiet passions: turf, the Irish language, nuclear non-proliferation, peaceful decolonization. He died in St Vincent's Hospital, Dublin, on 18 May 1983. His wife predeceased him.   EUNAN O'HALPIN

Sources L. C. Skinner, 'Frank Aiken', *Politicians by accident* (1946), 151–80 · C. S. Andrews, *Man of no property: an autobiography*, 2 (1982) · J. M. Skelley, *Irish policy at the United Nations, 1945–65* (1996) · *WWW* · b. cert. · m. cert. · d. cert. · *CGPLA Ire.* (1984) · *The Times* (20 May 1983)
Archives FILM BFI NFTVA, news footage
Wealth at death £149,756: probate, 1984, Ireland

Aikenhead, Mary Frances (1787–1858), Roman Catholic nun, was born on 19 January 1787, in the house adjoining the Aikenhead and Dupont apothecary premises on the corner of Grand Parade and Castle Street in Cork. She was the eldest of four children of Dr David Aikenhead, a physician and apothecary, and his wife, Mary, *née* Stackpole. Her father, who came from a Scottish military background, was first-generation Irish, and a member of the Church of Ireland; her mother came from an old recusant merchant family in Cork. Although Aikenhead was baptized in her father's religion at Shandon Protestant Church in Cork, her parents followed Irish custom by fostering her out to the Catholic couple Mary and John Rorke of Eason's Hill. After returning to her city home at six years of age, Aikenhead accompanied her father to Shandon church on Sundays, but Roman Catholic influences persisted in her life as her maternal grandmother and a widowed aunt introduced her to Ursuline and Presentation nuns in Cork. Her father's deathbed reception into the Catholic church led her to take instruction and make her confirmation in the Catholic faith on 2 July 1802.

Aikenhead assumed the management of family concerns and by the age of seventeen was attracted to the service of the poor. Through the connections of Anna Maria O'Brien (1785–1871), a close friend, Aikenhead came to Dublin and was introduced to a circle of philanthropic Catholic women engaged in ministering to the increasing numbers of Dublin poor. Aware of Aikenhead's resolution

Mary Frances Aikenhead (1787–1858), by unknown artist, c.1807

to serve the poor, Daniel Murray, who was then co-adjutor Roman Catholic bishop of Dublin, persuaded Aikenhead to found a religious congregation for that purpose and arranged authorization from the Vatican.

With a companion, Alicia Walsh, Aikenhead commenced a three-year novitiate at the Bar Convent of the Institute of the Blessed Virgin Mary in York, on 6 June 1812. She was formally nominated superior-general of the order of the Irish Sisters of Charity on 7 September 1815, and took possession of the North William Street orphanage in Dublin, where her new congregation opened a convent. Despite financial strain Aikenhead opened a second convent in Stanhope Street in 1819, where she personally instructed the novices in the regulations of her congregation. An official invitation to extend the mission of the Irish Sisters of Charity to prison visitation was issued by the prison authorities of Kilmainham gaol: Aikenhead visited two young women convicted of murder until they were executed.

Steady increase in the number of recruits assisted new foundations. Aikenhead was foremost in offering free education to poor Catholic girls and in 1834 she opened St Vincent's Hospital, the first Catholic hospital in Dublin. Despite increasingly poor health Aikenhead made foundations in Peacock Lane, Cork, in Lady Lane, Waterford, in Clonmel, co. Tipperary, and in Clarinbridge, co. Galway, and she sent five sisters to establish a foundation in Sydney, Australia, in 1838. For the last twenty-seven years of her life Aikenhead was an invalid, suffering from chronic spinal disease, dropsy, and eventual paralysis. Her last years were spent in Our Lady's Hospice for the Dying at Harold's Cross, Dublin, which she founded in 1845 and where she died on 22 July 1858. She was buried in the cemetery of St Mary Magdalen's Convent in Donnybrook, Dublin. After her death the Irish Sisters of Charity spread to England, Scotland, the United States, and Africa. They continued to expand Aikenhead's founding ministry to the schooling and housing of poor children and orphans, and to tending the sick and dying. Still vigorous at the end

of the twentieth century, the Irish Sisters of Charity administer large schools, orphanages, hospitals, and hospices for the dying. The decree introducing Aikenhead's cause for beatification in Rome was issued in 1921.   MARGARET MAC CURTAIN

Sources S. A. [S. Atkinson], *Mary Aikenhead: her life, her work and her friends* (1879) · M. Bayley Butler, *A candle was lit: the life of Mother M. Aikenhead* (1953) · M. Donovan, *Apostolate of love: Mary Aikenhead, 1787–1858, foundress of the Irish Sisters of Charity* (1979) · P. M. Mac Sweeney, *Letters of Mary Aikenhead* (1914) · *The life and work of Mary Aikenhead, foundress of Irish Sisters of Charity, 1787–1858* (1925) · M. Nethercott, *The story of Mary Aikenhead, foundress of the Irish Sisters of Charity* (1897) · Milltown convent, Milltown, Dublin, Ireland, Archives of the Irish Sisters of Charity

Archives Dublin Roman Catholic archdiocese, 'Positoi' MSS · Milltown convent, Milltown, Dublin, archives of the Irish Sisters of Charity

Likenesses miniature, c.1807, repro. in S. A., *Mary Aikenhead* [see illus.] · N. J. Crowley, oils, exh. RA 1845, St Vincent's Hospital, Dublin · Crawley, portrait, Milltown convent, Milltown, Dublin, archives of the Irish Sisters of Charity

Wealth at death £450: resworn probate, May 1863, *CGPLA Ire.* (1858)

Aikenhead, Thomas (*bap.* 1676, *d.* 1697), freethinker and blasphemer, was baptized on 28 March 1676, the son of James Aikenhead (*d.* in or before 1683), apothecary and burgess of Edinburgh, and his wife, Helen (*d.* 1685), daughter of Thomas Ramsey, former minister of Foulden. He matriculated at the University of Edinburgh in 1693 and was in his third year of studies when he came to the attention of the authorities for his heterodox opinions. On 10 November 1696 he was summoned before the Scottish privy council, charged with blasphemy, and remitted for prosecution in the courts. The privy council was clearly influenced not only by the outrageousness of what had been reported of Aikenhead's views, but also by the fact that irreligious opinions seemed to be becoming commoner in Edinburgh at this time.

The indictment at Aikenhead's trial itemizes the extreme anti-Christian views that he was accused of expressing. He was said to have ridiculed the scriptures as 'stuffed with maddness, nonsense, and contradictions', describing the Old Testament as 'Ezra's fables', an opinion possibly derived from Spinoza. The New Testament he labelled 'the History of the Impostor Christ', denying Christ's divinity and describing his miracles as 'pranks'; he also compared him unfavourably with both Moses and Muhammad as a manipulative politician. He was said to have rejected the doctrine of the Trinity, seeing the notion of spirit as a contradiction, and maintaining 'that God, the world, and nature, are but one thing, and that the world was from eternity'. In all Aikenhead was as complete a freethinker as any in early modern Europe, and he went further than most in averring that Christianity would soon 'be utterly extirpat', possibly as early as 1800 (*State trials*, 13.919–20).

Aikenhead's trial took place on 23 December 1696. The indictment against him invoked two acts of the Scottish parliament, one, of 1661, prescribing the death penalty for blasphemous utterances, and a further act passed in 1695 which prescribed milder punishments for the first and second such offences, with death only following a third. At his trial Aikenhead pleaded various mitigating circumstances, and these were repeated in two petitions that he addressed to the privy council. But doubt about the sincerity of his repentance meant that all attempts to apply leniency failed. In addition the public, almost proselytizing, nature of Aikenhead's expression of irreligious opinions clearly counted against him. The penalty prescribed in the 1661 act was therefore imposed and Aikenhead was executed on 8 January 1697, having been marched from Edinburgh to Leith 'between a strong Guard of Fuzileers, drawn up in two Lines' (Hunter, 314); this possibly reflected anxiety that popular sympathy—already apparently illustrated by the fact that six of the twelve jurors chosen to adjudicate the case refused to serve—might lead to an insurrection on his behalf. He left a paper, or speech, in which he gave an account of his heterodoxy and the route by which he had reached it, presenting himself as a puzzled freethinker rather than an outrageous blasphemer, but taking a strongly relativist line on moral issues, and reiterating his difficulties with the doctrine of the Trinity.

Among the sources relating to the case are two pamphlets by a fellow student, Mungo Craig, who may originally have informed on Aikenhead to the authorities. These give significant detail of the affair while also throwing interesting light on the advanced intellectual milieu from which Aikenhead emanated.

Aikenhead's trial and execution aroused strong contrasting opinions both in Scotland and in England. North of the border certain clergymen spoke out strongly in favour of his punishment, believing that 'God was glorified by such ane awful & exemplary punishment' (Hunter, 321); others claimed to share the reservations experienced by some of those on the privy council. In London the case was reported in the newspapers and clearly shocked many, including John Locke, who preserved among his papers the fullest collection of material relating to the case, which formed the basis of its early nineteenth-century publication.   MICHAEL HUNTER

Sources *State trials*, 13.917–40 · M. Hunter, '"Aikenhead the atheist": the context and consequences of articulate irreligion in the late 17th century', in M. Hunter, *Science and the shape of orthodoxy: intellectual change in late seventeenth-century Britain* (1995), 308–32 · M. Craig, *A lye is no scandal* (1697) · M. Craig, *A satyr against atheistical deism* (1696) · W. Lorimer, *Two discourses* (1713), v–viii · I. Bostridge, *Witchcraft and its transformations, c.1650–c.1750* (1997), 24–32
Archives Bodl. Oxf., Lovelace collection of Locke MSS, MS Locke b. 4, fols. 86–106 · NA Scot., sources relating to the case

Aikin, Arthur (1773–1854), natural scientist and author, was born on 19 May 1773 at Warrington, Lancashire, the eldest son of John *Aikin (1747–1822) and his wife, Martha (c.1746–1830), daughter of Arthur Jennings of Cheapside, London. His brothers were Charles Rochemont *Aikin and Edmund *Aikin; Lucy *Aikin was his sister. He was educated at Warrington Free School and from 1784 at the school at Palgrave, Suffolk, where his uncle Rochemont Barbauld (1749–1808) was principal. He trained for the Unitarian ministry at Hackney College from 1786, and it

Arthur Aikin (1773–1854), by William Brockedon, 1826

was there that Joseph Priestley (1733–1804) inspired him to take an interest in science. He was assistant minister at the High Street (Unitarian) church, Shrewsbury, from September 1793 to June 1795 at a salary of £130 a year. He left the ministry because of religious doubts to devote himself to science and authorship; in literary circles he was later known as 'King Arthur'.

Aikin's introduction to geology came in summer 1795 when he made a short excursion into north Wales. His journal was published in the first three numbers of his father's new *Monthly Magazine* in 1796. The romantic (including mining) and the botanic were then his main interests. In the autumn and winter of 1795–6 Aikin was at Edinburgh, where he attended lectures at the university and met P. M. Roget (1779–1869), Dugald Stewart (1753–1828), and Thomas Young (1773–1829).

In the summer of 1796, after settling in London, Aikin undertook another month-long, more geological, walking tour through north Wales and Shropshire, with his surgeon brother, Charles Rochemont (1775–1847), and cousin Charles Kinder (d. 1838). Their *Journal* was published in 1797. It had been inspired by De Saussure's *Voyage dans les Alpes*, had a lithological bias, but showed very little interest yet in details of stratigraphy or fossils. With the Unitarian George Dyer (1755–1841), Aikin made a pedestrian tour to Scotland in 1797, 'the leading object of which was a mineralogy survey' (*Monthly Magazine*, 5, 1798, 123). A paper on his visit to Portsoy was read to the Newcastle Literary and Philosophical Society in 1798. In the same year S. T. Coleridge (1772–1834) reported that Aikin 'had been a sullen cold-blooded fellow, but very acute' at Edinburgh (*Collected Letters*, ed. E. L. Griggs, 1956, 1.393).

Aikin's need to earn a living from writing led him to edit seven editions of one of his father's books for children as *The Natural History of the Year*, from 1798 to 1834. In 1823 and 1826 he revised at least two editions of the popular, multi-volume *Evenings at Home … for Young Children* produced by his father and his aunt Anna Barbauld.

Early in 1799 Aikin, with his brother Charles, started giving public lectures on chemistry and chemical manufactures at their home in London and later at the General Dispensary, Aldersgate Street. In 1799 they also joined the British Mineralogical Society, established to promote mineralogical surveys. In 1801 and 1802 Aikin and Wilson Lowry (1762–1824) were collecting materials for a mineralogical map of Great Britain. In the same year Aikin was the first to find 'a specimen of argillite full of [fossil] shells at the very summit' of Snowdon (Rodgers, 224).

In 1802 Aikin founded and edited the first six volumes of the *Annual Review*, published between 1803 and 1808. He also became a contributor on chemistry, geology, and mineralogy to Abraham Rees's *Cyclopaedia* and translated Vivant Denon's *Voyage dans la Basse et la Haute Égypte pendant les campagnes du Général Bonaparte*. In 1803 he edited an abridgement of John Pinkerton's *Modern Geography*. In 1807 he and his brother published two volumes of their influential *Dictionary of Chemistry and Mineralogy*, which concentrated on the processes involved in chemical manufacture. The third volume (1814) detailed the most important discoveries made in these fields.

Late in 1807, after another tour through Wales, Aikin became one of the founding members of the Geological Society of London and turned more to science. He helped compile the society's *Geological Inquiries*, issued in March 1808, and in May 1810 published his *Prospectus for a Mineralogical Survey of Shropshire*, with geological map and stratigraphic section. It was the first such publication by any member of the fledgeling Geological Society; Aikin had been busy with this project since his days in Shrewsbury but insufficient subscribers were forthcoming and it had to be abandoned in the 1816 depression. Aikin instead published a number of memoirs in the *Transactions of the Geological Society*, in which he was using palaeontological evidence from 1812. From 1812 to 1817 he was honorary secretary of the society. In 1813 he declined to compete for the new Dublin chair in mineralogy, writing to G. B. Greenough (1778–1855) how 'hitherto I have followed Geological pursuits only as the occupation of my leisure hours, deriving from other sources all the income required for the supply of my wants' (Aiken to Greenough, 17 May 1813, Greenough MSS). In the winter of 1813–14 Aikin delivered lectures on mineralogy to the Geological Society, which became the basis for his popular *Manual of Mineralogy* (two edns, 1814 and 1815).

In 1817 Aikin was appointed paid secretary to the Society of Arts, a post he held until 1840. His first two annual addresses to it were published and his book *Illustrations of Art and Manufactures* (1841) was based on the more than forty lectures he had read to the society. As secretary he

laid the groundwork for the transformation of the society from a premium-giving to a paper-reading one. He was also the first, if inactive, honorary secretary of the Institution of Civil Engineers (1818). From this period on Aikin was highly active as patent agent and industrial consultant. In 1818 he was also elected a fellow of the Linnean Society, having long retained the botanical interests shown by his contributions to the 1805 *Botanist's Guide* of Dawson Turner and L. W. Dillwyn. In 1821 he was appointed to lecture on the theory and practice of chemistry at Guy's Hospital, which he did until 1851.

In 1828 W. D. Conybeare had written to Adam Sedgwick that 'we ought to make a push to urge Aikin to publish his Shropshire materials, which would be very important … but [he] wants stirring up' (J. W. Clark and T. H. Hughes, *Life and Letters of Adam Sedgwick*, 1890, 1.324–5). Instead, between 1832 and 1835, Aikin passed the manuscripts of all these geological materials to Roderick Murchison (1792–1871), who made good use of them (if inadequately acknowledged) in his *magnum opus*, *The Silurian System* (1839).

Aikin was a founder member and treasurer (1841), and second president (1843–5), of the Chemical Society. In 1843 the mineral Aikinite was named after him by E. J. Chapman, as the plant *Aikinia* had been by Nathaniel Wallich (1784–1854) in 1832. Aikin died, unmarried, at his London home, 7 Bloomsbury Square, on 15 April 1854 after a life of enormous diversity and ubiquitous clubbability.

H. S. TORRENS

Sources B. Rodgers, *Georgian chronicle: Mrs Barbauld and her family* (1958) · H. S. Torrens, 'Arthur Aikin's mineralogical survey of Shropshire, 1796–1816', *British Journal for the History of Science*, 16 (1983), 111–53 · *PICE*, 14 (1854–5), 120–23 · *Christian Reformer*, 3rd ser., 10 (1854), 379–80 · *Quarterly Journal of the Geological Society*, 11 (1855), xli–xlii · A. Kent, 'Arthur Aikin, 1773–1854, and other presidents', *Proceedings of the Chemical Society* (1962), 133–4 · *Proceedings of the Linnean Society*, 2 (1848–55), 304–6 · P. Weindling, 'The British Mineralogical Society', *Metropolis and province*, ed. I. Inkster and J. Morrell (1983), 120–50 · D. Hudson and K. W. Luckhurst, *The Royal Society of Arts* (1954) · H. B. Woodward, *The history of the Geological Society of London* (1907) · J. Golinski, *Science as public culture* (1992) · W. P. W. Phillimore, ed., *Shropshire parish registers: nonconformist registers*, Shropshire Parish Registers (1903), vii · I. Inkster, 'Science and society in the metropolis: a preliminary examination of the social and institutional context of the Askesian Society of London, 1796–1807', *Annals of Science*, 34 (1977), 1–32 · UCL, Greenough MSS

Archives GS Lond., archives · Hackney Central Library, London · Stoke Newington Library, London · Warrington Library, Cheshire | UCL, Greenough MSS

Likenesses W. Brockedon, chalk drawing, 1826, NPG [*see illus.*] · J. Thomson, stipple (after S. Drummond), BM, NPG; repro. in *European Magazine* (1819)

Aikin, Charles Rochemont (1775–1847), surgeon, was born at Warrington, Lancashire, the second son of John *Aikin (1747–1822), physician, author, and religious dissenter, and Martha Jennings (*c*.1746–1830); he was the grandson of John *Aikin (1713–1780), and brother of Lucy *Aikin (1781–1864) and Edmund *Aikin. At the age of two he was adopted by his childless aunt, the author Anna Letitia *Barbauld (1743–1825), and he was educated at the school run by his uncle, the Revd Rochemont Barbauld, at Palgrave, Suffolk. Although adopted, Aikin remained close to his eldest brother, Arthur *Aikin (1773–1854): in the 1790s they shared a house in Broad Street Buildings, London, and Charles later married Anne (d. 1821), the daughter of Gilbert *Wakefield (1756–1801), one of Arthur's teachers and a friend of his father. Aikin matriculated at Edinburgh University in 1795 and gained the diploma of the Company of Surgeons in July 1799. He worked in London throughout his life, taking over his father's practice in 1798. He also served as secretary to the Medical and Chirurgical Society of London from 1809 to 1812, and was a member until 1818. Among his and Anne's children was the writer Anna Letitia *Le Breton.

Aikin's career was distinguished chiefly by his long involvement with smallpox vaccination. In 1800, less than two years after the appearance of Edward Jenner's first pamphlet on vaccination, Aikin published *A concise view of all the most important facts that have hitherto appeared respecting the cow pox*. As the title suggests, the work contained little new information but was a digest of contemporary knowledge of vaccination procedure, drawn from the writings of Jenner, George Pearson, and William Woodville. On the strength of this, in 1803 Aikin was appointed as one of the eight vaccinators of the Royal Jennerian Society, a London-based charity providing free vaccination to the poor, and he worked for a few hours each week at its Bishopsgate station. In 1809, through Jenner's patronage, he was appointed as a vaccinator at the new National Vaccine Establishment, a part-time post he held until his death. Though now largely forgotten, the establishment was one of the government's first and longest-surviving public health institutions. Until the development of calf-lymph in the late nineteenth century, smallpox vaccine was obtained from the lesions of vaccinated persons. The National Vaccine Establishment ensured a constant supply of vaccine by offering free vaccination at various stations in London and taking lymph from these poor patients. This work made Aikin's reputation as an expert, and in 1840 he was called in by the poor-law commissioners to advise them on implementation of the first vaccination act, which instituted free vaccination in England and Wales.

Aikin also had a long-standing interest in chemistry, which reflected his family's links to a group of distinguished dissenting scientists, including Joseph Priestley. Aikin collaborated with his brother Arthur on a *Dictionary of Chemistry and Mineralogy* (1807) and published papers on pharmaceutical chemistry.

Aikin died of 'dropsy after asthma of several years duration' (d. cert.) on 20 March 1847 at his house, 7 Bloomsbury Square, London. His work was continued by his son, Charles Arthur Aikin, who was also a vaccinator at the National Vaccine Establishment from 1848 and was a member of the Epidemiological Society committee which prompted parliament to introduce compulsory vaccination in England and Wales in 1853.

DEBORAH BRUNTON

Sources *London Medical Gazette*, [3rd] ser., 4 (1847), 572 · R. B. Fisher, *Edward Jenner* (1991) · *Medico-Chirurgical Transactions*, 1–10 (1809–19) · 'Return of sums voted for National Vaccine Institution', *Parl. papers* (1856), 52.521, no. 145 · 'Establishment of the vaccine board', *Parl. papers* (1831–2), 45.41, no. 712 · 'Copy of a letter from Dr. Edward Seaton to Viscount Palmerston', *Parl. papers* (1852–3), 101.75, no. 434 [incl. report on vaccination from Epidemiological Society] · A. L. Le Breton, *Memoir of Mrs Barbauld* (1874) · *Memoir of John Aikin*, ed. L. Aikin, 2 vols. (1823) · correspondence of the poor-law commissioners, 29 June 1840, 7 July 1840, 16 Oct 1840, PRO, MH 25.1 · d. cert. · *DNB*

Aikin, Edmund (1780–1820), architect, was born on 2 October 1780 at Warrington, Lancashire, the youngest son of John *Aikin (1747–1822), physician and author, and his wife, Martha, *née* Jennings (c.1746–1830). His two brothers, Charles Rochemont *Aikin and Arthur *Aikin, achieved prominence in the fields of surgery and natural science respectively. A shy, nervous, and physically delicate child, he was educated at home until, following the family's move to London in 1792, he was articled to the surveyor and builder James Carr, and entered the Royal Academy Schools in 1801. Between 1801 and 1812 he was a regular exhibitor at the Royal Academy and his drawings included *A Design for a Pantheon* (1801), *An Edifice for British Valour* (1802), *An Enchanted Palace* (1802), *A Design for a Monument* (1803), *An Interior of a Bath* (1804), *A Hall of Venus* (1806), *A Design for a Cenotaph* (1809), *A Monument to a Poet* (1811), *The Naval Arsenal, Sheerness*, and *A Design for a Monument to Burns* (1812).

Constitutionally more inclined towards literary and scholarly projects than the rigours of architectural practice, Aikin became a founding member of the London Architectural Society in 1806, and his 'Essay on modern architecture' formed the principal interest of their first publication in 1808. In the same year he published *Designs for Villas and other Rural Buildings*, with a dedication to the author and collector Thomas Hope, by whom he had been previously employed (together with the artist George Dawe) to prepare the finished drawings for Hope's *Household Furniture* (1807). He disapproved of the Gothic revival, and the publication of Thomas and William Daniell's *Oriental Scenery* (1808) aroused his interest in Islamic architecture as a possible alternative. In her memoir of her brother Lucy *Aikin drew attention to his *Essay on the Doric Order* (1810) as the first work to provide comparative illustrations to the text drawn to the same scale. Aikin's account of St Paul's Cathedral, which accompanied designs by James Elmes, appeared in John Britton's *Fine Arts of the English School* (1812), and his essay on Elizabethan architecture was appended to Lucy Aikin's *Memoirs of the Court of Queen Elizabeth* (1818).

Between c.1810 and 1813 Aikin assisted General Sir Samuel Bentham, naval engineer and architect, in his designs for works, principally at Sheerness and Portsmouth. Together they published designs for a bridge over the River Swale. In 1814, following his success in the competition for the Wellington assembly rooms, 127 Mount Pleasant (1815–16; now the Irish Centre), Aikin moved to Liverpool, where he also adapted an existing house in Colquitt Street for the premises of the Liverpool Royal Institution (opened 1817; dem.), and designed various other buildings, including some small villas. Though he was reluctantly induced to design a row of Gothic shop fronts in

Bold Street, his more important designs for the assembly rooms showed him to be 'a fastidious and scholarly Greek Revival architect' (Colvin, *Archs.*, 67). His essays helped to popularize knowledge of Greek architecture among surveyors and builders, though his comment, in *Designs for Villas*, that 'the age of invention has gone by, and that of criticism has succeeded … every style of architecture is open to our choice, there is no *prima facie* reason why one should be preferred to another' (*Designs for Villas*, 6–7) is of more lasting interest to architectural historians as an indication of

> a new historical approach [which] was felt only towards the end of the eighteenth century. By then the concept of a plurality of styles had taken hold. And with plurality went relativism—the collapse of implicit belief in the authority of any one style. (Crook, 110)

On the breakdown of his health in 1819 Aikin returned to London and died at his father's house in Stoke Newington on 11 March 1820.   ANNETTE PEACH

Sources Colvin, *Archs.* · *Memoir of John Aikin*, ed. L. Aikin, 2 vols. (1823), vol. 1, pp. 267–72 · Graves, *RA exhibitors* · W. J. Pinks, *The history of Clerkenwell*, ed. E. J. Wood, 2nd edn (1881), 268 · M. McMordie, 'Picturesque pattern books and pre-Victorian designers', *Architectural History*, 18 (1975), 44–60 · J. M. Crook, *The Greek revival: neoclassical attitudes in British architecture, 1760–1870*, rev. edn (1995) · J. S. Curl, *Georgian architecture* (1993) · *DNB* · *GM*, 1st ser., 90/1 (1820), 286 · *GM*, 1st ser., 92/2 (1822), 572 · *IGI*

Aikin, John (1713–1780), tutor and theological scholar, was born on 28 December 1713 in London. His father, John Aikin (1664–1756), a linen draper from Kirkcudbright, Scotland, had settled there some time previously; his mother, Anne Bentall, is described as the daughter of a London citizen. Aikin attended a school in St Albans kept by a former actor who exercised pupils in theatrical discourse. He also spent time in his father's shop, the initial intention being that he would enter the linen trade. This was followed by a period in the house of a foreign merchant, where he became fluent in French. Law was also considered as a likely career; he became a skilled courthand writer and acquired extensive knowledge of the constitution and laws of England. However in 1732 he entered Philip Doddridge's Northampton academy as a candidate for the dissenting ministry. This was followed by a period as a divinity student at King's College, Aberdeen, where he also studied classics. On 5 July 1737 he received an MA degree, 'having resided in the College for a considerable time past' (Anderson, *Officers and Graduates*, 232). In 1744 Marischal College, Aberdeen, also awarded him an MA.

Having graduated Aikin returned to Northampton, as assistant tutor in Doddridge's academy. In 1739 he entered the dissenting ministry in Leicester; a riding accident shortly afterwards damaged his lungs, made preaching difficult, and led to his resigning the ministry. He was prone to asthmatic attacks for the rest of his life. For a short time he taught in a school, as partner to Mr Lee of Farndon, near Harborough, Leicestershire. During this period he married Jane (Jenny; 1714–1785), daughter of the Revd John *Jennings (1687/8–1723), dissenting minister at Kibworth, and his second wife, Anna Letitia Wingate. Her maternal grandparents were Sir Francis Wingate and Lady

Ann Annesley, daughter of the first earl of Anglesey. Jennings had opened an academy in Kibworth in 1715 and one of his pupils had been Philip Doddridge, who boarded with the family; on 29 May 1730 he wrote a love letter, proposing marriage, to the young Jenny. Following their marriage the Aikins settled in Kibworth, where John ran a school. Although damaged lungs made extended speaking difficult he was a successful schoolmaster. Wakefield refers to 'some mortifying instances of severity in the castigation of his pupils' (*Memoirs of the Life of Gilbert Wakefield*, 218), but it would appear that he was comparatively less draconian than was common in those days. The Aikins' children were born at Kibworth—Anna Letitia Aikin, later *Barbauld (1743–1825) and John *Aikin (1747–1822)—both of whom became well-known literary figures. During this period Aikin developed a friendship with the botanist Richard Pulteney MD FRS; letters from Aikin to Pulteney between 1757 and 1764 survive and are held at the Linnean Society, London. They attest to Aikin's interest in the study of botany; Pulteney lent him books on the subject and supplied him with dried specimens.

In August 1758 Aikin embarked on the most significant period of his teaching career, on accepting the post of classics tutor at the new dissenting academy in Warrington. His lectures, designed to illustrate the history and literature of the Greeks and Romans, were invariably preceded by information about the author, 'the occasion of his writing, and the manner in which he treated his subject' (Turner, 16). He tended to avoid books usually read in schools and to select those with some relevance to other areas of study; for example, for students studying law Justinian's institutes might be chosen. He also taught French and lectured on grammar, oratory and criticism, logic, and history.

When Dr John Taylor died in 1761 Aikin was unanimously chosen to succeed him in the theology chair and as head of the academy. Characteristically reluctant, he tried to persuade his friend Mr Clark of Birmingham to take the place; finally he acceded, however, and Joseph Priestley replaced him as lecturer in languages and *belles-lettres*. Priestley notes:

> tutors … lived in the most perfect harmony. We drank tea together every Saturday, and our conversation was equally instructive and pleasing … We were all likewise Arians; and the only subject of much consequence on which we differed respected the doctrine of Atonement, concerning which Dr Aikin held some obscure notions. (Bright, 733)

A former student, writing in the *Monthly Repository* (vol. 8, 1813), comments on Aikin's extensive acquaintance with theology, impartiality in presenting evidence, variety of methods in pursuit of students' fuller comprehension, and lack of censorship when opinions differed. Wykes has suggested that Aikin was a good scholar but lacked an innovative approach in his teaching.

On 12 and 30 May 1774 respectively King's and Marischal colleges in Aberdeen awarded Aikin an honorary DD. In the same year *The Bill of Mortality of the Town of Warrington, for the Year 1773. By the Rev J. Aikin* appeared in *Philosophical Transactions* (64/1). McLachlan refers to a few articles by

Aikin published in the *Monthly Review* but apart from the preface to *Selecta quaedam ex C. Plinii secundi historia naturali, ad usum scholarum accomodata,* edited by his son, these were his only publications.

From 1778 Aikin's asthmatic attacks became more frequent and violent, and for a short time a former student, Mr Houghton, assisted him; in 1779 Gilbert Wakefield was appointed a regular tutor. On 14 December 1780 Aikin died at Warrington. The following Sunday William Enfield preached a funeral sermon, later published, extolling the extent of his learning; from literature to the natural sciences 'there is scarcely a province … of human knowledge which his philosophic and inquisitive mind did not visit' (Enfield, 7). Aikin was buried on the north side of the parish church in Warrington; a monument to his memory was erected in Cairo Street Unitarian Chapel. Thomas Barnes, a former student, wrote of Aikin:

> few have had mental treasures, more various, or more valuable … Though not known to the world at large as an author, his modesty having unhappily prevented him from appearing in print, he was uncommonly revered by all that knew him, for the wonderful extent of his knowledge, for the mild dignity of his character, and for the various excellencies which adorned the Scholar, the Tutor, and the Man. (Barnes, 76, 76n.)

DIANA K. JONES

Sources *Monthly Repository,* 8 (1813) · W. Turner, *The Warrington Academy* (1957) · H. McLachlan, *Warrington Academy: its history and influence,* Chetham Society, 107, new ser. (1943) · *DNB* · H. A. Bright, 'A historical sketch of Warrington Academy', *Christian Reformer, or, Unitarian Magazine and Review,* new ser., 17 (1861) · T. Barnes, 'On the affinity subsisting between the arts, with a plan for promoting and extending manufactures, by encouraging those arts, on which manufactures principally depend', *Memoirs of the Literary and Philosophical Society of Manchester,* 1 (1785), 72–89 · W. Enfield, *A funeral sermon occasioned by the death of the late Rev. John Aikin DD* (1781) · *Christian Reformer, or, Unitarian Magazine and Review,* new ser., 11 (1855) · P. J. Anderson, ed., *Officers and graduates of University and King's College, Aberdeen, MVD–MDCCCLX,* New Spalding Club, 11 (1893) · P. J. Anderson and J. F. K. Johnstone, eds., *Fasti academiae Mariscallanae Aberdonensis: selections from the records of the Marischal College and University, MDXCIII–MDCCCLX,* 3 vols., New Spalding Club, 4, 18–19 (1889–98) · J. Hunter, *Familiae minorum gentium,* ed. J. W. Clay, 1, Harleian Society, 37 (1894) · Watt, *Bibl. Brit.,* vol. 1 · *GM,* 1st ser., 50 (1780), 591 · H. L. Short, 'Warrington Academy', *Hibbert Journal,* 56 (1957), 1–7 · *Memoirs of the life of Gilbert Wakefield,* ed. J. T. Rutt and A. Wainewright, 2 vols. (1804), vol. 1 · Mrs H. Martin, ed., *Memories of seventy years* (1883) · D. L. Wykes, 'The contribution of the dissenting academy to the emergence of rational dissent', *Enlightenment and religion: rational dissent in eighteenth-century Britain,* ed. K. Haakonssen (1996), 99–139 · P. O'Brien, *Warrington Academy, 1757–86: its predecessors and successors* (1989) · I. Parker, *Dissenting academies in England* (1914) · A. Kippis and others, eds., *Biographia Britannica, or, The lives of the most eminent persons who have flourished in Great Britain and Ireland,* 2nd edn, 5 (1793) · D. L. Wykes, 'The reluctant businessman: John Colman of St Nicholas Street, Leicester (1727–1808)', *Transactions of the Leicester Archaeological and Historical Society,* 69 (1995), 71–85 · R. H. Jeffers, 'Richard Pulteney, MD, FRS (1730–1801), and his correspondents', *Proceedings of the Linnean Society of London,* 177th session (1958–9), 15–26 · *Calendar of the correspondence of Philip Doddridge,* ed. G. F. Nuttall, HMC, JP 26 (1979) · will, proved, 15 Jan 1781, Lancs. RO, WCW

Archives Linn. Soc., letters to Richard Pulteney and correspondents

Wealth at death £300—personal estate: will, 15 Jan 1781, Lancs. RO, WCW

Aikin, John (1747–1822), physician and writer, was born on 15 January 1747 at Kibworth Harcourt, Leicestershire, the younger child and only son of John *Aikin (1713–1780), theologian, and his wife, Jane Jennings (1714–1785). He had an elder sister, who, under her married name of Anna Letitia *Barbauld (1743–1825), was to become a renowned educationist. Aikin was educated at home until the age of eleven, after which he attended Warrington Academy, the well-known school for the children of dissenters at which his father was the classics tutor. In 1761 he was apprenticed to a surgeon and apothecary in Uppingham and remained there for three years. He entered Edinburgh University in 1764, but he left in 1766 without taking his degree. He continued his professional studies in Manchester (1766–9) and London (1769–70) before establishing a surgical practice in Chester. In 1771, however, he returned to Warrington and established a surgical practice there. On 8 July 1772 he married Martha (c.1746–1830), daughter of Arthur Jennings of Cheapside, London; they had three sons, the natural scientist and author Arthur *Aikin, the surgeon Charles Rochemont *Aikin, and the architect Edmund *Aikin, and a daughter, Lucy *Aikin, who published a memoir of her father in 1823.

Finding a surgical career unprofitable, Aikin decided to turn to medicine. He graduated MD of Leiden in 1784 and returned to England to establish a medical practice at Great Yarmouth, before moving to Norwich to be near his sister at Thetford. Divisions in Yarmouth society between dissenters on the one hand and the corporation and Church of England clergy on the other were exacerbated by the agitation in 1790 for the repeal of the Corporation and Test Acts. Aikin's circle of friends was dominated by members of the established church who shared his literary tastes, but he felt acutely the injustice of excluding dissenters from office and in 1790 published two pamphlets on this subject entitled *The Spirit of the Constitution and that of the Church of England Compared …* and *An Address to the Dissidents of England on their Late Defeat.* Although these were published anonymously, Aikin's authorship was soon discovered, and he lost the support of most of his Church of England friends and patients. The publications, combined with his wholehearted approval of the French Revolution in its early stages and his rejection of any form of 'puffing and elbowing' to increase his practice, resulted in the virtual ruin of his professional prospects in Yarmouth. Throughout his life he was to demonstrate a characteristic 'hatred of every thing unfair and unequitable which was his leading principle and almost his ruling passion' (Aikin, 176).

Aikin's position at Yarmouth became untenable, and in 1792 he moved to Broad Street Buildings in London. He found a more agreeable field for his medical and literary work in this close proximity to Hackney, where many dissenters lived. Lucy Aikin, his daughter, described this migration as a 'blessed change', as the dissenters regarded her father as 'a kind of confessor in the cause' (Aikin, 152), and in London he found a warm welcome, and became a minor literary success. His circle of friends included

John Aikin (1747–1822), by George Engleheart, pubd 1823 (after Wright)

Thomas Pennant, the naturalist; Erasmus Darwin; James Montgomery; John Howard, the philanthropist; and, for a time, Robert Southey. He was John Howard's literary executor, and had often been employed by him to write reports on prisons, and other documents; in 1792 he published a biography of Howard.

Aikin continued to practise as a physician, devoting his spare time to literature, but in 1796 he suffered a stroke of paralysis that effectively ended his medical career. In 1798 he gave up his house and practice to his son, and retired to Stoke Newington, where his sister lived. There he spent the last twenty-four years of his life in his favourite studies and occupations, and went on to produce a wide range of works.

Aikin is now better known as a literary figure than as a physician. His early works included *Biographical Memoirs of Medicine in Great Britain* (1780), and the *Monthly Magazine* had great praise for his later, more extensive *General Biography* (8 vols., 1799–1813), calling it 'not the most popular, but beyond question the best in the language' (*Monthly Magazine*, 520). Among his most original productions was *Evenings at Home, or, The Juvenile Budget Opened* (1792–6), written with his sister, which was reprinted many times and remained popular for years. Some of his other well-received publications were also written for children, including *Miscellaneous Pieces in Prose* (1773), *Letters from a father to his son on various topics relative to literature and the conduct of life* (1793), and *Letters to a Young Lady on a Course of English Poetry* (1804). His *Description of the Country from Thirty to Forty Miles Round Manchester* (1795) is a valuable account of this rapidly industrializing district.

In addition to his writing, Aikin also engaged in work as an editor and reviewer. In 1796 he became literary editor of the *Monthly Magazine* until he was dismissed summarily in 1806 after a dispute with the proprietor. He also wrote for the *Monthly Review* in the 1790s, and he assisted in the *Annual Review* edited by his son. He edited *The Athenaeum* for a brief run, and in 1811 he became editor of Dodsley's *Annual Register*. Aikin also became one of the circle surrounding the radical publisher Joseph Johnson, who published several of Aikin's works; he wrote Johnson's obituary for the *Gentleman's Magazine*.

Aikin's daughter supplied the following description:

> He was of the middle stature, and well proportioned, though spare; his carriage was erect, his step light and active. His eyes were grey and lively, his skin naturally fair, but, in his face, much pitted with the small pox. The expression of his countenance was mild, intelligent, and cheerful, and its effect was aided in conversation by the tones of a voice clear and agreeable, though not powerful. (Aikin, 275)

Aikin died at home in Stoke Newington on 7 December 1822 and was buried in Stoke Newington churchyard; he was survived by his wife. MARILYN L. BROOKS

Sources Memoir of John Aikin, ed. L. Aikin, 2 vols. (1823) · 'Dr. Aikin', *Monthly Magazine*, 54 (1822), 520–21 · *GM*, 1st ser., 93/1 (1823), 85–9 · *BDMBR*, vol. 1
Archives DWL · Hackney Archives, London, corresp. | JRL, Methodist Archives and Research Centre, letters to James Montgomery · Lpool RO, corresp. with William Roscoe · Sheff. Arch., corresp. with James Montgomery
Likenesses N. Branwhite, group portrait, stipple, pubd 1801 (*Institutes of the Medical Society of London*; after S. Medley), BM · G. Engleheart, engraving, pubd 1823 (after Wright), NPG [*see illus.*] · C. Knight, stipple (after J. Donaldson), BM

Aikin, Lucy (1781–1864), historian, the fourth child and only daughter of John *Aikin MD (1747–1822), and his wife, Martha Jennings (d. 1830), was born in Warrington on 6 November 1781. Her three brothers were Arthur *Aikin, Charles Rochemont *Aikin, and Edmund *Aikin. Her father moved the family to Yarmouth in 1784 and then to London in 1792. Dr Aikin retired from medical practice in 1797; with his wife and daughter he settled in Stoke Newington, Middlesex, where they lived until his death in 1822. Lucy, who never married, then moved with her mother to Hampstead, where she lived as a householder until 1844. She briefly resided with a nephew in London before joining the household of her niece Anna LeBreton in Wimbledon; in 1852 they returned to Hampstead. Lucy Aikin died from influenza on 29 January 1864 at her home, Milford House, Hampstead; she was buried in Hampstead.

Except for brief attendance at a day school in Yarmouth, Aikin was educated entirely at home. Her father and her aunt Anna Letitia Aikin *Barbauld were particularly important influences. She read widely in English, French, Italian, and Latin literature and history. She was encouraged to write; her first periodical contributions appeared when she was seventeen. Her early works were surely influenced by those of her father and aunt. She published

Lucy Aikin (1781–1864), by unknown photographer

two translations, *The Life of Ulrich Zwingli* (1812) and *The Travels of Rolando* (1823), as well as compilations of poetry and readings and English lessons for children. In 1810 *Epistles on Women, Exemplifying their Character and Condition in Various Ages and Nations* appeared. This work argued, in a series of poetical accounts, that women should be valued for themselves and not simply treated as inferior to men and thus unimportant. Her only work of fiction was *Lorimer, a Tale* (1814).

Aikin's most important publications were her histories and biographies. *Memoirs of the Court of Queen Elizabeth* (1818) is an account that concentrates on the art, literature, manners, and morals of Elizabeth's reign, with brief biographies of leading figures. It was followed by *Memoirs of the Court of King James the First* (1822) and *Memoirs of the Court of King Charles the First* (1833). Aikin used the available printed sources, quoting when relevant but always drawing her material together into a coherent narrative. In the preface to the work on Charles I she also acknowledged the use of various manuscript collections. These pioneering histories were well received; each was reprinted several times. The volumes were not uncritical. As a dissenting Liberal, Aikin condemned all religious persecution. She also clearly disapproved of both arbitrary royal actions and scheming and ambitious court favourites. She was not willing to continue her series to include either Cromwell or Charles II. She did project a work on the

social history of women in the eighteenth century, but this was never completed.

Aikin's works emphasized the artistic, social, and literary aspects of the period rather than its religious, military, or parliamentary history. Her choice of social history, as it was understood in the early nineteenth century, was one made by most women historians, from her contemporaries Mary Berry and Elizabeth Benger through to such mid-century writers as Agnes and Elizabeth Strickland. Female education stressed the literary and cultural achievements of society; therefore, their writing on these subjects could be regarded as serious. Their subject matter and emphases were limited by what was regarded as important in their time. Courtly life and high culture fill their pages; little or nothing is said about how ordinary people lived and worked. But unlike the standard histories written by men, Aikin and her fellow female historians stressed that the lives and actions of women were also an important part of history.

Aikin's other major publications were edited volumes of the works of several authors, each of which also included a biography of the author by the editor. *Memoir of John Aikin, MD* (1823) and *The Works of Anna Laetitia Barbauld* (1825) are the primary contemporary sources for the lives of Aikin's father and aunt. Her biography of Elizabeth Ogilvy Benger, published with Benger's *Memoirs of the Life of Anne Boleyn* (1827), is the primary account of that secondary writer. Benger, a member of Anna Barbauld's circle, wrote biographies of several Tudor and Stuart women; her work was similar to Aikin's though never as successful. Aikin, like her aunt, encouraged and publicized women writers when possible. Aikin's *The Life of Joseph Addison* (1843) printed a number of Addison's letters not previously available, and was the first biography of the essayist and poet to be published. It was reviewed unfavourably by Thomas Babington Macaulay, who, unlike Aikin, did not approve of Addison.

Aikin's own letters are as important as her formal publications. Her correspondents included members of her family, dissenting leaders on both sides of the Atlantic, and both male and female writers. The letters reveal a witty and appreciative reader of older and current literature and a perceptive observer of current events. As a woman and a Unitarian, Aikin was critical of much of the existing political and educational establishment in Britain. Although in no sense a radical, she advocated better education and more civil rights for women as well as more complete religious freedom for all.

BARBARA BRANDON SCHNORRENBERG

Sources P. H. Le Breton, *Memoirs, miscellanies, and letters of the late Lucy Aikin* (1864) · *Memoir of John Aikin*, ed. L. Aikin, 2 vols. (1823) · *DNB* · *CGPLA Eng. & Wales* (1864)
Archives priv. colls. | Lpool RO, Roscoe MSS
Likenesses photograph, priv. coll. [*see illus.*]
Wealth at death under £9000: probate, 26 Feb 1864, *CGPLA Eng. & Wales*

Aikman, George (1830–1905), painter and engraver, was born in Warriston Close, off the High Street, Edinburgh, on 20 May 1830, the ninth child of George Aikman, engraver, and Alison Mackay (*d.* in or before 1859), his wife. His father had been an engraver for William Home Lizars but established his own business in 1825 where he continued the Lizars tradition by producing all the plates and illustrations for the seventh edition of the *Encyclopaedia Britannica*. Many of these were drawn and engraved by his son George, who was educated privately and then sent to the Royal High School, Edinburgh. Thereafter he was apprenticed to his father and, after a journeyman period during which he worked in London and Manchester, he joined his father's firm as a partner. During his apprenticeship, Aikman attended classes at the Trustees' Academy, then under the directorship of Robert Scott Lauder. Much later, between 1868 and 1871, he attended the life school of the Royal Scottish Academy. He first exhibited there in 1850 and thereafter became a regular exhibitor, his subjects ranging between landscapes, architectural studies, figure studies, and portraits. On 2 December 1859 Aikman married Elizabeth Barnett (*c.*1833–1912) of Greenock and they had two sons and three daughters.

In 1872 Aikman abandoned his business as an engraver and turned his full attention to landscape painting in oils and watercolours. He worked mostly in Scotland, the north of England, and Warwickshire. Concentrating on moorland and woodland scenes, these oil paintings tend to be sombre in colour, for example *Scotch Firs* (exh. RA, 1878). He also painted harbour and coastal subjects in both oils and watercolours. These, with their use of silvery grey tones, show the influence of the Dutch painters of The Hague school. Aikman was a founder member of the Royal Scottish Society of Painters in Watercolour in 1878 and three years later he was elected an associate of the Royal Scottish Academy. In addition to his landscapes, Aikman was also deeply interested in the architecture of Edinburgh and he produced a series of finely worked drawings of the threatened buildings of the old town, for example *Bakehouse Close, Canongate* (Edinburgh City Art Collections).

Although Aikman first received recognition as a painter he also worked extensively as a printmaker. For most of his life he etched, and in this medium produced fine portraits, for example *Portrait of Thomas Carlyle* (1889; Royal Scottish Academy, Edinburgh). He also experimented with mezzotints, for example, *Portrait of Lord Blackburn after Daniel Macnee* (1888; Royal Scottish Academy, Edinburgh). In addition, Aikman produced *A Round of the Links: the Golf Greens of Scotland* (1893) with twenty etchings after John Smart, and he illustrated Thomas Chapman and John Southesk's book *The Midlothian Esks and their Associations from the Source to the Sea* (1895) with a series of full-plate etchings and smaller text illustrations. Through his father and from his own study, Aikman acquired a wide-ranging knowledge of engravers and engraving and he contributed to various publications on the subject as well as to the *Art Journal*.

Aikman died at home, 22 Scotland Street, Edinburgh, on 8 January 1905 and was buried in Warriston cemetery, Edinburgh, on 11 January. He was survived by his wife and family. JOANNA SODEN

Sources DNB · *Annual Report of the Council of the Royal Scottish Academy of Painting, Sculpture, and Architecture*, 78 (1905), 9–10 · C. B. de Laperriere, ed., *The Royal Scottish Academy exhibitors, 1826–1990*, 4 vols. (1991), vol. 1, pp. 15–18 · Graves, *RA exhibitors*, 2.358 · P. J. M. McEwan, *Dictionary of Scottish art and architecture* (1994), 38 · b. cert. · d. cert. · Royal Scot. Acad.
Archives Royal Scot. Acad., letter collection · Royal Scot. Acad., life school records
Likenesses photograph, Royal Scot. Acad.

Aikman, William, of Cairnie (1682–1731), portrait painter, was born on 24 October 1682 at Cairnie, Forfarshire, the second son and fifth child of William Aikman (1646–1699), laird of Cairnie and advocate, and his wife, Margaret Clerk (*d.* after 1729), daughter of John Clerk of Penicuik, Edinburghshire. Educated at Edinburgh University, he went on to study painting, working for the Flemish portrait painter John de Medina, who had a successful practice in Edinburgh, and then attending one of the London academies, possibly at the Rose and Crown. By August 1705 he was not only copying pictures in the Royal Collection but had been asked to 'draw Mrs Hill's picture, who is one of the Queen's greatest favourites' and was 'in good hopes to have the honour to draw both Queen [Anne] and Prince [George of Denmark]' (letter, 23 Aug 1705, Robertson Aikman MSS).

Following the deaths of his father and elder brother Aikman inherited Cairnie, but he had no desire to settle down as a country laird. After much anxious deliberation he sold the estate and set off for Italy, leaving behind with friends Marion Lawson of Cairnmuir, Peeblesshire, whom he had married in 1707 without his family's knowledge. Having visited Florence and copied the works of Carlo Maratta in Rome, he travelled to Turkey and Smyrna, went back to Rome, and then visited Naples before returning to Scotland in 1711. As Medina had recently died, he inherited his former master's clients and was soon accepting public commissions from Edinburgh town council and the Incorporation of Surgeons as well as painting the leading members of Scottish society.

John, second duke of Argyll, one of Aikman's appreciative patrons, then urged him to move to London. Apprehensive about the highly competitive atmosphere in the capital, the expense of premises, and the cost of drapery painters, Aikman was reluctant to move, but agreed to a trial period of six months. His sensitive, perceptive portraits were immediately popular, and in 1722 he settled permanently in London with his wife and children, living at first in Suffolk Street and painting not only the Scottish aristocracy in town but also prominent English figures such as Sir Robert Walpole, the prime minister, and the fourth earl of Chesterfield (Blickling Hall, Norfolk). Further examples of his work are at Blickling Hall. His two self-portraits, in the Galleria degli Uffizi, Florence, and the Scottish National Portrait Gallery, Edinburgh, are considered to be good examples of his work.

In view of his success, Aikman's admirers urged him to move to more fashionable premises, but he dreaded the expense, declaring that he had 'no courage to go into it, tho' every body would push me to it as the only means of cutting a figur, as they call it here' (Clerk of Penicuik MSS,

William Aikman of Cairnie (1682–1731), self-portrait

GD18/4583). Although his real ambition was to retire to Scotland, he did eventually move to a large house and studio in Leicester Fields. During a brief visit to Scotland in 1730 his friends were alarmed by his emaciated appearance: he had contracted tuberculosis. Back in London once more, too weak to paint, he was heart-broken by the death of his only son, John, a promising young artist, early in 1731. He himself died on 4 or 7 June that year, in his house in Leicester Fields, and father and son were buried together in Greyfriars churchyard, Edinburgh. Two daughters survived him.   ROSALIND K. MARSHALL

Sources Vertue, *Note books*, 3.22, 43, 51 · Redgrave, *Artists*, 2nd edn, 4 · [J. Anderson], 'Memoirs of Mr W. Aikman, with a portrait', *The Bee*, 18 (1793), 1–10 · J. Holloway, *William Aikman (1682–1731)*, Scottish Masters (1988) · F. Moücke, *Museum florentinum*, 11 (1762) · D. Irwin and F. Irwin, *Scottish painters at home and abroad, 1700–1900* (1975) · D. Macmillan, *Painting in Scotland: the golden age* (1986) [exhibition catalogue, U. Edin., Talbot Rice Gallery, and Tate Gallery, London, 1986] · J. Ingamells, ed., *A dictionary of British and Irish travellers in Italy, 1701–1800* (1997), 11 · priv. coll., Robertson Aikman MSS · NA Scot., Clerk of Penicuik MS, GD18/4583 · Scot. NPG
Archives NRA Scotland, priv. coll., commonplace book, corresp., and MSS | NA Scot., Clerk of Penicuik MSS, corresp. with Sir John Clerk, GD18 · NRA Scotland, priv. coll., Robertson Aikman MSS
Likenesses W. Aikman, self-portraits, oils, before 1707–*c.*1720, priv. coll. · W. Aikman, self-portrait, oils, Scot. NPG [*see illus.*] · W. Aikman, self-portrait, oils, Uffizi Gallery · W. Aikman, self-portraits, priv. colls. · L. Freeman, engraving (after self-portrait), repro. in Chambers, *Scots.* · P. A. Pazzi, line engraving (after self-portrait, Uffizi Gallery), BM · R. Scott, engraving (after self-portrait, Scot. NPG), repro. in Anderson, 'Memoirs of Mr W. Aikman'

Ailbe (*d.* 534?). *See under* Munster, saints of (*act. c.*450–*c.*700).

Ailean Dall. *See* Macdougall, Allan (1750?–1829).

Ailerán [Aileranus Sapiens] (*d.* **665**), scholar, usually called 'the Wise' (Aileranus Sapiens), was a teacher in the monastery of Clonard, Meath, and wrote at least two works to assist students in interpreting the gospels. Apart from his being a monk and teacher in Clonard, one of the more important early Irish monasteries, nothing is known of Ailerán's background, life, or career. His connection with Clonard has indeed been questioned, since it is first attested only in an Irish text of the late eighth or early ninth century; however, that it is also found in a continental poem of roughly similar date has inclined recent writers to accept the link as being based in fact.

The longer of Ailerán's works (twenty-six pages in a late twentieth-century edition) is the *Interpretatio mystica et moralis progenitorum domini Iesu Christi* ('A mystical and moral explanation of [the names] of the ancestors of [our] Lord Jesus Christ'). The 'genealogy of Jesus Christ' from Abraham, found in Matthew 1: 1–17, was a significant element in early medieval writing about the coming of Jesus, and consequently many works were dedicated to its interpretation. Ailerán's approach used the method of studying the meaning of each name found in the gospel text to point up other passages in the scriptures which he believed gave an insight into the gospel's hidden, and more important, meanings. Moreover, he believed that knowing, through an understanding of their names, what each of these people represented, made it possible to see divine providence preparing the way for the coming of the Christ.

Ailerán goes through the list of names first 'figuratively' and then 'morally'. 'Figurative' explanation informs the Christian of truths about the person, life, mission, and death of Jesus (and of the mysteries of the church) which should be understood and believed. Then 'moral' explanation holds up Christ's forebears as models for imitation, or as object lessons of what should be avoided ('moral' here should be taken as referring to the activities suited to believers, such as prayer, rather than as pointing to morality as a category broader than religion), and these various lessons are 'encoded' in their individual names.

Handbooks explaining biblical names already existed (Eusebius as reworked by Jerome was the most famous in Latin and a key source for the *Interpretatio*) and Ailerán interwove such information with material from a wide range of other patristic sources to produce a short and consistent tract. The work is simultaneously an explanation of one scriptural passage, and a statement of his belief that God foretold the coming of Jesus and in the course of this preparation hid a key to a deeper understanding of his Son. Thus Ailerán was read, in all probability, more often as a book directly on what Christians should believe about Jesus than as a work of exegesis. In form and structure it exhibits all the characteristics of early medieval handbooks for interpreting scripture. That the work survives in only three manuscripts (two from St Gallen and one from Reichenau) indicates that it was not influential and perhaps that it was not considered particularly useful.

Ailerán's other work is a didactic poem of forty lines on

the Eusebian canons entitled 'Kanon evangeliorum rhythmica'. The Eusebian canons are ten lists, keyed by marginal numbers to the four gospels, which enable the reader to find parallel passages in the other gospels where such exist. The lists (canons) note passages common to all four gospels, then combinations of three, then two, and finally items unique to individual gospels. The poem not only enables a student to understand the general theory of the canons, but once committed to memory constitutes a tool of continuous utility. The canons are easier to use if one remembers the gospels to which each relates, and this is conveyed in pen-pictures by Ailerán. Moreover, by giving the number of parallels in each canon, it conveys numerically a sense that the four gospels can be closely harmonized, along with the means of checking whether the actual tables in a gospel book are complete. Students' aids, by their very nature, do not survive in large numbers; consequently, that eleven manuscripts are known (early eighth to eleventh century in date and from across Europe) should be regarded as relative abundance, demonstrating the enduring utility of Ailerán's poem and its appeal within the academic environment before universities.

Modern assessments of Ailerán's stature as a writer have varied according to the overall view taken of the literary significance of Irish monasticism, ranging from exaggerated claims for his knowledge of Hebrew and Greek to dismissals of Ailerán as an academic hack reusing the onomastic work of Jerome. A balanced judgement should be based on the recognition that Ailerán belonged to a period when new works were praised in so far as they were useful in teaching and preaching: on this criterion he displays skill combined with ingenuity. The proof of this is that his works continued to be copied, even if not always under Ailerán's name; and he is praised in a short poem (mid-ninth century) on the scholars of Clonard. Ailerán is listed among the saints in two ninth-century Irish martyrologies: his feast day is given as 29 December, and the annals of Ulster record that he died in the great plague of 665.   THOMAS O'LOUGHLIN

Sources Ailerani Interpretatio mystica et moralis progenitorum domini Jesu Christi, ed. A. Breen (1995) · J. F. Kenney, The sources for the early history of Ireland (1929); repr. (1979), 279–81 · M. Lapidge and R. Sharpe, A bibliography of Celtic-Latin literature, 400–1200 (1985), 82–3 · M. Esposito, 'Hiberno-Latin manuscripts in the libraries of Switzerland: pt II', Proceedings of the Royal Irish Academy, 30C (1912–13), 1–14, esp. 1–5 · D. De Bruyne, 'Une poésie inconnue d'Aileran le Sage', Revue Bénédictine, 29 (1912), 339–40 · D. R. Howlett, The Celtic Latin tradition of Biblical style (1995), 129–31 · P. Ó Riain, 'The Tallaght martyrologies redated', Cambridge Medieval Celtic Studies, 20 (1990), 21–38, esp. 26–7 · E. Dekkers, Clavis patrum latinorum, 3rd edn (1995), nn. 1120–1121 · D. R. Howlett, 'Seven studies in seventh-century texts', Peritia, 10 (1996), 1–70, esp. 6–20

Ailesbury. For this title name see Bruce, Robert, second earl of Elgin and first earl of Ailesbury (bap. 1626, d. 1685); Bruce, Thomas, second earl of Ailesbury (1656–1741).

Ailill Molt (d. c.482), high-king of Ireland, was one of the five or more sons of *Nath Í mac Fiachrach (supp. d. 445?), ancestor of many of the Uí Fhiachrach kings of Connacht. His mother was said to have been Ethne ingen Chonrach

Cais. According to the mainstream medieval king-lists, Ailill Molt was the last high-king of Ireland for 500 years not to be a descendant of Niall Noígiallach (ancestor of the Uí Néill dynasty). His epithet molt means 'ram' or 'wether', though how this came to be attached to him is not known.

During the twenty years up to 482 Ailill Molt appears regularly in the annals of Ulster (the best chronicle for this period), yet it is hard to make many secure statements about his life or death. All the entries which refer to him are either glosses, or borrowings from the lost Book of Cuanu, or are written mainly in Irish rather than Latin— all symptoms of delayed arrival into the annals. It is unlikely that any of these entries were part of the chronicle sooner than the beginning of the eighth century at the earliest. Surprisingly for a high-king of Ireland, he receives no mention in the early writings about St Patrick. So elusive is Ailill Molt that some have suggested he was never high-king at all, and that his reign was a medieval concoction devised to absorb the chronological discrepancies caused by the misdating of the mission of St Patrick.

However, against this is the testimony of the earliest list of the kings of Tara (the formal title of the high-kings), Baile Chuinn Chétchathaig, composed about 700; this, in common with all subsequent lists, includes Ailill Molt as a king. The lists carry with them the baggage of Uí Néill dynastic propaganda, and it is improbable that Baile Chuinn Chétchathaig would have accepted Ailill Molt, who was not numbered with that dynasty, had he not been considered a high-king of Ireland of good standing.

If the reign is genuine, it is likely that there is a genuine base to the annal entries concerning Ailill Molt. These say that about 467 he held the 'Feast of Tara', a royal prerogative with pagan and sexual overtones. He was defeated in battle by the Leinstermen about 470 and again a few years later. He fell in or about 482 in a battle at Faughan Hill, near Kells (Meath), against descendants of Niall. He is said to have been married to Uchdelb, a daughter of Óengus, king of Munster. They had two sons, Mac Ercae (d. 543) and Cellach.   PHILIP IRWIN

Sources Ann. Ulster · A. P. Smyth, 'The Húi Néill and the Leinstermen in the Annals of Ulster, 431–516', Études Celtiques, 14 (1974–5), 121–43 · F. J. Byrne, Irish kings and high-kings (1973) · G. Murphy, 'On the dates of two sources used in Thurneysen's Heldensage: 1. Baile Chuind and the date of Cin Dromma Snechtai', Ériu, 16 (1952), 145–56 · M. C. Dobbs, ed. and trans., 'The Ban-shenchus [pt 2]', Revue Celtique, 48 (1931), 163–234, esp. 179–80

Ailnoth [Ælnoth] (fl. c.1085–c.1122), Benedictine monk and hagiographer, was an Englishman, from Canterbury, who spent his ecclesiastical career in Denmark. He was perhaps prior of the community of St Cnut at Odense, which was founded in 1095 as a daughter house of the Benedictine abbey of Evesham. He may have arrived in Denmark at the time of the establishment of this monastic house, one of the first in Scandinavia, or alternatively he may have accompanied relics of St Alban which arrived in Denmark somewhat earlier, perhaps c.1085. Most of the English churchmen of this period who laboured in Scandinavia are not known by name, but Ailnoth can be identified thanks to his authorship of an account of recent Danish history, including a *passio* of King Cnut. Cnut, who became king in 1080, was murdered in Odense in 1086 by political opponents and was canonized by the pope *c.*1099; his remains were translated the following year to a shrine in the cathedral church, and the hagiographical and liturgical support required by his cult was modelled on the liturgy of Anglo-Saxon royal saints, supplied presumably by Ailnoth and his fellow countrymen. His is the earliest work of history and hagiography known from a Scandinavian context. In the preface Ailnoth dedicated his composition to King Niels (*r.* 1104–34) and spoke of having lived twenty-four years in Denmark; dates of composition from *c.*1109 to 1122 have been proposed. The work was a partisan interpretation of the Danish political scene, upholding the ambitions of the sons of Swein Estrithson (particularly Cnut, Erik, and Niels) and claiming divine support for their plans for Denmark, which included the final stages of its conversion and Christianization and the extension of royal authority.   L. ABRAMS

Sources M. C. Gertz, ed., *Vitae sanctorum Danorum* (Copenhagen, 1908–12), 60–136 [incl. *passio* of Cnut] · *Ælnoths Krønike*, trans. E. Albrectsen (1984) · P. King, 'The cathedral priory of Odense in the middle ages', *Saga-Book of the Viking Society*, 16 (1962–5), 192–214 · E. Hoffmann, *Die heiligen Könige bei den Angelsachsen und den skandinavischen Völkern: Königsheiliger und Königshaus*, Quellen und Forschungen zur Geschichte Schleswig-Holsteins, 69 (1975) · C. Breengaard, *Muren om Israels hus. Regnum og sacerdotiumi Denmark, 1050–1170* (Copenhagen, 1982)
Archives Municipal Library, Saint-Omer, MS 716 · Public Library, Bruges, MS 403

Ailred [Ælred, Æthelred] **of Rievaulx** (1110–1167), religious writer and abbot of Rievaulx, was probably the youngest of the three sons of Eilaf, the last hereditary priest of the church of St Andrew at Hexham, grandson of Eilaf, treasurer of Durham, and great-grandson of the learned Alfred, son of Westou, sacristan of Durham and guardian of the shrine of St Cuthbert.

Early years Ailred was born at Hexham early in 1110 and, as a youth, was said to have been as intelligent as he was eloquent. He received a basic classical and literary education at Hexham and, probably, at Durham, but some time after 1124 he joined the court of David I, king of Scots, as a companion to David's eldest son, Henry, with whom he developed a deep friendship, and David's stepson, Waldef, another saint in the making. Here he sowed his wild oats, and here too he was elevated to the position of David's seneschal and was employed by his royal master on numerous diplomatic missions in Scotland and northern England.

It was on one such mission to Archbishop Thurstan of York about 1134 that Ailred first learned of the Cistercians of Rievaulx. The abbey had been founded in 1132 by Walter Espec and, according to Walter Daniel in his life of Ailred, it took but a single visit to persuade Ailred to relinquish the court for the cloister. Whether his decision was really as precipitate as Walter describes may perhaps be questioned, for the *Vita Ailredi*, important though it is, is a hagiographical work and its author was not averse to manipulating the truth to suit his purposes. But whatever the facts of the matter, with his entry into Rievaulx there is no doubt that Ailred had found his true home.

The new postulant, however, was unusual: he was familiar with the court, accustomed to power, and practised in diplomacy; and it would have been strange had William, abbot of Rievaulx, not profited from his talents. Thus, in 1138, during the war between Stephen and Matilda, Ailred probably accompanied William to Wark on the Scottish border to negotiate the surrender of Walter Espec's castle to King David; and in 1142, as William's representative, he journeyed to Rome to present to Innocent II the Cistercian objections to the election of Archbishop William of York.

Abbot of Revesby and then Rievaulx On his return from Rome, Ailred was appointed novice master at Rievaulx—he was tender and compassionate with his charges, though there are indications that he was also somewhat lax—but shortly thereafter, in 1143, he was appointed first abbot of Revesby in Lincolnshire. He governed the new abbey with a combination of deep spirituality and hardheaded business acumen, and as the religious life of the house grew in fervour, so its wealth and possessions grew in quantity.

Meanwhile, in 1145, William of Rievaulx had died and his successor, Maurice, found the abbatial burden too heavy. He therefore resigned in 1147 and Ailred was elected to succeed him: he would hold the office for the next twenty years. His election, however, was not unopposed, for there were some who thought him ambitious, self-indulgent, and too involved with worldly affairs. But once elected, Ailred brought to Rievaulx all the talents he had displayed at Revesby, and under his guidance Rievaulx 'doubled its monks, lay-brothers, laymen, granges, lands, and goods, and trebled its religious life' (*Life*, §30).

The new abbot, however, was hardly a model of monastic stability. He was much in demand as a fine preacher and was regularly sought out as an effective mediator in conflicts both secular and monastic. Thus, in the early 1160s he played an important role—perhaps a decisive role—in persuading Henry II to support the papacy of Alexander III; on 13 October 1163 he preached at Westminster at the translation of St Edward the Confessor; on 20 March in the following year—it was St Cuthbert's day, a saint to whom he had a particular devotion and to whom he composed a (lost) eulogy—he was preaching in a church in Kirkcudbright; and at about the same time (the year is uncertain) he negotiated peace between Fergus of Galloway and his contumacious sons. It was neither his first nor his last visit to Scotland, and on his way he would sometimes spend the night with his friend Godric of Finchale whose life, by Reginald of Durham, was written at Ailred's request. As abbot of Rievaulx he was also required to attend the annual general chapter at Cîteaux and to make annual visitations of Rievaulx's five daughter houses: Wardon, Melrose, Dundrennan, Revesby, and Rufford. As a consequence he was often away from his monastery, but even when he was within its walls his influence spread far and wide: he was in contact with the pope, kings, archbishops and bishops, and the most distinguished men in the realm, and the loss of his collected letters has deprived scholars of a wealth of literary evidence for the period.

Illness and death For the last ten years of his life Ailred was plagued by serious and painful illness: he suffered from arthritis, gout, and kidney stones; and, for the twelve months before his death, from some chronic bronchial disorder. So severe were his sufferings (which were exacerbated by his own austerities) that in 1157 the general chapter gave him leave to move into the infirmary at Rievaulx and to conduct the business of the house from there. This he did for a short time, but then moved from the infirmary to a small hut nearby. There he read and worked, and there too he received visitors, both heavenly (according to Walter Daniel) and earthly, though the latter were surely the more importunate. The monks came to him in dozens—even up to a hundred, says Walter—and it seems that the Rievaulx community intended to reap all the benefit it could from the enforced presence of its ailing abbot.

By January 1167 Ailred knew that he was dying. On the third of the month he spoke to his monks for the last time, advised them how best to choose his successor, and asked for certain relics and three books: his glossed psalter (it was preserved in the library after his death), Augustine's *Confessions*, and the gospel of St John. On 5 January he was anointed *in extremis* and given the viaticum by Roger of Byland, and as his body became ever feebler he grew impatient for death. 'Festinate [Hasten], for Crist luve', he would say (*Life*, §54), yet he lingered on for another week before he died on 12 January 1167 at about 10.30 p.m. He was fifty-seven. He was buried the next day in the chapter house at Rievaulx (his body was later translated to the church), and although never formally canonized, he became the centre of a local cult in the north of England which was recognized officially by the Cistercians in 1476.

Ailred as author Ailred was an accomplished writer of historical, hagiographical, spiritual, and theological works. He had lived in troubled times and, as a man who had enjoyed the trust of kings, was well placed to write of current events. That he did so with apologetic interest is only to be expected.

His earliest historical work is the *Vita Davidis Scotorum regis* written in 1153 on the death of his friend and former patron. The work is a paean in praise of David's virtues and a plea for loyalty to his grandson and heir, Malcolm IV. Ailred then made the *Vita* the first chapter of his *Genealogia regum Anglorum* (1153–4), a work that is partly advice on how to be a good king and partly a careful (if tenuous) argument for accepting the young Henry II as a lineal descendant of Edward the Confessor and for seeing the Norman kingship as the true successor to the Anglo-Saxon royal line. The same intent appears in the *Vita S. Eduardi regis et confessoris* (1162–3) written at the request of Lawrence of Westminster and dedicated to Henry II. It

is not a particularly original work, being heavily dependent on an earlier biography by Osbert of Clare, but with Ailred's additions the book proved immensely popular and played an important role both in advancing the cult of the Confessor in England and in establishing the myth of Plantagenet legitimacy.

Between the *Genealogia* and the *Vita* came *De bello standardii* (1155–7), an account of the battle of the Standard fought near Northallerton between the Scots and the English on 22 August 1138. Ailred's account, however, was written at least seventeen years after the affray and the roles played by certain of the protagonists were not quite as Ailred wished to remember them.

In the *Vita S. Niniani* (1154–60) and *De miraculis Hagustaldensis ecclesiae* (on the saints of Hexham, begun in 1155), history mingles with hagiography, for little definite was known of any of the saints in question. But although both works amalgamate earlier traditions with pious imagination, the story of the saints of Hexham is enriched by personal reminiscences of Ailred's own family—the saints of Hexham were, after all, his family's saints—and his comments are an important source for his own biography.

The extraordinary and horrible story of the nun of Watton is contained in a letter written by Ailred (*De sanctimoniali de Watton*) c.1160, after he had been asked by Gilbert of Sempringham to investigate events at Watton Priory. There a young novice, having taken the veil despite showing little inclination towards the religious life, had an affair with a man of the house and became pregnant. When this was discovered, the nuns forced her to castrate her lover, and placed her in irons in a cell. She then claimed to have been restored to her virginal condition through the miraculous intervention of the now deceased archbishop of York, Henry Murdac, who had placed her in the convent as a young girl. Ailred, dismayed at the ease with which male and female religious could meet, was undoubtedly relieved when the investigation was over.

Of Ailred's surviving spiritual treatises much has been written. The earliest (and finest) was the *Speculum caritatis*, a work requested by Bernard of Clairvaux whom Ailred had undoubtedly met on his way to Rome in 1142. It was begun when the author was novice master at Rievaulx and perhaps completed at Revesby. The last was the Augustinian *De anima* (not one of his best works) which was composed during the last two or three years of his life. Between these came *De Iesu puero duodenni* (1153–7), an allegorical exposition of Luke 2:41–52; the Ciceronian dialogue *De spiritali amicitia* (c.1160), a very popular work; the influential *De institutione inclusarum* (1160–62) addressed to his sister (for whose existence this is our only evidence); the brief but very personal *Oratio pastoralis* (c.1163–6); and a whole variety of sermons—about 200 according to Walter Daniel's conservative estimate—delivered at different times on different occasions: sermons that are in many ways more important than the treatises and certainly more neglected.

In these works Ailred emerges as a theologian and spiritual director, and as a man wholly consumed with a love for the incarnate Christ. Much of his thought is rooted in the writings of the standard Western authorities (especially Augustine and Gregory the Great) and in the Cistercian tradition of which, in England, he was the foremost representative; but in his discussion of human and divine relationships and in his conception of God as friendship (*amicitia*) he made important and original contributions to spiritual theology.

Not all Ailred's works have survived. The loss of his letters and his eulogy to St Cuthbert have already been mentioned, but the Rievaulx library catalogue also lists an otherwise unknown *De fasciculo frondium*, and Walter Daniel notes that he composed a liturgical homily on Luke 11:33 to be read on the feast day of St Edward the Confessor. A number of other treatises, both historical and spiritual, have at times been attributed to him (they are listed in Anselme Hoste's *Bibliotheca Aelrediana*), but none is certainly from his pen and some are clearly spurious. And as to Charles Dumont's suggestion that Ailred was the author of the pseudo-Bernardine *Jubilus rhythmicus de nomine Iesu*, that remains no more than an attractive hypothesis.   DAVID N. BELL

Sources *The life of Ailred of Rievaulx by Walter Daniel*, ed. and trans. F. M. Powicke (1950); repr. (1978); repr. with a new introduction by M. Dutton (1994) · J. Raine, ed., *The priory of Hexham*, 1, SurtS, 44 (1864) · A. Hoste, *Bibliotheca Aelrediana: a survey of the manuscripts, old catalogues, editions and studies concerning St Aelred of Rievaulx* (1962) · A. Squire, *Aelred of Rievaulx: a study* (1981) · Ailred of Rievaulx, *De anima*, ed. C. H. Talbot (1952), 1–62 · M. L. Dutton, 'Ælred, historian: two portraits in Plantagenet myth', *Cistercian Studies Quarterly*, 28 (1993), 113–44 · M. L. Dutton, 'The conversion and vocation of Aelred of Rievaulx: a historical hypothesis', *England in the twelfth century* [Harlaxton 1988], ed. D. Williams (1990), 31–49 · C. Dumont, 'L'hymne *Dulcis Jesu memoria*: le *Jubilus* serait-il d'Aelred de Rievaulx?', *Collectanea Cisterciensia*, 55 (1993), 233–43 · C. Dumont, introduction, in Aelred of Rievaulx, *The mirror of charity*, trans. E. Connor (1990), 11–67 · T. E. Harvey, *Saint Aelred of Rievaulx* (1932) · A. Hallier, *The monastic theology of Aelred of Rievaulx*, trans. C. Heaney (1969) · *Aelredus Rievallensis: opera ascetica*, ed. A. Hoste and C. H. Talbot (1971); repr. (1989)

Aimer, Philippe (*fl.* 1180–1181). *See under* Moneyers (*act. c.*1180–*c.*1500).

Ainfcellach (*d.* 719). *See under* Dál Riata, kings of (*act. c.*500–*c.*850).

Ainger, Alfred [*pseud.* Doubleday] (1837–1904), writer and Church of England clergyman, born at 10 Doughty Street, London, on 9 February 1837, was the youngest of the four children of Alfred Ainger (1797–1859) and his first wife, Marianne Jagger (*d.* 1839) of Liverpool. His father, an architect of scientific tastes, who designed the first University College Hospital in London (demolished and rebuilt 1900–06), was a Unitarian of Huguenot descent. His mother, who was musically gifted, died two years after her son Alfred's birth; his father married again and had a second family. After attending University College School the younger Alfred went in 1849 to Joseph King's boarding-school at Carlton Hill, London, where he fell under the two potent influences of Charles Dickens and Frederick Denison Maurice. His schoolmaster took him to hear Maurice preach, and he turned from his father's Unitarianism to the Church of England. Dickens's sons were

Alfred Ainger (1837–1904), by George Du Maurier, *c.*1881

Ainger's schoolfellows at King's school, and with them he visited their father. Dickens early discovered the boy's dramatic gift, and for several years Ainger was his favourite dramatic pupil, acting with him and Mark Lemon in the amateur performances which Dickens organized at his home, Tavistock House. At sixteen Ainger went to King's College, London, where Maurice was professor both of divinity and of English literature. Literature now absorbed him, particularly the writings of Charles Lamb and George Crabbe. Devotion to Shakespeare manifested itself early and in 1855 he became the first president of the college's Shakespeare Society. In October 1856 he matriculated at Trinity Hall, Cambridge, with a view to a legal career. Henry Latham and Leslie Stephen were tutors of his college, and Henry Fawcett—soon to be Ainger's close friend—was elected a fellow in the year of Ainger's entrance. At Cambridge, Ainger became the leading spirit of a literary circle which included Hugh Reginald Haweis, Horace Smith, and A. W. Ward. He was a foremost contributor to *The Lion*, a short-lived undergraduate magazine (3 nos., 1857–8) which Haweis edited. His Shakespearian criticism and his skit there on Thomas Babington Macaulay attested to his literary gifts and brilliant humour. Also at Cambridge he came to know Alexander Macmillan, at that time a bookseller in Trinity Street and afterwards the famous London publisher.

Ainger's health allowed him to do no more than take the ordinary law examination (in June 1859). He graduated BA in 1860 and MA in 1865. After his father's death in November 1859, and partly on the advice of his friends, Leslie

Stephen among them, he took holy orders. In 1860 he was ordained deacon and soon after became curate to Richard Haslehurst, vicar of Alrewas, in Staffordshire. In 1863 he was ordained priest, and from 1864 to 1866 was assistant master in the Collegiate School at Sheffield. In the autumn of 1865 he competed successfully for the readership at the Temple, London, and held the post for twenty-seven years.

Both Ainger's sisters married early, the younger, Marianne, to a German named Wiss, and the elder, Adeline, to Dr Roscow of Sandgate, who died in 1865. Shortly after Ainger's resettlement in London (1867) he experienced the greatest sorrow of his life at the sudden death of Adeline, his widowed sister. The shock aged him prematurely and turned his hair white. He became the guardian of his sister's four children—two girls and two boys—and devoted himself to their care. In 1876 he moved to Hampstead, where he lived with his two nieces, Ada and Margaret Roscow, and where he became friends with the artist of *Punch*, George Du Maurier. That companionship provided him with a definite field for his wit, and he constantly suggested the jests which Du Maurier illustrated. The poet Tennyson, and Charles John Vaughan, the master of the Temple from 1869, also formed part of his circle, and he was elected a member of the Literary Club, which had been founded by Samuel Johnson.

Ainger's own position in literature became established by his publications. At twenty-two he contributed his first successful article, 'Books and their uses', to an early number of *Macmillan's Magazine* (1, 1859–60, 110). He took the whimsical pseudonym Doubleday (doubled A). Eleven other articles appeared under the same friendly auspices between 1871 and 1896. From 1900 to 1904—the last years of his life—he was a regular contributor to *The Pilot*, a weekly journal edited by D. C. Lathbury.

Ainger's chief writings dealt with the life and work of Charles Lamb. His monograph on Lamb was published in 1882, in the English Men of Letters series (rev. and enlarged, 1888). There followed editions of *Lamb's Essays* (1883), *Lamb's Poems, Plays, and Miscellaneous Essays* (1884), and *Lamb's Letters* (1888; new edn, 1904), the last the only collection which at the time of publication could lay claim to completeness. His life of Lamb and his edition of Lamb's writings were carefully researched, but he omitted passages from the collection of writings which jarred with his view of Lamb's character. He contributed the articles on Charles and Mary Lamb, Tennyson, and George Du Maurier to the *Dictionary of National Biography*. In a remark which became famous, he summed up, in a speech at a dinner of the contributors (8 July 1897), the dictionary's character in the motto, 'No flowers, by request'.

As a lecturer on literary subjects Ainger was popular with cultivated audiences throughout the country, and from 1889 he frequently lectured at the Royal Institution; his titles included 'True and false humour in literature', 'Euphuism, past and present', and 'The three stages of Shakespeare's art'. In 1885 the University of Glasgow conferred upon him the honorary degree of LLD, and he was made an honorary fellow of his college, Trinity Hall.

During his last twenty years Ainger's influence as a preacher grew steadily. In 1887 he became a canon of Bristol. He was appointed select preacher of Oxford in 1893, and in the same year bad health compelled him to resign his readership at the Temple. He consequently accepted the living of St Edward's at Cambridge. Again illness speedily forced him to retire, and he spent two months travelling in Egypt and Greece. In June 1894, on Lord Rosebery's recommendation, he was appointed master of the Temple in succession to Charles Vaughan. Subsequently his duties of preacher became the main concern of his life. In 1895 he was made honorary chaplain, in 1896 chaplain-in-ordinary, to Queen Victoria, and in 1901 chaplain-in-ordinary to Edward VII. His sermons in the Temple were marked by beauty of language and by a quiet, practical piety, impatient of excess. Neither high-church nor low-church, he professed an unaggressive, moderate evangelicalism.

In 1903 Ainger's health deteriorated after an attack of influenza, and at the end of the year he resigned his canonry at Bristol. He died of pneumonia on 8 February 1904 at Darley Abbey, near Derby, the home of his younger niece, Ada Roscow, who in 1896 had married an old friend, Walter Evans. He was buried in the churchyard of Darley Abbey.

Apart from the works already mentioned and articles in periodicals, Ainger was the author of a volume of sermons (1870), a selection of Tennyson's works for the young (1891), a biographical preface to an edition of Thomas Hood's poems (1893, 1897), an introduction to an edition of John Galt's *Annals of the Parish* (1895), and a monograph on Crabbe (1903) in the English Men of Letters series. After his death a volume of sermons, *The Gospel of Human Life* (1904), and *Lectures and Essays* (2 vols., 1905) were edited by H. C. Beeching, dean of Norwich.

EDITH SICHEL, rev. NILANJANA BANERJI

Sources *The Times* (9 Feb 1904) • E. Sichel, *The life and letters of Alfred Ainger* (1906) • *WWW*, 1897–1915 • Venn, *Alum. Cant.* • E. Sichel, 'Canon Ainger', *QR*, 202 (1905), 169–96 • E. Sichel, 'Canon Ainger, a personal impression', *Monthly Review*, 14 (March 1904), 64–74 • L. A. Tollemache, *Old and odd memories* (1908) • A. W. Ward, 'Alfred Ainger', *Macmillan's Magazine*, 89 (1903–4), 470–80 • H. C. Beeching, preface, in A. Ainger, *The gospel of human life* (1904) • H. C. Beeching, preface, in A. Ainger, *Lectures and essays*, 2 vols. (1905) • *CGPLA Eng. & Wales* (1904)
Archives NRA, corresp. and papers | BL, corresp. with Macmillans, Add. MS 55097 • BL, letters to James Dykes Campbell, Add. MS 49524 • Bodl. Oxf., letters to Sidney Lee • LUL, letters to Austin Dobson • U. St Andr. L., letters to Leonora Blanche Lange
Likenesses G. Du Maurier, watercolour drawing, c.1881, NPG [see illus.] • H. G. Riviere, oils, 1904 (posthumous), Trinity Hall, Cambridge • Mrs S. G. Bainsmith, bust, Bristol Cathedral • Spy [L. Ward], caricature, NPG; repro. in *VF* (13 Feb 1892) • photographs, repro. in Sichel, *Life and letters of Alfred Ainger*
Wealth at death £9916 7s. 3d.: resworn probate, 18 March 1904, *CGPLA Eng. & Wales*

Ainger, Thomas (1799–1863), Church of England clergyman, was born on 1 August 1799 at Whittlesey, Cambridgeshire, the son of William Ainger and his wife, Mary, *née* Boyce. He was the youngest of their six children. He was educated at Norwich grammar school and St John's College, Cambridge. He graduated in 1821, became curate at St Giles's, Reading, in 1822, under Sir Henry Dukinfield, and after about three years became assistant minister at St Mary's, Greenwich. He married Frances, only daughter of William Barnard, in 1828; they had eight children. In 1841 Ainger was presented by Sir Thomas Maryon Wilson to the perpetual curacy of St John's, Hampstead, which he held until his death. On 19 February 1859 he became prebendary of St Paul's Cathedral. Ainger was energetic as a parish clergyman and poor-law guardian; he enlarged his church, abolished pew rents, and helped to found schools and a dispensary and to provide new churches in the rapidly developing district around Hampstead. He was 'a loyal Church man' (*Memoir*, xiv) who co-operated with members of other churches without any concession of Anglican principles. Ainger was ill from 1860, and died on 15 November 1863 in Hampstead; he was buried in Hampstead parish churchyard. He published four volumes and a number of single sermons.   H. C. G. MATTHEW

Sources *The last sermons of the Rev. Thomas Ainger…with a memoir* (1864) · *Clergy List* (1860) · Venn, *Alum. Cant.*

Wealth at death under £4000: resworn probate, Aug 1864, *CGPLA Eng. & Wales* (1863)

Ainley, Henry Hinchliffe (1879–1945), actor, was born at Morley, near Leeds, on 21 August 1879, the only son and eldest child of Richard Ainley, cloth finisher, and his wife, Ada Hinchliffe. After education at the church school of St Peter's, Morley, he became clerk in a bank at Sheffield, where he took part in amateur dramatics. When George Alexander and his company were on tour in 1899 young Ainley was permitted to 'walk on'. He then joined Frank Benson's company, making his first London appearance at the Lyceum Theatre in 1900 when he played Gloucester in *Henry V*. He was still a Bensonian when Alexander saw him as Lorenzo in *The Merchant of Venice* and chose him for Paolo in *Paolo and Francesca* by Stephen Phillips. So perfectly fitted was Ainley, both in looks and voice—from which the north country accent had gone during his training under Benson—that he became famous on the first night, 6 March 1902. His manner at that time was gently, though eagerly, romantic—in complete contrast to the masterfulness that he afterwards acquired.

In 1903 Ainley went to the United States and made his first appearance in New York as leading man to Maude Adams, playing, among other parts, the Revd Gavin Dishart in *The Little Minister*. That year he married Suzanne (1875–1924), actress, daughter of Richard Sheldon of New York. The marriage ended in divorce. In 1904 he returned to London to appear as Lancelot in Israel Zangwill's *Merely Mary Ann* and in 1905 he paid a short visit to Paris, where he was seen as Romeo in the balcony scene at the Opéra Comique. In 1906 he returned to the St James's Theatre to play Orlando in *As You Like It* to the Rosalind of Lilian Braithwaite, and he later joined the Vedrenne-Barker Company at the Royal Court Theatre, appearing as Orestes in Euripides' *Electra* and as Hippolytus. He gave a fine performance as Cassio in the production of *Othello* by Lewis Waller in May 1906. He was for several periods in the company of Sir Herbert Tree at His Majesty's Theatre, where in 1910 he took part in six plays during the Shakespeare festival.

It was in a production by Harley Granville Barker at the Savoy Theatre in 1912 that Ainley made one of his biggest and most original Shakespearian successes as Malvolio in *Twelfth Night*, giving the character an altogether new power and appeal. He also appeared memorably as Leontes in *The Winter's Tale*. Another remarkable development in the direction of strong character was his creation (1913) of Ilam Carve in Arnold Bennett's *The Great Adventure*, which ran for nearly two years at the Kingsway Theatre. Another notable character part which he made his own was Joseph Quinney in H. A. Vachell's *Quinneys'* at the Haymarket Theatre in 1915. In 1916 he joined the army with a commission in the Royal Garrison Artillery and served in England, France, and Italy. In 1917 he married Elaine Fearon, daughter of J. Willis Titus; this marriage was also dissolved. He was demobilized in 1919 and went into management at the St James's Theatre, opening as Fedya in *Reparation*, an adaptation of Tolstoy's *The Living Corpse*, and playing Mark Antony in a revival of *Julius Caesar* (1920). At His Majesty's Theatre in 1923 he gave a superb performance in the title part of J. E. Flecker's *Hassan*. At the Prince's Theatre in 1926 he played Macbeth to Sybil Thorndike's Lady Macbeth. After two years' illness he returned in July 1929 to play one of the most successful of all of his characters, as James Fraser in St John Ervine's *The First Mrs Fraser* at the Haymarket Theatre. In 1930 he appeared as Hamlet in a revival that was chosen for a royal command performance in the same year. At the Westminster Theatre in 1931 he did excellent work as Dr Knox in James Bridie's *The Anatomist* and in 1932 as the archangel in Bridie's *Tobias and the Angel*.

After an absence from the stage of six years, caused by illness, Ainley gave a single performance in 1938 at the Vaudeville Theatre of a scene from *Hassan*. After 1915 he appeared in a number of films, mostly theatrically conceived adaptations of Victorian novels and plays, but he made no deep impression in that medium. His broadcasts, on the other hand, were specially preserved by the British Broadcasting Corporation as examples of fine diction. No other actor of his time was better equipped for greatness than Ainley. In the romantic charm of his early performances and in the forceful but appealing character-creations of his later years he remained unexcelled. His Hamlet and Macbeth were not wholly satisfactory in construction and relation to the other characters, but they had magnificent moments. Whatever the type of play, Ainley's personality gave distinction to every part he took.

Henry Ainley had four children, two daughters and two sons, the elder of whom, Richard (1910–1956), also proved himself an actor of high ability. Henry Ainley died in London on 31 October 1945.

S. R. LITTLEWOOD, rev. K. D. REYNOLDS

Sources *The Times* (1 Nov 1945) · J. Parker, ed., *Who's who in the theatre*, 6th edn (1930) · R. Low, *The history of the British film*, 4: *1918–1929*

(1971) • personal knowledge (1959) • private information (1959) • *CGPLA Eng. & Wales* (1946)

Likenesses Foulsham & Banfield, photograph, *c.*1908, NPG • H. L. Oakley, silhouette, 1920, NPG • H. Coster, photographs, 1929, NPG • E. Kapp, drawing, 1932, Barber Institute of Fine Arts, Birmingham • R. G. Eves, chalk drawing, priv. coll. • H. Furniss, pen-and-ink caricature, NPG

Wealth at death £3306 1s. 11d.: probate, 22 Jan 1946, *CGPLA Eng. & Wales*

Ainslie, Charlotte Edith (1863–1960), headmistress and educationist, was born at Lauriston Place, Edinburgh, on 15 February 1863, the second daughter of William Ainslie, a pharmaceutical chemist, and his wife, Mary Ann Wood. She attended the Merchant Company's endowed George Watson's Ladies' College, Edinburgh, then under the headship of Alex Thompson, from 1873 to 1880. She later described herself as a shy pupil, but in her last year she obtained second place in the Edinburgh University senior local examinations. She spent the next two to three years in France, Germany, and Switzerland, teaching privately, to gain insight into foreign methods of study and education, and while abroad she began working for the St Andrews University higher certificate for women, the LLA diploma, which she gained with honours in 1885.

In January 1889 Ainslie was appointed head of the modern languages department at Dunheved College, Launceston, Cornwall. While teaching there she studied for and passed the London University matriculation examination, gaining the Reid scholarship awarded by the Bedford trustees. She attended Bedford College 1892–5, winning the Gilchrist scholarship for the best candidate of the year in 1893, and in 1895 she obtained the degree of BA division 1. She also studied psychology, ethics, and logic under J. H. Muirhead.

The following year Ainslie was appointed assistant mistress at the Skinners' Company's School for Girls, Stamford Hill, London. In 1901 she became senior lecturer in psychology and education, Cambridge Training College, and in 1902 she lectured at the Cambridge University extension summer meeting on the application of direct method and phonetics to modern language teaching. That year she was appointed headmistress of her former school, George Watson's Ladies' College. The first woman to be appointed head of any prestigious Scottish secondary school, Ainslie held the post until 1926 when she retired at the age of sixty-three. A small, white-haired woman, always elegantly dressed, she was reserved in manner and seemed somewhat unapproachable to her pupils and even to her staff, but her quiet competence gained her prominence in Scottish educational circles.

Ainslie was also actively involved in wider educational developments. In 1909 she became a governor of Bedford College, London. She was a member, and in 1912–13 president, of the Secondary Education Association of Scotland. She was also elected a member of the Scottish education reform committee, acting as convener of the subcommittee which reported on the education of women and also as a member of the professional training and status committee.

Ainslie wrote on the secondary education of girls, on domestic science in secondary schools, and on the position and status of female teachers, particularly in Scotland. She believed that educational aims should transcend gender, but that various gender differences, especially biological and behavioural, were significant. Ainslie promoted high academic standards, but she was also concerned that all pupils should be successful, since this developed self-confidence. The option should therefore be provided for them to develop intelligence and powers of reasoning through the study of problems connected with home life, such as economic history, social work, local government, and aspects of paid work. But she also believed that such courses, to encourage less academic girls, should never be compulsory, and that girls should always have the option of taking identical courses with boys. The widespread introduction of such domestic courses would require 'a revolution in the attitude of women generally to home life in its relation to society, and in the methods of domestic management' (C. E. Ainslie, 'Domestic science for girls in secondary schools', *Secondary School Journal*, 4/1, 1911, 3–5), which in turn would require a higher status and more academic training (including history, economics, and science) for domestic science teachers.

Given the existence of co-education in most Scottish schools, Ainslie wanted to see a female deputy headteacher with overall responsibility for the girls appointed in every secondary school. She was also critical of the existing career prospects, salary scales, and retirement rights for female teachers, primary and secondary.

Ainslie was regarded as one of the leading Scottish experts on girls' education. She appears to have abstained from any public pronouncements on the position of women or on women's suffrage, but she was present at the inaugural meeting of the Edinburgh Women Citizens' Association in 1918, was one of the twenty-one executive committee members subsequently elected from sixty-five candidates, and was elected a vice-president in 1921.

On her retirement in 1926 Ainslie received an honorary degree from Edinburgh University and in 1933 she was appointed OBE for services to education. She was co-opted onto the Merchant Company education board, 1929–36. Her leisure interests were travel, art, and music. Throughout her years as headmistress and subsequent retirement she lived at 12 Mayfield Terrace, Edinburgh. Charlotte Ainslie died on 24 August 1960, in a nursing home at 23 Eildon Street, Edinburgh. LINDY MOORE

Sources *George Square Chronicle* (July 1926), 88–102 • 'Dr C. E. Ainslie', *The Scotsman* (16 June 1938) • 'Appointment of headmistress to George Watson's Ladies College', *The Scotsman* (11 July 1902) • *The Scotsman* (27 Aug 1960) • *The Times* (3 Sept 1960) • *Scottish biographies* (1938) • George Watson's College archives, George Watson's Hospital minutes, 1901–3 • Merchant Company education board minutes, 1925–6, 1929–30, 1936–7 • 'A George Square retrospect', *George Square Chronicle* (1934), 32–3 • 'Edinburgh University graduation ceremony', *The Scotsman* (21 July 1926) • NA Scot., Edinburgh Women Citizens' Association MSS, GD 333, GD 333/6/1, GD 333/7/219, GD 333/7/1 • *Reform in Scottish education: being the report of the Scottish education reform committee* (1917) • 'LLA candidates, 1883–

1886', U. St Andr. L., special collections department, MS 680 • K. M. Hammond, 'George Square: sixty years ago', *University of Edinburgh Journal*, 29 (1979–80), 57–9 • b. cert. • d. cert.

Archives George Watson's College, Edinburgh, George Watson Ladies' College collection, archives

Likenesses S. Cursiter, oils, 1938, George Watson's College, Edinburgh • S. Cursiter, small replica portrait, oils, 1938, George Watson's College, Edinburgh • photograph, George Watson's College, Edinburgh • photograph, repro. in *George Square Chronicle* (July 1926), 88

Wealth at death £33,147 8s. 2d.: confirmation, 20 Dec 1960, *CCI*

Ainslie, George Robert (1776–1839), army officer and numismatist, was born near Edinburgh, the eldest son of Sir Philip Ainslie and his wife, the Hon. Elizabeth Gray, fifth daughter of John, twelfth Lord Gray. He entered the army as an ensign in the 19th regiment in 1793. His mother's political influence as a daughter of Lord Gray was instrumental in Ainslie's promotion to lieutenant during the same year. In 1794 he was made a captain in the 85th regiment. With his regiment he saw service in Flanders, and in 1799, when he was promoted major, was engaged in the short and disastrous expedition to The Helder. Ainslie did not display any real ardour for military life, failing to distinguish himself in any capacity. Consequently in 1800 he was promoted to a lieutenant-colonelcy in a fencible regiment.

In December 1802 Ainslie married the only daughter of Christopher Nevile of Wellingore, Lincolnshire, and niece of the earl of Gainsborough. They had two sons and three daughters; she survived her husband. Despite failing to re-apply for active service, Ainslie was made lieutenant-colonel of the 25th regiment in 1807, and promoted to brevet colonel in 1810. His influential relatives then secured for him the governorship, first of St Eustatius in the West Indies in 1812, and then of Dominica in June of the same year. His period in Dominica was controversial. Critics alleged that he became the puppet of a planter clique and for them cruelly crushed the maroons. However, his supporters claimed that the maroons were ferocious savages, and that in defeating them Ainslie performed a public service. In 1814 the island legislature thanked him and presented him with a 200 guinea sword, and inhabitants gave him addresses of support. He was criticized in parliament and in 1814 called to London to explain his conduct, then was permitted to return to Dominica, finishing as governor in 1815.

Ainslie was promoted major-general in 1813 and lieutenant-general in 1825, but was never actively employed again. He was unsuited to a military career, his great passion being collecting coins, an occupation which had been relatively neglected in England since the time of Addison. Ainslie specialized in Anglo-Norman coins, travelling all over England, and, what was then unusual, all over the rural districts of Normandy and Brittany, in search of coins. In 1830 he published the result of his work in a magnificent quarto entitled *Anglo-French Coinage*. Ainslie's was a unique collection of rare coins, and, absorbed in his pursuit, he died in Edinburgh on 16 April 1839.

H. M. STEPHENS, *rev.* S. KINROSS

Sources J. Philippart, ed., *The royal military calendar*, 3rd edn, 3 (1820) • *GM*, 2nd ser., 11 (1839), 555 [obit. of J. P. Ainslie] • D. P. Henige, *Colonial governors from the fifteenth century to the present* (1970)

Archives JRL, corresp. with William Murray • NL Scot., letters to Sir Walter Scott • U. Edin. L., letters to David Laing

Likenesses B. W. Crombie, coloured etching, 1838, NPG; repro. in *Modern Alterians* (1882) • J. T. Wedgwood, line engraving (after C. Hayter), BM

Ainslie, Henry (1760–1834), physician, the second son of James Ainslie, a physician of Kendal, was born on 21 March 1760 at Carlisle, Cumberland. After a sound education in Kendal he entered Pembroke College, Cambridge, in 1777; he was senior wrangler and second Smith's prizeman in 1781, and became a fellow of his college in 1782. In 1787 he obtained the university licence to practise physic and was elected physician to Addenbrooke's Hospital in Cambridge, a post he resigned in 1788. He was married to Agnes, daughter of William Ford of Waterhead, Coniston, on 9 August 1785. They had several children, one of whom, Gilbert, later became vice-chancellor of Cambridge University.

Ainslie took his MD degree in 1793 and left Cambridge for London, where in 1795 he was elected a fellow of the Royal College of Physicians. Also in 1795 he became assistant physician to St Thomas's Hospital; soon after he was elected physician in full. He delivered the Harveian oration in 1802, but it was not printed. He resigned his hospital post in 1800, and, though taking some part in the business of the Royal College of Physicians, he attained to no great fame or practice as a physician. He died on 26 October 1834 at Grizedale Hall, Northumberland, and was commemorated with his father and elder brother on a tablet in the church of Over Kellet, Lancashire.

NORMAN MOORE, *rev.* PATRICK WALLIS

Sources Venn, *Alum. Cant.* • Munk, *Roll* • *GM*, 2nd ser., 2 (1834), 657 • A. Rook, M. Carlton, and W. G. Cannon, *The history of Addenbrooke's Hospital, Cambridge* (1991) • F. G. Parsons, *The history of St Thomas's Hospital*, 3 vols. (1932–6)

Ainslie, Hew (1792–1878), brewer and poet, was born on 5 April 1792 at Bargeny Mains in the parish of Dailly, Ayrshire, only son of the three children of George Ainslie, a butler on the estate of Sir Hew Dalrymple Hamilton. His mother's name is unknown, but Ainslie praised her in many of his poems. Educated by a dominie at home, then at Ballantrae parish school and Ayr Academy, he finished formal schooling at fourteen. He was influenced by the colourful past of his family, by his mother's songs and lore, and by his father's small collection of Scottish literature, including Burns and Fergusson. For a time Ainslie worked for Hamilton, participating in the improvement of the estate's landscape and learning many of the skills that he used in later life as a construction consultant. His father ended his association with Hamilton in 1809 and moved the family to Roslin, near Edinburgh. Ainslie began to study law at Glasgow. In 1810 he became a clerk at Register House, Edinburgh, and became acquainted with many literary figures. He contributed to *Scottish ballads* by Robert Chambers and for a while he was amanuensis to

Dugald Stewart. Ainslie married his cousin, Janet (*d.* 1863), daughter of William Ainslie, on 1 August 1812.

In 1822 Ainslie published anonymously *A pilgrimage to the land of Burns … with … poetry.* Consisting of a narrative interspersed with spirited lyrics, it was his most successful book. *A pilgrimage* received a good review from Thomas Campbell in *New Monthly Magazine*, but Walter Scott was not impressed. With low prospects in Scotland, Ainslie emigrated to America in 1822 in order to make a better life for his family. At this time he and Janet had three children. They were to have seven more. On his arrival in America he tried his hand at farming the land which he had purchased in Rensselaer County, New York, but when that did not succeed as he had hoped he moved in 1825 to Robert Owen's social experiment at New Harmony, Indiana. He left after one year and in 1827 became associated with a firm of brewers, Price and Wood, of Cincinnati, Ohio. Here he was instrumental in establishing various breweries, mills, and factories in the western states. In 1829 Ainslie opened a branch of Price and Wood in Louisville, Kentucky, but this was destroyed by flood. A second brewery, of Bottomley and Ainslie, opened in 1840 in New Albany, Indiana, was destroyed by fire, but despite these disasters Ainslie learned many skills and established his reputation as a consultant on brewery and factory construction.

Ainslie retired in the early 1850s. He was one of the group of minor Scottish songwriters to be represented in *Whistle-Binkie* (1853). In New York in 1855 he published *Scottish songs, ballads and poems*, of which the most popular was 'The Rover of Loch Ryan'. Written in Scots this volume was not very popular in America but was a success in Scotland. It was followed by a selection of his poems with a memoir in 1857. Janet died in 1863 and shortly afterwards Ainslie journeyed to his homeland for a tour marked by 'unexpected acclaim' (*ANB*). He also travelled for three years around England, Ireland, and the continent, but it was in Scotland that he attracted the greatest interest, being touted in the Scottish press as an emigrant success story. Distinguished by his 6 feet 4 inches height, as a young man he was described as tall and lanky and he remained a lean figure in maturity; his hair, though grey, was 'as thick and wildly tousled as in his youth' (ibid.). He never lost his Scottish accent.

Hew Ainslie lived during his final years at his son's home on Chestnut Street in Louisville, Kentucky. He died there on 11 March 1878 and was buried with his wife at Cave Hill cemetery, Louisville.

The centenary of Ainslie's birth was celebrated in Scotland with the republication of *A pilgrimage to the land of Burns, and poems*, which contained a memoir of the author by Thomas C. Latto.

T. W. Bayne, *rev.* Douglas Brown

Sources Irving, *Scots.* · Boase, *Mod. Eng. biog.* · D. Baptie, ed., *Musical Scotland, past and present: being a dictionary of Scottish musicians from about 1400 till the present time* (1894) · J. G. Wilson, ed., *The poets and poetry of Scotland*, 2 vols. (1876–7) · *Who was who in America: historical volume, 1607–1896*, rev. edn (1967) · *ANB* · C. Selle, 'Brewer and poet Hew Ainslie: from the land of Burns to Kentuckiana', www.fossils.org/1995/54HewAinslie.htm · bap. reg. Scot. · m. reg. Scot.

Archives Filson Club Historical Society, Louisville, Kentucky, Ainslie (Hew) papers, 1834–1902 · Filson Club Historical Society, Louisville, Kentucky, misc. papers, 1869–70
Likenesses W. Wellstood, engraved portrait, repro. in H. Ainslie, *Scottish songs, ballads and poems* (1855) · portrait, repro. in H. Ainslie, *A pilgrimage to the land of Burns, and poems* (1892)

Ainslie, John (1745–1828), cartographer and land surveyor, was born on 22 April 1745 in Jedburgh, the younger son and younger child of John Ainslie, druggist in Jedburgh, writer to the signet, and burgess of the burgh. He may have been educated at Jedburgh grammar school and was later apprenticed to Thomas Jefferys, for whom he continued to work thereafter. He was employed by him to survey Bedfordshire with Thomas Donald, Buckinghamshire in 1766 to 1768, and Yorkshire from 1767 to 1770.

After Jefferys's death on 20 November 1771 Ainslie returned home and shortly thereafter made a map of Jedburgh and its environs. This plan was dogged by misfortune, and the loss of the plates on a trip to London was never rectified. Lean times followed, and three years later he was using the backs of sheets of his Jedburgh map to draw a privately commissioned plan. On 27 October 1776 he married Christian, daughter and heiress of Thomas Caverhill of Jedburgh, merchant. Ainslie's mind was still fixed on making large-scale county maps: he proposed to survey Selkirkshire, Fife, and Kinross-shire, Stirlingshire and Clackmannanshire, Perthshire, the Lothians, Wigtownshire, Angus, Renfrewshire, Kirkcudbrightshire, and Berwickshire. The surveys of Stirlingshire and of Perthshire were never embarked upon, for want of subscribers, and Berwickshire was surveyed by John Blackadder, Ainslie being responsible only for the engraving; but the other counties were surveyed and a first edition of the resultant maps was published in 1797. A new edition was brought out in 1801.

Ainslie settled in Edinburgh and had premises at St Andrew Street, Parliament Square, Rose Street, South Hanover Street, and latterly at Nicolson Street. From Parliament Square he published on 1 March 1778 a map of eastern Scotland from Moffat to Arbroath. He then published four charts covering the south-west coast from Saltcoats to Whitehaven in Cumberland, before turning to the east coast of Scotland, producing a general chart in 1785 and in May 1786 three separate charts of the same coast. Henceforth, the sheer variety of his cartographic output was impressive. In 1785 alone, not only did he survey and engrave the series of charts mentioned above, but he also made a series of estate plans for Patrick Kerr of Abbotrule (which Kerr failed to pay for), surveyed a line for a canal from the Forth to the Clyde for Robert Whitworth, and engraved several plans for the court of session in Edinburgh.

During 1787 and 1788 Ainslie devoted most of his time to preparing his great map of Scotland. On 1 January 1788 the first of nine sheets was complete. This map was a landmark in the improvement of the outline of Scotland, which was not superseded for twenty years. For the first time the Great Glen is shown as a straight line, and Skye, Mull, and Islay are shown with some degree of accuracy. In

1789–90 he made a book of plans of the earl of Eglinton's estates in Ayrshire (now in the National Archives of Scotland). He then worked again with Whitworth, surveying lines for the Edinburgh to Glasgow canal. With Charles Rennie, the civil engineer, he surveyed the new harbour for Saltcoats and the line for the Glasgow to Ardrossan canal. With the turn of the century Ainslie turned to agricultural improvement, publishing *The Gentleman and Farmer's Pocket Book, Companion and Assistant* in 1805 and a *Comprehensive Treatise on Land Surveying* in 1812. At the time of his death he had amassed £8976 7s. 6d. He died on 29 February 1828 at his house in Nicolson Street, Edinburgh; he had lived since 1804 at various addresses on that street.

IAN ADAMS, rev. ELIZABETH BAIGENT

Sources I. H. Adams, *John Ainslie: map maker* (1970) · J. B. Harley and J. C. Harvey, introduction, *Facsimile edition of a survey of the county of Yorkshire by Thomas Jefferys, 1775* (1973), 1–4 · W. Cowan, *The maps of Edinburgh, 1544–1929*, rev. C. B. B. Watson, 2nd edn (1932) · *Caledonian Mercury* (16 Nov 1816) · J. Donaldson, *Agricultural biography* (1854) · *Edinburgh Evening Courant* (1 Feb 1776) · *Edinburgh Evening Courant* (4 Dec 1794) · *The mapping of Scotland* (1971) · E. G. R. Taylor, *The mathematical practitioners of Hanoverian England, 1714–1840* (1966) · F. W. Steer and others, *Dictionary of land surveyors and local map-makers of Great Britain and Ireland, 1530–1850*, ed. P. Eden, 2nd edn, ed. S. Bendall, 2 vols. (1997)
Wealth at death £8976 7s. 6d.: DNB

Ainslie, Sir Robert, first baronet (1729/30–1812), diplomatist and numismatist, was the third son of George Ainslie (d. 1773), merchant, and his wife, Jean, daughter of Sir Philip Anstruther of Anstrutherfield, Fife. He grew up with his two brothers and five sisters in Bordeaux, France, where his father had traded as a merchant for some time. His father had returned to Scotland in 1727, when he purchased the estate of Pilton in Edinburghshire. His elder brothers were Philip (1728–1802), who was knighted, and George Ainslie (d. 1804), an army general and lieutenant-governor of the Isles of Scilly.

Nothing is known of Ainslie's education or early career, but he seems to have worked as a spy, for he is said to have intercepted correspondence from the duc d'Aiguillon to the Spanish court during the Falklands crisis of 1770–71. In January 1772, in Paris, he compiled some 'Anecdotes of the court of France' for George III, which the king copied out in his own hand. On 20 September 1775 Ainslie was appointed to succeed John Murray as British ambassador to the Ottoman Porte, and he was knighted on the same day. After receiving his official instructions he left England in May 1776 for Constantinople, where he arrived in the following October. Ainslie's two principal objectives were to further British trading interests, represented by the Levant Company, who paid his salary, and to maintain peace in the region. France dominated the Levant trade, and relations between Britain and the Ottoman empire had worsened in the Russo-Turkish War (1768–74), when Britain had lent support to the Russian fleet. However, the new sultan, ʿAbd-ul-hamid, who succeeded in 1774, advocated closer political and commercial ties with Britain to offset the latter's long-established interests in Russia, and he struck up an excellent relationship with Ainslie.

Unlike some of his predecessors, Ainslie adapted well to life in Constantinople:

> being strongly attached to the manner of the people … in his house, his garden, and his table he assumed the style and fashion of a Musselman of rank; in fine, he lived *en Turk*, and pleased the natives so much by this seeming policy … that he became more popular than any of the Christian ministers. (*St James's Chronicle*, 9 Dec 1790)

He certainly took advantage of the opportunity to purchase Ottoman and Byzantine antiquities and amassed a collection of drawings, many of which he commissioned from Luigi Mayer (d. 1803). Three volumes of drawings of Egyptian, Turkish, and Palestine views were engraved and published in London after Ainslie's return to England.

Throughout his embassy Ainslie was sceptical about improving Britain's trading position in the Black Sea, and he reported in 1781 that 'business was in a most deplorable state' (Bağiş, 'British economic policy', 42). Though in 1784 he won British merchants the same privilege of tax exemption that had been enjoyed by French merchants since 1740, Ainslie concentrated his efforts on political rather than commercial issues, a strategy that failed to please his paymasters, the Levant Company. Ainslie's diplomatic activities were always constrained by the fact that he played second fiddle to his counterpart in St Petersburg, Sir Robert Keith. Thus Britain's failure in 1786 to renew her commercial treaty of 1766 with Russia, who entered into a similar treaty with France instead, brought a change in policy towards the Turks. Ainslie was instructed to encourage the Ottoman empire, now ruled by the more belligerent Selim III, to declare war on Russia. War between the two states broke out on 14 August 1787, and continuing British fears that Russia would dominate the Mediterranean culminated in the Ochakov crisis in 1791. The parliamentary opposition to a war over Ochakov forced the prime minister, William Pitt, to climb down, and Ainslie ended all negotiations for an alliance with the Turks.

Ainslie spent his remaining time in Constantinople persuading Selim III to send the first Ottoman ambassador to London, Yusuf Agah Efendi, and adding to his valuable collection of coins from eastern Europe, Asia Minor, and north Africa. His collection was recorded by l'Abate Domenico Sestini in two publications: *Lettere e dissertazioni numismatiche sopra alcune medaglie rare della collezione Ainslieana* (9 vols., 1789–1806) and *Dissertazione sopra alcune monete armene dei principi Rupinensi della collezione Ainslieana* (1790). Ainslie was replaced as ambassador by Robert Liston in August 1793, but did not leave Constantinople until June 1794. He was awarded a pension of £1000 on the civil list on 8 September 1796. Supported by the earl of Leicester, Ainslie sought a parliamentary seat, and, after failing to be nominated at Great Yarmouth, he was returned for Milborne Port, Somerset, in May 1796. He was connected to Sir William Coles Medlycott, by the marriage of his kinsman Philip Ainslie to Medlycott's sister Jane. Ainslie supported Pitt in the Commons, albeit silently, and did not stand for re-election in 1802.

Ainslie was married and had one son, who died suddenly on 20 December 1796, a few days before he was to marry the daughter of William Baldwin MP. Ainslie was living in Great Torrington Street, London, when he was created a baronet on 13 October 1804, with remainder to his nephew Robert Sharpe Ainslie (1777–1853), the eldest son of George Ainslie. He died in Bath on 21 July 1812 after a long illness, aged eighty-two. His nephew inherited his estates in Lincolnshire and Huntingdonshire.

ARTHUR H. GRANT, rev. S. J. SKEDD

Sources A. I. Bağiş, Britain and the struggle for the integrity of the Ottoman empire: Sir Robert Ainslie's embassy to Istanbul, 1776–1794 (1984) • A. I. Bağiş, 'British economic policy in the Ottoman empire under George III', Four centuries of Turco-British relations, ed. W. Hale and A. I. Bağiş (1984) • D. B. Horn, The British diplomatic service, 1689–1789 (1961) • R. G. Thorne, 'Ainslie, Sir Robert', HoP, Commons, 1790–1820 • The barony of Scotland, 1 (1798) • GM, 1st ser., 43 (1773), 469 • GM, 1st ser., 82/2 (1812), 93
Archives PRO, corresp., FO 261/1–7 • PRO, entry book of corresp. with Levant Company, PRO 30/26/72 | BL, corresp. with Lord Grenville, Add. MSS 34429–34452 • BL, corresp. with Sir Robert Keith, Add. MSS 35511–35579 • CKS, corresp. with duke of Dorset • Lincs. Arch., corresp. with George Tennyson • NL Scot., corresp. with Sir Robert Liston • NL Wales, letters to Lord Hereford

Ainslie, Robert (1766–1838), writer, was born on 13 January 1766, at Berrywell, near Duns, Berwickshire, the son of Robert Ainslie (1734–1795), factor to Lord Douglas, and his wife, Catharine Whitelaw. His younger brother was Sir Whitelaw *Ainslie (1767–1837). In 1787, while apprenticed to Samuel Mitchison, a writer to the signet in Edinburgh, Ainslie met Burns, and in May of that year went on an excursion with the poet in Teviotdale and Berwickshire. One of Ainslie's sisters, whom Burns met at this time, was the subject of the impromptu beginning of 'Fair Maid'. The two young men were well suited, Burns appreciating Ainslie's 'carefree disposition and his zestful pleasure in wine, women, and the poet's song' (Lindsay, 5). A lifelong and very close friendship was established, with Burns proclaiming in 1787:

> There is one thing for which I set great store by you as a friend, and it is this, that I have not a friend upon earth, besides yourself, to whom I can talk nonsense without forfeiting some degree of his esteem. (Letters, 1.121)

According to W. S. Douglas, Burns based the ballad 'Robin Shure in Hairst' upon a love affair of Ainslie's youth (Works, 2.188).

Ainslie became a writer to the signet on 9 July 1798. On 22 December 1798, he married Jean (d. 1817), the daughter of Colonel James Cunningham of Balbougie, Fife, and of the Scots brigade in the Dutch service. (His brother Whitelaw was to marry her sister.) There were several children of the marriage. In his later life, Ainslie became more conservative and religious than might have been predicted from the exploits of his youth. He served as an elder in the Church of Scotland, and was the author of two devotional works, A Father's Gift to his Children (1818), which ran to two editions, and Reasons for the Hope that is in Us (1831). He also wrote The life, adventures, and serious remonstrances of a Scotch guinea note, containing a defence of the Scotch system of banking in 1826, and contributed to the Edinburgh Review and other

magazines. After the death of his first wife, he married on 18 October 1837 Isabella (1789/90–1862), the eldest daughter of the Revd Robert Munro of Ullapool.

Ainslie's intimacy with Burns and his genial manners won him a cordial welcome in the literary circles of Edinburgh. James Hogg referred to him as 'honest Ainslie', and remarked that his one failing was 'constitutional sleepiness'. Twenty of Burns's letters to Ainslie are included in the poet's correspondence. Ainslie presented Sir Walter Scott with a manuscript copy of 'Tam o' Shanter', which he had received from Burns at Ellisland. Ainslie died on 11 April 1838.

T. F. HENDERSON, rev. DOUGLAS BROWN

Sources Anderson, Scot. nat. • The life and works of Robert Burns, ed. R. Chambers, 4 vols. (1851–4) • The works of Robert Burns, another edn, ed. W. S. Douglas, 6 vols. (1877–9) • Register of the Society of Writers to Her Majesty's Signet (1983) • The letters of Robert Burns, ed. J. de Lancey Ferguson, 2nd edn, ed. G. Ross Roy, 2 vols. (1985) • M. Lindsay, The Burns encyclopedia, 2nd edn (1970) • m. cert.

Ainslie, Sir Whitelaw (1767–1837), surgeon, the son of Robert Ainslie (1734–1795) and Catharine Whitelaw, and brother of Robert *Ainslie (1766–1838), was born on 17 February 1767 at Duns, Berwickshire, where his father was factor to Lord Douglas. He was nominated assistant surgeon in the East India Company's service on 17 June 1788, and on his arrival in India he was appointed garrison surgeon of Chingleput. On 17 October 1794 he was promoted to the grade of surgeon, and in 1809 he served as president of the three-man committee appointed by the Madras government to investigate the causes of recent epidemics. In 1810 he was appointed superintending surgeon and served with the southern division of the Madras army. He retired to England on 26 February 1815 and was awarded 600 guineas by the East India Company in recognition of his services. He then immersed himself in writing on medicine and the history of India.

Ainslie's major work was published in 1813 as the Materia medica of Hindustan and was expanded to the two-volume Materia Indica in 1826. This was the first book-length study of Indian medicines to be published by a British writer. Ainslie was elected a fellow of the Royal Society of Edinburgh on 7 December 1829 and was knighted on 10 June 1835.

Ainslie married a daughter of Colonel James Cunningham, of Balbougie, Fife. Their only child, Jane Catharine, married James C. Grant-Duff; Ainslie Douglas Grant-Duff, the second son of the marriage, assumed in 1866 the surname of Ainslie. Whitelaw Ainslie died on 29 April 1837. His widow survived him until 17 March 1840.

B. D. JACKSON, rev. JAMES MILLS

Sources D. G. Crawford, ed., Roll of the Indian Medical Service, 1615–1930 (1930) • F. Bennet and M. Melrose, Index of fellows of the Royal Society of Edinburgh: elected November 1783 – July 1883, ed. H. Frew, rev. edn (1984) • M. Harrison, Public health in British India: Anglo-Indian preventive medicine, 1859–1914 (1994), 41 • D. Arnold, Colonizing the body: state medicine and epidemic disease in nineteenth-century India (1993), 45, 47

Ainsworth, Geoffrey Clough (1905–1998), mycologist, was born at 26 South Street, Handsworth, Birmingham, on 9 October 1905, the only son of Percy Clough Ainsworth, Wesleyan minister, and his wife, Gertrude (née Fisk). Like many ministers' families they moved around the country, and Ainsworth was educated at Ipswich grammar school and Kingswood School, Bath, before studying at University College, Nottingham. There he obtained a certificate in pharmacy and was awarded the silver medal and Harrison prize of the Pharmaceutical Society before graduating with first-class honours in botany in 1930. He then embarked on the parallel and overlapping disciplines of plant pathology and mycology that were to be his life's work. His first position was as an assistant at the Rothamsted Experimental Station at Harpenden in 1930–31, followed by a period from 1931 to 1939 at the Experimental and Research Station in Cheshunt. There he studied the virus diseases of plants at a time when the subject was at a most exciting stage, with new research techniques rapidly becoming available. On 30 September 1931 he married Frances Hilda Bryan, a Nottingham solicitor's daughter; they had two daughters, Judith and Sarah Frances. Ainsworth obtained a PhD from London University in 1934 and in 1937 published his first book, *The Plant Diseases of Great Britain*.

The British Mycological Society was always close to Ainsworth's heart. He served it in numerous capacities and was its president in 1950. As a member of its plant pathology committee in 1932 he first visited an organization that featured significantly in his later career—the Imperial Mycological Institute (later the Commonwealth Mycological Institute) at Kew. He joined its staff in 1939 as an assistant mycologist and remained there during the Second World War, when he became an important contributor to the institute's abstracting journal, *Review of Applied Mycology*. While on night-time fire-watching duty Ainsworth and his colleague Guy Bisby trawled through the institute library to obtain the raw material for a publication that became an enduring standard work of reference for every mycologist: *A Dictionary of the Fungi* was first published in 1943 following a special wartime allocation of paper.

When the war ended Ainsworth was lured into commercial mycology as head of the mycological department of the Wellcome Research Laboratories at Beckenham, Kent, where he became responsible for overseeing important research into fungal-produced antibiotics such as streptomycin and penicillin. In 1947–8 he worked as the Wellcome Trust's research fellow in medical mycology based at the London School of Hygiene and Tropical Medicine. He was an obvious choice as its director when the post fell vacant, but he was debarred because he had no medical qualification. From 1948 to 1957 he was a lecturer and then reader at the University of the South West (later the University of Exeter), arguably his most productive period. He published *British Smut Fungi* (with Kathleen Sampson) in 1950 and *Medical Mycology* in 1952 and became closely involved with thinking on mycological taxonomy. He also developed an interest in the history of science and of mycology in particular that remained with him; he later published standard works on the subject—*Introduction to the History of Mycology* (1976), *Introduction to the History of Plant Pathology* (1981), and *Introduction to the History of Medical and Veterinary Mycology* (1987).

Ainsworth returned to the Commonwealth Mycological Institute in 1957 and remained there until he retired in 1968—successively as assistant editor, assistant director, and director. During this period he co-edited with the Americans A. S. Sussman and F. K. Sparrow the most comprehensive multi-volume, multi-author work ever published on mycology: *The Fungi: an Advanced Treatise* (1965–73). In retirement Ainsworth moved first to Cornwall, then to Devon, and finally to be close to one of his daughters in Derby. He continued to write and work untiringly, especially in mycological history, and was ever willing to give of his time to others who shared what was then an unfashionable interest. Stefan Buczacki, whose own presidential address to the British Mycological Society was on a historical theme, later paid fond tribute to his stimulating conversations on the subject with Ainsworth in the library of the Linnean Society.

Probably Ainsworth's most enduring achievement was his role in establishing the International Mycological Association (IMA) and the six-yearly International Mycological Congresses of which the first was at Exeter in 1971. In 1996 the IMA instituted the Ainsworth medal in his honour and among his own awards were an honorary DSc from Exeter (1978), the Linnean medal for botany (1968), the Lucille K. Georg medal of the International Society for Human and Animal Mycology (1982 and 1997), and honorary membership of the British, American, and Indian mycological societies.

Geoffrey Ainsworth was a small, slight man and in later life had a pronounced stoop. He had a rich, firm, scholarly voice although with a slight stammer. He was a committed Quaker and socialist. He died in the Abbeydale Nursing Home, 182 Duffield Road, Derby, on 25 October 1998 of cerebral arteriosclerosis. His wife survived him.

STEFAN BUCZACKI

Sources D. L. Hawksworth, 'Obituary: Geoffrey Clough Ainsworth (1905–1998): mycological scholar, campaigner and visionary', *Mycological Research*, 104/1 (2000), 110–16 • *The Times* (20 Nov 1998) • personal knowledge (2004) • b. cert. • m. cert. • d. cert.
Likenesses photograph, repro. in Hawksworth, 'Obituary: Geoffrey Clough Ainsworth'
Wealth at death under £200,000: probate, 2 Dec 1998, *CGPLA Eng. & Wales*

Ainsworth, Henry (1569–1622), separatist minister and religious controversialist, was baptized on 15 January 1570 at Swanton Morley, Norfolk, son of Thomas Ainsworth, yeoman; he may have had a sister named Anna. He attended school at Swanton Morley for three years under a Mr Clephamson. In December 1586 he matriculated as a pensioner from St John's College, Cambridge, where his tutor was Ralph Furness, a member of the college's strong godly faction. On 15 December 1587, when he was aged eighteen, he moved to Gonville and Caius College, where he remained for three and a half years as a scholar under Dr Stephen Perse. While at Cambridge he appears to have been strongly attracted to learning, but he left without a degree in early 1591.

Soon after his departure Ainsworth espoused separatist opinions, which included rejection of the Church of England as false and anti-Christian, and refusal to attend its services. Instead, separatists assembled in gathered, covenanted, visibly godly congregations, where they sought to recreate the life of the primitive church as revealed in the scriptures. They also practised a rigorous system of discipline based on Matthew 18: 15–17. Separatism was illegal, and Ainsworth was soon apprehended in London. Under pressure, he agreed to attend public worship. Later, after he was freed, he returned to separatism and journeyed to Ireland, where in another brush with authorities he again temporarily submitted.

Teacher of the Ancient Separatist church, Amsterdam In the mid-1590s Ainsworth settled in Amsterdam. His early life there was one of extreme privation, but he bore the hardship without complaint, because his 'modest and bashfull' nature led him to hide it (Bradford, 132). Afterwards, when others realized his need, they provided for him. Resuming his former allegiance to separatism, some time before September 1597 Ainsworth joined the Ancient Separatist Church of Amsterdam. He became its 'teacher' or 'doctor', whose task it was to study the word of God and formulate sound doctrine based on it. The church, whose membership consisted almost entirely of English exiles, saw itself as 'a light upon an hil' for godly radicals who shared its members' principles of separating from outward sin, shunning non-biblical corruptions in worship, and watching over each other's spiritual welfare (Johnson, 156).

However, frequent contentions made attaining this ideal difficult. The most notorious occurred following the arrival of the pastor, Francis Johnson, and his brother George in late September 1597. The Johnsons already had a long-running dispute with each other over the seemliness of Francis's wife Tomison's dress and deportment. Their relations were becoming increasingly embittered, and their animosity divided the church. Ainsworth wavered: initially, he tried to intervene when George appealed to him for fair treatment, but Francis rebuked him sharply. Thereafter, he moved first to a mediatory stance and later toward a more prosecutorial position. On 15 January 1598 he persuaded the congregation to ratify the elders' rulings against George on three points concerning Tomison's speech and behaviour. Nevertheless, when Francis excommunicated George in late 1598 or early 1599 he offered no support.

Another major church controversy affected Ainsworth directly. Some time before late 1601 evidence of his earlier submissions to the established church came to light. This news caused a sensation because separatists believed that attending Church of England services constituted 'apostasy', and that, even if the apostate repented, he must be barred from holding church office. Francis Johnson and the other officers had previously attempted to persuade the congregation to modify this prohibition, but traditionalists in the congregation blocked them and, refusing

to recognize Ainsworth as their teacher, separated from him. Ultimately, however, the elders' view prevailed and Ainsworth was retained as teacher. Those who remained intransigently opposed to Ainsworth were accused of schism and excommunicated, among them John Johnson, Francis's and George's father.

Now firmly in office, Ainsworth joined the pastor in a publishing campaign to promote separatist beliefs and principles, which were anchored in the writings of Henry Barrow and John Greenwood and summarized by Johnson in *A True Confession of the Faith* (1596). Ainsworth's earliest works were collaborative. They probably included a letter to Thomas Wolsey condemning his 'judaizing' tendencies, written in 1602 but not published until 1657 as *A Seasonable Treatise for this Age*, and *An Apologie or Defence of such True Christians as are Commonly called Brownists* (1604), which contained a reprinting of Johnson's 1596 confession together with petitions for toleration addressed to James I.

Controversialist Ainsworth's first book published under his own name appeared in 1607, the year in which he married, on 29 March, Marjory (*née* Halie or Haley), widow of Richard Appelbey, formerly of Ipswich. *The Communion of Saincts* outlined the proper relationship of true visible church members to God and to each other, and gave advice about how these relationships should be nurtured and maintained. Speaking from experience, Ainsworth cited two things that hinder people from communion with God—one was the taking of too much liberty in faith and obedience to the gospel, and the other was 'over much straytnes which some men hav … both with their own and others infirmities' (*Communion of Saincts*, 'To the Christian Reader', fol. *3v). The following year he published *Counterpoyson*, in which he defended separatism against opponents who maintained that the best Church of England assemblies were true visible churches, and that their preachers were true ministers of Christ. He replied that the established church was a miscellaneous 'multitude of beleevers and infidels, holy and profane' (H. Ainsworth, *Counterpoyson*, 'A fore-speech', fol. ***3v), and added that it possessed a corrupt liturgy grounded upon the popish Book of Common Prayer, together with an anti-Christian ruling hierarchy that included lord bishops and other prelates. By contrast, he defined a true church as a gathered, covenanted congregation of saints drawn together to profess the gospel—'a company of faithfull people that truely worship Christ, and readily obey him' (H. Ainsworth, *Counterpoyson*, 208). That same year Ainsworth also began writing against more radical foes. He denounced Hendrik Niclaes, founder of the Family of Love, in *An Epistle Sent unto Two Daughters of Warwick* (1608). He asked his readers to try all of Niclaes's teachings by the scriptures, and decried his doctrines of inward baptism, the invisible church, and outward conformity with all kinds of religious services and ceremonies. Ainsworth's *A defence of the holy scriptures, worship, and ministerie used in the Christian churches separated from antichrist* (1609) was aimed at John Smyth, who had renounced communion with the Ancient church and was moving rapidly toward Anabaptism. Smyth initially broke with the separatists because of their use of English scriptural translations in worship, rather than extemporaneously translating from the original Hebrew and Greek texts, but later expanded his indictment to include allegations that internal and external financial contributions must be kept separate and that the role of the church's elders was wrongly defined. In reply Ainsworth defended the use of translations and dismissed Smyth's financial concerns as scripturally unclear. In the matter of church governance Ainsworth asserted that Christ had 'ordeyned a presbyterie or eldership … in every church: for to teach and rule'. However, he added that the people were obligated to submit to the elders only as long as they 'doe teach, rule and direct … in the wayes of Christ, by his owne word and lawes … and no further' (H. Ainsworth, *A Defence*, 120, 130).

Also in 1609 Ainsworth began a sporadic five-year correspondence with John Ainsworth, an English Catholic. In this exchange, published under the title *The Trying out of the Truth* (1615), Henry contended that all religious disputes should be resolved solely from the scriptures, while his opponent argued that the Bible alone provided an insufficient rule of faith. Ainsworth again displayed his confidence in the Bible in *An Arrow Against Idolatrie* (1610). He defined idolatry as 'mixing mens own inventions with the ordinances of God in the service of him' (p. 5). Using the Old Testament example of King Jeroboam, he denounced those who had changed the 'frame and constitution' of the church from God's scriptural plan and warned that God's righteous could not communicate with the unrighteous (p. 125).

The end of the Ancient church While Ainsworth was writing, the Ancient church again became embroiled in divisive disputes. The principal cause was a shift in Francis Johnson's views. Tired of the vicissitudes of traditional separatist church government and frightened by Smyth's insistence that the eldership must be subordinate to the congregation, the imperious pastor declared that the ultimate authority in the church resided with the eldership alone, both in theory and in practice. Because Johnson's new doctrine contravened both the church's confession of faith and God's word as he understood it, Ainsworth led a dissident faction. Still, even with some of his most fundamental beliefs at stake, he was reluctant to make his opposition publicly known, because he correctly feared that conflict would lead to schism. As contention increased, Ainsworth travelled to Leiden and appealed to the separatist church there for mediation. That congregation sent John Robinson, its pastor, and William Brewster, its elder, to attempt a reconciliation, but no compromise could be had. As a result, Ainsworth and his party felt compelled to secede, and a formal dissolution took place on the night of 15–16 December 1610.

Lingering ill feeling between the Ainsworthians and their Johnsonian opponents caused both sides to write apologias defending their principles and conduct. The first was Richard Clyfton's *Advertisement* (1612), which was followed by Ainsworth's *An Animadversion* (1613). Conflicts with the Johnsonians subsided when they lost the title to the former church's building in a lawsuit and departed for Emden in Germany about 1613.

Pastor of the 'Ainsworthians' Members of Ainsworth's group chose him as their new pastor, and he served for more than a decade, trying to promote unity, peace, and harmony despite declining health. Relations with the Dutch Reformed church, which the separatists had long regarded as true but corrupt, remained strained. They were particularly difficult with the Dutch-affiliated English Reformed church of Amsterdam (formed in 1607), partly because its minister, John Paget, was a militant foe of separatism. Confrontations sometimes occurred as these two congregations denounced each other and competed for members. One of these clashes provoked an eighteen-month correspondence, which Paget published as *An Arrow Against the Separation of the Brownists* (1618). At the outset he challenged Ainsworth to prove that the English Reformed church was too corrupt for Christian communion to exist between the two groups. The subsequent debate revolved around four issues: separatist refusal to recite the Lord's prayer during worship, their assertion that Paget was unlawfully called to his pulpit, their charge that the English Reformed church did not differ from the Church of England, and their contention the former nunnery chapel where the English Reformed church met was one of many popish 'idol-temples' that should be destroyed (pp. 211, 226). The result was a stalemate, and bitterness on both sides continued.

Some time in 1617 Francis Johnson reappeared in Amsterdam and published *A Christian Plea*, in which he continued his criticism of Anabaptism and reiterated his earlier published position that Catholic baptism was valid. Ainsworth's rejoinder was *A Reply to a Pretended Christian Plea* (1620), where he reduced the points at issue to one question: is Rome the true church of Christ, and its sacraments regarded as the seals of the covenant of grace? 'I deny it', he declared, because the true Church of Rome had been 'destroyed long since' (pp. 1, 38).

During the last years of Ainsworth's life internal tensions produced serious threats to church unity and tranquillity. He had to tread carefully between extreme exclusivists, who wanted total separation from any church that obstinately tolerated the least non-biblical 'corruptions', and more liberal members, who seem to have favoured Robinson's broader views about communion with the godly in England. Although Ainsworth probably agreed personally with his colleague on some points, he appears to have kept his opinions to himself, while working to find a middle way wherever possible.

Ainsworth's diplomacy preserved the peace for several years, but discord clouded his final days. Sabine Staresmore, a former member of Henry Jacob's London semi-separatist congregation who had gained membership in Robinson's church, came to Amsterdam and applied for Ainsworthian membership. At first he was admitted, but when questioned later he refused to renounce his Jacobite opinions. Struggling for compromise, Ainsworth agreed that Staresmore's church status should be re-examined, but death took the pastor before any resolution could be reached. The exclusivists then got the upper hand and Staresmore was expelled, along with all of those who sided with him.

Hebrew translator and annotator Many consider Ainsworth one of the finest Hebrew scholars of his day. His interest in languages may have begun at Cambridge. If so, it was powerfully strengthened when he arrived in Amsterdam, which had a large Jewish population living near the Ancient church. By 1605 Ainsworth had become part of an Amsterdam circle of English Hebraists that included Hugh Broughton, Matthew Slade, and later John Paget. These men sought to further their understanding of the Bible by learning its original tongues. Personally Ainsworth believed that by studying the Hebrew texts carefully and translating them as literally as possible, 'the mysteries of godlynes therin implied, may the better be discerned' (H. Ainsworth, *Annotations upon the Book of Genesis*, preface, 1616, fol. ***2v). He utilized the knowledge he acquired in his pastoral work, as well as in scholarly translations, accompanied by annotations.

Ainsworth and his fellow scholars sometimes quarrelled over details of translation and interpretation. He and Broughton debated translational issues and their effect on religion in a correspondence published in 1605 under the title *Certayne Questions*. Broughton bitterly charged that Ainsworth was a poor linguist whose mistakes were causing him to mislead his followers; Ainsworth refuted this. Paget attacked Ainsworth's methodology in 'An admonition touching talmudique and rabbinical allegations' appended to his *Arrow*. He claimed that Ainsworth's use of both the Old Testament text and marginal notes sometimes made the scriptures seem inconsistent. Responding in 'An advertisement' placed at the end of his *Annotations upon the Book of Deuteronomie* (1619), Ainsworth maintained that, where notes or text were incomprehensible, readers should in humility 'seek for further light' (Ainsworth, 'Advertisement', fol. Mm3r).

Despite these disagreements Ainsworth translated and annotated a substantial portion of the Old Testament. He began with *Annotations upon the Psalms* (1612), to which he added a metrical version that he set to selected tunes. The Amsterdam separatists used this psalter, as did the Pilgrim Fathers of Plymouth, Massachusetts. Next Ainsworth turned to the Pentateuch. *Annotations upon the Book of Genesis* appeared in 1616, *Exodus* in 1617, *Leviticus* in 1618, *Numbers* in 1619, and *Deuteronomie* in 1619. A collected edition, *Annotation upon the Five Books of Moses and the Psalmes*, came out in 1622. The last work in the series, *Solomons Song of Songs. In English Metre with Annotations*, appeared in 1623, and another composite edition that included the *Song of Songs* was issued in 1627.

Death and reputation Ainsworth died in 1622. According to Staresmore, who published *Certain Notes of M. Henry Aynesworth his Last Sermon* (1630), the cause was 'that sore, perplexing and tedious disease of the stone' (sig. B1v). It is not known if his wife survived him. John Ainsworth, who married at Leiden on 24 December 1636, may have been their son.

Controversial and edificatory works from Ainsworth's pen continued to appear in print after his death. *A Censure upon a Dialogue of the Anabaptists* (1623) reaffirmed Calvinist predestination by stating that Christian faith and obedience are the effects, not the cause, of election. *The Orthodox Foundation of Religion* (1641), a two-part work prepared for the use of the Ainsworthian congregation, consisted of short summaries of separatist doctrine, belief, and theology. *A Guide unto Sion* (1638), possibly by Ainsworth, set forth the nature of a 'true visible church' and pointed out the differences between it and 'false assemblies' (title-page).

Ainsworth was a diffident, eirenic scholar who ministered to strong-willed individualists. Therefore, he tended to keep his private opinions to himself if he thought they might disturb the peace and unity of the church. Although contemporaries state that he was a beloved pastor and gifted preacher, he was almost certainly more at ease sitting in his study than standing in the pulpit or presiding at congregational meetings. He meant well, but he lacked the strength of character to deal successfully with those bent on obeying every dictate of conscience no matter what the cost. William Bradford was probably right when he asserted that, 'the times and place in which hee lived were not worthy of such a man', but there is also truth in the proposition that Ainsworth's shortcomings prevented him from effectively meeting the challenges of church leadership during separatism's turbulent formative period in Amsterdam (Bradford, 137).

MICHAEL E. MOODY

Sources parish records, Swanton Morley, Norfolk RO, PD 539/1 · G. Johnson, *A discourse of some troubles and excommunications in the banished English church at Amsterdam* (1603) · W. Bradford, 'A dialogue, or, The sume of a conference between som younge men borne in New England and sundery ancient men that came out of Holland and old England anno domini 1648', *Publications of the Colonial Society of Massachusetts*, 22 (1920), 115–41 · M. Moody, '"A man of a thousand": the reputation and character of Henry Ainsworth, 1569/70–1622', *Huntington Library Quarterly*, 45 (1982), 200–14 · M. Moody, 'The apostasy of Henry Ainsworth: a case study in early separatist historiography', *Proceedings of the American Philosophical Society*, 131 (1987), 15–31 · M. Moody, 'A critical edition of George Johnson's *Discourse* (1603)', PhD diss., Claremont Graduate School, 1979 · W. Axon and E. Axon, 'Henry Ainsworth, the puritan commentator', *Transactions of the Lancashire and Cheshire Antiquarian Society*, 6 (1888), 42–57 · K. Sprunger, *Dutch puritanism* (1982) · K. Sprunger, *Trumpets from the tower* (1994) · C. Burrage, *Early English dissenters*, 2 vols. (1912) · H. Dexter, *The Congregationalism of the last three hundred years as seen in its literature* (1880) · H. M. Dexter and M. Dexter, *The England and Holland of the pilgrims* (1906) · S. Brachlow, *The communion of saints* (1988) · Venn, *Alum. Cant.*

Ainsworth, Robert (1660–1743), lexicographer and schoolmaster, was born in September 1660, probably at Wordsall, which, in the seventeenth century, was a collection of gentlemen's houses, in the parish of Eccles, about 4 miles from Manchester, the location cited by Dr Samuel Patrick in his preface to the second edition of Ainsworth's *Thesaurus* (1746). However, Wordsall, as a settlement, was no longer marked on eighteenth-century maps, and Patrick's 'Woodyale' is probably a misinterpretation of notes (Ainsworth, 1.xxvi). Today Clifton in Salford claims the honour of being his birthplace, but as Clifton is rather more than 4 miles from Manchester this is no doubt based on parish records, as, according to Speed's map of 1611, Wordsall had no church. Nothing is known of Ainsworth's parents, nor is there any evidence of his ever having attended a university or become a clergyman, but it is clear that he received an education.

Ideas on education After a period of teaching at a school in Bolton, Ainsworth moved to London in or before 1698. There he became the 'master of a considerable boarding school at Bethnal Green' (Nichols, *Lit. anecdotes*, 5.248), where, according to Patrick's preface, 'he wrote and published a short treatise of grammatical institution' (Ainsworth, 1.xxvi). In effect both an advertisement for the benefits of a privately run school not unlike his own and a proposal for educational reform, this tract—*The Most Natural and Easie Way of Institution*—rejected the learning of texts by heart before and unless they had been thoroughly understood, and expressed the author's surprise that parents allowed anyone knowing a little Greek and Latin to use the birch on their children. Ainsworth also diffidently noted the difficulties and inaccuracies of Lily's *Grammar* at several points, but did point out that the preface to the *Grammar* provided a guide to learning for children of lesser ability. He went on to offer a basic approach for learning Latin, to make a plea for small class-sizes for children of similar ages, and to outline high minimum requirements for the quality of the teachers. He was a very early proponent of the total immersion method of teaching languages, proposing that Latin be spoken at all times, '*i.e.* that no other Language be us'd in presence of the boys' (p. 16). The boys were to be accommodated in a convenient house near London with a 'large garden and other conveniences', with at least one master always in attendance (p. 17). His proposed principle of never punishing pupils but rewarding them instead for their proficiency seems to have been an attempt to change the natural aims of a class which, in his view, would more readily sink to the level of the least able rather than rise to that of the most competent. *The most Natural and Easie Way of Institution* was first published in 1698, but was enough of a success to be reissued in the following year; it was republished in 1736 by Curll and Wilford, probably with the intention of capitalizing on the success of Ainsworth's *Thesaurus*, which was first published in that same year.

Hackney and recognition From Bethnal Green, Ainsworth is said to have moved to Hackney and 'successively to other villages near London'. In April 1701 he was based at Grove Street, Hackney, and at the same time had a private school in the area, where 'he taught with good reputation many years' (Nichols, *Lit. anecdotes*, 5.248). The epistle dedicatory of Ainsworth's translation *J. Casa his Galateus, or, Treatise of Manners* (1701) provides evidence that he put his educational philosophy into practice. He persuaded a group of his pupils to translate the text, edifying in its own right, not from the original Italian but from a good Latin translation, thus working simultaneously on their social and linguistic skills. A prefatory letter is addressed to Samuel Nash, merchant and father of Robert, one of the 'pretty lisping translators' (p. xiii). One of the other translators was William Hustler, who was no doubt the son of the William Hustler MP to whom Ainsworth had addressed an epistle in *The most Natural and Easie Way of Institution* three years earlier.

Ainsworth's reputation as a learned man seems to have been well established by 1714, when he was first nominated as the right person to undertake a new English and Latin dictionary. In 1723, by which time Ainsworth had married, William Hearne described him as a 'mighty modest man' and an 'excellent' scholar, while in the following year Hearne wrote that 'he is well spoken of in Westminster School'—probably in consequence of Ainsworth's involvement in a projected major revision of Lily's *Grammar* by a large group of London schoolmasters (*Remains*, 251, 432). In 1724 he was elected fellow of the Society of Antiquaries, presumably in recognition of his interest in coin collecting. He had published a catalogue of John Kemp's classical antiquities in 1720 as *Monumenta vetustatis Kempiana, ex vetustis scriptoribus illustrata, eosque vicissim illustrantia*, while John Nichols later reported that Ainsworth:

> used to employ himself very much in rummaging the shops of obscure brokers in every quarter of the town; by which means he often picked up old coins and other valuable curiosities at a small expense; and became possessed of a very fine collection of English coins, which he sold singly to several gentlemen a short time before his death. (Nichols, *Lit. anecdotes*, 5.252)

This was also the collection from which a maidservant stole many gold and silver coins in 1734. Ainsworth was involved in two antiquarian publications following his election to the society: he superintended and partly wrote a description of John Woodward's antiquarian collection (published in 1728, after Woodward's death), and, together with Roger Gale, he produced a four-page account of Roman coins, *Iseion, sive, Ex veteris monumenti Isiace descriptione: Isidis delubrum reseratum*, in 1729.

Ainsworth's dictionary Ainsworth's remarkably enlightened views on education were too far in advance of his time to be generally accepted, so it is his English–Latin/ Latin–English dictionary which was the crowning glory of his career. It seems that Ainsworth encountered a number of difficulties in producing the dictionary, which hint at more obstacles than his failing eyesight. In 1723 Hearne reported Ainsworth had been writing it for 'about seven year'; by 1728 Ainsworth had 'at last finished it, though 'tis not printed for want of encouragement' (*Remains*, 251, 347). It was printed by 1734 but ''tis not yet published' (ibid., 432). (Ainsworth's wife had evidently died in the interim, as in the same year Hearne attributed the amount of free time at Ainsworth's disposal to his widowed status.) The dictionary finally appeared in 1736 as *Thesaurus linguae Latinae compendiarius, or, A compendious dictionary of the Latin tongue: designed for the use of the British nations*, a quarto edition in two volumes. In addition to its linguistic content, the third part of the work consisted of a number of lists relating to Roman civilization: Latin names of people and places, with a short account of them; the Roman calendar; Roman coins, weights, and measures; a chronology of Roman kings, consuls, and events; notes of Latin abbreviations; and a short list of 'the more common Latin words occurring in our ancient Laws' (vol. 1, title-page). In the preface Ainsworth wrote that he would have liked the letter size to be larger since it might discourage some older readers, but resignedly admitted that the font was probably large enough for young people, for whom his *Thesaurus* was mainly intended.

Although all dictionaries of the time were eclectic rather than innovatory, there were at least two points on which Ainsworth's *Thesaurus* marked a major advance in English lexicography. In the English–Latin section Ainsworth greatly facilitated the task of the young translator by systematically providing explanations of homonyms so that the reader could select the appropriate word for his purpose, as in Credit [authority], Credit [honour, reputation], Credit [belief], Credit [in traffick] (sig. O3r). He further provided several collocations and translations from Latin, including, 'To buy, *or* sell upon credit', 'Can you credit him?', 'To be in credit', 'To touch one's credit', and 'One out of credit', thereby underlining the statement in his own original preface that 'certain forms of English speech usually called *phrases* … are much more difficult to be translated into another language, than single words' (vol. 1, p. xii). In the Latin–English section his citation of illustrative quotations from classical authors helped move the *Thesaurus* towards becoming an authority for classical Latin. Ainsworth's contemporaries hailed it as 'the best Latin dictionary this kingdom hath ever produced', and felt that, in conjunction with Lily's *Grammar*, one 'need no longer have recourse to the treacherous aids of French translations' (Nichols, *Lit. anecdotes*, 2.88, 2.448).

A full account of the dictionary, its effect and antecedents, is given by Starnes. The work, however, took its definitive form only with the posthumous second edition of 1746, the text of which had been revised and corrected by Samuel Patrick. In the preface Patrick explained that, during the preparation of the first edition, after about a dozen sheets of the English–Latin section had been printed off, he was asked to assist in revising the copy on account of Ainsworth's advanced age and 'a disorder which affected his eyes' (Ainsworth, 1.xxvi). Although it was not to appear until three years after his death, Ainsworth had sufficient confidence in Patrick's skills and commitment, and the dictionary's general viability, to bequeath three copies, two to private schools, in his will of 1743. The *Thesaurus* became extremely popular and its subsequent printing history is complex in the extreme: the British Library alone holds over thirty editions and abridgements, the last published in 1882.

Final years Hearne is responsible for recording the rumour that Ainsworth was a nonjuror, though he adds 'I think he is rather a Calvinist', as if the two were mutually exclusive (*Remains*, 432). At his death Ainsworth's bequest

of £12 to 'six poor families not receiving alms of the parish' provides some further circumstantial evidence, and if Ainsworth had indeed refused to take the appropriate oaths that would help to explain the lack of information about his presence in established society (will, fol. 8r). Apart from one Dr Middleton Massey who was acquainted with him, there was a Mr Chishull, who described Ainsworth as 'doctissimus R. Ainsworth, amicus meus et vicinus, ob singularem eruditionem et humanitatem inter paucos aestimandus' ('the most learned R. Ainsworth, my friend and neighbour, highly esteemed on account of his singular erudition and humanity'), presumably the Edmund Chishull thanked by Ainsworth in the preface to the dictionary as 'vir eruditissimus, et dum vixit mihi amicissimus' ('most erudite of men, and, while he lived, my greatest friend'), and to whom it was reputed that Ainsworth had written an unpublished Latin poem (Nichols, *Lit. anecdotes*, 5.252; Ainsworth, *Thesaurus*, 1736, 1.iv). Intriguingly, the publication of both the first and second editions of Ainsworth's *Thesaurus* went completely unreported by the *Gentleman's Magazine*. Ainsworth's later religious beliefs seem to have been Methodist, as Charles Wesley, in his journal for 12 and 24 May 1738, noted Ainsworth's presence at meetings as 'a man, above seventy, who like old Simeon, was waiting to see the Lord's salvation, that he might die in peace. His tears and vehemence and childlike simplicity showed him upon the entrance of the kingdom of heaven' (*Journal*, 87).

Patrick and Nichols both claim that Ainsworth's teaching career was remunerative in that 'having acquired a moderate fortune, he left off and lived privately', but Hearne noted that he was still teaching in 1728 when Ainsworth would have been sixty-eight (Ainsworth, xxvi). However, although Ainsworth is reputed to have received £666 17s. 6d. for the first edition of his dictionary, there is little evidence of fortune in his will of seven years later. A possible explanation is given by Hearne, who wrote that Ainsworth, having no close family (his wife was dead and they had had no children), visited Lancashire in 1734 to 'make a settlement … for the poor forever' (*Remains*, 432). When Ainsworth drew up his will in April 1743, he possessed no land, and, though he made bequests to his kinsmen Robert, John, Peter, and Richard Ainsworth and their children, his disposable fortune, including outstanding bonds and credits, could have been as little as £252 2s. 0d. The estate would, therefore, have been considerably augmented by the £250 said to have been paid to his executor, Richard Ainsworth, for the second edition.

Ainsworth died at Stepney, Middlesex, where he was resident. The date of his death in the preface to the second edition of the *Thesaurus* is given as 4 April 1743, but this is evidently slightly inaccurate as he signed his will in the presence of witnesses the following day. However, he had died by 26 April, when the will was proved. He was buried, as he requested, in the cemetery of Poplar chapel. He composed his own poignant Latin epitaph:

> Rob. Ainsworth et uxor eius admodum senes
> dormituri vestem detritam hic exuerunt,
> novam primo mane surgentes induturi.

Dum fas, mortalis, sapias, et respice finem.
Hoc suadent manes, hoc canit Amramides.

(Rob. Ainsworth and his wife, both quite old, are about to sleep and have taken off their worn clothes; rising on the first morning, they will put on new ones. While you may, mortal, be wise, and consider your end. This is commended by the deified departed, this sung by Amramides.)

To thy reflexion, mortal friend
Th' advice of Moses I commend:
Be wise and meditate thy end.
(monument)

R. D. SMITH

Sources R. Ainsworth, *Thesaurus linguae Latinae compendiarius, or, A compendious dictionary of the Latin tongue*, ed. S. Patrick, 2nd edn (1746) · will, PRO, PROB 11/725, sig. 96 · *The remains of Thomas Hearne: Reliquiae Hernianae*, ed. J. Bliss, rev. edn, rev. J. Buchanan-Brown (1966) · Nichols, *Lit. anecdotes* · J. Speed, *The theatre of the empire of Great Britaine: presenting an exact geography of … England, Scotland and Wales* (1611) · 'City of Salford–Salford local history–Swinton and Pendlebury', www.salford.gov.uk/about/hswinton. asp, 12 March 2001 · *The journal of the Rev. Charles Wesley, M.A.*, ed. T. Jackson, 2 vols. (1849); repr. (1980) · De W. T. Starnes, *Renaissance dictionaries: English–Latin and Latin–English* (1954) · monument, Poplar chapel cemetery, London
Archives BL, letters to J. Strype and MSS, Add. MSS 5853, 6127, 6218
Wealth at death will, PRO, PROB 11/725, sig. 96 · could have been as little as £252 2s.

Ainsworth, William Francis (1807–1896), geographer and geologist, was born on 9 November 1807, in Exeter, the third son of John Ainsworth of Rostherne, Cheshire, army officer. At the suggestion of his cousin, the novelist William Harrison Ainsworth, he adopted the additional forename Francis to avoid confusion. In 1827 he became a licentiate of the Royal College of Surgeons, Edinburgh. He then went to London and Paris, where he studied at the School of Mines. After studying in Brussels he returned to Edinburgh in 1829. In 1830 he was a founder fellow of the Royal Geographical Society. In 1831 he studied cholera in Sunderland, and his book on the disease, published in 1832, led to his appointment as surgeon to the cholera hospital of St George's, Hanover Square. He later held similar appointments in Ireland.

In 1835 Ainsworth was appointed surgeon and geologist to the expedition to the Euphrates under Francis Rawdon Chesney to examine the feasibility of opening up the Mesopotamian rivers to steam navigation as a new route to India, as well as asserting British political presence in the area, promoting British commercial ties, and gathering scientific and archaeological data. Ainsworth constructed geological sections across northern Syria and the Taurus Mountains, discovered several deposits of commercially important minerals in Mesopotamia and Anatolia, and explored a substantial part of south-east Persia. With Chesney, Ainsworth published the first account of the expedition in the *Journal of the Royal Geographical Society* (1837) and the next year wrote his own fuller account as *Researches in Assyria, Babylonia and Chaldaea* (1838).

Ainsworth's next venture, the Kurdistan expedition, was altogether less successful. The Royal Geographical Society, one of the supporters of the Euphrates expedition, and the Society for Promoting Christian Knowledge undertook an expedition to the survivors of the Nestorian church to purchase or transcribe ancient manuscripts in their possession. An ulterior motive was to map and explore remote areas which were politically sensitive and possibly contained mineral deposits. Ainsworth was put in charge and went to Mesopotamia, through Asia Minor, the passes of the Taurus Mountains, and northern Syria, where he was arrested as he observed the battle of Nasib in 1839. Although the British ambassador secured his release, his maps and plans were confiscated and their irrelevance to the Nestorian church made public the real motives of the expedition. Ainsworth returned via the Kurdistan Mountains and Lake Orumiyyeh in Persia, continuing through Armenia and reaching Constantinople late in 1840. Ainsworth, remembering the unusually well-funded Euphrates expedition, borrowed much money on the credit of the Royal Geographical Society and regularly importuned it for help, eventually leaving it with a bill nearly four times the size of its agreed contribution, and with no great scientific results to show. His mismanagement led the society to be far more cautious in funding subsequent expeditions, as his 'wretched' performance (Mill, 54) not only drained its funds but soured its proceedings for years afterwards. It also showed the dangers, as well as the potential, of mixing political and strategic operations and overtly scientific expeditions. Ainsworth's own account of the expedition, *Travels and Researches in Asia Minor, Mesopotamia, Chaldaea and Armenia* (2 vols.), appeared in 1842.

Ainsworth then turned to writing. He settled at Hammersmith, helping his cousin to run magazines including the *New Monthly Magazine*, of which he became editor in 1871. He wrote some popular travel books which were of little importance. Using his knowledge of the geography of the Middle East he published *Travels in the Track of the Ten Thousand Greeks* (1844), thought by some to be his best work, and a geographical commentary to John Selby Watson's translation of Xenophon's *Anabasis* (1851). He was also secretary of the Syro-Egyptian Society, and a founder and treasurer of the West London Hospital. He died at 11 Wolverton Gardens, Hammersmith, on 27 November 1896. He was survived by a son and two daughters. Nothing is known of his wife.

ELIZABETH BAIGENT

Sources *Biograph and Review*, 6 (1881), 350–52 · R. A. Stafford, *Scientist of empire: Sir Roderick Murchison, scientific exploration and Victorian imperialism* (1989) · H. R. Mill, *The record of the Royal Geographical Society, 1830–1930* (1930) · *GJ*, 9 (1897), 98 · *The Times* (30 Nov 1896) · *The Athenaeum* (5 Dec 1896), 799–800 · *The Lancet* (19 Dec 1896), 1798 · *Provincial Medical Journal*, 8 (1889), 577
Archives RGS, travel notes and journal | RGS, letters to Royal Geographical Society · U. Durham L., letters to Viscount Ponsonby · U. Edin. L., letters to Sir John Philippart · Yale U., Beinecke L., letters to T. J. Pettigrew
Likenesses portrait, repro. in *Provincial Medical Journal*
Wealth at death £186 19s. 0d.: probate, 29 Dec 1896, CGPLA Eng. & Wales

Ainsworth, William Harrison (1805–1882), novelist, was born on 4 February 1805 at 21 King Street, Manchester, the elder of two sons of Thomas Ainsworth (1778–1824), a solicitor, and his wife, Ann (1778–1842), daughter of the Revd Ralph *Harrison (1748–1810), a nonconformist minister and tutor of languages and literature at the Manchester Academy. His parents both belonged to old Lancashire families, on his mother's side including prosperous merchants and members of the peerage; and his paternal grandfather was the noted mathematician Jeremiah Ainsworth. In his youth Ainsworth attended the Unitarian chapel where his maternal grandfather had preached, but in later life he was a 'staunch supporter' of the Church of England (Ellis, 1.24n.).

After being tutored privately until the age of twelve, Ainsworth attended the Manchester Free Grammar School from 1817 to 1822. During this period he produced his first literary works, including melodramas that he staged at home as well as poems, stories, and essays. His first known published work was a composition in rhymed couplets entitled *The Rivals: a Serio-Comic Tragedy*, which appeared in *Arliss's Pocket Magazine* in 1821 under the pseudonym T. Hall. He also wrote for other publications, including the *New Monthly Magazine* and the *London Magazine*, and even brought out his own publication, *The Boeotian*, which lasted for six numbers in 1824. In 1822 he published his first book, *Poems*, under the pseudonym Cheviot Ticheburn.

His father desiring him to follow a legal career, in the early 1820s Ainsworth was articled as a clerk with Alexander Kay, a Manchester solicitor. On his father's sudden death in 1824, Ainsworth inherited his law partnership and went to London for further legal training at the chambers of Jacob Phillips in the Inner Temple. In 1826 he was admitted as a solicitor in the court of king's bench. However, the law had never been his real interest—his father had called him an 'idle dog' (Ellis, 1.74) where his legal studies were concerned—and in 1826 he entered into the publishing business with John Ebers, an established publisher who was also manager of the Italian Opera House. Ebers had already published Ainsworth's first novel, a collaborative effort with J. P. Aston called *Sir John Chiverton* (1826), which won praise from Sir Walter Scott. Scott later contributed a ballad to one of Ainsworth's publishing ventures, a literary annual called *The Christmas Box* (1828), laughingly accepting the small payment Ainsworth offered him.

Ainsworth meanwhile had married his business partner's daughter, Anne Frances (Fanny) Ebers (1804/5–1838), on 11 October 1826, and he and his new wife moved in temporarily with her father at 8 Sussex Place. (Ainsworth had previously resided at 6 Devereux Court and 25 Great Ormond Street after moving to London.) The married couple moved into their own residence at 4 Sussex Place in 1827, then again shared a residence with John Ebers in the early 1830s at a house called The Elms in Kilburn High Road. The marriage produced three daughters, but ended in separation in 1835.

Ainsworth did not prosper in his partnership with Ebers

William Harrison Ainsworth (1805–1882), by Daniel Maclise, c.1834

and withdrew from it in 1829. Ellis attributes this development to Ainsworth's 'artistic temperament', which he says made him unsuited to a business career (Ellis, 1.181), but Ainsworth did return to the business side of literature in later years, owning several periodicals, and he has been noted for his astuteness in negotiating contracts for his novels (Sutherland, 158).

After leaving the partnership with Ebers, Ainsworth spent some time travelling in Europe and returned briefly to the law, opening chambers at 12 Grafton Street in 1830. He also became associated with the newly established *Fraser's Magazine* (he is one of the 'Fraserians' depicted in Maclise's 1834 group portrait of the contributors) and in 1831 began work on a new novel, *Rookwood*. This work was an instant success when it was published in 1834, not least because of its depiction of the legendary ride of the highwayman Dick Turpin from London to York, a ride which became accepted as historical fact even though it was an invention of Ainsworth's.

Ainsworth's next great success was with *Jack Sheppard* (1839), another 'Newgate novel' featuring a criminal. Praised for its vivid writing, especially its depiction of a storm on the Thames and its account of Jack Sheppard's escape from Newgate prison, the novel became so popular that by the end of 1839 nine different theatrical versions of it had appeared on the London stage. One of these versions introduced the hit song of the season ('Nix my Dolly, Pals'), based on a 'flash song' of criminal slang that Ainsworth had written for *Rookwood*. But *Jack Sheppard* also provoked criticism. John Forster attacked it in *The Examiner* for glorifying criminals, William Makepeace Thackeray did the same in his novel *Catherine*, and there were even suggestions that the notorious murder committed by Courvoisier in 1840 had been inspired by a reading of Ainsworth's novel.

Perhaps as a result of this furore, Ainsworth abandoned criminal romances for historical novels, quickly producing three successful works in this genre: *Guy Fawkes* (1840), *The Tower of London* (1840), and *Old Saint Paul's* (1841). During this period, Ainsworth also took over the editing of *Bentley's Miscellany* from Dickens, then left *Bentley's* at the end of 1841 to begin his own publication, *Ainsworth's Magazine*, which lasted until 1854. Ainsworth returned to *Bentley's* in 1854 as its proprietor, having purchased it for £1700, and he owned it until 1868. He also owned and edited the *New Monthly Magazine* from 1845 until 1870.

In the early days of his fame, at the time of *Rookwood*, Ainsworth was renowned not only for his writing, but also for his dashing good looks and fashionable clothes. Lady Blessington, whose salon he attended, said he and Count D'Orsay were the two handsomest men in London, and his dandyish appearance was captured in a much reprinted drawing by Maclise for *Fraser's* in 1834.

Ainsworth was also noted for playing host to writers and artists, first at Kensal Lodge and then at Kensal Manor House, his residences on the fringe of London on Harrow Road, where he moved after separating from his wife. Dickens, Thackeray, and Forster were among his guests. He was especially close to Dickens, introducing the younger novelist to his future biographer (Forster), his first illustrator (George Cruikshank), and his first publisher (John Macrone). But the friendship waned in later years.

Ainsworth's popularity also waned. His style of historical romances went out of fashion, and his occasional attempts in other forms, such as the autobiographical *Mervyn Clitheroe* (1851, 1857), were not successful. He thus fell back on his historical novels, producing them at an increasing pace but for decreasing profit. The declining popularity of his novels can be traced in his contracts with Chapman and Hall, who initially gave Ainsworth excellent terms but became less and less generous as his sales steadily declined throughout the 1860s, prompting his eventual move to the less prestigious publishing house of Tinsley in the 1870s. John Sutherland assesses Ainsworth's decline in this way: 'Many would have backed Ainsworth's talent against Dickens's in 1840. In the 1860s Dickens was earning £10,000 a novel, Ainsworth a hundredth of that sum; Dickens was buying Gadshill, Ainsworth was forced to sell his property piecemeal' (Sutherland, 160).

In 1853 Ainsworth had moved away from the London area, and became more and more of a recluse as he took up residence in Brighton at 5 Arundel Terrace. It was here, on 11 August 1866, that he married his second wife, Sarah (1835–1901), the daughter of Job Wells, a steward. There was one daughter of this marriage, born in 1867. Ainsworth is next recorded as living in Tunbridge Wells (at 1 St James's Villas), later in Hurtspierpoint in Sussex (at Little Rockley), and finally in Reigate (first at Hill View Lodge, then at 57 St Mary's Road).

Ainsworth's disappearance from public life is indicated by an often reported exchange between Forster and Robert Browning at a dinner party in the 1860s. Browning said, 'A sad, forlorn-looking being stopped me to-day, and reminded me of old times. He presently resolved himself into—whom do you think?—Harrison Ainsworth!' To which Forster replied, 'Good heavens! is he still alive?' (Ellis, 2.264).

But Ainsworth did win some recognition in his later years. In 1856 he was granted an annual civil-list pension of £100. A year earlier he had been invited to preside over a revival of the medieval custom of awarding a 'flitch' or side of bacon to a model married couple, a revival inspired by his novel *The Flitch of Bacon* (1853). And in 1881, just months before his death, he was honoured with a banquet hosted by the mayor of Manchester, at which he was celebrated as the 'Lancashire novelist' for depicting his native county in such works as *The Lancashire Witches* (1848) and *The Manchester Rebels of the Fatal '45* (1873).

Even at the height of his popularity Ainsworth was criticized for producing historical 'picture books' lacking in seriousness (Horne, 2.219), and in the twentieth century, though some critics (Ligocki, Worth) detected serious themes in his works, he was generally dismissed as a producer of potboilers of interest only to boys—perhaps reflecting the boyishness of his character, which Ellis says persisted into his old age (2.275). Ainsworth wrote some forty novels altogether, many of them historical romances about the Tudors and Stuarts, focusing especially on the royalist cause in the English civil war and the Jacobite cause in the eighteenth century. The novels are characterized by their attention to historical detail, but also introduce supernatural elements characteristic of the Gothic tradition. Often compared to Hugo, Dumas, and Scott, Ainsworth is said to lack their complexity and scope, and he has been criticized for his weak characterizations, clumsy plotting, and stilted dialogue. His one generally acknowledged virtue—his vivid narrative style—has not been enough to preserve his reputation with either critics or the general public.

Ainsworth died at his home, 57 St Mary's Road, Reigate, on 3 January 1882 of congestion of the lungs after suffering from what Ellis calls 'senile nerve degeneration' (2.341). Ainsworth himself said he had been suffering from neuralgia following an attack of shingles. He was buried on 9 January at Kensal Green cemetery.

SHELDON GOLDFARB

Sources S. M. Ellis, *William Harrison Ainsworth and his friends*, 2 vols. (1911) • K. Hollingsworth, *The Newgate novel, 1830–1847: Bulwer, Ainsworth, Dickens, and Thackeray* (1963) • J. A. Sutherland, 'Lever and Ainsworth: missing the first rank', *Victorian novelists and publishers* (1976), 152–65 • A. H. Joline, 'William Harrison Ainsworth', *At the library table* (Boston, MA, 1910), 83–123 • J. Evans, 'The early life of William Harrison Ainsworth', *Manchester Quarterly*, 8 (1882), 136–55 • G. Worth, *William Harrison Ainsworth* (1972) • A. Sanders, 'A Gothic revival: William Harrison Ainsworth's *The Tower of London*', *The Victorian historical novel* (1978), 32–46 • L. Ligocki, 'Ainsworth's Tudor novels: history as theme', *Studies in the Novel*, 4 (1972), 364–

77 · J. Biles, 'William Harrison Ainsworth: his artistry and signifi-cance', PhD diss. abstract, Emory University, 1954 · R. H. Horne, ed., *A new spirit of the age*, 2 vols. (1844); repr. (1971) · F. Gribble, 'Harrison Ainsworth', *Fortnightly Review*, 83 (1905), 533–42 · H. Locke, *A bibliographical catalogue of the published novels and ballads of Ainsworth* (1925) · d. cert. · J. W. T. Ley, 'Dickens and Ainsworth: Boz's first friend', *Dickensian*, 9 (1913), 285–8, 315–18

Archives BL, letters, as sponsor, to the Royal Literary Fund · Chetham's Library, Manchester, MSS · Hunt. L., corresp., journals, literary MSS, and papers · Man. CL, Manchester Archives and Local Studies, corresp. and papers · Morgan L. · Princeton University Library, New Jersey, corresp. and literary MSS · Ransom HRC · University of Iowa Libraries, Iowa City, corresp. | BL, agreements with and letters to R. Bentley, etc., Add. MSS 46612–46618, 46649–46652 · Man. CL, Manchester Archives and Local Studies, letters to J. Crossley, etc. · Museum of Science and Industry, Manchester, letters to William Scott · New York University, Fales Library, Fales Manuscript Collection · University of Illinois, Urbana–Champaign, Bentley MSS

Likenesses portraits, 1826–69, repro. in Ellis, *William Harrison Ainsworth* · D. Maclise, drawings, 1827–34, V&A · D. Maclise, drawing, 1834, repro. in *Fraser's Magazine* (July 1834), facing p. 48 · D. Maclise, oils, c.1834, NPG [*see illus.*] · D. Maclise, oils, 1834, Walker Art Gallery, Liverpool · R. J. Lane, lithograph, pubd 1839 (after W. Greatbach), BM · H. W. Pickersgill, oils, exh. RA 1841, Chetham's Hospital and Library, Manchester · R. J. Lane, lithograph, 1844 (after Count D'Orsay), NPG · H. Watkins, albumen print, 1856–9, NPG · G. Cruikshank, group portrait, etching (*Sir Lionel Flamstead and his friends*), V&A · G. Cruikshank, pencil drawing, BM · Hennah & Kent, carte-de-visite, NPG · Lock & Whitfield, woodburytype, NPG; repro. in T. Cooper, *Men of mark: a gallery of contemporary portraits* (1881) · London Stereoscopic Company, carte-de-visite, NPG · Southwell Bros., carte-de-visite, NPG

Wealth at death £4203 2s. 9d.: administration, 24 March 1882, *CGPLA Eng. & Wales*

Aio (*supp. fl.* 950x75), supposed historian, is said to have been a monk in the abbey of Crowland, Lincolnshire, and is mentioned only in the forged *Historia Croylandensis* attributed to Ingulf, a genuine eleventh-century abbot of the same monastery. This work was probably written in the mid-fifteenth century and professed to make use of material collected by two monks of Crowland, Aio and Brun, who, it claimed, had begun to compile a history of the abbey in the third quarter of the tenth century. There is no evidence that such a history, or its compilers, ever existed. C. F. KEARY, *rev.* MARIOS COSTAMBEYS

Sources Ordericus Vitalis, *Eccl. hist.*, 2.344–7 · A. Gransden, *Historical writing in England*, 2 (1982), appx C · W. G. Searle, *Ingulf and the Historia Croylandensis: an investigation*, Cambridge Antiquarian RS, 27 (1894)

Airay, Christopher (1600x03–1670), philosopher, was born at Clifton, Westmorland, and matriculated from Queen's College, Oxford, aged eighteen (Foster) on 9 November 1621. He graduated BA on 16 December 1625, was created a fellow in 1627, and proceeded MA on 29 January 1629. He was created BD on 1 or 2 November 1642 and was subsequently vicar of Milford, Hampshire, until his death, presumably at Milford, on 18 October 1670, aged sixty-nine (Foster). He was buried in the chancel of his church. Airay was the author of a textbook on logic, *Fasciculus praeceptorum logicorum*, published anonymously in 1628. The six books of this work show traditional scholastic origins in that Airay divides logic into propositions, which may be true or false, and discourse, which deals with the truth or falsity of particular propositions and the interrelationship between propositions as set out in syllogistic form. His discussion of the nature of discourse shows that he was, to some extent, influenced by the Ramists, particularly in emphasizing the laws of demonstration. Airay's son John graduated from Queen's in 1671. JOHN STEPHENS

Sources Foster, *Alum. Oxon.* · *DNB* · W. S. Howell, *Logic and rhetoric in England* (Princeton, 1956) · J. R. Magrath, *The Queen's College* (1921) · Wood, *Ath. Oxon.*, new edn · A. Pyle, ed., *The dictionary of seventeenth-century British philosophers*, 1 (2000)

Airay, Henry (1558x60–1616), college head, was born, probably at Kentmere, Westmorland, the son of William Airay (d. 1596?), who was either the brother-in-law or the favourite servant to Bernard Gilpin (1517–1583), the Apostle of the North, so called for his notable preaching and charitable activities. The Gilpin and Airay families had, in any event, much intermarried. He was educated at the grammar school of Kepier, in Gilpin's parish of Houghton-le-Spring, Durham, under direct influence of Gilpin, who sent him to Oxford in 1579, maintained him there, and remembered him later in his will. Airay matriculated from St Edmund Hall on 29 March 1580, aged twenty, but migrated as a 'poor boy' on 20 May 1582 to Queen's College. He graduated BA on 19 June 1583, and held office as college lecturer in dialectic. Having proceeded MA on 15 June 1586, he was chosen a fellow on 3 November, and over the next thirteen years held several college offices. After ordination he became an active and zealous preacher around Oxford, especially in the church of St Peter-in-the-East. His posthumously published sermons seem to have been preached mostly during this period. They attacked a perceived resurgence of Pelagianism and ideas of universal grace, as well as pleasure-seeking. Characteristic of his teaching was unambiguous predestinarianism, assertion of the possibility of experimental knowledge of election, and belief in salvation through preaching. He took the BTh degree on 16 November 1594, by which time he was senior fellow.

Airay became the closest friend of John Reynolds (1549–1607), the leading Oxford puritan, who was resident at Queen's College from 1586 to 1598, although Airay was more circumspect in rejecting ecclesiastical forms than Reynolds. A mentor in these years was the college provost from 1581, Henry Robinson. Robinson was chosen bishop of Carlisle in 1598, but held on to office at Queen's long enough to thwart interference in the succession by the earl of Essex and to ensure that Airay was elected provost on 9 March 1599. He took his DD degree on 17 June 1600. The following year Airay annoyed Bishop Richard Bancroft of London by supporting George Abbot's negative attitude to the renovation of Cheapside cross. In contrast, at Queen's substantial building works and repairs were undertaken, and so many students were attracted that, according to a survey made in summer 1612, the college had become the largest society in the university. Airay successfully defended the college's right to elect the principal of St Edmund Hall against the university's chancellor, Lord Buckhurst.

At the university level Airay had a running battle with John Howson of Christ Church. The most senior figure rebelling against Vice-Chancellor Howson's critique of over-emphasis on the pulpit, he assailed him in preaching during 1602. Howson attempted to use his authority to silence Airay, but ran into trouble with congregation. When Howson took the matter beyond the university, crown commissioners ordered Airay to submit, but, unlike junior men accused alongside him, he successfully evaded this. He was to clash with Howson again in 1612 over a sermon in which his old adversary had detected Arianism in the annotations of the Geneva Bible.

Airay was probably one of only two or three Oxford heads who did not approve the university's *Answere*, or refutation, of the puritan millenary petition to King James in 1603. In 1604, true to his principles, he jumped at an opportunity afforded by the king's desire for commemoration of his escape from the Gowrie conspiracy, and helped establish a new series of Tuesday sermons in the university. Authorities outside Oxford remained keen to keep the anti-separatist provost on side. Chancellor Buckhurst, probably encouraged by George Abbot, his chaplain, and supported by Richard Bancroft, explicitly assumed his ecclesiastical conformity in offering him the vice-chancellorship in 1605. Although Airay then refused, he did serve for a year from 17 July 1606. During his vice-chancellorship he called William Laud of St John's College to account for preaching matter he regarded as tantamount to popery in St Mary's, although Laud, by the intervention of Sir William Paddy with the chancellor and by threatening to take his case outside Oxford, managed, like Airay himself on a previous occasion, to avoid formal recantation. A few months later, when his friend Reynolds died, Airay preached the funeral sermon.

Airay had accepted in 1606 the impoverished college rectory of Charlton-on-Otmoor with a view to freeing it of a detrimental lease. The college refunded legal expenses during the long but ultimately successful struggle, and Airay remitted in his will any outstanding debt. In 1609 he received a prebend of Canterbury Cathedral in the gift of Archbishop Bancroft, and in 1615 he became rector of Bletchington, Oxfordshire. Airay died on 10 October 1616, aged fifty-seven, according to his funeral monument in Queen's College chapel, where he was buried. The monument, depicting him as Elisha to Henry Robinson's Elijah, was erected by Christopher Potter, a 'cousin' whom Airay had made his executor. By his will, proved at Oxford on 21 December 1616, Airay left land in Garsington which he had bought for £230 to the college; £40 to support the schoolmaster of Kendal; £40 for a preacher in Kentmere chapel; a gilt bowl of 30 ounces to his successors in the provostship; his books to the college according to his executor's discretion; and a number of lesser legacies.

Airay seems to have published nothing in his lifetime, although Anthony Wood mentions doubtfully a *Treatise Against Bowing at the Name of Jesus*. It was his executor, Christopher Potter, who published in 1618 ninety-five of Airay's sermons as *Lectures upon the Whole Epistle of Saint Paul to the Philippians*, with a laudatory preface and a dedication to Archbishop Abbot, and in 1621 his *Just and necessary apology touching his suit in law for the rectory of Charlton on Otmore, in Oxfordshire*. Airay had been an eminent promoter and defender of evangelical Calvinism in Oxford. Only a few months after his death, however, King James issued instructions to both the universities that were a considerable blow to the party he had represented.

A. J. HEGARTY

Sources Wood, *Ath. Oxon.*, new edn • A. Wood, *The history and antiquities of the University of Oxford*, ed. J. Gutch, 2 vols. in 3 pts (1792–6) • A. Wood, *The history and antiquities of the colleges and halls in the University of Oxford*, ed. J. Gutch (1786); appx (1790) • J. R. Magrath, *The Queen's College*, 2 vols. (1921) • J. R. Magrath, ed., *Liber obituarius aulae reginae in Oxonia*, OHS, 56 (1910) • C. M. Dent, *Protestant reformers in Elizabethan Oxford* (1983) • Foster, *Alum. Oxon.* • *Transactions of the Cumberland and Westmorland Antiquarian and Archaeological Society*, new ser., 34 (1933–4), 194–5 • E. Mackenzie and M. Ross, *An historical, topographical, and descriptive view of the county palatine of Durham*, 1 (1834) • *Fasti Angl.*, 1541–1857, [Canterbury] • Bodl. Oxf., MS Rawl. A. 289, fols. 76r–80r • [H. M. Wood], *Index of wills, etc., in the probate registry, Durham, and from other sources*, 1540–1599 (1928)

Likenesses brass effigy, Queen's College, Oxford • line engraving, BM, NPG • portrait, Queen's College, Oxford

Airbertach mac Cosse Dobráin (d. 1016), poet, was lector or *fer légind* (head of the school) and later superior of Ros Ailithir (Ross Carbery, in the south-west of what is now co. Cork). He belonged to the tradition of learned poetry that flourished in Ireland in the tenth and eleventh centuries. His importance is indicated by the only known event of his life other than his obit, an entry in the annals of Inisfallen recording that in 990 Brían Bóruma, king of Munster, ransomed him from vikings who attacked Ros Ailithir; in this entry he is named just by his patronymic, mac Cosse Dobráin, without his first name, Airbertach. The negotiations for his release were conducted at the island monastery of Inis Cathaig (Scattery Island in the estuary of the Shannon).

In spite of a distinction recognized by contemporaries, only four poems are generally agreed to be the work of Airbertach, all of them didactic. *Rofessa i curp domuin dúir* ('In the body of the hard world were known') is a poem of sixty-eight stanzas on the geography of the world; it appears to be derived from Isidore of Seville (d. 636) via some epitome. The other three are all aids to remembering biblical information, reflecting the biblically based learning of the ecclesiastical school. *Fichi ríg cía rím as ferr* ('Twenty kings according to the best reckoning') deals, in sixty-one stanzas, with the kings of Israel and Judah. *A dé dúlig, atat-teoch* ('O God the creator, I implore you') is a four-part poem, covering the psalms, biblical chronology, the elements from which Adam was created, and a commemoration of an apocryphal prophecy by St Thomas. *Ro-chúala crecha is tír thair* ('I have heard of plunderings in a land in the east') summarizes part of the historical books of the Old Testament in twenty-five stanzas.

The extant corpus of Airbertach's verse would be very much bigger if an argument put forward by Gearóid Mac Eoin were accepted. He has suggested that Airbertach was also the author of a long summary of biblical history entitled *Saltair na Rann* ('The psalter of the stanzas'), perhaps the most important work of the medieval Irish learned poets. This attribution, made on grounds of style and language, has been disputed by James Carney who would date *Saltair na Rann* more than a century earlier. However, the attribution to Airbertach still remains plausible.

Airbertach is not to be confused with Airard mac Coisse to whom a Middle Irish prose text has been attributed (*Airec Menman Airaird meic Coisse*), and who died in 990. The obit in the annals of the four masters (s.a. 1023) appears to stem from confusing the two authors.

PETER J. SMITH

Sources R. I. Best and others, eds., *The Book of Leinster, formerly Lebar na Núachongbála*, 6 vols. (1954–83), vol. 3 · J. Carney, 'The dating of early Irish verse texts, 500–1100', *Éigse*, 19 (1982–3), 177–216 · J. F. Kenney, *The sources for the early history of Ireland* (1929) · Ann. *Ulster*, s.a. 1016 · S. Mac Airt, ed. and trans., *The annals of Inisfallen* (1951), s.a. 990 · G. Mac Eoin, 'The date and authorship of *Saltair na Rann*', *Zeitschrift für Celtische Philologie*, 28 (1960–61), 51–67 · G. Mac Eoin, ed. and trans., 'A poem by Airbertach Mac Cosse', *Ériu*, 20 (1966), 112–39 · K. Meyer, 'Mitteilungen aus irischen Handschriften', *Zeitschrift für Celtische Philologie*, 3 (1899–1901), 17–39, esp. 20–24 · AFM, s.a. 1015, 1023 · P. Ó Néill, 'Airbertach mac Cosse's poem on the psalter', *Éigse*, 17 (1977–9), 19–46 · T. Olden, ed. and trans., 'The geography of Ros Ailithir', *Proceedings of the Royal Irish Academy*, 2nd ser., 2: Literature (1879–88), 219–52 · W. Stokes, ed. and trans., *Saltair na Rann*, Anecdota Oxoniensia, Medieval and Modern Series, 1/3 (1893) · J. Carney, 'The dating of early Irish verse texts, 500–1100', *Éigse*, 19 (1982–3), 177–216 · P. J. Smith, 'Early Irish historical verse: the evolution of a genre', *Irland und Europa im früheren Mittelalter / Ireland and Europe in the early Middle Ages: texts and transmission* [Konstanz 1998], ed. P. Ní Chatháin and M. Richter (Dublin, 2002), 326–41

Aird, Ian (1905–1962), surgeon, was born on 4 July 1905 at Belgrave Terrace, Corstorphine, Edinburgh, the first of two sons of William Aird (*b*. 1872), master tailor, and his wife, Jean Elizabeth Ogle (formerly Binnie). Both parents were lowland Scots, the father's forebears from Maybole and the mother's from Carstairs. Aird attended George Watson's College, Edinburgh, from 1914 to 1923. His reputation was bookish—he took Russian as an extra subject. At Edinburgh University he read medicine and graduated MB ChB in 1928. Apart from a continental tour most of his postgraduate training continued in Edinburgh under David Wilkie, Henry Wade, Norman Dott, and James Graham. He became FRCS (Edin.) in 1932. In 1934 the Medical Research Council awarded him a Rockefeller scholarship to Washington University (St Louis) with Evarts Graham, and he also spent a month at the Mayo Clinic. During his absence he was appointed assistant surgeon at the Royal Edinburgh Hospital for Sick Children. He took the degree of ChM (with high commendation) in 1936 and in December that year married (Beatrice) Margaret Cowes (1907–1992), of Kinghorn, Fife; there was a daughter, Heather, and a son, Ian Alisdair.

As a Territorial Force volunteer Aird was mobilized in October 1939; he was eventually to command the first mobile surgical unit in the western desert and was twice mentioned in dispatches, once after he had apparently confronted General Erwin Rommel in the surgeon's operating tent during a brief period of captivity. After an attack of renal colic in 1943 he was repatriated with the rank of lieutenant-colonel and returned to civilian surgery in Edinburgh, where he was assistant to Professor James Learmonth and assistant director of the Wilkie Research Laboratory. In 1946 he succeeded Grey Turner as professor of surgery in London University at the postgraduate medical school at Hammersmith, taking over a department of surgery which was not well provided with accommodation or equipment.

In the ensuing fifteen years Aird devoted himself to creating a research and clinical organization which came to possess international renown. Prominent among the themes he supported and supervised were: the development of heart–lung bypass and cardiac surgery; renal transplantation; and the early identification of the association of blood groups with a number of diseases. In the United Kingdom the clinical applications of the advances in the first two areas were somewhat slow because of a 'non-surgical' attitude among some of his medical colleagues, but eventually, with the zeal of his associates in the UK, Europe, and North America, both flourished in the late 1950s and after Aird's death. In the public mind Aird was linked with the separation of conjoint twins, which confirmed him as a surgical planner of high ability (though not with outstanding surgical performance unless the problem interested him) but also led to confrontations with the British popular press. He was much admired as a teacher and his single-author, unillustrated work, *A Companion in Surgical Studies* (1949; 2nd edn, 1953)—a development of lecture notes for a successful tutorial course in Edinburgh—became well-nigh essential for surgical trainees. It is arguable that the force of his personality and the undoubted clarity of writing in the *Companion* helped to set the post-war syllabus for the fellowship examinations of the British colleges of surgeons. He was also a pioneer of the use of film and closed-circuit television in surgical education.

Aird's contemporaries remember him as one with 'almost a foghorn voice, which combined with his short stature produced a commanding presence'; as 'having a good debating mind and [someone] who never liked to be defeated in argument'; as 'an inspiring leader, ruthlessly honest and without circumlocution'; as of 'consummate loyalty to his trainees'; as 'a scintillating teacher with incredible off-the-cuff ideas and shafts of wisdom'; and as having 'a combination of external bonhomie and inner turmoil' (private information). His obvious pleasure in the company of others (on his own terms) made him an internationally popular figure and, coupled with his linguistic ability in both the Romance languages and Russian, he was much in demand for lecturing and visiting, to which he tirelessly responded. In addition to his exceptional knowledge of his profession, he was a gifted pianist and kept a concert grand in his flat at the hospital.

In 1953 Aird was elected to the council of the Royal College of Surgeons, London (FRCS *ad eundem*, 1946), which he served until his death. He was particularly valued for his advice on surgical education. In 1957, at the time of his appointment as an honorary fellow of the American College of Surgeons together with John Bruce, he and Bruce were responsible with J. William Hinton for founding the James IV Association, a charitable foundation to finance international travel for young surgeons. Aird became its first president. In 1962 he received the Liston Victoria jubilee prize of the Royal College of Surgeons of Edinburgh. A project to which he devoted much effort—ahead of his time—was an attempt to form international surgical teams for disaster relief from the staff of academic departments.

The incessant peripatetic activity and self-demanding lifestyle probably affected Aird's mental and physical health. He much enjoyed entertaining others and had a fondness for Scotch whisky, but the latter did not seem to affect his intellectual or surgical ability. It came as a surprise to his professional acquaintances, therefore, when on 17 September 1962 he committed suicide by barbiturate poisoning at his flat in the Hammersmith Hospital, Du Cane Road, London. His note to the coroner expressed disappointment in the reception of his department's achievements by his peers and by grant-giving bodies, and commented on personal depression and intellectual decline; both, however, were scarcely apparent to others. Aird was cremated at Mortlake crematorium and his ashes were scattered there; a memorial service was held in the church of St Columba in London. He is remembered at the Royal Postgraduate Medical School (later a division of Imperial College school of medicine) by an annual lecture.

HUGH DUDLEY

Sources H. McLeave, *A time to heal—the life of Ian Aird, the surgeon* (1964) • R. H. O. B. Robinson and W. R. Le Fanu, *Lives of the fellows of the Royal College of Surgeons of England, 1952–1964* (1970) • J. Bruce, 'Introductory history', *Handbook of the James IV Association of Surgeons* (1996) • *The Times* (19 Sept 1962) • *The Scotsman* (18 Sept 1962) • *BMJ* (22 Sept 1962), 802; (29 Sept 1962), 864–5 • *The Lancet* (29 Sept 1962), 667–9 • personal knowledge (2004) • private information (2004) • m. cert. • *CGPLA Eng. & Wales* (1963) • d. cert.
Likenesses BCW, drawing, 1942, priv. coll. • T. Cuneo, group portrait (Council of Royal College of Surgeons), RCS Eng.
Wealth at death £7394 7s. 0d.: probate, 21 Jan 1963, *CGPLA Eng. & Wales*

Aird, Sir John, first baronet (1833–1911), civil engineering contractor, was born on 3 December 1833 in Greenwich, the second son of eight children of John Aird (1800–1876), contractor, and Agnes (d. 1869), daughter of Charles Bennett of Lambeth. His grandfather Robert Aird went south from Fortrose, Ross-shire, early in the nineteenth century, and worked for Hugh McIntosh, the civil engineering contractor. After Robert's death in an earth fall on the Regent's Canal works, John Aird senior continued to work for McIntosh until 1827. McIntosh had a large number of pipe-laying contracts for the metropolitan gas companies, and this probably helped Aird obtain a position with the Phoenix Gas Company, initially as an inspector and subsequently as manager of their works in Greenwich. During the 1840s he took an increasing number of private contracts, and in 1848 left the Phoenix Gas Company which,

Sir John Aird, first baronet (1833–1911), by Sir Benjamin Stone, 1897

however, continued to provide him with pipe-laying work. John Aird junior, who was privately educated in Greenwich and Southgate, joined his father when he was eighteen; his elder brother, Charles, was also part of the firm, which became known as John Aird & Sons. Aird senior had obtained contracts for pipe-laying and building work for the Great Exhibition of 1851, and one of Aird junior's first tasks was to assist in its demolition and the re-erection of the Crystal Palace at Sydenham.

On 6 September 1855 Aird married Sarah (1835–1909), daughter of Benjamin Smith, a Deptford wharfinger. They had two sons and seven daughters. Three of the daughters were to marry into families with civil engineering links. The eldest, Sarah, married Basil Pym Ellis who eventually became a partner in the firms of Aird & Sons and Lucas Brothers. Jessie, the second, married George Neill Abernethy, and Kate, the third, Alfred William Thomas Bean. In the 1850s the activities of John Aird & Sons expanded rapidly. Building on mains laying experience for the east London waterworks in the previous decade the Airds obtained contracts for the new waterworks of the Southwark and Vauxhall, Grand Junction, and west Middlesex water companies near Hampton in the 1850s. On the continent, where British-owned utility companies were often involved, the Airds began mains laying in the Netherlands, before building waterworks in Rotterdam, Amsterdam, Hamburg, Altona, Schiedam, Brunswick, Riga, Archangel, and Moscow. In Copenhagen, in addition to the waterworks, John Aird senior built the first major outfall sewer, which nearly bankrupted the firm. The Airds formed a partnership with Charles Fox and Thomas Crompton to establish the Berlin Water Company. Aird's brother-in-law Henry Gill was the engineer. Alexander, John Aird's younger brother, was the contractor's agent on many of these schemes, and remained in Germany for forty years.

The firm continued to work on gasworks contracts throughout the 1850s. John Aird senior took shares in the Crystal Palace Gas Company, whose works were built in 1854; Charles increasingly took responsibility for this side of the family's business. John Aird junior worked on a variety of schemes at this time, including South Staffordshire waterworks, Berlin waterworks, Palermo gasworks, and contracts in Ottawa, Brazil, and Singapore.

In the 1860s the Airds began railway contracting. In the Thames Valley Railway they took an entrepreneurial role with nearly 90 per cent of the share capital. They also became increasingly involved with other contractors. In addition to waterworks schemes at Calcutta, with Brassey and Wythes, and works with Peto and Betts in Cagliari, they partnered Sir John Kelk in the construction of Millwall docks (1863–8), which they helped finance. Their most lasting connection was with Charles Thomas and Thomas Lucas, who shared their premises in Belvedere Road, Lambeth, in the 1860s.

The Lucas brothers had begun their careers with Sir Samuel Morton Peto before branching off on their own, particularly as building contractors. In the wake of the Overend Gurney banking failure in 1866 both Airds and Lucas Brothers were ideally placed to fill the vacuum left by the bankruptcy of many of the leading contracting firms. Between them they completed many of Peto's contracts. From 1870 the two families operated as three firms: Lucas Brothers, who carried out building works, Lucas and Aird, who carried out railway and civil engineering contracts, and John Aird & Sons, who continued to specialize in water and gas contracts. Aird took increasing responsibility within the family firm at this time, having supervised the massive Beckton gasworks contract, completed in 1870. Following his father's death the firm was reorganized. In early 1877 it was in serious financial trouble with the Nottingham and Melton contract for the Midland Railway, and Lucas Brothers had to rescue it. Charles Aird retired, leaving Aird to continue with the Lucas brothers. Although their junior in years, his strength of personality made him a dominant force within the firms.

Over twenty years the various firms undertook more than seventy contracts, many on a grand scale, such as the Royal Albert and Tilbury docks schemes in the Port of London, Hodbarrow sea wall, works on the Midland, Metropolitan, and Great Eastern railways, including Liverpool Street Station, and an extensive railway system around Hull docks. Docks were also built at Portsmouth, Southampton, Newport, and Newhaven. They continued to build gasworks, with further extensions at Beckton, and their waterworks involvement included Thirlmere aqueduct for Manchester, part of the Elan valley aqueduct for Birmingham, and several reservoirs for the East London Waterworks Company.

As Aird's sons became old enough they were brought into the business. The elder, John (1861–1934), joined in 1879, and became a partner in 1886. One early scheme he worked on was the 1885 Suakim–Berber military railway. The younger, Malcolm (1872–1934), followed in 1892. Members of the Lucas family had been similarly brought in. After the death of Sir Charles Thomas Lucas in 1895 the firms of Lucas Brothers and Lucas and Aird were dissolved, almost all the Lucas family having retired, and a new firm of John Aird & Co. was set up to carry on the railway and civil engineering work; Aird & Sons continued the water and gas contracts. John Aird remained very active. Nearly fifty more contracts were taken by the two Aird firms before his death.

Aird's greatest works, for which he became a grand lord of the order of the Mejidiye in 1902, were in Egypt. In the 1890s plans for improving irrigation and control on the Nile had been frustrated by the cost. Aird offered to accept a deferred payment for the Aswan Dam and Asyut barrage, and was awarded the contract in 1898. Further contracts for raising the Aswan Dam and building the Esna barrage followed. Other large contracts were obtained at the Royal Edward Dock, Avonmouth, and finally at Tanjong Pagar docks in Singapore. This was the last major contract undertaken by the Airds. Aird suffered a stroke in 1908, and this prompted his retirement. The Singapore contract proved a financial disaster, in part due to misleading site investigations, and the firm lost around £1 million by the time the affair had been settled after Aird's death. It was left to Malcom Aird to wind the business up.

Sir John's baronetcy, awarded on 5 March 1901, was a public recognition of his considerable achievements. His organization was, after the death of Thomas Brassey, the largest contracting firm in the country, employing 30,000 men in December 1874, and as many as 20,000 men on the Aswan Dam alone twenty years later. It had its headquarters at 37 Great George Street, London, with depots in Lambeth and Fulham, and made great use of mechanical plant with a fleet of over a hundred locomotives. Aird himself helped develop the steam navvy.

Like many engineers of the Victorian period Aird entered politics and was MP for North Paddington in 1887–1902. He took his responsibilities seriously. Although his speeches were unremarkable he attended public functions as a matter of course and played a leading role in the public library movement in Paddington. He was the first mayor of Paddington in 1900–01. His portrait by Sidney Paget decorated the council chamber and shows him in mayoral robes with characteristic flowing beard.

Aird's other chief interest was in the arts. He had a theatre installed at his home at 14 Hyde Park Terrace, London, which also housed his important art collection. The works included early English and Dutch painters and a large number of works by late Victorian artists, including the Pre-Raphaelites. Aird's varied interests were reflected in his membership of a large number of professional and voluntary organizations. He was elected associate of the Institution of Civil Engineers in 1859, and member of the Iron and Steel Institute in 1887. He was a liveryman of the Needlemakers' Company, and its master 1890–92 and 1897–8. He was one of the first contractors to be appointed to the engineer and railway volunteer staff corps, being a major and subsequently honorary lieutenant-colonel. A leading freemason, he was master of the Prince of Wales Lodge, and a grand deacon. He was a member of the Junior Carlton Club. He was churchwarden at St John's, Southwick Gardens, where the Revd E. P. Anderson, who married his daughter Vida, was vicar. He was appointed to the royal commission on the depression in trade (1886), and his other chief public appointment was as commissioner of lieutenancy of the City of London. Aird retired to Wilton Park, Beaconsfield, Buckinghamshire, where he died on 6 January 1911. He was buried in a vault alongside his wife in St Anne's Church, at Littleworth, near Dropmore, Beaconsfield.

MIKE CHRIMES

Sources R. K. Middlemas, *The master builders* (1963), 121–59 · *Engineering* (13 Jan 1911), 59 · *PICE*, 184 (1910–11), 351–2 · 'Death of Sir John Aird Bart', *Kensington and Bayswater Chronicle* (14 Jan 1911) · P. Guillery, 'Building the Millwall docks', *Construction History*, 6 (1990), 3–21 · *The Times* (7 Jan 1911) · *The Times* (12 Jan 1911) · *The Times* (23 March 1911) · *Strand Magazine*, 30 (1905), 433–4 · *The Builder*, 100 (1911), 51–2 · J. Grant, ed., *Buckinghamshire: a short history with genealogies and current biographies* (1911) · *The Statesman*, 579 · *Cassier's Magazine*, 20 (Aug 1901), 266, 343–4 · d. cert. · *Engineering* (23 March 1906), 380 [obit. of Joseph Aird] · *The Builder*, 34 (1876), 393 [obit. of John Aird sen.] · *Engineering* (12 May 1876) [obit. of John Aird sen.]
Archives Museum of London | LMA, water companies' records · NA Scot., west highland railway · PRO, railway records
Likenesses J. Orchard, portrait, c.1849 · B. Stone, photograph, 1897, NPG [*see illus.*] · L. Fildes, portrait, 1898 · S. Paget, portrait, 1902; formerly in Paddington town hall, 1912 · O. Ford, bust · Spy [L. Ward], caricature, watercolour study, NPG; repro. in *VF* (20 June 1891) · photographs; copies, Inst. CE · portrait, repro. in *Engineering* · portrait, repro. in *Strand Magazine*, 30 (1908)
Wealth at death £1,057,859 1s. 2d.: resworn probate, 20 March 1911, CGPLA Eng. & Wales

Aird, Thomas (1802–1876), poet, was born on 28 August 1802 at Bowden, Roxburghshire, the second son of James Aird, builder, and his wife, Isabella Paisley. He was educated at the parish school of Bowden, where he combined an enthusiasm for literature and sports. In 1816 he began undergraduate studies at the University of Edinburgh, and while still a student he became private tutor in the family of a Mr Anderson, farmer, of Crosscleugh, Selkirkshire, where he frequently met James Hogg, the Ettrick Shepherd.

After graduation, although urged to become a minister in the Church of Scotland, Aird chose to stay in Edinburgh to pursue a writing career. In 1826 he published his first work, *Martzoufle: a Tragedy in Three Acts, with other Poems*. The lines entitled 'My Mother's Grave' have much genuine poetic feeling; but the volume did not attract much

notice. In the following year he contributed several articles to *Blackwood's Magazine*, and also produced his *Religious Characteristics*, a series of fervent prose essays, which John Wilson reviewed in very laudatory terms in *Blackwood's Magazine* for June 1827. The critic was soon afterwards introduced to Aird, and proved of great service to him. In 1830 Aird published *Captive of Fez*, a long narrative poem in five cantos.

When James Ballantyne died in 1832 Aird was chosen to succeed him in the editorship of the *Edinburgh Weekly Journal*; but he held the post for only a year. During his tenure as editor, he became acquainted with the Carlyles, who were in Edinburgh at the time. Thomas Carlyle spoke of him as a 'person of decided innocence, openness almost genius without the smallest culture, except from Blackwood's backshop' (*Carlyle Letters*, 6.361). In 1835 he left Edinburgh for Dumfries to undertake the editorship of the *Dumfriesshire and Galloway Herald*, to which Wilson had recommended him, and he continued in that office for twenty-eight years. He performed his editorial duties with great vigour, ardently supporting the Conservative interest in politics and church matters; but he was able to write at the same time a variety of poems, many of which he published in his paper. In 1845 he published *The Old Bachelor in the Scottish Village*, a prose delineation of Scottish character, with descriptive sketches of the seasons. The book proved popular in Scotland, and was reprinted in 1857.

In 1848 Aird prepared for press a collected edition of his poems, which enhanced his reputation. Many of them appealed to the religious instincts of his countrymen; others showed a vivid imagination at work, although the longer narrative poems were weakly plotted and constructed. In 1852 Aird edited, with a memoir, the works of his friend David Macbeth Moir; but after that date he suffered much ill health, and his literary efforts were confined to contributions to his newspaper. In 1863 he retired from his post as editor of the *Herald*; but he survived for thirteen years, dying in Castlebank, Dumfries, on 25 April 1876. He was buried in St Michael's churchyard, Dumfries.

Aird's poetry focuses mainly on nature, and is imitative of Wordsworth. As Carlyle was later to remark, Aird 'found everywhere a healthy breath as of mountain breezes', and translated this into works that sold well during his time, but did not survive well after his death.

SIDNEY LEE, rev. DAVID FINKELSTEIN

Sources J. Wallace, 'Memoir', in T. Aird, *The poetical works of Thomas Aird*, 5th edn (1878) · *The collected letters of Thomas and Jane Welsh Carlyle*, ed. C. R. Sanders and K. J. Fielding, 6 (1977), 361 · NL Scot. · d. cert. · CGPLA Eng. & Wales (1876)
Archives NL Scot., letters to Blackwoods · NL Scot., corresp. with Samuel Brown · NL Scot., letters to D. M. Moir and Catherine Moir
Wealth at death £9063 14s. 1d.: confirmation, 24 May 1876, CCI

Aird, William (d. 1606/7), Church of Scotland minister, worked as a mason until twenty years old. His wife, whose name is not known, taught him to read, and he later acquired Latin, Greek, and Hebrew. He studied theology for several years, probably at Edinburgh, and may have attended the university there during the first year after its opening in 1583, as he was called to the ministry in 1584. Shortly afterwards he fled to England with other ministers who opposed the passing by parliament in May of the Black Acts, which asserted the king's supremacy over the kirk. He remained in Berwick upon Tweed in the company of James Melville, but had returned to Edinburgh by October 1585, when the town council requested the return of John Cairns, reader, to St Giles, whom failing, either Michael Cranston, minister of Selkirk, or William Aird. The latter was eventually admitted minister of the collegiate charge of St Cuthbert's, Edinburgh, on 13 September 1586, as colleague of Robert Pont.

Aird remained close to the ministers opposed to the ecclesiastical policy of the crown and was in no way as cautious as Pont. In December 1592 he was one of the Edinburgh ministers vehemently opposed to Francis Stewart, first earl of Bothwell, and it was he who pronounced Bothwell's excommunication in February 1595. At the beginning of 1598 Robert Bruce, minister of Edinburgh and a prominent opponent of James VI, attempted to have Aird as one of his colleagues. This did not happen. At that year's general assembly Aird, along with Bruce, James Melville, and others, opposed the king's wishes in maintaining that ministers ought not to have the right to vote in parliament. There is no record of Aird's having been involved in the proceedings of any other general assembly and his name is listed only among the commissioners of the assembly of 1602. James VI is said to have sent him a purse of gold, probably during this assembly, but although Aird was impoverished he refused to accept it, considering it to be a bribe. However, an unknown hand left some sacks of meal the following day at his manse.

Exactly when Aird died is not known. He was present at a kirk session meeting at St Cuthbert's on 19 July 1606, but was dead by 20 September 1607, when his successor, William Arthur, was called. Aird's son John assisted his father after graduating MA at the University of Edinburgh in 1604, and was minister of Newton in 1614 before becoming minister of Newbattle the following year. He had the same attitude towards royal authority as his father, signing the protestation for the liberties of the kirk in 1617.

DUNCAN SHAW

Sources *Fasti Scot.*, new edn, 1.100 · D. Calderwood, *The history of the Kirk of Scotland*, ed. T. Thomson and D. Laing, 8 vols., Wodrow Society, 7 (1842–9), vol. 4, p. 236; vol. 5

Airedale. For this title name *see* Kitson, James, first Baron Airedale (1835–1911).

Airey, Diana Josceline Barbara Neave, Baroness Airey of Abingdon (1919–1992). *See under* Neave, Airey Middleton Sheffield (1916–1979).

Airey, Sir George (1761–1833), army officer, entered the army as ensign in the 91st regiment in 1779, and was promoted lieutenant in 1781; on 2 January 1782 he transferred to the 48th regiment, and went with it to the West Indies. Airey was almost certainly attracted to this unappealing station by the prospect of better pay, and he inadvertently laid the foundation for his future advancement through his perceptive observation of the military features of the islands.

In 1788 Airey was promoted captain and might have remained at that rank but for the outbreak of war with France in 1793. He was then thirty-two years old, which, at a time when men became lieutenant-colonels at twenty-three, should have ensured that he would have little opportunity of rising any further. However, his topographical knowledge enabled him to be of great assistance to Sir Charles Grey, who in 1793 captured the French West Indies with the aid of Sir John Jervis. Grey was so impressed with Airey that he recommended him to General Tonyn, who made him his aide-de-camp, and to Sir Ralph Abercromby. The latter appointed him assistant adjutant-general to his force which set out to recover the French West Indies, which had been recaptured by the enemy. Abercromby was greatly impressed by Airey's conduct, and being one who always recognized merit ahead of influence, he secured for Airey a majority in the 68th regiment in 1796 and a lieutenant-colonelcy in the 8th regiment in 1798. Abercromby was also influential in Airey's selection as deputy adjutant-general to the garrison of Minorca. This appointment prevented his accompanying the expedition to Egypt, where his patron was killed in 1801; but his ability soon came to the attention of the influential General Henry Fox, the brother of the politician and at this time governor and commander-in-chief in Minorca. The rather indolent general enjoyed having such an energetic man to save him trouble, and took him as military secretary to Ireland, when he was appointed commander-in-chief there in 1802. There, he married the Hon. Catherine Talbot, third daughter of Lord Talbot de Malahide: they had a large family, including Richard *Airey (1803–1881) and Sir James Talbot *Airey (1812–1898).

Airey accompanied Fox to Sicily as military secretary in 1805, and was deputy adjutant-general and military secretary to General Fraser during the disastrous expedition to Damietta in 1807. He was promoted colonel in 1808, commanded the 2nd brigade during the expedition to Ischia in Sicily in 1809, was promoted major-general on 4 June 1811, and was appointed commandant of the forces in the Ionian Islands in 1812. He was then appointed quartermaster-general to the forces in Ireland in 1813, a post he held for many years, became a lieutenant-general on 19 July 1821, received the command of the 39th regiment in 1823, was made a KCH in 1820 by George IV, and died in Paris on 18 February 1833.

Despite his limited active service, the value of Airey's services to the army cannot be underrated. His ability is illustrated by the way in which Sir Ralph Abercromby, a strict judge of staff officers, took him under his wing when he was only a captain, and also by his unfailing popularity with every chief that he served under. 'It is more rare to find an able staff officer', the duke of Wellington stated, 'than a good regimental officer' (*DNB*), and Airey can certainly be numbered among those few.

H. M. STEPHENS, *rev.* S. KINROSS

Sources Fortescue, *Brit. army*, vol. 8 · J. Haydn, *The book of dignities: containing rolls of the official personages of the British empire* (1851) · J. Philippart, ed., *The royal military calendar*, 3rd edn, 3 (1820) · *GM*, 1st ser., 103/2 (1833), 560–61 · GEC, *Peerage*
Archives Herefs. RO, corresp. and papers | BL, corresp. with Sir Hudson Lowe, Add. MSS 20107–20191 · U. Nott. L., corresp. with Lord William Bentinck

Airey, Sir James Talbot (1812–1898), army officer, born on 6 September 1812, was the son of Lieutenant-General Sir George *Airey (1761–1833) and his wife, Catherine, sister of the second Baron Talbot de Malahide. Richard *Airey was his brother. He was commissioned ensign in the 30th foot on 11 February 1830, became lieutenant on 3 May 1833, and exchanged to the 3rd Buffs on 23 August. He was aide-de-camp to the governor of Madras from May 1834 to July 1837.

On 26 January 1841 Airey was appointed extra aide-de-camp to Major-General Elphinstone, and accompanied him to Afghanistan. In the latter part of 1841 he was present at the forcing of the Khurd Kabul Pass and the actions near Kabul, and on 21 December he volunteered to be given up to Akbar Khan as a hostage. He was released with the other captives on 21 September 1842, joined the force sent into Kohistan under Brigadier M'Caskill, and was present at the capture of Istalif. He was mentioned in dispatches. He was promoted captain on 22 July 1842, and took part with his regiment in the 1843 Gwalior campaign. He was aide-de-camp to the governor of Ceylon from April 1847 to March 1851. On 11 November 1851 he became regimental major, and on 17 July 1854 exchanged to the Coldstream Guards as captain and lieutenant-colonel.

Airey served throughout the Crimean War with the light division as assistant quartermaster-general, being present at the Alma, Balaklava, Inkerman, and the assault of the Redan, and he accompanied the expedition to Kerch. He was mentioned in dispatches, and received the Légion d'honneur (fifth class) and the Mejidiye (fourth class). He was made CB on 5 July 1855.

Airey was promoted colonel on 26 December 1859, and became regimental major in the Coldstream Guards on 22 May 1866. He was promoted major-general on 6 March 1868, and commanded the troops at Malta from 21 August 1875 to 31 December 1878. He became lieutenant-general on 1 October 1877, and was placed on the retired list on 1 July 1881, with the honorary rank of general. He was made KCB on 2 June 1877, and colonel of the Royal Inniskilling Fusiliers on 13 March 1886. He died, unmarried, at his home, 114 Victoria Street, Westminster, on 1 January 1898. E. M. LLOYD, *rev.* JAMES LUNT

Sources *Hart's Army List* (1897) · *The Times* (3 Jan 1898) · J. T. Airey, 'The Cabool captives', *Colburn's United Service Magazine*, 3 (1845); 1 (1846) · V. Eyre, *Journal of an Afghanistan prisoner* (1976) · A. W. Kinglake, *The invasion of the Crimea*, 8 vols. (1863–87) · C. Hibbert, *The destruction of Lord Raglan* [1961] · Boase, *Mod. Eng. biog.* · d. cert.
Likenesses wood-engraving, NPG; repro. in *ILN* (13 July 1878)
Wealth at death £35,486 14s. 7d.: probate, 29 Jan 1898, CGPLA Eng. & Wales

Airey, Richard, Baron Airey (1803–1881), army officer, was born at Newcastle upon Tyne in April 1803, the eldest son from the six boys and three girls of Lieutenant-General Sir

Richard Airey, Baron Airey (1803–1881), by Lock & Whitfield, pubd 1878

George *Airey (1761–1833) and his wife, Catherine Talbot (*d.* 1852), third daughter of Richard Talbot of Malahide Castle, co. Dublin, and Margaret, *suo jure* Baroness Talbot of Malahide. He attended the junior department of the Royal Military College, Sandhurst, from 13 August 1815 to 31 March 1821, was appointed ensign without purchase in the 34th foot on 15 March 1821, and purchased advancement to lieutenant in the regiment on 4 December 1823. Airey went on half pay as a captain (22 October 1825) and re-entered the 34th in that rank through purchase (11 June 1826). Meanwhile, he had joined the senior department at Sandhurst on 6 February 1826, gaining his certificate of qualification on 14 December. Airey served as aide-de-camp to Lieutenant-General Sir Frederick Adam in the Ionian Isles (1827–30), then as military secretary to the governor- and commander-in-chief of British North America, Lieutenant-General Lord Aylmer, until 1832. He purchased his majority in the 34th (9 May 1834), and similarly became lieutenant-colonel (10 February 1838). While commanding his regiment in Canada, he introduced an evening meal for the men and opened a regimental canteen, innovations later adopted throughout the army. On 31 January 1838 Airey married his cousin the Hon. Harriett Mary Everard, third daughter of his maternal uncle, James Talbot, third Lord Talbot of Malahide, and his wife, Anne Sarah, *née* Rodbard. He relinquished command of the 34th to go on half pay on 13 February 1847. Probably at this time, and possibly after a short spell at the Horse Guards in London, at the request of his uncle Colonel the Hon. Thomas Talbot, who had no heir for his extensive estate there, Airey settled his family in the 'backwoods' of Ontario, but found the life 'not to his taste' (Wolseley, 2.244).

Airey returned to full-time service at the Horse Guards on 1 February 1851 as assistant adjutant-general, then as deputy quartermaster-general. Promoted colonel (11 November 1851), he was appointed military secretary to the commander-in-chief, Lieutenant-General Lord Hardinge, the following year. Offered a post on Lieutenant-General Lord Raglan's staff at the outset of the Crimean expedition in the spring of 1854, he opted instead for command of a brigade in the light division. Raglan recorded that, when Airey visited him in Bulgaria during June 1854, he was 'quite well but the air and the sun have made sad havoc with his complexion and he is very, very grey' (Sweetman, 199). Major-General Lord Ros fell ill shortly before the troops landed in the Crimea, so on 1 September 1854 Brigadier-General Airey was appointed quartermaster-general at Raglan's headquarters, with responsibility for 'the quartering, encamping, marching, embarking and disembarking of troops', together with the enforcement of camp regulations, production of maps and surveys, and gathering information about enemy troop deployments and intentions (Airey, 32). During the skirmish at the Bulganek River on 19 September 1854 and the battle of the Alma the next day, in accordance with accepted practice, he issued orders on Raglan's behalf. As the commander and his staff rode east of Sevastopol on 25 September during the allied flank march towards Balaklava, Airey's quick thinking prevented Raglan from stumbling into a Russian force marching out of the city. Once the British and French armies took possession of upland to the south of Sevastopol, Airey favoured an immediate assault, fearing (correctly, as it transpired) that otherwise they would be stranded on exposed heights for the winter. Following Raglan's instructions, he wrote out the order which led to the fateful charge of the light brigade on 25 October 1854, but unfortunately in the heat of battle kept no duplicate. Subsequently, he had to request a copy from Lieutenant-General Lord Lucan, the cavalry division's commander, to whom the order was addressed and who strongly resented implications that he was at fault. In writing and in person Airey attempted to placate Lucan, reputedly arguing that 'it is nothing to Chillianwallah' (Woodham-Smith, 269), a disaster in India five years previously caused by misinterpretation of an order to the cavalry. During the battle of Inkerman on 5 November 1854 and several actions in co-operation with the French against the fortifications of Sevastopol in the early months of 1855, Airey issued orders on Raglan's authority, and he frequently attended allied planning conferences as British representative. After a storm on 14 November 1854 destroyed crucial supplies and equipment, the British commander commended Airey for his 'unceasing energy and indefatigable exertions' to make good the deficiencies (Hibbert, 216). To Raglan's daughter Charlotte in April 1855, however, Airey admitted strain: 'My eyes are almost out—very dim indeed … I am really as weak as an old cat' (Sweetman, 302). Two months earlier

Raglan had praised Airey's devotion to duty when 'suffering under severe illness … caught on a wet and tempestuous night' (Hibbert, 255).

Airey was promoted major-general on 12 December 1854, and local lieutenant-general on 30 July 1855. In press and parliament, however, he was attacked for doing nothing to ease the sufferings of men and horses before Sevastopol during the bitter winter of 1854–5, and his removal from office demanded. Raglan, to whom Airey in turn was fiercely loyal, defended him by emphasizing that provision of food and forage was the exclusive province of the civilian commissariat, over which his quartermaster-general had no control: 'I consider his services invaluable' (Hibbert, 232). Airey was at Raglan's bedside when he died on 28 June 1855, and may have been the last to speak to him before he lapsed into unconsciousness. Raglan's successor in command, Lieutenant-General Sir James Simpson, declared Airey 'very much vilified … nor do I have any fault to find' with him (Sweetman, 300). Airey left the Crimea in November 1855 at his own request, subsequently being made a member of the Légion d'honneur (third class), and receiving the military order of Savoy (first class) and the Mejidiye (second class). A financial award of £100 per annum for 'distinguished services' in the Crimea dated from 23 October 1854, and he was appointed KCB on 5 July 1855.

On 26 December 1855 Airey went back to the Horse Guards as quartermaster-general and swiftly faced 'blame … inferentially cast upon me' (Airey, 1) in the second of two reports (dated 1 January 1856) from Sir John McNeill and Colonel Sir Alexander Tulloch, who had been sent out to investigate allegations of incompetence in the provision of supplies and transport in the Crimea. Airey and others 'animadverted upon' (ibid., viii) demanded an inquiry, and a board of general officers under Lord Seaton consequently met at Chelsea Hospital in May 1856. Before it, Airey challenged the competence of authors who erroneously believed 'the functions of my department extended to almost every kind of business connected with the army administration' (ibid., 34) and the validity of conclusions 'obtained by collating numerous intricate accounts and statements, without the advantage of oral explanation by the persons concerned' (ibid., 24). Taking each allegation in turn, he demonstrated either its dubious foundation or its irrelevance to his department. The board exonerated him, though embittered critics denounced the findings as a whitewash. Privately, Airey dismissed McNeill and Tulloch as 'a damned doctor and a colonel who had never been under any hotter fire than that of his own office fire in London' (Wolseley, 2.240).

Airey remained at the Horse Guards as quartermaster-general until 1 November 1865, then went to Gibraltar as governor and commander-in-chief for five years. Meanwhile, he had advanced to substantive lieutenant-general (14 October 1862), and been appointed GCB in March 1867 and colonel of the 17th foot (20 July 1860), moving to the 7th foot in the same capacity (1 May 1868). He returned to the Horse Guards as adjutant-general from 1 October 1870 to 1 November 1876, was promoted general on 9 April 1871, and on 29 October 1876 created Baron Airey of Killingworth, Northumberland, on retirement from office. Three years later he presided over a committee on the operation of the short-service system, recently introduced. Its report, presented in 1880, reflected Airey's military conservatism by recommending a minimum eight years with the colours, which would have undermined the new arrangement. As colonel of the 7th foot Airey also strongly opposed replacement of numerical titles for regiments by geographical designations. Airey died on 14 September 1881 at The Grange, Great Bookham, Leatherhead, Surrey, home of Lieutenant-General Sir Garnet Wolseley, survived by his daughter Katherine Margaret, wife of Sir George Cotterell. Airey and his wife, who died on 28 July 1881, were buried in Kensal Green cemetery, London; his title became extinct.

William Howard Russell, the war correspondent, describing Airey's frequent visits to the camps, trenches, and defence works in the Crimea during April 1855, noted that his 'presence and direction infused an amount of energy' into those around (Bentley, 177). Wolseley, who joined Airey's department in the Crimea, later served under him at the Horse Guards, and became a personal friend, believed him 'the wisest and ablest soldier it was ever my lot to do business with … thoroughly educated in the science, as well as conversant with the practice of his profession … cool, collected, never excited' (Wolseley, 2.242–3). He also referred to his 'courtly and reserved dignity … his old-world and stately manners' (ibid., 2.242) coupled with a self-deprecating sense of humour. Professionally, Airey demanded high standards; and, once orders had been delivered, expected officers to show initiative in carrying them out.   JOHN SWEETMAN

Sources Army List · Viscount Wolseley [G. Wolseley], *The story of a soldier's life*, 2 vols. (1903) · R. Airey, *Opening address before the board of general officers assembled at the Royal Hospital Chelsea* (1856) · C. Hibbert, *The destruction of Lord Raglan* [1961] · C. Woodham-Smith, *The reason why* (1957) · J. Sweetman, *Raglan: from the Peninsula to the Crimea* (1993) · D. Sutherland, *Tried and valiant: the history of the border regiment, 1702–1959* (1972) · Burke, *Peerage* (1887) · N. Bentley, ed., *Russell's despatches from the Crimea, 1854–1856* (1966) · GEC, *Peerage* · cadet registers, Royal Military College, Sandhurst · M. Adkin, *The charge: why the Light Brigade was lost* (1996) · M. Foss, *The royal fusiliers* (1967) · E. A. H. Webb, *A history of the services of the 17th (the Leicestershire regiment)* (1912) · Fortescue, *Brit. army*, vol. 13 · d. cert. · *CGPLA Eng. & Wales* (1881)
Archives Herefs. RO, corresp. and papers · University of Western Ontario, London, Ontario, corresp. and papers relating to Canada | BL, corresp. with Sir Austen Layard, Add. MSS 38997–38998 · BL, corresp. with Lord Strathnairn, Add. MS 42805 · Bodl. Oxf., corresp. with Talbot family de Malahide · CUL, letters to Lord Hardinge relating to Crimean War · NAM, corresp. with Lord Raglan · NL Scot., corresp. with Sir George Brown
Likenesses oils, *c*.1870, The Convent, Gibraltar · Lock & Whitfield, woodburytype, NPG; repro. in T. Cooper, *Men of mark: a gallery of contemporary portraits* (1878) [*see illus.*] · photograph (after portrait), IWM
Wealth at death £136,630 16*s*. 10*d*.: resworn probate, June 1882, *CGPLA Eng. & Wales* (1881)

Airlie. For this title name *see* Ogilvy, James, first earl of Airlie (1586–1666); Ogilvy, James, second earl of Airlie (1611–1704); Ogilvy, David, styled sixth earl of Airlie (1725–

1803); Ogilvy, Mabell Frances Elizabeth, countess of Airlie (1866–1956).

Airmyn [Ayreminne], **Richard** (*c*.1290–1340), administrator, came of a family that derived its name from the village of Airmyn on the River Aire in Yorkshire. Richard seems to have been a son of Adam and Matilda Airmyn and a younger brother of William *Airmyn (d. 1336), bishop of Norwich, although in his episcopal register the latter does not address him as such. On the other hand, Master Adam Airmyn, rector of Gargrave, later archdeacon of Norfolk, is regularly addressed as *carissime frater*. All three were trained as chancery clerks and both Richard and Adam owed much to the patronage of William, and in Richard's case to that of Robert Baldock (d. 1327). Richard was a clerk of the privy seal from about 1315 until 1323. Eventually he received higher wages than his colleagues, suggesting that he may have become chief clerk. In October 1318, with William Airmyn, he attended the important reforming parliament at York which confirmed the articles drawn up by Lancaster's supporters at Leake the previous August. According to the Pauline annalist William and his brother, presumably Richard, were captured by the Scots at Myton in Swaledale in 1319, a heavy ransom being paid for their release. Richard succeeded William as keeper of the rolls of chancery in 1324, an office he retained for a year. When in 1323–4 the temporalities of Winchester diocese were withheld from John Stratford (d. 1348), Richard Airmyn was appointed one of the administrators. During November and December 1324, owing to Chancellor Baldock's absence, he acted as a temporary keeper of the great seal.

Following William Airmyn's acceptance of provision to Norwich in 1325, Richard became involved in diocesan administration. He was appointed vicar-general of the diocese from Paris (20 September 1325) and shortly thereafter was deputed with his brother Adam to administer oaths of canonical obedience. At the time he held the valuable Yorkshire rectory of Kirk Ella. Such duties did not detain him long, for the following year he was succeeded as vicar-general by Adam. Edward II's growing hostility to William now affected Richard's career, and in March 1326 royal writs were issued for his and Adam's pursuit and arrest. It has been suggested that they took refuge on the continent and returned with Queen Isabella. All that is known for certain is that on 14 October 1326—Bishop William having returned to Norwich—Adam was reappointed vicar-general.

The first keeper of the privy seal in the reign of Edward III, Richard Airmyn held office from 1 March 1327 until the following 18 February. In 1327 he was made keeper for life of the Domus Conversorum (house of converts)—a domicile for converted Jews in Chancery Lane, probably already used for the storage of chancery records. He surrendered the office in 1339. But Isabella's irritation with Bishop Airmyn, on account of his alleged responsibility for the oath of homage performed to the French king by the future Edward III in 1325, may have damaged Richard's prospects, for he did not hold high office again.

His administrative career nevertheless brought ecclesiastical rewards. At Edward II's request he was granted (March 1320) an annual pension of £5 from Christ Church, Canterbury. The royal grant of a Lichfield prebend in 1328 proved abortive, but an expectative grace of 23 March in that year enabled him to secure collation to the chancellorship of Salisbury Cathedral (16 July 1329), a dignity held until his death, between 3 April and 9 May 1340. He also held prebends in York (from 1316), Chichester, and Lincoln, in addition to a prebendal portion in the royal chapel of Wimborne.

ROY MARTIN HAINES

Sources register of Bishop William Ayrmyn, Norfolk RO, Reg. 1/2 · notarial instrument, Norfolk RO, episcopal charters Box 1, no. 1228 [attesting appointment of Richard and Adam Airmyn to receive oaths of canonical obedience] · Historia Roffensis, BL, MS Cotton Faustina B.v., fols. 44v–45r, 55v · Chancery records · CEPR letters, vol. 2 · W. Stubbs, ed., 'Annales Paulini', Chronicles of the reigns of Edward I and Edward II, 1, Rolls Series, 76 (1882), 253–370 · J. C. Davies, The baronial opposition to Edward II (1918) · Tout, Admin. hist., vols. 2–3, 5–6 · J. L. Grassi, 'Royal clerks from the archdiocese of York in the fourteenth century', Northern History, 5 (1970), 12–33 · J. L. Grassi, 'William Airmyn and the bishopric of Norwich', EngHR, 70 (1955), 550–61 · Hemingby's register, ed. H. M. Chew, Wiltshire Archaeological and Natural History Society, Records Branch, 18 (1963) · R. M. Haines, The church and politics in fourteenth-century England: the career of Adam Orleton, c. 1275–1345, Cambridge Studies in Medieval Life and Thought, 3rd ser., 10 (1978) · J. R. Wright, The church and the English crown, 1305–1334: a study based on the register of Archbishop Walter Reynolds (1980) · Fasti Angl., 1300–1541, [Lincoln; Salisbury; York; Chichester; Coventry] · Fasti Angl., 1300–1541, [Coventry] · Fasti Angl., 1300–1541, [Chichester] · Fasti Angl., 1300–1541, [York] · Fasti Angl., 1300–1541, [Salisbury]

Airmyn [Ayreminne], **William** (d. 1336), administrator and bishop of Norwich, was the son of Adam and Matilda Airmyn, and probably came from the hamlet of Airmyn, near Selby, in Yorkshire, one of a large group of men from that region to obtain prominence in government service. First recorded as an attorney in chancery in April 1300, he obtained royal presentation to benefices in July 1304 and October 1306, and a royal gift of timber through the agency of Walter Langton in June 1307. He was proctor for St Augustine's, Canterbury, at the Carlisle parliament of January 1307. In Edward II's reign, especially after the appointment of Walter Reynolds as chancellor in 1310, Airmyn became one of those most responsible for the routine work of chancery. A steady stream of ecclesiastical patronage followed, including canonries in six cathedrals. In 1312 he spent six months at the papal curia on royal business, and was granted a papal dispensation at the king's request in October. In 1316 he was specially deputed to draw up the parliament roll of the Lincoln parliament. Distinguished by its being a chronological record of parliamentary proceedings, this set a pattern that was taken up again in the 1330s. In August 1316 he succeeded his fellow Yorkshireman, Adam Osgodby, as keeper of the rolls of chancery and of the house of converts, and in later years was variously described as vice cancellaries, and as the king's special clerk and secretary of the chancery. In May 1317 he and two royal justices were charged with the partition of the Gloucester inheritance. In September 1319 he and his brother Richard *Airmyn (d. 1340) were captured

by the Scots at the battle of Myton; they obtained their release with a ransom of 2000 marks. In March 1321 he was one of those who negotiated a truce with the Scots. His administrative expertise led V. H. Galbraith to suggest that he is the author of the Modus tenendi parliamentum, which may have been written at this time.

In February 1322 the king warmly commended Airmyn to the pope, while urging that the keeper of the privy seal, Robert Baldock, be promoted to the next available bishopric. Airmyn was one of those commissioned to negotiate a truce with Robert I in May 1323. In May 1324 he resigned his post as keeper of the rolls of chancery to his brother, Richard, and became keeper of the privy seal, an office he held until early 1325. On 7 January 1325 Airmyn was elected bishop of Carlisle, with support from both Edward II and Queen Isabella. The election was set aside by the papal provision of John Ross, but the pope promised to promote Airmyn in due course. Accordingly, on 19 July 1325, the day after hearing of the vacancy at Norwich, the pope provided Airmyn to that bishopric. The king, however, having determined upon the appointment of Baldock, now chancellor, angrily sequestered Airmyn's temporalities. Airmyn was accused of having obtained the see through the influence of Queen Isabella and her brother, the French king Charles IV. He was the more vulnerable to this charge in that he had been one of the envoys who had secured the terms of 31 May 1325 to end the War of St Sardos, terms viewed unfavourably with hindsight, although Edward had himself ratified the treaty in June 1325. Airmyn secured papal help in seeking to assuage the king's wrath. He had returned to England by December 1325 but did not respond to royal summonses in early 1326. The arrest of two of his brothers was ordered in March, and he soon fled abroad.

Airmyn supported the queen in her invasion in September 1326, and was with her at Bristol when Prince Edward was proclaimed custos of the realm. He was given charge of the great seal from 30 November until Hotham's appointment as chancellor on 28 January 1327. His temporalities were restored in early December 1326, and two months later he recovered the issues which had been confiscated between December 1325 and November 1326. From 1327 to 1335 Airmyn was prominent in diplomacy. He was one of those responsible for the settlement with France in March 1327, and for the peace with Scotland in March 1328. He played a large role in 1331 in negotiating the terms of Edward III's homage to Philippe VI and in the inconclusive process of Agen, and subsequently helped arrange the marriage of the king's sister, Eleanor, to Reginald (II), count of Gueldres, which took place in 1332. From 1 April 1331 to 29 March 1332 he held office as treasurer. His personal wealth, partly derived from property concentrated in Durham, Yorkshire, and Lincolnshire, must have been great, and he was able to advance the king £1000 for the Scottish wars in November 1334. He died at his house in Charing, London, on 27 March 1336, and was buried in Norwich Cathedral.

M. C. BUCK

Sources Chancery records · J. L. Grassi, 'William Airmyn and the bishopric of Norwich', EngHR, 70 (1955), 550–61 · Fasti Angl., 1300–

1541 • V. H. Galbraith, 'The *Modus tenendi parliamentum*', *Journal of the Warburg and Courtauld Institutes*, 16 (1953), 81–99 • E. Deprez, *Les préliminaires de la Guerre de Cent Ans* (1902) • J. L. Grassi, 'Royal clerks from the archdiocese of York in the fourteenth century', *Northern History*, 5 (1970), 12–33 • F. Blomefield and C. Parkin, *An essay towards a topographical history of the county of Norfolk*, 5 vols. (1739–75) • *CEPR letters*, vol. 2 • [R. E. Latham], ed., *Calendar of memoranda rolls (exchequer) …: Michaelmas 1326 – Michaelmas 1327*, PRO (1968) • *The liber epistolaris of Richard de Bury*, ed. N. Denholm-Young, Roxburghe Club (1950) • Historia Roffensis, BL, MS Cotton Faustina B.v • *RotP* • H. R. Luard, ed., *Flores historiarum*, 3 vols., Rolls Series, 95 (1890) • W. Stubbs, ed., *Chronicles of the reigns of Edward I and Edward II*, 2 vols., Rolls Series, 76 (1882–3)
Archives Norfolk RO, episcopal register

Airth. For this title name *see* Graham, William, first earl of Airth and seventh earl of Menteith (1591–1661).

Airy, Sir George Biddell (1801–1892), astronomer, was born at Alnwick, Northumberland, on 27 July 1801, the eldest of the four children of William Airy (1749–1827), of Luddington in Lincolnshire. His mother, Ann Biddell (*d.* 1841), a woman of strong character and natural abilities, was the daughter of a well-to-do farmer from near Bury St Edmunds, Suffolk. The Airys were an old family claiming descent from Thomas Ayray (*fl. c.*1350), but which had fallen on hard times by the eighteenth century. William Airy was a man of extraordinary gifts, and memory, who had risen from being a farm labourer to collector of excise in Northumberland, whence he was transferred to Hereford in 1802, and to Essex in 1810. Three years later he lost his appointment and lapsed into poverty. These events deeply influenced his son, and it is likely that the concern with public accountability which was such a trait in the latter's career stemmed from it.

When he was ten years old Airy took first place in Byatt Walker's school at Colchester. From 1812 he spent his holidays at Playford, near Ipswich, with his uncle Arthur Biddell, a farmer and valuer, whose influence on his career proved decisive. In Biddell's library he was able to study optics, chemistry, and mechanics, and he met there Thomas Clarkson, Bernard Barton, William Cubitt, and Robert and James Ransome. From 1814 to 1819 Airy attended the grammar school at Colchester, where he was noted for his memory, repeating at one examination 1394 lines of Latin verse; in his teens he garnered much miscellaneous information from his father's books. On Clarkson's advice he was sent to Cambridge, and entered as a sizar of Trinity College in October 1819. In 1822 he took a scholarship, and in 1823 graduated as senior wrangler and first Smith's prizeman. On his election to a fellowship of his college in October 1824 he became assistant mathematical tutor. He delivered lectures, took pupils, and pursued original scientific investigation.

Teaching at Cambridge Airy's *Mathematical Tracts on Physical Astronomy* was published in 1826, and it immediately became a textbook in the university. An essay on the wave theory of light was appended to the second edition in 1831. For his various optical researches, chiefly contained in papers laid before the Cambridge Philosophical Society, Airy received in 1831 the Copley medal from the Royal

Sir George Biddell Airy (1801–1892), by Maull & Polyblank, *c.*1864

Society. He was admitted to membership of the Astronomical and Geological societies respectively in 1828 and 1829, and was awarded in 1833 the gold medal of the former body for his detection of the 'long inequality' in the orbits of Venus and the earth, communicated to the Royal Society on 24 November 1831. The Lalande prize followed in 1834, and on 9 January 1835 Airy was elected a correspondent of the Académie Royale des Sciences. But he was not elected FRS until 21 January 1836 (after becoming astronomer royal); he was then immediately taken on to the council. It is hard to explain his long-delayed election to the Royal Society, for he already enjoyed an international scientific reputation and had many close friends who were fellows. It is likely that the high cost of fellowship (£50) was the main obstacle, for Airy was always fastidious about money and perceived himself as a relatively poor man.

In the winter of 1823–4 Airy stayed in London with James South, met Sir Humphry Davy and John Herschel, and had his first experience of practical astronomy at South's large private observatory at Blackman Street, Southwark. During a walking tour in Derbyshire in July 1824 he proposed, after two days' acquaintance, to Richarda (1804–1875), the eldest daughter of the Revd Richard Smith, a former fellow of Trinity and incumbent of Edensor, near Chatsworth. Richarda was a great beauty, and Airy later recorded: 'Our eyes met … and my fate was sealed … I felt irresistibly that we must be united' ('Family history of G. B. Airy', Enid Airy MSS, 41). He was gently refused, pending the improvement of his permanent financial prospects. Thenceforth he concentrated his efforts upon securing a position in life and an income. In 1825 and 1826 he led reading parties to Keswick, Swansea, and Orléans, usually at a fee of about £42 per student; on the first occasion he saw much of the poets Southey and Wordsworth, and on the second made the acquaintance in Paris of Laplace, Arago, Pouillet, and Bouvard.

Chairs at Cambridge On 7 December 1826 Airy was elected Lucasian professor of mathematics at Cambridge, but the emoluments of the office—£99 per annum, with £100 as *ex officio* member of the board of longitude—only slightly exceeded those of his relinquished college tutorship. Airy was anxious to obtain a chair in so far as it offered release from his bachelor fellowship, with the prospect of making a sufficient income to marry. He renewed the prestige of the Lucasian chair by his ardour for the promotion of experimental physics in the university. In his lectures on light he first drew attention to the defect of vision subsequently called 'astigmatism', from which he personally suffered. As a deeply practical man, Airy went on to develop an early form of spectacles with which to correct this condition. A trip to Dublin in 1827 in quest of the vacant post of astronomer royal in Ireland was fruitless. But on 6 February 1828, and after an adroit act of brinkmanship with the Cambridge University senate, he succeeded Robert Woodhouse as Plumian professor of astronomy and director of the newly established Cambridge University observatory, with the salary increased from £300 to £500 per annum. He now had an income and a residence that was sufficient to persuade Revd Smith of his ability to maintain his daughter, and Airy married Richarda Smith on 24 March 1830. At the Cambridge observatory he introduced an improved system of meridian observations, afterwards continued at Greenwich and partially adopted abroad, and set the example of thoroughly reducing them before publication.

In addition to superintending the erection of the meridian instruments at Cambridge, Airy devised the equatorial mount for the Cauchoix 12 inch object glass, which was presented in 1833 to the observatory by the duke of Northumberland—the famous Northumberland refractor. In February 1835 Sir Robert Peel offered Airy a civil-list pension of £300 a year, which, by his request, was settled on his wife. And on 18 June that year he accepted the post of astronomer royal, for which Lord Melbourne designated him in succession to John Pond, after much negotiation. Airy insisted that the salary should be increased from £600 to £800 per annum.

Astronomer royal Airy's tenure of the office of astronomer royal lasted forty-six years, and was marked by extraordinary energy. Although he bargained hard for his salaries, he gave total and devoted service in return, seeing himself as a thoroughly professional scientist. He completely re-equipped the Royal Greenwich Observatory with instruments designed by himself. The erection in 1847 of an altazimuth instrument for observing the position of the moon in every part of the sky proved of great importance for the correction of lunar tables. A new meridian transit circle of unprecedented optical power and mechanical stability was mounted in 1851, and a reflex zenith tube replaced Troughton's zenith sector in the same year.

Airy saw the 'staple and standard' work of the Greenwich observatory as the construction of critically accurate tables and maps of stellar and planetary positions. These tables, recorded to fractions of a single second of arc, could then be used by the Royal Navy and by other scientific bodies involved in navigation or astronomical research. But by 1859 other branches of astronomy, requiring great telescopic power rather than just positional measurement, were becoming important in international astronomy, and in that year Airy inaugurated the installation of a 13 inch aperture equatorial refracting telescope, with optics by Merz of Munich, to give Greenwich an enhanced capacity in physical astronomy. While Airy believed that 'by both reason and tradition' Greenwich was a meridian observatory, he was assiduous in keeping up to date. In 1838 he created at Greenwich a magnetic and meteorological department, where from 1848 he employed Brooke's system of photographic registration, as superior to the earlier and immensely tedious method of manual recording. From 1854 the meridian transit of stars was recorded electrically, thereby greatly reducing the personal errors of the individual astronomers who made the observations, and from the same time the observatory began to send electrical signals down the commercial telegraph network to broadcast Greenwich mean time signals across Britain. Spectroscopic observations were organized in 1868, and the prismatic mapping of solar prominences began in 1874. The Kew photoheliograph began a daily record of sunspots in 1873. One of Airy's abiding precepts was that an astronomical observation that had not been mathematically reduced was useless, and when he came into office at Greenwich he resolved to reduce and publish the backlog of outstanding lunar and planetary observations made at the observatory between 1750 and 1830. For this he received the gold medal of the Royal Astronomical Society in 1846 and a testimonial in 1848. The resulting body of published data would provide an invaluable source for researches into celestial mechanics.

Expeditions Airy observed the total solar eclipse of 8 July 1842 from Mount Superga, near Turin, and it was this eclipse which provided astronomers with the decisive confirmation of the existence of the solar prominences. Airy also observed the total eclipse of 28 July 1851 from Göteborg in Sweden. He then visited Uppsala, was received in audience by King Oscar at Stockholm, and on the return journey inspected the pumping engines at Haarlem. For the eclipse of 18 July 1860 in Spain he organized a cosmopolitan expedition, which he conveyed to Bilbao and Santander in the troopship *Himalaya*, placed at his disposal by the Admiralty.

In the autumn of 1854 Airy superintended an elaborate series of pendulum experiments for the purpose of measuring the increase of gravity with descent below the earth's surface. Similar attempts made by him in the Dolcoath mine, Cornwall, in 1826 and 1828, with the co-operation of William Whewell and Richard Sheepshanks, had been accidentally frustrated. He now renewed them in the Harton colliery, near South Shields, at a depth of 1260 feet. Although his value for 'G', the gravitational constant, was excessive, Airy used telegraphic apparatus to obtain a consistent time signal between the pendulums at the top and bottom of Harton pit.

The preparations for the observations of the transit of Venus in 1874 were laborious; Airy had control of the various British expeditions, and he provided twenty-three telescopes and undertook the preliminary work at the Greenwich observatory and the subsequent reduction of the vast mass of collected data. The volume embodying them was issued in 1881.

Greenwich meridian Airy was always assiduous in maintaining the primacy of the Greenwich observatory in matters pertaining to navigation. In 1838, the same year as he set up a magnetic department, he commenced a series of experiments to study the influence of the hulls of iron ships upon their compasses, and the system of correction which he devised remained in use for decades thereafter. He was keen to determine the longitudes of as many places as possible with reference to the Greenwich meridian. At first he used chronometers, and by the mid-1850s was employing the instantaneous signals of the electric telegraph to relate to Greenwich not only important maritime places in the British Isles, such as Valentia in western Ireland, but the state observatories of Paris, Brussels, Vienna, Washington, and elsewhere. The primacy of the Greenwich meridian which developed from Airy's astronomical and geodetic work played a major part in its being accepted in 1884 as the international zero longitude and prime meridian of the world.

Adviser to government His extraordinary industry and capacity for business enabled Airy to accomplish a wide range of official tasks. Indeed, he became something of a universal adviser to the government on matters involving physical science. These included the weights and measures commission (1838–42), of which he was chairman, and the tidal harbours commission. He was actively involved in the improvement of lighthouses, and advised and sometimes trained the officers who surveyed the Maine, New Brunswick, and Oregon boundaries. In 1845 his work on the railway gauge commission helped to provide the evidence from which parliament decided upon the 'standard gauge' of 4 feet 8½ inches for future British railways. He settled the provisions for the sale of gas, reduced the tidal observations of Ireland and India, and was consulted on the launch of the steamship *Great Eastern*, Charles Babbage's calculating engine, the smoky chimneys of the palace of Westminster, the design of Big Ben, and the laying of the Atlantic telegraph cable. Airy's work on the stresses within beams still has a major place in modern civil engineering design, and his paper on suspension bridges to the Institution of Civil Engineers in 1867 gained him the Telford medal. One of his few failures came in

1850, when he was refused the superintendentship of the *Nautical Almanac*, in spite of being 'willing to take it at a low rate for the addition to my salary' of astronomer royal. The job went to his former assistant, John Russell Hind. Airy was constantly active as a lecturer and an author. His published works, including books, official reports, major research papers, authoritative encyclopaedia chapters, and high-quality articles for *The Athenaeum* and other magazines, exceeded 500 items.

Honours and awards Airy was president of the Royal Society during 1872–3. He presided over the Royal Astronomical Society for four terms, and over the British Association at its Ipswich meeting in 1851. He became a member of the Cambridge Philosophical Society in 1823, and later of the Institution of Civil Engineers, of the Royal Society of Edinburgh, of the Royal Irish Academy, and of several foreign scientific bodies. On 18 March 1872 he succeeded Sir John Herschel as one of eight foreign members of the French Institute. In 1875 he was proud to be presented with the freedom of the City of London. He was created a DCL of Oxford on 20 June 1844 (though he refused to pay the fee of 6 guineas) and an LLD of Cambridge (1862) and Edinburgh, and was elected honorary fellow of Trinity College, Cambridge. Tsar Nicholas sent him a gold medal specially struck, and the foreign honours conferred upon him included the order of merit of Prussia, the Légion d'honneur, the North Star of Sweden, the Dannebrog, and the Rose of Brazil. On 17 May 1871 he was appointed companion of the Bath, and a year later (17 June 1872) was promoted to knight commander. But these honours came only after Airy had turned down three previous offers of a knighthood, in 1835 (on the grounds that he was too poor), in 1847, and in 1863 (because a £30 fee was involved).

Airy was an indefatigable traveller. In 1829 he inspected the observatories of Turin, Milan, Bologna, and Florence. In 1835 he examined the new 13.3 inch refractor at Markree, co. Sligo, and in 1848 elaborately tested the great Birr Castle reflector, also in Ireland. In 1846 he visited Hans Pieter Hansen at Gotha, Johann Gauss at Göttingen, and Caroline Lucretia Herschel at Hanover; in 1847 he spent a month at Pulkovo, St Petersburg, with Otto Struve, and, returning by Berlin and Hamburg, saw Alexander von Humboldt, Johann Galle, Adolf Repsold, and Carl Rumker. He entered into correspondence with Jean J. U. Le Verrier in June 1846 about the still unseen planet Neptune, and on 9 July suggested to Professor James Challis at Cambridge a plan of search. It is unfortunate, however, that Airy became posterity's scapegoat for Britain's failure to discover Neptune in 1845 on the basis of John Couch Adams's calculations, a year before its actual discovery in Berlin using Le Verrier's co-ordinates. But it must not be forgotten that Adams failed to supply Airy with adequate data in 1845, and did not reply to Airy's letters requesting them.

Retirement Airy resigned the office of astronomer royal on 15 August 1881, and resided thereafter with his two unmarried daughters at the White House, Croom's Hill, close to Greenwich Park, and at Playford, where he had bought a cottage in 1845. His wife had died on 13 August

1875, after several years of illness following a stroke. On the lapse of her civil-list pension Airy's salary was augmented to £1200 per annum. His main desire in retirement was to complete the 'numerical lunar theory', upon which he had been engaged from 1872. Although it was printed in 1886, the work was soon after recognized by Airy to be seriously flawed, so 'that the equations are not satisfied'. He continued to enjoy excursions to Cumberland and Playford, but a fall on 11 November 1891 produced an internal injury necessitating a surgical operation, which he survived only a few days. He died at the White House on 2 January 1892, and was buried on 7 January alongside his wife and three deceased children in Playford churchyard. Six children survived him.

In appearance, Airy was of medium stature and, while not powerfully built, possessed great powers of endurance. Even his infirmities became subjects for investigation, however; in *Philosophical Transactions of the Royal Society* (1870) Airy and his son Hubert, a physician, wrote one of the clinically definitive papers on migraine. The image of Airy which has come down from his *Autobiography* (1896), and from the reminiscences of some of his contemporaries, is that of a stern workaholic. An acquaintance with Greenwich observatory archives and with private family papers, however, adds depth to this two-dimensional view. His love of poetry, literature, and landscape, and his sustained romantic devotion to his wife, Richarda, indicate a remarkable warmth. The formality of letters to colleagues and even friends contrasts very markedly with those that were intended for members of his family. Although he derived obvious professional satisfaction from the efficient running of the Greenwich observatory, he kept strict office hours, and preferred to devote the remaining time not to learned societies or to clubs, but to family activities.

ALLAN CHAPMAN

Sources G. B. Airy, *Autobiography of Sir George Biddell Airy*, ed. W. Airy (1896) • E. J. R. [E. J. Routh], *PRS*, 51 (1892), i–xii • H. H. T. [H. H. Turner], *Monthly Notices of the Royal Astronomical Society*, 52 (1891–2), 212–29 • *The Times* (5 Jan 1892) • *East Anglian Daily Times* (11 Jan 1892) • *Suffolk Chronicle* (9 Jan 1892) • *Daily Times* (5 Jan 1892) • *PICE*, 108 (1891–2), 391–4 • Airy MSS, CUL, Royal Greenwich Observatory papers, RGO6 • Enid Airy MSS, priv. coll. • Milne–Read MSS, priv. coll. • private information (2004) • d. cert.
Archives Birr Castle, Offaly, archives, letters to earls of Rosse • CUL, Royal Greenwich Observatory papers, corresp. and papers as astronomer royal, RGO6 • Inst. EE, archives, corresp. with Sir Francis Ronalds • LUL, corresp. relating to London University • MHS Oxf., letters to Baden Powell • NHM, biography with his MS notes • NMM, letters to Professor Sedgwick and his daughter • Pembroke College, Oxford, letters to Bartholomew Price • PRO, letters to Sir Edward Sabine • RS, corresp. with Sir John Herschel • RS, letters to Sir John Lubbock • Trinity Cam., corresp. with William Whewell • U. Cam., department of manuscripts and university archives, journals, diaries, and memoranda • U. Cam., Institute of Astronomy Library, corresp. and papers • U. Edin. L., corresp. with Sir Charles Lyell • U. Lpool L., letters • U. St Andr. L., corresp. with James Forbes • University of Exeter Library, Lockyer Observatory archives, letters to Sir Norman Lockyer • Wellcome L., corresp. | American Philosophical Society, Philadelphia, letters to Admiral W. H. Smyth • BL, letters to Charles Babbage, Add. MSS 37183–37186, 37194, 37196 • BL, letters to S. Grimaldi, Add. MS 34189 • BL, corresp. with Sir Robert Peel, Add. MSS 40414–40593, *passim* • Bodl.

Oxf., letters to Lord Arthur Charles Hervey • Bucks. RLSS, corresp. with John Lee • CUL, letters to Sir George Stokes • Mitchell L., Glas., Glasgow City Archives, letters to Archibald Smith • NL Wales, letters to Sir George Cornewall Lewis • priv. coll., Enid Airy MSS • priv. coll., Milne–Read MSS • PRO, corresp. with Lord Ellenborough, PRO 30/12 • Ransom HRC, corresp. with Sir John Herschel • RAS, letters to James Bosanquet • RAS, letters to James Glaisher • RAS, letters to Royal Astronomical Society • RAS, letters to Richard Sheepshanks • RGS, letters to Sir David Gill • Royal Institution of Great Britain, London, letters to John Tyndall, etc.
Likenesses J. Deville, plaster bust, 1823, Observatories Syndicate, Cambridge • J. Pardon, oils, 1833–4, Observatories Syndicate, Cambridge • portrait, c.1835, RS • T. H. Maguire, lithograph, 1852, BM, NPG • E. Edwards, photograph, 1860–69, NPG • G. B. Black, lithograph, 1864 (after unknown portrait), NPG • Maull & Polyblank, photograph, c.1864, NPG [*see illus.*] • Lock & Whitfield, woodburytype photograph, c.1877, NPG • W. T. Morgan & Co., group portrait, photograph, 1891, NPG • Morgan & Kidd, group portrait, photograph, c.1891–1892, NPG • Miss A. Airy, watercolour drawing (after J. Collier, 1884), RAS • F. Artus, lithograph, BM, NPG • Maull & Polyblank, carte-de-visite, NPG • W. T. Morgan & Co., group portrait, photograph, NPG • I. W. Slater, lithograph (after T. C. Wageman), BM • J. Watkins, carte-de-visite, NPG • photographs, CUL • pictures and photographs, priv. coll.
Wealth at death £27,713 9s. 9d.: probate, 5 March 1892, CGPLA Eng. & Wales

Aiscough [Ayscough], **William** (c.1395–1450), administrator and bishop of Salisbury, was the son of Robert Aiscough, of Potgrange, near Masham, Yorkshire, and brother of Robert, who became dean of the Chapel Royal. Ordained in 1415, he was master of arts by 1423 and doctor of theology by 1432, both probably of Cambridge. From 1429, as the court of Henry VI was increasingly the focus of his activities, he was presented to a number of benefices, including prebends of Lincoln Cathedral, the king's free chapel of Bridgworth, and St Stephen's Chapel, Westminster. His post of royal chaplain must have assisted him in his elevation, by papal provision, to the bishopric of Salisbury on 12 February 1438. He was consecrated on 20 July at Windsor. He subsequently became the king's confessor, an unprecedented post for one who was already a bishop: frequently in the royal presence, he may have been a principal source of edifying information for John Blacman's life of Henry VI. During the 1440s he loaned the king £1602 and was active in making arrangements for the twin royal foundations of Eton and King's College—he was one of the compilers of the latter's statutes. He provided prebends in his diocese for several servants of the royal household and made Adam Moleyns (d. 1450), another leading royal councillor, an archdeacon and canon at Salisbury in 1439. His unpublished register shows him to have concerned himself regularly with diocesan affairs and the maintenance of orthodoxy, a different picture from the one often painted of the courtier-bishop.

As a regular member of the royal council he was inevitably associated with some of the government's most sensitive policies: in 1441 he was involved in the arraignment of the duchess of Gloucester and her associates for witchcraft. He accompanied Suffolk on an embassy to France in 1444 'in the mater of pees', and the following year he officiated at the marriage of Henry VI and Margaret of Anjou at Titchfield Abbey, Hampshire. In 1447 he was implicated in the arrest of Humphrey, duke of Gloucester, and was one of those blamed by the people for the duke's suspicious death. His membership of the inner circle of royal advisers made him dangerously unpopular. In 1447 it was alleged that he had endangered the succession to the throne, by discouraging the king from having 'his sport' with Queen Margaret, and in January 1450 he was one of those whom a yeoman of Westminster had plotted to behead. He was threatened in a gloating poem on the death of Suffolk; '"Heu mei", saith Salisbury "this gothe to ferre forthe"' (Wright, 2.232), and in several of Cade's manifestos was among those roundly condemned as the king's evil councillors. This climate of hatred seems to have persuaded him to leave London for the apparent safety of his castle in Sherborne. On his way there his baggage was plundered and then, on 29 June, he was captured by a large group of local men while celebrating mass at the church of the Bonshommes, Edington, Wiltshire. He was dragged out onto a hill, hacked to death, and despoiled. In the following days his palace at Salisbury and several episcopal manors were ransacked. The goods taken were valued at 10,000 marks, 'as thay saide that knewe it' (*An English Chronicle*, 64). His death can be seen less as a manifestation of anti-clericalism or a protest against absenteeism than as a major incident in a series of provincial revolts that followed the Kentish rising of Cade. He also appears to have had, like his predecessors, an uneasy relationship with the civic authorities of Salisbury, who resented his assertion of ecclesiastical property rights. Leland records that he was buried at the Bonshommes but no memorial survives, nor does a will, but he gave two manuscripts to Eton and owned a copy of the *Sermones* of Richard Fitzralph.

MARGARET LUCILLE KEKEWICH

Sources J. M. George, 'The English episcopate and the crown, 1437–50', PhD diss., University of Columbia, 1976 · J. N. Hare, 'The Wiltshire risings of 1450: political and economic discontent in mid-fifteenth century England', *Southern History*, 4 (1982), 13–31 · T. Wright, ed., *Political poems and songs relating to English history*, 2, Rolls Series, 14 (1861), 232 · J. S. Davies, ed., *An English chronicle of the reigns of Richard II, Henry IV, Henry V, and Henry VI*, CS, 64 (1856) · R. A. Griffiths, *The reign of King Henry VI: the exercise of royal authority, 1422–1461* (1981) · R. Somerville, *History of the duchy of Lancaster, 1265–1603* (1953) · A. Steele, *The receipt of the exchequer, 1377–1485* (1954), 253 · A. C. Reeves, *Lancastrian Englishmen* (1981) · *Francisci Godwini primo Landavensis dein Herefordensis Episcopi De praesulibus Angliae commentarius*, ed. G. Richardson (1743) · J. E. Jackson, 'Edington monastery', *Wiltshire Archaeological and Natural History Magazine*, 20 (1882), 241–306 · G. L. Harriss, *Cardinal Beaufort: a study of Lancastrian ascendancy and decline* (1988) · Chancery records · Emden, *Cam.*, 28
Archives Wilts. & Swindon RO, register, MS D1/2/10
Likenesses miniature, repro. in register of William Ayscough, bishop of Salisbury, Wilts. & Swindon RO, D1/2/10, fol. 5*r*
Wealth at death estates and income of bishopric of Salisbury; plus (probably considerable) personal wealth; quite a lot of chattels pilfered by rebels soon after his murder

Aislabie, Benjamin (1774–1842), wine merchant and cricket administrator, was born on 14 January 1774 in Newington Green, Middlesex, the third son, and sixth and last child, of Rawson Aislabie, soap and wine merchant of Newington Green, and his wife, Frances Rayson, of

Benjamin Aislabie (1774–1842), by Henry Edward Dawe

Dunham, Nottinghamshire. He was a descendant of John Aislabie, a Yorkshire MP and chancellor of the exchequer at the time of the South Sea Bubble.

Educated at Eton College, Aislabie was a wealthy West India merchant with a well-established wine business in the Minories in London. Little is known about his professional life and he is remembered for his lifelong interest in cricket.

On 13 March 1798 Aislabie married Anne, eldest child of William Hodgson, merchant, of the City of London. They had twelve children, of whom only six daughters and one son survived infancy. In 1802 Aislabie joined the Marylebone Cricket Club at its Dorset Square venue. Thenceforth he played many games, not only for the MCC, but for a variety of sides. He was a notoriously bad player. Throughout his career of some forty years he barely averaged four runs an innings and took a total of eight wickets. A big, heavy man (probably 17 stone), he had a substitute, not only to run for him when batting, but also to field for him. None the less, such was his amiable nature that all welcomed him as a playing companion.

Aislabie's great contribution was as a cricket administrator. Cricket was somewhat unco-ordinated before the early nineteenth century; many fixtures were impromptu and piecemeal, despite the use of rather grandiose labels. In 1822, eight years after Thomas Lord had moved his famous turf to its last resting place at St John's Wood, Aislabie became the first secretary of the MCC, the first sign of any real formality of organization. The following year he was also made president. With the game tainted by gambling and violent disputes, Aislabie's popularity was instrumental in attracting and retaining members, and by the time of his death the membership of fewer than 200 had almost doubled. He organized matches, collected subscriptions, and became central to the MCC's task of developing a legislative and administrative framework for the game. He presided over the club, as cricket was transformed into a well-regulated, even quasi-religious, pastime and a symbol of 'muscular Christianity'; it was Aislabie who, in 1841, took the MCC team to Rugby for the match celebrated in *Tom Brown's School Days* by Thomas Hughes.

Aislabie lived for most of his life at Lee Place, Eltham, Kent, and at East Park Place, Regent's Park, London, where he died from a throat abscess on 2 June 1842.

ERIC MIDWINTER, *rev.* CHRISTINE CLARK

Sources Aislabie MSS · A. Cochrane, 'Mr Aislabie', *Country Life*, 89 (1941), 558 · H. C. Smith, 'The centenary of Benjamin Aislabie', *Country Life*, 91 (1942), 1095 · J. Ford, *Cricket: a social history, 1700–1835* (1972) · C. Brookes, *English cricket, the game and its players through the ages* (1978)

Archives priv. coll., MSS

Likenesses N. Freese, miniature, 1798, repro. in *Country Life* · T. Atkinson, silhouette, 1818, repro. in *Country Life* · bust, 1838, Marylebone Cricket Club, London, Lord's Pavilion · H. E. Dawe, mezzotint, NPG [*see illus.*] · H. E. Dawe, oils, Marylebone Cricket Club, London, Lord's Pavilion

Aislabie, John (1670–1742), politician, was born on 4 December 1670 and baptized three days later at Holy Trinity Church, Goodramgate, York. He was the fourth son of George Aislabie (1630?–1675), the principal registrar of the archiepiscopal court of York, and his second wife, Mary, the eldest daughter of Sir John Mallory of Studley Royal, near Ripon. His father was killed by Jonathan Jennings in a duel on 10 January 1675, after Jennings had called him 'the scum of the county' (Darwin, 263). He was educated at Mr Tomlinson's school in York and he then attended St John's College (1687) and Trinity Hall, Cambridge (1692). In 1693 the death of his elder brother, George, left him in possession of Studley Royal. On 2 June 1694 he married, with a portion of £5000, Anne (*d.* 1700), the daughter of Sir William Rawlinson of Hendon, Middlesex. They had one son and three daughters. Fortunately for his political ambitions, his wife was also the niece of the archbishop of York, John Sharp, and the interest of the church allied to that of his estate enabled him to secure election to parliament for Ripon in 1695.

No doubt because of his relationship to Archbishop Sharp, Aislabie was accounted a tory in politics, but his career was to develop in such a way as to defy consistent party labelling. He signed the Association in February 1696, but on 25 November he voted against the attainder of the Jacobite conspirator Sir John Fenwick. Tragedy struck in January 1700 when his wife and a daughter perished in a fire at his house in Red Lion Square, London, reportedly begun by a servant to conceal the theft of some jewels. His election as mayor of Ripon in 1702, while no doubt strengthening his political interest, unfortunately made him ineligible to stand for the constituency in the election of that year. Instead he made an agreement to represent Northallerton, while maintaining his interest

at Ripon through the judicious dispersal of gifts to the corporation. At the 1705 election, the minor inconvenience of the mayoralty having been overcome, he was returned as MP for Ripon. By now he was an active parliamentarian, particularly over matters of trade, but he was still difficult to pin down politically. Indeed, on two extant parliamentary analyses in 1708, one listed him as a whig and the other as a tory. Such a lack of rigid party loyalty was likely to find favour from Robert Harley when the latter came to power in 1710, and on 4 October Aislabie achieved office as an Admiralty lord. However, he was one of the first to express misgivings about the direction of the ministry's policies, particularly with regard to the peace negotiations with France and the attacks on the duke of Marlborough.

On 25 April 1713 Aislabie was licensed to marry Judith (1676–1738x40), the daughter of Sir Thomas Vernon, a London merchant and MP, and the widow of Dr Stephen Waller; they had no children. In the 1713 parliamentary session Aislabie opposed the commercial treaty with France, despite which he retained office until 9 April 1714. Freed from the shackles of his position in the 1714 session, he was soon one of those leading the attack on the ministry for its perceived ambivalent attitude to the Hanoverian succession. His move into overt opposition was very timely, coming as it did just a few months before Queen Anne's death in August 1714.

Following the change of ministry on the accession of George I, Aislabie received office in October as treasurer of the navy, a post he had coveted in 1710. Further honours followed, including appointment to the privy council on 12 July 1716 and elevation to the chancellorship of the exchequer on 20 March 1718. As chancellor he was a manager of ministerial business in the Commons, a post for which he was well suited, if Arthur Onslow's assessment of him as a man of 'good understanding, no ill-speaker in parliament, and very capable of business' (*Buckinghamshire MSS*, 510–11) can be trusted. However, Onslow added that, in his role as chancellor, 'although he understood the business of the revenue better than any other person then employed, he was of a very little weight in the House of Commons' (ibid.). Onslow's judgement may have reflected the fact that Aislabie's duties as chancellor included managing the legislation designed to reduce the national debt by grafting it on to the South Sea Company. Aislabie was involved in operating subscription lists and profited by the rise in the stock price. When the bubble burst his actions came under the close scrutiny of the Commons, and he was forced to resign on 23 January 1721. The report of the investigation into the South Sea Company came before the Commons on 8 March 1721. Aislabie's long defence of his conduct did not deflect the house from voting him guilty of 'most notorious, dangerous, and infamous corruption' in promoting the South Sea scheme and in profiting therefrom. He was duly expelled and ordered to be confined in the Tower. Although he defended himself before the Lords, his name was included in the legislation confiscating the estates of those deemed responsible for the bubble in order to compensate those who had lost out during the speculation. However, he was allowed to keep all the property he had possessed on 20 October 1718, namely £119,000 out of an estate estimated at £164,000.

Upon his release from the Tower, Aislabie retired to Studley Royal and the pursuits of a country gentleman, in particular the laying out of his gardens according to his own plans. He died on 18 June 1742 and was buried in the family chapel in Ripon Minster. He was succeeded by his son, William, who had replaced him at Ripon and continued to represent the borough for sixty years until his death in 1781.   STUART HANDLEY

Sources HoP, *Commons* · K. Darwin, 'John Aislabie (1670–1742)', *Yorkshire Archaeological Journal*, 37 (1948–51), 262–324 · J. R. Walbran, ed., *Memorials of the abbey of St Mary of Fountains*, 2, SurtS, 67 (1878) · *The manuscripts of the earl of Buckinghamshire, the earl of Lindsey … and James Round*, HMC, 38 (1895), 510–11 [Onslow MSS] · will, PRO, PROB 11/719, sig. 206 · will, PRO, PROB 11/702, sig. 129 [2nd wife's will] · IGI · *GM*, 1st ser., 12 (1742), 331

Archives W. Yorks. AS, Leeds, corresp.

Likenesses portrait, Ripon town hall · portrait, Studley Royal, near Ripon · portrait, repro. in M. Pettman, *National Portrait Gallery: complete illustrated catalogue, 1856–1679*, ed. K. K. Yung (1980), 6, 707

Aisner, Julienne (1900–1947). *See under* Women agents on active service in France (*act.* 1942–1945).

Aitchison, Sir Charles Umpherston (1832–1896), administrator in India, born in Edinburgh on 20 May 1832, was the son of Hugh Aitchison of that city, and his wife, Elizabeth, daughter of Charles Umpherston of Loanhead, near Edinburgh. He was educated at Edinburgh high school and at Edinburgh University, where he took the degree of MA on 23 April 1853. While a student at the university Aitchison attended the lectures of Sir William Hamilton on logic and metaphysics. He afterwards passed some time in Germany, where he studied the works of Fichte and attended the lectures of Tholuck at the University of Halle. In 1855 he passed fifth at the first competitive examination for the Indian Civil Service, and after spending a year in England in the study of law and oriental languages, he reached India on 26 September 1856. In March 1857 he was appointed an assistant in Hissar, a district of the North-Western Provinces, and in the following month was transferred to the Punjab, shortly after the outbreak of the mutiny, thereby escaping the massacre of Europeans which took place at Hissar on 29 May. His first station in his new province was Amritsar, and immediately on arrival he was employed under the orders of the deputy commissioner in carrying out measures to prevent the Jullundur rebels from crossing the Beas River. Shortly afterwards he was appointed personal assistant to the judicial commissioner, in which capacity he compiled *A Manual of the Criminal Law of the Panjab* (1860). While thus employed, he associated with Sir John Laird Mair Lawrence, by whose policy, especially on the central Asian question, and on British relations with Afghanistan, he was strongly influenced during the remainder of his life. In 1892 he contributed a memoir of Lord Lawrence to Sir William Hunter's Rulers of India series.

In 1859 he joined the secretariat of the government of India as under-secretary in the political department, and

served there until 1865. On 2 February 1863 he married Beatrice Lyell, daughter of James Cox of Clement Park, Forfarshire; they had at least one surviving daughter, Winifred. In 1865 he took up administrative work in the Punjab, at the suggestion of Sir John Lawrence, serving first as deputy commissioner and then as commissioner of Lahore. In 1868 he rejoined the secretariat as foreign secretary, and retained that appointment until 1878.

As secretary Aitchison was extremely industrious and thorough in his work. He exercised a marked influence on successive governors-general, who trusted him for advice. During the earlier part of his service in the Indian foreign office he commenced a compilation entitled *A Collection of Treaties, Engagements, and Sanads Relating to India and Neighbouring Countries*; the first volume appeared at Calcutta in 1862, and eleven volumes were issued by 1892; each treaty was prefaced by a detailed historical narrative. In 1875 he published a treatise entitled *The Native States of India*, with the leading cases illustrating the principles which sustained their relations with the British raj. He regarded with grave apprehension the measures which, carried out under the government of Lord Lytton, culminated in the Anglo-Afghan War of 1878–9.

Before the war broke out in 1878, he accepted the appointment of chief commissioner of British Burma. When holding that office he raised two questions of considerable importance. The first concerned the opium trade as it affected Burma. The second referred to the liaisons of certain English public servants with Burmese women. Neither of these questions was dealt with officially by Lytton's government; but with reference to the second the viceroy intimated semi-officially that he disapproved of a circular which Aitchison had issued to the deputy commissioners and assistant commissioners as mixing up morals with politics. After Aitchison's departure from the province both these questions were taken up by his successor, who received the support of Lord Ripon's government in dealing with them. The number of licensed opium shops was then reduced to one-third of those previously licensed, and the legal consumption of opium was reduced by two-fifths, involving a loss of revenue of 4 lakhs of rupees. On the other question, the principle of Aitchison's circular stopping the promotion of officers who maintained alliances with Burmese women was enforced.

In 1881 Aitchison left Burma and assumed the post of lieutenant-governor of the Punjab on 4 April 1882. His government there was very successful. He advocated the policy of the Indianization of the civil service. On this issue he upheld a more liberal approach than that proposed by Lord Ripon's government at the time of the Ilbert Bill controversy. He had intended to leave India for good when his lieutenant-governorship came to an end in 1887, but he returned for another nineteen months to lend his experience to Lord Dufferin's council on the issues following from the annexation of Upper Burma. During the latter part of his government of the Punjab he had discharged the additional duty of presiding over the public service commission which examined the increasingly controversial issue of Indian representation in the higher ranks of the imperial bureaucracy. He continued to perform this duty after joining the governor-general's council. He gave unremitting attention to this work, and ensured the production of a unanimous report. It recommended the cessation of the practice of appointing to the highest posts a handful of Indians who had not entered the competitive examinations held annually in London. At the same time the commission successfully argued for the creation of a less powerful and prestigious provincial civil service open to indigenous appointees.

Aitchison retired and finally left India in November 1888. Early the following year he settled in London, but subsequently moved to Oxford. In 1881 he was nominated KCSI and in 1882 CIE. He received the degree of LLD from the University of Edinburgh in 1877, and that of honorary MA from Oxford University in 1895.

Aitchison, an essentially religious man, was a consistent and warm supporter of Christian missions while in India, and after his retirement was an active member of the committee of the Church Missionary Society. He died at St Christopher's, 100 Banbury Road, Oxford, on 18 February 1896, and was survived by his wife and daughter.

A. J. ARBUTHNOT, *rev.* IAN TALBOT

Sources G. Smith, *Twelve Indian statesmen, 1849–75* (1898) · Y. B. Mathur, *British administration of Punjab* (1974) · P. H. M. van den Dungen, *The Punjab tradition: influence and authority in nineteenth-century India* (1972) · N. G. Barrier, 'The Punjab government and communal politics, 1870–1908', *Journal of Asian Studies*, 27 (1968), 523–40 · Zafur-ul-Islam and R. Jensen, 'Indian Muslims and the public services, 1871–1915', *Journal of the Asiatic Society of Pakistan*, 4 (1964), 85–93 · C. E. Buckland, *Dictionary of Indian biography* (1906) · I. Ali, *The Punjab under imperialism, 1885–1947* (1988) · I. Talbot, *Punjab and the raj, 1849–1947* (1988) · d. cert.
Archives BL OIOC, corresp. and papers, MS Eur. F 166 · BL OIOC, papers relating to relations with Indian states, MS Eur. D 708 | BL, corresp. with H. Bruce, Add. MSS 43997–43998 · BL OIOC, Clerk MSS · BL OIOC, Dunlop-Smith MSS · BL OIOC, corresp. with Sir Frederick Goldsmid, MS Eur. F 134, nos. 10, 11, 38 · BL OIOC, corresp. with Sir Alfred Lyall, MS Eur. F 132 · BL OIOC, Lytton MSS · BL OIOC, letters to Sir Lewis Pelly, MS Eur. F 126 · BL OIOC, letters to Sir E. B. Sladen, MS Eur. E 290 · CUL, corresp. with Lord Mayo
Wealth at death no value given: confirmation sealed in London, 20 April 1896, CGPLA Eng. & Wales

Craigie Mason Aitchison, Lord Aitchison (1882–1941), by Stanley Cursiter, 1937

Aitchison, Craigie Mason, Lord Aitchison (1882–1941), judge, was born at the manse, Erskine, Falkirk, on 26 January 1882, the second son of the Revd James Aitchison, minister of the United Presbyterian church, and his wife, Elizabeth Mason Craigie. He was educated at Falkirk high school and went with a scholarship to the University of Edinburgh, where he graduated MA in 1903. He was a Vans Dunlop scholar in logic and metaphysics, and Muirhead prizeman in civil law. In 1906 he graduated as LLB with distinction. He was called to the Scottish bar in 1907 and took silk in 1923. In 1919 he married Charlotte Forbes, daughter of James Jones JP, of Torwood Hall, Larbert, Stirlingshire; they had two sons.

In 1929 Aitchison was appointed lord advocate—the first socialist to hold that great office—and sworn of the privy council. In 1929 he entered parliament as Labour member for the Kilmarnock division of Ayrshire; he subsequently sat from 1931 as a National Labour member, and had a distinguished career in the House of Commons. In 1933 the degree of LLD was conferred upon him by the University of Edinburgh, and in the same year he became lord justice-clerk of Scotland, with the judicial title of Lord Aitchison. The bare recital of these facts fails, however, to present a true picture of Aitchison's personality and achievements. At the bar he specialized in criminal work. It is not too much to say that he was the greatest criminal advocate in Scotland of his time. He appeared for the defence in many murder trials, and in none of them did the crown secure a verdict. His forensic eloquence, coupled with a pleasing voice and a gracious personality, was unmatched by any of his contemporaries. The cases of John Donald Merrett (1927), of the Oscar Slater appeal (1928), and of Scottish Amalgamated Silks Ltd (1932)—all well known to Scottish lawyers—were the highlights of his career at the bar. The Merrett case was one of alleged matricide, in which, on that charge, he secured a verdict of not proven. In the Slater appeal he succeeded in quashing a twenty-year-old conviction recorded against the accused man. The Silks case, an alleged long term fraud, lasted for thirty-three days.

In the office of lord justice-clerk Aitchison amply justified the expectations entertained regarding him by his colleagues and friends. He was a just and merciful judge. His opinions were luminous and convincing, and they stood well with the House of Lords. Their literary form was unimpeachable. In his later years Aitchison seemed to become in appearance, manner, and personality the embodiment of the old Scottish judges whom Sir Henry Raeburn loved to paint, with their characteristic combination of massive dignity, kindly good humour, and broad humanity. With a love of art and good literature, he was liberally endowed with the gift of friendship, and his friendship was loyal and abiding. A contemporary commentator and friend wrote of him after his death, quoting what Sir Walter Scott said to Lockhart at John Ballantyne's funeral: 'I feel as if there would be less sunshine for me from this day forth' (private information, 1959). Aitchison died in Edinburgh on 2 May 1941. His wife survived him.

ALNESS, rev.

Sources *The Scotsman* (3 May 1941) · *Scots Law Times: News* (10 May 1941) · personal knowledge (1959) · *WWW* · private information (1959) · *CGPLA Eng. & Wales* (1941)
Likenesses S. Cursiter, oils, 1937, Parliament Hall, Edinburgh [*see illus.*]
Wealth at death £10,036 18s. 6d.: confirmation, 29 Aug 1941, *CCI*

Aitchison, George (1825–1910), architect, was born in London on 7 November 1825, the son of George Aitchison (1792–1861) and his wife, Maria Freeman. After education at Merchant Taylors' School, London (1835–41), he was articled in 1841 to his father, then architect to the St Katherine Dock Company. He entered the Royal Academy Schools in 1847, graduated BA at University College, London, in 1851, and began in 1853 an architectural tour which led to his acquaintance in Rome with George Heming Mason. Mason introduced him to Frederick Leighton. After concluding the tour with William Burges, Aitchison returned to London in 1855 and four years later he was taken into partnership by his father, to whose practice and appointment he succeeded in 1861; he subsequently became joint architect to the London and St Katherine Dock Company. Aitchison's father was reputed to have designed 'the first incombustible building of iron and brick' (*RIBA Transactions*, 14, 1863–4, 107), Irongate wharf on the Thames (*c*.1845).

As a young man, Aitchison himself was also much involved with wharves, warehouses, and offices along the Thames, notably the depository for Messrs Hubbock and the tobacco warehouse for Victoria Dock. But it was Leighton, his lifelong friend, who gave him the opportunity to design one of the most innovative houses of the Victorian period, Leighton's own house and studio in Holland Road, South Kensington (1864–6; now Leighton House), to which the Arab Hall (1877–89) was later added. Aitchison's other principal works were: the hall of the Founders' Company (1877); offices for the Royal Exchange Company, Pall Mall (1886); decorations for the apartments of the Princess Louise at Kensington Palace; the board-room of the Thames conservancy (1868), with a frieze by Leighton; and a warehouse in Mark Lane, City of London (1864), the construction of which made ingenious use of cast iron. He was examiner in architecture and the principles of ornament in the Department of Science and Art, South Kensington, and for many years district surveyor for East Wandsworth and Tooting. Aitchison was elected ARA in 1881 and RA in

George Aitchison (1825–1910), by Sir Lawrence Alma-Tadema, 1900

1898. He acted from 1881 as lecturer, then from 1887 as professor of architecture, at the Royal Academy, a post which he resigned in 1905. From 1896 to 1899 he was president of the Royal Institute of British Architects (RIBA), and during his presidency (1898) was awarded the royal gold medal. For many years he was very much part of the inner circle of the RIBA.

As a lecturer and public speaker Aitchison was prolific, in particular at the RIBA and RA. His style was literary, discursive, and genial. And yet, over a period of half a century, there is in his lectures a manifest sense of doubt, even of despair. For decades he wrestled in public with the Victorian dilemma of style. Looking backwards and forwards at the same time, how could architects square art and science, utility and beauty? How could they serve two masters, history and progress? The fact that he could never quite admit that eclecticism—modern materials and historic forms—was indeed the Victorian style, makes him an appealing, and representative, figure.

Aitchison resided and worked at 150 Harley Street, London, where he died, unmarried, on 16 May 1910. He left a little over £13,000. His RIBA portrait by Alma-Tadema (1900) catches the style of the man: scholarly, gregarious, and perhaps a little garrulous.   J. MORDAUNT CROOK

Sources J. Mordaunt Crook, 'Groping in the dark: George Aitchison and the burden of history', *The study of the past in the Victorian age*, ed. C. Brooks (1997) · *CGPLA Eng. & Wales* (1910) · d. cert. · *DNB*
Archives Bodl. Oxf., letters to F. G. Stephens
Likenesses L. Alma-Tadema, oils, 1900, RIBA BAL, Drawings Collection [*see illus.*] · R. W. Robinson, photograph, NPG; repro. in *Members and associates of the Royal Academy of Arts, 1891*

Wealth at death £13,284 10s. 1d.: Principal Registry of the Family Division, London, probate records, CPR 1910, A–C, 13

Aitchison, Sir John (1789–1875), army officer, was the third son of William Aitchison of Drummore, East Lothian, and his wife, Jane, eldest daughter of James Mylne of Langridge, East Lothian. He was commissioned into the 3rd guards as ensign on 25 October 1805, served at the siege and capture of Copenhagen in 1807, and sailed with the regiment from Spithead for Portugal on 15 January 1809. In the Peninsula he quickly took part in the passage of the Douro, the capture of Oporto, and the subsequent pursuit of French forces under Marshal Soult. At Talavera on 28 July 1809 he suffered an arm wound while carrying the king's colour, as the regiment incurred heavy casualties.

Aitchison again distinguished himself at Busaco on 27 September 1810, and advanced to lieutenant and captain (22 November) before returning to England. In 1812 he once more saw action under Wellington at Salamanca (22 July), the capture of Madrid (12 August), and the unsuccessful siege of Burgos (September–October) before the withdrawal to winter quarters in Portugal. The following year he fought in the skirmishes at Osma and Tolosa, at the battles of Vitoria (21 June), Nivelle, and Nive (November–December), and the siege of San Sebastian (July–August). During February 1814 Aitchison took part in the crossing of the Adour and investment of Bayonne. Later editions of the *Army List* state without further detail that, for his services in the Peninsula, he received 'the War Medal with six clasps'. Although never again active in the field, he purchased advance to captain and lieutenant-colonel (15 December 1814), major and colonel (20 May 1836). He similarly secured command of 1st battalion, 3rd guards (in 1831 renamed Scots Fusilier Guards), as lieutenant-colonel on 11 August 1837, retaining that post until appointed major-general on 23 November 1841. During his period in command the Scots Fusilier Guards were used as auxiliary firemen when the houses of parliament burnt down in 1834, receiving the thanks of the home secretary for their efforts, and acted in a similar capacity two years later when the Foreign Office caught alight. In 1841 a serious fire broke out in the Tower of London, where Aitchison's battalion saved the royal regalia and secured the approbation of the constable, the duke of Wellington. From July 1836 Aitchison sat on the committee that planned creation of a 3rd Guards Club for serving and retired officers, formally established on 17 December.

From June 1845 until November 1851, as a major-general on the staff of the Madras presidency, in India Aitchison commanded the Mysore division (including Coorg) and the provinces of Malabar and Kanara. Promoted lieutenant-general on 11 November 1851, Aitchison was appointed colonel of the 72nd foot (29 December)—becoming KCB on 21 June 1859—and general (30 July 1860); he was made a GCB on 13 March 1867. He transferred to the colonelcy of the Scots Fusilier Guards on 27 August 1870, holding that appointment until his death.

Aitchison married Ellen Elizabeth, youngest daughter of Thomas Mayhew of Fairfield House, Saxmundham, Suffolk, on 31 October 1857. He died at his residence, 4 Devonshire Place, London, on 12 May 1875; his wife survived him.

JAMES LUNT

Sources Boase, *Mod. Eng. biog.* · *Hart's Army List* · F. Maurice, *The history of the Scots guards, from the creation of the regiment to the eve of the Great War*, 2 vols. (1934) · J. M. Brereton, *Guide to the regiments and corps of the British Army* (1985) · A. Goodinge, *The Scots guards*, Famous Regiments (1969) · C. W. C. Oman, *Wellington's army, 1809–1814* (1912); repr. (1968) · J. Weller, *Wellington in the Peninsula, 1808–1814*, new edn (1992) · J. Paget, *Wellington's Peninsular War* (1990) · W. J. Wilson, ed., *History of the Madras army*, 4 vols. (1882–8) · E. G. Phythian-Adams, *The Madras regiment, 1758–1958* (1958) · *CGPLA Eng. & Wales* (1875)
Archives BL OIOC, letters to Lord Tweeddale, MS Eur. F 96 · NL Scot., letters to John Rennie
Wealth at death under £40,000: probate, 15 Dec 1875, *CGPLA Eng. & Wales*

Aitken, Alexander Craig (1895–1967), mathematician, was born at Dunedin, New Zealand, on 1 April 1895, the eldest of the seven children of William Aitken and his wife, Elizabeth Towers. His grandfather Alexander Aitken had emigrated from Lanarkshire to Otago in 1868 and farmed in the neighbourhood of Dunedin. Aitken's father, one of fourteen children, left the farm to work as a grocer in Dunedin, and subsequently acquired the business. Aitken's mother was born in Wolverhampton and went to New Zealand at the age of eight.

Aitken became head boy of Otago Boys' High School in 1912 and won first place in the entrance scholarship examination to Otago University. His most striking characteristic at this stage was a phenomenal memory, and he had not shown any special bent for mathematics. He decided on a course combining languages with mathematics, but this was soon interrupted by the outbreak of war in 1914. He enlisted as a private soldier in the New Zealand expeditionary force and reached Gallipoli in November 1915 with the 6th infantry reinforcements, five weeks before the evacuation. Subsequently he served in France and was commissioned on the field of battle. He was badly wounded in a raid during the battle of the Somme and in March 1917 was invalided home to New Zealand. Before resuming his interrupted university career he wrote an account of his wartime experiences. His continuing anguish about those experiences caused him, forty-five years later with but little revision, to publish the work as *Gallipoli to the Somme: Recollections of a New Zealand Infantryman* (1963), which won the Hawthornden prize. In 1920 Aitken married Mary Winifred, daughter of Alfred Betts, of Nelson, New Zealand. She was a lecturer in botany at Otago University from 1916 to 1923. They had two children, a boy and a girl.

Mathematics was at a low ebb in Otago because there was no professor until R. J. T. Bell arrived from Glasgow in 1920. This may explain why in 1920 Aitken gained only a second-class degree in mathematics, although he achieved a first class in languages and literature (Latin and French). Nevertheless he decided to pursue mathematics: after three years as a master at his old school, in 1923 he was awarded a postgraduate scholarship and went to be discovered without having to find the polynomial explicitly.

In 1925 Aitken was appointed as lecturer in actuarial mathematics at Edinburgh and in 1936 he became a reader in statistics. Much of his later work belongs to statistics, and the mathematics to which it gives rise. Aitken was also interested in decimal coinage, and broadcast on the subject. He succeeded Whittaker in the Edinburgh chair of mathematics when the latter retired in 1946. He himself retired in 1965.

Aitken was renowned for his powers of mental calculation. They were the subject of a paper by the psychologist I. M. L. Hunter, who concluded that his skill possibly exceeded that of any other person for whom precise authenticated records existed. Aitken, a violinist and close friend of the musician Sir D. F. Tovey, said that he gave roughly four times as much thought to music as to mathematics. Physically he was short and slight; he was a leading high-jumper in his youth and a keen hill walker in his Edinburgh days.

Aitken was elected FRS in 1936 and for several terms was a vice-president of the Royal Society of Edinburgh, to which he had been elected in 1925. The universities of Glasgow and New Zealand awarded him honorary degrees. He was also a fellow of the Royal Society of Literature, and an honorary fellow of the Royal Society of New Zealand and of the Faculty of Actuaries. Aitken died at 153 Morningside Drive, Edinburgh, on 3 November 1967. He was survived by his wife.

J. M. WHITTAKER, rev. ANITA McCONNELL

Sources J. M. Whittaker and M. S. Bartlett, *Memoirs FRS*, 14 (1968), 1–14 · *Proceedings of the Edinburgh Mathematical Society*, 16 (1968), 151–76 · *The Times* (6 Nov 1967), 10g · *The Times* (7 Nov 1967), 12h · *The Times* (22 Nov 1967), 12h · I. M. L. Hunter, 'An exceptional talent for calculative thinking', *British Journal of Psychology*, 53 (1962), 243–58 · d. cert.
Archives Trinity Cam., corresp. with Harold Davenport · U. Edin. L., letters to I. Hunter · U. St Andr. L., corresp. with Sir D'Arcy Thompson
Likenesses P. Shillabeer, photograph, 1925, RS; repro. in Whittaker and Bartlett, *Memoirs FRS* · W. Stoneman, photograph, 1945, NPG [*see illus.*] · photograph, repro. in *Proceedings of the Royal Edinburgh Mathematical Society*
Wealth at death £34,124 17s.: confirmation, 13 Dec 1967, CCI

Alexander Craig Aitken (1895–1967), by Walter Stoneman, 1945

Edinburgh University to work under E. T. Whittaker, who was greatly interested in numerical mathematics and in 1913 had founded the only mathematical laboratory in the country. Since one of Whittaker's closest friends was G. J. Lidstone, the leading actuary of his time, Aitken was given a problem of actuarial interest as his doctoral subject: the graduation or the fitting of a smooth curve to a set of points subject to statistical error. Whittaker had taken the first step towards providing the subject with a rational basis but his formula was unsuited to numerical calculation. Aitken overcame the difficulty, an achievement for which he was awarded a DSc in 1926. The rest of his life, all of which was spent in Edinburgh, was devoted to the closely linked disciplines of numerical mathematics, statistics, and the algebra of matrices.

Numerical mathematics is a difficult subject to appraise since it is dependent on the characteristics of the machines or tables in use at the time. Mechanical calculating machines were in common use in industry and commerce but their cost, and not less their noise, precluded their use in a class of fifty students. Whittaker considered that a properly trained student could do nearly as well with tables. It was on this basis that Aitken took over the conduct of the laboratory. He discovered two new devices which have passed into general use: 'Aitken's δ-process', by which a sequence may be transformed into one more rapidly convergent; and the Neville–Aitken method in finite difference theory, by which the values of the interpolating polynomial at a series of equidistant points can

Aitken, Edith (1861–1940), headmistress, was born at Bishophill, Bishophill Junior, York, on 16 June 1861, the third child of Henry Martin Aitken, surgical instrument manufacturer, and his wife, Elizabeth Atkinson. She and her elder siblings were baptized at St Mary Minor, Bishophill, on 8 July 1861. Their father had advanced views on the education of girls, and the eldest daughter, Rose (1849–1922), went to Girton College, then at Hitchin, in 1871, before becoming a schoolmistress. Edith was educated at Lendal House, and privately until her father's death in 1875. His wishes were respected and she was sent as a boarder, at the age of fourteen, to North London Collegiate School, under Miss Buss, and where her elder sister was already teaching classics.

In 1879 Aitken went to Girton College, Cambridge, where she read for the natural sciences tripos and achieved first-class honours in part one in 1882, later (1904) taking her MA from Trinity College, Dublin, as Cambridge degrees remained closed to women. She was eventually able to take her Cambridge MA in 1925. She began her teaching career at Manchester Girls' High School, then moved to Nottingham Girls' High School in 1883. She joined the staff of Notting Hill high school three years later and returned to North London Collegiate School as science mistress in 1892. From 1899 to 1902 she was lecturer in chemistry at Bedford College, London. Her *Elementary Textbook of Botany*, first published in 1891, went through three editions.

In 1902, immediately after the end of the Second South African War, Aitken went out to South Africa to take up a position as the first headmistress of Pretoria High School for Girls, following in the footsteps of Ellen Constance Steedman, a fellow Girtonian scientist of her year, who became headmistress of Eunice High School, Bloemfontein, in 1901. Miss Aitken inherited the buildings of a school which had closed in 1899, but little else. She was well suited to the challenge. Although she modelled the new school on the North London Collegiate, even to the point of giving it the same motto ('We work in hope'), she was alert to the need for adaptation in South Africa. She herself qualified to teach Dutch and was adamant that both English- and Dutch-speaking pupils should be taught and received on the same footing, and appointed Dutch speakers as well as English. The school opened in 1902 with 106 pupils; in 1904 there were 167 on the roll, and by December 1908 the old buildings were too small for the 194 pupils, of whom 60 were boarders. From then on 'EA', as she was affectionately known, continually badgered the director of education for new premises further out of town. As a result, the school moved to its new buildings in 1915, though it took Miss Aitken another two years of persistence before she acquired adjacent playing fields. When she retired in 1923, the school had long been known as the best of its kind in South Africa. She last visited it in 1938, when she had the satisfaction of seeing how it thrived in every way. Not least, she was able to see how the pines and jacarandas she had planted stood high around the buildings.

Aitken's interests were wide. As well as enjoying riding, sport, music, and drama, her enthusiasm for art was a great bond with her brother Charles Aitken (1869–1936), director of the Tate collection. She was deeply saddened by his death, which left her isolated. After retiring to England she lived in a London flat, but later moved to Abbot's Holt, Tilford, Surrey. She died suddenly at the Grange Nursing Home, Wrecclesham, Farnham, Surrey, on 2 November 1940, after suffering a coronary thrombosis.

BARBARA E. MEGSON

Sources K. T. Butler and H. I. McMorran, eds., *Girton College register, 1869–1946* (1948) · *The Times* (12 Nov 1940) · b. cert. · d. cert. · L. Becker and S. van Putten, 'We work in hope': a history of Pretoria high school (1992) · York parish records, 1871
Likenesses portraits, repro. in Becker and van Putten, 'We work in hope'

Wealth at death £1500: probate, 9 July 1941, *CGPLA Eng. & Wales*

Aitken, (Adam) Jack (1921–1998), lexicographer and philologist, was born on 19 June 1921 in Edinburgh, the only son and eldest of the three children of Adam Aitken (1896–1958), miner, and his first wife, Alexandrina Sutherland (1896–1931). He was baptized into the Church of Scotland at Bonnyrigg at the age of six, but as an adult was agnostic. He was educated at Lasswade secondary school, Midlothian. With the support of the school and his minister, the Revd Oliver Dryer, he left home at the age of sixteen together with his younger sister Hope. He was able to continue his education thanks to a school bursary, and as the son of a miner he was able to obtain further bursaries that allowed him to enter the University of Edinburgh in 1939. His higher education was interrupted by the Second World War. Although philosophically a pacifist he served from 1941 to 1945 in the Royal Artillery and took part in the Normandy landings and in the war in north Africa, rising to the rank of sergeant-major. He was commended for bravery by Field Marshal Montgomery in 1944.

Aitken graduated MA with first-class honours in English language and literature from Edinburgh in 1947. In 1948 he was appointed assistant to the editor of *A Dictionary of the Older Scottish Tongue* (DOST), Sir William Craigie; assistant lecturer in English language at the University of Edinburgh; and research fellow at the universities of Edinburgh, Glasgow, and Aberdeen. On 19 June 1952 he married Norma Ward (later known as Chandra) Manson (b. 1927), a teacher for the National Childbirth Trust, with whom he had three sons and a daughter.

From 1954 to 1964 Aitken was lecturer at Edinburgh and Glasgow; he was promoted to senior lecturer at Edinburgh in 1965, and reader in 1975. From 1971 these positions were part-time, and from 1979 he devoted himself full-time to DOST, of which he was editor from 1956 until his retirement in 1986. In 1981 the British Academy awarded him the biennial Sir Israel Gollancz prize. In 1983 he was awarded a DLitt by the University of Edinburgh, and he was appointed honorary professor in 1984. In 1987 he was presented with a Festschrift: *The Nuttis Schell: Essays on the Scots Language Presented to A. J. Aitken*, edited by Caroline Macafee and Iseabail Macleod.

A. J. Aitken's major achievements were his work on DOST, which became a much more inclusive and more sophisticated work under his direction (vol. 3 onwards) than it had previously been, and his other publications on the Scots language. He also effectively established Scots as a university teaching subject. He was an early adopter of computer-assisted methods in the arts: with others he created the Older Scottish Textual Archive of over 1 million words of running text. He published numerous articles and edited collections of papers on Older and Modern Scots and on lexicography. He was editorial consultant and pronunciation editor of the definitive one-volume dictionary of Scots, *The Concise Scots Dictionary* (1985). Revised versions of three of his most important contributions, on Older Scots orthography, phonology, and stylistics, are included in the preface to volume 12 of DOST, and his posthumous monograph *The Older Scots Vowels* was prepared for publication by the Scottish Text Society. A cassette tape *How to Pronounce Older Scots*, with accompanying booklet, was published by Scotsoun in 1996. His name is attached to a sound law, Aitken's law, which he himself called the 'Scottish vowel-length rule'.

Aitken was active in the institutions of his disciplines. He chaired the language committee of the Association for Scottish Literary Studies from 1971 to 1976. Of the Forum for Research on the Languages of Scotland he was chairman from 1978 to 1981, and honorary president from 1994 to 1997. He was also vice-president of the Scottish Text Society from 1985, honorary preses of the Scots Language Society from 1994, honorary vice-president of the Scottish National Dictionary Association from 1995, and honorary vice-president of the Robert Henryson Society from 1996. His influence was international: he served variously as adviser and consultant on several major dictionary projects, including the *Dictionary of Sanskrit on Historical Principles*, the *Dictionary of Middle English*, the *Dictionary of Early Modern English Pronunciation*, and the *Dictionary of Old English*. He was looked to as the leading expert on Scots, and gave generously of his time in talks to the public and expert advice to colleagues all over the world. Aitken was known as a man of great personal integrity as well as scholarly dedication. For a period after the war and up to 1956, he was a member of the Communist Party. He was also a member of the ex-services branch of the Campaign for Nuclear Disarmament.

Apart from brief stays in Iceland in 1951 and India in the late 1960s, Jack Aitken lived in Edinburgh all his adult life. He died of ischaemia at his home, 5 Bellevue Crescent, on 11 February 1998, having had a heart by-pass operation twenty years previously, and was cremated at Warriston crematorium, Edinburgh, on 18 February 1998. His wife survived him.   CAROLINE MACAFEE

Sources *Who's Who in Scotland* (1992–8) · C. Macafee and I. Macleod, eds., *The nuttis schell: essays on the Scots language presented to A. J. Aitken* (1987) · *Glasgow Herald* (14 Feb 1998) · *The Scotsman* (17 Feb 1998) · *The Independent* (18 Feb 1998) · *Arran Banner* (21 Feb 1998) · *The Times* (3 March 1998) · *The Guardian* (10 March 1998) · *University of Edinburgh Bulletin* (17 March 1998) · C. Macafee, *English World-Wide*, 19/2 (1998), 275–85 · *Scottish Language*, 17 (1998) · *Medieval English Studies Newsletter*, 38 (June 1998) · private information (2004) [Chandra Aitken, widow; Hope Baker, sister]
Archives priv. coll., papers · U. Edin., Institute of Historical Dialectology, books and papers
Likenesses I. F. Mackenzie, photograph, repro. in Macafee and Macleod, eds., *The nuttis schell*, frontispiece

Aitken [Atkine], **James** (1612/13–1687), bishop of Galloway, was born in Kirkwall, Orkney, the third son of Henry Aitken, commissary and sheriff of Orkney and Shetland, and Elizabeth Buchanan. He attended Kirkwall grammar school before moving on to the University of Edinburgh, where he graduated MA on 23 July 1636. During the next two turbulent years of the covenanting revolution he completed his formal education at Oxford, where he studied divinity under John Prideaux of Exeter College. He returned to Scotland as chaplain to James, marquess of Hamilton, who was high commissioner to the Glasgow

assembly of 1638 that abolished episcopacy and the royal supremacy in the Church of Scotland. Aitken was presented to the charge of Harray and Birsay, Orkney, on 27 July 1641 and officially admitted on 26 June 1642. He married Alison, daughter of Thomas Rutherford of Hunthill; they had four daughters.

Alerted to an order for his deposition and apprehension by his kinsman Sir Archibald Primrose, the clerk of council and later lord register, for his pledge of loyalty to the crown and support for the ill-fated royalist military campaign led by the marquess of Montrose in 1650, Aitken sought refuge in the Netherlands between 1650 and 1653. He returned to Scotland during the relative calm of the Cromwellian interregnum and lived in Edinburgh between 1653 and 1660. After the Restoration his fidelity to the royalist cause was rewarded, on 15 May 1661, by a grant of £100. After accompanying Thomas Sydserf, the bishop of Orkney, to the court of Charles II in 1661 he was presented to the rectory of Winfrith, Dorset, by the bishop of Winchester. According to Anthony Wood he remained there for the next sixteen years.

On 1 November 1676 Aitken was appointed bishop of Moray. A letter patent to that effect was issued on 5 June 1677; episcopal consecration, however, was delayed until 28 October 1679. This did not prevent him from playing a conspicuous role in the convention of estates that met in Edinburgh in June 1678. He was translated to the see of Galloway on 6 February 1680 but received a dispensation permitting him to live in Edinburgh 'because it was thought unreasonable to oblige a reverend prelate of his years to live among such a rebellious and turbulent people' (Keith, 282). He took a prominent part in the parliaments that met in the capital in July 1681, April 1685, and April 1686, where he vociferously opposed repeal of the penal laws against Roman Catholics. Aitken died of apoplexy in Edinburgh on 15 November 1687 aged seventy-four, and was interred in Greyfriars Church; his funeral sermon was preached by Bishop John Hamilton of Dunkeld.   A. S. WAYNE PEARCE

Sources *Fasti Scot.*, new edn, vol. 7 · R. Keith and J. Spottiswoode, *An historical catalogue of the Scottish bishops, down to the year 1688*, new edn, ed. M. Russel [M. Russell] (1824), 153, 282 · *DNB* · *APS* · *The diary of Alexander Brodie of Brodie … and of his son James Brodie*, ed. D. Laing, Spalding Club, 33 (1863) · Wood, *Ath. Oxon.*, new edn, 4.871–2
Archives NL Scot., personal account book as rector of Winfrith, Dorset · NL Scot., corresp. and papers
Wealth at death £667 13s. 3d.; bequeathed fishing rights on River Spey, a library and dwelling house: inventory, NA Scot., CC 8/8/78, 252; CC 8/8/89, 47

Aitken, James [alias John the Painter] (1752–1777), radical and arsonist, was born in Edinburgh on 28 September 1752 to George Aitken, a blacksmith, and his wife, Magdalen. The eighth of twelve children, James qualified for admission as an impoverished student to Heriot's Hospital, Edinburgh, in April 1761. School records show that he remained until February 1767, when he was apprenticed to John Bonnar, an Edinburgh painter. Aitken completed his apprenticeship in 1774 and left for London carrying his journeyman's papers. Instead of plying his

James Aitken (1752–1777), by unknown engraver, pubd 1777 (after W. Cave)

trade, however, he drifted into a life of crime, burgling shops and homes and committing highway robberies. Looking for but not finding a new start in Virginia he sailed back to England in the spring of 1775 and resumed his thievery.

By the summer of 1776 Aitken had decided to strike a blow for the American revolutionary cause and destroy all six of the royal dockyards. Designing an ingenious incendiary device that would enable him to set fires, as he claimed, virtually undetected, he travelled to Paris and laid his plans before American commissioner Silas Deane the following October. Deane gave him a small sum of money and his half-hearted endorsement. With fire-starters made by an unsuspecting Canterbury tinsmith concealed in his bundle, Aitken returned to Portsmouth, where he had worked for a time known only as John. On 7 December he placed one of his devices in a dockyard hemphouse; it failed to ignite. A fire started in the neighbouring ropehouse by cruder methods did catch and Aitken hurried off to London. Although flames gutted the ropehouse it was rebuilt within months and damage to other buildings was minor.

In London Aitken met Dr Edward Bancroft, Deane's contact. Unbeknown to both Aitken and Deane, Bancroft was an opportunistic double agent; he did nothing to encourage Aitken and yet he did not report Aitken's visit to the authorities. Aitken headed west, intending to incinerate the royal dockyards at Plymouth. Thwarted by bad luck he turned away from the royal yards, went to Bristol, and lit fires along the waterfront on the night of 15–16 January, followed by more fires three nights later that caused greater damage than that produced at Portsmouth.

Before the end of December 1776 Portsmouth commissioner James Gambier had informed the Admiralty and the Navy Board that a man known only as John the Painter was the leading suspect in the ropehouse fire. The Admiralty and the Navy Board offered rewards of up to £1000 and had placed notices in newspapers throughout southern England describing the suspect as twenty-five or twenty-six years old, thin, 5 feet 7 inches tall, with a fair complexion and sandy hair, last seen wearing a faded brown surtout coat and cocked hat. Much to the relief of a distressed Whitehall the peripatetic Aitken was finally apprehended on 27 January in Hook, Hampshire, and held in the nearby Odiham gaol. The authorities were fortunate that John Dalby, keeper of the Andover bridewell, read the notices, made enquiries, and picked up the trail. Dalby had no sooner detained John than he was joined by shopkeeper James Lowe of Calne, Wiltshire. Lowe was in pursuit because his shop had been burgled and the man he chased fitted the thief's description. Only after he and Dalby deposited their captive in the Odiham gaol did Lowe realize they had bagged the notorious John.

Aitken, still known only by that alias and a couple of others he had lived under, was taken to London and examined by Sir John Fielding at his Bow Street court. Fielding got nowhere until the suspect foolishly confided many of his secrets to John Baldwin, a painter who visited him in his Clerkenwell cell, won his trust, and reported everything he learned to the Admiralty. Because of the evidence amassed through Baldwin's leads, Aitken was transferred to Winchester, formally indicted, and bound over for trial in the assize court there on 6 March. Joseph Gurney and William Blanchard of London each produced transcripts, and Gurney's was accepted as the official version and later published in the *State Trials*. Other, briefer accounts of this, the most celebrated court case of the decade, appeared in various pamphlets, magazines, and newspapers.

Aitken acted as his own counsel. In a very long proceeding by the standards of the day—some seven hours— twenty witnesses testified against Aitken; he called none of his own. Baldwin was the most important of Aitken's accusers. Prosecutors, led by William Davy, used the others to corroborate independently what Baldwin claimed John had told him. Aitken pleaded to have Baldwin's testimony struck, but the judge, Beaumont Hotham, refused, and with that his fate was sealed. Though condemned to be taken to Portsmouth and hanged on 10 March, with no hope of clemency, an unbroken Aitken left Winchester's Great Hall still refusing to acknowledge his guilt. He experienced a change of heart while awaiting execution—to the immense satisfaction, no doubt, of those who had seen to his prosecution. His confession, which was dictated to Winchester's gaoler, was rushed to press by local printer J. Wilkes as *The Life of James Aitken* (1777). Even though he may not have been completely candid in the *Life*, this version is more reliable than other purportedly true renditions that appeared at the same time, and it was pirated by others, notably *A Genuine Account of the Life of James Aitken* (1777). Through his confession and final conciliatory words just before he was hanged from the mizzen mast of the *Arethusa*, which had been erected on Portsmouth Common just for the occasion, Aitken gave the authorities everything they had sought but feared they would not get. Thomas Lawrence, who befriended Aitken after his capture, believed that he confessed in the false hope that his body would be buried instead of displayed on a gibbet.

Through all of this Silas Deane, safely in Paris, admitted that he had met Aitken but denied he had had anything to do with a plot to destroy the royal dockyards. After the war he confided to Edward Bancroft—whose own duplicity he never discovered—that he had indeed been a party to Aitken's scheme. Members of the political opposition attempted to exploit Aitken posthumously and embarrass the North ministry. They largely failed, whether in speeches on the floor of the Commons, or in the spoof *John the Painter's Ghost*, or in the spurious *History*, the *Short Account*, and the *Whole Life* of the now dead arsonist. In a most bizarre incident, confidence man David Brown Dignam linked Aitken to what Dignam claimed was a plot to assassinate George III. Dignam's hoax was soon enough exposed. Aitken's body remained on its gibbet for years, its exact fate now unknown. Supposed relics from the arsonist's life—an awl, a vial of turpentine, a pistol, and even a mummified finger turned into a tobacco stopper—were passed down the centuries, and those that survive are kept at the Portsmouth City Museum. Reviled by contemporaries as deluded, even demented, Aitken has long since been transformed by local folklore into a quaint, colourful figure.   NEIL L. YORK

Sources *The life of James Aitken, commonly called John the Painter* (1777) · J. Gurney, *The trial (at large) of James Hill, otherwise John Hinde, otherwise James Actzen* (1777); repr. in *State trials* · *The whole of the proceedings upon the trial of James Hill* [1777] · T. Lawrence, *A narrative of certain facts* (1777) · NMM, Sandwich MSS, SAN F/10, F/45c · NMM, Portsmouth Dockyard MSS, C POR/A/27; POR/C/22; POR/D/19, 20; POR/F/15, 16; POR/G/1; POR/H/9, 10 · navy board minute book, PRO, PRO/Admiralty 106/2594 · gaol books, western circuit, assize 23, PRO, vol. 8, pt. 1 · *A short account of the motives which determined the man, called John the Painter* (1777) · N. L. York, *Burning the dockyard: John the Painter and the American Revolution* (2001)
Archives NMM, Portsmouth Dockyard MSS · NMM, Sandwich MSS, SAN F/10, F/45c · PRO, navy board minute book, PRO/Admiralty 106/2594 · PRO, gaol books, western circuit, assize 23, vol. 8, pt. 1
Likenesses engraving, pubd 1777 (after W. Cave), BM [*see illus.*] · portrait, 1777, repro. in J. Wilkes, *The life of James Aitken* (1777), frontispiece · portrait, 1777, repro. in *London Magazine* (March 1777), 115 · portrait, 1777, repro. in J. Gurney, *The trial of James Hill* (1777) · line engraving, BM, NPG

Aitken, John (1793–1833), writer, was born at the village of Camelon, Stirlingshire, on 25 March 1793. After a good elementary school education, he became a clerk in the East Lothian Bank, from where he was transferred to the bank of Mr Park (one of the brothers of Mungo Park, the traveller) at Selkirk. Subsequently he became a teller in the East Lothian Bank, but when it failed in 1822 he moved to Edinburgh, where he set up as a bookseller, and published the *Cabinet*, a selection of miscellaneous pieces in prose and verse, which ran to three volumes, and met with considerable success. Shortly after this he was appointed editor of *Constable's Miscellany* in 1827. When Archibald Constable died later that year Aitken, Messrs Hurst, Chance & Co., of London, and Henry Constable purchased the title, but his connection with it ceased after the failure of the London firm in 1831. He had established a printing office, with the intention of starting a publication similar to the *Miscellany*, when he died unexpectedly on 15 February 1833. Aitken took an active part in founding the *Edinburgh Literary Journal*. He was an occasional contributor to periodicals, and wrote verse with elegance and taste.   T. F. HENDERSON, rev. H. C. G. MATTHEW

Sources W. C. Taylor, ed., *The cabinet of friendship* (1834) · Anderson, *Scot. nat.* · Irving, *Scots.*
Archives NL Scot., corresp. with Archibald Constable · U. Edin. L., letters to David Laing
Likenesses W. H. Lizars, line engraving (after J. Chrisholm), NPG

Aitken, John (1839–1919), meteorologist and experimental scientist, was born on 18 September 1839 at Falkirk, Stirlingshire, the fourth son of Henry Aitken of Darroch, the head of a well-known legal firm, and his wife, Margaret Russell. He was educated at Falkirk grammar school and the University of Glasgow, where he studied natural philosophy under William Thomson as well as engineering. Intending to pursue a career in engineering, he served two years' apprenticeship in Dundee, followed by a further three years with Napier & Sons, a Glasgow shipbuilding firm. After completing his apprenticeship, however, he suffered a breakdown in health, causing him to abandon his chosen profession. He had inherited sufficient wealth to live a life of leisure but elected to pursue his earlier interest in natural philosophy. His training as an engineer proved invaluable for his purpose, for he was able not only to devise the experiments he wanted to make, but also to construct the apparatus needed to perform them. He never married, and he converted much of his Falkirk home into a scientific laboratory and workshop.

Aitken's interests extended across a wide spectrum of physical science although his first contribution to the scientific literature was an article on an engineering subject—that of safety valves—published in *Engineering* (3 May 1867). His later work covered a broad range. His outstanding experimental skills were first exhibited in a paper on colour sensation that he presented to the Royal Scottish Society of Arts in 1872. He tried to co-ordinate his results into a modified form of Young's three-colour theory, introducing considerations of a physiological rather than a physical character and emphasizing the influence of the surrounding background, and also fatigue, in affecting the apparent colour perceived.

Aitken's early work on colour theory was followed by investigations into oceanic circulation, glacier motion, and changes of state, and the latter led him to a study of condensation in the earth's atmosphere. It was here that Aitken was to make the greatest impact. He designed an ingenious instrument, the Aitken dust counter, with which he showed that it was possible to count the number of dust particles (by which he meant condensation nuclei) in a closed sample of saturated air. Aitken expanded the air slightly using an air pump, thereby causing cooling and consequent condensation onto the dust particles, and so forming water droplets. The droplets then fell onto a silvered surface which had been ruled into squares, and the number of the droplets could easily be counted. He developed the instrument into a final portable form that was capable of considerable precision in the hands of a skilful operator.

Using his dust counter Aitken showed that condensation does not take place under normal atmospheric conditions, even at high supersaturations, without the presence of dust particles to act as nuclei, and he also performed an exemplary series of control experiments to counter any possible objections to his theory. He then took his experiments a stage further by showing that a more sudden expansion can result in condensation occurring in air from which dust has been removed by filtration. C. T. R. Wilson later demonstrated that under these circumstances the condensation takes place on ions in the free air, but this effect can only be achieved in the laboratory using a greater and more rapid degree of expansion, and hence cooling, than occurs naturally in the atmosphere. It is also worth noting that J. J. Thomson, in his classical experiments on mass and charge of an electron, made use of Aitken's condensation method in obtaining some of the measurements on which the determination of these small quantities depended.

Subsequent work by Aitken was largely within the field of meteorology, although he did maintain other interests. He made significant contributions to the study of dew formation, showing that the vapour which condenses as dew on cold surfaces comes from the ground below as well as from the air above, and that the 'dewdrop' on leaves of plants is actually exuded sap. He also disagreed with Sir Napier Shaw regarding the probable causes of cyclonic development (1917), although he acknowledged that he was himself handicapped by a lack of 'mathematical equipment' for this sort of investigation, and at his death he left behind a paper pointing to inadequacies in the standard Stevenson thermometer screen which, he considered, gave readings in calm and sunny conditions that were too high.

Following publication of his paper on dust, fog, and clouds (*Transactions of the Royal Society of Edinburgh*, 30, 1883, 337–68), Aitken was recognized as one of the great experimenters of the day. He was on intimate terms with Lord Kelvin and corresponded with Rayleigh and William Ramsay. Bearded and dignified, he was an original thinker who remained outside the mainstream of scientific activity. This had some disadvantages, but it helped him take an individual approach to problems; he remained in touch with other workers, and his findings were always made available. Although he lived a quiet country life, with country pursuits his main recreation, and never lived away from Falkirk, he was not a recluse and travelled widely within Europe.

Honours awarded to Aitken included fellowship of the Royal Society of Edinburgh in 1875 and its Keith (1883) and Gunning (1895) prizes; fellowship of the Royal Society in 1889 and its royal medal in 1917; and LLD from the University of Glasgow in 1899. He died at his home, Ardenlea, Arnothill, Falkirk, on 13 November 1919.

JIM BURTON

Sources *Collected scientific papers of John Aitken*, ed. C. G. Knott (1923), vi–xviii · C. G. Knott, *Proceedings of the Royal Society of Edinburgh*, 41 (1920–21), 177–81 · *Nature*, 104 (1919–20), 318, 337–8, 376 · *The Scotsman* (15 Nov 1919) · *British Weekly* (20 Nov 1919) · WWW · d. cert.
Archives NL Scot., corresp. and papers | U. Leeds, Brotherton L., letters to A. Smithells
Likenesses photograph, RS
Wealth at death £99,329 2s. 10d.: confirmation, 13 March 1920, CCI

Aitken, Marcia Anastasia, Lady Beaverbrook (1909–1994). *See under* Aitken, William Maxwell, first Baron Beaverbrook (1879–1964).

Aitken, Robert (1800–1873), Church of England clergyman, was born on 22 January 1800 at Crailing, near Jedburgh, a son of Robert Aitken, schoolmaster, and his wife, Ann Heron. He was educated at Jedburgh grammar school and the University of Edinburgh. As a young man he felt dissatisfaction with the presbyterianism of his upbringing and, under the influence of Bishop Jolly, was drawn to Anglicanism. Aitken first worked for his brother Mark, teaching at a private school in Whitburn, near Sunderland. In 1823 he was ordained deacon. At this time he married Anna Elizabeth Eyres; they had two sons and five daughters. Much of Aitken's early ministerial career was spent in the Isle of Man, but disputes with his bishop led him to leave the Church of England. Although Aitken was never formally received into the Wesleyan ministry, he was permitted to occupy the pulpits of that body, and remained in sympathy with them until the Warren controversy arose in 1834. Subsequently he preached at Liverpool and elsewhere in chapels of his own, but finally took leave of his congregation at Zion Chapel, Waterloo Road, Liverpool, and returned to the Church of England in 1840.

Aitken was curate of Perranuthnoe, near Marazion, Cornwall, from 1842 to 1844. He then became the incumbent of St James's, Leeds. After the death of his first wife Aitken married again in 1839, his second wife being Wilhelmina Day MacDowall (*née* Grant). They had two sons and a daughter. Aitken returned to Cornwall as the first incumbent of the new parish of Pendeen in 1849. Here a fine cruciform church on the model of the ancient cathedral of Iona was erected from Aitken's own design. The labour was supplied by the local people, chiefly in their leisure hours. Aitken remained at Pendeen until his death; but his services were often sought by the incumbents of churches in large towns, and he was well known as a preacher of almost unrivalled fervour. A fine presence and a commanding voice, combined with untiring zeal and sympathy for others, concealed his rashness of judgement. His religious creed was partly evangelical and partly Tractarian: on the one hand he emphasized conversion, on the other sacramental doctrines. Whether his opinions were in accord with the principles of the established church or not was fiercely disputed both before and after his death. His sermons and pamphlets, as well as the replies which they provoked, are listed in the first and third volumes of Boase and Courtney's *Bibliotheca cornubiensis*. Aitken died suddenly at Paddington Station on 11 July 1873, and was buried in Pendeen churchyard on 18 July. He was the father of Canon William Hay Mac-Dowall Hunter Aitken (1841–1927), the founder of the Parochial Missions Society.

W. P. COURTNEY, rev. I. T. FOSTER

Sources C. E. Woods, *Memoirs and letters of Canon Hay Aitken; with an introductory memoir of his father, the Rev. Robert Aitken of Pendeen* (1928) · *Cornish Telegraph* (16 July 1873) · *Cornish Telegraph* (23 July 1873) · *The Guardian* (23 July 1873) · Crockford · private information (2004) · Boase & Courtney, *Bibl. Corn.* · *Record* (16 July 1873) · Allibone, *Dict.* · Boase, *Mod. Eng. biog.* · IGI
Likenesses photograph, repro. in Woods, *Memoirs and letters of Canon Hay Aitken*
Wealth at death under £800: resworn probate, July 1874, CGPLA Eng. & Wales

Aitken, Sir William (1825–1892), pathologist, eldest son of William Aitken, a medical practitioner, was born in Dundee on 23 April 1825. He was educated at the high school in Dundee, and was subsequently apprenticed to his father and at the same time undertook further training at the Dundee Royal Infirmary. In 1842 he matriculated at the University of Edinburgh, and in 1848 he graduated MD, obtaining a gold medal for his thesis, 'On inflammatory effusions into the substance of the lungs as modified by contagious fevers' (*Edinburgh Medical and Surgical Journal*, 1849). In October of the same year Aitken was appointed demonstrator of anatomy at the University of Glasgow under Allen Thomson, and also pathologist to the royal infirmary. He held both posts until 1855, when he was sent to the Crimea under Robert S. D. Lyons, as assistant pathologist to the commission appointed to investigate the diseases from which the British troops were suffering. In 1860 Aitken was made professor of pathology in the newly constituted army medical school at Fort Pitt, Chatham, Kent, which was later moved to Netley, Hampshire. He held this appointment until April 1892, when failing health forced him to retire.

Aitken was elected FRS in 1873, and in 1884 he married Emily Clara, daughter of Henry Allen. He was knighted at the jubilee of 1887, and the following year he received the honorary degrees of LLD from the universities of Edinburgh and Glasgow. During his professional career, Aitken wrote a number of books which were well received and ran to several editions after their initial publication.

These included the *Handbook of the Science and Practice of Medicine* (1857), which had seven editions by 1880; *An Essay on the Growth of the Recruit and Young Soldier* (1862); and an unfinished 'Catalogue of the pathological museum at Netley Hospital'.

Aitken died at his home, Grove Cottage, Woolston, Hampshire, on 25 June 1892. He was survived by his wife.

J. B. NIAS, rev. JEFFREY S. REZNICK

Sources *The Lancet* (2 July 1892), 60–61 · *BMJ* (2 July 1892), 54–5 · *Men and women of the time* (1891) · private information (1901) · CGPLA Eng. & Wales (1892)
Archives BL, corresp. with Florence Nightingale, Add. MS 45773
Likenesses W. R. Symonds, oils, exh. RA 1888, Royal Victoria Hospital, Netley, Hampshire; replica, Royal Army Medical Corps, Camberley, Surrey
Wealth at death £2403 0s. 4d.: probate, 12 Aug 1892, CGPLA Eng. & Wales

Aitken, William Maxwell, first Baron Beaverbrook (1879–1964), newspaper proprietor and politician, was born on 25 May 1879 at the manse, Vaughan, Maple, Ontario, Canada. He was the third son and fifth member of a family of ten children, whose father, William Cuthbert Aitken (1834–1913), was a Presbyterian minister who had emigrated from Torphichen, Linlithgowshire, to Canada in 1864. His mother was Jane (1849–1927), daughter of Joseph Noble, a prosperous storekeeper and farmer in Vaughan. In 1880 William Cuthbert Aitken received the 'call' to St James's Church, Newcastle, New Brunswick, where Max Aitken spent his boyhood. Until he was sixteen he attended the local school, where he was described as a bright but idle boy and (an epithet which he was to relish later in life) mischievous. He was also sensitive and nervous and harboured a fear of death that remained with him. If it is true that the child is the father of the man, then Aitken's later character was discernible early on: his school principal noted his ability to size him up 'so accurately that he knew exactly every weak point in my character' (Chisholm and Davie, 24). At sixteen he took the examination for Dalhousie University, but declined to sit the Latin and Greek papers and was refused entrance, which was why he later helped build up the University of New Brunswick as a rival.

Making money While at school Aitken did various jobs to make money: he acquired a newspaper round and then became the St John *Daily Sun*'s Newcastle correspondent, being paid a dollar a column. He sold subscriptions for the *Sun* and founded a school newspaper, *The Leader*. After his failure to get into university he worked in a local drugstore, but escaped from drudgery by borrowing money from a local lumberjack and moved to Chatham with the intention of qualifying as a lawyer. He was restless and energetic, and showed initiative: he became local correspondent of the *Montreal Star* and an agent for the Great West Life insurance company; he also collected debts for a Newcastle doctor. While in Chatham he gained his first experience in politics, persuading a friend to stand for election as an alderman, but when his colleague Richard Redford Bennett (later prime minister of Canada) left the law firm for which they both worked, Aitken was passed

William Maxwell Aitken, first Baron Beaverbrook (1879–1964), by Walter Sickert, 1935

over for promotion. He moved to St John, still intending to become a lawyer, and sold insurance to pay his board. He then followed Bennett to Calgary, where he helped run Bennett's campaign for election to the legislative assembly of the Northwest Territories. Aitken again showed a talent for many things, but to no successful end; in Edmonton he sold meat at a loss, and returned to St John to set up as a full-time insurance agent.

Aitken was now twenty-one and still his restless energy had found no profitable outlet. In 1900 he decided to go to Halifax, where he resolved to do no more 'loafing' (Chisholm and Davie, 33). He was fortunate in his resolve, for at that time Halifax was entering a boom phase, as a growing town that was developing an infrastructure of gas, telephones, and tramways. Aitken sold bonds and became friendly with the family of John F. Stairs, a financial expert and local Conservative who supported the protectionist views then being expounded in England by Joseph Chamberlain. Aitken was an apt pupil, showing powers of flattery and persuasion, and also a certain lack of scruple. Stairs was impressed by Aitken's ability to drive staff and spot talent. Aitken learned the value of using the press to promote his business dealings, and he

was good at acquiring inside information and assessing his fellow businessmen. As he became richer he showed his later habit of distributing largesse to his family, but he counted every penny when he paid hotel or shop bills; he seemed to resent it when he was not making money, but he was no miser. On 29 January 1906 he married Gladys Henderson Drury (1887/8–1927), who was then eighteen years old. She was the daughter of Lieutenant-Colonel Charles Drury, the first Canadian to command the Halifax garrison. Aitken wrote, rather ambiguously, in his diary of his hopes that the 'experiment' would succeed (ibid., 56). It did, on Aitken's own terms, but he was to be an unfaithful husband and inveterate pursuer of women, famous or otherwise. It was typical of him to set off, the day after his wedding, to the Royal Security Bank in St John to check up on office management. Aitken and his wife left Halifax for good and moved to Montreal, where he worked as vice-president of Royal Securities. His business dealing reached new levels of intensity: he put money to work, buying and selling companies, starting a weekly magazine, nearly buying the *Montreal Gazette*, dealing in stock markets, and becoming involved in Cuba and Puerto Rico.

Aitken's ventures were not always successful, but he won more often than he lost, though he suffered from bouts of depression and illness. Their first child, Janet, was born on 9 July 1908, an event which Aitken reckoned increased the intimacy of his relationship with his wife; but he continued to please himself about when and where he went. In September 1908 he made his first visit to England. Soon after he was embroiled in controversy over his creation of a merger of Canada's cement industry; this was widely criticized in the press, and Aitken showed his anxiety over this when he wrote his little book *Success* in 1922. In it he discussed the Canada Cement Company affair, pleading that if he had shown 'pliability' then it might have turned into a habit (Beaverbrook, 74–6). In spring 1910 he paid a second visit to England to raise money to finance the acquisition of a steel company, and his decision to make his life there was probably influenced by the bad odour surrounding the cement merger.

Politics and war Aitken's interest in politics was quickened by what he called the 'exciting political situation over Chamberlain's plea for a united Empire' (Chisholm and Davie, 69). This involved the United Kingdom setting a tariff on foreign goods, but giving empire countries a special preferential rate. This policy deeply split the Conservative and Unionist Party when Chamberlain launched his tariff reform crusade in 1903, and the divisions threatened to keep the party in the political wilderness; but the Liberals were certainly going to remain the party of free trade, and Aitken's political ambitions could lie nowhere else than with the Unionists, at least if they could be persuaded to adopt tariff reform. Aitken met the future Unionist leader Andrew Bonar Law, and on his third visit to England in autumn 1910 he met Law again. The two men got on well, despite their very different individual temperaments: both had Scots-Canadian connections, both were sons of the manse, both were businessmen.

In the world of Edwardian politics Aitken's chief talents—his ability to cultivate friendships, influence people, and make money—were at a premium. In November 1910 Law recommended him as a possible parliamentary candidate for Ashton under Lyne. Aitken hesitated, thinking he was being offered a seat really intended for a working-class Conservative candidate, but he finally agreed to stand if he were given sufficient political support from leading Unionists such as F. E. Smith. Aitken was an efficient campaign organizer and he had money to spend on publicity. His wife was an able helper and Aitken, though not a natural public speaker—he acknowledged that his wife was better at this—won the seat by 196 votes. His victory was given added value by the fact that it was one of the few Unionist successes in the general election of December 1910.

Aitken was neither an effective nor a comfortable member of parliament. He rarely spoke in the House of Commons, and made little mark. He was knighted in 1911, not because of his political achievements, but in expectation of future contributions to Unionist Party funds. Aitken bought Cherkley Court, a large house near Leatherhead, Surrey, which became a centre of political gatherings. When Law replaced A. J. Balfour as leader of the Unionists in 1911, Aitken's stock rose accordingly. His delight in acting as a political go-between found outlet in 1913 when he offered his house for negotiations on the Ulster question and Irish home rule then being conducted between Law and H. H. Asquith, the Liberal prime minister.

Meanwhile Aitken made his first serious move into what was to be the real love of his life: journalism. He had already dabbled in the trade in Canada, founding the weekly *Canadian Century* in 1910 and saving the *Montreal Herald* from collapse by giving it $150,000 (and decisively influencing its change from a Liberal to a Conservative newspaper). In the same year he met R. D. Blumenfeld, editor of the *Daily Express*, whose newspaper also needed an injection of funds. Aitken wrote a cheque for £25,000 without collateral, thus beginning his long connection with the *Express* on terms highly favourable to himself. He tried to buy *The Standard*, but failed, but he got effective control of *The Globe*, which, though it proved an unsuccessful newspaper, gave him experience in journalism and its practitioners. The *Express* was still failing to pay its way, and Aitken was involved in yet another salvage operation on behalf of the Unionist Party; more importantly, he realized that the impact of the 'new journalism' launched by Lord Northcliffe had come to stay, and that this popular paper was the kind he wanted to own. He had to wait until November 1916 before finally getting his desire, paying £17,500 for shares which enabled him to take control of the *Express*, retaining Blumenfeld as editor. He kept the deal secret because he had learned by now that politicians, though they cultivated the press and even subsidized it, also resented its claim to speak to the people over their heads.

The outbreak of war in August 1914 gave Aitken his chance to demonstrate that he was (to his own satisfaction at any rate) a significant political player. But at first it was his publicity skills that were most useful. In January 1915 he became honorary lieutenant-colonel and was appointed to 'take charge of the work connected with records generally appertaining to the Canadian Overseas Expeditionary Force' (Chisholm and Davie, 125–6). He was made Canadian record officer, and in January 1916 published his first book, *Canada in Flanders*, vol. 1. His utter commitment to the war effort aroused his hostility to Asquith, who by 1915 was under attack for his mismanaging of the war. When Asquith reconstructed his cabinet in May 1915, Aitken did not get a post, and his antipathy to Asquith increased when Law tried to get Aitken appointed KCMG on the colonial list, but was prevented by Asquith. In the political intrigue that ended in Asquith's being replaced as prime minister by David Lloyd George in December 1916, Aitken was credited then and later (not least by himself) as a key figure in the business, but his account of the affair is at certain points debatable or wrong, and his use of the *Daily Express* to undermine Asquith may have been counter-productive. However, there is no doubt about his enjoyment of the crisis, and his role as go-between. Aitken later claimed that he expected to be included in Lloyd George's administration as president of the Board of Trade, but it seems unlikely that such an offer would have been made; in any event, no job emerged, but Aitken acquired a peerage, despite the king's objections, and Lord Beaverbrook, as he became, had collected material for his first major excursion into writing history, his *Politicians and the War* (1928). He was clearly a man to be reckoned with, and he would not be kept out of places of power for long. But he had to be careful: when in 1917 his control of the *Daily Express* became known, he was criticized by Conservative central office because, instead of doing the respectable thing and subsidizing loyal party newspapers, he was putting his money into an independent and, in central office's view, irresponsible non-party publication.

Beaverbrook's understanding of the key role of publicity in wartime secured him the position as head of the propaganda committee under the control of the department of information, and in February 1918 he became the first ever minister of information. He was also made chancellor of the duchy of Lancaster, with a seat in the cabinet. The appointment of a press lord, whose ranks Beaverbrook now openly joined, provoked political criticism, with Austen Chamberlain leading the attack. Beaverbrook decided to concentrate his propaganda efforts on using the press as the best means of promoting the British and allied cause. He made contact with people who had knowledge of foreign countries, but he met opposition from ministers, including Balfour, who resented his attempts to use their departments and networks for his own purposes. Beaverbrook was not a man to live long under frustrating circumstances, and he offered to resign in June 1918. His ministerial demise came, not over this, but from a leader in the *Daily Express* on 29 August 1918 declaring that, unless Lloyd George gave pledges on tariff reform and imperial preference, the *Express* would no longer support him. Lloyd George was furious, and the episode seemed to demonstrate the arrogance of the press barons. Beaverbrook stayed on until October 1918, and even after he went, pleading ill health, he threw the *Express* behind Lloyd George in the general election that Lloyd George and Law planned for December 1918.

Press lord Beaverbrook now threw his energies into making his newspaper business as successful as he had his other concerns. In 1919 the *Daily Express* circulation was under 400,000; but by 1930 it was 1,693,000 and in 1937 it stood at 2,329,000, the largest circulation of any newspaper in the British Isles. This was because of its popular, aggressive tone, but also its optimism, enthusiasm, and claim to speak for those who were, like Beaverbrook himself, determined to stand up for themselves and take control of their own lives. There were also lively features, and all this in the style of the new journalism. Beaverbrook, like his great predecessor Northcliffe, was careful to keep up with the new technology and to experiment with layout. Unlike Northcliffe he did not use stunts to promote sales: his success was based on his belief in the importance of the words on the page, and to this end he hired first-rate staff—financial writers like Francis Williams and the great cartoonist David Low. He kept tight control of his editors. One of the *Express*'s long-serving editors, Arthur Christiansen, recollected 'feeling sick when Neville Chamberlain described Czechoslovakia as "a far away country"' but when he expressed his opinion Beaverbrook said 'Well, isn't Czechoslovakia a far away country?' and 'I agreed that it was and got on with my job of producing an exciting newspaper' (Chester and Fenby, 23). Yet Beaverbrook allowed Low, in the words of the Political and Economic Planning *Report on the British Press* published in 1938, to 'hold up the whole of capitalist society to ridicule' (p. 178).

The paper stressed optimism. Francis Williams reminded Arthur Christiansen of his desire to 'make everyone feel it was a sunny day' (Christiansen, 151). The *Express* was ever-vigilant on behalf of the British people; in its coverage of the food shortage of 1946, and bread rationing, it complained that 'ex-enemies get more' and printed pictures of a beauty treatment in Paris which required using eight eggs and two double cognacs ('Report of the royal commission on the press', 331). A. J. P. Taylor put the *Express*'s success down to the fact that its owner was indifferent to the British class system, holding that 'there was no difference between rich and poor except that the rich had more money' (Taylor, *English History*, 310). But the *Express* did have its roots in what at the end of the twentieth century has been called 'middle England'. The Political and Economic Planning *Report on the British Press* carried out a survey of British newspaper readership, revealing that the bulk of the *Daily Express* readers were from social groups whose chief earner in the family brought in between £125 and £500 a year, concluding that 'in the middle grade of the population, the *Daily Mail* and the *Daily Express* held sway' (pp. 231, 235).

Beaverbrook made mistakes: the *Sunday Express*, which he launched in December 1918, failed to attract good circulation and soon used up the £500,000 that he put into it;

but when he made John Junor editor in 1928 it began to make money. Beaverbrook enjoyed the newspaper world. He liked attacking his enemies and supporting his friends. He loved picking up gossip to use in his newspapers, but he would also suppress a story if he were asked to by his wide circle of friends. Equally, he enjoyed playing fast and loose with the Conservative Party, broadly supporting it while finding fault with its policies and leaders when he saw fit. However, he did not seek to expand his empire indefinitely. In 1923 he bought the *Evening Standard* for himself and Lord Rothermere, and got a controlling influence in the Glasgow *Evening Citizen*. He installed machinery so that he could print the *Daily Express* in Manchester, and in 1928 he started the *Scottish Daily Express*; but that was as far as he went.

Beaverbrook was less successful in his direct political campaigns. Between 1919 and 1922 he followed Northcliffe's example in claiming to speak for the people, and he attacked Lloyd George's coalition government on a whole range of issues, from British intervention in Russia to the question of London slums. His interest in politics quickened after the death of Bonar Law in October 1923. Beaverbrook claimed that he had been the key figure in persuading Law to attend the Carlton Club meeting in 1922 which brought down the Lloyd George administration, but his relations with Law were troubled by the latter's refusal fully to endorse tariff reform. Beaverbrook funded and supported independent Conservative candidates, and once Law had gone he was able to take the gloves off. For the next fifteen years he devoted his political will to endeavouring to remove Stanley Baldwin from the Conservative leadership. Partly this was because Beaverbrook soon realized that he had no hold over Baldwin when Baldwin called a general election in the autumn of 1923 against Beaverbrook's advice. His anger grew when Baldwin fought the election on the issue of protection, but without special terms for the empire. Nevertheless, he supported the Conservatives' election campaign, but, the election lost, he wrote disparagingly of Baldwin in the *Sunday Express*: Baldwin, the paper wrote, was now stripped of his power and patronage and must rely on his own capabilities which had so far 'proved of second rank' (Koss, 2.434). Beaverbrook and Rothermere persuaded Winston Churchill to stand as an independent constitutionalist in a by-election in the Abbey division of Westminster on a platform of imperial preference. In May 1925 the *Daily Express* warned that independent Conservatives would again 'arise' and that it was quite likely that the *Express* would support them (Boyce, 'Crusaders without chains', 106). By 1929 he was ready to launch his bid for power, a bid he felt sure must succeed for, as he wrote in 1926, 'when skilfully employed at the psychological moment no politician of any party can resist (the press)' (Chisholm and Davie, 276).

Clearly Beaverbrook saw himself as the reincarnation of the great Northcliffe. There was another passing resemblance, and that was Beaverbrook's inability to remain faithful to his wife. It is hard to see how his marriage would have avoided strain, given Beaverbrook's lifestyle, but matters became more fraught in 1925 when he began to see Jane Norton (d. 1945), a society lady of considerable beauty, whom Lady Beaverbrook saw as at any rate an improvement on the 'actresses' who had attracted her husband hitherto. Old friends began to invite Beaverbrook and Jane Norton together, and some noticed an increasing coarseness in his treatment of his wife. Lady Beaverbrook and her daughter Janet spent some time in Canada in the winter of 1926 and summer 1927, when Lady Beaverbrook began to show signs of illness. In April 1927 she returned to England, still unwell; doctors could find nothing wrong with her, but she died from a brain tumour on 1 December. Beaverbrook retained enough of his Presbyterian upbringing to feel guilty, and he destroyed all his wife's papers, including her letters to him. Some said he ensured that her nurse would remain silent, lest his wife had let slip some damaging revelation. Beaverbrook told a friend that he wished he could turn the clock back twenty years, but he was soon to find consolation in the world that he now lived in, one dominated for the next decade by economic turmoil and political danger.

Empire crusader Characteristically, Beaverbrook rode out the great financial crash of 1929, selling shares before it struck. But he saw the opportunity for mobilizing opinion behind an empire crusade—a crusade for protection and imperial preference—in the crisis that overtook the world's markets. His brief, and not particularly happy, experience of cabinet government in 1917–18 had not dulled his appetite for political power, and while he would not have looked as far as Lord Rothermere, who hoped to see Beaverbrook in 10 Downing Street, he certainly believed that press lords had the power to 'coerce politicians' (Chisholm and Davie, 275).

Beaverbrook now set his sights firmly on the moving target of Stanley Baldwin, whom he believed to be a stubborn man and therefore weak and vacillating. Beaverbrook launched his crusade on 8 July 1929; it would not only be a newspaper campaign, but would involve creating a new political party. The new party started well: it enrolled 173,000 members in a fortnight and one Conservative noted that his party's rank and file were 'seething with uncertainty and unrest' (Boyce, 'Crusaders without chains', 107). In July 1929 Conservative central office repudiated Sir John Ferguson as candidate for the Twickenham by-election because of his open support for empire free trade; Ferguson won the seat anyway. Thus encouraged, Beaverbrook put his own party's candidate forward in the West Fulham by-election of May 1930 and won, and in October an Empire Free Trade candidate won in South Paddington. But Beaverbrook's ambitions were damaged as much as enhanced by these successes. To unseat Baldwin he must, in the end, pressurize the Conservative Party into accepting his doctrine; but setting his candidates against official Conservatives angered the party, and when one success, in East Islington in January–February 1931, let in the Labour candidate through a Conservative split vote, then it was clear to most Conservatives that Beaverbrook posed a threat to that most essential political

need: party unity. The downfall followed remarkably quickly. In the St George's Westminster by-election in March 1931 Baldwin counter-attacked, accusing the press lords of seeking 'power without responsibility' (Boyce, 'The fourth estate', 35). The words were Kipling's and they hit home. Baldwin's candidate, Duff Cooper, won; and in September 1931 Sir Robert Bruce Lockhart wrote in his diary that Brendan Bracken 'thinks that Max will be the last of his trade and that the reign of the great press lords is coming to an end' (Boyce, 'Crusaders without chains', 108).

The empire crusade was effectively over. Now Beaverbrook seemed to be an inveterate picker of lost causes. He backed Edward VIII in his attempt to retain the throne, hardly realizing that the king did not want to be saved at the expense of losing Mrs Simpson (whom Beaverbrook did not find attractive). Beaverbrook, who was no monarchist and confessed that he 'scarcely knew the King', was motivated by his desire, as he put it, to 'bugger Baldwin' (Birkenhead, 138). His strong support of appeasement in the late 1930s was more in line with political as well as public opinion; few people in Britain wanted to admit that war on the continent of Europe was inevitable. Beaverbrook no doubt spoke for many when he supported the Munich agreement, with the *Daily Express* claiming on 22 September 1938 that Britain had made no pledge to protect the frontiers of Czechoslovakia, but he pushed the point too far. In March 1939 he denied that Neville Chamberlain had made any absolute guarantee to Poland, and when war broke out in September Beaverbrook's confident assurances over the past few years that there would be no war this year or the next looked, to say the least, hollow. Beaverbrook's hostility to the war was compounded by his notion that the renamed duke of Windsor might be persuaded to stump the country calling for a compromise peace. However, the British failure in an expedition to Norway in April 1940 changed his mind. On 10 May he lunched with Churchill and thereafter threw his energy behind the war effort. Churchill asked the king to appoint Beaverbrook minister of aircraft production, knowing how good Beaverbrook was at inspiring and driving staff. On 14 May, aged sixty, Beaverbrook took over responsibility for repairs to damaged aircraft, as well as production of new planes. On 2 August he became a member of the war cabinet.

In and out of power There can be no doubt about Beaverbrook's commitment to the task, which he approached in his usual energetic and domineering style. Characteristically, he exaggerated his contribution to the increase in aircraft production, the numbers of which had been rising before he took up his position. He made some mistakes, for example in reducing the production of aircraft suitable for the vital role of photo-reconnaissance. His abrasive methods annoyed other departments and especially the Air Ministry, and he soon found his job irksome. He intimated to Churchill that he wished to go, and on 30 April 1941 his resignation was accepted. However, he now became minister of state because Churchill wanted to retain him in the cabinet; in addition he was made deputy chairman of the defence committee (supply), but with no executive function. He found this frustrating and in June 1941 got the Ministry of Supply for himself. But now a new crusade was on the horizon.

In September 1941 Beaverbrook went to Moscow to persuade the USSR to stay in the war. He met Stalin and believed that the two of them had established a rapport. He was certain that Stalin could be trusted, and urged Britain to help the USSR in every way it could. To this end he approved of the USSR's retaining much of eastern Poland, the Baltic states, part of Romania, and some of Finland after the war. His political position in Britain was strengthened when Churchill made him minister of production in February 1942. Beaverbrook's temperament was not suitable for the task, however, and he quarrelled with Ernest Bevin over control of shipbuilding and labour. His resignation came after only twelve days in office, on 20 February; but at least he was now free to devote himself to the cause of supporting the USSR in the war. In June 1942 he addressed a large crowd in Birmingham, calling for the allies to open a second front in Europe, and he pushed this cause with his usual energy and single-mindedness. Nevertheless, the suspicion that dogged Beaverbrook's motives persisted, for some thought that he was really scheming to supplant Churchill as prime minister. In September 1943 he returned to the cabinet as lord privy seal, where he used his business acumen to better effect in planning post-war air routes across the Atlantic; but he became bored with the detail of negotiations and decided that he would devote himself to assisting Churchill to win the general election that would follow the end of the war. Any notion that press lords could swing the electorate was damaged by the large Labour Party victory in 1945; and the *Daily Express*'s claim that there would be 'Gestapo in Britain' if Labour won was a misjudgement of the public mood (Chisholm and Davie, 453–4).

Beaverbrook's loss of touch was revealed also by his advice to Churchill in 1945 not to publish the Conservative Party's proposals for the health service, on the grounds that it was 'inexpedient' (Thomas, 38). He argued that free enterprise was the way forward, but he was not a consistently right-wing thinker: the cold war was, he thought, unnecessary. He still clung to the ideas of imperial unity, freedom from foreign entanglements, and a distant relationship with the United States of America, all of which—though not necessarily mistaken—were out of touch with the times. He remained the empire crusader, opposing British acceptance of an American loan in 1947, and, above all, against the British application to join the European Common Market (EEC) in 1961. His bitter attack on Europe derived its venom from his hatred of Germany. He complained that the EEC was 'an American device to put us alongside Germany. As our power was broken and lost by two German wars, it is very hard on us now to be asked to align ourselves with those villains' (Horne, 2.262).

Beaverbrook's press power continued to be the object of criticism, not least from the 1947 royal commission on the press. He maintained that this was intent on persecuting him, provoked by what was regarded—justifiably—as his policy of using his papers to blacklist people he did not like, and of retaining too tight a control over his editors. As usual, Beaverbrook adopted attack as the best means of defence, telling an astonished commission that he ran his papers for propaganda purposes, and that if an editor opposed a policy that was dear to his heart, such as empire free trade, then he 'talked' him out of it ('Report of the royal commission on the press', 43). Beaverbrook went on to say: 'No paper is any good at all for propaganda unless it has a thoroughly good financial position. So we worked very hard to build up a commercial position on that account' (ibid., 26). He admitted that the *Daily Express*'s commercial position was built on its ability to give its readers what they liked; and the Political and Economic Planning *Report on the British Press* had noted in 1938 that the chief subjects covered in the *Express* in a chosen period (28 February–6 March 1938) were indeed law (including crime, police, divorce, and suicide), accidents, film stars and films, and sport. Such topics as industry, science, medicine, education, and labour relations came well down the list, and unemployment was completely absent. More evasively, Beaverbrook told the royal commission that editors must have a degree of latitude, but must also be carried along with the proprietor's views. The commission noted that Beaverbrook picked staff who shared his views and policies, and controlled the newspapers even when his presence was removed.

Last years and reputation In 1951 Beaverbrook ceased to renew his membership of the Conservative Party and it was from that year that the empire crusader on the *Daily Express* masthead was draped in chains. This was significant. Beaverbrook's Presbyterian upbringing, though it seems to have exercised no influence on his private life, was perhaps manifested in his restless quest for a crusade—for a great cause that could be given a moral as well as political dimension. But from now on there were no great causes, or at least none that held any possibility of success: opposition to Europe was an example. Yet Beaverbrook was excited by the recognition of his role as a historian of his own times. When A. J. P. Taylor reviewed Beaverbrook's *Men and Power* in 1956, describing it as 'one of the most exciting works of history' he had ever read and its author as a great historian, comparable to Tacitus, Beaverbrook was delighted (Chisholm and Davie, 502). This was the start of a close friendship between the two, with Taylor witnessing to Beaverbrook's charm, and his ability to 'steal the hearts of men' (ibid., 503). Taylor remarked on Beaverbrook's restlessness in old age, with journeys to Jamaica, the Bahamas, France, New York, and Canada. He still ran the *Daily Express* as a very successful newspaper, with talented staff. A collector of political papers, his purchases included those of Lloyd George and Bonar Law, which were later opened to historians in the Beaverbrook Library in the *Daily Express* building, under the benign gaze of A. J. P. Taylor, its director. The University of New Brunswick, of which he became chancellor in 1953, received an endowment from him, as well as funding for founding scholarships and a new library and art gallery. He still aroused controversy, even in old age, with accusations of vendettas and sexual misbehaviour. Still accused of being unable to treat women with dignity, Beaverbrook nevertheless found a regular companion in Marcia Anastasia Dunn [see below], widow of Sir James Dunn, whom he married on 7 June 1963. Just over a year later, on 9 June 1964, he died of cancer at Cherkley. Beaverbrook's elder son, (John William) Max Aitken (1910–1985), succeeded to the baronetcy but disclaimed the barony, maintaining that 'there will be only one Lord Beaverbrook'.

Beaverbrook's reputation was controversial in his day, and has remained so, as new information has emerged. He made gifts to many people, some famous, some obscure; but this was seen by many as his way of controlling and corrupting. Cecil King, who like Clement Attlee described Beaverbrook as 'evil', wrote that 'he seemed to take pleasure in humiliating and corrupting his young men, preventing them from breaking loose by absurdly overpaying them' (Gourley, 40). Yet this might also be regarded as sound business sense: keeping talented staff by paying them well was hardly unusual. The question was whether this went further, and was a means of buying, not simply employing, people; but Beaverbrook employed David Low, whose cartoons were entirely of Low's own creation. He also gave money to those whose political ideas he did not agree with, and whom he did not control. Notably, Michael Foot was given £3000 to help save the left-wing journal *Tribune* from extinction. Yet even this could be construed as having a personal, or at least political, motive, that of promoting discord within the Labour Party.

Many bore witness to his charm, especially A. J. P. Taylor. Among his unlikely conquests was Aneurin Bevan, who enjoyed both Beaverbrook's hospitality and his conversation, and—to the disgust of Tom Clarke of the *News Chronicle*—'addressed Beaverbrook familiarly as Max' (Campbell, 64). Yet Bevan carefully avoided Beaverbrook's efforts to place him directly in his debt, by way of offers of money to pay for medical treatment, and of a cottage on the Cherkley estate. Beaverbrook's appearance was most unprepossessing. One journalist described him as looking 'like some genial spider' (*Fleet Street*, 93), while others were less complimentary.

Beaverbrook seems to have possessed the gift of making those to whom he spoke feel that he was solely interested in them. But he was sensitive and nervous about his own image, and his self-absorption was seen in his efforts to exercise control over one of his biographers, Tom Driberg. Beaverbrook influenced the text, yet managed to keep this secret, so that what was in reality a vetted work was regarded by many at the time as a highly critical biography, though the perceptive Evelyn Waugh dismissed it as a 'honeyed eulogy', and complained that 'you give little impression of the deep malevolence of the man' (*Letters*, 467). Beaverbrook disliked yielding centre stage, even to his first wife and his eldest son. His political adventures ended largely in failure. He made his career in England, but he remained devoted to the Canada he left for good in 1910, and he estimated that he had given $16 million to various causes and institutions in New Brunswick. He formally renounced his United Kingdom citizenship on 17 December 1951, and his ashes were laid to rest at Newcastle, New Brunswick, Canada, on 25 September 1964.

Some even regarded Beaverbrook as essentially an outsider: the Canadian who, whatever his wealth and ambitions, remained outside the establishment. But his significance does not lie in his political ambitions and causes, which largely failed, nor in his financial acumen, but in his talent for producing a brilliant newspaper. The *Daily Express* may not have exercised the political influence that Beaverbrook aspired to, but it represented a certain kind of Britain, or more properly England, at a particular era in its history. Beaverbrook was a shrewd picker of staff who recognized a first-rate journalist when he saw one. But he owed his success mainly to what he himself described as 'prejudice and breadth of vision. It's a rare combination' (Chisholm and Davie, 7–8). And one that Beaverbrook possessed, though in what proportions will always be a matter of controversy.

Marcia Anastasia Aitken [*née* Christoforides], Lady Beaverbrook [*other married name* Marcia Anastasia Dunn, Lady Dunn] (1909–1994), racehorse owner and Beaverbrook's second wife, was born on 27 July 1909 at Kaisaria, Cheam Road, Sutton, Surrey, the daughter of John Christoforides (or Christoforidi), a Greek-Cypriot tobacco merchant, and his wife, Mildred, *née* Boys. Educated partly at Roedean School, in 1930 she became secretary—initially paid 30s. a week—to Sir James Hamet *Dunn, first baronet (1874–1956), a London-based Canadian financier, who bought his baronetcy via the Lloyd George political fund. He returned to Canada and in 1935 took charge of the Algoma Steel Corporation of Ontario (gaining full control in 1944); she followed and became its assistant secretary. After his second wife divorced him, and after she had nursed him through a near fatal illness, he married her on 7 June 1942. Following his death, on 1 January 1956, she inherited half his fortune (estimated at nearly C$70 million). She gave a science block and endowed law scholarships at Dalhousie University, New Brunswick, of which Dunn had been a graduate. Griefstricken, she talked of entering a convent. Instead she became the constant companion of Lord Beaverbrook, a friend of Dunn since boyhood. He used her diary in writing his memoir of Dunn, *Courage* (1961), which she disliked. Reportedly she and Beaverbrook secretly plighted their troth at the church at Torphichen, West Lothian, in 1961. On 7 June 1963 he married her at Epsom register office. He repeatedly said that she was richer than he was, and it was conjectured that he hoped—though in vain—that she might divert funds to his Beaverbrook foundation at the University of New Brunswick. She became a trustee of the Beaverbrook foundations and was put on the board of Beaverbrook newspapers. On 9 June 1964 Beaverbrook died in her arms. She was bequeathed none of his fortune. According to A. J. P. Taylor, 'Beaverbrook had no doubt planned to play off Christofor against Max after his own death' (Taylor, *Beaverbrook*, 671), but she ended her connection with his newspapers.

Through her friendship with Lord Rosebery—and although both her husbands had deplored the racing world—Lady Beaverbrook became a leading racehorse owner and supporter of British racing. She was known in racing circles as Lady B, and her colours were beaver brown with maple-leaf green cross-belts. Devoted to her horses, she habitually gave them seven-letter names. Her pride and joy was Boldboy, who won more prize money than any other gelding trained in Britain: she made provision for him in her will. At the zenith of her career she employed Sir Gordon Richards as her racing manager. In total she owned more than 250 winners, and she was twice second in the owners' table. Following Beaverbrook's death she also renewed her interest in Dalhousie, which awarded her an honorary LLD degree in 1967 and of which she became chancellor in 1968. The university welcomed her money but resented her interference. Despite her wealth, some aspects of her life were austere. She died, childless, of liver failure and cancer at her Surrey home, Cherkley Court, Leatherhead, on 28 October 1994.

D. GEORGE BOYCE

Sources A. Chisholm and M. Davie, *Beaverbrook: a life* (1992); repr. (1993) · A. J. P. Taylor, *Beaverbrook* (1972) · L. Gourley, ed., *The Beaverbrook I knew* (1984) · S. E. Koss, *The rise and fall of the political press in Britain*, 2 (1984) · T. Driberg, *Beaverbrook: a study in power and frustration* (1956) · A. Christiansen, *Headlines all my life* (1961) · P. Howard, *Beaverbrook: a study of Max the unknown* (1964) · C. M. Vines, *A little nut-brown man: my three years with Beaverbrook* (1968) · 'Royal commission on the press, 1947–49: report', *Parl. papers* (1948–9), vol. 20, Cmd 7700 · J. Thomas, 'A bad press? Popular newspapers, the labour party, and British politics from Northcliffe to Blair', PhD diss., University College, Swansea, 1999 · L. Chester and J. Fenby, *The fall of the house of Beaverbrook* (1979) · *Report on the British press*, Political and Economic Planning (1938) · *Fleet Street, press barons and politics: the journals of Collin Brooks, 1932–1940*, ed. N. J. Crowson, CS, 5th ser., 11 (1998) · G. Boyce, 'The fourth estate: the reappraisal of a concept', *Newspaper history: from the seventeenth century to the present day*, ed. J. Curran, P. Wingate, and G. Boyce (1978), 19–40 · Lord Beaverbrook, *Success* (1922) · D. G. Boyce, 'Crusaders without chains: power and the press barons, 1896–1951', *Impacts and influences: essays on media power in the twentieth century*, ed. J. Curran, A. Smith, and P. Wingate (1987), 97–112 · Lord Birkenhead, *Walter Monckton: the life of Viscount Monckton of Brenchley* (1969) · A. Horne, *Macmillan*, 2 vols. (1988–9) · J. Campbell, *Nye Bevan and the mirage of British socialism* (1987) · *CGPLA Eng. & Wales* (1965) · A. J. P. Taylor, *English history, 1919–1945* (1997) · *The letters of Evelyn Waugh*, ed. M. Amory (1981) · Burke, *Peerage* · *The Times* (31 Oct 1994) · *Daily Telegraph* (31 Oct 1994) · *The Independent* (31 Oct 1994) · *The Guardian* (5 Nov 1994) · *CGPLA Eng. & Wales* (1997)

Archives HLRO, corresp. and papers · NA Canada, Canadian corresp. · News Int. RO, papers · NRA, priv. coll., letters · PRO, papers, CAB 127/239–258 · University of New Brunswick, Fredericton, Canadian corresp. | BL, corresp. with Lord Northcliffe, Add. MS 62161 · BL, corresp. with Marie Stopes, Add. MS 58555 · BLPES, corresp. with Lady Rhys Williams · Bodl. Oxf., corresp. with H. A. Gwynne · Bodl. Oxf., corresp. with Lord Monckton · Bodl. Oxf., corresp. with third earl of Selborne · Borth. Inst., corresp. with Lord Halifax · CAC Cam., corresp. with A. V. Alexander · CAC Cam., corresp. with Duff Cooper · CAC Cam., corresp. with Lord Croft · CAC Cam., corresp. with Lord Halifax [copies] · CKS, corresp. with J. H. Thomas · CUL, corresp. with W. A. Gerhardie · CUL, corresp. with Samuel Hoare · HLRO, corresp. with Geoffrey Bocca · HLRO, corresp. with Viscount Davidson · HLRO, letters to Charles Graves · HLRO, corresp. with Andrew Bonar Law · HLRO, corresp. with David Lloyd George · HLRO, corresp. with Herbert Samuel ·

HLRO, corresp. with John St Loe Strachey · JRL, letters to *Manchester Guardian* · King's Lond., Liddell Hart C., corresp. with Sir B. H. Liddell Hart · Liverpool RO, corresp. with seventeenth earl of Derby · NA Scot., corresp. with A. J. Balfour relating to *Politicians and the war* · NA Scot., corresp. with Lord Elibank · NL Wales, letters to Desmond Donnelly · Nuffield Oxf., corresp. with Lord Cherwell · U. Birm. L., corresp. with Lord Avon · U. Birm. L., corresp. with Austen Chamberlain relating to formation of Lloyd George government · U. Leeds, Brotherton L., corresp. with Henry Drummond-Wolff · U. Newcastle, Robinson L., corresp. with Walter Runciman relating to international loans · UCL, corresp. with Arnold Bennett's solicitors | FILM BFI NFTVA, *Reputations*, Channel 4, 28 June 1981 · BFI NFTVA, *Secret lives*, Channel 4, 2 Dec 1996 · BFI NFTVA, home footage · BFI NFTVA, news footage · BFI NFTVA, propaganda film footage (ministry of information) | SOUND BL NSA, current affairs recording

Likenesses print, 1926 (after D. Low, 1926) · H. Coster, photograph, *c*.1930, NPG · photograph, *c*.1930, NPG · W. R. Sickert, oils, 1935, NPG [*see illus.*] · G. Sutherland, study head, 1950, Beaverbrook Art Gallery, Fredericton, New Brunswick, Canada · F. Man, photograph, *c*.1951, NPG · G. Sutherland, oils, 1951, Beaverbrook Art Gallery, Fredericton, New Brunswick, Canada · G. Sutherland, oils, 1952, priv. coll. · G. Sutherland, oils, 1952, NPG · D. Low, caricature, repro. in D. Low, *Lions and lambs* (1928) · A. P. F. Ritchie, cigarette card · photographs, Beaverbrook Archive · photographs, Hult. Arch.

Wealth at death £379,530 effects in England: administration with will, 9 Sept 1965, *CGPLA Eng. & Wales* · £891,266—Marcia Anastasia Aitken [Lady Beaverbrook]: probate, 1997, *CGPLA Eng. & Wales*

Aitkin, John (*d.* 1790), surgeon, the date of whose birth is not recorded, must have studied medicine at Edinburgh, where he became a member of the College of Surgeons in 1770. In 1779 he is described as surgeon and lecturer on surgery in Edinburgh. Either at that time or later his lectures included, besides the practice of physic, anatomy, midwifery, and chemistry. He appears to have been a successful teacher, and wrote several books, chiefly as textbooks for his lectures. These include *Essays on Several Important Subjects in Surgery, Chiefly with Regard to the Nature and Cure of Fractures* (1771); *Elements of the Theory and Practice of Surgery* (1779), republished with the *Elements of the Theory and Practice of Physic*, thus forming two volumes entitled *Elements of the Theory and Practice of Physic and Surgery* (1783); *Outlines of the Theory and Cure of Fever* (1781), and *Principles of Midwifery or Puerperal Medicine* (1784).

Aitkin made certain practical improvements in surgery. He introduced an alteration in the mode of locking the midwifery forceps. He also invented a flexible blade to the lever. He likewise invented and described in his *Essays and Cases in Surgery* a pair of forceps for dividing and diminishing the stone in the bladder when too large to remove entire by lithotomy. He died at Edinburgh on 22 September 1790.

J. F. PAYNE, *rev.* MICHAEL BEVAN

Sources G. Long, ed., *The biographical dictionary of the Society for the Diffusion of Useful Knowledge*, 4 vols. in 7 (1842–4) · *GM*, 1st ser., 60 (1790), 866 · P. J. Wallis and R. V. Wallis, *Eighteenth century medics*, 2nd edn (1988)

Aiton, John (1797–1863), Church of Scotland minister and author, was born at Strathaven in June 1797, the youngest son of William *Aiton (1760–1848), authority on Scottish husbandry, and Margaret Borland (*d.* 1820). He studied theology at Edinburgh University and was licensed by the presbytery of Hamilton on 30 November 1819. He published, in 1824, *A Refutation of Mr Robert Owen's Objections to Christianity*. For this pamphlet he was presented by Lord Douglas to the benefice of Dolphinton, south Lanarkshire, and was its minister from April 1825 until his death. He published variously, including a biography of Alexander Henderson (1836), *Clerical Economics* (1842) (a handbook of clerical rights and duties), *Eight Weeks in Germany* (1842), *The Lands of the Messiah, Mahomet, and the Pope* (1852), *The Drying-up of the Euphrates* (1853), and *St Paul and his Localities in their Past and Present Condition* (1856). He died at Pyrgo Park, Havering, Essex, on 15 May 1863.

THOMAS JOHNSTONE, *rev.* H. C. G. MATTHEW

Sources *Fasti Scot.* · Boase, *Mod. Eng. biog.*
Archives U. Edin., New Coll. L., letters to Thomas Chalmers

Aiton, William (1731–1793), horticulturist, was born at Boghall, Carnwath, Lanarkshire, the son of John Aiton, farmer, and his wife, Jean Weir. With his two brothers he trained as a gardener on the Shawfield estate at Woodhall near Airdrie. In 1754 he settled in England and the next year became assistant to Philip Miller at the Physic Garden at Chelsea. In 1759 he was recruited by John Haverfield (*c.*1694–1784), gardener to Augusta, dowager princess of Wales, at Kew, to manage her small physic garden: his annual salary by 1770 was £120.

In 1764 Aiton met Joseph Banks, who was to have increasing influence over Kew through his friendship with George III. From about 1773 Banks oversaw day-to-day running of the gardens and, with Aiton, raised their scientific and horticultural stature, forming the foundation for the modern Royal Botanic Gardens. Seeds and plants were sent from expeditions to the growing network of botanical gardens projected by Banks with Kew at its centre: Banks appointed and sometimes supported collectors, though Aiton himself suggested sending Francis Masson to the Cape as early as 1772. Largely under Kew's aegis, almost 7000 plant species were introduced to British horticulture during the reign of George III.

On Haverfield's resignation Aiton took over the kitchen garden and pleasure grounds on 1 January 1783, becoming the first superintendent of the entire Kew estate. As early as 1773 a plant catalogue was begun and this list was the basis for Aiton's *Hortus Kewensis* (three volumes, published August to October 1789), which effectively covered all plants in cultivation in southern England, with engravings, some from drawings by Franz Bauer and Georg Ehret. Aiton took plants for identification to Banks's curator–librarians Daniel Solander and Jonas Dryander in Soho Square. Latin manuscript species descriptions by Solander were used by Dryander, who contributed most of the third volume himself, to make up the scientific text of the book, which is a major scholarly work dealing with some 5600 species arranged according to the Linnaean system. Although it appeared under Aiton's name, as Aiton was 'Gardener to His Majesty', he merely added the plants' dates of introduction and other horticultural matter: he had no botanical expertise or bibliographical skills.

Specimens on which the new species in the book were based are in the Natural History Museum, London.

Aiton's wife, Elizabeth (*c.*1740–1826), bore him four daughters and two sons, the elder of whom, William Townsend *Aiton (1766–1849), succeeded his father at Kew and brought out, with the help of Dryander and Robert Brown, a second edition of *Hortus Kewensis* (1810–13); the younger, John Townsend Aiton (1777–1851), became royal gardener at Windsor, and later at Frogmore and Kensington Palace. Aiton died, apparently of liver failure, on 2 February 1793; his pallbearers included the artist Zoffany as well as Banks and Dryander, and his remains were buried in an elaborate family tomb at St Anne's, Kew. The funeral sermon delivered at Brentford on 17 February by the Revd W. Smith was published as *Silent Submission to the Will of God* (1793), and Aiton's widow petitioned Banks to seek a pension: £150 per annum was granted.

Aiton's achievement was the consolidation of Kew Gardens under the supervision of Banks. He was commemorated in names of a genus of bryophytes, *Aitonia* (*Aytonia*), and, later, of the South African shrub *Aitonia* (= *Nymania*) *capensis* (Meliaceae), though neither name is in current use. Aiton House at Kew, built on part of the site of George III's Castellated Palace and opened in June 1977, accommodates the office of the curator, his deputy, and the plant records.

D. J. MABBERLEY

Sources R. Desmond, *Kew: the history of the Royal Botanic Gardens* (1995) · 'The tomb of William Aiton', *Bulletin of Miscellaneous Information* [RBG Kew] (1910), 306–7 · W. T. Thiselton-Dyer, 'The elder Aiton', *Bulletin of Miscellaneous Information* [RBG Kew] (1891), 298–9 · D. J. Mabberley, *Jupiter botanicus: Robert Brown of the British Museum* (1985) · *The Banks letters*, ed. W. R. Dawson (1958) · F. Pagnamenta, 'The Aitons: gardeners to their majesties', *Richmond History*, 18 (1997), 8–19; 19 (1998), 36–47; 20 (1999), 37–49 · will, PRO, PROB 11/1241, sig. 59
Likenesses G. Engleheart, oils, 1786–7, RBG Kew · G. Engleheart, engraving, repro. in Desmond, *Kew*, 36 · attrib. J. Zoffany, oils, RBG Kew

Aiton, William (1760–1848), genealogist, was born in Silverwood, Kilmarnock, in January 1760, the eldest son of Andrew Aiton (1722–1809) of Woodhead, farmer, and his wife, Jean Brown (*d.* 1809). He was a distant relative of the botanist William Aiton (1731–1793). In June 1778 he married Margaret Borland (*d.* 1820); they had eight sons, including the Church of Scotland minister and author John *Aiton, and four daughters; six of the children died in infancy. Aiton commenced as a messenger at arms in Strathaven, Lanarkshire, in 1785. He became a notary in 1788 and then, in 1816, sheriff-substitute in the town of Hamilton. He held this position, which included a remit over the county court, until 1822, being forced out, as he thought, by the Hamilton clan, who apparently disliked relinquishing their accustomed sway over the court. Aiton nursed a grudge thereafter, describing his grievances in *An Inquiry into the Origin, Pedigree and History of the Family … of Aitons in Scotland* (1830), and joyfully recounting his discovery that the Aiton pedigree was far older and better authenticated than that of the Hamiltons. This fact, he said, had become apparent while researching his *Inquiry into the Pedigree of the Hamilton Family* (1821).

In his day, Aiton was a well-known authority on Scottish husbandry, especially moss-earth or peat, combining this interest with antiquarian and historical researches. His study on peat was first published in Glasgow in 1805, and doubled in length for a new edition in 1811. He further wrote on the agriculture of Ayr and Bute, and made a study of the battle of Drumclog, which included an analysis of Walter Scott's *Old Mortality*. He was by nature a generous man, though never earning more than £100 a year. He died in 1848.   JANET BROWNE

Sources DNB · W. Aiton, *An inquiry into the origin, pedigree and history of the family or clan of Aitons in Scotland* (1830)

Aiton, William Townsend (1766–1849), horticulturist, was born at 199 Kew Road, Kew, Surrey, on 2 February 1766, the elder son of the horticulturist William *Aiton (1731–1793) and his wife, Elizabeth (c.1740–1826), whose maiden name was possibly Townsend. He was educated privately in Chiswick and at Bower House school in Camberwell. Through the influence of Sir Joseph Banks he was apprenticed at the age of sixteen to his father; he also undertook private commissions as a landscape gardener. On the death of his father he succeeded the latter in the royal gardens at Kew, and on the resignation of John Haverfield the younger in 1795 those at Richmond. In 1804 Aiton took control of the gardens of Kensington and St James's palaces in succession to William Forsyth, and by 1827 he was styled—at his own suggestion—director-general of his majesty's gardens. He was held in high esteem by George III and the royal family, and conducted a confidential correspondence with the duke of Kent until the time of his death. John Nash consulted him over the planting scheme for St James's Palace and the Brighton Pavilion. He landscaped 40 acres at Buckingham Palace, uniting two small ponds into a grand lake, and supervised many extensive and important alterations at Windsor.

Aiton succeeded in getting his brother John appointed to the charge of the Hampton Court Gardens over the gardener to the duke of Clarence, but the result was the reduction of his own authority, on the duke's accession as William IV, to the charge of the Kew and Buckingham Palace gardens. Although he supervised the construction of a £6000 greenhouse at Kew in 1839, his management of Kew was severely criticized in John Lindley's report on the royal gardens: his reign was seen as one of procrastination, characterized by his failure to deal with correspondence and his lack of any clear policy. The gardens were transferred to the state and in June 1840 W. J. Hooker was appointed director, although only in November did Aiton agree to relinquish control. He surrendered his post on 25 March 1841, but retained the management of the pleasure grounds at Kew until 1845. He received a generous pension of £1000 per annum (Hooker's salary, by comparison, was £300, with a £200 housing allowance).

Between 1796 and 1802 Aiton published an edition of Franz Bauer's *Delineations of Exotick Plants* and in 1810–13 a second edition of 1250 copies of his father's *Hortus Kewensis*, in five volumes. The scientific content in the *Hortus Kewensis* is attributable to Sir Joseph Banks's librarians, Jonas Dryander and Robert Brown, who contributed much original work to the last two volumes. Aiton checked the dates of introduction of plants, of which over 11,000 are listed, and he also supervised production of an *Epitome*, in one volume, published in 1814. His papers and the draft of a second edition of the *Epitome* were burnt by his brother John, although part of the manuscript of the *Hortus Kewensis*, in the hand of Aiton's amanuensis, Richard Cunningham, survives at Kew, while Brown's drafts are at the Natural History Museum. Aiton's herbarium relating to the work, with Robert Teesdale's herbarium, which he had bought in 1805, were auctioned at his death. His library, with that of John, was auctioned in 1851: Kew was forbidden to bid.

Aiton was elected a fellow of the Linnean Society in 1797 and was one of the founders and an active fellow of the Horticultural Society. To its *Transactions* he contributed a paper on the cultivation of the cucumber, for which he was awarded a silver medal in 1817. He died at 199 Kew Road, unmarried, on 9 October 1849, and was buried at St Anne's, Kew Green, where there is a plaque. His heir was his illegitimate son, William Atwell Smith (b. 1808).

Aiton, an able landscape gardener, was too inflexible to appreciate the changing role of botanic gardens, a role which Hooker understood and which was, paradoxically, promoted by Banks, Aiton's patron. His legacy is therefore largely in the royal gardens other than Kew and in the names of a number of garden plants commemorating him, one not yet relegated to synonymy being Robert Brown's name *Serruria aitonii* (Proteaceae).

D. J. MABBERLEY

Sources R. Desmond, *Kew: the history of the Royal Botanic Gardens* (1995) · D. J. Mabberley, *Jupiter botanicus: Robert Brown of the British Museum* (1985) · H. R. Fletcher, *The story of the Royal Horticultural Society, 1804–1968* (1969) · J. Britten, 'The history of Aiton's *Hortus Kewensis*', *Journal of Botany, British and Foreign*, 50 (1912), 3rd suppl., 1–16
Archives RBG Kew, notebook | BL, letters to Sir Joseph Banks, Add. MSS 33980–33982 · NHM, corresp.
Likenesses L. Poyot, lithograph, 1829, RBG Kew · portrait, Royal Horticultural Society, London; repro. in Fletcher, *The story of the Royal Horticultural Society*
Wealth at death £7000: PRO, PROB 11/2102

Akbar [*née* Hasib], **Shireen Nishat** (1944–1997), educationist, was born on 30 July 1944 in Calcutta, India, the daughter of F. A. Hasib and Selina Hasib, who also had two sons. Among her forebears was Begum Rokeya Hussain (1880–1923), an early worker for women's emancipation in Bengal. In 1957 her family moved to East Pakistan. Shireen Hasib was educated in Dacca at Viqarunisa School, Holy Cross College, and Dacca University. In 1968 she married Anwar Akbar; they had one daughter, Sameena. In the same year she moved to England, where she attended New Hall, Cambridge, graduating in 1970 with a second-class degree in English. She then moved on to the Cambridge

Shireen Nishat Akbar (1944–1997), by unknown photographer [third from left, in the Nehru Gallery of Indian Art, Victoria and Albert Museum]

including demonstrations by weavers from Bangladesh. Through all of her exhibition work she sought to inspire creative energy as well as inform a wider audience of the beauty and depth of tradition in Asian arts.

In 1991 Akbar joined the Victoria and Albert Museum as south Asian arts education officer. It was during her time at the V&A that she embarked upon the Mughal tent project, her greatest achievement. She encouraged south Asian groups throughout Britain, many of whom had never visited a museum before, to visit the museum and to see the relevance of the museum collections to their own lives. She organized workshops for women to collaboratively create tent hangings which would illustrate their aspirations. Participants were encouraged to learn textile techniques from each other as well as from the museum collections. The women gained a sense of ownership of their work and many made lifelong friendships with other participants. Each group created hangings of extraordinary beauty, which were exhibited together within one tent at the V&A in 1997. She conceived the Mughal tent project with an emphasis on group learning and the development of existing networks, which extended far beyond initial expectations as new groups set up in other countries. Her project had deep roots in the educational traditions of south Asia as well as Britain, and offered a commitment to social change, self-directed learning, and long-term rather than short-term goals. The Mughal tent project received international acclaim throughout the museum and education world, and stood as a model for community-education initiatives.

Akbar was an elegant woman with natural authority and charm. In pursuit of her vision she was often stubborn and unrelenting, but her eloquence and beauty always persuaded those around her to follow her lead. Through her own example she spent most of her life encouraging south Asian women to aspire to improving their own lives, to gain confidence, and to reach for new opportunities. For her contribution to arts and community education she was made MBE. Her marriage to Anwar Akbar ended in divorce. In 1994 she developed breast cancer, but bravely fought to recover and continued developing projects until her death at the Royal Free Hospital, Camden, London, on 8 March 1997. She was survived by her daughter, Sameena.   JULIE CORNISH

Sources *The Times* (19 March 1997) · *The Independent* (1 April 1997) · personal knowledge (2004) · private information (2004) · d. cert. **Likenesses** photograph, repro. in *The Times* · photograph, repro. in *The Independent* · photograph, V&A [*see illus.*] **Wealth at death** under £180,000: probate, 2 June 1997, *CGPLA Eng. & Wales*

Institute of Education, where she gained a teaching qualification in primary education. She remained in Britain to become a teacher in London.

In 1978 Akbar was employed by the inner London education authority to work with young Bangladeshi women in Tower Hamlets as a language tutor. She quickly developed other aspects to her work as she sought to address the problems of racial abuse experienced by Asian women, and the restrictions placed upon them by their own community. She acted as an interpreter for Bangladeshi families who did not speak English, and she took the children on visits to places they had no other opportunity of seeing. She was one of few people doing this type of work at the time and her initiatives helped to redefine community education in London.

Akbar's highly innovative approach led her to develop a series of increasingly ambitious community arts projects. To ensure that children gained as much as possible from an introduction to Asian arts she collected resource material from Asia to support the work carried out by teachers in east London. She helped to organize 'Crafts of Bangladesh', an exhibition at the Crafts Council in 1986, and later raised funds to purchase the exhibition as a permanent resource for east London educational institutions. In 1988, following the success of her previous exhibitions, the Whitechapel Art Gallery employed her to help organize 'Woven Air', an exhibition celebrating traditional and contemporary textile techniques. In parallel she developed an acclaimed educational programme,

Aken, Joseph van (*c.*1699–1749), drapery painter and painter of genre and conversation pieces, was born probably in Antwerp, where he first practised as a painter. The title to a mezzotint of him by John Faber after Thomas Hudson gives his name as Vanhaeken, under which spelling of his name, rendered 'Van Haeken', he appeared in the *Dictionary of National Biography*. He moved to London about 1720 with his artist brothers Arnold and Alexander. His Flemish-style conversation pieces, such as *An English*

Family at Tea (Tate Gallery, London) and *Schoolmaster with a Class of Boys* (City Museum and Art Gallery, Hereford), painted on arrival in England, are of considerable interest to the social historian, as are his crowded city scenes, *The Stocks Market* (Bank of England, London) and *Covent Garden Market* (Museum of London). His powers of observation were most profitably employed when he turned his hand to the depiction of 'silks satins Velvets, gold & embroideryes' for a number of London's leading portrait painters, including Thomas Hudson and Allan Ramsay (Vertue, 3.117). His particular skill in differentiating between fabrics and in delineating jewels, so accurately as to enable identification of, for example, a Spitalfields silk or a paste necklace, make the portraits on which he worked a rich resource for the study of costume.

Hogarth bitterly remarked that an industrious drapery painter could not 'fail of getting a fortune' and often painted nine-tenths of a portrait, though 'all the reputation is engrossed by the fizmonger' (Kitson, 100–01). Van Aken's services were jealously guarded by those fortunate enough to secure them. Many portraitists sent their canvases out to his studio (Reynolds is said to have left his apprenticeship to Hudson after refusing to carry a canvas to van Aken's house in the rain), but a few provincial painters such as Henry Winstanley and the amateur Rhoda Delaval sent painted heads on small pieces of cloth to be let in to full-size canvases on arrival in London.

Neither Hogarth nor Stephen Slaughter employed a drapery painter, but the majority of portraitists were willing to pay approximately 4 to 5s. a day to a run-of-the-mill practitioner and much more to someone of van Aken's ability. It appears that Jeremiah Davison, Henry Pickering, and Isaac Whood, as well as Hudson and Ramsay, all used van Aken's services, some giving guidelines as to hands, pose, and background, and others not. His earnings enabled him to form his own collection of works of art, which included Rembrandt's *The Entombment* (Hunterian Art Gallery, University of Glasgow) and three 'models in clay' by Michael Rysbrack (Vertue, 3.90). He won the respect and friendship of fellow artists and joined Hogarth, Hudson, Francis Hayman, and the sculptor Henry Cheere on a trip to Paris in 1748, going on to Flanders and the northern Netherlands with Hudson and Cheere to visit some of the leading continental painters of the day. Van Aken died in London on 4 July 1749, leaving a widow but no children. He was buried in St Pancras Church in London. At his death Hudson and Ramsay were joint executors of his will.   SUSAN SLOMAN

Sources Vertue, *Note books*, vol. 3 · R. Edwards, 'The conversation pictures of Joseph van Aken', *Apollo*, 23 (1936), 79–85 · J. Steegman, 'A drapery painter of the eighteenth century', *The Connoisseur*, 97 (1936), 309–15 · D. H. Solkin, *Painting for money: the visual arts and the public sphere in eighteenth-century England* (1993) · E. Einberg, *Manners and morals: Hogarth and British painting, 1700–1760* (1987) [exhibition catalogue, Tate Gallery, London, 15 Oct 1987 – 3 Jan 1988] · M. Kitson, ed., 'Hogarth's "Apology for painters"', *Walpole Society*, 41 (1966–8), 46–111 · H. Walpole, *Anecdotes of painting in England: with some account of the principal artists*, ed. R. N. Wornum, new edn, 3 vols. (1888), vol. 2, p. 331 · L. Lippincott, *Selling art in Georgian London: the rise of Arthur Pond* (1983) · C. White, D. Alexander, and E. D'Oench, *Rembrandt in eighteenth century England* (1983) [exhibition catalogue, Yale U. CBA] · J. C. Smith, *British mezzotinto portraits*, 4 vols. in 5 (1878–84) · J. Reynolds, *The works of Sir Joshua Reynolds ... to which is prefixed an account of the life and writings of the author by Edmond Malone*, 5th edn (1819) [with additional memoir by Joseph Farington] · Paul Mellon Centre for Studies in British Art, London, photographic J.

Likenesses J. Faber, mezzotint (after portrait by T. Hudson)

Wealth at death left widow £40 p.a. for life, and remainder to his brother: Vertue, *Note books*

Akenside, Mark (1721–1770), poet and physician, was born on 9 November 1721 in Butcher Bank, St Nicholas, Newcastle upon Tyne, the sixth of seven children of Mark Akenside (*b*. 1676), butcher, and his wife, Mary (1685–1760), daughter of William Lumsden. He was baptized on 30 November in the nonconformist meeting-house which his parents attended in Close Gate, Newcastle. On 11 October 1722 his father registered him in the Newcastle Butchers' Company ledgers as a freeman by right of paternity.

Education, and early literary career Akenside attended Newcastle Royal Grammar School, but is believed also to have received instruction from William Wilson, who was attached to the nonconformist meeting-house, established from 1727 at Hanover Square. He was so studious that a lamp is said to have been fitted in the Akenside family pew to enable him to take notes during sermons more easily (M. Phillips, 'The meeting house at Horsley-upon-Tyne', *Archaeologia Aeliana*, new ser., 13, 1889, 59). He also read widely in literature, and by his mid-teens was already writing poetry: his first published work, 'The Virtuoso', a ninety-line burlesque poem in Spenserian stanzas, appeared anonymously in the *Gentleman's Magazine* for April 1737. This was followed later in the year by 'Ambition and Content: a Fable' and 'The Poet: a Rhapsody'; by *A British Philippic* in 1738; and by 'Hymn to Science' in 1739. Edward Cave, the editor of the *Gentleman's Magazine*, was sufficiently impressed by the potential political impact of *A British Philippic* (an outspoken call to war against Spain, in opposition to Walpole's policy of peace) to publish the poem in a sixpenny folio as well as in the magazine itself; in one variant state, the pamphlet bears the title *The Voice of Liberty*, and sports a full-page engraving as frontispiece.

Akenside received sponsorship from the Dissenters' Society in London to study at Edinburgh University as a preparation for becoming a nonconformist clergyman: he enrolled at the university library on 24 November 1738 and matriculated on 23 March 1739. But within a year he switched to the study of medicine, and was elected to the Medical Society on 30 December 1740, where he contributed memorably to the society's debates.

By mid-1742, Akenside had returned to Newcastle, and refunded his grant to the Dissenters' Society. He apparently lived with his elder brother, Thomas, who was a barber–surgeon. From here he began corresponding with Jeremiah Dyson, an Edinburgh law student who was to become his lifelong friend and patron; he also composed his first major work, *The Pleasures of Imagination*, a philosophical poem in blank verse, totalling over 2000 lines. In

Mark Akenside (1721–1770), by Edward Fisher, 1772 (after Arthur Pond, 1754)

summer 1743 he went to London, and negotiated with Robert Dodsley for its publication. He asked £120—a large amount for an unknown author—and Dodsley consulted Alexander Pope, who, according to Samuel Johnson, advised that a good offer should be made for the work, 'for this was no every-day writer'. It appeared on 17 January 1744, and went through three further authorized editions before the end of the year.

Two literary quarrels arose from its publication. Richard Dawes, who became master of Newcastle Royal Grammar School shortly after Akenside left, construed a passage describing a facetious pedant as an attack on him and retaliated in *Extracts from a MS. Pamphlet Intitled 'The Tittle-Tattle-Mongers', number 1* (1747), a handwritten transcript of which is preserved in the British Library (BL, Burney MS 388); but Akenside denied that Dawes had been his target (ibid., fol. 52). The more serious dispute was with William Warburton, who in the preface to his *Remarks on Several Occasional Reflections* (1744) attacked Akenside for his acceptance of Shaftesbury's theory that ridicule is a test of truth, and who also construed some of Akenside's lines as an attack on the clergy in general and himself in particular. Although there is no reference to Warburton in the published poem, we know from a letter to David Fordyce, 30 July 1743, that Akenside had Warburton in mind as he wrote the offending lines (Dyce, xc). Nevertheless, a defence of Akenside, usually attributed to the poet himself, *An epistle to the Rev. Mr Warburton, occasioned by his treatment of the author of the 'Pleasures of imagination'*, was published anonymously in May 1744. Although there are signs that bad feeling continued as a result of this dispute—Akenside, for instance, drafted a hostile poem called 'Epode' when Warburton was preparing his edition of

Pope—public hostilities ceased until 1766, when Warburton reprinted the preface attacking Akenside in a new edition of *The Divine Legation of Moses*.

Like many Edinburgh students Akenside went to Leiden University to complete his medical studies, enrolling there on 7 April 1744 (27 March in England), and graduating MD on 16 May, when his thesis, *De ortu et incremento foetus humani*, was published. He returned to England almost immediately, and on the advice of the eminent physician Richard Mead sought to establish himself in a medical practice at Northampton. He attempted to enlist Philip Doddridge's support in this enterprise, but Doddridge was already committed to support the resident practitioner, James Stonhouse. After what is rumoured to have been bitter rivalry, Akenside moved to Hampstead, at that date a little outside London, where Jeremiah Dyson, now a barrister, bought Golder's Hill House at North End, and apparently tried to help Akenside gain a practice. However, Akenside again failed to establish himself, being perhaps insufficiently unctuous to obtain the approval of prospective clients (J. Hawkins, *Life of Johnson*, 2nd edn., 1787, 243–4). He therefore moved again, this time to Bloomsbury Square, London, where he lived until 1759 on income deriving in part from his literary works, but mainly from a substantial allowance (rumoured to amount to some £300 per annum) from Dyson.

During this unsettled period Akenside continued to revise *The Pleasures of Imagination* for successive editions, and, in November 1744, published a stinging satire, *An Epistle to Curio*, directed against William Pulteney, who, rather than leading the new government when Walpole fell from power in 1742, had disappointed his followers by instead accepting the earldom of Bath. The following year Akenside published *Odes on Several Subjects*, a collection of ten lyrics, predating similar collections by Joseph Warton, William Collins, and others, and so establishing an important literary trend. But his major source of earned income at this date seems to have been the editorship of Dodsley's periodical, *The Museum*, for which he received £100 per annum according to the contract, preserved in the National Library of Scotland (NL Scot., MS 582). This publication ran in thirty-nine fortnightly numbers from 29 March 1746 to 12 September 1747, publishing work by Samuel Johnson, William Collins, Joseph and Thomas Warton, Christopher Smart, and other significant mid-century figures.

Maturity Following the demise of *The Museum*, Akenside published *An Ode to the Right Honourable the Earl of Huntingdon* in 1748, and revised *The Pleasures of Imagination* more extensively than before for the fifth authorized edition (1754). But he appears from about this time to have devoted a greater proportion of his energies to furthering his medical career. He became a licentiate of the Royal College of Physicians on 25 June 1751, thereby becoming eligible to practise medicine in London; and in 1753 he received the degree of MD by mandamus from Cambridge (a degree of Oxford or Cambridge being a prerequisite for fellowship, which he obtained in 1754, of the Royal College of Physicians). He was also elected to a fellowship of the Royal Society (1753). In 1755 he gave the Goulstonian lectures to the college (on the lymphatic vessels in animals), and the Croonian lectures (on the revival of learning) there in 1756; but in 1757, when an extract from his Goulstonian lectures was printed in the *Philosophical Transactions of the Royal Society*, he was accused of plagiarism by Alexander Monro, whose father had taught him at Edinburgh, and who had recently published a pamphlet on the same subject. The dispute ended when Akenside protested that his work had been presented to the Royal College of Physicians two years previously. In 1759 he was appointed Harveian orator at the college, delivering an address in Latin on 18 October; he was also appointed assistant physician at St Thomas's Hospital, London (a post from which he was promoted to principal physician three months later) and assistant physician at the school of Christ's Hospital. In the same year he moved from Bloomsbury Square to Craven Street, and from there to Old Burlington Street in 1762, where he remained until his death.

Akenside continued to revise his poetry: he began to rewrite completely *The Pleasures of Imagination* on what Dyson called 'a somewhat different and an enlarged Plan', using the slightly changed title *The Pleasures of the Imagination*. The heavily revised book 1 was completed in 1757, and the rewritten book 2 in 1765; 540 lines of a new book 3 and 120 of a new book 5 had also been written by the time of his death. Additionally, he substantially revised *Odes on Several Subjects* for a second edition in 1760, and continued to revise them thereafter. He advised John Dyer, who speaks (J. Duncombe, ed., *Letters, by Several Eminent Persons Deceased*, 3 vols., 1772, 2.241) of the 'helps' he received from Akenside in giving 'a sort of finishing' to his georgic poem, *The Fleece* (1757). New poetry of his own, though, was limited in quantity: he wrote some new odes, which remained unpublished until his death; *An Ode to the Country Gentlemen of England* (1758); and in the same year he contributed a set of six inscriptions, several previously published odes, and the 'Hymn to the Naiads' (written 1746) to the sixth volume of Dodsley's *A Collection of Poems by Several Hands*. Finally, in 1766, following the reprinting of Warburton's 1744 attack on him, he published *An Ode to the Late Thomas Edwards, Esq*, a poem written in 1751, accusing Warburton of editorial incompetence, and of hypocrisy as well, in that it exposed Warburton's early intimacy with Pope's enemy Matthew Concanen.

Meanwhile, Akenside's medical career continued to progress. In 1761 he was appointed physician-in-ordinary to Queen Charlotte (an appointment often attributed to the influence of Dyson). He also published further medical works: in 1763 he read 'An account of a blow upon the heart' to the Royal Society; in 1764 he published *De dysenteria commentarius*; and in 1766, under the auspices of the Royal College of Physicians, he brought out an edition of William Harvey's works. He also contributed three essays to the first volume of the college's *Medical Transactions* (1768), and was said to be drafting an essay on erysipelas when he died of a 'putrid sore throat' on 23 June 1770. He was buried on 28 June at St James's, Piccadilly, leaving his entire estate and effects to his friend and patron, Jeremiah Dyson. Dyson edited a posthumous collection of Akenside's poetry in 1772.

Reputation and achievement Considering the extent of Akenside's literary fame and his longstanding business relationship with Robert and James Dodsley, there is surprisingly little by way of reminiscence or anecdote about him in the literary circles of the day, and what reports there are, seem contradictory. To some, he appeared stiff and formal in both demeanour and dress: Dyce records the actor John Henderson saying that 'when he walked in the streets, he looked for all the world like one of his own Alexandrines set upright' (Dyce, lxxvi); Nicholas Hardinge called him 'irritable' (Dyce, lv); and Thomas Coakley Lettsom deplored his apparently unfeeling behaviour towards patients and his violent objection to spitting in hospital wards (T. J. Pettigrew, *Memoirs of … Lettsom*, 3 vols., 1817, 1.22–4). Others found his company delightful: his long friendship with Dyson speaks for itself; letters in the British Library suggest an informal and genuine friendship with Joseph Warton and Thomas Birch; and Sir John Hawkins (*Life of Johnson*, 247) describes him at ease in congenial society. Possibly his strained demeanour among those he did not know well resulted from self-consciousness about the fact that one of his legs was substantially shorter than the other. Such a feeling may have been exacerbated by rumours that this was owing to an accident he had suffered when playing with one of his father's meat cleavers as a child. The unequal length of Akenside's legs is more probably explained by a broken bone which healed badly, but the story of the cleaver would serve to draw attention both to his physique and to his humble origins, of which he is said to have been ashamed. Whether for these reasons, or for comfort, he attempted to disguise the problem by wearing an artificial heel, which in turn may have contributed to the awkward gait that contemporaries sometimes commented on.

In addition to the matter of physique, there are two other stories about Akenside for which no evidence is discoverable. The first, which dates from the eighteenth century, is that upon the accession of George III in 1760, both he and Dyson, who had been opposition, or patriot, whigs, became committed tories, as a result of which conversion Akenside obtained his post as physician-in-ordinary to the queen. Whatever the truth about Dyson's political career, there is no known evidence, either biographical or literary, to suggest any change of political principle on Akenside's part. The other unprovable claim, by G. S. Rousseau, is that Akenside and Dyson were homosexual. While it is true that the relationship with Dyson was long and close, there is no evidence to support the claim of homosexuality; indeed, there is no evidence to suggest that Akenside ever had a sexual relationship with anyone.

Even Akenside's contemporaries were unsure how extensive his medical practice was, although latterly he clearly attained considerable professional prestige. G. R. Potter made a case for the originality of his MD thesis, which challenged the prevailing orthodoxy in embryology by outlining a theory based on epigenesis rather than preformation, although Potter's other claim, that he anticipated evolutionary theories, is not tenable. Akenside's other medical works are primarily descriptive, and while those written in Latin have been appreciated for their elegance, they were not scientifically groundbreaking.

Akenside was recognized as a major poet as soon as *The Pleasures of Imagination* appeared, and this work exerted considerable influence on his contemporaries and subsequently on the Romantic writers, as did his innovations in publishing groups of related odes in a single volume, and developing the genre of the poetic inscription. The Romantics were particularly attracted by the emphasis Akenside placed on the imagination and his active engagement with aesthetic and epistemological theory. Editions of his works appeared frequently until the last quarter of the nineteenth century, when philosophical and didactic poetry lost its popularity. A complete edition of his poems was published in 1996, but Akenside never regained the literary status he had formerly enjoyed, when Johnson and others had praised his versification, when Wordsworth and Coleridge had been deeply influenced by him, and when Anna Barbauld had predicted 'that his work, which is not formed on any local or temporary subject, will continue to be a classic in our language' (*The Pleasures of Imagination. By Mark Akenside, M. D. to which is Prefixed a Critical Essay on the Poem, by Mrs. Barbauld*, [1794], 36).   ROBIN DIX

Sources C. T. Houpt, 'Mark Akenside: a biographical and critical study', Ph.D diss., University of Pennsylvania, 1944; repr. (1970) • A. Dyce, 'The life of Akenside', in *The poetical works of Mark Akenside*, ed. A. Dyce (1835) • *The poetical works of Mark Akenside*, ed. R. Dix (1996) • S. Johnson, *The works of the English poets, with prefaces, biographical and critical, by Samuel Johnson*, 70 vols. (1779–81) • R. Mahony, 'Akenside, Mark', *Eighteenth-century British poets: second series*, ed. J. Sitter, DLitB, 109 (1991), 3–11 • R. Dix, ed., *Mark Akenside: a reassessment* (2000) • *DNB* • R. Dix, 'Mark Akenside: unpublished manuscripts', *Durham University Journal*, 86 (1994), 219–26 • G. S. Rousseau, '"In the house of Madam Vander Tasse, on the Long Bridge": a homosocial university club in early modern Europe', *Journal of Homosexuality*, 11 (1986), 311–47 • R. Dix, 'The pleasures of speculation: scholarly methodology in eighteenth-century literary studies', *British Journal for Eighteenth-Century Studies*, 23 (2000), 85–103 • R. Dix, 'Akenside's university career: the manuscript evidence', *N&Q*, 230 (1985), 212–15 • R. Dix, 'Relations between Mark Akenside and Sir James Stonhouse in Northampton, 1744', *N&Q*, 240 (1995), 68–70 • G. R. Potter, 'Mark Akenside, prophet of evolution', *Modern Philology*, 24 (1926–7), 55–64
Archives BL, autograph letters, Add. MSS • BL, letter, Stowe MS 748, fol. 163 • Hist. Soc. Penn., autograph letters | Amherst College, Massachusetts, Ralph M. Williams collection
Likenesses oils, c.1743–1747, RCP Lond.; repro. in R. Dix, ed., *The poetical works of Mark Akenside* (1996) • E. Fisher, mezzotint, 1772 (after lost portrait by A. Pond, 1754), BM, NPG; repro. in J. Dyson, ed., *The poems of Mark Akenside* (1772) [see illus.]
Wealth at death 'whole estate and effects of whatever kind' left to friend and patron Jeremiah Dyson: will, Dix, 'Mark Akenside', 244

Akerman, John Yonge (1806–1873), numismatist and antiquary, was born in London on 12 June 1806, the son of John Ackerman, a merchant, and his wife, Elizabeth Harriet Yonge. He married on 20 August 1826 Emma Mary Matthews of Bethnal Green, Middlesex. Ackerman became secretary at an early age to the radical writer and politician William Cobbett, in 1838 to the London and Greenwich Railway Company, and subsequently to Lord Albert Conyngham (later Lord Londesborough). In January 1834 Akerman was elected a fellow of the Society of Antiquaries. In the autumn of 1848 he became joint secretary of the society with Sir Henry Ellis; and five years later he became the sole secretary. He held that post until 1860, when he was forced by ill health to resign it and the editorship of *Archaeologia*. Akerman, although interested in the study of antiquities in general, specialized in numismatics. In 1836 he started, largely at his own expense, the first English periodical to focus on his favoured field, the *Numismatic Journal*, two volumes of which appeared under his editorship. He helped to establish the Numismatic Society of London, which held its first regular meeting on 22 December 1836; Akerman was its secretary from this date until 1860, and editor of the society's journal (a continuation of his own *Numismatic Journal*), first published in 1838 as the *Numismatic Chronicle*.

Akerman's contributions to numismatic and antiquarian literature originated frequently as papers appearing in the *Numismatic Journal*, the *Numismatic Chronicle*, and *Archaeologia*. A list of them was published in the *Numismatic Chronicle* in 1874: in 1841, for instance, he gave an account of the important Crondall find in the *Chronicle*. His publications included a *Descriptive Catalogue of Rare and Unedited Roman Coins* (1834), *Coins of the Romans Relating to Britain* (1836), *Numismatic Illustrations of the New Testament* (1846), an *Archaeological Index for Celtic, Romano-British and Anglo-Saxon Remains* (1847), a *Glossary of Provincial Words and Phrases in Use in Wiltshire* (1842), and *Spring Tide, or, The Angler and his Friends* (1850). In recognition of Akerman's published works and papers, especially of the series on the coins of the Romans relating to Britain, the gold medal of the French Institute was awarded to him, and he was also created an honorary member of several learned societies, among which were the Royal Academy of St Petersburg and the Istituto di Corrispondenza Archeologica of Rome. However, Akerman's main contribution to numismatics lay in popularizing the study of coins in England and establishing the Numismatic Society and its journal, rather than in his rapidly superseded publications.

After 1860 Akerman lived at Abingdon, where he died on 18 November 1873.

W. W. WROTH, *rev.* NILANJANA BANERJI

Sources 'Proceedings of the Numismatic Society, 1873–1874', *Numismatic Chronicle*, new ser., 14 (1874), 13–19 • R. A. G. Carson and H. Pagan, *A history of the Royal Numismatic Society, 1836–1986* (1986), 53, 79 [honorary members' list] • d. cert. • parish register, Bethnal Green, St Matthew, LMA, 20 Aug 1826 [marriage]
Archives S. Antiquaries, Lond., collections | Bodl. Oxf., corresp. with Sir Thomas Phillipps • Nuffield Oxf., corresp. and papers as secretary to William Cobbett • U. Edin. L., letters to James Halliwell-Phillipps • Yale U., Beinecke L., letters to T. J. Pettigrew
Likenesses H. A. Ogg, etching, BM, NPG

Akers, Sir Wallace Alan (1888–1954), chemist and industrialist, was born on 9 September 1888 at Walthamstow, the second child of Charles Akers, a chartered accountant, and his wife, Mary Ethelreda Brown. He was educated at Lake House School in Bexhill, and at Aldenham School. From there he went to Christ Church, Oxford, where he studied chemistry and obtained first-class honours in 1909.

In 1911 Akers joined Brunner Mond & Co. in Cheshire, the leading British firm of alkali manufacturers. Apart from a brief spell in the research laboratory, he was occupied with work in process technology. He was by training a physical chemist—one of the first Oxford produced—and the type of work he had in Cheshire suited him very well.

In 1924 Akers went for some three years to the Far East in the employment of the Borneo Company Ltd. Meanwhile, Imperial Chemical Industries had been formed in 1926, absorbing, among others, Brunner Mond, and in 1928 he returned to London to work in close conjunction with Colonel George Paton Pollitt who was then ICI's technical director. This work gave Akers wide experience in many branches of chemical technology, and in 1931 he was made chairman of ICI's Billingham division. Work there was essentially concerned with high pressure techniques using hydrogen. Ammonia synthesis was a major interest at this time.

From 1933 to 1936 Akers was responsible for an interesting project at Billingham which aimed to produce 100,000 tons of petrol a year by the hydrogenation of coal. At their most ambitious the executives at ICI saw this project as the beginning of a new industry which would compete with the oil companies in the production of petrol. The expense of the process and the commercial power of the oil companies made this a very risky undertaking, and Akers had been closely involved in negotiations intended to procure financial support from the government to set up this experimental industry. In the spring of 1931 he met a strong rebuff from the civil servant responsible, Sir John Anderson, whose skilful investigation had brought out the fact that ICI had already made a substantial investment in the project, which it was seeking to rescue. Akers and his colleagues resumed their negotiations with the government after the election of October 1931, obtaining some measure of success by 1933.

After a reorganization of the company in 1937, Akers's chairmanship of the Billingham division came to an end and he returned to ICI headquarters. There he worked with Holbrook Gaskell, especially in connection with the enormous wartime factory expansion programme. In 1939 he was appointed an executive manager. In this capacity he was involved early on in secret informal co-operation between the company and the government on the project to prepare an atomic bomb. In 1941 he took part in a bid by the company to take over the entire nuclear project and run it on behalf of the Ministry of Aircraft Production; indeed according to one civil servant he was

the plan's 'chief protagonist' (Gowing, 109). Though this takeover attempt was firmly rejected, he was nevertheless selected to become the director of the atomic project, working as a temporary civil servant responsible to Anderson, who was now a senior minister in the war cabinet.

Akers's appointment in 1941 as director of Tube Alloys (the code name for atomic research) in the Department of Scientific and Industrial Research caused some resentment among civil servants and scientists who were suspicious of his connections with ICI, but this soon dissipated once they got to know him. Things were, however, more difficult in the United States, where his involvement created the suspicion that Britain might be using the research with an eye to post-war economic gain. General Leslie Groves, who was placed in charge of the Manhattan project, was unwilling to deal with him, and this was a significant factor in the temporary breakdown of co-operation over nuclear matters. After the re-establishment of the partnership in August 1943, the United States government made it clear that it considered him unsuitable to be in charge of liaison between the British and American ends of the project, and Sir James Chadwick was given this responsibility in his stead (as technical adviser to the Combined Policy Committee). Contemporaries noted that Akers responded to this difficult situation with characteristic good grace. He remained head of Tube Alloys in Britain, retaining an important role in co-ordinating the activities of scientists engaged in nuclear research in Britain, but as he no longer had access to all the information on joint research being conducted in the United States, his input to decision making was much reduced.

Akers returned to full-time employment in ICI in 1946. In 1944 he had been appointed the company's first director to be specifically responsible for research, a post which he held until he retired in 1953. His juniors found him 'warm and friendly, with something of a donnish touch' (Reader, 447–8). He was strongly associated with ICI's post-war efforts to support fundamental research, 'freed from the urgencies and distractions of [the] applied research' already being carried out by the divisions (ibid., 447), and the laboratory complex set up for this purpose was renamed the Akers Research Laboratories in 1955. As part of the same policy he introduced ICI research fellowships, by which the company became involved in research carried out in university laboratories.

Akers was made CBE for his war services in 1944, and knighted in 1946. He was elected a fellow of the Royal Society in 1952. He was a most clubbable man. For many years he resided in the Royal Thames Yacht Club where he delighted in having friends and acquaintances to dine. A hard worker, he readily occupied himself reading and writing to the small hours. In April 1953 he served as one of the three members of the committee that devised the Atomic Energy Authority. He was interested in music and art, and a good pianist until he suffered a hand injury. He was a member of the scientific advisory committee, and subsequently a trustee, of the National Gallery.

Akers received the honorary degrees of DSc from Durham (1949) and DCL from Oxford (1952), and was elected FRS in 1952. He was treasurer of the Chemical Society from 1948 until 1954. He has been described as a 'tall, lean figure', with a 'blind eye' (*Chemistry and Industry*, 1449). On his retirement in 1953 he married Mademoiselle Bernadette Marie La Marre. This surprised all who knew him, for he had been considered a confirmed bachelor. The couple made their home at Yledyn, King's Road, Alton, Hampshire, where he died, on 1 November 1954. His widow returned to France where she survived him by nearly six years. FLECK, *rev.* JOSEPH GROSS

Sources *The Times* (6 April 1953), 6 · W. J. Reader, *Imperial Chemical Industries, a history*, 2 (1975) · M. Gowing, *Britain and atomic energy, 1939–1945* (1964) · J. I. Watts, *The first fifty years of Brunner, Mond and Company* (1923) · *Chemistry and Industry* (20 Nov 1954), 1449 · Lord Waverley and A. Fleck, *Memoirs FRS*, 1 (1955), 1–4 · Imperial Chemical Industries Billingham division, *Billingham* · WWW
Archives CAC Cam., corresp. with Sir James Chadwick
Likenesses photograph, 1913, repro. in Watts, *First fifty years of Brunner, Mond and Company*, facing p. 45 · W. Stoneman, photograph, 1947, NPG · W. Stoneman, sepia photograph, RS · photograph, repro. in *Memoirs FRS*, facing p. 1
Wealth at death £36,554 17s. 6d.: probate, 9 Dec 1954, CGPLA Eng. & Wales

Akroyd, Edward (1810–1887), industrialist and philanthropist, was born on 28 November 1810 at Brockholes, near Brookhouse, Ovenden, Halifax, the eldest of the ten children of Jonathan Akroyd (1782–1847) and his wife, Sarah, daughter of David Wright of Ovenden. Educated locally by an Anglican clergyman and at the Barkisland endowed school, he and his younger brother Henry became partners in the expanding family firm of James Akroyd & Son in 1839. Founded by their grandfather, James Akroyd (1753–1830), an enterprising yeoman clothier, who developed an extensive putting-out trade to spinners in the upland villages around Halifax and erected a water-powered worsted spinning mill at Brookhouse in 1805, the firm quickly diversified into weaving. Within a decade, both James Akroyd's sons, Jonathan and James (1785–1836), had successfully made the transition to urban industrialists, utilizing, from the 1820s, imported steam-powered Jacquard looms to manufacture a wide range of fabrics at their Halifax mills.

In 1847, on the death of their father, Edward and Henry inherited estate valued at £300,000 and one of the most successful textile firms in the country. They managed the firm jointly from 1847 until 1853, when the partnership was dissolved by mutual consent. Edward thereafter assumed sole responsibility and, when he re-formed the firm as a limited liability company in 1871, became chairman of the board of directors. He was regarded as a formidable commercial rival by Samuel Cunliffe Lister in the early 1850s and, although the demands of public life subsequently distanced him from the day-to-day management of the firm, he retained an interest in the details of its business, writing from Westminster, for example, in March 1873, commending his nephew's initiative in utilizing 'as much of our own yarn at present as possible', expediting 'the completion of our China orders', and

exploring the commercial potential of 'the electric telegraph' (E. Akroyd to J. Champneys, 19 March 1873, W. Yorks. AS, Calderdale, MS misc. 380/10). However, the firm experienced increasing commercial difficulties after 1850, losing its pre-eminence in the local economy to the rival Crossley carpet empire, and its dismemberment commenced within six years of Edward Akroyd's death.

Edward Akroyd appears to have lived at North Parade, and Woodside in Halifax from 1818 until his marriage on 10 October 1838 to Elizabeth (*d.* 25 Sept 1884), daughter of John Fearby of Poppleton Lodge, York. There were no children. They purchased Bankfield, a modest Regency villa in Halifax, which he extended over the next three decades, ultimately transforming it into a magnificent Gothic Italianate palazzo. Notwithstanding this domestic extravagance, Edward devoted much of his considerable disposable wealth to philanthropic, political, and religious causes, most notably his development of local model industrial communities. Indeed, when he died in 1887 he left an estate valued at little more than £1200, having, as his obituarist in the *Halifax Courier* of 26 November surmised, 'in one way or another' spent or given away 'his whole income'. His private generosity to the erstwhile factory reformer Richard Oastler and the veteran Halifax Chartist John Snowden in their declining years was paralleled by a profusion of public benefactions, epitomizing his growing commitment to class conciliation after 1850.

Akroyd later acknowledged that he first recognized the necessity 'for the manifestation on the part of employers of an interest in the physical well-being of the factory operatives' at the time of the passing of the Factory Act of 1833, which he had opposed. After serious disturbances in 1842, when his home and mills were attacked by Chartist rioters, he sought to develop 'a kindly feeling between the opposing classes of employer and employed' (*History of James Akroyd*, 1874, 14) by promoting allotment schemes for his employees in the 1840s; retraining redundant handcombers as weavers in the 1850s; encouraging his workers to become shareholders after the firm became a limited liability company in 1871; and providing pensions for former employees. Moreover, he was instrumental in the development of the penny savings movement 'to help the poor to help themselves', and the founding of the Yorkshire Penny Bank in 1859, serving as its vice-president from 1859 to 1870 and president until 1878.

The acquisition of a rural industrial site at Copley, some 2 miles south west of Halifax, in 1844, and the practical necessity of recruiting and retaining a reliable workforce, induced his provision between 1849 and 1865 of some 136 picturesque, terraced houses, the majority of them back-to-back, for rent by his workers, and his promotion of such amenities as allotment gardens; burial and clothing clubs; co-operative store, factory canteen, and school; cricket club and recreation ground; horticultural and floral society; lending library and newsroom; savings bank and spacious new parish church. He then proceeded to develop a fully integrated community, with the paternalist employer in residence, near his Bankfield mansion at Akroydon, and George Gilbert Scott's magnificent All

Souls Church, commissioned by Akroyd in 1856 and completed in 1859. During the period from 1861 to 1868 ninety-two superior, through-terraced houses, designed by George Gilbert Scott and W. H. Crossland in 'domestic Gothic', were constructed around a central park, with financial assistance from the Halifax Permanent Building Society. However, the mortgages remained prohibitive for the majority of his workers, and the vision of a socially mixed residential estate was never fully realized. The significance of the development, however, lay in its promotion of home ownership, which Akroyd believed to be the key to self-improvement; its concern for the residential environment, which foreshadowed the garden-city movement; and its range of community and welfare facilities. The last included schools, evening classes for women, and a working men's college; horticultural, floral, literary, and scientific societies; recreation club with bowling ground; clothing club, life annuity insurance scheme, mutual improvement society, and savings bank.

Akroyd entered parliament as whig member for Huddersfield in 1857 after a famous victory over Richard Cobden, whose censure motion had precipitated the fall of Palmerston's government. Although he narrowly lost the seat in 1859, he was subsequently returned without a contest for Halifax in 1865, and re-elected in 1868, holding the seat until his retirement in 1874. By the time he entered parliament, he had already abandoned his radical Methodist New Connexion roots, and subsequently espoused an increasingly militant anglicanism as he sought to defend the established church against its nonconformist critics, and by 1874 was regularly entering the division lobbies with the Conservatives. Moreover, his patriotic association with the volunteer movement after 1859 culminated in his appointment as honorary colonel of the 4th West Yorkshire rifle volunteers in 1870. Following his retirement from parliament, a bronze statue, paid for by public subscription, was erected in his honour in Halifax in 1876. Designed by J. Birnie Philip, it was considered an excellent likeness, tall, erect and dignified, in the easy attitude he frequently adopted when addressing public meetings.

Failing health, exacerbated by a serious riding accident, and financial worries, occasioned Akroyd's retirement to St Leonards, Sussex, attended, after the death of his wife in 1884, only by his valet. He died suddenly, from a malfunction of the aortic valve, on 19 November 1887 at his home, 59 Eversfield Place, St Leonards. After one of the largest funerals ever witnessed in Halifax, he was interred on 23 November with the remains of his parents, which he had had exhumed from Salem Methodist New Connexion Chapel in the 1850s, in the Gothic mortuary chapel of All Souls burial-ground at Akroydon.

JOHN A. HARGREAVES

Sources R. Bretton, 'Colonel Edward Akroyd', *Transactions of the Halifax Antiquarian Society* (1948), 60–100 · *History of James Akroyd and Son Ltd* (1874) · E. Akroyd, *On improved dwellings for the working classes* (1862) · E. Akroyd, *The church in its relation to the state and to the Nonconformists* (1872) · E. Akroyd, *The Yorkshire Penny Bank* (1872) · E. Akroyd, *An address to the parishioners of Copley on the pastoral letter and ritualism of the vicar* (1873) · E. Akroyd, *On the present state of political parties* (1874) · J. A. Jowitt, ed., *Model industrial communities in mid-nineteenth century Yorkshire* (1986) · E. Akroyd, *On the plan of juvenile and adult education adopted in the writer's manufactory* (1957) · D. Findlay, *All Souls, Haley Hill, Halifax* (1978) · E. Webster, 'Edward Akroyd (1810–1887)', *Transactions of the Halifax Antiquarian Society* (1987), 19–45 · J. Hole, *The homes of the working classes* (1866) · E. Baines, *Yorkshire Past and Present*, 11 (1875) · W. L. Creese, *The search for the environment* (1966) · V. Parker, *The English house in the nineteenth century* (1970) · R. Brook, *The story of Huddersfield* (1968) · G. Sheeran, *Brass castles* (1993) · L. Caffyn, *Workers' housing in West Yorkshire, 1750–1920* (1986) · *Halifax Courier* (26 Nov 1887) · *Halifax Guardian* (26 Nov 1887) · *CGPLA Eng. & Wales* (1888) · d. cert. [Elizabeth Akroyd] · J. A. Hargreaves, *Halifax* (1999)

Archives Bankfield Museum, Halifax, corresp. [fragments] · W. Yorks. AS, Calderdale, Calderdale District Archives, ephemera incl. invitation cards and passport, and corresp. [fragments] | Borth. Inst., letters to Sir Charles Wood

Likenesses election cartoons, 1868, Bankfield Museum, Halifax · election cartoons, 1868, Calderdale Central Library, Halifax · oils, 1868, Bankfield Museum, Halifax · J. B. Philip and Signor Fucigna, bronze statue, 1876, Haley Hill, Halifax · R. B. Joy, marble bust, 1890, Bankfield Museum, Halifax · D. Hardy, bronze bust, 1936, Yorkshire Bank, Halifax · plaque, Yorkshire Bank, Leeds

Wealth at death £1234 1s. 10d.: probate, 30 Jan 1888, *CGPLA Eng. & Wales*

Alabaster, William (1568–1640), Church of England clergyman and writer, was born in Hadleigh, Suffolk, on 27 February 1568, the son of Roger Alabaster (d. after 1606), a merchant; his mother was Bridget Winthrop (1543–1614), whose father had been master of the Clothworkers and lord of Groton Manor in Suffolk. William's uncle Thomas Alabaster was a London merchant engaged in the Spanish trade and an occasional agent for William Cecil.

John Still, later bishop of Bath and Wells, was Alabaster's first cousin and was rector of Hadleigh and dean of Bocking when Alabaster was born, and provided opportunities for his young kinsman. As a canon of Westminster he arranged in the early 1580s for William to attend Westminster School. In 1583 Alabaster was chosen one of the queen's scholars from Westminster to Trinity College, Cambridge, where Still was master. He graduated BA in 1587/8 and was elected a fellow of the college. Alabaster had already shown a flair for literature, and it is thought that his Latin tragedy *Roxana* (largely adapted from a work by Luigi Groto) was first performed at this time in the college. He was also working on an epic poem in praise of Queen Elizabeth, the 'Elisaeis' (never completed), which he showed to Still's friend Edmund Spenser when the latter visited Cambridge in 1591. Spenser subsequently praised Alabaster in *Colin Clouts Comes Home Again*, and it is possible that when Alabaster's parents and siblings migrated to the Munster plantation in Ireland in 1595 they did so to settle on Spenser's Kilcoman seigniory.

Alabaster received his MA in 1591 and was incorporated at Oxford in the following year. In 1595 he played a prominent role in a set of academic disputations organized by the earl of Essex for the Cambridge commencement. In 1596 he was appointed catechist at Trinity College, Cambridge, and in the same year joined the earl of Essex as a chaplain on the Cadiz expedition. In that captured city he

William Alabaster (1568–1640), by John Payne (after Cornelius Johnson)

references to it in two published answers, by John Racster and Roger Fenton.

Through the winter of 1597–8 Alabaster was visited in London by various church leaders—including Bancroft, Still, and Lancelot Andrewes—who attempted to sway him. These efforts failed, and he was deprived of his orders and benefices on 20 February. Denied both a martyr's fate and a public chance to defend his views, Alabaster took advantage of loose security to escape the Clink in Southwark. A warrant for his apprehension describes him at this stage of his life as 'a tall young man about the age thirty, sallow coloured, long visadged, lean faced, black haired, and speaketh somewhat thick' (journals of mayor and aldermen of London, 24, fol. 296*v*). He was sheltered for a time by the Revd Francis Gerard, who introduced him to the spiritual exercises of Ignatius of Loyola and arranged for him to travel to Rome via Douai. In November 1598 he took up residence at the English College in Rome; there he prepared a lengthy manuscript narrative of his conversion.

Early in 1599 Alabaster was in Spain, and in the summer he set out for England. Captured by English agents in La Rochelle, he was transported to London and lodged in the Tower. There he was eventually seen by William Cecil, and claimed to have been sent to England to conspire on behalf of the pope with the earl of Essex, charges which played into the hands of the earl's enemies and surfaced at Essex's trial in 1601.

Alabaster was moved to Framlingham Castle in 1601, was pardoned at James I's accession in 1603, but was then arrested again in 1604. While there is no evidence that at this point he had abandoned his conversion to catholicism, he was clearly troubled by the conflicts within the English Catholic community, and he offered to spy for Cecil on Catholic priests acting against the crown. He was released and returned to Europe. In 1607 he published, without an imprimatur, his *Apparatus in revelationem Jesu Christi*, a book of cabbalistic divinity that some considered heretical. In 1609 he was back at the English College in Rome where he became alienated from Father Robert Persons, then head of the college. He became involved in college plots and denounced Persons to the Inquisition. But it was Alabaster who was brought before that tribunal, which condemned his *Apparatus* in 1610 and ordered him to remain in Rome.

Disenchanted, Alabaster fled to Amsterdam and then returned to England, where in 1611 he was in the custody of Dr John Overall, the dean of St Paul's and another protégé of John Still. He made his peace with the Church of England, won the king's favour with a Latin epithalamium presented to the monarch on the marriage of the royal favourite Robert Carr in 1613, and at the king's command was absolved of past irregularity and created DD at Cambridge in 1614. He was also granted the living of Therfield, Hertfordshire. In 1615 he preached before the king at Whitehall and two years later preached a sermon at St Paul's which some felt smacked of popery (according to a report by Oliver Cromwell in his maiden speech to parliament in 1629). In 1618 Alabaster was admitted to Gray's

had his first contacts with Catholics and Catholic worship. On his return to England he turned down the living at Brettenham, Suffolk (which was given to his cousin Humfry Munning), but accepted the wealthy living of Landulph, Cornwall, from the earl of Essex. His cousin Joshua Winthrop was one of the guarantors for the first fruits.

At Eastertide in 1597 Alabaster travelled to London in search of further preferment, on which he based his plans for marriage. But while staying with Dean Gabriel Goodman of Westminster he encountered Father Thomas Wright, a Roman Catholic priest under house arrest. It was hoped that the brilliant Alabaster would convert Wright, but the reverse appears to have happened. Alabaster returned to Cambridge, broke off his planned marriage, and began to share with friends his attraction to Roman Catholicism. It was during this summer that he wrote many of his religious sonnets. In September intercepted letters of Wright indicated Alabaster's conversion and Richard Bancroft, the bishop of London, sent orders to Cambridge ordering that Alabaster be placed under close confinement. The following month Alabaster was sent to London when efforts by the various college heads failed to move him. Meanwhile he had expressed his views in a manuscript referred to as the 'Seven motives' which was intercepted when he tried to have it delivered to Essex, who he hoped would protect him. Although never published, the 'Seven motives' can be reconstructed from

Inn and was referred to as a royal chaplain; in the same year he married the widow Katherine Fludd, sister-in-law of Dr Robert Fludd. In 1625 he received the living of Little Shelford in Cambridgeshire.

Alabaster spent the rest of his life in publishing various works. He was interested in the world of John Dee and others, where the occult, medicine, cabbalism, and alchemy blended. In 1621 he published *De bestia apocalyptica*, a commentary on the book of Revelation. In 1632 he finally published *Roxana* after a pirated edition of the play had appeared earlier that year. Then came his *Ecce sponsus venit* (1633), a Latin treatise setting out what he saw as the signs given by Christ for knowing the state of the church and the second coming, and his *Spiraculum tubarum* (1633), which included a lexicon of Hebrew words to aid in the mystical interpretation of prophecy. In 1635 he published an abridgement of Schindler's Hebrew lexicon.

In 1637 Alabaster is reported to have taken up lodgings near the Tower of London in order to spend time with his friend Bishop John Williams (to whom he had dedicated one of his poems), who was incarcerated in the Tower. Alabaster died in London in April 1640 and was buried in the churchyard of St Dunstan-in-the-West. Nicholas Bacon of Gray's Inn was named executor of his will. In that year Samuel Hartlib wrote of Alabaster in his 'Ephemerides' that the:

> Dr is an universall schollar of a stupendous memory, ... an excellent Latinist, ... Poet. A great Linguist. The best Hebrician in England. Though hee bee Antick and Phantastical in some things in his Cabalistic writings yet even in that booke there are many excellent choice spiritually and morally allegorized Notions. A papist formerly now a zealous Protestant against them.
> (S. Hartlib, 'Ephemerides', 1640, part 1, Hartlib MS (Sheffield), 30/4/38B)

Among contemporaries he was praised for Latin verse which displayed academic learning and rhetorical virtuosity. His style in these works has been regarded as a forerunner of mannerist or metaphysical expression. But his modern reputation as a poet rests primarily on his vernacular religious sonnets, which circulated in manuscript and were not widely known until the twentieth century. They have been praised for their controlled, clear expression of interior belief and emotion, and for their clever conceits.   FRANCIS J. BREMER

Sources 'Alabaster's conversion', MSS, English College, Rome · E. Coutts, 'Life and works of William Alabaster', PhD diss., University of Wisconsin, 1956 · *The sonnets of William Alabaster*, ed. G. M. Story and H. Gardner (1959) · *The Elisaeis of William Alabaster*, ed. and trans. M. O'Connell (1979) · *The Winthrop papers*, ed. W. C. Ford and others, 1 (1929) · L. I. Guiney, *Recusant poets* (1939) · D. Sutton, ed., *Unpublished works by William Alabaster* (1997) · J. Hacket, *Scrinia reserata: a memorial offer'd to the great deservings of John Williams*, 2 pts (1693) · private information (2004) [Michael Questier, Ariel Hessayon, and Paul Hammer] · *Old Westminsters* · GL, journals of mayor and aldermen of London, 24, fol. 296v · J. W. Binns, *Intellectual culture in Elizabethan and Jacobean England: the Latin writings of the age* (1990)
Archives English College, Rome, autobiography | BL, Cotton MSS · BL, Harley MSS · BL, Lansdowne MSS · Bodl. Oxf., Ashmole MSS · Bodl. Oxf., collections by L. I. Guiney for edition of sonnets ·

Bodl. Oxf., MSS Rawl. · CCC Oxf., MS CCCIX and CCCXI · CUL, EDR · CUL, MSMm · Hunt. L., HM 39464
Likenesses J. Payne, line engraving (after C. Johnson), BM [*see illus.*] · portrait, repro. in W. Alabaster, *Ecce sponsus venit* (1633), frontispiece

Alain de Lille. *See* Lille, Alain de (1116/17–1202?).

Alan, lord of Galloway (*b.* before 1199, *d.* 1234), magnate, was the eldest son of *Roland, lord of Galloway (*d.* 1200), and Helen de Morville (*d.* 1217), sister and heir of William de Morville, lord of Lauderdale and Cunningham and royal constable. He had two brothers and two sisters, of whom *Thomas (*d.* 1231) became earl of Atholl in right of his wife, Ada married Walter Bisset of Aboyne, and Dervorguilla married Nicholas de Stuteville of Liddel in Cumbria.

Alan contracted three marriages: to a daughter of Roger de Lacy, constable of Chester; to Margaret (*d.* before 1228), eldest daughter of *David, earl of Huntingdon, in 1209; and, *c.*1229, to Rose, daughter of Hugh de *Lacy, earl of Ulster. The first two marriages produced children, but only daughters attained adulthood. Helen, his daughter by his first marriage, married Roger de *Quincy, while Christina (or Christiana) and Dervorguilla [*see* Balliol, Dervorguilla de], the children of Alan and Margaret, married William de *Forz and John de *Balliol respectively. Alan had one bastard son, Thomas.

Cross-border landholding and kinship with King John of England made Alan a man of consequence in both realms. His relationship with the king of Scots, based on loose overlordship rather than feudal subordination, allowed freedom of manoeuvre where his actions did not conflict with Scottish interests. Galloway's military resources and substantial fleet gave added influence; Alan's aid was courted unsuccessfully by John for his 1210 campaign against the Ulster Lacys, but he agreed to send one thousand men for the abortive Welsh campaign of 1212. A grant of estates in Antrim in 1212 was designed to draw him actively into the defence of Angevin Ulster against the native Irish. Despite such favours from John, when Alexander II entered the civil war in England in 1215, aligning himself with John's baronial opponents, Alan joined the Scottish king and was his chief lieutenant in the occupation of Cumberland and Westmorland from 1215 to 1217.

From 1225 Alan used the freedom afforded by the loose overlordship of the Scottish crown to interfere in the feud between King Ragnvald of Man and his half-brother, Olaf. His private interest, arising from efforts to secure Antrim with Ragnvald's support against the threat of a Lacy restoration, coincided at first with Anglo-Scottish policy towards the region and received the tacit support of his Scottish overlord. The prospect of a pro-Scottish client in Man led Alexander II to acquiesce to the marriage in 1226 of Alan's bastard son, Thomas, to Ragnvald's daughter, but the marriage provoked revolt against Ragnvald. Despite the support of Galwegian galleys and warriors, Ragnvald was overthrown and slain in 1229 by Olaf. Alan's ensuing attempts to conquer Man for Thomas destabilized the Hebrides and western highlands, thereby threatening

Scottish territorial interests, and in 1230–31 prompted active Norwegian support for Olaf. Joint action by Alan and Alexander averted catastrophe, but Scottish and Galwegian interests had diverged and the 1231 campaign marked the end of further Galwegian involvement in the Manx succession; Alan's dynastic ambitions had caused an undesirable war with a major foreign power.

Uncertainty over the succession to Galloway shadowed Alan's later years. His nearest legitimate male heir was *Patrick of Atholl [see under Thomas, earl of Atholl], son of his younger brother, Thomas, who had died in 1231, but, although Celtic practice did not debar his bastard son, Thomas, Alan's closest heirs by feudal law were his three daughters, all married to important Anglo-Scottish noblemen. To King Alexander, the crisis precipitated by Alan's Manx ventures made partition, and the attendant opportunity to replace the loose overlordship enjoyed by Alan with a more tightly defined relationship, an attractive proposition, for succession by Thomas threatened a revival of Galwegian interests in Man and so of risks to Scottish security. Alan died about 2 February 1234 and was buried in Dundrennan Abbey, where his mutilated tomb effigy survives. Partition of the lordship followed and, despite a rebellion in 1235 in favour of Thomas, was successfully enforced.　RICHARD D. ORAM

Sources *Scots peerage*, 4.139–43 · K. J. Stringer, 'Periphery and core in thirteenth-century Scotland: Alan, son of Roland, lord of Galloway and constable of Scotland', *Medieval Scotland: crown, lordship and community: essays presented to G. W. S. Barrow*, ed. A. Grant and K. J. Stringer (1993), 82–113 · G. W. S. Barrow, ed., *Regesta regum Scottorum*, 2 (1971), 37 · A. A. M. Duncan, *Scotland: the making of the kingdom* (1975), vol. 1 of *The Edinburgh history of Scotland*, ed. G. Donaldson (1965–75), 186–7, 250–53, 529–30, 543–4 · K. J. Stringer, 'The early lords of Lauderdale, Dryburgh Abbey and St Andrew's Priory at Northampton', *Essays on the nobility of medieval Scotland*, ed. K. J. Stringer (1985), 44–71, esp. 50–52 · J. Stevenson, ed., *Chronicon de Lanercost, 1201–1346*, Bannatyne Club, 65 (1839) · K. J. Stringer, 'Acts of lordship: the records of the lords of Galloway to 1234', *Freedom and authority: historical and historiographical essays presented to Grant G. Simpson*, ed. T. Brotherstone and D. Ditchburn (2000) · K. J. Stringer, 'Reform monasticism and Celtic Scotland: Galloway, c.1140–c.1240', *Alloa: Celtic Scotland in the middle ages*, ed. E. J. Cowan and R. A. McDonald (2000)

Likenesses effigy, Dundrennan Abbey

Alan of Beccles. See Beccles, Alan of (d. 1240).

Alan of Lynn. See Lynn, Alan (1347/8–1432).

Alan of Tewkesbury. See Tewkesbury, Alan of (b. before 1150, d. 1202).

Alan of Walsingham. See Walsingham, Alan (d. 1363).

Alan Rufus (d. 1093), magnate, was the second of at least seven legitimate sons of Count Eudo, regent of Brittany from 1040 to 1047, and Orguen, or Agnes, his Angevin wife. Alan was called Rufus ('the Red') to distinguish him from a younger brother, Alan Niger ('the Black'). His father, Eudo, was a brother of the Breton duke Alan III; the mother of Eudo and Alan III was an aunt of William the Conqueror. Eudo's status entitled his legitimate sons to bear the honorific title *comes* ('count'). Alan first occurs, with his father and some of his brothers, in an Angevin

charter given c.1050. He was probably recruited into the service of his second cousin William of Normandy before 1066. A Breton contingent, probably including Alan and his brother Brien, played an important role at the battle of Hastings and settled in England thereafter. The list of Alan's brothers in the above-mentioned charter does not include Brien, nor either of Alan's successors, Alan Niger and Stephen. Alan Rufus was therefore probably older than Brien. Brien was certainly given lands in Suffolk, and probably also in Cornwall.

After helping to defeat an attack on Exeter by the sons of Harold in 1069, Brien apparently returned to Brittany, leaving Alan as indisputably the most senior of the Bretons in England. Alan's position was further enhanced by the fall of Ralph de Gael in 1075, much of whose forfeited land in East Anglia he acquired. He held a great deal of land in Cambridgeshire, Suffolk, and Norfolk, and the earliest grants to him were probably in Cambridgeshire. Alan and two of his men, Aubrey de Vere and Harduin de Scales, figure prominently in two preliminary records of the Domesday survey, the *Inquisitio comitatus Cantabrigiensis*, and the *Inquisitio Eliensis*. The kernel of the vast honour of Richmond (based upon land in Yorkshire and Lincolnshire and extending to Northampton and London), for which Alan and his successors are best known, was granted only after the revolt of the north in 1070.

By 1086 Alan had settled some forty tenants on his lands, of whom all but two were Bretons. The grant of the northern lands was a measure of the Conqueror's trust. By 1086 Alan was one of the richest and most powerful men in England. He remained close to William I, accompanying him to Normandy and Maine on several occasions after 1066, and attested many of his charters. His importance is sometimes overlooked because his intense loyalty to William I, and subsequently to William II, meant that he was usually ignored by chroniclers, though he figures among those mentioned as helping William II keep his throne during 1087–8. He played an important role in the proceedings against William of St Calais, bishop of Durham. At his death in 1093 (perhaps in August) he was succeeded by his brother Alan Niger, of whom there is no trace in English documents before this date. Alan Niger died in 1098 and was succeeded by another brother, Stephen, who had also succeeded to their father's Breton lands.

The obit dates for Alan Rufus and Alan Niger have caused much confusion, but can be established by reconciling references in documents of St Mary's Abbey at York with a letter written by Anselm, archbishop of Canterbury. The letter reveals that both Alans had an affair with Gunnhild, daughter of the former King Harold and living in retirement at Wilton Abbey. Because Anselm regarded Gunnhild as a nun, it is not known whether she was legally married to either brother, though clearly she willingly entered each relationship. Eadmer later alleged that Matilda, wife of Henry I, had been intended by her father, Malcolm, king of Scots, as the wife of Alan Rufus. No recognized wife, nor any children, is known for either Alan, though the tenants of both in England included three of their illegitimate brothers, Ribald, Bodin, and Bardulf, and their wet-nurse, Orwen. Alan Rufus was the founder of St Mary's, York (based upon an earlier refoundation of St Olave), and of a priory at Swavesey, Cambridgeshire, which was a cell of St Serge and St Bacchus, Angers. He was also a benefactor of St Edmund's at Bury and was buried there, though he was later translated to St Mary's, York, at the request of St Mary's monks.

K. S. B. KEATS-ROHAN

Sources B. de Broussillon, ed., *Cartulaire de Saint-Aubin d'Angers*, 2 (1896), no. 677 · *Reg. RAN*, vol. 1 · Ordericus Vitalis, *Eccl. hist.*, vol. 2 · 'De injusta vexatione', Symeon of Durham, *Opera*, vol. 2 · T. Arnold, ed., *Memorials of St Edmund's Abbey*, 1, Rolls Series, 96 (1890), 35 · 'Epistolae Anselmi', ed. F. S. Schmitt, *S. Anselmi Cantuariensis archiepiscopi opera omnia*, 3–5 (1938–61), *epp.* 168–9 · A. Farley, ed., *Domesday Book*, 2 vols. (1783), vols. 1–2 · N. E. S. A. Hamilton, ed., *Inquisitio comitatus Cantabrigiensis … subjicitur inquisitio Eliensis* (1876) · A. Wilmart, 'Alain le Roux et Alain le Noir', *Annales de Bretagne*, 38 (1929), 576–95 · P. Jeulin, 'Aperçus sur le comté de Richmond en Angleterre … 1066/71–1398', *Annnales de Bretagne*, 42 (1935), 265–302 · K. S. B. Keats-Rohan, 'The Bretons and Normans of England, 1066–1154: the family, the fief and the feudal monarchy', *Nottingham Medieval Studies*, 36 (1992), 42–78 · K. S. B. Keats-Rohan, 'Le rôle des Bretons dans la politique de colonisation normande d'Angleterre (1042–1135)', *Mémoires de la Société d'Histoire et d'Archéologie de Bretagne*, 74 (1996), 181–215 · W. J. Corbett, 'The development of the duchy of Normandy and the Norman conquest of England', *Cambridge medieval history*, 5, ed. J. R. Tanner, C. W. Previté-Orton, and Z. N. Brooke (1926), 481–520, esp. 508–11

Wealth at death over £1100 p.a.: W. J. Corbett, 'The development of the duchy', 508–11

Alan son of Walter (*c*.1150–1204). *See under* Stewart family (*per. c*.1110–*c*.1350).

Alan, A. J. *See* Lambert, Leslie Harrison (1883–1941).

Alanbrooke. For this title name *see* Brooke, Alan Francis, first Viscount Alanbrooke (1883–1963).

Aland, John Fortescue, **first Baron Fortescue of Credan** (**1670–1746**), judge, was born on 7 March 1670, the second son of Edmund Fortescue of Bierton, Buckinghamshire, and his wife, Sarah, daughter (and ultimately heir) of Henry Aland of Waterford. On his father's side he was a descendant of Sir John Fortescue, chief justice during the reign of Henry VI and the author of the classic *De laudibus legum Angliae*. In recognition of his maternal inheritance he assumed the additional name Aland after succeeding his elder brother in 1704, although he was usually known by his paternal surname. He was admitted to the Middle Temple on 3 July 1688 and called to the bar there in 1695, but transferred to the Inner Temple in 1712.

Little is known about Fortescue Aland's early career at the bar. His reports include a learned argument in *Serle* v. *Blackmore* (6 Anne; 1707 or 1708), in king's bench, where he spoke against a plea for damages arising out of imprisonment at the suit of the defendant; and he also appeared as junior for the crown in *Attorney-General* v. *East India Company*, heard in the exchequer (1712), which turned partly upon the mathematics of computing customs duties. He followed the western circuit, presumably to take advantage of his connections among the main branch of the Fortescue family. There he forged useful alliances with some leading western lawyers: on 19 December 1707 he married

John Fortescue Aland, first Baron Fortescue of Credan (1670–1746), by John Faber junior, 1733 (after Sir Godfrey Kneller, *c*.1720)

Grace, daughter of Serjeant John Pratt, and he later acknowledged the patronage of Sir Thomas Parker, the queen's serjeant. As a 'favourite' of Parker, Fortescue Aland had high hopes on the occasion of his patron's promotion (in 1710) to lord chief justice of king's bench, and after 1714, when Parker was in great credit at the Hanoverian court, he secured a series of crown appointments, becoming king's counsel and solicitor-general to the prince of Wales in January 1715, and solicitor-general to the king in December, upon the dismissal of Nicholas Lechmere. His edition of Sir John Fortescue's *Difference between an Absolute and Limited Monarchy* (1714) included a fulsome dedication to Parker.

As a principal crown lawyer Fortescue Aland was brought into parliament via the duke of Somerset's interest at Midhurst in Sussex. He proved a disappointment, however; in 1716 Lord Chancellor Cowper wrote of him 'this gentleman wanting spirit equal to his learning and probity, … the king's business in the House of Commons was not so well sustained' (Lemmings, 'Lord Chancellor Cowper and the whigs', 170). In the event, since there was a vacancy in the court of exchequer, Cowper and his fellow ministers agreed to make room for a more 'useful' man (ibid., 171). He became a baron of exchequer on 7 February 1717, having been knighted two weeks earlier. During his brief tenure as solicitor-general he appeared in only one state trial, the unsuccessful prosecution of Francis Francia for allegedly treasonous correspondence with the agents of the Pretender (James Stuart) at the time of the Jacobite rising of 1715. His career on the judicial bench was equally undistinguished, partly because of political difficulties. In January 1718 he was called, with the rest of the judges, to give his opinion on the question as to the king's legal rights over the education and marriage of the royal grandchildren, relations between the king and the prince having broken down. Being the most junior, Fortescue Aland spoke first, and quoted many authorities, including his ancestor Sir John Fortescue, to verify the king's prerogative. Although all except two of the judges agreed with him, he later claimed the prince was offended that his former solicitor-general did not take his part. His fortunes were not affected immediately: he was promoted to the king's bench on 19 May 1718, and on 29 December 1721 he married for the second time. His second wife was Elizabeth (1691–1748), who was twenty years his junior and daughter and coheir of Sir Robert Dormer, a judge of common pleas. But on the accession of George II in 1727 he was the only judge not reappointed, and he spent more than a year out of office before becoming a puisne justice of common pleas on 23 January 1729. Indeed, he seems never to have overcome the disgrace, for his last years on the bench were punctuated by a series of complaining letters to Lord Chancellor Hardwicke, wherein he represented himself as a victim of royal injustice despite loyal services, and begged to retire with a pension and some honour. Although age and infirmities prevented him from going on circuit after 1740, the request was not granted until June 1746, when he resigned, becoming an Irish peer in August. He died on 19 December of that year, aged seventy-six, and was buried at Stapleford Abbots, Essex. He was succeeded in the barony by his only son from his second marriage, Dormer Fortescue-Aland (d. 1780). His only son from his first marriage, John Fortescue-Aland (b. 1711/12), predeceased him in 1743.

Although a learned lawyer, Fortescue Aland admitted to 'want of assurance', and seems to have been happier in his study than among 'the noise and trouble of the world' (BL, Stowe MS 750, fol. 28). In addition to researches in legal history, his scholarly work demonstrated an admiration for logic and mathematics. He was elected a fellow of the Royal Society on 20 March 1712 and became an honorary doctor of civil law at Oxford in 1733. His *Reports of Select Cases in All the Courts of Westminster-Hall* was published in 1748. DAVID LEMMINGS

Sources BL, Stowe MS 750; Add. MSS 35585–35588 · J. B. Lawson, 'Fortescue Aland, John', HoP, *Commons, 1715–54* · E. Foss, *Biographia juridica: a biographical dictionary of the judges of England … 1066–1870* (1870) · ER, 92.734–92, 842–7, 909–26 · *State trials*, 15.897–994, 1198–1230 · D. Lemmings, 'Lord Chancellor Cowper and the whigs, 1714–16', *Parliamentary History*, 9 (1990), 164–73 · D. Lemmings, *Gentlemen and barristers: the inns of court and the English bar, 1680–1730* (1990) · DNB · Sainty, *King's counsel* · Sainty, *Judges* · 'Fortescue of Credan', GEC, *Peerage*

Archives BL, Stowe MSS, legal papers, 403, 1011–1012 · S. Antiquaries, Lond., papers as solicitor-general | BL, letters to Lord Hardwicke, Add. MSS 35585–35588 · BL, letters to Lord Macclesfield, MS 750

Likenesses J. Faber junior, mezzotint, 1733 (after G. Kneller, c.1720), BM, NPG [*see illus.*] · G. Vertue, line engraving, 1750 (after G. Kneller), BM, NPG

Alanson, Edward (1747–1823), surgeon, was born on 23 October 1747 in Newton-le-Willows, Lancashire, the son of John and Margaret Alanson. He was apprenticed to William Pickering, a surgeon to the Liverpool Infirmary, in 1763. In 1768 he went to London and became a house pupil of the surgeon and natural scientist, John Hunter. In 1770 he became a surgeon to the Liverpool Infirmary. Four years later he left the house of William Pickering and moved to Cable Street, Liverpool. In 1777 he became a partner of Henry Park, who was also a surgeon to the infirmary, and in the same year he moved to Basnett Street. Alanson became one of the first three surgeons appointed to the Liverpool Dispensary in 1778. In 1779 he published *Practical Observations on Amputation and the After-Treatment*. At about the same time he helped to found the Liverpool Medical Library and the Liverpool Blind Asylum. In 1790 he moved to Wavertree, near Liverpool. He resigned his post at the infirmary on the grounds of poor health four years later and moved to Aughton, near Ormskirk, where he continued to practise surgery. In 1808 he returned to Wavertree.

Alanson is best-known for his improvements in the technique of amputation, and his important suggestions for hospital reform were a vital adjunct to his new surgical methods. In the early part of the eighteenth century amputations were generally performed by a circular incision perpendicular to the limb. A large open wound remained which was dressed by dry lint and the arteries were tied off by passing a ligature around the entire mass of vessels. Alanson urged that operations be carefully planned in advance. He championed the flap technique, which had recently been revived by a few English surgeons. In this procedure the surgeon cut obliquely inwards towards the bone. The muscles were divided so that the cut end of the bone was covered and a flap of skin was left that could be used to cover the wound. Alanson suggested that the wound be cleansed with warm water and bandaged so that the edges formed a straight line across the stump: no dressings were to be used. He also urged that the arteries be drawn out and tied individually. Although it had been common for surgeons to expect suppuration of the wound as an inevitable concomitant of amputation, Alanson demonstrated that by these methods it was possible for these wounds to heal 'by the first intention', that is, without significant infection. Wounds healed with little fever or discharge and patients seldom needed opium to control post-operative pain. Moreover, the cushion of muscle provided a more useful and less vulnerable stump.

Alanson reported that, of forty-six traditional amputations that he had witnessed, ten patients died and the survivors suffered prolonged complications. Following his adoption of the new methods, there were no deaths and only a few minor complications in thirty-five patients treated without selection at the Liverpool Infirmary. This was the best record until the development of antisepsis by Joseph Lister.

Alanson and his colleagues obtained these results by making hospital reform an important part of their work. It is reported that he never performed an operation without washing his hands. He also urged that hospital wards be vacated and thoroughly cleansed every four months, that iron beds be used, that patients be washed on admission and dressed in clean clothes and that their own clothing be cleaned before discharge, that infectious patients be denied admission, that patients with offensive sores and surgical patients be placed in separate rooms, that hospitals remain uncrowded, that the windows of each ward be opened daily, and that infirmaries remove patients to country houses for recovery.

Alanson's innovations evolved in close consultation with his gifted colleagues at the Liverpool Infirmary—the surgeons Henry Park and John Lyon, and the physicians Matthew Dobson, Henry Richmond, and Thomas Houlston—as well as with several other innovative surgeons and local reformers. He himself did not claim to have originated many of his improvements, but his work is notable for the way in which many details of care and technique were combined to produce a dramatically improved outcome, and for the rigour with which he analysed his work. Together, these amounted to a significant advance in the practice of surgery.

In June 1775 Alanson married the daughter of Nehemiah Holland, a Liverpool merchant. Alanson died on 12 December 1823 in Wavertree. His wife died a year later; they were survived by five of their twelve children.

MARGARET DeLACY, rev.

Sources R. W. Murray, *Edward Alanson and his times* (1914) · T. H. Bickerton and R. M. B. MacKenna, *A medical history of Liverpool from the earliest days to the year 1920*, ed. H. R. Bickerton (1936) · J. A. Shepherd, *A history of the Liverpool Medical Institution* (1979)

Alanus Anglicus (*fl. c.*1190–*c.*1210), canonist, was an Englishman who studied and taught canon law at Bologna. Little is known of his life. There is no firm evidence to support the speculation that he was identical with the 'Alanus, clerk of the lord pope Innocent III' who held the prebend of Chiswick in St Paul's Cathedral some time about 1200. About 1192 he produced the first recension of his *Apparatus*, or commentary, on Gratian's *Decretum*. He was again in Bologna in the years from 1202, and produced a second recension of his *Apparatus* (*c.*1205). The apparatus to *De consecratione* (in four manuscripts of the *Apparatus*) is not certainly by Alanus. Following the work of Gilbertus Anglicus (an English canonist studying and teaching at Bologna at the end of the twelfth and the beginning of the thirteenth century), Alanus assembled a decretal collection: of 484 decretals, 345 were by Innocent III, pope from 1198 to 1216. The first recension was rapidly succeeded by a second, which, with its glosses, was influential at Bologna. He also wrote an *Apparatus* on the decretal collection *compilatio prima*. Alanus's most famous students were Albertus and John Galensis. Alanus's academic activity ceases to be recorded before 1210. There is no firm evidence that he became a Dominican, or that a document, dated 1238, in the archive of the Dominican convent in Bologna refers to this Alanus.

Alanus made substantial contributions to political and legal thought. He was an originator of the well-known formula, 'the king in his kingdom is the emperor of his kingdom', a way of expressing the territorial sovereignty of kings. As he said in his apparatus on the *compilatio prima*, 'What is said of the emperor is held to be said of any king or prince who is subject to no one. For each one has as much right in his kingdom as the emperor has in the empire' (Stickler, 364). Alanus's English origins may have led him in part to the development of this idea, which should be understood against the background of the Roman law model of the emperor as universal temporal sovereign.

Alanus also developed the idea that spiritual power was superior to temporal. The trend among canonists commenting on Gratian's *Decretum* may be termed dualist: they presented temporal and spiritual power as being derived from God but existing in parallel. In the first recension of his *Apparatus* to the *Decretum* Alanus followed such an interpretation. However in his second, and better known, recension he expounded what may be termed a hierocratic argument: that the emperor derived his power from the pope. Alanus used the established 'two swords' imagery: both swords, 'spiritual' and 'material', were possessed by the pope, from whom the emperor derived his 'material' one. The pope could judge and depose the emperor, who was his subject in both temporal and spiritual matters, though because Christ had divided the functions of clergy and laity, the pope could not directly exercise the material sword. During the thirteenth century, the hierocratic interpretation increasingly supplanted the dualist in canonist thought.

Alanus did place some limit on papal monarchy. He said that a general council of the church was greater than the pope in matters of faith, and that a heretical pope could be judged against his will. It was, however, as an exponent of the idea of papal sovereignty that Alanus was remembered.

JOSEPH CANNING

Sources A. M. Stickler, 'Alanus Anglicus als Verteidiger des monarchischen Papsttums', *Salesianum*, 21 (1959), 346–406 · S. Kuttner, 'The collection of Alanus: a concordance of its two recensions', *Rivista di Storia del Diritto Italiano*, 26 (1953), 37–53 · S. Kuttner, 'Universal pope or servant of God's servants', *Revue de Droit Canonique*, 32 (1981), 109–49 · R. Weigand, *Die Naturrechtslehre der Legisten und Dekretisten von Irnerius bis Accursius und von Gratian bis Johannes Teutonicus* (Munich, 1967) · P. Landau, 'Alanus Anglicus', *Lexikon des Mittelalters*, 1 (1980), 267–8 · *Fasti Angl., 1066–1300*, [St Paul's, London], 41–2

Alanus, J. *See* Aleyn, John (d. 1373).

À Lasco [Laski], **John** (1499–1560), evangelical reformer, was born in Lask, Poland, the second of three sons and brother to four daughters of Jarslov Laski (d. 1521?), voivode of Sieradz, and Susanna Bak (*fl.* 1484–1510), daughter of the Bakova-Gora councilman Zbigniew Bak. His birth coincided with a rise in the family's fortune. His uncle Jan Laski (d. 1531) rose quickly in the ranks of the Polish nobility, becoming royal secretary, chancellor, and finally, in 1510, archbishop of Gnesen and primate of the Polish Roman Catholic church. In that same year Jan Laski brought his three nephews to Cracow to provide for their education.

Education and early career In March 1513 the primate travelled to Rome to participate in the fifth Lateran Council.

His two older nephews, Jerome and John, accompanied him on this journey, and were joined the following year by their youngest brother, Stanislaw. While the primate engaged in ecclesiastical and diplomatic discussions, the three young men continued their education under the watchful eye of their tutor, Jan Branicki. Early in 1515 they took up residence in Bologna, along with other Polish students. They pursued a private course of study, focusing on Latin, Italian, ecclesiastical law, and history. Apparently they were not enrolled in the university. According to his tutor, John was an exemplary student, 'in whom there is virtue that I have before never seen in a boy' (Dalton, 63). While in Bologna, à Lasco became acquainted with Reginald Pole, who later led the Catholic reformation in England. He just missed the German humanist Ulrich von Hutten, who probably left Bologna a few months before à Lasco's arrival.

In 1518 à Lasco moved to Padua, where for a short time he took on a diplomatic role as counsellor for the Polish nation. In March 1519 he went back to Poland. At some point during this period, à Lasco suffered the embarrassment of excommunication when his cousin defaulted on a loan that he had secured with John's name. The archbishop, however, made good the debt, and John was reconciled with the church. Meanwhile the primate had begun to advance the career of his protégé, who on 30 November 1517 was summarily named custodian of Leczyca, a canon of Plock, and coadjutor to the deacon of Gnesen. The following month he became deacon of Gnesen, and in May 1518 was appointed a canon of Cracow. In 1521 he was ordained to the priesthood, appointed dean of Gnesen, and named royal secretary. In 1525 he became provost of Leczyca, that is, head of the cathedral chapter, and in the following year was appointed to the same office for Gnesen.

In 1524 à Lasco accompanied his older brother, Jerome, on a diplomatic mission to France. Jerome had been introduced earlier to the French court during his student days in Bologna. *En route* they stopped briefly in Basel, where à Lasco first met Erasmus. He was immediately drawn to the humanist and would later return for a more extended visit. The brothers pushed on to Paris where à Lasco met some of the leading French humanists, including Marguerite de Valois, sister of François I, and Faber Staupulenses (Lefèvre d'Étaples). He may also have attended lectures at the Sorbonne.

In the spring of 1525 à Lasco returned to Basel, where he lodged with Erasmus in quarters provided by the publisher Johann Froben. During his stay he also met Beatus Rhenanus, the publisher Oporin, Heinrich Glarenius, Zwingli, Guillaume Farel, and Conrad Pellican, with the last of whom he briefly studied Hebrew. Funds supplied from Poland supported Erasmus's household during this period. À Lasco even purchased the master's library for 300 gulden, allowing Erasmus to use it until his death. Later Erasmus tried to terminate the agreement when à Lasco failed to make a second payment on time, and the dispute continued until Erasmus's death in 1536. Then in the following spring à Lasco made a final payment to the executor of Erasmus's estate through his messenger, Boniface Amerbach. He began to receive books in April 1537, but eventually sold most of them and virtually dissolved the collection.

Political engagements In June 1525 the primate, Jan Laski, summoned à Lasco back to Poland by way of Italy. John spent a few months in Padua and Venice, where he called upon the doge, Andrea Gritti, who would later be an important diplomatic ally. Then, after requesting additional funds from Poland, he continued his trip home, arriving in Poznan in April 1526. He spent the next several years immersed in the affairs of Poland's political and ecclesiastical hierarchy, while lamenting the loss of his student days in Basel.

From 1527 the Laski family was plunged into a complicated and ominous political intrigue. After the death of Lajos II Jagiellon in 1526, a bitter dispute arose over succession to the Hungarian throne. Ferdinand von Habsburg was perhaps the strongest contender, but János Zápolya was the local favourite. Jerome à Lasco secretly committed himself and his family to Zápolya's cause, continuing the anti-Habsburg policies of his uncle. Meanwhile the Polish king remained officially neutral in the affair. In 1528 Jerome travelled to Istanbul where, misrepresenting himself as an official ambassador, he concluded a treaty between Zápolya and Sultan Suleiman the Magnificent. The Turkish forces then attacked Hungary and in 1529 laid siege to Vienna. John à Lasco's role in this agreement is not clear, but he was often called upon to raise financial support. As a reward for his efforts, Zápolya named him bishop of Veszprém in 1529, a post in which he was never confirmed by the papacy. In March 1530 he delivered a speech before a Polish council of nobles, defending both his brother and Zápolya. This blatant opposition to the Habsburgs and the papacy, and the unpopular alliance with non-Christian Turks, brought ecclesiastical censure to the aged primate in Poland. He escaped further torment only through his death on 19 May 1531 in Kalisz; John à Lasco accompanied his uncle's body to Gnesen for burial.

The conflict over Hungary continued, with neither side gaining a decisive victory. In October 1530 the claimants met with other interested leaders in order to resolve the issue diplomatically. They agreed to a year-long armistice but found no permanent resolution. When conflict broke out again, Ferdinand gradually gained the upper hand. Suspicious and desperate, Zápolya turned on his former ally, Jerome à Lasco, who may have been asking for repayment of his debts. When Zápolya threw Jerome into prison, John immediately went to Kasemark in Hungary in order to secure his release. He sought support from important acquaintances, including the king of Poland, the king of France, and the duke of Prussia. Eventually Jan Tarnowski, a nobleman and confidant of Zápolya, took matters into his own hands and secured Jerome's release. Jerome immediately switched his allegiance to Ferdinand and sent his brother John to make the humiliating request for reconciliation. The entire affair plunged the Laski family deeply into debt and effectively ended its short-lived political power.

Changing allegiances After this débâcle, à Lasco withdrew for a time from public life, often residing with his sister-in-law, Anna von Kurozaek, in Rytwiany, Poland. Although he frequently complained of poverty he managed to support a young pupil, Nikolaus Anian Burgonius, sending him to Wittenburg in 1534 to study with Melanchthon. The two men were devastated when Burgonius died in Leipzig the following year. During the same period, à Lasco retained Andreas Frycz Modrzewski as his personal secretary. Modrzewski too resided for a time with Melanchthon and later contributed significantly to the protestant movement in Poland. These connections with Melanchthon are remarkable at a time when à Lasco had not yet declared himself for the protestant reformation.

After the death of his uncle à Lasco's place in the ecclesiastical hierarchy diminished rapidly. Several attempts to have him appointed to a bishop's see came to nothing. Declining career prospects and increasing contact with reforming impulses on the continent brought à Lasco closer to a momentous decision, one which would change his life. In April 1537 he travelled briefly to Frankfurt am Main, probably to test his prospects abroad. During this trip Duke Georg of Saxony imprisoned him briefly in Leipzig, on charges stemming from the Hungarian affair, regarding him as an enemy of Ferdinand von Habsburg. When a letter from the Habsburgs testified to John's new allegiance to Ferdinand, the duke released him. He spent a few days with Melanchthon and then visited the home of the noted German theologian and statesman Julius Pflug. In 1538 he returned to Poland where King Sigismund offered him the small bishopric of Kujawien. À Lasco politely refused; apparently he had already decided to emigrate.

In 1539 à Lasco set out for western Europe with his brother Jerome. He first returned to Frankfurt where he met Albrecht Hardenburg. He then accompanied his friend to Mainz and to Louvain, where Hardenburg served on the theological faculty. In Louvain he joined a small group devoted to biblical study that had its roots in the *devotio moderna*, a late medieval pietistic movement most famously represented by the *Imitatio Christi* of Thomas à Kempis. There he met the daughter of a Louvain weaver, whom he married in the spring of 1540; her name remains unknown. He defends his decision in a letter to a Polish bishop, citing the scriptural injunction (1 Corinthians 7: 9) to marry if one cannot remain chaste. To avoid possible persecution, the couple moved a few months later to Emden in East Friesland. Meanwhile Jerome returned to Poland and took to what proved to be his deathbed near the end of 1541. À Lasco quickly returned home and was with his brother when he died in December. When word of his homecoming spread abroad, à Lasco's enemies seized their opportunity. Using reports of his recent marriage, he was challenged to sign an oath testifying his allegiance to the Roman Catholic church. An archivist's note states that à Lasco actually signed the oath to deny that he had taken a wife and declared that he had not abandoned the doctrine of the gospel, but the oath itself makes no mention of the marriage. Nevertheless the sincerity of his religious allegiance had been called into question, and he was officially deprived of his benefices.

Returning to Emden, à Lasco now moved more decidedly into the protestant camp. In 1543 he accepted an invitation from Countess Anna of Oldenburg to be pastor of the Emden church and superintendent of all East Friesian churches. He followed the Swiss models for reform laid out by John Calvin and Heinrich Bullinger, although he repeatedly emphasized his independence from these leaders. He soon denied the physical presence of Christ's body and blood in the Lord's supper and stressed the importance of rigorous ecclesiastical discipline within the life of the church. He instituted a *coetus*, or synod of pastors and lay elders, to assist in church government. He hammered out his theology in the context of disputation, including dialogues with the Anabaptist leaders Menno Simons and David Joris. In 1549 East Friesland came under pressure to accept the Augsburg interim, the religious agreement forced by the emperor Charles V on the protestant princes of Germany in the previous year. For East Friesland this meant the danger of a return to Roman Catholic rule, and ultimately led to à Lasco's expulsion from Emden. He had anticipated this fate, however, and crossed to England to make arrangements for his being sheltered there. Ostensibly he made the journey to participate in a doctrinal colloquy summoned by Archbishop Thomas Cranmer as part of his programme of religious reform. Cranmer had written at least three times to à Lasco, inviting him to this conference, while à Lasco himself corresponded at intervals with Bullinger, Bucer, Melanchthon, and Calvin, all key components in Cranmer's plan. Cranmer even wrote to à Lasco urging him to bring Melanchthon to the conference. The invitation would also have had the support of William Turner, the king's physician and Protector Somerset's confidant, who had spent some time in Emden under à Lasco's spiritual direction. As nephew of the late archbishop of Gnesen, moreover, and an acquaintance of the duke of Prussia, à Lasco was also well known in English political circles, and he was later accused of having used this trip to negotiate a treaty between England and Prussia against Charles V, a charge he consistently denied.

À Lasco arrived in England in September 1548 and departed in late February or early March 1549. In the event the colloquy never took place, but this brief visit was none the less beneficial, for he had secured a place of refuge for his East Friesian congregations, should they be forced to leave the continent. On his return to Emden his earlier fears were realized. The countess had accepted a version of the interim and she asked à Lasco to resign. He rebuked her for a lack of courage but consented to depart. After a tearful farewell, he left Emden and set out for Bremen, where Hardenburg was serving as pastor. In April 1550 he continued his journey, arriving in England the following month. For a short time he resided with Cranmer in Lambeth but soon purchased his own home on Bow Lane, in the city of London. In June he, his wife, and his children (John, Jerome, and Barbara) were made English denizens.

Years in England In England, à Lasco served as superintendent of the Strangers' Church of London, which was officially incorporated by letters patent on 24 July 1550. The royal charter, still preserved in London's Guildhall, grants to the strangers the old church of the Austin friars off Threadneedle Street, which was renamed the 'Temple of the Lord Jesus'. À Lasco is named as superintendent, along with four additional pastors; two of these would oversee the Dutch church, which to this day continues to meet in Austin Friars, and two would direct the French/Walloon church, which would meet in St Anthony's Chapel on Threadneedle Street. The charter granted them freedom to use their own rites and ceremonies, 'not withstanding that they do not conform with the rites and ceremonies used in our Kingdom' (Lindeboom, 202). This was an extraordinary privilege, especially given the fact that a religious Act of Uniformity had just been passed the previous year. In his most famous work, *Forma ac ratio* (1555), à Lasco gives an account of the 'Form and Rationale' of the ceremonies used by these immigrants, which may have had some influence upon the 1552 Book of Common Prayer, especially on penitential rites associated with the morning and evening prayer services. More direct lines of influence can be traced to John Knox's Scottish order (1560–61) and to the Middleburg ordinal (1602), later used by English puritans. On the continent traces of the Strangers' Church's order can be found in the 1563 German Palatinate order and in the 'forms and prayers' attached to Pieter Dathenus's 1566 psalter, which in turn influenced liturgies in the Dutch reformed churches.

Opposition to these novel rites came almost immediately, most notably from Nicholas Ridley, bishop of London, in whose diocese the churches were established and who endeavoured to limit the independence of their congregations. This opposition was no doubt linked to the controversy over John Hooper's refusal to wear the requisite ecclesiastical vestments to his consecration as bishop of Gloucester. À Lasco took an active role in this controversy, vocally supporting Hooper in his opposition to the vestments. He was quite disappointed when Martin Bucer and Pietro Martire Vermigli finally persuaded Hooper that he should accept the prescribed ecclesiastical garb and be consecrated bishop.

At the same time there were disputes between the Dutch and the French congregations as to the ownership of property and the diversity of rites. When accused of departing from Calvin's example, à Lasco wrote directly to the Genevan reformer, asking for his assistance in the dispute. Meanwhile, a small Italian congregation joined the stranger group. Its minister charged à Lasco with departing from Calvin's teaching on predestination, but the superintendent responded simply that Calvin had spoken 'too harshly' in this matter (À Lasco, *Opera*, 2.676). In addition to professional struggles, à Lasco also experienced personal tragedy. His three-month-old son Paul died in November 1550, and in 1552 he lost his wife to the sweating sickness. He himself contracted the sickness and suffered from chronic headaches thereafter. In 1553, however, he announced plans to remarry. His second wife,

Katherina, accompanied him for the rest of his life and with her he had five more children, one of whom, Samuel, gained some notoriety as a soldier.

Return to Emden and Poland When Queen Mary ascended the English throne in 1553, à Lasco and most of his associates were forced to find refuge elsewhere. At first they sought a home in Denmark, but they were soon turned away, ostensibly because of their Zwinglian views on the sacraments. Late in 1553 à Lasco returned to Emden, where he found it necessary to rebuke a former colleague, Gellius Faber, for publishing a catechism that was too Lutheran in its content. He also began a literary war against the Lutheran theologian Joachim Westphal over sacramental issues. In the meantime he continued to involve himself in the affairs of returning exiles, advising congregations in both Wesel and Frankfurt am Main. In both cases he consulted Calvin. In April 1555 à Lasco went to Frankfurt, where he finally met Calvin personally. There he drew the fire of another Lutheran theologian, Johann Timann. In his response à Lasco argued unpersuasively that he agreed in substance with the standard Lutheran confession, the *confessio Augustana*.

In 1556 à Lasco's career came full circle, and he was allowed to return to Poland. He immediately came under attack for his sacramental teaching, most notably from a former colleague, Bishop Hosius. In 1557 he addressed a defence of his doctrine to the Polish king and appended a copy of the *confessio Augustana*. As the king read the confession, à Lasco's defence fell on the floor where a dog started to devour it. A sympathetic servant rescued the document and transcribed it for the king's reading.

During his final years à Lasco attended numerous meetings and synods aimed at achieving a religious consensus among the Polish people, and especially among Polish protestants. His efforts failed in 1558, when the Prussian Lutherans refused to sign a common confession at a conference in Königsberg. In the autumn of 1559 he fell sick, and by Christmas he was desperately ill. On 8 January 1560 he died at Pinczow in the presence of his wife and children. The funeral was held on 29 January, and his body was buried at the high altar in the church at Pinczow; the site of the grave was destroyed in 1884 by the bishop of Cracow. Soon after his death a certain Grzegorz Orszak began to circulate rumours that the lips on à Lasco's corpse had fused together, in divine judgment upon his heresy. The synod decided to reopen the grave to dispel the rumour. À Lasco left his family in relative poverty, though the local nobility granted them a gift of 289 gulden. In 1564 his wife wrote a touching letter to Duke Albrecht of east Prussia, requesting further support. The Laski family as a whole soon reverted to Roman Catholicism, before disappearing from the historical record.

Religious significance Throughout his career John à Lasco demonstrated a curious mixture of ecumenism and fierce independence. As an ecclesiastical diplomat he believed strongly that for protestantism to succeed upon the continent it was essential for the various evangelical factions to unite. The means to this end was a common confession of eucharistic doctrine. Hitherto the debate had centred upon the presence of Christ's body and blood in the elements of bread and wine. On this point à Lasco was decidedly Zwinglian, believing that Christ's body remained in heaven. However, he cleverly, though unsuccessfully, tried to refocus the discussion, drawing attention to the entire action of the ceremony rather than viewing the elements as the focal point. In this perspective the benefit of the eucharist does not lie in the bread and wine alone, but rather it depends upon participation in the rite as a whole. By such participation believers are 'sealed' by the Holy Spirit in the spiritual communion with Christ. They should therefore remain seated while receiving communion, because in this way the sacrament testifies to 'our Sabbath rest in Christ' (À Lasco, Opera, 2.658). As a seal, this rite carries divine authority, causing à Lasco to reject the Zwinglian analogy for the eucharist, as a soldier's oath of allegiance. He likewise opposed what he understood of Calvin's position, that Christ was somehow spiritually present in the elements.

À Lasco also made notable contributions to the formation of church polities. As superintendent of churches in East Friesland he was instrumental in establishing the *coetus*, the governing body consisting of ministers and lay elders, and perhaps more than any other leading reformer he insisted that both groups formed a single 'order', albeit with the important distinction that only ministers could teach and administer the sacraments. When he moved to England he instituted something like a synod, in which ministers and elders from the various stranger congregations supervised the entire organization of their churches. These incipient forms of presbyterianism would not be unknown to later Elizabethan puritans. Nor did they forget that the crown had once granted to these immigrants a right of legal nonconformity, something which in their own time it would not grant to England's own citizens.   DIRK W. RODGERS

Sources O. Bartel, *Jan Laski*, trans. A. Starke (1981) · H. Dalton, *Johannes à Lasco* (1881) · J. à Lasco, *Opera tam edita quam inedita recensuit*, ed. A. Kuyper, 2 vols. (1866) · J. Lindeboom, *Austin Friars: history of the Dutch Reformed church in London, 1550–1950*, trans. D. de Inough (1950) · D. Rodgers, *John à Lasco in England* (1994) · J. à Lasco, *Lasciana nebst den altesten evang. Synodalprotokollen Polēns, 1555–61*, ed. H. Dalton (1898) · J. à Lasco, *Miscellaneen zur Geschichte der evangelischen Kirche in Russland nebst Lasciana neue Folge*, ed. H. Dalton (1905) · A. Pettegree, *Foreign protestant communities in sixteenth-century London* (1986) · A. Sprengler-Ruppenthal, *Mysterium und Riten nach der Londoner Kirchenordnung der Niederländer* (1967) · K. Hein, *Die Sakramentslehre des Johannes a Lasco* (1904) · K. A. R. Kruske, *Johannes a Lasco und der Sacramentsstreit* (1901) · D. MacCulloch, *Thomas Cranmer: a life* (1996) · W. R. D. Jones, *William Turner: Tudor naturalist, physician and divine* (1998) · R. Leaver, 'Goostly psalmes and spirituall songs': English and Dutch metrical psalms from Coverdale to Utenhove, 1535–1561 (1991)
Archives Bodl. Oxf., MS Barlow 19 · Bodl. Oxf., Th. Seld 8 vo. 7.12. · GL
Likenesses glass plate, 1552?, Austin Friars Church, London; priv. coll. · H. Hondius, line engraving, BM, NPG; repro. in I. Verheiden, *Praestantium aligout theologorum … effigies* (The Hague, 1602) · line engraving, NPG

Wealth at death widow forced to solicit support from church at Pinczow and duke of Prussia: her letter to duke of Prussia, *Opera*, ed. Kuyper, 765 ff.; Bartel, *Jan Laski*, 263

Alasdair Mac Mhaighstir Alasdair. *See* MacDonald, Alexander (c.1695–c.1770).

Alban [St Alban, Albanus] (*d. c.*303?), Christian martyr in Roman Britain, was known from at least the tenth century as *protomartyr Anglorum* (*sic*); but the earliest reference to him is in 429 (the date is given by Prosper of Aquitaine writing a few years later), when the bishops Germanus of Auxerre (*d.* 445/6) and Lupus of Troyes were sent to Britain to combat the heresy of Pelagius. Constantius of Lyons, in his life of Germanus, written *c.*460–480, records that at the end of their mission 'the priests went to the tomb of the blessed martyr Alban to give thanks through him to God' (Constantius of Lyons, 262). A century later Venantius Fortunatus, bishop of Poitiers (*d. c.*610), in his poem *De virginitate*, placed 'illustrious Alban whom fertile Britannia bore' among the principal saints of the west who had died for their faith (Venantius Fortunatus, ed. Leo, 185).

The *De excidio* of Gildas, written at some time in the middle of the sixth century, is the earliest surviving British source to reveal anything more about Alban. Gildas was long thought to be relying on an earlier *passio* of the saint, but in 2001 Richard Sharpe identified this text as a substantially shorter version of the *passio* preserved in manuscripts in Turin and Paris. This shorter version, preserved in four manuscripts, the earliest of the ninth century and now in London, represents the oldest known text of the *passio*. It appears that it may have been composed for display on placards in the basilica in Auxerre dedicated to Alban and built by Germanus between his visit to Britain in 429 and his death in or about 446. This text may be the version perhaps known to Constantius of Lyons and was possibly the form of the *passio* known to Gildas. It served in turn as the base upon which editors in Merovingian Gaul embroidered the two different but related versions now preserved in Turin and Paris. In writing his *Historia ecclesiastica*, completed in 731, Bede drew both upon Gildas and on a form of the *passio* close to that in the Paris manuscript to compose what remained the basic account of Alban until the fanciful additions of the twelfth century Bede (*Hist. eccl.*, 1.7). Since the material added independently by each of the Merovingian editors can have no basis in fact, it is the shorter text that preserves what is likely to be in historical terms the most reliable version, although even here the introduction of miraculous elements shows that we are dealing with hagiography. It reveals the following sequence of events.

In the time of persecution (*tempore persecutionis*) a nameless Christian cleric fleeing from his persecutors was received as a guest by Alban, then still a pagan. Alban put on the man's cloak (*caracalla*), handed himself over in his place, and was taken at once to the judge (*iudex*). Under questioning Alban declared that he was a Christian, and was ordered to be put to the sword. Led away to sacrifice, he came to the river which divided the city wall (*murus*) from the arena where he was to die. Alban saw that the bridge over the river was so crowded with those who had come to see him die that he would scarcely be able to get across that evening. The judge would not permit him to die in the city. Alban entered the river which then dried up to let him pass (first miracle). When he came to the place where he was to die (the arena), the executioner ran up to him with drawn sword begging to take his place, and throwing away his sword cast himself at Alban's feet. While the (other) executioners were delaying, Alban and the crowd climbed a gentle flower-covered hill almost five hundred paces from the arena. At the top Alban asked for water and immediately a living spring (*fons perennis*) rose at his feet and having done its duty disappeared (second miracle). An executioner beheaded Alban but the executioner's eyes fell to the ground (third miracle) together with the martyr's head. The first executioner was then put to the sword. Amazed by these wonders and without waiting for the command of the emperors (*iniussu principum*), the judge ordered the persecution to cease. When St Germanus the bishop went to the basilica of Alban he ordered the tomb to be opened. He placed in it relics of all the apostles and various martyrs so that the limbs of saints collected from different places and equal in the sight of heaven should be gathered together in the security of one tomb. From the very place where the martyr's blood had poured out Germanus then took some dust (*massam pulveris*) from the earth which had been reddened by the martyr's blood. A huge multitude was that same day converted to God.

The text cannot be quite in its original state since Germanus is described as *sanctus* and the description of his visit is clearly an insertion, coming between the account of Alban's execution and the final sentence recording the consequent conversions. Yet it provides a clear and distinctive topographical setting, without in its present state saying where or precisely when the events took place. The Turin manuscript alone relates that the persecution took place in the time of the emperor Severus (*r*. 193–211), allowing John Morris to argue that the martyrdom took place in 209. Sharpe's recognition that this statement is an addition to the original text and inconsistent with it has removed the basis of Morris's suggestion. Gildas conjectured (*ut concimus*) that the martyrdom took place at the time of the great persecution under Diocletian at the beginning of the fourth century, presumably relying on the words *tempore persecutionis* at the start of the short text quoted above, and Bede accepted this as a fact. It has been argued that there is no sign that Diocletian's persecution had any impact in the western provinces, and that it is more likely that Alban suffered in one of the persecutions in the middle of the third century, under Decius (*r*. 249–51) or Valerian (*r*. 257–60). The mention of the city wall in the short text may however be decisive: the walls of Verulamium were not built until 260 at the earliest and probably rather later, in which case the traditional view that Alban was martyred under Diocletian, in the persecution that began in 303, is likely to be correct. The Turin manuscript gives the day and month (22 June) at the end of the text. Bede also has this date but appears to have used a text

closer to the Paris manuscript which agrees with the short version in having a date in the title at the start of the text. This title appears to have read 'De passione sancti Albani XI Kal. Iul', or 21 June.

Gildas is the first to identify Alban as *Verolamiensis*, a man from Verulamium (St Albans), the third-largest city of Roman Britain, on Watling Street, about 20 miles northwest of London. Bede went further in stating that the martyrdom took place 'near the city of Verulamium' (*Hist. eccl.*, 1.7), but he clearly had local information. The identification is plausible because, as has long been recognized, the setting of the martyrdom as described in the *passio* reflects the actual relationship between the site of Roman Verulamium and that of the ancient abbey dedicated to St Alban on the hill outside the walls, approximately 500 paces from the north-east gate and the River Ver (although no arena is known outside the walls; if the amphitheatre-like theatre inside the walls is meant, the topography is confused). It has become even more plausible in recent years, because excavation in the Roman city has shown that organized town life continued well into the fifth century, providing a context for the religious debates and structured society encountered by Germanus in 429, and because excavation outside the walls has shown that the abbey occupies the site of one of the cemeteries of the Roman city. This brings into sharp focus the one contemporary comment which Bede added to his account of Alban, that to his day (*usque ad hanc diem*) sick people were healed in a church on the site of the martyrdom (*in quo videlicet loco*) and 'the working of frequent miracles continues to bring it renown' (*Hist. eccl.*, 1.7). Although this appears to conflate the place of execution and the place of the saint's burial, it strongly suggests that the abbey of St Alban had its origin in a cemetery basilica erected over the site of the saint's grave in a pattern, as Wilhelm Levison first argued in 1941, characteristic of the empire as a whole but otherwise unrecognized in Roman Britain. The discovery of the cemetery below the abbey thus provides a context for the burial of Alban in a location which agrees with that which the *passio* describes.

The place of execution has never been clearly distinguished in St Albans tradition from the place of burial, as the earliest text shows in recording the removal apparently from the tomb of soil supposed to have been reddened by the out-pouring of the martyr's blood. The two sites are most unlikely to have been the same and the place of execution may now perhaps be identified with the Roman temple and associated head cult investigated by Rosalind Niblett in 1991–3 at Folly Lane on the hill to the north of the hill on which the abbey stands. The topographical details given in the *passio* agree as well with this site as with the site of the burial in the area of the abbey.

Towards the end of the eighth century (perhaps *c*.793) Offa, king of Mercia (*r*. 757–96), established or re-endowed a religious community at the place of Alban's burial, in a dominant setting beside Watling Street, the principal highway of his kingdom. In the course of this he apparently found what was believed to be the body of the saint; translated from shrine to shrine over the centuries, St

Alban remained the principal treasure of the abbey until its suppression by Henry VIII in 1539. In the late tenth century Alban was described in a charter of King Æthelred as *protomartyr Anglorum* (AS chart., S 888), 'by anticipation, as the English had not yet come to Britain', as Thomas Elmham (d. 1427) justly commented (Elmham, 182). In 1135 Geoffrey of Monmouth provided a name for the cleric Alban had sheltered, translating the word *caracalla* by its Latinized Greek equivalent *amphibalus* which he had read in Gildas and misunderstood as the name of a saint. Forty years later, in 1178, the bodies of 'St Cloak' and his companions were duly found at Redbourn, a few miles from St Albans, and brought to the abbey. By this time St Albans had been recognized by Pope Adrian IV (r. 1154–9; Nicholas Breakspear) as the premier abbey of England, partly in recognition of the protomartyr, partly no doubt because his own father, Robert of the Chamber, had entered the house and become a priest there. This new status led in the time of Abbot Simon (r. 1167–83) not only to the discoveries at Redbourn but also to the production by William of St Albans in Latin prose of a greatly enlarged and fanciful *Alia acta* of Sts Alban and Amphibalus and their companions, soon rewritten in Latin verse by Ralph of Dunstable, and before 1240 translated almost word for word into Anglo-Norman doggerel by Matthew Paris, monk and historian of the abbey (d. 1259). By the early fifteenth century these texts seem to have led to the production of a yet more fanciful Latin version (now apparently lost), the fullest of all the 'lives' of the two saints. This was used for the English prose life in the *Gilte Legende*, later abridged and revised by William Caxton (1415–1492) and printed c.1483–5. It was also used by John Lydgate as the basis for the 4621 lines of his English verse 'Livis and Passiouns of Seynt Albon and Seynt Amphibal', commissioned by Abbot John Whethamstede and completed in 1439. This was printed in 1534 at the request of Abbot Robert Catton, probably at St Albans by John Hertford.

The first known representation of Alban in art is the picture of his execution in the Albani psalter of c.1120–30 (Thomson, 1.416, 2.pl.72). The golden outer reliquary, made in the time of Abbot Simon but now lost, bore on one end, so that it could be seen by the celebrant at the high altar, the beheading of the saint, and on both sides in relief a series of scenes from his life and passion. These, or another series made by Walter of Colchester (d. 1248), may have been the inspiration of the definitive narrative sequence drawn by Matthew Paris c.1245–8 to illustrate his *Vie de Seint Auban*: fifty-four drawings of the lives and deaths of Sts Alban and Amphibalus, the visit of Sts Germanus and Lupus, the invention of the relics of St Alban by Offa, and the king's foundation of the abbey (TCD, MS E.1.40 (177)). Paris repeatedly shows Alban with a distinctive round-headed cross of Coptic type, suggesting that a cross preserved at St Albans and believed to be a relic of the saint was of Late Antique origin. The beheading of Alban is shown again in the finest style in a triangular panel of Purbeck marble on the west end of the shrine pedestal of 1308 still standing in the abbey (restored 1872,

1993). It was also the subject of the pewter badges made for sale to pilgrims.

Three centres abroad have some claim to Alban. Relics of the saint were removed from England c.1070, probably from Ely, by Cnut the Holy, king of Denmark, and placed in his newly founded monastery of Odense. The city still boasts an Alban Square, Albani beer, and the MacAlban bar. A parish church at Cologne was dedicated to Alban by at least the twelfth century, and from the late tenth century the church of St Pantaleon in the same city had relics of St Albinus which are still identified as belonging to St Alban. A church dedicated to St Alban is recorded at Mainz as early as 756. Although the legend of the Mainz saint indicates that they are not the same, his feast day on 21 June suggests that he is to be identified with the British martyr celebrated on 22 June.

MARTIN BIDDLE

Sources 'Prosperi Tironis epitoma chronicon', *Chronica minora saec. IV. V. VI. VII.*, ed. T. Mommsen, 1, MGH Auctores Antiquissimi, 9 (Berlin, 1892), 341–499 · Constantius of Lyons, 'Vita Germani episcopi Autissiodorensis', *Passiones vitaeque sanctorum aevi Merovingici*, ed. B. Krusch and W. Levison, MGH Scriptores Rerum Merovingicarum, 7/1 (Hanover, 1919) · *Venanti Honori Clementiani Fortunati presbyteri Italici opera poetica*, ed. F. Leo, MGH Auctores Antiquissimi, 4/1 (Berlin, 1881) · Gildas, 'De excidio et conquestu Britanniae', *Gildas: 'The ruin of Britain', and other works*, ed. and trans. M. Winterbottom (1978) · W. Meyer, ed., *Die Legende des heiligen Albanus, des Protomartyr Angliae, in Texten vor Beda*, Abhandlungen der Königlichen Gesellschaft der Wissenschaften zu Göttingen, new ser., 8/1 (Berlin, 1904), 1–82 · R. Sharpe, 'The late antique passion of St Alban', *Alban and St Albans: Roman and medieval architecture, art and archaeology* [University of Hertfordshire 1999], ed. M. Henig and P. Lindley (2001), 30–37 · Bede, *Hist. eccl.*, 1.7, 18, 20 · Thomas of Elmham, *Historia monasterii S. Augustini Cantuariensis*, ed. C. Hardwick, Rolls Series, 8 (1858) · *The Historia regum Britanniae of Geoffrey of Monmouth*, ed. and trans. L. Thorpe (1966) · William of St Albans, *Alia acta SS Albani et Amphibali*, ed. and trans. L. Simpson, *Hertfordshire Archaeology*, 8 (1980–82), 67–77 · M. Paris, *La vie de Seint Auban: an Anglo-Norman poem of the thirteenth century*, ed. A. R. Harden, Anglo-Norman Text Society, 19 (1968) · J. Lydgate, *The life of Saint Alban and Saint Amphibal*, ed. G. F. Reinecke (1985) · M. Biddle, 'Alban and the Anglo-Saxon church', *Cathedral and city: St Albans ancient and modern*, ed. R. Runcie (1977), 23–42, 138–42 · S. S. Frere and M. G. Wilson, *Verulamium excavations*, 2 (1983), 20–25, 93–101, 220–26 · R. Niblett, *The excavation of a ceremonial site at Folly Lane, Verulamium*, Britannia Monograph Series, 14 (1999) · W. Levison, 'St Alban and St Albans', *Antiquity*, 15 (1941), 337–59 · J. R. Morris, 'The date of Saint Alban', *Hertfordshire Archaeology*, 1 (1968), 1–8 · L. F. R. Williams, *History of the abbey of St Alban* (1917), 3–16, 239–43 · M. Biddle, 'Remembering St Alban: the site of the shrine and the discovery of the twelfth-century Purbeck marble shrine table', *Alban and St Albans: Roman and medieval architecture, art and archaeology* [University of Hertfordshire 1999], ed. M. Henig and P. Lindley (2001), 124–61, esp. 146–51 · B. Kjølbye-Biddle, 'The Alban Cross', *Alban and St Albans: Roman and medieval architecture, art and archaeology* [University of Hertfordshire 1999], ed. M. Henig and P. Lindley (2001), 85–110 · R. Niblett, *Verulamium: the Roman city of St Albans* (2001), 127–47 · G. R. Stephens, 'A note on the martyrdom of St Alban', *Hertfordshire Archaeology*, 9 (1983–6), 20–21 · R. M. Thomson, *Manuscripts from St Albans Abbey, 1066–1235*, 2 vols. (1982) · M. Biddle and B. Kjølbye-Biddle, 'The origins of St Albans Abbey: Romano-British cemetery and Anglo-Saxon monastery', *Alban and St Albans: Roman and medieval architecture, art and archaeology* [University of Hertfordshire 1999], ed. M. Henig and P. Lindley (2001), 45–77 · E. A. Thompson, *Saint Germanus of Auxerre and the end of Roman Britain*, Studies in Celtic History, 6 (1994) · E. P. Baker, 'The cult of St Alban at Cologne', *Archaeological Journal*, 94 (1937), 207–56 · W. McLeod,

'Alban and Amphibal: some extant lives and a lost life', *Mediaeval Studies*, 42 (1980), 407–30 • W. Levison, 'Bischof Germanus von Auxerre und die Quellen zu seiner Geschichte', *Neues Archiv der Gesellschaft für Ältere Deutsche Geschichtskunde*, 29/1 (1903–4), 95–175, at 147–60, 162 • C. C. Oman, 'The goldsmiths at St Albans Abbey during the 12th and 13th centuries', *Transactions of the St Albans and Hertfordshire Architectural and Archaeological Society* (1932), 215–36 • S. Keynes, 'Changing faces: Offa, king of Mercia', *History Today*, 40/11 (1990), 14–19 • *AS chart.*, S 888 • S. Lewis, *The art of Matthew Paris in the 'Chronica Majora'* (1987), 9–10, 106–15, 380–87, 413, 422, 425, 435–6 • P. Salway, *The Oxford illustrated history of Roman Britain* (1993), 321, 515–16

Alban [St Albans], **Roger** (*d.* after **1461**), genealogist, copyist, and Carmelite friar, was born in St Albans, Hertfordshire, and joined his order in London. He was ordained acolyte on 17 December 1401 and deacon on 19 December 1405. His name occurs as the copyist on three manuscripts, BL, Harley MS 3138 (dated 1424), Harley MS 211, and Stowe MS 8, and it has also been claimed that he copied BL, Stowe MS 38 and, in 1439, the anti-Wyclif treatise *Fasciculi zizaniorum* (Bodl. Oxf., MS e Museo 86). Alban was the author of a celebrated genealogical work in two parts, *Progenies regum Brytannie*, tracing the descent of Christ from Adam through the Hebrew kings, and then the succession of the English kings from Brutus and the Saxon kings down to Henry VI in 1461, and he is thought to have presented a copy of his work to Henry VI. A number of copies survive, some containing only the first part. Complete texts may be found in Winchester College, MS 13A, Oxford, Queen's College, MS 168, and Oxford, St John's College, MS 23. Bale records that Alban compiled as well a 'large, big volume' of extracts from Thomas Netter's *Doctrinale*, now lost.   RICHARD COPSEY

Sources Bale, *Cat.*, 2.94 • W. E. L. Smith, ed., *The register of Richard Clifford, bishop of Worcester, 1401–1407: a calendar*, Pontifical Institute of Medieval Studies: Subsidia Mediaevalis, 6 (1976), 67 • register of Roger Walden, bishop of London, 1405–6, GL, fol. 17 • R. Lavenham, *A litil tretys on the seven deadly sins*, ed. J. Van Zutphen, Institutum Carmelitanum, 35 (1956) • J. Pits, *Relationum historicarum de rebus Anglicis*, ed. [W. Bishop] (Paris, 1619), 643–4 • A. de la Mare, ed., *Catalogue of the collection of medieval manuscripts bequeathed to the Bodleian Library, Oxford, by James P. R. Lyell* (1971), 82–5 • V. Edden, 'Marian devotions in a Carmelite sermon collection of the late middle ages', *Mediaeval Studies*, 57 (1995), 101–29
Archives BL, Harley MSS 211, 3138; Stowe MSS 8, 38 • Bodl. Oxf., MS e Museo 86 • Queen's College, Oxford, MS 168 • St John's College, Oxford, MS 23 • Winchester College, MS 13A

Albani [*married name* Gye], **Dame Emma** [*née* Marie Louise Cécile Emma Lajeunesse] (**1847–1930**), singer, was born on 1 November 1847 at Chambly, Quebec, Canada, one of three surviving children of Joseph Lajeunesse, organist, and his wife, Mélina Mignault (*d.* 1856), from a better-off, half-Scottish family. (Albani later gave her date of birth as 1852.) Her father, whose own career was modest, had high ambitions for Emma. He trained her in singing, piano, and harp from the age of five, made her practise five hours a day, and showed her off in music shops; this led to her giving a public concert in Montreal at the age of eight, the first of several. According to H. Charbonneau, a biographer with local sources, Lajeunesse overworked Emma and beat her if she fell asleep or played badly, and she

Dame Emma Albani (1847–1930), by Walery, pubd 1889

feared him; she herself recorded that she 'never had a doll'.

After working in upper New York state, her father returned to the Montreal area and entered Emma in 1858 as a pupil in the Sacré-Coeur Convent, where she played the organ, composed, sang solos, and was encouraged by the Italian mother superior to think of a singing career. Following successful Montreal concerts in 1862, she was taken by her father to perform at Saratoga Springs and then Albany, New York; this led to her appointment at the age of sixteen as soloist, organist, and choirmaster of St Joseph's Roman Catholic Church, Albany. Four successful years there in turn resulted in her departure—subsidized by well-wishers—for Paris and then Milan. Here she studied (1868–70) first with Gilbert-Louis Duprez, later with Francesco Lamperti, both leading teachers of would-be opera singers. On Lamperti's advice she made her opera début in 1870 at Messina as Amina in Bellini's *La sonnambula*; this and later engagements at Acireale, Cento, Malta, and Florence were highly successful.

Aspiring young singers, especially British and American women, at that time might win prestige by appearing in Italy—the homeland of opera—without a fee; some took a stage name Italianized from their home town. Emma, however, promised so well that she was paid something from the start, and she maintained that the name she adopted, Albani, had nothing to do with Albany but was taken from the noble papal family, then nearly extinct. She always thought her early Italian experience had been well worth while, in part because 'the British do not understand Italian music' (letter to Eva Gauthier, 30 Oct 1905). It led to her engagement by Frederick Gye to sing for five seasons, starting in 1872, at Covent Garden. She was to appear there nearly every spring until her retirement from opera in 1896, taking, for the rest of the year, engagements in Paris, Brussels, Berlin, St Petersburg, and North America. On 6 August 1878 she married Gye's son Ernest (1839–1926), who then took over Covent Garden from his father and ran it in adverse economic circumstances until 1884. The couple had one son.

At first Albani sang mainly the coloratura soprano repertory (Amina, Lucia di Lammermoor, Linda di Chamounix, Gilda in *Rigoletto*), but also the dramatic part of Mignon in its soprano version. She was so successful as to alternate with the reigning 'queen' Adelina Patti. The Italian works, however, were losing esteem; from 1875 (1874 in New York) Albani started to sing Wagner's lighter parts, in *Lohengrin*, *Tannhäuser*, *The Flying Dutchman*, and ultimately (1889) *Die Meistersinger*. By London custom, she sang them in Italian—just as she did her roles in French works, even in Brussels, and notwithstanding the fact that she was a native French speaker; all she sang in German were a *Lohengrin* in Berlin, and *Tristan und Isolde* in her last Covent Garden season. According to Bernard Shaw, in Wagner she was 'always at her sincerest—that is, her best'. The shining high notes her Italian technique secured were what the composer had wanted; Shaw, however, scoffed at her lingering on these notes ('like a woman who will not come downstairs sensibly because she wants to show off her diamonds') and at her phlegmatic acting in Italian works.

In Britain Albani appeared regularly in oratorio at the Norwich, Crystal Palace, Birmingham, Leeds, and Three Choirs festivals, singing the staple Handel and Mendelssohn works, Gounod's *Redemption* and *Mors et vita* (on which she worked with the composer), Liszt's *St Elisabeth*, and other new works. Until her retirement in 1911 she went on lengthy concert tours to empire countries. Though highly paid in her best years, she was in financial trouble in 1908 and again in 1925, the year in which she was made DBE, and was helped in London and Canada with a benefit matinée, a subscription, and a civil-list pension of £100. She died at 61 Tregunter Road, Kensington, London, on 3 April 1930 and was buried in Brompton cemetery. As a leading singer with an irreproachable private life she had been a favourite of royalty, much decorated; in her last years she received visitors in 1890s dress and wearing her medals.   JOHN ROSSELLI

Sources H. Charbonneau, *L'Albani* (1938) · E. Albani, *Forty years of song* (1911) · H. Rosenthal, *Two centuries of opera at Covent Garden* (1958) · G. B. Shaw, *Music in London, 1890–94*, 3 vols. (1932) · G. B. Shaw, *London music as heard in 1888–89 by Corno di Bassetto* (1937) · *The Times* (4 April 1930) · m. cert. · d. cert.
Archives NYPL, Library for the Performing Arts, Eva Gauthier MSS · Royal Opera House, London, archives
Likenesses Walery, photograph, pubd 1889, NPG [*see illus.*] · P. Pinsonneault, photograph, *c.*1897, NPG · Lafayette, postcard, 1905, NPG · J. Russell & Sons, photograph, NPG · photograph, repro. in J. W. Davison, *From Mendelssohn to Wagner: memoirs of J. W. Davison* (1912) · photographs, repro. in Albani, *Forty years of song* · photographs, repro. in Charbonneau, *L'Albani* · woodburytype carte-de-visite, NPG
Wealth at death £1410 16s. 6d.: resworn probate, 21 Feb 1931, CGPLA Eng. & Wales

Albany. For this title name *see* Stewart, Robert, first duke of Albany (*c.*1340–1420); Stewart, Murdoch, second duke of Albany (*c.*1362–1425); Stewart, Alexander, duke of Albany (1454?–1485); Stewart, John, second duke of Albany (*c.*1482–1536); Stewart, Henry, duke of Albany (1545/6–1567); Louisa, styled countess of Albany (1752–1824); Leopold, Prince, first duke of Albany (1853–1884); Charles Edward, Prince, second duke of Albany (1884–1954).

Albemarle. For this title name *see* Monck, George, first duke of Albemarle (1608–1670); Monck, Christopher, second duke of Albemarle (1653–1688); Granville, George, Baron Lansdowne and Jacobite duke of Albemarle (1666–1735); Keppel, Arnold Joost van, first earl of Albemarle (1669/70–1718); Keppel, William Anne, second earl of Albemarle (1702–1754); Keppel, George, third earl of Albemarle (1724–1772); Keppel, George Thomas, sixth earl of Albemarle (1799–1891); Keppel, William Coutts, seventh earl of Albemarle and Viscount Bury (1832–1894).

Albert [Prince Albert of Saxe-Coburg and Gotha] (1819–1861), prince consort, consort of Queen Victoria, was born on 26 August 1819 at the ducal summer residence of the duchy of Saxe-Coburg-Saalfeld, the Rosenau, on the southern edge of the forest of Thuringen, about 4 miles from Coburg. On 19 September 1819 in the marble hall at the Rosenau he was baptized Franz Karl August Albrecht Immanuel with water from the River Itze, which flowed through the duchy. His name was immediately Anglicized by his family to Albert, the only one of his given names that was ever used. The reigning duke was his father, Ernest (1784–1844), who had named his first son and heir, born a year earlier, after himself. The mother of the boys, who would be their only children, was the former Princess Louise (1800–1831) of neighbouring, but larger and richer, Saxe-Gotha-Altenburg. Seventeen years younger than her husband, she had married him at sixteen on 31 July 1817.

The duke's rakish ways were unreformed by his marriage. After the birth of his sons he resumed his earlier sports of hunting and wenching. Louise consoled herself with flirtations, the last with a young lieutenant, Baron Alexander von Hanstein. On 4 September 1824 the unhappy duchess was banished from Coburg and left her small sons forever. The legal separation which Ernest had demanded was followed by formal divorce in 1826, after which Louise married Hanstein. She died of uterine cancer in August 1831.

By 1826 the duchy and the princelings had new names, as the death of the last eligible male descendant in Saxe-Gotha-Altenburg meant a rearrangement of mini-states. Ernest added Gotha in exchange for Saalfeld (which went to the duke of Meiningen), creating the hyphenated designation by which the young Albert was later identified.

Childhood and education Although abandoned at five, Albert understood—much later—the circumstances of

Albert [Prince Albert of Saxe-Coburg and Gotha] (**1819–1861**), by Franz Xaver Winterhalter, 1846

the studies of both boys for fifteen years in ducal residences from which their father was often absent. Until Albert was eleven (and Ernest twelve), Florschütz stolidly tutored the boys each day, taking his midday meal with them. Only their grandmother and step-grandmother furnished a softer presence. When the boys visited Louise's stepmother, they encountered music and theatre and even novels. Grandmother Augusta, a political liberal, flexible even in her Lutheranism, educated Albert in her own way. Two men were even more influential. Prince *Leopold (1790–1865), widower of Princess Charlotte of Wales, was Duke Ernest's youngest brother. After Louise's departure from Coburg, Leopold sent his private secretary, the one-time physician Baron Christian Friedrich *Stockmar, to report on the welfare of the children. He had recommended Florschütz and returned regularly to check on his charges, as Duke Ernest was, in Leopold's tart words, 'much occupied with his new and splendid possession of Gotha' and seeking a replacement duchess.

By 1831 the ambitious Leopold had been offered the throne of the new Belgian state. From Brussels he was also able to continue his oversight of the daughter of his sister Victoire, the widowed duchess of Kent. The Princess Victoria [*see* Victoria (1819–1901)], only a few months older than Albert, appeared likely to be queen in Great Britain after her childless uncle, now William IV. Through Stockmar, Leopold also kept watch over Ernest and Albert, who studied, exercised, played, dined, and even slept under the supervision of Florschütz. At six, Albert had lessons for one hour per day; two additional hours were added at seven, and at ten masters in mathematics and German were brought in. At twelve, instruction in history, philosophy, geography, Latin, and religion was extended to five hours. Exercises and games, sometimes with visiting cousins or local boys, filled what was left of the day. Lessons in shooting were deemed important, and Albert became an excellent marksman.

Early in the Florschütz programme, it became obvious that Albert did not have the hardy constitution of his elder brother, although he was slightly taller and seemed sturdy. He needed to retire earlier, and sometimes fell asleep in corners before bedtime. In later years he would find late-starting social occasions tedious and the effort to pretend otherwise wearying.

Rites of passage The major event of the home years was the confirmation of the brothers on Palm Sunday (12 April) 1835. By then Florschütz was enriching the traditional German curriculum with English and French, and cultivating the boys' interests in science. They began rock-collecting outings, classified specimens, and were instructed on occasion by a mineralogist imported from Frankfurt. Encouraged by Grandmother Caroline, they also moved beyond their tutor. Each loved music. They studied with a local church organist, using their own pennies for lessons when Duke Ernest refused to 'waste money' on the frivolity. Both sang and learned the rudiments of composition.

Following Lutheran confirmation, the duke took his sons on the traditional visit to Berlin for presentation to

his mother's departure and never doubted her affection; her loss could hardly have been repaired by the attentions of Christoph Florschütz, who in his mid-twenties had been engaged as tutor to the brothers. Albert became quiet and subdued, subject to fits of weeping which he confessed candidly in a journal begun, precociously, when he was less than six. Early on, Florschütz was not quite the benign influence he was later to become. On 26 March 1825 Albert wrote that he had 'made so many mistakes' in a letter that 'the Rath'—his tutor—'tore it up and threw it into the fire. I cried about it' (Grey, 34).

Albert's awkwardness with, and dislike of, his father, whom he had good reason to blame for a lonely and insecure childhood, was blunted by time, as were his impressions of Florschütz, who became, as Albert grew up, an affectionate companion and devoted teacher. Tutorial impatience, however, emerges in Albert's notation when not yet six, 'I cried at my lesson today, because I could not find a verb: and the Rath pinched me, to show me what a verb was. And I cried about it' (Grey, 34).

At first Albert fled from strangers, retreating into the arms of his brother, the two sharing an affection not reciprocated by their aloof father. Florschütz was to supervise the Prussian court. (Prussia and Austria dominated the German confederation.) With Florschütz replacing the duke, the miniature grand tour continued on to Dresden, Prague, Vienna, and Budapest, each with its ritual of dinners, parades, presentations, and concerts, Albert dutifully writing to his stepmother (Ernest had married his own niece, Princess Mary of Württemberg, in 1832) that the regimen took 'a giant's strength' but that he was bearing up under the fatigue.

The next rite of passage was tutelage by Dr Seebode, director of the high school at Coburg, in lieu of residence there. That became preparation for a stay in Belgium with Leopold, who wanted to validate the reports of Stockmar about the readiness of Albert for the goal both had set for him. By early 1836 it was clear that his English cousin would soon be queen. The childless William IV was often ill, and fading. The crucial matter was whether he would survive into May 1837, when his niece would be eighteen, and of age. If not, the duchess of Kent would be regent for her daughter, and very probably would arrange her marriage. Given the duchess's ambition, a political solution might supplant the family strategy for which Leopold hoped.

A Coburg alliance Albert's future lay in his being a marriageable protestant princeling. The Coburg succession was Ernest's. Without possessions or promise of title, there was almost no occupation possible for Albert other than a military commission in some appropriate service, or becoming a royal—or at worst aristocratic—husband. The future queen of England remained the ideal match. Leopold, however, was cautious about overt intervention. Although a father figure to Victoria, he was out of favour in England because, although a reigning sovereign of another state, he continued to pocket the £50,000 a year granted when he was married to Princess Charlotte of Wales. Unacceptable as it was to parliament, the stipend was legally his. He was also married, out of political necessity, to a French Catholic bride.

Although he could not be seen pulling the strings, with prospective consorts already making approaches now that Princess Victoria was nearly seventeen, Leopold rushed Duke Ernest to England with his sons. At the invitation of William IV, the prince of Orange had preceded them with his two sons, and the king, who disliked the duchess of Kent and the entire Coburg clan, tried in vain to prevent the visit.

On 18 May 1836, six days before her seventeenth birthday, the princess met her Coburg cousins for the first time. Three months her junior, Albert was handsome in a still immature way, but easily fatigued by ceremony. 'You can well imagine', he wrote to his stepmother, who did not accompany the duke, 'that I had many hard battles to fight against sleepiness during these late entertainments' (Grey, 131). Victoria confided to her journal that Albert was 'extremely good-looking', enjoyed—as she did—music, and seemed full of gaiety. Yet at her birthday ball, exhausted by the continual late hours, he 'turned as pale as ashes' (Woodham-Smith, 120), Victoria wrote, and took to his bed for a night and a day.

While the first encounter with the prince seemed unpromising on the surface, Victoria wrote to Leopold on Albert's departure, 'I have only now to beg you, my dearest Uncle, to take care of one, now *so dear* to me' (*Letters of Queen Victoria*, 1.62). The visiting tsarevich Alexander, tall and manly and heir to Nicholas I, was of the wrong faith and would some day rule Russia, where the future queen could not live. She could not even consider a home in cousin Ernest's Coburg or in the Netherlands of the Oranges, however protestant—and its princes looked 'Kalmuck' (Mongol) to her. Despite his apparent delicacy, Albert held unexpectedly high cards—and Victoria was highly susceptible to a pleasing male exterior. Her intimation to Leopold implied no obligation: another potential suitor might emerge. Still, Leopold felt it expedient to acquaint Albert with his prospects and seek the counsel of Stockmar.

Albert's ten months in Brussels were preparation for entrance into the University of Bonn for the 1837–8 academic year. No tutorial expertise was spared, and the director of the Royal Observatory, the mathematician and astronomer Laubert Adolphe Jacques Quetelet, oversaw the education of the young Coburgers. Although Florschütz remained in attendance with Albert's Swiss valet, Cart, the prince's schooling in Bonn was supervised by Baron von Wiechmann, a retired colonel, with instruction at the university supplied by August Wilhelm von Schlegel, the poet and critic, privately derided by his students for his vanity, and Immanuel Hermann von Fichte, the anthropologist and philosopher, among others in a distinguished professoriat. Albert and Ernest also involved themselves in fencing, songfests, dramatics, and student friendships—although they lived in a house rented for their small entourage rather than common undergraduate digs. It was the happiest year of both brothers' lives.

William IV died on 20 June 1837, four weeks after Victoria's coming of age. Albert wrote to her in rather stiff English to wish for a 'long, happy, and glorious' reign, and prayed her to think sometimes 'of your cousins in Bonn'. In cautious code about their future he added, 'I will not be indiscreet and abuse your time' (Grey, 147–8). As politicians and aristocrats sought to broker the inevitable royal marriage, however, Albert's name arose publicly, and, both to deflect matchmakers and to furnish herself with time to enjoy her elevated new status without domestic hindrance, the queen announced that she had no present interest in matrimony.

With Albert's situation in Bonn compromised by the rumours, Leopold advised him to delay his return to the university and 'disappear' into unpublicized but useful travel. Albert concurred that the reasons were 'imperative and conclusive'. Leaving on 28 August 1837, Ernest, Albert, and Florschütz travelled south into Switzerland, Austria, and Italy, going as far as Venice. Once home he prepared an album of scenes from the journey, a dried 'Rose des Alpes', and a scrap of Voltaire's handwriting he had obtained at Verney, and posted it to Victoria. Years later she described it as 'one of her greatest treasures'.

The brothers returned to Bonn in early November to

resume their studies while Albert, as he wrote to his father, began to reconsider 'the arrangement of my mode of life' (Grey, 165). As the academic year ended in mid-1838, the duke left for London to attend his niece's coronation. Neither he nor Stockmar saw there any improvement in Albert's prospects. At best no new rival had materialized. Enjoying power, position, and the freedom both afforded, Victoria seemed uninterested in marrying, and had even begun to complain coldly of the interference of Uncle Leopold, who was trying to rule her 'roast' (roost).

Albert's situation was precarious. Even his potential as protestant husband in a lesser court was compromised by his marital limbo in London. In Belgium, Leopold discussed the dilemma with the prince, who told him that he was prepared to submit to reasonable delay 'if I have only some certain assurance to go upon'. If after waiting for three years 'I should find that the Queen no longer desired the marriage, it would place me in a very ridiculous position, and would, to a certain extent, ruin all the prospects of my future life' (Grey, 218).

In Victoria's family letters Albert went unmentioned. Events in her own life, however, pushed her from her independent perch. She was nineteen, inadequately educated for her role, and both imperious and unsophisticated. Her relations with the witty, widowed prime minister, Viscount Melbourne, who had already been the subject of extramarital scandal, were themselves a potential scandal. Although he seemed avuncular, Melbourne was too much in her presence for wagging tongues. Further, the impolitic 'bedchamber' crisis and the embarrassing Lady Flora Hastings affair, which both broke in the spring of 1839, showed the queen as precipitate and petty, much in need of guidance she did not have. And looming across the North Sea was her allegedly wicked uncle, the duke of Cumberland, who in 1837 had become king of Hanover, since Salic law prevented her own succession there. Should she die without issue, he would succeed her.

Someone with an appropriate bloodline, preferably of mature years, was needed to rescue the girl-queen from herself and ensure the succession. Victoria wanted no husband to reign over her. Preferably, then, since a consort seemed inevitable and, in early 1839, soon, why not young Albert, who was handsome and merry, and—given his penniless and youthful state—malleable? The 'roast' would then remain her own.

Engagement and marriage In August 1839 Victoria was revisited by her Coburg uncles amid press speculation that the gathering was preliminary to the arrival of Ernest and Albert. She had tried to delay both confrontations on grounds of exhaustion—'from all I have gone through', she explained to Leopold (*Letters of Queen Victoria*, 1.232). However, the queen's uncles, Ferdinand, Ernest, and Leopold, overcame her resistance, and young Ernest and Albert arrived at Windsor on 10 October after a rough channel crossing and without their baggage, which had gone astray. 'Having no clothes', Victoria wrote to Leopold on 12 October, 'they could not appear at dinner but nevertheless *débutéd* after dinner in their *négligé*'. Ernest had

'grown quite handsome' but the young queen was overwhelmed by his brother, writing breathlessly with many underlinings, 'Albert's *beauty* is *most striking*, and he is so amiable and unaffected—in short, very *fascinating*; he is excessively admired here' (ibid., 1.237). From Victoria's side the matter was no longer a political arrangement. She had fallen in love.

Had the king of the Belgians been privy to Victoria's journal he would have had no doubts. 'It was with some emotion that I beheld Albert—who is *beautiful*', she wrote (Esher, 2.262). Her heart, she added, was 'quite *going*'. On 14 October she told Melbourne that she had changed her mind about marrying, and the prime minister wrote to Lord John Russell with real relief, 'I do not know that anything better could be done. He seems a very agreeable young man, he certainly is a very good looking one, and as to character, that, we must always take our chance of' (Woodham-Smith, 184).

Etiquette forbade the prince from speaking his mind before being spoken to, but from his side, relief as much as romance was involved. Soon after noon the next day, Victoria sent for Albert and asked him 'to consent to what I wished', and they embraced. 'Oh! *how* I adore and love him', she told her diary, 'I cannot say!! *how* I will strive to make him feel as little as possible the great sacrifice he has made; I told him it was a great sacrifice,—which he wouldn't allow' (Woodham-Smith, 184).

Albert responded, forgetting his English lessons, that he would be happy 'das Leben mit dir zu zubringen' ('to share life with you'), realizing that his new role would be an awkward one. On 16 October he wrote to Baron Stockmar of his joy in being 'the object of so much affection', and Stockmar responded with pleasure accompanied by earnest counsel. In reply Albert agreed that winning 'the respect, the love, and the confidence of the queen and of the nation' was crucial to his position (Grey, 235–6). Victoria was won, but the public, in the form of press comment, was quick to express doubts about the influence of a foreign prince upon a young sovereign. Albert understood, he confided to his stepmother, that 'life has its thorns in every position, and the consciousness of having used one's powers and endeavours for an object so great as that of promoting the welfare of so many will surely be sufficient to support me' (ibid., 238).

Albert had his first sense of his new role from the standpoint of the crown when, on 27 October, he was still a guest at Windsor and with the betrothal not yet public knowledge. Victoria wrote in her journal, 'I signed some papers and warrants etc. and he was so kind as to dry them with blotting paper for me. We talked … and he clasped me so tenderly in his arms, and kissed me again and again' (Woodham-Smith, 188).

On 14 November Albert returned to Coburg to conclude his affairs prior to a wedding in early February, discovering new disappointments about his status and authority by letter even before the queen read her declaration of intent to the privy council on 23 November. The government would not agree to make him a peer; the prime minister insisted on imposing his own private secretary,

George Anson, upon Albert, and parliament began wrangling over an annual allowance drastically reduced from that granted to Leopold in 1816: to Victoria's outrage the grant was pared to £30,000.

The dismayed prince was permitted little more than to import a personal establishment of librarian, groom, and valet. Even a bill for his naturalization was hotly debated (but passed), while legislation about his precedence after the queen was dropped after objections by the stuffy royal dukes. More stinging rebuffs came from the press, which questioned his protestantism (as other Coburgs had married Catholics in furthering their ambitions), his German background (in a street ballad he was 'Prince Hallbert'), and his mercenary motives (in another broadside he was after 'England's fat queen and England's fatter purse').

The best Victoria could do was to bestow on him the ribbon of the Garter before the wedding on 10 February 1840, held in the Chapel Royal of St James's Palace, at which he wore a British field marshal's uniform without insignia, since he was invested with no rank. Even the wedding journey was abbreviated—two days at Windsor. 'You forget, my dearest love', Victoria admonished with much underlining, 'that I am the Sovereign, and that business can stop and wait for nothing. Parliament is sitting' (*Letters of Queen Victoria*, 1.269). Albert and his Coburg entourage entered for the ceremony to the incongruous strains of 'See the conquering hero come'. He was pale and twenty.

On the morning after the bridal night ('we did not sleep much', Victoria noted in her diary), the queen awakened to revel in the 'beautiful angelic face' at her side. Her sensual Hanoverian temperament bloomed, and Albert remained sensitive to it. 'My dearest Albert put on my stockings for me', she confided to her diary on 13 February. 'I went in and saw him shave; a great delight for me.' Laurence Housman would imagine the scene in his charming series of royal vignettes, *Victoria Regina* (1934). From the start, two tables set up in the queen's rooms enabled them to work side by side, but the work remained the sovereign's. Sometimes she involved him enough to record a journal entry, 'Rested and read Despatches—some of which I read to Albert.'

'Master in the house'? The 'dual monarchy' Despite instant mutual affection, Albert and Victoria's temperaments were opposed and often collided, requiring forbearance which the young pair often did not have. Albert's Germanic discipline and reaction against the sexual profligacy of his father were at odds with Victoria's enthusiasm for food and drink, dancing and balls, court society and long nights. 'Prince Albert slept' was a common entry in the journals and letters of guests at Buckingham Palace who remained into the late hours. Albert's initial frustration and unease at his peripheral place, as Victoria clung to the prerogatives and powers which had been hers before the marriage, caused him to complain to a schoolfriend, 'I am only the husband, and not the master in the house' (Grey, 320). Quickly, biology altered the marital and political balance. Within weeks of the wedding, Victoria was pregnant.

'I must say that I could not be more unhappy', she complained to the dowager duchess of Saxe-Coburg and Gotha. In her journal she had written that pregnancy was 'the ONLY thing I *dread*'. Dread also ensured Albert his first victory in parliament. A Regency Bill empowered him, without an advisory council, to act in the event of the impairment of the queen or the survival only of a minor child. The prince crowed to his brother that it gave his position 'a fresh significance'. The red dispatch boxes arrived daily, whether or not the queen was up to them, and Albert's informal authority and influence grew. He had already begun to find a cultural role as one of the directors of the Ancient Concerts, presided—and spoke briefly—at a public meeting on abolition of the slave trade, and became a patron and purchaser of art and sculpture, influencing taste by his own. But his real work became the administration of what would be an informal dual monarchy.

In his final year at Bonn he had studied English language and history. Now he began the study, in earnest, of English law and constitutional history. He also pursued foreign affairs, a subject of little interest to him earlier. Before his marriage he had seldom even read a newspaper beyond the *Augsburger Allgemeine*.

As another pregnancy quickly followed the first—*Victoria, the princess royal, was born three weeks early, on 21 November 1840—Albert realized his domestic base was less secure than his political one had become. The household was still being run by the capable, if domineering, Baroness Lehzen, the queen's former governess—to Albert in letters to his brother the 'old hag' ('die Blaste'). Proper care of 'Vicky' became the cause about which Albert planned Lehzen's removal, but he bided his time.

In 1841 a Conservative government under Sir Robert Peel replaced Melbourne's whigs. Peel, to whom Albert would become almost as close as Victoria had been to Melbourne, placed the prince at the head of a royal commission appointed in October 1841, taking advantage of the rebuilding of the houses of parliament, gutted by fire in 1834, to promote and encourage the fine arts in the United Kingdom. The new Palace of Westminster, designed by Charles Barry, on which work began in 1837, would be the first major 'Victorian' building. Its decoration, overseen by leading men in the political and cultural milieu, was, Albert felt, his real initiation into public life. Compared to the suave Melbourne, Victoria found Peel, son of a cotton manufacturer, 'awkward'. To Albert he became informal mentor.

On 9 November 1841 Albert Edward [*see* Edward VII], to be created prince of Wales, was born, the first such since the future George IV in 1762. With Victoria recovering slowly early in 1842 from the difficult pregnancy and birth, and in post-partum depression, Albert began blaming Lehzen for meddlesome nursery management and urging her retirement. Victoria was distraught at relinquishing a confidant and companion with whom she had shared much of her life, but Stockmar and Albert made it clear that Lehzen's presence exacerbated tensions in the relationship between husband and wife. The baroness loyally departed in September 1842, taking her pension of £800 a year to Bückeburg in Hanover, where she lived until 1870.

Supreme in the royal household, Albert began putting affairs into Germanic order. Although Lehzen had no official status and was innocent of administrative detail, she had accrued a proliferation of duties and responsibilities. Beneath her sightless gaze, wasteful sinecures and perquisites flourished. With Anson as deputy, Albert consolidated household functions within existing regulations, squeezing corruption as well as inefficiency out of the system. Pursuing his interest in agriculture, he set up a model dairy farm at Windsor that was soon making a profit, and he multiplied the revenues from the duchy of Cornwall estates held in trust for the prince of Wales. Not all of the reforms sat easily with Victoria, who was comfortable with the traditional ways and, moreover, saw her authority being eroded, but, as Albert confided to the duke of Wellington, his goal was

> to be the natural head of the family, superintendent of her household, manager of her private affairs, her sole confidential adviser in politics, and only assistant in her communications with the officers of the Government, her private secretary and permanent Minister.   (Helps, 76)

And he would do so without English title or rank, submerging, as he put it, 'his directing individuality' in the queen's position and personality.

While the prince wished Victoria to perceive his actions as a sacrifice of personal ambition on her behalf, he was acquiring power in ways that became public: she held audiences with Albert at her side, and even at the opening or proroguing of parliament had him seated with her. Yet within the domestic apartments at Buckingham Palace or Windsor, royal tempers often flared. 'Victoria is too hasty and passionate', Albert explained. 'She will not hear me out but flies into a rage and overwhelms me with reproaches of … want of trust, ambition, envy, etc. etc.' (Longford, 161). He would often resort to long silences, then write admonitory notes in which he would address her as 'Dear Child'. Still, the marriage prospered as Victoria began to see advantages in a managing husband in whom she could take pride and who responded to her physical and emotional needs.

Although much of what has been called Victorianism emanates from the climate of evangelical Christianity—the strict, even dreary, moral fervour and the ethic of hard work—its equivalent at court was due more to Albert than to Victoria. With the loose reputation of the Regency to assuage in the new reign, and his own experience of Ernestine laxity in Coburg, the prince wanted to emphasize family and religious values. Even what became accepted as the Victorian Christmas was largely imported from Germany, the illustrated press making much of Albert's Christmas trees and gift-giving.

Short of abstinence—and Victoria was too sensual a being for that—the royal couple had no idea how to limit their family, and despite the queen's revulsion for pregnancy a surfeit of royal children followed the princess royal and the prince of Wales. *Alice was born in 1843, *Alfred in 1844, and *Helena in 1846. *Louise followed in 1848 and *Arthur in 1850. *Leopold was born in 1853 and *Beatrice, the last child, in 1857. Each necessary withdrawal from public life on Victoria's part increased Albert's actual and visible roles.

The burgeoning brood of children impelled Albert's search for private royal retreats free from the public gaze and from the bureaucracy of the Office of Woods and Forests, which oversaw not only Buckingham Palace and Windsor but the summer retreat at crowded Brighton, the rococo Royal Pavilion. Buckingham Palace, aside from its bleak formality, was subject to the fetid air of London. Unsuitable for family living, Windsor Castle was also known as a cave of the winds. In addition, an antique yacht was available, the *Royal George*, a cumbersome sailing ship in the new age of steam. The managerial prince, prone to seasickness anyway, suffered badly on his first voyage to Scotland and refused to embark for home on it. A modern vessel, the *Albert*, was constructed for royal use. The pavilion was abandoned and most of its furnishings sold at auction, the prince arranging to purchase, after driving a hard bargain, Osborne House on the Isle of Wight. There, supervising London master builder Thomas Cubitt, Albert had erected an Italianate home with campanile tower that might have graced the Bay of Naples rather than the Solent. The family moved in, construction still unfinished, in May 1845, with the prince, not yet twenty-six, still overseeing building and landscaping.

The visits of the royal couple to Scotland led to a second personal estate. Victoria enjoyed the bracing air. Her underactive thyroid, evidenced by her bulging eyes, left her always feeling too warm. For Albert, the lakes, hills, and woodlands off the Dee recalled his native Thuringia. When Balmoral Castle became available after the queen's first visit to it in 1848, it was a castle only in the Scottish sense of a large home, although it had turrets and round towers and gables. The royal couple paid for it from their privy purse, eased by the unexpected inheritance in 1852 of £250,000 from James Camden Nield. Some funds were returned by Victoria in the form of increased legacies to minor beneficiaries, and to restore the chancel of the church in which Nield was buried, and the remainder became the core of the building funds for the Frogmore mausoleum at Windsor; but in effect it freed royal funds for expanding and extending Balmoral. Stockmar, hearing the news from Albert, wished the otherwise uncharitable Nield 'a joyful resurrection'.

There would be less joy in government circles. The Isle of Wight was a longish journey by railway and steam packet. 600 miles from London by rail and coach, Balmoral was a night and a day away. Custom required a minister in residence while the queen was distant from parliament. The cabinet dreaded inhospitable Balmoral, but the queen had a right to live anywhere in her kingdom she wished.

Among royal travels were visits to stately homes of the influential peerage and, in 1843, visits to the French and Belgian courts. In October the pair were in Cambridge, where Albert received an honorary degree and began a fruitful association with a university he considered intellectually superior to somnolent Oxford. In December they visited Chatsworth, where the duke of Devonshire displayed his new greenhouse, designed by Joseph Paxton. Seeing it illuminated, Victoria described it as 'the finest thing imaginable of its kind', while Albert called it 'magnificent and beautiful', a work of genius. In 1851 he would employ Paxton to rescue the Great Exhibition.

The death of Duke Ernest in early 1844 caused Albert to revisit Coburg, with the queen, again pregnant, remaining at home. Extravagant mourning was customary, and Albert indulged in continental fashion, weeping and displaying his emotions in a manner considered unmanly by Englishmen. Revisiting his childhood evoked more genuine feeling, but Albert was relieved to get away from the financial importunities of his dissolute brother, the new duke, and return to Windsor, where on 6 August Victoria gave birth to Alfred, the future duke of Coburg.

As further royal children arrived, the press carried hostile comments and satirical cartoons, criticizing the cost of maintaining establishments for the growing family as each child came of age, yet the brood also created a sense of stability and continuity. State visits to Prussia and France were successes, except for a *battue* of game at which Victoria and Albert were guests, a style of shooting which was more slaughter than sport, and left newspapers carping about Albert's inability to adapt to the ways of English gentlemen. Never taking to Albert except during his highly visible but temporary successes, the press appeared to seek opportunities to strike at his foreignness—and would have been all the more outraged had it been more generally known that in the privacy of their personal apartments he and the queen usually conversed in German, in which Albert was always more comfortable.

During Peel's ministry, the prince was the primary intermediary between prime minister and queen. In meetings with ministers, the clerk of the privy council, Charles Greville, wrote on 16 December 1845, wife and husband received them together, and each said 'We'—'We think, or wish, to do so and so'. They were 'one person, and as he likes business, it is obvious that while she has the title he is really discharging the functions of the Sovereign. He is King to all intents and purposes' (Woodham-Smith, 239). Albert's informal authority became a royal embarrassment only when, on 27 January 1846, Peel's resolutions on financial policy were debated in the Commons while the prince was in the gallery. Lord George Bentinck, representing the conservative faction of Peel's party, accused him from the floor of appearing in the house to

> give éclat, and, as it were, by reflection from the Queen, to give the semblance of a personal sanction of Her Majesty to a measure which, be it for good or evil, a great majority at least of the landed aristocracy … imagine fraught with deep injury, if not ruin to them.

The seemingly unconstitutional partiality was questioned further in the press. Although Victoria considered the criticism outrageous, Albert never went to the house again.

After Peel's death in July 1850, the queen wrote to King Leopold that Albert 'feels as if he has lost a second father'. Another senior figure who meant much to Albert was the duke of Wellington, who died in September 1852. The royal couple's seventh child and third son, Arthur, had been born on the hero of Waterloo's eighty-first birthday, on 1 May 1850, and named for him. On the duke's impending retirement as commander-in-chief of the army that year, he proposed that Albert—who was a field marshal by grace of the queen—accept the post, with an experienced general as chief of staff, but the prince, now wary of overt intrusion into governmental affairs, wisely declined. Apart from the indelicacy of the appointment, he was already busy on the major project of his life, which would be realized as the Great Exhibition of 1851.

The Great Exhibition of 1851 Albert had become president of the Society of Arts on 2 June 1843. Founded in 1754 'for the Encouragement of Arts, Manufactures and Commerce', it had been in decline under the torpid presidency of the duke of Sussex. The prince's involvement was more than nominal. The Scientific Societies Act of 1843 (6 & 7 Vict. c. 36), to exempt from rates 'Land and Buildings occupied by Scientific and Literary Societies [provided that they] … shall be supported wholly or in part by annual voluntary contributions', was promoted by Albert and later known as the Prince Consort's Act.

In 1844 the secretary of the society, Francis Whishaw, proposed to revive the Society of Arts through annual exhibitions of manufactures, modelled upon French and north German precedents. It took until March 1847, even with Albert's encouragement and connections, to mount an exhibit at the society's premises in John Adam Street, London. Each display had been national in character, and Francis Fuller of the society's steering committee suggested in June 1849 to Thomas Cubitt, who was still working on Osborne House, that the London exhibition become international, and that, 'if Prince Albert would take the lead', it could be brought off. Cubitt took the idea to Albert. By the end of the month the prince had convened a committee to outline the more ambitious undertaking.

A memorandum almost entirely drafted by the prince declared that the productions of 'Machinery, Science, and Art … are of no country, but belong, as a whole, to the civilised world', and that it would be of advantage to Britain to have its products seen 'in fair competition with that of other nations'. Financing, initiated by donations of £1000 from the queen and £500 from the prince, came painfully slowly, and it was largely left to Albert to raise the money; he was caricatured in *Punch*, cap in hand, as 'The Industrious Boy'. A month later, in July 1850, when the project seemed doomed by lack of support and by the public outcry about desecrating the elms of Hyde Park, the proposed venue, *Punch* satirized the building plans with 'a simple design for the proposed building', a smoke-belching monstrosity. Albert lamented to Stockmar, still his sounding board, 'If we are driven out of the Park, the work is done for!! Never was anything so foolish' (Martin, 2.286).

While Albert suffered, as he confided to Stockmar, 'from sleeplessness and exhaustion' fending off adversaries, appealing for funds, and reviewing 245 unattractive architectural plans, Joseph Paxton unveiled his own design in the *Illustrated London News* on 6 July 1850. Based upon the Chatsworth conservatory but vast in scope, it was immediately admired. Nine days later Albert's committee accepted it, and the 1848 foot long structure of iron and glass went up over 18 acres of park, safely enclosing within its 293,655 panes of glass the threatened elms. A prefabricated engineering marvel, it was the most advanced building of the nineteenth century. A 'Crystal Palace', *Punch* declared with uncharacteristic enthusiasm.

The selection, transport, and arrangement of over 100,000 exhibits from 13,937 exhibitors was a diplomatic as well as a logistical challenge, and took all the managerial skills of Henry Cole, the prince's deputy. Cole, however, recognized that it was the 'generalship' of the prince in adjudicating the dizzying problems, raising the funds, and settling the controversies among participants that made the Great Exhibition of 1851—the first world fair—a spectacular success. He was the only one, Earl Granville, then vice-president of the Board of Trade, wrote, 'who has considered the subject both as a whole and in its details'. To his grandmother in Coburg, to whom he wrote often, Albert confided, 'I am more dead than alive of overwork. The opponents of the Exhibition work with might and main to throw all the old women into panic and to drive myself crazy' (Martin, 2.359). To the king of Prussia, Albert noted sardonically, 'Mathematicians have calculated that the Crystal Palace will blow down in the first strong gale. Engineers that the Galleries would crash in and destroy the visitors' (Jagow, 176). The 4500 tons of iron framework held, and 6,063,986 enthralled visitors, equal to a third of the kingdom, poured through over 140 days (no Sundays) from 1 May 1851 until the formal closing on 15 October. At thirty-two, Albert had achieved a visionary triumph—and turned a profit of £186,000 even after reducing entrance fees. And he had confounded such persistent critics as Lord Brougham, who claimed that a man in Albert's 'peculiar position' (of royal spouse) 'should have the sense to know that repose and inaction is his only security against ridicule'.

Inaction was impossible for Albert. Aside from his role in the dual monarchy he put his nervous energy to work on new problems and new concepts. The Crystal Palace, for example, had to be dismantled and moved, rather than demolished. The London, Brighton, and South Coast Railway purchased it for £70,000 and moved it to the Kent countryside at Sydenham, where it continued as an exhibition hall until destroyed by fire in 1936. Albert wanted to use the considerable profits to acquire property in South Kensington to further the goals of the Great Exhibition. Sceptics would denounce his plan as 'Albertopolis', but the educational, cultural, and scientific institutions initiated by the prince's foresight would materialize into a great complex of museums, colleges, and concert halls,

keeping Victoria busy at dedications for decades. The Great Exhibition would be the summit of Albert's public career, but at a cost. He had often complained of a 'weak stomach', and was subject increasingly to severe stomach cramps, blamed by himself on the tension of his crush of responsibilities and by his biographers on his Teutonic conscientiousness about detail. He drove himself nevertheless.

Uncrowned king With the collapse of the Chartist movement in the later 1840s, foreign policy came to dominate the succeeding decade and the attention of the prince. By early 1850 reaction to the revolutions of 1848 was sweeping Europe. Louis-Napoleon Bonaparte seized imperial power in historically hostile France, and Austria and Prussia resumed their old monarchist ways. Tsarist Russia sought further expansion at the expense of Ottoman territories in the Balkans. On almost every issue the queen and Albert seemed at odds with Lord Palmerston, the dominant influence on foreign policy until his death in 1865, who had the overt or covert support of the liberal-minded press. In a revealing memorandum Albert insisted, 'Nowhere does the Constitution demand an indifference on the part of the sovereign to the march of political events.' He saw no special 'House of Coburg' interests at stake, only those of England.

> Why are Princes alone to be denied the credit for having political opinions based upon an anxiety for the national interests and honour of their country and the welfare of mankind? Are they not more independently placed than any other politician in the State?

The sovereign—and he continued to use the masculine form—was '*necessarily*' a politician.

By late 1853 the press and the politicians had orchestrated emotional commitments which pitted Britain against Russian aggrandizement. The queen's warnings that the nation was unprepared and that war was not in Britain's interest were interpreted as Albert's ventriloquism. Palmerston fed newspapers with what the *Daily News* called 'Courtly distastes and Coburg intrigues'. The press charged Albert with meddling in public affairs, with promoting the interest of his Coburg relations, with behaving as a German rather than as an Englishman, and with conspiring—as a Russian agent—with foreign princes. Rumours spread early in 1854 that Albert had even been arrested for treason. 'You will scarcely credit it,' he wrote to Stockmar on 24 January, 'that my being committed to the Tower of London was believed all over the country—nay, even "that the Queen has been arrested!"' (Martin, 2.562). Lord Aberdeen, then prime minister, felt impelled to declare to parliament the prince's 'unimpeachable loyalty'.

The Crimean War officially began on 28 March 1854, by which time newspapers had other distractions, and Albert arose amid the bellicosity from the nadir of his reputation. Citing British unpreparedness, he pressed for realistic training with simulated combat and for a military instructional camp, which led to the establishment of Aldershot. Now representing an ally of France against Russia, Victoria and Albert exchanged state visits and military inspections with Napoleon III, leading to a period of *rapprochement*; and there was also a truce with Palmerston, who became prime minister for the first time at seventy-one in 1855. Mutual admiration even developed, Palmerston confiding that until his premiership, with its opportunities to see the prince (with Victoria) on a regular basis, 'I had no idea of his possessing such eminent qualities ...', and how fortunate it has been for the country that the queen married such a prince' (Martin, 2.429). In 1856 the queen wrote, 'Albert and I agreed that of all the Prime Ministers we have had, Lord Palmerston is the one who gives the least trouble and is most amenable to reason and most ready to adopt suggestions' (Longford, 247). Part of the reason was that Palmerston had yielded foreign affairs, where he had been a firebrand, to Lord Clarendon, an experienced diplomat, and 'everything is quite different'.

With peace and the stabilization of Turkey, Albert turned his attention to the education of the prince of Wales, who seemed unadaptable to a training of Albertine intellectual rigour, and to the betrothal of Princess Victoria to the future crown prince of Prussia, Frederick. While he hoped for placid, happy childhoods, out of the public eye at Balmoral or Osborne, for his family, exceptions were made of the heir, Albert Edward (Bertie), and 'Vicky', who was to be a political bridge to Germany. The queen was made desolate when Albert, as head of the family, permitted their second son, Alfred, to be sent to sea as a naval cadet at fourteen.

Albert's external domestic concentration in the middle 1850s remained English culture—the scientific and artistic complex planned for South Kensington, the National Gallery, and his efforts to raise public consciousness about the appalling cost to the nation of child labour ('an evil') and the failure of the educational system to reach half of Britain's children. Military matters again intervened with the outbreak of the Sepoy mutiny in India in 1857, causing Albert as well as the queen to press Palmerston about the government's apparent eagerness to relax military preparedness. Both supported conciliation rather than punishment in India, and Albert's role was significant in the royal proclamation establishing new governance for India. He and the queen rejected the government's draft and proposed a text that

> should breathe feelings of generosity, benevolence, and religious feeling, pointing out the privileges which the Indians will receive in being placed on an equality with the subjects of the British Crown, and the prosperity following in the train of civilisation. (Martin, 4.285)

The later 1850s were years of increasing depression for Albert. He parted from the newly wed princess royal 'in tears and snowdrift' early in 1858. In mid-pregnancy later that year Vicky suffered a fall upon which was blamed the foetal positioning which necessitated a forceps delivery, and led to an injured and useless left arm for the future William II of Germany. Albert pretended all was well. William was 'a living child, ... a strong, healthy boy'. With the birth of their youngest daughter, Beatrice, the miseducation of Bertie, the dynastic exile of Vicky—and her difficulties—and the increasing illness of the queen's mother,

Victoria herself underwent a long period of emotional imbalance. She and Albert endured arguments, long silences, and further chastising notes that unreasonably absolved him of any guilt. The queen's long-postponed letters patent on 25 July 1857 creating him prince consort improved nothing. Albert's title was ridiculed in the press, and the prince confided to his brother, 'This ought to have been done, as you thought yourself, at our wedding, but you also know in what state affairs were at the time.' Still, Albert explained, the matter had become urgent as his children as adults would otherwise outrank their father, 'a *foreign* prince'.

Foreign affairs continued to deteriorate as Napoleon III agitated for Italian unification at the expense of Austria, and sought Nice and Savoy for his pains. Victoria and Albert supported existing regimes and boundaries, seeing European stability as the highest good, but the country feared war from across the channel as France pressed its territorial claims. In 1860 Albert, with Victoria, revisited Coburg for what he was certain would be the last time. Only forty, the prince consort looked more like sixty. He no longer went shooting or even deer-stalking, blaming press of business, and was paunchy and overweight from lack of exercise. His hairline had receded and his moustache and sidewhiskers had become heavier. He remained prone to stomach pain and exhaustion, but loved his work, even when comparing himself, in a letter to Vicky, to the mill donkey near Osborne turning its wheel round and round. He knew he was doing his job well, the job he created for himself, and he lavished his hours on it. 'Lese recht aufmerksam, und sage wenn irgend ein Fehler da ist!' he would advise the queen about draft memoranda— 'Read carefully, and tell me if there is any fault in this!' Or 'Ich hab Dir hier ein Draft gemacht, lese es mal! Ich dächte es wäre recht so.' ('Here is a draft for you; read it. I should think this will do.') Under such conditions he was still Victoria's 'beloved and perfect Albert'.

Last years On 1 October 1860 the queen's journal opens, 'Before proceeding, I must thank God for having preserved my adored one!' Visiting Coburg, Albert had met with a carriage accident when his horses took fright and galloped off into the bar of a railway crossing. The prince jumped for his life and was only cut and bruised. Having perceived Albert's persistent despondency from letters and from the prince himself, the now aged Stockmar confided to Duke Ernest, 'God have mercy on us! If anything serious should ever happen to him, he will die.' Stockmar may have known, as a physician, the import of Albert's chronic cramps and chills, symptoms which were largely concealed from Victoria.

On Albert's last afternoon in Coburg, Ernest took his brother for a walk. 'At one of the most beautiful spots', Ernest recalled, 'Albert stood still, and suddenly felt for his pocket handkerchief.' The duke assumed that Albert's facial bruises had begun to bleed afresh, and went to help, but Ernest discovered instead 'that tears were trickling down his cheeks ... [and] he persisted in declaring that he was well aware that he had been here for the last time in his life' (Ernest II, duke of Saxe-Coburg and Gotha, *Memoirs*, 1888, 4.55).

At the same time the prince of Wales was on his first trip abroad, to Canada and the United States. His parents feared a public relations catastrophe, but it was a triumph. Only nineteen, and impervious to formal education, Bertie had proved to be socially adept. But Albert thought that his son could benefit from military training at the Curragh military grounds near Dublin. The royal pair even went to Ireland to observe the results, which would demonstrate that their son could wear a uniform admirably but was unfit to command a company, let alone a battalion.

After their annual early autumn stay at Balmoral in 1861, Victoria and Albert returned to Windsor to disquieting news that Bertie, whose education had been overseen meticulously if ineffectively, had acquired some unexpected instruction overseen by his brother subalterns. A young woman had been procured for his bed, and Bertie had imported her afterwards to amuse him further at his mockery of a university stint at Cambridge.

Albert worried that the prince of Wales would have to be hastened into an early marriage to channel such libertine impulses. Rushing an anguished letter to Bertie, Albert proceeded to a prearranged inspection at Sandhurst and a railway journey to Cambridge to have it out with his son. At a low ebb physically, made worse by worry and sleeplessness, Albert confessed to Victoria, 'Ich hänge gar nicht am Leben; du hängst sehr daran' ('I do not cling to life; you do; but I set no store by it'). 'I am sure that if I had a severe illness', he continued in German, 'I should give up at once, I should not struggle for life. I have no tenacity of life' (Martin, 5.415).

The prince consort returned in the cold, drenching rain of late November. He was so weak that the court physician, Edward Jenner, decided to stay the night. On 27 November, two days later, the queen wrote to Vicky that 'a great sorrow and worry', and 'a cold with neuralgia', had broken 'Dearest Papa' down. 'I never saw him so low.' Jenner, she added on 30 November, expected Albert to be 'quite well in two or three days—but he is not inclined himself ever to admit he is better!'

Later, on the 30th, the queen received a draft message from Palmerston which was to be rushed to Washington. Civil war in America had broken out in April and Britain had issued a proclamation of neutrality that in effect assisted the slave-owning south. Opinion was divided; many, especially in the cotton-manufacturing north of England, largely liberal in politics, supported their economic interest over an ethical one. Palmerston himself, and his chancellor of the exchequer, W. E. Gladstone, favoured the south both to protect industry and to weaken a burgeoning manufacturing colossus and commercial rival. To seek formal recognition by European powers, particularly Britain and France, the Confederacy sent two envoys, James Mason and John Slidell, via the West Indies on the British packet *Trent*. When a Federal warship intercepted the *Trent*, boarded it, and removed the rebel emissaries, the Palmerston government denied

that a belligerent had the right to search a neutral vessel, and declared the seizure a gross breach of international law. As press indignation grew about the insult to the flag, Lord John Russell, then foreign minister, drafted a bellicose, uncompromising message for Palmerston to the American secretary of state, demanding release of the men and an apology. A threat to break diplomatic relations was implicit. Reinforcements were shipped to Canada.

When Victoria brought the draft to Albert he read it and exclaimed, 'This means war!' The strident tone reflected Palmerstonian eagerness to confront the growing power of the United States, but not the anti-slavery views of Victoria and Albert. In the early morning light of 1 December, the prince tottered to his study and rewrote the ultimatum to give Washington a way out without concessions to the Confederacy, suggesting that the American captain had been overly zealous and had acted on his own initiative. Any other interpretation might have committed Britain to war.

The prince could eat no breakfast—he could no longer hold food down. He could hardly find the strength to write. But he brought his drafts to Victoria, observing, 'I am so weak; I have hardly been able to hold the pen.' In the margin of Albert's manuscript the queen wrote, later, 'This draft was the last the beloved Prince ever wrote' (Longford, 422). The conciliatory language was accepted as 'excellent' by Palmerston, and altered only in being recast in officialese. Washington backed down, apologized for the initiative of Captain Charles Wilkes, and released Mason, Slidell, and two companions.

In the first days of December, Albert's condition worsened. Jenner and his colleague, Dr James Clark, offered such reassurances that when the sincerely concerned Palmerston suggested that another physician be consulted, Victoria was uninterested. The lack of alarm at Windsor was apparent in the casualness of the prince's treatment, or lack of it. When he could, he paced about his dressing room and sometimes changed bedrooms. 'His manner was so unlike himself and he sometimes had a strange, wild look', Victoria wrote in her journal on 5 December. Two days later Jenner told the queen that he and Clark had found a slight eruption on the lower part of the stomach, unmistakable signs, they claimed, of 'gastric and bowel fever'. It was a euphemism for typhoid.

Albert grew more listless; his mind wandered. Palmerston urged the queen's aides to call in other physicians, saying, 'If it is unavoidable that the highest interest of the nation be sacrificed to personal and professional jealousy, there is no help for it and so it must be.' Only then, in the face of resentment from the attending doctors, Thomas Watson and Sir Henry Holland were summoned. Both supported the therapy in progress. (Holland and Clark, both septuagenarians, were derided by Lord Clarendon as 'not fit to attend a sick cat'.)

They were 'so fortunate in the doctors', the queen claimed to Vicky while preparing her for the worst. Albert was becoming 'sadly thin. It is a dreadful trial to witness this, and requires all my strength of mind and courage not to be overcome.' Sedated with brandy and given little else, he was failing rapidly. He imagined hearing the birds singing at the Rosenau, and when again lucid told his daughter Alice, eighteen and effectively nurse-in-attendance, that he knew he was dying. The public knew almost nothing other than that the prince was ill with a fever. By the 13th he was being drugged with brandy every half-hour, his doctors over the two weeks of his decline offering no other remedies. They may have understood more than they were willing to say as Albert lay bedridden—that his condition was irreversible.

If the prince's affliction were a slow, deteriorating one—something of the order of stomach cancer, which fits his symptoms over at least four years before December 1861—he had no resources left to fight the terminal episode of pneumonia, typhoid, or whatever. (There was no other reported typhoid in the vicinity.) Medicine in the mid-century was helpless, and in Albert's darkened room at Windsor the physicians merely watched his pulse weaken. As his rapid breathing became alarming, the queen bent over him to ask for 'einen Kuss', and Albert was able to kiss her. With a terrible calm Victoria held his thin, cold hand until her misery became overwhelming. Leaving the room she broke down.

Shortly before eleven on the night of 14 December, Albert's breathing began to change, and the queen was summoned. 'Oh, yes, this is death!' she cried on seeing Albert. She fell upon the still, cold body and called him by every endearing name she could recall from their life together. Then she permitted herself to be led away.

Albert was buried in the mausoleum at Frogmore, Windsor, on 23 December 1861. Victoria in widow's cap had been conducted to Osborne on the 19th, still too much in shock to be in attendance at the funeral in Wolsey's Chapel at which the twenty-year-old prince of Wales was chief mourner. Victoria learned from her private secretary, Sir Charles Phipps, that the obsequies had been managed 'as she could have wished, with due solemnity and every mark of profound respect, and yet without any unnecessary form or state'.

Two days before the funeral, Dr Jenner filed a death certificate fixing the cause as 'typhoid fever, duration 21 days', the first time that the label was publicly applied. Although questions were raised in *The Lancet* and in the *British Medical Journal* about discrepancies between the medical bulletins and the belated diagnosis, there was no autopsy and typhoid was accepted as fact. More honest, if evasive, Dr Clark later explained to the queen that overwork and worry had affected Albert—and 'exposure to chill when already sick'. In 1877 Jenner defended himself by explaining that '*no one* can diagnose typhoid at first'. Whatever the rationalizations, the prince died neither of misdiagnosis nor medical incompetence. He had apparently intuited, just as had Dr Stockmar, that he was suffering from an inoperable and incurable malignancy, and that melancholy understanding had contributed to the mixture of despondency and frenzied activity which characterized his last years.

Albert's death ushered in the lengthy retreat into mourning and seclusion which earned Victoria her lasting popular image as the archetypal widow. More significantly, the excesses of the queen's grief and her long exit from public life undermined Albert's efforts to assert the sovereign's role in a constitutional monarchy. The cult of memorializing the prince consort, perhaps the only major public issue to engage Victoria's enthusiasm during the decade after his death, gave Albert more major monuments in the capital of his adopted nation than any other non-monarch. The Albert Memorial in Hyde Park, on the site of the Great Exhibition, was designed by George Gilbert Scott; it was completed in 1872, though not unveiled until 1876. The Royal Albert Hall, designed by Captain Francis Fowke and Major-General Henry Scott, developed an idea adumbrated by Albert himself. Opened in 1872 it is, next to the Palace of Westminster, Victorian London's most striking building. The whole of the museum complex in South Kensington is in a sense a monument to Albert; he is especially commemorated in the Victoria and Albert Museum (as the South Kensington Museum was renamed in 1899) and in its Prince Consort Gallery. These and other metropolitan memorials were echoed in statues, halls, monuments, schools, hospitals, and even bridges bearing his name in many British and imperial towns and villages. The name Albert was until the mid-twentieth century a common boy's name, especially among the working classes. Albert's views were recorded in his posthumously published *Principal Speeches and Addresses* (1862). His wife commissioned Charles Grey, who had been secretary to both Albert and herself, as her husband's biographer. Grey's book, initially written for private circulation, was published as *Early years of his royal highness the prince consort. Compiled for and annotated by Queen Victoria* (1867). Theodore Martin was pressed 'with extreme diffidence—I might even say reluctance' into completing Grey's book (Martin, 1.v). In fact he began again at the beginning, publishing five volumes (1875–80). The queen intended Martin's biography to be a monument, but it has proved a mausoleum, though useful as a storehouse of letters and memoranda. Reviewing Martin's book, Gladstone considered 'Every statue and memorial of the Prince Consort may in some sense be considered a sermon made visible' (W. E. Gladstone, *Gleanings of Past Years*, 1, 1879, 97–8). This widely shared pietistic view proved too much for the twentieth century and Albert suffered more, perhaps, than anyone else from the reaction against Victorianism. Only recently has he again been treated sympathetically, notably by Robert Rhodes James in *Prince Albert* (1984) and Stanley Weintraub in *Albert: Uncrowned King* (1997).

Disraeli's private comment in December 1861 has remained valid. 'With Prince Albert we have buried our Sovereign. This German Prince has governed England for twenty-one years with a wisdom and energy such as none of our kings has ever shown' (G. E. Buckle, *Life of Benjamin Disraeli*, 4, 1916, 383). Beneath the rhetoric lay the reality that Albert had been a working partner in a dual monarchy. In an era of burgeoning parliamentary supremacy under an expanding electorate, he furnished the throne with a political and cultural influence which, after Victoria's withdrawal into woe, it would never recover. Unwritten powers accrue only to those who use them effectively, and the ceremonial and symbolic monarchy which gradually evolved after 1861 may well have been the result of the loss of Albert at the height of his intellectual powers; his vision of an activist role for Windsor Castle died with him.

Having come to a foreign country as a sire for the succession, Albert remained always the alien. His ways were not English ways, and although he arrived aged twenty with much to learn—and learned it, and more—he never adapted to English society and culture, and his adopted people never fully accepted him. Yet his mark upon Britain was far greater than that of most monarchs, and his marriage, arranged as it was, and stormy as at times it could be, remains one of the greatest love stories outside fiction.   STANLEY WEINTRAUB

Sources C. Grey, *The early years of his royal highness the prince consort: compiled for and annotated by Queen Victoria* (1867) • T. Martin, *The life of … the prince consort*, 5 vols. (1875–80) • *The letters of Queen Victoria*, ed. A. C. Benson and Lord Esher [R. B. Brett], 3 vols., 1st ser. (1907), vols. 1–3 • K. Jagow, ed., *Letters of the prince consort* (1938) • *The girlhood of Queen Victoria: a selection from her majesty's diaries between the years 1832 and 1840*, ed. Viscount Esher [R. B. Brett], 2 vols. (1912) • H. Bolitho, ed., *The prince consort and his brother* (1933) • S. Weintraub, *Albert: uncrowned king* (1997) • H. Hobhouse, *Prince Albert, his life and work* (1983) • R. R. James, *Prince Albert* (1984) • M. Charlot, *The young queen* (1991) • D. Bennett, *King without a crown* (1977) • S. Weintraub, *Victoria: biography of a queen* (1987) • A. Helps, ed., *The principal speeches and addresses of the prince consort* (1862) • R. Fulford, *The prince consort* (1949) • C. Woodham-Smith, *Queen Victoria: her life and times*, 1: *1819–1861* (1972) • E. Longford, *Victoria RI* (1964) • W. Ames, *Prince Albert and Victorian taste* (1967)

Archives Bayerisches Staatsarchiv, Schloss Ehrenburg, Coburg • Royal Arch., papers • Schloss Friedrichshof, Kronberg | BL, Aberdeen MSS • BL, corresp. with W. E. Gladstone, loan 73 • BL, corresp. with Sir Robert Peel, Add. MSS 40432–40441 • BL, corresp. with Lord Ripon, Add. MSS 40864–40877, *passim* • Bodl. Oxf., Disraeli MSS, letters to Benjamin Disraeli • Bodl. Oxf., Wilberforce MSS, letters to Samuel Wilberforce, Don e 164–5 • Borth. Inst., Halifax papers, corresp. with Sir Charles Wood • Chatsworth House, Derbyshire, Paxton MSS • CUL, corresp. relating to University of Cambridge • Herts. ALS, letters to E. B. Lytton • ICL, corresp. with Lord Playfair, B/Playfair • Lpool RO, letters to fourteenth earl of Derby, 920 Der 14, boxes 136, 143 • McGill University, Montreal, corresp. with Lord Hardinge • NA Scot., corresp. with Lord Panmure, GD45 • NL Scot., corresp. with George Combe • NRA, priv. coll., corresp. with Lord Seymour, 10 • PRO, corresp. with Lord Ellenborough, PRO 30/12 • PRO, corresp. relating to Germany, FO 95/714 717 • PRO, corresp. with Lord John Russell, PRO 30/22 • RSA • U. Durham L., Grey of Howick collection, corresp. with third Earl Grey; corresp. with Charles Grey • U. Nott. L., corresp. with duke of Newcastle • U. Southampton L., corresp. with Lord Palmerston, MS 62 • U. Southampton L., letters to duke of Wellington, MS 61 • V&A, Cole MSS • V&A NAL, letters to Sir Charles Eastlake • Wilts. & Swindon RO, corresp. with Sidney Herbert and Elizabeth Herbert, 1422 2057 • Worcs. RO, letters to Sir John Pakington, 705:8/705:349

Likenesses group portrait, oils, 19th cent. (after Winterhalter), Osborne House, Isle of Wight • G. E. van Ebart, oils, *c*.1824, Royal Collection • H. Kundmueller, ceramic, 1825–50, Osborne House, Isle of Wight • C. L. Muller, oils, 1825–50, Osborne House, Isle of Wight • J. Doyle, lithograph, pubd 1839 (after his earlier work), NG Ire. • L. von Meyern Hohenberg, drawing, 1839, RSA • W. C. Ross, miniature, 1839, Royal Collection • E. Wolff, marble bust, 1839, Royal Collection • J. Haslem, miniature, *c*.1840, Derby Art Gallery •

G. Hayter, group portrait, oils, 1840 (*The marriage of Queen Victoria and Prince Albert*), Royal Collection • J. Partridge, oils, 1840, Royal Collection • W. C. Ross, oils, 1840 (aged twenty), Royal Collection • W. E. Wagstaff, mezzotint, pubd 1840 (after oil painting by G. Patten, exh. RA 1840), NG Ire. • E. Landseer, group portrait, oils, 1840–45 (*Windsor Castle in modern times*), Royal Collection • E. H. Baily, marble bust, 1841, V&A • C. R. Leslie, group portrait, oils, 1841 (*The christening of the princess royal at Buckingham Palace*), Royal Collection • L. von Meyern, oils, 1841, Osborne House, Isle of Wight • J. Partridge, oils, 1841, Royal Collection • W. C. Ross, miniature, 1841, Royal Collection • W. C. Ross, oils, 1841 (aged twenty-two), Royal Collection • G. Hayter, group portrait, oils, 1842 (*The christening of the prince of Wales*), Royal Collection • E. Landseer, double portrait, oils, 1842 (with Queen Victoria), Royal Collection • J. Lucas, oils, 1842, Musée de Versailles et des Trianons; version, formerly United Service Club, London, in care of Crown Commissioners • R. W. Sievier, bust, exh. RA 1842, Royal Collection • F. X. Winterhalter, oils, 1842, Royal Collection • E. Lami, group portrait, oils, 1843 (*Reception of Queen Victoria at the Château d'Eu*), Musée de Versailles • R. Thorburn, miniature, 1843, Royal Collection • W. Allan, group portrait, oils, 1844, Scot. NPG • J. Francis, marble bust, exh. RA 1844, Guildhall Museum, London; related plaster bust, NPG • F. X. Winterhalter, oils, 1845, Royal Collection • A. E. Beranger, pigment on porcelain, 1846, Osborne House, Isle of Wight • F. Grant, oils, exh. RA 1846, Christ's Hospital, Horsham • J. G. Lough, statue, 1846, Royal Exchange, London • F. X. Winterhalter, group portrait, oils, 1846, Royal Collection • F. X. Winterhalter, oils, 1846, Lady Lever Art Gallery, Port Sunlight [*see illus.*] • W. E. Kilburn, photograph, 1848, Royal Collection • Baron Marochetti, marble bust, 1849, Royal Collection • F. R. Say, oils, exh. RA 1849, Examination Schools, Cambridge • E. Wolff, marble statue, 1849, Osborne House, Isle of Wight • J. Francis, marble bust, 1850 (with Queen Victoria), Geological Museum, London • Corden, oils, 1850–75 (after Macleay), Osborne House, Isle of Wight • oils, 1850–75, Osborne House, Isle of Wight • oils, 1850–75 (after Mayall), Osborne House, Isle of Wight • H. C. Selous, group portrait, oils, 1851 (*Royal opening of the Great Exhibition*), Royal Collection • B. E. Duppa, photograph, 1854, Royal Collection • R. Fenton, photograph, 1854, V&A • A. Blaikley, group portrait, lithograph coloured in oils, 1855 (*Faraday lecturing at the Royal Institution*), Hunterian Museum and Art Gallery, Glasgow • E. M. Ward, group portrait, oils, 1855 (*The queen investing Napoleon III with the order of the Garter*), Royal Collection • J. Barrett, oils, 1856, NPG • E. Boutibonne and J. F. Herring, oils, 1856, Royal Collection • J. Mahony, watercolour on paper, exh. 1856, NG Ire. • J. Phillip, oils, 1856, Royal Collection • L. Caldesi, group portrait, photograph, 1857, NPG • J. Phillip, group portrait, oils, 1858 (*The marriage of the princess royal*), Royal Collection • J. Phillip, oils, exh. RA 1858, Aberdeen Corporation • W. Boxall, oils, exh. RA 1859, Trinity House, London • M. Noble, marble bust, 1859, City Hall, Manchester • E. H. Thomas, group portrait, oils, 1859 (*Queen Victoria at a military review in Aldershot*), Royal Collection • F. X. Winterhalter, oils, 1859 (*The prince consort*), Royal Collection; version, NPG • S. Durant, medallion, 1860, Royal Collection • J. J. E. Mayall, photograph, 1860, Royal Collection • W. Theed, bust, 1860, Grocers' Company, London • J. Thomas, marble bust, 1860, Midland Institute, Birmingham • T. J. Barker, group portrait, oils, *c*.1861 (*Queen Victoria presenting a bible in the Audience Chamber at Windsor*), NPG • Mayall, photograph, 1861, NPG • group portrait, oils, 1861 (*The last minutes of the prince consort*), Wellcome L. • oils, 1861, Osborne House, Isle of Wight • Holl, line and stipple engraving, pubd 1862 (after photograph by E. Day), NG Ire. • J. C. Horsley, oils, *c*.1862, RSA • Baron Marochetti, marble effigy on tomb, 1862, Royal Mausoleum, Windsor Castle • J. G. Middleton, oils, exh. RA 1862, Hon. Artillery Company • W. Theed, marble statue, 1862, Osborne House, Isle of Wight • T. Woolner, marble statue, 1864, Oxf. U. Mus. NH, Prince Albert Memorial • M. Noble, statue, 1865, Peel Park, Salford • M. Noble, statue, 1865, Manchester • M. Noble, statue, 1865, Leeds • T. Thornycroft, bronze statue, 1866, Liverpool • W. Theed, marble statue, 1868, Royal Collection •

J. H. Foley, marble statue, 1871, Prince Albert Memorial, Dublin · C. Bacon, statue, 1874, Holborn Circus, London · G. G. Scott, marble statue, 1876, Albert Memorial, London · J. Steel, marble statue, 1876, Prince Albert Memorial, Edinburgh · G. Koberwein, oils, 1882, Osborne House, Isle of Wight · T. O. Barlow, mixed-method engraving (after J. Phillip), NPG · W. Bell, enamel on gold, NG Ire. · C. Haag, watercolours, Royal Collection · possibly by L. Haghe, coloured lithograph (after possibly his earlier work), BM, NPG · E. Landseer, group portrait, oils (*Royal sports on hill and loch*), Royal Collection · J. Mahony, watercolour on paper, NG Ire. · H. W. Phillips, group portrait, oils (*The royal commissioners for the Great Exhibition, 1851*), V&A · W. Simpson, enamel on copper (after Winterhalter, 1846), NG Ire. · H. J. Stewart, group portrait (*The landing of Queen Victoria at Dumbarton in 1847*), Dumbarton District Council; pencil and watercolour study, 1849, Scot. NPG · F. X. Winterhalter, double portrait, drawing (with Queen Victoria), Royal Collection · F. X. Winterhalter, group portrait, oils (*The first of May, 1851*), Royal Collection · caricatures, BM, NPG · coloured lithograph (after unknown artist), BM, NPG · coloured lithograph (after J. Pollard), NPG · memorial, St George's Chapel, Windsor · mezzotint (after V. Gortz), BM, NPG · oils (as a boy), Osborne House, Isle of Wight · photographs, Royal Collection · plaster cameo, NPG

Albert Victor, Prince, duke of Clarence and Avondale

(1864–1892), was born Albert Victor Christian Edward at Frogmore, near Windsor Castle, Berkshire, on 8 January 1864, the eldest son of the prince and princess of Wales (later *Edward VII and Queen *Alexandra). He was baptized in Buckingham Palace chapel on 10 March, and throughout his life he was second in succession to the throne after his father. Born two months prematurely, he was a sickly child, and inherited his mother's deafness. He and his brother Prince George (later *George V) were mutually devoted, and it was deemed inadvisable for the lethargic Prince Albert Victor (known as Eddy in the family) to be separated from George, whose 'lively presence is his mainstay and chief incentive to exertion' (H. Nicolson, *King George V*, 1952, 13), according to their tutor, the Revd John Neale Dalton. The brothers became naval cadets on the training ship *Britannia* in 1877.

In 1879, both princes joined HMS *Bacchante* on a three-year cruise, visiting many of the British colonies. In October 1883, Prince Albert Victor was entered at Trinity College, Cambridge, and studied during vacations at Heidelberg. This education had little effect, as according to one despairing tutor, 'he hardly knows the meaning of the words *to read*' (Magnus, 178). After hearing rumours of his immoral behaviour, the prince of Wales took him away from college and he joined the army. He resented the rigours of military discipline, and his great-uncle George, duke of Cambridge, commander-in-chief, found him 'an inveterate and incurable dawdler' (St Aubyn, 299). He left the service in 1891 after attaining the rank of major.

As an adult, Prince Albert Victor was tall and languid looking, with a carefully waxed moustache, receding hairline, and unnaturally long neck and arms. His father nicknamed him Collar-and-Cuffs; his grandmother Queen Victoria was worried by his unsuitability for the throne. His health had been undermined by heavy drinking, gout, and probably venereal disease; his dissipated lifestyle was unrelieved by any serious interests. He was said to be a regular patron of a homosexual brothel in Cleveland Street, central London, raided by the police in 1889,

Prince Albert Victor, duke of Clarence and Avondale (1864–1892), by W. & D. Downey, pubd 1891

though his apparent involvement was kept a closely guarded secret for many years afterwards. He was also suspected, albeit on the flimsiest evidence, of being Jack the Ripper, responsible for murdering several East End prostitutes in 1888.

On 24 May 1890 Prince Albert Victor was created duke of Clarence and Avondale, and earl of Athlone. His father and grandmother decided to send him on a tour of Europe or the more remote colonies, or to arrange his marriage to a princess with sufficient strength of character to compensate for his inadequacies. After becoming briefly (and unofficially) engaged to Princess Hélène d'Orléans (who was ineligible as a Catholic and daughter of the pretender to the French throne), on 7 December 1891 he was officially betrothed to Princess Victoria Mary of Teck (later Queen *Mary). The wedding was arranged for 27 February 1892, but the duke succumbed to pneumonia, following influenza, at Sandringham on 14 January 1892. He was buried in St George's Chapel, Windsor, on 20 January. Although deeply mourned by the family, his brother's promotion to the position of heir presumptive was 'a merciful act of providence' (Magnus, 239).

JOHN VAN DER KISTE

Sources J. Van der Kiste, *Edward VII's children* (1989) · M. Harrison, *Clarence* (1972) · P. Magnus, *King Edward the Seventh* (1964) · G. St Aubyn, *Edward VII, prince and king* (1979) · J. Van der Kiste, 'The duke of Clarence', *Royalty Digest* (1991–2), vol. 1, pp. 194–6 • J. Pope-Hennessy, *Queen Mary* (1959) • T. Aronson, *Prince Eddy and the homosexual underworld* (1994) • *DNB* • *The Times* (15 Jan 1882)

Archives PRO • Royal Arch.

Likenesses Hill & Saunders, photograph, postcard, 1865, NPG • K. W. F. Bauerle, group portrait, oils, *c*.1871, Royal Collection • J. Sant, group portrait, oils, *c*.1872 (*Victoria with three of her grandchildren*), Royal Collection • N. Chevalier, group portrait, oils, 1874 (*The marriage of the duke of Edinburgh*), Royal Collection • J. Sant, oil study for *Victoria and her grandchildren*, 1874, Royal Collection • H. von Angeli, oils, 1875, Royal Collection • H. von Angeli, group portrait, oils, 1876 (*Prince and princess of Wales and Albert Victor and Maud*), Royal Collection • W. & D. Downey, photograph, carte, *c*.1877, NPG • Count Gleichen, bronze statuette, 1877, Royal Collection • F. J. Williamson, marble statue and bust, 1877, Royal Collection • C. John junior, double portrait, 1882 (with Prince George), Royal Collection • L. Tuxen, group portrait, oils, 1884 (*Prince and princess of Wales and Albert Victor*), Det Nationalhistoriske Museum Paa Frederiksborg, Hillerod, Denmark • F. Tuttle, oils, 1885, Trinity Cam. • L. Tuxen, group portrait, oils, 1887 (*The royal family at the time of the jubilee*), Royal Collection • W. J. S. Webber, marble bust, 1890, Royal College of Music, London • G. Cooper, postcard, *c*.1890–1899, NPG • Lafayette, three postcards, *c*.1890–1899, NPG • W. & D. Downey, cabinet photograph, pubd 1891, NPG [*see illus.*] • Gunn & Stewart, postcard, 1891, NPG • Hill & Saunders, photograph, 1891, NPG • J. Russell, photogravure, 1891, NPG • F. Thurston, photograph, 1891, NPG • H. von Herkomer, watercolour drawing, 1892, Royal Collection • A. Gilbert, marble and bronze effigy on tomb, 1892–9, Windsor Castle, Albert Memorial Chapel • L. Fildes, oils, 1895?, Royal Collection • Chancellor, postcard (as a young man), NPG • Judd & Co., lithograph, NPG; repro. in *Whitehall Review* (16 Aug 1879) • photographs (as an infant), NPG • photographs, Royal Collection • prints, NPG • watercolour and other drawings, Royal Collection

Albert, Charles (*b*. 1767, *d*. in or after 1834). *See under* Industrial spies (*act. c*.1700–*c*.1800).

Albert, Harold [*formerly* Harold Albert Kemp; *pseud.* Helen Cathcart] (**1909–1997**), author and journalist, was born on 15 April 1909 at 48 Marsala Road, Lewisham, the son of Albert William Kemp, builder, and his wife, Mabel, the daughter of Frederick Read, dramatic reciter. He was educated at Upton Manor high school, Lewisham, and later at a dame-school. His parents separated during his childhood, his father setting up home with another woman in Bristol, while his mother married, possibly bigamously, George Spratley, a despised stepfather who beat young Harold to the point that he ran away from home. He did not see his father until he was twenty-one, and, though estranged from his mother, continued to answer pleas for financial help from his stepfather. In 1927 he dropped the surname Kemp, and was henceforth known as Harold Albert.

Albert's first work was in a packing factory, where he stamped prices on the soles of shoes. But by reading Dickens, Arnold Bennett, and Hugh Walpole, his eyes were opened to wider possibilities. By the age of twenty-one he had escaped from the factory and become a prolific journalist, writing for papers such as the *Sunday Sun*, the *Evening News*, and the *Daily Mirror*. His pieces ranged from 'Is success worthwhile?' to 'Dusting skeletons', and profiles of Queen Alexandra and the Elephant Man. Sometimes he wrote under his own name, but often he used one of a variety of pseudonyms, including Mark Priestley, Peter Davis,

and Webster Fawcett. He persuaded famous people to tell him how they were spending Easter, or their views on the youth of today. Some were kind to him, notably Frank Swinnerton, who took him to the Reform Club, but others rebuffed him sternly—Bernard Shaw, predictably, and A. A. Milne with undue severity.

Albert prospered. In the late 1920s he was taken up by the literary agent Rupert Crew, and he remained a client of the agency until his death. By 1931 he was renting a flat in Westbourne Terrace, Bayswater. He travelled extensively, even to Hollywood, where he interviewed Clark Gable on the set of *Gone with the Wind*, and was photographed with Mickey Rooney. By 1933 he had secured interviews with Hitler and Mussolini. The former was sitting under a portrait of Frederick the Great, and told him: 'Already we Nazis are masters of the street. Soon we shall be masters of the state.' The latter was dressed in black with 'a pallid face, the only luminosity his eyes'.

On 28 August 1932 Harold Albert married, in Paris, Winifred (1908–1996), the daughter of Richard Evans, a machinist (or engine fitter), of Toronto, Canada. Theirs was at times a troubled relationship, and there were no children of the marriage. In later life he indicated to a friend whether they were on speaking terms by the direction in which a pair of porcelain elephants faced on the mantelpiece of their cottage at Milland.

In 1933 Albert published his only novel, *Café People*, a more than readable account of the lives of several characters working in the Café Great. This was well reviewed, though eclipsed by Arnold Bennett's *Imperial Palace*. Albert became aware that he would not succeed as a novelist and after rejecting various ideas returned to the steadier income of journalism.

During the Second World War, Albert was a conscientious objector. He declared that he disapproved of war and would write only to amuse or divert the troops. He was indicted for inciting others to fight while refusing to do so himself, and was sentenced to six months' hard labour at Wormwood Scrubs in 1941 and to a further custodial sentence in 1943.

In the late 1940s Albert invented Mrs Helen Cathcart, and she proved his most lasting disguise. At first 'she' wrote articles about the royal family, and later a stream of books. These were all successful, often well received, and went into many editions. Early on, Albert claimed that Mrs Cathcart had worked for George V in some capacity, but her details were allowed to become gradually more obscure as she 'aged'. Of course she was never seen, and attempts to interview her were rebuffed by Albert, her 'literary representative', on her behalf. The ruse was suspected, but never proven: sometimes journalists visited Albert hoping to trap him into an admission, but they never succeeded. Occasionally, in a nice touch of detail, Helen Cathcart acknowledged the kind help of Harold Albert in her prefaces.

Cathcart biographies were written of the queen, the queen mother, Prince Charles, Princess Margaret, Lord Snowdon, Princess Alexandra, and the duchess of Kent.

There were histories of Sandringham, the queen's race-horses, and Prince Philip's sporting activities. By the standards of the late twentieth century the books were tame, but Albert was viewed with deep disfavour in the press office of Buckingham Palace, particularly on account of his more speculative journalism.

Albert also ghosted Queen Alexandra of Yugoslavia's book *Prince Philip—a Family Portrait* (1959), basing this on a few conversations with the former queen and on press reports. The duke of Edinburgh was shown the manuscript and did not disguise his irritation at being betrayed by his cousin. Ironically the book of which Albert was proudest was one written under his own name, *Queen Victoria's Sister: the Life and Letters of Princess Feodora* (1967).

The Cathcart books secured a good living for the Alberts, who bought a lovely cottage at Milland, Hampshire, cultivating an unusual spring garden on the slopes behind it, with rare species of azalea and rhododendron. Here they lived within their means, maintaining a small *pied-à-terre* in Earls Court. Winnie typed the books, and they had few friends, though Harold enjoyed an *amitié amoureuse* with a lady in America.

In time Helen Cathcart's books were overtaken by more prurient and revelatory books on the royal family and her market dwindled. In the 1980s and early 1990s she wrote a column for *Majesty* magazine. A work on the queen mother, for posthumous publication, lurked for many years in the office of Rupert Crew and was not published.

In old age the Alberts sensed approaching infirmity and retired to the same nursing home. Winnie died at Vine House, Easebourne Lane, Easebourne, Midhurst, Sussex, aged eighty-eight on 20 December 1996, and Harold died there on 20 October 1997, also aged eighty-eight, by which time his memory had gone. He was cremated in Chichester on 31 October and his ashes were scattered at his home in Milland. After Albert's death Helen Cathcart's true identity was finally exposed, catching the imagination of the world's press.   HUGO VICKERS

Sources The Times (4 Nov 1997) · Hampshire, Vickers Collection, private papers of Harold Albert · b. cert. · m. cert. · d. cert.
Archives priv. coll.
Likenesses photograph, Hampshire, Vickers Collection, Harold Albert papers
Wealth at death £595,724: administration, 17 April 1998, *CGPLA Eng. & Wales*

Albertazzi, Emma (*c*.1813–1847), singer, the daughter of Francis Howson, a London music teacher, was trained as a pianist and in 1827 articled to Andrea Costa, in whose house she met a fellow pupil, Francesco Albertazzi; they were married in November 1829. She appeared first in concert, then went to Milan and sang contralto parts in comic operas at the Cannobiana and one opera at La Scala (February 1833). She spent the next decade as leading contralto in both comic and serious opera at the Italian opera houses of Madrid (1833–5), London, and Paris (1835–42), making her London début in *La Cenerentola* on 19 April 1837. In 1838 she sang Anne Page in Balfe's *Falstaff* alongside Giulia Grisi, G. B. Rubini, Antonio Tamburini, and Luigi Lablache, the most famous singers of the day; in the

same company (with Giovanni Mario replacing Rubini) she won high praise in the first complete performance of Rossini's *Stabat mater* (Paris, 7 January 1842). At Drury Lane she was a success in an English version of *La gazza ladra* (1838). She was no actress, and was best suited to florid Rossinian singing, then going out of favour. By 1846 her voice was much weakened, perhaps by repeated pregnancy; she died of 'rapid consumption' at 30 North Bank, Marylebone, Middlesex, on 25 September 1847, leaving five children.   E. M. CLERKE, *rev.* JOHN ROSSELLI

Sources *Musical World* (2 Oct 1847) · G. Radiciotti, *Gioacchino Rossini: vita documentata*, 3 vols. (1927–9), 2.247–50 · A. Soubies, *Le Théâtre-Italien de Paris de 1801 à 1913* (1913), 80–3, 94 · H. Chorley, *Thirty years' musical recollections*, 1 (1862), 123, 143, 243–4 · J. E. Cox, *Musical recollections of the last half-century*, 1 (1872), 91 · G. Tintori, 'Cronologia', in C. Gatti, *Il Teatro alla Scala nella storia e nell'arte* (1964) · L. C. y Millán, *Crónica de la ópera italiana en Madrid* (1878) · d. cert.
Archives Archives Nationales, Paris, Archives de l'Opéra, contracts and corresp., series AJ[13]
Likenesses F. Corbaux, lithograph, pubd 1837 (as Zerlina in *Don Giovanni*), BM · Bayot, lithograph (as Cenerentola; after Bard), NPG · E. Fechner, lithograph (as Rosina in *Barbier de Seville*), BM · W. Taylor, lithograph (after F. Salabert), BM · drawing, repro. in Soubies, *Le Théâtre-Italien de Paris*, 83 · five prints, Harvard TC
Wealth at death left five children destitute: *DNB*

Alberti, Georg Wilhelm [*pseud.* Alethophilus Gottingensis] (*bap.* 1724, *d.* 1758), theologian and essayist, was baptized on 17 August 1724 NS at the church of St Aegidien, Osterode am Harz, in the electorate of Hanover; he was the son of August Christoph Alberti, brewer and burgher, and his wife, Catharina Margaretha, daughter of Henrich Georg Schimpf, builder and burgher of Osterode. On 4 January 1742 he matriculated at the University of Göttingen as a student of theology; he graduated MA on 12 December 1744 NS, and licentiate and doctor in philosophy on 9 September 1745 NS. On the advice of his teacher Joachim Oporin he went on an academic tour to Britain, where he arrived on 1 December/12 December 1745 NS. Though few details are known about his stay he was so disturbed by the advance of deism or freethinking in England that in 1747 he published a reply to a pamphlet written by Charles Blount but attributed to John Dryden. Writing under the pseudonym of Alethophilus Gottingensis, Alberti dedicated his reply to Princess Augusta. It is not known when he returned to Germany or which posts he held immediately afterwards, but in 1753 a vacancy arose in the Lutheran parish of Tündern, near Hameln, and in June 1754 NS he was introduced as its minister. His role in the parish became much more difficult after the sacking of the village by the French army in 1757.

Alberti was a man of conservative theological views, and was opposed to the Socinian and liberal views then current in the Church of England and in the dissenting churches. Religious and intellectual liberalism was still fairly unknown in Germany, particularly in the Lutheran church; his *Briefe über den allerneuesten Zustand der Religion in Gross-Britannien* ('Letters about the latest state of religion in Great Britain'), published in four parts from 1752 to 1754, together with his history of the Quakers, were the chief sources of information about British religious and intellectual movements for the reading public in eighteenth-century Germany. Alberti also wrote two small academic theses or pamphlets and a largely unpublished parish chronicle of Tündern. Alberti died in Tündern, probably on 3 September 1758 NS, but the date of his death can no longer be verified since there is a gap in the parish registers from 1730 to 1794.   G. H. THOMANN

Sources Kreiskirchenamt Osterode, parish registers, St Aegiduen, 1724 · Pfarrbestellungsakten, Landeskirchliches Archiv, Hannover, A 6, no. 8130 · Pfarrbestellungsakten, Niedersächsisches Hauptstaatsarchiv Hannover, Konsistorium Hannover, Han 83, III, no. 710 · G. von Selle, *Die Matrikel der Georg-August-Universität zu Göttingen, 1734–1837* (1932), 37 · G. W. Alberti, *Briefe über den allerneuesten Zustand der Religion in Groß-Britannien* (1752), 1.21, 23, and preface · Tündern parish archives, letter by Alberti's successor at Tündern as preface to the parish chronicle written by Alberti · Wagenmann, 'Alberti, Georg Wilhelm', *Allgemeine deutsche Biographie*, ed. R. von Liliencron and others, 1 (Leipzig, 1875), 213 · *DNB* · private information (2004) [M. Plasse]
Wealth at death Tündern looted by French army 1757

Albery, **Sir Bronson James** (1881–1971), theatre director, was born at Greenhithe, Kent, on 6 March 1881, the second in the family of three sons of James *Albery (1838–1889), dramatist, and his wife, Mary Charlotte *Moore (1861–1931), actress, later Lady Wyndham. He was named after the American dramatist Bronson Howard. His father died when he was eight and he and his two brothers were brought up by their mother, who had returned to the stage when James Albery was no longer able to write. He was educated at Uppingham School and at Balliol College, Oxford, where he obtained a second class in modern history in 1903. He was called to the bar at the Inner Temple in 1904 but his legal career was brief, though the intricacies of theatrical contracts would never defeat him. He married in 1912 Una Gwynn (d. 1981), daughter of Thomas William Rolleston, of Glasshouse, Shinrone, Irish scholar, poet, and friend of W. B. Yeats. They had two sons and two daughters.

Albery's first theatrical venture, with Allan Aynesworth at the Criterion in 1914, was Cyril Harcourt's comedy, *A Pair of Silk Stockings*; they put on two other plays that year. The war, in which he served in the Royal Naval Volunteer Reserve from 1917 to 1919, ended, for the time being, his connection with the theatre, but this resumed in 1920 with a revival at the Kingsway of *The Knight of the Burning Pestle* by Francis Beaumont and John Fletcher. In this production by Nigel Playfair, which originated at the Birmingham repertory theatre and ran for ninety-seven performances, the very young Noël Coward surprisingly played the grocer's apprentice.

From his mother Albery inherited his business sense, for, although Mary Moore was primarily a comedienne, it was her drive that led Sir Charles Wyndham to enlarge his theatrical empire—which began at the Criterion—and to build Wyndham's in 1899 and the New in 1903. Mary Moore had played in *David Garrick* with Charles Wyndham in many revivals, so it was understandable that Bronson Albery's next choice of production should be a musical version of the play at the Queen's in 1922. He would now be of great help to his mother in the running of the three

Sir Bronson James Albery (1881–1971), by Howard Coster, 1935

family theatres, and in 1922 Lewis Casson and Sybil Thorndike began their association with him. Sybil Thorndike's performance in *The Cenci* at a special matinée at the New convinced G. B. Shaw that she would be perfect for Saint Joan. With some misgivings, as it had a long cast and was, unfashionably, a costume play, in 1924 Albery agreed to do *Saint Joan*, which presently broke all existing records at the theatre.

When Albery found the family theatres' atmosphere restricting he was glad to help to establish the Arts Theatre Club in 1927. Nor was he obsessively commercial; when he saw the Compagnie des Quinze at the Vieux-Colombier in Paris he decided that discerning London audiences should be given a chance to see these actors. In 1931 he brought them, in *Noë*, to the Arts and then to the Ambassador's realizing, as he told W. A. Darlington, that 'the venture must lose'. After his mother's death in that year, he and Wyndham's son, Howard, were in joint command of the three theatres. From the Arts he transferred to the Criterion in 1932 in Ronald Mackenzie's *Musical Chairs*, with John Gielgud. This was the beginning of an association that would do much for both actor and manager. During his years at the New—in *Richard of Bordeaux*, *Hamlet*, *Romeo and Juliet*, *Noah*, and *The Seagull*—Gielgud built his unchallenged position, and Albery would be regarded as a manager of distinction and taste. Though after 1935 they no longer worked together, they remained friends; Gielgud had always found Bronnie to be encouraging and never unduly interfering, but he was also shrewd enough to withdraw from the production of a play by Emlyn Williams in which Gielgud appeared and which ran a week.

During the Second World War, while the New Theatre housed the Old Vic Company in seasons of classical acting at its best, Albery was its joint administrator from 1942 to 1944 with Tyrone Guthrie. After this he would be increasingly a theatre committee man, serving on such bodies as the Arts Council from 1948, the British Council drama advisory committee (1952–61), and the Society of West End Theatre Managers, of which he was president from 1941 to 1945 and 1952 to 1953. As a reader of plays his wife was of great help; perhaps through her influence he presented in 1946 the semi-autobiographical *Red Roses for Me* by Sean O'Casey. His manner was quiet; he gave an impression of shyness, though at the Garrick Club he was a popular member and a particularly keen bridge player. He was knighted in 1949 and was a chevalier of the Légion d'honneur. His son, Sir Donald Arthur Rolleston *Albery, succeeded him in management. Albery died in London on 21 July 1971. On 1 January 1973 the New Theatre, the home of his greatest successes, was renamed the Albery.

WENDY TREWIN

Sources *The Times* (22 July 1971) • Albery family MSS • W. Trewin, *All on stage: Charles Wyndham and the Alberys* (1980) • personal knowledge (2004) • *CGPLA Eng. & Wales* (1971)
Archives priv. coll., Albery family MSS
Likenesses H. Coster, photographs, 1930–39, NPG [*see illus.*] • photograph, repro. in Trewin, *All on stage*, facing p. 167
Wealth at death £72,784: probate, 10 Nov 1971, *CGPLA Eng. & Wales*

Albery, Sir Donald Arthur Rolleston (1914–1988), theatre manager, was born on 19 June 1914 at 33 Cumberland Terrace, Regent's Park, London, the elder son and second of the four children of Sir Bronson James *Albery (1881–1971), theatre director, and his wife, Una Gwynn (d. 1981), daughter of Thomas William Rolleston, Irish scholar and poet. He was educated at Alpine College, Switzerland, and joined the family firm of Wyndham and Albery, owners and managers of three London theatres: the Criterion in Piccadilly Circus, and Wyndham's and the New (after 1972 the Albery), both built by his grandmother, the actress Mary Charlotte *Moore, and Sir Charles *Wyndham, her partner and second husband. His first position of importance, as general manager of Sadler's Wells Ballet in London (1941–5), was complicated by wartime emergencies. On one occasion he arrived in Bath to find that the trucks containing scenery and costumes were immobilized in a siding close to unexploded bombs.

On first nights at his theatres Donald Albery, a tall lean figure, would be seen walking about the auditorium with a slight limp. He was prematurely bald and had a long narrow face, and in later years his resemblance to his father became more marked. He inherited the family business sense, though his taste in plays was modern, whereas Sir Bronson Albery was known for his classical productions. In 1953 he formed his own company, Donmar, and his choice of dramatists included Graham Greene, Tennessee Williams, Edward Albee, Jean Anouilh, and Iris Murdoch (adapted by J. B. Priestley). Greene's *The Living Room*, with

Sir Donald Arthur Rolleston Albery (1914–1988), by unknown photographer [right, with his son Ian B. Albery]

Dorothy Tutin, was his favourite production, and *I am a Camera*, John van Druten's adaptation from Christopher Isherwood, gave him 'enormous pleasure'.

Although he ran his theatres with an eye to commercial success, Albery could spring surprises and on occasion was prepared to take risks. He had youthful memories of going to Paris with his parents to see the Compagnie des Quinze, which Bronson admired and brought to London knowing that their appeal would be limited. On hearing about Samuel Beckett's *Waiting for Godot*, Albery went to Paris and decided to put it on in London. He hoped to cast star names in the roles of the tramps, but after two years of failing to persuade any of them—including Laurence Olivier and Ralph Richardson—the play opened at the Arts Theatre Club in 1955, directed by the young Peter Hall and without stars. In a daring move, he transferred it to the Criterion in the heart of the West End, where it survived for nearly 300 performances, though the audiences were frankly puzzled. Many left at the interval; the performances were disturbed by shouts of 'Take it off!', 'Rubbish!', and 'It's a disgrace!' The run was dogged by illness in the cast and inadequate understudies. In these unhappy circumstances the high teas provided by the management between the Saturday performances were greatly appreciated.

During the late 1950s and the 1960s the idiosyncratic productions of Joan Littlewood at the Theatre Royal, Stratford East, appealed to Albery. Under his management they moved to the West End and some even went to New York—another example of his adventurous spirit. These included *A Taste of Honey* and Brendan Behan's *The Hostage* (both 1959) and *Fings ain't what they used t'be* (1960). Out of gratitude to Joan Littlewood he presented a crystal chandelier to the Theatre Royal. This connection brought him his greatest success, the musical *Oliver!* (1960) by Lionel Bart (who also wrote the score of *Fings ain't*). *Oliver!* had been turned down by three managements and opened so disastrously at Wimbledon that doubts were expressed about the wisdom of taking it to the West End, where advance bookings (at the New) amounted to just £145. A new musical director had to be found at the last moment, but the first night changed these gloomy expectations, and Sean Kenny's revolving set, on which everything took place, was rapturously received. *Oliver!* ran for 2618 performances and has since been revived.

In 1960, against strong competition from Bernard Delfont, Albery added the Piccadilly to the Wyndham–Albery empire. Thus 3360 seats were offered to the public at every performance in these four theatres. At one point, when it looked as if the Criterion, the oldest of them, would be endangered by a Piccadilly Circus development scheme, Albery leapt eagerly into the fray and fought hard—enjoying the battle—and finally won. After *Oliver!* he produced several other musicals: in 1966 a failure, *Jorrocks*, which lost £70,000; and in 1968 a success, *Man of La Mancha*, which called for extensive structural alterations to the Piccadilly stage, and so, by special permission of the lord chamberlain, the safety curtain was never lowered during the run. Albery was the first manager to investigate the tourist trade in relation to the theatre. This pioneering survey proved beyond doubt that without overseas visitors the theatres would suffer irreparably (though this situation had been suspected for years).

When Sir Bronson Albery died in 1971 Donald Albery took control. In 1977 he became the third member of his family to receive a knighthood; in the following year he sold the theatres and retired to Monte Carlo. His son Ian carried on for a time, later becoming chief executive of the rebuilt Sadler's Wells Theatre. During the Albery regime their theatres were regarded as being among the best run in London, and the two back-to-back theatres, Wyndham's in Charing Cross Road and the Albery in St Martin's Lane, housed some of the most interesting productions of the period. From 1958 to 1978 Donald Albery was also a director of Anglia Television.

Albery was married three times. On 7 July 1934 he married Rubina (Ruby), daughter of Archibald Curie Macgilchrist, medical officer in India; she died in 1956 as a result of injuries incurred in a Second World War air raid. Ian Albery was their only son. In 1946, the year of his divorce from Ruby, he married, on 1 February, (Cicely Margaret) Heather (*b.* 1915/16), daughter of Brigadier-General Reginald Harvey Henderson Boys. They had two sons and a daughter. The marriage was dissolved in 1974, and in 1978 in New York he married Nobuko, daughter of Keiji Uenishi, businessman, and former wife of Professor Ivan Morris. Albery died in Monte Carlo on 14 September 1988.

WENDY TREWIN, *rev.*

Sources W. Trewin, *All on stage: Charles Wyndham and the Alberys* (1980) · P. Bull, *I know the face, but …* (1959) · m. certs. · personal knowledge (1996) · b. cert.
Likenesses photograph (with Ian Albery), unknown collection; copyprint, NPG [*see illus.*]

Albery, James [Jim] (1838–1889), playwright, eldest of the six children of James Albery (*d.* 1859), rope maker and cotton-waste dealer, and his wife, Amelia Eleanor (*d.* 1870), was born in Swan Street, Trinity Square, Southwark, London, on 4 May 1838. After private schooling, from 1852 to 1859 he trained as an architect with a firm in Fenchurch Street, but on his father's death joined the family business in Blackfriars Road. With his brother-in-law, Usher Back, as partner, he retained a direct interest until 1878, long after playwriting had become his principal income.

Albery began writing about 1860 when he was a member of the Southwark Literary Society and the Ingoldsby Club. His one-act farce *Alexander the Great* (with Joseph Dilley), staged at the Walworth Literary Institute in London in 1864, was subsequently performed professionally, after alteration, as *Chiselling* (1870). His friend Hermann Vezin staged and starred in Albery's drama on David Garrick, adapted from the German (Greenwich Theatre, 1865), and arranged its reincarnation as *Doctor Davy* (Lyceum, 1866). Albery's greatest triumph came early: the comedy *Two Roses* (1870), which put him for a decade into the dramatic first rank, and gave Henry Irving, as the humbug Digby Grant, his first major success. Although slight in plot, its characters were vivid and the language energetic. It ran for 249 performances, was revived several times, toured worldwide into the early 1880s, and was anthologized as late as 1953. Nothing ever matched it. Albery's next comedy, *Two Thorns* (1871; as *Coquettes*, Liverpool, 1870, and the USA, 1870–71), was criticized as vague in construction and indulgently epigrammatic. *Apple Blossoms* (1871), much superior, offered strong dialogue and several good comic roles, and lasted 100 performances. His scissors-and-paste Dickensian adaptation, *Pickwick* (1871), fared best in the version *Jingle*, as adapted and toured by Irving in 1878. He was constantly at work until 1880, with, among others, *Tweedie's Rights* (1871), *Forgiven* (1872), *Oriana* (1873)—an ambitious but unsuccessful verse drama—and *Jacks and Jills* (1880), his last original play, which encountered first-night hostility and closed after eight performances.

Albery claimed that, except once, he always wrote to commission. After *Two Roses*, the slow drift of his career was from original work to adaptation. His best in this vein was *Pink Dominos* (Criterion, 1877), described as in some ways 'better than the original [by Alfred Delacour and Alfred-Néoclès Hennequin]' (Knight, 178). Its 'fast' subject matter—a wife in pink domino disguise testing suspicions of her husband's infidelity—provoked instant press outrage and complaints to the censor. The scandal, however, ensured an exceptional 555 nights' run. Albery was forty when he astonished his friends at the Savage Club by marrying, on 12 June 1878, Mary Charlotte *Moore (1861–1931), a sixteen-year-old actress with the Criterion Theatre, and the youngest daughter of Charles Moore, a London parliamentary agent. Coincidentally, his playwriting career was degenerating. In the early 1880s Charles Wyndham engaged him in adaptations—notably *Little Miss Muffet* (1882)—but new work was not forthcoming, and his imprudent reliance on diminishing returns from revivals generated financial problems. In 1884 he fell ill, partly through excessive drinking, and one year later suffered a breakdown. His wife then took charge and, with Wyndham's help, returned to the stage as Mary Moore. Their home in Regent's Park was sold and Albery was marginalized in lodgings in Ramsgate, Kent. Mary cajoled him to continue writing, but to little avail, and she quickly adjusted to a new role as breadwinner. From 1885 the couple effectively lived separate lives.

Witty and clubbable, Albery was fascinated by the bohemian side of theatrical life. His widow described him as 'decidedly good-looking', but with 'prominent eyes' that gave him 'rather an aggressive appearance' (Moore, 33). He could be quarrelsome and sometimes unconventional, not to say peculiar. They had three children—Irving Albery (1879–1967), Bronson James *Albery (1881–1971), and Wyndham Albery (d. 1940)—and Mary recalled that, as an infant, Irving was made to swim from a rowing-boat off Broadstairs by being dangled in a sling made from a large handkerchief secured to a walking-stick. Irving Albery followed an army career and was subsequently MP for Gravesend from 1924 to 1945.

Few of Albery's plays were published in his lifetime, which made critical assessment difficult. But his youngest son's elegant and comprehensive edition (2 vols., 1939) tends to reinforce the judgement of Albery's contemporaries that he never fulfilled his true potential. Albery died of cirrhosis of the liver on 15 August 1889, in rooms in St Martin's Lane, London, and was buried on 20 August in Kensal Green cemetery. His widow continued to act to support her family, and in 1896 she went into partnership with Charles Wyndham, resulting in the opening in 1899 of Wyndham's Theatre in London. In 1916 she married him, becoming Lady Wyndham. Bronson James Albery went on to become a theatre manager, and was knighted in 1949.   JOHN RUSSELL STEPHENS

Sources Daily News (19 Aug 1889) · [W. Archer], The World (21 Aug 1889) · The Athenaeum (24 Aug 1889), 268 · The Theatre, 4th ser., 14 (1889), 164–5 · The dramatic works of James Albery, ed. W. Albery, 2 vols. (1939) · W. Trewin, All on stage: Charles Wyndham and the Alberys (1980) · Lady Wyndham [M. Moore], Charles Wyndham and Mary Moore (privately printed, Edinburgh, 1925) · W. Archer, English dramatists of to-day (1882) · J. Knight, Dramatic notes (1893) · The Theatre, 2 (1877), 103–4 · The Era (28 June 1884) · A. Nicoll, Late nineteenth century drama, 1850–1900, 2nd edn (1959), vol. 5 of A history of English drama, 1660–1900 (1952–9) · J. R. Stephens, The censorship of English drama, 1824–1901 (1980) · G. Rowell, ed., Nineteenth-century plays (1953) · The Theatre, 4th ser., 8 (1886), 332–3 [memoir of Mary Moore] · The life and reminiscences of E. L. Blanchard, with notes from the diary of Wm. Blanchard, ed. C. W. Scott and C. Howard, 2 vols. (1891) · DNB · Boase, Mod. Eng. biog.
Archives priv. coll. | BL, family papers, MS of play Jingle, Add. MS 43506
Likenesses photograph, c.1872–1873, repro. in Albery, ed., Dramatic works of James Albery, vol. 1, frontispiece · A. Bryan, cartoon (as Hamlet), repro. in Trewin, All on stage, facing p. 167 · woodburytype photograph, NPG

Albestroff. For this title name see Walkinshaw, Clementine, styled countess of Albestroff (c.1720–1802).

Albin, Eleazar (d. 1742?), naturalist and watercolour painter, may have been born somewhere in the German states to a family named Weiss. Nothing is known of his early life, although he later claimed, in his Natural History of Birds (1731–8), to have been 'at Jamaica' in 1701 (3.45). By 1708 he had adopted the surname Albin, had married, and was living in or near the parish of St James's, Piccadilly, where his daughter (named Elizabeth after her mother) was baptized on 21 June of that year. Five sons and four

daughters followed; the youngest, Judith (d. 1758), was baptized in St Pancras in April 1725.

According to the account he gave in his Natural History of English Insects (1720) Albin was well established as a teacher of watercolour painting by the time he met the silk weaver and naturalist Joseph Dandridge (in or about 1709), and had already developed an interest in flowers and insects. It is probable that Albin then received some form of instruction in natural history from Dandridge before being recommended to a Mrs How, a widow for whom he painted 'a great Number of both Caterpillars and Flies' (Insects, preface).

At about this time Albin also met Mary, dowager duchess of Beaufort, a keen botanist who encouraged him to begin work on a natural history of insects. The first plates were engraved in 1713 and work proceeded apace until the onset of financial difficulties caused by the death of his patroness in January 1715. Although Albin had by this time already issued Proposals for Printing by Subscription 'A Natural History of English Insects' ([1714?]) from his premises, 'next the Green Man near Maggots Brew House' (Bristowe, 'Life', 82) in Golden Square, subscriptions were slow to come in and as a result the work was not finally published until 1720. Ultimately attracting 170 subscribers, A Natural History of English Insects contained 100 copper plates which were hand-coloured by the author on request. Albin stressed that the insects depicted were copied 'exactly after the Life' as he had 'observed it as a great Fault of those who have gone before me in this Way, that they either did not look often enough at their Pattern, or affected to make the Picture outdo Nature'.

By the mid-1720s Albin was living in St Pancras and cultivating connections with gentlemen naturalists, connections which he put to great use for his A Natural History of Birds (3 vols., 1731–8). The first two volumes were printed under the patronage of Sir Robert Abdy of Albins (Albyns), Essex (from which village Albin may earlier have taken his Anglicized surname), and the third was greatly supported by Richard Mead (1673–1754), physician to the king. In addition to patronage Albin's connections also provided him with access to the large collections of exotic birds owned by the duke of Chandos, Thomas Lowther, and Joseph Dandridge. Other specimens were often obtained from the Newgate market or a Mr Bland's at the Tiger on Tower Hill, and still others were supplied by sea captains and foreign merchants. A number of live specimens were painted in several London apothecaries' shops and coffee houses. Additionally, in the preface to the first volume, Albin appealed to his readers for specimens, asking that 'Gentlemen … send any curious Birds … to Eleazar Albin near the Dog and Duck in Tottenham-Court Road' (Birds, vol. 1).

The three volumes of A Natural History of Birds contained a total of 306 plates. Although a number were unsigned, all except one (signed by Albin's son Fortin) were probably the work of either Albin or his daughter Elizabeth. The drawings by both father and daughter were generally accurate and well coloured, but the poses of the birds were often stiff and lifeless, and the accompanying text was sometimes directed more at gentlemen readers than at naturalists (an example is his comments on the taste of a number of the specimens). Nevertheless, the work was the first on birds to use coloured plates and made Albin one of the first successful compilers of the genre of profusely illustrated natural history books for the non-specialist reader.

Albin published *A Natural History of Spiders* in 1736. Although it contains the only known likeness of him, it has been claimed that many of the other plates in it were simply 'inferior copies' (Bristowe, 'Life', 84) of an earlier series of 119 pictures by Joseph Dandridge. Albin also illustrated (and possibly wrote) *A Natural History of English Song-Birds* (1737); it proved a popular work and a third edition was published in 1759.

It is not known precisely when Albin died but it was probably early in 1742; no illustrations after 1741 bear his name and the *Daily Advertiser* of 22 February 1742 carried an advertisement by John Robinson of Southampton Street, Covent Garden, for the sale of 'scarce and uncommon Books, in most Languages and Faculties; Being the Collection of Mr. Eleazar Albin, (the curious Drawer of Birds, Insects & c.) lately deceased, and of two private Gentlemen gone abroad'. Parish registers at St Pancras for this period record only the death of an Ebenezer Allcorn on 1 December 1741—an unlikely but possible corruption of Albin's name. Albin's daughter Elizabeth married John Jones at St Giles Cripplegate on 28 March 1730, so it is likely that she is the 'Elizabeth of John Jones' who died in St Giles parish on 1 August 1741. Three plates by Fortin Albin (two dated 1740) appeared in Roger North's *Treatise on Fish and Fish Ponds* ([1835?]), but nothing further is known of him.

PETER OSBORNE

Sources E. Albin, *A natural history of English insects* (1720) · E. Albin, *A natural history of birds*, 3 vols. (1731–8) · C. E. Jackson, *Bird etchings: the illustrators and their books, 1655–1855* (1985) · private information (2004) [J. Gross] · W. S. Bristowe, 'The life and work of a great English naturalist, Joseph Dandridge, 1664–1746', *Entomologist's Gazette*, 18 (1967), 73–89 · W. S. Bristowe, 'More about Joseph Dandridge and his friends James Petiver and Eleazer Albin', *Entomologist's Gazette*, 18 (1967), 197–201 · E. Albin, *Proposals for printing by subscription 'A natural history of English insects'* (1714?) · parish registers (baptism), London, St Pancras, June 1708–April 1725 · *Daily Advertiser* [London] (22 Feb 1742)

Likenesses engraving, repro. in E. Albin, *A natural history of spiders* (1736)

Albin, Henry (1624–1696), clergyman and ejected minister, was born at Batcombe, Somerset, on 20 June 1624 to parents whose names are as yet not known; he attended the grammar school at Glastonbury and is said by Edmund Calamy to have been a student at Oxford University. No record remains of this, however, and the Henry Albyne who matriculated as a pensioner from Trinity Hall, Cambridge, in 1648 may appear too young to be the man of Somerset. By this time, according to Calamy, Albin had been instituted to the rectory of West Camel in that county, in place of Anthony Richardson, sequestered probably in 1646. In March 1648 a list of elders of the classis of Wells and Bruton in Somerset includes the name of Henry Alben of Upton, almost certainly Upton Noble, a small parish adjoining Batcombe. This was surely Albin,

who in the same year signed the attestation issued by supporters of presbyterianism among the clergy of Somerset.

Nothing is known of Albin's life during the 1650s, but he was ejected from West Camel and, perhaps just after the Restoration, acquired a curacy at Donyatt, near Ilminster, Somerset. Having paid a clerical subsidy there in 1661 he was ejected the following year. In 1665 he was at his native Batcombe, teaching four or five boys. In 1669 he was reported to be preaching in several west-country meeting-places, notably the house of Thomas Moore, MP for Heytesbury, and at Glastonbury, where meetings of 300 people were said to take place 'in a barne belonging to John Austin, where a pulpit and seats are built' (*Calamy rev.*, 4). In 1672 he was licensed to preach at Spargrove, where Moore's house also received a licence.

All that is known of Albin's personal life is that his second wife, Mary, died in or before 1699, and that they had a daughter, Rachel, who married a Thomas Syms. Albin was listed as a preacher at Bruton and other places in 1687. His preface to *The dying pastor's last farewell to his friends in Froome Selwood, Shepton Mallet, Brewton, Wincalton and the adjacent parts* (1697) referred to 'his beloved friends and frequent hearers' in those places. Albin was living at Batcombe on 19 September 1696 when he signed his will, which left 20s. a year for five years towards the maintenance of ministers preaching in the house of his brother Samuel at Hengrove; his goods were valued at £214 9s. He died six days later at Batcombe and was probably buried there; the funeral sermon was preached by William Hopkins (d. 1700), also an ejected Somerset clergyman. Calamy wrote of Henry Albin as 'one of a large acquaintance and a very friendly temper … He had a majesty in his countenance, and yet was clothed in humility' (Calamy, *Abridgement*, 2.600).

STEPHEN WRIGHT

Sources *Calamy rev.* · E. Calamy, ed., *An abridgement of Mr. Baxter's history of his life and times, with an account of the ministers, &c., who were ejected after the Restauration of King Charles II*, 2nd edn, 2 vols. (1713) · Venn, *Alum. Cant.* · A. Gordon, ed., *Freedom after ejection: a review (1690–1692) of presbyterian and congregational nonconformity in England and Wales* (1917) · W. A. Shaw, *A history of the English church during the civil wars and under the Commonwealth, 1640–1660*, 2 vols. (1900) · G. L. Turner, ed., *Original records of early nonconformity under persecution and indulgence*, 3 vols. (1911–14) · Foster, *Alum. Oxon.* · H. Albin, *The dying pastor's last farewell to his friends in Froome Selwood, Shepton Mallet, Brewton, Wincalton and the adjacent parts* (1697) · M. W. Helms and J. P. Ferris, 'Moore, Thomas', HoP, *Commons, 1660–90*

Wealth at death £214 9s.: *Calamy rev.*

Albini, William de. *See* Aubigny, William d' (d. 1139); Aubigné, William d' (d. in or after 1148); Aubigny, William d', first earl of Arundel (d. 1176); Aubigny, William d' (c.1174–1221); Aubigné, William d' (d. 1236).

Albinus (d. 732), abbot of St Peter's and St Paul's, Canterbury, was an informant of Bede. What is known of him is derived almost entirely from Bede's *Historia ecclesiastica gentis Anglorum*. Albinus was a pupil of Archbishop Theodore and his coadjutor Hadrian, abbot of St Peter's and St Paul's. Their instruction of Albinus to a high standard in both Greek and Latin scriptures testifies to the depth of learning which the two had brought to England. On the death of Hadrian in 709 or 710, Albinus succeeded to the abbacy, being the first native Englishman who filled that post.

In two prefatory epistles to his *Historia ecclesiastica*, addressed to Albinus and to King Ceolwulf, Bede acknowledged the abbot's considerable contribution to his work, stating not only that he had received all his information about the Augustinian mission in Kent, and much of that on the East and West Saxons, East Anglia, and Northumbria, through Albinus, but that it was in fact through Albinus's prompting that he had undertaken the *Historia ecclesiastica* at all. However, Bede and Albinus probably never met, since they communicated both orally and in writing through the medium of Nothhelm, a priest of London. It is highly likely that the information that Nothhelm transmitted orally from Albinus to Bede included the Kentish royal genealogy which Bede gives (*Hist. eccl.*, 2.5), and probably also the account of the flight of Paulinus with Æthelburh and her children from Northumbria to Kent—Albinus would have seen the church treasure they brought with them (*Hist. eccl.*, 2.20). Among the written sources, Nothhelm himself caused to be copied Gregorian and other papal letters in Rome, and delivered these to Bede on Albinus's advice. Bede's use of the archaic 'Uurtigernus' for Vortigern (*Hist. eccl.*, 1.14) shows that Albinus had also provided a glossed Canterbury text of Gildas's *De excidio et conquestu Britanniae*—a text which, on linguistic grounds, must have been based on British sources from before *c.*600. This work must have reached Bede before 725, since a similar archaic form of the name Vortigern appears in his *De temporum ratione*, written in that year. Albinus died in 732, and was buried beside his master, Hadrian, at Canterbury.

MARIOS COSTAMBEYS

Sources *Venerabilis Baedae opera historica*, ed. C. Plummer, 1 (1896), 3 · Bede, *Hist. eccl.*, preface; 1.14; 2.5, 20; 4.2; 5.20 · 'Bedae chronica majora ad a. DCCXXV, eiusdem chronica minora ad a. DCCIII', *Chronica minora saec. IV. V. VI. VII.*, ed. T. Mommsen, 3, MGH Auctores Antiquissimi, 13 (Berlin, 1898), 223–354, esp. 303 · *William Thorne's chronicle of St Augustine's Abbey, Canterbury*, trans. A. H. Davis (1934), 24–5, 54 · J. M. Wallace-Hadrill, *Bede's Ecclesiastical history of the English people: a historical commentary*, OMT (1988), 20–21, 211–12 · K. Harrison, *The framework of Anglo-Saxon history* (1976), 123 · G. Henderson, *Bede and the visual arts* (1980), 4–5 [Jarrow Lecture] · D. N. Dumville, 'Sub-Roman Britain: history and legend', *History*, new ser., 62 (1977), 173–92 · M. Miller, 'Bede's use of Gildas', *EngHR*, 90 (1975), 241–61

Albright, Arthur (1811–1900), chemist and phosphorus manufacturer, was born on 3 March 1811 in Charlbury, Oxfordshire, into a Quaker family, the second son and sixth of ten children of William Albright, grocer and mercer of Charlbury, and his wife, Rachel Tanner of Woodborough, Somerset. He was educated at schools in Rochester and privately at home, and then at the age of sixteen became apprenticed to his uncle, a chemist and druggist in Bristol. He did not settle to this life and had a number of activities, including travel to France and Belgium, studying other industries such as beet growing. For a while he worked for a Bristol printer and publisher.

In 1842 Albright joined the firm of John and Edward Sturge, manufacturing chemists in Birmingham, a town congenial to enterprising dissenters because it did not tolerate the limitations on the holding of municipal office imposed on them in the older charter cities. The firm expanded its scope in 1844 to make white phosphorus (from bone-ash), the main outlet for which was the making of matches. The match, as a simple, reliable source of fire, was one of the great technical innovations of the nineteenth century, a fact which explains the importance of Albright's industrial activity. However, the white phosphorus matches were dangerous and their manufacture a serious danger to health. In the course of travels to find sources of bone-ash Albright met Anton Schrötter (1802–1875), who had published in 1850 a good method of making the red, or amorphous, form of phosphorus, which was much less reactive than the white form. Albright purchased the patents, and then took out his own on improvements to Schrötter's method. He was thus able to make, economically, this form of phosphorus which was a main factor in bringing about the widespread use of safety matches.

In September 1848 Albright married Rachel (*d.* 1899), daughter of George Stacey of Tottenham. They had four sons and four daughters. They lived mainly in fine houses not far from his factories. In 1851, in an area already much industrialized (Oldbury in Worcestershire), the Sturge brothers opened a new phosphorus plant, which Albright took over at the end of 1854. In 1856 he went into partnership with J. W. Wilson (1834–1907), who married his wife's sister, Catherine Stacey, in 1857. The firm Albright and Wilson survived until the middle of the twentieth century. Albright travelled all through his working life, in eastern Europe in the early 1850s and in western Europe thereafter, promoting the use of red phosphorus, for example by showing specimens at exhibitions, first in the 1851 Great Exhibition, then in the Paris *expositions* from 1855 onwards. In his widespread business dealings for an expanding export business he developed a good command of several European languages, for which he had shown a facility in childhood. Seeking sources of raw materials and expanding his export trade he visited Europe more than a hundred times, Egypt once, and the USA several times.

Albright was a dedicated and effective philanthropist, his early interest in phosphorus having grown out of a concern for the health of match workers. He concerned himself with alleviating the slave-like conditions of black people in the West Indies, and when war broke out in the United States in 1861 he worked at getting financial and material support for emancipated slaves. He was also active in alleviating distress in France following the devastation of the Franco-Prussian War. In later life he expanded this social interest, even attempting to enter parliament; he stood as a candidate for East Worcestershire in 1874, but his platform, based on proposals to deal with the health problems of prostitution near garrisons and naval establishments, attracted little support. He was an active member of the Arbitration Society, believing that the kind of process which proved successful in settling some international disputes, such as the Alabama arbitration of 1871, should become general. He supported Gladstone in opposing the jingoistic agitation of 1877–8 when a Russo-Turkish war was feared, but parted from him on some of his domestic policies. Albright died in Cheyne Walk, Chelsea, London, while on a visit to his daughter Dora (Lady Scott-Moncrieff), on 3 July 1900. He was buried at Witton, Birmingham.

FRANK GREENAWAY

Sources R. E. Threlfall, *The story of 100 years of phosphorus making, 1851–1951* (1951) • P. J. T. Morris and C. A. Russell, *Archives of the British chemical industry, 1750–1914: a handlist* (1988)
Archives Albright and Wilson Ltd, Oldbury, Birmingham • Birm. CA, family papers of Albrights of Edgbaston • Birm. CA, letters to his family, mainly while on business trips abroad
Likenesses P. Bigland, oils, repro. in Threlfall, *Story of 100 years of phosphorus making*, frontispiece
Wealth at death £112,305 9s. 5d.: probate, 7 Aug 1900, CGPLA Eng. & Wales

Alcester. For this title name *see* Seymour, Frederick Beauchamp Paget, Baron Alcester (1821–1895).

Alchfrith [Ealhfrith] (*fl. c.*655–*c.*665), sub-king of Deira, was the son of *Oswiu, king of Northumbria (d. 670), and of Rhiainfellt, granddaughter of Rhun, king of Rheged. He became sub-king of the Deirans under Oswiu, c.655, after the battle of Winwæd. In the 650s he married Cyneburh, the daughter of Penda, king of the Mercians, no doubt in an attempt by the two previously warring kingdoms to cement a peaceful alliance.

Alchfrith's involvement in ecclesiastical politics probably brought about his downfall. Initially, like his father, he adhered to the customs of the Ionan church in matters such as the keeping of Easter, but, after he became sub-king of the Deirans (and no doubt also as a result of his marriage), he came into contact with the rulers of southern kingdoms who adhered to the Roman tradition. Cenwalh, king of the Gewisse of the Thames valley (a tribe converted by the Frankish Bishop Agilbert), was his friend, and, c.658, recommended Wilfrid to him. Thereby Alchfrith was brought under the charismatic influence of someone whose recent continental travels had caused him to embrace Roman orthodoxy and to despise the different observance of the Irish and Britons as practically schismatic.

By the 660s the divisions of ecclesiastical custom in the Northumbrian church had become an acute problem. Alchfrith had presented to monks trained at Lindisfarne an estate of 40 hides for a monastic foundation at Ripon; but soon afterwards they renounced the site rather than change their Irish customs, as Alchfrith desired, and the foundation was given to Wilfrid. At that time, and perhaps not uninvolved in the transactions, Bishop Agilbert of the West Saxons was staying with Alchfrith and so was at hand to ordain the monk Wilfrid as a priest. At the Synod of Whitby which succeeded this event, in 664, Alchfrith, with Wilfrid and Agilbert, supported the protagonists of Roman custom; and after the success of their cause, Alchfrith sent Wilfrid to Francia to be consecrated as bishop for his people. At that point Alchfrith disappears from history.

Much of Alchfrith's life remains a mystery. At some stage in the 660s he wished to travel to Rome with Benedict Biscop, but his father forbade this. Bede tells that at one point Alchfrith waged war on his father, but whether this was after the Synod of Whitby and resulted in his death, or long before, is unknown. It seems unlikely that he disappeared into monastic life, since neither Bede nor Stephen of Ripon (Eddius Stephanus) mentions this; but his name has been read, together with that of his wife, on the famous cross at Bewcastle in Cumbria, and it is possible that he died either in banishment or in battle near to the border of his mother's kingdom. He would appear to have been succeeded in Deira by his half-brother *Ecgfrith.

ROSEMARY CRAMP

Sources Bede, *Hist. eccl.*, 3.14, 21, 25, 28 • E. Stephanus, *The life of Bishop Wilfrid*, ed. and trans. B. Colgrave (1927) • *Venerabilis Baedae opera historica*, ed. C. Plummer, 2 vols. (1896) • John of Worcester, *Chron.*

Alchin, William Turner (1790–1865), antiquary, was born at St Mary-at-Hill, Billingsgate, London. For some years he practised as a solicitor at Winchester, and during the latter part of his residence there (c.1825–1845) he compiled indexes to the ecclesiastical registers of that city and of Salisbury. These indexes have been of considerable importance to genealogists and antiquaries. Upon the retirement of William Herbert from the Guildhall Library, London, in 1845, Alchin was appointed to the office of librarian there, and he continued to hold it until his death (apparently unmarried) at his home, Whitehead's Grove, Chelsea, London, on 3 February 1865. His indexes to the ancient records of the corporation of London, and his calendar of the wills enrolled in the court of hustings of London, were of great value to scholars.

THOMPSON COOPER, *rev.* H. C. G. MATTHEW

Sources *City Press* (11 Feb 1865) • *ILN* (25 Feb 1865), 191 • Boase, *Mod. Eng. biog.*
Archives BL, indexes to the episcopal registers of Winchester, Egerton MSS 2031–2034 • Bodl. Oxf., corresp.
Wealth at death under £1500: probate, 31 May 1865, CGPLA Eng. & Wales

Alchmund. *See* Alhmund (d. 781).

Alcindor, John (1873–1924), general practitioner and leader of the African Progress Union, was born on 8 or 9 July 1873 in Port of Spain, Trinidad, the son of Francis Alcindor, cocoa planter. Almost nothing is known of his parents, though there were funds to pay for his schooling and medical studies. The family's African ancestry was suggested by Alcindor's dark complexion. Educated at St Mary's College, Port of Spain, Alcindor won an island scholarship in 1892, which paid for his fare to Britain and three years of studies. He was at Edinburgh University from October 1893, and in Glasgow—at the fever and eye hospitals, and at Anderson's College, to study mental diseases—graduating MB BCh in July 1899.

Alcindor worked in a series of London hospitals from October 1899, including Paddington Infirmary (1899), St Mary's, Plaistow (1900), the North London Hospital for Consumption (1901), and the hospital of St Francis (1902), and also in west London, before establishing his practice in Paddington about 1907. In 1911 he married the journalist Minnie Amy Clara Mary Martin (*b.* 1879), daughter of Louis Martin, architect; they had three sons who were educated at Catholic schools, despite their mother's free-thinking beliefs. Alcindor remained a staunch Catholic and regular churchgoer.

Alcindor's research on influenza was published in the *General Practitioner* in 1907, on cancer in the *British Medical Journal* in 1908, and on tuberculosis in *The Practitioner* in 1913. Known locally as 'the black doctor', he was one of Paddington's four district medical officers between 1917 and 1923. In this capacity he visited the poor in their homes or saw them at his Harrow Road practice. This personal service was under review by the Ministry of Health, which preferred such patients to be treated as out-patients at hospital. Despite the British Medical Association's support for Alcindor and his colleagues, he resigned in 1923.

By 1924 Alcindor had become secretary of the Poor Law Medical Officers' Association. He was a member of the National Council for Combating Venereal Disease, the American Anti-Tuberculosis Society, and the Catholic doctors' society. He was also awarded the Red Cross war medal for the considerable time he had spent meeting trainloads of wounded soldiers in London.

Alcindor attended the London Pan-African Conference in 1900 and was a friend of the Anglo-African composer Samuel Coleridge-Taylor. He met the composer's musical friends from America and attended his funeral in 1912. In mid-1921 Alcindor became publicly linked to the African Progress Union, a black-led London group founded in 1918. Alcindor led the union between 1921 and 1924, guiding students and protesting against ignorance and bigotry in business, politics, and the press. He also formed connections with black Americans and Africans who met in London, most notably at the Pan-African congresses of 1921 and 1923.

In 1923 Alcindor's protests to the Colonial Office focused its attention on the death of Kitosh, a servant of Jasper Abraham, a farmer in Kenya who had beaten Kitosh but who was found innocent of his death by a white jury. Information had reached Alcindor through an old London contact, Joseph Agard, born in British Guiana and trained in England as a barrister, who now worked in Mombasa. Alcindor referred to an earlier death and told the colonial secretary, 'We press for some investigation into these verdicts' (Alcindor to the duke of Devonshire, 17 Sept 1923, PRO).

Alcindor's African Progress Union committee included the American composer Edmund Jenkins, who settled in London in 1914; John Barbour-James, born in British Guiana and an officer in the postal service in colonial Ghana (1901–17); Agatha Acham Chen from Martinique, the wife of the lawyer Eugene Chen, whose children were completing their education in London while her husband worked for Chinese republican causes; Emma Smith from Sierra Leone, who had been a London resident for some decades; and Dr Alanu Ojo Olaribigbe, a Glasgow-educated Sierra Leonean whose practice was in London. Alcindor also had links with black people from the French colonies and with white liberal groups such as the Anti-Slavery Society and the International Bureau for the Protection of Native Races.

Alcindor died on 25 October 1924 in St Mary's Hospital, Paddington. His widow then ran residential accommodation for Africans in London. JEFFREY GREEN

Sources J. Green, 'West Indian doctors in London', *Journal of Caribbean History*, 20 (1986), 49–77 · J. Green, 'John Alcindor, 1873–1924: a migrant's biography', *Immigrants and Minorities*, 6 (1987), 174–89 · *The medical who's who* (1925) · private information (2004) · letter from Alcindor to the duke of Devonshire, 17 Sept 1923, PRO, CO 533/305/46261 · medical examination book, 1899, U. Edin.
Archives U. Edin., MSS
Likenesses photograph, *c.*1915, repro. in *British sports and sportsmen: cricket and football* (1917), 352 · photographs, *c.*1922, repro. in A. Ali, ed., *Third world impact* (1988), 234, 240
Wealth at death £3781 19s. 6d.: probate, 3 Feb 1925, *CGPLA Eng. & Wales*

Alcock, Charles William (1842–1907), sports administrator and writer, was born on 2 December 1842 at 10 Norfolk Street, Sunderland, the second child of six sons and three daughters of Charles Alcock (*d.* 1881), a shipowner and later a shipbroker and insurance broker, and his wife, Elizabeth Alcock, *née* Forster (*d.* 1890). He was educated at Walter Todd preparatory school in Woodford, and from 1855 to 1859 at Harrow School, following his elder brother, John Forster Alcock. Both were keen footballers and in 1859 the two formed the Forest club. John attended the inaugural meeting of the Football Association (FA) in 1863. In the same year *Bell's Life* noted that 'the play of Mr C. Alcock of the Forest club elicited great applause'. He stood just under 6 feet and weighed 13 stone 6 lb, and he was 'an excellent dribbler and goal getter, very hard to knock off the ball, and as hard a worker as he was enthusiastic'. He took a lead in founding the Wanderers in 1863, an Old Harrovian side which replaced Forest and won the FA cup five times between 1872 and 1878. He represented England against Scotland at the Oval in 1870 and captained them in the same fixture in 1875, acting as the cup final referee a week later. As a referee he was reputed to be good-natured and indulgent to offenders, and he was the first president of the Referees Association. 'A jovial comrade full of football anecdote', he also enjoyed athletics and golf, and played cricket for the Gentlemen of Essex. Wisden (1908) records that he was 'a steady bat, a fair change fast bowler, and an excellent long stop' and that he once had 'the curious experience of captaining France against Germany at a match in Hamburg'.

However, it is less as a player than as a prodigiously energetic sports administrator and journalist that Alcock is now remembered. He was undoubtedly the most important figure of his time in the shaping of association football and almost as influential in the development of cricket. As the only official with real power in both emergent summer and winter national sports during their formative years, he was the *éminence grise* of English sport. He was elected to the committee of the recently formed FA in 1866 at the age of twenty-three, and became its secretary in 1870, a position he held for twenty-five years, the first

Charles William Alcock (1842–1907), by James Russell & Sons

seventeen of which were unpaid. He was also the president of the Surrey FA, vice-president of the London FA and, in addition to his extensive responsibilities as secretary of Surrey County Cricket Club, he was also chairman of the Richmond Athletic Association and vice-president of Royal Mid-Surrey Golf Club.

Alcock's first love was football, which was then just emerging, as he later recalled, from 'the rough and semi-barbarous sport' of the previous century. The game was remarkably fortunate in its young advocate, who after scarcely a year in office devised the rules for the FA cup on the basis of the knock-out house competitions he had known at Harrow. He also took a lead in organizing the first unofficial international match between England and Scotland at the Oval in November 1870 and umpired the first official encounter two years later in Glasgow. Although quite badly injured two weeks before the game, he travelled with the team at his own expense 'through the night in draughty carriages with hard seats' to attend a goalless draw played at the West of Scotland cricket club at Partick.

The sport prospered mightily. 'What was ten or fifteen years ago the recreation of a few has now become the pursuit of thousands', Alcock observed on receiving a testimonial from the FA committee in April 1881 'in consideration of his having been the founder of the Association game'. Recalling the early opposition to football in the medical journal The Lancet and elsewhere, he moved on

with typical directness to the new problems of success, of gate money, professionalism, and the relations between north and south. 'The time had arrived to settle the question', for it was evident in the Lancashire cotton towns that players were being paid and 'Scotch professors' imported by teams such as Preston North End, who were suspended by the FA in 1884. The FA committee, mostly staunch public school amateurs, were for a firm line against professionalism. Alcock took a different view: calm, practical, genial, and effective, and drawing on his extensive experience of cricket, he saw the inevitability of the advent of the professional player. Although an amateur himself, he objected to the argument 'that it is immoral to work for a living'—even if that work took the form of sport. He twice proposed the legalizing of professionalism under strict controls before it was accepted in July 1885, thus averting a schism of the kind that afflicted rugby ten years later. Professionalism was permitted under strict controls and amateur influence preserved. When in 1888 a professional football league was proposed—almost the only major innovation of the time that was not of his devising—Alcock proved agreeable, his journalistic instinct for the commercial spectacle overcoming his residual amateur scruples. It was thus that the distinctive and durable dual structure of English football was born.

Remarkably, Alcock was just as active in cricket as in football. In 1872, the year of the first cup final and official international, he became secretary of Surrey, a post he held for the rest of his life. During this time the county enjoyed great success, winning eight county championships between 1887 and 1895. Alcock, a shrewd and flexible man, appointed the amateur W. W. Read as assistant secretary to 'secure the services of one of the very best cricketers Surrey ever had'. But he also took care to keep the professionals happy, encouraging crowd collections for great performances and introducing innovative 'star contracts' for top players such as Tom Hayward, George Lohmann, George Richardson, and Bobby Abel. Generous and pragmatic though he was, he expected deference from professionals and bridled when these four threatened to strike on the eve of the third test against Australia at the Oval in 1896 unless their match fee of £10 was doubled. The players backed down and apologized; Alcock admitted they had a case but rejected what he saw as 'a peremptory demand not a request for consideration'. His power within association football ensured that big FA fixtures came to the Oval, providing Surrey with a valuable source of income until 1895, when he supervised the building of a new pavilion and tavern. Completed within six months at a cost of £38,000, these helped to ensure the ground's future as a test venue.

Alcock always had an eye for the great event. Drawing on his experience in promoting international football, he arranged the first test match held in England, against Australia at the Oval in 1880. Two years later, again at the Oval under Alcock, the Australians returned with F. R. Spofforth, whose demolition of England inspired the legend of the Ashes. After the match N. L. Jackson, the founder of the Corinthians, saw Alcock 'sitting down on a huge iron safe, burying his head in his hands, oblivious to everything'. His breathless description of the defeat is memorable: 'Men who were noted for their coolness at critical moments were trembling like a leaf; some were shivering with cold; some even fainted. At times there was an awful silence' (W. A. Bettesworth, *Chats on the Cricket Field*, 1910, 23). Despite the England team's failure, the general arrangements for test matches were henceforth left in his hands by the MCC.

Alcock witnessed the Ashes test of 1882 as both an official and a journalist. Presumably reliant at first on family money, he soon established himself in the latter role and promoted the better conventions of what was then a new genre of writing. Although tending at times towards hyperbole, he was never crass and always readable. Writing not only supplemented his earnings as an administrator but also gave an outlet to his opinions and his feelings for the sports he loved. For thirty-five years he both made and reported the sporting news, exploiting his exceptional position to the full not just for his own ends—he was comfortably off and left over £3000 without making a large fortune—but also for the unity and prosperity of football and cricket. He began his journalistic career in his twenties, writing for *The Field* and *The Sportsman* before founding his own specialist magazines including a *Football Annual*, a *Football* magazine, and in 1882 the weekly *Cricket*. This has been described as 'the first viable national magazine solely devoted to cricket' (Sissons) and provided a model for future publications, mixing match reports with gossip and player profiles. Alcock also published several books, including *Football: the Association Game* (1890) and, with Viscount Alverstone, one of the first notable works of sports history, *Surrey Cricket: its History and Associations* (1902), known at the Oval as 'the Old Testament'.

Alcock married, on 19 December 1864, Eliza Caroline (1841–1937), daughter of Francis Webb Ovenden, watercolourist and marine painter. They had two sons and six daughters. He died on 26 February 1907 at his home at 7 Arundel Road, Brighton, and was survived by his wife and two of their daughters. He was buried on 2 March at Norwood cemetery in a plot acquired for his second son, Charles Ernest, who died at five months in 1874. In 1992 the Football Association agreed to adopt the grave of the man who, in the words of their official historian, was 'the forgotten father of English sport'. RICHARD HOLT

Sources A. Gibson and W. Pickford, *Association football and the men who made it*, 4 vols. [1905–6], vol. 3, pp. 135–7 • *The Times* (27 Feb 1907) • *Wisden* (1908), 132–3 • K. Booth, *The father of modern sport: the life and times of Charles W. Alcock* (2002) • B. Flanagan, *West Norwood's cemetery's sportsmen* (1995), 22–7 • B. Butler, *The official history of the Football Association* (1991), 5–20 • R. Sissons, *The players: a social history of the professional cricketer* (1988), 81, 105 • Lord Alverstone and C. W. Alcock, *Surrey cricket: its history and associations* (1902) • 'FA pay homage to forgotten father of English sport', *Daily Telegraph* (4 Dec 1992) • T. Mason, *Association football and English society, 1863–1915* (1980) • private information (2004) [K. R. Booth]
Likenesses postcard, 1893–7, Friends of Norwood cemetery, 79 Durban Road, London • J. Russell & Sons, photograph, Marylebone Cricket Club, Lord's, London [*see illus.*] • photograph, repro. in Butler, *Official history of the Football Association* • portrait, FA headquarters, Lancaster Gate
Wealth at death £3186 15s. 2d.: administration, 22 March 1907, CGPLA Eng. & Wales

Alcock, Edward (*fl.* 1745–1778), portrait and miniature painter, is first recorded in 1745, living in Liverpool with his mother. Nothing is known of his early life. In Liverpool he met the young carver and gilder Thomas Johnson, to whom he advanced money to set up in business *c.*1747; he later converted the loan into a short-lived partnership in Johnson's business as a carver. Alcock was next recorded in Bath in 1757. He led a peripatetic life; indeed the poet and landscape gardener William Shenstone described the painter as 'the most volatile of all creatures that have not wings' (NPG archive, Shenstone to Graves, 2 May 1761). He lived from 1759 to 1760 in Birmingham, where he may have been responsible for the portrait of George III displayed during the illuminations held there for the coronation. His patrons there included Mr Hylton, Captain Wight, and Shenstone. In 1760 he painted a full-length oil portrait of Shenstone (NPG), whose farming estate, The Leasowes, was close by. Alcock is mentioned in letters written by the poet in connection with a number of commissions. On 9 February 1760 Shenstone wrote to the Revd R. Graves:

> Alcock's portrait of me is in a manner finished … They say it is a likeness, allowing for the diminution of size. Indeed, if I can conclude any thing from the strong resemblance which he has produced of others here, I may conclude that he has not failed me. (*Letters*, 549)

Poet and painter were evidently well acquainted by this date and the letter continues 'I believe Alcock would go and settle at Bath, if Amos Green could be induced to join him' (ibid., 550). Shenstone's letter further implies that Green, a still-life painter who 'was esteemed inferior to no one in England for fruit' (ibid.), possibly worked closely with Alcock. Alcock was working once again for Shenstone in May 1761, 'improving the picture I [Shenstone] meant for Dodsley' (NPG archive, Shenstone to Graves, 2 May 1761). However, Shenstone did not think it would be easy to get Alcock to return to The Leasowes, implying that he had already moved, or intended to move soon.

It is not known whether Alcock returned to Bath, but he may well have travelled in the area as Thomas Chatterton wrote a poem entitled 'Mr Alcock of Bristol, an Excellent Miniature Painter' in 1769. By 1778 he was in London, where from 2 Craig's Court, Charing Cross, he exhibited a number of small portraits and genre paintings at the Royal Academy and Free Society of Artists. However, his connections with Birmingham remained strong, for in June of that year he wrote to the Birmingham manufacturer Matthew Bolton about a portrait commission and he was also evidently making pictures to be reproduced at Bolton's factory using the polygraph method. The date and place of Alcock's death are not known.

DEBORAH GRAHAM-VERNON

Sources Waterhouse, *18c painters* • artist's file, NPG, Heinz Archive and Library • *The letters of William Shenstone*, ed. M. Williams (1939) • Graves, *RA exhibitors* • *The complete poetical works of Thomas*

Chatterton, ed. H. D. Roberts, 2 vols. (1906) • J. Kerslake, *National Portrait Gallery: early Georgian portraits*, 2 vols. (1977) • private information (2004)

Alcock, George Eric Deacon (1912–2000), astronomer, was born on 28 August 1912 at 59 London Road, Fletton, Peterborough, the eldest of the four sons of George William Alcock (1880/81–1958), railwayman, and his wife, Jane (Jennie) Deacon (1875/6–1943), dressmaker. He was educated in Peterborough at Oundle Road infant school (1917–20) and New Fletton council school (1920–25), from whose playground he watched the partial solar eclipse of 8 April 1921. This inspired him with such enthusiasm for astronomy and natural history that his parents (serious-minded Baptists) economized so that he might attend Fletton grammar school (1925–9). After a year as a student teacher he completed a teaching course at the City of Leeds Training College (1930–32).

Until 1937, when Alcock secured a permanent job at Old Fletton council school, he did such supply teaching as was available locally while living at home and keeping himself busy with his studies of flora, fauna, church architecture, and the cosmos. Having joined the British Astronomical Association (BAA) in 1931 he borrowed a telescope, made a weather station in his back garden to predict clear skies, and began to survey heavenly bodies on a regular basis. His precise observation of meteor paths helped the BAA compute the orbit of dust streams around the sun.

Enlisting in the RAF in 1940 Alcock served in north Africa and Italy as a radio telegraph operator and meteorologist with the rank of corporal. His marriage to Mary Green (1907–1991), an infant school teacher, took place on 7 June 1941. The couple moved into a newly built house called Antares in Farcet, Huntingdonshire, 2 miles south of Peterborough, in 1947, after he had reclaimed his job at Old Fletton school on demobilization the previous year. A strict yet cheerful and popular master Alcock taught mainly ten- and eleven-year olds and organized many extra-curricular activities. He was a history and geography teacher at Fletton secondary modern school (1959–65) and later worked at Southfields county junior school before retiring in 1977.

Throughout these years Alcock continued his methodical stargazing. On coming home from school he would sleep for a few hours and then, weather permitting, sit in a deckchair in the garden and view the night sky from 8.15 p.m. until 1 a.m. or 3 a.m. He realized that the new radio telescope at Jodrell Bank had made tracking meteors by eye superfluous for scientific purposes, so in 1953 he set himself the new challenge of spotting an unknown comet. This was ambitious, for none had been discovered from Britain since 1894. Many times he came close to giving up, especially after his wife was crippled by a fall in December 1958 (they had no children to help with her care). Patient and dogged, George acquired a pair of 25 × 105 mm binoculars in January 1959 that crucially broadened his field of vision. On 25 August 1959 a fuzzy patch in the evening sky in the constellation of Corona Borealis signified success: it was the tenth magnitude comet, henceforth to be known as Comet Alcock 1959e. Just five

days later, on 30 August, he identified a second one, this time in Cancer. Press and television interviews followed—not that he ever courted publicity; his goal was to increase knowledge.

Alcock detected a third comet, in Cygnus, on 19 March 1963 and a fourth, in Hercules, on 26 September 1965. By then, however, his chief ambition was to discover a nova (an exploding star). Visual nova discoveries were extremely uncommon: astronomers normally found them only by analysing survey photographs long after their appearance, which was regrettable, for the period immediately following the explosion was the most valuable for observation. Such was Alcock's familiarity with the night sky that he believed himself capable of recognizing any star that began to shine more brightly than usual. Confounding sceptics he found his first nova in Delphinus on 8 July 1967. Then came Nova Vulpeculae (15 April 1968), Nova Scuti (31 July 1970), and another in Vulpecula (21 October 1976).

In his seventies, against conventional advice, Alcock decided to observe the sky from indoors on frosty nights, so it was through a double-glazed bedroom window that he sighted Comet IRAS-Araki-Alcock on 3 May 1983. Eight days later it passed closer to the earth than any comet since 1770. Nova Herculis, his final major find, on 25 March 1991, excited scientists by fading remarkably fast.

George Alcock set a British record by discovering five comets and five novae. He received BAA and Royal Astronomical Society awards and was appointed MBE in 1979. In 1987 the International Astronomical Union named asteroid 3174 after him. Many astronomers declared that his photographic memory of the patterns of some 30,000 stars was unique. He died at the District Hospital, Peterborough, on 15 December 2000.   JASON TOMES

Sources K. Williams, *Under an English heaven: the life of George Alcock* (1996) • *The Times* (6 Jan 2001) • *The Guardian* (26 Jan 2001) • D. Buczynski, 'The passing of a legend', *Astronomy Now* (June 2001), 33–4 • b. cert. • m. cert. • d. cert. • *CGPLA Eng. & Wales* (2001)
Likenesses photographs, repro. in Williams, *Under an English heaven*
Wealth at death under £210,000—gross; under £25,000—net: probate, 13 March 2001, *CGPLA Eng. & Wales*

Alcock, John (1430–1500), administrator and bishop of Ely, was born at Beverley, Yorkshire, the son of William Alcock of Hull. Alcock received his early schooling in the grammar school attached to Beverley Minster, and then attended Cambridge University. DCL by 1459, he began his career in local diocesan administration in London. On 16 December 1468 he was admitted to the prebend of Browneswood in St Paul's, but possibly more noteworthy was his admission to the prebend of North Alton in Salisbury Cathedral, the first sign that he had attracted any wider attention. On 20 April 1469 the crown appointed him to a panel to hear an appeal in a debt case, and on 13 and 20 January 1470 similarly in cases from the court of admiralty.

Hitherto Alcock had enjoyed a respectable but largely anonymous career: now it accelerated dramatically, for reasons probably relating to the readeption of Henry VI or, more precisely, to Edward IV's recovery. On 26 April 1471, by which date Edward had defeated the earl of Warwick but had still to defeat Margaret of Anjou, Alcock was appointed dean of the royal free chapel of St Stephen, Westminster. On 29 April, with the king still away on campaign, Alcock was appointed keeper of the rolls of chancery, despite no known experience in royal government. These were two, obviously linked, marks of strong favour, bringing Alcock from the fringes of royal circles into somewhere near their heart. It must be speculated that his behaviour during the readeption had in some way earned him the warm approval of the exiled king, whether as an exile himself or perhaps after the fashion of Thomas Millyng, abbot of Westminster, whose sympathy towards Queen Elizabeth Woodville while she was in his sanctuary, won him very similar preferment and promotion in his career at this time. Following involvement in Anglo-Scottish diplomacy later in 1471 Alcock was papally provided to Rochester on 8 January 1472 and consecrated on 15 March. Although he resigned as keeper of the rolls, he was now an active servant of the king, especially in the heavy preparations for the proposed invasion of France. From 20 September 1472 to 18 June 1473 he had the keeping of the great seal; Bishop Robert Stillington of Bath and Wells, who was chancellor, 'did nothing except through his pupil [discipulum], John Alcock' (Pronay and Cox, 133), as another leading official would recall. From 10 June to 29 September 1475, while the expedition finally took place, Alcock acted as chancellor in England, since Bishop Thomas Rotherham of Lincoln, the incumbent, accompanied the king into France; for this Alcock received £100.

Meantime Alcock had taken on a longer-term responsibility. As early as 8 July 1471 he had been appointed an administrator of the infant Prince Edward's holdings in Wales, Cornwall, and Cheshire, last but one of the fifteen nominees, but only behind the greatest in the realm who were unlikely to pay much close attention. Now, on 10 November 1473 he was appointed tutor to the three-year-old Prince Edward, and also president of his council which was being set up at Ludlow to oversee the marches and the principality of Wales. To this he gave most of his attention for the next decade. On 15 July 1476 Alcock was translated to the see of Worcester, allowing him some easier access to oversee his diocese even while so much at Ludlow.

Nothing is known of Alcock's reaction to the deposition of his pupil in June 1483 by Richard of Gloucester; he was not arrested, but it seems unlikely that he enjoyed the confidence of the new king. That he helped negotiate the marriage alliance with Scotland at Nottingham in September 1484 did not make him a traitorous collaborator in the eyes of the king's enemies, and Henry VII's accession saw confirmation of the esteem Alcock enjoyed in old Edwardian and new Tudor circles. On 7 October 1485 he was appointed chancellor of the realm, and on 7 November opened the king's first parliament with a sermon. In June and July 1486 in London he led a delegation that agreed a three-year truce with Scotland. On 6 October 1486 he was translated to the very rich and easily managed

see of Ely. He was selected to perform the baptism of Arthur, first son of Henry VII and Elizabeth. On 6 March 1487 Archbishop John Morton, now returned from exile, took over the great seal, but Alcock remained a trusted royal councillor.

Ely, however, provided special pleasures. As early as November 1486 the prior and monks obtained certain rights from the king in relation to choosing their own coroners—privileges derived, they were to understand, from Henry's personal affection for their new bishop. Cambridge University, of which Alcock was now visitor ex officio, saw much of him. On the first Sunday in Lent (23 February) 1488 he preached in Great St Mary's, starting at 1 p.m. and finishing after 3 p.m. In 1491–2 and 1492–3 he even took up extended residence in Peterhouse, of which he was ex officio patron. However, his affection for the college preceded this official connection: as far back as 1481 he had presented it with fifty-five manuscripts (of which forty-five are still there). Alcock shared in the current vogue for enlarging Cambridge University. He secured the site and buildings of a dissolved nunnery, St Radegund's, restored and converted the buildings, scattered his rebus liberally, endowed £70 p.a. in lands, and on 12 June 1496 established a college to support six priest fellows and 'a certain number of boys' (VCH Cambridgeshire, 3.421), dedicated to Radegund, the Blessed Virgin, and St John the Evangelist, but commonly known as Jesus College.

Alcock enjoyed building projects and endowments. On 22 November 1479 he received a royal licence to found a chantry and school in the grounds of Holy Trinity, Hull, where his father was buried; handsomely endowed, it was to become Hull grammar school. While at Worcester he had led the rebuilding of the church of Little Malvern Priory. He built a new great hall for the episcopal palace in Ely, and improved considerably the bishop's manor house at Downham. After he died on 1 October 1500 at Wisbech Castle, he was buried in his best-known building, his glorious chantry chapel towards the east end of Ely Cathedral, which he had designed and started, although it took until 1508 to complete.

Alcock was the author of a number of works, four published by Wynkyn de Worde in 1496–7: Mons perfeccionis, the Hyll of Perfeccion (STC, 1475–1640, 278–81); In die innocencium sermo pro episcopo puerorum (ibid., 282–3); an English sermon on the text, 'Qui habet aures audiendi, audiat' (Luke 8: 8; STC, 1475–1640, 284–5); and Desponsacio virginis Christo: Spousage of a Virgin to Cryste, being an 'exhortacyon made to relygyous systers' (STC, 1475–1640, 286–7). Other works included Gallicantus ad confratres suos curatos in sinodo apud Barnwell (25 September 1499), a charge to his diocese but deemed worthy of publication by Richard Pynson (ibid., 277), and 'The Abbay of the Holy Gost' (BL, Harley MSS 1704 art. 9, 2406 art. 41). He is associated with the translation of Pierre Gringore's Château de Labour, with which the name of Alexander Barclay, a monk of Ely, is linked; Alcock may have sponsored or encouraged his effort, and Barclay in his Eclogues 1 and 3 later recalled and lamented the bishop.

Alcock was of a generation of churchmen who sought to

renovate contemporary faith and religion within a strictly Catholic frame. Even the censorious protestant John Bale recalled him as one who 'having devoted himself from childhood to learning and piety, made such a proficiency in virtue that no one in England had a greater reputation for sanctity'; he had spent his life in vigils, study, abstinence, and in the subjugation of the temptations of the flesh (Bale, *Cat.*, x.xx). Alcock's register as bishop of Worcester is in that diocese's record office, while his Ely register is in Cambridge University Library (calendar by J. H. Crosby, *Ely Diocesan Remembrancer*, 1908–10).

R. J. SCHOECK

Sources *Chancery records* · Emden, *Cam.*, 5–6 · J. Gairdner, ed., *Letters and papers illustrative of the reigns of Richard III and Henry VII*, 2 vols., Rolls Series, 24 (1861–3) · W. Campbell, ed., *Materials for a history of the reign of Henry VII*, 2 vols., Rolls Series, 60 (1873–7) · Fuller, *Worthies* (1811) · C. L. Scofield, *The life and reign of Edward the Fourth*, 2 vols. (1923) · C. A. J. Skeel, *The council in the marches of Wales: a study in local government during the 16th and 17th centuries* (1904), 21–9 · *Fasti Angl.*, *1300–1541*, [Monastic cathedrals] · *VCH Cambridgeshire and the Isle of Ely*, vol. 3 · T. A. Walker, *A biographical register of Peterhouse men*, 2 vols. (1927–30) · J. Bale, *Illustrium Maioris Britannie scriptorum … summarium* (1548) · *The eclogues of Alexander Barclay*, ed. B. White, EETS, original ser., 175 (1928) · J. B. Mullinger, *The University of Cambridge*, 1 (1873) · W. D. Sweeting, *The cathedral church of Ely* (1901) · J. H. Crosby, ed., 'Ely episcopal registers', *Ely Diocesan Remembrancer* (1908–10), 277–304 [orig. CUL, MS EDK G/1/6] · J. Alcock, bishop's register, Worcs. RO · N. Pronay and J. Cox, eds., *The Crowland chronicle continuations, 1459–1486* (1986) · Bale, *Cat.*
Archives BL, Add. MS 5827 · BL, Harley MSS 1704 art. 9, 2406 art. 41 · Inner Temple, London, papers · Worcs. RO, register | CUL, MS EDK G/1/6
Likenesses J. Faber senior, mezzotint, 1714 (after unknown portrait), BM, NPG · oils, Jesus College, Cambridge

Alcock, John (1715–1806), organist and composer, was born at the family home, Crane Court, St Peter's Hill, London, on 11 April 1715, the third of the eight children of Daniel Alcock (*bap.* 1686) and his wife, Mary. They lived only a stone's throw from St Paul's Cathedral, and it was there at the age of seven that the boy was admitted as a chorister under Charles King. In 1727 he sang at the coronation of George II, and, two years later, was formally apprenticed to the blind organist John Stanley, only three years his senior, whose friendship and support he enjoyed until May 1786 when Stanley died.

When his articles expired in 1736, Alcock tried unsuccessfully for a couple of City organistships, but it was to be another twelve months before he gained his first professional appointment, as organist of St Andrew's Church in Plymouth. With a job in the offing, he married Margaret Beaumont (1711–1792) on 20 May 1737, and it was in Plymouth that the first three of their children were born. There too he produced *Six Suites of Lessons* for the harpsichord (1741), which, like almost all his later works, was published by subscription. In January 1742 the Alcocks moved to Reading where the mayor and corporation, acting on the advice of Stanley, had invited him to take over the new organ in St Laurence's Church. *Twelve English Songs* came out in 1743 and was followed seven years later by a set of *Six Concerto's in Seven Parts*, by which time too another five children had been born (with four more yet to

come); at least half of them died in infancy however. In 1746, with the backing of Stanley, Pepusch, William Turner, and John Robinson (organist of Westminster Abbey), Alcock applied for the vacant organistship of Salisbury Cathedral. He did not get it, but four years later he moved again (and again it seems by invitation), this time to Lichfield, where on 22 January 1750 he was installed as a vicar-choral of the cathedral and shortly afterwards made organist and master of the choristers as well. In both the Lichfield and Reading appointments it is clear that not only were his professional qualifications under consideration but his politics too. Fortunately, Alcock was a tory supporter, as is evident not only from the poll books of the 1753, 1754, 1755, and 1761 Lichfield elections, but also from his willingness to play the organ at the politically charged opening of the Radcliffe Camera at Oxford in April 1749. The borough of Reading too had an influential tory interest.

On his arrival in Staffordshire, Alcock found the music at a very low ebb, and, being the pedantic (and somewhat irascible) perfectionist he was, it was not long before he had fallen out rather disastrously with his Lichfield colleagues. A vivid impression of the problems as he saw them (and of the current state of cathedral music generally) is gained not only from the various essays with which he prefaced the several volumes of church music later produced, but also from his semi-autobiographical novel, *The Life of Miss Fanny Brown*, published under the pseudonym John Piper in 1761. Matters evidently came to a head in 1758 when the men of the choir petitioned the dean and chapter to admonish him for his general behaviour and 'Splenetic Tricks upon the Organ to expose or confound the Performers, or burlesque their Manner of Singing' (Shaw). But Alcock got the better of them in the end since, without risking his freehold place as vicar-choral, he nevertheless managed to divest himself of his more onerous duties as organist and master of the choristers. Quite when this happened is not entirely clear, but as vicar-choral he would remain a thorn in the flesh until his dying day.

In June 1755 Alcock took the BMus degree at Oxford, and he followed this up with the doctorate in 1766. From 1761 to 1786 (and with the periodic assistance of his sons) he served as organist of Sutton Coldfield parish church, and from 1766 to 1790 of Tamworth parish church as well. He was also sometime private organist to Arthur Chichester, fifth earl and first marquess of Donegal. Among several published volumes of church music, the most important, if only for its argumentative and self-justificatory preface, is his *Six and Twenty Select Anthems* (1771). Though hardly a very sociable man himself, he also turned out a large number of catches, canons, and glees (four of which won him Catch Club prizes at intervals during the 1770s), and a collection of such pieces (*Harmonia festi*) was issued in 1791. Alcock was also an ardent antiquary and collector of manuscripts. In 1752 he issued proposals for the quarterly publication in score of various services by Tallis, Byrd, and Gibbons, among others (with the possibility of anthems to follow), but, on learning that Maurice Greene had already embarked on a similar scheme (and was moreover planning to give one free copy to every cathedral and collegiate foundation in the land), Alcock backed off and generously handed his materials over to his rival. After fifty-five years of marriage his wife died (on 10 September 1792); Alcock himself, plagued by gout but still resident at 11 Vicars' Close, lived on until his death there on 23 February 1806. He was buried at Lichfield Cathedral.

John Alcock (*bap.* 1740, *d.* 1791), the eldest son of John and Margaret Alcock, was born in Plymouth and baptized there on 28 January 1740. As a chorister under his father at Lichfield Cathedral he learned to play the organ, and by the age of twelve he was evidently sufficiently accomplished to deputize for him on occasion. From 1758 to 1768 he was organist and master of the song school at Newark-on-Trent parish church. In 1766 he accompanied his father to Oxford, where, as John Alcock senior proceeded to his doctorate, he himself took a BMus degree. He also composed (and published) a number of songs and cantatas, together with some church music, various instrumental pieces, and other convivial items, and was from 1773 until his death in March 1791 organist of St Matthew's Church in Walsall. William, the youngest son (born 6 December 1756), was also a musician and organist of Newcastle under Lyme from 1781; the last surviving child of John and Margaret Alcock, he died at Liverpool on 16 December 1833.   H. DIACK JOHNSTONE

Sources P. Marr, 'The life and works of John Alcock (1715–1806)', PhD diss., U. Reading, 1978 · Eugenius [R. Bellamy], 'Biographical sketch of Dr. Alcock', *Monthly Mirror*, 4 (1797), 137–40 · J. Piper [J. Alcock], *The life of Miss Fanny Brown* (1761) · *GM*, 1st ser., 61 (1791), 383 [John Alcock jun.] · *GM*, 1st ser., 76 (1806), 286, 377 [John Alcock sen.] · H. W. Shaw, *The succession of organists of the Chapel Royal and the cathedrals of England and Wales from c.1538* (1991) · *New Grove* · W. Bingley, *Musical biography*, 2 (1814); repr. (1971), 236–40 · [Clarke], *The Georgian era: memoirs of the most eminent persons*, 4 vols. (1832–4) · P. Marr, 'John Alcock and Fanny Brown', *MT*, 118 (1977), 118–20 · P. Marr, 'John Alcock (1715–1806), vicar choral and organist at Lichfield Cathedral: a frustrated reformer', *Transactions of the South Staff. Archaeological and Historical Society*, 21 (1980), 25–33 · D. Dawe, *Organists of the City of London, 1666–1850* (1983)

Likenesses oils, *c.*1766, Royal College of Music, London · W. Newman, print (after stipple oval by R. Cooper), BM, NPG

Wealth at death valuable library to Revd John Parker, rector of St Botolph, Billingsgate

Alcock, John (*bap.* 1740, *d.* 1791). *See under* Alcock, John (1715–1806).

Alcock, Sir John William (1892–1919), aviator, was born at Basford House Cottage, Seymour Grove, Old Trafford, Manchester, on 6 November 1892, the eldest son of John Alcock, a domestic coachman and later a horsedealer, and his wife, Mary Whitelegg. He had a boyhood fascination with machines, and after attending the parish school at St Anne's on the Sea, Lancashire, he gained an apprenticeship at the Empress motor works in 1909. For a period in 1911 he worked for Norman Crossland, one of the founders of the Manchester Aero Club. When an aero engine was sent to Manchester for repair, Alcock had the opportunity to return with it to Brooklands in Surrey, where he became mechanic to the French pilot Maurice Ducrocq.

Sir John William Alcock (1892–1919), by Ambrose McEvoy, 1919

Taught to fly by Ducrocq, Alcock took his Royal Aero Club aviator's certificate (no. 368) at Brooklands in a Farman biplane on 26 November 1912. He was then employed by the Sunbeam motor-car company as a racing pilot, and regularly took part in races at Hendon. In July 1914 he competed against Harry Hawker and Frederick Raynham in a race from London to Manchester and back sponsored by the *Daily Mail*.

In November 1914 Alcock joined the Royal Naval Air Service as a warrant officer instructor, serving mostly at the Royal Naval Flying School at Eastchurch, Kent. Although he received his commission as a flight sub-lieutenant in December 1915, and was anxious to see active service, his flying experience was so valuable that he was retained at Eastchurch for another year. Among the pilots whom he trained during his two years as an instructor was Reginald Alexander John Warneford, the first naval pilot to be awarded the Victoria Cross.

In December 1916 Alcock was posted to 2 wing, royal naval air station, in the eastern Mediterranean. From the allied base at Mudros on the island of Lemnos he took part in long-distance bombing raids on targets in Turkish territory and on German targets in Macedonia. On 30 September 1917, flying a single-seater Sopwith F1 Camel, he earned the Distinguished Service Cross for a brave and skilful attack on three German seaplanes, two of which crashed into the sea. At 8.15 p.m. on the same day he set out in a Handley Page 0/100 bomber to attack Constantinople. One of his two engines failed over the Gallipoli peninsula, forcing him to turn back. After covering 60 miles with only one engine, he ditched in the sea, near Suvla Bay, where he and his two crew members remained afloat in the craft for two hours. Their Very lights failed to attract the attention of British destroyers, and as the plane began to sink they swam ashore. After hiding overnight, they were captured by the Turks the following noon, and held prisoner at Seraskerat prison in Constantinople. Alcock was later moved to the prisoner-of-war camp for officers at Kedos in Anatolia.

At the time of his capture Jack Alcock had devised the single-seat Alcock Scout biplane, which consisted of components from the Sopwith Triplane, Pup, and, according to some accounts, the Sopwith Camel. Armed with a single Lewis gun, it was intended to be powered by either a 100 hp Monosoupape or 100 hp Clerget rotary motor. Its first flight was made in the hands of another pilot, since Alcock was held captive, although news of its success was smuggled to him in prison. It was afterwards operated by 2 wing at Mudros during 1917–18.

Alcock was released by the Turks in September 1918 and reached London in December. He was passionate about flying and always hoped to do something outstanding. While imprisoned, he resolved to make an attempt to fly the Atlantic. In 1913 the *Daily Mail*, whose proprietor, Lord Northcliffe, was keen to promote aviation, had offered a prize of £10,000 to the first person to cross the Atlantic within seventy-two continuous hours. Competition was suspended during the war, but Northcliffe renewed the offer in July 1918; once hostilities ended in November, several manufacturers made plans to enter their aircraft. On demobilization in March 1919 Alcock approached the Vickers firm at Weybridge, who had considered entering their Vimy bomber (a twin-engined biplane powered by two Rolls-Royce 350 hp Eagle engines) but had not yet found a pilot. His enthusiasm quickly persuaded them to take up his proposition and work began on converting the Vimy for the long flight, replacing the bomb carriers with extra petrol tanks. Shortly afterwards a former Royal Flying Corps observer, Arthur Whitten Brown, was taken on as navigator, his first meeting with Alcock taking place in a hangar at Weybridge. Both were Mancunians by upbringing. Their shared determination to make the flight overcame marked differences in their personalities: Alcock, who was unmarried, was extrovert and sociable, with a boisterous sense of humour, while Brown, who was engaged, was quiet, nervous, and more intense. Together they tested the Vimy at Weybridge before leaving Southampton by sea on 4 May 1919 to join the other competitors assembled in Newfoundland to make the attempt from west to east (taking advantage of the prevailing winds). They arrived on 13 May, followed a fortnight later by the Vimy, which was transported in crates to be assembled and tested on site. 'Machine absolutely tophole', Alcock cabled to Vickers on 9 June after successfully completing the tests (Wallace, 71).

By the end of May 1919 the Atlantic air crossing had become a matter of national prestige. A United States navy flying-boat, commanded by Lieutenant-Commander Albert Cushing Read, left Newfoundland on 16 May and, after stopping off in the Azores for several days, reached Lisbon on 27 May, completing the stage-by-stage crossing in eleven days. Meanwhile an attempt at the non-stop crossing by Harry Hawker and Kenneth Mackenzie-Grieve ended when their Sopwith Atlantic ditched into the sea 500 miles off the Irish coast after the plane's engine overheated. Alcock and Brown continued their preparations, levelling an airfield, known as Lester's Field, near St John's, Newfoundland, in readiness for their attempt on the record.

Having eaten a final meal under the wings of the Vimy, loaded with 865 gallons of fuel, Alcock and Brown climbed into the cockpit at 16.00 Greenwich mean time (GMT) on Saturday 14 June 1919. Beneath his electrically heated flying suit Alcock wore a blue serge suit, Brown his Royal Flying Corps uniform. Two toy black cats, Twinkletoes and Lucky Jim, accompanied them as mascots. Seated side by side, Brown to port and Alcock, at the controls, to starboard, they took off at 16.13 and crossed the Newfoundland coast at 16.28. Their flight was beset by problems. The rupture of an inner exhaust pipe exposed them to the roar of the engines for most of the way, radio contact was lost, heavy cloud cover hindered navigation, and there was a continual danger of ice blocking the engines' air intakes and freezing the instrument gauges. Flying overnight, at one stage through a snowstorm, they crossed the coast of Ireland at 08.25 GMT the following morning and landed at 08.40 on what they took to be a field, but was in fact a marshy bog, at Clifden, Galway, where they were greeted by F. H. Teague, from the nearby Marconi wireless station. Coast to coast they flew 1890 miles in 15 hours 57 minutes at an average (wind-assisted) speed of 118.5 m.p.h., the actual journey from take-off to landing taking 16 hours 27 minutes.

At the Savoy hotel, on 20 June, Winston Churchill presented Alcock and Brown with the *Daily Mail*'s prize of £10,000 for the first non-stop flight across the Atlantic. Northcliffe, who was unable through illness to attend the presentation, sent a message to Alcock: 'Your journey with your companion Whitten Brown is a typical example of British courage and organizing efficiency', and went on to hope that following the flight, 'The American and British people will understand each other better as they are brought into closer daily contact' (Wallace, 278–9). On 21 June Alcock and Brown were received by George V at Windsor Castle and created KBE. Their Vimy aeroplane was brought back from Galway and presented to the nation by the manufacturers, Vickers and Rolls-Royce, to be exhibited in the Science Museum, South Kensington, London.

Alcock returned to Vickers at Weybridge as a staff pilot, testing and delivering new aircraft. On 18 December 1919 he set out to fly to Paris to deliver a Vickers Viking amphibian aeroplane which was to be shown off at the Aeronautical Exhibition. Flying solo (and therefore without a navigator) in fog, he came down at Côte d'Evrard, about 25 miles from Rouen. The plane tipped onto its nose and Alcock was thrown forward, sustaining a fracture of the skull. He was taken to no. 6 general hospital, Rouen, where he died on the same day without regaining consciousness. His body was brought back to England and after a service at Manchester Cathedral was buried in the southern cemetery, Manchester, on 27 December.

Despite the publicity which their Atlantic crossing attracted, and the honours bestowed in its aftermath, Alcock and Brown's flight did not herald an immediate development of aerial traffic between Europe and North America. The significance of their feat began to be discounted. Writing in the *Dictionary of National Biography* in 1927, Henry Albert Jones, the official air historian, suggested that 'the least eventful part' of Alcock's flying career, his period as an instructor during the early years of the First World War, was 'the most fruitful' (*DNB*). The Air Ministry, which was unenthusiastic about the newspaper-sponsored record-breaking attempts by commercial constructors, and gave no support to Alcock and Brown other than the loan of wireless and navigation equipment, preferred to develop airships as a safe and reliable means of long-distance air travel. In July 1919, less than a month after their flight, the Air Ministry's R34 airship, commanded by George Herbert Scott, accomplished the Atlantic crossing in both directions, though inevitably in a much slower time than Alcock and Brown had managed. No further successful Atlantic air crossing was achieved until the American Charles Lindbergh single-handedly flew a single-engine monoplane non-stop from New York to Paris in May 1927, and further losses of life on transatlantic crossings continued to cast doubt on the viability of heavier-than-air machines. Commercial flights across the Atlantic did not begin until twenty years after Alcock and Brown's record-breaking flight, and it was not until after the Second World War that their achievement was commemorated by a plaque near Lester's Field, Newfoundland, and by a statue at the foot of the control tower at London's Heathrow airport, erected at the suggestion of the aviator James Mollison, and unveiled in June 1954.

PETER G. COOKSLEY

Sources DNB · G. Wallace, *The flight of Alcock and Brown* (1955) · J. Pudney, *Six great aviators* (1955) · *The story of Alcock and Brown*, City of Manchester publicity office (1969) · b. cert. · *The Times* (22 Dec 1919), 12 · *The Times* (29 Dec 1919), 29 · D. Beaty, *The water jump: the story of transatlantic flight* (1976) · H. Penrose, *British aviation: the Great War and armistice, 1915–1919* (1969) · *Flight International* (12 July 1969), 959–61 · O. G. Thetford, *British naval aircraft, 1912–58* (1958), 335 · *Jane's all the world's aircraft* (1918), 59b · W. H. Longyard, *Who's who in aviation history* (1994), 9–10

Archives Museum of Science and Industry, Manchester, papers relating to his and W. A. Brown's transatlantic flight · Sci. Mus., Vickers Vimy aircraft used in transatlantic flight | FILM BFI NFTVA, documentary footage · BFI NFTVA, news footage · IWM FVA, documentary footage | SOUND IWM SA, oral history interview

Likenesses photographs, c.1914–1919, Hult. Arch. · A. McEvoy, oils, 1919, NPG [see illus.] · J. Lavery, oils, Royal Aero Club; on loan to RAF Museum, Hendon · memorial statue, London Airport · photographs, Marconi Wireless Telegraph Co. Ltd · photographs, Royal Aeronautical Society, London · photographs, British Aerospace · plaque, Manchester Town Hall

Wealth at death £9275 9s. 9d.: probate, 27 Feb 1920, CGPLA Eng. & Wales

Alcock [*née* Cumberland], **Mary** (1741?–1798), writer, was the youngest of four children of Bishop Denison Cumberland (1705/6–1774) and Joanna Bentley (1704/5–1775), daughter of Dr Richard *Bentley, classical scholar and master of Trinity College, Cambridge. The third of three daughters, and the sister of Richard *Cumberland (1732–1811), playwright and novelist, she was raised with her family at her father's rural rectory in Stanwick, near Higham Ferrars, Northamptonshire, until 1757, and thereafter in Fulham. In 1761 Denison Cumberland was appointed chaplain to Lord Halifax, lord lieutenant of Ireland, and her brother was made Ulster secretary. In 1763 her father was appointed by Halifax to the Church of Ireland see of Clonfert, Galway, where he was joined by his wife and Mary, and in 1772 translated to the more comfortable bishopric of Kilmore. About 1770 Mary Cumberland married, in Ireland, a man described by her brother as 'Mr Alcock, a young gentleman of good family, fortune and preferment', who quickly gave signs of being in precarious mental health, 'arising from a violent nervous affection on his spirits' (*Letters*, 68). At her death, she was described as the widow of Archdeacon Alcock, but her husband's identity has not been traced (he was not, as is sometimes reported, John Alcock, archdeacon of Raphoe, c.1733–1817). The marriage was probably unhappy: Richard Cumberland wrote to Garrick on 2 October 1771 that he had 'at length closed the uneasy transaction of my Sister's marriage, much to my satisfaction and to that of my family' (ibid., 84). During the period of her father's Irish residence, Mary Alcock also spent extended periods with her parents at her brother's house at Tyringham, on the banks of the River Ouse, near Newport Pagnell, Buckinghamshire. Alcock nursed her parents through long illness in Clonfert and later in Kilmore, until her father died in 1774 and mother soon after in 1775. After the bishop's death, Richard Cumberland lobbied for the recovery, for his sister's use, of arrears and money spent on improvements beneficial to the new bishop.

Evidence in her later poetry suggests Mary Alcock was resident in Bath from at least May 1783. There she announced to her relatives that she had 'turn'd out a poet' (*Poems*, 146), through her participation in the celebrated literary salon of Lady Anne Miller (1741–1781) at her villa in Batheaston, 2 miles outside Bath. The poetical compositions of Miller's friends were deposited anonymously in a large Roman vase, to be read out in front of the assembled company. Perhaps through this encouragement, Alcock permitted the anonymous publication in 1784 of a seven-page poem, *The Air Balloon, or, Flying Mortal*, which reflected the public enthusiasm for ballooning in England initiated by Lunardi's ascent from Moorfields, London, on 15 September 1784. Little is known of her later life, although it is apparent that Alcock engaged herself in charitable and benevolent schemes, and cared for the seven dependent orphans of her sister Elizabeth Hughes (d. 1770). Among her good works was a poem, 'The Confined Debtor: a Fragment from a Prison', written for the relief of the debtors confined in the county gaol at Ilchester, Somerset. Through the proceeds of the poem, which describes the miseries of the prison, 'many debtors were liberated out of their confinement at Ilchester, and fourteen out of Newgate'. As noted by her niece Joanna Hughes, Mary Alcock was a physically frail woman with 'a corporeal frame ... extremely feeble and defenceless', and visited by 'afflictions' of 'a very peculiar nature' (Hughes, iv–vi). Mary Alcock died on 28 May 1798, in her fifty-seventh year, at the home of her cousin, George Ashby, at Haselbeach Hall, Northamptonshire (6 miles south of Market Harborough), having fallen ill while on a journey from Yorkshire to Bath. She was buried in the parish church of that village. Her brother Richard Cumberland remembered her as 'the best and most benevolent of human beings' (Cumberland, *Memoirs*, 191).

Mary Alcock's works were collected after her death and published as *Poems ... by the Late Mrs Mary Alcock* in 1799. The volume was edited by her niece Joanna Hughes, whose preface records most of the available biographical information. The 183-page book comprised her extant poetry, published and unpublished, together with some pious essays on marital conduct, and a short series of Scriblerian-inspired satirical essays criticizing the debased taste of novel readers. Her niece relates that:

> She never held herself up as a writer: when she resorted to her pen it was either to amuse a leisure hour, to gratify an absent friend, or for the sublimer purpose of pouring out her heart in praises and thanksgivings to her God. (Hughes, iii)

The poems are not without merit, assaying sentimental piety and gentle satire in a variety of metrical forms, and on occasion treat serious political issues (such as civil discord in Ireland or the debate on the suspension of habeas corpus in the House of Lords). The volume met with no critical notice, but attracted 652 subscribers, among them royalty and many literary and artistic figures, including Charles Burney, Elizabeth Carter, William Cowper, Thomas Day, George Foote, Hannah More, George Romney, Samuel Rogers, and William Stockdale.

MARKMAN ELLIS

Sources J. Hughes, 'To the reader', in *Poems &c. &c. by the late Mrs Mary Alcock*, ed. J. Hughes (1799), iii–vii [preface] · R. Cumberland, *Memoirs of Richard Cumberland written by himself* (1806) · *The letters of Richard Cumberland*, ed. R. J. Dircks (1988) · *GM*, 1st ser., 68 (1798), 539 · *European Magazine and London Review*, 33 (1798), 431 · W. Mudford, *A critical examination of the writings of Richard Cumberland* (1812) · *Fasti Angl., 1541–1857*, [St Paul's, London] · J. B. Leslie, *Raphoe clergy and parishes* (1940) · H. Cotton, *Fasti ecclesiae Hibernicae*, 2nd edn, 1 (1851) · R. A. Hesselgrave, *Lady Miller and the Batheaston literary circle* (1927)

Alcock, Nathan (1709–1779), physician, was born in Runcorn, Cheshire, the second son of David Alcock (*bap.* 1675, *d.* 1750?) and Mary (*d.* 1747), whose maiden name was Breck, and was a descendant of Bishop Alcock, founder of Jesus College, Cambridge. His brother was Thomas *Alcock (1709–1798), clergyman and writer. A dislike of his schoolmaster seems to have interrupted his classical education. Later, in exchange for a small estate at Wirral, Cheshire, Alcock promised his father that he would take up medicine. He studied first at Edinburgh and then under

Boerhaave at Leiden, where he not only learned his subject but how to teach it; he graduated MD in 1742.

From Leiden, Alcock went to Oxford, where one professor of the medical faculty gave no lectures, and another did not reside. Alcock gave unauthorized lectures on anatomy and on chemistry, rousing a storm of opposition against him. Public readers were appointed to counter Alcock but they were unable to compete with his knowledge or his lecturing skills; so while Alcock's lectures were crowded, no one went to hear his opponents. Other methods of opposition were tried; for example, it was suggested that his residence in the Netherlands had probably made him unsound in theological opinions, and when it was proposed to give him a degree the heads of houses refused their consent. His friends, among whom were Sir William Blackstone and Robert Lowth, afterwards bishop of London, supported him, however, and in 1741 he was granted the degree of MA at Oxford by decree of convocation and incorporated from Jesus College. He graduated MB in 1744. He became MD in 1749, was elected FRS in the same year, and in 1754 became a fellow of the College of Physicians.

Alcock's practice in Oxford was extensive but, following the death of the woman he was planning to marry, he retired to Runcorn. Here, despite bouts of illness, his practice soon became as extensive as it had been at Oxford and he worked on for nearly twenty years. He died of apoplexy in Runcorn on 8 December 1779 and was buried in the parish church there.

Alcock was a tall man of dark complexion and athletic build. A letter of his shows him to have been a resolute whig in politics, and in religion he was a follower of Bishop Hoadly. His Leiden thesis was on pneumonia. He published no other work during his lifetime, but told his biographer (his brother Thomas, vicar of Runcorn) that he had begun to arrange some cases and to write on air and on the effects of climate. Alcock's *The Rise of Mahomet, Accounted for on Natural and Civil Principles* was edited by Thomas Alcock and published in 1796.

NORMAN MOORE, *rev.* CAROLINE OVERY

Sources Munk, *Roll* · T. Alcock, *Some memoirs of the life of Dr Nathan Alcock* (1780) · Foster, *Alum. Oxon.* · R. W. Innes Smith, *English-speaking students of medicine at the University of Leyden* (1932)

Alcock, Sir (John) Rutherford (1809–1897), diplomatist, was born in Ealing in May 1809, the son of Thomas Alcock, a doctor practising at Ealing. He was educated at a school at Hexham, Northumberland, and as a medical student at Westminster Hospital and Royal Westminster Ophthalmic Hospital (*c.*1824–1828), and also studied art in Paris in 1826. For a time he was house surgeon at Westminster Hospital, and in 1832 he was appointed surgeon to the British–Portuguese forces operating in Portugal. In 1836 he was transferred to the marine brigade engaged in the Carlist War in Spain, and rose rapidly to become deputy inspector-general of hospitals. He returned to England in 1838 and became lecturer in surgery at Sydenham College, publishing *Notes on the Medical History and Statistics of the British Legion in Spain*. On 17 May 1841 he married Henrietta (*d.* 1853), daughter of Thomas Bacon, a sculptor. Soon

Sir (John) Rutherford Alcock (1809–1897), by Lock & Whitfield, pubd 1877

afterwards he began to suffer from muscular trouble in his hands, which forced him to end his career as a surgeon.

In 1844 Alcock was appointed British consul at Foochow (Fuzhou), one of the Chinese ports newly opened to foreign trade by the treaty of Nanking (Nanjing). On his way to his new post he briefly acted as consul at Amoy (Xiamen). There his dignified presence (he was about 6 feet tall) and his firmness in demanding that the Chinese authorities should provide the British consul with appropriate accommodation deeply impressed his young interpreter, Harry Parkes, also to have a distinguished career in China and Japan. While consul at Foochow, Alcock asserted British interests and wrote voluminous reports on the prospects for British trade. After a year and a half at Foochow he was transferred to Shanghai, with Parkes following him. Over the next nine years he set the standard for consular activity in China. He insisted that the Chinese should observe treaty obligations and this led to some sharp conflicts with officials. A notable instance of this occurred in 1848, when three missionaries were attacked by a crowd of sailors. As the intendant had failed to punish the rioters, Alcock proclaimed that, until the criminals had been dealt with, no customs duties would be paid by British ships, and that the 1400 grain junks waiting to sail north would not be allowed to leave. Although there were fifty war junks in the harbour and only one British sloop-of-war, the threat apparently succeeded. The rioters were punished and the intendant was removed from office. While Alcock was at Shanghai the municipal regulations

for the government of the British community there were established, and the foundations of what was to become the International Settlement were laid. In March 1853 Alcock's wife died, and later that year Shanghai was captured by Small Sword rebels. Imperial control collapsed, and with it the collection of customs duties. This led Alcock to set up the 'provisional system', under which foreign ships were required to give promissory notes for the duty for which they were liable. From this initiative the imperial maritime customs service was to derive.

In 1858 Alcock was appointed the first consul-general in Japan. His principal concern was the implementation of the rights gained by Lord Elgin under the treaty of Edo, of 26 August 1858. Using the methods he had employed in China, he insisted that the Japanese government comply strictly with the agreement on the opening of treaty ports. Alcock, like other Westerners in Japan at that time, did not fully comprehend the relationship between the Bakufu, the government of the shogun, and the imperial court in Kyoto. The Bakufu, forced to make concessions to the Western powers, had earned the hostility of many Japanese, including the ronin, masterless samurai, who adopted the slogan 'Revere the emperor, expel the foreigner'. They committed a series of attacks on foreigners, and on 5 July 1861 a group of ronin attacked the British legation. Alcock was unharmed, but the incident convinced him of the merit of allowing the Bakufu to postpone the opening of the ports.

In 1862 Alcock returned to England on leave. He was knighted, and on 8 July he married Lucy Lowder (d. 1899), widow of the former Anglican chaplain of Shanghai. He contributed to the display of Japanese arts and crafts at the 1862 exhibition, and his own collection of Japanese art was later on show in London. In the following year he published *The Capital of the Tycoon*, an account of his three years' residence in Japan and of his journeys to the interior. He suffered the embarrassment of being criticized in parliament for his alleged indifference to Japanese religious feelings. In 1864 he returned to Edo. It was mainly due to his influence that a naval attack was made on the batteries of Choshu, the fief most openly opposed to the Bakufu. These batteries guarded the Strait of Shimonoseki, the entrance to the Inland sea. This event played an important part in convincing Choshu loyalists that the expulsion of the foreigners was impossible, and that in future they should direct their actions against the Bakufu. Soon afterwards Alcock was recalled to London for consultations.

In 1865 Alcock was appointed minister-plenipotentiary at Peking (Beijing). There he conducted many delicate negotiations with the Zongli Yamen, the prototype foreign office. In 1868 he reluctantly sanctioned the use of British gunboats to support Hudson Taylor of the China Inland Mission, whose mission had been attacked. His main concern was treaty revision. In October 1869 he concluded the Alcock convention, a draft agreement which recognized Chinese interests and set the relationship between the two countries on a more equal footing. It was denounced by British merchants as too favourable to China, and was not ratified by the British government.

In 1871 Sir Rutherford retired and settled in London. In his retirement he interested himself in hospital nursing establishments and actively supported many charitable institutions. He was president of the Royal Geographical Society from 1876 to 1878 and vice-president of the Royal Asiatic Society from 1875 to 1878. He continued to write, and in 1878 published *Art and Art Industry in Japan*. In 1881 he became the first chairman of the British North Borneo Company. Sir Rutherford died at his home, 30 Old Queen Street, London, on 2 November 1897, and was buried four days later at Merstham, Surrey. He left no children, but his stepdaughter, Amy Lowder, married Sir Lewis Pelly.

R. K. DOUGLAS, rev. J. A. G. ROBERTS

Sources A. Michie, *The Englishman in China during the Victorian era as illustrated in the career of Sir Rutherford Alcock, KCB, DCL*, 2 vols. (1900) • *The Times* (3 Nov 1897) • *The Times* (8 Nov 1897) • P. D. Coates, *The China consuls: British consular officers, 1843–1943* (1988) • G. Fox, *Britain and Japan, 1858–1883* (1969) • J. K. Fairbank, *Trade and diplomacy on the China coast: the opening of the treaty ports, 1842–1854*, 2 vols. (1953); repr. in 1 vol. (Cambridge, MA, 1969), 410–38 • R. Alcock, *The capital of the tycoon: a narrative of three years' residence in Japan*, 2 vols. (1863) • *CGPLA Eng. & Wales* (1897)
Archives University of Bristol Library, corresp. and papers | Bodl. Oxf., corresp. with Sir Henry Burdett • Bodl. Oxf., letters to Lord Kimberley • PRO, Foreign Office records • PRO, letters to Lord Hammond, FO391
Likenesses Lock & Whitfield, photograph, pubd 1877, NPG [*see illus.*] • L. A. de Fabeck, sketch, repro. in Michie, *Englishman in China* • photograph, Mansell collection; repro. in Coates, *China consuls* • photograph, repro. in Michie, *Englishman in China*
Wealth at death £8544 11s. 1d.: probate, 25 Nov 1897, *CGPLA Eng. & Wales*

Alcock, Simon (d. 1459), scholastic author, was educated at Oxford, where he had proceeded MA by 1422 and DD by 1427, at which date he composed the *De arte dictaminis*, now MS 184.4 of the library of St John's College, Oxford. He may also have composed the *De arte scribendi epistolas* which immediately follows it. His only other extant work is the *Tractatus de modo dividendi thema pro materia sermonis dilatanda*, which survives in three copies (BL, Harley MS 635, fols. 1–5; Bodl. Oxf., MS Bodley 52, fols. 102–108; and Oxford, Lincoln College, MS 101, item 2). Following an earlier conjecture of John Leland, Bale credited Alcock—perhaps rather implausibly—with a commentary on Lombard's *Sentences*, adding 'many sermons' on his own authority. Alcock owned a copy of Thomas de Hibernia's early fourteenth-century *Manipulus florum* (now Magd. Oxf., MS Lat. 87), and donated a copy of St Bonaventure's *Pharetra* to Oriel College, Oxford (MS 50). His earliest known preferment was to the rectory of West Tilbury, Essex, which he held by 1422, and resigned in 1428 for the rectory of Lamarsh in the same county. He held the rectory of Ufford, Northamptonshire, by 1435, and that of Cawston, Norfolk, from 1436. He held prebends at Ripon (1435–6), Hereford Cathedral (1436–59), and Lincoln Cathedral (1451–9). Alcock was buried in Lincoln Cathedral, where a monument records his death on 10 August 1459.

RICHARD REX

Sources Emden, *Oxf.* • H. Anstey, ed., *Epistolae academicae Oxon.*, 1, OHS, 35 (1898) • Bale, *Cat.*, 1.482 • *Fasti Angl., 1300–1541* • *Commentarii de scriptoribus Britannicis, auctore Joanne Lelando*, ed. A. Hall, 2 (1709), 417
Archives BL, Harley MS 635, fols. 1–5 • Bodl. Oxf., MS Bodley 52, fols. 102–108 • Lincoln College, Oxford, MS 101, item 2 • St John's College, Oxford, MS 184.4

Alcock, Thomas (d. 1564), merchant, was one of ten apprentices who had spent their early years in England before being sent to Russia by the Muscovy Company in 1557. At this time Russia's western neighbours were anxious to prevent the Muscovy Company exporting armaments to Russia, and on his way back from Moscow via Smolensk to Danzig, Alcock was arrested on 26 February 1558 near Turovli, in Poland. At Turovli his papers and money were confiscated and he was kept in fetters until Easter. He was questioned at length about the export of arms, but admitted only to having delivered 100 refurbished old coats of mail. He was then released, but without his possessions, and returned to England.

It is not known when Alcock was sent back to Russia, but he and Richard Cheinie, accompanied by some Russian merchants, set out from Yaroslavl on 10 May 1564 for Persia, where trading privileges had been granted the previous year by Abdullah Khan, king of Shirvan. They reached Astrakhan on 24 July, and took ship on the Caspian, arriving at Shemakha on 12 August, where they engaged in trade. On 20 October Alcock proceeded south alone, to Qazvin. He was only the second Englishman to make the journey from Astrakhan to Qazvin.

On his return Alcock had reached Jevat when Cheinie, learning of his whereabouts, went to join him in pursuing various debts owed to the company. One of the Russian merchants had recently killed a Muslim, and, fearing retribution, Alcock sent Cheinie back to Shemakha with their possessions. Three days later news came that Alcock had been killed a short distance from Shemakha, at a place called Levvacta, not now identifiable. The Muscovy Company later wrote to its agents, saying that Alcock might have been killed for offending against some local custom or religion; others thought it probable that he was attacked by robbers. The narrative of his journey was written by Cheinie.

ANITA McCONNELL

Sources T. S. Willan, *The early history of the Russia Company, 1553–1603* (1956) • 'A letter of Thomas Alcocke to the worshipfull Richard Gray, and Henrie Lane Agents in Moscovia from Tirwill in Polonia, written in Tirwill the 26. of April 1558', in R. Hakluyt, *The principal navigations, voyages, traffiques and discoveries of the English nation*, 2, Hakluyt Society, extra ser., 2 (1903), 396–9 • [R. Cheinie], 'The second voyage into Persia made by Thomas Alcocke, which was slayne there', *Early voyages and travels to Russia and Persia*, ed. E. D. Morgan and C. H. Coote, 2, Hakluyt Society, 73 (1886), 378–81

Alcock, Thomas (1709–1798), Church of England clergyman and writer, was baptized at Aston by Sutton, Cheshire, on 27 October 1709, the third son of David Alcock (bap. 1675, d. 1750?) and Mary Breck (d. 1747), of Aston and Higher Runcorn, Cheshire. He matriculated from Brasenose College, Oxford, on 1 March 1728 and proceeded BA in 1731 and MA in 1741. Although he was instituted as vicar of Runcorn on 17 July 1756 and became a Cheshire JP, all but his final years were spent in the Plymouth area of Devon. He was licensed as curate of Stonehouse on 30 December 1731, but in November 1732 began acting as minister of nearby St Budeaux to which he was officially licensed on 29 December 1733. In 1769 Alcock was disappointed in his expectations of succeeding to the vicarage of St Andrew's, Plymouth, which carried with it the nomination to St Budeaux. He thereafter refused to comply with the custom to preach in St Andrew's every ninth Wednesday, but on 21 May 1790 was prompted by an archidiaconal visitation there to deliver his hour-and-a-half long sermon 'An apology for Esau' which was subsequently published.

On 5 December 1737 Alcock married, at St Budeaux, Mary Harwood (bap. 1702, d. 1777), the only child and heir of Philip Harwood (d. 1713) of Ernesettle, Plymouth. Through this marriage, which was childless, Alcock obtained considerable property in St Budeaux. His local popularity was ensured when he ceased to collect tithes for the remainder of his life. Contemporaries noted his eccentric habits, spartan lifestyle, and kindness to the poor to whom he also acted as doctor and lawyer. In 1752 he published two pamphlets, *Observations on the Defects of the Poor Laws* and *Remarks on Two Bills for the Better Maintenance of the Poor*. In 1771 he contributed to the purchase of land at Weston Peverel to provide a master for the St Budeaux charity school and to clothe the poor. With his two elder brothers, Matthew (1705–1785) and Nathan *Alcock, the eminent physician, he similarly endowed Alcock's Charity at Runcorn which was also designed to promote psalmody in Runcorn church.

Alcock farmed at Ernesettle and in 1763, describing himself as 'A Cydermaker', he wrote *Observations on that Part of the Late Act of Parliament which Lays an Additional Duty on Cider*. As well as attacking the excise system, this pamphlet outlined the anticipated detrimental economic consequences of the measure and contributed to its repeal in 1766. Alcock's pamphleteering skills were also deployed in defence of local cidermakers in 1767 when George Baker suggested that the severe colic then peculiar to Devon was the result of lead poisoning from the presses, pipework, and storage vessels. *Cursory Remarks on Dr. Baker's Essay on the Endemial Colic in Devon* (1767) was followed by *The Endemial Colic of Devon not Caused by a Solution of Lead in the Cyder* (1769). Baker's empirical evidence was refuted by the assertion that the colic resulted only from the small shot used in bottle cleansing. These writings probably contributed to the decision to present Alcock with the freedom of the borough of Plymouth in a silver box on 16 October 1769.

When Nathan Alcock died in 1779 he left the residue of his estate, estimated at £15,000, to be divided equally between his surviving brothers, Matthew and Thomas. The latter produced *Some Memoirs of the Life of Dr Nathan Alcock* the following year and in 1796 also arranged the publication of Nathan's *The Rise of Mahomet, Accounted for on Natural and Civil Principles*. Thomas Alcock died at Runcorn on 24 August 1798 and was buried there three days later. PATRICK WOODLAND

Sources parish registers, Runcorn, Ches. & Chester ALSS, PAR RUN · baptismal records, parochial chapelry of Aston by Sutton, Ches. & Chester ALSS, P128/1/1 · act books of the bishop of Chester, Ches. & Chester ALSS, EDA 1/6, 1/8 · testimonial and deed of presentation to Runcorn, Ches. & Chester ALSS, EDP 234/1/2 · wills, Ches. & Chester ALSS, WS 1780, 1785 [Nathan and Matthew Alcock] · parish registers, St Budeaux, Plymouth and West Devon Record Office, Plymouth, MF3, 4; MF4 · presentations of freedom to borough of Plymouth, Plymouth and West Devon Record Office, Plymouth, W77f.9 · 'History of St Budeaux church', Plymouth and West Devon Record Office, Plymouth, 815/4 · J. Brooking-Rowe, *The ecclesiastica history of old Plymouth; and the parish, vicars and church of St Andrew*, [3 pts] (1876) · Foster, *Alum. Oxon.* · P. T. M. Woodland, 'The cider excise, 1763–1766', DPhil diss., U. Oxf., 1982, pt 3 · R. K. French, *The history and virtues of cyder* (1982) · D. Lysons and S. Lysons, *Magna Britannia: being a concise topographical account of the several counties of Great Britain*, 6 (1822) · B. F. Cresswell, *Notes on Devonshire churches* (1925) [privately printed]
Wealth at death over £7500?; incl. property in Plymouth area: will, Nathan Alcock, Ches. & Chester ALSS, WS1780

Alcock, Thomas (1784–1833), surgeon, was born in Rothbury, Northumberland. After serving an apprenticeship as a surgeon with John Anderson in Newcastle, he became in 1805 resident medical officer at the Sunderland Dispensary. In 1806 or 1807 he moved to London and studied at Joshua Brookes's school of anatomy and at the Westminster Hospital. After gaining his diploma from the Royal College of Surgeons he became a general practitioner.

From 1825 Alcock devoted himself solely to surgery. From 1813 to 1828 he worked as a surgeon to St James's workhouse. In 1828 he began giving lectures on surgery at a school in Little Dean Street, London. A visit to Paris in 1823 led him to publish in 1827 an essay on the use of the chlorides of soda and lime in cases of hospital gangrene, the practice having been extensively applied in France by Labarraque. A course of lectures on practical and medical surgery, delivered by Alcock to the students of the Borough Dispensary in 1824, appeared in *The Lancet* in 1825–6 and were republished with additions in 1830. Alcock published several other books and contributed many papers to medical journals. He died on 21 August 1833, at his home in New Burlington Street, London.

[ANON.], rev. KAYE BAGSHAW

Sources G. Long, ed., *The biographical dictionary of the Society for the Diffusion of Useful Knowledge*, 4 vols. in 7 (1842–4) · P. J. Wallis and R. V. Wallis, *Eighteenth century medics*, 2nd edn (1988) · *GM*, 1st ser., 103/2 (1833), 283
Likenesses B. R. Haydon, oils, *c*.1825, RCS Eng.

Alcuin [Albinus, Flaccus] (*c*.740–804), abbot of St Martin's, Tours, and royal adviser, was a major figure in the revival of learning and letters under the Frankish king and emperor, Charlemagne (*r*. 768–814).

Childhood and youth The approximate year of Alcuin's birth depends entirely on his retrospective allusions to episodes in his early life and on reported reminiscences included in a life written in the 820s, for which a favourite disciple, Sigwulf, seems to be the principal intermediate

Alcuin (c.740–804), medallion drawing

years. In all his works Alcuin reveals his reverence for 'Bede the teacher', whom he knew only at second hand, in his books and through Ecgberht; he also makes clear the enduring influence of Ælberht, *magister* (teacher) in York in the late 750s and early 760s and subsequently bishop. Alcuin's long poem on York, its place in the history of the Northumbrian kingdom and its saints, written probably in the early or mid-780s (although a later date is not absolutely excluded), includes an unusually full account of Ælberht's teaching programme, presented in terms of the seven liberal arts as defined by sixth-century scholars. The same poem devotes many lines to the Christian and pagan authors represented in the book collection Ælberht had assembled at York, of which Alcuin always regarded himself as the legitimate heir. In the early 760s he travelled with Ælberht to Rome, on a journey that also took them to Murbach Abbey (Alsace) and to the Lombard 'capital' at Pavia. While they were there a debate took place between a Jewish scholar and the Italian Pietro da Pisa, whom Alcuin was to re-encounter later at the Frankish royal court; but he does not claim that he was present, and he certainly learned nothing from it.

Early adulthood at York Alcuin's third and fourth decades were ones in which the kingship of Northumbria was violently contested by claimants from several different family lines, who typically behaved ruthlessly to defeated opponents and their magnate supporters; later evidence suggests that Alcuin, and perhaps the kindred to which he belonged, had connections with the line that attained the throne for the first time in 759, in the person of Æthelwald Moll, and again, after a break, in 774 (Æthelred I). But from the late 760s Alcuin was himself earning a reputation as a teacher of adolescents: among these was Liudger, future founder of Werden and first bishop of Münster (Westfalen), where a memory of Alcuin's teaching at York was still alive in the 840s.

The first didactic text attributable to Alcuin, a short computistic one with concluding verses, comes from the 770s. Plausibly, too, he was also helping his bishop to compose admonitory letters to the leading figures in the Northumbrian kingdom. In the last years of Ælberht's pontificate, Alcuin was (it was later reported) sent on a mission, of unknown purpose, to the Frankish king Charlemagne. This is the most likely, although not the certain, background of a lively letter-poem which was dispatched after his return home to some of the prominent clerics and royal courtiers whom he had met while travelling up the Rhine and at the court, including Pietro da Pisa and the arch-chaplain Fulrad. Alcuin was also working with his fellow cleric Eanbald (I) (who was elected as Ælberht's successor before the latter's death) in the construction of a splendid new church in York, on an unknown site; its highly unusual dedication to Alma Sophia (beneficent wisdom) suggests that it was in some way connected with the cathedral *scola*, the community of tonsured boys and young clerics. In 780 or 781 Alcuin again journeyed to Rome, to obtain the archiepiscopal pallium for Eanbald but possibly also taking with him to Italy a sister (perhaps stepsister) of the recently deposed king

source; a modern attempt to arrive at a more precise date in the late 740s is based on a demonstrably mistaken interpretation of one of the retrospective references. Nothing is known of Alcuin's parents or close kin. Modern literature generally speaks of him as 'noble-born'; his own references to collateral relatives (and notably to Wilgils, father of the missionary Willibrord whose life he wrote about 796) indicate that his family (*paterfamilias* is his word) was *ceorlisc*, that is, free but often subordinated to others of higher standing, and had a modest landholding, almost certainly in the Northumbrian south-east (southeast Yorkshire). From Wilgils and unnamed younger kin Alcuin inherited an oratory and well-endowed 'monastery' near the Humber estuary, founded early in the century; other and more distant relatives such as Beornred, who became abbot of Echternach and bishop (later archbishop) of Sens, had established themselves in Francia before Alcuin left Northumbria. As a very small child, he was handed over to the cathedral church of York and its clerical, non-monastic, community under Archbishop Ecgberht; stories in the life purport to show his mastery of the Psalms by the age of eleven, a precocious interest in Virgil, and an emotional response to part of St John's gospel in, perhaps, his late teens. Alcuin was to remain there for more than forty years, at first with the simple clerical tonsure which was remembered as having been imposed on 2 February in an unspecified year, and eventually—but only from c.770—as a deacon; he never proceeded to higher orders.

The greatest single influence from these years was evidently the daily liturgy of the cathedral, in which Alcuin participated from early boyhood. Some characteristic features of this can be reconstructed, both from a four-book florilegium *De laude Dei* (preserved in two continental manuscripts and only partly published), which also provides evidence of his early reading in the fathers (theology, history, and poetry) and other Christian texts, and also from the letters and other writings of his continental

Æthelred. The life of Alcuin records that it was at Parma during the return journey that Alcuin again met the Frankish king (perhaps in March 781) and was invited to join his court.

It has always been assumed that Alcuin left Northumbria for Francia almost immediately and most accounts of Carolingian court culture and of Alcuin's contributions to it are posited on that assumption. In fact, there are strong arguments for believing that Alcuin's earliest surviving letters (in which he already used the Latin name-form Albinus, although not yet his unexplained nickname Flaccus) were written at York c.784, and that he was still there when a papal legate arrived in 786. The decrees of the legatine synod were subsequently promulgated again in the Mercian kingdom, to which Alcuin and another York deacon had accompanied the legate, and where an English-language version (of which nothing survives) was additionally read out. It is not unlikely that Alcuin was responsible for the content and phraseology of those decrees that dealt with specifically English issues and perhaps of some others; if so, they provide some further indications of the older writings (of the fathers, and so on) with which he was familiar before he left his homeland. Later, mostly indirect, evidence suggests that Alcuin had also compiled other compendia from the (for its time) extensive range of books available to him at York and perhaps elsewhere in Northumbria; among them was one on computus, which, with other books, he evidently included in his baggage when he travelled to Charlemagne's court in summer or autumn 786, although whether it can be approximately reconstructed from items included in later compilations on the continent is disputed.

At the Frankish royal court Alcuin's first period of association with the court, which when he joined it was still itinerant and from which several of the first generation of resident foreign scholars had already departed, lasted three and a half years. For most of that time there is no direct and contemporary evidence of what he contributed, and it is unlikely that he was in any sense head of a palace school, as has commonly been supposed. Clearly, however, he shared literary and intellectual exchanges with men close to him in age, to some of whom (notably Arno, bishop and, from 798, archbishop of Salzburg and abbot of St Amand) he formed a lifelong attachment; he seems also to have enjoyed a close association with women in the royal family, although not with the queen, Fastrada (d. 794). He began to seek out and circulate short, predominantly late antique, works that had been neglected for centuries but had potential value as text books. Among these was the influential pseudo-Augustinian *De categoriis decem*; another was probably the even more enduring *De imagine Dei*, an exposition of the nature of man in terms of a simplified Augustinian psychology, which has sometimes been credited to Alcuin himself or to Alcuin and a pupil.

Almost certainly it was in this period that Alcuin, with others, composed a sequence of virtuosic figured poems and his own first extant work of exegesis, *Interrogationes et*

Responsiones in Genesin ('Questions and answers on Genesis'), which concisely presented largely inherited wisdom, with emphasis on a literal interpretation but also exploiting number symbolism. His imprint on the Frankish king's great capitulary or 'general admonition' of March 789, a programme for the reform and better ordering of both the Frankish church and secular society, is apparent in some of the content and language. The first royal grants of religious houses to Alcuin as sources of income seem to belong to these years: he is subsequently documented, mostly in his own letters, as *rector* (abbot) of an unlocated monastery dedicated to St John the Baptist, and of Ferrières, St Josse-sur-Mer, St Lupus's at Troyes, St Servatius's at Maastricht, and, perhaps, of Flavigny, as well as of St Martin's at Tours (from 796) and its dependencies. There is evidence also that before 790 he had aroused jealousy or irritation at the court, whether among lowly chaplains or established councillors.

Return to Northumbria and letter collection Early in 790 Alcuin returned to York. He had expected (he claims) that he would be sent to Britain to resolve a dispute between the Frankish king and King Offa of Mercia; but its resolution was almost certainly the work of others. It was at York that, highly unusually, he or anonymous amanuenses now began to keep texts of outgoing letters, which together with the small number retained and copies by their recipients (almost exclusively at Salzburg) ensured the preservation of around 275 from the last fourteen years of Alcuin's life. A very few of those written from Tours are strictly business or administrative letters, evidently representative of many others in that category which were not copied. Letters to English kings, bishops, abbots, and occasionally laymen are overwhelmingly admonitory; letters to the Frankish king (later emperor), to Arno, archbishop of Salzburg, and to a few others are sometimes of considerable length, dealing with a topic or, more often, with a number of topics of current interest or concern. The repeated commonplaces and stylistic pretensions of many of them, particularly in the later 790s, do not exclude adaptation to the occasion and to the recipient. Their not infrequent autobiographical references, paralleled in a small number of Alcuin's poems (which circulated less widely), reveal him as uncertain of himself even when he was being most authoritative and assertive, sensitive to slights—real or imagined—and to betrayal, especially by one-time pupils on whom he had lavished care and attention; they also reveal him as not merely acquisitive but, in the opinion of contemporaries, unacceptably avaricious, an accusation that he was always eager to rebut!

During his three-year return visit to Northumbria (790–93) Alcuin evidently had little or no success in checking the chronic violence associated with the exercise of royal power there. Nevertheless, his advice was sought by both the Mercian and the Frankish kings. In response to the latter, as revealed by a passage for which he may have been personally responsible in the contemporary Northumbrian (perhaps York) annals preserved in the *Historia regum* wrongly credited to Symeon of Durham, he contributed to the Frankish court text (the so-called *Libri Carolini*) designed to rebut the Greek position on the worship of images, probably on the topic of synodal authority. Before he departed from Northumbria, for the last time, in early summer 793, it is likely that Alcuin was already assembling a collection of patristic texts that demonstrated the falsity of the understanding of Christ's relationship with God the Father (Adoptionism) currently professed by Spanish and Pyrenean bishops. It is not improbable that the first of two versions of a work on spelling (*De orthographia*), which made extensive use of Bede's work of the same name and was perhaps intended to replace it, also belongs to these years.

Teaching and writing at the court of Charlemagne Alcuin was back in Francia when vikings sacked Lindisfarne on 8 June 793. The event, which is not recorded in any Frankish annalistic or other text, provoked him to a series of letters over the period of at least a year, in which he criticized the Northumbrian king and people, as well as bishops and other clerics in both southern and northern England, for the faithlessness and gross misconduct which had brought down the wrath of God; it also inspired a major verse lament addressed to the Lindisfarne community, in which the note of pessimism is particularly strong. Having finally rejoined the Carolingian court at or on its way to Frankfurt, Alcuin made a significant contribution to the proceedings of the synod assembled there early in 794. Stylistic and other features indicate that he was the principal author of two letters addressed to the Spanish bishops, respectively in the king's name and in that of the Frankish bishops. In the second of these Alcuin challenged their Adoptionist views with a long sequence of citations (not always apposite) from the fathers and from the liturgy, and seems to have been convinced that he had provided a definitive rebuttal. His reward was formal admission, although he was still only a deacon, to the bishop's *consortium* and confraternity of prayer.

When the Frankish court finally established itself at the new palace at Aachen, Alcuin was one of its resident members. Unlike others among the royal counsellors, loyal servants, and scholar-poets, vividly characterized in verse exchanges (for reading aloud) to which Alcuin was a party, he remained there for only two years; and for many months in those years Charlemagne himself was absent on military campaigns, from which Alcuin then and later excused himself. The king's biographer Einhard, at this time a boy, later briefly recalled Alcuin's presence and activity at the Aachen court; and there is a single contemporary reference to him in a fellow resident's poem. All the other evidence is in his own writings, directly in his letters (but written for the most part after he had left) and poems, indirectly in his pedagogic works. It nevertheless substantially justifies the modern image of a teacher, both of the king and some members of his family, and of adolescents at the court, lay and clerical. While he was there a beginning was made to the production of definitive written versions of his hitherto oral teaching in the areas of grammar, rhetoric, and dialectic, and perhaps also of music and arithmetic. An introduction to the first

of these (and by extension to the whole group), titled in later copies *De vera philosophia* ('Of true knowledge') and which draws heavily on the sixth-century Boethius's *Consolatio philosophiae*, links them with the understanding of scripture and the Christian's ascent to heaven. The other writings show a familiarity (perhaps owed to the court library) with several substantial works from pre-Christian and late antiquity, including Cicero's *De inventione*, Priscian's *Institutio grammatica* (of which also he made an excerpt which had only a limited circulation), the rare *Ars rhetorica* of Julius Victor, and an interpolated version of Cassiodorus's *Institutiones* with diagrams which he later imitated in his own teaching. Later letters to the king indicate that a knowledge and imitation of the Christian and pre-Christian poets whose works were available at the court were an integral part of grammatical studies there. A very active royal interest was in astronomy and calendar calculation, which prompted several queries to an absent Alcuin, and complaints from him about other scholars' misunderstandings, in future years. Alcuin's verses while he was at the court include a long epitaph for the recently deceased Pope Hadrian I (*d.* 795), incised (perhaps at Aachen) on a decorated marble slab still extant at St Peter's in Rome.

Letters written by Alcuin in 795 or 796 imply that he was still hoping, even intending, to return to York. He may have been led to believe that he was a possible successor to the first Archbishop Eanbald when he resigned or died; if so he was disappointed, even perhaps acknowledging that he was debarred by some past misconduct (sexual or other), as letters intended for Pope Hadrian and sent to Pope Leo III suggest. In April 796, when the Northumbrian king Æthelred, to whom he had once given adherence, was murdered (which, according to Alcuin, aroused the Frankish king to great anger), he finally acknowledged that return was impossible. Nor do his letters of this period to addressees in Mercia suggest that he saw that kingdom as a possible alternative home. Reluctantly, in the summer of 796, he accepted the abbacy of St Martin's at Tours, which had not in recent years been a religious community closely associated with the Frankish royal court or family, although he himself had written letters both to its community (on the subject of true confession) and to its abbot.

Last years at St Martin's, Tours The greatest number of Alcuin's extant letters and most of his major writings other than the earliest pedagogic ones belong to his final eight years. Early letters show a particular concern with the establishment of the Christian faith among the recently conquered Avars, on Francia's south-eastern border, and the missionary responsibility of his two friends, Arno, archbishop of Salzburg, and Paulinus, patriarch of Aquileia. He was concerned that what he regarded as the mistakes made in the (questionably effective) conversion of the Saxons a decade previously should not be repeated: admission to the Christian community in the ceremonies of baptism was of major importance, and he wrote on the subject more than once, adapting or incorporating older texts on the subject; but adult converts must be persuaded of the truths of the faith by good teaching. 'What avails baptism without faith?'; 'a man can be forced into baptism but not into belief' (Alcuin, *Epistolae*, 164).

During the next twelve months, to autumn 797, Alcuin seems to have had surprisingly little contact with the court; and his sadness at having left it is expressed in poems intended for another friend, Angilbert, abbot of St Riquier. Letters to England, however, were frequent and equally critical of the king and former kings of Northumbria, of the deceased Offa and his reigning son, and of Æthelheard, archbishop of Canterbury, who had abandoned his see following a Kentish repudiation of Mercian rule. After a first burst of enthusiasm, he was also critical of the behaviour of the new archbishop of York, his one-time pupil Eanbald (II). His other preoccupations were, first, raising the community of St Martin's (and probably other clergy and monks in the Tours region) from what he perceived to be their 'rusticity'. In fact, quite quickly he developed a substantially reconstructable advanced teaching programme based on his own and older didactic texts, although the main beneficiaries seem to have been adolescents attracted or sent from elsewhere, to the annoyance of the established residents. Second, he took in hand the organization and exploitation of the monastery's very extensive estates, without much sympathy for tenants and dependants.

Nothing engaged Alcuin more, however, than the Spanish Christological heresy, which he may for a time have believed to have been finally dealt with at Frankfurt, but which since then had apparently extended its infection (he made much use over the years of medical metaphors) to the south-western regions of the Frankish dominions. To combat it and to refute the counter-arguments of its two major exponents, Archbishop Elipand of Toledo and Bishop Felix of Urgel, Alcuin first wrote personal letters—in very different tone and form—during 797; and he followed these up in 798–800 with a succession of three substantial treatises, directed to one or other of his opponents and their counter-arguments but intended for wider circulation, which was never really achieved. In each of his treatises (for only the first of which is there a good modern edition) Alcuin supported the orthodox position with substantial patristic and liturgical testimony that he was progressively adding to with the help of his Tours disciples. The most accomplished and convincing was the second, *Libri septem contra Felicem* ('Seven books against Felix'). Augustine is used with discrimination, perhaps because Alcuin felt that in that father's major statement of Trinitarian doctrine he might seem to overstress Christ's humanity; and in several passages, as in other writings, Alcuin takes a firm stand on Mary's motherhood of the Son of God. Yet as letters make clear, he never got the backing from the king which he felt should have been forthcoming. In (probably) May or June 799, however, Alcuin was again at the Aachen court to dispute the controversial doctrines with Felix in the king's presence and he believed he had secured his opponent's admission of error and adherence to the teaching of the universal church.

Alcuin was subsequently to complain that he had not had sufficient opportunity to discuss 'other matters' with the king, who, by this time, like Alcuin himself, had other preoccupations. The pope, Leo III, had been attacked and mutilated by Roman enemies and had fled to the Frankish court while it was at Paderborn in Saxony. Alcuin expressed shock and an insistence that the king should take action against the miscreants: this would certainly involve an expedition to Rome, in which, however, he would not be taking part because of his age and ill health (the descriptions of his symptoms suggest that he suffered from recurrent malaria as well as cataracts). He also complained that he was not being kept informed about what was going on. Since 797 at the latest, a very few of Alcuin's letters addressed to the king or to friends who were also royal councillors and which are mainly concerned with very different topics, including astronomical and exegetic ones, refer in passing to a 'Christian authority' or a 'Christian Empire' which the Frankish king exercised or ruled over and the territorial bounds of which he had extended. Alcuin never attempts to explain what these terms signified for him (although modern scholars have speculated freely) nor directly to link them with, for example, Augustine's notions of 'empire' and the City of God; only in a poem of 799 or 800 does he speak of Charlemagne's right and duty to restore the 'ruler of the church' to his position of lawful authority in Rome.

In April 800 Charlemagne was at St Martin's, declaredly for the purpose of prayer. What passed between Alcuin and the king on that occasion is irrecoverable; the only reflection of the visit in his writings is the inclusion among his letters of a distinctive funerary oration for 'the lady Liutgard' (probably never formally queen) who died there. The further claim that Alcuin's preparation of a revised text of the Vulgate Bible already had the Frankish king's assumption of the imperial title in view similarly does not stand up to critical enquiry. Alcuin's supposed initiative or leading voice in the events leading to Charlemagne's acclamation and coronation as emperor at St Peter's, Rome, on 25 December 800 is much less clear than has sometimes been claimed.

Alcuin's subsequent approval and enthusiasm for Charlemagne's new dignity is unmistakable. Yet very soon after the emperor's return to Francia they came into open and at times bitter conflict, recorded in written exchanges of 801–2, which were for the most part preserved only by a successor with court connections. The occasion was a supposed violation of the right of sanctuary at St Martin's by officials of Theodulf, archbishop of Orléans, who had sought to recover a fugitive criminous cleric. The emperor's wrath was aroused by the violent counter-measures taken by the abbey's community and dependants; and although he accepted that Alcuin was not personally guilty of sedition, he was neither convinced nor appeased by his citation of both civil and canon law in defence of the Turonians' behaviour. They were brought before an imperial *missus* (a judge with delegated authority), whose conduct of the proceedings was in turn sharply criticized by Alcuin.

All this notwithstanding, the achievements of his last years, when Alcuin was over sixty, are substantial and remarkable. His earlier exegetical writings, only rarely datable but apparently extending over the whole period from the late 780s to his last years, were probably more important in his estimate of himself—filling in gaps left by the much-admired Bede—than that of modern scholars, who have been content to note their dependence on the great fathers (Jerome, Augustine, John Chrysostom in Latin translation, Cassiodorus). The implied range of reading is, however, impressive; his selection and abbreviation are far from arbitrary and allow Alcuin to give a different emphasis from his models or sources; and the greater concision was obviously welcome to succeeding generations. In 801 he completed his great commentary on St John's gospel which still found readers in twelfth-century Cistercian houses. Shortly afterwards he wrote a three-book *De fide sanctae trinitatis* with a strong Christological bias, dedicated to the emperor and claiming (not very justifiably) to use the methods of dialectic; it enjoyed early acclaim, and continued to have a wide readership in later centuries.

The substantial corpus of Alcuin's verse, much of it without any internal evidence of date and not clearly showing any stylistic or linguistic development, seems to have had few medieval readers and has been variously but usually negatively judged by modern scholars. Recently, however, its variety and the various techniques employed by its author to imitate and improve on the work of earlier poets have been stressed.

A high regard for Alcuin as a liturgist is evident in clerics of the next generation, who were themselves liturgical innovators or commentators, such as the chancellor Helisachar and Bishop Amalarius: for the latter Alcuin was 'the most learned teacher of our country' whose authority in such matters was unchallengeable (Amalarius, 3.94, 99). His *De laude* includes office chant-texts for which there is no other pre-800 record; perhaps during his years at court he 'revised' and supplemented an older Roman list of Old Testament and epistle mass readings; his composition (or organization) of a substantial series of votive masses which established themselves in later liturgy and of masses for new commemorations (notably All Saints but also the saints of particular churches) is well established. That he was responsible for the supplement(s) to the (papal) Gregorian sacramentary, as was believed for much of the twentieth century, has effectively been disproved. Alcuin had, however, a lifelong commitment to the importance and power of prayer, whether personal or collective, and its associated angelic presence. He made a not precisely definable but certainly major contribution to the compilation and early continental dissemination of books of private prayers (*libelli precum*) of which the oldest copy now extant is associated in manuscript with the Tours-written earliest copy of his *De vitiis et virtutum*, a moral treatise dedicated to the defender of the Breton frontier, Count Wido. Another and related work of his last years, prepared originally for Archbishop Arno but

known only from copies made after his death, is a devotional handbook made up predominantly of meditational comments on parts of the psalter.

The creation of a distinctive and outstanding minuscule script at Tours cannot be credited to Alcuin personally—his own handwriting, of which there are a very few examples, was essentially 'insular' in its forms. If, however, the earliest Tours-written books in which it is used, including both a rare Virgil commentary and the earliest complete Bibles (which reflect Alcuin's personal orthography), are correctly dated to the years immediately either side of 800, then it is difficult not to accept his personal influence on the fine sense of page layout and the adoption of a hierarchy of scripts, as well as on the forms of punctuation in which he was certainly interested, in the products of the monastery's scriptorium.

Death and reputation Alcuin died at St Martin's on 19 May 804, his last days being recorded in a largely conventional way in his life; but the same text records a vision in Italy of his death and admission to heaven as well as one closer at hand. Over his burial-place in the abbey a tomb was erected with an epitaph composed by himself. It was destroyed in viking attacks on Tours in mid-century and nothing certain is known of its appearance, but the text of the epitaph is widely preserved in manuscript copies. At least one of his disciples (perhaps named Candidus) included what seems to be a deliberately uncomplimentary reference to him in a sermon preached not long after his death. In general, however, Alcuin was held in high regard by those who had been taught by him or were pupils of his pupils; and only at the end of the century are there signs that his reputation was diminishing. At the end of the eleventh century and in the early twelfth century his achievements were lauded in different ways by Sigebert of Gembloux and William of Malmesbury. Although he was of little interest to the schools and universities of the high and later middle ages, a surprising number of his works continued to be copied in other centres; the *De fide sanctae trinitatis* was printed at Basel in 1493 as part of a widely used homiliary and reprinted many times in the next century; and some of the pedagogical and exegetical works were also printed in the sixteenth century. Alcuin's modern reputation, however, may be said to have begun in the second quarter of the nineteenth century, when the French historian and politician Guizot saw him as his own precursor, as 'Charlemagne's Minister of Education'.

D. A. BULLOUGH

Sources E. Dümmler, ed., *Epistolae Karolini aevi*, MGH Epistolae [quarto], 4 (Berlin, 1895) · Alcuinus, *Patrologia Latina*, 100–01 (1863) [reproduces *B. Flacci Albini seu Alcuini… opera omnia*, ed. F. Forster (1777); still the only edn of most of Alcuin's exegetic, dogmatic and pedagogic writings] · 'Vita Alcuini', ed. W. Arndt, [*Supplementa tomorum I–XII, pars III*], ed. G. Waitz, MGH Scriptores [folio], 15/1 (Hanover, 1887), 184–97 · Alcuin, 'Carmina', *Poetae Latini aevi Carolini*, ed. E. Dümmler, MGH Poetae Latini Medii Aevi, 1 (Berlin, 1881), 160–351, 631–3 · Alcuin, *The bishops, kings, and saints of York*, ed. and trans. P. Godman, OMT (1982) · Alcuin, *Libri IV de laude Dei et de confessione orationibusque sanctorum collecti*, extracts only published, edn in preparation · A. Werminghoff, ed., *Concilia aevi Karolini*, MGH Concilia, 2/1 (Hanover, 1906), 110–71, 220–5 · G. B.

Blumenshine, ed., *Liber Alcuini contra haeresim Felicis*, Studi e Testi, 285 (1980) · Alcuin, *De orthographia*, ed. H. Keil, *Grammatici Latini*, 7 (1880), 295–312 · *The rhetoric of Alcuin and Charlemagne*, trans. W. S. Howell (1941) [text with Eng. trans.] · Alcuin, 'Vita Willibrordi', ed. W. Levison, *Passiones vitaeque sanctorum aevi Merovingici*, MGH Scriptores Rerum Merovingicarum, 7/2 (Hanover, 1920), 81–141 · *Precum libelli quattuor aevi Karolini*, ed. D. Wilmart (1940) · Amalarius, *Opera liturgica omnia*, ed. J. Hanssens, 3 vols., Studi e Testi, 138–40 (1948–50) · L. Wallach, *Alcuin and Charlemagne* (1959) · J. Marenbon, *From the circle of Alcuin to the school of Auxerre: logic, theology, and philosophy in the early middle ages*, Cambridge Studies in Medieval Life and Thought (1981) · D. A. Bullough, *Carolingian renewal: sources and heritage* (1991) · D. A. Bullough, *Alcuin: achievement and reputation* [forthcoming]
Archives Bayerische Staatsbibliothek, Munich, MSS of writings · Biblioteca Apostolica Vaticana, Vatican City, MSS of writings · Bibliothèque Nationale, Paris, MSS of writings · BL, MSS of writings · Royal Library of Belgium, Brussels, MSS of writings · Stiftsbibliothek, St Gallen, MSS of writings | Bibliothèque Nationale, Paris, acta concilii Ephesi, MS lat. 1572
Likenesses manuscript illumination, 12th cent., Trinity Cam. · medallion drawing, Staatsbibliothek, Bamberg, Bamberg Bible, MS Bibl. 1, fol. 5*v* [*see illus.*] · portrait, Biblioteca Apostolica Vaticana, Vatican City, Fulda dedication pictures, MS Reg. lat. 124, fols. 2*v*, 3*v*

Aldam, Thomas (1616?–1660), Quaker preacher and writer, was born in Warmsworth, near Doncaster, although no further details of his parentage are known. He was a relatively affluent yeoman. He married Mary Killam (*d.* 1660) in 1644, and the couple had at least one child, Thomas (1652?–1723).

Thomas Aldam was probably a puritan before his discontent led him to find religious guidance in the nascent Quaker movement. Indeed Aldam was one of the very first to be 'convinced', joining with other radical separatists in 1651 or 1652 after hearing the future Quaker leader George Fox preach. His activities as a Quaker preacher and writer soon led to trouble. In 1652, after preaching against a minister of the established church, Aldam suffered arrest. Magistrates subsequently imposed a custodial sentence which they supplemented with fines totalling £93 for his refusal to remove his hat before 'superiors', and for failing to pay taxes to the state church. Aldam was also physically attacked by non-Quakers in 1654, 1655, and 1658.

Aldam put his time in prison to good use—particularly during the long stretch between 1652 and December 1654. His letters of the time exhibit an interest in wider Quaker affairs, as he set about establishing links between northern Quakers and printers in London. Later he generated interest for the first general Quaker fund intended to aid the movement's missionary work. His political and religious ideas were sometimes quite theatrically expressed. A parliamentarian sympathizer, he nevertheless once tore his hat into shreds when he was granted an audience with Oliver Cromwell, indicating, it seems, the certain belief that the protector would soon be torn from power. He was outraged at what he perceived to be the wrongful imprisonment of Quakers, doing much to document their plight. He was similarly dismissive of Charles II, being recorded as saying, 'I find nothing to this Man' (Aldam, 12).

Aldam died in June 1660, aged about forty-four, presumably in Warmsworth, after a period of illness. The date of his burial is unknown, but he was able to pass on a considerable estate at his death. Mary, his wife, died three months after her husband, and the tender testimony of her son reveals 'a Woman that truly feared God, and served him in her Day and Generation' (Aldam, 12). In his lifetime Aldam had seen Quakerism grow from a small gathering of northern separatists to a national movement. His was not an insignificant contribution; as a writer, preacher, administrator, and willing 'sufferer', Thomas Aldam made a valued commitment.

CATIE GILL

Sources T. Aldam, *A short testimony concerning … Thomas Aldam* (1690) · J. Besse, *A collection of the sufferings of the people called Quakers*, 2 vols. (1753) · W. C. Braithwaite, *The beginnings of Quakerism*, ed. H. J. Cadbury, 2nd edn (1955); repr. (1981) · 'Dictionary of Quaker biography', RS Friends, Lond. [card index] · R. Moore, *The light in their consciences: early Quakers in Britain, 1646–1666* (2000) · *The journal of George Fox*, ed. N. Penney, 2 vols. (1911) · M. K. Peters, 'Quaker pamphleteering and the development of the Quaker movement, 1652–1656', PhD diss., U. Cam., 1996 · J. Smith, *A descriptive catalogue of Friends' books*, 2 vols. (1867) · H. Tuke, *Biographical notices* (1815)
Archives RS Friends, Lond., corresp. and papers

Alday, John (*fl.* 1566–1579), translator, whose origins are obscure, is described by Tanner as a resident in London (Tanner, *Bibl. Brit.-hib.*, 25). He seems to have been preoccupied in particular with the state of man, as evidenced by his principal work, *Theatrum mundi: the Theatre or Rule of the Worlde*. It is undated, but is licensed to Thomas Hacket towards the end of 1566 (Arber, *Regs. Stationers*, 1.336) and therefore probably published early in the next year. The title-page continues: 'wherein may be sene the running race and course of every mans life, as touching miserie and felicity', yet the book touches considerably more misery than felicity. Essentially a long account of 'what miseries all humain creatures are subject to', it is small wonder that, among his multitudinous other references, Robert Burton draws on it in his *Anatomy of Melancholy*. After a dedication to Sir William Chester, Alday makes a lively address to the reader, complaining of man's condition, and inserts an explanatory note on his vocabulary: 'The cause why we have added unto this title the word *Rule* was for that this word *Theatre* was not known but of the learned'. The work contains five small specimens of verse, the longest of which, based on the ecclesiastical collect *Da pacem domine in diebus nostris*, is entitled 'A Complaint of the Pore Husbandmen in Metre' and ends on an uncharacteristically optimistic note:

When pilferie shall cease,
when reason and good policie
In justice shall take place,
then the good time shall be.

Otherwise, the book is made up of fabulous assertions: 'in Italy … they did not only drink themselves out of all measure but also they constrained their mares and horses to do the like' and instructions such as 'man child ought not to be too much effeminated, women children suffered to learne dauncing nor to paint their faces'. To the *Theatre* is appended *Of the Excellencie of Mankinde*, a tapestry of classical myth, which, in its fanciful subject matter and shorter length, can barely temper the preceding tract's melancholia at the human condition. The whole volume is a translation of two French pamphlets by Pierre Boaistuau, published in 1558. Another translation of the same two pamphlets was published by Francis Farrer in 1663 but does not acknowledge Alday's version.

Also from French was taken *A summarie of the antiquities and wonders of the worlde, abstracted out of the sixtene first bookes of the excellente Historiographer Plinie* (n.d.), licensed in July 1566 (Arber, *Regs. Stationers*, 1.314). This is a slim, curious volume, an arbitrary collocation of random sentences lifted from Pliny's *Natural History* for their oddity: 'There is also in the Indias, Apple trees which have the leaves three cubits long and two brode, bearing suche great fruit, that foure men can scarce eate one Apple'. It is remarkable for Alday's professed credulousness of his matter, based on the credo 'nothing is unpossible unto God', and for its sudden leaps of subject in successive sentences: 'The *Heliotropum* in his floure doth turne every day to follow the sunne. The Ant doth never begin to hourd up but in the full Mone.' Translated at the beginning of the book is a dedication to the Cardinall of Meuldon by Blayse of Changy, son of the original author. Alday's assertion in *Theatrum mundi* 'That a vertuous woman is God's gift from heaven to man' anticipates his third translation from French, *Praise and dispraise of women: gathered out of sundrye authors, as well sacred as prophane, with plentee of wonderfull examples … brought into our vulgar by John Allday* (1579).

ROSS KENNEDY

Sources E. Brydges, *Censura literaria: containing titles, abstracts, and opinions of old English books*, 2nd edn, 10 (1815), 1 · Tanner, *Bibl. Brit.-Hib.*, 25 · W. C. Hazlitt, *Collections and notes, 1867–1876* (1876), 466 · Arber, *Regs. Stationers*, 1.314, 366 · *DNB*

Aldborough. For this title name *see* Stratford, Edward Augustus, second earl of Aldborough (1733/4–1801).

Alden, Sir Percy (1865–1944), social worker and politician, was born at Walton Street, in St Thomas's parish, Oxford, on 6 June 1865, the third of six sons (there was also a daughter) of Isaac Alden (b. 1834), a master butcher, and his wife, Harriett Elizabeth, *née* Kemp. It is not known where he received his schooling, though by 1881 he was a pupil teacher in Oxford. At fifteen, while acting as a messenger for the Oxford local examinations delegacy, he met the philosopher T. H. Green, who encouraged him to pursue his studies at Balliol College, Oxford. He was admitted there in October 1884 as one of the talented local boys whom Benjamin Jowett brought into the college during his later years as master. After graduating with thirds in classical moderations (1886) and *literae humaniores* (1888), he embarked on a course at Mansfield College, the Congregationalist theological college which had recently been founded at Oxford, with the aim of becoming a Baptist minister. His studies were interrupted when, through the influence of A. M. Fairbairn, Mansfield's first principal, he was appointed in 1891 the first warden of the Mansfield House settlement. Inspired by the ideas of T. H. Green

and Arnold Toynbee, Mansfield House had been established at Canning Town in West Ham, to the east of London, to enable university men to undertake social work and live among the inhabitants in one of the most deprived areas serving the capital. Its objective was 'to provide the conditions for a good life, economically, socially, aesthetically, intellectually, and spiritually for all groups in society' (Kaye, 134).

Alden, who remained at Canning Town for ten years, was recognized as a pioneer of the settlement movement, adept at generating enthusiasm for the venture both among helpers and local people. His distinctive contribution was to involve the settlement in the municipal politics of West Ham, believing that such political activity was essential to improve social conditions. He set out his views on the role of settlements in local government in a contribution to *University and Social Settlements* (1898) edited by his friend the Christian socialist Will Reason. Mansfield House backed candidates for the school board and board of guardians; as a member of the school board, Alden developed provision for children with special educational needs. He was also elected a member of West Ham borough council (1892–1901), of which he was deputy mayor in 1898. In 1895 he organized a census of unemployment in the borough, which led the council to petition parliament that it was the duty of the state to provide employment for able-bodied persons who were out of work. Although not a member of the Independent Labour Party (ILP), Alden supported the Labour group in West Ham, which in 1898 became the first in Britain to run a local council. An exponent of co-operation between middle-class and working-class radicalism, he was labelled a 'kid-gloved sort of socialist' by one critic (Fink, 297).

Alden married on 14 September 1899 Margaret Elizabeth Pearse (1867–1958), a doctor of medicine, the daughter of Joseph Pearse, a missionary. They had four daughters. Margaret Alden, who had been educated at Walthamstow Hall, the school for the daughters of nonconformist missionaries, studied medicine at Edinburgh, Bern, and Geneva. She was senior resident physician of the Canning Town Medical Mission Hospital, part of the Canning Town Women's Settlement, a sister organization to Mansfield House. The author of *Child Life and Labour* (1908), she became in the 1920s a medical officer at infant welfare centres.

Alden's political activities grew out of his strong commitment to the Christian inspiration of the Mansfield settlement. 'I regard the Labour movement as a religious movement', he wrote, 'and can honestly say that I have found more unselfishness among working men than among any other class' (Kaye, 145). During the 1890s he became involved in a number of Christian socialist organizations, including the Christian Socialist League and Christian Social Brotherhood. He was concerned, however, at the alienation of working people from organized religion. This he described in his contribution to R. Mudie-Smith's *The Religious Life of London* (1904), based on the *Daily News* survey of attendance at public worship in London during 1902–3. He viewed the institutional church movement, whose success he had witnessed on travels in the USA, as the most promising way to bring Christian influences to bear upon working-class life. Non-sectarian churches would function as centres of social and educational as well as religious activity for their communities.

Alden stepped down as warden of Mansfield House in 1901, though he retained links as honorary warden and vice-president. He became a Quaker and organized social work for the Society of Friends. During 1901–2 he edited the Liberal daily paper *The Echo*, whose writers included Ramsay MacDonald. Alden was a member of the Fabian Society, and in 1903 joined the progressive Liberal discussion group in London the Rainbow Circle, which promoted collectivist causes. The topics of the papers which he read to the circle included property redistribution and peasant proprietorship, local-government reform and rural housing. In 1904, with other members of the Rainbow Circle, he helped to found the British Institute of Social Service, whose object was principally to gather and distribute data relevant to social service projects, but which in practice became a co-ordinating agency for social reformers.

Alden's own most influential contribution to social policy making was on unemployment. He became secretary of the National Unemployed Committee, created after a meeting in December 1902 sponsored by the ILP and attended by both Labour and radical Liberal figures, to put forward a programme for government action. Alden's book *The Unemployed: a National Question* (1905) drew both upon his experience in Canning Town and upon travels in Germany, the Netherlands, and Belgium to investigate continental approaches to the problem. He insisted that the state had a responsibility towards the unemployed. His prescriptions included the creation of a minister of commerce and industry, the provision of labour colonies to deal with vagrancy, state subsidies to insurance schemes run by trade unions, and public works to provide employment for those made jobless during trade depressions. His account of the German network of labour exchanges contributed to the development of William Beveridge's ideas on the subject. To Alden, the problem of unemployment exposed the inefficiency and damaging effects of the free market, which needed to be addressed by an ethical reorganization of industry.

Alden was one of the progressive politicians with an appeal to Labour voters for whom Herbert Gladstone, the Liberal whip, found a constituency and provided finance following the electoral pact with MacDonald, on behalf of the Labour Representation Committee, in 1903. He won the Tottenham division of Middlesex from the Conservatives at the general election of 1906 and held it until 1918. Before 1914 he was a leading exponent of the 'new Liberalism', and was among the critics of the failure of John Burns, president of the Local Government Board, to produce radical initiatives to deal with unemployment. Among the many radical causes which he advocated in parliament, he was notable as a defender of the land rights of the indigenous peoples of South Africa. During the First World War he undertook relief work for the Belgian Relief Committee in London, with which his wife was also involved, and was a government commissioner for the relief of Belgian refugees in the Netherlands, for which he was later decorated by the king of Belgium.

A breach between Alden and the Liberal leadership opened up when he opposed military conscription in a parliamentary debate on 6 January 1916. He remained within the party, however, and contributed the chapter on housing to the manifesto *Liberal Policy* (1918) put forward by the Asquith Liberals at the general election of 1918. On standing for Tottenham North he was defeated by a coalition Conservative at that election. His sympathy towards ethical socialism and his advanced views on public ownership, set out in an article in the *Contemporary Review* in April 1919, led him into the Labour Party. After unsuccessfully contesting Luton as a Labour candidate in 1922 he was elected for Tottenham South in 1923, but lost the seat in the general election of 1924. Disappointed with the performance of Ramsay MacDonald's first Labour government, and attracted by the innovative proposals for tackling unemployment developed by the Liberal industrial inquiry, he resumed his affiliation to the Liberal Party late in 1927.

Apart from his brief interval in parliament, Alden's principal post-war activity was as a charity administrator. He became chairman of the Save the Children Fund, taking part in refugee relief work in the Balkans, for which he received Hungarian and Bulgarian honours. He was bursar of the trust founded by his friend Sir Richard Stapley (1842–1920), a businessman, philanthropist, supporter of the Liberal Party, and stalwart of the Rainbow Circle, to help those who were too poor to pursue studies at university or at other institutions of higher education. He also chaired the Christian Social Research Trust founded in 1924 by Sir Halley Stewart, his own Halley Stewart lectures for 1936 being published as *Aspects of a Changing Social Structure* (1937). Their theme, 'the growing interest of the State in social and industrial problems', had been Alden's lifelong concern. In 1933 he was knighted on the recommendation of Ramsay MacDonald. He was killed during an air raid by a German flying bomb in Tottenham Court Road, London, on 30 June 1944.

M. C. CURTHOYS and TIM WALES

Sources *The Times* (3 July 1944), 6 · W. Blackshaw, *Mansfield College Magazine*, 15 (July 1945), 137–9 · *DLB*, 3.3–5 · I. Elliott, ed., *The Balliol College register, 1900–1950*, 3rd edn (privately printed, Oxford, 1953) · *The Labour who's who* (1927) · Burke, *Peerage* (1939) · *WWW* · b. cert. · m. cert. · d. cert. · census returns, 1881 · *BMJ* (17 May 1958), 1183–4 · E. Kaye, *Mansfield College, Oxford: its origin, history and significance* (1996) · L. Fink, 'The forward march of Labour started? Building a politicized class culture in West Ham, 1898–1900', *Protest and survival: the historical experience*, ed. J. Rule and R. Malcolmson (1993), 279–321 · M. Freeden, ed., *Minutes of the Rainbow Circle, 1894–1924* (1989) · M. Freeden, *The new liberalism: an ideology of social reform* (1989) · J. Harris, *Unemployment and politics: a study in English social policy* (1972) · J. Harris, *William Beveridge* (1977) · K. D. Brown, *Labour and unemployment, 1900–1914* (1971) · M. Pugh, *The making of modern British politics, 1867–1939* (1982) · P. Thompson, *Socialists, liberals and labour: the struggle for London, 1885–1914* (1967) · C. A. Cline, *Recruits to labour: the British labour party, 1914–1931* (1963)

Archives Labour History Archive and Study Centre, Manchester, papers
Wealth at death £21,628 10s. 5d.: 5 Oct 1944, *CGPLA Eng. & Wales*

Aldenham. For this title name *see* Gibbs, Henry Hucks, first Baron Aldenham (1819–1907).

Alder, Joshua (1792–1867), zoologist, was born on 7 April 1792 at Dean Street, Newcastle upon Tyne, the son of provision merchants. He was educated at Tanfield School, under a relative, the Revd Joseph Simpson. On his father's death in November 1808, he left school to help his mother run the family business. An early acquaintance with the wood-engraver Thomas Bewick (1753–1828) helped him to develop his talent for drawing; he was fond of sketching on the kitchen walls with a burnt stick, and of holding dramatic performances with puppets that he had made.

In 1815 Alder became a member of the Literary and Philosophical Society of Newcastle, which stimulated his interest in natural history; gradually he devoted himself to British conchology and zoophytology. From 1840 he gave up business and devoted himself exclusively to science. The loss of all his property by the failure of a local bank in 1857 was irreparable; however, with the aid of a civil-list pension of £70, supplemented by friends, he was able to continue his work until his death.

For over forty years, accompanied and helped by his sister, Alder made summer visits to the coasts of Britain, acquiring an extensive collection of shells and zoophytes. He was active in the Natural History Society of Northumberland, Durham, and Newcastle upon Tyne, and in the Tyneside Naturalists' Field Club, founded in 1846. His most important publication, *On the British Nudibranchiate Mollusca* (1845–55), was co-written with the marine zoologist Albany Hancock (1806–1873). His various papers (some of which were also written with Hancock) numbered over fifty.

Alder was noted not only for his geniality and decency, but also for his powers of observation and accuracy as a draughtsman. He was acknowledged to be an authority in species identification. He died at 11 Summerhill Terrace, Newcastle upon Tyne, on 21 January 1867.

G. T. BETTANY, *rev.* YOLANDA FOOTE

Sources *Natural History Transactions of Northumberland and Durham*, 1 (1867), 324–37 · Boase, *Mod. Eng. biog.* · d. cert.
Archives NHM, London, letterbooks and notebook · NMG Wales, drawings · U. Newcastle, Hancock Museum, drawings of marine animals | NHM, corresp. with Alfred Merle Norman · NMG Wales, letters to George Sowerby
Likenesses Maull & Polyblank, photograph, 1855, NPG [*see illus.*]

Aldersey, Laurence (1546–1597/8), sea captain, was born at Aldersey Hall, Spurstow, Cheshire, the son of Thomas Aldersey (*d.* 1557), sheriff of Chester in 1539 and mayor in 1549, and his wife, Cecilia Garnet (*fl.* 1513–1594), also of Chester. As the sixth in a family of at least eight children, in the mid-1560s he looked to London and to the merchant Thomas *Aldersey (1521/2–1598) for a career in Baltic and international trade. By 1589 Laurence, for whom there is

Joshua Alder (1792–1867), by Maull & Polyblank, 1855

no record of marriage, described himself to Richard Hakluyt as a merchant of London, but to the herald conducting the visitation of Kent in 1580–81 he was just a traveller in Ethiopia.

Two of Aldersey's travel accounts 'set down by himself' were published by Richard Hakluyt in the 1589 edition of *Principall Navigations*. The first shows that Laurence set out in April 1581 to travel through Holland and Germany to Venice, where he embarked for Cyprus before sailing on in a smaller barque to Jaffa. Thence he travelled overland to Jerusalem, visiting its sights from 12 to 22 August 1581. His whole trip took nine months and five days.

On 4 August 1586, the privy council considered how 'the 100 turkes brought by Sir Francis Drake out of the West Indyes, may upon their arrival at Woolwich and Blackwall' be 'conveyed home and presented to [William Harborne] the Ambassador unto the Grand Seigneur' (*APC*, 1586–7, 205–6). Commissioned to take them home, Laurence Aldersey left Bristol on 21 February 1587 in command of the *Hercules of London*, sailing via Malta and Zante. His second journal shows that on arrival in Patras in 1587:

> they brought us to the house of Cady, who was made then to understand of the 20 Turks that we had aboard, which were to go to Constantinople, being redeemed out of captivity by Sir Francis Drake, in the West Indies, and now … brought before him, that he might see them and when he had talked with them, and understood how strangely they were delivered, he marvailed much, and admired the Queen's Majestie of England.   (Hakluyt, 1589 edn, 225)

But the Greeks of Sio (Chios) were not so pleased, for 'there grew a great controversie between the marriners of the Hercules, and the Greeks of the towne of Sio, about the bringing home of the Turks, which the Greeks tooke in ill part, and so a broile beganne' (ibid., 226). Following more calls around the Grecian archipelago, and a second visit to Cyprus, Aldersey landed at Tripoli in Lebanon. Thence he took passage until 28 July 1587 for Bichieri, near Alexandria. Thomas Rickman, master of the *Tyger of London*, showed him Alexandria's buildings, while William Alday and William Caesar showed him respectively the sights of Cairo and the pyramids. Sailing homewards via Alexandria and Tunis, he visited John Tipton in Algiers before re-embarking on 7 January 1588 to reach Dartmouth on 1 February, and London on 7 February.

In 1597 Sir William Dethick granted arms to Laurence Aldersey, who died soon afterwards on a diplomatic mission carrying letters from Queen Elizabeth to the emperor of Ethiopia. Hakluyt in the 1598 edition of his *Principal Navigations* provides the text of the letters Aldersey carried in May 1597. Under Thomas Aldersey's will of 1595, Laurence was due just £5, and the forgiveness of large debts and behaviour 'dyvers waies offensive to me' (PRO, PROB 11/93, sig. 10).

R. C. D. BALDWIN

Sources R. Hakluyt, *The principal navigations, voyages, traffiques and discoveries of the English nation*, 2nd edn, 2 (1599), 150–54, 282–5; 3 (1600), 203 · R. Hakluyt, *The principall navigations, voiages and discoveries of the English nation* (1589), 177, 187, 224–7 · APC, 1586–7, 205–6 · *The visitation of London, anno Domini 1633, 1634, and 1635, made by Sir Henry St George*, 1, ed. J. J. Howard and J. L. Chester, Harleian Society, 15 (1880), 8 · BL, Harley MSS 1424; 1505; 1535, fol. 39; 2119 · C. G. O. Bridgeman, *A genealogical account of the family of Aldersey, of Aldersey and Spurstow, co. Cheshire* (privately printed, London, 1899) · D. B. Quinn, 'Turks, blacks and others in Drake's West Indian voyage', *Explorers and colonies: America, 1500–1625* (1990), 197–206 · BL, Add. MS 39925, fol. 19 · will, PRO, PROB 11/93, sig. 10 [Thomas Aldersey]

Wealth at death heavily indebted in 1597: will, PRO, PROB 11/93, sig. 10 [Thomas Aldersey]

Aldersey, Thomas (1521/2–1598), merchant, was born at Bunbury, near Spurstow in Cheshire, the second of five sons of John Aldersey (*c*.1494–1554), landowner, and Anne Bird of Colton near Chester. After an education in Bunbury, probably at Chantry House, Aldersey's apprenticeship began in London under Thomas Bingham in 1541. Bingham introduced him to London's protestant booksellers, and to a new breed of preachers including John à Lasco and Christopher Goodman whose family had also hailed from Chester. Aldersey's freedom of the city and livery of the Haberdashers' Company was conferred on 13 July 1548. As a young merchant he became concerned about the shaky trading economy that would have to sustain the congregation of protestant exiles that set itself up in Emden in August 1554. However, the presence in Emden during 1554 of John à Lasco and Sir John Cheke provided him with ways to reach another influential Marian exile, William Cecil, who proved concerned to advance such trading links after the loss of the Calais staple in 1558.

Aldersey suffered the suspicion of the Marian authorities as a leading protestant and an active supporter of Princess Elizabeth. His interest in Goodman's published work led to his being indicted in London on 29 April 1555,

Thomas Aldersey (1521/2–1598), by Robert Peake the elder, 1588

although his marriage to Alice Calthorpe (1526–1589×95) in 1554 seems to have helped him concentrate on commerce. He was accused again in Brussels in 1566 of extreme protestant belief, together with John Marsh, then governor of the Merchant Adventurers. Aldersey turned such problems to his advantage, for these same religious sympathies brought him into supportive contact with German protestants and the merchants of Emden, and thus into a circle conducting diplomatic and trading negotiations with Countess Anna of Emden.

On 3 May 1564 Aldersey wrote to Cecil that he was ready to sail to Emden as the trade mission's deputy governor. Cecil helped further by insisting that departure of the forty ships be delayed by a fortnight for diplomatic reasons, and to provide time to gather a larger naval escort. As a result all but one had arrived safely on 23 May 1564. Aldersey next reported to Cecil on his trading success at Emden, namely the sale of 5000 cloths by 24 June, but also noted attempts by the Hanseatic merchants to begin a trade boycott of Emden's mart. As Aldersey had convinced Cecil that the Emden mart could be built up to rival Antwerp if the smuggling of English cloth via France were curtailed, a new charter giving such powers to the Merchant Adventurers' Company followed on 18 July 1564, specifying Aldersey as a deputy governor.

Knowing the limitations of London's markets Aldersey had thrilled to Sir Thomas Gresham's vision of the Royal Exchange scheme and contributed a £4 subscription through the Haberdashers' Company in 1566. The support of Cecil and the Calthorpes set him on a rapid rise within London's merchant circles. In 1572 the privy council made him responsible for the sale of the goods and shipping seized from Spanish merchants in 1568. On 26 January 1574 the council gave a special commission to a number of merchants, mainly from Dublin, to act with Aldersey to search for illegal linen yarn exports from Ireland and to curtail smuggling by gaoling the culprits until they could be brought for trial. The council also asked Aldersey to report on those with claims for reprisals against Spain. His status to act arose from long involvement in Anglo-Spanish trade, which had begun with his advocacy to Cecil of the Bristolian John Frampton's claim for compensation for wrongful imprisonment in Seville in 1558–9. Having done this effectively Aldersey became a leading merchant or assistant in the Spanish Company after its rechartering for trade in 1578, although this trade proved intermittent for wider diplomatic reasons. In October 1580 he served with Julius Caesar on an admiralty court commission investigating piracy, and in 1582 on a privy council inquiry into overseas trade, inflation, and the recent rapid increase in gold exports. In 1582 he stood guarantor of the trade debts of three London Grocers, while proposing two other London merchants for election as aldermen.

The successful Emden initiative subsequently gave Thomas Aldersey a considerable status in city and privy council discussions of new Baltic marts for English woollen cloths. As a result he became the Eastland Company's leading assistant under its new charter of 1579. At first he promoted the growing trade in coloured cloths and naval stores with Danzig (where the annual sale of unfinished white cloths had been limited to just 200 rolls) before advocating that the Eastland trade transfer into the safer roads of Elbing from 1583. His own political career originated in the same merchanting circles with his election in 1571 as a common councillor for Cripplegate ward of the city of London. He became auditor of the city in 1571–2, and serjeant to the sheriff of London in 1576. In the 1570s he also served as one of the city's collectors of subscriptions to poor scholars at Oxford and Cambridge. As a highly respected assistant of the Haberdashers' Company by 1579, he was elected as the fourth of London's MPs on 7 October. Aldersey was active on various Commons committees until 1589 but did not seek re-election for parliament in November 1592. In 1584 he joined 119 others in signing a city petition in support of the puritan lecturer at St Mary-le-Bow suspended by Archbishop Whitgift. On 22 March 1590 he was asked by the city's court of aldermen to help in the governance of the Bridewell Hospital and of Christ's Hospital, accepting the work along with seven city appointees for six years.

Aldersey's house in Cripplegate was assessed for £100 towards the subsidy of 1589—the year his wife's brother, Martin Calthorpe, died in office as lord mayor of London. The heralds' visitation of London in 1568 recorded that Thomas and Alice Calthorpe's union was childless. This explains his subsequent generous treatment of Laurence *Aldersey, whose large debts and occasional offensive behaviour he forgave in his will, and the concern for his wider family apparent in his landed investments. Thomas

conducted a series of lucrative land deals in Kent, Middlesex, and Essex, with his elder brother John, acting as his attorney from 1554 until the latter's death on 17 October 1582. Following his brother's death Thomas (who had inherited most of John's property and goods) arranged that the family's Cheshire estates be administered by Randle Aldersey, John's eldest son. In 1593 Thomas arranged for the leasing of the large Christ's Hospital estate at Berden and Clavering in Essex to his eldest surviving nephew, John Aldersey (d. 1616). He had the estate mapped in 1597 by Ralph Treswell senior, his brother-in-law.

Aldersey never forgot his Cheshire roots. In 1582 he contributed to the installation of a new conduit from the Shambles to the High Cross in Chester. In 1584 he became treasurer of the Nantwich fire disaster relief fund, raising over £5300 inside two years. In 1575 he began his dearest scheme, to endow a grammar school at Bunbury, and soon appointed a teacher. It was incorporated by letters patent on 2 January 1594. His plans and landed endowments for the school were approved by the Haberdashers' court of assistants on 21 October 1594, for he intended that after his death they should operate the Free Grammar School of Thomas Aldersey at Bunbury as their first company school.

Thomas Aldersey's will, dated 20 February 1595, made provision for the poor of Bunbury and of the London parishes of St Mary Magdalen, St Lawrence Jewry, St Michael Bassishaw, and St Alban, Wood Street; and of Putney, Surrey, and of Barking, Essex. He also provided £20 for the poor of the city of Chester to be distributed by William Aldersey and Christopher Goodman—the latter a famous Oxford puritan often deprived of a licence to preach, but latterly resident in Chester. He died at Aldersey Hall, Spurstow, in December 1598 and was buried at the church of St Boniface, Bunbury. His will, proved on 23 February 1599, allocated £800 in cash to his family, while his propertied estate was divided almost equally between his school and John Aldersey of Berden, Essex. A portrait of Thomas Aldersey by Robert Peake the elder (now in the Grosvenor Museum, Chester) gives his age as sixty-six in 1588.

R. C. D. BALDWIN

Sources P. Rutter, *The Haberdashers' oldest school: a history of the Aldersey School, 1594–1994*, Bunbury (1993), 1–25 • BL, Add. MS 39925 • GL, MS 15885, nos. 1, 17, 31, 44 • GL, MS 115842 • Ches. & Chester ALSS, CR469/179, 180, 190, 271, 272, 273, 274, 275 • G. Ormerod, *The history of the county palatine and city of Chester*, ed. T. Helsby, 2 (1882), 198, 739–40 • G. Ormerod, ed., *The king's vale of England* (1656), 4, 8, 54, 103, 104 • I. W. Archer, *The history of the Haberdashers' Company* (1991), 75–6 and fig. 3 • GL, Noble collection, C 78 T [Thomas Aldersey] • will, PRO, PROB 11/93, sig. 10 • G. D. Ramsay, *The City of London in international politics at the accession of Elizabeth Tudor* (1975), 156, 242, 248, 262, 266–71 • C. G. O. Bridgeman, *A genealogical account of the family of Aldersey, of Aldersey and Spurstow, co. Cheshire* (privately printed, London, 1899), 15, 17, 125, 394, 426 • A. B. Beaven, ed., *The aldermen of the City of London, temp. Henry III– [1912]*, 1 (1908), 289 • S. E. Åström, *From cloth to iron: the Anglo-Baltic trade in the late seventeenth century*, 1 (1963), 22–8 • HoP, *Commons, 1558–1603*, 1.332 • CSP dom., 1581–90, 86, 591–2, 627 • Baron Kervyn de Lettenhove [J. M. B. C. Kervyn de Lettenhove] and L. Gilliodts-van Severen, eds., *Relations politiques des Pays-Bas et de l'Angleterre sous le règne de Philippe II*, 4 (Brussels, 1885), 276 • S. D'Ewes, *A compleat* journal of the … House of Lords & House of Commons (1693), 300–308 · R. Cooke, Visitation of London, 1568, ed. H. Stanford London and S. W. Rawlins, [new edn], 2 vols. in one, Harleian Society, 109–10 (1963), 37, 156 · PRO, SP11/5/8 · PRO, SP12/34/3, SP12/70/435, SP12/18/1 [Cecil's correspondence] · PRO, C66/1083 M46, C66/1007 M24, C66/1102, C66/1112, C66/1109 M4/5, C66/1158 M1, C66/1150 M31–2, C66/1 · BL, Lansdowne MS 112/1, fol. 3 · BL, Lansdowne MS 23, fol. 116 · BL, Lansdowne MS 146, fol. 43 · BL, Lansdowne MS 683, fol. 62 · BL, Lansdowne MS 56, fol. 1 · BL, Lansdowne MS 79, fol. 107 **Likenesses** R. Peake the elder, oils, 1588, Grosvenor Museum, Chester [see illus.] · R. Peake, oils, Haberdashers' Company Hall, London **Wealth at death** see will, PRO, PROB 11/43, sig. 10

Aldersey, William (1543–1616), merchant and antiquary, was baptized at St Oswald's, Chester, on 15 December 1543, the son of Ralph Aldersey (d. 1555) and Jane Goodman (d. c.1555). He followed in his father's footsteps as a successful merchant ironmonger. He married Mary, daughter of John Brereton of Wattenhall and Eccleston, Cheshire, on 22 December 1578, before being elected lord mayor of Chester twice, in 1595–6 and 1613–14. The mayoralty and associated civic administration was of considerable strategic importance because Chester was the principal port operating in support of the standing army in Ireland. Aldersey himself recorded the number and counties of origin of the troops and horses dispatched between 1594 and 1616. His pride in this related to a special barracks he had built for that traffic and to the city's ability efficiently to revictual warships such as HMS Moon. Thomas *Aldersey in his will of 1595 (proved in 1599) had recognized his distant cousin's civic concern and envisaged William working with the preacher Christopher Goodman for the sake of Chester's poor. In 1603 Aldersey administered Goodman's will, disposing of his fine theological library with help from another antiquarian bibliophile, Archbishop James Ussher.

Aldersey was so successful in overseas trade that he was included in the patent incorporating the East India Company on 31 December 1600. This too was lucrative, for although he had to subscribe £240 per share during 1601, the distributed profit on the first voyage by 1603 was nearly 300 per cent, and over all the East India voyages up to 1616 was never less than 220 per cent. Between his work and civic duties Aldersey studied the city's Roman archaeology and the documentation of its medieval re-emergence, writing 'A collection of the mayors who governed the cittie of Chester with the antiquities of the same' (BL, Add. MS 39925, fols. 32–164). The bulk of the draft was finished in 1594 but he extended it annually in the style of a chronicle until 1616. It incorporated separate lists of all the justices, aldermen, and sheriffs of Chester and their activities, written up in 1602. Aldersey extended backwards the historical studies of Archdeacon Rogers (d. 1595) on the bishopric of Chester. He took a keen familial interest in the Brereton family since Henry VII's time, especially in William Brereton, knighted after a skirmish in Kilkenny in 1588. He knew too the published work of John Brereton, who had sailed to Cape Cod in 1602 before resuming his priestly duties in York and then Suffolk.

Aldersey outlived his eldest son, David, but not his favoured nephew Thomas (1600–1675). The latter after attending Queens' College, Cambridge, became a distinguished lawyer of Gray's Inn and escheator of Cheshire from 1629, whereupon he extended Aldersey's civic histories beyond 1616 and similarly updated and copied his work on the justices of Chester while leaving intact all his uncle's entries. Thomas also recorded Aldersey's reputation as a 'lover of all good preachers' and as 'a wise and grave citizen'. Aldersey's last honour was to attend a civic dinner when James I visited Chester on 22 August 1616; as the most senior alderman he presented the king with a cup of gold on the city's behalf. He died at Chester on 26 October 1616 and was buried at St Oswald's, Chester, on 28 October. His will was proved in Chester later in 1616. An inquisition post mortem followed on 25 April 1617.

R. C. D. BALDWIN

Sources A. Kennet, 'The origins and early history of the mayors of Chester', monograph, Ches. & Chester ALSS, CR 942/714 352 048 KEN · Ches. & Chester ALSS, CR 489/452 · BL, Add. MS 29780, fols. 43–158 · BL, Add. MS 39925 · C. G. O. Bridgeman, A genealogical account of the family of Aldersey, of Aldersey and Spurstow, co. Cheshire (privately printed, London, 1899), 15–20, tables 1 and 2 **Archives** BL, Add. MS 29780, fols. 43–158 · BL, Add. MS 39925, fols. 32–164

Alderson, Sir Edward Hall (bap. 1787, d. 1857), law reporter and judge, was baptized on 10 September 1787 at Great Yarmouth Presbyterian Old Meeting Chapel, the eldest son of Robert Alderson (d. 1833), barrister and recorder, and his first wife, Elizabeth, daughter of Samuel Hurry of Great Yarmouth. Alderson's mother died of consumption in 1791 and he was sent to live with his maternal grandfather. His varied schooling included an unhappy stay at Charterhouse in 1800, and, more successfully, private tuition under Edward Maltby, afterwards bishop of Durham, in 1804–5. He entered Gonville and Caius College, Cambridge, in October 1805, and showed great proficiency in both mathematics and classics. In 1809 he was senior wrangler, first Smith's prizeman, and first chancellor's medallist; and as a result he was elected fellow of his college.

In 1811 Alderson was called to the bar of the Inner Temple, where he had been a pupil of Joseph Chitty. He joined the northern circuit and Yorkshire sessions and his career soon grew to remarkable proportions. He was co-editor (with Richard *Barnewall) of reports from the king's bench division covering the period from 1817 to 1822. On 26 October 1823 he married Georgina Catherine (d. 1871), daughter of the Revd Edward Drewe, with whom he had a substantial family. Parliamentary work was a major part of his practice: in 1825, his cross-examination of George Stephenson on the practicability of the latter's engine designs was highly instrumental in defeating the first bill to authorize the Liverpool and Manchester Railway, thus delaying that project for several years. Plainly destined for high office, despite holding neither silk nor (apparently by disinclination) any political post, Alderson was appointed a common law commissioner in 1828.

In November 1830 Alderson was appointed judge of the

court of common pleas, and thereupon knighted. In February 1834 he became a baron of the exchequer, specializing in equity matters until that jurisdiction was transferred to the court of chancery in 1841. He was later remembered, with varying degrees of enthusiasm, as a clever, analytical, and forthright judge, with little patience for those of lesser abilities; he was particularly astute in finding technical reasons to avoid the application of the death penalty. He was quick to take a view of a case, and exceedingly hard to talk out of it. As judge of assize, he was prominent in the attempts to suppress the Luddites in 1831 and the Chartists in 1842. He was popular with the bar and juries, if not always with his colleagues, not least because of his relentless jocularity, on the bench and off. Several of his charges to grand juries, in which he discoursed on the issues of the day, were published.

Alderson was a great exponent of the flexibility of the common law when in the right hands, and accordingly was an enemy of codification. He seems to have been dubious of the deterrent effect of the criminal law long before reaching the bench, and on many occasions argued for a reduction in the scope of the death penalty; he also argued that prison should be a means for reforming the criminal, even though this might be incompatible with deterrence.

An active churchman of moderate views and a lifelong friend of C. J. Blomfield, bishop of London, Alderson was prominent in seeking to reconcile the Church of England to the Gorham judgment of 1850. He opposed secular education, believing that the mere communication of knowledge without religious values was of little value. Yet he was a noted advocate of allowing Quakers, Jews, and others who felt unable to swear on the Christian Bible to affirm instead. A Conservative, yet with no parliamentary ambitions, he was suspicious of the 'tyranny' he saw in democracy.

A review of the leading civil cases in which Alderson gave judgment, either for himself or *per curiam*, reads like a broad survey of the legal problems of emerging capitalism. In *Russell* v. *Cowley* (1835) he gave vocal support to would-be patentees of new inventions; *Bligh* v. *Brent* (1837) was a major contribution to the legal understanding of company shares; *Hutchinson* v. *York etc. Railway Co.* (1850) firmly established the doctrine of common employment, though Alderson's *per curiam* judgment contained enough qualifications to enable later judges to begin the work of extirpating it; in *Egerton* v. *Brownlow* (1853) he argued strongly that public policy, while a necessary foundation for common law, was distinct from it and should remain so; and *Hilton* v. *Eckersley* (1855) was a major development of the law on trade combinations. His *per curiam* judgment in *Hadley* v. *Baxendale* (1854) was still required reading in basic law in the late twentieth century, and the same could be said up to a short time before this of *Wood* v. *Leadbitter* (1845), where he upheld the Jockey Club's effort to free Epsom racecourse of those they considered undesirables.

When not on circuit, Alderson divided his time between London and Lowestoft. He continued to compose classical and English poetry throughout his life, much of which has survived. He maintained a correspondence with his cousin, the novelist Amelia Opie, until her death in 1853. His last sitting was at the Liverpool winter assizes in December 1856, after which he was suddenly struck down on hearing of a serious injury to one of his sons. He died on 27 January 1857, from a brain disease, at his home at Park Crescent, London. He was buried on 2 February 1857 at St Mary Magdalen's Church, Risby, near Bury St Edmunds, a church of which he had himself laid the foundation stone.

STEVE HEDLEY

Sources C. H. Alderson, *Selection from the changes, charges, and other detached papers of Baron Alderson* (1858) · *Law Times* (31 Jan 1857), 255; (7 Feb 1857), 266 · *Law Times* (7 April 1894), 532–3 · Boase, *Mod. Eng. biog.* · Venn, *Alum. Cant.*
Likenesses W. Skelton, line engraving, pubd 1832 (after H. P. Briggs), BM, NPG · H. P. Briggs, oils, Inner Temple, London · oils, Gon. & Caius Cam.

Alderson, Sir Edwin Alfred Hervey (1859–1927), army officer, was born at Capel St Mary, Suffolk, on 8 April 1859, the eldest son of Lieutenant-Colonel Edward Mott Alderson, of Poyle House, Ipswich, and his wife, Catherine Harriett Swainson. In 1876 he joined the Prince of Wales's Own Norfolk artillery militia, and in 1878 was gazetted to the 97th foot, later the Queen's Own Royal West Kent regiment, joining his unit in Halifax, Nova Scotia. After a short term there he went with the regiment to Gibraltar, then in 1881 to Natal. There he was detached for service with the mounted infantry at Laing's Nek, and it was with the mounted infantry that he was identified for much of his career. In 1882 he served with them in the Egyptian campaign, including at Qassasin (26 August and 9 September) and Tell al-Kebir (13 September). He took part in the Gordon relief expedition (1884–5) with the mounted (camel) regiment. For saving a private from drowning in the Nile in 1885 he was awarded the bronze medal of the Royal Humane Society. Alderson married in 1886 Alice Mary, second daughter of the Revd Oswald P. Sergeant, vicar of Chesterton, Oxfordshire. They had one son, and Alice survived her husband.

In 1887 Alderson was appointed adjutant to the mounted infantry at Aldershot, having been promoted to captain in the previous year; he was given the same appointment in the Royal West Kent regiment in 1890, and retained it for four years. He passed out of the Staff College, Camberley, in 1895, and in 1896, with the substantive rank of major, went in command of the mounted infantry to Rhodesia, where he was prominent in defeating the Matabele (Ndebele) revolt (1896). He was then given command of all troops in Mashonaland, and received the brevet of lieutenant-colonel. He then served at Aldershot as deputy assistant adjutant-general and in command of the mounted infantry. In 1900 he was made brevet colonel and inspector-general of mounted infantry with the rank of brigadier-general. During the Second South African War he commanded the mounted infantry in 1901–2, his force including Canadian, Australian, New Zealand, and other colonial troops. He was mentioned in dispatches, subsequently receiving the CB (1900); he was also appointed successively aide-de-camp to Queen Victoria and to Edward VII. In 1903 he was promoted to the substantive rank of colonel, and for four years commanded the 2nd infantry brigade at Aldershot with the rank of brigadier-general. He was promoted major-general in 1907. From 1908 to 1912 in India he commanded the 6th (Poona) division.

On the outbreak of the First World War in 1914, Alderson was appointed (4 August) to command the 1st mounted division, all troops in the counties of Norfolk and Suffolk. In October, with the rank of lieutenant-general, he was given the command of the 1st Canadian division, which embarked for France in February 1915. The division fought at Neuve Chapelle (10–13 March), second Ypres (22 April–25 May), Festubert (15–25 May), and second Givenchy (15–16 June). In August the 2nd Canadian division arrived in France, and the two divisions became the Canadian army corps, with Alderson in command. A third division was added in January 1916, and in the following May, when Sir Julian Byng took over the command, Alderson became inspector-general, Canadian forces, and held that appointment until the end of hostilities. He was promoted KCB in 1916. In 1921 he was made colonel of the Royal West Kent regiment.

Alderson retired in 1920, and devoted himself to his two main recreations, hunting and yachting. A noted horseman, and a great believer in hunting as training for officers, he wrote *Pink and Scarlet, or, Hunting as a School for Soldiering* (1900); wherever he was stationed he hunted. He owned several racing and other craft, and was commodore of the Broads Cruising Association. He published several other books, among them *With the Mounted Infantry and Mashonaland Field Force, 1896* (1898). Alderson died at the Royal Hotel, Lowestoft, on 14 December 1927, and was buried three days later in Chesterton.

C. V. OWEN, rev. JAMES LUNT

Sources *The Times* (15 Dec 1927) · *The Times* (19 Dec 1927) · *Hart's Army List* (1897) · "*Queen's Own*" *Gazette* (Jan 1928) · J. F. Maurice and M. H. Grant, eds., *History of the war in South Africa, 1899–1902*, 4 vols. (1906–10) · J. E. Edmonds, ed., *Military operations, France and Belgium, 1915*, 2, History of the Great War (1928) · E. A. H. Alderson, *With the mounted infantry and the Mashonaland field force, 1896* (1898) · E. A. Alderson, *Pink and scarlet, or, Hunting as a school for soldiering* (1900) · E. A. Alderson, *Lessons from 100 notes made in peace and war* (1902) · G. W. L. Nicholson, *Canadian expeditionary force, 1914–1919: official history of the Canadian army in the First World War* (1962) · WWW
Archives National Archives of Zimbabwe, Harare, staff diary and papers | BL, corresp. with E. T. H. Hutton, Add. MS 50088, *passim*
Likenesses W. Stoneman, photograph, 1917, NPG
Wealth at death £44,894 17s.: resworn probate, 8 Feb 1928, CGPLA Eng. & Wales

Alderson, Sir Henry James (1834–1909), army officer, was born at Quebec on 22 May 1834, the son of Lieutenant-Colonel Ralph Carr Alderson (1793–1849), Royal Engineers, and his wife, Maria, daughter of Henry Thorold of Cuxwold, Lincolnshire. John *Alderson (*bap.* 1757, *d.* 1829), physician, was his grandfather. Educated at Stoton and Mayer's school at Wimbledon (1844–8), he entered the Royal Military Academy, Woolwich, in May 1848. He was commissioned second lieutenant in the Royal Artillery on 23 June 1852, and served in Canada until 1854, when, on promotion to lieutenant, he returned to England. Serving

through the Crimean War, he was at the Alma, Inkerman, and the siege and fall of Sevastopol. He was mentioned in dispatches, and received the Légion d'honneur (third class). He was promoted second captain on 1 April 1859 and from February to June 1864 was attached on special mission to the headquarters of the Federal army under General O. A. Gillmor during the American Civil War, being present at the bombardment of Charleston.

On his return to England, Alderson joined the experimental department of the School of Gunnery, Shoeburyness, and became successively captain on 6 July 1867, major on 3 July 1872, lieutenant-colonel on 1 October 1877, brevet colonel on 1 October 1881, and major-general on 9 July 1892. He married in 1877 his second cousin, Florence (b. 1844/5), youngest daughter of Sir Edward Hall *Alderson (*bap.* 1787, *d.* 1857), baron of the exchequer. They had one son, and Florence survived her husband.

From 1871 Alderson held various appointments in the department of the director of artillery at the War Office. From 1891 to 1896 he was president of the ordnance committee. He retired on 22 May 1896, and from 1897 until his death was a director of Sir W. G. Armstrong, Whitworth & Co., an armaments manufacturer. He was made CB on 21 June 1887, KCB on 30 May 1891, and was appointed colonel-commandant in the Royal Artillery on 4 November 1905. He died at Durham on 10 September 1909.

J. H. LESLIE, rev. JAMES LUNT

Sources *The Times* (11 Sept 1909) · *The Times* (2 Nov 1909) · *R. A. Institution Leaflet* (Oct 1909) · *Hart's Army List* · d. cert. · CGPLA Eng. & Wales (1909)
Wealth at death £13,243 5s. 10d.: resworn probate, 29 Oct 1909, CGPLA Eng. & Wales

Alderson, Sir James (1794–1882), physician, was born in Hull on 30 December 1794, the fourth son of Dr John *Alderson and his wife, Sarah Isabella (*née* Scott; *d.* 1805), and was baptized in the Bowl Alley Presbyterian Church, Hull, on 18 April 1795. He received his early education at the school of the Revd George Lee, Unitarian minister at Hull. While still in his teens he went to Portugal as clerk in the army commissariat, before the end of the Peninsular War. After his return to Britain, in 1818 he entered Pembroke College, Cambridge, where he was later made a fellow. He took his BA degree in 1822 as sixth wrangler; he became MA in 1825, and the following year he was incorporated at Magdalen Hall, Oxford, as MB. The degree of DM, Oxford, followed in 1829. To the Royal College of Physicians he was admitted inceptor candidate on 26 June 1826, candidate on 30 September 1829, and fellow on 30 September 1830. On 24 June 1828 he married Mary Anne, daughter of Peter Berthon of Glanadda, Caernarvonshire. He settled for a short time in London, and was physician to the Public Dispensary, Carey Street. On the death of his father Alderson succeeded to a large and lucrative practice in Hull and the neighbouring parts of Lincolnshire and the East Riding of Yorkshire. He was also elected physician to the Hull Infirmary. He took a close interest in promoting education in the town.

About 1850 Alderson left Hull once more for London, and settled in Berkeley Square. On the foundation of St

Sir James Alderson (1794–1882), by Edward Richard Whitfield (after John Edward Jones, 1847)

Mary's Hospital, Paddington, in 1851, he was appointed senior physician, a post which he held until elected president of the Royal College of Physicians in 1867, when the governors unanimously elected him consulting physician. He was treasurer of the college from 1854 to 1867, and took great interest in its administration. He was especially proud of having unearthed the original charter granted by Henry VIII, which had long been lost. He held the office of president until 1870. Alderson was the representative of the college at the General Council of Medical Education and Registration from 1864 to 1866. He was appointed physician-extraordinary to Queen Victoria in 1874, having received a knighthood in 1869. Alderson, who was a fellow of the Royal Society, contributed occasional papers to its *Transactions*, and to the *Transactions* of the Medico-Chirurgical Society; he delivered the Lumleian lectures in 1852 and 1853, and, unusually, was twice appointed to deliver the Harveian oration, in 1854 and 1867.

Alderson met Bishop Wilberforce when the latter was ill in Italy, and the two travelled home together. The journey provided Alderson with a fund of entertaining reminiscences. According to a contemporary Alderson was 'a man of cultivated mind, kindly disposition, and correct and courteous deportment. He was spare and erect in figure, and reserved in manner, conservative in his opinions, little disposed to scientific novelties or collegiate reforms'

(*BMJ*, 545). He died at his home, 17 Berkeley Square, London, on 13 September 1882, and was buried in Norwood cemetery.   ROBERT HARRISON, *rev.* MICHAEL BEVAN

Sources *BMJ* (16 Sept 1882), 545 · *The Lancet* (23 Sept 1882), 510 · private information (2004) · Venn, *Alum. Cant.* · *GM*, 1st ser., 98/1 (1828), 640 · R. G. Wilberforce, *Life of the right reverend Samuel Wilberforce … with selections from his diary and correspondence*, 2 (1881), 121 · *PRS*, 34 (1882–3), vi–vii

Likenesses wood-engraving, 1854, Wellcome L. · E. R. Whitfield, line engraving (after J. E. Jones, 1847), Wellcome L. [*see illus.*]

Wealth at death £15,690 4*s.* 11*d.*: probate, 11 Dec 1882, CGPLA Eng. & Wales

Alderson, John (*bap.* 1757, *d.* 1829), physician, was baptized on 4 June 1757 at Lowestoft, Suffolk, the youngest child of the Revd James Alderson (1713/14–1760), a dissenting minister, and his wife, Judith, *née* Mewse. He was only about three years old when his father died and he was brought up by an aunt and uncle in Ravenstonedale, Westmorland. Educated at the free grammar school there, he later inherited land and property from his uncle's manor at Ravenstonedale.

Alderson trained as a surgeon under his elder brother James, in Norwich, where he was for a time a lieutenant and surgeon to the West Norfolk militia, which also served at Hull in 1780. He studied medicine at Edinburgh for a year before starting in practice in Whitby, Yorkshire North Riding. He was awarded his MD by Marischal College, Aberdeen, in 1785. In 1786 he married Sarah Isabella Scott (*d.* 1805), daughter of Christopher Scott, of Beverley, East Riding of Yorkshire; the first of their eleven children (of whom five survived infancy) was born in Whitby.

The family moved to Hull in 1787, and Alderson was elected physician to Hull General Infirmary in 1792; he was also lecturer in physiology, as well as consulting physician to Hull lying-in charity. In 1814 he founded the Sculcoates refuge for the insane, whose prospectus stated, 'every attempt consistent with humanity will be made to restore the patient' (Luffingham, 'On apparitions', 11). Alderson also took a leading part in the life of the town, being made freeman in 1813, and he worked for thirty years towards the provision of commercial education in Hull. He was president of the Hull Subscription Library in 1801 and of the new literary and philosophical society in 1822, and he was the founder and first president of the Hull Mechanics' Institute in 1825. A man of many interests, a friend referred to his 'hobbyhorsism' (Bickford and Bickford, *Lunatic Asylums*, 14).

Alderson's many published works included *An Essay on the Nature and Origin of the Contagion of Fever* (1788), *An Essay on … Sumach with Cases Showing it's Efficacy in the Cure of Paralysis* (4 edns, 1794–1811), *A Treatise on Improvement of Poor Soils* (2 edns, 1802, 1807); and an 1805 lecture on apparitions (1810–23), which was concerned to show by case studies that illusions or hallucinations could often be removed by treating an underlying illness.

Alderson died on 16 September 1829 and was buried in the family vault at St Mary's, Sculcoates; an estimated 12,000–15,000 people attended his funeral. His statue was moved from the old to the new Hull Royal Infirmary in

1972. His surviving children were Christopher Richard (1787–1829), a physician at Hull General Infirmary and at Sculcoates; John (1790–1829); Ralph Carr (1793–1849), of the Royal Engineers and Royal Hospital, Chelsea; Sir James *Alderson (1794–1882), physician, who succeeded to his father's practice at Hull; and Margaret, wife of J. V. Thompson, barrister of Beverley.   JEAN LOUDON

Sources J. A. R. Bickford and M. E. Bickford, *The medical profession in Hull, 1400–1900: a biographical dictionary* (1983) · *GM*, 1st ser., 100/2 (1830), 346, 450 · *GM*, 2nd ser., 32 (1849), 664 · [R. L. Luffingham], *John Alderson and his family* (1995) · *GM*, 1st ser., 99/2 (1829), 285 · private information (2004) · R. L. Luffingham, 'On apparitions by John Alderson, M.D.', *Hull Medical Society, Historical Book Reviews*, 16 (Jan 1996) · J. A. R. Bickford and M. E. Bickford, *The private lunatic asylums of the East Riding* (1976) · *Fasti academiae Mariscallanae Aberdonensis: selections from the records of the Marischal College and University, MDXCIII–MDCCCLX*, 2, ed. P. J. Anderson, New Spalding Club, 18 (1898); 3, ed. J. F. K. Johnstone, New Spalding Club, 19 (1898) · E. Gillingswater, *An historical account of the ancient town of Lowestoft in the county of Suffolk* (1790)

Likenesses W. Behnes, marble memorial tablet, 1831, Holy Trinity, Hull · Earle, Roche Abbey stone statue, 1831–42, City Hall, Hull · R. Westmacott, stone statue, 1833, Hull Royal Infirmary · possibly by H. Cheney, oils, Wilberforce House Museum, Hull · portrait, Hull Royal Infirmary, Alderson House

Wealth at death Cottingham estate; several houses and some land; Sculcoates; industrial premises with wharf: Bickford and Bickford, *Medical profession*.

Aldfrith (d. **704/5**), king of Northumbria, was the illegitimate son of *Oswiu (611/12–670) and an Irish princess, Fin, of the Uí Néill dynasty, whom Irish sources describe as the daughter of Colmán Rímid who died c.604. This attribution has difficulties, in that it would put Aldfrith in his fifties at the time of his accession in 685, and his marriage and subsequent fathering of a son, *Osred I (c.696), very late in life. The chronology of his life has been plausibly resolved by suggesting that his mother was the granddaughter of Colmán Rímid.

During the reign of his half-brother, *Ecgfrith (645/6–685), Aldfrith lived in exile in Ireland and western Britain, and he seems to have been recalled from Ireland after Cuthbert had pointed out to his half-sister, the abbess *Ælfflæd, that he was a potential heir to the childless Ecgfrith. When he succeeded Ecgfrith, after the latter's death at the hands of the Picts at the disastrous battle of Nechtansmere (Dunnichen Moss, near Forfar), Aldfrith seems to have accepted that he would rule a Northumbrian kingdom within narrower bounds, and indeed the Northumbrians never retrieved their previous extensive overlordship of the Britons, Irish, and Picts. Nevertheless, during his reign of nearly twenty years, he maintained his kingdom in peace and political stability, so that scholarship and art could flourish as under no previous ruler.

The economic and political strength of Aldfrith's kingdom is reflected in his marriage alliance with a West Saxon princess, *Cuthburh (fl. c.700–718), sister of the powerful king *Ine, as well as in the introduction of a silver currency in Northumbria. The cultural strength in the creative blend of Anglo-Saxon, Celtic, and Mediterranean art which flourished in his reign produced outstanding manuscripts, such as the Lindisfarne gospels, and the architectural sculpture at Wearmouth–Jarrow and Hexham.

His early life in exile, which Bede said was for study, had provided Aldfrith with firsthand knowledge of the Celtic kingdoms in the west, and he retained friendships there. In Ireland he had a considerable reputation as a teacher and scholar, a reputation endorsed by a wide range of his contemporaries: Bede praised his learning and the community of Wearmouth–Jarrow benefited from his love of books, in that he gave them 8 hides of land in exchange for 'a codex of the cosmographers of miraculous workmanship' ('Historia abbatum auctore Baeda', p. 380); Aldhelm, whom he probably met in Wessex, wrote congratulating him on his learning and dedicated a treatise on poetic metre to him, addressing him by the learned pseudonym Acircius. According to the anonymous life of Cuthbert, Aldfrith was in Iona before 685 and, according to Irish sources, he had been a pupil of Adomnán, abbot of Iona. Certainly Adomnán seems to have paid him two official visits: the first to obtain the release of Irish prisoners captured in the wars of Ecgfrith's reign, the second when he stayed for two years studying the ways of the Northumbrian church. On that occasion he gave Aldfrith his book, *De locis sanctis*, which the king, in Bede's words, 'had copied for lesser folk to read' (Bede, *Hist. eccl.*, 5.15).

Aldfrith's sympathetic knowledge of the British and Irish churches must have made him an ideal mediator in their disputes with the English, and it is significant that Adomnán came away from a visit to his court converted to the customs of the Northumbrian church. On the other hand Aldfrith was no more successful than his predecessors in dealing with the controversial Northumbrian bishop, Wilfrid. He may have been alienated by Wilfrid's legalistic appeals to the hierarchy in Rome in the lengthy dispute over the division of the northern diocese, but, for whatever reason, despite an attempt at reparation to Wilfrid, early in his reign, Aldfrith soon supported the view that he should be stripped of his bishopric and landholdings. In 692 the king banished the bishop and they were never reconciled, although according to the abbess Ælfflæd, Aldfrith's dying wish was that his successor should make peace and a settlement with Wilfrid.

It is possible that the scholarly Aldfrith was equally unsuccessful in dealing with his own family life. At an unknown date, but 'during their lifetime', his wife, Cuthburh, separated from him and became a nun at Barking, and then, in 718, founded the monastery of Wimborne (*ASC*, s.a. 718). When Aldfrith became ill in 704 the succession to the throne was in no way secure, since his son Osred (who may or may not have been Cuthburh's child) was only about eight years old. Aldfrith's death, on 14 December in either 704 or 705, then ushered in a period of great instability for Northumbria: the throne was claimed by Eadwulf, of unknown descent, but possibly from the Deiran royal line, and for some months there was a struggle for power between Eadwulf and those who supported Osred's claim. Although Osred succeeded to his father's throne, thus preserving the Bernician royal line, dynastic struggles in Northumbria were only briefly buried in his reign and he and his supporters were unable either to sustain the economy by retaining a silver currency, or to provide the peace which encouraged learning. Bede, in his letter to Bishop Ecgberht of York, in 734, saw a decline in ecclesiastical standards as beginning after Aldfrith's reign, and certainly none of his successors in the independent kingdom of Northumbria achieved his status. Alcuin fittingly summed up Aldfrith as one who loved sacred learning from his earliest youth and was an eloquent scholar with a piercing intellect, 'a king and teacher at the same time' (Alcuin, 71). ROSEMARY CRAMP

Sources Bede, *Hist. eccl.* • *ASC*, s.a. 685, 705, 718 • B. Colgrave, ed. and trans., *Two lives of Saint Cuthbert* (1940) • E. Stephanus, *The life of Bishop Wilfrid*, ed. and trans. B. Colgrave (1927) • 'Historia abbatum auctore Baeda', *Venerabilis Baedae opera historica*, ed. C. Plummer, 1 (1896), 364–87 • Alcuin, *The bishops, kings, and saints of York*, ed. and trans. P. Godman, OMT (1982) • K. Grabowski and D. Dumville, *Chronicles and annals of mediaeval Ireland and Wales: the Clonmacnoise-group texts* (1984) • D. P. Kirby, *The earliest English kings* (1991) • *Aldhelm: the prose works*, trans. M. Lapidge and M. Herren (1979) • *Ann. Ulster* • K. Harrison, *The framework of Anglo-Saxon history* (1976) • D. P. Kirby, 'Bede, Eddius Stephanus and the "Life of Wilfrid"', *EngHR*, 98 (1983), 101–14

Aldgyth. *See* Ealdgyth (*fl. c.*1057–1066).

Aldhelm [St Aldhelm] (*d.* **709/10**), abbot of Malmesbury, bishop of Sherborne, and scholar, was a prolific Latin author whose idiosyncratic style of composition in the media of prose and verse, both metrical and rhythmical, was profoundly influential both in England and on the continent up to the Norman conquest. His life is moderately well documented: Bede devotes a brief paragraph to Aldhelm's achievement (Bede, *Hist. eccl.*, 5.18); and in the early twelfth century two authors composed lives of Aldhelm, Faricius, an Italian from Arezzo who served as physician to Henry I, and William of Malmesbury, who devoted the entire fifth book of his *Gesta pontificum* to Aldhelm. In addition, Aldhelm's own writings, particularly his letters, supply valuable details. Despite these, many aspects of his life remain obscure.

Origins and connections It is not known when or where Aldhelm was born. William of Malmesbury conjectures that, when he died, Aldhelm was 'not less than seventy years old' (*De gestis pontificum*, 332), which would place his birth about 639; but this is no more than a conjecture, based on the biblical notion of a life of three score years and ten, since William elsewhere states that 'no written source assigns a number to his age' (*De gestis pontificum*, 385). It is in any case likely that he was born in Wessex soon after it was converted to Christianity through the efforts of the Italian bishop, Birinus, and various sources imply that he was from an aristocratic family, perhaps even related to the West Saxon king. Faricius states that he was descended from royal stock (*regia stirpe*) and was the son of one Kenten, allegedly a brother of King Ine (*d.* 726). The name Kenten looks suspiciously like that of Centwine, king of the West Saxons (*d.* 685); but Faricius's statement is unverifiable, and William of Malmesbury cast doubt on it by pointing out that Ine apparently had no brother Centwine. In any event Aldhelm seems to have

Aldhelm [St Aldhelm] (*d.* **709/10**), drawing

been well connected to the royal court: he composed a poem in honour of a church constructed by Bugga, a well-authenticated daughter of King Centwine; he stood as sponsor in baptism to Aldfrith, king of Northumbria (685–705) and dedicated to him his massive *Epistola ad Acircium*; and Cuthburh, the sometime queen of this King Aldfrith and a sister of King Ine, was a member of the community of nuns at Barking Abbey to whom Aldhelm addressed his prose *De virginitate* (she subsequently became abbess of the minster at Wimborne in Aldhelm's diocese of Sherborne).

Education and influences There is similar uncertainty about Aldhelm's early education. A letter addressed to him by an anonymous Irish student mentions that Aldhelm had been 'nourished by a certain holy man of our [*sc.* Irish] race' (letter 6, *Prose Works*, 164). There is no doubt that Aldhelm was impressively familiar with contemporary Hiberno-Latin literature, and may have derived this from an Irish master. But the identity of this putative Irish master is unknown. Since Bede refers to Malmesbury as the *Maildubi urbs*, 'the *urbs* [that is, monastery] of Máeldub', William of Malmesbury deduced that Aldhelm's unknown Irish master was this very Máeldub; but William's deduction cannot be tested. Aldhelm's education only becomes a matter of established fact after the arrival in England of Archbishop Theodore in 669, and of Abbot Hadrian the following year, and the establishment of their school in Canterbury, to which (in Bede's words) 'they attracted a crowd of students into whose minds they daily poured the streams of wholesome learning' (Bede, *Hist. eccl.*, 4.2). Aldhelm was certainly among this crowd of students: in one letter (letter 5, *Prose Works*, 163) he speaks with firsthand knowledge of Archbishop Theodore's teaching, and in another (letter 2, *Prose Works*, 153) addressed to Abbot Hadrian, he speaks warmly of the 'intimate fellowship' (*sodali contubernio*) which existed between them. Various evidence confirms the fact of Aldhelm's study at the Canterbury school. The so-called Leiden glossary, for example, which is a later (*c.*800) copy of a set of glosses designed to explain various texts studied at Canterbury, and is as such a record of the teaching of Theodore and Hadrian, has many points of contact with the writings of Aldhelm, including both the list of texts glossed in the Leiden glossary and the particular interpretations placed on words which recur in the writings of Aldhelm.

Appointment as abbot of Malmesbury What is not clear, however, is how many years Aldhelm spent in uninterrupted study at Canterbury; and this question is linked with that of when he was appointed abbot. It seems clear that he would have had to relinquish his studies in order to undertake the responsibilities of an abbacy. In his letter to Hadrian (letter 2, *Prose Works*, 153) he apologizes for the fact that, 'after leaving Kent three years ago', he has been detained by illness and administration and has been unable to return; it would appear, therefore, that his letter dates from the period of his abbacy. By the same token, he mentions in his letter to Geraint, king of Dumnonia (roughly, modern Devon and Cornwall), that he is 'performing the office of abbot', and that, when he had 'recently' attended an episcopal synod, he had been commanded to write to Geraint concerning the orthodox method of dating Easter (letter 4, *Prose Works*, 155). It is known from Bede's account that the synod convened by Archbishop Theodore at Hertford in 672 gave its attention *inter alia* to the correct observance of Easter day (Bede, *Hist. eccl.*, 4.5). If the episcopal synod attended 'recently' by Aldhelm was that of Hertford in 672, then Aldhelm would have been appointed to the abbacy of Malmesbury very soon afterwards. William of Malmesbury gives the date of Aldhelm's appointment as 675, and he appears to have taken this date from a charter of Leuthere, bishop of the West Saxons (*AS chart.*, S 1245), which he quotes, granting land at Malmesbury for the establishment of a monastery. If Aldhelm was appointed abbot in 675, then, taking account of the three years referred to in his letter to Hadrian, he must have left the school of Canterbury in 672. Given that Hadrian did not arrive in England until 670, Aldhelm can have studied with the great Mediterranean master for two years at most. Two years seems a very short period in which to have acquired the immense range of learning which Aldhelm deploys.

However, the evidence is not irrefragable. The Synod of Hertford established that national synods were to take place semi-annually at 'Clofesho', and, given that Easter dating was a recurring issue, any synod subsequent to 672

might have commissioned Aldhelm to write to King Geraint. Furthermore, the charter of Bishop Leuthere is regarded as highly suspicious by students of diplomatic; if its evidence is set aside, there is no reliable means of dating Aldhelm's becoming abbot of Malmesbury. Some light is thrown on the question by twelve other Anglo-Saxon charters in which Aldhelm appears as a witness. Many of these are demonstrably spurious (and none is an original document), but some are thought to have an authentic basis. With the exception of one obviously spurious document dated 670 which Aldhelm witnesses as abbot (*AS chart.*, S 227) and the aforementioned foundation charter of Bishop Leuthere, none of the charters witnessed by Aldhelm carries a date earlier than 680; those which are thought to contain genuine elements date from between 681 (S 236) and 688 (S 235, 1170). The total number of charters which survive from this period is limited; but such as it is, the charter evidence fails to prove that Aldhelm was already abbot of Malmesbury in the 670s. If Malmesbury was founded (and he became its first abbot) *c.*680, then it is possible to envisage a longer period of study at the Canterbury school—up to (say) ten years—a figure which would square much better with the extent of his learning.

From whatever date he was appointed, Aldhelm as abbot was very active on Malmesbury's behalf. In his prose *De virginitate*, written some time during the period of his abbacy, he describes himself as weighed down with the burden of pastoral care. Two charters, of which Malmesbury and Aldhelm are beneficiaries, are thought to have an authentic basis (*AS chart.*, S 1169, 1170); they reveal that Aldhelm was successful in increasing his monastery's endowment. According to William of Malmesbury, he rebuilt a church in Malmesbury dedicated to St Peter and St Paul. One of Aldhelm's own *Carmina ecclesiastica* (no. 1) is a *titulus* (that is, a dedicatory epigram intended to be inscribed in a church or on an altar) on the dedication of a church in honour of the same apostles, and presumably pertains to his own church. This church was still standing in William's day (*c.*1125). Aldhelm also built a second church at Malmesbury, this time dedicated to the Virgin Mary. His second *Carmen ecclesiasticum*, a *titulus* for a church of St Mary, may pertain to this second Malmesbury church, which, too, was still in existence in William's day. William adds that traces remained of a third church built by Aldhelm, adjacent to that of St Mary and dedicated to St Michael. At some point during his abbacy he composed the aforementioned letter to Geraint, king of Dumnonia, setting out the correct Roman principles for calculating Easter. This letter (letter 4, *Prose Works*, 155) was much admired by Bede, who described it as 'an excellent book' (*liber egregius*) which led many Britons to adopt the catholic celebration of Easter (Bede, *Hist. eccl.*, 5.18). Aldhelm may also have been abbot of Malmesbury when he wrote to the abbots in the diocese of Bishop Wilfrid to express his sympathy with their position following Wilfrid's banishment (letter 12, *Prose Works*, 169); but since Wilfrid was banished from England on three separate occasions, it is not possible to date the letter confidently.

From the letter addressed to Aldhelm by the anonymous

Irish student (letter 6, *Prose Works*, 164) we know that Aldhelm had visited Rome at some point in his career. William of Malmesbury preserves the text of a papal privilege issued by Pope Sergius (687–701) in favour of Malmesbury, and deduces that Aldhelm had gone to Rome for the express purpose of obtaining this privilege for his monastery, as well as for a church which he had built on the River Frome, dedicated to St John the Baptist. The text of the papal privilege is not beyond suspicion (it is preserved solely in Malmesbury's archives) but, if genuine, it would be consonant with Aldhelm's ambitions on Malmesbury's behalf. William also describes various other activities of Aldhelm in Rome, but these are all manifestly legendary. The date and purpose of Aldhelm's trip to Rome remain uncertain, therefore.

Bishop of Sherborne In 706, following the death of Bishop Hædde, the vast West Saxon see was divided into what henceforth became the dioceses of Winchester and Sherborne, with the forest of Selwood serving as the point of division. Perhaps as a result of his experience negotiating with King Geraint, Aldhelm was made bishop of the western diocese (Wiltshire, Somerset, Dorset, and probably part of Devon), adjacent to Geraint's kingdom of Dumnonia. His activities during his brief bishopric are difficult to determine. William of Malmesbury reports that he built a marvellous church at Sherborne, which William had seen with his own eyes, but which no longer exists. Possibly it was at this time that he built churches at Bradford-on-Avon, dedicated to St Laurence, and at Wareham, both of which are mentioned by William of Malmesbury, who adds that the walls (but not the roof) of that at Wareham were standing in his own day. In his role as bishop of Sherborne, Aldhelm appears as witness to three surviving charters, dated 706 and 709. Two of these are spurious (*AS chart.*, S 79, 1175), though the witness list of the first might derive from a genuine document; the third (S 248), dated 705 (for 706) and arguably genuine, is witnessed by nine bishops, Aldhelm among them, and was perhaps issued by a synod otherwise unrecorded. Beyond these documents, nothing is known of Aldhelm's activity as bishop. According to Bede, Aldhelm presided energetically (*strenuissime*) over his diocese for four years; given that he was elected bishop in 706, his death may be placed in 709 (or possibly 710). In later liturgical sources, the date of his deposition is given as 25 May. William of Malmesbury also reports that Aldhelm died at Doulting, and that his body was taken back to Malmesbury by Ecgwine, bishop of Worcester, who erected a stone cross every 7 miles along the route from Doulting to Malmesbury. As with many details of Aldhelm's life, it is impossible to verify this report. According to Faricius, Aldhelm was buried in his own church of St Michael.

Aldhelm's works: an Anglo-Saxon literary pioneer What is not in doubt, however, is the extent of Aldhelm's literary estate. In nearly every aspect of his literary activity, he was a pioneer: as he proudly stated in his *Epistola ad Acircium*, no one before him, born of the English race or Germanic peoples, had toiled so mightily in pursuit of Latin poetry

and letters. The corpus of his writing (which is accessible in an excellent edition by Rudolf Ehwald) includes: a group of *tituli* intended for churches and altars (these *tituli* go by the editorial title of *Carmina ecclesiastica*); a collection of one hundred metrical riddles, or, as he himself calls them, *enigmata*; a lengthy poem consisting of some 2900 hexameters on the subject, the *Carmen de virginitate*; and a rhythmical poem describing a journey through the west of England and the effects on a wooden church of a mighty storm which had taken place during the journey (the *Carmen rhythmicum*). His prose writings include: the composite work *Epistola ad Acircium*; the massive prose *De virginitate*; and a small corpus of letters. Unfortunately, none of Aldhelm's writings can be dated precisely; they may be described briefly in the sequence which they occupy in Ehwald's edition.

The *Carmina ecclesiastica* consist of the following *tituli*: no. 1, for a church dedicated to St Peter and St Paul, presumably Aldhelm's own church at Malmesbury; no. 2, for a church dedicated to St Mary (again, probably intended for Aldhelm's second church at Malmesbury); no. 3, for a church built at an unknown location by Bugga, a daughter of King Centwine; no. 4, a collection of twelve *tituli* intended perhaps for altars, each one dedicated to one of the apostles and each containing brief notice of how the apostle in question lived and died (the twelve poems are followed by a metrical epilogue); and no. 5, a *titulus* on St Matthias (it is clear that this poem belonged originally to the collection of twelve *tituli* on the apostles). Of these, nos. 1–3 reveal that Aldhelm was familiar with the practice of providing metrical inscriptions for churches, a practice which in his day was fully in evidence in the numerous churches of Rome (Aldhelm shows familiarity in his verse with an anonymous collection of *tituli* from churches in Rome, perhaps compiled by an Anglo-Saxon pilgrim). Nos. 4–5 are drawn from the treatise of Isidore of Seville (570–636), *De ortu et obitu patrum*, and the fact that no. 4 includes a metrical epilogue suggests that their purpose was literary rather than dedicatory.

The *Epistola ad Acircium* was dedicated to Aldfrith, king of Northumbria (685–705), for whom Aldhelm stood as sponsor in baptism, and whose *quondam* queen Cuthburh became head of a community of women religious at Wimborne, within Aldhelm's diocese. After an exordium to Aldfrith, Aldhelm treats the arithmological significance of the number seven, with abundant biblical references. Then follows a treatise on metre (*De metris*), including discussion of the varieties of metrical feet and the construction of the hexameter, based on various Late Latin grammarians and illustrated by many quotations from classical and Christian poets. Ostensibly to illustrate the properties of the hexameter, Aldhelm inserts at this point his collection of one hundred hexametrical *Enigmata*; but these have value far beyond that of mere metrical examples. As a collection they offer a poetic cosmology, in which the 'mysteries' (*enigmata*) of God's creation are revealed in his creatures, animate and inanimate. All creatures are shown in a constant process of gestation and birth, all animated by a vital spirit which penetrates their being, and which can be understood figuratively even in man-made objects. The final part of the *Epistola ad Acircium* is a treatise *De pedum regulis*, which consists of a metrical *gradus* for non-Latin speakers, in which Aldhelm provides long lists of words constituting various metrical feet (spondees, iambs, trochees, and so on) which could be plundered by prospective poets seeking to fill out their hexameters. The main importance of these two metrical treatises is that they are the first to be composed by a non-native speaker of Latin.

Aldhelm's longest work is the prose *De virginitate*, an extended treatment of virginity dedicated to Abbess Hildelith and her community of nuns at Barking Abbey, Essex. A number of these nuns had previously been married: Aldhelm tailors his theoretical discussion of virginity (based on earlier treatises by Ambrose, Augustine, Jerome, and others) to the English nuns' circumstances, so that, of the three states, virginity, chastity, and marriage, Aldhelm especially praises the second (chastity), by which he understands someone who has once been married, but has rejected marriage in favour of the chaste life, as many of his addressees had apparently done. The theoretical argument is then illustrated by a long catalogue of examples arranged in approximate chronological order, beginning with Old Testament patriarchs, John the Baptist, apostles, then fathers of the church, martyrs, and confessors. The list of male confessors includes such universal saints as Martin, Basil, Antony, and Benedict (*fl.* 550), who is the latest saint to be commemorated by Aldhelm. Then follows a sequence of female martyrs, beginning with St Cecilia, then Agatha, Lucy, Agnes, and so on. The work concludes with an exhortation (based on an earlier treatise by Cyprian) to the nuns of Barking not to dress ostentatiously. In compiling his prose *De virginitate*, Aldhelm drew on an impressively wide range of hagiographical sources; his intention was to provide an anthology of edifying reading for his audience. But his selection of saints is idiosyncratic (it bears no relationship to the saints commemorated in Anglo-Saxon liturgical calendars, for example), as is his choice of incidents from the lives of the saints he was describing.

Aldhelm subsequently provided a verse counterpart to his prose treatise on virginity, on the model of the Late Latin poet Caelius Sedulius, whose *Carmen paschale* (a meditation on the typological significance of events in the life of Christ) was followed by a prose account of the same subject (*Opus paschale*). Bede refers to Aldhelm's essay in the genre as a 'twinned work (*opus geminatum*) after the example of Sedulius' (Bede, *Hist. eccl.*, 5.18). The resulting *Carmen de virginitate* is, at 2900 hexameter lines, one of the longest surviving pre-conquest Anglo-Latin poems. Although it basically follows the structure of the prose work, it incorporates a number of saints not treated in the earlier work, and omits some others. The tone of the poem is also strikingly different, in that virginity is portrayed as a vigorously aggressive virtue, trampling down the filth of the vices. The conflict between virtue and vice, which is latent throughout, emerges clearly in the final section of the poem, which describes an allegorical battle between the eight vices and their corresponding virtues.

A small collection of thirteen letters, addressed by and to Aldhelm, also survives; of these, seven are preserved only as extracts (sometimes very brief ones) by William of Malmesbury, so it is difficult to evaluate the context in which they were composed. (These extracts include the brief fragment of Aldhelm's letter to Abbot Hadrian, and the snippet of his correspondence with Cellán of Péronne, as well as his letter of solidarity to the abbots of Bishop Wilfrid.) The remaining letters are preserved intact, and include the aforementioned letter to Geraint, king of Dumnonia (no. 4) on the orthodox method of calculating the date of Easter, as well as a letter to a colleague named Heahfrith (no. 5), on the advantages of English schools, particularly that at Canterbury under the direction of Archbishop Theodore, over those of the Irish; the collection also includes several letters by various students seeking the opportunity to study with Aldhelm.

Finally there is a poem composed in continuous octosyllables (in a rhythmical form characteristic of Hiberno-Latin hymns) addressed to an unidentified colleague named Helmgils. The poem describes a violent storm which was witnessed by Aldhelm as he was travelling back (to Malmesbury or Sherborne) from the west of England, and was staying at an unspecified minster church (perhaps at Exeter). The violence of the storm tore off the roof of the church but, miraculously, the congregation of monks, who were celebrating the night office, was unscathed.

Assessment and reputation In all these Latin writings Aldhelm displays immense learning and a highly individual sense of style. Although he studied with Theodore and Hadrian, both of whom were native speakers of Greek, he seems to have known very little Greek, though he often used Greek words (extracted from Greek–Latin glossaries) to adorn his Latin style. He certainly knew no Hebrew. But his knowledge of Latin texts, both classical and patristic, was extraordinarily wide, and not matched by any other pre-conquest Anglo-Latin author (including Bede). He quotes from numerous classical texts not otherwise known to have been read in Anglo-Saxon England, such as Cicero, Claudian, Juvenal, and Seneca; and in fact he shows familiarity with certain texts which have not been preserved, such as Lucan's lost poem *Orpheus*, from which he quotes two lines. His Latin prose style is like no other: long, almost Joycean sentences, built up coherently from parallel subordinate clauses consisting of clusters of nouns and adjectives (often interlaced and frequently pleonastic) and alliterating phrases, all decorated with various kinds of arcane vocabulary, including grecisms and archaisms drawn from glossaries, and measured out in carefully observed rhythmical patterns. His quantitative verse is similarly distinctive: because he was the first non-native speaker of Latin to compose extensively in Latin metre, he adopted various strategies to facilitate composition, such as the repetitive use of certain favourite metrical patterns and of prefabricated formulas (often linked by alliteration) within hexameter lines, which are almost always end-stopped (unlike the verse of a classical Latin poet). The monotony of Aldhelm's metre is compensated by the brilliance of his poetic vocabulary. He was also a pioneer in the field of rhythmical Latin verse: he adapted the octosyllabic verse-form used by Hiberno-Latin authors for their stanzaic hymns into a form of continuous octosyllables suitable for narrative purposes; and he linked pairs of octosyllables together by means of alliteration, in the manner of Old English verse.

In all of these media, Aldhelm had eager imitators, both during his own lifetime and for several centuries afterwards. His writings became instant classics. His pupil Æthilwald imitated Aldhelm's continuous octosyllables, especially their patterns of alliteration, in several *carmina rhythmica*. The prose of the earliest letters of the Englishman Wynfrith, later known as Boniface, is modelled unmistakably on Aldhelm's prose, as is that of various English authors who went to Germany as missionaries during the eighth century, such as the nun of Heidenheim, Hugeburc, and Boniface's hagiographer Willibald and his successor Lul. It was presumably through these missionaries that Aldhelm's writings were carried to the continent: before 706 an Irishman at Péronne named Cellán wrote to Aldhelm praising his prose style. Manuscripts of Aldhelm's writings multiplied on the continent. In eighth-century England, the *enigmata* of Tatwine, Eusebius, and Boniface were all indebted to Aldhelm's *Enigmata*, both in structure and diction; and several of Aldhelm's *Enigmata* were translated at some point into Old English.

Aldhelm's *Carmina ecclesiastica* served as models for later Anglo-Latin *tituli*, and some of them were included by Milred, bishop of Worcester (*d.* 775), in his *sylloge* of epigrams. The style and diction of Aldhelm's Latin hexameters were imitated by eighth-century Northumbrian poets such as Bede, Alcuin, and the anonymous author(s) of the *Miracula S. Nyniae*, and in the early ninth century the Northumbrian poet Ædiluulf drew heavily on the diction of the *Carmina ecclesiastica* in his own *Carmen de abbatibus*. Another ninth-century author, the anonymous compiler of the Old English martyrology, laid Aldhelm's prose *De virginitate* heavily under contribution. But the tenth century in England saw the apogee of Aldhelm's influence. By then, he was studied as a curriculum author in Anglo-Saxon schools, and the intensity of this study is reflected in the dense glossing which accompanies his writings, particularly the prose *De virginitate*, in manuscripts of the period. It is also reflected in nearly all Anglo-Latin prose of that century, beginning with the royal charters of King Æthelstan (924–39), and including the *Regularis concordia* of Bishop Æthelwold and the entire corpus of Latin prose by Byrhtferth of Ramsey. Only with the Norman conquest did the influence of Aldhelm begin to wane.

As far as can be ascertained, the corpus of Aldhelm's Latin writings has remained more or less intact (with the exception of the letters preserved only partially by William of Malmesbury). However, he also enjoyed a considerable reputation as a vernacular poet: William of Malmesbury quoted an opinion derived from King Alfred's lost *Handboc* to the effect that Aldhelm had no rival as a poet in his native language, and that one of the best-known Old English poems was a composition by Aldhelm and was still being sung in Alfred's own day. Of Aldhelm's Old English poetry, unfortunately, nothing remains (or has been convincingly identified as such). But the originality and importance of his corpus of Latin writings well justifies his status as the first English man of letters.

From the tenth century onwards, a modest cult of St Aldhelm grew up, which apparently had its origin in Malmesbury, where the saint was buried. Aldhelm's name is invoked in some Anglo-Saxon litanies of the saints, and his deposition on 25 May is frequently entered in liturgical calendars. Faricius and William of Malmesbury record a number of miracles which took place at Malmesbury through Aldhelm's intercession. According to Faricius, Aldhelm's remains were translated to a new shrine during the reign of King Eadwig (955–9), at the instigation of Dunstan; Faricius gives the feast of this translation as 5 May, but it is not recorded in any Anglo-Saxon calendar. A second translation took place in 1078 at the instigation of Osmund, bishop of Salisbury; this second translation is commemorated on 3 October.   MICHAEL LAPIDGE

Sources Bede, *Hist. eccl.* · Faricius, 'Vita s. Aldhelmi', *Vita quorundam Anglo-Saxonum: original lives of Anglo-Saxons and others who lived before the conquest*, ed. J. A. Giles, Caxton Society, 16 (1854), 119–52 · *Willelmi Malmesbiriensis monachi de gestis pontificum Anglorum libri quinque*, ed. N. E. S. A. Hamilton, Rolls Series, 52 (1870), 332–443 · *AS chart.*, S 71, 73, 79, 227, 230, 231, 232, 235, 236, 237, 248, 1166, 1169, 1170, 1175, 1245 · *Aldhelm: the prose works*, trans. M. Lapidge and M. Herren (1979) [incl. *Epistolae*] · *Aldhelm: the poetic works*, trans. M. Lapidge and J. Rosier (1985) · *Aldhelmi opera*, ed. R. Ehwald, MGH Auctores Antiquissimi, 15 (Berlin, 1919) · A. Orchard, *The poetic art of Aldhelm* (1994) · A. Orchard, 'After Aldhelm: the teaching and transmission of the Anglo-Latin hexameter', *Journal of Medieval Latin*, 2 (1992), 96–133 · M. Lapidge, 'The hermeneutic style in tenth-century Anglo-Latin literature', *Anglo-Saxon England*, 4 (1975), 67–111

Likenesses drawing, BL, Royal MS 7 D.xxiv, fol. 85*v* [*see illus.*]

Aldhun (*d.* 1018), bishop of Durham, is documented chiefly in the *Libellus de exordio atque procursu istius hoc est Dunelmensis ecclesie*, which discusses the origins and development of the church of Durham and was written by Symeon of Durham between 1104 and 1107, and the *De obsessione Dunelmi et de probabite Ucthredi comitis, et de comitibus qui ei successerunt*, which is about the siege of Durham, belongs to the late eleventh or early twelfth century, and may also have been written in Durham. Aldhun held the bishopric of Chester-le-Street before that of Durham and Symeon dates his accession there to 990, which is probably correct, and refers to him as being of noble birth and a monk; but this last point may not be accurate, since the writer was anxious to present all the bishops of St Cuthbert's Church as monks as a means of justifying the fact that in his own age the church was governed by a monastic chapter. Symeon then tells the story of how in 995, faced with the threat of renewed viking attack, Aldhun moved the religious community of Chester-le-Street and the undecayed body of its principal saint, Cuthbert, to temporary shelter at Ripon. Once the danger was passed, they set out to return to Chester-le-Street, but at an unidentified place called 'Wrdelau' 'near Durham on the east side' the cart on which the body of St Cuthbert was being carried could not be moved. 'This occurrence', Symeon observed, 'clearly revealed to all that the saint did not wish to be taken back to his former resting-place.' Three days of fasting, prayers, and vigils were instituted to determine where the saint did want to rest, with the result that it was revealed to a 'certain religious man' called Eadmer that the saint wished to be translated to Durham, which was accordingly done, and the saint, bishopric, and religious community were established on the peninsula in the River Wear where they were to remain (Symeon of Durham, *Opera*, 1.78–9). This account is clearly a miracle-story and its details should not be taken literally; but there is no reason to doubt that the episcopal church of Chester-le-Street was indeed transferred to Durham at this time. The future earl of Northumbria, Uhtred of Bamburgh, is said to have assisted in clearing the peninsula of vegetation, and it appears from the *De obsessione Dunelmi* that he married Aldhun's daughter Ecgfritha, although he later repudiated her, nevertheless retaining the lands of the church of Durham which Aldhun had given him on condition of his remaining married to his daughter. Little is known of Aldhun's episcopate at Durham. His only appearance in a document is as a witness to a charter of Æthelred dated 1009, but it appears from Durham sources that he gave lands not only to Uhtred but also to the Northumbrian earls Æthelred and Northman. He built a small church of wattles on arrival at Durham and he then began construction of a stone church, into which the body of St Cuthbert was translated on 4 September 998 and which Aldhun lived to complete except for the west tower. (This church was later confused with the White Church, which Symeon says housed the body of St Cuthbert from 995 to 998 and which may have been a pre-existing church on or near the peninsula of Durham.) According to Symeon, Aldhun died in 1018, apparently heartbroken at the defeat of the Northumbrians by the Scots at the battle of Carham.   DAVID ROLLASON

Sources Symeon of Durham, *Libellus de exordio atque procursu istius, hoc est Dunhelmensis, ecclesie / Tract on the origins and progress of this the church of Durham*, ed. and trans. D. W. Rollason, OMT (2000) · C. J. Morris, *Marriage and murder in eleventh-century Northumbria: a study of De obsessione Dunelmi*, Borthwick Papers, 82 (1992) · C. R. Hart, *The early charters of northern England and the north midlands* (1975) · Symeon of Durham, *Opera*

Aldington. For this title name *see* Low, Austin Richard William, first Baron Aldington (1914–2000).

Aldington, Edward Godfree [Richard] (1892–1962), writer, was born on 8 July 1892 at 50 High Street, Portsea, Portsmouth, the eldest among the two sons and two daughters of Albert Edward Aldington (1864–1921), solicitor's clerk and amateur author, and Jessie May Godfree (1872–1954), novelist and keeper of the Mermaid inn at Rye. After preparatory schools at Walmer and St Margaret's Bay, Aldington, known from a young age as Richard, attended Dover College from 1904 to 1906. He started to write poetry in the following year, aged fifteen, after reading Wilde and Keats. In 1910 he enrolled at University College, London, where he encountered W. P. Ker and A. E. Housman, but he had to leave before taking his degree after his father's speculations failed.

Aldington worked briefly as assistant to a newspaper sports editor, but was soon making a living from his literary journalism and poetry. In 1912 he was introduced by Ethel Elizabeth (Brigit) Patmore (1882–1965) to avant-garde writers, including Yeats; Ford Madox Hueffer (later Ford); Ezra Pound, who became his close friend and literary ally; and the American poet Hilda *Doolittle, known as H. D. (1886–1961). Pound, H. D., and Aldington founded the influential imagist movement in 1912, rejecting regular stanzaic forms in favour of *vers libre*, and nineteenth-century poetical language in favour of sparse, concrete, highly visual presentation. Aldington's work appeared in *Des imagistes* (1914, edited by Pound), and he helped Amy Lowell edit the three volumes called *Some Imagist Poets* (1915, 1916, 1917). His first book of poems, *Images, 1910–1915*, was published by Harold Monro's Poetry Bookshop in 1915. He became literary editor of Dora Marsden's feminist magazine *New Freewoman* (later *The Egoist*), to which Pound also contributed. Aldington and H. D. became lovers in 1912, while in Paris with Pound. In the following year they spent eight months in Italy and France, and were married on 18 October 1913 in Kensington register office.

On the outbreak of the First World War, Aldington tried to join up in the Honourable Artillery Company, but was told he would be refused because of a childhood hernia operation. He worked instead as secretary to Ford, assisting with his propaganda writing and Ford's novel *The Good Soldier*. H. D. had discovered she was pregnant on the day war was declared. A daughter was stillborn on 21 May 1915. On 24 June 1916 Aldington joined the 11th battalion of the Devonshire regiment at Wareham, Dorset. He embarked on 21 December 1916, and saw active service in France and Flanders, first attached to the 6th battalion of the Leicestershire regiment as a private, and transferred to the 11th battalion in January 1917. He stayed in France until the end of May, and was back in England for officer training from June to the end of November, when he got his commission in the Royal Sussex regiment. In London he met T. S. Eliot, who took over his editorial duties for *The Egoist*, and also the American art student Dorothy (Arabella) Yorke (1891–1971), who lived above the Aldingtons at 44 Mecklenburgh Square, and with whom Richard began an affair. He and H. D. had separated by autumn 1919 although they continued to write to each other until H. D.'s death.

Aldington was back in the trenches from April 1918; by November he was signals officer to battalion headquarters, with the rank of acting captain. After the armistice he was in Belgium teaching arithmetic and English grammar to the troops, before being gazetted out in February 1919. Besides traumatic stress, he suffered from chronic bronchitis due to exposure to gas.

In 1919 Aldington's poems *War and Love* were published. He began to work for the *Times Literary Supplement* as a regular reviewer of French books. From autumn 1919 to

1927 he and Arabella were based in Berkshire, though they travelled frequently, especially in France. He was assistant editor for Eliot's *Criterion* from 1921, specializing in reviews of French poetry. He produced over twenty books of criticism and thirty books of translation, especially from the French, such as *Les liaisons dangereuses* (1924) and *Candide* (1927). His biographical study *Voltaire* (1925) was praised for objectivity and masterly concision.

During the general strike of 1926 Aldington was asked to help deliver *The Times* and obliged. However, though his friendships were predominantly with right-inclined writers such as Eliot, Pound, Wyndham Lewis, and later Roy Campbell, Aldington was equally scathing about all political or religious systems. He was an epicurean individualist, who resented any threat to individual fulfilment, whether from communism, capitalism, bureaucracy, or Christianity.

Aldington was expected to become editor of the *Times Literary Supplement* but after a visit from D. H. Lawrence—whom he had known since 1914, and who was the modern novelist he most admired—he decided he needed to write more personally, and to make a decisive break with England, and with Eliot's influence. Aldington spent most of the next decade in France. He became friendly with Nancy Cunard, with whom he discovered a new young writer called Samuel Beckett.

In autumn 1928 Aldington stayed at Port-Cros (an island near Hyères) with the Lawrences, and with Brigit Patmore, his new love. They visited the Pounds at Rapallo, where the Yeatses were also staying. Aldington wrote little poetry after his late thirties but entered a new phase as a novelist, writing seven novels from 1929 to 1939. His first, the anti-war book *Death of a Hero* (1929), made him famous: George Orwell thought it 'much the best of the English war books' (Doyle, 128) while Aldington thought of it as a 'jazz novel' (ibid., 129). It was a watershed in Aldington's career, and also the first real intimation of his satirical power: an angry denunciation of Victorian hypocrisy and social stupidity crushing individual happiness. These were his main fictional targets. *Death of a Hero* is also a rawly autobiographical work, expressing his anger towards his parents (especially his mother), the war, and the literary establishment, with recognizable satiric portraits of Eliot, Ford, Lawrence, and Pound.

Aldington's satire of modernist friends intensified in *Soft Answers* (1932), with biting caricatures of Pound and Eliot. Aldington objected to what he saw as Eliot's death wish; 'the War despair which involved so many of us and from which the healthy-minded have been struggling to escape' (Doyle, 148–9). In *Artifex* (1935) he elaborated his attack on the modernist movement as 'the art of exasperated neurasthenics' (pp. 33–4), on the grounds that art should intensify and enrich life. The satire of his second novel, *The Colonel's Daughter* (1931), is aimed at a similar target: the life-denying stupidity of English village society.

Aldington spent the early 1930s in Mediterranean Europe: he was with Patmore at the Villa Koeclin, Le Canadel (Var); then at Anacapri, where he worked on his third novel, *All Men are Enemies* (1933). His habit of overwork undermined his health, yet he was continually on the move: in Portugal; in France for most of 1933, mainly at Villa Devos, near Le Lavandou; motoring around Spain. He broke his knee in a car accident in Austria. One of his best novels dates from this period: *Women must Work* (1934). But during the depression he found it hard to repeat the success of *Death of a Hero*; though he became one of Russia's favourite contemporary English writers, thanks partly to Gorky's interest.

By 1935 Aldington felt finished even with Europe, and after a brief stay on a derelict plantation on Tobago he sailed for America in June, where he was based for the next decade, though his semi-nomadic existence regularly returned him to Europe before the Second World War. In winter 1935–6 he was back in London, then touring in Portugal, Spain, and Austria. He became involved with Patmore's daughter-in-law, Netta (1911–1977), daughter of James McCulloch, a lawyer, of Pinner, Middlesex. Early in 1937 Netta went with him to visit Italy and Nice, and to settle at the Villa Koeclin. His divorce from H. D. was finalized on 22 June 1938, and three days later Aldington and Netta married in London. Their daughter, Catherine (Catha), was born on 6 July 1938. In January 1939 they took an apartment on West 115th Street, New York. Aldington gave some lectures at Columbia and other east-coast universities. Late in 1940 they moved to Washington, DC. After the reception of his poem-sequence *The Crystal World* (1937) Aldington said: 'I promised myself I would never write another line of poetry' (Doyle, 240). Instead he obtained access to the Library of Congress to edit the substantial *Viking Book of Poetry of the English-Speaking World* (1941), which he intended to rival *The Oxford Book of English Verse*, and to offer alternative poetic traditions from those defined by Pound and Eliot. Aldington was happy and productive in America, saying 'our best time began' there (ibid., 204). He turned to life-writing for a last creative phase: eight biographical books, starting with his autobiography *Life for Life's Sake* (1941). The travelling continued: Jamay Beach, Nokomis, in Florida; Taos, New Mexico, to stay with Frieda Lawrence.

During much of the Second World War, Aldington, who had the appearance of a matinée idol, worked as a freelance screenwriter in Hollywood, where he befriended William Faulkner. His biography of the duke of Wellington (1943) won the James Tait Black memorial prize when it was published in the United Kingdom (1946). His last novel, *The Romance of Casanova* (1946) was a half-hearted potboiler (written for the movies), but Aldington still needed to pay damages to the Patmores. (The courts awarded damages as part of Netta's divorce from her husband, Michael Patmore.) After the war he left America, saying 'the place has nothing to offer but money' (Doyle, 226–7), and returned to his beloved France: first Paris, where he met the young Australian poet Alister Kershaw, who admired his work and offered loyal friendship, assistance, and financial support for the rest of his life, then from August 1947 the Villa Aucassin, Le Lavandou.

Aldington had edited Lawrence's *Selected Poems* (1932), and was now influential in getting Lawrence's prose republished, writing fourteen introductions for Heinemann and Penguin. He also produced the important first biography of Lawrence, *D. H. Lawrence: Portrait of a Genius, but …* (1950). His anthology of the aesthetes, *The Religion of Beauty*, appeared in the same year. That autumn Netta left him, and Aldington had what he called 'a sort of crack-up' (Doyle, 252). Unusually for him he did not produce a full-length book for the next four years. *Pinorman*, a biography of Norman Douglas and his friends Pino Orioli and Charles Prentice, appeared in 1954, as did the French edition of the book that was to have devastating personal consequences: *Lawrence of Arabia: a Biographical Enquiry* (1955). He had intended to produce a study of war-heroism to follow *Wellington*, but his careful research produced instead another death of a hero: the first systematic debunking of the legend of T. E. Lawrence, whom Aldington found a liar and fraud. It was, he said, 'more than a mere biography—it is the showing up and repudiation of a whole phase of our national life' (ibid., 274). The British establishment was scandalized. Attempts were made to prevent publication, then to ensure hostile reviews. Aldington's reputation and sales never recovered in the English-speaking world, and he lived in poverty, mainly on translation rights to his own books and his translations of others. In April 1951 Aldington and his daughter Catha left the Villa Aucassin, moving to a *pension*, Les Rosiers, Montpellier. Lawrence Durrell visited him here, and became another close friend. In 1957 Aldington was able to move to a cottage bought by Alister Kershaw, in the hamlet of Maison Sallé, Sury-en-Vaux, Cher, which provided his home for the rest of his life—though he continued to travel. His last trip was in summer 1962 to attend celebrations in the USSR for his seventieth birthday, where he was overwhelmed by admiration. He died on 27 July 1962 back at Maison Sallé, and was buried at Sury-en-Vaux.

The *Times* obituary showed how Aldington's scathing criticisms of England remained unforgiven: 'He was an angry young man of the generation before they became fashionable'; 'There were times when his anger betrayed him' (30 July 1962). The *Daily Telegraph* was more magnanimous: 'Aldington's brilliance in so many fields of literature has been rivalled by few of his generation and is indeed rare at any time' (30 July 1962).

Richard Aldington was extraordinarily prolific and versatile: a poet, novelist, translator, critic, biographer, editor, and anthologist. C. P. Snow called him 'a writer of great gifts', giving his readers 'a glow of power and vitality' (Doyle, xiii). He was an important contributor to modernist poetics, and a significant post-war novelist, though his subsequent repudiation of modernism and reputation for *ad hominem* denunciations have rather obscured his merits. In many ways a divided figure, he was characterized by acute sensitivity to beauty, passion for truth, and anger at hypocrisy. MAX SAUNDERS

Sources C. Doyle, *Richard Aldington* (1989) · N. Gates, *Richard Aldington* (1992) · C. Zilboorg, ed., *Richard Aldington and H. D.: the early years in letters* (1992) · R. Aldington, *Life for life's sake* (1941) · The *Times* (30 July 1962) · *Daily Telegraph* (30 July 1962) · H. D., *Bid me to live* (1960) · R. Aldington, *Death of a hero* (1929) · T. F. Staley, ed., *British novelists, 1890–1929: modernists*, DLitB, 36 (1985) · R. Aldington, *Artifex* (1935) · b. cert. · *CGPLA Eng. & Wales* (1963)

Archives Hunt. L., letters · NRA, corresp. and literary papers · Ransom HRC, corresp. and papers relating to T. E. Lawrence · Temple University, Philadelphia, Paley Library, corresp. and papers · Yale U., Beinecke L., corresp. and literary papers | BL, letters to Netta Aldington, Add. MS 54211 · BL, letters to Sydney Schiff and Violet Schiff, Add. MS 52916 · Harvard U., Houghton L., letters to John Cournos · Harvard U., Houghton L., letters to Amy Lowell · Hunt. L., letters · JRL, corresp. with Basil Dean · Lpool RO, corresp. with James Hanley · LUL, letters to Thomas Sturge Moore · Southern Illinois University, Carbondale, Morris Library, letters to P. A. G. Aldington · Southern Illinois University, Carbondale, Morris Library, letters to Ralph Pinker · Southern Illinois University, Carbondale, Morris Library, letters to Count Potocki de Montalk · Southern Illinois University, Carbondale, Morris Library, letters to Henry Slonimsky · Southern Illinois University, Carbondale, Morris Library, letters to Eric Warman · TCD, corresp. with Thomas McGreevy · U. Leeds, Brotherton L., letters to Clement Shorter · University of Bristol Library, corresp. and statements relating to trial of *Lady Chatterley's lover*

Likenesses H. Coster, photographs, 1931, NPG · photographs, repro. in Doyle, *Richard Aldington* · photographs, repro. in Zilboorg, ed., *Richard Aldington and H. D.*

Wealth at death £500—in England: administration with will, 30 Oct 1963, *CGPLA Eng. & Wales*

Aldis, Sir Charles (1776–1863), surgeon, the seventh son and one of the twenty-two children of Daniel Aldis, a medical practitioner of Aslacton, Norfolk, and his wife, Mary, was born at Aslacton on 16 March 1776. Apprenticed to his father in 1789, he travelled to London in 1794 and studied at Guy's and St Bartholomew's hospitals.

In 1797 or 1798 Aldis was made surgeon to the sick and wounded prisoners of war at Norman Cross barracks, Huntingdonshire (where 10,000–12,000 French and Dutch prisoners were then detained). In 1800 he moved to Hertford, where he introduced vaccination into three parishes in spite of opposition from other doctors, and then in 1802 he began to practise in Old Burlington Street, London. In 1803 he became a member of the Royal College of Surgeons. Aldis also became surgeon to the New Finsbury Dispensary, and he founded a special hospital, called the Glandular Institution for the Cure of Cancer, in Clifford Street. His *Observations on the Nature and Treatment of Glandular Diseases* appeared in 1820. Aldis was known as an antiquary as well as a surgeon and medical writer, and he was knighted by the lord lieutenant of Ireland for his contributions to medical literature. He had also won a reputation as a philanthropist, having been for many years 'connected with benevolent objects in the metropolis and elsewhere' (GM, 689). He died on 28 March 1863 at his home, 13 Old Burlington Street. He was survived by his son Charles James Berridge *Aldis (1808–1872).

J. F. PAYNE, rev. PATRICK WALLIS

Sources *GM*, 3rd ser., 14 (1863), 689 · *Medical Circular* (1 April 1863) · *London and Provincial Medical Directory* (1863) · P. J. Wallis and R. V. Wallis, *Eighteenth century medics*, 2nd edn (1988) · C. Aldis, *Memoirs of Sir Charles Aldis and Dr Aldis* (1852) · *CGPLA Eng. & Wales* (1863) · Boase, *Mod. Eng. biog.* · IGI

Likenesses T. Wageman, stipple, BM, NPG; repro. in *European Magazine* (1817) · T. Wageman, stipples (after his portrait), Wellcome L.

Wealth at death under £300: administration with will, 19 June 1863, *CGPLA Eng. & Wales*

Aldis, Charles James Berridge (1808–1872), physician and public health reformer, and the eldest son of Sir Charles *Aldis (1776–1863), surgeon, was born in London on 16 January 1808. He was educated at St Paul's School and matriculated from Trinity College, Cambridge, in 1828; he graduated BA (1831), MB (1832), and MA (1834). Aldis studied medicine at Addenbrooke's Hospital, Cambridge, and St George's Hospital, London, before gaining his MD from Cambridge in 1837. Two years earlier he had married Emily Arabella (d. 1863), daughter of the Revd John Brome of Trinity College, Cambridge: there were two daughters and a son. He became a fellow of the Royal College of Physicians in 1838 and lectured at his own house, at the Hunterian School of Medicine, and at the Aldersgate Street School. He delivered the Harveian oration at the Royal College of Physicians in 1859.

A versatile practitioner and writer, with interests ranging from noise pollution to the self-management of melancholia, Aldis specialized in detailed public health investigation in some of the most deprived areas of the capital. He was appointed medical officer of health for St George's, Hanover Square, in 1855, a position that he held until his death. Aldis was appointed physician at a number of working-class dispensaries, including the Farringdon and the Surrey. These posts involved him in the care of around 10,000 patients.

An influential critic of grossly overcrowded and insanitary housing, Aldis was an early supporter of the atmospheric theory of disease. He was convinced that adverse environmental conditions generated fevers which revealed themselves in a wide variety of interchangeable symptomological forms. An earnest moralist, he believed intemperance and incest to be endemic in the poorest sections of the capital, and that the latter practice predisposed women to insanity. Aldis was adamant that ventilation held the key to good health: an absence of fresh air invariably produced 'physical depression, functional disorder and ultimately organic change' (*State of Large Towns, Parl. papers*, 1844, 17.410). Committed to the practice of bleeding for country-dwellers and suburbanites, he insisted that a majority of the urban working class had been constitutionally weakened up to a point at which they would be harmed rather than helped by such radical treatment.

A Conservative in local politics, Aldis criticized rack-renting landlords, employers of sweated labour, and, on occasion, the lassitude of the sanitary committee by which he was employed. For many years his letters to The *Times* were 'incessant in their exposure of exacting employers of milliners and lethargic vestrymen' (*The Lancet*, 171). At a time when it was unfashionable and financially counter-productive for doctors to become involved in progressive causes, Aldis campaigned throughout the 1860s for reduced hours of work for female employees in dressmaking establishments. His lobbying played an important part in the successful passage of the Workshops Regulation Act of 1867. Taken in conjunction with the Sanitary Act of 1866, this measure, which was enforceable in relation to businesses employing fifty or fewer persons 'gave the … authorities ample opportunity for surveillance of industrial working conditions in London' (Hardy, 232). Like other metropolitan medical officers of the 1850s and 1860s, Aldis accepted that the entrenched power of local cliques of landlords and manufacturers would invariably militate against co-ordinated environmental intervention. Nevertheless, the publicity generated by city-wide campaigns for permissive legislation in the fields of employment, housing, and disease prevention created a framework in which an increasing minority of miscreants could be shamed into obeying the law. As an active member of the Association of Medical Officers of Health, Aldis played a significant role in ensuring that this organization became more adept at goading reactionary authorities into acquainting themselves with the best existing bureaucratic practice.

Aldis completed his first work, *An Introduction to Hospital Practice* (1835), before reaching the age of thirty. For the next twenty-five years he published on an extraordinarily wide and eclectic range of subjects, including interactions between the respiration of coal gas and chest diseases, predisposing factors in the onset of depression and madness, the mode of transmission and changing virulence of scarlet fever, and the eighteenth-century origins of the nineteenth-century public health movement. Neither an original nor penetrating stylist, Aldis nevertheless displayed an impressive range of cultural and linguistic references. At his most incisive he was a compelling witness to novel and disturbing aspects of metropolitan existence. Very few upper-middle-class doctors ventured as frequently or deeply into the *terra incognita* of the East End and inner city districts. Indeed the *Medical Times and Gazette* dismissed Aldis's work on the grounds that no occupation was 'so noisome, monotonous, thankless, useless, and hopeless as that of attending the dregs of the pauperised classes in Spitalfields, in the Borough, and in the Westminster Broadway' (Munk, *Roll*). That Aldis sacrificed the possibility of a safe and lucrative private practice for work involving daily contact with the poor and socially excluded is substantiated by the fact that in 1867 friends and associates felt it necessary to organize a testimonial on his behalf. Reading between the lines of his numerous articles in *The Lancet* and in other periodicals, one derives the impression of a man who gained recompense enough from scholarship and writing.

Aldis died at his home, 45B Chester Square, London, on 26 July 1872.   BILL LUCKIN

Sources *The Lancet* (3 Aug 1872), 171 · A. Hardy, *The epidemic streets: infectious disease and the rise of preventive medicine, 1856–1900* (1993) · *Medical Times and Gazette* (3 Aug 1872), 134–5 · Venn, *Alum. Cant.* · d. cert. · *DNB* · Munk, *Roll* · Boase, *Mod. Eng. biog.*

Archives LMA, archive, bound archive

Likenesses W. H. A., wood-engraving, Wellcome L. · W. H. A. (after Claudet), Wellcome L.

Wealth at death under £4000: probate, 16 Aug 1872, *CGPLA Eng. & Wales*

Aldred (*fl. c.*970), provost of Chester-le-Street and glossator, is known through three manuscripts. He added an interlinear Old English gloss and a colophon to the Lindisfarne gospels of *c.*698 (BL, Cotton MS Nero D.iv), four collects in honour of St Cuthbert and two colophons to the early tenth-century Durham ritual (Durham Cathedral Library, MS A.IV.19), and biblical extracts and exegetical notes to an early eighth-century copy of Bede's commentary on Proverbs (Bodl. Oxf., MS Bodley 819). All three manuscripts were at Durham in the twelfth century.

The first colophon in the Durham ritual records that the collects for St Cuthbert were written out for a bishop named Ælfsige by Aldred the provost at a place named Oakley, on a Wednesday which was both the feast of St Laurence and the fifth night of the moon. Ælfsige was bishop of Chester-le-Street between 968 and 990. The feast of St Laurence (10 August) fell on a Wednesday which was the fifth night of the moon in 970. Oakley has been identified as a place in Wessex, on the road between Salisbury and Blandford. Ælfsige was probably in the company of King Edgar in that year, attended by Aldred, whose title of provost indicates that he was the second highest-ranking member of the religious community at Chester-le-Street, where the relics of St Cuthbert then lay. The gloss to the Lindisfarne gospels must have been added before 970, as in its colophon Aldred describes himself simply as a priest. Canonical requirements mean that he must have been at least thirty years of age at that time. A marginal note beside the Lindisfarne colophon records that his father's name was Alfred.

Aldred was not an uncommon name in pre-conquest England and the forms of script which appear in the additions to the three manuscripts are occasionally sufficiently dissimilar to have led some scholars to argue that a single scribe could not have been responsible for all. Humfrey Wanley (1705) was able to compare the gospels and the ritual side by side and was fully convinced of their identity. Almost two centuries later Edward Maunde Thompson (in the *Dictionary of National Biography*) forcefully presented the opposite view. Modern scholarship, based on a more refined system of palaeographical analysis, has sided with Wanley. Neil Ker (1943) and Julian Brown (1960 and 1969) have put forward convincing arguments for believing Aldred the provost to be the scribe of the additions to all three manuscripts.

The word for word Old English gloss in the Lindisfarne gospels is Aldred's most significant work. It represents the earliest surviving version of the gospels in any form of the English language. It preserves a wide range of variant forms and has been characterized as displaying archaisms and innovations side by side, with some features which are to be found in much later forms of the language. It is of northern rather than West Saxon origin and shares features with Norse and with continental Germanic languages. Why Aldred might have thought it necessary or appropriate to gloss this magnificent manuscript in English is ultimately an unanswerable question. The language of the gloss may owe something to King Alfred's translations of some key Christian texts into English, which helped to engender a general shift towards the vernacular from the beginning of the tenth century. The use of English may have increased *faute de mieux*, however, as the standard of Latin letters declined. Aldred may have glossed the gospels simply in response to the need for those without Latin—but with English—to understand them.

JANET BACKHOUSE

Sources H. Wanley, 'Librorum vett. septentrionalium, qui in Angliae bibliothecis extant, catalogue historico-criticum', *Antiquae literaturae septentrionalis libri duo*, ed. G. Hickes, 2 (1705), 250–03 · N. R. Ker, 'Aldred the scribe', *Essays and Studies by Members of the English Association*, 28 (1943), 7–12 · A. S. C. Ross, E. G. Stanley, and T. J. Brown, *The Anglo-Saxon gloss in Codex Lindisfarnensis*, ed. T. D. Kendrick and others, 2 (1960) · T. J. Brown, *The Durham ritual: a southern English collectar of the tenth century with Northumbrian additions. Durham Cathedral Library A.IV.19* (1969)
Archives BL, Cotton MS Nero D.iv · Bodl. Oxf., MS Bodley 819 · Durham Cathedral, MS A.IV.19

Aldred, Cyril (1914–1991), Egyptologist and art historian, was born on 19 February 1914 at 41 Beltran Road, Fulham, London, the fifth of the six children of Frederick Aldred, a civil servant, and his wife, Lilian Ethel Underwood. Educated at the Sloane School, Chelsea, he then read English for a year at King's College, London, and art history at the Courtauld Institute of Art. He took his BA degree in 1936. In the following year he was appointed an assistant keeper in the Royal Scottish Museum, Edinburgh, where he remained until his retirement in 1974, apart from the years of the Second World War when he served in the RAF. He was keeper of art and archaeology from 1961 to 1974. On 28 May 1938 he married Jessie Kennedy Morton (*b.* 1908/9), masseuse, with whom he had a daughter.

In 1949 Aldred published a small popular monograph, *Old Kingdom Art in Ancient Egypt*, a seemingly modest survey of the first important period of Egyptian art. Two subsequent volumes on the art of the middle kingdom and the new kingdom (1950, 1952) established him as an art historian of significant potential. His interest in Egypt dated back to his schooldays. Meetings with Howard Carter, discoverer of the tomb of Tutankhamun, in 1933 led to an invitation to spend a season with him in Egypt. Carter wrote: 'I have found him to have a very fair knowledge of Egyptological subjects especially that of Egyptian Art' (priv. coll.).

Aldred did not take up Carter's offer, but he retained his interest in Egyptian art and began to develop it seriously when he returned to Edinburgh in 1946. The Egyptian collection in the Royal Scottish Museum was small but diverse, containing some important pieces which gave Aldred the scope to mount unusually good exhibitions. He took a special interest in materials and technologies, and was invited to write chapters on fine woodwork and furniture in the Oxford *History of Technology* (2 vols., 1954–6), significant and innovative studies, based on a close examination of original Egyptian material. His later *Jewels of the Pharaohs* (1971), although written for a popular readership, contained an authoritative examination of materials, techniques, and designs which was again based on close study of originals, especially those in Cairo and New York, and on his own experience as a practical jeweller.

By establishing friendly and fruitful contacts with colleagues throughout the Egyptological world Aldred was able to pursue vigorously his developing sculptural studies, at the same time enhancing his international standing. In 1955 he accepted an invitation to spend a year as an associate curator in the department of Egyptian art in the Metropolitan Museum of Art in New York. There he had the opportunity to enlarge his experience of Egyptian antiquities in one of the best Egyptian collections in the world, with a fine library and very congenial colleagues. William C. Hayes, the departmental curator, had hopes that Aldred might be groomed as his successor, but the latter's attachment to Edinburgh drew him back to Scotland in 1956, a substantially more mature scholar with particular interests in Egyptian sculpture and in the controversial Amarna period, the reign of the so-called heretic king Akhenaten.

It was in Egyptian sculpture that Cyril Aldred made his most enduring contributions to Egyptian art history. His articles were well argued and elegantly written, but it is a matter of great regret that he never wrote a comprehensive work on Egyptian statuary. His *Egyptian Art* (1980) was a popular account with little room for close argument. Essays on Egyptian sculpture in the three Egyptian volumes of André Malraux's *L'univers des formes* (1978, 1979, 1980) represent his most complete exposition of the subject. But his most important art-historical writing is contained in *Akhenaten and Nefertiti*, the volume which accompanied an exhibition in the Brooklyn Museum in 1973. Here he brought a systematization to a confused subject, Amarna art, and in so doing contributed substantially to the elucidation of many of the historical problems of that vexed period.

The Amarna period engrossed Aldred's scholarly attention for much of his active career. Particular aspects of the period and its protagonist Akhenaten were explored in articles and in *Akhenaten, Pharaoh of Egypt* (1968): the pathology of Akhenaten, family relationships, and the question of coregency. His views were restated with vigour in his last work, *Akhenaten, King of Egypt* (1988).

Beyond Egyptology and his duties in the Royal Scottish Museum, Cyril Aldred pursued many private interests, not least of which was the writing of occasional light verse, much of it composed for meetings of the Monks of St Giles, an Edinburgh dining club. He did not enjoy conventional lecturing, but excelled in less formal presentations, as on Nile cruises on which, as guest lecturer, he delighted his fellow travellers with his witty and well-informed talks. His distinction in Scottish intellectual life was recognized in 1978 when he was elected a fellow of the Royal Society of Edinburgh. A volume of essays, *Chief of Seers* (1997), written for him by colleagues, was published some years after his death. Cyril Aldred died at his home, 4A Polwarth Terrace, Edinburgh, on 23 June 1991, survived by his wife and their daughter.   T. G. H. JAMES

Sources T. G. H. James, 'Cyril Aldred', *Journal of Egyptian Archaeology*, 78 (1992), 258–66 [incl. portrait] · C. D. Waterston, 'Cyril Aldred', *Year Book of the Royal Society of Edinburgh* (1990–91), 32–4 · E. Goring, N. Reeves, and J. Ruffle, eds., *Chief of seers: Egyptian studies in memory of Cyril Aldred* (1997) [incl. appreciations by B. V. Bothmer, E. Goring, and N. Scott, bibliography by D. Magee, and portrait] · *The Independent* (6 July 1991) · *The Times* (6 July 1991) · b. cert. · m. cert. · d. cert.

Archives National Museums of Scotland, photographic archive · priv. coll., papers and photographs | U. Oxf., Griffith Institute, corresp. with J. Černý

Likenesses photograph, repro. in *The Times*

Wealth at death £282,284.83: confirmation, 1991, *CCI*

Aldred, Guy Alfred (1886–1963), anarchist and political propagandist, was born on 5 November 1886 at 24 Corporation Buildings, Farringdon Road, Clerkenwell, London, the son of Arthur Alfred Aldred (*b.* 1864/5), a dramatist, and his wife, Ada Caroline Holdsworth (*b.* 1866/7). His father had deserted his family by 1892, and he was brought up by his mother, a parasol maker; his maternal grandfather, Charles William Holdsworth, a radical bookbinder, was a strong early influence. Aldred was educated in Clerkenwell at the Iron infants' school (1891–3) and the Hugh Myddleton School (1893–1901). After leaving school he soon became a penny-a-line journalist with the National Press Agency (1901–6) and briefly with the *Daily Chronicle* (1907), before leaving to engage full-time in socialist propaganda. For the next fifty-six years, as a major figure in the British anarchist and anti-parliamentary communist movements, he wrote and published a stream of pamphlets, books, and journals, and set up a number of printing presses, from the Bakunin Press in London (1907) to the Strickland Press in Glasgow (1939–68).

Aldred's early political career was spent in London among dissident left groups, including the Social Democratic Federation (1905–6), but he soon moved towards anarchism. He quickly fell out with the Freedom group of anarchists, and set up instead his own group to promote industrial unionism and direct action. In 1908 he left his mother's home at 133 Goswell Road, London, to set up a free union with Rose Lillian *Witcop (1890–1932), a milliner. A son, Annesley, was born in 1909. Aldred's visit to Glasgow in 1912 at the invitation of the Glasgow Clarion Scouts was a great success, and he was invited back for several speaking tours of Scotland, although these were curtailed by war. In 1916 he spent his first spell of almost continuous imprisonment as a conscientious objector. On his release (March 1919) he returned to Glasgow, his base for the rest of his life.

Aldred now played a central part in efforts to realign the communist left on an anti-parliamentary basis, notably through the formation of the Communist League in 1919, but these foundered with the establishment in 1920 of the centralized Communist Party of Great Britain, backed by Moscow. Aldred and some remaining comrades defiantly formed the Anti-Parliamentary Communist Federation in 1921, based at 13 Burnbank Gardens, Glasgow (Bakunin House). By now Aldred and Witcop had separated, and he formed another free union with Jane Hamilton (Jenny) *Patrick (1884–1971). Despite a marriage of convenience with Witcop on 2 February 1926 at Glasgow register office to thwart her threatened deportation, the union with Jenny Patrick was lifelong and, after Witcop's death on 4 July 1932, constituted a valid marriage under Scottish common law. In 1933 Aldred's resignation from the Anti-Parliamentary Communist Federation over the divisive ballot-box tactic forced their move to 5 Baliol Street, which was their home for the rest of their lives.

Aldred's new organization, the United Socialist Movement, founded in 1934, marked a change in philosophy and tactics from an exclusively anti-parliamentary focus to the need for socialist unity to defeat fascism, notably through support of the anarchists in the Spanish Civil War. Street-corner meetings were held almost nightly in 1936–7, accompanied, despite extreme poverty, by a stream of papers and pamphlets. Two of Aldred's closest comrades, Ethel *MacDonald and Jenny Patrick, went to Spain to assist the propaganda effort of the anarchist federation, enabling Aldred to publish firsthand information on events such as the communist attack on the anarchists in Barcelona. In 1939 a £3000 legacy from Sir Walter Strickland enabled him to set up the Strickland Press at 104–6 George Street. Throughout the Second World War he was again active in the struggle against conscription.

Aldred made major contributions to anti-parliamentary communist theory, combining the ideas of Marx and Bakunin and giving priority to self-organized working-class activity. Also, by keeping his press and journals in almost continuous existence for over fifty years, he maintained an open forum for the libertarian left. His most important journals, the *Herald of Revolt* (1910–14) and *The Spur* (1914–21), enabled different elements of the rebel movement to exchange ideas, while *The Word* (1938/9–63) stubbornly proclaimed the anti-parliamentary and anti-militarist message in a hostile world. His many biographical studies rescued from neglect 'pioneers' of the movement.

As an anti-militarist and anti-war activist in two world wars, furthermore, Aldred offered uncompromising resistance to conscription—he even held meetings and published a newspaper while imprisoned for conscientious objection during the first, and used his experience and self-taught legal expertise to inspire and assist fellow resisters in the second. In addition he revived interest in an earlier generation of freethinkers, particularly Richard Carlile and Robert Taylor, situating them in a radical political tradition. Aldred was also significant for championing free speech. He received a prison sentence for publishing the banned *Indian Sociologist* (1909) and incurred prosecution for publishing Margaret Sanger's 'obscene' *Family Limitation* (1922). Between the wars he campaigned for the right to public speaking in Glasgow; he was also responsible for the controversial publication of the duke of Bedford's pacifist views in the Second World War.

After the war Aldred campaigned on a number of issues, including world government, neo-colonialism, and American use of UK military bases. In their pursuit he stood as a parliamentary candidate in six post-war elections in Glasgow, the last of which was the Woodside by-election in November 1962. Shortly afterwards, in January 1963, he suffered a heart attack. He resumed speaking and writing, but grew weaker and died in the Western Infirmary, Glasgow, on 16 October 1963. As he had bequeathed his body for research, his funeral, at Maryhill crematorium, was delayed until 4 May 1964.

BOB JONES

Sources G. A. Aldred, *No traitor's gate!*, 3 vols. in 1 (1955–63) • J. T. Caldwell, *Come dungeons dark* (1988) • J. T. Caldwell, 'The red evangel: a biography of Guy A. Aldred', unpublished typescript, 1976 [copy at Stirling University Library] • J. T. Caldwell, *With fate conspire* (1999) [includes full bibliography of Strickland Press titles] • *The Word*, 1–25 (1938–65) [vols. 24 and 25 include obituaries and tributes] • *The Spur*, 1–7 (1914–21) • *Herald of Revolt*, 1–4 (1910–14) • M. Shipway, *Anti-parliamentary communism: the movement for workers' councils in Britain, 1917–45* (1988) • B. Jones, *Left-wing communism in Britain, 1917–21* (1991) • G. A. Aldred, *Dogmas discarded*, 2 vols. (1940) • b. cert. • d. cert. • personal knowledge (2004)

Archives Glasgow Caledonian University • Mitchell L., Glas., corresp. and papers • University of Strathclyde, Glasgow | Internationaal Instituut voor Sociale Geschiedenis, Amsterdam, Freedom and Freedom Press archive and Andre Prudhommeaux collection • U. Hull, Brynmor Jones L., letters to C. W. Brook | S O U N D priv. coll., reel to reel tape recordings of lectures played at meetings in 1963

Likenesses photographs, 1902–7, repro. in G. A. Aldred, *No traitor's gait* (1956) • photograph, 1909, repro. in *Daily Mirror* (27 Aug 1909) • J. Parkes, oils, *c*.1927, People's Palace, Glasgow; repro. in Caldwell, *With fate conspire* • photograph, 1938, repro. in Caldwell, *Come dungeons dark*; priv. coll. • *News Chronicle*, photograph, 1946, repro. in Caldwell, *With fate conspire*; priv. coll. • P. Miller, drawings, 1961–3, repro. in Caldwell, *Come dungeons dark*; priv. coll. • photograph, 1962, repro. in *The Scotsman* (16 Nov 1962)

Aldrich, Henry (1648–1710), dean of Christ Church, Oxford, was born at Westminster on 15 January 1648 and baptized on 22 January 1648 at St Margaret's, Westminster, the eldest son of Henry Aldrich (d. 1683) and his wife, Judith Francis. After the Restoration, Aldrich's father became a retainer of the Berkeley family, serving in 1664 as clerk to the royalist soldier, John, first Baron Berkeley of Stratton, extraordinary commissioner of the navy. Pepys refers to the elder Aldrich in 1667 as 'Captain Aldrich that belongs to my Lord Berkeley' (Pepys, 8.255), and in 1679 Aldrich himself referred to his father serving Berkeley for 'many years before his death, and is still of that family' (*Ormonde MSS*, new ser., 5.11–13). In 1682 Aldrich's father was referred to as 'auditor' to James, duke of York (afterwards James II).

Aldrich's name appears in the school lists at Westminster in 1656 and he was elected a king's scholar in 1658. From there he matriculated from Christ Church, Oxford, on 19 July 1662. He graduated BA in 1666, proceeding MA in 1669. He became a tutor at Christ Church, which, under John Fell, dean from 1660, attracted many scions of the aristocracy. While a young man he may have received musical tuition from Edward Lowe, professor of music at the university. By 1670 he had probably come into possession of the collection of books and manuscripts assembled by Christopher Hatton, first Baron Hatton, which included several printed music scores, which

Henry Aldrich (1648–1710), by Sir Godfrey Kneller, 1696

became the core of his music collection. At the university festivity of encaenia in 1672 Aldrich set to music some verses written by Fell, the start of a long association with music at Oxford University ceremonies. He was also a humorist, gaining a reputation as a 'punner of the first value' (Suttle, 128) and in 1673 wrote perhaps his most famous catch, 'O the bonny Christ Church bells'. That year he was recommended to Henry Oldenburg for his 'kindness, learning and scholarship beyond his years I cannot sufficiently commend' (*Hist. U. Oxf.* 4: 17th-cent. *Oxf.*, 371). Aldrich's many talents ensured that he served as tutor to many noble students, including Charles Fitzroy earl and later duke of Southampton (1674), James Butler, the future second duke of Ormond (1676), and Charles Boyle, afterwards fourth earl of Orrery. In 1674 Aldrich published *Elementa geometricae*, which may explain John Perceval's description of him in 1675 as 'a great mathematician of our house' (Suttle, 120). He had by this stage developed a practical interest in architecture, and in 1675 and 1676 supervised the repair of St Mary's Church, Oxford, alongside Maurice Wheeler, rector of another Oxford church, St Ebbe's. From 1676 Aldrich was probably responsible for the design of most of the *Oxford Almanacks*, published annually, with much of the engraving also being done under his supervision.

Aldrich's role as tutor to the tory peerage bore fruit when the commission of ecclesiastical affairs appointed him on 4 February 1682 to the vacant canonry at Christ Church. He was installed on 15 February. On 2 March he proceeded BD and DD. One of his first tasks was to join in the attack on Samuel Johnson's tract opposing the succession of the duke of York to the throne, *Julian the Apostate*

(1682), preaching a sermon on 29 October 1682. In October 1683 he became a founder member of the Oxford Philosophical Society and spoke on hearing and the ear at a meeting. In 1685 five catches composed by Aldrich were published in a collection entitled *Catch that Catch Can*. By this time Aldrich was leading weekly music meetings in his rooms at Christ Church that continued until his death. They were connected to rehearsals of the Christ Church Cathedral choir, where Aldrich sang and was the leading force, but broadened to include informal music performances that reflected his wide range of musical interests. The circle of friends included Christ Church senior members, fellows of other colleges, laymen, and a series of undergraduates, not exclusively confined to Christ Church men. The gatherings were remembered for their conviviality; Aldrich was a renowned drinker and pipe smoker. He was 'a highly competent composer', although the four services that survive in manuscript have been described as 'rather routine in style' (*New Grove*). Many of his works were recompositions of earlier works by other composers, including Thomas Tallis, Orlando Gibbons, or Palestrina. His work circulated outside Oxford and was included in the Chapel Royal and Westminster Abbey repertoires by the late 1670s. Aldrich's intention was probably to adapt music from non-English sources for the English cathedral tradition, as well as adapting polyphonic music for contemporary homophonic performance. His interest in what was becoming known as ancient music has been described as a 'kind of musical Toryism' (Weber, 36), in which Aldrich sought to reinforce the place of the church in the state and in society by restoring the Church of England's musical tradition, which had suffered since the civil war.

As subdean Aldrich had increasingly taken over the day-to-day running of Christ Church from the ageing Dean Fell. However, when Fell died in summer 1686 James II did not appoint Aldrich in Fell's place but John Massey, a Catholic fellow of Merton College, Oxford, with no previous connection to Christ Church, who had received royal dispensation from taking the sacrament and the oaths required from a new dean. Aldrich did however succeed Fell on 5 January 1687 as curator of the Sheldonian Theatre. He dutifully installed Massey as dean but then led an unsuccessful attempt to have Massey's appointment ruled illegal, a proceeding quashed by James II. He was the only Christ Church canon actively to oppose James's Catholicizing policies in the university, organizing a group of students of Christ Church to rebut Roman Catholic tracts circulating in Oxford as they were published. He himself took to print with *A reply to two discourses lately printed at Oxford concerning the adoration of our blessed saviour in the holy eucharist* (1687) to rebut Abraham Woodhead's work which had been published under the auspices of Obadiah Walker, the Catholic master of University College. Aldrich was also active in supporting the fellows of Magdalen College in their refusal to elect another Catholic, Anthony Farmer, as master. Quick action by Aldrich also ensured that in July 1688 the new duke of Ormond was elected as chancellor of the university before James II could nominate the lord chancellor, George Jeffreys, first Baron Jeffreys.

The revolution of 1688 saw the departure of Massey from Christ Church and Aldrich's appointment as dean in April 1689. He was in London from Christmas 1688 and did not return to Oxford until the eve of his installation on 17 June 1689, perhaps acclimatizing to the new political order. As dean of Christ Church and rector of Wem, Shropshire (it has been questioned whether he held this living), Aldrich enjoyed an income of about £1200 per annum. In the politics of the new reign of William III and Mary II, Aldrich was a conservative tory, a clerical lieutenant of Laurence Hyde, first earl of Rochester. On 4 September 1689 Aldrich was named to an ecclesiastical commission charged with revising the liturgy, canons, and discipline of the church so that proposals for comprehension of protestant dissenters could be laid before convocation. Aldrich was one of the few present opposed to comprehension, and he challenged the legal basis of the commission and then walked out when the commission began to discuss what ceremonies might be omitted to meet dissenters' grievances. When convocation met, plans to elect John Tillotson prolocutor of the lower house were defeated when Aldrich proposed William Jane, who was chosen 55 to 28. Aldrich and Jane then dominated proceedings until convocation was adjourned on 13 December 1689.

In the reign of William III, Christ Church was the centre of conservative tory opposition to the new regime. Rochester, and his brother Henry Hyde, second earl of Clarendon, often visited the college and it was in Christ Church that Clarendon's *History of the Great Rebellion* was edited for publication. In 1691 Aldrich published *Artis logicae compendium*, a small treatise on logic which remained a standard textbook at Oxford into the late nineteenth century. On 4 October 1692 Aldrich was installed as vice-chancellor of the university. He retained the post for three years, during which time he acted to reimpose discipline and in July 1693 revived the institution of the Act as the university's principal ceremonial occasion, ensuring that specially composed music (often by himself) was performed throughout, in addition to works offered for music degrees. His practice of encouraging a young scholar to edit a classical text for distribution as a new year's gift provoked controversy in 1693 when Charles Boyle criticized Dr Richard Bentley of Trinity College, Cambridge, in the preface of his *Epistles of Phalaris* for denying him proper access to the manuscripts in his possession as librarian of the king's library in St James's Palace. Aldrich stayed out of the printed exchanges that followed. In March 1694 he ensured that Simon Adams was installed as principal of Magdalen, despite the opposition of the fellows. In January 1695 he went up to London with an address of condolence for the king following the death of Mary II, and in May John Evelyn heard him preach against Socinians at Whitehall. In the 1690s he also experimented with music printing, employing a moveable type devised by the university printer, Peter de Walpergen, and

also engraved many plates himself; the results survive among his manuscripts at Christ Church.

In 1701, with Rochester back in royal favour and convocation allowed to meet in February, Aldrich was a leading speaker in that assembly. However, Aldrich's toryism was of a more conservative kind than the fiery radicalism of Francis Atterbury. This can be seen in the publication in September 1701 of Aldrich and George Hooper's tract, *A Narrative of the Proceedings of the Lower House of Convocation Relating to Prorogations and Adjournments*, which was less assertive than Atterbury's *The Power of the Lower House of Convocation to Adjourn itself*. When convocation met again in December 1701 it was Aldrich who was chosen on 12 February 1702 to replace the ailing prolocutor, Robert Woodward. By the time convocation met for the first time under Queen Anne, Aldrich had become part of Robert Harley's strategy to tame the more extreme elements among the tories. Before his election as prolocutor on 20 October 1702 Aldrich had a private audience with the queen, when he was told that he would be elected prolocutor and should use his influence towards moderation. Thus the efforts of Atterbury to raise the political temperature failed. Many felt that Aldrich would be rewarded for his efforts with the bishopric of Bath and Wells, but, according to Atterbury, Aldrich faced 'such an objection as, being entertained, will equally hinder him in his pretensions to any other bishopric whatsoever' (*Epistolary Correspondence*, 3.145). William Nicolson, bishop of Carlisle, viewed Aldrich as firmly in the Rochester camp, but it seems that he was less concerned with procedural disputes with the bishops than with the growth of heresies. He even wrote circular letters in 1705 in favour of William Binckes, dean of Lichfield, as his successor as prolocutor, rather than Atterbury.

Throughout his period as dean of Christ Church, Aldrich continued to practise architecture, although little can definitely be attributed to him. He was probably the original architect of All Saints' Church, Oxford, constructed between 1701 and 1710, and was certainly the designer of the Peckwater quadrangle in Christ Church, begun in 1706 but not finished until 1714, after Aldrich's death. He encouraged Charles Brandon Fairfax to translate Palladio's *Antichità di Roma* into Latin, and on its publication in 1709 Fairfax stated that Aldrich regarded Palladio as his example in architecture, a statement supported by the classicism of the Peckwater quadrangle which entitles 'Aldrich to be regarded as one of the forerunners of the Palladian movement which he did not live to see' (Colvin, *Archs.*). Aldrich also prepared a history of architecture, written and illustrated by himself, divided into civil and military sections. Only the first and part of the second volume of the civil section were completed; they were eventually published as *Elementa architecturae civilis* in 1789.

Aldrich was reported to be ill in November 1707, but in October 1708 he was well enough to visit Henry St John (later Viscount Bolingbroke) at St John's Oxfordshire seat. Aldrich died unmarried on 14 December 1710 in London, where he had gone to seek treatment on 8 December from

Dr Radcliffe for 'an ulcer in the bladder' (*Remarks*, 3.90). He was brought back to Oxford on 22 December and buried in Christ Church that day. His will ordered all his personal papers to be burnt, but he left his collections of books (3000), prints (more than 2000 engravings), and musical manuscripts (estimated at more than 8000 compositions, including many pieces of Italian origin) to the college. He specified that no one was to consult the manuscripts without the permission of the dean and chapter, 'because they are things of value in themselves and to be found in very few Libraries' (Wollenberg, 86). The collection was used by Charles Burney and Sir John Hawkins when they researched their histories of music later in the eighteenth century. He gave duplicate copies of his books to his nephew, Charles, the son of his brother, Edward.

STUART HANDLEY

Sources Foster, *Alum. Oxon.* · *Old Westminsters*, 1.10 · *Remarks and collections of Thomas Hearne*, ed. C. E. Doble and others, 11 vols., OHS, 2, 7, 13, 34, 42–3, 48, 50, 65, 67, 72 (1885–1921) · W. G. Hiscock, *Henry Aldrich of Christ Church, 1648–1710* (1960) · G. V. Bennett, *The tory crisis in church and state, 1688–1730* (1975) · *Hist. U. Oxf.*, vols 4–5 · A. M. Burke, ed., *Memorials of St Margaret's Church, Westminster* (1914), 206 · H. M. Petter, *The Oxford Almanacks* (1974) · W. G. Hiscock, *A Christ Church miscellany* (1946) · E. F. A. Suttle, 'Henry Aldrich, dean of Christ Church', *Oxoniensia*, 5 (1940), 115–39 · *The life and times of Anthony Wood*, ed. A. Clark, 2, OHS, 21 (1892), 250, 308; 3, OHS, 26 (1894) · *The epistolary correspondence, visitation charges, speeches, and miscellanies of Francis Atterbury*, ed. J. Nichols, 5 vols. (1783–90) · Pepys, *Diary* · will, Oxf. UA · *Calendar of the manuscripts of the marquess of Ormonde*, new ser., 8 vols., HMC, 36 (1902–20) · *The London diaries of William Nicolson, bishop of Carlisle, 1702–1718*, ed. C. Jones and G. Holmes (1985) · *Report on the manuscripts of the marquis of Downshire*, 6 vols. in 7, HMC, 75 (1924–95) · *CSP dom.*, 1682, p. 61 · W. M. Marshall, *George Hooper, 1640–1727, bishop of Bath and Wells* (1976), 79–84 · *New Grove*, online edn, 17 May 2002 · Colvin, *Archs.* · W. Weber, *The rise of musical classics in eighteenth-century England* (1992) · S. Wollenberg, *Music at Oxford in the eighteenth and nineteenth centuries* (2001)

Likenesses G. Kneller, oils, 1696, Christ Church Oxf. [*see illus.*] · J. Smith, mezzotint, 1696 (after portrait by G. Kneller), BM, NPG · J. Smith, mezzotint, after 1710 (after G. Kneller), BM · marble busts, Christ Church Oxf.

Wealth at death see will proved by court of chancellor of University of Oxford, 5 Nov 1711, now held by Oxford University Archives

Aldrich, Robert (1488/9–1556), bishop of Carlisle, was born at Burnham, Buckinghamshire, probably the son of Richard Aldryge; his brother John, a London grocer, died early in 1518. Robert was educated at Eton College, and was admitted as a scholar of King's College, Cambridge, on 24 May 1507, aged eighteen, and as a fellow on 27 May 1510. The college records indicate that he retained his fellowship until Michaelmas 1528, so disproving claims that he was master of Eton for several years after 1515. At Cambridge he graduated BA in 1511–12, subsequently proceeding MA in 1515 and BTh in 1517. Ordained deacon on 15 March 1522 and priest (to the title of his fellowship) on 5 April 1522, he was a university preacher in 1522–3 and senior proctor in 1524–5, while in 1526–7 he was paid by the university for writing three letters to the king. On 15 March 1530 his BTh was incorporated at Oxford, where on 3 April following he was awarded the degree of DTh.

During his years in Cambridge, Aldrich befriended and worked with Desiderius Erasmus, whom he accompanied on his famous journey to the shrine of Walsingham in May 1512, and with whom he remained friends after Erasmus had left England. In 1527 Erasmus dedicated a book to Aldrich as a reward for the latter's services in collating manuscripts for a new edition of Seneca. No doubt it was with Erasmus's encouragement that Aldrich pursued a career both as a humanist and as a cleric. He was the author of 'Epigrammata varia', found in William Horman's *Vulgaria* (1519), and of 'Epistola ad Gul. Hormannum', a preface in verse to Horman's *Antibossicon* (1521), the latter having itself been composed with Aldrich's encouragement in order to attack the grammatical writings of Robert Whittington.

Aldrich began to accumulate benefices from the late 1520s, under the patronage of John Longland, bishop of Lincoln, who was encouraged in this by Erasmus—on 1 September 1528 Erasmus wrote to the bishop expressing pleasure in the favour Longland had shown his friend, whom he refers to as 'tuus Aldrisius', and urging him to extend it. On 18 April in that year Longland had collated Aldrich to the vicarage of Stanton Harcourt, Oxfordshire, and followed this up with two prebends in Lincoln cathedral, Centum Solidorum (18 July 1528) and Decem Librarum (6 May 1529). Aldrich also became Longland's chaplain. But his career took off in earnest in 1531 when he came to the attention of Henry VIII. He had already been presented to the living of Cheriton (3 January) when he preached before the king on 12 March in that year; on 30 December he became archdeacon of Colchester as well. Henry's favour subsequently brought him a prebend in St George's Chapel, Windsor (3 May 1534), and the position of royal chaplain (by 5 June 1535). He also obtained the vicarage of Welford-on-Avon, Gloucestershire (March 1535), and the Lincolnshire rectory of Gedney (by 1535). On 17 March 1536 he was appointed provost of Eton, a position he held until 29 December 1547. It was probably also in 1536 that he became almoner to Queen Jane Seymour. Finally, on 10 July 1537 the king nominated him to be bishop of Carlisle. Formal election took place on the 18th; the royal assent was given on 9 August, the temporalities were restored the following day, and Aldrich was consecrated on 19 August.

In addition to his academic and ecclesiastical duties Aldrich was engaged in various secular employments. In 1533 he formed part of an embassy sent to François I and Clement VII, and on 17 May 1534 he was appointed registrar of the Order of the Garter. In the latter capacity he compiled the order's register, known as the back book. On 1 February 1539 he was appointed to a committee set up to deal with debtors in Ludgate gaol who wished to compound with their creditors. Later that year he was one of the conservative bishops named to the committee for the revision of doctrine, and when it failed to agree predictably gave his support to the Act of Six Articles. From then until 1553 he appears to have remained a true Henrician Catholic in his beliefs, under Edward VI voting in parliament against every significant measure for further reformation, and above all against the Acts of Uniformity of 1549 and 1552. But perhaps because he did not go beyond opposition to outright resistance he was able to retain his bishopric, when half his fellow conservatives lost theirs. Following Mary's accession he accepted England's reunion with Rome, and he remained bishop of Carlisle until his death.

Little can be said about Aldrich's episcopate for lack of a register and other evidence. He certainly showed no enthusiasm for residence in his diocese. On 22 November 1540 the privy council noted that although he had been appointed treasurer for works on the defences of his cathedral city, he had none the less 'come hither rather to linger at Eton than for any just cause'; he was accordingly instructed to proceed to his diocese 'for the feeding of the people both with his preaching and good hospitality' (*LP Henry VIII*, vol. 16, no. 286). Later he entrusted the task of collecting ecclesiastical taxation to servants who embezzled the money, probably for lack of adequate supervision. Under Mary he served on the commission which examined the protestant martyrs John Hooper, Rowland Taylor, and John Rogers, but no executions for heresy are recorded in his doctrinally conservative diocese, and only three incumbents are known to have been deprived. As bishop he benefited from Mary's accession, through the annulment of the lease which he had been compelled in 1552 to grant to Lord Clinton of the soke of Horncastle in Lincolnshire at a ruinously low rent; the soke had for centuries been a pillar of his see's finances. It also provided an alternative residence, and it was at Horncastle that Aldrich died, probably on 5 May (some sources give 5 March) 1556, and was probably buried.

ANGELO J. LOUISA

Sources Emden, *Oxf.*, 4.4–5 · Cooper, *Ath. Cantab.*, 1.142–3, 547 · Wood, *Ath. Oxon.*, new edn, 1.232–4 · Wood, *Ath. Oxon.: Fasti* (1815), 83, 85 · M. A. R. Graves, *The House of Lords in the parliaments of Edward VI and Mary I* (1981), 90, 207, 220 · *LP Henry VIII* · Venn, *Alum. Cant.*, 1/1.14 · Foster, *Alum. Oxon.*, *1500–1714*, 1.13 · *Reg. Oxf.*, 1.159 · *Fasti Angl., 1300–1541*, [Lincoln], 52, 61 · *Fasti Angl., 1300–1541*, [St Paul's, London], 14 · *Fasti Angl., 1300–1541*, [York], 99 · *Fasti Angl., 1300–1541*, [Introduction], 23 · will, PRO, PROB 11/38, sig. 8; sentence, PRO, PROB 11/42A, sig. 49 · J. Strype, *Ecclesiastical memorials*, 3/1 (1822), 286, 290, 330 · *The acts and monuments of John Foxe*, ed. S. R. Cattley, 8 vols. (1837–41), vol. 6, pp. 126, 598 · commons books; mundum books; protocol books, King's Cam. · M. Bateson, ed., *Grace book B*, 2 vols. (1903–5) · W. G. Searle, ed., *Grace book Γ* (1908) · R. E. G. Cole, ed., *Chapter acts of the cathedral church of St Mary of Lincoln*, 1, Lincoln RS, 12 (1915) · L. B. Smith, *Tudor prelates and politics, 1536–1558* (1953) · F. Heal, *Of prelates and princes: a study of the economic and social position of the Tudor episcopate* (1980) · C. M. L. Bouch, *Prelates and people of the lake counties: a history of the diocese of Carlisle, 1133–1933* (1948)

Wealth at death PRO, PROB 11/42A, sig. 49 · 'chappell stuf to be given … to my coleage churche of Carlisle': will, PRO, PROB 11/38, fol. 157v

Aldridge, Amanda Christina Elizabeth [*pseud.* Montague Ring] (**1866–1956**), singer and composer, was born on 10 March 1866 at Luranah Villa, Hamlet Road, Penge, Surrey, the second of three daughters and third of four children of Ira Frederick *Aldridge (1807?–1867), the distinguished African-American tragedian, and his second wife, Swedish opera singer Amanda Pauline, *née* von

Brandt (*d.* 1915). Ira Aldridge died on tour in Łódź, Poland, on 7 August 1867, leaving his widow with three young children: Irene (Luranah; 1860–1932), Ira Frederick (1862–1886), and Amanda. A fourth, Rachel Margaret Frederika (*b.* 1868), was born after her father's death. The Aldridge children showed great musical promise from childhood and their mother encouraged them to have a sense of pride in their African heritage. In honour of her father Amanda added the name Ira to her own. She and her elder sister, Luranah, were educated at a convent school in Belgium. One of her earliest appearances as a singer was at a concert in Crystal Palace in 1881, when she sang Beethoven's 'Creation's hymn' and a ballad. Two years later, at the age of seventeen, she won a foundation scholarship to the newly opened Royal College of Music, where she studied singing (from 1883 to 1887) with Jenny Lind, known as the Swedish Nightingale, and Sir George Henschel. She was also a pupil of Dame Madge Kendal, who had played Desdemona to her father's Othello in 1865.

For many years Amanda Aldridge enjoyed success as a contralto, and often appeared with her brother, Ira Frederick, as her accompanist until his early death in 1886. In June 1905, after hearing a recital at Steinway Hall, a reviewer in *The Times* wrote:

> Miss Ira Aldridge held the attention of a large audience on Saturday afternoon … Dvorak's gipsy songs call for the exercise of a great deal of art … Miss Aldridge's style is excellent, her voice warm and mellow, and her intelligence far beyond dispute; the combination may well serve to explain the measure of her success.

When her singing career ended after an attack of laryngitis damaged her throat, Aldridge remembered what Jenny Lind had once told her: 'Never mind what happens to your throat. … You can always earn a livelihood as a singing teacher, because you have a good insight into voice theory and practice'.

Until she died Amanda Aldridge played an important part in the musical life of London's black middle class: after her singing career had ended she turned her attention to composing and teaching voice production and piano. She started composing when she was in her thirties and always published under the name Montague Ring, to separate her work as a composer from that as singer and instructor. She composed love songs, suites, sambas, and light orchestral pieces. Sophie Fuller summed up her work as a composer thus:

> Most of her music is in a popular style, often using syncopated dance rhythms. Her best-known work is *Three African Dances* (1913) … The slow, central movement, 'Luleta's Dance', uses themes reminiscent of music from West Africa … Aldridge also published over 25 songs [and] wrote her own words for many of her earliest songs. (Fuller, 37)

As a teacher, Aldridge's singing pupils included three distinguished African-Americans: tenor Roland Hayes, contralto Marian Anderson, and Paul Robeson. Hayes went on to perform her songs throughout England and Europe. In 1925 she befriended the African-American singer and actor Paul Robeson and his wife, Eslanda, when they visited London. That same year she composed music for the poem 'Summah is de lovin' Time', written by the

African-American Paul Laurence Dunbar, and dedicated it to the Robesons. She also presented Robeson with the earrings her father had worn on stage as Othello, expressing the hope that he would one day wear them when he too played the role. After settling in London in 1928, Robeson turned to Aldridge for elocution lessons before making his first appearance as Othello at London's Savoy Theatre with Peggy Ashcroft in 1930.

Although Aldridge appears to have stopped writing (or at least publishing) music by the end of the 1920s, she continued to teach and play an important part in musical life. She never married, partly because—in addition to her teaching work and composition—she had to look after her elderly, bedridden mother, who died in 1915, and her sister Luranah, whose own musical career had ended when she developed severe rheumatism. Luranah spent the last twenty years of her life as an invalid, before killing herself in 1932.

When Bermuda-born actor Earl Cameron began his professional career in Britain in the 1940s, there were few openings for young black actors in drama schools. On the advice of a friend, he turned to Aldridge for help. Much later he recalled:

> Miss Aldridge was about eighty at this time but still giving elocution lessons and instructing people in voice projection. She was light-skinned, rather short and stocky. She was a lovely, well-spoken, delicate and dignified lady with a tremendous sense of humour. She could laugh about most things. She was a courteous, beautiful human being, but not wealthy. I had the highest regard for her, and we got on extremely well. She helped me tremendously and I continued having lessons with her for at least two years. She told me all about her father, and showed me pictures of him. She did not like Herbert Marshall who later published a biography of her father. She didn't have a high opinion of Paul Robeson, either. She had given Robeson elocution lessons when he was preparing for his first appearance as Othello at the Savoy. She helped him greatly but, in later years, she was hurt when he failed to give her any credit. (Bourne, 156–7)

Aldridge died the day before her ninetieth birthday, in 1956, at Cave Hill Hospital in Coulsdon, Surrey. She was buried in an unmarked grave in Streatham Park cemetery.   STEPHEN BOURNE

Sources S. Bourne, *Black in the British frame: black people in British film and television, 1896–1996* (1998) · S. Fuller, *The Pandora guide to women composers: Britain and the United States, 1629–present* (1994) · J. Green, *Black Edwardians: black people in Britain, 1901–1914* (1998) · Z. Alexander, 'Black entertainers of the Edwardian era', *Weekend Voice* (17–21 Dec 1987) · H. Marshall and M. Stock, *Ira Aldridge: the negro tragedian* (1958) · b. cert. · CGPLA Eng. & Wales (1956) · d. cert.
Wealth at death £440 16s. 9d.: probate, 17 Aug 1956, *CGPLA Eng. & Wales*

Aldridge, Ira Frederick (1807?–1867), actor, was probably born on 24 July 1807 in New York city, the son of Daniel Aldridge, a lay preacher. Little is known of his mother, Lurona, who died when he was a youth. He was the first major African-American actor, although virtually all of his appearances were in Britain or on the continent; best known for his tragic roles, he was also successful in a variety of comic parts.

Aldridge's origins have often been romanticized: an

Ira Frederick Aldridge (1807?–1867), by Henry Perronet Briggs, *c*.1830 [as Othello]

anonymous 1849 publication, *Memoir and Theatrical Career of Ira Aldridge*, tells a tale, often repeated, that he was born in Senegal, the son of a royal family of the Fulah tribe. Based on the evidence, it seems most likely that he and his father were both free-born African-Americans. The *Memoir* is sometimes attributed to Aldridge, who may have had a hand in creating such a marketably romantic 'history'.

Aldridge was attracted to the theatre as a child, and attended performances at New York's Park Theatre. While a student at the city's African Free School he became involved in the short-lived African Theatre, where, according to the *Memoir*, he first played the part of Rolla in Sheridan's *Pizarro*, a part to which he would later return. After the closing of the African Theatre, when it became apparent that the opportunities for roles would be severely limited in the United States, Aldridge sailed for England some time around 1824. According to another popular but unconfirmed tale he travelled as a servant to the American actor Henry Wallack.

Aldridge made his London début on 10 October 1825, at the Royal Coburg Theatre, playing the part of Oronooko in *The Revolt of Surinam, or, A Slave's Revenge* (an adaptation of Thomas Southern's *Oronooko*). During his time at the Royal Coburg he performed in such other works as Thomas Morton's *The Slave* and J. H. Amherst's *The Death of Christophe*. From the beginning of his career, reviewers focused on his appearance: he was generally described as tall and well built; it was common for critics to note, with some surprise, that he was not as dark-skinned as actors in 'blackface', but rather was 'almost a light brown', with a 'mulatto tint'. His voice was described as 'rich and melodious', but some reviewers considered it nasal or whiny; the contradiction may be on account of varying responses to an American accent (many critics comment on his 'strikingly un-English' pronunciation, and George Eliot found it intolerable). He was given the sobriquet 'the African Roscius'.

Much of Aldridge's early career in Britain, when he was known as 'Mr Keene', found him in the provincial theatres, including those at Hull, Brighton, Manchester, Newcastle, Liverpool, and Edinburgh, and in the theatres of London's East End. *Othello*, *The Slave*, and Bickerstaffe's *The Padlock* were the staples of his repertory. He was married for the first time shortly after his arrival in England, to Margaret Gill (*c*.1800–1864).

Aldridge made his West End début at the Theatre Royal, Covent Garden, in 1833, when he played *Othello* barely two weeks after the death of Kean, who had been playing the Moor on that very stage. Aldridge was forced to circulate handbills defending his adoption of Kean's part. The reviews were a fascinating mix, indicative of the feelings Aldridge inspired in critics. Some, as in *The Athenaeum*, were unable to get beyond a consideration of his race; the *Theatrical Observer*, in a typical pun, noted that his performance was 'very *fair* for a *black*'. In general the more even-tempered reviewers focused on his 'naturalness'. Notably, they mention the overwhelmingly favourable response from the audience. After two performances Covent Garden closed for five days, and Aldridge's remaining performances were cancelled, possibly as a result of the hostility of the press. Aldridge sought out new roles beyond those of his standard repertory, and he in fact revived Shakespeare's rarely produced *Titus Andronicus* at the Britannia Theatre in 1852; in his revision the Moor Aaron became an unlikely tragic hero.

After continuing his work in the provinces and in Ireland, Aldridge began his first continental tour in 1852, and it was here that he received his warmest welcome from the theatrical community. Appearances in Switzerland and Germany, where he played in *Othello*, *The Padlock*, and *Macbeth*, were met with great acclaim; there and in various parts of the Austro-Hungarian empire he was able to move with ease among aristocrats and artists. On his visits to Russia in 1858 and 1862 he was credited with introducing a more naturalistic acting style and encouraging the production of Shakespeare's plays. It was on one such European tour, in 1857 or 1858, that he met the woman who was to become his second wife, Amanda Pauline von Brandt (*d*. 1915). They married on 20 April 1865, after Margaret Aldridge's death the previous year, and had four children: Irene (1860–1932), Ira Frederick Olaff (1862–1886), Amanda Christina Elizabeth *Aldridge (1866–1956), and Rachel Margaret Frederika (*b*. 1868, after her father's death). Aldridge's eldest child, Ira Daniel, was born in May 1847, when his first wife was nearly fifty and already in ill health; the child apparently was not hers.

Having returned to England in 1855, Aldridge again toured the provinces and appeared in the East End. After a second continental tour had enhanced his reputation he

was offered work at the Lyceum, and the response of the London press this time was much more respectful. Still, the theatres and audiences on the continent evidently offered Aldridge greater artistic range and freedom. It was on one such continental tour, when in Łódź, Poland, that he died of an apparent lung infection on 7 August 1867. He was buried on 9 August in the city's Evangelical cemetery.   HEIDI J. HOLDER

Sources H. Marshall and M. Stock, *Ira Aldridge: the negro tragedian* (1958) · E. Hill, *Shakespeare in sable: a history of black Shakespearean actors* (1984) · *Memoir and theatrical career of Ira Aldridge, the African Roscius* (1849) · S. Durilin, 'Ira Aldridge', trans. E. Blum, *Shakespeare Association Bulletin*, 17 (1942), 33–9 · O. Mortimer, 'Ira Aldridge, Shakespearean actor', *The Crisis*, 62 (1955), 203–14 · R. Cowhig, 'Ira Aldridge in Manchester', *Theatre Research International*, 11 (1987), 239–47 · F. Gaffney, 'A forgotten man: Ira Aldridge in Zagreb, Yugoslavia', *South African Theatre Journal*, 2 (1988), 3–15 · Adams, *Drama* · T. A. Brown, *History of the American stage* (1870) · *The George Eliot letters*, ed. G. S. Haight, 2 (1954), 301–2 · *The Era* (25 Nov 1846) · *The Era* (2 Feb 1863) · *The Era* (18 Aug 1867) · *Theatrical Observer* (11 April 1833)

Archives Harvard TC · Northwestern University, Illinois · NYPL, Schomburg Center for Research in Black Culture · NYPL for the Performing Arts · Theatre Museum, London

Likenesses J. Northcote, oils, 1826, Man. City Gall. · H. P. Briggs, oils, *c*.1830, Smithsonian Institution, Washington, DC, National Portrait Gallery [*see illus.*] · oils, *c*.1833 (as Mungo in *The padlock*), Theatre Museum, London · engraving, 1852 (as Aaron in *Titus Andronicus*; after photograph), Jerwood Library of the Performing Arts, London, Mander and Mitchenson collection · Barabas, lithograph, 1853, Bakhrushin State Central Theatrical Museum, Moscow, Russia · B. Feston, lithograph, 1853 · oils, *c*.1860, Bakhrushin State Central Theatrical Museum, Moscow, Russia · P. Calvi, bronze bust, NYPL, Schomburg Center for Research in Black Culture · more than sixty portraits, NYPL, Schomburg Center for Research in Black Culture, photographic collection

Wealth at death under £9000: resworn probate, Sept 1873, *CGPLA Eng. & Wales* (1867)

Aldridge, John Arthur Malcolm (1905–1983), painter and gardener, was born near Woolwich, London, on 26 July 1905, the second of the three sons (there were no daughters) of Major John Barttelot Aldridge DSO of the Royal Field Artillery and his wife, Margaret Jessica Goddard, the daughter of a Leicester architect. His father died when he was three, and his mother subsequently married again and had a daughter. He won scholarships both to Uppingham School and Corpus Christi College, Oxford, where he obtained a second in classical honour moderations (1926) and a third in *literae humaniores* (1928). At Oxford his diverse activities included both rugby and the Opera Club, but his interest in painting was already strong; with the intention of teaching himself to paint, he moved to Hammersmith in 1928. His work came to the attention of Ben Nicholson, who in 1930 invited him to exhibit in London with the Seven and Five Society. In 1933 he held his first one-man show, and a year later some of his paintings were chosen for the Venice Biennale.

During the 1930s Aldridge was closely associated with a group which included Robert Graves, Norman Cameron, Laura Riding, Len Lye, and Lucie Brown, whom he was later to marry. Both Deya, Majorca, which Graves made his home, and Place House, Great Bardfield, Essex, bought by

Aldridge in 1933, were centres of vigorous literary and artistic activity; these included productions of the Seizin Press. Aldridge notably illustrated Laura Riding's *The Life of the Dead* (1934), and also designed the dust-jackets for most of Graves's novels. Towards the end of the decade he began to design wallpapers, as did Edward Bawden, then also living in Great Bardfield. In 1939 Aldridge's name was included among those artists whom the third Viscount Esher proposed should be exempted from military service. In 1940 he married (Cecilia) Lucie (Leeds) Brown, daughter of Isaac Ebenezer Leeds Saunders, a farmer of Clayhithe, near Cambridge.

Between 1941 and 1945 Aldridge served in the Royal Army Service Corps and, after being commissioned, in the intelligence corps. During his time in north Africa and Italy, he made many drawings and watercolours, some of which are a valuable record of army and civilian life in wartime. He did distinguished work as an interpreter of air photographs.

After demobilization, Aldridge returned to Great Bardfield and resumed both his painting in oils and the care of his garden. In 1949 William Coldstream, recently appointed head of the Slade School of Fine Art, invited him to become a part-time member of staff at the school. For the next twenty-one years, until his retirement in 1970, and although without any formal art school training himself, Aldridge proved a successful and much-liked teacher. In 1948 he first exhibited at the Royal Academy; he was elected an associate in 1954, and Royal Academician in 1963. He played an active part in the academy's affairs, serving several times on the hanging committee. Locally, he was one of the principal organizers of an interesting experiment in the 1950s, when a number of painters and designers living in or near Great Bardfield exhibited their work in their own houses.

As a painter, Aldridge was primarily interested in landscape and vernacular buildings, particularly in Essex, abroad in Italy and France, and in Majorca, on visits to Robert Graves. He also produced some noteworthy still-life paintings, and a few portraits, including one of Robert Graves, which was later acquired by the National Portrait Gallery. His early work made a considerable impression; it had a freshness and directness, and the description 'stark and wiry' suits it well. This economical formality began to change during the 1930s and, after the war, he became more concerned with detailed, accurate representation, perhaps in part because he had little liking for the then fashionable abstract and decorative painting. His interest in gardening and painting ran closely together; as he wrote in 1959, he saw the development of a garden as 'a process which combines selection, precision and an understanding of the nature and possibilities of the materials in a way which is analogous to painting'. His friendship with the classical architect Raymond Erith was an important influence on him; a common passion for gardening drew him to near neighbours such as Sir Cedric Morris and John Nash. Following the dissolution of his first marriage in 1970 he married that year Margareta (Gretl) Anna Maria Cameron, widow of the poet (John)

Norman Cameron and daughter of Dr Friederich Viktor Bajardi, Hofrat at Graz. She died early in 1983. There were no children of either marriage.

Aldridge was a gentle, friendly man, of great charm, with a scholarly interest in painting, architecture, and gardening. In appearance he was tall and spare. He was a generous host in his beautiful Tudor house, in itself a work of art which owed much to the taste of his first wife, Lucie. It was there that he died on 3 May 1983. Examples of his work are in the Tate collection and in public galleries in Manchester, Leeds, and Aberdeen.

ANNE WHITEMAN, *rev.*

Sources *TLS* (2 Jan 1987) · personal knowledge (1990) · private information (1990)

Aldridge, William (1737–1797), Independent minister, was born at Warminster, in Wiltshire. He spent his youth in the pursuit of pleasure, but in his twenties he was affected by a passionate desire to be a preacher of the gospel. He joined the Countess of Huntingdon's Connexion and was admitted in 1768 to her college at Trefeca in south Wales. There he remained as a student and supply preacher until 1771.

Aldridge unsuccessfully sought episcopal ordination in 1771, and in September of that year was sent by Lady Huntingdon, with Joseph Cook, a fellow student, to Margate in the Isle of Thanet. They were total strangers in the place and began to address, in the open air, any who would listen to them. The numbers increased from month to month. Despite opposition from some locals and Anglican clergy, Aldridge and Cook preached at various places in Kent, including Folkestone, Deal, Canterbury, and Maidstone. A number of connexion chapels were opened and Aldridge took over with remarkable success a moribund presbyterian meeting-house in Dover. Later the two preachers supplied Margate and Dover alternately. Cook subsequently travelled as a missionary to South Carolina and Georgia in America.

Lady Huntingdon, who seldom permitted her preachers to stay long in any one place, sent Aldridge about 1775 to supply the Mulberry Garden Chapel in Wapping. There his ministry proved so remarkably successful that the large congregation petitioned Lady Huntingdon to allow him to continue as minister. Her refusal led him to leave the connexion in 1776.

Aldridge then accepted an invitation to become the minister at the Independent congregation in Jewry Street, London, where he remained until his death. His reputation as a preacher was great, and while at Jewry Street he was, according to Walter Wilson, 'greatly beloved by an affectionate congregation' (Wilson, 1.130). He died on 28 February 1797 in Jewry Street, London, and, like so many nonconformist ministers, was buried in Bunhill Fields. The Revd George Gold delivered the address at his interment on 7 March, and on the following Sunday the funeral sermons were preached for him by Revds Anthony Cole and Thomas Bryson.

Aldridge was not a prolific writer and has left only three published works, his *Doctrine of the Trinity, Stated, Proved and Defended*, a funeral sermon on the death of the countess of Huntingdon, and a collection of hymns, published in 1776, which reached a fifth edition in 1789.

A. B. GROSART, rev. M. J. MERCER

Sources W. Wilson, *The history and antiquities of the dissenting churches and meeting houses in London, Westminster and Southwark*, 4 vols. (1808–14), vol. 1, pp. 129–32 · C. Surman, index of dissenting ministers, DWL · D. M. Lewis, ed., *The Blackwell dictionary of evangelical biography, 1730–1860*, 2 vols. (1995) · [A. C. H. Seymour], *The life and times of Selina, countess of Huntingdon*, 2 (1840), 130–36 · T. Bryson, *Sermon on the death of the Rev. W. Aldridge* [n.d.], 14, 16 · J. A. Jones, ed., *Bunhill memorials* (1849), 5 · J. Julian, ed., *A dictionary of hymnology*, rev. edn (1907), 38 · 'Memoir of the late Rev. William Aldridge', *Evangelical Magazine*, 19 (1811), 409–12 · E. Welch, *Spiritual pilgrim: a reassessment of the life of the countess of Huntingdon* (1995)
Likenesses Pollard, line engraving, NPG · engraving, repro. in Wilson, *History and antiquities*, facing p. 129

Aldulf. *See* Ealdwulf (*d.* 1002).

Aled, Tudur. *See* Tudur Aled (*c.*1465–1525×7).

Alefounder, John (1757–1794), portrait and miniature painter, was born in September 1757, probably in Colchester, Essex, the son of an architect and surveyor. He entered the Royal Academy Schools, as an architect, on 4 October 1776, aged nineteen 'Sept last' (Hutchison, 142) and gained a silver medal in 1782 and in 1784. He exhibited first, in 1777, an architectural design for a lunatic hospital, and was granted the freedom of Colchester in the same year. By 1784 he had married and was living in Covent Garden. That year he exhibited some theatrical portraits and portrait groups, executed in chalks and oil paint. Bartolozzi engraved after Alefounder's miniature *Peter the Wild Boy* (exh. RA, 1783) in 1784, and in the same year Alefounder's portrait of the comic actor John Edwin, as Lingo in John O'Keefe's *The Agreeable Surprise* (1783), was engraved by C. N. Hodges.

After making his will in January 1785 Alefounder left England, in February, aboard the *Montagu*, arriving in Calcutta the following October; his wife and son remained in England. His decision to work in India was in defiance of East India Company policy, which aimed to regulate the number of artists working in India at any one time in a particular area. On arrival in India, Alefounder was anxious about establishing himself successfully and went 'melancholy mad' (Cotton, 'A Calcutta painter', 117). During his illness his pictures, paints, and equipment were sold, without his consent, on Mr Devis's order at Burrell and Goulds, Calcutta. Alefounder's advertisement in the *Calcutta Gazette* of 17 October 1786 thanked those who helped him recover some of his pictures and announced that he would 'continue to take likenesses'. He met with little success, however, and depended on the support of his compatriots for his subsistence. Records in the vestry of St John's Church, Calcutta, show that in 1787 he was responsible for cleaning the altarpiece, *The Last Supper*, by John Zoffany. In 1788, after an earlier suggestion from John David Patterson (of the civil service), he painted a series of thirty-six pictures, and sent drawings of these to be engraved; they included portraits of nawabs and 'remarkable characters' as well as portraits of local people, customs, and ceremonies. Though the scheme appears to have failed, due to lack of support, it was the first of its kind and provided a model which other British artists in India later adopted. In that year he was living at 4 Larkins's Lane, Calcutta, with a fellow portrait painter, Richard Miller.

While in India, Alefounder made several attempts on his life. The miniature painter Ozias Humphry stated that 'he has attempted to hang himself two or three times, but before he was quite dead was discover'd and cut down' (Humphry MSS, 3.58). While living with the painter Balthazar Solvyns, who befriended him, Alefounder finally succeeded in taking his own life, by cutting his throat with a penknife, in Calcutta on 25 December 1794. The donation by the Royal Academy of 5 guineas to 'Alefounder' in July 1796 was almost certainly for the relief of his widow and child (Farington, *Diary*, 2.599).

ERNEST RADFORD, rev. EMMA RUTHERFORD

Sources D. Foskett, *A dictionary of British miniature painters*, 2 vols. (1972) · B. S. Long, *British miniaturists* (1929) · G. C. Williamson, *Life and works of Ozias Humphry* (1918) · W. Foster, 'British artists in India, 1760–1820', *Walpole Society*, 19 (1930–31), 1–88, esp. 5–7 · artist's notes, NPG, Heinz Archive and Library · *The exhibition of the Royal Academy* (1771–93) [exhibition catalogues] · Redgrave, *Artists* · H. Blättel, *International dictionary miniature painters / Internationales Lexikon Miniatur-Maler* (1992) · RA, Ozias Humphry MSS, vols. 3, 4 · S. C. Hutchison, 'The Royal Academy Schools, 1768–1830', *Walpole Society*, 38 (1960–62), 123–91, esp. 142 · E. Cotton, 'British artists in India, 1760–1820', *Bengal Past and Present*, 42 (1931), 136–43, esp. 138 · E. Cotton, 'A Calcutta painter (John Alefounder)', *Bengal Past and Present*, 34 (1927), 116–19 · Farington, *Diary*, 2.599 · M. Archer, *India and British portraiture, 1770–1825* (1979), 270–72

Alemoor. For this title name *see* Pringle, Andrew, Lord Alemoor (*d.* 1776).

Alen, John (1476–1534), archbishop of Dublin, is of unknown parentage. He received his undergraduate training at Gonville Hall, Cambridge, between 1491 and 1495, although there is an unverified tradition that he studied at the University of Oxford before migrating to Cambridge. After receiving his BA in 1494–5, he obtained a fellowship from Peterhouse in 1496, which he held until 1503–4, and proceeded MA in 1498. He was ordained priest on 25 August 1499, having been granted a dispensation on 8 March to take priestly orders while under the canonical age.

The year 1499 also marked the beginning of Alen's career as a canon lawyer, with his appointment as commissary to Richard FitzJames, bishop of Rochester. By about 1502 or 1503, however, he had transferred to the service of William Warham, archbishop of Canterbury, for whom he worked for the next eleven years as a proctor at the papal curia. While in Rome, Alen was admitted to the confraternity of the English Hospice, serving successively as a chaplain, warden, chamberlain, and auditor from 1502 to about 1512, although he was expelled at the end of this period for contention and defiance of Cardinal Christopher Bainbridge, the English resident at the papal court. During the same period he also secured collation to a number of English benefices, including the prebend of Asgarby in the diocese of Lincoln, held from 1503 to 1528, and the rectories of Sundridge, held from 1508 to 1528, and Aldington, held from 1511 to 1512, both in Kent. The most important legacy of Alen's continental sojourn, however, was the development of his expertise as a canon lawyer. Honed and refined at the papal curia, and given formal recognition by 1508 through his procurement of a doctorate in canon and civil law from a foreign university, it was this expertise which brought him to the notice of Cardinal Thomas Wolsey, archbishop of York; and which marked him out as a potential contributor to the task of extending the cardinal's legatine jurisdiction throughout the English church.

Alen's relationship with Wolsey appears to have begun in 1518. In this year he was indicted by the cardinal on a charge of *praemunire* in the court of Star Chamber. The reason for the charge is now unknown, but it has been reasonably argued that it represented a display of power on the cardinal's part aimed at Warham, of whom Alen had been a protégé. It is also reasonable to assume that the case represented the first step in Wolsey's recruitment of Alen for, in the following year, he appointed him his commissary-general. From this point on, until his election to the see of Dublin in autumn 1528, he worked unceasingly and energetically to achieve the full and practical realization of the cardinal's legateship throughout both provinces of the English church, and was well rewarded for his efforts in the form of numerous ecclesiastical benefices. These included the rectory of Gaulby in Leicestershire, in 1523, and canonries in Southwell, from 1526 to 1528, St Paul's Cathedral, from 1527 to 1528, and Exeter, from March to November 1528, and the precentorship of St Mary's, Southampton, from 1527 to 1528.

Alen's particular role in the legatine project was to effect the intrusion of the cardinal's authority upon competing ecclesiastical jurisdictions. Thus, as commissary-general of the legatine court, he was involved closely in the usurpation of Canterbury testamentary jurisdiction and other attacks on Warham's prerogatives. He also led the assault on episcopal independence by carrying out, in Wolsey's name, the much resented legatine visitations in certain dioceses, and by compounding with the bishops for tributes to the cardinal in order that they might be permitted to exercise their own jurisdictions. The reduction of monastic independence was also a key strategic aim of the cardinal's legatine policy. Again, Alen played a central role in the proceedings by ensuring that Wolsey's preferred choices as monastic heads were elected, whether through dictate or intrigue; and by conducting the legatine visitations of religious houses, whether they were exempt or non-exempt. In addition, in 1524, along with Thomas Cromwell, he organized the suppression of some lesser monasteries for the endowment of Wolsey's projected colleges at Oxford and Ipswich, Suffolk.

In pursuing all of these objectives, Alen displayed the same determined and pugnacious streak to his character, which had first been revealed in his spat with Bainbridge. At this juncture, however, it earned him considerable notoriety, provoking a rash of criticism from both anti-clerical writers and Henry VIII's courtiers alike. Thus, in his *Supplication for the Beggars* (1529), Simon Fish tendentiously queried why Alen had gone unpunished by the king even though he had usurped crown pleas in Wolsey's legatine court (Fish, fol. 7r). In a subtler pasquinade, Jerome Barlow criticized his alleged corruption and cupidity during monastic visitations as a function of the cardinal's need to raise cash to fund his garish ostentation (Roy and Barlow, 57). More seriously, on 19 August 1527, the king's secretary, William Knight, advised Wolsey not to send Alen as his messenger to Henry as he had 'heard the king and noble men speak things incredible of the acts of Mr Alen and Cromwell' (*State Papers, Henry VIII*, 1.261). Despite all this, Wolsey stood by his commissary. Indeed, following the death of the archbishop of Dublin and lord chancellor of Ireland, Hugh Inge, on 3 August 1528, he instantly singled him out as the candidate most suited to be Inge's successor, conceiving his appointment as the opening move of a new initiative to institute reforms in the lordship of Ireland.

That Alen's elevation to the episcopate heralded a significant initiative in Ireland on Wolsey's part is evident from the terms of his appointment. Not only was he provided to the richest and, from an English perspective, most strategically important Irish archdiocese, but he was also designated, by personal decree, as Wolsey's vicelegate in Ireland. The clear implication of this was that the cardinal intended Alen to pursue the extension of his legateship in Ireland, with the same centralizing vigour that he had himself practised in England. In a similar vein, he also wished Alen to play a leading role in the sphere of secular politics. By nominating him as lord chancellor of Ireland and, from September 1529, a member of the three man 'secret council' appointed to exercise the executive powers of the chief governor in the lordship, the cardinal envisaged that his trusted servant would act as his agent on the Irish council as he experimented with various administrative alternatives to the overmighty rule of the earls of Kildare. However, these ambitious plans never came to fruition. Only six months after Alen arrived in Ireland, Wolsey fell from power because he failed to deliver a speedy and favourable resolution to the king's divorce proceedings against Katherine of Aragon. The consequences for Alen were clear and stark. Not only did his vice-legateship fall into abeyance, but the entire basis upon which he hoped to exercise political influence in Ireland—his relationship with the cardinal—was completely destroyed.

Yet Alen remained undaunted. Within his own archdiocese and province he proceeded with an energetic programme of reform, which had commenced before Wolsey's disgrace, and whose essence is neatly summed up in a phrase he coined himself 'winning bread and increasing honour' (Murray, 'Archbishop Alen', 4). 'Winning bread' meant realizing all potential revenues from his archbishopric, and was to be achieved through the augmentation or recovery of the see's ancient rents, and the exploitation of ancient feudal privileges. 'Increasing honour' meant the maximization of his jurisdictional competence, and was to be achieved by eliminating or subjugating competing ecclesiastical jurisdictions, and by extending his ecclesiastical patronage. The programme was clearly a mirroring in miniature of Wolsey's approach, and had been originally conceived as a means of making the cardinal's legateship a reality in Ireland. In the wake of his master's fall, however, Alen had to construct an alternative justification for it. This he did by formulating a newly articulated, ideological vision of his spiritual patrimony. Adapting the traditional primatial style of the see of Dublin, and emphasizing its traditional English politico-cultural character—he described the archdiocese of Dublin as the 'handmaid' of the English church—he cast himself as the 'primate of his [the king's] church in Ireland', and proceeded to carry out his reform programme in Henry's name.

But the king was unappreciative of Alen's efforts. This was most clearly seen in spring 1531, when he fined the archbishop the massive sum of £1466 13s. 4d. (about four times the annual income of his see), for offences against the statutes of *praemunire* and provisors, namely, his involvement in the exercise of Wolsey's legatine jurisdiction. The fine threw Alen's plans for reviving the financial fortunes of his archdiocese into disarray. All his efforts at 'winning bread' would now have to be redoubled just to meet the schedule of payments on his fine. Worse, this involved him in the dangerous business of attempting to recover see property and other rights from the powerful Geraldine interest, including coming into conflict with Gerald Fitzgerald, ninth earl of Kildare. As a result, his relations with the Fitzgeralds—which were already sour because of his earlier efforts under Wolsey to find an alternative to the Kildare system of governing the lordship—reached a particularly low point. This conflict was evinced by the decision, on the earl's reappointment as lord deputy in 1532, to replace Alen as lord chancellor of Ireland but did not end there. The rise of Cromwell at this time—Alen's former colleague in Wolsey's household—raised the very real possibility that the archbishop would receive a full political rehabilitation, and join the former's burgeoning movement of political and religious reform, which encompassed plans to curb the Fitzgeralds' traditional hegemony in the lordship. Thus, when the Fitzgeralds rose in revolt against Cromwell's innovations in summer 1534, the archbishop knew that he was a marked man. On 26 July he boarded a barque at Dublin and attempted to flee Ireland, but the ship ran aground on the sands near Clontarf, co. Dublin. The following morning Alen, his chaplains, and his servants were apprehended by Kildare's son, Thomas Fitzgerald, Baron Offaly, and forty of his men at the home of Master Howth in Artane. There, by Offaly's 'commandment', they were 'cruelly and shamefully murdered' (*State Papers, Henry VIII*, 2.201). The archbishop's death was as ignominious as it was shocking. Despite his former association with the pomp and glory of the great cardinal, and his relationship with the new star of English politics, Cromwell, Alen died in a foreign land

in which few mourned his passing. Nothing would signify this ignominious ending more than the fact that he was buried in a pauper's grave. JAMES MURRAY

Sources J. Murray, 'Archbishop Alen, Tudor reform and the Kildare rebellion', *Proceedings of the Royal Irish Academy*, 89C (1989), 1–16 • C. McNeill, ed., *Calendar of Archbishop Alen's register, c.1172–1534* (1950) • Emden, *Oxf.*, 1.20–21 • A. F. Pollard, *Wolsey*, 1st edn (1929); 3rd edn (1965) • P. Gwyn, *The king's cardinal: the rise and fall of Thomas Wolsey* (1990) • *LP Henry VIII*, vols. 1–2 • J. Guy, *The cardinal's court: the impact of Thomas Wolsey in star chamber* (1977) • D. Chambers, *Cardinal Bainbridge in the court of Rome* (1965) • S. Fish, *A supplication for the beggars* (1529); facs. edn (1973) • W. Roy and J. Barlow, 'Rede me and be nott wrote', *English reprints*, ed. E. Arber (1871) • J. Murray, 'The Tudor diocese of Dublin: episcopal government, ecclesiastical politics and the enforcement of the reformation, c.1534–1590', PhD diss., TCD, 1997 • *State papers published under … Henry VIII*, 11 vols. (1830–52)

Archives PRO, state papers, Henry VIII, SP 1 • PRO, state papers Ireland, Henry VIII, SP 60 • Representative Church Body Library, Dublin, Dublin diocesan registry CD6, register and roll of churches, MSS 3, 4, 9

Wealth at death insubstantial: PRO, SP 60/2, no. 25

Alesius [*formerly* Allane or Alan], **Alexander** (1500–1565), Lutheran theologian and reformer, was born at Edinburgh on 23 April 1500. He is sometimes referred to as Ales, Aless, or Alesse, but the matriculation roll of St Andrews University records his native family name as Allane or Alan. After his adventurous escape from Scotland he acquired a pseudonym in humanist fashion, Alesius—adopted about 1531—being a Latinized Greek construction meaning exile or refugee.

Early career: Scotland, 1500–1530 Of the parents and childhood of Alesius little is known except that he came from an important urban family and that his mother was Christina Bigholm. At the age of twelve he was sent to the University of St Andrews and enrolled as one of the first students of St Leonard's College. The foundation of this college was the joint venture of Alexander Stewart, archbishop of St Andrews, and John Hepburn, prior of the large Augustinian house there. While the former intended it as a means of introducing humanist studies into the university, the prior hoped to renew the spiritual and intellectual life of his order through a steady supply of well-educated novices. Life in the college was therefore very strict, both in terms of monastic discipline and educational demands. After three years Alesius graduated BA and probably joined the canons regular as a novice. His MA is not recorded, but may be assumed as he changed to the theological faculty and became himself a tutor at St Leonard's. Alesius's theological training was essentially conservative. The curriculum was heavily influenced by the close links that existed with the University of Paris, not least through the person of John Mair. Through Mair and his pupils at the Sorbonne, scholasticism experienced a late flowering; theologically he was a nominalist and orthodox, but constitutionally he was a conciliarist and an advocate of church reform, which he saw constantly thwarted by the papacy. Many years later Alesius spoke respectfully of his teacher as one to whom he owed his profound knowledge of scholastic theology, canon law, and conciliarist theories.

During the early 1520s St Andrews University gradually became exposed to the ideas of the Wittenberg reformers. Busy trading links between the Scottish North Sea ports and the continent facilitated the introduction of evangelical books, provoking acts of parliament in 1525 and 1527 directed against the importation or distribution of Lutheran books. At St Andrews this challenge became acute through the arrival in 1523 of the young humanist Patrick Hamilton. In 1527, suspected of heresy, Hamilton left the country for the new Lutheran University of Marburg, where he defended a series of academic theses which expounded Luther's theology on law and gospel, and which came to be known as 'Patrick's places'. Yet within a few months he was back in Scotland preaching in his home parish of Linlithgow. In the meantime Alesius had distinguished himself in a public debate, in which he refuted Luther's theology by making use of John Fisher's *Assertionis Lutheranae confutatio*. When Hamilton was summoned by the archbishop of St Andrews early in 1528 to answer charges of heresy, Alesius was one of the university's theologians chosen to bring about a recantation. Hamilton, however, was able to stand his ground, impressing both sympathizers and many opponents with his arguments and courageous death at the stake on 28 February 1528. The execution caused a storm of indignation in many parts of Scotland and had a particularly profound impact on St Leonard's College and among the Augustinian canons, many of whom refused to accept Hamilton's condemnation and now discussed his beliefs with even greater urgency.

In the events following Hamilton's death Alesius again played a prominent part. He is also by far the most detailed source of information for this important, but sparsely documented, chapter in the history of pre-Reformation Scotland, giving vivid accounts of the Hamilton incident and its aftermath in *Alexandri Alesii Scotti responsio ad Cochlei calumnias* (1534) and *Primus liber psalmorum* (1554). In March 1529, having been commissioned to deliver an oration before the provincial council, Alesius reprehended moral failings among the clergy, calling on the prelates to exercise their pastoral duties and to set an example of good conduct. He thereby incurred the particular wrath of his new prior, Patrick Hepburn, a man known for his violent temper and adulterous affairs, who saw the canon's address as an attack on himself. There followed a period of some eighteen months during which Alesius suffered violent persecution and incarceration at the hands of his prior. Eventually, fearing for his life, he was persuaded to flee the country. He narrowly escaped to Dundee where he boarded a merchant vessel bound for the continent, probably Flanders or France, but a gale drove the ship across the North Sea to Malmö in Scandinavia. While repairs were being carried out Alesius was able to witness at first hand the effects of the Reformation, which the self-confident magistrates of this wealthy trading port had introduced in 1528, and met such leading Danish reformers as Palladius, Wormordsen, and Chrysostomos. He finally resumed his journey to France, from where he travelled via Brussels and Cologne to Wittenberg. He never returned to Scotland, though he did contribute to Sebastian Münster's *Cosmographia universalis* (1550), an account of Edinburgh, written from memory, which constitutes the earliest known description of the city.

Wittenberg, c.1532–1535 Alesius arrived at Wittenberg in late 1531 or early 1532, and on 29 October 1532 was enrolled in the university. He seems to have struck up an immediate friendship with Philipp Melanchthon and immersed himself in the theology and academic methods of the German reformers. Subsequent events show that he studied Melanchthon's rhetorics, dialectics, and *Loci communes* of the early 1530s, Luther's interpretations of the Psalms, and Hebrew under Aurogallus. He was evidently held in high esteem at the university, for within twelve months he became a lecturer in the faculty of arts. He also contributed to academic disputations on several occasions and was elected dean of the arts faculty for the summer term of 1534.

During his Wittenberg years Alesius became involved in a literary feud with the Catholic polemicist Johannes Cochlaeus, which at once made him known throughout Germany and beyond. In March or April 1533 he published an open letter to James V, in which he appealed to his sovereign to annul a recent decree by the Scottish bishops prohibiting the possession and distribution of the New Testament in the vernacular (*Alexandri Alesii epistola contra decretum quoddam episcoporum in Scotia*). Although it is not certain to which decree he referred, there is evidence to show that William Tyndale's translations of the New Testament were secretly shipped to Scotland and that individuals were prosecuted for its possession. The publication of this elegantly written work may have been Melanchthon's idea, who at this time strove to further reform movements in other countries by appealing to their rulers. In June Cochlaeus reacted likewise with an open letter to the Scottish monarch, claiming that Alesius was translating Luther's New Testament and other works into Scots with the intention of shipping them to Scotland, and warning that free access to the scriptures in the vernacular would not only lead the people into error, but incite political and social unrest.

These claims provoked a second publication by Alesius in the summer of 1534: *Alexandri Alesii Scotti responsio ad Cochlei calumnias*, a masterpiece of Reformation apologetic. Avoiding all reference to specific theological tenets of the German reformers, it presented their endeavours as an attempt to lead the people back to the scriptures and to the original teaching of the early church. In August Cochlaeus once more retorted with *Pro Scotiae regno apologia Johannis Cochlei*, which is remarkable above all for its suggestion that Melanchthon, not Alesius, was the author of the two Wittenberg publications. Cochlaeus may have been right in so far as Melanchthon was probably responsible for the final editing of these works. His warnings may also have resulted in the act of parliament of 1535 which further tightened import controls for all people and goods arriving in Scotland.

England, 1535–1539 The year 1535 offered the prospect of an alliance between the German Lutherans and England. The cessation of hostilities between France and Spain had increased the likelihood of a Catholic alliance and of a general council proceeding against Henry VIII and his efforts to establish an independent church in England. The king therefore looked for support from the protestant Schmalkaldic League, though he may also have been genuine in his desire to receive advice, especially from Melanchthon, in finding a theological settlement for the church of which he was now head. The Germans, however, doubted Henry's motives, and Melanchthon was neither willing nor permitted to travel to England. Instead, Alesius was dispatched in August 1535 with copies of Melanchthon's latest edition of the *Loci communes* for the king and for Archbishop Cranmer. He seems to have made a favourable impression on the archbishop and on Thomas Cromwell, who invited him to put his abilities and experience to good use for the reform of the church in England. Having returned to Wittenberg in October with Henry's reply and a gift of 300 crowns for Melanchthon, Alesius once more set out to England in late December, whereupon Cromwell secured him a lectureship as 'king's scholar' at Cambridge University. This fitted in well with Cromwell's measures for university reform as outlined in the royal injunctions of October 1535, ordering the suspension of all teaching of scholastic theology in favour of lectures 'upon the scriptures of the Old and New Testaments according to the true sense thereof' (Leader, 332).

Residing at Queens' College, Cambridge, Alesius began to lecture on the Psalms; he may well have been the first scholar at the university to lecture on the Old Testament from the Hebrew text. A fair copy of this lecture, dedicated to Henry VIII, survives in Hatfield House (Cecil papers, 268, no. 3); it is evidence of the speed and thoroughness with which he had absorbed the principles of Lutheran theology and hermeneutics. Resistance to the new theology was, however, still considerable even at Cambridge. By late spring 1536 Alesius was put under such pressure from an obscurantist opponent that he had reason to fear for his life. Lack of support from the university, and the fact that the stipend promised by Cromwell was not paid, eventually forced him to leave Cambridge. Cromwell's failure to provide him with the necessary support may have been connected to the fall of Anne Boleyn and its consequences for the reform movement in England. In a long letter written to Queen Elizabeth twenty-three years later (PRO, SP 70/7, 1–11), Alesius provides fascinating glimpses of the events and rumours surrounding her mother's tragic end and describes the alarm it caused among English reformers.

In London, now training and practising as a physician under the eminent Dr Nicholas (Encolius?), Alesius remained in close contact with reformers such as Hugh Latimer and John Bale, and enjoyed above all the trust and friendship of Thomas Cranmer. Like the archbishop he opposed the wholesale secularization of the monasteries, proposing instead that they should in part be turned into schools and training colleges for the clergy. Cromwell,

too, continued to consult the Scot as an adviser to the crown or for his own political purposes, drawing on his theological expertise and firsthand experience of the Reformation in Germany. A well-known episode occurred in the summer of 1537, when Cromwell invited Alesius to a meeting of the bishops to participate in a debate on the sacraments. Having been introduced as the king's scholar, he delivered his opinion insisting that this matter, as all theological principles, ought to be decided by reference to scripture alone and that on these grounds there could be only two sacraments. This provoked an angry protest from John Stokesley, bishop of London, who made an appeal to tradition. The incident is interesting as it sheds light on the divisions among the English bishops at the time and on the way in which Cromwell, as vicar-general, attempted to direct their decisions in favour of reform. Alesius later published his debate with Stokesley in *De authoritate verbi Dei* (1542; partial translation as *Of the Auctorite of the Word of God*, undated), one of the clearest and most comprehensive statements of the Reformation on the subject of scriptural authority. Other evidence of Alesius's role as a theological adviser is found in an instruction of 7 April 1538 to the king's ambassadors Simon Heynes and Edmund Bonner, sent to Spain to remonstrate before the emperor against the general council, then summoned to Vicenza, making use of the king's writings against the council and of the books of Alesius and Henry Cole. It is possible, but by no means certain, that Alesius's tract was the one printed by Berthelet in 1538 under the title *A Treatise Concernynge Generall Councilles, the Byshoppes of Rome and the Clergy.*

Alesius's departure from England was as abrupt as it was unexpected. In June 1539, on the eve of the passing of the Act of Six Articles, Cranmer summoned his Scottish friend to warn of the dangers which the act posed for reformers like him since it demanded among other things the keeping of vows of celibacy and, as a token of his friendship, the archbishop gave him a ring, formerly Cardinal Wolsey's, which Cranmer had himself received from the king. Alesius, who by now had married Katherine Mayne, a fugitive from Edinburgh, was urged to leave the country without delay. He immediately sold his belongings and in disguise boarded a German vessel.

Frankfurt an der Oder, 1540–1542 By 9 July 1539 Alesius was back in Wittenberg. In the autumn of that year Joachim II, elector of Brandenburg, requested Melanchthon's assistance in implementing the Reformation in his territory. Alesius was recommended for a theological professorship at Frankfurt an der Oder, where he began lecturing in the summer term of 1540. Through his academic disputations and lectures on Romans and the Psalms he made an essential contribution to the reorganization of the university's curriculum. In early November he was dispatched with Konrad Keller and Johannes Lüdecke to the Colloquy of Worms. Their position there was difficult, since Joachim II had not joined the Schmalkaldic League, choosing instead to support the emperor's policy of conciliation between Roman Catholics and protestants. His delegates were therefore instructed to negotiate on the Catholic side.

Unwilling to compromise their evangelical consciences, Alesius and his co-delegates upheld the cause of the Reformation, thus provoking the anger of the imperial agent Antoine Perrenot de Granvelle and the Catholic delegates. A similarly difficult situation existed for Alesius at the Diet of Regensburg which he attended during the spring of 1541. Not much is known of his activity there, but it is recorded that he debated with Martin Bucer against Stephen Gardiner on celibacy and apparently prevented the Strasbourg reformer from making significant concessions. On 2 June, when the negotiations had practically broken down, Joachim II sent an official delegation including Alesius to Wittenberg to elicit a more conciliatory line from Luther and the elector of Saxony. Again, Alesius foiled his ruler's plans; if anything he contributed to a hardening of Wittenberg's attitude by warning of Joachim's lack of commitment to their cause. By now Alesius felt distinctly uneasy in Brandenburg. Matters came to a head in the summer of 1542: Christoph von der Strassen, professor of law and one of Joachim's chief advisers, declared in a lecture that the use of prostitution was not a legal crime that called for civil punishment. Alesius made a formal complaint to the senate and announced a public disputation to debate the issue. The senate, however, sided with von der Strassen, forbade the proposed disputation, and even imposed a publishing ban on Alesius's writings. Unable to work under such circumstances, Alesius left Frankfurt and turned to Leipzig in Saxony in the hope of new employment.

Leipzig, 1542–1565: professor of theology In Leipzig Alesius finally found favourable conditions for a lasting and productive career, enjoying the trust of both his rulers, Duke Moritz and Duke August, and the esteem of leading men in the university and in government. In 1544, on the resignation of Jakob Schenk, he was appointed professor of theology alongside Johannes Pfeffinger, Bernhard Ziegler, and Wolfgang Schirrmeister, thus completing the new team of evangelical theologians at the university. Pfeffinger, who held the first theological chair in the faculty and was superintendent of Leipzig, has often been regarded as the leading theologian of the university. When considering literary output or participation at religious and political negotiations, however, Alesius clearly emerges as its most capable and productive theologian, contributing enormously to the growing reputation of the university. Camerarius called him 'very dear to Melanchthon, extremely learned in theological matters, superbly skilled in crafting fitting disputations, a man distinguished by his dignity and academic rigour' (Camerarius, 134). Alesius produced biblical commentaries and disputations on Romans (1540–53), 1 and 2 Timothy (1550, 1551), Titus (1552), the gospel according to St John (1553), and a monumental commentary on the first book of Psalms (1554), all of which were greatly esteemed and enjoyed wide circulation. He reacted to most of the theological challenges of his time with a large number of disputations for which he had a particular skill. Several times he acted as dean of the faculty (1546–7, 1551, and 1554), and he was twice elected rector of the university (1555 and 1561).

As for other reformers at the time, the Schmalkaldic War (1546–7) and the interim of Augsburg (1548) were momentous events for Alesius. During the siege of Leipzig in early 1547 his house and library were completely destroyed. In the summer of 1548 the Diet of Augsburg imposed the interim on all protestant territories of the empire, ordering the reintroduction of most Roman Catholic rites and doctrines until final settlement at the resumed Council of Trent. The debate about the implementation of the interim was particularly acrimonious in Saxony, because Duke Moritz, though a protestant himself, had helped to defeat the Schmalkaldic League as the emperor's ally in order to obtain the electoral title of Saxony. In reality he had no intention of yielding to the demands of the Augsburg decree and was playing for time, but this was not apparent for about two years. His attempt to water down the interim by guaranteeing the integrity of Lutheran doctrine in the Saxon church, proposing only to introduce certain Roman rites as non-essential ceremonies (even these were never imposed), was viewed by many with suspicion or exasperation. While Pfeffinger and Ziegler were prepared to accept the Leipzig version of the interim, Alesius openly attacked it in at least two disputations. He took particular exception to the misuse of the distinction between essentials and non-essentials which Melanchthon had unwillingly proposed to Duke Moritz in order to legitimize his policy of prevarication. His most outspoken condemnation occurred in 1550 during his lectures on 1 Timothy, notes from which were sent by students to Matthias Flacius at Magdeburg, who published them as part of his campaign against the compromisers at Leipzig and Wittenberg. The long friendship between Alesius and Melanchthon probably reached a low point during this period.

Leipzig, 1542–1565: religious controversialist While in Germany the Reformation was in crisis, in England it was making rapid progress under Edward VI. Reformers such as Alesius, Melanchthon, and Bucer looked to Archbishop Cranmer as an additional voice of weight in the chorus of evangelical churches calling for a free general council. Melanchthon suggested that Cranmer should supervise the compilation and publication of a summary of essential doctrine to be agreed by all reformers. In an attempt to publicize Cranmer's doctrinal and liturgical projects Alesius published in the spring of 1548 a Latin translation of the *Order of Communion* (*Ordo distributionis sacramenti altaris*), and in late spring 1551 translated the first prayer book (*Ordinatio ecclesiae seu, Ministerii ecclesiastici in florentissimo regno Angliae*). By October 1552 he had also translated the first Book of Homilies, to be printed by Oporin at Basel, though publication does not seem to have followed. These translations were intended for the use of delegates at the hoped-for free general council. For Alesius the prayer book represented a model of territorial reformation, in which a secular ruler exercised his right and duty to restore the church within his realm according to the precepts of God's word. Although it in many ways fell short of his expectations, containing several 'Romish customs'—some of these, such as chrism in baptism and extreme unction, were tacitly omitted in the translation—the conservative character of the first prayer book is defended as an appropriate first step in introducing church reform.

In addition to the debate about the interim, Alesius was drawn into several other doctrinal controversies arising after Luther's death about the correct interpretation of his theology. Between 1552 and 1554 he aimed several disputations at Osiander's notion of a substantial rather than imputed righteousness. At Melanchthon's request he joined a delegation of theologians sent to Nuremberg in September 1555 to settle this issue. There is little evidence that he participated in the synergistic controversy which Pfeffinger unleashed in 1555 with his theses on free will, but concerning the necessity of good works there was a change or readjustment of position: in 1554 he had firmly rejected George Major's statement that good works were necessary for salvation, whereas he reconsidered his position in *De necessitate bonorum operum* (1560), agreeing that good works, though in no way meritorious, were necessary in so far as faith would inevitably lead to good works. It was perhaps over the doctrine of the eucharist that he was most critical of Luther. The correspondence of Albrecht Hardenberg and Hermann Hamelmann during the mid-1550s reveals that some reformed theologians regarded Alesius and Camerarius, like Melanchthon, as allies on the issue of real presence, even though none of these went as far as accepting Calvin's, and certainly rejected Zwingli's, eucharistic theology. In April 1563 Alesius intended to publish a disputation on the real presence, a reply to Ruard Tapper's defence of the Louvain articles of 1544. The theology presented there is essentially identical with that of the formula of concord which Melanchthon composed in November 1559 for Friedrich III, elector of the Palatinate. Alesius also claims to have rejected as early as 1531 Luther's doctrine of the ubiquity of the two natures of Christ as an unheard-of innovation, and reiterates the story, circulated first by Hardenberg, of Luther's confession to Melanchthon shortly before his death that he had gone too far in the controversy about the real presence. It was probably for this reason that Pfeffinger suppressed the publication of the tract, but a student smuggled a copy of the manuscript to Heidelberg where it was published soon after Alesius's death.

Outside the protestant camp Alesius participated in the continuing debate with Roman Catholic theologians. His most important writings here are *Ad duos et triginta articulos … aeditos a theologis Lovaniensibus brevis & moderata responsio* (1545), his refutation of an important pre-Tridentine statement of Catholic doctrine which appeared in 1544; *Ad libellum Ludovici Nogarolae … de traditionibus apostolicis & earum necessitate responsio* (1556/1567), directed against the writing of a lay theologian at the Council of Trent; and a series of disputations published between 1559 and 1564 in which he argued against Ruard Tapper's monumental defence of the Louvain articles. Through his excellent knowledge of the church fathers, canon law, and the scholastics, and by applying the methods of historical and literary criticism, Alesius attempted to show the unreliability and contradictory nature of much of the church's tradition, especially of its oral traditions and customs. In December 1551 he was chosen as a delegate to the Council of Trent, but was unable to attend owing to illness. Alesius also took issue with contemporary anti-Trinitarians, publishing four disputations against Michael Servetus (1554–5) and a refutation of Valentin Gentilis (1564). He died on 17 March 1565, probably at Leipzig, and was survived by his wife, Katherine, his daughters Christina and Anna, and his two sons Caspar and Alexander; a previous son, Caspar, had died in childhood.

Alesius is one of the more colourful characters of the Reformation. His gregarious nature and eagerness to be involved in the important issues of his age made him a valuable firsthand witness of many contemporary events. Through his international career he became a reformer of truly metropolitan stature, always maintaining his vision of the universal church and rising above the personal polemic or petty confessionalism that characterized many of his contemporaries. He was not an original thinker, but an effective and influential propagator of the Wittenberg school of exegesis and theology, which he represented at several universities, in religious negotiations, and through his many writings.

GOTTHELF WIEDERMANN

Sources G. Wiedermann, 'Der Reformator Alexander Alesius als Ausleger der Psalmen', PhD diss., Erlangen University, 1988 · G. Wiedermann, 'Alexander Alesius' lectures on the Psalms at Cambridge, 1536', *Journal of Ecclesiastical History*, 37 (1986), 15–41 · G. Wiedermann, 'Martin Luther versus John Fisher: some ideas concerning the debate on Lutheran theology at the University of St Andrews, 1525–30', *Records of the Scottish Church History Society*, 22 (1984–6), 13–34 · J. T. McNeill, 'Alexander Alesius, Scottish Lutheran (1500–1565)', *Archiv für Reformationsgeschichte*, 55 (1964), 161–91 · A. F. S. Pearson, 'Alesius and the English Reformation', *Records of the Scottish Church History Society*, 10 (1948–50), 57–87 · A. F. Mitchell, *The Scottish Reformation*, ed. D. H. Fleming (1900) · O. Clemen, 'Melanchthon und Alexander Alesius', *Archiv für Reformationsgeschichte*, Ergänzungsband, 5 (1929), 17–31 · G. Kawerau, 'Berichte vom Wormser Religionsgespräch 1540', *Archiv für Reformationsgeschichte*, 8 (1911), 403–8 · G. Kawerau, 'Alexander Alesius' Fortgang von der Frankfurter Universität', *Jahrbuch für Brandenburgische Kirchengeschichte*, 14 (1916), 89–100 · N. Müller, 'Zur Geschichte des Reichstags zu Regensburg 1541', *Jahrbuch für Brandenburgische Kirchengeschichte*, 4 (1907), 175–248 · G. Wartenberg, 'Zum Kommentar des Alexander Alesius zum Johannesevangelium', *Théorie et pratique de l'exégèse*, ed. I. Backus and F. Higman (Geneva, 1990), 329–42 · H. Tollin, 'Alex. Alesii Widerlegung von Servet's Restitutio Christianismi', *Jahrbücher für Protestantische Theologie*, 3 (1877), 631–52 · J. Camerarius, 'De vita Philippi Melanchthonis Joachimi Camerarii narratio', *Vitae quatuor reformatorum*, ed. A. F. Neander (Berlin, 1841), 1–164 · H.-G. Roloff, ed., *Die deutsche Literatur: biographisches und bibliographisches Lexikon*, 2/1 (Bern, [1979]), 140–62 [incl. bibliography of Alesius's works] · edn of Alesius's MSS and correspondence, [forthcoming] · PRO, state papers, secretaries of state, state papers foreign, Elizabeth I, SP 70/7, 1–11 · Hatfield House, Hertfordshire, Cecil papers 268, no. 3 · J. J. Vogel, *Leipzigisches Geschicht-Buch oder Annales* (1714) · T. Thomson, ed., *A diurnal of remarkable occurrents that have passed within the country of Scotland*, Bannatyne Club, 43 (1833) · 'Edinburgi regiae Scotorum urbis descriptio, per Alexandrum Alesium Scotum', *The Bannatyne miscellany*, ed. W. Scott and D. Laing, 1/2, Bannatyne Club, 19 (1827) · D. R. Leader, *A history of the University of Cambridge*, 1: *The university to 1546*, ed. C. N. L. Brooke and others (1988) · J. M. Anderson, ed., *Early records of the University of St Andrews*, Scottish History

Society, 3rd ser., 8 (1926), 320 • university records, Frankfurt an der Oder, 1540–42 • matriculation book, 1555, Leipzig University • matriculation roll, 1512, U. St Andr.

Archives Österreichische Nationalbibliothek, Vienna, MSS • Archives Municipales, Strasbourg, MSS • Bayersiche Staatsbibliothek, Munich, MSS • BL, MSS • Forschungs- und Landesbibliothek, Gotha, MSS • Hatfield House, Hertfordshire, MS • Herzog-August-Bibliothek, Wolfenbüttel, MSS • PRO, MSS • Sächsisches Hauptstaatsarchiv, Dresden, MSS • Staats- und Universitätsbibliothek, Göttingen, MSS • Staatsarchiv Preussischer Kulturbesitz, Berlin, MSS • Thüringisches Staatsarchiv, Weimar, MSS

Likenesses relief on tombstone, Mölkau church, near Leipzig

Alex, (Edward) Ephraim (1800–1882), founder of the Jewish Board of Guardians, was born on 12 December 1800 in St Katherine in the City of London. He was the eldest surviving son of Solomon Alex, dentist, of 11 Finsbury Place, Finsbury, and 21 Jewry Street, Aldgate, who was born abroad; his mother's name was probably Rachel. On 15 March 1840 Alex married Catherine, widow of Barron Jones and the daughter of Aaron Jones. They had no children and Catherine died on 16 June 1858. Alex practised as a dental surgeon at Bridge Street, Blackfriars, from 1829, and then at 35 Lower Brook Street, Westminster.

At the beginning of the nineteenth century the charitable system for poor Jews of German and Polish descent operated under a system which had been established in 1753 to meet the needs of a community of 8000, but by 1858 this had grown to 40,000. Alex was overseer of the Great Synagogue, London, and it was due to his efforts that the Jewish Board of Guardians was founded. On 12 January 1858 the committee of the Great Synagogue, largely at Alex's insistence, resolved that a board of guardians be appointed to relieve the strange and foreign poor. Delegates from the three main German congregations agreed on 15 July 1858 to recommend to their synagogues the establishment of a board of guardians. In early 1859 Alex sent out for private circulation an eight-page pamphlet on the subject, and on 22 February 1859 called the attention of his vestry to the state of the foreign poor. At the preliminary meeting of the board of guardians, on 25 February 1859, Alex was requested to act as temporary chairman. Finally, on 16 March 1859, the first meeting of the board was held at the Great Synagogue chambers and Alex was unanimously elected president for twelve months. He remained president for ten years, and retired only because of failing health. In April 1866, at a special meeting of the board at which the lord mayor of London and the chief rabbi were present, a public address of thanks was given to him for his services, and in June 1869 the board resolved that he be elected a life member and his name be recorded in all proceedings as founder and first president. His portrait, which had been painted by Professor Hart, was purchased by voluntary subscribers and hung in the offices of the board of guardians. In May 1869 Alex was elected a member of the Society of Arts.

After suffering from cancer of the bladder for nine months, but still an active member of the board, Alex died on 13 November 1882 at his home, 5 Chichester Street, Harrow Road. On his death a resolution of sympathy was passed by the Jewish Board of Guardians to his sisters. In a letter to the *Jewish Chronicle* dated 17 November 1882, Lionel Cohen, president of the Jewish Board of Guardians, described the gentleness of disposition and suavity of manner, which, combined with firmness of purpose, enabled Alex to surmount difficulties. Laurie Magnus's *The Jewish Welfare Board and the Men who Made it, 1859–1909* (1909) mentioned Alex's qualities of address, tact, and enthusiasm, which were invaluable to the long negotiations out of which this board had sprung. V. D. Lipman's *A Century of Social Service, 1859–1959: the Jewish Board of Guardians* (1959) noted Alex's tactical skill in seizing an opportunity, which was responsible for the board's foundation.

Alex's funeral took place at Willesden Jewish cemetery on 17 November 1882. His memorial stone, erected by his colleagues as a tribute of respect and esteem, was consecrated on Sunday 11 March 1883 by his friend the Revd A. L. Green, who died suddenly the same day. In 1963 the Jewish Board of Guardians became the Jewish Welfare Board, and in 1990 merged with the Jewish Blind Society to become Jewish Care, Anglo-Jewry's largest social services organization. DOREEN BERGER

Sources Jewish Board of Guardians, Jewish Board of Guardians Annual Reports (1879–88), 21–30 • Jewish Board of Guardians, First half yearly report 1st July to 31 December (1859) • L. Magnus, *The Jewish Welfare Board and the men who made it, 1859–1909: an illustrated record* (1909) • V. D. Lipman, *A century of social service, 1859–1959: the Jewish Board of Guardians* (1959) • *Reprint of the Book of Remembrance, 1859–1929*, Jewish Board of Guardians [1931] • editorial, *Jewish Chronicle* (25 June 1869) • 'Presentation to Ephraim Alex', *Jewish Chronicle* (4 May 1866) • *Jewish Chronicle* (17 Nov 1882) [letter from Lionel L. Cohen, president, Jewish Board of Guardians] • *Jewish World* (17 Nov 1882) • 'Meeting of Board of Guardians', *Jewish Chronicle* (22 Dec 1882) • *Jewish Year Book* (1996), 92–5 [Valentine Mitchell] • census returns, 1841, 1871, 1881 • marriage records, 15 March 1840, Great Synagogue, Duke's Place, London • d. cert.

Archives U. Southampton L., records of the Jewish Board of Guardians

Likenesses J. Faed, portrait • Hart, oils, Jewish Museum, London • portrait, repro. in Magnus, *Jewish Welfare Board and the men who made it*

Wealth at death £343: probate, 27 Nov 1882, *CGPLA Eng. & Wales*

Alexander [called Alexander the Magnificent] (d. 1148), bishop of Lincoln, came from the ecclesiastical dynasty established by his kinsman Roger, bishop of *Salisbury (d. 1139).

Family background and political involvement Roger originated from the Norman diocese of Avranches and both Alexander and *Nigel, later royal treasurer and bishop of Ely (d. 1169), are described as nephews (*nepotes*) of Bishop Roger; it has been conjectured that they were indeed nephews rather than illegitimate sons of the bishop, as has also been suggested. This was certainly the case with Alexander, who mentions his mother and father, as well as his uncle Roger, in the foundation charter for Haverholme Priory, Lincolnshire. Alexander's mother's name was Ada and his father was possibly Humphrey, the brother of Bishop Roger. It is probable that Alexander and Nigel were brothers, but definite proof is not forthcoming; certainly another brother of Bishop Alexander, David, became archdeacon of Buckingham in the Lincoln diocese, and a nephew of Alexander called William also held an archdeaconry, that of Northampton, in his uncle's gift. Another relative, Adelelm or Adelm, nephew or possibly son of Bishop Roger, who acted as royal treasurer in the early years of Stephen's reign, held the archdeaconry of Dorset in the Salisbury diocese, and then was appointed to the deanery of Lincoln Cathedral in the time of Bishop Alexander.

The date of Alexander's birth is not known but he was educated, along with Nigel, in the schools of Laon, and by 1121 he was an archdeacon in his uncle's church of Salisbury. While he was an archdeacon he is said to have composed an Anglo-Norman glossary of Old English legal terms. On 10 January 1123 Bishop Robert Bloet of Lincoln suffered an apoplectic fit while riding with Henry I and Bishop Roger of Salisbury in Woodstock deer park, and died in the royal presence. At Eastertide of that year, while the court was at Winchester, the king gave the vacant bishopric to Alexander 'out of love for the bishop [of Salisbury]' (ASC, s.a. 1123), and it is clear that Bishop Roger's important place in the royal government affected the choice of a new bishop. Alexander was consecrated at Canterbury on 22 July 1123. For the next sixteen years Bishop Roger and his kinsmen continued to maintain their pre-eminence in the administration first of Henry I and then of his successor Stephen, but as far as Alexander is concerned, although he frequently attested royal charters, he is not known to have held actual office in the king's government at this period (Bishop Roger's son, also Roger, was chancellor, and his nephew Adelelm was treasurer). Nevertheless he did not escape the dramatic downfall of Bishop Roger and his kin in 1139. On vague accusations by lay magnates, that Roger and his episcopal nephews were plotting treason, King Stephen summoned the three bishops to a council at Oxford in June. When they had arrived there, a quarrel, possibly contrived, over accommodation between them and the men of Count Alan of Brittany (an old enemy of Bishop Alexander, it is recorded) led to a riot, and was the pretext for the arrest and imprisonment of bishops Roger and Alexander and Roger the chancellor. Nigel of Ely and Adelelm the treasurer escaped to Bishop Roger's castle at Devizes.

The king ordered the bishops to hand over their castles; they hesitated and Stephen marched off to besiege Devizes, leaving Alexander, according to one account, imprisoned at Oxford. In due course the castle was surrendered, and the other Salisbury episcopal castles were invested. The king then moved northwards with Alexander to compel the surrender of the episcopal castles of Newark-on-Trent and Sleaford (and later Banbury in Oxfordshire)—quickly effected, chronicles relate, following royal threats to starve Bishop Alexander in the event of resistance. Although he was one of the bishops criticized by the author of the *Gesta Stephani* for their warlike demeanour during Stephen's reign, none the less, after the downfall of Bishop Roger's curialist dynasty, Alexander seems to have devoted most of his attention to his diocese for the remainder of his episcopate. In the contest

between Stephen and Matilda, he followed the lead of Henry de Blois, bishop of Winchester and legate (d. 1171), in his changing allegiances. He attested few of Stephen's charters, although understandably he was present in Lincoln in 1141 before Stephen's defeat and capture, and presided at the solemn mass in his cathedral preceding the battle.

Bishop of Lincoln Just over fifty charters or mentions of charters survive to shed a little light on Alexander's activities as a diocesan. Obviously with such a small collection of documentary sources the evidence is selective, and as might be expected from archival survivals is concerned chiefly with his cathedral church and with religious houses in the diocese. In these spheres, at least, Alexander made a significant contribution. The prebendal organization of the cathedral church developed during his episcopate. In a general confirmation issued by Pope Eugenius III (r. 1145–53) in 1146, ten prebendal churches are mentioned for the first time—Ketton, Gretton, Banbury, Buckden, Cropredy, Lafford (Sleaford), Leicester St Margaret, Leighton Bromswold (Ecclesia), Louth, and Thame—and it has been conjectured convincingly that since the last eight are episcopal manors the creation of these particular prebends can be ascribed to either Robert Bloet or Alexander. It is known for certain that Alexander established the prebend of Dunham (Dunholme) and Newport before 1145, the prebend of South Scarle in 1146 or 1147, and before 1146 added the manor of Milton to Binbrook to form the prebend of Milton Manor; he also probably annexed the church of Great Milton to the prebend of Aylesbury. He assigned the prebend of Leighton Ecclesia (the church of Leighton Bromswold, with the chapel of Salome Wood) to the subdeanery of Lincoln, and at the end of his episcopate he confirmed to the precentorship of the cathedral all the churches in the borough of Lincoln, of the demesne and gift of the late king, Henry I, that had not as yet been assigned as prebends or given to the common fund, together with the song school.

Alexander was probably present at the council held at Westminster by the papal legate, Giovanni da Crema, in September 1125, for shortly afterwards he left England in the company of the legate on his way to Rome, where the bishop remained for the winter of 1125–6 while the claims of Canterbury and York were being discussed in the curia. He certainly attended the legatine council of Archbishop William of Canterbury held at Westminster in May 1127, and was at the archbishop's council at London in late 1129, after Henry I's return from a long stay in Normandy. In 1143 he was present in Winchester at the legatine council convened by Henry de Blois, when the dispute between Archbishop Theobald of Canterbury (d. 1161) and the monks of St Augustine's, Canterbury, was settled, and two years later was numbered among those bishops and abbots who joined the legate Imar, cardinal-bishop of Tusculum, in settling a case between the bishops and monks of Rochester. In 1133 and 1134 he was personally in conflict with William de Corbeil, archbishop of Canterbury (d.

1136), over certain diocesan customs and rights; the precise nature of the quarrel is uncertain, but both prelates crossed to Normandy in 1134 to see the king about the dispute.

Dealings with monasteries In the establishment of monastic houses in his diocese Alexander played an active part as a founder as well as the confirmatory role of a diocesan (in all, thirteen Cistercian abbeys were founded in the Lincoln diocese during his episcopate), and to him are ascribed the foundations of the Cistercian houses of Louth Park, Lincolnshire, and Thame, Oxfordshire, the Arrouaisian abbey of Dorchester, Oxfordshire, and the Gilbertine house of Haverholme, as well as the leper hospital of St Leonard at Newark-on-Trent (in the York diocese). In June 1139 Alexander provided a new site at Thame for the Cistercian monks of Waverley, Surrey, who had failed in their attempt to establish a house at Otley, Oxfordshire, in the preceding year; likewise in 1139 he diverted Cistercian monks of Fountains who were trying to set up a monastic house at Haverholme to an alternative location in the episcopal manor of Louth. About 1140 he converted the existing collegiate church of secular canons at Dorchester, Oxfordshire, into an abbey of the Arrouaisian order and transferred the college's estates to the new house. With the new order of Sempringham he had close personal contacts—Gilbert of Sempringham (d. 1189) had been a member of the episcopal household until 1131, and enclosed the first seven women at Sempringham in that year—and it is probable that he was much concerned with advice and assistance in the early years of Gilbert's activities. Late in 1139 or possibly early 1140 he made over to Gilbert the site of Haverholme, rejected by the Cistercians, for a nunnery (although whether it was really suited for a nunnery if the Cistercians did not want it is an open question). The bishop was apparently much involved with the establishment of other female religious foundations in his diocese (in all seven nunneries were founded in the Lincoln diocese in his time), if not as actual founder. About 1140 Alexander attended the consecration of Christina of Markyate's cell at Sopwell, Hertfordshire, and in 1145 he obtained permission to consecrate the church of Holy Trinity, Markyate, also in Hertfordshire, for Christina and her nuns: in January 1139 the nuns of Godstow, Oxfordshire, were given 100s. a year from the episcopal market at Banbury, and the abbey was freed from the local archidiaconal jurisdiction, and given the right to elect its own abbesses.

Builder and artistic patron In the early 1130s Henry I granted to Alexander for his episcopal residence in Lincoln the gate of Eastgate with the tower over it; in 1137 Stephen gave him the land south of the cathedral, stipulating that if the bishop should build a house on this land as a residence for himself, then the church of Lincoln and the bishop and his successors should have the land in perpetual possession quit of all customary dues. This is the site of what is now known as the Old Palace, although it is uncertain whether Alexander actually commenced the

construction of the residence or whether this was left to Bishop Robert Chesney (1148–66) and his successors. More certain evidence of building in Alexander's time survives in relation to the episcopal castles of Newark-on-Trent in Nottinghamshire and Sleaford in Lincolnshire and probably also Banbury in Oxfordshire, but it was during his episcopate that Lincoln Cathedral became one of the first completely vaulted churches in the country (a recent study argues that it was possibly the first major English church to have been so vaulted). Gerald of Wales records that following a fire (the date of which is still debated by historians) Alexander caused the cathedral to be strengthened with stone vaults, and recent architectural study has suggested that Alexander was certainly responsible for the nave vaulting, if not more. The beginning of the transformation of the west front is also attributed to the bishop, and was completed in the time of his successor. Henry of Huntingdon (d. c.1155), recording the restoration and embellishment of the cathedral under Alexander, claims that it was 'not surpassed by any building in all England' (Huntingdon, 748).

Alexander was well known as a patron of learning, and contemporary writers praised the bishop's wisdom and munificence. Henry, archdeacon of Huntingdon, was commissioned by his episcopal patron to write his *Historia Anglorum*, and Geoffrey of Monmouth's translation of the 'Prophecies of Merlin' was produced at the bishop's request. Of the bishop's household little is known beyond information from the witness lists to episcopal charters and chronicle sources: as well as the future saint, Gilbert of Sempringham, who was an episcopal chaplain, Ralph Gubion acted as the bishop's treasurer before his elevation as abbot of St Albans in 1146, and a teacher and companion of his in the bishop's entourage was the Italian, Master Guido or Wido, who lectured on Holy Scripture. Henry of Huntingdon records that Alexander was called by contemporaries 'the Magnificent' on account of his lavishness and luxury (such behaviour calling down upon the bishop of Lincoln the expected criticism from Bernard of Clairvaux), and although he later chides his former patron with having spent well beyond his means, yet Henry clearly retains for the bishop a fondness and appreciation of many aspects of his character.

Death and burial Alexander was in Rome for a great part of 1145 and 1146, and in August 1147 he again set off, this time for Auxerre, to see Pope Eugenius III. The papal court was at Auxerre until mid-October that year but it is not known precisely when the bishop returned to England, although Henry of Huntingdon records that on account of the excessive heat he brought back with him the seeds of an illness that shortly afterwards led to his death. Alexander was buried in Lincoln Cathedral on 25 February 1148, and since his obit was celebrated at Lincoln on 20 February it is probable that he died on that day. No tomb or memorial now exists. A twelfth-century catalogue of books in Lincoln Cathedral records that the bishop gave the cathedral a number of works: a Genesis (incomplete), the gospels of

St Luke and St John, and the book of Job, all glossed, the canonical epistles, the Apocalypse, and a volume containing Proverbs, Ecclesiastes, and Canticles.

DAVID M. SMITH

Sources E. J. Kealey, *Roger of Salisbury, viceroy of England* (1972) · D. M. Smith, ed., *Lincoln, 1067–1185*, English Episcopal Acta, 1 (1980) · A. G. Dyson, 'The career, family and influence of Alexander le Poer, bishop of Lincoln, 1123–1148', BLitt diss., U. Oxf., 1971 · A. G. Dyson, 'The monastic patronage of Bishop Alexander of Lincoln', *Journal of Ecclesiastical History*, 26 (1975), 1–24 · Henry, archdeacon of Huntingdon, *Historia Anglorum*, ed. D. E. Greenway, OMT (1996) · *The book of John de Schalby: canon of Lincoln, 1299–1333, concerning the bishops of Lincoln and their acts*, trans. J. H. Srawley, another edn (1966) · G. Zarnecki, *Romanesque sculpture at Lincoln Cathedral* [1965] · E. C. Fernie, 'Alexander's frieze on Lincoln Minster', *Lincolnshire History and Archaeology*, 12 (1977), 19–28 · *Fasti Angl., 1066–1300*, [Lincoln] · *Fasti Angl., 1066–1300*, [Salisbury] · C. W. Foster and K. Major, eds., *The registrum antiquissimum of the cathedral church of Lincoln*, 10 vols. in 12, Lincoln RS, 27–9, 32, 34, 41–2, 46, 51, 62, 67–8 (1931–73) · *Gir. Camb. opera* · H. Chapman, G. Coppack, and P. Drewett, *Excavations at the Bishop's Palace, Lincoln, 1968–72* (1975) · D. Owen, ed., *A history of Lincoln Minster* (1994) · B. Golding, *Gilbert of Sempringham and the Gilbertine order, c.1130–c.1300* (1995) · *DNB* · *Reg. RAN* · M. Brett, *The English church under Henry I* (1975) · F. Barlow, *The English church, 1066–1154: a history of the Anglo-Norman church* (1979) · E. U. Crosby, *Bishop and chapter in twelfth-century England* (1994) · D. Whitelock, M. Brett, and C. N. L. Brooke, eds., *Councils and synods with other documents relating to the English church, 871–1204*, 2 vols. (1981) · *ASC* · K. R. Potter and R. H. C. Davis, eds., *Gesta Stephani*, OMT (1976)

Likenesses seal, 1145, BL; Birch, *Seals*, 1685

Wealth at death bequest of books

Alexander, Mrs. *See* Hector, Annie (1825–1902).

Alexander I (*d.* 1124), king of Scots, was the fifth son of *Malcolm III (*d.* 1093) and his second wife, *Margaret (*d.* 1093), and was possibly named after Pope Alexander II (*r.* 1061–73). He is presumed to have left Scotland when his father and mother died in 1093 and to have returned when his older brother *Edgar was placed on the throne in 1097. But Alexander is not mentioned by any source until the account of the opening of the tomb of St Cuthbert in 1104, when he was the only layman present and paid for a new shrine with generous gifts of cash—a remarkable testimony to his standing with the monks of Durham. Some accounts call him 'earl', but his endowment before 1107 is a matter of conjecture; it could have been that which Edgar prescribed in his will for *David, their youngest brother. Alexander's succession in 1107, according to the Peterborough chronicle, was 'as King Henry granted him' (Anderson, *Scottish Annals*, 128), but it is difficult to believe that the enthronement could be held up for weeks to allow consultation in France with Henry I. The latter's approval probably came soon after the succession, when Alexander was given as wife Sibylla, illegitimate daughter of the English king, a lady lacking in modesty and refinement, according to William of Malmesbury.

Alexander sought to deny to his youngest brother, David, the appanage of Strathclyde and Teviotdale bequeathed by Edgar, which David, with the help of the English and Normans, forced him to release; the relationship between them thereafter is something of a puzzle, for both took a hand in the affairs of Durham Priory and

Alexander I (*d.* 1124), seal

its lands in Berwickshire, yet Earl David's charters referred only once to his brother—when he founded Selkirk Abbey in 1113 for the souls of his parents and 'brothers', at a time when Henry reigned in England, Alexander in *Scotia*. David restored the see of Glasgow and rebutted the claims of Durham to authority in Teviotdale.

By contrast Alexander was only partially successful in his efforts to restore the see of St Andrews; his first nominee, Turgot, archdeacon and prior of Durham, who had written a biography for Alexander's sister Matilda of their mother, Margaret, was approved by Henry I and eventually consecrated at York on 1 August 1109, apparently without profession of obedience. The subsequent quarrels between Turgot and Alexander are not documented; it is known only that Turgot sought to go to Rome, and retired to Durham, where he died on 31 August 1115. Alexander, who appointed a monk of Bury St Edmund's to administer (it was later alleged, to plunder) the see, decided that his rights in the Scottish church would be better respected if a new bishop were consecrated by the archbishop of Canterbury, a see which had supported with monks his mother's foundation of Dunfermline Priory. After negotiations he requested in writing Eadmer, monk of Canterbury, for the see of St Andrews; the archbishop referred the request to Henry I who gave his approval in three lines—the whole correspondence is very revealing of relations between the kings and their churches. On 29 June 1120 Eadmer was elected and probably given the ring, but certainly not the staff, by the king—a reference to the contemporary investiture controversy between lay and ecclesiastical powers. A month later, because he was about to go to war, the king compromised, and Eadmer took the pastoral staff from the altar at St Andrews. But his consecration was another matter, a tussle between Canterbury, claimed by Eadmer, and York, supported by the pope;

Alexander would have neither, since a profession of obedience was demanded. Eadmer consulted the bishop of Glasgow and two Canterbury monks (perhaps at Dunfermline) and, restoring staff and ring, withdrew to Canterbury, probably in 1121; he made an abortive attempt at reinstatement in 1122.

This dismal tale, largely documented from Canterbury sources, illuminates Alexander's motives: he was determined to protect royal rights in the church, and the freedom of the churches in his kingdom from those in England. He did not interfere with the ties between Canterbury and Dunfermline, to which priory he and his wife were strikingly generous. Royal rights enabled him to bring Augustinian canons from Nostell and to establish them as a priory at Scone, probably as late as 1122. In January 1124 the king followed this up by nominating their prior, Robert, to the vacant see of St Andrews. Alexander also gave extensive lands, the Boar's Raik in eastern Fife, to the church of St Andrews 'so that the religious life might be established in that church', a plan which he could not enforce and which was completed by his successor through the establishment of the Augustinian priory there in 1144. He also took steps which seem to have been intended to establish Augustinians at the cathedral of Dunkeld, again frustrated by established clergy and resulting later in the abbey of Inchcolm; and finally he planned (fruitlessly, it seems) a cell of Scone on the island in Loch Tay where his wife had died on 12 July 1122. Thus he was a determined protagonist of the Augustinians, upon whom he conferred extensive resources, listed in the charter by himself and Sibylla (which may be a later working up of an authentic list of gifts) to Scone Priory. It seems likely that Scone was intended by Alexander to be the source of a wide Scottish dispersal of the order, but that he came to this purpose too late in life to be able to implement it.

That charter shows the primitive character of the Scottish economy, for it deals in lands, town houses, and fractions of the produce paid as rents to the king; Alexander did not dispose of readily available cash, but he may have had a following of knights of Anglo-French background, for he had a constable, Edward, who was said by Orderic Vitalis, improbably, to be the son of Earl Siward of 'Mercia'. Alexander certainly took a contingent to support Henry I against Welsh princes in 1114, and he clearly had to fight domestic enemies also. He has left three original charters at Durham and four or five copies from Scone Priory; they show that he had a chancellor, the first known in Scotland, and a double-sided seal, closely based on that of William Rufus but with an uncrowned king in majesty. But the only long witness list is on the dubious charter endowing Scone Priory; it lists bishops, earls, and six others, none evidence of a cohort of 'Normans' such as attended his brother David.

Alexander I was described by Ailred in conventional terms as pious; but also as 'beyond measure awesome to his [lay] subjects' (Anderson, Scottish Annals, 155), and the fifteenth-century vernacular chronicler, Wyntoun, called him 'the fierce'. Alexander had no surviving children with his wife, Sibylla. Orderic Vitalis alone tells that Malcolm, illegitimate son of Alexander, opposed the succession of David I in 1124; but Robert de Torigni identified Orderic's rebel Malcolm of 1130 as this illegitimate son, while Ailred identifies a Malcolm as 'heir of his father's [perhaps Alexander's] hatred and persecution' (Anderson, Scottish Annals, 193). Alexander died at Stirling on 27 April 1124 and was buried in Dunfermline Abbey. He was succeeded by his brother David I.

A. A. M. DUNCAN

Sources A. O. Anderson, ed., *Scottish annals from English chroniclers, AD 500 to 1286* (1908), 128–58, 167, 193 · A. O. Anderson, ed. and trans., *Early sources of Scottish history, AD 500 to 1286*, 2 (1922), 142–68 · A. C. Lawrie, ed., *Early Scottish charters prior to AD 1153* (1905), 20–48 · O. Engels and others, eds., *Series episcoporum ecclesiae Catholicae occidentalis*, 6th ser., 1, ed. D. E. R. Watt (1991), 81–3 · A. A. M. Duncan, *Scotland: the making of the kingdom* (1975), vol. 1 of *The Edinburgh history of Scotland*, ed. G. Donaldson (1965–75), 128–32 · G. W. S. Barrow, *The kingdom of the Scots: government, church and society from the eleventh to the fourteenth century* (1973), 169–73 · J. Wilson, 'The foundation of the Austin priories of Nostell and Scone', *SHR*, 7 (1909–10), 141–60 · T. N. Burrows, 'The foundation of Nostell Priory', *Yorkshire Archaeological Journal*, 53 (1981), 31–5 · I. B. Cowan and D. E. Easson, *Medieval religious houses: Scotland*, 2nd edn (1976), 91, 96–9 · A. H. Dunbar, *Scottish kings*, 2nd edn (1906)

Likenesses seal, U. Durham L., Durham dean and chapter archives · seal, BL; Birch, *Seals*, 14,769 [see illus.]

Alexander II (1198–1249), king of Scots, was born on 24 August 1198 at Haddington, the only son (there were also three daughters) of *William (William the Lion), king of Scots (c.1142–1214), and his wife, *Ermengarde (d. 1233), daughter of Richard, vicomte de Beaumont-sur-Sarthe and lord of Le Lude in Maine.

Prelude to kingship Alexander was recognized as heir to the throne by the Scottish élite at Musselburgh on 12 October 1201, and figured prominently in the treaties of 1209 and 1212 between his father and King John of England. Although their precise terms are unknown, under the first treaty Alexander offered John homage probably for the lands and rights King William held of the English crown (that is, not Northumberland, as has been argued, but Tynedale and superiority over the Huntingdon honour); and William also handed over his elder daughters, *Margaret and Isabel, to be married under John's control, in the expectation that at least one would become John's daughter-in-law. Under the 1212 treaty John granted Alexander's marriage, perhaps on the promise of a union with John's eldest daughter, *Joan (1210–1238), whom Alexander married in 1221, and of Northumberland as her dower.

After his knighting by John at Clerkenwell, Middlesex, on 4 March 1212, Alexander was carefully groomed for kingship by his ageing father, who involved him in government business and appointed him as an army commander in the campaign of summer 1212 against the pretender Guthred MacWilliam in Moray and Ross. During his final illness at Stirling, King William had his courtiers renew their support for Alexander's succession, and he was inaugurated at Scone on 5 December 1214, the day after his father's death. The sixteen-year-old king succeeded at a critical juncture. In the strongly Gaelic-Norse

Alexander II (1198–1249), seal

extremities of the realm respect for Scottish royal authority was the exception rather than the norm. Furthermore, King John, who had won major concessions in return for promises he had little intention of honouring, was behaving as overlord of Scotland in all but name. Alexander's reign was, nevertheless, marked by his resolute defence of his regal rights and dignity, by the steady expansion of his control over peripheral regions, and by the final emergence of the Scottish kingdom as one of medieval Europe's stronger medium-sized states.

War with England Until the mid-1220s Alexander relied heavily on his father's advisers, but there was no formal royal minority, and early in 1215 he reappointed the major officers of state to ensure governmental continuity and avoid any question of a regency. Another MacWilliam uprising in Moray or Ross was swiftly suppressed by the native northern magnate Farquhar MacTaggart, who presented Alexander with his enemies' heads on 15 June 1215. Asserting himself against King John, the young king exploited increasing baronial discontent in England to renew Scottish claims to the English border counties, whose recovery had been William the Lion's guiding aim; and in Magna Carta (chapter 59) John was obliged to offer justice to Alexander concerning not only his elder sisters (who remained unmarried) but his 'liberties and rights'. After John's repudiation of the charter, Alexander invaded Northumberland and besieged Norham on 19 October 1215. The Scots enjoyed unprecedented military advantages. At least twenty-five English castles north of the Humber already opposed John, and Alexander had the full support of the English barons of the region, the so-called 'Northerners', whose leaders, Robert de Ros (d. 1226/7) and Eustace de Vescy, had married illegitimate daughters of William the Lion. Inventories of the Scottish royal archives in 1282 and 1291 reveal that negotiations between Alexander and the 'barons of England' resulted

in a treaty, an agreement concerning his sisters' marriages, a judgment acknowledging his right to Northumberland, Cumberland, and Westmorland, and baronial mandates instructing the county communities to recognize his lordship. Vescy invested him with Northumberland at the siege of Norham, and many of the shire's élite gave him homage at Felton, near Alnwick, on 22 October 1215.

After Alexander's burning of Newcastle in December, King John marched north, took a heavy toll of rebel castles, including Carlisle and Richmond, and forced disloyal Yorkshire barons to flee to Scotland, where they entered Alexander's allegiance at Melrose on 11 January 1216. The English chronicler Matthew Paris records that, in a bombastic play on Alexander's youth and shock of red hair, John vowed to hunt the 'fox-cub' from his lair and, after seizing Berwick on 15 January, he devastated Lothian as far as Haddington. The fox-cub survived unscathed, and it was John's turn to be hunted in February when Alexander pursued him all the way to Richmond. He besieged Carlisle in July 1216, took the town on 8 August (the castle fell at an unspecified later date), and then marched his army some 350 miles to the Kent coast, an outstanding feat of Scottish arms. About mid-September he paid homage at Dover, for both the Huntingdon honour and the three northern shires, to the claimant to the English crown, Prince Louis of France, in return for the promise of an enduring alliance. Alexander then successfully came home, despite John's best efforts to intercept him—and in the process sacked the encampment of John's army, which had taken up ambush positions alongside the River Trent.

Alexander had agreed with Louis that his war gains would remain part of England; but this concession was rapidly overtaken by his wish to emulate King David I, who had effectively ruled the 'English' borders as part of a single Scoto-Northumbrian realm. Although firm control of Northumberland eluded him, Alexander established the constable of Scotland, Alan of Galloway, as lord of north Westmorland, and gave him general viceregal powers over all Cumbria. By April 1217 Alexander had also asserted his royal authority by imposing his nominee as bishop of Carlisle. But when, seven months after John's death, the French and English rebel army lost at Lincoln (20 May 1217), the ground was cut from beneath Alexander's feet. His raids on Northumberland in May and July 1217 served only to accelerate the Anglo-French peace negotiations culminating in the treaty of Kingston (12 September 1217). Moreover, since England enjoyed the pope's protection as a papal fief, Honorius III's legate Guala Bicchieri placed Alexander and his leading subjects under the full rigour of interdict and excommunication. Bereft of allies, Alexander bowed to the inevitable: at Berwick on 1 December 1217 he surrendered Carlisle in return for absolution for himself and his lay advisers, and at Northampton, on or before 19 December, he submitted in person to the young King Henry III, who, ignoring Alexander's claims to the border counties, took his homage for Tynedale and the Huntingdon honour. Early in 1218 the interdict on Scotland began to be relaxed, though senior Scottish churchmen remained unabsolved until later in that year.

Anglo-Scottish relations, 1218–1249 Despite the Scots' initial advantages, as in the war of 1173–4 they had fallen far short of matching the English crown's resources, and out of the wreckage of Alexander's fortunes came a new realism in the conduct of Anglo-Scottish relations. Their history from December 1217 to March 1296 is one of unbroken peace, and this long period of stability, unparalleled in the middle ages, owed much to Alexander's readiness to settle or play down his political differences with Henry III. Alexander's marriage to Joan of England at York in 1221, almost certainly on 19 June, was followed by the wedding of Margaret of Scotland to the English justiciar, Hubert de *Burgh, earl of Kent, in the same year, and by that of Isabel to Roger (III) *Bigod, future earl of Norfolk, in 1225. The Scottish princesses had been shabbily treated, and Hubert was later accused of helping himself to Margaret when she had been King Henry's intended queen—in accordance, that is, with the treaty of 1209. But Alexander evidently gave his approval to their marriages, and he imposed an aid of £10,000 on Scotland to raise their dowries. He visited Henry's court in friendship at Worcester in July 1223 and at York in December 1229. In 1235 he gave in marriage to Gilbert Marshal, earl of Pembroke, his youngest sister, another Margaret, for whom marriages had previously been contemplated to Count Thibault (IV) of Champagne (1219), Richard of Cornwall (1227), and King Henry himself (1231).

Most significant for the new *modus vivendi* between the kingdoms was the treaty of York (25 September 1237). Besides freeing Henry from any obligation concerning the marriage proposals of 1209, Alexander solemnly yielded in perpetuity Scottish royal claims to Northumberland, Cumberland, and Westmorland, for long the main stumbling-block to peace. In compensation he was promised lands in northern England worth £200 annually, and by 1242 he had been given a cluster of Cumberland manors centred on Penrith. He was ready enough to anger Henry by looking to France for his second wife, *Marie de Coucy (d. 1284), whom he married at Roxburgh on 15 May 1239, and it was primarily exaggerated English fears of an alliance between Alexander and Louis IX that brought the kingdoms to the brink of war in 1244. Alexander mustered his army in response to English mobilization, but then swiftly defused the crisis by agreeing to the treaty of Newcastle (14 August 1244), under which he promised to refrain from any hostile act against Henry unless in defence of Scottish interests (an important proviso), and betrothed his son, the future *Alexander III, to Henry's first-born daughter, Margaret.

Consolidation of the kingdom Although Anglo-Scottish tensions were never wholly eradicated, the importance of Alexander's conciliatory policies for the making of the Scots kingdom cannot be overstated. He had both the appetite and the opportunity to project royal power into northern and western Scotland with unprecedented

forcefulness. Early in 1221 he went to Inverness to quell the revolt of a highland chieftain, Donald MacNeil. In 1221–2 he conducted major campaigns against Argyll which seem to have resulted in the transfer of Kintyre, and perhaps Cowal, into safer hands, and in the fortification of Tarbert as a pivotal royal strongpoint. After his chief agent in the far north, Bishop Adam of Caithness, had been murdered in September 1222 in retaliation for zealously bringing his diocese into closer conformity with European norms, he mounted a punitive expedition in the autumn of that year, had the perpetrators mutilated, and temporarily confiscated half the earldom territories of the unreliable John Haraldsson, earl of Caithness. He returned north to confront another MacWilliam rising probably in 1228, when he appointed William Comyn, earl of Buchan, to complete the pacification of Moray on his behalf. The heads of the rebel leaders were delivered to the king, and in 1230 a MacWilliam baby girl had her brains dashed out against the market cross at Forfar.

The north had been decisively disciplined, and Alexander brought it definitively within the ambit of royal authority in the 1230s by establishing the great highland lordships of Badenoch and Lochaber, reviving the earldom of Ross, creating the earldom of Sutherland, and introducing a new line of pro-Scottish earls of Caithness. In the south-west a no less categoric assertion of royal power followed the death in 1234 of Alan of Galloway, who left a bastard, Thomas, and three legitimate daughters. Determined to snuff out the vestiges of Galwegian independence, Alexander ignored Celtic succession customs and insisted on partitioning the province among the daughters and their English husbands. The Galwegians rose in Thomas's support, and the king advanced into Galloway on 15 July 1235 with the indispensable Farquhar MacTaggart, now earl of Ross, who routed the rebel army in a counter-attack as it assaulted the royal camp. Alexander left behind Walter Comyn, earl of Menteith, as his military governor and before the year's end Thomas had surrendered, two of his Irish allies being torn apart by horses at Edinburgh.

With Galloway's 200-strong armada of galleys at his command, Alexander's attention returned to the problems of Scotland's west highland seaboard. In this volatile world, mighty Hebridean sea-lords holding island (Norwegian) and mainland (Scottish) territories continued to play largely for their own hand, and their feuding was easily exploited by the increasingly formidable King Haakon IV of Norway for his own power-building purposes. In the 1220s Alan of Galloway had campaigned with Alexander's encouragement against Skye, Lewis, and Man, but had achieved little apart from provoking Haakon to retaliate, and when in 1230–31 a combined Norwegian, Orcadian, and Hebridean fleet attacked Scottish-held Bute and Kintyre, Scotland faced its gravest crisis since King John's invasion in 1216. The only effective solution, as Alexander keenly appreciated, was to incorporate the whole of the Western Isles within his kingdom, and in 1244 he made the first of several offers to purchase them from Haakon. When these came to nothing, and Haakon commissioned

Ewen of Argyll to reinforce his authority over the Isles in 1249, Alexander launched a full-scale summer expedition with fleet and army. He made a bold start by ejecting Ewen from the mainland, and had the king's sudden death not brought matters to a premature halt, it is possible that the winning of the Isles for Scotland would not have been delayed until 1266.

Kingship, governance, and church In general a highly successful monarch, Alexander bequeathed to his successors a far stronger basis for effective kingship. He firmly understood the primacy of wealth for a ruler's strength, and the efficiency of his fiscal regime is amply demonstrated by his ability to provide his sisters with vast sums in dowry-money and to accumulate sufficient silver bullion to contemplate buying the Isles. An important law maker, he reaffirmed and extended his judicial superiority, and one of his most significant enactments provided a swift remedy for unjust dissasine (dispossession). He almost certainly introduced mortancestry to protect the rights of lawful heirs against intruders; and he gave fresh impetus to the use of a jury at the expense of the ordeal and combat, old forms of proof now largely discredited. The new processes of royal justice were popular, checked the expanding jurisdiction of the church courts, and played a vital part in the intensification of the Scottish king's role in governance.

Alexander's stern insistence on the overriding rights of royal lordship was encapsulated in his famous riposte to Ewen of Argyll that 'no one could serve two masters' (Paris, *Chron.*, 5.89), and he was more firmly the sovereign lord of mainland Scotland than any previous ruler had been. Dominance of the periphery depended crucially on the support of Scotland's Anglicized east-coast core where, by comparison with the recurrent instability of English politics, Alexander's relations with his magnates were remarkably trouble-free. Even the bitter feud between the powerful Comyns and the Bissets in 1242, though a severe test of his skills as a political manager, was kept within bounds, and thereafter a better balance was held between noble factions. He had no qualms about maiming or executing enemies beyond his heartlands; some lost lands to members of the Anglo-continental court nobility, notably the Comyns, Murrays, and Stewarts. In consequence he was often perceived as an ironhanded modernizing king who ruthlessly persecuted native Celtic society; and even Matthew Paris qualified his evident admiration for Alexander's piety and love of justice by interpreting his unexpected death as well-merited divine vengeance for ousting Ewen of Argyll. Nevertheless, the brutal side of his character should not be exaggerated. According to the Melrose chronicler, he was merciful to the Galwegians who submitted in 1235; and he was prepared in 1245 to acknowledge that Galloway had its own special laws. Nor, after Bishop Adam's slaughter, did he disinherit the families of the Caithness men implicated in the crime, for they were allowed to redeem their lands by paying fines. Thus aggressive state-building policies were not the only way Alexander won respect for his authority in the north and west; and above all he created a stronger sense of loyalty, even of Scottishness, by co-opting into the governing class Gaelic-Norse potentates like Farquhar MacTaggart and Alan of Galloway.

If a large part of the context for Alexander's achievements in Scotland was provided by Anglo-Scottish peace, his dealings with Henry III from 1217 reflected not only pragmatism but also an unshakeable determination to safeguard Scottish independence. His attempts in 1221 and 1233 to secure papal permission to be anointed and crowned, though foiled by English lobbying, reveal a deep conviction that his kingship was second to none, and he secured more recognition of Scotland's separate identity as an autonomous realm than his father had ever achieved. When in 1235 the papacy, at Henry III's bidding, commanded him to accept Scotland's feudal subjection to England, its injunctions were scorned. The treaty of York took the form of an honourable compromise between sovereign states, and his submissions in 1217 and 1244 entailed no acknowledgement of English overlordship. Unwelcome English influence was also kept at bay when with his backing the Scottish bishops won from Honorius III a confirmation of the liberties of the Scottish church (1218) and the right to establish their own provincial council (1225).

As a benefactor of the church, Alexander displayed a characteristic admixture of royal policy and piety, and his religious preferences were both conventional and innovative. He endowed or otherwise favoured the bishoprics of Argyll, Caithness, Moray, and Whithorn (Galloway), and brought them all under stricter Scottish control. He was a generous supporter of the Augustinian canons of Scone, the Benedictine monks of Coldingham and Dunfermline, the Cistercian monks of Coupar Angus, Melrose, and Newbattle, the Cistercian nuns of Manuel, and the Tironensian monks of Arbroath. In 1227–9 he founded with his mother, Queen Ermengarde, a Cistercian monastery at Balmerino, Fife, the last of Melrose's four Scottish daughter houses. About 1230 he set up a priory at Pluscarden, Moray, for the Valliscaulians, a new Burgundian monastic order which never reached England or Wales; in 1230–31 he introduced the mendicant orders to Scotland, the earliest Dominicans perhaps being brought from Paris, and by his death nine Dominican and at least three Franciscan friaries had been established, almost all apparently royal foundations.

Alexander had no children with Joan of England, and Alexander III, born on 4 September 1241, was the only child of his marriage to Marie de Coucy. He also had an illegitimate daughter, Margaret, who married Alan *Durward, a mainstay of his administration from 1244. Alexander's formative thirty-five-year reign ended when he died of a fever on the island of Kerrera, in Oban Bay, on 8 July 1249; his burial place was Melrose Abbey.

KEITH STRINGER

Sources A. O. Anderson, ed., *Scottish annals from English chroniclers, AD 500 to 1286* (1908); repr. (1991) · A. O. Anderson, ed. and trans., *Early sources of Scottish history, AD 500 to 1286*, 2 (1922); repr. with corrections (1990) · Paris, *Chron.*, vols. 2–5 · W. Bower, *Scotichronicon*, ed. D. E. R. Watt and others, new edn, 9 vols. (1987–98), vols. 4, 5 ·

Johannis de Fordun Chronica gentis Scotorum / John of Fordun's Chronicle of the Scottish nation, ed. W. F. Skene, trans. F. J. H. Skene, 2 vols. (1871–2) · G. W. S. Barrow and others, eds., *Regesta regum Scottorum*, 2–3, ed. G. W. S. Barrow and K. J. Stringer (1959–71) · *CDS*, vol. 1 · A. A. M. Duncan, *Scotland: the making of the kingdom* (1975), vol. 1 of *The Edinburgh history of Scotland*, ed. G. Donaldson (1965–75) · G. W. S. Barrow, *Kingship and unity: Scotland, 1000–1306*, rev. edn (1989) · K. J. Stringer, 'Scottish foundations: thirteenth-century perspectives', *Uniting the kingdom? The making of British history*, ed. A. Grant and K. J. Stringer (1995), 85–96 · A. A. M. Duncan, 'John king of England and the kings of Scots', *King John: new interpretations*, ed. S. D. Church (1999), 247–71 · J. C. Holt, *The northerners: a study in the reign of King John*, new edn (1992) · D. A. Carpenter, *The minority of Henry III* (1990) · K. J. Stringer, 'Periphery and core in thirteenth-century Scotland: Alan, son of Roland, lord of Galloway and constable of Scotland', *Medieval Scotland: crown, lordship and community: essays presented to G. W. S. Barrow*, ed. A. Grant and K. J. Stringer (1993), 82–113 · A. A. M. Duncan and A. L. Brown, 'Argyll and the Isles in the earlier middle ages', *Proceedings of the Society of Antiquaries of Scotland*, 90 (1956–7), 192–220 · B. E. Crawford, 'The earldom of Caithness and the kingdom of Scotland, 1150–1266', *Essays on the nobility of medieval Scotland*, ed. K. J. Stringer (1984), 25–43 · G. W. S. Barrow, 'Badenoch and Strathspey, 1130–1312, 1: secular and political', *Northern Scotland*, 8 (1988), 1–15 · H. L. MacQueen, *Common law and feudal society in medieval Scotland* (1993) · *The letters and charters of Cardinal Guala Bicchieri, papal legate in England, 1216–1218*, ed. N. Vincent, CYS, 83 (1996) · D. W. H. Marshall, 'A proposed marriage-alliance between Scotland and Champagne', *Scottish Notes and Queries*, 3rd ser., 7 (1929), 207–9 · R. A. MacDonald, *The kingdom of the isles: Scotland's western seaboard, c.1100–c.1336* (1997) · A. Young, *Robert the Bruce's rivals: the Comyns, 1212–1314* (1997)
Likenesses coins, AM Oxf., BM · coins, National Museum of Antiquities of Scotland, Edinburgh · seal, BL, NA Scot., NL Scot. · seal, U. Durham L., Durham Cathedral muniments, Misc. ch. 617 [*see illus.*]

Alexander III

Alexander III (1241–1286), king of Scots, was the only son of *Alexander II (1198–1249) and *Marie de Coucy (d. 1284). When Alexander II died on 8 July 1249, the Scottish crown passed to his son. Born at Roxburgh on 4 September 1241, and so aged just a little under eight years, this child was inaugurated as Alexander III on 13 July. In the traditional ceremony at Scone the young king was acclaimed by the community of Scots, enthroned on the ancient and symbolic 'stone of destiny', consecrated, invested with a mantle, and had his genealogy proclaimed by a Gaelic bard. Thereafter, the magnates of the kingdom made obeisance to him.

Problems of the minority In 1249, he who gained control of the king controlled the government (and revenue) of the kingdom. Alan Durward (d. 1275), at the head of a family which had wielded much influence under Alexander II, apparently tried to establish his own supremacy by claiming the right personally to knight Alexander III before his inauguration. Durward's attempt failed, but none the less, perhaps by virtue of some deal with the king's mother, Marie de Coucy, he did, in the first instance, gain control. The administration of the kingdom weathered the establishment of this new regime with a remarkable degree of continuity, and the business of government seems to have continued unimpeded. However, instability soon became apparent, most clearly in friction between Durward and his followers and their main baronial rivals, the Comyns. This resulted in a weakening of the government and the loosening of its grasp on the realm.

Presumably at the instigation of the Comyn faction, an appeal was made to Henry III of England for assistance against the Durward government. This provided Henry with an opportunity to revive the old claim to English sovereignty over Scotland; the approaches made to the papal curia by the Scots in search of the rites of unction and coronation for their king found no favour with the English monarch. The weak Durward regime was forced to curry favour with Henry, and effected a marriage between Alexander and Henry's daughter *Margaret (d. 1275). On Christmas day 1251 Alexander was knighted by Henry III, and on the following day the marriage took place at York. One English chronicle relates that, following the ceremony, the English king demanded homage of Alexander both for the lands which he held in England and for his Scottish kingdom. The homage for Scotland was refused, and no further discussion took place.

English interference Henry III none the less involved himself fully in the affairs of Scotland. It seems that Durward may have been the author of a devious plot to gain a right to the succession for himself or his heirs, and Henry used this to justify forcing the resignation of all the main officials of the Scottish household and appointing two of his own barons to represent his interests at the Scottish court. His interest was expressed purely in terms of his concern for the welfare of his daughter and son-in-law, but while such concern may well have been genuine enough, it can hardly be doubted that there were other motives for his involvement. Although Henry's name is nowhere associated with the appointment of the new Scottish royal council (comprised predominantly of Comyn supporters), his influence must nevertheless have been great.

The new government, however, soon became even less pleasing to Henry III than the one it had replaced. Either his representatives were powerless, or they co-operated with the Scottish magnates, who showed little respect for the interfering English king. His demands for military assistance in Gascony in 1253 fell on deaf ears in Scotland; only the ousted Alan Durward, who had made his peace with Henry III, went on campaign with the English magnates. Another source of contention was the money ordered to be levied by the papacy in Scotland to support an English crusade. The latter enterprise was intended to win the throne of Sicily for Henry III's second son, Edmund, and the Scots refused to pay.

By the summer of 1255 the situation had become intolerable to Henry. The Scottish government (including his own nominees) was foiling his attempts to have Scotland administered in England's interest, and in August 1255 he went to the border. On this occasion there was no formal dissociation of Henry III from the replacement of Alexander III's counsellors: 'at the instance of' the English king, and with the advice of named Scottish magnates, the Comyn party were removed from office. It was further 'agreed' between the kings that unless by reason of major trespass, the new council (named) would remain in office for seven years (that is, until Alexander was twenty-one), or for a shorter period as dictated by Henry and Alexander.

However, by 1257 the ousted Comyn faction had regained a strong enough position to force Alexander and the new government to negotiate with them, talks in which Henry III involved himself fully. These talks aimed at ensuring peace in Scotland, but failed, and in October 1257 the Comyns, led by Walter, earl of Menteith (d. 1258), seized Alexander and tried to gain control once more. Henry III prepared an invasion force to quell the rebellion, but other affairs diverted his attention, and on this occasion his influence was much more limited.

Coming of age The Comyns, too, experienced problems. Freed from the power of Alan Durward's faction, Alexander III, now aged seventeen, seems to have been more of a force to reckon with, and was no longer prepared to be dictated to by any of the rival parties. In a treaty which the Comyns made with the Welsh, who were rebelling against Henry III, reference is made to the possibility that Alexander might force them into a truce with Henry III, or that he might be persuaded to join their agreement. This confirms that Alexander refused to be ruled by the Comyns. His actions against Durward's supporters show that he was equally independent of them. Henry III's political defeat by his own barons left him unable to control events in Scotland, and the resultant settlement of September 1258 was one which probably reflected the wishes of Alexander III himself. The Scottish king had come to terms with both factions, and a new council was appointed which comprised men of both camps. Probably because it was the only way of retaining any influence, the English king promised to give help and advice to this council. He successfully requested a visit of the Scottish king and queen to England, which took place in November 1260. By that time it is clear that Alexander, now aged nineteen, was in personal control of the Scottish government, and that his minority had, de facto, ended.

Margaret was allowed to remain in England after Alexander's return, to give birth to her first child (a daughter, Margaret, who later married Erik, king of Norway), on the condition that if Alexander should die before her return, she and the child would be handed over without delay to a committee of, in effect, guardians, no matter what conditions prevailed in the two kingdoms.

Affairs in the west For the most part, the rest of Alexander III's reign saw a fairly steady growth, politically and economically, which rendered Scotland strong, stable, and prosperous by the last quarter of the century. An important element in this growth was the consolidation of the western boundaries of the kingdom. The Western Isles had for long owed nominal allegiance to the Norwegian king, although there was more than an element of imperialism in the attempts by either crown to control this area and the far west of the mainland. The independence of the western seaboard, as well as the interest of the Norwegians, posed a threat to the kings of Scots; the area was frequently troublesome also for the kings of Norway, who exercised little or no effective control. For some time, the Scots had entertained ambitions to take the isles, which had figured significantly in Scottish politics at various times. It was thus a policy of the thirteenth-century kings of Scots to bring the west more completely under their control. Alexander II had died during such an attempt, and Alexander III was fully aware of the advantages to be gained by extending his authority to the logical confines of the kingdom.

This policy, naturally, led to conflict both with the isles themselves and with the kings of Norway. In 1261 a Scottish embassy went to Norway to discuss the isles, and was held by the Norwegians. A Scottish force, led by the earl of Ross on the king's behalf, attacked the isles in the following year, and Haakon IV's reaction was personally to lead a fleet, which arrived on the west coast in the late summer of 1263. The Norwegian campaign, however, was to find only lukewarm support from the islesmen, a fact which seriously undermined its effectiveness. None the less, Rothesay Castle was taken, and Haakon redistributed lands in an attempt to bolster his authority; then, in order to encourage Alexander III to negotiate more favourably, the Norwegians penetrated into Loch Lomond and devastated the Lennox. The negotiations were fruitless, however, and the invasion came to an untimely end in the autumn, when storms drove some of the ships ashore, and a battle was fought between a Scottish force and the Norwegians. Both sides claimed victory in the battle of Largs; probably neither suffered badly, but it was enough, combined with the worsening weather, to convince Haakon IV of the futility of extending the campaign. He sailed northwards, exacting tribute from the islands as he went, and arrived in Orkney in October. Here he fell ill, and died in December.

The failure of the western campaign, the death of Haakon IV, the unwillingness of many of the islesmen to antagonize the Scottish crown, further aggressive Scottish action in Caithness and the west which brought many of the nobles of the area to King Alexander's 'peace', and above all the surrender of the king of Man to Alexander III, who threatened the island with invasion in 1264, persuaded the new Norwegian king, Magnus IV, to negotiate. After prolonged negotiation, peace was made in July 1266, in the treaty of Perth, which ceded the Western Isles to the Scottish crown in return for a down payment of 4000 merks, and an annual rent of 100 merks in perpetuity. This treaty, removing the threat of international conflict in connection with the Scottish crown's attempts to control and assimilate the Western Isles, made available the area's financial and military resources, without which it is doubtful if Robert I could successfully have waged his war against the English early in the next century.

Later dealings with England Following Scottish noble involvement in the English barons' wars, mainly, but not exclusively, on the royalist side, in 1265 Alexander III prepared to give Henry III aid against his rival, Simon de Montfort, but the forces he had gathered were not required. John Fordun also tells of the Scots king and clergy's refusal to bow to papal demands for a tax of the Scottish church in aid of the English crusading effort, although Scots did apparently take part in Louis IX's second crusade of 1270, in which David, earl of Atholl, Adam, earl of Carrick, 'and a great many other Scottish and English nobles' died (*Chronica gentis Scottorum*, 2.299). Also on crusade was Prince Edward, the heir to the English throne, when, in November 1272, Henry III died. Edward I was crowned at Westminster in August 1274, an occasion which Alexander III, his queen, and many Scots nobles attended.

Alexander III went to Westminster as an English baron, in virtue of his English lands. He did not, however, perform homage for those lands, a matter which was a point of discussion for several years. In October 1278 Alexander went south again, to perform the homage, having first obtained the necessary guarantees that his attendance would in no way prejudice the rights and liberties of his realm. On 28 October, at Westminster, the king of Scots performed the homage for his English lands, but denied strongly that any homage was due to Edward for the Scottish kingdom.

Last years: problems and achievements The later years of Alexander's reign, which appear to have been characterized by peace, good relations with other kingdoms, and strong rule, were blighted by problems in relation to the succession. Early in 1275 Alexander's queen, the English king's sister, had died, leaving Alexander with a daughter, Margaret, and two sons, Alexander and David (born in 1261, 1264, and 1273 respectively). The last five years of Alexander's own life saw the death of all three children: David in 1281, Margaret in 1283, and Alexander (married, but childless) in 1284. In 1281 Margaret had married Erik II of Norway, and at her death she left an infant daughter, the only heir in direct line to Alexander III after 1284. At Scone in February 1284 an impressive array of the baronial leaders of the Scottish community swore to accept and uphold *Margaret, the Maid of Norway, as the heir to the king, should no further child be born to the king or his late son. On 14 October 1285 the king married Yolande, the daughter of Robert, count of Dreux. But the marriage was short-lived, since in the following year, on 19 March, Alexander III died: after a council in Edinburgh, he was returning to his recently wed wife, when according to tradition his horse stumbled and threw him. A monument near Kinghorn in Fife marks the spot where he is said to have fallen. He was buried in Dunfermline Abbey.

Traditionally, Alexander III's reign has been viewed as a 'golden age' for Scotland. It has come to be perceived, however, that this picture is, at least in part, an exaggeration of the fourteenth- and fifteenth-century chroniclers, who wrote with hindsight, comparing the peaceful later thirteenth century with the war-torn years which followed and, further, who wrote with a propagandist message for their own times. None the less, it does seem to have been a relatively prosperous period: climatic conditions were good and the prolonged peace and increasing population were favourable both to agriculture and to foreign trade. The wool trade in particular flourished in this period, and was one factor which encouraged a relatively healthy money supply; it also, through the imposition,

some time between 1275 and 1282, of a new export custom on wool and hides, did much to bolster the royal income. There is also architectural evidence of a healthy economy: significant work on some of Scotland's most important ecclesiastical buildings, including the cathedrals of Dunblane, Dunfermline, Glasgow, and St Andrews, dates from this reign. The consistent message of the sources is that Alexander III's personal reign lived up to the expectations of good kingly rule as expressed by the political theory of the period.

NORMAN H. REID

Sources N. H. Reid, ed., *Scotland in the reign of Alexander III, 1249–1286* (1990) · *Johannis de Fordun Chronica gentis Scotorum* / *John of Fordun's Chronicle of the Scottish nation*, ed. W. F. Skene, trans. F. J. H. Skene, 1 (1871), 293–309 · *APS*, 1124–1423, 420–21, 424, 425 · *CDS*, vol. 1, nos. 1768, 1985, 2080, 2103, 2155, 2198, 2225, 2229; vol. 2, nos. 37, 44, 120, 122, 247, 250 · *Close rolls of the reign of Henry III*, 14 vols., PRO (1902–38), vol. 6, pp. 356–7, 430; vol. 8, pp. 2, 108; vol. 9, pp. 8–9; vol. 10, pp. 134, 168, 311, 329; vol. 12, p. 165 · E. L. G. Stones, ed. and trans., *Anglo-Scottish relations, 1174–1328: some select documents*, 2nd edn, OMT (1970), [29], [30–36], [38–41] · Rymer, *Foedera*, 1.279, 303, 322, 348–9, 353, 362, 402, 422 · 'Hakonar saga', *Icelandic sagas and other historical documents*, 2, ed. G. Vigfússon, Rolls Series, 88 (1887), 339–40, 344–67 · G. W. Dasent, trans., 'The saga of Hacon', *Icelandic sagas and other historical documents*, 4, Rolls Series, 88 (1894) · J. Stevenson, ed., *Chronicon de Lanercost, 1201–1346*, Bannatyne Club, 65 (1839), 57, 304–5 · A. O. Anderson and M. O. Anderson, eds., *The chronicle of Melrose* (1936), 109–10 · *Paris, Chron.*, 2.68 · A. A. M. Duncan, *Scotland: the making of the kingdom* (1975), vol. 1 of *The Edinburgh history of Scotland*, ed. G. Donaldson (1965–75), 561, 572–3, 577

Likenesses seals, repro. in J. H. Stevenson and M. Wood, *Scottish heraldic seals*, 3 vols. (1940)

Alexander of Ashby. *See* Ashby, Alexander of (1148/1154–1208/1214).

Alexander of Canterbury. *See* Canterbury, Alexander of (*fl.* 1100–1109).

Alexander of Dundonald (*c*.1220–1282). *See under* Stewart family (*per. c*.1110–*c*.1350).

Alexander of Hales. *See* Hales, Alexander of (*c*.1185–1245).

Alexander of Stainby. *See* Stainsby, Alexander of (*d.* 1238).

Alexander the Mason. *See* Newport, Alexander of (*fl. c*.1235–1257).

Alexander, Albert Victor, Earl Alexander of Hillsborough (1885–1965), politician and co-operator, was born at 59 George Street, Weston-super-Mare, Somerset, on 1 May 1885, the son of Albert Alexander (*d.* 1886), a blacksmith, and his wife, Eliza Jane, *née* Thatcher. On his father's death his mother moved back to her parents' house in Bristol, and provided for her four children by returning to her trade as a maker of surgical belts and corsets. For several years times were difficult, but eventually this determined and energetic woman owned a successful business.

Local government officer Alexander was educated at Barton Hill elementary school in Bristol, but ended his formal education at the age of thirteen to supplement the family income. His first job was in the office of a leather merchant, but he soon became employed as a boy clerk in the office of the Bristol school board. In 1903 he shifted to the school management department of the Somerset county council and returned to live at Weston-super-Mare. Apart from war service he remained in educational administration until 1920.

Alexander's marriage on 6 June 1908 to Esther Ellen (1877/8–1969), a schoolteacher, daughter of George Chapple of Tiverton, Devon, was the prelude to some significant shifts in his activities. His first religious affiliation had been to the Church of England; under his wife's influence, he became a Baptist. As a lay preacher he became an exponent of militant protestantism. 'If you want salvation, you have to be born again. You have to go to the life-giving Word of God; the Word made flesh' (*Hansard 5L*, 231, 1961, 242). His religious shift was accompanied by support for the Liberal Party, in contrast to his mother who was a stalwart Conservative. He joined the Weston Co-operative Society and became active in the National Association of Local Government Officers. In addition he continued his education at evening classes. Such activities located him very much in the culture of respectable Edwardian Liberalism. As an activist he developed political skills; his work as a lay preacher made him an effective public speaker. In this last field he emulated his maternal grandfather, Francis Thatcher, a well-known Bristol evangelist.

This stability was broken, perhaps decisively, by the First World War. Alexander volunteered in 1914, but was not called up until 1916, when he joined the Artists' Rifles. Military training affected his health and he saw no active service. Instead he became a posting officer, allocated recruits to their units, and following the armistice served as an education officer. He was demobilized with the rank of captain. A return to Weston-super-Mare and the Somerset education department perhaps seemed a move back to a narrower world. On holiday in London in 1920 he read an advertisement for a parliamentary secretary to the Co-operative Congress. In September 1920 he accepted the post; in November he began work in London.

Co-operator and Labour MP Within a year Alexander was associated with a great parliamentary victory. The Lloyd George coalition proposed to impose a corporation profit tax on the undistributed dividends of co-operative societies. Alexander's patient lobbying influenced some government back-benchers. On 19 July 1921 the tax proposal was defeated by 137 votes to 135. This parliamentary success raised Alexander's political status. He was approached by the Co-operative Party in Sheffield to be their parliamentary candidate. The Co-operative Party had emerged in 1917–18; its candidates normally enjoyed Labour Party support. In the general election of November 1922 Alexander was returned as the Labour and Co-operative member for Sheffield Hillsborough.

Alexander's achievement was distinctive. He had not been a member of any trade union affiliated to the Labour Party, nor had he been active in any socialist organization. Arguably his beliefs showed much continuity with his pre-war Liberalism; he proved a competent and well-informed parliamentary speaker. His administrative skills were evident, and in January 1924 he obtained a junior post in the first Labour government. As parliamentary secretary to the Board of Trade, he worked under another dedicated administrator, Sidney Webb. Beatrice Webb described him as

> a new discovery—a hard-headed administrative socialist, graduating in municipal service and recently identified with the Consumers' Co-operative Movement. He is a singularly good-tempered, sane-minded, direct-speaking person, alike in private and on the platform, with a strain of intellectual curiosity, of great value in social reconstruction. (22 March 1924, *The Diary of Beatrice Webb*, ed. N. I. MacKenzie and J. MacKenzie, 4, 1985, 22)

In the years of opposition from 1924 to 1929 Alexander never stood for election to the executive committee of the Parliamentary Labour Party (PLP). Dividing his time between parliament and the Co-operative Congress, he

Albert Victor Alexander, Earl Alexander of Hillsborough (1885–1965), by Howard Coster, 1942

stood therefore outside the formal leadership group. But as an effective parliamentarian he was tipped increasingly for high office in any future Labour government.

Board of Admiralty Whatever the distinctive character of his route to Labour politics, Alexander participated enthusiastically in the Sheffield labour movement. From 1922 the city had three Labour MPs, rising to five in 1929; Labour gained control of the city council in 1926. Alexander's campaigns in Sheffield included a strong co-operative element, but his work there and at Westminster was dominated by the depression in the Sheffield steel industry. It might have been expected that any ministerial advancement for Alexander might reflect his economic and social concerns; but the formation of the second Labour government in June 1929 saw him enter the cabinet as first lord of the Admiralty. Cabinet membership indicated his reputation for competence both in parliament and in administration. Beatrice Webb, an admirer, summarized the assessment that brought him to high office: 'a vigorous and masterful personality; with good physique, alert mind, straightforward manner, but without charm or brilliance. Somewhat of the Arthur Henderson build and temperament' (14 Sept 1929, *Beatrice Webb's Diaries*, ed. Cole, 219).

Alexander's appointment to the Admiralty did not arise from any prior interest in naval matters. Yet this became his specialism for over two decades. Contemporary and historical judgements have varied on how far Alexander acted as much more than the political representative of naval interests. Yet he rapidly developed a mastery over detail—so much so, that after a meeting in Rome with Mussolini in 1930, the latter assumed that Alexander had been a naval officer. Moreover he was an effective advocate for his case both in cabinet and in the Commons. Within his first year at the Admiralty he was involved in the London Naval Conference. The resulting treaty between Britain, the United States, and Japan presented agreement on both numerical and qualitative limitations on construction. He replied effectively to opposition criticism that the outcome would result in an erosion of British naval supremacy.

Alexander's departmental commitments meant that he had little involvement in the Labour government's desperate attempts to deal with rapidly rising unemployment. In August 1931, along with other cabinet members, he confronted the crisis precipitated by the publication of the May report on public expenditure and the flight of Britain's gold reserves. His basically liberal sentiments remained powerful. When the cabinet debated the possibility of a revenue tariff, Alexander was one of the five free-traders who backed the thorough opposition of the chancellor of the exchequer, Philip Snowden. He did not question the need for a balanced budget and cuts in public expenditure. A paper from him accepted cuts in naval pay provided that equivalent reductions were made elsewhere in the public services and in unemployment benefit. Alexander seemed impeccably orthodox; and yet in the symbolic cabinet vote on a 10 per cent cut in unemployment benefit he stood with Arthur Henderson and the dissenting minority.

With the formation of the National Government, Alexander became a prominent member of the Labour opposition. He was elected to the executive committee of the PLP and made a notably vigorous Commons speech opposing the new government's economy measures. Like other former members of the Labour cabinet, he distanced himself from any suggestion that they had been prepared to endorse many of the economies that they now criticized. Together with most of his colleagues Alexander was defeated in the October 1931 general election, and for the next four years concentrated on his work for the co-operative movement. In contrast to his success in 1921, he failed to persuade the National Government not to tax the surpluses of co-operative societies, a change introduced in 1933.

Prior to his election defeat in 1931 Alexander had been seen, for example by Arthur Henderson, as a possible future leader of the Labour Party. Yet when he regained his Sheffield seat in the general election of 1935 he did not stand for the leadership, and instead backed Herbert Morrison. During his years out of parliament he had tended to concentrate on co-operative affairs at a time when Attlee had strengthened his own position in the parliamentary party, and Morrison had been prominent both as a party policy maker and as leader of the successful Labour group on the London county council. In contrast, Alexander never established a dominant role in the broader Labour Party. He was not a star at party conferences and his increasing concentration on defence issues struck few chords with back-benchers and party activists. From 1935 he was a valued member of the party's Commons leadership; he played a significant part along with Hugh Dalton in shifting the PLP away from its opposition to defence estimates. Within the controversies of the late 1930s he endorsed collective security through the League of Nations, criticized the Munich settlement and the application of the non-intervention policy in Spain, and attacked any hint of a popular front.

Return to the Admiralty The formation of the Churchill coalition in May 1940 brought Alexander back to the Admiralty. He succeeded the new prime minister, with whom he had been in regular contact on naval matters since the latter's return to the Admiralty in September 1939. Churchill and the chiefs of staff continued to direct operations, and Alexander was denied access to the most secret materials. However, within his allotted sphere he acted with his customary energy and competence. His relationship with the sea lords was good, and his knowledge and zeal made him an effective advocate of the navy's case in the battle for resources. He was also an effective propagandist, speaking at 'warship weeks' to maintain public enthusiasm for the war. Critics suggested that he was too enamoured of naval tradition and too responsive to flattery by the sea lords, but his wartime ministerial career was generally reckoned a success.

Alexander would have preferred a continuation of the

coalition until the defeat of Japan, but the Labour victory in the 1945 election meant that his absence from the Admiralty was brief. His final stint covered the transition from a war to a peace footing. It also involved his absence from Whitehall between March and June 1946 as a member of the cabinet mission to India. His two colleagues were the secretary of state, Lord Pethick-Lawrence, and Sir Stafford Cripps, who had been involved in an earlier Indian initiative in 1942. Alexander was involved as the custodian of British defence interests; he began with slight knowledge of Indian affairs and was at first largely silent. As he became more familiar with the issues his interventions became vigorous, and he tended to side with the viceroy, Lord Wavell, sometimes in opposition to his cabinet colleagues. His responses could be thoroughly imperialist as he encountered Congress politicians. 'I was not prepared to sit down under the humiliation of my country and therefore something better than a policy of scuttle would have to be thought up' (Alexander, diary, 20 May 1946, quoted in Morgan, 221). Along with Ernest Bevin he was unhappy about the eventual decision to withdraw.

Minister of defence Alexander finally left the Admiralty in October 1946; until December he sat in the cabinet as minister without portfolio, but then became minister of defence in charge of a new department created to reorganize the direction of defence policy. In general he was less successful at defence than at the Admiralty. His old post had harnessed his talents for vigorous advocacy of a departmental case. The strategic perspective necessitated by his new responsibility proved more difficult. He also faced problems in arbitrating between the competing claims of the services. This friction over resources meant that his relationships with the service chiefs were more problematic than had been the case at the Admiralty. This was particularly the case with the chief of the Imperial General Staff, Field Marshal Montgomery, who felt that Alexander 'always sat on the fence' (Montgomery, 483). Away from the recriminations Alexander was a member of the secret cabinet committee concerned with the development of a British atomic bomb.

Some of Alexander's problems reflected broader political and economic pressures upon the government. He was a thorough supporter of Bevin's foreign policy, a position that provoked criticism among some co-operators, but military spending was necessarily constrained by economic difficulties, not least in summer 1947, when Alexander fought a long battle to limit cuts in defence expenditure. There were also problems with Labour backbenchers. Legislation to introduce peacetime national service for an eighteen-month period was introduced by the government in spring 1947. Opposition came not only from customary Labour critics of government foreign policy but from those influenced by pacifist or broader anti-militarist sentiments. The government responded by reducing the period of service from eighteen months to twelve, an announcement made by Alexander during the bill's committee stage (*Hansard 5C*, 437, 1947, 441–53). However, the intensification of the cold war produced a

reversal of the policy; further legislation in December 1948 restored the eighteen-month requirement.

Alexander expressed firm positions in some cabinet debates beyond his own ministerial responsibilities. His constituency interests helped to ensure that he initially supported the early nationalization of the iron and steel industry. On this divisive issue he stood at first, unusually, with what could broadly be characterized as the left within the cabinet. Subsequently, however, he favoured a compromise that fell short of full nationalization. In discussions on the National Health Service he was critical of the proposed dependence of hospitals on central government funds. His support of municipal involvement perhaps indicated the decentralizing strand within the co-operative tradition.

House of Lords Alexander took a peerage in the new year's honours list of 1950 and became chancellor of the duchy of Lancaster until the government lost office in the 1951 election. In this last ministerial phase he was a strong supporter of United States policy during the Korean War. He backed American moves to brand China as an aggressor in a United Nations resolution. A Foreign Office minister noted that Alexander and another supporter of the American line, Lord Jowitt, were 'like good old High Tories' (Kenneth Younger, quoted in Morgan, 431). In opposition, Alexander became deputy leader of the Labour group in the Lords and succeeded Jowitt as leader in 1955. He was a regular and conscientious participant in Lords debates until his retirement in autumn 1964. He died in Manor House Hospital, Hendon, Middlesex, on 11 January 1965, and was buried three days later at West Mersea, Essex. He was survived by his wife (who was made CBE in 1947) and by a daughter. A son died in infancy, and his title therefore became extinct.

Alexander was a committed co-operator, a fervent protestant, an energetic administrator, an uncomplicated patriot, and an enthusiast for traditions, especially those of the navy. His route into the upper echelons of the Labour Party was unusual; his contribution above all was to help make the party credible as a potential government, especially in an area such as defence, where Conservatives had traditionally claimed a special competence. Apart from his commitment to co-operation, he articulated little that was ideologically distinctive to the Labour cause. He retained legacies of his Liberal past, and in his later career his views on foreign policy and defence were little different from those of the Conservative leadership.

Beyond his extensive political activities Alexander was a convivial figure, with several friendships outside the labour movement. A self-taught pianist, his repertory of music-hall tunes provided the basis for relaxation in diverse settings, not least the vice-regal lodge. A second enthusiasm was football. In December 1946 Lord Wavell, increasingly at odds with the Attlee government over Indian policy, visited London. Towards the end of his visit Wavell went with Alexander to watch the minister's team, Chelsea, at home to Wolverhampton Wanderers. The viceroy, in his official discussions, had seen Alexander the defender of empire; at Stamford Bridge he saw Alexander as everyman: 'He is an enthusiastic football fan, shouting "foul", "play the game", "don't mess about" etc as loudly as anyone' (24 Dec 1946, *Wavell: the Viceroy's Journal*, 399).

DAVID HOWELL

Sources J. Tilley, *Churchill's favourite socialist: a life of A. V. Alexander* (1995) · *DNB* · *DLB* · T. F. Carbery, *Consumers in politics: a history and general review of the co-operative party* (1969) · Reports of the Co-operative Party · *Beatrice Webb's diaries, 1924–1932*, ed. M. Cole (1956) · H. Dalton, *Memoirs*, 3 vols. (1952–62) · *The political diary of Hugh Dalton, 1918–1940, 1945–1960*, ed. B. Pimlott (1986) · *The Second World War diary of Hugh Dalton, 1940–1945*, ed. B. Pimlott (1986) · K. Morgan, *Labour in power* (1984) · P. Williamson, *National crisis and national government: British politics, the economy and empire, 1926–1932* (1992) · A. Thorpe, *The British general election of 1931* (1991) · *Wavell: the viceroy's journal*, ed. P. Moon (1973) · *Hansard 5L* (1961), 231.238–52 · B. L. Montgomery, *The memoirs of field-marshal the Viscount Montgomery of Alamein* (1958) · b. cert. · *Hansard 5C* (1947), vols. 436–7 [National Service Bill] · P. Clarke, *The Cripps version: the life of Sir Stafford Cripps* (2002)
Archives CAC Cam., corresp. and papers · Plunkett Foundation, Long Hanborough, Oxfordshire, papers relating to Co-operative movement · Sheff. Arch., constituency papers | Bodl. Oxf., corresp. with Clement Attlee · HLRO, corresp. with Lord Beaverbrook · Nuffield Oxf., corresp. with Lord Cherwell
Likenesses W. Stoneman, photographs, 1929–42, NPG · H. Coster, photographs, c.1940–1949, NPG [*see illus.*] · F. Lion, portrait · E. Moore, portrait, priv. coll. · E. Moore, portrait; on loan to Admiralty · photographs, repro. in Tilley, *Churchill's favourite socialist*
Wealth at death £51,874: probate, 29 March 1965, CGPLA Eng. & Wales

Alexander, Alexander [Alick] (1849–1928), promoter of physical education, was born in Liverpool on 14 May 1849, the second son of W. C. Alexander, a chief carpenter in the Royal Navy who had settled in Liverpool at the end of his period of service. Following an education at Liverpool College and the Liverpool Institute, he was apprenticed to the well-known gymnast John Hulley, the first director of the Liverpool Gymnasium. After completing his training he became a demonstrator of physical training there. The Liverpool Gymnasium at that time was one of the acknowledged centres of sporting life in Britain, attracting pupils from all over Britain, and from as far afield as America. Representatives of the local medical profession co-operated in directing the classes on a sound theoretical basis. The gymnasium was also made available to all the leading artistes who visited the city, and it was from these performers that Alexander acquired many of his skills. He became a highly skilled performer in all the branches of his art, a quality he possessed in common with that other great pioneer of gymnastics Per Henryk Ling. His speciality was what later became known as agility exercises; these were not in fashion in the gymnasiums at the time because they were not thought to be essential to general health. Alexander, on the other hand, maintained that they were useful because they developed such qualities as pluck, skill, endurance, and the art of co-ordinating mind and muscle. After the temporary closure of the gymnasium in 1870, Alexander travelled around Britain and Ireland giving demonstrations of his physical prowess and offering his services teaching fencing and gymnastics skills to public schools and military establishments. For a period his services were employed at various institutions in Ireland, including Trinity College, Dublin (1875). While in Ireland he met his eventual wife, Emily Adelaide, daughter of John and Mary Smith of Dublin.

In 1880 Alexander returned to his native Liverpool to take over directorship of the ailing Liverpool Gymnasium, which had been purchased by the philanthropist Samuel Smith and was run by the Young Men's Christian Association. With considerable energy and enthusiasm he taught classes in health and fitness, staged numerous public displays, and prepared teams to compete and exhibit their skills around Britain and occasionally abroad. He led a team visit to Stockholm in 1896 at the invitation of King Oscar of Sweden, and at the invitation of Quintin Hogg mounted a display to celebrate the opening of the gymnasium at Regent Street Polytechnic in London.

Alexander, who was Britain's answer to the renowned German strongman Eugen Sandow, achieved notoriety for feats of strength such as crushing an apple with one hand, bending pokers and bars of iron, and raising his entire body weight by means of one finger only, and by performing a variety of somersaults and tumbling tricks on the ground and on the rafters of the Liverpool Gymnasium. It was claimed that he could out-perform any of his contemporaries in these feats. Other regular stunts included placing an apple on the back of an assistant's neck and then slicing it in two with a single blow of a sword while his assistant remained unharmed. Notables impressed by these feats were often invited to feel his muscles. Accidents resulting from acquiring, rehearsing, and performing these tricks eventually took their toll, however, and are thought to have been responsible for his eventual blindness in later life.

Alexander championed what he termed a British system of physical training, and published at least sixteen books describing its methods. The system consisted of free movements and breathing exercises, military and musical drill, gymnastics, outdoor games, and swimming. He advocated that the system should be taught in elementary schools and gave evidence to the royal commission on teacher education in 1887. His ideas, which became popular at the time of the Edwardian movement for national efficiency, were later aired before the royal commission on physical training (Scotland) in 1902. With his wife, who was also a physical training instructor, he opened the physical training college for women at Southport in 1891 to produce teachers scientifically trained in its techniques; they jointly wrote *British Physical Education for Girls* (1910). In 1886 he helped to found the National Physical Recreation Society, of which Herbert Gladstone was president and Arthur Kinnaird the secretary, with the object of promoting physical recreation among the working classes. He also claimed to have invented bent handlebars for racing bicycles. Alexander (or Alick) Alexander died at his home, Innisfallen, 8 York Road, Birkdale, Southport, Lancashire, on 23 May 1928, and was buried on 29 May in Birkdale cemetery. He was survived by his wife.

RICHARD WILLIAM COX

Sources A. Alexander, *A wayfarer's log* (1919) · N. A. Parry, 'The Liverpool Gymnasium', MEd diss., University of Manchester, 1974 ·

D. P. McPherson, 'Mr Alexander Alexander: an appreciation', *Liverpool Daily Post and Mercury* (29 May 1928) • 'Country's oldest cyclist? Death of Mr A. Alexander', *Liverpool Daily Post and Mercury* (24 May 1928) • *The Times* (26 May 1928), 17 • N. A. Parry, 'Pioneers of physical education in the nineteenth century: Alexander Alexander', *History of Education Society Bulletin*, 22 (1978), 21–38 • B. A. Furlong, 'Alexander Alexander, 1849–1928: building the foundations of health and strength in Liverpool and Southport', *History of Education*, 21 (1992), 179–87 • WWW • d. cert.
Archives BL, corresp. with Lord Gladstone, Add. MSS 46052–46059
Likenesses photograph, repro. in A. Alexander and E. A. Edwards, *British physical education for girls* (1910)
Wealth at death £12,095: probate, 6 July 1928, CGPLA Eng. & Wales

Alexander [*née* Barber], **Ann** (1774/5–1861), banker and bill broker, was born in Eckington, Derbyshire, the daughter of William and Mary Barber. Little is known about her life until the point when, while working in a Quaker milliner's in the City of London, she met William Alexander (1769–1819), a bank clerk. They were married on 13 February 1801 at Doncaster. There is no evidence that Ann was a Quaker by birth, so she must have become one by 'convincement', for the Alexanders were a Quaker family and mixed marriages were not permitted at that time.

The couple's first home was in Bunhill Row, off the City Road, but as their family grew in size they moved south of the Thames to 2 Kennington Terrace, Kennington Lane, and then to Kennington Place, Lambeth. Between 1802 and 1817 Ann and William had nine children, of whom eight survived to maturity. To provide for his family her enterprising husband combined his regular job as clerk (later head clerk) in a banking house with ventures of his own, including from 1806, partnership in a bill-broking business with his brother-in-law, John Rickman. In 1810 he launched out as a bill broker on his own account and founded the firm of Alexander & Co.

It was a momentous step—and a risky one given Alexander's responsibilities—and despite early success the business suffered from the effects of the Napoleonic war and post-war uncertainties. Then in 1819 disaster struck when William, weakened by business worries, became ill following a fall from a coach and died within a few weeks at the age of fifty.

In a world in which the penalties for ill fortune were unmitigated, the first priority was to secure a livelihood for Ann and the children. The family business was in a weak condition and required an injection of capital to enable it to continue. On the other hand, Ann was determined that it should be kept going until her eldest son, George William *Alexander (1802–1890), came of age. She was also willing to provide the element of continuity by herself taking over as principal of the bill-broking firm, at a time when such employment for a woman was entirely unknown. On this basis William's executors decided to allow the proceeds of a life assurance policy to be used to supply the necessary funds.

Precisely what part Ann Alexander played in the running of the business is unclear—but there is no doubt that it was her firm. The name was changed to A. M. Alexander and she took all the profits. George William Alexander, who worked without respite in the early years and who was to become the architect of the firm's future greatness, was admitted into partnership in 1823, when he came of age, and from 1824 the firm traded as A. & G. W. Alexander. Ann Alexander remained the senior partner but over time her influence waned as that of her son increased. Between 1823 and 1828 she took two-thirds of the profits and her son one-third. Then from 1828 to 1831 the partners took half each. Thereafter as new partners were admitted Ann Alexander's share declined, first to three-eighths and later to one-third. From 1838 when she retired at the age of sixty-four, she received £1000 per annum, paid at the rate of 4 per cent.

Over the years the Alexander family migrated from Lambeth to Stoke Newington and then to Reigate in Surrey. Ann Alexander died at London Road, Reigate, on 15 January 1861 aged eighty-six. GORDON FLETCHER

Sources 'Dictionary of Quaker biography', RS Friends, Lond. [card index] [see also Alexander, William (1769–1819)] • M. F. Lloyd Prichard, 'The Alexander family's discount company', *Journal of the Friends' Historical Society*, 49 (1960), 157–64 • K. F. Dixon, *The story of Alexanders Discount Company Ltd, 1810–1960* • 'Mr F. Newcomb', *Bankers' Magazine* (1924), 474–7 • K. F. Dixon, 'The development of the London money market, 1780–1830', PhD diss., U. Lond., 1962, appx 4 • W. T. C. King, *History of the London discount market* (1936), 117–18, 118 n4 • D. Kynaston, *The City of London*, 1 (1994), 25–6, 60–61, 88 • d. cert.
Wealth at death under £14,000: resworn probate, Feb 1862, CGPLA Eng. & Wales (1861)

Alexander, Boyd (1873–1910), traveller and ornithologist, born at Willesley Place, Cranbrook, Kent, on 16 January 1873, was a twin son (with Robert Alexander) of Colonel Boyd Francis Alexander, of an Ayrshire family, and his wife, Mary Wilson. After education at Radley College (1887–91) he passed into the army in 1893, joining the seventh battalion rifle brigade. Devoting himself to travel and ornithology, he made two excursions to the little-visited Cape Verde Islands in 1897 to study their ornithology. It was there that he met José Lopes, who became invaluable to him as a taxidermist and general assistant, accompanying him in all of his travels. Alexander went, in 1898, on an ornithological expedition to the Zambezi River and its tributary the Kafue, and in 1899 he joined the Gold Coast constabulary. He took part in the relief of Kumasi in 1900, for which he received the medal and clasp, and on his return to England he was offered and accepted a commission in the rifle brigade. Keeping up his studies of bird life in west Africa, he visited Fernando Po in 1902, and made there not only ornithological but also ethnological investigations and a map, and gathered material for a review of Spanish missionary work.

In 1904 Alexander started on a remarkable expedition from the mouth of the Niger to the Nile delta. It was designed to survey Northern Nigeria and to show that Africa could be crossed from west to east by means of its waterways. Accompanied by his younger brother, Captain Claud Alexander, and by Captain G. B. Gosling, P. A. Talbot, and José Lopes, Alexander left Lokoja on the Niger on 31

March, and travelled to Ibi on the Benue. There the party separated for a time. Gosling, a zoologist, went off to shoot big game. Claud Alexander and Talbot carried out a valuable survey of the Murchison Mountains in spite of sickness, scarcity of food, and difficulties with carriers and hostile indigenous peoples; they finally reached Maifoni, where Claud Alexander died of fever, after six weeks' illness, on 13 November 1904, at the age of twenty-six. Boyd Alexander meanwhile travelled alone by Loko on the Benue, Keffi, the Kachia and Panda Hills, and Bauchi to Yo (arriving on 26 October), some 30 miles from Lake Chad. He succeeded in visiting his dying brother at Maifoni, and thence he (now with Talbot, Gosling, and Lopes as companions) reached Lake Chad by way of Kukawa and Kaddai. Some months were spent in the difficult exploration of the lake. Their valuable surveys of the lake, when compared with other surveys, enabled geographers to form an idea of the remarkable periodic variations of level and other physical conditions to which the lake is liable in sympathy with periods of drought or heavy rainfall.

On 26 May 1905 Alexander, Gosling, and Lopes (Talbot having returned to the west) started up the Shari, making a detailed survey of the Bamingi tributary in September. They then traversed the watershed to the Ubangi, and proceeded across the centre of the continent, following that river and the Welle. At Niangara on the Welle, Gosling died of blackwater fever. Alexander now travelled to N'Soro, turned north to the Lado country, and followed the Yei River and Bahr al-Jebel downward through Anglo-Egyptian Sudan. He surveyed the Kibali tributary of the Welle in July and the Yei in October 1906, besides carrying out important zoological studies. He reached the Nile in December 1906 and from there returned to England.

For his journey across the continent Alexander received the gold medal of the Royal Geographical Society of Antwerp in 1907, and the founder's medal of the Royal Geographical Society of London in 1908, as well as the thanks of his colonel, the duke of Connaught, on behalf of his regiment. At the close of 1908 Alexander, with Lopes, left England again for west Africa. He visited the islands of São Thomé, Príncipe, and Annobón, and, in March 1909, the Kamerun Mountain, whence he proceeded to Lake Chad by way of the upper Benue, intending thereafter to make for Egypt through Wadai and Darfur. The country was known to be in a disturbed condition, and Alexander, on reaching Nyeri, 70 miles north of Abeshr, the capital of Wadai, was murdered by Muslim tribesmen on 2 April 1910. He was buried at Maifoni, by the grave of his brother Claud. Lopes was able to escape and relayed the news of Alexander's death through the French administration in the region. A memorial to Boyd and his brother Claud was placed in the parish church of Cranbrook, Kent. Alexander was an 'astute and persevering naturalist-explorer' (GJ, 110) who was modest about his remarkable exploits, and showed a 'brotherly willingness' (ibid.) to share the information that he acquired. He published an account of his journey of 1904–7 in From the Niger to the Nile (2 vols.,

1907). He also contributed a detailed account of Fernando Po to the Ibis (1903), and a paper 'From the Niger, by Lake Chad, to the Nile', to the Geographical Journal (30.119).

O. J. R. HOWARTH, rev. MARK POTTLE

Sources private information (1912) · GJ, 36 (1910), 108–10 · b. cert.
Archives Bodl. RH, diary · NHM, diaries | NRA, priv. coll., corresp. with Olive Macleod
Likenesses Godbold, portrait (as a boy); known to be in family possession in 1912
Wealth at death £7712 6s. 5d.: administration, 2 July 1910, CGPLA Eng. & Wales

Alexander [née Humphreys], **Cecil Frances** [Fanny] (1818–1895), hymn writer and poet, was born at 25 Eccles Street, Dublin, the second daughter of John Humphreys, major in the Royal Marines, and his wife, Elizabeth Frances Reed, daughter of Captain Reed of Dublin, and niece of General Sir Thomas Reed. While her father was living at Ballykeane, co. Wicklow, a warm friendship developed between Fanny (as she was often known) and Lady Harriott Howard, the daughter of the earl of Wicklow, who later became an author herself. Their intimacy continued after the family moved in 1833 to Milltown House, Strabane, co. Tyrone, where Major Humphreys served as agent to the marquess of Abercorn. Cecil Humphreys and Lady Harriott were both attracted to the teachings of the Oxford Movement, and began writing tracts, with Harriott supplying the prose and Cecil the verse. These tracts were published individually from 1842, and collected into a volume in 1848. The influence of the Tractarians remained deep and constant throughout Cecil's life, and was evident both in her literary endeavours and in her parish work. She had the opportunity to meet some of the movement's leaders, including Edward Pusey, Henry Manning, and John Keble.

It was while she lived at Milltown House that Cecil Humphreys published her best known poetry and hymns. In 1846 she published Verses for Holy Seasons, with a preface by Walter Farquhar Hook; it was followed in 1848 by Hymns for Little Children, for which John Keble wrote the preface. The purpose of this volume, which went through nearly a hundred editions, was to explain to children, by means of simple, concrete images, the articles of the apostles' creed. Its widespread success was due to her ability to understand the questions children asked: 'Where was Jesus born?' was answered by 'Once in royal David's city'; the answer to 'Why did he have to die?' was found in 'There is a green hill far away'; her response to 'Who made the world?' was 'All things bright and beautiful'. The proceeds from these early publications helped to finance a project in which Cecil took a special interest: the building of the Derry and Raphoe Diocesan Institution for the Deaf and Dumb.

On 15 October 1850 Cecil Humphreys was married at the parish church in Strabane to the Revd William *Alexander, an adherent of the Oxford Movement and newly appointed rector of Termonamongan, near Castlederg in co. Tyrone. She took an immediate interest in parish work, and carried food to the sick in remote parts of the

Cecil Frances Alexander (1818–1895), by Charles Napier Kennedy, 1894

Cecil Alexander's last years were marked by declining health: she was unable to accompany her husband on a visit to New York in 1891 and on a trip to South Africa in 1893 for her daughter's wedding. By 1895 she had become seriously ill, and died at the palace, Londonderry, on 12 October of that year, and was buried on 18 October at the city cemetery. She left two sons—Robert Jocelyn and Cecil John Francis—and two daughters, Eleanor Jane and Dorothea Agnes, who married George John Bowen. Bishop Alexander remained in the diocese of Derry and Raphoe until 1896, when he was appointed archbishop of Armagh and primate of all Ireland. In the same year he published a collective edition of his wife's work, with a biographical preface, as *Poems by Cecil Frances Alexander*.

LEON LITVACK

Sources E. Lovell, *A green hill far away: the life of Mrs C. F. Alexander* (1970) · W. Alexander, preface, *Poems by Cecil Frances Alexander* (1896) · E. Alexander, *Primate Alexander, archbishop of Armagh: a memoir* (1913) · V. Wallace, *Mrs Alexander: a life of the hymn-writer Cecil Frances Alexander* (1995) · R. F. Newton, 'A delicate question (Mrs Alexander)', *Hymn Society Bulletin*, 74 (winter 1955–6), 11–12 · H. Martin, *They wrote our hymns* (1961) · J. Julian, ed., *A dictionary of hymnology*, rev. edn (1907); repr. in 2 vols. (1915) · E. Routley, *A panorama of Christian hymnody* (1979) · E. Routley, *An English-speaking hymnal guide* (1979) · M. Frost, ed., *Historical companion to 'Hymns ancient and modern'* (1962)

Archives BL, letter to Mrs D. M. Craik, Add. MS 81896

Likenesses C. N. Kennedy, oils, 1894, Derry deanery, Londonderry [*see illus.*] · E. Lutyens, oils (after C. N. Kennedy), Church House, 46 Abbey Street, Armagh, Northern Ireland · photograph, Hymns Ancient and Modern Ltd, St Mary's Works, St Mary's Place, Norwich

district. In 1853 the couple travelled to Oxford, where Cecil was given a warm welcome on account of the popularity of her poems and hymns. In 1855 William Alexander became rector of Upper Fahan on Lough Swilly (a place which formed the setting for some of her poems). In 1860 he was appointed to the living of Camus-juxta-Mourne, Strabane. Owing to demanding parish work, and health problems which necessitated frequent trips to Dublin, Cecil Alexander's literary output decreased markedly. Her previous work was, however, highly regarded: she was consulted by Sir Henry Baker about the structure of *Hymns Ancient and Modern*, and the inclusion of her hymns helped to boost both her reputation and the popularity of the collection.

On 11 October 1867 William Alexander was enthroned as bishop of Derry and Raphoe, and the family moved to the bishop's palace in Londonderry. Cecil turned down many invitations to compose hymns and poems, including one from Edward Pusey in March 1871. She could not find the time for literary endeavours, owing to her heavy involvement in visiting the sick and to the active role her husband played in overseeing the disestablishment of the Church of Ireland in the years up to 1871. Despite this decline in publication the success of her earlier pieces ensured her a prominent place in the *Church of Ireland Hymnal*. Indeed, the honesty and straightforwardness of expression embodied in her verses, and their immediate appeal to the imagination, contributed to the extraordinary longevity of her achievement.

Alexander, Cosmo (1724–1772), portrait painter and traveller, was born probably in Aberdeen, the son and pupil of the Aberdonian painter and engraver John Alexander (1686–*c*.1766), who had worked in Rome from 1711 to 1719, and his wife, Isobel Innes. John Alexander named his son after Cosmo, son of the duke of Gordon, himself named after his godfather Cosimo III, grand duke of Tuscany.

Although he pursued a lifelong career as a portrait painter, the defining element of Cosmo Alexander's life was his support of the Jacobite cause. He was declared a wanted man after the battle of Culloden in 1745 and first went to London. He then left for Rome, arriving by Easter 1747 and staying in the strada Felice with two other Scots, the Jesuit priest Patrick Leith and George Gray. He began painting portraits of the Jacobite community in the city, including that year a commission from the Old Pretender, James Stuart, for a portrait of his son, Charles Edward Stuart, and subsequently received further commissions from the Pretender's family, the dates on the completed works covering his time in Rome and his subsequent stay in Paris. In June 1751 he left Rome for Leghorn, where he painted William Aikman (priv. coll.), and he then visited Bologna, Venice, Dresden, and Paris (1752), where he continued to paint members of the Scottish community.

In 1754 Alexander settled in Henrietta Street, London, in a furnished house bequeathed to him by the architect James Gibbs (1682–1754), a friend and fellow Aberdonian Catholic. He made frequent trips to Scotland and in 1755

Cosmo Alexander (1724–1772), self-portrait, before 1745?

the town council of Aberdeen employed him to paint portraits of the earl and countess of Findlater. In 1763–4 he worked in Rotterdam, The Hague, and Amsterdam, where his main patrons were the Hopes, a business family of Scottish descent.

In 1765 Alexander was admitted into the Incorporated Society of Artists, but in 1766 he left for the American colonies, painting portraits of the Scottish community in Philadelphia and joining the St Andrew's Society. He moved to New York in 1767, staying with the governor of New Jersey, William Franklin, during the winter of 1768–9 and then moving to Newport, Rhode Island, where he painted portraits of (among others) the Hunter, Keith, Ferguson, Grant, and Hamilton families. In Newport he met the Stuart family, whose fourteen-year-old son Gilbert (later to be famous for his portraits of George Washington) became Alexander's assistant, accompanying him on a tour of the southern states, on a route following churches designed by or after James Gibbs. They both arrived in Edinburgh in 1771. Alexander died in the following year, leaving Stuart in the care of his brother-in-law, the portraitist Sir George Chalmers.

Cosmo Alexander's work is competent but unoriginal. In historical terms he merits interest as much for his travel as for his role as the principal portraitist of leading Catholic and Jacobite Scottish families. There are examples of his work in Aberdeen Art Gallery, the National Galleries of Scotland, Edinburgh, and in the collection of the National Trust for Scotland.

PATRICIA R. ANDREW

Sources J. Ingamells, ed., *A dictionary of British and Irish travellers in Italy, 1701–1800* (1997) · G. M. Goodfellow, 'The art, life and times of Cosmo Alexander (1724–1772): portrait painter in Scotland and America', MA diss., Oberlin College, Ohio, 1961 · J. Holloway, *Patrons and painters: art in Scotland, 1650–1760* (1989) [exhibition catalogue, Scot. NPG, 17 July – 8 Oct 1989] · P. McLellan Geddy, 'Cosmo Alexander's travels and patrons in America', *Antiques*, 112 (Nov 1977), 972–9 · W. Dunlap, *History of the rise and progress of the arts of design in the United States*, 2 vols. (New York, 1834) · G. M. Goodfellow, 'Cosmo Alexander in America', *Art Quarterly*, 26 (autumn 1963), 309–22 · G. M. Goodfellow, 'Cosmo Alexander in Holland', *Oud Holland*, 79 (1964), 85–7

Archives Scot. NPG, archive folder, compilation of cuttings, photocopies, photographs, and MSS notes | Rome, AVR SA S. Andrea delle Fratte (Ford)

Likenesses C. Alexander, self-portrait, oils, probably before 1745, Aberdeen Art Gallery [*see illus.*]

Alexander, Daniel Asher (1768–1846), architect and engineer, was born on 6 May 1768 in the parish of St Olave, Southwark, London, the son of Daniel Alexander, broker, and his wife, Elizabeth. He was educated at St Paul's School and in 1782 he became a student at the Royal Academy, where after two months' study he gained a silver medal, and where, from 1788 to 1818, many of his designs were exhibited. He was a pupil of Samuel Robinson in Finsbury Circus, who taught him the principles of heavy construction. On 22 March 1792 he married Catherine Pattenden, with whom he set up home in Rockingham Row, Newington Butts. They had a son, but Catherine died in 1798, at the age of thirty-one, at East Farleigh. In 1800 Alexander married Anna Maria Broadley, the daughter of Peter Broadley JP, of Clapham and Southwark. They had five girls and three boys, and the family lived at 10 Eliot Place, Blackheath, Kent, which Alexander leased from 1805. In 1826 they moved to Yarmouth, Isle of Wight, and in 1837 to Baring Crescent, Exeter, where Alexander remained for the rest of his life.

Alexander's specialized knowledge of construction is evident in many of his works, one of the earliest of which was the widening, at Rochester, of the bridge over the Medway, where he accomplished the difficult task of forming the two middle arches of that bridge into one. In 1796 he was made surveyor to the London Dock Company, and until 1831 all the buildings in the docks were from his designs. He was surveyor also to the Trinity House, and in that capacity built lighthouses at Harwich, Lundy island, and elsewhere. He designed both Dartmoor prison (1805–12) and the old county prison at Maidstone (1810–17). The former generated much public interest when the original design was published in *Ackermann's Repository* (1810). Later historians have noted the influence of G. B. Piranesi's *Carceri d'invenzione* (1745?) on Alexander's designs.

Alexander reached the peak of his profession, and had many pupils, including W. H. Ashpitel, James Beck, Joseph Woods, James Savage, John Whichcord, James Pritchett, Edward I'Anson, John Wallen, and Richard Suter. Edward I'Anson went on to become Alexander's assistant and then partner until 1816. Alexander was publicly complimented by Sir John Soane from the chair of the Royal Academy for the finely conservative spirit he had shown in repairing two works of Inigo Jones—the Royal Naval Asylum at Greenwich, and Coleshill House, Berkshire. This work brought him into contact with the sculptors Sir Francis

Chantrey and John Flaxman, with whom he formed life-long friendships and with whom he made annual trips to France and the Southern Netherlands to draw and study. His views of Rouen, Leiden, and Antwerp were exhibited at the Royal Academy in 1816 and 1818.

Alexander was a member of the Architects' Club and treasurer of the Artists' Benevolent Fund. At a time when the professional status of architects was in the process of foundation, he was frequently called on as an expert witness. He was, in one case, asked by counsel to confirm whether he was a builder, to which he responded, 'I am more than that, I am an architect.' On being asked the difference he explained that, 'a builder supplies the bricks, and an architect supplies the brains.' Challenged by counsel to name the architect of the Tower of Babel, Alexander instantly replied, 'There was no architect; hence the confusion' (*The Builder*, 795).

Alexander died at Baring Crescent, Exeter, on 2 March 1846, and was buried at Yarmouth church in the Isle of Wight; he had raised the church tower, at his own expense, the better to mark the channel at that part. His eldest son, Daniel, who trained under his father, practised as an architect, but in 1820 gave up that profession for the church, and died vicar of Bickleigh, in Devon, in 1843.

ANNETTE PEACH

Sources Colvin, *Archs.* · *GM*, 2nd ser., 26 (1846), 210 · A. E. Richardson, 'The architect of Dartmoor', *ArchR*, 43 (1918), 77–80 · *The Builder*, 20 (1862), 795 · Graves, *RA exhibitors* · *IGI* · S. C. Hutchison, 'The Royal Academy Schools, 1768–1830', *Walpole Society*, 38 (1960–62), 123–91 · J. Harris, *A catalogue of British drawings for architecture, decoration, sculpture and landscape gardening, 1550–1900, in American collections* (1972) · [W. Papworth], ed., *The dictionary of architecture*, 11 vols. (1853–92) · J. B. Harris, 'Daniel Asher Alexander, 1768–1846: architect and engineer', MA diss., University of Manchester, 1967
Archives CKS, corresp. and papers relating to Mote Park · Col. U., Avery Architectural and Fine Arts Library, IB Box · Hydrographic Office, Taunton, admiralty records · priv. coll., papers relating to Longford Castle
Likenesses F. Chantrey, sketch, *c.*1818, V&A · attrib. J. Partridge, oils, *c.*1818, NPG · Masquerier, oils, 1819, RA · J. W. Cook, print, 1843, NPG · portrait, Port of London Authority building
Wealth at death £40,000

Alexander, David Lindo (1842–1922), lawyer and Jewish community leader, was born at 6 South Street, London, on 5 October 1842, second son in the large family of solicitor Joshua Alexander and his wife, Jemima (*b.* 1819), one of eighteen children of David Abarbanel Lindo (1772–1852) and Sarah Mocatta (1777–1852). He was educated at the City of London School and Trinity College, Cambridge, from where he graduated in mathematics among the wranglers in 1864. He was one of the first Jews to benefit from legislation passed in 1856 which abolished the Anglican religious test at Cambridge that had prevented Jews from matriculating. His obvious aptitude for mathematics notwithstanding (he had won prizes for this subject throughout his scholastic career), Alexander was elected by his college to a three-year studentship in law. He was destined to follow in the professional footsteps of his father and, like him, to enter Jewish communal life.

Alexander was called to the bar at Lincoln's Inn in 1866, took silk in 1892, was elected a bencher of his inn in 1895,

and retired from legal practice around 1907. His family were well connected to the élite 'cousinhood' of Anglo-Jewry, a fortunate advantage for a specialist in conveyancing law. In his youth the family were resident in South Street, Finsbury, and later moved to Wimpole Street in the heart of the West End. Two of his sisters married into the wealthy Beddington clan. Alexander never moved outside the smarter parts of London.

In 1886 the eligible bachelor married Hester (1845–1913), daughter of Simeon Joseph, a member of the London stock exchange. The couple, who lived at York Gate, Regent's Park, had three children, two sons and a daughter. The promising younger son, George Simeon, died young after being called to the bar at Lincoln's Inn. Hester herself became 'a confirmed invalid' soon after their marriage, and her husband cared for her with great devotion until her death on 29 May 1913.

Alexander was the product of an Ashkenazi–Sephardi union. On the maternal side he was a direct descendant of Isaac Lindo (*d.* 1712), one of the earliest 'Jew brokers' on the London stock exchange. His maternal grandfather, David Abarbanel Lindo (an uncle of Benjamin Disraeli), was prominent in the affairs of the Bevis Marks Spanish and Portuguese Synagogue, the oldest congregation in Britain, and was a staunch opponent of Jewish religious reform. Alexander's parents were apparently traditional in outlook. While he was at Cambridge his father arranged for him to dine with a local Jewish family rather than in hall, thus enabling Alexander to observe the Jewish dietary laws. His parents were members of the Ashkenazi Central Synagogue in Great Portland Street, London, and he started his own forty-year communal career in 1877 as one of its representatives on the Board of Deputies of British Jews. He was also associated with the New West End Synagogue in Bayswater. Both of these synagogues were prestigious 'cathedrals' of the establishment United Synagogue. Among other communal posts, Alexander served as vice-president of the Anglo-Jewish Association, on the council of Jews' College, and, most importantly, as president of the Board of Deputies between 1903 and 1917. His youngest brother, Lionel, was a president of the Jewish Board of Guardians, the premier welfare agency within the Jewish community.

As board president, Alexander was closely identified with the native Anglo-Jewish 'establishment' at a time when its hegemony was being increasingly challenged by the mass immigration of Jewish refugees from eastern Europe. Yiddish-speaking foreign-born Jews, crowded into the slums of the East End and equivalent metropolitan districts, had little in common with their English-speaking acculturated co-religionists, whose élite Alexander typified.

Almost from the beginning Alexander's presidency was criticized for being out of touch. On foreign policy matters dear to the heart of the immigrants, Alexander protested with reticence against atrocities in Russia at the time of the Kishinyov pogrom (1903) and he half-heartedly welcomed the liberal February revolution in 1917. Nearer home Alexander was attacked for the evidence he gave before the royal commission on divorce (1910). Rather than uphold freedom of religious conscience, he preferred to denounce 'foreign rabbis' in Britain who granted religious divorces (*gittin*) to couples still married according to civil law. He consistently adopted what the *Jewish Chronicle* dismissed as a 'no khaki, no soup' policy towards immigrant Russian Jews who refused to serve in the British army during the First World War.

Alexander is best remembered as co-signatory of a letter to *The Times* on 24 May 1917, framed by the leading Anglo-Jewish ideologue of Liberal Judaism and anti-Zionism, Claude G. Montefiore, president of the Anglo-Jewish Association. The letter stated that 'Emancipated Jews in this country regard themselves primarily as a religious community' with 'no separate aspirations in a political sense'. They were not 'a homeless nationality' that aimed to set up its own territorial centre. Indeed, such an aspiration would only undermine the struggle for equal rights everywhere and would brand all Jews 'as strangers in their native lands'. This manifesto was intended as a riposte to the Zionists who, led by the Russian-born Chaim Weizmann, were then conducting negotiations with the British government which resulted in the Balfour declaration on Palestine of 2 November 1917. The letter provoked a 'communal revolution' in Anglo-Jewry. The issue at stake was less the well-known anti-Zionism of the communal grandees than the manner in which their broadside had been delivered, without reference to ordinary members of the board. Alexander's presidency was denounced as secretive and autocratic. On 17 June the letter was condemned in a vote of censure by fifty-six votes to fifty-one, and Alexander was forced to resign. His departure did not mean that Zionist ascendancy of the board had been achieved. It did mean that the time for constitutional reform was at hand. The representative base of the Board of Deputies was broadened in 1919.

Although he joined the anti-Zionist League of British Jews formed in the aftermath of the declaration, Alexander's resignation in 1917 effectively marked the end of his political career. He died on 29 April 1922, aged seventy-nine, at his home, 50 Harrington Gardens, South Kensington, London, and was buried next to his wife at Willesden Jewish cemetery on 2 May.   SHARMAN KADISH

Sources *The Times* (3 May 1922) · *The Times* (22 June 1922) · *Jewish Chronicle* (6 June 1913) · *Jewish Chronicle* (5 May 1922) · *Jewish Encyclopedia* (1904) · *Jewish Year Book* · A. Hyamson, *History of the Ancient Synagogue of Spanish and Portuguese Jews* (1901), 172–5 · C. Roth, ed., *Encyclopaedia Judaica*, 16 vols. (Jerusalem, 1971–2) · D. Abrahams, 'Jew brokers of the City of London', *Miscellanies of the Jewish Historical Society of England*, 3 (1937), 80–94 · G. Alderman, *Modern British Jewry* (1992) · S. A. Cohen, *English Zionists and British Jews: the communal politics of Anglo-Jewry, 1895–1920* (1982) · S. Kadish, *Bolsheviks and British Jews* (1992) · CGPLA Eng. & Wales (1922) · b. cert. · d. cert. · d. cert. [Hester Alexander] · burial records, Willesden Jewish cemetery

Likenesses portrait, 1907; commissioned by the Board of Deputies of British Jews · photograph

Wealth at death £52,472 4s. 3d.: probate, 16 June 1922, CGPLA Eng. & Wales

Alexander, Frederick Matthias (1869–1955), originator of the Alexander technique and teacher, was born on 20

Frederick Matthias Alexander (1869–1955), by Anthony Ludovici, 1926

January 1869 at Wynyard, north-west Tasmania, the eldest of seven children of John Alexander (1843–1936), farmer and blacksmith, and his wife, Betsy Brown (d. 1923), a nurse.

Born prematurely at seven months, young Alexander was prevented by physical delicacy from full participation in all the pioneering activities of his family but he shared their enthusiasm for riding, shooting, fishing, and hunting, and especially their love of horses. School attendance was restricted but he had a sharp questioning mind, readily mastering basic skills and acquiring a thorough knowledge and love of Shakespeare and the Bible. This limited background did not preclude his recognition of certain principles, with regard to the working of the human organism, previously unconsidered. These principles concern the control of habits of thought and action, and particularly the critical significance of head carriage in the balanced working of the human postural mechanisms which are fundamental to efficient overall functioning. Alexander's later work attracted the favourable attention of the eminent neuro-physiologist Sir Charles Sherrington, while the American educationist John Dewey and the anatomist George Ellett Coghill spoke of their high regard for the practical value and scientific basis of his technique.

As a young man Alexander aspired to a career as an actor. His early work showed promise but recurrent hoarseness and loss of voice frustrated his ambition. He undertook a painstaking course of self-observation and experiment to discover what he was doing wrong. The outcome was the evolution of a practical technique that he successfully applied to himself and which he then began demonstrating to amateur performers who were impressed by the quality of his respiratory and vocal performance. His reputation led to the local press referring to him as 'the breathing man'.

Among Alexander's early pupils were medical men who benefited not only themselves, but were quick to see the possibility of benefit for their patients who suffered from such respiratory conditions as bronchitis and asthma. Most influential in Alexander's career were his own doctor, Dr Charles Bage, and the surgeon W. J. Steward McKay (1866–1948), who became a close friend and encouraged him to take his technique to a wider audience in London.

It was from this beginning that Alexander's work expanded. People came to him from all walks of life and all backgrounds, but it was the medical men who had enjoyed personal experience of his teaching who supported and encouraged him to publicize his work. He went to London in 1904 and was soon teaching some of the leading personalities in the theatrical and medical professions. In his first book, *Man's Supreme Inheritance* (1910), Alexander proposed that man's future success depends on his ability to evolve greater consciousness in the employment of motivating factors that determine his manner of personal use. On 10 August 1914 he married the Australian actress Edith Mary Parsons Young, *née* Page (1865–1938); they adopted Edith's niece, Peggy Piddock (1917–2001). Alexander also had a son, John Graham Vicary (*b.* 1931), by Gladys Edith (Jack) Vicary, *née* Johnson, his wife's niece by marriage.

Alexander regularly visited America (especially Boston and New York), and it was there that the distinguished philosopher and educationist Professor John Dewey became his pupil and friend. *Constructive Conscious Control of the Individual* (1924) contains the most complete exposition of Alexander's method. *The Use of the Self* (1931) followed and it includes a description of how Alexander came by his discoveries.

Alexander's Little School for children aged three to sixteen was opened in 1924, and in 1931 he established a training course for young men and women to become teachers of his method. In London his technique continued to attract more pupils including Aldous Huxley who modelled a central character (Dr Miller) in his novel *Eyeless in Gaza* (1936) on Alexander. In May 1937 a letter in the *BMJ*, signed by nineteen medical men, urged that 'the new field of knowledge and experience which has been opened up through Alexander's work' be included in the curriculum for medical students (*BMJ*, 1.1137). In 1940 Alexander evacuated the school, first to Canada and then to Stowe, Massachusetts. He returned to London in the summer of 1943 having published his fourth book, *The Universal Constant in Living* (1941).

Shortly before the Second World War, Alexander's work spread to South Africa, where it interested prominent people. In March 1944 a scurrilous attack on Alexander and many of his distinguished pupils and friends—including the earl of Lytton and Stafford Cripps, then British chancellor of the exchequer—was published in the official journal *Volksragte* (Manpower). Alexander successfully sued for libel in a case which attracted wide public interest. The South African government's defence was conducted by the attorney-general. It so happened that expert witnesses for the defendants lacked any practical knowledge of Alexander's technique, whereas those for Alexander could testify to the personal benefits that they had received from it.

In appearance FM (as Alexander was known to students and friends) was of medium height (1.7 metres) and build, light and deft in movement with a sharp, observant eye; in dress he was elegant and conventional, always with well-polished shoes. His cultured voice had no trace of regional accent. He was capable of great fun and humour with a gift for mimicry and impersonation and had a winning way with children. Above all, he was observant of everything around him and he certainly practised his own technique. He was genuinely modest about his achievements and contended that anyone could do what he did if they took the trouble. He asserted that anyone who could show him where he was wrong was his friend for life.

Alexander continued to teach and train his student teachers in London well into his eighty-seventh year. He died of heart failure on 10 October 1955 at 13A Morpeth Mansions, Westminster, London, following a respiratory infection; he was cremated at South London crematorium. The Alexander technique has continued to flourish, especially in the theatrical world.

MALCOLM WILLIAMSON

Sources F. M. Alexander, 'Autobiographical sketch', *F. Matthias Alexander articles and letters*, ed. J. M. O. Fischer (1995), 221–49 [*c*.1950] · private information (2004) [Walter Carrington; Marjory Barlow] · CGPLA Eng. & Wales (1956) · letter, *BMJ* (29 May 1937), 1137 · J. A. Evans, *Frederick Matthias Alexander: a family history* (2001)
Archives priv. coll., MSS · Tisch Library, Medford, Massachusetts, F. Matthias Alexander and Frank Pierce Jones archival collection | priv. coll., Constructive Teaching Centre archive collection · Society of Teachers of the Alexander Technique archive collection, London | FILM BFI NFTVA, documentary footage
Likenesses A. Ludovici, drawing, 1926, priv. coll. [*see illus.*] · photographs, News Int. RO, *The Times* photograph collection · photographs, Society of Teachers of the Alexander Technique, London · photographs, Constructive Teaching Centre Archives, London
Wealth at death £21,426 10s. 8d.: probate, 5 April 1956, CGPLA Eng. & Wales

Alexander, Sir George [*real name* George Alexander Gibb Samson] (**1858–1918**), actor and theatre manager, was born on 19 June 1858 at 1 Russell Villas, Russell Street, Reading, the only son of two children of William Murray Samson, a Scottish commercial traveller, and his wife, Mary Ann Hine, *née* Longman. He was educated at private schools in Clifton, near Bristol, and at Ealing in London, but mostly at Stirling high school, which he left when he was fifteen. His intensely anti-theatrical father wanted him to succeed him in commerce, while George himself toyed briefly with a career in medicine. Instead, he was apprenticed as a clerk to the London drapery firm of Leaf

Sir George Alexander (1858–1918), by Ellis & Walery

& Co. However, this did not dampen his ardour for the theatre and he was soon acting in amateur theatricals. In 1874 and again in 1876 he participated in a benefit performance for the Royal Hospital for Consumption given at the St James's Theatre. He also appeared as Henri de Neuville in *Plot and Passion* at the Cabinet Theatre, King's Cross, in 1875. These and other early theatrical forays were watched over with avuncular concern by his former Scottish dominie at Stirling, Duncan MacDougall, with whom George Samson corresponded regularly.

Professional actor Having abandoned the conventionality of trade in 1879, joined Ada Swanborough and W. H. Vernon's repertory company at the Theatre Royal, Nottingham, and dropped his last two names as being too biblical for the stage, plain George Alexander made his professional début on 7 September 1879 as Charles in W. B. Bernard's *His Last Legs* and Harry Prendergast in Sydney Grundy's *The Snowball*. A few more roles in Nottingham resulted in an engagement for 1879–80 with the T. W. Robertson provincial touring company and juvenile leads in Robertson's *Caste*, *Ours*, *School*, *Home*, *Society*, and *MP*. Alexander's London début followed on 4 April 1881 at the Standard, Shoreditch, where he was Freddy Butterscotch in Robert Reece's *The Guv'nor*. Henry Irving must have discerned some potential in this early, mundane career because he hired Alexander for the Lyceum, over, it must

be said, the fledgeling actor's own objections: Alexander thought he would benefit from further experience in the provinces before attempting the West End stage. Irving's perception proved to be acute, since Alexander's performance as Caleb Deecie in the revival of James Albery's *The Two Roses* (26 December 1881) was an immediate success. Irving was probably drawn by his handsome features, sense of humour, and manliness, since he also cast Alexander as Paris in *Romeo and Juliet* (8 March 1882).

Alexander's experience broadened as he bounced among several engagements. First he was at the Court Theatre, followed by provincial tours and Shakespearian roles (Orlando, Romeo, and Benedick) with Ellen Lancaster Wallis. A brief stint at the Adelphi in 1883 led to appearances with Kendal and Hare at the St James's, where one of his roles was Octave in *The Ironmaster* (1884) by Pinero, later a collaborator and friend.

Irving then rehired Alexander to play De Mauprat in Bulwer-Lytton's *Richelieu* (19 July 1884), and Alexander remained with Irving for the next six years, receiving invaluable training from the acknowledged master of the profession. However, Alexander found Irving's methods with his company extremely arduous and verging on the tyrannical: five or six hours of rehearsing with Irving often left him on the brink of tears. He vowed he would be much kinder to his own company when he ventured into management. Alexander accompanied Irving on two American tours, in 1884–5 and 1887–8, on one occasion deputizing for Irving when he fell ill in Boston. He scored a particular success on 9 January 1886 when he took over the title role (which he had coveted initially) in W. G. Wills's *Faust* from the ailing H. B. Conway, and played it for 384 performances. His other roles (such as Shakespeare's Orsino, Laertes, and Macduff) did not garner any accolades, although his salary increased gradually.

Early managerial enterprises Doubtless chafing under Irving's regime, and entertaining his own managerial aspirations, Alexander secured the rights to Hamilton Aïdé's *Dr Bill*, while marking time in *London Day by Day* (14 September 1889) at the Adelphi for the Gatti brothers. Soon afterwards he leased the Avenue Theatre and launched into management with *Dr Bill*, which opened on 1 February 1890. Once the Gattis finally released him, Alexander assumed the title role in *Dr Bill* and so joined the ranks of London's actor–managers. His other productions at the Avenue were *The Grandsire* (21 May 1890), *The Struggle for Life* (25 September 1890), and *Sunlight and Shadow* (7 November 1890). The results were mixed, and at one point he had to cope with a business manager who absconded with the box-office takings. Undeterred, however, in November 1890 Alexander signed the lease of the St James's Theatre, which began the most significant phase of his career and that theatre's history. He was to remain there until his death in 1918.

Alexander's methods At this juncture Alexander had only eleven years' professional experience; nevertheless, his managerial policy, production methods, and overall philosophy were already determined. He wanted the best acting, which he achieved by carefully casting performers of high ability; significantly Alexander did not reserve choice roles or the spotlight for himself as did other actor–managers. Stage management had to be thoughtful and natural, and backed by appropriate scenery. Another objective was the encouragement of British dramatists, and of eighty-one productions at the St James's only eight were devoted to foreign writers. Alexander practised careful financial management (perhaps a reflection of his Scottish heritage), but he paid both good salaries and royalties for the finest results. From one perspective, Alexander presented a range of plays: comedy, drama, modern romances, farce, costume drama, tragedy, history plays, the occasional play about provincial life, all found a place on the St James's stage. Nevertheless, his major concern was to present plays which would attract and retain a fashionable society audience, or playgoers interested in the doings of the smart and fashionable. Hesketh Pearson characterized aptly Alexander's productions:

> In a typical St James's play the humorous characters were delightfully playful, the serious characters charmingly sentimental, and the plot savoured of scandal without being objectionably truthful. Adultery was invariably touched on and inevitably touched up; theft was made thrilling and murder romantic.   (Pearson, 23)

In these endeavours Alexander was abetted by his able wife, Florence Jane Théleur (1857/8–1946), the daughter of Edward Théleur, whom he had married on 8 August 1882. She acted as his fashion and artistic director, as well as general adviser. She would scout for potential performers, and helped to manage Alexander's affairs, while maintaining a deceptively charming façade. In fact, she possessed a strong personality and was a firm friend.

Alexander's other methods were similarly focused on success. He consulted with dramatists, often working on their scripts with them, Pinero and R. C. Carton being noteworthy exceptions to this practice. Prior to rehearsal Alexander established the necessary blocking, envisioning exactly what he wanted. Rehearsals began promptly and lasted only three hours (from eleven to two o'clock) since Alexander believed longer rehearsals were unprofitable: his painful memories of Irving lingered on. This also reflected his concern for the welfare of the members of his company, with many of whom he worked repeatedly, for his was virtually a stock company. And, always, he saw himself as but one piece in the theatrical jigsaw puzzle, never the star.

The St James's Theatre Alexander opened his St James's management on 31 January 1891 by transferring *Sunlight and Shadow*, followed by several other offerings. His first major achievement came with Oscar Wilde's *Lady Windermere's Fan* (20 February 1892). Their association was somewhat surprising given Wilde's flamboyancy and Alexander's own intrinsic modesty and fastidiousness. But Alexander could draw on all his diplomatic skills when working with such acerbic, egotistical people. He cajoled Wilde with practical advice for improving the piece, some of which Wilde ignored, until first-night critics justified Alexander's judgement. In the end Wilde

enjoyed success and controversy, and went home £7000 richer.

Equally brilliant was Wilde's *The Importance of being Earnest* which Alexander produced on 4 February 1895, and which incidentally demonstrated that Alexander, as John Worthing, could act in farcical comedy. Again Alexander advised Wilde about the text itself: for example, he convinced Wilde to compress acts two and three into a single one. Unfortunately, the success was shortlived: Wilde's trial and conviction on charges of homosexual behaviour brought unwonted attention to the St James's. Alexander tried to keep the production going by removing Wilde's name from the production, but the ruse failed and Alexander had to withdraw the play. The incident caused a breach between the two men for several years, although Alexander later paid Wilde small monthly sums, and bequeathed his rights in Wilde's plays to the latter's son, Vyvian Holland. *Earnest* was successful eventually in 1909, when Alexander revived it and reprised Jack Worthing for 316 performances. Interestingly, in November 1895, Alexander himself skirted the law and social obloquy when he was arrested for soliciting a prostitute. He maintained stoutly he had merely given half a crown to an importunate beggar woman: a reluctant magistrate gave Alexander the benefit of the doubt.

More compatible in temperament, style, and method was Alexander's association with A. W. *Pinero. Their first play together was *The Second Mrs Tanqueray* (27 May 1893), considered at the time a daring treatment of the 'woman with a past', although it did not really exceed the social purview of its audience. The play was significant in establishing the career of the temperamental and caustic Mrs Patrick Campbell (scouted by Mrs Alexander), who was cast as Paula Tanqueray. Alexander played opposite her as her insincere, spineless husband. While the carefully mounted production proved highly successful, Mrs Campbell irritated and annoyed Alexander: she found him distant and too dignified; Alexander thought her insufficiently decorous. They performed together again only rarely.

Pinero's second St James's piece, *The Princess and the Butterfly* (29 March 1897), was less successful: it achieved a respectable run, but was expensive to produce. Alexander appeared in one of his typical *raisonneur* roles, Sir George Lamorant. The production also caused a rift between the two men, largely because Pinero insisted on autocratic rights as a playwright–director. When they eventually became reconciled, the result was *His House in Order* (1 February 1906), for which Alexander gave Pinero the free directorial hand he required. Its 427 performances provided Alexander with a resounding artistic and financial hit. Interestingly, Alexander, ever closely followed in such matters, set a new men's fashion by wearing a soft-collared shirt with a lounge suit as he played Hilary Jesson. Later collaborations with Pinero were *The Thunderbolt* (9 May 1908) and *Mid-Channel* (2 September 1909), both deserving better receptions, the delightful one-act *Playgoers* (31 March 1913), and the somewhat uninspired *The Big Drum* (1 September 1915).

Alexander's association with H. A. Jones produced similarly mixed results. *The Masqueraders* (28 April 1894) was successful (the cast included Mrs Campbell, capitalizing on her feat as Paula Tanqueray), while *The Triumph of the Philistines* (11 May 1895) flopped. More sensationally disastrous was *Guy Domville* (5 January 1895), Henry James's attempt to break into the potentially lucrative theatrical market. While well staged with a good cast, the play itself (despite praise from sympathetic critics) lacked congruity, and when Alexander mistakenly led James forward in response to first-night cries for the author, James was soundly booed off the stage by a segment of the audience. He never wrote another play.

However, Alexander was undeterred by such set-backs, and pressed ahead with other interests. He encouraged Stephen Phillips, whose work was rather in vogue, to write a poetic tragedy. The result was *Paolo and Francesca* (6 March 1902), which was received enthusiastically and, incidentally, launched Henry Ainley's career as a Shakespearian and romantic actor, while Alexander himself was a hit as Giovanni Malatesta. The piece ran for 134 performances. However, Alexander's interest in poetic drama was not extensive: he produced only two Shakespearian plays, *As You Like It* (2 December 1896) and *Much Ado about Nothing* (16 February 1898), both successful productions.

Later career, death, and reputation Alexander was at his best on stage in such costume romances as Edward Rose's dramatization of Anthony Hope's novel *The Prisoner of Zenda* (7 January 1896). For 255 performances Alexander was splendid in the dual roles of Rudolf and Rassendyll, roles matched perfectly with his persona as the ultimate matinée idol, projecting immaculate refinement. Audience, play, and actor were similarly suited with J. O. Hobbes's *The Ambassador* (2 June 1898), with Alexander in the title role. However, there were also notable failures, particularly the £6000 loss Alexander incurred with Jethro Bethell's musical version of *Turandot* (18 January 1913), given a lavish production. Altogether twenty-seven of his productions actually resulted in losses; nevertheless, he left an estate of more than £90,000 at his death.

Alexander gave other notable performances. On 16 September 1895 he appeared in a royal command performance of Carton's *Liberty Hall* at Balmoral and received a silver cigar box from Queen Victoria. For the royal command performance for Edward VII on 4 December 1908 Alexander was Edward Thursfield in Alfred Sutro's *The Builder of Bridges*, while on 17 May 1911 he played Alfred Evelyn in Bulwer-Lytton's *Money* in a royal command performance for the German emperor given at Drury Lane. Also at Drury Lane, Alexander played, at the playwright's request, in Hall Caine's *The Prodigal Son* (1905), for which he received £250 weekly.

Outside the theatre, Alexander found other outlets for his organizational abilities. From March 1907 he represented the South St Pancras division on the London county council for six years, and served diligently on several committees. But for ill health, he might have run for parliament. There was also committee work for the Actors' Benevolent Fund, the Royal General Theatrical Fund, and

the Coronation Gala Performance in 1911 (given at His Majesty's), while he was also vice-president of the Actors' Association and president of the Actresses' Franchise League. Only his considerable diplomacy as chairman of the organizing committee for the Shakespearian tercentenary celebration at Drury Lane in 1916 kept the whole affair together. Characteristically he put forward F. R. Benson's name for the knighthood he received on that occasion. Alexander's own knighthood in 1911 had proved a popular award and eminently appropriate for such a dignified leader of the theatre. An honorary LLD from the University of Bristol followed in 1912.

When the First World War broke out, Alexander's health was already in decline. However, he continued his work at the St James's and also toiled unflaggingly for several charities, notably the Red Cross Society, the League of Mercy, and the order of St John of Jerusalem, organizing fund-raising matinées, fêtes, and garden parties. His health failed finally on 16 March 1918, when he died of consumption and diabetes at his country home, Little Court, Chorley Wood, Hertfordshire. He was buried there four days later, mourned by such friends as Pinero, Ellen Terry, Irene Vanbrugh, Lillian Braithwaite, and C. Aubrey Smith. The staff of the St James's carried his coffin. A much larger, society-studded congregation attended his memorial service in London on 22 March 1918.

Alexander was no revolutionary, although a handful of his productions had a contemporary, albeit passing daring aura. However, he applied high standards to every aspect of his art and profession, and he insisted on dignity, refinement, and respectability. He nurtured his performers and encouraged native playwrights, although always with a careful business eye. In short, he knew what a St James's audience wanted and satisfied that demand thoroughly.

J. P. Wearing

Sources A. E. W. Mason, *Sir George Alexander and the St James' Theatre* (1935) · B. Duncan, *The St James's Theatre: its strange and complete history, 1835–1957* (1964) · *Who was who in the theatre, 1912–1976*, 1 (1978) · *The Times* (16 March 1918) · H. Pearson, 'Sir George Alexander', *The last actor-managers* (1950), 23–32 · F. Donaldson, 'Sir George Alexander', *The actor–managers* (1970), 108–22 · G. Rowell, 'The role of the reasoner (Charles Wyndham and George Alexander)', *The rise and fall of the matinee idol: past deities of stage and screen, their roles, their magic, and their worshippers*, ed. A. Curtis (1974), 20–30 · W. Macqueen-Pope, *St James's: theatre of distinction* (1958) · W. Archer, 'Conversation X with Mr George Alexander', *Real conversations* (1904), 197–215 · 'Mr George Alexander at home', *The Era* (3 June 1893), 9 · R. Weiss, 'Alexander, Sir George', *Actors, directors, and designers*, ed. D. Pickering (1996), vol. 3 of *International dictionary of theatre*, ed. M. Hawkins-Dady, 10–13 · b. cert. · m. cert. · d. cert.

Archives Theatre Museum, London, corresp. | BL, corresp. with George Bernard Shaw, Add. MS 50528 · University of Rochester Library, New York | FILM BFI NFTVA

Likenesses Falk, photograph, c.1885, NPG · W. H. Margetson, oils, 1885, Theatre Museum, London · Ellis & Walery, photograph, 1900 (in *Rupert of Hentzau*), NPG · H. Furniss, pen-and-ink caricature, 1905, NPG; repro. in *The Garrick Club* · B. Partridge, watercolour caricature, 1909, NPG · C. Buchel, lithograph, 1917, NPG · M. Beerbohm, caricature, V&A · R. Brough, portrait, Garr. Club · Dover Street Studios, postcard, NPG · Ellis & Walery, photograph, NPG [*see illus.*] · L. Fildes, portrait, Green Room Club · Max [M. Beerbohm], caricature, Hentschel-colourtype, NPG; repro. in *VF* (20 Jan 1909) · photograph, repro. in A. Curtis, ed., *The rise and fall of the* matinee idol (1974), 20–30 • photographs, NPG • print, NPG • ten photographs, repro. in Macqueen-Pope, *St James's: theatre of distinction* • ten photographs, repro. in *The last actor-managers* • thirteen photographs, repro. in Mason, *Sir George Alexander and the St James' Theatre* • three photographs, repro. in Duncan, *St James's Theatre* • three photographs, repro. in Donaldson, 'Sir George Alexander'

Wealth at death £90,672 10s. 3d.: probate, 4 June 1918, CGPLA Eng. & Wales

Alexander, George William (1802–1890), banker and philanthropist, was born on 25 April 1802 in Bunhill Row, London, the first of nine children, eight of whom survived to maturity, of William Alexander (1769–1819), bill broker, and his wife, Ann *Alexander, née Barber (1774/5–1861), of Eckington, east Derbyshire. At the age of four he was sent away to a boys' school in Rochester kept by his uncle, William Rickman, who maintained discipline by the use of the birch. Leaving school shortly before he was fourteen, he joined his father's firm of Alexander & Co. in Lombard Street in the City of London. He worked half-days until he was fourteen and a half, and then became a regular full-time clerk. Part of his daily round was to take down the shutters and to sweep out the offices.

It was not a propitious time. Trading conditions were generally difficult in the aftermath of war with Napoleon and many firms failed. Then in 1819 William Alexander died and it was decided to carry on the business in the name of his widow. Ann was aided and advised by a former colleague of William's and by her eldest son, who was already showing promise of being a successful bill broker. From the age of seventeen until he was almost twenty-one he worked without a day's holiday, with the consequence that he suffered a severe breakdown for a time. On coming of age he was made a partner, and became head of the firm when his mother Ann retired in 1838.

Like many other bill brokers and bankers in the early years of the nineteenth century, the Alexanders were Quakers, and George William followed the example of the great Quaker entrepreneurs in taking over an existing, modest-sized family business and transforming it into a much larger enterprise. Bill brokers originally acted purely as agents, buying and selling bills of exchange on commission. Gradually, in the wake of the financial crisis of 1825, changed circumstances led Alexanders and other of the more significant houses to begin to trade as principals, buying bills for their own portfolio and financing them with balances left by bankers 'at call'. In 1831 the firm obtained the right to discount bills for cash at the Bank of England and so could guarantee to repay loans taken. Thereafter progress was rapid and by 1847 the firm was sufficiently well known to be referred to in W. M. Thackeray's novel *Vanity Fair*, in which John Sedley asserts that 'Alexander would cash my bill, down sir, down on the counter, sir' (Thackeray, *Vanity Fair*, 373).

Under George William's direction Alexanders acquired a reputation for being prudently managed, and this undoubtedly helped him to bring the firm through the periodic financial crises that caused so many others to fail—not least because official and other help was encouraged in time of need. In the crisis of 1866, their giant rival, Overend, Gurney & Co., was refused accommodation by the Bank of England on the grounds that its business was unsound, and the company consequently collapsed. By taking advantage of the opportunities thus presented, Alexanders was able to establish itself as the leading private firm in the market. When the rise of the joint-stock discount companies posed a threat to the existence of the private firms, George William responded by amalgamating Alexanders for a period (1864–77) with Cunliffes & Co. Subsequently Alexanders came to rank alongside the National and the Union discount companies as one of the three leading discount houses.

George William followed Quaker tradition in his support for one of the great Victorian philanthropic movements, being for nearly forty years the 'indefatigable' treasurer of the British and Foreign Anti-Slavery Society (Isichei, 184). Not content with the routine obligation to be included in a published list of subscribers, he opened his home—'An abode of spotless order and of industry and hospitality' (Dixon, 4)—to a succession of runaway slaves and political refugees. He opposed moves towards free trade that would allow the import of cheap slave-grown sugar and in 1842 published his *Letters on the Slave Trade, Slavery and Emancipation*. In 1849–50 he toured the West Indies to investigate conditions at first hand. He also had charitable interests closer to home and in 1848 was one of the founders of Victoria Park Hospital, London.

Alexander was married twice, first in 1835 to Sarah Cleverly Horsnaill (1801–1843), with whom he had two sons and two daughters, and second in 1845 to Catherine Horsnaill (1806–1878), possibly his first wife's cousin; they had a daughter. Both sons became partners in the firm. He lived first at The Willows, Stoke Newington, Middlesex, and then, from 1853, at Reigate, Surrey. He retired from business in 1883. Alexander died at his home, Woodhatch, Reigate, on 24 November 1890.

The firm that Alexander inherited and transformed was the only private discount house to convert successfully to a limited company before 1914: it became a public company in 1911, operating as Alexanders Discount Co. Ltd. It was still trading in 1995, as Alexanders Discount plc, the longest-surviving discount house.

GORDON FLETCHER

Sources K. F. Dixon, *The story of Alexanders Discount Company Ltd, 1810–1960* • M. F. Lloyd Prichard, 'The Alexander family's discount company', *Journal of the Friends' Historical Society*, 49 (1960), 157–64 • *Alexander, George William, (1802–1890)*, Friends House Library • J. Smith, ed., *A descriptive catalogue of Friends' books*, 1 (1867), 9–10 • E. Isichei, *Victorian Quakers* (1970) • P. H. Emden, *Quakers in commerce: a record of business achievement* (1939) • W. T. C. King, *History of the London discount market* (1936) • D. H. Pratt, *English Quakers and the industrial revolution* (1985), chap. 5 • G. W. Alexander, *Letters on the slave trade, slavery and emancipation* (1842) • W. M. Thackeray, *Vanity Fair: a novel without a hero*, ed. G. Tillotson and K. Tillotson (1963)

Archives Alexanders Discount plc, London | Bodl. RH, corresp. as treasurer of the British and Foreign Anti-Slavery Society • Wellcome L., letters to John Hodgkin

Likenesses B. Haydon, portrait (*A meeting of the Anti-Slavery Society, 1840*), NPG

Wealth at death £227,610 10s. 10d.: probate, 24 Dec 1890, CGPLA Eng. & Wales

Alexander, Harold Rupert Leofric George, first Earl Alexander of Tunis (1891–1969), army officer, was born in London on 10 December 1891, the third son of James Alexander, fourth earl of Caledon (1846–1898) and his wife, Lady Elizabeth Graham-Toler (*d.* 1939), daughter of the third earl of Norbury. Alexander's youth was spent at the family estate, Caledon Castle, in co. Tyrone. His father, who had served briefly in the Life Guards but was better known as an adventurous deep-water yachtsman, died when Alexander was six; his mother, eccentric and imperious, held aloof from her children; but their four sons were perfectly happy in one another's company. It was in northern Ireland that Alexander developed both the athletic and the aesthetic sides of his character; he trained himself as a runner and enjoyed all the usual country sports, but he also taught himself to carve in wood and stone and began one of the main passions of his life: painting. After reading Sir Joshua Reynolds's *Discourses on Art* he decided that what he wanted most in the world was to be president of the Royal Academy. At Harrow School he worked well enough to rise smoothly. His games were cricket, athletics, rackets, rugby, boxing, fencing, and gymnastics and he won distinction at all of them; he is best remembered as nearly saving the game for Harrow in what *Wisden* called the most extraordinary cricket match ever played, at Lord's in 1910. He also won a school prize for drawing.

War and pacification Alexander went on to the Royal Military College, Sandhurst, and was commissioned in the Irish Guards in 1911. Although pleased at the idea of spending a few years in a guards battalion, he intended to retire before long and make a living as an artist. These plans were upset by the outbreak of war in 1914. Alexander's battalion went to France in August and he served there continuously until early 1919, being in action throughout except when recovering from wounds or on courses. He was twice wounded, awarded the MC (1915), and appointed to the DSO (1916). Promotion was rapid. A lieutenant when he arrived, he became a captain in February 1915; eight months later one of the youngest majors in the army, with the acting command of the 1st battalion of his own regiment; and in October 1917 a lieutenant-colonel, commanding the 2nd battalion. During the retreat from Arras in March 1918 he was acting brigadier-general in command of the 4th guards brigade.

The war was a turning point in Alexander's character and career. He had painted in the trenches, and he continued to paint throughout his life, reaching at times a standard only just short of the professional; but during the war he had come to realize the fascination of the profession of arms, and proved to himself and others that he was outstandingly competent at it. His reputation stood very high for courage but also for being cheerfully imperturbable in all circumstances. For four years he lived the life of a regimental officer, without any staff service; he later criticized senior commanders of that war for never seeking to share the conditions of the fighting troops.

Not wishing to go back to barracks or to the army of

Harold Rupert Leofric George Alexander, first Earl Alexander of Tunis (1891–1969), by Sir Oswald Birley, 1946

occupation in Germany, Alexander applied in 1919 for an appointment to one of the many military missions in eastern Europe. He was first posted as a member of the allied relief commission in Poland under Stephen Tallents and later went with Tallents to Latvia, which was in danger of falling either to Russia or to Germany. The allies had no troops in the Baltic and only a small naval detachment under Sir Walter Cowan. Tallents placed the *Landwehr*, composed of Baltic Germans, under Alexander's command. At the age of twenty-seven he found himself at the head of a brigade-sized formation with mainly German officers. He was good at languages and had taught himself German and Russian; his authority derived from his charm and sincerity and his obvious professionalism. He kept his men steady and resistant to the attractions of the German expeditionary force under von der Goltz and led them to victory in the campaign which drove the Red Army from Latvia.

Alexander retained all his life a keen interest in Russia. During the First World War he designed a new uniform cap for himself with a high visor and flat peak, on the model of one he had seen a Russian officer wearing. He always wore the order of St Anne with swords which Yudenich awarded him in 1919; when he met Rokossovsky in 1945 the Russian general muttered to him in an aside that he had once had it too. In the Second World War, like Churchill, he admired Stalin and was enthusiastic about the Soviet army.

After the Soviet Union recognized Latvia's independence in 1920 Alexander returned to England to become second in command of his regiment. In 1922 he was given command and took it to Constantinople as part of the army of occupation. In 1923, after the treaty of Lausanne, the regiment went to Gibraltar and in 1924 it returned to England. In 1926–7 he was at the Staff College, Camberley. He was very senior in rank, a full colonel, but for the duration of the course he was temporarily reduced to the rank of major. After commanding the regiment and regimental district of the Irish Guards (1928–30), he attended the imperial defence college. This was followed by the only two staff appointments in his career: GSO 2 at the War Office (1931–2) and GSO 1 at northern command (1932–4). He was already widely regarded as likely to make the outstanding fighting commander of a future war; the other name mentioned, from the Indian army, was that of Claude Auchinleck. Alexander married in 1931 Lady Margaret Diana Bingham (d. 1977), younger daughter of the fifth earl of Lucan; she was appointed GBE in 1954. They had two sons, one daughter, and an adopted daughter.

In 1934 Alexander was appointed to command the Nowshera brigade on the north-west frontier, one of the most coveted in India. Auchinleck commanded the next brigade, in Peshawar. Alexander surprised and delighted his Indian troops by learning Urdu as rapidly and fluently as he had Russian and German. Next year he commanded the brigade in the Loc Agra campaign (called after a small village north of the Malakand Pass) against invading tribesmen; and not long after, under Auchinleck's command as the senior brigadier, in the Mohmand campaign. Both operations were successful; roads were built, large regions pacified; Alexander was appointed CSI (1936). It was noted not only that he had mastered the difficult techniques of fighting in mountainous country but also that he was always to be seen with the foremost troops. This reflected both his personal courage and his revulsion from the way his senior commanders had behaved in the First World War; it remained to the end a characteristic of his style of leadership.

Dunkirk and Burma Alexander's promotion to major-general in 1937, at the age of forty-five, made him the youngest general in the British army; in 1938 he received command of the 1st division at Aldershot. In 1939 he took the division to France as one of the two in 1st corps under Sir John Dill. In the retreat to Dunkirk his division only once fought a serious if brief battle, when he successfully defended the Scheldt for two days, throwing back all German penetrations; for the rest of the time he was obliged to fall back with other divisions. It was Dunkirk which first brought his name prominently before the public. 1st corps was to form the final rearguard and Lord Gort superseded the corps commander and put Alexander in command. His orders were definite: to withdraw all the British troops who could be saved. The French commander, Admiral Abrial, favoured different tactics, and Alexander confessed that to carry out his orders while leaving the French still fighting made him feel that he had never been in such a terrible situation. During the three days in which he commanded, 20,000 British and 98,000 French were evacuated: Alexander left on the last motor launch, touring the beaches to see that there were no British troops remaining.

On returning to England, Alexander was confirmed in command of 1st corps, which was responsible for the defence of the east coast from Scarborough to the Wash. Promoted lieutenant-general, he succeeded Auchinleck at southern command in December 1940. He was an admirable trainer of troops, the first to introduce the realistic 'battle-schools' which became so prominent a feature of military life from 1940 to 1944. He was also put in command of a nominal 'Force 110' which was to be used for amphibious operations; he and his staff planned several which never came off, such as the invasion of the Canaries and of Sicily.

In February 1942 Alexander was suddenly informed that he was to take command of the army in Burma, where the situation was already desperate. The key battle had been lost before Alexander arrived; the Japanese were across the Sittang River in a position to encircle and capture Rangoon. The greatest good fortune, together with the oversight of a Japanese divisional commander, left open one narrow escape route, so Alexander and the bulk of his forces escaped from Rangoon which, obeying ill-considered orders from Sir A. P. Wavell, he had tried to hold almost beyond the last reasonable moment. After its fall Burma had no future military value except as a glacis for the defence of India. Alexander decided that the only success he could snatch from unmitigated defeat was to rescue the army under his command by withdrawing it to India. It was a campaign of which he always spoke with compunction and distaste, except for his admiration for General Slim. Left entirely without guidance after the fall of Rangoon—not that the guidance he had received previously had been of any value—Alexander did the best he could. As a further sign of the gifts he was to display as an allied commander, he got on the best of terms not only with Chiang Kai-shek but also with the American General J. W. Stilwell.

It might be thought that two successive defeats would have ended Alexander's hopes of high command. Churchill had shown no mercy to Gort or Wavell, and was to show none to Auchinleck. But as he wrote in *The Hinge of Fate* (1951), in sending Alexander to Burma 'never have I taken the responsibility for sending a general on a more forlorn hope' (Nicolson, 126). So greatly did he appreciate Alexander's ability that he immediately confirmed his designation as commander-in-chief of the First Army, which was to invade north Africa under Eisenhower's command in November 1942, when the allies for the first time seized the strategic initiative. But before that could take effect, Churchill felt impelled in early August to visit Egypt. Auchinleck was more impressive in the field than in conversation in his caravan; Churchill decided to replace him with Alexander. It is ironical that one of the main reasons why Auchinleck was replaced was that he declared himself unable to take the offensive until September: Churchill was to accept from Alexander, with but little remonstrance, a postponement until late October.

Egypt and Tunis Alexander took over as commander-in-chief, Middle East, on 15 August 1942. For the first time he found himself in a position which was not only not desperate but full of promise. He had a numerical superiority, and at last equality of equipment, against an army fighting at the end of a long and precarious line of communication with its bases and debilitated by sickness. General Gott, who was to have been his army commander, was killed; but he was replaced immediately by General Montgomery, who had been one of Alexander's corps commanders in southern command and whose skill in training and inspiring men was well known to him. He had a sound defensive position, strongly manned, and plans had been prepared for the expected enemy assault; they were based on a partial refusal of the left flank while holding the strong position of Alam Halfa, fortified and prepared by Auchinleck to block an advance on Alexandria. Reinforcements in men and tanks continued to arrive. Nevertheless there was a problem of morale, since the Eighth Army had been fighting in retreat since May and had lost one position after another; it was natural for the troops to wonder whether they might not find themselves retreating once more. The first step towards victory in Egypt was when Alexander made it known, as soon as he assumed command, that there was to be no further retreat; the decisive battle was to be fought on the Alamein line.

The defensive battle of Alam Halfa and the offensive battle of El Alamein were, as Alexander always insisted, Montgomery's victories. Alexander was good at delegating, and generously acknowledged the merits of his subordinates. Indeed, after the failure of the first plan at El Alamein, Lightfoot, Alexander may deserve part of the credit for Supercharge, the modified version. In truth the two generals, the commander-in-chief and the army commander, were aptly suited to their respective roles and played them well. The successful campaign in Egypt, won at almost the lowest point in the allied fortunes, marked the beginning of a period in which British and allied armies knew scarcely anything but success.

The invasion of north Africa in November meant that after two months a British army—the First, with a French and an American corps—was fighting in northern and central Tunisia against a mixed German–Italian army. Meanwhile the German–Italian armoured army of Africa, defeated at El Alamein, withdrew towards southern Tunisia pursued by the Eighth Army. A headquarters was required to command and co-ordinate the two allied armies. Alexander was summoned to the Casablanca conference of January 1943. He greatly impressed President Roosevelt, General Marshall, and the American chiefs of staff; his reputation at home had never been higher. The conference decided to appoint him deputy commander-in-chief to General Eisenhower, with command over all the forces actually fighting the enemy. He set up a very small headquarters, called the Eighteenth Army group from the numbers of the two British armies which made up the bulk of his command; this was originally located in the town of Constantine, but Alexander moved out into the field as soon as he could and operated from a mobile tented camp.

The Tunisian campaign proves Alexander's capacity as a strategist. It also demonstrates his great gift of boosting the morale of the troops he commanded, as well as his skill in co-ordinating the efforts of different nationalities. At the beginning he faced a difficult task. The southern flank of his western front had been driven in by a bold enemy thrust which threatened the communications of the whole deployment. Alexander was on the spot, even before the date at which he was officially to assume command (20 February 1943); he was seen directing the siting of gun positions at the approaches to the Kasserine Pass. This was a flash of his old style, but it was not long before he took a firm grip on higher things and reorganized the whole direction of the campaign. He sorted out the confusion into which rapid changes had thrown the First Army, mobilized the ponderous but skilful thrust of the Eighth Army, and directed both in the final victory of Tunis. In this last battle in Africa he employed an elaborate and successful plan of deception, based on an accurate knowledge of enemy dispositions and intentions, and broke through their strong defensive front with a powerful and well-concealed offensive blow. In two days all was over. A quarter of a million enemy were captured. On 13 May he made his historic signal to the prime minister: 'Sir, it is my duty to report that the Tunisian campaign is over. All enemy resistance has ceased. We are masters of the North African shores' (Nicolson, 192).

The Italian front Sicily was the next objective on which the Casablanca conference had decided. The forces commanded by Alexander, as commander-in-chief of Fifteenth Army group, consisted of the American Seventh and British Eighth armies. The principal interest in the campaign lies in the immense size of the amphibious effort required, larger in the assault phase even than for the invasion of Normandy, and in the elaborate planning which preceded it. It fell to Alexander to decide on the final form of the plan, a concentrated assault on the south-eastern corner of the island, rather than, as originally proposed by the planning staff, two separate attacks in the south-east and the north-west. In this decision he was vindicated, mainly because he correctly assessed the new possibilities of beach maintenance produced by recently acquired amphibious equipment. In the first few days, however, he made one of his few strategic errors by yielding to Montgomery's insistence that the Eighth Army could finish off the campaign by itself if the American Seventh Army were kept out of its way; admittedly Alexander was deceived by inaccurate reports of the progress that the Eighth Army was making. As a result the reduction of the island took rather longer than expected and many German defenders managed to withdraw into Calabria. Nevertheless the capture of Sicily in thirty-eight days was a notable strategic gain. It also encouragingly vindicated the methods of amphibious warfare soon to be used in invading France.

That invasion was the principal factor affecting the last two years of Alexander's career as a commander in the field, during which he was engaged on the mainland of Italy. His troops were now no longer the spearhead of the allied military effort in Europe. He was required to give up, for the benefit of the western front, many divisions of his best troops on three occasions and his task was defined as to eliminate Italy from the war and to contain the maximum number of German divisions. The first part of this directive was rapidly achieved. In his second task also, which from September 1943 onwards represented the sole object of the campaign, he was strikingly successful. So far from diverting troops from Italy to the decisive front, the Germans continuously reinforced it, not only robbing the Russian front but even sending divisions from the west. To obtain this success, however, in a terrain always favouring the defence, Alexander was obliged to maintain the offensive and to compensate for the lack of superior force by using all the arts of generalship.

The campaign in Italy was a great holding attack, Alexander stated later in an official dispatch. As is the nature of holding attacks, it was directed against a secondary theatre. Nevertheless it gave scope for daring strategic planning, despite the odds and the forbidding and mountainous nature of the ground. The initial assault at Salerno, simultaneous with the announcement of the Italian surrender, was a good example; a force of only three divisions, all that could be carried in the landing craft allotted to the theatre, was thrown on shore at the extreme limit of air cover. The landing at Anzio was a masterpiece of deception which caught the enemy off balance and forced him to send reinforcements to Italy. It made a vital contribution to the offensive of May and June 1944 in which the Germans were driven north of Rome, with disproportionately heavy losses in men and equipment. For this offensive Alexander secretly redeployed his two armies and mounted a most ingenious plan of deception; his opponent, Field Marshal Kesselring, was unable to react in time, for all that his defensive positions were strong both by nature and artificially. The capture of Rome just before the landing in Normandy boosted allied morale. More importantly for allied grand strategy, this crushing defeat obliged the Germans to reinforce Italy with eight fresh divisions, some taken from their western garrisons; a month later, in contrast, Alexander was ordered to surrender seven of his divisions for the campaign in France. The final battle, in April 1945, again exemplified Alexander's skill in deployment and in deception; by 2 May he had routed the most coherent enemy group of armies still resisting; all Italy had been overrun, and a million Germans had laid down their arms in the first big surrender of the war.

The Italian campaign showed Alexander at the height of his powers. These included, besides the skill of a strategist, a thorough grasp of the principles of administration. As an allied commander he was supreme; there were no instances of friction anywhere in his command in spite of its varied composition, including at one time or another troops from Britain, the United States, India, Canada, New Zealand, South Africa, France, Poland, Italy, Brazil, and Greece. For most of the campaign, as commander-in-chief of Fifteenth Army group (later renamed allied armies in Italy), he acted as an independent commander; it had been agreed that the commander-in-chief, Mediterranean, Sir Maitland Wilson, should concern himself primarily with the general maintenance of the Italian campaign and with the security of the other areas of the command.

Later life   On 12 December 1944 Alexander succeeded Wilson. He was appointed to the rank of field marshal, to date from 4 June 1944, when the allied armies entered Rome. But for all his high rank and heavy responsibilities he remembered his criticism of the commanders in the First World War. He always spent more time with the forward troops than in his headquarters. His popularity was immense, and his strategic planning benefited because he knew what the war was like at the point that counted.

After the war some thought Alexander would become chief of the Imperial General Staff. But W. L. Mackenzie King invited him to be governor-general of Canada, and Churchill pressed him to accept. Alexander's sense of duty was reinforced by a strong attraction to the idea of serving Canada. His extended tenure of office ran from 1946 to 1952. He was the last British governor-general, as popular as any of his predecessors. He was comparatively young and brought a young family with him; he toured the whole country, played games, skied, and painted. To his dignity as the representative of the king of Canada and his reputation as a war leader he added an informal friendliness and charm. While in Canada he produced his official dispatches on his campaigns published in the *London Gazette*; they have been described by his biographer as 'among the great state papers of our military history' (Nicolson, 295).

In January 1952 Churchill visited Ottawa and invited Alexander to be minister of defence in his government. When a friend remonstrated he replied: 'Of course I accepted. It's my duty' (Nicolson, 301). To another friend he said, 'I simply can't refuse Winston' (ibid., 302). As he entered on his first political post in that frame of mind it is not surprising that he did not much enjoy his period of office. He was not temperamentally suited to political life, and in any case had few real powers to exercise. Churchill continued to behave as though it was he who was the minister of defence and Alexander his spokesman in the Lords. Nevertheless, Alexander had the assets of his great personal popularity, his charm, and the fact that he numbered so many personal friends among foreign statesmen and military men—especially in the United States, and especially after the election of President Eisenhower. He made no particular mark as minister of defence because he preferred to rely on discreet persuasion and guidance; but he led a good team and suffered no diminution of his reputation. After two and a half years he resigned at his own request, in autumn 1954.

In the last fifteen years of his life Alexander accepted

several directorates. He was most active as director of Alcan, travelling extensively for the firm. He also served on the boards of Barclay's Bank and Phoenix Assurance. He devoted more and more time to painting. In 1960 the *Sunday Times* persuaded him to allow his memoirs to be ghosted. They were edited by John North and published in 1962, but were not very favourably received because of their curiously disorganized and anecdotal form. He had agreed to publish because he wanted justice done to the armies in Italy; for himself he preferred to be judged on the basis of his dispatches. For the rest, he devoted himself to his garden and to reunions with old comrades. He died suddenly after a heart attack on 16 July 1969, in hospital in Slough. His funeral service was held in St George's Chapel, Windsor, and he was buried in the churchyard of Ridge, near Tyttenhanger, his family's Hertfordshire home. The headstone of his grave bears at the top the single world Alex, the name by which he was known to his friends and his soldiers. He was succeeded by his elder son, Shane William Desmond (*b*. 1935).

Alexander was created a viscount in 1946 and an earl in 1952 on his return from Canada. He was appointed CB (1938), KCB and GCB (1942), GCMG on his appointment to Canada, and in the same year (1946) KG. He was sworn of the privy council in 1952 and also of the Canadian privy council. In 1959 he was admitted to the Order of Merit. He was colonel of the Irish Guards from 1946 to his death, constable of the Tower of London from 1960 to 1965. From 1957 to 1965 he was lieutenant of the county of London, and for a further year of Greater London. He was chancellor and then grand master of the Order of St Michael and St George, an elder brother of Trinity House, and in 1955 president of the MCC. He was a freeman of the City of London and of many other cities. His numerous foreign decorations included the grand cross of the Légion d'honneur, and the Legion of Merit and Distinguished Service Medal of the United States.

Alexander was 5 feet 10 inches tall, slim, muscular, and handsome. His features were regular in the style which was regarded as typical of the army officer when he was young; he wore a trim guardsman's moustache all his life. He dressed with careful and unaffected elegance on all occasions; his Russian-style cap was only the precursor of several variations on uniform regulations, whereas in plain clothes he favoured neatness, fashion, and the avoidance of the elaborate.   DAVID HUNT, rev.

Sources N. Nicolson, *Alex* (1973) • *LondG* (5 Feb 1948) • *LondG* (12 Feb 1948) • *LondG* (12 June 1950) • personal knowledge (1981) • *CGPLA Eng. & Wales* (1969) • *The Times* (17 June 1969) • I. S. O. Playfair and C. J. C. Molony, *The Mediterranean and Middle East*, 4–5 (1966–73) • Burke, *Peerage* (1980)

Archives NA Canada, accounts of campaigns, corresp., and papers relating to Brazil • PRO, corresp. and papers, WO214 | CAC Cam., corresp. with Edward Seago • King's Lond., Liddell Hart C., corresp. with Lord Alanbrooke • King's Lond., Liddell Hart C., corresp. with Sir B. H. Liddell Hart • Nuffield Oxf., corresp. with Lord Cherwell • PRO, corresp. with Sir Stafford Cripps, CAB127/118 | FILM BFI NFTVA, 'Victory in Africa: the entry of our armies into Tunis', *British News*, 24 May 1943 • BFI NFTVA, 'Lord Alexander leaves for Canada', *British News*, 15 April 1940 • BFI NFTVA, current affairs footage • BFI NFTVA, documentary footage • BFI NFTVA, news footage • IWM FVA, 'Prelude to Africa', Alexander surveying the victory parades at Tunis, 1942–3, MOI, 1943 • IWM FVA, 'London honours Alexander', *World Pictorial News*, footage of Alexander receiving the freedom of the city, 22 April 1946 • IWM FVA, 'Statesman on the move', Welt IM film • IWM FVA, actuality footage • IWM FVA, documentary footage • IWM FVA, news footage • IWM FVA, propaganda film footage (Central Office of Information) | SOUND BL NSA, current affairs recordings • BL NSA, recorded lecture • IWM SA, oral history interview • IWM SA, recorded lecture • IWM SA, recorded talk

Likenesses R. G. Eves, oils, 1940, IWM • R. G. Eves, oils, 1940, IWM • S. Morse-Brown, crayon drawing, 1943, IWM • O. Birley, oils, 1946, Harrow School, Middlesex [*see illus.*] • D. Gilbert, bronze bust, 1946, Harrow School, Middlesex • H. Carr, oils, 1947, IWM; version, Cavalry and Guards Club, London • J. Gilroy, oils, *c*.1957, McGill University, Montreal • O. Nemon, bronze bust, 1973, Old Radcliffe Observatory, Oxford • O. Birley, oils, White's Club, Montreal • M. Codner, oils, NPG • H. Coster, photographs, NPG • D. Gilbert, bust, NPG • J. Gilroy, oils; in possession of the Irish guards • A. Gray, bronze bust, priv. coll. • R. Jack, oils; in possession of the Irish guards • E. Seago, oils, NPG • oil study, NPG

Wealth at death £144,926: probate, 18 Aug 1969, *CGPLA Eng. & Wales*

Alexander [*other married names* Umpherston, Currie], **Helen** (1653/4–1729), covenanter, was born in the parish of Linton, probably in Haddingtonshire. Owing to her mother's early death and her father's remarriage she went to stay with her sister in Dirleton parish, Haddingtonshire. About 1672 she married Charles Umpherston (1646–1681), a tenant in Pentland, Edinburghshire, and moved to Pentland. There she met nonconformist presbyterians and was drawn to hear preachers such as John Welsh, Donald Cargill, and David Williamson, though, as yet, she was not 'thoroughly convinced' of the evil of attending the preaching of the (conformist) curates. After hearing David Williamson preach at a communion in Ormiston, and a visit to her sister, her religious conscience was awakened and she began to embrace covenanting principles, subsequently recording the year 1678 as a time of spiritual conviction and refreshment. It was much to her annoyance that her husband, through fear and ill counsel, submitted to the pressure of the 1678 'highland host', and paid his contribution to them.

Following the covenanters' defeat at the battle of Bothwell Bridge (22 June 1679) Alexander saw it as her 'duty to concern myself with the Lord's people' (Simpson, 350), collecting money and clothes for the prisoners brought to Edinburgh. At a later date she provided shelter and a place of refuge for fugitive nonconformists. The death of her husband in 1681 left her with three small children, and her attendance at a preaching in Pentland brought her before the courts. She was fined £50 Scots in her absence, at a court held by Skeen of Hallyard about 1681 or 1682, having judged it wrong to appear before such a court. Instead she chose to leave her home and belongings and shortly afterwards, fearing apprehension, was forced to leave her three young children.

About 1682 Alexander sheltered Andrew Guillan, one of those present at the murder of Archbishop Sharp in 1679. After Guillan was imprisoned she was apprehended (*c*.1683) by Sir Alexander Gibson, laird of Pentland, who ordered her to attend the established kirk. On her refusal she was taken prisoner and later sent to the Canongate Tolbooth, where she remained for eleven weeks. The official account of her release reports a caution of 3000 merks to appear before the council when called and her denial of any knowledge of Guillan's deed. As such, it is contrary to the traditional family account, where she claimed to have been released 'without the least compliance' (Simpson, 356) and that her reaction to the suggestion that she might be put to death was to send word to her home to have her grave clothes prepared. Her subsequent actions and manner of life also contradict it.

Alexander became acquainted with the prominent preacher James Renwick after his return from the Netherlands in 1683, and her home became a regular place of refuge for him. After the 1687 indulgence, the acceptance of which she opposed, she could not risk being seen around Pentland and stayed with her father in Linton for a period of time. About this time she was engaged in gathering money and clothes for prisoners in Dunnottar Castle. Her second husband, James Currie (*d.* after 1729), was a merchant in Pentland and a more resolute nonconformist than her first husband, being one of those to whom she gave refuge. About 1687 or 1688 some nonconformist writings were deposited in their home to be sold. This was discovered and reported, although they were not apprehended for it. Renwick had conducted their marriage on 30 November 1687, less than three months before his execution (17 February 1688) when Alexander assisted in the preparation of his body for burial. She had two children from her second marriage, as well as the three by her first. Two of her children died young. Late in life she dictated to her second husband an account of her experiences, the resulting manuscript being published in 1856 and providing most of the information about her activities and religious experiences. She died in March 1729, aged seventy-five. Her reputation as a heroic figure of the covenanting period long survived her, particularly in the west of Scotland.   ALISON G. MUIR

Sources R. Simpson, 'Helen Alexander', *Covenanters from the south, or, The church in the wilderness* (1856), 340–65 · R. Simpson, 'Helen Alexander', *A voice from the desert, or, The church in the wilderness*, 2 pts (1856), 340–65 [alternative title] · C. U. Aitchison, ed., *Passages in the lives of Helen Alexander and James Currie of Pentland, and other papers, printed for family use, from original manuscripts and papers in the possession of Francis Umpherston, esq., Elmswood, Loanhead* (1869) · Reg. PCS, 3rd ser., 8.239, 251

Alexander, Horace Gundry (1889–1989), Quaker envoy and mediator, was born on 18 April 1889 at Croydon, Surrey, the youngest of four sons of Joseph Gundry Alexander (1848–1918), a Quaker barrister and advocate of international arbitration, and of Josephine Crosfield Alexander. He was educated at Bootham School in York and at King's College, Cambridge, where he gained first-class honours in history in 1912. After the outbreak of war in 1914 he served as secretary to a succession of anti-war committees. When conscription came in 1916 he was required, as a conscientious objector, to take up school-teaching, working in Warwick and then in Cranbrook, Kent. On 30 July 1918 he married Olive Graham (1892–

Horace Gundry Alexander (1889–1989), by Morland Braithwaite

1942), and the following year joined the staff of Woodbrooke, the Quaker college in Selly Oak, Birmingham, where he remained until 1944, teaching international relations, with a special emphasis on the League of Nations and associated institutions. He was apt to express impatience with what he felt to be the vague pietism of some Quaker peace witness, and based his own teaching firmly on practical activity.

Alexander's father had long worked for the suppression of the opium trade between India and China, and in 1927–8 his son visited India and other parts of south-east Asia on behalf of the Selly Oak college to assess how controls on the trade worked. This visit convinced him of the need for Indian independence, a conviction confirmed by his first meeting with M. K. Gandhi in March 1928. In a later visit supported by the Quakers in 1930 he acted as an intermediary between Gandhi and the viceroy of India, Lord Irwin (later Lord Halifax), helping to make possible Gandhi's participation in the round-table conference in London in 1931. After the conference Alexander, along with Agatha Harrison and Carl Heath, initiated the India Conciliation Group, which aimed to create a better understanding of Indian political aspirations.

Throughout the 1930s Alexander was preoccupied with the threatening situation in Europe. He was secretary of the Anglo-German Society, a group of politicians and journalists who, while keenly aware of Nazi barbarities, sought to change the situation by peaceful means. His efforts at conciliation continued up to and after the outbreak of war in 1939.

For many years Alexander's wife had been disabled by a paralysis confining her to a wheelchair, though she took an active part in the work of the college. In January 1942 she died, and later that year he returned to India with a section of the Friends Ambulance Unit, which undertook air-raid protection work in areas threatened by advancing Japanese forces. This enabled him to renew and extend his acquaintance with public figures in India, the more so since, with the onset of the great Bengal famine, relief work became the most pressing concern, raising urgent questions about the effectiveness of British administration. He was back in Britain in September 1943, advocating a relaxation of the stringent measures which had been the government's response to Gandhi's Quit India campaign.

In 1945 Alexander visited the United States, and was present in San Francisco as an accredited press representative for *The Friend* when the United Nations was established. Following the election of a Labour government in Britain, he and Agatha Harrison operated in the background of Indian pre-independence negotiations to help unofficially at difficult moments. He was much involved in efforts to control the violence between Muslims and Hindus that marred the transfer of power, and was with Gandhi in Calcutta when independence was declared on 15 August 1947. With his Friends Ambulance Unit colleague Richard Symonds he served as an observer monitoring the situation of refugees in the partitioned province of the Punjab, and in subsequent years undertook a number of similar tasks. His personal dignity and immense patience admirably qualified him for such work. After 1951 he was based mainly in England again, and for many years in books and articles interpreted Gandhian ideas, and especially Indian policies in world affairs, to a Western audience. In 1984 his services were rather belatedly recognized with the award of India's Padma Bhushan medal.

Alexander had a lifelong passion for bird-watching. He and his elder brothers Wilfrid and Christopher belonged to the group of pioneers who substituted observation of the living bird for the collection of museum specimens. They are among the founding fathers of bird-watching, now the hobby of thousands. They also set those high standards of field identification, by both ear and eye, which have enabled the amateur bird-watcher to make an important contribution to the science of ornithology. Alexander's own contribution was recognized by the British Ornithologists' Union, whose records committee he chaired from 1957 to 1969. In 1958 he had married his second wife, Rebecca Bradbeer, *née* Biddle (1901–1991), and in 1969 went to live in Pennsylvania, where he died, at a retirement home in Crosslands, on 30 September 1989.

GEOFFREY CARNALL and J. DUNCAN WOOD

Sources H. Alexander, *The Indian ferment* (1929) · H. Alexander, *Gandhi through Western eyes* (1969) · H. Alexander, *Seventy years of birdwatching* (1974) · H. Alexander, autobiography, Woodbrooke College, Selly Oak, Birmingham · private information (2004)
Archives RS Friends, Lond., papers · Woodbrooke Quaker Study Centre, Birmingham | RS Friends, Lond., India Conciliation Group MSS · U. Oxf., Edward Grey Institute of Field Ornithology, ornithological archive | SOUND BL NSA, documentary recordings · IWM SA, 'British civilian alternativist conscientious objector worked as a teacher under home office scheme', IWM, 1974, 376 · IWM SA, oral history interviews
Likenesses M. Braithwaite, photograph, priv. coll. [*see illus.*] · photographs, priv. coll.

Alexander, (Conel) Hugh O'Donel (1909–1974), chess player and cryptanalyst, was born in Cork on 19 April 1909, the eldest of four children of Conel William Long Alexander (1879–1920), professor of engineering at University College, Cork, and his wife, Hilda Barbara Bennett (1881–1964), of Birmingham. On his father's death the family moved to Birmingham, where he attended King Edward's School. After winning the British boys' championship in 1926, he was soon recognized as one of the future hopes of British chess.

In 1928 Alexander went up to King's College, Cambridge, on a mathematics scholarship. By 1931 he was playing on top board for Cambridge, winning eleven games in succession. In 1932 he came second in the British championship. He left Cambridge with a first in 1931, but without the star indicating special distinction and so did not get a fellowship. This he rightly attributed to playing too much chess. However, Professor G. H. Hardy described him as the only genuine mathematician he knew who did not become a professional mathematician. Alexander married Enid Constance Crichton (1900–1982), daughter of Ronald William Neate, sea captain, on 22 December 1934. They had two sons (the elder of whom, Michael, was British ambassador to NATO from 1986 to 1992).

From 1932 to 1938 Alexander taught mathematics at Winchester and made his name in international chess. He played with success for England in the biennial international team tournaments, rising to first board at Buenos Aires in 1939. He came equal second with Paul Keres ahead of some of the world's best players at the Hastings Christmas congress in 1938 and won the British championship in the same year. He then became head of research in the John Lewis Partnership, London.

In February 1940 Alexander joined Hut 6 (army and air force Enigma) at the Government Code and Cypher School (GCCS) at Bletchley Park, and he was quickly placed in charge of a watch. He moved to Hut 8 (naval Enigma) in March 1941, as deputy head under Alan Turing. Documents captured in the spring led to breakthroughs which enabled Hut 8 to solve the main Kriegsmarine cipher, code-named Dolphin by GCCS, from August onwards.

Alexander was outstanding at a Bayesian probability system invented by Turing, called Banburismus, which he considerably improved. Banburismus made the production of operationally useful decodes possible by greatly reducing the number of tests on the 'bombes' (high-speed key-finding aids), which were in very short supply until mid-1943. On Trafalgar day (21 October) 1941, with Turing and two colleagues, he made a very unconventional, but successful, appeal direct to Winston Churchill for some junior clerks, who 'for some mysterious reason seemed to be scarcer than University mathematicians' (Alexander, 30); without them, the breaking of Dolphin was being delayed for about twelve critical hours each day.

Alexander became head of Hut 8 about November 1942, when Turing was in America, but had been the *de facto* head for some time, since Turing was uninterested in administration. Alexander transformed Hut 8 into a highly efficient instrument for delivering decodes speedily to Hut 4 (naval section). He was 'a quite splendid head of Hut 8' (private information, S. Wylie) and 'a model manager [who] treated us cryptographers as colleagues and was remarkably tolerant of our foibles' (private information, R. Noskwith). But he also led the way in many technical developments, such as using U-boat short signals as 'cribs' (probable plain text, needed for bombe 'menus'), which solved a potentially catastrophic crisis in mid-March 1943, at the height of the battle of the Atlantic. Stuart Milner-Barry, from Hut 6, found him 'an ideal colleague' who 'always took the broadest view of the issues involved' (private information, S. Milner-Barry).

When the US navy code-breaking unit, OP-20-G, assumed responsibility for breaking Shark (the Atlantic U-boats' cipher) at the end of 1943, Alexander undertook a range of tasks, mainly on machine ciphers. He played a major role, with OP-20-G, in solving traffic on the complex Coral cipher machine (JNA 20) used by Japanese naval attachés. Deciphered Coral signals from the Japanese naval mission in Germany yielded vital intelligence, especially on technical developments such as the advanced high-speed type XXI and XXIII U-boats and German jet aircraft. He was also chairman of an important committee dealing with a rewirable reflecting rotor ('D') for Enigma, which the Luftwaffe introduced in January 1944, and maintained a watching brief on Hut 8.

Alexander formally transferred to the naval section in October 1944, to carry out research on the principal Japanese naval code, JN 25, which was something of an anticlimax after the excitement of naval Enigma. Although GCCS was largely left to tackle virtually obsolete versions of JN 25, which OP-20-G, being the leader in this area, decided to bypass, Alexander still put his best into the work, and devised new Bayesian scoring methods to counter the increasing complexities of the code. In mid-1945 he spent about six weeks as the head of the code-breaking section of HMS *Anderson* in Colombo, where he helped to accelerate the supply of signals intelligence for the Eastern Fleet and to improve morale.

Much is owed to Alexander and the Hut 8 code-breakers. Although without intelligence from naval Enigma the Kriegsmarine would still have been defeated in the long run, the cost in human life in the global conflict would have been even more terrible than it was.

Alexander returned to John Lewis in late 1945 but, realizing that cryptanalysis was his true vocation, joined the Government Communications Headquarters (GCHQ) (as GCCS became) in mid-1946. He was promoted to head of section H (cryptanalysis) in 1949 and, refusing promotion, remained in that post until his retirement. He promoted several new cryptanalytic techniques, and was a strong advocate of GCHQ's massive investment in computers. In chess, he was first at Hastings in 1946–7 and joint first with

the grand master of the USSR, David Bronstein, in Hastings in 1953. But gradually his work lessened his participation in chess.

GCHQ was very reluctant to let him go until 1971, when he was two years over retirement age. The National Security Agency (NSA), GCHQ's United States counterpart, held him in such high esteem that it then tried hard to recruit him. Fortunately, although tempted, he declined. The director of NSA recalled that he had already made a 'monumental' contribution to Anglo-American work on signals intelligence (private information, N. Gayler), and to this crucial part of 'the special relationship' between Britain and the United States.

On retiring from GCHQ Alexander concentrated on writing about chess. He wrote several excellent books, and was chess correspondent of the *Sunday Times*, the *Financial Times*, the *Evening News*, and *The Spectator*. A chess amateur all his life, had it not been for the war he might well have aspired to the world championship title. Mikhail Botvinnik (the world champion from 1948 to 1963, except for two brief periods) considered that 'with his urge for overcoming and taming opposition, with his enthusiasm for uncompromising struggle, Alexander pioneered the way for British players to modern, complicated and daring chess; chess players will never forget him' (private information).

Alexander was that rarest of men: a superbly skilled cryptanalyst who was also an excellent manager. He also combined a razor-keen intelligence with considerable energy and enthusiasm. His exceptional technical skills, and his gifts of leadership, man management, and administrative ability, made him an inspiring head of both Hut 8 at Bletchley and section H in GCHQ. He became an almost legendary figure to the intelligence communities of Great Britain and the USA. He was appointed OBE (1946), CBE (1955), and CMG (1970). Hugh Alexander was a most vivid and attractive personality, who delighted his friends with his gaiety, humour, and warmth. A magnificent talker, he loved to argue but was ever ready to see his opponent's point of view. Alexander died at Cheltenham on 15 February 1974 and was buried at Solihull.

HARRY GOLOMBEK, *rev.* RALPH ERSKINE

Sources private information (2004) [M. Alexander, son; R. Noskwith; S. Wylie] · R. Erskine, 'Kriegsmarine short signal systems—and how Bletchley Park exploited them', *Cryptologia*, 23/1 (1999), 65–92 · R. Erskine, 'Naval Enigma: the breaking of Heimisch and Triton', *Intelligence and National Security*, 3/1 (1988), 162–83 · H. Golombek, *The encyclopedia of chess* (1977) · F. H. Hinsley and others, *British intelligence in the Second World War*, 2 (1981) · S. Milner-Barry, 'Memoir', in H. Golombek and W. R. Hartson, *The best games of C. H. O'D. Alexander* (1976), 1–9 · P. S. Milner-Barry, '"Action this day": the letter from Bletchley Park cryptanalysts to the prime minister, 21 October 1941', *Intelligence and National Security*, 1/2 (1986), 272–6 · C. H. O'D. Alexander, 'Cryptographic history of work on the German naval Enigma', PRO, HW 25/1 · personal knowledge (1986) · private information (1986) · A. P. Mahon, 'The history of Hut Eight', PRO, HW 25/2 · history of Japanese code JNA 20 Coral, National Archives and Records Administration, College Park, Maryland, Historic Cryptographic Collection, RG 457, no. 4424 · *CGPLA Eng. & Wales* (1974)

Archives National Archives and Records Administration, College Park, Maryland, Crane Naval Security Group files, RG 38 ·

PRO, Government Code and Cypher School: directorate, Second World War policy papers, HW 14
Wealth at death £15,722: probate, 1 April 1974, *CGPLA Eng. & Wales*

Alexander, James (1691–1756), lawyer and politician, was born on 27 May 1691 at Muthill, Perthshire, Scotland, the son of David Alexander. His mother's name is unknown. His grandfather was a descendant of the first earl of Stirling, but his father had no claim to be counted among the nobility. Alexander was educated as an engineer, receiving instruction in mathematics and surveying. He moved to America in 1715, apparently in order to take advantage of the shortage of engineers in the colonies, and settled in Perth Amboy, New Jersey. Although his political enemies would later charge that he had supported the Jacobites in Scotland and had fled for his life when the Hanoverians prevailed, there was no substance to the allegation. His family had been supporters of Hanover, and he was a strong whig with political views entirely incompatible with those of the Jacobites.

In America, Alexander apparently received patronage from an influential Briton, possibly John, duke of Argyll, a family friend, for in the next few years he secured many favours from well-placed persons in New York and New Jersey. His mathematical ability also worked to his advantage. On 7 November 1715 he was appointed surveyor-general of East Jersey and within two years had secured the same office in West Jersey and in New York. He used these positions to gain title to lands before they could be acquired by other speculators. In 1718 he became recorder of Perth Amboy and deputy secretary of New York. Meantime he studied for the law; in 1720 he was admitted to the bar in New York and three years later began a practice in New Jersey. In March 1719 he was appointed commissioner to survey the boundary between New York and New Jersey. He became a councillor in New York in 1721 and a councillor in New Jersey in 1722. In the latter year he became attorney-general of New Jersey, and held the position until 1727.

In 1721 Alexander married Mary Spratt Provoost (1693–1760), daughter of John Spratt and Maria DePeyster. She was a wealthy New York widow who ran a successful mercantile business. They had seven children, one of whom, William *Alexander (styled sixth earl of Stirling), served as an army officer under George Washington. After moving to New York, James Alexander became a vestryman in Trinity Church and helped found the American Philosophical Society, the New York Library Society, and King's College (Columbia University). In 1732 he began a troubled relationship with Governor William Cosby, who had just assumed office in New York. Alexander and his law partner, William Smith, defended Councillor Rip Van Dam against attempts by Cosby to seize half of Van Dam's salary. For their pains, they were challenged by the governor on some of their land claims in upstate New York. Also, Alexander was removed from the council of New York. Three years later he was discharged from the council of New Jersey.

Alexander reciprocated against Cosby by organizing and leading opposition to him in New York. In 1733 Alexander and his friends hired a newspaperman, John Peter Zenger, to publish a newspaper that was critical of the governor. Cosby retaliated by charging Zenger with libel and sedition, and had him thrown in gaol. Alexander and Smith volunteered to defend Zenger in court, intending to turn the trial into an attack on Cosby. But the judge, declaring the two lawyers to be in contempt, disbarred them from the practice of law. Zenger was acquitted in 1735, with Alexander assisting Zenger's lawyer, Alexander Hamilton, outside the courtroom. When Cosby died in 1736 Alexander was readmitted to the bar and restored to the councils of New York and New Jersey.

Alexander died in Albany on 2 April 1756, and was buried the same day at Trinity Church, Lower Manhattan, New York. He was a powerful and substantial figure in the middle colonies and one of the foremost patrons of the arts. His wealth was estimated at £100,000. He was regarded as the most prominent lawyer in New Jersey and was considered one of the best attorneys in New York. Perhaps his most lasting legacy was his firm and courageous stand against Governor Cosby in defence of freedom of the press.

PAUL DAVID NELSON

Sources T. L. Purvis, 'Alexander, James', *ANB* · E. B. O'Callaghan and B. Fernow, eds. and trans., *Documents relative to the colonial history of the state of New York*, 15 vols. (1853–87), vols. 4–6 · W. A. Whitehead and others, eds., *Documents relating to the colonial, revolutionary and post-revolutionary history of the state of New Jersey*, 5–7 (1882) · A. Valentine, *Lord Stirling* (1969) · *New-York Gazette, or, The Weekly Post-Boy* (5 April 1756) · G. P. D. Nelson, *William Alexander, Lord Stirling* (1987) · C. A. Ditmas, *The life and services of Major-General William Alexander also called the earl of Stirling* (1920) · T. Russell, 'Alexander, Mary Spratt Provoost', *ANB*
Archives New York Historical Society, MSS
Wealth at death £100,000: Purvis, 'Alexander, James'

Alexander, Sir James Edward (1803–1885), army officer, born on 16 October 1803, was the eldest son of Edward Alexander of Powis, Clackmannanshire, and Catherine, daughter of John Bryce Glass, provost of Stirling. He was educated at the universities of Edinburgh and Glasgow, and at the Royal Military College, Sandhurst. He obtained a Madras cadetship in 1820, and a cornetcy in the 1st Madras light cavalry on 13 February 1821. He was made adjutant of the bodyguard by Sir Thomas Munro, and served in the First Anglo-Burmese War. On leaving the East India Company's service he joined the 13th light dragoons as cornet on 20 January 1825. He was given a lieutenancy on half pay on 26 November. As aide-de-camp to Colonel Kinneir, British envoy to Persia, he was present with the Persian army during the war of 1826 with Russia, and received the Persian order of the Lion and Sun (second class). On 26 October 1827 he was gazetted to the 16th lancers. He went to the Balkans during the Russo-Turkish War of 1829, and received the Turkish order of the Crescent (second class).

Alexander was promoted captain on half pay on 18 June 1830, and exchanged to the 42nd highlanders (the Black Watch) on 9 March 1832. He went to Portugal during the Miguelite War (1832–4), and afterwards visited South America and explored the Essiquibo. Passing next to

South Africa, he served in the Cape Frontier War of 1835 as aide-de-camp to Sir Benjamin D'Urban. He led an exploring party into Nama Land and Damaraland, for which he was knighted in 1838. He married in 1837 Eveline Marie, third daughter of Lieutenant-Colonel Charles Cornwallis *Michell. They had four sons and a daughter.

Alexander went on half pay on 24 April 1838. He exchanged to the 14th foot on 11 September 1840, and went to Canada with the regiment in 1841. From 1847 to 1855 he was aide-de-camp to D'Urban and to Sir William Rowan, who succeeded D'Urban in command of the troops in Canada. He became major in the army on 9 November 1846, lieutenant-colonel on 20 June 1854, and regimental major on 29 December 1854.

His regiment having been ordered to the Crimea, Alexander rejoined it there in May 1855, and remained there until June 1856, receiving the Mejidiye (fifth class). On his return to England he was appointed to a depot battalion, but on 30 March 1858 he returned to the 14th to raise and command its 2nd battalion, which he took to New Zealand in 1860. He commanded the troops at Auckland during the war there until 1862. He had become colonel in the army on 26 October 1858, and was granted a pension for distinguished service in February 1864. He was promoted major-general on 6 March 1868, and made CB on 24 May 1873. On 1 October 1877 he became lieutenant-general and was placed on the retired list, and on 1 July 1881 he was given the honorary rank of general. He inherited the estate of Westerton, near Bridge of Allan, and was a magistrate, a deputy lieutenant for Stirlingshire, and a fellow of the Geographical and other societies. He saved Cleopatra's Needle from destruction, and had much to do with its transfer to England in 1877. At its base he buried, among other artefacts, photographs of the twelve best-looking English women of the day. His extensive travels provided material for his varied publications, which included *Travels from India to England* (1827) and *Cleopatra's Needle* (1879). Alexander died at Surrey Lodge, Barfield, Ryde, Isle of Wight, on 2 April 1885 from chronic cystitis and bronchitis.   E. M. LLOYD, rev. JAMES LUNT

Sources *The Times* (7 April 1885) • Boase, *Mod. Eng. biog.* • H. O'Donnell, *Historical records of the 14th regiment* (1893) • R. Cannon, ed., *Historical record of the fourteenth, or the Buckinghamshire regiment of foot* (1845) • J. E. Alexander, *Travels from India to England* (1827) • J. E. Alexander, *Travels to the seat of war in the east, through Russia and the Crimea, in 1829*, 2 vols. (1830) • J. E. Alexander, *Narrative of a voyage of observation among the colonies of north Africa, and of a campaign in Kaffirland in 1835* (1837) • J. E. Alexander, *An expedition of discovery into the interior of Africa, through the countries of the Great Namaquas, Boschmans and Hill Damaras*, 2 vols. (1838) • J. E. Alexander, *L'Acadie, or, Seven years exploration in British America* (1849) • J. E. Alexander, *Passages in the life of a soldier*, 2 vols. (1857) • J. E. Alexander, *Incidents of the Maori War in New Zealand* (1873) • J. E. Alexander, *Cleopatra's Needle, the obelisk of Alexandria, its acquisition and removal to England described* (1879) • Burke, *Gen. GB* • d. cert.

Archives NA Canada, notes on British North American boundary dispute • RGS, corresp. and papers | U. Edin. L., letters to David Laing

Likenesses R. J. Lane, lithograph, 1827, NPG • photograph, repro. in O'Donnell, *Historical records of the 14th regiment*, 321 • portrait, repro. in *Colburn's New Monthly Magazine*, 117 (1880)

Alexander, John (1686–1743), minister of the Presbyterian General Synod of Ulster, was born on 30 September 1686 at Temple Patrick, co. Antrim, the son of John Alexander (d. 1712), and his wife, Mary Hamilton. His father was the fourth son of William Alexander, first earl of Stirling. He was educated at Glasgow University where he matriculated on 3 March 1701. He subsequently trained for the ministry, probably under Samuel Jones at Gloucester and later at Tewkesbury. About 1713 he became the first minister of the newly opened Independent chapel in Gloucester and in 1723 or 1724 he was appointed minister of the dissenting congregation at Stratford upon Avon. While at Gloucester he began training men for the ministry and continued this practice at Stratford. A manuscript in Dr Williams's Library gives the names of eleven students trained by him.

In 1730 Alexander accepted an invitation to become minister at the Presbyterian chapel in Plunket Street, Dublin, and commenced his ministry there on 15 November. During the year 1734 he served as moderator of the General Synod of Ulster. Although a classical scholar of some renown and described by Robert MacMaster as 'no stranger to any branch of polite or useful learning' (Witherow, 351–2), he is credited with only one publication, *The Primitive Doctrine of Christ's Divinity* (1727). On 8 August 1732 he married Hannah Higgs (1704/5–1768), daughter of the Revd John Higgs of Evesham. They had four children: Mary (b. 1734), John *Alexander (1736–1765), Benjamin (1737–1768), and Hannah (b. 1742). He died in Dublin on 1 November 1743 and was buried in Dublin. Shortly afterwards his widow and young family returned to England and settled in Birmingham.

ALEXANDER GORDON, rev. M. J. MERCER

Sources DWL, Wilson MS A 13 • T. Witherow, *Historical and literary memorials of presbyterianism in Ireland, 1623–1731* (1879) • C. Surman, index, DWL • H. McLachlan, *English education under the Test Acts: being the history of the nonconformist academies, 1662–1820* (1931) • DWL, Wilson MS D* 13 • R. MacMaster, *Funeral sermon for John Alexander* (1743) • J. Murch, *A history of the Presbyterian and General Baptist churches in the west of England* (1835)

Alexander, John (1736–1765), Presbyterian minister and writer, was born in Dublin on 26 January 1736, the second of four children of John *Alexander (1686–1743), dissenting minister, and Hannah (1704/5–1768), daughter of the Revd John Higgs, of Evesham. John's brother Benjamin (1737–1768) was a physician and translator. After the death of his father on 1 November 1743 John's family moved back to England and settled in Birmingham. In 1751 he entered Daventry Academy, established by Caleb Ashworth to educate nonconformists barred from admission to English universities. Alexander shared a room with Joseph Priestley; aware of the inadequacy of language teaching at Daventry, they became hard students of Greek together. Alexander emerged as one of the best Greek scholars of his time. He also studied biblical criticism under George Benson in London, and became Presbyterian minister of Longdon, 12 miles from Birmingham.

Alexander contributed to *The Library, or, Moral and Critical Magazine*, edited by Andrew Kippis (1761–2), essays entitled 'Defence of persecution', 'Dulness', 'Common sense', 'Misanthropy', and the 'Present state of wit in Britain'. He died suddenly on the night of 28 December 1765, at his home in Longdon, just after finishing a sermon on death. This was posthumously published along with his *Paraphrase on 1 Cor. xv* and *Commentary on Rom. vi., vii., viii., with Sermon (Ecc. ix. 10)*, edited by the Revd John Palmer (1766). Another of his sermons appears in the first volume of J. H. Bransby's *Sermons for the Use of Families* (1808).

ALEXANDER GORDON, rev. PHILIP CARTER

Sources A. Kippis and others, eds., *Biographia Britannica, or, The lives of the most eminent persons who have flourished in Great Britain and Ireland*, 2nd edn, 2 (1780), 207 · *Life and correspondence of Joseph Priestley*, ed. J. T. Rutt, 1 (1831) · C. H. Beale, *Memorials of the old meeting house and burial ground, Birmingham* (1882) · *Monthly Repository*, 17 (1822) · DWL, Wilson MS A 13
Archives DWL, Wilson MS A 13

Alexander, Mary (1760–1809), Quaker minister, was born on 7 February 1760 at Needham Market, Suffolk, the third of the eight children of Dykes Alexander (c.1724–1786), shopkeeper, and his wife, Martha Biddle (1727–1775), of whom five survived childhood. Both her parents were established Quakers, her father being an elder and her mother a minister. Mary was conscious when young of the possibility that she too might be called to the ministry and she tried to prepare herself. She began to read the Bible, instead of the plays and romances that she had earlier enjoyed, and learned from several British and American travelling ministers visiting her area. In 1786 Mary's father died and this blow was followed only nine weeks later by the death of Elizabeth, the wife of her eldest brother, Samuel. The family agreed that Mary should continue to live in her father's house with her youngest brother, William, while Samuel and his four children were looked after by his wife's aunt Mary Gurney.

Mary Alexander struggled between her call to the ministry and her family obligations, especially after Mary Gurney's death in 1788. But confirmation of her calling came one night in 1789 when, she says, 'a light shone round my bed and I heard a voice intelligibly say "Thou art appointed to preach the Gospel"' (Alexander, 24). She first spoke in meeting in July 1789 and was formally recognized as a Quaker minister in 1791. Her first journeys as a minister were mainly local but in 1794 she ventured further afield, to Lincoln, where she met and travelled with another minister, Ann Tuke (1767–1849) of York, who became a close friend. Their friendship developed further when Ann married Mary's brother William in September 1796. William and Ann asked Mary to live with them in the family home but she decided to find a house nearby instead. A ministerial journey to Wales with Ann and William in 1797 was continually interrupted by Mary's illnesses. She struggled on but at Cirencester she felt close to death; she dreamed that she was dead but was sent back to life as her time had not yet come.

Eventually, at the beginning of 1798, Mary returned to Needham Market and moved into her own 'very peaceful home' (Alexander, 74) but her ministerial obligations gave her little time to enjoy it. She travelled extensively with Elizabeth Coggeshall of Newport, Rhode Island, returning home at the end of 1800. For the next few years most of Mary's travels were in her own area. She also acted as 'an affectionate nurse and attendant' (ibid., 194) to her sister-in-law Hannah, the wife of her younger brother Dykes, at the birth of their daughter but the experience depressed her and she described it as 'a season of peculiar withdrawing of all substantial comfort' (ibid., 116). 1808 brought another change in her life when her brother William and his family moved to York, where he went into business as a bookseller and publisher. For Mary this was 'a closely trying separation' and made 'a chasm' in her domestic circle (ibid., 189–90).

At the end of October 1809 Mary went, with her older sister Martha Jesup, to visit Friends' families in Worcester. There she was joined by another minister, William Forster, with whom she attended two crowded public meetings. She was obviously ill and as soon as she had done her duty she went back to Worcester to the care of her relative Thomas Burlingham. At first her illness was thought to be another attack of the bilious complaint from which she had often suffered before but it soon became obvious that she had smallpox and she gradually grew worse. Her brothers Samuel and Dykes were sent for and she died, in Worcester, surrounded by her family, on 4 December 1809, at the age of forty-nine. She was buried in Worcester. Her brother William could not be with her at her death but he made sure that her account of her spiritual life was published. On hearing of Mary's death Deborah Darby wrote in her journal: 'thus the Church is stripped of its Pillars, may the great Lord of the Harvest be pleased to raise up and set forth more faithful labourers' (Labouchere, 336).

As the only unmarried woman in her family Mary Alexander might have spent her life seeing to the needs of her brothers' and sister's children, and she did take some share in this. But as a Quaker minister her family and friends accepted that she had a higher call, to which she was faithful in spite of her physical weakness.

GIL SKIDMORE

Sources W. Alexander, ed., *Some account of the life and religious experience of Mary Alexander* (1811) · 'Dictionary of Quaker biography', RS Friends, Lond. [card index] · R. Labouchere, *Deborah Darby of Coalbrookdale, 1754–1810* (1993)

Alexander, Michael Solomon (1799–1845), first bishop of the United Church of England and Ireland and of the Protestant Church of Germany in Jerusalem, was born on 1 May 1799 in the town of Schönlanke in the grand duchy of Posen in Prussian Poland (today Trzcianka in Poland) as the second son of a Jewish rabbi. At sixteen he held the position of teacher of the Talmud and the German language. His father died in 1817 and differences of opinion arose between him and his elder brother, who was nominated rabbi in place of their father. The disagreement caused Alexander to leave his country in 1820 to find his living in England.

In London Alexander became acquainted with the chief rabbi who found him a position as private tutor for a Jewish family in Colchester, where he was exposed for the first time to the Christian holy scriptures. In order to avoid succumbing to his inner promptings and accepting the new faith, he began wandering through the cities of England, serving as a rabbi in Norwich and, from 1823, as *shochet* and prayer-reciter in Plymouth. On his arrival in Plymouth he was invited to the house of a Jewish widow where he met her daughter Deborah Levy (1804–1872), whom he married on 3 November 1824. Deborah gave birth to two sons and twelve daughters.

Alexander decided to convert to Christianity and was baptized on 22 June 1825 at St Andrew's Church, Plymouth (Deborah was baptized on 9 November 1825 at All Hallows Church in Exeter). On the following day they left for Exeter, and shortly after that for Dublin, where Alexander acted as the secretary to the Church of Ireland Jews' Society. He was ordained deacon on Trinity Sunday 1827 in St Anne's Church, Dublin, and in December that year he was ordained priest by letters emissary from the archbishop of Dublin. During 1827 he became acquainted with Joseph Wolff, an emissary of the London Society for Promoting Christianity amongst the Jews, and followed him to join that society in London.

In 1827 Alexander was sent to serve as a missionary in Danzig, West Prussia, where he opened a school for the children of the Jewish community. This institute was abandoned in April 1830 when he was recalled to serve in England. During the 1830s he undertook the revision of the London Jews' Society's edition of the Hebrew Bible and the revision of the Hebrew translation of the New Testament which had been produced by the same society. In 1832 he was nominated professor of Hebrew and rabbinical literature at King's College, London, and held the title of doctor of divinity of Trinity College, Dublin.

In 1841 Alexander was consecrated in London as the first protestant bishop in Jerusalem. The originator of the idea to establish a protestant bishopric in Palestine, the aim of which was to bolster the position of protestants in the Holy Land, was Christian Karl Josias von Bunsen, the friend and confidant of the king of Prussia, Friedrich Wilhelm IV. Bunsen had developed his ideas as early as 1838 and 1839, during a stay in London, with certain prominent British personalities among whom were leading members of the London Jews' Society. In 1840 Bunsen returned to England for another visit and began working on the 'Jerusalem plan' in greater detail. Knowing that the sultan would probably oppose the establishment of such an institute in his territory, he made the land recently acquired in Jerusalem by the London Jews' Society and the establishment of their mission station there a central factor in his discussions with his English friends. These ideas and the steps taken to promote them were in harmony with the general outlook of Friedrich Wilhelm, who supported the plan in its entirety. The king therefore suggested that the British establish a joint bishopric for the two countries on the basis of the society's mission station in Jerusalem.

In order to enable Alexander, not a British subject, to extend his protective authority over the Anglican members of the Jerusalem congregation, parliament passed a special law—the Jerusalem Bishopric Act (5 October 1841)—which was ratified by Queen Victoria (queen's licence for consecration, 6 November 1841). His authority was defined in a statement of proceedings:

> His spiritual jurisdiction will extend over the English clergy and congregations, and over those who may join his Church and place themselves under his Episcopal authority in Palestine, and, for the present in the rest of Syria, in Chaldea, Egypt, and Abyssinia ... His chief missionary care will be directed to the conversion of the Jews, to their protection, and to their useful employment. (Statement of proceedings relating to the establishment of a bishopric ... in Jerusalem)

The consecration of Alexander by the archbishop of Canterbury took place on Sunday 11 November 1841 in Lambeth Palace chapel. On 7 December 1841 he sailed from Portsmouth on board the frigate *Devastation*—a warship which her majesty had placed at his disposal. On 21 January 1842, with an escort of 100 horsemen, Bishop Alexander entered the Jaffa Gate to fulfil his mission in Jerusalem. His arrival stirred great excitement among the local population. What impressed them more than anything else, in view of their familiarity with the lifestyle of the Catholic high clergy, was the fact that the new bishop was married to a 'bishopess', as they put it. Their amazement increased at the sight of the bishop's children riding on donkeys at the tail end of the procession, drawing loud exclamations from the onlookers: 'Vescovini, Santa Maria!' ('Little bishops, Holy Mary!'; K. von Hase, *Kirchengeschichte auf der Grundlage akademischer Vorlesungen*, Leipzig, 1892, 3.556).

Since Alexander had come to Palestine without a permit from the Turkish authorities, he presented himself before the pasha of Jerusalem. At the end of the meeting an explicit directive was issued that proclamations should be made from the minarets that: 'He who touches the Anglican bishop touches the apple of the pasha's eye.' But this formal visit and its outcome did not prevent the governor of Jerusalem from putting obstacles in the path of the bishopric later on, and the pasha 'seems to have forgotten all about the apple of his eye' (Corey, 69, 81).

Immediately after his arrival Alexander began to turn the bishopric into a concrete reality and paved its way by establishing institutions and deepening the ties with the Jewish communities in Palestine. On 28 February 1842 he laid the first row of stones at the site of the first protestant church to be built in the East, and on 1 November 1842 the ceremony for laying the corner-stone was held. On this festive occasion Alexander's wife, Deborah, inserted in the corner-stone a parchment scroll on which was written:

> The foundation stone of this church erected on Mount Zion Jerusalem by the London Society for Promoting Christianity Amongst the Jews was laid this first day of November (All Saints Day) in the year of our Lord MDCCCXLII [1842] and the seventh year of Her Majesty Queen Victoria by Mistress Alexander the lady of the Right Reverend the Anglican Lord Bishop of the United Church of England and Ireland in Jerusalem (Johns)

Christ Church was inaugurated on 21 January 1849, seven years to the day after Alexander entered the Holy City.

In May 1843 Alexander consecrated the New Hebrew College in the Christian quarter near Damascus Gate. This institution was intended to provide a framework for training new converts and those still in the process of conversion as potential missionaries. Besides religious studies they were taught the English language and introduced to the rules of Hebrew grammar. In the same year he assisted the London Jews' Society to set up a school of industry in order to train converts in carpentry work and to teach them acceptable working habits. Another institution founded at his initiative was the book depot, which was opened a year later at the edge of the Jewish quarter. Its purpose was to sell the Jewish sacred scriptures in many languages and to distribute the Christian scriptures free. The depot was run by converted Jews who were engaged in reading passages from the Bible and the New Testament to unlettered Jews.

During Alexander's episcopate, on 12 December 1844, the London Jews' Society opened the Jews' Hospital on the eastern slopes of Mount Zion near the Jewish quarter. The hospital was planned to hold twelve beds on two separate floors, for men and for women, and within days the institute was filled to capacity. Soon enough it contained dozens of beds and became the flagship of the entire British enterprise in Palestine in those days.

The joint bishopric, headed by Alexander and his successors, laid the basis for all Christian activity in Palestine during the nineteenth century. The legal status of protestants in the Ottoman empire improved, and the sentiment was that the time was finally ripe for raising Palestine from its ruins. Completely new protestant communities were springing up. Health, education, charity, and welfare institutions were established, attracting thousands of travellers, pilgrims, scholars, and scientists to Palestine.

At the end of 1845 Alexander went down to visit the Jewish community in Egypt on his way to England. On 23 November, near the village of Ras el-Wadi, before he could reach Cairo, the bishop died from a rupture of the largest blood vessel close to the heart. Those accompanying him brought his body back to Jerusalem and buried him on Saturday night, 20 December 1845, by the light of torch flames in the former London Jews' Society cemetery near Jaffa Gate. Three years later the protestant congregation acquired its permanent cemetery on Mount Zion and his remains were moved there.

After Alexander's death a feeling of depression overcame the protestants in Palestine. The experienced missionary Erasmus Scott Calman (1796–1890) articulated this feeling in his letter to Alexander's widow written a few months after her husband's death:

The Jerusalem mission has lost much in my estimation and judgement of what is really true and valuable, by the removal of the Bishop your late beloved husband who acted as a connected link between Jews and Gentile. Since that event, I am sorry to say, everything here has assumed a form of isolation and separation.

If this situation did not change quickly, he wrote, the 'thaw in the sun will freeze again in the shade' (Calman to Deborah Alexander, 4 Aug 1846, LPL, MS 3397).

YARON PERRY

Sources LPL, Alexander papers, MSS 3393–3397 · Y. Perry, *British mission to the Jews in nineteenth-century Palestine* (2002) · M. W. Corey, *From rabbi to bishop: the biography of the Right Reverend Michael Solomon Alexander, bishop in Jerusalem* [1956] · *Two sermons, preached … on occasion of the death of the Right Rev. Michael Solomon Alexander, D.D.* (1846) · Bodl. Oxf., CMJ archive · J. F. A. de le Roi, *Michael Solomon Alexander der erste evangelische Bischof in Jerusalem. Ein Beitrag zur orientalischen Frage* (Gütersloh, 1897) · F. C. Ewald, *Journal of missionary labours in the city of Jerusalem during the years 1842–3–4*, 2nd edn (1846) · *Jewish Intelligence, Monthly Account of the Proceedings of the London Society for Promoting Christianity amongst the Jews* (1846) · [H. Abeken], *The protestant bishopric in Jerusalem: its origin and progress. From the official documents published by command of his majesty the king of Prussia and from other authentic sources* (1847) · W. Ayerst, *The Jews of the nineteenth century: a collection of essays, reviews, and historical notices* (1848) · W. T. Gidney, *The history of the London Society for Promoting Christianity amongst the Jews, from 1809 to 1908* (1908) · F. Bunsen, *Memoirs of Baron Bunsen … drawn chiefly from family papers*, 2nd edn, 2 vols. (1869) · J. W. Johns, *The Anglican cathedral church of Saint James Mount Zion, Jerusalem* (1844), hand-drawn illustration, no. 6

Archives LPL, papers, MSS 3393–3397 · St Ant. Oxf., Middle East Centre, corresp.

Likenesses J. W. Cook, stipple, pubd 1843 (after E. Fancourt), NPG · drawing, repro. in *The Jerusalem bishopric and its connection with the London Society for Promoting Christianity amongst the Jews* (1887), 6

Alexander, Peter (1893–1969), literary editor and scholar, was born on 19 September 1893, at 3 Great George Street, Hillhead, Glasgow, the only son of Robert Alexander (1844–1900) of Glasgow, schoolmaster and later head teacher, and Christina Cameron McDonald Munn (1863–1949), schoolmistress. After his father's death in 1900 Alexander attended John Watson's school, Edinburgh, and, from 1907, Whitehill higher grade school in the east of Glasgow. In October 1911 he entered the University of Glasgow, enrolling in Latin and mathematics. In his second year at university, he joined the English and moral philosophy classes. The English literature department consisted of the regius professor, W. Macneile Dixon, Dr John Semple Smart, and two assistants. Alexander always regarded Smart as a determining influence and much later was to edit his posthumous book *Shakespeare: Truth and Tradition* (1928).

In 1914 Alexander interrupted his studies to enlist with the Cameron Highlanders and was in July 1916 commissioned as second lieutenant in the Royal Field Artillery. He spent these war years on the western front, ending as a captain and returning to the university in 1919. He took an honours degree in 1920, gaining the most distinguished first of the year, and was awarded the valuable George A. Clark scholarship. This would have enabled him to research into his particular topic of interest, 2 and 3 *Henry VI*, for a further four years. He used that scholarship as a means of financing travel in Italy and had meant to spend a subsequent period in France. In the event, a vacancy occurred in the department, and Alexander was appointed lecturer in English literature as from October 1921.

On 15 June 1923 Alexander married Agnes Effie Macdonald, who had been his fellow student in the honours school. She was the daughter of the late Revd Angus Macdonald, minister of the United Free Church of Scotland. There were three sons: Peter, who, as a lieutenant in the Royal Tank regiment, was killed in Normandy in July 1944; Donald, who was reader in medicine at Glasgow University; and Nigel, who became a professor of English in the University of London.

Alexander's most original work was *Shakespeare's 'Henry VI' and 'Richard III'* (1929) in which he argued that plays long taken to have been crude sources for Shakespeare, such as *The Contention betwixt the Two Famous Houses of Yorke and Lancaster* (1594) and *The True Tragedie of Richard Duke of Yorke* (1595), were in fact inaccurate transcriptions of the already existing 2 and 3 *Henry VI*. This gives us a more sophisticated Shakespeare—as, indeed, the relatively polished early plays *Titus Andronicus* and *The Comedy of Errors* might have led us to suspect.

In his various Shakespeare books, such as *Shakespeare's Life and Art* (1939) and his replacement for John Masefield's *Shakespeare* in the Home University Library (1964), Alexander showed little awareness of the principles of interpretation as evinced by his contemporary G. Wilson Knight. Rather than acknowledging the new criticism or anticipating cultural materialism, he built upon his predecessor, A. C. Bradley. His most lasting achievement was an edition of Shakespeare prepared for Collins (1951). This one-volume collection proved convenient for professors speaking at conferences or visiting other universities. It could frequently be seen in the hands of Shakespearians such as L. C. Knights, who might well have found Alexander's ventures into the critical field simplistic. There can be no doubt that it had popular appeal for students and for the literate public at large.

However, the very accessibility of this edition was somewhat misleading. It conflated the quarto and folio versions of *Hamlet* and *Othello*, producing centos rather than texts. Alexander omitted such works as *Edward III* and *The Two Noble Kinsmen* that have as much of Shakespeare in them as 1 *Henry VI*, which he included. He promulgated readings which some have found problematic, such as ''a babbl'd of green fields' (*Henry V*, II.iii) and 'arm-gaunt steed' (*Antony and Cleopatra*, I.iv) without due comment. However, how could he have found room for extensive annotation in a popular edition of Shakespeare's works? Compromise was inherent in the undertaking.

Upon the retirement of Macneile Dixon in 1935, Alexander assumed the regius professorship, which he held until 1963. This tenure was temporarily interrupted when, at the outbreak of the Second World War, he re-enlisted in the army, being posted to the Middle East in 1940 and returning to Glasgow as a major in 1943. He made few reforms to the syllabus, other than removing the study of history from the English honours school. It was mostly his own graduates that he appointed to lectureships, and even then he revealed a prejudice against appointing women. His solitary lady lecturer, a temporary appointment, found herself rebuked for 'wasting the time of his young men'. Stricture from such a source would have been formidable. An impressive lecturer, with his square

jaw and bushy eyebrows, Alexander seemed to regard research as a subsidiary activity. In that whole tenure, only one scholar of note, Ernst Honigmann, emerged from his department.

In retirement Alexander was invited to lecture at New York University and Trinity College, Dublin, and he returned to New York, where he had proved especially effective, from 1965 to 1967. He had been elected a fellow of the British Academy in 1951, appointed CBE in 1964, and awarded an honorary degree of LLD by the University of Aberdeen in 1966. Alexander died of lung cancer in hospital in Alexandria, Dunbartonshire, on 18 June 1969. He was survived by his wife. PHILIP HOBSBAUM

Sources J. C. Bryce, *Peter Alexander (1893–1969)* (1982) · personal knowledge (2004) · private information (2004) [Nigel Alexander, son; H. Buchan, colleague] · d. cert. · *CCI* (1970)
Archives U. Glas. L., MSS, Accession Numbers 4593, 2376
Likenesses photograph, 1951 (with members of his department), U. Glas., department of English literature · photograph, repro. in Bryce, *Peter Alexander* (1982)
Wealth at death £26,981 12s. 11d.: confirmation, 31 March 1970, *CCI*

Alexander, Samuel (1859–1938), philosopher, the third son and fourth child of Samuel Alexander, an Australian, and his wife, Eliza Sloman, who came from Cape Town, was born at Sydney, New South Wales, on 6 January 1859. His father, a saddler, died of consumption at the age of thirty-eight, shortly before his birth. His mother died in his house at Manchester in 1917, having gone to live with him there, with the rest of her family, in 1903.

About 1863 the family left Sydney for St Kilda, a suburb of Melbourne. Alexander was educated at home and at private schools before entering Wesley College, Melbourne, in 1871. There, and in his two years at the University of Melbourne, where he held an exhibition, he gained all the distinctions open to him. In 1877, without completing his degree, he sailed for Britain on a voyage lasting 108 days, with the express purpose, bold in view of the family finances, of winning a scholarship at Oxford or Cambridge. He was advised that a scholarship at Balliol College, Oxford, might be beyond his reach, and so prudently entered for one at Lincoln College as well, and did not succeed. But he won his scholarship at Balliol, where he graduated BA in 1881. Lincoln made amends by electing him to a fellowship in 1882. Its choice was amply justified by the sustained distinction of Alexander's undergraduate career, for he obtained firsts in mathematical and classical moderations (1879) and in *literae humaniores* (1881). According to the *Jewish Chronicle* this was the first election of a professing Jew to a fellowship in either of the ancient English universities.

Alexander retained his fellowship for eleven years, living in Oxford except for the period between the end of 1888 and June 1891. The break, originally designed to be permanent, was due partly to his desire to mingle with a wider world, partly to his determination to increase his proficiency in experimental psychology. In pursuit of the latter aim he studied under Hugo Müsterberg at Freiburg-

Samuel Alexander (1859–1938), by Francis Dodd, 1932

im-Breisgau; in pursuit of the former, he lectured at Toynbee Hall, Whitechapel, and busied himself in other ways with the popularization of academic subjects. These activities were indicative of firmly held beliefs. In Oxford he was one of the rebels who thought that the course in Greats needed quickening from modern science, especially psychology. He lectured on that subject to any, dons or undergraduates, who were sufficiently interested to attend supernumerary courses. The same policy directed Alexander's occasional writings and his first book, *Moral Order and Progress* (1889), an expansion of his essay for the Green moral philosophy prize which he had won in 1887. In its day it was widely believed to be the best systematic general treatise on evolutionary ethics in the English language. In the preface Alexander expressed his 'present dissent from [T. H.] Green's fundamental principles' (Alexander, *Moral Order and Progress*, vii) and added: 'I have come to the ideas, borrowed from biology and the theory of evolution, which are prevalent in modern ethics, with a training derived from Aristotle and Hegel, and I have found, not antagonism but, on the whole, fulfilment' (ibid., viii).

In 1893 Alexander became professor of philosophy at the University of Manchester, where he taught for thirty-one years. It was a happy appointment. Even the physical climate of 'dear old sooty Manchester' was tolerably congenial to him. In its university, while he had rather too many courses to give, their variety stimulated him, and, his classes being small, he could think aloud as he lectured. His academic influence soon extended far beyond

his lecture-room. His width of interests, his unstudied, notorious, picturesque untidiness, his catholic understanding of whatever was young almost compelled this result. Long before he reached the peak of his fame he had become a focus for admiration and for vast affection in the university and in the city. He was prominent in the university's more public activities, especially in the movement for providing university residences for women. In an extra-academic way his feminist principles made him favour the cause, although not always the tactics, of the local advocates of women's suffrage. He was a left-wing Liberal and an early supporter of Zionism. He was a friend of Chaim Weizmann, whom he introduced to A. J. Balfour.

As the years passed, many of his friends began to fear that Alexander's wide knowledge and his highly original powers would never find expression in print. A very few articles and an admirable little book on Locke (1908) were inadequate counter-evidence. By 1907, however, according to his own modest statement, he had come to believe that he might have something to say. He took his cue, in a measure, from the realist principle of G. E. Moore's 'Refutation of idealism' (*Mind*, 1903) but unlike many contemporary realists he was never content with polemical forays into the theory of knowledge. He was always bent upon a comprehensive system of ontological metaphysics, and this attitude, at the time, raised exceptional interest and expectation in the small world of technical British philosophy. The interest grew as Alexander in a series of presidential addresses to the Aristotelian Society (1908–11: he was again president, 1936–7) and in articles in *Mind* (1912–13) attempted the exploratory work which, as he always maintained, should precede the composition of a serious philosophical treatise. When the University of Glasgow, shortly before the First World War, invited him to become its Gifford lecturer, there was a general belief that he would use the opportunity to complete the huge task for which he had been preparing so sedulously for at least seven years.

An elaborate essay, 'The basis of realism' (*Proceedings of the British Academy*, 1914), the year after he had been elected a fellow of that body, is an admirable summary of the results that Alexander had reached during this preparatory period. The Gifford lectures themselves, given in the war years 1917 and 1918, were called 'Space, time, and deity'. Strenuously revised, but not very much altered, they were published under the same title (although Alexander much preferred the hyphenated form 'space-time') in two substantial volumes in 1920. By that time the issue of realism had become subordinate in the author's philosophy, although he remained a realist, holding that mind takes its place among the differentiated comprents in space-time. Primarily, Alexander was a metaphysician who attempted to describe and 'identify in concrete experience' 'the ultimates which the sciences left over'. Whatever is, he maintained, is a specification of space-time, either a 'categorial' (or wholly pervasive) attribute of space-time, or, like the neural process which is 'enjoyed' as personal experience, something 'empirical' (that is, non-pervasive) which nevertheless evolves or 'emerges' from the 'continuum of motions' which is the ultimate matrix space-time. Deity is the stage beyond mind, as yet unaccomplished but descriptive of a *nisus* in space-time towards a specific accomplishment which, just because it expresses the march of things, should receive the reverent acquiescence of 'natural piety'.

The value of the book has to be estimated by the vision, skill, and resolution with which it pursued its sweeping design. It is only accurate to say that, since Hobbes, no English philosopher, before Alexander, had built in accordance with so ambitious an architectural plan or had given comparable attention to the proportion and solidity of all the parts of his edifice. In less than a decade the general opinion was that the book marked the end of an epoch rather than a fresh beginning, and Alexander himself considered that the future was with A. N. Whitehead, rather than with himself, so far as such a philosophy had a future. He preferred to let his book stand with very few published afterthoughts, although his essay *Spinoza and Time* (1921) is an important supplement.

Alexander is acknowledged to be the first in a group of Anglo-American philosophers, comprising most notably Whitehead and John Dewey, who wrote in the first half of the twentieth century and who attempted to construct a metaphysics of experience that would resolve the dualisms of modern philosophy—such as mind and body, and subject and object—without resorting to the completed harmonies of idealistic philosophy. The search for an open system that embraces diversity in noncoercive and transmuting unities continues today in such successors of empirical metaphysics as process philosophy and antifoundationalism. In the period following the Second World War books were written on Alexander's philosophy from the viewpoints of process philosophy, idealism, naturalism, and empirical dualism, reflecting the complexity and the potentialities of his thought for productive reinterpretation. In each case, the commentators drew upon a different strand of Alexander's philosophy and showed its implications, allowing his thought to inform schools with which he had kinship, but with which he could not be fully identified.

Alexander was modest, although not self-depreciating. He wrote and planned in the grand manner simply because no other manner suited this theme. He resigned his chair in 1924, but continued to live in Manchester in honoured and busy tranquillity. Manchester's pride in him seemed to increase with his years. In its university he presented for honorary degrees until 1930, in a memorably delightful way. His fairly frequent public lectures were eagerly attended in Manchester and elsewhere. At philosophical congresses he held as of right the unofficial position of the foremost British philosopher, distinguished in matter, manner, and beauty of voice, sensitive to the meeting's mind, and overcoming the lifelong handicap of his deafness with charm. His striking head, Roman–Jewish profile, and beard gave him an impressive appearance. His main interest in these closing years was in literature and aesthetic theory. This is shown in several

of the essays published after his death in *Philosophical and Literary Pieces* (1939) and in his last book, *Beauty and other Forms of Value* (1933). Often humorous, always beautifully written and vividly informed by his psychological interest, his literary pieces include discussions of Dr Johnson, Jane Austen, Molière, and Pascal. *Beauty and other Forms of Value* marks a break with Alexander's interest in speculative, albeit scientifically chastened, metaphysical unity, substituting for it concern with analysing the structure of the finite, partial, and heterogeneous syntheses achieved by such cultural activities as the arts, sciences, and moral disciplines. Here Alexander falls in with the governing tendencies toward analysis in the British philosophy of his time, contributing to them cogently and with clarity and elegance. R. G. Collingwood commented in 1928 that Alexander's late writings on aesthetics were the most significant contribution to the philosophy of art in English philosophy since the eighteenth century.

Alexander's valedictory work, 'The historicity of things', in *Philosophy and History: Essays Presented to Ernst Cassirer*, edited by R. Klibansky and H. J. Paton (1936), is a beautiful and fully mature wisdom essay. Surrendering the last vestiges of rationalism in his doctrine of space-time, Alexander embraces Plato's 'wandering cause', which dooms rationalistic systems to failure.

Alexander died at Manchester on 13 September 1938, and his ashes lie in the section reserved for the British Jewish Reform congregation in Manchester southern cemetery. He was unmarried. He received honorary degrees from the universities of St Andrews, Durham, Oxford, Birmingham, Liverpool, and Cambridge, and was appointed to the Order of Merit in 1930. He was elected an honorary fellow of Lincoln College in 1918 and of Balliol College in 1925.

JOHN LAIRD, rev. MICHAEL A. WEINSTEIN

Sources *Philosophical and literary pieces*, ed. J. Laird (1939) · *The Times* (14 Sept 1938) · J. L., 'Samuel Alexander, 1859–1938', *PBA*, 24 (1938), 378–95 · M. A. Weinstein, *Unity and variety in the philosophy of Samuel Alexander* (1984) · B. D. Brettschneider, *The philosophy of Samuel Alexander* (1964) · S. Alexander, *Moral order and progress* (1889) · A. P. Stiernotte, *God and space-time: deity in the philosophy of Samuel Alexander* (1954) · J. W. McCarthy, *The naturalism of Samuel Alexander* (1948) · M. R. Konvitz, *On the nature of value: the philosophy of Samuel Alexander* (1946) · R. G. Collingwood, 'Review of S. Alexander, *Art and instinct*', *Journal of Philosophical Studies*, 3 (1928), 370–73 · private information (1949) · personal knowledge (1949) · *AusDB* · *CGPLA Eng. & Wales* (1938)

Archives JRL, corresp. and papers | BL, corresp. with Macmillans, Add. MS 55167 · BL, corresp. with Marie Stopes, Add. MS 58476 · Bodl. Oxf., corresp. relating to Society for the Protection of Science and Learning · U. Glas. L., letters to D. S. MacColl

Likenesses W. Stoneman, two photographs, 1917–31, NPG · J. Epstein, bust, 1925, Manchester University, Arts Building · F. Dodd, chalk drawing, 1932, NPG [see illus.]

Wealth at death £16,103 4s. 11d.: probate, 14 Nov 1938, *CGPLA Eng. & Wales*

Alexander, Stanley Walter (1895–1980), financial journalist and editor, was born on 16 November 1895 at 35 Harcourt Road, Deptford, London, the son of Walter Henry Alexander, board of works clerk, and his wife, Alice Maude Mary Kemp. He left the Roan School, Greenwich, in 1910 at the age of fourteen to work as a clerk for

W. Maxwell Aitken (later first Baron Beaverbrook), and moved to the London office of Royal Securities Corporation, the Canadian investment bank owned by Aitken, later becoming his private secretary, entrusted with all his affairs. Alexander enlisted in the army in 1915, rising to the rank of sergeant-major, but was classified unfit for active service because of a heart condition—he was also only 5 feet 1 inch tall—and from 1915 to 1917 worked as a clerk in the Canadian war records office, set up by Aitken, moving with him to the Ministry of Information in 1918. He was appointed MBE in 1918. In 1919 he married Doris Emily Kibble, a bank clerk: they had two sons. After the war he got a job as a journalist on the *Daily Express*, and became a highly respected financial journalist, holding, at various times from 1923 to 1946, the post of City editor of all three Beaverbrook newspapers: the *Daily Express*, the *Sunday Express*, and the *Evening Standard*. He had to put up with a lot of interference from Beaverbrook, who wanted to control the financial policies of his newspapers.

In the 1930s Alexander began to campaign for free trade, publishing a series of pamphlets under the name of Hannibal. In these, which included *The Economic War* (1932), *Tariffs Mean War* (1933), *Justice for All Workers* (1936), *The Price we Pay* (1940), and *The Kingdom of Bevin* (1941), he declared his conviction that tariffs weakened the economy and made war more likely. He also attacked government expenditure on social services and 'the rise of the sentimentalists who wanted more and more social services and more and more of the nation's income and capital given away' (*The Price we Pay*, 18), opposed the trade unions as a protectionist force, argued that children were kept at school too long, and blamed many of the country's problems on women's suffrage: after the war, 'we must never again see the mass votes of women deciding the course of events' (ibid., 24). He also shared Beaverbrook's opposition to the League of Nations.

In *The Kingdom of Bevin* Alexander wrote that Britain could not afford socialism, and what was needed was a revival of the spirit of individualism, self-reliance, and freedom. He was a member of a group centred on the Individualist Bookshop in Charing Cross Road, started by Sir Ernest Benn in 1926 as a focus for discussion on the dangers of the growing powers of the state, and he was one of those who signed a manifesto on British liberty in 1942. He was a founding member of the Society of Individualists in November 1942, which grew out of lunches at the Reform Club, of which he was a member. Under Benn's presidency the society waged a press campaign, and continued to hold regular lunches after it became the Society for Individual Freedom in 1947.

Alexander stood unsuccessfully as a free trade candidate for the City of London in the 1945 parliamentary election, and again for North Ilford in 1950. He had left the *Evening Standard* in 1946, and now bought the *City Press*, a City of London newspaper which had been struggling since the printing works had been bombed during the war. He edited it until 1966 (it survived until 1976), campaigning through its columns for free trade and sound money, and

conducting a vigorous campaign against Britain's entry into the Common Market.

A liveryman of the Worshipful Company of Tallow Chandlers, Alexander stood for election to the court of common council of the City of London in 1974, as an anti-dear food candidate: the Anti-Dear Food Campaign saw itself as the successor to the Anti-Corn Law League, and opposed government maintenance of food prices and the regulation of food production. He was the founder of the City of London Free Trade Club, chairman of the Sound Currency Association, and president of the Free Trade League and of the Cobden Club. He was also on the council of the Kipling Society from 1967, and chairman from 1971 to 1973: he had met Kipling in Beaverbrook's company before the First World War. He published *Save the Pound—Save the People*, a collection of pamphlets, in 1974. Alexander died on 24 March 1980 at St Bartholomew's Hospital, Smithfield, London.   ANNE PIMLOTT BAKER

Sources D. Abel, *Ernest Benn: counsel for liberty* (1960) · A. J. P. Taylor, *Beaverbrook* (1972) · S. W. Alexander, *Address to the electors of Cripplegate ward* (1974) · *The Times* (25 March 1980) · *Kipling Journal* (June 1980) · WWW · HLRO, Beaverbrook papers · b. cert. · d. cert. · CGPLA Eng. & Wales (1980)
Archives BLPES, papers, Coll. Misc. 565 | HLRO, corresp. with Lord Beaverbrook
Wealth at death £133,718: probate, 20 June 1980, CGPLA Eng. & Wales

Alexander, Walter (1879–1959), bus operator, was born on 2 May 1879 at Bonnybridge, Falkirk, son of Robert Alexander, a carter, and his wife, Elizabeth, née Stirling. In 1902 the family opened a general store at Camelon, near Falkirk, which also sold, hired, and repaired bicycles. In 1913 Walter bought a chain-driven Belhaven lorry, which was used in the cartage business during the week and, by substituting a charabanc body, carried passengers at the weekend. A second Belhaven was acquired in 1916.

Alexander married Isabella Daly in 1898 at Falkirk. They had at least one son, also called Walter. **Walter Alexander** (1902–1979) was born at Bonnybridge on 16 February 1902, left school at fourteen and joined his father in the business. When their first bus was obtained in 1919 he drove it on an extension of the Falkirk–Bonnybridge route to Kilsyth. Tours were advertised, and a private party was taken on an extended tour to John o' Groats in 1920; probably this was the first time a charabanc had made the journey.

The family shop was sold in 1921, and by the time the business was incorporated in 1924 the two men were in full partnership. They were more like brothers than father and son. By 1928 the fleet had grown to more than 100 vehicles, and services reached Glasgow and Aberdeen, with a co-ordination agreement with the Scottish Motor Traction company (SMT) between Perth and Dundee. A coach-building works was established at Stirling (removed to Falkirk in 1959).

After the main-line railway companies obtained road powers in 1928 a considerable consolidation of bus company ownership took place in Scotland. The London and North Eastern Railway (LNER) and the London Midland

and Scottish Railway (LMS), invested in SMT, which, while remaining an operator, became a holding company, among its interests being a two-thirds share in W. Alexander & Sons Ltd. In the more settled market of the 1930s the Alexanders were able to expand further (taking over some SMT services in the process), and when the SMT group was sold to the British Transport Commission in January 1949 roughly half its fleet of more than 5000 vehicles were in Alexander's 'Bluebird' livery; a famous emblem in Scotland, still to be seen there.

Father and son Alexander continued to serve on the board of Scottish Omnibuses Ltd, the state-owned holding company, the older man until his death. His son joined the board of the successor Scottish Transport Group in 1969, and retired in 1971. They were not alone among the founders of the Scottish bus industry in making this transition to public ownership while remaining in control. They bought out the coach-building side of the business in 1948, and formed Walter Alexander & Co. (Coachbuilders) Ltd, which became one of the largest bodybuilding firms in the UK.

Walter Alexander, senior, was a JP, and a football enthusiast, becoming chairman of Falkirk FC in 1951. After the death of his first wife he married on 2 October 1936 Clarissa May Brookes and thirdly, on 12 December 1953, Anne Cooper Elder, or Strachan, who survived him. He died of heart failure at Edinburgh Royal Infirmary on 19 June 1959. His son, who had married Katherine Mary Turnbull, died after a stroke at the family home, Solsgirth House, near Dollar, on 5 March 1979. There is no doubt that the contribution of the two men, through what remained almost a family business for so long, was of outstanding value to travellers in Scotland, from the midlands to Inverness.   JOHN HIBBS

Sources private information · *Transport Journal*, 13/136 (3 July 1959) · *DSBB* · b. cert. · b. cert. [Walter Alexander, jun.] · d. cert. · d. cert. [Walter Alexander, jun.]

Alexander, Walter (1902–1979). *See under* Alexander, Walter (1879–1959).

Alexander, William, first earl of Stirling (1577–1640), poet and politician, was born probably at Menstrie Castle in Clackmannanshire, the only son (there were four daughters) of Alexander Alexander (*d.* 1581) and Marion, daughter of Gilbert Graham of Gartavertane. His descent has been traced from the lords of the Isles through the Macalisters or MacAlexanders of Kintyre, but the name was too common in the lowlands for much weight to be attached to this conjectural lineage. The earliest record of the Alexanders as holders of land from the earl of Argyll in Menstrie is the choosing in 1506 of Thomas Alexander to act in a boundary dispute between the abbot of Cambuskenneth and Sir David Bruce of Clackmannan. William Alexander was of the fifth generation descended from Thomas.

Early life The dates between which Alexander must have been born are given by the words, 'Aetatis suae LVII', on the portrait that appears in some copies of his *Recreations*

William Alexander, first earl of Stirling (1577–1640), by unknown artist

with the Muses of 1637, a portrait that must have been drawn in 1633 or after, since it was in that year that he was made earl of Stirling and the portrait is titled a likeness of the 'Comitis de Sterlin'. He was therefore fifty-seven between 1633 and 1637. McGrail argues that his birth was in 1577 from Alexander's having written to William Vaughan that 'wee were borne both under the same *Horoscope*' (McGrail, 4). The *Dictionary of National Biography* gives 1577 as the year of Vaughan's birth.

On the death of his father, on 10 February 1581, Alexander was left in the tutelage of his father's brother James, burgess of Stirling. He may have attended the grammar school in Stirling, whose rector was then Dr Thomas Buchanan, nephew of George Buchanan, the humanist poet, historian, and political theorist. As for his further education, his future benefactions to the University of Glasgow suggest that he studied there (McGrail, 6). His friend William Drummond of Hawthornden says that he was educated in the University of Leiden; there is no record of his taking a degree, but he may have studied there too.

Alexander went on the grand tour in the company of Archibald Campbell, seventh earl of Argyll, and if settings of sonnets in *Aurora* by the Loire (Sonnet 36), by the Po (Sonnet 53), and in the Apennines (Sonnet 57) record occasions of his journeying, he must have taken in France and Italy anyway. But it must be said that from such hints in *Aurora* it is not easy to make out a coherent itinerary. Alexander would have been back in Scotland in 1600 if he wrote the anonymous pamphlet *A short discourse of the good ends of the higher providence, in the late attemptat against his maiesties person* (Edinburgh, 1600). James VI had been rescued by his attendants in Gowrie House, Perth. His rescuers had killed the earl of Gowrie and his brother, who had probably been trying to seize James and with him the power to govern Scotland. Gowrie belonged to a family distinguished for taking the ultra-protestant side against the monarch, and five prominent members of the kirk refused to accept the king's story that he was being abducted. In this situation *A short discourse* would have been a welcome support to the king, though its arguments are declamatory rather than forensic. And if it had been known that Alexander had written it, it would have helped to attract the royal favour he so remarkably came to enjoy. The grounds for thinking that Alexander was the author are, however, only matters of style (McGrail, 21–2) and the royalism of his connections and later career. It is curious that he did not take credit publicly for so ingratiating a piece.

In 1601 Alexander married Janet, daughter of Sir William Erskine, titular parson of Campsie, with whom he had at least eight sons and three daughters. He probably wrote most of his sonnet sequence *Aurora* before his marriage (though it was published only in 1604). *Aurora* ends with his turning from love to marriage: 'Hymen's torch hath bur'nd out all thy [love's] darts' (Song 10, 16), he declares, and looks forward with complacency to becoming a husband, 'Since that I must command when I have yeelded' (ibid., 46), sentiments that, though correct enough when he wrote them, could never have pleased in a bridegroom. The history of an emotion that a sonnet sequence sketches may have little to do with actual events in a poet's life. Still, according to Alexander's friend John Leech, the love that inspired the sonnets was for a real woman, Elizabeth, daughter of Sir John Shaw of Sauchie. Alexander says in Sonnet 99 that he found his Aurora in the arms of one 'in the evening of his age': Elizabeth Shaw married John Murray, first earl of Annandale, who was probably about forty at the time. If we did not have Leech's story it would be possible to read the sequence as going through conventional vicissitudes of love to end in marriage to the person who had caused the pains the poet loved to feel.

Writings When *Aurora* came out (London, 1604) Alexander was making a name as a man of letters in more ambitious ways. In 1603 he had published the first of his tragedies, *Darius* (Edinburgh, 1603), and followed that with *The Monarchick Tragedies* (London, 1604), comprising *Darius* and *Croesus* together with *Paraenesis*, *Aurora*, and a number of occasional pieces. *Darius* and *Croesus* are written in what was one of the most highly regarded genres of the Renaissance, the Senecan closet tragedy in verse. They share with *Paraenesis* an interest in how a prince should rule. *Paraenesis*, which also came out separately in 1604, is advice to Henry, prince of Wales; when Alexander published it again, in *Recreations with the Muses*, he dedicated it to Charles, eldest son of Charles I. It has been praised for honest forthrightness, for instance for its recommendations that a prince should read books, love virtue, seek advice from counsellors that he has chosen, and promote justice. But nothing in all these worthy commonplaces goes against what James had said in his *Basilikon Doron*. What *Paraenesis* does show is that Alexander is putting himself forward as a good adviser to a prince, an ideal courtier and royal servant. Besides, his literary effort would have commended him to James, who in his younger days in Scotland wrote verse, laid down how it should be written, and liked the company of poets. James appears in Alexander's verse as Apollo, the god of poetry and inspirer of poets. So, for example, in 'Some verses written shortly thereafter [that is, after James's leaving for England in 1603] by reason of inundation of Doven, a water neere unto the authors house, whereupon his maiestie was sometimes wont to hawke', Alexander pictures Scotland in mourning for the king's departure and adds:

> This hath discourag'd my high-bended minde,
> And still in doale my drouping Muse arrayes:
> Which if my *Phoebus* once upon me shin'd,
> Might raise her flight to build amidst his rayes.
> (*Poetical Works*, 2.538)

Again, he declares in a sonnet that when James writes poetry, 'He *Phoebus* seems, his Lines *Castalian* Streams' (ibid., 2.541). He is saying that James not only writes but also inspires poetry. And certainly the idea of monarchy is his master-theme. Moreover, like William Drummond of Hawthornden, he seems to have experienced the absence of James and the court in London as a personal bereavement, the loss of the crown of all personal and social projects.

James himself wrote as royal critic an uncomplimentary sonnet on Alexander's *Doomes-Day* (1614), 'The complainte of the muses to Alexander upon himselfe, for his ingratitude towards them, by hurting them with his hard hammered wordes, fitter to be used upon his mineralles' (Rogers, *Memorials*, 1.48). Others appreciated him more generously. His neighbour Alexander Hume, poet and minister of Logie, appointed him in 1609 by his will one of the counsellors to his wife and children and 'tutor testamentary' to his children if his wife should remarry or die. There is no reason to think that Drummond of Hawthornden met Alexander before 1612, but after that their correspondence is an interesting example of how Renaissance friendship might be carried on with the help of literature. Each admires the other's work, each writes complimentary poems for the other's volumes. When Alexander was involved in the project of getting together an edition of James's (and his own) translations of the Psalms, he let fall in a letter (18 April 1620)—with a servant's sharp eye for the foibles of his master—that the king would not welcome Drummond's translation of a psalm:

> which I think very well done: I had done the same, long before it came, but he [James] prefers his own to all else, tho' perchance when you see it, you will think it the worst of the Three. No man must meddle with that Subject. (*Works of William Drummond*, 151)

A number of Drummond's letters to Alexander are preserved, which besides treating literary matters condole in Alexander's griefs with as much feeling as Drummond's rather elaborate manner allows. Drummond imitated and borrowed some of Alexander's poetry, a mark of admiration he extended to many, but a genuine one. Alexander enjoyed the admiration of other contemporary poets. Sir Robert Aytoun supplied one of the commendatory poems to *The Monarchick Tragedies* (1604; *Poetical Works*, 1.ccvi–ccvii). The Scots Latin poets Arthur Johnstone and Andrew Ramsay celebrated him (ibid., 1.ccxiii–ccxvii). He was praised by English poets, among others by Michael Drayton, in Pastoral 6, *Pastorals Contayning Eglogues* (1619; *Works*, 2.549–50) and in 'To my most Dearely-Loved Friend Henry Reynolds Esquire, of Poets and Poesie' (1627; *Works*, 3.230), by Samuel Daniel in 'The epistle dedicatory to the prince', *Philotas* (1605; *Complete Works*, 3.101), and by Sir John Davies of Hereford in *The Scourge of Folly* (1611; *Poetical Works*, 1.ccvii). Aytoun, Daniel, and Davies anyway praised him while his interest to men of letters was as a poet rather than as a figure of some importance at court. Drayton was a friend for whom Alexander supplied a complimentary sonnet prefixed to *England's Heroicall Epistles* (1619; ibid., 2.538) and the recipient of Drummond's epistolary friendship as well as its subject when he wrote to Alexander.

Alexander, in short, made a successful career as a poet. He followed up those publications already mentioned with *The Monarchicke Tragedies* (London, 1607), which added to *Croesus* and *Darius*, *The Alexandraean* and *Julius Caesar*. *An Elegie on the Death of Prince Henrie* (1612) was his contribution to the general deluge of poetic tears, and he brought out a first version of *Doomes-Day, or, The Great Day of the Lords Judgement* (Edinburgh, 1614; London, 1620). A third edition of *The Monarchicke Tragedies* came out in 1616 in London. Finally, in 1637, he published in London an edition of the works he wished to be known by, *Recreations with the Muses*. From this he excluded *Aurora*, as immature, and *An Elegie on ... Prince Henrie*; he added twenty 'Houres' to the original four of *Doomes-Day*, and there was an entirely new work, *Jonathan*.

In addition to his poetry, Alexander wrote 'Anacrisis', probably in 1634, an undistinguished and probably unfinished essay on criticism, which he sent to Drummond. His 'Supplement to a defect in the third book of "Arcadia"' was published in the Dublin edition of Philip Sidney's *Arcadia* (1621) and all subsequent seventeenth-century English editions. It is an accomplished imitation of Sidney's average style.

Alexander had many admirers in the early seventeenth century. By the eighteenth century there are only sporadic notices of his work and publication of excerpts, as for instance in Thomas Heyward's *The British Muse* (1738). In the nineteenth century there was some continuing interest. His poetry is included in Alexander Chalmers's *Works of the English Poets* (1810), but lopped of the plays, except for the choral speeches. A complete edition of only 350 copies appeared in three volumes in Edinburgh in 1870–72 (McGrail, 218–20). And Palgrave anthologized Sonnet 33 from *Aurora*, a pleasant fancy about mutuality in love. Kastner and Charlton's two-volume edition of Alexander's *Poetical Works*, for the Scottish Text Society, came out in 1922 and 1929; it includes his drama.

Alexander's work has elicited little critical commentary. It would be agreeable to dissent from the prevalent view that it is insufferably dull. At the very least, it can be said that his versifying is generally competent and his expression clear, though coloured with some mannerisms of Sidney and, in *Doomes-Day*, of Sylvester. Occasionally in *Aurora* a detail seems more than just Petrarchan literary currency, such as this simile—drawn from the river meanders known as the Links of Forth—with its skilful turns of rhyme and line:

> As Forth at Sterling glides as 'twere in doubt,
> What way she should direct her course;
> If to the sea, or to the source,
> And sporting with her selfe, her selfe doth flout:
> So wandered I about
> In th'intricated way.
> (Song 3, 97–102)

But the sequence, despite its occasional felicities, fails to generate intensity of feeling or imagination. Alexander wrote some admirable couplets on the return of Charles from Spain in 1623 when, to the heartfelt rejoicing of the country, the proposed match to the infanta had fallen through. In their neat antitheses and graceful mythological turns, they strikingly resemble Edmund Waller's verse.

The Monarchicke Tragedies, like all essays in their kind, lack dramatic interest, whether of character or plot development. They are constructed to give occasions for speeches or tirades on mutability, empire, or counsel. Alexander's thoughts on those subjects are not new; his expression is fairly clear of the eccentricity, but also of the confused magnificence, of other Jacobean writers. He does not have an interesting mind, as does Fulke Greville, with whose Senecan closet dramas his have been compared. A note of asperity is sometimes heard among his commentators, not least Kastner and Charlton, the note of men who have been obliged to read with attention long tracts where attention is rarely aroused naturally. There are moments of interest but no sustained interest. The expression of grief is particularly bombastic. Women declare their involvement in their men's fortunes with gratifying absoluteness. In all these plays the characters display magnanimous minds, even those, such as Darius, Croesus, or Caesar, who have uttered base or foolish thoughts.

Doomes-Day, Alexander's most ambitious project in verse, is not so much an account of the sublimely odd events that will end the world as a moralizing declamation on them. His imagination is too equable for his subject, so that while *Doomes-Day* makes a very respectable complement to Du Bartas's *La sepmaine*, only persistent readers of what in its final version runs to over 11,000 lines will find much to divert them. The first 'Hour' was translated into French by John Wodroeph and printed opposite the original in his *The Spared Houres of a Souldier in his Travells, or, The True Marrowe of the French Tongue* (1623, 1625).

Royal servant and projector Alexander's career as man of letters was well under way by the time James left Scotland for England, but it is not known when his career as a courtier began. Probably he had been introduced to the Scottish court by the seventh earl of Argyll, but given his lament for the king's desertion of his native land, it is unlikely that he was among the crowd of Scottish gentlemen who accompanied James to London in 1603. The earliest signs of his advancing his fortunes are Scottish and even tied to his own locality. On 8 May 1607 his father-in-law, William Erskine, secured a life pension from the exchequer of £200 yearly, half of which was to revert to Alexander while he lived. And in 1609 Erskine bought the duties payable to the earl of Argyll on Alexander's lands of Menstrie. These were now paid to him but would revert to Alexander on his death. Meanwhile, Alexander hatched the first of his money-making schemes. In September 1607 he and his heirs were granted the mining rights of the barony of Menstrie, a tenth of the profits being reserved to the king. He consolidated this venture in 1611 when he got the right for twenty-one years to refine the silver he mined. Again in 1607, he undertook with a kinsman, Walter Alexander, to gather the arrears of taxes due to the crown throughout Scotland from 1547 to 1588. The king was to receive half of what was brought in up to £6000. But little could be wrung from the Scots. The royal authorization for this unprofitable venture shows that Alexander had been made gentleman to the privy chamber of Prince Henry by 1607. On Prince Henry's death in 1612 he was made gentleman usher to Prince Charles. That and a more significant honour, his knighting in 1608 or 1609, indicate that he had gained entry to the court in England. But it probably required little influence to gain the right in March 1613 to mine and refine the silver ore of Hilderston in Linlithgowshire, Alexander's last mining scheme. The rich vein was known to be exhausted. He evidently hoped to make a profit on the inferior ore that remained, but it seems to have yielded less than the expenses of mining and refining, and the project collapsed.

A more solid source of advancement was Alexander's appointment early in 1614 as master of requests for Scotland, a job that he was fitted for by his position in Scotland and at the court in London. His business was to deal with the minor matters arising between the kingdoms, above all to see to it that the plague of beggarly Scots wandering from their native land did not 'trouble [the King] and discredit their countrey' (Rogers, *Register*, 1.3). Both his office and his conduct in it recommended him for admission to the privy council of Scotland on 1 July 1615. In 1617 he accompanied James on his triumphant visit to Scotland. As an officer of the crown he seems to have played the part of diplomat and peacemaker. And so one finds him trying to soothe the abrasions of Stuart ecclesiastical policy in Scotland. The five articles of Perth (1618) were imposed by James on the kirk through a packed assembly. They required various liturgical reforms, such as kneeling at communion, which were widely resented in predominantly Genevan Scotland. And in 1619 they provoked an acerbic pamphlet from David Calderwood, *Perth Asemblie*. The printer was found, hailed before Alexander and John Spottiswoode, brother of the archbishop of St Andrews,

in London, and imprisoned. Typically, Alexander worked for his release, but he was resisted by the archbishop. He was, however, successful in the case of another protester in 1622. David Forrester had been evicted from his charge for refusing to kneel at communion. Alexander succeeded in patching matters up and Forrester was reinstated.

While his career as crown servant was prospering, Alexander began to entertain a grand design for colonizing the New World. England laid claim to the eastern coast of North America by right of John Cabot's landfall in Newfoundland in the reign of Henry VIII. Between New England and Newfoundland, the territories actively exploited, there lay what is now New Brunswick and Nova Scotia, untouched by English enterprise. It was there that Alexander hoped to found a colony of New Scotland, but in doing so took no account that this territory had already been claimed by France, named 'La Cadia', and to some extent colonized. Even though the French do not seem to have been active in the area in the 1620s, the grant that Alexander secured from James on 29 August 1621 of the lands not only of the future Nova Scotia and New Brunswick but also of the Gaspé peninsula and the islands of the Gulf of St Lawrence posed a threat to the colony of New France about Quebec. It was, however, Scottish indifference rather than French hostility that obstructed Alexander's scheme. A ship finally left Kirkcudbright in June 1622, but a storm drove it back from Cape Breton to St John's, Newfoundland, where the party decided to winter. He dispatched a second ship with supplies in March 1623, which arrived to find the key members of the expedition, the minister and the blacksmith of the first boatload, dead. Immediate settlement was postponed, and after some prospecting of the coast for future settlement the ships returned to Britain.

Alexander was now £6000 out of pocket but could not afford to give up. In 1624 he published *An Encouragement to Colonies*, a treatise recommending his scheme as one that would 'spread the gospel and secure lawful increase of commerce' (sig. A4). His ideas are general and show little acquaintance with the realities of settling in America. He recommends its solitude, for example, to those who would pursue the contemplative life. At the same time he hoped to make settling more attractive to the Scots by carving up the territory into baronetcies. He persuaded James to issue a proclamation in November 1624 founding the knights baronets of Nova Scotia. This provided that 100 gentlemen, on the payment of 1000 merks to Alexander and the furnishing of six men to the colony, would gain a hereditary title and 30,000 acres of land to be held in free baronetcy under the king, of which 14,000 acres 'were for the use of the Crown as sites for churches, schools etc' (McGrail, 91). Few took advantage of the offer and the new order ran up against jealousy of the Scots feudal orders about precedency. Sir Thomas Urquhart's jibe 'He was born a poet and aimed to be a king' expressed the disdain and fear aroused among his class (Urquhart, 168). But Alexander had remarkable backing from James and then from Charles. Objections were rebuffed and the process of getting patents to baronetcies expedited. And still the response fell miserably short of the required complement.

In 1628 Alexander sent out a third expedition with his eldest son (also Sir William) in charge. A report of that expedition, 'A voyage to New Scotland', presumably taken down by Drummond of Hawthornden from conversation with Sir William (NL Scot., Hawthornden MS 2061, fols. 148–50) records the setting up of two forts, the second near the remains of an abandoned French one at Annapolis. Sir William returned to Britain in November and then set off again for New Scotland in March 1629, where he spent the winter. But all this activity had been undertaken while England was at war with France and had been associated with hostile designs on Quebec. Indeed, his father's patent in the New World had been enlarged in February 1628 to take in both banks of the St Lawrence almost up to Quebec. The war ended in April 1629, and Charles had to deal with a French government now actively interested in its American dominions. He found that the dowry for Henrietta Maria would not be paid unless New Scotland was ceded to France, and in March 1632, by the treaty of St Germaine-en-Laye, Alexander's New World possessions were made over.

Secretaryship of state for Scotland and further projects While Alexander's New World schemes came to nothing, he advanced as a servant of the crown in the early years of Charles's reign. On 28 January 1626 he was made Scottish secretary of state. That office had been held by the earl of Melrose, who had led the opposition to the institution of knights baronets of Nova Scotia. While Melrose was not ejected from office (he remained secretary in Scotland, while Alexander was secretary in London), the promotion nevertheless impaired his rank and was felt as a slight, a typical consequence of Charles's peremptory dealings. Alexander went on to acquire more offices and their dues, partly because he was near the king and conspicuously eager to serve and partly perhaps because he was not without emollient diplomatic skills. He remained on the privy council and sat on the commission on teinds, or tithes (1627), which was to negotiate the necessary but extremely intricate and delicate matter of reappropriating for the kirk some of the revenue of the lands that had been seized by landowners following the Reformation. And on 6 November 1627 he was also made keeper of the signet, which brought the emoluments that came from ratifying all legal and official documents. By 1629 he had been given powers to nominate not only the clerks of the signet but also the clerks of the shires and clerks of the peace. He was naturally an important figure in the preparations for Charles's coronation in Scotland, already under way in 1630. In that year, in recognition of his services, he was raised to the peerage on 4 September as Viscount Stirling and Lord Alexander of Tullibody. Perhaps in anticipation of this dignity he had already begun to build a mansion in Stirling in the French style, far grander than the family seat at Menstrie; it was designed by his second son, Anthony, and known after it passed out of the hands of the Alexander family to the ninth earl of Argyll as Argyle's Lodging. To set the seal on his importance, on 14 June he was created among the coronation honours of 1633 earl of Stirling and viscount of Canada.

Stirling's position, however, was financially embarrassed. He had not recouped his losses in New Scotland and his outlays in the service of his kings exceeded the income of his offices. He had been involved in a design to exploit the fish in the British seas. But the Association for Fishing, chartered in 1632 and centred in Lewis, failed, like all the projects he engaged on, to realize great profits. As a means by which Charles might repay the £16,000 he owed him, another scheme presented itself, but this in the upshot made Stirling as unpopular with the lower classes in Scotland as his position of secretary and agent of Charles made him with the landed ones. There was a dearth of small coin in Scotland. As a remedy, copper coinage was introduced, and on 26 August 1631 he was put in charge of its administration; the royal dues for coining were made over to him. The profits were small, far too small to satisfy his creditors or pay off what was owing him from the king. The coins, called 'turners', were minted vastly in excess of requirements and possibly deliberately struck in metal not worth the 2d. at which they were valued. Instead of encouraging trade, they caused the flight of silver from currency. Charles backed his creditor against the protests of the country and Stirling got the blame for misgovernment, if not corruption. Yet even in 1639 when his hour had passed, the Scottish parliament was unable to deal with the problem posed by the need for small coin and quickly followed up a proclamation devaluing the 'turners' with one re-establishing their value. Stirling was probably not so much inept or unusually venal as a victim of monetary laws and trends nobody understood. However it was, he failed to profit substantially from his enterprise.

Another project was equally unprofitable. Stirling and James had worked on a rendering of the Psalms into metre. Now Stirling felt that his work as collaborator (he had probably translated more than James, polished the royal efforts, and exercised great tact in the whole business) might be rewarded. If his and James's renderings could be ordained for public use in the churches of the three kingdoms, he stood to make a tidy sum. Charles granted him the right to print *The Psalmes of David Translated by King James* for twenty-one years and the first edition came out in 1631. In spite of Charles's injunctions, it was not accepted by the bishops of the Church of England, a body generally favourable to motions from Charles. The general assembly of the kirk in 1631 emphatically rejected it. Charles met that protest with a decree that no other metrical psalms should be sold in Scotland. In 1636 Stirling brought out a second edition, incorporating, with his usual attempt at conciliation, revisions in response to criticisms of the first edition. But at this point the *Psalmes* and Stirling's importance in affairs were overwhelmed by the wave of resistance to Charles's ecclesiastical policy in Scotland.

Bishops' wars and death Charles had long designed to bring the government and services of the kirk into harmony with the Laudian order now regulating the Church of England, and in consultation with the Scottish bishops drew up a book of ecclesiastical canons and a prayer book. The Book of Common Prayer was published in 1637, and bound up with it were Stirling's revised *Psalmes*. Rioting in Edinburgh greeted the first use of the prayer book on 23 August and several petitions from all classes were presented to the privy council for its withdrawal. Stirling, out of touch with Scottish feeling, played down the agitation to Charles. Charles in any case was not someone to respond skilfully to the opposition of his subjects. He dismissed the petitions out of hand, with the result that he exasperated a large part of the country sufficiently for it to band together in the national covenant of 1638 and in the end to embark on the armed resistance of the bishops' wars. This successful opposition ended the years of Charles's personal rule and set in train those events that brought England to civil war. Stirling, eminently the creature of Charles's personal rule, was suddenly inconsequential and seen to be of insufficient weight to manage the broils in Scotland.

During the bishops' wars Stirling was with the king and still enough involved in affairs to play some part in the treaty of Berwick (1639). But rather like the monarchs deserted by fortune in his tragedies, he was beset by calamities. His second son, Sir Anthony, died in 1637. Then in May 1638 his eldest son, Sir William, who had been his deputy in New Scotland and in the secretaryship of Scotland during the troubles following the imposition of the prayer book, died of a fever. Deprived of these supports, Stirling himself began to fail. He had to make away large parts of his estates and emoluments to satisfy his creditors in January 1640 and died on 12 February at his Covent Garden house in London in debt to the enormous sum of approximately £136,000 Scots. In April his body was brought back to Scotland and buried on the 12th in Bowie's aisle in the Holy Rude Church in Stirling, it is said by night to avoid the crowd of angry creditors. In the eighteenth century Bowie's aisle was used as a saw-pit and the lead of the coffin was picked away by schoolboys to write with. The aisle itself was demolished in the nineteenth century and with it all memorial of the first earl of Stirling. He was succeeded by the infant son of his eldest son, who survived his grandfather by only a few months; the earldom then passed to Alexander's third son, Henry. His wife survived at least until May 1649.

Stirling had imagined the role of counsellor with great persistence in the years when he wrote *Paraenesis* and *The Monarchicke Tragedies*. From these imaginings he brought to the part an ideal of service and a fund of unexceptionable commonplaces, with perhaps a certain forthrightness in delivering them that may have carried an air of manly honesty. In practice, to judge from his letters, tact and a way of conciliating opponents seem to have been his greatest assets. He was not a bad choice as intermediary between Charles and the Scots in the earlier part of the reign. As a projector, he was no doubt self-seeking and inflamed with the great expectations of a successful and lavish courtier. But he could with some justice represent his schemes to himself as leading to the public good. New

Scotland, following New England, was an obvious place for colonial development and the failure of the project may be put down to the conservatism or narrowness of the Scots as much as to Charles's selling out to France. Fish in the Scottish seas were still an unexploited source of wealth in 1730, as James Thomson laments (*Autumn*, 920–23). A copper coinage was needed in Scotland. And James's and Stirling's metrical Psalms could only have improved on the doggerel versions of Sternhold and Hopkins. That these schemes failed was partly bad luck; they were both imaginative and, in outline, apt. But perhaps their failure was owing also to a certain diffuseness in Stirling's energy. That is the trouble with his poetry. It makes the right noises but rarely achieves concentrated effect in words.

Three portraits of Stirling survive. The earliest is the engraving, probably by William Marshall, prefixed to a few copies of the *Monarchicke Tragedies* of 1616. The second is the Marshall engraving prefixed to a few copies of *Recreations with the Muses* (1637); it was probably drawn in 1634. The third is the oil portrait in the Scottish National Portrait Gallery, in which the badge of Stirling's earldom hangs at his breast; the frame bears the date 1636. From the painting, one gathers that his hair and beard were dark and that his looks in middle age were all that could be desired of a counsellor in point of gravity.

DAVID REID

Sources T. H. McGrail, *Sir William Alexander, first earl of Stirling* (1940) · C. Rogers, *Memorials of the earl of Stirling and of the house of Alexander*, 2 vols. (1877) · C. Rogers, ed., *The earl of Stirling's register of royal letters relative to the affairs of Scotland and Nova Scotia from 1615 to 1635*, 2 vols. (1885) · W. Alexander, *An encouragement to colonies* (1624) · *The poetical works of Sir William Alexander, earl of Stirling*, ed. L. E. Kastner and H. B. Charlton, 2 vols., STS, new ser., 11, 24 (1922–9) · *The works of William Drummond, of Hawthornden*, ed. J. Sage and T. Ruddiman, [3 pts] (1711) · *Scots peerage* · W. Fraser, ed., *Registrum monasterii S. Marie de Cambuskenneth*, Grampian Club, 4 (1872) · *DNB* · D. Laing, 'A brief account of the Hawthornden MSS in the possession of the Society of Antiquaries of Scotland', *Archaeologia Scotica: Transactions of the Society of Antiquaries of Scotland*, 4 (1857) · W. Alexander, *A short discourse of the good ends of the higher providence, in the late attemptat against his maiesties person* (1600) · W. K. Leask, ed., *Musa Latina Aberdonensis*, 3: *Poetae minores*, New Spalding Club, 37 (1910) · R. M. Fergusson, *Alexander Hume … and his intimates* (1899) · NL Scot., Hawthornden MS 2061 · *The works of Michael Drayton*, ed. J. W. Hebbel, 5 vols. (1931–41) · *The complete works … of Samuel Daniel*, ed. A. B. Grosart, 5 vols. (1885–96) · *CSP dom.*, 1603–10 · J. M. Thomson and others, eds., *Registrum magni sigilli regum Scotorum / The register of the great seal of Scotland*, 11 vols. (1882–1914), vols. 6, 8 · *Reg. PCS*, 1st ser., vol. 10 · *Reg. PCS*, 2nd ser., vol. 4 · T. Urquhart, *The jewel*, ed. R. D. S. Jack and R. J. Lyall (1983) · *The letters and journals of Robert Baillie*, ed. D. Laing, 1 (1841) · *The Stirling Antiquary* (1904), 3 · GEC, *Peerage* · private information (2004) [J. G. Harrison]
Archives NA Scot., register of royal letters · NL Scot., corresp. · NL Scot., official letters | NA Scot., letters to seventh earl of Menteith · NL Scot., Hawthornden MS 2061 · NRA, priv. coll., corresp. with John, first earl of Traquair
Likenesses W. Marshall, line engraving, 1634?, BM; repro. in W. Alexander, *Recreations with the muses* (1637) · attrib. W. Marshall, line engraving, BM, NPG; repro. in W. Alexander, *Monarchicke tragedies*, 3rd edn (1616) · oils, Scot. NPG [*see illus.*]
Wealth at death owed approx. £136,000 Scots; owed to him £9983 Scots: Edinburgh commissariat testaments, vol. 60, 1641

Alexander, William, styled sixth earl of Stirling (1726–1783), army officer in America, was born on 25 December 1726 in New York city, one of seven children of James *Alexander (1691–1756), a surveyor, lawyer, and politician, and Mary Spratt Provoost (1693–1760), a rich merchant and the daughter of John Spratt and Maria DePeyster. He was reared in privilege and received an education from his father and tutors. Although in awe of his wealthy and powerful parents, he assumed a clerkship in his mother's mercantile business and subsequently became a co-partner. In 1748 he married Sarah (*d.* in or after 1783), daughter of Philip Livingston; they had two children.

Having obtained a contract for supplying the king's troops in New York during the Niagara campaign of 1755–6, Alexander joined the commissariat of the army. Shortly afterward he attracted the notice of General William Shirley, the commander-in-chief and governor of Massachusetts, who made him his aide-de-camp and private secretary. He went to England in 1756 to pursue payment of bills owed him, and to give evidence on behalf of Shirley after the latter had been charged with neglect of duty. Successful in forwarding his financial claims, he was less so in defending Shirley, who was removed from the governorship of Massachusetts.

Alexander became enamoured of the style of life of the landed gentry, and asserted a claim to the lapsed Scottish earldom of Stirling. After spending a fortune pursuing the title, he finally had to rely on the evidence of two old men to affirm his descent from John Alexander, uncle of the first earl. A jury at Edinburgh declared him heir male of Henry, fifth earl of Stirling, but in March 1762 the Lords committee on privileges decided against his claims. Before this he had returned to America, where he continued to make use of the title to the close of his life. He succeeded his father, who died in 1756, as surveyor-general of New York and New Jersey, and was subsequently chosen as a member of the provincial councils of both colonies. He was also appointed a governor of King's College (later Columbia University), an institution that he had actively supported for many years.

Living as a country gentleman, Stirling wasted a fortune of more than £100,000 in the next twenty years. He also developed a drinking problem, according to both friends and enemies. In the disputes that led to the revolt of the American colonies he initially favoured British policies of tightening control over them. In the 1760s he even encouraged the Board of Trade to enforce mercantile laws that his fellow citizens found onerous. When the rupture finally took place, however, he sided with the American rebels, and was promoted colonel and chosen to command a New Jersey militia regiment. In January 1776 he distinguished himself by the brilliant capture of a British armed transport and was made a brigadier-general of the middle department. Shortly afterwards he assumed the chief command at New York and began improving the city's defences. He was relieved of this duty by the arrival of General George Washington in April. At the battle of Long Island on 26 August he was taken prisoner but was soon exchanged. He served with Washington at the battle

of White Plains, the march across New Jersey, and the defeat of the Hessians at Trenton on 25 December. In February 1777 he was promoted major-general.

Although Stirling's subsequent military achievements were not of a strikingly brilliant character, they were solid and substantial. At Metuchen in June 1777 he was pummelled by the British army, but in the battles of Brandywine and Germantown he conducted himself with great discretion. At the battle of Monmouth on 28 June 1778 he placed the batteries of his division with great effect to retard advancing British troops, and he also repulsed with heavy loss an attempt to turn his flank. After this battle, he chaired the court martial of General Charles Lee, and in 1779 he assisted Major Henry Lee in attacking British troops at Paulus Hook. Early in 1780 he conducted an ineffectual raid on Staten Island and in June helped Nathanael Greene repulse enemy forces at Springfield. In 1781 he was appointed to the command in Albany, under orders to thwart an expected enemy attack at Saratoga. No attack came, and his duty for the remainder of the war was easy. He died at Albany on 15 January 1783 of a violent attack of gout, and was buried the following day at the Dutch church, Albany. He was remembered by his family, friends, and military colleagues as a genuinely likeable, decent, trustworthy man, whose ebullient personality expressed itself in buoyant optimism and good humour.   PAUL DAVID NELSON

Sources P. D. Nelson, *William Alexander, Lord Stirling* (1987) • P. D. Nelson, 'Alexander, William', *ANB* • W. A. Duer, *The life of William Alexander, earl of Stirling* (1847) • A. Valentine, *Lord Stirling* (1969) • L. Schumacher, *Major-General the earl of Stirling: an essay in biography* (1897) • C. A. Ditmas, *Life and service of Major-General William Alexander* (1920) • T. Thayer, 'The army contractor for the Niagara campaign', *William and Mary Quarterly*, 14 (1957), 31–46 • T. L. Purvis, 'Alexander, James', *ANB* • T. Russell, 'Alexander, Mary Spratt Provoost', *ANB*
Archives National Archives and Records Administration, Washington, DC • New York Historical Society • NYPL | L. Cong., Washington MSS
Likenesses B. Otis, oils, Independence National Historical Park, Philadelphia

Alexander, William (*bap.* 1742?, *d.* 1788?), physician and author, was probably the son of William Alexander and Elizabeth Allanson of Halifax who was baptized at Halifax on 6 January 1742; much about his life remains obscure. In the 1760s he attended medical classes at the University of Edinburgh including those of William Cullen in chemistry and James Russell in natural philosophy. By then he had already seen service with the Surrey militia, and he appears to have practised in Edinburgh for some years before taking his MD in 1769. On 26 January 1765 he was admitted to the Medical Society of Edinburgh and on 28 December 1766 he married Eliza Thomson in the college kirk, Edinburgh. By 1768 he had moved to London, where in that year he published his *Experimental Essays*, in which he described experiments he had conducted in Edinburgh and London, in a 'free and liberal spirit of enquiry' in opposition to 'blind deference to rules' (W. Alexander, *Experimental Essays*, 1768, vi–vii). His *Experimental Enquiry concerning the causes which have generally been said to produce* *putrid diseases* (1771) details experiments conducted with 'the stinking water of the North Loch' and from other marshes and locations around Edinburgh, and in London (W. Alexander, *An Experimental Enquiry*, 1771, 65–73). On 16 October 1771 he married for a second time, at Haughton-le-Skerne, co. Durham; his second wife was the widowed Elizabeth Bendlowes.

The tone of Alexander's medical writing is of an impatience with inherited wisdom, an urgent preoccupation with experiment, and an insistence on investigation. His range of interests, in natural history, in medical science, and in travel literature, placed him at the heart of new approaches to the 'natural history of man' pioneered by Claude Buffon. His best-known work, the *History of Women* (1779), draws upon these interests but also deserves to take a place among Enlightenment histories of civil society. Though Alexander clearly knew and was influenced by Montesquieu and the *encyclopédistes*, it was to contemporary Scottish historians such as John Millar, Lord Kames, and Gilbert Stuart that he owed his greatest debts. Like them, he attempted to place the history of women and gender roles firmly within the history of civil society, though he also perpetuated their disagreements and inconsistencies. The *History* is long, rambling, and inconsistent, and omits any scholarly references. In it, Alexander drew widely and indiscriminately upon biblical history, theological studies, classical and medieval histories, and travel literature to construct narratives of women's employment, marriage, child-rearing patterns, customs and ceremonies, and the status and public power of women. He explored the relative influences of nature, or biology, and education, or environment, in shaping the manners of women; the potential for the moral corruption of nations in the absence of female chastity; the relationship between the progress of 'civilization' and the condition of women; and the distinctive characteristics of both 'northern' and British women. On the whole Alexander was inclined to give little weight to the influence of Christianity in the improvement of the condition of women, and there is an anti-Catholic and anti-clerical tinge to much of his discussion. The work received broadly favourable reviews, although the *Gentleman's Magazine* criticized his treatment of the women of the Bible and the *Monthly Review* judged it frivolous, inelegant, and obscene, entirely inappropriate for female readers. Alexander appears to have made some amendments to meet these comments in the third edition of 1782. The work was sufficiently successful to be translated into German in 1780–81, and into French in 1791.

Very little is known of Alexander's last years. He was admitted as a non-resident fellow of the Royal Society of Edinburgh on 3 November 1783, when his address was given as London. Obituaries vary on his date of death; it is not clear whether he can be identified with the Dr Alexander who kept an academy in Hampstead and died in Margate on 9 September 1788.　　JANE RENDALL

Sources J. Rendall, introduction, in W. Alexander, *History of women, from the earliest antiquity to the present time*, 2 vols. (1995), v–xxvi · *Medical Register* (1779) · *Medical Register* (1780) · *Medical Register* (1783) · *Transactions of the Royal Society of Edinburgh*, 1/1 (1788), 88 · *European Magazine and London Review*, 14 (1788), 232 · *GM*, 1st ser., 58 (1788), 840 · *Scots Magazine*, 33 (1771), 558 · F. J. Grant, ed., *Register of marriages of the city of Edinburgh, 1751–1800*, Scottish RS, 53 (1922) · E. G. Forbes, ed., *Index of fellows of the Royal Society of Edinburgh, elected from 1783 to 1882, containing their dates of birth, death and election to that society* (1980) · medical matriculation registers, U. Edin. L. · *IGI*

Archives U. Edin. L., MSS · U. Edin. L., medical matriculation registers

Alexander, William (1767–1816), artist and museum curator, was born at Maidstone, Kent, on 10 April 1767, one of the three sons and one daughter of Harry Alexander, a coachbuilder. A pencil and watercolour sketch by Alexander of the street where he was born is in Maidstone Museum and Art Gallery. He attended Maidstone grammar school, and moved to London in 1782, enrolling as a student at the Royal Academy Schools in 1784. He may have studied with J. C. Ibbetson (1759–1817), who probably recommended him for the post of junior draughtsman in Lord Macartney's embassy to China in 1792–4. A self-portrait sketched during the voyage (with a fanciful piratical eyepatch) is in the British Museum.

The enriching encounter with China provided a source of inspiration for Alexander's exhibiting and publishing career. His drawings illustrative of the expedition were engraved for the official record (G. Staunton, *An Authentic Account of an Embassy from the King of Great Britain to the Emperor of China*, 1797). Alexander's own publications included *Views of the headlands, islands, etc., taken during a voyage to, and along the eastern coast of China, in the years 1792 & 1793* (1798). His designs were used for the aquatints in John Barrow's *A Voyage to Cochin China, in the Years 1792, and 1793* (1806).

On his return from China Alexander married on 10 April 1795 Jane Wogan or Wagan, but she died shortly afterwards. They had no children. Between 1795 and 1804 Alexander worked up many of his preliminary studies and sketches of Chinese landscape and costume for the exhibition at the Royal Academy. Characteristic are: *The Emperor of China's Garden, the Imperial Palace, Pekin* (1793; V&A) and *The Pagoda of Lin-ching-shih, Peking* (exh. RA, 1796; priv. coll.). Resident in London between 1795 and 1801, Alexander was an active member of Girtin's Sketching Club (founded 1799) and visited the physician and patron of watercolour painters Dr Thomas Monro at his house at Fetcham, Surrey. On 29 August 1802 he was appointed master of landscape drawing at the Royal Military College in Great Marlow, Buckinghamshire; he resigned in 1808. Having completed work on Daniell's sketches for George Vancouver, *A voyage of discovery to the North Pacific Ocean, and round the world … in the years 1790–1795* (3 vols., 1798), he published *The Costume of the Russian Empire* (1802), illustrated with seventy-three engravings, and in 1805 *The Costume of China*, containing forty-eight coloured engravings; he also produced drawings engraved by T. Medland as illustrations to *Egyptian monuments from the collection formed by the National Institute … deposited in the British Museum* (1805–7).

On 11 June 1808 Alexander was appointed assistant librarian and first keeper of prints and drawings at the British Museum. In 1810, commissioned by the trustees, he began the first inventory of the museum's collection of prints and drawings. Principally appointed for his skills of draughtsmanship, Alexander was soon engaged by the trustees to illustrate items from the Townley collection, in Taylor Combe's *A Description of the Collection of Ancient Terracottas in the British Museum* (1810) and *A Description of the Collection of Ancient Marbles in the British Museum* (parts 1–4, 1812–18). Alexander was a member of the Society of Antiquaries.

Alexander is best remembered for his work on China in a period in which the Chinese style greatly influenced the decorative arts in Britain. His meticulous, highly finished technique using pen, ink, and tinted wash is distinctive, his watercolours delicate, his engravings and soft ground etchings were much admired. His other significant publications include a collection of etchings *Chinese Life* (1798–1805); a lithograph facsimile of his journal (1837); and his narrative *A journey to Beresford Hall, the seat of Charles Cotton esqre, the celebrated author and angler* (1841). Some of his collection of eighteenth-century British paintings and drawings were sold at Sothebys in February and March 1817. Alexander died of a brain fever on 23 July 1816 at his uncle's house in Maidstone. He was buried at Boxley, Kent. Examples of his drawings are in the Victoria and Albert Museum, London; the Ashmolean Museum, Oxford; the Fitzwilliam Museum, Cambridge; the India Office Library, London; Leeds City Art Gallery; Maidstone Museum and Art Gallery; and other regional museums.

RICHARD GARNETT, rev. HEATHER M. MACLENNAN

Sources P. Conner and S. L. Sloman, *William Alexander: an English artist in imperial China* (1981), incl. bibliography and list of works [exhibition catalogue, Brighton and Nottingham, 8 Sept – 17 Dec 1981] · *GM*, 1st ser., 86/2 (1816), 94 · A. Griffiths, ed., *Landmarks in print collecting: connoisseurs and donors at the British Museum since 1753* (British Museum Press, 1996) [exhibition catalogue, Museum of Fine Arts, Houston, TX, 1996, and elsewhere] · Farington, *Diary* · M. Hardie, *Water-colour painting in Britain*, ed. D. Snelgrove, J. Mayne, and B. Taylor, 2–3 (1967–8) · *IGI* · Mallalieu, *Watercolour artists* · Graves, *RA exhibitors* · L. Binyon, *Catalogue of drawings by British artists and artists of foreign origin working in Great Britain*, 4 vols. (1898–1907) · Redgrave, *Artists* · R. Parkinson, *British watercolours at the Victoria and Albert Museum* (1998) · A. Wilton and A. Lyles, *The great age of British watercolours, 1750–1880* (1993) [exhibition catalogue, RA, 15 Jan – 12 April 1993, and National Gallery of Art, Washington, DC, 9 May – 25 July 1993] · P. Conner, 'Alexander, William', *The dictionary of art*, ed. J. Turner (1996) · T. Dodd, *The connoisseur's repertory, or, A biographical history of painters, engravers, sculptors, and architects ... from the twelfth century to the end of the eighteenth* (1825) · S. C. Hutchison, 'The Royal Academy Schools, 1768–1830', *Walpole Society*, 38 (1960–62), 123–91, esp. 148

Archives BL, journals of voyage to Beijing, Add. MSS 35174–35175 · BL OIOC, drawings of China · CKS, MS on Alexander family

Likenesses W. Alexander, self-portrait, pencil, pen, and ink drawing, 1792–4, BM; repro. in Conner and Sloman, *William Alexander*, 2 · S. Cousins, pencil drawing, 1815, BM · C. Picart, stipple (aged forty-one; after H. Edridge), BM, NPG

Alexander, William (1824–1911), archbishop of Armagh, was born in Derry on 13 April 1824. His father, Robert Alexander, rector of Termoneeney, Derry, at the time, later to be prebendary of Aghadowey, Derry, was a nephew of Nathanael Alexander, bishop of Meath, and great-nephew

William Alexander (1824–1911), by Charles Napier Kennedy, 1894

of James Alexander, first earl of Caledon. His mother was Dorothea, daughter of Henry McClintock of Ballyarton, co. Londonderry. William was the eldest son in a family of three boys: Henry rose to the rank of rear-admiral and Robert, a soldier, was killed at the siege of Delhi.

William was educated at Tonbridge School, Kent, winning an exhibition to Exeter College, Oxford, where he matriculated on 19 November 1841, graduating (fourth class) in classical honours in 1847. He left Oxford for a time, returning to New Hall and thence to Brasenose College, from which he took the degree of BA in 1854. He distinguished himself by winning the Denyer prize for an essay on the divinity of Christ (1850), and in 1853 received an award for his congratulatory ode to Lord Derby, the new chancellor. His poem 'The Waters of Babylon' received the university prize in 1860, and in 1867 he was a candidate for the professorship of poetry, being narrowly defeated by Sir Francis H. Doyle. In 1867, on his preferment to the episcopate, Oxford awarded him the degree of DD, followed by an honorary DLitt in 1907, the year in which he was elected an honorary fellow of Brasenose. He had already been conferred with an honorary LLD by Dublin.

Alexander was ordained deacon in 1847 for the curacy of Templemore, Derry Cathedral, where he served until 1850, having been ordained priest in 1848. From 1850 to 1855 he was rector of Termonamongan, co. Tyrone, becoming rector of Upper Fahan (then in the diocese of

Derry) in 1850. From 1855 to 1860 he served as rector of Fahan and from 1860 as rector of Camus-juxta-Mourne until his appointment to the see of Derry in 1867. He held the sinecure of dean of Emly from 1864. In 1896 he was translated to the see of Armagh. On 15 October 1850 he married Cecil Frances, née Humphreys [see Alexander, Cecil Frances], the hymn writer; they had two sons and two daughters. Mrs Alexander died on 12 October 1895.

Much in demand as preacher and lecturer, in both Britain and America (where he carried out a speaking tour in 1891 in aid of Derry Cathedral), Alexander was select preacher at Oxford on four occasions, twice at Cambridge and once at Dublin. His Bampton lectures appeared in a third edition in 1898, and his published works also included two books of verse: *Specimens* (1867), privately circulated as part of his canvass for the Oxford chair of poetry, and *St Augustine's Confessions and other Pieces* (1886). He was capable of some telling phrases, for instance attributing to Swift the capacity to 'carve out a tumour in alabaster' and 'enshrine putrescence under a crystal case'. Yet neither his poetry nor his theological writing has stood the test of time, though as an orator he made significant contributions to several important contemporary debates.

Alexander's Tractarian outlook, dating from his undergraduate years at Oxford, made him suspect in some Church of Ireland quarters. He took a minority position as a member of the court of the general synod when the court found against the vicar of St Bartholomew's, Dublin, in a case related to an alleged infringement of the canons of the Church of Ireland. His proposals for a diocesan conference in Derry in 1890, when the Revd R. R. Dolling was to be a speaker, caused such a furore that the occasion had to be cancelled.

Yet Alexander's churchmanship would in a later era be generally regarded as having stood the Church of Ireland in good stead. Forcefully, yet with tact, he argued for the integrity of Anglican formularies at a time when attempts were made from within the newly disestablished church radically to revise the Book of Common Prayer. A contemporary wrote of 'the impassioned rhetoric of the great poet-preacher, with the innate witchery of his superb voice'.

Alexander was very much in tune with Church of Ireland opinion when he contributed with equal skill, but less success, to two other, and perhaps more important, debates. Disestablishment was abhorrent to him and he spoke vigorously against it in the House of Lords. 'You are condemning the Irish Church of the last century because it did not act upon principles not then recognised.' He also pointed out, with some justification, that since the Act of Union had joined the established churches of England and Ireland 'for ever', the government disestablishment bill struck at a fundamental condition of the union of the two kingdoms. He made an impassioned speech against home rule for Ireland in the Albert Hall, London, in 1893, regarding the proposal with grave apprehension so far as the future of the Church of Ireland was concerned.

Though a high-churchman Alexander was not insensitive to the feelings of other churches. He deprecated it when terms such as 'apostolic succession' were used in such a way as to cause offence, and he maintained cordial relations with Cardinal Logue, the Roman Catholic primate.

Archbishop Alexander resigned from his see on 30 January 1911, and lived in Torquay, Devon, until his death at his home, Belton Lodge, Torquay, on 12 September of that year. He was buried on 16 September 1911, beside his wife, in the churchyard of Derry Cathedral. The Synod Hall in Armagh is dedicated in his memory.

KENNETH MILNE

Sources J. B. Leslie, *Derry clergy and parishes* (1937) · *The Guardian* (15 Sept 1911) · *The Times* (13 Sept 1911) · E. Alexander, *Primate Alexander, archbishop of Armagh: a memoir* (1913) · *Hansard 3*, cols. 1728, 1740 · *Journal of the General Convention of 1870* (1870) · *Journal of the General Synod of the Church of Ireland, 1895* · H. E. Patton, *Fifty years of disestablishment* (1922) · G. F. Seaver, *John Allen Fitzgerald Gregg, archbishop* (1963) · Foster, *Alum. Oxon.* · W. A. Phillips, ed., *History of the Church of Ireland*, 3 (1933) · R. B. McDowell, *The Church of Ireland, 1869–1969* (1975) · letter by William Alexander, 10 June 1867, Representative Church Body Library, Dublin [soliciting support for his candidacy for chair of poetry] · *Irish Ecclesiastical Gazette* (17 May 1895) · *CGPLA Ire.* (1911) · *The Times* (18 Sept 1911)
Archives Representative Church Body Library, Dublin, letters to Thomas Cooke-Trench | BL, letters to Mrs D. M. Craik
Likenesses C. N. Kennedy, oils, 1894, Derry deanery, Londonderry [see illus.] · W. Osborne, oils, 1896, Synod Hall, Armagh · H. H. Browne, oils, c.1911, NG Ire. · Elliott & Fry, photograph, NPG · J. Russell & Sons, photograph, London · Spy [L. Ward], caricature, NG Ire.; repro. in *VF* (1895)
Wealth at death £33,569 1s. 8d.: resworn probate, 18 Dec 1911, *CGPLA Ire.* · £29,099 13s. 8d. in England: Irish probate sealed in England, 28 Dec 1911, *CGPLA Eng. & Wales*

Alexander, William (1826–1894), novelist and journalist, was born on 12 June 1826 at the farm of Westerhouses, Rescivet, in the parish of Chapel of Garioch, Aberdeenshire. He was the eldest son of the ten children of James Alexander (1789–1856), blacksmith and tenant farmer, and his wife, Anne Wilson of Old Rayne (1802–1889). He received the normal course of instruction for a country boy at the parish school of Daviot, but the real education of this deeply cerebral man began within the pioneering educational self-help movement then spreading throughout the north-east of Scotland.

Alexander's enthusiastic beginnings in the family farming tradition ended abruptly when, at about the age of twenty, he lost a leg in an accident. During the long recuperation period he taught himself shorthand and became active in the Aberdeenshire and Banffshire Mutual Instruction Union. This won him the friendship and support of William McCombie of Cairnballoch, political economist and moral philosopher, and one of the most impressive autodidacts in Scotland in a generation which included Robert Chambers and Hugh Miller. McCombie gave Alexander a thorough grounding in 'the leading philosophical tendencies of the age' and a job on his newspaper, a struggling radical weekly called the *Aberdeen Free Press*. Alexander was the main support of his late father's young family, and he was forty-one when he married

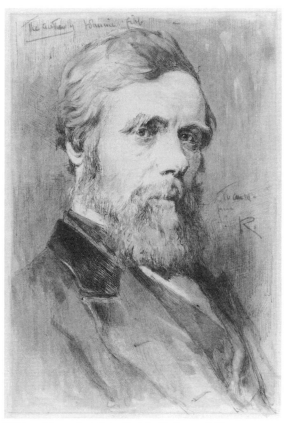

William Alexander (1826–1894), by Sir George Reid

Anne Allan, a schoolteacher, at Oldmachar, Aberdeen, on 22 May 1867. They had no children.

McCombie was largely an absentee editor, so that Alexander effectively ran the *Free Press* for many years before he officially succeeded to the editorial chair in 1870. He was one of the pioneering generation of professional journalists that created the Scottish popular press after the repeal of the Stamp Act in 1855. A lifetime of reporting politics at city and parliamentary level nourished his fascination with power. He was effective in gaining access for the press to the centres of decision making, and was intimately familiar with every aspect of newspaper work, from agriculture—in which he was an authority in his own right—to fine art. His shorthand was renowned, and he was famous for his ability to reproduce people vividly and economically on the page. His professional achievements were recognized when he was made vice-president of the Institute of Journalists. Alexander was active in liberal politics in the north-east of Scotland and also in the civic life of the city of Aberdeen. He was a council member of the New Spalding Club and the Aberdeen Philosophical Society, and was active in many projects for the benefit of the city. In 1887 he was awarded an honorary LLD by the University of Aberdeen.

As a writer, Alexander's most famous work is the novel *Johnny Gibb of Gushetneuk*, begun as a serial in the *Free Press* on 28 September 1869. It was published in book form in 1871 and went through more than twenty editions thereafter, seldom being out of print. The novel long enjoyed a merely regional reputation because of the radical demotic Scots in which it is written, as, for example, in the famous opening apostrophe:

> Heely, heely, Tam, ye glaiket stirk—ye hinna on the hin shelvin o' the cairt. Fat hae ye been haiverin at min? That cauff saick'll be tint owre the back door afore we win a mile fae hame. See't yer belly ban' be ticht aneuch noo. Woo, lassie! Man, ye been makin' a hantle mair adee aboot blaikin that graith o' yours, an' kaimin the mear's tail, nor balancin' yer cairt, an' gettin' the things packit in till't.
> (W. Alexander, *Johnny Gibb*, 1871, 1)

It later came to be regarded as a classic of nineteenth-century Scottish fiction. A masterly study of power and its ramifications at every social level, the work deals with the struggle to control the land and the impact of the great Disruption of 1843, the most dramatic event of nineteenth-century Scottish history. It centres on the eponymous hero, Johnny Gibb, tenant farmer of Gushetneuk in Aberdeenshire, a man conceived in epic Courbet-like proportions, who leads the successful revolt of the small farmers against established authority in politics and religion. The novel takes a revolutionary view of the centrality and significance of the common man, and offers a radical solution to the crisis in land ownership, being influenced by John Stuart Mill as well as by contemporary French socialist thinking.

It was not Alexander's intention that *Johnny Gibb* should appear in book form at all; it was deliberately addressed to a plebeian audience, the high-quality Scottish common readers among whom he himself had grown up, and it was only at the insistence of friends that it was launched into the heavily Anglicized middle-class book market. Because the market for books within the United Kingdom was at that time dominated by England, Scottish novelists, from Scott to Barrie and beyond, had to accommodate themselves to this fact, and present a view of Scotland and Scottish life that fitted English prejudices and expectations. Some of Alexander's other writings were also published in book form—his short-story collection *Life amongst my Ain Folk* (1875) and the brilliant social history *Notes and Sketches Illustrative of Northern Rural Life* (1877).

Most of Alexander's work, including a further five novels, remained until the mid-1980s in the obscurity of the newspaper columns in which it had originally been published, so that his full range and power only then began to be appreciated. The 'lost' novels (two of which, *The Laird of Drammochdyle* and *My Uncle the Baillie*, were published in book form in 1986 and 1995 respectively) deal powerfully with city as well as country life, with the plight of the urban poor as well as with farmers and cotters; they draw upon a complex of advanced social, economic, and scientific theory, and taken together form an ambitious imaginative sequence covering more than a century of social and economic change.

Alexander's work demonstrates the presence of a sophisticated literary realism in a tradition previously dismissed as having dwindled into kailyard sentimentality. It was central to the re-evaluation of nineteenth-century Scottish literature that took place in the last decades of the twentieth century. Alexander died of pneumonia at his home, 3 Belvidere Street, Aberdeen, on 19 February 1894 and was buried on 24 February in the city's Nellfield cemetery. WILLIAM DONALDSON

Sources W. Donaldson, *Popular literature in Victorian Scotland* (1986), 101–44 · W. Donaldson, 'Introduction', in W. Alexander, *Johnny Gibb of Gushetneuk* (1995), vii–xxiii · W. Alexander, *My uncle the baillie*, ed. W. Donaldson (1995), introduction, 1–17 · W. Donaldson, 'William Alexander and north-east literature', *Aberdeen University Review*, 55 (1993–4), 260–70 · A. Mackilligan, 'Johnny Gibb of Gushetneuk', *Buchan Club Transactions*, 13 (1926), 96–120 · W. Alexander, *Rural life in Victorian Aberdeenshire*, ed. I. Carter (1992), introduction, 5–25 · W. Alexander, *The Laird of Drammochdyle*, ed. W. Donaldson (1986), introduction, vii–xxi · parish records (birth), Chapel of Garioch, Aberdeenshire, 12 June 1826 · private information (2004)
Likenesses G. Reid, oils, *c.*1880, Aberdeen Art Gallery · G. Reid, sketch, *c.*1880, Aberdeen Art Gallery · J. Pittendrigh Macgillivray, bronze effigy on monument, *c.*1895, Nellfield cemetery, Aberdeen · G. Reid, pen, ink, and wash on paper, Scot. NPG [*see illus.*]
Wealth at death £4678 13s. 11d.: confirmation, 31 March 1894, CCI

Alexander, William (1845–1919), surgeon, was born on 29 April 1845 at Holestone, co. Antrim, Ireland, one of eight known children of James Alexander (*d.* 1887), tenant farmer, and his wife, Elizabeth (*d.* 1906). After schooling in nearby Doagh, Alexander studied medicine from 1866 to 1870 at Queen's College, Belfast, winning many prizes and scholarships. In 1870 he graduated MD MCh (Royal University of Ireland), as gold medallist and exhibitioner; in 1877 he obtained his FRCS in London. Alexander moved to Liverpool in the early 1870s to become resident surgeon at the Liverpool select vestry's huge Brownlow Hill workhouse infirmary. On establishing a general practice in 1875, he became visiting surgeon. About this time he married Alice Cooper Caey, daughter of David Moore MD, of Belfast. Their only child, David Moore Alexander (1878–1915), became a bacteriologist. Mrs Alexander died a few years after the birth of their son.

Brownlow Hill offered Alexander plenty of opportunity for pathological experiment and, in addition to performing his routine surgical work, he was able to perfect several innovative operations, including a new way of excising advanced cancer of the rectum, the radical cure of hernia, cholecystostomy (on which he made the first Liverpool report in 1888), surgery for epilepsy, and the correction of uterine displacement.

In 1888 Alexander was appointed honorary surgeon to the Royal Southern Hospital in Liverpool's dockland. A former colleague described Alexander as one of the last of the old school of general practitioner surgeons, whose career, encompassing medicine, general surgery, gynaecology, midwifery, paediatrics, and pharmacy, was of a kind becoming unusual in an age of increasing specialization. Physically and mentally Alexander was an extraordinary worker whose day generally began with a pre-breakfast visit to Brownlow Hill and ended with a night-time check on his post-operative patients at the Royal Southern. Alexander was a diehard in his adherence to Listerian antisepsis and later to aseptic principles; in 1889 he led a surgical revolt at the Royal Southern by refusing to operate in a theatre lying immediately above the mortuary; this resulted in the building of a separate block containing a mortuary, a post-mortem room, and laboratories.

Alexander regularly presented papers and demonstrated pathological specimens to fellow members of the Liverpool Medical Institution, and he wrote articles for the *Liverpool Medico-Chirurgical Journal* and other publications. He also lectured in clinical surgery at Liverpool University, and when time allowed he carried out his own research. In 1881 he won the Jacksonian prize for his essay 'The pathology and surgical treatment of diseases of the hip joint'. This was based on case histories of boys with strumous (tubercular) bone disease who were cared for at the select vestry's convalescent home in Maghull, which though only 7 miles from Liverpool provided an environment of fresh air and green fields that Alexander insisted upon for the treatment of these patients. In 1883 Alexander won the Guy's Hospital Sir Astley Cooper prize for his essay 'The pathology and pathological relations of chronic rheumatoid arthritis'.

Alexander was also interested in those workhouse inmates who suffered from epilepsy. In his *Treatment of Epilepsy* (1889) he described their aimless and stigmatized lives, deplored the widespread use of bromides which had debilitating side-effects, and outlined his attempts to reduce seizures by trephining, removal of the superior cervical ganglia, and ligature of the vertebral arteries. In *Brain* (July 1882), Alexander claimed considerable success for the last of these procedures, but in his *Treatment of Epilepsy* he admitted that the improvement was only temporary and that he no longer recommended it. After this date Alexander seldom operated for epilepsy. A rare criticism of Alexander's work had appeared in the *Liverpool Review* of June 1887, when 'Scrutator' decried the procedures as useless, unethical, and experimental. Having considered the limited options Alexander concluded that a communal country life would be best for his patients, and with financial backing from a Liverpool merchant and the support of the Liverpool Central Relief and Charity Organization Society (to which he was medical officer) he began to plan a suitable scheme. After visiting a well-known epileptic 'colony' in Bielefeld, Germany, Alexander and a small committee launched a home for epileptics in the Manor House, Maghull, in 1888. At the Manor House, capable epileptics were provided with simple, nourishing food, warm clothing, and regular hours of sleep, recreation, and work in agriculture or a choice of trades. Men and women were segregated and no lunatic or hopeless cases were accepted. The Manor House proved to be the first of several epileptic homes and colonies in Britain which were later known as the Maghull Homes, one of which was named the Alexander Home.

Alexander, who did most of the gynaecological work at

the Royal Southern and who became president of the British Gynaecological Association, is also remembered in the Alexander–Adams operation to correct the retroverted uterus, sharing the honour with James Adams of Glasgow, whose first report followed two months after Alexander's in 1882. Alexander wrote numerous papers on the operation as well as two books, *The treatment of backward displacements of the uterus and of prolapsus uteri by the new method of shortening the round ligaments* (1884), and *Practical gynaecology with fifteen years' experience of the operation of shortening the round ligaments* (1899).

In 1894 Alexander published *The Results of Twenty Years' Experience in Practical Surgery*. He began to run down his lucrative Rodney Street practice and he retired in 1910, after nearly forty years at Brownlow Hill and twenty-two years at the Royal Southern, retaining links with the latter as honorary consulting surgeon. With the niece who shared his home he moved to a new house, Holestone, Tower Road, Heswall, on the Wirral peninsula. A lieutenant-colonel in the Territorial Army, he joined the staff of the 1st Western General Hospital when war broke out in 1914. Alexander died of influenza and heart failure at home on 9 March 1919. After a service on 13 March in the local Presbyterian church at Heswall, where he was a regular worshipper, he was buried on the same day at Heswall, at St Peter's parish church.

JEAN BARCLAY

Sources C. J. Macalister, *The origin and history of the Liverpool Royal Southern Hospital* (1936) · J. A. Shepherd, *A history of the Liverpool Medical Institution* (1979) · V. G. Plarr, *Plarr's Lives of the fellows of the Royal College of Surgeons of England*, rev. D'A. Power, 2 vols. (1930) · W. T. Pike, *Liverpool and Birkenhead in the twentieth century: contemporary biographies* (1911) · J. A. Barclay, *The first epileptic home in England: a centenary history of the Maghull Homes, 1888–1988* (1990) · *Liverpool Review* (11 June 1887) · *Liverpool Review* (25 June 1887) · *The Lancet* (23 March 1919) · *BMJ* (22 March 1919), 362 · *Liverpool Daily Post and Mercury* (15 March 1919) · S. Ridland, 'Poor-law administration by the Select Vestry of Liverpool, 1871–1922', Liverpool College of Higher Education, 1978 · *Calendar* [Queen's College, Belfast] (1865–70) · d. cert.

Likenesses F. T. Copnall, oils, repro. in Macalister, *Origin and history of the Liverpool Royal Southern Hospital*, facing p. 121 · photograph, repro. in Pike, *Liverpool and Birkenhead in the twentieth century*, 193

Wealth at death £59,371 1s. 7d.: probate, 17 June 1919, *CGPLA Eng. & Wales*

Alexander, William Lindsay (1808–1884), Congregational minister, eldest son of William Alexander (1781–1866), wine merchant, and his wife, Elizabeth Lindsay (d. 1848), was born at Leith on 24 August 1808. Having attended Leith high school and a boarding-school at East Linton, he entered Edinburgh University in October 1822, but completed his studies from 1825 to 1827 at the University of St Andrews, whither the reputation of Thomas Chalmers had drawn him. His parents were Baptists, but on 29 October 1826 he became a member of the Leith Congregational Church.

In September 1827 Alexander became a student for the ministry at the Glasgow Theological Academy, under Ralph Wardlaw and Greville Ewing; by the end of the year he was appointed classical tutor in the Blackburn theological academy, teaching also Hebrew and other subjects except theology until December 1831. After an abortive attempt to study medicine at Edinburgh, he became minister of Newington Independent Church, Liverpool, in 1832. Here he remained until May 1834, but was never formally inducted to the pastorate.

After a short visit to Germany, followed by some literary work in London, Alexander was called to the pastorate of North College Street Congregational Church, Edinburgh, and was ordained there on 5 February 1835. He was soon recognized as a powerful preacher and remained in this post for over forty years. On 24 August 1837 he married Mary (d. 1875), daughter of James Marsden of Liverpool; they had thirteen children, of whom eight survived him.

Alexander's meeting-house, improved in 1840, when the name was changed to Argyle Square Chapel, was bought by the government in 1855. The congregation then met in Queen Street Hall until 8 November 1861, when a new building, named Augustine Church, was opened on George IV Bridge. Alexander published a book of hymns in 1849, subsequently known as *The Augustine Hymn Book*, and his congregation enjoyed a high reputation for singing. An organ was installed in the Augustine Church in 1863, the same year in which the first organ was introduced into the church of an Edinburgh Presbyterian congregation—that of the nearby Old Greyfriars Church.

In 1861 the University of St Andrews made Alexander examiner in mental philosophy. In 1870 he joined the committee preparing the Revised Version of the Old Testament. In 1871 he was made assessor of the Edinburgh University court, having in 1852 been an unsuccessful candidate for the chair of moral philosophy. He resigned his pastorate on 6 June 1877, and in the same year was made principal of the Theological Hall, Edinburgh, where he had held the chair of theology since 1854; he retained the former office until July 1881. He died at Pinkieburn House, near Musselburgh, on 20 December 1884, and was buried on 24 December at Inveresk.

Alexander was perhaps the best-known non-Presbyterian minister in Scotland. A member of many of Edinburgh's learned societies, and the recipient of doctorates from the universities of St Andrews (1846) and Edinburgh (1884), his congregation was drawn from the city's political and professional élites. He published extensively on theology, church history, and biography, and translated Dorner's *History of the Doctrine of the Person of Christ* (1864). He was a frequent contributor to the *British Quarterly Review* and the *British and Foreign Evangelical Review*, and wrote articles for the eighth edition of the *Encyclopaedia Britannica*, whose publisher, Adam Black, was a member of his congregation. He edited the *Scottish Congregational Magazine* in 1835–40 and 1847–51. Perhaps his most substantial work was the two-volume *A System of Biblical Theology*, which was published posthumously in 1888.

ALEXANDER GORDON, rev. DAVID HUDDLESTON

Sources J. Ross, *W. L. Alexander: his life and work* (1887) · E. T. McLaren, *Dr Lindsay Alexander* (1911) · W. D. McNaughton, *The Scottish Congregational ministry, 1794–1993* (1993) · A. Peel, *The Congregational two* *hundred, 1530–1948* (1948) · H. Escott, *A history of Scottish Congregationalism* (1960)

Archives U. Edin., New Coll. L., occasional discourses
Likenesses N. Macbeth, oils, exh. RA 1874?, Scot. NPG · Hutchinson, marble bust, 1895, Augustine Church, Edinburgh · Annan & Swan, photogravure, repro. in Ross, *W. L. Alexander*, frontispiece · J. Moffat, carte-de-visite, NPG
Wealth at death £20,466 6s. 6d.: Scottish confirmation sealed in England, 17 Feb 1885, CGPLA Eng. & Wales

Alexander, William Picken, Baron Alexander of Potterhill (1905–1993), educationist, was born on 13 December 1905 at 27 Caledonia Street, Paisley, the younger son of Thomas Alexander, then manager of a firewood factory, later director of a sports goods manufacturer, and his wife, Joan, *née* Brown. His parents were both Scottish. He attended Paisley grammar school, then Glasgow University (where he read mathematics), and Jordanhill Training College. From 1929 to 1931 he taught in schools in Renfrewshire before taking up an assistant lectureship in the department of education at Glasgow University. There he was able to pursue his interest in educational psychology, especially IQ testing and factorial analysis. He spent the year 1932/3 as a Rockefeller research fellow in the United States. After his return he married Mary Cochrane (Maisie) McLauchlan, a teacher and daughter of Thomas McLauchlan, joiner, in Paisley on 25 December 1933. The marriage was to last until 1949, when it was dissolved.

Educational administrator Alexander's interest in psychology—he later became a fellow of the British Psychological Society—led him to try out various occupational guidance tests, and these indicated that he should turn to educational administration. In 1934 he became deputy director of education for Walthamstow, and in 1935 director of education for Margate. In the same year his first book, *Intelligence, Concrete and Abstract*, which contained the outcome of some of his research, was published. At a time when intelligence testing as a means of classifying children was seen as the way forward he was invited to give evidence to the Spens committee on secondary education, where he greatly impressed Percival Sharp, secretary of the Association of Education Committees (AEC) and former director of education for Sheffield. In 1939 he was appointed director of education for Sheffield, where he remained until the end of 1944. His resourcefulness in handling the wartime situation in that city attracted attention, for he established the earliest large-scale home service education system for pupils whose schools were closed but who had not been evacuated. On the retirement of Sir Percival Sharp he succeeded him as secretary of the AEC at the beginning of 1945. For the next quarter of a century he was to be the most influential single figure in the administration of education in England and Wales.

Secretary of the AEC Until 1945 the membership of the AEC had consisted largely of part III authorities (the authorities for elementary education in non-county boroughs with populations over 10,000 and in urban districts with populations over 20,000) and county boroughs, while many counties did not join. With the abolition of the part III elementary authorities under the Education Act of 1944, Alexander sought to bring into membership education committees of all counties in England and Wales, and they did in fact join. Only the London county council, with its unique position, remained outside. This achievement of unified representation of all county and county borough education committees served to strengthen greatly the national position of the AEC. By the early 1970s the association was itself represented on nearly 100 national and international bodies, ranging from examination boards to broadcasting organizations. The success of this association owed much to Alexander, whose weekly articles in *Education* became a source of influence, and whose ability quickly came to be recognized as outstanding by those he had dealings with in the Ministry of Education, in local authorities, and in teachers' organizations, even though they might not always agree with his views.

From 1945 the ministry, faced with implementing the Education Act of 1944, placed great emphasis on achieving consensus between the partners—education authorities, teachers' organizations, and itself. The senior officers at the ministry soon found that of the local authority bodies they needed to consult, the County Councils Association, the Association of Municipal Corporations, and the AEC, it was Alexander for the AEC who would provide quickly a coherent and logical view, and they came to turn to him most frequently. In 1946 the other organizations complained about this to the permanent secretary, Sir John Maud. An internal minute commented that if 'we frequently call upon Dr Alexander, that is because his wider experience and interest are specially valuable, and not because he represents the AEC rather than the AMC or any other body' (PRO, Ed 136/807, WLR to permanent secretary, 16 Jan 1947).

One of the most difficult problems of the post-war years was school building. The promise of a secondary school place for every child over eleven lay at the centre of the Butler act. There were fears in the ministry that this principal reform might not be achieved for an indefinite period. By the time it had been achieved in the 1960s there were a further million pupils to provide places for, and success in handling such a large building programme was due to the development of a close working relationship with the local authorities. In informal discussions among ministry and AEC members early in 1946 it became clear that so much building would be needed that both speedy methods of construction and a much more expeditious approach to planning and administrative procedures than had existed pre-war would be essential. The ministry decided to set up a small committee to look at sites and building procedures, and asked Alexander for the names of a few local authority people who would be knowledgeable rather than representative of the various associations. It reported in November 1946 and established an approach to sites and buildings for schools which made possible a building achievement greater than any since Forster's Elementary Education Act of 1870. Strong support was needed to sustain an adequate building programme against economic and political vagaries and negative Treasury pressure. The emergence of an effective and vigorously led AEC went far to provide that support.

A vital role which Alexander took over as secretary of the AEC was that of leader for the local education authorities in the Burnham committee, which for many years determined teachers' salaries. Before negotiations began Alexander would have a private session with the ministry officials who then knew how things stood when the committee met. On occasion he made common cause with the unions and at other times would support the ministry's views against the teachers. His strong personality and keen perception of the current situation meant that he was indispensable in producing agreed settlements. Until 1963 the minister had always accepted and given effect to the agreed report of the committee. In that year there was a clash with the minister, Sir Edward Boyle, who felt justified in seeking legislation to strengthen his position. Alexander continued as leader of the authorities panel until 1973. The commentary on each Burnham report, which he wrote and published at the conclusion of negotiations, became the guide by which the recommendations were applied.

Government policy for school examinations and the curriculum was challenged and reversed by Alexander on a number of occasions in the middle years of the century. The Norwood report (1943) had proposed the abolition of external examinations apart from one for those seeking entry to higher education at the age of eighteen. This represented the opinions of her majesty's inspectorate and of Ellen Wilkinson, the minister who issued a draft circular to local authorities in 1946 supporting this and stating that she would assume full responsibility for the direction of examination policy. The AEC strongly opposed this attempt to enlarge ministerial powers, and the circular was changed so that she would only act with the assistance of a reconstituted Secondary Schools Examinations Council, on which local authority representation was increased from five to eight members. These became the driving force in the council, which replaced the embattled school certificate and higher school certificate examinations with the general certificate of education at O and A levels, which met the needs of grammar school pupils. By 1953 Alexander was convinced of the need for a leaving examination for average pupils from the whole age group. Although supported by teachers' associations, this was resisted by the ministry for some years. Eventually the council decided that it would set up a subcommittee of its own to take forward the project, and a new minister, Geoffrey Lloyd, said that he would not wish to stand in its way. The outcome was, however, only accepted 'reluctantly' by the minister, for the recommendation was to establish a certificate of secondary education as the leaving examination for the middle ability range of each age group. It would be run by regional boards whose members would be nominated by local authorities and teachers' associations.

By 1962 ministry officials were bringing forward proposals for policy making machinery for curriculum and examinations by an internal curriculum studies group.

Local authority and teacher organizations saw this as an attempt to take over an area where they had the principal interest, and made clear their opposition. Alexander was largely responsible for the negotiations which led to the ministry's agreeing to establish the Schools Council for the Curriculum and Examinations, consisting of representatives of local authorities and teachers' organizations, to control this field of policy making.

Political change and the later years The continued success of a system of educational government in which matters of vital national concern such as content, buildings, and staffing were largely left to local education committees operating when necessary through their national organization—Alexander's 'national service locally administered'—depended above all on a measure of general agreement and support for education policy among the different political parties. After the Butler act of 1944 this existed but from the 1960s it broke up, largely round the issue of comprehensive secondary education, the school reorganizations which this often required, and the increasing anxieties over the standards which pupils were achieving. In retrospect Alexander's strong opposition to the Local Government Act of 1958 on the grounds that its abolition of the specific government grant for education in favour of a general grant to local authorities would weaken the position of education at the local level undoubtedly proved to be true, although his fears took some years to become reality. Political party fighting in local authorities became more widespread, and the parties became more inclined to instruct their local people on town and county hall issues. It seemed impossible that a non-party organization of members and officers such as the AEC should be allowed to continue to lead such an important local service as education. The local government reorganization of 1974 greatly weakened the position of education committees and officers. The metropolitan council and county council associations—as the Association of Municipal Corporations and County Councils Association became—seized the opportunity to end the position of the AEC. Although some committees tried to continue the AEC, many others were blocked from membership by their parent authorities. It ceased to exist in 1977, by which year Alexander was well beyond retirement age.

After the dissolution of his first marriage Alexander married Joan Mary Williamson, daughter of Robert Baxter Williamson, a company director, in Marylebone, London, on 27 September 1949. There were two sons. In retirement he and his wife continued to live at Moor Park, Northwood, Middlesex. He had been knighted in 1961, and elevated to the peerage as Baron Alexander of Potterhill (a life peer) in 1974. He enjoyed his membership of the House of Lords but remained an observer of, rather than a participant in, affairs while the weakened position of education in local authorities led to a great increase in central government control. He died on 8 September 1993 at Bishopswood Private Hospital, Rickmansworth Road, Northwood, of pulmonary embolism, deep vein thrombosis, and atrial fibrillation. He was survived by his second wife and one of their two sons. A memorial service was held in the chapel of St Mary Undercroft, in the Palace of Westminster, on 9 December 1993.

Lord Boyle considered Alexander the most influential educationist of the post-war period. That was an accurate assessment, for it was Alexander whose expertise, energy, and strength of personality did more than any other single individual to push through the implementation of the Education Act of 1944 by both central and local authorities within a 'national service locally administered'.

PETER GOSDEN

Sources G. Cooke and P. Gosden, *Education committees* (1986) · U. Leeds, Brotherton L., archives of the Association of Education Committees · *The Independent* (9 Sept 1993) · *The Times* (9 Sept 1993) · *The Guardian* (9 Sept 1993) · personal knowledge (2004) · *WWW*, 1991–5 · d. cert. · b. cert. · m. cert.
Archives U. Leeds, Brotherton L., archives of the Association of Education Committees
Likenesses photograph, 1922, U. Leeds, school of education · photograph, repro. in *The Times* · photograph, repro. in *The Guardian* · photograph, repro. in *The Independent*
Wealth at death £226,785: probate, 16 Dec 1993, CGPLA Eng. & Wales

Alexander, William Whiteway (1852–1933), athletics administrator, was born on 3 December 1852 at Park Hill Farm, Andover, Hampshire. Most of his boyhood was spent on the Isle of Wight. In his teens, certainly before he was eighteen, he left home and made his way to the mainland, apparently distressed when his father remarried soon after his mother's death. He was interested in horses and worked for some years as a stable boy. At Brewood, Staffordshire, he began to compete in local athletics meetings, and after moving to Birmingham to take a job with the Post Office, he joined Birchfield Harriers in 1879. He developed into a good cross-country runner and finished fourth in the English championship of 1881. But after becoming secretary to the Birchfield club in 1882 and taking a place on the committee of the Midland Counties Cross Country Association, his running took second place to administration and an ambition to make Birchfield a successful club. The national and area associations had recently been formed and many new clubs were being founded. Within Birmingham there was intense rivalry between Birchfield and Moseley Harriers, and also between the men who were the driving forces behind these clubs, Alexander and Harry Oliver. The most prestigious prize in inter-club competition was the English cross-country championship, which Birchfield won for the first time in 1880. Inspired by Oliver, Moseley took the title the following four years, using the strategy of importing good runners from outside the Birmingham area.

When Moseley disbanded in 1886 it left Birchfield as the top club in the midlands, and Alexander set about making it the top club in the country. He did so by copying Moseley's policy and signing up some of the best runners from all around the midlands, and then, at the turn of the century, setting up club branches and feeding runners to the parent club. It proved extremely effective. Birchfield enjoyed a prolonged run of success in the cross-country championship that a century later remained the most outstanding in any branch of inter-club competition in Britain; of the forty-nine championships held from 1886 to 1939 the club won twenty-seven of them, and finished outside the first three only six times.

Although primarily interested in the fortunes of Birchfield, Alexander had an abiding love for cross-country and all those who took part in it. He claimed it was the purest and healthiest of pastimes, with no material reward for weekly toil and strict training. In this, he was certainly drawing a comparison with the track handicap races, where the lure of attractive prizes caused some chicanery. He was official handicapper in the midlands from 1886 until the authorities formed a handicapping board in 1901. In 1930 the Amateur Athletic Association produced a book detailing the first fifty years of organized athletics in England, and Alexander wrote the section on cross-country. He was secretary of the Midland Counties Cross Country Association (1888–98), and its treasurer (1888–95) and president (1903–4); he was also secretary of the English Cross Country Union (1890–93 and 1896–8).

On 20 September 1926 Birchfield members were called to a meeting 'to consider the purchase of land for an athletics track and sports ground which will perpetuate the life work of Mr W. W. Alexander and commemorate the club's jubilee in December 1927'. The motion was passed, the money raised from club funds and public subscription, and the Alexander Stadium was officially opened on 27 July 1929. It was Birchfield's home until the club moved to a new stadium (named the Birmingham Alexander Stadium) in 1977.

Alexander married twice, had six children with his first wife (Mary Ann Lucy Hancock, whom he married in 1877), and four with the second, the last child being born when he was seventy-eight. Alexander, who became a subpostmaster, died from bronchial pneumonia at his home, 176 Gooch Street, Birmingham, on 6 October 1933 and was buried in the cemetery of Aston parish church, Birmingham.

WILFRED MORGAN

Sources *Stagbearer* (Nov 1933) · *History of Birchfield Harriers, 1877–1988* · *Sport and Play and Wheel Life* (25 Dec 1920) · E. L. Levy, *Autobiography of an athlete* (1913) · H. F. Pash, ed., *Fifty years of progress, 1880–1930: the jubilee souvenir of the Amateur Athletic Association* [1930] · *100 years of midland cross-country running, 1879–1979*, Midland Counties Cross-Country Association (1980) · d. cert.
Likenesses photograph, c.1925, Birchfield Harriers
Wealth at death £526 11s. 8d.: probate, 30 June 1934, CGPLA Eng. & Wales

Alexandra [Princess Alexandra of Denmark] (**1844–1925**), queen of the United Kingdom of Great Britain and Ireland, and the British dominions beyond the seas, and empress of India, consort of Edward VII, was born at the Gule or Yellow Palace in Copenhagen, Denmark, on 1 December 1844 and was given the names Alexandra Caroline Mary Charlotte Louisa Julia. She was the eldest daughter and the second of the six children of Prince Christian of Schleswig-Holstein-Sonderburg-Glücksburg (1818–1906) and his wife, Louise, princess of Hesse-Cassel (1817–1898).

Although unimpeachably royal, the family lived in modest circumstances, the prince having little income beyond his pay as an officer in the Danish guards. Prince Christian's position, if not his finances, changed in 1852 when he became heir to the Danish throne. King Frederick VII had succeeded his father Christian VIII in 1848 and he had no children. Prince Christian was far from being in direct line of succession but the choice of him as heir was greatly helped by the fact that, unlike other members of his family, he was a sound supporter of Denmark on the Schleswig-Holstein question.

The young princess's childhood was a happy one, within the security of a loving family. Prince Christian, although devoid of intellectual interests, was a fond husband and father while Princess Christian, the more dominant figure in the family, presided over a domestic world marked by music, a rather hearty gaiety, and simple religious faith. Alix, as she was known within the family, was not particularly close to her elder brother, Prince Frederick, later King Frederick VIII (1843–1912), and there was a big age gap between her and the youngest children, Princess Thyra (1853–1933) and Prince Waldemar (1858–1939). With her second brother, William, later king of the Hellenes (1845–1913), and Princess Dagmar (or Minny), later empress of Russia (1847–1928), Alexandra made up an intimate group within the family. The education the children received was limited, but the princess acquired a reasonable command of French and German, was carefully instructed in religion, and developed her aptitude for music.

Engagement In 1858 Queen Victoria and Prince Albert began to consider the question of a bride for their eldest son, Albert Edward, the prince of Wales [see Edward VII]. It had been decided that, as the carefully planned education given to 'Bertie' had not produced a paragon of virtue, an early marriage was the best hope of curbing his wayward inclinations. There seemed little likelihood of Princess Alexandra being seriously considered. On political grounds she appeared to be ruled out as the sympathies of Queen Victoria and Prince Albert were pro-German on the Schleswig-Holstein question. They also considered the Danish royal family to be unsuitable, largely because of the personal life of the thrice-married Frederick VII. The prince of Wales's refusal of a merely dynastic marriage and the shortage of eligible, attractive, protestant princesses led, nevertheless, to the contemplation of a match with the beautiful Danish princess. She was, as the prince's elder sister, *Victoria, the crown princess of Prussia, observed to Queen Victoria, 'outrageously beautiful' (Woodham-Smith, 407). A stilted and formal courtship was choreographed by the crown princess, who introduced the potential couple in September 1861 at the cathedral town of Speyer. It was not until the following September that the prince of Wales proposed, and was accepted by Alexandra, at the palace of Laeken outside Brussels. During the year much had happened: the prince's affair with the actress Nellie Clifton had made an early marriage seem even more desirable to his parents, and the prince consort had died in December 1861.

The princess was immediately approved by Queen Victoria, who had accompanied her son to Brussels, and whose impression of her as a 'dear, lovely being' (Fulford, 2.105) was reinforced by Alexandra's first visit to Britain. Staying at Osborne and Windsor in November 1862, the princess was undaunted by the atmosphere of deepest mourning, and effortlessly charmed the queen. When she returned to Britain for the wedding she was received with

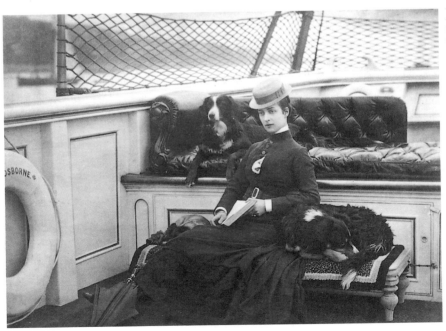

Alexandra (1844–1925), by Symonds & Co., 1880 [on the royal yacht *Osborne*]

great enthusiasm by the public and by the ringing verses of the poet laureate, Alfred Tennyson:

Sea King's daughter from over the sea,
Alexandra!
Saxon and Norman and Dane are we,
But all of us Danes in our welcome of thee,
Alexandra!

The wedding, in deference to the mourning for the prince consort, took place, not in London, but in St George's Chapel, Windsor, on 10 March 1863. It was, however, preceded by a carriage procession through London which attracted enormous crowds.

Society and politics Queen Victoria had hoped that marriage would have a steadying effect on the prince of Wales and that the princess would be 'his salvation'. In the short term marriage did indeed see a faithful and uxorious prince, but the queen found much to disapprove of in the lifestyle of the newly married couple. A court in prolonged mourning found itself a foil to a prince and princess of Wales who epitomized all that was glamorous and fashionable and who were the acknowledged leaders of a high society which the queen disdained. The princess, not unnaturally, revelled in her acclamation as the most beautiful and elegant woman of the day. The invention of photography and the coming of illustrated magazines gave her image a currency denied to beauties of previous eras; her dresses, her hair styles, and the jewelled collars she wore to hide a scar on her neck were widely copied. In the early years of the marriage she was by no means retiring and was as eager as her husband for the round of fashionable occasions that centred on their London home, Marlborough House.

The couple also devoted much time to the rebuilding of Sandringham House in Norfolk, acquired by the prince a few months before their marriage. It was to become a much loved home for both of them, though the expense of its restoration led the prince into financial difficulties. He was in any case inclined to overspend and his extravagance was matched by that of Alexandra who had no money sense. Any doubts that Queen Victoria had about her daughter-in-law were assuaged, and the princess's popularity with the British public increased, by the birth of a son, Prince *Albert Victor (known to the family as Eddy), afterwards duke of Clarence (1864–1892), on 8 January 1864.

Alexandra's Danish patriotism and loyalty to her family were, however, to cause problems. Throughout her life she was to return frequently to her native land and identified strongly with its interests. Her father succeeded to the Danish throne as Christian IX in November 1863 and in 1864 Denmark was at war with Austria and Prussia over Schleswig-Holstein. Queen Victoria and the crown princess of Prussia were outraged by Alexandra's open support for the Danish cause, especially as the prince of Wales associated himself with that support. The princess was to be, thereafter, vehemently anti-Prussian. So bitter were her feelings that in 1866, during a visit to Germany, she refused to meet the king of Prussia until forced to do so, in an atmosphere of great tension. The incident exacerbated

difficulties in the relationship between Queen Victoria and her daughter-in-law. The queen already disapproved of the prince and princess of Wales's role as leaders of the fashionable Marlborough House set, and Alexandra's furious disapproval of Princess Helena's marriage with Christian of Schleswig-Holstein-Sonderburg-Augustenburg, who had sided with Prussia in the recent war in Schleswig-Holstein, had further infuriated the queen.

Prior to her father's accession to the Danish throne, Alexandra's brother William had become King George of the Hellenes in June 1863 and this provided the princess with a second foreign policy interest; she was, to the occasional embarrassment of the Foreign Office, to be the earnest advocate of British support for her brother and his kingdom.

Married life On 3 June 1865 the princess gave birth to a second son, George, later *George V (1865–1936). Four other children were to be born to the prince and princess of Wales: *Louise, afterwards duchess of Fife and princess royal (1867–1931); *Victoria (1868–1935); *Maud, afterwards queen of Norway (1869–1938); and John (born 6, died 7 April 1871).

The princess of Wales's third confinement, that of Princess Louise in 1867, was complicated by rheumatic fever that left her with a limp. The fever and pregnancy seem to have accelerated otosclerosis, a form of deafness she had inherited from her mother. The limp she was able to cope with, developing a glide rather than a walk and managing to skate, to ride, and to dance; but her increasing deafness was to change her life. She did not curtail her public duties but she could no longer enjoy the social world and withdrew into a private milieu of her family, close friends, and retainers. This resulted in the prince and princess of Wales living rather separate lives. The prince was not a faithful husband and perhaps this did not greatly worry the princess, who was more sentimental than passionate. But her husband's affairs might well not have been so open or on such a scale had it not been for the princess's withdrawal from the social round, which was so important to the restless prince who was denied any real responsibilities by the queen. One beneficial result of the princess's withdrawal into family life was the restoration of the good opinion of Queen Victoria, to whom she became once more a 'real devoted sympathizing daughter' (Hibbert, 150).

Alexandra's relations with her children were marked by a gushing affection that became less appropriate as they got older. When Prince George was a 25-year-old naval officer, her letters to him concluded: 'With a great big kiss for your lovely little face'. To all her children she was 'Motherdear'. She recreated much of the atmosphere of her own childhood in her family circle: a simple and uncomplicated Christianity, no great pride in being royal, and a sense of fun, much reliant on practical jokes. It was not an environment which provided her children with intellectual curiosity and it was perhaps too suffocatingly cosy, but it was secure and loving, in contrast to the family life of so many royal children.

The simplicity of the princess of Wales contrasted with

her ability to get her own way. Her beauty and elegance and even her unpretentiousness and kindness could all be called upon as assets. Even her disabilities, her limp and her deafness, could be used to advantage. When called to account for her extravagance (in part due to generosity and in part to a self-indulgence that contrasted with her modest Danish upbringing), she would simply not hear. She ostensibly ignored her husband's barely concealed infidelities and gave him public support when he was involved in scandals. She herself attracted loyal male admirers, including her husband's younger brother, Prince Alfred, and Oliver Montagu, the brother of Lord Sandwich, but gave no cause for scandal.

The death of Alexandra's eldest son, the duke of Clarence, on 13 January 1892, shortly before he was to be married to Princess May of Teck, was a heavy blow. Prince Eddy had not been an adequate heir to the throne, but his mother had loved him dearly. In July 1893 Prince George, who had become duke of York the previous year, himself married Princess May. The duke and duchess of York lived for most of the year at York Cottage, in the shade of Sandringham House, and the shy and serious Princess May (later Queen Mary) did not fit easily into the close, but far from cerebral, family circle of her husband's demanding mother and proprietorial sisters.

The prince of Wales, notoriously, spent the greater part of his life waiting to ascend the throne, and his wife had to wait thirty-four years from her marriage until she became queen consort. By the nineties Alexandra, having brought up her family, had settled into a quiet domestic routine, delighting in her grandchildren. Although still beautiful, she was fifty-six and very deaf when Queen Victoria died on 22 January 1901.

On the throne Queen Alexandra rose to the challenge of her new position with aplomb and determination. She brooked no interference when it came to choosing her coronation robes, nor would she use the title 'queen consort', preferring to be simply 'the queen'. Her only failing in her new position was her lack of punctuality, which had irritated her husband considerably for many years. Despite the king's reluctance to allow her to take a full share in the social and ceremonial duties of the monarchy, there can be no doubt that Queen Alexandra contributed greatly to the standing of the monarchy during his reign. If the king's taste made his court formal and splendid, the queen added a lighter and gayer touch. Her popularity with the public was enhanced by her association with charitable work. Queen Alexandra's Imperial Military Nursing Service was established in 1902, and she presided over the first council meeting of the British Red Cross Society in 1905. A favourite charity was the London Hospital, which she referred to as 'my hospital'. The Alexandra Rose day in aid of hospitals was instituted in 1913 and continues to commemorate her work. Alexandra must be given much credit for her part in developing one of the most important roles of the modern monarchy, the patronage and encouragement of charitable institutions and societies.

The king and queen led largely independent lives for much of every year but this was a tacit acceptance of their different tastes—the king's for a crowded social life and the queen's for a quiet domesticity at Sandringham and holidays in Denmark—rather than an estrangement. The king's association with Alice Keppel, mistress and companion of his later years, was quietly accepted by Alexandra, who ensured that it did not detract from her position as queen nor encroach on her own harmonious relationship with her husband.

Widowhood Edward VII's death in 1910 was a bitter blow and left Queen Alexandra miserable. Influenced by her sister, the dowager empress of Russia, who enjoyed precedence at St Petersburg over the wife of the reigning sovereign, she was reluctant to accept the diminution of her position in the new reign. George V and Queen Mary tactfully acquiesced in breaches of protocol such as taking precedence at her husband's funeral, continuing to fly the royal standard over Buckingham Palace (which she was slow to vacate), and addressing her letters to her son to 'King George' rather than to 'The king'. She took the new title of queen mother, and in her widowhood she lived once more at Marlborough House and retained Sandringham. The upkeep of two large houses would have been beyond her income, even if she had not continued to be extravagant and generous. As it was, the king had to make her a private allowance; her finances improved in 1920 when the Treasury reduced the tax it levied on her income.

The First World War brought out all Alexandra's fervent anti-German feeling, despite the fact that she had relatives fighting on both sides of the conflict. She was aghast at the shabby treatment of the first sea lord, Prince Louis of Battenberg, because of his German origins; but demanded that the king take down the Garter banners of the enemy sovereigns in St George's Chapel. As her war work, she took on hospital visiting, an activity for which her charm and sympathy made her well suited. Revolution in Russia resulted in the murder of her nephew, the tsar, and his family and concern for the safety of her sister, Empress Maria, who was rescued by a British warship from Yalta.

By this time Queen Alexandra had become very frail and was completely deaf and almost blind. In the last years of her life she had frequent visits from the Empress Maria and was looked after devotedly by her unmarried daughter, Princess Victoria, and two elderly courtiers, Sir Dighton Probyn and the Hon. Charlotte Knollys. She died of a heart attack at Sandringham House on 20 November 1925, and was buried at Windsor.

Queen Alexandra remains an icon of feminine beauty. She was described by her prospective sister-in-law in 1861 as having:

a lovely figure but very thin, a complexion as beautiful as possible. Very fine white regular teeth and very fine large eyes—with extremely prettily marked eyebrows. A very fine well-shaped nose, very narrow but a little long—her whole face is very narrow, her forehead too but well shaped and not at all flat. Her voice, her walk, carriage and manner are perfect, she is one of the most ladylike and aristocratic looking people I ever saw! (Fulford, 1.337–8)

Her beauty, which remained remarkably unaltered throughout her life, was probably her best-known characteristic. Far from clever, married to a notorious philanderer, increasingly isolated from all but her family by her deafness, perhaps more than any other royal consort she embodied the importance of the image over the substance of royalty.

A. W. PURDUE

Sources G. Battiscombe, *Queen Alexandra* (1969) · P. Magnus, *King Edward the Seventh* (1964) · A. McNaughton, *The book of kings: a royal genealogy*, 3 vols. (1973) · F. Ponsonby, *Recollections of three reigns* (1951) · K. Rose, *George V* (1983) · K. Rose, *Kings, queens and courtiers* (1985) · C. Woodham-Smith, *Queen Victoria: her life and times*, 1: 1819–1861 (1972) · *Dearest child: letters between Queen Victoria and the princess royal, 1858–1861*, ed. R. Fulford (1964) · *Dearest mama: letters between Queen Victoria and the crown princess of Prussia, 1861–1864*, ed. R. Fulford (1968) · C. Hibbert, *Edward VII* (1976)

Archives Central Archives, Moscow · NL Scot., corresp. · NRA Scotland, priv. coll., letters · Royal Arch., personal papers and letters, engagement diaries · Wolferton Station Museum, letters and drawings from her and her children to a former nanny | BL, letters to Carpenter, Add. MS 46722 · BL, letters to Lady Holland, Add. MS 52113 · Bodl. Oxf., letters to Herbert Asquith · Bodl. Oxf., letters to Sir Henry Burdett · CAC Cam., corresp. with Lord Esher · CAC Cam., corresp. with Lord Fisher · CAC Cam., corresp. with Lord and Lady Hardinge · NA Scot., letters to sixth duchess of Buccleuch · NAM, letters to Earl Roberts · Staffs. RO, letters to duchess of Sutherland

Likenesses W. P. Frith, group portrait, oils, 1863 (*The marriage of the prince of Wales*), Royal Collection · J. Gibson, marble bust, 1863, Royal Collection · R. Lauchert, oils, 1863, Royal Collection · G. H. Thomas, group portrait, oils, 1863 (*The marriage of the prince of Wales*), Royal Collection · A. Graefle, oils, 1864, Royal Collection · H. N. O'Neil, oils, 1864, NPG · F. X. Winterhalter, oils, 1864, Royal Collection · M. Noble, marble bust, 1866, Gowsworth House, Cheshire · W. P. Frith, oil miniature, 1867, Royal Collection · P. D'Epinay, marble bust, 1868, Gov. Art Coll. · M. Thornycroft, marble bust, 1868, Royal Collection; repro. in Battiscombe, *Queen Alexandra* · Count Gleichen, marble bust, 1875, Royal Collection · H. von Angeli, group portrait, oils, 1876, Royal Collection · Count Gleichen, marble bust, 1879, Walker Art Gallery, Liverpool · Symonds & Co., photograph, 1880, NPG [*see illus.*] · H. Garland, marble bust, 1883, NPG · C. J. Turrell, miniature, exh. RA 1884, Royal Collection · L. Tuxen, group portrait, oils, 1884, Det Nationalhistoriske Museum paa Frederiksborg, Hillerod, Denmark · L. Tuxen, group portrait, oils, 1887 (*The royal family at the time of the jubilee*), Royal Collection · Count Gleichen, marble statue, 1891, Royal College of Music, London · W. B. Richmond, oils, 1892?, Royal Collection · L. Fildes, portrait, 1893, Royal Collection · L. Fildes, oils, 1894, NPG; replica, NPG · F. G. M. Gleichen, marble bust, exh. RA 1895, Constitutional Club, London · Lafayette Ltd, print, 1901, NPG · J. Gilbert, double portrait, oils, *c.*1902 (with Edward VII), Royal Collection · G. W. de Saulles, bronze medal, 1902, Scot. NPG · L. Tuxen, sketch, 1902, Det Nationalhistoriske Museum paa Frederiksborg, Hillerod, Denmark · J. H. F. Bacon, oils, 1903, NPG · L. Fildes, oils, 1905, Royal Collection · F. Flaming, oils, 1908, Royal Collection · G. E. Wade, bronze bust, 1908, Whitechapel High Street, London · E. Hughes, three oil paintings, Royal Collection · oils (after L. Fildes), Osborne House, Isle of Wight · photographs, Royal Collection · photographs, NPG · prints, BM, NPG · two photographs, Royal Library, Copenhagen, Denmark

Alexandra, Princess [*married name* Princess Arthur of Connaught], *suo jure* **duchess of Fife** (1891–1959), was born Alexandra Victoria Alberta Edwina Louise Duff on 17 May 1891 at East Sheen Lodge, Richmond, Surrey. She was the elder daughter and second child of Alexander William George Duff, first duke of Fife (1849–1912), and of Princess *Louise

Princess Alexandra, *suo jure* duchess of Fife (1891–1959), by Alexander Corbett, pubd 1913

Victoria Alexandra Dagmar (1867–1931), eldest daughter of Edward VII. Her birth followed that of a stillborn son the year before. Her father, formerly the sixth earl of Fife, was created a duke by Queen Victoria when he married in 1889, and in 1900 he was granted letters patent to enable his dukedom to be inherited by Alexandra and then by her sister Maud (born in 1893).

Alexandra was known as Lady Alexandra Duff until 1905, when the king declared that she and Maud should bear the title of princess and style of highness with precedence after the royal highnesses. Her mother, being reclusive, kept Alexandra and Maud away from the rest of the royal family and they were brought up quietly at home.

In August 1910 Alexandra's meddlesome spinster aunt Princess Victoria arranged for her first cousin, the myopic Prince Christopher of Greece, to be invited to Mar Lodge, the Fifes' estate near Braemar. Princess Victoria assured the duke of Fife that Christopher would not propose, but neglected to inform the hopeful suitor. During the visit the young couple became secretly betrothed, though the duke of Fife soon forbade the union. Prince Christopher concluded that they were both 'more in love with love than with each other' (Christopher, prince of Greece, 97).

In November 1911 the Fife family set off aboard the P. & O. liner *Delhi* for their annual winter holiday in Egypt. In the early hours of 13 December their ship ran ashore off Cape Spartel. They were rescued, but the rescue boat sank and Alexandra was struck by a wave full in the face. She felt the water rush up her nose and swallowed it in gulps. As she wrote later, 'This is death, I thought' (Alexandra, *Egypt and Khartoum*, 9). However, she was rescued by a doctor and dragged, 'a soaking, sodden mess' (ibid., 10), to the beach. They then undertook a 10 mile ride on mules to Tangier, where they rested before continuing to Egypt and the Sudan.

On their way to Khartoum, Alexandra's father caught a chill and died at Aswan on 29 January 1912. Alexandra succeeded her father as duchess of Fife in her own right. She later wrote: 'I could never have the same love or admiration for any other man, and I never did' (Alexandra, *Egypt and Khartoum*, 54). She assumed responsibility for her mother and sister, and took a keen interest in the welfare of her tenants in Scotland.

On 15 October 1913, at the Chapel Royal, St James's Palace, she married her cousin *Arthur Frederick Patrick Albert, Prince Arthur of Connaught (1883–1938), and on 9 August 1914, their son, Alastair Arthur, earl of Macduff, was born. The outbreak of the First World War gave her the opportunity to realize a childhood ambition to nurse. She worked at St Mary's, Paddington, and qualified as a state registered nurse in 1919. She was awarded first prize for a paper on eclampsia (convulsions in late pregnancy), and especially enjoyed working in casualty.

In 1920 Alexandra accompanied Prince Arthur to South Africa, where he served as governor-general until 1923. She found life there restricting, and hated having to be polite when she was shown round badly run hospitals. Her only relief was their annual holiday, hunting big game in Rhodesia.

In 1923 the Fife family suffered serious financial repercussions from the death of the duke's business partner Lord Farquhar, who had left Princess Arthur a large bequest, including 7 Grosvenor Square, a diamond necklace, and the residue of his property. But Farquhar proved to be bankrupt and, as a co-trustee of the Fife estates, Alexandra's mother was obliged to sell a great number of pictures and other possessions to make good an £80,000 shortfall. Alexandra herself remained a rich woman and continued to run the Mar Lodge estate, near Braemar, where she spent her summers. She became a keen angler and field-sports enthusiast: in 1939 she killed seventy-five stags in a week. Eventually she bequeathed the estate to her husband's nephew Captain Alexander Ramsay, but the furniture to her own nephew Lord Carnegie, who succeeded her as the third duke of Fife.

On her return to London in 1923, Alexandra became a nurse at University College Hospital and Charing Cross Hospital, using the name Nurse Marjorie. She performed minor operations as well as being a competent operating theatre nurse, and once amputated a patient's thumb. In July 1925 she was appointed a lady of the Royal Red Cross. In the Second World War, by which time she was a widow, Alexandra became sister in charge of the casualty clearing station of the 2nd London General Hospital. Subsequently she opened the Fife Nursing Home in Bentinck Street, which she equipped and financed herself. She served as matron for ten years, caring for patients who included

actors, acrobats, film critics, dressmakers, and, as she put it, enigmatically, 'a (great) Prime Minister' (Alexandra, *A Nurse's Story*).

After the early death of her husband on 12 September 1938, the tragic death of her son in 1943, and that of her sister in 1945, Alexandra fell victim to crippling rheumatoid arthritis and took no further part in public life after March 1946. She continued to live in Avenue Road, north of Regent's Park, and was taken for drives in her special ambulance car. In the 1950s she renewed a childhood friendship with her first cousin the duke of Windsor, who visited her and arranged for supplies of the drugs hydrocortone and meticorten to be delivered to her from the Schering Corporation in America, with the approval of her doctor, Sir Horace Evans. These alleviated her suffering, though she adjured the duke that her name must not be used for publicity by the manufacturer. During these years, Alexandra was able to publish the volumes of memoirs *A Nurse's Story* (1955) and *Egypt and Khartoum* (1956). At the time of her death she was working on a history of big game hunting.

Princess Alexandra could have been one of the most prominent members of the royal family, but her preference for nursing and a certain inherent shyness kept her largely out of the public gaze, although she did serve as counsellor of state during the absences abroad of George VI in 1939, 1943, and 1944. Her official title, Princess Arthur of Connaught, retained a certain resonance and even scored a mention in Sandy Wilson's popular musical *The Boyfriend*.

Alexandra died at her home, 64 Avenue Road, St John's Wood, London, on 26 February 1959. She was cremated and her ashes were buried in the chapel at Mar Lodge on 3 March.   HUGO VICKERS

Sources DNB · *Burke's guide to the royal family* (1973) · Alexandra, *A nurse's story* (1955) · Alexandra, *Egypt and Khartoum* (1956) · *The Times* (27 Feb 1959) · *The Times* (28 Feb 1959) · *The Times* (4 March 1959) · K. Rose, *King George V* (1983) · G. Aston and E. Graham, *His royal highness the duke of Connaught and Strathearn: a life and intimate study* (1929) · N. Frankland, *Witness to a century* (1993) · Christopher, prince of Greece, *Memoirs* (1938)

Archives Royal Arch., letters to the duke of Windsor | FILM BFI NFTVA, current affairs footage · BFI NFTVA, news footage

Likenesses W. & D. Downey, group portrait, photograph, c.1891, NPG · W. & D. Downey, group portrait, photograph, c.1892, NPG · A. Hughes, photograph, 1894, NPG · A. Corbett, group portrait, photograph, c.1910, NPG · L. Charles, two group portraits, photographs, c.1911, NPG · A. Corbett, photograph, NPG; repro. in *ILN* (18 Oct 1913) [suppl.] [*see illus.*] · H. Wrightson, photographs · various photographs, Royal Collection

Wealth at death £86,217 4s. 8d.: probate, 23 April 1959, *CGPLA Eng. & Wales*

Alexandre, Pierre [*pseud.* Simon Alexius] (*c.*1498–1563), prior of Arras and theologian, was born in Arras where he entered the Carmelite priory. He studied theology at Paris, gaining his doctorate there on 11 December 1534. This suggests he was born about 1498. Having become Carmelite prior at Arras he was responsible for extensive rebuilding of the friary. A noted preacher, he was chaplain to Mary of Hungary, regent in the Netherlands, by early 1541. His developing evangelical views led to a trial for heresy by the Inquisition in 1543–4, but he fled to Strasbourg before sentence of excommunication was passed on 2 January 1545. By November 1545 he was lecturing at Heidelberg, where it was said the 'hardiesse' of his teaching surprised even Calvin. The Schmalkaldic war interrupted his teaching, and in February 1548 he travelled with Pietro Martire Vermigli (Peter Martyr) to England, where they found employment with Thomas Cranmer at Lambeth Palace. Alexandre received the living of All Hallows Church, Lombard Street, and in 1551 was installed in the eighth prebend of Canterbury Cathedral. In 1549, acting on Cranmer's behalf, he helped persuade Martin Bucer to come to England. During 1552–3, in line with Cranmer's plans for higher education at Canterbury, Alexandre gave four lecture courses there. At some point he married, though the identity of his wife is unknown.

On the accession of Mary Tudor, Alexandre was summoned to appear before the ecclesiastical commission. He was also forced to separate from his wife. Once more he fled to Strasbourg, where he was appointed pastor on 27 July 1555. While there he gave lodgings in his house to the future archbishop of Canterbury, Edmund Grindal. Alexandre's violent opinions aroused dissension, however, and in 1559 he was expelled. He returned to England, where he recovered his Canterbury prebend and ministered to the French church until Nicholas des Gallars arrived from Geneva in June 1560. The two men soon quarrelled, especially over Alexandre's more liberal view of church discipline. Grindal, as bishop of London, attempted to mediate during an increasingly bitter conflict, exacerbated by the intemperate language in which Alexandre expressed his deeply held views. Finally, early in 1562, Gallars called on the congregation to choose between Alexandre and himself. Anticipating a negative verdict Alexandre left London, to die of gout in January 1563. His last work, written in 1562, was an apologia for his beliefs (edited in P. Denis, 'Pierre Alexandre et la discipline ecclésiastique', *Bibliothèque d'Humanisme et Renaissance*, 39, 1977, 555–560).

Alexandre had been a valuable assistant to Cranmer, as can be seen from his surviving notebooks: these contain material on the church fathers (CUL, MS Ee 2.8; Paris, Bibliothèque Nationale, MSS latin 1624, 1647), on protestant theology (Cambridge, Corpus Christi College, MS 102; Paris, Bibliothèque Nationale, MSS latin 1624, 3396, MSS Dupuy 424, 614), on scripture for Cranmer's projected commentary (Cambridge, Corpus Christi College, MS 104; Paris, Bibliothèque Nationale MS Dupuy 614), and his Canterbury lectures (Cambridge, Corpus Christi College, MSS 115, 126; BL, Add. MS 48040, Bodl. Oxf., MS Bodley 28). Some earlier works, including three volumes of sermons, perished as a result of his condemnation by the Inquisition. He published two works while in Strasbourg: *Une epistre consolatoire aux freres et membres de l'eglise de Jesu Christ qui fut en Angleterre durant le regne du bon roy Eduoard* (Geneva, 1556, 1558), and *De origine novi dei missatici … dialogi vii* (Geneva, 1558). The latter was published under the pseudonym Simon Alexius. RICHARD COPSEY

Sources J. K. Farge, *Biographical register of Paris doctors of theology, 1500–1536* (1980), 8.12–14 · O. Michotte, *Un réformateur, Pierre Alexandre* (Nessonvaux, 1913) · P. Denis, 'Pierre Alexandre et la discipline ecclésiastique', *Bibliothèque d'Humanisme et Renaissance*, 39 (1977), 551–60 · A. de Saint-Paul, 'Pierre Alexandre', *Dictionnaire de théologie catholique*, ed. A. Vacant and others (Paris, 1903–72) · F. de Schickler, *Les églises du réfuge en Angleterre*, 3 vols. (Paris, 1892) · P. Collinson, *Archbishop Grindal, 1519–1583: the struggle for a reformed church* (1979) · D. MacCulloch, *Thomas Cranmer: a life* (1996) · A. Pettegree, *Foreign protestant communities in sixteenth-century London* (1986) · J. F. Gilmont, 'Un pseudonyme de Pierre Alexandre: Simon Alexius', *Bulletin de la Société d'Histoire du Protestantisme Belge*, 5/6 (1970–71), 179–88 · R. Peter and J. Rott, eds., *Les lettres à Jean Calvin de la collection Sarrau* (Paris, 1972), 82–4 [n. 9] · *Fasti Angl., 1541–1857*, [Canterbury]

Archives Bibliothèque Nationale, Paris, MSS latin 1624, 1647, 3396 · Bibliothèque Nationale, Paris, MSS Dupuy 424, 614 · BL, Add. MS 48040 · Bodl. Oxf., MS 32 · CCC Cam., MSS 102, 104, 115, 126, 340 · CUL, MS Ee 2.8

Alexis Master (*fl. c.*1120–*c.*1140), manuscript artist, was active at St Albans Abbey, and probably at Bury St Edmunds Abbey, in the 1120s and 1130s. The name 'Alexis Master', first coined in German by the art historian Adolph Goldschmidt, derives from the illustrations of the life of St Alexis which this artist contributed to the great St Albans psalter now in Hildesheim Cathedral. Otto Pächt suggested that the Alexis Master should be identified as Anketil, a monk-goldsmith of St Albans Abbey, who completed a new shrine for the relics of St Alban in 1129 and spent part of his career at the Danish court as royal moneyer; this identification, however, has not met with general acceptance. C. R. Dodwell proposed that the Alexis Master was a secular artist hired by Geoffrey of Gorham, abbot of St Albans between 1119 and 1146.

The surviving corpus of the Alexis Master's work comprises historiated initials, full-page paintings, and tinted drawings. It is believed to span six manuscripts, being concentrated in two: the St Albans psalter, and the life and miracles of St Edmund in the Pierpont Morgan Library, New York. His chief monument is his work in the St Albans psalter: forty full-page prefatory paintings illustrating the life of Christ and other subjects; tinted drawings of the life of St Alexis and of Christ at Emmaus; the historiated initial at the beginning of Psalm 1; and underdrawings for other historiated initials. Made in the 1120s, the manuscript was originally intended for the St Albans monastic community. During production, or soon afterwards, the Alexis Master adapted it for the use of the recluse Christina of Markyate by adding the Alexis and Emmaus drawings, intended to echo incidents in Christina's own life.

The master probably travelled to Bury St Edmunds Abbey at some time between 1130 and 1135 to provide the cycle of thirty-two full-page pictures which prefaces the New York manuscript. These pictures illustrate the life, passion, and posthumous miracles of the Anglo-Saxon martyr-king Edmund. The sacrifice of formal organization to dramatic tension in the pictures has raised doubts about their attribution to the Alexis Master, but this characteristic can probably be ascribed to the natural evolution of his style.

The Alexis Master's full-page narrative pictures show stylistic and iconographic links with Anglo-Saxon and Ottonian art and the monumental art of Italy, which he may have visited. His pictures represent a new departure in post-conquest English manuscript art, which until his time had been largely confined to decorative initials. Through his stimulus, the art of pictorial narrative experienced a major revival in twelfth-century England. His style was inherited and perpetuated at St Albans, Bury St Edmunds, Canterbury, and Winchester. Apart perhaps from Master Hugo of Bury St Edmunds, he was the most influential English artist of his generation.

TIMOTHY GRAHAM, rev.

Sources O. Pächt, C. R. Dodwell, and F. Wormald, *The St Albans psalter* (1960) · R. M. Thomson, *Manuscripts from St Albans Abbey, 1066–1235*, 2 vols. (1982) · C. R. Dodwell, *The pictorial arts of the West, 800–1200* (1993), 327–36 · A. Goldschmidt, *Der Albanipsalter in Hildesheim* (1895)

Alexius, Simon. *See* Alexandre, Pierre (*c.*1498–1563).

Aleyn, Charles (*d.* **1640**), poet, was born in Cambridgeshire, and was admitted sizar at Sidney Sussex College, Cambridge, on 26 January 1618. He proceeded BA in 1621–2, and MA in 1625. He became a master in the school of Thomas Farnaby in Cripplegate, London, and was subsequently private tutor to Edward Sherburne (1618–1702), a former pupil at Farnaby's school.

In 1631 Aleyn published *The Battailes of Cresey, and Poictiers*, a verse history of the campaigns. A second, much enlarged edition came out two years later. Thomas May wrote one of the commendatory verses (in Latin) to the first edition, and a verse by Henry Blount was added in the second. In 1638 Aleyn published a verse history of Henry VII's reign, *The Historie of that Wise and Fortunate Prince, Henrie of that Name the Seventh*, with a commendatory poem by his pupil. Aleyn's third publication, *The Historie of Eurialus and Lucretia* (1639), was a prose romance, a translation of the Latin *De duobus amantibus*, by Pope Pius II.

Aleyn died in 1640 and was buried in the churchyard of St Andrew's, Holborn. William Winstanley, writing in 1687 in his *Lives of the most Famous English Poets*, declared that Aleyn was 'no despicable Poet, as may be seen by his Works, which still live in Fame and Reputation'. This is no longer the case.

ELERI LARKUM

Sources Venn, *Alum. Cant.* · DNB · W. Winstanley, *The lives of the most famous English poets* (1687)

Likenesses line engraving, 1638 (after W. Marshall), NPG; repro. in C. Aleyn, *The historie of that wise and fortunate prince, Henrie* (1638)

Aleyn, John [J. Alanus] (*d.* **1373**), composer, probably came from Pattishall, Northamptonshire. He is first recorded on 29 April 1361 in possession of a chantry in the church of St James Garlickhythe, London. By Michaelmas 1362 he was a clerk and chaplain in the household chapel of Edward III, and on 25 September of that year he was presented to a canonry at Windsor, which he held until his death. This was the most important of his numerous ecclesiastical preferments · and he bequeathed to St George's Chapel at Windsor a roll of music (*unus rotulus de cantu musicali*) which may well have contained polyphonic works. Aleyn

also appears to have undertaken a number of administrative tasks in royal service. In 1366 he was sent to Oxford by Queen Philippa to seek out one of her own clerks; he was paid on 20 October 1367 for transporting a quantity of the king's money to Westminster; and he later served as a receiver of loans from religious houses in Kent. Aleyn's most important work is the three-voice Latin motet *Sub Arturo plebs / Fons citharizancium / In omnem terram* (*Motets of French Provenance*, ed. F. L. Harrison, 172ff.). Each voice carries a different verbal text: one of the two upper voices (which are of equal range) names fourteen contemporary singers and musicians, nine of whom served in the household chapels of Edward III or of the Black Prince during the 1360s; the other names four music theorists, beginning with Tubal, and identifies the motet's composer as Alani, J. This work is the only complete English representative of the mid- and late fourteenth-century tradition of 'musicians' motets', and it was almost certainly inspired by earlier French models. Composed probably in the late 1360s or early 1370s (it was once thought to be earlier), *Sub Arturo plebs* enjoyed an extensive continental circulation well into the fifteenth century. Four secular songs which survive in a variety of contrafact versions (that is, in versions where new sets of words have replaced the originals, but the music remains unchanged), variously attributed to 'Alanus' and to 'Magister Alanus', may also be the work of Aleyn, as may a three-voice Gloria setting in the Old Hall manuscript (BL, Add. MS 57950) attributed to 'Aleyn'. Aleyn, who is commonly identified with the composer J. Alanus, died between 29 September and 7 December 1373.

ANDREW WATHEY

Sources A. Wathey, 'The peace of 1360–1369 and Anglo-French musical relations', *Early Music History*, 9 (1990), 129–74 · D. Fallows, 'Alanus, Johannes', *New Grove* · M. Bent, 'Aleyn', *New Grove* · B. Trowell, 'A fourteenth-century ceremonial motet and its composer', *Acta Musicologica*, 29 (1957), 65–75

Archives Bibliothèque Nationale, Paris, MS n.a.fr. 6771 · BL, Add. MS 57950 · Conservatorio, Bologna, Q.15 · Musée Condé, Chantilly, MS 564 · Suffolk RO, Ipswich, HA30: 50/22/13.15

Alfield, Thomas (1552–1585), Roman Catholic priest and martyr, was born in Gloucester, the son of Robert Alfield (*b. c.*1514), who was a fellow of King's College, Cambridge, between 1535 and about 1539, and a master at Eton College and Gloucester School. Robert Alfield has been described as 'doubtless Provost Lupton's gentleman' at Eton (Sterry, 4). His son is listed as a king's scholar at Eton (1565–8) in the name of Thomas Aufield or Alfield. On 8 September 1568 Alfield was admitted as a scholar at King's College, Cambridge. He graduated BA in 1573 and was a fellow of King's from 1571 to 1575. A William Aufield, possibly a nephew, was also a king's scholar at Eton, and likewise of King's College in 1618.

Alfield was brought up a protestant but was reconciled to Roman Catholicism, and accordingly crossed the channel to the English College, Douai, on 8 September 1576. Diocesan returns of 1577 for the diocese of Gloucester recorded a long list of recusants who 'come not to churche'. Among them was 'Thomas Awfeld of the Trinite in Gloucester' (*Miscellanea*, 82). Alfield was from the parish of the Holy Trinity. On 18 September 1580 Alfield returned to the English College, then at Rheims, with a relative, Thomas Evans, a goldsmith, and Nicholas Smith, a Jesuit novice. On 4 March 1581 he was ordained a priest at Châlons. On 29 March he returned to England, using the alias Badger, accompanied by John Ballard and a future martyr, John Adams. He then converted another future martyr, William Deane, to his religion.

On 1 December 1581 Alfield witnessed the execution of Edmund Campion at Tyburn. He himself was arrested on 7 April 1582 and tortured. Alfield then agreed to go to protestant services and was accordingly set free the same year. He then went back to his father's house in Gloucester until about Christmas 1582. After this Alfield lived 'mostly at Hasfield co. Gloucester with John Pauncefote and his wife Dorothy dau. of William Lord Windsor and aunt of the two Pawlets' (Sterry, 4). The 'two Pawlets' overlapped with Alfield at Eton. John Pauncefoot, a fellow recusant from Hasfield, fled to Rouen in 1584, and his wife, Dorothy, was committed to Newgate prison in 1585. His brother Robert, meanwhile, is recorded as a servant of the Jesuit Robert Persons. In 1583 Alfield again refused to go to protestant services. State papers record that his brother-in-law John Mynors, of Aldersgate Street, London, was questioned 'as to his knowledge of Thomas Alfield, who had lived in the house of Thomas Pauncefoot' (*CSP dom., 1581–90*, 153).

Early in 1584 a 'book penned, as it was supposed by Cecil, Lord Treasurer, entitled *The Execution of Justice … to persuade the world that Catholics … had not suffered for Religion, but for Treason*' (Challoner, 168) was answered by William Allen's book *Modest Defence of the English Catholiques*. Alfield and Thomas Webley, a dyer, imported Allen's book and distributed five to six hundred copies in September 1584 in the parish of All Saints, Bread Street, London, and were then arrested. The 'chief crime laid against him [Alfield] was the bringing into the Realm Dr Allen's book, writ in Defence of the English Catholicks' (Strype, 3.309–11). Alfield protested that the book was a loyal book, 'tendering powerfully to induce the English Catholics to remain attached to Elizabeth in spite of all the cruelties' (Pollen, 112). Both Alfield and Webley were terribly tortured to make them reveal the names of the people to whom they had distributed the books. They were committed to Newgate prison on 14 June 1585 and were tried under the statute 23 Eliz. c.2 s.2, which made publication of any book against the queen a felony punishable by death, and convicted on 5 July at the Old Bailey. Alfield was tried before the recorder of London, William Fleetwood, a fellow Etonian. They were offered their lives if they would renounce the pope and acknowledge Elizabeth's ecclesiastical supremacy. Both refused and were hanged at Tyburn on 6 July 1585. As they were not convicted of treason, they were not, additionally, quartered. The next day Fleetwood wrote to Sir Francis Walsingham: 'thank you for the furthering of the execucion of Awfeld' (Pollen, 120). Robert Persons commented at the time: 'It is

thus that these men answer our books—by hanging us' (Burton and Pollen, 163).

Thomas Alfield was one of the 136 martyrs formally beatified by the pope in 1929.

ANTONY CHARLES RYAN

Sources CSP dom., 1581–90, pp. 153, 168, 242–3, 249 · PRO, SP 12/167, no. 28 · Venn, *Alum. Cant.* · G. Anstruther, *The seminary priests*, 4 vols. (1969–77), vols. 1, 3 · Gillow, *Lit. biog. hist.*, 1.12 · *Miscellanea, XII*, Catholic RS, 22 (1921) · J. H. Pollen, ed., *Unpublished documents relating to the English martyrs*, 1, Catholic RS, 5 (1908) · R. Challoner, *Memoirs of missionary priests*, 2 vols. (1741–2), vol. 1, p. 168 · W. Sterry, ed., *The Eton College register, 1441–1698* (1943), 4 · J. Strype, *Annals of the Reformation and establishment of religion … during Queen Elizabeth's happy reign*, 2nd edn, 3 (1728), 309–11 · T. F. Knox and others, eds., *The first and second diaries of the English College, Douay* (1878) · *The letters and memorials of William, Cardinal Allen (1532–1594)*, ed. T. F. Knox (1882), vol. 2 of *Records of the English Catholics under the penal laws* (1878–82) · E. H. Burton and J. H. Pollen, eds., *Lives of the English martyrs: the martyrs declared venerable, 1583–88*, 2nd ser., 1 (1914), 145–63 · H. Foley, ed., *Records of the English province of the Society of Jesus*, 3 (1878), 44 · A. F. Allison and D. M. Rogers, eds., *The contemporary printed literature of the English Counter-Reformation between 1558 and 1640*, 2 vols. (1989–94)

Archives BL, Lansdowne collection, Lansdowne MS 33 art. 58 (1819) · BL, Lansdowne MSS, record of transfer of subject to Newgate prison, his indictment, and trial, vol. xlv, no. 74

Alfonsi, Petrus (*fl.* **1106–1126**), scholar and translator of scientific works, was born in northern Spain, to Jewish parents. He was baptized a Christian on 29 June 1106 in Huesca, Aragon, with the names of the apostle on whose feast day the baptism took place and of his godfather, Alfonso I of Aragon (r. 1104–34). To his contemporaries he was sometimes known as Petrus Ebreus, but Petrus Alfonsi and Petrus Alfonsus are the forms of his name commonly found in modern scholarship, though the manuscripts favour Alfunsus, Anfulsus, Anfusus, or Anfus (all with -f- or -ph-) and also Amdefunsus, for the second element. Until his baptism, according to his own testimony and that of another Jewish scholar from Huesca, Abraham bar Hiyya, Alfonsi had been a prominent member of the Jewish community of Huesca, a city which, until its capture in 1096, had been in Islamic territory. His educational and cultural background, therefore, was in secular sciences of ultimately Greek origin, but read in Arabic, and in the Hebrew scriptures. It was this background that put him in a unique position to impart the knowledge of Arabic science to a European audience. Although he addresses 'all the Peripatetics in France' in a letter in which he advertises his teaching skills, the only country in which his presence is attested is England. The belief that he was 'a doctor of king Henry I of England' rests on the evidence of just one fourteenth-century manuscript of his *Disciplina clericalis* (CUL, MS Ii.6.11). More secure is the evidence of a work on the times when the moon's orbit crosses that of the sun, which is entitled 'The opinion of Peter the Hebrew, surnamed Anphus, concerning the Dragon, which the lord Walcher, prior of the church of Malvern translated into Latin', and which refers in its text to conversations between Alfonsi and Walcher (Bodl. Oxf., MS Auct. F.1.9, fol. 96).

Prior Walcher died in 1135 and the presence of Alfonsi in

the west country in the years before that date might have been a contributing factor to the remarkable efflorescence of Arabic science in that region from the 1120s onwards. One example of this is the knowledge (for the first time in the Latin West) of a complete set of astronomical tables. The mid-ninth-century tables (*Zij*) of al-Khwarizmi were translated by Alfonsi and included the starting date (or radix) of 1 October 1116. No integral version of Alfonsi's translation appears to have survived, for at an early date some chapters from a version by Adelard of Bath were added to, or replaced, Alfonsi's canons (rules for using the tables). Adelard's own version of the tables (without Alfonsi's chapters) includes the date 1126, and it is clear that the one version is closely related to the other, though this relationship is obscured by the several variant versions given by the manuscripts. In any case, these versions bear witness to a close association between Alfonsi and Adelard in the west country (where Adelard was writing) and the lively interest in astronomy in that area: probably Alfonsi was one of the 'magistri' in 'Arabum studia' to whom Adelard expresses his debt. It is possible that he subsequently returned to Spain, but so far it has proved impossible to identify Alfonsi with any certainty in Iberian records.

Petrus Alfonsi wrote two major literary works. The first is the *Dialogi*, a set of twelve conversations between Alfonsi's new Christian self and his old Jewish self, Moses, in which his purpose is to justify his conversion to Christianity. His criticisms of Judaism are backed up by copious references to the Talmud and the work quickly became, and remained, a popular work for Christian apologists and missionaries dealing with Judaism, and, through its description of Jewish mystical ideas, had an influence on Joachism and the Christian Cabbala. But the *Dialogi* also explores what Islam has to offer (here Alfonsi uses the Arabic text of the *Apologia* of Pseudo-al-Kindi, which was later to be translated by Pedro de Toledo) and digresses quite widely, and explicitly, on medical, astronomical, and cosmological topics. The second work is the *Disciplina clericalis*, an equally popular collection of proverbs, exemplary tales, and animal fables, loosely strung together to provide an education for a 'gentleman' (including table manners), and taken from Arabic and Hebrew sources. This was translated into European vernaculars several times and influenced Boccaccio and Chaucer.

The digressions in the *Dialogi* point to Alfonsi's principal interest in medicine and astronomy. No medical work of his survives and it is rather as a teacher of astronomy that he advertises himself in his letter to the peripatetics of France. Here he claims astronomy as the culmination of the seven liberal arts, which he classifies differently from Boethius and the main Latin tradition, throwing out grammar and logic and substituting medicine and necromancy. He gives as an example of his competence in astronomy a portion of his introduction to the astronomical tables of al-Khwarizmi.

Other works have been attributed to Petrus Alfonsi. One which was probably correctly attributed, but is no longer extant, is 'three books of dialogues of which the first is

about the seven arts, the second about religions, [religious] laws and faiths, and the third about man's advantage [*humanum proficuum*]', mentioned in the late fourteenth-century *Catalogus scriptorum ecclesiae* of Henry Kirkestede (R. H. Rouse, ed., 'Catalogus de libris authenticis et apocryphis', PhD diss., Cornell University, 1963, 221). The third book is also cited by Peter of Cornwall in the late twelfth century. But the *Liber Marii de elementis*, whose author refers to a book of his own called *De proficuo humano*, is probably not by Alfonsi, but rather by the Marius Salernitanus who was a teacher of Gottfried of Viterbo (*d.* 1192×1200). Similarly the *Liber ysagogarum Alchorismi in artem astronomicam*, attributed in one manuscript to 'magister A' and featuring the table of eras from Alfonsi's translation of al-Khwarizmi's *Zij*, is probably not by Alfonsi but rather by another Jewish scholar, Avendauth.

In spite of strenuously denying his Jewishness in the *Dialogi*, Alfonsi had the typical interests of Jewish scholars of his time: in theology on the one hand, and in astronomy, astrology, and other mathematical topics on the other. By being one of the first Jewish scholars to transfer this knowledge into a Christian context, he has an important place in the history of culture.

CHARLES BURNETT

Sources CUL, MS Ii.6.11 • Bodl. Oxf., MS Auct.F.1.9 • M.-J. Lacarra, *Estudios sobre Pedro Alfonso de Huesca* (1996) • J.-M. Millás Vallicrosa, 'La aportación astronómica de Pedro Alfonso', *Sefarad*, 3 (1943), 65–105 [incl. edns of *Sententia Petri Ebrei* and 'Letter to the Peripatetics of France' with preface to trans. of al-Khwarizmi's *Zij*] • J. Tolan, *Petrus Alfonsi and his medieval readers* (1993) [incl. edn of 'Letter to the Peripatetics of France'] • C. Burnett, 'The works of Petrus Alfonsi: questions of authenticity', *Medium Aevum*, 66 (1997), 42–79 [incl. edn of the preface to al-Khwarizmi's *Zij*] • P. Sj. van Koningsveld, 'La *Apologia* de Al-Kindi en la España del siglo XII: Huellas toledanas de un "animal disputax"', *Estudios sobre Alfonso VI y la reconquista de Toledo: actas del II Congreso Internacional de Estudios Mozárabes* [Toledo 1985], 3 (Toledo, 1989), 107–29 • *Der Dialog des Petrus Alfonsi: seine Überlieferung im Druck und in den Handschriften: Textedition*, ed. K.-P. Mieth (Berlin, 1982) • P. Alfonsi, *Disciplina clericalis I: Lateinischer Text*, ed. A. Hilka and W. Söderhjelm, Acta Societatis Scientiarum Fennicae, 38/4 (1911) • O. Neugebauer, ed. and trans., *The astronomical tables of al-Khwārizmī* (1962)
Archives Bodl. Oxf., MS Auct. F.1.9 • CUL, MS Ii.6.11

Alford. For this title name *see* Egerton, Marianne Margaret, Viscountess Alford (1817–1888).

Alford, Edward (1565/6–1631/2), politician, was born in London the only surviving son of Roger Alford (*d.* 1580) and his wife, Elizabeth (*d.* 1598), daughter and heir of Thomas Ramsey, esquire, of London and Hitcham, Buckinghamshire, and widow of Thomas Clerke of North Weston, Oxfordshire. The Alfords were Sussex gentry who traced their origins back to Richard, lord of Aldford, Cheshire, who held Newton manor in Sussex in 1200; another ancestor fought at Agincourt. Edward's direct line came into the county in the fifteenth century. His grandfather, Robert Alford (*d.* 1546), married Anne Brydges, a member of the prominent Gloucestershire and Somerset family, while his father made the transition from the local to the national stage as secretary to Sir William Cecil and as MP (for Bletchingley, Surrey, in 1558 and for Preston, Sussex, in 1559). Roger's brother, Sir Francis *Alford, was also an MP in Elizabeth's parliaments.

In his will Roger Alford left instructions for Edward to pursue his studies at Oxford and Lincoln's Inn, and to seek service in Cecil's entourage thereafter. Alford duly matriculated at Trinity College, Oxford, in 1581, aged fifteen, and subsequently entered Lincoln's Inn in 1583. He did not enter government service, but the durability of the Cecil connection was suggested in 1610 when the earl of Salisbury, the son of his father's patron, included him among a 'select number' of MPs with whom he had a private meeting about the levying of impositions, customs duties imposed under the royal prerogative (Foster, *Proceedings*, 2.274n.).

On 11 April 1589 Alford married Judith Downing of Suffolk, with whom he had six sons and a daughter. He sat for Beverley, Yorkshire, in the parliament of 1593, and though no record of his activity in it has survived, he harked back to his service under Elizabeth in later years. He served in no other Elizabethan parliament, however, and his effective career began in 1604 with his election for Colchester, Essex, which he represented in the four succeeding parliaments of 1614, 1621, 1624, and 1625 as well. Alford faithfully reflected the interests of the town corporation which controlled the parliamentary franchise, advancing bills for it in 1621 and 1624, but by the session of 1606–7 he was also the acknowledged leader of the delegation from Sussex where his seat at Offington, near Worthing, lay.

Alford soon adopted a third constituency, parliament itself. Throughout his long career, few MPs were as consistent in their defence of the privileges and autonomy of the House of Commons, and none stouter. In 1610 it was Alford's initiative which secured the ruling that all matters concerning the privileges of the Commons should be perused by the committee for privileges before being entered in the journal of the house. In 1607 he brandished a precedent for expelling a privy councillor who had revealed matters before the house to the king, and in 1621 he rebuked James I for interfering in another pending issue, complaining that there were 'Eyes over him to observe' (Tyrwhitt, 1.32). That same year he claimed for the house the right to adjourn itself on its own authority, and in 1628 he protested against the forced Easter sitting of parliament as an infringement of its liberty. In 1624 he objected strenuously when the Lords debated supply and in 1628 he opposed their admitting the testimony of judges. Royal councillors in the House of Commons had traditionally set the legislative agenda, but in 1625 Alford opposed having the solicitor-general, Sir Robert Heath, chair a committee 'because he was sworn to the King and of his fee' (Jansson and Bidwell, 234). Similarly he objected to the speaker's attending the presentation of the petition on billeting to Charles I in 1628; he had been sharply critical of what he regarded as a previous speaker's obsequious deportment at a conference with the Lords in 1621. At the end of the first session in 1621 he urged that a committee be set up to maintain parliamentary privileges during the summer recess, and when sittings resumed in the

autumn he protested the detention of his fellow MP, Sir Edwin Sandys. In 1624 he moved a bill for the preservation of parliament's liberties, and tried to attach a rider to the subsidy bill providing that parliament should meet after adjournment 'at a specified time'.

Alford was equally vigilant against other extensions of royal prerogative, including impositions, monopolies, proclamations, and purveyances, both as abuses in themselves and as encroachments on local commerce and governance. After joining the general parliamentary attack on increased customs rates in 1610 and 1614, he blamed them for the trade depression in 1621 and sought to have them added as grievances to the petition of right. Proclamations were another source of evil. Alford attacked the Lenten proclamation against killing meat in 1621 as a prime example of government meddling that raised the price of victuals for the poor in a time of dearth, and he continued to complain of Star Chamber prosecutions for violations of similar decrees in 1624 and 1628. That proclamations were typically enforced in prerogative courts such as Star Chamber suggested to him a sinister pattern in which conciliar decrees bypassed both statutes and the subject's redress at the common law. Particularly obnoxious among proclamations were those for patents of monopoly, which Alford saw as conspiracies to enrich London-based trading companies such as the Merchant Adventurers at the expense of the outports of the southern coast, and particularly abusive among courts was that of chancery, a perennial target of common lawyers. In 1621 Alford introduced a seventeen-point bill to halve the number of masters of chancery, curb their powers, and appoint two common-law 'judges assistant' to oversee them. In addition he proposed to erect a new court of appeal empowered to reverse chancery decrees by writ of error. In 1624 he spoke to no fewer than eight bills concerning chancery, enjoining the house to consider them 'with as much expedition as may be'.

Alford stubbornly resisted the drift to war in the parliaments of 1624 and 1625, and characteristically opposed grants of subsidy. Along with other dissidents he was pricked for sheriff to disable him from sitting in parliament in 1626, but, although removed from the bench, he retained the position of deputy lieutenant for Sussex, probably through the influence of the earls of Arundel and Dorset, and remained a receiver of admiralty droits. His return to parliament in 1628 was marred by a disputed election, and despite the support of the Colchester corporation he was forced to accept a seat at Steyning, Sussex. Alford's service in this, his last parliament, was perhaps his most significant. Rejecting a mere confirmation of Magna Carta in the dispute with Charles over the forced loan and billeting, he proposed to proceed by petition of right on 6 May and to incorporate the king's response as a preamble to the subsidy bill, thus firmly tying redress of grievances to supply. Alert to the symbolic significance of the moment, he proposed that Charles receive the petition in parliament rather than at Whitehall. The house did not immediately pick up his suggestion, but as reformulated by Sir Edward Coke it became the basis of the most important affirmation of personal liberty yet made by an English parliament.

Alford, who had so often clashed with councillors from Sir Francis Bacon to Sir Robert Heath, sounded a rare and perhaps valedictory note of conciliation at the end of the session: 'I hope we may recede and find a better world at our next meeting' (Johnson and others, 4.320). Such a hope proved forlorn, and after the dissolution of parliament in March 1629 he retired to his estate at Offington. His last recorded parliamentary address was another protest against the imprisonment of a fellow MP. Alford died, probably at Offington, late in 1631 or early the following year (his will was proved on 26 January 1632). He was buried in the chancel of Hamsey church near Lewes, where he owned a manor. Two of his sons, Sir Edward (1592–1653), knighted 1632, and John (1590–1649), sat in parliament; the former was heavily fined for his service in the king's cause during the civil war. Alford's other sons were Henry, Lancelot, Robert, and William; the last-named became vicar of Purton, Wiltshire. Alford's daughter Elizabeth was an executor of his will.

Alford was the quintessential county backbencher of his era. His core views were conservative and insular, and his resistance to the extension of prerogative government, from the Act of Union to the forced loan, was principled and unremitting. He believed in a balanced polity, and although he had no wish to magnify parliament's powers as such, he came to see them as the last bulwark of a system whose co-ordinate institutions had become increasingly impotent in the face of royal pressure. It was parliament, then, that by curbing prerogative courts and conciliar lawmaking, by asserting its privileges to defend the subject's liberties, by reining in government spending and rejecting all non-parliamentary taxation, and by functioning generally as the watchdog of the realm, would preserve the constitution. Such a view was to animate the Long Parliament in its first great spate of reform. No one articulated it more clearly, consistently, and fearlessly in the decades before 1640 than Edward Alford.

ROBERT ZALLER

Sources J. Alford and W. P. W. Phillimore, eds., *Alford family notes* (1908) · A. Fletcher, *A county community in peace and war: Sussex, 1600–1660* (1975) · E. R. Foster, ed., *Proceedings in parliament, 1610*, 2 vols. (1966) · Greaves & Zaller, *BDBR*, 5–7 · J. K. Gruenfelder, *Influence in early Stuart elections, 1604–1640* (1981) · N. M. Fuidge, 'Alford, Edward', HoP, *Commons, 1558–1603* · N. M. Fuidge and A. Davidson, 'Alford, Roger', HoP, *Commons, 1558–1603* · R. C. Johnson and others, eds., *Commons debates, 1628*, 6 vols. (1977–83) · Keeler, *Long Parliament* · W. Notestein, F. H. Relf, and H. Simpson, eds., *Commons debates, 1621*, 7 vols. (1935) · M. Jansson and W. B. Bidwell, eds., *Proceedings in parliament, 1625* (1987) · W. Notestein, *The House of Commons, 1604–1610* (1971) · R. E. Ruigh, *The parliament of 1624: politics and foreign policy* (1971) · C. Russell, *Parliaments and English politics, 1621–1629* (1979) · [E. Nicholas], *Proceedings and debates of the House of Commons, in 1620 and 1621*, ed. [T. Tyrwhitt], 2 vols. (1766) · *The parliamentary diary of Robert Bowyer*, ed. D. H. Willson (1971) · parliamentary transcripts, 1624, Yale U., Yale Center for Parliamentary History · R. Zaller, *The parliament of 1621: a study in constitutional conflict* (1971) · R. Zaller, 'Edward Alford and the making of country radicalism', *Journal of British Studies*, 22/2 (spring 1983), 59–79 · *DNB* · Foster,

Alum. Oxon. · *IGI* · W. P. Baildon, ed., *The records of the Honorable Society of Lincoln's Inn: admissions*, 1 (1896), 98

Alford, Francis (*c.*1530–1592), civil lawyer and member of parliament, was the second son of Robert Alford (*d.* 1546) and his wife, Anne Brydges. He gained a BA degree at Trinity College, Cambridge, in 1549 and was admitted to Christ Church, Oxford, in 1550. Until 1555 he was clerk of the market in Oxford and a proctor in the vice-chancellor's court. The civil law was apparently his chosen career, and during 1557–9 he studied in Italy. He wrote some short works, for instance on legal reform and trading corporations, but later hopes to be allowed to write an account of Elizabeth I's reign, with access to the papers of Lord Burghley, were never fulfilled. By 1562 he had married Agnes, widow of Augustine de Augustinis, physician to Thomas Wolsey; they appear to have had one son.

With Thomas *Sackville, Lord Buckhurst, as a cousin and constant support, perhaps even financially, Alford was ostensibly well placed for advancement, and he was able to secure election to borough seats in Lancashire, Cornwall, Berkshire, and Sussex so that he sat in nine of the thirteen parliamentary sessions of Elizabeth's reign. Beyond this, the minor offices of rector in Croxton, Cambridgeshire, and chanter at Lincoln Cathedral were the only posts to come his way. Alford obviously aroused distrust. He may have gone to Italy in order to escape the regime of Queen Mary, and his support of the protestant settlement of 1559 was clear, but his credit suffered because his Catholic wife practised her faith within his household. A visit to France, the details of which remain unclear, also led to the accusation that he had associated with the supporters of Mary, queen of Scots, there: this may account for the apparent loss of royal favour by the mid-1570s.

Alford was probably not popular in parliament. He was unsympathetic to frequent and widely supported calls for reform of the church. In the parliament of 1584–5 he opposed a bill for improving the quality of the clergy, arguing that the Commons should not take it upon themselves to interfere in church matters, but also pointing out that many benefices were too poor to support well-qualified men. In the next parliament too (1586–7) he made his hostility to parliamentary involvement clear and argued that the problem of clerical inadequacy be left to the church itself.

For some time Alford was in a minority on the question of what to do about Mary Stuart. While most members were unreservedly against Mary by 1572, Alford insisted that her being privy to the plots against Elizabeth was a necessary condition of her guilt. He was also uncertain of the propriety of trying her, a foreign sovereign, in England. This was anathema to the predominant mentality of the time, and a stark contrast to the later argument of Job Throckmorton that parliament had full competence in the matter. The hostile reception of Alford's views led him to reflect that he was being denied the parliamentary right of free speech. Though he shared this caution about the Scottish queen with Elizabeth herself, by 1586–7 he had come to support the general clamour for Mary's execution. He was also in favour of the view that Elizabeth should accept the sovereignty of the Netherlands.

These were major issues of continuing importance. Yet Alford, in common with many of his fellow members of parliament, made a more broadly based contribution to the business of the House of Commons. He claimed later in life that he had 'done my country some good, whereunto we are called' (HoP, *Commons, 1558–1603*, 1.335). He appears to have sat on Commons committees which dealt with a wide range of bills, and a particular concern with vagabonds and the poor was sustained in the 1570s and 1580s. Though (typically) unsympathetic to vagabonds, he was also anxious in the 1584–5 parliament to preserve what he called the liberties of the common subjects. He thought that a bill that proposed to limit the keeping of hawks, ferrets, and so on to substantial landholders would threaten these. The measure, he feared, would cause discontent because it would deny 'our poor neighbours' their traditional pastimes. Alford was buried at St Dunstan-in-the-West, London, on 3 September 1592.

T. E. HARTLEY

Sources J. G. Alford, *Alford family notes*, ed. W. P. W. Phillimore (1908) · D. Dean, *Law-making and society in late Elizabethan England: the parliament of England, 1584–1601* (1996) · G. R. Elton, *The parliament of England, 1559–1581* (1986) · T. E. Hartley, ed., *Proceedings in the parliaments of Elizabeth I*, 1 (1981) · T. E. Hartley, ed., *Proceedings in the parliaments of Elizabeth I*, 2 (1995) · HoP, *Commons, 1558–1603*

Archives Inner Temple, London, letter-book, Petyt MS 538/10

Alford, Henry (1810–1871), dean of Canterbury and biblical scholar, was born at 25 Alfred Place, Bedford Square, London, on 10 October 1810, the son of the Revd Henry Alford (1782–1852), an evangelical and the son and grandson of evangelical clergy, and his first wife, Sarah Eliza (d. 1810), daughter of Thomas Bradley Paget, banker, of Tamworth, Staffordshire. His father was rector of Ampton, near Bury St Edmunds (1826–42), and Aston Sandford, Buckinghamshire (1836–50), but his mother died at his birth, and Henry spent much of his boyhood with relations, especially the family of his uncle, the Revd Samuel Alford, also an evangelical, of Heale House, in the parish of Curry Rivell near Taunton—the parish where two previous generations of the family had been vicars. At nine Alford was sent to a school kept by the Revd B. Jeanes, Congregationalist minister at Charmouth, Dorset, after which he went to a private school at Hammersmith; to Ilminster grammar school, Somerset, from 1824; and to Aston, Suffolk, from 1827, as a private pupil of the Revd John Bickersteth, an evangelical, with whose sons (later dean of Lichfield and bishop of Ripon) he formed a close friendship. Alford entered Trinity College, Cambridge, in October 1829, gained the Bell scholarship in March 1831, and graduated eighth classic and thirty-fourth wrangler in January 1832; he became MA (1835), BD (1850), and DD (1859), and was president of the union in 1832.

In October 1833 Alford was ordained as curate to his father's parish of Ampton, Suffolk, and he began at once to take pupils. He was elected fellow of Trinity College in October 1834 and was ordained priest in November. In

Henry Alford (1810–1871), by unknown photographer

March 1835 he became vicar of Wymeswold, Leicestershire, a Trinity living, and on 10 March he married his cousin Frances (Fanny) Oke Alford (1810/11–1878), daughter of Samuel Alford, of Heale House; they had four children, of whom both the sons died in childhood. Alford continued for eighteen years at Wymeswold, engaged in parish work and in tuition. In 1845 he began his Greek Testament; the first volume was published in 1849 and the last in 1861. In 1853 he moved to London, and became minister of Quebec Chapel, Portman Square, Marylebone. In each of his appointments he improved the pastoral care, preaching, and music. In March 1857, during Palmerston's first ministry, he was appointed by the crown as dean of Canterbury, which office he continued until his death. He disagreed with the canons and, frustrated by them, recommended to the archbishop the abolition of canons.

Although delicate as a child Alford as a man had extraordinary powers of mental work, and also travelled much in England and on the continent. With little or no private income he made his own way. Towards the end of his life he bought a house, Vine's Gate, near Sevenoaks, as a summer home; his domestic life was happy, and he had many friends, among whom the closest were the Revd E. T. Vaughan, of Harpenden, Hertfordshire, and the Revd J. H. Hamilton, vicar of St Michael's, Chester Square, London, and afterwards canon of Rochester.

Alford had a poetical temperament, and his talents were drawn out by those with whom he mixed at Cambridge, including the Tennysons—he had a lasting friendship with Alfred Tennyson—Arthur Hallam, and Christopher Wordsworth. He published *Poems and Poetical Fragments* (1831), *The Abbot of Muchelnaye* (1841), with sonnets, and later a translation of *The Odyssey*, in blank verse. His poems were commended by William Wordsworth, with whom he was acquainted, and were received favourably in the *Edinburgh Review* and elsewhere. He wrote many hymns: 'Come, ye thankful people, come', 'In token that thou shalt not fear', and 'Ten thousand times ten thousand' were particularly highly regarded. He composed piano, organ, and vocal music, sang and played, carved in wood, painted in watercolours, and published a book on the Riviera, with coloured lithographs from his watercolours.

Alford's religious development was precocious. At ten he wrote a short sermon, and from childhood he had looked forward to ordination. He worked earnestly in his parish, built schools, and restored the church. He was a successful preacher in various styles from the serious to the extempore, with a clear baritone voice, and he published various volumes of sermons. He was Hulsean lecturer at Cambridge in 1841–2, and published the addresses as *The Consistency of the Divine Conduct in Revealing the Doctrines of Redemption* in two volumes. His early training was evangelical, and he was to some extent influenced by the clericalist movement of 1835–42. However, he rejected this and adopted distinctly protestant convictions, and he enjoyed good relations with leading nonconformist ministers (including Unitarians). Although he did not take a leading role in any church party, he ably defended evangelicalism against ritualism and rationalism. In 1865 he wrote to a friend, 'I trust we are doing good service against Ritualism' (Alford, 386). At Canterbury he instituted Sunday afternoon sermons, and he regularly lectured and preached there and in London. He also founded a choral society for the performance of oratorios in the cathedral, and took great interest in the restoration of the buildings. The new King's School, the uncovering of the infirmary arches, and the restoration of the south Norman tower and the porch, were done under his direction; the statues in the porch and west front were obtained by subscriptions he raised; and the Roman columns from Reculver were placed by him in the baptistery garden.

Alford's Greek Testament and other biblical works constituted his chief claim to fame. He recognized the superiority of the German scholars, and went to Bonn in 1847 for three months to master the German language. For his Testament he adopted a text taken mainly from Bultmann and Lachmann, but corrected later using the works of Tregelles and Tischendorf. His theological standpoint included a liberal belief in inspiration; he dissociated himself from mechanical and verbal theory, and from the freer handling of the New Testament by writers such as Jowett. His work formed an epoch in biblical studies in England, and his pioneering edition introduced German scholarship into English textual studies. Disliking German rationalism, he regarded his work as an attempt to provide 'students of Scripture [with] fitting weapons for the coming struggle with infidelity' (Alford, 196). He was later a leader of the revisers of the English New Testament. In his last year he started, but never finished, an Old Testament commentary.

Alford's works were very miscellaneous, and included his New Testament works, a book on the Greek poets, lectures on English descriptive poetry, and many other subjects. He was editor of *Dearden's Magazine*, published at Nottingham. From 1866 to 1870 he was the first editor of Alexander Strahan's *Contemporary Review*, and to this and two other Strahan publications, *Good Words* and the *Sunday Magazine*, he was a regular contributor. Under his editorship a tone of scholarly Christianity typified the *Contemporary Review*. One of the most voluminous writers of his age, he published forty-eight volumes, and many articles, hymns, sermons, and tracts.

When Alford began his New Testament in 1845 he was working seven hours a day with pupils, besides having the responsibilities of his parish and family; and throughout life his work was on a similar scale. He had extraordinary buoyancy, but overstrain began to affect him some ten years before his death, and he had to take frequent breaks, mostly as foreign tours, which became longer and more frequent. His death was sudden, apparently from exhaustion. He died at the deanery, Canterbury, on 12 January 1871, and was buried in the churchyard of St Martin's, Canterbury, on 17 January. Later that year a statue to his memory was placed at the west front of Canterbury Cathedral.

W. H. FREMANTLE, *rev.* ROGER T. STEARN

Sources F. Alford, *The life, journals and letters of Henry Alford* (1873) • private information (1885) • Boase, *Mod. Eng. biog.* • O. Chadwick, *The Victorian church*, 2nd edn, 2 (1972) • *Wellesley index* • Venn, *Alum. Cant.* • D. M. Lewis, ed., *The Blackwell dictionary of evangelical biography, 1730–1860*, 2 vols. (1995)
Archives Canterbury Cathedral, archives, notebook • Hergest Trust, Kingston, Herefordshire, archives, corresp. | Durham Cath. CL, letters to J. B. Lightfoot • DWL, letters to Henry Allon • LPL, corresp. with A. C. Tait
Likenesses L. Dickinson, oils, 1857, deanery, Canterbury • J. H. Baker, line engraving, BM • London Stereoscopic Co., carte-de-visite, NPG • Maull & Polyblank, carte-de-visite, NPG • photograph, NPG [see illus.]
Wealth at death under £25,000: probate, 7 March 1871, *CGPLA Eng. & Wales*

Alford, Kenneth J. See Ricketts, Frederick Joseph (1881–1945).

Alford, Lady Marian. See Egerton, Marianne Margaret, Viscountess Alford (1817–1888).

Alford, Michael. See Griffith, Michael (1584/5–1652).

Alfred [Ælfred] (848/9–899), king of the West Saxons and of the Anglo-Saxons, was born at Wantage. He was the youngest of at least six children of King *Æthelwulf of Wessex (d. 858) and of *Osburh, daughter of Oslac, the king's butler (said to be descended from the family that founded the kingdom of the Isle of Wight). Three of his elder brothers, *Æthelbald, *Æthelberht, and *Æthelred, were successively kings of Wessex before him; his sister, Æthelswith, was wife to *Burgred, king of the Mercians.

Alfred (848/9–899), silver penny, 871–99

In 868 he married *Ealhswith (d. 902), daughter of a Mercian ealdorman, Æthelred Mucel, and of Eadburh. Their children were *Æthelflæd, 'lady of the Mercians', *Edward the Elder, king of the Anglo-Saxons, Æthelgifu, abbess of Shaftesbury, *Ælfthryth, wife to Baudouin (II), count of Flanders, and Æthelweard. Among their grandsons were *Æthelstan, *Edmund, and *Eadred, kings of the English; their many granddaughters were married into half the princely houses of Europe. Alfred's grandfather, *Ecgberht, had been the first of his line since the later seventh century to be king of Wessex. His family vividly documents the ability of early medieval aristocrats to move in quite a short time from apparent obscurity to unprecedented power and glory.

Sources From the perspective of a modern biography, the central point about King Alfred's life is that so much information is not available for any earlier Englishman, nor for any in the next two centuries. It is not usually possible to identify the birthplace or daughters of Anglo-Saxon kings, still less their in-laws. So high a level of documentation carries a danger of magnifying the king's image, and must itself be explained. The pre-eminent source is a seemingly contemporary life by his teacher and counsellor, the Welsh Bishop Asser. Although known to a few eleventh- and twelfth-century writers, it survived into modern times in only a single manuscript that was destroyed in 1731 by the fire in the Cotton Library. The sole access to it since the development of modern standards of scholarly enquiry has been through transcripts and editions made between c.1570 and 1722. For that reason, but also because of oddities in its presentation, and above all distaste for its account of the king's behaviour, the authenticity of the life has often been challenged. Yet to do so raises such problems in turn that there is really no option but to take it, with all its imperfections and difficulties, as the work of a man who came to know Alfred

very well. That does not mean accepting all it says as literal truth. It does mean coming to terms with the fact that these things could be said by someone who influenced the king and was vastly impressed by him.

Second, and linked to Asser in that it was the main ingredient of his narrative, is a set of annals known as the Anglo-Saxon Chronicle. This is itself a much debated source. It is extant in a series of vernacular manuscripts and in Latin renditions like Asser's. The versions that seem closest to its original form blend the chronological summary in Bede's *Historia ecclesiastica gentis Anglorum* with materials like the West Saxon genealogical regnal list (which prefaces some chronicle texts but was also transmitted separately), and with other annalistic information on the early church, the English settlements, and Wessex from the seventh to ninth centuries. There is a marked break in the chronicle's transmission in the early 890s, with the hand changing in the only contemporary copy, and the sundry texts tending to go separate ways thereafter; it is reasonably deduced that the 'core' chronicle was assembled about then. Linguistic analysis suggests that a series of compilers was involved. But it is hard to resist the suspicion that royal patronage stands somewhere behind a work whose theme may be read, and for many centuries was read, as the rise of the house of Alfred to the leadership of the English struggle with their Danish enemy. The activity of Danish armies increasingly dominates events as the story proceeds, with the first great battles following the alleged recognition of Ecgberht as *Brytenwalda* ('Britain-ruler') in succession to the kings said by Bede to have held *imperium* over the southern English; and with the first continuation of the 'core' chronicle offering a close account of Alfred's campaigns in 893–6. Most telling of all, perhaps, is the way that the annals of the 880s almost abandon English history to follow the continental progress of the Danish army that in 892 crossed to attack the English. It follows from all this that the chronicle, like Asser, is as good or bad a source as anything connected with Alfred would be. It may be trusted for insight into royal views but was hardly disinterested.

Other sources pose less risk of a massaged record but still tend to raise Alfred's profile. His 'law book' is the first English legislation of its type for at least one century and perhaps two. It is matched by a short statement of the legal terms agreed between Alfred's realm and the Danes to the east. Each is a further sign of determination that his rule be recorded in writing. On the other hand, the surviving charters of his reign are strangely few: a mere twenty-one for the area he directly ruled, of which just fifteen (ignoring a few palpable forgeries) are records featuring Alfred's name, six from Kent and nine from Wessex. The contrast with his immediate predecessors is clear: the reigns of his elder brothers produced twenty-one extant charters, eleven Kentish, in under thirteen years; his father's nineteen-year rule saw a minimum of twenty-five. The dearth of Alfredian records is, however, more than compensated by the document known as the Burghal Hidage, which shows every sign of being an official memorandum (though at one or more removes from the original) of the chain of forts that the king organized, together with arrangements for their upkeep and defence. Moreover, a text of the king's will was preserved. Quite apart from the important light it sheds on the politics of Alfred's close family, and one or two intriguing *personalia*, this is the earliest record of the resources in money and land at the disposal of an early English king.

Lastly, but above all, there is what Alfred wrote himself. Not all the works sometimes attributed to him were his: some, like the Anglo-Saxon Chronicle itself, were clearly by other hands, if probably done under his aegis. But there is no good reason to doubt that the four books that stand in his name, plus one other, were in a real sense composed by him: these are his law book, together with more or less free translations of Pope Gregory's *Book of Pastoral Rule*, of Boethius's *Consolation of Philosophy*, of Augustine's *Soliloquies*, and of the first fifty psalms. The only books for centuries either way to express the ideas of a secular monarch, they on their own establish that there was something extraordinary about Alfred. They would be grounds enough to study him closely, even if his other achievements were less epoch-making.

'Deeds' and their setting: Ecgberht's dynasty Early medieval kings and their historians inherited from the Roman empire the notion that a ruler's *gesta*, by which was especially meant his victories, were the most important thing about him. Alfred's were of quite special importance, because they were the foundation for the eventual emergence of a kingdom of the English. But any account of them should begin with notice of their background. The near monopoly exerted by the Danish wars over the ninth-century English narrative has obscured the politics that set the pattern of Alfred's career and perhaps of his character.

The kingdom ruled by Alfred's predecessors was almost certainly a more loose-knit structure than appears from the Anglo-Saxon Chronicle's retrospect. Its kings from the mid-seventh century to the early ninth were all credited with descent from the alleged founders of the kingdom; but there is little to suggest any close relationship between successive kings. The evidence is at least compatible with a kingship disputed and/or exchanged between the realm's chief families. That might help to explain one of the strangest things about Alfred's grandfather, Ecgberht (r. 802–39): the hints, none in itself conclusive but cumulatively persuasive, that whatever his West Saxon ancestry, his background was essentially Kentish; his father seems to have been among Kent's last independent kings. After they wrested south-east England from Mercian control (825–7), Ecgberht and his son Æthelwulf were more careful of Kentish sensitivities than were Mercian overlords. Whether or not they were outsiders, they did break with West Saxon tradition in another way: Ecgberht insisted on being succeeded by his son, as no West Saxon ruler since 641 demonstrably had. Æthelwulf's accession was perhaps buttressed by his unction at the Council of Kingston in Ecgberht's final year; until at least 979, Kingston would remain the site for royal inaugurations, just as after 1066 kings were (preferably)

crowned at Westminster since it was thence that English kingship took its new direction. One reason for Æthelwulf's marriage to Osburh was no doubt to strengthen his position by an alliance with one of the chief West Saxon princely families.

If this is the correct construction to put upon the policy of Ecgberht and Æthelwulf, it very nearly failed. Asser reveals, though the Anglo-Saxon Chronicle perhaps typically does not, that when Æthelwulf came back in 856 from a journey to Rome and the West Frankish court (accompanied by the young Alfred), he was faced with a revolt by his eldest surviving son. Æthelbald may have been alienated by his father's return with a fresh royal bride, Judith, daughter of Charles the Bald (d. 877), and potential mother of illustrious competitors for the throne: Æthelbald eventually married her himself. But his supporters were the ealdorman of Somerset and the bishop of Sherborne, pillars of the West Saxon establishment; and the outcome could have effectively broken the Kentish connection. By what Asser thought superhuman forbearance, but what looks as much like an admission of defeat, Æthelwulf left Wessex to Æthelbald, and settled for rule of his family's original south-eastern base. Partition was to continue on his death in 858, with the accession to Kent of his next son, Æthelberht.

Nevertheless, Æthelwulf did not forget the dynastic imperative. Two years before they journeyed together to Rome, he had sent four-year-old Alfred on a visit to the pope. The chronicle's story that Leo IV had consecrated him to kingship has naturally raised doubts. But a letter of Leo survives to show that he did make Alfred a 'consul'; a procedure that in other early medieval contexts was easily confused with royal ceremony. The inspiration for the episode was pretty clearly the papal unction in 781 of two infant sons of Charlemagne (742–814), Pippin and Louis, who went on to rule Italy and Aquitaine respectively. Yet had Æthelwulf meant to subdivide his kingdom in 853, he should have sent all junior sons. His move is best read as an effort to underpin his dynasty by a gesture in favour of its youngest and least secure scion. A complex scheme in his will as relayed by Alfred's own seems to have bestowed on his younger sons enough of the land that was his to dispose of (his 'bookland') to maintain them in strength and style. From the perspective of the 850s, the danger of a fraternally disputed throne may have paled beside that of the displacement of the whole dynasty by one of the lineages that had previously aspired to kingship of Wessex.

Alfred's accession As it turned out, Æthelbald's childless death in 860 gave Ecgberhtian strategy a second chance. Æthelred and Alfred temporarily transferred their endowments to Æthelberht, so endorsing his rule over Wessex as well as Kent. When Æthelberht too died heirless, in 865, the arrangement was repeated in Æthelred's favour, though not without hesitation on Alfred's part. Æthelred did leave sons at his own early death in 871, but they were so young that, in the dire emergency of the moment, Alfred's accession could not be challenged. He was, however, obliged to guarantee his nephews' previously agreed property rights; and here lay a foretaste of the trouble that would erupt between his son and nephew when he died. Alfred's dynasty, therefore, was neither monolithic nor stable. The Anglo-Saxon Chronicle, and still more Asser, liked to dwell on the disastrous outcome of dynastic splintering in other kingdoms under Scandinavian attack. The problem could have imperilled Alfred too, as it did his heir.

A second corollary of Alfred's background is more elusive but possibly more important. In the nature of ninth-century politics, there were at least two views as to what to do with younger sons. If Æthelwulf were bent on maintaining Alfred's kingly potential, others (most obviously his elder brothers and their contacts) would wish to steer him in other directions. The counter-influences may have included the boys' mother, who in Asser's famous tale gave Alfred a book of 'Saxon' poems as reward for precociously memorizing it, thereby prefiguring his scholarship. Alfred, in other words, may very well have grown up under conflicting impulses. The life of a warrior and of a clerk had never yet been fully blended in the Germanic kingdoms of northern Europe. In Alfred they were. But he paid a price in loss of inner peace. One of Asser's most obscure—and to doubters of his authenticity suspect—chapters gives a long account of a series of illnesses that Alfred actually prayed to be inflicted upon him as a penitential discipline, though not so as to disfigure him or impede the performance of his duties. (These disorders are now diagnosed as culminating in Crohn's disease.) Since the disorder flared again on his wedding day, it is a fair deduction that it was fuelled by a conflict in Alfred's mind between secular and clerical callings. If so, the conflict was never resolved. But it was arguably the key to his unique creativity.

The Danish assault Over the last generation, studies of ninth-century Scandinavian action have been driven by debate as to whether 'vikings' were as destructive of life and property as is suggested in sources produced by their Christian victims. There is no doubt that Scandinavian expansion, like most of history's major developments, was a complex process with many-sided effects. Nor is there much doubt that *the* typical activity of vikings, properly so-called, was raiding in quest of moveable wealth, whether in the form of treasure itself or of captives for ransom or sale as slaves. Most of those who experienced such visitations did indeed recover from them in due course. None the less, there were times when raiders consolidated their efforts under formidable leadership, and on those occasions the outcome could be something like a conquest. There is reason to believe that the armies which descended on Anglo-Saxon Britain from 865 were expeditions of this more ambitious type. A persistent but elusive tradition represents the first 'great army' as led by Ivarr the Boneless, a hero of later Scandinavian saga, and his brothers Hálfdan and Ubba.

To appreciate the threat that Alfred faced, it is only necessary to contemplate this army's record in other Anglo-Saxon kingdoms. Northumbria was overrun and its kings killed in 866–7. East Anglia followed suit in 869–70. Mercia was reduced to a west midlands rump after attacks

in 868–9 and 872–4, and King Burgred departed for Rome. Native kings were initially replaced by indigenous rivals, but before long Scandinavian kings and 'earls' took control. The Anglo-Saxon Chronicle explicitly records the organized settlement of armies in Northumbria (876), Mercia (877), and East Anglia (880). There is ample linguistic and toponymic evidence for a Danish and Norwegian presence in Yorkshire, the east midlands, East Anglia, and also the Lake District. Scandinavian political ascendancy in these areas lasted at most for eighty years, so it is hard to imagine what could have had that effect if not relatively numerous settlers. Many stories of the desecration of churches are late and unreliable; Christianity survived and soon enough spread to the invaders. But the succession to all bishoprics bar York and Lindisfarne was disrupted, and nearly every church lost all its muniments. Whether or not Scandinavians took their paganism seriously, and the family of Ivarr seems to have done, their arrival clearly did not make for a thriving church.

If, therefore, Alfred was not fighting for the existence of English identity and Christian civilization, as Victorians thought, much was at stake for his people, for their spiritual guides, and for himself. Contemporary Anglo-Saxons could indeed have had as strong a sense of impending catastrophe as Victorians thought appropriate. They did not need to know much about their past to be aware of what a pagan people, their very selves, had once done to the Britons; the word *wealh*, which increasingly meant 'slave' as well as 'Welshman', was a reminder. Scandinavians for their part wanted what Germanic invaders usually wanted: a political context they could dominate, land on which to settle their followers, and treasure with which to cement their warbands and prime their less predatory enterprises. They would take as much of lowland Britain as they could get at less than ruinous cost. If these objectives made them difficult to get rid of, steady resistance could induce them to go off in search of easier targets.

In the winter and early spring of 870–71, before Alfred became king of the West Saxons, their forces fought five times against the Danish enemy and lost thrice. A month after his accession, Alfred fought again and again lost. The clashes included one on the Berkshire downs (then called Ashdown) which English sources represent as a spectacular victory, perhaps because it was Alfred's first; but the ensuing defeats took the Danes into the heartland of Wessex, into what is now Wiltshire. It was not because they were beaten in battle or outmanoeuvred that they left Wessex alone for the next five years. They were simply sufficiently discouraged by months of fighting to come to terms—not improbably in return for what other ages would call danegeld. But the real crisis had merely been put off.

In early 871 the first 'great army' had been joined by a second force under Guthrum. It was this army, when Hálfdan had settled the first in the north, that conquered Mercia. Alfred, who may well have thought that the West Saxons had invited the 870–71 assault by the assistance they had given Burgred in 868, took no steps to stop them.

But Guthrum's force had not yet lost its momentum. From a base in Cambridge it launched attacks on Wareham and then on Exeter (876-7). The upshot was another fragile peace: oaths were sworn, hostages given, and silver paid. As a result, it was what was left of Mercia that was shared out. But almost at once Guthrum (using knowledge of the church calendar that was one viking asset) nearly captured Alfred in twelfth night carousal at Chippenham. The situation may have looked more serious in retrospect than it really was. The ealdorman of Devon was able to repel a further attack from the north. Alfred himself made his refuge in the Somerset wetlands a base for guerrilla operations. Yet the crisis was grave enough. The varying texts of the Anglo-Saxon Chronicle add up to the assertion that much of Wessex was subjected and settled; analogy with the fate of other Anglo-Saxon kingdoms shows what that could have meant.

There is thus a symbolic truth in the *mélange* of legends that associated this period with the consolatory ministrations of saints. One of these stories, in an eleventh-century life of St Neot, was the origin of the tale of how, brooding on 'God's just judgment', Alfred was berated by the wife of a swineherd for letting her loaves (or 'cakes') burn. In any event, he did draw fresh inspiration from somewhere. By early May 878 he had rallied enough of an army from the shires of Somerset, Wiltshire, and West Hampshire to rout a Danish force at Edington and put Guthrum under siege. The Danish king was probably as completely surprised as Alfred had been at another Wiltshire royal estate four months before. He surrendered and was baptized with thirty leading followers.

The final crisis There is an obvious case for seeing Edington as a decisive victory. On 9 May 957 King Eadwig's council gathered there to issue a charter which (in a unique formula) invoked divine goodness to his ancestors (*AS chart.*, S 646). It looks like an anniversary celebration. But the problem with making so much of a single battle is that Scandinavian assailants were often beaten and baptized elsewhere without much effect on their behaviour, let alone the entire national history of the victors. Guthrum's army was still intact enough to be 'honoured with goods' (*ASC*, s.a. 878), and to stage a leisurely withdrawal which for a whole year took it no further than Cirencester. But it did at last retire to East Anglia, which was now itself shared out, Guthrum becoming king with the baptismal name of Æthelstan. The crucial point about Edington was that it once and for all established that Wessex could not be so easily conquered as the other English kingdoms. The Danes did better to be content with what they had. Settlement released the steam from the second Danish army, as it had from the first.

Unfortunately, it was the way of the viking world that a third army was immediately at hand. After exploratory contact with Guthrum's army in the aftermath of Alfred's victory, its significant reaction was to transfer its attention to the continent. Its movements in the fragmenting Frankish empire over the next dozen years were duly noted by the Anglo-Saxon Chronicle, as if in awareness that it might return. So, in late 892, it did. But there were

major differences between the war that followed, anyway as described by the chronicle, and that of the 870s. The first was that the Danes found it harder to break into Wessex or west Mercia. Early in 893 they were within 10 miles of where they had been victorious just before Alfred's accession, but were beaten back and besieged on an islet in the Thames by an army under Alfred's son. In 877 they had had to be negotiated out of an occupied Exeter, but in 893 they took so long besieging it that the king came up with a relieving force. A second point was that this army was almost continuously shadowed by English troops. Even at Buttington, on the upper Severn, an alliance of West Saxons, Mercians, and Welsh bottled it up and drove it back to the Thames estuary. The cycle was repeated twice more all along the Anglo-Danish border. This time around, it was besieged English who sallied out to attack, Danes who were successfully blockaded. Their very ships became a wasting asset as a fortified bridge blocked their descent of the Lea in 895. The emerging impression, and it may not be much exaggerated, is of the hunters hunted. In the end, the third army gave up the struggle, as had the other two. The difference was that they had no new kingdom in lowland Britain to show for it. Those not accommodated among their predecessors in the north and east went back to Francia. If, as is likely, they formed the nucleus of the future duchy of Normandy, the English would one day hear from them again; but not before they had formed their own kingdom.

Military initiatives The course of the 893-6 campaigns shows quite clearly that much had been done since the 870s to stiffen resistance. Historians isolate three military 'reforms' of Alfred as making all the difference. One, reported in the Anglo-Saxon Chronicle's annal for 893, is the division of the *fyrd* ('militia') into two 'so that always half were at home and half on service'. Nothing is here said to imply an interchange of swords and ploughshares. It is not stated that the policy was new. But the arrangement does betray a cast of mind which will reappear in the next section. A second, with a special appeal to later patriots, was the king's naval initiative. The 896 annal is emphatic that he built ships to an enlarged sixty-oar design of his own. Presumably because of their very size and lack of manoeuvrability, they ran aground on their first outing, their crews incurring heavy losses from the ensuing struggle in the mud. The Anglo-Saxons, themselves the vikings of the post-Roman era, hardly needed lessons in the value of maritime operations. But in so far as the naval system of later Saxon England was certainly predicated on sixty-oared ships, Alfred was the father of *an* English navy.

Much the most important of Alfred's strategic departures, however, both in immediate effects and in longer-term results, was the third: the chain of forts around his kingdom, from Devon and Somerset to Sussex and Surrey, which is recorded in the Burghal Hidage. The hidage as it stands certainly dates from his son Edward's second decade. But it was no less clearly undergoing revision as it took its extant form. That Alfred initiated the scheme it attests is strongly implied by what Asser says and generally agreed by archaeologists. The scheme provided a fortified site, whether built more or less from scratch or reused Roman or Iron Age defences, within 20 miles of every West Saxon settlement, and in particular along Wessex's coastal or riverine perimeter. Each was allotted a number of 'hides', which meant in this context the service of an equivalent number of individuals on the building, maintenance, and defence of the wall. One version supplies a formula to calculate the personnel needed for any given length of wall; it is a striking and now famous fact that the defensive circuit of most (if not all) of the list's sites is about what the manpower yielded by the hidage formula would have covered. Some of these places look like emergency refuges that could never have been viable settlements. Others, like Winchester, seem to have been planned as the towns they did become. Upwards of 27,000 men, if the figures are credible, could be mobilized to implement the scheme. One need look no further for the reason why the Danes of the 890s made so little headway in Alfred's kingdom; nor for proof of his organizing ability.

The making of England Alfred's success also had a political dimension. The mangled Mercian kingdom was handled with both firmness and tact. Its ruler from the early 880s was *Æthelred, who was in no formal context allowed the title of king. But he did not always have to defer to his 'lord' King Alfred, whose daughter he married and who (it is said) gave him responsibility for the long-since Mercian town of London. Æthelred played a crucial role in the fighting of 893–6, not just in defence of Mercia but in reinforcing his brother-in-law Edward. Asser gives the outline of a complex web of alliances that brought most Welsh kings into Alfred's camp; like Æthelred, Welshmen fought at Buttington. Less immediately productive feelers were put out towards the north, to the Danes of what is now Yorkshire and perhaps to the community of St Cuthbert. But Alfred's most important (or best recorded) negotiations were with Guthrum. A text of some date after Edington and before Guthrum's death in 890 traces a frontier between their peoples and fixes terms for their relationship in matters of homicide, trade, and fugitives. Importantly, it was a treaty of equals. But here Alfred also took a major further step. He headed 'the councillors of all the English people [*Angelcynnes*]' (*English Historical Documents*, 1.380).

Likewise, at the time when London was ceded to Æthelred, the Anglo-Saxon Chronicle asserts of Alfred that 'all *Angelcyn* except what was under subjection to the Danes submitted to him' (*ASC*, s.a. 886). Some of his charters now called him 'king of the Anglo-Saxons', the point presumably being that he was lord of (Anglian) west Mercians as well as West Saxons. But 'Angelcyn' has a deeper resonance than that. In Alfred's writings of the 890s, it in effect translated Bede's *gens Anglorum*—'the English people'. Asser went further yet (perhaps beyond even the king's vision) in hailing him as 'ruler of all Christians of the island of Britain'. The priority in the wars of the 870s and in the burghal system of the 880s was of course the

defence of the kingdom he inherited. But his success, in combination with that of Danish armies everywhere else, opened the road to a hegemony of which his grandfather could only dream; and rule of 'the English' had all the ideological impetus of Bede's great history of how that people had first come to God. From the near disaster of 878 to the vision of the 890s was a transformation to stir the blood, even had it not led on to the creation of a state that still endures.

Government: administration and household Part of the foundation for Alfred's military success thus lay in skilled administration. The hide, key component of the burghal scheme, was, with its Celtic and continental counterparts, the portent of pre-bureaucratic rule in Europe. It involved sophisticated assessment of the resources in men and materials extractable from units of land: a calculation that in its earlier days can only have been done in the head. Totals, multiples, and fractions of hidage measured services due and payments owed. The indispensable skill of early medieval government was mental arithmetic. Alfred's government was good at it. The symmetry in his will's disposal of money between his family, churchmen, and magnates bears out Asser's highly coloured account of the allocation of his revenue and of the duty roster in his household. Here (as in Charlemagne's will, known to Asser, so presumably to Alfred, through its quotation by Einhard, the emperor's biographer), is a complex parcelling of labour and reward whose logic stands out when put down on paper in figures. Of the sums bequeathed by his will, half is split between his two sons. The other half is distributed in a ratio of 9:6:5 among his close family, secular following, and Christian causes respectively. It is the same sort of scheme as Asser describes, the main difference being that Christian causes got an eighth rather than Asser's half (though the four causes that divide God's share are similar in the will and in Asser).

Asser's record of the cyclical allotment of household tasks may also err on the visionary side: it owes something to the account of Solomon's arrangements in the book of Kings. But it also corresponds to the Anglo-Saxon Chronicle's report of Alfred's *fyrd* organization; and a post-conquest source preserves a garbled account of how the care of the royal chapel and relics was arranged in triple shifts, just like the deployment of Alfred's retainers according to Asser. That there were some important changes in the royal household appears from the witness lists of his family's charters. 'Priests' are unusually evident already under his father and brothers, and in Edward's early years they become plentiful; among their names are those said by Asser to have been Alfred's recruits. The assumption would be that they served the king's chapel and 'school'.

Resources and enrichment Two other aspects of Alfred's government come in here. One is his accumulating wealth. A total of 2000 silver pounds is distributed by his will. This is only what he was free to bequeath, but is even so twenty-five times the size of the period's largest known silver hoard. A king's wealth in the early middle ages might have a variety of sources. Alfred must have been milking his erstwhile Scandinavian enemies as they had once milked him. Some of his south-western forts were well placed to exploit the local tin, lead, and silver mines. Rents from 'borough' tenures would be a main source of revenue for his successors. Clearing vikings from the western seas fostered commerce that paid toll at West Saxon ports. In any event, the change in Alfred's political fortunes is vividly revealed by his coinage. In the 870s it was heavily debased, like that of Mercia with which it was closely linked. There is then (one would think after Edington, though numismatists incline to date it a bit before) recovery to a real silver standard, and from about the time of the 886 'submission' a silver penny heavier than any before.

This evidence for Alfred's wealth is in marked counterpoint to a feature of his government noted in the discussion of sources: the paucity of his charters. Some of the blame for the dearth must lie with the decline of learning that Alfred bemoaned: west midland churches, home of several of the scholars he enrolled, had a relatively healthier charter output. By contrast, Kent, the source of most earlier ninth-century documents, was entering a phase when its clerks were evidently unable to draft them properly. But there may also be a foretaste of his son's reign: after a dozen charters in Edward's early years, most linked with Winchester, the series ceases altogether until after his death—a development with no parallel in Anglo-Saxon history. Particularly suggestive is that many of the charters of Alfred and Edward are of the same type: exchanges of lands with churches, from which the churches were far from obviously gainers. One remarkable transaction (*AS chart.*, S 354) saw Alfred deferring the implementation of his father's bequests to Winchester in return for letting them off the share of the 'tribute that our whole people was accustomed to pay the pagans' in the 870s; then allowing the bequest to go ahead after 879 in exchange for a large (and highly strategic) estate along the northern scarp of the Berkshire downs. Æthelwulf's one-time bequest was also just about all the land that Winchester got from Alfred's will. According to Asser, he founded a monastery at Athelney and a convent at Shaftesbury. But Athelney was always a rather marginal foundation and Shaftesbury came to regard its true founder as Alfred's granddaughter-in-law. Overall, the evidence for Alfred's husbanding of his resources creates the suspicion that when Asser hymned his generosity to God, it was what he (and perhaps the king) wished were possible, not what was done in fact.

Law making The king's law book is quite another matter. Here, the laws laid down by Alfred and his councillors are followed by those in the name of his predecessor *Ine, and prefaced by a translation of those given by God to Moses. With one or two important exceptions, Alfred's own laws are, as he claimed in his preface, traditional both in subject matter and expression. In several ways they are more like the very earliest Anglo-Saxon legislation than Ine's, and they look like statements of custom only marginally, if at all, adjusted. But the whole of

Alfred's law book was greater than the sum of its parts. By appending Ine's code, despite the contradictions arising from his own revisions of it, he highlighted the distinguished legislative record of his dynasty and of his people. In his preface, he also acknowledged the inspiration of laws made in the time of Æthelberht of Kent and Offa of Mercia: the former was the first English king to be baptized and his code is extant; the latter received the legates of Pope Gregory's successor in 786, and the edict they issued may well be what Alfred had in mind. Crucial moments in English relations with God were subtly evoked at the same time as tribute was paid to other than West Saxon law makers. But in addition, West Saxon and other English legislation is juxtaposed with that of God himself; and the linking passage in Alfred's preface is so constructed as to bring out the continuity as well as the contrasts between the dispensations of the present and of Sinai. What is at least implied is that the laws of Angelcyn are themselves laws of God, as befitted those of another 'chosen people' that had received its own 'land of promise' in return for its obedience to the divine will. The ideological charge inherent in the idea of Angelcyn is given new and legally binding force.

That explains the most important innovation amid so much that was traditional in Alfred's laws: the opening clauses on the keeping of 'oath and pledge'. A code of Edward just a few years later shows that oath and pledge was something sworn by 'the whole people', and that it covered not just fidelity to the king but obedience to his law and God's: criminals were perjured. From the final years of Alfred's reign come the first hints of the fierce criminal jurisdiction enforced by his successors, and itself the germ of the cruel notion of felony: that all serious crime is in effect treasonable. Such severity was condign. God's law for God's people deserved no less. It was with Alfred's law making and its ideology that English law began to become a system set apart from every other.

The reading and writing of books Asser's last chapter describes Alfred's dealings with his judicial officers. They were to remedy their shortcomings by learning *sapientia* ('wisdom'), which was to say that they were to learn to read, as the king had. 'Wisdom' did not mean knowledge of the law book: Asser does not mention it. The language used in this chapter is the same as that which earlier describes Alfred's own quest for a *sapientia* that is unambiguously the wisdom of Solomon. Solomon was wise because he knew that wisdom itself was more important than the good things of this world, which flowed only from knowledge of their strictly relative value. To be wise was to adopt God's priorities, as revealed above all in the Bible. That idea of wisdom observably drove Alfred's programme of spiritual and cultural revival and inspired his own astonishing writings.

These writings, like the law book, are not described by Asser, who was writing in 893 and who does refer to a version of Pope Gregory's *Dialogues* by Werferth, bishop of Worcester (which is extant). Presumably, then, most of the Alfredian *œuvre* was the work of his last years. The programme's objectives are set out in a preface to a translation of Gregory's *Pastoral Rule*, whose relatively unevolved style suggests that, apart perhaps from the law book, it was Alfred's first work. The argument (*English Historical Documents*, 1.818) is that learning had once flourished among Angelcyn, who as a result 'prospered in warfare and wisdom'. Now it had declined to the point that very few could render Latin into English; and 'remember what temporal punishments came upon us when we neither loved [wisdom] … nor allowed it to others'. The critical issue here is not whether Alfred drew a blacker picture of contemporary learning than was truly warranted, but that he was looking back to the golden outlines of the one drawn by Bede. For Alfred, as implicitly for Bede, it was the wisdom and so warfare of all Englishmen that was at stake. The English really would go the way of the Britons and Israelites if, like Britons and Israelites, they forgot what God expected of them. The revival of learning was as badly needed as the building of forts.

The preface shows how Alfred proposed to set about this revival. An initial stage was to establish a court of scholars, as Charlemagne had; and the preface acknowledges the help of four visitors. One was Asser himself; the way that his account of his summons follows the lines of Charlemagne's recruitment of Alcuin (d. 804) in Alcuin's life suggests that such parallels were in the air. Another was Alfred's archbishop, Plegemund, like Werferth a product of the evidently superior Mercian sphere of learning. But the two most important actually were from the Carolingian realm: John the Old Saxon who, as such, is likely to have known what the Carolingian Renaissance did for the development of Saxon and High German vernaculars; and Grimbald of St Bertin, who was sent to the king by Fulk, archbishop of Rheims, and who should thus have been conscious of the profuse writings of Fulk's predecessor, Hincmar (d. 882), on Frankish law, government, and history.

Another Carolingian expedient was an educational system. But Alfred's differed in three ways from Charlemagne's. First, the emphasis was on a school at court itself rather than in the kingdom's major churches. Second, what is attested for Charlemagne only by later stories is stated by Asser and implied by Alfred's preface: children of lesser as well as noble birth were schooled there. And third, above all, schooling was to begin in the vernacular, not for its own sake but, as Alfred said, to lay foundations on which Latin learning could then be built in those continuing to 'higher rank'. There is some reason to think that the 'Alfredian Renaissance', like its Carolingian counterpart, went part of the way towards producing a cadre of educated aristocrats. More obvious was an effect somewhat other than that intended: the vernacular received such a boost that English now became a language of prose literature, with all that was to mean for its survival when its place was taken for three centuries after 1066 by Latin and French.

The most obvious outcome of Alfred's movement, however, was Alfredian literature. Asser finds his niche here.

First and foremost a work of insular learning, the life was also influenced by Carolingian writings on kingship, including Einhard and the 'mirror of princes' by the Irishman Sedulius Scottus (*fl.* 840x51–860x74). The Anglo-Saxon Chronicle, though not very like the Frankish royal annals, may derive general inspiration from their Rheims continuation by Hincmar. Neither of these works comes in the category of what Alfred says that he was having translated as 'books necessary for all men to know' (*English Historical Documents*, 1.819). The *Pastoral Rule*, whose preface lays out his whole scheme, clearly did. So, presumably, did two complementary works of history that are not attributed to the king himself and were probably by court scholars: a translation of Orosius's *History Against Pagans*, which gives world history a strongly confessional slant; and one (by a Mercian) of Bede's *Historia ecclesiastica*, where the underlying thesis of the *Pastoral Rule* preface receives full expression. Equally significant are artefacts. The 'Alfred jewel' was found in Somerset in 1693; it bears the legend '+AELFRED MEC HEHT GEWYRCAN' ('Alfred had me made'), is in the style of the court atelier, and shows a figure most plausibly interpreted as Christ personifying wisdom. A no less characteristic piece that could be from the same workshop was a sword found at Abingdon in 1874; the hilt is adorned with the evangelist symbols, as befitted a weapon for God's soldiers. A third such work is the Fuller brooch, its iconography very clearly linked with ideas conveyed by Alfredian literature.

But important and fascinating as are all these works, they hardly compare with the record of the Carolingian Renaissance. What gives Alfred's movement its unique distinction is his own part in it. No Carolingian king is known to have put quill to parchment; Einhard explicitly says that Charlemagne was unable to do so. But the four books which have a preface or epilogue that ascribes them to Alfred share a consistent (if perceptibly developing) vocabulary and syntax. To argue that Alfred may not actually have *written* these books is to split hairs; more certainly than any other work of Europe's middle ages, they bear the impress of a single, royal, mind. The two that most merit notice are the Gregory and the Boethius. The first is a fairly literal translation of Gregory's treatise on the life and tasks of the bishop. But it has been observed that the line between episcopal and secular government, already eroded by Gregory's regular references to Old Testament kings (especially Solomon), is further blurred by Alfred. A book about how to be a bishop becomes one about how to be a king. The king's pursuit of learning and wish to impart it to others is thereby clarified. That was just what Gregory expected of bishops.

But much of the *Pastoral Rule* is devoted to the officeholder's besetting sin: the temptations of worldly pomp. Gregory's remedy was contemplation of true, other-worldly, values. It may well be that Alfred's other works were not 'for all men to know', but (as implied by a manuscript transmission more restricted than the Gregory) studies for personal use. Augustine's *Soliloquies* is professedly contemplative; the psalms were the staple of monastic meditation. As for the Boethius: what could be a better reminder of the transitoriness of glory than a book written by a fallen minister under sentence of death? The main strands picked out by the justly intensive study given to Alfred's Boethius are its debt to Carolingian (even perhaps Welsh) commentaries on the *Consolation*, which is clear enough but can be exaggerated; and the realism, even secularity, of Alfred's paraphrase compared with the original. Alfred of course wrote as a Germanic aristocrat with a full appreciation of power's imperatives. But his objective remains a focus on a good greater than power. Where Boethius turned a nice Hellenistic phrase about honour being given not to virtues by office but to office by virtue, Alfred is moved to the Solomonic observation that power is wisdom's reward. In a sense, therefore, Alfred's books hold the answer to why he wrote them. They instructed him to do so. Gregory the Great was, after God, the first maker of Angelcyn in that he was the architect of its conversion. Would-be kings of Angelcyn must rule and live as he had taught.

Significance and character   Alfred died on 26 October 899. He was barely fifty. His successor was his son Edward, though only after a challenge from Æthelwold, son of Æthelred, who called in the Danes of the north and east. about 901 Edward buried his father in the New Minster which he was founding at Winchester; the story went that Alfred planned the foundation and that his ghost insisted that he be moved there from the cathedral, where he had first been buried. It is needless to endorse all that has been thought of Alfred as history transmuted into myth. The historical record plainly establishes that he was among the most remarkable rulers in the annals of human government. Posterity required what it seeks of any national hero: a figure matching the preoccupations of the moment. The late medieval Alfred founds a college, like other monarchs of that age. The sixteenth-century Alfred's fosterage of vernacular devotion led Archbishop Parker, Queen Elizabeth's first archbishop of Canterbury, to collect Alfredian manuscripts and publish Asser: an early step in Alfred's climb to an eminence where 'the Great' follows his name almost as automatically as in that of Charlemagne. The eighteenth- and nineteenth-century Alfred of course builds ships (and makes clocks): 'Rule Britannia' was written for *Alfred: a Masque* in 1740 (with works by James Thomson and David Mallet and music by Thomas Arne). The Alfred of E. A. Freeman in the *Dictionary of National Biography* did more than save, build, and enlighten the English nation. An embodiment of Victorian virtues, he met 'with triumph and disaster', and treated 'those two impostors just the same'. The story of Alfred and the cakes is one of the best known in English history.

Yet there is more to all this than a need to father present values on past heroes. Most of the Alfreds of later ages are to be found in the sources. The encomium nearest his own time, that of his kinsman *Æthelweard, stresses just what Asser singled out as abnormal: his learning. Rather than reject the Victorian icon, as modern scholars so typically have, its pigments should be explored. That Alfred was out of the ordinary is argued by the amount that is known,

and put beyond doubt by what is known of his own mind. The clue to the phenomenon of Alfred lies squarely in its extreme rarity. When stories like Asser's were told elsewhere in the ninth and tenth centuries, it was in saints' lives like that of the eccentric Count Gerald of Aurillac. Asser's is not a saint's life, because Alfred chose to be less (or more) than a saint. But his biography testifies to the pressures that might have made him one. Throughout the Carolingian era, intellectuals framed a programme for secular life which, Einhard apart, made scant concessions to the norms of the battlefield or bedroom. The laymen who took it on board needed upbringings as ambiguous as Alfred's perhaps was; they were predictably few and strange. Alfred attained the standards of the intelligentsia in that he wrote books. But the culture of classical and patristic Rome was not easily reconciled with that of the northern warrior, to which he was also called, and which was at a premium in the prolonged crisis of his reign. The resulting tensions readily explain the disciplinary bodily affliction for which he prayed. Yet Alfred absorbed those tensions. The resilient intellectual in politics who could glimpse the political potential of Bede's ideal of Englishness also fathered five children. And it was to Ealhswith that, in an unmistakably personal touch, he bequeathed the places of his birth and of his two greatest victories.

PATRICK WORMALD

Sources *Asser's Life of King Alfred: together with the 'Annals of Saint Neots' erroneously ascribed to Asser*, ed. W. H. Stevenson (1904); repr. with a supplementary article by D. Whitelock (1959) · *ASC*, s.a. 853–901 · *English historical documents*, 1, ed. D. Whitelock (1955), no. 33 · F. Liebermann, ed., *Die Gesetze der Angelsachsen*, 3 vols. (Halle, 1903–16), vol. 1, pp. 16–129 · *AS chart.*, S 217–23, 287, 319, 342a–357, 1202–3, 1275–9, 1415–16, 1441–2, 1445, 1507–8, 1513, 1627–8, 1652, 1819 · H. Sweet, ed., *King Alfred's West Saxon version of Gregory's 'Pastoral care'* (1871) · W. Sedgefield, ed. and trans., *King Alfred's version of the 'Consolations' of Boethius: done into modern English* (1900) · J. Bately, ed., *The Old English Orosius* (1980) · *Alfred the Great: Asser's Life of King Alfred and other contemporary sources*, ed. and trans. S. Keynes and M. Lapidge (1983) [incl. trans. of all major sources] · D. Hinton, *Catalogue of the Anglo-Saxon ornamental metalwork, 700–1100, in the department of antiquities, Ashmolean Museum* (1974) · F. M. Stenton, *Anglo-Saxon England*, 3rd edn (1971) · J. Campbell, ed., *The Anglo-Saxons* (1982) · C. Plummer, *The life and times of Alfred the Great* (1902) · A. P. Smyth, *Alfred the Great* (1995) · D. N. Dumville, 'The Ætheling: a study in Anglo-Saxon constitutional history', *Anglo-Saxon England*, 8 (1979), 1–33 · P. A. Stafford, 'The king's wife in Wessex, 800–1066', *Past and Present*, 91 (1981), 3–27 · S. Keynes, 'The control of Kent in the ninth century', *Early Medieval Europe*, 2 (1993), 111–32 · J. L. Nelson, 'Reconstructing a royal family: reflections on Alfred, from Asser', *People and places in northern Europe, 500–1600: essays in honour of Peter Hayes Sawyer*, ed. I. Wood and N. Lund, [another edn] (1991), 47–66 · D. Hinton, *Alfred's kingdom* (1977) · D. Hill and A. Rumble, eds., *The defence of Wessex: the Burghal Hidage and Anglo-Saxon fortifications* (1996) · N. P. Brooks, 'England in the ninth century: the crucible of defeat', *TRHS*, 5th ser., 29 (1979), 1–20 · D. N. Dumville, *Wessex and England from Alfred to Edgar* (1992) · R. Abels, 'King Alfred's peace-making strategies with the vikings', *Haskins Society Journal*, 3 (1991), 23–34 · J. Maddicott, 'Trade, industry, and the wealth of King Alfred', *Past and Present*, 123 (1989), 3–51 · J. Maddicott, R. Balzaretti, and J. L. Nelson, 'Trade, industry, and the wealth of King Alfred: debate', *Past and Present*, 135 (1992), 142–88 · M. A. S. Blackburn and D. N. Dumville, eds., *Kings, currency and alliances: the history and coinage of southern England in the ninth century* (1998) · S. Keynes, 'The West Saxon charters of King Æthelwulf and his sons', *EngHR*, 109 (1994), 1109–49 · J. M. Wallace-Hadrill, 'The Franks and the English in the ninth century: some common historical interests', *Early medieval history* (1975), 201–16 · J. Bately, 'The compilation of the Anglo-Saxon Chronicle, 60 BC to AD 890: vocabulary as evidence', *PBA*, 64 (1978), 93–129 [1980 for 1978] · J. Campbell, 'Asser's Life of Alfred', *The inheritance of historiography*, ed. C. Holdsworth and T. P. Wiseman (1986), 115–35 · A. Scharer, 'The writing of history at King Alfred's court', *Early Medieval Europe*, 5 (1996), 177–206 · A. Frantzen, *King Alfred* (1986) · J. M. Wallace-Hadrill, *Early Germanic kingship in England and on the continent* (1971) · D. A. Bullough, 'The educational tradition in England from Alfred to Ælfric: teaching *utriusque linguae*', *Settimane di studio del Centro Italiano di Studi sull' Alto Medioevo*, 19 (1972), 453–94 · P. Szarmach, ed., *Studies in earlier Old English prose* (1986), pt 1 · K. Sisam, 'The publication of Alfred's Pastoral care', *Studies in the history of Old English literature* (1953), 140–47 · J. Bately, 'Lexical evidence for the authorship of the prose psalms in the Paris psalter', *Anglo-Saxon England*, 10 (1982), 69–95 · J. Wittig, 'King Alfred's *Boethius* and its Latin sources: a reconsideration', *Anglo-Saxon England*, 11 (1983), 157–98 · J. Nelson, 'The political ideas of Alfred of Wessex', *Kings and kingship in medieval Europe*, ed. A. J. Duggan (1993) · J. Nelson, 'The Franks and the English in the ninth century revisited', *The preservation and transmission of Anglo-Saxon culture*, ed. J. T. Rosenthal and P. Szarmach (1996) · D. Pratt, 'The illnesses of King Alfred the Great', *Anglo-Saxon England*, 30 (2001), 39–90 · *Willelmi Malmesbiriensis monachi de gestis regum Anglorum*, ed. W. Stubbs, 2 vols., Rolls Series (1887–9), vol. 2, p. 124 · R. Abels, *Alfred the Great* (1998) · P. Kershaw, 'Illness, power, and prayer in Asser's *Life of King Alfred*', *Early Medieval Europe*, 10 (2001), 201–24

Archives BL, Add. MS 47967 · CCC Cam., MS 173 | Bodl. Oxf., MS Hatton 20 [copy]

Likenesses silver penny, 871–99, BM [*see illus.*] · miniature in historiated initial, 1321, BL, Cotton MS Claudius D.ii, fol. 5*r* · portrait, 17th cent. · Count Gleichen, statue, 1877, market place, Wantage · H. Thornycroft, statue, 1901, Winchester

Wealth at death 2000 silver pounds; also lands: will, S 1507; *Domesday book*

Prince Alfred, duke of Edinburgh (1844–1900), by Abel Lewis, *c.*1875–80

Alfred, Prince, duke of Edinburgh (1844–1900), duke of Saxe-Coburg and Gotha and naval officer, second son of Queen *Victoria and Prince *Albert, was born Alfred Ernest Albert at Windsor Castle on 6 August 1844. An extroverted child, his capacity for learning delighted his parents. They feared that the comparative academic weakness of his elder brother *Edward, the prince of Wales, would have an adverse effect on him, and at fourteen—the earliest possible age—he joined the navy in August 1858, and was appointed to the *Euryalus*. His first naval journey was to the Mediterranean, South Africa, and the West Indies, returning home in August 1861. He was then appointed to the *St George* for service in the channel, North America, West Indies, and the Mediterranean.

In November 1862, the citizens of Greece deposed the unpopular King Otho and held a plebiscite to choose his successor. Of 241,202 votes cast for various members of European royal houses, Prince Alfred received 230,016. Acceptance of the Greek crown by a British prince, however, was contrary to the terms of the London protocol of 1830, and his election was declared invalid. The Greek throne was accepted by Prince William, second son of the future Christian IX of Denmark. The prince of Wales, the heir presumptive to Ernest, duke of Saxe-Coburg and Gotha, renounced his title in the duchy in favour of Prince Alfred in 1863.

Meanwhile, Prince Alfred pursued his naval career. In February 1863 he was promoted to lieutenant. In February 1866 he was promoted to captain (passing over the immediate rank of commander), and was granted an annual income of £15,000 by parliament. On the queen's birthday (24 May 1866) he was created duke of Edinburgh and earl of Ulster and Kent. In January 1867 he commissioned the *Galatea*, and undertook an extensive world tour including South America, the Cape, and Australia. On 12 March 1868, while at Sydney, he was wounded in an assassination attempt by James O'Farrell, a Fenian sympathizer, who shot him in the back. The tour was curtailed to allow him time to recover, and the *Galatea* returned to England that summer. Later the same year the duke sailed for China, India, and Japan, returning to England in 1871.

In February 1876 the duke was appointed to the ironclad *Sultan*, part of the Mediterranean Fleet. In 1878 there was a threat of war between Russia and the powers of western Europe, and he was at the centre of controversy when he invited Alexander of Battenberg (recently nominated as sovereign prince of Bulgaria and an officer in the Russian fleet) on board *Sultan* for a rendezvous with his brother Louis, a junior officer under the duke. The queen and Admiralty were horrified by the duke's indiscretion, and he threatened to demand a court martial in order to clear his name, but the storm soon blew over. In December 1878 he was promoted to rear-admiral, and in November 1879 was appointed to the command of the naval reserve, which he held for three years. In November 1882 he was promoted to vice-admiral, and from December 1883 to December 1884 commanded the channel squadron. From 1886 to 1889 he was commander-in-chief in the Mediterranean, based on Malta. In October 1887 he was made an admiral; from 1890 to 1893 he was commander-in-chief at Devonport; and in June 1893 he was promoted to admiral of the fleet. He discharged his naval duties with zeal and efficiency, took a well-informed interest in the details of all the ships in his squadron, and not only his own officers but also captains of other European naval powers were greatly impressed by his ability as a fleet leader on manoeuvres.

On the death of his uncle Ernest on 22 August 1893, the duke became reigning duke of Saxe-Coburg and Gotha. As a German sovereign prince, he was permitted—after a bitter political dispute involving the queen, Gladstone, and the radicals—to remain an English admiral of the fleet, but he no longer had a seat or voice in the House of Lords. Resident in Coburg, he maintained Clarence House in London, which he visited each year.

The duke's personal interests were varied. The first member of the royal family to collect stamps, he began the royal philatelic collection, and encouraged his nephew, later George V, to take up the hobby. A lifelong friend of the composer Arthur Sullivan, his patronage of musical education helped to establish the Royal College of Music, Kensington. In childhood he had taught himself the violin, which he played throughout his life, though his niece Princess Alice of Albany (later countess of Athlone) recalled 'the erratic movements of his bow over the strings, which he fingered with exuberant originality but with little regard for the score' (For my Grandchildren, 1966, 86).

The duke was an intensely shy man and his reserve was often mistaken for rudeness by those who did not know him well. Although the prince of Wales was devoted to him, other members of the family (especially his brother-in-law Prince Henry of Battenberg) found him a bore. Queen Victoria sometimes had occasion to deplore his 'hard, selfish, uncertain character' (Later Letters of Lady Augusta Stanley, 150–51), and was furious when he argued with her devoted (if frequently rude and drunken) highland servant John Brown.

After paying court in his younger days to his cousin Princess Frederica of Hanover, and the eccentric Princess Elizabeth of Wied (later queen of Romania), the duke married the Grand Duchess Marie Alexandrovna (1853–1920), daughter of Alexander II, tsar of Russia, at St Petersburg, on 23 January 1874. It was a controversial match, partly on account of uneasy Anglo-Russian relations, and partly as the Romanovs belong to the Russian Orthodox church; but the queen was assured that the Church of England would not refuse to acknowledge a creed other than their own, and that Marie would be a more suitable bride than an English subject or a Roman Catholic. Always conscious of her imperial superiority, Marie disliked her British relatives, and after the birth of their children, husband and wife drifted apart. They had four daughters: Princess Marie (1875–1938), who married Ferdinand, later king of Romania; Princess Victoria Melita (1876–1936), who married Ernest, grand duke of Hesse and by Rhine (and, after their divorce, Cyril, grand duke of Russia); Princess Alexandra (1878–1942), who married Ernest, hereditary prince of Hohenlohe-Langenburg; and Princess Beatrice (1884–1966), who married Prince Alfonso of Bourbon-Orléans, infante of Spain.

The duke's only son, Prince Alfred (1874–1899), committed suicide. He had apparently married a commoner, Mabel Fitzgerald, contrary to the Royal Marriages Act, and shot himself after his mother insisted on the annulment of their union, though he lingered for several days. The duke's heavy drinking and indifferent health had concerned family and friends for some time. He held his wife responsible for their son's death; relations between them worsened, and his condition deteriorated. In June 1900, cancer of the tongue and throat was diagnosed, and he died at Rosenau, near Coburg, on 30 July 1900. He was buried on 4 August at Coburg, and was succeeded as duke by his nephew Charles, duke of Albany, son of *Leopold, Queen Victoria's youngest son. JOHN VAN DER KISTE

Sources J. Van der Kiste and B. Jordaan, Dearest Affie (1984) • The letters of Queen Victoria, ed. G. E. Buckle, 3 vols., 3rd ser. (1930–32), vol. 3 • The Times (1 Aug 1900) • R. A. Hough, Louis and Victoria: the family history of the Mountbattens (1974) • J. Van der Kiste, 'My dear Ludwig', Royalty Digest, 1 (1991–2), 322–5 • Dearest child: letters between Queen Victoria and the princess royal, 1858–1861, ed. R. Fulford (1964) • Dearest mama: letters between Queen Victoria and the crown princess of Prussia, 1861–1864, ed. R. Fulford (1968) • Your dear letter: private correspondence of Queen Victoria and the crown princess of Prussia, 1865–1871, ed. R. Fulford (1971) • Darling child: private correspondence of Queen Victoria and the crown princess of Prussia, 1871–1878, ed. R. Fulford (1976) • Beloved mama: private correspondence of Queen Victoria and the German crown princess, 1878–1885, ed. R. Fulford (1981) • Beloved and darling child: last letters between Queen Victoria and her eldest daughter, 1886–1901, ed. A. Ramm (1990) • M. Reid, Ask Sir James (1987) • E. Longford, ed., Darling Loosy: letters to Princess Louise, 1856–1939 (1991) • E. Longford, Victoria RI (1964) • Later letters of Lady Augusta Stanley, 1864–1876, ed. A. V. Baillie and H. Bolitho [1929] • Gladstone, Diaries • T. Martin, The life of … the prince consort, 5 vols. (1875–80), vol. 1

Archives Royal Arch., corresp. and papers • Schloss Ehrenburg, Coburg, Bayerisches Staatsarchiv • Staffs. RO, letters to duchess of Sutherland • Wellcome L., diary of his illness by his physician • Worcs. RO, letters to Sir John Pakington | BL, corresp. with W. E. Gladstone, loan 73 • BL, corresp. with Lord Ripon, Add. MS 43510 • Lpool RO, letters to fourteenth earl of Derby • U. Southampton L., Broadlands MSS

Likenesses W. C. Ross, miniature, 1845, Royal Collection • M. Thornycroft, statue, 1846 (Prince Alfred as a boy as 'Autumn'), Osborne House • F. X. Winterhalter, group portrait, watercolour, 1847, Royal Collection • F. X. Winterhalter, oils, 1852, Royal Collection • L. Caldesi, photograph, 1857, NPG • J. Phillip, group portrait, oils, 1858, Royal Collection • W. and D. Downey, double portrait, carte, 1860–69 (with Edward VII), NPG • F. R. Say, oils, 1861, South African Library, Cape Town, South Africa • W. Bambridge, photograph, 1862, NPG • G. H. Thomas, group portrait, oils, 1862, Royal Collection • Ape [C. Pellegrini], chromolithograph, 1873, NPG • C. Summers, marble bust, exh. RA 1873, Melbourne Art Gallery, Australia • N. Chevalier, group portrait, oils, 1874, Royal Collection • A. Lewis, photograph, c.1875–1880, NPG [see illus.] • G. Koberwein, oils, exh. RA 1876, Trinity House, London • J. E. Boehm, marble bust, 1879, Royal Collection • H. von Angeli, oils, 1892, Windsor Castle, Windsor, Berkshire • H. von Angeli, oils, probably c.1892,

Royal Collection · A. L. Bambridge, oils, c.1893, Admiralty, Devonport · Ape [C. Pellegrini], chromolithograph caricature, NPG; repro. in VF (10 Jan 1874); study, Carrington Album, Royal Collection · N. Chevalier, three portraits, Royal Collection · Russell & Sons, photograph, NPG · J. Steell, plaster bust, Scot. NPG · H. Thornycroft, marble bust (as a child), Royal Collection · F. X. Winterhalter, drawing, Royal Collection · F. X. Winterhalter, group portrait, oils (The royal family, 1846), Royal Collection · prints, BM, NPG · prints, NPG · prints, Royal Collection

Alfred Ætheling (d. 1036/7), prince, was the second son of *Æthelred II (c.966x8–1016) and his second consort, *Emma of Normandy (d. 1052). He was the brother of *Edward the Confessor and they had a sister, Godgifu; he was also half-brother to *Harthacnut and to Gunnhild. He first witnesses a royal charter in 1013, when he was exiled to Normandy with his family, presumably returning on Æthelred's restoration in 1014. However, he and Edward sought Normandy again, probably late in 1016 after the conquest of England by *Cnut, who in 1017 married their mother. Emma long committed herself to the children of this second match.

The brothers remained under the protection of the Norman dukes Richard (II) (996–1026), Richard (III) (1026–7), and Robert (1027–35); their sister married Drogo, count of the Vexin. The Norman chronicler William of Jumièges says that Robert (who married, then repudiated, Cnut's sister) treated them with honour, adopted them as brothers, and sent messengers to Cnut asking that they be restored to their own. On his refusal, Robert assembled a fleet at Fécamp which sailed against England but was driven by a gale to Jersey. Nevertheless, Cnut then offered to restore half England to the princes, whereupon Robert decided to go on pilgrimage to Jerusalem. Of doubtful reliability, this story need not be totally fictitious, as Edward and Alfred witness two of Robert's charters, probably both issued at Fécamp in 1033, and other charter evidence suggests that Edward was being accorded the title king.

The princes' real chance came with Cnut's death (12 November 1035). The most detailed account of what followed is in the Encomium Emmae, written for Alfred's mother c.1040–42. It says that Harold Harefoot (allegedly the son of Cnut and Ælfgifu of Northampton), who opposed Emma and her son Harthacnut in the ensuing succession dispute, forged a letter to Normandy in her name alleging that the English would prefer Edward or Alfred as king. Alfred set out with companions via Flanders and landed in England, where he met Earl Godwine while attempting to reach his mother. Godwine swore loyalty, and arranged accommodation at Guildford; but Harold's men captured them during the night, executed most, but took Alfred to Ely, where he was tried, blinded, killed, and buried at the abbey. William of Jumièges broadly agrees, though here Godwine sends Alfred to Harold in London, who orders that he be taken to Ely and blinded. William of Poitiers largely follows Jumièges, but hints that death was unintentional, the knife accidentally entering Alfred's brain during the blinding. This is plausible, as blindness would have sufficed to remove him from political contention. The C and D texts of the Anglo-Saxon Chronicle for 1036 also record his tribulations and death, which an Ely calendar shows occurred on 5 February (probably in 1036, but conceivably, if events were prolonged, in 1037). The chronicle also stresses his innocence: he was apparently attempting a military coup, but one of little interest to the English. Efforts to sanctify him, alluded to by both encomiast and chronicler, failed.

M. K. LAWSON

Sources ASC, s.a. 1036 [texts C, D] · A. Campbell, ed. and trans., Encomium Emmae reginae, CS, 3rd ser., 72 (1949), 40–47 · The Gesta Normannorum ducum of William of Jumièges, Orderic Vitalis, and Robert of Torigni, ed. and trans. E. M. C. van Houts, 2, OMT (1995) · The Gesta Guillelmi of William of Poitiers, ed. and trans. R. H. C. Davis and M. Chibnall, OMT (1998) · E. O. Blake, ed., Liber Eliensis, CS, 3rd ser., 92 (1962), 158–60 · English historical documents, 1, ed. D. Whitelock (1955) · F. Barlow, Edward the Confessor (1970), 44–7 · S. Keynes, 'The æthelings in Normandy', Anglo-Norman Studies, 13 (1990), 173–205 · S. D. Keynes, 'The Crowland psalter and the sons of King Edmund Ironside', Bodleian Library Record, 11 (1982–5), 359–70

Alfred of Beverley. See Beverley, Alfred of (d. 1154x7?).

Alfred the Englishman. See Shareshill, Alfred of (fl. c.1197–c.1222).

Algarotti, Francesco, Count Algarotti in the Prussian nobility (1712–1764), poet and scholar, was born on 11 December 1712 in the family home in Venice on the Fondamenta Nuove, the second son of Rocco Algarotti (d. 1726) and his wife, Maria Mercati. His father was a prosperous merchant of Paduan origin, settled in Venice. His elder brother, Bonomo, was very close to him throughout his lifetime, both as a partner in many of his undertakings and as his main link with Venice during many years of absence.

Algarotti's education began in Venice, under the tutorship of Carlo Lodoli, but on his father's death in 1726 he was sent to Bologna, where he studied natural science and mathematics and established lifelong friendships with his tutors, Eustachio Manfredi and the Zanottis. It was here that Algarotti was first introduced to Newtonian optics. On leaving Bologna he went to Rome, where he met Martin Folkes, vice-president of the Royal Society of Arts, whose introductions facilitated his stay on his first visit to London in 1736. It was on his way to England that he met Mme du Châtelet and Voltaire, both of whom shared his Newtonian interests and were impressed by the young Venetian.

Algarotti's first London visit was a triumph. Through Voltaire he met Lord Hervey, who opened many doors for him, including that of Queen Caroline, and his other introductions led to a fellowship of the Royal Society and of the Society of Antiquaries. During his lifetime Algarotti enjoyed a vast acquaintance with contemporaries throughout Europe, but his appreciation of England was of a special nature. His relationship with England originated from his Newtonian studies in the 1720s and 1730s, culminating in his Newtonianismo per le dame (1737), translated into English two years later by Elizabeth Carter. It developed during his three visits to London into an involvement in the English literary and artistic milieu of the period, and a lasting correspondence with many of its

Francesco Algarotti, Count Algarotti in the Prussian nobility (1712–1764), by Jean-Étienne Liotard, c.1745

leading figures. Several of his works were dedicated to Englishmen, including the politicians Thomas Hollis and William Pitt and the diplomat Thomas Villiers; another was dedicated to W. T. How, through whom he became acquainted with the poet Thomas Gray. Algarotti's admiration for Palladio made him a natural friend of Lord Burlington, and he stayed at Chiswick House in 1739.

The youthful Algarotti was considered to be an engaging and outstandingly good-looking young man. The courtier Lord Hervey especially appreciated his combination of vivacity and mature taste. Algarotti's charm smoothed his way into the highest social circles (Voltaire called him the Swan of Padua) and into the affections of both men and women. Lord Hervey and Lady Mary Wortley Montagu were both deeply attracted to him and quickly became rivals for his affection. Lady Mary's infatuation for Algarotti subsequently directed the course of her life, prompting her move to Venice (1739) and Turin two years later. Here the relationship ended before a correspondence and friendship resumed fifteen years later. Despite his attractions, Algarotti's weaknesses did not escape the attention of his critics: his supposed snobbery, apparent frivolity, and the standard of his scholarship aroused criticism. His indecision and unwillingness to displease left his conclusions surrounded by qualifications. Such qualities did not sit comfortably with nineteenth-century English sensibilities. Thomas Carlyle, for example, dismissed him as 'a wearisome literary man … one of those half-remembered men whose books seem to claim a reading and do not pay you when given' (T. Carlyle, *History of Frederick the Great*, 1897, 3.327).

After his initial visit to England, Algarotti withdrew to France to complete his *Newtonianismo* and later to Italy to arrange for its publication in 1737. One of the best-known of Algarotti's works, the *Newtonianismo* appeared in Italy (the Naples edition of 1737 had a commissioned frontispiece by Piazzetta), in France, and in England (in Carter's translation). Despite its sound scholarship, this elegant popularization met with some complaints of inadequacy and of frivolity—not unexpectedly from Horace Walpole. Disappointed, Algarotti did nothing serious until his return to England in 1739, facilitated by the generosity of Lady Mary. Here he repeated his earlier successes, culminating in an invitation from Lord Baltimore to accompany him on a diplomatic mission to Russia. This trip produced not only a series of letters to Lord Hervey (later to appear as *Viaggi di Russia*) but also, on his return journey, an introduction to Crown Prince Frederick of Prussia. Frederick was much taken with him, and on succeeding to the throne in 1740 immediately entreated him to return to Berlin. Welcomed into the king's inner circle, he was created a count in December and sent on a diplomatic mission to Turin in 1741. This proved unsuccessful, and when misunderstandings with the king arose in 1742 he left Berlin for several years.

It was now Algarotti's good fortune to be invited to Dresden by Augustus III, elector of Saxony and king of Poland, who created him a councillor of war and entrusted him with the reorganization and extension of the Dresden Gallery of Paintings. This involved spending time in Venice acquiring existing works and commissioning new ones, not least from Tiepolo. Algarotti's approach to the reorganization was highly innovative: rather than follow the personal tastes of the sovereign, he selected works to illustrate the development of the history of painting. The newly commissioned works were based on Algarotti's scholarship and on his assessment of each painter's individual style.

In 1746 Algarotti returned to Berlin; welcomed by the king, he was then made a chamberlain and a knight of the Order of Merit. His years here were a period of literary activity, which continued after his return in 1753 to Italy: to Venice, Bologna, and finally Pisa, where he found the climate beneficial to his failing health. It was in these later years that he encouraged and supported the young painter Mauro Tesi, of whom he was particularly fond, and to whom he left a generous bequest.

Algarotti died in Pisa on 23 May 1764 and was buried there in the campo Santo. His tomb was designed by Tesi and paid for by Frederick the Great, bearing the significant motto 'Algarottus non omnis' (Haskell, 360). His will included bequests to the eminent, including William Pitt and Frederick the Great, as well as to servants and friends. His collection of paintings, drawings, and books acquired jointly with his brother became the property of his niece Maria Corniani Algarotti and were catalogued for sale in 1776.

Algarotti's was a many-sided personality: he was both poet and scientist, scholar and writer. He remained in sympathy with the past yet was very conscious of the current trends of the Enlightenment and of neo-classicism, and it was these interests, together with his charming physical presence, which made him such a figure of both celebrity and controversy within the English cultural élite of the mid-eighteenth century. Algarotti enjoyed considerable fame during his lifetime, and his works continue to be read with interest by historians of art and literature. Scholarship on him is vast and continuing, expanding far beyond the *aemulus Ovidii* and *Neutoni discipulus* of Frederick the Great's epitaph on him.   DAVID PARKER

Sources I. Treat, *Un cosmopolite italien au XVIIIème siècle* (Trévoux, 1913) · A. M. Ghisalberti, ed., *Dizionario biografico degli Italiani*, 2 (Rome, 1960) · D. Michelessi, *Memoire intamo alla vita ed agli scritti del conte Francesco Algarotti* (Venice, 1770) · *Francesco Algarotti saggi*, ed. G. da Pozzo (Bari, 1963) · F. Haskell, *Patrons and painters: a study in the relations between Italian art and society in the age of the baroque*, 2nd edn (1980) · I. Grundy, *Lady Mary Wortley Montagu* (1999) · G. da Pozzo, *Il testamento dell'Algarotti* (Venice, 1964)
Archives Archivio Communale, Treviso, MS 1256
Likenesses J.-E. Liotard, pastel drawing, *c*.1745, Rijksmuseum, Amsterdam [*see illus.*] · J. Richardson, two drawings, V&A · portrait, Museo di Roma, Pinacoteca dell'Arcadia

Alger, John Goldworth (*bap.* 1836, *d.* 1907), journalist and historian, born at Diss, Norfolk, and baptized on 7 August 1836, was the only son of John Alger, a corn merchant of that town, and his wife, Jemima, daughter of Salem Goldworth, yeoman, of Morningthorpe, Norfolk. Mary Jemima *Alger was his younger sister. Educated at Diss, Alger became a journalist at the age of sixteen. At first he wrote for the *Norfolk News*, afterwards transferring his services to the *Oxford Journal*. In 1866 he joined the parliamentary reporting staff of *The Times*, and after eight years in that capacity was sent to Paris in 1874 to act as assistant to Henri de Blowitz, the paper's Paris correspondent. There he remained for twenty-eight years, very much the second fiddle to Blowitz's first violin.

Alger's leisure was chiefly devoted to historical research in the Bibliothèque Nationale and Archives Nationales. He made himself thoroughly familiar with the topographical history of Paris, and threw new light on byways of the French Revolution, investigating with especial thoroughness the part that Britons played in the great movement. His chief publications were *Englishmen in the French Revolution* (1889); *Glimpses of the French Revolution* (1894); *Paris in 1789–94: Farewell Letters of Victims of the Guillotine* (1902); and *Napoleon's British Visitors and Captives* (1904). He also published *The Paris Sketch Book* (1887)—a description of current Parisian life—contributed historical articles to several leading magazines, and was an occasional contributor to the *Dictionary of National Biography*. In 1902 Alger retired from *The Times* on a pension, and settled in London. He died from mitral disease, at 7 Holland Park Court, Addison Road, West Kensington, on 23 May 1907; he was unmarried.   S. E. FRYER, *rev.* H. C. G. MATTHEW

Sources *The Times* (25 May 1907) · H. G. S. A. de Blowitz, *My memories* (1903)
Wealth at death £15,815 7*s.* 4*d.*: administration, 30 Aug 1907, *CGPLA Eng. & Wales*

Alger, Mary Jemima (1838–1894), headmistress, was born on 4 February 1838 at Diss, in Norfolk, daughter of John Alger, corn merchant, and his wife, Jemima, *née* Goldworth, of yeoman stock. Mary had sisters and an only brother, John Goldworth *Alger, who became a journalist. Mary's education was private, and she then taught in several private schools. Such education—by its nature unexamined—varied widely in quality, but Mary's must be judged by its results. When she was thirty-seven, in 1875, she was appointed first headmistress of the Girls' Public Day School Company (GPDSC) (later Trust) school at Clapham in south-west London—its fifth venture. These schools were the turning point in what has been called the 'renaissance of girls' education'. Financed by investment, managed by a powerful council with strong academic and social support, and under royal patronage, they were to consolidate and disseminate the new kind of school for girls.

Experience of organizing large girls' schools, with a broad academic curriculum, leading to public examinations and, for some, careers and higher education, was slowly accumulating, and could succeed only if women of the right calibre and qualities could be found to run them. These early headmistresses were of necessity without professional preparation, but many of them, unlike Miss Alger, came from academic backgrounds, had scholastic connections, or were of some social standing. Miss Alger became 'by common consent one of the greatest of all the headmistresses who have served the Trust' (Magnus, 117).

Clapham was to be a 'middle school' founded by the company to comply with the findings of the recent schools' inquiry (Taunton) commission that the various levels of the Victorian middle classes required schools with different leaving ages and charging different fees. But while Clapham catered for a middle range of middle-class girls, it was still a public school providing a broad curriculum, with Latin, German, music, algebra, elementary mathematics, and physical science as 'extras'. Under the eye of the powerful council Miss Alger presided over this establishment on Clapham Common until, in 1878, she was transferred to Sheffield to open what was to become one of the most famous of the company's high schools. This began with thirty-seven pupils and under Miss Alger rapidly grew to sixty-eight. The system of teaching, she explained to a meeting of parents and shareholders, 'should be liberal in the widest sense' for the 'education of girls was assuming a broader aspect' (*The Times*, 1878, GPDST press cuttings collection). But at this same meeting Miss Alger's resignation was announced, as she had been appointed by the company, skilfully deploying its scarce resources, to open its high school at Dulwich. At Sheffield she was succeeded by Mrs Woodhouse, who had come with her from Clapham, and to whom the founding of the school is usually accredited.

The choice of Miss Alger to open a third company school in succession implies a high opinion of her organizational abilities. The GPDSC opened a school only where local demand was demonstrated by the taking up of sufficient shares, and in Dulwich, where the education of boys had been well supplied by the reorganization of the great Alleyn charity, the need for a girls' school was keen. The high school opened in September 1875 with forty-seven girls; a year later there were 179 pupils and by 1885 there were 400 on the books. The organization and management of such a number of girls of all ages and attainments, following a wide curriculum, was formidable and still experimental. It was made more difficult by the erratic attendance of some pupils who came only for short periods—a common problem in girls' schools of the period. Miss Alger also had to persuade many parents to commit their daughters to the new curriculum. She regretted that they did not always take advantage of the callisthenics course provided by a woman teacher, replacing the usual drill sergeant, and that botany remained the chief science subject, few girls taking chemistry.

Miss Alger was 'a most successful mistress not only in organizing her school as a whole, but in making each girl feel that her education was an object of individual attention to the headmistress' (*Journal of Education*, 1 May 1894, 270–71). She inspired the girls, as one of them at Clapham remembered, with a sense of 'the importance of life and of our share in it' (Magnus, 74). On her leaving them the girls at Sheffield thanked her for her great kindness: 'she had made school like home' (*The Times*, n.d., GPDST press cuttings collection). Dulwich was remembered as 'such a comfortable school' (Magnus, 117). This emphasizes the continuity between the old-style domestic and private schooling and the new-style public schools—a particularly feminine contribution to the concept of secondary education. The style of teaching, however, was markedly different. A Clapham pupil recalled her first lesson with Miss Alger—on Carlyle's *Past and Present*: 'To be led to think, to judge, to ponder, was a new delight to a girl who had hitherto only "done lessons"' (Magnus, 74). Miss Alger gave the same individual attention to her staff, at Dulwich seeing each of them alone every week and encouraging their individuality. She had 'a noteworthy tolerance of varying methods, so that her school was distinguished alike by orderliness and freedom' (Magnus, 117). The resulting academic standard was high—between 1882 and 1892 many university scholarships were gained by Dulwich girls, including nine to Girton College, Cambridge. The supply of good entrants to the women's colleges was one of the chief contributions and functions of GPDSC schools to the general advance of girls' education, one which eventually provided them with qualified teachers.

The prosperity of the Dulwich school was however declining by 1891. Miss Alger reported that the numbers were down, following changes in the population of Dulwich, fewer of the new inhabitants being able to afford the high-school fees. The establishment of James Allen's Girls' School as part of the Dulwich foundation, with 'remarkably low fees', and the opening of other GPDSC schools at Brixton (1889) and Sydenham (1887) had brought too much competition. By this time, too, Miss Alger's health was faltering. She was granted a term's sick leave in 1891, and although she recovered and returned to

work in the next year, hoping to 'continue a little longer', in March 1894 it was reported 'with regret that she was ill without hope of recovery' (finance committee, 17 March 1894, GPDST records). She died of chronic kidney failure on 17 March 1894 at her home next door to the school, 55 Lancaster Road, Dulwich, made available by the council thirteen years before, on terms accepted by Miss Alger as long as venetian blinds and gas fittings were provided. Her funeral service was held at the church she attended, St Peter's, Streatham, and she was buried on 25 March in Norwood cemetery. An Alger Memorial Fund was raised by the GPDSC to provide two scholarships to the school for two years, a fitting way to commemorate a woman who had played a key part in the transformation of girls' education during the reign of Queen Victoria.

MARGARET BRYANT

Sources Boase, *Mod. Eng. biog.* · *Journal of Education*, new ser., 16 (1894), 270–71 · *The Times* (19 March 1894) · records of Girls' Public Day School Trust, 26 Queen Anne's Gate, London · L. Magnus, *The jubilee book of the Girls' Public Day School Trust, 1873–1923* (1923) · press cuttings, GPDST collections · *Norwood Press* (24 March 1894) · *South London Press* (31 March 1894) · J. Kamm, *Indicative past: one hundred years of the Girls' Public Day School Trust* (1971) · b. cert. · d. cert.
Archives 26 Queen Anne's Gate, London, minutes of the council and committee of Girls' Public Day School Trust
Wealth at death £5895 16s. 10d.: administration, 10 April 1894, CGPLA Eng. & Wales

Algeranoff, Harcourt [*real name* Harcourt Algernon Leighton Essex] (**1903–1967**), dancer and ballet master, was born in London on 18 April 1903, the son of Thomas Richard Essex, a sculptor, and his wife, Alice Kendall. He was named Harcourt Algernon Leighton Essex. He dropped his original name and assumed that of Algeranoff when he joined Anna Pavlova's company in 1921. It was as though he had not only taken on a Russian stage name—as was usual enough at the time when, in the world of ballet, to be British was to be nothing much whereas to be Russian was to be in the height of fashion—but had largely assumed a Russian identity; Algeranoff, it seemed, became the most persistent of the many character roles in which he excelled.

Algeranoff studied at one time or another under the Russians Nicholas Legat and Lubov Chernicheva, but his most formative period was that of the far-ranging tours which he undertook as 'character soloist' with Pavlova. It was then that he became interested in Indian and Japanese dance, about which he subsequently lectured. His experiences of that period, remembered with nostalgia, were eventually put into a book, *My Years with Pavlova* (1957). Algeranoff married the French dancer Claudie Léonard (*b.* 1924); they had a son, Noel, who, following in parental footsteps, became a mime. Claudie Algeranova later became ballet mistress at the Bavarian State Opera in Munich.

Algeranoff was a founder member of the Markova–Dolin Company in 1935, joined the De Basil Ballet Russe, the company with the best claim to be the successor to the great Diaghilev ballet, in 1936, and the International Ballet, under Mona Inglesby, in 1943. It was with De Basil and the International that he chiefly made, and consolidated, his considerable reputation as a character dancer or, more specifically, as a character actor; for the roles with which he was memorably associated were those in which dancing counted for less than acting. Algeranoff learned the traditional character roles (Carabosse, Rothbart, Hilarion) from a colleague of his in the International, Nikolay Sergeyev, the one-time regisseur of the Maryinsky Ballet in St Petersburg. Sergeyev's notation of the nineteenth-century classics, which he brought with him when he left the Soviet Union, had enabled the Sadler's Wells (subsequently the Royal) Ballet to present exceptionally authentic versions of those basic works. He had then transferred his allegiance from the Sadler's Wells Ballet to the International. Among the character roles in which Algeranoff excelled were the astrologer in *Le coq d'or*, the magician Kastchei in *Firebird*, Pierrot in *Carnaval*, Dr Coppélius in *Coppélia*, the master of ceremonies in *Gaieté Parisienne*, Carabosse in *The Sleeping Beauty*, and Death in Mona Inglesby's choreographic version of *Everyman*.

Algeranoff also conducted outstanding classes in character and national dancing at the International Ballet. However, the ballet *For Love or Money*, which he made for the company in 1951, is remembered only as indicating that, for all his stagecraft, his ability as a teacher, and his exceptional skill as a performer, he lacked the inventiveness of movement which bespeaks a true choreographer.

After the International Ballet ceased to exist, Algeranoff went to Australia in 1954. There he worked at first in the Australian Children's Theatre. He then became ballet master to the Borovansky Ballet (1959) and a guest artist (1962–3) in the Australian Ballet, which at that time was beginning to take shape under the guidance of Peggy van Praagh. For a time Algeranoff returned to Europe, becoming director of the Norwegian State Opera and Ballet Company. But in 1959 he decided to settle in Australia, making his home in Mildura, where he opened a dance studio. In contemporary Australia there was scarcely the opportunity for Algeranoff's career to prosper conspicuously; but he was one of the pioneers whose example and influence contributed to the growth of an indigenous company in that country where ballet had been previously an intermittent import only. Algeranoff became ballet master for Australia's North Western Ballet Society.

Algeranoff did not belong to the native and nascent British ballet which, young though it was, sent its missionaries, such as Peggy van Praagh, to the dominions. He was one of the last of those few British dancers who made their way in a world of cosmopolitan ballet still dominated by expatriate Russians. But they too have their place in the story of the widening popularity of ballet in the mid-twentieth century.

Algeranoff was dapper, talented, youthfully handsome, and took himself very seriously. He played his Russian character role with zest, in public at least, and loved to tell stories about Pavlova. Algeranoff died in a road accident in Robinvale, Australia, on 7 April 1967.

JAMES MONAHAN, rev.

Sources H. Algeranoff, *My years with Pavlova* (1957) · *The Times* (19 April 1967) · private information (1981) · H. Koegler, *The concise Oxford dictionary of ballet*, 2nd edn (1982) · CGPLA Eng. & Wales (1967) **Wealth at death** £1728 effects in England: probate, 25 July 1967, CGPLA Eng. & Wales

Alhmund [Alchmund] (*d.* **781**), bishop of Hexham, was consecrated in 767. He died in 781, and was buried near his more famous predecessor, Acca, outside the walls of the church of his see. The translation of Alhmund's body to a tomb within the church took place about 1030. Alhmund should not be confused with the boy martyr *Ealhmund (*d.* 800). WILLIAM HUNT, *rev.* MARIOS COSTAMBEYS

Sources Symeon of Durham, *Opera*, vol. 1

Alhred (*fl.* **765–774**). *See under* Oswulf (*d.* 759).

Ali, (Chaudhri) Muhammad (**1905–1980**), prime minister of Pakistan, 1955–6, was born on 15 July 1905 in Nangalambia village, Jullundur district, Punjab province, India. His father was Chaudhri Khairuddin, a farmer and member of the Arain community, his mother, Ayesha Khairdin; he was the third of five children, with two elder sisters and two younger brothers. Muhammad Ali was educated at Nangalambia high school and at the University of the Punjab, Lahore, where he gained an MSc. He had the reputation of being an outstanding student and for the year after he graduated taught chemistry at Islamia College, Lahore.

In 1928 Muhammad Ali entered the Indian audit and accounts service. In 1932 he was seconded as accountant-general to Bahawalpur state, where he set the finances on a sound footing and planned the repayment of the state's debts to the government of India. In 1936 he joined the finance department of the government of India, rising to become deputy financial adviser on military finance in 1939, joint financial adviser on military finance and additional financial adviser, department of war and supply, in 1943, and financial adviser, department of war and supply, in 1945. He was only the second Indian to hold this last post. In 1942 he toured the war fronts in the Middle East, visiting El Alamein, Tobruk, and Iran. In 1945 he was a member of the Hydari commission to negotiate an agreement over items in short supply in the United Kingdom; in 1946 he was a member of the Indian lend-lease mission to the United States; and from June 1947 he was the member representing Pakistan, alongside H. M. Patel representing India, of the two-man steering committee which worked out the details of the division of the assets of British India. In this capacity he also worked with Patel as secretary to the partition committee, which presided over the whole process.

From 1947 to 1956 Muhammad Ali was a major figure in the establishment of the Pakistani state. From August 1947 to October 1951 he was secretary-general of the civil service. Acutely aware of the enormous problems which confronted the government of the new state, he set out to establish a greater degree of administrative centralization than had existed in British India. His post was to be the key link between the cabinet and the bureaucracy; he appointed officials not just at the central but also at the provincial levels and was the decision maker in all matters to do with the administration. During these years he acquired considerable influence over the affairs of Pakistan. The prime minister, Liaquat Ali Khan, 'was very much under the influence of Chaudhri Mohammad Ali' (Khan, 40), noted the future martial law ruler Ayub Khan. Muhammad Ali left his own record of the difficulties of these founding years in his book *The Emergence of Pakistan* (1967).

After the assassination of Liaquat Ali Khan in October 1951 Muhammad Ali joined the cabinet as minister of finance and economic affairs. During the years 1952–4 he led Pakistan's delegation to the Commonwealth Finance Ministers' Conference and the annual meetings of the International Monetary Fund and of the International Bank for Reconstruction and Development. Over the same period he laid the foundations of Pakistan's planning commission. On 7 August 1954 he was elected leader of the Muslim League party in the constituent assembly. On 11 August 1955 he became prime minister, leading a coalition between the Muslim League and the United Front of East Pakistan.

The crowning achievement of Muhammad Ali's premiership was to bring to an end the nine-year period of constitution making with the promulgation on 23 March 1956 of the first constitution of the Islamic Republic of Pakistan. He had been closely involved in the negotiations leading up to this moment. The key issue in this process was how to create a constitution in which the Bengalis, who formed the majority of the country's population, would not dominate the state at the centre. Under the so-called Muhammad Ali formula the five provinces of the west wing of Pakistan would agree to form one unit while the Bengali east wing would agree to a status of parity with the west. The first stage of the process was achieved with the passage of the One Unit Bill on 14 October 1955, and the second with the adoption of a federal and parliamentary constitution for the country in March 1956. Unfortunately, Muhammad Ali was keener to make a constitution than to make one which would work. His constitution weighted power too much in favour of the president and exacerbated relations between centre and province, and province and province. On 8 September 1956, despairing of being able to govern, he resigned. No elections were held under the constitution. Politics became increasingly chaotic until, in October 1958, Ayub Khan declared martial law.

Muhammad Ali was a dedicated constitutionalist and devoted himself to opposing the martial law regime. In 1958 he founded the Tahrik-I-Istehkam-I-Pakistan Party for the consolidation of Pakistan, the protection of the constitution, separate elections for non-Muslims, and the establishment of a welfare state. In 1959 he merged his party with the Nizam-i-Islam Party. In 1960 he stirred up much controversy through his widely publicized reply to Ayub Khan's constitutional commission, in which he urged the restoration of parliamentary democracy and expressed his fears that the presidential system would lead to dictatorship. In 1964 he played the leading part,

along with Khwaja Nazimuddin, in bringing together utterly dissimilar parties in the Combined Opposition Party, which sought to restore parliamentary democracy and to remove within ten years the economic disparity between East and West Pakistan. The party's candidate for the presidency was Fatima Jinnah, the sister of the founder of Pakistan; despite having the full weight of the government machine ranged against her, she gave Ayub Khan a good fight in the elections of January 1965.

In October 1969, six months after the fall of Ayub Khan, Muhammad Ali retired from politics. He became a deeply religious man, devoting much of his time to reciting the Koran and reading Islamic literature. His wife, who survived him, was Razia Sultana, daughter of Dr Muhammad Jan of Amritsar. They had four sons and one daughter. He died at his home in Karachi from heart failure on 1 December 1980.

Muhammad Ali was primarily an administrator. As a politician he had no following and did not seek one. He was of equable temperament and adopted a rational and pragmatic approach to issues. If his contemporaries assessed him as a major contributor to the consolidation of the Pakistani state, subsequent comment has tended to focus on his contributions, through both his successes and his failures, towards establishing the dominance of a military-bureaucratic élite in the governance of that state. FRANCIS ROBINSON

Sources *Dawn* (2–3 Dec 1980) · N. K. Jain, ed., *Muslims in India: a biographical dictionary*, 2 vols. (1979–83) · C. M. Ali, *The emergence of Pakistan* (1967) · A. Jalal, *The state of martial rule* (1990) · M. Ayub Khan, *Friends not masters: a political autobiography* (1967) · private information (2004)

Archives priv. coll. | FILM IWM FVA, actuality footage
Likenesses photographs, priv. coll. · photographs, Hult. Arch.

Alice [married name Alice de Lusignan], *suo jure* **countess of Eu** (*d.* 1246), magnate, was the daughter of Henri, count of Eu and lord of Hastings, and Matilda, the daughter of Hamelin (de *Warenne), earl of Surrey, and Countess Isabel de *Warenne. On the death of her brother Raoul d'Eu in 1186 Alice became the sole heir of the Eu lands. About 1191 she married Raoul de Lusignan, taking the great estates of Eu to a powerful lord of Poitou. She had one son, also Raoul, and a daughter, Mathilde. Her lands were forfeit in 1201–2, when King John's marriage to Isabella of Angoulême led to a dispute with the Lusignan family. After the death of her husband on 1 May 1219 Alice was thrust into the centre of contemporary politics: she was now a powerful dowager with the task of administering the Eu inheritance, to which she was more than equal. In 1219 she paid 15,000 silver marks (£10,000) to the king of France to receive the county of Eu and took steps to regain control of her English inheritance which had been entrusted to the earl of Surrey in England as her representative on the death of her husband. In 1220 she was successful in her defence of her claim to the castle of Tickhill in a case that had been brought against her in the previous year. Alice was rich enough to lend 140 marks to the count of Aumale, who still owed her the sum in 1223. In a shrewd political move she handed her custody of Tickhill to

Henry III in 1225 for the duration of Anglo-French hostilities in an agreement that ensured that her lands would not suffer loss. She lost Tickhill on 18 February 1244 when Henry III seized it on account of her support for the French king, Louis IX, for whom she was responsible for levying troops. Louis twice ordered her to appear with her forces to fight for him.

Alice left a large number of charters that testify to her secular and religious patronage. She was, for example, a benefactor of English and French religious houses including St Martin's, Battle, Christ Church, Canterbury, Robertsbridge, St Michael's, Tréport, St Mary's, Eu, and Foucarmont. She granted an annual allowance to the recluse of Hackington, Loretta, countess of Leicester. She died, probably between 13 and 15 May, in 1246, at La Mothe St Héray in Poitou. She left a will and may have been buried at her husband's foundation of Fontblanche Priory at Exoudun.   SUSAN M. JOHNS

Sources GEC, *Peerage* · *CPR, 1216–25* · *Curia regis rolls preserved in the Public Record Office* (1922–), vol. 9 · *Close rolls of the reign of Henry III*, 1, PRO (1902) · *Calendar of charters & documents relating to the abbey of Robertsbridge, W. Sussex* (1873) · P. Laffleur and D. E. Kermignani, eds., *Cartulaire de l'abbaye de S-Michel de Tréport* (1880) · cartulary of Foucarmont, Bibliothèque Municipale, Rouen, Y13 · cartulary of counts of Eu, Bibliothèque Nationale, Paris, MS latin 13904 · Merton Oxf., muniments 1006, 952, 953 · *Pipe rolls*, 29 Henry III, 31 Henry III
Archives Merton Oxf., muniments 952, 953, 1006 | Bibliothèque Municipale, Rouen, Y13 · Bibliothèque Nationale, Paris, MS Latin 13904
Wealth at death bequeathed land to Foucarmont: will, GEC, *Peerage*

Alice, Princess [*married name* Princess Louis of Hesse] (1843–1878), grand duchess of Hesse, consort of Louis IV, the third child and second daughter of Queen *Victoria and Prince *Albert, was born Alice Maud Mary at Buckingham Palace in the early morning of 25 April 1843. Overshadowed by her elder sister, Vicky, the princess royal, she developed a close bond of affection with Bertie, the prince of Wales, frequently acting as intermediary between him and the queen. Her reputation for sweetness of disposition, which gave her the role of peacemaker in the often stormy royal household, was enhanced following her early death: in a popular edition of Alice's letters to the queen published in 1885, Princess Helena described her as 'loving Daughter and Sister, the devoted Wife and Mother, and a perfect, true Woman'. Such fulsome tributes have served to disguise the more complex character of the princess, and to diminish the importance of her public life.

The marriage of the princess royal in 1858 left Alice as the eldest daughter at home, and the queen came to rely on her for companionship, while the prince consort turned to her as a substitute for his eldest child, with whom he had enjoyed a particularly close relationship. Alice was thus introduced to his ideas for a liberal Europe led by a united Germany, and gained from him an interest in the arts and sciences. Plans for her marriage were advanced in the traditional royal manner, and, following the rejection by her parents of the prince of Orange as a

Princess Alice (1843–1878), by Franz Xaver Winterhalter, 1861

suitable candidate, she was introduced to Prince Louis of Hesse (1837–1892), and a marriage was arranged. Before the wedding could take place, the family was convulsed by the deaths of the duchess of Kent and the prince consort. During Albert's illness, Alice was in constant attendance, recognizing the seriousness of his condition when Victoria refused such knowledge. It was Alice who sent for the prince of Wales when the queen would have kept him away, and she who constantly attended her mother during the traumatic weeks following Albert's death. Thereafter, the eighteen-year-old princess acted informally as the queen's agent in household and ministerial affairs, all communications from the government passing through her hands while Victoria remained incapacitated. Her conduct under these trying circumstances won her the praise of all, including Lord Clarendon, who wrote that 'there is not such another girl in a thousand', adding, with accuracy, that 'she is going with a dull boy to a dull family in a dull country and I have a presentiment that she won't be happy' (Noel, 87). Her marriage to Louis of Hesse took place, as planned, on 1 July 1862 at Osborne in surroundings of unrelieved gloom—the queen described it as 'more like a funeral than a wedding' (Fulford, 85). The marriage was not unsuccessful, but Alice increasingly felt at an emotional and intellectual distance from her husband, despite the continuance of a strong affection between them. They had two sons and five daughters, among them the future Tsarina Alexandra Feodorovna, and the Grand Duchess Serge, both of whom were to die at the hands of Russian revolutionaries, and Victoria [*see* Mountbatten, Victoria Alberta Elisabeth Mathilde Marie].

The couple removed to Darmstadt shortly after the marriage; their residence in Germany was a constant source of tension with Victoria, who had expected them to spend most of their time in England. Alice found the small German court stifling, and made herself unpopular with court officials by her disregard for their strict etiquette. At the same time, her relationship with her mother deteriorated over her strong disapproval of the marriage of her sister Helena with Christian of Schleswig-Holstein, and over Alice's practice of breast-feeding her children.

An interest in child welfare propelled the princess towards a more general interest in the welfare of her subjects, and she made the Neues Palais in Darmstadt a centre of philanthropic activity. Beginning with plans for a home for the mentally ill, in 1866 Alice organized a vast bazaar in the newly constructed palace to raise funds; this proved highly successful and the home opened in October 1869. Meanwhile the Austro-Prussian War had started and Darmstadt filled with the wounded. Alice, pregnant with her third child, became deeply involved in the administration of field hospitals and nursing the injured. A disciple of Florence Nightingale, with whom she engaged in a detailed professional correspondence, she continued to be greatly preoccupied with the care of the sick and wounded after the war ended. In 1867 she set up a national organization, the Alice-Frauenverein ('Alice women's guild') to train nurses, professional and auxiliary, for wartime and other emergencies. At the same time, she developed a deep interest in the position of women, and particularly in their capacity to earn an independent living, to promote which she created the Alice-Verein für Frauenbildung und Erwerb ('Alice guild for the education and training of women'). The success of the Frauenverein was early put to the test in the Franco-Prussian War, which again found Alice deeply involved in the care of the wounded, turning the Neues Palais into a medical depot. In 1871 she nursed her favourite brother, the prince of Wales, through typhoid fever.

Alice's health began to deteriorate in the late 1860s, when she began to suffer from rheumatism, neuralgia, and eye strain. Her seven pregnancies in ten years, the strain of two wars, tensions within her family, and the unremitting pressure of the work in which she engaged contributed to the decline. Moreover, during the same period she underwent a crisis of faith. Encouraged by Prince Albert to think deeply on religious matters, she found herself repelled by the unreflective sentimentality of much Victorian religion, and while she did not cease to believe, she sought an intellectual basis for her faith. This she seems to have found in the theology of David Friedrich Strauss, who was living in Darmstadt, and with whom she developed a close friendship. He dedicated his volume of lectures on Voltaire to her. The death of her three-year-old younger son, after a fall from a window, restored her faith in the necessary existence of God and the afterlife, but she never fully recovered from the loss.

When Louis and Alice succeeded as grand duke and duchess on 13 June 1877, the burdens of Alice's public duties increased, adding to the weariness of spirit which was so similar to that suffered by her father. None the less, she continued in her self-appointed tasks, including having Octavia Hill's pamphlets on organized charity translated into German and contributing a foreword to them. In the summer of 1878 the family took a holiday at Eastbourne, paid for by Victoria, but even here Alice continued to visit hospitals and the sick, apparently unable to pause in her exertions. Towards the end of the year, her children and husband fell ill with diphtheria, from which her youngest daughter, May, died on 16 November. Alice herself succumbed to the disease, and died on 14 December 1878, the anniversary of her father's death. She was buried in the mausoleum at Rosenhöhe, Darmstadt, where a memorial by Sir Joseph Edgar Boehm of Alice and May was erected.   K. D. REYNOLDS

Sources G. Noel, *Princess Alice: Queen Victoria's forgotten daughter* (1974) · Alice, grand duchess of Hesse-Darmstadt, *Letters to her majesty the queen*, ed. Princess Christian (1885) · *The letters of Queen Victoria*, ed. A. C. Benson, Lord Esher [R. B. Brett], and G. E. Buckle, 9 vols. (1907–32) · *Dearest mama: letters between Queen Victoria and the crown princess of Prussia, 1861–1864*, ed. R. Fulford (1968) · J. Van der Kiste, *Queen Victoria's children* (1986) · M. Charlot, *Victoria: the young queen* (1991)

Archives Hessisches Staatsarchiv, Darmstadt, Germany · Royal Arch. · U. Nott. L., papers relating to marriage | BL, letters to Florence Nightingale

Likenesses E. Landseer, oils, 1843, Royal Collection · portrait, 1843 (after E. Landseer), Osborne House, Isle of Wight · M. Thornycroft, portraits, 1843–61, Osborne House, Isle of Wight · M. Thornycroft, portrait, 1845, Osborne House, Isle of Wight · F. X. Winterhalter, group portrait, watercolour, 1847, Royal Collection · F. X. Winterhalter, group portrait, oils, 1849 (*The four daughters of Queen Victoria*), Royal Collection · L. Caldesi, photograph, 1857, NPG · J. Phillip, group portrait, oils, 1858 (*The marriage of the princess royal*), Royal Collection · E. Moira, miniature, exh. RA 1860?, Royal Collection · W. & D. Downey, photograph, 1860–69 · Mayall & Co., photograph, 1861, NPG · M. Thornycroft, marble bust, 1861, Royal Collection · F. X. Winterhalter, oils, 1861, Royal Collection [*see illus.*] · W. & D. Downey, carte-de-visite, 1862?, NPG · G. H. Thomas, group portrait, oils, 1862 (*The marriage of Princess Alice to Prince Louis of Hesse*), Royal Collection · J. Kopf, marble bust, 1874, Royal Collection · H. von Angeli, portrait, 1877–8 · J. E. Boehm, marble bust, 1879, Royal Collection · W. Bambridge, photograph, NPG · E. Boehm, funeral monument, Rosenhöhe, Darmstadt, Germany, mausoleum · S. D. Durant, medallion, NPG · E. Landseer, oils (as a child), Royal Collection · M. Thornycroft, statuette (as a child), Royal Collection · Queen Victoria, drawings, Royal Collection · F. X. Winterhalter, double portrait, watercolour drawing (with princess royal), Royal Collection · F. X. Winterhalter, group portrait, oils (*The royal family, 1846*), Royal Collection · Winterhalter and Koberwein, oils, Osborne House, Isle of Wight · photographs, NPG · photographs, Royal Collection · portrait, Osborne House, Isle of Wight · prints, BM, NPG

Alice, Princess [Princess Alice of Albany], **countess of Athlone** (1883–1981), was born Alice Mary Victoria Augusta Pauline at Windsor Castle on 25 February 1883. She was the elder child and only daughter of Prince *Leopold George Duncan Albert, first duke of Albany (1853–1884), Queen Victoria's fourth and youngest son, and his wife, Princess Helen of Waldeck-Pyrmont (1861–1922). Her father died of haemophilia little more than a year after her birth and she was brought up by her mother at Claremont House, near Esher. Lewis Carroll, who met this other Alice with the Cecil family at Hatfield House when she was six, described her as 'a sweet little girl, though with rather unruly spirits' (*Letters*, 2.743). She, too, had her reservations about their supposed friendship: 'He was always making grown-up jokes to us,' she confided, 'and we thought him awfully silly' (personal knowledge).

On 10 February 1904 Princess Alice was married to the younger brother of the future Queen Mary, Prince Alexander of Teck (1874–1957) [see Cambridge, Alexander Augustus Frederick William Alfred George]. A serving officer in the British army, he abandoned his German princely title in 1917, adopted by royal licence the family name of Cambridge, and was created earl of Athlone.

Princess Alice's lifelong vivacity concealed anxiety and sorrow. Her brother, Prince *Charles Edward, second duke of Albany, had at the age of fifteen been taken away from Eton College to be brought up in Germany as heir to his uncle, the reigning duke of Coburg. He entered on his unfortunate inheritance in 1900, fought for his adopted country during the First World War, and was deposed in 1918. He later became a fervent supporter of the Nazi regime. These events naturally distressed Princess Alice, whose heart was torn between patriotism and affection for an only brother.

As wife of the governor-general of South Africa in 1923–31 and of Canada in 1940–46, Princess Alice proved a memorable proconsul in her own right: graceful, sympathetic, and perpetually amused. But tragedy struck again in 1928. Her son, Rupert Alexander George Augustus, Viscount Trematon (b. 1907), had inherited the haemophilia of his grandfather, Prince Leopold. He died of injuries in a motoring accident from which others might have recovered. A younger son, Maurice Francis George, had died in 1910 before he was six months old. There was also one daughter of the marriage, Lady May Helen Emma Cambridge (b. 1906), who married a soldier, Henry Abel Smith, governor of Queensland from 1958 to 1966.

From their marriage until 1923 the princess and her husband lived in Henry III Tower, Windsor Castle. Later they had an apartment in Kensington Palace, with a country place at Brantridge Park, Sussex. Lord Athlone's death in 1957 dissolved a partnership of more than half a century but did not deflect his widow from a way of life both industrious and convivial. Well into her tenth decade, she remained an active patron of many institutions; the Royal School of Needlework and the Women's Transport Service earned her particular interest. Princess Alice's leisure hours were no less productive, and she would continue to knit even while walking up a mountain at Balmoral.

A sense of adventure as well as of thrift led Princess Alice to travel about London by bus. For many years she similarly crossed the Atlantic each winter in a banana boat, combining her duties as chancellor (1950–71) of the University of the West Indies with a holiday in Jamaica. Several times she revisited South Africa and made the long journey to stay with her son-in-law and daughter in Australia.

Although below middle height, Princess Alice had a patrician presence, with aquiline features, observant eyes, and a stylish sense of fashion. She was an engaging talker and needed little prompting to recall life at Windsor under Queen Victoria, whose unsuspected laughter still rang in the ears of her last surviving granddaughter almost a century later. Not all her memories were benign. She never forgave W. E. Gladstone for having cheated her family of a whole year's civil list when her father died a few days before the start of the fiscal year; or Sir Winston Churchill for filling her drawing-room with pungent cigar smoke during the Quebec conference of 1943. Some of these recollections she confided to an entertaining volume of memoirs, *For my Grandchildren* (1966). Her views on public affairs were emphatic and not always predictable. When a colonial governor of radical bent expressed his belief in universal suffrage, she replied: 'Foot, I have never heard such balderdash in my life.' Yet she was the first member of the royal family publicly to advocate birth control, and like her cousin George V did not harbour a trace of racial prejudice.

Princess Alice, the last surviving member of the Royal Order of Victoria and Albert, was also appointed GBE in 1937 and GCVO in 1948. She had many honorary degrees. She died on 3 January 1981 at Kensington Palace in her ninety-eighth year. After a funeral service in St George's Chapel, Windsor, her remains were buried at Frogmore.

KENNETH ROSE, rev.

Sources Princess Alice, *For my grandchildren* (1966) · T. Aronson, *Princess Alice* (1981) · personal knowledge (1990) · *The letters of Lewis Carroll*, ed. M. N. Cohen and R. L. Green, 2 vols. (1979) · *The Times* (5 Jan 1981) · *The Times* (9 Jan 1981)
Archives University of Cape Town Library, letters to J. Newton Thompson
Likenesses Hill & Saunders, double portrait, photograph, c.1883–1884 (with father, duke of Albany), NPG · L. Tuxen, group portrait, oils, 1887 (*The royal family at the time of the Jubilee*), Royal Collection · L. Tuxen, oils, 1893 (*Marriage of King George V and Queen Mary*), Royal Collection · P. de Laszlo, oils, c.1929, priv. coll. · N. Hepple, oils, c.1954, priv. coll. · Snowdon, photograph, 1978, NPG · Madame Yevonde, photographs, NPG · photograph, repro. in *Burke's guide to the royal family* (1973) · photographs (several royal groups), NPG · photographs, Royal Collection
Wealth at death £182,125: probate, 13 July 1981, CGPLA Eng. & Wales

Alice, Princess [Princess Alice of Battenberg; *married name* Princess Andrew of Greece] (1885–1969), was born (in the presence of Queen Victoria, her great-grandmother) on 25 February 1885 at Windsor Castle. Named Victoria Alice Elizabeth Julie Marie, she was the eldest of the four children, including Louis *Mountbatten (1900–1979) and George *Mountbatten (1892–1938), of Prince Louis of Battenberg, later first marquess of Milford Haven [see Mountbatten, Louis Alexander (1854–1921)], and his wife, Victoria [see Mountbatten, Victoria Alberta Elisabeth Mathilde Marie (1863–1950)], daughter of Ludwig IV, grand duke of Hesse and by Rhine (1837–1892).

Princess Alice began a life of travel at once, being taken to Darmstadt for her baptism and then back to Portsmouth. Before she was six months old she had made five sea voyages. She was deemed slow to learn until congenital deafness—caused by thickening of the Eustachian tubes—was detected by her grandmother Princess Battenberg (the morganatic wife of Prince Alexander of Hesse). A resourceful, intelligent child, she was both remote and independent because of her deafness, able to spend hours absorbed in her own company, a trait that continued throughout her life. Proficient in several languages, she could lip-read in more than one. Her brown eyes and golden hair attracted the attention of her great-aunt, the Empress Frederick, who described her as having 'the most perfect face … so interesting and picturesque'.

Alice was educated privately in Germany, at her parents' homes in Darmstadt and Schloss Heiligenberg, Jugenheim; in Malta, where her father, a naval officer, was stationed for several winters; and in London, where her father was periodically based at the Admiralty. In 1902, when attending the coronation of Edward VII in London, she met Prince Andrew of Greece (1882–1944), the fourth son of George I of Greece (1845–1913). They were married in Darmstadt on 7 October 1903; the occasion was one of the last great pre-war gatherings of European royalty, for many of whom a dismal fate awaited.

Prince and Princess Andrew went to live in Greece, partly at the royal palace in Athens and partly at Tatoï. In 1913 they inherited the villa Mon Repos on Corfu from George I of Greece. While Prince Andrew was a full-time professional army officer, Alice learned Greek, and worked at the School of Embroidery and at a number of other charitable endeavours. They had four daughters—Margarita (b. 1905), Theodora (b. 1906), Cécile (b. 1911), and Sophie (b. 1914). Prince and Princess Andrew travelled extensively in Europe and to Russia, where Alice was much taken with the nursing order founded by her aunt Elizabeth, Grand Duchess Serge of Russia (1864–1918).

Greece was beset by political problems between 1912 and 1922. During the Balkan wars of 1912–13 Alice threw herself into the task of nursing, assisting at operations, setting up hospitals near the front, and organizing supplies. This was perhaps her finest hour, and in 1913 George V awarded her the Royal Red Cross. In 1916 Alice hid with her children in the cellars of the Royal Palace during the allied bombardment of Athens. In 1917 the Greek royal family were forced into exile and lived mainly in Switzerland. During this time Alice became interested in spirituality and religion, being particularly influenced by a popular history of religions, Les grands initiés by Édouard Schuré. In the aftermath of the Russian revolution she suffered the tragic loss by murder of two aunts, the tsarina and Grand Duchess Serge.

In 1920 Alice and her family returned to Athens when her brother-in-law King Constantine I was restored to the throne. In June 1921 her son Philip was born at their Corfu villa, Mon Repos. Prince Andrew commanded an army division in the disastrous Asia Minor campaign of 1921–2, in the aftermath of which King Constantine was driven into exile and Andrew himself was the victim of a show trial. Six former ministers were executed, but Prince Andrew, following appeals from his wife, was rescued by the timely intervention of Gerald Talbot, a secret-service man sent to Athens by the Greek prime minister Venizelos. Andrew, Alice, and their family left Greece in a British warship.

Years of exile followed, spent mainly at a small house in St Cloud, near Paris, lent them by Andrew's sister-in-law, Princess George of Greece (1882–1962), and in London, where Alice launched her two elder daughters in English society. During these years she was politically active; and at one point, believing that she enjoyed the support of George V, she nearly put to the League of Nations the proposal that her husband be made president of Greece. In the winter of 1928–9 she translated Prince Andrew's book, published as Towards Disaster in London in 1930.

Remaining impressed by the spiritual and practical work undertaken by her late aunt Elizabeth, Alice moved towards religion, converting, in October 1928, to Greek Orthodoxy. Soon after this she suffered a serious religious crisis which required treatment, first at the clinic of Dr Ernst Simmel at Tegel, near Berlin, and later at the clinic of Dr Ludwig Binswanger at Kreuzlingen in Switzerland, where she was a patient for two and a half years. Subsequently she led a migratory life in various places in Italy and Germany before settling in Cologne between 1933 and 1937, where she pursued religious studies with help from some academic friends. During this period she occasionally saw her mother, but no other members of her family. Her marriage to Prince Andrew was effectively at an end, for they had separated in 1930. In 1930 and 1931 all her four daughters were married to German princes.

In 1937 Alice resumed contact with her family in Darmstadt, following the death of her uncle, Grand Duke Ernst Ludwig of Hesse and by Rhine. Shortly afterwards her daughter Cécile was killed in an aeroplane accident with her husband, two sons, and mother-in-law. Thereafter Alice resumed full contact with all her relations, spending time with her mother in London and then in 1938 returning to Athens, which she made her home until 1967. During the Second World War she worked in soup kitchens and, putting herself in considerable personal danger, hid a Jewish family in her house for several months in 1943. She was still in Athens at the time of the communist invasion in December 1944, at which time she also learned of the death of Prince Andrew in Monte Carlo.

In November 1947 Alice was present at the wedding of her son, Philip, to Princess Elizabeth (later Queen Elizabeth II), and as a wedding present she designed the bride's engagement ring. Soon afterwards she pursued her long-held dream of founding her own sisterhood in Greece, the order of Martha and Mary, which aimed to provide practical nursing help. She trained on the island of Tinos, and set up a house for nursing sisters in Athens. This occupied her for a number of years and involved her in two fundraising tours of the United States in 1950 and 1952, but the project eventually failed because suitable candidates for the sisterhood were not forthcoming.

Princess Alice travelled considerably in her last years, visiting her daughters in Germany and going as far afield as India in 1960 as the guest of Rajkumari Amrit Kaur, and to Bahrain in 1961. She was present at Queen Elizabeth II's coronation in 1953, wearing a version of the grey nun's habit that she wore from 1949 onwards. By 1967 her health was failing and the political situation worsening for the Greek royal family. Alice accepted the queen's invitation to live at Buckingham Palace, where she died on 5 December 1969. Her funeral was held on 10 December in St George's Chapel, Windsor, and her coffin laid in the royal vault, though she had wished to be buried close to her aunt Elizabeth (now a Russian Orthodox saint) in Jerusalem. In 1988, after prolonged negotiations by the dean of Windsor, Bishop Michael Mann, her coffin was taken to Jerusalem and placed, on 3 August, in a vault under the Russian Orthodox church of St Mary Magdalene. In 1994 Alice was awarded the posthumous Yad Vashem title of Righteous Among the Nations for hiding the Jewish family in 1943.

HUGO VICKERS

Sources H. Vickers, *Alice, Princess Andrew of Greece* (2000) · private papers, Mountbatten Archives, Broadlands, Hampshire · private papers, U. Southampton, Hartley Library, Mountbatten archives · correspondence, Royal Arch. · papers of the duke of Edinburgh, Buckingham Palace · private information (2004) [duke of Edinburgh; Princess George of Hanover] · *The Times* (6 Dec 1969) · *Burke's guide to the royal family* (1973) · Queen Victoria, journal, Royal Arch. · papers, in possession of Princess Bagration, New York, USA

Archives Royal Arch., corresp., etc. · U. Southampton, Hartley Library, Mountbatten papers, corresp., etc. · Broadlands, Hampshire, Mountbatten papers, corresp., etc.

Likenesses P. A. de Laszlo, oils, 1907, priv. coll. · photographs, U. Southampton, Hartley Library

Wealth at death no possessions

Alington. For this title name *see* Sturt, Henry Gerard, first Baron Alington (1825–1904).

Alington, Cyril Argentine (1872–1955), headmaster and dean of Durham, was born in Ipswich, Suffolk, on 22 October 1872, the second son of the Revd Henry Giles Alington (1837–1928), an inspector of schools, and his wife, Jane Margaret Booth (d. 1910). In 1886 he went with classical scholarships to Marlborough College, where he was in the cricket eleven, and in 1891 he proceeded to Trinity College, Oxford. A first class in honour moderations (1893) and in *literae humaniores* (1895) was followed by his election at the second attempt to a fellowship at All Souls College, Oxford, in November 1896. In that year he had returned, as sixth-form master, to Marlborough. He was ordained deacon in 1899 and priest in 1901, and in the former year moved to Eton College where in 1904 he became master in college with a particularly gifted set of boys in his charge. He married, on 5 April 1904, Hester Margaret (d. 1958), youngest daughter of George William *Lyttelton, the fourth Lord Lyttelton. Of her it is impossible to find any comment but affectionate praise. She kept open house and her advice was available to all. She was devoted to Alington, as he was to her.

In 1908 Alington was appointed headmaster of Shrewsbury School; he was younger than all except two of his staff. The school was down to 240 boys, but by the end of 1916 the number had recovered to 394. In January 1917 he succeeded his brother-in-law, Edward *Lyttelton, as headmaster of Eton; again he was to preside over a recovery of numbers, from just under 1000 to 1150. He retired from Eton in 1933.

Alington was endowed with almost every gift to ensure a successful career. Extraordinarily handsome, especially in later years when robed and in the pulpit, he impressed the great majority of boys at Shrewsbury and Eton. As a young man he was a very successful cricketer and for years afterwards he maintained a high standard as a player of fives and rackets. He possessed a wide and extraordinarily retentive memory which enabled him to produce the apt quotation for any occasion. He was a most facile and brilliant versifier and he composed some admirable hymns. He was interested in political history and wrote some historical works; probably the best is *Twenty Years* (1921), a study of the party system, 1815–1835. *A Schoolmaster's Apology* (1914) gives his views on education and religion at one of the most active stages of his career; he claims that he spent a week on it. Sermons and verses were published. He also wrote a number of detective stories and other novels: clever, witty, but quickly perishable. All these varied publications bear witness to the incredible speed at which his mind, his imagination, and his pen worked. He dispatched the routine business of a headmaster so rapidly that he did not require a full-time secretary either at Shrewsbury, where he employed a young cricket professional, Neville Cardus, or at Eton. He readily dominated masters' meetings, and his conversation was brilliant.

Alington was not a scholar in any true sense. As a teacher he was least successful with the ablest boys, who recognized his weaknesses. He would prepare lessons in classics where he knew his grasp was shaky, but he felt he could teach English and divinity off the cuff, with unfortunate results. Lack of self-criticism encouraged him to preach too often, with fables at the end of evensong as well as sermons. Yet he was at his best in the pulpit, and he could influence boys even to the end of his life. His Holy Week addresses at Eton indelibly impressed the hushed and crowded chapel; in these addresses his striking presence, his melodious voice, and his theatrical tricks were all at the service of convincing material.

As a headmaster Alington was not an innovator. He did not regard maths and science as educational disciplines of much value except to scientists. He was a considerable builder at Shrewsbury, though not all his projects were soundly financed. At Eton he brought about less physical change, but at both schools he cared for and improved the environment. His impact as headmaster, however, was above all personal. He knew surprisingly many boys, and took an interest in them; his own zest for life infected them. He was a firm disciplinarian (he reintroduced birching, which had been dropped by his predecessor), but severity could be tempered: boys in trouble and good boys could experience his kindness alike.

In 1933 Alington was appointed dean of Durham and transferred these qualities to his new job; he displayed the same affection and ready friendship towards Durham miners that he had shown to his pupils. The warmth with which he writes of his time at Durham makes that section the most appealing part of his very brief memoir, *A Dean's Apology* (1952).

Alington had two sons and four daughters. The eldest daughter died aged thirty, and the younger son was killed at Salerno, Italy, in 1943—losses which were met with Christian fortitude. The elder son, Giles, also died before his mother; he was a much loved and respected senior tutor and dean of University College, Oxford. The three other daughters married Sir Alec Douglas-Home, Sir Roger Mynors, and the Revd John Wilkes, warden of Radley College, Abingdon, Berkshire, all of whom had been Etonians under his charge.

Alington, who had become DD at Oxford in 1917, received other honours: he was chaplain to the king from 1921 to 1933, and he was made an honorary fellow of Trinity College, Oxford, in 1926, and an honorary DCL at Durham in 1937. He died at his home, Treago, St Weonards, Herefordshire, on 16 May 1955 and was buried at Durham Cathedral.   TIM CARD

Sources *DNB* · C. A. Alington, *A dean's apology* (1952) · R. C. Martineau, *Eton College Chronicle* (27 May 1955) · G. Madan, memoir, Eton, archives · *The Times* (17 May 1955) · *The Salopian* (24 July 1955) [memoirs by J. M. Peterson, R. A. Knox, N. Cardus and an historical note by J. B. Oldham] · J. H. C. Leach, *A school at Shrewsbury* (1990) · T. Card, *Eton renewed: a history from 1860 to the present day* (1994) · Burke, *Gen. GB* (1937)

Archives Bodl. Oxf., letters to Sir William Anson · Bodl. Oxf., corresp. with Geoffrey Dawson · Bodl. Oxf., letters to J. L. L. Hammond · U. Reading L., corresp. with George Bell & Sons | FILM BFI NFTVA, news footage

Likenesses F. Dodd, drawing, Eton · G. Fiddes Watt, oils, priv. coll.

Wealth at death £7431 11s. 5d.: probate, 30 July 1955, *CGPLA Eng. & Wales*

Alison, Archibald (1757–1839), Scottish Episcopal clergyman and writer on aesthetics, was born in Edinburgh, the son of Patrick Alison, lord provost of the city, originally of Newhall, Coupar Angus; his mother's family, the Harts, came from Listerick, near Edinburgh. Alison was educated at Glasgow University, where he met his lifelong friend Dugald Stewart (1753–1828), later that university's professor of moral philosophy, and at Balliol College, Oxford, where he matriculated on 9 November 1775 and graduated LLB in 1784. At Oxford he was an acquaintance of the physician Matthew Baillie (1761–1823) and another Edinburgh man, William Gregory. It was through the latter that in late 1782 Alison met Dorothea *Gregory (*bap.* 1754, *d.* 1830), daughter of John *Gregory, an Edinburgh professor of medicine, and his wife, Elizabeth, *née* Forbes, and sister of the physician James *Gregory.

Alison was at this time a lowly paid curate at Brancepeth, co. Durham, and his status evidently failed to impress Dorothea Gregory's patron, the eminent literary hostess Elizabeth Montagu, who intended her charge to marry a nephew of hers, Matthew Robinson Montagu. An eighteen-month stand-off between Dorothea and Montagu ended with Alison's marriage to Gregory on 19 June 1784 at Thrapston, Northamptonshire; the couple had six children, including the physician William Pulteney *Alison and the historian and lawyer Sir Archibald *Alison,

Archibald Alison (1757–1839), by William Walker, pubd 1823 (after Sir Henry Raeburn)

first baronet. As part of the original marriage agreement Alison had been promised a more prosperous living at Sudborough, Northamptonshire, by Sir William Pulteney, whose agent was one of Gregory's guardians. That the living went to another was due either to Pulteney's considerate deception—the promise of a more lucrative position being his attempt to convince Montagu of Alison's increasing financial security—or to Montagu's intervention with Robert Lowth, bishop of London. Despite this setback, the couple did move to Sudborough, where Alison served as curate for six years. Regular visitors included Dugald Stewart, James Gregory, the mathematician John Playfair, and the engineer Thomas Telford whom Alison met when Telford was employed to carry out repairs to the parsonage.

It was while at Sudborough that Alison wrote a study of aesthetics, his *Essays on the Nature and Principles of Taste* (1790), for which he is now best known. Alison's analysis, which he dedicated to Dugald Stewart, is regarded as one of the most readily accessible and best illustrated contributions to an eighteenth-century English and Scottish tradition of associationist psychology. Following Edmund Burke, Alison argued that taste was a consequence of the imagination's response to viewed objects, though he differed from Burke in suggesting that this response is based not on an instinctive sense but on David Hartley's thesis, commonly known as the 'association of ideas', in which ideas or perceptions—in Alison's work those concerned with determining the beautiful and the sublime—are generated by mental associations prompted by observation. For Alison, therefore, the aesthetic quality of an art work, a music composition, an architectural or natural form, physiognomy, or physical movement is the result of a complex 'emotion of taste'—itself subdivided into the emotions of the beautiful and the sublime—prompted by personal association rather than by a quality integral to the studied entity. Different entities arouse a variety of emotions and prompt distinctive associations to determine their respective beauty or sublimity, with the collapse of a train of ideas preventing any possibility of judging these qualities. To achieve a complete aesthetic response required that the association of ideas in turn stimulate what Alison termed the 'exercise of the imagination'. In its most intense form a comprehensive response enabled the imagination to achieve a dreamlike 'state of reverie' which, distanced from daily reality, offers a gateway to romantic ecstasy. Only in a state of 'aesthetic disinterestedness', Alison argued, was it possible to achieve a pure reaction based on an unfettered combination of emotion, ideas, and imagination. Yet the disinterested state remained subject to competing factors, such as physical pain or the pressing nature of daily responsibilities, which inhibit the full exercise of the imagination; in addition Alison realized it to be further conditioned by relative characteristics such as a person's age, experience, or education. However, while initially and persuasively stating the relativity of the aesthetic response, Alison also argued counter to the implications of this proposal by advocating the possibility of, and indeed need for, shared standards of 'good' taste broadly commensurate with the classical unities of high art favoured by an educated upper class.

It has been suggested by one commentator (Rizzo) that Alison's wife may have encouraged him to write the *Essays* as a means of convincing Elizabeth Montagu of her husband's intellectual credentials. Despite at first having little scholarly impact, the work gained a favourable response from Montagu, prompted improved relations, and led William Pulteney to bestow on Alison the curacy of Kenley, Shropshire, in 1790. Here, according to his son Archibald, he enjoyed the happiest period of a life dedicated to a combination of 'literary study with active beneficence and easy independence' (Alison, 1.9). In addition to his essays on taste, Alison studied botany, zoology, and ornithology and, while at Kenley, advocated the development of an allotment system for impoverished parishioners, a theme reiterated in a later sermon 'On summer' in which he identified land ownership as the 'most honourable, the most important, and the most fruitful' condition in society (A. Alison, *Sermons*, 1814, 200). In 1794 he became vicar of another Shropshire parish, High Ercal, to which he added the rectory of Roddington three years later.

In 1800 Alison and his family returned to Prestonfield, near Edinburgh; he became minister of the Episcopal church in the city's Cowgate, where he remained for the rest of his career. During this period Alison published a two-volume collection of *Sermons, Chiefly on Particular Occasions* (1814) which included a well-regarded series on the seasons which, optimistic and eloquent in tone, recalls

the work of the Edinburgh professor of *belles-lettres* Hugh Blair, and other 'moderate' eighteenth-century Scottish churchmen. The *Sermons* were followed by the publication of another pulpit discourse on the peace of 1815 and a memoir of the historian Alexander Fraser Tytler, Lord Woodhouselee, in the *Transactions of the Royal Society of Edinburgh* (1818). Alison's comfortable lifestyle at Edinburgh was disrupted in 1812 and 1819 by the death of two of his daughters, and by that of his wife, Dorothea, in July 1830. He retired from the ministry in November of that year after a period of serious ill health. Alison died in Edinburgh on 17 May 1839, aged eighty-one, and was buried at the city's St John's Church. A monument, with an inscription by Francis, Lord Jeffrey, was erected at St Paul's Chapel, Edinburgh.

The success of his *Essays on Taste* ensured Alison a degree of celebrity during his lifetime, though the popularity of his principal study owed much to Lord Jeffrey whose 'Essay on beauty' in the *Edinburgh Review* (vol. 18, May 1811) provided a largely positive interpretation of an expanded second edition (1810) of Alison's thesis. In the wake of Jeffrey's review the *Essays* ran to a sixth Edinburgh edition in 1825 and to further economy editions in England and the United States. In contrast to the *Essays*' early nineteenth-century success, later commentators, among them Leslie Stephen in the *Dictionary of National Biography*, thought the work dated and down-played Alison's lasting influence on the philosophy of aesthetics. Contemporary reviews, while largely positive, also questioned elements of the *Essays*: for Jeffrey, for example, Alison's identification of taste with imagination paid too little attention to the quality of the original object while, at the same time, arguing for an independently determinable aesthetic hierarchy from high to folk art, a point also made in Martin Kallich's more recent analysis. Notwithstanding Jeffrey's or Stephens's opinion, Alison's work has again been considered worthy of detailed study, particular attention being paid by W. P. Albrecht (*The Sublime Pleasure of Tragedy*, 1975) and John Hayden ('Wordsworth, Hartley and the revisionists', *Studies in Philology*, 81, 1984), to the *Essays*' impact on the work of Hazlitt, Keats, and Wordsworth.

PHILIP CARTER

Sources DNB · M. Kallich, 'Alison, Archibald', *The dictionary of eighteenth-century British philosophers*, 2 vols. (1999) · B. Rizzo, *Companions without vows: relationships among eighteenth-century British women* (1994) · A. Alison, *Some account of my life and writings*, 2 vols. (1883) · I. Ross, 'Aesthetic philosophy: Hutcheson and Hume to Alison', *The history of Scottish literature*, ed. C. Craig, 2: 1660–1800, ed. A. Hook (1987), 239–57 · GM, 2nd ser., 12 (1839), 319–20 · Foster, *Alum. Oxon.*

Archives NL Scot., letters to Sir William Forbes

Likenesses J. Henning, porcelain medallion, 1802, Scot. NPG · W. Walker, stipple, pubd 1823 (after H. Raeburn), BM, NPG [*see illus.*] · S. Joseph, marble bust, 1841, Scot. NPG · W. H. Lizors, etching (after 'P. Morris'), BM, NPG; repro. in P. Morris [J. G. Lockhart], *Peter's letters to his kinsfolk*, 2nd edn, 3 vols. (1819)

Alison, Sir Archibald, first baronet (1792–1867), historian and lawyer, was born on 29 December 1792 at Kenley, Shropshire, in the parsonage of his father, Archibald *Alison (1757–1839), son of Patrick Alison, lord provost of

Sir Archibald Alison, first baronet (1792–1867), by Sir John Watson-Gordon, 1839

Edinburgh. The elder Archibald married in 1784 Dorothea (*d.* 1830) [*see* Gregory, Dorothea], daughter of John *Gregory, of a line of eminent Scottish mathematicians and scientists. They had six children, the younger Archibald being the second son. With blood entirely Scottish, he owed the accident of English birth to his father's profession as an Episcopalian minister, and so in Scottish terms a dissenter, to whom few clerical charges were available north of the border.

Not until 1800, when the elder Archibald was appointed to the chapel in the Cowgate, Edinburgh, could he move his family home. The younger Archibald had a private tutor before going to the University of Edinburgh in 1805. He studied law from 1810, and was called to the bar on 8 December 1814. The end of the European wars let him go touring, first to Paris to see the victorious allied forces, then in 1816 to the Alps, in 1817 to Ireland, in 1818 to Italy, in 1821 to Germany and Switzerland. He travelled not just for pleasure, but collected original sources later used in his historical work. In 1822 the tory lord advocate, Sir William Rae, made Alison an advocate-depute, most junior of the Scottish law officers. He found the job demanding, and 'worked like a galley-slave' (*Some Account*, 1.216). On 21 March 1825 he married Elizabeth Glencairn Tytler (1799–1873), youngest daughter of Lieutenant-Colonel William Tytler and niece of Alexander Fraser Tytler, Lord Woodhouselee (1747–1813). They had two sons, Sir Archibald *Alison, second baronet, and Frederick, who entered the army, and a daughter, Eliza, who married Robert Cutlar Fergusson.

Promises of promotion came to nothing, so Alison was still at his post when in 1830 the whigs took office and dismissed all appointees of the previous government. With his income vanished he turned to writing, notably in *Blackwood's Edinburgh Magazine*, to which during two decades he contributed at least fifty articles. They ranged over high tory themes, with emphasis on an anti-Malthusian view of population, on the doctrines of the banking school and—above all—on the French Revolution. Alison declared it his life's work 'to oppose the erroneous opinions which, since the French Revolution and in consequence of it, had, as I conceived, overspread the world, in political, economical and social concerns' (*Some Account*, 1.244–5). It was through the gloomy foreboding with which he greeted all suggestion of constitutional change in Britain that he first came to public notice. On seeing that this was what the whigs intended, he made his name with a series of thirteen articles in *Blackwood's*, from January 1831 to January 1832 which, inevitably, linked parliamentary reform with the French revolution of 1830.

Alison elaborated these sombre theses in the ten volumes of his *History of Europe during the French Revolution* (1833–42). The central failure he identified in the France of the *ancien régime*, as in present-day Britain, was the ruling class's reluctance to stand up to popular intimidation. Britain might have been spared the fate of France, but had no grounds for confidence in the future: whig ministries were practically treasonable, and 1832 heralded an era of democracy and the descent into anarchy. Despite the heavy political baggage, his work offered the first survey of the revolution in English, and several editions won huge sales on both sides of the Atlantic, with translations into French, German, and even Arabic. The purple prose did lighten the cumbersome apparatus of Scottish philosophical history, which in his hands grew ponderous with long citations of authorities. Benjamin Disraeli pilloried him in *Coningsby* (1844, bk 3, chap. 2) as Mr Wordy, who 'proves that Providence is on the side of the Tories'. But success spurred him on. Determined to bring out the concluding volume on the anniversary of the battle of Waterloo, he began dictating the final pages at 10 a.m. on 6 June 1842, went on until 3 a.m. the next day, when his amanuensis broke down, and finished the last line by himself at 6 a.m. In emulation of Gibbon, he then opened his windows and looked out complacently at a summer's morning.

As a Conservative without romantic excess, and in the Scottish context without a trace of Jacobitism, Alison contrived to become, in this golden age of whig historiography, influential in the cause of the opposing ideology. His *History* was 'the Bible of the Tory party, which found in it the comfort it needed during the early years of the reformed Parliament' (Gooch, 305). What he propounded, notably in a wide-ranging introduction, was the moderate, antiquarian pragmatism underlying English liberty. Linked with nostalgia for an ancient constitution, he wrote:

> struggles for freedom in England … acquired a *definite and practicable object*, and, instead of being wasted in aspirations after visionary schemes, settled down into a strong and inextinguishable desire for the restoration of an order of

things once *actually established*. (A. Alison, *History of Europe during the French Revolution*, 2.20)

Here lay a contrast with Scotland: in John Knox's reformation a spirit of freedom 'wasted itself … in visionary and impracticable schemes', after which the country 'returned to its pristine servitude' (ibid., 33). The struggles of the 1640s even anticipated the French Revolution:

The mild and humane conduct of the Civil War in England forms the most striking contrast to the cruelty of the royalists, or the severity of the covenant in Scotland. The horrors of the Vendée insurrection were anticipated in the massacres of Montrose's followers; and the Noyades of the Loire are not without parallel in the atrocious revenge of the popular faction. (ibid., 38)

None the less, Alison thought a tory interpretation of Scottish history might yet be constructed on the benevolent paternalism seen at work in education, the poor law, and legal reform. In a *Blackwood's* article, 'The old Scottish parliament', he even defended this object of derision to Anglicizing whigs because it 'gave a full and fair representation to the whole property of the nation, and entirely excluded that selfish and partial legislation which never fails to follow the ascendancy of mere numbers' (*Blackwood*, 36, Nov 1834, 661). He thus rejected the standard contemporary view that 'the original institutions of Scotland were the height of human absurdity, a compound of feudal tyranny and savage violence, and that all the prosperity which now distinguishes its surface is to be ascribed to the Union with England' (ibid., 663). Sadly, since 1832 there remained 'not one vestige of the ancient Scottish constitution' (ibid., 672).

In other books, where Alison had not the grand sweep of events to sustain his narrative, he made heavy weather of it. His attack on *Population* by Thomas Malthus (1840) was later judged 'long, heavy, pompous and irrelevant' (*DNB*), but none the less hinted at a progressive tory programme of poor relief, diffusion of property, and penal reform. Alison published a *Life of Marlborough* in 1847, an expanded second edition of which appeared in 1852. After publishing lives of Lord Castlereagh and of Sir Charles Stewart in 1861, he completed his autobiography, published after his death as *Some Account of my Life and Writings* (2 vols., 1862). Then he laid down his pen, thinking it useless to provoke hostility by his resolute refusal to 'worship the Dagon of Liberalism' (*Some Account*, 2.375).

Meanwhile, in spite of this copious literary production, Alison had resumed a public career. He did so not in national politics, having turned down the job of solicitor-general after the tories returned to power briefly in 1834, but at a local level in the west of Scotland. He accepted the post of sheriff of Lanarkshire, with an income of £1400 a year. In February 1835 he moved to Glasgow and took up residence at Possil House, where he would stay until his death. Active in many charities and institutions of his adopted city, he became a vocal champion of its virtues. This was Scotland's busiest sheriffdom, in a burgeoning industrial region with the associated social problems reflected in the pressure of work in the courts.

Alison vigorously upheld the authority of the state, especially against the early Scottish trade unions. They fitted into his demonology as examples of 'democratic ambition on a large scale' (*Some Account*, 2.374). In 1837 recession brought a wave of strikes round Glasgow, above all among weavers. When a strike-breaker was murdered, Alison arrested the whole leadership of the weavers' union and had them successfully tried in January 1838. He drew sweeping conclusions in an article entitled 'The practical working of trades unions' (*Blackwood*, 43, 1838). On the evidence of the twenty years of violence for which he held them responsible in the west of Scotland, he claimed that they inevitably turned into conspiracies 'exceeding in the tyranny which they exercise, the widespread misery which they produce, anything attempted by the Czar Peter or Sultan Mahmoud in the plenitude of their power' (ibid., 288). From their activities, he foresaw 'a civil war of the worst and most appalling kind' (ibid., 301). By his actions in 1837–8 Alison all but succeeded in strangling the Scottish unions at birth, and they never really recovered until the end of the century. If Chartism too turned out a damp squib in Glasgow, the credit must largely be laid at the sheriff's door. The danger appeared to Alison to be at its most acute in Scotland, whereas unions might be 'perfectly innocuous yet in London' (ibid.).

On a broader view his condemnation of labour was not absolute:

I think that in fifty or a hundred years, when wealth is more generally diffused, and the enjoyments and artificial wants of society consequent upon wealth have taken root in the lower classes of society, we may then be prepared for liberal institutions, such as those connected with combinations. ('Select Committee on … Combinations of Workmen: First Report', 179–80)

Against Alison's severe views on organized labour must be set his distress at the callousness of contemporary capitalism, which he also wished to correct. His brother, William Pulteney *Alison (1790–1859), pioneer of the reform of public health in Scotland, proposed that relief should be extended to the children of the able-bodied unemployed, contrary to the Scottish poor law. Archibald agreed, and tried to give effect to the idea by his own judgments in test cases, but the court of session overturned them in 1852.

For all his hair-raising opinions, Alison was a witty, high-spirited man, his sense of humour contributing to an evenness of temper not always immediately apparent. While he seems to have taken his eternal forecasts of disaster seriously, they merely endeared him to a wide circle of friends and the public at large. He won election as rector of Marischal College, Aberdeen, against Lord Macaulay in 1845, and as rector of the University of Glasgow against Lord Palmerston in 1850. He was made a baronet in 1852. To many of his countrymen, his proud patriotism made up for other foibles. In 1853 he joined the National Association for the Vindication of Scottish Rights, a proto-nationalist body. But Alison and his friends resigned when they discovered 'elements of a dangerous character beginning to work in it. We soon found that other more ardent and hot-headed patriots not obscurely aimed at a *dissolution of the Union*' (*Some Account*, 2.31). Scottish nationalism was unlikely to flourish except as the kind of popular movement that Alison could not stomach.

Alison remained active to the end of his life. He took a close interest in the American Civil War, as a defender of slavery and partisan of the Confederacy despite his humanitarian instincts. He noted on 9 September 1863, when aged seventy, that he had walked 20 miles in five hours without fatigue. He attended to his duties on 19 May 1867, was taken ill next day, and died on 23 May at Possil House. A crowd of more than 100,000 Glaswegians attended a lavish public funeral on 30 May, as he was sent to be buried in Dean cemetery, Edinburgh. E. B. Hamley reported:

> Of these, who numbered half the working population of the city, at least three-fourths were artisans, mill-girls, and iron-foundry workers, swarthy with toil. These were the attendants who, at the sacrifice of some of their means of livelihood, assembled to pay a last respect to the most unbending Conservative in Great Britain. (*Blackwood*, 102, 1867, 127)

Yet it was as a practical man, dealing with their everyday problems, that he had best served such people.

MICHAEL FRY

Sources *Some account of my life and writings: an autobiography by the late Sir Archibald Alison*, ed. Lady Alison, 2 vols. (1883) · M. Michie, 'Enlightenment and conservatism in Victorian Scotland: the career of Sir Archibald Alison', PhD diss., Atkinson College, USA, 1995 · 'Select committee on trades' unions or combinations of workmen: first report', *Parl. papers* (1837–8), vol. 8, no. 488 · *Wellesley index* · G. P. Gooch, *History and historians in the nineteenth century*, 2nd edn (1913), 304–5 · M. Milne, 'Archibald Alison, conservative controversialist', *Albion*, 27 (1995), 420–30 · H. Ben-Israel, *English historians on the French Revolution* (1968) · *DNB* · *Blackwood*, 102 (1867), 127

Archives NL Scot., legal works with MS additions [copies] · U. Edin. L., lecture notes | BL, corresp. with Sir Robert Peel, Add. MSS 40407–40425, 40500–40503 · Durham RO, letters to Lady Londonderry, D/LO/c 167, 524 · Herts. ALS, letters to E. B. Lytton · NA Scot., Lord Advocate's MSS · NL Scot., corresp. with Blackwoods · NL Scot., letters, MSS 9817, 10997 · NL Scot., letters to R. M. Martin

Likenesses J. Watson-Gordon, portrait, 1839; Christies, 2–3 April 1969, lot 46 [*see illus.*] · R. S. Lauder, two oil paintings, *c*.1840, Scot. NPG · L. Ghémar, lithograph, BM · Maull & Polyblank, photograph, NPG · P. Park, marble bust, Scot. NPG · D. J. Pound, stipple and line engraving (after Werge), NPG · two cartes-de-visite, NPG

Wealth at death £14,745 13*s.* 2*d.*: inventory, 4 Oct 1867, NA Scot., SC36/48/58/178

Alison, Sir Archibald, second baronet (1826–1907), army officer, was born at Edinburgh on 21 January 1826, the eldest son of Sir Archibald *Alison, first baronet (1792–1867), historian, and his wife, Elizabeth Glencairn (1799–1873), youngest daughter of Lieutenant-Colonel William Tytler. In 1835 Possil House, near Glasgow, became the family home. The father educated his son privately, until he went to Glasgow University. There, at the age of fifteen, he gained the first prize for an English essay on Sulla, and reviewed Thierry's *History of the Gauls* in *Blackwood's Edinburgh Magazine*. Between Alison and his father there was always a very close relationship. They shared the same tastes, and the son replied in *Blackwood's Magazine* (May

Sir Archibald Alison, second baronet (1826–1907), by Maclure & Macdonald, pubd 1882

1850) to the criticisms in the *Edinburgh Review* on the later volumes of his father's *History of Europe*.

On 3 November 1846 Alison was commissioned ensign in the 72nd foot (later Seaforth Highlanders); he was promoted lieutenant on 11 September 1849, and joined the headquarters of the regiment in Barbados. Yellow fever was raging there, and his father had arranged for an exchange, but Alison refused to leave his regiment at such a time. He went with it to Nova Scotia in 1851, and came home with it in October 1854, having been promoted captain on 11 November 1853.

After some months at Malta the regiment went to the Crimea in May 1855 and, having taken part in the expedition to Kerch, was placed in the Highland brigade at the end of June. While serving with the regiment in the trenches before Sevastopol, Alison attracted the notice of Sir Colin Campbell by opportunely producing a sketch plan of the trenches, which he had drawn on an envelope, as well as by his coolness under fire. He was mentioned in dispatches and was made brevet major on 6 June 1856. On 19 December 1856 he left the 72nd for an unattached majority.

When Sir Colin Campbell left England at twenty-four hours' notice on 12 July 1857 to suppress the Indian mutiny, he took Alison with him as his military secretary, and his younger brother, Frederick, as his aide-de-camp.

In the second relief of Lucknow both brothers were wounded, Archibald losing his left arm. He returned to duty early in 1858, but the stump became inflamed, and he was invalided home (10 March). He had been mentioned in dispatches, and was made brevet lieutenant-colonel and CB (28 February 1861). On his arrival in England he dined with Queen Victoria. He published 'Lord Clyde's campaign in India' in *Blackwood's Magazine* (October 1858), and later other articles.

Alison was unemployed for the next four years. On 18 November 1858 he married Jane, daughter of James Black of Dalmonach, a Glasgow merchant. She died on 15 July 1909. Jane edited her father-in-law's autobiography, and was a woman of many gifts. They had two sons and four daughters. From 17 March 1862 to 19 October 1867 Alison was an assistant adjutant-general, first with the inspector-general of infantry at headquarters, and three years afterwards in the south-western district. He became brevet colonel on 17 March 1867, and succeeded his father as baronet in May 1867. On 1 October 1870 he was placed on the staff at Aldershot as assistant adjutant-general.

At the end of 1873 Alison went to the west coast of Africa in command of the British brigade in the Second Anglo-Asante War, with the local rank of brigadier-general. He took part in the battle of Amoaful, the capture of Bequah, the action at Ordahsu, and the capture of Kumasi. At Amoaful the enemy fire was very heavy, and the dense growth made direction difficult, but his staff were struck by his self-possession and the precision of his orders. When abscesses in his only hand made him nearly helpless, he bore his suffering without complaint. He was mentioned in dispatches, received the thanks of parliament, and was made KCB on 31 March 1874. After a few months at Aldershot, he went to Ireland as deputy adjutant-general on 17 October 1874, and was promoted major-general on 1 October 1877. After four months as commandant of the Staff College at Camberley, he was appointed deputy quartermaster-general for intelligence, and helped the headquarters staff to meet the Egyptian crisis of 1882.

On 6 July 1882 Alison left England to command a force which was assembled at Cyprus to secure the Suez Canal. The bombardment of Alexandria took place on the 11th, and Alison landed there on the 17th with two battalions which were soon reinforced. On the 24th he occupied Ramlah and, receiving instructions to 'keep Arabi Pasha constantly alarmed', made repeated demonstrations towards Kafr el Dauwar, especially on 5 August. Thus Arabi was led to expect that the British advance on Cairo would be from Alexandria, and not from Isma'iliyyah, as was planned. In that advance Alison commanded the Highland brigade, the leading brigade of the 2nd (Hamley's) division in the storming of the trenches at Tell al-Kebir; Alison took a personal part, revolver in hand, in the confused fighting inside. After the surrender of Cairo he was sent to occupy Tanta with half a battalion of the Gordon Highlanders (17 September). He found there an Egyptian force disposed to resist, but by coolness and tact

he induced them to surrender. He was mentioned in dispatches, received the thanks of parliament, and was promoted lieutenant-general for distinguished service on 18 November 1882. After Wolseley's departure Alison was in command of the British force in Egypt until 17 May 1883. On his return a sword of honour was presented to him by the citizens of Glasgow, with a tiara for Lady Alison.

Alison commanded the Aldershot division from 1 August 1883 until the end of 1888, except for part of 1885, when he acted as adjutant-general during Wolseley's absence in Egypt. He received the GCB on 21 June 1887, was promoted general on 20 February 1889, and retired on 12 January 1893.

He was given the colonelcy of the Essex regiment on 24 November 1896, and was transferred to his former regiment, the Seaforth Highlanders, on 30 March 1897. He was also honorary colonel of the 1st volunteer battalion of the Highland light infantry, and was honorary LLD of Cambridge, Edinburgh, and Glasgow. From 1889 to 1899 he was a member of the Indian council. Alison died at his London home, 93 Eaton Place, on 5 February 1907, and was buried at Dean cemetery, Edinburgh, four days later. He was characterized as a man who knew how to combine courtesy with insistence on duty. E. M. LLOYD, rev. JAMES LUNT

Sources The Times (6 Feb 1907) · The Times (9 Feb 1907) · *Autobiography of Sir Archibald Alison (1st Baronet)*, ed. J. Alison (1883) · *Hart's Army List* · Blackwood, 181 (1907) · 'Some military memories of Sir Archibald Alison', *Cornhill Magazine*, [3rd] ser., 22 (1907), 307–16 · J. F. Maurice, *Military history of the campaign of 1882 in Egypt*, rev. edn (1908) · H. Brackenbury, *The Ashanti war*, 2 vols. (1874) · A. I. Shand, *Life of Sir E. Hamley*, 2 vols. (1895) · Burke, *Peerage* · d. cert.
Archives Bodl. Oxf., journals and letter-books · NL Scot., mathematical notes | BL OIOC, corresp. with Sir Frederic Goldsmid, MS Eur. F 134, no. 10 · NL Scot., corresp. with Blackwoods, MSS 4063–4709
Likenesses T. J. Barker, oils, 1859, NPG · S. West, portrait, 1865, priv. coll. · K. A. Fraser Tytler, plaster bust, 1883, Scot. NPG · Monroe, portrait, 1900, priv. coll. · Maclure & Macdonald, chromolithograph, NPG; repro. in *Pictorial World* (28 Oct 1882) [see illus.] · engraving, repro. in Alison, ed., *Autobiography of Sir Archibald Alison*, 1 · portraits, BL OIOC

Alison, Dorothea. See Gregory, Dorothea (*bap.* 1754, *d.* 1830).

Alison, Francis (1705–1779), Presbyterian minister and college principal in America, was born in the parish of Leck in co. Donegal, the son of Robert Alison, a weaver descended from emigrants from Scotland. His mother's name and ancestry are unknown. He may have received his early education at Francis Hutchinson's Presbyterian academy in Dublin. Later he went to Scotland where he graduated MA at the University of Edinburgh in 1733. He completed his preparation for the ministry by studying for the next two years, possibly at the University of Glasgow. Thereafter, he returned to Ireland where he was licensed to preach by the presbytery of Letterkenny. In 1735 Alison joined the large-scale Scots-Irish emigration to British America where he earned prominence as a minister, teacher, and citizen.

After serving for two years as a tutor in Talbot county,

Maryland, Alison was ordained to the Presbyterian ministry and was installed as pastor of the New London congregation in Chester county, Pennsylvania, which he served from 1737 to 1752. Shortly after settling in New London in 1737, Alison married Hannah Armitage of New Castle, Delaware, who survived him. They had a daughter and three sons, two of whom predeceased him. The other, also Francis Alison, became a prominent physician. Alison's sermons demonstrated his reconciliation of Scottish Enlightenment philosophy with moderate Calvinistic theology. He preached clearly from notes that included numerous references to the scriptures. His parishioners appreciated his ministry. Most supported him against a revivalistic intruder into his parish and tried to prevent his departure in 1752. As the allegedly excessive emotionalism of the so-called 'great awakening of religion' divided Presbyterians in America during the late 1730s and 1740s, Alison became a leader of the anti-revivalistic Old Side. Nevertheless, he worked for the reunification of the Old and New Side synods, which occurred in 1758.

Important as Alison's ministry was, he was even more significant in the field of education. Shortly after beginning his ministry he opened the New London Academy. The curriculum included Latin, logic, metaphysics, ethics, science, mathematics, and moral philosophy which Alison taught, basing his lectures on Hutchinson's teachings from the Scottish Enlightenment. The Old Side synod adopted the school as its seminary. It became so well known that it attracted and trained capable students who later became ministers, state governors, congressmen, teachers, and physicians. In 1752 Alison left New London to take charge of the Academy of Philadelphia. In 1755 he and the Scottish Anglican William Smith added a college, of which he became academic vice-provost. In 1779 the state's legislature changed the college's name to the University of Pennsylvania. The curriculum that he installed was similar to that of his New London Academy. Because of disagreements with Smith and other problems, in 1766 he obtained funds for and chartered an academy in Newark, Delaware, which became the basis for that state's university.

During Alison's years in Philadelphia he served also as assistant minister of the city's Old Side First Presbyterian Church. His concern for his denomination's clergy and their dependants led him to establish in the mid-1750s the Presbyterian Ministers Fund, America's first life insurance company. With most other Presbyterians he worked against Benjamin Franklin's campaign of the mid-1760s to transform proprietary Pennsylvania into a royal colony, fearing that the change would lead to the legal establishment of the Church of England. As a Presbyterian, he also opposed the Church of England's attempt to secure the appointment of a bishop for the colonies, remembering that in his native Ireland bishops, who exercised not only ecclesiastical but also political powers, had discriminated against dissenters. In 1766 he formulated, with Connecticut Congregationalists, the 'convention for religious liberty'. As a staunch supporter of religious freedom, he opened his schools to students of all denominations and nationalities. When the leading German Lutheran pastor in Pennsylvania, Henry Melchior Muhlenberg, attempted to have inserted into Pennsylvania's 1776 constitution a clause to exclude Jews from voting, Alison successfully opposed him.

During and after Alison's lifetime he received numerous honours and testimonies to his achievements and character. In 1756 the University of Glasgow awarded him the honorary degree of doctor of divinity. Ezra Stiles, president of Yale College, called him America's most learned scholar of the classics. According to William Smith, provost of the College of Philadelphia, he was capable of holding any academic post in the country. Bishop William White emphasized his impeccable integrity. Never strong physically, Alison died in Philadelphia on 28 November 1779.   JOHN B. FRANTZ

Sources E. Ingersoll, 'Francis Alison: American philosopher, 1705–1779', PhD diss., University of Delaware, 1974 · D. Sloan, *The Scottish Enlightenment and the American college ideal* (New York, 1971) · T. C. Pears, 'Francis Alison', *Journal of Presbyterian History*, 29 (1951), 13–25 · W. B. Sprague, 'Francis Alison, 1736–1779', *Annals of the American pulpit*, 3 (1859), 73–6, 78 · G. S. Klett, *Presbyterians in colonial Pennsylvania* (1937) · L. J. Trinterud, *The forming of an American tradition: a re-examination of colonial Presbyterianism* [1949] · W. Turner, 'The College, Academy, and Charity School of Philadelphia … 1740–1779', PhD diss., University of Pennsylvania, 1952 · E. Ingersoll, 'Alison, Francis', *ANB* · J. L. McAllister, 'Francis Alison and John Witherspoon: political philosophers of the American revolution', *Journal of Presbyterian History*, 29 (1976), 33–60 · W. I. Addison, *A roll of graduates of the University of Glasgow from 31st December 1727 to 31st December 1897* (1898), 12
Archives Hist. Soc. Penn., collection · Pittsburgh Theological Seminary, Pennsylvania, volume of sermons in MS · Presbyterian Historical Society, Philadelphia, Pennsylvania, papers incl. sermons, record group 294, 0.25 cu.ft | University of Delaware, Newark, Hugh M. Morris Library, Moyerman collection, collection of letters · University of Pennsylvania Library, Philadelphia, University Archives, collection of class notes · Yale U., Ezra Stiles collection, corresp. with Ezra Stiles
Likenesses oils, Presbyterian Historical Society, Philadelphia, Pennsylvania
Wealth at death 'above poverty' since arrival in America; hoped to leave inheritance to children: Pears, 'Francis Alison'

Alison, William Pulteney (1790–1859), physician and social reformer, born at Boroughmuirhead near Edinburgh on 12 November 1790, was the son of Archibald *Alison (1757–1839), who was in charge of the Episcopal congregation in Edinburgh as well as being a noted author, and his wife, Dorothea *Gregory (*bap.* 1754, *d.* 1830), daughter of John *Gregory (1724–1773), a member of a leading literary and academic family in Scotland. His younger brother was the historian Sir Archibald *Alison (1792–1867). Alison received a private education and then entered Edinburgh University in 1803; there he took arts classes before proceeding to medicine. He received his MD in 1811 with a dissertation entitled 'De viribus naturae medicatricibus'. As a student Alison became a warm advocate of the ideas of Dugald Stewart, professor of moral philosophy at Edinburgh. In later life among his other accomplishments he continued to aspire to some

William Pulteney Alison (1790–1859), by John Henry Robinson, pubd 1849 (after George Richmond, 1847)

competence in the field of metaphysics. In the phrenological controversies that agitated the Edinburgh intellectual community during his lifetime, Alison was a strong advocate of the claims of 'Scottish' philosophy over those of the new system propounded most notably by George Combe. In 1836 Alison supported William Hamilton against Combe in the contest for the chair of logic at Edinburgh.

In 1815 Alison was appointed physician to the recently established New Town Dispensary in Edinburgh, and the post brought him into regular contact with patients drawn from the poorest sections of the population. This experience, together with that which he subsequently gained at the Royal Infirmary, was the stimulus to the active interest that he took in the health and conditions of the poor. He published quarterly reports in the *Edinburgh Medical Journal* on outbreaks of epidemic disease in the city. At the same time he developed a career in academic medicine; he was appointed to the regius chair of medical jurisprudence at Edinburgh in 1820, his first step on the path to preferment within the university medical school. Alison's family connections were of service to him in his quest for advancement: for a time he assisted his uncle, James *Gregory (1753–1821), in teaching the practice of medicine. Alison's steady progress up the academic hierarchy continued when in 1822 he became professor of the institutes of medicine, a post he was to hold for twenty years, during which he exercised the right it carried of also serving as a clinical professor at the Royal Infirmary.

On 6 September 1832 Alison married his cousin Margaret Crawford Gregory, James Gregory's daughter. The marriage was childless. In 1842 Alison attained the pinnacle of the professorial hierarchy when he was appointed to the chair of the practice of medicine.

Although the chair of the institutes of medicine later became confined to the teaching of physiology, during Alison's tenure it also encompassed the fields of pathology and therapeutics. He resisted the tendency among his contemporaries to equate pathology with morbid anatomy; in Alison's view the study of the lesions responsible for certain forms of disease far from exhausted the scope of the subject. Alison's principal focus in his teaching was, however, on the science of physiology. His lectures were published in 1831 as *Outlines of Physiology* and expanded in subsequent editions to *Outlines of Physiology and Pathology*. As a physiologist Alison was less concerned with describing the outcome of detailed experimental procedures than with presenting certain broad principles from which it was supposedly possible to derive an understanding of the actions of the living body in health and disease. These principles were also to supply the basis for a rational therapeutics. A merely empirical approach to the administration of medicines was, in Alison's view, bound to lead to fallacy.

Alison held that the phenomena of life, in so far as they were incompatible with the normal laws of physics and chemistry, had to be referred to the actions of a 'vital principle'. This vital principle was not to be confused with mind, which Alison viewed as an entirely separate entity. Physiological explanation had always to terminate with reference to some 'laws of vitality'; it was possible to give no further account of these laws other than to say that 'they depend on the will of the Author of Nature' (W. P. Alison, *Heads of Lectures on the Institutes of Medicine*, 1828, 2). In Alison's view physiology, more than any other science, 'contributes to give us more precise information as to the existence and attributes of this First Cause, by enabling us to perceive the adaptation of means to ends, in the laws by which these changes are regulated' (W. P. Alison, *Outlines of Human Physiology*, 1839, 8). Alison resisted any suggestion that life might depend upon the material organization of the body: vitality, he insisted, 'is found not only to precede [organization], but to be essential to its development' (ibid., 3).

Although Alison was a hospital physician who gave clinical lectures on individual cases seen on the wards, he impressed on his students 'the peculiar value of observations made on large and organized bodies of men, as in the experience of military and naval practitioners' (W. P. Alison, *Outlines of Physiology and Pathology*, 1833, 28). More generally he was much concerned with questions of the action of morbid influences on populations rather than on individuals. Knowledge of this kind was essential to the prevention of disease through measures of public health or 'medical police'. Alison maintained that there were many diseases that were:

nearly beyond the power of medicine, but the causes of which are known, and under certain circumstances may be avoided; and the conditions necessary for avoiding them are in a great measure in the power of communities, though beyond the power of many of the individuals composing them. (ibid., 29)

Alison was, in particular, exercised during the latter part of his career with the issue of the relationship between poverty and disease. He recognized that it might seem incongruous for someone in his position to become involved in the heated debates on this question that occurred in the 1840s. He pointed out, however, that when:

in the two greatest cities in Scotland, where the science and civilization of the country might be supposed to have attained their highest development, and where medical schools exist, claiming as high a rank in point of practical usefulness as any in Europe, the annual proportions of deaths to the population is not only much beyond the average in Britain, but very considerably greater than that of London, it surely cannot be thought beyond the province of one who is honoured with a situation of trust and responsibility in the greatest of these medical schools, to endeavour to investigate the causes of this mortality, and the means by which it may be diminished. (W. P. Alison, *Observations on the Management of the Poor in Scotland*, 1840, iv–v)

Qua physician used to treating other ills, Alison therefore proposed to extend his enquiries to the relief of 'the grand evil of Poverty itself' (ibid., vii).

Alison maintained that there was a strong link between poverty and the virulence of the outbreaks of fever that occurred in Edinburgh and other Scottish cities. He did not contend that 'destitution is an adequate cause for the *generation* of fever, nor that it is the *sole* cause of its *extension*,—but that it is *one* cause of the diffusion of fever' (W. P. Alison, *Observations on the Epidemic Fever of MDCCCXL III in Scotland …*, 1844, 1). He dismissed Edwin Chadwick's claim that fever tended to strike healthy, employed individuals. In Alison's view there was a clear correlation between the incidence of epidemic disease and the degree of economic deprivation. Indeed, the rapidity with which an outbreak spreads, Alison claimed, 'may even be held as *a test* of the inadequacy and inefficacy' of the measures of poor relief adopted by a community (ibid., 2).

This conclusion led Alison to review the provisions for the relief of poverty that currently obtained in Scotland. He alleged that the upper classes in Scotland did less in this regard than those of any other well-regulated European nation. He was in particular critical of the prejudice of the Scottish ruling class that 'all legal provision for the poor is a great evil' (*Observations*, 1840, 37). While in England there was a long-established legislative framework to ensure minimum standards of poor relief, in Scotland voluntary charity was supposed to suffice. This state of affairs was justified on the grounds that legal guarantees of support would sap the moral fibre and self-reliance of the poor and so increase the incidence of indigence. Malthusian notions were often invoked to assert that with such guarantees of support the poor were likely to multiply more rapidly, thus adding to the demands on the system. These arguments were used by the 1844 commission on provision for the poor in Scotland to justify the retention of the voluntary system. Alison acknowledged that there was also a reluctance on the part of the Scottish élite to accept that any English system of administration might be superior to their traditional methods of dealing with indigence.

In reply Alison contended that it was unrelieved indigence that truly sapped the morality of the poor. It not only made them more prone to disease, but also more short-sighted and reckless; in this state they were more likely to indulge in early marriage and produce large families. There was no evidence that the English system of relief had brought the evil consequences imputed to it. On the contrary 'the English people receive a temporal reward for their more humane and merciful management of the poor, in the comparative exemption of most of their great towns from the curse of contagious fever' (*Observations*, 1840, 43–4). As a result of the publication of these views Alison engaged in a controversy with the leading Scottish clergyman Thomas Chalmers, who argued for a retention of the system of parochial provision for the poor.

Alison did not rely solely upon appeals to altruism to impress on his readers the need for reform. While contagion might arise among the poorest sections of society, experience showed that it soon spread to strike down even the most respectable members of the community. It could not, moreover, be in the interests of society to allow the growth of a disaffected and unregulated underclass. Alison pointed out that 'this concession of the right of relief naturally involves the *counter right* of inspection, by duly qualified and *responsible* agents' (W. P. Alison, *Observations on the Epidemic Fever*, 1844, 31). As part of the proposed system of administration the poor would therefore have to submit to constant surveillance. By 1845 much of what Alison had proposed had passed into legislation.

In the winter of 1855–6 Alison suffered from frequent epileptic attacks. This led him to resign his chair and to withdraw from practice. His wife had predeceased him and he spent his last days living at a retreat at Woodville near Colinton. He died there on 22 September 1859. The interment took place at St John's Episcopal Church burial-ground.

Alison's physiological views enjoyed considerable popularity during his lifetime; they were, however, soon superseded and acquired an archaic aspect. His work in public health enjoyed more enduring influence, largely because his views accorded with wider movements of the time. As well as his intellectual attainments, Alison's contemporaries made much of his character: his piety and philanthropy were seen as setting an example to others of his station.   L. S. JACYNA

Sources *Edinburgh Medical Journal*, 5 (1859–60), 469–86 · *DNB* · parish register (birth), 12 Nov 1790, Edinburgh, St Cuthbert's · parish register (marriage), 6 Sept 1832, Colinton, St Paul's · d. cert.
Archives Royal College of Physicians of Edinburgh, medical papers · U. Edin., Lothian Health Services Archive, lecture notes | Mitchell L., Glas., Glasgow City Archives, corresp. with John Strang · NL Scot., letters to Blackwoods · U. St Andr. L., corresp. with James Forbes

Likenesses J. H. Robinson, stipple, pubd 1849 (after G. Richmond, 1847), BM, NPG, Wellcome L. [*see illus.*] · lithograph, Wellcome L. · photograph, Wellcome L.

Alken family (*per.* **1745–1852**), engravers and painters of sporting scenes, may have originated in Denmark, perhaps from the village of Alken in north Jutland. According to family tradition they moved to England to escape the political disturbances during the reign of King Christian VII. However, the first representative to reach England was **Sefferein** [i] **Alken** (1717–1782), who is known to have been in London by 1745, a year before Christian VII came to the throne. Sefferein was a carver in wood and stone who worked for Sir William Chambers at Somerset House and Marlborough House. He married, first, Eleanor (*d.* 1752) and, second, Anne, whose children were Mary (*b.* 1754), Anne (*b.* 1755), **Samuel** [i] **Alken** (1756–1815), Oliver (*b.* 1759), and Martin (*b.* 1761).

Samuel [i] Alken was born on 22 October 1756 at 3 Dufours Place, near Golden Square, Westminster, and trained as an architect. His earliest publication was *A New Book of Ornaments* (1779), but after his marriage in 1780 to Lydia Woodley he seems to have lived by watercolours, aquatints, and etchings, although he may have had another occupation as a drawing-master or craftsman. In 1784 he published a set of sporting landscapes after Samuel Howitt and later issued a series of excellent aquatints after caricature drawings by Thomas Rowlandson, such as the university scene *O tempora, o mores* (1787), and *Studious Gluttons* (1788). In 1789 he added the aquatint to Rowlandson's etchings of a set of shooting scenes designed by George Morland. The chief beauty of many sporting scenes was the landscape, and Alken became a respected master. His aquatint landscape was combined with Bartolozzi's stippled figures in a large portrait of the duke of Newcastle, *Return from Shooting*, after Francis Wheatley (1792). During the 1790s he aquatinted a large number of plates for sets and books of picturesque views in the lakes, Wales, Ireland, Switzerland, and other places. These included some of his own compositions and a set of aquatints of drawings by the great popularizer of picturesque scenery William Gilpin, published in 1794. In 1801 he aquatinted a view near Exeter after the satirical poet and amateur painter John Wolcot (Peter Pindar). It seems likely that he also mixed socially with the convivial set whose drawings he reproduced. By 1796 he had moved to 2 Francis Street, near Bedford Square.

Besides two daughters who died young, Samuel and Lydia Alken had three sons, **Henry Thomas Alken** (1785–1851), **Sefferein John Alken** (1796–1873), and Samuel [ii] Alken (1784–1824?), who were all sporting artists. Another son, **George Alken** (*d.* 1862?), a designer and lithographer of sporting prints, drowned near Woolwich, possibly in 1862. Sefferein John, latterly resident at Newington, Lambeth, habitually signed his work 'S. Alken', so that it is easily confused with that of his father and brother. Sporting designs dating from after the elder Samuel's death in November 1815 are evidently by one or other of the sons. They differed from the father in that they painted in oils

and specialized in sport rather than landscape, but a considerable number of their paintings and designs were published.

Henry Thomas Alken, born on 12 October 1785 at 3 Dufours Place, was the dominant sporting artist of the early nineteenth century. After receiving his first lessons from his father, the boy was sent at an early age to J. T. Barber, a painter of miniatures. He exhibited twice at the Royal Academy, in each case miniatures of ladies (painted in 1801 and 1802), and showed an early liking for depicting animals, especially dogs and horses. Henry married on 14 October 1809 Maria Gordon (*d.* 1841) of Ipswich, Suffolk, and for a while lived in that town, where their children Sefferein [ii] (1821–1873), **Samuel Henry Gordon Alken** (1810–1894), Lydia Anne, Elizabeth, and Ellen were born. Henry's first sporting prints were published in 1813, and he demonstrated his expertise in the book *The Beauties and Defects in the Figure of the Horse Comparatively Delineated* (1816). From then on he delivered a long series of designs to the leading sporting printsellers—S. and J. Fuller, Thomas McLean, and Rudolph Ackermann among others. He issued many sets of prints in wrappers and provided illustrations to a series of books, employing the pseudonym Ben Tally Ho for his mildly satirical sallies, and often collaborating with his friend the sporting journalist Charles James Apperley (1779–1843), known as Nimrod. Alken was very well informed about horses and riding, and he appeared to be an insider among the wealthy young set who gathered at Melton Mowbray to hunt and drink and (on at least one occasion literally) paint the town red. His familiarity with sporting lore gave rise to the story (put forward in the *Dictionary of National Biography*) that he might have been a hunt servant to the duke of Beaufort. Henry maintained a connection with Ipswich, evident in *A Cockney's Shooting Season in Suffolk* (1822) and *The First Steeple-Chase on Record* (1839), which recorded a nocturnal romp by cavalry officers stationed at Ipswich in 1803 and became the single most popular set of sporting prints. *The Beaufort Hunt* (1833) and *The Quorn Hunt* (1835) were his most distinguished hunting sets. He was also a prolific designer, etcher, and lithographer of scenes relating to racing, shooting, coaching, and other sports, and in 1820 he issued a series entitled *National Sports of Great Britain*. He wrote several books on aspects of engraving, including *The Art and Practice of Engraving* (1849). Alken never used his second name, leading to confusion with his son Samuel Henry Gordon, who also signed designs and paintings 'H. Alken'. Indeed, H. Alken may have been less a person than a family industry, and precise authorship of the resulting prolific output remains difficult to disentangle. The better sporting paintings have usually been attributed to Henry Thomas.

Out and about from his residence in Spring Place, Kentish Town, Henry Alken appeared:

> quaintly countrified, oddly old fashioned … His hat was ugly, low-crowned and broad-brimmed; his frock of Kendal green was dotted with large gilt buttons; and his gaiters and kickseys of brown cloth were in accord with a rustic waistcoat cut low, having ample pockets out of date but

convenient for carrying sketch-books. His shoes were thick and solid, and he preferred a walking staff to a walking stick. (Sparrow, 12)

In later life he drifted into ill health, consumption, and poverty. After his wife died, in 1841, he was cared for by an unmarried daughter and lived at Ivy Cottage, Highgate, where he died in the early summer of 1851. His funeral expenses were met by his daughter Lydia, who had married the animal painter and engraver J. C. Zitter.

Samuel Henry Gordon, born in Ipswich, also returned to London, where he worked as an artist and specialized in painting animals; he executed many of the horses depicted in George Sala's 60 foot long panorama of the funeral procession of the duke of Wellington in 1852. At the time of the 1881 census he was unmarried and living at 62 High Street, Shadwell. He died in a workhouse in 1894.

TIMOTHY CLAYTON and ANITA MCCONNELL

Sources W. S. Sparrow, Henry Alken (1827) · A. Noakes, The world of Henry Alken (1952) · W. Gilbey, Animal painters of England, 3 vols. (1900–11), vol. 1, pp. 1–28, 331–2 · D. Snelgrove, British sporting and animal prints, 1658–1874 (1978) · J. Egerton and D. Snelgrove, The Paul Mellon collection: British sporting and animal drawings, c.1500–1850 (1978) · J. Egerton, The Paul Mellon collection: British sporting and animal paintings, 1655–1867 (1978) · F. Siltzer, The story of British sporting prints (1929) · J. R. Abbey, Scenery of Great Britain and Ireland, 1770–1860 (1952) · J. R. Abbey, Life in England, 1770–1860 (1953) · J. R. Abbey, Travel, 1770–1860, 2 vols. (1956) · F. G. Stephens and M. D. George, eds., Catalogue of political and personal satires preserved … in the British Museum, 5–11 (1935–54) · C. Lane, Sporting aquatints and their engravers, 2 vols. (1978) · Boase, Mod. Eng. biog., 4.82–3 · parish register, St James, Piccadilly, City Westm. AC [baptism, burial; Samuel [i] Alken] · City Westm. AC, parish register [baptism; Sefferein John Alken]

Alken, George (d. 1862?). See under Alken family (per. 1745–1852).

Alken, Henry Thomas (1785–1851). See under Alken family (per. 1745–1852).

Alken, Samuel (1756–1815). See under Alken family (per. 1745–1852).

Alken, Samuel Henry Gordon (1810–1894). See under Alken family (per. 1745–1852).

Alken, Sefferein (1717–1782). See under Alken family (per. 1745–1852).

Alken, Sefferein John (1796–1873). See under Alken family (per. 1745–1852).

Alkin, Elizabeth [nicknamed Parliament Joan] (c.1600–1655?), nurse and spy, was the wife of Francis Alkin, who was hanged as a spy in Oxford by royalist forces during the civil war. Alkin's activities are known largely from her surviving petitions for payment and relief (many of them undated or misattributed in CSP dom.) and from references in contemporary newsbooks.

Employed from the beginning of the civil war as a spy by the earl of Essex, Sir William Waller, and Thomas Fairfax, in 1645 and 1647 Alkin received payments from the committee for the advancement of money for several 'discoveries', including information about the activities of George Mynnes, a Surrey ironmaster who was supplying royalist forces with iron and wire. Increasingly she seems to have concentrated her intelligencing activity on the London news press: in 1648 she was on the trail of *Mercurius Melancholicus* and the *Parliament Kite*, and in February 1649 *Mercurius Pragmaticus* called her an 'old Bitch' who could 'smell out a Loyall-hearted man as soon as the best Blood-hound in the Army' (*Mercurius Pragmaticus*, sig. 2v). She appears in *A Perfect Diurnall* (2–9 July 1649) as 'One Jone (a clamerous woman) whose husband was hang'd at Oxford for a spie, & she sometimes imployed in finding out the presses of scandalous pamphlets' (Nevitt, 91).

In June 1649 Alkin was sent to 'the house of correction' for 'great incivilities' to Sir James Harrington MP, and the following month was involved in a fracas in the Salutation tavern in Holborn with some soldiers who apparently suspected her of being a royalist (Williams, 131–3). A dispute in the same year over her occupation of the house of Stephen Fosett, surgeon to Sir Arthur Aston (governor of Oxford during the first war and responsible, she claimed, for her husband's death), resulted in a grant of £50 and a house.

The newspaper the *Man in the Moon*, whose printer Edward Crouch was arrested in December 1649, warned its readers of Alkin's activities, describing 'Parliament Jone' as 'a fat woman, aged about fifty' (Nevitt, 91). She was involved not only in the detection of royalist newspapers but also in the publication of several short-lived parliamentarian titles. In June 1650 she was apparently one of the publishers of the *Impartial Scout*; and between then and September 1651 she was involved in several issues of newsbooks associated with Henry Walker: the *Moderne Intelligencer*, *Mercurius Anglicus* (October 1650; a royalist title appropriated by anti-royalists), and the *Modern Intelligencer* (26 August–3 September 1651). Three weeks later *Mercurius Scoticus, or, The Royal Messenger* appeared with her imprint (23–30 September 1651). The colourful assumption (by Joseph Frank and J. B. Williams) that her publication of pseudo-royalist titles was a means of flushing out royalist buyers of newsbooks remains unsubstantiated, and Nevitt argues for her more complex editorial involvement in a process of 're-appropriating Royalist titles for Parliamentarian consumption' (ibid., 101).

Alkin claimed recompense for the discovery of four presses run by William Dugard at the Merchant Taylors' School, the incident leading to Dugard's committal to Newgate (20 February 1650) for his publication of Salmasius's *Defensio regia* and *Eikon basilike* the previous year. Lodgings in Whitehall may have been her reward. In November 1651 she was again pursuing printers, being paid £10 for the discovery of Edward Hall's *Manus testium lingua testium*; and in the following year she received similar sums for unspecified acts of good service. Often payment was slow, and many of her petitions in pursuit of arrears emphasize the financial distress of her three children and the expenses of her work.

During the First Anglo-Dutch War (1652–4) Alkin pursued new ways in which to serve the state. On 22 February 1653 she petitioned for a position as nurse to maimed seamen in Dover. On 4 April she received £13 6s. 8d. for her care of the sick and wounded in Portsmouth, and on 2 June she claimed expenses for caring for the wounded at Harwich. By November she was apparently back in London: her evidence about a murderous incident involving the brother of the Portuguese ambassador, which occurred at the New Exchange in November 1653, led to the setting up of a committee of investigation by the council of state. In 1654 she was still pursuing payment for her nursing, and in February she asked for a grant from the navy commissioners for her expenses in relieving Dutch prisoners as well as English seamen at Harwich and Ipswich. Her letter reports her financial distress (she had sold her bed and household goods), her terminal illness, and consequent charges for medicine and attendance. A note of 11 May 1655, referring her petition for relief to the committee for petitions, is the last documentary record of her existence, and she presumably died that year. An undated petition requests her burial in the cloisters of Westminster Abbey.

MAUREEN BELL

Sources CSP dom. · M. Nevitt, 'Women in the business of revolutionary news: Elizabeth Alkin, "Parliament Joan", and the Commonwealth newsbook', News, newspapers, and society in early modern Britain, ed. J. Raymond (1999), 84–108 · J. McElligott, 'Propaganda and censorship: the underground royalist newsbook, 1647–1650', PhD diss., U. Cam., 2000 · J. Frank, The beginnings of the English newspaper, 1620–1660 (1961) · J. B. Williams, A history of English journalism (1908) · I. MacDonald, Elizabeth Alkin: a Florence Nightingale of the Commonwealth (1935) · G. E. Manwaring, 'Parliament Joan: the Florence Nightingale of the seventeenth century', United Service Magazine, 3rd ser., 57 (1918), 301–10 · Mercurius Pragmaticus, 45 (13–20 Feb 1649), sig. 2v · Fourth report, HMC, 3 (1874), 180 n. 56

Allam, Andrew (*bap.* 1655, *d.* 1685), antiquary, was baptized on 23 April 1655 at Garsington, Oxfordshire, the second of four surviving children of Andrew Allam (*d.* 1674) and his wife, Bridget, *née* Darling (*d.* 1680). He was educated at a private grammar school in Denton, near Cuddesdon, Oxfordshire, by William Wildgoose. In 1671 he entered St Edmund Hall, Oxford, with the lowly status of batteler, and graduated BA in 1675 and MA in 1677 (incorporated at Cambridge, 1675). In 1680 he took holy orders. His academic career culminated in his appointment as vice-principal of St Edmund Hall in 1682, and his election as one of the masters of the schools in 1683.

Allam is chiefly known as a colleague of Anthony Wood, with whom he exchanged research and information on contemporary events from the late 1670s onwards, greatly assisting Wood in the compilation of his *Athenae Oxonienses*. In 1680 he provided much information on Oxford gossip to Wood while he was absent from the town, and in 1685 undertook work for him in London. Wood valued both Allam's friendship and scholarship, as Allam was one of his most reliable correspondents. They shared a dislike for the apathy widespread among their peers towards the history of the university and its members.

Due to his early death, Allam's only known large-scale work was a projected history of English cathedrals, the notes for which were later used by Bishop Kennett. He produced a few minor publications, mostly epistles dedicatory, prefaces, and the like. Of more substance were his translation of Nepos, *Life of Iphicrates*, and a biographical account of Dr Richard Cosin prefaced to his *Ecclesiae Anglicanae politeia*, both published in 1684. According to Wood, Allam's additions to Edward Chamberlain's *Angliae notitia* of 1684 were incorporated into the 1687 edition without acknowledgement, although his work extending *The Historical and Chronological Theatre of Christopher Helvicus* was printed with due attribution in the 1687 English edition.

Allam contracted smallpox and died unmarried on 17 June 1685 at St Edmund Hall. He was buried that evening at St Peter-in-the-East, Oxford. His premature death was much lamented by Wood, who claimed that 'he understood the world of men well, authors better, and nothing but years and experience were wanting to make him a compleat walking library' (Wood, *Ath. Oxon.*, 4.175). Many of Allam's books and papers were acquired by Wood. His almanac, incorporated into Wood's diaries, includes a detailed account of the death of Charles II.

PETER SHERLOCK

Sources Wood, *Ath. Oxon.*, new edn, 4.174–6 · The life and times of Anthony Wood, ed. A. Clark, 5 vols., OHS, 19, 21, 26, 30, 40 (1891–1900) · Foster, *Alum. Oxon.* · parish registers, Garsington, Oxon. RO · parish register, Oxford, St Peter-in-the-East, 17 June 1685 [burial]

Archives Bodl. Oxf., Tanner MS 454 · Bodl. Oxf., letters to Anthony Wood

Allan, David (1744–1796), portrait and genre painter, was born at Alloa, Clackmannanshire, on 13 February 1744, the son of David Allan, shoremaster, and Janet Gullan. Allan, who was born prematurely, seems to have been asthmatic and never enjoyed good health. He showed an early proclivity to art, and was dismissed from school for caricaturing his teacher. At eleven, on 23 February 1755, he was apprenticed to the Glasgow printers Robert and Andrew Foulis and attended the drawing academy they had established earlier that year in the University of Glasgow. He remained at the academy until 1762. A drawing of the interior of the academy (Glasgow University) is attributed to Allan. Lord and Lady Cathcart, whose house, Shaw Park, was near Alloa, took an interest in the young artist and raised a subscription to send him to Rome to continue his studies. He travelled via Genoa and Leghorn in late summer 1767 (not, as previously supposed, in 1764) and remained in Italy for ten years. However, he seems to have returned home several times during this period as there are portraits of individuals not known to have travelled to Italy, painted by Allan and dated 1768, 1770, 1773, and 1774. In Rome, Allan joined the circle of Gavin Hamilton, whose example he endeavoured to follow in a series of paintings with classical subjects such as *The Continence of Scipio* (1774; NG Scot.) and *The Origin of Painting* (1775; NG Scot.). He also sent similar pictures to the Royal Academy exhibitions of 1771 and 1773. In 1773 he won the Concorso Balestra, the gold medal for history painting awarded by the Accademia di San Luca, Rome. As its president, Hamilton probably awarded the prize and certainly set the subject, *Hector's Farewell to Andromache*, and Allan's winning entry

David Allan (1744–1796), self-portrait, 1770

(Accademia di San Luca, Rome) is strikingly close to Hamilton's own painting.

Although resident in Rome, Allan visited Naples annually from 1768 to 1770, and certainly also at other times, as is demonstrated by a number of dated works and a sketchbook of 1770. There he enjoyed the patronage of Sir William Hamilton, British envoy to the Neapolitan court and brother of Lady Cathcart, whose full-length portrait he presented to the British Museum in 1775. He had earlier painted a charming domestic portrait of Sir William and the first Lady Hamilton (1770; priv. coll.). The work of the Neapolitan genre painter Pietro Fabris, also patronized by Sir William, shaped Allan's own genre style. Fabris's paintings offered a humorous, observational account of ordinary life, but for Allan this approach also had important antiquarian and documentary purposes. Allan's paintings and numerous drawings recorded antiquities, customs, games, and costumes in which he sought to express continuity with the remote past; for example *The Seven Sacraments* is concerned with popular religious practice and *A Neapolitan Dance* (both NG Scot.) with traditional music and dance. In a similar way he sought echoes of the graceful movements seen in the decoration of the antique vases collected by Sir William in the gestures and attitudes of local people. Allan also travelled to the islands of Malta, Ischia, Procida, and Minorca on the same quest under the influence of his fellow Italian-based Scot, the antiquary James Byres. Byres believed that these Mediterranean islands had been refuges from the flood, and were therefore sites where antediluvian survivals were most likely to be found. Allan also recorded contemporary events, and a

set of large drawings of the Roman carnival (exh. RA, 1779; Royal Collection), later engraved in aquatint and published by Paul Sandby in 1781, is among the most ambitious of his Italian works.

Allan finally returned to Britain via northern Italy in 1777 and spent two years in London. According to the anonymous author of the first biography of the artist (possibly Robert Brown), 'Memoir of David Allan', included in the 1808 edition of Allan Ramsay's *Gentle Shepherd*, Allan returned to Scotland in 1779 because of his poor health. He exhibited several genre works at the Royal Academy in 1777; however, he was evidently also trying to establish himself as a portrait painter and the strength of the competition in London may have been another factor. Allan practised a style of informal conversation portrait closely based on Zoffany, which met with some success in Scotland. He worked extensively for the Hopes of Hopetoun, painting portraits of both them and various connected families such as those of the earl of Mar and the duke of Atholl. A portrait of his first patrons, the Cathcarts (priv. coll.), is characteristically set during a cricket match.

In 1781 Allan exhibited a large picture, *A Highland Dance*, at the Royal Academy. This work bears close comparison with his earlier *A Neapolitan Dance* and exemplifies Allan's adaptation of the Neapolitan genre style to Scottish manners and customs. His work also has an affinity with the Scottish vernacular poetry of Allan Ramsay and Robert Burns in its direct response to scenes of ordinary life; in this he set an example followed by a number of later Scottish painters, most notably David Wilkie. Allan's Scottish works—usually drawings which were occasionally made into prints—record the street life of Edinburgh, local customs, for example *A Highland Wedding* (NG Scot.), and festivals, for example *A Miner's Gala* (priv. coll.). They are informed with the same blend of documentary, even antiquarian interest and sympathetic humour as his Italian works. Allan's most famous works of this type were a set of twelve aquatints illustrating an edition of the poet Allan Ramsay's pastoral *The Gentle Shepherd*, published by the Foulis Press in 1788. Notably, he dedicated these illustrations to Gavin Hamilton, acknowledging his debt to the older artist. In this dedication he claims that his images were studies from nature; by this he seems to mean that their style echoes the simple and unspoilt manners of the country people who were his subjects. Further, he remarks that though he lacks skill in handling aquatint this lack of sophistication actually gives his work greater expression. This claim also throws light on the naïvety of his style generally; though this may reflect the limitation of his talent, it seems that it was also a self-conscious attempt to emulate the naïvety of unaffected country manners or indeed the reflection in them of an imagined continuity with a supposed earlier, unspoiled condition of human society.

Such a view is supported by Allan's collaboration with Robert Burns through the intermediary of the music publisher George Thomson. In 1793 Thomson commissioned Allan to make illustrations to the songs that Burns wrote to traditional Scottish tunes. Allan produced more than

100 drawings, all in the same small oval format, the majority of which are in the National Gallery of Scotland and Royal Scottish Academy, as well as a number of etchings. Burns felt that Allan's illustrations exactly matched what he was trying to do and wrote to Thomson: 'I am highly delighted with Mr Allan's etchings. The expression of the figures … is absolutely faultless perfection'. However, the project was never realized, though Allan himself published twenty-five etchings in 1796, *Etchings Illustrative of some Celebrated Scottish Songs*. Thomson later published a number in his six-volume *Songs of Burns* (Edinburgh, 1822) and the composer Alexander Campbell published several in his *Introduction to the History of Poetry in Scotland* (1798). One of Allan's most characteristic works, *The Penny Wedding* (1795; NG Scot.), is in the same spirit—celebrating, just as Burns does, the carefree life of ordinary people, unencumbered by property. The scene is light-hearted, but Allan's intention was fundamentally serious, and reflected a particular view of the nature and history of society. Allan's other, antiquarian, concern with seeking out an authentic past is reflected in his approach to the small number of history paintings he made, which survive only in the form of drawings. For example, in *The Abdication of Mary Queen of Scots* (NG Scot.) he endeavoured to incorporate likenesses copied from surviving contemporary portraits of the subjects. Similarly, he helped David Steuart Erskine, eleventh earl of Buchan, in his search for authentic portraits of Scottish historical figures.

In 1786 Allan succeeded Alexander Runciman as master of the Trustees' Academy in Edinburgh, a post which he held until his death. On 28 October 1788 he married Shirley Welsh; they had a son, David, and a daughter, Barbara. Describing the artist, his first biographer, who evidently knew him personally, was not flattering: 'He was under the middle size; of a slender feeble make, with a long, sharp, lean, white coarse face, much pitted by the small pox, and fair hair' ('Memoir of David Allan', 628). He does add, however, that in company Allan's lively manner and humour belied his appearance. Allan himself was more flattering in his self-portrait painted in Italy in 1770, as also was Domenico Corvi, who painted him in 1774 (both Scot. NPG). Allan died in Edinburgh of 'a dropsy preceded by an asthma' on 6 August 1796.

W. C. MONKHOUSE, *rev.* DUNCAN MACMILLAN

Sources 'Memoir of David Allan', A. Ramsay, *The gentle shepherd*, Newhall edn, 2 vols. (1808), vol. 2, pp. 619–31 • B. Skinner, *The indefatigable Mr Allan* (1973) • D. Ridgeway, 'James Byers and the ancient state of Italy', *Secondo congresso internazionale etrusco* (Florence, 1985) • J. Ingamells, *British and Irish travellers in Italy, 1701–1800* (1997) • A. Ramsay, *The gentle shepherd* (1788) • T. Crouther Gordon, *David Allan: the Scottish Hogarth* (1951)

Likenesses D. Allan, self-portrait, oils, 1770, Scot. NPG [*see illus.*] • D. Corvi, oils, 1774, Scot. NPG • J. Tassie, paste medallion, 1781, Scot. NPG • J. Medina, oils (after D. Allan), Scot. NPG

Allan, Eliza MacNaughton Luke [Dot] (1886–1964), novelist, was born on 13 May 1886 at Headswood House, Denny, Stirlingshire, the only child of Alexander Allan, iron merchant, and his wife, Jean, daughter of John Luke,

founder of the Vale paper works in Denny. She was educated privately and attended classes at Glasgow University.

Allan is described as small, soft-voiced, of a retiring disposition, with dark hair and grey eyes. While still a young woman she moved to Glasgow with her widowed mother, never marrying and remaining there for the rest of her life. Although the archetypal 'daughter at home', who largely abandoned writing during both world wars to concentrate on nursing and charity work, she was nevertheless a prolific freelance journalist, wrote several plays (theatregoing was one of her main interests), and published ten novels between 1921 and 1958.

Allan once said in an interview: 'I don't believe in the localisation of a writer's talent. One ought to take the world for one's field if one wants to' (Kyle). Glasgow provides the setting for her earlier novels, and the theme of *Deepening River* (1932) is the development of Clyde shipbuilding from the eighteenth to the early twentieth century. However, her characters, as in her first novel, *The Syrens* (1921; published simultaneously in Britain and the USA and translated into Dutch), often reject the conventions of their place and time. *Makeshift* (1928), though uneven in quality, is notable for its young heroine's determination that her life, unlike her mother's, shall not be 'second best—makeshift all the time' and that she will not be 'used', practically or emotionally. Her sexual awareness, too, is identified and expressed with unexpected frankness.

Allan's best-known novel, *Hunger March* (1934), follows the events of one day in a depression-hit city, unnamed but recognizable as Glasgow. Through contrasting but linked characters, including a merchant facing bankruptcy, his office cleaner and her long-term unemployed son, and an enthusiastic middle-class radical, Allan presents the great hunger march which swamps the city centre during the afternoon and evening of her chosen day. Her sympathies are with the marchers, but she acknowledges equally the despair of the conscientious employer. There is a clear indictment throughout of the apathy and insensitivity she sees in the prosperous middle class to which she herself belonged.

Allan published little or nothing during the Second World War, and her post-war novels, most of which have historical settings, did not attract great attention. *John Mathew, Papermaker* (1948) is closely based on her mother's family, papermakers since 1780. She was a member of Scottish PEN and in her later years gave unobtrusive financial support to a number of aspiring writers. She died of cancer at her home, 5 Hamilton Drive, Glasgow, on 3 December 1964, and a private funeral took place two days later, after a service at Belhaven Westbourne church.

MOIRA BURGESS

Sources E. Kyle, 'Modern women authors, 3: Dot Allan', *Scots Observer* (25 June 1931) • *Glasgow Herald* (4 Dec 1964) • *The Scotsman* (4 Dec 1964) • *Falkirk Herald* (5 Dec 1964) • *Stirling Observer* (10 Dec 1964)

Likenesses photograph, 1931, repro. in *Scots Observer* • photograph, 1933, repro. in R. D. MacLeod, ed., *Modern Scottish literature* (1933), 20 • photograph, 1964, repro. in *Stirling Observer*

Wealth at death £448,983 4s. 4d.: confirmation, 17 Feb 1965, CCI

Allan, George (1736–1800), antiquary and topographer, was born on 7 June 1736 in Darlington, co. Durham, the eldest son of James Allan (1712–1790) and Elizabeth Pemberton (1710–1756). His father, 'Auld Jem', fourth son of Nicholas Allan of Staindrop, had trained as an attorney, and in 1738 was appointed bailiff of Darlington by Bishop Chandler. 'A good lawyer and a very accurate antiquary', he was also said, while affable to acquaintances, to be 'peevish and austere to an excess' (Nichols, *Lit. anecdotes*, 344). The immediate ancestor of this family was George Allan, who lived in Yarm in 1651, and whose eldest son, Thomas, was linked with the Tyneside coal trade. A fifth son, George, settled in Darlington, co. Durham, and his heir married Thomasine Prescott, coheir to Blackwell Grange, outside Darlington. Through lack of further children their property was bequeathed by the surviving grandchild, Anne, to her cousin 'Auld Jem', who thereby acquired Blackwell Grange while continuing to practise in the Durham courts. He was reputed to be a wealthy man: the rental of his estates in 1812 was estimated to exceed £10,000 a year.

Although relations between 'Auld Jem' and his sons were bad, it would appear that George Allan the antiquary had little need to earn a living, despite being described as a lawyer with an extensive practice in Darlington. He was reputed to have paid considerable sums for the manuscript collections of Dr Christopher Hunter and of various Durham lawyers such as Thomas Gyll, John Mann, Ralph Hodgson, and Gabriel Swainston. Other items acquired by him ran the gamut from fossils and shells to insects, reptiles, and birds. His special interests were heraldry, genealogy, and the history of Darlington itself. In 1764 he was said to have been offered the place of Richmond herald, which he declined as incompatible with his professional standing and future prospects. Between 18 and 24 September 1766 he married Anne (1741–1787), only daughter and heir of James Colling Nicholson of Scruton, Yorkshire. Their eldest son, George (1767–1828), a fellow-commoner of Trinity Hall, Cambridge (1784), was admitted to the Middle Temple in 1785. He graduated BA in 1789, and was called to the bar in 1790; he served as MP for Durham City from 1813 to 1818. A second son, James (1772–1795), also admitted to Trinity Hall, was captain in the 29th regiment of foot, and died of yellow fever at Grenada in 1795 at the age of twenty-three. There were also four daughters.

About 1768 Allan set up a private press at Blackwell Grange, his father's home, in order to print many of his manuscript treasures, such as the charter granted by Queen Elizabeth founding the free grammar school at Darlington in 1567, collections relating to St Edmund's Hospital at Gateshead (1769), and the hospitals at Greatham (1770) and Sherburn (1771). He also engraved several charters in facsimile, and seals of bishops. As early as 1763 he had issued a prospectus for a peerage to be printed in forty-two numbers but, on finding the cost would reach several thousand pounds, he relinquished

the scheme after publishing the first number. In 1774 he was elected a fellow of the Society of Antiquaries, to whose library he presented twenty (or twenty-six) manuscript volumes of collections relating to the University of Oxford, made by William Smith, rector of Melsonby, Yorkshire. He was generous with his collections, and made them available to fellow antiquarians; he encouraged William Hutchinson, a fellow lawyer based at Barnard Castle, to make them the basis for a *History of the County Palatine of Durham* (3 vols., 1785–94). Later Robert Surtees made similar use of the material for his county history (4 vols., 1816–40), as did Sir Cuthbert Sharp for his work on Hartlepool.

Allan retired from the law in 1790, shortly after the death of his father. At the same time he purchased for £700 the entire museum of natural history of his lately deceased friend Marmaduke Tunstall of Wycliffe, which included stuffed birds said to have cost £5000 (which had been used as models by Thomas Bewick), in addition to curiosities brought by Captain Cook from Otaheite and other places, a collection of Indian armour, and Chinese antiques. His son George wrote of him: 'He was warm in his affections, but very keen in resentment, and though I believe as temperate a man as ever existed, he was extremely irritable during the latter years of his life' (Nichols, *Lit. anecdotes*, 368).

> He rose at half past seven, ate a hearty breakfast at eight, very seldom took any exercise, and scarce ate any animal food at all. About three glasses of wine was his allowance after dinner. He drank tea, but seldom ate supper … It was generally two o'clock before he retired to his room; and although I will not take upon me to say it was the last office he performed, he always read the Newspaper in bed, by a reflecting lamp, which burnt all night.   (ibid., 368)

Allan suffered a paralytic stroke in July 1797, and on 18 May 1800 died suddenly of a second stroke at Blackwell Grange. He was buried in the family vault in St Cuthbert's Church, Darlington, six days later. After his death his library and the museum pieces were bought by his eldest son under the terms of his will. Subsequently the Newcastle upon Tyne Literary and Philosophical Society acquired for £400 his museum items, including bronze Roman statues, altars, crosses, seals, and the like. Part of his heraldic, genealogical, and Darlington material, together with the collection of manuscripts bequeathed to Allan by Thomas Randall, master of Durham grammar school, was bought by the dean and chapter of Durham for £150, and remains in the cathedral library. His collection of pictures, 'which filled every pannel [*sic*], gradually insinuated themselves along the passages, and clothed the walls of the great staircase' (Surtees, 3.371) was also dispersed. It contained a portrait of Anne Boleyn attributed to Holbein, several by Sir Peter Lely of such notabilities as Lord Fairfax, Sir Henry Wotton, and Lady Castlemaine, and a pastel portrait by Gainsborough of a companion of Lady Seaforth.

C. M. FRASER

Sources Nichols, *Lit. anecdotes*, 8.344–68, 697–757 · R. Surtees, *The history and antiquities of the county palatine of Durham*, 1 (1816), 8; 3 (1823), 370–73 · W. H. D. Longstaffe, *The history and antiquities of the parish of Darlington*, new edn (1909), 383–418 · PRO, Durham 13/125,

145 • W. Hutchinson, introduction, *The history and antiquities of the county palatine of Durham*, 1 (1785), 9 • Venn, *Alum. Cant.* • DNB
Archives Bodl. Oxf., corresp. • Bodl. Oxf., list of references to northern counties • Durham Cath. CL, antiquarian collections • N. Yorks. CRO, personal papers • S. Antiquaries, Lond., corresp. of various antiquaries transcribed by him
Likenesses J. Collyer the younger, line engraving (with William Hutchinson; after J. Hay), BM, NPG; repro. in Nichols, *Lit. anecdotes*, frontispiece; *see illus. in* Hutchinson, William (1732–1814) • engraving (with William Hutchinson), Bodl. Oxf., MS Don 87 • pastel drawing, NPG

Allan, Sir Henry Marshman Havelock-, first baronet (1830–1897), army officer and politician, eldest of eight children (four surviving) of Major-General Sir Henry *Havelock (1795–1857) and his wife, Hannah (*d.* 1882), daughter of Dr Joshua *Marshman, was born at Chinsura, India, on 6 August 1830. He assumed the additional surname of Allan on 17 March 1880, in compliance with the terms of the will of his cousin, Henry Allan of Blackwall Grange, Durham.

Educated at the Revd Dr Cuthbert's school in St John's Wood, London, Havelock was commissioned as ensign in the 39th foot on 31 March 1846, and became lieutenant (by purchase) in the 86th foot on 23 June 1848. On his way out to join his regiment in Bombay in the autumn of 1848 Havelock suffered severe sunstroke, which obliged him to return to England on sick leave. Contemporaries blamed this incident for his subsequent fits of eccentricity. After his sick leave Havelock returned to India, where he transferred to the 10th foot as adjutant on 13 February 1852. In 1856 he returned to England, hoping to be employed in the war with Russia. In this he was not successful, but he went to the Staff College, and returned to the East in time to take part in the Anglo-Persian War.

Havelock was appointed, from 22 January 1857, acting deputy assistant quartermaster-general of his father's division in the expedition under Sir James Outram against Persia, and took part in the bombardment and capture on 26 March of Muhammarah. He was mentioned in dispatches.

From Persia, Havelock accompanied his father to Calcutta, where he arrived after the outbreak of the mutiny. On his father's appointment to command a column for the relief of Cawnpore and Lucknow, Havelock went with him as aide-de-camp. He took part in the actions at Fatehpur on 12 July, Aong and Pandu Nadi on the 15th, and Cawnpore on the 16th, where he distinguished himself, riding in front of the 64th foot towards a 24-pounder gun, which was firing first roundshot and then grape. The gun was captured by a gallant charge. For this he received the Victoria Cross on 15 January 1858. Despite controversy over the general recommending his son, there was no question as to young Havelock's gallantry.

On 21 July Havelock was appointed deputy assistant adjutant-general to the force. On the first advance from Cawnpore to Lucknow he was present at the actions at Unao on 29 July, Basiratganj on 5 August, when his horse was shot under him, and Bithur on 16 August. In the second advance from Cawnpore, after Outram had joined the

force with reinforcements, he took part in the actions at Mangalwar on 21 September and at the Alambagh on 23 September, where, reportedly, he twice saved Outram's life. Two days later he displayed great gallantry at the successful attack on the Charbagh Bridge of Lucknow, where an entrance to the city was gained; during the attack he was dangerously wounded, and was recommended by Outram for the Victoria Cross.

As soon as he was convalescent Havelock took part in the defence of the residency at Lucknow until its relief by Sir Colin Campbell. While in Lucknow, he transferred to the 18th foot (the Royal Irish regiment), as captain, on 9 October 1857. On 17 November he was again severely wounded, when accompanying his father and Outram across the open space between the residency and Sir Colin's relieving forces at the Moti Mahal. In spite of his wound he attended his father's deathbed on 24 November. On 22 January 1858 the baronetcy and pension of £1000 a year proposed to be conferred on his father were bestowed on him.

In December 1857, though still suffering from his wounds, Havelock was appointed, at his own request, deputy assistant adjutant-general to the Azamgarh and Jaunpur field force under Brigadier-General Franks. He took part in the successful actions at Nasratpur on 23 January 1858, Chanda and Hamirpur on 19 February, Sultanpur on 23rd, and Dhaorara on 4 March. He distinguished himself on 14 March at the storming of the *imambara* in Lucknow, taking part the same day in the storming and capture of the *kaisarbagh*. On 19 March Lucknow was finally won.

On 29 March, as deputy assistant adjutant-general to the field force in the Bihar and Ghazipur districts, Havelock accompanied Sir Edward Lugard's column to the relief of Azamgarh, and was present at the successful actions of Metahi on 11 April and 15 April. The rebels were then pursued into the jungles of Jagdispur. In October Havelock proposed to mount some infantry to make up for the deficiency in cavalry, and was given the command of a small column of mounted infantry. He pursued the Shahabad rebels for 200 miles in five days, fighting three actions on 19, 20, and 21 October, finally driving them into the Kaimur hills, and was again wounded.

On 25 November 1858 Havelock was appointed to command the 1st regiment of Hodson's Horse, which he held until March 1859. He led it through the campaign in Oudh under Lord Clyde, including the successful action at Bajadua on 26 December, the capture of Masjadua on the following day, and the defeat of the rebels near Bandi on the Rapti on 31 December. He was frequently mentioned in dispatches for his services during the mutiny. He received a year's service for Lucknow, and the brevets of major (19 January 1858) and lieutenant-colonel (26 April 1859).

On Havelock's return home in 1860 he joined his regiment at Shorncliffe. On 1 October 1861 he was appointed deputy assistant adjutant-general at Aldershot. In August 1863 he accompanied his regiment to New Zealand, and on 25 October was appointed deputy assistant quartermaster-general to the forces in that colony, serving throughout 1863–4 under Major-General Duncan Cameron. He took part in the Waikato campaign and was present at the storming and capture of Rangiriri on 20 and 21 November 1863. He commanded the troops engaged in the action at Waiari in January 1864, was present at the actions at Paterangi and Rangiawhia on 20 and 21 February, and at the siege and capture on 2 April of Orakau. For his services he was mentioned in dispatches, promoted major (28 June 1864), and made a CB military division, on 10 August 1866.

Havelock returned to England at the beginning of 1865. On 10 May that year he married Lady Alice Moreton, daughter of Henry George Francis *Moreton, second earl of Ducie (d. 1853), and his wife, Elizabeth (d. 1865). They had three children: Ethel (b. 1867), who married Joseph Albert Pease MP (later Lord Gainford), Henry Spencer Moreton (1872–1953), who succeeded his father in the baronetcy and served as Liberal MP for Durham from 1910 to 1918, and Allan (b. 1874).

In 1867 Havelock published *Three Main Military Questions of the Day*, which included a highly regarded and influential disquisition on mounted infantry tactics. From 13 March 1867 until 31 March 1869 he served as assistant quartermaster-general in Canada, and from 1 August 1869 to 30 September 1872 he served in the same capacity in Dublin. He obtained leave of absence to see part of the Franco-Prussian War and was present at Sedan. In 1877 he visited the theatre of the Russo-Turkish War, acting as a newspaper 'occasional correspondent'.

In January 1874 Havelock unsuccessfully contested Stroud as a Liberal, but in July he was returned as MP for Sunderland, for which he sat until 1881, when he resigned to take command, on 1 April, of the 3rd infantry brigade at Aldershot. He had already been given the brevet of colonel on 17 June 1868, and was promoted major-general on 18 March 1878.

Ill health compelled Havelock-Allan to retire from the active list on 9 December 1881, with the honorary rank of lieutenant-general. Nevertheless he visited Sir Garnet Wolseley's headquarters at Isma'iliyyah in 1882, and was present at the battles of Qassasin and Tell al-Kebir, when he reputedly led a charge armed only with a riding crop.

In December 1885 Havelock-Allan became Liberal MP for the south-east division of Durham county, but the following year his concern for the integrity of the empire led him to join the Liberal Unionists. He was re-elected in July 1886, narrowly defeated in July 1892, and again elected in July 1895. His pluck and energy were as evident in his political career as in his military. Shrewd and well-meaning, but impetuous and choleric, he held strong opinions on many subjects. He was a good speaker, and was held in high esteem by his Durham mining constituents. He spoke often on army questions, and was chairman of the parliamentary naval and military service committee. He was made KCB on 21 June 1887, and was a JP for the North Riding and for the county of Durham, of which he was a deputy lieutenant. He was also an alderman of Durham county council, honorary colonel of the Durham militia artillery, commander of the Tyne and Tees voluntary brigade, and (from 27 November 1895) colonel of the Royal Irish regiment.

In the recess of 1897 Havelock-Allan went to India to inquire into complaints of indiscipline in the 2nd battalion, Royal Irish regiment, and visited the Afghan frontier. He was moving down the Khyber Pass on 30 December after a visit to Landi Kotal when a fresh horse gave him some trouble, and in giving it a good gallop to steady it he got into broken ground on the flank, where some Afridis were waiting. One of them fired at the horse (hoping to capture Havelock-Allan and put him to ransom) but the ball passed through Havelock-Allan's leg, cutting an artery, and he bled to death. When his body was found, it was taken to Rawalpindi, where his regiment, the Royal Irish, was then quartered. He was survived by his wife.

R. H. VETCH, rev. ALEX MAY

Sources Army List · Hart's Army List · Burke, *Peerage* · *The Times* (1 Jan 1898) · *The Times* (7 Jan 1898) · O'M. Creagh and E. M. Humphris, *The V.C. and D.S.O.*, 1 [1920] · J. W. Kaye, *A history of the Sepoy War in India, 1857–1858*, 9th edn, 3 vols. (1880) · G. B. Malleson, *History of the Indian mutiny, 1857–1858: commencing from the close of the second volume of Sir John Kaye's History of the Sepoy War*, 3 vols. (1878–80) · J. E. Alexander, *Bush fighting, illustrated by remarkable actions and incidents of the Maori war in New Zealand* (1873) · G. le M. Gretton, *The campaigns and history of the royal Irish regiment* (1911) · J. C. Marshman, *Memoirs of Major-General Sir Henry Havelock* (1860) · J. C. Pollock, *Way to glory: the life of Havelock of Lucknow* (1957) · C. Hibbert, *The great mutiny, India, 1857* (1978) · B. Farwell, *Queen Victoria's little wars* (1973)
Archives N. Yorks. CRO, corresp. and papers | BL OIOC, Havelock MSS
Likenesses oils, c.1881, NAM · chromolithograph, c.1890, NAM · Bassano, photographs, 1897, NPG · Bassano, photograph, repro. in P. A. Wilkins, *The history of the Victoria cross* (1904), 85 · Spy [L. Ward], caricature, chromolithograph, NPG; repro. in *VF* (29 March 1879) · portrait, repro. in G. T. Denison, *Soldiering in Canada* (1900) · portrait, repro. in T. E. Toomey, *Heroes of the Victoria cross* (1895)
Wealth at death £11,806 8s. 3d.: probate, 15 March 1898, CGPLA Eng. & Wales

Allan, John Robertson (1906–1986), novelist and journalist, was born on 4 September 1906 at Auchnashag, Udny, Aberdeenshire, the son of Eliza Jane Allan, a domestic servant. Allan was brought up on his grandfather's farm, Bodachra, near Aberdeen. He attended Robert Gordon's College and the University of Aberdeen, and graduated with honours in English in 1928. Denied the prospect of a university lectureship, he worked as a sub-editor on the *Glasgow Herald*.

Allan's first novel, *Farmer's Boy* (1935), an imaginative reconstruction of life at Bodachra, won comparison with the work of James Leslie Mitchell in its evocation of the spirit of the north-east of Scotland. *Summer in Scotland* followed in 1938, a charming and provocative introduction to the country, based on the principle that 'It is one of the best pleasures of travel to sharpen the wits' (p. 5). Allan's masterpiece, *North-East Lowlands of Scotland* (1952), knits together geology, climate, social and economic organization, language, and culture into a single profoundly understood and memorably expressed whole. One has to go back to the founder of the genre, the great French historian Jules Michelet, to find work of similar authority and panache.

After war service as a captain in the Gordon Highlanders, Allan began dairy farming at Little Ardo, Methlick, Aberdeenshire, described in *The Seasons Return* (1955). The demands of broadcasting and declining health effectively brought his writing career to a close in the later 1950s. The few commentaries on Allan's work tend to present him as a simple figure, a man of the bothy with a pen in his hand; but he was a complex and sophisticated writer, hard-headed, practical, and worldly, yet with a poet's sensitivity, inventiveness of language, and imaginative sweep. John R. Allan died of pneumonia at his home, Ivydean, Blairlogie, near Stirling, on 4 October 1986. He was survived by his wife, Jean (*née* Mackie).

WILLIAM DONALDSON

Sources J. R. Allan, *Farmer's boy* (1935) · J. R. Allan, *Summer in Scotland* (1938) · J. R. Allan, *North-east lowlands of Scotland* (1952) · J. R. Allan, *The seasons return* (1955) · J. R. Allan, *A new song to the Lord* (1931) · J. R. Allan, ed., *Scotland 1938: twenty-five impressions* (1938) · J. R. Allan, *Green heritage* (1991) · J. Webster, *Aberdeen University Review*, 52 (1987–8), 84–5 · R. F. Mackenzie, 'John R. Allan', *Leopard*, 45 (Dec 1978–Jan 1979), 24–7 · b. cert. · d. cert.
Archives BBC Scotland, Glasgow, broadcast scripts
Likenesses photograph, repro. in Mackenzie, 'John R. Allan', 25

Allan, Mary Miller (1869–1947), college head, was born at 12 Commerce Street, Glasgow, on 12 August 1869, the youngest of the six children of William Allan, a grain mill manager and his wife, Margaret. Educated at Glasgow high school and Dundas Vale Training College, Glasgow, she obtained her government teacher's certificate in 1891 and the LLA diploma of St Andrews University (by external study) in 1894. A lectureship at Dundas Vale was followed in 1895 by the headship of Leeds Higher Grade School for Girls. In 1903 she was appointed first woman principal of Homerton College, Cambridge.

Mary Allan was tall and well built with an attractive Scottish accent and a good dress sense. A woman of outstanding ability and determination, by her forceful leadership at Homerton she set new standards of academic and professional excellence for the training of women teachers. Her students found her an awe inspiring, unapproachable figure and nicknamed her 'stern daughter of the voice of God', after the Wordsworth ode which she would declaim at her Sunday evening poetry readings. She maintained strict control over every aspect of the college's life and was particularly concerned with the sexual and social respectability of her students. Her annual homily that her 200 women students lived in the same town as 4000 male undergraduates and that there had never been any trouble between them became legendary.

Mary Allan gathered around her a staff of women graduates, all of whom shared her high ideals of service and commitment to women's education. She formed a close professional and personal relationship with her vice-principal, Edith Waterhouse. They shared the same sense of humour and enjoyed going to Gilbert and Sullivan operas together. In 1919–20 she visited America and Japan before touring India as the only woman member of the commission of inquiry into village education. This enriching experience deepened her religious faith which led her to urge students to see the finger of God in everything they did. She herself was a regular worshipper at the Emmanuel Street Congregational Church in Cambridge.

There is no evidence that Mary Allan was actively involved in the suffrage movement, but her work at Homerton in advancing the academic attainment and social status of women teachers was important for feminism. A socialist, she was one of the signatories in 1918 for the nomination of Cambridge's first Labour parliamentary candidate. She was elected first woman president of the Training College Association in 1916 and was always concerned with the salaries and conditions of service of the teaching profession. She served on both the Cambridge and Cambridgeshire education committees.

Mary Allan was unmarried and after her retirement in 1935 she lived with her sister and nieces at 8 Dean Court, Holbroke Road, Cambridge. She died from cancer on 2 November 1947 in the Hope Nursing Home, Brooklands Avenue, Cambridge. The large attendance at her funeral, including representatives of the local and national institutions with which she had been connected, bore witness to the outstanding contribution which she had made to education in general and to the training of women teachers in particular.

ELIZABETH EDWARDS

Sources Homerton College Archive, Cambridge · E. Edwards, 'Educational institutions or extended families? The reconstruction of gender in women's colleges in the late nineteenth and early twentieth centuries', *Gender and Education*, 2 (1990), 17–35 · local records collection, Mitchell L., Glas. · *CGPLA Eng. & Wales* (1948) · b. cert.
Likenesses H. Riviere, oils, 1913, Homerton College, Cambridge
Wealth at death £2749 2s. 4d.: probate, 3 Jan 1948, *CGPLA Eng. & Wales*

Allan, Peter (1799–1849), recluse, was born on 6 September 1799, the son of Peter Allan, shoemaker in Gladsmuir, and Jane Renny, daughter of Archibald Kenley of Tranent. In early life he was in domestic service as a valet to William Williamson. Afterwards he became gamekeeper to the marquess of Londonderry, and was reputed to be an unerring shot and to possess exceptional physical strength. At a later date he opened a tavern at Whitburn, a village on the Durham coast. He married Elizabeth (1801/2–1870). The acquisition of some small property near his inn drew his attention to the quarries in the neighbourhood; he exhibited so much practical skill in works of excavation that several quarries were placed under his superintendence. About 1827 he formed an eccentric plan for colonizing the wild rocks round the Bay of Marsden, 5 miles to the north of Sunderland. After many months spent in carrying out his project, he moved there in July 1828, with his wife, children, and parents, and lived there for the rest of his life.

The Marsden Rocks were known as a rendezvous of smugglers, but the place seemed uninhabitable. Nevertheless, Allan's superhuman energy and industry transformed the limestone cliff into a large dwelling house.

Having hollowed a wide ledge on the face of the rock and connected it with the land above, he built upon it a large timber hut, part of which formed a tavern called The Grotto, and part a farmhouse. Within the adjoining rock, on the same level, Allan dug out fifteen large rooms, most of which were lighted by windows hewn in the cliff overlooking the sea. The total length of the excavated chambers, each of which received a name, such as the 'gaol room', the 'devil's chamber', the 'circular room', and so forth, was 120 feet, their greatest height 20 feet, and their greatest breadth 30 feet. On the waste ground above the excavations Allan introduced rabbits for shooting, and the farmhouse and ledge he stocked with domestic animals.

During the twenty-one years that Allan lived with his family in the rock he rarely visited neighbouring towns. He rescued several vessels in distress off the coast, and in 1844 he saved from drowning some boys who had wandered into the caves below his dwelling; an act commemorated in a poem entitled 'The Mercy at Marsden Rock'. Allan was nevertheless regarded by his neighbours with many misgivings, and the excise officers, suspecting him to be a smuggler, frequently molested him. In 1848 the lord of the manor claimed rent from him as the owner of the surface ground, and on his denial of his liability served him with a process of ejectment. Allan refused to quit, and brought a suit against the landlord, by which his right of habitation was upheld, but each side had to pay its own costs. Amid these anxieties Allan's health gave way, and he died on 31 August 1849, in his fifty-first year. He was buried in the presence of his parents, who had lived with him and who survived him, in Whitburn churchyard, and his tombstone bore the inscription, 'The Lord is my rock and my salvation'.

Allan's family continued to live for some years at Marsden after his death. One of his sons inherited his passion for excavation, and his daughter, from the readiness with which she aided distressed ships, was compared to Grace Darling. The strange structure was for many years 'one of the principal curiosities of the north of England', and many descriptions of it were published by local writers. It lasted until February 1865, when it was destroyed by a cliff fall. The Marsden Grotto remains in use, linked to a hotel.

SIDNEY LEE, *rev.* H. C. G. MATTHEW

Sources *N&Q*, 8 (1853), 539, 630, 647 · *GM*, 2nd ser., 32 (1849), 440 · *Marsden rock, or, The story of Peter Allan and Marsden marine grotto* (1848) · J. Latimer, *Local records, or, Historical register of remarkable events which have occurred in Northumberland and Durham ... 1832–57* (1857) · J. Murray, *A handbook for travellers in Durham and Northumberland* (1873) · private information (2004)

Allan, Peter John (1825–1848), poet, was born at York on 6 June 1825, the third son of Dr Colin Allan and Jane Gibbon. His father became the chief medical officer of Halifax, Nova Scotia, and so Allan spent the majority of his childhood there, before moving to Fredericton, New Brunswick, on his father's retirement in 1836. For a time Allan studied at King's College, New Brunswick, but left without taking a degree in order to study law. Encouraged, however, by the publication of several of his early poems in two local newspapers, he abandoned his studies and

devoted himself to the preparation of a volume of poetry. Having secured sufficient subscriptions to underwrite the cost, Allan sent the manuscript to England for publication. Before the book was printed, however, he was seized with fever, and died in Fredericton on 21 October 1848, at the age of twenty-three.

In 1853, the *Poetical Remains of Peter John Allan, Esq.* was published in London. The volume contains a short biographical notice of the poet, written by his brother J. McGrigor Allan. Allan's verse was indebted to the intellectual and stylistic influence of the Romantic poets, Lord Byron in particular. Among the most effective of his poems are 'The Isles of the Blest', 'The Land of Dreams', and 'Sonnet to Nature', all of which attempt to describe the ideal reality that is revealed to the poet through his imaginative engagement with the natural world. Although it received unenthusiastic reviews in its day, more recently Allan's poetry has been praised for its 'intellectual toughness' in eschewing 'the moralistic attitudes and sentimental tone' of mid-nineteenth-century provincial Canadian verse (Vincent). CHARLES BRAYNE

Sources T. B. Vincent, 'Allan, Peter John', *DCB*, vol. 7 · *Poetical remains of Peter John Allan, Esq.*, ed. H. Christmas (1853)

Allan, Robert (1774–1841), poet, was born on 4 November 1774, at Kilbarchan, Renfrewshire, the third of ten children of William Allan, a flax dresser, and his wife, Mary Loudon. He became a muslin-weaver by trade, and on 14 February 1801 he married Janet Lang of Kilbarchan.

Allan also wrote songs, which earned the praise of Robert Tannahill, like him a Renfrewshire weaver and songwriter. R. A. Smith set some to music in his *Scottish Minstrel* (1820), and a number of them appeared in the *Harp of Renfrewshire* published the same year. A collection of Allan's poems entitled *Evening Hours* was printed by subscription in 1836, without great success. He had reared a large family, and was poor and discontented, when he sailed to the United States, where his youngest son was a portrait painter. He died at New York on 1 June 1841, six days after landing, from a cold caught during the journey.

FRANCIS ESPINASSE, *rev.* SARAH COUPER

Sources C. Rogers, *The modern Scottish minstrel, or, The songs of Scotland of the past half-century*, 2 (1856), 169–88 · W. Anderson, *The Scottish nation*, 1 (1866), 116–17 · J. G. Wilson, ed., *The poets and poetry of Scotland*, 1 (1876), 510–11 · Chambers, *Scots.* (1868–70), 1.32 · D. Baptie, ed., *Musical Scotland, past and present: being a dictionary of Scottish musicians from about 1400 till the present time* (1894) · bap. reg. Scot. · m. reg. Scot.

Allan, Robert (1806–1863). *See under* Allan, Thomas (1777–1833).

Allan, (Maria Caterina) Rosalbina Caradori- [Caradori-] (1800–1865), singer, was born in Milan. Her father, Baron de Munck, was an Alsatian and a colonel in the French army. Her mother, whose maiden name, Carradori, she adopted (and always so spelt in Italy), came from St Petersburg. Owing to her father's death Rosalbina had, like several other people of 'good' family whose fortunes had suffered in the revolutionary wars, to adopt music as a profession. She was trained by her mother,

(Maria Caterina) **Rosalbina Caradori-Allan** (1800–1865), by John Hayter, pubd 1827 [as Cresea in *Medea in Corinto* by Simone Mayr]

spoke four languages, and was always considered a perfect lady. After a tour in France and Germany she was engaged for the King's Theatre, London, where she first appeared as Cherubino in *Le nozze di Figaro* on 12 January 1822. Her salary for this season was £300, rising, over the following four seasons, ultimately to £1200. In 1822–7 she sang leading soprano parts, among them Vitellia in Mozart's *La clemenza di Tito*, Zerlina in his *Don Giovanni*, and Rosina in *Il barbiere di Siviglia*, alongside some of the greatest singers of the day—Angelica Catalani, G. B. Velluti, and Giuditta Pasta. In 1824 she married Edward Thomas Allan, the secretary of the King's Theatre; they had one son, from whom at her death she was painfully estranged. Allan predeceased her, at an unknown date.

Rosalbina Caradori-Allan spent the years 1830–32 singing leading parts in Venice, Milan, and Paris. At Venice she created Juliet in Bellini's *I Capuleti e i Montecchi* (11 March 1830); at La Scala she performed the hero's part in Meyerbeer's *Il crociato in Egitto*, originally written for the castrato Velluti, rather than the heroine's role which she had undertaken in London. She then returned to Britain for good, sang one more season of Italian opera in 1834, and afterwards limited herself almost wholly to concerts and oratorio, which suited her better at a time when opera singing was growing more energetic, even violent. She had already sung the soprano solo at the first British performance of Beethoven's ninth symphony (21 March 1825), had taken part in the York, Leicester, and Three Choirs festivals, and performed in the 1834 Handel festival in Westminster Abbey. In 1836 she sang at the Manchester festival with Maria Malibran, and in 1846 took part in the first performance of Mendelssohn's *Elijah* at Birmingham. She took occasional engagements overseas, in New York (1838, first US performance of Donizetti's *L'elisir d'amore*) and, as late as 1852, when she was semi-retired, in St Petersburg in concert with Balfe. She developed cancer of the neck glands, a painful illness, and died at Elm Lodge, Surbiton Hill Road, Kingston, Surrey, on 15 October 1865.

Contemporary estimates were much affected by Caradori-Allan's standing as a well-born person. Her singing was said to be most musicianly and tasteful but lacking in force; her voice, sweet but small, could be expressive, but she failed when she attempted grandeur in Spontini's *La vestale* (London, 1826). For Chorley she was 'one of those first-class singers of the second class with whom it would be hard to find fault, save want of fire'.

W. B. SQUIRE, *rev.* JOHN ROSSELLI

Sources J. Ebers, *Seven years of the King's Theatre* (1828) · J. E. Cox, *Musical recollections of the last half-century*, 2 vols. (1872) · R. Edgcumbe, *Musical reminiscences, containing an account of the Italian opera in England from 1773*, 4th edn (1834) · *The Times* (19 Oct 1865) · *Vincenzo Bellini: epistolario*, ed. L. Cambi (Milan, 1943) · M. Girardi and F. Rossi, eds., *Il Teatro La Fenice: cronologia degli spettacoli*, 2 vols. (1989) · G. Tintori, 'Cronologia', in C. Gatti, *Il Teatro alla Scala* (1964) · Castil-Blaze [F. H.-J. Blaze], *L'opéra-italien de 1548 à 1856* (Paris, 1856) · H. F. Chorley, *Thirty years' musical recollections*, 2 vols. (1862) · B. Labat-Poussin, ed., *Archives du Théâtre National de l'Opéra* (Paris, 1977) · d. cert.

Archives Archives Nationales, Paris, AJ¹³ · Biblioteca Nazionale Centrale, Florence, Fondo Lanari, Carteggi Vari · Fondazione Levi, Venice, Archivio del Teatro La Fenice

Likenesses J. Hayter, lithograph, 1827, BM, NPG [*see illus.*] · Hullmandel (as Cresea in *Medea* by S. Mayr; after Hayter) · engraving, repro. in Ebers, *Seven years of the King's Theatre* · ten prints, Harvard TC

Wealth at death under £4000: resworn probate, Sept 1866, *CGPLA Eng. & Wales* (1865)

Allan, Thomas (1777–1833), mineralogist, was born at Edinburgh on 17 July 1777, the eldest of ten children born to Robert Allan (1740–1818), a partner in Allan and Stewart, bankers and merchants, and his wife, Anne, daughter of William Learmonth. After education at Edinburgh high school he entered his father's bank, but took to scientific pursuits from his childhood. At the peace of Amiens he visited Paris, made scientific acquaintances, and began a mineralogical collection in Dauphiné. He married, on 1 January 1806, Christian (1778–1817), daughter of George and Juliet Smith of Burnhall, co. Durham. They had five children; Christian died at Turin, Italy, on 14 May 1817.

In 1808 Allan published an *Alphabetical list of the names of minerals at present most familiar in the English, French, and German languages* and he was the reputed author of a *Sketch of Mr. Davy's Lectures in Geology, from Notes Taken by a Private Gentleman* (concerning Humphry Davy), which appeared about 1811. He afterwards travelled in Ireland and England; in 1812 he visited the Faeroe Islands, and sent an account of their mineralogy to the Royal Society of Edinburgh. In 1811 the Bavarian mineralogist Karl Giesecke shipped to Denmark a collection of minerals, formed during six years' residence in Greenland. The ship was captured by a French privateer and retaken by an English frigate, and the boxes, their contents considered to be of little value, were sold at Leith to Allan for £40. They contained a quantity of the rare mineral cryolite, worth some £5000, and a new mineral, later named, after the purchaser, allanite. Allan discovered the identity of the collector and the provenance of the samples only in 1812, and was pleased to meet Giesecke when he returned to Leith with a fresh collection from Greenland.

The following year Allan supported Giesecke's successful application for the professorship of mineralogy at Dublin. Allan continued to increase his collection, with the assistance of W. Haidinger, a German geologist, until it became the finest in Scotland. Allan was an admirer of Hutton, and published papers on his theories in the Edinburgh *Transactions*. He also wrote the article 'Diamond' for the *Encyclopaedia Britannica*. He was elected to the Royal Society of Edinburgh in 1805, and to the Royal Society of London in 1815. He was a public-spirited citizen, filled many municipal offices, and was a liberal contributor to Edinburgh charities. He took over from his father as the proprietor of the *Caledonian Mercury*. He died of apoplexy on 12 September 1833, at Linden Hall, Northumberland, and was buried at St Cuthbert's churchyard, Edinburgh. His eldest son, **Robert Allan** (1806–1863), advocate and banker, also took an interest in mineralogy. He accompanied his father on a geological excursion to Cornwall and travelled widely in Europe. His *Manual of Mineralogy* (1834) was illustrated by his own fine drawings of crystals.

[ANON.], *rev.* ANITA MCCONNELL

Sources W. V. Farrar, 'Thomas Allan, mineralogist: an autobiographical fragment', *Annals of Science*, 24 (1968), 115–20 · A. L. Reade, 'Pedigree XVIII: Anderson of Clough ... with Reid, Allan', *The Reades of Blackwood Hill in the parish of Horton, Staffordshire: a record of their descendants* (privately printed, London, 1906), 65–9 · *GM*, 1st ser., 103/2 (1833), 382 · Burke, *Gen. GB* (1846–9) · *The Scotsman* (18 Sept 1833) · private information (2004)

Archives NHM, catalogue of mineral collection · NHM, notebooks

Likenesses H. Raeburn, portrait, 1801 · H. Raeburn, portrait, 1805 · portrait, National Museum of Scotland

Wealth at death £2190 5s. 6d.—Robert Allan: confirmation, 1863, NA Scot., SC 70/1/118

Allan, Thomas (*fl.* 1800–1840), lawyer and political adviser to the Wesleyan Methodists, was one of the most important laymen of his generation, but his biographical details remain unknown. When in 1799–1800 parliamentary attempts were made to exclude itinerant preaching and Sunday schools from the protection of the Toleration Act, Methodists could not remain unpolitical; in 1803 they appointed a committee of privileges to guard their rights, and a connexional solicitor to advise on the sudden propensity of magistrates, it was thought *ultra vires*, to refuse licences to dissenting preachers. Thomas Allan was appointed solicitor and a founder member of the committee. In 1811 Lord Sidmouth took advantage of disorder in the country to launch another bill to restrict the scope of the Toleration Act. He hoped to circumvent Methodist

opposition by a private negotiation with Thomas Coke and Adam Clarke, but he was routed by a vivid agitation in the country masterminded by Allan in alliance with the dissenters. At the crucial point (9 May 1812) Allan personally pressed the prime minister, Spencer Perceval, for legislation unequivocally to establish the rights evangelicals had long believed they possessed. Two days later Perceval was dead, but Allan lobbied his successor, Lord Liverpool, and members of both houses of parliament, and secured the passing of the Toleration Act 1812, drafted by himself.

Allan based his case on the conservative, disciplined, loyal, and protestant character of the connexion, and in that spirit he watched its interests in the troubled years before and after Peterloo. Allan was too protestant to want equal rights for all religious communities: a founder (in 1813) and leading propagandist of the Protestant Union and much involved in the estate affairs of his 'old friend glorious John Lord Eldon' (Allan to his son Thomas, 9 March 1829, Thomas Allan MSS), he was indeed an Eldonian, a committed supporter of the protestant settlement. At the Catholic emancipation crisis in 1829, however, Allan accepted Jabez Bunting's argument that Methodists should take no corporate stand, whatever they did individually. Allan's protestantism also turned him against Lord John Russell's education proposals in 1839. He felt that, unless the government were kept out of national education, there would be no preventing public money going to support popery and other bad causes; Bunting felt, rightly in the short term, that he could establish a position of privilege for Wesleyanism.

In 1810 Allan had presented Bunting with a memorandum calling for major reorganization in the financing and administration of missions, the selection and training of preachers, the spiritual instruction of Methodist children, and the clarification of Methodism's legal position. Bunting made this programme his life's work, but the two drifted ever further apart, and the obliteration of Allan's memory was the work of the Bunting party, a work frustrated only by the modern recovery of Allan's papers. A scholarly man, Allan left a large theological library to the Methodist conference; but as a local preacher he chose to minister in workhouses and small chapels, and had no use for the high doctrine of the pastoral office with which Bunting identified himself. When the latter introduced seminary training for ministers Allan opposed it, foreseeing the divisions it would create within the ministry; and by 1840 he had concluded, again rightly, that the great age of Wesleyan expansion was over. Thomas Allan disappears from the record at this time; details of his death have not been traced.

W. R. WARD

Sources JRL, Methodist Archives and Research Centre, Thomas Allan MSS · D. Hempton, 'Thomas Allan and Methodist politics, 1800–1840', *History*, new ser., 67 (1982), 13–31; repr. in D. Hempton, *The religion of the people* (1996), 109–29 · D. N. Hempton, 'Allan, Thomas', *The Blackwell dictionary of evangelical biography, 1730–1860*, ed. D. M. Lewis (1995) · W. R. Ward, *Religion and society in England, 1790–1850* (1972) · *The early correspondence of Jabez Bunting, 1820–1829*, ed. W. R. Ward, CS, 4th ser., 11 (1972) · *Early Victorian Methodism: the correspondence of Jabez Bunting, 1830–1858*, ed. W. R. Ward (1976)

Archives JRL, Methodist Archives and Research Centre | JRL, Jabez Bunting MSS

Allan, (Babette Louisa) Valerie. *See* Hobson, (Babette Louisa) Valerie (1917–1998).

Allan, Sir William (1782–1850), painter, was born on 4 October 1782 and baptized on 11 October in the Old Kirk, Edinburgh, one of the three children of William Allan, the macer at the court of session and his wife, Mary, *née* Cram. The family lived at 19 Parliament Square. He was educated at Edinburgh high school before, about 1795, being apprenticed to Walter Smeaton or Smiton, a coach painter on Leith Walk, and on his death to Messrs Crichton and Field, also coachmakers of Leith Walk. His skill at painting coats-of-arms on carriage panels led him to be commissioned to paint anatomical preparations in the Edinburgh Surgeons' Square Hall. In 1799 he enrolled at the Trustees' Academy, where he studied under John Graham. There Allan met fellow student David Wilkie, an artist with whom he was to show considerable affinity and maintain close, lifelong relations. About 1803 he moved to London. His early historical subjects included *Paul and Virginia*, which, together with the landscape *Inver, Near Dunkeld*, was shown at the Royal Academy in 1803. This début commenced a lifelong association with the institution which was to be marked by participation in almost all of its annual exhibitions between 1815 and 1849, a zenith being reached in 1835 when he was elected a Royal Academician. In 1805 Allan showed *Gipsy Boy and Ass*, reputedly in the manner of Opie, though a lack of recognition and employment meant that in the same year he set sail for Russia. His ship damaged in a storm, he disembarked at Memel, East Prussia (now Klaipeda, Lithuania), and there spent the summer painting portraits of the diplomatic community, including the Danish consul. Thereafter he travelled overland to St Petersburg, encountering the Russian army on its way to Austerlitz. Through the agency of Sir Alexander Crichton, the brother of his former employer, then physician to Tsar Alexander's family, Allan acquired a number of patrons from the Russian court. Foremost among these were members of the Potocki family, influential members of the Polish landed gentry, for whom Allan painted *The Raising of Lazarus*, and with whom Allan resided at their Ukrainian estates of Zofiówka and Tulchin. At the first he executed six views of the Ukraine's most renowned picturesque park, which were to be reproduced as engravings by Wilhelm Friedrich Schlotterbeck in *Sophiowka* (Vienna, 1815), a poem by the leading Polish Romantic Stanislaw Trembecki. For this work he collaborated with Trembecki's French translator, the Comte Auguste de La Garde-Chambonas, whom he had met at Zofiówka in 1811. Allan's illustrations comprised six small views of the park, featuring the grottoes, cascades, and Island of Love. At Tulchin, in 1813, he painted his self-portrait in the costume of a Circassian (exh. Edinburgh Exhibition Society, 1814; engraved by W. H. Lizars).

In 1808 Allan was in Odessa and travelled across the Crimea and into the Kuban region. He joined the entourage of the duc de Richelieu, then governor of Odessa, through

Sir William Allan (1782–1850), by William Nicholson, 1818 [in Circassian dress]

whom he was introduced to Arslan Giray, a surviving member of the Crimean Tartar Khan family. Allan painted Giray's portrait and chose the story of the prince's elopement as the subject of one of several major oil paintings on the picturesque tragedy of life of the peoples of the southern parts of the Russian empire that he was to create after his return to Scotland in 1814: *Haslan Gheray Conducting Alkazia across the Kuban* (1816; Makhachkala Museum, Dagestan; variant, priv. coll.). This, together with *Circassian Prince on Horseback Selling Two Boys* (also known as 'Border Guards') and *Bashkirs Conducting Convicts* (both 1815; State Hermitage Museum, St Petersburg), was bought by the future Tsar Nicholas I, after a visit to Allan's Edinburgh studio in 1816. A further, contemporary, work with a similar theme, though larger scale and an interior with neoclassical groupings, was *Circassian Chief Selling Captives to a Turkish Bashaw*, which was won by the earl of Wemyss in a lottery organized by James Gibson Lockhart.

Following his return to Edinburgh, Allan held a one-man exhibition there in January 1817 and established his studio, replete with his collection of exotic arms and costumes, some of which he wore himself, as one of the most fashionable in the Scottish capital. He published *Haslan Gheray: a Narrative Illustrative of the Subject of a Painting* (Edinburgh, 1817), with his own etching derived from the oil as a frontispiece. It reveals the moment of escape as the young prince leads his bride and horse across the river and away from the pursuers sent by her father. His early oils of this period reveal increased theatricality and a sense of humour or even Dutch burlesque (he was renowned as an entertainer and mimic) while still concentrating on eastern romantic genre. Examples included *Jewish Wedding in Poland*, *The Cossack Courtship*, and *Tatar banditti Dividing the Spoil* (1817; Tate collection). His *A Press Gang* (exh. Royal Academy, 1818) was regarded by many as his finest genre painting. He became the preferred artist of Lockhart and Walter Scott, painting the latter's portrait on several occasions, as well as those of his children and circle, and executing drawings of the interior of Abbotsford. His subjects included the poets William Laidlaw and James Hogg, the actors William Murray, Charles Mackay, and James Russell, the Leeds surgeon William Hey, and the publisher William Blackwood. Many of these works survive in the Abbotsford House collection, and the National Portrait galleries in London and Edinburgh. He also established himself as a leading graphic artist, illustrating the Waverley novels (published 1820) and appearing with David Roberts and Owen Jones as an illustrator of *Ancient Spanish Ballads Historical and Romantic* (1842). Under Lockhart's and Scott's influence he was encouraged to take up Scottish history subjects. His first such painting was *The Murder of Archbishop Sharp on Magus Moor* (exh. RA, 1821), this being followed by such works as *John Knox Admonishing Mary Queen of Scots* (exh. Royal Scottish Academy, 1823; priv. coll.) and *Regent Moray Shot by Hamilton* (exh. RA, 1825; priv. coll.). In 1826 he was appointed master of the Trustees' Academy, Edinburgh; his pupils included Sir George Harvey, Robert Scott Lauder, Thomas Duncan, James Drummond, William Bell Scott, and John Crawford Wintour. In 1829 he was afflicted by an illness of the eyes which led him to travel to Italy and the western parts of the Ottoman empire to recuperate. Upon his return to Edinburgh he continued with a mix of national and eastern romantic narrative visions, his principal canvases including dramas such as *Lord Byron Reposing in the House of a Turkish Fisherman after Swimming the Hellespont* (exh. 1831; priv. coll.), *The Slave Market, Constantinople* (exh. RA, 1838; National Gallery of Scotland, Edinburgh), *Christmas Eve* (undated; Aberdeen Art Gallery), and *The Murder of David Rizzio* (1833; National Gallery of Scotland, Edinburgh).

In 1834 Allan visited Spain and Morocco, his works from this trip including the watercolour *A Street in Cadiz* (British Museum) and studies of the Alhambra. In 1838 he was appointed president of the Royal Scottish Academy, having been influential in its establishment; and in 1841 succeeded Wilkie as queen's limner in Scotland, a post which brought with it a knighthood. He knew Charles Dickens, was the first artist to paint a scene from *Nicholas Nickleby*, and drew Dickens's portrait when Dickens received the freedom of Edinburgh in 1841. He was also an honorary member of the academies of New York and Philadelphia. In 1843, after several visits to France and Belgium, Allan extended his concern with battle scenes with the panoramic *Waterloo from the French Side* (V&A, Apsley House, London), which was purchased by the duke of Wellington. A large-scale companion to this, 'from the British side' (Royal Military College, Sandhurst), was entered unsuccessfully by Allan in the Westminster Hall competition of

1846. In 1844 he revisited St Petersburg where Tsar Nicholas commissioned him to paint *Peter the Great Teaching his Subjects the Art of Shipbuilding* (exh. RA, 1845). In the mid-1840s he was on intimate terms with David Octavius Hill, who made several striking calotype portraits of Allan (Scot. NPG and City Library, Edinburgh). In 1847 he visited Germany and France. He died of bronchitis, after years of a chronic windpipe disease, in his studio at 72 Great King Street, Edinburgh, on 23 February 1850 and was buried in the Dean cemetery on 1 March. At the time of his death he was painting his last patriotic epic, *The Battle of Bannockburn* (NG Scot.). Unmarried, he was survived by a niece, Catherine Allan, who had served as his housekeeper for much of his life. An auction sale of his paintings, drawings, engravings, books, armour, and costumes, held by C. B. Tait and T. Nisbet on 18–20 April 1850, was followed by a posthumous exhibition in 1851. This was curated by David Octavius Hill and held at Alexander Hill's Galleries, 67 Princes Street, Edinburgh. JEREMY HOWARD

Sources J. Howard and others, *William Allan: artist adventurer* (2001) [exhibition catalogue, City Art Centre, Edinburgh, 30 June – 6 Oct 2001] · D. Irwin and F. Irwin, *Scottish painters at home and abroad, 1700–1900* (1975), 204–13 · D. Macmillan, *Painting in Scotland: the golden age* (1986), 179–80 [exhibition catalogue, U. Edin., Talbot Rice Gallery, and Tate Gallery, London, 1986] · *Art Journal*, 11 (1849), 108–9 · B. Allen and L. Dukelskaya, eds., *British art treasures from the Russian imperial collections in the Hermitage* (1996), 108–10, 190–91 [exhibition catalogue, Yale U. CBA, 5 Oct 1996 – 5 Jan 1997] · W. Allan, 'Sir William Allan', *The Connoisseur*, 186 (1974), 88–93 · A. Bivar, 'Mohammed Ali, son of Kazem-Beq: Scottish missionaries and Russian orientalism', *Bulletin of the School of Oriental and African Studies*, 57 (1994), 283–302 · W. Allan, *Haslan Gheray: a narrative illustrative of the subject of a painting* (1817) · W. D. McKay and F. Rinder, *The Royal Scottish Academy, 1826–1916* (1917), 13–15 · Graves, *RA exhibitors* · Chambers, *Scots.* (1868–70) · Anderson, *Scot. nat.* · [J. G. Lockhart], *Peter's letters to his kinsfolk*, ed. W. Ruddick (1977), 115–23 · J. L. Caw, *Scottish painting past and present, 1620–1908* (1908), 108–10 · W. D. McKay, *The Scottish school of painting* (1906), 141–6 · C. Ferrard and others, *Visions of the Ottoman empire* (1994), 24–5 [exhibition catalogue, Scot. NPG, 16 Aug – 6 Nov 1994] · J. Cannizzo, *O Caledonia! Sir Walter Scott and the creation of Scotland* (1999) [CD-ROM] · b. cert. · J. Howard and A. Szczerski, 'William Allan, Greek beauty and Polish romanticism', *Apollo*, 153 (2001), 47–55

Archives NL Scot., corresp. · U. Edin. L., corresp.

Likenesses W. Nicholson, oils, 1818, Scot. NPG [*see illus.*] · W. Bewick, chalk drawing, 1824, Scot. NPG · W. Allan, self-portrait, oils, 1835, Royal Scot. Acad. · D. O. Hill, calotypes, c.1843–1849, Scot. NPG · D. O. Hill, calotypes, c.1843–1849, Edinburgh City Library · T. Faed, group portrait, oils, 1849 (*Sir Walter Scott and his friends at Abbotsford*), Scot. NPG · R. Adamson, photographs, NPG · A. Geddes, etchings, BM · D. O. Hill, photographs, NPG · J. Watson-Gordon, oils, Royal Academy · prints, repro. in *Art Journal*, 11

Allan, William (1813–1874), trade unionist, was born at Carrickfergus in Antrim, the son of a Scottish cotton-mill manager. His parents soon moved back to Scotland where at the age of twelve he began work as a cotton piecer, but then shifted to an engineering apprenticeship at Holdsworths in Glasgow. He married Holdsworth's niece, and on finishing his apprenticeship moved to Liverpool and then to the railway works at Crewe, where he became an active member of the Journeymen Steam Engine and Machine Makers' Friendly Society, also known as the 'Old Mechanics' and one of the strongest engineering unions at the time. In 1848 the general secretary of the union resigned, having been involved in a long court case over the legality of giving financial assistance to strikers in the railway works at Newton-le-Willows in Manchester, and Allan, who had been active in this dispute, was appointed in his place. In this capacity and then as general secretary of the Amalgamated Society of Engineers, Allan was to be until his death in 1874 the undisputed leader of the skilled engineers and one of the most prominent trade unionists in the country.

At the time of his appointment as secretary of the Steam Engine Makers Allan was already well known as an advocate of the wider amalgamation of the engineering unions, and in 1850 he took the initiative in organizing a major conference on the subject in Birmingham attended by delegates from thirty-seven societies. Although this conference not only approved the principle, but also worked out many of the practical details and appointed a committee headed by Allan to set up a new permanent organization, the actual launch of the Amalgamated Society of Engineers (ASE) in January 1851 was a rather uncertain affair. A large number of the local branches of the Steam Engine Makers refused to join and only a few branches of the other societies affiliated; indeed initially the ASE had only 5000 members, fewer than the Steam Engine Makers had had on its own. Allan persisted and, with strong support from William Newton of the London Steam Engine Makers, managed gradually to build up the strength of the new union. This development was not at first at all welcome to the employers, and the ASE's attempt to limit the spread of overtime and piecework led to a major national lock-out in 1852, ending in a humiliating defeat for the union which included the signing of an anti-union pledge on the return to work.

However, this turned out to be only a short-term setback, for both the general economic climate and the expansion of the engineering industry were highly favourable to skilled trade unionism in this period, and within a few years the ASE had established a formidable bargaining position and secured recognition from the employers. By the mid-1860s the union had over 30,000 members (about 75 per cent of those eligible), organized in over 300 branches, with an annual income of over £80,000 and financial reserves of around £140,000. This unprecedented achievement led many other unions to adopt the methods and even the exact constitution of the ASE, eventually leading to the coining of the phrase 'new model union' for this type of organization. Most of the methods used by Allan within the ASE were, however, the long-established methods of the Steam Engine Makers, albeit now practised at the level of a major national industry. In particular, high levels of individual subscription combined with tight central control of branch spending made it possible to provide generous welfare benefits, and to use these both to tie the membership more closely to the union and to finance major industrial disputes. Allan's own contribution was his outstanding ability as a trade union officer: cautious over industrial disputes, expert in negotiation, with an immense capacity for hard work on

points of administrative detail and an unimpeachable personal integrity. He was elected unopposed as general secretary in every election over a 24-year period and steered the union's affairs very ably through the ups and downs of cyclical unemployment.

Allan also took part in wider trade union and political movements. He was the original proposer of the establishment of the London Trades Council in 1859 and became one of its most influential leaders. He was also active in the Reform League from 1865 and in the campaign for reform of trade union law which reached its peak at the time of the royal commission on trade unions of 1867–9, before which, as a member of the 'junta' or five-member Conference of Amalgamated Trades, he was an important witness. He was a major speaker at the first Co-operative Congress in 1869 and served as treasurer of the Trades Union Congress in 1871. He also became a practising Anglican, serving as churchwarden for the parish of Christchurch, London, as a member of the St Saviour's board of works, and as vice-president of the National Sunday League.

Allan was a central figure in the early development of British craft unionism. He was a dark, vigorous-looking man, with a shrewd judgement of his peers and a blunt way of expressing himself, but also a reputation for being kind-hearted and generous. Little is recorded of his personal life other than that he and his wife had five children. He suffered from Bright's disease for some years before his death on 15 October 1874 at his home, 90 Blackfriars Road, London; he was buried in Norwood cemetery.

ALASTAIR J. REID

Sources 'Allan, William', *DLB*, vol. 1 · J. B. Jefferys, *The story of the engineers, 1800–1945* [1946] · H. Pelling, *A history of British trade unionism* (1963) · *CGPLA Eng. & Wales* (1874)
Wealth at death under £3000: probate, 4 Nov 1874, *CGPLA Eng. & Wales*

Allan, Sir William (1837–1903), engineer and politician, born at Dundee on 29 November 1837, was the third son of James Allan (d. 1883), machine maker, and his wife, Margaret Dickson (d. 1879). After being educated in local schools, Allan served his apprenticeship as an engineer at his father's Seabraes foundry, Dundee. As a journeyman he moved to Glasgow, and in 1856 he went for a short time to Paterson, New Jersey. In 1857 he joined the Royal Navy as engineer, and spent the next three years mainly at foreign stations. In 1861, when the civil war broke out in America, it was said that Allan's 'love of adventure' led him to become chief engineer on board a ship seeking to break through the North's blockade of southern ports. He was in Charleston harbour when ships of the federal government bombarded the city on 21 December 1861, and was captured and taken to the Old Capitol Prison, Washington. Released on parole, he returned to Dundee, resuming work at Seabraes foundry. His varied experience had made him a competent workman, and when the North-Eastern Engineering Company was formed at Sunderland in 1866 he was engaged as foreman over one of the departments. However, by 1868 the company was in difficulties, and Allan was appointed manager. Under his control the concern flourished, especially after its removal to Wallsend-on-Tyne. Allan married, in 1870, Jane, daughter of Walter Beattie of Lockerbie. They had at least one son, Walter B. Allan.

In 1886 Allan founded his own company, the Scotia Engine Works, at Sunderland, and he remained active head of the firm until 1900. The business was then amalgamated with the firm of Richardson, Westgarth & Co. Ltd, of which Allan became a director. He was also until his death chairman of the Albyn Line Ltd, shipowners of Sunderland.

From his youth Allan was an advanced radical, and showed practical sympathy with the working classes. He was the first large employer to introduce an eight-hour day in his own works. At a by-election at Gateshead on 24 February 1893 Allan was returned as a Liberal, and continued to represent the town until his death. His speeches in the Commons were known more for their force than their elegance, but were said to display sincerity and common sense. His practical knowledge led him to oppose strenuously the introduction of the Belleville type of boiler into the navy.

In addition to his other activities Allan was, from 1871, a prolific writer of patriotic Scottish songs and poems, publishing volumes such as *Heather-Bells* (1875), *Roses and Thistles* (1878), *Northern Lights* (1889), and *Democratic Chants* (1892). His only technical publication was 'The shipowners' and engineers' guide to the marine engine' (Sunderland, 1880). Allan served as a JP and deputy lieutenant for co. Durham, and was knighted in 1902. He died from heart disease on 28 December 1903 at Scotland House, Sunderland, and was buried in Ryhope Road cemetery, Sunderland. A. H. MILLAR, *rev.* IAN ST JOHN

Sources *Dundee Yearbook* (1903) · *Dundee Advertiser* (29 Dec 1903) · A. Reid, *The bards of Angus and the Mearns* (1897) · *WWW*, 1897–1915 · *WWBMP*, vol. 2 · H. W. Lucy, *A diary of the Unionist parliament, 1895–1900* (1901) · H. W. Lucy, *The Balfourian parliament, 1900–1905* (1906) · *Hansard 4* (1896), 42.80 · d. cert.
Archives Bodl. Oxf., corresp. with Lord Selborne · PRO NIre., corresp. with Castlereagh
Likenesses B. Stone, photograph, 1897, NPG · T. Haddon, oils, probably exh. RA 1899, National Liberal Club, London · P. May, sketch, repro. in Lucy, *The Balfourian parliament*, 109 · Spy [L. Ward], cartoon, repro. in *VF* (1893)
Wealth at death £6957 16s. 7d.: probate, 21 Jan 1904, CGPLA Eng. & Wales

Allanson, Peter [name in religion Athanasius] (1804–1876), historian and abbot of Glastonbury, was born on 11 June 1804 in Castle Street, Holborn, London, the second son of William Walter Allanson and his wife, Mary Ann Barber, from Lambeth. The family was Roman Catholic and Allanson was sent to Ampleforth College in Yorkshire in 1812. The headmaster of Ampleforth at that time was Father Augustine Baines (a future bishop), and the school, though small, was a good one. Allanson senior's business suffered, as many did, with the coming of peace, and Allanson was withdrawn from school in 1816. Realizing that he had a vocation, he returned to Ampleforth to join the Benedictines and he made his solemn profession on 2 June 1821.

In 1825 a problem arose about money when Allanson inherited £1000. Until 1858, in the special conditions of the mission, monks retained their own money. Prior Burgess wanted the money for Ampleforth, but Allanson appealed to the president-general, Richard Marsh, who supported him. To make peace Marsh accepted Allanson at St Edmund's, Douai, France, at that time in his care, then later sent him home. Burgess received Allanson back in peace and he resumed his ordination course, being made priest on 27 June 1828. He was called to the mission in November and he was placed with the Riddells at Swinburne, about 19 miles north-west of Newcastle upon Tyne. The mission was small and scattered. At first the chapel was in the house, but the present church, which stands nearby, was built in 1842. Allanson continued to live in a house on the estate, Swinburne Hermitage.

In 1842 general chapter made Allanson historiographer of the congregation; this work occupied most of his time for the next sixteen years and renders him a figure of substantial importance in English monastic history. His work consists of five volumes of *Records*, transcriptions of documents, largely in Latin; two volumes of *Acts of General Chapter* of the English Benedictine congregation, which has met, with minor variations, every four years since 1621; three volumes of *History*, arranged for the most part to correspond with the four-year cycle of general chapters; two volumes of *Biography*; and finally a much thinner volume giving a history of the various Benedictine missions in England. The whole manuscript was produced by a secretary, Glendinning, a shadowy figure about whom little is known. Allanson says that he first assembled the records and documents, then wrote the *History*, and only at the end put together the two volumes of *Biography*, although these had been the original project and, for the reader, they are the best starting point. The work was nearly complete by 1854. He persuaded other monks to lend him documents, but he also quotes letters and documents still kept at Lille and Douai in France, which he probably visited. His use of sources was careful and critical, and there are many lengthy footnotes, as well as the huge collection of *Records*. If he was uncertain, he said so, explaining why. The manuscript is undated, but the work was clearly slow; his writings show that he found it wearisome. Allanson seems to have wanted his work to remain unpublished during his life. Two copies exist, one at Ampleforth, and the other, a slight revision, at Downside. The whole was published on microfiche in 1978, in only about thirty copies.

In 1858 Allanson was elected northern provincial, that is superior of all the monk missioners in the province of York; in 1862 he became titular cathedral prior of Norwich and, in 1874, abbot of Glastonbury. He engaged energetically in missionary affairs and gave financial support to his monastery. He seems to have suffered for many years a disease whose known symptoms are tremulous handwriting and dizziness, which he sometimes found disabling. He remained an active missioner, however, until he died at Swinburne on 13 January 1876. He was buried at Ampleforth. ANSELM CRAMER

Sources A. Allanson, *Biography of the English Benedictines* (1999) · B. Green, ed., *A history of the English Benedictine congregation, 1558–1850* (1978) · P. J. McCann, obituary, *c.*1940, Ampleforth Abbey, Yorkshire · letters, Ampleforth Abbey, Yorkshire · letters, Downside Abbey, near Bath, Birt collection · *Acta Capitulorum Generalium*, 1842, vol. 2, 460 · parish register, Holborn, St Andrew's, LMA, 1804 · *Lincoln's Inn Fields registers*, 19 (1917)

Archives Ampleforth Abbey, Yorkshire, historical collections and works relating to the Benedictines · Downside Abbey, near Bath, historical collections and works relating to the Benedictines

Likenesses drawing, 1947 (after photograph) · photograph, Ampleforth Abbey

Allardice, Robert Barclay [*known as* Captain Barclay] (**1779–1854**), pedestrian, was the son of Robert Barclay (1731–1797) of Ury, Kincardineshire, founder of the town of Stonehaven, who took the name of Allardice upon his marriage to Sarah Ann Allardice (*d.* 1833) in 1776. The marriage was dissolved in 1793, and Mrs Allardice married John Nudd in 1795. Robert was born at Ury, on 25 August 1779, and was educated at Richmond School and Brixton Causeway before succeeding to the family estate after his father's death in 1797. He went into the 23rd regiment in 1805, was promoted captain in 1806, and served in the Walcheren expedition in 1809 as aide-de-camp to the marquess of Huntly. He was promoted major in January 1814, but resigned in March that year. He devoted himself to agriculture and improved the local breed of cattle. He married, on 19 July 1819, Mary (*d.* 1820), daughter of Alexander Dalgarno, of Aberdeen. Their only child, Margaret, married S. Ritchie in 1840, and settled in America.

After his mother's death in July 1833, Captain Barclay claimed the earldom of Airth on the ground of his descent from William, earl of Monteith (*d.* 1694). The case was heard before the House of Lords in 1839; and in 1840 Captain Barclay claimed also the earldoms of Strathearn and Monteith, but proceedings were ultimately dropped.

Captain Barclay was known for his extraordinary pedestrian performances. Powerful physique was a hallmark of the family. His ancestor, the first Barclay of Ury, was one of the strongest men in the kingdom, and his sword, too heavy for ordinary men, was preserved in the family; his grandfather (great-grandson of this first Barclay) was known as 'the Strong', and his father was a 'noted pedestrian', who walked from Ury to London (510 miles) in ten days.

Captain Barclay's most noted feat was walking 1 mile in each of 1000 successive hours. This feat was performed at Newmarket from 1 June to 12 July 1809. His average time of walking the mile varied from 14 min. 54 sec. in the first week to 21 min. 4 sec. in the last, and his weight was reduced from 13 stone 4 lb to 11 stone. He was so little exhausted that he started for the Walcheren expedition on 17 July in perfect health. He had previously accomplished many similar if less dramatic feats, starting at the age of seventeen, when he walked 6 miles within an hour on the London to Croydon road for a wager of 100 guineas. Another outstanding—and rewarding—achievement was to walk 90 miles in 21½ hours in 1801 for 5000 guineas. He also competed in a 24-hour race against the professional

Robert Barclay Allardice [Captain Barclay] (**1779–1854**), by Solomon? Williams, pubd 1809

Abraham Wood, an unusual match, from which Wood had to withdraw with injured feet after six hours. Wagers and challenges aside, Barclay's own lifestyle was one of extraordinary vigour. In 1808, for instance, he started at 5 a.m., walked 30 miles grouse shooting, dined at 5 p.m., walked 60 miles to his house at Ury in eleven hours, then after attending to business walked 16 miles to Laurence Kirk, danced at a ball, returned to Ury by 7 a.m., and spent the next day partridge shooting, having travelled 130 miles and been without sleep for two nights and three days. In 1810–11 he rode twice a week 51 miles to hunt, and after hunting returned the same night. A year later he went 33 miles out and home three times a week for the same purpose.

Barclay had trained under John Smith, the Yorkshire pedestrian, and Will Ward, the pugilist. He earned a high reputation as a trainer himself after preparing Tom Cribb for his second fight with the American Tom Molyneaux. In their first contest in 1810 Cribb, unfit and overweight, had come close to losing. Barclay then took him up to Scotland and gradually put him through a regime similar to his own, with the result that he won the return fight in September 1811 with comparative ease. Barclay described his methods in a pamphlet, *Training for Pedestrianism and Boxing* (1816). Less happily, his attempt to do the same for the Scottish fighter Sandy M'Kay nearly twenty years later ended in tragedy, with M'Kay killed in his return fight with Sandy Byrne in June 1830. Barclay's pedestrian career appears to have ended after his defeat by an officer of the

7th dragoons in a 2 mile race in Hyde Park, London, in 1813, though his achievement of 1000 miles in 1000 hours remained a standard challenge long after his retirement. In 1842 he published a short account of an agricultural tour made in the United States in the preceding spring. He was a strong protectionist, discussing the matter with W. E. Gladstone (the Gladstones were his neighbours at Ury). He died on 8 May 1854, at Ury, having been injured three days previously by a kick from a horse; he was buried at the family burial-ground, known as the Houff, in Ury.   LESLIE STEPHEN, rev. DENNIS BRAILSFORD

Sources H. D. Miles, *Pugilistica: the history of British boxing*, 3 vols. (1906) · *Sporting Magazine* (Nov 1801) · *Sporting Magazine* (Sept 1804) · *Sporting Magazine* (Nov 1804) · *Sporting Magazine* (July 1807) · *Sporting Magazine* (Sept 1807) · *Sporting Magazine* (Oct 1807) · *Sporting Magazine* (Dec 1807) · *Sporting Magazine* (Oct 1808) · *Sporting Magazine* (June 1809) · *Sporting Magazine* (June 1813) · *Sporting Magazine* (Jan 1823) · *Sporting Magazine* (March 1830) · *Sporting Magazine* (July 1830) · *The Times* (16 May 1854) · P. F. Radford, 'From oral tradition to printed record: British sports science in transition, 1805–7', *Proceedings of the XIIth HISPA Congress* (1987), 295–304 · W. Thom, *Pedestrianism* (1813) · Gladstone, *Diaries* · Boase, *Mod. Eng. biog.*
Likenesses R. Dighton, coloured etching, pubd 1809, NPG · S.? Williams, coloured aquatint, pubd 1809, BM, NPG [*see illus.*] · line engraving, pubd 1813, BM · R. M. Hodgetts, mezzotint, pubd 1843 (after J. Giles), NPG · R. M. Hodgetts, mezzotints (after J. Giles), NPG · engraving (after a miniature, 1798), repro. in Miles, *Pugilistica*, 1, facing p. 436

Allardyce, Alexander (1846–1896), journalist and historian, son of James Allardyce, farmer, was born on 21 January 1846 at Tillyminit, Gartly, in the parish of Rhynie, Aberdeenshire. He received his first lessons in Latin from his maternal grandmother and was then educated at Rhynie parish school, Aberdeen grammar school, and the University of Aberdeen. In 1868 he became a sub-editor on the *Friend of India* at Serampore, Bengal. The viceroy, Lord Mayo, appreciated him so highly that he offered him an assistant commissionership, but he kept to journalism. He was on the *Friend of India* until 1875, having apparently at the same time written for the *Indian Statesman*. In 1875 he succeeded John Capper as editor of the *Ceylon Times*, and one of his early experiences of office was tendering an apology to the judicial bench for contempt (*The Times*, London, 25 April 1896). Returning to Europe, he was for a time in Berlin and afterwards in London, where he wrote for *Fraser's Magazine*, the *Spectator*, and other periodicals. In 1877 he settled at Edinburgh as reader to the house of William Blackwood & Sons, and assistant editor of *Blackwood's Magazine*, for which he also wrote quite regularly.

Allardyce was a competent historian, editing the Ochtertyre MSS of John Ramsay as *Scotland and Scotsmen in the Eighteenth Century* (2 vols., 1888), and *Letters from and to Charles Kirkpatrick Sharpe* (2 vols., 1888). He also wrote novels on Indian and Scottish themes. When comparatively young Allardyce had married his cousin, Barbara Anderson, who survived him; there was no family. He died at Portobello, Edinburgh, on 23 April 1896, and was buried in Rhynie parish churchyard.

T. W. BAYNE, rev. H. C. G. MATTHEW

Sources *The Times* (24 April 1896) · *The Scotsman* (24 April 1896) · *Daily Free Press* [Aberdeen] (24 April 1896) · *The Athenaeum* (2 May

1896), 584 · R. H. Smith, *An Aberdeenshire village propaganda forty years ago* (1889)
Archives NL Scot., corresp. with Blackwoods

Allbutt, Sir Thomas Clifford (1836–1925), physician, born at Dewsbury, Yorkshire, on 20 July 1836, was the only son of the Revd Thomas Allbutt, vicar of Dewsbury, and his wife, Marianne, daughter of Robert Wooler, of Dewsbury. Allbutt was sent to St Peter's School, York, from where he entered Gonville and Caius College, Cambridge, in 1855; he gained a classical scholarship there a year later. Profoundly influenced by his reading of Auguste Comte's works on positivism, he turned from studying the classics to medicine. In 1860 he obtained a first-class degree (the only one of the year) in the natural sciences tripos, with distinction in chemistry and geology. After studying medicine at St George's Hospital, London, and taking the Cambridge MB degree in 1861, he went to Paris and attended the clinics of Armand Trousseau, G. B. A. Duchenne, Bazin, and Hardy.

Allbutt's active professional life falls into three periods: from 1861 to 1889 he was an extremely successful consulting physician in Leeds; from 1889 to 1892 he was a commissioner in lunacy in London; and for the remainder of his long life he was regius professor of physic at Cambridge. At Leeds he utilized the early lean years in wide reading, writing medical essays, and pursuing clinical work at the fever hospital, the general infirmary, where he was physician from 1864 to 1884, and the West Riding asylum. During 1865 and 1866 he treated victims of an outbreak of typhus fever by open-air methods, a management which he later advocated for consumption.

During his time at Leeds, Allbutt invented a short clinical thermometer, greatly facilitating the routine taking of temperatures. The early thermometers had been extremely cumbersome, approximately 25 centimetres in length, and taking 20–25 minutes to register, whether placed in the mouth or axilla. In 1870 Allbutt wrote an extensive review entitled *Medical Thermometry*, in which he outlined the history of thermometry and described his own contribution to it: a thermometer approximately 6 inches in length that, as he put it, 'Could live habitually in my pocket, and have as constantly with me as a stethoscope'. His version of the thermometer, devised in 1867, was quickly adopted elsewhere. In 1871 Allbutt also wrote a pioneering monograph on the use of the ophthalmoscope in nervous and other diseases, and he contributed equally significant papers on syphilitic disease of the cerebral arteries (1868), the effect of strain on the heart (1870, 1873), and anxiety as a cause of kidney disease (1876). He was elected a fellow of the Royal Society in 1880, and, in addition, he initiated and encouraged the practice of consultation between medical witnesses before the hearing of legal cases. He delivered the Goulstonian lectures entitled 'Chapters on visceral neuroses' at the Royal College of Physicians in 1884, and in 1885 he introduced the surgical treatment of tuberculous glands in the neck. In an address at Glasgow in 1888 he began pleading for the study of comparative medicine, believing that a great deal

Sir Thomas Clifford Allbutt (1836–1925), by Sir William Orpen, 1919–20

could be learned by observing the physiology and diseases of animals, and that information gained thereby could often be applied to human medicine. Allbutt had the gratification of seeing a professorship of comparative medicine established at Cambridge in 1923.

The fatigue of consulting practice prompted Allbutt to move to London, to accept a commissionership in lunacy, in 1889. In London he greatly enjoyed the company of the literary and artistic lions of the day. However, in 1892 he was appointed regius professor of physic at Cambridge, though being the first regius professor not previously a resident in Cambridge he did not obtain a footing in Addenbrooke's Hospital until 1900.

Probably Allbutt's greatest service to contemporary medicine was his *System of Medicine* in eight volumes (1896–1899), which went into a second edition in eleven volumes (1905–1911). His most outstanding scientific contributions to medicine were his descriptions in 1895 of hyperpiesia or high blood pressure in the absence of kidney disease. In his time he was equally known for his paper in 1894 on the aortic origin of angina pectoris, and he stubbornly held to his views on the subject despite increasing evidence to the contrary. He gave numerous addresses and in his eightieth year he published *Diseases of the Arteries and Angina Pectoris* (1915), an encyclopaedic but not lasting volume, of only modest consequence; six years later, in 1921, he published *Greek Medicine in Rome*. These essays were widely acclaimed and can be read with advantage today. His scholarly and meticulous care in the use of words was shown in his *Notes on the Composition of Scientific Papers* (1904; 3rd edn, 1923), an enduring and still useful volume, if somewhat dated.

Allbutt was married to Susan, daughter of Thomas England, merchant, of Headingley, Leeds, on 15 September 1869. They had no children. He was created KCB in 1907. He was president of the British Medical Association in 1920 and in the same year was admitted a member of the privy council, a rare if not unique honour for a practising physician. There is good evidence that George Eliot drew on him, in part at least, for the character of Lydgate in *Middlemarch* (1872). A serious, somewhat humourless man, Allbutt died suddenly on 22 February 1925 at his home, St Radegunds, 5 Chaucer Road, Cambridge; he was buried in the nearby churchyard at Trumpington.

H. D. ROLLESTON, *rev.* ALEXANDER G. BEARN

Sources H. D. Rolleston, *The Right Honorable Sir Thomas Clifford Allbutt KCB: a memoir* (1929) · b. cert. · m. cert. · d. cert. · personal knowledge (1937)
Archives BL, corresp. with Macmillans, Add. MS 55248 · Bodl. Oxf., corresp. with Viscount Addison · King's AC Cam., letters to Oscar Browning
Likenesses W. Orpen, oils, 1919–20, U. Cam., medical school library; on loan from FM Cam. [*see illus.*] · M. G. Gillick, bronze relief plaque, 1928, U. Cam., department of medicine · J. Russell & Sons, photograph, NPG · mezzotint (after W. Orpen) · photograph, Wellcome L.
Wealth at death £56,963 14s. 7d.: probate, 24 April 1925, CGPLA Eng. & Wales

Allchurch, Ivor John (1929–1997), footballer, was born on 16 October 1929 at 66 Waunwen Road, Swansea, the sixth of the seven children of Charles Wilfred (Charlie) Allchurch, furnaceman, and his wife, Mabel, formerly Miller, *née* Smith. His parents were natives of Dudley who had moved to Swansea. He was educated at Plasmarl School, Swansea, but left at fourteen to work first in an office, then as a fish market porter.

Allchurch's extraordinary football talents, which in peacetime would have earned schoolboy representative honours, were spotted in September 1944 by a scout from Swansea Town. He became a member of the club's ground staff in 1945 and a full professional two years later. National service with the army from 1947 to 1949 delayed his entry into league football, although he played at a high non-league standard as a guest with Shrewsbury Town and Wellington Town. He made his Football League second-division début on 26 December 1949, away to West Ham United, and made an immediate impact as an elegant, ball-playing inside-forward. Roy Paul, a Swansea team-mate, recalled that 'Even as a youngster he had the hallmark of greatness' (Paul, 79). Within weeks of his début Allchurch was the subject of transfer speculation, and in less than a year he was a Welsh international, capped against Ireland at Sunderland on 15 November 1950.

Among the most gifted of a remarkable generation of footballers who emerged from Swansea in the decade following the Second World War, Allchurch was without question the one most cherished by his home town. In part this was because he was more closely identified with Swansea Town than the others. Jack Kelsey and John

Charles spent their careers with other clubs, Trevor Ford played little more than a season, and Cliff Jones played five seasons with Swansea before passing the bulk of his career elsewhere. Allchurch's popularity also reflected his quality as a footballer. Tall, slim, and fair-haired—characteristics that led to his being described as Swansea's 'Golden Boy' (Farmer and Stead, 12)—he was described by the Scottish journalist Bob Ferrier as 'the complete natural intuitive inside-forward—the Mozart of football' (ibid., 49). Jimmy Hill, who played against him, said 'he had elegance … the game never seemed to be going too fast for him' (ibid., 163). Jimmy Murphy, who managed the Wales national team in the late 1950s, said: 'Ivor had the lot. He was two-footed: a superb runner on the ball with a glorious body swerve. He could shoot hard and accurately with both feet, and he was very good in the air' (Murphy, 102).

On 13 June 1953 Allchurch married Esmé Thomas, an eighteen-year-old accountant machine operator in a toy factory, and daughter of Richard Thomas, labourer in a steel works. They had two sons; three other children were stillborn. Allchurch continued to play for Swansea until 1958. Some observers argued that his decision to stay with second-division Swansea led to his not fulfilling a remarkable talent. Before the abolition of the maximum wage in 1961 there was no financial pressure on players to move to leading clubs. Allchurch was described by John Charles as 'a loyal Swansea lad. All he wanted to do was play football' (South Wales Evening Post, 11 July 1997). He was content to stay, hoping Swansea might win promotion. There were years of press speculation, much predicting that his transfer would set a new British record. In 1952 he nearly did leave, for Wolverhampton Wanderers, but as a consequence of the club's financial situation—which was improved in time to negate the transfer—rather than any desire on his part. Any suggestion of underachievement was belied by his international performances, particularly in the 1958 world cup, when Wales, after qualifying for the first time, reached the quarter-final before losing to the eventual winners, Brazil. Santiago Bernabeu, president of Real Madrid, then the dominant club in Europe, called him 'the greatest inside-forward in the world' (Murphy, 103).

In October 1958 Allchurch left Swansea for Newcastle United, saying 'it is now or never' (Farmer and Stead, 85). He stayed at Newcastle until 1962, then moved to Cardiff City before returning to Swansea Town in 1965. He played his 694th and last Football League match—at the time the third-highest career total—in May 1968. These included 103 first-division matches, all for Newcastle. He scored 245 goals, including 160 (a club record) for Swansea. The first man to play more than fifty times for Wales, his sixty-eight caps and twenty-three goals remained national records for many years following his last cap in 1966. He was appointed MBE in the new year's honours list of 1966.

Allchurch went on playing non-league football until the age of fifty, when his wife demanded that he burn his boots. He then worked as a storeman. He was mild-mannered and unpretentious, diffident to the point of shyness. In company he was 'modest, reserved, quietly elegant and circumspect', and in later life took on 'something of a clerical air' with a 'refined manner and somewhat nervous smile' (Farmer and Stead, 164). He died at his home, 12 Whitestone Road, Bishopston, Swansea, on 9 July 1997, of cancer. He was survived by his wife and their two sons. His funeral, at Morriston crematorium, near Swansea, on 16 July 1997, attracted more than 500 mourners. His younger brother, Len (b. 1933), was also a successful footballer, who played for Swansea (in 1953–4 the club's playing staff included four sets of brothers), Sheffield United, and Stockport. He won eleven Wales caps between 1955 and 1964.

HUW RICHARDS

Sources D. Farmer and P. Stead, *Ivor Allchurch MBE* (1998) · J. Murphy, *Matt, United and me* (1968) · R. Paul, *Red dragon of Wales* (1956) · R. Shepherd, 'Swansea Town FC', 1912–64 (1998) · D. Farmer, *Swansea City, 1912–82* (1982) · *South Wales Evening Post* (1949–97) · G. Lloyd, *C'mon City* (1999) · M. Risoli, *When Pele broke our hearts* (1998) · H. Richards, '…Ivor Allchurch', *For club and country*, ed. P. Stead and H. Richards (2000) · b. cert. · m. cert. · d. cert.
Wealth at death £180,000: administration, 4 March 1998, *CGPLA Eng. & Wales*

Allcroft, John Derby (1822–1893), glove manufacturer and entrepreneur, was born in Worcester on 19 July 1822, only son and elder child of Jeremiah Macklin Allcroft (1791–1867), who was a partner in the glove manufacturing firm of J. and W. Dent & Co. His mother, Hannah (1801–1836), was the daughter of Thomas Derby of Birmingham, and niece of the artist William Derby. In 1854 Allcroft married Mary Annette, daughter of the Revd Thomas Martin, but she died childless in 1857. His second wife was Mary Ann Jewell (1833–1895), daughter of John Blundell of Timsbury Manor, Hampshire. The couple were married in August 1864; they had four sons and two daughters.

After completing his education, Allcroft joined his father's firm, building up the London end of the business with such diligence and success that, when the partners retired in 1846, he and three other employees bought the company. With the name changed to Dent, Allcroft & Co., the metropolitan end was further expanded, moving from small premises in Friday Street to a new warehouse and headquarters in Wood Street, Cheapside. Under Allcroft's direction the organization flourished and, anticipating the growing demand for gloves, he centralized and streamlined the three Worcester factories to concentrate on the efficient production of quality goods. The advent of the railway to the town in the 1850s aided the growth of the business, and Allcroft eventually became a shareholder in seven different railway companies. By the 1870s his British employees numbered over 1000, and more factories had been opened. With new outlets and factories in New York and continental cities, the company became the pre-eminent glove manufacturers in the world. Allcroft ran the business until his retirement in 1873 when, as sole partner, his capital holding was £500,000.

As a devout evangelical Christian, Allcroft's religious faith was central to his life. He built and endowed three churches in London: St Martin's, Gospel Oak (1865), St

John Derby Allcroft (1822–1893), by Sir Francis Grant, 1873

Jude's, South Kensington (1870), and St Matthew's, Bayswater (1881), together with mission rooms in Worcester and Stokesay village. He donated funds for the founding and repair of several other churches, including Onibury church on his Shropshire estate. On his retirement from business he became the treasurer of Christ's Hospital, of which he had been a governor since 1849. He was chairman of the Church Pastoral Aid Society, vice-president of the Church Association, and was instrumental in the founding of the YMCA.

Allcroft's London home was in Lancaster Gate, but in 1869 he acquired the estate of Stokesay Castle, Shropshire. After the subsequent purchase of two neighbouring estates, Allcroft commissioned Thomas Harris in 1887 to design a great Jacobean-style mansion. Furnished and fitted by well-known, mainly metropolitan companies, and including such innovative features as integral electric light, the mansion cost a total of about £500,000. The family moved into the new Stokesay Court in 1892, but Allcroft himself died before the interior was properly completed.

Allcroft regularly bought paintings at the Royal Academy summer exhibition. He chose works by established contemporary painters, such as T. S. Cooper, from whom he purchased and commissioned nine major works. He was known as a benevolent patron of artists he particularly admired.

Allcroft was Conservative MP for Worcester from 1878 to 1880, and served as lieutenant for the City of London from 1879 to his death. He was a JP for Shropshire and its sheriff

in 1893, and was elected a fellow of the Royal Geographical and Royal Astronomical societies. Initiated into freemasonry in 1846, he belonged to four lodges. In 1883 he was elected to the office of grand treasurer and became chairman for the anniversary festival of the Royal Masonic Benevolent Institution. He helped found the Derby Allcroft Lodge, Worcester, becoming worshipful master in 1886.

Allcroft died at 108 Lancaster Gate, London, on 29 July 1893. A preliminary funeral service was held at St Matthew's Church, Bayswater; following a second service he was buried at St Michael's Church, Onibury. He was survived by his second wife.　POLLY HAMILTON

Sources J. M. Robinson, 'Stokesay Court & the Allcroft family', *Stokesay Court: Ludlow, Shropshire*, 1 [1994], 12–20 [sale catalogue, Sothebys, London, 1994 (sale LN4585)] · C. Newell, 'The paintings', *Stokesay Court: Ludow, Shropshire*, 2 [1994] [sale catalogue, Sothebys, London, 1994 (sale LN4585)] · M. Hall, 'Stokesay Court, Shropshire [pt 1]', *Country Life* (18 Aug 1994), 32–7 · M. Hall, 'Stokesay Court, Shropshire [pt 2]', *Country Life* (25 Aug 1994), 38 · R. H. G. Ring, 'Allcroft, John Derby', *DBB* · J. N. Summerson, *Victorian architecture: four studies in evaluation* (1970), 50–53 · *ILN* (7 Oct 1893) · *The Times* (1 Aug 1893) · *Association News: The Journal of the Young Men's Christian Association*, 8/83 (Oct 1893), 1 · Boase, *Mod. Eng. biog.* · family register, Stokesay Archive · b. cert., Stokesay Archive · d. cert.
Archives Stokesay Archive, Stokesay Court, Onibury, Shropshire · Stokesay Photographic Archive, Stokesay Court, Onibury, Shropshire
Likenesses F. Grant, oils, 1873; Sotheby's, 29 Sept 1994, lot 537 [*see illus.*] · photograph, 1883, repro. in *The contents of Stokesay Court* · H. von Herkomer, oils, 1884, Christ's Hospital, London · photograph, repro. in *The contents of Stokesay Court*
Wealth at death £492,063 8s. 4d.: resworn probate, Feb 1894, *CGPLA Eng. & Wales* (1893)

Allde [Alldee], **Edward** (1555×63–1627), printer, son of John *Allde (d. 1584), printer, and his wife, Margaret (d. after 1603), was made free of the Stationers' Company by patrimony on 18 February 1584. His name appeared on book imprints from the year of his freedom, and he entered his first copy in the Stationers' register in 1586. The *Short-Title Catalogue* associates him with the production of over 700 items during his career; however, he mostly acted as a 'trade printer', printing material for others. In 1586 he was recorded as operating only one press, but he had expanded his business to two presses by 1615. Between 1612 and 1620 he was one of five appointed printers responsible for the printing of all ballads; in the earlier year he was also granted a twenty-one-year patent over the production and importation of all printed songs other than ballads, and of ruled music paper. In the early 1620s he acted as an assign for Roger Wood and Thomas Symcock, the beneficiaries of a controversial patent for all single-sided printing.

Allde's name appears frequently in the Stationers' Company's records, binding and freeing apprentices (including a son, Jonathan, by patrimony), entering books in the register, and airing his disputes with other members; on three occasions he represented the company at mayoral dinners, and he was twice elected as one of the auditors of the company's English stock. In 1611 he was elected to the livery, and in 1619 he turned down the office of renter warden. In addition to several fines for relatively minor offences, Allde occasionally faced more drastic punishment: in 1597 his press and type were seized and defaced for printing a Catholic book, forcing him to petition the archbishop of Canterbury for reinstatement as a licensed printer; in 1600 he escaped imprisonment for printing a 'Disorderly ballad' (Arber, *Regs. Stationers*, 2.831); three years later his press was once again defaced, and Allde himself was imprisoned for his involvement in an illegal edition of James I's *Basilikon Doron*; and in 1621 he was sent to prison again for printing a book about the king of Bohemia, and was subsequently suspended from the livery for two years for 'verie unfitting wordes and scandalous speeches' (Jackson, 138).

For the first four years of his career Allde was based at his parents' establishment, the Long Shop in the Poultry, but, perhaps in consequence of his marriage to Rose Mason in St Giles Cripplegate parish, on 1 December 1588, he moved to the Golden Cup in Fore Street, outside Cripplegate, and remained there probably until 1596. During that time the parish register notes the christening of five children, along with the burial of one child whose baptism was otherwise not recorded; five servants were also buried. In 1597 Allde was recorded as dwelling in Aldersgate; between 1604 and 1612 he was resident on Lambeth Hill, near Old Fish Street; and from probably 1612 onwards he was based in Christchurch parish. At some point during this time he married his second wife, Elizabeth, whose surname was probably Oulton.

Allde's presence at the August 1627 meeting of the company's governing court of assistants suggests that he had been elected to that body, but by the time of the next meeting he was dead, having died some time between 20 August and 3 September. He was buried probably at Christ Church Greyfriars (according to the request in his will) on or before 3 September. He left substantial sums to his grandson, granddaughter and stepson; his sister, niece, servant, the vicar and poor of Christchurch parish, and a Northamptonshire parson were also all named beneficiaries. The Stationers' Company was left £6; it managed to supplement this by fining five stationers who had been 'absent at mʳ Alldees funerall, having ben warned' (Jackson, 475). Allde's widow continued as printer until her own death in 1636, when she was succeeded by Richard Oulton, her son from her previous marriage.

I. GADD

Sources STC, 1475–1640 · Arber, *Regs. Stationers* · W. W. Greg and E. Boswell, eds., *Records of the court of the Stationers' Company, 1576 to 1602, from register B* (1930) · W. A. Jackson, ed., *Records of the court of the Stationers' Company, 1602 to 1640* (1957) · liber A, Stationers' Company, London, fols. 51r, 68r, 70r, 72v · calls on livery, 1606–1737, Stationers' Company, London, 4 · GL, MS 9171/25, fols. 196r–196v · W. W. Greg, ed., *A companion to Arber* (1967) · D. F. McKenzie, ed., *Stationers' Company apprentices*, [1]: 1605–1640 (1961) · W. E. Miller, 'Printers and stationers in the parish of St Giles Cripplegate, 1561–1640', *Studies in Bibliography*, 19 (1966), 15–38 · A. Hunt, 'Book trade patents, 1603–1640', *The book trade and its customers, 1450–1900: historical essays for Robin Myers*, ed. A. Hunt, G. Mandelbrote, and A. Shell (1997), 27–54 · H. R. Plomer, 'The Long Shop in the Poultry', *Bibliographica*, 2 (1896), 61–80 · R. B. McKerrow, 'Edward Allde as a

typical trade printer', *The Library*, 4th ser., 10 (1929–30), 121–62 · H. R. Plomer, 'Some petitions for appointment as master printers called forth by the star chamber decree of 1637', *The Library*, 3rd ser., 10 (1919), 101–16

Allde, John (*b.* in or before **1531**, *d.* **1584**), printer and bookseller, took up his freedom of the Stationers' Company in January 1555. He had been apprenticed to the bookseller Richard Kele until Kele's death in 1552, and was left 'fyve pounds in wares' in Kele's will (Plomer, *Abstracts*, 9–11).

Allde was listed in the letters patent incorporating the company in 1557. From 1560 to 1567 he registered many ballads and almanacs, but little else; he then began to print more books, chiefly of a popular nature, but continued his production of ballads. Henry Plomer characterized him as 'essentially a popular … but by no means an indifferent printer', possessing 'a considerable variety of types' (Plomer, 'Long Shop', 72–3). From at least 1561 to his death Allde lived at the Long Shop next to St Mildred Poultry, London; and, judging from the considerable number of apprentices he bound during that time (including Anthony Munday in 1576), he carried on a flourishing trade. In 1568 he was imprisoned in the counter with two Dutch-born stationers for printing a book about the duke of Alva.

Allde's son Edward *Allde was freed as a stationer by patrimony in February 1584. John Allde was buried at St Mildred Poultry in May 1584. He left no will, but the administration of his estate was granted to his widow, Margaret, in June. She continued the business at the Long Shop, registering books and binding apprentices until 1603; in 1589 Edward moved to separate premises in Fore Street, Cripplegate, London.

H. R. TEDDER, *rev.* I. GADD

Sources Arber, *Regs. Stationers* · STC, 1475–1640 · CSP dom., 1547–80, 320, 332 · E. G. Duff, *A century of the English book trade* (1905) · H. R. Plomer, 'The Long Shop in the Poultry', *Bibliographica*, 2 (1896), 61–80 · H. R. Plomer, *Abstracts from the wills of English printers and stationers from 1492 to 1630* (1903), 9–11 [will of Richard Kele, Allde's master] · R. B. McKerrow, 'Edward Allde as a typical trade printer', *The Library*, 4th ser., 10 (1929–30), 121–62 · administration, London commissary court, GL, GL 9168/14, fol. 51v · parish register, London, St Mildred Poultry, May 1584 [burial]

Allectus (*d.* 296), Roman emperor in Britain, first appears in the records of the revolt of his predecessor Carausius (286–93). What little can be established about him derives from hostile contemporary, or near contemporary, accounts of that revolt, in which Carausius rose against the joint emperors Diocletian and Maximian and maintained a separatist regime in Britain and parts of Gaul from 286 until his death in 293. The name Allectus appears to mean 'selected' or 'chosen' and has no strict contemporary parallels. There is no record of any other name for him, and his career before his appearance with Carausius is unknown. That he was 'chief financial officer' (*summae rei praeesset*) to Carausius (*Liber de caesaribus*, 39) suggests that he was experienced in financial affairs either through an imperial administrative career or in private life; it is

Allectus (d. 296), coin

of panegyrists or imperial historians recourse has to be made to evidence of Allectus's coinage, itself tendentious. The chosen types are banal, invoking the normal administrative virtues of peace, foresight, even-handedness, and justice. Unlike the coinage of his predecessor, that of Allectus places no emphasis on the loyalty of the army, nor were there special issues to celebrate individual units, further emphasizing that the transfer of power was accomplished without resistance from the military. Exceptionally, the coins introduced as part of a currency reform depict warships from the imperial fleet. Allectus issued a large gold coinage and there is every evidence of monetary stability during the brief period of his rule.

Two further events can be ascribed to the years between the assumption of power by Allectus and his defeat in 296: a reform of the coinage system and the start of construction of what may have been intended as a palace or administrative centre on the north bank of the Thames in London. The coin reform is characterized by the introduction of a new denomination, probably valued as a 2-denarius piece, possibly introduced to permit parity with the new coinage system being introduced in the rest of the empire at this time. The London building work, represented by massive masonry foundations supported on a raft of oak piles, has been dated by tree ring analysis to 294.

The collapse of Allectus's regime is recounted in two panegyrics, the earlier addressed to Constantius in 297 and the later to his son in 310. Very slight differences between the accounts may be attributed to the discretion normally shown by orators recounting recent historical events to participating rulers. These sources claim that the army of Britain was supplemented by Frankish mercenaries; that Allectus, terrified by the approach of imperial vengeance, abandoned his coastal defences, misused his naval forces, and in confronting Asclepiodotus and Constantius did not marshal all of the forces available to him. Allectus died on the battlefield, his body being found stripped of imperial regalia, possibly discarded in an attempt to avoid recognition during the last phase of the conflict. Coin evidence indicates that the coastal forts, later known as the Saxon Shore forts, which stretch from the Wash to the Severn, were occupied during the reigns of Carausius and Allectus but appear to have played no significant part in hampering the success of the invasion. The long-held view that Allectus stripped the garrison troops from Hadrian's Wall, thus inaugurating a destructive invasion of the province by northern tribesmen, has been undermined by modern archaeological research. The relations of Allectus with the population of Britain are painted darkly in the contemporary, hostile, sources. On the other hand, slender evidence which suggests that London lost its administrative primacy immediately after the reconquest of Britain may hint at a less than wholehearted acceptance of reincorporation into the empire by the population. No epigraphic evidence has come to light for the reign, suggesting that exceptional efforts were made to expunge memory of the revolt in the period following the recovery of the island.

very likely that he served on the administrative staff of Carausius before the revolt, though his conduct during the final stages of this suggests that he lacked military experience. The wording of the ancient sources suggests that Allectus held a position akin to the later office of *comes sacrarum largitionum*, and as such managed the raising of taxes to pay the army and to fund the regular imperial gifts to the troops which did so much to sustain loyalty to the emperor. In such a position he would have been responsible for the issue of the silver donative coins marked RSR (perhaps *rationalis summae rei* or, as has been suggested, *redeunt Saturnia regna*, a Virgilian allusion to the return of a golden age) which characterize the start of Carausius's reign. Other sources simply describe Allectus as Carausius's 'henchman' or 'ally'.

The defeat of his forces at Gesoriacum (Boulogne) in 293 has been seen as the occasion for the death of Carausius, at the hands of Allectus or his agents. The circumstances of the killing of Carausius are not known, though negotiation with his opponents to the detriment of his immediate circle of conspirators may have been contributory. In any event there is no evidence for resistance to Allectus's assumption of power and whatever the feelings of the army at the fall of their erstwhile commander they appear to have fought loyally for Allectus in 296. Coin evidence shows that Allectus celebrated a self-bestowed consulship some time in the period 293 to 295.

While it is normally assumed that the fall of Gesoriacum marked the end of hostilities in Gaul, a study of the distribution of Allectus's coins on the continent points to a more complicated series of events. The three years which elapsed before an attempt was made to recover Britain for Rome may have seen continued resistance by forces loyal to Allectus in Gaul itself.

In the absence of sources uncontaminated by the views

Allectus's well-struck coins show a portrait of a man in early middle age, of slender features with a distinctive retroussé nose, wavy hair, and a curled beard.

P. J. CASEY

Sources R. A. B. Mynors, ed., *XII panegyrici Latini* (1964) · *Sexti Aurelii Victoris liber de caesaribus*, ed. F. Pichlmayr, rev. edn, rev. R. Gruendel (Leipzig, 1961) · Eutropius, *Breviarum ab urbe conditam*, ed. C. Santini (1979) · A. Burnett, 'The coinage of Allectus: chronology and interpretation', *British Numismatic Journal*, 54 (1984), 21–40 · P. J. Casey, *Carausius and Allectus: the British usurpers* (1994)
Likenesses coin, BM [*see illus.*] · coins, repro. in Burnett, 'Coinage of Allectus'

Alleine, Joseph (*bap.* 1634, *d.* 1668), ejected minister and devotional writer, was born in a house next to the Poultry Market, Devizes, Wiltshire, and baptized on 8 April 1634, at St John's Church, there, the fourth child of Tobias Alleine (*d.* 1667), tradesman, and his first wife, Elizabeth, daughter of Edward Northie, who was at least twice mayor of Devizes. He was educated in classics at Poulshot by William Spinage, fellow of Exeter College, Oxford. He went in 1649 to Lincoln College, Oxford, but transferred, as a scholar, to Corpus Christi College in 1651. The example of his elder brother, Edward, a minister who had died in 1645 aged twenty-six, inspired Joseph to want to replace him in the ministry. On graduating BA in 1653 he was elected chaplain of Corpus Christi College, preferring that to a fellowship.

Two years later Alleine was invited by George Newton, the puritan vicar of St Mary Magdalene Church, Taunton, Somerset, to become his assistant. He accepted, and after examination was ordained by the presbyterian fourth Somerset Taunton classis. On 4 October 1655, after his ordination, he married his cousin Theodosia *Alleine (*fl.* 1654–1677), daughter of Richard *Alleine (1610/11–1681), minister of Batcombe, Somerset. Joseph's salary was £80 a year, raised by voluntary subscription. In *The Life and Death of Joseph Allein* Newton described Alleine as 'a young man of singular accomplishments, natural and acquired, his intellectuals solid, his affections lively, his learning much beyond the ordinary size, and above all, his holiness eminent. He had a good head and a better heart' (Baxter, Alleine, and Newton, 44). Joseph and Theodosia lived with Newton for two years and when they moved into a house of their own Theodosia, helped by Joseph, began a school with about fifty scholars, half of them boarders. Newton and Alleine were popular pastors, diligent in visiting the congregation, and their Sunday and Wednesday sermons were frequently written down by the listeners.

Newton and Alleine were ejected from the living on 24 August 1662 by the terms of the Act of Uniformity, which also required Alleine to be reordained. They stayed in Taunton, holding their congregation together, meeting in groups and worshipping in private houses in an endeavour to avoid arrest. Alleine regularly preached six times a week and sometimes ten and even fourteen times in and around Taunton. Under such conditions he considered going to China as a missionary, but was dissuaded. He was arrested on suspicion of preaching at a service held on 17 May 1663, and committed to Ilchester gaol. At his trial in the great hall of Taunton Castle on 14 July nothing was found against him, but instead of being released, he was indicted again and found guilty, on the same weak evidence, by lord chief justice Sir Robert Foster. He was fined 100 marks, and ordered to be confined in prison until it was paid. Refusing to pay he remained in gaol where he spent his time writing pastoral letters to the people of Taunton, and theological articles. His writing on covenanting, together with that of his father-in-law, later inspired John Wesley to institute the Methodist covenant service. A number of ejected ministers came to Taunton to help Newton and Alleine, including in 1663 John Wesley from Whitchurch in Dorset, grandfather of the founder of Methodism.

Alleine was released from prison on 20 May 1664, and resumed his forbidden ministry, but persecution was affecting his health. In August he became ill but recovered by the spring of 1665. Later that year the provisions of the Five Mile Act compelled him to move to Wellington and then to various secret places in and around Taunton. He found a home with John Mallack at Fullands, a mile out of Taunton on the Corfe road. It was probably here that Alleine took part in the ordination of George Trosse. Alleine was arrested as he conducted a service at Fullands on 10 July 1665 and was convicted of holding a conventicle by the justices meeting at the Castle tavern. Those involved, including his wife, father, and seven ministers were each ordered to pay £3 or serve sixty days in prison. Nearly all refused to pay and served their time in Ilchester gaol. Alleine's health deteriorated despite visiting his home town Devizes, for its waters, and Dorchester, to seek the advice of Dr Losse. He returned to Taunton in February 1668, and became very ill. He was taken to Bath in the hope of a cure, but despite a temporary improvement, died there at 6 p.m. on Saturday 17 November 1668, leaving significant sums to his wife and a number of other relatives. He was buried later that month within the sanctuary of St Mary Magdalene, Taunton, as was his wish. His funeral sermon, which was published, was preached by George Newton. His memorial in the church, which described him as a burnt offering for Taunton, was replaced by a similar one in the 1840s. Alleine's most famous book, *Alarm to the Unconverted*, was published posthumously in 1671, when 20,000 copies were sold. Twenty years later, under the title *Sure Guide to Heaven*, a further 50,000 copies were sold. It became an evangelical classic and was still in print in 1998.

BRIAN W. KIRK

Sources C. Stanford, *Joseph Alleine: his companions and times* [1861] · *The nonconformist's memorial … originally written by … Edmund Calamy*, ed. S. Palmer, [3rd edn], 3 (1803), 206–12 · *Calamy rev.* · R. Baxter, T. Alleine, and G. Newton, *The life and death of that excellent minister of Christ, Mr Joseph Alleine* (1822) · E. Calamy, ed., *An abridgement of Mr. Baxter's history of his life and times, with an account of the ministers, &c., who were ejected after the Restauration of King Charles II*, 2nd edn, 2 vols. (1713), vol. 2, pp. 299–301 · *Eclectic Review*, new ser., 1 (Dec 1861), 611 · Wood, *Ath. Oxon.*, 1st edn, 2.299–301 · A. Gordon, ed., *Freedom after ejection: a review (1690–1692) of presbyterian and congregational nonconformity in England and Wales* (1917) · Foster, *Alum. Oxon.* · J. Waylen, *A history, military and municipal of the ancient borough of the Devizes* (1857), 338–40 · J. Toulmin, *The history of the town of Taunton*, ed. J. Savage (1822), 149 · will, PRO, PROB 11/329, fols. 91–2

Likenesses engraving · oils, Taunton United Reformed Church
Wealth at death personalty, £600 to wife; bequests to members of family and various ejected ministers: *Calamy rev.*; will, PRO, PROB 11/329, fols. 91–2

Alleine, Richard (1610/11–1681), clergyman and ejected minister, was named after his father, Richard Alleine (*d. c.*1655?), the rector of the Somerset parish of Ditcheat for over fifty years, who supervised his early education. Richard was sent to Oxford, where he matriculated at St Alban Hall on 15 October 1630 aged nineteen; he graduated BA on 20 June 1631 and proceeded MA at New Inn Hall on 29 April 1634. On 2 March 1634 he was ordained priest in the diocese of Salisbury, and was licensed to preach in that diocese on 25 May in the following year. In 1635 he was appointed chaplain to Sir Ralph Hopton. It is ironic that Hopton was a chief architect of the royalist supremacy in Somerset in 1643–5 which the Alleine family united in opposing.

Already, before the civil war, Alleine was assisting his aged father in pastoral duties in Somerset. It was Alleine senior who, following the death of the famous Richard Bernard, its long-standing incumbent, presented his son to the rectory of Batcombe, Somerset. Instituted on 18 March 1642, Alleine was reported to have been 'a zealous person for the blessed cause then driving on' (Wood, *Ath. Oxon.*, 4.13). The assertion is given colour by a report that at Alleine's induction service one of his friends from London, taking offence at 'a very fair crucifix' in the church, 'most maliciously threw a stone at it and broke it' while Richard, 'a great precisian', and his younger brother William *Alleine (1613/14–1677) looked on (*Calamy rev.*, 7).

During the civil wars, Wood reported, Alleine was 'a preacher up of sedition, a zealous convenanteer' (Wood, *Ath. Oxon.*, 4.13). In 1648 he signed the presbyterian-inspired *Attestation of the Ministers of Somerset* and in 1654 became an assistant to the commission for the approval of parish ministers in Somerset. Alleine is reported to have had great difficulties extracting tithes from many at Batcombe in the early 1650s. He married twice, but little is known of either woman other than the fact that Frances, his second wife, and five children survived him. A daughter, Theodosia *Alleine (*fl.* 1654–1677), was the wife and biographer of Joseph *Alleine.

Alleine was ejected after the Restoration, but continued for a time to live at Batcombe, where in 1661 he issued a defence of presbyterian ordination. The passage of the Five Mile Act made it necessary to move to Frome Selwood, but he seems not to have been otherwise much constrained by the Clarendon code. In 1669 he was reported to be preaching in his house at Frome Selwood, at Batcombe, Beckington, and elsewhere in Somerset and also in Wiltshire and Dorset. He was several times fined for preaching but these impositions were paid by Thomas Moore, the sympathetic MP for Heytesbury, Wiltshire. Such was Alleine's grave and pious reputation that the magistrates hesitated to respond with a term of imprisonment for fear of the outcry which might result.

Alleine's *Vindiciae pietatis, or, A Vindication of Godliness*, first published in 1663, went through several editions despite its being refused a licence. According to Calamy copies were 'greedily bought up and read by sober people', proving so saleable that the king's bookseller, Roger Norton:

> caused a great part of the impression to be seized, because unlicensed, and so to be sent to the king's kitchen. Thence he bought them for an Old Song, bound them up and sold them in his own shop. This was at length complained of: and he was forced to beg pardon upon his knees at the council table, and send them back to the King's kitchen to be … rubbed over with an inky brush. (Calamy, *Abridgement*, 2.580–81)

Alleine corresponded with Richard Baxter in 1671, and on 20 April 1672 was licensed to preach as a presbyterian at Beckington. He is said to have continued to preach at the house of Robert Smith in Frome until the day of his death on 22 December 1681. He was buried at Frome church, where the Anglican vicar, Richard Jenkins, delivered a respectful sermon in his memory.

STEPHEN WRIGHT

Sources E. Calamy, ed., *An abridgement of Mr. Baxter's history of his life and times, with an account of the ministers, &c., who were ejected after the Restauration of King Charles II*, 2nd edn, 2 vols. (1713) · *Calamy rev.* · Wood, *Ath. Oxon.*, new edn · D. Underdown, *Somerset in the civil war and interregnum* (1973) · *Calendar of the correspondence of Richard Baxter*, ed. N. H. Keeble and G. F. Nuttall, 2 (1991)
Wealth at death £394 13s. 8d.: inventory, *Calamy rev.*

Alleine, Theodosia (*fl.* 1654–1677), nonconformist writer, was a daughter of Richard *Alleine (1610/11–1681), rector of Batcombe, Somerset. Whether her mother was his first wife (whose name is unrecorded) or his second, Frances, is not known. Both her father and her paternal uncle, William *Alleine, vicar of Blandford Forum, Dorset, were to be nonconformist ministers following the Restoration. In August 1654 she became acquainted with her future husband, Joseph *Alleine (*bap.* 1634, *d.* 1668), who was presumably a cousin, though of what degree is not known, then tutor and chaplain at Corpus Christi College, Oxford. She supported him when, rejecting other offers of preferment and despite the 'meanness of the maintenance' (*Life and Death of Mr. Joseph Alleine*, appended letters, p. 7), in 1655 he received presbyterian ordination at Taunton, Somerset, to become assistant to George Newton, vicar of St Mary Magdalene, Taunton. 'Mr. Newton … seeing him restless in his spirit, and putting himself to many tedious Journeys to visit me (as he did once a Fortnight Twenty Five Miles) he perswaded him to marry, contrary to our purpose, we resolving to have lived much longer single' (ibid., 91). The marriage took place on 4 October 1655.

Husband and wife lived for two years with Newton, and then took a house in Taunton, where Theodosia Alleine, 'having been always bred to work', ran a school, 'and had many Tablers [boarders], and Scholars, our Family being seldome less than Twenty, and many times Thirty; My School usually Fifty or Sixty of the Town and other places' (*Life and Death*, 91). Ejected from the established church by the Act of Uniformity in 1662, Joseph Alleine, like Newton, committed himself to an illegal nonconformist ministry, in which he was fully supported by his wife. The couple:

sold off all our goods, preparing for a Goal [gaol], or Banishment, where he was desirous I should attend him, as I was willing to do, it always having been more grievous to me to think of being absent from him, than to suffer with him. (ibid., 63)

From May 1663 Theodosia Alleine attended her husband during his twelve-month imprisonment at Ilchester, Somerset, and, following the passage of the Five Mile Act in 1665, moved with him to Wellington, near Taunton, 'to a Dyers House, in a very obscure place' (ibid., 65). When still harassed and pursued, they moved to a house just outside Taunton, Fullands (which still stands), the home of John Mallack, merchant (d. 23 November 1678), also staying by turns with different friends, 'though it was troublesome for us to be so unsetled' (ibid., 68). Theodosia Alleine again attended her husband when he was imprisoned in July 1665 for holding a conventicle at Mallack's house, and she nursed him attentively during his prolonged last illness (from the summer of 1667 until his death on 17 November 1668). In search of a cure she took him to drink the waters at Devizes, to Dorchester (where they lodged with Mrs Bartlet, 'a Ministers Widdow' (ibid., 80–81)) to consult the physician Frederick Losse, and to take the waters at Bath, where they were visited by a number of friends including Richard Fairclough and his wife, and John Howe.

Theodosia Alleine's reputation derives from *The Life and Death of Mr. Joseph Alleine* (1672), a composite work consisting of contributions by Richard Baxter, Richard Alleine, Newton, Fairclough, and unidentified friends, and 'A full narrative of his life from his silencing to his death; by his widow, Mrs. Theodosia Alleine, in her own words: wherein is notably set forth with what patience he ran the race that was set before him', which occupies the greater part of the book. A prefatory note explains that this 'was sent up by her to a worthy Divine, by him to be published in his own Stile, not imagining it should be put forth in her own words'. The 'worthy divine' was probably Baxter, as Anthony Wood supposed (Wood, 3.822): Baxter admired Joseph Alleine, he firmly believed in the usefulness of exemplary biography, and his publisher, Nevil Simmons, is identified by their imprints as responsible for two of the 1672 editions of the work. (There were also two editions dated 1671 and one in 1672 with blank imprints.) It was an exceptionally successful work, enjoying seven editions within six years of its appearance. Theodosia Alleine's circumstantially detailed account of her husband's determination to continue his ministry despite persecution and illness confirmed his reputation for exceptional piety and pastoral commitment. Unremarked at the time was the picture it also gives of a no less resilient and resourceful wife.

Joseph Alleine bequeathed his widow £320, his plate, household goods, horse and watch. On 17 March 1673 she married Robert Taylor, widower of Elizabeth Gamlen, a nonconformist and witness of Newton's will, and a constable of Taunton. Wood's assertion that after Joseph Alleine's death his widow 'courted a lusty chaundler of Taunton', and married him, is of a piece with his description of the 'Narrative of his life' as a 'canting farce' and its

author as 'a prating gossip and a meer Xantippe' who snared Joseph Alleine with her wiles (Wood, 3.822), for which he was reproved by Edmund Calamy (Calamy, 2.577). Even Wood, however, allows she 'was accounted by her partie a religious woman' (Wood, 3.822). The last firm reference to Theodosia Alleine is as a beneficiary of her father's will (made in July 1677 and proved four years later). Wood states that she died before Monmouth's rebellion.

N. H. KEEBLE

Sources *The life and death of Mr Joseph Alleine, late teacher of the church at Taunton … whereunto are annexed diverse Christian letters … and his funeral sermon preached by Mr Newton* (1672) • E. Calamy, ed., *An abridgement of Mr. Baxter's history of his life and times, with an account of the ministers, &c., who were ejected after the Restauration of King Charles II*, 2nd edn, 2 vols. (1713), vol. 2, pp. 574–7 • *Calamy rev.* • C. Stanford, *Joseph Alleine: his companions and times* [1861] • Wood, *Ath. Oxon.*, new edn, 3.819–22 • private information (2004) [B. Kirk] • Foster, *Alum. Oxon.* • PRO, PROB 11/329, fols. 91r–92r [will of Joseph Alleine]

Alleine, William (1613/14–1677), clergyman and ejected minister, was the son of Richard Alleine (d. c.1655?), rector of the Somerset parish of Ditcheat, and younger brother of Richard *Alleine (1610/11–1681) of Batcombe and Frome Selwood. He attended Oxford University, after matriculating aged seventeen on 4 November 1631 at New Inn Hall, where he graduated BA on 29 April 1634 and MA on 19 January 1637. Alleine then served as chaplain to Lord Digby in London, but at the outbreak of the civil war he was back in Somerset, at Ilchester, where he collaborated with the parliamentarian forces and was plundered by cavaliers. Seeking to avoid further such attentions he went to Bristol but, on the fall of that city, was plundered again. He moved to London, but soon returned to the west country. On 28 January 1647, by order of the standing committee of Dorset but on request of 'the inhabitants' of Blandford Forum, Alleine, 'an able godly and orthodox divine', was admitted to the vicarage of the town at the generous yearly salary of £80 (Mayo, 192); he served as an assistant to the county commissioners for approving parish ministers in 1654. He married first a widow, Mary Sterr, née Hillard, who died before 10 November 1657, when a deposition in a chancery suit refers to her as dead; his second wife, Katherine, survived him, but it appears from his will that his relationship with her became distant.

After the Restoration, Alleine was ejected from Blandford; his successor was instituted in 1661. In 1665 at his native Ditcheat it was charged that he refused to attend church, and that he 'doth often keep private meetings for the sowing seeds of rebellion' (*Calamy rev.*, 8). For Calamy, by contrast, he was a 'true, patient labourer in the Gospel, and a most happy comforter of many dejected souls and wounded spirits' (Calamy, *Abridgement*, 2.263). He was probably the William Alleine, resident of Marshfield, Gloucestershire, reported in 1669 to have been preaching in St Laurence Chapel and in a house at Warminster, Wiltshire.

About this time Alleine returned to Bristol, where he seems to have become convinced that the sufferings of the saints would soon be at an end. He wrote two books on this theme, *The Mystery of the Temple*, which promises on its title-page to review 'some signs of the times when the fall of Babylon is near', and *Some Discovery of the New Heavens*, both published posthumously. A collection of six of his sermons was issued at Bristol by his eldest son, Joseph, as *Several Discourses on the Unsearchable Riches of Christ* (1697). Calamy records that William Alleine spent his last years at Yeovil, but his will, signed on 13 June 1677, gives his residence as Ditcheat, and it is likely that it was there that he died, aged sixty-three, in October of the same year.

STEPHEN WRIGHT

Sources E. Calamy, ed., *An abridgement of Mr. Baxter's history of his life and times, with an account of the ministers, &c., who were ejected after the Restauration of King Charles II*, 2nd edn, 2 vols. (1713) · *Calamy rev.*, 7–8 · C. H. Mayo, ed., *The minute books of the Dorset standing committee* (1902) · will, PRO, PROB 11/355, sig. 112
Wealth at death see will, PRO, PROB 11/355, sig. 112

Allen. *See also* Allan, Alleyn.

Allen, Alexander (1814–1842), philologist and classical scholar, was born at Hackney, Middlesex, on 23 September 1814, the son of John *Allen (1771–1839), a dissenting layman and author of *A History of Modern Judaism* (1816), and his wife, Charlotte Jane. He was educated at his father's school and at University College, London, where he was distinguished in Greek and Latin. On his father's death he carried on the Madras House Grammar School, at Hackney. He obtained, in 1840, the degree of doctor of philosophy from the University of Leipzig. His kind disposition and natural wisdom made him an excellent teacher. In the dedication of his *Etymological Analysis of Latin Verbs* (1836) to Thomas Hewitt Key, he acknowledges that many of his philological principles were derived from Key. He also acknowledges, in his *Essay on Teaching Greek* (*Papers of the Central Society of Education*, vol. 1), his obligations to his friend W. Wittich, teacher of German in University College, London. In the two or three years before his death he studied Old English, Swedish, Danish, Icelandic, and German, with a view to a comprehensive work on the history and structure of the English language, but the notes he left were not in a state ready for publication. His other works included: *Constructive Greek Exercises, for Teaching Greek from the Beginning by Writing* (1839); several more works on Latin and Greek; *A New English Grammar* (1841); and essays on writing Latin and Greek exercises and on parsing in the *Journal of Education*. He also contributed articles to the *Penny Cyclopaedia* and Smith's *Dictionary of Greek and Roman Antiquities* and *Dictionary of Greek and Roman Biography and Mythology*. Allen died, of pneumonia, on 6 November 1842, at Marc Street, Hackney, Middlesex.

JAMES MEW, rev. JOHN D. HAIGH

Sources BL cat. · *The Athenaeum* (12 Nov 1842), 972 · *Papers of the Central Society of Education*, 1.257 · G. Long, ed., *The biographical dictionary of the Society for the Diffusion of Useful Knowledge*, 4 vols. in 7 (1842–4) · A. Allen, 'Dedication', *An etymological analysis of Latin verbs* (1836) · d. cert. · IGI

Allen, Anthony (1685–1754), barrister and antiquary, was born on 3 June 1685 and baptized at Much Hadham, Hertfordshire, two days later, the fourth surviving son of William Allen (d. 1698), of Much Hadham, and his wife, Bridget James. After attending Bishop's Stortford School,

he was sent to Eton College in 1699. He was admitted to King's College, Cambridge, on 18 April 1703 and to the Middle Temple on 26 October 1704. He obtained his BA in 1707/8, was called to the bar on 22 June 1710, and proceeded MA in 1711. He was a fellow of King's from 1706 to 1717. One source suggests that he married on 4 October 1717, which would account for the termination of his fellowship at King's in that year.

On 17 January 1726 Allen was admitted a freeman of Guildford, at that time represented in parliament by Arthur Onslow, whom he described in his will as 'my patron' (will, fol. 367v). Apparently through the influence of Onslow, now MP for Surrey and speaker of the House of Commons, Allen became a master in chancery in 1728. He was made an associate bencher of the Middle Temple on 27 November 1730 and a bencher on 12 February 1741, and served as reader in 1745 and treasurer in 1749. On 11 November 1746 he married Rebecca Collier (d. 1778). They had no children.

Allen's chief pursuit aside from the law seems to have been antiquarianism. By his will of 22 October 1753 he left to Onslow his unpublished work on the churches in Surrey and his account of the Middle Temple. His junior clerk, Thomas Sibthorpe, was bequeathed £120 to transcribe Allen's catalogues of scholars educated at Eton College and at King's College, Cambridge. Two copies were to be made of the resultant five folio volumes, laid out according to Allen's plans, one to be presented to Onslow and the other to King's. Sibthorpe was bequeathed Allen's manuscript material on 'the degeneracy of words' (an English dictionary of obsolete words and those which have changed their meaning or assumed a proverbial usage), his law dictionary, and his law reports. Allen also left £200 to the hospital 'for exposed and deserted young children' in lieu of what he had originally promised such a foundation before 'that indefatigable schemist Captain Thomas Coram' (will, fol. 367v) had pressed upon the foundation plans with which he had disagreed.

Allen died on 11 or 12 April 1754 and was buried on 16 April in the Temple Church. He ordered a quiet burial, 'having ever entertained an utter contempt of all costly and ostentatious internments' (will, fol. 368).

STUART HANDLEY

Sources R. A. Austen-Leigh, ed., *The Eton College register, 1698–1752* (1927), 3 · will, PRO, PROB 11/807, sig. 97 · H. A. C. Sturgess, ed., *Register of admissions to the Honourable Society of the Middle Temple, from the fifteenth century to the year 1944*, 1 (1949), 256 · IGI · *Register of burials at the Temple Church, 1628–1853* (1905), 58 [with introduction by H. G. Woods] · H. Carter, ed., *Guildford freemen's books, 1655–1933* (1963), 9 · GM, 1st ser., 24 (1754), 191 · will, PRO, PROB 11/448, fols. 25v–26v [will of William Allen, father] · will, PRO, PROB 11/1044, fol. 213 [will of Rebecca Allen, second wife]
Archives NL Wales, lexicographical papers

Allen, Bennet (bap. 1736, d. 1819), Church of England clergyman and journalist, was born at Yazor, Herefordshire, where he was baptized on 26 August 1736, the second son of James Allen (c.1700–1776), vicar of Yazor, and of his wife, Elizabeth, née Bennet. His father and elder brother, also James Allen, had been educated at Balliol College, Oxford, but Bennet Allen matriculated as a commoner at Wadham

College, Oxford, on 27 March 1754. He became a scholar on 26 September 1754, and was Hody (Greek) exhibitioner from 1755 to 1760, taking his BA in 1757 and MA in 1760. He was ordained deacon in 1759, and priest in 1761. He became probationary fellow of Wadham in June 1759, and fellow in July 1760, immediately applying for leave on grounds of ill health; indefinite leave was unofficially granted. Until 1766 he appears spasmodically in the college records, being appointed to a succession of college offices which were undertaken by deputies.

During this period Allen was making his career as a journalist in London, producing *inter alia* the fawning *Poem Inscribed to his Majesty* (1761) and, in 1764, the satirical *Poem of the Peace*, as well as *Satirical Trifles*, and a free treatment of Boileau's *Fourth Satire*. His talents commended him to Frederick Calvert, sixth Lord Baltimore. Allen is sometimes said to have written the pamphlet *Modern Chastity, or, The Agreeable Rape*, telling in lubricious detail how Baltimore was entrapped by a 'methodistical milliner', Sarah Woodcock, and wrongly charged with abduction and rape. His authorship is unlikely, since the trial took place in 1768, after Allen's departure to America. He did, however, defend Baltimore in similar terms in the American press.

Allen had left for Maryland in October 1766, with instructions from Lord Baltimore, the colony's 'proprietor', to the governor, Horatio Sharpe, to provide his 'particular friend … one of the best' ecclesiastical livings available (*Archives of Maryland*, 14.323). He was appointed in 1767 to the rectory of St Anne, Annapolis, described by his rival and successor, Jonathan Boucher, as 'pleasant but of small value' (Boucher, 54). He declined a richer but more remote living, telling Baltimore that 'my constitution and education have spoiled me for a good savage' (Fisher, 38.305); however, he was heard to say that £300 p.a. 'will hardly supply me with Liquors' (Haw, 141). His attempts to acquire another living in plurality (in the course of which he exaggerated both his social and his ecclesiastical position in England) and his activities as Lord Baltimore's agent and receiver-general (he was appointed in July 1768, and dismissed in November of the same year after refusing to produce his accounts) alienated leading figures in the colony, most notably the powerful Dulany family, and earned him wide notoriety. Allen wrote for the Philadelphia press against the growing patriot movement, and was involved in controversy about the right to tithe in tobacco. There were challenges to duels, one at least initiated by Allen himself. In 1768 he was the victim of a public 'caning' by Walter Dulany in the streets of Annapolis. The same year Governor Sharpe appointed him to the wealthiest living in the colony, All Saints, Frederick, worth some £800 to £1000 p.a. To counter the expected opposition of his parishioners, Allen forced his way into a locked church to 'read himself in', and held a pistol to the head of one of the mob who tried to pull him out of the pulpit. 'They accuse me of swearing by God I would shoot … I believe I did swear. It was better than praying just then' (*Archives of Maryland*, 14.501–2). Exasperated, Baltimore tried to have his former friend arrested at

Annapolis races in May 1769. Baltimore's dismissal of Sharpe as governor in 1769 was in part a result of the controversies stirred up by Allen.

Allen made concessions to the parishioners and retained his incumbency at Frederick, although frequently absent. In 1775 he was living comfortably with his sister Elizabeth, two slaves, a fine library, and extensive wine-cellar (Fisher, 39.61, 63–4). Stories circulated about his taste for drink and women, based at least in part on what he said himself. With the outbreak of the American War of Independence Allen returned to England, in September 1775, leaving his sister to look after his affairs. He resumed his fellowship at Wadham until it expired under the statutory time limit in 1780. He wrote anonymously on American affairs for the *Morning Post*, in which on 29 June 1779 he libelled Daniel Dulany, formerly secretary of Maryland, accusing him of surreptitiously keeping contact with the rebels while professing loyalty to the king. The newspaper published a retraction, but Dulany's brother Lloyd issued a challenge. Allen eventually admitted to authorship, and a duel with pistols took place in Hyde Park, London, in June 1782. Dulany was fatally wounded. Allen was tried at the Old Bailey for murder. In spite of a strong directive by the judge, the jury would convict him only of manslaughter, and Allen received a prison sentence of six months. His second, the Wilkesite barrister Robert Morris, was acquitted. No ecclesiastical sanction seems to have been inflicted. A subscription was raised to relieve Allen's misfortunes, said to be occasioned by 'his loyalty to the King and attachment to the British constitution' (Fisher, 39.64). The subscribers included Lord North, the duke of Montague, and Bamber Gascoyne, in whose house at Ilford Allen was living, and who gave him the chaplaincy of St Mary's Hospital, Ilford, said by Allen to be worth only £20 p.a. (Fisher, 39.64, 71).

Elizabeth Allen was driven out of Maryland in 1780, and received a small Treasury pension. Allen himself received £100 p.a. from the Treasury from 1785, increased to £300 by parliament in 1788. In 1802 he claimed no less than £90,000 compensation from the £600,000 made available by the USA for debts owed to British subjects; he received £1106. British negotiators at the treaty of Ghent in 1814 declined to press a further claim for £53,000 (Fisher, 39.65). Allen spent his final years at 12 Gee Street, Somers Town, London, where, according to the *Gentleman's Magazine*, he died on 18 April 1819, aged eighty-three. He was still unmarried and was survived by his sister. He was buried at the new church of St Mary's, Marylebone, on 26 April. His reputation lived on in lurid terms in Maryland; he features large in the novel *Richard Carvel* by the Maryland author Winston Churchill (1899).

C. S. L. DAVIES

Sources J. Fisher, 'Bennet Allen, fighting parson', *Maryland Historical Magazine*, 38 (1943), 299–322; 39 (1944), 49–72 · J. Haw, 'The patronage follies: Bennet Allen, John Morton Jordan, and the fall of Horatio Sharpe', *Maryland Historical Magazine*, 71 (1976), 134–50 · J. Boucher, *Reminiscences of an American loyalist, 1738–1789*, ed. J. Bouchier [sic] (1925) · H. H. Lockwood, *The Revd Bennet Allen: chaplain extraordinary* (privately printed, 2001) · R. B. Gardiner, ed., *The* registers of Wadham College, Oxford, 2 (1895) · Wadham College Muniments, 2/3 [convention bk] · 'Correspondence of Governor Horatio Sharpe, 1761–1771', ed. W. H. Browne, Archives of Maryland, 14 (1895), esp. 323, 501–2 · W. H. Browne, ed., 'Proceedings of the council of Maryland, April 15, 1761–September 24, 1770', Archives of Maryland, 32 (1912) · B. Allen, An address to the vestrymen, church-wardens and parishioners of All Saints, Frederick County (1768) · GM, 1st ser., 38 (1768), 180–88 · Annual Register (1782) · Foster, Alum. Oxon. · will, PRO, PROB 11/1616, fol. 4

Wealth at death approx. £3500 in Bank of England stock and sterling: will, PRO, PROB 11/1616, fol. 4

Allen, Sir Carleton Kemp (1887–1966), jurist and warden of Rhodes House, was born on 7 September 1887 in Carlton, Melbourne, the youngest of the three sons of the Revd William Allen, nonconformist minister, whose own father, a civil engineer, had emigrated from England in the 1850s. Allen's mother, Martha Jane Holdsworth, of Yorkshire stock, was an Australian born at Maryborough, Victoria. The family moved to New South Wales in 1900 where Allen's father was for many years the minister of the flourishing Congregational church in the Sydney suburb of Petersham. The two elder sons were to spend their lives in the academic profession in Australia but 'C. K.'—he was always known by his initials—went to and stayed in England.

Allen was educated at Newington College, Sydney, and the University of Sydney where he obtained prizes in classics and English. In 1909 he went up on a travelling scholarship to New College, Oxford, and joined a group of able young lawyers, pupils of Francis de Zulueta. Allen gained a first in jurisprudence in 1912. In 1913 he was elected Eldon law scholar. His main outside interests were music and acting. In the Oxford Dramatic Society production he was a memorable Julius Caesar to the Mark Antony of Philip Guedalla and in 1913 he produced and played a leading part in Thomas Dekker's The Shoemaker's Holiday. Before the First World War he rejected several offers to become a professional actor, and he long retained an interest in the Oxford University Dramatic Society, through which he met his wife. After the war he became the society's senior treasurer, producing and playing Jaques in As You Like It and inaugurating the summer productions which became a feature of the Oxford Trinity term. He was, along with J. B. Fagan, a founding member of the Oxford Playhouse theatre.

Commissioned in January 1915 in the 13th battalion of the Middlesex regiment, Allen was almost immediately thrown into the battle of Loos, in which the battalion had severe losses, and was badly wounded during the attack on the Hohenzollern redoubt. On sick leave he revisited Australia, as it turned out for the last time. He rejoined his battalion in February 1916 and was then almost continuously engaged in battle, being wounded again on the Somme in July 1916, before becoming captain and adjutant of his regiment. In the March 1918 retreat he was awarded the Military Cross. These savage experiences left a deep imprint upon a stoical nature.

On demobilization Allen was appointed lecturer in law at University College, Oxford. He also acted as assistant to

Sir Carleton Kemp Allen (1887–1966), by Walter Stoneman, 1945

Sir Paul Vinogradoff, whose Outlines of Historical Jurisprudence (1920–22) he helped to see through the press and from whom he derived his interest in legal theory. He was called to the bar at Lincoln's Inn in 1919 but did not practise, for in 1920 he was elected Stowell civil law fellow at University College. In 1924–5 he was the Oxford University junior proctor. He also reviewed novels, and for fifteen years wrote under a pseudonym regular columns in the Illustrated London News and The Sketch. In 1925 his light comedy, The Judgment of Paris, was accepted for a London production but never staged, so he converted it to a novel which was published by the Bodley Head and sold reasonably well.

In 1926 Allen went to India for six months to deliver the Tagore lectures in Calcutta. These formed the core of his Law in the Making, published by the Clarendon Press in 1927. To his surprise the book went into seven editions, his last words, as he put it, appearing in 1964. It began with a judicious and well informed sketch of the schools of legal philosophy in the English-speaking world and in Europe. But its core was an account, both historical and comparative, of the way in which law has changed and grown in the past, whether through custom, equity, precedent or legislation, and how those agencies of change operated in England at the time of writing. Composed with verve, it instructed and enlivened two generations of law students and their seniors. In the 1960s, however, jurisprudence took a more philosophical turn, so that Allen's contribution to the subject, as he foresaw, became dated.

Allen's incursions into public law had more lasting effects. As early as 1923, when most lawyers denied the existence of administrative law in Britain and deplored its existence in France, he was publishing articles to the contrary, later collected as *Bureaucracy Triumphant* (1931), and arguing that the new system should be rationally thought through. He attacked the growth of administrative tribunals and the obstruction faced by those wishing to sue government departments. In *Law and Orders* (1945), which went into three editions, he attacked what he called the 'creeping bindweed' of delegated legislation. The tone of his writings, driven by his respect for lawyers and judges, was polemical but also ironical. 'It is only the lawyer who knows how to temper the fierce legalism of the layman' (*Bureaucracy Triumphant*, 73). His needling did much to spur on the reforms that have since been made in all these areas.

Law in the Making had led in 1929 to Allen's election to the Oxford chair of jurisprudence in succession to Walter Ashburner, the chair that Vinogradoff had earlier held. He was able to continue as a fellow of University College, Oxford, with which he remained closely associated to the end of his days; on retirement he became an honorary fellow of the college in 1963. His tenure of the chair was, however, brief. He surprised many when in 1931 he resigned it to accept the invitation of the Rhodes trustees to succeed Sir Francis Wylie as Oxford secretary to the trustees and only the second warden of Rhodes House, Oxford. At the time this seemed a loss to the law, since he had been an admirable teacher and most lucid lecturer, who combined serious thought with a light touch. But at Rhodes House administration did not take up too much of his time. He was not primarily concerned with the Rhodes Trust's activities overseas, although he kept in touch with the selection committees in the constituencies from which the Rhodes scholars were drawn and he and his wife travelled widely in consequence. His writings on administrative law continued unabated: *Legal Duties* appeared in 1931, *Law and Disorders* in 1954, and *Administrative Jurisdiction* in 1956. In *Aspects of Justice* (1958) his combination of practical and theoretical interests and his classical background again showed to advantage.

As warden of Rhodes House, Allen's own experience of the difficulties of the young who arrive at Oxford from overseas, allied to a shrewdly dispassionate common sense, qualified him to guide Rhodes scholars with the keenest sympathy in their hopes and disappointments. To them he extended an imaginative fair-mindedness along with an exceptional gift for staying outside his own firmly conservative, not to say reactionary, prejudices. He declined, for example, to make use of the National Health Service.

Hospitality was in the capable hands of Allen's wife, whom he had married in 1922: Dorothy Frances, youngest daughter of Edward Halford, retired customs and excise official, of Oxford. They had a daughter and a son. That she was the more outgoing member of a happy partnership— C. K. suffered in his later years from a heart condition—is manifest in her *Sunlight and Shadow* (1960), which she scribbled for her grandchildren just before her death in 1959 and which Allen subsequently edited for publication.

The Allens saw three distinct phases of the history of Rhodes House: the spacious and well staffed hospitality of the time before the Second World War; the exhilarating improvisation, with C. K. himself sometimes at the piano, of wartime Oxford with the courses for soldiers on leave for which Dorothy Allen was awarded a British Empire Medal; then, after the war, the return of former servicemen with their wives, while food rationing continued. To each period they brought a note of quiet enjoyment and, particularly on Dorothy Allen's part, a gift of greeting the unexpected combined with a shared sense of community and subdued adventure.

Allen's own account of his 21-year stewardship of Rhodes House may be found in his contribution to *The First Fifty Years of the Rhodes Scholarships* (1955), edited by Lord Elton. It was typical of C. K. that when he came to hand over Rhodes House to his successor E. T. Williams in 1952 he secured for him those advantages of which he had felt deprived during his own tenure.

In the Second World War, Allen undertook civil defence duties and was a member of the appellate tribunal for conscientious objectors. He was appointed a justice of the peace for Oxford late in 1941, took silk in 1945, and was chairman of the Oxford bench from 1952 to 1956. His appearance and learning lent him authority, but his deafness led to criticism as he continued on the bench in his later years. Allen's experience there provided material for his Hamlyn lectures which were published under the title *The Queen's Peace* (1953). He received various honours: an Oxford DCL in 1932 and an honorary LLD at Glasgow University. He was elected FBA in 1944 and knighted in 1952. His club was the Reform.

Allen's strength as a legal scholar and propagandist derived from his sound classical education, his ability to relate theory to practice, and his vivid style. He believed in the individual and had a deep distrust for the increasing power of the state. In later years he was uneasily reconciled to giving ministers and government departments limited powers to legislate, but he maintained an eagle-eyed readiness to expose, often in the correspondence columns of *The Times*, the tendency to overbear to which he felt public servants were prone.

Allen was of short, stocky build but impressive appearance. His strong eyes, striking nose, clipped moustache, and magnificent crop of lint-white hair (he greyed early) reminded one that he had been a soldier. If he came to absorb some, perhaps more than he was aware, of the prejudices of the English with whom he spent most of his life, he retained his quizzical right to poke fun at them. Increasing deafness made him harder to convince but he continued to make his points with the same deliberation with which he would tap away ash from his ever-present cigarette by way of emphasis. Persuaded to give up smoking at the age of seventy-five, he continued to enjoy bridge, at which he did not greatly like losing, and wine, of which he was a good judge. Until his last illness he took little notice of the regimen that his doctors recommended. Austere in appearance, jaunty in carriage, he was a charming companion and staunch colleague. The essence of integrity, a good judge of Oxford and Surrey cricket, Allen was a man of great determination. Beneath a tolerantly wry scepticism lay a solid core of stern, almost puritanical devotion to truth and justice.

The stoical way in which Allen set about coping with a new existence after Dorothy Allen's death, for they had been a devoted pair, was impressive. To the delight of their friends C. K. remarried in 1962. His second wife, Hilda Mary (d. 1969), daughter of Arthur Grose, had been Dorothy Allen's closest friend. The second marriage was also exceptionally contented and 114 Banbury Road, Oxford, where they lived, warm in its welcome. Allen died at home in Oxford on 11 December 1966.

E. T. WILLIAMS, rev. TONY HONORÉ

Sources A. L. Goodhart, 'Sir Carleton Kemp Allen, 1887–1966', *PBA*, 53 (1967), 391–8 · C. K. Allen, preface, *Bureaucracy triumphant* (1931) · personal knowledge (1981, 2004) · 'Preface', C. K. Allen, *Law in the making*, 7th edn (1964) · *WWW*, 1961–1970 · *The Times* (12 Dec 1966) · *CGPLA Eng. & Wales* (1967)
Archives Bodl. Oxf., corresp. with A. L. Goodhart; corresp. with J. L. Myres
Likenesses W. Stoneman, photograph, 1945, NPG [*see illus.*] · J. Gunn, oils, Bodl. RH · photograph, repro. in Goodhart, 'Sir Carleton Kemp Allen, 1887–1966'
Wealth at death £51,554: probate, 20 Jan 1967, *CGPLA Eng. & Wales*

Allen, Charles (*fl.* 1685–1687), writer on dentistry, published while living in Stonegate, York, the earliest known book in English devoted exclusively to treatment of the teeth: *The operator for the teeth, shewing how to preserve the teeth and gums from all the accidents they are subject to* (1685). Two copies are known, one in the library of York Minster, the other in the College of Dentistry of New York University. A second edition of the book appeared in 1686 in Dublin, where Allen was currently lodging at Essex Street. This version contains some modification to the original text, with *Particular Directions for Children's Teeth and Use of the Polican, Never Published before*. A 'polican' or 'pelican' was a contemporary extraction instrument. The book was bound together with a treatise by an 'unknown hand' (continuously paginated with Allen's), entitled *A physical discourse, wherein the reasons of the beating of the pulse, or pulsation of the arteries, together with those of the circulation of the blood, are mechanically explained; which was never done before.* Only five copies of this 1686 edition have currently been located.

In 1687 the main text of the Dublin edition of Allen's work was reprinted for sale in London but with a new title page: *Curious observations in that difficult part of chirurgery, relating to the teeth. Shewing how to preserve the teeth and gums from all accidents they are subject to.* Fourteen copies of this London edition are known. That any copies at all survived is due partly to the fact that they were collected as examples of seventeenth-century printing in Dublin, London, and York. It was not until B. W. Weinberger acquired a copy of the 1687 edition, in 1923, that the significance of Allen's book for the history of dental treatment in Britain was appreciated and that further copies were sought out. Different editions have subsequently been found, variously listed in a number of bibliographies published between 1824 and 1905.

Little is known about Charles Allen except what can be deduced from his book. He refers to an unidentified 'master', but never calls himself a barber surgeon. In March 1686 Allen presented a copy of his *Operator for the Teeth* to the Dublin Philosophical Society but no definite connection can be shown between Allen and either that city or York; his presence in either place may have been purely for the purpose of having his book printed. The book reveals a high degree of literacy, if not very wide reading. The text of approximately forty pages is addressed to the general reader and deals, *inter alia*, with the anatomy of the teeth, and with gum diseases, oral hygiene, toothache remedies, decay, and extraction. Allen speaks of filling cavities and replacing missing teeth with artificial or transplanted substitutes, but he is sparing in the detail he gives of techniques and materials. Some of his suggestions are decidedly fanciful and seem unlikely to have been the product of practical experience. Allen claimed to have invented a number of instruments which would be described in the next edition. No such work has yet been found.

CHRISTINE HILLAM

Sources C. Allen, *The operator for the teeth* [1685], ed. R. A. Cohen (1969) · B. W. Weinberger, 'Charles Allen's *The operator for the teeth*, York, 1685: the history of the first English dental publication, with corrections', *Journal of the American Dental Association*, 18 (1931), 67–76 · C. Allen, *Curious observations on the teeth* [1687], ed. L. Lindsay (1924) · B. W. Weinberger, 'The first English dental publication', *Journal of the American Dental Association*, 11 (1924), 506–22 · Dublin Philosophical Society minutes, 8 March 1686, Royal College of Surgeons in Ireland, Dublin

Allen, (William Ernest) Chesney (1894?–1982), comedian and singer, was probably born in Brighton on 5 April 1894. The son of a prosperous builder, Allen's first employment on leaving school was as a solicitor's clerk. In 1912, at the age of eighteen, he made his début as an actor in repertory at the Grand Theatre, West Hartlepool. His first appearance as an actor on the London stage came the following year when he appeared at the Bedford, Camden Town. During the First World War he was commissioned in the cavalry and served on the western front with the Royal West Kents, meeting his future partner Bud *Flanagan in Flanders, at an *estaminet* in Poperinghe in 1917. After the war he returned to the stage. He had a brief spell as a hypnotist's stooge and appeared as Rugby in the farce *You Never Know you Know* at the Criterion Theatre in London before joining the touring variety company of Florrie Forde as a straight man to Stan Stanford in the double act of Stanford and Allen. In 1922 he married Aleta Turner, a variety artist and principal boy in Forde's company.

After Stanford's departure from the double act in 1924, Allen met Flanagan again in Glasgow and the two formed a double act which first appeared at the Keighley Hippodrome in 1926. Flanagan and Allen toured with Forde's company, Flo and Co., until its dissolution in 1930. Temporarily short of engagements, the two considered leaving the stage to go into business as bookmakers. However, after a triumphant appearance in variety at the Argyle Theatre, Birkenhead, in January 1931 they found themselves in demand in London. Appearances at the Holborn Empire and the London Palladium consolidated their reputations and established them as the 'Oi!' comedians, working an act of sentimental songs and a cross-talk routine in which Allen's corrections of Flanagan's ridiculous periphrases would be met with an 'Oi!' from Flanagan, orchestra, and audience.

In 1932 Flanagan and Allen were invited to join the cast of a successful 'crazy week' at the Palladium to form what would come to be the *Crazy Gang. Allen appeared with the Crazy Gang in a series of highly popular variety shows and revues throughout the thirties and into the early war years. With Flanagan, he added a dimension of emotional warmth to the robust vulgarity and slapstick of the gang. Allen was a dapper, sophisticated straightman to Flanagan's streetwise but tender-hearted scamp; their enormous appeal was based in a warm companionability that transcended the obviously wide difference in social class between them. Their songs, sung in a characteristic soft, syncopated manner as they swayed together on stage, were sentimental affirmations of the persistence of human warmth in troubled times: Allen's *Times* obituary called their most celebrated hit, 'Underneath the Arches', 'the theme-song of the depression'.

Flanagan and Allen continued their enormous pre-war success as recording artists and as performers on stage and screen throughout the Second World War. Allen appeared in the wartime films *Gasbags* (1940) with the Crazy Gang and *We'll Smile Again* (1942), *Theatre Royal* (1943), and *Here Comes the Sun* (1945) with Flanagan, and appeared with Flanagan on stage, popularizing songs such as 'Run, rabbit run', 'We're gonna Hang out the Washing on the Siegfried Line', and 'Umbrella Man'. He toured with Flanagan in the Entertainments National Service Association, including a spell in France shortly after D-day.

At the end of 1945 Allen announced his retirement from the stage, citing ill health and particularly arthritis as his reason. He did not, however, sever his connections with the Crazy Gang, who re-formed in 1947. Allen, who had acted as business manager for Florrie Forde and had looked after many of the affairs of the Crazy Gang, became their agent and manager. He continued in this role, and appeared on stage with the gang in their frequent royal variety performances, until the group's final show in 1962. He was the last survivor of the Crazy Gang and late in life benefited from revived interest in the group—appearing as himself in a nostalgic musical tribute, *Underneath the Arches*, at the Chichester Festival Theatre in 1981 and the Prince of Wales Theatre, London, in 1982 and making his seventeenth appearance in a royal variety show. He died on 13 November 1982 in the King Edward VII Hospital, Easebourne, Midhurst, Sussex.

DAVID GOLDIE

Sources M. Owen, *The Crazy Gang: a personal reminiscence* (1986) · J. Fisher, *Funny way to be a hero* (1973) · R. Wilmut, *Kindly leave the stage!* (1985) · B. Flanagan, *My crazy life* (1961) · *The Times* (15 Nov 1982) · *Sunday Times* (14 Nov 1982) · R. Busby, *British music hall: an illustrated who's who from 1850 to the present day* (1976) · R. Hudd, *Roy Hudd's cavalcade of variety acts* (1997) · I. Bevan, *Top of the bill* (1952) · B. Green, ed., *The last empires: a music hall companion* (1986) · *Who's who in the theatre* · *CGPLA Eng. & Wales* (1983) · d. cert.
Archives FILM BFI NFTVA, documentary footage · BFI NFTVA, performance footage | SOUND BL NSA, oral history interviews · BL NSA, performance recordings
Likenesses photographs, 1933–82, Hult. Arch.
Wealth at death £92,823: probate, 5 May 1983, *CGPLA Eng. & Wales*

Allen, (Reginald) Clifford, Baron Allen of Hurtwood (1889–1939), politician and peace campaigner, was born at St Olave's, Slow Park, Newport, Monmouthshire, on 9 May 1889. As an adult he was always known as Clifford Allen, or by close friends as CA. He had a brother, Walter Godfrey Allen (1891–1986), who became an architect, and two sisters. His father, Walter Allen (1855–1913), owned a drapery business; his mother, Frances Augusta, née Baker, died in 1903 aged thirty-five and left her son two legacies—precarious health and moral seriousness. Allen was educated at Berkhamsted School, at University College, Bristol, and from 1908 to 1911 at Peterhouse, Cambridge. He intended to take holy orders but at Cambridge his Anglicanism gave way to secularism and his political Conservatism to socialism, which found expression in the university Fabian society. After leaving Cambridge, Allen remained an active Fabian and joined the City of London branch of the Independent Labour Party (ILP). He was heavily involved in the emergence of a Labour newspaper, the *Daily Citizen*, demonstrating a flair for organizational work and making many significant contacts within the labour movement, not least with Ramsay MacDonald. The newspaper first appeared on 8 October 1912 but, after the outbreak of war, its persistent financial difficulties led to its demise in May 1915.

The war transformed Allen's political reputation. His position was uncompromisingly anti-war. He published a speech under the title *Is Germany Right and Britain Wrong?* Most significantly, he was involved centrally in the formation of the No-Conscription Fellowship (NCF) late in 1914 and identified thoroughly with the ILP's defence of internationalism and its criticism of militarism. With the introduction of military conscription in 1916, the NCF dedicated itself to support for individual resisters. Allen would have been exempted from military service on health grounds, but chose to contest his conscription with the claim that his position as NCF chairman qualified as essential war work. But in August 1916 he was arrested, court-martialled, and gaoled. He chose the absolutist position, and refused to accept the option of non-combatant work. Released twice and rearrested, he was finally sentenced to two years' hard labour. His health deteriorated radically and he was released in December 1917, following an agitation on behalf of the imprisoned absolutists.

Allen left prison with severely damaged lungs. The remainder of his life alternated between periods of

(Reginald) Clifford Allen, Baron Allen of Hurtwood (1889–1939), by Elliott & Fry

intense political activity and bouts of illness followed by convalescence. Within the ILP Allen's war record gave him a heroic status. His experiences symbolized the principled commitment and suffering of many party members. In 1920 he visited the Soviet Union as a member of a joint Labour Party–Trades Union Congress delegation. He was attracted by the egalitarianism of the Soviet experiment but was also concerned about the threat of bureaucratization.

Allen thought that in British conditions the transition to socialism could be made without violence. In the early 1920s he saw the ILP as a viable instrument, and he promoted the idea of the ILP as a socialist think-tank developing detailed policies for the wider labour movement. Such an ambition necessitated funds. Allen was elected ILP treasurer in 1922 and demonstrated a talent for raising money from a wide range of progressive sympathizers. Party organization was made more professional; the party newspaper, *Labour Leader*, became the *New Leader*. Edited by H. N. Brailsford, this became renowned for socialist journalism of a very high quality. The unexpected advent of a Labour government in January 1924 with prominent ILP members in key posts, including MacDonald as prime minister, suggested that Allen's strategy might be effective.

Allen became ILP chairman in 1923, and at the party conferences of 1924 and 1925 he emphasized the need to develop detailed policies based on thoroughly scientific investigation combined with a strongly moral commitment. The most famous product of this agenda was the doctrine of the *Living Wage*, published by the ILP in 1926. This powerful, if ambiguous, policy represented a serious attempt to provide a response to poverty and unemployment, an alternative to the dominant economic orthodoxy. But Allen had already ceased to count within the ILP, and resigned as chairman, ostensibly on the ground of ill health, in October 1925. In reality, his resignation stemmed from personal and political differences. Experience of Labour in office had deepened the antagonism of many on the left of the ILP towards MacDonald. For such critics, Allen's approach seemed too conciliatory and too remote from working-class experience. Allen, however, felt that a more adversarial policy would damage the prospects for socialism. He became exasperated with some ILP members who indulged in socialist rhetoric but avoided serious thinking. His resignation marked a significant moment in the leftward shift of the ILP.

Nevertheless, Allen continued his involvement in the labour movement, not least as a director of the *Daily Herald* from 1925 to 1930. These links were effectively destroyed in the crisis of 1931. Although ill, Allen supported MacDonald in deciding to lead a national government and then in the subsequent election campaign. In letters to *The Times* he emphasized the need to restore confidence, and criticized the Labour Party for refusing to join a national government. The argument failed to appreciate the sense of solidarity that had kept almost all Labour politicians and many Labour sympathizers united through the crisis. His rarely reciprocated admiration for MacDonald was a powerful factor. Allen's apostasy was confirmed for many former associates when he accepted a peerage as Baron Allen of Hurtwood in the new year's honours list of 1932. His subsequent attempt to develop a significant political presence for the small National Labour group was disillusioning. MacDonald was largely inaccessible, and Allen's view that National Labour could be the socialist leaven in the National Government ignored its numerical weakness in the Commons. Eventually Allen shifted his focus to developing a broad cross-party progressive programme centred on the idea of planning. In February 1935 he played a central role in setting up the Next Five Years group. His most significant collaborators were a dissident Conservative member, Harold Macmillan, and the economist Sir Arthur Salter. The result was the publication in July 1935 of *The Next Five Years*. Subtitled *An Essay in Political Agreement*, it was supported by 153 political and literary figures. The legacy of 1931 remained potent and the labour movement was almost unrepresented. Allen, in turn, remained hostile to the Labour Party and was suspicious of any collaboration with Lloyd George's Council of Action for Peace and Reconstruction. He still saw the National Government as the only plausible administration. The Next Five Years group offered an agenda without an instrument, a manifestation of the unsuccessful quest for a British new deal.

Predictably, Allen opposed the Versailles settlement and argued consistently that German grievances should be responded to sympathetically. Late in 1934 he joined the Anglo-German group with the purpose of improving relations between the two countries. He visited Hitler in January 1935 and the following year attended the Nuremburg rally. His search for a peaceful European settlement did not entail blindness to the brutality of the Nazi regime. He campaigned on behalf of political prisoners; his last speech to the Lords, on 27 July 1938, included an indictment of Nazi antisemitism. As the agitation by Czechoslovakia's Sudeten Germans threatened serious international consequences, Allen claimed that they should be allowed to join Germany. He travelled to Berlin and Prague in August 1938 to meet Ribbentrop, the German foreign minister, and the Czech president, Benes, and prime minister, Hodza. The prospect emerged of a four-power conference to settle the issue, and Allen reported this to the British foreign secretary, Lord Halifax. Subsequently Allen was a thorough defender of the Munich agreement. It was his last political intervention. Exhausted and ill, he died in a sanatorium at Montana, Switzerland, on 3 March 1939. His body was cremated at Lausanne three days later and the ashes scattered on Lake Geneva.

Allen was survived by his wife, Marjory Gill (1897–1976) [see Allen, Marjory], and by their daughter, Polly. They had married on 17 December 1921; she was the sister of Colin Gill, and cousin of Eric Gill, and was a landscape architect. They shared a commitment to experimental education and founded a nursery school in their local village. Allen felt that his wife's support had prolonged his life.

Allen was a complex figure. His appearance was striking: the handsome head, the auburn hair, the frailty. The impact was deepened by his reasoned yet passionate advocacy. Yet this man of austere principle and firm purpose was an effective organizer and, for some, an assured practitioner of the politician's machiavellian arts. He had a genius for friendship, but broke with political organizations and erstwhile colleagues rather than compromise his principles. One characterization presents him as a Labour renegade whose choice in 1931 condemned him to political marginality. An alternative presentation—more sympathetic and perhaps more apposite—identifies him as one committed to liberal, rational, humane values who believed in the feasibility of a better society but who found no effective organization for furtherance of this agenda.   DAVID HOWELL

Sources *Plough my own furrow: the story of Lord Allen of Hurtwood as told through his writings and correspondence*, ed. M. Gilbert (1965) · A. Marwick, *Clifford Allen: the open conspirator* (1964) · *DLB* · M. Allen and M. Nicholson, *Memoirs of an uneducated lady: Lady Allen of Hurtwood* (1975) · b. cert. · m. cert. · D. Ritschel, *The politics of planning: the debate on economic planning in Britain in the 1930s* (1997), chap. 6 · M. A. Hamilton, *Remembering my good friends* (1944) · J. Paton, *Left turn* (1936) · F. M. Leventhal, *The last dissenter: H. N. Brailsford and his world* (1985) · F. Brockway, *Inside the left* (1942) · D. Marquand, *Ramsay MacDonald* (1977) · H. Macmillan, *Winds of change, 1914–1939* (1966) [vol. 1 of autobiography] · R. Monk, *Bertrand Russell: the spirit of solitude* (1996) · *The Times* (4 March 1939) · *Manchester Guardian* (4 March 1939) · *New Statesman* (11 March 1939) · Burke, *Peerage* (1939) · D. Howell, *MacDonald's party: Labour identities and crisis, 1922–1931* (2002)

Archives U. Warwick Mod. RC, press cuttings · University of South Carolina, Columbia, South Carolinian Library, corresp. and papers | BLPES, corresp. with the Independent Labour Party · BLPES, Francis Johnson MSS · Bodl. Oxf., corresp. with Gilbert Murray · Cumbria AS, Carlisle, Catherine Marshall MSS · HLRO, letters to Herbert Samuel · McMaster University, Hamilton, Ontario, William Ready division of archives and research collections, corresp. with Bertrand Russell · NA Scot., corresp. with Lord Lothian · Ruskin College, Oxford, letters to James Middleton
Likenesses W. Stoneman, photograph, 1932, NPG · Elliott & Fry, photograph, NPG [see illus.] · C. Gill, cartoons, repro. in Gilbert, ed., *Plough my own furrow*
Wealth at death £7500 12s. 6d.: probate, 26 April 1939, CGPLA Eng. & Wales

Allen, Edgar Johnson (1866–1942), marine zoologist and scientific administrator, was born on 6 April 1866 at 6 Havelock Terrace, Preston, Lancashire, the son of the Revd Richard Allen, a Wesleyan Methodist minister, and his wife, Emma Johnson, daughter of a Bideford shipbuilder. They had three daughters and five sons, of whom Allen was the second. He was educated at the Grove School near Leeds and Kingswood School, Bath, before studying chemistry and physics at the Yorkshire College, Leeds, where he graduated with an external London honours BSc degree in 1885.

Allen briefly taught science at Dunheved College, Launceston, before being appointed first headmaster of Coke College, Antigua. He returned to Europe in 1890 and spent a year studying under F. E. Schultze at the Zoological Institute in Berlin before undertaking postgraduate research in zoology under W. F. R. Weldon at University College, London. During the summers of 1892 and 1893, assisted by grants from the British Association for the Advancement of Science and the Royal Society, he visited the laboratory of the Marine Biological Association (MBA) of the United Kingdom at Plymouth to work on the nervous system of Crustacea. In December 1894 he was appointed the laboratory's director, its fifth in eight years of existence. This instability was partly due to strained relations with the parent body, and this situation improved when Allen also became secretary of the association in 1895 (from 1902 secretary to the council). Chronic underfunding was a more long-term problem and Allen, too, contemplated resignation at one stage but weathered the difficult years, remaining as director until his retirement in 1936. During this time, under his outstanding scientific and administrative leadership, the previously small and struggling laboratory developed into a leading centre for marine research.

Allen was immediately concerned to expand the scope of the laboratory offshore and to undertake more extensive oceanographic surveys of the region. Through the support of members of the association such as G. P. Bidder, and others, these began in a hired vessel in 1899–1900 and were developed during the following decade into 'regular investigation of the physics, chemistry and biology of the Western Channel and Approaches', carried out in the association's own yacht *Oithona* (Southward and Roberts, 168).

During the first decade of the twentieth century the Plymouth laboratory undertook government-sponsored fisheries research as part of the British contribution to the work of the International Council for the Exploration of the Sea. However, in 1910 the fisheries work was taken over by the government, and the laboratory again found itself without adequate funding. During the First World War its work was largely suspended and Allen was employed on other projects, including experiments on the hearing of sea lions under water and whether they could be employed to track submarines.

It was not until 1919 that renewal of support from the Development Commission enabled the laboratory to expand, and undertake research which had an important bearing on the subsequent development of biological oceanography. Allen believed that 'the problems of marine fisheries were most likely to be solved with physics and chemistry' (Mills, 5). He felt that the broad questions of fisheries could be settled only by comprehensive knowledge not only of the fish themselves but also of the conditions in which they lived. This view grew out of work he had begun in 1905 on the laboratory culture of phytoplankton. He demonstrated that growth was proportional to the amount of nitrate present, and that phosphate was also essential. He further showed that marine productivity had a direct effect on fish populations (using mackerel catches as an example), and that stocks were boosted when conditions were good for phytoplankton growth, the microscopic plants of this 'blue pasture' being 'grazed' by zooplankton, which then in turn became food for many of the commercial fishes.

After 1910 'both Allen's work and his philosophy of research dominated the way scientists' at Plymouth approached problems (Mills, 203). In the work carried on at the laboratory during the 1920s and 1930s, which developed both from these ideas and from work carried out before the First World War by German fisheries scientists at Kiel, he achieved his aims partly by ensuring that the physical sciences, as well as biology, were strongly represented. However, he did not believe in heading a team, preferring rather, having recruited staff, to allow individuals to work on problems that interested them—though these may well have been suggested by Allen's leading questions. As one of them, L. H. N. Cooper, later said: 'Allen never directed. He just planted seeds' (Mills, 206).

During these years Allen himself was principally engaged in projects connected with both the local and national standing of the laboratory. He was continually seeking to extend its influence, by, for example, introducing Easter and summer classes for students. He never married, and much of the space in the director's house, which formed part of the laboratory building, was given over to its work. The habits of economy instilled in the lean early years remained with him and he used his considerable business acumen to support the laboratory and operation of its research vessels. He paid particular attention to developing the library, much of it through exchange of scientific periodicals, and throughout the period of his directorship acted as editor of the association's own journal. For much of his time at Plymouth opportunities for personal scientific work were limited, but Allen's research was well regarded. He worked extensively on Polychaeta but published few of his results, instead making them available to W. C. M'Intosh for his monograph for the Ray Society. At different times he also studied aspects of amphipod genetics (eye colour in *Gammarus*), and fish biology.

Allen's contribution to science was recognized both at home and overseas. He was elected a fellow of the Royal Society in 1914, and awarded its Darwin medal in 1936. He was a foreign member of the Royal Academy of Denmark and was awarded the Hansen memorial medal and prize in 1923. The Linnean Society awarded him its gold medal in 1926, and in 1938 he received the Agassiz medal for oceanography from the US National Academy of Sciences. He was made a CBE in 1935, and a fellow of University College, London, in 1938. He was awarded a DSc degree by the University of London, and that of LLD by Edinburgh.

Allen was also active in both local and national societies, serving as president of the Devonshire Association in 1916, of the Plymouth and District Field Club, and of the Plymouth Institution. In 1922 he chaired one of the sections of the British Association for the Advancement of Science meeting in Plymouth. For many years he was a member of the Devon and Cornwall sea fisheries committee. From 1929 to 1937 he served on the Tees and Mersey survey committees of the Department of Scientific and Industrial Research, and was on the Water Pollution Board from 1932 to 1937. As a member of the British delegation he served on several committees of the International Council for the Exploration of the Sea.

In 1912 a colleague, feeling that scientists should be more forceful in negotiations with the Board of Agriculture and Fisheries, wrote of him 'Allen is ... so frightfully retiring' (A. E. Shipley to G. P. Bidder, MBA archives), but in 1923, when he received the Hansen medal, a Danish newspaper commented (in translation) 'Dr Allen is a sympathetic, tall and slender figure, with a congenial man-of-the-world appearance' (MBA archives).

On retirement in 1936 he was persuaded to stay in Plymouth, and spent his last few years still involved in scientific interests until failing memory obliged him to give up research. He died suddenly on 7 December 1942 at his home, Reservoir House, Skardon Place, Plymouth.

MARGARET DEACON

Sources S. W. Kemp and A. V. Hill, *Obits. FRS*, 4 (1942–4), 357–67 · G. P. Bidder, 'Edgar Johnson Allen, 1866–1942', *Journal of the Marine Biological Association of the United Kingdom*, 25 (1943), 671–84 · A. J. Southward and E. K. Roberts, 'One hundred years of marine research at Plymouth', *Journal of the Marine Biological Association of the United Kingdom*, 67 (1987), 465–506 · E. L. Mills, *Biological oceanography: an early history, 1870–1960* (1989) · *WW* (1942) · A. Varley, *Catalogue of the archives of the Marine Biological Association* [1997] · *The Times* (8 Dec 1942), 6d · b. cert. · d. cert. · Marine Biological Association of the United Kingdom, Plymouth, E. J. Allen MSS
Archives Marine Biological Association of the United Kingdom, Plymouth, personal and scientific papers | Rice University, Houston, Texas, corresp. with Sir Julian Huxley · U. St Andr. L., corresp. with Sir D'Arcy Thompson

Likenesses R. Schwabe, portrait, photographic copy, Marine Biological Association Laboratory, Plymouth · photograph, RS; repro. in Kemp and Hill, *Obits. FRS*, facing p. 357 · two photographs, Marine Biological Association Laboratory, Plymouth

Wealth at death £9744 18s. 7d.: probate, 18 June 1943, *CGPLA Eng. & Wales*

Allen, Edmund (1510s–1559), protestant reformer, was born in Norfolk some time in the 1510s. He took his BA at Corpus Christi College, Cambridge, in 1535, and his MA in 1537. He was ordained deacon in Lincoln diocese in April 1536. In the same year he was elected a fellow of Corpus, rising to become steward in 1539. Within the next few years he went abroad, having been given formal permission to study elsewhere by his college. His choice of Germany suggests that he already had reformed sympathies, and that his departure may have coincided with the change towards conservatism in the religious atmosphere at home. In the next few years he seems to have travelled to various centres of reform: his Landau letter of 1546 describes how he had to move frequently to hear 'the divers Gifts of God in good men' (Masters, 214). He must, however, have remained in one situation long enough to acquire both a BTh and a wife (whose identity is unknown). The existence of the latter probably explains his wish to remain abroad while Henry VIII was alive. In 1545 his patron, Sir Henry Knyvett, wrote from court to the master of Corpus asking that Allen be allowed to extend his stay overseas for two or three years, since the wars made travel dangerous and he was benefiting from his studies. Mr Porie responded that two more years were acceptable, but the fellowship expected Allen to 'use himselfe pristelike in holinesse and devocion, whereof we here otherwise' (Masters, 213), indicating perhaps that rumours of the wife had reached Cambridge. It was in response to this that Allen wrote his only known letter from the continent, from the city of Landau, thanking the fellowship and asking urgently for his stipend because of 'the extreme dearth that hath bene here so great thes three yearys' (Masters, 214).

The death of Henry VIII was apparently the signal for Allen to return to England, though he never returned to his college. He had already been commissioned by Queen Katherine Parr as one of the team of godly divines to translate Erasmus's *Paraphrases*, and ultimately he contributed the last section of this work with his translation of Leo Juda's paraphrase of Revelation, produced in 1549. On his return he was brought to the attention of Princess Elizabeth, to whom he became chaplain quite early in Edward VI's reign. He was one of the group of preachers licensed to preach throughout the realm in 1547–8, and in February 1548 he acquired the benefice of Welford in Berkshire from Thomas Seymour, Lord Sudeley. Elizabeth had asked Seymour for this favour, a request that caused her problems at the time of his arrest the following year. Allen's importance in this period lay first in his proximity to the princess: he was active in her household for much of the reign, and his influence on her was recognized by Martin Bucer, who in 1549 asked him to persuade her to take a young German reformer into her establishment. Second

he played a significant part in promoting protestant catechizing by publishing in 1548 *A catechisme, that is to saie, a familiar introduction and trainyng of the simple in the commaundements of God*, which was augmented and reprinted in 1551. He also published *A Shorte Cathecisme* in 1550, a volume that went through two printings in its first year. Like Calvin he seems to have believed that 'catechism is the seed that multiplies from age to age' (*CSP dom.*, 1547–53, no. 419), and he was one of a handful of authors who determined this key form of English protestant instruction.

Allen's catechisms offer one of the earliest examples of the confident use of the question and answer form in English, 'to aid', as he puts it, 'those who do not have the Latin tongue' (Allen, *A Catechisme*, sig. A1). The first of the catechisms is described as 'gathered', and depends largely upon continental sources, including elements of Leo Juda's short catechism and possibly some Bucerian influence. Allen's sources may be German, but his concerns with Reformation at home are constantly evident: the king and council, for example, are praised for 'the true planting and setting forth of Christ's pure religion in this realm' (sig. B1). Only his last appended section on congregational discipline, cast in the language of the German reformed communities, appears deracinated. His eucharistic doctrine conforms better to the circumstances of 1548–9 than of 1551: the rite is memorialist, but faithful men are inwardly partakers of Christ's body and blood; real presence, in the spiritual sense of that term, is upheld. This view is intriguingly close to that which Elizabeth seems to have espoused in her adulthood, and it has been suggested that Allen's instruction was a key element in fixing her ideological views at an impressionable age. In 1553 he went into exile once again, a key reason presumably being his marriage; a year earlier he had undertaken the costly task of sharing a private act of naturalization, for his wife and the children born overseas, with the reformer John Rogers and others. Nothing is known about his second exile, but on Mary's death he must have returned very promptly to England, because he was sent abroad on embassy in June 1559. Elizabeth had remained loyal to her household chaplain, and by the time of his embassy he had already been offered the bishopric of Rochester. Was Rochester chosen so that Allen might some day become royal almoner, as did several of his successors? The *congé d'élire* was issued on 27 July 1559, but a month later he was dead. On 30 August the diarist Henry Machyn reported on his funeral, which took place in the London church of St Thomas the Apostle, and on the wife and eight children that Allen left behind. FELICITY HEAL

Sources E. Allen, *A catechisme, that is to saie, a familiar introduction and trainyng of the simple in the commaundements of God* (1548) · E. Allen, *A shorte cathecisme* (1550) · R. Masters, *The history of the College of Corpus Christi and the B. Virgin Mary ... in the University of Cambridge* (1753) · *The diary of Henry Machyn, citizen and merchant-taylor of London, from AD 1550 to AD 1563*, ed. J. G. Nichols, CS, 42 (1848) · H. Robinson, ed. and trans., *Original letters relative to the English Reformation*, 1, Parker Society, [26] (1846) · J. L. Chester, *John Rogers* (1861) · *CPR, 1547–60* · register of Bishop Longland, Lincs. Arch. · register of Bishop Sallot alias Capon, Wilts. & Swindon RO · C. H.

Garrett, *The Marian exiles: a study in the origins of Elizabethan puritanism* (1938) · I. Green, *The Christian's ABC: catechisms and catechising in England, c.1530–1740* (1996) · *Fasti Angl., 1541–1857,* [Canterbury] · private information (2004) [R. Bowers, Jesus College, Cambridge] · *CSP dom.*, 1547–53, no. 419

Allen, Edward Heron- (1861–1943), lawyer and scholar, was born in London on 17 December 1861, the fourth child of George Allen (1823–1911), head of the firm of Allen & Son, Solicitors, Soho, London, and his wife, Catherine Herring or Heron (*b.* 1830). His father's firm, of which Heron-Allen became the senior partner in 1889, had been founded by his grandfather Emmanuel Allen in 1788, and acquired many county and parochial appointments, which were held in succession by his descendants down to Heron-Allen himself.

Educated at Harrow School from 1876, where he developed an interest in classics, music (particularly violin playing), and science, Heron-Allen entered articles at his father's firm in 1879. The office being temptingly placed in the violin-making district of Soho, Heron-Allen attached himself at the same time to the distinguished French émigré maker nearby, Georges Chanot, and made there two accomplished violins. Keeping careful notes he then produced in 1884, the year of his admission as a solicitor, *Violin-Making as it Was and Is*, a comprehensive and pioneering treatise still in print a century later. At the same time he developed an interest in reading personality through a study of hand and finger formation (as well as palmistry), and his *Manual of Cheirosophy* (1885) and *The Science of the Hand* (1886) also went through many subsequent editions. Becoming well known at a young age in these two disparate fields, he contributed violin-related articles for the second edition of Grove's *Dictionary of Music and Musicians* and for the *Dictionary of National Biography* on British violin-makers and astrologers. In 1886 he was invited to the United States on an extended lecture tour, the subject being cheirosophy. This was hugely successful and remunerative. He spoke and demonstrated in New York, Boston, Chicago, and other American cities. While there he published under various pen-names the first three of a number of short novels or stories of an early science fiction type which have become collector's pieces. They also reflect his fascination with the borderline between science and the occult.

Returning to the more mundane world of legal practice in London after three years of living a literary and bohemian existence, Heron-Allen nevertheless found time to develop other interests. Notably, following on from his study of Persian, he published in 1898 a literal translation of the 'Rubaiyat of Omar Khayyam' from the then earliest manuscript in the Bodleian Library, followed by other studies of various versions up to 1908. Fascinated by whether Khayyam was a mere voluptuary or a sublime philosopher, he lectured widely on the place of the rubai in Persian poetry. He also published a translation entitled *The Lament of Baba Tahir* (1901) from a little-known Persian dialect, Luri.

The death of his father in 1911 enabled Heron-Allen to retire from practice at the age of fifty to Large Acres, the house he had built at Selsey Bill, Sussex. There he produced a large quarto volume on the history of Selsey Bill (1911), built a library for his connoisseur's collection of 12,000 books (the rare violin book content of which was bequeathed to the Royal College of Music), and devoted himself in the main to an intensive study of the foraminifera of the local coast. He published, often with Arthur Earland, numerous studies of a proto-zoological nature, and put together over the rest of his life what the British Museum, to which the collection was donated, describes as one of the two most important type slide collections of recent foraminifera extant in England. It was largely in recognition of his work in this field that he was elected a fellow of the Royal Society in 1919. He had served during the First World War in intelligence, playing a significant part in the production of propaganda, facilitated by his linguistic abilities. *Edward Heron-Allen's Journal of the Great War* was published in 2002, with a biographical introduction by the editors, Brian W. Harvey and Carol Fitzgerald. The original typescript of this, together with much other unpublished source material, has been deposited at the West Sussex Record Office, Chichester.

Heron-Allen was twice married, first on 1 July 1891 to Marianna, daughter of the artist Rudolf Lehmann. She died in 1902. In November 1903 he married Edith Emily (1872–1943), daughter of William Brown Pepler MD, with whom he had two daughters. The younger one, Armorel, a fortnight after graduating with a first in zoology at Lady Margaret Hall, Oxford, in 1930, died tragically in a car crash, a catastrophe which he had forecast and secretly recorded in writing many years previously after unwittingly observing her hands. Much affected, he nevertheless completed some of his scientific work, presenting various collections and items to appropriate museums before his death on 28 March 1943 at Large Acres, survived by his elder daughter and, for some two months only, his widow. His ashes were interred at Church Norton, in Selsey.

BRIAN W. HARVEY

Sources B. W. Harvey, 'The power of the pen', in B. W. Harvey, *The violin family and its makers in the British Isles: an illustrated history and directory* (1995), 269–80 · W. M. Morris, *British violin makers: classical and modern, being a biographical and critical dictionary* (1904), 58–62 · R. L. Hodgkinson, 'The Heron-Allen and Earland type slide collection of foraminifera in the British Museum (Natural History)', *Journal of Micropalaeontology*, 8/2 (1989), 149–56 · B. W. Harvey, 'Heron-Allen's fidiculana', *The Strad*, 104 (1993), 484–6 · R. A. Gregory, *Obits. FRS*, 4 (1942–4), 447–54 · *WWW*, 1941–50 · private information (2004)

Archives NHM, corresp., drawings, papers · NMM, naval autograph collection · priv. coll., MS journals | BL, corresp. relating to motto for City of Westminster, Add. MS 40166h · Bodl. Oxf., corresp. with John Johnson · U. Reading L., letters in files of Bodley Head Ltd · U. St Andr. L., letters to Sir D'Arcy Wentworth Thompson · W. Sussex RO, papers incl. typescript of *Edward Heron-Allen's journal of the Great War* and source materials

Likenesses Van der Weyde, photograph, 1884, repro. in E. H. Allen, *Violin-making as it was and is*, frontispiece · Hardman, portrait, 1928, repro. in Harvey, *Violin family and its makers*, pl. 19

Wealth at death £75,810 15s. 3d.: probate, 2 Oct 1943, *CGPLA Eng. & Wales*

Allen, Elias (*c*.1588–1653), maker of mathematical instruments, was born near Tonbridge, Kent, probably in Ashurst, of unknown parentage. Apprenticed in 1602 to London instrument maker Charles Whitwell in the Grocers' Company, he served his master for nine years. Following Whitwell's death in 1611, Allen, then resident in Black Horse Alley, took his freedom on 7 July 1612, at the same time binding his first apprentice. His reputation was already sufficiently high for him to be recommended in Hopton's *Speculum topographicum* of 1611.

Allen soon moved to a workshop beside St Clement Danes Church, the Strand, probably the premises of his former master. He consolidated his position as foremost among the London makers of mathematical instruments, working mainly in brass but occasionally in silver. He won the patronage of various members of the aristocracy and made instruments for James I and Charles I. He also benefited from close association with leading contemporary mathematicians, in particular Edmund Gunter and William Oughtred. These two provided the instrument maker with many of his most popular designs—the Gunter quadrant and sector, and Oughtred's circles of proportion (a logarithmic calculating device), double horizontal instrument (an astronomical instrument), and universal equinoctial ring dial. Surviving examples bear witness to Allen's skill in dividing scales and his artistry as an engraver.

Allen became an associate of the Clockmakers' Company soon after its foundation in 1631, and was appointed as an assistant on 3 October 1633. On 18 January 1636 he assumed the responsibilities of renter warden (treasurer); he was master of the company from 19 January 1637 until 29 July 1638.

This was the peak of Allen's career. Through hard work combined with notable ability he had created a thriving business, becoming the first English instrument maker not to be forced to supplement his income by engraving maps or practising as a surveyor. He was highly respected within London's mathematical community, his workshop being both a centre for discussions and a post office for various correspondences. His skill was esteemed by the most able mathematicians of his day, who were even prepared to alter instrument designs to accommodate his suggestions. He was also courted by his peers in the City: the master of the Vintners' Company commissioned Allen to produce a new gauging instrument. Meanwhile he profited from the increased amateur interest in mathematics which enabled him to develop a market for his wares among the gentry. His skill further showed itself in his ability to train his apprentices to the same high standards. Several of them proceeded to eminent positions in the trade; Ralph Greatorex is perhaps the best-known, by virtue of his association with Pepys. Through Robert Davenport (who settled in Edinburgh) and John Prujean (in Oxford), Allen's craft succession was spread across the country. However, it was the task of another pupil, John Allen, to train Walter Hayes, the instrument maker who inherited Allen's mantle in the latter half of the century.

Elias Allen's achievement is celebrated most clearly in the wealth of instruments he left, but is also commemorated by his portrait—an extremely unusual accolade for a seventeenth-century artisan. The painting (known only through a later engraving by Wenceslaus Hollar) was the work of the Dutch artist Hendrik van der Borcht, and dated from about 1640. Allen's trade suffered during the civil war, forcing him to petition the Clockmakers for funds in January 1649. However, he continued to work until his death in late March 1653. He left one surviving daughter, Elizabeth; his wife, also Elizabeth, whom he married about 1606, died in 1642. He was buried on 1 April 1653 in St Clement Danes, London. H. K. HIGTON

Sources H. K. Higton, 'Elias Allen and the role of instruments in shaping the mathematical culture of seventeenth-century England', PhD diss., U. Cam., 1996 · J. Brown, *Mathematical instrument-makers in the Grocers' Company, 1688–1800* (1979) · E. G. R. Taylor, *The mathematical practitioners of Tudor and Stuart England* (1954) · A. J. Turner, 'William Oughtred, Richard Delamain and the horizontal instrument in seventeenth-century England', *Annali dell'Istituto e Museo di Storia della Scienza di Firenze*, 6 (1981), 99–125 · B. Loomes, *The early clockmakers of Great Britain* (1981) · administration of estate, PRO, PROB 6/28, fol. 83 · parish registers, St Clement Danes, City Westm. AC · parish register, St Bride's, GL · portrait inscription

Archives BM, mathematical instruments · MHS Oxf., mathematical instruments · NMM, mathematical instruments · Sci. Mus., mathematical instruments · Whipple Museum of the History of Science, Cambridge, mathematical instruments

Likenesses W. Hollar, engraving, 1660? (after H. van der Borcht, *c*.1640), Sci. Mus. · W. Hollar, print, 1666 (after H. van der Borcht), BM

Allen, Ethan (1738–1789), revolutionary army officer and politician in America, was born on 10 January 1738 in Litchfield, Connecticut, the eldest of the seven children of Joseph Allen (1708–1755) and Mary Baker (1708–1774), farmers. The Allen family lived in what was then a frontier region of New England.

Allen served briefly in the French and Indian War, though he did not experience combat. In 1762 he married Mary Brownson (1732–1783), farmer, with whom he had five children, and opened a productive iron forge in Salisbury, Connecticut. Allen's unusual religious opinions (as a deist) and outrageous personal conduct ruined this early promise, as he was warned out of Salisbury in 1765 and Northampton, Massachusetts, in 1767.

Allen turned next to hunting, at which he excelled, becoming one of the most notable professional hunters in New England. In 1770 he moved to the Green Mountains and began investing in New Hampshire titles to these lands, which were nearly worthless as New York claimed the region. Within a year he became the leader and chief propagandist of the largely bloodless resistance to New York's jurisdiction. In 1771 he founded the Green Mountain Boys to resist authority in the region of settlers backed by New York, and as a result a £100 reward for his capture was announced in the province of New York.

In his many newspaper articles and books Allen extended John Locke's ideas to a logical extreme. He argued that the land belonged to those who worked it, with or without proper legal title, and denied the right of any government to interfere with this labour theory of land value. Frontier farmers, Allen held, were therefore entirely justified in resisting those who tried to steal the land they worked. As Allen wrote in the *Connecticut Courant* (31 March 1772), 'we mean no more by that which is called the Mob, but to defend our just Rights and Properties'. After four years in which he had successfully nullified New York's rule in the Green Mountains, he used this line of thought to justify a call for the settlers in the region to create their own state and formulate its government according to their desires. The British government realized the radical danger in Allen's political theory, and the privy council made plans to send troops against the Green Mountain Boys in May 1775.

The outbreak of the American War of Independence prevented the planned military action against Allen's forces. Instead, on 10 May 1775, Ethan Allen led his Green Mountain Boys in a bold surprise attack on Fort Ticonderoga. Within two days his forces had taken control of Lake Champlain without a single casualty, taking captive every British soldier in the area and capturing valuable stores of munitions. News of this first offensive victory made Allen an instant national hero, and the continental congress awarded him command of the Green Mountain regiment of the continental army. The elderly leaders of the Green Mountain towns, however, distrusted Allen as too radical, and gave the command to his cousin Seth Warner.

Undeterred, Allen joined the staff of the patriot general Richard Montgomery as a recruiter, enlisting American Indians and French Canadians to join the forces invading Canada. Allen made a serious miscalculation in launching a daring and unsupported attack on a weakly defended Montreal. He was taken prisoner and spent the next two years in brutal captivity in British prisons, aboard prison ships, and in the New York city gaol. Allen's family transformed his cruel treatment at the hands of the British into a *cause célèbre* in Britain and America. Having finally been exchanged in May 1778 for Lieutenant-Colonel Archibald Campbell, Allen wrote a narrative of his captivity that lacerated the British as vindictive monsters, while calling on Americans to abandon any thought of compromise. The work was an enormous success, going through eight editions in two years, and is rated the second best-selling book of the American revolutionary period after Thomas Paine's *Common Sense* (1776).

In Allen's absence from the Green Mountains the region had declared its independence to become the state of Vermont, though in the face of unrelenting opposition from New York. Between 1778 and 1784 Allen operated as commander-in-chief of Vermont's forces, unofficial member of its legislature, chief diplomat, adviser to Governor Thomas Chittenden, and *ex officio* judge of Vermont's court of confiscation. He devoted his energies in these years to defending Vermont, in the process adopting policies that permanently tarnished his fame as a patriot.

From 1778 to 1781 Allen tried to convince congress to accept Vermont's statehood. Twice congress promised to admit Vermont into the union, only to renege on these

engagements when the government of New York threatened to abandon the revolutionary struggle. In a dangerous gambit, Allen opened negotiations with the British commander in Canada, General Frederick Haldimand, to determine possible grounds for Vermont's joining the British empire as an autonomous province. Over the next three years Allen moved adroitly between congress and Britain, keeping each just slightly informed of his dialogue with the other. Allen stopped negotiations with the British in 1784, when passions within New York to retain Vermont died down. In 1786, in response to Allen's refusal to lead Shays's rebellion, New York's legislature finally gave up its effort to reclaim Vermont, though the state's governor, George Clinton, refused to approve Vermont's entry into the union until 1791.

Although he lacked a formal education, Ethan Allen had aspirations to be accepted as an Enlightenment philosopher. From 1781 to 1785 he worked to reach these ambitions in *Reason the Only Oracle of Man* (1785), the first known deistic work by an American. One-third of this long theological study is dedicated to showing the perceived fallacies of Christianity, the other two-thirds to putting forth a deistic religion of nature. Most copies of *Reason* were destroyed in a fire, traditionally assumed to have been set intentionally by religious opponents. Those who read *Reason* were generally shocked by its contents, and dismissed it and its author as 'atheist'. This book faded from sight, though not without further undermining Allen's reputation.

Many Americans were repelled by Allen's religious heresies, agreeing with the Revd Lemuel Hopkins's portrait of Allen as a frontier thug:

> One hand is clench'd to batter noses,
> While t'other scrawls 'gainst Paul and Moses.
> (Smith, 142)

Others found his political views reprehensible. The loyalist Peter Oliver thought Allen was 'of a bad Character, & had been guilty of Actions bad enough to forfeit even a good one' (Oliver, 138). But despite Allen's deism, even political opponents shared George Washington's estimation in 1778 that 'There is an original something in him that commands admiration'. Allen himself gloried in the controversies he raised as a 'clodhopper philosopher' (Allen to Crevecoeur, 2 March 1786, Ethan Allen papers, Vermont State Archives, Montpelier).

Despite his disappointment that *Reason* did not raise more of a firestorm, Allen enjoyed his brief retirement. In 1786 he made a successful journey to the Wyoming valley of Pennsylvania, in support of the squatters there who proclaimed their right to the land they worked. He spent his final years just outside Burlington with his family. He had three children with his second wife, Frances Montresor Buchanan (1760–1834), whom he married in 1784. Allen died near his home in Colchester, Vermont, on 12 February 1789, and was buried in Colchester four days later.

MICHAEL A. BELLESÎLES

Sources M. A. Bellesîles, *Revolutionary outlaws* (1993) · J. L. Barr and S. Caswell, *The genealogy of Ethan Allen and his brothers and sisters*, ed. L. P. Krawitt and others (Burlington, VT, 1991) · J. Pell, *Ethan Allen*

(1929) • E. Allen, *Narrative of Colonel Ethan Allen's captivity* (1779) • P. Oliver, *Origin and progress of the American revolution: a tory view*, ed. D. Adair and J. A. Shutz (1961) • E. H. Smith, *American poems* (1793) • IGI • J. Duffy and others, eds., *Ethan Allen and his kin: correspondence, 1772–1819*, 2 vols. (1998)

Archives University of Vermont, Burlington, Bailey–Howe Library, family papers • Vermont State Archives, Montpelier, papers

Wealth at death $70,000: Chittenden county probate records, Burlington, vol. 1 (1789)

Allen, Francis (*c*.1583–1658), politician and regicide, was probably born in London, though nothing is as yet known of his early life or parentage. He first appears in the mid-1630s as a liveryman of the Goldsmiths' Company living on Fleet Street. He was one of those goldsmiths living in 'remote' places who opposed attempts to force them back into the City by crown and company and to settle them in Goldsmiths' Row in Cheapside. Allen, a successful banker and financier with business interests in the Atlantic trade (he was an active member of the Bermuda Company), no doubt had good material reasons to resist. Suspended from the livery, when he refused the offer to rejoin in 1638 he explained that he was 'ready to doe the company' service but 'desired to be excused if it were so that he must leave his dwellinge which he could no wayes consent unto without his undoing' (Griffiths, 189). However, his objection was also ideological. His original withdrawal, he maintained in 1644 (by when the company was more than happy to welcome back a man upon whom 'Parliament hath cast an eye of favour'), had been because he conceived the order to return to the City 'to be altogether illegal and againste the right and liberty of the subject' (Griffiths, 190).

Allen was elected 'recruiter' MP to the Long Parliament for Cockermouth in April 1642, and certified as such in April 1646. He became a commissioner of customs for parliament from 1643 to 1645 and was appointed one of the treasurers-at-war in March 1645, when the civil war was at a critical point, taking an active part in the financial administration of the war and in liaison with the Scottish army. In politics he was a radical figure, best labelled as a political Independent by the late 1640s. During the wardmote elections of 1642 he was active in the attempt to broaden the franchise in his ward of Farringdon Without upon which officers were elected. In January 1644 he was part of a hostile demonstration against the earl of Essex. In February 1646 he fell victim to the increasing tensions between parliament and the City when he was attacked for reporting to the Commons the details of a meeting between the Scottish commissioners and the presbyterian-dominated London common council (of which he was a member). The Scots had in barely coded terms denounced (and received a sympathetic hearing from their City allies) political and religious Independents for seeking to disturb the unity between the two kingdoms. At the end of the year, when the presbyterians triumphed in the wardmote elections, Allen lost his seat as councillor. He was from 1646 a presbyterian elder of St Dunstan-in-the-West, Fleet Street, the church of the prominent Independent William Strong. It has been suggested that in these years Allen is best thought of as a 'parochial Independent', one happy to maintain the parochial structure of the church, but Erastian in outlook and tolerant of gathered congregations (Lindley, 278). In the later stages of his life he could well be described as an Independent.

Allen was nominated as one of the 135 commissioners (MPs and others) to form the high court of justice to conduct the trial of Charles I. The meetings of the court started on 8 January 1649 but Allen did not attend at the painted chamber in Whitehall until 17 January. Thereafter, however, he was in regular attendance, being recorded as present at nine out of twelve private meetings in the painted chamber and at all four sessions of the actual trial in Westminster Hall, including the final session on Saturday 27 January, in which the sentence of death was passed by all present (though he did not sign the death warrant). On 30 January (the day of the king's execution) he was appointed a member of the committee of the high court to arrange payments for the court and prepare its accounts [*see also* Regicides].

Allen became one of the most active members of the Rump Parliament, often in alliance with his fellow London merchant, Richard Salwey. With Salwey he sat on the committee for establishing the Commonwealth's council of trade. He was by this time a very rich financier; he was elected alderman in 1649 and sheriff in 1651 and 1652. Throughout most of the history of the Rump he was a close political supporter of Oliver Cromwell, but in 1653 he fell out with him in the complicated debates about the dissolution of the house. When the parliament was dissolved by military force, Allen was one of the opponents bitterly attacked by Cromwell, and he was arrested by the army for a short time. Thereafter he dropped out of active politics. He died on 6 September 1658: an unnamed wife but no children are mentioned in his will. In the Act of Indemnity passed in August 1660 after the Restoration the name of Francis Allen appears with those of other deceased regicides exempted from indemnity in respect of 'all rights and properties'.   A. W. McINTOSH, *rev.*

Sources A. B. Beaven, ed., *The aldermen of the City of London, temp. Henry III–[1912]*, 2 vols. (1908–13) • HLRO, MS 3676 • P. Griffiths, 'Politics made visible: order, residence and uniformity in Cheapside, 1600–1645', *Londinopolis: essays in the social and cultural history of early modern London*, ed. P. Griffiths and M. S. R. Jenner (2000), 176–96 • K. Lindley, *Popular politics and religion in civil war London* (1997) • R. Brenner, *Merchants and revolution: commercial change, political conflict, and London's overseas traders, 1550–1653* (1993) • D. Underdown, *Pride's Purge: politics in the puritan revolution* (1971) • B. Worden, *The Rump Parliament, 1648–1653* (1974) • D. Brunton and D. H. Pennington, *Members of the Long Parliament* (1954) • G. Yule, *The independents in the English civil war* (1958) • will, PRO, PROB 11/281, sig. 472

Allen, George (1832–1907), engraver and publisher, was born on 26 March 1832 at Newark-on-Trent, Nottinghamshire, the son of John Allen, a publican, and his wife, Rebecca. He was educated at a private grammar school in Newark, and on his father's death in 1849 he was apprenticed for four years to an uncle (his mother's brother), a builder in Clerkenwell. After becoming a skilled joiner he was employed for three and a half years (1853–7) upon the interior woodwork of Dorchester House, Park Lane, and

George Allen (1832–1907), by Fred Yates, 1890

with another workman spent seventy-nine days on the construction of just one of its interior doors. Ruskin referred to this work in *Munera pulveris* and used to show a model of it to his friends as a specimen of English craftsmanship. Following the foundation of the Working Men's College in Red Lion Square in 1854, Allen attended Ruskin's lectures and joined the drawing class there; under Ruskin and D. G. Rossetti, he became one of its most promising pupils. Ruskin stated that 'the transference to the pen and pencil of the fine qualities of finger that had been acquired by handling the carpenter's tools', coupled with an 'innate disposition to art', enabled Allen to achieve precise draughtsmanship with great rapidity. Allen was drawn more closely to Ruskin by marrying, on 25 December 1856 at St Jude's Church, Whitechapel, his mother's maid, Ann Eliza Hobbes (known as Hannah). (His occupation was recorded on the marriage certificate as 'carpenter'.)

From 1 February 1857 Allen acted as an assistant drawing-master under Ruskin at the college (after its move to Great Ormond Street). Following his appointment he was offered the posts of superintendent of the furnishing of the royal palaces of Queen Victoria and, at Rossetti's suggestion, of partner in charge of furniture with Morris & Co., but these he declined in order to devote himself to Ruskin's service, in which he remained successively as general assistant, engraver, and publisher for fifty years. One of his first jobs with Ruskin, late in 1857, was to sort and arrange the drawings and sketches that J. M. W. Turner had given to the nation and which were held at the National Gallery, London. William Ward acted

as copyist and Allen as engraver. Ruskin encouraged Allen to specialize in engraving, and he studied line engraving under John Henry Le Keux (the engraver of many of the finest plates in Ruskin's *Modern Painters*) and mezzotint under Thomas Goff Lupton (who engraved some of the *Liber Studiorum* plates for Turner). Allen demonstrated his knowledge of the two techniques by producing mixed plates for Ruskin's later books, and in all executed more than ninety plates for Ruskin.

In 1862, when Ruskin thought of settling in Savoy, Switzerland, Allen with his family went out to join him at Mornex, and during this time they travelled together in Italy. His main work in Switzerland was to copy and engrave the work of Turner at full size. He also proved an excellent geologist and mineralogist, so that Ruskin often trusted to his observations; after his death the University of Oxford acquired his mineral collection. Ruskin took no offence when on Sundays Allen engaged in his favourite recreation of rifle-shooting. The death of Ruskin's father, in 1864, ended the Swiss interlude, and through the remainder of the decade Allen acted as a general servant to Ruskin. Many of his reminiscences were of distinguished visitors to Ruskin's house at Denmark Hill to whom he was instructed to show the collection of Turner's drawings.

Late in 1870 Ruskin decided to set Allen up as his own publisher, and through him developed plans to 'attack what he saw as the three great evils of the bookselling trade: the discount system, underselling and the monopoly of London-based publishers and booksellers over the trade' (Maidment, 'Allen', 6–7). At a week's notice, and without any previous experience, Allen started upon this enterprise at his home at Heathfield Cottage, Keston, Kent, so giving rise to a sarcastic journalistic reference to Ruskin's idea of publishing 'in a field in Kent'. At first he worked mainly as a distributor, especially of Ruskin's *Fors Clavigera*, a monthly publication aimed at 'the workmen and labourers of Great Britain'. However, he was also authorized to launch the 'revised and enlarged' edition of Ruskin's works, which focused attention on his social, cultural, and economic theories rather than his views on the visual arts; this he did in 1871 with *Sesame and Lilies*, in conjunction with Ruskin's existing publisher Smith, Elder. In 1874 Allen secured a loan from Ruskin in order to build himself Sunnyside Villa at Orpington, Kent; he developed his business in an outhouse on the property and tended its garden in his spare time. From that time Ruskin officially dubbed him his publisher, and publication of all of Ruskin's books was gradually transferred to him.

By then a familiar figure at Ruskinian gatherings, Allen became one of the first 'companions' of Ruskin's Guild of St George. His responsibilities became all the more serious after 1878, when Ruskin began to suffer from bouts of insanity. Ruskin was then less able to control his own interests and became increasingly dependent on income from his books. Allen tried to develop the firm in commercially sound directions while remaining true to Ruskin's ideological objections to mainstream practices. However, concessions were inevitable. In 1882 he was sanctioned by

Ruskin to enter into an agreement with booksellers which established fixed discounts and consistent prices for Ruskin's works, and in 1886 he drew up his own agreement with Ruskin according to which he worked for proportionate profits rather than on commission. The resulting expansion of the business necessitated the addition of premises in London. In February 1890 Allen opened a publishing house at 8 Bell Yard, Chancery Lane, and from January 1894 he operated at larger premises at 156 Charing Cross Road.

Although Ruskin's works remained the principal part of his business, Allen engaged there in general publishing, issuing biographies and travel books and reprinting fairy tales and standard literary works. His approach to books reflected his earlier career as an engraver, for he emphasized illustration and fine printing. He commissioned such leading illustrators as C. E. Brock, Walter Crane, Hugh Thomson, Arthur Gaskin, Phil May, and Thomas Heath Robinson. Despite falling sales, he also persisted in producing lavish editions. A decline in this luxury market made him rely again on the sale of Ruskin's books at a time when they had ceased to appear radical. He was too late to make much money out of the cheaper editions of Ruskin that he had reluctantly introduced in the late 1880s, yet he persuaded both himself and Ruskin's guardians that economically priced volumes best served Ruskin's general purpose and his publishing venture. This led him to issue three publications which were, financially and historically, his most important achievements of the 1890s: a four-volume edition of *Fors Clavigera* (1896), *Modern Painters* (1897), and *The Stones of Venice* (1898).

Allen's last enterprise was the great library edition, edited by E. T. Cook and A. Wedderburn, of Ruskin's works (1903–11), of which, however, he did not live to see the completion. He died at his home in Orpington, aged seventy-five, on 5 September 1907, and was buried in the parish churchyard. His wife had died, in her eightieth year, eight months before him. They had four sons and four daughters. The eldest daughter, Grace, and the two eldest sons, William and Hugh, continued the business at 44 Rathbone Place, Oxford Street. The firm entered into receivership in 1913, and a year later its assets were sold to Stanley Unwin, so leading to the formation of a new company, George Allen and Unwin.

E. T. COOK, rev. DAVID WOOTTON

Sources B. Maidment, 'John Ruskin and George Allen', PhD diss., University of Leicester, 1973 · B. Maidment, 'Author and publisher: John Ruskin and George Allen, 1890–1900', *Business Archives*, 36 (June 1972), 21–32 · B. Maidment, 'Ruskin, *Fors Clavigera* and Ruskinism', *New approaches to Ruskin*, ed. R. Hewison (1981), 194–213 · B. Maidment, 'George Allen: George Allen and Company Limited', *British literary publishing houses, 1820–1880*, ed. P. J. Anderson and J. Rose, DLitB, 106 (1991), 6–11 · personal knowledge (1912) · E. T. Cook, 'Ruskin and his books: an interview with his publisher', *Strand Magazine*, 24 (1902), 709–19 · 'Publishers of to-day: Mr George Allen', *Publishers' Circular* (12 May 1894), 508–11 · correspondence with John Ruskin, accounts of George Allen, Lancaster University, Ruskin Library · B. Maidment, 'Only print—Ruskin and the publishers', *Durham University Journal*, 63/3 (1970–71), 196–207 · m. cert. · d. cert. · *CGPLA Eng. & Wales* (1907)

Archives George Allen and Unwin Ltd, London, MSS | Bodl. Oxf., corresp. with John Ruskin [transcripts]
Likenesses F. Yates, oils, 1890, unknown collection; copyprint, NPG [*see illus.*] · E. Vieler, photograph, c.1902, repro. in Cook, 'Ruskin and his books'
Wealth at death £10,187 19s. 8d.: probate, 11 Oct 1907, *CGPLA Eng. & Wales*

Allen, George Cyril (1900–1982), economist, was born on 28 June 1900, at 5 Bertie Terrace, Park Road, Kenilworth, Warwickshire, the only child of George Henry Allen (*fl.* c.1875–1940), a coachman and domestic servant who later became dispatch foreman at the Humber motor works, Coventry, and his wife, Elizabeth Sharman, daughter of a baker in Harpenden, Hertfordshire. He was educated at King Henry VIII School, Coventry (c.1911–18), and the University of Birmingham (1918–21), where he was a student in the faculty of commerce. There the economic historian Sir William Ashley, with his blend of economics and history, had an important influence on him. Allen wrote an MComm thesis, 'Restrictive practices in the copper mining industry', which was the first sign of his lifelong interest in the economics of industry. Ashley thought sufficiently well of it to send a copy to Keynes, then editor of the *Economic Journal*. Keynes asked Allen to write a paper on the subject, and this appeared in the *Economic Journal* in 1923.

Ashley was also instrumental in giving Allen the opportunity of a teaching post in Japan. In 1922 he urged Allen to accept a two-year appointment as a lecturer in economics at the new Nagoya high school (later part of the University of Nagoya) in central Japan. Thus began Allen's lifelong study of Japanese economic affairs, and of Japan as a nation. Henceforward his academic work and his publications were shared between the study of the economics of British industry and the study of Japan. On his return to Britain, he took up a research fellowship and then a lectureship at his old university, Birmingham. In 1925 his article on Japan's currency and exchange rate policy was published in the *Economic Journal*. His first book, *Modern Japan and its Problems*, was published in 1928, and the next year he published *The Industrial Development of Birmingham and the Black Country, 1860–1927*. Both books were innovatory in their fields, and that on Japan was especially original, linking as it did a study of Japan's political and social organization with its financial and industrial systems.

On the basis of these achievements Allen was appointed in 1929 the first holder of the chair of economics and commerce at Hull University College, at the age of twenty-eight. In the same year he married Eleanora (Nell) Shanks (d. 1972), daughter of David Shanks JP of Moseley, Birmingham; they had no children. From 1933 to 1947 Allen was Brunner professor of economic science at the University of Liverpool, and from 1947 to 1967 professor of political economy at University College, London. In 1975 he retired to Oxford, and in 1980 was made a supernumerary fellow of St Antony's College, where he welcomed the foundation of the new Nissan Institute for Japanese Studies.

Allen also had experience outside the university. In 1930 he served briefly as economic adviser to Lloyd George.

During the war years he served in the Board of Trade, where he was mainly concerned with work on post-war reconstruction. He was an active member of the group of economists anxious to introduce legislation to control monopoly and restrictive practices. This led to the prominence given to the subject in the 1944 white paper on employment policy, and eventually to the legislation of 1948. From 1950 to 1962 he was a member of the Monopolies and Restrictive Practices Commission (from 1956 the Monopolies Commission). He also served on the Central Price Regulation Committee (1944–53) and on several other official committees.

In 1945 Allen's Japanese expertise was called upon by the Foreign Office, where for six months he was in charge of the Japanese section of the economic and industrial planning staff. There his unique knowledge of the Japanese economy contributed to the formulation by the allied powers of policy towards Japan during the occupation. His optimism about Japan's economic prospects was almost unique in Britain at that time.

In his last year at Hull, Allen published what was perhaps his best-known work, *British Industries and their Organization* (1933), which was to go through five editions, the last in 1970. It combined a historical account of the industries covered with an analysis of their current economic problems. For many years this was by far the most valuable book on British industry. Allen continued to be a prolific author in his two chosen fields, but from 1938 the books he wrote were mainly about Japan and the Far East, though his articles, pamphlets, and other publications show a rough balance between his interests in Britain and Japan. His work was pragmatic rather than ideological, relying on detailed knowledge of the subject and emphasizing the importance of institutional and social factors.

Allen made many visits to Japan, where he was much respected. He received the order of the Rising Sun in 1961 and the Japan Foundation award in 1980. His genial personality and acute analytical mind made him very well liked and regarded wherever he worked. He was appointed CBE in 1958 and elected a fellow of the British Academy in 1965. He died at his home, 15 Ritchie Court, 380 Banbury Road, Oxford, on 31 July 1982.

AUBREY SILBERSTON

Sources M. Gowing, 'George Cyril Allen, 1900–1982', *PBA*, 71 (1985), 473–91 · *WWW* · *The Times* (10 Aug 1982) · b. cert. · personal knowledge (2004)
Archives UCL, memoranda and papers; additional papers | BLPES, corresp. with the editors of the *Economic Journal*
Wealth at death £181,124: probate, 25 Nov 1982, CGPLA Eng. & Wales

Allen, Sir George Oswald Browning [Gubby] (1902–1989), cricketer and cricket administrator, was born on 31 July 1902 in Sydney, Australia, the younger son and second of the three children of Sir Walter Macarthur Allen (1870–1943) and his wife, Marguerite Julie (Pearl), daughter of Edward Lamb, of Sydney, minister of lands in Queensland. His sister married Sir William Dickson, marshal of the Royal Air Force. His brother died on active service in 1940. Although by birth a third-generation Australian—

Sir George Oswald Browning [Gubby] **Allen** (1902–1989), by unknown photographer, c.1932–3

his father's brother had played cricket for Australia against England at Sydney in 1887—Allen was taken to England at the age of six, so that he could be educated there. In the event, his parents chose to settle in England, his father becoming commandant-in-chief of the metropolitan special constabulary, in which post he was appointed KBE in 1926.

It was not long before Gubby, as he came to be known, was resolutely English. After showing early promise as a cricketer at Summer Fields School, Oxford, he had three years in the Eton eleven (1919–21) before winning a blue at Cambridge in 1922 and 1923. After two years at Trinity College, Cambridge, he left without a degree and became a stockbroker in the City of London. By 1923 he was making the occasional appearance for Middlesex and gaining a reputation as a genuinely fast bowler and no mean batsman. Of no more than medium build, Allen achieved his pace through timing, thrust, and a fine follow through. He made the most of an elastic strength, while managing, at the same time, to play the game with style. Between the late 1920s and the mid-1930s there was no English fast bowler, apart from Harold Larwood, capable of more dangerous spells.

Allen was essentially an amateur. Even when, in 1929, he took all ten Lancashire wickets for forty runs for Middlesex at Lord's, he had done some stockbroking in the City first and arrived on the ground too late to open the bowling. He never played first-class cricket regularly enough in England to score 1000 runs or take 100 wickets in a season.

Not surprisingly, perhaps, it was in Australia, to which he went back as a member of the MCC sides of 1932–3 and 1936–7 and had plenty of bowling, that he was at his most consistent.

On the first of these tours Allen's refusal to resort to 'leg theory' distanced him from his captain, Douglas Jardine. Despite that, he took twenty-one wickets in the five test matches. Four years later he took another seventeen test wickets at the same time as enduring, as England's captain, the mortification of seeing Australia recover from the loss of the first two test matches so effectively that they won the last three and, with them, the Ashes. On the tour of 1936–7 a friendship developed between Allen and his opposite number, Donald Bradman, which was to last for over fifty years and to have a major influence within the corridors of cricketing power.

In the seventeen years which passed between the last of Allen's twenty-five test matches, at Melbourne in 1937, and his last first-class match, against Cambridge University at Fenner's in 1954, he played very little first-class cricket, even for Middlesex. This was partly because of the Second World War, during which he served, to the rank of lieutenant-colonel, in military intelligence (MI5) at the War Office, partly because of the time he gave to the City, and partly through choice. He did, however, accept an invitation to take a somewhat experimental MCC side to the West Indies in 1947–8, a decision which he considered afterwards to have been a mistake. By then he was forty-four—older than any England captain since W. G. Grace in 1899—and he tore his hamstring (the first instance of many) on the outward voyage.

Elected to the MCC committee for the first time in 1935, at what was then an unusually young age, Allen became in time the *éminence grise*. As a cricket administrator of dominance and durability he ranks with the seventh Baron Hawke of Towton (1860–1938), the fourth Baron Harris (1851–1932), and Sir Pelham Warner (1873–1963). For half a century there was scarcely an issue connected with the game in which he was not closely involved. He was chairman of the England selectors from 1955 to 1961, president of the MCC in 1963–4, treasurer of the MCC from 1964 to 1976, a member of the Cricket Council from its formation in 1968 until 1982, a prime mover in founding the national coaching scheme, and co-author, with H. S. Altham, of the *MCC Cricket Coaching Book* (1952), the standard work of its kind.

Allen's other main sporting interest was golf, a game to which he applied himself diligently and which he played well enough to have, at his best, a handicap of four. His own account of a good round, stroke by stroke, was always something of a ceremony. As a source of cricketing reference he had no equal, and in the summers after his retirement from the City (he was a member of the stock exchange from 1933 to 1972) there was never much doubt where to find him: he would be in his customary place in the window of the committee room at Lord's.

Allen was appointed CBE in 1962 and knighted in 1986. He was awarded the Territorial Decoration of Ireland (1945) and the American Legion of Merit (1946) for his war services. Although he never allowed himself to be talked into marriage, he always enjoyed feminine company. Allen died on 29 November 1989 at his home, 4 Grove End Road, overlooking the Lord's pavilion in St John's Wood, London.   JOHN WOODCOCK, *rev.*

Sources E. W. Swanton, *Gubby Allen: man of cricket* (1985) · CGPLA Eng. & Wales (1990) · Wisden
Likenesses photograph, c.1932–1933, Marylebone Cricket Club, Lord's, London [see illus.] · J. A. Hampton, black and white photograph, 19 July 1939, Hult. Arch. · Ward, portrait, Lord's cricket ground, London
Wealth at death £977,589: probate, 19 April 1990, CGPLA Eng. & Wales

Allen, (Charles) Grant Blairfindie (1848–1899), writer on science and novelist, was born at Alwington, near Kingston, Ontario, Canada, on 24 February 1848, the second but only surviving son of Joseph Antisell Allen, a clergyman of the Church of Ireland who had emigrated to Canada in 1840 and who survived his son by eleven months, dying at Alwington on 6 October 1900. His mother, Charlotte Catherine Ann, was the only daughter of Charles William Grant, fifth Baron de Longueuil.

Grant Allen (as he always styled himself) spent the first thirteen years of his life in the Thousand Islands region, on the upper St Lawrence River, where he developed a love of animals and flowers under the tutelage of his father. About 1861 the family moved to New Haven, Connecticut, where Allen had a tutor from Yale University. A year later the family went to France. Allen studied first at the Collège Impérial at Dieppe and later transferred to King Edward's School at Birmingham. In 1867 he was elected to a postmastership at Merton College, Oxford. His undergraduate career was interrupted by his marriage, at the age of twenty, to Caroline Ann Bootheway (b. 1844/5), daughter of William Bootheway, a labourer, on 30 September 1868. The marriage was a short one, however, as his wife, who had always been an invalid, soon died. Allen went on to gain a first class in classical moderations and a second class in the final classical school after only a year's reading. In 1871 he graduated BA but proceeded to no further degree. For the next three years he undertook what was to him the uncongenial work of a schoolmaster at Brighton, Cheltenham, and Reading.

On 20 May 1873 Allen married Ellen (b. 1852/3), the youngest daughter of Thomas Jerrard, a butcher, of Lyme Regis, Dorset, and shortly thereafter he accepted an appointment as professor of mental and moral philosophy at a college at Spanish Town in Jamaica, founded by the government for the education of native peoples. The experiment was a failure, and in 1876 the college was finally closed. Allen returned to England with a small sum of money in compensation for the loss of his post. His three years' experience in Jamaica, however, had an important influence on the development of his mind, having given him time to read and to allow his ideas to clarify. It was during this time that he, always proud of his Scottish blood, acquired a fair knowledge of Old English. He also studied philosophy and physical science and framed an evolutionary system of his own, based mainly

(Charles) **Grant Blairfindie Allen** (1848–1899), by Sir William Rothenstein, 1897

on the works of Herbert Spencer. This period marked the end of his formal studies.

While at Oxford, Allen had contributed to a short-lived periodical, the *Oxford University Magazine*, of which only two numbers appeared (December 1869 and January 1870). When he returned from Jamaica in 1876, he resolved to support himself by his writing. His first book was an essay, *Physiological Aesthetics* (1877), which he dedicated to Spencer and published at his own risk. It did not sell, but it won for him some reputation and introduced his name to the editors of magazines and newspapers. At this time he began to publish popular scientific articles, always with an evolutionary moral, in *The Cornhill*, the *St James's Gazette*, and elsewhere. He also assisted Sir William Wilson Hunter in the compilation of the twelve-volume *Imperial Gazetteer of India*, in which he wrote the greater part of the articles on the North-Western Provinces, the Punjab, and Sind. For a short time he was on the staff of the *Daily News* and was also one of the regular contributors to *London* (1878–9), a short-lived periodical. During this early period (1879–83) his publications were scientific, such as his essay *The Colour Sense* (1879), which won high approval from Alfred Russel Wallace; three collections of popular scientific articles (*Vignettes from Nature*, 1881; *The Evolutionist at Large*, 1881; and *Colin Clout's Calendar*, 1883), the value and accuracy of which are attested by letters from Charles Darwin and T. H. Huxley; two series of botanical studies on flowers (*Colours of Flowers*, 1882, and *Flowers*

and their *Pedigrees*, 1883); and a short monograph, *Anglo-Saxon Britain* (1881).

During 1884 Allen began to contribute short stories to such periodicals as *Longman's Magazine*, *Belgravia*, and *The Cornhill* under the pseudonym of J. Arbuthnot Wilson; these were later collected under the title of *Strange Stories* (1884). His first novel, *Philistia*, originally appeared as a serial in the *Gentleman's Magazine* and then was published in the standard three-volume edition in 1884, again under a pseudonym, Cecil Power. The book, a satire on socialism and modern journalism, was largely autobiographical. Although it was not a success with the public, he was encouraged to continue writing, and during the next fifteen years he brought out more than thirty works of fiction, which were both popular and profitable. In addition to healthy sales, in 1891 he won a prize of £1000 from *Tit-Bits* magazine for his novel *What's Bred in the Bone*. He had a knack for devising ingenious plots based on contemporary issues and on his wide experience. *In All Shades* (1886), set in Jamaica, deals with multicultural love; *The Tents of Shem* (1891) is set in Algeria; *The Type-Writer Girl* (1897), written under the pseudonym of Olive Pratt Rayner, seized upon the very topical subject of a university-educated woman struggling with the reality of earning her own living; *The British Barbarians* (1895) is a satire on British society seen from the vantage point of the twenty-fifth century.

Perhaps Allen's most notable and lasting achievement was the novel *The Woman who Did* (1895), the story of Herminia Barton, a Girton College girl who falls deeply in love with Alan Merrick but decides not to marry him on the grounds of female emancipation. They cohabit and she gives birth to a daughter, but after Merrick's sudden death tragedy overwhelms her life with remorseless precision. Allen honestly intended the novel as a polemic on the position of women and dedicated it to his wife, with whom he passed 'my twenty happiest years'. It caused a great sensation, and the public read it eagerly, but they were shocked and also puzzled by its lack of humour. Allen wrote two novels in direct response (*The Woman who Didn't*, 1895, and *The Woman who Wouldn't*, 1895), and the notoriety of *The Woman who Did* helped establish the 'new woman' novel as a genre. The novel also claimed the notice of many late twentieth-century feminists for its outspoken analysis of the female dilemma.

Allen's intellectual activity was not confined to novel-writing. He made regular contributions to newspapers, magazines, and reviews, some of which were collected and reprinted in *Falling in Love, with other Essays on More Exact Branches of Science* (1889) and *Postprandial Philosophy* (1894). He returned twice to the more abstruse science of his earlier days. In 1888 he brought out *Force and Energy*, which embodies the results of his lonely reading and cogitations in Jamaica (the first draft had been privately printed in 1876). Contemporary physicists generally declined to discuss his novel theory of dynamics, considering it that of an amateur. He nevertheless persisted in it, and when the book passed into the remainder market in 1894, he presented a copy to a friend with the inscription: 'It contains my main contribution to human thought. And I desire here to state that, when you and I have passed away, I believe its doctrine will gradually be arrived at by other thinkers'. His other serious work was *The Evolution of the Idea of God* (1897), an enquiry into the origin of religions. The book is crowded with anthropological lore and contains numerous brilliant *aperçus*, but it labours under the defect of attempting to explain everything by means of a single theory. In 1894 he issued *The Lower Slopes*, an unremarkable volume of poems written in his youth. More successful were the detective stories, written later in his life, many of which appeared in the *Strand Magazine*, and volumes of detective fiction, of which the most notable is *An African Millionaire: Episodes in the Life of the Illustrious Colonel Clay* (1897). Allen at this time also found a fresh interest in art. He had always been attracted to art as a handicraft, but the appreciation of painting and architecture came later, as the result of repeated visits to Italy. To his scientific mind they fell into their place as branches of human evolution. It is this unifying conception of art, as well as of history, that inspired the series of guidebooks on Paris, Florence, Venice, and the cities of Belgium (1897, 1898) which he wrote in his last years. Throughout all his mature work his interest in science and evolution informs his fiction:

> As a scientist Allen was an evolutionist, and as a novelist one of his most persistent themes was the effect of heredity. Even his lighter and more popular works evidence not only his scientific outlook but also his persistent questioning of established convention and of institutions and officials that uphold it. (Christou, 11)

Allen never enjoyed robust health, and London was always distasteful to him. In 1881 he settled at Dorking in Surrey, where he delighted in botanical walks in the woods and on sandy heaths. However, nearly every year he was compelled to winter in southern Europe, usually at Antibes, though once or twice he went as far as Algiers and Egypt. In 1892 he bought a plot of land almost on the summit of Hindhead, Haslemere, Surrey, and built himself a cottage which he called The Croft. Here he found that he could endure the severity of an English winter amid surroundings wilder than at Dorking, and with the society of a few congenial friends. He still made trips to the continent, chiefly to prepare his guidebooks. His favourite British holiday resort was on the River Thames, near Marlow. On 25 October 1899 he died of liver cancer at his home at Hindhead. His body was cremated at Woking, Surrey, the only ceremony being a memorial address by Frederic Harrison. He was survived by his second wife, and his only child, Jerrard Grant Allen.

J. S. Cotton, rev. Rosemary T. Van Arsdel

Sources E. Clodd, *Grant Allen, a memoir with a bibliography* (1900) • J. Sutherland, 'Allen, (Charles) Grant (Blairfindie)', *The Stanford companion to Victorian fiction* (1989), 20–21 • A. Christou, 'Allen, Grant', *The 1890s: an encyclopedia of British literature, art, and culture*, ed. G. A. Cevasco (1993) • BL cat. • R. LeGallienne, 'Grant Allen', *Fortnightly Review*, 72 (1899), 1005–25 • C. K. Shorter, 'Grant Allen: life and work', *The Critic*, 38 (1900) • W. J. Harvey, 'Grant Allen', *The new Cambridge bibliography of English literature*, [2nd edn], 3, ed. G. Watson (1969), 1031–3 • m. certs. • d. cert. • *CGPLA Eng. & Wales* (1899)

Archives LUL, letters to Herbert Spencer • Richmond Local Studies Library, London, corresp. with Douglas Sladen • U. Leeds, Brotherton L., letters to Edward Clodd

Likenesses W. Rothenstein, lithograph, 1897, NPG [*see illus.*] • Barraud, print, NPG; repro. in *Men and Women of the day*, 4 (1891)

Wealth at death £6455 3s. 3d.: probate, 14 Dec 1899, *CGPLA Eng. & Wales*

Allen [*née* Howse; *other married name* Chapman], **Hannah** (*fl.* 1632–1664), bookseller, was probably the daughter of Robert Howes, bookseller and bookbinder, and his wife, Anne, who baptized a daughter, Anne, on 26 December 1619 in St Botolph, Aldgate, London. She married the bookseller Benjamin Allen (d. 1646) on 2 April 1632 at St Katharine by the Tower and a son, Benjamin, was baptized on 9 August 1635 at St Olave, Hart Street. A daughter, mentioned in Benjamin's will, has not been traced.

After her first marriage Hannah lived and worked in London at The Crown in Pope's Head Alley, an area known for its radical bookshops. Her brother may have been the bookbinder Samuel Howes, who was apprenticed to the Allens' neighbour Henry Overton and who used a Pope's Head Alley address. It is not until after Benjamin's death in May 1646 that Hannah's role in the business becomes prominent. Left £150 in Benjamin's will, and with two children to support, she inherited a business already established as sympathetic to Baptist, Independent, and millenarian publishing. She kept on Benjamin's apprentice of three years, Livewell *Chapman (*fl.* 1643–1665), bound John Allen in 1646, and took a third apprentice, John Garfield, in 1647. Chapman was freed as a stationer in November 1650 and by 12 September of the following year he and Hannah were married. A son, Livewell, was baptized on 2 June 1652 and a daughter, Patience, on 6 December 1653, both at St Mary Abchurch.

Between August 1646 and January 1651 Hannah issued about sixty books and pamphlets. Many of her imprints show her working with other stationers, notably Matthew Simmons, Henry Overton, and John Rothwell. Her publications with the printer Simmons suggest some kind of partnership in the early phase of her career, but from the beginning of 1649 her use of a great variety of printers suggests increasing financial independence and confidence. Leona Rostenberg's presentation of her is thoroughly misleading in ignoring her development of the business. While some of the works published by Hannah Allen were by authors previously published by Benjamin (such as Jeremiah Burroughes, Nicholas Lockyer, William Greenhill, Samuel Richardson, Samuel Chidley, John Cotton, and Richard Mather), her total output suggests that Hannah moved the business in a more millenarian, radical, and eventually Fifth Monarchist direction. She was the first publisher of William Cradock, Henry Jessey, and Vavasour Powell, and brought out books by, among others, Thomas Manton, Thomas Brookes, Richard Kentish, and John Robotham. She published several topical pamphlets relating to the army, reports of Indian conversions in New England and Formosa, and Mannasseh ben Israel's plea for readmission of the Jews, *The Hope of Israel* (1650). In Jessey's *The Exceeding Riches of Grace* (1647) she is reported as visiting Sarah Wight's bedside in the company of other local tradeswomen; Wight's other visitors included the prophet Anna Trapnel, the religious leaders Thomas Goodwin, John Simpson, Nicholas Lockyer, and Walter Cradock, and Captain Harrison and Praisegod Barbon.

After her second marriage Hannah's name disappears from imprints and from Stationers' Company records, except for the freeing of apprentices in 1654 and 1655, but it is likely that she still played an important role. She was perhaps ten years older and certainly much more experienced in bookselling than Livewell Chapman. Chapman was often absent in the late 1650s and early 1660s, imprisoned in Ludgate or the Gatehouse and, in 1662, fleeing abroad. At such times she was no doubt in sole charge of the business. In 1663 she was suspected of managing the printing of *The Face of the Times* by Sir Henry Vane, and when Chapman was released from prison in May 1664 it was on security that 'neither he nor his wife' publish or disperse illegal books (PRO, SP 29/98/25). Imprisonments and fines ruined Chapman's business, his last publication appearing in 1664. If Hannah can be identified as the 'widow Hannah Chapman' listed in the Stationers' Company poor book from 1678 to 1705, then she lived in poverty to a great age.   MAUREEN BELL

Sources M. Bell, 'Hannah Allen and the development of a puritan publishing business, 1646–51', *Publishing History*, 26 (1989), 5–66 · ESTC · G. E. B. Eyre, ed., *A transcript of the registers of the Worshipful Company of Stationers from 1640 to 1708*, 3 vols. (1913–14) · H. Jessey, *The exceeding riches of grace advanced by the spirit of grace, in an empty nothing creature, viz. Mris Sarah Wight* (1647) · L. Rostenberg, 'Sectarianism and revolt: Livewell Chapman, publisher to the Fifth Monarchy', *Literary, political, scientific, religious and legal publishing, printing and bookselling in England, 1551–1700: twelve studies* (1965), 203–36 · PRO, state papers · will, PRO, PROB 11/196, sig. 57 [Benjamin Allen] · Greaves & Zaller, *BDBR* · IGI

Allen [*née* Archer], **Hannah** (*c.*1638–1668x1708), nonconformist writer, was the daughter of John Archer of Snelston, Derbyshire, and his wife, the daughter of William Hart of Uttoxeter Woodland in nearby Staffordshire. Her father, who was from a family of tanners and tailors, died when Hannah was 'very young' and her mother brought her up 'in the fear of God' (Allen, 1). Most of the information concerning her life is derived from her later work, a spiritual narrative of melancholy and temptation, *A Narrative of God's Gracious Dealings with that Choice Christian Mrs Hannah Allen* (1683). In 1650, aged 'about twelve' (ibid., 2), Hannah was sent to live with her aunt Ann and uncle Samuel Wilson, a merchant, in the parish of St Mary Aldermanbury, London. She went to school there but, after an illness, decided to return to her mother. This seems to have been the start of her torments, as 'the enemy of my Soul'—Satan—began a campaign of temptation, casting into her mind 'horrible blasphemous thoughts' (ibid., 2–3).

Back at Snelston Hannah was comforted by reading a book by 'Mr Bolton' (possibly either Robert or Samuel, clergymen) and, throughout her later text, writing and reading mark key moments in her spiritual and psychological journey. Returning to her aunt's house in London

after about two years, on 23 December 1654 she married Hannibal Allen (d. 1664), merchant, a widower, and was 'admitted to the sacrament' (Allen, 6) by Edmund Calamy, the well-known presbyterian minister of St Mary Aldermanbury. She and her husband had at least one child. She was at this time 'frequently exercised with a variety of Temptations' (Allen, 7), and 'much inclined to Melancholy' (ibid.) because her husband was away. Having returned to Snelston while her husband was overseas, in February 1664 Hannah heard of Hannibal's death and from this moment she writes of intensified and more dramatic temptations. At first she was comforted by a minister, her relative by marriage, John Shorthose. She also used to 'write in a Book I kept for that purpose in Shorthand' (ibid., 12) and a few passages from this book, written in her 'deep distress' (ibid.) in 1663–4, were published in her 1683 work. After 26 May 1664 Hannah 'writ no more' (ibid., 21) as, overcome by despair, her 'language and condition' (ibid.) grew worse than ever. Her condition deteriorating, she was taken to London and lodged with her brother where she attempted suicide by taking spiders 'one at a time in a Pipe with Tobacco' (ibid., 32–3) and was removed to the house of her kinsman Peter Walker. She was later unable to remember much about this period, a spiritual nadir which preceded her gradual recovery, but later recalled saying '*the hottest place in hell must be mine*' (ibid., 48).

Hannah stayed with Walker until summer 1665 when, as she was no better, her aunt took her back to Snelston. After another year of illness Hannah gradually began to recover and by spring 1668 was well again. At that time she married Charles Hatt (d. 1709), a widower then living in Warwickshire and one 'that truly fears God' (Allen, 71). Hannah had previously met him in the company of her aunt at his house in Old Jewry, London. This was probably the same Charles Hatt who had his house in Great Warley, Essex, licensed for presbyterian preaching in 1672. Hannah then wrote her narrative describing her spiritual trajectory from intensifying temptation to despair ('I was perswaded I had sinned the Unpardonable Sin'; ibid., 4) and on to an eventual recovery of faith and calm. The modes of her writing, retrospective but incorporating written fragments from the time of her collapse, and the nature of the temptations to which she was subject, as well as the cures proposed by relations, have led the text to be interpreted as a narrative of madness and depression as well as religious belief. The circumstances surrounding the composition of the text are unclear but it is possible that the Hatts were connected with a network of puritan friends which included their neighbours, the nonconformist couple Nathaniel Rich and his wife, Elizabeth, of Stondon Hall, Essex, and Hannah's narrative may have been written for that circle. At one point in the text Hannah addresses 'your Ladyship' (ibid., 34), perhaps intending Lady Elizabeth, who had shown an interest in nonconformist religious works, having transcribed in shorthand and been involved in publishing the sermons of the independent minister William Strong in 1656. Certainly Charles Hatt knew the Riches later in life.

It is unknown when Hannah died. Her husband wrote his will on 28 January 1708, naming his wife at that time as Sarah and mentioning three children (although it is unclear how many of these where his and Hannah's), and property in Snelston. The will was proved on 4 April 1709.

S. J. WISEMAN

Sources H. Allen, *A narrative of God's gracious dealings with that choice Christian Mrs Hannah Allen, (afterwards married to Mr Hatt), reciting the great advantages the Devil made of her deep melancholy, and the triumphant victories, rich and sovereign graces, God gave her over all his strategems and devices* (1683) · R. Baxter, *The certainty of the world of spirits* (1691), 71–3 · *Calendar of the correspondence of Richard Baxter*, ed. N. H. Keeble and G. F. Nuttall, 2 (1991) · W. Strong, *XXXI select sermons* (1656) · F. Bate, *The declaration of indulgence, 1672* (1908) · parish registers, Snelston, 1575–1684, Derbys. RO, 20 C transcript microfilm M149, vol. 9 · *The collected works of Katherine Philips the matchless Orinda*, ed. P. Thomas, 2 (1992), 2–12 · *Correspondence of Sir Robert Kerr, first earl of Ancram, and his son William, third earl of Lothian*, ed. D. Laing, 2 vols., Roxburghe Club, 100 (1875) · C. H. Firth and G. Davies, *The regimental history of Cromwell's army*, 1 (1940) · *Familiar letters: written by the right honourable John late earl of Rochester and several other persons of honour and quality* (1697) · R. Bolton, *Instructions for a right comforting afflicted consciences, with speciall antidotes against some grievous temptations* (1631) · S. Bolton, *The guard of the tree of life* (1656) · administration, PRO, PROB 6/39, fol. 92 · will, PRO, PROB 11/507, sig. 76 · *IGI*

Allen, Sir Hugh Percy (1869–1946), university professor and conductor, was born at Reading on 23 December 1869, the youngest of the seven children of John Herbert Allen, who was in business with Huntley and Palmers of Reading. His mother, Rebecca, was the daughter of Samuel Bevan Stevens, a member of the firm of Huntley, Bourne, and Stevens, which made the tins for biscuits manufactured by Huntley and Palmers.

There is not much evidence that music was seriously cultivated in the home, nor that any particular success was achieved by the boy at Kendrick School, Reading, but the arrival of Dr Frederick John Read as organist of Christ Church, Reading, when Allen was eight, was a milestone in his life. Determined to have lessons from Read, Allen played the organ at local churches—Coley (1880), Tilehurst (1884), Eversley (1886)—and in 1887 he combined his post at the last of these with some teaching at Wellington College. In that year he went as assistant to Read, who had been appointed organist of Chichester Cathedral. This provided valuable experience in cathedral services, the training of a choir, and the responsibilities of a cathedral organist. As yet, however, he had no paper qualifications. He therefore took his BMus examinations at Oxford in 1892, and in the same year was appointed organ scholar of Christ's College, Cambridge. Here appeared the first signs of his power to influence others musically when he gave performances of Bach cantatas in the college chapel. The college music society, the college orchestra, the university musical club, performances of Greek plays: all these gained by his infectious enthusiasm and his drive. He graduated in 1895 and in 1896 took his DMus examinations at Oxford, although he was prevented by regulations from taking the degree until 1898.

In 1897 Allen was appointed organist of St Asaph Cathedral, and in his one year there he vastly improved the standard of singing and radically altered the repertory. The next year he went to Ely Cathedral, where he forged musical links with Cambridge. While there he conducted notable performances of Bach's St Matthew passion and Brahms's Requiem and *Schicksalslied*. In 1902 Allen married Edith Winifred, daughter of Oliver Hall, of Dedham, Essex; they had one son and one daughter.

In 1901 Allen was appointed organist of New College, Oxford. Like those at St Asaph and Ely, the choir at New College was soon required to sing much difficult music, and the weekly service lists show both progressiveness and catholicity. In 1908 the college showed its appreciation of Allen's work by offering him a fellowship. But research was not his métier, and he soon resigned the fellowship. More importantly, it was at this time that he was responsible for amalgamating two choral societies (of different traditions and understandable rivalry) into the Oxford Bach Choir, which developed a great reputation; and he formed an orchestra to accompany it. Both choir and orchestra became important in both the university and the city. Appointed choragus to the university in 1909, he began to introduce a new scheme of practical training for Oxford's music students.

Such was Allen's reputation that he was frequently approached by musical authorities outside Oxford. He became director of the Petersfield Festival (1906), conductor of the London Bach Choir (1907–20), director of music at University College, Reading (1908–18), and director of music at Cheltenham Ladies' College (1910–18). In 1913, 1922, 1925, and 1928 he conducted at the Leeds Festival. In 1918 Sir Walter Parratt resigned the professorship of music at Oxford, and there was no doubt about the identity of his successor. Oxford was glad to have at last a resident professor. But when Sir Hubert Parry died later in the year Allen was appointed director of the Royal College of Music in London, and Oxford thought it would lose him. As usual with Allen, nothing of the sort occurred. He retained his professorship, kept his rooms at New College, and for another seven years conducted the Oxford Bach Choir. However, he undertook practically no other performing engagements.

Allen's arrival at the Royal College of Music coincided with post-war expansion. The number of students rose from 200 to 600, and many of the director's plans for extension of work, which were made quickly and, as it seemed, temporarily, eventually became permanent. For nineteen years he directed the affairs of the college, but in 1937 he felt he ought to retire. Retirement with Allen meant a change of occupation; to the end of his life he retained his Oxford professorship and made Oxford his headquarters. He continued to press for the creation of a music faculty, which the university granted in 1944. New premises and the setting up of a music school occupied him continuously from this time until his death.

In Oxford, Allen galvanized generations of undergraduates into musical action. He was criticized for being content with less than perfect performances, but his critics, while having a modicum of truth on their side, failed to perceive his aim. In Allen's mind, rehearsals (where he could talk and teach) were more important than performances.

In addition, his advice and help were sought by many musical organizations. The Incorporated Society of Musicians owes its reconstitution and its revivification chiefly to him; Kneller Hall sought his help; he was a member of the council of the corporation of the Royal Albert Hall; the Royal Philharmonic Society needed, and got, his advice; the British Broadcasting Corporation made him chairman of its music advisory committee in 1936. There was a time, just before he retired from the Royal College of Music, when it could be safely said that there were few musical happenings in the country about which Allen had not been consulted.

Although a gifted conductor, Allen undoubtedly 'owed his position less to his musical than to his organizing abilities, and to sheer energy and driving force' (Colles and Turner, 281). He received many honours, being knighted in 1920, appointed CVO in 1926, and promoted KCVO in 1928 and GCVO in 1935. Besides receiving his Oxford doctorate he was made an honorary MusD of Cambridge (1925), DLitt of Reading (1938), LittD of Sheffield (1926), and DPhil of Berlin. He was also an honorary fellow of Christ's College, Cambridge (1926); and in 1937 he was master of the Worshipful Company of Musicians.

On 17 February 1946 Allen was knocked down by a motorcyclist in Oxford, and the severe injuries which he received caused his death three days later on 20 February in the Radcliffe Infirmary, Oxford.

W. K. STANTON, rev.

Sources C. Bailey, *Hugh Percy Allen* (1948) · personal knowledge (1959) · T. A. B. Corley, *Quaker enterprise in biscuits: Huntley and Palmer of Reading, 1822–1972* (1972) · *CGPLA Eng. & Wales* (1946) · H. C. Colles and M. Turner, 'Allen, Sir Hugh (Percy)', *New Grove*
Archives New College, Oxford, notebooks | SOUND BL NSA, 'Impression of the life and work of a great musician', NP 3582R
Likenesses J. S. Sargent, pencil drawing, 1925, New College, Oxford · L. Campbell Taylor, oils, 1937, Royal College of Music, London · plaster bust, Royal College of Music, London
Wealth at death £6334 13s. 3d.: probate, 28 May 1946, *CGPLA Eng. & Wales*

Allen, Sir James (1855–1942), politician in New Zealand, was born on 10 February 1855 in Adelaide, South Australia, the son of James Allen and his wife, Esther, *née* Bax. His mother died when he was very young and his father, a New Zealand businessman and property speculator, soon took him to Dunedin, the provincial capital of Otago, New Zealand. In the early 1860s he and his brother Charles were sent to England and placed in the care of an uncle in Cockhill, Somerset. Their father returned to Dunedin, where he died in 1865.

After attending a boarding-school in Somerset with his brother, Allen was educated at Clifton College, Bristol (1869–74). He went on to St John's College, Cambridge (followed by his brother), where he specialized in mineralogy and graduated with a third-class degree in the natural sciences tripos in 1878. At university he excelled in rowing and rugby. On 23 August 1877 he had married, at Evercreech, his cousin Mary Jane Hill Richards (d. 1939), the

daughter of John Richards, a farmer of Alford in Somerset. They had three daughters and three sons.

Following a teaching stint at Harrow School, Allen returned to Dunedin, where he had inherited considerable property. He gained his first political experience with a seat on the city council from 1880 to 1883, during which time he became a well-known local figure. Back in England between 1884 and 1887, he spent three successful years in London at the Normal School of Science and the Royal School of Mines. When his businesses in Otago called him back to New Zealand he used his new knowledge to add coal- and goldmining to his interests. In 1887 he rose rapidly to national prominence by dramatically seizing the Dunedin East seat in the house of representatives from the premier, Sir Robert Stout.

Allen was among the conservatives who lost their seats in the Liberal victory of 1890, but two years later he was returned as the member for Bruce at a by-election. His reputation for integrity and hard-working soundness and solidity was eventually rewarded, and in 1903 he was generally recognized as the only possible rival to William Massey when the leadership of the opposition fell vacant. His lack of charisma, even compared with that of Massey, ensured however that he stood no chance; and he slipped easily into the role of the new leader's loyal and dependable deputy.

Allen became the leading opposition spokesman on defence matters, pursuing an interest long held through training in volunteer defence units (in which he ultimately reached the rank of colonel). He also developed a long-standing interest in education at all levels. His vigorous personal support of the 'bibles-in-schools' movement reflected a lifelong interest in religion. He was the last life member appointed to Otago University's council (1887) and served as its vice-chancellor (1903–9) and chancellor (1909–12). As a member of the senate of the University of New Zealand Allen would—unusually for him—take up some progressive causes, such as the appointment of examiners from within New Zealand. But he was more usually to be found attacking the Liberal government's radicalism and its alleged profligacy in spending and borrowing.

Allen became deputy to the premier when Massey established the Reform ministry in July 1912. In view of his interests he was selected to take up the defence, education, and finance portfolios. In these he found it difficult—especially in economic matters—to live up to promises of fundamental change. However, there were initiatives in education, including statutory funding for university colleges and a general educational restructuring in 1914, and developments in defence, such as efforts to increase efficiency in the compulsory military training programme. His most important achievement in peacetime was the procurement in 1913, in the face of 'bullying' opposition by the first lord of the Admiralty, Winston Churchill (diary, 21 April 1914, Grant-Duff MSS, CAC Cam.), of Britain's consent to dedicated naval forces for New Zealand. Later that year, after initial doubts, he acquiesced in the government's sometimes clandestine use of the military in its determination to crush organized labour during the 'great strike'.

Allen's particular strength was organization, and his careful shepherding of defence administration enabled the dominion to make a quick and easy adjustment to war-time mode in 1914. A New Zealand expeditionary force seized German Samoa shortly after the outbreak of the First World War in August, and by mid-October the bulk of the main New Zealand expeditionary force had left for the Middle East, in line with Allen's war contingency plans. (Previously, he had vigorously championed the idea of a force ready to react to disturbance anywhere in the empire, a concept even right-wing observers felt to be imperialist 'militarism run mad' (Weitzel, 138).) The creation of a national coalition government in August 1915, the month his youngest son died at Gallipoli, left him able to concentrate solely on the defence portfolio.

Not only was Allen New Zealand's war leader from August 1916, he was also acting prime minister for a total of nearly two years. This resulted from the frequent absences overseas (on imperial, war, and peace business) of Massey and his *de facto* co-leader in the National Government, Sir Joseph Ward. His wartime role was, however, punctuated by controversies. In particular, serious opposition to the government's initial reliance on voluntary war service was targeted at the defence minister. Then from 1916 he was under severe attack from the opposite perspective when cabinet did endorse his arguments for the introduction of conscription—including for the draconian way in which he applied the system. But the views of the commander of the expeditionary force (who did not like his reserved, humourless demeanour) sum up his overall reputation in this period: his pre-war 'efforts to improve the status and organisation of the New Zealand forces' had provided an 'invaluable' base for the war effort. 'I cannot say enough of all the help and support that he gave to me and to all the units of the force' during the conflict (General Sir Alexander Godley, archives of St John's College, Cambridge, ref. 4257).

Weary of the problems posed by post-war rehabilitation, Allen prepared to leave politics at the 1919 general election. But with the demise of the coalition government in August of that year he was persuaded to stay on and also to take up the finance portfolio again. On narrowly retaining his seat he added to his defence and financial portfolios that of New Zealand's first minister of external affairs. His acceptance of this position, that of administering the dominion's interests in the Pacific, reflected a long-standing fascination in the region; in 1903 he had published *New Zealand's Possessions in the South Seas*. He now instituted arrangements for exercising his country's League of Nations mandate in Western Samoa.

But in 1920 Allen finally relinquished politics for diplomacy to become New Zealand's high-profile high commissioner in the United Kingdom. He now championed imperial co-operation and the sanctity of British imperialism with the same enthusiastic conviction which had led him during wartime to secure the highest proportion of men in uniform in the empire. After his return to Dunedin in

1926 he continued to pursue his international interests, presiding for example for a dozen years over the new dominion branch of the Institute of Pacific Relations, as well as serving on its Pacific council.

As high commissioner Allen had represented his country at the League of Nations, where he had displayed a frugality over financial policy which had increasingly become his characteristic during his years of ministerial responsibilities. His essential conservatism, coupled with his practical experiences, had, however, brought him to believe that international co-operation was a vain hope: the best one could hope for was a *pax Britannica* resting on the Royal Navy and the might of the British empire. As an active legislative councillor after his appointment to the second chamber on 1 June 1927, he focused on imperial and international affairs.

Allen was appointed KCB in 1917, for his contribution to the war effort, and GCMG in 1926. He ceased to attend legislative council meetings a year before his wife's death in 1939, and his appointment as a councillor lapsed in 1941. He died on 28 July 1942 at his home, Arana, Clyde Street, Dunedin, and was buried at the city's northern cemetery. He had been a highly efficient—if unglamorous—statesman and administrator. He was unfazed by criticism, and his reputation rests principally on his firm organizational control over New Zealand's preparations for and operations of war. It might be said that he epitomized the rather dull conservatism of many New Zealand politicians of the post-pioneering period; it might also be said that he embodied, at a high level of probity and effectiveness, a cautiousness and consolidationism that was virtually inevitable given the temper of his times. Either way, a recent assessment that he 'deserves a more prominent place in New Zealand history than he has hitherto been given' (Baker, 224) is vindicated by a reassessment of the evidence. RICHARD S. HILL

Sources I. McGibbon, 'Allen, James', *DNZB*, vol. 3 · St John Cam., Archives · P. Baker, *King and country call: New Zealanders, conscription and the Great War* (1988) · J. Allen, National Archives of New Zealand · R. S. Hill, *The iron hand in the velvet glove: the modernisation of policing in New Zealand, 1886–1917* (1995) · I. McGibbon, *Blue-water rationale: the naval defence of New Zealand, 1914–1942* (1981) · *DNB* · L. C. Voller, 'Colonel the honourable Sir James Allen, GCMG KCB TD MA Cantab., statesman', MA thesis, University of Otago, 1943 · *DNZB* database printouts · CAC Cam., Grant-Duff MSS · G. Howard, *The navy in New Zealand* (1981) · A. H. McLintock, ed., *An encyclopaedia of New Zealand*, 3 vols. (1966) · J. O. Wilson, *New Zealand parliamentary record, 1840–1984* (1985) · G. H. Scholefield, ed., *Who's who in New Zealand*, 3rd edn · R. L. Weitzel, 'Pacifists and anti-militarists in New Zealand', *New Zealand Journal of History*, 7 (1973), 128–47
Archives NL NZ, MSS
Likenesses W. Stoneman, two photographs, 1921–6, NPG · photograph, repro. in Baker, *King and country call*, 35

Allen, James Baylis (1803–1876), engraver, was born in Birmingham on 18 April 1803. He was the son of a button manufacturer and, as a boy, he followed his father's business but about 1818 he was articled to his elder brother Josiah, a general engraver at 3 Colmore Row, Birmingham, working on needle labels and patterns. From 1821 he attended drawing classes run by Joseph Vincent Barber and Samuel Lines. In 1824 he went to London and worked for several years for the Bank of England, engraving Britannia on banknotes as a test of his line engraving skill. He also worked for the Findens, Charles Heath, and Robert Wallis, and again met Joseph Goodyear and John Pye, friends from his apprenticeship days in Birmingham.

Most of Allen's work was engraved in line and on steel; his subject was primarily landscape. His earliest published and dated work appeared in S. W. H. Ireland's *England's Topographer* (1828). Contributions were also made to T. H. Shepherd's volumes of 1829–30 and to the annuals. Allen engraved a total of sixteen plates after J. M. W. Turner between 1830 and 1859, two of which were on copper; they include four for Turner's *Rivers of France* (1833–5) and six for his *England and Wales* (1827–32). These are regarded as his best plates. His work after W. H. Bartlett included four plates each for William Beattie's *Switzerland* (1836) and J. S. Coyne's *Scenery and Antiquities of Ireland* (1840), and two for Julia Pardoe's *The Beauties of the Bosphorus* (1839). In 1838 he engraved the landscape portions of C. L. Eastlake's *Greek Fugitives* to help his friend Goodyear, who had been exhausted by the undertaking.

Allen married Mary Jennings on 26 June 1845 at St Pancras Old Church, London. Their youngest child, Walter J. Allen, became a draughtsman, wood-engraver, and a member of the *Art Journal* staff. Allen engraved eighteen plates for the *Art Journal* between 1850 and 1864, and he suggested to the editor, Samuel Carter Hall, the idea of producing an illustrated catalogue of the Great Exhibition of 1851. His last plates were done for E. C. Booth's *Australia* (1873–6) after J. S. Prout. His plates were usually signed J. B. Allen but variants include J. B. Allan, Jas. B. Allen, J. Allen, J. B. Allon, and, probably, James Allen.

Allen died on 11 January 1876 at his home, 3 Stratford Place, Rochester Square, Camden Town, after a long and painful illness, and was buried in Highgate cemetery, close to the vault of his friend Goodyear. His will, proved on 7 February 1876, showed the value of his estate at under £100. In 1877 the exhibition of engravings by Birmingham men included thirty-seven of Allen's engravings from 1829 to 1863 from the stock of Henry Graves, priced between 15s. and £4 1s.   B. HUNNISETT

Sources *Art Journal*, 38 (1876), 106 • Redgrave, *Artists* • *Exhibition of engravings by 19 Birmingham men* (1877), 9, 10, 23–4 [exhibition catalogue, Royal Birmingham Society of Artists, 1877] • B. Hunnisett, *An illustrated dictionary of British steel engravers*, new edn (1989), 10–11 • IGI • CGPLA Eng. & Wales (1876) • DNB
Wealth at death under £100: probate, 7 Feb 1876, CGPLA Eng. & Wales

Allen, James Charles (*bap.* 1790?, *d.* 1833), engraver, was the son of a Smithfield salesman and a native of London. Nothing else is known of his parentage or early life but he may perhaps be identified with James Charles, the son of William and Elizabeth Allen, baptized on 31 August 1790 at St Sepulchre, London. He was a pupil of William Bernard Cooke, to whom he was apprenticed and in whose studio he worked for several years after the termination of his apprenticeship. Most of his work was done on copper in the field of book illustration, and among the earliest engravings appearing over his name were some after

J. M. W. Turner, with whom he worked most closely over a cover design for *Views of Sussex*, published between 1816 and 1819. Allen engraved a total of fourteen plates after Turner, the last eight of which, for the projected *East Coast of England*, were unfinished and unpublished about 1830. Six of Allen's engravings were exhibited in Cooke's exhibition of engravings of living British artists in 1821, three of which, after J. P. Cockburn, were published in *Views of the Colosseum* (1821). Allen's address was given in the catalogue as 132 Goswell Street, London. In 1825 *Views in the South of France, Chiefly on the Rhône* contained engravings by him after Peter DeWint, based on sketches by John Hughes.

Allen's work on steel included twelve plates after W. H. Bartlett, David Cox, and Henry Gastineau for *The Watering Places of Great Britain and Fashionable Directory* (1831), followed by a portrait of Cuthbert, Lord Collingwood, vice-admiral, and the *Defeat of the Spanish Armada, 1588*, after P. J. de Loutherbourg, for Edward Hawke Locker's *Memoirs of celebrated naval commanders illustrated … from original pictures in the naval gallery of Greenwich Hospital* (1832). These were probably among Allen's last works, executed at a time when he was departing from his usual landscape subjects with greater skill than he had done previously. This greater independence from his master's influence was a promising development but, weak in health and 'eccentric in his habits' (*DNB*), he died, in middle age, in 1833. His plates were signed J. C. Allen.

On 9 November 1833 administration of the estate of James Charles Allen was granted to his only son, also named James Charles Allen, in which the elder Allen was described as a gentleman and widower, his estate being worth £450. His address was given as 161 Goswell Street, London.   B. HUNNISETT

Sources Redgrave, *Artists* • IGI • L. Herrmann, *Turner prints: the engraved work of J. M. W. Turner* (1990), 90, 93 • *Collected correspondence of J. M. W. Turner*, ed. J. Gage (1980), 81 • W. G. Rawlinson, *The engraved work of J. M. W. Turner*, 2 (1913) • administration, PRO, PROB 6/209, fol. 311v
Wealth at death £450: administration, 1833, PRO, PROB 6/209, fol. 311v

Allen, James John [Jim] (1926–1999), playwright and scriptwriter, was born on 7 October 1926 at 31 Higher Duke Street, Miles Platting, Manchester, the second child of John (Jack) Allen, a railway labourer, and his wife, Catherine (Kitty) Lee. The family was of Irish descent. After attending local Roman Catholic schools, Jim dropped out of education in 1939 and lied about his age in order to work in a wire factory. He was conscripted into the Seaforth Highlanders in 1944 and served in Germany with the occupation forces. A brawl outside a public house earned him three months in prison, where a fellow inmate introduced him to revolutionary politics. Allen began reading Marx and Lenin, and also Upton Sinclair and Jack London. On leaving the army in 1947 he was briefly a hospital cleaner in London, but could not settle. Temporarily using the identity of his brother John to conceal his prison record, he entered the merchant navy and worked on Jamaican banana boats until 1949. Unskilled jobs at docks and building sites followed before he became a miner at Bradford colliery, Manchester.

In the 1950s Allen joined the Revolutionary Communist Party, a small Trotskyite movement that turned into the Socialist Labour League in 1958, led by Gerry Healy. In its struggle for the 'dictatorship of the proletariat', the league set store by first rejecting revisionists and Stalinists whom it accused of betraying the workers: the Labour Party, Trades Union Congress, and Communist Party of Great Britain. In 1958 Allen helped found *The Miner*, a weekly newspaper attacking the leadership of the National Union of Mineworkers. This provided his first experience of writing. He lost his job in the pit after four years and alternated between labouring on construction sites and campaigning for the Socialist Labour League. Barred from the shop stewards' movement by the Communist Party of Great Britain, he had the idea of subverting the 'bourgeois' medium of television to convey his revolutionary message.

Allen offered his first play (about a hod carrier) to the Manchester-based independent television company Granada in 1964. Although they rejected it, they perceived his flair for capturing the rhythm and humour of working-class speech and recruited him to the writing team of the popular serial *Coronation Street*. He contributed three dozen episodes between January 1965 and July 1966, but the editing-out of political content infuriated him. After getting his half-hour drama 'The Hard Word' onto BBC2 (15 June 1966), he left Granada to work with Tony Garnett, a radical television producer engaged on broadening the range of the weekly *Wednesday Play* on BBC1. Allen achieved his breakthrough with 'The Lump' (BBC1, 1 February 1967), about the exploitation of casual labour in the building trade. Garnett then introduced him to director Ken Loach, whose political views were similar, and the two men collaborated on a succession of controversial plays in a naturalistic semi-documentary style. Set in Liverpool docks, 'The Big Flame' (BBC1, 19 February 1969) was intended to provoke strikes. A quotation from Trotsky ended 'Rank and File' (BBC1, 20 May 1971). For ITV, meanwhile, Allen wrote 'The Man Beneath' (Rediffusion, 7 December 1967) about pit closures, 'The Pub Fighter' (Rediffusion, 27 February 1968), and 'The Talking Head' (London Weekend Television, 30 August 1968). For authenticity he drew on his own experiences of sit-ins and picket lines, and his plays gained resonance from the deterioration of industrial relations in the 1970s.

Allen continued to live in north Manchester. His wife, Clare, a schoolteacher, was the family's regular breadwinner. He stayed at home and looked after their young children (three girls and two boys), regularly getting up at five o'clock in the morning in order to write undisturbed. Prickly and suspicious, he kept his distance from television colleagues in order to avoid being corrupted by bourgeois influence. Trips to London were sometimes necessary: he crammed appointments into a single day and took everything required in a plastic carrier bag.

With *Days of Hope* (BBC1, 11 September – 2 October 1976), a four-part series lasting for over six hours, Allen and Loach sought to reawaken the revolutionary spirit by depicting major events in British class politics between 1916 and 1926. The plays stimulated passionate argument: some left-wing drama critics thought their naturalism reduced their ideological impact; Conservatives accused the BBC of spending licence payers' money on Trotskyite agitprop. Allen claimed to speak for the oppressed. 'A Choice of Evils' (BBC1, 19 April 1977) castigated the Catholic church.

Roland Joffé directed Allen's next two plays. In 'The Spongers' (BBC1, 24 January 1978), a young mother falls into the 'poverty trap' and kills herself. 'United Kingdom' (BBC1, 8 December 1981) showed local-government spending cuts sparking a popular uprising. Opinion was turning against such seditious material, and Allen protested that BBC producers went in fear of the Thatcher government. Scripts on the Irish civil war and the rise of Hitler remained unfilmed. Moreover the pre-publicity for his stage play *Perdition*, to be produced by Loach, caused a furore in April 1987 with its allegations of collusion between Hungarian Zionists and Nazis to secure the freedom of a few Jews in return for silence about the fate of all those in concentration camps. The Royal Court Theatre cancelled the production after accusations of antisemitism, and Allen and his publishers faced a libel action. They won but at a cost of £30,000 in legal and research fees. *Perdition* was finally premièred at the Gate Theatre, Notting Hill, in June 1999, just before Allen's death.

Allen reached a low ebb in 1987–8, shunned by television, embroiled in the libel suit, and widowed. His writing found a fresh outlet, however, in three ambitious low-budget films made with Loach. *Hidden Agenda* (1990) purported to uncover British death squads in Northern Ireland. The critically acclaimed *Raining Stones* (1993) portrayed life on a tough Manchester council estate. At his best, Allen did succeed in combining ideology with moving drama. *Land and Freedom* (1995), designed to expose Stalinist perfidy in the Spanish Civil War, won an award at the Cannes Film Festival.

Never outflanked on the left, Allen firmly rejected suggestions that communism had failed: real communism had still to be tried. He died of cancer at his home, 1 Parkside, Alkrington, Middleton, Manchester, on 24 June 1999, and was buried in Manchester on 3 July.

JASON TOMES

Sources B. Slaughter, 'Jim Allen: a lifetime's commitment to historical truth', www.wsws.org/articles/1999/aug1999/obit-a11. shtml [*World Socialist* website], 10 June 2002 · P. Madden, 'Jim Allen', *British television drama*, ed. G. Brandt (1981), 36–55 · *The Guardian* (25 June 1999) · *The Independent* (6 July 1999) · *The Times* (7 July 1999) · K. Loach, *Loach on Loach*, ed. G. Fuller (1998) · B. Behan, 'Jim Allen', *The Independent* (16 July 1999) · d. cert.
Archives FILM BFI NFTVA, documentary footage
Likenesses photograph, repro. in *The Times*
Wealth at death under £200,000 gross; under £40,000 net: administration, 4 Oct 1999, *CGPLA Eng. & Wales*

Allen, James Mountford (1809–1883), architect, was born on 14 August 1809 at Crewkerne, Somerset, the son of the Revd John Allen, vicar of Bleddington, Gloucestershire, formerly headmaster of Crewkerne grammar school, and his wife, Jane Ann, *née* Butler. At the age of sixteen he left Crewkerne to study at Exeter under Mr Cornish—either Robert Cornish (*c*.1760–1844), surveyor to Exeter Cathedral, or his son Robert Stribling Cornish (1788–1871)—until at twenty-one he went to London, where he worked in the office of Charles Fowler. Reference to the catalogues of exhibitions at the Royal Academy confirms that Allen was erroneously identified as John M. Allen by Algernon Graves in compiling his *Dictionary of Royal Academy Contributors*. Allen exhibited in 1839 a 'view of Honiton Church, Devon, just completed from the designs of Mr Fowler' (*The Exhibition of the Royal Academy*, 1839), and also in 1844 and 1845 designs for a new rectory house at Stepney and a parsonage house at Barnton, and for All Saints' Church, Thelwall, Cheshire, and the east end of All Saints' Church, Shadwell. After several years of general practice he returned at the age of forty-seven to Crewkerne, where he established an extensive practice as a church architect. He also designed or restored rectories, schools, and private houses in the area. A contemporary (*The Builder*, 863) noted that St Mary Magdalene's Church at Cricket Malherbie, near Ilminster (1855), and the reredos at St Andrew's Church, Chardstock (1863–4), were his best-known designs, and that the latter served as a model for other local churches. Allen died at the Home Hospital, 16 Fitzroy Square, St Pancras, on 27 February 1883, while on a visit to London.

ANNETTE PEACH

Sources *The Builder*, 44 (1883), 863 · *IGI* · Colvin, *Archs.* · Graves, *RA exhibitors* · *The exhibition of the Royal Academy* (1839) [exhibition catalogue] · *The exhibition of the Royal Academy* (1844) [exhibition catalogue] · *The exhibition of the Royal Academy* (1845) [exhibition catalogue] · *Devon*, Pevsner (1989) · *Somerset*, Pevsner · d. cert.

Archives RIBA BAL, biography file

Wealth at death £1584 5*s*. 9*d*.: probate, 30 July 1883, *CGPLA Eng. & Wales*

Allen, Sir John (*c*.1470–1544), mayor of London, was born in Thaxted, Essex, into an agrarian family of moderate means. His father, Richard Allen, apprenticed him to Roger Bourchier of the London Mercers' Company, to which he was admitted in 1497. Allen was elected a warden of the Mercers in 1509, making him eligible for ward office, and in 1515 he was nominated alderman from Langbourn and Vintry wards. When Allen's nomination was rejected by the court of aldermen, the freemen from Vintry ward, where the Mercers maintained an almshouse, elected him anyway. Allen was nominated alderman from eight other wards during a civic career that spanned three decades. He rose to the status of master mercer in 1518, and was designated one of two London sheriffs by Lord Mayor Thomas Exmew that same year. In 1523 Allen translated from Vintry to Lime Street ward and in 1525 the court of common council elected him lord mayor of London. As was customary, Henry VIII knighted the new officer.

During Allen's first term, following a decision in Star Chamber that aliens must contribute to the king's treasury just as natural-born citizens did, foreigners were ordered to come before the mayor, swear allegiance to the monarch, and indicate their wealth. At the same time the city ordered a boycott of immigrant merchants who imported woad, simultaneously damaging their businesses while taxing them. Thus Allen's first mayoralty, called 'distinguished' by Lyell and Watney (p. xxiii), has been branded as xenophobic by others.

In late 1525 or early 1526 Allen was sworn as a councillor to the king, part of the outer ring of advisers stationed at Westminster that dealt with criminal matters. Allen served on a number of government commissions for the jurisdiction of London, including those for the peace, tax collection, and the property of lunatics. In August 1532 he and Thomas Cromwell were examiners in a treason trial; two months later Allen was among a dozen signatories to a letter 'from Council Chamber, Westminster', sent to the king advising him of plague around the inns of court (*LP Henry VIII*, 5, no. 1421). Stow refers to Allen in 1536 as 'one of the king's council' (Stow, 242). As a councillor Allen was the recipient of many gifts from the monarch and purchased a suppressed priory at Hatfield Peverel in Essex. Allen also adjudicated disputes involving the Merchant Adventurers, of which he was a member, during the decade after his first mayoralty.

Allen no doubt anticipated a peaceful retirement from municipal duties and bought a large house in Sything Lane in Tower Street ward. In 1535, however, the king proclaimed to common council his preference for Allen to serve as mayor again in the coming year. Despite the custom of a single-term limit for London mayors during Tudor times and Allen's sincere reluctance to accept the office, he was elected, one of only two men to serve twice during the reign of Henry VIII. Allen was instrumental in keeping London calm during the tumultuous events of 1536 and personally arranged for the supplying of horses to the king's men during the Pilgrimage of Grace. Fearful of economic depression in the city after the dissolution of the monasteries, Allen asked Cromwell to allocate £10,000 as a subsidy for St Bartholomew's fair in Smithfield. By royal command, the lord mayor and a deputation of aldermen attended the arraignment and trial of Anne Boleyn. They also witnessed her execution; Allen ordered all foreigners excluded from the vicinity. During his second mayoralty King Henry and Jane Seymour attended the marching watch of the city on St Peter's night from the vantage point of the newly built Mercers' Hall. In late 1536 Allen received the designation 'Father of the City' from the court of aldermen.

Allen contended with Thomas Barnaby, a fellow mercer, over a loan of £100 made by Allen to Barnaby in 1537 for the lease of his house in security. Cromwell urged Allen to be patient with Barnaby, but Allen's misgivings proved prescient. In the autumn of 1541, after Cromwell's fall and Allen's retirement from government service, Barnaby convinced the privy council to act against the former mayor; Allen was ordered to 'compound with Thomas Barnaby for his debt and to restore the lease of a house Barnaby had given him in caution' (*LP Henry VIII*, 16, no. 1155).

Allen has been described as a bachelor by some sources, and his sons are labelled illegitimate by official records.

However, the Mercers' records indicate that his tomb contained enough room 'for him and his wife' (Watney, 103). This was probably the Elizabeth Jay who was the major beneficiary of Allen's will. Allen also had a romance with a much younger woman, the sister of Lady Sidney, and gossip about his behaviour was relayed to Cromwell, who lamented Allen's indiscreet conduct.

Allen died in London in September 1544, and was initially buried in a 'fair and beautiful chapel, arched over with stone, by him built' adjacent to the former St Thomas of Acon Hospital and to the Mercers' Hall in Cheape ward (Stow, 103, 242). By Stow's time Allen's tomb had been removed to the main Mercers' church and his chapel had been divided into leased shops; vandals had defaced many of the funerary monuments in the Mercers' church including Allen's. Allen left portions of his sizeable estate throughout England to three sons, John, Christopher, and Lazarus. Sir William Paget had the right to wardship and marriage of Christopher and Lazarus Allen; the brothers eventually married Paget's daughters Margaret and Agnes. Allen consigned his London house and lands in Middlesex to Elizabeth Jay, probably his mistress and the mother of Christopher and Lazarus; he also entrusted her with 'the keeping of John, my fool', during his natural life. He bestowed large amounts for poor relief, including £50 to be shared among the poor at 10s. per week, £10 for poor maidens' marriages, and 500 marks to stock sea coal, financed by rent from his Essex estate. Stow included Allen in his roll of honourable citizens, noting that Allen gave to the city of London 'a rich collar of gold' to be worn by the mayor (Stow, 103). The lord mayor's collar, composed of twenty-eight ornate SS links joined by alternate enamel Tudor roses and gold knots, was first worn by Sir William Laxton, mayor in 1548.

ELIZABETH LANE FURDELL

Sources E. L. Furdell, 'The king's man in London: the career of Sir John Allen', *Proceedings of the Montana Academy of Sciences*, 37 (1977), 185–91 · *LP Henry VIII* · J. Stow, *The survey of London* (1912) [with introduction by H. B. Wheatley] · J. Watney, *History of the Mercers' Company* (1914) · L. Lyell and F. D. Watney, eds., *Acts of court of the Mercers' Company, 1453–1527* (1936) · will, PRO, PROB 11/31, sig. 1 · journals, CLRO, court of common council · repertories of the court of aldermen, CLRO · C. J. Kitching, ed., *London and Middlesex chantry certificate, 1548*, London RS, 16 (1980) · C. Wriothesley, *A chronicle of England during the reigns of the Tudors from AD 1485 to 1559*, ed. W. D. Hamilton, 1, CS, new ser., 11 (1875)

Allen, John (*c.*1596–1671), minister in America, was born to unknown parents. He matriculated as a pensioner at Christ's College, Cambridge, in July 1613, graduating BA in 1617 and proceeding MA in 1620 (not, as Venn says, from Gonville and Caius College). He was ordained priest at Peterborough on 6 August 1620 and by 1623, when their only surviving child, John, was born, had married his first wife, Margaret. From about 1624 he was rector of Saxlingham-juxta-mare, Norfolk. His sister Elizabeth also lived in that parish and in 1629 married Thomas Fisher.

In 1635 Allen displayed an interest in New England when he donated £25 to the Massachusetts Bay Colony treasury. In 1637 he migrated with his wife, sister, and brother-in-law to that colony, where he became one of the initial settlers of the town of Dedham. Allen was chosen one of the pillars of the church who wrote the covenant whereby the church was formed in accordance with congregationalist principles. He was then chosen pastor and ordained in 1639. Margaret Allen died in 1653, by which time their son, who had accompanied his parents to New England and graduated from Harvard in 1643, had journeyed to England, where he served as vicar of Rye from 1653. That year Allen married his second wife, Catherine, the widow of former governor Thomas Dudley. They had three children.

Allen occasionally assisted the Revd John Eliot in the mission to the Indians, and he served the colony as an overseer of Harvard College. He collaborated with the Revd Thomas Shepard in defending the New England way against presbyterian critics in the 1640s. In 1637 thirteen English divines, probably led by John Dod, had sent nine questions to the colonial clergy enquiring about church practices in the region. The New Englanders had replied and, with the prospect of church reform in England moving to the fore in 1643, the English clergyman John Ball had written a critique of the colonists' answer, published as *A Tryall of the New-Church Way in New England and Old* (1644). Shepard and Allen responded with *A Defense of the Answer Made unto the Nine Questions* (1648). This was part of a broadening debate over church polity which engaged the transatlantic puritan community in the 1640s and 1650s. In it the two colonial clergymen defended the colonists against charges that they had deserted England, arguing that they had come to the New World to save the mother country, and they defended the New England way against criticisms from both presbyterian and sectarian critics. They stressed, for example in *A Treatise of Liturgies* (1653), the depth of spiritual searching and preparation that lay behind the whole enterprise: the Lord 'knowes what prayers and teares have been poured out to God by many alone, and in dayes of fasting and prayer with Gods servants together for his counsell, direction, assistance, blessing in this worke' (Webster, 58).

In the 1660s Allen became involved in another debate over church practices that raged in New England. The half-way covenant was a reform of membership policies that proposed expanding membership in the colonial churches to more than those who had an experience of conversion, by allowing children of such 'saints' to be admitted to a partial, or half-way, membership. This proposal was recommended to the churches by the synod of 1662 and Allen was one of the advocates of the change. His *Animadversions upon the Antisynodalia Americana* (1664) was a response to an attack on the half-way covenant published by Charles Chauncy. Despite his support for the reform Allen was unable to persuade his own congregation to adopt it, but he remained a respected figure in Dedham and throughout the region until his death at Dedham on 26 August 1671. His son John, who after his ejection from Rye in 1662 had practised medicine in London, returned to America in 1680 to minister to a congregation at Woodbridge, New Jersey.

FRANCIS J. BREMER

Sources private information (2004) [R. C. Anderson, New England Historical and Genealogical Society] · K. Lockridge, *A New England town* (1985) · F. J. Bremer, *Congregational communion: clerical friendship in the Anglo-American puritan community, 1610–1692* (1994) · W. B. Sprague, *Annals of the American pulpit*, 1 (1857) · *DNB* · Dedham town records, Dedham, Massachusetts · T. Webster, *Godly clergy in early Stuart England: the Caroline puritan movement, c.1620–1643* (1997)
Archives Dedham, Massachusetts, town records

Allen, John (1660?–1741), physician, whose origins and early life are unknown, was admitted extra-licentiate of the Royal College of Physicians on 13 September 1692. He practised at Bridgwater, Somerset, and was married, though the name of his wife is unknown, with at least one son. Allen was known in the medical world for his *Synopsis universae medicinae practicae, sive, Doctissimorum virorum de morbis eorumque causis ac remediis judicia* (1719). Assembled from Allen's own notes it was an exhaustive and clearly presented catalogue of diseases, set out with classical and modern opinions, symptoms, and prescriptions. There were indexes of dispensaries and suppliers of drugs, and an index of 'distempers'. The book rapidly found favour: it went through three Latin editions before it was translated into English, French, and German, sometimes with additions. The author is described as MD, but it is not known where Allen acquired this qualification, and this may have led to the belief among continental writers, and documented in the *Dictionary of National Biography*, that Allen was a pseudonym.

Allen's other learned pursuits included astronomy—he and John Milner of Yeovil observed the solar eclipse of 1725—and mechanical engineering. In 1729 he patented several ingenious ideas (no. 513), some of which revived those patented by Thomas Togood in 1662. Allen envisaged an economical boiler, which would save fuel by putting the fire centrally within the boiler; propelling a ship by means of jets of water expelled below the water by the force of gunpowder and adapting a similar explosive force to pumps for draining mines; and drying malt in a kiln by the passage of heated water. He expanded on these ideas in his pamphlet *Specimina ichnographica* (1730), and claimed to have propelled a boat on the River Parret by setting up a pump to take in water and expel it at the stern. On this trial run the pump was, however, operated by two men.

Munk's *Roll* states that Allen presented a copy of *Specimina* to the king in May 1730; the book was certainly presented to the Royal Society, where his communication on the advantages of wooden bridges, with the plans for 'a new model for bridges over large rivers' (Royal Society, RBC 14.229–30), was read on 8 May 1730. The date of his election to the Royal Society is uncertain, but he was admitted on 26 October 1732. The reading of Allen's letter on 'a proposition in gunnery, to reduce a larger piece of ordnance to a more moderate size' (RBC 18.67–76) in December 1732 was followed at the January meeting by his extension of the idea to cannon. His proposition was the impractical one of fitting a wooden slide within the muzzle, thereby effectively extending the barrel while economizing on metal and reducing weight.

In *Specimina* Allen mentioned having sent to the Royal Society in 1716 a description of his hodometer, or ship's log. An example had been made by John Rowley and put on board a ship commanded by a Captain Chander, sailing to the West Indies. According to Allen nothing more was heard of it until Henry de Saumarez described it as his own 'marine surveyor' in the *Philosophical Transactions* of 1725. De Saumarez's log consisted of a four-armed flyer towed through the water, its revolutions driving a counter fixed on deck. As no trace of Allen's log survives among the society's records its resemblence to that of de Saumarez remains unknown. Allen died at Bridgwater on 16 September 1741. His ownership of Dunwear Manor, in Somerset, passed to his son Benjamin (d. 1791), and thence to Benjamin's son Jeffrey Allen (d. 1844).

J. F. PAYNE, *rev.* ANITA McCONNELL

Sources H. P. Spratt, 'The prenatal history of the steamboat', *Transactions* [Newcomen Society], 30 (1955–7), 13–23 · *VCH Somerset*, 6.206, 222, 294 · *Marten Triewald's Short description of the atmospheric engine, published at Stockholm, 1734*, ed. and trans. R. Jenkins (1928) · Munk, *Roll*, 2.485–6 · *GM*, 1st ser., 11 (1741), 500 · RS, LBC 20.187, 25.139–148; RBC 14.229–30, 18.67–76, 18.77–86
Archives RS
Likenesses T. Frye, oils, 1739, RCP Lond. · G. Vandergucht, line engraving, Wellcome L.

Allen, John [*pseud.* Junius junior] (d. 1783×8), Particular Baptist minister and writer, became minister in 1764 of the Particular Baptist church in Petticoat Lane, London, having previously preached at Salisbury. On settling in London he opened a linen-draper's shop in Shoreditch, which soon failed. He fell into debt and in 1767 was confined in the king's bench. His church left him. His next congregation, at Broadstairs, near Newcastle, also dismissed him for bad behaviour. By 1768 he was back in London, living as a schoolteacher in Virginia Street. His financial difficulties continued, however, and in January 1769 he was tried at the Old Bailey for forging a £50 note. Although acquitted, his reputation was shattered.

About 1770 Allen left for America. After a short stay in New York, he was invited by the Second Baptist Church in Boston to preach in 1772. His thanksgiving sermon, *An Oration, upon the Beauties of Liberty*, became one of the best-selling pamphlets of the day, with seven editions printed in four cities between 1773 and 1775. In it he charged George III with violating the rights of Englishmen and urged that such 'arbitrary despotic power in a prince … must be feared, abhorred, detested and destroyed' (*Oration*, 25). But while denouncing British tyranny he also exposed the hypocrisy of the colonists' claims for a liberty which they denied to Baptists and slaves. He pursued this argument in *The Watchman's Alarm* (1774): 'Blush ye pretended votaries for freedom! … who are thus making a mockery of your profession by trampling on the sacred natural rights … of Africans' (*Watchman's Alarm*, 27). Until recently his American pamphlets were attributed to Isaac Skillman.

Allen had a considerable reputation, particularly among high Calvinists, as an author of religious works, many of which, such as the *Royal Spiritual Magazine* (3 vols., 1752), were frequently reprinted. The Boston Baptist John Proctor considered his *Spirit of Liberty* (1770), published under the name Junius junior, 'the best defence of Believer's Baptism' he ever read. Although he thought Allen 'far exceeds Whitefield and … most men' as a preacher, Proctor worried that his erratic conduct would hinder his usefulness. Indeed, some even suspected Allen 'made too free with spiritous liquers' (Davies, 116, 118). He seems to have wandered to New Hampshire in 1774, where he died some time between 1783 and 1788. According to one account, he wished to be buried in the middle of a remote orchard: 'as I have stood alone through life, let me lie alone after death' (ibid., 119).   JIM BENEDICT

Sources W. Wilson, *The history and antiquities of the dissenting churches and meeting houses in London, Westminster and Southwark*, 4 vols. (1808–14), vol. 4, pp. 426–8 · J. Bumsted and C. Clark, 'New England's Tom Paine: John Allen and the spirit of liberty', *William and Mary Quarterly*, 21 (1964), 561–70 · H. M. Davies, *Transatlantic brethren: Rev. Samuel Jones (1735–1814) and his friends* (1995), 115–19 · W. G. McLoughlin, *New England dissent* (1971), vol. 1, p. 584; vol. 2, pp. 723–4, 766–7 · W. G. McLoughlin, *Soul liberty: the Baptists' struggle in New England, 1630–1833* (1991), 147–9, 153 · B. Bailyn, *Pamphlets of the American revolution, 1750–1776*, 1 (1965), 16–17, 146, 165–6 · B. Bailyn, *The ideological origins of the American revolution* (1967) · J. Ivimey, *A history of the English Baptists*, 4 vols. (1811–30), vol. 4, pp. 237–8 · H. Stout, *The New England soul* (1986), 314 · *The trial of the Revd John Allen, taken exact from the proceedings of the King's commission of the peace, oyer and terminer, and gaol-delivery for the city of London* [1773] · *DNB*

Allen, John (1771–1839), religious writer, was born at Truro and educated there by Dr Cardue. For thirty years he kept the Madras House Grammar School at Hackney. With his wife, Charlotte Jane, he had at least one son and one daughter. His chief work was *Modern Judaism, or, A brief account of the opinions, traditions, rites, and ceremonies of the Jews in modern times* (1816). It was reprinted in 1830; twenty-five years later it was described as 'still the best book on this subject in the English language' (Waller). A twentieth-century commentator considered that Allen 'showed a surprising amount of knowledge … of … arcane subjects' (Katz, 355). He published anonymously *The fathers, the reformers, and the public formularies of the Church of England in harmony with Calvin and against the bishop of Lincoln* (1812). In 1815 he edited the journals of the evangelical propagandist Major-General Andrew Burn, and in the same year translated Calvin's *Institutes* (1815; 2nd edn, 1838). He also translated the sermons of Daniel de Superville (1816) and *Two Dissertations on Sacrifices* from the Latin of William Owtram (1817). Allen died on 17 June 1839 in Hackney, and his school was continued by his son, Alexander *Allen (1814–1842).   K. D. REYNOLDS

Sources G. Long, ed., *The biographical dictionary of the Society for the Diffusion of Useful Knowledge*, 4 vols. in 7 (1842–4) · Boase & Courtney, *Bibl. Corn.* · J. F. Waller, ed., *The imperial dictionary of universal biography*, 3 vols. (1857–63) · *GM*, 2nd ser., 12 (1839), 210 · D. S. Katz, *The Jews in the history of England, 1485–1850* (1994); pbk edn (1996) · *IGI*

Allen, John (1771–1843), political and historical writer, was born at Redford, in the parish of Colinton, near Edinburgh, on 3 February 1771. His father, James Allen, a writer to the signet and the owner of the small estate of Redford, became bankrupt; but after his death the son, through the aid of his mother's family and the liberality of her second husband, was educated privately. He was apprenticed to an Edinburgh surgeon named Arnot (in whose house his lifelong friend, John Thomson, was his companion in instruction), and in 1791 became MD of the University of Edinburgh. While living in Edinburgh, waiting for a practice, he added to his resources by lecturing on medical topics—Francis Horner being one of the students who were attracted to his course—and translated Cuvier's *Introduction to the Study of the Animal Economy* (1801). In private life he was known for his zeal in promoting the cause of political reform in Scotland, and through his sympathy with the principles of the whig party and his deep knowledge of constitutional history, he was one of the select few to whom the plan of the *Edinburgh Review* was communicated by Francis Jeffrey and his coadjutors.

In 1801 Lord Holland desired the services of 'a clever young Scotch medical man to accompany him to Spain', and Allen was recommended, according to one account by Lord Lauderdale, and according to another by Sydney Smith. Allen remained abroad with the Holland family until 1805, and on his return to England became a regular inmate of Holland House. For a few months in 1806 he was under-secretary to the commissioners for treating with America; but that was the only official position which he ever held. Two years later Allen accompanied Lord Holland on a tour in Spain, and while there made a close and accurate study of the history and social characteristics of the Spanish people. He made some progress towards a volume 'on the interior economy and administration of Spain under the different periods of her history', with the object of illustrating the different causes that have checked her progress; but it was never finished. Spanish topics predominated in the early articles he wrote for the *Edinburgh Review*, to which he contributed thirty-five articles between 1804 and 1843.

It is as a figure in the social life of Holland House that Allen is best known, and his diary is an important source for it. He helped Lord Holland to research the materials for his speeches, and to Allen's acute criticism Holland submitted the historic protests which appeared in the journals of the House of Lords. Allen sat at the bottom of the table and carved, went out with the family to dinner parties, and had a room of his own in the house. Macaulay styles him 'a man of vast information and great conversational powers', but notes that Lady Holland treated him like 'a negro slave'. Lord Byron said that he was 'the best informed and one of the ablest men' that he knew. Lord Brougham appended a warm eulogy of Allen to the third series of the *Historic Sketches of Statesmen who Flourished in the Time of George III* (1845 edn, 2.175–82), and there are frequent and laudatory notices of him in Greville's journals in his description of the famous dinner parties at Holland House.

Had it not been for the luxurious retreat offered by Holland House, Allen's contributions to literature might have been more numerous. The historical portion of the *Annual Register* for 1806–7 was written by him. His articles in the *Edinburgh Review* included a review (December 1816) of Warden's letters from St Helena, a contribution which is said to have surprised Napoleon by its intimate knowledge of his early life, and a critique of Lingard which led to a controversy, Allen defending himself in a much-reprinted *Vindication* (1826). Allen's best-known work was an *Inquiry into the Rise and Growth of the Royal Prerogative in England* (1830), which was reprinted after his death with biographical notices by Sir James Gibson Craig and Major-General Fox. Together with some of his articles for the *Edinburgh Review*, it represented an attack on radical views about parliament and a 'Norman yoke', but also an emphasis on the limitations to the monarchy. In 1831 he published *A Short History of the House of Commons*, sceptical about the use of history made by both sides during the Reform Bill controversy. As a Scot he resented Sir Francis Palgrave's opinion, that from the seventh century to the reign of Edward I Scotland was a dependent member of the English monarchy, and he issued in 1833 a *Vindication of the Ancient Independence of Scotland*. Considerable portions of the *Memorials and Correspondence of Charles James Fox*, a work which bears the name of Lord John Russell as editor, were left by Allen in a state ready for the press, and the life of Fox in the seventh and eighth editions of the *Encyclopaedia Britannica* was his composition. Allen was steeped in the history and traditions of the whigs, which led him, unusually for his time, to study Anglo-Saxon, although his writings played down the radical emphasis on a mythic Anglo-Saxon representational system.

Allen was warden of Dulwich College from 1811 to 1820, and master from that year until his death. He was also auditor of the duchy of Lancaster from 1841 until his death. It seems he never married. He died in London at 33 South Street, Lady Holland's residence, on 10 April 1843, and was buried at Millbrook, near Ampthill, Bedfordshire, close by the third Lord Holland. He left his medical books and manuscripts to Dr John Thomson, his other manuscript journals and diaries to Major-General Charles Richard Fox, and his Spanish and Italian books to Dulwich College.   W. P. COURTNEY, rev. H. C. G. MATTHEW

Sources GM, 2nd ser., 20 (1843), 96 · *Wellesley index* · Lord Holland [H. R. V. Fox] and J. Allen, *The Holland House diaries, 1831–1840*, ed. A. D. Kriegel (1977) · P. B. M. Blaas, *Continuity and anachronism* (1978) · *The Horner papers: selections from the letters and miscellaneous writings of Francis Horner, MP, 1795–1817*, ed. K. Bourne and W. B. Taylor (1994) **Archives** BL, corresp. and papers · PRO, corresp. and papers, PRO 30/26/109 · U. Glas. L., journal of a tour in France | All Souls Oxf., letters to Sir Charles Richard Vaughan · BL, corresp. with Sir Henry Ellis, Add. MS 32514 · BL, letters to Sir Henry Ellis, Add. MS 65155 · BL, corresp. and papers relating to C. J. Fox · BL, letters to Macvey Napier, Add. MSS 34612–34623, *passim* · Dulwich College, London, corresp. with Dulwich College and tenants · Glos. RO, letters to Daniel Ellis · JRL, lecture notes · U. Glas. L., Allen MSS · U. Lpool L., letters to Joseph Blanco White **Likenesses** E. Landseer, oils, 1836, NPG

Allen, John (1789–1829), bookseller and antiquary, was born 'about' 27 July 1789, and baptized on 4 August 1789 at Hereford, the eldest son of John Allen (c.1754–1828), a leading bookseller in the city, and his wife, Mary (c.1754–1827), daughter of Francis Thomas of Hereford. By the age of fifteen Allen showed interest in matters antiquarian and in 1807 visited Richard Gough at Enfield. He began early to

collect materials towards a history of his native county that was never to be written. His most notable accomplishment is the substantially complete bibliography of Herefordshire books, pamphlets, and printed ephemera entitled *Bibliotheca Herefordiensis* (1821), which he printed on his father's press in only twenty-five copies. This work is perhaps the earliest county bibliography published in England. He translated and printed in 1820 the royal charter granted to the city of Hereford in 1696 by William III, the title-page giving the incorrect year 1697. A miscellany entitled *Collectanea Herefordensia* (1825) comprised pieces written by him for the *Hereford Independent*. A young man of definite opinions, tending to reform in politics and to liberal thinking in religious matters, Allen never married.

Among the books Allen presented to Hereford's Permanent Library, an institution he was instrumental in forming, was a pamphlet which had been the subject of a successful suit for libel. By depositing it Allen reiterated the libel. He was proceeded against at Hereford in April 1822 and, despite public sympathy, found guilty, with nominal damages of £5 being awarded against him. Though his solicitors waived their fees, the Allens had to pay over £400 in costs. In 1823 Allen's father sold his business, while Allen himself left Hereford to live in London, apparently in reduced financial circumstances. In March 1827 he was briefly held in Clerkenwell prison and on 12 April he was admitted to Bethlem Hospital a lunatic. He was discharged on 3 January 1828 but on 28 May was admitted to Hereford Asylum, where he died on 16 August 1829; he was buried four days later at Hereford. Existing records do not reveal the nature of his mental disorder, nor do they shed light on his cause of death.   PAUL LATCHAM

Sources J. Allen, *Bibliotheca Herefordiensis, or, A descriptive catalogue of books, pamphlets, maps, prints, &c. relating to the county of Hereford* (1821) [Allen's own annotated copy in Hereford Library incl. bibliographical information] · admission registers of the Bethlem Royal Hospital, Beckenham, Kent · records, Herefs. RO, Hereford Asylum, Q/AL/128 · 'Trial report of Williams Esq. *v* Allen Esq. in a case of libel', *Hereford Journal* (3 April 1822) · autograph letter dated 21 March 1827 from Allen at Clerkenwell prison to William Upcott, librarian of the London Institution, tipped in to a copy of *Bibliotheca Herefordiensis*, Hereford Library, Pilley collection · parish register (birth), 1789, Hereford, St Peter's · parish register (baptism), 4/8/1789, Hereford, St Peter's · P. Latcham, 'John Allen jr and his Bibliotheca Herefordiensis', *A Herefordshire miscellany* (2000) **Likenesses** T. Leeming, group portrait, 1815 (*The Hereford chess club, 1815*), Hereford Museum and Art Gallery

Allen, John (d. 1855), Irish nationalist and army officer, was a native of Dublin, where he was also for some time a partner in a drapery business. His participation in the United Irish movement brought him the unwanted attention of the authorities and he left Dublin, through the assistance of Lord Edward Fitzgerald, to work with Arthur O'Connor in the preparation of the projected rising and French invasion of 1798. Along with O'Connor he was tried for high treason at Maidstone in February 1798, but was acquitted. The aftermath of the failed 1798 rebellion found him serving as a United Irish agent in France, where he remained until he joined Robert Emmet in the aborted rising in Dublin in 1803. Allen escaped from Dublin in the uniform of the Trinity College yeomanry corps, and obtained a passage in a vessel to France. Like several veterans of the United Irish movement, he entered the French service. He was promoted to colonel for leading the storming party at the capture of Ciudad Rodrigo in Spain in 1810. During the second occupation of Paris in 1815 his surrender was demanded by the British government; but while being conducted to the frontier, he made his escape, with the connivance of the gendarmes who had him in their charge, at the last station on French territory. Subsequently he lived at Caen, in Normandy, with his sisters. Allen, a protestant, died at Caen on 10 February 1855.

NANCY J. CURTIN

Sources R. R. Madden, *The United Irishmen: their lives and times*, 3rd ser., 7 vols. (1842–6) · M. Elliott, *Partners in revolution: the United Irishmen and France* (1982) · *Memoirs of Miles Byrne*, ed. F. Byrne, 3 vols. (1863), 190 · R. Hayes, *Biographical dictionary of Irishmen in France* (1949)

Allen, John Romilly (1847–1907), archaeologist, born at Park Village West, Regent's Park, London, on 9 June 1847, was the eldest son of George Baugh Allen (1821–1898), a well-known special pleader of the Inner Temple, of Cilrhiw, near Narberth, Pembrokeshire, and his wife, Dorothea Hannah (d. 1868), third daughter of Roger Eaton of Parc Glas, Pembrokeshire. Allen was educated at King's College School, London (1857–60), Rugby School (1860–63), and King's College, London (1864–6). In 1867 he was articled to G. F. Lyster, engineer in chief to the Mersey Docks and Harbour Board, with whom he remained until 1870. He was next employed as resident engineer to the Persian railways of Baron Julius de Reuter and then in supervising the construction of docks at Leith, near Edinburgh, and at Boston, Lincolnshire. Meanwhile he was interested in archaeology, and to this pursuit, and particularly to the study of prehistoric antiquities and of pre-Norman art in Great Britain, he devoted the rest of his life. His earliest contribution to *Archaeologia Cambrensis*, the journal of the Cambrian Archaeological Association, appeared in April 1873; he joined the association in 1875, was elected a member of the general committee in 1877, became joint editor of the journal in 1889, and was sole editor from 1892 until his death. The extent of his influence on the standards of the *Archaeologia Cambrensis* is documented and acknowledged in its pages over twenty years. His article on 'Early Christian art in Wales', which appeared in the January 1899 issue, was the first systematic account of the subject.

Allen's time at Leith gave him the opportunity to visit Scottish archaeological sites; in 1883 he was elected fellow of the Society of Antiquaries of Scotland (honorary fellow, 1900), and in 1885 was the society's Rhind lecturer in archaeology. His Rhind lectures, on *Early Christian Symbolism in Great Britain and Ireland*, were published in 1887. In England he became FSA in 1896, editor of the *Reliquary and Illustrated Archaeologist* in 1893, and Yates lecturer in archaeology in University College, London, for 1898. Allen was comfortably off, but not rich, and it was largely through the support of the Society of Antiquaries of Scotland and its jubilee research fellowship, endowed by Dr R. H. Gunning, that he was able to fund his work in Scotland. Allen's only salaried employment, after he left civil engineering, was as an editor. Allen's great work *The Early Christian Monuments of Scotland* (1903, with Joseph Anderson) gave him scope for a general analysis and classification of ornament which put the study of early medieval sculpture throughout the British Isles on a new footing. His unrivalled knowledge of the visual material, and the soundness of his approach, widely acknowledged by fellow workers in his lifetime, continue to command respect. Allen was a tireless fieldworker; in his last book, *Celtic Art in Pagan and Christian Times* (1904), he was able to claim that he had personally examined nearly all the early Christian monuments of Scotland, England, Wales, and Ireland. Allen pioneered scientific methods of description, but because he was himself an accomplished artist he never lost sight of the aesthetic quality of patterns, and his descriptive writing was fluent and evocative. A passionate advocate of the preservation of monuments, he urged the creation of collections of casts, photographs, and drawings before the monuments themselves had weathered away. Such collections, he pointed out, would not only record the appearance of rapidly disintegrating works of art, but could also be used for study and education at all levels. These views, trenchantly expressed, cropped up regularly in his many contributions to archaeological journals.

Allen's scholarly expertise extended beyond sculpture. He was what would now be called an art historian, as well as an archaeologist. His detailed knowledge of metalwork and manuscript illumination enabled him to show how comparative study of art in various media could help establish chronology. His iconographical research resulted in his listing examples, anticipating the creation of art indices. Allen's more general interests, particularly in the technical appliances of all cultures, found an outlet in his work for the *Reliquary and Illustrated Archaeologist*.

As a freelance scholar, Allen was able to express his views without inhibition. He had hard words to say in print of the curators of the London museums, who he thought neglected early Christian archaeology in Britain and were remote from the general public. But his hot indignation was matched by a keen sense of humour and a kind heart. Well-read and a noted conversationalist, he was regarded with great affection by all who worked with him or benefited from his advice. For most of his life Allen lived in London. He died there, unmarried, at his home, 28 Great Ormond Street, on 5 July 1907.

I. B. HENDERSON

Sources *Archaeologia Cambrensis*, 6th ser., 7 (1907), 441–2 · *The Times* (13 July 1907) · *WW* · Burke, *Gen. GB* · I. Henderson, 'The making of *The early Christian monuments of Scotland*', in J. R. Allen and J. Anderson, *The early Christian monuments of Scotland*, 1 (1993), 13–40 · T. C. Hughes, *Journal of the British Archaeological Association*, new ser., 13 (1907), 207–8 · 'A classified list of papers and articles by J. Romilly Allen, 1876–1896', BL, Add. MS 37628 · b. cert. · d. cert.

Archives BL, collections relating to archaeology and art history, Add. MSS 37539–37628 · NL Wales · NMG Wales · Pembrokeshire RO, Haverfordwest · Royal Museum, Edinburgh
Likenesses photograph, NMG Wales; repro. in Allen and Anderson, *Early Christian monuments of Scotland* · photograph, repro. in *Archaeologia Cambrensis*, 6th ser., 8 (1908)

Allen, John Willoughby Tarleton (1904–1979), colonial educationist and Swahili scholar, was born on 14 November 1904 at the vicarage, Chalfont St Peter, Buckinghamshire, the second of the two children of Roland *Allen (1868–1947), theologian, and his wife, Mary Beatrice (1863–1960), daughter of John Walter Tarleton and his wife, Finetta. The children of elderly and domineering parents, both Allen and his sister, Priscilla Mary Allen (1903–1987), had an isolated childhood and difficult school years. Allen was educated at Marlborough College, Westminster School, and St John's College, Oxford (second class honours in *literae humaniores*, 1927). After graduation he joined the colonial service, and worked in administration and education, mainly in east Africa. In 1958 he left the colonial service and moved to Makerere University College, Kampala, Uganda. Latterly he was attached to the Institute of Swahili Research at the University of Dar es Salaam, and then taught Swahili to Danish volunteers in Tengeru, Tanzania. On 29 September 1930 Allen had married, in Tanga, Tanganyika, Winifred Ethel Emma (Winkie) Brooke (1902–1991), a teacher. They had four children: one son and three daughters, one of whom died in childhood.

Allen was generally known as John, despite having been formally (and somewhat idiosyncratically) registered as Iohn by his father. This perhaps trivial fact may seem to characterize his life, in that his official career in the colonial service and in education was far less important than his mainly unofficial work with Swahili. He was an amateur in the truest and best sense of the word: a lover of Swahili (Kiswahili). He spent all the time he could spare on promoting Swahili as a national and international language, on standardizing it, and on popularizing its classical and modern literature. He was active in the work of the Inter-territorial Language Committee (later the East African Swahili Committee), which eventually became the Institute of Swahili Research at the University of Dar es Salaam. He edited the journal *Swahili* (later renamed *Kiswahili*) published by this succession of organizations, and also edited many books and pamphlets, translating and writing papers on Swahili language studies.

The long tradition of literature, and particularly of poetry, in Swahili was largely unknown in the rest of the world until the efforts of many dedicated expatriates such as Allen brought it to light. It was unknown because it was either orally transmitted or, if written, was in manuscript form in the Arabic script, and Swahili poets and scholars tended to keep such manuscripts in their private collections. Allen was acquainted with many Swahili poets, writers, and intellectuals, and his work in collecting and bringing to light much traditional and modern literature was most valuable. He initiated and edited the traditional poetry series Johari za Kiswahili ('Swahili jewels') published by the East African Literature Bureau, and the collected works of the great contemporary poet Shaaban Robert, *Diwani ya Shaaban* ('The poetic works of Shaaban'), published by Nelson as a series of fourteen volumes during the 1960s. He also brought to light and edited the first major prose work in Swahili, *Habari za Wakilindi* ('The history of the Wakilindi people') by Abdallah bin Hemedi'l-Ajjemi (1962). Latterly, a large number of manuscripts in Swahili having been deposited in the library of the University of Dar es Salaam by the efforts of many interested parties, Allen undertook the enormous task of microfilming, cataloguing, and making notes of these manuscripts in nineteen volumes (1970). Many of the works he edited and published he also transliterated from Arabic to roman script, and translated with notes. John Allen had not himself the gift of poetry or great literary prowess, but he had the insight to recognize greatness in the compositions of others, and the energy and generosity to bring them to public knowledge. Swahili writers and scholars owe him a considerable debt.

On retirement in 1968 Allen and his wife returned to England, where he died on 6 April 1979 of emphysema at his home at Halford, 8 Boults Lane, Old Marston, Oxfordshire. He was buried at Old Marston.   JOAN MAW

Sources H. J. B. Allen, *Roland Allen, pioneer, priest and prophet* (1995), 180–81 · *Kiswahili*, 49/1 (March 1982) · private information (2004) [H. J. B. Allen, son] · *CGPLA Eng. & Wales* (1979) · b. cert. · d. cert.
Archives SOAS, corresp. and papers
Wealth at death £22,371: probate, 16 July 1979, *CGPLA Eng. & Wales*

Allen, Joseph William (1803–1852), landscape painter, was born in Lambeth, London, the son of Joseph William Allen, a schoolmaster, and his wife, Isabella, and was baptized on 27 November 1803. He attended St Paul's School and also worked there as an assistant master. He was an usher in a school at Taunton but turned from teaching to art, initially painting watercolours and then adding oils and etchings to his repertory. His first employer was a dealer and he subsequently painted theatrical scenery with Clarkson Stanfield (1793–1867) and Calvin F. Tomkins (1798–1844) at the Olympic Theatre, London, during Madame Vestris's tenure there. Allen became a member of the Society of British Artists in 1830 where he exhibited 329 works, and over time served as its secretary, treasurer, vice-president, and president. He exhibited eleven pictures at the Royal Academy of Arts from 1826 to 1833 and further works at the British Institution and the New Society of Painters in Water Colours. In addition, he served as drawing-master at the City of London School from its inception in 1834; he presented a portrait of the school's founder, *Warren Stormes Hule*, in 1841. Allen's subjects were largely idealized views of scenery in north Wales, Cheshire, Yorkshire, and midland counties. *The Vale of Clyde—Seen from the Hills Dividing Flintshire from Denbighshire* (exh. Society of British Artists, 1847) was often cited by contemporaries as one of his finest efforts and was purchased as a prize by the Art Union. His watercolours have been likened to those of David Cox (1783–1859) and Samuel

Prout (1783–1852), and his oils were described by Samuel Redgrave and the *Art Journal* as lacking finish and bearing evidence of haste, often attributed to the need to sustain a particularly large family. Lord Northwick was frequently cited as the leader of his patrons, and Prince Albert purchased three works for the Royal Collection, including a fine oil entitled *The Castle at Reihardsbrunn* (1840; Royal Collection, Osborne House). Allen died at his home, Priory Cottage, Lower Mall, Hammersmith, Middlesex, on 26 August 1852 of a heart complaint, leaving a wife and eight children destitute, since his medical condition rendered him unable to procure life insurance. Friends and colleagues established a subscription to aid his family, the council of the City of London School contributing 50 guineas and Queen Victoria and Prince Albert £25. There are portraits by Allen in Eton College and the corporation of the City of London collections; the Victoria and Albert Museum, the Tate collection, the British Museum, and the Wolverhampton Central Art Gallery hold examples of his work.   JASON ROSENFELD

Sources *Art Journal*, 14 (1852), 316 · *GM*, 2nd ser., 38 (1852) · O. Millar, *The Victorian pictures in the collection of her majesty the queen*, 2 vols. (1992) · R. Parkinson, ed., *Catalogue of British oil paintings, 1820–1860* (1990) [catalogue of V&A] · Wood, *Vic. painters*, 3rd edn · J. Johnson, ed., *Works exhibited at the Royal Society of British Artists, 1824–1893, and the New English Art Club, 1888–1917*, 2 vols. (1975) · M. Bradshaw, ed., *Royal Society of British Artists: members exhibiting, 1824–1892* (1973) · Graves, *RA exhibitors*, 1 (1905), 25 · Redgrave, *Artists* · L. Lambourne and J. Hamilton, eds., *British watercolours in the Victoria and Albert Museum* (1980) · M. Hardie, *Water-colour painting in Britain*, ed. D. Snelgrove, J. Mayne, and B. Taylor, 2nd edn, 3 vols. [1967–8] · D. Brook-Hart, *British 19th century marine painting* (1974) · M. H. Grant, *A dictionary of British landscape painters, from the 16th century to the early 20th century* (1952) · H. M. Cundall, *A history of British water colour painting* (1908) · [W. H. Overhall], ed., *Catalogue of sculpture, paintings, engravings and other works of art belonging to the corporation of London*, 2 vols. (1867–8) · IGI

Wealth at death destitute

Allen [*née* Gill], **Marjory, Lady Allen of Hurtwood** (1897–1976), landscape architect and promoter of child welfare, was born on 10 May 1897 at Hazelstubbs, Gravel Hill, Bexleyheath, the daughter of George Joseph Gill (*c*.1860–1947), a water-rate collector, and his wife, Sarah Shorey (Sala) Driver (1864–1953), who worked for the press section of the Inland Revenue. George Gill was a cousin of Eric Gill, and temperamentally a reformer. In 1908 he took his family of four sons and Marjory to live on a smallholding, Brambletye Farm, Cudham, Kent. From 1910 to 1916 Marjory was educated at Bedales School in Hampshire (of which she subsequently became a governor), where she was encouraged to experiment in garden design and was free to explore the surrounding downland. She took a horticultural diploma course at University College, Reading, between 1918 and 1920. On 17 December 1921 she married the socialist politician and pacifist (Reginald) Clifford *Allen, later Baron Allen of Hurtwood (1889–1939); they had a daughter. They were very happy, sharing a common attitude to life and a deep love of the countryside around their home on Abinger Common near Guildford. Marjory

Allen was known to her close friends as Joan. She was a stocky woman, with square shoulders and a strong face, not much interested in dressiness.

Marjory Allen was closely involved with the small group of people who were practising the art of landscape architecture in the 1920s and 1930s and was elected the first fellow of the new Institute of Landscape Architects on 25 March 1930. This was on the strength of the roof garden she was then creating at Selfridges, the idea for which she had herself put forward. This was followed by a series of other commissions to design London gardens, such as the BBC balcony gardens in Portland Place, and a roof-top nursery school playground in St Pancras, all designed from home. She was chairman of the coronation planting committee, 1937–9. After Lord Allen's death in 1939 she moved to London where her formidable energy and her warmth were turned to the promotion of landscape architecture, her chosen career, and to the wellbeing of children. In retrospect her achievements in the latter field may seem the more memorable, even though these were so vividly informed by a feeling for landscape design.

In 1939 Allen was elected vice-president of the Institute of Landscape Architects, a position which she sustained through the war years until 1946. She lectured about the future of the profession, promoting the role of landscape architects in the design of parks, housing, roads, factories, and other areas of the human environment. She believed that:

> landscape architecture is essentially a fine art, which embraces the wide field of physical planning of the land for human use and enjoyment. It is concerned … with developing and promoting an environment that will bring refreshment, delight and health to the urban population. (*Wartime Journal of the Institute of Landscape Architects*, 3, April 1943, 4)

Her jauntiness is illustrated by the words attributed to her—'let's call an international meeting and possibly have an international federation arising from it'—which led in August 1948 to a conference in London and Cambridge where the International Federation of Landscape Architects was founded (Harvey, 11).

In parallel with this work on behalf of her profession, Allen became increasingly interested in the wellbeing of children, both in Britain and beyond. In 1944 she ran a single-handed campaign to expose the conditions under which children in institutions were living; this led to the passing of the Children's Act in 1948; her publication *Whose Children?* of 1944 was part of this effort. She was chairman of the Nursery School Association of Great Britain (1942–8), then its president (1948–51). She was founder president of the World Organisation for Early Childhood Education, a member of the Central Advisory Council for Education (1945–9), and chairman of the Advisory Council on Children's Entertainment Films (1944–50). In 1950, as liaison officer with UNICEF, she developed programmes for handicapped children in Europe and the Middle East.

Allen's ideas began to focus particularly upon the plight of children growing up in cities, bereft of opportunities to release the natural energies of youth. She was early to recognize the deadening effect upon children of high-rise living; she wrote of new tower blocks being built in Glasgow as 'a kind of psychological pollution' (Allen, *Planning for Play*, 14). Practically minded as ever, she promoted the idea of adventure playgrounds, junk playgrounds where the young, lightly supervised to limit danger, could indulge in risky, messy, and untidy activities and could do their own thing, whether energetic, creative, or peaceful.

Allen wrote a series of illustrated books: *The Things we See: Gardens* (1953) and *The New Small Garden* (1956), both with her old friend Susan Jellicoe, *Adventure Playgrounds* (1954), *Play Parks* (1960), *Design for Play* (1962), *New Playgrounds* (1964), and finally *Planning for Play* (1968). Pictures, painstakingly assembled from numerous sources, some overseas, were often as powerful as the carefully researched script. The image of a child leaping through the air from a pile of loose soil with an expression of concentrated enjoyment won over many of the sceptical and cautious. At the same time, inspired by the Emdrup waste material playground in Copenhagen, she imitated the idea of adventure playgrounds, chairing the Lollard Adventure Playground Association between 1954 and 1960 and the London Adventure Playground Association. Later she extended these ideas to become chair of the Handicapped Adventure Playground Association, which particularly provided play opportunities for disabled children. She wrote in *Planning for Play* that:

> the purpose of this book is to explore some of the ways of keeping alive and of sustaining, the innate curiosity and natural gaiety of children. Gifts that are so vivid and creative have importance for future careers and happiness ... we should never forget that play is not a passive occupation. For children and young people it is an expression of their desire to make their own discoveries in their own time and at their own pace. At its best, play is a kind of research ... an adventure and an experiment that are greatly enjoyed. (Allen, *Planning for Play*, 10–11)

She died on 11 April 1976.   HAL MOGGRIDGE

Sources Lady Allen of Hurtwood, *Planning for play* (1968) · M. Allen and M. Nicholson, *Memoirs of an uneducated lady: Lady Allen of Hurtwood* (1975) · S. Harvey and S. Rettig, *Fifty years of landscape design* (1985) · *Landscape and Garden* (1934–9) · *Wartime Journal of the Institute of Landscape Architects* (1941–6) · *Journal of the Institute of Landscape Architects* (1946–70) · *Landscape Design* (1970–76) · G. Jellicoe, *Landscape Design*, 115 (Aug 1976), 7 · S. Harvey, ed., *Reflections on landscape* (1987) · WWW

Archives U. Warwick Mod. RC, corresp. and papers

Likenesses group photograph, repro. in Harvey and Rettig, *Fifty years of landscape design*, p. 155 · photographs, repro. in Allen and Nicholson, *Memoirs of an uneducated lady*

Allen, Mary Sophia (1878–1964), police officer, was born on 12 March 1878 at 2 Marlborough Terrace, Newport Road, Roath, Glamorgan, the daughter of Thomas Isaac Allen, a superintendent of the Great Western Railway, and his wife, Margaret Sophia Carlyle. Her sister, Mrs Hampton, was an early member of the Women Police Volunteers. Mary Allen was educated at home and at Princess Helena College, Ealing. In her memoirs she describes herself as a delicate child who was often ill and was therefore forced to lead a rather cloistered childhood.

In 1909, inspired by Annie Kenney, Allen left home for London to join the campaign for women's suffrage. She served three prison terms for her suffragette activities, during which she went on hunger strikes and was forcibly fed. She was awarded a hunger strike medal from Mrs Pethick-Lawrence in August 1909. In her book *Lady in Blue* Mary Allen wrote that while in prison she 'first envisaged the idea of women police, to arrest women offenders, attend them at police stations, and escort them to prison and give them proper care' (Allen, *Lady*, 16).

Following a period of illness (as a result of being force-fed during her final prison term) Allen was forbidden by Mrs Pankhurst from participating in any further militant activities. Instead she moved to Edinburgh, where she acted as an organizer. Shortly afterwards, just before the outbreak of war, she joined the Women Police Volunteers as sub-commandant. The Women Police Volunteers was an independent organization whose members were trained, uniformed, and prepared to work full time. It was founded by Margaret Damer Dawson, and funded by subscription and private donation. In November 1914 Mary Allen and a colleague began their service in Grantham, Lincolnshire, where the population had almost doubled since military troops had taken up residence. In May 1915 she was transferred to Hull, where she and her colleagues maintained order through several Zeppelin raids. After a period of service in Hull she returned to London to assist in the training of policewomen for munitions factories all over the country. She was appointed OBE in February 1918 for her services during the war.

When Margaret Damer Dawson died in May 1920 Mary Allen succeeded her as commandant of the Women's Auxiliary Service, as her force was now called. Members of the Women's Auxiliary Service initiated women police forces abroad, notably in Ireland and Cologne, Germany. Her first book, *The Pioneer Policewoman* (1925), describes her work and adventures during this period. Subsequently Mary Allen travelled extensively on lecture tours and inspected the training methods and administration of women police forces in many countries, including Egypt, Brazil, and Finland. About this time the National Council of Women wrote letters of complaint to the Home Office, stating that Mary Allen was masquerading abroad as an official policewoman, whereas in fact she was a purely independent agent. The fact that she continued to wear her uniform—riding breeches, skirted coat, overcoat, flat cap, and military boots—together with her authoritative manner and considerable skill in self-advertisement, undoubtedly contributed to her success in this venture.

In 1927 she founded and edited the *Policewoman's Review*, which ran until 1937. It was here, in December 1933, that she advertised for recruits to her newly formed women's reserve, the object of which was to train women for service in any national emergency. Members were to be trained in first aid, fire drill, and lorry driving, among other things. The idea of a women's reserve generated a number of protests to the press, as well as complaints to the Home Office, which pointed out that many of the aims of the women's reserve were already covered by existing organizations such as the British Red Cross, the order of St John, and the Voluntary Aid Detachment.

On her first visit to Berlin, in 1934, Allen met Hitler and Goering. With Goering she discussed whether police-women should wear uniform and was glad to report that his reply (strongly in the affirmative) exactly summed up her own views on the subject, which she considered to be one of the 'most controversial matters concerning police-women all over the world' (Allen, *Lady*, 155). In the same year her second book, *Woman at the Crossroads*, was published, followed by *Lady in Blue* (1936). By the late 1930s her concern with the issues of prostitution, white slave traffic, and the illegal drug trade was well established and in April–May 1940 she contributed a series of articles on vice in *Action*, the organ of the British Union of Fascists (BUF). She had joined the BUF in December 1939. Her membership, as well as her involvement with other prominent members such as Sir Oswald Mosley, resulted in a suspension order under defence regulation 18B on 11 July 1940. This involved restrictions on her movement and communications, but she was not imprisoned. Although she repeatedly asked for the removal of these restrictions, the Home Office saw no grounds for granting her request.

Little is known of Allen from this time until her death, although it appears that she was received into the Roman Catholic church in 1953. She did not marry and had no children. In 1959 she became a patient at Birdhurst Nursing Home, 4 Birdhurst Road, South Croydon, where she remained until her death there from cerebral thrombosis and cerebral arteriosclerosis on 16 December 1964.

VERA DI CAMPLI SAN VITO

Sources M. S. Allen, *Lady in blue* (1936) · M. S. Allen, *The pioneer policewoman*, ed. J. H. Heyneman (1925) · *The Times* (18 Dec 1964) · *Daily Telegraph* (18 Dec 1964) · *Croydon Advertiser* (25 Dec 1964) · E. Crawford, *The women's suffrage movement: a reference guide, 1866–1928* (1999), pp. 8–9 · J. Lock, *The British policewoman: her story* (1979) · 'The hunger-strikers at St James's Hall', *Votes for Women* (6 Aug 1909) · PRO, microfilm, HO 144/21993 · *Policewoman's Review*, 7/8 (Dec 1933) · *CGPLA Eng. & Wales* (1965) · b. cert. · d. cert.

Archives BL, Newspaper Library · BL · PRO, HO 144/21993 · Women's Library, London

Likenesses Mrs A. Broom, photograph, 1916, NPG [*see illus.*] · photographs, repro. in Allen, *Lady in blue*, frontispiece · photographs, repro. in Allen, *Pioneer policewoman*

Wealth at death £289: administration with will, 13 Dec 1965, *CGPLA Eng. & Wales*

Allen, Norman Percy (1903–1972), metallurgist, was born in Wrexham, north Wales, on 5 June 1903, the fifth of ten children, seven girls and three boys, of Sidney Edward Allen, an accountant in the borough treasurer's department at Wrexham, and his wife, Emily Eliza Davis. He was educated at Burton upon Trent Boys' Grammar School from 1913 to 1920. He was awarded the prestigious Linley open scholarship at Sheffield University, studied metallurgy there under Professor C. H. Desch, and graduated with a second-class honours degree in 1923. After a two-year spell in the university working on low melting point zinc base die-casting alloys he joined Swansea University College in 1925 to work on the porosity of copper and copper alloys. There he met Olive Gwendolen Williams, his future wife. She was a native of Swansea, where her father, J. H. Williams, was a tin-plate and metal merchant. In 1928 Allen joined Birmingham University as assistant lecturer, and he was married in 1929. There were two sons and one daughter of the marriage.

At Birmingham, Allen studied the mechanism responsible for the porosity of commercial tough pitch copper. Allen showed that this was related to the presence of hydrogen in the melt in thermodynamical equilibrium with copper oxide present, and that on solidification this would lead to the evolution of hydrogen gas or steam,

Mary Sophia Allen (1878–1964), by Mrs Albert Broom, 1916 [centre, with members of the women police]

forming small blowholes. On the basis of this work Allen was awarded the DSc degree by Birmingham University in 1934.

In 1933 Allen joined the Mond Nickel Research Laboratory in Birmingham, where he remained until 1944. He was second in command to Dr L. B. Pfeil. Apart from his administrative duties for the research programme as a whole, he was involved in a major research project on the transformation characteristics of low alloy steels, in particular on the effect of alloying elements such as nickel and chromium, which enabled steel to be hardened in thick sections on cooling from high temperature; this helped to economize on these strategic elements which were in short supply during the war. From 1939 he and his colleagues developed the Nimonic alloys suitable for high temperature applications in gas turbines. These alloys transformed the Whittle engine into practical reality, and even today remain the standard blading material for many aircraft and land-based gas turbine installations throughout the world. Allen made a major contribution to the speed with which these alloys became available for exploitation by engine designers.

In 1944 Allen joined the National Physical Laboratory (NPL) as superintendent of the metallurgy division, and initiated a good mix of programmes, ranging from the academic to the applied. While he was conversant with the whole of the work going on, he was personally involved with a number of the projects. In 1963 Allen initiated the superconductivity project, aimed at promoting the application of superconductors in industry.

The NPL was also very much involved in the development of materials for high temperature service. Systematic studies were carried out in the division on creep of Nimonic alloys for gas turbines, and on a variety of alloys used in power station components—for example, superheater tubes and steam pipes. These careful and objective researches were a major factor which enabled the turbine designer to increase continually the size, operating temperature, and efficiency of the turbine units.

Following the catastrophic failures of certain welded ships during the war, a long-term investigation was initiated in 1946 under Allen's leadership to determine the effects of alloying elements on the mechanical properties of pure iron. This work contributed significantly to improved steel making procedures in the late 1950s, and to an understanding of the complex mechanical properties.

In 1966 Allen was appointed deputy director of the NPL and until he retired at the end of 1969 he was concerned with the administrative changes needed in the formation of the materials group which absorbed the metallurgy division. He received many honours, including election to the Royal Society in 1956, the Bessemer medal of the Iron and Steel Institute in 1965, and the platinum medal of the Institute of Metals in 1967. He was president of the Institution of Metallurgists in 1961–2, was made an honorary fellow of the Institute of Metals in 1971, and was appointed CB in 1966. He had honorary doctorates from Prague (1964) and Sheffield (1966).

Allen was short and stockily built and his face was notable for the bushy eyebrows, the owlish glasses, and an ever present smile. He was full of energy, and worked at a pace which his staff sometimes found difficult to match. He was very good at stating a case, and he appeared to enjoy an argument. He was conscientious and a very hard worker, who set high standards. He did not tolerate anything slipshod in experimental work or argument. At home he took a full interest in his family and their development. He enjoyed walking and gardening and in his later years became an enthusiastic amateur painter. Allen died suddenly on 23 February 1972, at his home, 10 Firlands, Ellesmere Road, Weybridge, Surrey, when influenza brought on the failure of an already weakened heart. P. B. HIRSCH, rev.

Sources C. Sykes, *Memoirs FRS*, 19 (1973), 1–18 · *The Times* (26 Feb 1972) · personal knowledge (1986) · *CGPLA Eng. & Wales* (1972)

Wealth at death £22,428: probate, 3 May 1972, *CGPLA Eng. & Wales*

Allen, Percy Stafford (1869–1933), Erasmian scholar, was born at 2 Twickenham Park, Twickenham, Middlesex, on 7 July 1869, the younger son and fourth child of Joseph A. Allen (1825–1910), a London bill broker. The Allens were a distinguished and old-established Quaker family, but Joseph Allen had been obliged to leave the Society of Friends on marrying 'out' to Mary Mason (d. 1892), youngest daughter of Hans David Christopher Satow and sister of the Anglican diplomat and historian Sir E. M. Satow. Percy Allen was educated at Clifton College (1882–8) and at Corpus Christi College, Oxford, where he was a scholar (1888–92), taking a first class in classical moderations (1890) and a second in *literae humaniores* (1892).

In 1884 Allen had accompanied his father on a visit to Gibraltar, Morocco, and Malta for the Anti-Slavery Society; in 1893 he travelled with a pupil in Australia and New Zealand. After returning to Oxford at the end of that year, he won the chancellor's prize for a Latin essay (on the character of Alcibiades) in the summer of 1894. In 1896 he took his MA and became a master at Magdalen College School. Appointed professor of history in the government college at Lahore in 1897, he visited England in the summer of 1898, to marry on 20 September his cousin Helen Mary (1872–1952), daughter of Arthur John and Agneta Allen, of Chislehurst, where Joseph Allen had built himself a house. They had one child, a daughter, who died at birth in 1906.

The climate of India seriously affected the health of both Allen and his wife, and in 1901 he resigned his Lahore professorship and returned to Oxford, where the rest of the Allens' life was spent. Initially they were supported by an annual £250 from Allen's father and by small earnings from minor academic and administrative chores; the death of Joseph Allen in 1910 relieved financial pressure. In 1906 a project to make Allen a research fellow of Corpus Christi failed, but in 1908 he was elected to a fellowship of Merton College, which he held until 1924, becoming an honorary fellow in 1925. He filled various college offices, notably that of librarian (1915–24), bringing order into the college archives and early holdings, as well as publishing

Merton Muniments, a facsimile and edition of some of its earliest documents, with his friend H. W. Garrod in 1928 and having a large part in similar publications by others. The fellowship carried no teaching duties, but for many years Allen continued the lectures he had first given in 1906 on the tradition of the classics. In 1924 he was elected president of Corpus Christi College; he retained this office until his death.

Allen's name will always be associated with his masterly edition of the correspondence of Erasmus, *Opus epistolarum Des. Erasmi Roterodami*. His interest in Erasmus dated from 1892 when, immediately after taking his first degree, he competed unsuccessfully for the chancellor's English essay prize. The subject was Erasmus. In 1893–4 he attended the lectures on the life and letters of Erasmus by James Anthony Froude, who influenced him profoundly: he always maintained that *The Life and Letters* (1894) was better than any other book on Erasmus, and on the day on which Froude died he began to read his *History of England*, which he would never willingly hear disparaged. Allen's first published book was *Selections from the Writings of James Anthony Froude* (1901). His virtually flawless scholarship and his gentle, impartial temper make his admiration for Froude seem paradoxical. But he was a man incapable of paradox and, on the main issues of the Reformation, he believed Froude to have been right.

During his four years in India, Erasmus's correspondence continuously preoccupied Allen. On 22 June 1901 he and his wife were cutting up earlier printings of the letters to form, along with the extensive collections he had made in the Netherlands and Germany between 1893 and 1896, a basis for a new edition. After the Allens' return to Oxford in 1901 they regularly (the 1914–18 war years excepted) spent spring and summer in European libraries, collating the known material and bringing to light an immense amount of material hitherto unknown. They were aided in 1904 by a small private gift, part of which was spent on a typewriter, and later by modest financial support from the Clarendon Press, which also intervened to allay anxieties about putative rivals. Every letter was copied fair in the library where the manuscript (or the first printed text) was to be found. The copy so made became the 'printer's copy', with no intervening transcript. The proof of each letter was corrected in the library where the original copy had been made. In the decipherment of difficult fifteenth- and sixteenth-century hands Allen had no rival. Nobody knew the texts of the Reformation as well as he; to nobody were the lives of the great and little men of the Reformation so intimately familiar; he knew them and their writings, and anything that anybody else had written about them, at first hand. Ingram Bywater called him 'the most learned man in Oxford' (*DNB*), and the *Opus epistolarum* is one of the great monuments of English learning.

The first volume in this first critical edition of Erasmus's correspondence appeared in 1906, and the eighth was published posthumously in 1934, with Allen's portrait for a frontispiece and his life by Garrod, in Latin, by way of introduction. Allen had left it to his wife, his collaborator since the beginning, and to Garrod to complete the last three volumes; for these he had collected the materials, but without furnishing commentary and introductions. Volumes 9–11 appeared between 1938 and 1947; an index compiled by Barbara Flower, completed and edited by Elisabeth Rosenbaum, was published as volume 12 in 1958. Reissued in the 1960s and reprinted entire in 1992, the edition still holds the field unchallenged for accuracy and comprehensiveness. Text apart, 'Allen' is, in its commentary and introductions, 'a treasure-house of unborrowed learning' (*DNB*), the beginning of a new era in Erasmus scholarship, in which Erasmus is presented, in his own words, fully but sparely and impartially. Moral and historical judgement is left to the reader, who is deemed to share the familiarity of Allen with language, persons, and issues, as well as his affection for Erasmus and his appreciation of Erasmus's situation. The most important single printed source for the intellectual history of western Europe during pre-Reformation and Reformation times, the *Opus epistolarum* contains more than 3100 letters, 1600 of them by Erasmus himself, as against the 1800 in total printed by Jean Leclerc in 1706. Its texts are based almost entirely on known manuscripts, where Leclerc had often to rely on printed texts. Its datings, on which Erasmus chronology often depends, have stood the test of time remarkably: only a handful of finished letters, with a number of drafts, have since come to light. Its commentary (Leclerc had effectively none), though inevitably now dated, is still indispensable. 'Allen' is the starting point for the correspondence, and for much else, in the edition of the complete works of Erasmus in English issued by Toronto University Press (1974–) and for Toronto's companion biographical register, *Contemporaries of Erasmus* (1985–7), while in the Amsterdam edition of the complete works in Latin, also in progress, the correspondence has been judged less in need of immediate attention because of 'Allen'.

Besides the *Opus epistolarum*, Allen published his prize essay (1894), some single lectures, a little volume of *Selections from Erasmus* (1908), and eleven lectures in *The Age of Erasmus* (1914). In 1924 he and his wife published jointly *Sir Thomas More: Selections from his English Writings and from the Lives by Erasmus and Roper* (presenting a view of More which, like their view of Erasmus, was somewhat sentimental); and in 1929 they edited the *Letters of Richard Fox, 1486–1527*, the correspondence of the founder of Corpus. In 1934 there appeared posthumously another volume of Erasmian studies by Allen, *Erasmus: Lectures and Wayfaring Sketches*.

Allen received honorary degrees from the universities of Leiden (1922), Birmingham and Louvain (1927), and Durham (1931); between 1909 and 1930 he became, by invitation, foreign, honorary, or extraordinary member of academies or learned societies in Amsterdam, Antwerp, Ghent, Leiden, and Utrecht; in 1923 he was elected fellow of the British Academy. In 1925 his sense of what was required of the head of a college led him to take his DLitt at Oxford.

Allen was himself an indefatigable letter writer: he

wrote easily and copiously, in a minute and precise hand, to family and friends and was prompt in dealing with official correspondence. To Sir Aurel Stein, his closest friend since their meeting at Lahore, he wrote weekly until Stein begged him to write only fortnightly. The selection of letters published in 1939 by Mrs Allen exhibits happily a single-minded scholar of simple tastes, regular habits, personal modesty, care for his friends, and devotion to Erasmus, his works, and his ideals—Allen was a supporter of the League of Nations—a man of moral principle and lovable and saintly character. They give only a superficial impression of his presidency of Corpus Christi, election to which the Allens privately called 'the miracle'. The election process was protracted, and Allen's eventual appointment was controversial among both undergraduates and influential fellows. He was well-meaning and conscientious, but he had neither taste nor aptitude for debate or for university administration. To individual undergraduates he was kind, presenting them all with his edition of the letters written by the founder, Bishop Fox. Yet he and his wife seemed remote and unworldly, entertainments at the lodgings were stiff and for some even painful, and there were embarrassing disciplinary problems. There could be no question, however, that Allen's devotion to the college rested upon a deep knowledge of its origins, and his *Times* obituarist thought that on scholarly grounds he was 'almost the ideal Head of a House'.

Besides his Latin and Greek, Allen had excellent French and German and could converse in Italian, Spanish, Dutch, and Hindustani. Personally frugal though unobtrusively generous and considerate to others, he defined his recreations as foreign travel and bicycling; both were pursued with a degree of hardiness. In youth he had rowed for his college, and he remained supportive of its boat club. Tall and spare, upright and unhurried but unpompous in carriage as in all things, careful in dress, pale in complexion, he wore his dark hair cut short; like his small moustache it greyed in later life. His eyes were hazel and he habitually wore spectacles.

For thirty years Allen occupied seat S8 in Selden End of the Bodleian Library, of which he was a curator from 1913 and a benefactor; from 1915 to 1924 he was a curator of the Indian Institute. He died in the president's lodgings at Corpus Christi, after a protracted illness, on 16 June 1933. After a funeral service on 20 June he was cremated at Reading; his ashes were buried near the altar in Corpus Christi chapel, which, as an Anglican with doctrinal reservations, he believed should be the centre of college life. The P. S. Allen junior research fellowship in history at Corpus Christi was founded by a bequest from his widow. Her own contribution to their scholarly collaboration was acknowledged by several honours: she received honorary doctorates from the universities of Basel (1946) and Amsterdam (1948) and an honorary MA degree from Oxford (1932), and was elected an honorary fellow of St Hilda's College, Oxford (1944). J. B. TRAPP

Sources DNB · H. W. Garrod, 'Percy Stafford Allen, 1869–1933', *PBA*, 19 (1933), 381–407 · *The letters of P. S. Allen*, ed. H. M. Allen (1939) · Bodl. Oxf., MSS P. S. Allen 1–271 [*Summary catalogue*, nos. 37512–37783] · CCC Oxf., nos. 570, 574 · R. Symonds, 'The world behind Erasmus: P. S. Allen as president of Corpus, 1924–1933', *Pelican Record* [Corpus Christi College, Oxford], 41 (2000), 21–34; repr. in *The fox, the bees and the pelican: some worthies and noteworthies of Corpus Christi College, Oxford* (2002), 79–88 · WWW, 1929–40 · b. cert. · m. cert. · d. cert. · *The Times* (16 Sept 1952), 8 · *Pelican Record*, 30 (Dec 1952), 71–2

Archives Bodl. Oxf., corresp. and papers · CCC Oxf., papers · Merton Oxf., papers | Bodl. Oxf., corresp. with Sir Aurel Stein · JRL, letters to the *Manchester Guardian*

Likenesses drawing, 1877, Bodl. Oxf., Allen papers, 268 · photograph, 1923, Bodl. Oxf., Allen papers, 268 (Sc 276780) · photograph, 1927, repro. in *Letters of P. S. Allen*, ed. Allen · H. A. Olivier, oils, 1929, CCC Oxf., President's Lodgings · H. A. Olivier, portrait, 1929 (after his earlier portrait), Merton Oxf.; repro. in *Letters of P. S. Allen*, ed. Allen · drawing (after photograph, 1927?), Bodl. Oxf., Allen papers; repro. in H. de Vocht, *Monumenta humanistica Lovaniensia: texts and studies about Louvain humanists* (1934) · photographs, Bodl. Oxf., Allen papers 271

Wealth at death £12,566 12s. 4d.: probate, 22 Nov 1933, CGPLA Eng. & Wales

Allen, Sir Peter Christopher (1905–1993), chemist and industrialist, was born at Mawmead, Ashtead, Surrey, on 8 September 1905, the son of Sir Ernest King Allen (1864–1937), barrister and later assistant public trustee, and his wife, Florence Mary, née Gellatly. After Harrow School (1919–24) he studied natural sciences at Trinity College, Oxford (1925–8), then joined Brunner Mond, part of newly formed Imperial Chemical Industries (ICI) as a chemist. His first book on his lifelong obsession, *Railways of the Isle of Wight* came out the same year. On 27 June 1931 he married Violet Sylvester Wingate-Saul (1908/9–1951); they had two daughters.

Allen opted for management and was soon in ICI's alkali division at Winnington, a thrusting and cosmopolitan outfit whose outstanding research unit discovered polythene, a foundation of modern plastics, in 1933. A large self-confident man who radiated enthusiasm, Allen relished the atmosphere. 'We were good and we knew it … rather brash and not very popular; we didn't care' (Reader, 2.80). Allen's work was crucial in the commercial development of polythene. He insisted, against opposition, on doubling its original production capacity, expressing frustration when it became a key component of wartime radar sets and ICI was unable to supply demand. 'It maddens me that night fighter equipment should wait on our incompetence', Allen wrote in his diary on 29 August 1941 (ibid., 2.358). As managing director of the new plastics division from 1942 and chairman from 1948, he oversaw the development of ICI's discoveries for wartime use and the domestic revolution they brought. 'Chemically, it is a good and exciting time to be alive', he wrote in 1943 (ibid., 2.349). 1951 brought inevitable promotion to the ICI board but personal tragedy with the death of his wife after twenty years of marriage.

A year later came remarriage—on 21 October 1952; his second wife was Consuelo Maria Linares Rivas (1924/5–1991)—and a growing fascination with Spain, culminating in his chairmanship of the Anglo-Spanish Society from 1973 to 1980. Allen's responsibilities on ICI's board included growth sectors—paint, plastics, and the new

Terylene fibre. As the company's involvement in synthetic fibres mushroomed, he became a director of British Nylon Spinners. But he increasingly fretted over the lack of hands-on engagement of board members and jumped at the chance to become president (1959) and chairman (1962) of Canadian Industries Ltd, ICI's subsidiary in Canada.

It was a turning point, fostering a driving interest in improving productivity and a belief in the importance of ICI's involvement in North America that flowered when Allen became chairman. It also fed his passion for golf and, with wide connections with American business, he was elected as the first British member at Augusta. Returning to oversee ICI's European operation in 1962, he became deputy chairman in 1963 at a time of controversy. There was growing economic pressure on British industry. ICI was shaken by its high-profile failure to take over Courtaulds. Allen was heavily involved in export promotion and was knighted in 1967. But when a disillusioned ICI board forced the retirement of Sir Paul Chambers in 1968, he was planning retirement. His colleagues thought differently. Disliking the front runner, Richard Beeching, who had made few friends after returning from rationalizing the railways, and feeling that two younger candidates were not ready, they turned to Allen, to his surprise. He was chairman from 1968 to 1971.

Allen's successor, Jack Callard, encapsulated his contemporaries' view of Allen's 'rock-like stature, his warm and jovial manner, his openness to other people's views, his interest in everyone and all things, his decisiveness, his love of games, particularly golf' (*The Independent*, 2 Feb 1993). Others marked the rapidity with which he could crystallize a lengthy document or discussion, his efforts to improve productivity, and his criticism of ICI offices for 'collecting useless statistics and disseminating useless knowledge' (*Daily Telegraph*, 1 Feb 1993). Others noted impatience; when he visited a site he always seemed eager to get to the next engagement, often something to do with railways. And the books flowed—four on railways and one each on golf and Spain before he became chairman and more afterwards.

Allen's period in office was difficult but set markers for the future. He steadied the board. He presided over, but was not much involved in, complex and ultimately disastrous moves to extend ICI's profitable fibres operation downstream by buying textile companies like Viyella. His productivity drive was prescient but not initially successful: ICI profits, to his chagrin, shrank. His crucial legacy was to encourage, against considerable opposition from heavy chemical traditionalists, a strategic move to establish ICI in the USA with a major acquisition.

By the end of the century, when 40 per cent of ICI's business and even more of Zeneca's, its successful offspring, came from the USA, the significance of Allen's strategy was obvious. But in 1971 the board wobbled. The key decision came only days after he retired. In an unprecedented move, he was asked back for a pre-board discussion at which his weight helped sway the decision. As a result

Britain's biggest manufacturer became a genuine multinational. Allen's incisive thinking was missed as the company was slow to reshape itself in the seventies.

On retirement, surrounded by railway memorabilia which included a full-size Spanish shunting engine, there were more books and more travel, but Allen's golf was hampered by a failed hip replacement. He became a director of British Insulated Callender's Cables. The British Transport Trust recognized his work by naming a building at the York Railway Museum after him.

Allen's second wife died in 1991. He died on 24 January 1993 at his home, Telham Hill House, Telham Lane, Battle, Sussex.   MARTIN ADENEY

Sources J. Callard, *The Independent* (2 Feb 1993) · *Daily Telegraph* (1 Feb 1993) · *The Times* (28 Jan 1993) · W. J. Reader, *Imperial Chemical Industries: a history*, 2 vols. (1975), vol. 2 · private information (2004) [interviews with former directors of ICI] · C. Kennedy, *ICI, the company that changed our lives* (1986) · *CGPLA Eng. & Wales* (1993) · b. cert. · m. certs. · d. cert.

Likenesses R. Spear, oils, Imperial Chemical Industries Headquarters, Manchester Square, London · portrait, The Times Picture Library · portrait, Telegraph Picture Library · portrait, Independent Picture Library

Wealth at death £773,927: probate, 1993, *CGPLA Eng. & Wales*

Allen, Ralph (*bap.* 1693, *d.* 1764), postal entrepreneur and philanthropist, was baptized on 24 July 1693 in the parish church of St Columb Major in Cornwall, one of four children of Philip Allen (*d.* 1728). Much remains obscure about his early life, but his father is reputed to have kept an inn in nearby St Blazey, and his mother came from St Austell. The satirist Alexander Pope referred to him in a poem of 1738 as 'low-born'. This was later changed to 'humble' (*Epilogue to the Satires*) and excused as indicating manner rather than origins, but the episode suggests a condescension towards the 'self-made' man of quiet demeanour and simple dress.

Allen later showed an affectionate concern for his immediate family, perhaps due to an awareness of the benefits he had derived from their association with the post office established at St Columb in 1704, on the new post road to Falmouth, which his grandmother was said to keep. His aptitude for business, which was first shown there, led to his move about 1708 to the office at Exeter, and in 1710 to that at Bath, where in 1712 he became the salaried deputy postmaster.

In the early eighteenth century almost all mail travelled via London, on six main post roads. By a successful experiment at the Exeter post office, started in 1696 by Joseph Quash, the Bristol mail was sent directly to that city across the main post roads. This system of 'cross-post' was extended to Chester in 1700, and to Oxford via Bath in 1709–10. Ralph Allen's move to Bath was probably associated with the latter development. His experience there enabled him, in 1720, to secure the right to farm the cross-post, and the bye-way post which was delivered along the line of the post roads and to towns nearby. This bid was a bold move, for Allen agreed to pay £6000 per year to operate services from which the annual revenue was then less than £4000. His anticipation of great profit was correct, especially as the renewable contracts permitted the expansion of the system over England and Wales. Allen's success was not due to any major innovation, but to a business acumen allied to a meticulous attention to detail, and a determination to prevent fraud, which in time realized profits in the order of £12,000 per year.

Such a contract required strong backing, and this Allen was able to secure 'on his own personal Character alone' (Hopkins, 22–3). It is probable that the strongest support came from Major-General George Wade, sent to Bath to quell the disaffection in the west country arising from the succession of George I in 1714. Intelligence gained through Allen's official duties provided information on Jacobite preparations. This service to the Hanoverian government introduced him into more cosmopolitan circles than hitherto, as well as providing a firm basis for the friendship between the two men that was strengthened when Wade became member of parliament for Bath in 1722. A scheme to make the River Avon navigable to Bristol was revived, and the first meeting of the proprietors in December 1724 was attended by Allen in his own right, and as Wade's representative. In January 1725 Allen became chief treasurer of the navigation with control of the iron chest, in which were placed the proprietors' funds. Later that year his acceptance by the borough was signified by his becoming a freeman and member of the common council, for which he sometimes acted as banker. Completed in three years, the Avon navigation allowed the carriage of building materials between Bristol and Bath, enabling the needs of the spa to be met as it grew in importance as a resort for the rich and fashionable.

On 26 August 1721 Allen married Elizabeth Buckeridge, the daughter of a London merchant, and her dowry may have helped his finances; but there was to be no family dynasty, for an only child, born in 1725, and named George, died in infancy. A house near the abbey, bought in 1726, became office and home. The large circle of relations provided a supportive network, and it was from Elizabeth's brother that in 1728 the land, which was to provide the site for the mansion at Prior Park, and to give access to fine building stone on Combe Down, was purchased. The height of the downland, and the steepness of the slope, made it difficult for stone to be carted to river level, and so an ingenious wooden railway was built, and equipped with wagons and cranes. Allen acquired a near monopoly of the Bath building-stone industry, and became a major local employer. From the quay the stone was shipped across river to sites in Bath, or down the Avon for use elsewhere. These profitable developments provided Allen with sources of income that were independent of the renewal of his Post Office contract.

With his amiable temperament Allen formed many fruitful professional partnerships, especially that with the architect John Wood the elder, who added a new Palladian front to Allen's town house and then from the mid-1730s created the fine mansion at Prior Park, of which the main apartments were ready for occupation in 1741. The new house had a new mistress, for Ralph Allen's first wife died in February or March 1736, and a year later, on 24 March 1737, he married Elizabeth Holder (d. 1766), of the Manor House at Bathampton. In 1742 Allen completed the purchase of this property, which was to become the family home of Philip, his younger brother and colleague.

Prior Park became not only a fine architectural feature but also a centre of hospitality and culture. The house and grounds overlook Bath, in a position of natural advantage on the southern slopes, which was enhanced by Alexander Pope's advice on the planning of the garden features. Writers, poets, and painters were regular visitors—commemorating Allen in such characters as Henry Fielding's Squire Allworthy in *Tom Jones* (1749). Fielding also dedicated his *Amelia* (1751) to Allen and after his death Allen took charge of his family, and provided for the education of his children. Allen's friendship with Pope dated from about 1736.

Well-read clergymen spent time at Prior Park, especially William Warburton, who married Gertrude Tucker, Allen's favourite niece: preferment was secured for him, eventually to the bishopric of Gloucester. Politicians of the whig persuasion were welcomed, Bath's mid-century members of parliament, William Pitt the elder and Sir John Ligonier, in particular. Royalty such as Princess Amelia were also entertained. The less privileged were helped by Allen's generous financial and practical support—individuals such as workmen, for whom housing was built, and institutions such as the Bath General Hospital, for which funds and building stone were provided. Allen was said to give away more than £1000 a year. From 1750 he spent the late summer of every year in a house he had built in Weymouth, where business and hospitality continued.

Allen served as mayor of Bath in 1742, and acted as a justice of the peace for Somerset from 1749. His support for the Hanoverians remained staunch, and at the time of the 1745 rebellion he raised and funded a volunteer force. However, his lack of understanding of the finer points of politics was exposed in 1763, when he promoted a congratulatory address from the corporation to the king, on the 'adequate' peace already castigated by Pitt as 'inadequate' (Peach, 175–85). Allen had to suffer the scorn of the caricaturists, and although the corporation rallied to his support he resigned as alderman.

Allen died on 29 June 1764 at Prior Park having suffered for some time from 'gravel' stones in the urinary tract (Boyce, 251, 255). He was buried on 5 July at nearby Claverton church, the manor (subsequently demolished) having been added to his possessions in 1758. After his death William Pitt wrote to Mrs Allen that, 'I fear not all the examples of his virtues will have power to raise up to the world his like again' (Taylor and Pringle, 2.290). Pitt was also left £1000 in Allen's will, where he was described 'as the best of friends, as well as the most upright and ablest of Ministers that has adorned our Country' (Boyce, 284).

Deprived of his commercial talents, and with large bequests to meet, Allen's heirs found it difficult to maintain Prior Park after his death. The contents were sold in 1769, the mansion itself in 1807. Ralph Allen had shown an acute aptitude for business, tempered by a genuine largeness of spirit. He had found ways to serve both public good and private profit, and had achieved the notable feat of making few enemies while amassing a great fortune.

BRENDA J. BUCHANAN

Sources B. Boyce, *The benevolent man: a life of Ralph Allen of Bath* (1967) · R. E. M. Peach, *The life and times of Ralph Allen* (1895) · R. Allen, *Ralph Allen's own narrative, 1720–1761*, ed. A. E. Hopkins (1960) · S. Davis, *Ralph Allen: benefactor and postal reformer* (1985) [Bath Postal Museum booklet] · T. Mowl and B. Earnshaw, *John Wood, architect of obsession* (1988) · G. Clarke, *Prior Park: a compleat landscape* (1987) · M. Chapman, *A guide to the estates of Ralph Allen around Bath* (1996) [survey of Old Bath, booklet] · R. S. Neale, *Bath, 1680–1850: a social history, or, A valley of pleasure, yet a sink of iniquity* (1981) · B. J. Buchanan, 'The Avon navigation and the inland port of Bath', *Bath History*, 6 (1996), 63–87 · S. McIntyre, 'Towns as health and pleasure resorts: Bath, Scarborough and Weymouth, 1700–1815', DPhil diss., U. Oxf., 1973 · J. Wood, *A description of Bath*, 2nd edn (1765); repr. (1969) · A. Pope, *One thousand seven hundred and thirty eight: a dialogue something like Horace* (1738) · H. Robinson, *The British Post Office: a history* (1948) · *GM*, 1st ser., 34 (1764), 350 · *Correspondence of William Pitt, earl of Chatham*, ed. W. S. Taylor and J. H. Pringle, 4 vols. (1838–40), vol. 2, p. 290 · parish register (burial), Bath RO

Archives Bath Central Library, accounts, corresp., estate map, and papers · Bath City RO, Bath, estate map, papers relating to his estate, and reference book · Post Office Archives, London, instructions issued by Allen | BL, letters to duke of Newcastle, Add. MSS 32732–33053, *passim* · BL, corresp. with Alexander Pope, Egerton MS 1947 · BL, letters to Charles Yorke, Egerton MS 1952 · Emmanuel College, Cambridge, letters to George Dyer · PRO, letters to first earl of Chatham, PRO 30/8

Likenesses J. van Diest, oils, *c*.1728, Guildhall, Bath, Victoria Art Gallery Collection · T. Hudson, oils, *c*.1740, Bath Preservation Trust; versions, Hurd Episcopal Library, Hartlebury, priv. coll; modern copy, GPO · medal, 1752, Post Office Archives, London; repro. in R. C. Tombs, *The king's post* (1905), facing p. 49 · J. Faber junior, mezzotint, 1754 (after T. Hudson), BM, NPG · P. Hoare, marble bust, 1757, Royal National Hospital for Rheumatic Diseases, Bath · P. Hoare, marble bust, 1757, Guildhall, Bath · A. Pond, oils, *c*.1757, Hurd Episcopal Library, Hartlebury; version, Guildhall, Bath, Victoria Art Gallery Collection; formerly in possession of Gertrude Allen · W. Hoare, oils, *c*.1758, Royal Devon and Exeter Hospital; copy, Guildhall, Bath, Victoria Art Gallery Collection · W. Hibbart, caricature, etching, 1763, repro. in Boyce, *Benevolent man*, pl. 13 · W. Hoare, etching, 1764 (after his oil painting, *c*.1758), BM, NPG · I. Gosset senior, sculpture, wax profile, Hurd Episcopal Library, Hartlebury · T. Worlidge?, portrait, Royal National Hospital for Rheumatic Diseases, Bath · oils, NPG

Wealth at death probable rental value of estates £3606 p.a.: *GM*, 350 · shares amounting to £40,000; mines and equipment; legacies of £60,000: will, repr. in Peach, *Life and times*, 226–41; *GM*; 'General account of the personal estate of Ralph Allen, 1764–7', Bath RO · mansion at Prior Park, two manor houses, several town houses, and summer residence at Weymouth; but executors and trustees struggled to meet £60,000 bequest: *GM*; 'General account of the personal estate of Ralph Allen, 1764–7', Bath RO; will, repr. in Peach, *Life and times*, 226–41

Allen, Robert (*fl.* 1582–1612), Church of England clergyman and religious writer, was probably the Robert Alen who matriculated as a sizar at Pembroke College, Cambridge, at Easter 1582 and graduated BA in 1585–6 and MA in 1589. In the epistle dedicatory to *The Doctrine of the Gospel* (1606) he says that he has been catechizing during a ministry of twenty years, which accords with a graduation date of 1585–6. During his career he ministered to churches in small villages, including Culford, Suffolk, north of Bury St Edmunds, of which he had been deprived for nonconformity by 7 August 1605, when his successor was installed.

Allen was one of at least fifteen Suffolk ministers who were authors in the years round 1600. His first book, *An Alphabet of the Holy Proverbs of King Salomon* (1596), which was intended for household use, provides brief expositions of the more difficult proverbs, compares translations of selected ones, and includes an epistle dedicatory to Thomas, fourth Lord Wentworth, and Robert Rich, the future second earl of Warwick. Allen published two works in 1600, one of which, *A Treatise of Beneficence*, was completed at Culford in May and dedicated to Sir John Popham, lord chief justice and privy councillor. In it Allen praises the Vagrancy Act of 1598, castigates vagabonds as dangerous and unworthy of relief, urges charity for deserving poor, and buttresses his argument with mostly classical quotations, especially from Seneca. This book was reprinted in 1603 as *The Oderifferous Garden of Charitie*. In 1600 Allen also published *A Treasurie of Catechisme, or, Christian Instruction*, with an epistle dedicatory to his patron, Sir Nicholas Bacon, and his wife, Lady Anne. A substantial book of 308 pages, *A Treasurie* was intended for catechists and mature Christians rather than children and uneducated believers. Its coverage includes social themes ranging from marriage and sexual matters to landlord–tenant relations and appropriate conduct for lawyers.

Bacon was still Allen's patron when the latter completed *The Doctrine of the Gospel*, a work of 998 pages in three parts, which explicates 'what those things are which the faithful Ministers of Jesus Christ doe beate their wittes about' (sig. *4*v). Dedicated to the Bacons (Sir Nicholas, Lady Anne, Sir Nathaniel, Sir Francis, Sir Edmund, and Edward JP) this book too was written for mature believers, and also for fellow ministers, many of whom Allen had heard preach—he likens himself to a bee that has extracted honey from their works. One of those ministers, Richard Blackerby, contributed verses to conclude Allen's mammoth undertaking. By this time Allen was suffering from ill health, but he continued to write. In 1608 he saw a work by a deceased fellow minister, Robert Pricke, through the press; entitled *A Verie Godlie and Learned Sermon*, it had been preached at the funeral of Sir Edward and Lady Susan Lewkenor. Allen contributed an epistle to Pricke's son Timothy, a fellow pastor. The following year Allen shepherded another of Robert Pricke's works, *The Doctrine of Superioritie, and of Subjection*, through to publication. In an epistle to Sir Edward Lewkenor the younger, Sir Robert Lewkenor, Sir Robert Quarles, and four other gentlemen, Allen describes himself as a friend of Pricke's former congregation at Denham, Suffolk. Allen completed his final work, *Concordances of the Holy Proverbs of King Salomon: and of his Like Sentences in Ecclesiastes*, on 20 July 1612; it groups verses according to a wide variety of themes. There is no further reference to him, and it is not known when he died.

RICHARD L. GREAVES

Sources Venn, *Alum. Cant.*, 1/1.19 · K. Fincham, *Prelate as pastor: the episcopate of James I* (1990) · P. Collinson, *The religion of protestants* (1982) · R. L. Greaves, *Society and religion in Elizabethan England*

(1981) • I. Green, *The Christian's ABC: catechisms and catechising in England, c.1530–1740* (1996) • P. Collinson, *Godly people: essays on English protestantism and puritanism* (1983)

Allen, Robert Calder (1812–1903), naval officer, born on 8 August 1812, was the son of William Allen, a master in the navy and presumably a follower of Admiral Sir Robert Calder. He entered the navy as a second-class volunteer in July 1827. In that grade and as second master he served with credit, principally on the west coast of Africa and in China. On 26 August 1841 he was advanced to be master, and in 1842–5 was master of the *Dido* under Captain Henry Keppel, during her celebrated cruises against the Malay pirates of Borneo. Here Allen demonstrated both courage and high seamanship. In 1850–51 he was master of the *Resolute* in the Arctic, under Captain Horatio Austin, whom he followed from the *Blenheim*, and had charge of the magnetic observations. In 1854–5 he was master of the blockship *Hogue* in the Baltic, and rendered efficient service by his survey, often under fire, of the approaches to Bomarsund. In June 1863 he was promoted to the then new rank of staff commander, and in July 1867 to that of staff captain. In 1866–7 he was master attendant and harbour-master at Malta and in 1867 he was appointed in the same capacity to Devonport, before being transferred to Deptford. When that dockyard was closed in October 1870 he retired with the rank of captain. He was a silent, thoughtful man, modest and retiring. The subordinate position in which so much of his service was passed prevented his name from coming prominently before the public but in the navy his reputation as a sound and skilful navigator and pilot stood very high, and was officially recognized by a CB in 1877.

Allen was twice married. With his first wife he had a daughter and four sons, who all entered the public service, navy, army or marines. His second wife survived him. He died at his home, 72 Shirland Road, Paddington, London on 29 January 1903.

J. K. LAUGHTON, rev. ANDREW LAMBERT

Sources V. Stuart, *The beloved little admiral* (1967) • *CGPLA Eng. & Wales* (1903) • private information (1912) • *Navy List* • G. S. Ritchie, *The Admiralty chart: British naval hydrography in the nineteenth century* (1967) • d. cert.
Wealth at death £701 18s. 11d.: probate, 25 March 1903, *CGPLA Eng. & Wales*

Allen, Sir Roger (1909–1972), diplomatist, was born on 17 August 1909 at 12 Primrose Hill Studios, Fitzroy Road, St Pancras, London, the only son of Major Herbert Charles Goodeve Allen (b. 1878), artist, and officer in the special reserve of the Royal Engineers, and his wife, Winifred Frances, daughter of the Revd Francis Hoare, vicar of Trinity Church, Derby. On his father's side he was descended from a long-established Pembrokeshire family with a tradition of overseas service; his paternal great-grandfather, Charles Allen (1808–1884), was a member of the Bengal civil service and of the legislative council of India, and his paternal grandfather, Herbert James Allen (1841–1912), was HM consul at Newchwang (Yingkou), China.

Allen was educated at Repton School, Derbyshire,

between 1923 and 1928 before reading modern languages at Corpus Christi College, Cambridge. After graduating with an upper second-class degree, in 1932 he trained as a lawyer at the Inner Temple, and was called to the bar in 1937. In April 1940 he joined the Foreign Office on a temporary basis, and he remained there for the duration of the war. Thereafter legal practice seemed dull in comparison and he stayed on in the foreign service, becoming a grade 7 officer in January 1946. His first overseas posting—at the relatively late age of thirty-nine—was to the Soviet Union. Arriving in Moscow in April 1946, his time at the embassy coincided with the deepening of the cold war. The breadth of experience gained was immense. He returned to the Foreign Office in May 1948, and in January 1949 became head of the United Nations political department, with the rank of counsellor. The dominant issue was China's permanent seat on the Security Council in the light of Mao's communist victory over Chiang Kai-shek in 1949.

Allen's next focus was Egypt. As head of the African department from February 1950 to September 1953 he advocated the evacuation of Britain's garrison in the Suez Canal zone, the largest military base in the world. Keeping 80,000 troops in an area the size of Wales made little sense financially, diplomatically, or strategically. After a battle against Egyptian policemen in Isma'iliyyah in January 1952 Britain's senior military officers gradually came to the same conclusion. Their pace, however, did not match Allen's, and frustration occasionally got the better of him. 'The British soldier', he wrote to a colleague at the Cairo embassy in February 1952, 'seems willing to put up with a great deal of sniping and bomb-throwing for the sake of a few tennis courts and amenities such as a place to have his pre-prandial drink' (Kent, 2.348). But it was the 'Suez group' of Conservative backbench rebels, secretly encouraged by the prime minister, Winston Churchill, that caused the most trouble for Allen. Churchill and the Suez group held that the canal was the 'jugular vein of empire' and as such was of great psychological importance. The foreign secretary, Anthony Eden, on the other hand agreed with the realism of Allen's recommendations—while also admiring their crisp, forceful style—and he staked his political future on the policy of withdrawal. In order to press home the reasons for evacuation Allen was promoted assistant secretary of state in charge of Middle Eastern affairs in September 1953. The Anglo-Egyptian defence agreement of July 1954, by which the last British troops pulled out of Egypt in June 1956, owed more to Allen than to any other official. On 9 January 1954 he married Jocelyn, daughter of Commander Arthur Henry de Kantzow, Royal Navy officer. They had two children: Georgina (b. 1954) and Charles (b. 1956).

In June 1954 (a month before the Egyptian agreement was concluded) Allen was appointed deputy high commissioner in Bonn. His reputation as a no-nonsense troubleshooter preceded him. Germany's relationship with the Western powers was in the balance when France rejected the European Defence Community treaty on 30 August. The crisis that followed was all the graver because the

United States had threatened an 'agonizing reappraisal' of its European commitments should the Germans not be integrated into a suitable defensive arrangement. Britain responded—with Allen a key figure—by securing Germany's inclusion in the Western European Union in October 1954. This arrangement was coupled with the full restoration of German sovereignty, thus paving the way for its accession into NATO in May 1955. Due to the changed status of the government Allen assumed the title of minister, and the high commission became an embassy. He was made KCMG in January 1957.

In May 1957 Allen was given his first mission: the ambassadorship to Greece. Despite being based in Athens the future of Cyprus was at the top of his agenda. A Greek–Cypriot revolt against British rule had begun in 1954 with nationalists demanding union with Greece (Enosis). London resisted this because Cyprus had been earmarked as the new headquarters for Britain's Middle East forces following the evacuation from Egypt. However, the Suez debacle of 1956 wrecked these plans, making disengagement from Cyprus appear inevitable. Ever the realist, Allen urged that the Greek–Cypriot leader, Archbishop Makarios, be returned to Cyprus without delay (having been forcibly exiled in March 1956). The Macmillan government eventually relented, in February 1959, and an independent republic of Cyprus was established in August 1960.

In November 1961 Allen became ambassador to Iraq, one of the most difficult and dangerous of all missions. Three years earlier Iraq's pro-British monarchy had been brutally overthrown. Another coup was a distinct possibility owing to the fragile position of the military junta led by Brigadier Abdul Karim Qasim. Qasim had alienated the Arab world in 1960 by threatening to annex Kuwait, while his domestic opponents were emboldened by his failure to suppress a Kurdish insurrection. His overthrow in February 1963 was therefore not a surprise, but the show trial and execution—the corpse was displayed on television—shocked the world. Allen's coolness in the crisis (by now his trademark) was evident in his reports back home. During a picnic by the Euphrates he explained to an Iraqi minister that there was no danger of Sir Alec Douglas-Home being hanged should he lose the next general election in Britain.

A relief from the rough house politics of Baghdad came in August 1965, when Allen was promoted deputy under-secretary of state in the Foreign Office. The permanent head, Paul Gore-Booth, respected Allen's clear-headed and forthright approach. But the calm was soon upset when George Brown arrived as foreign secretary in August 1966 with two preconceptions: that all his officials had been educated at Eton and Winchester colleges, and that they all dined in white ties. Allen was unable to hide his annoyance with Brown's prejudices, let alone with his heavy drinking. Brown responded by freezing Allen out of his inner circle. The situation grew so tense that Allen requested an overseas appointment. He ended his foreign service as ambassador to Turkey, from March 1967 to September 1969. Ill health dogged these years, brought on by the stresses of his previous job.

On retirement Allen returned to his London home—5 William Street House, William Street—and became director-general of the Middle East Association. He died on 9 February 1972, and was survived by his wife, Jocelyn, and their two children. His diplomatic career had coincided with Britain's retreat as a global power. Above all he was an accomplished professional who understood the realities of imperial decline and the need to adjust accordingly.   MICHAEL T. THORNHILL

Sources E. Shuckburgh, *Descent to Suez: diaries, 1951–56* (1986) • J. Kent, ed., *Egypt and the defence of the Middle East*, 3 vols. (1998), ser. B/4 of *British documents on the end of empire* • R. Holland, *Britain and the revolt in Cyprus* (1998) • P. Gore-Booth, *With great truth and respect* (1974) • private information (2004) • *The Times* (10 Feb 1972); (12 Feb 1972); (19 Feb 1972) • *WWW* • Burke, *Peerage* • Burke, *Gen. GB* • *Law list* (1938) • *FO List* (1960) • will, principal registry of the probate department, London • b. cert. • m. cert.
Archives PRO, FO 371 series
Wealth at death £196,682: probate, 1972, *CGPLA Eng. & Wales* • £34,550: further grant, 1972, *CGPLA Eng. & Wales*

Allen, Roland (1868–1947), missionary, was born at The Friary, Derby, on 29 December 1868, third son of the Revd Charles Fletcher Allen (1835–1873), curate and schoolmaster, and Priscilla Malpas (1839–1935). Only Reginald (b. 1863) and Willoughby (b. 1867) attended the Clergy Orphan School, Canterbury. Both became Church of England clergymen. Willoughby, a Hebrew scholar, was twice archdeacon. They had one surviving sister.

A scholarship took Roland from Bristol grammar school (1884–7) to St John's College, Oxford (BA, 1889). He proceeded, with a second in classics and modern history, and the Lothian prize, to Leeds Clergy Training School. But he barely sampled a conventional career, discovering instead the sting of Christ's reference to the prophet without honour in his own country and his own house. His radical understanding of evangelization met with incomprehension in his time. It is acknowledged in diverse denominations today as a seminal response to the post-colonial dissolution of political and religious structures.

In 1895 Allen joined the north China mission of the Society for the Propagation of the Gospel and in 1900, as chaplain to the British legation, was trapped in Peking (Beijing) by the Boxer uprising. His diary furnished an evocative narrative, *The Siege of the Peking Legations* (1901), but two articles in the *Cornhill Magazine* (July–December 1900) on the causes of the siege and of the 'providential' preservation of the legations clarify his reflections on the experience. He accepts the necessity for social change in China, and is blunt about the folly of the court and the superstitious popular ignorance it exploited in its encounter with the foreign pressure for 'concessions'. But he is appalled by the imperial brutality of that pressure, and laments the corrupting entanglement of competing missions; for instance the French legation's insistence on political status for the Catholic hierarchy, the abuse of landlord power by missions, and their provocative misuse of political influence with local officials to protect converts involved in private litigation.

On furlough in 1901 Allen married Mary Beatrice Tarleton (1863–1960), daughter of Admiral Sir John Tarleton, and returned briefly to China, but left on health grounds. He took his only living, Chalfont St Peter in Buckinghamshire, in 1904, but resigned in 1907 rather than continue extending the sacraments of the church to parishioners who gave no evidence of faith. Briefly a naval chaplain, he was torpedoed and invalided, worked for the Young Men's Christian Association, taught at King's College, Worcester, and thereafter collaborated in the Survey Application Trust, funded by an evangelical businessman whose insights into the contradictions of missionary organization he clarified (Allen, *James Sidney Wells Clark*).

Allen's first significant 'prophetic' text, *Missionary Methods: St Paul's or ours?* (1912), established the position he reiterated in a long succession of publications, mostly from the World Dominion Press and in church periodicals: Christ commanded, St Luke focuses, and St Paul pursued an *apostolic* mission, communicating the redeeming energy of the Holy Spirit and helping believers submit themselves to it; Christ said nothing about a trained, professional priesthood, about institutional structures, or about providing health and education; hospitals and schools, though good in themselves, are irrelevant to the Pentecostal message; missions, exhausted by competition for funds, doctors, and teachers, idolize a 'progress' to which the Holy Spirit is indifferent; above all, patronizing insistence on a salaried priesthood, however 'native', replicates a deadening past. Christian communities open to the Holy Spirit, however, will identify their own 'priests' and thrive in independence.

Allen visited India in the late 1920s. An exasperated George Hubback, bishop of Assam, writing in 1928, finally acknowledged the gulf dividing them. He had been more patient than most, but spoke for other churchmen tormented by Allen's monotonic attentions: 'You may hear the voice of our Lord speaking direct to you; others like myself are less highly honoured and have to depend for guidance on those in authority over us' (D. M. Paton, 1968, 155). A decade after his death, however, Bishop Lesslie Newbigin was drawing attention to the slow but steady increase in the number of those who felt compelled to listen to his message for modern missiology (Yates, 63).

Travels in east and southern Africa confirmed Allen's alienation from the church as an institution (*Le Zoute: a Critical Review of Christian Mission in Africa*, 1927). In 1932, following his son and daughter, he settled in Kenya. He died at his home in Hurlingham Road, Nairobi, on 9 June 1947, and was survived by his wife and two children, Priscilla Mary Allen (1903–1987) and John Willoughby Tarleton *Allen (1904–1979), a colonial educationist and Swahili scholar.   GERALD STUDDERT-KENNEDY

Sources D. M. Paton, ed., *Reform of the ministry: selected work and correspondence of Roland Allen, with biographical essay by D. Paton* (1968) • R. Allen, *The ministry of the spirit: selected writings*, ed. D. M. Paton (1960) [incl. a memoir by A. McLeish] • R. Allen, *Missionary methods: St Paul's or ours?* (1912) • T. Yates, *Christian mission in the twentieth century* (1994) • R. Allen, 'Of some of the causes which led to the siege of the foreign legations at Peking', *Cornhill Magazine*, [3rd] ser., 9 (1900), 669–80 • R. Allen, 'Of some of the causes which led to the preservation of the foreign legations in Peking', *Cornhill Magazine*, [3rd] ser., 9 (1900), 754–76 • L. R. Marchant, 'Chinese antiforeignism and the Boxer uprising', in L. Giles, *The siege of the Peking legations: a diary*, ed. L. R. Marchant (1970) • R. Allen, *The siege of the Peking legations* (1901) • R. Allen, *Le Zoute: a critical review of Christian mission in Africa* (1927) • R. Allen, *James Sidney Wells Clark* (1937) • b. cert. • *CGPLA Eng. & Wales* (1948)

Archives Bodl. RH, United Society for the Propagation of the Gospel archive

Likenesses photograph, repro. in Paton, ed., *The ministry of the spirit*

Wealth at death £5175 18s. 4d.—in England: Kenyan probate sealed in England, 18 March 1948, *CGPLA Eng. & Wales*

Allen, Sir Roy George Douglas (1906–1983), economist, was born on 3 June 1906 at 24 Gladstone Street, Stoke-on-Trent, Staffordshire, but grew up in Worcester. He was the elder son of George Henry Allen, a steelworks manager, and his wife, Jessie Callcott Hill. His father was an all-England angling champion and later ran a fishing tackle shop above which the family lived. He was educated at a local primary school in Worcester before winning a scholarship to the Royal Grammar School, Worcester. From there he went in 1924 to Sidney Sussex College, Cambridge, as a mathematics scholar. He obtained a first in part one of his degree in 1925 and became a wrangler in 1927. He was awarded a research scholarship and stayed on in Cambridge for a fourth year, which he spent mainly reading economics and philosophy.

Except for a period in the United States in 1937 on a Fulbright scholarship, his war service, and a sabbatical year spent in Berkeley, California, in 1957, Allen's working life was spent at the London School of Economics and Political Science (LSE), which he joined as an assistant in statistics on 1 August 1928, initially on a one-year contract. He was made assistant lecturer in statistics in 1934, and on 28 March 1936 married a former student, Kathleen Lily (b. 1912/13), statistician, daughter of Arthur Nash, an oil company's costing clerk; they had two sons and a daughter. Allen was promoted to lecturer in 1938 and reader in economic statistics with special reference to mathematical economics in 1939. He was appointed professor of statistics at the University of London in October 1944, though he did not return to the LSE until November 1945. He became emeritus professor in 1973 and continued teaching at the LSE until shortly before his death.

The interest in economics that Allen had shown during his final year at Cambridge blossomed at the LSE, and he published a number of articles in *Economica*, the *Economic Journal*, and the *Review of Economic Studies* between 1932 and 1934. His collaboration with J. R. Hicks led to two pathbreaking articles on the theory of value, utility, and consumers' behaviour, 'A reconsideration of the theory of value', published in two parts in *Economica* in 1934.

Allen's first major work on statistics was *Family Expenditure*, written jointly with A. L. Bowley and published in 1935. This study incorporated his theoretical work on consumer theory and represented a major contribution to the econometric analysis of household budgets. He was an early pioneer in the teaching of econometrics and presented courses in this subject from 1935 to 1939 and again in 1946 and 1947. After his statistical work during the Second World War his interest in the subject was evident in his academic work, and he developed courses on index numbers and national income accounting that he taught for many years. It must be said that the students' enthusiasm for these subjects was never as great as that of the lecturer, though they enjoyed his humour and style.

Allen was active in developing courses for teaching mathematics to economists, and his *Mathematical Analysis for Economists* (1938) was a pioneering work that was translated into over twenty languages; it remained the chosen text for many teachers until well into the 1960s. Having published *Mathematical Economics* in 1956 he undertook the responsibility for developing a new introductory course when the economics department at the LSE decided that all economics students must study some mathematics. The result was *Basic Mathematics*, published in 1962. His final textbook on economics, *Macro-Economic Theory*, was published in 1967: while not universally adopted by teachers, it brought control theory and the closed loop systems developed by Allen's colleague A. W. Phillips to a wide audience.

Allen's war service lasted from 29 September 1939 to 1 November 1945. He was a statistician in the Treasury from 1939 to 1941, before becoming director of records and statistics for the British supply council in Washington from 1941 to 1942. He then became British director of research and statistics for the combined production and resources board in Washington from 1942 to 1945.

Allen's public service continued in peacetime and he was a statistical adviser to the Treasury from 1947 to 1948 during the crisis after the suspension of convertibility in 1947, when his skills were in demand to provide improved data on the outflow of dollars. He was also a consultant at the United Nations Statistical Office in 1949–50 and 1952, as well as a member of the Air Transport Licensing Board from 1960 to 1972 and a member of the Civil Aviation Authority from 1972 to 1973. He was a member of the committee of inquiry on decimal currency in 1962–3, and expressed some private reservations when the government introduced a decimal currency that was based on the pound at the expense of introducing a halfpenny coin, rather than using 10s. as the basic decimal unit. He was chairman of the impact of rates committee from 1963 to 1965 and a member of the royal commission on civil liability in 1974–8. For many years he was economic adviser to the British Medical Association.

Allen's academic and public service achievements were justly recognized. He was made a DSc (Econ.) by the University of London in 1943. He was president of the Econometric Society in 1951 and, having been elected a fellow of the British Academy in 1952, served as treasurer from 1954 to 1973. He was president of the Royal Statistical Society in 1969–70, and received the Guy gold medal of the society in 1979. He also served as treasurer of the International Statistical Institute, was made an OBE in 1946 and a CBE in 1954, and was knighted in 1966. He became an honorary fellow of Sidney Sussex College in 1971 and was made an honorary fellow of the LSE in the same year.

Allen was a modest man, with a gentle voice, a twinkling eye, a taste for quiet bow-ties, and a great love of music. Always approachable, he was a good friend to colleagues and students alike in giving unsparingly of his time. He died of a heart attack at his home, Greyfriars, South Green, Southwold, Suffolk, on 29 September 1983, a few days before a party that was to have been held at the LSE to mark his retirement after fifty-five years of teaching there.

J. J. THOMAS

Sources WWW · J. Eatwell, M. Milgate, and P. Newman, eds., *The new Palgrave: a dictionary of economics*, 4 vols. (1987) · 'Memorial meeting for Professor Sir Roy Allen', 1 March 1984, BLPES, London School of Economics history collection · A. Cairncross, 'Roy Allen, 1906–1983', *PBA*, 70 (1984), 379–85 · E. Grebenik, *Journal of the Royal Statistical Society: series A*, 147 (1984), 706–7 · b. cert. · m. cert. · personal knowledge (2004) · private information (2004)
Archives BLPES, archive collection, history of the LSE project
Likenesses B. Lessware, photograph, repro. in *LSE Magazine*, 46 (Nov 1973), 9 · W. Stoneman, photograph, repro. in Cairncross, *PBA* (1984), facing p. 379
Wealth at death £194,134: probate, 1 Aug 1984, *CGPLA Eng. & Wales*

Allen, (Herbert) Stanley (1873–1954), physicist, was born at Turf Street, Bodmin, Cornwall, on 29 December 1873, the fifth son of Richard Allen, Wesleyan minister in Bodmin, and his wife, Emma Johnson. In 1886 he went to Kingswood School, Bath, where he gained several scholarships and became senior prefect. In 1893 he entered Trinity College, Cambridge, holding a foundation sizarship.

Allen studied mathematics, was tutored by R. R. Webb, and graduated in 1896 as tenth wrangler. A year later he attained a first class in part two of the natural sciences tripos, studying physics, and received an exhibition and the Walker prize. After a brief spell at Aberystwyth he returned to Cambridge to the Cavendish Laboratory under J. J. Thomson. There he studied the motion of spheres in viscous fluids, which had implications for the measurement of electron charge. In 'On the motion of a sphere in a viscous fluid' (*Philosophical Magazine*, 50, 1900, 519–33) he introduced snap photography to record his results. He subsequently investigated the relation between the energy of primary and secondary X-rays.

In 1900 Allen became superintendent of Lord Blythswood's laboratory in Renfrew, helping to perfect the Blythswood dividing engine for ruling accurate diffraction gratings, and investigating spectra and natural radioactivity. He was appointed to a lectureship at King's College, London, in 1905. On 6 August 1907 he married Jessie Euphemia Macturk (1882/3–1943), daughter of a Free Church minister, Andrew Macturk, whom he had met in Renfrew. The couple lived at New Malden, Surrey, where their son and daughter were born. Allen experimented on gaseous discharge and photoelectric fatigue, receiving a London DSc degree in 1909; he published *Photoelectricity* in 1913. He was a member of the Physical Society for forty-nine years, and from 1916 to 1921 was its honorary secretary.

In 1919 Allen moved to a lectureship at Edinburgh. He was elected a fellow of the Royal Society of Edinburgh in 1920, received the society's MacDougal Brisbane medal for

1922–4, and served on its council. He was appointed professor of natural philosophy at St Andrews University in 1923 and established his family at Lamorna, Hepburn Gardens. As head of department he displayed a quiet sense of humour and concern for the conditions of his staff. He twice oversaw substantial enlargements of the physics laboratory, the first extension being largely destroyed by fire in 1931. Having been nominated as a candidate each year since 1922, Allen was at last, in 1930, elected a fellow of the Royal Society, where his brother E. J. Allen was already a fellow.

Allen's interest in quantum physics began while he was at King's College and continued at St Andrews. Pointing out that Rutherford, in deducing the atomic nucleus, had assumed that either together or separately the electrons and atomic core had no intrinsic magnetic moment, Allen explored how such moments might arise and their implications for atomic spectra. At a discussion at the Royal Society on 19 March 1914 he anticipated, tentatively, the idea of a spinning electron, but he concentrated instead on the alternative of a magnetic core. He subsequently became the chief proponent in Britain of A. Parson's (1915) spinning annular ring electron, propounded in 'The case for the ring electron' (*Proceedings of the Physical Society*, 31, 1919, 49–68). In the 1920s he investigated E. Whittaker's 'calamoids' (four-dimensional tubes of electromagnetic force) as the basis of quantum physics. From this he published *The Quantum and its Interpretation* in 1928 and *Electrons and Waves* in 1932.

A keen cyclist when young, Allen's health deteriorated following pneumonia in 1932. He retired early, in 1944, after a period of anxiety about his son who had been wounded at the battle of El Alamein, and the death of his wife the previous year. He remained in St Andrews with his daughter until her marriage in 1953 when the family moved to the Manse of Resolis, Balblais, Conon Bridge, Ross-shire. There he died of senile decay on 27 April 1954.

ISOBEL FALCONER

Sources W. Wilson, *Memoirs FRS*, 1 (1955), 5–10 · D. Jack, *Nature*, 174 (1954), 108–9 · H. W. Turnbull, *Year Book of the Royal Society of Edinburgh* (1953–4), 6–8 · senate minutes and minutes of university court, 1923–44, U. St Andr. · R. H. Stuewer, *The Compton effect: turning point in physics* (1975) · b. cert. · m. cert. · d. cert.
Likenesses photograph, repro. in Wilson, *Memoirs FRS*, facing p. 5
Wealth at death £9189 7s. 6d.: confirmation, 6 July 1954, CCI

Allen, Thomas (1540–1632), mathematician and antiquary, was born on 21 December 1540 at Uttoxeter, Staffordshire, the son of William Allen. His family were local gentry who are known to have had Roman Catholic connections. Two of his four uncles also lived at Uttoxeter. Nothing is known of his activities and education before he matriculated as a scholar at Trinity College, Oxford, on 4 June 1561. He proceeded BA in 1563, became a fellow of his college in 1565, and took his MA in 1567. Though formally an adherent of the Church of England, his own beliefs and inclinations tended towards Roman Catholicism, with an Erasmian tinge. About 1570, not wishing to take the oath of supremacy and allegiance incumbent upon fellows on

college foundations, he joined the independent Gloucester Hall (which provided a home for notionally conforming church papists).

Allen spent his life at Gloucester Hall, together with several other members of Trinity College who had similar beliefs. It is not known when he first became interested in mathematics and astrology. As early as 1563 he had begun acquiring manuscripts and he gradually built up one of the largest private manuscript collections in Oxford, from which something over 250 titles are still extant. He was particularly orientated towards mathematical and scientific manuscripts, and is primarily responsible for the preservation of the works of Roger Bacon and of the Merton school of astronomers and mathematicians.

Allen had a lively, affable, and sociable disposition and took an active part in university affairs. In 1598, with the vice-chancellor and the two proctors, he served on a commission of four charged to reorder the university statutes and to have them copied. In the same year he was appointed to the committee set up to assist Thomas Bodley in the establishment of his library. He played a major role in this undertaking, soliciting gifts from his patrons, pupils, and friends, besides presenting twenty-one volumes to the library himself.

Although he wrote little and published nothing, it is clear that Allen was an active and successful teacher of mathematics. Lectures that he gave on the subject were so popular 'that it was feared the rooms would burst' (Burton and Bathurst, 5). Among his pupils were Sir Philip Sydney, Robert Fludd, and Sir Kenelm Digby. His influence as a mathematician was also exerted through his contacts with Thomas Harriot, John Dee, and a number of other mathematical practitioners and scholars.

Allen was well known to scholars outside Oxford. Among his acquaintances and correspondents were Camden, Selden, William Gent, Robert, earl of Leicester, Henry Percy, ninth earl of Northumberland, and Sir John Scudamore of Holme Lang. However, he consistently refused honours (such as a bishopric from Leicester) which would remove him from his studious life at Oxford. In 1583 he was strongly solicited to join the circle of Albert Laski in Poland but declined to do so. He may nevertheless have spent some time residing with the circle of mathematical practitioners supported by Northumberland, which, as well as Harriot, included others with whom he is known to have been acquainted, such as the geographer Robert Hues. In addition he made a regular tour through the country to Staffordshire each summer, visiting fellow lovers of antiquities, mathematicians, and Catholics *en route*.

Like a number of other mathematicians, Allen was popularly supposed to be a necromancer—an impression actively encouraged by his college servant, John Thuragh. He did indeed have a high reputation as an astrologer, and this was enhanced by the remarkable accuracy of his prognostications concerning William Herbert, earl of Pembroke (1580–1630), and Robert Pierrepoint, earl of Kingston. He was also consulted on other matters relating to the occult such as the laying of ghosts. His only extant extended piece of writing is a commentary on the second and third books of Ptolemy's *Tetrabiblos*, an astrological text. In his will he left a large concave mirror, given to him by John Dee, to Sir Thomas Aylesbury, and probably also his other instruments and some manuscripts. The bulk of his book collection, however, was left to Sir Kenelm Digby who, after having them bound, was two years later persuaded to present them to the Bodleian Library where they remain. Allen died at Gloucester Hall on 30 September 1632 and was buried the following day in Trinity College chapel.　　　　　　　　　　　　　　　A. J. TURNER

Sources Wood, *Ath. Oxon.* · *Brief lives, chiefly of contemporaries, set down by John Aubrey, between the years 1669 and 1696*, ed. A. Clark, 1 (1898), 26–8 · J. Aubrey, *Letters from eminent persons* (1813), 2.202 · W. Burton and G. Bathurst, *Orationes binae* (1632) · W. Camden, *Epistolae* (1691) · M. Foster, 'Thomas Allen (1540–1632), Gloucester Hall and the survival of Catholicism in post-Reformation Oxford', *Oxoniensia*, 46 (1982), 99–128 · A. G. Watson, 'Thomas Allen of Oxford and his manuscripts', *Medieval scribes, manuscripts and libraries: essays presented to N. R. Ker*, ed. M. B. Parkes and A. G. Watson (1978) · M. Feingold, *The mathematicians' apprenticeship: science, universities and society in England, 1560–1640* (1984)
Archives BL, Cotton MS Julius C.V., fol. 353 · Bodl. Oxf., Ashmole MSS · Bodl. Oxf., Digby MSS
Likenesses stained or painted glass, 1632 (after portrait, 1628), Oriel College, Oxford · oils, 1633 (after portrait, 1628), Trinity College, Oxford · J. Bretherton, engraving (after oil painting, 1633), repro. in R. T. Gunther, ed., *Early science in Oxford*, 11: *Oxford colleges and their men of science* (1937), 286 · pastel drawing, Bodl. Oxf. · portrait (after oil painting, 1633), Bodl. Oxf.

Allen, Thomas (1608–1673), clergyman and ejected minister, was born in Norwich, son of John Allen, a dyer there. He went to school in the city before being admitted to Gonville and Caius College, Cambridge, on 6 July 1624, aged fifteen. A scholar of the college from 1625 to 1629, he graduated BA in 1628 and proceeded MA in 1631. On 26 February 1634 he was appointed to the parish church of St Edmund's, Norwich; he was ordained priest on 2 March. Bishop Matthew Wren deprived Allen and others of their posts in 1636 for refusing to read the Book of Sports. It was said that Allen would have resigned in any case, since he had become ill and 'his living being a small one, and himself having large temporal means' (Bodl. Oxf., MS Tanner 68.155).

It was reported in 1636 that Allen had gone to the Netherlands, and by 1638 he had arrived in New England. He became a teacher of a Congregational church at Charlestown, Massachusetts, and married Ann, widow of John *Harvard (1607–1638). Cotton Mather described Allen as a 'pious and painful minister of the Gospel' (*Magnalia*, bk 3, 215). By the winter of 1651/2 he had returned to Norwich, where he became a city preacher, giving the Sunday sermon before the mayor and aldermen in the Dutch chapel. On 25 February 1652 he received a £10 gratuity for his services, and on 2 April was awarded a stipend of £20 a quarter. In 1655 he prepared for publication three of the works of his 'most Honoured friend' John Cotton (Cotton, *Covenant*, introduction). On 12 January the next year he was noted as a pastor of a congregationalist meeting at St George's parish in Norwich. That same year he married Joanna, widow of Robert *Sedgwick (*bap.* 1613,

d. 1656), former soldier in New England and governor of Jamaica; they had two children, Thomas and Mary. On 12 June 1657 Allen was also admitted rector of St George, Tombland.

Allen published his most celebrated work, *A Chain of Scripture Chronology: from the Creation of the World to the Death of Jesus Christ*, in 1659, with an introduction by William Greenhill. Using the scriptures, he calculated that Jesus died approximately 3968 years after Adam and the creation. He was ejected from St George's in 1662, and by 1669 was reportedly preaching twice a week in St Clement's parish, Norwich. He received a licence as an Independent in St Andrew's parish on 10 June 1672, but died the next year, in Norwich, on 21 September. Ten of his sermons were published posthumously as *The Way of the Spirit in Bringing Souls to Christ* (1676).　　　MARK ROBERT BELL

Sources *Calamy rev.*, 7 · *DNB* · C. Mather, *Magnalia Christi Americana*, 7 bks in 1 vol. (1702), bk 3, p. 215 · Venn, *Alum. Cant.* · Bodl. Oxf., MS Tanner 68.155 [concerning Bishop Wren's removal of certain ministers] · J. Cotton, *The covenant of grace: discovering the great work of a sinners reconciliation to God* (1655) · J. Cotton, *An exposition upon the thirteenth chapter of the Revelation* (1655) · J. T. Evans, *Seventeenth-century Norwich: politics, religion and government, 1620–1690* (1979), 195–6, 220, 234 · *BL cat.*

Allen, Thomas (1681–1755), Church of England clergyman and writer, son of Thomas Allen (*d.* 1699), was born at Oxford on 25 December 1681 and baptized there at St Peter-in-the-East on 1 January 1682. He was educated at New College School, Oxford, until the death of his father in 1699, and matriculated from Wadham College, as a commoner, on 8 July 1699; he graduated BA on 2 July 1705. He worked as a clerk in Lincoln's Inn, London, then became schoolmaster of the Chantry School, Brook Street, St Andrew, Holborn, for about three years. He was ordained deacon on 23 September 1705 and priest on 30 December. On 5 February 1706 he became vicar of Irchester, Northamptonshire, after its squire, Samuel Collins, offered him the vicarage at half stipend and required a £200 bond. He married Dorothy Plowman, daughter of Richard and Dorothy Plowman of Blisworth, Northamptonshire. Five of their children were born in Irchester: John (*b.* 8 Dec 1707) and Thomas (*b.* March 1709), who both died of smallpox; Timothy (*b.* May 1710, *d.* c.1730); Elizabeth (*b.* May 1712); and Samuel (*b.* April 1713). During these years in Irchester, Allen 'kept a school' and published a sermon preached at St Dunstan's Church, Fleet Street, London (Bodl. Oxf., MS Rawl. J, fols. 2, 26).

In 1714 Mr Watkins, rector of Kettering, offered to 'exchange profits' with Allen, and the congregation offered him the post when Watkins retired (Bodl. Oxf., MS Rawl. J, fols. 2, 27). Although the rectory was worth about half of the Irchester living, Allen and his former patron, Collins, bore each other resentment. Thus Allen went to London in 1715 to persuade the earl of Rockingham to grant him the office, and to publish what proved to be his most popular work, *The Practice of a Holy Life*, a collection of prayers and meditations. While in London, his wife, 'in a fit of despair', murdered their son Samuel and cut her own throat; she recovered, and was tried and acquitted at the next assizes (Bodl. Oxf., MS Rawl. J, fols. 2, 28). Allen nevertheless resigned the Irchester vicarage and took up the rectory of Kettering on 18 May 1715, where he and his wife had five more children: Mary (*b.* 1716), Edmund (*b.* 5 Aug 1718), Dorothy (*b.* 1719), Lucetia (*b.* 11 June 1721), and Hester (*b.* 15 May 1723).

Allen wrote various religious works at Kettering, including a reply to Thomas Woolston's controversial *A Free-Gift to the Clergy* that was entitled *An Apology for the Church of England, and Vindication of her Learned Clergy* (1725). He also published *The Christian's Sure Guide to Eternal Glory* (1733), which, together with his *Practice of a Holy Life*, was translated into Russian; *The Travels of … Jesus Christ* (1735, illustrated); a sermon preached at Newgate in 1744 to twenty-one condemned criminals; and *The New-Birth, or, Christian Regeneration … in Blank or Miltonian Verse* (1753). In the preface to this last work Allen claims, with characteristic exaggeration, to have improved on Milton's *Paradise Regained*.

Allen died, as he was reading prayers in his church, on 31 May 1755. His correspondence with Richard Rawlinson includes some Latin verses on the church steeple at Irchester and an eccentric autobiography written in August 1738, a fair copy of some Latin verses he presented to the royal family, and numerous proposals for printing various works by subscription which were never published. There is a sale catalogue of his books in the British Library.   LESLIE STEPHEN, *rev.* ADAM JACOB LEVIN

Sources Bodl. Oxf., MS Rawl. J, fols. 2, 23–54 · Bodl. Oxf., MS Rawl. J, 4°5, fols. 183–5, 189 · Foster, *Alum. Oxon.* · parish register (baptism), St Peter-in-the-East, 1681, Centre for Oxfordshire Studies, Oxford · A. Chalmers, ed., *The general biographical dictionary*, new edn, 1 (1812), 481 · Watt, *Bibl. Brit.*, 1.22a–23a · F. J. G. Robinson and others, *Eighteenth-century British books: an author union catalogue*, 1 (1981), 50 · *GM*, 1st ser., 25 (1755), 284
Archives Bodl. Oxf., MS Rawl. J, 4°5, fols. 183, 184, 184*, 185, 189 · Bodl. Oxf., MS Rawl. J, fols. 2, 23–54
Likenesses line engraving, NPG
Wealth at death see administration, PRO, PROB 6/131, fol. 99

Allen, Thomas (1803–1833), topographer, son of J. Allen, map engraver, was probably born in London. In 1827 he published *The History and Antiquities of the Parish of Lambeth and the Archiepiscopal Palace*, with illustrations, chiefly drawn and etched by himself. He afterwards published: *The History and Antiquities of London, Westminster, and Southwark* (1827 and 1828), illustrated by his own engravings on copper and woodcuts; *A New and Complete History of the County of York* (1828–31), with engravings after Nathaniel Whittock; and *A History of the Counties of Surrey and Sussex* (1829–30), with engravings after Whittock. In 1830 he began publication of *A History of the County of Lincoln*, with engravings after his own drawings. It was suspended on his death and two volumes were finally completed and published (1833–4). Allen also published guidebooks to London (1830) and the zoological gardens, and contributed some plates and articles to the *Gentleman's Magazine*. He projected a historical and topographical atlas of England and Wales in twenty-three parts, but he did not live to attempt it, as he died prematurely of cholera in the City Road, London, on 7 July 1833. He was buried on 24 July in St Luke's churchyard, Old Street, London.

In the year of his death Allen turned to the manufacture of filters, thus combining publishing and medicine in a way common at the time. His books were almost all published in several parts, to satisfy the demand for cheap, illustrated topographies from a public eager for historical details enlivened by romantic and picturesque scenery. He was an industrious compiler, although even his *Gentleman's Magazine* obituarist, a former collaborator, admitted that accuracy was often sacrificed to speed (*GM*, 103/2, 1833, 86). Similarly, his illustrations were neat rather than inspired. His *History of York*, for example, was described in 1869 as a 'catchpenny work' by the Yorkshire bibliographer William Boyne, and in 1994 as 'perfunctory and derivative' (Currie and Lewis, 435). However, Allen's works were no worse than many other contemporary popular histories, and his *Lincoln* was thought worthy of reprinting in 1995.   ELIZABETH BAIGENT

Sources *GM*, 1st ser., 99/2 (1829), 356 · *GM*, 1st ser., 103/2 (1833), 86 · C. R. J. Currie and C. P. Lewis, eds., *English county histories: a guide* (1994) · J. T. S. [J. T. Stanesby], 'Allen, Thomas', *The biographical dictionary of the Society for the Diffusion of Useful Knowledge*, ed. G. Long, 2 (1843) · Redgrave, *Artists*, 2nd edn · *DNB*

Allen, Thomas William (1862–1950), Greek scholar and palaeographer, was born on 9 May 1862 at 103 Camden Road Villas, Camden New Town, London, the eldest of five children of Thomas Bull Allen, wholesale tea dealer, and his wife, Amelia Le Lacheur. One of his sisters married the classical scholar John Percival Postgate. He was educated privately and went up to University College, London, for one year, but in 1881 was elected to a scholarship at the Queen's College, Oxford, and read classics there, graduating with a double first in 1885. In 1887 he was elected by the Craven committee to a travelling fellowship, which enabled him to spend nearly two years working in Italian libraries, where he acquired a wide and detailed knowledge of Greek palaeography, designed partly to assist in the preparation of a new text of Homer. In 1890 he became a fellow of his Oxford college; the appointment was made without an examination, in the words of the then senior tutor, 'a compliment which has never before been paid to anyone by this college' (Wilson, 313). Allen remained in Oxford, twice making unsuccessful applications for chairs at Scottish universities. He was for a time senior tutor of his college, and was generous in his entertainment of pupils, even if the style of his tutorials was somewhat dry and old-fashioned. He took a vigorous part in the social life of the senior common room, and was a connoisseur of food and drink.

In 1894 Allen married Laura Hope (*d.* 1936), whom he had met in Florence at the end of 1889. The marriage was not a great success, and their daughter Charlotte, born in 1896, died at the age of twenty-three, a tragedy from which Allen never quite recovered.

Allen's best-known scholarly work was the large edition of the *Iliad* prepared for the Clarendon Press (1931); he had previously collaborated with D. B. Monro to issue a text in the series of Oxford Classical Texts, and he also prepared the *Odyssey* for the same series. These editions were the product of his extensive labours collating numerous manuscripts, but it has become clear that his work of collation was not as meticulous as it seemed. On the other hand his palaeographical publications retain their importance for specialists, in particular his *Notes on Abbreviations in Greek Manuscripts* (1889). In 1922 he was elected a fellow of the British Academy. He died at his home, 24 St Michael's Street, Oxford, on 30 April 1950.

N. G. WILSON

Sources N. G. Wilson, 'Thomas William Allen, 1862–1950', *PBA*, 76 (1990), 311–19 · personal knowledge (2004) · private information (2004) [archivist, the Queen's College, Oxford] · b. cert. · d. cert.
Likenesses M. J. Lancaster, photograph, repro. in Wilson, 'Thomas William Allen', 312
Wealth at death £1262 15s. 11d.: probate, 29 June 1950, *CGPLA Eng. & Wales*

Allen, Walter Ernest (1911–1995), novelist and literary scholar, was born on 23 February 1911 at Aston, Birmingham, the youngest of the four children, all sons, of Charles Henry Allen (*fl.* 1870–1950), silversmith's designer, and his wife, Annie Maria Thomas. His father's family came from the Staffordshire Black Country and his mother's from Wales, but he did not know either of his grandfathers, who died before he was born. Allen grew up in a working-class home in Birmingham; his father, a skilled craftsman, was a man with wide interests who encouraged his son's aspirations, despite material hardships. Allen was a clever child with a gift for writing, who won scholarships to King Edward's Grammar School, Aston, and subsequently to Birmingham University, where he read English. He graduated in 1932 at a time of high unemployment, but scraped a living by contributing articles, stories, and reviews to the several newspapers then published in Birmingham. He also wrote radio scripts for the midland region of the BBC, laying the foundations of his later career as a broadcaster.

Allen became a close friend of Louis MacNeice, then a young lecturer in classics at Birmingham University, and came to know W. H. Auden and Henry Green and local writers such as John Hampson, Peter Chamberlain, and Leslie Halward. In 1935 Allen's horizons were broadened when he went to the United States as a visiting lecturer at the summer session of the University of Iowa. As a young man, his father had spent some months in America in an unsuccessful attempt at emigration, and he fascinated his son with accounts of the country. Allen continued this fascination throughout his own life; he came to know the United States well and was never able to regard it as 'abroad'. Back in Birmingham he returned to journalistic work, this time as part of a two-man news agency. But he had higher literary ambitions; he wrote a novel which remained unpublished (the typescript is in his papers at Birmingham University Library), but his next novel, *Innocence is Drowned* (1938), was accepted for publication by Michael Joseph. On the strength of this success, Allen moved to London to become a man of letters. He managed narrowly to survive by writing book reviews and reports for publishers, and making summaries of novels for an American film company, which he described as the lowest form of literary life.

Innocence is Drowned attracted some respectful reviews when it appeared but sold few copies. It, and its successors, *Blind Man's Ditch* (1939) and *Living Space* (1940), draw on Allen's experience of working-class life in Birmingham and his own hopes and disappointments as a socially mobile scholarship boy. They also show his interest in literary form, in the careful development of narrative and the treatment of time. In *Blind Man's Ditch* Allen seems to be presenting his young self as the precocious schoolboy Arnold Hipkiss: 'an undersized boy with solemn horn spectacles, like a wise owl' (W. Allen, *Blind Man's Ditch*, 1939, 218)—'[t]here wasn't any subject that he could not write about' (ibid., 226).

Allen spent the war years as a technical writer in armaments factories, first in Bristol and then in his native Birmingham. On 8 April 1944, after a three-week courtship, he married Peggy Yorke Joy (*b.* 1915), a physiotherapist serving with the Red Cross; he wrote 'Marrying her was far and away the wisest thing I have ever done' (Allen, 146). They had four children. During the war years Allen contributed regular literary essays to the widely read periodical *Penguin New Writing*. As he ruefully acknowledged, they made him known as a critic rather than as a novelist; modestly, he preferred to describe himself as a literary journalist. At the end of the war Allen and his wife returned to London and he picked up the threads of his literary career. He made an adequate but precarious living as a freelance writer, reviewer, and publisher's adviser; his most regular work was as a radio broadcaster on literary and cultural topics. Between 1948 and 1960 Allen and his family lived first in Kent, on Romney Marsh, and then in Devon before he returned to London, where he lived for the rest of his life. During those years he published a succession of books on the novel and novelists, including studies of George Eliot and Arnold Bennett. Allen's most enduring and best-known book is *The English Novel* (1954), which provides a lucid, well-informed, and critically perceptive history of the subject from Bunyan to Lawrence and Joyce.

Allen continued to write novels himself, and *All in a Lifetime* (1959) has been generally admired; in this novel Allen returns to working-class Birmingham and traces the life and times of his father, from the 1870s to the 1950s. Between 1959 and 1961 he acted first as assistant literary editor and then as literary editor of the *New Statesman*. Looking back on his career, Allen recognized that his traditional kind of literary journalist was being replaced by critics based in universities. He made his own forays into the academic world as a visiting professor in North American colleges and universities and came to think of himself as a 'transatlantic man'. His survey of British and American fiction from the 1920s to the 1960s, *Tradition and Dream*, was published in 1964. Allen entered the academy full-time in 1967 when he was appointed founding professor of English at the New University of Ulster, where he served until he retired in 1973.

In 1975 Allen was physically disabled by a severe stroke,

but his mental powers were unaffected and he continued to write. His memoir of his literary life, *As I Walked Down New Grub Street* (1981), is light-hearted and informative. In 1989 he published his last novel, *Accosting Profiles*, more than fifty years after his first; it draws on his experience of British and American universities.

Walter Allen died at his home, 4B Alwyne Road, London, on 28 February 1995 of bronchopneumonia and cerebrovascular accident. His funeral and cremation took place at Golders Green crematorium early in March 1995.

BERNARD BERGONZI

Sources W. Allen, *As I walked down New Grub Street* (1981) · *WW* (1995) · *The Times* (2 March 1995) · T. Cooper, 'Walter Allen (1911–1995)', *Reports of the Royal Society of Literature* (1994–6), 28–9 · 'Catalogue of the papers of Walter Ernest Allen (1911–1995)', 1997, U. Birm. L., special collections department · private information (2004)
Archives U. Birm. L., contracts, literary MSS, and other papers · University of Bristol Library, corresp. and statements relating to trial of *Lady Chatterley's Lover* | Derbys. RO, letters to Walter Brierley | SOUND BL NSA
Likenesses photographs

Allen, (Herbert) Warner (1881–1968), journalist and writer, was born at Godalming on 8 March 1881, the elder son of Captain George Woronzow Allen RN, and his wife, Ethel Harriet, daughter of the Revd Canon John Manuel Echalaz (1801–1877), rector of Appleby in Derbyshire and fellow of Trinity College, Oxford. He was educated at Charterhouse School, where he came under the influence of the classicist T. E. Page. He won a scholarship to University College, Oxford, and obtained a first class in classical honour moderations in 1902, and a third in *literae humaniores* in 1904. Having had some disinclination towards metaphysics, and a leaning towards a literary career, he had meanwhile taken up modern languages and won the Taylorian Spanish scholarship in 1903.

When writing his first book, an edition of the translation by James Mabbe of the Spanish *Celestina* (1908) Allen supported himself by journalism. In 1908 he married Ethel, the daughter of Warwick Pembleton, and they had one son, G. Warner Allen. Also in 1908 he was appointed to the position of Paris correspondent of the *Morning Post*. He thus became immersed in French life at the end of the *belle époque*, and reported the sensational trial of Mme Caillaux. Shortly after the outbreak of the First World War in 1914 he was made an official representative of the British press at the French front. In 1917 he accompanied the British divisions diverted to support the Italians, and remained in Italy until the following year, when he was transferred to the American expeditionary force in France, and accompanied it in its occupation of Germany, where he stayed until March 1919. Out of these experiences he published *The Unbroken Line* (1916) and, with the paintings of Captain Martin Hardie, *Our Italian Front* (1920). He was made CBE (1920) and chevalier of the Légion d'honneur for his war services.

As an extramural obligation to his proprietor Allen participated in the cross-channel flight of the *Morning Post* dirigible, which ended in disaster; but he fortunately escaped almost unscathed. He was foreign editor of the *Morning Post* (1925–8), and London editor of the *Yorkshire Post* (1928–30), while at the same time he made many contributions to the *Saturday Review*. He then retired to Brightwell-cum-Sotwell, in Berkshire, to concentrate on writing books, and produced some of his best and well-respected works on wine, including *The Romance of Wine* (1931) and *Sherry* (1934); he had already published *The Wines of France* (1924). It was also at this time that he produced the first of his detective novels, *The Uncounted Hour: a Crime Story* (1936), and collaborated with E. C. Bentley on *Trent's Own Case* (1936), a sequel to Bentley's earlier mystery novel, *Trent's Last Case* (1913). His writing was interrupted, however, by the outbreak of the Second World War in 1939. Although fifty-eight years old, he was then gazetted acting wing commander, Royal Air Force Volunteer Reserve, and he served as assistant deputy director in the foreign division of the Ministry of Information from 1940 to 1941.

After the war, Allen returned to writing about wine, publishing *A Contemplation of Wine* and *Natural Red Wines* (1951), *White Wines and Cognac* and *Sherry and Port* (1952), and ending with *A History of Wine: Great Vintage Wines from the Homeric Age to the Present Day* (1961). In all of his publications on the subject, vinous information was nicely interwoven with literary and historical allusions. He travelled widely among the European vineyards; his accurate judgement of wine was recognized by all amateurs qualified to assess this, and he was greatly respected by the leaders of the wine trade.

Allen himself, however, set greatest value on a series of mystical writings such as *The Timeless Moment* (1946) and *The Uncurtained Throne* (1951). As a youth Allen had abandoned formal Anglicanism, but T. E. Page had imbued him with the spirit of Plato, and later reading of Plotinus and acquaintance with, among others, T. S. Eliot and Dean W. R. Inge evoked in him a perception of transcendental values and a faith in the immortality of the soul—attuned to an ethic that was certainly Christian. This gave him great personal serenity and an outward gentleness of address which made him deeply loved, particularly by the young.

Warner, as everyone called Allen, was a man of rather above average height, with kindly features and, as the French politely put it, a *léger embonpoint* of the true gourmet. He was a keen Savage in the heyday of the Savage Club, and was naturally elected to the Saintsbury Club, founded in oenophilist memory of Professor George Saintsbury, with its limited membership and precious cellar. At home and at his club he went to great pains to select food and wines that would gratify his guests, who were usually considerable connoisseurs. Although he lived long as a countryman and had a fine garden, he was not addicted to field sports. But with his vast reading, undimmed memory, and facility with words, he had a quick draw and a flawless aim for the clues of the *Times* crossword puzzles.

Allen died at his Berkshire home, Iden House, Brightwell-cum-Sotwell, on 12 January 1968, and was mourned by a large circle of friends, and a school of young disciples who were perhaps more attracted by his philosophy of the table than by his spiritual intimations.

H. W. YOXALL, *rev.*

Sources unpublished autobiography · personal knowledge (1981) · d. cert. · *The Times* (13 Jan 1968)
Wealth at death £20,018: probate, 27 March 1968, *CGPLA Eng. & Wales*

Allen, William (1532–1594), cardinal, was born at Rossall Grange in the parish of Poulton-le-Fylde in Lancashire, the third of four sons of John Allen (*d. c.*1566) and Jane, the daughter of Thomas Lister of Westbury, Yorkshire; there were three younger sisters. The family were minor gentry, leasing Rossall from the Staffordshire Cistercian abbey of Dieulacres. Allen was baptized at All Hallows, Bispham, where his grandfather and great-grandfather were buried. One of the most religiously conservative regions of England, the Fylde would remain Allen's fundamental 'England of the mind': until the early 1580s up to three masses a day were celebrated in his sister-in-law's household at Rossall, colouring Allen's perceptions of the impact of the Reformation during his long years of exile. To the end of his life he contrasted this rural Catholic England with the effete world of merchants, shopkeepers, and courtiers who were sustained in heresy, he thought, only by 'the partiality of a few powerable persons' (Allen, *Modest Defence*, 56).

Early years: from Oxford to exile, 1532–1567 Nothing is known of Allen's life before he matriculated at Oriel College, Oxford, in 1547. He graduated BA in 1550 and was elected a fellow the same year. The extent of his legal conformity to the Reformation is unknown, but the university, and Oriel, proved highly resistant to the Edwardian regime's attempts to impose the new religion. From 1548 religious controversy was fuelled by the appointment of the Italian reformer Pietro Martire Vermigli (known as Peter Martyr) as regius professor of theology. Allen's tutor, Morgan Phillips (nicknamed the Sophister for his debating skills), was one of the three Catholic disputants against Peter Martyr in the public debate of May 1549, and Allen cannot have avoided the rancid atmosphere of religious controversy within the university.

The accession of Queen Mary in 1553 triggered a heady period of Catholic restoration, into which Allen was drawn. He proceeded MA on 16 July 1554 along with two future pillars of the Catholic cause, Thomas Harding and Nicholas Harpsfield. Two new Catholic colleges, Trinity and St John's, were founded, and Catholic scholars ousted under the Edwardian regime were restored. The queen's marriage to Philip II internationalized the Oxford Counter-Reformation, bringing a series of distinguished Spanish theologians, including the Dominicans Fray Bartolomé Carranza, future archbishop of Toledo and primate of Spain, who deputized as visitor of the university for Cardinal Pole, and Peter de Soto, credited with restoring Oxford theology single-handed to a state of shining orthodoxy. Allen was never to share the suspicion which many even of his Catholic fellow countrymen felt towards Spain, nor to budge from the perception of the Spaniards as champions of Catholic truth which he formed in these years.

In 1556 Allen succeeded Morgan Phillips as principal of St Mary Hall, Oxford. There, and in the key office of university proctor in 1556 and 1557, he must have been actively involved in the Marian purge of the university and the religious revival which was to produce a remarkable generation of Catholic students, thirty-seven of whom became Jesuits or seminary priests, among them Gregory Martin, translator of the Rheims–Douai Bible. Allen wholeheartedly endorsed the uncompromising religious vision of Marian Catholicism, including the persecution of protestants. He almost certainly witnessed Cranmer's Oxford trial and burning. If so, he felt no pity for the old man's agonized indecision, describing him later as that 'notorious perjured and oft relapsed apostate, recanting, swearing, and forswearing at every turn' (Allen, *Modest Defence*, 104).

The accession of Queen Elizabeth put an end to Allen's Oxford career. Between 1559 and 1561 all but one of the Catholic heads of colleges were ejected, and, though Allen lingered in the university, he resigned his post at St Mary Hall in 1560. In 1561 he joined the drift of displaced academics to the Low Countries. There are no firm dates for his activities at this time, except that he matriculated in the University of Malines on 27 May 1563, continuing his theological studies and supplementing his income by becoming private tutor to Christopher Blount, youngest son of the fifth Lord Mountjoy and future Irish adventurer and plotter. A severe wasting illness which attacked both pupil and tutor soon brought Allen home to Lancashire to convalesce, and it was here that his view of the Elizabethan Reformation took its decisive form.

Allen was horrified to discover that many Catholics in Lancashire were attending prayer-book services, some even communicating, and also that some priests celebrated both mass and the communion service on the same day. Though still a layman, he launched a vigorous propaganda campaign against attendance at the parish churches, travelling from one gentry household to another, in order to prove 'by popular but invincible arguments that the truth was to be found nowhere else save with us Catholics' (Knox, *Douay Diaries*, xxiii–xxiv; Knox, *Memorials*, 56–7).

It is not known how long Allen remained in England, though his polemical activities made even Lancashire too hot to hold him. According to his secretary and first biographer, Nicholas Fitzherbert, he spent some time in the Oxford area, where he was able to contribute at first hand to the persistence of Catholicism within the university, and later in the household of the conformist but fellow-travelling duke of Norfolk. By 2 May 1565, however, the year in which he was finally deprived of his Oriel fellowship for non-residence, he had left England for the last time, since his treatise on purgatory is dated at Antwerp on that day. He settled at Malines, where he was ordained to the minor orders and the priesthood, and where he found a teaching post in theology at the Benedictine college.

Simultaneously, Allen was establishing himself as an apologetic writer. The polemical programme he developed in Lancashire and afterwards was distilled into a 'Scroll of articles', which circulated in manuscript and which was adopted as the basis for controversial treatises by several other writers, especially his colleague and assistant, Richard Bristow. In May 1565 Allen himself published *A Defense and Declaration of the Catholike Churchies Doctrine, Touching Purgatory*, begun three years before as a contribution to the controversy stirred up by John Jewel's *Apology*. It is a thorough and vigorous book, whose salty phrasing shows the ferocity of Allen's rejection of protestantism. It drew the attention of the Elizabethan regime: Allen's name, identified as the author of 'the late booke of purgatory', heads the list of priests singled out for special mention in a writ directed to the sheriff of Lancaster early in 1568. On 26 April 1567 Allen published his second apologetic work at Louvain, a defence of priestly absolution and the doctrine of indulgences, *A Treatise Made in Defence of the Lawful Power and Authoritie of Priesthod to Remitte Sinnes*.

Douai College and the English mission, 1567 By now Allen's mind was turning to more practical measures. The Elizabethan purge of the universities had created a remarkable Catholic diaspora in France and the Low Countries. More than a hundred senior members left the University of Oxford in the first decade of Elizabeth's reign, gravitating to university towns like Louvain and Douai. Two short-lived houses of study nicknamed Oxford and Cambridge were formed at Louvain, while Douai University, which received its charter in 1559 just as this stream of refugees was beginning, availed itself of the sudden flood of academic talent and became something of an English institution. Many of the exiles had no visible means of support; many were young and in need of academic and moral guidance. Allen felt intensely the lack of any institution offering 'regiment, discipline, and education most agreable to our Countrimens natures, and for prevention of al disorders that youth and companies of scholers (namely in banishment) are subject unto' (Allen, *Apologie*, 19). Out of this concern Douai College emerged, and in its wake the rest of the English seminaries abroad.

Founding the English College at Douai was Allen's greatest achievement, though his precise intentions have been variously understood. By the 1580s Douai was being seen, and saw itself, as the first Tridentine seminary, a forcing ground for missionary storm troopers in the fight against Elizabethan protestantism. It has been doubted by John Bossy and others whether in 1568 Allen contemplated any such outcome. In the autumn of 1567 he and Morgan Phillips made a pilgrimage to Rome with a Belgian friend, John Vendeville, regius professor of canon law at Douai and future bishop of Tournai. Vendeville, a pious Counter-Reformation activist, was seeking papal approval for a missionary enterprise to the Muslim world, but he evidently did not have the right Roman connections, and was refused an audience with Pius V. On their return journey Allen persuaded him to devote his influence and financial backing instead to a college for English students of theology in the Low Countries. To begin with, the objective

was to provide a single institution in which the scattered scholarly exiles might study 'more profitably than apart', to secure a continuity of clerical and theological training, so that there would be theologically competent clergy on hand for the good times when England returned to Catholic communion, and meanwhile to provide an orthodox alternative to Oxford and Cambridge. But Vendeville would hardly have adopted this substitute for his Barbary mission unless he felt that Douai College would have some missionary dimension. As early as 1568 he told the Spanish authorities in the Netherlands that the students were to be specially trained in religious controversy and, after a two-year preparation, sent back to England to promote the Catholic cause 'even at the peril of their lives' (Knox, *Douay Diaries*, xxviii; Knox, *Memorials*, 22). Allen himself understood the damaging consequences of any merely passive 'waiting game': in the 1567 preface to his treatise on the priesthood he lamented the 'great desolation of christian comfort and all spiritual functions' which the Elizabethan settlement had brought to the parishes, and the dangers of leaving the people to the ministrations of schismatic and heretical parish clergy. It was a short step from this sort of awareness to the activist frame of mind reflected in the saying recorded by the preacher at his funeral—'Better times don't come by waiting: they have to be made' (Knox, *Memorials*, 367).

The college began in a rented house near the theological schools in Douai at Michaelmas 1568, and received papal approval the same year. Allen was joined by a handful of former Oxford academics and a couple of Belgian theology students, though the Belgians soon tired of the spartan conditions in the house and took themselves off. Funding was precarious, and largely dependent on Allen's own resources. He became public catechist at Douai in 1568, took the BTh degree in 1569 and the licentiate in 1570, and in the same year was appointed regius professor of divinity in the university, with a stipend of 200 crowns, which he put into the common purse. This appointment marks the beginning of Philip II's support, a patronage which shaped all Allen's subsequent thinking and loyalties. The college quickly began to attract other exiles, including celebrities like Thomas Stapleton, who became a 'tabler' or paying guest in 1569: Stapleton and Allen took the DTh degree at Douai on 10 July 1571. In 1570 Morgan Phillips died and left his entire estate to the college. On the strength of the legacy eight new students were taken in, including Gregory Martin and Edmund Campion. On 17 May 1576 Allen's income was further augmented when he became twelfth prebendary at Cambrai Cathedral, for which he needed a papal dispensation, since the post was reserved for graduates in medicine.

The growing numbers and the mixed character of the community called for miracles of tact on Allen's part. Some of the former senior dignitaries among the exiles resented his prominence and suspected him of self-aggrandizement, or of designs on the alms and pensions for which they jostled: the grant of a papal pension of 100 crowns a month to the college in 1575 (increased to 150 crowns in 1579) rankled particularly. Nor was finance the only nightmare: the political upheavals of the Low Countries, and the suspicion that the English exiles were a Spanish fifth column, provoked local hostility, and Calvinist advances in the region led to the banishment of the college from Douai on 22 March 1578. They settled at Rheims, returning to Douai only in 1593.

Despite these troubles the college grew remarkably between 1570 and 1580, sustained partly by Spanish and papal subsidies, and partly by Allen's tireless charm, energy, and optimism. The continuing haemorrhage from Oxford brought to Douai not only Martin and Campion, but the protomartyr of the seminaries, Cuthbert Mayne, a graduate of St John's College and, like a good many of the early recruits, sometime priest of the new church. Allen rejoiced in this despoiling of the protestant universities and set himself 'to draw into this College the best wittes out of England' (Allen, *Apologie*, 22v; Ryan, 66–7). He exploited the evangelistic potential of these young men, setting them to write to friends, family, and former teachers and colleagues to urge them to become Catholics. As part of this campaign Edmund Campion wrote to his friend and patron Bishop Cheney of Gloucester, urging the old man to renounce heresy and 'make trial of our banishment' (Simpson, 509–13). The college acted as a magnet for other English exiles in the Low Countries, attracting a satellite community which included a number of gentry families and a stream of visitors ranging from the casually curious to relatives or friends of the students. By May 1576 there were eighty students in the college, by September the same year 120. The growing numbers created constant problems of accommodation and finance, and the foundation of the English College in Rome in 1576 was, among other things, an attempt simply to deal with the overflow. At the end of the decade Allen reckoned that there were on average 100 students in the college in any one year, and that they were ordaining twenty men to the priesthood annually. The first ordinations came in 1573, four priests left the college for England in 1574, and by 1580 about 100 had been sent on the mission. Allen's open-door policy was a security nightmare, and an increasingly hostile English government had little difficulty in planting spies within the college itself: there were at least two assassination attempts against him in the late 1570s.

The academic regime devised by Allen had much in common with that pursued in the Society of Jesus, but differed in several important ways both from university theology courses and from the normal seminary syllabus of the late sixteenth century. Allen insisted on a thorough grounding in dogmatic theology through the study of St Thomas Aquinas (using Jesuit commentaries), and constant practice in preaching and disputation. But above all he was determined to eliminate the advantage the English Bible gave to protestants. The publication of Gregory Martin's translation of the New Testament in 1582, for which Allen raised the finance and supplied many of the doctrinal notes, was part of this project. Between three and five chapters of the Old or New Testaments were read aloud at each of the two main meals daily. There were

daily lectures on the New Testament, Hebrew and Greek classes, and regular disputations on controverted points of scripture. There was a special emphasis on English church history, the canons and decrees of Trent, and the catechisms of Trent and of the Jesuit Peter Canisius, and on the reconciliation of penitents in confession, based on cases of conscience specially devised with the English mission in mind. Allen's own lectures as regius professor were polemics against 'the heretics of our time': his course on the eucharist was published at Antwerp from student notes in 1576.

To this new style of theological training Allen added a new spirituality, focused on daily mass and regular weekly communion, twice weekly fasting for the conversion of England, regular meditation on the mysteries of the rosary, and the use of the Jesuit *Spiritual Exercises*. Allen was a devoted admirer of the Jesuits: he wholeheartedly approved placing the English College in Rome under Jesuit management in 1578, and he procured the society's decision to send Edmund Campion and Robert Persons to England in 1580. He understood that his regime was producing a different kind of priest, altogether more formidable than 'the common sort of curates had in old tyme' (Knox, *Memorials*, 32). He believed in the special value of a graduate clergy, and academic distinction was prized at Douai: masters of arts and doctors sat in due order of precedence at high table, and Cuthbert Mayne kept the exercise for his baccalaureate in theology just days before returning to England and martyrdom in 1575. This emphasis on academic excellence was part of the legacy of Marian Oxford to the Elizabethan mission.

Of the 471 seminary priests known to have been active in England in Elizabeth's reign, at least 294, 62 per cent, were imprisoned at some time or another; 116 were executed, 17 died in gaol, and 91 were banished. Allen worried about the power of life and death he exercised over these men, yet persecution was fundamental to the spirituality he encouraged among the seminarians. The likelihood of martyrdom was one of the inducements Allen offered to persuade Campion to go to England, and in the wake of his and his companions' executions Allen declared that 'Ten thousand sermons would not have published our apostolic faith and religion so winningly as the fragrance of these victims, most sweet both to God and men' (Allen, *Briefe Historie*, ix; Knox, *Memorials*, 135). He was distributing fragments of Campion's 'holy ribbe' as relics by May 1582. Allen's whole seminary project was in a sense heroic, confrontational, its objective the separation of the Catholic community from an acquiescent conformity which he feared would ultimately absorb and undo them.

Yet Allen also understood the pressures Catholics in England were under. His gentleness and pastoral sensitivity are evident in the briefing he gave each of his priests on their departure for the mission:

> how and where to condiscende withowt synne to certain feablenesse growne in manns lyfe and manners these ill tymes, not always to be rigorous, never over scrupulous, so that the churche discipline be not evidently infringed, nor

no acte of schisme or synne plainly committed. (Knox, *Memorials*, 34)

As persecution mounted in the early 1590s he instructed his priests to hold the line on the sinfulness of outward conformity, yet to deal gently with those who fell into it through fear—'be not hard nor roughe nor rigorous … in receavinge againe and absolving them … which mercie you must use, thoughe they fall more than once, and though perhaps you have some probable feare that they will of like infirmity fall againe' (ibid., 354).

The creation and success of Douai College established Allen as the unchallenged spiritual leader of the English exiles. In 1572 Pope Gregory XIII gave him wide faculties to delegate missionary powers to priests bound for England. These powers of delegation and dispensation were greatly extended in August 1575, and by successive popes thereafter. In the absence of a bishop, Allen had become the effective head of the English recusant community.

Political activity, 1572–1587 Allen never doubted that what was needed for the reconversion of England was, in essence, the repetition of the Marian restoration. In 1588, when the Armada was about to sail, he sent for the complete Vatican files on the legatine mission of Cardinal Pole. So his blueprint for the reconversion went beyond writing and training priests: it included removing Queen Elizabeth and implementing a sternly Catholic political regime. He did not believe in tolerating error, nor that Catholics and protestants could live in peace together. North-western Europe from the 1560s seemed to be falling apart over religion—France was descending into religious civil war and Allen's arrival in the Low Countries coincided with the outbreak of the Calvinist revolt there. Allen's personal safety, the existence of his college, and the future of his projects for the reconversion of England were inextricably involved with the political dominance of Spain, as he discovered when in 1578 the English College was forced by the ebb and flow of the Dutch revolt to abandon Douai and take up temporary residence at Rheims.

In the early 1560s the loyalty of English Catholics was hardly an issue. But after the arrival of Mary, queen of Scots, in England in 1568, the rising of the northern earls in 1569, and the excommunication of the queen by Pope Pius V, the Elizabethan regime was bound to treat Catholicism as a political threat, and Catholics were bound to take stock of the courses of action open to them. By now it was clear to everyone that the Elizabethan settlement was not just going to go away. Something would have to be done, and the key to action was the bull of excommunication.

Regnans in excelsis solemnly declared Elizabeth an apostate from the Catholic faith, a heretic, and a tyrant, and it absolved English Catholics of their allegiance to her. But it was issued without any serious attempt to secure political backing to enforce it. It therefore exposed English Catholics to charges of treason, without offering any compensating hope of liberation. In 1580 a ruling was secured from Gregory XIII which absolved Catholics from obeying the bull until its enforcement became practicable, and in the meantime it was tacitly allowed to drop. Some theologians indeed questioned the extent of the pope's authority in matters of civil allegiance, and therefore the legitimacy of the bull.

Allen, however, was an ardent papalist, who saw in the pope the surest defence of the church and the 'rocke of refuge in doubtful daies and doctrines'. He was to place the excommunication and deposition of Elizabeth, and the right of the pope to perform such an act, at the centre of his political thinking (Allen, *Apologie*, 17). In 1572 he was one of the exiles at Louvain who petitioned Pope Gregory XIII to implement the bull against the 'pretended Queen', and to extirpate protestantism in England, from which the infection of heresy was spreading like cancer to the surrounding nations. In 1584, in a pamphlet defending the loyalty of English Catholics, he devoted three chapters to an extended defence of the deposing power of the pope.

Yet it was one thing to accept *Regnans in excelsis*, another thing to act on it, and here the only realistic hope was to involve the king of Spain. Allen was in any case in constant touch with Spain and with Spanish officials in northern Europe: the management of pensions, the procurement of ecclesiastical and civil preferment for his growing circle of supplicants and clients, above all the protection of his college, demanded it. But he went beyond this, and throughout the 1570s and early 1580s Allen was a key figure in a succession of plans for Spanish or French invasions of England. Early in 1576 he took part in a consultation in Rome on English affairs; the foundation of the English College there was one outcome. But that was a by-product of a council of war, whose main objective was to plan an invasion of England by a papal force led by Don John of Austria to set Mary on the throne. In collaboration with the Spanish pensioner Sir Francis Englefield, Allen prepared a lengthy memorial of advice for this invasion, the first of many. Spanish setbacks in the Netherlands meant that in the event nothing was done, and Allen was increasingly aware that simple reliance on Spain would be a mistake. However zealous for religion he might be, Philip II was a politician first—as Allen's friend Nicholas Sander told him, 'wee shall have no stedy comfort but from God, in the Pope not the King of Spain. Therefore I beseech you, take hold of the Pope' (Knox, *Memorials*, 38).

Allen's involvement in the invasion plans of 1576 was almost certainly provoked by an attempt by Elizabeth's ministers to secure the expulsion of the exiles, in particular the college, from the Low Countries. The wave of persecution which followed the arrival in England of the Jesuit missionaries Campion and Persons in 1580 pushed him in this direction again. His letters in the wake of Campion's martyrdom are a curious mixture of grief, anger, and exaltation, but there is no mistaking the growth of his hostility to Elizabeth, 'our Herodias', who had bathed her hands in the 'brightest and best blood' of Catholics (Knox, *Memorials*, 131; *Letters*, ed. Renold, 75). In 1583 he was named as papal legate and bishop of Durham if the proposed invasion led by the duc de Guise succeeded, but the discovery of the Throckmorton plot prevented its implementation. 'If [the invasion of England] be not carried out this year', he told Cardinal Galli in April 1584, 'I give up all hope in man and the rest of my life will be bitter to me' (Knox, *Memorials*, 233). He collaborated closely with the political Jesuit Robert Persons, and was in regular correspondence with Mary, queen of Scots, throughout the early 1580s. His involvement in the fight against international protestantism deepened, and he was drawn into the negotiations which led to the formation of the Catholic Holy League in France in 1584 and 1585. Despite his Spanish loyalties he was also a Guise client, and to the end of his life remained hostile towards Henri IV of France, whom he regarded even after his conversion as a crypto-protestant. In these years Allen exerted all his influence to commit the king of Spain and the pope to the 'enterprise of England', and his postbag was stuffed with the explosive matter of high espionage. When he fell seriously ill with urine retention in late July 1585 he panicked and burnt everything, including his cipher books.

The election of a new pope, Sixtus V, brought the still convalescent Allen from Spa to Rome in November 1585, partly to secure continued support for the college, partly to help settle the animosities dividing the English students in Rome against the Jesuits who managed the college there, but largely for political reasons. If the enterprise of England was to become a reality, the new pope had to be persuaded of its importance. Allen worked hard to scotch rumours of the easing of persecution in England, and in September 1585 drafted an elaborate memorial for the pope, describing the religious geography of England, pressing on him the widespread Catholicism of the north and west, the unwarlike character of the urban supporters of protestantism, and the ease with which an invasion might be carried through.

The formidable and volatile Franciscan Pope Sixtus V, though deeply committed to re-Catholicizing Europe, distrusted the dominance of Spain and resented the interference of Philip II in ecclesiastical affairs. If he was to be brought to back—and to help finance—the enterprise of England, every ounce of pressure and persuasion would be needed. The Spanish ambassador in Rome, Count Olivares, recognized the role Allen could play in this, and detained him in Rome. Allen became, to all intents and purposes, a Spanish servant, receiving detailed briefings from the maladroit Olivares on handling the pope. Allen's own centrality to the enterprise, in any case, was obvious, and became critical after the execution of Mary, queen of Scots, in February 1587. As the unquestioned religious leader of the English Catholics, he was now the only conceivable figurehead for a crusade. Despite vigorous opposition from the French, Sixtus V bowed to unrelenting Spanish pressure, orchestrated in part by Robert Persons, Allen's closest Jesuit collaborator. He created Allen cardinal-priest on 7 August 1587, with the title of San Martino ai Monti. The Roman bookmakers, who had given high odds against his promotion, lost a fortune. Elaborate plans for his role in the invasion of England were drawn up, in part at least based on Pole's legatine mission. Interestingly however, unlike Pole, who believed in separating religious and secular roles, Allen intended to hold the office of lord chancellor as well as that of archbishop of Canterbury. Yet the pope undoubtedly saw Allen as a Spanish stooge, and when, in October 1588, at Philip II's command, Allen sought permission to go to the Netherlands to be in readiness when the call to England came, Sixtus V threw a series of spectacular tantrums.

Political thought and the Elizabethan martyrs It is against these developments that Allen's role in the martyrdom of his priests has to be viewed. In the face of the Elizabethan regime's insistence that the priests died for treason, Allen consistently maintained their total innocence. In his most impressive work, the eloquent *Apologie and true declaration of the institution and endevours of the two English colleges, the one in Rome the other now resident in Rhemes*, published in 1581 to allay the animosities aroused by the Jesuit mission, and again in *A True, Sincere and Modest Defence of English Catholics that Suffer for their Faith*, published in 1584 as a reply to Burghley's *The Execution of Justice in England*, he claimed that none of the priests had any political involvement whatever. In both these works and in his account of the martyrdoms of Campion and his companions, *A Briefe Historie of the Glorious Martyrdom of xii Reverend Priests*, published in 1582, he insisted that it was the government, not the Catholics, who were making an issue of the bull of excommunication, which Catholics had allowed to fall into a harmless oblivion. He claimed that no discussion of the bull was allowed at Douai, and this was certainly true.

Allen was nevertheless being economical with the truth. He himself repeatedly defended the validity of the bull in the writings which his priests helped circulate in England, and he actively sought the armed implementation of the bull and the deposition of Elizabeth in 1572, 1576, 1583, 1586, and 1588. In 1586 he told the pope that the 'daily exhortations, teaching, writing and administration of the sacraments … of our priests' had made the Catholics in England 'much more ready' for an invasion, and that no good Catholic now 'thinks he ought to obey the queen as a matter of conscience, although he may do so through fear, which fear will be removed when they see the force from without'. The priests, he added, 'will direct the consciences and actions of the Catholics … when the time comes' (Mattingley, 336–7).

Yet Allen was not lying: he rigorously kept from all but a handful of his friends and his pupils any knowledge of his own political activities, and certainly approved of the breve of Gregory XIII formally allowing the excommunication to be held in abeyance indefinitely, which Campion and Persons took with them to England in 1580. He himself observed a scrupulous distinction in his writings between the work of priests—which was to preach the gospel and to endure martyrdom for it when the time came—and the role of princes and fighting-men: 'the spiritual [sword] by the hand of the priest, the [material sword] by the hand of the soldier' (Allen, *Modest Defence*, 196). The 'readiness' his priests contributed to, therefore, was indirect, a strengthening of loyalty to the papacy, and a willingness to choose God rather than man when put to the test, as the Henrician and Edwardian Catholics had so signally failed to do. The English Reformation was for him a sacrilegious invasion of the spiritual sphere by the secular power. It followed that any recovery of Catholic understanding and commitment—however apolitical and spiritual its ministers, methods, and aims—must inevitably lead to a confrontation with the protestant state. The more clearly the people saw in the light of the gospel, the more resolutely they would reject the claims of the royal supremacy over their consciences.

But in any case, the notion that a Catholic might be rebellious seemed to Allen nonsense. It was the protestants who were rebels, following 'their own deceiptful wils and uncertaine opinions, without rule or reason', stirring up civil war in France and rebellion against the lawful sovereign in the Netherlands and in Scotland, fastening on the weakness of the body politic—'they make their market most', he claimed, 'in the minority of princes or of their infirmity' (Allen, *Modest Defence*, 141–6). Catholics, by contrast, as men of 'order and obedience', took no such liberties, but 'commit the direction of matters so important to the Church and to the chief governors of their souls'. The deposing power was a God-appointed safeguard, stretching back to Old Testament priests and prophets, and entrusted to the pope for the preservation of the prince and people in due obedience to the law of Christ. Catholics therefore proceed by reason and conscience, protestants by 'fury and frenzy' (ibid., 141–2). It was the Elizabethan government, with its murder of priests and war against Catholic truth, which sinned in forcing men and women to choose between civil and religious obedience, between God and the prince.

These views were never concealed by Allen, but their consequences were at length spelt out in open calls to resistance. In 1587 an English commander with the earl of Leicester's expedition to help the rebels in Holland, Sir William Stanley, surrendered the town of Deventer to the Spanish forces. Allen published a defence of Stanley's action, claiming that the English involvement in a war against Philip was sinful and unjust, Stanley's action that of an informed conscience, and that any Catholic should do the same. He further declared that:

> al actes of justice within the realme, done by the Quenes authoritie, ever since she was, by publike sentence of the Church, and Sea Apostoloke, declared an Haeretike … and deposed from al regal dignitie … al is voide, by the lawe of God and man.

He called for the formation of companies of English soldiers on the continent to be trained 'in Catholike and old godly militare discipline', just as the seminaries were training priests, to undo the evil of the Reformation: 'it is as lawful, godly and glorious for you to fight, as for us Priestes to suffer, and to die'. To labour in either of these ways for the defence of the faith 'is alwaies in the sight of God, a most precious death, and martyrdom' (Allen, *Copie of a Letter*, 17, 29). This book caused consternation among loyalist Catholics in England, who hoped he would disown it as a forgery. In the following year, however, Allen

burnt his boats with his *Admonition to the Nobility and People of England*, written as part of the preparation for the Armada, calling on English Catholics to overthrow Elizabeth, whom he denounced as a sacrilegious heretic and incestuously begotten bastard, guilty of ruining the commonwealth by a whole range of ills, from the promotion of base-born upstarts to the enjoyment of nameless acts of debauchery with her young courtiers.

In the conditions of his own time, Allen's animosity to Elizabeth is easy to understand. Yet he cannot entirely be absolved of responsibility for the disasters of Catholicism in the 1580s and 1590s, above all for being unrealistic in his hopes for any such attempts. Despite the spoliation of his old family home, Rossall Grange, by pursuivants in 1584, and the exile of his sister-in-law and her daughters, Allen naïvely persisted in the conviction that two-thirds of the English people were Catholics in their hearts and discontented with Elizabeth's rule, the 'pure zelous heretikes' 'very few' and 'effeminate, delicate and least expert in the wars' (Allen, *Admonition*, sig. D5). Dazzled by the extraordinary impact of his priests, he never allowed himself to acknowledge the extent of anti-Spanish feeling in England, or the unlikelihood of the population of late Elizabethan England flocking to the pope's banner. And he consistently underestimated his enemy, declaring in 1581 that no intelligent person could be a protestant: even the promoters of reformation were mere *politiques* 'who, because they be wise, can not be Protestants 23 yeres, that is to say, any long time together' (Allen, *Apologie*, 4v). Successive popes and the most experienced king in Christendom, of course, took the same optimistic view, and Philip II committed the seaborne might of the world's greatest power to it. Allen had at least the excuse of seeking the restoration of the lost greatness of a Catholic England, and above all the longing of one who had spent 'al or most of our serviceable yeres out of our natural countrie'. In 1580, as Campion set out for England, Allen told him that he and his like 'will procure for me and mine the power of returning' (Allen, *Apologie*, 7; Simpson, 134).

The cardinal of England, 1587–1594 Allen had a high understanding of the office of cardinal as an instrument of the papacy he so much revered. He was the poorest of the cardinals, with an income made up of a Spanish pension of 1000 ducats, charged on the archbishopric of Palermo, the titular abbacy of San Lorenzo di Capua, a Calabrian monastery worth 2000 ducats, and a papal dole of 100 crowns a month, the so-called 'piatto del Cardinale povero'. Despite shaky Italian (he preferred to talk in Latin) he was an active and effective member of the curia, involved in two congregations: that responsible for the missionary affairs of Germany, and the congregation of the index, for which he undertook an edition of the works of St Augustine, barely begun before his death. In 1591 the pro-Spanish Pope Gregory XIV appointed him apostolic librarian, and made him a member of the commission for the revision of the Vulgate (where he was a conservative influence, resisting textual change). He enjoyed the friendship of, and was treated as an equal by, the greatest men of his age—Philip

Neri and Cardinal Bellarmine in his last years, as Borromeo earlier. He lived in a modest house beside the English College in the via Monserrato, sleeping in a room without tapestries on a bed borrowed from the Spanish ambassador, and keeping open house to English visitors. The protestant traveller Fynes Moryson was one of many who sought his protection while viewing the antiquities of the city, in 1593: Allen gave him a safe conduct on condition that he refrain from openly offensive speech and attend a course of instruction on the Catholic faith while he remained in the city. Allen's household included his exiled brother Gabriel; Thomas Hesketh, son of his sister Elizabeth; and another kinsman, the priest Richard Haydock. It was the hub of a network of English information, clientage, and organization. More than ever he was the central figure in the concerns of the English Catholics, Gregory XIV and Clement VIII extending his jurisdictional powers over the mission in 1591 and 1594. Allen's eirenical nature and passionate concern for unity were exerted to the full in supporting the English seminaries, and in holding together a community increasingly riven by the bitterness of defeat, in particular the ancient rivalry of Welsh and English clergy in Rome, and the ominous gap opening between the secular clergy and his revered Jesuits. After his death the anti-Jesuit party among the secular clergy claimed that Allen had come to regret his earlier overreliance on the Society of Jesus. There is no hint of this in his last urgently pacific letter on the subject, written in March 1594, but it is perhaps confirmed by the remark of the Jesuit rector of the English College, Alfonso Agazzari, in 1596, that while Allen had been 'in union with and fidelity to' the society, God had preserved and exalted him, but 'when he began to leave this path … the thread of his plans and his life were cut short together' (Knox, *Douay Diaries*, 387).

On 10 November 1589 Philip II nominated Allen to the archbishopric of Malines. Allen was attracted by the proximity to England and by the opportunity to lead the Counter-Reformation in the familiar Low Countries, but the see was too impoverished for him to be able to afford to go. The nomination was renewed in 1591, and again in 1594, when Allen's death put an end to it. By the early 1590s Allen himself was in any case a disappointed man, aware that there was little chance now of a dramatic restoration of Catholicism. By then he was forced to consider seriously the notion, which he had half-heartedly canvassed in the early 1580s, of securing some minimal toleration for Catholics in a protestant England. In a world in which nobody believed in toleration, it was a project as hopeless as invasion, but a remarkable glimpse of his changed perceptions in spring and autumn 1593 can be caught through the eyes of an English government go-between. John Arden, the brother of Allen's Jesuit confessor and closest English friend in Rome, was encouraged by the cardinal to broker a protracted negotiation for the granting of freedom of conscience to Catholics and a marriage between 'one of Elizabeth's blood' and a Spaniard, to secure the succession. In return, Allen would call off the pope, the king of Spain, and the Catholic League, and all

the Catholics would 'do that duty that is due to the Queen, religion excepted, and would take arms in defence of her person and realm against the King of Spain or whosoever'. A striking feature of the whole negotiation was Allen's declared willingness to shrug off his Spanish involvements. When Arden asked him why he was so keen to unite an English heir with a Spaniard, Allen replied that 'he would never wish it if they might have liberty of conscience', and he excused his writings against Elizabeth with 'alas, it was to get favour of the King of Spain who maintained them'. Allen may have been tailoring his words to his hearer, but a key to his deepest feelings appeared from an impassioned outburst, when he snatched up a Bible and swore 'as I am a priest' that to secure the free practice of Catholicism he would rather 'leave here and all … and be content to live in prison all the days of my life' in England (Wernham, vol. 1, no. 627; vol. 4, nos. 638–43; vol. 5, no. 627).

Allen died painfully after a fifteen-day illness from a strangury on the morning of 16 October 1594, at his home in the via Monserrato. He was 7000 ducats in debt, and the pope paid his doctor's bills: his will displays considerable financial anxiety about his many English dependants. His sole surviving brother and companion, Gabriel, was his principal heir. Characteristically, he left the vestments and ornaments of his chapel to the parish church of Rossall 'if the kingdom of England should ever revert to the Catholic faith'. He was buried in the English College's church of the Holy Trinity, but his tomb was desecrated and his bones scattered during the French revolutionary occupation of Rome.

Allen was tall and thin with a prominent nose, deep-set eyes, and reddish hair and beard, cut short for most of his life but worn long in his last years in Rome. A spy in 1580 described his face as 'full of wrinkles; under his right eye a mole, not very big. Longhanded, the nails of his fingers long and growing up' (Anstruther, 1.5).

Assessment Allen died as the first, heroic, phase of the mission was drawing to its close. English colleges on the continent were multiplying and the succession of martyrs continued—Robert Southwell going to Tyburn within six months of Allen's death. But the excitement and creative verve of the 1580s were never quite equalled, just as the opportunities which had faced the mission then were slipping away. The first seminary priests and their Jesuit colleagues represented one of the most effective experiments of an exceptionally innovative and turbulent period of Christian history, and it was Allen's vision that they incarnated. No English protestant attempt to rethink ministry, or to equip men for ministry, was half so radical, or so professional. No one else in that age conceived so exalted nor so demanding a role for the secular priesthood, and no one else apart from the great religious founders produced a body of men who rose to that ideal so eagerly, and at such cost. 'The quarrell is God's', he had told one of his critics, 'and but for Hys holy glory and honor I myght sleepe att ease, and let the worlde wagge and other men worke' (Knox, *Memorials*, 37). Allen's creation of storm troopers for counter-reformation, and the energy, humanity, and management of men by which he preserved them, showed pastoral resource and vision on a par with that of Cardinal Borromeo in his own generation, or Vincent de Paul in the next. Allen understood perfectly well what he had achieved, and six months before his death wrote of 'the semynarie of Doway, which is as deere to me as my owne life, and which hath next to God beene the beginning and ground of all the good and salvation which is wrought in England' (Knox, *Memorials*, 358).

EAMON DUFFY

Sources *The letters and memorials of William, Cardinal Allen (1532–1594)*, ed. T. F. Knox (1882), vol. 2 of *Records of the English Catholics under the penal laws (1878–82)* · T. F. Knox and others, eds., *The first and second diaries of the English College, Douay* (1878) · *Letters of William Allen and Richard Barret, 1572–1598*, ed. P. Renold, Catholic RS, 58 (1967) · P. J. Ryan, ed., 'Some correspondence of Cardinal Allen, 1597–85: from the Jesuit archives', *Catholic Record Society Miscellanea*, 7 (1911), 12–105 · W. Allen, *A true, sincere and modest defence of English Catholiques that suffer for their faith at home and abrode* (1584); repr., ed. R. M. Kingdon (1965) · W. Allen, *An apologie and true declaration of the institution and endevours of the two English colleges* (Henault (Rheims), 1581) · W. Allen, *The copie of a letter written by M. Doctor Allen: concerning the yeelding up, of the citie of Daventrie, unto his Catholike majestie, by Sir William Stanley* (Antwerp, 1587) · W. Allen, *An admonition to the nobility and people of England . . . made for the execution of his holines sentence, by the highe and mightie kinge Catholike of Spain: by the cardinal of Englande* (1588) · R. B. Wernham, ed., *Lists and analyses of state papers foreign series Elizabeth I*, 1 (1964); 4 (1984); 5 (1989) · P. J. Holmes, ed., *Elizabethan casuistry*, Catholic RS (1981) · M. Haile, *An Elizabethan cardinal, William Allen* (1914) · A. Bellesheim, *Wilhelm Cardinal Allen und die Englischen Seminare auf dem Festlande* (Mainz, 1885) · B. Camm, *William Cardinal Allen, founder of the seminaries* (1908) · E. Duffy, 'William Allen, 1532–1594', *Recusant History* (April 1995), 265–90 · G. Mattingly, 'William Allen and Catholic propaganda in England', *Travaux d'Humanisme et Renaissance*, 28 (1957), 325–39 · A. C. Southern, *Elizabethan recusant prose, 1559–1582* (1950) · A. F. Allison and D. M. Rogers, eds., *The contemporary printed literature of the English Counter-Reformation between 1558 and 1640*, 1 (1989) · P. Milward, *Religious controversies of the Jacobean age* (1978) · J. Bossy, *The English Catholic community, 1570–1850* (1975) · P. Guilday, *The English Catholic refugees on the continent, 1558–1795* (1914) · P. McGrath and J. Rowe, 'Anstruther analysed: the Elizabethan seminary priests', *Recusant History*, 18 (1986), 1–13 · P. Holmes, *Resistance and compromise: the political thought of the English Catholics* (1982) · G. Anstruther, *The seminary priests*, 1 (1969) · T. H. Clancy, *Papist pamphleteers* (Chicago, 1964) · A. Kenny, 'From hospice to college', *The Venerabile*, 21 (1962), 218–73, 269–70 [sexcentenary issue: *The English hospice in Rome*] · *Hist. U. Oxf.* 3: *Colleg. univ.* · R. Simpson, *Edmund Campion* (1896) · L. F. Von Pastor, *The history of the popes* (St Louis, 1930) · W. Allen, *A briefe historie of the glorious martyrdom of XII reverend priests, executed within these twelve monethes for confession and defence of the Catholicke faith* (1582); repr., ed. J. H. Pollen (1908)
Archives Archivio Vaticano, Vatican City, MSS · Archivum Romanum Societatis Iesu, Rome, letters · Georgetown University, Washington, DC, letters · Venerable English College, Rome, accounts · Westm. DA, MSS | Archivo General de Simancas, Valladolid, Secretaría de Estado Legajo, corresp. with Spanish court
Likenesses portrait, 1594, Ushaw College, Durham; repro. in Haile, *Elizabethan cardinal*; copy, English College at Rome · E. de Boulonois, line engraving, BM, NPG; repro. in I. Bullart, *Académie des Sciences et des Arts* (Amsterdam, 1682) · T. A. Dean, stipple (after Moysten), NPG · portrait, Douai Abbey, Woolhampton, Berkshire; repro. in Haile, *Elizabethan cardinal*
Wealth at death personal debts of 2000 scudi, with a further 5000 scudi of debts incurred on behalf of English College at Rheims, relatives, and dependants · debts of 7000 ducats

Allen, William (*d.* **1686**), religious writer and controversialist, went to London about 1630. Nothing is known of his earlier life. In 1640 or 1641 he joined the church ministered to by John Goodwin, vicar of St Stephen, Coleman Street, London. He continued as a member when in 1645 it adopted congregational principles, and subsequently he became an elder. Allen married the sister of Robert Abbot or Abbott, the puritan pastor and friend and correspondent of Richard Baxter, and their son, also named William, stayed for a time in the early 1650s at Kidderminster under Baxter's care. In a letter to Baxter of 7 January 1652 Abbot confesses that 'noe great matter of learning' can be expected from his nephew, but he is pleased to hear that 'he doe keep within his traces' when he was 'so wild heere' in London. He speaks of the boy's mother as having been 'a very good woman' and of his father as one of Goodwin's 'gifted preachers' (*Correspondence of Richard Baxter*, 1.73).

In 1653 Allen was convinced by Samuel Fisher (the future Quaker) of the justness of believers' baptism. With some twenty other members of the congregation he separated from Goodwin's church and formed a Baptist congregation which, meeting in Lothbury, not far from Goodwin's Coleman Street church, within five years had grown to over a hundred members. In *Philadelphia, or, XL Queries* (1653) Goodwin argued that those committed to believers' baptism need not separate from those who practised infant baptism, but he received from Allen an uncompromising *Answer* (1653) which rejected the possibility of mixed communion. The controversy continued in Goodwin's response, *Water-Dipping No Firm Footing for Church-Communion* (1653), Allen's *Some Baptismal Abuses Chiefly Discovered* (1653), and Goodwin's *Cata-Baptism* (1655).

Goodwin held Barbara Lambe, the wife of Allen's close friend Thomas Lambe, largely responsible for the separation, though she herself stated that it was Allen who converted Lambe. Whichever was the case, in September 1654, when the first general assembly of the General (that is, Arminian or non-Calvinist) Baptists was held in London, both Allen and Lambe were prominent among the elders attending. By August 1658, however, Lambe was entertaining doubts about both separation and believers' baptism, as Barbara Lambe explained when she wrote, though a stranger, to seek the advice of Richard Baxter on whether or not her husband should return to Goodwin's church. In subsequent correspondence with Barbara—'an extraordinary intelligent Woman' (*Reliquiae Baxterianae*, 2.180, para. 45)—and Thomas Lambe and, at Barbara Lambe's prompting, with Allen, whom Baxter already knew, Baxter argued against separation and for parish churches, and he put forward 'a Model of Agreement' between paedobaptists and Anabaptists (ibid., 2.186–8, para. 45). Allen showed himself sympathetic to these arguments and, in a letter of 29 October 1658, he acknowledged 'strong inclinations to a free communion with all

Saints as Saints' (*Correspondence of Richard Baxter*, 1.357). During the period of 'strange Confusions that swarm in this City about things both Civil and Divine' (ibid., 1.414) following Cromwell's death, Allen was involved in negotiations among London ministers and such grandees as Edward Whalley and William Goffe to promote co-operation between different ecclesiastical traditions, at which Baxter's proposals were discussed. These discussions came to nothing, but by the summer of 1659 the Lothbury church had been dissolved. In a letter of 6 September 1659 Baxter reports that Allen and Lambe 'have renounct their separation, & dissolved their church ... & are all for peace' (ibid., 1.408). The day before Allen had dated the preface to his *A Retractation of Separation* (1660), in which he rejected his own earlier arguments for separation and argued for 'generall communion' (title page). By November, Baptists were numbering Allen among the presbyterians.

Although 'taken in the Snare of Separation for a time' and 'in that of *Antinomianism*' soon after going to London, from which he credited Goodwin with having recovered him (*Correspondence of Richard Baxter*, 2.133), Allen was no radical. He was dismayed at any suggestion that Baptists were implicated either in the death of Charles I or in the overthrow of Richard Cromwell. In 1659 he took pleasure in the declining influence of Sir Henry Vane (though he did not then share Baxter's fierce opposition to all Vane stood for), he had foreknowledge of the rising of Sir George Booth, and he was sympathetic to the case for the return of the secluded members to the restored Rump. That he welcomed the Restoration, and was in favour of the new regime, is indicated by his being elected a London common councilman for Broad Street ward in the autumn of 1660. With these conservative leanings he became a member of the established church following the Restoration and as zealous a conformist as he had been separatist. In *A Perswasive to Peace & Unity* (1672; 2nd edn 1680) and *A Serious and Friendly Address to the Non-Conformists* (1676) he argued that, since private opinion should be 'in subordination to the publick good' (1672, 33), nonconformists are obliged to accept the terms of church communion which 'our Superiours have thought fit to appoint' (1680, iii) and that they should comply with the laws of the land and the practices of the established church. Lambe, too, was publishing similar ideas in the 1670s, so that, though he had a hand in turning both men 'from Anabaptistry and Separation', Baxter came to regret that the two 'are now more zealous than other Men against Independency and Separation' and 'in Sense of their old Errour, run now into the other Extreme' (*Reliquiae Baxterianae*, 2.180–81, para. 45; 3.180, para. 11). In June 1673 he prefaced Allen's treatise defending the place of works in justification, *A Discourse of the Nature, Ends and Differences of the Two Covenants* (1673), but his bitter disappointment at the *Serious and Friendly Address* appears to have brought their long friendship to an abrupt conclusion.

Allen died in 1686. His funeral sermon, preached on 17 August by Richard Kidder, then rector of St Mary Outwich and afterwards bishop of Bath and Wells, described Allen as 'a Citizen of this great City' who 'was for a very considerable part of his life a Man of Trade, and worldly Business', 'exactly just to all men in his Dealings and Trade'. The exact nature of his commercial activity is not specified, though in 1678 he was elected master of the Company of Upholders, but from Kidder's comment that 'God blessed his endeavours' it appears that Allen enjoyed success as a merchant (Kidder, 21, 25, 30). In his will of 2 February 1686 Allen mentions property in London, Hertfordshire, and Buckinghamshire. Baxter's pupil, the younger William Allen, seems to have followed his mother into the grave before his father's death, as had another son, John. Allen was survived by three children, Thomas, Mary, and Sarah, and by his grandchildren, William and Elizabeth. Allen had remarried, and in his will remembered 'my deare and loveinge wife', Alice, whom he appointed his executor (PRO, PROB 11/384, fol. 107r), and to whom Kidder dedicated his funeral sermon. N. H. KEEBLE

Sources *An apologeticall account of some brethren of the church whereof John Goodwin is pastor* (1647) · *The humble representation and vindication of many ... belonging to severall of the baptized churches in this nation* (1654) · *Reliquiae Baxterianae, or, Mr Richard Baxter's narrative of the most memorable passages of his life and times*, ed. M. Sylvester, 1 vol. in 3 pts (1696), pt 2, pp. 180–81; pt 3, p. 180; appx 3, pp. 51–66; appx 4, pp. 67–107 · *Calendar of the correspondence of Richard Baxter*, ed. N. H. Keeble and G. F. Nuttall, 2 vols. (1991) · W. Kennett, *A register and chronicle ecclesiastical and civil* (1728), 519 · R. Kidder, *A sermon preached at the funeral of Mr William Allen, August 17 1686* (1686) · E. S. More, 'Congregationalism and the social order: John Goodwin's gathered church, 1640–60', *Journal of Ecclesiastical History*, 38 (1987), 210–35 · G. F. Nuttall, 'Thomas Lambe, William Allen and Richard Baxter: an additional note', *Baptist Quarterly*, 27 (1977–8), 139–40 · M. Tolmie, 'Thomas Lambe, soapboiler, and Thomas Lambe, merchant, General Baptists', *Baptist Quarterly*, 27 (1977–8), 4–13 · J. R. Woodhead, *The rulers of London, 1660–1689* (1965), 17 · J. F. Houston, *Featherbedds and flock bedds: notes on the history of the Worshipful Company of Upholders of the City of London* (1993), 39 · PRO, PROB 11/384, quire 104, fols. 106v–107r

Archives DWL, Baxter letters

Allen, William (1704–1780), landowner and politician in America, was born on 5 August 1704 in Philadelphia, Pennsylvania, to William Allen (d. c.1725), merchant, and his wife, known only by her maiden name, Budd. They were Presbyterians from Dungannon, Tyrone, to whom William Penn granted land. Allen in 1720 went to England to study at the Middle Temple (August 1720) and at Clare College, Cambridge (September 1720), and then toured France. He returned to Philadelphia in 1725 to take over his late father's business. Allen eventually owned ships, ironworks, and copper mines besides his mercantile establishment, but it was through his land speculations that he became the wealthiest resident of the colony. He left at death an estate of £100,000. Tall, handsome, and a smart dresser, Allen in 1734 married Margaret Hamilton, daughter of Andrew *Hamilton, the noted Pennsylvania lawyer. They had nine children. One daughter married Governor John Penn of Pennsylvania, another married James DeLancey jun. of New York.

The Allens lived ostentatiously, but William was also very philanthropic, supporting the Pennsylvania Hospital and the College of Philadelphia. He was an active trustee of the college until 1779 and also gave substantial funds to poor relief in Philadelphia. His loan enabled the government to purchase the land for the construction of what became Independence Hall. He supported the artists Benjamin West and John Singleton Copley, and he owned several of West's paintings, but no portrait of him is known.

Allen began his political career in the Philadelphia city government in 1727. In 1730 he was elected to the Pennsylvania House. Here he supported William Penn's sons, the proprietors of the colony, and their chief advocate, Allen's future father-in-law, who had become speaker in 1729. Andrew Hamilton and Allen led the Proprietary Party, which dominated the house for most of the 1730s. Allen corresponded with Proprietor Thomas Penn about political affairs in the colony. When in 1739 both Hamilton and Allen unwisely decided to retire from the house, the opposition Quaker Party rose up again, displeased with the Proprietors' paper money policy and with the governor's support for the war with Spain, and took control of the house for the next seventeen years. Allen failed to win a seat in the house in 1740, and in 1742 he was accused by the Quakers of encouraging sailors to foment a riot during the Philadelphia election to scare away Quaker Party voters. The riot failed to oust the Quakers, and Allen was never again able to stand as a legislative candidate from Philadelphia.

Although out of the legislature until 1755, Allen continued his political efforts. He tried and failed to bring Benjamin Franklin over to the Penns' side. In 1750 he was appointed chief justice of the supreme court by his brother-in-law, Governor James Hamilton. Here he upheld Pennsylvania practice against British precedent in the numerous land claim cases that the courts handled.

Allen played a prominent political role in the attacks on the Quaker government for its failure to defend the colony in 1754–6. He obtained election as a non-resident representative from a western county in 1755. Benjamin Franklin's allies then dominated the house, and Allen remained in a small minority of Proprietary supporters there. During his next twenty years in the house he was never assigned to bring in a bill and performed only superficial committee tasks. Despite his efforts in the elections of 1764–6, he remained a marginalized legislator.

When Allen went to England in the summer of 1763, he joined the colonial agents in opposing the Sugar Act and the proposed Stamp Act, and praised John Wilkes's stand against the Bute ministry. He continued his opposition to imperial impositions for the next twelve years, but did not serve on any of the committees directing resistance in Philadelphia. He remained in the house until about 30 October 1775, when the agitation for independence became too great. He publicly condemned independence in the Philadelphia coffee houses in the spring of 1776, but after July stayed out of political debate. He died in Philadelphia on 6 September 1780, freeing his slaves in his will.

BENJAMIN H. NEWCOMB

Sources N. S. Cohen, 'Allen, William (1704–1780)', *ANB* • *The papers of Benjamin Franklin*, 3, ed. L. W. Labaree and W. J. Bell (1961), 296–7n. • C. Bridenbaugh and J. Bridenbaugh, *Rebels and gentlemen: Philadelphia in the age of Franklin* (1942) • J. E. Illick, *Colonial Pennsylvania: a history* (1976) • N. S. Cohen, 'William Allen, chief justice of Pennsylvania', PhD diss., U. Cal., 1966 • G. Mackinney and C. F. Hoban, eds., *Votes and proceedings of the house of representatives of the province of Pennsylvania*, 8 vols. (1754–76), vols. 3–6 [Oct 1726 – June 1776] • W. T. Parsons, 'The bloody election of 1742', *Pennsylvania History*, 36 (1969), 290–306 • T. Thayer, *Pennsylvania politics and the growth of democracy, 1740–1776* (1953) • J. J. Kelley, *Pennsylvania: the colonial years, 1681–1776* (1980) • R. A. Ryerson, *The revolution is now begun: the radical committees of Philadelphia* (1978) • P. Thompson, *Rum punch and revolution: taverngoing and public life in revolutionary Philadelphia* (1999) • Venn, *Alum. Cant.*

Archives Hist. Soc. Penn., Thomas Penn papers • Hist. Soc. Penn., Burd Shippen Hubly family papers

Wealth at death £100,000: Illick, *Colonial Pennsylvania*, 180

Allen, William (1770–1843), philanthropist and scientist, was born on 29 August 1770 at Stewart Street, the Old Artillery Ground, Spitalfields, London, the eldest of the six sons of Job Allen (1734–1800) and his wife, Margaret Stafford (d. 1830). His father, a silk manufacturer, was a member of the Society of Friends. William Allen grew up, and remained, a committed Friend, and became a leading member of the Gracechurch Street meeting. After going to a Quaker boarding-school at Rochester for a brief period, he was employed in his father's business; but his interest in chemistry led him to enter J. G. Bevan's chemical establishment at Plough Court. On Bevan's retirement in 1795 he took over the business and opened a laboratory at Plaistow. He later formed a partnership with his second wife's two nephews (Messrs Allen and Hanbury). His position enabled him to make many scientific experiments, and he associated with like-minded friends, including the surgeon Astley Paston Cooper, in the Askesian Society. He gave lectures to his fellow members at Plough Court, and became a fellow of the Linnean Society in 1801 and of the Royal Society in 1807. He was appointed lecturer at Guy's Hospital in 1802, and lectured there until 1826. At the request of his friend Humphry Davy he also lectured at the Royal Institution.

Allen's interests, however, moved from science to philanthropy. He had been interested from childhood in the anti-slavery campaign; in 1794 Thomas Clarkson became his friend, and both he and Wilberforce remained close friends throughout Allen's life. On the abolition of the slave trade in 1807, Allen became an active member of the African Institution, and shared in the agitation for the abolition of black slavery in Sierra Leone and the West Indies. He was equally active in promoting education and was a member of the committee formed in 1808 for the support of Joseph Lancaster, the founder of the monitorial school at Borough Road, Southwark, which in 1814 became the British and Foreign School Society. Allen was its treasurer and steady supporter. Under his guidance, the committee paid Lancaster's debts, pruned the monitorial institution at Borough Road of extravagances, set up an enlarged committee to raise subscriptions, warded off the challenge of the Anglican National Society, and, after more extravagances and indiscretions, ousted Lancaster from control of the institution. Allen played a leading part in the production of the British Society's teaching manual

William Allen (1770–1843), by Henry Perronet Briggs, exh. RA 1844

and wrote the preface to *Scripture Lessons* (1820, based on extracts from the Bible), which was for many years the only permitted reading book in British Society schools. The controversy between Lancaster and Andrew Bell, mainly over their respective roles in monitorial education, was one of the topics of *The Philanthropist*, a quarterly journal which Allen started in 1811 and maintained until 1817, and in which many other social reforms were discussed. James Mill was his chief contributor, and their friendly relations were initially undisturbed by radical religious differences.

In 1814, Allen, with Jeremy Bentham, Robert Owen, and four other partners, bought the New Lanark mills from Owen's previous partners in order to establish a model industrial community. Differences arose over the issue of management; in 1824, Allen—who was alarmed by Owen's avowed atheism—succeeded in enforcing biblical instruction in the New Lanark schools, and in banning the teaching of singing, dancing, and drawing. Owen consequently withdrew from the management and gave up his partnership in 1829, though Allen retained his interest until 1835. Allen was generally admired but Owen considered him narrow-minded and 'a very bustling, meddling character' (Owen, 95, 141), though anxious to do good in his own way. He thought that familiarity with great men had turned the worthy Quaker's head. However unkind this conclusion may seem, it is undeniable that Allen was moving in exalted circles. The duke of Kent was interested in both Owen's and Lancaster's schemes, and served as chairman of the committee appointed to look into Lancaster's muddled affairs. His own financial situation had become embarrassed, and Allen undertook to act as trustee for his estates; the duke consented to live upon a fixed allowance until his debts were discharged. Allen continued to act until the duke's death and the final settlement of his affairs. When the allied sovereigns visited England in 1814, Alexander I of Russia was introduced to Allen as a model Quaker. The tsar attended a Quaker meeting and visited Friends' houses, and evidently regarded Allen with considerable respect and sympathy.

In August 1818 Allen left England on a tour: after travelling through Sweden and Finland to Russia, he visited Alexander at St Petersburg, then moved to Moscow and Odessa. He reached Constantinople in July 1819, and returned by the Greek islands, Italy, and France to England in February 1820. In 1822 he went to Vienna to see Alexander again, chiefly in a vain attempt to obtain a declaration from the powers that the slave trade should be piracy. The tsar and Quaker parted, after several interviews, with prayers and embraces. Allen made other journeys to the continent in 1816, 1832, and 1833, when he examined schools, prisons, and social institutions. In interviews with statesmen and rulers, including the crown prince of Prussia, the king of Bavaria, and the king and queen of Spain, he encouraged them to adopt his ideas for reforms. In Britain he took an interest in many philanthropic causes: he promoted schools and district visiting societies, and gave evidence on the education of the poor to two parliamentary select committees. He also campaigned for the abolition of capital punishment and the protection of the Greeks, corresponding with the duke of Wellington and other political leaders. In 1841 he was appointed president of the Pharmaceutical Society's council. His chief interest in later years was in an 'agricultural colony' with industrial schools, which he helped to found at Lindfield in Sussex, and which he frequently visited to superintend its working.

Allen married, in 1796, Mary Hamilton (b. 1771), who died ten months later; she left a daughter, who in 1822 married Cornelius Hanbury, and herself died in 1823 after the birth of a son. Allen married again in 1806; his second wife was Charlotte Hanbury (b. 1762), who died in 1816. In 1827 he married Grizell Birkbeck, *née* Hoare (b. 1757), who died in 1835. Allen himself died on 30 December 1843 at Lindfield, and was buried in the Quaker burial-ground, Stoke Newington.   LESLIE STEPHEN, rev. G. F. BARTLE

Sources *Diary and correspondence of William Allen*, ed. L. Bradshaw, 3 vols. (1846) · H. Hall, *William Allen* (1953) · G. F. Bartle, 'William Allen: friend of humanity', *History of Education Society Bulletin*, 50 (1992), 15–28 · M. Braithwaite, ed., *Memorials of Christine Majolier Alsop* (1881) · J. Muckle, 'Alexander I and William Allen: a tour of Russian schools in 1819', *History of Education*, 15 (1986), 137–45 · J. Sherman, *Life of William Allen* (1851) · A. Bain, *Life of James Mill* (1882) · R. Owen, *Life of Robert Owen written by himself* (1867) · G. F. Bartle, 'Benthamites and Lancasterians', *Utilitas*, 3/2 (1991), 275–88 · J. Foyle, *The Spitalfields genius* (1884) · *The Philanthropist* (1811–17) · F. Place, autobiography and correspondence, BL, Add. MSS 35152 and 27823 · D. Salmon, *William Allen* (1905) · 'Select committee on the state of education', *Parl. papers* (1834), 9.83, no. 572 ·

'Select committee on the education of the lower orders of the metropolis', *Parl. papers* (1816), 4.216, no. 495

Archives Glaxo Smith Kline, Greenford, Middlesex, letter-book entitled 'African correspondence' and account books relating to the Lindfield settlement • Royal Pharmaceutical Society, London • RS Friends, Lond., corresp. and papers | Brunel University, Middlesex, British and Foreign School Society archives • RS, letters to R. W. Fox • UCL, letters to Society for the Diffusion of Useful Knowledge

Likenesses P. E. Bovet, engraving, 1823 (after Mme Munier-Romilly), Geneva • B. R. Haydon, group portrait, oils, 1840 (*The Anti-Slavery Society convention*), NPG • group portrait, engraving, 1840 (Borough Road monitorial school; visitors to the school include Allen, marked E, wearing his hat), repro. in J. Hamel, *Mutual instruction* (1818) • T. F. Dicksee, oils, 1842, Hanbury Manor Hotel, Ware, Hertfordshire • H. P. Briggs, oils, exh. RA 1844, Royal Pharmaceutical Society, London [*see illus.*] • C. Baugniet, lithograph (after T. F. Dicksee), NPG • J. Gilbert, group portrait, oils (*Men of science living in 1807–8*), NPG • H. C. Shenton, engraving, Royal Pharmaceutical Society, London, Library • photograph, RS Friends, Lond.

Allen, William (1792–1864), naval officer and writer, was born at Weymouth in November 1792, entered the navy as a volunteer in October 1805, and as midshipman was present at the passage of the Dardanelles in 1807. On the *Leda* (36 guns), he served at the capture of Java (August 1811) and the successful attack on the pirate base at Sambas, Borneo (June 1813). He was promoted lieutenant on 25 March 1815, commander on 20 June 1836, and captain on 31 January 1842. He took part in the Niger expedition of Richard Lander and Oldfield, 1832; but he was best-known for commanding the steamer *Wilberforce* in the disastrous Niger expedition of 1841–2. Though Allen could not be blamed for the misfortunes of this expedition, he was on his return placed on half pay. He retired from the service as a captain in December 1855. He was promoted to retired rear-admiral in April 1862.

It is difficult to account for Allen's sudden promotion between 1836 and 1842, and his subsequent retirement. His wide-ranging interests and modest private means may have been sufficient to keep him ashore. The effects of disease proved singularly long-lasting among his fellow officers from the 1841–2 expedition.

With T. R. H. Thomson, the surgeon, Allen published *A Narrative of the Expedition Sent by H.M.'s Government to the River Niger in 1841* (2 vols., 1848). In 1849 he travelled through Syria and Palestine, and published the results in *The Dead Sea, a New Route to India* (2 vols., 1855), in which he advocated the construction of a canal between the Mediterranean and the Red Sea by the Jordan valley and Dead Sea, and compared that route with the proposed Suez Canal: this 'attracted considerable attention' (*GM*). His other publications included a pamphlet, *Mutual Improvement* (1846), advocating good-conduct prizes to be awarded by ballot by the community divided for the purpose into small groups; in 1849 a *Plan for the immediate extinction of the slave trade, for the relief of the West India colonies, and for the diffusion of civilisation and Christianity in Africa by the co-operation of Mammon with philanthropy*, a chimerical scheme of compulsory 'apprenticeship' or 'temporary bondage'; and papers in the *Journal of the Royal Geographical Society* (vols. 7, 8, 13, and 23). He was an FRGS (1835) and a

fellow of the Royal Society (1844), and an accomplished musician; some of his landscape paintings were exhibited at the Royal Academy from 1828 to 1847. He was described as 'rather under middle height, with very handsome features ... beaming with benevolence and good humour', with 'an excessive love of children, of whom he was the idol' (*GM*). He died, unmarried, at his residence, Bank House, Weymouth, Dorset, on 23 January 1864.

J. S. KELTIE, rev. ANDREW LAMBERT

Sources D. Syrett and R. L. DiNardo, *The commissioned sea officers of the Royal Navy, 1660–1815*, rev. edn, Occasional Publications of the Navy RS, 1 (1994) • O'Byrne, *Naval biog. dict.* • Boase, *Mod. Eng. biog.* • *GM*, 3rd ser., 16 (1864) • D. A. Farnie, *East and west of Suez: the Suez Canal in history, 1854–1956* (1969)

Likenesses W. Brockedon, black and red chalk drawing, 1834, NPG • G. Cook, line and stipple (after W. Barclay), BM, NPG; repro. in W. Allen, *A narrative of the expedition ... to the River Niger in 1841*, 2 vols. (1848)

Wealth at death under £1500: probate, 3 March 1864, *CGPLA Eng. & Wales*

Allen, William Edward David [*pseuds.* James Drennan, Liam Pawle] (1901–1973), historian and businessman, was born on 6 January 1901 at 12 Sussex Place, Regent's Park, London, the eldest of the three sons of William Edward Allen (1860–1919), printer and theatre owner, and his wife, Sarah Collett (1863–1944), daughter of Thomas Phinn QC, who had some success on the stage as Cissie Grahame. His father was born in Belfast, the third son of David Allen, who had founded the printing business of David Allen & Sons, which under William senior's guidance moved its headquarters to London, where it became the nerve centre of theatrical advertising in Britain and a major force in bill-posting. His remarkable mother later went into theatrical management and became, after her husband's death, both chairman and majority shareholder of the Allen business. W. E. D. (Bill) Allen was baptized into the Church of England (despite his family's Presbyterian origins), was educated in Mr Goodhart's house at Eton College (1914–18), and published his first book, *The Turks in Europe* (1919), when he was eighteen.

Instead of going to Oxford after his father's death, Allen briefly studied commerce and accounting, joined the family firm as a 'canvasser' in 1920 and was made a director in 1922. He became chairman in 1927, retaining that position until 1970. His *David Allens: the History of a Family Firm, 1857–1957* (1957) gives a vivid account of family tensions, the move out of printing and theatrical advertising, and the unsuccessful attempts to make the firm an advertising agency in its own right and to become a force in radio advertising from a base in Andorra. The business was highly sensitive to changes in national prosperity, and suffered considerably from restrictions imposed in each of the world wars, but it recovered rapidly after 1945.

The business gave Bill Allen financial independence, but never wholly absorbed him. In the 1920s he travelled extensively and acted as a special correspondent for the *Morning Post* during the Riff and Graeco-Turkish wars. He published a sober study of the Caucasus in the Nations of Today series (1923), and a mannered book called *Beled-es-*

Siba (1925): mainly about Morocco, it also includes an affectionate and brilliant essay on the Orangemen of west Tyrone which has much historical value. On visits to Constantinople and the countries of the Black Sea he made a remarkable collection of icons, dispersed from former Greek churches in Turkey, and from the Soviet Union. Twenty-four of the icons were later acquired by the National Gallery of Ireland.

On 6 December 1922 Allen married Lady Phyllis Edith King (1897–1947), daughter of the third earl of Lovelace, and their daughter was born in 1925. The marriage was not a success and ended in divorce in 1932. Until about 1935 Cissie Allen financed her son's personal enterprises. She also provided a home at Commonwood House, Chipperfield, Hertfordshire, where he and his brothers could bring their guests at weekends: in Bill's case, he wrote later, these would include 'bizarre intellectuals, Caucasian philologists and exiled national leaders from the remoter parts of Central Asia' (Allen, 262).

In 1929 Allen's career took a controversial turn. He had always identified with the Ulster origins of his family, and although there was a strong family tradition against mixing business and politics, he became Ulster Unionist MP for West Belfast. He used his time in parliament to raise topics from China to Central America, but he was less good as a speaker than as a writer. He became one of Sir Oswald Mosley's closest associates, and, alone among those taking the Conservative whip, joined Mosley's New Party. Although Allen ceased to be an MP in 1931 he wrote the 'Letters of Lucifer' for *The Blackshirt*, attacking tory plutocracy, and in 1934 published a full-scale defence of British fascism, *BUF: Oswald Mosley and British Fascism*, under the pseudonym James Drennan. In it he argued for a collectivist 'Elizabethan' model of society, instead of the liberal bourgeois system which he considered to have failed, and that parliament needed streamlining if the drastic action required to cure the evils of the depression was to be taken. The book presented Mosley's career in heroic terms, and contrasted it with the cowardice of the MPs who might have joined him. It was British fascism's most systematic defence. Later Allen withdrew from Mosley in disillusionment.

In 1932 Allen had published his lively and respected *History of the Georgian People* and that July married Paula Alexandra Gellibrand (1893–1981), formerly wife of the marquès de Casa Maury. She was a society beauty, much photographed by Cecil Beaton, and may have been the model for the heroine of Enid Bagnold's *Serena Blandish*. They lived partly at Mullagh Cottage, near Killyleagh, co. Down, and jointly wrote *Strange Coast* (1936), a novel of romance and adventure set in a fictionalized Georgia of the 1920s, which appeared under the pseudonym Liam Pawle. The marriage was dissolved in 1939.

Between 1939 and 1949, Allen was mainly in Africa and the Middle East. He wrote a valuable history of Ukraine, prepared with the collaboration of several Russian and Ukrainian scholars, which appeared in 1940, dedicated to N. M., 'half Ukrainian, half Angel'—Nataliya (Natasha)

Maksimovna (c.1900–1966), daughter of Maksim Kossovsky, late of the imperial Moscow bar. She became his third wife on 6 March 1943. During the Second World War, Allen first served with the Household Cavalry. In 1941 he was a captain with Orde Wingate's military mission to Abyssinia where, as transport officer, he successfully took Sudanese camels over mountain terrain. He was invalided out of the army and held a series of civilian posts as press attaché and information officer, and became information counsellor at Ankara during the critical period between 1947 and 1949. He was appointed OBE in 1948. Penguin published his book *Guerrilla War in Abyssinia* (1943) and his accounts, with Pavel Muratov, *The Russian Campaigns of 1941–43* (1944) and *The Russian Campaigns of 1944–1945* (1946). The book on Abyssinia is autobiographical and has inimitable period atmosphere. It is also a classic study of the conditions for successful guerrilla war.

In 1946 Allen acquired Whitechurch House, Cappagh, co. Waterford, and from 1949 Natasha Allen's talents turned the derelict mansion and gardens into a home which welcomed a constant stream of guests. Allen now divided his working time between the affairs of David Allens, the estate at Whitechurch, and the two major books which he completed during the 1950s. *Caucasian Battlefields* (1953), written with Pavel Muratov, remains a classic study. *David Allens* (1957) is a fine piece of business history and a stylish collective biography of the Allen family. He also wrote a short study, *The Poet and the Spae Wife* (1960), which linked his interest in the history of the Maghrib with his affection for Ireland, and in 1963 published a powerful essay, *Problems of Turkish Power in the Sixteenth Century*. He continued to travel widely, to Iran, to Alaska, and to Yucatan, accompanied by Natasha, though her health had begun to fail. She died in 1966 after a lengthy illness. In 1969 he married (Gertrude) Anne Pentland, a nurse. A son was born in 1972.

Allen's final historical study, prepared with Anthony Mango as translator, was an edition of the records of the Russian embassies to the Georgian kings between 1589 and 1605, which was published by the Hakluyt Society in 1970. He died on 18 September 1973 at 96 Lower Leeson Street, Dublin, and was buried at Chipperfield parish church, Hertfordshire.

Allen was a man of many talents: a gentleman, a businessman, a philosopher, an adventurer, but continuously and most powerfully an energetic historian and linguist. He made his library, later held by the University of Indiana, the finest private collection of books on Georgia and the Caucasus in the Western world. Throughout his life he travelled extensively in remote places and may be the only person to have walked the entire length of the Turkish-Russian frontier. Personally he was exceedingly loyal and generous. His history of David Allens brings out the depth of his affection for his family and its Ulster origins, and for those who had worked for the enterprise.

ARTHUR GREEN

Sources W. E. D. Allen, *David Allens: the history of a family firm, 1857–1957* (1957) · private information (2004) · *WWW* · *The Times* (21 Sept

1973) · *Irish Times* (25 Sept 1973) · will, proved Dublin, 8 May 1974 · b. cert. · m. cert.

Archives NRA, priv. coll., MSS | CAC Cam., corresp. with Sir E. L. Spears · LPL, corresp. with John A. Douglas

Likenesses Mak, oils, *c*.1930, priv. coll. · N. Hepple, group portrait, 1959 (David Allen board)

Wealth at death £305,311—value of aggregable property; incl. library valued at more than £30,000: estate duty affidavit, 1974, Dublin

Allen, William Frederick. *See* Leo, Alan (1860–1917).

Allenby, Edmund Henry Hynman, first Viscount Allenby of Megiddo (1861–1936), army officer, was born on 23 April 1861, St George's day, on the estate of his mother's family at Brackenhurst Hall, near Southwell, Nottinghamshire, the second child and eldest son of six children (three boys, three girls) of Hynman Allenby (*c*.1822–1878), a country gentleman, and his wife, Catherine Anne (1829x31–1922), daughter of the Revd Thomas Coats Cane of Nottinghamshire. Married in 1859, Allenby's parents, after the death of Hynman Allenby's father in 1861, established the family home at Felixstowe House, Felixstowe, Suffolk (subsequently demolished); they also bought an estate in Norfolk of some 2000 acres. Brought up the son of a country squire in the countryside, away from the cities, Allenby loved nature and developed a keen knowledge of flora and fauna, a passion that would remain with him all his life. In 1935, aged seventy-four, he went to wildest Patagonia in Argentina on a final fishing trip to see if the salmon really were as big as in his beloved River Tay.

Early life and career Allenby's family background and early years did not suggest a military career. After being tutored at home by a governess Allenby went in 1871 to Ashbocking vicarage to be educated by the Revd Maurice Cowell. He then went in 1875 to Haileybury College in Hertfordshire, a former training school for the East India Company resurrected as a public school in 1862. While Allenby showed no remarkable aptitude in schoolwork or sport, his schooling in the classrooms and on the playing fields of Haileybury left its imprint. Rather than intelligence, the public schools at this time emphasized courage, duty, fortitude, integrity, selflessness, self-control, and a 'manly' belief in the virtues of the Christian faith as the vital attributes for 'character' and for a successful career in positions of authority (James, 6). Considering Haileybury's connections with India, Allenby decided in 1878 on a career in the Indian Civil Service, and he went to several 'crammer' schools in London to prepare for the entrance exams. These he failed, twice. Only after this setback did he choose a career in the army. As he later recounted in a public speech, he went into the army in 1881 'because he was too big a fool for anything else' (Savage, 24).

Having passed out of Sandhurst in December 1881, Allenby was gazetted to the 6th (Inniskilling) dragoons, a not particularly fashionable cavalry regiment, on 10 May 1882. It is unclear why Allenby chose the mounted arm,

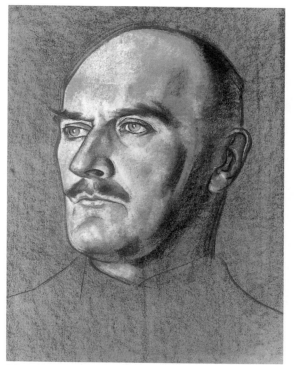

Edmund Henry Hynman Allenby, first Viscount Allenby of Megiddo (1861–1936), by Eric Kennington, pubd 1926

but it was as a cavalryman that he made his reputation. Military life suited Allenby. While not an automaton, he was loyal, accepted orders without question, and enjoyed outdoor physical activity. When Allenby joined the army, it was beginning a period of transition as the old army gradually reformed to meet the challenges of modern, industrialized warfare. It was, however, in old-style colonial soldiering in southern Africa that Allenby served his apprenticeship as a subaltern. He joined his regiment in South Africa in 1882 before embarking in 1884 on an expedition to eject Boer lodgements in Bechuanaland (now Botswana). In 1886 Allenby returned home for a two-year stint at the cavalry depot at Canterbury and two seasons' fox-hunting. He then returned to South Africa a captain, accompanied by some hounds, joined his regiment, now on active duty in Zululand, and was promoted adjutant. With this appointment there emerged a serious application to soldiering that replaced Allenby's previously good-natured insouciance. While he had seen no actual fighting in southern Africa, he learned much of the basic fieldcraft that he would need in later wars. In this period Allenby also became something of a martinet; when he assumed senior command his withering temper, imposing physical presence (matched by a voracious appetite), and obsession with discipline and orders earned him the nickname 'the Bull'.

In 1890, when the 6th dragoons returned home for garrison duties, Allenby settled into a rhythm of hunting, sport, socializing, and military duties. He also married: in

1895 he had met Adelaide Mabel Chapman (*c*.1868–1942), daughter of Horace Edward Chapman, and on 30 December 1896 the two were married at the bride's home at Donhead House, Salisbury, Wiltshire. Allenby's wife shared his love of the country and the marriage was intensely happy, lasting until his death in 1936. Adelaide Mabel, along with Allenby's mother, to whom he wrote regularly until her death in 1922, provided a solid foundation on which Allenby built his reputation as a soldier. In 1898 Adelaide Mabel gave birth to a son, Michael, the Allenbys' much loved only child. Michael's death on the western front in July 1917 shattered the typically marmoreal Allenby, who broke down and, inconsolable, wept in front of one of his divisional commanders (General Sir John Shea, recording, IWM SA, typescript, 5.41–2).

Allenby's reticence masked considerable ambition and drive, and in 1896 he passed by competition into the Staff College at Camberley, a notable achievement at a time when few cavalrymen entered Staff College except by nomination. Allenby's class included another future field marshal, Douglas Haig. The cerebral James Edmonds, another entrant of 1896, recalled that Allenby was 'curiously taciturn' at Staff College and 'rather out of his depth in the very medium company of 1896–7' (Gardner, 23). While Allenby was neither strikingly intellectual nor garrulous, he was more popular than Haig, over whom fellow officers elected him to the prestigious position of master of the drag hounds for the 1896–7 season. A solid rather than outstanding student at Staff College, Allenby showed himself to be tolerant and flexible and, while not a big debater, capable of interesting conversations on a range of topics. His willingness to listen and consider new ideas would prove to be assets as he rose to the pinnacle of his profession.

Promoted major in 1897, Allenby was made adjutant (equivalent to a brigade-major) to the 3rd cavalry brigade in 1898. The next year saw the outbreak of the Second South African War (1899–1902), and in October the Inniskillings shipped out for service in South Africa against the Boers. This was Allenby's first war. Given temporary command of the Inniskillings in 1900, he emerged at the war's end in 1902 with much credit, a brevet lieutenant-colonelcy, and useful contacts; and in 1902 he was created CB in recognition of his service. Allenby started the war as an unknown major; he ended it with a reputation as a competent, reliable leader, and as someone marked out for possible promotion. While not a brilliant commander, Allenby had suffered no major reverses and, physically tough, had proved himself in the field on lengthy, exacting operations during which British columns swept the veldt for Boer commandos. Allenby also worked well with an attached Australian cavalry regiment, the New South Wales lancers, a portent of future operations during the First World War, when he commanded Australian mounted troops in Palestine. After the Second South African War, Allenby became a full colonel and in 1905 was made a brigadier-general and given command of the 4th cavalry brigade. In 1909 he rose to the rank of major-general before, the following year, becoming inspector-general of cavalry, a post held until the outbreak of the First World War.

As Allenby coped with the pressures of senior command before and during the First World War, he became increasingly irascible, obsessive with discipline, and bad-tempered towards subordinates. Hubert Gough, his chief staff officer when inspector-general of cavalry, recalled that Allenby had a 'great regard for regulations and all sort of detail' and that if Allenby, when inspecting a unit, saw any neglect of detail or orders he was liable to explode (Gardner, 62). Cavalrymen who neglected to do up their chinstraps felt the full weight of Allenby's concern with obeying all orders to the letter. During one inspection an officer remarked 'Very good, Sir', to which Allenby barked back, 'I want none of your bloody approbation' (James, 81). As one of his officers recalled, while Allenby had been an easy-going young officer and a good-humoured squadron leader, he was a strict colonel, an irascible brigadier, and an explosive general (Wavell, *Study in Greatness*, 1.114). This bad temper got worse once war broke out in 1914. One senior western front commander willing to withstand one of Allenby's tirades earned himself the sobriquet 'toreador', before being dismissed (James, 84). Allenby's wicked temper was a result of his having to cope with the strains of command. He was also capable of great kindness, did not bear grudges, and was always willing to listen to his officers as long as they could provide convincing evidence for their arguments.

The First World War: France Allenby assumed command of the cavalry division on the outbreak of war in August 1914. However, the relationship with his commander, Haig, was far from ideal. While there was goodwill between the two men, both were uncommunicative in each other's company. This made discussions of strategy awkward. Allenby fumbled for words while Haig rambled through a series of unfinished sentences.

While questions were raised over his handling of the cavalry during the retreat from Mons, Allenby's defence of the Messines–Wytschaete ridge during the first battle of Ypres (October–November 1914), with what was now the cavalry corps of two divisions, showed him at his dogged best: unflappable, reliable, and determined to stick to his orders and hold his ground at all cost against overwhelming odds. In May 1915 Allenby took over 5th corps during the second battle of Ypres before taking charge of the Third Army in October 1915 with the temporary rank of general. He was made a KCB in the same year (a GCMG would follow in 1917, a GCB in 1918, and a GCVO in 1934). In the trying circumstances of the western front, unable to institute manoeuvre warfare, Allenby proved himself a competent rather than inspiring general.

Allenby's opportunity to prove himself came in April 1917 when his Third Army attacked at Arras. In the planning stages of the battle he reduced the preparatory bombardment to under 48 hours to give his assault troops the element of surprise. But Haig vetoed Allenby's 'hurricane' bombardment in favour of a longer five-day artillery barrage and, under pressure, Allenby acquiesced in the change of plan. While disadvantaged operationally, Allenby instituted a number of measures, such as using the sewers and cellars of Arras as a way of getting troops secretly to the jumping-off points, to achieve tactical surprise. The result was an impressive initial gain of almost 4 miles when the battle opened on 9 April 1917. Thereafter the fighting turned into a series of bitter and costly attritional battles as the Third Army engaged the German defence-in-depth system. Allenby's inability to change Haig's mind once the battle of Arras bogged down, and his willingness faithfully to carry out orders that he must have known would achieve little except cause heavy casualties, show some of his shortcomings. As was noted in his obituary: 'Allenby conscientiously, if clumsily, carried out an operation which, it was recognized, could hardly be decisive, and had been continued mainly with a view to giving the French time in which to recover' (*The Times*, 18). The assessment of Gough, commander of the Fifth Army, was that while Allenby's behaviour was 'very just' he also had 'no ideas and when in France would apply orders rigidly without reasoning' (King's Lond., Liddell Hart MSS, talk with Lloyd George and Gough, 28 Nov 1935, 11/1935/107).

Allenby came unstuck after Arras and, looking for a new commander for Palestine, the British leader, David Lloyd George, dispatched him to the Middle East to command the British-led Egyptian expeditionary force (EEF). While Allenby was desolate at being moved to Palestine, independent command in a peripheral war theatre away from the intrigues of the western front made his name and in October 1919 secured him a field marshal's baton, a viscountcy, and an award from parliament of £50,000.

The First World War: Palestine When Allenby arrived in Egypt on 27 June 1917 (he assumed command the following day), EEF morale had collapsed. Under the uninspiring leadership of General Archibald Murray the force had been defeated twice at the town of Gaza in spring 1917. Allenby set about rebuilding the EEF into a force capable of taking the offensive. He moved his headquarters to Khan Yunis, just behind the front line at Gaza, and embarked on a series of tours of EEF front-line troops. The tough Australian and New Zealand mounted troops that formed a mobile core to the EEF soon noticed the change in atmosphere. One Australian light horseman remembered how under Murray he and his comrades were 'fed up—we considered we hadn't had the leadership we were due for and it seemed to be one blunder after another. Then the arrival of Allenby, morale rose' (IWM SA, Trooper Pollock recording, 4200). Allenby's impact resonated through the EEF. Richard Meinertzhagen, an EEF staff officer, recorded how the force was finally awakening from its 'lethargic sleep under Murray' (Meinertzhagen diaries, 15 July 1917), while Ronald Storrs, a future military governor of Jerusalem, noted that under Allenby the EEF was advancing with 'exhilaration into new hope' (Storrs, 270). With the weight of the western front lifted from his shoulders, Allenby rose to meet the challenges of his new post. Unlike Murray, he was no office general and, physically fit, was willing and able to travel over bumpy

tracks in the stifling heat to visit units in the desert. Allenby's experience in field command of everything from a troop in southern Africa in the 1880s to an army in France gave him the standing to talk to rankers and lift their spirits. His sheer presence helped lift morale, and, like General Bernard Montgomery before the battle of Alamein in 1942, show his men that the impending battle was winnable (Hughes, 14–17).

While Allenby's personality remained fundamentally unchanged (Falls, *DNB*), the different circumstances in Palestine drew out his best qualities and emphasized a more sympathetic and thoughtful side. The Australian official historian Henry Gullett remembered Allenby visiting an Australian unit out in the desert where the canteen had been open for some time before he arrived, with the result that many of the men were drunk. The drunks struck matches on Allenby's car, 'almost leaned on him. The tighter they were the closer they wished to get to him' (Gullett papers, AWM40/69, 'Murray'). Allenby's reaction to this incident was afterwards to write an appreciative note to the unit commander. Major-General George de Symons Barrow, one of Allenby's divisional commanders, compared Allenby favourably to Haig, writing about how Allenby was happy to be contradicted as long as this was backed up by a cogent argument (G. de S. Barrow, *Fire of Life*, 1942, 46). Storrs recalled that being told off by Allenby was like being blown from the muzzle of a gun, but when the victim regained the ground Allenby bore him no malice (Storrs, 270). Allenby's mix of martinet and motivation infused new life into the EEF, transforming it into a fighting force. His first action opened in October 1917 with the third battle of Gaza, the objective being to capture Jerusalem.

Prior to third Gaza, artillery, aeroplanes, men, and equipment poured into Egypt, turning the EEF into a well-equipped force of ten divisions—seven infantry and three cavalry. On 12 August 1917 Allenby organized these units into three corps: the 20th and 21st infantry corps and the desert mounted corps. These reinforcements were vital for the offensive to break the Turkish lines that stretched in a ragged line from Gaza to Beersheba. For the third battle of Gaza, Allenby adopted a plan worked out by Murray's staff before his arrival. This plan involved shifting the emphasis of attack away from Gaza, with two of his three mounted divisions, plus four of the infantry divisions available, attacking the weaker eastern extremity of the Turkish lines at Beersheba, before rolling up the enemy defences from the east. The plan worked. Australian light horse troops charged in and took Beersheba on 31 October and moved west to join up with the force at Gaza prior to the push on Jerusalem. The city was finally captured on 9 December 1917. The surrender was taken by two 'cockney' privates from the 60th (London) division out looking for water; they were accosted by the mayor of Jerusalem bearing the keys to the city, and looking for someone to surrender to (James, 140).

Considering the weak nature of the Turkish defences at Gaza, it has been suggested (Hughes, 43–59) that Allenby would have done better to concentrate his augmented force, which included a substantial pool of artillery, for an assault on Gaza town rather than on Beersheba. This would have led to a more comprehensive victory. As it was, the Turks were allowed the space to retire in good order to a new defensive line across central Palestine just north of Jerusalem from which they were not dislodged until the war's end. This does not, however, diminish Allenby's success at third Gaza: he reversed the two earlier defeats at Gaza and captured the historic city of Jerusalem. While he was perhaps too cautious and methodical at third Gaza, he was also under intense pressure to invade Palestine and take Jerusalem, especially after his supposed failure at Arras. Having examined the plan offered to him on his arrival in Egypt, he felt that this offered the best likelihood of fulfilling the wishes of his political superiors in the time allotted for the task. He was also hampered by having to conduct operations within the context of a protracted struggle between Lloyd George and elements of the military, notably General William Robertson, over war strategy and the question of whether 'side-shows' such as Palestine were worthy of support. Caught in the middle of this acrimonious debate, Allenby had to tread carefully and please both sides.

With the capture of Jerusalem, Allenby was portrayed as a modern-day Richard Lionheart (*Punch*, 19 Dec 1917) finally recapturing the holy city lost to the Muslims in 1187. For Britain the fall of Jerusalem was a notable propaganda coup at a very difficult moment in the war; for Lloyd George it was the Christmas present for the nation that he had demanded of Allenby before he left for Palestine. Allenby's entry into the city on 11 December was a carefully stage-managed show. He entered on foot through the Jaffa Gate, having dismounted outside the walls, in a gesture that compared favourably to the German Kaiser's entry on horseback in 1898, read out a proclamation of martial law, and then left, again on foot.

After third Gaza the impending German (Ludendorff) offensives on the western front hampered Allenby's plans, as the EEF was a potential reserve force for France. When the offensives broke in March 1918 he lost the bulk of his infantry and some of his cavalry. They were replaced by untrained Indian troops who needed time to be absorbed into the EEF. This restricted Allenby's plans for 1918. From March to May 1918 he launched two 'raids'—the official nomenclature for multi-divisional attacks—across the River Jordan towards Amman. Their objectives were unclear and resulted in two comprehensive defeats by Turkish forces (Hughes, 71–88). These defeats shocked Allenby (Allenby MSS, 6/IX–X/40–41) and for a circumspect commander such as Allenby suggest a loss of grip on operations.

Allenby's finest hour, and the crowning triumph of the Palestine campaign, came with his final offensive against the Turkish armies in Palestine, launched on 19 September 1918 and ending with the armistice signed at Mudros on 30 October 1918. This final battle was given the name Megiddo as Allenby's forces pushed by the ancient mound of Megiddo, the supposed site of the final battle (or Armageddon) revealed in the book of Revelation (16: 16).

Megiddo was a cavalry triumph: once artillery and infantry had punched a hole in the Turkish lines, Allenby's British, Indian, Australian, and New Zealand cavalry swept out behind Turkish lines and advanced all the way to Aleppo in northern Syria. Having said this, the poor condition of the Turkish forces in Palestine must be allowed for in assessing Allenby's success at Megiddo. Debilitated by a lack of men and equipment, they were in a much weakened state by September 1918. The Turkish high command from late 1917 had starved the Palestine front of *matériel*, preferring to concentrate resources on a push in the Caucasus. By the battle of Megiddo the Turks in Palestine could do little to resist when overwhelmed by Allenby's superior forces. The scale of the triumph surprised Allenby, who was planning a methodical push into Palestine and Syria (Hughes, 97). While cavalry was used extensively in the Russian civil war, and even the Second World War, the battle of Megiddo marked the swansong of cavalry, and the end of the era of the horse as a decisive weapon of war.

Throughout the campaign Allenby liaised with Hashemite Arab forces allied to Britain. Directed by Colonel T. E. Lawrence (Lawrence of Arabia), the Arabs were deployed on Allenby's right flank. While Allenby approved Lawrence's operations, the considerable post-war interest in the enigmatic Lawrence should not detract from Allenby's concentration on the main push by the EEF west of the River Jordan. Allenby took little account of the Arab force militarily, although he accommodated the imperial need to promote the Hashemites by ordering his troops to allow the Arabs into Damascus 'first', even though EEF cavalry clearly entered the city on 30 September–1 October 1918 before Arab forces arrived.

Post-war The war's end presented Allenby with new challenges. He was the military commander of a swath of territory stretching from the Sudan to northern Syria before, in March 1919, becoming special high commissioner for Egypt, a post that was confirmed in October 1919 when he returned to London to be raised to the peerage, as first Viscount Allenby of Megiddo and Felixstowe, and promoted field marshal. Allenby was an able colonial administrator at a difficult time for the British empire. In 1919 Egypt rose in revolt and he had to deploy large numbers of troops to suppress the uprising with considerable force. Simultaneously his troops were clamouring to be demobilized, to the extent that some units effectively mutinied and refused to carry out orders (Hughes, 141–3). Meanwhile Australian and New Zealand troops went on the rampage through the Palestinian village of Surafend, beating to death some forty Arab villagers. On another occasion a paraded Australian unit shouted Allenby 'out' in an orchestrated example of disobedience (A. F. Nayton, letter, *The Times*, 29 May 1964). While he was furious at these acts of indiscipline, there was little Allenby could do now that the war was over. Worried by the threat of revolt, he urged the negotiators at the Paris peace conference to bear in mind the consequences of their decisions for the Middle East. Pressures within Egypt after the 1919 revolt for independence were a perennial problem for Allenby, temporarily solved by the granting of some self-rule in 1922. The end of his tenure in Egypt was marred by the assassination of Sir Lee Stack, the governor-general of Sudan, in 1924. He never resolved the dilemma of Egypt's status, an issue that rumbled on into the 1930s and beyond. It was, therefore, with some relief that in June 1925 Allenby left the official residency in Cairo with his wife and returned to Britain and retirement after a long period of service as a soldier and administrator.

While the king gave the Allenbys rent-free use of Deal Castle, by 1928 they had purchased a more manageable town house at 24 Wetherby Gardens, London, on the fringes of Kensington. Allenby's chief public work was as president of the British National Cadet Force. Otherwise he used the time afforded by his retirement to indulge in bird-watching and travelling. Indeed it was after a trip to buy material for the aviary in his garden that Allenby died at home of a burst blood vessel in his brain on 14 May 1936. He was cremated and buried in St George's chapel in Westminster Abbey on 19 May. MATTHEW HUGHES

Sources A. Wavell, *Allenby: a study in greatness*, 2 vols. (1940) · B. Gardner, *Allenby* (1965) · L. James, *Imperial warrior: the life and times of Field-Marshal Viscount Allenby, 1861–1936* (1993) · A. Wavell, *Allenby in Egypt* (1943) · M. Hughes, *Allenby and British strategy in the Middle East, 1917–1919* (1999) · R. Savage, *Allenby of Armageddon* (1925) · King's Lond., Liddell Hart C., Allenby MSS · *DNB* · *The Times* (15 May 1936) · Australian War Memorial, Canberra, Australia, Gullett papers · C. Falls and G. Macmunn, *Official history, military operations, Egypt and Palestine*, 2 vols. (1928–30) · J. Newell, 'Allenby and the Palestine campaign', *The First World War and British military history*, ed. B. Bond (1991) · C. Falls, *Armageddon, 1918* (1964) · H. S. Gullett, *The Australian imperial force in Sinai and Palestine, 1914–1918* (1923), vol. 7 of *The official history of Australia in the war of 1914–1918* · IWM SA, General Sir John Shea, ref. 4227; Trooper Pollock, ref. 4200 · King's Lond., Liddell Hart C., Liddell Hart MSS · R. Storrs, *The memoirs of Sir Ronald Storrs* (1937); repr. (New York, 1972) · Meinertzhagen diaries, Bodl. RH · C. S. Forester, *The general* (1936) · *CGPLA Eng. & Wales* · A. P. Wavell, *The Palestine campaigns* (1928)
Archives King's Lond., Liddell Hart C., corresp. and MSS · St Ant. Oxf., Middle East Centre, Allenby collection | HLRO, letters to H. Samuel · IWM, corresp. with H. Wilson · King's Lond., Robertson MSS · NA Scot., corresp. with P. Kerr · St Ant. Oxf., corresp. with R. MacInnes | FILM Australian War Memorial, Canberra · BFI NFTVA, 'With the crusaders in the Holy Land: Allenby—the conqueror', 1917 · BFI NFTVA, 'General Allenby's entry into Jerusalem', Topical Budget, 23 Feb 1918 · BFI NFTVA, 'With Allenby in Palestine', 1918 · BFI NFTVA, documentary footage · BFI NFTVA, news footage · IWM FVA, 'General Allenby's entry into Jerusalem', Topical Film Company, 21 Feb 1915, IWM 13 · IWM FVA, 'Allenby in Cairo (1917)', Topical Film Company, 1917, IWM 14 · IWM FVA, actuality footage · IWM FVA, documentary footage | SOUND BL NSA, current affairs recordings · IWM SA
Likenesses E. Kennington, pastel, pubd 1926, NPG [*see illus.*] · photograph, IWM · photograph, repro. in *The Times*
Wealth at death £30,249 19*s*. 7*d*.: probate, 1936, resworn (n.d.)

Allenson, John (*d.* 1619), Church of England clergyman and literary editor, was born in Durham. He matriculated from Trinity College, Cambridge, in 1576, and the same year moved to St John's College as an Ashton scholar. He graduated BA in 1580, was ordained deacon at Durham on 22 May 1581, and proceeded MA in 1583. His puritan views, influenced greatly by his college tutor, William Whitaker (1548–1595), brought him into conflict with the ecclesiastical authorities in Cambridgeshire. In 1583 he was suspended from his first curacy at Barnwell, near Cambridge, having refused to subscribe to Whitgift's articles of religion. He was later suspended again—from the curacy of Horningsea, Cambridgeshire. In both cases it seems that he was singled out because of his puritan convictions. Despite these troubles, he continued to preach the gospel faithfully.

On 20 March 1584 Allenson was elected Lady Margaret fellow of St John's, and he subsequently held numerous college posts, including sacrist and senior bursar, from 1586 to 1595 under Whitaker's mastership. He proceeded DD in 1590. Following his mentor's death, he devoted himself to meticulously editing Whitaker's works. These consisted of several lectures on the papacy, and controversies concerning the church, councils, and the sacraments of the Lord's supper and baptism, many of them recorded first in note form by Allenson. The *Praelectiones ... G. Whitakeri* was published in Cambridge in 1599 and 1600; other editions of his works appeared in Hanover between 1604 and 1608. Allenson also edited a further treatise on the nature of original sin, published by John Ward in Frankfurt in 1624. A man of devout piety and firm Calvinism, his scholarly work helped nurture puritanism within Cambridge in the early seventeenth century.

In 1611 Allenson returned to his native county, where he was appointed rector of Whickham, near Newcastle upon Tyne. He remained there until his death in the latter part of 1619. He was buried in Whickham on 11 December 1619. ROGER N. McDERMOTT

Sources Venn, *Alum. Cant.* · B. Brook, *The lives of the puritans*, 3 vols. (1813), vol. 2, pp. 72–85; vol. 3, p. 513 · *DNB*

Allerton. For this title name *see* Jackson, William Lawies, first Baron Allerton (1840–1917).

Allestree, Richard (*b.* before **1582**, *d. c.*1643), almanac maker and mathematician, was a younger son of William Allestree (*b.* before 1520, *d.* 1581) and his wife, Ellen. The family lived at Alvaston and Derby. Richard was an uncle of the famous royalist divine Richard Allestree. William Allestree was five times MP for Derby between 1542 and 1555, and five times bailiff of Derby (1541–79). Well educated, with a good grasp of Latin, Richard practised and probably taught mathematics, including surveying. His work *The Arithmathematicall Treasurie* was entered in the Stationers' register in July 1650 but is otherwise unknown. He published a series of well-known almanacs between 1617 and 1643, calculated for Derby and sometimes Coventry (where his younger brother, James, was a goldsmith); two earlier editions, for 1615 and 1616, were not published. The almanacs included information on some local topics, such as Derby's annual fairs and its first mayor, and a woodcut of a quadrant to be cut out and pasted on a board for use as a simple surveying instrument.

Allestree had practised astrology for twenty years before compiling almanacs, but came to believe—'God opening mine eyes' (Bretnor, sig. A3*v*)—that it was essentially fraudulent. His almanacs reflect this view and have a pious, even puritan flavour, with numerous biblical citations and attacks on popish idolatry. He conceded that the stars had some influence as secondary causes, for instance by altering the balance of the four humours, but judged it ungodly and unlawful to seek to predict the future. He stressed instead the role of free will and of divine providence. While accepting astrology's value in physic, especially for deciding the best time to draw blood from patients, he dismissed as heathenish the notion that parts of the body were governed by different zodiacal signs, and he brushed aside the use of astrology in farming as superstitious. In 1618 Thomas Bretnor, the leading almanac maker of the time, poured scorn on so-called 'Christian Almanackes', an allusion to Allestree's works; Allestree responded in his edition for 1619, repudiating the ten extreme positions Bretnor had fathered on him but repeating his condemnation of judicial astrology. On astronomical matters Allestree was a traditionalist, mocking the ideas of Copernicus and Tycho Brahe. His friend Robert Woodford, who wrote admiring verses in many editions, may have been the well-known Northamptonshire puritan diarist, who had connections with Coventry. Allestree, who is not known to have married, probably died about 1643.   BERNARD CAPP

Sources B. S. Capp, *Astrology and the popular press: English almanacs, 1500–1800* (1979) · W. D. Pink, 'Allestry, of Alvaston, co. Derby', *The Genealogist*, new ser., 32 (1915–16), 164–9 · G. D. Squibb, ed., *The visitation of Derbyshire, begun in 1662*, Harleian Society, new ser., 8 (1989) · C. J. Black, 'William Allestry', HoP, *Commons* · Arber, *Regs. Stationers*, vol. 4 · E. G. R. Taylor, *The mathematical practitioners of Tudor and Stuart England* (1954) · T. Bretnor, *A new almanack and prognostication* (1618) · W. P. W. Phillimore, *Calendars of wills and administrations ... of the bishop of Lichfield and Coventry, 1516–1652*, British RS, 7 (1892)

Allestree, Richard (1621/2–1681), Church of England clergyman, was born at Uppington, near the Wrekin, Shropshire. His father, Richard Allestree, was steward to Sir Richard (afterwards Lord) Newport. According to the hagiographic biography of Allestree by his friend Bishop John Fell, the Allestree family was of ancient stock and had formerly been prosperous: Anthony Wood associates them with the Allestree family of Derby, one of whom, William (d. 1655), was recorder of Derby, and another, Richard, the author of several almanacs between 1617 and 1643. The younger Richard Allestree of Uppington was educated locally and then under Philemon Holland at the free school, Coventry. He matriculated from Christ Church, Oxford, on 17 February 1637 aged fifteen (hence the preference for 1621/2 as his date of birth—also given by Wood—rather than Fell's assertion of March 1619). His tutor was Richard Busby, and after six months Dean Samuel Fell, 'observing his parts and industry', made him a student of the house (Fell, sig. a2). Allestree graduated BA on 24 October 1640 and soon afterwards was chosen moderator in philosophy.

In 1642 Allestree joined the royalist troop raised in Oxford by Sir John Byron, and therefore he may have participated in the skirmish at Brackley in August. He did not, however, accompany Byron's troop when it later withdrew from the city and so was present to witness the

Richard Allestree (1621/2–1681), by David Loggan, pubd 1684

arrival of Viscount Saye and Sele's parliamentarian force and the attempt to intimidate the citizens and university. According to his later biographers Allestree distinguished himself by his daring at this juncture. Saye's troops were seizing the treasure of the colleges and had locked the valuables found in the deanery at Christ Church in a chamber. Allestree, who had a key to the chamber, secretly removed these spoils overnight and would have been punished had not the parliamentarian forces left to join the earl of Essex's army. Allestree joined the royalist army and was present at the battle of Kineton Field in October 1642. On his way back to Oxford he was seized by a parliamentarian force from Broughton House, but was released when that garrison surrendered to the royalists. He had returned to Christ Church by 29 October, when Charles I arrived in Oxford, and took up lodgings in the deanery. Allestree proceeded MA on 2 June 1643 but, according to Wood, he suffered a severe bout of the sickness, possibly a form of typhus, which swept through the crowded garrison city. Once he had recovered he apparently took up arms for the king again and may have been in military service until the end of the civil war. Fell's 'Life of Allestree' describes how he sought ordination when 'carnal weapons proved frustrate, and Divine providence call'd his servants to the more christian exercises of praiers and tears for the defence of the king and the church' (Fell, sig. bv). Allestree had a hand in the University of Oxford's decree against the solemn league and covenant. He became censor of Christ Church, and was apparently 'a noted tutor' (Wood, *Ath. Oxon.*, 3.1270). The parliamentary visitation of the university brought his academic career to an end. On 5 May 1648 he refused to submit to the authority of the visitors and was expelled from the university.

Fell states that after leaving the university Allestree became chaplain to Francis Newport and was sent to France to resolve the affairs of his father, Lord Newport, who had died in exile there. On his return he remained with the Newport family in Shropshire until the defeat of the royalists at the battle of Worcester. He then once again visited France, this time taking royalist dispatches to Charles Stuart at Rouen. On his return he established contact with John Dolben and John Fell, who, having been ejected from the university, were now living privately in Oxford. Allestree, Fell, and Dolben read the common prayer of the Church of England in private at the house, known as Beam Hall, of Dr Thomas Willis in Merton Street. A later account by one of the worshippers, Leoline Jenkins, suggested that about 300 episcopalians attended these services. Their practice was memorialized at the Restoration in a triple portrait of Allestree, Fell, and Dolben by Sir Peter Lely which is now at Christ Church. During the 1650s Allestree lived with Sir Anthony Cope of Hanwell, near Banbury, but he was also a royalist agent and travelled to and from the exiled court several times. In June 1659 he brought the verbal proposal from the king that new bishops should be consecrated, and by November he had a list of names to discuss with English sympathizers.

Predictably the restoration of the monarchy brought about a transformation of Allestree's position. From April 1660 he was petitioning for a canonry at Christ Church, on 27 July 1660 he was elected a canon, and on 31 July he was nominated by Dean Morley to act as his proxy while Morley was away in London and at court. On 3 October Allestree was created DD by royal mandate along with Fell and Dolben. They then assumed powerful positions within the University of Oxford. A jaundiced Anthony Wood accused the three divines of attempting 'to reduce the University to that condition as it stood in Laud's time' (*Life and Times*, 1.348–9). Allestree served as treasurer of Christ Church and his administrative skills helped the college restore its finances; he was a personal donor to the rebuilding. In 1663 he was appointed a chaplain-in-ordinary to the king, and that December he was elevated to the position of regius professor of divinity. On 10 August 1665 Allestree was appointed provost of Eton College, and he held this post alongside his chair. Allestree built the west side of the college's outer court at his own expense and is credited with restoring the institution's prosperity.

Allestree took his academic duties seriously. He applied himself to study and worked each night until 8 p.m. with the result, claimed Fell, that 'few of his time had either a greater compass or deeper insight into all parts of learning; the modern and learned languages, rhetoric, philosophy, mathematics, history, antiquity, moral and polemical divinity' (Fell, sig. c2v–d). As leader of the theology faculty Allestree was keen to maintain the tenor of the king's 1662 instructions to preachers to avoid abstruse and speculative doctrines which might excite controversy.

Harmony within the university, which was after all one of the Church of England's two seminaries, would strengthen the church against its enemies, the Roman Catholics, the dissenters, the Socinians, and the Hobbists. This is apparent in his routine preaching as recorded in student notebooks: he preached against the fashionable notions of the Hobbesians and virtuosi who cast doubt on the immortality of the soul. John Evelyn judged his sermon on Romans 6: 3 ('the necessity of those who are baptised to die to sin') as 'a very excellent discourse, from an excellent Preacher' (Evelyn, 4.61). Fell wrote that his sermons show a 'spirit of persuasive rhetoric and ardent piety, whereby tho' dead he yet speaketh' (Fell, sig. e2). As professor, Allestree took the chair in the divinity school during examinations and could intervene to prevent heterodoxy or contention. But this did not prevent him from subtly advancing his own theological outlook. At the 1661 act, for example, while Thomas Barlow, Lady Margaret professor, asserted the idolatrous nature of the Roman church, Allestree argued for a distinction to be drawn between the false Catholic belief in purgatory and the ancient practice of prayer for the dead.

Allestree's influence on the late seventeenth-century church may owe less to his preaching or his university lectures than to the series of moral and devotional works initiated by *The Whole Duty of Man* (1657). *The Whole Duty of Man* was intended to show 'the very meanest readers' how 'to behave themselves so in this world that they may be happy for ever in the next'. This best-selling manual's prescription of morality and effort was balanced by an emphasis on divine grace and devotional practice: the result was sober, orthodox, common-sense advice pitched at the level of ordinary Anglican parishioners. This was an anonymous work and although it rapidly won acclaim among Allestree's peers, its authorship remained a mystery. Gilbert Sheldon did not know the author's identity; Henry Hammond praised 'two excellent pieces … from an unknown hand' (Peck, 53), the *Whole Duty* and *The Gentleman's Calling* (1660). The latter was 'by the author of the *Whole Duty*' (*Correspondence of … Duppa and … Isham*, 175–6), but Bishop Duppa doubted that both works were by the same writer. The *Whole Duty* was a publishing sensation, and Timothy Garthwait, the bookseller who had purchased it 'from the Author upon Valuable consideration', took steps to prevent pirate editions in London and Dublin (Bodl. Oxf., MS Carte 45, fol. 144). A total of six further works in this vein appeared as by the author of the *Whole Duty* between 1660 and 1678 and all were collected as a single folio, *The Works of the Author of 'The Whole Duty of Man'*, published by Bishop Fell at Oxford in 1684. Many names were canvassed as the author, including Fell and Dorothy, Lady Pakington, but Allestree is by far the most likely candidate. This series shows that Allestree was no prisoner of the ivory tower and that his Arminian theology was easily translated into a rigorous yet optimistic practical Christianity.

Although Allestree adopted no overt political role his loyalty to church and state was beyond question: occasionally there were references to his being 'against all

Indulgence and Accomodation' towards the nonconformists (Keeble and Nuttall, 2.68). In a curious episode in 1679 Richard Baxter reproached him for repeating in the 1660s a libellous story that Baxter had killed a man in cold blood during the civil wars. Allestree admitted as much and asked Baxter's forgiveness. Allestree's mind was probably on higher things: in 1679 his poor health and failing eyesight led him to resign his chair; and in August 1680 his friend John Evelyn did not think he was likely to recover from a recent fall. On his deathbed Allestree had the offices of the church constantly read to him. He died on 28 January 1681 in London and was buried in Eton College chapel.

JOHN SPURR

Sources Bodl. Oxf., MS Carte 45, fol. 144 · letter of Allestree to Fell, 29 April 1675, BL, Add. MS 4275, fol. 4 · *The works of the author of 'The whole duty of man'* (1684) · R. Allestree, *Forty sermons* (1684) · J. Fell, 'Life of Allestree', in R. Allestree, *Forty sermons* (1684) · H. Cary, ed., *Memorials of the great civil war in England from 1646 to 1652*, 2 vols. (1842) · P. Barwick, *The life of … Dr John Barwick*, ed. and trans. H. Bedford (1724) · *The letter-book of John, Viscount Mordaunt, 1658–1660*, ed. M. Coate, CS, 3rd ser., 69 (1945) · P. Elmen, 'Richard Allestree and *The whole duty of man*', *The Library*, 5th ser., 6 (1951–2) · I. Green, *Print and protestantism in early modern England* (2000) · *Calendar of the correspondence of Richard Baxter*, ed. N. H. Keeble and G. F. Nuttall, 2 vols. (1991) · *Calamy rev.* · *Walker rev.* · *Hist. U. Oxf.* 4: *17th-cent. Oxf.* · Wood, *Ath. Oxon.*, new edn, vol. 3 · Wood, *Ath. Oxon.*: *Fasti* (1815) · Foster, *Alum. Oxon.* · M. Burrows, ed., *The register of the visitors of the University of Oxford, from AD 1647 to AD 1658*, CS, new ser., 29 (1881) · W. Kennett, *A register and chronicle ecclesiastical and civil* (1728) · *Fasti Angl.* (Hardy), vol. 2 · *Nineteen letters of the truly reverend and learned Dr Henry Hammond*, ed. F. Peck (1739), 53 · *The correspondence of Bishop Brian Duppa and Sir Justinian Isham, 1650–1660*, ed. G. Isham, Northamptonshire RS, 17 (1951) · Evelyn, *Diary* · *The life and times of Anthony Wood*, ed. A. Clark, 1, OHS, 19 (1891) · BL, Harley MS 6621, fols. 42, 53

Likenesses P. Lely, group portrait, oils, Christ Church Oxf. · D. Loggan, line engraving, BM, NPG; repro. in Allestree, *Forty sermons* [see illus.] · oils, Eton

Allestry, Jacob (1653–1686), poet, was the son of James Allestry (*d.* 1670), the eminent London bookseller and printer to the Royal Society. He entered Westminster School (as captain of the election) in 1667 and continued his education at Christ Church, Oxford, where he matriculated on 3 July 1672. He was appointed reader of the music speech at the 1679 act, and *terrae filius* in 1682. Both offices he performed to acclaim. He wrote several poems, contributing the main hand to the 'Verses and Pastoral' spoken in the Sheldonian Theatre on 21 May 1681, before James, duke of York. Both the 'Verses and Pastoral' and an unrelated poem, 'What art thou, love?', were later published in *Examen poeticum* (1693). Allestry failed to further the reputation he had acquired, however, and fell into a life of indulgence. Laid low with a venereal disease, he passed the last seven weeks of his life incognito in a house in Fish Row, in the St Thomas's parish of Oxford, tended by a nurse. He died there of that condition on 15 October 1686 and was buried in the churchyard of St Thomas's the following day.

A. H. BULLEN, rev. JONATHAN PRITCHARD

Sources Wood, *Ath. Oxon.*, new edn, 4.202 · *The life and times of Anthony Wood*, ed. A. Clark, 2, OHS, 21 (1892), 490, 564; 3, OHS, 26 (1894), 24, 51–2, 198 · *Old Westminsters*, 1.14 · J. Welch, *The list of the queen's scholars of St Peter's College, Westminster*, ed. [C. B. Phillimore], new edn (1852), 163, 172, 532 · R. A. Beddard, 'Tory Oxford', *Hist. U. Oxf.* 4: *17th-cent. Oxf.*, 863–906 · H. R. Plomer and others, *A dictionary of the booksellers and printers who were at work in England, Scotland, and Ireland from 1641 to 1667* (1907), 2–3

Alley, William (1510/11–1570), bishop of Exeter, entered Eton College as a scholar from High Wycombe, Buckinghamshire, about 1524, and proceeded to King's College, Cambridge, where he was admitted a scholar on 12 August 1528, aged seventeen, and a fellow in 1530. He graduated BA early in 1533 and vacated his fellowship in 1534 on being ordained deacon, and probably also priest—presumably to take up an ecclesiastical post. At this time or later he acquired a mastery of Greek and Hebrew and a knowledge of theology which led him towards protestantism, but little is recorded about his life for the next twenty-five years. By 1544 he had proceeded MA, but from which university is unknown. The Exeter historian John Hooker, who knew him well during the 1560s, states that he took advantage of the permission for priests to marry, granted in 1549, and consequently had to abandon his vocation when clergy marriages were again forbidden in 1553. Alley's wife, Sybil, is said to have been of the Honacott family of Landkey, north Devon, which suggests that he may be identical with the William Alle who was instituted to the rectory of Oakford, also in north Devon, in 1544, and vacated it in 1554. Hooker goes on to say that, during the restoration of Catholicism under Queen Mary (1553–8):

> he travelled from place to place in the North countrie, where he was not knowne, and sometimes by practising of phisick, and sometimes by teaching of scholars, he picked out a poore living for himself and his wife, and so continued, being not knowne to have beene a preest. (Hooker, *Catalog*, sig. I.iiv)

Alley came to prominence in his late forties, following Mary's death. He was admitted to a canonry of St Paul's Cathedral, London, on 1 January 1559, with the prebend of Pancratius, and subsequently acted as reader in divinity at the cathedral at the invitation of the new bishop of London, Edmund Grindal. In February 1560 he gave a series of lectures there on the first epistle of Peter, which were later incorporated into his published work and in which he advocated conformity to the ceremonies practised in whatever church a worshipper happened to attend. In the following month he was nominated by the crown to be bishop of Exeter in place of James Turberville, who had been deprived in the previous summer. This nomination may have been influenced by his Devon connections, but Alley's reputation as a preacher is indicated by the report of the London diarist Henry Machyn that he preached at court on 2 April against blasphemy, dice, women, and drunkenness, as well as delivering three funeral sermons in the capital between June and August. He was elected bishop by the chapter of Exeter Cathedral on 21 May, received the royal assent on 8 June, was consecrated on 14 July, and was given the temporalities of the see on 26 August. On 11 November 1561 he was admitted to the degree of DD at Oxford.

Religious conservatism in the diocese of Exeter had led

to the western rebellion of 1549, and Alley faced potential opposition as a protestant bishop—having been preceded in this respect only by Miles Coverdale, who had briefly presided in 1551–3. Perhaps for this reason he was accompanied to Exeter in the summer of 1560 by the earl of Bedford, the chief protestant magnate in Devon. Hooker alleges that Alley was sometimes 'so despitefully dealt with' that two sympathetic local gentry, Sir Gawen and Sir Peter Carew, 'guarded him and brought him to the pulpit sundry times, and there countenanced and supported him against his adversaries' (Hooker, *Sir Peter Carew*, 111–12). He was also hampered by the decline in the bishop's income caused by surrenders of property during the Reformation, and complained in 1565 that his revenue was no more than £300 net. Notwithstanding these difficulties, he was an active bishop. He served as a justice of the peace in Devon in 1562, 1564, and 1569, and in Cornwall in 1564, although his attempt to exercise his powers in Exeter itself was firmly resisted by the city council. In 1560 he returned a list of all his clergy to Archbishop Matthew Parker, who had requested details of their scholarly attainments, marital status, and preaching abilities; his report survives in the library of Corpus Christi College, Cambridge, in MS 97. The records of his ordinations of clergy, preserved in his episcopal register, show that he resided in Devon for most of his episcopate, normally in the bishop's palace at Exeter except for periods in 1562 and 1564, when he was based at Honiton. In the summer of 1565 he travelled to Cornwall, visiting Budock, Truro, and Egloshayle, and in the following year to north Devon. In the summer of 1569 he was again in Cornwall, at Budock, Lostwithiel, and Mount Edgecumbe, as well as at Chawleigh and Plympton in Devon, and he visited Launceston as late as March 1570, when he was, in Hooker's words, 'somwhat grosse and his bodie full of humors' (Hooker, *Catalog*, sig. K.ir).

Alley was active in the Canterbury convocation which met in London in 1563, contributing one of the discussion papers outlining proposals to enhance discipline and clarify doctrine. Deploring controversy over 'adiophorus' matters—issues he regarded as of secondary importance—he called for such measures as an ambiguous credal statement on Christ's descent into hell, a ruling on compulsory vestments, more effective episcopal authority over penitents, excommunicates, criminals, simoniacs, and witches, and provision for godly preachers where they were lacking. In this official setting his programme fared no better than the others: the government implemented none of them. He also encouraged the clergy of his diocese to hold 'prophesyings'—organized religious discussions—and is said by his successor, William Bradbridge, to have taken trouble 'to travail in the work himself' (Collinson, 237).

Alley's scholarship exceeded that of most of his predecessors at Exeter. Hooker regarded him as 'well learned universallie, but his cheefe studie and profession was in divinitie and in the tongs' (Hooker, *Catalog*, sig. K.i), and asserts that he preached regularly on holy days, as well as

giving divinity lectures on weekdays. His chief publication, *Ptōchomuseion*, subtitled 'The poore mans librarie', was issued in London by John Day in two volumes in 1565 and reissued in 1571. It is a wide-ranging encyclopaedia of theology with linguistic and historical notes, based on his lectures of 1560 with copious additions, and dedicated to the earl of Bedford. Alley compiled a Hebrew grammar which he wished but failed to publish, and a short 'Judgment concerning the doctrine and discipline of the church'. He also revised the translation of the book of Deuteronomy for the Bishops' Bible of 1568. Hooker, who gives a warm and affectionate account of his character, described him as:

> loth to offend, readie to forgive, void of malice, full of love, bountifull in hospitalitie, liberall to the poore, and a succourer of the needie, faithful to his freend, and courteous to all men; a hater of covetousness, and an enimie to all evill and wicked men, and lived an honest, a godlie, and vertuous life. (ibid.)

He conceded, however, that the bishop might appear on first acquaintance to be both rough and austere, and could be credulous and hasty.

Alley's will, a brief document, was made on 1 April 1570. He bequeathed his divinity books to his son Roger, his books of philosophy and physic to his son-in-law Christopher Bodlegh, and his books of humanity (Latin or Greek) to his younger sons, who were apparently still receiving their education. He had himself promoted Roger to be archdeacon of Cornwall and Christopher to a canonry of Exeter Cathedral; another son or relative, Matthew Alley, was briefly vicar of Talland, Cornwall. The bishop left the residue of his goods to his wife, Sybil, whom he made his executor, subject to the supervision of the two Carews. She later married Richard Dillon of Chumhill in Bratton Fleming, north Devon. Hooker, a well-informed witness, twice states that Alley died on 1 April 1570. The date usually given, 15 April, comes from a later account of the Latin inscription (now illegible) on his monument in Exeter Cathedral, and cannot be true since Alley's will was proved on 12 April. The monument, a ledger stone, originally lay in the middle of the cathedral choir, 10 yards west of the high altar, but is now said to lie in the north choir aisle.

NICHOLAS ORME

Sources J. Hooker [J. Vowell], *A catalog of the bishops of Excester* (1584), sigs. I.iiv.–K.ir • Emden, *Oxf.* • episcopal register, Devon RO, Chanter XVIII–XIX • Venn, *Alum. Cant.* • *Report on the Pepys manuscripts*, HMC, 70 (1911), 50 • J. Hooker, annals of Exeter, Devon RO, Exeter city archives, book 51, fol. 353r • J. Hooker, *The life and times of Sir Peter Carew, kt.*, ed. J. Maclean (1857), 111–12 • J. Strype, *Annals of the Reformation and establishment of religion … during Queen Elizabeth's happy reign*, new edn, 4 vols. (1824), vol. 1/1, pp. 518–22 • W. P. Haugaard, *Elizabeth I and the English Reformation* (1968) • P. Collinson, *Archbishop Grindal, 1519–1583: the struggle for a reformed church* (1979) • V. Hope, 'Exeter Cathedral monumentarium', Exeter Cathedral Library, MS 1956 • *Correspondence of Matthew Parker*, ed. J. Bruce and T. T. Perowne, Parker Society, 42 (1853) • *The diary of Henry Machyn, citizen and merchant-taylor of London, from AD 1550 to AD 1563*, ed. J. G. Nichols, CS, 42 (1848), 230–41 • T. Westcote, *A view of Devonshire in MDXXX*, ed. G. Oliver and P. Jones (1845), 549 • D. J. Crankshaw, 'Preparations for the Canterbury provincial convocation of 1562–

63: a question of attribution', *Belief and practice in Reformation England: a tribute to Patrick Collinson from his students*, ed. S. Wabuda and C. Litzenberger (1998), 60–93
Archives Devon RO, episcopal register, Chanter XVIII–XIX

Alleyn, Edward (1566–1626), actor, theatre entrepreneur, and founder of Dulwich College, was born on 1 September 1566 in the London parish of St Botolph without Bishopsgate, 'near Devonshire House, where now is the sign of the Pye'. He was baptized the following day in the parish church, the son of Edward Alleyn (d. 1570), originally of Willen, Buckinghamshire, and Margaret Townley, who claimed descent from the family of that name of Townley, Lancashire. The Alleyn family's coat of arms consisted of a chevron between three cinquefoils gules. At some time before 1566 Alleyn's father migrated to London and purchased an inn in Bishopsgate. However, he came to hold a variety of posts at court and in local circles; in 1567 he was identified as porter to the queen. He also served for a time as head of Bethlem Hospital, which was located near the family inn. The date of his marriage is unknown but he and his wife had five sons (John, Edward, William, Oliver, and Percival), two of whom (John and Edward) lived into adulthood. In 1570, after a brief illness, he died, and was buried on 13 September. He left a brief will, in which he bequeathed everything to his wife. Although there is no inventory extant his legacy was probably substantial; in addition to the inn he held leases to prime properties in the Bishopsgate district that he had gained through his association with Bethlem Hospital (Cerasano, 'Edward Alleyn's early years', 237–8).

On 20 January 1571 Margaret Alleyn married Richard Christopher, alias Grove, at St Botolph without Bishopsgate, whereupon Christopher moved into his wife's house, probably to manage the inn. They had one child, a son, who did not live into adulthood, and seven and a half years into the marriage Christopher died. On 21 October 1579 Margaret entered into her third marriage, with John Browne, a haberdasher. Thus by the time that Edward turned thirteen years of age he would have known his natural father and two stepfathers. It is impossible to determine the success of the third marriage but it is clear that within the first few years Alleyn's brother John was in litigation with Browne. Browne claimed that certain leases to the Bethlem properties that had been acquired by Edward Alleyn senior had been stolen from the family home during the time that Margaret was married to Richard Christopher. Hence Browne went to court in order to recover the property from John Alleyn, who, he thought, was the thief. During the proceedings John concocted an elaborate explanation, claiming that his mother (who was illiterate) and his first stepfather had transferred the properties to him to clear a debt. Browne's claims seem never to have come to anything and John Alleyn later sold the leases to his brother Edward (Cerasano, 'Edward Alleyn's early years', 238–9).

Actor and businessman, 1583–1600 Alleyn was a silent presence in the early life of his family but by 1583, at the age of seventeen, he was performing with the Earl of Worcester's Men, a company that made its reputation

Edward Alleyn (1566–1626), by unknown artist

through provincial touring. From several documentary sources it is clear that John Alleyn helped to shape his younger brother's career. By 1580 John, then 'servant to the Lord Sheffield', was already a player, and in 1589 he was identified as 'servant to the Lord Admiral' (Chambers, 2.298–9). By this time, in addition to his interests in performing, John had also made a foray into theatrical investing. During the same year the Alleyn brothers, along with the player Robert Browne (not a relative of their stepfather), purchased 'playing apparel, playbooks, instruments, and other commodities', probably to furnish their company. Within the year John was serving as manager and leader of the Admiral's Men. In this capacity he is known to have gone to the Theatre (built by James Burbage in 1576) to collect money from its owner (Warner, 2–4).

By January 1592 Edward Alleyn was established as an actor; for an indeterminate time he acted with Lord Strange's Men, performing at the Rose Playhouse, which was owned by Philip *Henslowe, a dyer. By the autumn of 1592 he had begun to form a business partnership with Henslowe, whose stepdaughter Joan Woodward (d. 1623) he married on 22 October. Two years later he had achieved celebrity status on the London stage, by which time he was leader of the Admiral's Men, one of the two prominent London troupes and the primary competition for the Lord Chamberlain's Men, the company with which Shakespeare acted and for which he composed his early plays. Doubtless Alleyn performed many roles during his apprenticeship years but these have been lost to time. Therefore his best-known roles were those of the early 1590s, most of them found in Christopher Marlowe's plays. He played the thundering conqueror Tamburlaine

(*Tamburlaine the Great*), Doctor Faustus (in the play of the same name), and perhaps Barabas in *The Jew of Malta*. In addition he probably performed King Edgar (*A Knack to Know a Knave*), Orlando in Robert Greene's *Orlando Furioso*, Muly Mahamet (*The Battle of Alcazar*), Cutlack (*Cutlack the Dane*), Sebastian (*Frederick and Basilea*), and Tamar Cam in *1 Tamar Cam* (Chambers, 2.297–8). From contemporary comments and extant playbooks it would appear that Alleyn excelled in majestic roles and that some playwrights who worked with the Admiral's Men might well have written roles specifically with him in mind. Predictably he was most frequently compared with Richard Burbage, the lead actor in Shakespeare's troupe, though it would appear that the two actors had very different stage personalities. Ben Jonson, who worked with Alleyn's company in the late 1590s, stated that he should be remembered for all time because he lent eternity to the work of so many dramatists through his acting. But despite many enthusiastic descriptions of him as a performer theatre historians have little sense of the specifics of his style. Nevertheless he was apparently a man of exceptional physical stature, with a strong voice to match his size. These attributes, commentators implied, helped to create those roles in which he excelled (Cerasano, 'Tamburlaine', 171–9).

The 1590s also mark a period of domestic success for Alleyn. The marriage to Joan Woodward was apparently a good one. Several letters written by her to Edward while the latter was on tour attest to the closeness of their bond, and letters from Alleyn to her, addressing her as 'my good sweetheart and loving mouse', would suggest that the partnership was at least affectionate. Letters from Philip Henslowe to Alleyn written during the same period discuss both domestic matters and the business partnership that the two had formed. Several of the letters concern the spread of the plague in London, assuring Alleyn that the family was safe and well. One includes the sad news that a fellow actor's wife and family were plague victims: 'Robert Browne's wife in Shoreditch & all her children & household be dead & her doors shut up' (*Henslowe Papers*, 34–41).

From Henslowe's account book of the Rose Playhouse (commonly referred to as his diary) it would appear that he and Alleyn ran the theatre as a shared partnership. Alleyn presumably earned his share of the profits primarily from his work on stage; however, he also co-signed loans to, and for, the company, authorized the purchase of playbooks and costumes, witnessed loans for ready money advanced to individual players, and occasionally sold his own copies of playbooks to the company (*Henslowe's Diary*, 8, 32, 43, 49, 72–4).

1597 has been traditionally thought to be the year in which Alleyn retired from the stage. Historians have thought that at this point he took time away from playing in order to manage theatrical and other investments. It was, from all available evidence, a planned leave, during which time he performed specific duties, primarily associated with revivifying political alliances that he hoped would assist him in acquiring the court-appointed position of master of the bears, bulls, and mastiff dogs, an attractive position that was especially lucrative in London, as well as one concerned with certain court entertainments (Cerasano, 'Edward Alleyn's "retirement"', 98–112). By this time he was thoroughly an entrepreneur who, with his father-in-law, planned his investment strategies carefully. In the following decade he left playing entirely and became absorbed in the life of the court and in local politics.

In 1598 Alleyn and Henslowe made concrete plans to gain the mastership of the bears but it passed to someone else. When the office next became vacant they tried for it again but they were passed over in favour of Sir William Stewart, a friend of the new king. Finally, in 1604, they purchased the patent from Stewart and together held a joint patent for the office until 1616, when Henslowe died and his share passed to his son-in-law (Cerasano, 'The master of the bears', 195–209). Also in 1604 Alleyn played the part of the Genius of the City in the 'Magnificent Entertainment' presented to King James in the course of his formal passage through London. The patronage of his company had then passed to James's son, Prince Henry, and Alleyn—though not necessarily performing as an actor during these years—was frequently described as 'servant to the prince' right up until 1612, just before the prince's death.

The Fortune Playhouse, 1600 During the late 1590s Alleyn and Henslowe decided to build a new playhouse north of London Wall, in the parish of St Giles Cripplegate. The Rose was then thirteen years old and in need of repair, and the move to a new location gave the investors an opportunity to capitalize on a new market. The parish was well known to Alleyn, who regularly donated to poor relief there, and the parish in which he was born and raised was located not far to the east. On 8 January 1600 the men signed a contract for the new theatre with Peter Street, formerly master of the London Carpenters' Company, and construction began immediately. Soon afterwards local justices of the peace attempted to stay the construction, but Alleyn and Henslowe were confident that their political patrons would support them—and they judged accurately. On 12 January Charles Howard, then lord admiral and patron of Alleyn's playing company, issued a warrant offering his support for the playhouse and citing Alleyn's and his company's holiday entertainments for the queen. Shortly thereafter local inhabitants wrote to the privy council, reminding them of Alleyn's financial generosity towards the parish. Yet apparently the justices' resistance continued. On 8 April members of the privy council intervened by issuing their own warrant, again reminding the justices that 'her Majesty … [was] well pleased heretofore at times of recreation with the services of Edward Alleyn and his company' (*Henslowe Papers*, 49–52). The Fortune was finished by late summer and Alleyn returned to the stage, temporarily, in order to launch the new enterprise (*Henslowe's Diary*, 137). The Fortune seems to have found immediate success. It was known for its repertory of comedies, written by popular playwrights such as Thomas Dekker, and for its talented, experienced acting company, the Admiral's Men. John Chamberlain dubbed the theatre 'the fairest playhouse in this town'. Though some historians conclude that it was leased over to the company upon Henslowe's death it is clear that Alleyn was making a sizeable profit by renting the lease as late as 1618. The original playhouse was in operation for twenty-one years, until 9 December 1621, when it burnt down. In his diary Alleyn wrote: 'this night at 12 of the clock the Fortune was burnt' (Warner, 190). He built a second Fortune almost immediately, on the same site, in brick.

Entrepreneur, patron, and legacy builder, 1617–1626 With changing dramatic tastes and many players and playwrights retiring or dying, the conditions in the theatre began to change. Yet Alleyn continued to be effective in promoting his theatre and his bear-baiting business, which brought in a small fortune. In addition to his official duties he seems to have been called in occasionally to advise upon royal entertainments; he moved the baiting to court regularly, for special occasions, and he also baited lions before the king at the Tower of London. Upon the death of Philip Henslowe, in 1616, he became involved in a series of lawsuits in which Henslowe's nephew attempted to gain control of part of his uncle's estate. The conflict was waged in two courts and the precise outcome is uncertain. However, several deponents argued that Alleyn had been the prime mover in bringing all of his enterprises to their affluence, and virtually all of the deponents stated that the estate was meant to pass to Alleyn, which it did. Additionally Alleyn became involved in the construction of a private playhouse in the Blackfriars, near to Puddle Wharf. From its inception the investment presented a great risk, owing to the sad state of the property itself; also the residents of the Blackfriars were opposed to local entertainment, which, they argued, would bring daily annoyances and objectionable persons to the area. In the end, with the playhouse virtually complete, Alleyn was prohibited from opening its doors. He sued the owner of the property to regain his initial investment and won the case but, lacking the support of his most powerful political allies, he never got the private playhouse in the Blackfriars that he had wanted (Cerasano, 'Competition for the King's Men?', 173–86).

Other set-backs occurred. On 28 June 1623 Joan Alleyn died; she was buried in the chapel of the 'hospital', now Dulwich College, endowed four years earlier by Alleyn for twelve poor scholars and twelve poor pensioners. The impulse for this foundation had come from a variety of factors: Alleyn's childlessness; the current vogue for building such foundations, exemplified by such patrons as Thomas Sutton (who built Sutton's Hospital, that is, Charterhouse, in 1611); and the driving impulse to achieve fame and build a monumental legacy that seemed to be one of Alleyn's defining traits throughout his life. He had purchased the manor of Dulwich in 1605; the bargain was completed in late spring the next year and the entire estate passed into his hands in 1614. In May 1613 the physical construction of the college had begun (Alleyn having moved to Dulwich from his former house in Southwark) and in September 1616 the college chapel was consecrated by George Abbot, archbishop of Canterbury. Then, in 1618,

Alleyn encountered opposition from Francis Bacon, then lord chancellor, who attempted to stay the patent for the institution because he opposed the transfer of personal fortunes to foundations. Bacon commented: 'hospitals abound, and beggars abound never a whit less.' But Alleyn was not one to be easily beaten down. After almost a year of politicking he managed to convince Bacon to change his mind, and on 13 September 1619 he read the deed of foundation and statutes in the college. Distinguished statesmen attended the event, including Francis Bacon, Inigo Jones (the king's surveyor), Thomas Howard, earl of Arundel, Sir Thomas Grimes, John Finch (later lord keeper), and Sir John Bodley (Warner, 181–2).

Final days On 3 December 1623 Alleyn married, as his second wife, Constance, daughter of John *Donne, poet and dean of St Paul's Cathedral. Despite her relative youth the couple had no children, and Alleyn lived only another three years. During the autumn of 1626 Alleyn—who seems to have become ill earlier in the year during a journey to visit his property in Simonstone, York—weakened. He managed to return to Dulwich but by 13 November his condition was so precarious that he dictated his will. He died on 25 November 1626 and was buried two days later in the college chapel, just two months after his sixtieth birthday. Among his final wishes he ordered his executors to build ten almshouses in the parishes of St Saviour's Southwark and St Botolph without Bishopsgate, where he had spent much of his personal and professional life. (He had also served in local church government as vestryman, in 1607, and as auditor of token books, in 1608, at St Saviour's.) His widow received £100 and her jewels in addition to the exact sum of £1500 that was the totality of what Alleyn and Donne had settled upon when the couple married. Constance Alleyn went on to marry the Revd Samuel Harvey, of Abury Hatch, Essex. There is no known portrait of Constance; a full-length portrait of Alleyn (date of composition unknown) shows him in a pose typical of period fashion—wearing a long gown and holding a glove, which he has removed to show his signet ring. Both the ring and the portrait are held by Dulwich College (Cerasano, 'Tamburlaine', 171–9). A portrait of Joan Alleyn, also the property of Dulwich College, shows a well-to-do woman with gloves and Bible, wearing a hat. She—whom Alleyn referred to as his 'mouse'—seems aptly depicted.

In later life Alleyn's property holdings and his accumulated wealth were substantial, and this passed on to his foundation, which was formally called the College of God's Gift at Dulwich. Among Alleyn's material holdings were some books and pictures and the stave that he carried as master of the bears. Despite his worldly success he died still hoping for 'some further dignity', but he never was granted a knighthood, perhaps because of his earlier involvement in the theatre. In fact, at various times during his life he seemed to be forced into rationalizing his earlier professional involvement in the theatre. When, for instance, Sir Francis Calton had second thoughts about having sold the Dulwich properties to Alleyn the latter defended himself:

That I was a player I cannot deny; and I am sure I will not. My means of living were honest, and with the poor abilities wherewith God blessed me I was able to do something for myself, my relatives, and my friends. (Collier, 143–6)

Nevertheless regardless of Calton's poor opinion of him Alleyn managed to build an impressive legacy of friends and social contacts. The doors of many aristocrats and highly placed men of government were open to him, and most of his contemporaries thought of him as a generous, affable, God-fearing individual. In addition to those who identified him as the 'Roscius of his age' Alleyn was most often identified as the master of the bears and, alternatively, as the founder of Dulwich College. William Alexander, earl of Stirling, called him his 'deservedly honoured friend' and memorialized him in verse, praising him beyond those who were 'great by bulk or chance'. For Alexander, Fortune saw fit to reward Alleyn for his virtue.

S. P. CERASANO

Sources G. F. Warner, ed., Catalogue of the manuscripts and muniments of Alleyn's College of God's Gift at Dulwich (1881) · DNB · W. W. Greg, Henslowe papers: being documents supplementary to Henslowe's diary (1907) · Henslowe's diary, ed. R. A. Foakes and R. T. Rickert (1961) · E. K. Chambers, The Elizabethan stage, 4 vols. (1923) · S. P. Cerasano, 'Cheerful givers: Henslowe, Alleyn and the 1612 loan book to the crown', Shakespeare Studies, 28 (2000), 215–19 · S. P. Cerasano, 'Competition for the King's Men? Alleyn's Blackfriars venture', Medieval and Renaissance Drama in England, 4 (1989), 173–86 · S. P. Cerasano, 'Edward Alleyn's early years: his life and family', N&Q, 232 (1987), 237–43 · S. P. Cerasano, 'Edward Alleyn's "retirement", 1597–1600', Medieval and Renaissance Drama in England, 10 (1998), 98–112 · S. P. Cerasano, 'More on Edward Alleyn's "Shakespearean" portrait of Richard III', Shakespeare Quarterly, 33 (1982), 342–4 · S. P. Cerasano, 'Tamburlaine and Edward Alleyn's ring', Shakespeare Survey, 47 (1994), 171–9 · S. P. Cerasano, 'The master of the bears in art and enterprise', Medieval and Renaissance Drama in England, 5 (1991), 195–209 · J. Briley, 'Edward Alleyn and Henslowe's will', Shakespeare Quarterly, 9 (1958), 321–30 · will and related documents, PRO, PROB 11/150, sig. 146; PROB 10/443 · W. Rendle, 'Edward Alleyne', The Genealogist, new ser., 2 (1885), 241–55 · J. P. Collier, Memoirs of Edward Alleyn (1841) · J. P. Collier, The Alleyn papers (1843) · parish register, St Botolph without Bishopsgate, 2 Sept 1566 [baptism]

Archives Dulwich College, London, corresp., diary, and memorandum book | Dulwich College, London, Henslowe MSS

Likenesses oils, Dulwich Picture Gallery, London [see illus.]

Wealth at death see administration, PRO, PROB 10/443; will, PRO, PROB 11/150, sig. 146

Alleyne, Sir John Gay, first baronet (1724–1801), planter and politician, was born in the parish of St James, Barbados, on 28 April 1724, the second (but only surviving) son of John Alleyne (1695–1730), of Four Hills, Barbados, and his wife, Mary (d. 1742), the daughter of William Terrill of Cabbage Tree Hall, Barbados. He was the great-great-grandson of Reynold Allen or Alleyne (1609–1651), originally from Kent, who was a landowner in Barbados by 1638, and who was killed assisting the forces sent to Barbados in 1651 to secure the island's adherence to the authority of the Commonwealth. Over the several generations they had lived in the island, the Alleynes had intermarried with other planter families and acquired considerable wealth. They also had influential connections in Britain: one of John Gay Alleyne's sisters, Mary (1721–1742), married in 1740 Charles *Knowles (d. 1777), later governor of Jamaica,

a baronet, and rear-admiral, while another, Rebecca (1725–1764), married in 1754 William Bouverie, second Viscount Folkestone (later, from 1765, first earl of Radnor). On his father's death Alleyne inherited the Barbadian plantations of Four Hills, Bawdens, and Skeets, and on his mother's death a 'place in Gloucestershire called Langley and all the rest and residue of her estate' (Allen, 3.158). On 19 October 1746, at St James's, Barbados, he married Christian (d. 1782), the fourth daughter of Joseph Dottin of Black Rock and St Nicholas plantations, Barbados, and his wife, Anne, the daughter and heir of Major Edward Jordan of Black Rock. They had one son, Gay (bap. 20 April 1747), who died young.

His wealth and position ensured Alleyne a role in the political life of his native island. Although he seems to have spent almost all his life in Barbados, and there is no indication of where (if at all) he had any formal education, his 'great talents and extensive erudition' (Poyer, 338) certainly included wide reading in both English constitutional law and more general literature. He was first elected to the house of assembly of Barbados in 1757, as one of the members for the parish of St Andrew, where he owned the plantations Bawdens and The River (as well as other property elsewhere in the island). With the exception of the session of 1771–2, when he was out of the island, he was re-elected as a member for St Andrew, and from 1767 was chosen as speaker of the house for every annual session, until his resignation in 1797.

There can be no doubt of Alleyne's loyalty to the crown and to British sovereignty over Barbados, but it was as a specifically Barbadian patriot that he was long remembered in the island. This aspect of his career emerged in 1760, when he published A defence of the conduct of Barbadoes, during the late expedition to Martinique and Guadeloupe, in a letter to the Right Hon. Gen. Barrington. This was a response to a pamphlet published the previous year by Richard Gardiner, a captain in the marines. Alleyne vigorously refuted Gardiner's suggestions that Barbados had been less than enthusiastic in its support for Britain in its conflict with France in the Caribbean. Although his own pamphlet was published anonymously, described only (on the title-page) as 'By a Native, Resident in the Island', Alleyne's authorship was known, and he was formally thanked by the house of assembly.

On his election as speaker of the house of assembly in 1767, Alleyne was the first holder of that office to claim formally from the local representative of the crown the privileges traditionally claimed by the House of Commons in Britain, and more recently claimed as a right by the house of assembly of Jamaica. These were:

first, Security to their Persons and Servants from all Arrests and other Disturbances that might obstruct their regular Attendance on the House: Secondly, Freedom of Speech in their Assembly; and lastly, a free Access, at all Times, to the Representative of the Crown. (Alleyne, Remarks, 41)

Alleyne persuaded the house to agree to his making the claim, and Samuel Rous, the senior member of the island's council and the crown's representative in the interval between two governors, who had been fore-warned by Alleyne of his intentions, was happy to concur. Thereafter, the claim of privileges became a regular feature of each annually elected assembly. Alleyne's standing in Barbados was recognized by the crown when he was created a baronet on 8 April 1769.

In 1768 there was published in London *A short history of Barbados, from its first discovery and settlement, to the end of the year 1767*. This was anonymous, but it was known in Barbados to be the work of Henry Frere, a prominent member of the council. Frere belittled the claim of privileges, suggesting that they were pointless, or possibly even pernicious—the claim of freedom from arrest, he alleged, might easily be used to defraud lawful creditors. The same year there appeared in Barbados a pamphlet (soon afterwards reprinted in London) of *Remarks upon a book, intitled, A short history of Barbados: in which the partial and unfair representations of the author upon the subjects of his history in general, and upon that of the demand of privileges in particular, are detected and exposed*. The *Remarks* were anonymous, but Alleyne's authorship was easily discerned. He accused Frere of being a servile copyist, of falling into various errors of fact, of short-changing the reading public by the ludicrous brevity of his work, and, above all, of seeking 'to inculcate a Doctrine of the most abject and undistinguishing Submission to our Governors, by discouraging every Effort of Liberty, if it take the Form of Opposition, in the Representatives of the People' (Alleyne, *Remarks*, 7). In a second edition of his *History*, which was only slightly revised and largely ignored the *Remarks*, Frere dismissed them as 'written with the peevishness of a child, whose play-things have been disturbed' (Frere, new edn, xi). Alleyne gave some justification for this, but the *Remarks* nevertheless demonstrated that the claim for privileges was founded upon ample precedent, and that the often arbitrary conduct of earlier governors of Barbados suggested that they might indeed be a useful bastion against tyranny. The *Remarks* led to a duel between Frere and Alleyne, which ended without bloodshed but left a lasting enmity between the two 'literary antagonists' (Poyer, 340).

Alleyne proved a most active speaker in other ways. Contrary to precedent, he secured the acquiescence of the house in his claim to speak and vote on any matter, like any other member, while presiding over their deliberations. Those of his interventions singled out by John Poyer in *The History of Barbados* display occasional inconsistencies, but are distinguished by a concern for strict financial probity in public affairs (even on occasions when this worked to his own disadvantage), for the avoidance of all extravagance in public expenditure during what he considered to be the island's declining fortunes, and for the preservation of the rights of the house of assembly, particularly where these concerned control of the public purse, against real or imagined encroachments by the council or the governor. Nevertheless, about 1783, following the removal of a particularly obnoxious governor (James Cunninghame), Alleyne appears to have got his brother-in-law Lord Radnor to try to persuade the British

authorities that Alleyne himself was the ideal candidate for the vacant position. People born in the Caribbean were not often appointed to governorships in the eighteenth century, particularly in their own territories, and the application was unsuccessful.

Alleyne's first wife died in 1782, but he retained a life interest in her plantation of St Nicholas, where he may have been responsible for the great house, later called St Nicholas Abbey, modelled after an English manor house of the seventeenth century, and the only house of its type in Barbados. On 29 June 1786, at St James's, Barbados, he married his cousin Jane Abel (1765–1806), the daughter of Abel Alleyne MD, of Mount Standfast, Barbados, and his wife, Jane Skeet. They had two sons and five daughters. The elder son, John Gay Newton Alleyne (1787–1800), died while a schoolboy at Eton College, and it was the second son, Reynold Abel Alleyne (1789–1870), who succeeded to the baronetcy.

Alleyne resigned as speaker of the house of assembly on 11 July 1797 on the grounds of ill health, having already obtained leave of absence from the house for the remainder of its session. He travelled to England in the hope that a change of climate might improve his condition, and there made his will, dated from Albemarle Street, Westminster, on 13 October 1798. His health did not recover, and he returned to Barbados, where he died; he was buried in St James's, Barbados, on 7 December 1801.

Alleyne's work as speaker led Poyer to call him 'the venerable patriot' (Poyer, 348, 648) who was 'uniformly the noble, erect and zealous assertor of the rights of the people' (ibid., 440). This view of him remained traditional in Barbados well into the second half of the twentieth century, with his defence of the rights of the assembly being seen as an important step in the progress of Barbados to democracy. More recent opinion has tended to emphasize the fact that, while he might have referred to the assembly as the 'representative Body of a free People' (Alleyne, *Remarks*, 70), it was in his day (whatever it became two centuries later) representative only of an oligarchy based on class and race, and that its main function was the preservation of the system of plantation slavery on which the property of its members was based. In a Barbados three-quarters of whose population consisted of black slaves, the 'free People' to whom Alleyne referred was composed solely of white male landowners. He was capable of looking beyond his own class to some extent: he showed real concern for the distress caused to both poor whites and slaves by the scarcity of provisions when the American War of Independence interrupted imports, and between 1770 and 1783 he founded a school, known as the Seminary, for poor whites in the parish he represented. The school was opened to all races in the nineteenth century and still existed at the start of the twenty-first century, under the name Alleyne School. He reportedly referred to slavery as an 'unhappy sight' (Allen, in Brandow, 40), but as a slave owner himself he seems to have had little desire to upset the established order of things, and he could speak of 'that subordination which so happily subsisted, not less to the ease and comfort of the negroes than to the satisfaction of their masters' (Poyer, 646). When in 1998 a number of historical figures were officially declared to be national heroes by the government of Barbados, Alleyne's claims had been canvassed, but he was omitted from the list.

JOHN GILMORE

Sources L. R. Allen, 'Alleyne of Barbados', *Journal of the Barbados Museum and Historical Society*, 3 (1935–6), 100–14, 153–68, 223–34; 4 (1936–7), 34–46, 85–95, 134–40, 189–95; 5 (1937–8), 32–8, 101–08, 151–4, 190–93; repr. in *Genealogies of Barbados families*, ed. J. C. Brandow (Baltimore, 1983) · [J. G. Alleyne], *A defence of the conduct of Barbadoes, during the late expedition to Martinique and Guadeloupe, in a letter to the Right Hon. Gen. Barrington, by a native, residing in the island* (1760) · [J. G. Alleyne], *Remarks upon a book, intitled, A short history of Barbados: in which the partial and unfair representations of the author upon the subjects of his history in general, and upon that of the demand of privileges in particular, are detected and exposed* (Barbados, 1768) · [H. Frere], *A short history of Barbados, from its first discovery and settlement, to the end of the year 1767* (1768); new edn (1768) · J. S. Handler, *A guide to source materials for the study of Barbados history, 1627–1834* (Carbondale, 1971) · F. A. Hoyos, *Our common heritage* (Barbados, 1953) · F. A. Hoyos, *Builders of Barbados* (1972) · J. Poyer, *The history of Barbados, from the first discovery of the island, in the year 1605, till the accession of Lord Seaforth, 1801* (1808)
Likenesses portrait, repro. in Allen, 'Alleyne of Barbados', vol. 3, facing p. 223 · portrait, Barbados Museum and Historical Society

Allfrey, Phyllis Byam Shand (1908–1986), author and politician, was born in Roseau, Dominica, British West Indies, on 24 October 1908, the second daughter of Francis Byam Shand (*b.* 1879), a lawyer who had come to Dominica from England in the early 1900s, and Elfreda Millicent Crompton Nicholls, whose family had settled in the islands in the mid-seventeenth century. Phyllis Byam Shand was named after her ancestor William Byam, who first settled in Barbados, but eventually moved to Antigua, where he became governor. He was doubtless the Byam whom Aphra Behn describes with vehement negativity in *Oroonoko* (1688). Phyllis Shand's parents were married in St George's Church in Roseau on 27 March 1905, and had three other daughters: Marion (*b.* 1906), Celia (*b.* 1910), and Rosalind (*b.* 1912). Phyllis Shand and her sisters grew up in Roseau, where they were educated somewhat haphazardly at home, with various tutors educating them in poetry, arithmetic, religious studies, and French. Phyllis also practised drawing and music, and started writing plays at an early age. Her first short story was published in *Tiger Tim's Weekly* when she was thirteen.

Having followed her sister Celia to England when Celia married Jack Richmond Allfrey, Phyllis Shand met and married Jack's brother, Robert Edward Allfrey (1906–1986), on 22 May 1930. Shortly after the wedding they went to the United States, where Robert Allfrey had been offered a job as a hydraulic engineer. Their two children were born in Buffalo, New York: Josephine, nicknamed Phina, in February 1931, and Philip in April 1935. The family returned to England in June 1936. In London, Phyllis Allfrey took a job as secretary to the author Naomi Mitchison, a job that brought her into contact with prominent Fabian socialists of the time. She then served as London county council welfare officer to assist those whose homes had been bombed, and she offered her own home

as a haven for Dominicans migrating to England. During this period she began to write professionally, winning an international award for her poem 'While the Young Sleep'. In 1940 she published *In Circles*, a collection of thirteen poems she had written from 1936 to 1939. Three of the poems reflect West Indian themes. In 1942 she published 'Uncle Rufus', a short story about her childhood in Dominica, in the London *Tribune*.

Throughout the 1940s Phyllis Allfrey wrote numerous short stories, some of which were published in an assortment of magazines including *The Windmill*, *Pan Africa*, and the *Manchester Guardian*. By 1950 she had collected another set of poems, which she published under the title *Palm and Oak*. The two trees named in the title represented her own ancestry—West Indian and European—which she described as 'tropic' and 'nordic'. Increasing literary success encouraged her to more sustained writing. The Allfreys' two children were in school, and during this peaceful period Phyllis Allfrey wrote *The Orchid House*. The novel was published quickly, with a British edition from Constable in 1953, to be followed by an American edition from Dutton in the same year. In 1954 Librairie Stock published a French edition, *La maison des orchidées*. Writing the novel 'drove me towards my home island' (P. Allfrey to E. Campbell, n.d.), and the Allfreys returned to Dominica in 1954.

In Dominica, Phyllis Allfrey was caught up in the island's social and economic politics. She co-founded the Dominica Labour Party to help the island's underpaid tropical fruit workers, and for the next two decades her political activity overshadowed her creative writing. Her most significant political success occurred in 1958, when she won an all-island election for the cabinet of the newly created federal government of the West Indies. As minister of labour and social affairs, she moved with Robert and her adopted African-Caribbean daughter, Sonia, and Carib son, David, to federation headquarters in Trinidad. There they lived until 1961, when the West Indies Federation collapsed. Upon their return to Dominica, they ran the *Dominica Herald*, and then, in 1965, they founded a weekly newspaper, *The Star*.

The Orchid House was republished in London in 1982 by Virago Press, followed by an American edition in 1985 by Three Continents Press. During her newspaper years, Phyllis Allfrey continued to write poetry and short stories in addition to political essays and editorials for *The Star*. Poor health and poverty caused the Allfreys to give up *The Star* in February 1982, allowing time for Phyllis to work on her novel *In the Cabinet*. Phyllis Shand Allfrey died of malnutrition and colon cancer in the Princess Margaret Hospital, Roseau, Dominica, on 2 April 1986, *In the Cabinet* remaining unfinished. Although she died in great poverty, she was accorded a federal minister's funeral in Roseau, where she was buried in the Anglican cemetery. Robert, who died before the end of the year, was cared for in his final months by their adopted Carib son, Robbie. Robert lies in the cemetery in the Carib Reserve not far from the one-room cabin that he and Phyllis had built.

ELAINE CAMPBELL

Sources personal knowledge (2004) · E. Campbell, 'Phyllis Shand Allfrey', *Fifty Caribbean writers: a bio-bibliographical critical sourcebook*, ed. D. C. Dance (1986), 9–18 · E. Campbell, 'Introduction', in P. S. Allfrey, *The orchid house* (1982) · L. Paravisini-Gebert, *Phyllis Shand Allfrey: a Caribbean life* (1996) · E. Campbell, 'Report from Dominica, B.W.I.', *World Literature Written in English*, 17 (April 1978)
Archives Lennox Honeychurch Archives, Dominica
Likenesses photograph, repro. in D. E. Herdeck and others, eds., *Caribbean writers* (1979), 19 · photograph, repro. in *Observer Magazine* (22 July 1984), 23 · photograph, repro. in Paravisini-Gebert, *Phyllis Shand Allfrey*, cover

Allgood, Sara (1883–1950), actress, was born in Dublin on 31 October 1883, the second daughter of George Allgood (*d.* in or before 1911), a printing compositor, and his wife, Margaret Harold, a second-hand furniture seller.

Sara was educated at Marlborough Street Training College, Dublin, and was later apprenticed to an upholstery firm. Known as Sally, she joined Maude Gonne's revolutionary women's society, Inghinidhe na hEirean (the Daughters of Erin) about 1902 and became a member of the dramatic class. William Fay recruited her into the Irish National Theatre Society in 1903. Her first appearance was in Lady Gregory's *Twenty-Five* (1904); her first speaking parts were as Princess Buan in *The King's Threshold*, by W. B. Yeats, and Cathleen in *Riders to the Sea*, by J. M. Synge. When the Abbey Theatre, Dublin, opened on 27 December 1904 she also revealed a talent for comedy, as Mrs Fallon in Lady Gregory's *Spreading the News*. She became the undisputed leading lady of the company. Her glorious voice, her sheer stage presence, and the approach to acting that came to typify the Abbey were a marriage between her talent and the training that she received from the Fay brothers, William and Frank. Early exponents of naturalism, the Fays were influenced by Constant Coquelin's acting theories and André Antoine's production methods.

Sara Allgood's performances for the Irish National Theatre Society at the Abbey and on their annual London visits from 1904 to 1913 won acclaim; they included the title role in W. B. Yeats's *Deirdre*, Maurya in *Riders to the Sea*, Mrs Delane in Lady Gregory's *Hyacinth Halvey*, Widow Quin in Synge's *Playboy of the Western World*, and Kathleen in Yeats's *Cathleen ni Houlihan*. Lady Gregory became her ally and lifelong friend. She acted with Mrs Patrick Campbell in *Deirdre* (1908) and *Electra* (1909) in London. In 1908 she helped to open Miss Horniman's Gaiety Theatre, Manchester, and toured to Stratford in William Poel's production of *Measure for Measure*. 'Miss Allgood's Isabella was magnificent—rich, vehement, passionate', wrote Yeats (who earlier doubted her potential) to Synge (Saddlemyer, 277). She occasionally directed and she also taught acting. After a season at Liverpool Repertory Theatre in 1914 she made a hit as the unlikely comic lead in *Peg o' my Heart*, by J. Hartley Manners (1915). The play toured Australia in 1916, where she married Gerard Henson, her leading man. Her daughter, Mary, born 18 January 1918, lived for only an hour, and Henson himself died in the influenza epidemic in November 1918.

Back in London, Sara Allgood played Mrs Geoghegan in

Sara Allgood (1883–1950), attrib. Robert Gregory

The Whiteheaded Boy by Lennox Robinson and Mrs O'Flaherty in *O'Flaherty V.C.* by G. B. Shaw (1920). Formerly a key player for Yeats and Lady Gregory, her personal and artistic maturity was now equally important to Sean O'Casey; her Juno, in his *Juno and the Paycock* on 3 March 1924, became part of Irish theatrical history. In two other O'Casey dramas, as Bessie Burgess in *The Plough and the Stars* (1926) and Mrs Henderson in *The Shadow of a Gunman* (1927), she was unforgettable; she brought poetry to realism. Before and after the First World War she toured with the Abbey Theatre and the Irish Players in the USA—visits which affected the direction of American theatre. Other successes included Mrs Peachum in Sir Nigel Playfair's revival of John Gay's *Beggar's Opera* (London, 1925), Julia Hardy in *Things that are Caesar's* (London, 1933), Mme Raquin in *Thérèse Raquin* (Dublin, 1934), an adaptation of the novel by Émile Zola, and Honoria Flanaghan in *Storm in a Teacup* by James Bridie (London, 1936). However, she was never offered the great non-Irish classic roles. In 1940 she moved to Hollywood, and in 1945 became an American citizen. Among fifty films, she starred in Alfred Hitchcock's *Blackmail* (1929) and *Juno and the Paycock* (1930). Hollywood found her stage presence difficult, casting her in Irish character parts, but she was nominated for an Academy award as best supporting actress in John Ford's *How Green was my Valley* (1941). She died in Woodlands Hills, California, on 13 September 1950.

In Sara Allgood, seen as the Irish Eleonora Duse, critics praised the art that concealed art: simplicity, sincerity, depth of characterization, the haunting quality of her rich contralto voice, the ability to grip both audience and actors. Gabriel Fallon recalled that as she simply opened the door in act 3 of *Juno*, came in, and sat down, 'tragedy sat at the elbow of every member of the audience' (Coxhead, 212).

Maire O'Neill (1887–1952) was born Mary Agnes Allgood on 12 January 1887 in Dublin. The younger sister of Sara Allgood, she was known as Molly; she invented an Irish professional name in order to be distinct from Sally. In 1905 she joined the Irish National Theatre Society. A bewitching, rebellious, mischievous young woman, there was 'a fascination about her that commands attention' (Byrne, 91). She was engaged to John Millington *Synge, whose obvious affection for her scandalized Miss Horniman, and met disapproval from her sister and from the other directors of the Abbey Theatre. An unequal partnership, with continuous quarrels, it stimulated some of Synge's best writing: '*Playboy* is radiant with the triumph of winning her, *Deirdre* poignant with the anguish of losing her' (Coxhead, 194). Although Synge had already found elements of Pegeen Mike, Molly gave him the real impetus for the part that became her first major triumph when *The Playboy of the Western World* opened on 26 January 1907. Synge was writing *Deirdre* for Molly when he died in 1908; she collaborated with Yeats and Lady Gregory to finish the play. Critical responses to the production in 1910 suggest that it was too reverential, though Molly acted with pathos and beauty.

By 1910 Molly had equal billing with Sara on Abbey summer tours. On 15 July 1911 she married George Herbert Mair (1887–1926), political writer and reviewer of the *Manchester Guardian*; they had two children, Pegeen and John. Extending her range beyond Irish parts, she played Zerline in *Turandot*, adapted by Jethro Bethell (London, 1913). A season with Liverpool Repertory Company gave her the role of Mother in G. Hauptmann's *Hannele*, the title role in Shaw's *Candida*, and Nora Burke in Synge's *The Shadow of the Glen*. In June 1913 she played Nerissa in *The Merchant of Venice* in Tree's Shakespearian festival (London); she also played Mary Ellen in *General John Regan*, by G. A. Birmingham, in New York. 1914 saw her as Portia in *The Merchant of Venice*, in Paris and London. At the Abbey in 1916 she created Aunt Helen in *The Whiteheaded Boy*, but the need for money to keep open house for artists and writers in Chelsea meant that her leads in the Shaw season in 1917 were her last at the Abbey. Her range in the 1920s encompassed Mrs Beetle in *The Insect Play*, by the brothers Capek, in New York (1921), Widow Quin, and Mrs Gogan in O'Casey's *The Plough and the Stars* (1926). G. H. Mair died suddenly on 3 January 1926. On 22 June Molly married Arthur Sinclair (1883–1951), the Abbey's leading actor. They divorced after five years but remained friends and, with Sara, continued touring Irish plays to America. In later years O'Casey characters remained the staple of Molly's repertoire but she also played other roles, such as Aunt Judy in Shaw's *John Bull's Other Island*, in 1938. Her films included *Love on the Dole* (1941) and, posthumously, *The Horse's Mouth* (1953).

Molly's son died in a plane crash in 1942. She herself died in Basingstoke on 2 November 1952, following a fire at her home, 40 Redcliffe Square, Chelsea. Her obituary in *The Stage* (6 November 1952) praises her 'matchless interpretations of the Irish character' and 'the powerful impact of her personality in all the pathetic, bitter and humorous facets of these vivid characters'. Nobody who saw or worked with the Allgood sisters ever forgot them. Geniuses in a new theatre movement—of idealism and art—their acting was one definition of the Abbey's greatness. SUSAN C. TRIESMAN

Sources E. Coxhead, *Daughters of Erin: five women of the Irish renascence*, pbk edn (1979) · *Who was who in the theatre, 1912–1976*, 4 vols. (1978), vols. 1, 3 · E. M. Truitt, *Who was who on screen*, 3rd edn (1983) · A. Saddlemyer, ed., *Theatre business: correspondence of the first Abbey Theatre directors: William Butler Yeats, Lady Gregory, and J. M. Synge* (1982) · J. P. Wearing, *The London stage, 1900–1909: a calendar of plays and players*, 2 vols. (1981) · R. Hogan and M. J. O'Neill, eds., *Joseph Holloway's Abbey Theatre: a selection from his unpublished journal, Impressions of a Dublin playgoer* (1967) · E. H. Mikhail, *The Abbey Theatre: interviews and recollections* (1988) · D. Byrne, *The story of Ireland's national theatre: the Abbey Theatre, Dublin* (1929) · S. McCann, ed., *The story of the Abbey Theatre* (1967) · *Letters to Molly: John Millington Synge to Maire O'Neill, 1906–1909*, ed. A. Saddlemyer (1971) · *Irish Times* (3 Nov 1952) · *The Stage* (6 Nov 1952) · *The Stage* (21 Sept 1950) · m. cert. [Mary Agnes Allgood] · d. cert. [Maire O'Neill]

Archives NYPL, Berg collection, 'Memories' | Dublin City Library, Irish theatre archive · Jerwood Library of the Performing Arts, London, Mander and Mitchenson theatre collection · NL Ire., Henderson scrapbook of the Abbey Theatre | FILM BFI NFTVA · Los Angeles, California, Hollywood Film Archive

Likenesses photograph, 1907 (Molly Allgood), priv. coll. · photograph, 1924, priv. coll. · photograph, still, 1949 (Molly Allgood), NL Ire., Bord Fáilte Éireann · R. Gregory, drawing (when young), repro. in Lady Gregory, *Our Irish theatre* (1914) · attrib. R. Gregory, pencil and ink drawing, NG Ire. [*see illus.*] · P. Tuohy, portrait, NL Ire.

Wealth at death £18,000: *The Stage* (21 Sept 1950) · died in poverty; Mary Agnes Allgood: Coxhead, *Daughters of Erin*

Allhusen, Christian Augustus Henry (1806–1890), chemical manufacturer, was born on 2 December 1806 in Kiel, Germany, the fourth son in the family of five sons and two daughters of Carl Christian Allhusen, merchant of Kiel, and his wife, Anna Margaretha Schroder. The French occupation of Schleswig-Holstein caused the family to break up.

Allhusen's education is obscure; he worked in the grain trade, first at Rostock, then from 1825 at Newcastle upon Tyne with two older brothers. In 1827 his brothers left Newcastle and he invited Henry Bolckow, a Rostock friend, to join him in the grain trade; he was also involved in ship and insurance broking.

Allhusen married Anne, daughter of John Shield of Broomhaugh, in 1835; they had four sons and two daughters. His daughter Annie married twice, her second husband being Lord D'Arcy Godolphin Osborne, brother of the duke of Leeds.

Allhusen entered the Tyneside chemical industry at Gateshead in 1840 when he purchased the soap works of Charles Attwood & Co. He was not a chemist but adopted innovatory methods and used commercial skill to promote his products. In 1862 he began drilling for salt on Teesside for manufacturing alkali by the Leblanc process on Tyneside. However, this benefited the rival Solvay process, then expanding on the Tees, and so in practice hastened the decline of the Tyneside industry.

Allhusen was a member of Gateshead town council from 1849 to 1853, an early president of the Newcastle chamber of commerce, and a Tyne commissioner from 1852 to 1855. An Anglican and liberal (later Liberal Unionist), he amassed a large fortune and his influence in the north-east was considerable. As an advocate of free trade, he supported Richard Cobden in his scheme for a commercial treaty with France in 1860, and represented local chemical manufacturers at the Paris conferences. To celebrate the treaty he invited W. E. Gladstone, chancellor of the exchequer, to visit Newcastle in 1862. Allhusen's business interests were varied; he was a director of the Marine Insurance Company, the Northfleet Coal and Ballast Company, the Brazil Great Southern Railway, the British Land and Mortgage Company of America, the International Bank of London, the New Oriental Bank Corporation, the Metropole Hotel Company, and the Newcastle and Gateshead Water Company. A major shareholder in the Northumberland and Durham District Bank, which failed in 1857, he managed to avert the closure of the Derwent Iron-works Company, which owed the bank £1 million. In 1864 it was registered as the Consett Iron Company.

From 1842 Allhusen lived at Elswick Hall, Newcastle, but moved to Stoke Court, Stoke Poges, Buckinghamshire, in 1873 and died there on 13 January 1890, not long after his wife. Soon after Allhusen's death his Tyneside factory was amalgamated in the United Alkali Company.

N. G. COLEY, rev.

Sources R. W. Rennison, 'Allhusen, Christian Augustus Henry', *DBB* · J. Fenwick Allen, 'Industrial celebrities: Christian Allhusen', *Chemical Trade Journal* (5 April 1890), 222–3 · *Newcastle Daily Journal* (13 Jan 1890) · *Newcastle Daily Chronicle* (14 Jan 1890) · W. A. Campbell, *The old Tyneside chemical trade* (1964) · d. cert.
Likenesses photograph, repro. in Rennison, 'Allhusen, Christian Augustus Henry'
Wealth at death £1,126,852 1s. 10d.: probate, 28 Feb 1890, *CGPLA Eng. & Wales*

Allibond, John (1596/7–1658), Church of England clergyman and satirist, was born at Chenies, Buckinghamshire, the son of Peter *Allibond (1559/60–1629), rector of Chenies. He was a chorister at Magdalen College, Oxford, from 1612 to 1616, matriculated there on 7 June 1616, aged nineteen, and graduated BA on 3 July of the same year. While serving as clerk of Magdalen from 1617 to 1625 he proceeded MA on 9 June 1619. From 1625 to 1632 he was master of Magdalen grammar school, and following the establishment of the Heather endowment in 1627 he was appointed to read a lecture in English on music once a term in the music school. In July 1626 and July 1631 he lectured at the Act, when theses were defended, and his inclusion of jokes intended to amuse the women became a tradition that continued after the Restoration. A budding poet, he contributed to *Britanniae natalis* (Oxford, 1630), a collection of verse by academics celebrating the birth of Prince Charles. He also wrote 'Dulcissimis capitibus … Invitatio ad frugi prandiolum', in the clerks'

register, and 'Concio ad clerum Oxoniensium', preserved in the Taylor manuscripts at the Bodleian Library. He was rector of St Mary-de-Crypt, Gloucester, from 1634 to 1638 and perpetual curate at St Nicholas, Gloucester, from 1635 to 1645. He also became rector of Bradwell, Gloucestershire, in 1636, a position he held until his death, and on 17 October 1643 was awarded the degree of DD.

Allibond's caustic view of puritans, both lay and clerical, is evinced in part in his report to Peter Heylyn, a royal chaplain, on 24 March 1640, concerning the election in Gloucester of representatives to the Short Parliament. When supporters of the puritan Sir Robert Cooke reportedly reneged on their commitment to vote for Sir Robert Tracy, Allibond remarked that such men were 'the hands that have builded as much of this Troy as is up', and warned that if elected, men such as Cooke would 'hold the King's nose to the grindstone and ruin the Church' (*CSP dom.*, *1639–40*, 580–83). In the same letter Allibond satirized Thomas Wynell, lecturer at Gloucester, for his interest in Scottish divinity. Friends of Allibond urged him to stand for election to convocation, but he declined, citing personal reasons.

In his major work, *Rustica academiae Oxoniensis nuper reformatae descriptio* ('A rustic description of the Oxford academy recently reformed'), published anonymously on a single sheet in 1648, Allibond satirized the puritan-inspired parliamentary visitation of Oxford. He had heard that the university was to be reformed 'by dunces call'd the godly', including Daniel Greenwood, the 'dull Damn'd principal' of Brasenose, and the 'hum-drum dotard' John Wilkinson, president of Magdalen, whose walls

> Are now with dolesome dulness fill'd,
> And bats and howlets live there.

As he watched the visitors impose their alterations he was reminded of the story of those who had slept through the persecution of the Roman emperor Decius and awakened to find Constantine in power: they

> Sure never found such ill-look'd men,
> Or monsters of God's making.

Alas, the halls of the music school were silent, while in the Bodleian Library

> … piles of books, in woful case,
> Neglected lay at random,
> Because the saints had not the grace
> Or wit to understand 'em.

The plain style of preaching generally favoured by puritans likewise drew criticism,

> … for the style of saint,
> Was plunder'd by the roundhead.
> (Scott, 5.503–9)

Anthony Wood's manuscripts contain a key to the poem. *Rustica academiae Oxoniensis* was twice reprinted in 1648 and at least six times in the eighteenth century, including Edward Ward's English translation (1717) and its incorporation in the first volume of Edward Popham's *Selecta poemata Anglorum Latina* (1774).

Allibond, whom Wood praised as 'a most excellent Lat[in] poet and philologist' (Wood, *Ath. Oxon.: Fasti*, 2.69), died at Bradwell, Gloucestershire, in 1658. His brother

Peter (1607/8–1641) was a fellow of Lincoln College, Oxford, and proctor of the university from 1640 until his death on 19 February 1641. His other brother, Job (*d.* 1688), converted to Catholicism and was employed in the Post Office.　　　　　　　　　　　　RICHARD L. GREAVES

Sources Foster, *Alum. Oxon., 1500–1714*, 1.19 • Wood, *Ath. Oxon.: Fasti* (1815), 365; (1820), 69 • W. Scott, ed., *A collection of scarce and valuable tracts … Lord Somers*, 2nd edn, 13 vols. (1809–15), 5.503–9 • *CSP dom.*, 1639–40, pp. 580–83 • *DNB* • P. M. Gouk, 'Music', *Hist. U. Oxf.* 4: *17th-cent. Oxf.*, 621–40, esp. 624 • *The diary of Thomas Crosfield*, ed. F. S. Boas (1935) • Wood, *Ath. Oxon.*, new edn, 2.440–41 • K. Sharpe, *The personal rule of Charles I* (1992), 855 • *Walker rev.*, 179
Archives Oxf. UA, register N, fol. 236*v*

Allibond, Peter (1559/60–1629), Church of England clergyman and translator, was born at Wardington, Oxfordshire, where his family had lived for many generations; his parents' names are not known. He became a student at Magdalen Hall, Oxford, in 1578 (according to Anthony Wood): he matriculated from there, aged twenty, on 15 April 1580, graduated BA on 21 February 1582, and proceeded MA on 6 July 1585. After some years spent in foreign travel, he was ordained. In 1592 Bridget Russell, countess of Bedford, presented him to the rectory of Chenies in Buckinghamshire, where the mansion house of the Bedfords stood. At Chenies, says Wood, 'continuing many years, he did much improve the ignorant with his sound doctrine' (Wood, *Ath. Oxon.*, 2.440). There Allibond baptized twelve children as his between February 1595 and June 1613; as he entered only his own name as parent in the parish register, it is not possible to say whether his wife at the time of his death, Margaret Balham, was the mother of all or some of them.

In 1591 Allibond published a translation from the French of a work by the Huguenot Jean de l'Espine as *Comfort for an afflicted conscience, wherein is contained both consolation and instruction for the sicke, against the fearfull apprehension of their sinnes, of death and the devill, of the curse of the law, and of the anger and just judgement of God*. He dedicated the book to five Buckinghamshire gentlemen, including Sir Francis Goodwin. In the following year he published a translation, again from French, of a short tract, in part if not wholly by l'Espine, as *A confutation of the popish transubstantiation, together with a narration how that the masse was at sundrie times patched and peeced by sundrie popes. Wherein is contained a briefe summe of the reasons and arguments for those readers that will not receive the masse*. Allibond deplored, in a prefatory note, that 'at this time the papists are very rife and ready with their seducing seminaries and Jesuits', and displayed the bitterest hatred of Catholicism.

Allibond's theological views received their fullest exposition in a third work, which he translated from the Latin in 1604, *The golden chayne of salvation written by that reverend and learned man, Maister Herman Renecher*. The English version is dedicated to Edward Russell, third earl of Bedford, and his wife, Lucy, whom Allibond calls his neighbours and 'singular good lord and lady'. He thanks them and the countess's mother, Anne, Lady Harington, for their generosity and support 'when Death Gods Sergeant had as it were seized on me, had not the mercifull judge of

the world reprived me' (Rennecher, sig. A2*v*). He praises the earl and countess fulsomely as patrons and exemplars of godliness: 'I can testify to this by experience, as being the poore Minister of the place, where your Honors for some good space resided' (ibid., sig. A3*r*–A3*v*). Allibond speaks of having received aid from 'another who joyned with me in this small worke', but mentions no name (ibid., 'To the Gentle Reader').

Allibond died on 6 March 1629 and was buried in the chancel of his parish church. In his will he made his wife, Margaret, his executor and principal beneficiary. He left 20*s.* apiece to Chenies and Wardington to be given to their poor. The overseers of the will were his eldest son, his brother-in-law Richard Balham, and his son-in-law Dr Paul Hood, rector of Lincoln College, Oxford, and a man 'of the Antiarminian or Puritan party' in the politics of the university before the civil war (Wood, *History … of the University*, 2.424).

One of Allibond's daughters, Bridget (*bap.* 1609), who died at Chenies about the age of seventeen, was celebrated by the minor poet Sir Aston Cokayne. According to Cokayne (who had been at school under Allibond at Chenies), Bridget died of grief after the death of her lover, who had been sent abroad by his kin to keep them separate:

> Virgins should mourn her loss; And (by her) men
> May se how Maids belov'd can love agen.
> (Cokain)

At least three of her brothers survived Allibond. The eldest was John *Allibond, the anti-puritan satirist and friend of Peter Heylyn. Job Allibone (*bap.* 1599, *d.* 1672) converted to Catholicism and was the father of Richard *Allibone, one of the judges who tried the seven bishops in 1688. Peter (*bap.* 1607) became a fellow of Lincoln College. He died in London early in 1641, awaiting a hearing before the House of Commons to answer the complaints of the town authorities of Oxford for his actions, as university proctor, over the night-watch and over his release of an 'Irish footpost' imprisoned by the mayor (Green, 235).

SIDNEY LEE, *rev.* TIM WALES

Sources Foster, *Alum. Oxon.* • Wood, *Ath. Oxon.*, new edn, 2.440–41 • H. Rennecher, *The golden chayne of salvation*, trans. P. Allibond (1604) • will, PRO, PROB 11/155, sig. 23 • L. L. Peck, *Court patronage and corruption in early Stuart England* (1990), 79 • *IGI* • A. Wood, *The history and antiquities of the University of Oxford*, ed. J. Gutch, 2 vols. in 3 pts (1792–6) • V. H. H. Green, *The commonwealth of Lincoln College, 1427–1977* (1979) • A. Cokain [A. Cokayne], *Small poems of divers sorts* (1658), 124–5 [224–5] • *Corrections and additions to the Dictionary of National Biography*, Institute of Historical Research (1966)

Allibone [Allibond], **Sir Richard** (1636–1688), judge, was the son of Job Allibone (*bap.* 1599, *d.* 1672). Allibone's paternal grandfather, Peter *Allibond, served as rector of Chenies, Buckinghamshire, until his death in 1629, but Job Allibone broke with the family religion and converted to Roman Catholicism. For this act he was disinherited, but he managed to secure himself a place in the Post Office. Where the family lived during Richard Allibone's childhood is unclear, although his father was buried in Essex.

Allibone was raised as a Roman Catholic. On 24 March 1652 he began studies at the Catholic English College at Douai. When he returned to England is unknown, but on 27 April 1663 he entered Gray's Inn and began training as a barrister. He was called to the bar on 11 February 1670. Of his career during the reign of Charles II very little can be said. He apparently purchased a house near Gray's Inn and practised law. At some point he married Barbara, daughter of Sir Francis Blakiston, who outlived him. Early on, Allibone's Roman Catholicism probably hindered his career, but it proved a boon after the accession of James II in 1685. The king, naturally interested in promoting his co-religionists, showed favour to many prominent Roman Catholic families. One of Allibone's brothers was ordained as a Roman Catholic priest during these years, and Allibone himself began a meteoric rise through the legal profession. In January 1686 he reportedly boasted that he would 'do fine things in a great place' (Ellis, 1.5). Sure enough, James soon appointed Allibone to his council, and on 22 October 1686 he was knighted. Early in the following year rumours flew that he would be named attorney-general, or that he would succeed Sir John Travers as master of the rolls. He received material favours from the king, including the right to hold 'a yearly fair and weekly market' (CSP dom., 3.23). Allibone was made a serjeant-at-law on 28 April 1687 and was elevated to the king's bench, filling the vacancy created by the discharge of Justice Wythens. Allibone thus figured prominently in James's efforts to advance Roman Catholics within the government and to secure a compliant judiciary. Achieving these ends famously required the king to suspend the tests and penal laws against Catholics and use the dispensing power to advance individuals to office. Indeed, Allibone was among those listed in a July 1687 ordinance dispensing with the oath of royal supremacy for Roman Catholic office holders. Needless to say his promotion proved unpopular with many protestants. An observer of the 1687 assizes at York was stunned to find it presided over by a 'papist' named 'Alabon, the first that ever sate as judge of that persuasion' (Memoirs of Sir John Reresby, 461). Allibone was angered on this occasion by his failure to coax the Yorkshire grand jury into voting an address of thanks to James II for the declaration of indulgence. When the assize court reached Lancaster, it was boycotted by the gentry. It is said that while at Lancaster Allibone 'openly attended mass while his brother judge attended church to hear the assize sermon, attacked protestants in his charge, and then proceeded to weed them out of the commission' (Cockburn, 255).

Allibone's time on the king's bench was brief. He is remembered for one opinion only: his instructions to the jury in the trial of the seven bishops. When James brought seven English bishops before the king's bench on charges of seditious libel in June 1688 he undoubtedly counted on Allibone's support. Unsurprisingly, he received it. Allibone's interventions in the trial uniformly supported the position of the king. In his instructions to the jury he was the justice most favourable to the crown's case against the bishops. He advised the jury that 'no man can

taken upon him to write against the exercise of the government', and that petitions are properly delivered to parliament only and not to the king. He further opined that the truth or falsity of the bishops' petition was irrelevant, and that the petition constituted a libel merely because it touched on state affairs (State trials, 12.427–9). Speaking for generations of whigs, Lord Macaulay pronounced that Allibone's opinion showed 'gross ignorance of law and history', and 'brought on him the contempt of all who heard him'. The latter charge may have been true, but the former was not. Unpopular though it was, the settled law of 1688 did indeed prohibit even truthful petitions that touched on public affairs. Macaulay's indignation notwithstanding, the best recent authority has judged Allibone's remarks 'a perfectly valid summary of the law as it stood' in 1688 (W. A. Speck, *Reluctant revolutionaries: Englishmen and the Revolution of 1688*, 1989, 152).

In general, history has judged Allibone unfairly. True, he was 'strict and rigid', but he was also thought to be 'equall in giving his judgement' (*Memoirs of Sir John Reresby*, 461). His reputation seems to have suffered unduly for a charge to the 1688 assizes at Croydon in which he condemned the acquittal of the seven bishops. As a Roman Catholic, Allibone was roughly treated by the whig historians. He might perhaps have exhibited more objectivity during the trial of the seven bishops, but his legal opinions were sound. He would undoubtedly have faced difficult times had he survived the fall of James II, but on 22 August 1688 he died in his house in Brownlow Street, Holborn, London. Rumours blamed his death on 'vehemence in declaiming against the bishops in his charge to the juries' (Ellis, 2.137). Allibone was buried on 4 September in Dagenham, Essex, where he is remembered by a monumental inscription and a standing effigy in robes.   JEFFREY R. COLLINS

Sources Wood, *Ath. Oxon.*, 1st edn · Foss, *Judges*, 7.209–10 · *State trials*, vol. 12 · G. Agar-Ellis, ed., *The Ellis correspondence: letters written during the years 1686, 1687, 1688, and addressed to John Ellis*, 2 vols. (1829) · T. B. Macaulay, *The history of England from the accession of James II*, new edn, ed. C. H. Firth, 6 vols. (1913–15) · *CSP dom.*, 1687–9 · *Memoirs of Sir John Reresby*, ed. A. Browning (1936) · *DNB* · Holdsworth, *Eng. law*, vol. 6 · J. S. Cockburn, *A history of English assizes, 1558–1714* (1972) · Baker, *Serjeants*
Likenesses effigy, Dagenham, Essex

Allies, Jabez (*bap.* 1787, *d.* 1856), antiquary, the second son of William and Anne Allies, was baptized on 22 October 1787, at Lulsley, Worcestershire, where his family had lived for generations. As a youth, he was fascinated by Roman and Anglo-Saxon remains, and by the rural customs of the region. He served a clerkship in London, and practised there as a solicitor. He regularly read papers to the Society of Antiquaries, of which he was elected a fellow on 18 March 1841, and at meetings of the Archaeological Institute. He showed an aptitude for antiquarian research, and investigated the surviving Roman remains of Worcestershire, which had received little attention from earlier historians such as T. R. Nash.

After his marriage to Catherine (*d.* 1855), daughter of William Hartshorne of Clipstone, Northamptonshire, with whom he had an only child, William Hartshorne

Allies, Allies left London and lived for some years at Catherine Villa in Lower Wick, Worcester. He supported various activities connected with Worcestershire and its history, and published works on a variety of subjects. The first was *Observations on certain curious indentations in the Old Red Sandstone of Worcestershire and Herefordshire considered as the tracks of antediluvian animals* (1835), which was followed by *On the Causes of Planetary Motion* (1838) and two slight works on folklore and legend. However, the work for which he is chiefly remembered is his *On the Ancient British, Roman and Saxon Antiquities of Worcestershire* (1840), originally a slight work which appeared in a retitled and much enlarged second edition in 1852. This work was one of the first to recognize the importance of such evidence as field names. Allies also contributed papers to the *Archaeological Journal* and the correspondence columns of periodicals, and was always willing to give assistance to fellow antiquaries.

Allies died on 29 January 1856, at Tivoli House, Cheltenham, which he had purchased a few years earlier, and was buried in Leckhampton churchyard by the side of his wife.　　JOHN WESTBY-GIBSON, *rev.* ROBIN WHITTAKER

Sources GM, 2nd ser., 45 (1856), 316 · *Archaeological Journal*, 13 (1856), 396 · E. O. Browne and J. R. Burton, eds., *Short biographies of the worthies of Worcestershire* (1916), 4–5 · parish register, Lulsley, Worcestershire, 22 Oct 1787 [births]
Archives Bodl. Oxf., corresp. with Sir Thomas Phillipps

Allies, Mary Helen Agnes (1852–1927), historian and translator, was born possibly at St John's Wood, London, on 2 February 1852, the eldest daughter of Thomas William *Allies (1813–1903) and his wife, Eliza Hall (*d.* 1902), second daughter of Thomas Harding Newman of Nelmes, Essex. Allies and his wife were recent converts to Roman Catholicism, and at the time of their daughter's birth Allies was serving as the secretary of the Catholic poor school committee. With her five brothers and one sister, Mary Allies grew up in the family home at St John's Wood, and then Portman Square, London. In 1859 she was sent to school at the Convent of the Holy Child, at St Leonards, and then to the Visitation Convent in the rue d'Enfer, Paris.

Mary Allies was influenced and guided by her father: after her sister married in 1883, she alone was left at home to 'feed on the marrow of his mind' (Allies, 164). Her first published work, *The Life of Pius VII* (1875), a sympathetic portrait of the pope persecuted by Napoleon I, reflects her father's ultramontane sympathies and his opposition to state control of the Roman Catholic church. Based on a wide range of printed sources in German, French, and Italian, the *Life*, still the only English biography of Pius VII, remains a standard work. An abbreviated version was published in 1897.

Mary Allies's next publication was the *Three Catholic Reformers of the Fifteenth Century* (1878), which contained sketches of the lives of three religious: Vincent Ferrier, Bernardino of Siena, and John Capistran. It was a lightweight and uncritical work of piety: Allies seems to have heeded the advice of Newman, who warned her in 1876 of the dangers of writing about the religious orders and

exhorted her to concentrate on presenting 'pictures of saintliness, of spiritual beautifulness, and winning heroism' (*Letters and Diaries*, 28.130). Her next works were collections of extracts from Augustine (1886) and John Chrysostom (1889), which were followed by *Letters of St Augustine* (1890). The *History of the Church in England* (1892–7) was a readable and vehemently Catholic account of the English church before 1603. However, Allies dealt cannily with the legends of the early saints, and the survey of the devotional practices which closed the first volume is an original and striking piece of religious sociology. Later works included a translation from Greek of part of John of Damascus's *De fide orthodoxa* (1898) and a biography of her father (1907). She also contributed articles to the *Catholic World* and the *Dublin Review*.

In 1890 the Allies family moved back to St John's Wood. After the death of her parents, Mary Allies, who never married, looked after her brother's children. She died at home at Berkeley Lodge, 7 Melina Place, St John's Wood, on 27 January 1927.　　ROSEMARY MITCHELL

Sources *The letters and diaries of John Henry Newman*, ed. C. S. Dessain and others, [31 vols.] (1961–) · *WWW* · M. H. Allies, *Thomas William Allies* (1907) · F. C. Burnand, ed., *The Catholic who's who and year-book* (1909) · Allibone, *Dict.* · d. cert. · CGPLA Eng. & Wales (1927)
Wealth at death £36,300 8s. 0d.: resworn probate, 16 March 1927, CGPLA Eng. & Wales

Allies, Thomas William (1813–1903), theologian and Roman Catholic convert, born at Midsomer Norton, Somerset, on 12 February 1813, was the son of Thomas Allies, curate of Henbury, Bristol, and later rector of Wormington, and his wife, Frances Elizabeth Fripp, daughter of a Bristol merchant. His mother died a week after his birth, and he was brought up by his father's second wife, Caroline Hillhouse. After education at Bristol grammar school he entered Eton College in April 1827 under Edward Coleridge. There in 1829 he was the first winner of the Newcastle scholarship. He matriculated at Wadham College, Oxford, in 1828, where he was exhibitioner in 1830–33; he graduated BA with a first class in classics in 1832, proceeded MA in 1837, and was fellow from 1833 until 1841 and humanity lecturer in 1838–9.

After a religious conversion in 1837 Allies took holy orders the following year and, under the influence of William Dodsworth, became a committed Tractarian. From 1840 to 1842 he was examining chaplain to Dr Blomfield, bishop of London, but the latter found Allies's Tractarian sympathies uncongenial and in June 1842 relegated him to the living of Launton, near Bicester. His pugnacious disposition, which along with his small stature and dapper appearance won him among his friends the nickname of the Bantam Cock, did not endear him to his episcopal superiors. On 1 October 1840 he married Eliza Hall Newman, the sister of Thomas Harding Newman, a fellow student at Oxford. There were five sons and two daughters of the marriage. In June 1842 he first met J. H. Newman, to whom he increasingly turned for guidance. Travels in France in 1845 and 1847 with John Hungerford Pollen quickened his doubt of the validity of the Anglican position, and a statement of his views in his *Journal in France*

(1848) incurred the disapproval of Samuel Wilberforce, bishop of Oxford. Study of the fathers, and especially of Suárez's work *De erroribus sectae Anglicanae*, combined with the Gorham decision on baptismal regeneration in 1850, undermined his faith in the established church, and in his work *Royal Supremacy* (1850) he forcefully presented the Roman Catholic point of view.

In October 1850 Allies resigned his Launton living and joined the Roman Catholic church—a step which his wife had taken five months previously. He moved to Golden Square, London, where he took pupils, and then to The Priory, 21 North Bank, St John's Wood, later the residence of George Eliot. From August 1853 until his retirement on a pension in 1890 he was secretary of the Catholic poor school committee in John Street, Adelphi (instituted in 1847), and actively promoted Catholic primary education. To his energy was largely due the foundation of the Notre Dame Training College, Liverpool, in 1855, the Sacred Heart Training College for Women, Wandsworth, in 1874, and St Mary's Training College for Men at Hammersmith. As honorary secretary of the Education Crisis Fund (1870–73) he successfully raised £50,000 to enable the Catholic community to meet the demands of the 1870 Education Act. He was appointed in March 1855 the first professor of modern history at the new Catholic University of Ireland, Dublin, under Newman's rectorship. He soon resigned the post because of a dearth of students, but his proposed course of lectures formed the basis of his voluminous *The Formation of Christendom* (8 vols., 1865–95). The work trenchantly expounds the predominance in history of the see of Peter.

Among Allies's intimate friends in his last years were Lord Acton, the Catholic historian, and Aubrey de Vere, who addressed a sonnet to him on the publication of the sixth volume of *The Formation of Christendom* in 1888. In 1885 Pope Leo XIII created him knight commander of St Gregory, and in 1893 he received the pope's gold medal for merit. In 1897 his health declined; he died at his home, 3 Lodge Place, St John's Wood, on 17 June 1903, and was buried at St Mary Magdalene's, Mortlake, by the side of his wife. She had predeceased him on 24 January 1902. Allies, one of the most learned of the Oxford converts to Rome, keenly felt his marginalization: 'My malady has been that I have a mind and education above my station' (Allies, 79). He traced the growth of his opinions in his autobiography, *A Life's Decision* (1880). His principal works of controversy, in defence of the papal claims, were reprinted in *Per crucem ad lucem* (2 vols., 1879), and a memoir by his daughter, Mary *Allies, was published in 1907.

W. B. OWEN, rev. G. MARTIN MURPHY

Sources M. H. Allies, *Thomas William Allies* (1907) · A. Pollen, *John Hungerford Pollen, 1820–1902* (1912) · V. A. McClelland, *English Roman Catholics and higher education, 1830–1903* (1973), 137–8 · *The letters and diaries of John Henry Newman*, ed. C. S. Dessain and others, [31 vols.] (1961–), vols. 11–31 · H. P. Liddon, *The life of Edward Bouverie Pusey*, ed. J. O. Johnston and others, 4 vols. (1893–7), vol. 3 · *The Times* (2 July 1903) · *The Tablet* (20 June 1903) · G. Donald, *Men who left the movement* (1933), 74–152 · m. cert. · d. cert. · V. A. McClelland, 'The most turbulent priest of the Oxford diocese: T. W. Allies and the quest

for authority, 1837–50', *By whose authority?*, ed. V. A. McClelland (1996), 273–90

Archives Birmingham Oratory, letters to J. H. Newman · Bodl. Oxf., corresp. with H. E. Manning · Westm. DA, letters to Wiseman

Likenesses Mrs Carpenter, oils, repro. in Allies, *Thomas William Allies*

Wealth at death £39,359 13s. 1d.: probate, 27 July 1903, CGPLA Eng. & Wales

Allin, Sir Thomas, first baronet (*bap.* 1612, *d.* 1685), naval officer, was born at Lowestoft and baptized there on 8 November 1612, the younger son of Robert Allin (*d.* 1613) and his wife, Alice. Many of his family were seamen. Thomas may perhaps be identified with the Thomas Alling who married Rebecca Whiting at Redisham on 8 July 1635. When the civil war broke out he took a leading part in the local contest between his royalist birthplace and parliamentarian Yarmouth. He appears first as a privateer captain in 1644, later serving in the official royalist naval force. In 1648 the prince of Wales sent him from Holland to foster disaffection in the enemy's ships. Back at Helvoetsluys he helped to prevent Warwick's intended blockade. In January 1649, after leading (from the *Charles*) a detachment of six frigates, he sailed with the main royalist fleet to Kinsale. Following some successful prize taking, he was himself captured in April. Already recognized as one of the 'principal hinges' of the royalist navy (*Journals*, 2.215), his instructions from Rupert were published by parliament to expose him as a pirate. He spent some months in Peterhouse, a London prison, before escaping in August.

On arriving at Lisbon in March 1650 Allin was appointed flag captain to Prince Maurice in the *Convertine*. In October he transferred to the *Charles* prize, which was sunk by Blake off Cartagena on 6 November, along with all other royal ships sheltering there. Allin escaped to Toulon, only to find himself facing court martial and a death sentence for cowardice. Despite the reasonable defence that he was attempting to protect the king's hard-won prizes, Allin did not wait to debate the point but fled to Jersey, where he was received by Sir George Carteret but forced to leave following Rupert's protest. Though Allin continued to evade the temporary hostility of his comrades, he later fell into the hands of his real enemies. By 1653 he was in Newgate, and Olderings, his house near Lowestoft, was sold. Further detention followed in 1655. No more is heard of him until 24 June 1660 when he was made captain of the *Dover*. Allin's experience, however tarnished, made him one of the few sea officers on whom the government of Charles II could absolutely rely; Coventry said he was the only one on the king's side 'good for anything' (Pepys, *Diary*, 4.170).

Unsurprisingly Allin was continuously employed on missions of importance. The first was to convey a new ambassador, Lord Winchilsea, to Constantinople. For this purpose Allin was given command of the *Plymouth*, 'unkindly' displacing her existing captain (Pepys, *Diary*, 18 August, 1.224). While he was fitting out Allin petitioned for the grant of a baronetcy to reward past services and to sustain his new responsibilities; this was for the present

Sir Thomas Allin, first baronet (*bap.* 1612, *d.* 1685), by Sir Peter Lely, *c.*1665–6

denied him. He sailed on 20 October and, after some mishaps on the way, delivered his charge. In passing he called at Algiers and made the first of many attempts to represent his nation's interests there. He was home by September 1661. On 24 October he sailed again, as captain of the *Foresight*, for Cadiz; outbound, he took Sir Henry Vane to confinement in the Isles of Scilly. He returned in February 1662.

On 18 April, again in the *Foresight*, Allin began a voyage principally to escort Dunkirk troops going to aid the Portuguese against the Spanish. Allin lost contact with his convoy off Land's End, but continued to Lisbon anyway. He gave some assistance with coastal work to the Portuguese campaign, returning to England by 2 August. Just one week later he was commissioned to the *Lion*, in which he sailed again for Lisbon on 28 August, returning in December. From June to September 1663 he was commander in the Downs aboard the *Rainbow*, and again from April to June 1664 in the *St Andrew*. On 25 June he was commissioned to the *Plymouth* and on 11 July became vice-admiral to Sandwich. Remaining with the *Plymouth*, he was on 11 August instructed to relieve Lawson as commander in the Mediterranean, with the chief purpose of making a new treaty with Algiers. He was required to maintain a 'posture of defence' towards the Dutch (*Journals*, 2.216). He was in such a hurry to depart that he signed his own name wrongly on a seaman's ticket.

While still in the Downs on 19 August Allin had news of the Dutch spice fleet coming from Smyrna. He met Lawson at Gibraltar on 16 September, and on the 28th was left in command of the twelve ships on station. On 30 October he concluded a treaty with Algiers which mostly repeated Lawson's 1662 articles. Meanwhile on 16 October in London the rules of engagement were changed to permit an attack on the Smyrna fleet. Allin seems to have received his new orders at Ibiza on 14 November, and on 19 December, off Cadiz and with eight warships, he attacked the Dutch fleet of thirty merchantmen and three escorts. Despite advantages of surprise and superiority, he took only two prizes and sank two others. He blamed fretting wind for lack of greater success. Nevertheless the incident was celebrated as a triumph at home, compensating for earlier news that two of Allin's own ships had been lost by navigational error. Allin was home by April 1665, in time to participate in the war which his attack on the spice fleet had occasioned.

In the *Plymouth* Allin took part in the battle of Lowestoft on 3 June, when he had a two-hour contest with nine of the enemy. On 11 June he reluctantly transferred to the *Old James*, and on the 24th he was knighted. On 2 July he became admiral of the blue and later that month sailed with Sandwich to Bergen. In October he obtained command of the (first) *Royal James*, aboard which he hoisted his flag as admiral of the white in April 1666. On the division of the fleet it was expected that, with the *Royal James* becoming the flagship of Rupert's detachment, Allin would go to the *Triumph*. But when Rupert sailed on 29 May, he had Allin still aboard with him in a supernumerary capacity. This arrangement continued when the fleet reunited for the final day of the June battle (4th). Allin resumed his proper position by the time of the St James's day fight on 25 July, at which he led the attack and broke through the Dutch centre; the two ships he took then fired were the only ones the enemy lost that day. In a skirmish on the 26th Allin was slightly wounded. He was obliged to shift to the *Sovereign* when both generals subsequently commandeered the *Royal James*. Back on his own ship on 18 September he captured a Frenchman who mistook Allin's white flag for the French colour. Ashore once more, he was forced by illness to miss his own dining-in as elder brother of Trinity House on 24 November.

During 1667 Allin undertook police and defence work in the channel; from January to June 1668 he patrolled in the *Monmouth*. Having long been designated commander in the Mediterranean, he sailed in August 1668 with nine warships and two supports, and reached Algiers on 29 September. On 2 February he concluded an agreement and sailed for home immediately, apparently unaware that the government had ordered him to stay and impose firmer conditions. Despite or because of being 'extremely censured' for leaving English merchants unprotected in the Mediterranean, and for having no more than 'patched up a disadvantageous peace' (*Samuel Pepys and the Second Dutch War*, 199–200), Allin was sent back with orders (29 June) to open hostilities if necessary. He sailed on 17 July with the *Resolution*, seventeen other warships, and six supports. On his arrival at Algiers on 1 September he found the locals 'raving' (*Journals*, 2.111), and so made war on them. Ship to shore bombardment achieved little, but he had some success in his intermittent attacks on Algerine shipping. On 24 September 1670 he handed over his command to Spragge, and was back in Portsmouth by 5 November. On 15 April 1671 Allin became comptroller of the navy in succession to Mennes. In this year he also contested the parliamentary seat of Dunwich. During the Third Anglo-Dutch War, in which no active command was available to an officer of Allin's seniority, he was energetic in inspecting ships and defences. His services were honoured with a baronetcy on 7 February 1673. During 1678 he briefly returned to sea in command of the (third) *Royal James*. He had vacated the comptrollership by 28 January 1680.

Allin retired to the house he had acquired at Somerleyton, Suffolk, where he died in 1685 and was buried on 5 October. He left £500 for his own funeral and monument (the marble bust extant in Somerleyton church), £10 to the poor of Lowestoft, and the rest of his substantial estates in the county to his son Thomas (*c*.1651–1696), who had married Mary Caldwell in 1672, his grandsons Richard, Edmond, and Allin (children of his daughter Alice and Edmond Anguish), and his second wife, Elizabeth Anguish, whom he had married by about 1660. The baronetcy passed to his son Thomas, who left no heirs.

In an age when many profited handsomely from public service, Allin's rapacity was considered extreme. He was said to have established the Mediterranean commander's 50 per cent cut on all plate carried in the king's ships, and was in general derided as having practised 'more the trade of merchantmen' (*Samuel Pepys and the Second Dutch War*, 200). Allin cheerfully admitted he loved 'to get and to save' (Pepys, *Diary*, 6.314). He also knew that his 'ill' French would make Pepys laugh (*CSP dom.*, 1672, 221). But Pepys, who wrote patronizingly of Allin's simple domestic tastes, recognized him as 'in serious matters … a serious man' (Pepys, *Diary*, 9.274).   C. S. KNIGHTON

Sources *The journals of Sir Thomas Allin, 1660–1678*, ed. R. C. Anderson, 2 vols., Navy RS, 79–80 (1939–40) • Pepys, *Diary*, 1.153; 1.224; 4.170–71, 196, 405; 5.322; 6.8, 10, 12–14, 19–20, 62, 147, 287, 314; 7.93–4, 97, 102, 381; 8.149, 161, 479; 9.272–3, 374, 427–8, 473, 513, 516, 529; 10.7–8 • *Samuel Pepys and the Second Dutch War: Pepys's navy white book and Brooke House papers*, ed. R. Latham, Navy RS, 133 (1995), 114, 199–200, 230, 242–3 [transcribed by W. Matthews and C. Knighton] • *The Tangier papers of Samuel Pepys*, ed. E. Chappell, Navy RS, 73 (1935), 183 • *CSP dom.*, 1660–72 • J. R. Powell and E. K. Timings, eds., *Documents relating to the civil war, 1642–1648*, Navy RS, 105 (1963), 203–4 • J. M. Collinge, *Navy Board officials, 1660–1832* (1978), 81 • B. Capp, *Cromwell's navy: the fleet and the English revolution, 1648–1660* (1989), 167, 376 • J. D. Davies, *Gentlemen and tarpaulins: the officers and men of the Restoration navy* (1991), 24, 29, 51, 56, 63–4, 177, 183–4 • R. Ollard, *Man of war: Sir Robert Holmes and the Restoration navy* (1969), 29, 31, 38 • R. Ollard, *Cromwell's earl: a life of Edward Mountagu, 1st earl of Sandwich* (1994), 118, 122, 132 • F. Kitson, *Prince Rupert: admiral and general-at-sea* (1998), 45, 49, 53, 82, 84, 89, 143, 149, 150, 205, 209, 214, 219, 226, 250 • J. R. Powell and E. K. Timings, eds., *The Rupert and Monck letter book, 1666*, Navy RS, 112 (1969), 13, 54, 82, 87, 113, 132, 157, 197, 204, 215, 219, 237, 242, 267, 278 • *Memoirs of Prince Rupert and the cavaliers including their private correspondence*, ed. E. Warburton, 3 vols. (1849), vol. 3, p. 253 • R. C. Anderson, 'The royalists at sea', *Mariner's Mirror*, 14 (1928), 320–38, esp. 321 • R. C. Anderson, 'The royalists at sea', *Mariner's Mirror*, 21 (1935), 61–90, esp. 64 • J. B. Hattendorf and others, eds., *British naval documents, 1204–1960*, Navy RS, 131 (1993), 194–5 • E. Gillingwater, *An historical account of the ancient town of Lowestoft, in the county of Suffolk* (1790), 111, 112, 156–7, 376, 382–3, 418n. • W. A. Copinger, *The manors of Suffolk*, 7 vols. (1905–11), vol. 5, pp. 6, 12, 71; vol. 7, p. 288
Archives Bodl. Oxf., corresp. and journal, Tanner MSS 296, 297 | NMM, Dartmouth MSS • PRO, SP and ADM
Likenesses P. Lely, oils, *c*.1665–1666, NMM [*see illus.*] • G. Kneller, oils, 1680, NMM; repro. in Kitson, *Prince Rupert*, following p. 160 • Vanderbank, engraving (after Kneller), repro. in W. L. Clowes and others, *The Royal Navy*, 7 vols. (1897–1903), vol. 2, p. 424
Wealth at death left £500 for own funeral and monument; £500 from estates to eldest of his daughter's three sons (together with the customer's place already bought for him) at age of twenty-one; £1000 likewise to second grandson; owned eight principal manors; £50 p.a. to own daughter: will, PRO, PROB 11/381, fols. 68*v*–70; Copinger, *Manors of Suffolk*, vol. 7, p. 288

Alline, Henry (1748–1784), evangelist and hymn writer, was born in Newport, Rhode Island, on 14 June 1748, the second son of William Alline and Rebecca Clark. His father, who was probably a miller, responded to the announcements of free land in Nova Scotia, and in 1760 the Alline family immigrated to the township of Falmouth, receiving 1000 acres of land. Although young Henry had attended school in Newport, he received no further formal education in Nova Scotia. Resident in a remote farming village on the northern frontier, he spent his free time in youthful recreation and in reading, both the Bible and a small number of religious writings available to him. Especially influential would have been the Anglican theologian William Law. At the same time that Nova Scotia was experiencing the political turmoil leading to the American Rebellion, Alline struggled with his own internal conflicts and 'carnal' desires. His concern for the state of his soul came to consume him. He found partial release from his inner turmoil through a crisis conversion in 1775, when, as he later recorded, 'redeeming love broke into my soul with repeated scriptures with such a power that my whole soul seemed to be melted down with love' (Alline, *Life*, 34).

Conversion did not resolve all of Alline's concerns. His experiences and reading made him quite suspicious of the traditional teachings of the New England puritanism in which he had been raised. He was particularly critical of the vengeful God of puritanism and of the preordained election of the saints. Although he desperately desired to preach the gospel, his upbringing told him that only those with formal educational credentials were allowed to become clergymen. Having rejected the offer of a commission in the Nova Scotia militia, he decided that his only commission should be one 'from heaven to go forth, and enlist my fellow-mortals to fight under the banners of Jesus Christ' (Alline, *Life*, 44). On 18 April 1776, a day set aside by the Nova Scotia government for 'fasting and prayer' in the midst of the escalating American war—and perhaps not entirely coincidentally the first anniversary of the battle of Lexington and Concord that had begun the fighting—Henry Alline decided on a public preaching career.

As Alline would demonstrate, he had successfully rejected the troubles of the secular world. He offered to others what he had found for himself: a spiritual assurance that rejected and transcended the civil war all around. God had brought the planters to Nova Scotia to shelter them 'in this peaceable corner of the earth' (Alline, 'Sermon', 94). Like most of his hearers, he associated the coming of the American Rebellion with the judgement of God. For the first three years of his brief career as an itinerant preacher, Alline focused his efforts on the region around the Bay of Minas, including the Chignecto area that was so caught up in an American invasion in 1776. He sometimes also made occasional and controversial forays to the south-coast fishing villages, where he came into conflict with Jonathan Scott (1744–1819), the pastor of the puritan church at Jebogue (Yarmouth). Scott saw in Alline's anti-Calvinistic insistence on free will a dangerous alternative to New England orthodoxy. For Scott, Henry Alline was as radical and revolutionary as any rebel firebrand.

Alline began expanding his preaching territory in 1779. In 1781 his controversial *Two Mites on some of the most Important and much Disputed Points of Divinity* was published in Halifax. Like that of many another self-taught evangelists on the northern frontier, Alline's doctrine was mystical, ascetic, other-worldly, anti-intellectual, and egalitarian. He deliberately denied that 'earthy dignity, the esteem of man or a conspicuous station in the world' made a man of God (Alline, *Two Mites*, 109). He insisted that political leaders would have no special privileges on the day of judgement, and emphasized that Christ had commanded his followers 'to salute no man by the way'. For those who shared his vision and spiritual experience, Alline insisted on withdrawal from 'this ensnaring world' on the grounds that 'you have no continuing city here' (ibid., 243, 245). In a published critique of Alline, Jonathan Scott accused the evangelist of appealing to the 'Passions of the young, ignorant and inconsistent, who are influenced more by the Sound and Gingle of the words' (Scott, 168).

In his own way, Alline was a populist leveller. He travelled the countryside preaching and singing hymns, regarding music as a way to attract and hold an audience—as well as a useful vehicle on the road to salvation. He composed more than 500 hymns during his brief lifetime, most of them appearing in print only after his death. One, originally published in 1781, suggests Alline's approach to hymn writing:

> O that the Lord of life would come,
> And all my soul inflame
> With love, to walk with Christ the Lamb,
> And spread his worldly name.
> O Jesus, enter my heart,
> and write my name above;
> Make rocks remove, and guilt depart,
> And fill my soul with love.
> (Bumsted, *Hymns*, 13)

A few of his hymns remained in Baptist hymnals well into the twentieth century.

Alline died of tuberculosis at North-Hampton, New Hampshire, on 2 February 1784 at the start of a preaching tour of the United States. He was buried there the following day. *The Life and Journal of the Rev. Mr Henry Alline*, cited by William James in his *Varieties of Religious Experience* as a classic account of the 'sick soul', was published in Boston in 1806 from manuscripts he left behind at his death. In the Atlantic region of Canada, Alline left a legacy of evangelism and revivalism among his followers, who were called 'New Lights', many of whom later became Baptists. In the United States he was even more influential. His theology served as the basis for the important American frontier denomination called the Free Will Baptists founded by Benjamin Randall.   J. M. BUMSTED

Sources H. Alline, *The life and journal of the Rev. Mr Henry Alline* (1806) · H. Alline, *Two mites on some of the most important and much disputed points of divinity* (1781) · H. Alline, 'Sermon on a day of thanksgiving 1782', *The sermons of Henry Alline*, ed. G. Rawlyk (1986) · J. Scott, *A brief view of the religious tenets and sentiments … of Mr. Henry Alline* (1784) · J. M. Bumsted, *Henry Alline* (1970) · E. Clarke, *The siege of Fort Cumberland, 1776: an episode in the American Revolution* (1995) · J. M. Bumsted, ed., *Henry Alline's hymns and spiritual songs* (1987) · S. Marini, *Radical sects of revolutionary New England* (1982) · W. James, *The varieties of religious experience: a study in human nature* (1902)
Archives Acadia University, Wolfville, Nova Scotia, Maritime Baptist Historical collection
Wealth at death approx. $12 in money, besides a horse and sleigh, and apparel: Alline, *Life*, 179

Allingham [*née* Paterson], **Helen Mary Elizabeth** (1848–1926), watercolour painter, was born on 26 September 1848 at Swadlincote, Derbyshire, the eldest of the seven children (three boys and four girls) of Alexander Henry Paterson (1825–1862), medical practitioner and surgeon, and his wife, Mary Chance Herford (1824–1894), daughter of John Herford, a Manchester wine merchant. Both her parents came from staunchly Unitarian families with Unitarian ministers on both sides, although she was not especially observant herself. On her mother's side, Helen Paterson was related to eminent Unitarians such as Joseph Priestley, Elizabeth Gaskell, and Bessie Parkes. She inherited artistic talent from this side of her family too: her grandmother, Sarah Smith Herford, gained limited recognition for her oil painting, and Helen's aunt, Laura Herford, was the first woman to gain admission to the Royal Academy Schools in 1860.

Within a year of Helen's birth the Paterson family moved to Altrincham, Cheshire, where the Herfords lived. She grew up in an enlightened middle-class family environment and received her early education at the Unitarian School for Girls in Altrincham founded by her grandmother. Of medium height and thin, with fairish hair, she became a rather reserved character, very close to her family and a small circle of friends. Following the death of Helen's father and youngest sister in a diphtheria epidemic in 1862, the family moved to Birmingham to live with her paternal grandmother and aunts. Financial difficulties experienced during these years had a profound effect on her, teaching her the importance of thrift; she became a hard-working and consistent supporter of her family for the rest of her life. From 1862 to 1866 she attended the Government School of Design in Birmingham where she was awarded prizes for her art. In 1866 she enrolled at the Female School of Art in Bloomsbury, prior to entry to the Royal Academy Schools in 1868: nominally she remained a student until 1872 but she rarely attended after 1870 as she became disillusioned with the lack of tuition. Only the academician Frederick Walker encouraged her desire to paint in watercolour. His influence can be seen in her choice of subjects during the 1870s, in which a large figure dominated the picture and landscape is of secondary importance.

From mid-1868 Helen Paterson also worked as a freelance illustrator for various children's magazines such as *Once a Week* and *Little Folks*. In January 1870 this led to a permanent position as illustrator on a new weekly periodical, *The Graphic*, whose visual content was innovative. She was the only woman on the staff. That same year she started exhibiting with two drawings at the Dudley Gallery in Piccadilly. In 1872 she attended evening classes at the Slade School alongside Kate Greenaway, a lifelong friend. Helen illustrated Thomas Hardy's novel *Far from the Madding Crowd* when it was first serialized in *Cornhill* magazine in 1872, and Annie Thackeray's novel *Miss Angel* for the same journal in 1875. Hardy admired her illustrations for his first truly successful novel and later asked her to illustrate *A Laodicean*, an offer that she declined. She exhibited two paintings at the Royal Academy in 1874 entitled *Wait for me* and *The Milkmaid*.

On 22 August 1874 Helen Paterson married the Irish poet William *Allingham (1824–1889) at the Unitarian Chapel, Little Portland Place, London. There were three children of the marriage, Gerald Carlyle (b. 1875), Eva Margaret (b. 1877), and Henry William (b. 1882). After her marriage Helen Allingham relinquished her post on *The Graphic* and from 1874 concentrated on her painting. She moved into circles which included her husband's artistic friends such as Edward Burne-Jones and William Morris and literary figures including Thomas Carlyle and Alfred Lord Tennyson. She illustrated her husband's book of children's poetry *Rhymes for the Young Folk* (1885) using their children as models for the sketches. In 1875 her painting achieved recognition when she was elected associate of the Royal Society of Painters in Water Colours; she was the first woman to be granted full membership in 1890. She exhibited annually at the society from 1875 until 1925.

Although Allingham painted some seaside scenes in the late 1870s and early 1880s during family holidays in Kent and the Isle of Wight, it was rural life which really inspired her. In 1881 the family moved to Sandhills, near Witley, Surrey, where Birket Foster and Edmund Evans were already living. The surrounding cottages and countryside determined the work for which she is best known. From then on she rejected the use of bodycolour in favour of pure watercolour and followed Walker's lead in painting *en plein air* for most of the year. She depicted the cottages she saw around her in Sandhills with minute attention to detail such as the mortar round a chimney or moss on roof tiles. Children—often her own—appeared in her scenes, as did young women engaged in various gentle rural pursuits or just watching the world go by. During the 1880s her figures became smaller, taking their place in the landscape, while the cottages grew in significance. It was Helen Allingham's ability to paint a romantic view of rural life with exquisite precision that captured the public's imagination. Friendship with her Surrey neighbour

Gertrude Jekyll introduced garden scenes into Helen's pictures with the flowers painted in similar detail. Her cottage paintings were so popular that the Fine Art Society invited her to hold her first one-woman exhibition of sixty-six pictures entitled 'Surrey cottages' in 1886 and another six months later. Thereafter she generally exhibited twice a year at the Fine Art Society until 1913, as well as exhibiting elsewhere.

William Allingham's ill health brought the family back to London—this time Hampstead—in 1888 where Helen was left a widow a few months later at the height of her popularity but with little money and three children to support. She continued painting six days a week, travelling around Middlesex and Buckinghamshire and to the west country to paint the cottage scenes the public craved, though she herself was tiring of her subject matter. After 1900 when her popularity began to wane, Allingham searched for new subject matter. In 1901 and 1902 she visited Venice, but the sixty watercolours resulting from these tours have never been as popular as her English cottage scenes. She occasionally painted portraits of children and of her husband's friends including Thomas Carlyle and Alfred Lord Tennyson, but these were usually private commissions. Her paintings were used to illustrate books such as Marcus Huish's *Happy England* (1903), a description of her life and art; her brother Arthur Paterson's *Homes of Tennyson* (1905); and Stewart Dick's *Cottage Homes of England* (1909). She herself published editions of *William Allingham's Diaries* with Dollie Radford (1907) and *Letters to William Allingham* with Mrs E. Baumer Williams (1911).

After the First World War, Helen Allingham's scenes lost favour and were considered old-fashioned and sentimental, though she continued working as hard as ever producing cottage paintings. On 28 September 1926 she died of acute peritonitis while staying with a friend at Valewood House, Haslemere, Surrey, where she had gone to paint. She was cremated at Golders Green on 2 October 1926. A plaque commemorating her life was erected inside Rosslyn Hill Chapel, Hampstead, London. After her death, Allingham's works remained unfashionable until the 1980s. Viewed as overly sentimental and pretty, they were dismissed as the product of a woman artist. Allingham herself had no interest in the feminist movement (and her paintings showed country women enshrined in traditional domesticity), but her style and choice of subjects cannot be attributed entirely to a desire to remain within 'womanly' bounds. Financial considerations were clearly her prime motivation, and when her cottage scenes lost their commercial appeal, she exhibited an ability to explore new subjects. While it may seem strange that a pupil of Frederick Walker and an illustrator for *The Graphic* was so unaffected by the social realism of fellow artists of the 1870s, her paintings deserve to be assessed on their own merits and recognized as among the best of their genre. In her choice of subject matter, Helen Allingham—like the Pre-Raphaelites—harked back to an idyllic past that never really existed. She played an important role in the late nineteenth-century idealization of the English countryside and the growth of a nostalgic movement for the preservation of rural life and crafts. Her cottage scenes remain the most popular, but her finest works are considered to be the few domestic interiors that she painted, often using her own children as models. Many of her paintings can be found in the Hampstead Museum, Burgh House; the Victoria and Albert Museum; and the British Museum, London.

INA TAYLOR

Sources I. Taylor, *Helen Allingham's England* (1990) · M. Huish, *Happy England* (1903) · Patric Allingham bequest, Hampstead Museum, Burgh House, London · private information (2004) · *Hampstead and Highgate Express* (2 Oct 1926) · *The Times* (2 Oct 1926) · A. Lester, ed., *The exhibited works of Helen Allingham* (1979) · A. Watts, *Helen Allingham's cottage homes — revisited* (1994) · C. Newall, *Victorian watercolours* (1987) · A. Clayton-Payne, *Victorian cottages* (1993) · P. Gerrish Nunn, *Victorian women artists* (1987) · m. cert. · d. cert. · records, Government School of Design, Birmingham · records, Female School of Art, London · records, RA, Royal Academy Schools

Archives Hampstead Museum, Burgh House, London, Patric Allingham bequest

Likenesses H. M. E. Allingham, self-portrait, watercolour, 1885, Hampstead Museum, Burgh House, London · photographs, Hampstead Museum, Burgh House, London

Wealth at death £16,186 10s. 1d.: probate, 26 Nov 1926, CGPLA Eng. & Wales

Allingham, John Till (*fl.* 1799–1810), playwright, was the son of an Irish wine merchant in the City of London. He trained for the law, but made his name as a successful and prolific playwright. Both he and his sister appeared on the stage.

Allingham's farce *Fortune's Frolic*, first produced at Covent Garden in 1799, enjoyed great success, its leading character, Robin Roughhead, being played by many popular comedians. His second play, *'Tis All a Farce*, produced at the Haymarket in 1800, was less successful.

Other plays included the comedy *Hearts of Oak* (1803), *The Romantic Lover*, a comedy produced at Covent Garden in 1806, and the musical farces *The Weathercock* (1805) (which, according to T. Gilliland, was 'universally esteemed'), 'Who Wins? or, The Widow's Choice' (1808?, not printed), with music by Henry Condell, and *Transformation, or, Love and Law* (1810). His plays owed much to the ability and popularity of Charles Mathews, whom Harlow painted as Mr Wiggins in the farce *Mrs Wiggins* in 1803.

In his *Life of John Kemble* (1825), James Boaden writes of Allingham that 'with an agreeable person, and a jovial temper he … became dreadfully embarrassed in his circumstances, and died yet young, the victim of disease, brought on by intemperance.' He was said to have devoted his leisure to the study of mechanics, and to have invented a flying machine, by means of which he succeeded in 'fluttering about his apartments like a dabchick', but his attempt to rise in the air with the help of balloons filled with steam failed. He once fought a duel in a turnip field with one of his critics (Boaden, 2.349–50). John Till Allingham was a direct forebear of the twentieth-century novelist Margery Allingham (1904–1966).

E. D. COOK, *rev.* JOHN D. HAIGH

Sources Genest, *Eng. stage*, vol. 1 · J. Boaden, *Memoirs of the life of John Philip Kemble*, 2 vols. (1825) · D. E. Baker, *Biographia dramatica, or, A companion to the playhouse*, rev. I. Reed, new edn, rev. S. Jones, 3 vols. in 4 (1812) · T. Gilliland, *The dramatic mirror, containing the history of the stage from the earliest period, to the present time*, 2 vols. (1808) · D. J. O'Donoghue, *The poets of Ireland: a biographical dictionary with bibliographical particulars*, 1 vol. in 3 pts (1892–3) · C. Knight, ed., *The English cyclopaedia: biography*, 3 (1856) · *The thespian dictionary, or, Dramatic biography of the present age*, 2nd edn (1805) · J. T. Allingham, 'A sketch of "Who wins? or, The widow's choice": a new musical farce' [n.d., 1808?] · S. J. Kunitz and H. Haycraft, eds., *Twentieth century authors: a biographical dictionary of modern literature* (1942)

Likenesses W. Ridley, stipple (after S. De Wilde), BM, NPG; repro. in *Monthly Mirror* (1804)

Allingham, Margery Louise (1904–1966), writer, was born on 20 May 1904 in Ealing, London. She was the eldest of three children of the journalist and writer Herbert John Allingham (1867–1936), editor of the *London Journal*, and his wife, Emily Jane, *née* Hughes (1879–1960). Both parents, who were cousins, produced pulp fiction for serialization in popular magazines and journals. Margery's literary apprenticeship began on her seventh birthday, when she was assigned her own office in the family home at the Old Rectory in Layer Breton, Essex. While her beloved father's encouragement probably influenced Allingham's writerly development most significantly, her conventional education was not neglected, despite an illness which kept her from school for some years. She attended Endsleigh House School in Colchester from 1915 to 1918, then moved to the Perse School for Girls in Cambridge from 1919 to 1920, and completed her education at the Regent Street Polytechnic in London (1921–23), where she studied speech and drama and lost her childhood stammer.

Although her hope for a career in the theatre was disappointed, Allingham was already launched in what would be her lifelong professions of journalism and writing fiction. By 1922 she had published reviews, stories, and film synopses in the *Picture Show* and the *Girl's Cinema*, fan magazines edited by her maternal aunt, Maud Hughes, the first of their kind in Britain. Her first novel, *Blackkerchief Dick*, an adventure story, appeared in 1923. She met her future husband, Philip (Pip) Youngman Carter (1904–1969), an art student at the polytechnic, in 1921. The couple married on 29 September 1927. Their amiable, childless marriage was funded by Allingham's increasingly successful fiction. And, although Youngman Carter assisted his wife as a sounding board for plot design, and by producing covers and illustrations for her work, he found it difficult to sell his art. Allingham supported his increasingly expensive tastes until after the Second World War, when Pip came into his own writing society columns for *The Tatler*, which he edited from 1954.

While the couple retained a base in London, from 1931 their main home was in rural Essex, a region with which Allingham always felt a deep affinity. In 1937 they took up permanent residence at D'Arcy House at Tolleshunt D'Arcy just 5 miles from Allingham's childhood home at

Margery Louise Allingham (1904–1966), by Howard Coster, 1936

Layer Breton. Aside from her affection for her garden, and her first aid and air raid precautions work during the Second World War, Allingham's was a writer's life. During her long career she published twenty-five novels, as well as the posthumous *Cargo of Eagles* (1968), completed by her husband. In addition she produced four novellas, sixty-four stories, a wartime book on England for American readers, and a great number of reviews and other articles for such publications as *Time and Tide*, the *Daily Herald*, and *Homes and Gardens*.

Despite her sunny character, and her success as a novelist, the last part of Allingham's life also contained difficulties and disappointments. The thyroid condition from which she had suffered since her polytechnic days, and which was the reason for her corpulence, was finally diagnosed in 1940. By the 1950s she was increasingly ill, and her condition led to episodes of confusion and depression, for which she was hospitalized. Discovery of Pip's infidelity, and problems with the Inland Revenue caused her distress for many years. In the end, she suffered from breast cancer, and died at Severalls Hospital, Colchester, on 30 June 1966. She was buried at Tolleshunt D'Arcy five days later, in the graveyard of the fourteenth-century church of St Nicholas, and remembered for her warmth, vitality, and humour.

The significance of Allingham's contribution to the development of detective fiction becomes clearer as time passes. She is rightly judged to be one of the four queens of crime of the golden age of mystery writing along with Agatha Christie, Dorothy L. Sayers, and Ngaio Marsh. Her contribution to the genre is the foregrounding of the kinds of psychological interest which would lead later in the twentieth century to the psychological crime fiction of such exemplary practitioners as Ruth Rendell, P. D. James, and Minette Walters. Allingham's fiction displays a keen sense of place, and in this comparisons are often made between her work and that of Dickens and Robert Louis Stevenson. Her representation of houses and architecture is deft and resonant. She also shares a particular sense of fun and gaiety with P. G. Wodehouse, who is sometimes mentioned in discussions of her dialogue, with its breezy and often zany 1920s English taste for eccentricity, wit, and absurdity. Most of all, however, she is praised for her set of memorable recurring characters, who grow in depth as her career proceeds. The most important of these, her detective Albert Campion, made his first appearance in *The Crime at Black Dudley* (1929), her second mystery novel after her début in *The White Cottage Mystery* (1928). The diffident, languid, aristocratic Campion, with his sensitivity to evil and his passion for justice, becomes an increasingly complex figure over time. Campion's comic manservant, Magersfontein Lugg, an earthy former burglar, and Campion's associate, the earnest policeman Stanislaus Oates, both first appear in *Mystery Mile* (1930). Lady Amanda Fitton, who later marries Campion and who is one of Allingham's characteristically strong female characters, is introduced in *Sweet Danger* (1933) as a young woman who combines high spirits with high intelligence and, most unusually, electrical and engineering skills. Another interesting young policeman, Charlie Luke, appears in *More Work for the Undertaker* (1948). Allingham deploys her ensemble of characters to make intricate observations regarding political, class, gender, and family relations, as well as using them in more conventional ways in the service of her always entertaining mysteries.

Opinion differs as to Allingham's best book, though there is general consensus that her finest fiction appeared after the Second World War. Her own favourite was *The Beckoning Lady* (1955), which contained autobiographical elements. *More Work for the Undertaker*, featuring one of Allingham's absorbing eccentric fictional families, is also well regarded. However, it is *The Tiger in the Smoke* (1952), which has attracted the most critical esteem, with its killer on the loose in fog-bound London, its surreal touches, and its intense drama of good and evil.

Allingham's work has been adapted for audio cassette, radio, and television. The BBC television series based on her novels in 1989 and 1990 was particularly successful and brought her many new readers.

KATE FULLBROOK

Sources J. Thorogood, *Margery Allingham: a biography* (1991) • R. Martin, *Ink in her blood: the life and crime fiction of Margery Allingham* (1988) • B. A. Pike, 'Margery Allingham', *British mystery writers, 1920–1939*, ed. B. Benstock and T. F. Staley, DLitB, 77 (1989), 3–12 • *DNB* • C. Kaplan, 'Margery Allingham', *An encyclopedia of British women* writers, ed. P. Schlueter and J. Schlueter (1989), 3–4 • H. R. F. Keating, 'Margery Allingham', *Twentieth-Century Crime and Mystery Writers*, ed. J. M. Reilly, 2nd edn (1985), 16–18 • J. Jones, 'Allingham, Margery', *Dictionary of British women writers*, ed. J. Todd (1989) • P. Youngman Carter, preface, in M. Allingham, *Mr Campion's clowns* (1967)

Archives SOUND BBC Radio Archives, various interviews

Likenesses H. Coster, photograph, 1936, NPG [*see illus.*]

Wealth at death £11,428: probate, 1967, *CGPLA Eng. & Wales*

Allingham, William (1824–1889), poet, was born on 19 March 1824 in Ballyshannon, co. Donegal, the eldest of the five children of William Allingham and his wife, Elizabeth, *née* Crawford (*d*. 1833). His father ran a shipping business, plying cargo such as timber and slate, between North America, the Baltic, and Ireland; he also carried emigrants to the United States. Both his father and his mother were natives of Ballyshannon. William Allingham was educated locally, at Wray's School in Church Lane, where the language of instruction was Latin, and then boarded at Killeshandra, co. Cavan, in 1837. He was unhappy at school and his father, now a manager of the Provincial Bank in Ballyshannon, gave him a job soon after. He subsequently worked at branches of the Provincial in Armagh, Strabane, and Enniskillen, as well as at Ballyshannon. In 1843 he first visited London, enjoying the mixture of excitement, culture, and solitude. He secured the interest and support of the editor and essayist Leigh Hunt around this time, who encouraged him and helped him into print. In 1846 he entered the customs service after two months' training in Belfast, where he enthused about Tennyson, then at the height of his popularity, to his fellow trainees. His first posting was in the town of Donegal, as principal coast officer, at a salary of £80 a year.

Allingham had a keen appreciation of the English and Scots ballad, and of Irish folk-songs in English. Inspired by the Romantic and Victorian rediscovery of the ballad, and intrigued by its Irish varieties, he began to collect these words and songs, an interest facilitated by the nature of his work, which required a good deal of travel and contact with country people. He also began writing his own attempts at the ballad form, and went to the printers of broadsheets in Dublin and Belfast, where he had his own compositions set up on the long strips of white-brown paper (W. Allingham, 'Preface', *The Ballad Book*, 1865, xxxiii), with the typical woodcut decorations at the top and bottom from the printers' blocks. He then gave them away, or had them sold at markets and fair-days in the Donegal towns. By upbringing a member of the Church of Ireland, he exhibited a marked interest in the Gaelic and Catholic culture of his region, on one occasion taking part in the pilgrimage to Lough Derg, an occasion for singing and story-telling as well as for piety and silence.

Allingham continued to visit London, where, through Leigh Hunt's circle, he met Thomas Carlyle, Coventry Patmore, Tennyson, and Dante Gabriel Rossetti. Through Rossetti he came to appreciate the work of the Pre-Raphaelite school of painters and writers, finding its combination of medievalism and realism congenial to his observant sensibility and traditionalist temperament. In 1849 the customs service transferred him to Ramsey on

William Allingham (1824–1889), by Helen Allingham, 1876

the Isle of Man, and the following year he brought out his first book of verse, *Poems*, dedicated to Leigh Hunt, which although praised in private by Tennyson, sold poorly. It contained one of his best-known poems, 'The Fairies', which was written at Killybegs in Donegal in 1849. He was moved to Coleraine in 1850; in February 1854 he resigned briefly, hoping to make a living by writing. He quickly realized his mistake and rejoined the service, first being posted to New Ross in Wexford, before returning to Ballyshannon in 1855. Carlyle, for one, thought him lucky to escape the drudgery of hack-work in London. In 1854 he published *Day and Night Songs*, reissued the following year with illustrations by Rossetti, John Everett Millais, and Arthur Hughes, making this volume a notable one in the history of book illustration.

The routine of Allingham's life at Ballyshannon was varied by trips to London where he visited his artist and writer friends, and further afield. On one memorable occasion in Paris he had dinner with Thackeray, after which they visited 'Father Prout' (Francis Sylvester Mahony), author of 'The Bells of Shandon', and found him giving house-room to a fellow-Corkman who had run out of money. In 1863 Allingham transferred to the London docklands, where he suffered a nervous breakdown; after a period of convalescence back home he moved to Lymington, Hampshire, from where he could easily visit Tennyson, now living at Farringford on the Isle of Wight. Allingham was at work on two major projects: his anthology of British ballads, *The Ballad Book* (1865), and *Laurence Bloomfield in Ireland*, a verse novel in heroic couplets analysing the tensions in Irish society, particularly those generated by the land question. It was issued in 1863 in twelve parts in *Fraser's Magazine*, and was then edited by James Anthony Froude for volume publication in 1864. Its eponymous hero is an idealistic young landlord who returns to his estates intending to improve the conditions of his tenantry. One of these, Neal Doran, joins a secret society of agitators, and is almost ruined by these associations, but he is saved by the generosity and moral steadfastness of Bloomfield. The poem provides painterly encapsulations of mid-nineteenth-century Irish rural society in the aftermath of the great famine of 1845–50: there is a scene of eviction, powerfully evoked, and clearly etched from Allingham's personal experience; a round tower with a winding stair which symbolizes history; a flashy big house with gaudy and inelegant interiors which is contrasted sharply with rain-soaked hovels. When *Laurence Bloomfield* appeared, Gladstone quoted from it in the House of Commons, and Ivan Turgenev declared that he had never understood Ireland until he read it. Lord Palmerston rewarded Allingham with a civil-list pension of £60 for his poetry (18 June 1864), augmented in 1870 to £100.

In 1870 Allingham resigned from the customs service to become sub-editor under Froude of *Fraser's Magazine*. A collection of his pieces from that magazine, *Rambles by Patricius Walker* was published in 1873, and he took over the editorial chair in 1874. In that year, on 22 August, he married Helen (1848–1926), daughter of Dr Alexander Paterson, who as Helen Mary Elizabeth *Allingham enjoyed considerable success as a watercolourist, and whose reputation revived in the late twentieth century. They lived in Chelsea, where the friendship with Carlyle strengthened. Allingham resigned as editor of *Fraser's* in 1879 and went to live at Sandhills, near Witley, in Surrey. Tennyson was now at Aldworth, not far away, and his proximity was not unconnected to Allingham's choice of residence, but in 1881 Allingham moved back to London, to their house in Lyndhurst Road, Hampstead, so that he and his wife could be near the schools they had selected for their two sons and daughter.

Laurence Bloomfield in Ireland is Allingham's main literary achievement, but his poems about Ballyshannon and nature show both a Pre-Raphaelite taste for detail, as well as a talent for accurate and clear description which can carry emotional, and often quite complex, implications. In poems such as 'An Evil May-Day' (1882) he credits the material world with an underlying order and significance, but this confidence is troubled in other pieces, such as 'George Levison, or, The Schoolfellows' in *Fifty Modern Poems* (1865), where an idyllic marriage is disturbed by the visit of a ruined and broken friend of the husband. 'Bridegroom Park' in *Life and Phantasy* (1889) tells a Gothic tale of sexual betrayal, death, and ghostly presences, and even the charm and lightness of 'The Fairies' has a sinister underside. Allingham's diary and a fragment of an autobiography demonstrate his accuracy and patience, and contain vivid sketches of his literary friends; the diary remained in print well into the late twentieth century.

To his contemporaries in England, Allingham seemed to carry an atmosphere of Irish open spaces and vitality; Tennyson relished his ready wit and appreciative presence; and his reserve and dark good looks were remarked upon by Georgina Burne-Jones, the painter's wife. Later in life, however, his health was impaired by a fall from a horse, and after a period of illness he died at home in Hampstead on 18 November 1889. His remains were cremated at Woking, and his ashes were buried in Ballyshannon Church of Ireland graveyard, where there is a commemorative slab. A collection of *Varieties in Prose* was published posthumously in 1893, and a six-volume collected edition of his works was issued between 1888 and 1893.

ROBERT WELCH

Sources *William Allingham: a diary*, ed. H. Allingham and D. Radford (1907); repr. with introduction by G. Grigson (1967) • A. Warner, *William Allingham* (1975) • J. Hewitt, ed., *The poems of William Allingham* (1967) • T. Brown, *Northern voices* (1975) • R. Welch, *Irish poetry from Moore to Yeats* (1980) • G. B. N. Hill, ed., *The letters of Dante Gabriel Rossetti to William Allingham, 1854–1870* (1897)
Archives Hunt. L., corresp. • NL Ire., corresp. and literary papers • NL NZ, Turnbull L., notebook | BL, corresp. with Macmillans, Add. MS 55006 • Bodl. Oxf., corresp. with John Ruskin [transcripts] • NL Scot., corresp. with Carlyle family • Queen's University, Belfast, letters to Henry Sutton • U. Leeds, Brotherton L., letters to Henry Sutton • U. Reading L., letters to George Bell & Sons
Likenesses photographs, *c.*1857, NPG; copy negatives by E. Walker, NPG • H. Allingham, portraits, 1876–89, NPG, NG Ire. [*see illus.*] • portraits, 1888–93, repro. in W. Allingham, *Collected poems* (1893) • V. Breen, bust, 20th cent., Allied Irish Bank, Ballyshannon, co. Donegal, Ireland • A. Hughes, pen, ink, and pencil drawing, Whitworth Art Gallery, Manchester • A. Munro, plaster bust, NG Ire.; related portrait, exh. RA 1855 • C. F. Murray, drawing, FM Cam.
Wealth at death £269 16s. 9d.: probate, 26 Feb 1890, *CGPLA Eng. & Wales*

Allinson, Thomas Richard (1858–1918), dietitian and businessman, was born at 43 Rumford Street, Hulme, Lancashire, on 29 March 1858, the son of Thomas Allinson, a bookkeeper, and his wife, Ellen (formerly Sims). He left school at fifteen and, aiming to be a doctor, he subsidized his studies by becoming a chemist's assistant. In 1879 he graduated LRCP (Edinburgh) and LRCS (Edinburgh). Over the next six years Allinson gained an unusually broad medical experience, in hospitals and country practice, in the poor-law system, in club practice and the police service, and on board ship. In 1885 he set up his own practice in Spanish Place, near Manchester Square in London's West End; the practice was linked with a private hospital that treated patients according to Allinson's ideas. That year he also began writing a column for the *Weekly Times and Echo*; some of his articles were reprinted in his *Medical Essays* (2 vols., 1887) and revised in five volumes between 1889 and 1893.

In 1886 Allinson published *A System of Hygienic Medicine*. His philosophy sprang from the notion that the body contained a vital force which, if nourished by fresh air, exercise, and appropriate diet, would yield its owner good health. Allinson believed that meat, tea, coffee, tobacco, and alcohol on the other hand weakened the life force. As

Thomas Richard Allinson (1858–1918), by Ray, pubd 1911

bread formed an important part of ordinary people's subsistence fare, he insisted that white bread, with its noxious additives, should be avoided, in favour of the wholemeal kind, containing the bran fibre. His *Advantages of Wholemeal Bread* appeared in 1893. To produce and market wholewheat flour of the desired purity, Allinson established the Natural Food Company, later incorporated under his chairmanship. Allinson bread products continue to be sold today.

Allinson was a fierce critic of certain current medical practices. In a pamphlet of 1888, *How to Avoid Vaccination*, he condemned this 'nasty rite' (by then compulsory) and explained ways of circumventing the law. The medical authorities in Edinburgh at once compelled him to remove his name from the pamphlet, which none the less continued to circulate anonymously. Allinson also opposed surgical operations, and the wholesale prescribing of drugs, which he considered dealt merely with local areas of illness instead of paying regard to the body's entire system. In thirteen books, in his weekly column, and in more than 1000 pamphlets, as well as in lectures throughout the country, Allinson advocated some sensible ideas about hygiene, but incurred the hostility of the medical establishment.

After disregarding a caution by the Edinburgh authorities, in 1892 Allinson was charged by the General Medical Council in London with infamous conduct, namely advertising both his services as a doctor and his commercial products. He took his case to the Court of Appeal, but lost. In 1895 he was fined £20 for continuing to style himself LRCP. Five years later he was censured at the inquest on a small child who had died of malnutrition after being fed Dr Allinson's Food for Babies and Invalids, which was shown to consist mainly of pearl barley. In 1910 Allinson was convicted for sending indecent material through the post, though he won the case on appeal. This was probably a birth-control pamphlet, which argued that it was individually and socially wrong for too many children to be born. As early as 1891 he had fallen out over this issue with editors of *The Vegetarian*.

During the First World War, Allinson had the satisfaction of seeing the introduction of 'war bread' with a low rate of extraction that benefited health. Despite his love of a good scrap, he presented a sympathetic bedside manner towards the thousands who passed through what he claimed to be the largest medical practice in England. With a lofty brow and twinkly bespectacled eyes above a full beard, he dressed well in black jacket, striped trousers, and fancy waistcoat adorned with a thick, gold fobchain. His only known pastime was stamp collecting.

In the final two years of his life Allinson suffered from chronic bronchitis, and he died of tuberculosis at his home at 4 Spanish Place, on 29 November 1918; he was cremated at Golders Green, Middlesex, on 2 December. He left a wife, Anna, with whom he had three sons and a daughter, and his estate was valued at £26,048. One son, Dr Bertrand Allinson, a dietetic guru in London, remained in good standing with his medical colleagues; another son, Adrian Paul Allinson (1890–1959), designed posters for the Southern Railway.   T. A. B. CORLEY

Sources S. Pepper, 'Allinson's staff of life: health without medicine in the 1890s', *History Today*, 42/10 (1992), 30–35 · *The Times* (30 Nov 1918) · *The Lancet* (4 June 1892) · *The Lancet* (30 July 1892) · *The Lancet* (29 June 1895) · *The Lancet* (6 July 1895) · *The Lancet* (23 Nov 1895) · *The Lancet* (14 Dec 1895) · *Law reports: queen's bench division*, 1 (1894), 750–66 · *The Times* (5 March 1910) · *The Times* (9 April 1910) · J. R. Irons, *Breadcraft* (1848), 283–5 · *CGPLA Eng. & Wales* (1919) · b. cert. · d. cert.

Likenesses Ray, caricature, pubd 1911, NPG [*see illus.*]

Wealth at death £26,047 12s. 7d.: probate, 27 Feb 1919, *CGPLA Eng. & Wales*

Allison, John Drummond (1921–1943), poet, was born in Caterham, Surrey, on 31 July 1921, the youngest of the four sons of Harry Ashby Allison (1870–1946), a chartered accountant, and his wife, of Austrian descent, Gertrude Jane Mabel Wolfsberger (1877–1961). Baptized Drummond because his mother noted that he had the pugnacious chin of Sapper's popular fictional hero Bulldog Drummond, his boyhood was a happy one. The family home was filled with books and visitors including the author T. H. White. One friend remembers the atmosphere as 'utterly Betjeman' (private information). After attending Downside preparatory school, Purley, he won a scholarship in 1934 to Bishop's Stortford College, a liberal, nonconformist public school, where he flourished: acting, debating, and subscribing to the Left Book Club.

In 1939 Allison won an open exhibition at Queen's College, Oxford, forming productive friendships with Sidney Keyes and John Heath-Stubbs, with whom he founded a salon where other aspiring poets were persuaded to read and discuss their works. Allison contributed to *Eight Oxford Poets*, edited by Keyes and Michael Meyer and published by Routledge in 1941, *Poetry from Oxford in Wartime, 1942–3* (Basil Blackwell), and *Z: Oxford and Cambridge Writing* (John Lehmann, 1942). He gained a second class in the shortened honours school in modern history before moving on to Sandhurst and a commission in the East Surrey regiment. He trained in Plymouth and at the battle school in Northern Ireland, spending his leaves in Oxford and London, where he met Tambimuttu and Dylan Thomas in the Swiss Pub in Soho. He had time to correct the final proofs of his single volume of published poems, *The Yellow Night* (Fortune Press, 1944), before being seconded to the West Surreys and embarking for north Africa in October 1943. In November his regiment joined the Fifth Army in Italy and on the night of 2–3 December he was mortally wounded leading a platoon attack against a German machine-gun post on a mountain ridge overlooking the Garigliano River. He was buried in Italy, first in the divisional cemetery at Roccamonfina then in the war cemetery at Minturno, north of Naples, Italy.

Compact of stature, determined, energetic, moving and speaking at high speed, Allison had the appearance of a young James Cagney. Impulsive, ebullient, uninhibited, generous, and ingenuous, he gained the affection of a wide circle of friends, male and female. His poetic themes concerned love and longing and the quest for identity, certainty, and purpose in a world of widespread social and political instability and disillusionment. He also wrote about cricket (the subject of two of his most powerful poems 'Verity' and 'The Oval') and of his growing sense of foreboding as the war snatched him from unscathed and enchanted Oxford, forcing him to confront his own mortality. Though his is a raw talent and his poems are often uneven and wilfully obscure, his vocabulary is vibrant and illuminating. His tone is ironic and his language engagingly colloquial, steeped in Arthurian imagery, in political and historical reference, and in his own experience. His mature poems, among them 'Love's Milanese', 'The Brass Horse', 'O Sheriffs', 'A Funeral Oration', 'After Lyonesse', 'Yorktown Gate Guard', and 'The Yellow Night', have found favour in modern anthologies. Allison readily acknowledged his early debt to Swinburne and later to W. H. Auden yet he developed a highly individual and modern style. Echoes of Allison may be found in the early works of Thom Gunn. Though one should not claim too much, there are many who believe that Allison's poetry has stood the test of time better than that of more acclaimed contemporaries. He was, in the words of Ian Hamilton, 'perhaps the most absorbed and striking elegist of Auden's "low, dishonest decade"' (Hamilton, 74).

STEPHEN BENSON

Sources M. Sharp, introduction, in *The poems of Drummond Allison*, ed. M. Sharp (1978) [incl. notes] · A. Thwaite, 'The poetry of Drummond Allison', *Nimbus Magazine*, 3/2 (winter 1955), 43–7 · I. Hamilton, *A poetry chronicle: essays and reviews* (1973) · private information (2004) [N. Beerbohm]
Archives Bishop's Stortford College, archives · Ransom HRC
Likenesses D. Haughton, pencil drawing, repro. in D. Allison, *The yellow night: poems, 1940–41–42–43* (1944) · photograph, repro. in Liber vitae reginensium qui pro patria mortem obierunt MCMXXXIX–MCMXLV, 1951, Queen's College, Oxford

Allison, Thomas (*bap.* 1647, *d.* in or before 1706), Arctic explorer, was baptized on 6 June 1647 in Great Yarmouth, Norfolk, the son of Roger Allison and his wife, Elizabeth. He became a freeman in 1668, having served his apprenticeship to Nicolas Allen of Yarmouth whose trade is unknown. Allison and his wife, Eleanor, had a son, John, baptized in 1677, and a daughter, Anne, baptized the following year. His will refers to his wife, Mary (perhaps his second wife), and a daughter, 'Ann'. The one certain fact concerning Allison's career as a mariner is that for some time he was employed by the Russia Company trading between London and Archangel on the White Sea. On one of these voyages he and his crew were obliged to winter on Arctic shores. His journal detailing their sufferings and final escape was subsequently published at the suggestion of his employers as *An account of a voyage from Archangel in Russia in the year 1697 … published … chiefly for the benefit of those that sail that way, as well as for the satisfaction of the curious* (1699). The journal opens with the departure on 8 October 1697 of Allison's ship the *Ann* of Yarmouth (260 tons) bound for Gravesend. Ten days later the *Ann* became partially disabled in a storm, but after sighting land off North Cape (lat. 71°) Allison eventually found a safe anchorage on what is thought to be the west shore of Porsanger Fjord, just south of North Cape. At this juncture Allison's narrative proper begins with detailed day-to-day accounts of the problems facing him in maintaining the health and morale of his crew of twenty-four men and boys throughout the freezing conditions of a long, dark Arctic winter. The ship herself provided shelter though with limited stores and fuel. Fortunately the steep slopes of the fjord were well wooded with larch and willows, as Allison wrote: 'We happened well into a place so plentifully supplied with what we could not have lived without' (Allison, 518). Presented with an almost total absence of wildlife Allison organized regular foraging for shellfish, urchins, dills, and such scallops as could be dredged through the sea ice. But it was the intense cold that posed the main challenge to survival and caused even journal writing to become a major affliction, as Allison recorded: ''Twas vexatious enough to get my ink ready for use and no less to keep it so, a boy being forced to thaw it as oft as I had occasion to dip my pen' (ibid., 507). Several cases of frostbite are noted, some severe enough to require the services of the surgeon, William Brown, 'who had a good understanding of his business' (ibid., 504). With the approach of Christmas Allison took care to distribute extra rations including beer and honey to make drink. The discovery of a deserted fishing village in the neighbourhood, described in some detail, provided an interesting diversion. The months of January and February brought little relief, the occasional thaw raising hopes of release only to be dashed by a return of the frost. February saw the men on reduced rations, Allison taking pains to claim no more than his fair share 'to prevent all discontent and murmuring' (ibid., 508). Not until mid-March was relief at last assured by the unexpected arrival of a yawl from North Cape bearing provisions and news from Europe. There follow accounts of visits to a settlement named 'Swetwell' and to 'Colwitch', presumably the modern Kolvik, of which Allison gives a brief description and account of the inhabitants, their customs, and dwelling places. On 25 March 1698, free at last from her icy prison, the *Ann* was got ready for sea, finally reaching Gravesend on 24 April. From his own account Allison appears to have been not merely an experienced Arctic navigator and leader of men, but also something of an amateur naturalist, commenting on such northern phenomena as the aurora and the properties of ice. On returning to London he sought identification of specimens of shellfish and a commercial outlet for certain coloured rocks.

Allison's will was proved in the Norwich consistory court in 1706. In 1808 his journal was reprinted by John Pinkerton in volume 1 of his *Travels* and this brought the work to the notice of a wider public.   H. G. R. KING

Sources T. Allison, *An account of a voyage from Archangel in Russia in the year 1697* (1699); repr. in J. Pinkerton, ed., *A general collection of the best and most interesting voyages and travels in all parts of the world*, 1 (1808) [repr. in *A collection of travels*, ed. J. Pinkerton, 1 (1808), 491–521] · private information (2004) [Norfolk RO] · baptism registers, Great Yarmouth [transcript in Norfolk RO] · will, 1706, Norfolk RO, Norwich consistory court · *DNB*

Wealth at death lands in Yarmouth: will, 1706, Norwich consistory court, Norfolk RO

Allitsen, Frances [*real name* Mary Bumpus] (**1848–1912**), composer, was born on 30 December 1848 at 159 Oxford Street, London, one of the seven children of John Bumpus, a bookseller, and his wife, Emma Louisa Barton. Little is known about her early life other than that her parents were opposed to the idea of a woman entering the musical profession or studying music seriously. Mary Bumpus was initially interested in writing novels and stories, but with the encouragement of its principal, Weist Hill, studied at the Guildhall School of Music, where she was a corporation exhibitioner for at least four years when she was in her thirties (1881–5). Even as a student she was known as Frances Allitsen, a pseudonym doubtless chosen to assuage her parents' dismay at her choice of career. Nevertheless they may still have refused to help her financially, since she seems to have given singing lessons in order to pay for composition tuition.

Many of Allitsen's early works were performed at Guildhall concerts in the early 1880s, including a piano sonata, a 'Slavonic' overture for orchestra, and several songs. It was as a songwriter that she was to become best known, although she continued to write instrumental music throughout her life. Her songs are on a large scale, displaying formal inventiveness, complex harmonies (often with

an additional accompanying instrument as well as the piano), and a keen ear for detailed word painting.

Allitsen took great care over the financial details of her career, keeping a precise record of her transactions with various publishers from 1885 to 1896 (BL, Add. MS 50071). For most of her songs she received a 3*d*. royalty for every copy sold, sometimes with an additional down payment. By the 1890s her passionate and harmonically complex songs were being frequently performed all over Britain by the leading singers of the day, such as David Bispham and Clara Butt, often accompanied by Allitsen herself. A collection of *Six Songs* to poems by various authors, including Tennyson and Marie Corelli, was published in 1889 and sold well. But her most popular song was a setting of Charles Mackay's 'There's a land', published in 1896 and widely performed by Clara Butt during the Second South African War. Other of her bombastically patriotic songs also became particularly popular at this time, as did her religious songs, such as the psalm setting 'The Lord is my light' (1897). In addition, Allitsen wrote several works that she regarded as more 'artistic', including the song cycle for baritone and piano *Moods and Tenses* (1905).

Allitsen's cantata *For the Queen*, to a libretto by Frank Hyde, for baritone, mezzo-soprano, bass, chorus, and orchestra, was first heard at the Crystal Palace, London, in 1911. Several elements of this work, such as details of plot and aspects of musical style, can also be found in *Bindra the Minstrel* (1912), her only opera. This is a dramatically engaging work for which she wrote her own libretto, about how a deposed king in tenth-century Asia is saved by his trusty minstrel who rekindles the devotion of the people through the power of his songs.

In 1911 Allitsen kept a short diary (BL, Add. MS 50071) which shows her unsuccessful attempts at getting *Bindra the Minstrel* performed, as well as her depressed state of mind towards the end of her life. A typical entry reads: 'As usual—health delicate, people unkind, remiss and neglectful—professional anxieties and indecisions'. She died of pleurisy on 1 October 1912 at her home, 20 Queen's Terrace, St John's Wood Road, London, and was buried in Hampstead cemetery.   SOPHIE FULLER

Sources S. Fuller, *The Pandora guide to women composers: Britain and the United States, 1629 – present* (1994), 38–40 · H. Simpson, *A century of ballads, 1810–1910* (1910) · A. T. C. Pratt, ed., *People of the period: being a collection of the biographies of upwards of six thousand living celebrities*, 2 vols. (1897) · L. Ronald, 'Some lady song writers', *Lady's Realm* (1901), 474–80 · 'Popular lady composers: Miss Frances Allitsen', *Strand Musical Magazine*, 2 (1895), 251 · *The Times* (3 Oct 1912) · F. Allitsen, Book for entering musical and literary agreements, BL, Add. MS 50071 · CLRO, Guildhall School of Music and Drama archive · b. cert.

Likenesses portrait, repro. in 'Popular lady composers: Miss Frances Allitsen' · portrait, repro. in Ronald, 'Some lady song writers', 479 · portrait, repro. in Simpson, *Century of ballads, 1810–1910*, facing p. 311

Allix, Peter [Pierre] (**1641–1717**), Church of England clergyman and religious writer, was the son of Pierre Allix, pastor of the Reformed church at Alençon in Normandy. After education at the protestant academy at Saumur, where in 1664 he participated in a disputation published as *De*

ultimo judicio, he became pastor of the Reformed congregation at Grande-Quevilly, Rouen. Having gained a good reputation for learning and for his preaching, in 1670 he succeeded the renowned Jean Daillé on the pastorate of the main Huguenot church of Charenton, near Paris. An open and direct man he was brisk and effective in the pulpit, attracted teachers from the Sorbonne to his home, met English and Scottish visitors, and built up scholarly contacts with men such as the Oxford orientalist Robert Huntingdon. He published both theological treatises and, in *Les maximes du vrai Chrétien* (1678) and *Préparation à la sainte cène* (1682), manuals for godly living and for taking communion. However, although he at first collaborated with his colleague Jean Claude in a new French translation of the Bible, controversy over the ideas of Claude Payon in time divided the men and their congregation. Allix was labelled a Socinian for his support of Payonist fellow Norman Charles le Cène, whose probationary pastorate at Charenton was cut short after condemnation of his perceived Arminian tendencies. In April 1683 rumours were circulating that Allix was about to convert to Catholicism, but that year he was moderator of the last French protestant synod at Lisy, and often preached before it.

By this time Allix had become well known across the channel. Surviving letters of April 1684 reveal him in correspondence with Archbishop William Sancroft and, through Edinburgh minister Mr Fall, in contact with William Lloyd, bishop of St Asaph, who was known for his anti-popery and support for toleration but who was also working on a defence of episcopal government. By August, with the revocation of the edict of Nantes imminent, Allix had decided to accept an invitation from another tolerationist, Gilbert Burnet, to pursue his studies in England and dispatched his books there secretly. After a farewell sermon later published as *L'adieu de St Paul aux Ephésiens* (1688), he left Paris with the formalization of the revocation on 21 October, and travelled to England with his wife, Marguerite (later Margaret) Roger of Rouen, whom he had married in 1678, and three children, including Jean Pierre (John Peter; 1679–1758) and Jacques (James; d. 1703x6). By 17 November Robert Harley had noted his arrival in London, where he settled initially at the house of Mr Skey in Charterhouse Yard. As he was a high profile refugee, his flight prompted an instruction from Versailles on 9 February 1686 to Bonrepaux, the French envoy in London, to offer him a pension of 3000 or 4000 livres if he would convert and return. On 8 July, John Evelyn encountered him as a fellow dinner guest at Lambeth Palace, conversing fluently in Latin with the archbishop. Two days later his petition to Sancroft for the establishment of a new French church conforming to the Anglican rite was answered with a royal patent. Established in Jewin Street, Aldersgate, it had Allix as self-proclaimed rector and four other ministers as curates. He troubled many by being the first refugee minister to undergo reordination, although it is possible that he regarded the episcopal laying on of hands simply as institution to the living.

Allix soon demonstrated his gratitude for asylum. On 20 December 1686 he dedicated to James II his *Reflexions sur les cinq livres de Moyse* (1687), an exposition of the Pentateuch. The promised sequel, tracing through the historic and prophetic books of the Old Testament and through the New Testament God's plans to send the Messiah, followed later in the year as *Reflexions sur les livres de l'écriture sainte* (1687); an English edition appeared in 1688. With his wife and sons John Peter and James, Allix obtained denization on 16 December 1687, and, unlike some other Huguenot ministers, he rapidly learned English. Between April and August 1688 he published in his new language three anti-Catholic discourses, on good works, on the minister's intention in administering the sacrament, and on penance. Writing to Lady Russell on 19 September John Tillotson, dean of St Paul's, appended to a list of clerical appointments that uncertain autumn the regretful comment that 'Mr Allix is put by at present' (Agnew, 330).

The advent of William and Mary gave Allix a chance to flourish, although the fact that most of his barrage of pamphlets in 1689 appeared anonymously indicates some insecurity. In *An Examination of the Scruples of those who Refuse to Take the Oath of Allegiance*, licensed on 16 April, he stressed the contractual nature of government in England. *A Letter to a Friend*, licensed on 20 April, retreated to a position of passive acceptance of *de facto* power by the individual Christian and by the church, but acknowledged 'right of the Society and its Representatives to examine this question' (p. 7). *An Account of the Private League betwixt the Late King James the Second and the French King*, licensed on 2 May, was followed by *A Letter from a French Lawyer to an English Gentleman*, licensed on 27 May, which sought to justify the revolution from French history and to explain the muted French reaction to James's plight. *Reflections upon the Opinions of some Modern Divines Concerning the Nature of Government*, licensed on 29 June, praised the 'miraculous revolution' which 'hath already retrieved the State from Ruine' (preface) and asserted that 'the Rights of Sovereignty … have no Institution in the Law of Nature' (p. 1); sovereigns did not receive their power immediately from God. *Some Remarks upon the Ecclesiastical History of the Ancient Churches of Piedmont*, licensed on 23 September under his own name and dedicated to William III, a king who had done so much for the 'poor and afflicted church' was 'a kind of Apology for the Reformation' (p. A2). A complementary work, *Remarks upon the Ecclesiastical History of the Ancient Churches of the Albigenses* (1692), dedicated to Mary II, celebrated their independence from Rome and perceived apostolic purity.

Throughout his stay in England, Allix maintained his scholarly contacts. He corresponded regularly with Huntingdon, now at Trinity College, Dublin, and in the early days forged a friendship with Thomas Edward, the Oxford Coptic scholar. Allix seems to have matriculated pensioner from Trinity Hall, Cambridge, in Easter term 1689; the following year he was awarded a DD from Emmanuel College, incorporated at Oxford on 13 June 1692. On the recommendation of Burnet, as bishop of Salisbury, on 14 May 1690 he was collated as treasurer of the cathedral. On 12 September the ministers and elders of Jewin Street Church recorded an enthusiastic farewell testimonial, but he soon returned to visit and probably spent much of the next decade in London, immersed in his studies and unattached to a particular congregation. His daughter Marie was baptized by Claude Groteste de la Mothe at the Savoy Chapel on 16 September 1692 (with Burnet's wife Mary and Thomas Burnet, master of the Charterhouse, as godparents), while his son Gilbert was baptized on 1 January 1694 at St Sepulchre, Holborn, and his daughter Margaret on 1 May 1698 at St Botolph, Aldersgate. On 11 January 1695 he was admitted as a residentiary canon at Salisbury, but on 26 December 1697 the king, writing from Kensington, sent the dean and chapter a dispensation from residence, since he was 'engaged in a great and useful work relating to the History and Councills of the Gallican Church, which is now almost ready for the press, which necessarily requires his presence here' (*Various Collections*, 1.373).

The king was misinformed: Allix lived another twenty years, but the work never appeared. Instead, he published a succession of more modest works and encouraged the projects of scholars like Alexander Cunningham the jurist. Having reiterated his position on acceptance of *de facto* power in *A Letter to a Friend Concerning the Behaviour of Christians under Various Revolutions* (1693) and defended Burnet's position on the Trinity in *Animadversions on Mr Hills Book* (1695), he drew on his talents as a Hebraist for *The Judgement of the Ancient Jewish Church Against the Unitarians* (1699), *The Book of Psalms* (1701), and works on Messianic prophecy and the birth date of Jesus. These received a mixed reception: welcomed by Robert Harley, who found in Allix, the once suspected Socinian, a defender of orthodoxy, they evoked the rage of Stephen Nye and William Whiston, who felt their own orthodoxy unjustly impugned. Allix courted the patronage of high placed clergy and laymen, such as Thomas Herbert, eighth earl of Pembroke and fifth earl of Montgomery, both for himself and his sons. It was probably on behalf of James that he wrote gratefully in 1702 and 1703 to the young man's protector, Governor Thomas Pitt at Fort St George in Madras, while he made use of the Harleys' favour to beg for John Peter in 1705 the London lectureships of St Antholin or St John Baptist. However, his frequent visits to the Harleys' London house proved increasingly fruitless as Robert's patience seems to have run out over the non-appearance of Allix's *magnum opus*. Contrary to allegation he had not robbed the nation, Allix protested to Harley on 29 September 1707, 'my conscience doth not reproach me' (BL, Add. MS 4253, fol. 15*v*).

When Allix made his will in London on 18 February 1717 he reviewed a career in which 'I have endeavourd to edifye the faithfull by my Ministry, my workes and my Example' and 'I have always wished the welfare of this Nation and the Church of England' (will). Gratitude to King George for a pension, and to the archbishop of Canterbury and the bishop of Norwich, who had procured it for him, was matched by regret that, having left most of his wealth in France, there was insufficient to fulfil settlement obligations toward his wife, let alone his five surviving children. He died on 21 February and was buried at St Sepulchre. His widow remained in London, and was buried at St Antholin's on 24 October 1739. Of his two daughters, Margaret married Pierre Signoret, a merchant, the year of her father's death; Marie or Mary had already married Admiral Sir Charles Wager. Of his sons, John Peter (*d.* 1758) became a royal chaplain and successively dean of Gloucester and Ely, William (1688/9–1769) became a naval commissioner, and Gilbert (*d.* 1767?) a London merchant.

VIVIENNE LARMINIE

Sources Venn, *Alum. Cant.* · E. Haag and E. Haag, *La France protestante*, 10 vols. (Paris, 1846–59), vol. 1, pp. 61–3 · D. C. A. Agnew, *Protestant exiles from France, chiefly in the reign of Louis XIV, or, The Huguenot refugees and their descendants in Great Britain and Ireland*, 3rd edn, 2 vols. (1886), vol. 1, pp. 328–34; vol. 2, p. 131 · BL, Add. MSS 4253, fols. 12–19; 4277, fol. 3; 22851, fols. 48r–49r; 22852, fol. 142 · *The manuscripts of his grace the duke of Portland*, 10 vols., HMC, 29 (1891–1931), vol. 3, pp. 390, 583, 606; vol. 4, p. 240 · *Report on manuscripts in various collections*, 8 vols., HMC, 55 (1901–14), vol. 1, p. 373 · *Report on the manuscripts of the marquis of Downshire*, 6 vols. in 7, HMC, 75 (1924–95), vol. 1, pp. 42, 119, 499, 515 · *Manuscripts of the earl of Egmont: diary of Viscount Percival, afterwards first earl of Egmont*, 3 vols., HMC, 63 (1920–23), vol. 1, p. 200 · will, PRO, PROB 11/556, fols. 166–7 · W. Minet and S. Minet, eds., *Register of the church of St Martin Orgars*, Huguenot Society of London, quarto ser., 37 (1935) · W. A. Shaw, ed., *Denizations and naturalizations of aliens in England and Ireland, 1603–1700*, Huguenot Society, quarto ser., 18 (1911), 192–3 · W. Minet and S. Minet, eds., *Registers of the churches of the Chapel Royal, St James's and Swallow Street*, Huguenot Society, quarto ser., 28 (1924), 15 · *Fasti Angl., 1541–1857*, [Salisbury], 13, 100 · F. Layard, 'Huguenots in north Britain', *Proceedings of the Huguenot Society of London*, 3 (1888–91), 33–4 · E. G. Léonard, *A history of protestantism*, 2: *The Establishment*, ed. H. H. Rowley (1967), 392–3 · C. P. Allix, 'The escape of Dr Pierre Allix from France in 1685', *Proceedings of the Huguenot Society of London*, 13 (1924–9), 625–7 · E. Labrousse, 'Great Britain as envisaged by Huguenots of the seventeenth century', *Huguenots in Britain and their French background, 1550–1800*, ed. I. Scouloudi (1987), 149 · ESTC

Archives BL, letters and papers · CUL, religious treatises, sermons, etc.

Likenesses J. Freeman, oils (after unknown artist), Emmanuel College, Cambridge

Wealth at death property left behind in France: will, PRO, PROB 11/556, fols. 166–7

Allman, George James (1812–1898), naturalist, was born in February 1812 in Cork, the eldest son of James Allman of Bandon, co. Cork. He was educated at the Belfast Academical Institution and at Trinity College, Dublin, where he graduated BA in 1839 and MB in 1843. Although he subsequently graduated MD in 1847, having become a fellow of the Royal College of Surgeons in Ireland in 1844, his real interests lay in natural science—especially marine zoology.

Allman's first scientific paper—on Polyzoa—appeared in 1843; it was followed by one on Hydrozoa in 1844. In the latter year he was appointed, in succession to William Allman (no relation), professor of botany in Dublin University. On 1 June 1854 he was elected FRS, and in the following year he was appointed regius professor of natural history and keeper of the natural history museum in the University of Edinburgh.

Allman's reputation rests on his investigations into the classification and morphology of the Coelenterata and Polyzoa. Between 1844 and 1873 he published more than

100 papers in this area. His *Monograph of the Freshwater Polyzoa* was published by the Ray Society in 1856, and in 1871–2 the same society published in two fine folios Allman's most important work, *A Monograph of the Gymnoblastic or Tubularian Hydroids*. Six years later Allman was invited to report on the hydroids collected on behalf of the United States government, by L. F. de Pourtalès, in the Gulf Stream; Allman's report formed part two of the fifth volume of the *Memoirs of the Museum of Comparative Zoology at Harvard*. In 1883 he performed a similar service for the British government, contributing a report on hydroids to a series of *Challenger* reports edited by Sir Charles Wyville Thomson. For his work on hydroids Allman received the Brisbane medal of the Royal Society of Edinburgh in 1877, the Cunningham medal of the Royal Irish Academy in 1878, and the gold medal of the Linnean Society in 1896.

Meanwhile, in 1870, Allman retired from his professorship at Edinburgh, being presented with a testimonial on 29 July. In 1871 he was elected a member of the Athenaeum. From 1855 until the abolition of the board in 1881 he was a member of the royal commission on Scottish fisheries, and in 1876 he was appointed a member of the royal commission inquiring into the working of the queen's colleges in Ireland. He had always taken a keen interest in the popularization of science and was one of the early promoters of the British Association for the Advancement of Science; he presided over the biological section in 1873, and over the united association when it met at Sheffield in 1879. He served on the council of the Royal Society from 1871 to 1873, and in 1874 succeeded George Bentham as president of the Linnean Society, to the *Journal* of which he had contributed several papers, the most important being that on the freshwater medusa; he served in that office until 1883. He also acted for many years as examiner in natural history for the University of London and for the army, navy, and Indian medical and civil services.

On leaving Edinburgh, Allman had settled first at Weybridge and then near to Alfred Russel Wallace, at Ardmore, Parkstone, Dorset. There he devoted much time to his favourite hobby—horticulture—and in the last year of his life he printed a volume of poems for private circulation. He died at his home on 24 November 1898, and was buried on 29 November in Poole cemetery. His wife, Hannah Louisa, third daughter of Samuel Shaen of Crix, near Colchester, Essex, with whom he had no children, had died in 1890.   A. F. POLLARD, rev. PETER OSBORNE

Sources *Proceedings of the Linnean Society of London* (1895–6), 30 · *Nature*, 59 (1898–9), 202–4 · Foster, *Alum. Oxon.* · *Men and women of the time* (1895) · *WWW* · *The Times* (28 Nov 1898) · L. Huxley, *Life and letters of Thomas Henry Huxley*, 2 vols. (1900) · A. T. C. Pratt, ed., *People of the period: being a collection of the biographies of upwards of six thousand living celebrities*, 2 vols. (1897)
Archives ICL, letters to Thomas Huxley · Linn. Soc., letters to James Murie · Maison d'Auguste Comte, Paris, letters to Auguste Comte · Maison d'Auguste Comte, Paris, letters to Pierre Laffitte
Likenesses T. H. Maguire, lithograph, 1851 (one set of *Ipswich Museum Portraits*), BM, NPG · E. M. Busk, oils, 1897, Linn. Soc. · F. W. Burton, chalk drawing, NG Ire.

Wealth at death £13,296 15s. 10d.: probate, 14 Feb 1899, CGPLA Eng. & Wales

Allman, George Johnston (1824–1904), mathematician, was born on 28 September 1824 at Dublin. He was a younger son of William *Allman MD (1776–1846), professor of botany in Trinity College, Dublin, and his wife, Anne (d. 1831). He entered Trinity College and after a distinguished career graduated in 1844 as senior moderator and gold medallist in mathematics with Samuel Haughton. He was also Bishop Law's mathematical prizeman and graduated LLB in 1853 and LLD in 1854. He married in 1853 Louisa (d. 1864), daughter of John Smith Taylor of Dublin and Corballis, co. Meath.

Allman was elected professor of mathematics in Queen's College, Galway, in 1853, and remained in this post until he retired in 1893, having reached the age limit fixed by civil service regulations. He was elected a member of the senate of Queen's University in 1877, and in 1880, when the Royal University of Ireland was founded, he was nominated by the crown as a life senator. He was made FRS in 1884, and awarded an honorary degree of DSc by Dublin in 1882. He contributed a few papers on mathematical subjects to scientific periodicals, besides an account of Professor James McCullagh's lectures on 'The attraction of the ellipsoid', which appears in the latter's collected works. He also wrote a number of articles in the ninth edition of the *Encyclopaedia Britannica* on Greek mathematicians. His chief contribution to science is his *History of Greek Geometry from Thales to Euclid* (1889), which first appeared as articles in *Hermathena*. In this he traced the rise and progress of geometry and arithmetic, and threw new light on the history of the early development of mathematics. With his lifelong friend, John Kells Ingram, he was attracted to positivism, and entered into correspondence with Comte in 1852; in 1854 he went to Paris and made his personal acquaintance. His position at Galway prevented his taking any public part in the positivist movement, but his teaching was much influenced by Comte's mathematical work the *Synthèse subjective*, and his general theory of historical development. Allman died of pneumonia on 9 May 1904 at Farnham House, Finglas, Dublin. A son and two daughters survived him.

ROBERT STEELE, rev. ANITA McCONNELL

Sources B. W., *PRS*, 78A (1907), xii–xiii · *Positivist Review*, 12 (1904), 149 · *The Times* (13 May 1904)
Likenesses Schemboche, photograph, 1890, RS · M. A. Fox, photograph, RS

Allman, William (1776–1846), botanist, was born on 7 February 1776 at Kingston, Jamaica, the son of Thomas Allman. His mother was a native of Waterford, Ireland. Before William was four his parents returned to Ireland, and he was educated in Waterford. In 1792 he entered Trinity College, Dublin, where he was elected a scholar (1795), and graduated BA (1796) and MA (1801). Allman proceeded to study medicine, obtaining MB and MD (1804), and was admitted a licentiate of the King and Queen's College of Physicians in Ireland in December 1804; his thesis, *Disputatio medica de paralysi*, was published the same year. He practised medicine in Clonmel, co. Tipperary, until

1809. On 16 January 1809 he was elected professor of botany in the school of physic, University of Dublin, in succession to Dr Robert Scott. Before about 1814 Allman married; his wife's name was Anne and she died in 1831. Among their children was George Johnston *Allman, mathematician.

Allman became friendly with Robert Brown, botanist and librarian to Sir Joseph Banks, and consequently after 1812 taught his students the natural system of classification of plants. While he was perhaps the first professor in the British Isles to teach the natural system, Allman was overshadowed in Ireland by his contemporaries, and made no other significant contribution to botany. In *The Lancet* (12 March 1825), Erinensis (Dr Peter Hennis Green) satirically characterized Allman as 'far gone in swaddling … sedulously occupied in strewing the philosophy hall of the University with "green rushes", and constructing a new "railway" to heaven, out of flowers and scraps of scripture'.

Allman published two (now negligible) books on the classification of plants (*Analysis per differentias constantes viginti, inchoata, generum plantarum …*, 1828; and *Familiae plantarum*, 1836) and some minor papers on mathematics and botanical topics. His *Abstract of a memoir on the mathematical connexion between the parts of vegetables … read before the Royal Society* was privately printed (1844) because his essay, 'An attempt to illustrate a mathematical connection between the parts of vegetables', dated 31 January 1811 and communicated by Robert Brown to the Royal Society of London, remained unpublished; manuscript copies survive in the Royal Society and in the Natural History Museum, London.

Allman was elected an honorary fellow of the King and Queen's College of Physicians in Ireland (1813). He was a member of the botanical societies of London and Edinburgh, and occupied the chair of botany at Dublin until 1844 when he retired. He was succeeded by Dr George James Allman, who, despite the common surname, was not related. William Allman died on 8 December 1846. *Allmania*, a small genus of plants from tropical Asia belonging to the cockscomb family (Amaranthaceae), was named in his memory by his friend Robert Brown.

E. CHARLES NELSON

Sources Burtchaell & Sadleir, *Alum. Dubl.* • Royal College of Physicians of Ireland, Dublin, Archives • RS • Linn. Soc., archives • *DNB* • M. Fallon, ed., *The sketches of Erinensis: selections of Irish medical satire, 1824–1836* (1979)
Archives NHM, botany library, MS 'An attempt to illustrate a mathematical connection between the parts of vegetables' • NHM, department of botany, herbarium specimens • RS • RS, MS on mathematics

Allom, Thomas (1804–1872), architect and artist, was born on 13 March 1804 at Lambeth, the second of the two children of Thomas Allom (1770–1840), a coachman, and his wife, Martha Rampley (1771–1861), who were both originally from Suffolk. He was articled to the architect Francis Goodwin and attended the Royal Academy Schools as an architectural student from 1828. In 1834 he was a founder member of the Institute of British Architects, of which he

Thomas Allom (1804–1872), by Thomas Carrick, 1846

became a fellow in 1860. With his first wife, Mary Ann Rawlins (1806–1854), he had four children, and in 1856 he married, secondly, Eliza Fox (1813–1890). He lived at several addresses in central London before moving in 1852 to 1 Lonsdale Road, Barnes, Surrey. An obituary states that 'in his three fold capacity of architect, artist and draughtsman few men were more widely known in the art world' (*Art Journal*, 34, 1872, 300). It is upon about 1500 designs for albums of topographical steel-engravings that his more prominent and lasting reputation rests. This work, initially undertaken to support himself as a student, became his principal occupation between 1828 and 1845, and during these years he made extensive sketching tours in England, Scotland, France, Belgium, and Turkey, mainly for the publisher H. Fisher & Son. His *China: in a series of views, displaying the scenery, architecture and social habits of that ancient empire* (4 vols., 1843), with a letterpress by G. N. Wright, was the best-known nineteenth-century work on the subject, although he never visited the country and based his illustrations on the work of other artists.

Allom was a skilled lithographer and produced some book illustrations in this medium mostly after the work of other artists or architects. Possibly with the intention of gaining a wider audience, in the 1840s he offered for sale some single-issue lithographs and lithotints of topographical views, events, and celebrations. His finished watercolours and oil paintings were based mostly on his topographical designs, a notable exception being a large history painting, *The Burning of Corinth* (1871, priv. coll.; version ex Sothebys, New York, 18 March 1998). His work was usually signed 'T. Allom', and examples can be found in several public collections, including those in the Victoria and Albert Museum, the British Museum, and the Royal Institute of British Architects. He exhibited sixty-five works between 1824 and 1871 at the Society (later Royal Society) of British Artists and the Royal Academy, where 'his charming pencil always gained a place of honour' (*The Builder*, 26 Oct 1872, 840). Consequently his perspectives were much in demand by other architects, among them Charles Barry, for whom he made in 1844 two large watercolours of the new houses of parliament for presentation to the tsar following his visit to the site (Academy of Arts, St Petersburg).

In 1840 Allom returned to his original profession of architecture. His successful early partnership with H. F. Lockwood was brief, and after 1843 he generally worked on his own with occasional help from his son and pupil Arthur Allom (1829–1895, ARIBA 1851, FRIBA 1869). His architectural *œuvre*, though comparatively small, included a wide variety of different building types which in style reflected the eclecticism of his period; Jacobethan workhouses, the most successful of which was the Kensington workhouse (Stone Hall; 1847–8), and neo-Gothic churches such as Christchurch, Highbury (1847–8). His choice of the classical style for St Peter's, Kensington (1855–7), provoked contemporary criticism, though this was obviously dictated by the surrounding Ladbroke estate, where as surveyor he had designed about a hundred houses (1852–66) in a style based on freely treated Italian and empire sources. The picturesque layout of this estate demonstrates how successfully his artistic talent served and informed his architectural work. The William Brown Library, Liverpool (1857–60), was built to his classical design, though it was altered by John Weightman.

Allom died of heart disease at his home in Barnes on 21 October 1872 and was buried at Kensal Green cemetery.

DIANA BROOKS

Sources D. Brooks, *Thomas Allom (1804–1872)* (1998) [exhibition catalogue, Heinz Gallery, RIBA, 26 March – 9 May 1998] • *The Builder* (1843–72) [esp. 30 (1872), 840] • *The Architect* (26 Oct 1872) • *Art Journal*, 34 (1872) • *BL cat.* • V. Shuisky, 'The architectural graphics of Charles Barry and Thomas Allom in the USSR Academy of Arts', *Arkhitektura SSSR* (May 1987), 102–5 • LMA, Blake MSS, Ac.61.39 • Graves, *RA exhibitors*, 1 (1905), 27 • *Transactions of the Royal Institute of British Architects* (6 Jan 1835) • *Remaining works of Thomas Allom* (1873) [sale catalogue, Christies, 14 March 1873] • *Watercolours and drawings by Thomas Allom* (Christies, South Kensington, 28 Nov 1983) • *Watercolours and drawings by Thomas Allom* (Christies, South Kensington, 18 Nov 1985) • parish records • census returns • private information (2004) • d. cert. • *CGPLA Eng. & Wales* (1873)

Likenesses T. Carrick, miniature, 1846, priv. coll. [*see illus.*] • T. Carrick, photograph, *c*.1860, RIBA BAL • E. A. Olivieri, plaster, RIBA, drawings collection • woodcut (after photograph? by T. Carrick, *c*.1860), BM

Wealth at death under £1500: probate, 13 Jan 1873, *CGPLA Eng. & Wales*

Allon, Henry (1818–1892), Congregational minister and leader, was born at Welton, near Hull, on 13 October 1818, the son of William Allon (*d.* 1878), a builder and later estate steward, and Mary Allon. He followed his father in apprenticeship to a builder in Beverley. He first attended a Wesleyan Methodist chapel, then sought membership of the local Congregational church, and at about the age of nineteen began to preach. When his work took him to Hull, he attended Thomas Stratten's Congregational

Henry Allon (1818–1892), by Lock & Whitfield, pubd 1879

church, and was encouraged to consider a call to ministry. As a result he spent a year with Alexander Stewart, minister of High Barnet Congregational Church, who prepared him for entrance to Cheshunt College. In 1839 he began four years of education and training for ministry at Cheshunt, and came to the notice of two leading trustees, James Sherman and James Bennett, who encouraged him in his vocation. His loyalty to the college was lifelong; in later years he served as secretary and trustee.

In January 1844 Allon began his lifelong ministry at Union Chapel, Islington, London, as assistant to Thomas Lewis, and was ordained a few months later on 12 June 1844. When Lewis died in 1852 Allon became sole minister of the church, serving for the next forty years. Union Chapel had an unusual history in having been founded in 1802 by a group composed of both Anglicans and nonconformists, and in having used both Anglican and nonconformist forms of worship for many years; this tradition made the congregation sympathetic to Allon's efforts to raise the general standards of congregational worship.

Allon was endowed with many gifts, literary, artistic, and musical, and used them in the service of the church. Of striking appearance, he was an outstanding preacher, and attracted a large and distinguished congregation; during his ministry the membership of his church grew from 318 in 1844 to 758 in 1874. In spite of an extension to the church building in 1861, it proved to be too small, and in 1875 the decision was taken to rebuild on an enlarged site. The new church, designed by James Cubitt, was opened on 5 December 1877 in the presence of Gladstone (whom

Allon had met several times with other nonconformist ministers at Newman Hall's house), R. W. Dale, and other significant figures. It was designed, acoustically and architecturally, to express Allon's belief that every member of a congregation should be able to participate in the worship.

Allon represented the more cultured side of nonconformity. Thomas Binney, his senior by twenty years, set new standards of nonconformist worship during his long ministry at the King's Weigh House, and Allon developed this tradition further, insisting that worship should always represent the best that a minister and congregation can offer. He was fortunate in his church organists, principally H. J. Gauntlett, from 1853 until 1861, and Ebenezer Prout, from 1861 until 1873. In a decade in which several denominations produced new hymnbooks, Allon and Gauntlett produced in 1858 *The Congregational Psalmist*, which was reissued several times and widely used in Congregational churches throughout the country. It was innovative, not only in encouraging the use of chants, hitherto regarded with suspicion, in nonconformist worship, but in including music as well as words for general congregational use. Allon encouraged large numbers of his congregation to attend a weekly psalmody class, begun in 1848, believing that the music of worship could and should be shared by the whole congregation to the highest possible standard. He was editor of the *New Congregational Hymn Book* in 1868, *Anthems for Congregational Use* in 1872, and published *Hymns for Children's Worship* in 1878 and *The Congregational Psalmist Hymnal* in 1886. His essay entitled 'The worship of the church' in *Ecclesia* (1870, edited by H. R. Reynolds), set out the principles on which he believed worship should be based.

In 1860 Allon began writing and reviewing for journals, and in 1866 he was invited to join H. R. Reynolds as co-editor of the *British Quarterly Review*, a nonconformist journal of theology, literature, science, and politics. When Reynolds resigned in 1874, Allon continued as sole editor until the journal came to an end in 1886. He maintained the high standard set by his two predecessors, Robert Vaughan and H. R. Reynolds, and attracted a wide range of contributors, including many Anglicans (among them Gladstone, whose important article on evangelicalism appeared in July 1879). He published volumes of sermons, wrote a biography of his mentor, James Sherman, and edited, with a long introductory biographical and critical sketch, the sermons of his friend Thomas Binney. Albert Peel published a volume of his correspondence, as *Letters to a Victorian Editor*, in 1929.

On 12 October 1848 Allon married Eliza Goodman, daughter of Joseph Goodman, miller, of Witton, Huntingdonshire; they had four daughters and three sons. He was twice elected chairman of the Congregational Union of England and Wales (an unusual honour), for the years 1864 and 1881. In 1864 he used the second of his two chairman's addresses to call for a more highly educated Congregational ministry, a matter of continuing concern to him. Seventeen years later he was the union's choice as

chairman in the jubilee year. He was awarded the honorary degree of DD by Yale in 1871. He died at his home, 10 St Mary's Road, Islington, on 16 April 1892, survived by his wife. He was buried on 21 April in Abney Park cemetery.

His son, **Henry Erskine Allon** (1864–1897), composer, was born on 16 October 1864, educated at Amersham Hall School, near Reading, at University College, London, and at Trinity College, Cambridge. He studied music under William Henry Birch and Frederic Corder, and wrote chamber music, piano solos, and cantatas. He was a promoter of and frequent contributor to the *New Musical Quarterly Review*. He died on 3 April 1897 from cerebral meningitis, leaving his musical library to the Cambridge Union Society.   ELAINE KAYE

Sources W. Hardy Harwood, *Henry Allon DD* (1894) • A. Peel, *Letters to a Victorian editor* (1929) • *Congregational Year Book* (1893), 202–5 • *Memorial of the late Rev. Henry Allon* (1892) • *Sermons preached at the dedication of Union Chapel, Islington* (1878) • A. Argent, 'Henry Allon at Union Chapel, Islington', *Congregational History Circle Magazine*, 1/3 (1993) • *Congregational Year Book* (1865), 46–72 • I. Bradley, *Abide with me: the world of Victorian hymns* (1997) • Gladstone, *Diaries* • m. cert. • d. cert. • d. cert. [Henry Erskine Allon] • *DNB* • Venn, *Alum. Cant.* [Henry Erskine Allon] • *IGI* • Boase, *Mod. Eng. biog.*
Archives BL, letters to W. E. Gladstone, Add. MS 44095 • Union Chapel, Islington, London, records
Likenesses W. & D. Downey, woodburytype, *c.*1890, NPG; repro. in W. Downey and D. Downey, *The cabinet portrait gallery* (1890), vol. 1 • J. Cochran, stipple (after a photograph), NPG • J. Cochran, stipple and line engraving (after W. Gush), NPG • Lock & Whitfield, woodburytype photograph, NPG; repro. in *The Congregationalist* (1879) [*see illus.*] • Martin and Sallnow, photograph, repro. in *Memorial of the late Rev. Henry Allon* • F. Martyn, photograph, repro. in Hardy Harwood, *Henry Allon DD* • lithograph, NPG • portrait, repro. in Peel, *Letters to a Victorian editor*
Wealth at death £28,126 4s. 0d.: resworn probate, Feb 1893, *CGPLA Eng. & Wales* (1892) • £5966 13s. 8d.—Henry Erskine Allon: probate, 27 April 1897, *CGPLA Eng. & Wales*

Allon, Henry Erskine (1864–1897). *See under* Allon, Henry (1818–1892).

Allott, Kenneth Cyril Bruce (1912–1973), literary scholar and poet, was born on 29 August 1912 at Cynon surgery, Llanwynno, Mountain Ash, Glamorgan, the elder son of Hubert Cyril Willoughby Allott, a general practitioner, and his wife, Rose Finlay. About 1913 the family moved to Whitchurch, Shropshire, where Allott and his younger brother, (Denys Neville) Guy, attended local schools before being sent in 1923 to Beaumont College in Berkshire, a Jesuit-run Roman Catholic public school which later joined with Stonyhurst School. By the age of thirteen Allott was reading Kant, and he informed his younger brother that he had renounced his faith. While Allott was at Beaumont his parents separated and Allott's father went to live with a nurse whom he had met during the war. Allott's mother died a few years later—Allott believed from a broken heart. From the age of about fourteen Allott and his brother were brought up by his mother's sisters, Sarah and Mary Finlay. Following the wishes of his aunts, the boys attended St Cuthbert's Roman Catholic Grammar School in Newcastle upon Tyne, where Allott was known as Speedy because he spoke so quickly.

In 1934 Allott graduated with first-class honours from

Newcastle's Armstrong College. In 1935 he gained a diploma in education, and in 1936 he became a BLitt student at St Edmund Hall, Oxford. His BLitt dissertation, an edition of the poems of the seventeenth-century Catholic writer William Habington, was published by Liverpool University Press (1948). On 10 July 1936 Allott married Surya Kumari Lall (b. 1913/14), the daughter of Kundan Lall, a barrister. They had a daughter and a son. Soon after the awarding of his BLitt degree, in 1938, Allott began teaching at Burgess Hill School in London, and also at this time began reviewing for the *Morning Post* and working with Geoffrey Grigson on the poetry magazine *New Verse*. He was, along with many other young writers, an observer for Charles Madge's social survey group, Mass-Observation.

In 1940 Allott successfully applied as a conscientious objector and in 1942 he and his family moved to Gateshead, where he had been appointed an extramural lecturer. In 1943 he was appointed a staff tutor at Vaughan College, an extramural college in Leicester, and in 1945 an assistant lecturer in the English department at Liverpool University. In 1948 he was promoted to a lectureship at Liverpool. In November 1950 his first marriage was dissolved, and on 1 June 1951 he married Miriam Farris (b. 1920), a fellow lecturer in the English department. In 1955 he was appointed to a senior lectureship and, after a period (1962–3) as acting head of department, in 1964 he became the first holder of the university's newly established Andrew Cecil Bradley chair in modern English literature.

Throughout his academic career Allott was engaged in writing fiction and poetry. In 1937 he had published, in collaboration with Stephen Tait, a comic novel entitled *The Rhubarb Tree*, and also a play, *A Room with a View*, based on E. M. Forster's novel. He published two collections of poetry, *Poems* (1938) and *The Ventriloquist's Doll* (1943), and is perhaps best remembered for the widely anthologized 'Lament for a Cricket Eleven'. His poetry was influenced by Auden and Eliot, and is characterized by an elegiac tone, by flashes of surrealism, and by a keen sense of morality. He was regarded by many—including Francis Scarfe, who devotes an entire chapter on Allott's work in his *Auden and after: the Liberation of Poetry, 1930–41* (1942)—as one of the most promising young poets of his day.

During the 1960s and early 1970s Allott held several visiting professorships—at the University of Otago, and with the British Council in New Zealand and in India (New Delhi). During this period he was a member of the advisory boards of *Victorian Poetry* and *Victorian Studies*, and was also general editor of the five-volume anthology *The Pelican Book of English Prose* (1956), and a general editor of the *Oxford History of English Literature*.

Allott was an outstanding scholar and a leading authority on Victorian literature. He edited selections of the work of Winthrop Mackworth Praed and Robert Browning, wrote essays on Keats, Shelley, and Clough, and edited the standard Longmans annotated edition of Matthew Arnold's *Complete Poems* (1965). His other scholarly works include a biography of Jules Verne (1940) and a book written with Miriam Allott, *The Art of Graham Greene* (1951). He reviewed regularly for the *Times Literary Supplement*. Allott was always youthful in appearance, witty, enthusiastic, an extremely popular lecturer, and a great lover of cats. He was also a heavy smoker, believing wrongly that his lungs would be protected because of an earlier illness from tuberculosis (c.1949–50).

Besides his academic work on Victorian literature Allott was a champion of new writing. At Oxford he co-edited the literary magazine *Programme*, and was assistant editor of the influential poetry magazine *New Verse* from 1936 to 1939. His anthology *The Penguin Book of Contemporary Verse* (1950; revised and enlarged, 1962) was used widely in schools and colleges.

Kenneth Allot died at Broadgreen Hospital, Liverpool, on 23 May 1973, of lung cancer. He was cremated at Anfield cemetery, Liverpool. Miriam Allott succeeded her husband as Bradley professor at Liverpool. Allott's *Collected Poems* was published posthumously in 1975.

IAN SANSOM

Sources private information (2004) · b. cert. · m. certs. · d. cert. · F. Scarfe, *Auden and after: the liberation of poetry, 1930–41* (1942) · *CGPLA Eng. & Wales* (1973)
Archives University of Bristol Library, editorial corresp. relating to *Pelican book of English prose* | U. Lpool L., letters to L. C. Martin · U. Reading L., corresp. with George Bell & Sons
Wealth at death £51,588: administration with will, 9 Aug 1973, *CGPLA Eng. & Wales*

Allott, Robert (*fl.* **1599–1600**), literary compiler, was the editor of *Wits Theater* (1599) and *Englands Parnassus* (1600). There are two possible candidates for identification with the editor. Rollins, Eccles, and I favour the Robert Allott who was a gentleman from Driby, Lincolnshire, born about 1563–4, one of four sons of Robert Allott of Louth (d. 1564). This Allott matriculated at Corpus Christi College, Oxford, about 1581, and was subsequently admitted to the Inner Temple in November 1584. He was living in London in the parish of St Martin-in-the-Fields when, on 18 August 1598, he testified in a court case. The Bridget Alliatt who was baptized at St Martin-in-the-Fields on 14 November 1599 is probably his daughter. He seems to have been the Robert Allat who died of the plague and was buried on 7 November 1603 at St Ann Blackfriars. The will of his aunt Dame Anne Allott mentions his children—a son, Robert, and four daughters. Both Wagner (p. 466) and Woudhuysen (p. 282) identify this Allott with the person whose name and initials are subscribed to five poems added to BL, Harley MS 7392, a poetry anthology associated both with Oxford and London and with St Loe Kniveton and Humphrey Coningsby, the latter Allott's contemporary at Oxford. The Christopher Middleton for whom Allott wrote a commendatory Latin poem may have been the Middleton who was at Oxford with him.

Honigmann, however, identifies Robert Allott as the son of John Allott of Criggletstone, Yorkshire, the individual who matriculated as sizar from St John's College, Cambridge, about 1592, receiving his BA in 1595–6, his MA in 1599, his medical licence in 1606, and his MD in 1608. This

Allott was, according to Venn, a Linacre lecturer at the university and 'a celebrated physician', who died at Cambridge in 1642 (Venn, *Alum. Cant.*, 1.23). He was, Honigmann notes (p. 23), a fellow student of Christopher Middleton's at St John's (who may, however, be the same Christopher Middleton who was at Brasenose College, Oxford, in the early 1580s). Their Cambridge contemporary John Weever addressed them jointly in *Epigrammes* (1599, 4.4), complimenting their 'wits', 'conceits', and 'sweete [poetical] layes'. Honigmann argues that this Robert Allott was part of a literary circle that included, in addition to Weever and Middleton (for whose poem *The Legend of Humphrey, Duke of Gloucester*, 1600, both Allott and Weever supplied commendatory pieces), Michael Drayton and Frances Meres, another contemporary of Allott from Cambridge—a coterie that was connected with the publishing ventures of Nicholas Ling, Cuthbert Burbie, and Valentine Simmes. Honigmann sees 'the ex-student from Cambridge closing in on the publisher [Ling] from 1599, through his friends' as a member of a 'literary group … heavily involved in anthologies … [one that] could "puff" a struggling author's reputation' (Honigmann, 23). There is, however, no evidence that the Robert Allott who spent most of his life as a physician in Cambridge ever lived in London.

Robert Allott wrote two poems printed in the front matter of Gervase Markham's *Devereux* (1597). He is also probably the R. A. who contributed a Latin commendatory sonnet to Ling in *Politeuphuia, Wits Commonwealth* (1597), the prose collection Ling edited under the patronage of John Bodenham, who had gathered material for it and other prose and poetry publications that Bodenham sponsored. Allott himself edited a third volume in the Bodenham series, the prose commonplace book *Wits Theater of the Little World* (1599). His dedication to Bodenham, signed Robert Allott, in one of the British Library copies, acknowledges the patron's responsibility for initiating the project. The following year Allott compiled and edited *Englands Parnassus* (1600), a large poetical dictionary with 2350 items, a work Moss claims is 'an attempt to replace the ancient canon of authors and rewrite commonplaces in the language of a new canon of modern poets' (Moss, 210). Crawford produced a modern edition in 1913, identifying most of the (often mislabelled) pieces, suggesting that Allott was partial to the verse of his friends (Allott, *Englands Parnassus*, vii). Allott, then, was an important agent in the process of redirecting texts that normally circulated in manuscript and found their resting places in private collections of individual compilers into the more public world of print. The poetical and prose collections for which he was directly responsible and those with which he was otherwise connected represent an important moment of late Elizabethan literary anthologizing that signalled print's growing importance as the medium of literary transmission. ARTHUR F. MAROTTI

Sources M. Eccles, *Brief lives: Tudor and Stuart authors* (1982) · Foster, *Alum. Oxon.* · R. Allott, ed., *Englands Parnassus*, rev. C. Crawford (1913) · R. Allott, ed., *England's Helicon 1600, 1614*, rev. H. Rollins (1935) · E. A. J. Honigmann, *John Weever* (1987) · B. N. Wagner, 'New

poems by Sir Edward Dyer', *Review of English Studies*, 11 (1935), 466–71 · E. Pomeroy, *The Elizabethan miscellanies: their development and conventions* (1973) · A. Moss, *Printed commonplace-books and the structuring of Renaissance thought* (1996) · F. Williams, 'Notes on *Englands Parnassus*', *Modern Language Notes*, 52 (1937), 402–5 · Venn, *Alum. Cant.* · H. R. Woudhuysen, *Sir Philip Sidney and the circulation of manuscripts, 1558–1640* (1996) · BL, Harley MS 7392, fols. 77r–78v · C. T. Wright, 'Anthony Mundy and the Bodenham miscellanies', *Philological Quarterly*, 40 (1961), 449–61

Archives BL, Harley MS 7392, fols. 77r–78v

Allott, William (*d.* 1587), Roman Catholic priest, was a native of Lincolnshire and educated at Cambridge, but did not proceed to a degree. With the change in religious policy after the accession of Queen Elizabeth he withdrew to the continent. In April 1567 he matriculated at Louvain and was ordained there. He was for a time receiver to a Mr Redborne at Antwerp. He travelled to Rome in August 1579 and proceeded to England via Rheims the same year.

Allott was in high favour with Mary, queen of Scots, whom he served during her confinement. In June 1582 he was described as 'above 40 years of age, reddish and thick-haired of head and beard, using it cut finely' (Anstruther, 6). He worked on the clandestine English Catholic mission, and was arrested as a priest in the house of a widow named Lovell in Norwich. He was imprisoned at the Marshalsea on 24 February 1584. He was presumably banished in 1585, and was subsequently appointed canon of St Quentin on the intercession of Mary, queen of Scots; he also received a pension from the pope. While in the Low Countries he became acquainted with Lord Morley and under his patronage produced *Thesaurus bibliorum*, first published in Antwerp in 1577; subsequent editions appeared in Lyons (1580 and 1585), Antwerp (1581), and Cologne (1612). The book was dedicated to Pope Gregory XIII and Lord Morley.

William Allott died at Spa in the Spanish Netherlands in 1587. THOMPSON COOPER, *rev.* IAN DICKIE

Sources T. F. Knox and others, eds., *The first and second diaries of the English College, Douay* (1878) · G. Anstruther, *The seminary priests*, 1 (1969) · Venn, *Alum. Cant.* · BL, Add. MS 48023, fol. 98 · C. Talbot, ed., *Miscellanea: recusant records*, Catholic RS, 53 (1961), 194

Alloway. For this title name *see* Cathcart, David, Lord Alloway (1763–1829).

Allport, Sir James Joseph (1811–1892), railway manager, was born at Birmingham on 27 February 1811, the third son of William Allport (*d.* 1823) of Birmingham and his wife, Phoebe, daughter of Joseph Dickinson of Woodgreen, Staffordshire. His father was a manufacturer of small arms, and for a time prime warden of the Birmingham Proof House Company. James was educated in Belgium, and at an early age, on the death of his father, assisted his mother in the conduct of her business. He married in 1832 Ann (*d.* 1886), daughter of John Gold of Birmingham, and they had two sons and three daughters.

In 1839 Allport entered the service of the newly founded Birmingham and Derby Railway as chief clerk, and after filling the post of traffic manager was soon appointed manager of that railway. While in this employment, in

1841 he was one of the first to advocate and propose the establishment of a railway clearing-house system. On the amalgamation of his company with the North Midland and Midland Counties Railway on 1 January 1844, Allport was not selected as manager of the joint undertaking, which became the Midland Railway. However, through the influence of George Hudson, 'the railway king', who had marked his ability, Allport was appointed manager of the Newcastle and Darlington line. This line prospered under his six years' control, and developed into the York, Newcastle, and Berwick Railway. He was next chosen in 1850 to manage the Manchester, Sheffield, and Lincolnshire, then little more than a branch of the London and North Western; and three years later, on 1 October 1853, he was appointed general manager of the Midland Railway.

At this period the Midland possessed only 500 miles of railroad, consisting of little more than an agglomeration of local lines serving the midland counties, and was in a position of dependence on the London and North Western. The extension of this railway system and its conversion into a trunk line were the first great objects of the new manager, and the policy of securing independent approach to the centres of population was now inaugurated, and henceforth consistently followed. In 1857 this work began by the completion of the Midland line from Leicester to Hitchin, which thus became, instead of Rugby, the nearest point of connection with London.

In this same year Allport was induced to accept the position of managing director to Palmer's Shipbuilding Company at Jarrow, and resigned his office in the Midland on 25 May 1857, but was elected a director on 6 October 1857. Three years later it was, however, found to be to the interest of the Midland to recall him to the post of general manager, and his services were almost immediately successfully employed in opposing a proposed bill which would have enabled the London and North Western, the Great Northern, and the Manchester, Sheffield, and Lincolnshire railways by far-reaching agreements seriously to handicap traffic on the Midland. In 1862 the act of parliament was secured by means of which the company was enabled to reach Lancashire through the Derbyshire dales, and in the following year powers were granted to lay down the line between Bedford and London.

Not satisfied with this rapid extension, Allport in 1866 was mainly responsible for the introduction of the bill into parliament authorizing the creation of the Settle and Carlisle Railway line. Great perseverance and determination on the part of the manager were necessary after the railway panic in 1866 to maintain the company's resolve to establish an independent route to the north. The difficulties and expense of the enterprise were immense, and its construction gave Allport more anxiety than any other railway work he had ever undertaken. The line was not completed for passenger traffic to Carlisle before 1875. The St Pancras terminus of the Midland Railway had been opened on 1 October 1868. By the securing of a London terminus, and the creation of a new and independent route to Scotland, Allport's main purpose was accomplished, and the Midland line was established as one of the great railway systems of the country.

The development of the coalfields in mid-England by means of this line was an object always kept in view by the general manager, and eventually successfully accomplished. The process, however, led in 1871 to a severe coal-rate struggle with the Great Northern Railway, in which Allport's action in suddenly withdrawing through rates to all parts of the Great Northern system, besides being unsuccessful, proved subsequently somewhat prejudicial to the interests of his company.

Competition with the Great Northern was one of the chief reasons which in the first instance caused the Midland board to decide on running third-class carriages on all trains on and after 1 April 1872. But Allport was a firm believer from the first in the eventual success of a course regarded at the time by most railway managers as revolutionary, and in later life looked back on the improvement of the third-class passenger's lot as one of the most satisfactory episodes in his career. Three years later first-class fares were reduced to the rate of second-class, which was then abolished; and these changes were subsequently introduced by other railways.

Allport not only boosted traffic and offered improved and cheaper railway travel, but he also kept the Midland in the forefront of technological innovation. In particular, he rapidly introduced a number of American railway practices, including the employment of Westinghouse air brakes (which revolutionized rail safety). Allport also purchased for the Midland the first of the luxurious Pullman carriages, which were imported from the USA in kits and then assembled at Derby. The company's sleeping cars and drawing-room cars subsequently established a legendary reputation for their levels of comfort from their introduction in 1874.

Allport retired from his post as general manager on 17 February 1880, when he was presented with £10,000 by the shareholders, and elected as a director of the company. In 1884 he received the honour of knighthood, and in 1886 was created a member of the royal commission to report upon the state of railways in Ireland. He was a director of several important industrial undertakings. After his retirement he inspected the New York, Pennsylvania, and Ohio Railway system on behalf of the bondholders, and exposed its mismanagement.

Allport has been characterized as a railway general manager 'par excellence' (DBB). In collaboration with the chairman, John Ellis, he transformed a set of provincial coal lines into a great national railway. He built up a lucrative freight traffic in such midlands' commodities as coal, bricks, and Burton beer; and, through shrewd marketing and technical innovation, established the Midland's legendary reputation for speed *and* comfort. Allport was one of the first generation of the new breed of professional railway managers. He died on 25 April 1892 at the Midland Railway's own Grand Hotel at St Pancras, London. He was buried in Belper cemetery, Derby, on 29 April.

WILLIAM CARR, rev. ROBERT BROWN

Sources T. R. Gourish, 'Allport, Sir James Joseph', *DBB* · W. M. Acworth, *The railways of England* (1889) · R. Williams, *The Midland railway: a new history* (1988) · *The Times* (29 April 1892) · *Railway News* (30 April 1892) · *CGPLA Eng. & Wales* (1892)
Likenesses G. W. Emery, mezzotint (after J. E. Williams), BM
Wealth at death £194,032 15s. 7d.: resworn probate, April 1894, *CGPLA Eng. & Wales* (1892)

Allsop, Thomas (1795–1880), writer, was born on 10 April 1795 and baptized on 20 November 1795 at Wirksworth, Derbyshire, the son of William Allsop, farmer, and his wife, Elizabeth, *née* Harding, of Stainsborough Hall, near Wirksworth, a property which belonged to his grandfather. Allsop was educated at Wirksworth grammar school, and though originally intended to follow his father's profession, a desire to see more of the world led him to abandon farming for the experience of London. At the age of seventeen he entered the large silk mercery establishment of his uncle Mr Harding at Waterloo House, Pall Mall, with whom he remained some years. Ultimately he left for the stock exchange, where he made a fair amount of money during the early years of railway construction.

Allsop attended Coleridge's 1818 lectures, and was so impressed that he addressed a letter to him. Coleridge found it so 'manly, simple, and correct', that he asked to meet Allsop, and consequently established a friendship which lasted all the life of the poet, Coleridge becoming a frequent guest at Allsop's house. On the poet's death Allsop published in two volumes his most considerable work, entitled the *Letters, Conversations and Recollections of S. T. Coleridge* (1836). The collection's main virtue, that it was a product of an editor greatly devoted to and friendly with Coleridge, is also its main defect, as Allsop interpreted many of Coleridge's comments in light of his own character, and his edition therefore ran counter to the general impression of the poet. This was seized on by the reviewers of the time, and the finer points of Allsop's recollections went unremarked. It is impossible, however, to read Coleridge's letters and not perceive the personal value that he set on Allsop's companionship.

Allsop included other literary figures in his social circle; his wife worked to make their home attractive to her husband's friends, and it became a favourite resort of Charles Lamb, Barry Cornwall, and William Hazlitt, among others. Lamb's letters and Thomas Talfourd's *Memorials of Lamb* record a high personal estimation of Allsop, reflected in the fact that Lamb asked Allsop to be an executor of his will, in a letter dated 9 August 1823. Other visitors to his home included men as dissimilar as William Cobbett, Giuseppe Mazzini, and the emperor of Brazil, who, after a visit to Coleridge's grave, sent Allsop an expensive silver urn engraved with words of personal regard.

Allsop's foresight in the area of public affairs, as well as on intellectual matters, was demonstrated in his *Budget of Two Taxes Only*, addressed to the then chancellor of the exchequer in 1848. His last work was *California and its Gold Mines* (1852–3)—mines which he during two years personally explored. The book consists of letters addressed to his son Robert, after the manner of his friend Cobbett's letters to his son James. While Allsop's letters display remarkable practical judgement, similar to that of Cobbett on the subject of which he wrote, there is a brightness and vivacity of philosophic reflection in them without parallel in commercial reports.

Allsop's political sympathies were radical; when Feargus O'Connor was elected member for Nottingham, Allsop gave him his property qualification of £300 p.a. in land, then necessary by law, that Chartism might be represented in parliament. When on a grand jury about 1836, Allsop startled London by informing the commissioners at the Old Bailey that he should think it unjust 'to convict for offences having their origin in misgovernment', since society had made the crime, and he considered the state culpably insensitive to the condition of the people. He despaired of amelioration from the influence of the clergy, and, when needing a house in the country, stated in an advertisement that preference would be given to one situated where no church or clergyman was to be found within 5 miles.

Deploring the subjugation of France under the late emperor, Allsop, like Landor, entertained and showed sympathy for Orsini. On the trial of Dr Bernard for being concerned in what was called the 'attempt of Orsini', it transpired that the shells employed were ordered by Allsop in Birmingham; but as he used no concealment of any kind and gave his name and address openly, it did not appear that he had any other knowledge than that the shells were intended as an improvement in a weapon of military warfare. The government offered a reward of £500 for his apprehension, when George Jacob Holyoake and Dr Langley had an interview with the home secretary, and brought an offer from Allsop immediately to surrender himself if the reward was paid to them to be applied for the necessary expenses of his defence, as he did not at all object to be tried, but objected to be put to expense without just reason. The reward was withdrawn, and Allsop returned to England. By reason of his friendships, his social position, and his boldness, he was one of the unseen forces of revolution in his day, and his sentiments are instructive. His favourite ideal was the man who was 'thorough'—who saw the end he aimed at, and who knew the means and meant their employment. He had a perfect scorn for propitiation when a wrong had to be arrested. Without expecting much from violence, he thought it was merited when there was no other remedy.

On the night before the Chartist demonstration on 10 April 1848, Allsop, being the most trusted adviser of Feargus O'Connor, wrote to him as follows from the Bull and Mouth Hotel, St Martin's-le-Grand, London:

> Nothing rashly. The government must be met with calm and firm defiance. Violence may be overcome with violence, but a resolute determination not to submit cannot be overcome. To remain in front, *en face* of the government, to watch it, to take advantage of its blunders, is the part of an old general who will not be guided like a fish by its tail. Precipitate nothing, yield nothing. Aim not alone to destroy the government, but to render a class government impossible. No hesitation, no rash impulse, no egotism; but an earnest,

serious, unyielding progress. Nothing for self, nothing even for fame, present or posthumous. All for the cause. Upon the elevation of your course for the moment will depend the estimation in which you will henceforth be held; and the position you may attain and retain will be second to none of the reformers who have gone before you.

Yet in these seemingly revolutionary fervours Allsop was none the less in many ways still a conservative, and only sought the establishment of right and justice. He adopted no opinion which he had not himself well thought over, and he expressed none of the truth and relevance of which he was not well assured in his own mind. Allsop died on 12 April 1880 at Castle Park Gardens, Exmouth, and his body was removed for burial on 17 April to Brookwood cemetery, Woking, in order that Holyoake, to whom he left autobiographical papers, might speak at his grave, which could only be done on unconsecrated ground.

G. J. HOLYOAKE, rev. REBECCA MILLS

Sources T. Allsop, *Letters, conversations and recollections of S. T. Coleridge*, 2 vols. (1836) · P. Fitzgerald, ed., *The life, letters and writings of Charles Lamb* (1876), 3.79–102 · G. J. Holyoake, *Life of Joseph Rayner Stephens* (1881), 189–90 · T. N. Talfourd, *Memoirs of Charles Lamb*, ed. P. Fitzgerald (1892), 228n · T. Allsop, *California and its gold mines*, ed. R. Allsop (1853) · Allibone, *Dict.* · J. M. Wheeler, *A biographical dictionary of freethinkers of all ages and nations* (1889) · Boase, *Mod. Eng. biog.* · IGI · *Collected letters of Samuel Taylor Coleridge*, ed. E. L. Griggs, 6 vols. (1956–71) · d. cert. · *CGPLA Eng. & Wales* (1880)

Archives Tyne and Wear Archives Service, Newcastle upon Tyne, letters to Joseph Cowen

Wealth at death under £2000: administration, 3 May 1880, *CGPLA Eng. & Wales*

Allsopp, Henry, first Baron Hindlip (1811–1887), brewer, was born on 19 February 1811 at Burton upon Trent, the third but only surviving son of Samuel Allsopp of Burton upon Trent and his wife, Frances, only daughter and heir of Charles Fowler of Shrewsbury.

The firm of Samuel Allsopp & Sons had claims to be the oldest brewery in Burton: Samuel Allsopp's uncle and great-uncle (both named Benjamin Wilson) were the most prominent exporters of Burton ales to the Baltic from the 1740s to the 1800s. Like M. T. Bass, Allsopps were early entrants to the Indian trade and the firm was the first to brew India pale ale (IPA) in Burton in 1822. The firm flourished both in the Indian export trade and the English domestic market in the 1830s and 1840s. Virtually no records survive for the firm before its incorporation in 1887 and it is difficult to trace its growth. Although it always appears to have followed in the wake of its great rival, Bass, Allsopps was by any reckoning a spectacularly successful Victorian firm before the mid-1880s, acknowledged as the world's third biggest brewery in the 1870s. Henry Allsopp was the key figure in its development after he took over the direction of the firm from his father in 1838.

Relying on the burgeoning demand for premium Burton pale ales and constructing a network of agencies, stores, and bottling contracts, Allsopp saw production increase from a few thousand barrels a year in 1830 to a peak of 700,000 barrels in the mid-1870s. The firm's beers were sold in forty-four countries abroad, and the new brewery built in the late 1850s was *the* model British brewery of the third quarter of the nineteenth century, combining the most up-to-date machinery with convenience of layout. With its 'enormous dimensions, handsome elevations', Alfred Barnard ranked it in 1889 'equal to any in the Kingdom' (Weir and others, 133). The firm was also in the van of employing brewing scientists.

In February 1887 Allsopps was floated on the stock market and was sold by the family to the new company for £3.3 million. Following the wildly successful incorporation of Guinness as a public company in October 1886, the investing public's demand for brewery shares was insatiable, and the flotation seemed as triumphant as that of Guinness. There was said to be fighting in the street for prospectuses, and the chairman reported applications from 37,000 individuals for £105 million worth of capital, an over-subscription of some thirtyfold. The reality, as commentators in the know pointed out, was very different. Although profits over the previous five years had increased—owing solely to the lowest brewing material prices within memory—sales had declined by almost one-third of their 1875 peak. With Henry Allsopp's advancing years, the firm was losing its lead, especially exposed by its decision not to acquire a large tied-house estate. Goodwill in the new company balance sheet was inflated to a crazy eight times average net profits. The prospect of an 8 per cent dividend on ordinary shares was held out; in fact the company never paid more than 7 per cent in the next twenty-eight years, and in no fewer than twenty of them distributed no dividend at all. Henry Allsopp, an old and honourable man, was immensely hurt by accusations in the financial press that his family had sold to a gullible public a vastly overpriced pup on a false prospectus. Within six weeks of the flotation he was dead.

Oddly, given his wealth and his firm's prominence in the industry, Henry Allsopp cut a much smaller figure than M. T. Bass both in Burton and the national trade. Seemingly much less conscious of publicity, he nevertheless served as Conservative MP for East Worcestershire from 1874 to 1880. Moreover, although generous to brewing trade charities, he was a more modest benefactor to his home town than his rivals, the Bass family. The principals of the two firms might meet from time to time to discuss prices, gravities, discounts, and loans to publicans, but in general a historic, deep-seated rivalry existed between the two firms. When, like many a member of the Victorian new, super rich, the Allsopps claimed ancient descent (from a knight in Richard II's reign), the news caused mirth at Bass.

In May 1880 Henry Allsopp was created a baronet; in February 1886 he was elevated to a barony, the first fully signed-up member of the 'beerage'. He became a modest large landowner, in 1873 owning 1158 acres at Hindlip Hall, Worcestershire. On 21 August 1839 he married Elizabeth (d. 1906), second daughter of William Tongue of Comberford Hall, Staffordshire; they had six sons (two of whom were MPs at the time of their father's death) and two daughters. Lord Hindlip died on 2 April 1887 at Hindlip Hall, Worcestershire. None of his sons inherited his entrepreneurial abilities; although two remained on the board of the new company after 1887, the company came to have the reputation of being the worst managed big brewery in Britain before 1914.   R. G. WILSON

Sources C. C. Owen, *The development of industry in Burton-upon-Trent* (1978) · K. H. Hawkins, 'The conduct and development of the brewing industry in England and Wales, 1860–1930: a study of the role of entrepreneurship in determining business strategy, with particular reference to Samuel Allsopp & Sons Ltd', PhD diss., University of Bradford, 1981 · C. C. Owen, 'The greatest brewery in the world': a history of Bass, Ratcliff & Gretton, Derbyshire RS, 29 (1992) · T. R. Gourvish and R. G. Wilson, *The British brewing industry, 1830–1980* (1994) · A. Bernard, *Noted breweries of Great Britain and Ireland*, 1 (1889) · *Licensed Victuallers' Gazette and Hotel Courier* (7 June 1873) · *Brewers' Guardian* (5 April 1887) · CGPLA Eng. & Wales (1887) · GEC, *Peerage* · *Dod's Peerage*

Archives Allied Breweries, Burton upon Trent, Samuel Allsopp & Sons

Wealth at death £557,577 0s. 10d.: probate, 18 June 1887, *CGPLA Eng. & Wales*

Allston, Washington (1779–1843), painter and poet, was born on 5 November 1779 at Brook Green domain, All Saints' parish, in the district of Georgetown, South Carolina, the second of the two children of William Allston junior (d. 1781), a captain in General Francis Marion's brigade during the American War of Independence, and his second wife, Rachel, *née* Moore (d. 1839). He was brought up on his parents' South Carolina plantation until spring 1787, when he was sent to Robert Rogers's school in Newport, Rhode Island. In 1796 he entered Harvard University, and four years later he graduated having earned the distinction of class poet. Allston departed for England in 1801 and was admitted to the Royal Academy Schools, where he studied under Benjamin West. In November 1803 he began a tour of the continent, stopping for some time in Paris. There he became acquainted with William Hazlitt. He also spent much of his time in the Louvre and Luxembourg galleries, where he was able to absorb the light, colour, and space of the works by Venetian painters that had been looted by Napoleon. He then made his way through Switzerland to Italy, and in 1805 settled at the Villa Malta in Rome. While in Rome, Allston painted at least seventeen pictures, among them an unfinished portrait of Coleridge (1806), whose enthusiasm for the story of the Argonauts inspired him to paint *Jason Demanding to Return to his Father's Kingdom* (c.1807–8; both Fogg Art Museum, Harvard University). He also painted three scenes from Shakespeare and a number of classical landscapes, including *Diana and her Nymphs in the Chase* (1805; Fogg Art Museum). This painting was not only praised by his contemporaries for its composition and translucent colouring, but was a favourite of Coleridge, whose rendering of it in words can be found within the pages of his notebooks. While in Rome, Allston introduced Coleridge to artists who frequented the Caffè Greco and Villa Malta, among them the Danish sculptor Bertel Thorvaldsen, the German artist Asmus Jakob Carstens, and the German landscape painters Gottlieb Schick and Joseph Anton Koch. He also guided Coleridge's visits to see paintings in Rome and its surrounding areas. The two became close friends, and from February to March 1806 Coleridge

joined Allston at his lodgings in Olevano, a small town outside Rome, where they spent time 'sketching, talking, sampling the Albano wine and discussing art history and aesthetics' (Holmes, 55).

In spring 1808 Allston returned to Boston, where he remained for three years. In response to the lack of interest in historical painting in America, he turned to portraiture, painting mainly close friends and family; he was listed as a portrait painter in the *Boston City Directory* for 1810. Despite the lack of interested patrons, Allston experimented with ideas he refined through his discussions with Coleridge. The meditative cast of his work is reflected in the appearance of solitary, contemplative figures in states of reverie and atmospheric effects produced by the 'half-light' of early morning and evening. This is evident in paintings such as *Coast Scene on the Mediterranean* (1811; Columbia Museum of Art and Science, Columbia, South Carolina) and *The Valentine* (1809–11; priv. coll.). The extent to which Allston felt the lack of commissions clearly concerned his wife, Ann, *née* Channing (1778–1815), whom he had married on 19 June 1809. She wrote to her father that she 'feared there was too little taste for the arts in America to encourage him' (*Correspondence*, 58).

Frustrated with the lack of patrons in America, Allston departed once again for England and, with Ann and his student, Samuel F. B. Morse, settled in London in 1811. He immediately rekindled his friendship with Coleridge, who introduced him to William Wordsworth—the latter's *Ode Composed upon an Evening of Extraordinary Splendor and Beauty* was indebted in part to Allston's painting *Jacob's Dream* (1817; Petworth House, Sussex, National Trust collection)—and to Robert Southey, whose poetry he greatly admired. Wordsworth described Allston as 'slim somewhat dark delicate in appearance, seeming taller than he is with jet-black hair, and a complection out of which the colour seems to have been taken by a hot relaxing climate' (*Love Letters of William and Mary Wordsworth*, 135). In 1814 Allston painted portraits of both Coleridge (NPG) and Southey. Through Coleridge he also became acquainted with prominent art patrons such as George Beaumont and the third earl of Egremont. In 1811 Beaumont commissioned *The Angel Releasing St Peter from Prison* (1814–16; Museum of Fine Art, Boston) for the altar in the parish church at Ashby-de-la-Zouch, and had, on Coleridge's advice, acquired one of Allston's landscapes in 1816. According to Charles Leslie, next to Beaumont, Lord Egremont was 'first to appreciate Allston's merit' (*Correspondence*, 583). He owned three of Allston's works, *Jacob's Dream*, *The Repose in Egypt* (before 1818), and *Contemplation* (1817–18; Petworth). It was at this time that Allston became celebrated in the London art world for his painting *The Dead Man Restored to Life by Touching the Bones of the Prophet Elisha* (1811–14; Pennsylvania Academy of Fine Arts), which won a prize of 200 guineas at the British Institution. However, one of his most experimental and promising pieces, *Elijah in the Desert* (1817–18; Museum of Fine Arts, Boston), suffered critical neglect for privileging a bold and expressive landscape over its biblical subject. Yet this painting 'may well have made a lasting impression' on Bristol painters such as Francis Danby (Greenacre, 14). Allston considered it one of his 'best efforts' and regretted having to part with the picture when it was sold.

Allston's and Coleridge's intellectual exchanges on matters of art and poetry became increasingly significant for Allston in shaping a theoretical foundation for his own practice, and for Coleridge in realizing a system of practical criticism for the fine arts. This is evident not only in the fragmented set of essays *On the Principles of Genial Criticism*, which accompanied Allston's exhibition in Bristol in 1814, but also in his integration of Coleridge's critical principles into his *Lectures on Art* (1850), the first art treatise to be published in America. Their interest in the complex relationship between painting and poetry as sister arts is reflected in a painting by Allston, aptly titled *The Sisters* (c.1816–17; Fogg Art Museum) by Coleridge. Following the death of his wife, Ann, on 2 February 1815, Allston fell into a deep depression, through which he was supported by Coleridge.

In 1818 Allston rather suddenly decided to quit England for America, against the advice of both Coleridge and Beaumont, who argued 'you are quitting this country at a moment when the extent of your talents begins to be felt, and when the encouragement you are likely to receive will bring them to perfection' (Beaumont to Allston, 29 June 1818; *Correspondence*, 118). The circumstances of his departure are curious. In a rather reflective mood, Allston wrote to William Dunlap on 18 February 1834 that it was occasioned by a strong feeling of homesickness. However, in a letter to Charles Leslie on 28 August 1818, Allston urgently expressed a wish that no correspondence directed to his residence at Buckingham Place be accepted. He claimed that 'there are letters of this unpleasant kind I have had from Bristol and other places', and hoped that Leslie would excuse this request, knowing what he had 'already suffered' (*Correspondence*, 121–2). Leslie thought Allston's departure was due to the constant solicitations from beggars he had aided in the past.

After moving to Cambridgeport, Massachusetts, in 1830 Allston married, on 1 June of that year, Martha Remington Dana (1784–1862). Having lost the remainder of his patrimony through the mismanagement of his agent in South Carolina and the collapse of a London bank, he was forced to take on small commissions to meet their expenses. Time spent on these commissions and on his renewed interest in writing usurped that available for what many thought would be his masterpiece, *Belshazzar's Feast* (1817–43; Detroit Institute of Arts). A number of subscribers raised $10,000 to enable him to finish the work, but by then too great a distance had formed between his original idea and the fulfilment of a duty that left him uninspired. Guilt-ridden, he continued to work on the painting until his death, on 9 July 1843. He was buried on 10 July in the Dana family vault in the churchyard on the common in Cambridge, Massachusetts.

At a time when 'practical knowledge of the craft traditions of Italy and Flanders had … disappeared in England' Allston's innovative and sometimes experimental approach to the more technical aspects of glazing and colouring reflected his study of the 'indirect techniques of the Masters, whose surfaces were built up slowly from a number of layers of underpainting' (Kinnaird, 141–2). His interest in technique, and the theoretical aspects of art, enriched his friendship with Coleridge, to whom he acknowledged he owed more, intellectually, than any other man.

SHANNON R. McBRIAR

Sources *The correspondence of Washington Allston*, ed. N. Wright (1993) • E. P. Richardson, *Washington Allston: a study of the Romantic artist in America* (1948) • W. N. Gerdts and T. E. Stebbins, jun., *A man of genius: the art of Washington Allston, 1779–1843* (1979) • J. B. Flagg, *The life and letters of Washington Allston* (1892) • E. Zuccato, *Coleridge in Italy* (1996) • *William Wordsworth*, ed. S. Gill (1984) • F. Greenacre, *Francis Danby, 1793–1861* (1988) • *The love letters of William and Mary Wordsworth*, ed. B. Darlington (1982) • R. Holmes, *Coleridge: early visions* (1989) • J. Kinnaird, *William Hazlitt: critic of power* (1978)
Archives Longfellow National Historical Site, Cambridge, Massachusetts, papers • Mass. Hist. Soc., corresp., papers, literary MSS | Mass. Hist. Soc., letters to W. Channing • Mass. Hist. Soc., Dana family papers, notebooks, sketchbooks, and letters • Mass. Hist. Soc., corresp. with David Sears • Mass. Hist. Soc., Susan Powell Mason Warren papers, corresp. • Mass. Hist. Soc., Welles family, corresp.
Likenesses W. Allston, self-portrait, 1796–1800, Harvard U., Fogg Art Museum • W. Allston, self-portrait, 1805, Museum of Fine Arts, Boston • J. A. Ames, portrait, priv. coll. • E. A. Brackett, portrait, Worcester Art Museum, Massachusetts • S. V. Clevenger, portrait, Boston Athenaeum • G. W. Flagg, portrait, Kennedy Galleries, New York • C. Harding, portrait, Providence Athenaeum, Rhode Island • D. C. Johnston, portrait, Bowdoin College Museum of Art, Maine • C. B. King, engraving, repro. in W. Allston, *Outlines and sketches* (1850) • C. R. Leslie, portrait, National Academy of Design, New York • E. G. Malbone, portrait, Museum of Fine Arts, Boston • R. M. Staigg, portrait, Museum of Fine Arts, Boston • G. Stuart, portrait, Metropolitan Museum of Art, New York
Wealth at death In the administration of Allston's estate, Franklin Dexter and Richard Henry Dana posted $30,000 on 9 August 1843. His personal estate was inventoried as $1,004.75 on 9 Jan 1844, and $100.00 was added on 22 May 1844: Wright, ed. *Correspondence* (1993)

Ally Sloper group (*act.* 1867–1923), cartoonists, was founded by **Charles Henry** [Harry] **Ross** (1835–1897), magazine editor and cartoonist, the son of Charles Ross, chief of *The Times*'s parliamentary staff, and nephew of the miniature painter Sir William Ross RA. He followed his father into the reporters' gallery of the House of Commons, and began to decorate his notes there with caricatures of the members. Later he entered the civil service at Somerset House, and continued to write for both newspapers and magazines during his spare time. When the Somerset House staff was reduced, Ross was delighted to retire on his pension and concentrate on writing and drawing.

Ross wrote six novels in all, ranging from Gothic 'penny dreadfuls' to light romances. His *The Pretty Widow* (2 vols., 1868) won great praise, for example, 'We welcome heartily a new writer so fresh, so original, and so finished. How compact and how interesting the story! How dramatic and how powerful its stormier passages!' So did his children's books which he illustrated, his humorous compilations, and his plays, which he assisted by also managing no fewer than three theatres (the Surrey, the Strand, and the Holborn).

Ross was both editor and writer for the weekly humorous magazine *Judy* (subtitled 'The London Serio-Comic Journal') when he created Ally Sloper, the first continuing comic-strip hero born in Britain. Sloper's début was a full-page picture strip in the issue of 14 August 1867, entitled 'Some of the Mysteries of Loan and Discount'. His name, an abbreviation of Alexander Sloper, was actually a period pun: rent dodgers were apt to slope up an alley when the collector came calling. For a while Sloper had a partner in petty crime called Isaac Moses, known colloquially as Ikey Mo, but as his popularity grew and his appearances became a weekly fixture, he became a man of many parts including the first serialized strip which depicted his adventures as *Judy*'s war correspondent.

Ross later described the birth of Sloper:

> I cannot tell you what it was that suggested Ally, but about 1860 I wrote a book of his adventures for Ward & Lock, only then I called him 'the Great Gun'. These were afterwards published as *The Ups and Downs of Ally Sloper*. Previous to this I introduced the character into a romance I wrote called *Dead Acres*. (*St James's Budget*, 24 Aug 1894)

Sloper's physical appearance owed much to illustrations of Dickens's Mr Micawber: bulb-nosed, bald-headed, spindle-shanked, bespatted big boots, batter-hatted, and of course booze-nosed. Ross drew in a crude style, largely inspired by the strip drawings of the German Wilhelm Busch, whose picture stories were reprinted in England from 1860.

Ross lost control of his character in 1884 when he sold all rights to the famous publisher and engraver Gilbert Dalziel. Long before that, his huge workload had in fact led him to assign the inking of his pencilled roughs to his future artistic partner and wife, **Isabelle Emilie de Tessier** (*b.* 1850/51). Born in Paris and originally an actress, calling herself Marie Duval, she became a pioneering female cartoonist, and married Ross about 1869. Many of the Sloper reprint collections are credited to her, often signed with a simple 'M D'. The first of many such was *Ally Sloper: a Moral Lesson*, issued by the *Judy* office in November 1873, qualifying to be called the world's first comic book (American comic books all began by reprinting newspaper strips). The first regular publications starring Sloper were pocket-sized picture papers, first *Ally Sloper's Comic Kalendar* (1875–87, thirteen issues) and then *Ally Sloper's Summer Number* (1880–87, eight issues).

While the first issue of *Ally Sloper's Half-Holiday* (3 May 1884) contained mainly reprints of the Ross/Duval strips, the weekly's success was largely due to **William Giles Baxter** (1856–1888). Of English parentage, Baxter spent part of his childhood in America. He trained as an architect and had a detailed architectural draughtsman-like style which was far more sophisticated than Ross's scratchy work. Before his first cartoons appeared in *Judy* in 1883, Baxter had worked for the publisher J. A. Christie on a new satirical weekly in Manchester, *Momus*, of which he

became joint editor. On moving to London he also designed Christmas cards, but it is his large front-page cartoons for the new tabloid *Ally Sloper's Half-Holiday* that remain breathtaking, outclassed only by his centre spreads for the annual Christmas numbers. Baxter created a vast Sloper 'family' (which anticipates the 'family' Carl Giles was later to create for the *Daily Express*) including Mrs Sloper, her pretty showgirl daughter, Tootsie Sloper, her naughty son, Master Alexander Sloper, Bill Higgins, Dook Snook, Lord Bob, the Hon. Billy, all the way down to boozing-pal Mr McGooseley and the shaggy dog, Snatcher. The characters were brought to life by music-hall performers, a short film was made (1898), and ventriloquists used Sloper dummies. The characters were merchandised as household items including china busts, brass doorstops, fireguards, and medallions.

Following his early death (due to alcoholism), on 2 June 1888, at 44 Mornington Road, Regent's Park, London, Baxter was replaced on the staff by the almost equally brilliant W. F. Thomas, who drew Sloper up to the final issue of the *Half-Holiday* in 1923. Ross died on 12 October 1897, at 499 Wandsworth Road, Clapham, London, leaving a son, Charles. Later revivals included comics in 1948 and 1949 and the first 'adult comic' created by Denis Gifford in 1976. Incredibly, the latest (and last) appearance of Sloper was drawn by comic artist Walter Bell, who as a young man had assisted Thomas in the 1920s. Examples of Baxter's work are in the Victoria and Albert Museum, London.

DENIS GIFFORD

Sources *St James's Budget* (24 Aug 1894) · W. Andrews, *Modern merry men* (1904) · D. Gifford, *Victorian comics* (1976) · M. Horn, ed., *World encyclopædia of comics* (1976) · M. Bryant and S. Heneage, eds., *Dictionary of British cartoonists and caricaturists, 1730–1980* (1994) · D. Kunzle, 'The first Ally Sloper: the earliest popular cartoon character as a satire on the Victorian work ethic', *Oxford Art Journal*, 8/1 (1985), 40–48 · d. cert. [William Giles Baxter] · d. cert. [Charles Henry Ross]

Almack, William (*d.* 1781), founder of club and assembly rooms, was born in Thirsk, in the North Riding of Yorkshire—not, as was sometimes stated by his contemporaries, in Scotland. In his youth he moved to London to work as a valet to the fifth duke of Hamilton, in whose employment he met Elizabeth (*d.* in or after 1781), daughter of William Cullen of Sanches, Lancashire, and brother of the physician William *Cullen. The couple married at St George's, Mayfair, on 16 May 1752 and had two children: William (*d.* 1806), barrister, and Elizabeth, who later married the royal physician David Pitcairn.

At about the time of his marriage Almack left the duke's household to establish himself as a wine merchant and proprietor of the Thatched House tavern in St James's Street, London. He also purchased two properties on Pall Mall—nos. 49 and 50—recently built by the architect Henry Holland. In the former Almack set up his first gentleman's club, which was subsequently moved to St James's Street and took the name Boodle's after its manager, Edward Boodle. At no. 50 he established a second club, Almack's, which opened in 1764. From the start

William Almack (*d.* 1781), by Richard Josey (after Thomas Gainsborough)

Almack's gained a name as a haunt of the young, fashionable, and extremely well-to-do. Of the original membership of twenty-seven a sizeable number styled themselves 'macaronis', a band of élite Italophiles sporting fine clothes and monumental wigs. Within a year the club had accepted a further 141 members, many being drawn from Almack's well-established rival, White's, by the new club's reputation as a centre for gaming. Chief among the gamesters were Stephen Fox, a founder member, and his brother Charles James, who joined in 1765. Dressed in broad-brimmed straw hats to keep their faces clear of hair and in coats turned inside out for luck, men like the Foxes proposed huge wagers during sessions of 'deep play'. Horace Walpole, writing in 1770, thought the 'gaming at Almacks … worthy of the decline of an empire or commonwealth … The young men of the age lose five, ten, fifteen thousand pounds an evening' (to Horace Mann, Walpole, *Corr.*, 23.187–8). The composure demanded at the card table became the hallmark of the club's membership. 'O for the sang-froid of an Almackian, who pursues his delights "Though in the jaws of ruin and codille"', mused Walpole (ibid., 32.123). And for the fashionable, for whom Westminster remained the epitome of modish living, Almack's proved a haven while more boorish types left for the summer. To Viscount Nuneham, Walpole commented on a London near deserted save for 'macaronis lolling out of windows at Almack's like carpets waiting to be dusted' (27 July 1773, ibid., 35.458).

The club remained under William Almack's supervision until 1774. Four years later it was taken over by the then manager, William Brooks, renamed after its new owner, and moved to new premises built by the younger Henry Holland on St James's Street opposite Boodle's. With it went many of its members (then numbering 333). The socialite James Hare wrote,

> Brooks opens his new house, and invites all or as many as
> Please to come from the Club in Pall Mall. Almack desires us
> to stay but as there can be no reason for preferring a bad old
> house to a good new one, I imagine Brooks will be victorious.
> (Joliffe, 26)

Thereafter, gatherings at 50 Pall Mall dwindled, though the house later became the location for a new club, Goosetree's.

Since the mid-1760s Almack had divided his time between his club and a set of assembly rooms which he opened in 1765. Built by Robert Mylne on King Street, Westminster, the rooms were celebrated both as the venue for weekly 10 guinea subscription balls and as a meeting place for groups such as the Dilettanti Society and, from 1770, a mixed club where newcomers were elected by members of the opposite sex.

Club and assembly rooms earned Almack a sizeable fortune, part of which was spent on a residence in Hounslow, Middlesex. Following his death on 3 January 1781, the King Street rooms were bequeathed to Almack's niece and renamed Willis's, after her married name. The assembly retained its reputation as a centre of fashionable living and, like the club in the 1760s and 1770s, Willis's (or Almack's as it was still often called) remained a target for later generations of the modish and their critics. Novels such as Marianne Hudson's *Almack's* (1826) and *The Key to Almack's* (1827), and Charles White's *Almack's Revisited* (1828), sought to 'expose the vices of fashionable life in their original and proudest sphere' (M. Hudson, *Almack's*, preface), while satires such as *The Ball, or, A Glance at Almack's* (1829) by G. Yates nostalgically recalled the elegance of its founder's generation as a corrective to the loose posture and morals of contemporary ball-goers. By the following decade the rooms were in decline—'clear proof that the palmy days of exclusiveness are gone by' (*QR*, 1840, quoted in Timbs, 2.88–9)—and finally closed in 1863. Their original site at 28 King Street is now marked by an office complex, Almack House. The gentlemen of Brooks's celebrated 200 years of secluded clubbability in 1978.   PHILIP CARTER

Sources *DNB* · J. Timbs, *Club life of London: with anecdotes of the clubs, coffee-houses, and taverns of the metropolis, during the 17th, 18th, and 19th centuries*, 2 vols. (1866) · H. S. Eeles and Earl Spencer, *Brooks's, 1764–1964* (1964) · J. Joliffe, 'The birth of Brooks's', *Brooks's: a social history*, ed. P. Ziegler and D. Seward (1991) · Walpole, *Corr.* · will, PRO, PROB 11/1073, fols. 9r–10r · *GM*, 1st ser., 40 (1770), 414–15 · IGI
Likenesses R. Josey, mezzotint (after T. Gainsborough), NPG [*see illus.*]
Wealth at death over £5000; property in King Street, Westminster, and Hounslow: will, PRO, PROB 11/1073, fols. 9r–10r

Almain, Edmund of. See Edmund of Almain, second earl of Cornwall (1249–1300).

Almain, Henry of. See Henry of Almain (1235–1271).

Almeida, John. See D'Almeida, João (*c.*1572–1653).

Almon, John (1737–1805), bookseller and political journalist, was born on 17 December 1737 in Moore Street, Liverpool, to the Irish-born John Almon (*b.* 1706), seaman, and his wife, Isabella Thompson (*d.* 1744). Apprenticed to a Liverpool bookseller in March 1751, Almon left before completing his apprenticeship to become a common seaman. In London in 1759, he found work as a journeyman printer and quickly became part of the literary scene. Although much of his early work is unidentifiable, he appears to have been also a prolific writer and compiler. His earliest known works supported the policies of Newcastle and Pitt and attacked those who wrote in opposition to them, the first indications of his lifelong political views.

On 26 October 1760 Almon was married to Elizabeth Jackson (1737–1781) at St John the Evangelist, Westminster; together they had ten children. The following January he was working for *The Gazetteer*, a periodical whose editor Charles Say—who became Almon's mentor, friend, and business partner—had been called to appear before the House of Commons to apologize for reporting on the proceedings of parliament. Almon contributed significantly to *The Gazetteer*'s growing popularity by introducing innovations such as a daily summary of correspondence received and 'Articles of literature and entertainment' which abstracted articles taken from other publications and periodicals.

In the meantime, Almon's passionately partisan pamphlets made him a favourite with supporters of Pitt and opponents of the Bute ministry. In November 1762 Almon wrote *A Review of Mr. Pitt's Administration*, highlighting his almost fanatical distrust of Bute. The work was dedicated to Earl Temple, who asked to meet him, and Almon proudly became 'Temple's man', maintaining a lifelong devotion to the earl. Although Bute initiated the newspaper and pamphlet wars that enlivened the 1760s, the extremely wealthy Temple seems to have been the real master of the battles for public opinion. Temple was known to be a supporter of the opposition press, although Almon was always careful to note that Temple did not write anything himself, but provided information and 'lines of reasoning' (J. Almon, *Biographical, Literary and Political Anecdotes*, 2, 1797, 27–8). Almon later characterized Temple as the strongest, and at times only, supporter of the constitutional rights of the British people. While writing at Temple's behest, Almon continued his work for *The Gazetteer* and later for the *London Evening-Post*, run by Say's son-in-law John Miller. In 1763, with Temple's assurance of support, Almon set up shop at 178 Piccadilly, opposite Burlington House. Temple not only switched his own business to Almon, but persuaded many friends to do the same; as a result Almon's shop became a centre of information and activity for the opposition for twenty years.

While he continued to write and compile works of his own, Almon became noted for knowing how to publish and promote authors' works, and for his fearlessness in publishing works opposed to the government. As late as 1777 Thomas Paine sent copies of *The American Crisis* to Benjamin Franklin, suggesting that he take the pamphlet to Almon, who 'might venture' to publish it, but if Franklin

sent it to others, 'some republican expressions should be omitted' (*Papers*, 204–5). Almon is perhaps best-known as the friend and publisher of John Wilkes. He was one of Wilkes's most loyal adherents and helped to support him in exile. The two met in 1761 and, although they had their differences, remained friends until Wilkes's death in 1797. Among the many pamphlets Almon published in support of Wilkes was *A Letter on Libels, Warrants, Seizure of Papers, etc.* (1764), which prompted Almon's first appearance before Lord Chief Justice Mansfield, on a charge of contempt of court. The case was later dismissed on a technicality.

Almon's political interests had led him to collect parliamentary debates even before he wrote *An History of the Parliament of Great Britain from the Death of Queen Anne to the Death of King George* (1763). His parliamentary friends provided him with notes of their speeches and Almon collated these with the *Commons Journals* to ensure accuracy. In 1766 he began publishing *The Debates and Proceedings of the British House of Commons* in bound volumes, a work that can be a frustrating read due to uneven organization and its characteristic polemical tone. Between 1766 and 1774 Almon compiled eleven volumes of Commons debates, and from 1774 to 1780 published seventeen volumes of the *Parliamentary Register*, a journal which included the debates of the House of Lords.

In January 1770 Almon was once again before Lord Mansfield, charged with selling a copy of Miller's *London Museum* which contained a copy of Junius's *Letter to the King*, a work the government considered to be seditious libel. Despite being the least involved of the six printers charged, Almon was the first tried and only one convicted. Although his fine was nominal, he and two guarantors were required to post £500 surety of good behaviour for two years. Unrepentant, even as his case was being tried, Almon published and republished *The Trial of John Almon*, including the trial record's copy of the *Letter*, and he continued to write summaries of the debates for the *London Evening-Post*, which were in clear violation of parliamentary privilege.

In 1771 Almon assisted Wilkes in the scheme that established press reporting of parliament. Later Almon collected and published the *Protests of the House of Lords* (1772), and at the beginning of the parliamentary session in 1774 began the new monthly, the *Parliamentary Register*, in order to report on the events in the North American colonies. Almon had close ties to America, and was well known for printing both sides of the conflict, most notably in his monthly report of American news, *The Remembrancer, or, Impartial Repository of Public Events*, from 1775 to 1784.

In 1781, not long after the death of his patron, Lord Temple, Almon retired with a modest fortune to Boxmoor House, Hemel Hempstead, Hertfordshire. Soon after their move his wife died, and he occupied himself with projects, writing *The Revolution in MDCCLXXXII Impartially Considered* (1782) and working on a long-planned compilation, *The Anecdotes of the Life of the Right Hon. William Pitt, Earl of Chatham* (1792). He returned to London in 1784, residing at 182–3 Fleet Street, and on 2 September married Maria

Parker, widow of the proprietor of the *General Advertiser*. He served for two years as a conscientious common councilman in the city but the *General Advertiser* was not as successful as his former publications had been. In 1786 he once again came before Lord Mansfield, this time for a libel which had been planted by government agents. In contrast with the situation at his previous court appearances, he did not have the influential Lord Temple behind him, nor was he defended by the brilliant Serjeant John Glynn but by a lawyer who was later suspected of being in government pay. Almon fled to France and was outlawed. After returning to England in 1792, he spent a year in king's bench prison, much to the outrage of the London newspapers. He spent the rest of his life in semi-retirement at Boxmoor writing and compiling histories and memoirs. His later works include *Memoirs of a Late Eminent Bookseller* (1790); *The Causes of the Present Complaints* (1793); *Biographical, Literary and Political Anecdotes* (1797); *Correspondence of the Late John Wilkes* (1805); and *Letters of Junius* (1806).

Almon died at Boxmoor House on 12 December 1805, his wife surviving him. He bequeathed houses in Fleet Street and Jermyn Street, London, and the house, gardens, and orchards at Boxmoor to his spinster daughter Caroline and son Charles. Almon was in the centre of the political events of his time, controversial and passionately biased, yet remarkably consistent in his loyalties and commitments. Instrumental in shaping public opinion and a central figure in the decisions regarding libel laws and freedom of the press, he also helped to promote the public reporting of parliamentary debates.

LYNDA L. LEITNER

Sources J. Almon, *Memoirs of a late eminent bookseller* (1790) · [A. Stephens], *Public characters of 1803–1804* (1804), 120–38 · P. G. D. Thomas, 'The beginning of parliamentary reporting in newspapers, 1768–1774', *EngHR*, 74 (1959), 623–36 · P. D. G. Thomas, *John Wilkes: a friend to liberty* (1996) · R. Haig, 'The Gazetteer', 1735–1797: a study in the eighteenth century English newspaper (1960) · *GM*, 1st ser., 75 (1805), 1179–81 · *The papers of Benjamin Franklin*, 24 (1984) · *State trials*, 20.803–68 · *IGI* · journals, CLRO, court of common council · parish registers, Liverpool Public Library · parish register, Herts. ALS · parish registers, GL · parish registers, City Westm. AC · will, PRO, PROB 11/1434, fols. 161–2 · J. Almon, *New Foundling Hospital for wit* (1786) · L. Leitner, 'John Almon, (1737–1805), journalist and publisher', PhD diss., U. Wales, Aberystwyth

Archives BL, corresp., Add. MS 20733 · Duke U., Perkins L., MSS and letters · New York Historical Society, corresp. and MSS | BL, Grenville MSS · BL, letters to J. Wilkes, Add. MSS 30868–30875, *passim* · GL, public and parish records · Hunt. L., Grenville MSS

Likenesses caricature, repro. in *Town and Country Magazine*, 12 (1 April 1780), 127–8

Wealth at death bequeathed houses at 182 and 183 Fleet Street and another in Jermyn Street, St James, and lifetime use of Boxmoor House orchard, house, and garden to daughter Caroline, which then to go to son and heirs; mourning ring to daughter Mary Bourdillon; widow 'left in great distress' even though houses in Fleet Street came with her upon marriage: will, PRO, PROB 11/1434, fols. 161–2

Almond, Hely Hutchinson (1832–1903), headmaster, born in Glasgow on 12 August 1832, was the second son of George Almond, incumbent of St Mary's Episcopal

Hely Hutchinson Almond (1832–1903), by Elliott & Fry, 1895

Chapel, Glasgow, and his second wife, Christiana Georgina, eldest daughter of Thomas Smith, barrister, of London. His paternal great-grandfather was headmaster of Derby School, and his maternal great-grandfather was John Hely-*Hutchinson, provost of Trinity College, Dublin. Precociously clever, he began to learn his letters at sixteen months, and by the age of three was struggling with the multiplication table. After attending the collegiate school, Glasgow, in 1845 he entered the University of Glasgow. At the end of the session he gained the Cowan gold medal in the Blackstone Latin examination, and he also specially distinguished himself in the Greek, mathematics, and logic classes.

Having been elected in 1850 to a Snell exhibition, Almond proceeded to Balliol College, Oxford, where he obtained a first class in both classical and mathematical moderations, but, owing to ill health and other causes, gained only a second in the final examinations. He graduated BA in 1855 and MA in 1862. Almond's experience of Oxford was ambiguous; his impression of his tutors was not entirely favourable, and he underwent a period of religious apathy, which he later lamented. But his experience of college athletics (he rowed in the Balliol eight) made him an admirer of the English system of education for the upper classes with its emphasis on the training of character.

Almond had, however, no immediate vocation for teaching and became a schoolmaster rather by chance. In 1855 he left Oxford for Torquay, where his father was living in retirement; and it was only after failing to gain a position in the Indian Civil Service that he took his first teaching post. A friend who ran a private tutorial establishment sought Almond's help, and during this temporary appointment Almond acquired an enthusiasm for teaching. In 1857 he took up the offer of a tutorship at Loretto School at Musselburgh, near Edinburgh, made to him by Charles Langhorne, a Balliol contemporary, whose father founded the school. In 1858 he became second master at Merchiston Castle School, Edinburgh, where he took an active part in rugby football and introduced an English professional to instruct the boys in cricket.

In 1862, following the death of his father, Almond purchased Loretto School from the Langhorne family. It was then chiefly a preparatory school, and he began with only fourteen boys. In his early years there the financial prospects were bleak, but he gradually built up the school and by the end of the century Loretto had become recognized as a leading public school, catering for boys up to university entry. Almond's position as headmaster and proprietor gave him the opportunity to pursue his own distinctive educational aims. Pupil numbers never reached 150, which enabled him always to know every boy personally, and allowed him to evolve his guiding principle of rule by persuasion, not by force. 'Relations between master and boys were unusually sincere, and the place had rather the aspect of a family than a school' (Mackenzie, 160).

At Loretto, Almond pioneered the idea of systematic physical exercise and the cultivation of physical hardiness as essential to a healthy adolescence. He attached cardinal importance to fresh air, personal cleanliness, proper and regular diet, the regulation of the hours of sleep and study, and physical exercise in all weathers. Dormitory windows were left open at night, cold baths were the rule, and boys were forbidden to eat between meals. Participation in physical activity was compulsory. Almond also implemented his firm views on rational dress: instead of linen shirts and collars and close-fitting suits, boys wore loose-textured tweed knickerbocker suits and flannel shirts open at the neck, and changed into flannels for all forms of strenuous exercise. Almond's system fostered extraordinary stamina, as testified by the large proportion of Loretto boys who went on to gain athletic distinction at Oxford and Cambridge.

Almond publicized his views on physical nurture widely, acknowledging the influence at various times of Archibald Maclaren, Herbert Spencer, and John Ruskin. His biographer described his system as informed by a 'Sparto-Christian ideal' (Mackenzie, 247). A lay member of the Episcopalian church, having recovered his faith during his father's final illness, Almond published three volumes of school sermons. A chapel was erected at Loretto to mark his marriage in 1876 to Eleanora Frances, daughter of H. B. Tristram, canon of Durham. His views on the miraculous aspects of Christianity and the divinity of Christ were considerably altered under the influence of T. H. Huxley's writings, and he cannot be simply classified as a muscular Christian. Although, like other headmasters, he promoted team games because they encouraged unselfishness (see his article entitled 'Football as a moral agent', *Nineteenth Century*, 1893), he did not see games primarily as a means either of controlling boys or of moralizing them; rather, they were part of his 'gospel of good health' (Mangan, 54), which owed much to physiological Darwinism. Almond's ideas, which he described in his evidence to the royal commission on physical training (Scotland) (1903), became fashionable in the early twentieth century, in the context of contemporary anxieties about physical deterioration; in particular, his belief in the importance of fresh air anticipated the methods later used in the prevention and cure of consumption.

Almond's influence on the educational world was more limited, and the phenomenon of 'Lorettonianism' with which Almond was associated found few imitators. A critic of examinations, he spoke of developing in boys an independent interest in study. But his hostility to 'cramming' knowledge was not matched by much positive enthusiasm for alternative forms of intellectual activity—indeed, Almond disliked bookishness—and led in practice to low academic standards; and although an innovator in physical education, he was notably slow to develop science teaching. He spoke much of promoting individuality and of his aversion to uniformity, custom, and convention; yet there is little evidence that under his headmastership Loretto avoided the tendency to conformity which was characteristic of public schools of the period. It has been commented that Almond's 'crusade for independence of mind and rational living often appeared to be little more than a preference for open-necked flannel shirts and cold dormitories' (Roach, 189).

Almond was made an honorary LLD of Glasgow University in 1886. He died of a bronchial condition, after a few years of failing health, at his home, North Esk Lodge, Musselburgh, on 7 March 1903, and was buried in the churchyard at Inveresk. His wife survived him; they had three sons and three daughters.   M. C. CURTHOYS

Sources *DNB* · R. J. Mackenzie, *Almond of Loretto* (1905) · H. B. Tristram, *Loretto School past and present* (1911) · M. Lochhead, *Episcopal Scotland in the nineteenth century* (1966) · J. A. Mangan, *Athleticism in the Victorian and Edwardian public school* (1981) · J. Roach, *Secondary education in England, 1870–1902* (1991) · *WWW* · *CCI* (1904)
Likenesses Elliott & Fry, photogravure, 1895, repro. in Mackenzie, *Almond of Loretto* [see illus.] · photographs, repro. in Mackenzie, *Almond of Loretto*
Wealth at death £9480 6s. 5d.: confirmation, 23 Jan 1904, *CCI* · £652 8s.: additional estate, 29 April 1904, *CCI*

Alms, James (1728–1791), naval officer, was born on 15 July 1728 at Gosport, the son of John Alms, said to be a servant of the duke of Richmond, and his wife, Mary. After serving in merchant ships he entered the navy about 1740 in the *Namur*, and was rated midshipman by Captain Charles Watson of the *Dragon*, a ship in which he had his small share of the battle off Toulon on 11 February 1744. Afterwards he was with Edward Boscawen in the *Namur* in the action off Cape Finisterre on 3 May 1747, and also in the East Indies, when the ship was lost in a tremendous storm (12 April 1749), near Fort St David's, south of Madras, Alms being one of twenty-three survivors. On 14 May 1749 he was promoted lieutenant by Boscawen in the *Syren*, in which he continued on the East India station until she returned home in the spring of 1752.

With little interest, and being on very meagre half pay, he obtained the command of a former East Indiaman, the *Hardwick*, and was for some three or four years employed trading between Bombay and China. His ship being taken up by government for the carriage of stores, he was present at the capture of Gheria by his old captain, now Rear-

Admiral Watson, on 12–13 February 1756. In March 1759 he was appointed first lieutenant of the *Mars* (74 guns), commanded by Captain James Young, and in her took part in the blockade of Brest, which culminated on 20 November in the crushing defeat of the French at Quiberon Bay. He continued in the *Mars* for nearly two more years, during further operations on the coast of France. On 10 July 1761 Alms was made commander of the *Flamborough's Prize*, and in November he was moved as acting captain to the *Alarm*, in which he went to the West Indies with Admiral Sir George Pocock's fleet for the Havana expedition. On the passage to Havana the *Alarm* led the fleet and captured two Spanish ships. However, on arrival at Havana, Alms handed the *Alarm* over to the captain appointed to her, and reverted to commander in the sloop *Ferret*, and in August he moved to the *Cygnet*. During the operations he showed himself an 'alert, forceful man', to quote Keppel (Syrett, 266), being employed on various detached duties, including the clearance of wrecks from Mariel harbour. He took dispatches home in the *Cygnet* but, despite the strong recommendations of Keppel, he was not promoted to post rank until 20 June 1765.

Until 1770 Alms lived with his family at Chichester. He was married and is thought to have had five children. In the following three years, by the influence of Viscount Halifax, he commanded the *Montreal* in the Mediterranean. In 1776 he was employed as captain regulating the impress service for the Sussex district. He was at this time suffering from severe asthma, which prevented his accepting any more active service; nor did he feel equal to any appointment until, at the end of 1780, he was offered the *Monmouth* (60 guns), fitting for the East Indies. This he accepted, hoping that the warm climate might prove beneficial to his complaint. He sailed on 13 March 1781, as one of the squadron under Commodore George Johnstone, and was therefore at the action with bailli de Suffren's squadron in Praya Bay. At the Cape, Johnstone put Alms in command of the reinforcements and East India ships bound for India. He experienced a difficult passage with adverse winds leading to much sickness, and has been criticized for ignoring the advice of the East India commanders, although Alms clearly had much experience of the Eastern seas. In the end he had to leave the troopships on the coast of Arabia to enable the line-of-battle ships to reach India in time for the campaigning season, for Alms realized that Sir Edward Hughes would face Suffren's newly arrived squadron with a much weaker force. Alms finally joined Hughes on 11 February 1782 in time to take part in the battle off Sadras on 17 February, and also in that off Providien on 12 April, which included the episode for which he is remembered. By the skilful dispositions of the bailli de Suffren, the *Superb* and the little *Monmouth* had to sustain the concentrated attack of up to five of the French ships. The *Monmouth* was reduced to a wreck and lost 147 killed and wounded, out of an actual complement of a little over 400. Alms's eldest son, George Pigot, a lieutenant of the *Superb*, was killed in the same action; and, indeed, the *Superb*'s loss in men was somewhat greater than that of the *Monmouth*.

Notwithstanding the rigours of Providien, Alms, still commanding the *Monmouth*, had a full share of the battles off Negapatam on 6 July, and off Trincomalee on 3 September; however, his health broke down during the winter, and he was obliged to go on shore at Madras for several months. This was virtually the end of his active service. He arrived at Spithead in June 1784 and, after living in domestic retirement at Chichester for a few years, died on 8 June 1791, and was buried in the cathedral on 14 June.

J. K. LAUGHTON, *rev.* A. W. H. PEARSALL

Sources D. Syrett, ed., *The siege and capture of Havana, 1762*, Navy RS, 114 (1970) · H. W. Richmond, *The navy in India, 1763–1783* (1931) · J. Charnock, ed., *Biographia navalis*, 6 (1798), 546–52 · *Naval Chronicle*, 2 (1799), 549–79 · C. Hardy, *A register of ships* (1799) · Birr Castle, Earl of Rosse's MSS, H2, fol. 156 · logs, PRO, ADM 51/188, 223, 351, 595, 3757, 3836 · muster books, PRO, ADM 36/2095, 4153, 4949, 5593 · letters, PRO, ADM 1/1445, 1447
Archives PRO, letters, ADM 1/1445, 1447

Alnwick, Martin (*d.* 1336), Franciscan friar, theologian, and philosopher, doubtless came from Northumberland. Possibly the Martinus occasionally recorded as participating in Oxford disputations in the last years of the thirteenth century, he was certainly at Oxford by 1300, when he was among the friars presented to the bishop of Lincoln for licence to hear confessions—unsuccessfully in his case. He subsequently took the degree of DTh. About 1304 he became thirty-second regent master (or lector) of his order's Oxford schools. In 1311 he was summoned to Avignon to take part in the controversy over the issue of poverty between the conventual and spiritual Franciscans, as one of the four advisers of the general minister. He pleaded the cause of the conventuals, which eventually prevailed. On 1 October 1318 he was licensed to hear confessions in the diocese of York. A volume, now lost, containing his *Determinacio* and disputations was later recorded in the library of the Augustinian friars at York. According to Bale, Alnwick died in 1336 and was buried at Newcastle.

The last nineteen questions of the commentary on book 1 of the *Sentences* attributed to William Ware are in reality the work of Martin Alnwick. These questions are found in incomplete gatherings in five manuscripts (Bordeaux, Bibliothèque Municipale, MS 163; Troyes, Bibliothèque Municipale, MS 501; Vatican City, Biblioteca Apostolica Vaticana, MS Vat. lat. 4871, MS Vat. Chigi B. VII. 114; and Vienna, Nationalbibliothek, MS 1424). They deal with the issues of God's knowledge, power, and will. Although most of these questions place him in the tradition of the Franciscan school, he seems to have been strongly influenced by the secular master, Henri de Gand, following him especially in his teaching that God has both speculative and practical ideas. At times, however, he opposes Henri, as when he denies Henri's affirmation of the possibility of the divine ideas being infinite. Recently some of Alnwick's logical teaching has been discovered, especially in the area of the *Perihermenias* question concerning the truth and falsity of propositions. Other works once ascribed to him, such as the commentary on books 1 and 2 of the *Sentences* conserved at the library of San Antonio in

Padua, and a *Universal Chronicle* printed in 1750, really belong to William Alnwick and Martinus Polonus respectively.

S. F. BROWN

Sources L. M. de Rijk, 'Some 14th century tracts on the *Probationes terminorum*: Martin of Alnwick, OFM, Richard Billingham, Edward Lipton, and others', *Artistarium*, 3 (1982), 7–33 · V. Doucet, 'Commentaires sur les *Sentences*: supplément au répertoire de M. Frédéric Stegmueller', *Archivum Franciscanum Historicum*, 47 (1954), 88–170, esp. 144 · Emden, *Oxf.* · P. Glorieux, 'Jean de Saint-Germain, maître de Paris et copiste de Worcester', *Mélanges Auguste Pelzer* (1947), 527–8 · J. Lechner, 'Beiträge zum mittelalterlichen Franziskanerschrifttum vornehmlich der Oxforder Schule des 13/4 Jahrhunderts auf Grund einer Florentiner Wilhelm von Ware Ms.', *Franziskanische Studien*, 19 (1932), 1–12 · F. Pelster, 'Die Kommentare zum vierten Buch der *Sentenzen* von Wilhelm von Ware, zum ersten Buch von einem Unbekannten und von Martin von Alnwick in Cod. 501 Troyes', *Scholastik*, 27 (1952), 344–67 · *Fratris Thomae vulgo dicti de Eccleston tractatus de adventu Fratrum Minorum in Angliam*, ed. A. G. Little (1951), 54 · A. G. Little and F. Pelster, *Oxford theology and theologians*, OHS, 96 (1934) · A. G. Little, *The Grey friars in Oxford*, OHS, 20 (1892)
Archives Österreichische Nationalbibliothek, Vienna, MS 1424 · Biblioteca Apostolica Vaticana, Vatican City, MSS Vat. lat. 4871; Vat. Chigi B. VII.114 · Bibliothèque Municipale, Bordeaux, MS 163 · Bibliothèque Municipale, Troyes, MS 501

Alnwick, William (*c*.1275–1333), Franciscan friar and theologian, and bishop of Giovinazzo, took his name from Alnwick in Northumberland. The course of his later career suggests that he was born about 1275. Having become a Franciscan friar, he probably studied theology at his order's studium at Newcastle. However, by 1303 he was a licensed doctor of theology at Paris, being then listed among the few foreign masters who sided with Philippe IV, king of France, in his dispute with Pope Boniface VIII. Alnwick also lectured at other intellectual centres on the continent—at Montpellier, Bologna, and Naples. But he returned to England, for he is listed as the forty-second Franciscan regent master at Oxford. This would place him as a master at Oxford about 1316, during the years when Henry Harclay was chancellor of the university.

Notes in the margins of Alnwick's manuscripts indicate that he was in lively debate with the authors of his own and recent times, English and French, including Thomas Aquinas, Bonaventure, Henri de Gand, Pierre Aureole, Giacomo da Ascoli, Godefroi de Fontaines, Henry Harclay, and Thomas Wilton. Mainly, however, he was in conversation with John Duns Scotus, and it was this association that kept his memory alive, particularly among other Scotists, like Peter Thomas and the anonymous Scotist of Vatican City, Biblioteca Apostolica Vaticana, MS Vat. lat. 869, who disagreed with him. He collaborated with Scotus in the production of the latter's *Commentary on the 'Sentences'* (*Ordinatio*). He also served as the reporter for one of Scotus's *Collationes*, and compiled the long additions (*Additiones magnae*) which were meant to fill the lacunae left in books 1 and 2 of the *Ordinatio*. But although Alnwick based his philosophy and theology on the fundamental starting points of Scotus's teaching, he often followed his own star.

Alnwick's commentary on Peter Lombard's *Sentences* is preserved in whole or part in manuscripts found in Assisi,

Cracow, and Padua. A few questions of this commentary have been edited in journals, as have almost a dozen questions of his *Determinationes*, as well as a sermon on the beatific vision, and some questions from his commentary on the *De anima*. His *Quodlibet* and *Quaestiones de esse intelligibili* were published in 1937 as volume 10 of the Bibliotheca Franciscana Scholastica Medii Aevi.

Alnwick participated in the general chapter of the Franciscan order held at Perugia in 1322, where he joined the theologians who drew up and signed the decree *De paupertate Christi* attacking the position on apostolic poverty maintained by Pope John XXII. Alnwick may not have been actively involved in the formulation of the decree, but his commitment to it is shown by the public defence he subsequently gave of it in the last question of his *Determinationes*. There he argued that Christ and his apostles possessed nothing either personally or in common. This opposition to the papal thesis caused Pope John in 1323 to order the bishops of Bologna and Ferrara to initiate a process against Alnwick, who, however, fled to Naples, where King Robert of Sicily befriended him, and in 1330 had him canonically appointed and legitimately confirmed as bishop of Giovinazzo. He died in Avignon in March 1333.

S. F. BROWN

Sources W. Alnwick, *Quaestiones disputatae de esse intelligibili et de quodlibet*, ed. A. Ledoux (Florence, 1937), ix–xlvi · S. F. Brown, 'Sources for Ockham's prologue to the *Sentences* [pt 2]', *Franciscan Studies*, new ser., 27 (1967), 39–107 · S. D. Dumont, 'Univocity of the concept of being in the fourteenth century: John Duns Scotus and William of Alnwick', *Mediaeval Studies*, 49 (1987), 1–75 · S. D. Dumont, 'Univocity of the concept of being in the fourteenth century: the *De ente* of Peter Thomae', *Mediaeval Studies*, 50 (1988), 186–256 · S. F. Brown and S. D. Dumont, 'Univocity of the concept of being in the fourteenth century: an early Scotist', *Mediaeval Studies*, 51 (1989), 1–129 · R. Schönberger and B. Kible, *Repertorium edierter Texte des Mittelalters* (Berlin, 1994), nn. 13234–49 · J. D'Souza, 'William of Alnwick and the problem of faith and reason', *Salesianum*, 35 (1973), 425–88 · D. Veliath, 'The Scotism of William of Alnwick in his *Determinationes de anima*', *Salesianum*, 32 (1970), 93–134 · F. Prezioso, *L'evoluzione del volontarismo da Duns Scoto a Guglielmo Alnwick* (1964) · M. Schmaus, 'Guglielmi de Alnwick, O.F.M., doctrina de medio quo Deus cognoscit futura contingentia', *Bogoslovni vestnik*, 12 (1932), 201–25 · Emden, *Oxf.*

Alnwick, William (*d.* 1449), bishop of Norwich and Lincoln, was probably born in Alnwick, Northumberland. Of unknown parentage, he was described by the papal collector, Piero da Monte, a hostile witness, as *rusticanus homo … ex vili genere natus* ('a peasant … born of a low family'; Haller, 74). His first important patron was Stephen Scrope, archdeacon of Richmond and chancellor of Cambridge University, where Alnwick obtained a doctorate in civil law by 1419. In the previous year he had acted as Scrope's executor. His first benefice, Goldsborough in Scrope's archdeaconry, was secured before he was ordained acolyte in 1415; and he probably owed his next rectory (Hollingbourne, Kent, acquired in December 1419) to service to Archbishop Henry Chichele (*d.* 1443). By July 1420, when he was appointed to treat with ambassadors of the duke of Brittany, he had, like others from Chichele's administration, entered Henry V's service in France. About then he became the king's secretary and confessor, continuing in those offices until Henry's death. He also took his turn in the mundane work of arranging retinues. To this royal service he owed his promotion to the archdeaconry of Salisbury (7 December 1420) and prebends in York (1421) and Bayeux (1422) cathedrals. Alnwick accompanied Henry V on his last itinerary of England between February and June 1421, playing a part in the attempts of Bishop Richard Flemming (d. 1431) to settle conflicts at Lincoln Cathedral, and of the king to enforce reform on the Benedictines. He was with Henry when he died in France on 31 August 1422, and accompanied the body on its journey back to England.

On 16 December 1422 Alnwick joined the council established to rule during Henry VI's minority, as keeper of the privy seal, a post of central importance to conciliar rule and in which, according to his epitaph, *noluit ille pati falsum* ('he would not endure deceit'; Peck, 2.15). As well as participating in the day-to-day administration of England he served on several embassies to treat with Scotland between December 1423 and August 1425. He continued to collect benefices, becoming warden of St James's Hospital, Westminster, canon of St Paul's Cathedral (both in December 1422) and dean of St Martin's-le-Grand (1425). In the confused period following the death of Archbishop Henry Bowet of York in 1423 he was originally suggested by the government for the see of Ely, but was rejected by both chapter and pope; however, he was eventually provided (27 February 1426) to Norwich. The temporalities were restored on 4 May, and he was consecrated at Canterbury (18 August) by his erstwhile patron, Archbishop Chichele. Unlike most of his predecessors in the office he continued as keeper of the privy seal for several years after his promotion. In May 1427 he was sent on a delicate mission to the duke of Burgundy to try and patch up the alliance recently greatly strained by the behaviour of Humphrey, duke of Gloucester (d. 1447). In 1430 he treated with envoys of the king of Castile, concluding a truce on 15 November. In May 1431 Alnwick joined Henry VI on his coronation tour of France. He attended Jeanne d'Arc's abjuration in Rouen (24 May) and the king's coronation in Paris (16 December), returning to England with the royal party on 9 February 1432. Politically Alnwick was one of the majority of Henry V's former servants, led by Cardinal Henry Beaufort (d. 1447), who defended conciliar rule against Gloucester's ambitions. Most of them had accompanied Henry VI to France and, by their return, Gloucester was firmly in the ascendant. On 25 February Gloucester made a clean sweep of all royal officials, dismissing, among others, the chancellor, the treasurer, and the keeper of the privy seal, Bishop Alnwick.

Alnwick was readmitted to the council by December 1433, at about which time he became the young king's confessor. As confessor and local diocesan he waited intermittently on Henry VI during his extended visit to Bury St Edmunds between Christmas 1433 and April 1434. From July to September 1435 Alnwick served on the English embassy to the disastrous Congress of Arras, where English ambitions were overturned by the peace made between France and Burgundy. In February 1436 he was commissioned to treat with the Scots and in November 1436 he was appointed to deal with envoys from Prussia, Danzig, and the Hanseatic League, concluding a treaty with them on 22 March 1437. By now he was bishop of Lincoln for, in May 1436, Henry had written to the pope, praising Alnwick, the chapter's 'choice', in the highest terms, to request his translation there. Alnwick assisted Henry VI in founding both Eton College and King's College, Cambridge. He helped compile the latter's original statutes and was its designated visitor, as well as being commissioned by Archbishop John Stafford (d. 1452) to consecrate the chapel and cemetery in 1444. In 1441 he was one of those who presided at the trial and divorce of Eleanor Cobham, Gloucester's wife. On 24 April 1442 Alnwick received exemption from attendance at council and parliament, having cited his intention of devoting himself to his spiritual duties. He continued to make very occasional appearances at council meetings, and seems to have attended all but one (Bury St Edmunds, February 1447) of the meetings of parliament called before his death. However, he was no longer at the centre of politics.

No matter how important his contribution to royal government, the plethora of surviving records means that Alnwick is best remembered as a diocesan, first at Norwich and then at Lincoln. Recent scholarship has improved the general reputation of the fifteenth-century episcopate, and Alnwick is no longer regarded as unusually devoted to his spiritual duties. However, even during his greatest periods of political involvement, he was clearly conscientious and spent as much time in his dioceses as possible, perambulating them and carrying out his episcopal duties until his death. At Norwich his heresy proceedings are well known, because well recorded. Between September 1428 and March 1431 about a hundred suspected Lollards came before Alnwick's court, three of whom, William White, John Wadden, and Hugh Pye, who had reneged on previous recantations, were burnt. Among others brought to trial was Margery *Baxter, who hid White before his detention [*see under* Lollard women (*act. c.*1390–*c.*1520)]. Alnwick's determination to stamp out heresy in his diocese (which he shared with other bishops, led by Archbishop Chichele) engendered conflict with Bury St Edmunds Abbey. Alnwick's decision to conduct investigations within the town ensured that, henceforth, Abbot William Curteys (d. 1446) regarded him as a determined opponent of his monastery's privileges and exemption. The two were to clash over their respective jurisdictions on a number of occasions. Similarly, in 1433, Alnwick's attempt to appoint the prior of Binham, a cell of St Albans in Norfolk, as collector of the clerical subsidy caused conflict with Abbot John Whethamstede (d. 1465), who celebrated his victorious defence of the privileges of St Albans by placing verses lampooning the bishop in his abbatial register. However, both cases reflect the background of contemporary episcopal attacks on religious exemptions in the ecumenical councils as much as the personalities involved. After his translation to Lincoln, where he was enthroned on Maundy Thursday (28 March)

1437, Alnwick's relations with both abbots seem to have been cordial.

Alnwick's determination to uphold the discipline of religious life is witnessed by the extensive records of his visitations in the diocese of Lincoln. His primary visitation of his own cathedral revealed a lamentable state, physical and spiritual. This was largely caused by friction between the chapter and Dean John Macworth (d. 1452) who, since his installation in 1412, had been in dispute with many of his fellow canons, culminating in 1435 in his assault on the chancellor, Peter Partridge (d. 1451), in the cathedral choir. After much deliberation all agreed that Alnwick should arbitrate, and, because much conflict arose from ambiguities in the cathedral's statutes and customs, that he should also try to elucidate them. In June 1439 his *Laudum* ('Award'), a masterpiece of balance, was accepted by all parties, and from that time on all incoming canons swore to abide by it. In October 1440 he presented his draft *Novum registrum* ('New register'), a remarkably lucid document, encapsulating in content the statutes and customs of Lincoln Cathedral, but based in form on the statute book of St Paul's. (The *Laudum* and *Novum registrum* are both most conveniently found in *Statutes of Lincoln Cathedral*.) Despite much argument the chapter never formally adopted the *Novum registrum* (although the register was treated as though it had been, c.1690–1870). Macworth, who was excommunicated in 1445, continued to oppose Alnwick over various jurisdictional matters. Nevertheless the bishop was able to report in July 1449 that he had received the penitent dean back into the bosom of holy mother church.

Five months later, on 5 December 1449, Alnwick died suddenly in London. As requested in his will, made on 12 October 1445 while Macworth was excommunicate, he was buried at the west end of the nave of Lincoln Cathedral, 'in that place wherein the bishop makes his station at the time of the procession' (Thompson, 1.xxv). However, his tomb was destroyed in 1644. His will established a chantry, shared with his first patron, Stephen Scrope, which was to last five years. It was extended for a further twenty years in 1465 by his executor John Breton, a canon of Lincoln, who in making his own will requested burial 'at the side or feet of my most singular lord' (Lincoln Chapter Acts, A.2.35, fol. 97v). Alnwick, described by his epitaph as *pretiosarum domuum edificator*, 'a builder of costly edifices' (Peck, 2.15), also asked his executors to erect a great window above the western entrance to Norwich Cathedral. The entrance itself, which may have been built during his Norwich episcopate, still bears his arms (argent a cross moline sable) surrounded by a request for prayers for his soul. He left his more troublesome spouse, Lincoln Cathedral, only £20.

Other building works undertaken by Alnwick included the Norwich palace gateway; extensive alterations to the Lincoln episcopal palace whose three-storied gatehouse is still known as Alnwick Tower; and some work at both Buckden parish church, Huntingdonshire, where stone corbels in the shape of angels hold his arms, and the chamber block of the bishop's palace at Lyddington, Rutland, where the glass in the windows of the great chamber contains numerous depictions of his arms and his motto, *Delectare in Domino* ('To delight in the Lord'), and a portrait of a bishop who may be Alnwick himself. At Cambridge he is reputed to have contributed to the south part of the university schools, while in 1428 he joined with others in founding a residence there for Benedictine scholars. He helped found parish guilds in Thame, Oxfordshire, and Louth, Lincolnshire; and, in 1448, with the earl of Northumberland, he founded, in St Michael's Church, Alnwick, a chantry of two priests, one of whom was to teach grammar to poor boys. Those who opposed him might well have agreed with Monte that he was *duri capitis et inexorabilis* ('hard-headed and unyielding'; Haller, 74), while his household servants were said to have found him so tight-fisted a master that at his death they compensated themselves for his stinginess by taking 2000 marks from his executors, to distribute among themselves (Giles, 39). However, to his friends at Crowland Abbey he was not only 'a man of the most consummate skill in the transaction of business', but also 'singularly distinguished among his fellow bishops of England for bearing the highest character and an unblemished name' (Ingulph, 405–6).

ROSEMARY C. E. HAYES

Sources archives, PRO · R. C. E. Hayes, 'William Alnwick, bishop of Norwich (1426–37) and Lincoln (1437–49)', PhD diss., Bristol University, 1989 [and sources therein cited] · A. H. Thompson, ed., *Visitations of religious houses in the diocese of Lincoln*, 2–3, CYS, 24, 33 (1919–27) · H. Bradshaw and C. Wordsworth, eds., *Statutes of Lincoln Cathedral*, 3 vols. (1892–7) · A. H. Thompson, *The English clergy and their organization in the later middle ages* (1947) [incl. fragment of Alnwick's Lincoln court bk] · N. P. Tanner, ed., *Heresy trials in the diocese of Norwich, 1428–31*, CS, 4th ser., 20 (1977) · *The award of William Alnwick, bishop of Lincoln, AD 1439*, ed. and trans. R. M. Woolley (1913) · D. Knowles [M. C. Knowles], *The religious orders in England*, 3 vols. (1948–59) · R. Hayes, 'The "private life" of a late-medieval bishop: William Alnwick, bishop of Norwich and Lincoln', *England in the fifteenth century* [Harlaxton 1992], ed. N. Rogers (1994), 1–18 · F. Peck, ed., *Desiderata curiosa*, 2 vols. (1732–5) · J. Haller, ed., *Piero da Monte: ein Gelehrter und päpstlicher Beamter des 15. Jahrhunderts* (Rome, 1941) · *Ingulph's Chronicle of the abbey of Croyland*, ed. and trans. H. T. Riley (1854) · J. A. Giles, ed., *Incerti scriptoris chronicon Angliae de regnis trium regum Lancastrensium* (1848) · *Chancery records* · PRO, C84 147/14 · Reg. John Stafford, LPL · Emden, *Cam.*

Archives Lincs. Arch., Lincoln episcopal and chapter records · Norfolk RO, Norwich episcopal and chapter records | BL, Bury St Edmunds abbey registers, Add. MSS 7096, 14848 · CCC Cam., library, MS 108

Likenesses boss on gateway (of Alnwick?), bishop's palace, Norwich · corbel on gateway (of Alnwick?), bishop's palace, Norwich · glass (of Alnwick?), bishop's palace, Lyddington · portrait over entrance (of Alnwick?), Norwich Cathedral

Wealth at death approx. £1100—bequests; £700 and five-year chantry; also up to £400 to defend estate; also cost of great west window, Norwich Cathedral; residue to poor scholars and other good works: will, LPL, Reg. Stafford, fols. 178v–179v

Alpenny, Caroline Cadette. *See* Howard, Caroline Cadette (b. 1821, d. in or after 1901).

Alphege. *See* Ælfheah (d. 1012).

Alphery, Mickepher [Mikifor Olferyevich Grigoryev] (d. **1668**), Church of England clergyman, was asserted by

John Walker to have been descended from the Russian imperial line and sent to England by John Bedell, a Russian merchant, to be educated at Oxford, when his and his brothers' lives were in danger from a powerful faction in Russia. Reality seems to have been more complex. In June 1602 Alphery (described in Russian documents as Olfer'yev syn Grigor'yev) was one of four gentlemen's sons whom the tsar Boris Godunov confided to the care of the English ambassador, John Meyrick, for education in England. They arrived in November and according to John Chamberlain were 'to be dispersed to divers schooles at Winchester, Eaton, Cambridge and Oxford' (Cleminson, 400), although they do not appear in school registers.

On 10 April 1609 Alphery matriculated from St John's College, Cambridge, moving to Clare College, where he graduated BA in 1612. By the following year, when the Russian ambassador moved to repatriate the four young men, only Alphery could be found, and he argued successfully for permission to stay to complete his studies. He proceeded MA in 1615, and the same year was ordained deacon and priest in the Church of England. His conversion from the Orthodox church, which he now strongly rejected, breached the terms of Meyrick's original commission. Russian diplomats tried every means, including an unsuccessful kidnapping attempt, to induce him to return home, but Alphery remained obdurate and the authorities in England were apparently unmoved by threats of reprisals on English interests in Russia. Finally Meyrick arranged a meeting between the ambassador, Isaak or Ivan Pogozhev, and Alphery, held on 10 February 1622, but when the latter appealed to the king to be allowed to stay in England the privy council pronounced in his favour, asserting that the king would not 'send him away by force, when he hath received the true religion ... to a place where ... hee cannot enjoye the freedome of his conscience'. Such an action would be 'against the law of God and nations and soe unbeseemeing a just and sovereign prince' (Cleminson, 401). Thereafter Alphery seems to have been left undisturbed.

After his ordination Alphery had lived for a time in London, in close touch with merchants trading with Russia, including Bedell. In 1618 the latter presented him to the rectory of Woolley, Huntingdonshire. About this time he married Joanna (d. 1655); they had eight children baptized between 1619 and 1635. He was ejected in 1643. The fifths were belatedly paid to him by his successor. His poverty prompted his recommendation by the committee for plundered ministers to the charity of merchants trading with Russia, and in 1650 he supplied the pulpit at Easton for 2s. 6d. a sermon. When Joanna died in January 1655 she was buried at Woolley.

Alphery was reinstated at Woolley in 1660, but later left a curate there and retired to his daughter-in-law's house at Hammersmith. When he drew up his will on 15 April 1668 he was 'sicke and weake in body', with small debts to his son Francis and his son Stephen's wife. The executor, his son Mickepher (bap. 1620), obtained probate on 10 November 1668.   S. L. SADLER

Sources proceedings of the committee of plundered ministers, 1644–5, BL, Add. MS 15669, fols. 125, 188b • proceedings of the committee of plundered ministers, 1645–6, BL, Add. MS 15670, fols. 64, 80 • M. Alphery, petition, 23 June 1660, HLRO, main papers collection • Woolley parish register, Cambs. AS, Huntingdon, 2917/1 • J. Walker, *An attempt towards recovering an account of the numbers and sufferings of the clergy of the Church of England*, 2 pts in 1 (1714), 183 • *Walker rev.*, 206 • Venn, *Alum. Cant.*, 1/1.23 • *VCH Huntingdonshire*, 1.369, 370; 3.125, 127 • W. H. B. Saunders, *Legends and traditions of Huntingdonshire* (1888), 195–200 • *CSP dom.*, 1638–9, 245 • will, PRO, PROB 11/328, sig. 134 • R. Cleminson, 'Boris Godunov and the rector of Woolley: a tale of the unexpected', *Slavonic and East European Review*, 65 (1987), 399–403

Wealth at death £10 bond to be administered, quarterly rents due to Alphery: will, PRO, PROB 11/328, sig. 134

Alpin (d. 840). See under Dál Riata, kings of (act. c.500–c.850).

Alport, Cuthbert James McCall [Cub], **Baron Alport** (1912–1998), politician, was born on 22 March 1912 at Turffontein, near Johannesburg, South Africa, the only surviving child of (Arthur) Cecil Alport (1880–1959), doctor and later professor of medicine, and his wife, Janet (d. 1976), daughter of James McCall, of Caitloch, Dumfriesshire. An elder brother had died in infancy. The family shuttled between South Africa and England before settling in London in 1921. While at Wilkinson's School in Orme Square (1922–6), Cuthbert gained the nickname Cub by which he was known thereafter. He went to Haileybury College in 1926 and received tuition in oratory, as his father saw him as a future prime minister. At Pembroke College, Cambridge (1931–5), he gained a second-class degree in history and law and was elected vice-president of the Cambridge University Conservative Association and president of the Cambridge Union (1934–5).

Alport started work in 1936 as a junior tutor at the Bonar Law Memorial College at Ashridge, running courses for Conservative activists. He meanwhile studied for the bar and wrote *Kingdoms in Partnership* (1937), a paean to the British Commonwealth. Late in 1937 he entered Conservative central office as assistant secretary for political education, thanks to R. A. Butler, whose brother Jock (d. 1943) was his friend. Having joined the part-time Artists' Rifles in 1934, he was called up in 1939. Aldershot, the War Office, and staff college preceded service in east Africa with the King's African rifles. He ended the war as GSO1, east African command, with the rank of lieutenant-colonel. Shortly after demobilization he married, on 26 October 1945, Rachel Cecilia Bingham (1917–1983), only daughter of Lieutenant-Colonel Ralph Charles Bingham and great-granddaughter of the fourth earl of Lucan, who had lately served in the WRNS. They had three children: Cecilia (b. 1946), Lavender (b. 1950), and Arthur (b. 1954).

Alport returned to Conservative central office in October 1945 to be director of political education. By the end of the year this post had evolved into that of director of the Conservative Political Centre (CPC), a new semi-autonomous body designed to engage in 'the battle of ideas' over the role of government. Alport, already balding and avuncular, was thus the most senior of 'Rab's boys'—young men appointed by Butler to reform the Conservative Party after the election defeat of 1945. In dozens

Cuthbert James McCall Alport, Baron Alport (1912–1998), by Walter Stoneman, 1956

of CPC discussion papers he promoted centrist policies in tune with his own beliefs.

Alport left the CPC and entered the House of Commons on winning Colchester from Labour at the 1950 general election. Soon after he made his home in the constituency at The Cross House, Layer de la Haye, Essex. Dissatisfaction with Conservative social policy quickly led him and Angus Maude to gather a number of promising new Conservative MPs, including Iain Macleod, Edward Heath, Robert Carr, and Enoch Powell, into what became known as the 'one nation' group (so called after the pamphlet which they issued in autumn 1950). Alport's main interest, however, was the Commonwealth. His maiden speech urged the creation of a colonial army, and *Hope in Africa* (1952) aired his ideas on how to bring African society up to the standards of western civilization through multiracial partnership. He chaired the non-party Joint East and Central Africa Board (1953–5) and visited Kenya during the Mau Mau emergency. Passionately devoted to the liberal model of the Commonwealth, he nevertheless argued that full democracy could not succeed in Africa without economic and educational progress on a large scale—and he really wanted Britain to bring it about. This outlook later left him isolated in the crossfire between tory right-wingers hostile to African nationalism and left-wingers demanding swift decolonization.

As assistant postmaster-general from December 1955, Alport was responsible for introducing regional postage stamps for Scotland, Wales, and Northern Ireland. He then served as under-secretary of state at the Commonwealth Relations Office (CRO) from January 1957 until October 1959, when he was advanced to the new post of minister of state in the same department. Had his patron, Rab Butler, attained the premiership, his preferment might have been more dramatic, yet the CRO suited him well, especially as he was its chief spokesman in the Commons while Lord Home was secretary of state. By 1960, however, Alport worried that Macleod, as colonial secretary, was preparing colonies for independence too hastily. Being sworn of the privy council in May, moreover, was no compensation for playing second fiddle after July 1960 to Churchill's son-in-law, Duncan Sandys, a Commonwealth secretary who did not impress him.

Of British possessions in Africa at this time, the Federation of Rhodesia and Nyasaland (sometimes designated the Central African Federation) presented the most intractable problems. It had been judged to make economic sense in 1953 to unite Southern Rhodesia, Northern Rhodesia, and Nyasaland. Most of the black population opposed the federation as a device to extend the control of white settlers concentrated in Southern Rhodesia; the whites obstructed any but very gradual movement towards majority rule. Matters were complicated by the overlapping competencies of the CRO and Colonial Office. While British ministers feared the federation going the way of either of its neighbours (South Africa and the Congo), their uncertain response to unrest in Nyasaland exposed Conservative divisions over colonial policy.

Alport saw the Federation of Rhodesia and Nyasaland as a crucial test for his vision of African development, so he volunteered in January 1961 to leave parliament and become high commissioner in the territory. He aspired to help the British government towards a coherent policy; maybe he even flattered himself that he might rescue the federation from dissolution where another would fail. He took a life peerage on 16 February 1961 and, as Baron Alport, of Colchester in the county of Essex, flew to Salisbury, Southern Rhodesia, on 3 March. During two years of tortuous constitutional negotiations he struggled to reconcile Roy Welensky, Hastings Banda, and Kenneth Kaunda to a pluralist federal structure, but no compromise resulted. Butler, given special responsibility for central African affairs, decided in December 1962 to go against Alport's advice and grant Nyasaland the right to secede. Cub and Rab ceased to be friends. With the federation doomed (though it took a year to wind up), its high commissioner was accused of betrayal by angry whites, who already thought him patronizing (as he tended to cloak his diffidence with pomposity). The mission had failed; he left on 7 June 1963. *The Sudden Assignment* (1965) gave his account of his time as high commissioner.

Though earlier led to expect the resumption of his ministerial career, Alport was merely appointed British delegate to the Council of Europe (1964–5). He took employment as chairman of a unit trust administered by the Dawnay Day Group and tried to make the most of the House of Lords, where he became a deputy speaker (1971–82 and 1983–94). An adviser to Harold Wilson on the breakaway (Southern) Rhodesia, he went to Salisbury in June–July 1967 for fruitless talks about talks with Ian Smith. His involvement with the Labour government displeased fellow Conservatives, as did his repeated advocacy in the 1970s of an all-party coalition and proportional representation. From 1974 to 1982 he was an assessor of exclusion orders under the Prevention of Terrorism Act. Colchester and district profited from his work for numerous local voluntary organizations.

Viewing Thatcherism as despicable heresy, Alport spoke and voted in the House of Lords according to his 'one nation' principles, but criticism so indiscriminate failed to make much impact. The Conservative whip was withdrawn from him in 1984—a rare event in the upper house. Widowed in 1983, he latterly found happiness in a secret romance with Annie Patricia (Pat) Llewelyn-*Davies, Baroness Llewelyn-Davies of Hastoe (1915–1997), who had served as Labour chief whip in the Lords. He died of cancer at Abberton Manor Nursing Home, Abberton, Colchester, on 28 October 1998, and was buried in the churchyard at Layer de la Haye. He was survived by his three children.

The Conservative modernizer of the 1940s seemed old-fashioned by the 1970s. His political career was sacrificed without thanks to the Federation of Rhodesia and Nyasaland. While others abandoned them, he remained true to Commonwealth and 'Butskellite' ideals.

JASON TOMES

Sources M. Garnett, *Alport: a study in loyalty* (1999) • Lord Alport, *The sudden assignment* (1965) • *The Times* (29 Oct 1998) • *Daily Telegraph* (29 Oct 1998) • *The Guardian* (2 Nov 1998) • *The Independent* (4 Nov 1998) • Burke, *Peerage* • *WWW* • m. cert. • d. cert.
Archives University of Essex, Colchester, Albert Sloman Library | Bodl. Oxf., Conservative Party archives • Bodl. RH, corresp. with Sir Roy Welensky and papers • Essex RO, Colchester, papers relating to local affairs in north-east Essex • PRO, Commonwealth Relations Offices files • Trinity Cam., R. A. Butler papers
Likenesses W. Stoneman, photograph, 1956, NPG [*see illus.*] • photograph, 1959, repro. in *Daily Telegraph* • photograph, 1967, repro. in *The Independent* • photograph, repro. in *The Times* • photograph, repro. in *The Guardian* • photographs, repro. in Garnett, *Alport*

Alsager, Thomas Massa (1779–1846), financial journalist and businessman, was born on 27 September 1779, probably at Southwark, Surrey, the fifth of the nine or ten children of Thomas Alsager (1738?–1790), a setter in the cloth trade, and his wife, Mary, *née* Crosby (d. after 1790) of Southwark. The source of his unusual second name is unknown, but it may be derived from Massey, a common surname around Audley, Staffordshire, where the Alsager family originated.

Little is known of Alsager's formal education, though he probably attended school at Congleton, Cheshire, between the ages of five and eleven, returning to London after his father died. Three years later he began a seven-year apprenticeship as a setter in the family business at Southwark, stretching semi-finished cloth to the width then required by law. Alsager appears to have prospered in the twenty years or so after 1800, and his interests grew to include a bleaching works at Faringdon.

If, as seems likely, Alsager was largely self-educated, the results were remarkable. He was a first-rate scholar and linguist, and it was said that he could perform competently on all the instruments of the orchestra. By 1813, the date of his first recorded meeting with Charles Lamb, Alsager was clearly both comfortably situated and highly cultivated—doubly qualified to become an associate of the so-called Elian circle around Lamb. His contribution was not on a par with Coleridge or Wordsworth, but he was a congenial host and a good listener, qualities that were much appreciated. He was a good friend to Leigh Hunt when he was imprisoned in 1813. It was Alsager's copy of George Chapman's *Homer*, loaned to John Keats in 1816, which inspired the latter to write 'On First Looking into Chapman's Homer'. It was also Alsager, in 1818, who was largely responsible for persuading William Hazlitt to deliver his celebrated *Lectures on the English Poets*. On 30 May 1823 Alsager married Elizabeth Roper (d. 1845), when she was seventeen. They had thirteen children in all, eleven daughters and two sons, of whom eight daughters and one son survived infancy.

Alsager's closest friend, also from Southwark, was the journalist Thomas Barnes, who had been appointed editor of *The Times* in 1817. In the same year, at the age of thirty-eight, Alsager joined him, taking up the post of City correspondent and supplying music criticism from time to time. When John Walter (1776–1847), the chief proprietor, sold some of his shares in 1819 Alsager bought a modest interest in *The Times*. By the end of the year he was ensconced in the paper's newly established City of London office, from where he began to report and comment on the markets. Alsager 'appears to have been the world's first financial editor' ('Financial journalism').

The craze for financial speculation in 1825 stimulated the demand for news from the City, and most of the leading London dailies responded. *The Times*, which published Alsager's 'money article' on a daily basis from 1825, was soon regarded as 'the chief authority on these matters, and became the favourite medium for circulating official and semi-official communications' (Marks, 1904). Alsager's City intelligence was regarded as highly reliable; he had good connections and was close to the Rothschilds. His views, especially as they related to the currency, foreign investment, and joint-stock banking, were rather conservative.

Alsager became an increasingly important figure at Printing House Square after 1827, when he purchased a partnership in *The Times*. He was by then already known as the joint manager, with William Delane. *The Times* prospered under their stewardship until the mid-1840s. It seems likely that Alsager's most important contribution, apart from drawing in financial advertising through the prestige achieved by his money article, was to accelerate the flow of news from abroad by developing 'express' channels of communication exclusive to *The Times*.

As his career flourished, Alsager moved to the fashionable West End, first to a house in Mecklenburg Square, described by Lamb as 'almost too fine to visit', and then, in 1830, to 26 Queen Square, Bloomsbury. He also appears to have maintained a home in Kingston, Surrey. His lifelong devotion to music could now be indulged munificently, and Queen Square was the venue for an influential series of recitals which led eventually to the formation of the Beethoven Quartet Society. Alsager was particularly devoted to Beethoven's music, and sponsored, in 1832, the first performance in England of the mass in D. Mendelssohn was one of a number of distinguished European participants in Alsager's musical matinées.

Alsager's other great interest was the Worshipful Company of Clothworkers, which he entered after completing his apprenticeship, eventually becoming master in 1836–7. Having discovered that the company had neglected its duties in administering various charitable trusts, he undertook painstaking research to clarify the position and, despite some opposition, instituted a system of monitoring committees to ensure that the company avoided further embarrassments of this kind. It was transformed into one of the most efficiently run of the City livery companies.

Having achieved eminence as a journalist Alsager's demise was especially tragic. He was widely praised when *The Times* punctured the bubble of railway speculation in November 1845, though at least one rival newspaper claimed that he had a personal interest in creating a bear market. There were also damaging accusations that *The Times* had puffed the Direct London and Exeter line, in which Alsager and Delane held shares. A year later, in October 1846, Alsager left *The Times* under a cloud, having been accused by the chief proprietor of misrepresenting the financial position of the printing department. Though this did not amount to more than a complacent acceptance of Delane's creative accounting, the termination of his connection with the paper he had served for almost thirty years was a damaging blow. The depression which afflicted him following the death of his wife a year earlier intensified, and on the first anniversary of her funeral, 6 November 1846, he attempted to take his own life, using a knife to cut his throat and slash his left wrist. He lingered until 15 November, when he died exhausted. The coroner resisted pressure to declare that Alsager had been of unsound mind in his last days which would have spared his family the ignominy of a midnight burial. He was buried at Kensal Green. DILWYN PORTER

Sources News Int. RO, *The Times* archive · D. E. Wickham, 'Thomas Massa Alsager (1779–1846): an Elian shade illuminated', *Charles Lamb Bulletin*, n.s., 35 (1981) · [S. Morison and others], *The history of The Times*, 2 (1939) · T. Girtin, *The golden ram: a narrative history of the Clothworkers Company* (1958) · *Register of the trusts, charities and estates administered by and belonging to the Clothworkers Company* (1842) · H. H. Marks, 'The evolution of the City article', *Financial News* (14 June 1897) · 'Suicide of Mr. Alsager, the official assigner', *Morning Herald* (17 Nov 1846) · 'Financial journalism: when money makes news and news makes money', *The Economist* (26 Dec 1987) · IGI

Archives Clothworkers' Hall, London, Worshipful Company of Clothworkers archive · News Int. RO, *The Times* archive, papers | BL, corresp. with William Ayrton, Add. MS 52339, *passim*

Likenesses H. P. Briggs, oils, Worshipful Company of Clothworkers, London

Alsop, Anthony (*bap.* 1670, *d.* 1726), Latin poet, was born at Darley, Derbyshire, and was baptized on 4 January 1670 at

Anthony Alsop (*bap.* 1670, *d.* 1726), by unknown artist

St Helen's, Darley, the son of Anthony Alsop and his wife, Anne Lowe. He was educated at Westminster School (king's scholar, 1686), and was head of the list of students elected to Christ Church, Oxford, in 1690. A successful student (the equivalent of a fellow elsewhere) could hope for a long career in the college, followed by a more lucrative clerical living. Alsop graduated BA on 1 January 1695 and MA on 23 March 1697; he became BD in 1706, but never took the degree of DD. He was appointed to various college offices at Christ Church, most importantly that of senior censor (1703–5), in charge of discipline. He was an active tutor, enjoying the confidence of Dean Aldrich: among his pupils were several aristocrats, notably James Cecil, fifth earl of Salisbury.

Alsop must have begun to write Latin verse at school: the art was highly prized at both Westminster and Christ Church. At Oxford he established a reputation as one of the most accomplished of a group of poets. His long alcaic ode 'Britannia' was sung at the encaenia in 1693, and printed in the programme. He contributed to the university collection on the death of Queen Mary (1695; ode 1.2). These early poems focus on the horror of war, as does a hexameter dialogue for public recitation, 'Givetta ardens' (1696; poem 3.8), which also injects some black humour and exploding Frenchmen.

Aldrich commissioned from Alsop an edition of Aesop as a new year's present and a further salvo in the battle of the books between Christ Church and Richard Bentley, the great but graceless Cambridge scholar. Charles Boyle's *Phalaridis epistolae* (1695) had opened hostilities; Alsop's *Fabularum Aesopicarum delectus* (1698) offered a further selection of allegedly superior ancient wisdom. Alsop refers to 'Richardum quendam Bentleium Virum in volvendis Lexicis satis diligentem' ('some fellow called Richard Bentley, a man of fair diligence in turning the pages of dictionaries'; Money, 79)—not a bad description of the profession, but well calculated to wound Bentley's pride. A fable compares Bentley to the dog in the manger, alluding to the phrase 'singular humanity' which Boyle had sarcastically used of him.

As early as 1695 Alsop's political position was fixed: he was a Jacobite, and, though there is no evidence of active involvement in sedition, he finds Latin verse a convenient medium for the expression of subversive ideas, for an audience of sympathetic friends. One of these was David Gregory, the Scottish astronomer, for whose marriage Alsop wrote a powerful ode:

En! tempus instat, en! veniet dies,
Cum rursus in Coelum caput efferet
Nomen Stuartorum.
('Look—the time is at hand, look, the day will come, when the name of Stuart will again raise its head to heaven.' Ode 1.11.57–9, Money, 141)

Many of Alsop's most successful odes are humorous: he had great fun at the expense of Arthur Charlett, gossipy master of University College, Oxford, with a pair of poems published in broadsheet form (1706; odes 1.9 and 1.10). His own friends are gleefully lampooned: John Keill, another professorial follower of Newton, can't keep his trousers buttoned (ode 2.2). Alsop, in these personal letters, shows a distinct preference for the sapphic metre, which he handles with brilliance. Many poems are addressed to the physician John Freind and the musical clergyman Sir John Dolben. To Henry Brydges, brother of the duke of Chandos, he sends some sarcastic suggestions for seeking clerical preferment by abandoning doctrine. The lawyer Joseph Taylor is given advice on corrupting the electorate. Alsop was fond of drinking, smoking, and music: good humour shines through his work, but it is not without pointed political and sexual satire.

Alsop might easily have been Oxford's first professor of poetry, in 1708, but he ceased to 'stir for it now upon Account of the smallness of the Sallary' (Thomas Hearne, quoted in Pittock, 127). Alsop was a friend and protégé of Aldrich's abrasive successor as dean, Francis Atterbury, through whom he obtained the patronage of Sir Jonathan Trelawny, bishop of Winchester. Trelawny had many clerical appointments in his gift: he presented Alsop with those of Nursling and Alverstoke, in Hampshire, and then in 1715 the richer benefice of Brightwell, Berkshire, together with a prebend at Winchester. These provided him with a very comfortable living.

On 31 December 1716 Alsop married Mrs Margery Bernard (d. 1718), widow of his predecessor at Brightwell. Unfortunately he was then sued for breach of promise by his mistress of some twelve years' standing, Elizabeth Astrey, 'a very light body, even, as some say, a meer Whore', the suit being 'looked upon by honest Men [that is, tories] as a Party Business, carried on chiefly by one Dr Lasher, a notorious Whigg' (Remarks, 18 July 1717, quoted

in Money, 169). Canon William Stratford, much less sympathetic to his former colleague Alsop, was highly amused: 'it is said a little volume of love letters [between Alsop and Astrey] will be published' (letter to Edward Harley, 6 Jan 1717, quoted in Money, 168). The judge was (again, according to Hearne, himself far from unbiased), another 'notorious Whigg'; whatever the merits of the case, Alsop lost it, and the enormous sum of £2000 was awarded in damages against him. He fled to the Netherlands, after some delaying tactics and attempts to reach a compromise. Stratford thought he was ruined; Atterbury didn't. The period of his exile produced some entertaining poetry, describing his own predicament among the materialistic Dutch; it also saw the tragedy of his wife's death, in early 1718, which he laments most movingly, in heartfelt and deeply personal Latin verse. He and his wife were genuinely attached, despite the strange circumstances of their short marriage. By the autumn of 1719 Mrs Astrey had agreed to accept a reduced sum, and Alsop could return to a quieter life at Brightwell and Winchester.

Alsop wrote some agreeable light verse in English (good enough for Dodsley's Collection), but the Latin Horatian ode was his natural medium. Pope may poke a little fun at him (Dunciad, 4.224), but compared with the roasting Bentley's pedantry receives, he is treated sympathetically. Thomas Hearne summed him up with huge affection: 'He was a man of most ready wit, of excellent Learning, a fine Preacher, and of rare good nature. He was looked upon to be the best Writer of Lyric Verses in the World' (Money, 54).

Alsop died on 10 June 1726, as described in the Reading Post, or, Weekly Mercury: '[when Alsop] was walking by a small Brook called the Lock Bourne, near the college of Winchester, the ground gave way under his Feet, which threw him into the Brook, where he was found dead the next morning' (Money, 54). He had almost certainly been drinking to celebrate the birthday of the Pretender (James Stuart): a sad, but perhaps appropriate, end for such a convivial literary Jacobite.

Alsop left a will dated 22 February 1720 (probably 1721), proved on 3 May 1727, in which he requested burial at Lewknor. His handwriting was certified not by any academic friends but by a London hosier and a distiller (further evidence, perhaps, of his wide range of drinking companions). He appointed his sister Elizabeth Alsop as executor, mentioning also his late 'dearly beloved' wife and her son, Francis *Bernard. To his 'good and deare friend John Nicoll', second master of Westminster School, he bequeathed his manuscript sermons, desiring him 'neither to publish nor lett copies be taken'. He also made bequests to the poor of Darley, his birthplace, and Brightwell.

Most of Alsop's odes remained in manuscript; they were collected by his stepson, Francis Bernard (later governor of Massachusetts), who proposed their publication in 1748, declaring that Alsop was 'not unjustly esteemed inferior only to his master Horace' (Money, 65). Printed by Bowyer, they appeared in two books (Antonii Alsopi, Aedis

Christi olim alumni, odarum libri duo) in 1752. The edition prepared by David Money (1998) adds two further books: book
3 contains additional odes, and hexameter poems, reliably attributed to Alsop, while book 4 contains his English
poems, and a number of Latin works of doubtful attribution. The doubtful works vary in interest: some are skilful
but straightforward elegiac exercises, of the sort that
many contemporaries composed, while odes 4.8 and 4.9
are extremely risqué. Other uncollected odes may well be
in existence, though it is wise to be sceptical of some
manuscript attributions to Alsop.

If his poetic achievement is compared with the Latin
works of Milton, Gray, Addison, or Samuel Johnson (or
indeed any of the other famous English authors who have
written partly in Latin), Alsop seems to stand up very well
in their company, his elegance and wit at least the equal of
most rivals. The lack of a significant vernacular oeuvre
has inevitably sidelined him; there has been relatively little critical interest, much of it rather patronizing. He did
not seek fame for himself, and has not received it: it
remains to be seen whether scholars of the twenty-first
century, in reassessing the concept of an English 'canon',
and perhaps recognizing the historical significance of
neo-Latin in general, will view Alsop as anything more
than an entertaining eccentric. For at least some contemporaries, though, he was the best Latin poet in the world.

D. K. MONEY

Sources D. K. Money, *The English Horace: Anthony Alsop and the trad-
ition of British Latin verse* (1998) · *Remarks and collections of Thomas
Hearne*, ed. C. E. Doble and others, 11 vols., OHS, 2, 7, 13, 34, 42–3,
48, 50, 65, 67, 72 (1885–1921) · *The manuscripts of his grace the duke of
Portland*, 10 vols., HMC, 29 (1891–1931), vol. 7 · L. Bradner, *Musae
Anglicanae: a history of Anglo-Latin poetry, 1500–1925* (1940) · E. G. W.
Bill, *Education at Christ Church, Oxford, 1660–1800* (1988) · *Old Westminsters* · L. Bradner, 'Some notes on Anthony Alsop's *Odarum libri
duo*', *Bodleian Library Record*, 9 (1976), 231–4 · will, PRO, PROB 11/615,
sig. 104 · *Hist. U. Oxf.* 5: *18th-cent. Oxf.* · parish register, Darley, St
Helen, 4 Jan 1760, Derbys. RO [baptism] · parish register, Derbys.
RO, 13 Aug 1660 [marriage: Anthony Alsop and Anne Lowe, par-
ents] · K. Maslen and J. Lancaster, *The Bowyer ledgers* (1991) · *The epistolary correspondence, visitation charges, speeches, and miscellanies of
Francis Atterbury*, ed. J. Nichols, 5 vols. (1783–90) · J. H. Pittock, *Henry
Birkhead, founder of the Oxford chair of poetry* (1999)
Archives BL · Bodl. Oxf. · Christ Church Oxf. | U. Nott., Port-
land MSS
Likenesses portrait, Christ Church Oxf. [*see illus.*]

Alsop, Benjamin (*b. c.*1658, *d.* in or before **1703**), bookseller, was the only son of Vincent *Alsop (*bap.* 1630,
d. 1703), presbyterian minister, and his wife, Elizabeth,
daughter of Benjamin King of Oakham, Rutland. His
father, who was married on 1 May 1657, lived and
preached at Geddington and Wellingborough in Northamptonshire. On 27 November 1672 Alsop was apprenticed to the well-known nonconformist bookseller
Nathaniel Ponder; he gained the freedom of the Stationers' Company on 6 October 1679. He then set up in business on his own with a bookshop under the sign of the
Angel and Bible in the Poultry in London, and between
1679 and 1684 was involved in the publication of over
twenty books. His wife's name is not known, but they had

at least three children—Martha, Elizabeth, and Benjamin.

Many of the authors published by Alsop were nonconformists, the most celebrated being John Bunyan. In 1682,
together with Dorman Newman, Alsop published
Bunyan's allegory *The Holy War*. He subsequently went on
to publish four other works by Bunyan: *The Greatness of the
Soul* (1682 and 1683), *A Case of Conscience Resolved* (1683), *A
Holy Life, the Beauty of Christianity* (1684), and *Seasonable Counsel* (1684). Among other notable authors with whom he
was associated as sole or joint publisher were John Owen,
Richard Baxter, Nehemiah Coxe, Thomas Gouge, and
Stephen Lobb. He was also involved in the innovative practice of publishing by subscription, in 1680 undertaking
with booksellers Thomas Parkhurst, Jonathan Robinson,
and Brabazon Aylmer to publish the sermons of the celebrated presbyterian preacher Thomas Manton. He was
also joint publisher with the same men, as well as Thomas
Cockerill and Dorman Newman, of Matthew Poole's *Annotations upon the Holy Bible* (1683–5), a two-volume work
which Alsop's father helped to complete after Poole's
death in 1679. In 1683, along with Thomas Malthus, he
published a work by an anonymous woman, *Fifteen Real
Comforts of Matrimony*, and in the same year they also published *The Compleat Statesman*, a flattering account of the
whig leader Anthony Ashley Cooper, earl of Shaftesbury.

In 1685 Alsop gave up his business to become a captain
in the army raised by the duke of Monmouth to overthrow
the Catholic James II. Monmouth's revolt failed, but Alsop
escaped and went into exile in the Netherlands. John
Dunton, who later took over Alsop's shop in the Poultry,
described him as 'a first-rate bookseller', but also as 'a wild
sort of a spark' who had joined Monmouth in hopes of
being 'made an earl, or a baron at least' (Dunton, 290–91).
Alsop's background, however, strongly suggests that religious and political beliefs also motivated him to take this
radical step. In 1687 his father was a prominent supporter
of James II's declaration of indulgence and, perhaps as a
result, on 31 May 1687 obtained a pardon for his son. It is
unclear whether Alsop returned to England and nothing
is known of his later years except that his father, who died
on 8 May 1703, outlived him.   W. R. OWENS

Sources H. R. Plomer and others, *A dictionary of the printers and
booksellers who were at work in England, Scotland, and Ireland from 1668
to 1725* (1922) · Wing, *STC* · J. Dunton, *The life and errors of John Dunton
… written by himself* (1705) · G. E. B. Eyre, ed., *A transcript of the registers of the Worshipful Company of Stationers from 1640 to 1708*, 3 vols.
(1913–14) · *CSP dom.*, 1686–7 · *Calamy rev.* · D. F. McKenzie, ed., *Stationers' Company apprentices*, [2]: 1641–1700 (1974)

Alsop [Alsopp], **Thomas** (*d.* 1558), apothecary, is thought to
have been connected with the Alsop family of Alsop (now
Alsop-en-le-Dale) chapelry in Ashbourne, Derbyshire, but
his parentage remains unknown; and, although Alsops
from Alsop were living in London during the sixteenth
century, no link with Thomas has been found. His
brothers Robert and Reginald lived in Kent; he also had
two sisters, Joan and Margery. Nothing is known of Alsop's
early life, but as a citizen and grocer of London he would
have obtained his freedom of the City by patrimony (if his

father had been a member of the Grocers' Company, which embraced apothecaries), by redemption (by purchase), or, most likely, by serving an apprenticeship. He was established in business by 1538, when he supplied rose water, 'certain stuff', and 'medicine' for Prince Edward, later Edward VI (Madden, 65, 74, 78).

In 1539 the crown granted eight properties in the parish of St Stephen Walbrook, with an annual rental of 55s. (not £55 as Matthews states in *The Royal Apothecaries*, p. 68), to Alsop and his wife, Anne, for an outlay of £285. Shakespeare's Falstaff mentions 'Bucklersbury in simple-time' (*Merry Wives of Windsor*, act III, scene iii), referring to the seasonal aromas of herbs and spices emanating from the grocers' and apothecaries' shops abounding in that street. Alsop's residence was The Angel in Bucklersbury, in the adjacent parish of St Mary Woolchurch, where he was assessed on lands and fees valued at £60 in 1541. Later he acquired six other properties—two each in the parishes of St John the Evangelist, St Bride, and St Stephen Walbrook.

Holbein's painting shows Henry VIII granting the charter (*sic*: the union was effected by statute) uniting the Barbers' Company with the Fellowship of Surgeons (1540): it depicts members of the company, and Henry's physicians, William Butts and John Chambre, with Alsop, their apothecary. Alsop entered Henry VIII's service, under a warrant dated 1 September 1540, as a gentleman apothecary, with an annual fee of £26 13s. 4d. The following year he was joined by John Hemmingway, as yeoman apothecary, with £11 2s. 6d. By chance, some of Alsop's accounts, written in a mixture of English and Latin, with individual prices, survive in the Public Record Office (*LP Henry VIII*, 21, pt 2, no. 768). In 1544 Margaret Douglas, Henry VIII's niece, received several items including '*aqua lactis virginis* for the morphew', being 'water of virgin's milk', a medicinal wash for a skin complaint; lotion for her husband's eyes; and 'treacle', some kind of compound, for her monkey.

In 1546–7 'My lady Mary[']s grace' (later Mary I) received a pot of green ginger, and Mr (James) Hill, a singer, was given 'The King[']s julep *cum vino granatorum* ['with wine of grains': seeds—'grains of Paradise'—of the Melegueta pepper, *Aframomum melegueta*], double'. Another account illustrates Henry's failing health, with, for example, eyewash made from eyebright, *Euphrasia officinalis*; almond oil for the lips; rhubarb pills; '*nigella contusa in panno ligato*', 'fennel-flower [*Nigella sativa*] bruised in a tied cloth'; bags with sponges, herbs, musk, and civet for the *bayn* ('bath'); and 'fomentation' for piles. Also supplied were succade (candied fruit) on St Bartholomew's eve (23 August); licorice and sugar candy for Henry's hounds; and 'horehound water' for his hawks, made with 'white horehound' (*Marrubium vulgare*). A further account details items supplied for the king's funeral, such as the perfumed substances placed in the coffin. The accounts were signed by George Owen and Thomas Wendy, Henry's physicians, and two of them were receipted on the verso by Alsop.

Henry left Alsop, by then his chief apothecary, £66 13s. 4d. Edward VI's apothecaries were John de Soda (d. 1551), who had served Katherine of Aragon; Alsop, as serjeant of the royal 'confectionary [pharmacy]'; and—still with his lower status—Hemmingway. Mary appointed John de Soda, son of the deceased official, with effect from 24 June 1553; if she continued Alsop's serjeantry (as implied in Machyn's *Diary*, p. 163), no patent or payment has been noted.

Despite his royal appointment Alsop had maintained his business interests. He was elected one of the three wardens of the Grocers' Company in 1552 and remained on its court of assistants until 1557. A patient of his in 1555 was Sir William Petre, secretary of state.

'Sick of body by the visitation of Almighty God', Alsop made his will on 16 January 1558, asking for his body to be buried in St Mary Woolchurch. He left his sister, Margery Andleby, an annuity of 40s., but his properties, unspecified, in London and in Deptford and Greenwich, Kent, were bequeathed to his wife, Anne, with reversion to Margery's sons Richard and John Andleby; to William Gillott, Anne's son by a former marriage; to Alsop's brother Robert's sons Robert and John; to his brother Reginald's sons Robert and Thomas; and to his sister Joan Taylor's sons Lynne and John Taylor. Alsop died on the day he made his will, 16 January 1558, and was buried—presumably in St Mary Woolchurch—during that month. His reference to illness, and his sudden death and burial, suggest that he died of the 'sweating-sickness'. Nevertheless, his funeral was an impressive affair, with twenty-four escutcheons and many mourners, and, after the next day's 'morrow-mass', a great dinner. Probate was granted to William Gillott, as proctor for Anne Alsop, executrix, on 22 January 1558.

An inquisition post-mortem (1558) mentions the sixteen London properties that Alsop was holding when he died; his heir, for this purpose, was named as Robert Alsop, aged thirteen, son of his brother Reginald. Anne Alsop died in September 1560; administration was granted to her son, William Gillott, on 11 September, and she was buried within St Mary Woolchurch the following day.

JOHN BENNELL

Sources L. G. Matthews, *The royal apothecaries* (1967), 62, 67–8, 78, 73, 177, pl. 3 · will, 1558, PRO, PROB 11/40, sig. 3 · *LP Henry VIII*, 14/2, no. 619 (47); 16.192; 21/2, nos. 634 (p. 322), 768 · G. S. Fry, ed., *Abstracts of inquisitiones post mortem relating to the City of London*, 1: *1485–1561*, British RS, 15 (1896), 149–51 · F. Madden, *Privy purse expenses of the Princess Mary, daughter of King Henry the Eighth* (1831), 65, 74, 78, 242, 283 · Viscount Strangford, ed., 'Household expenses of Princess Elizabeth', *Camden miscellany, II*, CS, 55 (1853), 33 · *CPR, 1547–8*, 394; *1553–4*, 317 · R. M. Glencross, ed., *Administrations in the prerogative court of Canterbury, 1559–1571* (1912), 11 · parish register, London, St Mary Woolchurch, GL, MS 7644 [burial: Anne Alsop, wife] · R. G. Lang, ed., *Two Tudor subsidy assessment rolls for the city of London, 1541 and 1581*, London RS, 29 (1993), no. 163 (on p. 112) · churchwardens' accounts, London, St Mary Woolchurch, GL, MS 1013/1 [Anne Alsop's burial inside church] · H. Bayles, 'Notes on accounts paid to the royal apothecaries in 1546 and 1547', *Chemist and Druggist* (27 June 1931), 794–6 [from *LPH*, vol. 21, no. 768] · P. Hunting, *A history of the Society of Apothecaries* (1998) · T. Vicary, *A profitable treatise of the anatomy of mans body* (1577); F. J. Furnivall and P. Furnivall, eds., EETS, extra ser., 53 (1888), 108–9, 117–19, 121 · *The diary of Henry Machyn, citizen and merchant-taylor of London, from AD 1550 to AD 1563*, ed. J. G. Nichols, CS, 42 (1848), 163

Archives PRO, accounts, SP 1.228
Likenesses H. Holbein, oil on boards, 1541? (*Henry VIII granting charter to Barber-Surgeons' Company*), Barber–Surgeons' Hall, London; repro. in Matthews, *Royal apothecaries*, pl. 3 · B. Baron, etching, Wellcome L.
Wealth at death at least sixteen properties in London and Kent: will, PRO, PROB 11/40, sig. 3; Fry, ed., *Abstracts*

Alsop, Vincent (*bap.* 1630, *d.* 1703), clergyman and ejected minister, was the son of George and Judith Alsop. His father was rector of South Collingham, Nottinghamshire, and there Alsop was baptized on 30 August 1630. He attended Uppingham grammar school and in September 1647 was admitted sizar at St John's College, Cambridge, where he matriculated in 1648. There is no record of his having graduated.

Alsop became an assistant master at Oakham School, Rutland, and married Elizabeth, the daughter of the Oakham minister, Benjamin King, on 1 May 1657. It was his father-in-law, according to Calamy, who won Alsop to 'serious Piety and practical Godliness' (Calamy, *Abridgement*, 2.487); that is to say, to presbyterianism. Having been ordained deacon episcopally, presbyterian ordination now followed, and he obtained the curacy of Langham (a parish adjacent to Oakham) a fortnight before his wedding, on the nomination of his father-in-law. He was rector of Wilby, Northamptonshire, in 1662, but was ejected in the same year. He preached semi-privately at Oakham and Wellingborough. According to Calamy, it was 'for praying with a sick Person' that he served six months in gaol at Northampton (*Calamy rev.*, 8). In 1672 he obtained a licence under the declaration of indulgence to minister in his house at Geddington.

Alsop's career was made for him by his writings, which started in 1675 with his *Anti-Sozzo*, against the 'Socinianism' as he saw it of the doctrines of William Sherlock. Anthony Wood wrote it off as a crude Marvell imitation (Wood, *Ath. Oxon.*, 4.108), but it made an immediate impact upon fellow presbyterians. His characterization of Sherlock's writings has a truly Marvellian bite: 'they were like those gawdy signs which Encounter us upon the Road, whose promising Motto first invites the Traveller with Hopes of Horses-meat and Mans-meat, and then Baffles his hopes with Entertainment that would starve a Dog' (Alsop, *Anti-Sozzo*, 225). He turns the 'Enthusiast' sneer back on his critic: 'it is much reproached and little understood … Enthusiasm is when the Mind is wholly enlightened by God: In which sense I pray God make us all Enthusiasts' (ibid., 349). The presbyterian minister Thomas Cawton, of Tothill Street, Westminster, was impressed enough by what he read to designate Alsop as his successor; he was to minister there from 1677 until his death in 1703. Alsop's successor, in his turn, would be Edmund Calamy, not only to the living itself, but in the shaping of a radically different future for English presbyterianism.

The catalyst for change would be James II's first declaration of indulgence of April 1687, but the ideology was already there, in essence, a decade earlier, in Alsop's dedicatory epistle to *Melius inquirendum* of 1679, with its notable plea for 'Latitude', and a recognition that 'the variety which we behold in the Universe, is not its deformity, but its beauty'. To see beauty in variety meant for presbyterians the plotting of a different course from their traditional goal of comprehension; it meant presbyterians making common cause, not only with Independents, but even with Quakers and Baptists. Restoration dissent, therefore, had to break with what Beddard called 'the archaic ethos of Anglo-puritanism', give up thoughts of a 'national church', and settle for a sectarian future. Beddard believed that Alsop was the man who was the emancipator of Restoration dissent (Beddard, 166). Thus, when Edward Stillingfleet castigated the *Mischief of Separation* in 1680, Alsop countered with his own *Mischief of Impositions*: the enforcement of *adiaphora* was the cause of, not the response to, separatism. A collector of table-talk gossip captured Stillingfleet's personal response to his three main puritan adversaries: John Owen treated him like a 'gentleman', Richard Baxter like a 'clown', but Alsop like 'a jack-pudding' (Bodl. Oxf., MS Rawl. D 973, fol. 210v). With men of harder views even than Stillingfleet in the saddle, both at the end of Charles II's reign and for much of James II's reign, Alsop's main aim was survival. One way was by concealing his forename, which fooled Anthony Wood into giving him the wrong one, as well as at the same time putting would-be persecutors off the scent (Wood, *Ath. Oxon.*, 4.106). Another way was by dividing his Tothill Street congregation in two. Each half met separately in a private home once a fortnight to take the sacrament.

When James II dramatically reversed alliances with his first declaration of indulgence, he looked for a sympathetic response to the victims of high Anglican persecution. He got it from Penn's Quakers, he got it from Bunyan's Baptists, and—the biggest prize of all—he got it from Alsop and six or seven other presbyterians. Alsop not only drafted their crucial manifesto: *The humble address of divers of your majestie's loyal subjects dwelling in or near your city of Westminster, and the liberties thereof*; he also spent the whole of Friday 29 April 1687 hawking it up and down the streets of the neighbourhood, 'taking subscriptions' from all and sundry. In 'whig' politicking and the defence of the autonomy of the local church, Alsop's principles were now being put into practice. For this he earned Macaulay's displeasure. Alsop was the renegade, 'zealous for the dispensing power' (Macaulay, 2.1376). A common view of the time was that his actions were designed to win parole for his son, Benjamin *Alsop, who had burned his fingers badly in the Monmouth rebellion. James II gave him his pardon on 31 May 1687, but even Roger Morrice (no admirer of Alsop's tactics) did not see this as a total explanation for Alsop's stance (DWL, Morrice MS Q, fol. 118). What Alsop did in 1687, in fact, was what he had been urging his fellow nonconformists to do, for at least the previous decade. It was also a philosophy which he could put into practice with the change of regime. After the passing of the Toleration Act in 1689 many presbyterians had still hoped for inclusion within a modified national church, but the Alsop logic was beginning to make headway among others. Alsop was an original manager of the

Common Fund in July 1690, formed to help aged ministers and poor churches in the country and to provide theological education for ordinands. Of the original fourteen managers, seven were Independents, and seven (including Alsop) Presbyterians. He was a strong supporter of the 'Happy Union' formed on 6 April 1691 between the two denominations, which was not, however, destined to remain happy for long. A lecturer at the joint Congregationalist–Presbyterian Pinners' Hall lectures since 1685, Alsop resigned in 1694 on the expulsion of Daniel Williams, and was one of the founders of the Presbyterian Salters' Hall lectures. He took part in June 1694 in the first public ordination among dissenters in London since 1662.

Alsop died at Tothill Street on 8 May 1703. Both his wife and son had predeceased him, but his will provided for Benjamin's two daughters, Martha and Elizabeth, and son, Benjamin, drawing principally for his legacy upon the returns in 1694 from loans which he had initially made to William III and Mary for their prosecution of war against France. Edmund Calamy took over more than Alsop's ministry in Tothill Street after his death: in 1704 his 'Introduction' to the second part of his *Defence of Moderate Nonconformity* was acclaimed as a coming-of-age for his denomination. Presbyterian colleagues stood him a supper; John Howe and John Locke praised his contribution. Calamy's vision of a sectarian future under a protestant dynasty was one thing; the earlier readiness of Alsop to accept toleration, however, even from a popish king, was a much bolder and more imaginative risk. 1687, not 1689, was therefore the real nonconformist watershed and it was Alsop, not Calamy, who was the real emancipator of Restoration dissent. WILLIAM LAMONT

Sources *Calamy rev.*, 8–9 · E. Calamy, ed., *An abridgement of Mr. Baxter's history of his life and times, with an account of the ministers, &c., who were ejected after the Restauration of King Charles II*, 2nd edn, 2 vols. (1713), vol. 2, pp. 487–9 · Wood, *Ath. Oxon.*, new edn, 4.106 · 'Ent'ring book', DWL, Morrice MS Q, fol. 118 · Bodl. Oxf., MSS Rawl. · BL, Birch MS 4275 · R. A. Beddard, 'Vincent Alsop and the emancipation of Restoration dissent', *Journal of Ecclesiastical History*, 24 (1973), 161–84 · T. B. Macaulay, *The history of England from the accession of James II*, new edn, ed. C. H. Firth, 6 vols. (1913–15), vol. 2, pp. 873, 992; vol. 3, p. 1376 · W. M. Lamont, *Richard Baxter and the millennium: protestant imperialism and the English revolution* (1979), 210–84 · A. Gordon, ed., *Freedom after ejection: a review (1690–1692) of presbyterian and congregational nonconformity in England and Wales* (1917), 199 · V. Alsop, *Anti-Sozzo* (1675) · V. Alsop, *Melius inquirendum* (1679) · V. Alsop, *Mischief of impositions* (1680) · W. Wilson, *The history and antiquities of the dissenting churches and meeting houses in London, Westminster and Southwark*, 4 vols. (1808–14), vol. 4, pp. 63–6 · Venn, *Alum. Cant.* · IGI

Archives BL, Birch MS 4275 · Bodl. Oxf., MSS Rawlinson · Congregational Library, London, 'Of church government and ceremonyes', MS.1.7 [holograph MS]

Likenesses portrait, DWL

Wealth at death £100 annuities plus £200 and £600 to granddaughters; £400 for grandson; drew upon returns of loans made to William III and Mary in 1694: will, 8 May 1703

Alston, Charles (1685–1760), physician and botanist, was born on 24 October 1685 at Eddlewood, in the parish of Hamilton, Lanarkshire, the third son of Thomas Alston (d. 1703), a physician of Thrinacre Milne and Eddlewood.

According to family tradition his paternal ancestors came from England with the founders of the dukedom of Hamilton in the time of Robert the Bruce. After boyhood at Hamilton he entered Glasgow University, in 1700, but the death of his father in 1703 left the family impoverished and compelled him to forgo graduating. The duchess of Hamilton, however, recognizing his promise, arranged for him to receive some legal training under a writer to the signet, James Anderson, in Edinburgh; after three years the duchess then employed him as her 'principal servant' in her household at Hamilton.

By this time it had become apparent that medicine was Alston's preferred vocation, and with the duchess's encouragement he used his abundant leisure to study to that end. When the failure of the Jacobite rising in 1715 caused the superintendent of the physic garden at the palace of Holyrood, William Arthur, to flee to Italy, the duchess used her influence to obtain for her protégé the vacant post. This brought him the titles of king's botanist and regius professor of botany, a requirement to lecture at the garden, and a stipend of £50. Conscious that it was an appointment 'during the Sovereign's pleasure' only, the duchess instructed her executors to pay Alston £500 in the event of the stipend lapsing; as it turned out, he held the post for life.

What Alston still lacked were relevant qualifications. Accordingly, after putting the garden in such order as he could, he returned to Glasgow to obtain a degree and then absented himself for the academic year 1718–19 to study under Hermann Boerhaave at Leiden. He became MD at Glasgow in December 1719 and was elected to fellowship of the Royal College of Physicians of Edinburgh in August 1721, by which year his courses at the royal garden had begun. Before long his reputation was sufficient to gain him the secretaryship of the college, in 1725, an office he was to occupy for the impressive span of twenty-one years. At the instance of the new professor of anatomy at Edinburgh University, Alexander Monro, whose friendship Alston had made at Leiden, he was also induced to extend his teaching of botany and materia medica to that institution too, and thereafter he played a major part in bringing the Edinburgh medical school a reputation in Europe second only to Leiden's. When eventually its relevant professorship fell vacant in 1738, he was consequently the automatic choice to succeed—while retaining his royal posts—and in a strong position to ask its patrons, the town council, to attach to it a much enhanced stipend. When that materialized, in 1746, it was sizeable enough probably to engage some labour at last for the university's botanic garden at Trinity Hospital. For lack of assistance the garden had seriously deteriorated and to Alston belongs the credit for effecting a great revival, notably by improving the soil and initiating seed exchanges with Leiden and elsewhere. One of Alston's first steps, in 1740, was also to produce a printed index to the plants for the guidance of the students. However, his attempts to obtain funds for a new and larger garden less subject to atmospheric pollution repeatedly proved in vain.

Alston's research interests latterly became focused on

the medicinal virtues of lime water, on which he published three dissertations and corresponded at length with Stephen Hales. In botany Alston was a staunch adherent to the natural classification of J. P. de Tournefort; he used his one substantial publication, *Tirocinium botanicum Edinburgense* (1753, reissued in English in 1754), to make an ill-judged attack on the increasingly widely accepted sexual system of Linnaeus, following Tournefort in refusing to acknowledge the existence of sexuality in plants. In seeking to demonstrate that stamens are unnecessary for the development of good seed, however, the evidence he adduced was seemingly the first record of the phenomenon later recognized as apogamy.

At the time of his death, which occurred at Edinburgh on 22 November 1760 (his widow, Bethia, died on 31 January 1788), Alston was preparing for publication his lecture course on materia medica. That task was subsequently carried through by his successor, John Hope, who had been the most outstanding of his students. The book gives evidence of Alston's scepticism about the supposed efficacy of many simples, in the absence of experimental testing. In his memory, a genus of mainly tropical African pagoda trees was later named *Alstonia* by Robert Brown.

D. E. ALLEN

Sources H. R. Fletcher and W. H. Brown, *The Royal Botanic Garden, Edinburgh, 1670–1970* (1970), 37–45, 59 · I. B. Balfour, 'A sketch of the professors of botany in Edinburgh from 1670 until 1887', *Makers of British botany: a collection of biographies by living botanists*, ed. F. W. Oliver (1913), 280–301, esp. 284–6 · R. Pulteney, *Historical and biographical sketches of the progress of botany in England*, 2 (1790), 9–16 · B. Henrey, *British botanical and horticultural literature before 1800*, 2 (1975), 198–200 · *GM*, 1st ser., 30 (1760), 594 · W. S. Craig, *History of the Royal College of Physicians of Edinburgh* (1976) · autobiography of Charles Alston, U. Edin. · *Scots Magazine*, 50 (1788), 206

Archives RBG Kew, lecture notes and papers · RCS Eng., treatise on materia medica · Royal College of Physicians of Edinburgh, lecture notes · U. Edin. L., lectures, letters received, and papers; lectures on materia medica · U. Glas. L., lecture notes · Wellcome L., lecture notes; notes on materia medica

Alston, Sir Edward (1597–1669), physician, the eldest son and quite possibly the eldest child of the eight children of Edward Alston (*d.* 1651), a substantial yeoman of Edwardstone, Suffolk, and Margaret Penning (*d.* in or before 1648), daughter of Arthur Penning of Kettleborough, Suffolk, was born in Edwardstone on 24 June 1597. Alston's grandfather was Thomas Alston of Newton, Suffolk, where the Alstons were in continual possession of land since the reign of Edward III. Alston matriculated as a pensioner at St John's College, Cambridge, in 1612. He was awarded a BA in 1616 and an MA in 1619. He had by this time decided to practise medicine, and received a university medical licence in 1620. His movements after this are not clear, but he may have gone directly to London, as in 1624 he married Susan Hussey (*b. c.*1592), daughter of Christopher Hudson of Norwich, and widow of Jasper Hussey, citizen and fishmonger of London; they had two daughters, Mary (1627–1660) and Sarah (*b.* 1632). Through the marriage Alston gained possession of Hussey's lands and tenements in Billingsgate, although Alston's claim was challenged in 1629 and was still being challenged in 1662, indicating that the holdings were valuable.

Alston's marriage licence of 1624 identified him as a gentleman residing in the parish of St Mary Abchurch, perhaps eschewing the title of physician until he had taken an MD, which he did at Cambridge in 1626. With his degree and the requisite number of years of medical practice, Alston was elected a candidate of the College of Physicians on 10 December 1628. He was elevated to a fellowship on 4 April 1631. While he was very active in establishing his practice, raising his income, and managing his investments, he was relatively inactive in the college. Although he attended meetings regularly, he held no office in the college until he was chosen a censor in 1642.

Alston was also a leading Presbyterian, being a ruling elder of St Mary-at-Hill in 1646 and a regular attender of classis meetings. He had little reason to remain loyal to the Laudian Church of England: in 1636 his father was brought before the ecclesiastical court of high commission on the charge of desecrating the parish church of Edwardstone. Despite the testimony of many friends, Alston senior was found guilty and fined. In 1647 Alston's elder daughter, Mary, married James Langham, a wealthy merchant and a zealous Presbyterian. His younger daughter, Sarah, married into one of the most prominent puritan gentry families, that of Sir Harbottle Grimston; on her marriage to George Grimston in 1652, Alston provided a dowry of £6000, as he had done for her older sister. The young Grimston died in 1655; when Sarah later married John Seymour, fourth duke of Somerset, Alston gave her an additional portion of £10,000. After her father's death, she married Henry Hare, second Baron Coleraine. A contemporary portrait of Dr Alston descended in the nineteenth century to the travel writer Augustus J. C. Hare, but has since been lost.

A great deal is known about Alston's wealth, but very little about his medical practice, which took him into the homes of the wealthy and powerful, such as Sir Harbottle Grimston, whose haemorrhoids he claimed to cure with local issue. Alston's skill in making and managing money did not escape the College of Physicians, which elected him its treasurer in 1649. He served in that capacity until 1654. In the following year he was elected president of the college and was continuously re-elected until 1666, far and away the longest tenure of that office in the seventeenth century, and one of the longest in the entire history of the college. Like his Presbyterian sons-in-law, Langham and Grimston, Alston welcomed the restoration of Charles II and was knighted by the king in 1660 in an act of goodwill towards the College of Physicians. Alston was now a resident of the parish of St Helen, Bishopsgate, where his fellow parishioners were, like himself, among the wealthiest and most puritanical citizens of London, whose restored Anglican priest dared not ask them to kneel at communion.

As president, Alston kept the College of Physicians afloat during a period of extreme political upheaval and is credited with the creation of the honorary fellowship which, in effect, licensed seventy-three distinguished academic physicians in 1664 and filled the college coffers with their dues. After the great fire of London in 1666, which destroyed the college house, Alston took it upon himself to negotiate for a new site without sufficient consultation with the college fellows; as a result, he was removed from office in the following year. Alston found it difficult to come to terms with his removal. He was by now seventy years old, and became increasingly determined that the college should bear the financial brunt of his mistake. 'To speak briefly', wrote the college registrar on 30 September 1668, 'he had greatly dishonoured the good name earned by diligent administration of our Society for many years by his inauspicious discourtesy and bitterness' (*Annals*, iv, 141). Alston did not long survive this public embarrassment. He died in the parish of St Helen, Bishopsgate, on 24 December 1669. He left many bequests in his will: £200 a year to his wife, £100 to Sir Harbottle Grimston, and many smaller bequests to friends and family, widows and children. There was no mention of the College of Physicians, nor any fellow, nor any physician. Alston was involved with two publications, *A Paper Delivered by Dr Alston, etc. for Bathes and Bath-Stoves* (1648) and *A Collection of Acts of Parliament … College of Physicians* (1660).

WILLIAM BIRKEN

Sources L. Cresswell, *Stemmata Alstoniana* (1905) · W. Birken, 'The puritan connexions of Sir Edward Alston', *Medical History*, 18 (1974), 370–74 · Munk, *Roll* · G. Clark and A. M. Cooke, *A history of the Royal College of Physicians of London*, 1 (1964) · *The Winthrop papers*, ed. W. C. Ford and others, 1 (1929), 70 · J. L. Chester and J. Foster, eds., *London marriage licences, 1521–1869* (1887) · J. B. Whitmore and A. W. Hughes Clarke, eds., *London visitation pedigrees, 1664*, Harleian Society, 92 (1940) · J. Wilford, *Memorials and characters … of divers eminent and worthy persons* (1741), 242–3 · *The visitation of London, anno Domini 1633, 1634, and 1635, made by Sir Henry St George*, 2, ed. J. J. Howard, Harleian Society, 17 (1883) · J. T. Cliffe, *The puritan gentry besieged, 1650–1700* (1993) · *Diary of the Rev John Ward … from 1648 to 1679*, ed. C. Severn (1839) · V. Pearl, 'London, puritans and Scotch fifth columnists: a mid-seventeenth century phenomenon', *Studies in London history*, ed. A. E. J. Hollander (1969), 324 · N. King, *The Grimstons of Gorhambury* (1983) · R. Ashton, *Counter-revolution: the second civil war and its origins, 1646–8* (1994) · J. Spurr, *The Restoration Church of England, 1646–1689* (1991) · CSP dom., 1636–8 · wills, PRO, PROB 11/332, sig. 2; PROB 11/216, sig. 79 [Edward Alston the elder] · annals, RCP Lond., 4.141 · B. Hamey, 'Bustorum aliquot reliquiae…', 1699, RCP Lond. · LPL, MS 272, fol. 202 · W. J. Harvey, ed., *List of the principal inhabitants of the City of London, 1640* (1886)
Wealth at death 'very rich': DNB

Alston, Edward Richard (1845–1881), zoologist, was born at Stockbriggs House, near Lesmahagow, Lanarkshire, on 1 December 1845, the fifth son of Mr J. W. Alston of Stockbriggs, a wealthy merchant of Glasgow. A delicate child, probably suffering from early tuberculosis, he was educated at home. From his earliest years he was keenly interested in natural history, and kept tame animals at the family's country home at Stockbriggs. His first publication, at the age of twelve, was a letter to *The Field* on 9 January 1858 (under the pseudonym of Tomtit) on the food of the dipper. Various other short notices quickly followed, and his first contributions to *The Zoologist*, on the treecreeper and marsh tit, appeared in March 1860. A stay with family friends in Germany in the summer of 1862

was curtailed by illness, but after convalescence at home his general health became much more robust for some years.

Alston became a member of the Natural History Society of Glasgow in February 1863, and was for several years a member of council. Financially independent, he travelled throughout Scotland, and subsequently published a number of pieces on the vertebrate zoology of the country, many genuinely original in content, in the *Proceedings of the Natural History Society of Glasgow* and *The Zoologist*. During this period he kept extensive notebooks, some extracts from which appeared in his memorial notice in the society's *Proceedings* (5, 1882, 69–76).

In 1868 Alston moved to Glasgow to commence business in the family mercantile house of Mathieson and Alston. This was a part-time appointment: he usually spent the summer months in the country at Stockbriggs or away on natural history pursuits. He also made many visits to London, where he regularly attended meetings at the Royal College of Surgeons, British Museum (Natural History), and the Zoological Society. In 1871 and 1872 he visited Norway with his close friend J. A. Harvie-Brown. The second trip led to the publication in *The Ibis* of a paper on the geographical distribution of birds in northern Europe (1873). In the same year Alston moved to London. He acted initially as London representative of the family firm, but was soon devoting all his energies to zoological investigation. In 1876 the British Association held its annual meeting in Glasgow, and Alston contributed the section on the mammals of the west of Scotland to the association's handbook prepared for the occasion. In London his talents were soon recognized. A fellow of the Zoological Society from 1869, he served for many years on various committees and from 1880 on the society's council. He was also a fellow of the Linnean Society, edited the Mammalia section of the *Zoological Record* from 1873 to 1878, and was zoological secretary of the society from 1880 until his death.

Alston devoted his research in London to the study of the osteology of the Mammalia, initially under the guidance of Professor Flower at the Royal College of Surgeons. He assisted Professor Thomas Bell with the second edition of the latter's *British Quadrupeds* (1874), virtually rewriting the entire work (a fact well known to zoologists of the day, but one that Professor Bell, for legal reasons, 'was unable adequately to acknowledge in print'; *Proceedings of the Linnean Society*). In the same year Alston began contributing to the *Proceedings of the Zoological Society of London*; over the next seven years he published twenty-five papers on various mammal groups. These earned Alston the reputation of one of the foremost mammalian osteologists of his generation. As a result, in 1879 F. O. Godman and O. Salvin asked Alston to undertake the entire division on Mammalia for their immense work *Biologia Centrali-Americana*. Although now in failing health he managed to complete the section before he died. At the same time Alston was also working on an account of the mammals of Scotland. This was commissioned as part of the proposed Fauna of Scotland series by the Natural History Society of Glasgow.

Alston's *Fauna of Scotland: Mammalia* appeared in 1880, and was a volume on which much later work on Scottish mammals was based. In the same year he was elected to honorary membership of the society.

Alston continued to work until some three weeks before his death, from acute pulmonary tuberculosis, on 7 March 1881, at his home, 14 Maddox Street, off Regent Street, London. Given his tragically short life, frequently plagued with ill health, and his lack of formal early education, his achievements were astounding. It would be difficult to find any other zoologist of his day who achieved so much in so short a time under such adverse circumstances, and who was so universally highly regarded by his colleagues. According to his obituary notice in the *Proceedings of the Linnean Society* he was

> universally beloved; for to great force of character and to a frank outspokenness when he deemed that the occasion required it, he united an amiability of manner and a conciliatory mode of expression which precluded the possibility of giving offence. The lot of any man may justly be envied whose loss is so sincerely mourned.

J. A. GIBSON

Sources C. H. Alston, *Wild life in the west highlands* (1912) · [J. A. Harvie-Brown], 'In memoriam—E.R.A.—*obiit* March 7, 1881', *Proceedings of the Natural History Society of Glasgow*, 5 (1882), 69–76 · 'Obituary notice of Edward Richard Alston', *Proceedings of the Linnean Society of London* (1880–82), 16–17 · J. A. Harvie-Brown, *Travels of a naturalist in northern Europe* (1905) · *CGPLA Eng. & Wales* (1881)
Archives U. Edin. L., zoological papers · University of Bristol Library, anthropological notes relating to Barna Isle and Lesmahagow
Wealth at death under £14,000: probate, 10 May 1881, *CGPLA Eng. & Wales*

Alströmer, Jonas (1685–1761). *See under* Industrial spies (act. c.1700–c.1800).

Alten, Sir Charles von, Count von Alten in the Hanoverian nobility (1764–1840), army officer in the British and Hanoverian armies, is most famous for his service at the head of the famous light division of the British army during the Peninsular War. He was born on 12 October 1764 at Burgwedel, Hanover, the youngest son of Augustus Eberhardt, Baron Alten, of an ancient protestant family of Wilkenburg in Hanover. At the age of twelve he became a page of honour to George III in the electoral household, and in 1781 received a commission as ensign in the Hanoverian foot guards. As a captain in the Hanoverian service, Alten served under the duke of York during the campaigns in Flanders and Holland of 1793–5. It was during this period that he first displayed his abilities as a light infantry officer, particularly while employed to command an important line of posts on the Lys between Poperinghe and Wervicq in 1794.

In 1803, when the Hanoverian army was disbanded under the terms of the convention of Lauenburg, Alten was one of the first to leave Hanover and enrol himself in the force then being formed at Lymington, Hampshire, which was to become the King's German Legion (KGL). As commander of the light battalions of the legion, Alten served in the expedition to Hanover under Lord Cathcart,

in 1805; at Copenhagen in 1807; with Sir John Moore, in Sweden and Spain, in 1808; and in the Walcheren expedition of 1809. He then served with the army in the Peninsula, commanding a British brigade at the battle of Albuera in May 1811. The following April, Wellington, then preparing his final stroke, placed Alten at the head of the light division (composed of the British 43rd, 52nd, and 95th rifles, with some Portuguese troops, and light cavalry and artillery). It was in this role that Alten fought at Vitoria, the battles on the Nivelle and the Nive, Orthez, and Toulouse. When the peninsular army was broken up, Alten was presented with a sword of honour by the British officers under his command in recognition of his services, and in 1815 he was appointed one of the first knights commander of the Order of the Bath. Later in 1815 he commanded the 3rd division of the British army at Quatre-Bras and Waterloo, being severely wounded on the latter occasion. Alten's conduct earned him praise as 'a very gallant young fellow' on the part of a Captain Kincaird (Fitchett, 123). In acknowledgement of his services at Waterloo he was made a count in the Hanoverian nobility, and a knight of the order of St Anne by Tsar Alexander I.

The KGL was disbanded in 1816, and Alten, who was then placed on half pay, was appointed to command the contingent of the reorganized Hanoverian army, serving with the allied army of occupation in France. After his return to Hanover in 1818, he became minister of war and of foreign affairs and inspector-general of the Hanoverian army, posts which he held until his death. He rose to the rank of field marshal in the Hanoverian service, while retaining his major-general's rank on the British half-pay list. He died at Botzen, in the Tyrol, on 20 April 1840, and was honoured with a public funeral. His remains were interred at his seat at Wilkenburg.

H. M. CHICHESTER, *rev.* S. KINROSS

Sources Fortescue, *Brit. army*, vol. 6 · J. Haydn, *The book of dignities: containing rolls of the official personages of the British empire* (1851) · J. Thomas, *Universal pronouncing dictionary of biography and mythology*, 5th edn (1930) · W. H. Fitchett, ed., *Wellington's men: some soldier autobiographies* (1900), 116–25 · E. C. Joslin, A. R. Litherland, B. T. Simpkin, and others, eds., *British battles and medals*, 6th edn (1988) · W. F. P. Napier, *History of the war in the Peninsula and in the south of France*, 6 vols. (1828–40) · review of *Wellington despatches*, vols. 3–5, *GM*, 2nd ser., 13 (1840), 189 · D. Chandler, ed., *Great battles of the British army* (1991) · *GM*, 2nd ser., 14 (1840), 92–4 · *GM*, 1st ser., 85/1 (1815), 68, 627, 629, 632 · *GM*, 1st ser., 85/2 (1815), 451
Likenesses T. Heaphy, watercolour drawing, 1813–14, NPG · G. F. Reichmann, oils, 1836, Royal Collection · J. W. Pieneman, group portrait, oils (*The battle of Waterloo*), Rijksmuseum, Amsterdam

Altham, Harry Surtees (1888–1965), schoolmaster and cricket historian, was born at 8 The Terrace, York Town, Frimley, Surrey, on 30 November 1888, the younger son of Sir Edward Altham Altham (1856–1943), army officer, and his wife, Georgina Emily (1855–1945), daughter of W. Macpherson Nicol, of Inverness. His father was the first university candidate for the army, in 1876, and retired with the rank of lieutenant-general, having served as quartermaster-general in India (1917–19). Altham was educated at Repton School, where he showed himself a gifted cricketer and natural leader, and he remained devoted to the school for the rest of his life. In the opinion of a number of good judges, the side which he captained in 1908 challenges that of 1905 as the best English school cricket eleven ever. He made his début in first-class cricket, for Surrey against Leicestershire, at the Oval in August 1908, and after the First World War played also for Hampshire from 1919 to 1923. After going up to Trinity College, Oxford, where he obtained a second class in *literae humaniores* in 1912, he gained his cricket blue in 1911 and 1912. In May 1913 he became an assistant master at Winchester College, and apart from war service with the 5th King's Royal Rifle Corps, during which he was appointed to the DSO, awarded the MC, and three times mentioned in dispatches, he lived in Winchester for the rest of his life. On 27 June 1917 he married (Winifred) Alison (1889–1979), daughter of Somerville Reid Livingstone-Learmonth, sheep farmer in Australia; they had one son and two daughters.

In his chosen profession as schoolmaster Altham found supreme happiness and complete fulfilment. He felt an instinctive sympathy for the young, and for over fifty years infected young Wykehamists with his own vitality and optimism, and with his simple belief that life was there to be lived with zest, courage, and conviction. He had, too, the great teacher's priceless gift of being able to communicate to others his delight in the things he valued—a play by Shakespeare, maybe, or a poem by Browning or Housman, a trifid spoon, an illuminated capital, a well-executed on-drive, or a well-loved feature in the cathedral at Winchester, which he served as editor of its *Record* from 1948 onwards. When Altham was 'on form' and involved, his eyes would light up and his hands move, as he caught the humour or the happiness of the moment with an allusive comment, a warm reflection, or a lively quip.

Altham was, perhaps, most at home, apart from home itself, in the classroom, on the cricket field—though cricket was only *primus inter pares* of several games that he enjoyed and excelled at—and in Chernocke House, or Furley's, as it is known colloquially, of which, wonderfully supported by his wife, he was housemaster between 1927 and 1947. This was for him an especially happy period, when a whole set of shared assumptions had yet to be questioned and when those under him could react instinctively to his concern both for them and for the values he hoped they would accept.

Altham's influence on cricket was profound. On returning to Winchester after the war in 1919 he quickly showed that that influence would not be parochial, for he found time, while teaching in term and playing for Hampshire in the summer holidays, to write *A History of Cricket* (1926) which John Arlott found 'remarkable for its scope, perception and mature style'. Subsequent editions were published in collaboration with E. W. Swanton. Altham regarded as of great importance his editorship and authorship of large parts of *The M.C.C. Cricket Coaching Book* (1952), the outcome of the rhetorical question asked at a meeting of the MCC committee by him and G. O. Allen, 'What does MCC do to encourage and help the young to

play cricket?' It was thus a seminal work, used as the coach's bible for several decades. Altham was also joint author of *Hampshire County Cricket* (1957) and regularly contributed to *Wisden*, *The Cricketer* (in which his *History of Cricket* first appeared in serial form in 1922), *The Observer*, *World of Cricket* (1966), county cricket club handbooks, and various publications in Britain and abroad.

In addition Altham made a notable contribution to the cricketing scene as an administrator, an after-dinner speaker of real distinction—at, for instance, the centenary dinners of Hampshire County Cricket Club in 1962 and Yorkshire County Cricket Club in 1963—and an unrepentant advocate of what cricket could do for the young in terms of character and enjoyment. He was a successful MCC president in 1959–60, treasurer from 1950 until 1963, and member of the committee for close on a quarter of a century; he was chairman (in 1949) of the MCC cricket inquiry committee which pioneered *The M.C.C. Cricket Coaching Book* of 1952; and although not himself a test player, he was chairman of the test selection committee in 1954. He helped to found the MCC youth cricket association and became its first chairman (1952–65), being the 'head and right arm' of the coaching courses at Lilleshall, where he was in his element as companion, conversationalist, and coach. He was the first president of the English Schools' Cricket Association (1951–7); and, even more satisfying, perhaps, president of the Hampshire County Cricket Club from 1947 until his death. Hampshire's first county championship win in 1961 owed much to his inspiration. It is fair to say that few people can have given back to a game so much of what they have taken from it. He was appointed CBE in 1957.

Altham died suddenly at 363 Fulwood Road, Sheffield, on 11 March 1965, some two hours after addressing the Sheffield Cricket Lovers' Society. He was buried on 20 March at Morn Hill cemetery, Winchester. There is a tablet to his memory in the memorial gallery at Lord's.

HUBERT DOGGART

Sources G. H. G. Doggart, ed., *The heart of cricket: a memoir of H. S. Altham* (1967) · personal knowledge (2004) · b. cert. · m. cert. · d. cert. · *WWW*
Likenesses P. Bell, oils, 1959, Lord's, Marylebone Cricket Club pavilion · E. Nelson, oils, 1976, Lord's, Marylebone Cricket Club pavilion
Wealth at death £7389: probate, 19 May 1965, *CGPLA Eng. & Wales*

Altham, Sir James (*c.*1555–1617), judge, was the third son of James Altham (1525?–1583), a prosperous London merchant, and his first wife, Elizabeth, the sister of Sir Thomas Blank, lord mayor of London in 1582. His mother died in 1558; his father then married the formidable widow of Sir Andrew Judd, lord mayor in 1550. In 1562 the family settled at Mark Hall, Latton, Essex. Breaking with family tradition, James chose to enter the law. After a short period from 1571 without taking a degree at Trinity College, Cambridge, he was admitted to Gray's Inn in 1575, called to the bar in 1581, and made an ancient of the inn in 1595. In 1599 he was made bencher, the first non-reader to be granted this distinction. He was reader at

Staple Inn in 1591, and at Gray's Inn in 1600 and 1603. In 1603 he was created serjeant-at-law, and in 1607 he was knighted and became a baron of the exchequer, which office he held until his death.

Altham was a very sound technical lawyer, 'a good, learned and discreet judge, of great estimation for his wisdom, gravity, affability and order' (*Diary of Richard Hutton*, 17). A volume of law reports attributed to him, though never printed, survives in the Inner Temple. Altham played a relatively minor part in public affairs. He represented Bramber, Sussex, in the parliament of 1589, but seems to have taken no active part in its proceedings; although he sat as a member of the court in several of the more important constitutional cases of the early seventeenth century, his role in them was insignificant; and in 1610 he used the influence of Sir Julius Caesar to ensure that his name was struck off a commission of judges to go into Ireland.

Altham was married three times: to Margaret Skinner (d. 1597), in 1584; to Mary Grimes, *née* Stapers, in 1598; and, at an unknown date, to Helen Hyde, *née* Saunderson (d. 1638). He had a son, James, from his first marriage and a son (Richard) and two daughters (Elizabeth and Mary) from his second. His third marriage was childless. Altham maintained strong links with the City of London, drawing up on its behalf seven bills for the parliament of 1601. He owned property there, and his first and second wives were buried there. In 1604 he purchased Oxhey, near Watford in Hertfordshire; here he built a fine house, at a cost of £3000, and, in 1612, a chapel. Earnest in matters of religion, Altham was the dedicatee of *Iaphets First Publique Perswasion*, written by the puritan divine Thomas Taylor; he decried religious vanity, and in his will he expressed the desire that his funeral should take place at night without any pomp.

Altham died at Serjeants' Inn, London, on 21 February 1617, and was buried at his own request in Oxhey chapel, where he had already erected a monument to himself and his third wife, who—despite having borne seventeen children in her first marriage, to John Hyde of London—survived until 1638. He died a wealthy man, leaving lands in London, Essex, and Yorkshire as well as in Hertfordshire.   DAVID IBBETSON

Sources J. E. Cussans, *History of Hertfordshire*, 3 vols. (1870–81) · W. R. Prest, *The rise of the barristers: a social history of the English bar, 1590–1640* (1986), 230–31, 340 · HoP, *Commons, 1558–1603*, 1.341 · J. Edmunds, *History of Latton* (1980), 20, 23 · W. W. Rouse Ball and J. A. Venn, eds., *Admissions to Trinity College, Cambridge*, 2 (1913), 84 · J. Foster, *The register of admissions to Gray's Inn, 1521–1889, together with the register of marriages in Gray's Inn chapel, 1695–1754* (privately printed, London, 1889), 48 · R. J. Fletcher, ed., *The pension book of Gray's Inn*, 2 vols. (1901–10) · A. W. Simpson, *Legal theory and legal history* (1987), 43 · Baker, *Serjeants*, 496 · Sainty, *Judges*, 123 · *VCH Essex*, 8.189 · *VCH Hertfordshire*, 2.456–7 · G. J. Armytage, ed., *Middlesex pedigrees*, Harleian Society, 65 (1914), 158 · A. W. Hughes Clarke, ed., *The register of St Dunstan in the East, London*, 1, Harleian Society, register section, 69 (1939), 102, 161 · J. L. Chester and J. Foster, eds., *London marriage licences, 1521–1869* (1887), 23 · J. Stow, *A survey of London*, rev. edn (1603); repr. with introduction by C. L. Kingsford as *A survey of London*, 2 vols. (1908), vol. 2, pp. 182, 185 · will, PRO, PROB 11/129, fol. 209 · F. G. Emmison, ed., *Elizabethan life: wills of Essex gentry and merchants* (1978), 51 [father's will] · inquisition post mortem, PRO, C142/362/187 · father's inquisition post mortem, PRO, C142/202/176 · *The diary of Sir Richard Hutton, 1614–1639*, ed. W. R. Prest, SeldS, suppl. ser., 9 (1991), 17 · BL, Add. MS 12497, fol. 446

Archives BL, corresp. and MSS, Add. MSS 12497, 40746; Harley MS 1546; Lansdowne MS 87 · Essex RO, Chelmsford, deeds and estate records · Inner Temple, London, MSS

Likenesses monumental effigy, Oxhey, Hertfordshire

Wealth at death approx. £350 p.a. in lands: will, PRO, PROB 11/129, fol. 209

Althans, (Andrew) Henry (1784–1855), educationist, was born on 22 October 1784 at Whitechapel in the East End of London. He was the eldest son of Frederick Charles Althans, a corn factor, and his second wife, Margaretta Magdalen Jasper (1752–1789), who was partly of German origin. His mother's piety was commemorated by the posthumous publication of her papers, *The Christian Character Exemplified* (1791). After attending a boarding-school at Greenwich run by John Bitterman, he conducted a business as a corn factor in London, having premises at Tower Hill from 1822 until his death. He probably married before 1805, but no details of his wife are known.

Like his mother, who died when he was a child, Althans was devout; in 1811 he became a Sunday school teacher at the Sion Congregational Chapel in Whitechapel, and a little later he opened a school for pauper children near the Tower of London. When this school was forced to close he transferred his efforts to a Sunday school at Bethnal Green. In 1814 he helped to establish the east London auxiliary of the Sunday School Union, remaining a leading committee member for many years and editing tracts and magazines. In 1831, when Henry Dunn became secretary of the British and Foreign School Society, with its headquarters in Southwark, Althans was appointed half-time agent and inspector for the society's metropolitan schools within 12 miles of central London, at a salary of £80 a year. As he informed the parliamentary select committee on the state of education in 1834, it was his duty to visit schools 'unexpectedly' and keep in touch with teachers and committee members. His 1837 report on the Borough Road model school at Southwark contained a detailed description of the monitorial system and was the most informative account of Borough Road since Joseph Lancaster's day.

In 1838, Althans gave evidence to the select committee on education of the poorer classes. He also wrote two reports on education in London, one on Whitechapel and the East End, and one on the south London parishes. He played a prominent part in the opening of the Abbey Street British day schools at Bethnal Green in 1840, becoming superintendent of the Sunday school section. A strong supporter of the monitorial system and of scriptural education, he was opposed to free education for the children of the poor, believing it would be little valued. On his retirement in 1854, he was presented with a portrait of himself which was later engraved in his memorial testimonial. Little is known about his family life: several of his sons worked as clerks at their father's corn factor business in George Street, Tower Hill; one of them, John (d. 1882), was prominent in the Religious Tract Society. Althans died from hepatitis at his home, 12 Great Cambridge Street, Shoreditch, on 4 March 1855 and was interred at Abney Park cemetery, Stoke Newington.   G. F. BARTLE

Sources Address … at the grave … a brief memoir of H. Althans (1855) · G. F. Bartle, 'The role of the British and Foreign School Society in the education of poor children', Journal of Educational Administration and History, 24 (1992), 74–90 · G. F. Bartle, 'The agents and inspectors of the British and Foreign School Society', History of Education Society Bulletin, 34 (1984), 74–90 · Boase, Mod. Eng. biog. · d. cert. · will, 1855, PRO, PROB 11/2213 · The Christian character exemplified, from the papers of Mrs M. M. A–ns, ed. J. Newton, [new edn] (1818)
Likenesses engraving, repro. in Address … at the grave
Wealth at death see will, PRO, PROB 11/2213

Althaus, Julius (1833–1900), physician and neurologist, born in Lippe-Detmold, Germany, on 31 March 1833, was the fourth and youngest son of Friedrich Althaus and Julie Draescke. His father was Lutheran general superintendent of Lippe-Detmold, a dignitary equivalent to the Anglican rural dean; his mother was a daughter of the last protestant bishop of Magdeburg. Althaus received a classical education at the University of Bonn, and began his medical studies at Göttingen in 1851. He proceeded to Heidelberg and graduated MD at Berlin in 1855 with a thesis 'De pneumothorace'. He then proceeded to Sicily with Professor Johannes Mueller, and from there to Paris, where he worked under Professor Jean Martin Charcot.

Althaus afterwards settled in London, when Robert Bentley Todd gave him opportunities of undertaking the electrical treatment of patients at King's College Hospital. In 1866 he was mainly instrumental in founding the Hospital for Epilepsy and Paralysis in Regent's Park (which later moved to become the Maida Vale Hospital for Nervous Diseases), to which he was attached as physician until his resignation in 1894, when he was appointed to the honorary office of consulting physician. He was admitted a member of the Royal College of Physicians of London in 1860. At the time of his death he was a corresponding fellow of the New York Academy of Medicine, and he had received the insignia of the order of the Crown of Italy.

Althaus was greatly interested in the therapeutic effects of electricity and published works on the subject including A Treatise of Medical Electricity in 1859. He also wrote on the spas of Europe, sclerosis of the spinal cord, and influenza. His most popular book was On Failure of Brain Power (1882). Althaus married Anna Wilhelmina Pelzer in June 1859; both had great musical talent. They had two sons and a daughter. He died at his home, 26 Queen Anne Street, London, on 11 June 1900, and was buried at Woking. He was survived by his daughter.

D'A. POWER, rev. CAROLINE OVERY

Sources J. Pagel, Biographisches Lexikon (1901) · The Lancet (16 June 1900), 1763 · BMJ (16 June 1900), 1508 · A. Fielding, A history of the Maida Vale Hospital for Nervous Diseases (1958) · 'Centenary of Maida Vale Hospital', BMJ (9 July 1966), 108–9 · private information (1901)
Likenesses bust, repro. in Fielding, History, frontispiece · photograph, repro. in BMJ (9 July 1966)
Wealth at death £2158 5s. 11d.: probate, 25 July 1900, CGPLA Eng. & Wales

Althorp. For this title name see Spencer, John Charles, Viscount Althorp and third Earl Spencer (1782–1845).

Altounyan, Roger Edward Collingwood (1922–1987), physician, was born on 24 October 1922 at Aleppo, Syria, the only son and fourth of the five children of Ernest Haig Riddell Altounyan (1889–1962), surgeon, and his wife, Dora Susie (1886–1964), artist and daughter of William Gershom *Collingwood (1854–1932), poet and secretary of John Ruskin, of Lanehead, Coniston. Ernest Altounyan had been educated at Rugby School, Cambridge University, and the Middlesex Hospital, London. Having qualified in 1915, he married and then served with the Royal Army Medical Corps in France, where he was severely wounded and won the Military Cross. After the war he and his wife went to the Altounyan Hospital, Aleppo, which had been founded by his Armenian father, Assadour Aram Altounyan. About 1955 Ernest Altounyan's fortunes changed; the hospital and his other property were confiscated and he was turned out of Syria. The family returned to Britain and subsided on a small property in the Lake District inherited through Dora's family.

Roger Altounyan's childhood was spent at Aleppo and at Lanehead, where Arthur Ransome, a family friend and neighbour, taught the children to sail their dinghy Swallow on Lake Coniston. When Ransome later wrote his book Swallows and Amazons, Roger and his sisters were the originals for the characters of the Walker family. Ransome dedicated the first edition to them, though he later disclaimed the connection.

Altounyan was educated at Abbotsholme School, Derbyshire, where his severe eczema made his life difficult and often unhappy. In 1941 he joined the RAF, where his ability as an instructor of bomber pilots was exceptional. He was appointed to the staff of a flying instructors' school in 1943 and was awarded the Air Force Cross for the dangerous work of developing low-level night-flying techniques.

After the war Altounyan read medicine at Cambridge and the Middlesex Hospital, where he first developed the asthma which was to trouble him for the rest of his life. On 8 September 1951 he married Hella-Christel Schumacher (b. 1925); they had five children. Altounyan qualified in August 1952 and went to Aleppo to help his father, but in 1955 the political situation created increasing difficulties and he returned to the UK. In 1956 he obtained a post with Bengers, a small pharmaceutical company, at Holmes Chapel, Cheshire, which was developing compounds to relax bronchial smooth muscle and help asthmatic subjects. New compounds were being tested in sensitized guinea pigs for their ability to relax contracted smooth muscle induced by allergic reactions. Altounyan noted that one otherwise inactive compound significantly diminished this allergic reaction, and saw its potential for the treatment of human asthma.

Because reactions in guinea pigs are clearly different from those in humans, studies on human asthma were essential. Altounyan therefore began careful studies on himself to see whether prior inhalation of the experimental compounds would prevent the development of attacks of asthma that he could induce by inhaling extracts of guinea-pig hair. Over the next seven years he gave himself more than 600 attacks, each lasting between two and three hours. The studies were done at Monsall Hospital, Manchester, where he also saw patients in his thrice-weekly outpatient clinics.

Although Altounyan eventually obtained encouraging results, these were only in himself, not in the guinea pigs. An independent expert's opinion did not support him, and the project was closed down in 1961. But Altounyan persuaded his colleagues to continue, initially in secret until, in January 1965, they synthesized the highly active disodium cromoglycate with the required properties. A small clinical trial in severe asthmatics using an ingenious inhalation device invented by Altounyan gave such encouraging results that a pilot production plant was commissioned. But three further trials by acknowledged asthma experts were not supportive and it was feared that Altounyan had produced a monumental commercial failure. Fortunately, senior management saw for themselves the undoubted benefit in a group of patients and had no further doubts. The drug was eventually marketed worldwide as Intal—interferes with allergy—a major new treatment for asthma. Over the next twenty years, ignoring advice, Altounyan continued testing further new drugs on himself even though he was increasingly disabled with breathlessness, and eventually required continuous oxygen therapy.

Altounyan lectured widely on asthma, with clarity and wit, and was admired and respected by colleagues throughout the world. His original and meticulous investigation of patients, which ahead of prevailing practice included provocation tests for bronchial hyper-reactivity, gave him an unsurpassed understanding of the nature and treatment of airways disease, as set out in his publication in *Thorax* in 1964. For his outstanding work Altounyan was elected FRCP in 1982, and he received an honorary doctorate of Southampton University. His major contributions to medicine, benefiting countless asthmatics, were made at great personal cost, and many felt that he did not receive adequate recognition.

Although blessed with an exceptionally clear and original mind, and possessing the leadership qualities so necessary for success, Altounyan had no personal ambition. His intellectual honesty was absolute so that at times he could be embarrassingly frank. He loved entertaining with Middle Eastern cuisine and copious amounts of home-made wine. He was an enthusiast who enjoyed life, but never more than when sailing *Amazon* on his beloved Lake Coniston. He died at his home, 2 Stanneylands Road, Wilmslow, Cheshire, on 10 December 1987, and was buried at Wilmslow parish church four days later. He was survived by his wife.   J. B. L. Howell

Sources T. S. C. Orr, 'Roger Altounyan: the man and his work', *Respiratory Medicine*, 83 (1989), suppl. 3–6 · S. G. Cohen, 'Roger Altounyan, 1922–1987, British physician and pharmacologist', *Allergy and Asthma Proceedings*, 19 (1998), 328–32 · private information (2004) · T. Altounyan, *In Aleppo once* (1969) · T. Altounyan, *Chimes from a wooden bell* (1990) · *CGPLA Eng. & Wales* (1988)
Likenesses photograph, repro. in Orr, 'Roger Altounyan'
Wealth at death £200,257: probate, 2 June 1988, *CGPLA Eng. & Wales*

Altrincham. For this title name *see* Grigg, Edward William Macleay, first Baron Altrincham (1879–1955); Grigg, Joan Alice Katherine, Lady Altrincham (1897–1987).

Alured, John (*bap.* 1607, *d.* 1651), army officer and regicide, was baptized in the parish of All Saints, Sculcoates, Hull, Yorkshire, on 4 April 1607, the eldest son of Henry Alured (*c.*1581–1628), gentleman landowner, and his wife, Frances (*d.* 1626), daughter of Francis Vaughan of Sutton upon Derwent, Yorkshire. The Alureds moved to Yorkshire from East Anglia during Henry VIII's reign, establishing their seat at the Hull Charterhouse, just north of the town. Alured belonged to the fourth, and last, generation of the family to sit in parliament; his great-grandfather and grandfather represented Hull in three of the Elizabethan parliaments, and his uncle, Thomas *Alured, sat for the nearby borough of Hedon in 1628–9. (Alured's father never served as an MP, as some authorities have claimed.) Alured's pedigree as a parliament-man was matched by his godly ancestry. The Alureds had supported further reformation in religion since the 1580s, and John's uncle, Thomas, was part of a high-powered puritan clique that opposed the crown over the Spanish match.

On 11 August 1628, a few months after inheriting the family estate (worth £400–£500 a year), Alured was admitted to Gray's Inn. Despite his godly background, he was described about 1630 as 'a most profane young gentleman' (*God's Plot*, 53). It was his marriage on 17 November 1631 to his second cousin Mary, daughter of the godly North Riding knight Sir Richard Darley of Buttercrambe (father of the future parliamentarians Henry and Richard Darley), and the influence of the Darleys' chaplain—the puritan divine, Thomas Shepard—that worked a 'great reformation' (ibid.) in his conduct. The marriage also had material benefits—Sir Richard settled a 'considerable sum[m]e of money' (PRO, C10/14/3) on his daughter as her marriage portion. The union produced two sons before Mary's death some time in or before 1635. Alured married again about June that year; his second wife was Mary, daughter of John Arnold, a London feltmaker, whom he later deserted along with their son and two daughters.

Alured consolidated his family's puritan connections, becoming an investor in the Providence Island Company, of which Viscount Saye and Sele and Henry Darley were leading members. In July 1638, as the kingdom began to mobilize for war against the Scottish covenanters, he was reported to the privy council for having declared that the Scots were 'brave boyes' and would 'reforme this land by a parlim[en]t … for the kinge would be forsed to lay downe his taxes by theire comminge in to England' (PRO, SP 16/395/29, fol. 56). In the elections to the Short Parliament in 1640, he was returned for Hedon—probably on the interest of his kinsman Henry, first Viscount Dunbar, from whom the Alureds leased the manor of Burstwick, near Hedon. Alured signed at least two of the three Yorkshire petitions of July, August, and September 1640, complaining about illegal billeting and requesting that the king summon parliament. Re-elected for Hedon in the autumn, he was a member of the committee that the Long Parliament sent to Hull in May 1642 to assist Sir John Hotham—who would later accuse Alured of plotting his downfall.

Alured and his younger brother Matthew *Alured (bap. 1615, d. 1694) were commissioned as captain and lieutenant of horse respectively under the earl of Essex in July 1642, but John spent most of the war as a colonel in Ferdinando, Lord Fairfax's northern parliamentarian army. He fought at several engagements, including Adwalton Moor (and probably Marston Moor), and was part of the entourage that Sir Thomas Fairfax took to London in February 1645 to take up his command of the New Model Army. Alured may well have been a patron of Philip Nye's Independent congregation at Hull—of which his own parish minister, Robert Luddington, was a member—and had certainly fallen out of sympathy with the Scots by 1645, signing numerous letters to parliament from the Yorkshire parliamentary committees in the summer and autumn of that year complaining about the 'oppressions' of the Scottish army in the north.

Never very active at Westminster, Alured virtually abandoned his seat altogether after May 1645. Despite his political inactivity, he was evidently thought well-affected by the army and its allies, for on 6 January 1649 he was appointed one of the commissioners for the king's trial. He attended numerous meetings of the trial commission, was present on 27 January when sentence was pronounced, and signed the death warrant [see also Regicides]. According to a Restoration pamphleteer, Alured was a man of 'turbulent spirit, and apt to take fire like gunpowder', although he could also be 'a cruel and close pursuer of whatsoever he intended to put in execution' (*Cromwell the Late Great Tirant*, 1660, 5). It was perhaps this last trait that steeled him for regicide. In the summer of 1649 he petitioned parliament for compensation for his losses—which he put at £5275—and arrears of pay amounting to £5494. In August 1649 the house ordered that he be paid £2000, but he probably saw none of this sum before his death in the autumn of 1651. His place of burial is not known. According to his widow, he died in possession of an estate of 'great yearly … value' (PRO, C10/465/3).

DAVID SCOTT

Sources D. Scott, 'Alured, John', HoP, *Commons, 1690–1715* [draft] · *JHC*, 2–7 (1640–59) · W. D. Pink, 'Alured of the Charterhouse, co. York', *Yorkshire Genealogist*, 1 (1888), 1–4 · *God's plot: the paradoxes of puritan piety, being the autobiography and journal of Thomas Shepard*, ed. M. McGiffert (1972) · W. L. F. Nuttall, 'The Yorkshire commissioners appointed for the trial of King Charles the First', *Yorkshire Archaeological Journal*, 43 (1971), 147–57 · J. G. Muddiman, *The trial of King Charles the First* (1928) · J. A. Jones, 'The war in the north: the northern parliamentarian army in the English civil war, 1642–1645', PhD diss., York University, Toronto, 1991 · A. E. Trout, 'Nonconformity in Hull', *Transactions of the Congregational Historical Society*, 9 (1924–6), 29–43, 78–85, esp. 31–2 · Bodl. Oxf., MS Nalson IV, fols. 60, 108, 187, 282, 309 · Bodl. Oxf., MS Nalson V, fol. 21 · I. Morgan, *Prince Charles's puritan chaplain* (1957) · D. Scott, 'Darley, Henry', HoP, *Commons* [draft] · D. Scott, '"Hannibal at our gates": loyalists and fifth-columnists during the bishops' wars—the case of Yorkshire', *Historical Research*, 70 (1997), 269–93 · court of chancery, PRO, C10/14/3 · court of chancery, PRO, C10/465/3 · state papers domestic, Charles I, PRO, SP 16/395/29, fol. 56 · *Oliver Cromwell the late great tirant his life-guard* (1660), 5

Alured, Matthew (*bap.* 1615, *d.* 1694), parliamentarian army officer, was baptized at Sculcoates, Yorkshire, on 3 January 1615, the sixth son of Henry Alured (*c.*1581–1628) of the Charterhouse, near Hull, and his wife, Frances (*d.* 1626), daughter of Francis Vaughan of Sutton upon Derwent. Alured's family had moved from East Anglia to Hull in the early sixteenth century. He belonged to the fourth, and last, generation of the family to sit in parliament. His great-grandfather and grandfather had represented Hull; his uncle, Thomas *Alured, had sat for Hedon in 1628–9; and his elder brother, John *Alured, was returned for Hedon to the Short and Long parliaments. Alured's pedigree as a parliament man was matched by his godly ancestry. The Alureds had supported further reformation in religion since the 1580s, prompting several members of the family to oppose royal policies during the 1620s and 1630s. Orphaned at thirteen, Alured was educated in the household of his uncle, Francis Darley of Kilnhurst—a kinsman of the godly North Riding parliamentarians Henry and Richard Darley. He married in 1642 Catherine Nelthorpe (*d.* 1671), daughter of Thomas Stephenson.

Alured entered public affairs in 1642, joining the Darleys and other Yorkshire gentlemen in their petitions to Charles asking him to return to Westminster, and to forbear from raising troops 'illegally' (*A Letter from … Committees of the Commons' House, Residing at Yorke*, 12 May 1642, BL, E148/4; Parliamentary Archives, main papers, 6/6/1642, fols. 84–5). Commissioned as a parliamentarian lieutenant of horse in July 1642, he was appointed a colonel in Ferdinando, Lord Fairfax's northern army, in April 1644. His regiment fought at Marston Moor and other engagements before being disbanded in February 1646. In March 1647 he and other reformado officers petitioned parliament in an unsuccessful attempt to curry favour with the presbyterians and so regain military employment. During the second civil war he commanded an East Riding militia regiment, but did not rejoin the regular army until 1650, when he was appointed colonel of a foot regiment raised for the Scottish service. In April 1654 Cromwell put him in charge of suppressing the Glencairn rising, but relieved him of command in May when it emerged that Alured had fallen in with Anabaptists and had denounced the Protector for behaving autocratically and favouring presbyterians and cavaliers over 'honest old Independents' (BL, Add. MS 25347, fols. 21v–25v). Recalled to London, he joined those 'that would stand right for a Commonwealth' (Thurloe, *State papers*, 3.147–8), and, with colonels John Okey and Thomas Saunders, signed a petition drafted by John Wildman attacking the protectorate. *The Petition of Several Colonels* demanded free and successive parliaments and that the government be settled according to the revised version of the *Agreement of the People* that the army had presented to the Rump in January 1649 (*The Humble*

Petition of Several Colonels of the Army, 18 Oct 1654, BL, 669 f. 19/21). Alured was court-martialled and cashiered in December 1654, and spent most of the next two years in prison.

Returned for Hedon in January 1659, Alured joined other republican MPs in attacking the protectoral settlement. He declared loudly against the royalist presence in the house, and denounced agents of Cromwellian 'tyranny'. He supported the army's overthrow of the protectorate, and during the summer the Rump appointed him captain of its life guard and a colonel of horse. Along with Okey, Saunders, and a small number of other senior officers, Alured opposed Lambert's dissolution of the restored Rump in October 1659. They petitioned General Fleetwood, demanding new parliamentary elections and that all standing forces be subordinate to parliament, but were removed from their commands (BL, Add. MS 4165, fols. 38–42). Alured played a leading role in bringing down the committee of safety in December, and the Rump appointed him a commissioner for management of the armed forces. Won over by General Monck's public commitment to preserving the republic and holding new elections, Alured persuaded Colonel Overton to surrender the garrison at Hull in March 1660. In April, however, Monck removed Alured from command after some of his troops had declared for Lambert. At the Restoration, Alured obtained a royal pardon, but lost the offices and the church and crown lands he had acquired during the 1650s. He was briefly imprisoned in 1661 and 1663 on suspicion of plotting against the crown, and in 1673 was disabled from serving as mayor of Hedon for refusing the required oaths. He was buried in St Mary's, Beverley, on 28 August 1694. His legatees included the dissenting minister William Foster and his congregation at Beverley. Alured left the bulk of his estate (which was probably worth less than £500 a year) to his daughter and grandson. DAVID SCOTT

Sources 'Alured, Matthew', HoP, *Commons* [draft] · *JHC*, 6–7 (1648–59) · *Diary of Thomas Burton*, ed. J. T. Rutt, 4 vols. (1828) · Thurloe, *State papers*, vols. 2–4 · C. H. Firth and G. Davies, *The regimental history of Cromwell's army*, 2 vols. (1940) · B. Taft, 'The humble petition of several colonels of the army', *Huntington Library Quarterly*, 42 (1978–9), 15–41 · *The memoirs of Edmund Ludlow*, ed. C. H. Firth, 2 vols. (1894) · W. D. Pink, 'Alured of the Charterhouse, co. York', *Yorkshire Genealogist*, 1 (1888), 1–4 · *Newes from Yorke, being a true relation of the proceedings of Sir Hugh Cholmley since his comming to Scarborough* (1643) [Thomason tract E 85(17)] · *A miraculous victory obtained by the Right Honourable Ferdinando Lord Fairfax against the army under the command of the earl of Newcastle at Wakefield in York-shire* (1643) [Thomason tract E 104(13)] · *A letter from the Right Honourable Ferdinando Lord Fairfax, Sir Hugh Cholmley … committees of the Commons' House of parliament residing at Yorke together with a relation of all the passages at the great meeting at Yorke, on Thursday the 12 of this instant May* (1642) [Thomason tract E 148(4)] · *Parliamentary Intelligencer*, 1 (19–26 Dec 1659) [Thomason tract E 182(15)] · *Packets of letters from Scotland, Berwick, Newcastle, and York to members of the House of Commons* [1648] [Thomason tract E 446(3)] · *Mercurius Politicus* (19–26 May 1659) [Thomason tract E 762(15)] · *The case of Colonel Matthew Alured* (1659) [Thomason tract E 983(25)] · *A true narrative of the proceedings in Parliament … from the 22 of Septemb. untill this present* (1659) [Thomason tract E 1010(24)] · T. Saunders, J. Okey, and M. Allured, *To his highness the lord protector … the humble petition of several colonels of the army* (1654) [Thomason tract 669.f.19(21)] · *CSP dom.*, 1637–80 · J. A. Jones, 'The war in the north: the northern parliamentarian army in the English civil war, 1642–1645', PhD diss., York University, Toronto, 1991 · wills in Harthill deanery, Sept 1694, Borth. Inst. · M. E. Ingram, ed., *The parish registers of Sculcoates, 1538–1772*, Yorkshire Parish Register Society, 103 (1959), 22

Archives BL, Add. MS 25347 · BL, Add. MS 4165, fols. 38–42 · East Riding of Yorkshire Archives Service, Beverley, MSS · Hull Central Library, Bench Book 6 · Palace of Westminster, Main MSS | BL, Stowe MS 189, fols. 60–61 · PRO, CRES 6/1, p. 196; E113/7, pt 2; E121/5/5/6, 16; E121/3/3/117; SP 28/34, fols. 399–400; SP 28/252, pt 1, fol. 178; SP 28/288, fols. 36, 38, 46

Wealth at death probably under £500 p.a.: *CSP dom., 1637–8*, p. 558

Alured, Thomas (*bap.* 1583, *d.* 1638), administrator, was baptized at Sculcoates, near Hull, Yorkshire, on 3 September 1583, the third son of John Alured (*c.*1545–1606) of the Charterhouse, Sculcoates, and his wife, Frances, daughter of Sir Henry Gates of Seamer, Yorkshire. The parliamentarian army officers John *Alured and Matthew *Alured were his nephews. Thomas was educated at Trinity College, Cambridge, where he was admitted scholar in Easter term 1602, and Gray's Inn, where he was admitted on 7 May 1604. At his father's death in 1606 he received a life annuity of £60 a year. Shortly thereafter he became a private secretary to Ralph Eure, Lord Eure, president of the council of the marches of Wales, who appointed him to several administrative posts, including the auditorship of the council. He lost his secretaryship upon Eure's death in 1617 but retained the other offices, probably as sinecures, as he kept his main residence at the Blackfriars in London. In April 1617 he married Mary Jones; their marriage left no known heirs and she predeceased him in 1632.

Alured earned instant notoriety in June 1620 as the author of a widely circulated letter urging the royal favourite George Villiers, marquess of Buckingham, to block the marriage then mooted between Prince Charles and the Spanish infanta Maria. Drawing attention to the dismal record of previous Anglo-Spanish matches between Henry VIII and Katherine of Aragon and Queen Mary and Philip II, the tract urged that Charles be found an English bride in the manner of Edward IV and Henry VIII, whose daughters, Elizabeth of York and Elizabeth Tudor, established 'peace in the land and religion in the church until his Majesty's happy coming [in 1603] who brought both with him' (BL, Harley MS 6021, fol. 137). The privy council took a dim view of Alured's intrusion into one of the most jealously guarded of royal prerogatives, and threw him into the Fleet prison until he submitted an abject apology; his disgrace presumably also explains his surrender in 1621 of all of his Welsh offices bar the auditorship.

Alured's considerable surviving correspondence hardly mentions the Spanish match, and it has been suggested that the polemic which bears his name may have been drafted by the puritan divine John Preston, who was closely associated with Sir Fulke Greville, then Alured's superior as secretary of the council in the marches. Alured's willingness to claim authorship may have represented a ham-fisted attempt to ingratiate himself with the anti-Spanish faction at court. This would explain why he spent the next few years cultivating the favours of Greville's former secretary Sir John Coke: in 1624 he helped with Coke's marriage negotiations; and in the following year he unsuccessfully asked Coke to intercede with his brother-in-law Valentine Cary, bishop of Exeter, for a seat in parliament. Subsequently recommended for seats at Rye in 1626 and Scarborough in 1628, Alured was finally returned in the latter year for Hedon in Holderness, where his eldest brother owned some land. He left little trace upon the parliament but wrote a series of newsletters to Coke detailing its proceedings.

Probably thanks to Coke, Alured became secretary to Lord Keeper Sir Thomas Coventry by 1631, and was a man of some means by the time of his death in May 1638, bestowing legacies of over £1000 in his will. He was buried in St Anne Blackfriars on 19 May 1638.   SIMON HEALY

Sources HoP, *Commons, 1604–29* [draft] · I. Morgan, *Prince Charles's puritan chaplain* (1957) · *The manuscripts of the Earl Cowper*, 3 vols., HMC, 23 (1888–9), vols. 1–2 · will, PRO, PROB 11/177, fol. 32 · Venn, *Alum. Cant.*
Archives BL, Harley MS 6021
Wealth at death approx. £1000–£2000—est. from size of bequests: will, PRO, PROB 11/177, fol. 32

Alva. For this title name *see* Erskine, James, Lord Alva (1722–1796) [*see under* Erskine, Charles, Lord Tinwald (*bap.* 1680, *d.* 1763)].

Alvanley. For this title name *see* Arden, Richard Pepper, first Baron Alvanley (1744–1804).

Alvares, Jacob Jessurun. *See* Fonseca, Alvaro da (1657?–1742).

Alvars, Elias Parish- (1808–1849), harpist and composer, was born on 28 February 1808 at Teignmouth, where his father was an organist. His earliest teachers on the harp were N. C. Bochsa (from 1820) and subsequently F. J. Dizi and Théodore Labarre in Paris. In his fifteenth year he made a short but successful concert tour of Germany, and then, after continuing his study of the harp, went in 1828 to Italy. There he concentrated on the theory of music, playing the piano (in which he was proficient), and singing under Guglielmo and Leidesdorf in Florence. Two years later he returned to England, and in 1831 revisited Germany and gave concerts in Denmark, Sweden, and Russia. From Russia he went to Constantinople to perform before the sultan, and in 1832 travelled through Austria and Hungary. He next joined John Field in a tour of Switzerland and Italy, and in 1834 obtained an engagement as solo harpist at La Scala in Milan. From there he travelled, via Munich, to Vienna, where in 1836 he studied counterpoint under Simon Sechter and Ignaz Seyfried, and married the harpist Melanie Lewy. He was also engaged as principal harpist at the court opera, and wrote much music for his own instrument with orchestra. From 1838 to around 1842 he travelled in the East and collected many eastern melodies, some of which he subsequently used in his compositions (for example, *Voyage d'un harpiste en Orient*, op. 79). In 1842 he returned to Europe and gave concerts in Dresden and Leipzig, and later (1843) in Prague. In Leipzig he made the acquaintance of Mendelssohn, who exercised a strong influence over his work.

Parish-Alvars eventually returned to England in 1842; on 16 May he played before the queen at Buckingham Palace, with Bernhard Molique and others, and two days later made his first appearance at the Philharmonic concerts. He apparently hoped to settle permanently in London, but, following the introduction of works such as his G minor concerto, op. 81, in 1844, he found the musical establishment unsympathetic to the harp as a solo instrument. As a result he returned to Vienna and then continued to travel, at first through Italy (including a performance in Naples) and then in Germany. He made a prolonged stay in Leipzig in 1846, benefiting from his contact with Mendelssohn. In the following year he returned to Vienna and was appointed 'chamber musician' to the emperor.

Parish-Alvars was unquestionably one of the most distinguished harpists of any period and was unsurpassed as a virtuoso. He was known in Vienna as 'der Paganini der Harfe', and contributed much to the development of new performance techniques on the double-action harp, which caused much enthusiasm among his contemporaries, including Berlioz, Liszt, and Mendelssohn, as well as providing inspiration and a model for all composers writing for the instrument. He excelled in the production of novel effects, and his works, which were well known during the period, rank high among compositions for the harp. His output includes more than eighty published compositions for solo harp, including numerous transcriptions and romances, many of which are of exceptional difficulty, in addition to two concertos, a concertino for two harps, and duos for harp and piano. Among his unpublished works are the fantasia *Sounds of Ossian*, which is one of the most demanding solos ever written for the harp, a symphony, two piano concertos, an opera, and an incomplete harp method. He is also reputed to have enjoyed playing on the harp such works as Beethoven's and Hummel's piano concertos, Spohr's violin compositions, and Chopin's studies. He died in Vienna on 25 January 1849.   R. H. LEGGE, *rev.* DAVID J. GOLBY

Sources A. Griffiths, 'Parish Alvars, Elias', *New Grove* · J. D. Brown, *Biographical dictionary of musicians: with a bibliography of English writings on music* (1886)

Alverstone. For this title name *see* Webster, Richard Everard, Viscount Alverstone (1842–1915).

Alves, Robert (1745–1794), poet, was born at Elgin on 11 December 1745. His father's circumstances were humble, and he was one of a large family but as a promising student he was placed at the Elgin grammar school. At Marischal College, Aberdeen, he won the highest bursary of the year in which he competed. An 'Elegy on Time', written during his second year at university and published in 1782, gained him the admiration and friendship of Dr Beattie, then one of the professors of Marischal College.

Though designated for the church, after leaving Aberdeen, Alves was successively master of a parish school in

Deskford, Banffshire, and tutor in the family of a gentleman in Bognie, Aberdeenshire, who offered him a living in the Church of Scotland. But he preferred the headmastership, with a lower stipend, of the Banff grammar school, which he held from 1773 until 1779, when, on the failure of his suit to the 'Delia' of his sonnets, he migrated to Edinburgh. There Alves taught the classics and several modern languages, occasionally translating and compiling for the Edinburgh booksellers.

In 1780 Alves's *Ode to Britannia* appeared, a celebration of the gallantry of Scottish troops in America. In 1782 he published a volume of *Poems*, and in 1789, *Edinburgh, a Poem in Two Parts*, which describes the topography and social aspects of the Scottish capital, together with the *Weeping Bard*, much of which is plaintively autobiographical. Alves died suddenly in Edinburgh on 1 June 1794, while seeing through the press *Sketches of the History of Literature* (1794), a work which shows that criticism was not his forte. In 1801 *The Banks of Esk and other Poems* was published, which included his vigorous refutation of the ridicule of Scottish poets by English literary writers.

FRANCIS ESPINASSE, *rev.* SAYONI BASU

Sources 'Memoir', R. Alves, *Sketches of the history of literature* (1794) · A. Campbell, *An introduction to the history of poetry in Scotland*, 2 pts in 1 (1798–9)

Alvey, Richard (*d.* 1584), Church of England clergyman, was a scholar of Christ's College, Cambridge, whence he migrated to St John's College, from which he graduated BA in 1528 or 1529, MA in 1532, and BD in 1543. He was elected a fellow of St John's in 1537 or 1538. On 12 March 1539 he was instituted to the rectory of Thorington, Essex, at the college's presentation. On 21 May 1546 he was dispensed to hold a further benefice, having already (11 May) been admitted to that of Greenstead-juxta-Colchester, Essex, by the crown's grant. On 13 November 1548 he was instituted to the rectory of Sandon, Essex, to which he had been presented by Sir John Gates. On 11 December 1552 Edward VI nominated him to a canonry of Westminster Cathedral, where he was installed on 16 December. He was deprived along with the other married canons on 30 March 1554. He and his wife, Emma (*née* Goodlad), joined the exile community at Frankfurt. Alvey supported Richard Cox in his defence of the 1552 prayer book there, and he signed the letter to Calvin of 5 April 1555, in which Cox and his party justified their recent victory over Knox, which had resulted in the Scot's withdrawal from the city. Alvey signed a further joint letter to Calvin on 20 September. Meanwhile, back in Essex, a linen draper from Billericay called Thomas Watts had been executed for adhering to what he 'was so taught to believe' by Alvey's preaching (*Acts and Monuments*, 7.121). In the spring of 1557 Alvey subscribed to the Book of Discipline by which the Frankfurt community broke with the episcopal and liturgical inheritance that had prevailed two years before. In June 1557 Alvey was living with Richard Luddington, perhaps also a Johnian, though of a later generation than Alvey; David Whitehead was resident in the same house.

Following Elizabeth's accession Alvey returned to England, and the queen appointed him master of the Temple on 13 February 1560. On 21 May he was reappointed a canon of Westminster on the abbey's reconstitution as a collegiate church; with his new colleagues he was installed there on 30 June. He was also restored to his living of Thorington, which he held until 1565. On 10 April 1571 he was collated by the bishop of London (Sandys) to the rectory of Little Burstead, Essex, which he held until 1576. At Westminster, Alvey was appointed *lector theologiae*, with an annual fee of £8 13s. 4d. in addition to his prebend of £28 5s., on 3 November 1561. Henry Machyn records that two days later Alvey gave a 'godly sermon' before a 'grett audyense' in the abbey (*Diary of Henry Machyn*, 272). Alvey was regularly reappointed to the lectureship during the tenure of his stall. In 1569 he and his wife took a lease of two of the dean and chapter's tenements in Tothill Street, Westminster. In 1583 Emma Alvey obtained a lease in her own right of another Westminster Abbey property, in nearby King Street. In October 1573 Alvey gave the dean and chapter a set of six silver spoons embellished with his monogram. He was one of the most assiduous attenders of chapter meetings, though on occasion he registered a dissenting voice to the grants made. He had resigned his canonry by 10 February 1574, when Thomas Aldrich was appointed to the vacancy, but Alvey was allowed to receive the emoluments up to the day of his successor's installation.

Alvey remained master of the Temple, and in March 1575 he consulted Archbishop Parker over the conduct of the controversial Spanish refugee Antonio del Corro (Corranus), who had been appointed reader of the Temple, and thus Alvey's subordinate, on the recommendation of the earl of Leicester. Despite this evangelical patronage Corro had upset the congregation in the Temple Church by 'affirming free will, and speaking not wisely of predestination' (Bruce and Perowne, 476). Corro was, in fact, articulating opinions which would later be termed Arminian, and Alvey's concern shows that he was himself solidly attached to the prevailing Calvinist orthodoxy.

Alvey subsequently acquired a more congenial assistant. In November 1580 the Middle Temple ordered £20 to be provided for a preacher to be selected by Alvey and three others. Alvey's health was declining (he made his will on 23 March 1581), and the man he chose to 'supply his weakness' was Walter Travers (Martin, 333). By choosing so prominent a radical as his successor, Alvey emphatically affirmed his own preferred brand of churchmanship. Alvey remained active; during 1581 he was troubled with securing possession of the master's official residence, petitioning the privy council for the matter to be 'quyeted and ended by reasonable composition' (PRO, SP 12/157, no. 6). Alvey was himself encouraged by the council to enforce church attendance in the Temple. On 9 February 1582 the Middle Temple parliament agreed to confer with their Inner Temple colleagues about Alvey's request for 'overseers and collectors … to take the view of all resident and in commons who do not resort to church, or being there, do not demean themselves according to the laws'. On 2 July Alvey was duly allowed to nominate 'such as he can persuade' among the Middle Templars (Martin, 248, 252).

It was not until 27 January 1583 that the Inner Temple made a similar order.

Alvey died in or before August 1584, when Whitgift notified the queen of the vacant mastership. Alvey had hoped Travers would succeed him, but the archbishop disapproved both of the latter's opinions and of his orders. The lawyers of the Temple, with whom Archbishop Sandys was dining, commended Alvey's 'saint-like life', and, 'as they bewail'd his death, so they wisht for a like pattern of virtue and learning to succeed him' (Walton, 46). Richard Hooker was appointed master in March 1585.

Alvey left all his 'humanitie' books to the scholars of Westminster School, to be distributed at the discretion of the dean and the headmaster; he had previously (1572) recommended the under-master, John Price, to the lord keeper for a Norfolk living. Alvey left his divinity books to such of his kin as might study the subject. His only asset of substance was a bond for £84 owed to him by his brother-in-law Richard Ferris; this sum was to be shared by his widow, their daughter Martha Sturrope, and Martha's children Audrey and Joshua. Plate and yet more spoons were left to others, including William Goodlad, one of the queen's butlers and presumably Emma Alvey's kinsman. In November 1584 the Inner Temple gave Mrs Alvey 5 marks 'for her relief' (Inderwick, 332).

Walton says of Alvey that he was 'a man of strict life, of great learning, and of so venerable behaviour as to gain such a degree of love and reverence from all men, that he was generally known by the name of Father Alvie' (Walton, 45).

C. S. KNIGHTON

Sources T. Baker, *History of the college of St John the Evangelist, Cambridge*, ed. J. E. B. Mayor, 1 (1869), 283 · C. H. Garrett, *The Marian exiles: a study in the origins of Elizabethan puritanism* (1938), 71–2 · *Fasti Angl., 1541–1857*, [Ely], 74, 75 · *The acts and monuments of John Foxe*, ed. S. R. Cattley, 8 vols. (1837–41), vol. 7, p. 121 · C. S. Knighton, ed., *Acts of the dean and chapter of Westminster*, 1 (1997), 85, 101; 2 (1999), 4, 22, 40, 54, 56–7, 65, 68, 101 · *The letter book of John Parkhurst, bishop of Norwich*, ed. R. A. Houlbrooke, Norfolk RS, 43 (1974–5), 115 · *The diary of Henry Machyn, citizen and merchant-taylor of London, from AD 1550 to AD 1563*, ed. J. G. Nichols, CS, 42 (1848), 272 · *Correspondence of Matthew Parker*, ed. J. Bruce and T. T. Perowne, Parker Society, 42 (1853), 476 · H. Robinson, ed. and trans., *Original letters relative to the English Reformation*, 1 vol. in 2, Parker Society, [26] (1846–7), 755, 763 · I. Walton, *The life of Mr. Rich. Hooker* (1665), 45–6 · *The works of … Richard Hooker*, ed. J. Keble, 7th edn, 1, rev. R. W. Church and F. Paget (1888), 26–9 · D. S. Chambers, ed., *Faculty office registers, 1534–1549* (1966), 275 · J. Venn, ed., *Grace book Δ* (1910), 6, 442 · Venn, *Alum. Cant.*, 1/1.26 · Cooper, *Ath. Cantab.*, 1.491 · S. J. Knox, *Walter Travers: paragon of Elizabethan puritanism* (1962), 56–9, 66, 70 · F. A. Inderwick and R. A. Roberts, eds., *A calendar of the Inner Temple records*, 1 (1896), 311, 320, 327, 331, 332, 333 · C. T. Martin, ed., *Minutes of parliament of the Middle Temple*, 4 vols. (1904–5), vol. 1, pp. 239, 245, 248, 252, 333 · state papers, domestic, Elizabeth I, PRO, SP 12/157, no. 6 · *CSP dom., 1581–90*, 81 · GL, MS 9531/11, fol. 46 · Westminster Abbey muniments, Reg 5, fol. 105 · City Westm. AC, Reg. Elsam, fols. 223v–224v

Wealth at death £84 owing to him: City Westm. AC, Reg. Elsam, fols. 223v–224v

Alvey, Thomas (1645–1704), physician, was born in St Faith's parish, London, on 4 May 1645, the son of Thomas Alvey, a merchant tailor. He was educated at Merchant Taylors' School, London, and at Merton College, Oxford (BA 1662, MA 1667, BM 1669, DM 1671). He became a fellow of the Royal College of Physicians, London, in 1676, censor in 1683, Harveian orator in 1684, and was appointed an elect in January 1704. Alvey wrote *Dissertatiuncula epistolaris, unde pateat urinae materiam potius e sero sanguinis quam e sero (quod succo alibili in nervis superest), ad renes transmitti* (1680). He died in 1704.

THOMPSON COOPER, *rev.* PATRICK WALLIS

Sources Foster, *Alum. Oxon.* · Munk, *Roll* · C. J. Robinson, ed., *A register of the scholars admitted into Merchant Taylors' School, from AD 1562 to 1874*, 2 vols. (1882–3) · Wood, *Ath. Oxon.*

Archives BL, corresp. with Dr T. Novell, Sloane MS 491

Alwyn, William (1905–1985), composer, was born William Alwyn Smith on 7 November 1905 at 54 Kettering Road, Northampton, the son of William James Smith and his wife, Ada Tyler Tompkins. Northampton was also the birthplace of the composers Edmund Rubbra and Malcolm Arnold. Though he was of humble background—his father was a grocer—Alwyn's gifts were apparent in childhood, when the gift of a piccolo at the age of nine launched him on the path to music. He attended Northampton grammar school, and by fifteen he had become a pupil at the Royal Academy of Music in London, studying composition as well as the flute and piccolo. A financial crisis on the death of his father two years later meant that Alwyn had to pay his own way by playing in cinema pit ensembles and giving elementary piano lessons in the impoverished East End of London.

Success was not long in coming, however. Alwyn was invited back to the Royal Academy to teach composition, and also became principal flautist of the London Symphony Orchestra. On 1 January 1929 he married Olive Mary Audrey, daughter of William Joseph Pull; they had two sons. As a composer he achieved an early breakthrough with the first performance, at the 1927 Promenade Concerts, of his *Five Preludes for Orchestra*. From the mid-1930s onwards he composed over 200 scores for films of various kinds: short documentary features were his initial terrain, but he later turned to feature films, and among his sixty or more in this genre scores such as those for *Odd Man Out* (1946), *The Fallen Idol* (1948), *The History of Mr. Polly* (1949), and the Disney version of *Swiss Family Robinson* (1960) all became classics of their kind. The composer once commented that he found film work a huge stimulus: it gave him the opportunity to experiment, to work with orchestras, and to confront in music a wide range of emotional scenarios.

During the Second World War these skills were put to good use in composing music for a string of propaganda films for the ministry of information and the army film unit. These included *Desert Victory*, *Fires were Started*, and *World of Plenty*, all made in 1943. Alwyn played the flute many times in the series of wartime concerts mounted at the National Gallery by Dame Myra Hess, and was also active as an air-raid warden. Though he continued to write film music until the early 1960s, he always refused the temptation to emigrate to Hollywood, a possibility that was regularly on offer.

Sensibly, Alwyn delayed embarking on a symphonic career until he was in his forties and ready for such a step. He then began what was always conceived as a cycle of four symphonies, a tetralogy with symphonic features in itself, such as a lighter-veined scherzo or an energetic finale. Sir John Barbirolli conducted the first symphony (1949) and encouraged him to continue in this vein. The birth of the third symphony (1955–6) was scrupulously recorded in a compositional diary which Alwyn later allowed to appear (in the *Adam International Review* for 1968) under the title 'Ariel to Miranda'. The 1950s were an immensely productive decade for Alwyn, in which he wrote music in a wide variety of orchestral and chamber forms. Some of his most immediately attractive music came in his concertos, such as *Autumn Legend* (1955), which was inspired by the paintings of the Pre-Raphaelites and features a solo cor anglais; and also in *Lyra angelica* (1954), where the harp is the solo instrument, evoking a vision of heaven.

By now Alwyn was regularly writing songs, occasionally using his own texts for the purpose, though he also set such writers as William Blake and Louis MacNeice; and in later years he was close to the poet Michael Armstrong, whose evocations of the night strongly appealed to him. Mention should also be made of Alwyn's work on behalf of his fellow composers. He campaigned for composers' rights as an active member of the Composers' Guild of Great Britain, the Performing Right Society, the Mechanical Copyright Protection Society, and the Society for the Promotion of New Music. He was appointed CBE in 1978.

Alwyn may have thought that with his fourth symphony he had written the last of his 'dramas of contrast and emotion'. There was to be an epilogue, though. In 1973, still adhering to this rubric, he added a comparatively short but powerful single-movement work, giving it the subtitle *Hydriotaphia*. This was a reference to the famous work of the seventeenth-century English religious writer Sir Thomas Browne.

The fifth symphony embraced the elegiac note that increasingly surfaces in the music of Alwyn's later years and that was an integral part of his aesthetic of modern Romanticism. He once identified Dante Gabriel Rossetti as an important model for him, while he claimed to have learned formal musical freedom from early exposure to the example of Liszt's 'Faust' symphony. The last twenty-five years of Alwyn's life were spent in Suffolk, at Blythburgh, within sight of the sea. His amanuensis and literary secretary from 1961 was Doreen Mary Carwithen (1922–2003), whom he had taught composition at the Royal Academy of Music. They later married. At Blythburgh he not only composed two operas to his own librettos, *Juan, or, The libertine*, and *Miss Julie*, based on Strindberg's play, but also found time to paint, to translate modern French poetry, and to dabble in autobiography (*Winged Chariot*, which was privately published in 1983).

In 1981 Alwyn was severely ill after a stroke, which made him unable to compose for two years. He died at the Southwold and District Hospital, Southwold, Suffolk, on 11 September 1985, just short of his eightieth birthday. The third quartet, which he wrote in the year before his death, demonstrated undiminished powers and is one of the works within a very large corpus that is destined to be remembered. His widow subsequently established the William Alwyn Foundation to promote her husband's works.   PIERS BURTON-PAGE

Sources W. Alwyn, *Winged chariot: an essay in autobiography* (1983) · S. Craggs and A. Poulton, *William Alwyn: a catalogue of his music* (1985) · H. Ottaway, 'Alwyn, William', *New Grove*, vol. 1, pp. 300–01 · *WWW, 1981–90* · *The Times* (13 Sept 1985) · *Daily Telegraph* (13 Sept 1985) · F. Routh, *Contemporary British music* (1972) · *CGPLA Eng. & Wales* (1986) · b. cert. · m. cert. [Olive Mary Audrey Pull] · d. cert. · J. Huntley, *British film music* (1947)
Archives Britten–Pears Library, Aldeburgh, scores, paintings, written works, MSS | SOUND BBC Sound Archives
Wealth at death £375,552: probate, 3 April 1986, *CGPLA Eng. & Wales*

Alypius (*fl.* 360–*c*.371). *See under* Roman officials (*act.* AD 43–410).

Aman, Dudley Leigh, first Baron Marley (1884–1952), marine officer and politician, was born on 16 May 1884 at Helsby, Cheshire, the son of Edward Godfrey Aman (1853–1939), the manager of a salt works, and his wife, Annie Florence Pitcairn (*d.* 1939), daughter of Henry James Pelham West. Educated at Marlborough College, he was commissioned in the Royal Marine Artillery in January 1902 and received his initial training at the Royal Naval College, Greenwich (1902–4). Until August 1914 he experienced a traditional Royal Marines career, combining schooling, sea duty, and shore duty at the Royal Marine Artillery barracks, Eastney. He acquired expertise in gunnery and torpedoes, but specialized in wireless telegraphy while also passing preliminary examinations for interpreter in French and Italian. In 1914 he graduated from the Army Staff College, Camberley. On 16 May 1910 he married Octable Turquet (1881–1969), daughter of Sir Hugh Gilzean-*Reid, the Gladstonian Liberal journalist and politician; they had one son.

During the First World War, Aman served on two ships (Third Fleet, wireless duties) in August and September 1914, and aboard HMS *Tiger* (Grand Fleet) in 1917. His main service was in France and Belgium between 1915 and 1917 with the anti-aircraft brigade (attached to various army units) of the Royal Marine Artillery; although commandant of a trench mortar school, his primary duty was as commander of the brigade's C battery. For his actions at the second battle of Ypres he received the Distinguished Service Cross in 1916: he had 'commanded two sections of anti-aircraft guns in the salient of YPRES since 3rd May 1915, with marked success, and has shewn great ability and zeal, and a fine example of coolness and courage under fire' (*London Gazette*, 24 Feb 1916). Aman was only one of thirty-five Royal Marines to receive this decoration during the First World War. Appointed in late 1917 to the Signal School, Portsmouth, for experimental and research work, he retired at his own request from the Royal Marines with the rank of major on 10 November 1920. During the emergency of the coal strike of 1921 he was recalled to active service for two months (8 April–4 June), his last duty with his corps.

In 1917, while still on active duty, Aman joined the Fabian Society. After the war he became active in the Labour Party, by his own account resigning from the Royal Marines in order to concentrate on political work for the party. Living at Rowlands Castle in Hampshire, he was the founder of the Hampshire and Isle of Wight Labour Federation, a member of the agricultural committee of Hampshire county council, and a JP. He was among several upper- and middle-class recruits to Labour during these years. Many were committed to anti-militarist and internationalist principles; few shared Aman's military background. Yet all were involved in the attempt to broaden the Labour Party into a progressive organization. He fought five parliamentary elections: Petersfield, Hampshire, in 1922 and 1923; the Isle of Thanet in 1924; and Faversham, Kent, in a by-election of January 1928 and again at the general election in 1929. His first three attempts were pioneer efforts in hopeless seats. Faversham was more promising but he lost narrowly in both contests. Nevertheless he established himself as an effective campaigner and a regular participant at Labour Party conferences.

In January 1930 Aman was created first Baron Marley to strengthen the very small Labour Party contingent in the House of Lords. He served as under-secretary of state for war until the collapse of the Labour government in August 1931. During 1930–31 he was a lord-in-waiting to King George V. Unlike several Labour peers, he stayed with the Labour Party through the 1931 crisis and for several years thereafter took a sizeable share of the party's work in the House of Lords, of which he was a deputy speaker (1930–41) and chief Labour Party whip (1930–37). He also chaired a ministry of health departmental committee on garden cities and satellite towns, whose report was issued in 1935.

Marley's principal concern through the 1930s was the deteriorating international situation. In 1933 he wrote the introduction to the *Brown Book of the Hitler Terror and the Burning of the Reichstag* prepared by the World Committee for the Victims of German Fascism. He described what he saw in Germany as 'well organized terror', with verified documentation provided by 'the tortured and martyred victims themselves'. He warned that 'the memory of the public is short' and that 'public opinion is unfortunately only too ready to reconcile itself to a *fait accompli*, as in the case of Italy'. Hence the need to keep 'alive the memory of the criminal acts of the Nazi government'. As he concluded, the struggle against 'Hitler Fascism' as such 'is a fight on behalf of the real Germany'. Later he insisted that the essence of Nazism was class oppression: 'The Nazi regime was not a persecution only of the Jews but of all German workers by the possessing classes' (*The Times*, 28 Oct 1935).

Marley's involvement with the World Committee was opposed by Herbert Morrison, who criticized any association with communists (*Labour Party Conference Report*, 1934, 136–8). Through his concern to prevent war and to support progressives Marley took part in an anti-war conference in Shanghai in 1933. *En route* for China, his entry to Japan was blocked by the authorities on the ground that the conference was a Comintern affair. He was able to stay for one night in Kyoto but was not allowed to contact Japanese sympathizers. Following the conference he travelled home via Vladivostok and Moscow. Like many other progressives, he was attracted to the development of the Soviet economy in contrast with what seemed to be the shortcomings of capitalist counterparts. His commitment to the Labour Party and socialism owed much to the belief that planning was the most effective route to an efficient modern economy.

In the late 1930s Marley's position seems to have been less firmly on the left. He responded to the Munich agreement with the assessment that, in the light of the military weakness of France and the difficulty of defending Czechoslovakia, Neville Chamberlain had no option, though he regretted that the Soviet Union had not been taken into consultation (*Hansard 5L*, 110, 5 Oct 1938, 1445). His House of Lords involvement became less central to his activities; between 1943 and 1945 he was attached to the Ministry of Aircraft Production. A vice-president of the Motion Study Society of Great Britain and an associate member of the Institute of Personnel Management, he took a particular interest in industrial efficiency and industrial psychology. He hoped that useful developments would be engendered by the Anglo-American Council on Productivity.

Marley's life and career are a salutary warning against stereotyped images. Although not drawn from the traditional sources—sons of clerics and military officers—for officers of the Royal Marines, he none the less had the education and talent to acquire a commission and excel in his corps. His assessment of society and ensuing conclusions led him into a career in politics which diverges from the standard image of a British military officer. His political career was one of success and disappointment, but his humanistic concerns were paramount. As his parliamentary colleague M. Phillips Price wrote in 1952, 'Lord Marley was one of those who joined the labour movement soon after the First World War out of conviction and idealism, although it must have been against his tradition, upbringing, and material interest to have done so.' Most important, with a keen sense of humour, 'he saw the human side of every situation' (*The Times*, 29 March 1952). He died at Manor House Hospital, London, on 29 February 1952 and was succeeded by his son, Godfrey Pelham Leigh Aman (1913–1990). DONALD F. BITTNER

Sources official record of service, PRO, ADM 196/63, p. 168 with attachments · H. E. Blumberg, *Britain's sea soldiers: a record of the royal marines during the war, 1914–1919* (1927), chap. 25 · E. Fraser and L. G. Carr-Laughton, *The royal marine artillery, 1804–1923*, 2 (1930), chap. 55 · *The Times* (3 March 1952); (29 March 1952) · *Globe and Laurel*, 55/2 (March–April 1952), 87 · WWW · Burke, *Peerage* (1970), 1766 · Kelly, *Handbk* (1952), 1412 · *Whitakers peerage, baronetage, and companionage* (1932), 414 · *The Labour who's who* (1927) · F. W. S. Craig, *British parliamentary election results, 1918–1949*, 3rd edn (1983), 367, 385, 387 · J. Thompson, *The royal marines: from sea soldiers to a special force* (2000) · *Navy List* · *Lean's the Royal Navy List and Naval Recorder* (1911) · *Hart's Army List* (1913) · *Army List* (1914); (1915); (1919) · m. cert.

Archives Royal Marines Museum, Eastney barracks, Southsea, Hampshire, personal medals | Bodl. Oxf., corresp. with Lord Ponsonby · Labour History Archive and Study Centre, Manchester, corresp. with J. S. Middleton

Likenesses photograph, repro. in *The Times* (27 Jan 1928) · photograph, repro. in *The Times* (1 Jan 1930) · photographs, Royal Marines Museum, Eastney barracks, Southsea, Hampshire, photographic archives

Wealth at death £5740 4s. 6d.: probate, 23 July 1952, *CGPLA Eng. & Wales*

Amanullah Khan (1892–1960), amir of Afghanistan, was born on 2 June 1892 at Paghman, Kabul. He was the third son of Amir (King) Habibullah (d. 1919), but his mother, Ulya Hazrat, was the 'first queen'. She used her considerable skill and intelligence to prepare him for the throne. However, Amanullah contracted two unhappy arranged marriages—with Peri Gul in 1908 and Shahzada Khanum (d. 1911) in 1910—while in his teens, at his mother's instigation. He also imbibed her Anglophobia. This was reinforced by the father of his third, and lifelong, wife, the talented Soraya Tarzi, whom he married in 1913. Mahmud Beg Tarzi, his father-in-law, had spent many years in exile and had been greatly influenced by the liberalism and anti-colonialism of the Young Turk movement. Tarzi encouraged Amanullah to support the so-called War Party of the Young Afghans during the First World War. The latter espoused pan-Islamic anti-British sentiments and were committed to modernizing Afghanistan.

Amir Habibullah was more pro-British, although Afghanistan remained neutral during the war. Amanullah and Mahmud Beg Tarzi fell into disfavour because of their pro-Turkish sentiments, as did many of the Young Afghans, who were gaoled. These circumstances aroused suspicion following Habibullah's mysterious murder on 19 February 1919 during a hunting expedition from his winter court at Jalalabad. Amanullah, who had remained in Kabul, seized the throne from his uncle Nasrullah. He was backed by the army, the Young Afghans, and the powerful figures of Tarzi and Ulya Hazrat.

Amanullah's position was strengthened by his assuming the mantle of Afghan nationalism in the Third Anglo-Afghan War, which he launched in May 1919. The peace treaty which followed the month-long conflict was a personal triumph: it guaranteed Afghanistan the right to control its own foreign affairs, something the British had denied to earlier amirs, who, in Lord Lytton's colourful phrase of 1877, were 'earthen pipkins' between the two iron pots of Britain and Russia. Amanullah was brought back to earth the following year by the disastrous hijrat episode. Indian Muslims began a religiously ordained flight to Afghanistan in response to British treatment of the defeated ruler of Turkey. By August 1920 about 50,000 *muhajirin* (refugees) had flocked to Afghanistan. The impoverished country could not absorb such an influx and had to expel the refugees.

In 1919 Amanullah embarked on a number of reforms, which included the abolition of forced labour, the granting to women of freedom of choice in marriage, and anti-corruption and anti-smuggling measures, and culminated in the promulgation of Afghanistan's first constitution in 1923. These reforms alienated his country's traditional tribal and religious leaders. The Mangal tribes, led by the Lame Mullah, responded by rising in revolt in Khost in 1923–4. Amanullah made some concessions to religious pressure in its aftermath. However, following his return from a successful European visit with Queen Soraya in July 1928, he embarked on further ambitious reforms. These included such controversial measures as the requirement of Western dress at court functions, the discouragement of purdah, the changing of the day of rest from Friday to Thursday, and the reduction of allowances and subsidies for mullahs (clerics). Such reforms were just part of a vast programme which would have revolutionized Afghan society. Before many could be implemented Amanullah faced another serious tribal revolt in November 1928, led by the Shinwaris. Many mullahs supported it, including the influential hazrat of Shor Bazaar, one of the most important commercial centres of Kabul. The hazrat's Mojadidi family claimed the hereditary right to crown Afghan kings at their coronation. Opposition also emerged in the north from the Tajik leader Bach-i-Saqao, who briefly supplanted Amanullah and reigned as King Habibullah.

Amanullah fled from Kabul on 14 January 1929 and abdicated in favour of his older half-brother Inayatullah. At Kandahar, Amanullah tried to rally Pashtun support against the Tajik ruler in Kabul, but his attempts were unavailing and he had to slip across the border to India. On 22 June 1929 he and most of his family sailed from Bombay to Europe. Exile in genteel poverty in Italy awaited him. Amanullah Khan never returned to Afghanistan before his death in Switzerland on 26 April 1960; he was buried in Jalalabad.

Amanullah was a sincere individual given to emotion. Despite the claims of his critics, he was a pious Muslim who placed importance on the substance, rather than the outward trappings, of religion. The overthrow of the modernizing shah of Iran, Reza Shah Pehlavi, in 1979 questions a too easy assumption that Amanullah was a man before his time. His judgement, however, that without a centralizing and modernizing ideology Afghanistan would break up into its constituent tribal elements appears prescient in the light of late twentieth-century developments.   IAN TALBOT

Sources L. B. Poullada, *Reform and rebellion in Afghanistan, 1919–1929* (1973) · R. T. Stewart, *Fire in Afghanistan, 1914–1929: faith, hope and the British empire* (1973) · I. A. Shah, *The tragedy of Amanullah* (1933) · S. K. H. Katrak, *Through Amanullah's Afghanistan* (1929) · L. W. Adamec, *Afghanistan, 1900–1923: a diplomatic history* (1967) · V. Gregorian, *The emergence of modern Afghanistan* (1969) · G. MacMunn, *Afghanistan from Darius to Amanullah* (1929) · G. N. Molesworth, *Afghanistan, 1919* (1962) · M. H. Kakar, *Afghanistan: a study in internal political developments, 1880–1896* (1971) · A. Guha, 'The economy of Afghanistan during Amanullah's reign, 1919–1929', *International Studies*, 9/2 (1967), 167–82

Archives BL OIOC, political and secret department files, LPS · National Archives of India, New Delhi | FILM BFI NFTVA, news footage · IWM FVA, actuality footage

Likenesses black and white photographs, March 1928, Hult. Arch. · black and white photographs, c.1929, Hult. Arch. · photographs, repro. in Poullada, *Reform and rebellion*

Ambedkar [*formerly* Ambavadekar], **Bhimrao Ramji** (1891–1956), politician, was born at Mhow in central India on 14 April 1891, the youngest of the fourteen children of Ramji Maloji Sakpal, a subahdar-major in the British Indian army and headmaster in a military school, and his wife, Bhimabai Murbadkar. When the boy was barely two his father retired and settled first at Dapoli, then at Satara, where he attended the high school. His family were untouchables, belonging to the community of Mahars, who, though of lowly caste, were reputed to be a spirited people from whom the Bombay army had obtained early recruits. The indignities, humiliations, and hardships to which he was subjected stirred in this proud, intelligent, and sensitive boy a bitter resentment which lingered with him to the end.

In 1900 he entered his surname in the government middle school enrolment lists as Ambedkar, from a teacher in Satara who had showed him kindness. He next attended Elphinstone high school in Bombay and later Elphinstone College with financial help from the Maharaja Gaikwar of Baroda. In 1906 he married Ramabai (*d.* 1935), daughter of Bhiku Dhutre, a railway porter at Dapoli. Of their four sons and one daughter, only the son survived. He graduated in 1912 and in the following year went with a three-year scholarship from the maharaja to Columbia University, New York, where he wrote his first publication, 'Castes in India' (*Indian Antiquary*, May 1917), and secured a PhD in economics. He then went to the London School of Economics and was admitted to Gray's Inn. Short of money, he returned to India, where the terms of his scholarship required him to enter the service of Baroda state. Although a junior administrative officer, as an untouchable he found himself treated with contempt by clerks and office boys, unable to obtain accommodation, and even denied food. Consequently, he left Baroda state in disgust and in November 1918 managed to secure a job as lecturer in political economy at Sydenham College, Bombay. Two years later he returned to England, where he was called to the bar in 1923 and in the same year obtained his DSc (London) for a thesis, subsequently published, entitled 'The problem of the rupee'. He returned to India in April 1923 and started legal practice in Bombay.

Ambedkar soon began to organize the untouchables and to make them socially and politically conscious through the first of a series of Marathi newspapers, a Society for the Welfare of the Depressed Classes with the motto 'Educate, agitate, organize', and *satyagrahas* (non-violent campaigns) for temple entry. Especially important were many conferences of the depressed classes, the most famous held in 1927 at Mahad, in which the traditional Hindu law book the *Manusmriti* was burned. Meanwhile, he testified on behalf of untouchables' rights to the franchise committee (1919) and to the Simon commission on constitutional reform (1928), was nominated to the Bombay legislative council (1925), and became a professor at the Government Law College (1928).

Bhimrao Ramji Ambedkar (1891–1956), by unknown photographer

In September 1930 Ambedkar was officially invited to attend the Indian round-table conference on constitutional reform in London as a representative of the so-called depressed classes. His appointment marked a milestone in the socio-political struggle of the untouchables, for never before had they been consulted in framing the future of India. Ambedkar became an all-India figure. He used this vantage-point successfully to question with blunt and militant doggedness the claim of M. K. Gandhi to represent all India including the untouchables. The British government in 1932 announced its own communal award in relation to the newly reformed constitution, which treated the untouchables as politically separate from the Hindus. Gandhi, then in prison, launched on a protest fast, which led ultimately to negotiations with Ambedkar that culminated in the Poona pact of 1932, which conceded far more parliamentary representation to the untouchables than they had been allotted under the British award, but allowed the general electorate to elect 'scheduled caste' representatives, a situation which still exists. Ambedkar's criticism of the Congress Party and of caste Hindus grew increasingly strong and in 1935 he announced his intention to convert, with the words 'I will not die a Hindu'. However, he gave his chief attention to politics and in the same year founded the Independent Labour Party, the forerunner of the Scheduled Castes Federation (1946) and the Republican Party (1956).

In 1940 Ambedkar published *Thoughts on Pakistan*, which,

though critical of some aspects of M. A. Jinnah's thinking, was not hostile to the idea of Pakistan. When in 1942 the viceroy, Lord Linlithgow, decided to expand his executive council, Ambedkar was invited to join it as the member in charge of labour. In 1945 he published his most critical book, *What Congress and Gandhi have done to the Untouchables*, and in the same year founded the People's Education Society, which still runs a broad spectrum of educational institutions.

As independence drew near, Ambedkar turned his attention and energies to the constructive constitutional tasks for which he was well equipped by training and temperament. He became a member of the constituent assembly in 1946 and as chair of the drafting committee became one of the principal architects of independent India's constitution. As law minister in Nehru's first cabinet he also contributed to the drafting of the Hindu Code Bill, in the process earning, not without some irony, the accolade of 'a modern Manu' after the legendary Hindu lawgiver. On 27 September 1951 he resigned from Jawaharlal Nehru's government, protesting at the slow pace of reform.

Ambedkar's first wife died in 1935, and in 1948 he married Sharada Kabir, a Saraswat Brahman by caste and a doctor by profession. In his later years ill health hampered the tempo of his normal activities, and his last days were occupied with the thought of embracing Buddhism, which he did, with many of his followers, at a ceremony in Nagpur in October 1956. In November he attended the fourth conference of the World Fellowship of Buddhists at Katmandu, Nepal. It was his last public appearance. He died in his sleep on the night of 5–6 December 1956 at Delhi, and was cremated, his ashes being interred in Chaitua Bhumi, Shivasi Park, Bombay .

Ambedkar's fame has increased since his death, with the publication of dozens of books extolling his life and thought and the reprinting of all his writings by the government of Maharashtra. A network of colleges in Maharashtra, Karnataka, and Andhra Pradesh are credited to his influence, and his followers have succeeded in forcing the renaming of a university as Dr Babasaheb Ambedkar Marathwada University. The conversion to Buddhism continues, although slowly, but *dalit sahitya*, the literature of the oppressed, flourishes in Marathi, Gujarati, and Kannada, a tribute to Ambedkar's inspiration.

FRANK MORAES, rev. ELEANOR ZELLIOT

Sources D. Keer, *Dr. Ambedkar: life and mission* (1962) · K. N. Kadam, *Dr Babasaheb Ambedkar and the significance of his movement: a chronology* (1991) · *Dr Babasaheb Ambedkar: writings and speeches*, ed. V. Moon, [16 vols.] (1979–) · E. Zelliot, *From untouchable to Dalit: essays on the Ambedkar movement* (1996) · A. K. Narain and D. C. Ahir, eds., *Dr. Ambedkar, Buddhism, and social change* (1994)

Archives Ambedkar Library, Nagpur, Vasant Moon MSS · Ambedkar Library, Bombay, Vasant Moon MSS · Bombay University Library, Khairmoday MSS | FILM BFI NFTVA, 'In the footsteps of Ambedkar', Channel 4, 6 Jan 1989 · priv. coll., Bombay · priv. coll., Hyderabad | SOUND BL NSA, documentary recordings

Likenesses P. B. Ramteke, portrait, 1988, priv. coll. · M. Wagh, bust, 1994, Col. U. · M. Wagh, bronze statue, Bombay Maidan · M. Wagh, bronze statue, Parliament Building, New Delhi · photograph, repro. in Keer, *Dr. Ambedkar* [see illus.]

Amberley. For this title name *see* Russell, John, Viscount Amberley (1842–1876); Russell, Katharine Louisa, Viscountess Amberley (1842–1874).

Ambler, Eric Clifford (1909–1998), writer, was born on 28 June 1909 at Wellington Road, Charlton, south-east London, the eldest child in the family of two sons and one daughter of Alfred Percy Ambler (1882–1929), an advertising executive and part-time entertainer whose family had moved to London from Salford in Lancashire, and Amy Madeleine Andrews (*b.* 1886), eldest daughter of a London cabinet-maker. Ambler's parents were musical and for a number of years performed as 'living marionettes' at concert parties. Although they discouraged Ambler from taking to the stage, he always said he learned far more from the theatre than from books: 'I was a failed playwright before I was any sort of novelist' (*Ambler at 80*).

Ambler described himself as 'a nasty little boy' (*Ambler at 80*) whose childhood was spent with a book in one hand and a catapult in the other. At the age of eight he won a scholarship to Colfe's grammar school in Lewisham. Although he loathed the school he was very well taught there, particularly in science—'I liked the discipline of science. The only discipline I did like' (ibid.). Aged fifteen he astonished everyone by winning the top scholarship to Northampton Engineering College, Islington, an associate college of London University. But engineering bored him and in 1926 he left without taking his degree. He then became a technical trainee at the Edison Swan Electrical Company, progressing from the shop floor to the publicity department. This led to a copywriting job with the firm's advertising agency, work at which he proved so proficient that by the age of twenty-six he had become a director.

The turning point in Ambler's life came in 1936, with the publication of his first novel, *The Dark Frontier*. Having failed to find a market for his plays, he 'set out to improve a shoddy article' (*The Guardian*). This was the British spy thriller, in thrall, as he saw it then, to the puerile 'snobbery with violence' of writers like Sapper and Dornford Yates. Ambler, who 'couldn't have been farther to the Left', decided he would make it 'grow up' (*Newsagent and Bookshop*, 22 Feb 1979). His aim was realism, particularly social realism. His protagonists met in dingy bars, not in posh gentlemen's clubs. They had a degree in science, not a private income. And they whistled the 'Internationale', not the 'Eton Boating Song'.

Ambler cheerfully admitted how 'clumsy' were *The Dark Frontier* and its successor, *Uncommon Danger* (1937). But they struck an immediate chord with intelligent young readers, many of whom shared his 'popular front' convictions. In 1937 he left advertising, having contracted to produce two books a year for £4 a week. He went to live in France, partly because his money went further there, but also because it was a more stimulating environment. 'France was full of *emigrés*, some living on their wits, others with the most lurid of pasts. These were the sort of people I wanted to write about' (personal knowledge). A chance encounter with some exiled Turks in Nice produced his Balkan masterpiece, *The Mask of Dimitrios*, the book on which his reputation as 'the father of the modern spy novel', as he was acclaimed in 1975, still rests. Despite being published 'inauspiciously' in August 1939, it has never been out of print.

On 5 October 1939 Ambler married Harriet Louise Crombie, *née* Smith (*b.* 1902/3), an American fashion artist, who had three children from a previous marriage. They were divorced in 1958. In 1940 he joined the Royal Artillery. Two years later he was transferred to the army film unit, for whom he made over ninety films, most notably *The Way Ahead* (1944) starring David Niven and Peter Ustinov. Once, filming in Italy with the American director John Huston and a US army crew, Ambler and his colleagues were shelled so fiercely that his unconscious 'played a nasty trick on him' (Ambler, *Here Lies*, 208). A confirmed atheist, he heard himself saying, 'Into thy hands I commend my spirit.' But Huston thought Ambler 'was one of the coolest men I've ever seen under fire'. He was awarded the US bronze star.

Ambler was demobbed in the rank of lieutenant-colonel. By now he had become fascinated with the process of film-making and for twenty years after the war worked as a writer–producer, first in England, later in Hollywood. There he met his second wife, **Joan Mary Harrison** (1907–1994), film and television producer, who was born at 12 Wodeland Road, Guildford, Surrey, on 20 June 1907, the daughter of Walter Harrison, a newspaper editor, and his wife, Amelia McWhir Mure, *née* Asher. After graduating BA in French from St Hugh's College, Oxford, she studied at the Sorbonne. In 1935 she was hired by Alfred Hitchcock as his secretary and soon became his friend and collaborator. She accompanied him to Hollywood in 1939 to work on *Rebecca* for David O. Selznick. Because Harrison so closely resembled the 'cool blonde' type of actress Hitchcock favoured, people wondered if they were more than simply colleagues. The answer was no. In 1942, following rumours of a romance with Clark Gable, Harrison decided to strike out on her own and for ten years was under contract as an independent producer to RKO. Harrison was not only beautiful and intelligent but also very tough—essential for a woman producer in Hollywood. Unsurprisingly, given her apprenticeship with Hitchcock, she was most at home with film-noir, producing such classics as *The Phantom Lady* (1944) and *Ride the Pink Horse* (1947). Then RKO was taken over by Howard Hughes, who had old-fashioned ideas about a woman's place. Harrison went to New York and became a 'live' television producer. In 1955 Hitchcock lured her back to Hollywood to work on *Alfred Hitchcock Presents*, the long-running television series. Soon she virtually ran Hitchcock television, selecting story material for the shows and hiring the writers, directors, and actors who would put it across. One of the writers she hired was Eric Ambler. They were married in 1958 and had no children. In 1969 they moved to Switzerland, for by then Ambler had had his fill of writing for films. After a wasted year spent working on *Mutiny on the Bounty*, in a fruitless attempt to make Fletcher

Christian (Marlon Brando) a more important figure than Captain Bligh (Trevor Howard), he concluded that 'no amount of money is worth the boredom of producing rubbish' (*Newsagent and Bookshop*, 22 Feb 1979).

If social realism had been Ambler's aim before the war, it was ideological realism that inspired his first post-war novel, *Judgement on Deltchev* (1951). The story of a Stalinist show trial in the Balkans, it marked his break with the left. But Ambler never became a cold war warrior. His later novels are almost as devoid of moral judgements as they are of gratuitous sex and violence. Something of an anarchist at heart, he writes about rootless nonconformists and their efforts to beat the system. One such is Arthur Abdel Simpson in *The Light of Day* (1962), the Levantine hustler whose life has been 'one long dirty story'; another is Paul Firman in *Send No More Roses* (1977), the plausible extortionist whose murky past is as well laundered as his bespoke shirts. 'Like most novelists I reproduce aspects of myself', Ambler once said. 'And I find myself equivocal' (*Ambler at 80*).

As a young man Ambler was sometimes mistaken for the future Edward VIII. In later life, always immaculately dressed—it was hard to imagine him without a tie—he looked more like a retired banker than like the man who had debagged the 'clubland heroes'. But his urbanity was mitigated by a taste for mild hamming: he liked to pull funny faces and talk in a stage whisper.

Ambler won numerous literary awards, including the Crime Writers Association gold dagger (1959, 1962, 1967) and diamond dagger (1986), and the Mystery Writers of America grand master award in 1975. He was made OBE in 1981.

Ambler and Joan Harrison, who had begun to suffer from a degenerative brain disease, moved to London in 1982, the better to arrange proper care for her. His autobiography, *Here Lies Eric Ambler*, was published in 1985. Joan Harrison died on 14 August 1994 at their London home, 14 Bryanston Square, and Ambler died there four years later on 23 October 1998. He was buried on 30 October in Hendon cemetery.   MICHAEL BARBER

Sources E. Ambler, *Here lies Eric Ambler* (1985) · *Ambler at 80*, Radio 4, 29 June 1989 · E. Ambler, *The story so far* (1993) · G. Lambert, *The dangerous edge* (1975) · C. James, 'Prisoners of Clarity—2', *New Review* (Sept 1974) · *The Guardian* (2 Feb 1970) · *The Times* (2 Sept 1994) · personal knowledge (2004) · d. cert. · b. cert. [Joan Mary Harrison] · d. cert. [Joan Mary Harrison] · m. cert. [Harriet Louise Crombie]

Archives Boston University, Massachusetts, corresp. and literary MSS

Wealth at death £30,586: probate, 1999, *CGPLA Eng. & Wales*

Ambroise (*fl.* 1188–1195), crusader and historian, was a Norman, possibly from the region of Évreux. His *Estoire de la guerre sainte* is a unique vernacular eyewitness account of the third crusade, and perhaps 'the best source for the crusade of Richard' (La Monte, 22). Ambroise never indicates his role in the crusade: the only detail he gives about himself is the remark 'nos autre qui a pié fumes' ('we who were on foot'; Ambroise, verse 12039). He seems, then, to have been a simple footslogger, one of the *gent menue* or small folk. It is unlikely that he was a soldier, as he makes no reference to any direct involvement in fighting. It has been suggested, from his mention of *chanson de geste* characters in his poem, that he was a professional *jongleur*. Nevertheless epic characters are mentioned infrequently, and they rub shoulders with classical, and even, occasionally, biblical, figures. As Ambroise also appears to be familiar with the rhetorical and literary culture taught in the schools, it is possible that he may have been a cleric, although when he mentions the priests accompanying the army he never places himself among them.

It is clear from his narrative that Ambroise was a subject of Richard I, who is the hero of his story and can do no wrong in his eyes. From the first-person sections of his history it can be concluded that he was present at the famous meeting between Henry II and Philip Augustus near Gisors on 21 January 1188 at which the third crusade was proclaimed, and that he was in London for Richard's coronation on 3 September 1189. He accompanied Richard's army from the time when it left Vézelay on 4 July 1190, two days after the truce between Richard and Philip. They travelled to Marseilles, and from there sailed to Messina, where quarrels between the crusaders and the townspeople ended with the occupation of the town by Richard in September. The army sailed on to Rhodes and then Cyprus, which Richard conquered, and arrived at Acre on 8 June 1191. Ambroise was present at the fall of Acre on 12 July, 'si com il vit a sa veüe' ('as he saw with his own eyes'; Ambroise, verse 4568), and describes many minor events of the fighting; he paints in graphic detail the army's trek along the coast from Acre to Ramlah, afflicted by the heat, assailed by hunger and thirst, and constantly skirmishing with Saladin's forces. He appears to have been present at the battle of Arsuf on 7 September 1191, a serious defeat for Saladin (again he gives no suggestion that he was fighting); and he was one of those who visited the holy places in and around Jerusalem after the truce agreed between Richard and Saladin on 2 September 1192.

Ambroise shows (for a crusader) a surprising interest in his surroundings. He refers to various local customs of the Turks, and also describes the equipment and tactics of their light cavalry, so different from those of the crusaders. He mentions local fauna such as camels, dromedaries, and crocodiles. He also gives the first attested Western examples of the words 'caravan' (*carvane*, verse 9948, from the Persian *kärawän*) and 'carob' (*quaroble*, verse 4362, Arabic *karrüba*), and several times uses the Arabic term *melek* ('king') which, he notes, was applied to Richard by the Turks (verses 6832–3 and 7123–5, for example). He has occasional vivid details: Richard returns from fighting on one occasion so covered with arrows that 'il resembloit un heriçon' ('he looked like a hedgehog'; Ambroise, verse 11630); a squadron of black warriors in their red turbans 'sembloient cerisiers meurs' ('looked like ripe cherry-trees'; ibid., verse 3357); the army is at one point attacked by swarms of midges nicknamed 'estinceles' ('sparks') and so badly bitten that they all looked like lepers (ibid., verses 9526–41). These touches contribute to the feel of eyewitness veracity, as does Ambroise's emotional description at the end of the poem of his visit to the holy places in and around Jerusalem. There is no doubting his piety: for him, the crusaders are either 'l'ost Deu' ('the army of God') or simply 'les pelerins' ('the pilgrims'), and if Jerusalem was not delivered it was due to the sins of the Christians, and particularly to the discord in the crusader army, which Ambroise contrasts poignantly if inaccurately with the harmony and unity of purpose of those taking part in the first crusade.

Scholars have remarked on the striking similarities between the narrative of Ambroise's *Estoire* and the *Itinerarium regis Ricardi* of the Augustinian canon and historian *Richard. Most of the evidence strongly suggests that the *Itinerarium* was largely a translation of the *Estoire*, and there is little doubt that Ambroise's multiple claims to be an eyewitness should be accepted. He is careful to indicate his sources for events he did not witness personally, and when he attacks the *jongleurs* as 'vilains conteors' ('second-rate story-tellers'), it is not for being poor rhymesters but for being so untrustworthy that he cannot tell what in them is true and what is lies (Ambroise, verses 4189–94). His emphasis on his truthfulness and authority resembles that of other vernacular historians of the twelfth century such as Wace and Benoît de Ste Maure; and although his presentation of his material is less sophisticated than theirs, he is technically competent and handles the standard rhetorical figures of the period with ease. His frequently unvarnished narrative style exemplifies a deliberately 'naïve' self-presentation as a simple, and therefore reliable, eyewitness.

Ambroise's narrative ends with Richard's departure from Syria; and as the last event he mentions dates from 1195, and there is nothing to indicate that he knows of Richard's death in 1199, it is assumed that the *Estoire de la guerre sainte* was finished before 1199, and probably in or shortly after 1195. Nothing is known about Ambroise's later life.   PETER DAMIAN-GRINT

Sources Ambroise, *L'estoire de la guerre sainte*, ed. G. Paris (1897) · P. Damian-Grint, 'Vernacular history in the making: twelfth-century historiography in the Anglo-Norman *regnum*', PhD diss., U. Lond., 1994 · H. Budde, 'Ambroise', *Grundriß der romanischen Literaturen des Mittelalters*, 11/2 (1993), 39–40 · J. L. La Monte, 'Introduction', in Ambroise, *The crusade of Richard Lion-Heart*, ed. J. L. La Monte, trans. M. J. Hubert, Records of Civilization: Sources and Studies, 34 (1941), 3–27 · P. Bancourt, 'De l'imagerie au réel: l'exotisme oriental d'Ambroise', *Images et signes de l'Orient dans l'Occident médiéval*, Senefiance, 11 (1982), 27–39 · M. Ailes, 'Epic and romance in the crusading chronicle of Ambroise', Oxford Old French graduate seminar, 1998 [unpublished paper] · W. Stubbs, ed., *Chronicles and memorials of the reign of Richard I*, 1: *Itinerarium peregrinorum et gesta regis Ricardi*, Rolls Series, 38 (1864) · K. Norgate, 'The *Itinerarium peregrinorum* and the "Song of Ambrose"', *EngHR*, 25 (1910), 523–47 · J. G. Edwards, 'The *Itinerarium regis Ricardi* and the *Estoire de la guerre sainte*', *Historical essays in honour of James Tait*, ed. J. G. Edwards, V. H. Galbraith, and E. F. Jacob (1933), 59–77

Archives Biblioteca Vaticana Apostolica, Vatican City, Vatican reg. 1659

Ambrose, Benjamin Baruch [Bert] (1896–1971), band leader and violinist, was born in London on 15 September 1896. As a musician he became well known to the world as

Bert Ambrose (or simply Ambrose). The full circumstances, exact birthplace, and details of his family are not available, and it is possible that the family's original name was not Ambrose. At the age of fifteen he went with an aunt to America and began an obscure early musical career there, studying the violin and playing in cinema orchestras in New York. He is first heard of playing the violin for six weeks at Reisenweber's Restaurant in a band led by Emil Coleman; after this he was in the orchestra at the Palais Royal. He became leader of the orchestra there, but came into real prominence as musical director of the Club de Vingt in New York from 1917 to 1920. Luigi Naintre, who opened the Embassy Club in London in 1920, discovered Ambrose on one of his American trips and took him back to London that year to organize the Embassy Club orchestra. In 1922 Ambrose returned to New York as musical director at the Clover Gardens, but Naintre persuaded him to return to London in 1922, when Ambrose and his seven-piece Embassy Club orchestra really began to make their mark. The original personnel, with Ambrose leading on the violin, were Arthur Aaronson (alto saxophone and clarinet), Joe Crossman (tenor saxophone), Max Raiderman (piano), Harry Edelson (banjo), Julius Mustaum (bass), and Eddie Grossbart (drums). Some early recordings were made for Columbia, and by 1926 two trumpets and a trombone had been added.

Ambrose left the Embassy Club in 1927 to take up a residence at the Mayfair Hotel. Joe Crossman went with him, the band at the Embassy Club continuing under Max Raiderman. Ambrose went to New York to recruit five American musicians to join the band, which opened at the Mayfair on 27 March 1927. He achieved his dance band supremacy over the coming years by regularly importing American musicians such as Sylvester Ahola and Danny Polo; by keeping his ear to the latest developments in America and the sounds of bands led by the Dorseys, Benny Goodman, and others; and by employing such talented arrangers as Lew Stone, Bert Barnes, Ronnie Munro, Bert Read, and Sid Phillips. The band performed regularly at the London Palladium, found a talented and individual vocalist in Sam Browne, and began to produce a regular output of top-class recordings. Throughout the ensuing years Ambrose employed a distinguished list of female vocalists who included Ella Logan, Elsie Carlisle, Anona Winn, Vera Lynn, and Anne Shelton.

In 1928 the BBC began a series of fortnightly broadcasts from the Mayfair Hotel, and it was this that finally made Ambrose into a truly national figure; also significant was the fact that the band was undoubtedly one of the best in the country with its inherent feeling for the new jazz idiom—an element that came out strongly, for example, in a 1930 recording, 'Eleven-Thirty, Saturday Night', which had a typical Lew Stone arrangement. From September 1933 to July 1936 Ambrose again played at the Embassy Club and during this period made some of his best recordings, including 'Embassy Stomp' (1935), 'Copenhagen' (1935), 'Champagne Cocktail' (1936), and 'Cotton Pickers' Congregation' (1937). The average number in the band at this time was eleven, but for broadcasting and recording purposes it was often augmented to as many as twenty-one, and included strings. In 1934 he made a trip to America and played a summer season in Biarritz. He organized in 1935 a small group which he called the Embassy Rhythm Eight and used mainly for recording and accompanying the vocalists Elsie Carlisle and Sam Browne.

From September 1936 to early 1937 Ambrose worked again at the Mayfair, and during the following summer he played in Paris and Cannes. At the end of the year he went into partnership with the band leader Jack Harris to buy Ciro's Club in London, where each band played a number of six-month stints. In between times he led a band at the Café de Paris in 1938, worked in films and radio, and continued to lead an eight-piece band in 1938–9. He re-formed his Mayfair Orchestra at the end of 1939 but had to limit his own activities owing to ill health. He led an octet for a stage show in 1940–41 and continued to lead pick-up bands through the war years, and played at Ciro's in 1945–7 and at the Nightingale Club in 1948–9. He led various groups during the 1950s, with a residency at the Café de Paris in 1955–6, and made a farewell tour from May to September 1956. He became increasingly active, and eventually wholly involved, in managing other performers.

The wonderfully integrated sound of the Ambrose orchestra in an arrangement by a master such as Sid Phillips, with its underlying swinging impulse (the 1936 classic 'Hors d'oeuvres', for example), is fondly remembered by many who grew up with its broadcasts and recordings for HMV and Decca in the 1930s; and they will happily recall the Ambrose signature tune 'When Day is Done'. Many distinguished British band musicians and leaders played with Ambrose in the 1930s—including Ted Heath, Lew Davis, Max Goldberg, Billy Amstell, Lew Stone, Stanley Black, George Chisholm, George Melachrino, and Sid Phillips. In 1936 Ambrose and the band were seen and heard in a British Lion film called *Soft Lights and Sweet Music*, with a strangely assorted supporting cast that included his current vocalist Evelyn Dall, Harry Tate, Turner Layton, the drummer Max Bacon, Donald Stewart, Elisabeth Welch, Billy Bennett, and the Western Brothers. In 1937 Vera Lynn joined the band as vocalist; she appeared on television with Ambrose in 1938 before marrying the band clarinettist Harry Lewis and leaving for a distinguished solo career in 1940. Challenged by the London visits of the Ellington band in 1933 and Louis Armstrong in 1935, leaders like Ambrose would dearly have liked to put even more jazz content into their playing. But the pre-war BBC and record companies were somewhat nervous of anything that was not deemed 'commercial', and most musicians had to satisfy their natural jazz leanings by appearing in small swing groups at an occasional 'jazz jamboree' at the Gaumont State in Kilburn.

Ambrose, in his quiet and ever modest way, always fought for the highest standards under whatever circumstances, and was ever a professional and perfectionist—and the perfect gentleman. In his last days he was on tour as manager for the singer Kathy Kirby when, after suffering a sudden haemorrhage and collapsing in a Leeds television studio, he died in the General Infirmary, Leeds, on 11 June 1971.

PETER GAMMOND

Sources B. Kernfeld, ed., *The new Grove dictionary of jazz*, 2 vols. (1988) · A. McCarthy, *The dance band era* (1971) · B. Amstell and R. T. Deal, *Don't fuss, Mr Ambrose* (1986) · B. Rust, *The dance bands* (1972) · B. Rust, disc notes, *Hits of 1931: Ambrose and his orchestra* (1981) [World Records SH 419] · *Melody Maker* · d. cert. · J. Chilton, *Who's who of British jazz* (1997) · B. Rust, disc notes, *Ambrose and his orchestra* (1974) [World Records SH B21] · F. Clayton, disc notes, *Ambrose, 1935–1937* (1988) [Harlequinn HQ 3016]
Likenesses photographs, EMI Records · photographs, Decca Record Co. · photographs, repro. in *Melody Maker*

Ambrose, Isaac (*bap.* 1604, *d.* 1664), Church of England clergyman and ejected minister, and author, was baptized on 29 May 1604 at Ormskirk, Lancashire, the son of the vicar, Richard Ambrose (*d.* 1613), and his wife, Marie. He entered Brasenose College, Oxford, in 1621 as a batteler and graduated BA in 1624. Having been ordained, Ambrose was presented by Bishop Morton to the 'little cure' of Castleton, Derbyshire, in 1627, and became vicar of Clapham, Yorkshire, in 1629.

Ambrose attracted the notice of William Russell, afterwards earl of Bedford, and was by the king's influence incorporated MA at Cambridge University in 1632. Having resigned his small living in 1631, he was made one of the king's four preachers in Lancashire and took up residence at Garstang. He married Judith (*d.* 1668) in 1633; her surname is unknown. About 1640, through the patronage of the pious Lady Margaret Hoghton, he obtained the vicarage of the corporate town of Preston in Amounderness, where at the level of gentry Catholics outnumbered protestants. In November 1642 Ambrose was briefly taken prisoner by the king's commissioners of array, and he was again arrested on 20 March 1643, but in both cases he was released by the influence of neighbouring gentlemen. On the taking of Bolton in May 1644 he took refuge in Leeds.

Ambrose played a prominent part in the establishment of presbyterianism in Lancashire in the 1640s. Empowered by parliament in 1644 to ordain ministers, he was several times moderator of the seventh Lancashire classis, and was a signatory of the harmonious consent (1648) of the Lancashire presbyterian clergy, expressing solidarity with the Westminster assembly and opposing calls for toleration. He also appears as an official disburser of relief after the ravages of the civil war campaigns in and around Preston. However, when he signed the 'Agreement of the people taken into consideration', the local committee for the relief of plundered ministers ordered him to be sent a prisoner to London; there, in April and May 1649, he made the acquaintance of and received assistance from, among others, Lady Mary Vere and the earl of Bedford. Subsequently Ambrose continued to exercise his ministry in Preston, described as 'painful' in the *Parliamentary Survey* of 1650, but in 1654, probably as a result of illness, he left and returned to Garstang as minister.

Although as a king's preacher Ambrose had been appointed to proclaim protestant doctrine to a county where recusancy was strong, his written works are largely free of controversy and doctrinal refutation—although he does refer to papacy as 'the common enemy' in the 'Epistle Dedicatory' to Sir Orlando Bridgeman in his *War with Devils* of 1661. They draw, instead, on the 'affectionate' strain of puritanism, weaving together such writers as Rutherford, Bolton, and Baxter with Ambrose's own particular style of warmth and urgency. His *Prima, media & ultima* (1650), while beginning with a call to new birth and ending with reflections on death and judgement that read like a collection of sermons, is largely concerned with the 'middle things', the means 'for continuance and increase of a Godly life'. These include a commitment to systematic meditation, which is reinforced by a few illustrations from his own diary, kept during his annual monthly retreat in May in the woods near Hoghton Tower. This central theme of identification with Jesus in thought and behaviour is further expanded in *Looking unto Jesus* (1658). His funeral sermon for Lady Margaret Hoghton, *Redeeming the Time* (1658), is a tribute to her personal piety and kindness. Rather different in approach is his twin text of 1661, *War with Devils and Ministration of and Communion with Angels*, which is more anecdotal and less systematic, but revealing of his desire to be accommodating after the Restoration. He commends Stillingfleet's approach to religious controversy, for example, and suggests Charles's escape from Worcester was 'almost miraculous'. Ambrose's works were highly regarded at the time, and continued to be reprinted after his death, appearing in Wesley's Christian Library. Alongside Ambrose's unwavering doctrinal Calvinism is a personal warmth that seems to have attracted both gentry and people, as well as his fellow ministers, of whom Henry Newcome was perhaps the closest. Ambrose contributed dedicatory epistles to Newcome's earlier works, and a few personal glimpses of Ambrose's friendship can be gained in turn from Newcome's published diary. It is a pity so little of Ambrose's own diary has survived.

Notwithstanding Ambrose's desire for accommodation, in 1662 he was ejected for nonconformity. Having retired to Preston, he died—quietly, according to the sympathetic Edmund Calamy, of a sudden apoplexy, according to the hostile Anthony Wood—on 23 January 1664, and was buried there two days later.

ROGER POOLEY

Sources E. Axon, 'The king's preachers in Lancashire, 1599–1845', *Transactions of the Lancashire and Cheshire Antiquarian Society*, 56 (1941–2), 67–104 · H. Fishwick, *The history of the parish of Garstang in the county of Lancaster*, 2, Chetham Society, 105 (1879) · B. Nightingale, *Lancashire nonconformity*, 6 vols. [1890–93], vol. 1 · *Calamy rev.* · I. Ambrose, *Compleat works* (1674) · *VCH Lancashire*, vol. 7 · W. A. Shaw, ed., *Minutes of the committee for the relief of plundered ministers and of the trustees for the maintenance of ministers … 1643–1660*, 2, Lancashire and Cheshire RS, 34 (1896), 54–217 · *The autobiography of Henry Newcome*, ed. R. Parkinson, 2 vols., Chetham Society, 26–7 (1852) · *The harmonious consent of the ministers of the province within the county palatine of Lancaster* (1648) · Wood, *Ath. Oxon.*, new edn, 3.659–61 · R. C. Richardson, *Puritanism in north-west England: a regional study of the diocese of Chester to 1642* (1972) · B. Nightingale, *Isaac Ambrose of Garstang and Preston* (1912) · parish register, Ormskirk, 29/5/1604 [baptism] · parish register, Preston, Lancashire, 25 Jan 1664 [burial]

Archives DWL, letter | DWL, Baxter corresp., 6.16
Likenesses line engraving, pubd 1674, BM, NPG · engraving (after effigy), repro. in Ambrose, *Compleat works*

Ambrose, John (*d.* 1771), naval officer, was commissioned fourth lieutenant of the *Lenox* on 20 June 1728, and from 27 March 1734 served as captain of the frigate *Greyhound* in Sir John Norris's fleet off Lisbon. As captain of the *Rupert* (60 guns) from 12 September 1740 he cruised the north coast of Spain and the coast of Portugal, intercepting several privateers, for which he received a silver cup and 'a piece of plate of one hundred guineas value' (Charnock, 4.255) in gratitude from the merchants of London. He enjoyed further success in the Mediterranean from 1743, including the capture (in company with the *Guernsey*) of the *Maria Fortune*, bound from Cadiz with a cargo worth £100,000.

Ambrose was, however, one of several officers made scapegoats for the disorder and confusion of the action off Toulon on 11 February 1744, following a parliamentary inquiry in March 1745. Found guilty by a court martial on 18 October 1745 of having neglected his duty; of firing and continuing to fire on the enemy while altogether out of range; of not having assisted the *Marlborough* when that vessel was in extreme danger; of failing to protect the fire-ship; and finally of 'disobedience to his majesty's instructions and the signals and commands of the admiral, neglect of naval military discipline, and being one of the principal causes of the miscarriage of his majesty's fleet' (Charnock, 4.256), he was cashiered and fined one year's pay, to be given to the chest at Chatham.

In 1748 Ambrose was restored to his rank and half pay, and in April 1750 he became a superannuated rear-admiral. He died at Bath on 25 March 1771.

J. K. LAUGHTON, *rev.* RANDOLPH COCK

Sources register of commissions and warrants, PRO, ADM 6/14,15 · J. Charnock, ed., *Biographia navalis*, 6 vols. (1794–8) · W. L. Clowes, *The Royal Navy: a history from the earliest times to the present*, 7 vols. (1897–1903) · *GM*, 1st ser., 41 (1771), 191 · *Copies of all the minutes and proceedings taken … before the court martial lately held at Chatham* (1746) · D. Syrett and R. L. DiNardo, *The commissioned sea officers of the Royal Navy, 1660–1815*, rev. edn, Occasional Publications of the Navy RS, 1 (1994)

Ambrosius Aurelianus [called Emrys Wledig] (*fl.* 5th cent.), military leader, successfully resisted the Anglo-Saxon advance across Britain. What little specific information can be established about him and his activities derives from chapter 25 of the *De excidio Britanniae* by Gildas, which was the source for Bede's account in his *Historia ecclesiastica gentis Anglorum*. Gildas describes Ambrosius Aurelianus as *dux* ('leader' or 'duke') and as a *vir modestus* ('gentleman'), and states that his parents 'had worn the purple'. The exact implications of this last phrase are difficult to determine with any certainty: it may indicate specifically that the family of Ambrosius had been of Roman senatorial rank, or it may simply mean that he was a member of the late Romano-British nobility. Bede, for instance, assumed Ambrosius's parents were 'of royal birth and title'. However, the modern suggestion that Ambrosius Aurelianus was a kinsman of St Ambrose of Milan, the son of a praetorian prefect called Aurelius

Ambrosius, cannot be substantiated beyond the obvious onomastic parallel. Nor is it easy to locate exactly where in Britain Ambrosius was active. Various attempts (some very unconvincing) have been made to identify English place names thought to contain the personal name Ambrosius and which therefore could have been associated with him: for example, Ambresbyrig, the Old English form of Amesbury in Wiltshire, which may mean 'the stronghold of Ambrosius'.

While Gildas does not give any absolute dates for Ambrosius, historians have either followed Bede and dated him *c.*495, or have argued that Gildas's relative chronology would suggest the 430s or 440s. According to Gildas, the young Ambrosius had survived a period of significant Anglo-Saxon advance, though it had claimed the lives of his parents. He later rallied the Britons and they defeated the enemy in battle, thus marking an improvement in British military fortunes. Subsequently, victory could go either way until the great British victory at 'Mount Badon', though neither Gildas nor Bede connect Ambrosius with this battle, which later tradition associated with the figure of *Arthur. It would seem that Ambrosius's own descendants (*suboles*) sought to maintain his leadership of the Britons (whether just militarily or otherwise is not clear) but, according to Gildas, those of his own day were certainly inferior to their ancestor.

By the early ninth century, the Welsh had developed Ambrosius Aurelianus into a figure of legend, bearing the vernacular name Emrys Wledig ('Emrys the Overlord'). Thus, there are various notices of him in the *Historia Brittonum*, where he is synchronized with and generally placed in opposition to Vortigern. The most clearly legendary passage describes how the orphan Emrys identifies a lake under Vortigern's fortress in Snowdonia where a red and a white worm, representing the Welsh and the English respectively, are in constant conflict. From this the boy predicts the ultimate victory of the Welsh and in return is granted all the kingdoms in western Britain by Vortigern. This story may have been composed to explain the origins of the Gildasian Ambrosius Aurelianus, though it does contain elements characteristic of medieval prophetic literature and had later echoes in Geoffrey of Monmouth's *Historia regum Britanniae* (where the role of Emrys is given to Merlin and the two 'worms' are called dragons) and also in the Welsh medieval vernacular tale *Lludd and Llefelys*.

DAVID E. THORNTON

Sources *Gildas: 'The ruin of Britain', and other works*, ed. and trans. M. Winterbottom (1978) · Bede, *Hist. eccl.*, 1.16 · T. Mommsen, ed., *Chronica minora saec. IV. V. VI. VII.*, 3, MGH Auctores Antiquissimi, 13 (Berlin, 1898) · Nennius, 'British history' and 'The Welsh annals', ed. and trans. J. Morris (1980) · *The Historia regum Britannie of Geoffrey of Monmouth*, ed. N. Wright, 1: *Bern, Bürgerbibliothek, MS 568* (1985) · *The Mabinogion*, trans. G. Jones and T. Jones, revision of 1974 edn (1984) · D. N. Dumville, *Histories and pseudo-histories of the insular middle ages* (1990) · J. N. L. Myres, *The English settlements* (1986)

Ameer Ali, Saiyid (1849–1928), judge and Muslim leader in India, was born on 6 April 1849 at Chinsura, Bengal, the fourth son of Saiyid Saadat Ali Khan (who died of cholera

Saiyid Ameer Ali (1849–1928), by Walter Stoneman, 1917

in 1856) of Mohan, Oudh, and his wife, the daughter of Shamsuddin Khan, landowner, of Sambalpur. Ali's family were Shi'i Muslims who claimed descent from the Prophet Muhammad through his daughter Fatimah and the eighth iman, Ali Raza; they were prosperous landowners of Persian descent who had come to India with Nadir Shah in 1739 and settled in Oudh. Ali's father had trained as a physician and was scholarly but restless, peripatetic, and apparently dilettante. Influenced by two British officials, he made the crucial decision to give his sons an English education.

Ali attended Hooghly College, where the principal, Robert Thwaytes, became 'one of the best friends of my life' (*Memoirs*, 16). He read much in English, graduated with distinction in 1867, and in 1868 was the first Muslim to receive a Calcutta University MA, in history and political economy. He also gained a BL degree. Awarded a Victoria scholarship, he left for England in December 1868, arriving in January 1869.

Early career The legal profession was at this time the favourite and most lucrative career of Calcutta graduates. Ali was admitted a student of the Inner Temple in May 1870, called to the bar in January 1873, and worked for an English law firm. The welcome and hospitality he received in England made him a lifelong Anglophile. He lived with an English family and was treated as 'one of themselves' (Gordon, 62). He told Napoleon III, whom he met at Brighton in 1872, that he loved England. He arrived with letters of introduction from British friends and from the viceroy, Lord Mayo, was admitted into London society, and then and on later visits to England became friendly with liberal politicians. These included the Fawcetts, whom he accompanied to women's suffrage meetings; journalists, including James Knowles of the *Nineteenth Century*; Captain Shaw of the London Fire Brigade; Lady Hobhouse; and others. John Bright proposed him for the Reform Club, of which he continued a member for nearly

half a century; he used the club's address in later life when writing to *The Times*.

In 1873 Ali returned to Calcutta. Of short stature, ambitious and capable, proud of his Saiyid and Persian heritage, he was primarily a Muslim devoted to his religion and his co-religionists: according to a fellow Muslim, he was 'a God-intoxicated man who lived by and with the Qur'an' (Aziz, vi). He was also a loyalist, who wrote of 'the necessity of British rule' (Gordon, 72). Although resident in Bengal, he never considered himself a Bengali. He spoke Urdu but wrote in English and published almost all his works in London. A Muslim modernist, influenced by Karamat Ali Jawnpuri (*d.* 1873), he believed that Islam was compatible with modern life and progress, and that Muslims should adopt Western education. He favoured educating Indian women and wanted polygamy prohibited. Indian Muslims were backward in terms of Western education, less literate and with a lower proportion of graduates than the Hindu majority. Ali saw the Hindus as threatening Muslim interests, and the Western-educated Hindus as competing with Muslims for government posts. In February 1873 Ali enrolled as an advocate in the Calcutta high court, and he built up a successful and lucrative practice. A fellow of Calcutta University (1874), he was a part-time lecturer on Muslim law (1875–9) and Tagore law professor (1884).

Ali believed that the condition of Muslims in India had declined, and that their fortunes could not be revived by their efforts alone; they needed government help, and to gain this they required their own political organization. In May 1877 he founded the Central National Mahommedan Association, of which he was secretary until 1890. A loyalist Muslim pressure group, asserting Muslim interests and wanting government posts filled by nomination not competitive examinations, this organization had members who were largely notables, mostly non-Bengali, and by 1888 it had more than fifty branches in different parts of India. In 1882 it presented a memorial, written by Ali, to the viceroy, Lord Ripon, requesting appointment of more Muslims to government service and more government assistance to Western education of Muslims, and alleging that Hindu prejudicial treatment often prevented Muslims from advancing. Like Sir Saiyid Ahmad Khan, Ali opposed the Indian National Congress, regarding it as a Hindu organization inimical to Muslim interests. The 'Congress-wallahs', especially Surendranath Banerjea and his *Bengalee*, criticized Ali. In 1883–4 Wilfrid Scawen Blunt visited India and was entertained by Ali. Later, in his book *India under Ripon*, he alleged that Ali fawned on the British and let down his compatriots. Ali wrote that Blunt had traduced and misrepresented him.

Ali was presidency magistrate from 1878, and chief magistrate from 1879 to 1881. He was a member of the Bengal legislative council from 1878 to 1883. A continuing issue was the relationship of the ryots (tenant farmers) with the zamindars (landlords) and officials' attempts to protect the former from the latter. The Bengal Tenancy Bill (1882), intended to protect ryots, aroused zamindari opposition and divided the legislative council, with

Indian non-officials including Ali advocating the zamindars' cause and the lieutenant-governor and other British officials arguing for the ryots. Although diluted in favour of the zamindars, the Bengal Tenancy Act (1885) was an important change in tenancy legislation. Babu (later Raja) Peary Mohan Mookerjee, the champion of the landlords, complimented Ali on his consideration for them.

In England in July 1880 Ali met 'the lady of my dreams' (*Memoirs*, 50), Isabelle Ida, second daughter of Heyman Konstam of 64 Gloucester Place, London, and sister of Gertrude *Kingston (d. 1937), the actress. They married on 21 October 1884 at the Unitarian church, Little Portland Street, London, and among the guests were Lord Stanley and Sir Ashley Eden. They had two sons. Ali's wife survived him. Their elder son (Saiyid) Waris (1886–1975), Wellington and Balliol, became a member of the Indian Civil Service and shot for India at Bisley. Their younger son, Sir Torick (1891–1975), Marlborough and Christ Church, became a Bengal high court judge. Both had British wives and retired to England.

High court judge and judge to the privy council From 1883 to 1885 Ali was a member of the viceroy's legislative council. He contributed to negotiating a compromise on the controversial Ilbert Bill (1883). In 1887 he was made CIE. Recommended by Sir Courtney Ilbert, he was a Calcutta high court judge from 1890 to 1904. He was the second Muslim appointed, and some considered his appointment political. Reportedly his merits as a judge were obscured by a conversational manner in court and a tendency to prolixity in judgment—superficial faults which increased with advancing years. He gave judgments of far-reaching importance including *Imambandi* v. *Mutsaddi* in Muslim law, *Ramachandra* v. *Vinayak*, *Buddha Singh* v. *Laltu Singh*, and *Girjabai* v. *Sadashiv* in Hindu law. Nevertheless Curzon did not have a high opinion of him as a judge. His publications included *Personal Law of the Mahommedans* (1880) and *Mahommedan Law* (2 vols., 1880 and 1884, and later editions).

During his judgeship Ali spent his vacations in England, and following his retirement in 1904 he settled there, residing at The Lambdens, near Theale, Berkshire, and later at his 'beautiful home', Pollingfold Manor, near Rudgwick, Sussex. He continued actively concerned with Muslim and Indian affairs. He was for some years chairman of the Woking mosque committee, and in 1910 was involved in the project, not then successful, of a London mosque. Muslims supported Curzon's partition in 1905 of Bengal and his creation of a Muslim-majority province. Ali praised Curzon and wrote to him expressing 'great regret' (*Memoirs*, 72) at his resignation. During the Swadeshi period Ali supported the forces of order and wanted firmer government action lest the government's authority be lost.

In 1905 the Unionist government appointed Lord Minto viceroy, and in the new Liberal government John Morley became secretary of state for India. Under pressure from the Hindu-dominated Indian National Congress, the administration wanted to introduce reforms, including more representative government. Alarmed at the perceived Hindu threat, Muslim leaders requested separate communal representation. In October 1906 a Muslim delegation, led by the Aga Khan, attended the viceroy, who agreed to their request for separate representation, more than proportional to their numbers. In December 1906 at Dacca the All-India Muslim League was established, with the Aga Khan as president. In May 1908 Ali and others established a London branch, with Ali as president, which had an important role in the following years. Morley agreed to separate representation but wanted a system of electoral colleges which Ali and other Muslims opposed, and there was further controversy and agitation, in which Ali took a leading role. In January 1909 he led a deputation to Morley. Finally Morley agreed to separate representation without electoral colleges and disproportional to numbers. So in the Indian Councils Act (1909) essentially the Muslims gained what they wanted, and thereafter the communal electoral system was a continuing feature of the raj. Neither Morley nor Minto thought highly of Ali. Morley wrote that he was 'a vain creature, with a certain gift of length' (Koss, 145), eager for a KCSI, a 'windbag' and 'conceited egotist' (Wasti, 183). Minto alleged he was frustrated at not being knighted. Nevertheless Morley, having decided to appoint an Indian judge to the privy council, appointed Ali to this unsalaried and onerous post in 1909. The first Indian member of the privy council, he applied himself keenly to the work of the judicial committee and attended Indian appeals almost until his death. In 1913 he resigned from the Muslim League, regarding it as too extreme.

Like other Indian Shi'a, Ali supported the Sunni Ottoman caliphate, which he accepted as a 'pontifical' or temporal caliphate. In India his pan-Islamism was quiescent, but in England he was more active. He supported the Turks in the Italo-Turkish War (1911–12), and with others formed the British Red Crescent which helped the Turks. However, in the First World War he was loyal to the British empire, and the Red Crescent supplied a motor field ambulance for Flanders and comforts to Indian troops there. After the war he unintentionally contributed to the abolition of the caliphate. In 1922 the new Turkish assembly abolished the sultanate but elected a new caliph without secular power. In late 1923 the Aga Khan and Ali wrote to the Turkish prime minister requesting enhancement of the caliph's position. This alarmed the Turkish government, which allegedly suspected a British plot, and gave Mustafa Kemal (Atatürk) his opportunity: he instigated the assembly's abolition of the caliphate in 1924. Latterly Ali mournfully reproached the Turks, whom for so many years he had defended in Britain.

Assessment A Muslim modernist and orthodox Shi'i, Ali was in the late nineteenth and early twentieth centuries a leading polemicist of Islam. His message was both for his co-religionists and for the British. In his publications, notably his *Spirit of Islam* (1891), developed from his *A Critical Examination of the Life and Teaching of Mohammed* (1873), and his *Short History of the Saracens* (1899), partly derived from Gibbon's *Decline and Fall*, both much reprinted, he restated the history of Islam for the West, and he influenced both British readers and Western-educated Muslims in India and Egypt. Like other modernists, he claimed that some Koranic injunctions were relevant only to the prophet's period, though his angelology was cautiously traditional. He argued that Christianity was an 'incomplete religion' and Islam the final stage in the evolution of religion. He claimed that it was superior to Christianity and Hinduism, dismissing the latter as idolatry and fetishism. He idealized the orthodox caliphate of the first four caliphs, and claimed the Muslim failure to conquer Europe was a tragedy, limiting its civilizing mission. He claimed 'the real history of India commences with the entry of the Mussulmans' (Gordon, 70), and that they brought culture to an idolatrous and backward land.

Ali was awarded honorary doctorates by Cambridge, Calcutta, and Aligarh universities. Following diabetes and a heart attack, he died on 3 August 1928 at his residence, Pollingfold Manor, near Rudgwick, Sussex, and was buried on 7 August at Brookwood cemetery, Surrey. After his death his widow and son compiled from his notes his 'Memoirs', which exaggerated the significance of his political role, and were published in *Islamic Culture* in 1931 and 1932. He has been called 'one of the greatest Muslims of India' (*Memoirs*, vii). Although he died before the concept of Pakistan developed in the 1930s, his Muslim separatism contributed to Pakistan's emergence. With Muslim separatism and partition probably the most contentious subjects in the historiography of the sub-continent, opinions on Saiyid Ameer Ali continue to differ.

S. V. FitzGerald, *rev.* Roger T. Stearn

Sources *Memoirs and other writings of Syed Ameer Ali*, ed. S. R. Wasti (1968) · M. Y. Abbasi, *The political biography of Syed Ameer Ali* (1989) · K. K. Aziz, *Ameer Ali: his life and work* (1968) · C. E. Buckland, *Dictionary of Indian biography* (1906) · S. E. Koss, *John Morley at the India Office, 1905–1910* (1969) · S. A. Wolpert, *Morley and India, 1906–1910* (1967) · B. B. Misra, *The administrative history of India, 1834–1947: general administration* (1970) · L. A. Gordon, *Bengal: the nationalist movement, 1876–1940* (1974) · B. R. Nanda, *Gokhale: the Indian moderates and the British raj* (1977) · A. Ahmad, *Islamic modernism in India and Pakistan, 1857–1964* (1967) · *The Times* (4 Aug 1928) · personal knowledge (2004) · *Calcutta Weekly* (13 Aug 1928) · A. Seal, *The emergence of Indian nationalism: competition and collaboration in the later nineteenth century* (1968) · S. R. Wasti, *Lord Minto and the Indian nationalist movement, 1905 to 1910* (1964) · R. Gopal, *Indian Muslims: a political history, 1858–1947* (1959) · J. Foster, *Men-at-the-bar: a biographical hand-list of the members of the various inns of court*, 2nd edn (1885) · *WWW*, 1916–1928; 1971–1980 · Kelly, *Handbk* (1914) · I. Stephens, *Pakistan* (1963) · J. M. Brown, *Modern India: the origins of an Asian democracy*, 2nd edn (1994) · A. Burton, *At the heart of the empire: Indians and the colonial encounter in late-Victorian Britain* (1998) · *CGPLA Eng. & Wales* (1928)

Likenesses photograph, *c.*1909, repro. in Abbasi, *Political biography* · W. Stoneman, photograph, 1917, NPG [*see illus.*] · O. Birley, portrait, Gov. Art Coll.

Wealth at death £4535 13s. 4d.: probate, 14 Nov 1928, *CGPLA Eng. & Wales*

Amelia [Emily], **Princess** (1711–1786), was born on 30 May/10 June 1711 at the palace of Herrenhausen in Hanover, Germany, the summer residence of her grandfather, Georg Ludwig, elector of Hanover (from 1714 King *George I of Great Britain), the second daughter of Georg August (1683–1760), electoral prince of Hanover (after

Princess Amelia (1711–1786), by unknown engraver (after Jacopo Amigoni)

1727 elector of Hanover and King *George II of Great Britain), and his wife, *Caroline of Brandenburg-Ansbach (1683–1737). Her full names were Amelia Sophia Eleonora. In October 1714, shortly after her grandfather acceded to the British throne, she and her sisters, *Anne (1709–1759) and Caroline Elizabeth [*see below*], accompanied their parents to England, where the family was installed in St James's Palace. Her brother *Frederick Lewis (1707–1751) remained in Hanover.

Formative influences Amelia's later taste for intrigue may well have been formed by the ongoing familial power struggles that involved her from as early as December 1717, when her parents were ordered to leave St James's Palace by George I. The king insisted, however, that the children remain. Although he and the prince and princess of Wales were fond of the children, they were pawns in the adults' power game. When the king granted the princess of Wales but not the prince easy access to the children, the prince promptly brought a lawsuit to try and secure their return to his care. He found to his chagrin that in England royal grandchildren belonged to the crown: he could not force the king to return them, nor could he even control their education. Tensions between the two royal households gradually receded after 1717, but the king and prince were not officially reconciled until 1720, and even then their relationship was never smooth. For Amelia and her sisters the reconciliation brought little change: they remained in the king's household at St James's, subject to every shift in family affections. In 1722 Amelia and Caroline attracted widespread public notice when they were inoculated against smallpox using a method only recently brought to England by Lady Mary Wortley Montagu. The process was still so new as to generate debate in England and be viewed with alarm by relatives on the continent. Fortunately, all went without incident.

Amelia (or Emily, as she was often called in Britain) benefited from the joint efforts of two intelligent women: her mother and Johanne Sophie, countess of Schaumburg-Lippe, whom the king had placed in charge of the princesses' household. Consequently she grew up well educated, trilingual (in English, German, and French), highly politicized, latitudinarian in religion, and fond of music, especially that of Handel. She was clever and articulate, but also, less flatteringly, bluntly outspoken, often to the point of tactlessness, impatient, and generally ill-suited to the machinations of a court and its politics. She particularly lacked the patient subtlety and flattering emollience needed to negotiate successfully the ever shifting alliances, deep family divisions, and contending political factions that came to dominate her father's court. Nor did her character lend itself to the prevailing ideals of passive submissive femininity. As a young woman, she was drawn far more to the stables than to the drawing-room or ballroom. She enjoyed fishing and loved horses. An avid hunter, she soon earned the reputation of being the hardest rider after stags in the royal family. Even when she was over forty she was still capable of shocking the 'good women' at Hampton Court by attending chapel on Sunday 'in riding clothes with a dog under her arm' (Walpole, *Corr.*, 37.341).

Social and political life Walpole's tone of studied amusement is reflective of his ambiguous feelings towards Amelia. A member of her inner circle of acquaintances for fifty years, he wavered continually between being inordinately proud and flattered to be a favourite and being sharply critical of her character and behaviour. He preferred pretty, pliant, conventional women who wore their intelligence lightly; it is not surprising that he found Amelia's forthright assertiveness, occasional arrogance, and tendency to disregard convention somewhat grating. More unfortunately for her historical reputation, however, she was also exactly the wrong sort of woman to appeal to the leading memoirist of George II's court, the exquisitely effeminate John, Lord Hervey. His dislike of her as a woman was exacerbated by the fact that he saw her as a rival, first for the attention of the prince of Wales and then, more importantly, for that of the queen. His description of her in 1734, when she was only twenty, paints her as darkly as possible for posterity:

> [she] was glad of any back to lash, and the sorer it was the gladder she was to strike. She had much the least sense (except her brother) of the whole family, but had for two years much the prettiest person. She was lively, false, and a great liar; did many ill offices to people and no good ones; and for want of prudence said almost as many shocking things to their faces as for want of a good-nature or truth she said disagreeable ones behind their backs. She had as many enemies as acquaintances, for nobody knew her without disliking her, nor was anybody acquainted with her without knowing her; and everybody in the Court being of the same opinion about her, people spoke their opinion with as little caution as variation. (Hervey, 81)

While Amelia's acerbic tongue could make enemies, it was also one of her attractions. Lady Louisa Stuart, who encountered her in old age, was more even-handed than Hervey when she described Amelia as:

> a woman of quick parts and warm feelings, but without Lady Yarmouth's *bonhommie*, [who] knew more of the world than princes usually do; partly from native sagacity, partly from keeping better company and having a mind above that jealous fear of the superior in understanding. (introduction, in *Letters and Journals*, 1.lxxxi)

However, even she noted that the inflated mock grandeur of her relative, Lady Mary Coke, could try the princess's patience sorely. Still, Amelia managed to stay on good terms with Lady Mary for over twenty years, quite a feat in itself. Indeed, over the years she gathered around her a group of intelligent, often witty, well-read and politically aware intimates, including ladies of her household such as Lady Cecilia Isabella (Bell) Finch, who became lifelong friends and acquaintances. While Walpole occasionally complained that her regular levées and private parties were stuffy and 'trist', he continued to attend and take part in their fine mixture of social and political gossip, their discussions of the latest political tracts and literature, and their never-ending games of loo.

Amelia's life would undoubtedly have been very different had George I lived long enough to carry out his plan for a double marriage between his Hanoverian and Prussian grandchildren. He had intended her to marry Prince Frederick of Prussia (after 1740 Frederick II, 'the Great'), but negotiations collapsed following the accession of George II to the throne in 1727. As there were few other suitable protestant princes and, it seems, marriage to a British commoner was never considered, Amelia had no choice but to remain single. She and Caroline remained unmarried while Anne married William, prince of Orange, in 1734; the younger sisters, *Mary (1723–1772) and *Louisa [see under Anne, princess royal], married respectively Landgrave Frederick of Hesse-Cassel in 1740 and Frederick V, king of Denmark, in 1743. Although Walpole suggests that Amelia held out hopes for a marriage as late as the peace of Aix-la-Chapelle in 1748, this seems unlikely given her age. As the first unmarried adult English princesses in living memory, she and Caroline, who maintained their own households, were both central and marginal to the court and its politics. Superfluous to the succession, they were doubly hampered by gender: traditional options open to younger sons were closed to them. Following the death of her mother in 1737, Amelia, as the eldest of the widowed king's daughters resident in Britain, became the highest-ranking woman at court. Her proximity to the king and his known reliance on female advisers in the past meant that she could have significant political influence. This situation would have been ideal for a woman with real political ability. Amelia, however, lacked the interpersonal skills and the necessary political sense to use to advantage the queen's death and the factional politics of the 1740s. Her jealousy of her father's politically astute mistress, Amalie von Wallmoden, countess of Yarmouth, limited her influence with her father and his ministers from the outset. Furthermore, in the late 1740s she aligned herself politically with her younger brother *William Augustus, duke of Cumberland (1721–1765), and his political cronies, the hot-headed John Russell, fourth duke of Bedford, and his supporters, thereby choosing allies who were distrusted by the king, the prime minister Henry Pelham, and the reversionary interest of her brother Frederick's court at Leicester House. Her continued support of her brother William after the death of the prince of Wales in 1751, and the part that she reputedly played in influencing the king against Augusta, dowager princess of Wales, in the subsequent regency debate, earned her the lasting dislike and distrust of both the princess of Wales and her son, the future George III.

The Richmond Park affair Amelia was appointed ranger of Richmond Park in 1751, gaining her own residence for the first time at New Lodge. Her period as ranger brought her notoriety and revealed her inability to see the political consequences of her actions. It resulted in a series of lawsuits as she tried, ultimately unsuccessfully, to limit public access to the park and traditional rights to gravel, wood, and water. In attempting to close the park to the public after 1751 and make it accessible only to a select group of friends and those neighbours who had been granted special passes, she also gained, for historians such as E. P. Thompson, a high place on the list of arrogant aristocratic landowners intent on removing common rights from the 'people'. She was by no means alone in what she was doing, however, and would probably have succeeded with a minimum amount of fuss had her estate been elsewhere. Like many contemporary landowners she was a firm believer that private property should be private— and that estates should be closed to the public. Even Walpole noted that in closing Richmond she was only 'imitating what the Duke has done at Windsor' (Walpole, *Corr.*, 20.322). The problem arose from a combination of factors: her rank—as a member of the royal family, she was expected to set an example for the rest of the country; her gender—her actions went against gender stereotypes which defined women as caring, considerate, and philanthropic by nature; the location of Richmond Park—it was far too close to London and the vocal London press for her actions to remain unnoticed; and the nature of the 'public' that she was excluding—not a group of untutored and impoverished rustics, but prosperous members of the middling sort and substantial tradesmen and artisans who felt that their traditional liberties were being threatened and who were more than ready to use all methods available to them to combat the perceived injustice.

Under the capable direction of a brewer, a stonemason, and a shoemaker, the closure of the park became a public issue. They organized public meetings, printed memorials in the press (particularly the *London Evening-Post*), and even gathered a substantial number of signatures on a petition which they had presented to the king. In the end, they had recourse to the law. In a series of judgments between 1754 and 1758, Amelia was forced to grant the public rights to use the ancient footways across the park. These cases, especially the last at the Surrey Lent assizes of 1758 before Sir Michael Foster, were high-profile affairs. In a society that was still highly deferential, the idea of trying a case against a member of the royal family posed particular concerns for the jurors. Foster was forced to put a talesman on the jury and fine absentees £20 each in order to ensure that they did their duty. And they did. As a result of the final verdict in 1758, the public was given access to the park via stepladders (gates could be closed; stiles and ladders could not so easily be stopped). When John Lewis, the brewer who had brought the successful case of 1758, returned to the court to complain that the rungs of the ladders were set too far apart for children and old men, Foster specified that they be changed so as to accommodate 'not only children and old men, but OLD WOMEN too' (Thompson, 113). After this ruling Amelia withdrew from active involvement in the park, so it is possible that she did not see the transfer of the rangership to John Stuart, third earl of Bute, in 1761 as a great loss.

Later years After her father's death in 1760, Amelia lost her apartments at St James's Palace, but received a pension of £1000 p.a. on the Irish establishment and a household of three ladies of the bedchamber. She took Sir Richard Lyttelton's house in Cavendish Square and, following the loss of New Lodge with the rangership of Richmond Park in 1761, she bought Gunnersbury House in Ealing, Middlesex. George III was hostile to female politicians and his ministers were opposed to Amelia, so she lost what special political influence she had enjoyed. However, her later years were perhaps her happiest, devoted as they were to her circle of acquaintances and her estate at Gunnersbury, where she improved the gardens and built a temple and shell grotto bath house. Although she became increasingly arthritic, deaf, and blind as an old woman, she remained interested in political developments and characteristically opinionated. Despite the poor relationship she had with George III, she refused to use her electoral interest as a landowner in Middlesex against the king. She was highly incensed when, during the Middlesex election of 1774, William Ponsonby, second earl of Bessborough, used her name without her permission to support Hervey Morres, second Viscount Mountmorres, an opposition candidate supported by her despised other nephew, William, duke of Gloucester. Amelia disapproved strongly of the behaviour of George III's younger brothers and later his sons, and this may have been behind her decision to leave her estate to her German nephews, the second and third sons of her sister Mary, landgravine of Hesse-Cassel.

Amelia died at her house in Cavendish Square, London, on 31 October 1786, and was buried on 11 November in the royal vault in Henry VII's chapel in Westminster Abbey. A frustrated politician, she was by temperament prevented from making the most of the possibilities open to her through gender, birth, and circumstance.

Princess Caroline Amelia's next youngest sister, **Princess Caroline Elizabeth** (1713–1757), enjoyed a similar but quieter life. She was born on 30 May/10 June 1713 at Herrenhausen, and moved to Britain with her sisters in 1714. After the death of Queen Caroline in 1737 she took some responsibility for the upbringing of her younger sisters Mary and Louisa. In the 1730s and early 1740s she enjoyed a close friendship with Lord Hervey. In 1743 Horace Walpole reported that her marriage to Duke Adolphus Frederick of Holstein-Gottorp, later king of Sweden, was being discussed at the initiative of Russia, but Caroline remained unmarried. She suffered increasingly from ill health and in the 1750s went into 'absolute confinement' (Walpole, *Corr.*, 21.165) in St James's Palace. She died on 28 December 1757 at St James's Palace, and was buried on 5 January 1758 in Henry VII's chapel, Westminster Abbey.

E. H. CHALUS

Sources A. Newman, ed., 'Leicester House politics, 1750–60, from the papers of John, second earl of Egmont', *Camden miscellany, XXIII*, CS, 4th ser., 7 (1969), 85–228 · 'Memoir on the events attending the death of George II and the accession of George III, by Henry Fox, first Lord Holland', in *The life and letters of Lady Sarah Lennox, 1745–1826*, ed. countess of Ilchester and Lord Stavordale, 2 vols. (1901), 1–81 · BL, Northumberland papers, Syon House manuscripts, reel 16, letters and papers, 31, 1752–4; reel 18, letters and papers, 35, July–September 1763 [microfilm M/295] · J. Brooke, *King George III* (1972) · W. Coxe, *Memoirs of the administration of the Right Honourable Henry Pelham, collected from the family papers and other original documents*, 2 vols. (1829) · R. Hatton, *George I: elector and king* (1978) · IGI · John, Lord Hervey, *Some materials towards memoirs of the reign of King George II*, ed. R. Sedgwick, new edn, 3 vols. (1952) · Newcastle papers, BL, Add. MSS 32876, 32919, 32923, 32941, 32949 · *The Grenville papers: being the correspondence of Richard Grenville ... and ... George Grenville*, ed. W. J. Smith, 4 vols. (1852–3) · *The letters and journals of Lady Mary Coke*, ed. J. A. Home, 4 vols. (1889–96) [incl. introduction by Lady Louisa Stuart] · Walpole, *Corr.*, vols. 9–12, 18–25, 28–39, 42 · E. P. Thompson, *Customs in common* (New York, 1991) · C. C. Trench, *George II* (1973) · P. C. Yorke, *The life and correspondence of Philip Yorke, earl of Hardwicke*, 3 vols. (1913) · letters to Lord Hardwicke, BL, Add. MS 35349, fols. 32–44 · letters of Queen Charlotte to Lady Holdernesse, etc., 1773–1808, BL, Add. MS 33131 · *GM*, 1st ser., 30 (1760), 538 · *GM*, 1st ser., 56 (1786), 1000–01 · *Letters from George III to Lord Bute, 1756–1766*, ed. R. Sedgwick (1939) · *Letters from Liselotte: Elisabeth Charlotte, princess palatine and duchess of Orléans*, ed. and trans. M. Kroll (1970) · T. Secker, *The autobiography of Thomas Secker, archbishop of Canterbury*, ed. J. S. Macauley and R. W. Greaves (Lawrence, Kansas, 1988), folio 53 (1758–64), 38–9 · *The royal kalendar of complete and correct annual register ... for the year 1770* (1770?) · Thomas Morrell (Handel's librettist) to an unknown addressee (*c.*1764), www.music.princeton.edu/~jeffery/HANDEL. html · M. H. Waldegrave, *Waldegrave family history*, 4 pts (1974–8), pt 3 · John, second earl of Ashburnham, personal diary, W. Sussex RO, ASH 934 (1774) · R. Whitworth, *William Augustus, duke of Cumberland* (1992) · will, PRO, PROB 11/1147, sig. 556 · *GM*, 1st ser., 28 (1758), 41

Archives BL, letters to Lord Hardwicke, Add. MS 35349 · BL, Holland House papers · BL, Newcastle papers · BL, letters to Stephen Poyntz · Suffolk RO, Bury St Edmunds, Hervey papers · Yale U., Walpole corresp.

Likenesses M. Maingaud, double portrait, oils, 1718 (with her sister Anne), Royal Collection · M. Maingaud, group portrait, oils, 1721 (with sisters), Royal Collection · P. Mercier, oils, 1728, Shire Hall, Hertford · W. Hogarth, group portrait, oils, *c.*1731–1732 (*The family of George II*), Royal Collection; version, NG Ire · P. Mercier, group portrait, oils, 1733, NPG; version, Royal Collection · J. B. van Loo, oils, *c.*1738, Royal Collection · oils, *c.*1740, Royal Collection · oils, *c.*1755, Royal Collection · Dorothy, countess of Burlington, oils, Chatsworth House, Derbyshire · J. Faber junior, mezzotint (after H. Hysing), BM, NPG · L. B. Roubiliac, bust, FM Cam. · J. Simon, mezzotint (aged nine; after Maingaud), BM · J. S. Tanner, medal, BM · line engraving (after J. Amigoni), BM, NPG [*see illus.*] · oils (with her sisters Anne and Mary at Hampton Court)

Wealth at death bequeathed at least £71,500, mainly from stocks; excl. value of sales of lands and estate at Gunnersbury and elsewhere: will, PRO, PROB 11/1147, sig. 556

Amelia, Princess (1783–1810). *See under* George III, daughters of (*act.* 1766–1857).

American Indians in England (*act. c.*1500–1609) included approximately twenty American natives, who lived for a time in England. The first were brought from the 'Newfound Island' by Sebastian Cabot in 1498 or, more likely, by Bristol seamen in 1501 or 1502. According to the *Chronicle* of Robert Fabyan (*d.* 1513), sheriff of London, as quoted by John Stow in 1580, Cabot brought back at least three inhabitants of Newfoundland who survived for a time in England, for 'This yeere [1502] also were brought to the king three men, taken in the new founde Island ... These were clothed in beastes skins, and ate raw fleshe, and spake such speach that no man could understand them, and in their demeanour like bruite beastes, whom the king kept a time after' (Hakluyt, 7.155). Two years later two of them were at Westminster Palace dressed in English garb. There is no record of their deaths in England or return to America.

No further American native is known to have reached England until 1532, when a Brazilian cacique voluntarily accompanied Captain William Hawkins to England. A member of Hawkins's crew, Martin Cockeram, was left as hostage. On his arrival, the Brazilian was taken to London and presented to Henry VIII, then at Whitehall, 'at the sight of whom the king and all the nobilitie did not a little marvaile', his 'apparel, behaviour, and gesture' being 'very strange' (Hakluyt, 11.24). After a year in England the Brazilian died en route to his homeland. Cockeram was however released, and returned eventually to his home at Plymouth.

The next American native did not arrive until 1576, when Sir Martin *Frobisher seized an Inuk man on Baffin Island in north-eastern Canada. The Inuk, while in his kayak, had been snatched from the water and held on board in the hope of getting back three of Frobisher's men who had been lost, presumed killed or captured by the Inuit. He reached London in October 1576, one 'whose like was never seen nor whose language was understood' (Best, 1.50). 'He was in good shape ... a very broad face and very fat and full his body ... His colour of skin all over a dark sallow, like the tawny Moors or rather Tatar nation, whereof I think he was. His countenance sullen or shurlish and sharp withal' (ibid., 1.166). In anger and frustration over his captivity, the unnamed Inuk severely bit his tongue; from that wound, or perhaps from a disease contracted on the voyage, he died in London two weeks after his arrival. He was then embalmed by the eminent surgeon William Crow (or Clowes), the intention being to return the body to the Inuit; however he was instead buried at St Olave's, Hart Street, London. A portrait for the queen is known to have been executed by a Dutch artist, though the only surviving likeness is a watercolour by Lucas de Heere now in the Rijksuniversiteit te Gent. In 1577 Frobisher took three more captives from Baffin Island: a man named Kalicho at one location and a woman and her infant child at another (called respectively Arnaq and Nutaaq, though the words may have meant woman and child), and carried them to Bristol. **Kalicho** (d. 1577), in a kayak, entertained crowds with his skill at darts but within a month succumbed to lung and brain damage incurred at his capture, and was buried in the town on 8 November. **Arnaq** (d. 1577) died a few days later, probably of measles, and was buried on 12 November; **Nutaaq** (d. 1577) was taken to London for display at the Three Swans Inn but died about a week later, probably of the same disease, and was buried at St Olave's.

English and continental artists created numerous images of the four Baffin Islanders. Most notably the Flemish artist Cornelius Ketel painted all four; John White drew the captives of 1577. Queen Elizabeth acquired two full-length portraits, which were hanging at Hampton Court a decade and a half later. Derivative renderings of the Inuit circulated widely in England and western Europe.

In 1584 the scouting expedition of captains Philip Amadas and Arthur Barlowe to what is now North Carolina, on Walter *Ralegh's behalf, brought back the Algonquians **Manteo** (fl. 1584–1587) and **Wanchese** (fl. 1584–1586). They were lodged in London at Durham House, where Thomas *Harriot taught them English while he learned their Algonquian dialect, and they helped to promote Ralegh's colonizing venture. Both of them accompanied the expedition of 1585 to Roanoke Island, where Manteo served the outpost as an interpreter and guide; Wanchese rejoined his people and opposed English settlement. A year later Manteo went again to England, then returned to Roanoke in 1587 with Ralegh's new colonial effort under John White and was baptized there in August. Accompanying Manteo on that journey was Towaye, also from the Roanoke area, who had probably gone to England in 1586. Another Roanoke Indian, later renamed **Rawly** (d. 1589), was captured by Sir Richard *Grenville in 1586; parish records from Bideford, Devon, show that he was baptized on 27 March 1587 and died there in April 1589.

In 1594 Ralegh sent a scouting expedition to Trinidad and Guiana under Captain Jacob *Whiddon, who returned with several natives. The number of Whiddon's recruits (possibly captives) is uncertain, but it probably included two from Trinidad, including one renamed **John Provost** (fl. 1595–1604), and two from the mainland. In 1595 Sir Walter Ralegh apparently took all four on his first Guiana expedition, with Provost serving as interpreter. Later that year Ralegh carried several Indians to England, including **Cayowaroco** (fl. 1595–1596), son of the local cacique Topiawari, who entrusted the lad to Ralegh. Cayowaroco returned to Guiana after his father's death in 1596. Other Indians who journeyed to England with Whiddon in 1594, Ralegh in 1595, or Lawrence Keymis in 1596

probably included Henry, William, and Martyn (no surname was given for these three), **Leonard Ragapo** (fl. 1595–1600), and **Anthony Canabre** (fl. 1595–1609). All served later English expeditions as interpreters or guides or for liaison with the area's natives.

The impact of these twenty or so Americans on English explorations and on attitudes towards Indians is arguable. Prior to 1584 they were viewed primarily as exotica. A witness of Frobisher's captive of 1576, for example, thought him 'such a wonder onto the whole city [of London] and to the rest of the realm that heard of yt as seemed never to have happened the like great matter to any man's knowledge' (Collinson, 87). But Frobisher had planned to train the adult Inuit as interpreters for future expeditions, much as Ralegh would later employ the Algonquians of the 1580s and the Guianans and Trinidadians of the 1590s. None of these American natives brought great success to England's overseas ventures, but with the exception of Wanchese, they helped rather than hindered English efforts.

Most of the American natives in England after 1584 survived the onslaught of European pathogens and were accepted as more than curiosities. Manteo was treated with considerable respect, at least by Ralegh's circle, during his two sojourns in England, and that seems to have been true also of Rawly and the Indians from Trinidad and Guiana. Some of them returned quickly to their homelands, but others—apparently by choice—extended their stays for many years, the longest resident being Anthony Canabre who stayed for fourteen years. Several, including Rawly, Leonard Ragapo, and Canabre, converted to Anglican Christianity. But modern knowledge of their actions and thoughts comes exclusively from English and other European sources. The travellers left no known records of their perceptions of England and its people, nor of how the experiences abroad influenced their own lives.

ALDEN T. VAUGHAN

Sources R. Hakluyt, *The principal navigations, voyages, traffiques and discoveries of the English nation*, 2nd edn, 3 vols. (1598–1600); repr. 12 vols., Hakluyt Society, extra ser., 1–12 (1903–5) · D. B. Quinn, ed., *The Roanoke voyages, 1584–1590*, 2 vols. (1955) · W. Ralegh, *The discoverie of the large, rich, and bewtiful empyre of Guiana*, ed. N. L. Whitehead (1997) · L. Keymis, *A relation of the second voyage to Guiana* (1596) · R. Harcourt, *A relation of a voyage to Guiana*, 2nd edn, ed. C. A. Harris (1928) · W. C. Sturtevant and D. B. Quinn, 'This new prey: Eskimos in Europe in 1567, 1576, and 1577', *Indians and Europe: an interdisciplinary collection of essays*, ed. C. F. Feest (1987) · R. Collinson, ed., *The three voyages of Martin Frobisher* (1867) · D. B. Quinn, ed., *New American world: a documentary history of North America to 1612*, 5 vols. (1979) · J. A. Williamson, ed., *The Cabot voyages and Bristol discovery under Henry VII* (1962)

Archives BL, Michael Lok (accounting of Frobisher's first voyage), Cotton MS, Otho EVIII · PRO, Cathay Company, financial records

Likenesses engraving (*Frobisher's captives* (1576–1577)), repro. in Sturtevant and Quinn, 'This new prey', 89–91

Amery, John (1912–1945), traitor, was born on 14 March 1912 at 9 Embankment Gardens, Chelsea, London, the elder son (there were no daughters) of Leopold Charles Maurice Stennett *Amery (1873–1955), politician, and his wife, Florence Louise Adeliza (Bryddie; 1885–1975), daughter of John Hamar Greenwood of Whitby, Ontario, and sister of (Thomas) Hamar (first Viscount) Greenwood. At sixteen he ran away from Harrow School, and set up as a film director, work which took him to central Europe and east Africa, but proved financially unrewarding. It combined ill with his taste for fast cars and high life; in 1936 he was declared bankrupt, and settled with his family that he had better live abroad. Two years earlier, experiences in Vienna on the verge of civil war had awakened in him vehement, if premature, anti-communism. Accordingly, he went to Spain when civil war broke out there in July 1936 to take an active part on the insurgent General Franco's side, smuggling arms across the Pyrenees and receiving the Italian medal for valour in action. In 1939 bad health drove him to a sanatorium in French Savoy.

Amery's first marriage (in Athens), which his parents disapproved, to Una Wing had rapidly broken down. He contracted a second, to Jeannine Barde, a Frenchwoman who had plenty of friends at Vichy. She died in April 1944; the following October he married another Frenchwoman, Michelle Thomas. There were no children.

During his gun-running activities Amery had met Jacques Doriot, a renegade French communist who had turned ardent fascist. Doriot summoned him to Paris in the autumn of 1942, convinced him that Germany was going to lose the war unless Great Britain joined against the USSR, and enlisted Amery's aid. For the next eighteen months Amery toured prisoner-of-war camps, seeking to recruit a Legion of St George—unromantically renamed by the Germans the British Free Corps—to fight alongside the Germans against the Russians and save Europe from bolshevism. From thousands of prisoners, thirty men elected to join him; they never went into action. He also broadcast to his fellow countrymen in England, seeking to persuade them to change sides, and gave anti-communist lectures, notably in Oslo and Belgrade.

In April 1945 Amery and his wife were in northern Italy, making for Switzerland, when they were captured by communist partisans. He was handed over to the British army and sent back to England. His brother, (Harold) Julian *Amery (later Lord Amery of Lustleigh), attempted to establish Spanish nationality for him, but failed. He was arraigned on eight counts of treason before Sir Travers Humphreys at the Old Bailey on 28 November 1945. He pleaded guilty, knowing this would mean execution, and was hanged at Wandsworth prison on 19 December 1945 by the famous executioner Albert Pierrepoint.

M. R. D. FOOT, rev.

Sources R. West, *The meaning of treason* (1949) · private information (1993) · M. Scriven, 'Why they hanged Amery's brother', *Evening Standard* (4 Sept 1996) · b. cert.
Likenesses photographs, 1932–c.1936, Hult. Arch.

Amery, (Harold) Julian, Baron Amery of Lustleigh (1919–1996), politician, was born on 27 March 1919 at 3 Embankment Gardens, Chelsea, London, the younger son (there were no daughters) of Leopold Charles Maurice Stennett *Amery (1873–1955), politician, and his wife, Florence

(Harold) Julian Amery, Baron Amery of Lustleigh (1919–1996), by Elliott & Fry, 1951

Louise Adeliza (known as Bryddie) Greenwood (1885–1975), one of ten children of John Hamar Greenwood of Whitby, Ontario, and sister of (Thomas) Hamar Greenwood, first Viscount Greenwood. Amery's father was for many years MP for Birmingham Sparkbrook, and was a close ally of the Chamberlain dynasty founded by Joseph Chamberlain: this friendship made all the more painful his famous (and witheringly effective) attack on the government of Neville Chamberlain in May 1940 in the House of Commons. Amery was, thus, bred to politics. However, after education at Summerfields School, Oxford (1928–32), Eton College (1932–7), and Balliol College, Oxford (1937–9), he joined the army.

Amery's military career—most engagingly described in his autobiography, *Approach March* (1973)—was not highly successful, but it was adventurous, and adventure was something he craved. He was also of a highly romantic disposition, and so in the Balkans favoured the forces of General Mihailovic in Serbia—because they were loyal to the king—and of King Zog in Albania. Unfortunately for Amery, the allied high command, under the influence of their principal operative in the Balkans, Fitzroy Maclean, decided to favour the communists, led by Josip Broz, later to be known to the world as Marshal Tito. After the war Amery was equally unsuccessful in his attempts to shore up the failing regime of General Chiang Kai-shek in China. None of this depressed an ever ebullient spirit, but it did lead him to a lifelong loathing and fear of communism, which he was to express over a long political career.

This career began in 1945, when he unsuccessfully contested the seat of Preston North. He stuck with the constituency, however, and in the general election of 1950 was victorious. He had spent the previous few years writing an account of his wartime experiences in Albania, *Sons of the Eagle* (1948), and the fourth volume of *The Life of Joseph Chamberlain* (1951), the first three volumes of which had been written by J. L. Garvin. On 26 January 1950 he married Catherine (*d*. 1991), younger daughter of a rapidly rising star in Conservative politics, (Maurice) Harold *Macmillan.

Like his father, Amery was an ardent imperialist, but unlike most of his ilk he was also a stout supporter of the nascent European Economic Community. To the end of his life he managed to juggle these positions, at least to his own satisfaction. Though generally regarded as being on the right wing of his party, he differed from his fellows in one other very important respect: he was staunchly opposed to capital punishment. This opposition arose from a particular family tragedy. His elder brother, John *Amery (1912–1945), had been a Nazi collaborator, and was executed on a charge of treason in December 1945. To the end of his own days, Amery believed that his brother had been more naïve than sinister, and that his offences had certainly not merited the death penalty.

In 1954 the Suez group of Conservative MPs was formed: its purpose was to resist the proposal of the government of Sir Anthony Eden to withdraw from the Suez Canal zone. Amery joined the group and became its secretary. When, in 1956, President Nasser of Egypt nationalized the canal, Eden felt constrained to take military action, and Amery was vociferous in his support. The expedition—not least because of American pressure—was a failure, and Eden resigned. This episode had two crucial consequences for Amery. First, it induced an anti-American feeling which reinforced his commitment to Europe. Second, it brought his father-in-law to power (in January 1957) and he was appointed a junior minister at the War Office. In November 1958, however, he was transferred to the Colonial Office, and found himself presiding over the British withdrawal from Cyprus. He justified his position to sceptical friends by saying that, since Cyprus was only a staging post for Suez, and since Britain had lost Suez, there was no point in retaining the island, which could only be done at great military and human cost. He served as secretary of state for air between October 1960 and July 1962, and then became minister for aviation. At that ministry he attracted considerable controversy by his passionate advocacy of the Anglo-French Concorde aircraft. This advocacy—and the considerable expense it entailed—he justified on the grounds that a close alliance between Britain and France was essential to the creation of a strong Europe. None of the posts he had held carried cabinet rank, and he always regretted that he never served in cabinet.

After the Conservative general election defeat of October 1964 Amery's fortunes dimmed. They revived somewhat when, having lost Preston in March 1966, he won Brighton Pavilion at a by-election in March 1969. Meanwhile, he published the last two volumes of *The Life of Joseph Chamberlain* (1969). When Edward Heath won the general election of June 1970, he made Amery successively minister of state at the Ministry of Public Building and Works (June–October 1970), at Housing (October 1970–November 1972), and, finally, at the Foreign Office (November 1972–March 1974). This last choice was interesting, for it showed that the prime minister was prepared to overlook Amery's implacable support for the white government in Rhodesia because of his equally implacable support for Britain's membership of the Common Market. This was to be Amery's last ministerial post. In 1975 Heath was overthrown by Margaret Thatcher, who steadfastly ignored Amery. As it turned out, this was wise of her. After her general election victory in May 1979 she faced a Commonwealth prime ministers' conference in Zambia; so it was natural that the last House of Commons debate before the summer recess would be on Rhodesia, the subject that most preoccupied the Commonwealth. Most Conservatives on the right believed they could trust her to preserve the *status quo*. She made a speech which, while ringing in tone, was opaque in argument. Only Amery saw through it, and deduced that she was prepared to accede to Commonwealth demands for a Rhodesia under black majority rule. He gave his judgement in forthright terms, but it availed him nothing. Effectively, his political career was over.

In 1992 Amery retired from the House of Commons to his splendid house at 112 Eaton Square, Westminster, which his family had occupied since 1924. John Major caused him to be given a life peerage, as Baron Amery of Lustleigh, in 1992. He promised to be active in the House of Lords, but the death of his wife in 1991 and increasing ill health prevented that. He died of heart failure at his home on 3 September 1996, a brave man, who did considerable service to his country, and who was remembered with love by many friends in all parts of the world. He was survived by his four children, (Caroline) Louise Michelle (*b*. 1951), Theresa Catherine Roxanne (*b*. 1954), and twins (*b*. 1956) Leopold Harold Hamar John and (Alexandra) Elizabeth Charmian.   PATRICK COSGRAVE

Sources J. Amery, *Approach march: a venture in autobiography* (1973) • *WWW* • Burke, *Peerage* • *The Times* (4 Sept 1996) • *The Independent* (4 Sept 1996) • *Daily Telegraph* (4 Sept 1996) • *The Guardian* (4 Sept 1996) • d. cert. • *Dod's Parliamentary Companion* (1996) • J. Jones and S. Viney, eds., *The Balliol College register, 1930–1980*, 5th edn (privately printed, Oxford, 1983?)

Archives CAC Cam., corresp. and papers • King's Lond., Liddell Hart C., military corresp. and papers | BLPES, corresp. relating to chairmanship of United Europe movement • Bodl. Oxf., corresp. with Barbara Pym • Bodl. RH, corresp. with Sir. R. R. Welensky • CAC Cam., corresp. with P. G. Buchan-Hepburn • CAC Cam., corresp. with Sir E. L. Spears • HLRO, letters to Beaverbrook • King's Lond., Liddell Hart C., corresp. with Sir B. H. Liddell Hart

Likenesses photographs, 1939–79, Hult. Arch. • Elliott & Fry, photograph, 1951, NPG [*see illus.*] • photograph, repro. in *The Times* • photograph, repro. in *The Independent* • photograph, repro. in *Daily Telegraph* • photograph, repro. in *The Guardian*

Wealth at death £4,375,875: probate, 23 Dec 1996, *CGPLA Eng. & Wales*

Amery, Leopold Charles Maurice Stennett (1873–1955), politician and journalist, was born on 22 November 1873 at Gorakhpur in the North-Western Provinces of India, the eldest of the three sons of Charles Frederick Amery (1833–1901), of Lustleigh in Devon, an official in the Indian forestry commission, and his wife, Elisabeth Johanna Leitner (c.1841–1908), the daughter of Leopold Saphir and Marie Henriette, *née* Herzberg (c.1812–1879), who as a child adopted the name of her stepfather, Johann Moritz Leitner (1800–1861), a physician of Budapest. In 1877 Elisabeth Amery returned from India to Britain, and in 1885 divorced her husband, who took up farming in Canada and had no further contact with his family. Many of Amery's maternal family converted to protestantism and migrated to Britain. His Jewish connections were known, but unremarked, by his contemporaries.

Education and early life Amery's early schooling took place in his aunt's library, and at small schools in Brighton, Cologne, and Folkestone. From 1887 at Harrow School he moved rapidly, taking the top place in the examinations for a number of years, winning scholarships and prizes, and representing the school at gymnastics. It was here that he first encountered Winston Churchill, a taller though junior contemporary, who pushed Amery into the school swimming pool; they were to be associated, in ever varying relationship (as Churchill put it), for the rest of Amery's political life. An exhibitioner at Balliol College, Oxford, in 1892, Amery went on to take first classes in classical moderations (1894) and *literae humaniores* (1896), was *proxime accessit* to the Craven scholar (1894) and Ouseley scholar in Turkish (1896), and won a half-blue in cross-country running. He also had a reputation for rejecting prevailing philosophical and economic orthodoxies.

In 1897 Amery was elected, at the second attempt, to a seven-year fellowship in history at All Souls College, which he actually held until 1912, studying the Austro-Hungarian and Turkish empires and acquiring a working knowledge of fourteen languages. (From 1939 the fellowship was renewed: for the rest of his life the college was his second home.) He joined the staff of *The Times* in 1899, and in covering the build-up to the Second South African War of 1899–1902 was the only correspondent to visit the Boer forces. After narrowly escaping capture with Winston Churchill, he was ordered away from the front to organize the paper's war correspondents. He remained a member of the editorial staff of *The Times* for the next ten years, having been called to the bar at the Inner Temple in 1902.

Commitment to empire In South Africa, Amery had come to regard Alfred Milner with filial devotion. He collaborated with the young men of Milner's staff (the 'Kindergarten') on an occasional basis and was spotted by Milner as a promising unofficial agent for empire in London to research the imperial economy and prepare material for the imperial conferences. Amery's commitment to the empire as 'the final object of patriotic emotion and action' (Amery, *Political Life*, 1.253) assumed the dimensions of a faith, staunchly defended for more than sixty years, and

Leopold Charles Maurice Stennett Amery (1873–1955), by Sir James Gunn, 1942

sustained by a fine mind and (sometimes obdurate) political courage. All Souls, *The Times*, and the patronage of Milner and Joseph Chamberlain gave him contacts and unusual influence, magnified by his appetite and capacity for work.

Over nine years Amery planned, edited, and largely wrote *The Times History of the War in South Africa* (7 vols., 1899–1909), which demonstrated the need for reform of the army and the War Office. After extensive discussions with the army chiefs, he advocated its reorganization in *The Problem of the Army* (1903) and became a forthright lobbyist for compulsory military training and national service. Under the pseudonym Tariff Reformer in *The Times* he attacked free trade, and he followed this with *The Fundamental Fallacies of Free Trade* (1906), which he described as a theoretical blast of economic heresy, including the proposition that the total volume of British trade mattered less than the function of trade in balancing the country's deficiency in raw materials and foodstuffs by the export of its surplus manufacturing, shipping, and financial skill. This analysis underlay Amery's lifelong drive for partnership with the empire's primary producers.

In 1910 Amery married Florence Louise Adeliza (Bryddie) Greenwood (1885–1975), the daughter of John Hamar Greenwood of Whitby, Ontario, and the sister of Hamar (later Viscount) Greenwood, a barrister and Liberal MP. They had two sons, John *Amery (1912–1945) and (Harold) Julian *Amery (1919–1996), and from 1924 lived in Eaton Square, London, in a large family house which seemed unchanging to those who came to know it over two generations.

Conservative politics Amery turned down the editorships of *The Observer* (1908) and *The Times* (1912) for politics and the struggle for a winnable seat. With the help of the Chamberlain connection he was adopted for the safe seat of South Birmingham (later Sparkbrook), where he was returned unopposed in May 1911. He held the seat until 1945, with his priorities largely unchanged—to persuade the Conservative Party to adopt a policy of economic and social progress rather than negative anti-socialism; and, for the Commonwealth, to insist on freedom and equality as the condition for effective unity, to be maintained and developed by the indispensable element of economic co-operation. Tariff reform came to have many different meanings for Conservatives; Amery was one of its central economic theorists, linking it to imperial consolidation over the vicissitudes of fifty years. He considered political federation of the empire, as advocated by Lionel Curtis, with whom Amery collaborated in the Round Table movement, both impractical and unhistorical. Union would evolve through co-operation and personal contact. Clear principles should be debated in new imperial institutions modelled on the committee of imperial defence, and each country left to reconcile them with popular consent and public opinion in its own way. (He was later to advance a similar strategy for India and for European union.)

Amery's diaries, kept more or less continuously from 1910 until his death, are a unique record of a Conservative who represented the imperialist wing of the party for forty years. With gusto, and something of a taste and reputation for intrigue, he threw himself into the thick of political controversy on the right wing of his party. In January 1914 he proposed a British covenant pledged to resist the coercion of Ulster. He served on the joint parliamentary committee investigating the Marconi scandal, and travelled to the southern hemisphere dominions with the first Empire Parliamentary Association in 1913.

In the First World War, Amery served as an intelligence officer in Flanders and then, on the strength of his languages, in the Balkans, Gallipoli, and Salonika. His analysis then would have held as good for him twenty years later:

> Our political object is the defence and welfare of the British Empire. … We are not a part of Europe. This war against a German domination in Europe was only necessary because we had failed to make ourselves sufficiently strong and united as an empire to be able to disregard the European balance. … We have got to get back to a British point of view. (Amery to Milner, 25 May 1915, Bodl. Oxf., MSS Milner, 350/142)

With Milner's patronage, in 1916 he was appointed assistant secretary to Maurice Hankey at the war cabinet secretariat, where he played a significant role in the successful experiment of dominion participation in an imperial cabinet and war conference, and in the creation of the Supreme Allied War Council. Amery's view of Britain's world role emphasized the Middle East as the link between the African and Asian empires and the southern dominions—essentially, 'the British geo-political system that endured until the crack-up at Suez in 1956' (Louis, 68). He was a lifelong Zionist—a supporter of the creation of the state of Israel, having drafted the agreed text of the Balfour declaration (1917) giving effect to a Jewish national home in Palestine, not as a nationalist state but one where (on the analogy of Canada) vigorous but mutually tolerant Jewish, non-Jewish, and Arab national cultures would co-exist with equal rights.

In 1919 Amery was appointed as Milner's parliamentary under-secretary at the Colonial Office. His scheme of land settlement and assisted empire migration (enacted in the Empire Settlement Act) showed his capacity for constructive thought and achievement on a limited budget. When Milner resigned in 1921, Amery was appointed parliamentary and financial secretary to the Admiralty, where he defended the ending of the Anglo-Japanese alliance while privately deploring the tripartite naval agreement between Britain, the United States, and Japan. He was prominent in 'the revolt of the under-secretaries' which played its part in ending Lloyd George's coalition, acting as a vigorous spokesman for the junior ministers at their meeting with Austen Chamberlain on 16 October 1922.

Admiralty and Colonial Office Amery achieved cabinet office when Bonar Law appointed him first lord of the Admiralty in October 1922. A tenacious defender of naval strength and autonomy, he presided over planning the complex Singapore naval base for the use of the fleet in the Far East. He played a significant role in the choice of Baldwin to succeed Law, and in persuading the Conservative leadership that the solution to Britain's industrial and unemployment problems lay in safeguarding British industry from unfair competition and stimulating a common market of the empire by reciprocal preferences. Like most of his colleagues, he was sceptical of Baldwin's impetuous decision to call an election on the issue prematurely in 1923. The election was lost, Amery believed, because the case had never been properly formulated or explained: he was instrumental in setting up a small policy secretariat (the forerunner of the Conservative Research Department) as a remedy.

Baldwin gave Amery the colonial secretaryship from 1924 to 1929, the office he coveted and which he held for long enough to record real achievements. Despite the constraints imposed by Churchill at the exchequer, a policy of colonial development was established—modest in scope, with the creation of an empire marketing board and a new co-ordinated agricultural research service for the colonies. Settler-led development at this time was accepted in Palestine, where Amery insisted on equal rights for all communities; in East Africa, by contrast, his support for white settler government was resisted as a breach of trusteeship obligations to Africans and Indians. In 1925 the achievement of Amery's long-projected institution of a separate Dominions Office with quasi-diplomatic status marked his determination to resolve the anomalies between theory and practice in the dominion relationship (from June 1925 to June 1929 he held the secretaryship of state for the dominions concurrent with the colonial secretaryship).

At the imperial conference of 1926 the final formula squaring dominion independence with Commonwealth unity was Balfour's, but much of the background thinking was Amery's. Yet the symbolism of Commonwealth was less important to Amery than its practical functioning as a strong British imperial economic and strategic unit, and he declared his intention to move in 1928 to a policy on empire trade with or without his colleagues. As the first colonial secretary to tour all the dominions, sitting with the various cabinets and (as he put it) 'quickening the consciousness of Empire' in more than 300 speeches (published as *The Empire in the New Era*, 1928), he believed he had 'strengthened my personal equipment in fact and in public esteem for tackling the really big job' (*Amery Diaries*, 1.529, 3 Feb 1928). He found little support from his colleagues.

Amery later argued that a cabinet of overworked ministers 'is quite incapable of either thinking out a definite policy, or of securing its effective and consistent execution' (*Thoughts on the Constitution*, 1946, 86). Few, if any, in the cabinet had his versatility and breadth of experience of the world, but he did not command commensurate influence. Contemporaries maintained that he was ineffective in discussion, speaking too often and for too long, the inherent interest of his content diminished by the unvarying pace and pitch of his delivery; it was said that he might have been prime minister had he been half a head taller and his speeches half an hour shorter. His face would carry the unchanging half-smile of a Buddha as he spoke in perfectly constructed sentences which somehow lacked edge. On occasions he appeared resolutely independent. No place was found for him in the governments of the 1930s; in any case, his inclusion would not have found favour among Labour members of the coalition. He alluded to this elliptically in his autobiography, with the hope that it might have

> its encouraging aspect [for younger men], in so far as it shows what appreciable results can be achieved even by an unknown young man, provided he knows what he wants done, and is well content that the actual doing and the credit should rest with others.   (Amery, *Political Life*, 1.14)

The copious detail of his diaries recorded a version of events that did not hesitate to explain his own role fully. He never bore grudges, and would easily shrug off disappointments by escaping from Westminster to climb a mountain. (Three were named in his honour.) Lord Brand later said of him, 'What courage and what simplicity and what strength, physical and other. He was all of one piece' (Brand to Bryddie Amery, 4 Dec 1955, CAC Cam., MSS Amery 454/2). He was also the last—and perhaps the only—privy councillor to knock another member to the floor of the House of Commons on a matter of honour.

The locust years On the back benches, Amery kept in political trim with sustained, purposeful activity—at first experimenting with fiction (*The Stranger of the Ulysses*, 1934), then updating the case for empire (*The Forward View*, 1935), and familiarizing himself with aircraft production and air defence, strategic raw materials, supply. In 1932 he rejoiced that tariff reform had at last been adopted as a policy; the imperial element would follow. He attended the Ottawa conference in a minor advisory capacity only, a

chained Prometheus who was acknowledged as one of the few people to understand the preference problem, but whose discussions with the dominion representatives were interpreted by his party colleagues as obstructive intrigue.

In the international confusions and dangers of the 1930s Amery has been absolved from the taint of appeasement. It is perhaps more accurate to say that he was deeply sceptical of idealistic internationalism and disarmament, of the League of Nations and later the United Nations, and took his stand on realities as he saw them: Britain had no further interest in Europe than to see peace and stability; the empire was over-committed, unable to face a challenge from both Germany and Japan together; America, inherently opposed to British protection and imperial economic consolidation, was at best an uncertain ally. The few cards Britain held must therefore be played to maximum advantage. Amery was sufficiently pragmatic to acknowledge that dominion self-government would ultimately come to India, placing strain on the 'frontier empire' from the Middle East to Afghanistan. The eastern Mediterranean was a weak link, but would be secure if Italy could be wooed from commitment to Germany, despite the invasion of Abyssinia. Germany might be given elbow room in eastern Europe, short of Yugoslavia and the Balkans, but there must be no surrender of colonies.

The fall of Austria and the Czechoslovak crisis in 1938 made it clear that Britain's involvement in Europe could not, after all, be avoided. Amery abstained in the Munich debate, torn between war and an ignominious peace; decision came in December when he analysed the facts of the military, naval, and air position. From then on he was committed to gearing the country for war, working with Churchill (their third war, he remarked) to press for a national government and war cabinet and then to harass the government on the conduct of the war. The moment for which he is best remembered came in the debate on the invasion of Norway on 7 May 1940. Speaking with the authority of a former first lord of the Admiralty and the advantage of a Birmingham political background, and sensing the sympathy of the house, he quoted Cromwell's injunction to the Long Parliament: 'Depart, I say, and let us have done with you. In the name of God, go' (*Hansard 5C*, vol. 360, 1940, col. 1150). The effect was annihilating. On the following day the government lost a division of the house; Neville Chamberlain resigned.

Amery, Churchill, and India Throughout their political lives, Amery and Churchill had seldom seen eye to eye—whether over free trade, the gold standard, naval strength, the empire, or America. Above all they diverged on Indian self-government, which Churchill passionately opposed. Amery had hoped to return to high office in defence or economic policy, and was deeply disappointed by Churchill's offer of the India Office—a position defined as cabinet rank minister outside the war cabinet—though he was to serve on the strategic Middle East and Indian committees. The Indian portfolio grew in importance and challenge as the struggle for Indian self-determination, and the danger of civil war between the Indian National

Congress and the Muslim League, interacted with the vital war role of the Indian army in the Middle and Far East. Amery entered office determined to cut through the uncertainties that beset the Government of India Act of 1935. The survival of the empire depended on the Indian war effort; India needed a resolute policy, consistently applied. He demanded the maximum expansion of Indian troops and production, proposing to reciprocate with a clear-cut statement promising Indian self-government, with a home-made constitution, at the end of the war.

The relationship between prime minister and secretary of state got off to a bad start and continued stormily. Churchill did not hide his mistrust of Amery, and demanded he modify his 'revolutionary' policy; Amery admired Churchill as a war leader sufficiently to comply, but otherwise regarded him as an incorrigible whig and resented his unprecedented interventions in the affairs of the department. Often goaded to the brink of resignation by what he called Winstonian harangues, he stuck to his post at the cost of his own health, tenacious rather than adroit, defending the authority of frustrated viceroys before a cabinet that did not scruple to override them, confronting Churchill and conciliating him by turns, endlessly redrafting documents in his own hand in the attempt to find a constructive way forward. Colleagues in the office remembered his tireless presence, his diminutive frame perched on a tall stool, adjusting his spectacles like an old man but with a very young mind that illumined new aspects of a question.

Amery personally prevented Linlithgow from banning the Indian National Congress and dissuaded Churchill from seeing India for himself. In order to secure Muslim support against the advancing Japanese after the fall of Singapore, Amery introduced the possibility of local secession from an Indian dominion into the terms authorized for the Cripps mission in 1942, thus inadvertently laying the basis for partition, which he deplored. He engineered Wavell's appointment as viceroy. While he agreed with the progressive Indianization of the viceroy's council and its evolution to something like a cabinet, his instincts were conservative: he would not dilute the powers of the viceroy and held no brief for the tactics of the Indian political parties; he deplored 'the internationalist tripe which has, of necessity perhaps, been talked during the war' (*Amery Diaries*, 2.864); he opposed concessions to Gandhi on hunger strike. He battled in cabinet, having to fight his corner even over the need to relieve the Bengal famine and to forestall the repudiation of Britain's wartime indebtedness to India.

In the hope of a dramatic gesture to break the deadlock caused, Amery believed, by nationalism and India's sense of subjection, he amended his original proposal: India should acquire full independence on the basis of her existing constitution on VE- (or VJ-) day, with the viceroy's powers reserved to prevent the Hindus on his council overriding the Muslims—'a superficially daring but really cautious and practical policy' (*Amery Diaries*, 2.1023). The interest of the plan lay in the fact that it did not presuppose (or rule out) a Westminster-style democracy for India.

It found no favour and was never put to the cabinet, although Amery believed the formula might have averted partition, and that his proposal later influenced Mountbatten's tactics. Thereafter he backed Wavell's plan for a conference of Indian leaders, but left office with the Indian question deadlocked after the Simla conference of June 1945 broke up over Jinnah's insistence that the Muslim members of the proposed executive council be drawn exclusively from the membership of the Muslim League.

Out of parliament In the landslide election of 1945 Amery lost Sparkbrook. He described the Conservative Party's election campaign as 'sordid': 'unless [the party] recovers an ideal and a method it will never again enthuse the country' (*Amery Diaries*, 2.1047, 1049). In the same year he was appointed Companion of Honour, having refused the offer of a peerage to leave the way open for his son Julian's parliamentary career. In October 1945 the Amery family faced the trial and execution for treason of John Amery, the elder son. His father afterwards circulated a pamphlet among friends, 'John Amery: an explanation'. Though a man of strong feelings and capable of deep affection, Amery was never demonstrative. His family life was unusually close, Julian's family living in the Eaton Square house, and father and son sharing a study. Bryddie's health gave way; his friends remarked on the extraordinary fortitude that enabled Leo to carry on apparently as before. At the age of seventy-one he could find election defeat rejuvenating, and hoped to find a new seat. He was to be seen on the platform of every Conservative Party conference, the conscience of the party, encouraging and gently directing youthful aspirants such as Peter Walker and Alan Lennox-Boyd, much as Milner had educated him. As late as 1948 he could still announce, 'We have got to be quite clear about it. Empire Preference is a foundation for our whole economic life' (Goldsworthy, 170). But according to his son Julian he came to accept that the analysis he had in the first place adopted from Joseph Chamberlain—the need for a wider area of trade and investment—might in some senses be met by the move into the European Economic Community.

In the twentieth century few, if any, British politicians who built their careers round a vision of a consolidated empire or Commonwealth gained recognition at the highest level, Amery among them. But Westminster had never bounded his life. In public he could seem austere; in private he was stimulating and lively company. He was a skilled mountaineer and skier (and wrote about his experiences in *Days of Fresh Air* [1939] and *In the Rain and the Sun*, 1946), and served as president of the Classical Association, the Alpine Club, and the Ski Club of Great Britain. He read and wrote prodigiously—from a treatise arguing that Goliath's Philistines were the remnants of Agamemnon's expeditionary force (*The Times*, 23 Nov 1973) to his stimulating and influential analysis of the constitution delivered in 1946 as the Chichele lectures in All Souls ('Thoughts on the Constitution'), commemorated there fifty years later as of enduring relevance. He produced four volumes of memoirs (three of which were published as *My Political Life*) and a stream of other works, on international trade, the balanced economy, and Britain's role between the Commonwealth and a more closely united Europe. He had served from 1919 on the Rhodes Trust (becoming chairman in 1933), where he had used his influence to bring research into closer relation with policy through the Beit, Smuts, and Rhodes chairs in imperial history that he had helped to found in Oxford, Cambridge, and London universities, as well as the Chichele chair of military history at All Souls. Balliol, his old college, rewarded him with an honorary fellowship. He died in London on 16 September 1955. On 22 November 1973 Julian Amery commemorated the hundredth anniversary of his father's birth with a dinner attended, as Isaiah Berlin put it, by 'some of those splendid pillars of the past, whose like, I suspect, we may never see again' (Berlin to Julian Amery, 26 Nov 1973, CAC Cam., MSS Julian Amery 578/1). DEBORAH LAVIN

Sources L. S. Amery, *My political life*, 3 vols. (1953–5) · *The Leo Amery diaries*, ed. J. Barnes and D. Nicholson, 2 vols. (1980–88) · W. R. Louis, *In the name of God, go! Leo Amery and the British empire in the age of Churchill* (1992) · D. Dilks, *Neville Chamberlain*, 1: 1869–1929 (1984) · P. Williamson, *National crisis and national government: British politics, the economy and empire, 1926–1932* (1992) · K. Middlemas and J. Barnes, *Baldwin: a biography* (1969) · J. Ramsden, *The age of Balfour and Baldwin, 1902–1940* (1978) · S. Constantine, *The making of British colonial development policy* (1984) · G. Rizvi, *Linlithgow and India* (1978) · R. J. Moore, *Churchill, Cripps and India* (1979) · D. Goldsworthy, *Colonial issues in British politics* (1971) · J. Ramsden, *The age of Churchill and Eden, 1940–1957* (1995) · *Baffy: the diaries of Blanche Dugdale, 1936–47*, ed. N. A. Rose (1973) · W. Rubenstein, 'The secret of Leopold Amery', *Historical Research*, 73 (2000), 175–96 · private information (2004) [Lord Walker, Sir Edward Forde, John Grigg, Sir Roger Cary] · W. R. Louis, 'Leo Amery and the post-war world, 1945–55', *Journal of Imperial and Commonwealth History*, 30 (2002), 71–90

Archives CAC Cam., corresp. and papers · LPL, corresp. and papers, incl. some relating to son's conversion to Orthodoxy | All Souls Oxf., letters to Sir William Anson · BL, corresp. with Lord Cecil · BL, corresp. with Arthur James Balfour · BL, corresp. with Lord Jellicoe · BL, corresp. with Lord Northcliffe · BL OIOC, corresp. with Sir Reginald Dorman-Smith · BLPES, letters to Violet Markham · BLPES, corresp. with Tariff Commission · BLPES, corresp. with Lady Rhys Williams · Bodl. Oxf., corresp. with Lionel Curtis · Bodl. Oxf., corresp. with Geoffrey Dawson · Bodl. Oxf., corresp. with H. A. Gwynne · Bodl. Oxf., letters to Lady Milner · Bodl. Oxf., letters to Lord Milner · Bodl. Oxf., corresp. with Lord Monckton · Bodl. Oxf., corresp. with Lord Selborne · Bodl. Oxf., corresp. with Lord Simon · Bodl. RH, corresp. with Sir Robert Coryndon · Bodl. RH, corresp. with Lord Lugard · Bodl. RH, corresp. with Joseph Oldham · Bodl. RH, corresp. with Charles Walker · CAC Cam., corresp. with Ernest Bevin · CAC Cam., corresp. with Sir Henry Page Croft · CUL, corresp. with Sir Samuel Hoare · Durham RO, corresp. with Lord and Lady Londonderry · HLRO, corresp. with Lord Beaverbrook · HLRO, letters to Andrew Bonar Law · HLRO, corresp. with David Lloyd George · HLRO, corresp. with Herbert Samuel · JRL, corresp. with Sir Claude Auchinleck · King's Lond., Liddell Hart C., corresp. with Sir Basil Liddell Hart · Lpool RO, corresp. with Lord Derby · NA Scot., corresp. with Lord Lothian · NAM, letters to Lord Roberts · NL Aus., letters to Alfred Deakin · NL Aus., corresp. with Lord Novar · NL Scot., corresp. with John Buchan [copies] · Nuffield Oxf., corresp. with Lord Cherwell · U. Birm. L., corresp. with Mrs Neville Chamberlain · U. Leeds, Brotherton L., corresp. with Henry Drummond-Wolff · U. Lond., Institute of Commonwealth Studies, corresp. with Richard Jebb · U. Warwick Mod. RC, letters to Sir Leslie Scott | FILM BFI NFTVA, *A tour of the dominions by the Right-Hon. L. S. Amery,* M.P., 1928; documentary footage; news footage; propaganda footage · IWM FVA, actuality footage · IWM FVA, news footage | SOUND IWM SA, recorded lecture

Likenesses D. Low, pencil drawing, 1928, NPG · J. Gunn, oils, 1942, NPG [*see illus.*] · C. Beaton, double portrait, photograph, 1944 (with Lady Amery), NPG · C. Beaton, photograph, 1944, NPG · S. Elwes, oils, *c.*1954, Bodl. RH · H. Coster, photographs, NPG · T. Cottrell, cigarette card, NPG · J. Gunn, oils, second version, Bodl. RH · oils, Balliol Oxf. · oils, All Souls Oxf.

Wealth at death £8820 8*s.* 9*d.*: probate, 7 Nov 1955, *CGPLA Eng. & Wales*

Ames, Jeremiah (1706–1776), banker and merchant, was born on 20 July 1706 at Evercreech, near Shepton Mallet, Somerset, one of eight children of Levi Ames (*d.* 1726), grocer, and his first wife, Hannah (*d.* 1711), daughter of John Watts of Doulting, Somerset. Ames was one of four brothers; he also had four sisters. Until his father's death in 1726, he worked as his apprentice in the grocery trade, acquiring the basic commercial skills which were to stand him in such good stead in later years. He was married to Phoebe Collins, the seventh of ten children of Robert Collins of Horton, near Ilminster, Somerset, probably around 1730. Together they had four sons and three daughters. From the 1730s onwards Ames was increasingly involved with the commercial, civic, and religious life of the city of Bristol, where he lived for many years at 17 Lower Maudlin Lane.

Ames was chiefly known as one of the six founding partners of the Harford Bank, the fourth oldest private banking house in Bristol, established in 1769. However, his interest in banking developed relatively late in life and no doubt stemmed directly from his long-standing commercial interests in Bristol and its hinterland. Indeed his business activities closely mirrored the diverse economy of the expanding metropolis of the west. Ames was active in sugar baking and refining, the manufacture of snuff and tobacco, gunpowder making, and dealing in iron goods; he also had extensive interests in shipping. He was a co-founder of the Bristol Fire Office, which underwrote fire insurance for domestic and commercial property and goods. Ames himself had extensive property interests, including mills, warehouses, and a considerable number of properties for private rental in Bristol. Together with his brother Samuel, he inherited land and property in and around Shepton Mallet.

Ames spent a lifetime serving the city of Bristol in a variety of civic capacities. For many years an alderman, he was elected sheriff of the city on 29 September 1742 and on 15 September 1759 was chosen as mayor. The high regard for the probity of his business dealings and the execution of his official duties no doubt stemmed, in part, from his involvement in nonconformist religious society, notably the Unitarian church.

Ames died in Bristol on 3 April 1776, aged sixty-nine, and was survived by his wife. An obituary notice in *Felix Farley's Bristol Journal* (6 April 1776) noted:

> Wednesday morning died Jeremiah Ames, Esq; Alderman of this city. His inviolable integrity in his commercial and judicial capacity rendered him a valuable member of society. And his domestic virtues endearing him to his relatives,

oblige them to lament their loss, and to venerate his memory.

He was buried shortly afterwards in the dissenting burial-ground, Brunswick Square, Bristol. The chief beneficiary of his complex legacy was his eldest surviving son, **Levi Ames** (*bap.* 1739, *d.* 1820), banker and merchant, whose life and career closely mirrored those of his father. He lived next door at 15 Lower Maudlin Lane and was a partner in the bank of Ames, Cave & Co. between 1786 and 1820. He was elected sheriff of Bristol in 1771 and became mayor in 1788. Ames was twice married: first, in 1770, to Anna Maria Poole, and later to a woman whose name was probably Elizabeth Wraxhall. He died on 16 December 1820.   IAIN S. BLACK

Sources C. H. Cave, *A history of banking in Bristol from 1750 to 1899* (privately printed, Bristol, 1899) · L. Tantum, *The Ames family and the divorce that shocked Bristol* (privately printed, Bristol, 1983) · *Felix Farley's Bristol Journal* (6 April 1776) · PRO, PROB 11/1054, sig. 283 · H. St V. Ames, 'Pedigrees and genealogical notes re: Ames, Lyde and related families', Bristol RO, MS 28591 34a and b · Unitarian birth registers, Bristol RO, FC 39461/R/1(a)1, FC 39461/R/2(a)6
Wealth at death £70,000: Cave, *History of banking* · £18,415 cash bequests: will, PRO, PROB 11/1054

Ames, Joseph (1619–1695), naval officer, was born at Great Yarmouth on 5 March 1619, the son of John Ames (*c.*1577–1647). Bred to the sea, Ames appears to have played no part in the civil war but he shared the puritan sentiments strong in the town and on 18 February 1647 was admitted to the congregationalist church led by William Bridge. Seven children born to Ames and his wife, Margaret, were baptized into the church between 1647 and 1656. Ames was drawn into naval service by the First Anglo-Dutch War (1652–4). Arriving back in England in January 1653 from a trading voyage to Barbados with a cargo of sugar, he was appointed to command the hired merchantman *Samuel Talbot*, which carried thirty guns. He served in John Lawson's squadron at the Gabbard in June, and played an important role in the battle off the Texel on 2 July, being awarded a gold medal by parliament for his service in saving the *Triumph*, the beleaguered flagship, from being fired. In recognition of his services against the Dutch he was appointed to the newly built *Winsby*, which he commanded continuously from 1654 to 1660. In 1655 he convoyed the fishing fleets to Newfoundland, bringing home a young deer as a present to Cromwell from the governor of Providence, New England. In 1656 he served with Robert Blake and Edward Mountagu on their expedition to Spain, and he remained on station with Blake to maintain the blockade through the winter. On 20 April 1657 the *Winsby* was one of the twelve ships selected for Richard Stayner's daring attack on the Spanish plate fleet at Santa Cruz in the Canaries, which resulted in the destruction of the Spanish force, though much of the treasure it carried had already been taken ashore. In spring 1659 Ames commanded the *Winsby* in Mountagu's expedition to the Baltic to protect English interests in the Swedish-Danish war and to deter Dutch intervention. In May 1660 Mountagu regarded him as sufficiently dependable to join the fleet which brought Charles II back to England, and a few weeks later he was sent to escort a convoy to the Sound.

Though Ames does not appear to have been politically militant the Restoration ended his naval career, for he was laid aside later in 1660 when he refused to take the oaths of allegiance and supremacy. He returned home to Yarmouth, where the family lived for many years in Middlegate Street, and resumed his mercantile career. After the death of his first wife he married again, and with his second wife, Ruth, had another son, who was baptized in the congregationalist church in 1663. Many of the letters which Ames, as master and part-owner of the *Return*, sent between 1663 and 1674 to the London agent of the consortium of owners have survived, documenting his commercial ventures to Newcastle and further afield to France and Italy. Sometimes he commanded the vessel, at others he hired a master. In one he sent his regards to Mr [William] Bridge, the former minister at Yarmouth, and another, in 1665, records that his family had moved to Gorleston, just outside Yarmouth. On retiring from the sea, probably about 1674, Ames is said to have established a brewery. He died at Yarmouth in December 1695.   BERNARD CAPP

Sources *CSP dom.*, 1652–60 · B. Capp, *Cromwell's navy: the fleet and the English revolution, 1648–1660* (1989) · C. J. Palmer, *The perlustration of Great Yarmouth*, 3 vols. (1872–5) · 'Baptisms and deaths recorded in the church book of the Great Yarmouth Independent Church, 1643–1705', *A miscellany*, ed. P. Millican, Norfolk RS, 22 (1951) · S. R. Gardiner and C. T. Atkinson, eds., *Letters and papers relating to the First Dutch War, 1652–1654*, 5, Navy RS, 41 (1912) · letters of Joseph Ames, 1663–74, BL, Add. MS 57491 · Thurloe, *State papers*, vol. 7 · J. R. Powell, *Robert Blake: general-at-sea* (1972) · *DNB*
Archives BL, letters, Add. MS 57491 · PRO, letters, SP 18

Ames, Joseph (1689–1759), bibliographer and antiquary, was born of a seafaring family in Great Yarmouth, Norfolk, on 23 January 1689. He was the son of John Ames (1651–1699?), master in the merchant service, and his wife, Esther (*d.* 1712?). The family moved to Wapping, where Joseph went to school. His father died when he was twelve years old, and he was apprenticed to a plane maker in King's Street, near Guildhall, London, but there is no record of his taking up his freedom. He set up as a ship's chandler and ironmonger in Wapping, near or in the Hermitage, where he lived and traded for the rest of his life. He married Mary Wrayford (*bap.* 1683, *d.* 1734), daughter of William Wrayford, a merchant in Bow Lane, and his wife, Ann, at St Botolph without Bishopsgate on 12 April 1714. Of the six children born to the couple, only one daughter, Mary, survived. She lived with her father for the rest of his life.

Some time before 1720 Ames attended the lectures of Dr John Theosophilus Desaguliers, a leader in the field of experimental philosophy and the inventor of the planetarium. There the Revd John Russel, preacher at St John-at-Wapping, introduced Ames to Peter, later Sir Peter, Thompson, merchant and antiquary, and to the Revd John Lewis, antiquary and vicar in Margate. All four men had connections with Thompson's home town of Poole in Dorset. They discussed the history of English printing, and Lewis put his extensive notes for a history of printing at Ames's disposal in the hope that he would continue the work. Ames lent Lewis examples of early title-pages, and they did their best to promote each other's books. Thompson was their Maecenas, encouraging them and helping to finance publication of Lewis's history of Thanet. Ames took a stock of the *History of Thanet*, of which eighteen copies were left when he died; the bookseller Thomas Payne of Round Court, who, with Ames's help, had bought all Lewis's books shortly before his death in 1746, purchased the six copies remaining at the posthumous sale of Ames's library.

In 1736 Ames was admitted fellow of the Society of Antiquaries, and from 1741 he was its secretary, from 1754 with the Revd William Norris as assistant secretary. When, in 1743, he was elected to the Royal Society, he wrote delightedly to make Lewis 'a partaker of [his] joy in being chosen a ffellow' (Lewis to Ames, 9 Feb 1743, BL). It may be significant that Ames only once contributed to the Thursday meetings of the Society of Antiquaries. He seems to have felt ill at ease with some of the grander fellows, and complained of a lack of interest and support for his researches: 'I assure you though I am in the midst of antiquaries they are so great men and their time so took up by the Gay World etc that one can't have that benefit from 'em one might expect or they be willing to give' (Ames to Ballard, c.1740, Bodl. Oxf.). Yet he had a wide circle of correspondents, some being fellows of the Society of Antiquaries and Royal Society. They included, as well as Lewis and Thompson, George Ballard, Dr Ducarel, Thomas Martin of Palgrave, Samuel Pegge the elder, Thomas Rawlinson, and William Oldys, Norroy king of arms. He supplied news of the concerns of the Society of Antiquaries, and the correspondents discussed their antiquarian and bibliographical research. He and Ballard corresponded from 1730 until the latter's death in 1755, and Ames continued to write to Ballard's son in much the same terms thereafter. He visited Ballard in Oxford and helped him in the publication of his study of *Some Learned Ladies of Great Britain*.

Ames combined visits to friends in the country with use of their libraries whenever he could. In the summer of 1755 he 'resorted to Poole to my good friend Sir Peter Thompson' (Ames to Ballard, 8 Nov 1755, Bodl. Oxf.). He made many trips to Oxford to use the Bodleian, and also to Cambridge to use the public library (now the University Library). Other private libraries open to him were those of John Anstis the younger and Sir Hans Sloane. When James West invited him to his seat in Ascot on his way to Oxford in 1752 he told Ballard that 'This is a temptation to one that loves rambling and very much desires to see … many old friends at Oxford' (Ames to Ballard, 14 March 1752, Bodl. Oxf.).

Ames was invited to be a trustee of the British Museum but declined, explaining to Samuel Pegge:

As to my being one of the persons appointed to take care of the British Museum I thought at first that it would have been a good thing, and agreeable to me. And which I am apt to think was also the mind of Sir Hans, when he made me one of his Trustees [of his will] … but when, after our great men thought fit to purchase it, they also thought fit to put in whom they pleased. Fit or not fit, I think never entered their thoughts, but how to shew or declare their power … so that

such company as are these I am as well pleased to be without.   (Ames to Pegge, 28 April 1757, BL)

Ames had intended to leave a great part of his own collection to the museum but explained, 'now my mind is so changed, that no publick body what so ever shall if I can prevent it ever be the better for any part of it as I find none is bestowed by the Publick bodies' (ibid.). The irony is that Ames's large collection of title-pages eventually went to the British Museum (collection now in the BL). The bookseller Mileson Hingeston acquired it after Ames's death and donated it to the museum after he left off business in 1778.

Ames formed what he termed his 'museum' of title-pages and stray leaves as specimens of early printing and a record of printers' marks. Such collecting was a fashionable eighteenth-century pastime and was considered a laudable way of saving printed matter for posterity; but a hundred years later William Blades denounced the 'biblioclasts who went about the country, from library to library, tearing away title pages from rare books of all sizes' (*The Enemies of Books*, 1896). John Bagford was the chief object of Blades's wrath, but he also blamed Ames, not realizing that Ames took most of the leaves from defective copies of books, saving them from destruction and often making use of them to complete imperfect copies. Ames, by his own admission, rescued 'from the flames a number of title pages in danger of destruction' (Ames to Ballard, 20 May 1734, Bodl. Oxf.). He described how he saved Thomas Hearne's library from dispersal and loss, and he and Ballard together managed to salvage the unpublished writings of the leading Anglo-Saxon scholars William and Elizabeth Elstob.

Ames also made a large collection of engraved portraits, following another fashion of the day, of which he made use in his *Catalogue of English heads, or, An account of about two thousand prints describing what is particular on each* (1747). For each subject he listed the 'name, title, or office of the person, the habit, posture, age or time when done, the name of the painter, graver, scraper etc, and some remarkable particulars relating to their lives' (preface). The Bible in English was another object of Ames's interests as a collector; he compiled a list which was later enlarged by Andrew Ducarel, Lambeth librarian, and published as *A list of various editions of the Bible and parts thereof in English, from the year 1526 to 1776, from a MS … much enlarged and improved* in 1777.

Thus Ames had plenty of material for a history of printing, including not only his own collections but also Lewis's notes passed on to him for that very purpose; but he was inhibited by others who were at work in the field. John Bagford too had collected specimens of printing with a view to writing a history, and the printer Samuel Palmer was halfway through a *General History of Printing* at the time of his death. During Palmer's lifetime Ames was unwilling to compete with him, for Palmer's knowledge of the practice of printing far outdid his own, and for many years he refused to put pen to paper despite being strongly urged by Lewis, Thompson, and others. Then Palmer died suddenly, leaving his work unfinished; it was taken over by George Psalmanazar—'the false Formosan'—a hack writer who knew nothing of the matter. When Psalmanazar's work came out in 1732 it turned out to be so inadequate and inaccurate that Ames relented and set to work on his own history, which was to be issued on subscription, the customary eighteenth-century way of defraying the cost of printing. During the next seventeen years he sent many a letter of apology to those who wrote with thinly disguised impatience enquiring when the work, to which they had subscribed, was going to appear.

At last, in 1749, two years too late for Lewis to see it, came Ames's *Typographical antiquities, being an historical account of printing in England, with some memoirs of our antient printers, and a register of the books printed by them, from the year 1471 to 1600, with an appendix concerning printing in Scotland and Ireland at the same time*. It was intended as an aid to book collectors: Ames was at pains to go back to source, 'for I did not chuse to copy into my book from catalogues, but from the books themselves', and he gave accurate transcripts of title-pages. This would also 'enable gentlemen to complete their antient books, which often are imperfect at the beginning, or end, by copying from this' (preface). The frontispiece, a collage of early printers' devices, could be used to identify defective copies, and the engraved portraits which head many of the biographical entries also served as visual aids. Ames:

> endeavoured to make my book as useful as I could, by shewing the rise, progress, and gradual improvement of this art. In my account of its most eminent men I have added all their privileges, licences, patents, etc, which were granted to them; together with the name of the place, and sign at which they dwelt, the inconveniences and disasters they met with, as also the charter of the Company of Stationers. (ibid.)

The *Typographical Antiquities* is the work on which Ames's lasting reputation rests and which has formed the basis of later histories of English printing. Ames's portrait, engraved by R. K. Laurie, shows him black-suited and bewigged, quill in hand, his library behind him, and a copy of the *Typographical Antiquities* open beside him. He was the first to attempt to use type identification for dating early books, trying to date Caxton's undated books in a more systematic way than previous bibliographers by identifying and classifying a few of the types he used. The method was developed more fully by William Blades, a practising printer with an infallible eye for type variation, in his *Life and Typography of William Caxton* (1863), and has been used by students of early books ever since.

After Ames's death Sir Peter Thompson acquired Ames's own annotated copy of the *Typographical Antiquities* together with the copyright and original blocks. He sold the copyright and blocks to William Herbert, who continued Ames's work and refined his methodology to produce a three-volume edition of the *Typographical Antiquities* (1785–96). This later came into the hands of Thomas Frognal Dibdin, who enlarged it further. It has been considered a key work ever since.

Ames built up, in addition to his type specimen 'museum', a working (rather than a bibliophile's) library of some two or three thousand books. These included English incunabula, at that time still worth very little, books about London and the City, bibles and books of psalms, a number of classical texts, and the works of friends and antiquarian acquaintances such as Lewis, Ballard, Stukeley, and Folkes.

Ames died of a 'seizure', after a fit of coughing on 7 October 1759 at the house of a friend in Clement Lane, near the Royal Exchange, London, and was buried in the churchyard of St George-in-the-East. He died intestate, but circumstantial evidence suggests that Thompson handled his posthumous affairs and arranged for the library and coin collection to be auctioned by William Langford in February 1760. Such an arrangement was not unknown in Ames's day. His collection of title-pages and 'paper marks', as already noted, and the heavily annotated copy of the *Typographical Antiquities* finally went to the British Museum together with Thompson's marked copy of the sale catalogue.   ROBIN MYERS

Sources [R. Gough], 'Memoir', in J. Ames, *Typographical antiquities, being an historical account of printing in England, with some memoirs of our antient printers, and a register of the books printed by them, from the year 1471 to the year 1600, with an appendix concerning printing in Scotland and Ireland at the same time*, 2nd edn, 1, rev. W. Herbert (1785) · Nichols, *Lit. anecdotes*, 5.256–9 · Nichols, *Illustrations* · *DNB* · corresp., BL, Add. MSS 5151, 5831, 5834, 6210, 6216, 6219, 6402 · *IGI* · W. Langford, *A catalogue of the genuine and entire collection of scarce printed books, manuscripts and coins of Mr Joseph Ames FRS and secretary of the Society of Antiquaries lately deceased which will be sold at auction by Mr Langford in his house in the Great Piazza, Covent Garden on Monday 5th May 1760 and the following seven evenings (Sunday excepted)* · F. Grose, *Olio* (1793), 133
Archives BL, corresp. and papers, Add. MSS 5151, 5831, 5834, 6210, 6216, 6219, 6402 · BL, minute books of Society of Antiquaries, Egerton MSS 1041–1042; Add. MS 18823 · Bodl. Oxf., notes of antiquarian journeys · Bodl. Oxf., extracts made from John Aubrey's *Monumenta Britannica* · S. Antiquaries, Lond., notebook and commonplace book | Norfolk RO, corresp. with T. Martin
Likenesses R. Laurie, engraving, after 1749, repro. in Nichols, *Lit. anecdotes* · T. Hodgetts, mezzotint (after R. Laurie), BM, NPG; repro. in J. Ames, *Typographical antiquities*, ed. W. Herbert and T. F. Dibdin, new edn, 1 (1810) · R. Laurie, mezzotint, NPG
Wealth at death library sold by auction 1760 (1350 lots, gross value £283 12s. 9d): Sir Peter Thompson's marked and priced copy of the sale catalogue, BL, 11904 q24

Ames, Leslie Ethelbert George (1905–1990), cricketer, was born at Fairfield House, Elham, Kent, on 3 December 1905, the son of Harold Ames, accountant, and his wife, Edith Broadbridge. He attended the Harvey Grammar School, Folkestone, and was unusual in his day in embarking on a career as a professional cricketer after a grammar school education. He left school at seventeen and was apprenticed in his cousin's grocery business, but a year later he joined the Kent staff and made his county début in 1926. His 1000 runs in 1927 led *Wisden* to see him as 'a likely England cricketer' (*Wisden*, 1928, 115). It was a prophecy soon to be fulfilled, especially after he scored 1919 runs and took twenty-one wickets behind the stumps in 1928. After virtually repeating the performance in 1929, he was selected for the MCC tour of the West Indies (1929–30), where he averaged almost 60 in the tests and established himself as the England wicket-keeper for the 1930s.

Leslie Ethelbert George Ames (1905–1990), by unknown photographer, 1930s

Ames played for England in forty-seven test matches, although he had to wait for the decline in ability by George Duckworth before he established himself in the MCC 'bodyline' tour of 1932–3. In the following summer, against the West Indies, he topped the averages (83.50) and set a record (since beaten) by dismissing eight West Indies batsmen in the third test at the Oval. His last test was against South Africa in the ten-day 'timeless match' at Durban in 1939. In all tests he made 2434 runs (average 40.56) with seventy-four catches and twenty-three stumpings. His wicket-keeping technique had been honed by 'keeping' to the Kent leg-spinner A. P. (Tich) Freeman, though he proved his abilities in standing back against Harold Larwood and Bill Voce on the hard Australian pitches in 1932–3. He was a hard-hitting, orthodox batsman, who excelled at the hook and the cut. His strength to England lay in the runs he could be relied on to make batting at number seven. He continued to score freely for Kent, making his highest score (295) on his home ground, Folkestone, against Gloucestershire in 1933—a year in which he amassed 3058 runs (average 58.80), with eight other centuries. Like many other professional cricketers of the period, he also excelled at football,

playing at outside-left for Folkestone, Clapton Orient, and Gillingham.

Ames, who reached the rank of squadron leader in the Royal Air Force during the Second World War, played for Kent purely as a batsman in the six post-war seasons. With a career record of 37,248 runs (average 43.51) and 1121 dismissals (704 caught and 417 stumped), he had established himself as the best batsman–wicket-keeper in the game. He remains as the only test wicket-keeper to have made 100 centuries in first-class cricket.

Afflicted by lumbago, Ames retired in 1951, but he still had much to give the game. He was a test selector (1950–56), the first professional to be appointed (apart from on overseas tours), and served his old county, Kent, as manager (1957–74) and secretary (1961–73), before ultimately becoming president (1975). He also managed three MCC tours, the most memorable of which was that to the West Indies in 1967–8, when England won the series. From the turmoil of that riot-torn tour of Pakistan in 1968–9 'one man emerged with much honour, Leslie Ames, [who] carried the burden' (E. M. Wellings, Wisden, 1970, 914). Kent, under his influence, improved considerably with Colin Cowdrey 'in the middle' and Ames behind the scenes. He was appointed CBE in 1973 for his services to cricket and was awarded an honorary MA by Kent University in 1988.

Following the death of his first wife, Leonie Muriel File (1907/8–1978), whom he had married on 30 April 1930, Ames married, on 29 January 1980, Jane Burgoyne Templeton Dingwall (1910/11–1995). He died at the Kent and Canterbury Hospital, Canterbury, on 27 February 1990. A memorial service was held in Canterbury Cathedral.

IVO TENNANT

Sources A. Hill, Les Ames (1990) · D. Moore, The history of Kent county cricket club (1988) · E. W. Swanton, The world of cricket (1966) · C. Cowdrey, MCC: the autobiography of a cricketer (1976) · b. cert. · m. certs. · d. cert.
Archives FILM BFI NFTVA, documentary footage · BFI NFTVA, sports footage
Likenesses photograph, 1930–39, Popperfoto, Northampton [see illus.] · photographs, repro. in Hill, Les Ames
Wealth at death £292,383: probate, 13 July 1990, CGPLA Eng. & Wales

Ames, Levi (bap. 1739, d. 1820). See under Ames, Jeremiah (1706–1776).

Ames, Richard (bap. 1664?, d. 1692), satirist, was born of 'Plebean Extraction' (Ames, Last Search, sig. A2v); he can probably be identified with a 'Richardus Emms', son of Richard and Maria, baptized in St Martin-in-the-Fields, Westminster, on 5 January 1664. He was apprenticed to a tailor in 1678. John Dunton the bookseller describes him as 'Mr Ames, originally a Coat-seller; but had always some Yammerings upon him after Learning and the Muses' (Dunton, 247). Both of his parents were dead before 1683, the date of a letter in which he expresses his dissatisfaction with his humble status as a 'Mechanick' and his love of learning:

> I … had rather have the possession of a Library, than be master of both the Indies … The current of my Inclinations never were, nor ever will be to a Trade, Business and my self being Antipodes … my thoughts are engaged in other affairs, which hath so great an influence over my actions, that I

often doe things diametrically opposite to the commands I receive. (Ames, 'Letter on education')

Ames's elegy on Richard Baxter, praising Baxter's 'Heavenly Piety' and efficacy as 'kind Physician of the sickly Soul' (Ames, *An Elegy on the Death of … Mr. Richard Baxter*, 1693), suggests that Ames was a dissenter; elsewhere he strongly attacks clergy who claim that 'none were to be Saved out of the Pale of the Church of England' (Ames, *Jacobite Conventicle*, sig. A2r). Several of his works are strongly anti-French and anti-Jacobite. His best-known poem, *Sylvia's Revenge, or, A Satyr Against Man* (1688), an answer to Robert Gould's violent misogynist satire *Love Given O're* (1683), went through twelve editions. Its sequel, *Sylvia's Complaint* (1692), similarly assumes a female persona defending 'her Injur'd Sex' against unjust allegations and criticizing the 'unbounded *Arbitrary Power*' husbands exercise over their wives (R. Ames, *Sylvia's Complaint*, 1692, sig. A2r, 14). Ames also wrote several poems arguing a contrary position, including *The Female Fire-Ships: a Satyr Against Whoring* (1691) and *The Folly of Love: a New Satyr Against Women* (1691). Dunton's claim that 'you might engage him upon what Project you pleas'd, if you'd but conceal him' (Dunton, 247) is borne out by Ames's authorship of *The Pleasures of Love and Marriage* (1691), an answer to his own poem *The Folly of Love*.

As well as these satires in heroic couplets, Ames is the author of a number of comic poems in anapests on the general theme of drinking and conviviality, whose common theme is the declining quality of the claret served in London taverns: *The Search after Claret* (1691), *A Farther Search after Claret* (1691), *The Last Search after Claret* (1691), and the posthumously published *The Bacchanalian Sessions* (1693), the last of which contains a prefatory poem 'To the Memory of Mr Richard Ames'. Two late poems, though largely conventional, can be seen to some extent as palinodes: *Fatal Friendship, or, The Drunkard's Misery* (1693), advertised as 'by a young Gentleman, a little before his Death; who lately fell an unhappy Sacrifice to the Bottle', and *The Rake, or, The Libertine's Religion* (1693), presenting its 'late Author' as a penitent. Dunton writes:

> *Wine and Women* were the great Bane of his Life and Happiness … a little before his Decease, he said to me, with a Deal of Concern: Ah Mr. *Dunton! with what another Face does the World appear, now that I have Death in View*. (Dunton, 247)

Ames died 'in a hospital' in London, some time before 25 October 1692.

Though he is listed in the British Library catalogue as 'Richard Ames of Lincoln's Inn', there is no reliable evidence linking him to the inns of court; his name does not appear in the register of admissions to Lincoln's Inn, and the attribution on the title-page of *Lawyerus bootatus & spurratus, or, The Long Vacation* (1691) to 'a Student of Lincolns-Inn' simply reflects the persona used in the poem, suitable for a satire on attorneys whose only concern is the size of the fees they receive. There is a useful essay by Hugh Amory on the canon of Ames's writings, which draws on extensive lists of 'Books written by the Author' in *The Bacchanalian Sessions* and *The Folly of Love*.

WARREN CHERNAIK

Sources R. Ames, 'Letter on education', Feb 1683, BL, Burney MS 393 · J. Dunton, *The life and errors of John Dunton … written by himself* (1705) · H. Amory, 'Richard Ames (d. 1692): a catalogue', *Essays in honor of James Edward Walsh*, ed. H. Amory and R. G. Dennis (1983), 196–220 · F. Nussbaum, *Satires on women: love given o're* [1682], *The female advocate* [1697], *The folly of love* [1691], Augustan Reprints, 180 (1976) · F. Nussbaum, *The brink of all we hate: English satires on women, 1660–1790* (1984) · W. Chernaik, *Sexual freedom in Restoration literature* (1995) · 'To the memory of Mr Richard Ames', R. Ames, *The Bacchanalian sessions* (1693) · R. Ames, *The Jacobite conventicle* (1692) · R. Ames, *The last search after claret* (1691) · IGI

Archives BL, Burney MS 393

Ames, William (1576–1633), theologian and university teacher, was born at Ipswich, the son of William Ames, merchant, and his wife, Joane Snelling, also from a Suffolk merchant family. Both of these families were substantial folk. William had one sister, Elizabeth. When the two were quite young, the parents died, and William went to live with an uncle, his mother's brother, Mr Snelling, at Boxford, Suffolk.

Early years and education Ames's uncle provided well for his religious training and education. Snelling was a puritan and Boxford was filled with people of strict Calvinistic religion. Nonconformism was the rule; two Boxford preachers of the time, Henry Sandes and William Bird, participated in the secretive presbyterian classis meetings at nearby Dedham. Young Ames breathed in all of this puritanical atmosphere and it moulded him. The tenets of puritan nonconformity, Ames declared in later life, were 'from my childhood … unanswerable' (W. Ames, *Reply to Dr. Mortons Generall Defence*, 1622, 27). Early in 1594 Snelling sent Ames to Christ's College, Cambridge, where he stayed for sixteen years. He matriculated as a pensioner, graduated BA in 1598, and proceeded MA in 1601. The college elected him as fellow, and he also at that time, according to college regulations, was ordained. Entering Christ's meant joining the stronghold of Cambridge puritanism. His most profound Christ's College influence was William Perkins (1558–1602), college fellow and powerful preacher. Perkins preached the necessity of conversion and a pious daily Christian walk; and although young Ames had always tried to follow the precepts of strict religion, Perkins called for him to go deeper. Under his spell, Ames 'was called out of his naturall estate of sin and misery, as Lazarus out of his grave' (Quick, fol. 2). This profound conversion convinced Ames that such an experience must be the starting point of all religion. All else was show. 'A man may be *bonus ethicus*' (a moral person) 'and yet not *bonus Theologus*' (a sincere-hearted converted Christian; W. Ames, *Fresh Suit Against Human Ceremonies*, 1633, 1.131).

As college fellow and disciple of Perkins, Ames opposed middle-of-the-road religion, but he exceeded Perkins's nonconformism by resisting the wearing of the surplice and all ceremonialism. In him was 'a concurrence of much non-conformity' (Fuller, 301). His charismatic teaching and preaching attracted a circle of young disciples; these he led into conversion and then directed in prayer

The Pourtracture of the Reverend and worthy Minifter of God, William Ames D.D. fometine of Chrifts Colledge in Cambridge. And Proffefor of Divinity in the Famous Univerfity of Franeker in Friefland.

Printed for Iohn Rothwell at the Swan in Pauls Church yard   Will: Marfhall fculpfi

William Ames (1576–1633), by William Marshall, pubd 1633

and devotions. In 1609, when Valentine Cary became master, with a mandate to produce religious conformity, the end was near for Ames. In a last fling he preached a stinging sermon on 21 December 1609 at St Mary's Church, in which he played the 'watchman' of the Lord, inveighing first against Christmas merriment, then against 'all playing at cards and dice' (which he knew Master Cary enjoyed). Playing with cards or dice was 'the device of the devil', akin to abusing the word, the sacraments, and providence; this sermon was the last straw of nonconformity. The vice-chancellor's court called in Ames, and after a perfunctory hearing suspended him from all ecclesiastical duties and from all his academic degrees, just short of an outright expulsion. Hereafter, because of his notorious puritanism, there was no future for him at Cambridge. Ames withdrew and looked for another position.

In a short time Ames found a place as city lecturer at Colchester, which he held briefly in 1610. Since the pay was from city and voluntary funds, he hoped to avoid close supervision from George Abbot, the bishop of London, but the bishop had already heard plenty about Ames's stubbornness, and he refused to give him a preaching licence. Abbot curtly dismissed him: 'How durst you (sayd he) preache in my Diocesse' (W. Ames, *Fresh Suit Against Human Ceremonies*, 1633, 2.409). His critics told him he would have a job if he would conform: 'What a man Ames would be if he were a son of the Church' and what a future

he would have (Nethenus). But not being an obedient, subservient son, Ames looked abroad. Before the end of the year he went into exile.

Exile and chaplaincy in the Netherlands, 1610–1619 Ames found a new career in the Dutch Netherlands, where he joined a sizable Anglo-Scottish community. Some were religious refugees like Ames, others were merchants carrying on their trade, and still others were soldiers fighting the Eighty Years' War against Spain, serving with the English and Scottish regiments in the employ of the Dutch states general. English-language chaplains were needed, and these positions were a God-given blessing for the deprived and silenced preachers from England. The English bishops could exert very little supervision over the English religion of the Low Countries. Ames first spent a short time at Leiden, where John Robinson's English congregation gave shelter to him and to fellow refugees of religion Henry Jacob and Robert Parker. Next, Ames found employment as chaplain to Sir Horace Vere, commander of English forces in the Netherlands, from 1611 to 1619. Ames had several duties: he presided over the little English congregation of The Hague; he acted as personal spiritual counsellor to Sir Horace Vere and his wife, Mary, Lady Vere; and during military campaigns he followed the troops out into the field.

In his ministry Ames selectively used the Church of England prayer book: 'Some things he left out' and other things he improvised with words of his own (Boswell MSS, 1.250–51). Freed from supervision, Ames practised the non-liturgical Reformed style. Although Sir Horace was pleased with the spiritual food Ames passed out to the troops, it was not according to the rule of the Church of England. Consequently, the bishops at home sent over word that he should be speedily removed. However, what called attention to Ames at this time was not so much his chaplaincy work but the publishing of a book, *Puritanismus Anglicanus* (1610), co-authored by Ames and William Bradshaw. The bulk of the text, by Bradshaw, had been printed earlier in English as *English Puritanisme*; now under Ames's hand, the book was put into Latin and prefaced with an essay by Ames himself. Bishop Abbot was distressed and declared that Ames deserved removal and 'some exemplary Punishment' (R. Winwood, *Memorials*, 1725, 3.346), but with Sir Horace's firm support Ames managed to ward off these threats for several years.

During this period Ames married twice. He first married a daughter of Ursula Sotherton and John *Burges, his predecessor as chaplain at The Hague, but this marriage was cut short owing to his wife's early death. He next married, by 1618, Joane Fletcher (1586/7–1644), daughter of Giles *Fletcher (*bap.* 1546, *d.* 1611) and sister to Phineas and Giles Fletcher, the poets. This second marriage produced three children, Ruth, William, and John.

Defender of Calvinism and adviser to the Synod of Dort, 1618–1619 About the same time that Ames arrived in the Netherlands, the Dutch Reformed church erupted into open controversy, with one faction, the Remonstrants (Arminians), promoting the doctrine of free will, and the opposing faction, the Contra-Remonstrants (the strict Calvinists), teaching the orthodox doctrines of predestination. Ames wholeheartedly supported the Calvinists and took up the pen on their behalf. Previously, he had spoken out on English ceremonies; now he tackled larger issues and revealed great skill as a systematic doctrinal theologian. The anti-Arminian books rolled forth: *De Arminii sententia* (1613), *Rescriptio scholastica & brevis* (1615), *Rescriptio contracta* (1617), *Coronis ad collationem hagiensem* (1618), and, somewhat later, *Anti-synodalia scripta remonstrantium* (1629). Nicolaas Grevinchoven of Rotterdam responded on behalf of the Dutch Arminians; they argued much about the doctrines of redemption, predestination, and election. This theological duel won Ames some acclaim as the Augustine of Holland and Hammer of the Arminians. An international theological conference called by the states general to try to resolve the divisive issues, the Synod of Dort, met at the south Netherlands city of Dordrecht in 1618 and 1619. By this time the Calvinist party was in control of the situation and arranged for a successful Calvinist outcome. Because of Ames's highly visible work as a defender of Calvinism his friends secured him the part-time appointment as paid adviser to Johannes Bogerman, the synod president. For a few months Ames travelled back and forth between The Hague and Dordrecht, but he had to leave his chaplain's post under pressure from England. At the conclusion, the synod produced a set of theological canons and expelled the Arminians from public positions. As a result, Ames hoped to gain a new position as professor of theology at Leiden University, but the post eluded him. King James of England, learning of the intended appointment, absolutely opposed him: 'for Ames his preferment, His Majesty doth utterly distaste it' (E. Arber, *Pilgrim Fathers*, 1897, 213). Under such pressure the Dutch authorities backed away from their offer. Instead of the prestigious professorship, Ames had to settle for an inconspicuous position as supervisor of a Leiden student burse (house college), where theological students roomed and ate their meals and received extra instruction. He held this job between 1619 and 1622.

Professor and writer at Franeker University, 1622–1633 On 21 March 1622 the curators of the University of Franeker, in the northern province of Friesland, invited Ames to their faculty as professor of theology. Within a few weeks the Ames family had moved to Franeker. The salary was set at 600 florins a year. On 23 May 1622 he gave his inaugural oration, sharing the occasion with Johannes Hachting, the new professor of logic. Ames's learned oration was on the theological significance of the urim and thummim of the high priest's breastplate (Exodus 28: 30). Four days later, on 27 May, Ames advanced to doctor of theology after defending his 'Theses de conscientia', a collection of thirty-eight theses and four corollaries on conscience. Hereafter, his friends liked to call him 'the learned Doctor Ames'. Although he was initially delighted to have a fixed professorship, the Franeker situation did not strike him as quite right. His fellow theological professors Sibrandus Lubbertus and Johannes Maccovius were very contentious. The students seemed to be disobedient and raucous.

Here was no quiet retreat for learning and piety. John Davenport's *Apologeticall Reply* (1636) had an 'eyewitness' report about Ames, revealing that he almost retreated. 'At first comming to Franeker, he found things in such a frame in the university, that he thought of departing thence before he was settled' (p. 83).

Nevertheless, Ames made his stand. The Franeker years were very productive for his scholarly achievements. Under his Latinized name of Guilielmus Amesius he published his magnum opus, the *Medulla theologiae* (a short version in 1623, followed by the full edition in 1627), and, nearly as famous, *De conscientia, et eius jure, vel casibus*, a reworking of his doctoral theses (1630). These books made an international reputation for him among Reformed theologians. Other large writings from this period were the *Bellarminus enervatus* against Cardinal Robert Bellarmine (4 vols., 1625–9) and the *Anti-synodalia scripta remonstrantium* (1629), a last blast against Arminianism. He also was preparing some biblical exegetical works: *Lectiones in CL. psalmos Davidis* (on the Psalms), *Explicatio analytica utriusque Epistolae Divi Petri Apostoli* (on the epistles of Peter), and *Christianae catecheseōs sciagraphia* (on the catechism). These latter three were all published posthumously, under the direction of Hugh Peter, in 1635. In his teaching Ames always emphasized biblical exegesis and practical theology; there must always be a balance of doctrine and the practical application.

In addition to teaching and writing, from June 1626 to June 1627 Ames took his turn as rector magnificus, the highest university office, a position which rotated every year among the professors based on seniority. The university motto was *Christo et ecclesiae* ('for Christ and the church'), and in assuming the office Ames delivered his Latin oration on the deep meaning of this motto. When he relinquished the rectorship a year later he orated on the rector's calling to be a moral 'watchman' against all educational irregularity and iniquity, based on Isaiah 21; this imagery and desire for moral policing at Franeker was reminiscent of his earlier Cambridge 'watchman' preaching (1609).

As Franeker professor, Ames was distressed to find much coldness of religion and little piety. Although theological orthodoxy was all that he could desire, in tune with the strict canons of Dort, still 'something necessary was lacking'. As the teacher of future preachers, he gave an 'Exhortation to the students of theology' (1623; published in *De conscientia*, 1630) which pleaded for less doctrinal wrangling and more zeal for 'life and practice ... conscience and its concerns'. Franeker needed more daily puritanical 'observance'. During his years as professor Ames often called for a 'reformation' to deliver professors and students from love of stage plays, oaths, dicing, masking, swearing, heavy drinking, and Sabbath breaking; instead, they would all work for personal godliness. He warned: unless the godly party acted decisively, the university motto might just as well be changed from *Christo et ecclesiae* ('for Christ and church') to *Bacchus et Bacchantibus* ('for Bacchus and the Bacchants'; 'Oration on becoming rector', 1626, *Opera omnia*, vol. 5). The Ames-inspired moral reforms, his 'reformation' of the 1620s, instituted some new strict rules of student conduct, but with very little lasting effect. The failure to cleanse the moral life of the university was one of the greatest disappointments of Ames's life. Indeed many students, and some of the professors, openly mocked him for his excessive zeal. He had 'continuall opposition, and suffering' (Davenport, 83).

As professor Ames instilled into his teaching and writing three great truths: Ramist philosophy, orthodox Calvinist theology, and puritan moral piety. Ramism, the philosophy of Pierre de la Ramée (1515–1572), provided the theoretical framework for his thought. Ramist method was an organizational principle by which any doctrine could be presented for effective teaching. As Ames understood it, the best Ramism meant defining all terms carefully, arranging all material into dichotomies, and showing practical applications. The Ramist hallmark of an Ames book was an outline chart (often on a fold-out page) with everything in dichotomies. Ames's philosophy also expanded into a general scheme of organizing an entire curriculum, which was once again laid out in charts and which he named *technometria* or *technologia*. His *Philosophemata* contains the Ramist philosophical essays of Ames and his Franeker students (1643; also in vol. 5 of his *Opera omnia*, 1658–61).

The *Medulla theologiae* ('Marrow of theology'; 1623, 1627) was Ames's summation of systematic religion. The opening sentence gave the essence, 'Theology is the doctrine of living to God'. Following Ramist methodology, he gave two parts, faith and observance. Under faith he summarized the doctrines of Calvinist religion. The second part was the practical, moral application (the observance). This two-pronged, balanced approach set him apart from many systematic theologians of the orthodox school. By highlighting both faith and observance, Ames helped to set a pattern for English and American puritan theology, and he hoped that it might also point a direction for Dutch Reformed theology. The *Medulla* had a wide readership in Latin and also went into English (as *The Marrow of Theology*), Dutch, and German.

Part two of the *Medulla* was a treatise on morality and ethics, but more teaching on this subject was needed. In 1630 Ames brought out his *De conscientia* as a full-scale treatise on ethical living, so that he could greatly elaborate on the 'observance' side of theology. The first part of *De conscientia* explained the workings of conscience, and the latter part of the book systematically treated the ten commandments and gave many specific applications for daily Christian living. In doing this, Ames became a casuist. He gave protestants a book of casuistry, which he called 'cases of conscience'. Although he was extremely critical of Catholic, and especially Jesuit, manuals of casuistry, he believed he had achieved a wholesome guide to godliness. All his ethics flowed from the Bible, not philosophy. 'Every precept of universal truth pertaining to living well in either economics, politics, or law very properly belongs to theology' (W. Ames, *Medulla*, 1623, thesis vii). Increase Mather of New England commended Ames: 'It is rare for a scholastical wit to be joined with an heart warm in religion, but in him it was so' (Mather, 1.245).

Ames's writing and teaching on behalf of conversion, piety, and moral reformation put him in contact with like-minded Dutch churchmen around the country. The Dutch puritans, the people of practical piety, formed a movement called the Nadere Reformatie (the 'further reformation'); Ames supported this in every way possible.

An English edition of Ames's *Works* appeared in 1643 (containing three of his books), and a comprehensive Latin collection, *Guilielmi Amesii opera omnia*, in five volumes, appeared at Amsterdam between 1658 and 1661.

Spokesman of English puritanism Even though removed from home, Ames kept his hand in nonconformist activities relating to England. Puritan exiles in the Low Countries wrote books, organized a synod of preachers, opened schools for students from England, and kept a steady communication with like-minded nonconformists back in England. Ames was at the forefront of this activity. In his *Puritanismus Anglicanus* of 1610, where he added a preface to William Bradshaw's earlier little tract, he described English puritans as devout people of three goals: they seek a pure church, they teach and practise personal godliness, and their authority is the Bible. The common maligning of their message, he believed, was the work of Satan, 'that old crafty fox' (*Puritanismus Anglicanus*, preface). He was never ashamed to call himself a puritan, even 'of the rigidest sort' (using a phrase from Bradshaw's 1605 *English Puritanism*), and he asked others to join him. His identification with Bradshaw, moreover, marked him as a certain kind of puritan—not only a moral reformer, but one who rejected all ecclesiastical hierarchy in favour of the independence of the congregations. Although he did not use the label of Congregationalist or Independent, he was a forerunner of that form of nonconformity.

Several of Ames's books were outright attacks upon the hierarchy and ritual of the Church of England. Two books attacked Bishop Thomas Morton of Lichfield and Coventry, *A Reply to Dr. Mortons Generall Defence of Three Nocent Ceremonies* (1622) and *A Reply to Dr. Mortons Particular Defence of Three Nocent Ceremonies* (1623). The 'three nocent ceremonies' in question were the wearing of the surplice, the sign of the cross in baptism, and kneeling at the communion service. As long as the institution of bishops and ceremonies corrupted the English church, 'wee deny utterly, that we have such a reformation therein, as may represent the face of the primitive Church' (W. Ames, *A Reply to Dr Mortons Generall Defence*, 63). At the end of his life Ames was working on the *Fresh Suit Against Human Ceremonies in God's Worship* (posthumously published, 1633). This book rebutted John Burgess, his father-in-law of his first marriage, who had conformed and become an apologist for the church. All his books were published by surreptitious puritan presses in the Netherlands and then smuggled back into England. Ames not only advanced his own books but arranged for Dutch presses to publish books of friends remaining in England.

Ames was of further service to the nonconformists by providing theological directions for organizing churches along Reformed, non-episcopal lines. In the Netherlands the English-language churches could do pretty much what they wanted. Ames defined the church as a local congregation of gathered believers joined together by confession of faith and a written and spoken covenant. Because each congregation was a true church, it had its own autonomy, apart from any synodal or episcopal supervision. Only such a local assembly 'and not larger' is properly signified by the word 'church' (W. Ames, *Marrow of Sacred Divinity* in *Works*, 1643, 187). The seventeenth-century Netherlands had twenty-five to thirty Anglo-Scottish churches, and most of these followed the lead of Ames by organizing themselves upon the basis of a written covenant designed by the congregation itself. Alexander Hodge of Amsterdam in 1681 (nearly fifty years after Ames's death) testified to his continuing influence on the making of covenants: 'for it was done by the advice of Dr. Ames … all the English Churches in the Netherlands, were founded upon such a written Federall transaction betwixt them and God' (Quick, fol. 46). While lauding the autonomy of congregations, Ames could also collaborate easily with presbyterial Reformed people, but he had little patience with outright separatists. He exchanged several writings with John Robinson, the separatist leader of the Pilgrim congregation of Leiden, in which he sharply opposed the Robinsonian position of separatism. Ames's concept of the autonomous, self-governing, but non-separatist, church was a middle position between conformity and separation, a kind of non-separatist Congregationalism.

Move to Rotterdam and death (1633) In 1633 Ames made a decision to leave his professorship at Franeker, with its attendant preoccupation with issues concerning the Dutch church, and to concern himself instead with controversies in the English church. By this time he discerned that his moral reformation at the university had stalled. He also complained about the damp Friesland climate, and he hoped for better health if he could move south. He received two invitations worthy of consideration. One was from John Winthrop in 1628 on behalf of settlers in America who asked him to go over and help plant churches. The other invitation was to go to Rotterdam and to become co-pastor with Hugh Peter at the English Reformed church; Peter had already re-organized it along independent, covenanted lines, as recommended by Ames. Peter and Ames also hatched a plan for establishing at Rotterdam a little English college or seminary, in connection with the church, with Ames as professor. Peter persuaded the Rotterdam magistrates to support Ames in this joint pastor–teacher appointment; the salary was to be 1000 florins. According to Peter, Ames's real motivation for moving was not ill health or discouragement but puritan vision. Ames 'left his professorship in *Friezland* to live with me because of my Churches Independency at *Rotterdam*' (H. Peter, *Mr. Peters Last Report*, 1646, 14). Ames had attracted a considerable number of English students to come to Franeker to study, and because of his learned and pious reputation he might well have succeeded in doing the same at Rotterdam.

In August or September 1633 the Ames family moved south to Rotterdam. Hardly had Ames settled in when he fell ill. His house flooded, and when he stepped out into the cold waters he caught pneumonia and died on 11 November. He was buried at Rotterdam on 14 November 1633, aged fifty-seven. Hugh Peter preached the funeral sermon. His widow and three children, Ruth, William, and John, were left nearly destitute. They raised some money by selling his books; an auction catalogue of his library was printed at Amsterdam in 1634, indicating that the family sold his library in the Netherlands, rather than sending it on to America, as was sometimes reported. Joane Ames and the three children initially returned to England, but in May 1637 they travelled to New England. There help was available since the reputation of Doctor Ames remained very high: had he lived to make the trip to America, there is great likelihood that he would have become the first president of Harvard College. In the event young William Ames (d. 1689) subsequently returned to England and became a Congregationalist minister.

Cotton Mather wrote, on behalf of American puritans, that Ames was their sublime, subtle, irrefragable, 'yea that angelical doctor' (Mather, 1.236). Americans appreciated the combination of methodical scholarship and warm-hearted religion in his *Medulla* and *Conscientia*, which served as valued textbooks at early Harvard and Yale. His teachings on congregational polity made him (along with William Bradshaw, Henry Jacob, and Robert Parker) a father of the New England churches. John Cotton said he brought 'light' to the Americans about the 'Way of Congregational churches' (J. Cotton, *Way of Congregational Churches*, 1648, 13). Recent interpretations of Ames see his influence in three arenas: as a leading voice of American and English puritanism; as a force in the development of Reformed pietism on the continent (in Germany and Hungary); and in the Netherlands, where he lived for twenty-three years, as a strong supporter of the Nadere ('further') Reformation.   KEITH L. SPRUNGER

Sources M. Nethenus, 'Praefatio introductoria', in *Guilielmi Amesii … opera … omnia*, ed. M. Nethenus, 1 (1658) • J. Quick, 'The life of William Ames' in 'Icones sacrae Anglicanae', DWL, MS 38.34, 35 • K. L. Sprunger, *The learned Doctor William Ames: Dutch backgrounds of English and American puritanism* (1972) • K. L. Sprunger, *Dutch puritanism: a history of English and Scottish churches of the Netherlands in the sixteenth and seventeenth centuries* (1982) • K. L. Sprunger, 'William Ames and the Franeker link to English and American puritanism', *Universiteit te Franeker, 1585–1811*, ed. G. Th. Jensma, F. R. H. Smit, and F. Westra (1985), 264–74 • K. L. Sprunger, introduction, *The auction catalogue of the library of William Ames* (1988) • H. Visscher, *Guilielmus Amesius* (1894) • K. Reuter, *Wilhelm Amesius* (1940) • D. Horton, trans., *William Ames by Matthew Nethenus, Hugo Visscher, and Karl Reuter* (1965) • J. Davenport, *Apologeticall reply to a booke called an 'Answer to the unjust complaint of W. B.'* (1636) • J. D. Eusden, ed. and trans., *The marrow of theology: William Ames, 1576–1633* (1968) • L. Gibbs, *William Ames technometry* (1979) • W. B. S. Boeles, *Frieslands Hoogeschool en het Rijks Athenaeum te Franeker*, 2 vols. (1878–9) • P. Miller, *Orthodoxy in Massachusetts, 1630–1650* (1933) • S. E. Morison, *The tercentennial history of Harvard College and University, 1636–1936*, 1: *The founding of Harvard College* (1935) • R. P. Stearns, *The strenuous puritan: Hugh Peter, 1598–1660* (1954) • T. Fuller, *The history of the University of Cambridge from the conquest to the year 1634*, ed. M. Prickett and T. Wright (1840) • J. R. Beeke, *Assurance of faith: Calvin, English puritanism, and* the *Dutch second reformation* (1991) • T. Brienen and others, *De nadere reformatie en het gereformeerd piëtisme* (The Hague, 1989) • T. Webster, *Godly clergy in early Stuart England: the Caroline puritan movement, c.1620–1643* (1997) • BL, Boswell MSS, Add. MS 6394 • State Papers 16, vol. 250, no. 28 • C. Mather, *Magnalia Christi Americana*, 3rd edn, 7 bks in 2 vols. (1853–5)

Archives Provinciale Bibliotheek van Friesland, letters, MS 408 **Likenesses** W. Marshall, line engraving, BM, NPG; repro. in W. Ames, *Fresh suit against human ceremonies in God's worship* (1633) [*see illus.*] • line engraving, BM, NPG • oils, Gemeentemuseum Coopmanshûs, Franeker

Wealth at death very little; friends had to make a plea for funds for the widow and orphaned children: Sprunger, *The learned Doctor Ames*, 250

Ames, William (*d.* 1662), Quaker preacher, was born at Frampton Cotterell, near Bristol; his parents' names are not known. He was not well educated and when young was prone to lying, drunkenness, and licentiousness. During the civil war he joined the king's army and later served as a marine under Prince Rupert in the admiral's own ship. The crew were Dutch and Ames learned to speak their language fluently, an accomplishment he was to make full use of in the future.

As he grew older Ames became more serious. Switching sides, presumably in 1649 when Rupert's ships were blockaded and many of them eventually captured at Kinsale, he served in the parliamentarian army in Ireland as a sergeant in a regiment of foot. Now it was the piety of the soldiers and the discipline of the army which attracted him and he was very strict with his men. He was also influenced by the many Baptists in the army and joined them, becoming a preacher and an elder. Although he was outwardly changed, Ames felt that within himself he was as bad as he had ever been, angry and untruthful: 'There was none so forward to condemn sin yet myself the greatest sinner' (Ames). This changed when Ames heard the preaching of Edward Burrough and Francis Howgill on their visit to Ireland, was convinced, and became a Quaker. He left the army and went to preach Quakerism in Essex, a stronghold of the Baptists. Ames was soon at the very centre of the Quaker movement and published an account of his spiritual journey in 1656, which was translated into Dutch, French, and Swedish. In that year he first went to the Netherlands as a Quaker, speaking and writing pamphlets in Dutch. From 1657 William spent most of his time in the Netherlands and other European countries, although he kept in close contact with Quakers in Britain by letter and visits in both directions. He had various companions including Humble Thatcher and William Caton and travelled with them to Germany and Friesland. William's preaching was effective and he convinced Jacob Sewel, a surgeon of Amsterdam, his wife, Judith Zinspenning, and their son young William, who later became a notable historian of Quakerism.

Ames was at first welcomed by the Mennonites but they later turned against him and he encountered opposition elsewhere. In 1659 he was set upon by a crowd and imprisoned in the hospital for the insane at Rotterdam. After three weeks the governor invited Ames to escape and when he refused released him the next day. When Ames realized that people believed he had broken out he went back and gave himself up, for as Sewel comments, 'I truly believe he would rather have died than to have spoken a lie'—a telling contrast to his youth (Sewel).

At the beginning of 1661 William travelled to the Palatinate through Bohemia then to Frankfurt and Danzig. In the winter of 1661–2 he was in Amsterdam where he became ill and was left unusually weak. At the beginning of 1662 he went back to London, was arrested and sent to Bridewell. He was severely treated there and became ill again. On his release he returned to Amsterdam, where he died in September of that year. He was buried on 1 October, attended to the grave by his old companion William Caton.

Ames was a man of strong passions which he eventually channelled in the service of Quakerism. His ability to speak and write Dutch was very valuable to the movement as it enabled him to advise George Fox on how best to translate and publish his writings. Ames wrote prolifically himself, although he should be distinguished from the William Ames (1576–1633) who also published in the Netherlands and whose works were reprinted in 1658, but who was not related to him or connected with Quakers. Ames's preaching 'in a piercing and energetic tone of voice' (Sewel) was memorable and effective and he gave everything he had to the truth he had found. As William Sewel says:

> He was indeed a zealous man, and though some were ready to think him too ardent yet he was discreet. He was also generous and lest he might seem to be burdensome to any he rather chose to work with his hands.

GIL SKIDMORE

Sources G. Croese, *The general history of the Quakers* (1696) • W. Ames, *A declaration of the witness of God manifested in me from my youth* (1656) • W. Sewel, *The history of the rise, increase and progress of the Christian people called Quakers* (1722) • 'Extracts from the A. R. B. MSS', *Journal of the Friends' Historical Society*, 27 (1930), 18–22 • W. C. Braithwaite, *The beginnings of Quakerism* (1912)

Archives RS Friends, Lond., letters and accounts of his travels

Amesbury. For this title name *see* Dundas, Charles, Baron Amesbury (1751–1832).

Amherst [*formerly* Tyssen-Amherst], **Alicia Margaret** [*married name* Alicia Margaret Cecil, Lady Rockley] (1865–1941), garden historian, was born on 30 July 1865 at Didlington Hall, Didlington, near Mundford, Norfolk, fifth of the seven children (all daughters) of William Amhurst Tyssen-*Amherst (1835–1909), landowner, and his wife, Margaret Susan Mitford (1835–1919). The surname was spelt Tyssen-Amhurst until 1877, when it became Tyssen-Amherst, and the double-barrel ceased to be used after her father, a Conservative MP (1880–92), became Baron Amherst of Hackney in 1892. He was a collector of rare books and manuscripts.

Alicia, educated by governesses, could not remember a time when she did not love gardening. Didlington Hall possessed extensive parkland and a large lake. Her mother, an eager horticulturist, set aside a semicircular flower bed, 40 feet in diameter, as a garden for the child. At ten, Alicia purchased her first rose bush; by thirteen, she was bringing back exotic plants from the Riviera. Flowers would always delight her, especially pansies.

Alicia took up writing in spring 1891 after meeting Percy Newberry, the Egyptologist, who visited Didlington Hall to study papyri in the Amherst Library. He had contributed a few articles about the history of English gardens to the *Gardener's Chronicle* in 1889, and at his suggestion Alicia decided to expand on them. Having learned to read old documents in her father's collection, she consulted the monastic rolls of Norwich and Ely and worked at the British Library, the Public Record Office, and Trinity College, Cambridge, where she uncovered *The Feate of Gardening* by 'Mayster Ion Gardener', the earliest known treatise on the subject in English, dating from about 1440.

A History of Gardening in England by the Hon. Alicia Amherst appeared in November 1895. It was an unprecedentedly thorough account of English horticulture from Roman times, complete with footnotes and bibliography. The initial print run of 700 copies sold out almost at once; a second edition immediately followed, and a third in 1910. Its author received both the freedom of the Worshipful Company of Gardeners in 1896 and the freedom of the City of London.

On 16 February 1898 Alicia Amherst married Evelyn *Cecil (1865–1941), an aspiring Conservative politician who entered parliament four months later. Their children were Robert (1901–76), Margaret, and Maud. A keen imperialist, like her husband, after a tour of South Africa in 1899–1900, Mrs Cecil attained prominence in the British Women's Emigration Association and served as vice-chairman of the South African Colonisation Society, which organized the subsidized settlement of women in the newly annexed Transvaal in order to boost the English speaking population. The scheme was not outstandingly successful. Typically, she wished to send educated women of high moral character to be schoolmistresses and lady farmers, while supply and demand both pointed to lower-class women prepared to work in domestic service.

As the Hon. Mrs Evelyn Cecil, Alicia published *Children's Gardens* in 1902, a volume that combined practical instruction for wealthy juveniles with homilies about patience, neatness, springtime, and youth. More substantial was *London Parks and Gardens* (1907), a historical and horticultural survey. The Edwardian period saw a rapid growth in the popularity of gardening as a pastime among fashionable ladies. Mrs Cecil sat on the board of the Chelsea Physic Garden from 1900 (when the City Parochial Foundation took it over from the Society of Apothecaries) and she helped stage the Country in Town exhibition in Whitechapel in 1906, which promoted the planting of smoke-resistant flowers in poor city districts. Her own London home being in Belgravia, it was at Lytchett Heath House, near Poole, Dorset, that most of her gardening took place.

From 1917 to 1919 Mrs Cecil was honorary assistant director of horticulture within the food production department of the Board of Agriculture and Fisheries, where she advocated more allotments and school gardens and investigated products such as gelozone (a gelatine substitute made from seaweed). Empire settlement again occupied her after the war, when various voluntary groups amalgamated at the behest of the Colonial Office to create the Society for the Oversea Settlement of British Women (SOSBW) in 1919. Already an MBE since 1918, as its vice-chairman (1919–38), she earned a CBE in 1922. That year she became Lady Cecil, when her husband was knighted. His barony made her Lady Rockley in 1934.

After much travel on behalf of the SOSBW, Lady Rockley was able to bring her two passions together in *Wild Flowers of the Great Dominions of the British Empire* (1935). Illustrated with some of her own watercolours, the book aimed to boost imperial unity by fostering common knowledge of the flora of bush, veld, and prairie. Ill health forced her retirement from public life in 1938; she died at Lytchett Heath, Dorset, on 14 September 1941 and was buried there four days later beside the family chapel (later St Aldhelm's Church). A flowering shrub, Hebe Alicia Amherst, was named to honour the woman whose *History of Gardening in England* provided a starting point for all later British garden historians. JASON TOMES

Sources J. Percy, 'Author by accident', *The Garden*, 114/3 (1989) · *The Times* (15 Sept 1941) · B. L. Blakeley, 'Women and imperialism: the colonial office and female emigration to South Africa, 1901–1910', *Albion*, 13 (1981), 131–49 · A. Amherst, *A history of gardening in England* (1895) · Lady Davson, 'The Dowager Lady Rockley', *The Times* (19 Sept 1941) · E. Cecil [A. Amherst], *Children's gardens* (1902) · b. cert.

Archives Chelsea Physic Garden, London, papers | U. Oxf., Griffith Institute, Percy Newberry papers · Women's Library, London, records of the British Women's Emigration Association, the South African Colonisation Society, and the Society for the Oversea Settlement of British Women

Wealth at death £9630 8s.: probate, 18 Nov 1941, *CGPLA Eng. & Wales*

Amherst, Francis Kerril (1819–1883), Roman Catholic bishop of Northampton, was born on 21 March 1819, at 13 Queen Anne Street, Marylebone, Middlesex, and baptized at St James's Church, Spanish Place. He was the eldest of the three sons and five daughters of William Kerril Amherst and his wife, Mary Louisa, daughter of Francis Fortescue-Turville of Bosworth Hall, Leicestershire. He spent his early youth in Little Parndon House, Essex, which was purchased by his father in 1822, and at Bosworth Hall. The family were very devout: two of his sisters eventually became nuns and his brother William a Jesuit. In 1829 Amherst was sent to a preparatory school in Northampton, kept by the Revd William Foley; in 1830, he went to St Mary's College, Oscott.

In the early 1830s Amherst's parents moved to Fieldgate at Kenilworth, where his father died on 8 January 1835. A bank failure in India added to the family's troubles, and Francis and William, the remaining sons, had to seek a profession. Amherst left Oscott for Belgium in 1839 with the intention of studying engineering, but by May 1840 he had determined to enter the church and to 'add my mite to the reconversion of England' (Roskell, 135). In 1841 he returned to Oscott to study divinity. He was ordained priest in June 1846, and remained at Oscott as a professor.

For some time Amherst had contemplated joining a religious order and, in April 1853, he entered the noviciate of the Dominicans at Woodchester; the austere life there damaged his health and he left the order. Shortly afterwards, in 1856, he was appointed missionary rector of St Augustine's in Salford. Here he sponsored a mission and visited the sick and prisoners, roundly rejecting any clerical contribution to social reform and declaring that the church's mission was to save souls, not sweep streets. He was consecrated bishop on 4 July 1858 and appointed to the diocese of Northampton, where there were few Catholics: Amherst once commented that he felt like St Simeon Stylites. Furthermore, the diocese was in 'the most destitute condition … I am in sad want of priests and money' (Roskell, 233). Like others, he struggled with the expenses of a new episcopal establishment, but nevertheless managed to build several schools as well as superintending the care of orphans. In 1863–4, he supervised the building of a cathedral at Northampton; he also worked at a favourite project for the rearrangement of the Birmingham, Northampton, and Westminster dioceses in accordance with new railway routes, which he felt would improve pastoral care. His activity was fuelled by the conviction that the Church of England was on the point of collapse, as all her best men were turning to Rome. His judgement that the future enemy of Catholicism was infidelity, rather than protestantism, was a more prescient one.

In 1862 Amherst was appointed assistant to the pontifical throne, a post to which he was well suited. In 1869–70, he attended the First Vatican Council with other English bishops, and, like them, was distressed by what he felt was the gross misrepresentation of the proceedings in the English press. Although concerned about the possible effects of an untimely declaration of papal infallibility, he believed it the duty of good Catholics to obey the decrees once they were issued.

By September 1879 Amherst was in such poor health that he resigned his see and retired to the family home at Fieldgate. In 1880 he was preconized to the titular see of Souza. He died at Fieldgate on 21 August 1883, probably of cancer, and was buried in his own cathedral of Northampton.

Amherst was a man of sincere piety, whose career was characterized by loyalty to his church. He was a keen lover of Gothic architecture: in 1877, he purchased and restored at his own expense the medieval hospital of St John at Northampton. His passion for all things ornithological and his competent but unoriginal poetry bear witness to his sensitivity to natural things. But he had little leisure for literary work; of the few works he published *Lenten Thoughts* (1873) was the best known.

ROSEMARY MITCHELL

Sources M. F. Roskell, *Memoirs of Francis Kerril Amherst, DD, lord bishop of Northampton*, ed. H. F. J. Vaughan (1903) · Gillow, *Lit. biog. hist.* · F. J. Cwiekowski, *The English bishops and the First Vatican Council* (1971)
Archives British Province of the Society of Jesus, London, Northampton Roman Catholic diocesan archives, corresp. · NRA, corresp. and papers
Likenesses photograph, 1860–70, repro. in Roskell, *Memoirs of Francis Kerril Amherst*
Wealth at death £13,346 5s. 1d.: resworn probate, Feb 1884, CGPLA Eng. & Wales (1883)

Amherst, Jeffrey, first Baron Amherst (1717–1797), army officer, was born on 29 January 1717 at Brooks Place, Riverhead, Kent, the second son of Jeffrey Amherst (*d.* 1750) and his wife, Elizabeth (*d.* 1751), daughter of Thomas Kerrill of Hadlow, Kent. John *Amherst, naval officer, was his younger brother. Descended from a line of Kentish lawyers, Amherst was sent as a boy to be a page for Lionel Cranfield Sackville, first duke of Dorset, at Knole. In 1731 Dorset procured for him through Sir John Ligonier a commission as an ensign in the 1st foot guards. Impressed by the young Amherst, Ligonier remained his patron.

Early career During the War of the Austrian Succession Amherst served as aide-de-camp to Ligonier and saw action at Dettingen (1743), Fontenoy (1745), and Rocoux (1746). He then joined the staff of William Augustus, duke of Cumberland, where he organized intelligence gathering efforts, and was present at Laffeldt in 1747. Amherst remained part of Cumberland's military family, serving under him on the outbreak of the Seven Years' War. In 1756 he was made colonel of the 15th foot. He was with the duke at Hastenbeck (1757) and, surviving Cumberland's subsequent disgrace, remained on the continent as commissary to German troops in British pay.

Amherst's great opportunity came in 1758 when, at the urging of Ligonier, William Pitt the elder selected him over the heads of numerous senior officers to command the expedition against the French fortress of Louisbourg on Cape Breton Island. Supported by a naval squadron under Admiral Edward Boscawen, Amherst got his 14,000 men ashore safely and conducted a conventional siege that brought the surrender of Louisbourg in seven weeks. Amherst was then named to succeed Sir James Abercromby—who had just spectacularly failed to dislodge the French from Fort Ticonderoga in New York—as commander-in-chief of British forces in North America. Amherst proved much more successful than had his predecessors in persuading the North American colonies to support the war effort with men and money. The efforts involved, however, led him to take a negative view of the colonists, especially as soldiers. The Americans, he noted, 'if left to themselves would eat fryed Pork and lay in their tents all day long' (Shy, 93). Amherst was, however, tactful in dealing with colonial officials and confined his complaints to fellow officers and to the ministry. Ignorant of his opinions, colonists in New Hampshire, Massachusetts, New York, and Virginia would name four towns and a county after him.

Canada, 1760–1763 In July 1759, after lengthy preparations, Amherst succeeded in taking Ticonderoga and began plans for an invasion of Canada. James Wolfe, who had served under Amherst at Louisbourg, had been given the task of taking Quebec, after which he was to place himself under Amherst's direction. News of Wolfe's success—and

Jeffrey Amherst, first Baron Amherst (1717–1797), by Sir Joshua Reynolds, 1765

death—did not reach Amherst until mid-October. By this time Amherst had postponed his invasion until the following year. Criticized for not moving in 1759, Amherst may have doubted the prospects of Wolfe's success; at any rate he preferred to minimize his own risks. He husbanded his resources and worked out a careful plan for the conquest of Canada. In August 1760 Amherst launched a three-pronged invasion. Commanding the largest column himself, he moved down the St Lawrence from Lake Ontario. His forces converged at Montreal. Summoned to surrender, Pierre de Rigaud de Vaudreuil de Cavagnial, marquis de Vaudreuil, the French governor-general, attempted to buy time by suggesting that they wait until word from Europe confirmed or denied rumours of peace. Amherst refused: 'I have come to take Canada, and I will take nothing less' (Long, 133). On 8 September 1760 Vaudreuil surrendered New France.

The conquest of Canada was Amherst's greatest achievement. The rest of his North American service was less dramatic though also indicative of his organizational abilities. In addition to establishing a military government for Canada, Amherst managed effectively the relatively thankless tasks of keeping colonial forces in the field after the French danger had been eliminated and meeting demands for troops to serve in the West Indies, seriously depleting his own forces in the process.

Amherst's most critical challenge, however, proved to be Indian relations, a task at which he was much less adept. Amherst held a low opinion of Native Americans. His characterization of the Cherokee as a 'perfidious race

of Savages' (Long, 128) typified his attitude. He underestimated and distrusted Indians as allies and was contemptuous of them as enemies. He particularly detested their practice of sometimes massacring or torturing prisoners and blamed the French for permitting such conduct. (For this reason he refused to grant the surrendering garrisons at Louisbourg and Montreal the honours of war.) He was slow to appreciate signs of Indian unrest as the war wound down in North America, and he worsened the situation by encouraging settlement around frontier forts and by stopping in 1761 the practice of giving gifts to friendly tribes. When a general Indian war—the Pontiac War—broke out in May 1763 Amherst at first dismissed it as 'Meer Bugbears' (Anderson, 538). When he eventually grasped the gravity of the situation he soon had troops moving into the interior (with orders to take no Indian prisoners), though he was recalled before the war was brought to an end. A particularly controversial aspect of Amherst's response was an attempt to infect the Indians threatening Fort Pitt with smallpox by providing them with contaminated blankets. Amherst enthusiastically approved the proposal by Colonel Henry Bouquet: 'You will Do well to try to Innoculate the Indians by means of Blanketts, as well as to try Every other method that can serve to Extirpate this Execreble Race' (Fenn, 1556–7). It is likely, however, that the Fort Pitt garrison had acted on its own before Amherst's approval arrived. The British government was taken aback by Pontiac's rising and tended to blame Amherst for lack of warning if not for the uprising itself. His long-standing request to be relieved of the American command was soon granted. The Pontiac War was to have significant consequences in encouraging the British government to keep a standing army in North America and to limit settlement east of the Appalachians, measures that helped to provoke colonial resistance in the post-war era.

Amherst's return to England was not the triumph his conquest of Canada had led him to expect. He had received some measure of recognition: in 1759 he had been named governor of Virginia (on a non-resident basis) and in 1761 he was appointed KB. He was also by this time colonel of the 60th foot (the Royal Americans). Amherst, however, felt compelled periodically to remind others of his achievements. George III, while noting Amherst's considerable services, once remarked that they 'would not be lessened if he left the appreciating them to others' (Patterson, 92).

Amherst's return from America saw major transitions in his personal life. His wife—Jane Dalison (b. 1722) whom he had married at Gray's Inn chapel, London, on 20 May 1753—went insane. After her death (7 January 1765) Amherst razed the family seat at Riverhead (which he had inherited on the death of his brother Sackville in 1763) and built a new house that he christened 'Montreal'. On 26 March 1767, at St James's, Westminster, he married Elizabeth Cary (1739/40–1830), the daughter of Lieutenant-General George Cary. Both marriages proved childless, though Amherst had a natural son and namesake (c.1752–

1814) who rose to the rank of major-general; the identity of his mother is unknown.

Later career Promoted lieutenant-general in 1765, Amherst pursued a career that had its peacetime ups and downs over the next decade. Few patrons were left to forward his interest: Cumberland died in 1765, and Ligonier was increasingly less influential until his own death in 1770. Respected by his fellow officers and sometimes consulted by ministers on military matters, Amherst was reserved and aloof by nature and generally shunned the company of politicians. He was shocked in 1768 when asked to resign as governor of Virginia so that the penurious Norborne Berkeley, fourth Baron Botetourt, could be sent out in his stead. Angry at 'having my pocket picked of the Government of Virginia' (Amherst MSS, U1350, C81/13), he reacted by resigning his colonelcies as well. Temporarily the darling of the opposition, who used his treatment as an occasion to attack the Chatham administration, Amherst was eventually mollified when George III intervened with promises of a peerage and an equivalent to the £1500 a year he had lost from his governorship. Adamantly refusing a pension, he was named in 1770 governor of Guernsey and in 1772 lieutenant-general of the ordnance. In 1776 he received his peerage as Baron Amherst of Holmesdale.

Amherst's American experience made him an obvious source of advice to the North ministry as relations with the colonies worsened in the early 1770s. Offered the American command in 1774, he refused. Some read into this sympathy for the Americans. Amherst, however, entirely supported the government's colonial policy; he simply had no desire to return to America. As a peer Amherst regularly attended the Lords where he consistently supported the North ministry and confined his infrequent verbal contributions to military matters. After the American victory at Saratoga in October 1777 Amherst declined the American command for the second time. In early 1778 he was promoted general and accepted the position of commander-in-chief (with the title general on the staff), a position something like a modern chief of staff that also included command of home forces and a seat in the cabinet. Uncomfortable in the presence of politicians, he was a taciturn cabinet colleague, generally expressing his approval or disapproval of propositions in as few words as possible. Lord George Germain (who as Lord George Sackville had been a boyhood friend) noted that Amherst 'never could, without great difficulty, be induced to assign the reasons or state the grounds of his opinion' (*Memoirs of … Wraxall*, 1.407). He consequently exerted relatively little influence on the overall direction of the war in America and did not attempt to dissuade the cabinet from decisions with which he disagreed. Amherst found more congenial the command of home forces. Here he was able to limit political influence in appointments and promotions, and he made it a policy that officers whose regiments were posted overseas should join them or resign. He also found a focus in preparing for a possible Franco-Spanish invasion, a serious prospect by 1779. Amherst methodically developed plans to meet the threat and frequently reviewed regular and militia regiments to improve their readiness. In general he became opposed to sending more troops overseas.

While Amherst's home defence plans were never put to the test, he did find himself forced into action when the Gordon riots shook London in June 1780. He was criticized variously for slowness in reacting, for neglecting the City in his troop dispositions, and for disarming law-abiding subjects as well as rioters. Careful to observe the law in using military force, he ended the riots in forty-eight hours once he had authorization to act without magistrates.

When the North administration fell in 1782 the politically unaware Amherst was surprised to find himself replaced as commander-in-chief by Henry Seymour Conway. He subsequently voted against Shelburne's peace preliminaries and the Fox–North India Bill. He became a supporter of the younger Pitt, and in 1788 was granted a second peerage, as first Baron Amherst of Montreal, with special remainder to William Pitt *Amherst, his nephew and heir. After war broke out with revolutionary France, Amherst was recalled as commander-in-chief in 1793. The army was unprepared for the conflict, and two years under Amherst's leadership did not noticeably improve its performance. In 1795 Pitt told George III:

> the feelings of personal regard and esteem which every one bears towards Lord Amherst cannot prevent a very general sense that his age and perhaps his natural temper are little suited to the activity and energy which the present moment seems to call for. (*The Later Correspondence of George III*, ed. A. Aspinall, 5 vols., 1962–70, 2.298)

Amherst was replaced by the king's son, Frederick, duke of York. Amherst declined an earldom but was made a field marshal in 1796. He died at his home, 'Montreal', Riverhead, Kent, on 3 August 1797, and was buried on 10 August at Sevenoaks.

Assessment One of the major figures in eighteenth-century military history, Amherst was a soldier whose career followed an uneven trajectory. While cautious and more likely to inspire respect than affection, he possessed sound judgement and organizational abilities of a high order. His great success came early, however, and even his conquest of Canada was clouded by his failures in Indian relations. His reticence and discomfort in the company of politicians later limited his influence on the direction of the American war, though he made useful contributions to the war effort at home. The last three and a half decades of Amherst's career were ultimately anti-climactic, and he came close to outliving his reputation.

WILLIAM C. LOWE

Sources J. C. Long, *Lord Jeffery Amherst: a soldier of the king* (1933) · R. Whitworth, *Field Marshal Lord Ligonier: a story of the British army, 1702–1770* (1958) · F. Anderson, *Crucible of war: the Seven Years' War and the fate of empire in British North America, 1754–1766* (2000) · J. Shy, *Toward Lexington: the role of the British army in the coming of the American Revolution* (1965) · P. Mackesy, *The war for America, 1775–1783* (1964) · R. H. Whitworth, 'Field-Marshal Lord Amherst: a military enigma', *History Today*, 9 (1959), 132–7 · A. T. Patterson, *The other armada: the Franco-Spanish attempt to invade Britain in 1779* (1960) · E. A. Fenn, 'Biological warfare in eighteenth-century America: beyond Jeffery Amherst', *Journal of American History*, 86 (2000),

1552–80 • [J. Amherst], *The journal of Jeffery Amherst*, ed. J. C. Webster (1930) • T. Hayter, *The army and the crowd in mid-Georgian England* (1978) • GEC, *Peerage*, new edn • *The historical and the posthumous memoirs of Sir Nathaniel William Wraxall, 1772–1784*, ed. H. B. Wheatley, 5 vols. (1884) • *The correspondence of George, prince of Wales, 1770–1812*, ed. A. Aspinall, 8 vols. (1963–71) • CKS, Amherst papers, U1350 [microfilm, Library of Virginia, Richmond, Virginia, USA] • W. R. Nester, *'Haughty conquerors': Amherst and the great Indian uprising of 1763* (2000)

Archives Amherst College Library, Massachusetts, corresp. and papers • BL, papers, RP288 [microfilm] • CKS, corresp. and papers • L. Cong., accounts • PRO, military corresp. and papers, WO 34 • U. Mich., Clements L., corresp. and papers | American Antiquarian Society, Worcester, Massachusetts, corresp. with John Bradstreet • BL, corresp. with Frederick Haldimand, Sir R. Burton, Charles Rainsford, and others, Add. MSS 21657–21737, *passim* • BL, letters to the earls of Hardwicke, Add. MSS 35613–35665, *passim* • CKS, letters to William Pitt • Hunt. L., corresp. with J. Abercromby; corresp. with Sir George Pocock • Legislative Library of Nova Scotia, Halifax, letters to Charles Lawrence • NMM, Sandwich MSS, letters to Lord Sandwich • PRO, letters to William Pitt, PRO 30/8 • U. Mich., Clements L., corresp. with T. Gage • U. Nott. L., letters to General Monckton

Likenesses F. Hayman, group portrait, oils, c.1760 (*The clemency of General Amherst*), Beaverbrook Art Gallery, Fredericton, New Brunswick, Canada • J. Reynolds, oils, 1765, Amherst College, Massachusetts, Mead Art Museum [*see illus.*] • J. Watson, mezzotint, 1766 (after J. Reynolds), BM, NPG • M. F. Quadal, group portrait, oils, 1772 (*George III at a review*), Royal Collection • J. Sayers, caricature, etching, pubd 1782 (after his earlier work), NPG • attrib. T. Lawranson, oils, c.1785, National Gallery of Canada, Ottawa • S. W. Reynolds, mezzotint, pubd 1820 (after J. Reynolds), BM • J. S. Copley, group portrait, oils (*The collapse of the earl of Chatham in the House of Lords, 7 July 1778*), Tate collection; on loan to NPG • T. Gainsborough, oils, Amherst College, Amherst, Massachusetts; version, NPG • plaster medallion (after J. Tassie), Scot. NPG

Wealth at death income c.£3100 p.a. in mid-1760s (£1500 from governorship of Virginia, £800 from two colonelcies, £800 from private means: Long, *Lord Jeffrey Amherst*, 197

Amherst, John (bap. **1717/18**, d. **1778**), naval officer, was baptized on either 6 January 1717 or 6 January 1718 at Sevenoaks, Kent, the son of Jeffrey Amherst of Riverhead, Kent, and Elizabeth Kerrill. His elder brother was Jeffrey *Amherst, first Baron Amherst. According to his passing certificate John Amherst went to sea in 1730 and passed on 6 January 1737. He served mainly with Captain Thomas Smith, his patron, and was promoted lieutenant on 24 July 1739. He was promoted captain on 29 December 1744. Amherst took a prominent part in the naval protest against the 1749 Navy Bill which, among other things, put officers on half pay under martial law. In May 1751 he wrote to a friend that he believed his career was being adversely affected by Admiralty resentment at his action (Wyndham, 2.45). Nevertheless he served as flag-captain to Rear-Admiral Thomas Griffin, on the *Princess Mary*, in the East Indies. In 1753 he commissioned the *Mars* (64 guns) as guardship at Portsmouth. With the threat of war in 1755 the *Mars* formed part of the fleet sent into North American waters under Vice-Admiral Edward Boscawen. In going into Halifax harbour the *Mars* ran aground and was totally lost, though her stores were saved. Amherst was acquitted of all blame at the resulting court martial, and on his return to England was appointed to the *Deptford* (50 guns), which sailed with Admiral John Byng to the

Mediterranean in March 1756. In the action off Cape Mola on 20 May Byng ordered the *Deptford* to quit the line of battle, and be ready to assist any ship, as she might be directed: Amherst's part was thus one of an onlooker until, late in the day, he was signalled to support the *Intrepid*, then much disabled. In the following year he commanded the *Captain* (64 guns) at Louisbourg, under Francis Holburne and Boscawen, and later he commanded the *Arrogant* (74 guns), first at the capture of Belle Île in 1761, and afterwards, in 1762, as senior officer at Gibraltar, with a broad pennant. He was advanced to flag-rank in 1764 and to vice-admiral of the blue on 24 October 1770; and in 1776 he was appointed commander-in-chief at Plymouth. Amherst married Anne, eldest daughter of Edward Linzee, mayor of Portsmouth. In February 1750 Amherst, known for his bad temper, informed Thomas Smith that 'we are parted by articles, and I never will see hir more' (Wyndham, 2.45).

Amherst died suddenly at Gosport on 14 February 1778, just two weeks after his promotion to admiral of the blue. He was buried in the parish church of Sevenoaks. In his will Amherst left everything to his brother; his widow then married Thomas Monday.

J. K. LAUGHTON, rev. NICHOLAS TRACY

Sources D. Syrett and R. L. DiNardo, *The commissioned sea officers of the Royal Navy, 1660–1815*, rev. edn, Occasional Publications of the Navy RS, 1 (1994) • M. Wyndham, *Chronicles of the eighteenth century*, 2 vols. (1924) • PROB 11/1039 • N. Surry and J. H. Thomas, eds., *Book of original entries, 1731–1751* (1976) • IGI

Amherst, William Amhurst Tyssen-, first Baron Amherst of Hackney (**1835–1909**), book collector, was born at Narford Hall, Swaffham, Norfolk, on 25 April 1835, the eldest son of William George Daniel-Tyssen (1801–1855), who had added Tyssen to his surname in 1814 on his marriage to Amelia, daughter of Captain John Amhurst RN, a native of Kent, and Mary, eldest daughter of Andrew Fountaine, of Narford. His maternal grandmother, Mary Tyssen, was daughter and heir of Francis John Tyssen, from whom the family inherited extensive property in Hackney. Together with his father he took by royal licence, on 6 August 1852, the name of Tyssen-Amhurst, for which he substituted Tyssen-Amherst on 16 August 1877.

A relationship with the Amhersts of Kent, descendants of the general, was remote. More direct was one with Sir Andrew Fountaine, the eighteenth-century virtuoso, among whose collections of books, coins, and works of art Tyssen-Amhurst grew up at Narford. He was educated at Eton College and matriculated from Christ Church, Oxford, on 19 May 1853. He was still an undergraduate when his father died in 1855, bequeathing him large properties in London and Norfolk. His country estates at Didlington Hall, near Brandon, and elsewhere totalled 9488 acres in the returns for 1881; he farmed on a large scale and was a noted breeder of Norfolk polled cattle. He was Conservative MP for West Norfolk (1880–85) and for South-West Norfolk (1885–92); he also served as high sheriff of his county in 1866. Tyssen-Amhurst married, on 4 June 1856, at Hunmanby, Yorkshire, Margaret Susan (1835–

1919), only child of Robert Mitford, of Mitford Castle, Northumberland, and of Hunmanby Hall. They had seven daughters, of whom six survived him. These included Alicia Margaret *Amherst (1865–1941).

Collecting books and antiquities was Tyssen-Amhurst's chief interest, and he gathered a library rich in ecclesiastical history, especially of the Reformation and the Church of England, and in editions of the English Bible (of which his collection was inferior only to that of Lord Ashburnham). Equally strong was his interest in the history of the spread of printing, and historic bookbindings. He bought steadily from the 1860s, often in friendly rivalry with the earl of Carysfort, and had the benefit in the saleroom of the regular agency of Bernard Quaritch. His library included seventeen Caxtons, in its day one of the two or three best collections in private hands, and his early printed books illustrated the spread of typography in practically every European country. He was a member of the Roxburghe Club and presented to his fellow members an edition (by I. H. Jeayes) of *Norfolk Letters of Philip Gawdy, 1579–1616* (1906); he also presented volumes to the Hakluyt Society and the Scottish Text Society.

A detailed catalogue of Tyssen-Amhurst's collection was in preparation by the distinguished bibliographer Seymour De Ricci, who gratefully recorded that he owed to Tyssen-Amhurst's 'kind lessons in English bibliography … my own earliest interest in that difficult science'. However, owing to the dishonesty of Charles Cheston, the solicitor entrusted with the administration of Tyssen-Amhurst's estate and trust funds, a sale of the library at Didlington proved urgently necessary. De Ricci's *catalogue raisonné* had to be reduced to a much abbreviated (though still substantial) hand-list, speedily produced for private circulation in 1906. A major sale by Sothebys was organized: its two sections commenced on 3 December 1908 and 24 March 1909, and the total realized was £32,592. The seventeen Caxtons were sold privately to John Pierpont Morgan for £24,000. (Later sales were held by Sothebys on 12 December 1911, and on 17 January and 14 November 1921.)

Tyssen-Amhurst also took a pioneering interest in Egyptian antiquities by collecting some important papyri, of which two catalogues were issued: by P. E. Newberry on the Egyptian papyri in 1899, and by B. P. Grenfell and A. S. Hunt on the Greek in 1900. Both sections were eventually bought by Pierpont Morgan in 1913. Tyssen-Amhurst's other antiquities included old Gobelins and other tapestries, French and English furniture, Limoges enamels, and English maiolica; these were sold by Christies on 11 December 1908 for £38,796, with a further £3500 being raised from prints and paintings.

Tyssen-Amhurst, who had made little mark in the House of Commons, but who was rich and well connected, was created Baron Amherst of Hackney in Lord Salisbury's dissolution honours in 1892, with a special remainder to his eldest daughter, Mary Rothes Margaret, wife of Lord William Cecil, a son of the third marquess of Exeter, and their children. Lord Amherst was 'of middle height and sturdy appearance, of genial and unassuming manners' (*DNB*).

He died suddenly on 16 January 1909 at 23 Queen's Gate Gardens, London, and was buried on 20 January in the family vault at Didlington.   ALAN BELL

Sources DNB · GEC, *Peerage* · *The Times* (18 Jan 1909) · *The Times* (21 Jan 1909) · S. De Ricci, *English collectors of books and manuscripts* (1930)
Archives Hackney Archives, London, corresp. and papers, incl. archaeological papers · Norfolk RO, corresp. and papers · Order of St John Library and Museum, London, papers as secretary-general, Order of St John of Jerusalem · University of Toronto, Thomas Fisher Rare Book Library, family and personal corresp. and papers, incl. genealogical notes | CUL, letters to Joseph Bonomi
Likenesses J. Collier, portrait, repro. in *Catalogue of old Gobelins and other tapestry … collected by the Rt. Hon. Lord Amherst of Hackney* [1908] · Spy [L. Ward], chromolithograph caricature, NPG; repro. in VF (10 March 1904) · engraving (after J. Collier)
Wealth at death £67,457 19s. 1d.: probate, 10 Feb 1909, CGPLA Eng. & Wales · £341—net: GEC, *Peerage*

Amherst, William Pitt, first Earl Amherst of Arracan (1773–1857), diplomatist and governor-general of Bengal, was born on 14 January 1773 in Bath, the first of three children of Lieutenant-General William Amherst (1732–1781), aide-de-camp to the king, governor of St John's, Newfoundland, and adjutant-general of the army, and his wife, Elizabeth Patterson (d. 1776/7). Amherst and his two sisters were brought up on the Isle of Wight until the deaths of their parents caused them to be transferred to Kent, where they were placed under the care of their uncle Jeffrey *Amherst, first Baron Amherst (1717–1797), commander-in-chief of the army.

Amherst attended Westminster School and afterwards went on to Christ Church, Oxford, where he graduated MA in 1797. His academic performance was unexceptional and contemporaries remembered him as quiet and inoffensive. However, Westminster and Christ Church introduced Amherst to several individuals who would figure prominently in his later career: George Canning, Charles Wynn, and John Parker, first earl of Morley. When his uncle died leaving no issue in 1797, Amherst succeeded to the title of Baron Amherst of Montreal. His first marriage was on 24 July 1800 to Sarah, countess dowager of Plymouth (1762–1838), widow of the fifth earl of Plymouth and daughter of Andrew, second Lord Archer, whom he had first met while touring the continent in 1793. They had three sons and one daughter: Jeffrey, Sarah, William, and Frederick. Jeffrey died in India in 1826; the second brother, William, succeeded to his father's titles on his father's death in 1857. After the death of his first wife Amherst married on 25 May 1839 Mary (1792–1864), widow of his stepson, the sixth earl of Plymouth, and eldest daughter and coheir of the third duke of Dorset. Amherst's second marriage was without issue.

Amherst had little political or diplomatic experience prior to his appointment as ambassador-extraordinary to the court of the Two Sicilies in 1809. He was by his own admission a poor and infrequent speaker in the House of Lords. Nevertheless, he did curry some favour at court and was lord of the bedchamber to George III from 1802 to 1804. His two years at the Sicilian court were fruitless as he tried, without sufficient support from London, to patch

William Pitt Amherst, first Earl Amherst of Arracan (1773–1857), by Sir Thomas Lawrence, 1821

over the rift between Sicilian constitutionalists and nationalists and the island's nominal rulers, the exiled Bourbon king of Naples and his wife, Maria Carolina, who fought tenaciously to defend their authority. Following his resignation and departure from Sicily in 1811 Amherst retreated from public life until he was called to lead an embassy to the court of the Chinese emperor in 1816. A recent spate of disturbances between European seamen and Chinese locals, together with concerns that the Chinese court might react adversely to British expansion into the borderlands between India and Tibet, led the British government to mount this embassy. With hindsight, it is clear that it was doomed from the start. The British had not learned from the failure of Lord Macartney's embassy of 1797 that their idea of diplomatic intercourse was fundamentally at odds with that of the Chinese court, particularly in the use and interpretation of symbols and ceremonies that reflected the Chinese court's perception of a hierarchically arranged world with their emperor at its apex. Following Amherst's refusal to perform the *kowtow* (a ritual that involved kneeling three times and touching one's head to the floor nine times), Amherst and his entourage were sent away from Peking (Beijing) without an audience with the Jiaqing emperor (1796–1820). Like Macartney, Amherst looked upon the *kowtow* as demeaning to both Britain and himself. There followed another period in the political wilderness until Amherst's appointment in 1823 as governor-general of Bengal in succession to the marquess of Hastings.

Amherst went to India anticipating peace and stability; instead he found India on the brink of a war with Burma that would ultimately prove to be the most expensive and controversial campaign fought to date. His briefings with senior officials in London prior to his departure had not even hinted that there was a remote chance of war breaking out in India. Rather, he was told that it was now time to implement the political and economic reforms, including sweeping changes to the military establishment, over which the marquess of Hastings had procrastinated. Amherst's intention to follow these instructions was dashed by the war. Tensions between British India and Burma had a long history, but Amherst's predecessors, preoccupied with troubles elsewhere in India, had generally ignored them. However, in 1823 there was an escalation in tensions, triggered primarily by Burmese moves into Arakan, Assam, and Cachar, semi-independent states which lay astride the frontier between British India and Burma. When the Burmese court refused to pull back from its forward positions, war was declared on 24 February 1824. Amherst was reluctant to engage in war; not only was he mindful of London's injunctions to bring back prosperity but he was conscious of his own limited experience. He confided to Lord Morley that 'I would not have you suppose that I deem myself a man of sufficient calibre to govern India in difficult times' (Amherst to Morley, 23 Aug 1825, BL, Add. MS 48225). Eventually Amherst was persuaded to mount an attack on Rangoon by the more experienced officials around him, including John Adam (acting governor-general, 1822–3, and member of the supreme council, 1823–5) and Thomas Munro (governor of Madras, 1819–27). To do otherwise, they argued, would give the impression that Britain had lost its resolve and that its military powers were diminished. What had been predicted to be a short and cheap war of no more than six weeks turned into two years of arduous campaigning that cost nearly £5 million, yielded little loot, gained the unprofitable territories of Arakan, Tenasserim, and Assam, and so demoralized the army that not only was there a spectacular rise in desertions but British troops were forced to put down brutally a mutiny of Indian sepoys at Barrackpore in October 1824. Even the short and victorious campaign against Bharatpur conducted between December 1825 and January 1826 could not expunge the memory of the First Anglo-Burmese War.

Neither historians nor his contemporaries and successors have been kind to Amherst; John Malcolm wrote to him that he was being compared to 'the person who brought the blue flies into the butcher's shop' (31 May 1826, MS Eur F140/137a). Nearly a hundred years later Lord Curzon described him as having left 'the most inconspicuous and impalpable of impressions' (G. Curzon, *British Government in India*, 1925, 2.172). Yet such judgements do not take into account how constrained Amherst was by forces beyond his control, nor the extent to which the campaigns mounted against him masked over partisan agendas within the government and the East India Company. Even his appointment had been a weak one. Of the nine names put forward to succeed Hastings, Amherst's was the one that alienated the fewest, but conversely it generated little enthusiasm, and was only approved by the East India Company by a narrow margin. His chief backer, George Canning, also intrigued against him once Canning had calculated that a vacancy in Calcutta could be put to his own political advantage. Amherst's stock at court had fallen owing to his support for Catholic emancipation and sympathies for Queen Caroline. In India his lack of proconsular style and his frugal ways won him few friends. He was too conciliatory and deferential to those around him, preferring to depend on others, like Thomas Munro, for advice, rather than act in an autocratic manner. Officials in India took this to be a sign of weakness and indecision and openly flouted his authority. Had it not been for the intervention of the duke of Wellington in 1825, who armed himself with up-to-date reports and assessments from Thomas Munro, Amherst might not have survived as governor-general.

Amherst was exhausted by the widespread criticism of his management of the war. The sudden death of his eldest son at Barrackpore towards the end of 1826 was the final blow. He resolved to return to England, even before the usual five-year term had elapsed, as soon as he returned from a lengthy upcountry tour in which he inaugurated the viceregal practice of taking refuge in Simla during the hot season. Before his departure from India in 1827 Amherst did begin to address some of the army reforms and economic retrenchments which the court of directors had earlier demanded, though William Bentinck, Amherst's successor, would later gain the credit as well as the opprobrium for them. Amherst received the customary promotion in the peerage and took the title of Earl Amherst of Arracan in the East Indies and Viscount Holmesdale of Holmesdale, Kent.

Amherst did not come away from India totally disgraced; he was named lord of the bedchamber by George IV (1829–30) and again by William IV (1830–37). Lord Ellenborough suggested that he succeed the marquess of Anglesey as lord lieutenant of Ireland, but this was rejected by Wellington. Seven years later he would have sailed to Canada in 1835 as governor-in-chief but for the collapse of Peel's ministry. Thereafter, he stayed clear of national and imperial politics, preferring instead to spend his time on his Kentish estates, where he occasionally took up local affairs, pushing for road improvements in the county and promoting the establishment of a savings bank in Sevenoaks. He died at his home, Knole House, near Sevenoaks, on 13 March 1857 and was buried eight days later in the church at Sevenoaks.

DOUGLAS M. PEERS

Sources A. T. Ritchie and R. Evans, *Lord Amherst and the British advance eastwards to Burma* (1894) · Burke, *Peerage* (1837) · D. M. Peers, *Between Mars and Mammon: colonial armies and the garrison state in India, 1819–1835* (1995) · H. Ellis, *Journal of the proceedings of the late embassy to China*, 2nd edn, 2 vols. (1818) · L. Kitzan, 'Lord Amherst and the declaration of war on Burma, 1824', *Journal of Asian History*, 9 (1975), 101–28 · L. Kitzan, 'Lord Amherst and Pegu: the annexation issue, 1824–1826', *Journal of Southeast Asian Studies*, 8 (1977), 176–95 · J. Dunlop, *The pleasant town of Sevenoaks: a history* (1964) · D. M. Peers, 'The duke of Wellington and British India during the Liverpool administration, 1819–1827', *Journal of Imperial and Commonwealth History*, 17 (1988–9), 5–25 · C. J. Phillips, *History of the Sackville family*, 2 [1929] · BL OIOC, Amherst MSS, MS Eur. F 140/137a
Archives BL OIOC, corresp. and papers, MS Eur. F 140 · BL OIOC, Home misc. series, corresp. and papers relating to India · BL OIOC, letters to his wife, MS Eur. B 363 · CKS, papers · NRA, priv. coll., journals · U. Nott. L., papers relating to India | BL, corresp. with Lord Morley, Add. MSS 48224–48225 · BL, corresp. with Sir Robert Peel, Add. MSS 40352–40388, 40560, *passim* · BL OIOC, letters to Sir Thomas Munro, MS Eur. F 151 · BL OIOC, letters to Sir G. A. Robinson, MS Eur. F 142 · NL Wales, Charles Wynn MSS · priv. coll., corresp. with Lady Sarah Williams-Hay · U. Nott. L., corresp. with Lord William Bentinck · U. Southampton L., Wellington MSS
Likenesses T. Lawrence, oils, 1821, Toledo Museum of Art, Ohio [*see illus.*] · J. Posselwhite, stipple, 1845 (after H. L. Smith), BM · G. Hayter, group portrait, oils (*The trial of Queen Caroline, 1820*), NPG · F. R. Say, oils, Christ Church Oxf. · oils, repro. in Ritchie and Evans, *Lord Amherst*, frontispiece · oils (after A. W. Devis), NPG

Amhurst, Nicholas (1697–1742), satirist and political writer, was born on 16 October 1697 at Marden, Kent, the first son of Edward Amhurst (*bap.* 1665, *d.* 1713), grazier, and grandson of George Amhurst, rector of Marden. His mother, Martha, *née* Simmonds (1664–1699), died before he was two years old. He was educated at Merchant Taylors' School, London, and at St John's College, Oxford. While at Oxford he became involved with a group of students and fellows hostile to the political (tory) and religious (high-church) commitments of the university, most notable of whom were Thomas Tooly (1688–1758), Samuel Downes (1697–1723), and James Welton (1699–1772). Amhurst was to have been elected to a fellowship of his college but on 29 June 1719 he was expelled from the university for what was described as misconduct and libertinism. His first considerable offence to the university was his satirical poem *Strephon's Revenge: a Satire on the Oxford Toasts*. In this work, written in 1718 and printed by his friend Richard Francklin (1699–1765), he accused the head of his college, assorted members of the university, and a number of the women of Oxford of, variously, vanity, sloth, fornication, embezzlement, drunkenness, slander, and irreligion. A number of the figures in the poem were readily identifiable. His attacks on high-churchmen at this time included *Protestant Popery, or, The Convocation: a Poem* and *A Congratulatory Epistle from his Holiness the Pope to the Revd. Dr. Snape* (both 1718). Thomas Hearne reported in January 1719 that Amhurst 'is said to have bought ten Pounds' worth of Pamphletts on purpose to qualifie himself to write in Defence of the Bp of Bangor's Principles' (*Remarks*, 6.287). Bishop Benjamin Hoadley was the leading low-church controversialist; Andrew Snape was one of his principal antagonists.

After his expulsion from the university Amhurst moved to London, became a professional writer, and went on to produce the *Terrae-filius*. Before being collected in two volumes, in 1726, and running to four editions, the *Terrae-*

filius was published in fifty numbers as a bi-weekly news-paper, from 11 January to 6 July 1721. It consisted of satires upon the life of Oxford, and though banned in the city it was much read by members of the university, being available from Mr Drew's ironmonger's shop in Abingdon. Amhurst's criticism of university life was undoubtedly bound up with his expulsion, his anger and contempt being précised in no. 45 of *Terrae-filius* and outlined in the mock dedication of his *Poems on Several Occasions* (1720) to William Delaune, the college head said to have been responsible for his expulsion from Oxford:

> *Imprimis*, For loving *foreign* Turnips and *Presbyterian* Bishops. *Item*, For believing that *Steeples* and *Organs* are not absolutely necessary to salvation. *Item*, For Ingratitude to his Benefactor, that spotless Martyr, St. WILIAM LAUD. *Item*, for *Preaching* without Orders, and *Praying* without a Commission. *Item*, For lampooning *Priestcraft* and *Petticoatcraft* … *Item*, For *not* lampooning the *Government* and the *Revolution*.   (p. xiii)

This work, with its biting attacks upon the authorities and its amusing essays on student idleness, displays Amhurst's trenchant satiric accomplishments and stern morality; his comedic sense of life at Oxford has no equal in the history of such satires. His prolonged and specific criticism on the manners, morals, and frequent unscholarly activities of eighteenth-century Oxford has become an important historical source for students of the history of the university. The *Terrae-filius*, the collected edition of which (1726) had a frontispiece by the young Hogarth, remains Amhurst's finest work. From this period his verses, in *Poems on Several Occasions* (1720) and *Oculus Britanniae* (1724), gained a wide readership.

That Amhurst, after the success of the *Terrae-filius*, with its whig sympathies, should then edit (for Bolingbroke and Pulteney) the leading anti-Walpole newspaper, *The Craftsman*, epitomizes not only a mercurial element in his personality but also a tendency to self-destructiveness and a rigid opposition to governing authorities. He conducted (under the pseudonym Caleb D'Anvers) *The Craftsman* from its inception in December 1726 until the Pulteney circle was accommodated to the government in 1737. Estimates of *The Craftsman*'s circulation vary from an improbable 10,000 to a niggardly 500 copies (Kramnick), but there is some agreement that it was the most important periodical of its day. While Bolingbroke and Pulteney were the major writers for the journal it is clear that Amhurst produced a good deal of the material himself. There is, further, some evidence that his Oxford tutor Thomas Tooly (expelled from St John's College in 1721) contributed pieces. On 2 July 1737 *The Craftsman* published a cod letter purportedly from Colly Cibber. This ironical epistle advocated that a new act for licensing plays be extended to past as well as contemporary works, pointing out that a good many old works could be construed as seditious and a danger to good order. Most notably mentioned in this light were the plays of Shakespeare. The letter concludes by suggesting that its author should be made the licensing authority for old plays. For this libel Henry Haines, who had reluctantly succeeded Francklin as printer of *The Craftsman* five years earlier, was immediately arrested,

and in August admitted to bail in recognizance of £600. In September Amhurst surrendered himself on account of the libel and was held for ten days but then released on a plea of habeas corpus. His printer, evidently deserted by all the crew of *The Craftsman*, was less fortunate: Haines was tried in February 1738 before a special jury and sentenced to one year's imprisonment, but in the event spent two years in the king's bench prison because he could not find bail. His own account of the affair, in *Treachery, Baseness, and Cruelty Display'd to the Full* (1740), complains bitterly about the negligence and malevolence of both Francklin and Amhurst. A contemporary satirist referred in 1738 to 'Poor *Haines*'s ears in pain for *Caleb*'s wit' (Plomer, 114).

Shortly after this affair, when his political allies made their peace within the government, Amhurst began to decline. The irony of his life is that he should have ended up a tenant of a Walpole. Deserted by most of his well-placed friends—most particularly Pulteney—he spent his last days in a cottage of his first printer, Francklin, on Horace Walpole's Strawberry Hill estate. He died there, unmarried, on 27 April 1742 and was buried, a gentleman, at Twickenham parish church; the cause of death has been variously stated as 'a fever' (Cibber, 337), 'immoderate drinking of Geneva' (Varey, xxx), and 'a broken heart' (ibid.). The best portrait of Amhurst (depicted as Caleb D'Anvers) is a mezzotint print of 1720 by Isaac Simon. It is not possible, given the paucity of evidence, to discern the balance in Amhurst between the changeable, embittered hothead and the loyal, if excitable, man of principle. It is clear that he had long-lasting friendships but equally clear that he offended many who might have been in a position to assist him.   MICHAEL ERBEN

Sources N. Amhurst, *Terrae-filius, or, The secret history of the University of Oxford*, 3rd edn (1754) · *The Country Journal, or, The Craftsman* (1726–37) · *GM*, 1st ser., 7 (1737), 430, 513, 573; 8 (1738), 108, 274; 9 (1739), 323 · S. Varey, *Lord Bolingbroke: contributions to The Craftsman* (1982), xv, xvi, xxx · *The manuscripts of his grace the duke of Portland*, 10 vols., HMC, 29 (1891–1931), vol. 7, p. 257 [letter from William Stratford to Harley] · H. R. Plomer and others, *A dictionary of the printers and booksellers who were at work in England, Scotland, and Ireland from 1726 to 1775* (1932), 113–14 · IGI · H. Haines, *Treachery, baseness, and cruelty display'd to the full* (1740) · I. Kramnick, *Bolingbroke and his circle* (1968), 19 · R. Shiels, *The lives of the poets of Great Britain and Ireland*, ed. T. Cibber, 5 (1753), 335–8 · *Remarks and collections of Thomas Hearne*, ed. C. E. Doble and others, 6, OHS, 43 (1902), 285–7 · J. Ralph, *The case of authors by profession or trade* (1758) · A. Kippis and others, eds., *Biographia Britannica, or, The lives of the most eminent persons who have flourished in Great Britain and Ireland*, 2nd edn, 5 vols. (1778–93), vol. 1 · Merchant Taylors' School, London, register · St John's College, Oxford, register
Archives Bodl. Oxf., MS Eng. misc. c. 107
Likenesses I. Simon, mezzotint, 1720, AM Oxf., BM · line engraving, 1737, BM, NPG; repro. in C. D'Anvers [N. Amhurst], *The Country Journal, or, The Craftsman*, 8 (1737) · J. Simon, mezzotint (after G. Kneller), BM
Wealth at death very small; may have died leaving possessions worth less than £5: Varey, *Lord Bolingbroke*, xxx; *Biographia Britannica*, 175

Amice, countess of Rochefort and *suo jure* countess of Leicester (*d.* **1215**). *See under* Breteuil, Robert de, fourth earl of Leicester (*d.* 1204).

Amiens, Hugues d'. *See* Hugh (d. 1164).

Amigo, Peter Emmanuel (1864–1949), Roman Catholic bishop of Southwark, was born on 26 May 1864 at Waterport Street, Gibraltar, the ninth of the eleven children of Peter Lawrence Amigo (*b.* 1825), flour merchant, and his wife, Emily Savignon, or Sabinon (*b.* 1827). His parents were both Roman Catholics who had been born in Gibraltar. Amigo was educated locally until he was fourteen, when he was sent to school in England at St Edmund's College, Old Hall Green, Ware, Hertfordshire. While he was still at school there he decided to become a priest and continued his studies in philosophy at St Edmund's. He completed his theological studies at St Thomas's Theological College, Hammersmith, London, and was ordained a priest at Our Lady of Victories, Kensington, on 25 February 1888. His first appointment took him back to St Edmund's, Ware, to teach classics, church history, and scripture. In 1892 he was transferred to become assistant priest at Holy Trinity Church, Brook Green, Hammersmith, and was transferred after four years to St Michael's Church, Commercial Road, Stepney. On the death of Canon Akers he became parish priest there in 1901. At this time his old friend Francis Bourne was bishop of Southwark and he arranged for him to be transferred to the diocese of Southwark. Amigo entered the diocese in 1901 and was appointed parish priest of the church of the English Martyrs, Walworth, south London. The following year he was appointed joint vicar-general of the diocese.

Following the elevation of Francis Bourne to the see of Westminster, Amigo was chosen to succeed him at Southwark, an appointment due entirely to the influence of Francis Bourne, who overruled the selection of the canons of the diocese. However, shortly after his consecration, which took place on 25 March 1904 at his cathedral of St George, Southwark, he fell out with Bourne over the administration of the diocesan seminary at Wonersh and later over financial irregularities which had occurred while Bourne was bishop of Southwark. As a result Bourne spent much time trying to have Amigo removed from Southwark and posted to another diocese, either Plymouth or Hexham. When that failed he tried to have Southwark divided up so that Amigo could be sent off to a new diocese in either Kent or Sussex. At about the same time the bishop also had to contend with the modernist crisis and he was personally responsible for having the well-known Jesuit George Tyrrell excommunicated by Rome for publishing an article attacking Pius X in *The Times* on 30 September 1907. Later he denied Tyrrell a Catholic burial.

During the First World War, Amigo gave much help to exiles from Belgium and also travelled twice to Spain with government backing to help persuade Alfonso XIII from siding with Germany during the war. At the end of the war the bishop became involved with Irish politics. He used his influence with John Walter, proprietor of *The Times*, in obtaining evidence to show to the British government of the atrocities being committed in Ireland by the Black and Tans. He then supported Terence McSweeney, lord mayor of Cork, who was imprisoned in Brixton prison as a member of the IRA. McSweeney went on hunger strike and at his death in prison he was given a grand requiem mass in St George's Cathedral.

In the 1930s Amigo befriended King Alfonso, then in exile, and backed General Franco in the Spanish Civil War. As a result, on one occasion someone daubed the walls of the cathedral with the word 'Fascist'. In 1930 he had become responsible for promoting the cause of canonization of Thomas More and John Fisher, bishop of Rochester, who were put to death by Henry VIII for refusing to acknowledge Henry as head of the church. When they were canonized in 1935 Amigo regarded the event as the high water mark of his episcopate. As a result of this success he was given the personal title of archbishop by Pius XI in 1938. During the Second World War Amigo remained in London and in 1941 suffered the tragic loss by enemy action of his beloved cathedral of St George. However, he maintained a full schedule of visitations to his far-flung diocese, which covered Surrey, Sussex, and Kent, using public transport whenever possible.

Though short of stature Amigo was gifted with a loud voice, albeit with a strong Spanish accent. He could be brusque and abrupt at times, even during major ceremonies, but his overriding interest was in the poor and underprivileged. He had a photographic memory and could remember the names of people after a gap of over forty years. He rarely took a holiday, but one of his favourite activities was to visit the Kentish hop fields during the hop picking season, where he would meet up with families whom he had known in the East End of London. As a character he was larger than life and was never afraid to dabble in political matters if he thought it could aid religion. He had little time for women's liberation and felt that a woman should stay at home and look after her children.

Archbishop Amigo died on 1 October 1949 at St George's Cathedral after a short illness, though he had been very frail indeed for the final three years of his life. He was buried on 6 October inside the ruins of his cathedral (later rebuilt), following a solemn requiem at Westminster Cathedral, which was marked by a spontaneous expression of grief by thousands gathered outside.

MICHAEL CLIFTON

Sources records collected by Bishop Fitzgerald of Gibraltar, *c.*1950, Archives of Roman Catholic Archdiocese of Southwark, Southwark, London · Archives of the Roman Catholic Archdiocese of Southwark, Southwark, London · Westm. DA · B. Bogan, *The great link: a history of St George's, Southwark, 1786–1848–1948* [1948] · W. F. Brown, *Through windows of memory* (1946) · M. de la Bedoyère, *The life of Baron von Hugel* (1950) · *The Southwark Record* (1921–49) · G. A. Beck, 'And so this man also died', 1962, Archives of the Roman Catholic Diocese of Southwark, Southwark, London · M. Clifton, *Amigo friend of the poor* (1987) · P. E. Amigo, *A bishop to his people: pronouncements selected from his pastoral letters*, ed. H. Rochford (1934) · private information (2004) · personal knowledge (2004) · *CGPLA Eng. & Wales* (1949)

Archives St George's Roman Catholic Cathedral, Southwark, London, Archives of the Roman Catholic Archdiocese of Southwark, corresp., diaries, and papers | St Edmund's College, Ware · Westm. DA, corresp. Cardinal Bourne · Westm. DA

Likenesses J. Lavery, oils, 1927, Southwark Catholic Cathedral House · photographs, Southwark Catholic Cathedral House
Wealth at death £200 10s. 0d.: probate, 21 Dec 1949, CGPLA Eng. & Wales

Amigoni, Jacopo (c.1680x85–1752). See under Venetian painters in Britain (act. 1708–c.1750).

Amir Chand [Omichund, Umichund] (d. 1758), merchant, was a major trading partner of the British in Bengal and deeply involved in the events that gave them political power there. Very little is known about his origins. He appears to have been a Nanakpanthi Sikh who came to Bengal early in the eighteenth century from Agra in north India with his brother Deep Chand, to seek his fortune. Both men prospered. Amir Chand seems to have begun business under a great Calcutta merchant, Bostom Das Sett, who supplied the East India Company with cotton cloth. By the 1730s Amir Chand had himself become the leading supplier of the company, undertaking to procure up to one-third of what they required to ship to Britain in any one year. He lived in Calcutta in great state, owning a number of houses and employing a huge retinue. He was described as 'the most opulent inhabitant of the colony', whose way of life 'resembled more the state of a prince than the condition of a merchant' (Orme, 2, pt 1, 50). As well as trading with the British, Amir Chand dealt with the nawabs, the rulers of Bengal, from whom he received grants to control certain trades in return for his services. He and his brother were particularly concerned with the province of Bihar, where they dominated the trade in salt-petre and opium.

In 1756 Bengal was thrown into crisis when the British provoked the nawabs to attack and take their settlement of Calcutta. Amir Chand had to make hard choices between the two sources of his wealth and influence and he played his cards badly. The British governor believed that he was at first siding with the nawab and confined him for a time. In 1757 the British under Robert Clive recaptured Calcutta and Amir Chand successfully sought a reconciliation. He is described as 'going up and embracing each member of the Council among whom Colonel Clive was sitting' (Sinha, 1.244). He involved himself in the plots to overthrow the nawab which followed the British recovery of Calcutta, backing a candidate who appeared to have far less chance than the one whom the British eventually chose to support. Nevertheless, he did his best to exploit the situation and to gain a huge reward for himself. He insisted that any agreement with the future nawab should contain clauses guaranteeing him 5 per cent of the Bengal nawabs' accumulated treasure and a quarter of their jewels. Since British estimates of the treasure put it at some £40 million, this meant that he was claiming at least £2 million. Clive had no intention of giving him what he wanted, but believed that he had kept in communication with the reigning nawab and might betray the conspiracy to him prematurely. He and his colleagues therefore decided to trick Amir Chand. A false treaty was drawn up to be shown to Amir Chand which included a generous provision for him. Because the British

admiral Charles Watson, whose signature was essential, had scruples about this piece of skulduggery, his name was added by somebody else. After the British victory at Plassey, in a scene immortalized in Macaulay's essay 'Lord Clive',

> Clive then turned to Mr Scrafton one of the servants of the Company, and said in English, 'It is now time to undeceive Omichund.' 'Omichund', said Mr Scrafton in Hindostanee, 'the red treaty is a trick. You are to have nothing.' Omichund fell back insensible into the arms of his attendants. He revived; but his mind was irreparably ruined.

Whatever the truth of the rest of the story, there is no evidence that disappointment drove Amir Chand insane. He continued to do business with the company for the short remainder of his life. He died in December 1758, apparently away from Calcutta, leaving a fortune estimated at some £450,000, the bulk of which, presumably since he died without issue, was bequeathed to a Sikh shrine. Much of his wealth was used up in litigation brought by his brother-in-law Huzuri Mal, who contested the management of the estate.   SOMENDRA C. NANDY

Sources N. K. Sinha, The economic history of Bengal from Plassey to the permanent settlement, 1 (privately printed, Calcutta, 1956) · P. Spear, Master of Bengal: Clive and his India (1975) · [R. Orme], A history of the military transactions of the British nation in Indostan, 2 vols. (1763–78) · S. C. Hill, Bengal in 1757, 3 vols. (1905) · K. Chatterjee, 'Trade and durbar politics in the Bengal subah, 1733–1757', Modern Asian Studies, 26 (1992), 233–73 · S. Chaudhury, From prosperity to decline: eighteenth century Bengal (1995) · K. Chatterjee, Merchants, politics and society in early-modern India: Bihar, 1733–1820 (1996) · T. B. Macaulay, EdinR, 70 (1840), 295–362
Wealth at death Rs4,200,000 [est. £450,000]: Sinha, Economic history of Bengal 238–44

Amis, Sir Kingsley William (1922–1995), writer, was born on 16 April 1922 at 102 South Side on the edge of Clapham Common in south London, the only child of William Robert Amis (1889–1963), a senior clerk in the London office of J. J. Colman & Co., the mustard manufacturer, and Rosa Annie (Peggy), née Lucas (1891–1957). The family milieu was suburban and lower-middle-class.

Education and early career Amis was raised in Norbury, a ward of the borough of Croydon, and educated at St Hilda's primary school and Norbury College, and, in 1934, as a fee-paying pupil at the City of London School, located at Victoria Embankment, which his father and two uncles had attended before him (from 1935 he attended the school on scholarship). In August 1939 City of London was evacuated to Wiltshire, where it shared facilities with Marlborough College. Here Amis spent the final two years of his secondary education as a boarder. In 1940 the family moved to Berkhamsted in Hertfordshire within commuting distance of London (and outside the flight path of enemy bombers).

In April 1941 Amis went up to St John's College, Oxford, to read English as an exhibitioner (during the war the university allowed undergraduates to matriculate at the beginning of Hilary or Trinity terms). A week after his arrival in Oxford he met Philip Larkin, also reading English at St John's, and quickly formed a friendship which

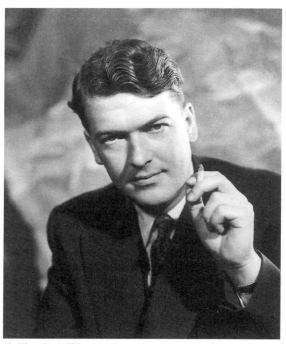

Sir Kingsley William Amis (1922–1995), by Mark Gerson, 1957

became the most important of both men's lives and a crucial shaping influence on post-war literature. At Oxford Amis was an open and active communist (he joined the party in June 1941), sang in the University Labour Club choir, and edited the club's *Bulletin* for a term. He also wrote poems for university periodicals and collaborated with Larkin on poems, stories, and parodies (often of writers on the Oxford syllabus). Amis's literary ambitions at Oxford were largely poetical. The most important contemporary influences on his early poetry, aside from Larkin, were W. H. Auden and William Empson; among living novelists, he and Larkin admired Christopher Isherwood, Graham Greene, Henry Green, and Julian Hall, author of *The Senior Commoner* (1933), 'a wonderful marsh-light of a novel whose influence in 1946 or so was to help to render unpublishable the predecessor of *Lucky Jim* [a novel entitled "The Legacy"]' (K. Amis, *Memoirs*, 55).

Amis's undergraduate education was interrupted by the war. In July 1942 he joined the Royal Signals and in November 1943 was commissioned as a second lieutenant in the Second Army headquarters signals, landing at Normandy in June 1944. He travelled with the Second Army through France, Belgium, and Germany, never once encountering enemy fire. During five months stationed at Sonnis in Belgium he attempted his first adult fiction, 'Who Else is Rank', an unfinished and unpublished 80,000-word novel jointly written with a fellow officer, E. Frank Coles, and closely based on the authors' wartime experiences (several stories in *My Enemy's Enemy*, 1962, his first collection of stories, were also inspired by the war). Amis was demobilized and returned to Oxford in October 1945.

Though Larkin had finished his studies at Oxford in June

1943 (he had been exempted from military service because of poor eyesight) the two friends kept in close touch by letter and through occasional visits, Larkin to Oxford and Amis to Leicester, where Larkin worked from 1946 to 1950 at the university library. Amis's first book of verse, *Bright November*, which drew on his wartime experience, was published in 1947. In December of that year he was awarded a first-class degree and began work on a BLitt thesis entitled 'English non-dramatic poetry 1840–1900 and the Victorian reading public', first under Lord David Cecil, then under F. W. Bateson (the thesis was not completed until May 1950 and was failed in November, partly, Amis suspected, because of opposition from Cecil, one of its examiners). On 21 January 1948 Amis married Hilary Ann (Hilly) Bardwell (*b*. 1929), an art student at Ruskin College, Oxford (and daughter of Leonard Sidney Bardwell, a retired staff officer at the Ministry of Agriculture), whom he had first met in January 1946. Their first child, Philip, was born on 15 August 1948; their second son, the writer Martin Amis, was born on 25 August 1949; a daughter, Sally, was born in 1954.

Lucky Jim   In October 1949, after several unsuccessful applications to universities in Britain and abroad, Amis was appointed an assistant lecturer in English at the University College of Swansea. Amis enjoyed teaching there and got on well with his colleagues, but the family had very little money. Amis had to supplement his income by outside examining and extramural teaching, while his wife took on part-time work as a cleaner. Despite his failure to find a publisher for his novel 'The Legacy', late in 1949 he embarked on a second novel, provisionally titled 'Dixon and Christine'. With Larkin's help and encouragement, plus Hilly's timely inheritance of a small legacy (enabling the family to move into a bigger house, one with a room of his own for writing), a first draft was finished in November 1951. In April 1953 a much revised version of this draft, retitled *Lucky Jim*, was accepted by Victor Gollancz and its publication in January 1954 transformed Amis's life. *Lucky Jim* was soon a financial and critical success: 7500 copies were in print by mid-February, 12,000 by the end of the year, in sixteen Gollancz-style mini-impressions; the American rights were sold to Doubleday, and film rights were sold to the Boulting Brothers.

Lucky Jim has been described as the finest comic novel of its generation, the earliest and most influential of 'campus' or 'redbrick' novels, and a key text both of the 'Movement', the pre-eminent poetical grouping of the period, and of the 'angry young men'. According to Amis, its success derived from traditional comic ingredients: 'a young man at odds with his surroundings, and trying to make his way, and suffering comic misfortunes, and getting the girl—it can't fail, really' (McDermott, 54). Others saw it as heralding important social changes. To the novelist David Lodge, Amis

> articulated through his hero, Jim Dixon, the feelings of a
> much larger number of people in the next generation (my
> own) who were products of the 1944 Education Act and the
> Welfare State. Through the comedy of Jim's private fantasies
> and accidental breaches of social decorum, Amis gave us, as

it were, permission not to be overawed by the social and cultural codes of the class to which we had been elevated by education. It was enormously liberating. (*The Independent*)

Amis was not always comfortable with such readings. Though Jim is often at odds with polite or established codes and norms, he is no rebel, which is in part why Amis consistently deplored the novel's association with the angry young men. 'There was no anger', Amis has declared, 'unless a mild, usually amused and very intermittent irritation can be called anger' (McDermott, 21). As for the angry young man phenomenon itself, Amis called it 'a phantom creation of literary journalists' (*Letters of Kingsley Amis*, 704). The novel's association with the 'Movement', in contrast, was more substantial. The term itself was coined in 1954 by J. D. Scott, literary editor of *The Spectator*, who applied it to Amis, John Wain, Elizabeth Jennings, Thom Gunn, John Holloway, Donald Davie, D. J. Enright, and Iris Murdoch (Larkin was a later addition). Movement writers, Scott claimed, were 'bored by the despair of the Forties, not much interested in suffering, and extremely impatient of poetic sensibility, especially poetic sensibility about "the writer and society"'. The Movement was 'anti-phoney', 'anti-wet', its prevailing tone was 'sceptical, robust, ironic, prepared to be as comfortable as possible' (*The Spectator*, 1 Oct 1954, 399–400). This description Amis characterized as 'useful up to a point' (*Letters of Kingsley Amis*, 405), and though he often resisted the Movement label also helped to publicize it.

Fame The success of *Lucky Jim* coincided with Amis's growing visibility as a poet. Both Amis and Larkin, as well as other poets soon to be associated with the Movement, were represented in *New Poems 1952*, a PEN publication. At a party to celebrate the book's launch, Amis met Robert Conquest, who became a lifelong friend and collaborator (notably as co-author of the 1965 novel *The Egyptologists*). John Wain, a former student and fellow at St John's, and lecturer in English at Reading, was the most energetic publicist both of Amis and of the Movement writers in general. Wain not only commissioned an extract from *Lucky Jim* to be broadcast on the first programme of the radio series *First Reading*, but helped to arrange for the publication at the end of the year of a second volume of Amis's poems, *A Frame of Mind*, as part of a series of limited editions of new poets. A third slim volume, *Kingsley Amis: No. 22, the Fantasy Poets*, was published in the same month as *Lucky Jim*. Despite Amis's association with the Movement, these early poems are often obscure, impersonal, 'difficult', unlike the more mature verse, which is closer in manner and subject matter to the fiction.

Amis's second novel, *That Uncertain Feeling* (1955), shared the provincial setting and subversive humour of *Lucky Jim*. It also contained a satirical portrait of a poet very much like Dylan Thomas, among the most prominent of Movement *bêtes noires*. It was published several months after Amis's return from a summer in Portugal, a trip financed by a Somerset Maugham award for *Lucky Jim*. Though Amis professed to hate foreign travel, his experiences in Portugal provided him with the materials for a third novel, *I Like it Here* (1958). Between 1955 and 1958 Amis published a

fourth volume of poems, *A Case of Samples: Poems 1946– 1956*, and appeared in two influential anthologies: D. J. Enright's *Poets of the 1950s*, considered something of a Movement manifesto, and Conquest's *New Lines*, both published in 1956. He also took on a number of literary and journalistic commissions: he published fiction reviews, essays, and short stories in *The Spectator* and elsewhere (for the most part Amis's literary criticism, collected in *What became of Jane Austen? and other questions* (1970) and *The Amis Collection* (1990) appeared initially in non-academic periodicals); edited *Oscar Wilde: Poems and Essays* (1956); began reviewing jazz records for *The Observer* (from 1956 to 1958); wrote a BBC radio play, *Touch and Go* (1957), the first of several commissions for radio and television; and a pamphlet for the Fabian Society, *Socialism and the Intellectuals* (1957).

After his return from the war Amis had allowed his membership in the Communist Party to lapse. The Soviet invasion of Hungary in 1956 turned him into a firm and total anti-communist. Though in March 1956 he publicly protested against the Anglo-French-Israeli invasion of Egypt, he described himself in *Socialism and the Intellectuals* (1957) as anti-activist. Self-interest, he now declared, was 'the best and most trustworthy political motive' (though he also lamented the absence of more respectable motives in the current political climate: 'no Spain, no fascism, no mass unemployment'; pp. 13, 7). In the years to follow, Amis moved steadily to the right, in part out of principle, in part out of a congenital opposition to fashion, though he continued to vote Labour until the general election of 1966, when he voted for the anti-Common Market candidate.

Chief among the offshoots of Amis's growing fame in the late 1950s was an invitation from R. P. Blackmur to spend a year at Princeton University as a visiting fellow in creative writing and to deliver the Christian Gauss seminars in criticism, in the spring of 1959. Somewhat to his surprise, Amis enjoyed his year at Princeton; he even enjoyed teaching creative writing. At Blackmur's suggestion, he chose science fiction, a lifelong interest, as the topic of his Gauss seminars. These were eventually published in 1960 as *New Maps of Hell: a Survey of Science Fiction*, the first book-length study of the genre to be written by a critic from an academic background. Amis kept up his association with science fiction both by reviewing it for *The Observer* (from 1960 to 1965) and by a five-year stint co-editing *Spectrum: a Science Fiction Anthology* (1961–5), with Robert Conquest. While at Princeton, Amis also lectured at a number of east coast universities, reviewed 'foreign' films for *Esquire*, and frequented jazz clubs in Manhattan. Though sorely tempted to stay on in the United States, he and his family returned to Swansea in July 1959.

In 1960 Amis published *Take a Girl Like You*, his fourth and longest novel, and mostly told, unlike its predecessors, from the heroine's point of view. This story, derived in part from Richardson's *Clarissa*, is of the protracted seduction of Jenny Bunn, a sexually and socially innocent primary schoolteacher. Jenny's seducer, Patrick Standish, is as clever, witty, and subversive as previous Amis heroes, but much more predatory. Patrick inaugurates a line of deeply flawed male characters in Amis's writing of the 1960s and early 1970s, one that includes Dai Evans, the hero of *The Evans Country* (1962), a sequence of six poems (expanded to eleven when it appeared in a subsequent volume, *A Look Round the Estate: Poems 1957–1967*); Roger Micheldene, in the novel *One Fat Englishman* (1963); Ronnie Appleyard, in *I Want it Now* (1968); and Sir Roy Vandervane, in *Girl, 20* (1971). Amis identified *Take a Girl Like You* as his favourite novel, but its cruelty, particularly that of its ending, in which a drunk Jenny is seduced by Patrick, shocked many readers, beginning with its American publisher (who sought to have the ending rewritten). The novel anticipates and dissects the new sexual morality of the 1960s, and may have been fuelled in part by tensions in Amis's private life. Amis's marriage had been stormy from the start, largely because of his compulsive philandering, but in the late 1950s and early 1960s it was especially troubled.

A new life In April 1961 Amis was offered a fellowship in English at Peterhouse, Cambridge, making him the college's first fellow and director of studies in English. Though largely content at Swansea, he accepted the new post in the hope that it would afford him more time for his own writing. This hope proved unfounded, and the life of a Cambridge don was not to his taste. In December 1962 he resigned his fellowship, though he continued teaching at Peterhouse until the end of the academic year. At the same time the tensions in his marriage came to a head. In the previous October he had begun an affair with the novelist Elizabeth Jane Howard (*b.* 1923), a much more serious affair than its predecessors, and one which precipitated a split with his wife and family the following summer. In September, Amis moved to London to live with Jane Howard (her name to friends and family) and to pursue a full-time writing career. They married on 29 June 1965.

Amis's fifth novel, *One Fat Englishman* (1963), set on a college campus in the United States, draws on his experiences at Princeton. Its obnoxious hero, Roger Micheldene, is pathologically aggressive: 'Of the seven deadly sins, Roger considered himself qualified in gluttony, sloth and lust but distinguished in anger' (p. 10). This anger is manifested in a sneering attitude to all things American, an attitude Amis meant to discredit, in part because it was so common among educated Englishmen. Roger is a lapsed Catholic, and beneath his anger sounds a note of metaphysical or religious despair, one Amis would develop in subsequent novels, in particular *The Anti-Death League* (1966). Amis's own religious upbringing had been low-church, 'strong in morality, rudimentary and quite uninsistent in matters of doctrine', and though he claimed never to have attended, 'voluntarily or otherwise, any act of worship as such', or to have consulted the Bible or any other religious writing 'in the hope of spiritual comfort or ethical guidance' (McDermott, 9), he was well versed both in scripture and in Christian doctrine.

The Anti-Death League mounts a ferocious attack not only on those who would deny or refuse to contemplate the evils of the world, but on the Christian God. It also marks a formal as well as thematic departure for Amis. Though the most self-consciously serious of his novels, its plot draws on elements from popular or genre fiction, including espionage, fantasy, and science fiction. This interest in popular fiction, heralded by two 'studies' of James Bond novels (*The James Bond Dossier* and *The Book of Bond, or, Every Man his Own 007*, both published in 1965), was developed in his own Bond thriller, *Colonel Sun* (1968), published under the pseudonym Robert Markham; in *The Green Man* (1969), a ghost story (as concerned with theological or religious questions as *The Anti-Death League*); in *The Riverside Villas Murder* (1973), a classic detective story; and in *The Alteration* (1976), an 'alternate world' novel. Of these experiments with genre fiction the most important are *The Alteration* and *The Riverside Villas Murder*. *The Alteration*, an attempt to imagine what England would have been like in 1976 had the Reformation never occurred, is among the most intricate and inventive of Amis's novels; *The Riverside Villas Murder*, while strictly honouring the conventions of the murder story, is also a loving and meticulous reconstruction of suburban life in the 1930s, drawing on many details from his own childhood.

Amis's oppositional character, and increasing conservatism, brought him much into the public eye in this period. With Robert Conquest, he contributed several articles to Brian Cox and A. E. Dyson's anti-progressive 'Black papers on education' (1969–77), opposing university expansion, as well as other educational reforms and trends (he had already published an influential article in *Encounter* in 1960 deploring the expansion of higher education, partly on the grounds that 'More will mean worse', a phrase which gained wide currency). He also became involved in a long and acrimonious correspondence in the popular and periodical press over the Vietnam War, which he supported. His anti-communism took on a new intensity in these years, inspired in part by Robert Conquest's powerful exposure of Stalinist atrocities in *The Great Terror* (1968). He spearheaded a campaign in 1968 against Yevgeny Yevtushenko's candidacy for the chair of poetry at Oxford University, an elective post. He publicly condemned the left totalitarianism of Che Guevara, Mao Zedong, and Ho Chi Minh. Yet he was also an outspoken opponent of racism and capital punishment. In 1967 Amis was invited to lecture for a term on modern British fiction at Vanderbilt University in Nashville, Tennessee, where the racism he and Jane Howard encountered distressed them not only for its own sake, but because of its likely effect on conservative causes: 'It would take some strength of mind not to say, in effect, "anybody who thinks like that about Negroes must be wrong about everything. Stop US murder in Vietnam!"' (*Letters of Kingsley Amis*, 689).

On their return from Tennessee (and a brief trip to Mexico) in March 1968, Amis and Howard purchased a large house in Barnet, Hertfordshire, the upkeep of which, both financial and physical, contributed to tensions in their marriage. These were the years when Amis's drinking became especially heavy. Amis was a lifelong drinker and connoisseur of drink, and though alcohol rarely interfered with his capacity to work, it could make him irascible and paranoid. It may also have impaired his sex drive. In the mid-1970s Amis and Howard consulted several sex therapists after what, in his *Memoirs* (1991), he describes as 'various difficulties had arisen between us' (p. 117). These difficulties, and the therapy sessions themselves, are drawn on to comic effect in *Jake's Thing* (1978), a novel marked by a newly pointed animus to women. In July 1976 he and Jane Howard moved to Gardnor House, in Flask Walk, Hampstead, but the marriage continued to deteriorate; in September 1979 Amis announced to Larkin a 'total loss of sex-drive' (*Letters of Kingsley Amis*, 876). Less than a year later, in November 1980, Jane Howard left him, refusing to return until he promised to give up drinking totally.

Later life The breakup of Amis's second marriage occasioned the longest gap between novels in his career. Two years after *Jake's Thing*, Amis published *Russian Hide-and-Seek* (1980), the second and weaker of his 'alternate world' novels (it is set in a twenty-first-century England ruled by the Soviets). Two years between novels was a standard interval for Amis. *Stanley and the Women* took him four years to complete, and, as his correspondence suggests, caused him uncharacteristic difficulty and self-doubt. During these years Amis busied himself with other projects: he campaigned in the press against arts subsidies, slovenly and incorrect language use, and a mentality labelled 'sod the public' ('the working slogan not only of government, the service industry and the retail trade, but also … of interior designers, providers of culture, playwrights, composers and many more'; *The Spectator*, 19 Oct 1985, reprinted in *The Amis Collection*, 229); he edited the anthology *The Golden Age of Science Fiction* (1981); started a column on drink in the *Daily Express* (1982), which became *Every Day Drinking* (1983); and was appointed poetry editor of the *Daily Mirror*, choosing and introducing a poem a day, Monday to Friday (both poems and introductions were reprinted in 1984 as *The Pleasures of Poetry*). Though he continued to write the occasional poem after the publication of *Collected Poems, 1944–1979* (1979), he produced no further collections of verse.

The darkness and aggression of *Stanley and the Women* mark a nadir in Amis's life. Though the novel had its defenders (even among female reviewers), the harshness of its treatment of women was much deplored, and rumour had it that its initial failure to find an American publisher derived from opposition among feminist editors. Amis was an increasingly embattled and embittered figure in these years. Though slim and handsome in youth and early middle age, he began to put on weight and his face grew puffy and red. Though a gregarious and clubbable man, as funny in person as on paper, he developed a reputation for rudeness and impatience, an impression he partly cultivated. Amis was prone to neuroses and hypochondria throughout his life, but was especially anxious during these years. Always frightened of flying and unable to drive a car, he now feared travelling of any sort, and was terrified of being left on his own at night. His life was ruled by an increasingly rigid and narrow routine: writing in the morning, drinks and lunch at his club, the Garrick, writing again in the late afternoon, perhaps after a nap, then supper, television, more drink, and a sleeping pill.

After the breakup of his second marriage, Amis's sons devised a remarkable plan for his living arrangements. They suggested that he move in with his first wife, Hilly, her third husband, Lord Kilmarnock, and their son Jaime. Much to the amazement of all concerned, the arrangement lasted. Amis paid the bills and the Kilmarnocks did the housework and cooking. The result, Martin Amis has suggested, was a return to creative health (M. Amis, 312–13). Two years after the publication of *Stanley and the Women*, Amis published *The Old Devils*, a work every bit as darkly comic, caustic, and clear-sighted as its predecessors (including *Ending Up* (1974) an earlier novel of old age), but also suffused with regret and affection, both for Wales and for lost (and recovered) love. *The Old Devils* won the Booker prize and was followed in customary two-yearly intervals by four other novels: *Difficulties with Girls* (1988), a sequel to *Take a Girl Like You* (in which Jenny Bunn is again a wholly sympathetic heroine); *The Folks that Live on the Hill* (1990), published in the same year Amis was knighted (he had been appointed CBE in 1981); *The Russian Girl* (1992); and *You Can't Do Both* (1994), perhaps Amis's most autobiographical novel. Amis's final novel, *The Biographer's Moustache*, was published in 1995 (to poor reviews, unlike its immediate predecessors). During this period of late productivity Amis also edited *The Great British Songbook* (1986) with James Cochrane; reissued an expanded version of his *Collected Short Stories* (1987, originally published 1980); edited *The Amis Anthology* (1989), described in the introduction as 'a collection of my favourite poems'; began several restaurant columns in magazines; published his *Memoirs*, *We are All Guilty*, a novel for young adults (both in 1991), and a final collection of short stories, *Mrs. Barrett's Secret and other Stories* (1993).

Late in August 1995, while on his annual summer holiday in Swansea, Amis had a fall and suspected stroke. He was hospitalized in London, his condition deteriorated, and on 22 October, after contracting pneumonia, he died in St Pancras Hospital. At the time of his death he was at work on a new novel, provisionally titled 'Black and White', and had all but completed the posthumously published *The King's English: a Guide to Modern Usage* (1997). His body was cremated at Golders Green crematorium on 31 October and a funeral service was held at St Mark's Church, near the home he shared with the Kilmarnocks in Primrose Hill. A year later, at a packed memorial service in St Martin-in-the-Fields, he was hailed as the funniest and most gifted British novelist of his generation. A selection of his letters was published in 2000.

ZACHARY LEADER

Sources *The letters of Kingsley Amis*, ed. Z. Leader (2000) · K. Amis, *Memoirs* (1991) · E. Jacobs, *Kingsley Amis: a biography* (1995) · M. Amis, *Experience* (2000) · *The Independent* (23 Oct 1995) · J. McDermott, *Kingsley Amis: an English moralist* (1989) · *The selected letters of Philip Larkin*, ed. A. Thwaite (1992) · B. Morrison, *The Movement* (1980) · P. Fussell, *The anti-egotist: Kingsley Amis man of letters* (1994) ·

A. Motion, *Philip Larkin: a writer's life* (1993) · J. Gohn, *Kingsley Amis: a checklist* (1976) · D. Salwak, *Kingsley Amis: a reference guide* (1978) · b. cert. · m. certs. · d. cert.

Archives Hunt. L., corresp. and literary MSS · Ransom HRC, notes for his works · University of Bristol Library, corresp. and statements relating to trial of *Lady Chatterley's Lover* | BBC WAC · Bodl. Oxf., corresp. with R. B. Montgomery · Princeton University, New Jersey · State University of New York, Buffalo · Victor Gollancz Ltd, London | FILM BFI NFTVA | SOUND BL NSA

Likenesses M. Gerson, photograph, 1957, NPG [*see illus.*] · photographs, repro. in Leader, ed., *Letters* · photographs, repro. in Jacobs, *Kingsley Amis* · photographs, repro. in Amis, *Memoirs* · photographs, repro. in Amis, *Experience* · photographs, repro. in Thwaite, ed., *Selected letters*

Wealth at death £616,503: probate, 27 Dec 1995, CGPLA Eng. & Wales

Ammon, Charles George (1873–1960), trade unionist and politician, was born on 22 April 1873 into a poor working-class family in White Street, Southwark, London. He was the eldest child of Charles George Ammon (*d.* 1887), cutler and toolmaker, and Mary Kempley (1851–1900) of Thanet, and had four younger sisters. Educated at Mawby Street board school, he continued his studies at Sunday school and the working men's college.

Ammon started work at the age of eleven in a bottle factory, and joined the Post Office as a telegraph messenger when he was fourteen. Promoted to sorter at the south-eastern district office in 1892 when Post Office trade unionism was taking hold, Ammon joined the Fawcett Association (the trade union for sorters) when chairman William Clery and secretary Wallace Cheesman were dismissed for lobbying MPs. Ammon was appointed a branch secretary before he was twenty, and joined the central executive of the association. In 1893 he was a founder member of the Independent Labour Party. In 1898 at Bermondsey parish church Ammon married Ada Eileen May (*d.* 1958). They had a son who died in 1909, and two daughters who outlived them both.

In 1901 Ammon became a Wesleyan lay preacher, failing to become a minister in 1902 only because he was married. His religious ideas remained important to him for the rest of his life. He was active in the Brotherhood Movement of idealistic socialism, and was its national president in 1920. Ammon was undogmatic in his advocacy of temperance and even stood drinks for others. In later years, however, he tried without success to persuade Clement Attlee, when prime minister, to bring his influence to bear to elevate the moral standards of younger Labour MPs.

Ammon was elected editor of the Fawcett Association journal, *The Post*, in 1904 and was chairman of the association from 1911 to 1919. During this period he was a dominant figure, working for greater unity not only among postmen, but also with the TUC and the Labour Party, whose conferences he attended from 1905. He was parliamentary secretary of the national joint committee of the Post Office Association, and played a decisive role in bringing about the merger of his union in 1920 with other groups of postal workers to form the amalgamated Union of Post Office Workers. With Ernest Bevin he visited the American Federation of Labor convention in San Francisco in 1915. In the following year he left the Post Office and became parliamentary secretary to the No-Conscription Fellowship. From August 1918 he was general secretary of the Port of London Staff Association, leaving in 1920 when he was elected organizing secretary of the Union of Post Office Workers. He retained this post until 1928, concentrating on the union's comprehensive general education programme. By this time Ammon's interests had already began to extend into local and national politics: he was a member of the London county council for North Camberwell from 1919 to 1925, and from February 1922 to 1931 was MP for the same division. Active on the education committee of the LCC, he became a Labour whip, and in the Labour governments of 1924 and 1929–31 was parliamentary secretary to the Admiralty, taking pride in his role in building five new cruisers. He was also on the Labour Party national executive from 1921 to 1927.

Ammon lost all his elected positions in 1931 but was voted back onto the first Labour LCC in 1934. He was re-elected MP for North Camberwell in November 1935, and continued to be active politically during the war, although he was by then nearly seventy. In 1941–2 he chaired the LCC and in 1944 he became the first trade union peer when he was created Baron Ammon of Camberwell. In April 1945, at Bevin's instigation, Ammon was appointed chairman of what was later to become the National Dock Labour Board. His trade union background made him a good choice for a body which was responsible, through the introduction of the national dock labour scheme in June 1947, for decasualizing dock labour by registering dockers and arranging their employment. The board included union representatives and employers. From August 1945 Ammon also served as government chief whip in the House of Lords.

During 1949, against the background of the cold war and talk of 'communist subversion'—from Ammon as much as anyone else—dockers at Avonmouth refused to unload a 'blackleg' ship at the request of the communist-led Canadian Seamen's Union. As the unofficial dispute spread, the dock labour board announced on 13 June that all those who supported sympathy action would be suspended from the labour scheme. The government, concerned to retain the support of trade union leaders, forced the board to withdraw this order, which prompted Ammon on 20 June to tell a journalist 'that's crazy' (Ammon, 42). In consequence, Attlee dismissed Ammon from the government and from the board, successfully appealing to the strikers to return. In later years Ammon defended his actions, pointing to widespread support, all of it from beyond the labour movement.

Ammon was mayor of Camberwell in 1950–51 and spoke frequently in the Lords until he was disabled by a stroke in February 1955. In his last years he was 'acutely conscious that [he had] not travelled so far as was sometimes foretold' (Ammon, 152). He belonged to a generation that rose from great poverty; the idealistic socialism of his youth, derived from his Wesleyan Methodism, had an abiding impact. Ammon died in King's College Hospital on 2 April 1960. The address at his funeral service on 7 April at Herne Hill Methodist Church was given by Donald Soper.

ALAN CLINTON

Sources J. Bellamy, B. Sadler, and J. Saville, 'Ammon, Charles (Charlie) George (Lord Ammon of Camberwell)', *DLB*, vol. 1 · A. Clinton, *Post Office workers: a trade union and social history* (1984) · P. Weller, 'British labour and the Cold War: the London dock strike of 1949', *Social conflict and the political order in modern Britain*, ed. J. E. Cronin and J. Schneer (1982), 146–78 · K. Harris, *Attlee* (1982) · K. O. Morgan, *Labour in power, 1945–1951* (1984) · G. A. Phillips and N. Whiteside, *Casual labour: the unemployment question in the port transport industry, 1880–1970* (1985) · R. Hyman, 'Praetorians and proletarians: unions and industrial relations', *Labour's high tide: the government and the economy, 1945–51*, ed. J. Fyrth (1993), 165–92 · *WWBMP* · C. G. Ammon, autobiography, U. Hull, Brynmor Jones L.

Archives Bodl. RH, corresp. on colonial questions · Southwark Local Studies Library, London, press cuttings and diaries relating to travels abroad · U. Hull, Brynmor Jones L., corresp. and papers | Bodl. Oxf., corresp. with Attlee · Bodl. RH, corresp. with Arthur Creech Jones · Post Office Archive, London · U. Warwick Mod. RC, Union of Communication Workers MSS · UCW House, London, Union of Communication Workers MSS

Wealth at death £15,640 13s. 3d.: probate, 14 June 1960, *CGPLA Eng. & Wales*

Ammonius, Andreas [Andrea della Rena] (*bap.* **1476**, *d.* **1517**), humanist scholar and poet, was the son of Elisabetta Vanni and her husband, Francesco della Rena (dell' Arena). Of a family long established as silk weavers at Lucca, he was baptized in the cathedral there on 13 October 1476. In preparation for an ecclesiastical career, he studied with Oliviero da Montegallo, professor of logic at the University of Bologna during 1494–5 and 1497–8; he was probably *magister* by February 1497. Oliviero, requested by the general of the Servites to revise the *Logica* of Stephanus de Flandria, entrusted the task to his pupil. It was printed at Bologna in 1495, with a prose dedication and prefatory Latin verses signed Andreas Arena. This Latinized form of his family name appears in his early extant work; by 1511, at latest, probably in imitation of his admired Erasmus, he had Graecized it to Ammonius (Greek *Ammos*).

When Ammonius left Bologna is unclear. Later, in Rome, he was a member of the Lucchese circle which included Silvestro Gigli (1463–1521), successor to his uncle Giovanni as Henry VII's ambassador in Rome and bishop of Worcester, and Nicolò Tegrimi, Lucca's ambassador to the papacy. The edition (Rome, 1503 or 1504) of Tegrimi's oration before the new Della Rovere Pope Julius II contains a laudatory Latin poem by Arena, who had become friendly with members of the Della Rovere family and also then got to know Pietro Griffo, who was in England in 1506 and, as papal sub-collector, from 1509 to 1512.

Ammonius was one of the second-rank Italian humanists who made a career in early Tudor England. He was in England by 1506, having probably travelled there with Gigli, always his protector. Gigli was bringing the papal cap and sword to Henry VII, who received them on 8 September 1505. Substantial patronage for Ammonius seems to have been slow to accrue. In 1509 he was secretary to

William Blount, Lord Mountjoy, and closely connected with Erasmus and with the 'new' Henrician London humanist circle. Erasmus recognized Ammonius's elegant Latin in the letter begging him to return to England, signed by Mountjoy on 27 May that year. Ammonius and Erasmus had first met during 1505–6, before Erasmus's visit to Italy, when Ammonius may have been welcomed by Thomas More, his closest English friend, and perhaps lodged with the Mores in Bucklersbury; he was there with Erasmus between 1509 and 1511, before leaving in October 1511, on More's remarriage, for the nearby hospital of St Thomas of Acon. He was also on good terms with Thomas Linacre, John Colet, Cuthbert Tunstal, Richard Pace, and others, and was admitted to Doctors' Commons on 22 September 1515.

On 18 November 1511, when Ammonius regretted to Erasmus that he had left Rome where his friends had prospered, he had been Latin secretary to Henry VIII since July, though Pietro Carmeliano also acted until 1513. Twenty brief and conventional Latin complimentary poems, apparently written by Ammonius between 1503 and 1511, had been printed at Paris, with an epistle dedicatory to Mountjoy dated from London, 18 May 1511, through the mediation of Erasmus and together with Erasmus's *De ratione studii*. A few similar poems are extant. With his substantial personal and official correspondence, these complete Ammonius's surviving works. Others referred to or summarized by Erasmus, such as his panegyric on Henry VIII's victories in France, on the defeat of the Scots in 1513, or ascribed to him, have perished.

On 3 February 1512 Ammonius was made canon and prebendary of St Stephen's, Westminster, with residence provided; on 17 July 1513 he was collated prebendary of Fordington and Writhlington in Salisbury and on 14 August 1517, of Compton Dunton in Bath and Wells. Benefices in Gloucester and Worcestershire were secured for him by Richard Fox and by Gigli respectively, but death prevented him from occupying them. In the summer and autumn of 1513 Ammonius accompanied Henry on his expedition against the French. Accorded English citizenship on 12 April 1514, he had already begun to intrigue for the papal collectorship. This brought him into acrimonious conflict in England with the sub-collector, Ammonius's fellow humanist Polydore Vergil of Urbino, and with Cardinal Adriano Castellesi, then collector, in Rome. At Henry's solicitation, Leo X made Ammonius collector (16 August 1514). After protests from Castellesi, reduction of Ammonius to sub-collector, Polydore's imprisonment by Wolsey and Wolsey's elevation to the cardinalate (1515), and, finally, detection of Castellesi in conspiracy against the pope, Gigli wrote in June 1517 to Ammonius that the collectorship was his.

Most current knowledge of Ammonius personally comes from the frank and intimate correspondence between him and Erasmus, to whom he was 'dearest of mortals': thirty-two surviving letters, some long, from Erasmus between 1511 and 1517 place Ammonius among the most frequent recipients, and Erasmus lamented his death in five more; fourteen from Ammonius to Erasmus are extant. Erasmus published some letters and attempted to recover others or have them destroyed after Ammonius's death. They exchanged Latin poems, Greek jokes, gossip, compliments, complaints about England, and visits in Cambridge and London; Ammonius supplied information about international affairs (Roman especially), Greek wine, and a white Irish horse, besides urging Erasmus's needs on Richard Foxe and Thomas Ruthall, and securing the living of Aldington for him from William Warham in 1512. When in 1516 Erasmus was seeking a new papal dispensation from his defect of birth, his monastic vows, and his failure to wear his Augustinian canon's religious habit, he returned to England in August to consult Ammonius, who busied himself in the matter, and at Westminster on 9 April 1517 transmitted the formula of absolution at their last recorded meeting.

Ammonius died suddenly in London of the sweating sickness, during the night of 17–18 August 1517; the epidemic which carried him off caused More to write to Erasmus that one was safer on the battlefield than in the city. Executors of his will, dated 17 August and requesting burial at St Stephen's, Westminster, were his cousin Pietro Vanni (d. 1563), Wolsey's and later Henry VIII's Latin secretary and Henry's ambassador, and two London Lucchese merchants; it was proved at Lambeth on 30 April 1518, Vanni and Ammonius's mother being the chief beneficiaries. Ammonius wrote an accomplished italic hand. No portrait is extant or recorded. J. B. TRAPP

Sources *Opus epistolarum Des. Erasmi Roterodami*, ed. P. S. Allen, 1–3 (1906–13) · *The correspondence of Erasmus*, ed. and trans. R. A. B. Mynors and others, 22 vols. (1974–94), vols. 2–6, letters 215, 218–21, 226, 228, 232–4, 236, 238–40, 243, 245–50, 255, 262, 273, 280–83, 288, 295, 338–9, 360, 378, 389, 414, 427, 429, 446–7, 451–3, 455–6, 466, 475, 478–9, 483, 498, 505, 517–18, 539, 543, 551–2, 566, 619, 623–4, 637, 639, 642–3, 649, 655–6, 658, 774–5, 822, 828, 855, 860 · *Andreae Ammonii carmina omnia*, ed. C. Pizzi (Florence, 1958) · G. Tournoy, 'The unrecorded poetical production of Andreas Ammonius', *Humanistica Lovaniensia*, 37 (1988), 255–64 · G. Tournoy, 'Two poems written by Erasmus for Bernard André', *Humanistica Lovaniensia*, 27 (1978), 45–51 · D. R. Carlson, 'Three Tudor epigrams: 1, another poem of Andreas Ammonius (Andrea Ammonio)', *Humanistica Lovaniensia*, 45 (1996), 189–91 · *LP Henry VIII*, vols. 1–2 · *CSP Venice, 1509–19* · *Fasti Angl., 1300–1541*, [Salisbury], 53 · *Fasti Angl., 1300–1541*, [Bath and Wells], 41 · G. D. Squibb, *Doctors' Commons: a history of the College of Advocates and Doctors of Law* (1977), 57–8, 134 · P. O. Kristeller, *Iter Italicum*, 7 vols. (1963–97), vol. 1, nos. 264; vol. 2, no. 525; vol. 3, nos. 290a, 349b; vol. 4, nos. 136a–b, 171b, 340b; vol. 5, nos. 77b, 78a, 82b · *The poems of Desiderius Erasmus*, ed. C. Reedijk (Leiden, 1956), 69–72, 291–2, 300–03 · G. Tournoy, 'Della Rena, Andrea', *Dizionario biografico degli Italiani*, ed. A. M. Ghisalberti and others, 37 (Rome, 1989) [see also 'Boschetti, Gian Galeazzo', 'Carmeliano, Pietro', 'Castellesi, Adriano'] · M. Monaco, 'Note per una biografia dell'umanista lucchese A. Ammonio (1476–1517)', *Annali dell'Università di Lecce, Facoltà di lettere e filosofia*, 7 (1975–6), 87–136 [1977] · C. Pizzi, *Un amico di Erasmo: l'umanista Andrea Ammonio* (1956) · T. B. Deutscher, 'Andrea Ammonio of Lucca', *Contemporaries of Erasmus: a biographical register*, ed. P. G. Bietenholz and T. B. Deutscher, 1 (1985), 48–50 · PRO, PROB 11/19, fol. 51
Archives BL, Cotton MSS · PRO, MSS
Wealth at death left 100 nobles to cousin and executor Pietro Vanni; 20 nobles to his chaplain; £20 to named *famulus* and smaller sums to others; vestment of 50 ducats to chapel of S. Crucis at Lucca; £20 for charitable distribution; residue to mother: will, PRO, PROB 11/19, fol. 51*r*

Amner, John (*d.* 1641), composer and organist, came from a family which was intimately associated with the music at Ely Cathedral for over half a century. Michael Amner, his uncle, was a lay clerk at the cathedral (1576–88), as was also Ralph Amner [*see below*], who may have been the composer's brother. John himself was a chorister at Ely in late 1593, since his name is included in a list of choristers compiled in connection with the episcopal visitation held on 22 October that year. Perhaps surprisingly (given the proximity of Cambridge), he later undertook a period of study at Oxford, where he enjoyed the patronage of William Bourchier, third earl of Bath (1557–1623). He received the Oxford bachelor of music degree in 1613, some three years after returning to Ely as *informator choristarum* (1610). He was later ordained deacon, and became a minor canon at Ely Cathedral, although he retained his post as *informator choristarum* there throughout his lifetime. In 1640 Amner incorporated his Oxford BMus degree at Cambridge, where he signed the university subscription book confirming his recognition of the Thirty-Nine Articles.

Amner was one of the most gifted and prolific provincial composers of sacred music of his day. Despite this, his music enjoyed only a limited popularity outside the Cambridge and Ely area. In his compositions he successfully exploited both the older 'full' form and the more fashionable 'verse' form (in which passages are allocated to solo singers, with organ accompaniment). He wrote two settings of the preces and four service settings, two of which are incomplete. His third service is described in the manuscript sources as 'Cesar's Service', and was presumably commissioned by Dr Henry Caesar, dean of Ely Cathedral from 1616 to 1636. He wrote over forty sacred works, not all of which were intended for liturgical use. There are, however, at least two dozen full and verse anthems which appear to have been intended for use within the liturgy, although several of these are incomplete.

Amner's most significant legacy is his *Sacred Hymnes of 3. 4. 5 and 6. Parts for Voyces & Vyols*, which was printed in 1615 by Edward Allde (*d.* 1634). It contains twenty-six compositions and is a late example from the English madrigalian tradition that embraces some fifty or so collections published between 1588 and 1627. It was intended primarily for domestic use by skilled amateurs, and was printed in exercise of the royal patent 'to print sett songes et al.' granted to Allde by James I. The collection was issued in six partbooks—*cantus primus, cantus secundus, tenor, bassus, quintus,* and *sextus*—copies of which survive in five English and four American libraries (although some of these copies are incomplete). Unlike some of the more popular madrigalian prints, it enjoyed only a single edition.

Although its title suggests liturgical intent, the overwhelming majority of the pieces in *Sacred Hymnes* are typical of the wide range of secular styles which characterizes most Elizabethan and Jacobean madrigalian collections. The eighteen three-, four-, and five-part pieces were probably intended for unaccompanied performance. By contrast, several of the six-part pieces are in the nature of 'consort anthems' and are provided with an accompaniment for a consort of viols (at this period the choristers at Ely Cathedral were routinely taught to play the viol). The high point of the collection is reached in 'O ye little flock', an extended consort anthem in three sections portraying the Christmas story. Some of the compositions in *Sacred Hymnes* exist also in liturgical versions at Ely Cathedral, Peterhouse (Cambridge), and elsewhere, and in some cases the liturgical versions were copied by Amner himself. No fewer than eleven of Amner's compositions in the Peterhouse 'Caroline' partbooks are in the hand of the composer.

Amner wrote a small quantity of instrumental music, which survives only in manuscript. An incomplete pavan and galliard for viols exists in the British Library. His only known keyboard music, 'O Lord, in thee is all my trust', is a substantial and technically demanding set of variations on a metrical psalm tune, and is preserved in the New York Public Library. Amner died in Ely, where he was buried on 28 July 1641. **Ralph Amner** (*d.* 1664), musician, was by Christmas 1605 a lay clerk at Ely Cathedral, in which capacity he continued until Easter 1609. He was noted among lay vicars at Westminster Abbey that year, but by 1614 had been ordained. From September 1614 he served in various capacities in the Chapel Royal at Windsor. In 1635 he became a member of the Corporation of Musick in Westminster. Having regained his place in the Chapel Royal at the Restoration, he attended Charles II's coronation on 23 April 1661. He died at Windsor on 3 March 1664 and was buried there the following day. William Child's catch commemorating Amner was published in Hilton's *Catch that Catch Can* (1667).　　　　　JOHN MOREHEN

Sources H. W. Shaw, *The succession of organists of the Chapel Royal and the cathedrals of England and Wales from c.1538* (1991) • A. J. Greening, 'Amner, John', *New Grove* • J. Morehen, 'A neglected East Anglian madrigalian collection of the Jacobean period', *Transactions of the Cambridge Bibliographical Society*, 11 (1996–9), 285–312 • *Sacred hymnes … John Amner*, ed. J. Morehen (2000), vol. 40 of *The English madrigalists* • P. Le Huray, *Music and the Reformation in England, 1549–1660* (1967); repr. with corrections (1978), 128–9, 390–91 • R. T. Daniel and P. le Huray, *The sources of English church music, 1549–1660* (1972) • I. Payne, 'British Library Add. MSS 30826–28: a set of partbooks from Trinity College, Cambridge?', *Chelys*, 17 (1988), 3–14 • A. Ashbee and D. Lasocki, eds., *A biographical dictionary of English court musicians, 1485–1714*, 1 (1998), 20–22

Amner, Ralph (*d.* 1664). *See under* Amner, John (*d.* 1641).

Amner, Richard (*bap.* 1737, *d.* 1803), Presbyterian minister and biblical critic, was born at Hinckley, Leicestershire, the third of five children of Richard Amner and Anne, his wife. He was baptized on 26 April 1737 at the Presbyterian Great Meeting, Hinckley. In 1755 he entered Daventry Academy under Caleb Ashworth to prepare for the dissenting ministry; five manuscript essays he wrote in shorthand as a student survive. He was chosen as minister of the Independent congregation, Middlegate, Great Yarmouth, and ordained on 21 July 1762, but his stay was brief. He must originally have been considered orthodox in his beliefs, since the congregation had been formed in 1732 by a secession from the Presbyterian Old Meeting,

after the departure of the minister from orthodox Calvinist preaching. Following the disclosure of Amner's Arian opinions casting doubt on the full divinity of Christ, he preached his last sermon at Yarmouth on 5 March 1764. From 1765 he was minister of the Presbyterian meeting, Red Lion Hill, Hampstead, Middlesex. In 1777 he became minister of the Old Meeting, Coseley, Staffordshire. He retired from the ministry in 1794 because of failing eyesight and returned to Hinckley, his native town, to devote himself entirely to study. He died there on 8 June 1803.

Amner published four works, the first anonymously in 1768 on observing the sabbath. His later essays on biblical criticism emphasized the sufficiency of scripture and reason. His rationalist approach to questions of revelation was disliked by orthodox critics, but such an approach was increasingly adopted by presbyterians during the second half of the eighteenth century. In his final work, *Considerations on the Doctrines of a Future State* (1797), he disclosed his early debt to Nathaniel Lardner, with whom he corresponded as a young man. Lardner and Ashworth were among the ministers sent presentation copies of his first book in 1768 (Bodl. Oxf., MS Montagu d. 6, fol. 36r). He was also a regular contributor to the *Gentleman's Magazine*. However, the most remarkable incident in Amner's personal history involved George Steevens, the Shakespearian commentator. When Steevens published his edition of Shakespeare's plays in 1793, it was found that he had put Amner's name to many of the obscene notes which he had inserted concerning the playwright's more bawdy passages; Amner supposedly earned Steevens's malignancy while they were both living in Hampstead.

DAVID L. WYKES

Sources J. Nichols, *The history and antiquities of the county of Leicester*, 4/2 (1811), 747 • *GM*, 1st ser., 73 (1803), 693 • DWL, Walter Wilson MSS, vol. E, p. 285; vol. I.2, fol. 59v; vol. I.5, fol. 376r • student essays, orations, and themes, 'Daventry I', DWL, New College collection, L12/1 • R. Amner, letter [to T. Cadell], 3 Feb 1768, Bodl. Oxf., MS Montagu d. 6 • 'A list of students educated at the academy at Daventry', *Monthly Repository*, 1st ser., 17 (1822), 165 • J. Browne, *A history of Congregationalism and memorials of the churches in Norfolk and Suffolk* (1877), 247 • H. Sharpe, *The meeting house on Red Lion Hill and Rosslyn Hill Chapel, Hampstead* (1914), 22–4 • G. E. Evans, *Midland churches: a history of the congregations on the roll of the Midland Christian Union* (1899), 86 • Nichols, *Illustrations*, 8.335 • *The plays of William Shakespeare … with the corrections and illustrations of various commentators. To which are added, notes by Samuel Johnson and G. Steevens* (1793), 12.427, 503; 14.395 • non-parochial registers, Great Meeting, Hinckley, 1706–82, PRO, RG4/3894
Archives DWL, New College MSS

Amoroso, Emmanuel Ciprian (1901–1982), veterinary embryologist and endocrinologist, was born on 16 September 1901 in Port of Spain, Trinidad, the third child in the family of eight sons (one of them adopted) and three daughters of Thomas Amoroso, bookkeeper and later estate owner, and his wife, Juliana Centeno. After attending St Thomas's preparatory school, Trinidad, in 1913 he entered St Mary's College, Trinidad, and took the junior Cambridge certificate examination in 1917. Amoroso left school early after suffering an attack of typhoid which left him virtually blind in one eye. At the age of twenty-one he nevertheless arrived in Dublin where he enrolled in University College at the National University in Ireland. He supported himself at first by selling newspapers outside the main railway station and later by teaching anatomy. An outstanding student, he won several prizes and in the final medical examination he achieved the highest marks ever attained. He graduated BSc in 1926 and MB BCh BAO (Dublin) in 1929. He also found time to become a useful amateur heavyweight boxer. In 1930 he was awarded a travelling studentship which enabled him to undertake postgraduate studies in Berlin and Freiburg. To ensure that he could read scientific publications in the original text and to avoid any bias introduced by another translator, Amo, as he was by then universally known, began to learn all the European languages. He was to become a highly competent linguist. After his period of study in Germany he moved to University College, London, where his interest in experimental embryology was excited and in 1934 he obtained his PhD degree, the first of a bewildering array of higher degrees and fellowships from many parts of the world.

In 1934 Amoroso joined the Royal Veterinary College as a senior assistant in charge of histology and embryology. Amoroso's most difficult task on joining the college was to overcome the racism of many of his academic colleagues who thought him 'not even the equal of that sprinkling of Asian students whom it was his duty to teach. Even his professor, James McCunn, turned against him, and the students were encouraged to do likewise' (Short, 7). The support of a handful of staff and outsiders helped Amoroso to survive this difficult period.

On 21 March 1936 Amoroso began a short-lived marriage to Elsie Mary ('Peter') Pole (or Harvey; b. 1903/4), daughter of Henry Pole, an accountant. There were no children. After his marriage failed he remained a private and rather lonely person.

In 1948 Amoroso was appointed to the chair of physiology at the Royal Veterinary College and for a while also acted as professor of anatomy. In 1950 he became professor of veterinary physiology at London University. In 1957 he was elected FRS; he also held fellowships of the Royal College of Physicians (1966), Royal College of Surgeons (1960), Royal College of Obstetricians and Gynaecologists (1965), and Royal College of Pathologists (1973). He became an honorary associate of the Royal College of Veterinary Surgeons (1959) and of the British Veterinary Association. In 1964 he was awarded the MD of the National University of Ireland. He held numerous honorary doctorates.

Amoroso's interests and research ranged over an extraordinarily diverse group of subjects including cancer and the first studies of the seried veins of the neck of the giraffe. However, his greatest contribution to knowledge lay in the field of reproductive biology, notably in studies of the structure and function of the placenta. He published many papers and stimulating reviews but much of his thought, philosophy, and work was encapsulated in his outstanding chapter in volume 2 of *Marshall's Physiology of Reproduction* (3rd edn, ed. A. S. Parkes, 1952). Amoroso was

awarded the Mary Marshall medal of the Society of Fertility and the Carl Hartman medal of the Society for the Study of Reproduction. It was, however, the presentation of the Dale medal by the Society for Endocrinology at the symposium on 29 September 1981 to honour his eightieth birthday which gave him particular pleasure and delighted his many friends and colleagues.

Amoroso was a practical supporter of the learned societies with which he concerned himself and several benefited from his financial acumen. As a chairman of scientific meetings he was outstanding. He possessed the ability to distil complex arguments and to identify key facts from which he presented a lucid and elegant summary. His mastery of the English language was complete and generations of students were captivated by the literary flair of this man who was slightly larger than life with a touch of flamboyance—cigar, pocket handkerchief, and bow-tie—who referred to himself as an Afro-Saxon. He was an inspired teacher as well as research worker and set many others on the road to scientific success. Yet he had time for the less successful and did not forget the difficulties he faced in his early life or the help he received. It was an indication of the impact he made on students and on veterinary preclinical teaching that twenty years after his retirement and six years after his death a new award for outstanding veterinary preclinical research should be designated the Amoroso award.

On Amoroso's retirement in 1968 the University of London conferred on him the title of emeritus professor and the Royal Veterinary College awarded him its highest honour by making him a fellow. In 1969 Amoroso was appointed CBE and in 1977 he received the Trinity cross, the highest national award of Trinidad and Tobago. Retirement only marked a further stage in his veterinary career and was followed by a series of visiting professorships and other posts in Santiago, Sydney, Nairobi, and Guelph and by a long period as special professor in the University of Nottingham. He was slowed only by incipient heart disease and continued to work at the Institute of Animal Physiology at Babraham before he died on 30 October 1982 at the home of some friends in Leeds. A memorial service was held at St Peter's Church, Babraham, on 6 January 1983 for his close friends and colleagues; this was followed by a memorial mass at the church of St Anselm and St Cecilia, Kingsway, London, on 28 February.

A. O. BETTS, rev. MICHAEL BEVAN

Sources P. Jewell, 'Journal of Zoology', 200 (1983), 1–4 · R. V. Short, *Memoirs FRS*, 31 (1985) · Munk, *Roll* · personal knowledge (1990) · private information (1990) · m. cert.
Archives Wellcome L., papers
Likenesses photograph, repro. in Short, *Memoirs FRS*
Wealth at death £85,030: administration with will, 28 Feb 1983, *CGPLA Eng. & Wales*

Amory, Derick Heathcoat, first Viscount Amory (1899–1981), industrialist and politician, was born on 26 December 1899 in London, the second son of Sir Ian Murray Heathcoat Heathcoat-Amory, second baronet (1865–1931),

Derick Heathcoat Amory, first Viscount Amory (1899–1981), by Walter Stoneman, 1955

and his wife, Alexandra Georgina (d. 1942), daughter of Vice-Admiral Henry George Seymour. Derry, as he was familiarly called, was educated at Eton College and at Christ Church, Oxford, where he achieved a third in modern history in 1921, and settled down to a business career in the family's textile business in Tiverton, Devon. In the course of the next quarter-century only war service really interrupted his work for John Heathcoat & Co., of which he became managing director, leading by example and—like Stanley Baldwin—placing a high value on traditional working relationships. His early biographer was, however, insistent that whereas Baldwin's Worcestershire inheritance was Anglican and feudal, Amory's in Tiverton was 'puritan, radical, nonconformist, squire-less'. The view from within the firm was that 'Mr Derry' was 'the born executive—slow-moving, tenacious, patient, never deflected by personal considerations from what he held to be the general good' (Gore Booth, 19, 44). This liberal view of owners' responsibility within modern industry was powerfully reinforced when he made over a large part of his personal capital (and persuaded his wealthier elder brother to do the same) in order to create a trust fund for the benefit of Heathcoats workers.

Amory's sense of duty took him on to the Devon county council for twenty years from 1932, where he chaired the education committee. He was also county commissioner for the Boy Scouts from 1930 to 1945. In the same spirit of support for the young he was later a leading advocate of the Outward Bound Trust, and secretary of the House of Commons' own scout troop. Amory served in the Territorial Army during the 1930s, and during the Second World War he was a staff lieutenant-colonel with the Royal Artillery, seeing action at Salerno. In 1944, responsible for training paratroops for the Arnhem landings, he insisted on taking part along with his trainees, and was injured and taken prisoner during the operation.

In 1945 Amory stepped into the vacancy left by a cousin killed in action to become Conservative MP for Tiverton, his earlier Liberalism now abandoned in admiration for Churchill and an anti-socialism that had been enhanced by Labour's upsurge. He remained, though, an extremely moderate man with little of the fire of party politics in him—the despair of Conservative Party image makers when he became chancellor. When appointed to his party's industrial policy committee in 1946 he moderated the conflicting views of other members, and transmitted to them the consensual, co-partnership approach to industrial relations that he had inherited and fostered at Heathcoats. He was thus an important, if inconspicuous, influence on the *Industrial Charter* which the Conservatives published in 1947, a landmark in their recovery from the election defeat in 1945. His moderation even more clearly signalled his support, throughout his parliamentary career, for the abolition of the death penalty, a view shared by few tory leaders of his generation.

Though Amory made only a limited impact within the opposition period of 1945–51, he was appointed to ministerial office as soon as Churchill regained power after the general election of 1951. His promotion was so surprising that he himself is said to have asked whether Churchill had really meant to send for Julian Amery. He served initially as minister of state for pensions (1951–3), where his moderate politics reassured voters fearing that the Conservatives intended to attack the new welfare state. He had already served as a representative of the war-disabled, on the pensions central advisory committee. Then after a short period as minister of state at the Board of Trade (1953–4), he joined the cabinet as minister of agriculture, fisheries, and food on 28 July 1954, after his predecessor Thomas Dugdale had been forced out over the Crichel Down affair.

Churchill needed a reassuring presence at agriculture, preferably someone versed in the priorities of the countryside, and he found this in the member for Tiverton. Amory, with added responsibility for food policy, carried through the final demolition of wartime rationing as economic conditions improved, a policy that did no harm at all to the Conservative Party's chances of re-election in 1955. He also introduced and passed the Agriculture Act (1957). This completed the long process of disengaging the industry from wartime controls and introducing the price support which remained in place for many years, a remarkable feat which was achieved without alienating either farmers or consumers. Eden kept him at agriculture throughout his premiership (1955–7), as more surprisingly did Macmillan when he succeeded Eden in January 1957. Though one of the cabinet critics of the Suez adventure, Amory loyally accepted the majority view. He was the only one of those whose names were mentioned in the press as Eden's ministerial critics who immediately denied the press reports and pledged his complete support for the prime minister and the invasion.

A year later Macmillan suffered the resignation of his chancellor of the exchequer, Peter Thorneycroft, after the cabinet refused in January 1958 to agree to expenditure cuts deemed necessary to reduce inflation. He turned to Amory to restore business and party confidence in government policy. Macmillan probably also saw Amory as a more biddable chancellor than Thorneycroft had been, and knew that he would not cause him real difficulties as the government proceeded to reflate the economy in advance of the next general election, due in about two years. Amory therefore took over the Treasury on 7 January 1958, only a few weeks before a budget that was bound to be contentious, and with the previous team of Thorneycroft, Nigel Birch, and Enoch Powell tempted to criticize in order to justify their own departures.

It says a good deal for the respect with which Amory was already regarded in the Commons and the financial press that the budget of 1958 was a personal triumph. He did enough to get the economy moving after a period of sluggish growth, but continued to proclaim his adherence to Thorneycroft's war on inflation. As his time at the Treasury went on, however, and under constant expansionist urgings from Macmillan, this hard-won early respect was partially lost, with a steady sequence of moves to free up credit. A second expansionist budget in 1959, cutting both interest and purchase tax when growth was already surging ahead, did something to ensure Conservative re-election in the following October, but reluctance to insist on remedial action when Macmillan still did not want to apply the brakes, either then or in his final budget in 1960, helped to prepare the way for the recession, credit squeeze, and major economic setbacks of 1961-3. It is only fair to add that Amory presided over a period of steady economic growth, low unemployment, and sustained business confidence, and that he shared with Macmillan, as a result of his experiences in Tiverton in the 1930s, an absolute abhorrence of unemployment.

Amory remained at the exchequer until July 1960, having made it clear at the time of the general election in 1959 that he would retire from ministerial office when he was sixty, and to general amazement insisting on actually doing so. This was surprising in part because some Conservative MPs by then saw him as a potential successor to Macmillan, though whether such support would have survived the economic consequences of his Treasury policies during 1961 is far from clear. The premiership was in any event an outcome well beyond the ambitions of Amory himself, who stepped down in 1960 not just from the government but from his Commons seat too, making the break irrevocable.

Amory was made a viscount in September 1960, on his departure from the Commons, and succeeded his brother as fourth baronet in 1972. He devoted the rest of his life mainly to public service, most prominently as chairman of the Medical Research Council (1960-61 and 1965-9) and as British high commissioner in Canada (1961-3). Latterly, his activities centred on Devon, where he became a deputy lieutenant in 1962, his other positions including the chancellorship of the University of Exeter, chairmanship of the Exeter Cathedral appeal, and presidency of the County Councils' Association. He also partially resumed his business career, as a director of ICI and chairman of Heathcoats. He died at his home, the Wooden House, Chevithorne, near Tiverton, on 20 January 1981. Since he was unmarried, the viscountcy became extinct, the baronetcy passing to his brother William (1901-1982).

During a visit to India in 1957, Amory explained to an audience in Bombay:

> I began as a businessman, and it took me almost twenty years to get over my initial distrust of politicians, whom I had heard defined as people who always looked for trouble and found it, generally made wrong diagnoses and consequently applied wrong remedies.

He was a stocky, bespectacled, modest, and earnest-minded man, and the celebration of his career in the naming of a Yorkshire pub as the Jolly Minister (the inn sign depicting him on horseback, as minister of agriculture) was among the most improbable events of the 1950s. Yet he was easily the most prominent of the patient, committed, moderate, and trustworthy men who did so much in office to restore the Conservatives' credibility in the generation after 1945. It was also highly symbolic of those conservative times when, on his appointment as chancellor in 1957, he refused to move into 11 Downing Street, preferring to remain in his tiny bachelor flat in Pimlico. When a journalist suggested that he would have to secure the help of a sister-in-law with official entertaining, he replied in tones of horror, 'Good gracious, no. They all have husbands and they are far too busy' (Gore Booth, 183).   JOHN RAMSDEN

Sources J. Barnes, 'Derick Heathcoat Amory', *Blackwell biographical dictionary of British political life in the twentieth century*, ed. K. Robbins (1990) · DNB · W. Gore Booth, *The reluctant politician: Derick Heathcoat Amory* (1958) · S. Brittan, *The Treasury under the tories, 1951-1964* (1964) · A. Horne, *Macmillan*, 2: *1957-1986* (1989) · J. Ramsden, *The age of Churchill and Eden, 1940-1957* (1995) · J. Ramsden, *The winds of change: Macmillan to Heath, 1957-1975* (1996) · A. Seldon, *Churchill's Indian summer* (1981) · *The Times* (12 Jan 1981) · Burke, *Peerage* (2000)
Archives CAC Cam., corresp. with A. V. Hill | FILM BFI NFTVA, news footage · BFI NFTVA, party political footage · BFI NFTVA, propaganda film footage
Likenesses W. Stoneman, photograph, 1955, NPG [*see illus.*]
Wealth at death £491,305: probate, 23 Feb 1981, *CGPLA Eng. & Wales*

Amory, Thomas (1690/91-1788), novelist, was according to his son, Dr Robert Amory, the son of Counsellor Amory who, accompanying William III to Ireland, was made secretary for the forfeited estates, and possessed 'very considerable property' in co. Clare (*GM*, 58.1062, 59.322). Subsequently disputed (*GM*, 59.107-8), Robert Amory's account would have Counsellor Amory to be Thomas Amory of Bunratty, son of another Thomas Amory and his wife,

Elizabeth, daughter to the nineteenth lord of Kerry. The difficulty of disentangling truthful information from the fictionalized account of himself Amory offers in his best-known work, *The Life of John Buncle, Esq.* (1756–66), is appropriately indicated by his son's reference to 'my father (John Buncle), Thomas Amory'.

The novelist was probably born in London but grew up from infancy in Ireland, where he claims to have learned Irish. In *John Buncle* Amory describes an education at Trinity College, Dublin, and offers vivid accounts of life in the Irish capital and among the Gaelic aristocracy in the west of Ireland. Amory alleged extensive acquaintance with leading Irish contemporaries including Jonathan Swift, Constantia Grierson, Hugh MacCurtin (Aodh Buí Mac Cruitín), and 'my friend, worthy John Toland' (T. Amory, *Memoirs of Several Ladies*, 1755, 75). Amory appears to have left Ireland about 1729 and to have toured extensively in the north of England; by 1755 he was living in Westminster.

An earlier manuscript entitled 'The antient and present state of Great Britain' having been destroyed by fire, Amory published *Memoirs of several ladies of Great Britain, interspersed with literary reflexions, and accounts of antiquities and curious things* (1755), set principally in the Western Isles and giving abundant evidence of its author's devotion to intellectual speculation, anti-Trinitarianism, and learned women. In 1756 he published the first and in 1766 the second volume of *The life of John Buncle, esq.: containing various observations and reflections made in several parts of the world and many extraordinary relations*. An extravagant fictional autobiography, lengthily praised in the *Monthly Review*, the work was contemptuously dismissed in a single sentence by the *Critical Review*.

John Buncle is an enthusiastic anti-Trinitarian who marries in rapid succession eight (short-lived) wives, each beautiful, learned, and a strict anti-Trinitarian; the personal qualities of all are well represented by the composite Miss Spence who has 'the *head* of *Aristotle*, the *heart* of a *primitive Christian*, and the *form* of *Venus de Medicis*' (T. Amory, *Buncle*, 2.162). His powerful advocacy of education for women produced scepticism even from Amory's admirers. As enthusiastic in learning as in religion, Buncle discourses on topics as varied as monogamy and microscopes, the Spanish fly and fluxions (dismissing George Berkeley's mathematical contribution as worthless). His familiarity with Irish antiquity Buncle attributes partly to knowledge of a manuscript of the 'Foras feasa ar Éirinn' by Geoffrey Keating (Seathrún Céitinn), though Dermod O'Connor's printed translation, *General History of Ireland* (1722) of Keating's work, was probably Amory's source for quotations. Though Buncle's travels from Astrakhan to Peru must be accounted fantastical, Amory seems to have had a first-hand knowledge of, as well as enthusiasm for, the wild beauties of the English Lake and Peak districts. *John Buncle* proved popular enough to be reprinted in 1770, and to be translated into German.

In later years Amory had a 'very peculiar look and aspect' and allegedly rarely stirred abroad, except 'like a bat, in the dusk of the evening' (*GM*, 58). He died at Westminster on 25 November 1788, aged ninety-seven. His work was admired by William Hazlitt, who considered Amory the 'English Rabelais' (Hazlitt), and by Leigh Hunt.

IAN CAMPBELL ROSS

Sources *GM*, 1st ser., 58 (1788), 1062 • *GM*, 1st ser., 59 (1789), 107–8, 322 • J. Lodge, *The peerage of Ireland*, 2 (1754), 114 • I. C. Ross, 'Thomas Amory, *John Buncle*, and the origins of Irish fiction', *Éire–Ireland*, 18/3 (1983), 71–85 • I. C. Ross, ed., 'Fiction to 1800', *The Field Day anthology of Irish writing*, ed. S. Deane, A. Carpenter, and J. Williams, 3 (1991), 682–759, esp. 694–704, 758 • W. Hazlitt, 'On John Buncle', *The round table* (1817) • L. Hunt, *A book for a corner* (1849) • J. O'Hart, *The Irish and Anglo-Irish landed gentry* (1884); facs. edn (1969), 452, 514 • Burtchaell & Sadleir, *Alum. Dubl.*, 2nd edn • *DNB* • *Monthly Review*, 15 (1756), 497–512, 585–604 • *Monthly Review*, 35 (1766), 33–43, 100–23 • *Critical Review*, 21 (1766), 470

Amory, Thomas (1701–1774), Presbyterian minister, was born at Taunton, Somerset, on 28 January 1701, the second son of John Amory (d. c.1740), grocer, and his wife, Anne (d. 1742), the elder sister of the Revd Henry Grove (1684–1738). He was brought up in Taunton as a dissenter at Paul Street meeting, where his father was a trustee from 1709 to 1733. Details of his earliest education are not known, but he was taught the classics by Thomas Chadwick, a Presbyterian minister at Taunton, from about 1712, interrupted by a period at Exeter to learn French.

Intended for the ministry from his earliest years, Amory joined the academy run by Stephen James and Henry Grove, his uncle, at Taunton in March 1717. In the summer of 1722 he was examined and approved as a candidate for the Presbyterian ministry. His father had the means to send him to London in November 1722 to study experimental science under John Eames at Moorfields. In 1725, on Stephen James's death, he became assistant to Robert Darch at Bishop's Hull meeting-house and assistant tutor at the Taunton academy. He also preached at dissenting chapels in the area, which included Lambrook and West Hatch, prior to his ordination on 3 October 1730 into a joint ministry with Edmund Batson at Pauls Meeting, Taunton. He was now recognized as a significant figure among the more theologically heterodox and non-Calvinist ministers in the west of England.

Theological and financial differences arose with Batson and the congregation, so in 1732 Amory's friends seceded and built a new meeting-house in Tancred Street, Taunton, in which he ministered for the next seventeen years. When his uncle Henry Grove died in 1738, Amory became principal of the Taunton academy; in the twenty-one years of his principalship he trained about twenty-five ministers. On 7 September 1741 he married Mary Baker, daughter of the Revd Samuel Baker of Parish Street Chapel, Southwark, at Taunton. They had six children, two of whom predeceased him.

Much influenced by Henry Grove, Amory, however, took a more heterodox view than his uncle and became Arian in his beliefs. He was a noted critic of the Calvinist position and of evangelical doctrine generally. Though seen as a radical thinker among the Presbyterians, he was widely respected by all dissenters in Taunton, as he consistently avoided adopting a partisan approach to religious issues. It was thought he would stay in Taunton for the rest of his life.

Nevertheless in October 1759 Amory moved with his family to the City of London and became afternoon preacher at the Old Jewry meeting-house. The reasons for the change included a decline in numbers of those attending the academy (it closed on his departure), the desire to improve the position of his children, and the wish to place himself in a wider sphere of influence than Taunton could provide. In 1766 he became co-pastor of Old Jewry on the death of Samuel Chandler, and in 1770 the colleague of Dr Richard Price as morning preacher at the meeting-house at Newington Green. His scholarship was recognized in 1768 when he was awarded the degree of DD by the University of Edinburgh, and in the same year was made one of the lecturers at Salter's Hall.

Amory did not achieve the success in London which he might have expected. 'His family benefited by many advantages peculiar to London, but the pastor himself never achieved any popularity in his more elevated station' (Pike, 151–2). His preaching was admired for its content but was not popular, as his voice was not strong. His friend Andrew Kippis admitted that 'his sermons though practical, serious and affecting to the attentive however, were rather too close, judicious and philosophical for the common run of congregations' (Kippis, 1.176).

By the 1770s Amory had become a leading figure among the Presbyterians, and took a strong stand in the agitation against the requirement laid on dissenting ministers to subscribe to the doctrinal articles of the established church. Personally he always refused to subscribe and did not live to see relief granted in 1779. D. Bogue and J. Bennett, the historians of dissent in the following century, and of a very different theological view, tacitly admit the strength of his theological influence within dissent:

> From his uncle, Dr Amory inherited the calvinophobia, and this disease, instead of being milder, grew more inveterate,

so that he sought relief in Arianism, a system which few of the Presbyterian ministers of London, in his day, professed so openly as himself. (Bogue and Bennett, 2.209)

Amory's numerous publications consisted of sermons, devotional works, and collections of the writings of Henry Grove, who was the principal influence on Amory's life and thought. He was a kindly man, who apparently in conversation told a fund of stories, and 'None could excel him as a husband, a father, a master, or a friend' (Kippis, 1.176). Amory died after a short illness in the parish of St Olave Jewry, on 24 June 1774, being active in his ministry to within days of his death; he was buried at Bunhill Fields on 5 July 1774. He was survived by his widow, who presented his portrait to Dr Williams's Library in April 1801.

ALAN RUSTON

Sources A. Kippis and others, eds., *Biographia Britannica, or, The lives of the most eminent persons who have flourished in Great Britain and Ireland*, 2nd edn, 1 (1778), 175–80 · W. Wilson, *The history and antiquities of the dissenting churches and meeting houses in London, Westminster and Southwark*, 4 vols. (1808–14), vol. 2, pp. 385–93 · J. Murch, *A history of the Presbyterian and General Baptist churches in the west of England* (1835), 208–10 · G. H. Pike, *Ancient meeting-houses, or, Memorial pictures of nonconformity in old London* (1870), 151–2 · parish register (baptism), Taunton, St Mary, 28 Feb 1701 · C. Surman, index of dissenting ministers, DWL · IGI · D. Bogue and J. Bennett, *History of dissenters, from the revolution in 1688, to … 1808*, 2 (1809), 209 · R. Flexman, *A crown of life, the gratuitous reward of the faithful Christian: a sermon preached at the Old Jewry, July 10, 1774, on occasion of the death of the Rev. Thomas Amory* (1774) · A. Brockett, *Nonconformity in Exeter, 1650–1875* (1962), 139, 240 · J. Manning, 'Memorial of dissenting academies in the west of England', *Monthly Repository*, 13 (1818), 89–90 · B. W. Kirk, *A history of Taunton United Reformed church* (1999) · will, PRO, PROB 11/999, 252

Archives DWL, MSS

Likenesses J. Wooding, line engraving, pubd 1789, NPG · J. Hopwood, stipple (after Baxter), BM, NPG · engraving, DWL · engravings, repro. in Wilson, *History and antiquities*, 385 · oils, DWL

Wealth at death see will, PRO, PROB 11/999

PICTURE CREDITS

Abbas Hilmi II (1874–1944)—© National Portrait Gallery, London

Abbot, Charles, first Baron Colchester (1757–1829)—Palace of Westminster Collection

Abbot, George (1562–1633)—© National Portrait Gallery, London

Abbot, Robert (1559/60–1618)—collection Maidstone Museum and Art Gallery; Photograph: The Paul Mellon Centre for Studies in British Art

Abbott, Charles, first Baron Tenterden (1762–1832)—© National Portrait Gallery, London

Abbott, Eric Symes (1906–1983)—© National Portrait Gallery, London

Abdul Rahman, Tunku (1902–1990)—© reserved

À Beckett, Arthur William (1844–1909)—© National Portrait Gallery, London

À Beckett, Gilbert Abbott (1811–1856)—© National Portrait Gallery, London

À Beckett, Gilbert Arthur (1837–1891)—© National Portrait Gallery, London

Abel, Sir Frederick Augustus, first baronet (1827–1902)—© National Portrait Gallery, London

Abel, Karl Friedrich (1723–1787)—The Huntington Library, Art Collections and Botanical Gardens, San Marino, CA, USA

Abell, Sir George Edmond Brackenbury (1904–1989)—© National Portrait Gallery, London

Abell, William (b. c.1584, d. in or after 1655)—© National Portrait Gallery, London

Abercrombie, Sir (Leslie) Patrick (1879–1957)—© National Portrait Gallery, London

Abercromby, James (1706–1781)—© National Portrait Gallery, London

Abercromby, Sir Ralph, of Tullibody (1734–1801)—Scottish National Portrait Gallery

Abernethy, John (1680–1740)—© National Portrait Gallery, London

Abernethy, John (1764–1831)—St Bartholomew's Hospital Archives and Museum. Photograph: Photographic Survey, Courtauld Institute of Art, London

Abington, Frances (1737–1815)—Yale Center for British Art, Paul Mellon Collection

Abraham, Charles John (1814–1903)—© National Portrait Gallery, London

Abraham, William [Mabon] (1842–1922)—© National Portrait Gallery, London

Abrahams, Harold Maurice (1899–1978)—Getty Images - A. R. Coster

Achilli, (Giovanni) Giacinto (b. c.1803)—© National Portrait Gallery, London

Achurch, Janet (1864?–1916)—© National Portrait Gallery, London

Ackermann, Rudolph (1764–1834)—© National Portrait Gallery, London

Acland, Sir Arthur Herbert Dyke, thirteenth baronet (1847–1926)—© National Portrait Gallery, London

Acland, Sir Henry Wentworth, first baronet (1815–1900)—Royal Photographic Society; photograph National Portrait Gallery, London

Acland, Sir Richard Thomas Dyke, fifteenth baronet (1906–1990)—© National Portrait Gallery, London

Acland, Sir Thomas Dyke, eleventh baronet (1809–1898)—© National Portrait Gallery, London

Acton, Sir Harold Mario Mitchell (1904–1994)—© National Portrait Gallery, London

Acton, John Adams- (1830–1910)—© National Portrait Gallery, London

Acton, John Emerich Edward Dalberg, first Baron Acton (1834–1902)—© National Portrait Gallery, London

Acton, Sir John Francis Edward, sixth baronet (1736–1811)—© National Portrait Gallery, London

Adair, Sir Robert (1763–1855)—The Baltimore Museum of Art: The Jacob Epstein Collection, BMA 1951.109

Adam, Alexander (1741–1809)—Scottish National Portrait Gallery

Adam, John (1721–1792)—© National Portrait Gallery, London

Adam, Robert (1728–1792)—© National Portrait Gallery, London

Adam, William (1751–1839)—photograph by courtesy Sotheby's Picture Library

Adam, William Patrick (1823–1881)—© National Portrait Gallery, London

Adams, James Williams (1839–1903)—courtesy of the Director, National Army Museum, London

Adams, John (1735–1826)—Gift of Mrs. Robert Homans, Photograph © 2004 Board of Trustees, National Gallery of Art, Washington

Adams, John (1768?–1829)—Phillips Picture Library

Adams, John Couch (1819–1892)—Pembroke College, Cambridge

Adams, (Wilfred) Robert (c.1900–1965)—Getty Images - Frank Lilley

Adams, Samuel (1722–1803)—Copyright 2004 Museum of Fine Arts, Boston; Deposited by the City of Boston

Adams, Sarah Flower (1805–1848)—© National Portrait Gallery, London

Adams, Sir Walter (1906–1975)—© National Portrait Gallery, London

Adamson, Patrick (1537–1592)—Scottish National Portrait Gallery

Adamson, William (1863–1936)—© National Portrait Gallery, London

Adderley, Charles Bowyer, first Baron Norton (1814–1905)—© National Portrait Gallery, London

Adderley, James Granville (1861–1942)—© National Portrait Gallery, London

Addington, Henry, first Viscount Sidmouth (1757–1844)—© National Portrait Gallery, London

Addison, Christopher, first Viscount Addison (1869–1951)—© National Portrait Gallery, London

Addison, Joseph (1672–1719)—© National Portrait Gallery, London

Addison, Laura (1822–1852)—© National Portrait Gallery, London

Addison, Thomas (1795–1860)—by permission of the Royal College of Physicians, London; photograph National Portrait Gallery, London

Adeane, Michael Edward, Baron Adeane (1910–1984)—© National Portrait Gallery, London

Adelaide (1792–1849)—© National Portrait Gallery, London

Adler, Hermann (1839–1911)—London College of Jewish Studies; photograph © National Portrait Gallery, London

Adler, Nathan Marcus (1803–1890)—© National Portrait Gallery, London

Adolphus Frederick, Prince, first duke of Cambridge (1774–1850)—The Royal Collection © 2004 HM Queen Elizabeth II

Adrian, Edgar Douglas, first Baron Adrian (1889–1977)—© National Portrait Gallery, London

Adrian, Richard Hume, second Baron Adrian (1927–1995)—photograph by Ian Fleming

Adye, Sir John Miller (1819–1900)—© National Portrait Gallery, London

Æthelberht [St Æthelberht] (779/80–794)—© Copyright The British Museum

Æthelberht (d. 865)—© Copyright The British Museum

Æthelred II (c.966x8–1016)—© Copyright The British Museum

Æthelstan (893/4–939)—Master and Fellows of Corpus Christi College, Cambridge

Æthelwulf (d. 858)—© Copyright The British Museum

Aga Khan III (1877–1957)—© Tom Hustler / National Portrait Gallery, London

Agar, Eileen Forrester (1899–1991)—© Estate of Eileen Agar; collection National Portrait Gallery, London

Agasse, Jacques-Laurent (1767–1849)—Museum Stiftung Oskar Reinhart; photograph National Portrait Gallery, London

Agate, James Evershed (1877–1947)—© National Portrait Gallery, London

Aickman, Robert Fordyce (1914–1981)—© National Portrait Gallery, London

Aigueblanche, Peter d' (d. 1268)—by permission of the Dean and Chapter of Hereford Cathedral

Aikenhead, Mary Frances (1787–1858)—© National Portrait Gallery, London

Aikin, Arthur (1773–1854)—© National Portrait Gallery, London

Aikin, John (1747–1822)—© National Portrait Gallery, London

Aikin, Lucy (1781–1864)—private collection; photograph National Portrait Gallery, London

Aikman, William, of Cairnie (1682–1731)—Scottish National Portrait Gallery

Ainger, Alfred (1837–1904)—© National Portrait Gallery, London

Ainsworth, William Harrison (1805–1882)—© National Portrait Gallery, London

Aird, Sir John, first baronet (1833–1911)—© National Portrait Gallery, London

Airey, Richard, Baron Airey (1803–1881)—© National Portrait Gallery, London

Airy, Sir George Biddell (1801–1892)—© National Portrait Gallery, London

Aislabie, Benjamin (1774–1842)—© National Portrait Gallery, London

Aitchison, Craigie Mason, Lord Aitchison (1882–1941)—in the collection of the Faculty of Advocates; photograph courtesy the Scottish National Portrait Gallery

Aitchison, George (1825–1910)—RIBA Library Drawings Collection, London

Aitken, Alexander Craig (1895–1967)—© National Portrait Gallery, London

Aitken, James (1752–1777)—© Copyright The British Museum

Aitken, William Maxwell, first Baron Beaverbrook (1879–1964)—© The Beaverbrook Foundation; collection National Portrait Gallery, London

Akbar, Shireen Nishat (1944–1997)—V&A Images, The Victoria and Albert Museum

Akenside, Mark (1721–1770)—© National Portrait Gallery, London

Alabaster, William (1568–1640)—© Copyright The British Museum

Aland, John Fortescue, first Baron Fortescue of Credan (1670–1746)—© National Portrait Gallery, London

Albani, Dame Emma (1847–1930)—© National Portrait Gallery, London

Albert [Prince Albert of Saxe-Coburg and Gotha] (1819–1861)—Board of Trustees of the National Museums and Galleries on Merseyside (Lady Lever Art Gallery, Port Sunlight)

Albert Victor, Prince, duke of Clarence and Avondale (1864–1892)—© National Portrait Gallery, London

Albery, Sir Bronson James (1881–1971)—© National Portrait Gallery, London

Albery, Sir Donald Arthur Rolleston (1914–1988)—© National Portrait Gallery, London

Alcock, Charles William (1842–1907)—Marylebone Cricket Club Photo Library

Alcock, Sir John William (1892–1919)—© National Portrait Gallery, London

Alcock, Sir (John) Rutherford (1809–1897)—© National Portrait Gallery, London

Alcuin (c.740–804)—Staatsbibliothek, Bamberg, MS Bibl. 1, fol. 5v

Alder, Joshua (1792–1867)—© National Portrait Gallery, London

Aldersey, Thomas (1521/2–1598)—© Chester City Council (Grosvenor Museum)

Alderson, Sir James (1794–1882)—Wellcome Library, London